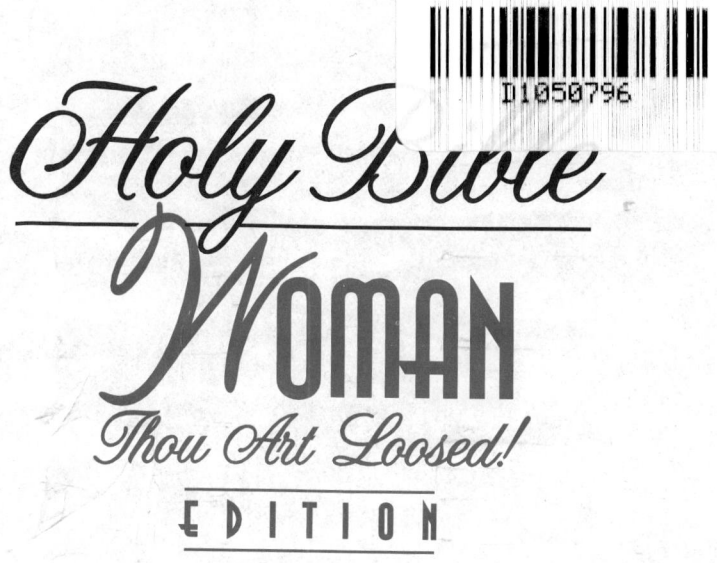

Holy Bible

Woman

Thou Art Loosed!

EDITION

T. D. JAKES
General Editor

NEW KING JAMES VERSION

Holy Bible

WOMAN

Thou Art Loosed!

EDITION

T. D. JAKES

General Editor

Thomas Nelson Publishers
Nashville

Contents

The Books of the Bible
The Old Testament

The New Testament

Welcome
from Bishop T.D. Jakes

Welcome to the *Holy Bible, Woman Thou Art Loosed Edition*. I am delighted that you are the proud owner of this excellent Book and I pray that it will bless you immensely. This Bible combines two of the most exciting things in my life: the mighty Word of God and the powerful message of His healing and wholeness.

In order for you to receive the full benefit of this Bible, you must use and understand it. May I take just a minute to acquaint you with some of its features? First, you may notice that some of the pages are pink. Most of the pink pages contain articles I have written to go along with specific Bible verses. These articles are drawn from my books and are intended to speak life to your spirit and to enhance your Bible study. On other pink pages you will find "Soul Secrets." These are prayers that deal with many of the sensitive issues in your life. Though these prayers can stand alone, I hope you will use them as starting places as you begin to pour out your heart before the Lord in prayer.

In the front of the Bible, there are a few things I would hate for you to miss. You'll find "The Victorious Woman's Guide to Bible Reading," which lists verses in 25 categories that are important to getting free and staying free in your life. Then, just preceding the Old Testament, you'll come across one of my favorite sections: "Leading Ladies." Here, I'll take you through a readable "portrait gallery" of ten of the Bible's key women. They are not necessarily the most famous biblical women, but in many ways they are some of the most real. You can enjoy an in-depth look at Naomi, Gomer, Michal, Mary, and others. As a special treat, I have included a written version of one of my most popular sermons, "The Woman with the Alabaster Box."

Throughout the *Holy Bible, Woman Thou Art Loosed Edition,* I have strung "Gospel Pearls"—bite-sized quotations that will encourage and inspire you all the way through the Bible. All of these elements exist along with the accurate, but easy-to-understand New King James Version of the Scriptures.

Finally, I have included an index to all of the supplemental material and an index entitled, "Where to Find Her," which tells you where to locate many women mentioned in the Bible. These will help you find your way through the Bible easily.

Nothing excites me more than seeing women healed and set free. Whoever you are, whatever your circumstances, I hope that your strength, your wholeness, your freedom, and your sense of destiny will increase as a result of your using this Bible. My sister, be blessed by the Word of God and by the God of the Word!

T. D. Jakes

Index to Articles

The Victorious Christian Woman's Guide to Bible Reading

The Basis for Victorious Living

The Bible—Your Source Book
Psalm 119
Proverbs 30:5
Isaiah 40:8
Mark 13:31
2 Timothy 3:16, 17
Hebrews 4:12

The Bible—Your Comfort
Psalm 19:7-10
Psalm 119:50
Psalm 119:165
Isaiah 49:13
Romans 15:4
2 Corinthians 1:3, 4

The Bible—Your Guide
Psalm 37:23, 24
Psalm 73:23, 24
Psalm 119:105
Proverbs 3:5, 6
Proverbs 6:22, 23
Isaiah 28:29

The Bible—Your Strength
2 Samuel 22:40
Job 12:13
Psalm 18:30
Isaiah 40:29-31
Acts 20:32
Ephesians 1:13, 14

The Victorious Woman

Loosed by God's Mercy
Numbers 14:18, 19
1 Chronicles 16:34
Psalm 103:8
Psalm 118
Isaiah 55:7
Daniel 9:9
Romans 9:14-16
Ephesians 2:4-7
James 5:11
1 Peter 1:3-5

Loosed by God's Love
Isaiah 43:4
Jeremiah 31:3
John 3:16, 17
Romans 5:5-8
Titus 3:4-7
1 John 4:8-11

Loosed by God's Faithfulness
Deuteronomy 31:6-8
1 Kings 8:56
Psalm 89:1, 2
Lamentations 3:22-24
1 Corinthians 1:9
Hebrews 13:5

Loosed from Fear
Joshua 1:9
2 Chronicles 20:15
Psalm 23
Psalm 91:1-12

Proverbs 29:25
Matthew 14:25-27
John 14:25-31
1 John 4:18

Loosed from Anger
Psalm 37:7, 8
Proverbs 15:1, 18
Proverbs 29:22
Ecclesiastes 7:9
Ephesians 4:26, 27
Colossians 3:5-10
James 1:19, 20

Loosed from Discouragement
Psalm 31:9-16
Psalm 42:5
Psalm 138:7
Isaiah 43:1, 2
2 Corinthians 4:8-10
Galatians 6:9
Philippians 1:3-6
Philippians 4:6, 7
Hebrews 10:35-37

Loosed from Frustration
Psalm 37:5-8
Isaiah 50:7
Isaiah 54:17
Ephesians 4:1-3
Philippians 1:3-6
2 Timothy 2:22-26
1 Peter 5:8-11

Guide to Bible Reading

Loosed from Depression
Psalm 34:6, 17, 18
Isaiah 61:1-3
Jeremiah 31:25
John 16:20-22
Philippians 4:8, 9
1 Peter 5:6, 7
Revelation 21:4

Loosed from Giving in to Temptation
Luke 22:31, 32
John 16:33
Romans 8:37
1 Corinthians 10:13
Ephesians 6:10-18
Hebrews 2:14-18
James 1:2, 3

Loosed from Marital Problems
Genesis 2:18, 21-25
Proverbs 10:12
Proverbs 31:10-31
1 Corinthians 7:2-5, 10, 11
Ephesians 5:22-28, 33
1 Peter 1:22
1 Peter 3:1, 2, 7

Loosed from Financial Stress
Psalm 34:9, 10
Malachi 3:10-12
Matthew 6:31-34
Luke 6:38
Romans 8:32
Philippians 4:19
3 John 2

Loosed to Find What God Wants
Psalm 32:8
Proverbs 3:5, 6; 16:3
Isaiah 42:16
John 16:13
1 Corinthians 2:16
James 1:5
1 John 5:20

Loosed to Forgive Others
Matthew 6:14, 15
Matthew 18:21-35
Mark 11:25, 26
Luke 6:37
Luke 17:3, 4
Ephesians 4:31, 32
Colossians 3:12, 13

Loosed to Grow in Faith
Luke 17:5, 6
Acts 16:25-31
Romans 10:8-10
Ephesians 2:8-10
Colossians 2:6, 7
1 Timothy 4:14-16
Hebrews 11:6

Loosed to Love
Leviticus 19:18
Deuteronomy 6:5
Matthew 5:43-48
John 13:34, 35
1 Corinthians 13
1 Peter 4:8
1 John 4:7-11

Loosed to Peace
Leviticus 26:6
Psalm 85:8, 9
Isaiah 26:3
John 14:27
Romans 15:13
Philippians 4:6, 7
2 Thessalonians 3:16

Loosed to Praise
2 Samuel 22:2-4
Psalm 34:1
Psalm 111
Psalm 150
Isaiah 25:1
Revelation 4:9-11
Revelation 5:8-14

Loosed to Pray
Psalm 86:1-7
Psalm 145:17-19
Jeremiah 33:3
Matthew 6:5-13
Matthew 18:19, 20
Romans 8:26
Hebrews 4:16

Loosed to Turn Back to God
2 Chronicles 7:14
Psalm 119:57-59
Isaiah 55:7
Acts 3:19
2 Corinthians 7:9
Ephesians 4:17-24
James 4:7-10

Loosed to Stand Strong
Psalm 31:23, 24
Isaiah 40:29-31
Zechariah 10:12
Ephesians 3:14-19
Ephesians 6:10-13
Colossians 2:6, 7
2 Peter 1:5-11

Loosed to Receive Eternal Life
John 3:16; 5:24; 10:27, 28
Romans 6:22, 23
Romans 10:9, 10
Titus 3:1-8
Hebrews 9:13-15
1 John 2:24, 25
1 John 5:11-13

Where to Find Her

Abigail
1 Sam. 25:2-44

Abigail (Daughter of Jesse)
1 Chr. 2:16

Abimelech's Killer
Judg. 9:22-54

Abishag
1 Kin. 1:2, 3, 15; 2:17, 21, 22

Abital
2 Sam. 3:4; 1 Chr. 3:3

Achsah
Josh. 15:16-19; Judg. 1:12-15;
1 Chr. 2:49

Ahinoam (wife of David)
1 Sam. 25:43

Ahinoam (wife of Saul)
1 Sam. 14:50

Anna
Luke 2:36-38

Apphia
Philem. 2

Athaliah
2 Kin. 8:26; 11:1, 13-20

Bathsheba
2 Sam. 11:3; 12:24; 1 Kin. 1:11-
31; 2:13, 18, 19

Bernice
Acts 25:13, 23

Bilhah
Gen. 29:29—30:7; 35:22, 25

Bithiah
1 Chr. 4:18

Candace
Acts 8:27

Chloe
1 Cor. 1:11

Claudia
2 Tim. 4:21

Cozbi
Num. 25:14, 15

Damaris
Acts 17:34

Daughter of Abraham
Luke 13:16

Daughter of Jerusalem
Song 3:5; Zeph. 3:14

Daughter of the King of the South
Dan. 11:6

Daughter of Meshullam
Neh. 6:18

Daughter of Pharaoh
Ex. 2:5, 6

Daughters of Philip
Acts 21:8, 9

Daughters of Shallum
Neh. 3:12

Daughters of Your People
Ezek. 13:17

Daughters of Zelophehad
Num. 26:23—27:7; 36:2, 6, 10,
11; Josh. 17:3; 1 Chr. 7:15

Deborah
Judg. 4:1—5:31

Delilah
Judg. 16:4-20

Diana
Acts 19:24, 27, 28, 34, 35

Dorcas
Acts 9:36-41

Drusilla
Acts 24:24

Eglah
2 Sam. 3:5; 1 Chr. 3:3

Elect Lady, The
2 John 1

Elizabeth
Luke 1:5-25, 39-45, 57-61

Esther
The Book of Esther

Eunice
2 Tim. 1:5

Euodia
Phil. 4:2

Leading Ladies

*T*he Bible is full of wonderful women! I have written and preached about many of them and have learned powerful lessons for my life from their lives. This "Leading Ladies" section is a sort of written portrait gallery of some of the key women in God's Word and in the history of our faith. The ten women on the following pages represent many of the trials and triumphs that women today can identify with and understand. In these articles, I have tried to offer pieces of hope for every woman who reads this book. You'll find something for older women, something for abused women, something for desperate women, something for women with health problems, and something for those who are broken and bitter.

I hope you'll gain strength and encouragement as you read about these women of God. I pray that you will see yourself as you wander through this gallery of leading ladies.

Naomi
Ruth 1-4

*S*ome women never find their reason for living until their latter years. Until she found her purpose, Naomi was a bitter woman. In fact, she said, "Do not call me Naomi [which means "my joy"]; call me Mara [which means "bitterness"]. I went out full, and the Lord has brought me home again empty" (see Ruth 1:20). When Naomi started out as a young wife, she had everything. But at the end, she had nothing.

She lost her husband and two sons, but she rediscovered her purpose and recycled her life. And look what happened! As she began to nurse her grandchild, Obed, and teach him her faith, she planted the seed of faith for future generations. Obed was the father of Jesse, and Jesse was the father of King David!

How could Naomi have known that Obed would be an ancestor of the Messiah? How could she have known that Ruth, the daughter-in-law who refused to leave her, was placed by God in the family tree of Jesus, His Son? How could this winter woman have known that her legacy would outlive her by thousands of years?

No doubt Naomi knew discouragement well. No doubt there were times she wanted to roll over and die. But if she had given in to the temptation to give up, she would have stopped short of God's restoration. She would have gone to her grave never knowing what blessing God was about to pour out for her. She would have died in bitterness without having tasted His joy.

My sister, the timing of the Lord defies human reason. To those of you whose dreams have been denied thus far in your life, hang on. To those whose past seems unredeemable, keep standing strong. To those for whom the future looks blank and empty, do not roll over and die. Stand against thoughts that whisper, "You're too old for this. God can't do anything else with you. You're all used up and all worn out." Whoever you are, whatever your situation, do not give up. Do not stop short of the Lord's plan for your life. You may be stuck in a rut today, but one touch of God in your life can bring unspeakable joy.

You may look like a little old lady to some people, but they just can't see your might. They don't know that little old ladies can move heaven and earth by the power of prayer. They don't know that some of God's toughest warriors are elderly women. They don't know that wrinkled hands can be lifted in powerful praise and feeble knees can march!

You are never too old for God. You are never too used up to be of service in His kingdom. A life's worth of lessons are yours. You have learned faith and practiced patience. You know how to listen. You have developed a friendship with God that can only exist because you have walked with Him day after day, year after year. You have stored the treasures of mercy and compassion in your heart and you possess the secrets of seasoned wisdom that only comes with time.

Like Naomi, perhaps the Lord has saved the best for last in your life. You must endure and not give in. God has more in store for you than you know. Life must go full-circle. God's plan must be worked out in God's time. Older women, you are jewels in the crown of heaven. You offer gifts that no one else can. Keep the light in your eyes and the fire in your hearts burning brightly. God isn't finished with you yet.

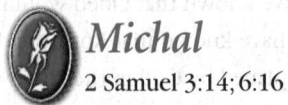

Michal
2 Samuel 3:14; 6:16

*V*ery few men would have been able to live with her. She was one of those women who can't get along with a man—any man.

She peers from the window of her palatial environment and looks with cold indifference down into the streets of the city to behold the man who is her husband. But she feels no connection with him. No bond. So it was with Michal and David. Two people living together but not joined together.

Michal is the sad seed of a callous father who failed to walk with God. Her eyes were dulled with the disillusionment that comes from having no model of godly marriage. Her relationship with her father had affected her perception of all men. His greed and ambition had taught her to be cynical rather than selfless, guarded rather than generous. And now her marriage yields only a harvest of bitterness and resentment. Planted firmly in the soil of her past, that root of bitterness now rises to haunt her and ruin her chances at happily-ever-after. In fact, she is so bitter that she resents her husband's happiness.

Almost any other woman would have been delighted to see the joy on her husband's face, the glide in his stride, the excitement in his eyes as he returns to her, wet with the precious anointing of an encounter with God. But Michal vividly reminds us that when a woman's heart is bitter, her eyes are blind.

Michal looks out the window, but she cannot see. She cannot see that God has given her another chance at peace and contentment. She cannot see that the man she married was in no way like the man she now beholds—that he has changed and that for the rest of her life, she can enjoy the fruit of that transformation. But she is blind, and the look she gives David is the mockery of a smile, a sneer.

It is a tragedy, but it is not all Michal's fault. Her father had failed her long before she failed David. Her father had planted that bitter root in sweet water that contaminated her perception and disrupted her peace. And now she cannot understand her husband.

I wish that all fathers knew how important it is to provide their daughters with the proper perception of masculinity. For long after the fathers are gone, the husbands will have to live with the fruit. Michal is fresh fruit gone bad, and she has left a bitter taste in David's mouth.

My sister, don't dampen your husband's desire to dance. If God has given him joy and peace, celebrate with him! If you want to be loved and adored, you must be able to celebrate his successes. If you fail to appreciate what God has given you, what you see coming *in* you may later see walking *out* because you haven't known how to receive the man God sent back home to you.

If you are one of those lonely, bitter wives, take heart, my sister. God is a God of new beginnings. If your past has limited you, shake it off before it destroys your future. And, start this day out new. The next time you see your anointed husband dancing toward you, clap your hands, open your doors, and tell him to come on in. It's time to celebrate!

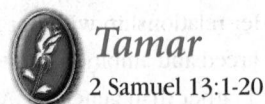

Tamar
2 Samuel 13:1-20

She lay among the soiled and wrinkled linen, the room in total disarray, her garments tattered and torn, her future changed forever. Her femininity had been crushed like a rosebud. Tears ran down her face like rain on a windowpane. She was weeping, not just because of her torn flesh, but because of her shattered trust. She had tried to help a man in need, and instead of receiving his gratitude, she had been brutally abused and assaulted.

She had entered into the relationship as his sister, but she had tried to be his friend. She was Tamar. Her brother Amnon was ill. He needed her, he said. You know how it is when a man needs you. Sometimes your maternal instincts take over, and reason goes out the window. Besides, Tamar thought she could cure her brother by caring for him. Little did she know that what ailed him could not be cured by any woman's gentle nurture.

While she stirred the soup and prepared to minister to him, he plotted her demise. Somewhere in the process of trying to help him, the tenor of the relationship changed. The tempo escalated, and before she knew what had happened, Amnon had raped her and left her bleeding and humiliated.

Be watchful, my sister. Be careful, because you may not realize the moment a relationship changes. It can happen in the blink of an eye, and you will wonder why you didn't see it coming.

Tamar wailed, but no one answered. She cried, but it seemed no one cared. She needed compassion and sympathy, but all she found was loneliness and despair. Bad enough that the one she had trusted had betrayed her. Worse still, that he had rejected her as well. "What you did at the end is worse than what you did in the beginning," she told him (see 2 Samuel 13:16). Who would have ever thought that something so innocent could have brought such evil results?

Just when it seemed she could not bear the shame and disgrace a moment longer, another man entered. It was Absalom. He lifted her from her crumpled state, wiped her hair from her face, kissed the tears from her eyes, and brought her into his house where she could recover.

Be wise, my sister. You may have the best of intentions, but I must tell you that good intentions may not prevent a broken heart. Still, every man is not like Amnon. And just because you were violated once doesn't mean you can't learn from your experience. It doesn't mean you can never be loved.

So take courage. If no man comes to assist you, pick yourself up and walk on. Walk right past the agony of the first man and listen for the knock of the second. It will come. The knock may not be delivered by a human hand, but it will come. It will be the knock of Jesus—your Bridegroom, coming for you, His beloved.

 ## Naaman's Little Maid
2 Kings 5:1-14

She's a common, ordinary woman—a very young woman at that. She works an insignificant job, going absolutely nowhere. But little does she know that she is a woman on a mission, placed there by God to represent Him and to speak His word boldly and without fear.

This little maid was on location for a moment that she could not have foreseen. She was not there merely to make the beds and clean the closets. From the beginning, God had orchestrated her life. All of her toil and troubles had prepared her. She may have considered herself poor and unworthy; her life, mediocre. But she was there by divine appointment—to be a witness in the house of a rich man. And one day made all the difference—the day she realized that she was there to deliver a life-changing message to a mighty man.

Can you imagine how she felt when those words leaped up in her heart? She had to have been a woman who could respond at a moment's notice. Tradition had taught her to be silent in the presence of a man. But there was a still, small voice inside her that challenged her to speak.

So she opened her mouth and cleared her throat and spoke deliverance to him. Her tender voice arrested her master's leprosy, and in that instant, she was the richest woman in the kingdom. For wealth is not determined by status or income. Her wealth was her wisdom, spoken under the inspiration of the Master Conductor of her life, far exceeding any earthly pay.

Just think of it—mighty men can be moved by little maids! Every woman must understand that she has a purpose for being in the place she's in. She may be a little maid, but she has a big message.

Many women will be world-shakers as they mother their children, nurture friendships, and encourage their men. They are the keepers of the flame and the guardians at the gate, and though they may never be famous, they will always be significant. Their contribution is too infinite to be calculated, their words too powerful to be recorded. They instill wisdom in their children, hope in the hearts of broken men, and terror in the heart of the enemy. It is their words of encouragement that ignite the flame of passion that produces kings and conquerors.

Now the world will see the Naamans and the presidents and the CEOs, but none of these would ever attain such heights if it were not for the little maids. The prophet Joel reminds us that in the last days, God will pour out His spirit upon His handmaidens (see Joel 2:29). There is an anointing for women to speak the right words at the right time and to turn their insignificant positions into mighty pulpits. They will be able to preach earth-shaking revivals in quiet rooms to one broken man who desperately needs to receive a word from God.

Take courage, my sister. Don't be intimidated by those around you. Don't allow subservient positions or poor wages to stifle your lips of praise. Be renewed in your mind. You are in the right place at the right time. God will use you as only He can. Listen carefully. The Master Conductor is about to give you your cue.

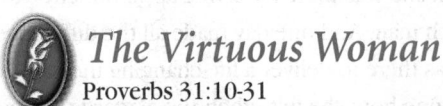

The Virtuous Woman
Proverbs 31:10-31

The writer of Proverbs tells us:"Charm is deceitful and beauty is passing, but a woman who fears the LORD, she shall be praised" (Proverbs 31:30). I am here to praise the Lord's excellent ladies. I am here to celebrate His women of virtue, His women of victory, His women of faith, His women of power.

Perhaps you are feeling left out just now. Maybe you do not feel like a lady of excellence. You may feel like a victim instead of a victor. You may feel like a woman of failure instead of a woman of faith. I am here to proclaim a new day to your life. I am here to remind you that our Heavenly Father calls you His beloved. He sees you robed in the righteousness of Christ Jesus. He sees that your sins have been paid for. He sings to you and dances over you as He quiets you with His love (see Zephaniah 3:17).

To those of you who think that excellence has escaped you, that virtue has vanished, it is time to change your mind. To those of you who are simply surviving, flipping the pages of your calendar without living your life, I say there is more. To those who are coasting comfortably through this present season, there is always room for improvement. Whatever your situation, I invite you to come. Join me for a journey through Proverbs 31 and see the kind of woman God has ordained you to be.

The Bible tells us that a virtuous woman is more precious than any jewel. As a jeweler admires, examines, and appreciates every facet of a diamond or a ruby, so the Lord looks at His daughters with the same sense of awe and wonder. When a son of God takes a virtuous woman as a wife, she is worth more to him than any treasure. The wealth of her spirit cannot be calculated and the riches within her cannot be counted. Her value is beyond appraisal both to her lover and to her Lord.

She is priceless to a man for many reasons, but most of all because "the heart of her husband safely trusts her" (Proverbs 31:11). Ladies, take it from a man. This is more important than you can imagine. You must be trustworthy and you must be safe. A man wants a resting place—a place where he can drop his guard and share his deepest hopes, fears, and dreams. You can be that place for him if you will keep his secrets and keep your mouth shut! A man will put up with almost anything when he knows he can safely trust a woman.

It is vital that you do him "good and not evil" all the days of your life. A man will not trust a malicious woman. If there is evil in your heart, it is time to be cleansed. Evil often results from unresolved hurt and bitterness that has become infected and left to fester in the human heart. Jesus is the Healer of hurts and He is able to turn even the hardest, most evil heart into a garden of love and grace. Look for ways to be good to your husband. Cook his favorite meal, refuse to nag, celebrate his gifts and talents, thank God for him—out loud. Encourage him in the hard places, talk less and listen longer . . . .

As we read on, we see that a virtuous woman is also a vigilant woman. She does not spend her days reading little romance novels on the couch, wishing for a storybook life. In fact, she does not engage in fantasy of any kind. She accepts the realities of her life and works hard. She is a cook, a home manager, a real estate buyer, an investor, a seamstress, a fitness buff! She's a fashion plate herself and makes sure that her family always looks sharp (see

Proverbs 31:21, 22). She is never lazy, but stays active in spirit, soul, and body.

The virtuous woman is a person of confidence and kindness. She "perceives that her merchandise is good," which tells me that this woman is not given to false humility, self-abasement, or the "you're no good, you're no good, you're no good" lie of the devil. Daughter of God, arrogance is ugly, but there are few things more attractive than a woman who knows exactly who God has made her to be, who can share her gifts unashamedly, and who can enjoy and celebrate who she is.

This woman is a giver. She cares for those around her who do not have as much as she does. She is aware of the needs of others and quick to respond. She knows that God is a generous God, the giver of every good and perfect gift (see James 1:17). She is eager to bless others as He has blessed her. In your quest to mature in Christ and to develop the character of a godly woman, do not neglect to cultivate generosity. Be assured, my sister, that selfishness will leave you lonely, so practice the ministry of sharing. A woman who has learned to live with an open hand and an open heart is a blessing to many.

In verse 23, the Bible speaks again of the virtuous woman's husband. It tells us that he "is known in the gates, when he sits among the elders of the land." I have sometimes wondered why the Scripture contains this one sentence about her husband in the middle of a lengthy description of the woman. I believe the writer knew a timeless secret that many people in our modern world seem to have forgotten: a woman can have tremendous impact on her man's success. She can inspire him like no one else. She is created to help him and encourage him and call forth his gifts. A former United States first lady was once asked, "What would you have done if you had married your high school sweetheart, who became a moderately successful farmer. You wouldn't have had the chance to be first lady." She replied, "Oh, of course I would have. That ol' farmer would have been the president of the United States." It is so true: Behind every good man, there is indeed a good woman.

The virtuous woman is decorated with strength and honor. By now you know that life is not for the fainthearted. To live well, you must develop strength spiritually, physically, mentally, and emotionally. But in your growing strong, be careful not to leave behind your femininity, your grace, your gentleness, and your tender heart. Strive for honor and integrity, remembering always that the truth makes you free (see John 8:32). You can lose a lot, but if you hold on to your honor, you will always be rich.

Stay cheerful and optimistic. That is what Proverbs 31:25 means when it says that this woman "shall rejoice in time to come." When you have placed your future in the hands of our loving Father, you can relax. His plan for your life is perfect, and so is His timing. Every person alive faces uncertainty in the days ahead. Look to those days and celebrate what God will do for you.

Speak with wisdom and kindness to everyone you meet, understanding that "death and life are in the power of the tongue" (Proverbs 18:21). A woman's words can be mighty, so choose them carefully. Speak health, speak victory, speak love, speak life.

I hope I have helped you, my sister, and set you on the course toward being the virtuous woman God wants you to be. I pray that your children will indeed "rise up and call [you] blessed" and that you will gain the praise of your husband (see Proverbs 31:28). Above all, I pray that you will grow in love and in the fear of the Lord. You shall be praised!

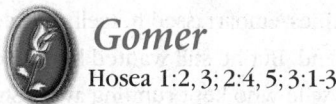

Gomer
Hosea 1:2, 3; 2:4, 5; 3:1-3

She had been around. And around. And around. And finally she had arrived. No one would believe how far she had traveled to become a respectable woman. Respectable, indeed. Who would have ever suspected that this woman who was now a wife and mother had once been a mistress of the night!

Only the Lord knew how far she had come. The Bible doesn't tell us what led to her indiscretion. For she was already in the sewers of sexual promiscuity when she stepped onto the pages of the text. Even *God* called her a harlot. This was no wild rumor bandied about by bored housewives who had nothing better to do. The Almighty Himself had labeled her.

Amazing, isn't it, that God can know you're a loose woman and still offer a candle to light your way from the darkness of the night into the brightness of the light.

And so this woman had begun her long, tempestuous journey—her movement from midnight to daylight. She moved with the slow and hesitant pace of a bride approaching her groom. Destiny was waiting for her. Since none of us are where we are without leaving where we were, she started the steps that were necessary for real transformation.

And what a long flight of steps. She left her ankle bracelets, her tingling bells, and her artifacts of prostitution along the way. She was snatched out of the arms of men who bought her like a piece of meat, into the arms of a Redeemer who procured her like a diamond in the rough.

How difficult it must have been for a woman who had been passed around to believe that someone could find her valuable and attractive.

People have a way of defining who we are by what we do. When God called her a harlot, He was speaking of her profession. But when He addresses her personally, He calls her Gomer, "Beloved." What a contradiction! Still, it lets us know that God calls those things that are not as though they are because He has the power to bring them into being.

Just about the time Gomer got to the top step and Hosea made her his wife, she reverted to her previous lifestyle. She slips out of the marital bed and slides into the night. She finds herself right back in the old rut, wondering if she'll ever be free of the mess she's in.

Now the Scriptures are quite candid about Gomer's sins. She made mistakes, ruined opportunities, embarrassed herself, disgraced her children, and disappointed her husband. But he still wanted her. He even searched the streets, looking for the wife who kept running away. She was his wife even when she didn't act like it. She was the mother of his children and perhaps someone else's children, but he wanted her. She had been molested and mauled by other men, but he still wanted her. So Hosea, whose name means "Salvation," kept calling her: "Gomer . . . my Beloved."

Other men might have seen her on the slave table, abused and battered, tattered and torn, her belly stretched from bearing children. She was no longer the glamour queen she had once been. They may have laughed and turned away.

But to Hosea, she was as lovely as a breeze singing from a mountain stream. And, standing afar off with tears in his eyes, he looked past the disheveled hair, the bruised skin, the lacerated flesh, the portly body, and he loved her. He could have said, "That woman has hurt me, humiliated me, failed me, even backslidden." He could have left her there on the auction block. Instead, he said, "I want her," and he emptied his pockets to redeem her. "Here," he said, "I will pay the price to buy her back."

Now perhaps you've been around the blocks a few times and made some mistakes and blown some chances, and the enemy has said to you that you are beyond repair. But God keeps calling you by your name and not your shame. Listen to Him. You must hear God call you by name until you are so filled with whose you are that you forget what you have done. He is saying, "Beloved, I want you. I've already paid the price to buy you back. Come home."

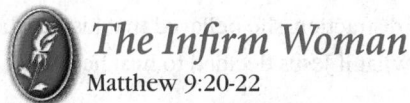

The Infirm Woman
Matthew 9:20-22

*T*he woman is ill. Every part of her is aching. Her pulse is weak. Her body, trembling. She tries desperately to hide her pain. She is a woman whose trauma has become so all-consuming that she stands alone in the midst of a crowd. Her problems are multiple, complex, and diverse. On one hand, she is impoverished. She has spent all she had on doctors. She is fresh out—out of finances, out of friends, and tragically, with her life's blood flowing out of her, almost out of time.

Even religion, as it were, has denied this woman's healing. The rabbinical laws had forbidden her to touch or be touched. What can a woman do when her mutiny is within? When she lives with a roommate of pain in a house of despair? What can she do when there's no friendly touch to serve as a sedative to ease her discomfort? When a woman is sick, her whole body wars against her.

Yet way down deep in the innermost part of her heart, a flickering flame defied the blowing wind of disease and refused to be extinguished. A passion to live refused to die. Oh, yes she was sick and broken and lonely, but she was a long way from dead. She knew it wasn't over. Her body didn't know it. Her finances didn't show it. Her family was gone. But she knew. Down in the chambers of her being, down in the basement of her feminine spirit whispered a hope that none could hear: If I may but touch the hem of His garment.

It is not what others say about her, nor even what is said to her that determines a woman's destiny—but what she says about herself. And although this woman's head was throbbing, her guts cramping, and she felt faint from an issue of blood, she kept whispering hope in the depths of her soul.

While death was stalking her, leering over her shoulder, it was the "if" that kept her alive. *"If* I may but touch. . . ."* No one dies as long as she's holding on to an "if." *If* I believe, there may be a change. *If* picked up that bleeding woman and caused her to press through the crowd, past the disdainful looks of prominent men. *If* gave her the courage to survive their stares and make her way toward the stranger called Jesus.

But when she got there, He wasn't even looking in her direction! What's a woman to do when she's in trouble and God is looking the other way? First of all, she refused to be discouraged. In spite of His distraction, she believed that just maybe she could still be made whole. What if Jesus decided to heal her? What if He changed her circumstances?

The waiting game was over. This was a woman who was taking charge of her life. No more standing around, hoping someone would get to her. She pressed through the crowd, defying the social dictates of her day that said it wasn't appropriate for a woman to touch a man—in fact, it was forbidden.

"If He won't touch me, then I'll touch Him," she decided. And before they knew it, she had slipped around the system, and climbed over the pain, and touched the hem of His garment.

Now it doesn't matter how you touch Him. And it doesn't matter where you touch Him. It only matters that you touch Him. The Scriptures say that we have not a High Priest who cannot be touched by the feeling of our infirmities. And on this particular day, Jesus knew He had been touched. Touched by a woman the law had declared unclean.

She touched Him. Without need for recognition, status, or fame. With no ulterior motive, no personal agenda. All she needed was relief from her terrible pain. She was not looking for approval. She was not worried about women's rights. She wasn't after a position on the board. All she sought was a position on her knees. And in response, His virtue came running down.

That virtue flowed down to her terrible secret and healed her. The Bible says that she knew within herself that she was healed. Isn't it amazing that her deliverance happened inside? Inside herself, she had whispered, "If I may but touch the hem of His garment." And in that same part of her inner self, she knew the instant she was healed.

But that's not the end of the story. Jesus asked, "Who touched me?" Now that woman could have kept quiet and never called attention to herself. She could have melted into the crowd, clutching her healing to herself. But she decided to go public. Perhaps, if she told her secret—her embarrassing secret—some other woman who was all bent over and bleeding could gather up the courage to let Jesus heal her.

Perhaps you are dealing with some issues that seem insurmountable. No matter how badly you are wounded, how sick, how lonely; no matter how many others have pushed past you on the way to the top, keep moving on toward Jesus, the Healer. And when He heals you, maybe you should go public and let the world know that an unclean woman—a woman without a dime in her pocket or a friend to her name—can touch a holy God. Let the world know you made it from disgrace to grace, carried to Him on whispers of hope.

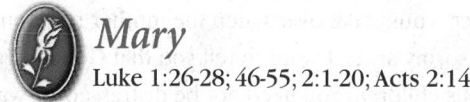 ## Mary
Luke 1:26-28; 46-55; 2:1-20; Acts 2:14

She stood at the foot of the Cross and gazed up at the oozing wounds of her baby. Those who stood with her saw a man—some, a teacher; some, a prophet. But she saw a child. She saw a baby wrapped in swaddling clothes. She saw the infant she had rocked to sleep night after night. She saw a little boy's first faltering steps. She had raised Him. She had loved Him. She had touched Him as only a mother can. And now she stands on Calvary's hill, giving Him up to His Father—the Father she has never seen.

What do you do when you outlive your child, and bury the one that you thought would bury you? Can you imagine standing by, hearing the clanging of steel against steel, the jeers and cheers of an angry crowd, the dull thud as the heavy timber drops home? Her arms are empty, her heart is aching, her mind, troubled as she watches Him writhe in agony, yet make not a single cry. He is both her Child and her Creator. He was the recipient of her milk and the Giver of her life. But as she stands at the foot of the Cross, she does not see a king, she sees a Child. And she gives Him back to His Father.

How do we say good-bye to love so young and tender? How do we dismiss a song in the middle of a stanza, a poem interrupted by prose? It didn't seem right. His life had stopped like a ballerina poised at the peak of a dance step. He had warned them it would happen. But He had promised to rise again.

She is Mary, the mother of Jesus. And yet she is every woman—black and white, red and brown, young and old. She possesses the wisdom that often takes years to attain. She has come to learn the art of losing what she loves and giving up what thought she owned. Her closest companions were her tears as she watched Him give His life away, one breath at a time.

There are no words of comfort to ease the pain of a

woman caught in such an impossible dilemma. Who can know her grief? What hands can wipe away her tears? What arms can hold her aching heart, or warm the icy chill of her fear? Only the Father. And so she trusted the Father that she couldn't see to care for the Child she could.

She never left Him. It was hard to stay, but impossible to go. It was painful to watch, but she would not turn her head. She went as far as her human feet could carry her, and looked as deep as earthly eyes can gaze. She had learned the art of loving at a distance and praying through silent lips that the Father would take over when the mother had done all she knew to do.

And so, my sister, I want to tell you that God is a Father who always takes care of His children. You need not be distressed, or walk in fear, wondering if the Father will provide. He may not always appear, but He will always provide. For those traumatic moments when everything that you love has been compromised, and all of your hopes have fallen short of reality, you must learn to stand and watch. You may even shed a tear, but you will know that you have given it back to the Father.

Many women have borne children. The women of the Scriptures prayed for children like a drought cries out for rain. But Mary stands far above all the others, for she is the only woman in the history of this world who ever carried inside her the same child twice. No wonder the Scriptures declare that she has been highly favored among women. Never before nor ever again has a woman had the privilege of bearing the same child more than once.

Mary has been His student and His teacher. She has watched Him grow from infancy to manhood. She has heard Him whisper prayers, and seen Him answer prayers. And now, when everyone else thinks He is gone, she is waiting for Him to come back!

She had been to the tomb, seen where they laid Him. She had heard the snickering of men who claimed He was a fraud. But none of the jeers of all the scoffers could rob her of what her heart knew about Him. She walked among His disciples and almost seemed out of place. But like all true women of faith, she refused to give up on what she believed. When she no longer could see her Son, she remembered Him. She loved Him, she cared for Him, and she went to the tomb where they laid Him. But she knew He would not stay there.

I think about the upper room on the day of Pentecost. What went through Mary's mind when the mighty wind began to blow? What did this mother think as she saw the fire fall? It must have been familiar when she heard the sound from heaven. Can you imagine her excitement as she stood among the 120 who were filled with His Spirit that day?

She was the only one who was not astounded by the fullness of His presence, for she had carried Him earlier. She would have recognized Him. She had felt Him leaping in her womb. As a young maiden, she had carried Him as a secret on the inside. And though time had passed, she would have known Him, for He had lived in her before. And when His Spirit came inside her, she would have been pregnant again—pregnant with promise.

On that day, they all praised and worshiped and exclaimed with exaltation. There was excitement in the city, for the very breath of Him had come again. For the first time ever, He lived inside many, where once, she had been His only home.

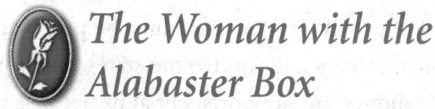

The Woman with the Alabaster Box
Luke 7:36-50

I can almost see her now. Gathering her shawl around her soft, smooth shoulders and walking quickly down the cobblestone streets of the city. She moved with the determination that is only seen in the gait of a lady who is on an important mission. She was on her way into an area where—according to the protocol of her culture—she would not be allowed. But who can think about tradition when an urgent unction commands a loving heart to move?

She bundled her shawl around herself, knowing better than to think it was the cool evening air that had caused the chill running down her spine. It was really the uncertainty that all of us feel when we know we are entering an environment where we are not invited and may not be well received. Yet, this woman was compelled to keep walking. Even if people rejected her and scoffed at her brazenness, she had to go.

She knew that the Stranger would be there. If she were ever going to tell Him what He had meant to her, she must do it now. Somehow she sensed that she was running out of opportunities. She almost found herself sprinting, racing to pick up her pace. She had to make it to the house in time. She did not know what she would say or how she would do it. And she didn't care.

True praise cannot be rehearsed. It is as spontaneous as the moment of inspiration that births it.

Adoration and adulation for Him compelled her to risk the taunts of the people around Him. She knew that they would not receive her warmly. But who were they to reject her because of who she used to be? How dare they whisper about her as if she were the only sinner in the room. Had they not also failed along the way? She was no different from them, but then again, she wasn't looking for them. If it meant passing through them to get to Him, she was willing to brave their stares—just to get close to the Stranger.

How easily we forget our own weaknesses when we start looking at someone else's. This woman's struggles had become the meal of the ravenous local gossips whose minds were filled with nothing but the memories of someone else's affairs. Though she knew that the Stranger had set her free, still she must have felt a bit intimidated as she drew nearer to the place where He was.

Isn't it strange that all of us who pursue God must be prepared to confront things? We must face our fears and survive the stares of our peers who either do not approve of who we are now, or sneer at us because of who we once were. If we are going to reach our goals in Christ, or in life, we must press through public opinion and intimidation. We must know that every step we take is moving us closer and closer to our destiny. The bitter taste of fear is neutralized by the sweet expectation of victory!

She was snatched away from her musings by the realization that her feet had taken her where her thoughts had already been. She was at the door of the Pharisee's house—the house where Jesus was. She stood at the door, her feet almost frozen to the floor. She felt paralyzed by the hesitation that always precedes the opening of a door that will unlock hidden destiny and change us forever. Her hand touched the door, and suddenly she knew that she was about to cross the threshold into her divine purpose. *I was compelled to come to this place,* she must have thought as she twisted the latch that unlocked her fate.

Before she could move away from the door, she stepped into the house, and found herself the object of a room full of unwelcome stares. She was the only woman in a seriously male-dominated environment. But sometimes maximizing a woman's potential requires her to walk into the presence of men, even when they would prefer that she stay outside. She had made it through the door and it was too late to constrain her with their traditions. She had come to see Jesus.

She entered a poorly lit room. Her nostrils caught the

scent of baked bread and fresh fish. It was obvious that the men had come for dinner. No one invited her to have a seat—much less a morsel of bread. But she had not come to see them, nor had she come to eat a fine meal. She had braved the evening air and bucked tradition with one thing on her mind. She had come to see Jesus.

No one even said hello as she walked into the room. She felt her blood throbbing through her veins. Her breathing was so shallow she could barely fill her lungs with air. She was tempted to run out of the house and retreat into the shadows of the night.

There is nothing quite as frightening for a "sinner woman" than to walk into a room full of self-righteous people. It would have been as scary for her as it would for a modern-day woman to walk through gunfire with no bullet-proof vest. As dangerous as it had been for her to travel alone in the darkness, that now seemed more inviting than the room. She might have walked back toward the door, but it was too late. She had seen Him.

O woman of God, when you see Jesus, all fear vanishes. Just one look into the warm eyes of a loving Savior can disarm everything life uses to assault our peace. Can you imagine Him in the room with you? Just knowing He is there clearly dispels any apprehensions you may have felt and leaves you in His wonderful presence. Though it sometimes happens in a public place, when we recognize the presence of God we are immediately alone with Him. And that is the most glorious place we can be.

There He was. The Master Himself. And He no longer seemed like a stranger. When she saw Him, all thoughts of sneers and jeers and whispers slipped from her mind like steam from a kettle. Her eyes locked on His. Something about Him commanded her attention. She had been in the company of many men. But none were like this Man. He was distinctly and remarkably different from anyone else. Everyone who had ever encountered Him had been changed forever. She was no different from the others. He had changed her life. He had spoken to her femininity. He had healed her self-esteem and altered her tragic path of failures and poor decisions. She had not come to ask anything of Him. She just wanted to say one thing to Him. She wanted to say thanks. But face to face, words failed her.

She tumbled to His feet. She had heard the men murmuring earlier—talking about her amongst themselves. But now her ears were filled with the roar of an inner excitement. The room was electrified by a power she could not even see. I can't help wondering how those who said they loved Him the most could stand with such indifference in the presence of such power. How could they make the foolish mistake of taking for granted the presence of an awesome God. They should have been lying at His feet, but they were too busy jockeying for earthly position. Herein is the greatest threat to those of us who have been Christians for a long time—our tendency to take for granted the presence of Christ. The Jesus we have become so accustomed to is the Jesus that others are striving so desperately to touch.

At the risk of being shunned and scoffed and mocked, the woman began to sob helplessly at His feet. True worship strips away pretense and reveals our naked need of the Lord. She lay at His feet and remembered where she had come from. She was so thankful to be with Him now. She had made many mistakes. She was an experienced woman. She now regretted so many of those experiences. She had stumbled and faltered through life, caught up in the storm of human error. In the midst of her tempestuous environment, He had saved her life from destruction. She had never known a love like this. In front of all of those men, she broke down and began to sob. It was the kind of sobbing that comes from a heart that had been through too much to talk about it. Every word escaped her, and her tears spoke what her lips could not say.

Each tear reminded her of another incident she had survived. It was as if everyone had left the room but this one woman and Jesus, her Lord. True praise is so intimate that even if someone else is in the room, His face is the only one we can see. And she began to lavish Him with praise—the kind of praise that only comes from someone who has been lavishly forgiven.

Her praise irritated the Pharisees. In fact, it even condemned them. Until she arrived, the atmosphere in the room had seemed quite normal. Business as usual. But when this woman began to thank Jesus from the depths of her heart, she unintentionally magnified their gross ingratitude. Their indignant stares would have been too much for her had she looked up. But this woman was literally lying on the floor. With trembling hands and tear-streaked face, she stretched forth her fingers and touched Him. It was as if lightning had bolted through her. She knew that one touch, that one intimate touch had changed her forever. She was alone with the Lover of her soul.

In that moment, a woman was able to give Jesus the praise that He always deserves but rarely receives. She knew what it was to be neglected and unappreciated. She knew what it was like to be surrounded by opportunistic and self-serving people who thrive on false intimacy. She wanted to protect Him from the pain of their betrayals and denials. She wanted to rock Him like a baby. She wanted to shield Him from any hurt that might await Him. She wanted to envelop Him with the same sense of safety He had given her; but all she could do was stroke Him gently and heave out the weeping sounds of adoration and exaltation that were born in the very core of her being. She had pressed her way through the dark night to be there. She was with Him and all was well for one solitary, stolen moment of history.

Oh, she had almost become so engrossed in the lavish love of the lonely Prince that she had forgotten to give Him His gift. It wasn't right to come before Him without a gift. He had done too much for her not give back to Him. She reached within the folds of fabric that made up her garments and found it where she had hidden it from the thieves of the night. Her alabaster box.

The box was worth the equivalent of one year's wages. When she pulled it from its hiding place, everyone in the room gasped. No doubt they thought she had come to hand it over. She had not.

The precious spikenard had been imported. It was very, very valuable. It would have brought an excellent price in the market had she put it on the table at the auction. But it was not for gain. It was for love. She raised the exquisite box designed to hold the exotic perfume and, as the men watched in disbelief, she broke it at His feet.

One of His disciples began to mutter angrily. He had wanted to sell it and pocket the money. But it was too late. The aroma of her praise had already begun to waft through the air. It drove back the smell of the dinner they were planning to eat.

This little sinner woman had taken over the place with her love. The fragrance filled the room until all of those around her could not help noticing it. They dropped their heads, one by one, as they realized how badly Jesus needed her ministry.

Dear lady, do you have any idea how badly the body of Christ needs *your* ministry? Your praise can make a difference in the entire atmosphere of a meeting. Men have a tendency to become engulfed with politics and position. We don't mean to, but many times we miss opportunities to be intimate with God. Sadly, we become so busy with His work that we fail to lie at His feet. When we do, it reminds us that we have failed to entertain Him and appreciate Him. As this woman lay at His feet, no man could deny that she had affected everything around them forever. And she had profoundly affected the Master. It was obvious to them, in that one act of kindness, that true praise is expensive. If you are going to have the kind of anointing that alters atmospheres, it comes at a great price.

They stood in awe as she bathed His feet with her precious ointment and tears. She untied her hair, which would have been socially improper in that day, but this wasn't about propriety. She *had* to bless him. She began to dry His feet—the ones that would soon be nailed to a tree—with her hair. This was the last gentle touch those feet would know. The next time, they would feel the rough hands of a Roman soldier forcing them together and drving a spike through them. Her tender caress was the closest thing He would ever know to a loving touch. She knelt at those feet and worshiped.

This woman effected massive change with her praise and her giving. She gave herself, her substance, and her time. She realized in the house of a Pharisee that true praise is not so much what you say; it is more aptly what you do. She is the official representative of every woman who has ever felt locked out of His presence by the traditions of men. She is the queen mother of every woman whose past sins should have kept her out of His presence, but ushered her in instead. She is the ambassador of every woman who praises under pressure and worships amidst criticism.

But the greatest legacy she leaves for women to understand is this: You have the ability to make a difference if you humble yourself under the mighty hand of God. You can make a difference if you give Him what you feel without regard for what other people think. We are not told what kind of sin this woman committed. It is enough for us to know that this kind of radical praise comes from a heart that is broken by the humility of failure and made whole by the honor of forgiveness. We can only speculate what this woman had done wrong, but there is one thing we know. Somewhere beneath the aroma of her expensive perfume, beyond her unbound hair, behind her praise, there was a story.

And so it is with all who love Him. We give Him public praise for the private things He's done for us. It is the secret things He has done that make us all weep at His feet. He said that whenever the gospel is preached, people would always remember this woman who traveled through the streets to thank Him for something neither of them ever told!

My sister, the Lord knows your secrets. He knows the secret desires of your heart and He knows the secret sins of your soul. May I tell you one more secret? Jesus is longing for you to sit at His feet and pour out your passion. He would love nothing more than for you to fall on your face and worship Him with the full force of a woman's emotion. Get your alabaster box. Round up that which is most precious to you. And break it before Him. Let the sweet perfume of your ministry fill the place where you are, and praise Him with extravagance.

Dorcas
Acts 9:36-41

*D*orcas had helped everybody but herself. She was the giving, caring kind of woman that the whole community sought out in times of crisis. She had built a reputation for being compassionate, resourceful, and generous. As is often the case with this type of person, she had given to others until she had broken herself down.

Have you ever given your courage to someone who was discouraged, then walked away discouraged yourself? Have you ever wondered when someone would come see about you? Yet the next time the need arises, you're the first one on the scene. If you are like Dorcas, you often find your-self helping others even when helping them is hurting you.

Now Dorcas was sick, and she died. Simply collapsed. Gave out. Her friends—the ones who had benefited from her kindness—gathered around, reminiscing about her loving and compassionate deeds. Thinking her life was over, they had laid Dorcas on a table and mourned her. They believed this was the end of her. It probably seemed to them that all her giving had been in vain.

But God never forgets a labor of love. My sister, God has not forgotten your ministry. You may help someone who rises up, walks away, and forgets to thank you for your sacrifice. But not God. He never forgets, and just when you need Him most, He will show up.

This time He sent Peter to show Dorcas's friends that God cares for care-ers, gives to givers, and loves lovers. When Peter came in, he sent everyone else out. All the spectators were removed, and Dorcas was left with the only One who could restore her.

You can't keep giving and be restored at the same time. Peter speaks to the women of our generation when he says that there comes a time when you must put all others out and allow God to refurbish you. Trees do not continue to bear fruit without rest. The ground will not continue to yield a harvest without replenishing the soil. And no matter how strong you are, there comes a time when everyone must leave you alone in the presence of the only One who can raise you up again. In the privacy of your prayer closet, allow Him to renew you and restore you. Ask Him to water the parched and barren places in you. The Scriptures say that Peter spoke a word to her: "Dorcas, arise."

I feel a resurrection coming to the distraught heart of empty women who have poured themselves out over and over. This is the time for you to arise. If you have become a martyr to your marriage, arise. If you have been a minister to your children, arise. If you are burned out, stressed out, laid out like Dorcas—cold and lifeless—arise! Expect God to show up and raise you up again. God is not through with you yet. He has a plan and a purpose for your life. And though you may be tired, weak, and weary, it is not over until God says it's over. My sister, put death on hold, and drive depression out, for the Word of the Lord comes to the woman who has given too much to everyone else. The Lord says, "Today is your day. Dorcas, arise!"

Old Testament

1 In the beginning God created the heavens and the earth. 2 The earth was without form, and void; and darkness *was*ª on the face of the deep. And the Spirit of God was hovering over the face of the waters.

3 Then God said, "Let there be light"; and there was light. 4 And God saw the light, that *it was* good; and God divided the light from the darkness. 5 God called the light Day, and the darkness He called Night. So the evening and the morning were the first day.

6 Then God said, "Let there be a firmament in the midst of the waters, and let it divide the waters from the waters." 7 Thus God made the firmament, and divided the waters which *were* under the firmament from the waters which *were* above the firmament; and it was so. 8 And God called the firmament Heaven. So the evening and the morning were the second day.

9 Then God said, "Let the waters under the heavens be gathered together into one place, and let the dry *land* appear"; and it was so. 10 And God called the dry *land* Earth, and the gathering together of the waters He called Seas. And God saw that *it was* good.

11 Then God said, "Let the earth bring forth grass, the herb *that* yields seed, *and* the fruit tree *that* yields fruit according to its kind, whose seed *is* in itself, on the earth"; and it was so. 12 And the earth brought forth grass, the herb *that* yields seed according to its kind, and the tree *that* yields fruit, whose seed *is* in itself according to its kind. And God saw that *it was* good. 13 So the evening and the morning were the third day.

14 Then God said, "Let there be lights in the firmament of the heavens to divide the day from the night; and let them be for signs and seasons, and for days and years; 15 and let them be for lights in the firmament of the heavens to give light on the earth"; and it was so. 16 Then God made two great lights:

the greater light to rule the day, and the lesser light to rule the night. *He made* the stars also. 17 God set them in the firmament of the heavens to give light on the earth, 18 and to rule over the day and over the night, and to divide the light from the darkness. And God saw that *it was* good. 19 So the evening and the morning were the fourth day.

20 Then God said, "Let the waters abound with an abundance of living creatures, and let birds fly above the earth across the face of the firmament of the heavens." 21 So God created great sea creatures and every living thing that moves, with which the waters abounded, according to their kind, and every winged bird according to its kind. And God saw that *it was* good. 22 And God blessed them, saying, "Be fruitful and multiply, and fill the waters in the seas, and let birds multiply on the earth." 23 So the evening and the morning were the fifth day.

24 Then God said, "Let the earth bring forth the living creature according to its kind: cattle and creeping thing and beast of the earth, *each* according to its kind"; and it was so. 25 And God made the beast of the earth according to its kind, cattle according to its kind, and everything that creeps on the earth according to its kind. And God saw that *it was* good.

26 Then God said, "Let Us make man in Our image, according to Our likeness; let them have dominion over the fish of the sea, over the birds of the air, and over the cattle, over allª the earth and over every creeping thing that creeps on the earth." 27 So God created man in His *own* image; in the image of God He created him; male and female He created them. 28 Then God blessed them, and God said to them, "Be fruitful and multiply; fill the earth and subdue it; have dominion over the fish of the sea, over the birds of the air, and over every living thing that moves on the earth." 29 And God said, "See, I have given

1:2 ªWords in italic type have been added for clarity. They are not found in the original Hebrew or Aramaic.   1:26 ªSyriac reads *all the wild animals of.*

*W*hen God restores you, He does so in a way that suddenly you are walking in the light and you can hardly recall how dark your life had been.

You Are Somebody

Genesis 1:27

G od looked out across eternity. He saw you. He saw everything He had created and everything He would create around you. He saw the specific need on this earth that He would make you to meet. He saw the full set of traits and abilities that you would need in order to complete His purpose for your life. He knew what kind of environment that would be necessary for you to properly develop the gifts He would give you.

God looked . . . and then He created. He created you. You! And God looked at you and said, "This is good."

Do you have the same opinion of yourself? Do you agree with God's opinion of you? It's important that you appreciate the way God created you because other people are going to treat you the way you treat yourself. They will respect you only to the degree that you respect yourself.

If you are attracting people who don't treat you well, I'm sorry but you are the prime suspect in that case. What kind of message are you sending that allows them to treat you poorly?

In order for people to treat you well, there must be something deep inside of you that sends out a signal saying, "I am somebody because God made me to be somebody. I may not be twenty-one and wear a size seven. I may be seventy-one and wear a size twenty-seven. But I am somebody." When you send out a signal like that, other people pick up on it.

There's something your spirit exudes that gives you presence with others. There's a quality of inner strength that makes you attractive. It causes other people to recognize you, to pay attention to you, to ask when you walk into a room, "Who is she?" They won't be asking because your dress is so stunning, but because your character is so magnetic. Projecting that kind of strength is not arrogance or pride. It is healthy self-esteem and the power of God's Spirit within you.

The way you appreciate yourself impacts everything you do. It affects the way you sit in a classroom, or apply for a job, or talk to people at a social function, or go about the ministry God has called you to undertake. It even affects the way you pray and the way you study God's Word. If you think that you are a nobody with no future and no value, you are going to pray with less power and suspect that the promises of God are for everybody else but you.

God wants you to appreciate who He made you to be and to develop what He gave you. He doesn't want you to try to exchange what He gave you for what He gave someone else. You are a unique blend of talents and giftings and character; and you have a unique destiny upon this earth. You are somebody!

you every herb *that* yields seed which *is* on the face of all the earth, and every tree whose fruit yields seed; to you it shall be for food. 30 Also, to every beast of the earth, to every bird of the air, and to everything that creeps on the earth, in which *there is* life, *I have given* every green herb for food"; and it was so. 31 Then God saw everything that He had made, and indeed *it was* very good. So the evening and the morning were the sixth day.

2 Thus the heavens and the earth, and all the host of them, were finished. 2 And on the seventh day God ended His work which He had done, and He rested on the seventh day from all His work which He had done. 3 Then God blessed the seventh day and sanctified it, because in it He rested from all His work which God had created and made.

4 This *is* the history*ᵃ* of the heavens and the earth when they were created, in the day that the LORD God made the earth and the heavens, 5 before any plant of the field was in the earth and before any herb of the field had grown. For the LORD God had not caused it to rain on the earth, and *there was* no man to till the ground; 6 but a mist went up from the earth and watered the whole face of the ground.

7 And the LORD God formed man *of* the dust of the ground, and breathed into his nostrils the breath of life; and man became a living being.

8 The LORD God planted a garden eastward in Eden, and there He put the man whom He had formed. 9 And out of the ground the LORD God made every tree grow that is pleasant to the sight and good for food. The tree of life *was* also in the midst of the garden, and the tree of the knowledge of good and evil.

10 Now a river went out of Eden to water the garden, and from there it parted and became four riverheads. 11 The name of the first *is* Pishon; it *is* the one which skirts the whole land of Havilah, where *there is* gold. 12 And the gold of that land *is* good. Bdellium and the onyx stone *are* there. 13 The name of the second river *is* Gihon; it *is* the one which

goes around the whole land of Cush. 14 The name of the third river *is* Hiddekel;*ᵃ* it *is* the one which goes toward the east of Assyria. The fourth river *is* the Euphrates.

15 Then the LORD God took the man and put him in the garden of Eden to tend and keep it. 16 And the LORD God commanded the man, saying, "Of every tree of the garden you may freely eat; 17 but of the tree of the knowledge of good and evil you shall not eat, for in the day that you eat of it you shall surely die."

18 And the LORD God said, "*It is* not good that man should be alone; I will make him a helper comparable to him." 19 Out of the ground the LORD God formed every beast of the field and every bird of the air, and brought *them* to Adam to see what he would call them. And whatever Adam called each living creature, that *was* its name. 20 So Adam gave names to all cattle, to the birds of the air, and to every beast of the field. But for Adam there was not found a helper comparable to him.

21 And the LORD God caused a deep sleep to fall on Adam, and he slept; and He took one of his ribs, and closed up the flesh in its place. 22 Then the rib which the LORD God had taken from man He made into a woman, and He brought her to the man.

23 And Adam said:

"This *is* now bone of my bones
And flesh of my flesh;
She shall be called Woman,
Because she was taken out of
Man."

24 Therefore a man shall leave his father and mother and be joined to his wife, and they shall become one flesh.

25 And they were both naked, the man and his wife, and were not ashamed.

3 Now the serpent was more cunning than any beast of the field which the LORD God had made. And he said to the woman, "Has God indeed said, 'You shall not eat of every tree of the garden'?"

2 And the woman said to the ser-

2:4 *ᵃ*Hebrew *toledoth*, literally *generations*   2:14 *ᵃ*Or *Tigris*

---

*W*hen you move into the fullness of your appointment with God's destiny for you, you won't think any more about those things in your past. You will be free. You will be loosed at last to do and be what it is that God has appointed you to do and to be!

Plug in to God's Power

Genesis 3:4, 5

Nearly every home in America is wired for electricity. Walls are covered with receptacles that deliver the electric current. In order to take advantage of the power, something must be plugged in to the receptacle. The receptacle is the female, and the plug is the male.

Like receptacles, women were made to be receivers. Men were made to be givers—physically, sexually, and emotionally.

The woman was fashioned out of the man to complete his purpose, to be a helpmeet. She helps him meet and accomplish his task. Take the power saw, for example. A power saw has great potential for cutting. However, it is ineffective until it is plugged in. The receptacle helps the power saw meet its purpose. Without the receptacle, the saw, though mighty, remains limited.

There is a certain vulnerability about being a receptacle. By nature, women are wide open; men are closed. You must be careful what you allow to plug in to you and draw strength from you. The wrong plugs can drain your power.

God recognizes your vulnerability; therefore, He has designed a plan whereby a man who plugs in to a woman sexually must have a covenant with her. God never intended for anyone to have casual sex. His design always included the commitment of a covenant. He planned for men and women who are joined together sexually to be committed for life. Nothing short of this commitment meets His standard.

God wants a woman to be covered like an outlet is covered, in order that no one tamper with her intended purpose. The married woman is covered by her husband. The single woman is covered by her chastity and morality. It is dangerous to be uncovered.

In Genesis 3, we see that Eve allowed herself to be uncovered by Satan, who plugged in to her desire to see, taste, and be wise. The enemy took advantage of her weakness. Be careful whom you let uncover you. The wrong person can lead you to complete destruction.

Be on your guard. There is a special conflict between women and the enemy. He is attracted to you because he knows that you were designed to help meet someone's purpose. If he can get you to help meet *his* purpose, you will belong to him and not to God.

If godly women do not learn how to start praying and doing effective spiritual warfare, they will never discern what is plugging in to them. Pray to be plugged in to the mighty power of God's Spirit. He alone can overcome the enemy's strategy to bring you down.

pent, "We may eat the fruit of the trees of the garden; 3 but of the fruit of the tree which *is* in the midst of the garden, God has said, 'You shall not eat it, nor shall you touch it, lest you die.'"

4 Then the serpent said to the woman, "You will not surely die. 5 For God knows that in the day you eat of it your eyes will be opened, and you will be like God, knowing good and evil."

6 So when the woman saw that the tree *was* good for food, that it *was* pleasant to the eyes, and a tree desirable to make *one* wise, she took of its fruit and ate. She also gave to her husband with her, and he ate. 7 Then the eyes of both of them were opened, and they knew that they *were* naked; and they sewed fig leaves together and made themselves coverings.

8 And they heard the sound of the LORD God walking in the garden in the cool of the day, and Adam and his wife hid themselves from the presence of the LORD God among the trees of the garden. 9 Then the LORD God called to Adam and said to him, "Where *are* you?"

10 So he said, "I heard Your voice in the garden, and I was afraid because I was naked; and I hid myself."

11 And He said, "Who told you that you *were* naked? Have you eaten from the tree of which I commanded you that you should not eat?"

12 Then the man said, "The woman whom You gave *to be* with me, she gave me of the tree, and I ate."

13 And the LORD God said to the woman, "What *is* this you have done?"

The woman said, "The serpent deceived me, and I ate."

14 So the LORD God said to the serpent:

"Because you have done this,
You *are* cursed more than all cattle,
And more than every beast of the field;
On your belly you shall go,
And you shall eat dust
All the days of your life.
15 And I will put enmity
Between you and the woman,
And between your seed and her Seed;

He shall bruise your head,
And you shall bruise His heel."

16 To the woman He said:

"I will greatly multiply your sorrow and your conception;
In pain you shall bring forth children;
Your desire *shall be* for your husband,
And he shall rule over you."

17 Then to Adam He said, "Because you have heeded the voice of your wife, and have eaten from the tree of which I commanded you, saying, 'You shall not eat of it':

"Cursed *is* the ground for your sake;
In toil you shall eat *of* it
All the days of your life.
18 Both thorns and thistles it shall bring forth for you,
And you shall eat the herb of the field.
19 In the sweat of your face you shall eat bread
Till you return to the ground,
For out of it you were taken;
For dust you *are,*
And to dust you shall return."

20 And Adam called his wife's name Eve, because she was the mother of all living. 21 Also for Adam and his wife the LORD God made tunics of skin, and clothed them. 22 Then the LORD God said, "Behold, the man has become like one of Us, to know good and evil. And now, lest he put out his hand and take also of the tree of life, and eat, and live forever"— 23 therefore the LORD God sent him out of the garden of Eden to till the ground from which he was taken. 24 So He drove out the man; and He placed cherubim at the east of the garden of Eden, and a flaming sword which turned every way, to guard the way to the tree of life.

4 Now Adam knew Eve his wife, and she conceived and bore Cain, and said, "I have acquired a man from the LORD." 2 Then she bore again, this time his brother Abel. Now Abel was a keeper of sheep, but Cain was a tiller of the ground.

*D*on't quit or give up. Give birth to that promise God has put in your life. Look for it to be born in you and to be a blessing.

Your Appointed Seed

Genesis 4:25

You have an appointment with God that has been set from the foundations of the earth, and that appointment isn't over until God says it's over. You may think that all of your good days are gone, but the very fact that you are alive says God wants you to be alive. He is not through with you yet. You have an appointment.

Even after all she had been through with Cain and Abel, Eve still had an appointment with God. In spite of everything she had experienced, all the heartache and hard times she had known, she had an appointed task. Eve said, "God has appointed another seed for me" (Genesis 4:25). Her appointment involved having another baby, another son.

When you make an appointment, you set a date and a time in the present for something that is going to happen in the future. And that's exactly what God has done in setting His appointment with you. God's destiny for you is preset. He has known all along that you would go through what you've been through to get to the place where you are right now. Even so, He still has an appointment with you. He has not canceled out. There's still something on His calendar that has your name on it.

The devil knows God has a plan for you. That's why he has worked so hard to wipe you out. He didn't want you to live long enough to receive all that God had in store for you. He knew there was more ahead. He knew it was good. He knew it had to do with life. That's why he tried so hard to deal you a deathblow early on. He sent trials, troubles, and tribulations to destroy you—and if you refused to be destroyed on the outside, he tried even harder to destroy you on the inside.

Start looking ahead. There's something coming up on God's calendar and it's got your name on it. There's something good just over the horizon of tomorrow—something good for your life, your marriage, your family, your work, your ministry. For everything you have loved and lost, God has another seed. For everything that has died or been stolen from you, God has another seed. For everything you can no longer hold, God has another seed.

Every time the devil tells you that you are going down, that you are going to die, that you are going to cave in, that there's nothing else for you, tell him, "You are a liar. There's got to be something else. I have an appointment with God. He has another seed for me to birth. He has another miracle for me to hold."

Where you are right now is not where you are going. If you are not on your deathbed, God still has an appointed task for you to finish. He has called you with an eternal purpose.

3 And in the process of time it came to pass that Cain brought an offering of the fruit of the ground to the LORD. 4 Abel also brought of the firstborn of his flock and of their fat. And the LORD respected Abel and his offering, 5 but He did not respect Cain and his offering. And Cain was very angry, and his countenance fell.

6 So the LORD said to Cain, "Why are you angry? And why has your countenance fallen? 7 If you do well, will you not be accepted? And if you do not do well, sin lies at the door. And its desire is for you, but you should rule over it."

8 Now Cain talked with Abel his brother;ᵃ and it came to pass, when they were in the field, that Cain rose up against Abel his brother and killed him.

9 Then the LORD said to Cain, "Where is Abel your brother?"

He said, "I do not know. Am I my brother's keeper?"

10 And He said, "What have you done? The voice of your brother's blood cries out to Me from the ground. 11 So now you are cursed from the earth, which has opened its mouth to receive your brother's blood from your hand. 12 When you till the ground, it shall no longer yield its strength to you. A fugitive and a vagabond you shall be on the earth."

13 And Cain said to the LORD, "My punishment is greater than I can bear! 14 Surely You have driven me out this day from the face of the ground; I shall be hidden from Your face; I shall be a fugitive and a vagabond on the earth, and it will happen that anyone who finds me will kill me."

15 And the LORD said to him, "Therefore,ᵃ whoever kills Cain, vengeance shall be taken on him sevenfold." And the LORD set a mark on Cain, lest anyone finding him should kill him.

16 Then Cain went out from the presence of the LORD and dwelt in the land of Nod on the east of Eden. 17 And Cain knew his wife, and she conceived and bore Enoch. And he built a city, and called the name of the city after the name of his son— Enoch. 18 To Enoch was born Irad;

and Irad begot Mehujael, and Mehujael begot Methushael, and Methushael begot Lamech.

19 Then Lamech took for himself two wives: the name of one was Adah, and the name of the second was Zillah. 20 And Adah bore Jabal. He was the father of those who dwell in tents and have livestock. 21 His brother's name was Jubal. He was the father of all those who play the harp and flute. 22 And as for Zillah, she also bore Tubal-Cain, an instructor of every craftsman in bronze and iron. And the sister of Tubal-Cain was Naamah.

23 Then Lamech said to his wives:

"Adah and Zillah, hear my
    voice;
Wives of Lamech, listen to my
    speech!
For I have killed a man for
    wounding me,
Even a young man for hurting
    me.
24   If Cain shall be avenged
    sevenfold,
Then Lamech seventy-
    sevenfold."

25 And Adam knew his wife again, and she bore a son and named him Seth, "For God has appointed another seed for me instead of Abel, whom Cain killed." 26 And as for Seth, to him also a son was born; and he named him Enosh.ᵃ Then men began to call on the name of the LORD.

5 This is the book of the genealogy of Adam. In the day that God created man, He made him in the likeness of God. 2 He created them male and female, and blessed them and called them Mankind in the day they were created. 3 And Adam lived one hundred and thirty years, and begot a son in his own likeness, after his image, and named him Seth. 4 After he begot Seth, the days of Adam were eight hundred years; and he had sons and daughters. 5 So all the days that Adam lived were nine hundred and thirty years; and he died.

6 Seth lived one hundred and five years, and begot Enosh. 7 After he

4:8 ᵃSamaritan Pentateuch, Septuagint, Syriac, and Vulgate add "Let us go out to the field."
4:15 ᵃFollowing Masoretic Text and Targum; Septuagint, Syriac, and Vulgate read Not so.
4:26 ᵃGreek Enos

God wants you to be alive. He is not through with you yet. Your appointment isn't over until God says it's over!

The Battle of the Sexes

Genesis 5:2

Many women are inflamed with the frustrations and the discontentment that come from their need to be affirmed by a man or a masculine image. Some have reached a point where they have become embittered by the lack of positive male examples. They throw themselves into careers, education, or some other demand in order to avoid the battle of the sexes. God never intended for it to be a battle. He intended for one to complement the other. But when complementing is deferred long enough, an irritation will develop. Eventually, the "un-complemented" people end up in a full-blown battle.

Thank God for Jesus! He medicates the things that frustrate, eventually eliminating the entire struggle in the hearts of those who trust in Him. His presence helps women and men alike to avoid obsessions and extremes that accompany disorders and dysfunctions. He is literally the balm that, if applied regularly and completely, can break the habits we all wrestle to control! He is balm for every woman and every man whose life has been injured by something they received. He provides even for those whose pain stems from the starving reminders of what they didn't receive. He is the bread of heaven, and if they take Him in, He will satisfy.

In addition to experiencing the wonders of the love of Jesus, women also need to understand how to love a man. They need to know that they can move a man more by smiling than by barking an order. They can melt his stern resolve with one gentle kiss. They can inspire him to perform simply by telling him how wonderful he is.

These basic realities are true with all men. That type of kindness is not challenging or threatening; any man responds well to positive reinforcement. Even God responds to praise! It is not manipulative to know this. It is manipulative only when you praise so that you can gain influence rather than praising from a sincere heart that appreciates the warm love of a giving God.

Men who love you will say no to you at one time or another. This includes a loving father, a loving husband, and your loving heavenly Father. The answer no to your question doesn't mean that you are rejected, just that your idea is.

This is invaluable in helping you deal with life. It is important that you have a point of reference for fatherhood. It takes the mystique away from masculinity. We are often intimidated by what we don't understand. That kind of intimidation can lead to the demise of an entire relationship. Lack of negotiation skills destroys the potential for long-range relationships. Even in your prayer life, you can better relate to your heavenly Father as you realize that a no to your request doesn't change His commitment to you or His affection for you. Understand these things, and you will make progress toward ceasing the battle of the sexes in your life.

begot Enosh, Seth lived eight hundred and seven years, and had sons and daughters. 8 So all the days of Seth were nine hundred and twelve years; and he died.

9 Enosh lived ninety years, and begot Cainan.ᵃ 10 After he begot Cainan, Enosh lived eight hundred and fifteen years, and had sons and daughters. 11 So all the days of Enosh were nine hundred and five years; and he died.

12 Cainan lived seventy years, and begot Mahalalel. 13 After he begot Mahalalel, Cainan lived eight hundred and forty years, and had sons and daughters. 14 So all the days of Cainan were nine hundred and ten years; and he died.

15 Mahalalel lived sixty-five years, and begot Jared. 16 After he begot Jared, Mahalalel lived eight hundred and thirty years, and had sons and daughters. 17 So all the days of Mahalalel were eight hundred and ninety-five years; and he died.

18 Jared lived one hundred and sixty-two years, and begot Enoch. 19 After he begot Enoch, Jared lived eight hundred years, and had sons and daughters. 20 So all the days of Jared were nine hundred and sixty-two years; and he died.

21 Enoch lived sixty-five years, and begot Methuselah. 22 After he begot Methuselah, Enoch walked with God three hundred years, and had sons and daughters. 23 So all the days of Enoch were three hundred and sixty-five years. 24 And Enoch walked with God; and he *was* not, for God took him.

25 Methuselah lived one hundred and eighty-seven years, and begot Lamech. 26 After he begot Lamech, Methuselah lived seven hundred and eighty-two years, and had sons and daughters. 27 So all the days of Methuselah were nine hundred and sixty-nine years; and he died.

28 Lamech lived one hundred and eighty-two years, and had a son. 29 And he called his name Noah, saying, "This *one* will comfort us concerning our work and the toil of our hands, because of the ground which the LORD has cursed." 30 After he begot Noah, Lamech lived five hundred and ninety-five years, and had sons

and daughters. 31 So all the days of Lamech were seven hundred and seventy-seven years; and he died.

32 And Noah was five hundred years old, and Noah begot Shem, Ham, and Japheth.

6 Now it came to pass, when men began to multiply on the face of the earth, and daughters were born to them, 2 that the sons of God saw the daughters of men, that they *were* beautiful; and they took wives for themselves of all whom they chose.

3 And the LORD said, "My Spirit shall not striveᵃ with man forever, for he *is* indeed flesh; yet his days shall be one hundred and twenty years."

4 There were giants on the earth in those days, and also afterward, when the sons of God came in to the daughters of men and they bore *children* to them. Those *were* the mighty men who *were* of old, men of renown.

5 Then the LORDᵃ saw that the wickedness of man *was* great in the earth, and *that* every intent of the thoughts of his heart *was* only evil continually. 6 And the LORD was sorry that He had made man on the earth, and He was grieved in His heart. 7 So the LORD said, "I will destroy man whom I have created from the face of the earth, both man and beast, creeping thing and birds of the air, for I am sorry that I have made them." 8 But Noah found grace in the eyes of the LORD.

9 This is the genealogy of Noah. Noah was a just man, perfect in his generations. Noah walked with God. 10 And Noah begot three sons: Shem, Ham, and Japheth.

11 The earth also was corrupt before God, and the earth was filled with violence. 12 So God looked upon the earth, and indeed it was corrupt; for all flesh had corrupted their way on the earth.

13 And God said to Noah, "The end of all flesh has come before Me, for the earth is filled with violence through them; and behold, I will destroy them with the earth. 14 Make yourself an ark of gopherwood; make rooms in the ark, and cover it inside and outside with pitch. 15 And this is how you shall make it: The length of the ark *shall be* three

5:9 ᵃHebrew *Qenan*   6:3 ᵃSeptuagint, Syriac, Targum, and Vulgate read *abide.*   6:5 ᵃFollowing Masoretic Text and Targum; Vulgate reads *God;* Septuagint reads LORD *God.*

*E*very child of God desperately needs a "Judas" to carry out certain aspects of divine providence in her life. Sometimes your friends can cause you the most pain, but through their betrayal, God's will can be executed.

hundred cubits, its width fifty cubits, and its height thirty cubits. 16 You shall make a window for the ark, and you shall finish it to a cubit from above; and set the door of the ark in its side. You shall make it *with* lower, second, and third *decks.* 17 And behold, I Myself am bringing floodwaters on the earth, to destroy from under heaven all flesh in which *is* the breath of life; everything that *is* on the earth shall die. 18 But I will establish My covenant with you; and you shall go into the ark—you, your sons, your wife, and your sons' wives with you. 19 And of every living thing of all flesh you shall bring two of every *sort* into the ark, to keep *them* alive with you; they shall be male and female. 20 Of the birds after their kind, of animals after their kind, and of every creeping thing of the earth after its kind, two of every *kind* will come to you to keep *them* alive. 21 And you shall take for yourself of all food that is eaten, and you shall gather *it* to yourself; and it shall be food for you and for them." 22 Thus Noah did; according to all that God commanded him, so he did.

7 Then the LORD said to Noah, "Come into the ark, you and all your household, because I have seen *that* you *are* righteous before Me in this generation. 2 You shall take with you seven each of every clean animal, a male and his female; two each of animals that *are* unclean, a male and his female; 3 also seven each of birds of the air, male and female, to keep the species alive on the face of all the earth. 4 For after seven more days I will cause it to rain on the earth forty days and forty nights, and I will destroy from the face of the earth all living things that I have made." 5 And Noah did according to all that the LORD commanded him. 6 Noah *was* six hundred years old when the floodwaters were on the earth.

7 So Noah, with his sons, his wife, and his sons' wives, went into the ark because of the waters of the flood. 8 Of clean animals, of animals that *are* unclean, of birds, and of everything that creeps on the earth, 9 two by two they went into the ark to Noah, male and female, as God had commanded Noah. 10 And it came to pass after seven days that the waters of the flood were on the earth. 11 In the six hundredth year of Noah's life, in the second month, the seventeenth day of the month, on that day all the fountains of the great deep were broken up, and the windows of heaven were opened. 12 And the rain was on the earth forty days and forty nights.

13 On the very same day Noah and Noah's sons, Shem, Ham, and Japheth, and Noah's wife and the three wives of his sons with them, entered the ark— 14 they and every beast after its kind, all cattle after their kind, every creeping thing that creeps on the earth after its kind, and every bird after its kind, every bird of every sort. 15 And they went into the ark to Noah, two by two, of all flesh in which *is* the breath of life. 16 So those that entered, male and female of all flesh, went in as God had commanded him; and the LORD shut him in.

17 Now the flood was on the earth forty days. The waters increased and lifted up the ark, and it rose high above the earth. 18 The waters prevailed and greatly increased on the earth, and the ark moved about on the surface of the waters. 19 And the waters prevailed exceedingly on the earth, and all the high hills under the whole heaven were covered. 20 The waters prevailed fifteen cubits upward, and the mountains were covered. 21 And all flesh died that moved on the earth: birds and cattle and beasts and every creeping thing that creeps on the earth, and every man. 22 All in whose nostrils *was* the breath of the spirit[a] of life, all that *was* on the dry *land,* died. 23 So He destroyed all living things which were on the face of the ground: both man and cattle, creeping thing and bird of the air. They were destroyed from the earth. Only Noah and those who *were* with him in the ark remained *alive.* 24 And the waters prevailed on the earth one hundred and fifty days.

8 Then God remembered Noah, and every living thing, and all the animals that *were* with him in the ark. And God made a wind to pass over

7:22 aSeptuagint and Vulgate omit *of the spirit.*

Gospel Pearls

the earth, and the waters subsided. 2 The fountains of the deep and the windows of heaven were also stopped, and the rain from heaven was restrained. 3 And the waters receded continually from the earth. At the end of the hundred and fifty days the waters decreased. 4 Then the ark rested in the seventh month, the seventeenth day of the month, on the mountains of Ararat. 5 And the waters decreased continually until the tenth month. In the tenth *month,* on the first *day* of the month, the tops of the mountains were seen.

6 So it came to pass, at the end of forty days, that Noah opened the window of the ark which he had made. 7 Then he sent out a raven, which kept going to and fro until the waters had dried up from the earth. 8 He also sent out from himself a dove, to see if the waters had receded from the face of the ground. 9 But the dove found no resting place for the sole of her foot, and she returned into the ark to him, for the waters *were* on the face of the whole earth. So he put out his hand and took her, and drew her into the ark to himself. 10 And he waited yet another seven days, and again he sent the dove out from the ark. 11 Then the dove came to him in the evening, and behold, a freshly plucked olive leaf *was* in her mouth; and Noah knew that the waters had receded from the earth. 12 So he waited yet another seven days and sent out the dove, which did not return again to him anymore.

13 And it came to pass in the six hundred and first year, in the first *month,* the first *day* of the month, that the waters were dried up from the earth; and Noah removed the covering of the ark and looked, and indeed the surface of the ground was dry. 14 And in the second month, on the twenty-seventh day of the month, the earth was dried.

15 Then God spoke to Noah, saying, 16 "Go out of the ark, you and your wife, and your sons and your sons' wives with you. 17 Bring out with you every living thing of all flesh that *is* with you: birds and cattle and every creeping thing that creeps on the earth, so that they may abound on the earth, and be fruitful and multiply on the earth." 18 So Noah went out, and his sons and his wife and his sons' wives with him. 19 Every animal, every creeping thing, every bird, *and* whatever creeps on the earth, according to their families, went out of the ark.

20 Then Noah built an altar to the LORD, and took of every clean animal and of every clean bird, and offered burnt offerings on the altar. 21 And the LORD smelled a soothing aroma. Then the LORD said in His heart, "I will never again curse the ground for man's sake, although the imagination of man's heart *is* evil from his youth; nor will I again destroy every living thing as I have done.

22 "While the earth remains,
Seedtime and harvest,
Cold and heat,
Winter and summer,
And day and night
Shall not cease."

9 So God blessed Noah and his sons, and said to them: "Be fruitful and multiply, and fill the earth.*ᵃ* 2 And the fear of you and the dread of you shall be on every beast of the earth, on every bird of the air, on all that move *on* the earth, and on all the fish of the sea. They are given into your hand. 3 Every moving thing that lives shall be food for you. I have given you all things, even as the green herbs. 4 But you shall not eat flesh with its life, *that is,* its blood. 5 Surely for your lifeblood I will demand *a reckoning;* from the hand of every beast I will require it, and from the hand of man. From the hand of every man's brother I will require the life of man.

6 "Whoever sheds man's blood,
By man his blood shall be shed;
For in the image of God
He made man.
7 And as for you, be fruitful and multiply;
Bring forth abundantly in the earth
And multiply in it."

8 Then God spoke to Noah and to his sons with him, saying: 9 "And as for Me, behold, I establish My covenant with you and with your descen-

9:1 ᵃCompare Genesis 1:28

*I*t is time for you to say to yourself and the world as a whole, "It's my time to conceive. It's time for the treasure God put inside me to come up. It's time for me to be *loosed* to do what God created me to do."

dants[a] after you, 10 and with every living creature that *is* with you: the birds, the cattle, and every beast of the earth with you, of all that go out of the ark, every beast of the earth. 11 Thus I establish My covenant with you: Never again shall all flesh be cut off by the waters of the flood; never again shall there be a flood to destroy the earth."

12 And God said: "This *is* the sign of the covenant which I make between Me and you, and every living creature that *is* with you, for perpetual generations: 13 I set My rainbow in the cloud, and it shall be for the sign of the covenant between Me and the earth. 14 It shall be, when I bring a cloud over the earth, that the rainbow shall be seen in the cloud; 15 and I will remember My covenant which *is* between Me and you and every living creature of all flesh; the waters shall never again become a flood to destroy all flesh. 16 The rainbow shall be in the cloud, and I will look on it to remember the everlasting covenant between God and every living creature of all flesh that *is* on the earth." 17 And God said to Noah, "This *is* the sign of the covenant which I have established between Me and all flesh that *is* on the earth."

18 Now the sons of Noah who went out of the ark were Shem, Ham, and Japheth. And Ham *was* the father of Canaan. 19 These three *were* the sons of Noah, and from these the whole earth was populated.

20 And Noah began *to be* a farmer, and he planted a vineyard. 21 Then he drank of the wine and was drunk, and became uncovered in his tent. 22 And Ham, the father of Canaan, saw the nakedness of his father, and told his two brothers outside. 23 But Shem and Japheth took a garment, laid *it* on both their shoulders, and went backward and covered the nakedness of their father. Their faces *were* turned away, and they did not see their father's nakedness.

24 So Noah awoke from his wine, and knew what his younger son had done to him. 25 Then he said:

"Cursed *be* Canaan;
A servant of servants
He shall be to his brethren."

26 And he said:

"Blessed *be* the LORD,
The God of Shem,
And may Canaan be his
servant.
27 May God enlarge Japheth,
And may he dwell in the tents
of Shem;
And may Canaan be his
servant."

28 And Noah lived after the flood three hundred and fifty years. 29 So all the days of Noah were nine hundred and fifty years; and he died.

10 Now this *is* the genealogy of the sons of Noah: Shem, Ham, and Japheth. And sons were born to them after the flood.

2 The sons of Japheth *were* Gomer, Magog, Madai, Javan, Tubal, Meshech, and Tiras. 3 The sons of Gomer *were* Ashkenaz, Riphath,[a] and Togarmah. 4 The sons of Javan *were* Elishah, Tarshish, Kittim, and Dodanim.[a] 5 From these the coastland *peoples* of the Gentiles were separated into their lands, everyone according to his language, according to their families, into their nations.

6 The sons of Ham *were* Cush, Mizraim, Put,[a] and Canaan. 7 The sons of Cush *were* Seba, Havilah, Sabtah, Raamah, and Sabtechah; and the sons of Raamah *were* Sheba and Dedan.

8 Cush begot Nimrod; he began to be a mighty one on the earth. 9 He was a mighty hunter before the LORD; therefore it is said, "Like Nimrod the mighty hunter before the LORD." 10 And the beginning of his kingdom was Babel, Erech, Accad, and Calneh, in the land of Shinar. 11 From that land he went to Assyria and built Nineveh, Rehoboth Ir, Calah, 12 and Resen between Nineveh and Calah (that *is* the principal city).

13 Mizraim begot Ludim, Anamim, Lehabim, Naphtuhim, 14 Pathrusim, and Casluhim (from whom came the Philistines and Caphtorim).

15 Canaan begot Sidon his firstborn, and Heth; 16 the Jebusite, the Amorite, and the Girgashite; 17 the Hivite, the Arkite, and the Si-

9:9 [a]Literally *seed*   10:3 [a]Spelled *Diphath* in 1 Chronicles 1:6   10:4 [a]Spelled *Rodanim* in Samaritan Pentateuch and 1 Chronicles 1:7   10:6 [a]Or *Phut*

Gospel Pearls

nite; 18 the Arvadite, the Zemarite, and the Hamathite. Afterward the families of the Canaanites were dispersed. 19 And the border of the Canaanites was from Sidon as you go toward Gerar, as far as Gaza; then as you go toward Sodom, Gomorrah, Admah, and Zeboiim, as far as Lasha. 20 These *were* the sons of Ham, according to their families, according to their languages, in their lands *and* in their nations.

21 And *children* were born also to Shem, the father of all the children of Eber, the brother of Japheth the elder. 22 The sons of Shem *were* Elam, Asshur, Arphaxad, Lud, and Aram. 23 The sons of Aram *were* Uz, Hul, Gether, and Mash.ᵃ 24 Arphaxad begot Salah,ᵃ and Salah begot Eber. 25 To Eber were born two sons: the name of one *was* Peleg, for in his days the earth was divided; and his brother's name *was* Joktan. 26 Joktan begot Almodad, Sheleph, Hazarmaveth, Jerah, 27 Hadoram, Uzal, Diklah, 28 Obal,ᵃ Abimael, Sheba, 29 Ophir, Havilah, and Jobab. All these *were* the sons of Joktan. 30 And their dwelling place was from Mesha as you go toward Sephar, the mountain of the east. 31 These *were* the sons of Shem, according to their families, according to their languages, in their lands, according to their nations.

32 These *were* the families of the sons of Noah, according to their generations, in their nations; and from these the nations were divided on the earth after the flood.

11 Now the whole earth had one language and one speech. 2 And it came to pass, as they journeyed from the east, that they found a plain in the land of Shinar, and they dwelt there. 3 Then they said to one another, "Come, let us make bricks and bake *them* thoroughly." They had brick for stone, and they had asphalt for mortar. 4 And they said, "Come, let us build ourselves a city, and a tower whose top *is* in the heavens; let us make a name for ourselves, lest we be scattered abroad over the face of the whole earth." 5 But the LORD came down to see

the city and the tower which the sons of men had built. 6 And the LORD said, "Indeed the people *are* one and they all have one language, and this is what they begin to do; now nothing that they propose to do will be withheld from them. 7 Come, let Us go down and there confuse their language, that they may not understand one another's speech." 8 So the LORD scattered them abroad from there over the face of all the earth, and they ceased building the city. 9 Therefore its name is called Babel, because there the LORD confused the language of all the earth; and from there the LORD scattered them abroad over the face of all the earth.

10 This *is* the genealogy of Shem: Shem *was* one hundred years old, and begot Arphaxad two years after the flood. 11 After he begot Arphaxad, Shem lived five hundred years, and begot sons and daughters.

12 Arphaxad lived thirty-five years, and begot Salah. 13 After he begot Salah, Arphaxad lived four hundred and three years, and begot sons and daughters.

14 Salah lived thirty years, and begot Eber. 15 After he begot Eber, Salah lived four hundred and three years, and begot sons and daughters.

16 Eber lived thirty-four years, and begot Peleg. 17 After he begot Peleg, Eber lived four hundred and thirty years, and begot sons and daughters.

18 Peleg lived thirty years, and begot Reu. 19 After he begot Reu, Peleg lived two hundred and nine years, and begot sons and daughters.

20 Reu lived thirty-two years, and begot Serug. 21 After he begot Serug, Reu lived two hundred and seven years, and begot sons and daughters.

22 Serug lived thirty years, and begot Nahor. 23 After he begot Nahor, Serug lived two hundred years, and begot sons and daughters.

24 Nahor lived twenty-nine years, and begot Terah. 25 After he begot Terah, Nahor lived one hundred and nineteen years, and begot sons and daughters.

26 Now Terah lived seventy years, and begot Abram, Nahor, and Haran. 27 This *is* the genealogy of Terah: Terah begot Abram, Nahor, and

10:23 ᵃCalled *Meshech* in Septuagint and 1 Chronicles 1:17   10:24 ᵃFollowing Masoretic Text, Vulgate, and Targum; Septuagint reads *Arphaxad begot Cainan, and Cainan begot Salah* (compare Luke 3:35,36).   10:28 ᵃSpelled *Ebal* in 1 Chronicles 1:22

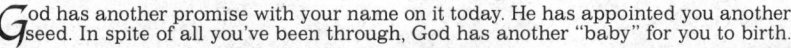
God has another promise with your name on it today. He has appointed you another seed. In spite of all you've been through, God has another "baby" for you to birth.

Speaking His Language

Genesis 11:7

Have you ever noticed that men and women sometimes seem to be speaking different languages? Women tend to be verbal while men tend to be physical. Women want to talk about everything; men don't always use words. Even male-to-male, men often communicate through touch. A pat on the back means "I like you." A coach's playful slap on a basketball player's rump says, "Good job!"

Men and women need to learn each other's method of communication. Whenever I feel affectionate, the first thing I want to do is buy my wife a gift. After we got married, I was shocked to find that although she enjoyed my gifts, she would go into orbit over cards! She keeps cards that are so old they've turned yellow. We spent the first few years of our marriage learning each other's language.

Instead of feeling neglected, ask your husband to share with you why he does what he does and says what he says. Or better still, observe his method of communication and teach him yours. Your spouse may think he's telling you one thing when you're hearing another. He may wonder, "What more does she want? I married her, didn't I? I did this and that and the other for her."

You may be living in the Tower of Babel. That was the place where families were divided because they could not understand each other's language. You'd better get busy and learn before frustration turns your household into Babel—babble! At Babel, all progress ceased and confusion took over.

When you approach your husband, do not corner him. Catch him at a time when he won't feel interrogated. You may be surprised that men tend to avoid open confrontation. I have seen big, burly, macho men intimidated by a hundred-pound woman. Even men who are physically abusive still have moments of anxiety when facing their wives. As the Bible says, "It is better to dwell in a corner of a housetop, than in a house shared with a contentious woman" (Proverbs 25:24). Unless you are deliberately trying to drive him away, remember that you could win the argument and lose the man.

Faith calls those things that are not as though they were (see Romans 4:17). Everything you were going to do for him when he changes, do it now and do it by faith. Then God will turn your Tower of Babel into a Pentecost. At Pentecost, each person heard the message in his own language (see Acts 2:6). I pray that God would interpret the language of your love so that your marriage will be powerful and productive.

Haran. Haran begot Lot. 28 And Haran died before his father Terah in his native land, in Ur of the Chaldeans. 29 Then Abram and Nahor took wives: the name of Abram's wife *was* Sarai, and the name of Nahor's wife, Milcah, the daughter of Haran the father of Milcah and the father of Iscah. 30 But Sarai was barren; she had no child.

31 And Terah took his son Abram and his grandson Lot, the son of Haran, and his daughter-in-law Sarai, his son Abram's wife, and they went out with them from Ur of the Chaldeans to go to the land of Canaan; and they came to Haran and dwelt there. 32 So the days of Terah were two hundred and five years, and Terah died in Haran.

12 Now the LORD had said to Abram:

"Get out of your country,
From your family
And from your father's house,
To a land that I will show you.
2 I will make you a great nation;
I will bless you
And make your name great;
And you shall be a blessing.
3 I will bless those who bless you,
And I will curse him who
curses you;
And in you all the families of
the earth shall be blessed."

4 So Abram departed as the LORD had spoken to him, and Lot went with him. And Abram *was* seventy-five years old when he departed from Haran. 5 Then Abram took Sarai his wife and Lot his brother's son, and all their possessions that they had gathered, and the people whom they had acquired in Haran, and they departed to go to the land of Canaan. So they came to the land of Canaan. 6 Abram passed through the land to the place of Shechem, as far as the terebinth tree of Moreh.*a* And the Canaanites *were* then in the land. 7 Then the LORD appeared to Abram and said, "To your descendants I will give this land." And there he built an altar to the LORD, who had appeared to him. 8 And he moved from there to the mountain east of Bethel, and he pitched his tent *with*

Bethel on the west and Ai on the east; there he built an altar to the LORD and called on the name of the LORD. 9 So Abram journeyed, going on still toward the South.*a*

10 Now there was a famine in the land, and Abram went down to Egypt to dwell there, for the famine *was* severe in the land. 11 And it came to pass, when he was close to entering Egypt, that he said to Sarai his wife, "Indeed I know that you *are* a woman of beautiful countenance. 12 Therefore it will happen, when the Egyptians see you, that they will say, 'This *is* his wife'; and they will kill me, but they will let you live. 13 Please say you *are* my sister, that it may be well with me for your sake, and that I*a* may live because of you."

14 So it was, when Abram came into Egypt, that the Egyptians saw the woman, that she *was* very beautiful. 15 The princes of Pharaoh also saw her and commended her to Pharaoh. And the woman was taken to Pharaoh's house. 16 He treated Abram well for her sake. He had sheep, oxen, male donkeys, male and female servants, female donkeys, and camels.

17 But the LORD plagued Pharaoh and his house with great plagues because of Sarai, Abram's wife. 18 And Pharaoh called Abram and said, "What *is* this you have done to me? Why did you not tell me that she *was* your wife? 19 Why did you say, 'She *is* my sister'? I might have taken her as my wife. Now therefore, here is your wife; take *her* and go your way." 20 So Pharaoh commanded *his* men concerning him; and they sent him away, with his wife and all that he had.

13 Then Abram went up from Egypt, he and his wife and all that he had, and Lot with him, to the South.*a* 2 Abram *was* very rich in livestock, in silver, and in gold. 3 And he went on his journey from the South as far as Bethel, to the place where his tent had been at the beginning, between Bethel and Ai, 4 to the place of the altar which he had made there at first. And there Abram called on the name of the LORD.

5 Lot also, who went with Abram,

12:6 *a*Hebrew *Alon Moreh*   12:9 *a*Hebrew *Negev*   12:13 *a*Literally *my soul*   13:1 *a*Hebrew *Negev*

---

*T*he treasure in you is filled with possibilities and potentialities. Your treasure is a blessing just waiting to be born. When you give birth to the treasure that God has put in you, your entire life is going to be changed.

had flocks and herds and tents. 6 Now the land was not able to support them, that they might dwell together, for their possessions were so great that they could not dwell together. 7 And there was strife between the herdsmen of Abram's livestock and the herdsmen of Lot's livestock. The Canaanites and the Perizzites then dwelt in the land.

8 So Abram said to Lot, "Please let there be no strife between you and me, and between my herdsmen and your herdsmen; for we *are* brethren. 9 *Is* not the whole land before you? Please separate from me. If *you take* the left, then I will go to the right; or, if *you go* to the right, then I will go to the left."

10 And Lot lifted his eyes and saw all the plain of Jordan, that it *was* well watered everywhere (before the LORD destroyed Sodom and Gomorrah) like the garden of the LORD, like the land of Egypt as you go toward Zoar. 11 Then Lot chose for himself all the plain of Jordan, and Lot journeyed east. And they separated from each other. 12 Abram dwelt in the land of Canaan, and Lot dwelt in the cities of the plain and pitched *his* tent even as far as Sodom. 13 But the men of Sodom *were* exceedingly wicked and sinful against the LORD.

14 And the LORD said to Abram, after Lot had separated from him: "Lift your eyes now and look from the place where you are—northward, southward, eastward, and westward; 15 for all the land which you see I give to you and your descendants*a* forever. 16 And I will make your descendants as the dust of the earth; so that if a man could number the dust of the earth, *then* your descendants also could be numbered. 17 Arise, walk in the land through its length and its width, for I give it to you."

18 Then Abram moved *his* tent, and went and dwelt by the terebinth trees of Mamre,*a* which *are* in Hebron, and built an altar there to the LORD.

14 And it came to pass in the days of Amraphel king of Shinar, Arioch king of Ellasar, Chedorlaomer king of Elam, and Tidal king of nations,*a* 2 *that* they made war with Bera king of Sodom, Birsha king of Gomorrah, Shinab king of Admah, Shemeber king of Zeboiim, and the king of Bela (that is, Zoar). 3 All these joined together in the Valley of Siddim (that is, the Salt Sea). 4 Twelve years they served Chedorlaomer, and in the thirteenth year they rebelled.

5 In the fourteenth year Chedorlaomer and the kings that *were* with him came and attacked the Rephaim in Ashteroth Karnaim, the Zuzim in Ham, the Emim in Shaveh Kiriathaim, 6 and the Horites in their mountain of Seir, as far as El Paran, which *is* by the wilderness. 7 Then they turned back and came to En Mishpat (that *is*, Kadesh), and attacked all the country of the Amalekites, and also the Amorites who dwelt in Hazezon Tamar.

8 And the king of Sodom, the king of Gomorrah, the king of Admah, the king of Zeboiim, and the king of Bela (that *is*, Zoar) went out and joined together in battle in the Valley of Siddim 9 against Chedorlaomer king of Elam, Tidal king of nations,*a* Amraphel king of Shinar, and Arioch king of Ellasar—four kings against five. 10 Now the Valley of Siddim *was full of* asphalt pits; and the kings of Sodom and Gomorrah fled; *some* fell there, and the remainder fled to the mountains. 11 Then they took all the goods of Sodom and Gomorrah, and all their provisions, and went their way. 12 They also took Lot, Abram's brother's son who dwelt in Sodom, and his goods, and departed.

13 Then one who had escaped came and told Abram the Hebrew, for he dwelt by the terebinth trees of Mamre*a* the Amorite, brother of Eshcol and brother of Aner; and they *were* allies with Abram. 14 Now when Abram heard that his brother was taken captive, he armed his three hundred and eighteen trained *servants* who were born in his own house, and went in pursuit as far as Dan. 15 He divided his forces against them by night, and he and his servants attacked them and pursued them as far as Hobah, which *is* north of Damascus. 16 So he brought back all the goods, and also brought back his brother Lot and his goods, as well as the women and the people.

13:15 *a*Literally *seed,* and so throughout the book   13:18 *a*Hebrew *Alon Mamre*
14:1 *a*Hebrew *goyim*   14:9 *a*Hebrew *goyim*   14:13 *a*Hebrew *Alon Mamre*

17 And the king of Sodom went out to meet him at the Valley of Shaveh (that *is*, the King's Valley), after his return from the defeat of Chedorlaomer and the kings who *were* with him.

18 Then Melchizedek king of Salem brought out bread and wine; he *was* the priest of God Most High. 19 And he blessed him and said:

"Blessed be Abram of God Most High,
Possessor of heaven and earth;
20 And blessed be God Most High,
Who has delivered your enemies into your hand."

And he gave him a tithe of all.

21 Now the king of Sodom said to Abram, "Give me the persons, and take the goods for yourself."

22 But Abram said to the king of Sodom, "I have raised my hand to the LORD, God Most High, the Possessor of heaven and earth, 23 that I *will take* nothing, from a thread to a sandal strap, and that I will not take anything that *is* yours, lest you should say, 'I have made Abram rich'— 24 except only what the young men have eaten, and the portion of the men who went with me: Aner, Eshcol, and Mamre; let them take their portion."

15 After these things the word of the LORD came to Abram in a vision, saying, "Do not be afraid, Abram. I *am* your shield, your exceedingly great reward."

2 But Abram said, "Lord GOD, what will You give me, seeing I go childless, and the heir of my house *is* Eliezer of Damascus?" 3 Then Abram said, "Look, You have given me no offspring; indeed one born in my house is my heir!"

4 And behold, the word of the LORD *came* to him, saying, "This one shall not be your heir, but one who will come from your own body shall be your heir." 5 Then He brought him outside and said, "Look now toward heaven, and count the stars if you are able to number them." And He said to him, "So shall your descendants be."

6 And he believed in the LORD, and He accounted it to him for righteousness.

7 Then He said to him, "I *am* the LORD, who brought you out of Ur of the Chaldeans, to give you this land to inherit it."

8 And he said, "Lord GOD, how shall I know that I will inherit it?"

9 So He said to him, "Bring Me a three-year-old heifer, a three-year-old female goat, a three-year-old ram, a turtledove, and a young pigeon." 10 Then he brought all these to Him and cut them in two, down the middle, and placed each piece opposite the other; but he did not cut the birds in two. 11 And when the vultures came down on the carcasses, Abram drove them away.

12 Now when the sun was going down, a deep sleep fell upon Abram; and behold, horror *and* great darkness fell upon him. 13 Then He said to Abram: "Know certainly that your descendants will be strangers in a land *that is* not theirs, and will serve them, and they will afflict them four hundred years. 14 And also the nation whom they serve I will judge; afterward they shall come out with great possessions. 15 Now as for you, you shall go to your fathers in peace; you shall be buried at a good old age. 16 But in the fourth generation they shall return here, for the iniquity of the Amorites *is* not yet complete."

17 And it came to pass, when the sun went down and it was dark, that behold, there appeared a smoking oven and a burning torch that passed between those pieces. 18 On the same day the LORD made a covenant with Abram, saying:

"To your descendants I have given this land, from the river of Egypt to the great river, the River Euphrates— 19 the Kenites, the Kenezzites, the Kadmonites, 20 the Hittites, the Perizzites, the Rephaim, 21 the Amorites, the Canaanites, the Girgashites, and the Jebusites."

16 Now Sarai, Abram's wife, had borne him no *children*. And she had an Egyptian maidservant whose name was Hagar. 2 So Sarai said to Abram, "See now, the LORD has restrained me from bearing *children*. Please, go in to my maid; perhaps I shall obtain children by her." And Abram heeded the voice of Sarai. 3 Then Sarai, Abram's wife, took Hagar her maid, the Egyptian, and gave her to her husband Abram to be his

God allows different people to come into your life to accomplish His purposes. Your friends are ultimately the ones who will help you become all that God wants you to be.

wife, after Abram had dwelt ten years in the land of Canaan. 4 So he went in to Hagar, and she conceived. And when she saw that she had conceived, her mistress became despised in her eyes. 5 Then Sarai said to Abram, "My wrong be upon you! I gave my maid into your embrace; and when she saw that she had conceived, I became despised in her eyes. The LORD judge between you and me."

6 So Abram said to Sarai, "Indeed your maid is in your hand; do to her as you please." And when Sarai dealt harshly with her, she fled from her presence.

7 Now the Angel of the LORD found her by a spring of water in the wilderness, by the spring on the way to Shur. 8 And He said, "Hagar, Sarai's maid, where have you come from, and where are you going?"

She said, "I am fleeing from the presence of my mistress Sarai."

9 The Angel of the LORD said to her, "Return to your mistress, and submit yourself under her hand." 10 Then the Angel of the LORD said to her, "I will multiply your descendants exceedingly, so that they shall not be counted for multitude." 11 And the Angel of the LORD said to her:

"Behold, you are with child,
And you shall bear a son.
You shall call his name
    Ishmael,
Because the LORD has heard
    your affliction.
12 He shall be a wild man;
His hand shall be against every
    man,
And every man's hand against
    him.
And he shall dwell in the
    presence of all his brethren."

13 Then she called the name of the LORD who spoke to her, You-Are-the-God-Who-Sees; for she said, "Have I also here seen Him who sees me?" 14 Therefore the well was called Beer Lahai Roi;ª observe, it is between Kadesh and Bered.

15 So Hagar bore Abram a son; and Abram named his son, whom Hagar bore, Ishmael. 16 Abram was eighty-six years old when Hagar bore Ishmael to Abram.

17 When Abram was ninety-nine years old, the LORD appeared to Abram and said to him, "I am Almighty God; walk before Me and be blameless. 2 And I will make My covenant between Me and you, and will multiply you exceedingly." 3 Then Abram fell on his face, and God talked with him, saying: 4 "As for Me, behold, My covenant is with you, and you shall be a father of many nations. 5 No longer shall your name be called Abram, but your name shall be Abraham; for I have made you a father of many nations. 6 I will make you exceedingly fruitful; and I will make nations of you, and kings shall come from you. 7 And I will establish My covenant between Me and you and your descendants after you in their generations, for an everlasting covenant, to be God to you and your descendants after you. 8 Also I give to you and your descendants after you the land in which you are a stranger, all the land of Canaan, as an everlasting possession; and I will be their God."

9 And God said to Abraham: "As for you, you shall keep My covenant, you and your descendants after you throughout their generations. 10 This is My covenant which you shall keep, between Me and you and your descendants after you: Every male child among you shall be circumcised; 11 and you shall be circumcised in the flesh of your foreskins, and it shall be a sign of the covenant between Me and you. 12 He who is eight days old among you shall be circumcised, every male child in your generations, he who is born in your house or bought with money from any foreigner who is not your descendant. 13 He who is born in your house and he who is bought with your money must be circumcised, and My covenant shall be in your flesh for an everlasting covenant. 14 And the uncircumcised male child, who is not circumcised in the flesh of his foreskin, that person shall be cut off from his people; he has broken My covenant."

15 Then God said to Abraham, "As for Sarai your wife, you shall not call her name Sarai, but Sarah shall be her name. 16 And I will bless her and also give you a son by her; then I will

16:14 ªLiterally *Well of the One Who Lives and Sees Me*

*D*on't give up. Don't give in. Don't give way. God has another method to bring you the blessing He has destined for you to receive.

No Need for a Vacuum

Genesis 16:6–9

I challenge you as a woman to resist the temptation to live in a vacuum. If your broken past has left you suspicious of the male gender as a whole, remember that wholeness will enable you to love the imperfect. To expect to find an ideal man—one who can be trusted not to disappoint—is neither true nor realistic. Nor is it true that if you demand such a man, that you yourself could live up to those standards. It is a trick the enemy uses to stop you from enjoying life. It is a lofty expectation that is fictitious and nonexistent. People do fail. Men fail. Women fail. Children fail. But thanks be to God, He does not fail!

His unfailing love, when graciously bestowed, will enable you to love the imperfect. He loves you in spite of what He knows about you. What a healing! What a lesson He teaches when He loves in spite of your failures and misalignments. The real challenge is to receive His love and learn to become secure enough to emulate that love in your relationships. Without that, you will have tremendous standards but absolutely no companionship. The walls that you build to protect yourself will actually imprison you, and time will escape like sand trickling through an hourglass.

God enables you to experience a level of faith that makes you a joy to be with. He heals you until you have no need to live in a vacuum. He brings you to the point where you can be free from broken beginnings. If your beginnings were less than what you hoped, God heals. Even if you had no father image or the father image you grew up with was distorted or perverted, Christ makes it possible to redefine what it means to have a father. He can assist you in your search to understand the masculine heart, to celebrate the unique differences that can enrich your life and your relationships.

If you have spent all your life in promiscuity, have suffered from low self-esteem, or are so starved for male attention that you will accept it by the hour, the night, or the weekend, you need to know that a real relationship with God will heal the void. Then, when you are ready to enter into a relationship with a man, it will be for the right reason and not because of that insatiable thirsting for affirmation that causes your relationships to be destroyed. After all, don't you want to be the best you can be for him?

bless her, and she shall be *a mother of* nations; kings of peoples shall be from her."

17 Then Abraham fell on his face and laughed, and said in his heart, "Shall *a child* be born to a man who is one hundred years old? And shall Sarah, who is ninety years old, bear *a child?*" 18 And Abraham said to God, "Oh, that Ishmael might live before You!"

19 Then God said: "No, Sarah your wife shall bear you a son, and you shall call his name Isaac; I will establish My covenant with him for an everlasting covenant, *and* with his descendants after him. 20 And as for Ishmael, I have heard you. Behold, I have blessed him, and will make him fruitful, and will multiply him exceedingly. He shall beget twelve princes, and I will make him a great nation. 21 But My covenant I will establish with Isaac, whom Sarah shall bear to you at this set time next year." 22 Then He finished talking with him, and God went up from Abraham.

23 So Abraham took Ishmael his son, all who were born in his house and all who were bought with his money, every male among the men of Abraham's house, and circumcised the flesh of their foreskins that very same day, as God had said to him. 24 Abraham *was* ninety-nine years old when he was circumcised in the flesh of his foreskin. 25 And Ishmael his son *was* thirteen years old when he was circumcised in the flesh of his foreskin. 26 That very same day Abraham was circumcised, and his son Ishmael; 27 and all the men of his house, born in the house or bought with money from a foreigner, were circumcised with him.

18 Then the LORD appeared to him by the terebinth trees of Mamre,*ª* as he was sitting in the tent door in the heat of the day. 2 So he lifted his eyes and looked, and behold, three men were standing by him; and when he saw *them,* he ran from the tent door to meet them, and bowed himself to the ground, 3 and said, "My Lord, if I have now found favor in Your sight, do not pass on by Your servant. 4 Please let a little water be brought, and wash

your feet, and rest yourselves under the tree. 5 And I will bring a morsel of bread, that you may refresh your hearts. After that you may pass by, inasmuch as you have come to your servant."

They said, "Do as you have said."

6 So Abraham hurried into the tent to Sarah and said, "Quickly, make ready three measures of fine meal; knead *it* and make cakes." 7 And Abraham ran to the herd, took a tender and good calf, gave *it* to a young man, and he hastened to prepare it. 8 So he took butter and milk and the calf which he had prepared, and set *it* before them; and he stood by them under the tree as they ate.

9 Then they said to him, "Where *is* Sarah your wife?"

So he said, "Here, in the tent."

10 And He said, "I will certainly return to you according to the time of life, and behold, Sarah your wife shall have a son."

(Sarah was listening in the tent door which *was* behind him.) 11 Now Abraham and Sarah were old, well advanced in age; *and* Sarah had passed the age of childbearing.*ª* 12 Therefore Sarah laughed within herself, saying, "After I have grown old, shall I have pleasure, my lord being old also?"

13 And the LORD said to Abraham, "Why did Sarah laugh, saying, 'Shall I surely bear *a child,* since I am old?' 14 Is anything too hard for the LORD? At the appointed time I will return to you, according to the time of life, and Sarah shall have a son."

15 But Sarah denied *it,* saying, "I did not laugh," for she was afraid.

And He said, "No, but you did laugh!"

16 Then the men rose from there and looked toward Sodom, and Abraham went with them to send them on the way. 17 And the LORD said, "Shall I hide from Abraham what I am doing, 18 since Abraham shall surely become a great and mighty nation, and all the nations of the earth shall be blessed in him? 19 For I have known him, in order that he may command his children and his household after him, that they keep the way of the LORD, to do righteousness and justice, that the LORD may bring to Abraham what He

18:1 *ª*Hebrew *Alon Mamre*   18:11 *ª*Literally *the manner of women had ceased to be with Sarah*

Gospel Pearls

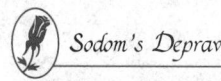
has spoken to him." 20 And the LORD said, "Because the outcry against Sodom and Gomorrah is great, and because their sin is very grave, 21 I will go down now and see whether they have done altogether according to the outcry against it that has come to Me; and if not, I will know."

22 Then the men turned away from there and went toward Sodom, but Abraham still stood before the LORD. 23 And Abraham came near and said, "Would You also destroy the righteous with the wicked? 24 Suppose there were fifty righteous within the city; would You also destroy the place and not spare *it* for the fifty righteous that were in it? 25 Far be it from You to do such a thing as this, to slay the righteous with the wicked, so that the righteous should be as the wicked; far be it from You! Shall not the Judge of all the earth do right?"

26 So the LORD said, "If I find in Sodom fifty righteous within the city, then I will spare all the place for their sakes."

27 Then Abraham answered and said, "Indeed now, I who *am but* dust and ashes have taken it upon myself to speak to the Lord: 28 Suppose there were five less than the fifty righteous; would You destroy all of the city for *lack of* five?"

So He said, "If I find there forty-five, I will not destroy *it.*"

29 And he spoke to Him yet again and said, "Suppose there should be forty found there?"

So He said, "I will not do *it* for the sake of forty."

30 Then he said, "Let not the Lord be angry, and I will speak: Suppose thirty should be found there?"

So He said, "I will not do *it* if I find thirty there."

31 And he said, "Indeed now, I have taken it upon myself to speak to the Lord: Suppose twenty should be found there?"

So He said, "I will not destroy *it* for the sake of twenty."

32 Then he said, "Let not the Lord be angry, and I will speak but once more: Suppose ten should be found there?"

And He said, "I will not destroy *it* for the sake of ten." 33 So the LORD went His way as soon as He had finished speaking with Abraham; and Abraham returned to his place.

19 Now the two angels came to Sodom in the evening, and Lot was sitting in the gate of Sodom. When Lot saw *them,* he rose to meet them, and he bowed himself with his face toward the ground. 2 And he said, "Here now, my lords, please turn in to your servant's house and spend the night, and wash your feet; then you may rise early and go on your way."

And they said, "No, but we will spend the night in the open square."

3 But he insisted strongly; so they turned in to him and entered his house. Then he made them a feast, and baked unleavened bread, and they ate.

4 Now before they lay down, the men of the city, the men of Sodom, both old and young, all the people from every quarter, surrounded the house. 5 And they called to Lot and said to him, "Where are the men who came to you tonight? Bring them out to us that we may know them *carnally.*"

6 So Lot went out to them through the doorway, shut the door behind him, 7 and said, "Please, my brethren, do not do so wickedly! 8 See now, I have two daughters who have not known a man; please, let me bring them out to you, and you may do to them as you wish; only do nothing to these men, since this is the reason they have come under the shadow of my roof."

9 And they said, "Stand back!" Then they said, "This one came in to stay *here,* and he keeps acting as a judge; now we will deal worse with you than with them." So they pressed hard against the man Lot, and came near to break down the door. 10 But the men reached out their hands and pulled Lot into the house with them, and shut the door. 11 And they struck the men who *were* at the doorway of the house with blindness, both small and great, so that they became weary *trying* to find the door.

12 Then the men said to Lot, "Have you anyone else here? Son-in-law, your sons, your daughters, and whomever you have in the city—take *them* out of this place! 13 For we will destroy this place, because the outcry against them has grown great before the face of the LORD, and the LORD has sent us to destroy it."

*D*o you really want to see God move? Really? Then touch God with your passion. Touch Him with your feelings, with your tears that flow like a flood from your eyes, with your groanings and wailings.

14 So Lot went out and spoke to his sons-in-law, who had married his daughters, and said, "Get up, get out of this place; for the LORD will destroy this city!" But to his sons-in-law he seemed to be joking.

15 When the morning dawned, the angels urged Lot to hurry, saying, "Arise, take your wife and your two daughters who are here, lest you be consumed in the punishment of the city." 16 And while he lingered, the men took hold of his hand, his wife's hand, and the hands of his two daughters, the LORD being merciful to him, and they brought him out and set him outside the city. 17 So it came to pass, when they had brought them outside, that he[a] said, "Escape for your life! Do not look behind you nor stay anywhere in the plain. Escape to the mountains, lest you be destroyed."

18 Then Lot said to them, "Please, no, my lords! 19 Indeed now, your servant has found favor in your sight, and you have increased your mercy which you have shown me by saving my life; but I cannot escape to the mountains, lest some evil overtake me and I die. 20 See now, this city is near enough to flee to, and it is a little one; please let me escape there (is it not a little one?) and my soul shall live."

21 And he said to him, "See, I have favored you concerning this thing also, in that I will not overthrow this city for which you have spoken. 22 Hurry, escape there. For I cannot do anything until you arrive there."

Therefore the name of the city was called Zoar.

23 The sun had risen upon the earth when Lot entered Zoar. 24 Then the LORD rained brimstone and fire on Sodom and Gomorrah, from the LORD out of the heavens. 25 So He overthrew those cities, all the plain, all the inhabitants of the cities, and what grew on the ground.

26 But his wife looked back behind him, and she became a pillar of salt.

27 And Abraham went early in the morning to the place where he had stood before the LORD. 28 Then he looked toward Sodom and Gomorrah, and toward all the land of the plain; and he saw, and behold, the smoke of the land which went up like

the smoke of a furnace. 29 And it came to pass, when God destroyed the cities of the plain, that God remembered Abraham, and sent Lot out of the midst of the overthrow, when He overthrew the cities in which Lot had dwelt.

30 Then Lot went up out of Zoar and dwelt in the mountains, and his two daughters were with him; for he was afraid to dwell in Zoar. And he and his two daughters dwelt in a cave. 31 Now the firstborn said to the younger, "Our father is old, and there is no man on the earth to come in to us as is the custom of all the earth. 32 Come, let us make our father drink wine, and we will lie with him, that we may preserve the lineage of our father." 33 So they made their father drink wine that night. And the firstborn went in and lay with her father, and he did not know when she lay down or when she arose.

34 It happened on the next day that the firstborn said to the younger, "Indeed I lay with my father last night; let us make him drink wine tonight also, and you go in and lie with him, that we may preserve the lineage of our father." 35 Then they made their father drink wine that night also. And the younger arose and lay with him, and he did not know when she lay down or when she arose.

36 Thus both the daughters of Lot were with child by their father. 37 The firstborn bore a son and called his name Moab; he is the father of the Moabites to this day. 38 And the younger, she also bore a son and called his name Ben-Ammi; he is the father of the people of Ammon to this day.

20 And Abraham journeyed from there to the South, and dwelt between Kadesh and Shur, and stayed in Gerar. 2 Now Abraham said of Sarah his wife, "She is my sister." And Abimelech king of Gerar sent and took Sarah.

3 But God came to Abimelech in a dream by night, and said to him, "Indeed you are a dead man because of the woman whom you have taken, for she is a man's wife."

4 But Abimelech had not come near her; and he said, "Lord, will You slay

19:17 [a]Septuagint, Syriac, and Vulgate read *they.*

Gospel Pearls

a righteous nation also? 5 Did he not say to me, 'She *is* my sister'? And she, even she herself said, 'He *is* my brother.' In the integrity of my heart and innocence of my hands I have done this.''

6 And God said to him in a dream, "Yes, I know that you did this in the integrity of your heart. For I also withheld you from sinning against Me; therefore I did not let you touch her. 7 Now therefore, restore the man's wife; for he *is* a prophet, and he will pray for you and you shall live. But if you do not restore *her,* know that you shall surely die, you and all who *are* yours."

8 So Abimelech rose early in the morning, called all his servants, and told all these things in their hearing; and the men were very much afraid. 9 And Abimelech called Abraham and said to him, "What have you done to us? How have I offended you, that you have brought on me and on my kingdom a great sin? You have done deeds to me that ought not to be done.'' 10 Then Abimelech said to Abraham, "What did you have in view, that you have done this thing?''

11 And Abraham said, "Because I thought, surely the fear of God *is* not in this place; and they will kill me on account of my wife. 12 But indeed *she is* truly my sister. She *is* the daughter of my father, but not the daughter of my mother; and she became my wife. 13 And it came to pass, when God caused me to wander from my father's house, that I said to her, 'This *is* your kindness that you should do for me: in every place, wherever we go, say of me, "He *is* my brother."''''

14 Then Abimelech took sheep, oxen, and male and female servants, and gave *them* to Abraham; and he restored Sarah his wife to him. 15 And Abimelech said, "See, my land *is* before you; dwell where it pleases you." 16 Then to Sarah he said, "Behold, I have given your brother a thousand *pieces* of silver; indeed this vindicates you[a] before all who *are* with you and before everybody." Thus she was rebuked.

17 So Abraham prayed to God; and God healed Abimelech, his wife, and his female servants. Then they bore *children;* 18 for the LORD had closed up all the wombs of the house of Abimelech because of Sarah, Abraham's wife.

21 And the LORD visited Sarah as He had said, and the LORD did for Sarah as He had spoken. 2 For Sarah conceived and bore Abraham a son in his old age, at the set time of which God had spoken to him. 3 And Abraham called the name of his son who was born to him—whom Sarah bore to him—Isaac. 4 Then Abraham circumcised his son Isaac when he was eight days old, as God had commanded him. 5 Now Abraham was one hundred years old when his son Isaac was born to him. 6 And Sarah said, "God has made me laugh, *and* all who hear will laugh with me." 7 She also said, "Who would have said to Abraham that Sarah would nurse children? For I have borne *him* a son in his old age."

8 So the child grew and was weaned. And Abraham made a great feast on the same day that Isaac was weaned.

9 And Sarah saw the son of Hagar the Egyptian, whom she had borne to Abraham, scoffing. 10 Therefore she said to Abraham, "Cast out this bondwoman and her son; for the son of this bondwoman shall not be heir with my son, *namely* with Isaac." 11 And the matter was very displeasing in Abraham's sight because of his son.

12 But God said to Abraham, "Do not let it be displeasing in your sight because of the lad or because of your bondwoman. Whatever Sarah has said to you, listen to her voice; for in Isaac your seed shall be called. 13 Yet I will also make a nation of the son of the bondwoman, because he *is* your seed."

14 So Abraham rose early in the morning, and took bread and a skin of water; and putting *it* on her shoulder, he gave *it* and the boy to Hagar, and sent her away. Then she departed and wandered in the Wilderness of Beersheba. 15 And the water in the skin was used up, and she placed the boy under one of the shrubs. 16 Then she went and sat down across from *him* at a distance of about a bowshot; for she said to

20:16 ᵃLiterally *it is a covering of the eyes for you*

Soul Secrets
when it seems too late

God, I have prayed for years. I have done everything I know to do in order to see my dreams come true. I have had seasons of working hard and seasons of "letting go and letting God" and, still, the things I have believed You for seem like they will never happen. I have had one disappointment after another. And it's almost too late.

I feel like Sarah—like it is impossible for me to ever hold the one thing I long for most.

God, do not let me miss my destiny! But do not let me hope for things that are not a part of Your plan for my life. Let me hear Your voice telling me what You really have for me. Give me glimpses of the gifts You have for me so that I might fight with faith to apprehend Your promises. Help me to understand the difference between what I must go after and what I must wait on You for. When it is up to me, give me the strength to demolish doubt and to march fearlessly into the new day You have prepared for me. When I must wait on You, give me grace and patience. Fill me with the holy anticipation that accompanies a perfectly timed present.

They say You are never, ever late. God, in these days when it seems like time is pressing in around me on every side, keep me firm in faith. Save me from giving up. Do not let me stop short of my blessing. Thank You for being faithful. Always faithful. It is never too late with You.

herself, "Let me not see the death of the boy." So she sat opposite *him,* and lifted her voice and wept.

17 And God heard the voice of the lad. Then the angel of God called to Hagar out of heaven, and said to her, "What ails you, Hagar? Fear not, for God has heard the voice of the lad where he *is.* 18 Arise, lift up the lad and hold him with your hand, for I will make him a great nation."

19 Then God opened her eyes, and she saw a well of water. And she went and filled the skin with water, and gave the lad a drink. 20 So God was with the lad; and he grew and dwelt in the wilderness, and became an archer. 21 He dwelt in the Wilderness of Paran; and his mother took a wife for him from the land of Egypt.

22 And it came to pass at that time that Abimelech and Phichol, the commander of his army, spoke to Abraham, saying, "God *is* with you in all that you do. 23 Now therefore, swear to me by God that you will not deal falsely with me, with my offspring, or with my posterity; but that according to the kindness that I have done to you, you will do to me and to the land in which you have dwelt."

24 And Abraham said, "I will swear."

25 Then Abraham rebuked Abimelech because of a well of water which Abimelech's servants had seized. 26 And Abimelech said, "I do not know who has done this thing; you did not tell me, nor had I heard *of it* until today." 27 So Abraham took sheep and oxen and gave them to Abimelech, and the two of them made a covenant. 28 And Abraham set seven ewe lambs of the flock by themselves.

29 Then Abimelech asked Abraham, "What *is the meaning of* these seven ewe lambs which you have set by themselves?"

30 And he said, "You will take *these* seven ewe lambs from my hand, that they may be my witness that I have dug this well." 31 Therefore he called that place Beersheba,^a because the two of them swore an oath there.

32 Thus they made a covenant at Beersheba. So Abimelech rose with Phichol, the commander of his army, and they returned to the land of the Philistines. 33 Then *Abraham* planted a tamarisk tree in Beersheba, and there called on the name of the LORD, the Everlasting God. 34 And Abraham stayed in the land of the Philistines many days.

22 Now it came to pass after these things that God tested Abraham, and said to him, "Abraham!"

And he said, "Here I am."

2 Then He said, "Take now your son, your only *son* Isaac, whom you love, and go to the land of Moriah, and offer him there as a burnt offering on one of the mountains of which I shall tell you."

3 So Abraham rose early in the morning and saddled his donkey, and took two of his young men with him, and Isaac his son; and he split the wood for the burnt offering, and arose and went to the place of which God had told him. 4 Then on the third day Abraham lifted his eyes and saw the place afar off. 5 And Abraham said to his young men, "Stay here with the donkey; the lad^a and I will go yonder and worship, and we will come back to you."

6 So Abraham took the wood of the burnt offering and laid *it* on Isaac his son; and he took the fire in his hand, and a knife, and the two of them went together. 7 But Isaac spoke to Abraham his father and said, "My father!"

And he said, "Here I am, my son."

Then he said, "Look, the fire and the wood, but where *is* the lamb for a burnt offering?"

8 And Abraham said, "My son, God will provide for Himself the lamb for a burnt offering." So the two of them went together.

9 Then they came to the place of which God had told him. And Abraham built an altar there and placed the wood in order; and he bound Isaac his son and laid him on the altar, upon the wood. 10 And Abraham stretched out his hand and took the knife to slay his son.

11 But the Angel of the LORD called to him from heaven and said, "Abraham, Abraham!"

So he said, "Here I am."

12 And He said, "Do not lay your hand on the lad, or do anything to him; for now I know that you fear God, since you have not withheld

21:31 ^aLiterally *Well of the Oath* or *Well of the Seven*   22:5 ^aOr *young man*

God has called you with an eternal purpose. Where you are right now is not where you are going. He still has an appointed task for you to finish.

your son, your only *son,* from Me."
13 Then Abraham lifted his eyes and looked, and there behind *him was* a ram caught in a thicket by its horns. So Abraham went and took the ram, and offered it up for a burnt offering instead of his son. 14 And Abraham called the name of the place, The-Lord-Will-Provide;*a* as it is said *to* this day, "In the Mount of the Lord it shall be provided."

15 Then the Angel of the Lord called to Abraham a second time out of heaven, 16 and said: "By Myself I have sworn, says the Lord, because you have done this thing, and have not withheld your son, your only son— 17 blessing I will bless you, and multiplying I will multiply your descendants as the stars of the heaven and as the sand which *is* on the seashore; and your descendants shall possess the gate of their enemies. 18 In your seed all the nations of the earth shall be blessed, because you have obeyed My voice." 19 So Abraham returned to his young men, and they rose and went together to Beersheba; and Abraham dwelt at Beersheba.

20 Now it came to pass after these things that it was told Abraham, saying, "Indeed Milcah also has borne children to your brother Nahor: 21 Huz his firstborn, Buz his brother, Kemuel the father of Aram, 22 Chesed, Hazo, Pildash, Jidlaph, and Bethuel." 23 And Bethuel begot Rebekah.*a* These eight Milcah bore to Nahor, Abraham's brother. 24 His concubine, whose name was Reumah, also bore Tebah, Gaham, Thahash, and Maachah.

23 Sarah lived one hundred and twenty-seven years; *these were* the years of the life of Sarah. 2 So Sarah died in Kirjath Arba (that *is,* Hebron) in the land of Canaan, and Abraham came to mourn for Sarah and to weep for her.

3 Then Abraham stood up from before his dead, and spoke to the sons of Heth, saying, 4 "I *am* a foreigner and a visitor among you. Give me property for a burial place among you, that I may bury my dead out of my sight."

5 And the sons of Heth answered Abraham, saying to him, 6 "Hear us, my lord: You *are* a mighty prince among us; bury your dead in the choicest of our burial places. None of us will withhold from you his burial place, that you may bury your dead."

7 Then Abraham stood up and bowed himself to the people of the land, the sons of Heth. 8 And he spoke with them, saying, "If it is your wish that I bury my dead out of my sight, hear me, and meet with Ephron the son of Zohar for me, 9 that he may give me the cave of Machpelah which he has, which *is* at the end of his field. Let him give it to me at the full price, as property for a burial place among you."

10 Now Ephron dwelt among the sons of Heth; and Ephron the Hittite answered Abraham in the presence of the sons of Heth, all who entered at the gate of his city, saying, 11 "No, my lord, hear me: I give you the field and the cave that *is* in it; I give it to you in the presence of the sons of my people. I give it to you. Bury your dead!"

12 Then Abraham bowed himself down before the people of the land; 13 and he spoke to Ephron in the hearing of the people of the land, saying, "If you *will give it,* please hear me. I will give you money for the field; take *it* from me and I will bury my dead there."

14 And Ephron answered Abraham, saying to him, 15 "My lord, listen to me; the land *is worth* four hundred shekels of silver. What *is* that between you and me? So bury your dead." 16 And Abraham listened to Ephron; and Abraham weighed out the silver for Ephron which he had named in the hearing of the sons of Heth, four hundred shekels of silver, currency of the merchants.

17 So the field of Ephron which *was* in Machpelah, which *was* before Mamre, the field and the cave which *was* in it, and all the trees that *were* in the field, which *were* within all the surrounding borders, were deeded 18 to Abraham as a possession in the presence of the sons of Heth, before all who went in at the gate of his city. 19 And after this, Abraham buried Sarah his wife in the cave of the field of Machpelah, before Mamre (that *is,* Hebron) in the land of Canaan.

22:14 *a*Hebrew *YHWH Yireh*   22:23 *a*Spelled *Rebecca* in Romans 9:10

Gospel Pearls

20 So the field and the cave that *is* in it were deeded to Abraham by the sons of Heth as property for a burial place.

24 Now Abraham was old, well advanced in age; and the LORD had blessed Abraham in all things. 2 So Abraham said to the oldest servant of his house, who ruled over all that he had, "Please, put your hand under my thigh, 3 and I will make you swear by the LORD, the God of heaven and the God of the earth, that you will not take a wife for my son from the daughters of the Canaanites, among whom I dwell; 4 but you shall go to my country and to my family, and take a wife for my son Isaac."

5 And the servant said to him, "Perhaps the woman will not be willing to follow me to this land. Must I take your son back to the land from which you came?"

6 But Abraham said to him, "Beware that you do not take my son back there. 7 The LORD God of heaven, who took me from my father's house and from the land of my family, and who spoke to me and swore to me, saying, 'To your descendants*a* I give this land,' He will send His angel before you, and you shall take a wife for my son from there. 8 And if the woman is not willing to follow you, then you will be released from this oath; only do not take my son back there." 9 So the servant put his hand under the thigh of Abraham his master, and swore to him concerning this matter.

10 Then the servant took ten of his master's camels and departed, for all his master's goods *were in* his hand. And he arose and went to Mesopotamia, to the city of Nahor. 11 And he made his camels kneel down outside the city by a well of water at evening time, the time when women go out to draw *water*. 12 Then he said, "O LORD God of my master Abraham, please give me success this day, and show kindness to my master Abraham. 13 Behold, *here* I stand by the well of water, and the daughters of the men of the city are coming out to draw water. 14 Now let it be that the young woman to whom I say, 'Please let down your pitcher that I may drink,' and she says, 'Drink, and

I will also give your camels a drink'— *let her be the one* You have appointed for Your servant Isaac. And by this I will know that You have shown kindness to my master."

15 And it happened, before he had finished speaking, that behold, Rebekah, who was born to Bethuel, son of Milcah, the wife of Nahor, Abraham's brother, came out with her pitcher on her shoulder. 16 Now the young woman *was* very beautiful to behold, a virgin; no man had known her. And she went down to the well, filled her pitcher, and came up. 17 And the servant ran to meet her and said, "Please let me drink a little water from your pitcher."

18 So she said, "Drink, my lord." Then she quickly let her pitcher down to her hand, and gave him a drink. 19 And when she had finished giving him a drink, she said, "I will draw *water* for your camels also, until they have finished drinking." 20 Then she quickly emptied her pitcher into the trough, ran back to the well to draw *water*, and drew for all his camels. 21 And the man, wondering at her, remained silent so as to know whether the LORD had made his journey prosperous or not.

22 So it was, when the camels had finished drinking, that the man took a golden nose ring weighing half a shekel, and two bracelets for her wrists weighing ten *shekels* of gold, 23 and said, "Whose daughter *are* you? Tell me, please, is there room *in* your father's house for us to lodge?"

24 So she said to him, "I *am* the daughter of Bethuel, Milcah's son, whom she bore to Nahor." 25 Moreover she said to him, "We have both straw and feed enough, and room to lodge."

26 Then the man bowed down his head and worshiped the LORD. 27 And he said, "Blessed *be* the LORD God of my master Abraham, who has not forsaken His mercy and His truth toward my master. As for me, being on the way, the LORD led me to the house of my master's brethren." 28 So the young woman ran and told her mother's household these things.

29 Now Rebekah had a brother whose name *was* Laban, and Laban ran out to the man by the well. 30 So it came to pass, when he saw

24:7 *a*Literally *seed*

*I*f you are going to hold on to your miracle, your dream, the fulfillment of God's plan for your life, then you are going to have to keep moving. Always keep moving toward what God has for you.

the nose ring, and the bracelets on his sister's wrists, and when he heard the words of his sister Rebekah, saying, "Thus the man spoke to me," that he went to the man. And there he stood by the camels at the well. 31 And he said, "Come in, O blessed of the LORD! Why do you stand outside? For I have prepared the house, and a place for the camels."

32 Then the man came to the house. And he unloaded the camels, and provided straw and feed for the camels, and water to wash his feet and the feet of the men who *were* with him. 33 *Food* was set before him to eat, but he said, "I will not eat until I have told about my errand."

And he said, "Speak on."

34 So he said, "I *am* Abraham's servant. 35 The LORD has blessed my master greatly, and he has become great; and He has given him flocks and herds, silver and gold, male and female servants, and camels and donkeys. 36 And Sarah my master's wife bore a son to my master when she was old; and to him he has given all that he has. 37 Now my master made me swear, saying, 'You shall not take a wife for my son from the daughters of the Canaanites, in whose land I dwell; 38 but you shall go to my father's house and to my family, and take a wife for my son.' 39 And I said to my master, 'Perhaps the woman will not follow me.' 40 But he said to me, 'The LORD, before whom I walk, will send His angel with you and prosper your way; and you shall take a wife for my son from my family and from my father's house. 41 You will be clear from this oath when you arrive among my family; for if they will not give *her* to you, then you will be released from my oath.'

42 "And this day I came to the well and said, 'O LORD God of my master Abraham, if You will now prosper the way in which I go, 43 behold, I stand by the well of water; and it shall come to pass that when the virgin comes out to draw *water,* and I say to her, "Please give me a little water from your pitcher to drink," 44 and she says to me, "Drink, and I will draw for your camels also,"—*let* her *be* the woman whom the LORD has appointed for my master's son.'

45 "But before I had finished speaking in my heart, there was Rebekah, coming out with her pitcher on her shoulder; and she went down to the well and drew *water.* And I said to her, 'Please let me drink.' 46 And she made haste and let her pitcher down from her *shoulder,* and said, 'Drink, and I will give your camels a drink also.' So I drank, and she gave the camels a drink also. 47 Then I asked her, and said, 'Whose daughter *are* you?' And she said, 'The daughter of Bethuel, Nahor's son, whom Milcah bore to him.' So I put the nose ring on her nose and the bracelets on her wrists. 48 And I bowed my head and worshiped the LORD, and blessed the LORD God of my master Abraham, who had led me in the way of truth to take the daughter of my master's brother for his son. 49 Now if you will deal kindly and truly with my master, tell me. And if not, tell me, that I may turn to the right hand or to the left."

50 Then Laban and Bethuel answered and said, "The thing comes from the LORD; we cannot speak to you either bad or good. 51 Here *is* Rebekah before you; take *her* and go, and let her be your master's son's wife, as the LORD has spoken."

52 And it came to pass, when Abraham's servant heard their words, that he worshiped the LORD, *bowing himself* to the earth. 53 Then the servant brought out jewelry of silver, jewelry of gold, and clothing, and gave *them* to Rebekah. He also gave precious things to her brother and to her mother.

54 And he and the men who *were* with him ate and drank and stayed all night. Then they arose in the morning, and he said, "Send me away to my master."

55 But her brother and her mother said, "Let the young woman stay with us *a few* days, at least ten; after that she may go."

56 And he said to them, "Do not hinder me, since the LORD has prospered my way; send me away so that I may go to my master."

57 So they said, "We will call the young woman and ask her personally." 58 Then they called Rebekah and said to her, "Will you go with this man?"

And she said, "I will go."

59 So they sent away Rebekah their sister and her nurse, and Abraham's servant and his men. 60 And they blessed Rebekah and said to her:

Gospel Pearls

"Our sister, *may* you *become*
The *mother of* thousands of ten
thousands;
And may your descendants
possess
The gates of those who hate
them."

61 Then Rebekah and her maids arose, and they rode on the camels and followed the man. So the servant took Rebekah and departed.

62 Now Isaac came from the way of Beer Lahai Roi, for he dwelt in the South. 63 And Isaac went out to meditate in the field in the evening; and he lifted his eyes and looked, and there, the camels *were* coming. 64 Then Rebekah lifted her eyes, and when she saw Isaac she dismounted from her camel; 65 for she had said to the servant, "Who *is* this man walking in the field to meet us?"

The servant said, "It *is* my master." So she took a veil and covered herself.

66 And the servant told Isaac all the things that he had done. 67 Then Isaac brought her into his mother Sarah's tent; and he took Rebekah and she became his wife, and he loved her. So Isaac was comforted after his mother's *death.*

25 Abraham again took a wife, and her name *was* Keturah. 2 And she bore him Zimran, Jokshan, Medan, Midian, Ishbak, and Shuah. 3 Jokshan begot Sheba and Dedan. And the sons of Dedan were Asshurim, Letushim, and Leummim. 4 And the sons of Midian *were* Ephah, Epher, Hanoch, Abidah, and Eldaah. All these *were* the children of Keturah.

5 And Abraham gave all that he had to Isaac. 6 But Abraham gave gifts to the sons of the concubines which Abraham had; and while he was still living he sent them eastward, away from Isaac his son, to the country of the east.

7 This *is* the sum of the years of Abraham's life which he lived: one hundred and seventy-five years. 8 Then Abraham breathed his last and died in a good old age, an old man and full *of years,* and was gathered to his people. 9 And his sons Isaac and Ishmael buried him in the cave of Machpelah, which *is* before Mamre, in the field of Ephron the son of Zohar the Hittite, 10 the field which Abraham purchased from the sons of Heth. There Abraham was buried, and Sarah his wife. 11 And it came to pass, after the death of Abraham, that God blessed his son Isaac. And Isaac dwelt at Beer Lahai Roi.

12 Now this *is* the genealogy of Ishmael, Abraham's son, whom Hagar the Egyptian, Sarah's maidservant, bore to Abraham. 13 And these *were* the names of the sons of Ishmael, by their names, according to their generations: The firstborn of Ishmael, Nebajoth; then Kedar, Adbeel, Mibsam, 14 Mishma, Dumah, Massa, 15 Hadar,*a* Tema, Jetur, Naphish, and Kedemah. 16 These *were* the sons of Ishmael and these *were* their names, by their towns and their settlements, twelve princes according to their nations. 17 These *were* the years of the life of Ishmael: one hundred and thirty-seven years; and he breathed his last and died, and was gathered to his people. 18 (They dwelt from Havilah as far as Shur, which *is* east of Egypt as you go toward Assyria.) He died in the presence of all his brethren.

19 This *is* the genealogy of Isaac, Abraham's son. Abraham begot Isaac. 20 Isaac was forty years old when he took Rebekah as wife, the daughter of Bethuel the Syrian of Padan Aram, the sister of Laban the Syrian. 21 Now Isaac pleaded with the LORD for his wife, because she *was* barren; and the LORD granted his plea, and Rebekah his wife conceived. 22 But the children struggled together within her; and she said, "If *all is* well, why *am I like* this?" So she went to inquire of the LORD.

23 And the LORD said to her:

"Two nations *are* in your womb,
Two peoples shall be separated
from your body;
One people shall be stronger
than the other,
And the older shall serve the
younger."

24 So when her days were fulfilled *for her* to give birth, indeed *there were* twins in her womb. 25 And the first came out red. *He was* like a

25:15 *a*Masoretic Text reads *Hadad.*

---

*T*he thing that God has for you must be done. That's the way God feels about His plan for you. Write yourself a note, "I have an appointment. It must be kept."

hairy garment all over; so they called his name Esau.[a] 26 Afterward his brother came out, and his hand took hold of Esau's heel; so his name was called Jacob.[a] Isaac *was* sixty years old when she bore them.

27 So the boys grew. And Esau was a skillful hunter, a man of the field; but Jacob was a mild man, dwelling in tents. 28 And Isaac loved Esau because he ate *of his* game, but Rebekah loved Jacob.

29 Now Jacob cooked a stew; and Esau came in from the field, and he *was* weary. 30 And Esau said to Jacob, "Please feed me with that same red *stew,* for I *am* weary." Therefore his name was called Edom.[a]

31 But Jacob said, "Sell me your birthright as of this day."

32 And Esau said, "Look, I *am* about to die; so what *is* this birthright to me?"

33 Then Jacob said, "Swear to me as of this day."

So he swore to him, and sold his birthright to Jacob. 34 And Jacob gave Esau bread and stew of lentils; then he ate and drank, arose, and went his way. Thus Esau despised *his* birthright.

26 There was a famine in the land, besides the first famine that was in the days of Abraham. And Isaac went to Abimelech king of the Philistines, in Gerar.

2 Then the LORD appeared to him and said: "Do not go down to Egypt; live in the land of which I shall tell you. 3 Dwell in this land, and I will be with you and bless you; for to you and your descendants I give all these lands, and I will perform the oath which I swore to Abraham your father. 4 And I will make your descendants multiply as the stars of heaven; I will give to your descendants all these lands; and in your seed all the nations of the earth shall be blessed; 5 because Abraham obeyed My voice and kept My charge, My commandments, My statutes, and My laws."

6 So Isaac dwelt in Gerar. 7 And the men of the place asked about his wife. And he said, "She *is* my sister"; for he was afraid to say, "*She is* my wife," *because he thought,* "lest the men of the place

kill me for Rebekah, because she *is* beautiful to behold." 8 Now it came to pass, when he had been there a long time, that Abimelech king of the Philistines looked through a window, and saw, and there was Isaac, showing endearment to Rebekah his wife. 9 Then Abimelech called Isaac and said, "Quite obviously she *is* your wife; so how could you say, 'She *is* my sister'?"

Isaac said to him, "Because I said, 'Lest I die on account of her.' "

10 And Abimelech said, "What *is* this you have done to us? One of the people might soon have lain with your wife, and you would have brought guilt on us." 11 So Abimelech charged all *his* people, saying, "He who touches this man or his wife shall surely be put to death."

12 Then Isaac sowed in that land, and reaped in the same year a hundredfold; and the LORD blessed him. 13 The man began to prosper, and continued prospering until he became very prosperous; 14 for he had possessions of flocks and possessions of herds and a great number of servants. So the Philistines envied him. 15 Now the Philistines had stopped up all the wells which his father's servants had dug in the days of Abraham his father, and they had filled them with earth. 16 And Abimelech said to Isaac, "Go away from us, for you are much mightier than we."

17 Then Isaac departed from there and pitched his tent in the Valley of Gerar, and dwelt there. 18 And Isaac dug again the wells of water which they had dug in the days of Abraham his father, for the Philistines had stopped them up after the death of Abraham. He called them by the names which his father had called them.

19 Also Isaac's servants dug in the valley, and found a well of running water there. 20 But the herdsmen of Gerar quarreled with Isaac's herdsmen, saying, "The water *is* ours." So he called the name of the well Esek,[a] because they quarreled with him. 21 Then they dug another well, and they quarreled over that *one* also. So he called its name Sitnah.[a] 22 And he moved from there and dug another well, and they did not quarrel over

---

25:25 [a]Literally *Hairy* 25:26 [a]Literally *Supplanter* 25:30 [a]Literally *Red* 26:20 [a]Literally *Quarrel*
26:21 [a]Literally *Enmity*

Gospel Pearls

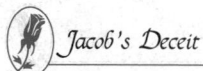

it. So he called its name Rehoboth,^a because he said, "For now the LORD has made room for us, and we shall be fruitful in the land."

23 Then he went up from there to Beersheba. 24 And the LORD appeared to him the same night and said, "I *am* the God of your father Abraham; do not fear, for I *am* with you. I will bless you and multiply your descendants for My servant Abraham's sake." 25 So he built an altar there and called on the name of the LORD, and he pitched his tent there; and there Isaac's servants dug a well.

26 Then Abimelech came to him from Gerar with Ahuzzath, one of his friends, and Phichol the commander of his army. 27 And Isaac said to them, "Why have you come to me, since you hate me and have sent me away from you?"

28 But they said, "We have certainly seen that the LORD is with you. So we said, 'Let there now be an oath between us, between you and us; and let us make a covenant with you, 29 that you will do us no harm, since we have not touched you, and since we have done nothing to you but good and have sent you away in peace. You *are* now the blessed of the LORD.' "

30 So he made them a feast, and they ate and drank. 31 Then they arose early in the morning and swore an oath with one another; and Isaac sent them away, and they departed from him in peace.

32 It came to pass the same day that Isaac's servants came and told him about the well which they had dug, and said to him, "We have found water." 33 So he called it Shebah.^a Therefore the name of the city *is* Beersheba^b to this day.

34 When Esau was forty years old, he took as wives Judith the daughter of Beeri the Hittite, and Basemath the daughter of Elon the Hittite. 35 And they were a grief of mind to Isaac and Rebekah.

27 Now it came to pass, when Isaac was old and his eyes were so dim that he could not see, that he called Esau his older son and said to him, "My son."

And he answered him, "Here I am."

2 Then he said, "Behold now, I am old. I do not know the day of my death. 3 Now therefore, please take your weapons, your quiver and your bow, and go out to the field and hunt game for me. 4 And make me savory food, such as I love, and bring *it* to me that I may eat, that my soul may bless you before I die."

5 Now Rebekah was listening when Isaac spoke to Esau his son. And Esau went to the field to hunt game and to bring *it.* 6 So Rebekah spoke to Jacob her son, saying, "Indeed I heard your father speak to Esau your brother, saying, 7 'Bring me game and make savory food for me, that I may eat it and bless you in the presence of the LORD before my death.' 8 Now therefore, my son, obey my voice according to what I command you. 9 Go now to the flock and bring me from there two choice kids of the goats, and I will make savory food from them for your father, such as he loves. 10 Then you shall take *it* to your father, that he may eat *it,* and that he may bless you before his death."

11 And Jacob said to Rebekah his mother, "Look, Esau my brother *is* a hairy man, and I *am* a smooth-skinned man. 12 Perhaps my father will feel me, and I shall seem to be a deceiver to him; and I shall bring a curse on myself and not a blessing."

13 But his mother said to him, "*Let* your curse *be* on me, my son; only obey my voice, and go, get *them* for me." 14 And he went and got *them* and brought *them* to his mother, and his mother made savory food, such as his father loved. 15 Then Rebekah took the choice clothes of her elder son Esau, which *were* with her in the house, and put them on Jacob her younger son. 16 And she put the skins of the kids of the goats on his hands and on the smooth part of his neck. 17 Then she gave the savory food and the bread, which she had prepared, into the hand of her son Jacob.

18 So he went to his father and said, "My father."

And he said, "Here I am. Who *are* you, my son?"

26:22 ^aLiterally *Spaciousness*   26:33 ^aLiterally *Oath* or *Seven*   ^bLiterally *Well of the Oath* or *Well of the Seven*

God made men and women very differently. The woman was at the peak of God's creative crescendo. God outdid Himself when He brought her forth.

19 Jacob said to his father, "I *am* Esau your firstborn; I have done just as you told me; please arise, sit and eat of my game, that your soul may bless me."
20 But Isaac said to his son, "How *is it* that you have found *it* so quickly, my son?"
And he said, "Because the LORD your God brought *it* to me."
21 Then Isaac said to Jacob, "Please come near, that I may feel you, my son, whether you *are* really my son Esau or not." 22 So Jacob went near to Isaac his father, and he felt him and said, "The voice *is* Jacob's voice, but the hands *are* the hands of Esau." 23 And he did not recognize him, because his hands were hairy like his brother Esau's hands; so he blessed him.
24 Then he said, "*Are* you really my son Esau?"
He said, "I *am*."
25 He said, "Bring *it* near to me, and I will eat of my son's game, so that my soul may bless you." So he brought *it* near to him, and he ate; and he brought him wine, and he drank. 26 Then his father Isaac said to him, "Come near now and kiss me, my son." 27 And he came near and kissed him; and he smelled the smell of his clothing, and blessed him and said:

"Surely, the smell of my son
Is like the smell of a field
Which the LORD has blessed.
28 Therefore may God give you
Of the dew of heaven,
Of the fatness of the earth,
And plenty of grain and wine.
29 Let peoples serve you,
And nations bow down to you.
Be master over your brethren,
And let your mother's sons bow
down to you.
Cursed *be* everyone who curses
you,
And blessed *be* those who bless
you!"

30 Now it happened, as soon as Isaac had finished blessing Jacob, and Jacob had scarcely gone out from the presence of Isaac his father, that Esau his brother came in from his hunting. 31 He also had made savory food, and brought it to his father, and said to his father, "Let my father arise and eat of his son's game, that your soul may bless me."
32 And his father Isaac said to him, "Who *are* you?"
So he said, "I *am* your son, your firstborn, Esau."
33 Then Isaac trembled exceedingly, and said, "Who? Where *is* the one who hunted game and brought *it* to me? I ate all *of it* before you came, and I have blessed him—*and* indeed he shall be blessed."
34 When Esau heard the words of his father, he cried with an exceedingly great and bitter cry, and said to his father, "Bless me—me also, O my father!"
35 But he said, "Your brother came with deceit and has taken away your blessing."
36 And *Esau* said, "Is he not rightly named Jacob? For he has supplanted me these two times. He took away my birthright, and now look, he has taken away my blessing!" And he said, "Have you not reserved a blessing for me?"
37 Then Isaac answered and said to Esau, "Indeed I have made him your master, and all his brethren I have given to him as servants; with grain and wine I have sustained him. What shall I do now for you, my son?"
38 And Esau said to his father, "Have you only one blessing, my father? Bless me—me also, O my father!" And Esau lifted up his voice and wept.
39 Then Isaac his father answered and said to him:

"Behold, your dwelling shall be
of the fatness of the earth,
And of the dew of heaven from
above.
40 By your sword you shall live,
And you shall serve your
brother;
And it shall come to pass, when
you become restless,
That you shall break his yoke
from your neck."

41 So Esau hated Jacob because of the blessing with which his father blessed him, and Esau said in his heart, "The days of mourning for my father are at hand; then I will kill my brother Jacob."
42 And the words of Esau her older son were told to Rebekah. So she

Gospel Pearls

sent and called Jacob her younger son, and said to him, "Surely your brother Esau comforts himself concerning you *by intending* to kill you. 43 Now therefore, my son, obey my voice: arise, flee to my brother Laban in Haran. 44 And stay with him a few days, until your brother's fury turns away, 45 until your brother's anger turns away from you, and he forgets what you have done to him; then I will send and bring you from there. Why should I be bereaved also of you both in one day?"

46 And Rebekah said to Isaac, "I am weary of my life because of the daughters of Heth; if Jacob takes a wife of the daughters of Heth, like these *who are* the daughters of the land, what good will my life be to me?"

28 Then Isaac called Jacob and blessed him, and charged him, and said to him: "You shall not take a wife from the daughters of Canaan. 2 Arise, go to Padan Aram, to the house of Bethuel your mother's father; and take yourself a wife from there of the daughters of Laban your mother's brother.

3 "May God Almighty bless you,
    And make you fruitful and
      multiply you,
    That you may be an assembly
      of peoples;
4   And give you the blessing of
      Abraham,
    To you and your descendants
      with you,
    That you may inherit the land
    In which you are a stranger,
    Which God gave to Abraham."

5 So Isaac sent Jacob away, and he went to Padan Aram, to Laban the son of Bethuel the Syrian, the brother of Rebekah, the mother of Jacob and Esau.

6 Esau saw that Isaac had blessed Jacob and sent him away to Padan Aram to take himself a wife from there, *and that* as he blessed him he gave him a charge, saying, "You shall not take a wife from the daughters of Canaan," 7 and that Jacob had obeyed his father and his mother and had gone to Padan Aram. 8 Also Esau saw that the daughters of Canaan did not please his father Isaac. 9 So Esau went to Ishmael and took Mahalath the daughter of Ishmael, Abraham's son, the sister of Nebajoth, to be his wife in addition to the wives he had.

10 Now Jacob went out from Beersheba and went toward Haran. 11 So he came to a certain place and stayed there all night, because the sun had set. And he took one of the stones of that place and put it at his head, and he lay down in that place to sleep. 12 Then he dreamed, and behold, a ladder *was* set up on the earth, and its top reached to heaven; and there the angels of God were ascending and descending on it.

13 And behold, the LORD stood above it and said: "I *am* the LORD God of Abraham your father and the God of Isaac; the land on which you lie I will give to you and your descendants. 14 Also your descendants shall be as the dust of the earth; you shall spread abroad to the west and the east, to the north and the south; and in you and in your seed all the families of the earth shall be blessed. 15 Behold, I *am* with you and will keep you wherever you go, and will bring you back to this land; for I will not leave you until I have done what I have spoken to you."

16 Then Jacob awoke from his sleep and said, "Surely the LORD is in this place, and I did not know *it*." 17 And he was afraid and said, "How awesome *is* this place! This *is* none other than the house of God, and this *is* the gate of heaven!"

18 Then Jacob rose early in the morning, and took the stone that he had put at his head, set it up as a pillar, and poured oil on top of it. 19 And he called the name of that place Bethel;*ª* but the name of that city had been Luz previously. 20 Then Jacob made a vow, saying, "If God will be with me, and keep me in this way that I am going, and give me bread to eat and clothing to put on, 21 so that I come back to my father's house in peace, then the LORD shall be my God. 22 And this stone which I have set as a pillar shall be God's house, and of all that You give me I will surely give a tenth to You."

29 So Jacob went on his journey and came to the land of the people of the East. 2 And he looked,

28:19 ªOr *House of God*

---

and saw a well in the field; and behold, there *were* three flocks of sheep lying by it; for out of that well they watered the flocks. A large stone *was* on the well's mouth. 3 Now all the flocks would be gathered there; and they would roll the stone from the well's mouth, water the sheep, and put the stone back in its place on the well's mouth.

4 And Jacob said to them, "My brethren, where *are* you from?"

And they said, "We *are* from Haran."

5 Then he said to them, "Do you know Laban the son of Nahor?"

And they said, "We know him."

6 So he said to them, "Is he well?"

And they said, "*He is* well. And look, his daughter Rachel is coming with the sheep."

7 Then he said, "Look, *it is* still high day; *it is* not time for the cattle to be gathered together. Water the sheep, and go and feed *them*."

8 But they said, "We cannot until all the flocks are gathered together, and they have rolled the stone from the well's mouth; then we water the sheep."

9 Now while he was still speaking with them, Rachel came with her father's sheep, for she was a shepherdess. 10 And it came to pass, when Jacob saw Rachel the daughter of Laban his mother's brother, and the sheep of Laban his mother's brother, that Jacob went near and rolled the stone from the well's mouth, and watered the flock of Laban his mother's brother. 11 Then Jacob kissed Rachel, and lifted up his voice and wept. 12 And Jacob told Rachel that he *was* her father's relative and that he *was* Rebekah's son. So she ran and told her father.

13 Then it came to pass, when Laban heard the report about Jacob his sister's son, that he ran to meet him, and embraced him and kissed him, and brought him to his house. So he told Laban all these things. 14 And Laban said to him, "Surely you *are* my bone and my flesh." And he stayed with him for a month.

15 Then Laban said to Jacob, "Because you *are* my relative, should you therefore serve me for nothing? Tell me, what *should* your wages be?" 16 Now Laban had two daugh-

ters: the name of the elder *was* Leah, and the name of the younger *was* Rachel. 17 Leah's eyes *were* delicate, but Rachel was beautiful of form and appearance.

18 Now Jacob loved Rachel; so he said, "I will serve you seven years for Rachel your younger daughter."

19 And Laban said, "*It is* better that I give her to you than that I should give her to another man. Stay with me." 20 So Jacob served seven years for Rachel, and they seemed *only* a few days to him because of the love he had for her.

21 Then Jacob said to Laban, "Give *me* my wife, for my days are fulfilled, that I may go in to her." 22 And Laban gathered together all the men of the place and made a feast. 23 Now it came to pass in the evening, that he took Leah his daughter and brought her to Jacob; and he went in to her. 24 And Laban gave his maid Zilpah to his daughter Leah *as* a maid. 25 So it came to pass in the morning, that behold, it *was* Leah. And he said to Laban, "What is this you have done to me? Was it not for Rachel that I served you? Why then have you deceived me?"

26 And Laban said, "It must not be done so in our country, to give the younger before the firstborn. 27 Fulfill her week, and we will give you this one also for the service which you will serve with me still another seven years."

28 Then Jacob did so and fulfilled her week. So he gave him his daughter Rachel as wife also. 29 And Laban gave his maid Bilhah to his daughter Rachel as a maid. 30 Then *Jacob* also went in to Rachel, and he also loved Rachel more than Leah. And he served with Laban still another seven years.

31 When the LORD saw that Leah *was* unloved, He opened her womb; but Rachel *was* barren. 32 So Leah conceived and bore a son, and she called his name Reuben;*a* for she said, "The LORD has surely looked on my affliction. Now therefore, my husband will love me." 33 Then she conceived again and bore a son, and said, "Because the LORD has heard that I *am* unloved, He has therefore given me this *son* also." And she called his name Simeon.*a* 34 She con-

29:32 *a*Literally *See, a Son*   29:33 *a*Literally *Heard*

*I*t's a part of our creation to express our emotions. Emotions are a key part of the way we relate to one another and to God.

No Comparison

People often compared Leah and Rachel, judging the two sisters by what they were on the outside. Not God. He never asks us to compare ourselves with any other person. In fact, it is a slap in God's face to look at someone else and say, "I wish I were more like her."

Why? Because God tenderly and uniquely designed you just the way He wanted you to be. He made you for Himself. He made you in a way that can never be duplicated.

When you begin to compare yourself with another person, you are saying, "God, You made a mistake. You failed. You could have done a better job creating me." None of us has the privilege of criticizing God. He is the Creator who looks at each of His created beings and says to Himself, "It is good."

Some women never cease to amaze me. They wouldn't be caught dead in the same dress some other woman is wearing. They will experiment with all kinds of hairstyles and makeup to be sure they don't appear to be copying someone else's "look." But they fail to apply that same principle to the way they view their own personalities, abilities, and inner beauty. They wouldn't dream of copying the way another woman dresses, but they desire to copy the way she is and to duplicate the way she acts, the way she talks, the way she performs, and the things she owns.

The fact is, everyone is attractive in one way or another. There's a twofold tragedy related to developing your own sense of beauty: First, you compare yourself to others; and then, you allow others to define what is attractive. It is dangerous to give so much power to another person that their opinion determines your self-esteem.

Get to the place where you hold a high opinion of yourself based on the fact that God made you exactly, precisely, intricately, wondrously, and uniquely the way you are. You are a one-of-a-kind creation for which there is no comparison!

God made you for His own purposes so that you might reflect a unique aspect of His glory. When you cease to compare yourself with others and refuse to be intimidated by what other people think and say, you are then in the position to birth that business, that ministry, that effort to change your community that God intended.

How dare you compare yourself with somebody else! God wanted you to be you. Nobody else. You!

ceived again and bore a son, and said, "Now this time my husband will become attached to me, because I have borne him three sons." Therefore his name was called Levi.ᵃ 35 And she conceived again and bore a son, and said, "Now I will praise the LORD." Therefore she called his name Judah.ᵃ Then she stopped bearing.

30 Now when Rachel saw that she bore Jacob no children, Rachel envied her sister, and said to Jacob, "Give me children, or else I die!"

2 And Jacob's anger was aroused against Rachel, and he said, "*Am* I in the place of God, who has withheld from you the fruit of the womb?"

3 So she said, "Here is my maid Bilhah; go in to her, and she will bear *a child* on my knees, that I also may have children by her." 4 Then she gave him Bilhah her maid as wife, and Jacob went in to her. 5 And Bilhah conceived and bore Jacob a son. 6 Then Rachel said, "God has judged my case; and He has also heard my voice and given me a son." Therefore she called his name Dan.ᵃ 7 And Rachel's maid Bilhah conceived again and bore Jacob a second son. 8 Then Rachel said, "With great wrestlings I have wrestled with my sister, *and* indeed I have prevailed." So she called his name Naphtali.ᵃ

9 When Leah saw that she had stopped bearing, she took Zilpah her maid and gave her to Jacob as wife. 10 And Leah's maid Zilpah bore Jacob a son. 11 Then Leah said, "A troop comes!"ᵃ So she called his name Gad.ᵇ 12 And Leah's maid Zilpah bore Jacob a second son. 13 Then Leah said, "I am happy, for the daughters will call me blessed." So she called his name Asher.ᵃ

14 Now Reuben went in the days of wheat harvest and found mandrakes in the field, and brought them to his mother Leah. Then Rachel said to Leah, "Please give me *some* of your son's mandrakes." 15 But she said to her, "*Is it* a small matter that you have taken away my

husband? Would you take away my son's mandrakes also?"

And Rachel said, "Therefore he will lie with you tonight for your son's mandrakes."

16 When Jacob came out of the field in the evening, Leah went out to meet him and said, "You must come in to me, for I have surely hired you with my son's mandrakes." And he lay with her that night.

17 And God listened to Leah, and she conceived and bore Jacob a fifth son. 18 Leah said, "God has given me my wages, because I have given my maid to my husband." So she called his name Issachar.ᵃ 19 Then Leah conceived again and bore Jacob a sixth son. 20 And Leah said, "God has endowed me *with* a good endowment; now my husband will dwell with me, because I have borne him six sons." So she called his name Zebulun.ᵃ 21 Afterward she bore a daughter, and called her name Dinah.

22 Then God remembered Rachel, and God listened to her and opened her womb. 23 And she conceived and bore a son, and said, "God has taken away my reproach." 24 So she called his name Joseph,ᵃ and said, "The LORD shall add to me another son."

25 And it came to pass, when Rachel had borne Joseph, that Jacob said to Laban, "Send me away, that I may go to my own place and to my country. 26 Give *me* my wives and my children for whom I have served you, and let me go; for you know my service which I have done for you."

27 And Laban said to him, "Please stay, if I have found favor in your eyes, *for* I have learned by experience that the LORD has blessed me for your sake." 28 Then he said, "Name me your wages, and I will give *it.*"

29 So *Jacob* said to him, "You know how I have served you and how your livestock has been with me. 30 For what you had before I *came was* little, and it has increased to a great amount; the LORD has blessed you since my coming. And now, when shall I also provide for my own house?"

29:34 ᵃLiterally *Attached*   29:35 ᵃLiterally *Praise*   30:6 ᵃLiterally *Judge*   30:8 ᵃLiterally *My Wrestling*   30:11 ᵃFollowing Qere, Syriac, and Targum; Kethib, Septuagint, and Vulgate read *in fortune.* ᵇLiterally *Troop* or *Fortune*   30:13 ᵃLiterally *Happy*   30:18 ᵃLiterally *Wages* 30:20 ᵃLiterally *Dwelling*   30:24 ᵃLiterally *He Will Add*

Gospel Pearls

31 So he said, "What shall I give you?"

And Jacob said, "You shall not give me anything. If you will do this thing for me, I will again feed and keep your flocks: 32 Let me pass through all your flock today, removing from there all the speckled and spotted sheep, and all the brown ones among the lambs, and the spotted and speckled among the goats; and *these* shall be my wages. 33 So my righteousness will answer for me in time to come, when the subject of my wages comes before you: every one that *is* not speckled and spotted among the goats, and brown among the lambs, will be considered stolen, if *it is* with me."

34 And Laban said, "Oh, that it were according to your word!" 35 So he removed that day the male goats that were speckled and spotted, all the female goats that were speckled and spotted, every one that had *some* white in it, and all the brown ones among the lambs, and gave *them* into the hand of his sons. 36 Then he put three days' journey between himself and Jacob, and Jacob fed the rest of Laban's flocks.

37 Now Jacob took for himself rods of green poplar and of the almond and chestnut trees, peeled white strips in them, and exposed the white which *was* in the rods. 38 And the rods which he had peeled, he set before the flocks in the gutters, in the watering troughs where the flocks came to drink, so that they should conceive when they came to drink. 39 So the flocks conceived before the rods, and the flocks brought forth streaked, speckled, and spotted. 40 Then Jacob separated the lambs, and made the flocks face toward the streaked and all the brown in the flock of Laban; but he put his own flocks by themselves and did not put them with Laban's flock.

41 And it came to pass, whenever the stronger livestock conceived, that Jacob placed the rods before the eyes of the livestock in the gutters, that they might conceive among the rods. 42 But when the flocks were feeble, he did not put *them* in; so the feebler were Laban's and the stronger Jacob's. 43 Thus the man became exceedingly prosperous, and had large flocks, female and male servants, and camels and donkeys.

31 Now *Jacob* heard the words of Laban's sons, saying, "Jacob has taken away all that was our father's, and from what was our father's he has acquired all this wealth." 2 And Jacob saw the countenance of Laban, and indeed it *was* not *favorable* toward him as before. 3 Then the LORD said to Jacob, "Return to the land of your fathers and to your family, and I will be with you."

4 So Jacob sent and called Rachel and Leah to the field, to his flock, 5 and said to them, "I see your father's countenance, that it *is* not *favorable* toward me as before; but the God of my father has been with me. 6 And you know that with all my might I have served your father. 7 Yet your father has deceived me and changed my wages ten times, but God did not allow him to hurt me. 8 If he said thus: 'The speckled shall be your wages,' then all the flocks bore speckled. And if he said thus: 'The streaked shall be your wages,' then all the flocks bore streaked. 9 So God has taken away the livestock of your father and given *them* to me.

10 "And it happened, at the time when the flocks conceived, that I lifted my eyes and saw in a dream, and behold, the rams which leaped upon the flocks *were* streaked, speckled, and gray-spotted. 11 Then the Angel of God spoke to me in a dream, saying, 'Jacob.' And I said, 'Here I am.' 12 And He said, 'Lift your eyes now and see, all the rams which leap on the flocks *are* streaked, speckled, and gray-spotted; for I have seen all that Laban is doing to you. 13 I *am* the God of Bethel, where you anointed the pillar *and* where you made a vow to Me. Now arise, get out of this land, and return to the land of your family.' "

14 Then Rachel and Leah answered and said to him, "Is there still any portion or inheritance for us in our father's house? 15 Are we not considered strangers by him? For he has sold us, and also completely consumed our money. 16 For all these riches which God has taken from our father are *really* ours and our children's; now then, whatever God has said to you, do it."

17 Then Jacob rose and set his sons and his wives on camels. 18 And he

---

*W*omen, don't let anyone convince you that you need to stifle your emotions. Don't let anything happen that makes you so cold you lose your ability to love.

carried away all his livestock and all his possessions which he had gained, his acquired livestock which he had gained in Padan Aram, to go to his father Isaac in the land of Canaan. 19 Now Laban had gone to shear his sheep, and Rachel had stolen the household idols that were her father's. 20 And Jacob stole away, unknown to Laban the Syrian, in that he did not tell him that he intended to flee. 21 So he fled with all that he had. He arose and crossed the river, and headed toward the mountains of Gilead.

22 And Laban was told on the third day that Jacob had fled. 23 Then he took his brethren with him and pursued him for seven days' journey, and he overtook him in the mountains of Gilead. 24 But God had come to Laban the Syrian in a dream by night, and said to him, "Be careful that you speak to Jacob neither good nor bad."

25 So Laban overtook Jacob. Now Jacob had pitched his tent in the mountains, and Laban with his brethren pitched in the mountains of Gilead.

26 And Laban said to Jacob: "What have you done, that you have stolen away unknown to me, and carried away my daughters like captives *taken* with the sword? 27 Why did you flee away secretly, and steal away from me, and not tell me; for I might have sent you away with joy and songs, with timbrel and harp? 28 And you did not allow me to kiss my sons and my daughters. Now you have done foolishly in *so* doing. 29 It is in my power to do you harm, but the God of your father spoke to me last night, saying, 'Be careful that you speak to Jacob neither good nor bad.' 30 And now you have surely gone because you greatly long for your father's house, *but* why did you steal my gods?"

31 Then Jacob answered and said to Laban, "Because I was afraid, for I said, 'Perhaps you would take your daughters from me by force.' 32 With whomever you find your gods, do not let him live. In the presence of our brethren, identify what I have of yours and take *it* with you." For Jacob did not know that Rachel had stolen them.

33 And Laban went into Jacob's tent, into Leah's tent, and into the two maids' tents, but he did not find *them.* Then he went out of Leah's tent and entered Rachel's tent. 34 Now Rachel had taken the household idols, put them in the camel's saddle, and sat on them. And Laban searched all about the tent but did not find *them.* 35 And she said to her father, "Let it not displease my lord that I cannot rise before you, for the manner of women *is* with me." And he searched but did not find the household idols.

36 Then Jacob was angry and rebuked Laban, and Jacob answered and said to Laban: "What *is* my trespass? What *is* my sin, that you have so hotly pursued me? 37 Although you have searched all my things, what part of your household things have you found? Set *it* here before my brethren and your brethren, that they may judge between us both! 38 These twenty years I *have been* with you; your ewes and your female goats have not miscarried their young, and I have not eaten the rams of your flock. 39 That which was torn *by beasts* I did not bring to you; I bore the loss of it. You required it from my hand, *whether* stolen by day or stolen by night. 40 *There* I was! In the day the drought consumed me, and the frost by night, and my sleep departed from my eyes. 41 Thus I have been in your house twenty years; I served you fourteen years for your two daughters, and six years for your flock, and you have changed my wages ten times. 42 Unless the God of my father, the God of Abraham and the Fear of Isaac, had been with me, surely now you would have sent me away empty-handed. God has seen my affliction and the labor of my hands, and rebuked *you* last night."

43 And Laban answered and said to Jacob, "*These* daughters *are* my daughters, and *these* children *are* my children, and *this* flock *is* my flock; all that you see *is* mine. But what can I do this day to these my daughters or to their children whom they have borne? 44 Now therefore, come, let us make a covenant, you and I, and let it be a witness between you and me."

45 So Jacob took a stone and set it up *as* a pillar. 46 Then Jacob said to his brethren, "Gather stones." And they took stones and made a heap, and they ate there on the heap.

Gospel Pearls

47 Laban called it Jegar Sahadutha,*a* but Jacob called it Galeed.*b* 48 And Laban said, "This heap *is* a witness between you and me this day." Therefore its name was called Galeed, 49 also Mizpah,*a* because he said, "May the LORD watch between you and me when we are absent one from another. 50 If you afflict my daughters, or if you take *other* wives besides my daughters, *although* no man *is* with us—see, God *is* witness between you and me!"

51 Then Laban said to Jacob, "Here is this heap and here is *this* pillar, which I have placed between you and me. 52 This heap *is* a witness, and *this* pillar *is* a witness, that I will not pass beyond this heap to you, and you will not pass beyond this heap and this pillar to me, for harm. 53 The God of Abraham, the God of Nahor, and the God of their father judge between us." And Jacob swore by the Fear of his father Isaac. 54 Then Jacob offered a sacrifice on the mountain, and called his brethren to eat bread. And they ate bread and stayed all night on the mountain. 55 And early in the morning Laban arose, and kissed his sons and daughters and blessed them. Then Laban departed and returned to his place.

32 So Jacob went on his way, and the angels of God met him. 2 When Jacob saw them, he said, "This *is* God's camp." And he called the name of that place Mahanaim.*a*

3 Then Jacob sent messengers before him to Esau his brother in the land of Seir, the country of Edom. 4 And he commanded them, saying, "Speak thus to my lord Esau, 'Thus your servant Jacob says: "I have dwelt with Laban and stayed there until now. 5 I have oxen, donkeys, flocks, and male and female servants; and I have sent to tell my lord, that I may find favor in your sight." ' "

6 Then the messengers returned to Jacob, saying, "We came to your brother Esau, and he also is coming to meet you, and four hundred men *are* with him." 7 So Jacob was greatly afraid and distressed; and he divided the people that *were* with him, and the flocks and herds and camels, into two companies. 8 And he said, "If Esau comes to the one company and attacks it, then the other company which is left will escape."

9 Then Jacob said, "O God of my father Abraham and God of my father Isaac, the LORD who said to me, 'Return to your country and to your family, and I will deal well with you': 10 I am not worthy of the least of all the mercies and of all the truth which You have shown Your servant; for I crossed over this Jordan with my staff, and now I have become two companies. 11 Deliver me, I pray, from the hand of my brother, from the hand of Esau; for I fear him, lest he come and attack me *and* the mother with the children. 12 For You said, 'I will surely treat you well, and make your descendants as the sand of the sea, which cannot be numbered for multitude.' "

13 So he lodged there that same night, and took what came to his hand as a present for Esau his brother: 14 two hundred female goats and twenty male goats, two hundred ewes and twenty rams, 15 thirty milk camels with their colts, forty cows and ten bulls, twenty female donkeys and ten foals. 16 Then he delivered *them* to the hand of his servants, every drove by itself, and said to his servants, "Pass over before me, and put some distance between successive droves." 17 And he commanded the first one, saying, "When Esau my brother meets you and asks you, saying, 'To whom do you belong, and where are you going? Whose *are* these in front of you?' 18 then you shall say, 'They *are* your servant Jacob's. It *is* a present sent to my lord Esau; and behold, he also *is* behind us.' " 19 So he commanded the second, the third, and all who followed the droves, saying, "In this manner you shall speak to Esau when you find him; 20 and also say, 'Behold, your servant Jacob *is* behind us.' " For he said, "I will appease him with the present that goes before me, and afterward I will see his face; perhaps he will accept me." 21 So the present went on over before him, but he himself lodged that night in the camp.

22 And he arose that night and took his two wives, his two female ser-

*H*ear me clearly: The time has come for you to come out of your shock! Allow yourself to feel again. Allow yourself to cry again. Allow yourself to cry out to God again.

vants, and his eleven sons, and crossed over the ford of Jabbok. 23 He took them, sent them over the brook, and sent over what he had. 24 Then Jacob was left alone; and a Man wrestled with him until the breaking of day. 25 Now when He saw that He did not prevail against him, He touched the socket of his hip; and the socket of Jacob's hip was out of joint as He wrestled with him. 26 And He said, "Let Me go, for the day breaks."

But he said, "I will not let You go unless You bless me!"

27 So He said to him, "What *is* your name?"

He said, "Jacob."

28 And He said, "Your name shall no longer be called Jacob, but Israel;*a* for you have struggled with God and with men, and have prevailed."

29 Then Jacob asked, saying, "Tell *me* Your name, I pray."

And He said, "Why *is* it *that* you ask about My name?" And He blessed him there.

30 So Jacob called the name of the place Peniel:*a* "For I have seen God face to face, and my life is preserved." 31 Just as he crossed over Penuel*a* the sun rose on him, and he limped on his hip. 32 Therefore to this day the children of Israel do not eat the muscle that shrank, which *is* on the hip socket, because He touched the socket of Jacob's hip in the muscle that shrank.

33 Now Jacob lifted his eyes and looked, and there, Esau was coming, and with him were four hundred men. So he divided the children among Leah, Rachel, and the two maidservants. 2 And he put the maidservants and their children in front, Leah and her children behind, and Rachel and Joseph last. 3 Then he crossed over before them and bowed himself to the ground seven times, until he came near to his brother.

4 But Esau ran to meet him, and embraced him, and fell on his neck and kissed him, and they wept. 5 And he lifted his eyes and saw the women and children, and said, "Who *are* these with you?"

So he said, "The children whom God has graciously given your ser-

vant." 6 Then the maidservants came near, they and their children, and bowed down. 7 And Leah also came near with her children, and they bowed down. Afterward Joseph and Rachel came near, and they bowed down.

8 Then Esau said, "What *do* you *mean by* all this company which I met?"

And he said, "*These are* to find favor in the sight of my lord."

9 But Esau said, "I have enough, my brother; keep what you have for yourself."

10 And Jacob said, "No, please, if I have now found favor in your sight, then receive my present from my hand, inasmuch as I have seen your face as though I had seen the face of God, and you were pleased with me. 11 Please, take my blessing that is brought to you, because God has dealt graciously with me, and because I have enough." So he urged him, and he took *it.*

12 Then Esau said, "Let us take our journey; let us go, and I will go before you."

13 But Jacob said to him, "My lord knows that the children *are* weak, and the flocks and herds which are nursing *are* with me. And if the men should drive them hard one day, all the flock will die. 14 Please let my lord go on ahead before his servant. I will lead on slowly at a pace which the livestock that go before me, and the children, are able to endure, until I come to my lord in Seir."

15 And Esau said, "Now let me leave with you *some* of the people who *are* with me."

But he said, "What need is there? Let me find favor in the sight of my lord." 16 So Esau returned that day on his way to Seir. 17 And Jacob journeyed to Succoth, built himself a house, and made booths for his livestock. Therefore the name of the place is called Succoth.*a*

18 Then Jacob came safely to the city of Shechem, which *is* in the land of Canaan, when he came from Padan Aram; and he pitched his tent before the city. 19 And he bought the parcel of land, where he had pitched his tent, from the children of Hamor, Shechem's father, for one hundred

---

32:28 *a*Literally *Prince with God*   32:30 *a*Literally *Face of God*   32:31 *a*Same as *Peniel,* verse 30
33:17 *a*Literally *Booths*

---

*I*f you have lost your tears, ask God to restore them to you. Ask Him to bring your femininity out of shock.

Don't Let the Limp Fool You

Genesis 32:31, 32

Jacob wrestled with an angel of the Lord one night and came out of that experience with two things: the blessing of God and a limp in his walk. He limped for the rest of his life. The limp didn't mean that Jacob hadn't been blessed by God. It meant only one thing—that he had a limp.

Your struggle with sin doesn't mean that you aren't saved in your spirit or healed in your soul. It only means that you still have a limp. And the fact is, you may never lose your limp entirely. You may learn to walk and even to skip and run. You may learn to get around so well that nothing about your limp slows you down. You may be able to get a built-up shoe that disguises the handicap and allows you to function as though you had never been injured. You may even forget all about your limp. When that happens, and you feel no pain and no self-consciousness about it, then you are healed, even though the limp remains.

My children recently saw a man who had lost the use of his legs. They said, "Why don't you come have our daddy pray for you?"

"Oh, I'm all right now," the man said. "I am healed."

They didn't understand what he meant, so he went on to explain. "You see, when this first happened, I was in pain all the time. I know I'm healed because it doesn't hurt anymore." Even though his injury was over, his agony had continued.

Don't let the limp fool you. You can be healed and still have a limp. The limp is only a sign that you have been through something, not that you are still struggling with something. If you can think about some insult or adversity and it doesn't hurt anymore, you can be certain that you have been healed. If you can talk about a painful experience in your past and it doesn't cause you to feel anger or hatred, you have been healed. If you can see the person who has wronged you or hurt you and not feel bitterness, then by God's grace, you have been healed.

You may still have scars on your body, tell-tale signs of your predicament. You may still be divorced. You may still have a need. You may still have the "limp," but on the inside you have been healed.

Don't confuse the scars with the inner work. The scars do not define the healing. What God has done in your innermost being proves that you've been healed.

pieces of money. 20 Then he erected an altar there and called it El Elohe Israel.*a*

34 Now Dinah the daughter of Leah, whom she had borne to Jacob, went out to see the daughters of the land. 2 And when Shechem the son of Hamor the Hivite, prince of the country, saw her, he took her and lay with her, and violated her. 3 His soul was strongly attracted to Dinah the daughter of Jacob, and he loved the young woman and spoke kindly to the young woman. 4 So Shechem spoke to his father Hamor, saying, "Get me this young woman as a wife."

5 And Jacob heard that he had defiled Dinah his daughter. Now his sons were with his livestock in the field; so Jacob held his peace until they came. 6 Then Hamor the father of Shechem went out to Jacob to speak with him. 7 And the sons of Jacob came in from the field when they heard *it;* and the men were grieved and very angry, because he had done a disgraceful thing in Israel by lying with Jacob's daughter, a thing which ought not to be done. 8 But Hamor spoke with them, saying, "The soul of my son Shechem longs for your daughter. Please give her to him as a wife. 9 And make marriages with us; give your daughters to us, and take our daughters to yourselves. 10 So you shall dwell with us, and the land shall be before you. Dwell and trade in it, and acquire possessions for yourselves in it."

11 Then Shechem said to her father and her brothers, "Let me find favor in your eyes, and whatever you say to me I will give. 12 Ask me ever so much dowry and gift, and I will give according to what you say to me; but give me the young woman as a wife."

13 But the sons of Jacob answered Shechem and Hamor his father, and spoke deceitfully, because he had defiled Dinah their sister. 14 And they said to them, "We cannot do this thing, to give our sister to one who is uncircumcised, for that *would be* a reproach to us. 15 But on this *condition* we will consent to you: If you will become as we *are,* if every male of you is circumcised, 16 then we will give our daughters to you, and we

will take your daughters to us; and we will dwell with you, and we will become one people. 17 But if you will not heed us and be circumcised, then we will take our daughter and be gone."

18 And their words pleased Hamor and Shechem, Hamor's son. 19 So the young man did not delay to do the thing, because he delighted in Jacob's daughter. He *was* more honorable than all the household of his father.

20 And Hamor and Shechem his son came to the gate of their city, and spoke with the men of their city, saying: 21 "These men *are* at peace with us. Therefore let them dwell in the land and trade in it. For indeed the land *is* large enough for them. Let us take their daughters to us as wives, and let us give them our daughters. 22 Only on this *condition* will the men consent to dwell with us, to be one people: if every male among us is circumcised as they *are* circumcised. 23 *Will* not their livestock, their property, and every animal of theirs *be* ours? Only let us consent to them, and they will dwell with us." 24 And all who went out of the gate of his city heeded Hamor and Shechem his son; every male was circumcised, all who went out of the gate of his city.

25 Now it came to pass on the third day, when they were in pain, that two of the sons of Jacob, Simeon and Levi, Dinah's brothers, each took his sword and came boldly upon the city and killed all the males. 26 And they killed Hamor and Shechem his son with the edge of the sword, and took Dinah from Shechem's house, and went out. 27 The sons of Jacob came upon the slain, and plundered the city, because their sister had been defiled. 28 They took their sheep, their oxen, and their donkeys, what *was* in the city and what *was* in the field, 29 and all their wealth. All their little ones and their wives they took captive; and they plundered even all that *was* in the houses.

30 Then Jacob said to Simeon and Levi, "You have troubled me by making me obnoxious among the inhabitants of the land, among the Canaanites and the Perizzites; and since I *am* few in number, they will gather

33:20 *a*Literally *God, the God of Israel*

Gospel Pearls

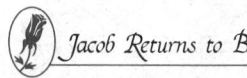

themselves together against me and kill me. I shall be destroyed, my household and I."

31 But they said, "Should he treat our sister like a harlot?"

35 Then God said to Jacob, "Arise, go up to Bethel and dwell there; and make an altar there to God, who appeared to you when you fled from the face of Esau your brother."

2 And Jacob said to his household and to all who *were* with him, "Put away the foreign gods that *are* among you, purify yourselves, and change your garments. 3 Then let us arise and go up to Bethel; and I will make an altar there to God, who answered me in the day of my distress and has been with me in the way which I have gone." 4 So they gave Jacob all the foreign gods which *were* in their hands, and the earrings which *were* in their ears; and Jacob hid them under the terebinth tree which *was* by Shechem.

5 And they journeyed, and the terror of God was upon the cities that *were* all around them, and they did not pursue the sons of Jacob. 6 So Jacob came to Luz (that *is,* Bethel), which *is* in the land of Canaan, he and all the people who *were* with him. 7 And he built an altar there and called the place El Bethel,*a* because there God appeared to him when he fled from the face of his brother.

8 Now Deborah, Rebekah's nurse, died, and she was buried below Bethel under the terebinth tree. So the name of it was called Allon Bachuth.*a*

9 Then God appeared to Jacob again, when he came from Padan Aram, and blessed him. 10 And God said to him, "Your name *is* Jacob; your name shall not be called Jacob anymore, but Israel shall be your name." So He called his name Israel. 11 Also God said to him: "I *am* God Almighty. Be fruitful and multiply; a nation and a company of nations shall proceed from you, and kings shall come from your body. 12 The land which I gave Abraham and Isaac I give to you; and to your descendants after you I give this land." 13 Then God went up from him

in the place where He talked with him. 14 So Jacob set up a pillar in the place where He talked with him, a pillar of stone; and he poured a drink offering on it, and he poured oil on it. 15 And Jacob called the name of the place where God spoke with him, Bethel.

16 Then they journeyed from Bethel. And when there was but a little distance to go to Ephrath, Rachel labored *in childbirth,* and she had hard labor. 17 Now it came to pass, when she was in hard labor, that the midwife said to her, "Do not fear; you will have this son also." 18 And so it was, as her soul was departing (for she died), that she called his name Ben-Oni;*a* but his father called him Benjamin.*b* 19 So Rachel died and was buried on the way to Ephrath (that *is,* Bethlehem). 20 And Jacob set a pillar on her grave, which *is* the pillar of Rachel's grave to this day.

21 Then Israel journeyed and pitched his tent beyond the tower of Eder. 22 And it happened, when Israel dwelt in that land, that Reuben went and lay with Bilhah his father's concubine; and Israel heard *about it.*

Now the sons of Jacob were twelve: 23 the sons of Leah *were* Reuben, Jacob's firstborn, and Simeon, Levi, Judah, Issachar, and Zebulun; 24 the sons of Rachel *were* Joseph and Benjamin; 25 the sons of Bilhah, Rachel's maidservant, *were* Dan and Naphtali; 26 and the sons of Zilpah, Leah's maidservant, *were* Gad and Asher. These *were* the sons of Jacob who were born to him in Padan Aram.

27 Then Jacob came to his father Isaac at Mamre, or Kirjath Arba*a* (that *is,* Hebron), where Abraham and Isaac had dwelt. 28 Now the days of Isaac were one hundred and eighty years. 29 So Isaac breathed his last and died, and was gathered to his people, *being* old and full of days. And his sons Esau and Jacob buried him.

36 Now this *is* the genealogy of Esau, who is Edom. 2 Esau took his wives from the daughters of Canaan: Adah the daughter of Elon the Hittite; Aholibamah the daughter of

35:7 *a*Literally *God of the House of God*   35:8 *a*Literally *Terebinth of Weeping*   35:18 *a*Literally *Son of My Sorrow*   *b*Literally *Son of the Right Hand*   35:27 *a*Literally *Town of Arbah*

*I*n our souls, we have self-consciousness. We know that we exist. We know we are alive because we have a soul. It is from our souls that we relate to one another as human beings.

Anah, the daughter of Zibeon the Hivite; 3 and Basemath, Ishmael's daughter, sister of Nebajoth. 4 Now Adah bore Eliphaz to Esau, and Basemath bore Reuel. 5 And Aholibamah bore Jeush, Jaalam, and Korah. These *were* the sons of Esau who were born to him in the land of Canaan.

6 Then Esau took his wives, his sons, his daughters, and all the persons of his household, his cattle and all his animals, and all his goods which he had gained in the land of Canaan, and went to a country away from the presence of his brother Jacob. 7 For their possessions were too great for them to dwell together, and · the land where they were strangers could not support them because of their livestock. 8 So Esau dwelt in Mount Seir. Esau *is* Edom.

9 And this *is* the genealogy of Esau the father of the Edomites in Mount Seir. 10 These *were* the names of Esau's sons: Eliphaz the son of Adah the wife of Esau, and Reuel the son of Basemath the wife of Esau. 11 And the sons of Eliphaz were Teman, Omar, Zepho,*ª* Gatam, and Kenaz.

12 Now Timna was the concubine of Eliphaz, Esau's son, and she bore Amalek to Eliphaz. These *were* the sons of Adah, Esau's wife.

13 These *were* the sons of Reuel: Nahath, Zerah, Shammah, and Mizzah. These were the sons of Basemath, Esau's wife.

14 These were the sons of Aholibamah, Esau's wife, the daughter of Anah, the daughter of Zibeon. And she bore to Esau: Jeush, Jaalam, and Korah.

15 These *were* the chiefs of the sons of Esau. The sons of Eliphaz, the firstborn *son* of Esau, were Chief Teman, Chief Omar, Chief Zepho, Chief Kenaz, 16 Chief Korah,*ª* Chief Gatam, *and* Chief Amalek. These *were* the chiefs of Eliphaz in the land of Edom. They *were* the sons of Adah.

17 These *were* the sons of Reuel, Esau's son: Chief Nahath, Chief Zerah, Chief Shammah, and Chief Mizzah. These *were* the chiefs of Reuel in the land of Edom. These

were the sons of Basemath, Esau's wife.

18 And these *were* the sons of Aholibamah, Esau's wife: Chief Jeush, Chief Jaalam, and Chief Korah. These *were* the chiefs *who* descended from Aholibamah, Esau's wife, the daughter of Anah.

19 These *were* the sons of Esau, who is Edom, and these *were* their chiefs.

20 These *were* the sons of Seir the Horite who inhabited the land: Lotan, Shobal, Zibeon, Anah, 21 Dishon, Ezer, and Dishan. These *were* the chiefs of the Horites, the sons of Seir, in the land of Edom.

22 And the sons of Lotan were Hori and Hemam.*ª* Lotan's sister *was* Timna.

23 These *were* the sons of Shobal: Alvan,*ª* Manahath, Ebal, Shepho,*b* and Onam.

24 These *were* the sons of Zibeon: both Ajah and Anah. This *was the* Anah who found the water*ª* in the wilderness as he pastured the donkeys of his father Zibeon. 25 These *were* the children of Anah: Dishon and Aholibamah the daughter of Anah.

26 These *were* the sons of Dishon:*ª* Hemdan,*b* Eshban, Ithran, and Cheran. 27 These *were* the sons of Ezer: Bilhan, Zaavan, and Akan.*ª* 28 These *were* the sons of Dishan: Uz and Aran.

29 These *were* the chiefs of the Horites: Chief Lotan, Chief Shobal, Chief Zibeon, Chief Anah, 30 Chief Dishon, Chief Ezer, and Chief Dishan. These *were* the chiefs of the Horites, according to their chiefs in the land of Seir.

31 Now these *were* the kings who reigned in the land of Edom before any king reigned over the children of Israel: 32 Bela the son of Beor reigned in Edom, and the name of his city *was* Dinhabah. 33 And when Bela died, Jobab the son of Zerah of Bozrah reigned in his place. 34 When Jobab died, Husham of the land of the Temanites reigned in his place. 35 And when Husham died, Hadad the son of Bedad, who attacked Midian in the field of Moab, reigned in his place. And the name

Gospel Pearls

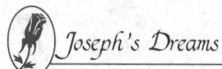

of his city *was* Avith. 36 When Hadad died, Samlah of Masrekah reigned in his place. 37 And when Samlah died, Saul of Rehoboth-by-the-River reigned in his place. 38 When Saul died, Baal-Hanan the son of Achbor reigned in his place. 39 And when Baal-Hanan the son of Achbor died, Hadar*ᵃ* reigned in his place; and the name of his city *was* Pau.*ᵇ* His wife's name *was* Mehetabel, the daughter of Matred, the daughter of Mezahab.

40 And these *were* the names of the chiefs of Esau, according to their families and their places, by their names: Chief Timnah, Chief Alvah,*ᵃ* Chief Jetheth, 41 Chief Aholibamah, Chief Elah, Chief Pinon, 42 Chief Kenaz, Chief Teman, Chief Mibzar, 43 Chief Magdiel, and Chief Iram. These *were* the chiefs of Edom, according to their dwelling places in the land of their possession. Esau *was* the father of the Edomites.

37 Now Jacob dwelt in the land where his father was a stranger, in the land of Canaan. 2 This *is* the history of Jacob.

Joseph, *being* seventeen years old, was feeding the flock with his brothers. And the lad *was* with the sons of Bilhah and the sons of Zilpah, his father's wives; and Joseph brought a bad report of them to his father.

3 Now Israel loved Joseph more than all his children, because he *was* the son of his old age. Also he made him a tunic of *many* colors. 4 But when his brothers saw that their father loved him more than all his brothers, they hated him and could not speak peaceably to him.

5 Now Joseph had a dream, and he told *it* to his brothers; and they hated him even more. 6 So he said to them, "Please hear this dream which I have dreamed: 7 There we were, binding sheaves in the field. Then behold, my sheaf arose and also stood upright; and indeed your sheaves stood all around and bowed down to my sheaf."

8 And his brothers said to him, "Shall you indeed reign over us? Or shall you indeed have dominion over us?" So they hated him even more for his dreams and for his words.

9 Then he dreamed still another dream and told it to his brothers, and said, "Look, I have dreamed another dream. And this time, the sun, the moon, and the eleven stars bowed down to me."

10 So he told *it* to his father and his brothers; and his father rebuked him and said to him, "What *is* this dream that you have dreamed? Shall your mother and I and your brothers indeed come to bow down to the earth before you?" 11 And his brothers envied him, but his father kept the matter *in mind*.

12 Then his brothers went to feed their father's flock in Shechem. 13 And Israel said to Joseph, "Are not your brothers feeding *the flock* in Shechem? Come, I will send you to them."

So he said to him, "Here I am."

14 Then he said to him, "Please go and see if it is well with your brothers and well with the flocks, and bring back word to me." So he sent him out of the Valley of Hebron, and he went to Shechem.

15 Now a certain man found him, and there he was, wandering in the field. And the man asked him, saying, "What are you seeking?"

16 So he said, "I am seeking my brothers. Please tell me where they are feeding *their flocks*."

17 And the man said, "They have departed from here, for I heard them say, 'Let us go to Dothan.' " So Joseph went after his brothers and found them in Dothan.

18 Now when they saw him afar off, even before he came near them, they conspired against him to kill him. 19 Then they said to one another, "Look, this dreamer is coming! 20 Come therefore, let us now kill him and cast him into some pit; and we shall say, 'Some wild beast has devoured him.' We shall see what will become of his dreams!"

21 But Reuben heard *it*, and he delivered him out of their hands, and said, "Let us not kill him." 22 And Reuben said to them, "Shed no blood, *but* cast him into this pit which *is* in the wilderness, and do not lay a hand on him"—that he might deliver him out of their hands, and bring him back to his father.

23 So it came to pass, when Joseph

36:39 *ᵃ*Spelled *Hadad* in Samaritan Pentateuch, Syriac, and 1 Chronicles 1:50   *ᵇ*Spelled *Pai* in 1 Chronicles 1:50   36:40 *ᵃ*Spelled *Aliah* in 1 Chronicles 1:51

---

*T*o tell a person not to be emotional is to tell a person not to be human. It is to deny that person's God-given right and privilege to enter into adoration of the Creator.

had come to his brothers, that they stripped Joseph *of* his tunic, the tunic of *many* colors that *was* on him. 24 Then they took him and cast him into a pit. And the pit *was* empty; *there was* no water in it.

25 And they sat down to eat a meal. Then they lifted their eyes and looked, and there was a company of Ishmaelites, coming from Gilead with their camels, bearing spices, balm, and myrrh, on their way to carry *them* down to Egypt. 26 So Judah said to his brothers, "What profit *is there* if we kill our brother and conceal his blood? 27 Come and let us sell him to the Ishmaelites, and let not our hand be upon him, for he *is* our brother *and* our flesh." And his brothers listened. 28 Then Midianite traders passed by; so *the brothers* pulled Joseph up and lifted him out of the pit, and sold him to the Ishmaelites for twenty *shekels* of silver. And they took Joseph to Egypt.

29 Then Reuben returned to the pit, and indeed Joseph *was* not in the pit; and he tore his clothes. 30 And he returned to his brothers and said, "The lad *is* no *more;* and I, where shall I go?"

31 So they took Joseph's tunic, killed a kid of the goats, and dipped the tunic in the blood. 32 Then they sent the tunic of *many* colors, and they brought *it* to their father and said, "We have found this. Do you know whether it *is* your son's tunic or not?"

33 And he recognized it and said, "*It is* my son's tunic. A wild beast has devoured him. Without doubt Joseph is torn to pieces." 34 Then Jacob tore his clothes, put sackcloth on his waist, and mourned for his son many days. 35 And all his sons and all his daughters arose to comfort him; but he refused to be comforted, and he said, "For I shall go down into the grave to my son in mourning." Thus his father wept for him.

36 Now the Midianites[a] had sold him in Egypt to Potiphar, an officer of Pharaoh *and* captain of the guard.

38 It came to pass at that time that Judah departed from his brothers, and visited a certain Adullamite whose name *was* Hirah. 2 And Judah saw there a daughter of a certain Ca-naanite whose name *was* Shua, and he married her and went in to her. 3 So she conceived and bore a son, and he called his name Er. 4 She conceived again and bore a son, and she called his name Onan. 5 And she conceived yet again and bore a son, and called his name Shelah. He was at Chezib when she bore him.

6 Then Judah took a wife for Er his firstborn, and her name *was* Tamar. 7 But Er, Judah's firstborn, was wicked in the sight of the LORD, and the LORD killed him. 8 And Judah said to Onan, "Go in to your brother's wife and marry her, and raise up an heir to your brother." 9 But Onan knew that the heir would not be his; and it came to pass, when he went in to his brother's wife, that he emitted on the ground, lest he should give an heir to his brother. 10 And the thing which he did displeased the LORD; therefore He killed him also.

11 Then Judah said to Tamar his daughter-in-law, "Remain a widow in your father's house till my son Shelah is grown." For he said, "Lest he also die like his brothers." And Tamar went and dwelt in her father's house.

12 Now in the process of time the daughter of Shua, Judah's wife, died; and Judah was comforted, and went up to his sheepshearers at Timnah, he and his friend Hirah the Adullam-ite. 13 And it was told Tamar, saying, "Look, your father-in-law is going up to Timnah to shear his sheep." 14 So she took off her widow's garments, covered *herself* with a veil and wrapped herself, and sat in an open place which *was* on the way to Timnah; for she saw that Shelah was grown, and she was not given to him as a wife. 15 When Judah saw her, he thought she *was* a harlot, because she had covered her face. 16 Then he turned to her by the way, and said, "Please let me come in to you"; for he did not know that she *was* his daughter-in-law.

So she said, "What will you give me, that you may come in to me?"

17 And he said, "I will send a young goat from the flock."

So she said, "Will you give *me* a pledge till you send *it?*"

18 Then he said, "What pledge shall I give you?"

37:36 aMasoretic Text reads *Medanites.*

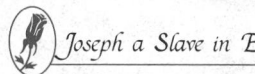

So she said, "Your signet and cord, and your staff that *is* in your hand." Then he gave *them* to her, and went in to her, and she conceived by him. 19 So she arose and went away, and laid aside her veil and put on the garments of her widowhood.

20 And Judah sent the young goat by the hand of his friend the Adullamite, to receive *his* pledge from the woman's hand, but he did not find her. 21 Then he asked the men of that place, saying, "Where is the harlot who *was* openly by the roadside?"

And they said, "There was no harlot in this *place.*"

22 So he returned to Judah and said, "I cannot find her. Also, the men of the place said there was no harlot in this *place.*"

23 Then Judah said, "Let her take *them* for herself, lest we be shamed; for I sent this young goat and you have not found her."

24 And it came to pass, about three months after, that Judah was told, saying, "Tamar your daughter-in-law has played the harlot; furthermore she *is* with child by harlotry."

So Judah said, "Bring her out and let her be burned!"

25 When she *was* brought out, she sent to her father-in-law, saying, "By the man to whom these belong, I *am* with child." And she said, "Please determine whose these *are*—the signet and cord, and staff."

26 So Judah acknowledged *them* and said, "She has been more righteous than I, because I did not give her to Shelah my son." And he never knew her again.

27 Now it came to pass, at the time for giving birth, that behold, twins *were* in her womb. 28 And so it was, when she was giving birth, that *the one* put out *his* hand; and the midwife took a scarlet *thread* and bound it on his hand, saying, "This one came out first." 29 Then it happened, as he drew back his hand, that his brother came out unexpectedly; and she said, "How did you break through? *This* breach *be* upon you!" Therefore his name was called Perez.*ᵃ* 30 Afterward his brother came out who had the scarlet *thread* on his hand. And his name was called Zerah.

39 Now Joseph had been taken down to Egypt. And Potiphar, an officer of Pharaoh, captain of the guard, an Egyptian, bought him from the Ishmaelites who had taken him down there. 2 The LORD was with Joseph, and he was a successful man; and he was in the house of his master the Egyptian. 3 And his master saw that the LORD *was* with him and that the LORD made all he did to prosper in his hand. 4 So Joseph found favor in his sight, and served him. Then he made him overseer of his house, and all *that* he had he put under his authority. 5 So it was, from the time *that* he had made him overseer of his house and all that he had, that the LORD blessed the Egyptian's house for Joseph's sake; and the blessing of the LORD was on all that he had in the house and in the field. 6 Thus he left all that he had in Joseph's hand, and he did not know what he had except for the bread which he ate.

Now Joseph was handsome in form and appearance.

7 And it came to pass after these things that his master's wife cast longing eyes on Joseph, and she said, "Lie with me."

8 But he refused and said to his master's wife, "Look, my master does not know what *is* with me in the house, and he has committed all that he has to my hand. 9 *There is* no one greater in this house than I, nor has he kept back anything from me but you, because you *are* his wife. How then can I do this great wickedness, and sin against God?"

10 So it was, as she spoke to Joseph day by day, that he did not heed her, to lie with her *or* to be with her.

11 But it happened about this time, when Joseph went into the house to do his work, and none of the men of the house *was* inside, 12 that she caught him by his garment, saying, "Lie with me." But he left his garment in her hand, and fled and ran outside. 13 And so it was, when she saw that he had left his garment in her hand and fled outside, 14 that she called to the men of her house and spoke to them, saying, "See, he has brought in to us a Hebrew to mock us. He came in to me to lie with me, and I cried out with a loud voice.

38:29 ᵃLiterally *Breach* or *Breakthrough*

*I*f we ever needed women to prostrate themselves on the altar and wail in response to God's people being taken into bondage, it is now!

Soul Secrets
in the midst of unjust accusations

L ord, I'm sick and tired of lies. Weary of dodging verbal
bullets and ducking under insults. You know I did not
do what they say I've done. They're out to get me, to
make me the butt of all their jokes. How could they be so
cruel? With friends like mine, who needs enemies?

And then I think of all the suffering You did while You were
walking on this earth. They made jokes about You too. You
were despised and rejected and ridiculed—and crucified. They
dared You to prove Yourself even while You were hanging on a
cross, taking Your dying breath—for them and for me! And
that's when You said, "Father, forgive them. They don't know
what they're doing."

Lord, forgive me for my pity party. Send the Spirit of Truth
into every aspect of this situation. Keep me strong in You and
keep me focused on the path You have set before me. Then
stretch my heart big enough to forgive others as You have forgiven me. I thank You, Father, that what others have meant for
evil, You will use for good.

15 And it happened, when he heard that I lifted my voice and cried out, that he left his garment with me, and fled and went outside."

16 So she kept his garment with her until his master came home. 17 Then she spoke to him with words like these, saying, "The Hebrew servant whom you brought to us came in to me to mock me; 18 so it happened, as I lifted my voice and cried out, that he left his garment with me and fled outside."

19 So it was, when his master heard the words which his wife spoke to him, saying, "Your servant did to me after this manner," that his anger was aroused. 20 Then Joseph's master took him and put him into the prison, a place where the king's prisoners *were* confined. And he was there in the prison. 21 But the LORD was with Joseph and showed him mercy, and He gave him favor in the sight of the keeper of the prison. 22 And the keeper of the prison committed to Joseph's hand all the prisoners who *were* in the prison; whatever they did there, it was his doing. 23 The keeper of the prison did not look into anything *that was* under *Joseph's* authority,^a because the LORD was with him; and whatever he did, the LORD made *it* prosper.

40 It came to pass after these things *that* the butler and the baker of the king of Egypt offended their lord, the king of Egypt. 2 And Pharaoh was angry with his two officers, the chief butler and the chief baker. 3 So he put them in custody in the house of the captain of the guard, in the prison, the place where Joseph *was* confined. 4 And the captain of the guard charged Joseph with them, and he served them; so they were in custody for a while.

5 Then the butler and the baker of the king of Egypt, who *were* confined in the prison, had a dream, both of them, each man's dream in one night *and* each man's dream with its *own* interpretation. 6 And Joseph came in to them in the morning and looked at them, and saw that they *were* sad. 7 So he asked Pharaoh's officers who *were* with him in the custody of his lord's house, saying, "Why do you look *so* sad today?"

8 And they said to him, "We each have had a dream, and *there is* no interpreter of it."

So Joseph said to them, "Do not interpretations belong to God? Tell *them* to me, please."

9 Then the chief butler told his dream to Joseph, and said to him, "Behold, in my dream a vine *was* before me, 10 and in the vine *were* three branches; it *was* as though it budded, its blossoms shot forth, and its clusters brought forth ripe grapes. 11 Then Pharaoh's cup *was* in my hand; and I took the grapes and pressed them into Pharaoh's cup, and placed the cup in Pharaoh's hand."

12 And Joseph said to him, "This *is* the interpretation of it: The three branches *are* three days. 13 Now within three days Pharaoh will lift up your head and restore you to your place, and you will put Pharaoh's cup in his hand according to the former manner, when you were his butler. 14 But remember me when it is well with you, and please show kindness to me; make mention of me to Pharaoh, and get me out of this house. 15 For indeed I was stolen away from the land of the Hebrews; and also I have done nothing here that they should put me into the dungeon."

16 When the chief baker saw that the interpretation was good, he said to Joseph, "I also *was* in my dream, and there *were* three white baskets on my head. 17 In the uppermost basket *were* all kinds of baked goods for Pharaoh, and the birds ate them out of the basket on my head."

18 So Joseph answered and said, "This *is* the interpretation of it: The three baskets *are* three days. 19 Within three days Pharaoh will lift off your head from you and hang you on a tree; and the birds will eat your flesh from you."

20 Now it came to pass on the third day, *which was* Pharaoh's birthday, that he made a feast for all his servants; and he lifted up the head of the chief butler and of the chief baker among his servants. 21 Then he restored the chief butler to his butlership again, and he placed the cup in Pharaoh's hand. 22 But he hanged the chief baker, as Joseph had inter-

39:23 ^aLiterally *his hand*

*M*an looks on the outer appearance but God looks on the heart. He is looking to see what we desire with all of our hearts, not what we want as a whim or an idea in our minds.

preted to them. 23 Yet the chief butler did not remember Joseph, but forgot him.

41 Then it came to pass, at the end of two full years, that Pharaoh had a dream; and behold, he stood by the river. 2 Suddenly there came up out of the river seven cows, fine looking and fat; and they fed in the meadow. 3 Then behold, seven other cows came up after them out of the river, ugly and gaunt, and stood by the *other* cows on the bank of the river. 4 And the ugly and gaunt cows ate up the seven fine looking and fat cows. So Pharaoh awoke. 5 He slept and dreamed a second time; and suddenly seven heads of grain came up on one stalk, plump and good. 6 Then behold, seven thin heads, blighted by the east wind, sprang up after them. 7 And the seven thin heads devoured the seven plump and full heads. So Pharaoh awoke, and indeed, *it was* a dream. 8 Now it came to pass in the morning that his spirit was troubled, and he sent and called for all the magicians of Egypt and all its wise men. And Pharaoh told them his dreams, but *there was* no one who could interpret them for Pharaoh.

9 Then the chief butler spoke to Pharaoh, saying: "I remember my faults this day. 10 When Pharaoh was angry with his servants, and put me in custody in the house of the captain of the guard, *both* me and the chief baker, 11 we each had a dream in one night, he and I. Each of us dreamed according to the interpretation of his *own* dream. 12 Now there *was* a young Hebrew man with us there, a servant of the captain of the guard. And we told him, and he interpreted our dreams for us; to each man he interpreted according to his *own* dream. 13 And it came to pass, just as he interpreted for us, so it happened. He restored me to my office, and he hanged him."

14 Then Pharaoh sent and called Joseph, and they brought him quickly out of the dungeon; and he shaved, changed his clothing, and came to Pharaoh. 15 And Pharaoh said to Joseph, "I have had a dream, and *there is* no one who can interpret it. But I have heard it said of you *that* you can understand a dream, to interpret it."

16 So Joseph answered Pharaoh, saying, "*It is* not in me; God will give Pharaoh an answer of peace."

17 Then Pharaoh said to Joseph: "Behold, in my dream I stood on the bank of the river. 18 Suddenly seven cows came up out of the river, fine looking and fat; and they fed in the meadow. 19 Then behold, seven other cows came up after them, poor and very ugly and gaunt, such ugliness as I have never seen in all the land of Egypt. 20 And the gaunt and ugly cows ate up the first seven, the fat cows. 21 When they had eaten them up, no one would have known that they had eaten them, for they *were* just as ugly as at the beginning. So I awoke. 22 Also I saw in my dream, and suddenly seven heads came up on one stalk, full and good. 23 Then behold, seven heads, withered, thin, *and* blighted by the east wind, sprang up after them. 24 And the thin heads devoured the seven good heads. So I told *this* to the magicians, but *there was* no one who could explain *it* to me."

25 Then Joseph said to Pharaoh, "The dreams of Pharaoh *are* one; God has shown Pharaoh what He *is* about to do: 26 The seven good cows *are* seven years, and the seven good heads *are* seven years; the dreams *are* one. 27 And the seven thin and ugly cows which came up after them *are* seven years, and the seven empty heads blighted by the east wind are seven years of famine. 28 This *is* the thing which I have spoken to Pharaoh. God has shown Pharaoh what He *is* about to do. 29 Indeed seven years of great plenty will come throughout all the land of Egypt; 30 but after them seven years of famine will arise, and all the plenty will be forgotten in the land of Egypt; and the famine will deplete the land. 31 So the plenty will not be known in the land because of the famine following, for it *will be* very severe. 32 And the dream was repeated to Pharaoh twice because the thing *is* established by God, and God will shortly bring it to pass.

33 "Now therefore, let Pharaoh select a discerning and wise man, and set him over the land of Egypt. 34 Let Pharaoh do *this,* and let him appoint officers over the land, to collect one-fifth *of the produce* of the land of Egypt in the seven plentiful

Gospel Pearls

years. 35 And let them gather all the food of those good years that are coming, and store up grain under the authority of Pharaoh, and let them keep food in the cities. 36 Then that food shall be as a reserve for the land for the seven years of famine which shall be in the land of Egypt, that the land may not perish during the famine."

37 So the advice was good in the eyes of Pharaoh and in the eyes of all his servants. 38 And Pharaoh said to his servants, "Can we find *such a one* as this, a man in whom *is* the Spirit of God?"

39 Then Pharaoh said to Joseph, "Inasmuch as God has shown you all this, *there is* no one as discerning and wise as you. 40 You shall be over my house, and all my people shall be ruled according to your word; only in regard to the throne will I be greater than you." 41 And Pharaoh said to Joseph, "See, I have set you over all the land of Egypt."

42 Then Pharaoh took his signet ring off his hand and put it on Joseph's hand; and he clothed him in garments of fine linen and put a gold chain around his neck. 43 And he had him ride in the second chariot which he had; and they cried out before him, "Bow the knee!" So he set him over all the land of Egypt. 44 Pharaoh also said to Joseph, "I *am* Pharaoh, and without your consent no man may lift his hand or foot in all the land of Egypt." 45 And Pharaoh called Joseph's name Zaphnath-Paaneah. And he gave him as a wife Asenath, the daughter of Poti-Pherah priest of On. So Joseph went out over *all* the land of Egypt.

46 Joseph was thirty years old when he stood before Pharaoh king of Egypt. And Joseph went out from the presence of Pharaoh, and went throughout all the land of Egypt. 47 Now in the seven plentiful years the ground brought forth abundantly. 48 So he gathered up all the food of the seven years which were in the land of Egypt, and laid up the food in the cities; he laid up in every city the food of the fields which surrounded them. 49 Joseph gathered very much grain, as the sand of the sea, until he stopped counting, for *it was* immeasurable.

50 And to Joseph were born two sons before the years of famine came, whom Asenath, the daughter of Poti-Pherah priest of On, bore to him. 51 Joseph called the name of the firstborn Manasseh:*a* "For God has made me forget all my toil and all my father's house." 52 And the name of the second he called Ephraim:*a* "For God has caused me to be fruitful in the land of my affliction."

53 Then the seven years of plenty which were in the land of Egypt ended, 54 and the seven years of famine began to come, as Joseph had said. The famine was in all lands, but in all the land of Egypt there was bread. 55 So when all the land of Egypt was famished, the people cried to Pharaoh for bread. Then Pharaoh said to all the Egyptians, "Go to Joseph; whatever he says to you, do." 56 The famine was over all the face of the earth, and Joseph opened all the storehouses*a* and sold to the Egyptians. And the famine became severe in the land of Egypt. 57 So all countries came to Joseph in Egypt to buy *grain,* because the famine was severe in all lands.

42 When Jacob saw that there was grain in Egypt, Jacob said to his sons, "Why do you look at one another?" 2 And he said, "Indeed I have heard that there is grain in Egypt; go down to that place and buy for us there, that we may live and not die."

3 So Joseph's ten brothers went down to buy grain in Egypt. 4 But Jacob did not send Joseph's brother Benjamin with his brothers, for he said, "Lest some calamity befall him." 5 And the sons of Israel went to buy *grain* among those who journeyed, for the famine was in the land of Canaan.

6 Now Joseph *was* governor over the land; and it was he who sold to all the people of the land. And Joseph's brothers came and bowed down before him with *their* faces to the earth. 7 Joseph saw his brothers and recognized them, but he acted as a stranger to them and spoke roughly to them. Then he said to them, "Where do you come from?"

And they said, "From the land of Canaan to buy food."

41:51 *a*Literally *Making Forgetful*   41:52 *a*Literally *Fruitfulness*   41:56 *a*Literally *all that was in them*

There are many things that God expects us to do, but there are some things that only God can do. And God expects us to call upon Him to do those things that are His job.

8 So Joseph recognized his brothers, but they did not recognize him. 9 Then Joseph remembered the dreams which he had dreamed about them, and said to them, "You *are* spies! You have come to see the nakedness of the land!"

10 And they said to him, "No, my lord, but your servants have come to buy food. 11 We *are* all one man's sons; we *are* honest *men;* your servants are not spies."

12 But he said to them, "No, but you have come to see the nakedness of the land."

13 And they said, "Your servants *are* twelve brothers, the sons of one man in the land of Canaan; and in fact, the youngest *is* with our father today, and one *is* no more."

14 But Joseph said to them, "It *is* as I spoke to you, saying, 'You *are* spies!' 15 In this *manner* you shall be tested: By the life of Pharaoh, you shall not leave this place unless your youngest brother comes here. 16 Send one of you, and let him bring your brother; and you shall be kept in prison, that your words may be tested to see whether *there is* any truth in you; or else, by the life of Pharaoh, surely you *are* spies!" 17 So he put them all together in prison three days.

18 Then Joseph said to them the third day, "Do this and live, *for* I fear God: 19 If you *are* honest *men,* let one of your brothers be confined to your prison house; but you, go and carry grain for the famine of your houses. 20 And bring your youngest brother to me; so your words will be verified, and you shall not die."

And they did so. 21 Then they said to one another, "We *are* truly guilty concerning our brother, for we saw the anguish of his soul when he pleaded with us, and we would not hear; therefore this distress has come upon us."

22 And Reuben answered them, saying, "Did I not speak to you, saying, 'Do not sin against the boy'; and you would not listen? Therefore behold, his blood is now required of us." 23 But they did not know that Joseph understood *them,* for he spoke to them through an interpreter. 24 And he turned himself away from them and wept. Then he returned to them again, and talked with them.

And he took Simeon from them and bound him before their eyes.

25 Then Joseph gave a command to fill their sacks with grain, to restore every man's money to his sack, and to give them provisions for the journey. Thus he did for them. 26 So they loaded their donkeys with the grain and departed from there. 27 But as one *of them* opened his sack to give his donkey feed at the encampment, he saw his money; and there it was, in the mouth of his sack. 28 So he said to his brothers, "My money has been restored, and there it is, in my sack!" Then their hearts failed *them* and they were afraid, saying to one another, "What *is* this *that* God has done to us?"

29 Then they went to Jacob their father in the land of Canaan and told him all that had happened to them, saying: 30 "The man *who is* lord of the land spoke roughly to us, and took us for spies of the country. 31 But we said to him, 'We *are* honest *men;* we are not spies. 32 We *are* twelve brothers, sons of our father; one *is* no *more,* and the youngest *is* with our father this day in the land of Canaan.' 33 Then the man, the lord of the country, said to us, 'By this I will know that you *are* honest *men:* Leave one of your brothers *here* with me, take *food for* the famine of your households, and be gone. 34 And bring your youngest brother to me; so I shall know that you *are* not spies, but *that* you *are* honest *men.* I will grant your brother to you, and you may trade in the land.' "

35 Then it happened as they emptied their sacks, that surprisingly each man's bundle of money *was* in his sack; and when they and their father saw the bundles of money, they were afraid. 36 And Jacob their father said to them, "You have bereaved me: Joseph is no *more,* Simeon is no *more,* and you want to take Benjamin. All these things are against me."

37 Then Reuben spoke to his father, saying, "Kill my two sons if I do not bring him *back* to you; put him in my hands, and I will bring him back to you."

38 But he said, "My son shall not go down with you, for his brother is dead, and he is left alone. If any calamity should befall him along the way in which you go, then you would

Gospel
Pearls

bring down my gray hair with sorrow to the grave."

43 Now the famine *was* severe in the land. 2 And it came to pass, when they had eaten up the grain which they had brought from Egypt, that their father said to them, "Go back, buy us a little food."

3 But Judah spoke to him, saying, "The man solemnly warned us, saying, 'You shall not see my face unless your brother *is* with you.' 4 If you send our brother with us, we will go down and buy you food. 5 But if you will not send *him*, we will not go down; for the man said to us, 'You shall not see my face unless your brother *is* with you.' "

6 And Israel said, "Why did you deal *so* wrongfully with me *as* to tell the man whether you had still *another* brother?"

7 But they said, "The man asked us pointedly about ourselves and our family, saying, '*Is* your father still alive? Have you *another* brother?' And we told him according to these words. Could we possibly have known that he would say, 'Bring your brother down'?"

8 Then Judah said to Israel his father, "Send the lad with me, and we will arise and go, that we may live and not die, both we and you *and* also our little ones. 9 I myself will be surety for him; from my hand you shall require him. If I do not bring him *back* to you and set him before you, then let me bear the blame forever. 10 For if we had not lingered, surely by now we would have returned this second time."

11 And their father Israel said to them, "If *it must be* so, then do this: Take some of the best fruits of the land in your vessels and carry down a present for the man—a little balm and a little honey, spices and myrrh, pistachio nuts and almonds. 12 Take double money in your hand, and take back in your hand the money that was returned in the mouth of your sacks; perhaps it was an oversight. 13 Take your brother also, and arise, go back to the man. 14 And may God Almighty give you mercy before the man, that he may release your other brother and Benjamin. If I am bereaved, I am bereaved!"

15 So the men took that present and

Benjamin, and they took double money in their hand, and arose and went down to Egypt; and they stood before Joseph. 16 When Joseph saw Benjamin with them, he said to the steward of his house, "Take *these* men to my home, and slaughter an animal and make ready; for *these* men will dine with me at noon." 17 Then the man did as Joseph ordered, and the man brought the men into Joseph's house.

18 Now the men were afraid because they were brought into Joseph's house; and they said, "*It is* because of the money, which was returned in our sacks the first time, that we are brought in, so that he may make a case against us and seize us, to take us as slaves with our donkeys."

19 When they drew near to the steward of Joseph's house, they talked with him at the door of the house, 20 and said, "O sir, we indeed came down the first time to buy food; 21 but it happened, when we came to the encampment, that we opened our sacks, and there, *each* man's money *was* in the mouth of his sack, our money in full weight; so we have brought it back in our hand. 22 And we have brought down other money in our hands to buy food. We do not know who put our money in our sacks."

23 But he said, "Peace *be* with you, do not be afraid. Your God and the God of your father has given you treasure in your sacks; I had your money." Then he brought Simeon out to them.

24 So the man brought the men into Joseph's house and gave *them* water, and they washed their feet; and he gave their donkeys feed. 25 Then they made the present ready for Joseph's coming at noon, for they heard that they would eat bread there.

26 And when Joseph came home, they brought him the present which *was* in their hand into the house, and bowed down before him to the earth. 27 Then he asked them about *their* well-being, and said, "*Is* your father well, the old man of whom you spoke? *Is* he still alive?"

28 And they answered, "Your servant our father *is* in good health; he *is* still alive." And they bowed their heads down and prostrated themselves.

---

*G*o to God. There are jobs that only God can do. Going to anybody else and trying any other method is a waste of your time. Go to the altar and cry out for God!

29 Then he lifted his eyes and saw his brother Benjamin, his mother's son, and said, "*Is* this your younger brother of whom you spoke to me?" And he said, "God be gracious to you, my son." 30 Now his heart yearned for his brother; so Joseph made haste and sought *somewhere* to weep. And he went into *his* chamber and wept there. 31 Then he washed his face and came out; and he restrained himself, and said, "Serve the bread."

32 So they set him a place by himself, and them by themselves, and the Egyptians who ate with him by themselves; because the Egyptians could not eat food with the Hebrews, for that *is* an abomination to the Egyptians. 33 And they sat before him, the firstborn according to his birthright and the youngest according to his youth; and the men looked in astonishment at one another. 34 Then he took servings to them from before him, but Benjamin's serving was five times as much as any of theirs. So they drank and were merry with him.

44 And he commanded the steward of his house, saying, "Fill the men's sacks with food, as much as they can carry, and put each man's money in the mouth of his sack. 2 Also put my cup, the silver cup, in the mouth of the sack of the youngest, and his grain money." So he did according to the word that Joseph had spoken. 3 As soon as the morning dawned, the men were sent away, they and their donkeys. 4 When they had gone out of the city, *and* were not *yet* far off, Joseph said to his steward, "Get up, follow the men; and when you overtake them, say to them, 'Why have you repaid evil for good? 5 *Is* not this *the one* from which my lord drinks, and with which he indeed practices divination? You have done evil in so doing.'"

6 So he overtook them, and he spoke to them these same words. 7 And they said to him, "Why does my lord say these words? Far be it from us that your servants should do such a thing. 8 Look, we brought back to you from the land of Canaan the money which we found in the mouth of our sacks. How then could we steal silver or gold from your lord's house? 9 With whomever of your servants it is found, let him die, and we also will be my lord's slaves."

10 And he said, "Now also *let* it *be* according to your words; he with whom it is found shall be my slave, and you shall be blameless." 11 Then each man speedily let down his sack to the ground, and each opened his sack. 12 So he searched. He began with the oldest and left off with the youngest; and the cup was found in Benjamin's sack. 13 Then they tore their clothes, and each man loaded his donkey and returned to the city.

14 So Judah and his brothers came to Joseph's house, and he *was* still there; and they fell before him on the ground. 15 And Joseph said to them, "What deed *is* this you have done? Did you not know that such a man as I can certainly practice divination?"

16 Then Judah said, "What shall we say to my lord? What shall we speak? Or how shall we clear ourselves? God has found out the iniquity of your servants; here we are, my lord's slaves, both we and *he* also with whom the cup was found."

17 But he said, "Far be it from me that I should do so; the man in whose hand the cup was found, he shall be my slave. And as for you, go up in peace to your father."

18 Then Judah came near to him and said: "O my lord, please let your servant speak a word in my lord's hearing, and do not let your anger burn against your servant; for you *are* even like Pharaoh. 19 My lord asked his servants, saying, 'Have you a father or a brother?' 20 And we said to my lord, 'We have a father, an old man, and a child of *his* old age, *who is* young; his brother is dead, and he alone is left of his mother's children, and his father loves him.' 21 Then you said to your servants, 'Bring him down to me, that I may set my eyes on him.' 22 And we said to my lord, 'The lad cannot leave his father, for if he should leave his father, *his* father would die.' 23 But you said to your servants, 'Unless your youngest brother comes down with you, you shall see my face no more.'

24 "So it was, when we went up to your servant my father, that we told him the words of my lord. 25 And our father said, 'Go back *and* buy us a little food.' 26 But we said, 'We can-

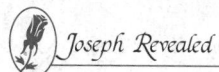

not go down; if our youngest brother is with us, then we will go down; for we may not see the man's face unless our youngest brother *is* with us.' 27 Then your servant my father said to us, 'You know that my wife bore me two sons; 28 and the one went out from me, and I said, "Surely he is torn to pieces"; and I have not seen him since. 29 But if you take this one also from me, and calamity befalls him, you shall bring down my gray hair with sorrow to the grave.'

30 "Now therefore, when I come to your servant my father, and the lad *is* not with us, since his life is bound up in the lad's life, 31 it will happen, when he sees that the lad *is* not *with us*, that he will die. So your servants will bring down the gray hair of your servant our father with sorrow to the grave. 32 For your servant became surety for the lad to my father, saying, 'If I do not bring him *back* to you, then I shall bear the blame before my father forever.' 33 Now therefore, please let your servant remain instead of the lad as a slave to my lord, and let the lad go up with his brothers. 34 For how shall I go up to my father if the lad *is* not with me, lest perhaps I see the evil that would come upon my father?"

45 Then Joseph could not restrain himself before all those who stood by him, and he cried out, "Make everyone go out from me!" So no one stood with him while Joseph made himself known to his brothers. 2 And he wept aloud, and the Egyptians and the house of Pharaoh heard *it.*

3 Then Joseph said to his brothers, "I *am* Joseph; does my father still live?" But his brothers could not answer him, for they were dismayed in his presence. 4 And Joseph said to his brothers, "Please come near to me." So they came near. Then he said: "I *am* Joseph your brother, whom you sold into Egypt. 5 But now, do not therefore be grieved or angry with yourselves because you sold me here; for God sent me before you to preserve life. 6 For these two years the famine *has been* in the land, and there *are* still five years in which *there will be* neither plowing nor harvesting. 7 And God sent me before you to preserve a posterity for you in the earth, and to save your lives

by a great deliverance. 8 So now *it was* not you *who* sent me here, but God; and He has made me a father to Pharaoh, and lord of all his house, and a ruler throughout all the land of Egypt.

9 "Hurry and go up to my father, and say to him, 'Thus says your son Joseph: "God has made me lord of all Egypt; come down to me, do not tarry. 10 You shall dwell in the land of Goshen, and you shall be near to me, you and your children, your children's children, your flocks and your herds, and all that you have. 11 There I will provide for you, lest you and your household, and all that you have, come to poverty; for *there are* still five years of famine." '

12 "And behold, your eyes and the eyes of my brother Benjamin see that *it is* my mouth that speaks to you. 13 So you shall tell my father of all my glory in Egypt, and of all that you have seen; and you shall hurry and bring my father down here."

14 Then he fell on his brother Benjamin's neck and wept, and Benjamin wept on his neck. 15 Moreover he kissed all his brothers and wept over them, and after that his brothers talked with him.

16 Now the report of it was heard in Pharaoh's house, saying, "Joseph's brothers have come." So it pleased Pharaoh and his servants well. 17 And Pharaoh said to Joseph, "Say to your brothers, 'Do this: Load your animals and depart; go to the land of Canaan. 18 Bring your father and your households and come to me; I will give you the best of the land of Egypt, and you will eat the fat of the land. 19 Now you are commanded—do this: Take carts out of the land of Egypt for your little ones and your wives; bring your father and come. 20 Also do not be concerned about your goods, for the best of all the land of Egypt *is* yours.' "

21 Then the sons of Israel did so; and Joseph gave them carts, according to the command of Pharaoh, and he gave them provisions for the journey. 22 He gave to all of them, to each man, changes of garments; but to Benjamin he gave three hundred *pieces* of silver and five changes of garments. 23 And he sent to his father these *things:* ten donkeys loaded with the good things of Egypt, and ten female donkeys loaded with

grain, bread, and food for his father for the journey. 24 So he sent his brothers away, and they departed; and he said to them, "See that you do not become troubled along the way."

25 Then they went up out of Egypt, and came to the land of Canaan to Jacob their father. 26 And they told him, saying, "Joseph *is* still alive, and he *is* governor over all the land of Egypt." And Jacob's heart stood still, because he did not believe them. 27 But when they told him all the words which Joseph had said to them, and when he saw the carts which Joseph had sent to carry him, the spirit of Jacob their father revived. 28 Then Israel said, "*It is* enough. Joseph my son *is* still alive. I will go and see him before I die."

46 So Israel took his journey with all that he had, and came to Beersheba, and offered sacrifices to the God of his father Isaac. 2 Then God spoke to Israel in the visions of the night, and said, "Jacob, Jacob!"

And he said, "Here I am."

3 So He said, "I *am* God, the God of your father; do not fear to go down to Egypt, for I will make of you a great nation there. 4 I will go down with you to Egypt, and I will also surely bring you up *again*; and Joseph will put his hand on your eyes."

5 Then Jacob arose from Beersheba; and the sons of Israel carried their father Jacob, their little ones, and their wives, in the carts which Pharaoh had sent to carry him. 6 So they took their livestock and their goods, which they had acquired in the land of Canaan, and went to Egypt, Jacob and all his descendants with him. 7 His sons and his sons' sons, his daughters and his sons' daughters, and all his descendants he brought with him to Egypt.

8 Now these *were* the names of the children of Israel, Jacob and his sons, who went to Egypt: Reuben *was* Jacob's firstborn. 9 The sons of Reuben *were* Hanoch, Pallu, Hezron, and Carmi. 10 The sons of Simeon *were* Jemuel,[a] Jamin, Ohad, Jachin,[b] Zo-

har,[c] and Shaul, the son of a Canaanite woman. 11 The sons of Levi *were* Gershon, Kohath, and Merari. 12 The sons of Judah *were* Er, Onan, Shelah, Perez, and Zerah (but Er and Onan died in the land of Canaan). The sons of Perez were Hezron and Hamul. 13 The sons of Issachar *were* Tola, Puvah,[a] Job,[b] and Shimron. 14 The sons of Zebulun *were* Sered, Elon, and Jahleel. 15 These *were* the sons of Leah, whom she bore to Jacob in Padan Aram, with his daughter Dinah. All the persons, his sons and his daughters, *were* thirty-three.

16 The sons of Gad *were* Ziphion,[a] Haggi, Shuni, Ezbon,[b] Eri, Arodi,[c] and Areli. 17 The sons of Asher *were* Jimnah, Ishuah, Isui, Beriah, and Serah, their sister. And the sons of Beriah *were* Heber and Malchiel. 18 These *were* the sons of Zilpah, whom Laban gave to Leah his daughter; and these she bore to Jacob: sixteen persons.

19 The sons of Rachel, Jacob's wife, *were* Joseph and Benjamin. 20 And to Joseph in the land of Egypt were born Manasseh and Ephraim, whom Asenath, the daughter of Poti-Pherah priest of On, bore to him. 21 The sons of Benjamin *were* Belah, Becher, Ashbel, Gera, Naaman, Ehi, Rosh, Muppim, Huppim,[a] and Ard. 22 These *were* the sons of Rachel, who were born to Jacob: fourteen persons in all.

23 The son of Dan *was* Hushim.[a] 24 The sons of Naphtali *were* Jahzeel,[a] Guni, Jezer, and Shillem.[b] 25 These *were* the sons of Bilhah, whom Laban gave to Rachel his daughter, and she bore these to Jacob: seven persons in all.

26 All the persons who went with Jacob to Egypt, who came from his body, besides Jacob's sons' wives, *were* sixty-six persons in all. 27 And the sons of Joseph who were born to him in Egypt *were* two persons. All the persons of the house of Jacob who went to Egypt were seventy.

28 Then he sent Judah before him to Joseph, to point out before him *the way* to Goshen. And they came to the

---

46:10 [a]Spelled *Nemuel* in 1 Chronicles 4:24　[b]Called *Jarib* in 1 Chronicles 4:24　[c]Called *Zerah* in 1 Chronicles 4:24　46:13 [a]Spelled *Puah* in 1 Chronicles 7:1　[b]Same as *Jashub* in Numbers 26:24 and 1 Chronicles 7:1　46:16 [a]Spelled *Zephon* in Samaritan Pentateuch, Septuagint, and Numbers 26:15 [b]Called *Ozni* in Numbers 26:16　[c]Spelled *Arod* in Numbers 26:17　46:21 [a]Called *Hupham* in Numbers 26:39　46:23 [a]Called *Shuham* in Numbers 26:42　46:24 [a]Spelled *Jahziel* in 1 Chronicles 7:13 [b]Spelled *Shallum* in 1 Chronicles 7:13

Gospel Pearls

land of Goshen. 29 So Joseph made ready his chariot and went up to Goshen to meet his father Israel; and he presented himself to him, and fell on his neck and wept on his neck a good while.

30 And Israel said to Joseph, "Now let me die, since I have seen your face, because you are still alive."

31 Then Joseph said to his brothers and to his father's household, "I will go up and tell Pharaoh, and say to him, 'My brothers and those of my father's house, who were in the land of Canaan, have come to me. 32 And the men are shepherds, for their occupation has been to feed livestock; and they have brought their flocks, their herds, and all that they have.' 33 So it shall be, when Pharaoh calls you and says, 'What is your occupation?' 34 that you shall say, 'Your servants' occupation has been with livestock from our youth even till now, both we and also our fathers,' that you may dwell in the land of Goshen; for every shepherd is an abomination to the Egyptians."

47 Then Joseph went and told Pharaoh, and said, "My father and my brothers, their flocks and their herds and all that they possess, have come from the land of Canaan; and indeed they are in the land of Goshen." 2 And he took five men from among his brothers and presented them to Pharaoh. 3 Then Pharaoh said to his brothers, "What is your occupation?"

And they said to Pharaoh, "Your servants are shepherds, both we and also our fathers." 4 And they said to Pharaoh, "We have come to dwell in the land, because your servants have no pasture for their flocks, for the famine is severe in the land of Canaan. Now therefore, please let your servants dwell in the land of Goshen."

5 Then Pharaoh spoke to Joseph, saying, "Your father and your brothers have come to you. 6 The land of Egypt is before you. Have your father and brothers dwell in the best of the land; let them dwell in the land of Goshen. And if you know any competent men among them, then make them chief herdsmen over my livestock."

7 Then Joseph brought in his father Jacob and set him before Pharaoh; and Jacob blessed Pharaoh. 8 Pharaoh said to Jacob, "How old are you?"

9 And Jacob said to Pharaoh, "The days of the years of my pilgrimage are one hundred and thirty years; few and evil have been the days of the years of my life, and they have not attained to the days of the years of the life of my fathers in the days of their pilgrimage." 10 So Jacob blessed Pharaoh, and went out from before Pharaoh.

11 And Joseph situated his father and his brothers, and gave them a possession in the land of Egypt, in the best of the land, in the land of Rameses, as Pharaoh had commanded. 12 Then Joseph provided his father, his brothers, and all his father's household with bread, according to the number in their families.

13 Now there was no bread in all the land; for the famine was very severe, so that the land of Egypt and the land of Canaan languished because of the famine. 14 And Joseph gathered up all the money that was found in the land of Egypt and in the land of Canaan, for the grain which they bought; and Joseph brought the money into Pharaoh's house.

15 So when the money failed in the land of Egypt and in the land of Canaan, all the Egyptians came to Joseph and said, "Give us bread, for why should we die in your presence? For the money has failed."

16 Then Joseph said, "Give your livestock, and I will give you bread for your livestock, if the money is gone." 17 So they brought their livestock to Joseph, and Joseph gave them bread in exchange for the horses, the flocks, the cattle of the herds, and for the donkeys. Thus he fed them with bread in exchange for all their livestock that year.

18 When that year had ended, they came to him the next year and said to him, "We will not hide from my lord that our money is gone; my lord also has our herds of livestock. There is nothing left in the sight of my lord but our bodies and our lands. 19 Why should we die before your eyes, both we and our land? Buy us and our land for bread, and we and our land will be servants of Pharaoh; give us seed, that we may live and

We have a High Priest, Jesus Christ, who is only touched by your boldness to come before His throne of grace and cry out with your faith for what you need from Him.

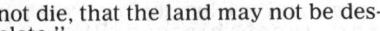
not die, that the land may not be desolate."

20 Then Joseph bought all the land of Egypt for Pharaoh; for every man of the Egyptians sold his field, because the famine was severe upon them. So the land became Pharaoh's. 21 And as for the people, he moved them into the cities,*a* from *one* end of the borders of Egypt to the *other* end. 22 Only the land of the priests he did not buy; for the priests had rations *allotted to them* by Pharaoh, and they ate their rations which Pharaoh gave them; therefore they did not sell their lands.

23 Then Joseph said to the people, "Indeed I have bought you and your land this day for Pharaoh. Look, *here is* seed for you, and you shall sow the land. 24 And it shall come to pass in the harvest that you shall give one-fifth to Pharaoh. Four-fifths shall be your own, as seed for the field and for your food, for those of your households and as food for your little ones."

25 So they said, "You have saved our lives; let us find favor in the sight of my lord, and we will be Pharaoh's servants." 26 And Joseph made it a law over the land of Egypt to this day, *that* Pharaoh should have one-fifth, except for the land of the priests only, *which* did not become Pharaoh's.

27 So Israel dwelt in the land of Egypt, in the country of Goshen; and they had possessions there and grew and multiplied exceedingly. 28 And Jacob lived in the land of Egypt seventeen years. So the length of Jacob's life was one hundred and forty-seven years. 29 When the time drew near that Israel must die, he called his son Joseph and said to him, "Now if I have found favor in your sight, please put your hand under my thigh, and deal kindly and truly with me. Please do not bury me in Egypt, 30 but let me lie with my fathers; you shall carry me out of Egypt and bury me in their burial place."

And he said, "I will do as you have said."

31 Then he said, "Swear to me." And he swore to him. So Israel bowed himself on the head of the bed.

48 Now it came to pass after these things that Joseph was told, "Indeed your father *is* sick"; and he took with him his two sons, Manasseh and Ephraim. 2 And Jacob was told, "Look, your son Joseph is coming to you"; and Israel strengthened himself and sat up on the bed. 3 Then Jacob said to Joseph: "God Almighty appeared to me at Luz in the land of Canaan and blessed me, 4 and said to me, 'Behold, I will make you fruitful and multiply you, and I will make of you a multitude of people, and give this land to your descendants after you *as* an everlasting possession.' 5 And now your two sons, Ephraim and Manasseh, who were born to you in the land of Egypt before I came to you in Egypt, *are* mine; as Reuben and Simeon, they shall be mine. 6 Your offspring whom you beget after them shall be yours; they will be called by the name of their brothers in their inheritance. 7 But as for me, when I came from Padan, Rachel died beside me in the land of Canaan on the way, when *there was* but a little distance to go to Ephrath; and I buried her there on the way to Ephrath (that is, Bethlehem)."

8 Then Israel saw Joseph's sons, and said, "Who *are* these?"

9 Joseph said to his father, "They *are* my sons, whom God has given me in this *place*."

And he said, "Please bring them to me, and I will bless them." 10 Now the eyes of Israel were dim with age, *so that* he could not see. Then Joseph brought them near him, and he kissed them and embraced them. 11 And Israel said to Joseph, "I had not thought to see your face; but in fact, God has also shown me your offspring!"

12 So Joseph brought them from beside his knees, and he bowed down with his face to the earth. 13 And Joseph took them both, Ephraim with his right hand toward Israel's left hand, and Manasseh with his left hand toward Israel's right hand, and brought *them* near him. 14 Then Israel stretched out his right hand and laid *it* on Ephraim's head, who *was* the younger, and his left hand on Manasseh's head, guiding his hands

47:21 *a*Following Masoretic Text and Targum; Samaritan Pentateuch, Septuagint, and Vulgate read *made the people virtual slaves.*

knowingly, for Manasseh *was* the firstborn. 15 And he blessed Joseph, and said:

> "God, before whom my fathers Abraham and Isaac walked, The God who has fed me all my life long to this day,
> 16 The Angel who has redeemed me from all evil, Bless the lads; Let my name be named upon them, And the name of my fathers Abraham and Isaac; And let them grow into a multitude in the midst of the earth."

17 Now when Joseph saw that his father laid his right hand on the head of Ephraim, it displeased him; so he took hold of his father's hand to remove it from Ephraim's head to Manasseh's head. 18 And Joseph said to his father, "Not so, my father, for this *one is* the firstborn; put your right hand on his head."

19 But his father refused and said, "I know, my son, I know. He also shall become a people, and he also shall be great; but truly his younger brother shall be greater than he, and his descendants shall become a multitude of nations." 20 So he blessed them that day, saying, "By you Israel will bless, saying, 'May God make you as Ephraim and as Manasseh!'" And thus he set Ephraim before Manasseh.

21 Then Israel said to Joseph, "Behold, I am dying, but God will be with you and bring you back to the land of your fathers. 22 Moreover I have given to you one portion above your brothers, which I took from the hand of the Amorite with my sword and my bow."

49 And Jacob called his sons and said, "Gather together, that I may tell you what shall befall you in the last days:

> 2 "Gather together and hear, you sons of Jacob, And listen to Israel your father.

> 3 "Reuben, you are my firstborn, My might and the beginning of my strength,

> The excellency of dignity and the excellency of power.
> 4 Unstable as water, you shall not excel, Because you went up to your father's bed; Then you defiled *it*— He went up to my couch.

> 5 "Simeon and Levi *are* brothers; Instruments of cruelty *are in* their dwelling place.
> 6 Let not my soul enter their council; Let not my honor be united to their assembly; For in their anger they slew a man, And in their self-will they hamstrung an ox.
> 7 Cursed *be* their anger, for *it is* fierce; And their wrath, for it is cruel! I will divide them in Jacob And scatter them in Israel.

> 8 "Judah, you *are he* whom your brothers shall praise; Your hand *shall be* on the neck of your enemies; Your father's children shall bow down before you.
> 9 Judah *is* a lion's whelp; From the prey, my son, you have gone up. He bows down, he lies down as a lion; And as a lion, who shall rouse him?
> 10 The scepter shall not depart from Judah, Nor a lawgiver from between his feet, Until Shiloh comes; And to Him *shall be* the obedience of the people.
> 11 Binding his donkey to the vine, And his donkey's colt to the choice vine, He washed his garments in wine, And his clothes in the blood of grapes.
> 12 His eyes *are* darker than wine, And his teeth whiter than milk.

> 13 "Zebulun shall dwell by the haven of the sea; He *shall become* a haven for ships, And his border shall adjoin Sidon.

*Y*ou may be weak. You may have failed. You may have sinned. But if you still have feeling toward God and you still have a desire in your heart to see God move on your behalf, then God can still be moved.

14 "Issachar is a strong donkey,
  Lying down between two
    burdens;
15 He saw that rest *was* good,
  And that the land *was* pleasant;
  He bowed his shoulder to bear
    a burden,
  And became a band of slaves.

16 "Dan shall judge his people
  As one of the tribes of Israel.
17 Dan shall be a serpent by the
    way,
  A viper by the path,
  That bites the horse's heels
  So that its rider shall fall
    backward.
18 I have waited for your
    salvation, O LORD!

19 "Gad, a troop shall tramp upon
    him,
  But he shall triumph at last.

20 "Bread from Asher *shall be* rich,
  And he shall yield royal
    dainties.

21 "Naphtali *is* a deer let loose;
  He uses beautiful words.

22 "Joseph *is* a fruitful bough,
  A fruitful bough by a well;
  His branches run over the wall.
23 The archers have bitterly
    grieved him,
  Shot *at him* and hated him.
24 But his bow remained in
    strength,
  And the arms of his hands were
    made strong
  By the hands of the Mighty *God*
    of Jacob
  (From there *is* the Shepherd,
    the Stone of Israel),
25 By the God of your father who
    will help you,
  And by the Almighty who will
    bless you
  With blessings of heaven
    above,
  Blessings of the deep that lies
    beneath,
  Blessings of the breasts and of
    the womb.
26 The blessings of your father
  Have excelled the blessings of
    my ancestors,
  Up to the utmost bound of the
    everlasting hills.
  They shall be on the head of
    Joseph,

And on the crown of the head
  of him who was separate
  from his brothers.

27 "Benjamin is a ravenous wolf;
  In the morning he shall devour
    the prey,
  And at night he shall divide the
    spoil."

28 All these *are* the twelve tribes of
Israel, and this *is* what their father
spoke to them. And he blessed them;
he blessed each one according to his
own blessing. 29 Then he charged them and said
to them: "I am to be gathered to my
people; bury me with my fathers in
the cave that *is* in the field of Ephron
the Hittite, 30 in the cave that *is* in
the field of Machpelah, which *is* before Mamre in the land of Canaan,
which Abraham bought with the field
of Ephron the Hittite as a possession
for a burial place. 31 There they buried Abraham and Sarah his wife,
there they buried Isaac and Rebekah
his wife, and there I buried Leah.
32 The field and the cave that *is* there
were purchased from the sons of
Heth." 33 And when Jacob had finished commanding his sons, he drew
his feet up into the bed and breathed
his last, and was gathered to his people.

50 Then Joseph fell on his father's
  face, and wept over him, and
kissed him. 2 And Joseph commanded his servants the physicians
to embalm his father. So the physicians embalmed Israel. 3 Forty days
were required for him, for such are
the days required for those who are
embalmed; and the Egyptians
mourned for him seventy days.

4 Now when the days of his mourning were past, Joseph spoke to the
household of Pharaoh, saying, "If
now I have found favor in your eyes,
please speak in the hearing of Pharaoh, saying, 5 'My father made me
swear, saying, "Behold, I am dying;
in my grave which I dug for myself
in the land of Canaan, there you shall
bury me." Now therefore, please let
me go up and bury my father, and I
will come back.' "

6 And Pharaoh said, "Go up and
bury your father, as he made you
swear."

7 So Joseph went up to bury his fa-

God is not moved by what you have. He is moved by how you feel about what you
don't have and what you need. He is moved by what you are believing for with your
faith.

The "Yes" Zone

Genesis 50:20

The art of surviving painful moments is living in the "yes" zone. We need to learn to respond to God with a yes when the doors are open and a yes when they are closed. Regarding relationships, our prayer must be:

> *I trust Your decisions, Lord, and I know that if this situation is good for me, You will allow it to continue. I also know that if the door is closed, it is also for my good. So I say yes to You as I go into the relationship.*

This is the epitome of trust in our living God. This kind of trust is seldom achieved, but greatly to be sought. In so doing, you will be able to savor the gift of companionship without fear of reprisal.

If God allows a relationship to continue, and some painful betrayals come from it, know that He will only allow what ultimately works for your good. Sometimes such a betrayal ushers you into the next level of consecration—a level you could never reach on your own. For that, you can give thanks! What a privilege to live in the assurance that God is in control of you and of everyone He allows behind the shield of His purposes for your life. The unique thing about God's parenting is that He sometimes uses a negative to bring about a positive just as He did in Joseph's life (see Genesis 50:20). This knowledge will set you free from internal struggle and allow you to be transparent.

It is very important to understand the sovereignty of God. There must be an awareness within your heart, a deep knowledge that God is in control and that He is able to reverse the adverse. When you come to believe in His sovereignty, you can overcome every human trial, knowing that each one is divinely permitted and supernaturally orchestrated. God arranges these trials in such a way that the things that could have paralyzed you will now motivate you.

God delights in bestowing His abundant grace so that you can live in the world without fear. You will like some of your relationships better than others. God creates different types of people, and all are His handiwork. Ultimately, your friends are the ones who will help you to become all that God wants you to be and to understand the many levels of His love.

ther; and with him went up all the servants of Pharaoh, the elders of his house, and all the elders of the land of Egypt, 8 as well as all the house of Joseph, his brothers, and his father's house. Only their little ones, their flocks, and their herds they left in the land of Goshen. 9 And there went up with him both chariots and horsemen, and it was a very great gathering.

10 Then they came to the threshing floor of Atad, which *is* beyond the Jordan, and they mourned there with a great and very solemn lamentation. He observed seven days of mourning for his father. 11 And when the inhabitants of the land, the Canaanites, saw the mourning at the threshing floor of Atad, they said, "This *is* a deep mourning of the Egyptians." Therefore its name was called Abel Mizraim,*a* which *is* beyond the Jordan.

12 So his sons did for him just as he had commanded them. 13 For his sons carried him to the land of Canaan, and buried him in the cave of the field of Machpelah, before Mamre, which Abraham bought with the field from Ephron the Hittite as property for a burial place. 14 And after he had buried his father, Joseph returned to Egypt, he and his brothers and all who went up with him to bury his father.

15 When Joseph's brothers saw that their father was dead, they said, "Perhaps Joseph will hate us, and may actually repay us for all the evil which we did to him." 16 So they sent

messengers to Joseph, saying, "Before your father died he commanded, saying, 17 'Thus you shall say to Joseph: "I beg you, please forgive the trespass of your brothers and their sin; for they did evil to you." ' Now, please, forgive the trespass of the servants of the God of your father." And Joseph wept when they spoke to him.

18 Then his brothers also went and fell down before his face, and they said, "Behold, we *are* your servants."

19 Joseph said to them, "Do not be afraid, for *am* I in the place of God? 20 But as for you, you meant evil against me; *but* God meant it for good, in order to bring it about as *it is* this day, to save many people alive. 21 Now therefore, do not be afraid; I will provide for you and your little ones." And he comforted them and spoke kindly to them.

22 So Joseph dwelt in Egypt, he and his father's household. And Joseph lived one hundred and ten years. 23 Joseph saw Ephraim's children to the third *generation.* The children of Machir, the son of Manasseh, were also brought up on Joseph's knees. 24 And Joseph said to his brethren, "I am dying; but God will surely visit you, and bring you out of this land to the land of which He swore to Abraham, to Isaac, and to Jacob." 25 Then Joseph took an oath from the children of Israel, saying, "God will surely visit you, and you shall carry up my bones from here." 26 So Joseph died, *being* one hundred and ten years old; and they embalmed him, and he was put in a coffin in Egypt.

50:11 *a*Literally *Mourning of Egypt*

The Second Book of Moses Called

EXODUS

1 Now these *are* the names of the children of Israel who came to Egypt; each man and his household came with Jacob: 2 Reuben, Simeon, Levi, and Judah; 3 Issachar, Zebulun, and Benjamin; 4 Dan, Naphtali, Gad, and Asher. 5 All those who were descendants*a* of Jacob were seventy*b*

1:5 *a*Literally *who came from the loins of*　*b*Dead Sea Scrolls and Septuagint read *seventy-five* (compare Acts 7:14).

Gospel
Pearls

persons (for Joseph was in Egypt *already*). 6 And Joseph died, all his brothers, and all that generation. 7 But the children of Israel were fruitful and increased abundantly, multiplied and grew exceedingly mighty; and the land was filled with them.

8 Now there arose a new king over Egypt, who did not know Joseph. 9 And he said to his people, "Look, the people of the children of Israel *are* more and mightier than we; 10 come, let us deal shrewdly with them, lest they multiply, and it happen, in the event of war, that they also join our enemies and fight against us, and *so* go up out of the land." 11 Therefore they set taskmasters over them to afflict them with their burdens. And they built for Pharaoh supply cities, Pithom and Raamses. 12 But the more they afflicted them, the more they multiplied and grew. And they were in dread of the children of Israel. 13 So the Egyptians made the children of Israel serve with rigor. 14 And they made their lives bitter with hard bondage—in mortar, in brick, and in all manner of service in the field. All their service in which they made them serve *was* with rigor.

15 Then the king of Egypt spoke to the Hebrew midwives, of whom the name of one *was* Shiphrah and the name of the other Puah; 16 and he said, "When you do the duties of a midwife for the Hebrew women, and see *them* on the birthstools, if it *is* a son, then you shall kill him; but if it *is* a daughter, then she shall live." 17 But the midwives feared God, and did not do as the king of Egypt commanded them, but saved the male children alive. 18 So the king of Egypt called for the midwives and said to them, "Why have you done this thing, and saved the male children alive?"

19 And the midwives said to Pharaoh, "Because the Hebrew women *are* not like the Egyptian women; for they *are* lively and give birth before the midwives come to them."

20 Therefore God dealt well with the midwives, and the people multiplied and grew very mighty. 21 And so it was, because the midwives feared God, that He provided households for them.

22 So Pharaoh commanded all his people, saying, "Every son who is born[a] you shall cast into the river, and every daughter you shall save alive."

2 And a man of the house of Levi went and took *as wife* a daughter of Levi. 2 So the woman conceived and bore a son. And when she saw that he *was* a beautiful *child,* she hid him three months. 3 But when she could no longer hide him, she took an ark of bulrushes for him, daubed it with asphalt and pitch, put the child in it, and laid *it* in the reeds by the river's bank. 4 And his sister stood afar off, to know what would be done to him.

5 Then the daughter of Pharaoh came down to bathe at the river. And her maidens walked along the riverside; and when she saw the ark among the reeds, she sent her maid to get it. 6 And when she opened *it,* she saw the child, and behold, the baby wept. So she had compassion on him, and said, "This is one of the Hebrews' children."

7 Then his sister said to Pharaoh's daughter, "Shall I go and call a nurse for you from the Hebrew women, that she may nurse the child for you?"

8 And Pharaoh's daughter said to her, "Go." So the maiden went and called the child's mother. 9 Then Pharaoh's daughter said to her, "Take this child away and nurse him for me, and I will give *you* your wages." So the woman took the child and nursed him. 10 And the child grew, and she brought him to Pharaoh's daughter, and he became her son. So she called his name Moses,[a] saying, "Because I drew him out of the water."

11 Now it came to pass in those days, when Moses was grown, that he went out to his brethren and looked at their burdens. And he saw an Egyptian beating a Hebrew, one of his brethren. 12 So he looked this way and that way, and when he saw no one, he killed the Egyptian and hid him in the sand. 13 And when he went out the second day, behold, two Hebrew men were fighting, and he said to the one who did the wrong,

---

1:22 [a]Samaritan Pentateuch, Septuagint, and Targum add *to the Hebrews.*   2:10 [a]Literally *Drawn Out*

Go to God today with your need and express your need to Him with the full force of your feelings and faith.

"Why are you striking your companion?"

14 Then he said, "Who made you a prince and a judge over us? Do you intend to kill me as you killed the Egyptian?"

So Moses feared and said, "Surely this thing is known!" 15 When Pharaoh heard of this matter, he sought to kill Moses. But Moses fled from the face of Pharaoh and dwelt in the land of Midian; and he sat down by a well.

16 Now the priest of Midian had seven daughters. And they came and drew water, and they filled the troughs to water their father's flock. 17 Then the shepherds came and drove them away; but Moses stood up and helped them, and watered their flock.

18 When they came to Reuel their father, he said, "How is it that you have come so soon today?"

19 And they said, "An Egyptian delivered us from the hand of the shepherds, and he also drew enough water for us and watered the flock."

20 So he said to his daughters, "And where is he? Why is it that you have left the man? Call him, that he may eat bread."

21 Then Moses was content to live with the man, and he gave Zipporah his daughter to Moses. 22 And she bore him a son. He called his name Gershom,*a* for he said, "I have been a stranger in a foreign land."

23 Now it happened in the process of time that the king of Egypt died. Then the children of Israel groaned because of the bondage, and they cried out; and their cry came up to God because of the bondage. 24 So God heard their groaning, and God remembered His covenant with Abraham, with Isaac, and with Jacob. 25 And God looked upon the children of Israel, and God acknowledged *them.*

3 Now Moses was tending the flock of Jethro his father-in-law, the priest of Midian. And he led the flock to the back of the desert, and came to Horeb, the mountain of God. 2 And the Angel of the LORD appeared to him in a flame of fire from the midst of a bush. So he looked, and behold, the bush was burning with fire, but the bush *was* not consumed. 3 Then Moses said, "I will now turn aside and see this great sight, why the bush does not burn."

4 So when the LORD saw that he turned aside to look, God called to him from the midst of the bush and said, "Moses, Moses!"

And he said, "Here I am."

5 Then He said, "Do not draw near this place. Take your sandals off your feet, for the place where you stand *is* holy ground." 6 Moreover He said, "I *am* the God of your father—the God of Abraham, the God of Isaac, and the God of Jacob." And Moses hid his face, for he was afraid to look upon God.

7 And the LORD said: "I have surely seen the oppression of My people who *are* in Egypt, and have heard their cry because of their taskmasters, for I know their sorrows. 8 So I have come down to deliver them out of the hand of the Egyptians, and to bring them up from that land to a good and large land, to a land flowing with milk and honey, to the place of the Canaanites and the Hittites and the Amorites and the Perizzites and the Hivites and the Jebusites. 9 Now therefore, behold, the cry of the children of Israel has come to Me, and I have also seen the oppression with which the Egyptians oppress them. 10 Come now, therefore, and I will send you to Pharaoh that you may bring My people, the children of Israel, out of Egypt."

11 But Moses said to God, "Who *am* I that I should go to Pharaoh, and that I should bring the children of Israel out of Egypt?"

12 So He said, "I will certainly be with you. And this *shall be* a sign to you that I have sent you: When you have brought the people out of Egypt, you shall serve God on this mountain."

13 Then Moses said to God, "Indeed, *when* I come to the children of Israel and say to them, 'The God of your fathers has sent me to you,' and they say to me, 'What *is* His name?' what shall I say to them?"

14 And God said to Moses, "I AM WHO I AM." And He said, "Thus you shall say to the children of Israel, 'I AM has sent me to you.'"

15 Moreover God said to Moses,

2:22 *a*Literally *Stranger There*

Gospel Pearls

"Thus you shall say to the children of Israel: 'The LORD God of your fathers, the God of Abraham, the God of Isaac, and the God of Jacob, has sent me to you. This *is* My name forever, and this *is* My memorial to all generations.' 16 Go and gather the elders of Israel together, and say to them, 'The LORD God of your fathers, the God of Abraham, of Isaac, and of Jacob, appeared to me, saying, "I have surely visited you and *seen* what is done to you in Egypt; 17 and I have said I will bring you up out of the affliction of Egypt to the land of the Canaanites and the Hittites and the Amorites and the Perizzites and the Hivites and the Jebusites, to a land flowing with milk and honey." ' 18 Then they will heed your voice; and you shall come, you and the elders of Israel, to the king of Egypt; and you shall say to him, 'The LORD God of the Hebrews has met with us; and now, please, let us go three days' journey into the wilderness, that we may sacrifice to the LORD our God.' 19 But I am sure that the king of Egypt will not let you go, no, not even by a mighty hand. 20 So I will stretch out My hand and strike Egypt with all My wonders which I will do in its midst; and after that he will let you go. 21 And I will give this people favor in the sight of the Egyptians; and it shall be, when you go, that you shall not go empty-handed. 22 But every woman shall ask of her neighbor, namely, of her who dwells near her house, articles of silver, articles of gold, and clothing; and you shall put *them* on your sons and on your daughters. So you shall plunder the Egyptians."

4 Then Moses answered and said, "But suppose they will not believe me or listen to my voice; suppose they say, 'The LORD has not appeared to you.' "
2 So the LORD said to him, "What *is* that in your hand?"
He said, "A rod."
3 And He said, "Cast it on the ground." So he cast it on the ground, and it became a serpent; and Moses fled from it. 4 Then the LORD said to Moses, "Reach out your hand and take *it* by the tail" (and he reached out his hand and caught it, and it be-

came a rod in his hand), 5 "that they may believe that the LORD God of their fathers, the God of Abraham, the God of Isaac, and the God of Jacob, has appeared to you."
6 Furthermore the LORD said to him, "Now put your hand in your bosom." And he put his hand in his bosom, and when he took it out, behold, his hand *was* leprous, like snow. 7 And He said, "Put your hand in your bosom again." So he put his hand in his bosom again, and drew it out of his bosom, and behold, it was restored like his *other* flesh. 8 "Then it will be, if they do not believe you, nor heed the message of the first sign, that they may believe the message of the latter sign. 9 And it shall be, if they do not believe even these two signs, or listen to your voice, that you shall take water from the river*a* and pour *it* on the dry *land.* The water which you take from the river will become blood on the dry *land.*"
10 Then Moses said to the LORD, "O my Lord, I *am* not eloquent, neither before nor since You have spoken to Your servant; but I *am* slow of speech and slow of tongue."
11 So the LORD said to him, "Who has made man's mouth? Or who makes the mute, the deaf, the seeing, or the blind? *Have* not I, the LORD? 12 Now therefore, go, and I will be with your mouth and teach you what you shall say."
13 But he said, "O my Lord, please send by the hand of whomever *else* You may send."
14 So the anger of the LORD was kindled against Moses, and He said: "Is not Aaron the Levite your brother? I know that he can speak well. And look, he is also coming out to meet you. When he sees you, he will be glad in his heart. 15 Now you shall speak to him and put the words in his mouth. And I will be with your mouth and with his mouth, and I will teach you what you shall do. 16 So he shall be your spokesman to the people. And he himself shall be as a mouth for you, and you shall be to him as God. 17 And you shall take this rod in your hand, with which you shall do the signs."
18 So Moses went and returned to Jethro his father-in-law, and said to

4:9 *a*That is, the Nile

*T*he depth of the trouble you have been experiencing is likely to be equal to the depth of the desire that drives you toward God. The greater your problem, the more intense your fear, the deeper your discouragement, the more you are willing to risk crying out to God.

him, "Please let me go and return to my brethren who *are* in Egypt, and see whether they are still alive."

And Jethro said to Moses, "Go in peace."

19 Now the LORD said to Moses in Midian, "Go, return to Egypt; for all the men who sought your life are dead." 20 Then Moses took his wife and his sons and set them on a donkey, and he returned to the land of Egypt. And Moses took the rod of God in his hand.

21 And the LORD said to Moses, "When you go back to Egypt, see that you do all those wonders before Pharaoh which I have put in your hand. But I will harden his heart, so that he will not let the people go. 22 Then you shall say to Pharaoh, 'Thus says the LORD: "Israel *is* My son, My firstborn. 23 So I say to you, let My son go that he may serve Me. But if you refuse to let him go, indeed I will kill your son, your first-born." ' "

24 And it came to pass on the way, at the encampment, that the LORD met him and sought to kill him. 25 Then Zipporah took a sharp stone and cut off the foreskin of her son and cast *it* at *Moses'*ª feet, and said, "Surely you *are* a husband of blood to me!" 26 So He let him go. Then she said, "*You are* a husband of blood!"—because of the circumcision.

27 And the LORD said to Aaron, "Go into the wilderness to meet Moses." So he went and met him on the mountain of God, and kissed him. 28 So Moses told Aaron all the words of the LORD who had sent him, and all the signs which He had commanded him. 29 Then Moses and Aaron went and gathered together all the elders of the children of Israel. 30 And Aaron spoke all the words which the LORD had spoken to Moses. Then he did the signs in the sight of the people. 31 So the people believed; and when they heard that the LORD had visited the children of Israel and that He had looked on their affliction, then they bowed their heads and worshiped.

5 Afterward Moses and Aaron went in and told Pharaoh, "Thus says the LORD God of Israel: 'Let My peo-ple go, that they may hold a feast to Me in the wilderness.' "

2 And Pharaoh said, "Who *is* the LORD, that I should obey His voice to let Israel go? I do not know the LORD, nor will I let Israel go."

3 So they said, "The God of the Hebrews has met with us. Please, let us go three days' journey into the desert and sacrifice to the LORD our God, lest He fall upon us with pestilence or with the sword."

4 Then the king of Egypt said to them, "Moses and Aaron, why do you take the people from their work? Get *back* to your labor." 5 And Pharaoh said, "Look, the people of the land *are* many now, and you make them rest from their labor!"

6 So the same day Pharaoh commanded the taskmasters of the people and their officers, saying, 7 "You shall no longer give the people straw to make brick as before. Let them go and gather straw for themselves. 8 And you shall lay on them the quota of bricks which they made before. You shall not reduce it. For they are idle; therefore they cry out, saying, 'Let us go *and* sacrifice to our God.' 9 Let more work be laid on the men, that they may labor in it, and let them not regard false words."

10 And the taskmasters of the people and their officers went out and spoke to the people, saying, "Thus says Pharaoh: 'I will not give you straw. 11 Go, get yourselves straw where you can find it; yet none of your work will be reduced.' "

12 So the people were scattered abroad throughout all the land of Egypt to gather stubble instead of straw. 13 And the taskmasters forced *them* to hurry, saying, "Fulfill your work, *your* daily quota, as when there was straw." 14 Also the officers of the children of Israel, whom Pharaoh's taskmasters had set over them, were beaten *and* were asked, "Why have you not fulfilled your task in making brick both yesterday and today, as before?"

15 Then the officers of the children of Israel came and cried out to Pharaoh, saying, "Why are you dealing thus with your servants? 16 There is no straw given to your servants, and they say to us, 'Make brick!' And

4:25 ªLiterally *his*

Gospel
Pearls

indeed your servants *are* beaten, but the fault *is* in your *own* people."

17 But he said, "You *are* idle! Idle! Therefore you say, 'Let us go *and* sacrifice to the LORD.' 18 Therefore go now *and* work; for no straw shall be given you, yet you shall deliver the quota of bricks." 19 And the officers of the children of Israel saw *that* they *were* in trouble after it was said, "You shall not reduce *any* bricks from your daily quota."

20 Then, as they came out from Pharaoh, they met Moses and Aaron who stood there to meet them. 21 And they said to them, "Let the LORD look on you and judge, because you have made us abhorrent in the sight of Pharaoh and in the sight of his servants, to put a sword in their hand to kill us."

22 So Moses returned to the LORD and said, "Lord, why have You brought trouble on this people? Why *is* it You have sent me? 23 For since I came to Pharaoh to speak in Your name, he has done evil to this people; neither have You delivered Your people at all."

6 Then the LORD said to Moses, "Now you shall see what I will do to Pharaoh. For with a strong hand he will let them go, and with a strong hand he will drive them out of his land."

2 And God spoke to Moses and said to him: "I *am* the LORD. 3 I appeared to Abraham, to Isaac, and to Jacob, as God Almighty, but *by* My name LORD*a* I was not known to them. 4 I have also established My covenant with them, to give them the land of Canaan, the land of their pilgrimage, in which they were strangers. 5 And I have also heard the groaning of the children of Israel whom the Egyptians keep in bondage, and I have remembered My covenant. 6 Therefore say to the children of Israel: 'I *am* the LORD; I will bring you out from under the burdens of the Egyptians, I will rescue you from their bondage, and I will redeem you with an outstretched arm and with great judgments. 7 I will take you as My people, and I will be your God. Then you shall know that I *am* the LORD your God who brings you out from under the burdens of the Egyp-

tians. 8 And I will bring you into the land which I swore to give to Abraham, Isaac, and Jacob; and I will give it to you *as* a heritage: I *am* the LORD.' " 9 So Moses spoke thus to the children of Israel; but they did not heed Moses, because of anguish of spirit and cruel bondage.

10 And the LORD spoke to Moses, saying, 11 "Go in, tell Pharaoh king of Egypt to let the children of Israel go out of his land."

12 And Moses spoke before the LORD, saying, "The children of Israel have not heeded me. How then shall Pharaoh heed me, for I *am* of uncircumcised lips?"

13 Then the LORD spoke to Moses and Aaron, and gave them a command for the children of Israel and for Pharaoh king of Egypt, to bring the children of Israel out of the land of Egypt.

14 These *are* the heads of their fathers' houses: The sons of Reuben, the firstborn of Israel, *were* Hanoch, Pallu, Hezron, and Carmi. These are the families of Reuben. 15 And the sons of Simeon *were* Jemuel,*a* Jamin, Ohad, Jachin, Zohar, and Shaul the son of a Canaanite woman. These *are* the families of Simeon. 16 These *are* the names of the sons of Levi according to their generations: Gershon, Kohath, and Merari. And the years of the life of Levi *were* one hundred and thirty-seven. 17 The sons of Gershon *were* Libni and Shimi according to their families. 18 And the sons of Kohath *were* Amram, Izhar, Hebron, and Uzziel. And the years of the life of Kohath *were* one hundred and thirty-three. 19 The sons of Merari *were* Mahli and Mushi. These *are* the families of Levi according to their generations.

20 Now Amram took for himself Jochebed, his father's sister, as wife; and she bore him Aaron and Moses. And the years of the life of Amram *were* one hundred and thirty-seven. 21 The sons of Izhar *were* Korah, Nepheg, and Zichri. 22 And the sons of Uzziel *were* Mishael, Elzaphan, and Zithri. 23 Aaron took to himself Elisheba, daughter of Amminadab, sister of Nahshon, as wife; and she bore him Nadab, Abihu, Eleazar, and Ithamar. 24 And the sons of Korah *were* Assir, Elkanah, and Abiasaph.

6:3 *a*Hebrew *YHWH*, traditionally *Jehovah*   6:15 *a*Spelled *Nemuel* in Numbers 26:12

God's blessing is an overflowing blessing. Give birth to the gifts and talents and powers and the ministries of the Holy Spirit inside you.

These are the families of the Korahites. 25 Eleazar, Aaron's son, took for himself one of the daughters of Putiel as wife; and she bore him Phinehas. These *are* the heads of the fathers' houses of the Levites according to their families.

26 These *are the same* Aaron and Moses to whom the LORD said, "Bring out the children of Israel from the land of Egypt according to their armies." 27 These *are* the ones who spoke to Pharaoh king of Egypt, to bring out the children of Israel from Egypt. These *are the same* Moses and Aaron.

28 And it came to pass, on the day the LORD spoke to Moses in the land of Egypt, 29 that the LORD spoke to Moses, saying, "I *am* the LORD. Speak to Pharaoh king of Egypt all that I say to you."

30 But Moses said before the LORD, "Behold, I *am* of uncircumcised lips, and how shall Pharaoh heed me?"

7 So the LORD said to Moses: "See, I have made you *as* God to Pharaoh, and Aaron your brother shall be your prophet. 2 You shall speak all that I command you. And Aaron your brother shall tell Pharaoh to send the children of Israel out of his land. 3 And I will harden Pharaoh's heart, and multiply My signs and My wonders in the land of Egypt. 4 But Pharaoh will not heed you, so that I may lay My hand on Egypt and bring My armies *and* My people, the children of Israel, out of the land of Egypt by great judgments. 5 And the Egyptians shall know that I *am* the LORD, when I stretch out My hand on Egypt and bring out the children of Israel from among them."

6 Then Moses and Aaron did *so;* just as the LORD commanded them, so they did. 7 And Moses *was* eighty years old and Aaron eighty-three years old when they spoke to Pharaoh.

8 Then the LORD spoke to Moses and Aaron, saying, 9 "When Pharaoh speaks to you, saying, 'Show a miracle for yourselves,' then you shall say to Aaron, 'Take your rod and cast *it* before Pharaoh, *and* let it become a serpent.'" 10 So Moses and Aaron went in to Pharaoh, and they did so, just as the LORD commanded. And Aaron cast down his rod before Pharaoh and before his servants, and it became a serpent.

11 But Pharaoh also called the wise men and the sorcerers; so the magicians of Egypt, they also did in like manner with their enchantments. 12 For every man threw down his rod, and they became serpents. But Aaron's rod swallowed up their rods. 13 And Pharaoh's heart grew hard, and he did not heed them, as the LORD had said.

14 So the LORD said to Moses: "Pharaoh's heart *is* hard; he refuses to let the people go. 15 Go to Pharaoh in the morning, when he goes out to the water, and you shall stand by the river's bank to meet him; and the rod which was turned to a serpent you shall take in your hand. 16 And you shall say to him, 'The LORD God of the Hebrews has sent me to you, saying, "Let My people go, that they may serve Me in the wilderness"; but indeed, until now you would not hear! 17 Thus says the LORD: "By this you shall know that I *am* the LORD. Behold, I will strike the waters which *are* in the river with the rod that *is* in my hand, and they shall be turned to blood. 18 And the fish that *are* in the river shall die, the river shall stink, and the Egyptians will loathe to drink the water of the river." ' "

19 Then the LORD spoke to Moses, "Say to Aaron, 'Take your rod and stretch out your hand over the waters of Egypt, over their streams, over their rivers, over their ponds, and over all their pools of water, that they may become blood. And there shall be blood throughout all the land of Egypt, both in *buckets of* wood and *pitchers of* stone.' " 20 And Moses and Aaron did so, just as the LORD commanded. So he lifted up the rod and struck the waters that *were* in the river, in the sight of Pharaoh and in the sight of his servants. And all the waters that *were* in the river were turned to blood. 21 The fish that *were* in the river died, the river stank, and the Egyptians could not drink the water of the river. So there was blood throughout all the land of Egypt.

22 Then the magicians of Egypt did so with their enchantments; and Pharaoh's heart grew hard, and he did not heed them, as the LORD had said. 23 And Pharaoh turned and went into his house. Neither was his heart moved by this. 24 So all the

Gospel Pearls

Egyptians dug all around the river for water to drink, because they could not drink the water of the river. 25 And seven days passed after the LORD had struck the river.

8 And the LORD spoke to Moses, "Go to Pharaoh and say to him, 'Thus says the LORD: "Let My people go, that they may serve Me. 2 But if you refuse to let *them* go, behold, I will smite all your territory with frogs. 3 So the river shall bring forth frogs abundantly, which shall go up and come into your house, into your bedroom, on your bed, into the houses of your servants, on your people, into your ovens, and into your kneading bowls. 4 And the frogs shall come up on you, on your people, and on all your servants." ' "

5 Then the LORD spoke to Moses, "Say to Aaron, 'Stretch out your hand with your rod over the streams, over the rivers, and over the ponds, and cause frogs to come up on the land of Egypt.' " 6 So Aaron stretched out his hand over the waters of Egypt, and the frogs came up and covered the land of Egypt. 7 And the magicians did so with their enchantments, and brought up frogs on the land of Egypt.

8 Then Pharaoh called for Moses and Aaron, and said, "Entreat the LORD that He may take away the frogs from me and from my people; and I will let the people go, that they may sacrifice to the LORD."

9 And Moses said to Pharaoh, "Accept the honor of saying when I shall intercede for you, for your servants, and for your people, to destroy the frogs from you and your houses, *that* they may remain in the river only."

10 So he said, "Tomorrow." And he said, "*Let it be* according to your word, that you may know that *there is* no one like the LORD our God. 11 And the frogs shall depart from you, from your houses, from your servants, and from your people. They shall remain in the river only."

12 Then Moses and Aaron went out from Pharaoh. And Moses cried out to the LORD concerning the frogs which He had brought against Pharaoh. 13 So the LORD did according to the word of Moses. And the frogs died out of the houses, out of the courtyards, and out of the fields. 14 They gathered them together in heaps, and the land stank. 15 But when Pharaoh saw that there was relief, he hardened his heart and did not heed them, as the LORD had said.

16 So the LORD said to Moses, "Say to Aaron, 'Stretch out your rod, and strike the dust of the land, so that it may become lice throughout all the land of Egypt.' " 17 And they did so. For Aaron stretched out his hand with his rod and struck the dust of the earth, and it became lice on man and beast. All the dust of the land became lice throughout all the land of Egypt.

18 Now the magicians so worked with their enchantments to bring forth lice, but they could not. So there were lice on man and beast. 19 Then the magicians said to Pharaoh, "This *is* the finger of God." But Pharaoh's heart grew hard, and he did not heed them, just as the LORD had said.

20 And the LORD said to Moses, "Rise early in the morning and stand before Pharaoh as he comes out to the water. Then say to him, 'Thus says the LORD: "Let My people go, that they may serve Me. 21 Or else, if you will not let My people go, behold, I will send swarms *of flies* on you and your servants, on your people and into your houses. The houses of the Egyptians shall be full of swarms *of flies,* and also the ground on which they *stand.* 22 And in that day I will set apart the land of Goshen, in which My people dwell, that no swarms *of flies* shall be there, in order that you may know that I *am* the LORD in the midst of the land. 23 I will make a difference[a] between My people and your people. Tomorrow this sign shall be." ' " 24 And the LORD did so. Thick swarms *of flies* came into the house of Pharaoh, *into* his servants' houses, and into all the land of Egypt. The land was corrupted because of the swarms *of flies.*

25 Then Pharaoh called for Moses and Aaron, and said, "Go, sacrifice to your God in the land."

26 And Moses said, "It is not right to do so, for we would be sacrificing the abomination of the Egyptians to the LORD our God. If we sacrifice the abomination of the Egyptians before

8:23 [a]Literally *set a ransom* (compare Exodus 9:4 and 11:7)

God wants to loose something in the souls of women today. There's something He desires to set free. I believe that today is the day God wants to loose you in your heart, your attitude, your emotions, your praise.

their eyes, then will they not stone us? 27 We will go three days' journey into the wilderness and sacrifice to the LORD our God as He will command us."

28 So Pharaoh said, "I will let you go, that you may sacrifice to the LORD your God in the wilderness; only you shall not go very far away. Intercede for me."

29 Then Moses said, "Indeed I am going out from you, and I will entreat the LORD, that the swarms *of flies* may depart tomorrow from Pharaoh, from his servants, and from his people. But let Pharaoh not deal deceitfully anymore in not letting the people go to sacrifice to the LORD."

30 So Moses went out from Pharaoh and entreated the LORD. 31 And the LORD did according to the word of Moses; He removed the swarms *of flies* from Pharaoh, from his servants, and from his people. Not one remained. 32 But Pharaoh hardened his heart at this time also; neither would he let the people go.

9 Then the LORD said to Moses, "Go in to Pharaoh and tell him, 'Thus says the LORD God of the Hebrews: "Let My people go, that they may serve Me. 2 For if you refuse to let *them* go, and still hold them, 3 behold, the hand of the LORD will be on your cattle in the field, on the horses, on the donkeys, on the camels, on the oxen, and on the sheep— a very severe pestilence. 4 And the LORD will make a difference between the livestock of Israel and the livestock of Egypt. So nothing shall die of all *that* belongs to the children of Israel." ' " 5 Then the LORD appointed a set time, saying, "Tomorrow the LORD will do this thing in the land."

6 So the LORD did this thing on the next day, and all the livestock of Egypt died; but of the livestock of the children of Israel, not one died. 7 Then Pharaoh sent, and indeed, not even one of the livestock of the Israelites was dead. But the heart of Pharaoh became hard, and he did not let the people go.

8 So the LORD said to Moses and Aaron, "Take for yourselves handfuls of ashes from a furnace, and let Moses scatter it toward the heavens in the sight of Pharaoh. 9 And it will become fine dust in all the land of Egypt, and it will cause boils that break out in sores on man and beast throughout all the land of Egypt."
10 Then they took ashes from the furnace and stood before Pharaoh, and Moses scattered *them* toward heaven. And *they* caused boils that break out in sores on man and beast. 11 And the magicians could not stand before Moses because of the boils, for the boils were on the magicians and on all the Egyptians. 12 But the LORD hardened the heart of Pharaoh; and he did not heed them, just as the LORD had spoken to Moses.

13 Then the LORD said to Moses, "Rise early in the morning and stand before Pharaoh, and say to him, 'Thus says the LORD God of the Hebrews: "Let My people go, that they may serve Me, 14 for at this time I will send all My plagues to your very heart, and on your servants and on your people, that you may know that *there is* none like Me in all the earth. 15 Now if I had stretched out My hand and struck you and your people with pestilence, then you would have been cut off from the earth. 16 But indeed for this *purpose* I have raised you up, that I may show My power *in* you, and that My name may be declared in all the earth. 17 As yet you exalt yourself against My people in that you will not let them go. 18 Behold, tomorrow about this time I will cause very heavy hail to rain down, such as has not been in Egypt since its founding until now. 19 Therefore send now *and* gather your livestock and all that you have in the field, for the hail shall come down on every man and every animal which is found in the field and is not brought home; and they shall die." ' "

20 He who feared the word of the LORD among the servants of Pharaoh made his servants and his livestock flee to the houses. 21 But he who did not regard the word of the LORD left his servants and his livestock in the field.

22 Then the LORD said to Moses, "Stretch out your hand toward heaven, that there may be hail in all the land of Egypt—on man, on beast, and on every herb of the field, throughout the land of Egypt." 23 And Moses stretched out his rod toward heaven; and the LORD sent thunder and hail, and fire darted to the ground. And the LORD rained hail

Gospel Pearls

on the land of Egypt. 24 So there was
hail, and fire mingled with the hail,
so very heavy that there was none
like it in all the land of Egypt since
it became a nation. 25 And the hail
struck throughout the whole land of
Egypt, all that *was* in the field, both
man and beast; and the hail struck
every herb of the field and broke every tree of the field. 26 Only in the
land of Goshen, where the children
of Israel *were*, there was no hail.

27 And Pharaoh sent and called for
Moses and Aaron, and said to them,
"I have sinned this time. The LORD
is righteous, and my people and I *are*
wicked. 28 Entreat the LORD, that
there may be no *more* mighty thun-
dering and hail, for *it is* enough. I
will let you go, and you shall stay no
longer."

29 So Moses said to him, "As soon
as I have gone out of the city, I will
spread out my hands to the LORD; the
thunder will cease, and there will be
no more hail, that you may know that
the earth *is* the LORD's. 30 But as for
you and your servants, I know that
you will not yet fear the LORD
God."

31 Now the flax and the barley
were struck, for the barley *was* in the
head and the flax *was* in bud.
32 But the wheat and the spelt were
not struck, for they *are* late crops.

33 So Moses went out of the city
from Pharaoh and spread out his
hands to the LORD; then the thunder
and the hail ceased, and the rain was
not poured on the earth. 34 And when
Pharaoh saw that the rain, the hail,
and the thunder had ceased, he
sinned yet more; and he hardened his
heart, he and his servants. 35 So the
heart of Pharaoh was hard; neither
would he let the children of Israel go,
as the LORD had spoken by Moses.

10 Now the LORD said to Moses,
"Go in to Pharaoh; for I have
hardened his heart and the hearts of
his servants, that I may show these
signs of Mine before him, 2 and that
you may tell in the hearing of your
son and your son's son the mighty
things I have done in Egypt, and My
signs which I have done among them,
that you may know that I *am* the
LORD."

3 So Moses and Aaron came in to
Pharaoh and said to him, "Thus says
the LORD God of the Hebrews: 'How

long will you refuse to humble yourself before Me? Let My people go,
that they may serve Me. 4 Or else, if
you refuse to let My people go, behold, tomorrow I will bring locusts
into your territory. 5 And they shall
cover the face of the earth, so that
no one will be able to see the earth;
and they shall eat the residue of what
is left, which remains to you from the
hail, and they shall eat every tree
which grows up for you out of the
field. 6 They shall fill your houses, the
houses of all your servants, and the
houses of all the Egyptians—which
neither your fathers nor your fathers'
fathers have seen, since the day that
they were on the earth to this day.' "
And he turned and went out from
Pharaoh.

7 Then Pharaoh's servants said to
him, "How long shall this man be a
snare to us? Let the men go, that they
may serve the LORD their God. Do
you not yet know that Egypt is destroyed?"

8 So Moses and Aaron were
brought again to Pharaoh, and he
said to them, "Go, serve the LORD
your God. Who *are* the ones that are
going?"

9 And Moses said, "We will go with
our young and our old; with our sons
and our daughters, with our flocks
and our herds we will go, for we must
hold a feast to the LORD."

10 Then he said to them, "The LORD
had better be with you when I let you
and your little ones go! Beware, for
evil is ahead of you. 11 Not so! Go
now, you *who are* men, and serve the
LORD, for that is what you desired."
And they were driven out from Pharaoh's presence.

12 Then the LORD said to Moses,
"Stretch out your hand over the land
of Egypt for the locusts, that they
may come upon the land of Egypt,
and eat every herb of the land—all
that the hail has left." 13 So Moses
stretched out his rod over the land
of Egypt, and the LORD brought an
east wind on the land all that day and
all *that* night. When it was morning,
the east wind brought the locusts.
14 And the locusts went up over all
the land of Egypt and rested on all
the territory of Egypt. *They were*
very severe; previously there had
been no such locusts as they, nor
shall there be such after them.
15 For they covered the face of the

whole earth, so that the land was darkened; and they ate every herb of the land and all the fruit of the trees which the hail had left. So there remained nothing green on the trees or on the plants of the field throughout all the land of Egypt.

16 Then Pharaoh called for Moses and Aaron in haste, and said, "I have sinned against the LORD your God and against you. 17 Now therefore, please forgive my sin only this once, and entreat the LORD your God, that He may take away from me this death only." 18 So he went out from Pharaoh and entreated the LORD. 19 And the LORD turned a very strong west wind, which took the locusts away and blew them into the Red Sea. There remained not one locust in all the territory of Egypt. 20 But the LORD hardened Pharaoh's heart, and he did not let the children of Israel go.

21 Then the LORD said to Moses, "Stretch out your hand toward heaven, that there may be darkness over the land of Egypt, darkness *which* may even be felt." 22 So Moses stretched out his hand toward heaven, and there was thick darkness in all the land of Egypt three days. 23 They did not see one another; nor did anyone rise from his place for three days. But all the children of Israel had light in their dwellings.

24 Then Pharaoh called to Moses and said, "Go, serve the LORD; only let your flocks and your herds be kept back. Let your little ones also go with you."

25 But Moses said, "You must also give us sacrifices and burnt offerings, that we may sacrifice to the LORD our God. 26 Our livestock also shall go with us; not a hoof shall be left behind. For we must take some of them to serve the LORD our God, and even we do not know with what we must serve the LORD until we arrive there."

27 But the LORD hardened Pharaoh's heart, and he would not let them go. 28 Then Pharaoh said to him, "Get away from me! Take heed to yourself and see my face no more! For in the day you see my face you shall die!"

29 So Moses said, "You have spoken well. I will never see your face again."

11 And the LORD said to Moses, "I will bring one more plague on Pharaoh and on Egypt. Afterward he will let you go from here. When he lets *you* go, he will surely drive you out of here altogether. 2 Speak now in the hearing of the people, and let every man ask from his neighbor and every woman from her neighbor, articles of silver and articles of gold." 3 And the LORD gave the people favor in the sight of the Egyptians. Moreover the man Moses *was* very great in the land of Egypt, in the sight of Pharaoh's servants and in the sight of the people.

4 Then Moses said, "Thus says the LORD: 'About midnight I will go out into the midst of Egypt; 5 and all the firstborn in the land of Egypt shall die, from the firstborn of Pharaoh who sits on his throne, even to the firstborn of the female servant who *is* behind the handmill, and all the firstborn of the animals. 6 Then there shall be a great cry throughout all the land of Egypt, such as was not like it *before,* nor shall be like it again. 7 But against none of the children of Israel shall a dog move its tongue, against man or beast, that you may know that the LORD does make a difference between the Egyptians and Israel.' 8 And all these your servants shall come down to me and bow down to me, saying, 'Get out, and all the people who follow you!' After that I will go out." Then he went out from Pharaoh in great anger.

9 But the LORD said to Moses, "Pharaoh will not heed you, so that My wonders may be multiplied in the land of Egypt." 10 So Moses and Aaron did all these wonders before Pharaoh; and the LORD hardened Pharaoh's heart, and he did not let the children of Israel go out of his land.

12 Now the LORD spoke to Moses and Aaron in the land of Egypt, saying, 2 "This month *shall be* your beginning of months; it *shall be* the first month of the year to you. 3 Speak to all the congregation of Israel, saying: 'On the tenth of this month every man shall take for himself a lamb, according to the house of *his* father, a lamb for a household. 4 And if the household is too small for the lamb, let him and his neighbor next to his house take *it* according

Gospel Pearls

to the number of the persons; according to each man's need you shall make your count for the lamb. 5 Your lamb shall be without blemish, a male of the first year. You may take *it* from the sheep or from the goats. 6 Now you shall keep it until the fourteenth day of the same month. Then the whole assembly of the congregation of Israel shall kill it at twilight. 7 And they shall take *some* of the blood and put *it* on the two doorposts and on the lintel of the houses where they eat it. 8 Then they shall eat the flesh on that night; roasted in fire, with unleavened bread *and* with bitter *herbs* they shall eat it. 9 Do not eat it raw, nor boiled at all with water, but roasted in fire— its head with its legs and its entrails. 10 You shall let none of it remain until morning, and what remains of it until morning you shall burn with fire. 11 And thus you shall eat it: *with* a belt on your waist, your sandals on your feet, and your staff in your hand. So you shall eat it in haste. It *is* the LORD's Passover.

12 'For I will pass through the land of Egypt on that night, and will strike all the firstborn in the land of Egypt, both man and beast; and against all the gods of Egypt I will execute judgment: I *am* the LORD. 13 Now the blood shall be a sign for you on the houses where you *are*. And when I see the blood, I will pass over you; and the plague shall not be on you to destroy *you* when I strike the land of Egypt.

14 'So this day shall be to you a memorial; and you shall keep it as a feast to the LORD throughout your generations. You shall keep it as a feast by an everlasting ordinance. 15 Seven days you shall eat unleavened bread. On the first day you shall remove leaven from your houses. For whoever eats leavened bread from the first day until the seventh day, that person shall be cut off from Israel. 16 On the first day *there shall be* a holy convocation, and on the seventh day there shall be a holy convocation for you. No manner of work shall be done on them; but *that* which everyone must eat—that only may be prepared by you. 17 So you shall observe *the Feast of* Unleavened Bread, for on this same day I will have brought your armies out of the land of Egypt. Therefore you

shall observe this day throughout your generations as an everlasting ordinance. 18 In the first *month,* on the fourteenth day of the month at evening, you shall eat unleavened bread, until the twenty-first day of the month at evening. 19 For seven days no leaven shall be found in your houses, since whoever eats what is leavened, that same person shall be cut off from the congregation of Israel, whether *he is* a stranger or a native of the land. 20 You shall eat nothing leavened; in all your dwellings you shall eat unleavened bread.' "

21 Then Moses called for all the elders of Israel and said to them, "Pick out and take lambs for yourselves according to your families, and kill the Passover *lamb*. 22 And you shall take a bunch of hyssop, dip *it* in the blood that *is* in the basin, and strike the lintel and the two doorposts with the blood that *is* in the basin. And none of you shall go out of the door of his house until morning. 23 For the LORD will pass through to strike the Egyptians; and when He sees the blood on the lintel and on the two doorposts, the LORD will pass over the door and not allow the destroyer to come into your houses to strike *you*. 24 And you shall observe this thing as an ordinance for you and your sons forever. 25 It will come to pass when you come to the land which the LORD will give you, just as He promised, that you shall keep this service. 26 And it shall be, when your children say to you, 'What do you mean by this service?' 27 that you shall say, 'It *is* the Passover sacrifice of the LORD, who passed over the houses of the children of Israel in Egypt when He struck the Egyptians and delivered our households.' " So the people bowed their heads and worshiped. 28 Then the children of Israel went away and did *so;* just as the LORD had commanded Moses and Aaron, so they did.

29 And it came to pass at midnight that the LORD struck all the firstborn in the land of Egypt, from the firstborn of Pharaoh who sat on his throne to the firstborn of the captive who *was* in the dungeon, and all the firstborn of livestock. 30 So Pharaoh rose in the night, he, all his servants, and all the Egyptians; and there was a great cry in Egypt, for *there was*

God tenderly and uniquely designed you to be just the way He wanted you to be. He made you for Himself. He made you in a way that can never be duplicated.

Soul Secrets
of a woman in bondage

Lord, I'm living in a house of bondage. And I feel trapped. The place in me that should be holy is haunted. I go from room to room within myself—from the den of depression and wrong decisions to the hallway of unhealed heartache. I feast at the table of frustrated ambition. I drag my wounded ego to bed each night and cover up with affliction. I wake up every morning to greet infirmity again—fear, anger, and bitter remorse.

Jesus, come quick! I can't live in this house anymore! Tear down all my wailing walls. Demolish my pride and my lust. Break the chains of resentment and rejection. Send the Holy Ghost in power. Spirit of Liberty, Spirit of Life, I cry for You! Spirit of Freedom, Spirit of Victory, fight for me! I am free in Jesus' name. I declare the Lord's release to every part of me—suffering spirit, beat-down body, messed-up mind.

The blood of Jesus has broken every bond. Holy Spirit, come and live in me. Be mighty in me, and let the sweet song of deliverance fill every room.

not a house where *there was* not one dead.

31 Then he called for Moses and Aaron by night, and said, "Rise, go out from among my people, both you and the children of Israel. And go, serve the LORD as you have said. 32 Also take your flocks and your herds, as you have said, and be gone; and bless me also."

33 And the Egyptians urged the people, that they might send them out of the land in haste. For they said, "We *shall* all *be* dead." 34 So the people took their dough before it was leavened, having their kneading bowls bound up in their clothes on their shoulders. 35 Now the children of Israel had done according to the word of Moses, and they had asked from the Egyptians articles of silver, articles of gold, and clothing. 36 And the LORD had given the people favor in the sight of the Egyptians, so that they granted them *what they requested.* Thus they plundered the Egyptians.

37 Then the children of Israel journeyed from Rameses to Succoth, about six hundred thousand men on foot, besides children. 38 A mixed multitude went up with them also, and flocks and herds—a great deal of livestock. 39 And they baked unleavened cakes of the dough which they had brought out of Egypt; for it was not leavened, because they were driven out of Egypt and could not wait, nor had they prepared provisions for themselves.

40 Now the sojourn of the children of Israel who lived in Egypt[a] *was* four hundred and thirty years. 41 And it came to pass at the end of the four hundred and thirty years—on that very same day—it came to pass that all the armies of the LORD went out from the land of Egypt. 42 It *is* a night of solemn observance to the LORD for bringing them out of the land of Egypt. This *is* that night of the LORD, a solemn observance for all the children of Israel throughout their generations.

43 And the LORD said to Moses and Aaron, "This *is* the ordinance of the Passover: No foreigner shall eat it. 44 But every man's servant who is bought for money, when you have circumcised him, then he may eat it.

45 A sojourner and a hired servant shall not eat it. 46 In one house it shall be eaten; you shall not carry any of the flesh outside the house, nor shall you break one of its bones. 47 All the congregation of Israel shall keep it. 48 And when a stranger dwells with you *and wants* to keep the Passover to the LORD, let all his males be circumcised, and then let him come near and keep it; and he shall be as a native of the land. For no uncircumcised person shall eat it. 49 One law shall be for the native-born and for the stranger who dwells among you."

50 Thus all the children of Israel did; as the LORD commanded Moses and Aaron, so they did. 51 And it came to pass, on that very same day, that the LORD brought the children of Israel out of the land of Egypt according to their armies.

13 Then the LORD spoke to Moses, saying, 2 "Consecrate to Me all the firstborn, whatever opens the womb among the children of Israel, *both* of man and beast; it is Mine."

3 And Moses said to the people: "Remember this day in which you went out of Egypt, out of the house of bondage; for by strength of hand the LORD brought you out of this *place.* No leavened bread shall be eaten. 4 On this day you are going out, in the month Abib. 5 And it shall be, when the LORD brings you into the land of the Canaanites and the Hittites and the Amorites and the Hivites and the Jebusites, which He swore to your fathers to give you, a land flowing with milk and honey, that you shall keep this service in this month. 6 Seven days you shall eat unleavened bread, and on the seventh day *there shall be* a feast to the LORD. 7 Unleavened bread shall be eaten seven days. And no leavened bread shall be seen among you, nor shall leaven be seen among you in all your quarters. 8 And you shall tell your son in that day, saying, 'This is done because of what the LORD did for me when I came up from Egypt.' 9 It shall be as a sign to you on your hand and as a memorial between your eyes, that the LORD's law may be in your mouth; for with a strong hand the LORD has brought you out of Egypt. 10 You shall therefore keep

---

12:40 [a]Samaritan Pentateuch and Septuagint read *Egypt and Canaan.*

We each must get to the place where we hold a high opinion of ourselves solely on the basis of the fact that God made us exactly, precisely, intricately, wondrously, and uniquely the way we are.

this ordinance in its season from year to year.

11 "And it shall be, when the LORD brings you into the land of the Canaanites, as He swore to you and your fathers, and gives it to you, 12 that you shall set apart to the LORD all that open the womb, that is, every firstborn that comes from an animal which you have; the males *shall be* the LORD's. 13 But every firstborn of a donkey you shall redeem with a lamb; and if you will not redeem *it,* then you shall break its neck. And all the firstborn of man among your sons you shall redeem. 14 So it shall be, when your son asks you in time to come, saying, 'What *is* this?' that you shall say to him, 'By strength of hand the LORD brought us out of Egypt, out of the house of bondage. 15 And it came to pass, when Pharaoh was stubborn about letting us go, that the LORD killed all the firstborn in the land of Egypt, both the firstborn of man and the firstborn of beast. Therefore I sacrifice to the LORD all males that open the womb, but all the firstborn of my sons I redeem.' 16 It shall be as a sign on your hand and as frontlets between your eyes, for by strength of hand the LORD brought us out of Egypt."

17 Then it came to pass, when Pharaoh had let the people go, that God did not lead them *by* way of the land of the Philistines, although that *was* near; for God said, "Lest perhaps the people change their minds when they see war, and return to Egypt." 18 So God led the people around *by* way of the wilderness of the Red Sea. And the children of Israel went up in orderly ranks out of the land of Egypt.

19 And Moses took the bones of Joseph with him, for he had placed the children of Israel under solemn oath, saying, "God will surely visit you, and you shall carry up my bones from here with you."[a]

20 So they took their journey from Succoth and camped in Etham at the edge of the wilderness. 21 And the LORD went before them by day in a pillar of cloud to lead the way, and by night in a pillar of fire to give them light, so as to go by day and night. 22 He did not take away the pillar of cloud by day or the pillar of fire by night *from* before the people.

14 Now the LORD spoke to Moses, saying: 2 "Speak to the children of Israel, that they turn and camp before Pi Hahiroth, between Migdol and the sea, opposite Baal Zephon; you shall camp before it by the sea. 3 For Pharaoh will say of the children of Israel, 'They *are* bewildered by the land; the wilderness has closed them in.' 4 Then I will harden Pharaoh's heart, so that he will pursue them; and I will gain honor over Pharaoh and over all his army, that the Egyptians may know that I *am* the LORD." And they did so.

5 Now it was told the king of Egypt that the people had fled, and the heart of Pharaoh and his servants was turned against the people; and they said, "Why have we done this, that we have let Israel go from serving us?" 6 So he made ready his chariot and took his people with him. 7 Also, he took six hundred choice chariots, and all the chariots of Egypt with captains over every one of them. 8 And the LORD hardened the heart of Pharaoh king of Egypt, and he pursued the children of Israel; and the children of Israel went out with boldness. 9 So the Egyptians pursued them, all the horses *and* chariots of Pharaoh, his horsemen and his army, and overtook them camping by the sea beside Pi Hahiroth, before Baal Zephon.

10 And when Pharaoh drew near, the children of Israel lifted their eyes, and behold, the Egyptians marched after them. So they were very afraid, and the children of Israel cried out to the LORD. 11 Then they said to Moses, "Because *there were* no graves in Egypt, have you taken us away to die in the wilderness? Why have you so dealt with us, to bring us up out of Egypt? 12 *Is* this not the word that we told you in Egypt, saying, 'Let us alone that we may serve the Egyptians?' For *it would have been* better for us to serve the Egyptians than that we should die in the wilderness."

13 And Moses said to the people, "Do not be afraid. Stand still, and see the salvation of the LORD, which He will accomplish for you today. For the Egyptians whom you see today,

13:19 [a]Genesis 50:25

Gospel Pearls

you shall see again no more forever. 14 The LORD will fight for you, and you shall hold your peace."

15 And the LORD said to Moses, "Why do you cry to Me? Tell the children of Israel to go forward. 16 "But lift up your rod, and stretch out your hand over the sea and divide it. And the children of Israel shall go on dry *ground* through the midst of the sea. 17 And I indeed will harden the hearts of the Egyptians, and they shall follow them. So I will gain honor over Pharaoh and over all his army, his chariots, and his horsemen. 18 Then the Egyptians shall know that I *am* the LORD, when I have gained honor for Myself over Pharaoh, his chariots, and his horsemen."

19 And the Angel of God, who went before the camp of Israel, moved and went behind them; and the pillar of cloud went from before them and stood behind them. 20 So it came between the camp of the Egyptians and the camp of Israel. Thus it was a cloud and darkness *to the one,* and it gave light by night *to the other,* so that the one did not come near the other all that night.

21 Then Moses stretched out his hand over the sea; and the LORD caused the sea to go *back* by a strong east wind all that night, and made the sea into dry *land,* and the waters were divided. 22 So the children of Israel went into the midst of the sea on the dry *ground,* and the waters *were* a wall to them on their right hand and on their left. 23 And the Egyptians pursued and went after them into the midst of the sea, all Pharaoh's horses, his chariots, and his horsemen.

24 Now it came to pass, in the morning watch, that the LORD looked down upon the army of the Egyptians through the pillar of fire and cloud, and He troubled the army of the Egyptians. 25 And He took off[a] their chariot wheels, so that they drove them with difficulty; and the Egyptians said, "Let us flee from the face of Israel, for the LORD fights for them against the Egyptians."

26 Then the LORD said to Moses, "Stretch out your hand over the sea, that the waters may come back upon the Egyptians, on their chariots, and

on their horsemen." 27 And Moses stretched out his hand over the sea; and when the morning appeared, the sea returned to its full depth, while the Egyptians were fleeing into it. So the LORD overthrew the Egyptians in the midst of the sea. 28 Then the waters returned and covered the chariots, the horsemen, *and* all the army of Pharaoh that came into the sea after them. Not so much as one of them remained. 29 But the children of Israel had walked on dry *land* in the midst of the sea, and the waters *were* a wall to them on their right hand and on their left.

30 So the LORD saved Israel that day out of the hand of the Egyptians, and Israel saw the Egyptians dead on the seashore. 31 Thus Israel saw the great work which the LORD had done in Egypt; so the people feared the LORD, and believed the LORD and His servant Moses.

15 Then Moses and the children of Israel sang this song to the LORD, and spoke, saying:

"I will sing to the LORD,
  For He has triumphed gloriously!
  The horse and its rider
  He has thrown into the sea!
2 The LORD *is* my strength and song,
  And He has become my salvation;
  He *is* my God, and I will praise Him;
  My father's God, and I will exalt Him.
3 The LORD *is* a man of war;
  The LORD *is* His name.
4 Pharaoh's chariots and his army He has cast into the sea;
  His chosen captains also are drowned in the Red Sea.
5 The depths have covered them;
  They sank to the bottom like a stone.

6 "Your right hand, O LORD, has become glorious in power;
  Your right hand, O LORD, has dashed the enemy in pieces.
7 And in the greatness of Your excellence

14:25 [a]Samaritan Pentateuch, Septuagint, and Syriac read *bound.*

*T*hank God today for making you exactly the way you are and for transforming you daily into exactly the woman He wants you to be. You are without comparison in His eyes!

You have overthrown those
who rose against You;
You sent forth Your wrath;
It consumed them like stubble.
8 And with the blast of Your
nostrils
The waters were gathered
together;
The floods stood upright like a
heap;
The depths congealed in the
heart of the sea.
9 The enemy said, 'I will pursue,
I will overtake,
I will divide the spoil;
My desire shall be satisfied on
them.
I will draw my sword,
My hand shall destroy them.'
10 You blew with Your wind,
The sea covered them;
They sank like lead in the
mighty waters.

11 "Who *is* like You, O Lord,
among the gods?
Who *is* like You, glorious in
holiness,
Fearful in praises, doing
wonders?
12 You stretched out Your right
hand;
The earth swallowed them.
13 You in Your mercy have led
forth
The people whom You have
redeemed;
You have guided *them* in Your
strength
To Your holy habitation.

14 "The people will hear *and* be
afraid;
Sorrow will take hold of the
inhabitants of Philistia.
15 Then the chiefs of Edom will be
dismayed;
The mighty men of Moab,
Trembling will take hold of
them;
All the inhabitants of Canaan
will melt away.
16 Fear and dread will fall on
them;
By the greatness of Your arm
They will be *as* still as a stone,
Till Your people pass over, O
Lord,
Till the people pass over
Whom You have purchased.

17 You will bring them in and
plant them
In the mountain of Your
inheritance,
In the place, O Lord, *which*
You have made
For Your own dwelling,
The sanctuary, O Lord, *which*
Your hands have established.

18 "The Lord shall reign forever
and ever."

19 For the horses of Pharaoh went
with his chariots and his horsemen
into the sea, and the Lord brought
back the waters of the sea upon
them. But the children of Israel went
on dry *land* in the midst of the sea.
20 Then Miriam the prophetess, the
sister of Aaron, took the timbrel in
her hand; and all the women went
out after her with timbrels and with
dances. 21 And Miriam answered
them:

"Sing to the Lord,
For He has triumphed
gloriously!
The horse and its rider
He has thrown into the sea!"

22 So Moses brought Israel from
the Red Sea; then they went out into
the Wilderness of Shur. And they
went three days in the wilderness
and found no water. 23 Now when
they came to Marah, they could not
drink the waters of Marah, for they
were bitter. Therefore the name of it
was called Marah.ᵃ 24 And the people
complained against Moses, saying,
"What shall we drink?" 25 So he
cried out to the Lord, and the Lord
showed him a tree. When he cast *it*
into the waters, the waters were
made sweet.
There He made a statute and an ordinance for them, and there He tested
them, 26 and said, "If you diligently
heed the voice of the Lord your God
and do what is right in His sight, give
ear to His commandments and keep
all His statutes, I will put none of the
diseases on you which I have brought
on the Egyptians. For I *am* the Lord
who heals you."
27 Then they came to Elim, where
there *were* twelve wells of water and

15:23 ᵃLiterally *Bitter*

Gospel
Pearls

seventy palm trees; so they camped there by the waters.

16 And they journeyed from Elim, and all the congregation of the children of Israel came to the Wilderness of Sin, which is between Elim and Sinai, on the fifteenth day of the second month after they departed from the land of Egypt. 2 Then the whole congregation of the children of Israel complained against Moses and Aaron in the wilderness. 3 And the children of Israel said to them, "Oh, that we had died by the hand of the LORD in the land of Egypt, when we sat by the pots of meat *and* when we ate bread to the full! For you have brought us out into this wilderness to kill this whole assembly with hunger."

4 Then the LORD said to Moses, "Behold, I will rain bread from heaven for you. And the people shall go out and gather a certain quota every day, that I may test them, whether they will walk in My law or not. 5 And it shall be on the sixth day that they shall prepare what they bring in, and it shall be twice as much as they gather daily."

6 Then Moses and Aaron said to all the children of Israel, "At evening you shall know that the LORD has brought you out of the land of Egypt. 7 And in the morning you shall see the glory of the LORD; for He hears your complaints against the LORD. But what *are* we, that you complain against us?" 8 Also Moses said, "*This shall be seen* when the LORD gives you meat to eat in the evening, and in the morning bread to the full; for the LORD hears your complaints which you make against Him. And what *are* we? Your complaints *are* not against us but against the LORD."

9 Then Moses spoke to Aaron, "Say to all the congregation of the children of Israel, 'Come near before the LORD, for He has heard your complaints.' " 10 Now it came to pass, as Aaron spoke to the whole congregation of the children of Israel, that they looked toward the wilderness, and behold, the glory of the LORD appeared in the cloud.

11 And the LORD spoke to Moses, saying, 12 "I have heard the complaints of the children of Israel. Speak to them, saying, 'At twilight you shall eat meat, and in the morn-

ing you shall be filled with bread. And you shall know that I *am* the LORD your God.' "

13 So it was that quails came up at evening and covered the camp, and in the morning the dew lay all around the camp. 14 And when the layer of dew lifted, there, on the surface of the wilderness, was a small round substance, *as* fine as frost on the ground. 15 So when the children of Israel saw *it,* they said to one another, "What is it?" For they did not know what it *was.*

And Moses said to them, "This *is* the bread which the LORD has given you to eat. 16 This is the thing which the LORD has commanded: 'Let every man gather it according to each one's need, one omer for each person, *according to the* number of persons; let every man take for *those* who *are* in his tent.' "

17 Then the children of Israel did so and gathered, some more, some less. 18 So when they measured *it* by omers, he who gathered much had nothing left over, and he who gathered little had no lack. Every man had gathered according to each one's need. 19 And Moses said, "Let no one leave any of it till morning." 20 Notwithstanding they did not heed Moses. But some of them left part of it until morning, and it bred worms and stank. And Moses was angry with them. 21 So they gathered it every morning, every man according to his need. And when the sun became hot, it melted.

22 And so it was, on the sixth day, *that* they gathered twice as much bread, two omers for each one. And all the rulers of the congregation came and told Moses. 23 Then he said to them, "This *is what* the LORD has said: 'Tomorrow *is* a Sabbath rest, a holy Sabbath to the LORD. Bake what you will bake *today,* and boil what you will boil; and lay up for yourselves all that remains, to be kept until morning.' " 24 So they laid it up till morning, as Moses commanded; and it did not stink, nor were there any worms in it. 25 Then Moses said, "Eat that today, for today *is* a Sabbath to the LORD; today you will not find it in the field. 26 Six days you shall gather it, but on the seventh day, the Sabbath, there will be none."

27 Now it happened *that some* of the people went out on the seventh

day to gather, but they found none. 28 And the LORD said to Moses, "How long do you refuse to keep My commandments and My laws? 29 See! For the LORD has given you the Sabbath; therefore He gives you on the sixth day bread for two days. Let every man remain in his place; let no man go out of his place on the seventh day." 30 So the people rested on the seventh day.

31 And the house of Israel called its name Manna.*a* And it *was* like white coriander seed, and the taste of it *was* like wafers *made* with honey.

32 Then Moses said, "This *is* the thing which the LORD has commanded: 'Fill an omer with it, to be kept for your generations, that they may see the bread with which I fed you in the wilderness, when I brought you out of the land of Egypt.' " 33 And Moses said to Aaron, "Take a pot and put an omer of manna in it, and lay it up before the LORD, to be kept for your generations." 34 As the LORD commanded Moses, so Aaron laid it up before the Testimony, to be kept. 35 And the children of Israel ate manna forty years, until they came to an inhabited land; they ate manna until they came to the border of the land of Canaan. 36 Now an omer *is* one-tenth of an ephah.

17 Then all the congregation of the children of Israel set out on their journey from the Wilderness of Sin, according to the commandment of the LORD, and camped in Rephidim; but *there was* no water for the people to drink. 2 Therefore the people contended with Moses, and said, "Give us water, that we may drink."

So Moses said to them, "Why do you contend with me? Why do you tempt the LORD?"

3 And the people thirsted there for water, and the people complained against Moses, and said, "Why *is* it you have brought us up out of Egypt, to kill us and our children and our livestock with thirst?"

4 So Moses cried out to the LORD, saying, "What shall I do with this people? They are almost ready to stone me!"

5 And the LORD said to Moses, "Go on before the people, and take with you some of the elders of Israel. Also take in your hand your rod with which you struck the river, and go. 6 Behold, I will stand before you there on the rock in Horeb; and you shall strike the rock, and water will come out of it, that the people may drink."

And Moses did so in the sight of the elders of Israel. 7 So he called the name of the place Massah*a* and Meribah,*b* because of the contention of the children of Israel, and because they tempted the LORD, saying, "Is the LORD among us or not?"

8 Now Amalek came and fought with Israel in Rephidim. 9 And Moses said to Joshua, "Choose us some men and go out, fight with Amalek. Tomorrow I will stand on the top of the hill with the rod of God in my hand." 10 So Joshua did as Moses said to him, and fought with Amalek. And Moses, Aaron, and Hur went up to the top of the hill. 11 And so it was, when Moses held up his hand, that Israel prevailed; and when he let down his hand, Amalek prevailed. 12 But Moses' hands *became* heavy; so they took a stone and put *it* under him, and he sat on it. And Aaron and Hur supported his hands, one on one side, and the other on the other side; and his hands were steady until the going down of the sun. 13 So Joshua defeated Amalek and his people with the edge of the sword.

14 Then the LORD said to Moses, "Write this *for* a memorial in the book and recount *it* in the hearing of Joshua, that I will utterly blot out the remembrance of Amalek from under heaven." 15 And Moses built an altar and called its name, The-LORD-Is-My-Banner;*a* 16 for he said, "Because the LORD has sworn: the LORD *will have* war with Amalek from generation to generation."

18 And Jethro, the priest of Midian, Moses' father-in-law, heard of all that God had done for Moses and for Israel His people—that the LORD had brought Israel out of Egypt. 2 Then Jethro, Moses' father-in-law, took Zipporah, Moses' wife, after he had sent her back, 3 with her

---

16:31 *a*Literally *What?* (compare Exodus 16:15)　　17:7 *a*Literally *Tempted* *b*Literally *Contention*
17:15 *a*Hebrew *YHWH Nissi*

Gospel Pearls

two sons, of whom the name of one *was* Gershom (for he said, "I have been a stranger in a foreign land")[a] 4 and the name of the other *was* Eliezer[a] (for *he said,* "The God of my father *was* my help, and delivered me from the sword of Pharaoh"); 5 and Jethro, Moses' father-in-law, came with his sons and his wife to Moses in the wilderness, where he was encamped at the mountain of God. 6 Now he had said to Moses, "I, your father-in-law Jethro, am coming to you with your wife and her two sons with her."

7 So Moses went out to meet his father-in-law, bowed down, and kissed him. And they asked each other about *their* well-being, and they went into the tent. 8 And Moses told his father-in-law all that the LORD had done to Pharaoh and to the Egyptians for Israel's sake, all the hardship that had come upon them on the way, and *how* the LORD had delivered them. 9 Then Jethro rejoiced for all the good which the LORD had done for Israel, whom He had delivered out of the hand of the Egyptians. 10 And Jethro said, "Blessed *be* the LORD, who has delivered you out of the hand of the Egyptians and out of the hand of Pharaoh, *and* who has delivered the people from under the hand of the Egyptians. 11 Now I know that the LORD *is* greater than all the gods; for in the very thing in which they behaved proudly, *He was* above them." 12 Then Jethro, Moses' father-in-law, took[a] a burnt offering and *other* sacrifices *to offer* to God. And Aaron came with all the elders of Israel to eat bread with Moses' father-in-law before God.

13 And so it was, on the next day, that Moses sat to judge the people; and the people stood before Moses from morning until evening. 14 So when Moses' father-in-law saw all that he did for the people, he said, "What *is* this thing that you are doing for the people? Why do you alone sit, and all the people stand before you from morning until evening?" 15 And Moses said to his father-in-law, "Because the people come to me to inquire of God. 16 When they have a difficulty, they come to me, and I judge between one and another; and

I make known the statutes of God and His laws."

17 So Moses' father-in-law said to him, "The thing that you do *is* not good. 18 Both you and these people who *are* with you will surely wear yourselves out. For this thing *is* too much for you; you are not able to perform it by yourself. 19 Listen now to my voice; I will give you counsel, and God will be with you: Stand before God for the people, so that you may bring the difficulties to God. 20 And you shall teach them the statutes and the laws, and show them the way in which they must walk and the work they must do. 21 Moreover you shall select from all the people able men, such as fear God, men of truth, hating covetousness; and place *such* over them *to be* rulers of thousands, rulers of hundreds, rulers of fifties, and rulers of tens. 22 And let them judge the people at all times. Then it will be *that* every great matter they shall bring to you, but every small matter they themselves shall judge. So it will be easier for you, for they will bear *the burden* with you. 23 If you do this thing, and God *so* commands you, then you will be able to endure, and all this people will also go to their place in peace."

24 So Moses heeded the voice of his father-in-law and did all that he had said. 25 And Moses chose able men out of all Israel, and made them heads over the people: rulers of thousands, rulers of hundreds, rulers of fifties, and rulers of tens. 26 So they judged the people at all times; the hard cases they brought to Moses, but they judged every small case themselves.

27 Then Moses let his father-in-law depart, and he went his way to his own land.

19 In the third month after the children of Israel had gone out of the land of Egypt, on the same day, they came *to* the Wilderness of Sinai. 2 For they had departed from Rephidim, had come *to* the Wilderness of Sinai, and camped in the wilderness. So Israel camped there before the mountain.

3 And Moses went up to God, and the LORD called to him from the

---

18:3 aCompare Exodus 2:22   18:4 aLiterally *My God Is Help*   18:12 aFollowing Masoretic Text and Septuagint; Syriac, Targum, and Vulgate read *offered.*

God doesn't make mistakes. He doesn't err. He doesn't have mishaps or incidents or accidents. God creates only what He wants to create.

mountain, saying, "Thus you shall say to the house of Jacob, and tell the children of Israel: 4 'You have seen what I did to the Egyptians, and how I bore you on eagles' wings and brought you to Myself. 5 Now therefore, if you will indeed obey My voice and keep My covenant, then you shall be a special treasure to Me above all people; for all the earth is Mine. 6 And you shall be to Me a kingdom of priests and a holy nation.' These are the words which you shall speak to the children of Israel."

7 So Moses came and called for the elders of the people, and laid before them all these words which the LORD commanded him. 8 Then all the people answered together and said, "All that the LORD has spoken we will do." So Moses brought back the words of the people to the LORD. 9 And the LORD said to Moses, "Behold, I come to you in the thick cloud, that the people may hear when I speak with you, and believe you forever."

So Moses told the words of the people to the LORD.

10 Then the LORD said to Moses, "Go to the people and consecrate them today and tomorrow, and let them wash their clothes. 11 And let them be ready for the third day. For on the third day the LORD will come down upon Mount Sinai in the sight of all the people. 12 You shall set bounds for the people all around, saying, 'Take heed to yourselves that you do not go up to the mountain or touch its base. Whoever touches the mountain shall surely be put to death. 13 Not a hand shall touch him, but he shall surely be stoned or shot with an arrow; whether man or beast, he shall not live.' When the trumpet sounds long, they shall come near the mountain."

14 So Moses went down from the mountain to the people and sanctified the people, and they washed their clothes. 15 And he said to the people, "Be ready for the third day; do not come near your wives."

16 Then it came to pass on the third day, in the morning, that there were thunderings and lightnings, and a thick cloud on the mountain; and the sound of the trumpet was very loud, so that all the people who were in the camp trembled. 17 And Moses

brought the people out of the camp to meet with God, and they stood at the foot of the mountain. 18 Now Mount Sinai was completely in smoke, because the LORD descended upon it in fire. Its smoke ascended like the smoke of a furnace, and the whole mountain*a* quaked greatly. 19 And when the blast of the trumpet sounded long and became louder and louder, Moses spoke, and God answered him by voice. 20 Then the LORD came down upon Mount Sinai, on the top of the mountain. And the LORD called Moses to the top of the mountain, and Moses went up.

21 And the LORD said to Moses, "Go down and warn the people, lest they break through to gaze at the LORD, and many of them perish. 22 Also let the priests who come near the LORD consecrate themselves, lest the LORD break out against them."

23 But Moses said to the LORD, "The people cannot come up to Mount Sinai; for You warned us, saying, 'Set bounds around the mountain and consecrate it.'"

24 Then the LORD said to him, "Away! Get down and then come up, you and Aaron with you. But do not let the priests and the people break through to come up to the LORD, lest He break out against them." 25 So Moses went down to the people and spoke to them.

20 And God spoke all these words, saying:

2 "I am the LORD your God, who brought you out of the land of Egypt, out of the house of bondage. 3 You shall have no other gods before Me.

4 "You shall not make for yourself a carved image—any likeness of anything that is in heaven above, or that is in the earth beneath, or that is in the water under the earth; 5 you shall not bow down to them nor serve them. For I, the LORD your God, am a jealous God, visiting the iniquity of the fathers upon the children to the third and fourth generations of those who hate Me, 6 but showing mercy to thousands, to those

19:18 *a*Septuagint reads all the people.

The greater part of our attractiveness lies within and it wells up from the inside and finds a creative and appropriate expression on the outside. God sees what no one else can see. And it's that part of you that He values the most.

No Other Gods

Exodus 20:1–4

*I*n our modern times, we think idols and their offerings are obsolete, but that is not true! Today, the idols have taken on a disguise. Let's disrobe them and expose their danger. Idols are the things you worship, the things to which you yield your strength. They are false gods.

I know that most of us have no physical shrines in our homes, but don't you realize you can worship things by paying them too much attention? You can worship them by dedicating your life to impressing them or by allowing their opinion to determine your self-worth or esteem. Those things are idols in your life.

You have shed tears over them. You have birthed blessings that you have not enjoyed because you did a right thing for a wrong reason. In Genesis 29:31–35, you'll see that Leah did that. She was trying to win Jacob with her successes instead of thanking God that He had given her an area of success to balance the many failures. Leah missed out on a real experience with God because her strength was sapped away through idolatry.

Finally, after a series of births, Leah has reached a degree of maturity, though she will struggle in this area again. Winning Jacob's love will always be an area of vulnerability for her. She has refocused her attention on the Giver of life and the Healer of hearts.

After this she births Judah. She has been resurrected, and she testifies in Genesis 29:35, "Now I will praise the LORD." *Judah* means "praise." You cannot praise and honor God for what He has given you until you have been weaned from the idols you have lived for in the past!

Now, can we confront the Jacob in your life? Is there an idol, the thing in your life that has stolen your attention and emotions from a God who keeps blessing you? Have you missed the sweet taste of God's favor because you took the successes that He gave you and paraded them before others whose minds you wanted to change? Is there an area or issue that you have allowed to become an idol? It may be an ex-husband. It may be a childhood rivalry. It could be the result of burning, painful words that scalded your heart and left you blistered inside!

This may be an area that God needs to heal in your life. I join you in faith and prayer, and I break the spirit of idolatry over your life. You will live for the Lord and no one else! I agree with you in prayer that God in His mercy would restore unto you the joy of your salvation. Lord, restore to Your daughter the joy of having You, the joy of being at peace within. I rebuke that spirit that drives and torments her—stealing precious moments from her. In Jesus' name, woman, be loosed!

who love Me and keep My commandments.

7 "You shall not take the name of the LORD your God in vain, for the LORD will not hold *him* guiltless who takes His name in vain.

8 "Remember the Sabbath day, to keep it holy. 9 Six days you shall labor and do all your work, 10 but the seventh day *is* the Sabbath of the LORD your God. *In it* you shall do no work: you, nor your son, nor your daughter, nor your male servant, nor your female servant, nor your cattle, nor your stranger who *is* within your gates.

11 For *in* six days the LORD made the heavens and the earth, the sea, and all that *is* in them, and rested the seventh day. Therefore the LORD blessed the Sabbath day and hallowed it.

12 "Honor your father and your mother, that your days may be long upon the land which the LORD your God is giving you.

13 "You shall not murder.

14 "You shall not commit adultery.

15 "You shall not steal.

16 "You shall not bear false witness against your neighbor.

17 "You shall not covet your neighbor's house; you shall not covet your neighbor's wife, nor his male servant, nor his female servant, nor his ox, nor his donkey, nor anything that *is* your neighbor's."

18 Now all the people witnessed the thunderings, the lightning flashes, the sound of the trumpet, and the mountain smoking; and when the people saw *it*, they trembled and stood afar off. 19 Then they said to Moses, "You speak with us, and we will hear; but let not God speak with us, lest we die."

20 And Moses said to the people, "Do not fear; for God has come to test you, and that His fear may be before you, so that you may not sin." 21 So the people stood afar off, but Moses drew near the thick darkness where God *was*.

22 Then the LORD said to Moses,

"Thus you shall say to the children of Israel: 'You have seen that I have talked with you from heaven. 23 You shall not make *anything to be* with Me—gods of silver or gods of gold you shall not make for yourselves. 24 An altar of earth you shall make for Me, and you shall sacrifice on it your burnt offerings and your peace offerings, your sheep and your oxen. In every place where I record My name I will come to you, and I will bless you. 25 And if you make Me an altar of stone, you shall not build it of hewn stone; for if you use your tool on it, you have profaned it. 26 Nor shall you go up by steps to My altar, that your nakedness may not be exposed on it.'

21 "Now these *are* the judgments which you shall set before them: 2 If you buy a Hebrew servant, he shall serve six years; and in the seventh he shall go out free and pay nothing. 3 If he comes in by himself, he shall go out by himself; if he *comes in* married, then his wife shall go out with him. 4 If his master has given him a wife, and she has borne him sons or daughters, the wife and her children shall be her master's, and he shall go out by himself. 5 But if the servant plainly says, 'I love my master, my wife, and my children; I will not go out free,' 6 then his master shall bring him to the judges. He shall also bring him to the door, or to the doorpost, and his master shall pierce his ear with an awl; and he shall serve him forever.

7 "And if a man sells his daughter to be a female slave, she shall not go out as the male slaves do. 8 If she does not please her master, who has betrothed her to himself, then he shall let her be redeemed. He shall have no right to sell her to a foreign people, since he has dealt deceitfully with her. 9 And if he has betrothed her to his son, he shall deal with her according to the custom of daughters. 10 If he takes another wife, he shall not diminish her food, her clothing, and her marriage rights. 11 And if he does not do these three for her, then she shall go out free, without *paying* money.

12 "He who strikes a man so that he dies shall surely be put to death. 13 However, if he did not lie in wait,

Gospel
Pearls

but God delivered *him* into his hand, then I will appoint for you a place where he may flee.

14 "But if a man acts with premeditation against his neighbor, to kill him by treachery, you shall take him from My altar, that he may die.

15 "And he who strikes his father or his mother shall surely be put to death.

16 "He who kidnaps a man and sells him, or if he is found in his hand, shall surely be put to death.

17 "And he who curses his father or his mother shall surely be put to death.

18 "If men contend with each other, and one strikes the other with a stone or with *his* fist, and he does not die but is confined to *his* bed, 19 if he rises again and walks about outside with his staff, then he who struck *him* shall be acquitted. He shall only pay *for* the loss of his time, and shall provide *for him* to be thoroughly healed.

20 "And if a man beats his male or female servant with a rod, so that he dies under his hand, he shall surely be punished. 21 Notwithstanding, if he remains alive a day or two, he shall not be punished; for he *is* his property.

22 "If men fight, and hurt a woman with child, so that she gives birth prematurely, yet no harm follows, he shall surely be punished accordingly as the woman's husband imposes on him; and he shall pay as the judges *determine.* 23 But if *any* harm follows, then you shall give life for life, 24 eye for eye, tooth for tooth, hand for hand, foot for foot, 25 burn for burn, wound for wound, stripe for stripe.

26 "If a man strikes the eye of his male or female servant, and destroys it, he shall let him go free for the sake of his eye. 27 And if he knocks out the tooth of his male or female servant, he shall let him go free for the sake of his tooth.

28 "If an ox gores a man or a woman to death, then the ox shall surely be stoned, and its flesh shall not be eaten; but the owner of the ox *shall be* acquitted. 29 But if the ox tended to thrust with its horn in times past, and it has been made known to his owner, and he has not kept it confined, so that it has killed a man or a woman, the ox shall be stoned and its owner also shall be put to

death. 30 If there is imposed on him a sum of money, then he shall pay to redeem his life, whatever is imposed on him. 31 Whether it has gored a son or gored a daughter, according to this judgment it shall be done to him. 32 If the ox gores a male or female servant, he shall give to their master thirty shekels of silver, and the ox shall be stoned.

33 "And if a man opens a pit, or if a man digs a pit and does not cover it, and an ox or a donkey falls in it, 34 the owner of the pit shall make *it* good; he shall give money to their owner, but the dead *animal* shall be his.

35 "If one man's ox hurts another's, so that it dies, then they shall sell the live ox and divide the money from it; and the dead *ox* they shall also divide. 36 Or if it was known that the ox tended to thrust in time past, and its owner has not kept it confined, he shall surely pay ox for ox, and the dead animal shall be his own.

22 "If a man steals an ox or a sheep, and slaughters it or sells it, he shall restore five oxen for an ox and four sheep for a sheep. 2 If the thief is found breaking in, and he is struck so that he dies, *there shall be* no guilt for his bloodshed. 3 If the sun has risen on him, *there shall be* guilt for his bloodshed. He should make full restitution; if he has nothing, then he shall be sold for his theft. 4 If the theft is certainly found alive in his hand, whether it is an ox or donkey or sheep, he shall restore double.

5 "If a man causes a field or vineyard to be grazed, and lets loose his animal, and it feeds in another man's field, he shall make restitution from the best of his own field and the best of his own vineyard.

6 "If fire breaks out and catches in thorns, so that stacked grain, standing grain, or the field is consumed, he who kindled the fire shall surely make restitution.

7 "If a man delivers to his neighbor money or articles to keep, and it is stolen out of the man's house, if the thief is found, he shall pay double. 8 If the thief is not found, then the master of the house shall be brought to the judges *to see* whether he has put his hand into his neighbor's goods.

Go back to the *source* of what makes you "attract" other people—the Source of your attractiveness is the Holy Spirit of God. He is the One who woos and wins the heart.

9 "For any kind of trespass, *whether it concerns* an ox, a donkey, a sheep, or clothing, *or* for any kind of lost thing which *another* claims to be his, the cause of both parties shall come before the judges; *and* whomever the judges condemn shall pay double to his neighbor. 10 If a man delivers to his neighbor a donkey, an ox, a sheep, or any animal to keep, and it dies, is hurt, or driven away, no one seeing *it,* 11 *then* an oath of the LORD shall be between them both, that he has not put his hand into his neighbor's goods; and the owner of it shall accept *that,* and he shall not make *it* good. 12 But if, in fact, it is stolen from him, he shall make restitution to the owner of it. 13 If it is torn to pieces *by a beast, then* he shall bring it as evidence, *and* he shall not make good what was torn.

14 "And if a man borrows *anything* from his neighbor, and it becomes injured or dies, the owner of it not *being* with it, he shall surely make *it* good. 15 If its owner *was* with it, he shall not make *it* good; if it *was* hired, it came for its hire.

16 "If a man entices a virgin who is not betrothed, and lies with her, he shall surely pay the bride-price for her *to be* his wife. 17 If her father utterly refuses to give her to him, he shall pay money according to the bride-price of virgins.

18 "You shall not permit a sorceress to live.

19 "Whoever lies with an animal shall surely be put to death.

20 "He who sacrifices to *any* god, except to the LORD only, he shall be utterly destroyed.

21 "You shall neither mistreat a stranger nor oppress him, for you were strangers in the land of Egypt. 22 "You shall not afflict any widow or fatherless child. 23 If you afflict them in any way, *and* they cry at all to Me, I will surely hear their cry; 24 and My wrath will become hot, and I will kill you with the sword; your wives shall be widows, and your children fatherless.

25 "If you lend money to *any of* My people *who are* poor among you, you shall not be like a moneylender to him; you shall not charge him interest. 26 If you ever take your neighbor's garment as a pledge, you shall return it to him before the sun goes down. 27 For that *is* his only covering, it *is* his garment for his skin. What will he sleep in? And it will be that when he cries to Me, I will hear, for I *am* gracious.

28 "You shall not revile God, nor curse a ruler of your people.

29 "You shall not delay *to offer* the first of your ripe produce and your juices. The firstborn of your sons you shall give to Me. 30 Likewise you shall do with your oxen *and* your sheep. It shall be with its mother seven days; on the eighth day you shall give it to Me.

31 "And you shall be holy men to Me: you shall not eat meat torn *by beasts* in the field; you shall throw it to the dogs.

23 "You shall not circulate a false report. Do not put your hand with the wicked to be an unrighteous witness. 2 You shall not follow a crowd to do evil; nor shall you testify in a dispute so as to turn aside after many to pervert *justice.* 3 You shall not show partiality to a poor man in his dispute.

4 "If you meet your enemy's ox or his donkey going astray, you shall surely bring it back to him again. 5 If you see the donkey of one who hates you lying under its burden, and you would refrain from helping it, you shall surely help him with it.

6 "You shall not pervert the judgment of your poor in his dispute. 7 Keep yourself far from a false matter; do not kill the innocent and righteous. For I will not justify the wicked. 8 And you shall take no bribe, for a bribe blinds the discerning and perverts the words of the righteous.

9 "Also you shall not oppress a stranger, for you know the heart of a stranger, because you were strangers in the land of Egypt.

10 "Six years you shall sow your land and gather in its produce, 11 but the seventh *year* you shall let it rest and lie fallow, that the poor of your people may eat; and what they leave, the beasts of the field may eat. In like manner you shall do with your vineyard *and* your olive grove. 12 Six days you shall do your work, and on the seventh day you shall rest, that your ox and your donkey may rest, and the son of your female servant and the stranger may be refreshed.

13 "And in all that I have said to you, be circumspect and make no mention of the name of other gods, nor let it be heard from your mouth. 14 "Three times you shall keep a feast to Me in the year: 15 You shall keep the Feast of Unleavened Bread (you shall eat unleavened bread seven days, as I commanded you, at the time appointed in the month of Abib, for in it you came out of Egypt; none shall appear before Me empty); 16 and the Feast of Harvest, the first-fruits of your labors which you have sown in the field; and the Feast of Ingathering at the end of the year, when you have gathered in *the fruit of* your labors from the field.

17 "Three times in the year all your males shall appear before the Lord GOD.[a]

18 "You shall not offer the blood of My sacrifice with leavened bread; nor shall the fat of My sacrifice remain until morning. 19 The first of the firstfruits of your land you shall bring into the house of the LORD your God. You shall not boil a young goat in its mother's milk.

20 "Behold, I send an Angel before you to keep you in the way and to bring you into the place which I have prepared. 21 Beware of Him and obey His voice; do not provoke Him, for He will not pardon your transgressions; for My name *is* in Him. 22 But if you indeed obey His voice and do all that I speak, then I will be an enemy to your enemies and an adversary to your adversaries. 23 For My Angel will go before you and bring you in to the Amorites and the Hittites and the Perizzites and the Canaanites and the Hivites and the Jebusites; and I will cut them off. 24 You shall not bow down to their gods, nor serve them, nor do according to their works; but you shall utterly overthrow them and completely break down their *sacred* pillars.

25 "So you shall serve the LORD your God, and He will bless your bread and your water. And I will take sickness away from the midst of you. 26 No one shall suffer miscarriage or be barren in your land; I will fulfill the number of your days.

27 "I will send My fear before you, I will cause confusion among all the people to whom you come, and will make all your enemies turn *their* backs to you. 28 And I will send hornets before you, which shall drive out the Hivite, the Canaanite, and the Hittite from before you. 29 I will not drive them out from before you in one year, lest the land become desolate and the beasts of the field become too numerous for you. 30 Little by little I will drive them out from before you, until you have increased, and you inherit the land. 31 And I will set your bounds from the Red Sea to the sea, Philistia, and from the desert to the River.[a] For I will deliver the inhabitants of the land into your hand, and you shall drive them out before you. 32 You shall make no covenant with them, nor with their gods. 33 They shall not dwell in your land, lest they make you sin against Me. For *if* you serve their gods, it will surely be a snare to you."

24 Now He said to Moses, "Come up to the LORD, you and Aaron, Nadab and Abihu, and seventy of the elders of Israel, and worship from afar. 2 And Moses alone shall come near the LORD, but they shall not come near; nor shall the people go up with him."

3 So Moses came and told the people all the words of the LORD and all the judgments. And all the people answered with one voice and said, "All the words which the LORD has said we will do." 4 And Moses wrote all the words of the LORD. And he rose early in the morning, and built an altar at the foot of the mountain, and twelve pillars according to the twelve tribes of Israel. 5 Then he sent young men of the children of Israel, who offered burnt offerings and sacrificed peace offerings of oxen to the LORD. 6 And Moses took half the blood and put *it* in basins, and half the blood he sprinkled on the altar. 7 Then he took the Book of the Covenant and read in the hearing of the people. And they said, "All that the LORD has said we will do, and be obedient." 8 And Moses took the blood, sprinkled *it* on the people, and said, "This is the blood of the covenant which the LORD has made with you according to all these words."

9 Then Moses went up, also Aaron,

23:17 [a]Hebrew *YHWH*, usually translated LORD   23:31 [a]Hebrew *Nahar*, the Euphrates

God looked, and then He created. He created you. *You!* And God looked at you and said, "This is *good.*" It's important that you come to appreciate the way God created you because other people are going to treat you the way you treat yourself.

Nadab, and Abihu, and seventy of the elders of Israel, 10 and they saw the God of Israel. And *there was* under His feet as it were a paved work of sapphire stone, and it was like the very heavens in *its* clarity. 11 But on the nobles of the children of Israel He did not lay His hand. So they saw God, and they ate and drank.

12 Then the LORD said to Moses, "Come up to Me on the mountain and be there; and I will give you tablets of stone, and the law and commandments which I have written, that you may teach them."

13 So Moses arose with his assistant Joshua, and Moses went up to the mountain of God. 14 And he said to the elders, "Wait here for us until we come back to you. Indeed, Aaron and Hur *are* with you. If any man has a difficulty, let him go to them." 15 Then Moses went up into the mountain, and a cloud covered the mountain.

16 Now the glory of the LORD rested on Mount Sinai, and the cloud covered it six days. And on the seventh day He called to Moses out of the midst of the cloud. 17 The sight of the glory of the LORD *was* like a consuming fire on the top of the mountain in the eyes of the children of Israel. 18 So Moses went into the midst of the cloud and went up into the mountain. And Moses was on the mountain forty days and forty nights.

25 Then the LORD spoke to Moses, saying: 2 "Speak to the children of Israel, that they bring Me an offering. From everyone who gives it willingly with his heart you shall take My offering. 3 And this *is* the offering which you shall take from them: gold, silver, and bronze; 4 blue, purple, and scarlet *thread*, fine linen, and goats' *hair;* 5 ram skins dyed red, badger skins, and acacia wood; 6 oil for the light, and spices for the anointing oil and for the sweet incense; 7 onyx stones, and stones to be set in the ephod and in the breastplate. 8 And let them make Me a sanctuary, that I may dwell among them. 9 According to all that I show you, *that is,* the pattern of the tabernacle and the pattern of all its furnishings, just so you shall make *it.*

10 "And they shall make an ark of acacia wood; two and a half cubits *shall be* its length, a cubit and a half its width, and a cubit and a half its height. 11 And you shall overlay it with pure gold, inside and out you shall overlay it, and shall make on it a molding of gold all around. 12 You shall cast four rings of gold for it, and put *them* in its four corners; two rings *shall be* on one side, and two rings on the other side. 13 And you shall make poles *of* acacia wood, and overlay them with gold. 14 You shall put the poles into the rings on the sides of the ark, that the ark may be carried by them. 15 The poles shall be in the rings of the ark; they shall not be taken from it. 16 And you shall put into the ark the Testimony which I will give you.

17 "You shall make a mercy seat of pure gold; two and a half cubits *shall be* its length and a cubit and a half its width. 18 And you shall make two cherubim of gold; of hammered work you shall make them at the two ends of the mercy seat. 19 Make one cherub at one end, and the other cherub at the other end; you shall make the cherubim at the two ends of it *of one piece* with the mercy seat. 20 And the cherubim shall stretch out *their* wings above, covering the mercy seat with their wings, and they shall face one another; the faces of the cherubim *shall be* toward the mercy seat. 21 You shall put the mercy seat on top of the ark, and in the ark you shall put the Testimony that I will give you. 22 And there I will meet with you, and I will speak with you from above the mercy seat, from between the two cherubim which *are* on the ark of the Testimony, about everything which I will give you in commandment to the children of Israel.

23 "You shall also make a table of acacia wood; two cubits *shall be* its length, a cubit its width, and a cubit and a half its height. 24 And you shall overlay it with pure gold, and make a molding of gold all around. 25 You shall make for it a frame of a handbreadth all around, and you shall make a gold molding for the frame all around. 26 And you shall make for it four rings of gold, and put the rings on the four corners that *are* at its four legs. 27 The rings shall be close to the frame, as holders for the poles to bear the table. 28 And you shall make the poles of acacia

Gospel
Pearls

wood, and overlay them with gold, that the table may be carried with them. 29 You shall make its dishes, its pans, its pitchers, and its bowls for pouring. You shall make them of pure gold. 30 And you shall set the showbread on the table before Me always.

31 "You shall also make a lampstand of pure gold; the lampstand shall be of hammered work. Its shaft, its branches, its bowls, its *ornamental* knobs, and flowers shall be *of one piece.* 32 And six branches shall come out of its sides: three branches of the lampstand out of one side, and three branches of the lampstand out of the other side. 33 Three bowls *shall be* made like almond *blossoms* on one branch, *with* an *ornamental* knob and a flower, and three bowls made like almond *blossoms* on the other branch, *with* an *ornamental* knob and a flower—and so for the six branches that come out of the lampstand. 34 On the lampstand itself four bowls *shall be* made like almond *blossoms, each with* its *ornamental* knob and flower. 35 And *there shall be* a knob under the *first* two branches of the same, a knob under the *second* two branches of the same, and a knob under the *third* two branches of the same, according to the six branches that extend from the lampstand. 36 Their knobs and their branches *shall be of one piece;* all of it *shall be* one hammered piece of pure gold. 37 You shall make seven lamps for it, and they shall arrange its lamps so that they give light in front of it. 38 And its wick-trimmers and their trays *shall be* of pure gold. 39 It shall be made of a talent of pure gold, with all these utensils. 40 And see to it that you make *them* according to the pattern which was shown you on the mountain.

26 "Moreover you shall make the tabernacle *with* ten curtains *of* fine woven linen and blue, purple, and scarlet *thread;* with artistic designs of cherubim you shall weave them. 2 The length of each curtain *shall be* twenty-eight cubits, and the width of each curtain four cubits. And every one of the curtains shall have the same measurements. 3 Five curtains shall be coupled to one another, and *the other* five curtains *shall be* coupled to one another.

4 And you shall make loops of blue *yarn* on the edge of the curtain on the selvedge of *one* set, and likewise you shall do on the outer edge of *the other* curtain of the second set. 5 Fifty loops you shall make in the one curtain, and fifty loops you shall make on the edge of the curtain that *is* on the end of the second set, that the loops may be clasped to one another. 6 And you shall make fifty clasps of gold, and couple the curtains together with the clasps, so that it may be one tabernacle.

7 "You shall also make curtains of goats' *hair,* to be a tent over the tabernacle. You shall make eleven curtains. 8 The length of each curtain *shall be* thirty cubits, and the width of each curtain four cubits; and the eleven curtains shall all have the same measurements. 9 And you shall couple five curtains by themselves and six curtains by themselves, and you shall double over the sixth curtain at the forefront of the tent. 10 You shall make fifty loops on the edge of the curtain that is outermost in *one* set, and fifty loops on the edge of the curtain of the second set. 11 And you shall make fifty bronze clasps, put the clasps into the loops, and couple the tent together, that it may be one. 12 The remnant that remains of the curtains of the tent, the half curtain that remains, shall hang over the back of the tabernacle. 13 And a cubit on one side and a cubit on the other side, of what remains of the length of the curtains of the tent, shall hang over the sides of the tabernacle, on this side and on that side, to cover it.

14 "You shall also make a covering of ram skins dyed red for the tent, and a covering of badger skins above that.

15 "And for the tabernacle you shall make the boards of acacia wood, standing upright. 16 Ten cubits *shall be* the length of a board, and a cubit and a half *shall be* the width of each board. 17 Two tenons *shall be* in each board for binding one to another. Thus you shall make for all the boards of the tabernacle. 18 And you shall make the boards for the tabernacle, twenty boards for the south side. 19 You shall make forty sockets of silver under the twenty boards: two sockets under each of the boards for its two tenons. 20 And for the sec-

ond side of the tabernacle, the north side, *there shall be* twenty boards 21 and their forty sockets of silver: two sockets under each of the boards. 22 For the far side of the tabernacle, westward, you shall make six boards. 23 And you shall also make two boards for the two back corners of the tabernacle. 24 They shall be coupled together at the bottom and they shall be coupled together at the top by one ring. Thus it shall be for both of them. They shall be for the two corners. 25 So there shall be eight boards with their sockets of silver—sixteen sockets—two sockets under each of the boards.

26 "And you shall make bars of acacia wood: five for the boards on one side of the tabernacle, 27 five bars for the boards on the other side of the tabernacle, and five bars for the boards of the side of the tabernacle, for the far side westward. 28 The middle bar shall pass through the midst of the boards from end to end. 29 You shall overlay the boards with gold, make their rings of gold *as* holders for the bars, and overlay the bars with gold. 30 And you shall raise up the tabernacle according to its pattern which you were shown on the mountain.

31 "You shall make a veil woven of blue, purple, and scarlet *thread,* and fine woven linen. It shall be woven with an artistic design of cherubim. 32 You shall hang it upon the four pillars of acacia *wood* overlaid with gold. Their hooks *shall be* gold, upon four sockets of silver. 33 And you shall hang the veil from the clasps. Then you shall bring the ark of the Testimony in there, behind the veil. The veil shall be a divider for you between the holy *place* and the Most Holy. 34 You shall put the mercy seat upon the ark of the Testimony in the Most Holy. 35 You shall set the table outside the veil, and the lampstand across from the table on the side of the tabernacle toward the south; and you shall put the table on the north side.

36 "You shall make a screen for the door of the tabernacle, *woven of* blue, purple, and scarlet *thread,* and fine woven linen, made by a weaver. 37 And you shall make for the screen five pillars of acacia *wood,* and overlay them with gold; their hooks *shall*

be gold, and you shall cast five sockets of bronze for them.

27 "You shall make an altar of acacia wood, five cubits long and five cubits wide—the altar shall be square—and its height *shall be* three cubits. 2 You shall make its horns on its four corners; its horns shall be of one piece with it. And you shall overlay it with bronze. 3 Also you shall make its pans to receive its ashes, and its shovels and its basins and its forks and its firepans; you shall make all its utensils of bronze. 4 You shall make a grate for it, a network of bronze; and on the network you shall make four bronze rings at its four corners. 5 You shall put it under the rim of the altar beneath, that the network may be midway up the altar. 6 And you shall make poles for the altar, poles of acacia wood, and overlay them with bronze. 7 The poles shall be put in the rings, and the poles shall be on the two sides of the altar to bear it. 8 You shall make it hollow with boards; as it was shown you on the mountain, so shall they make *it.*

9 "You shall also make the court of the tabernacle. For the south side *there shall be* hangings for the court *made of* fine woven linen, one hundred cubits long for one side. 10 And its twenty pillars and their twenty sockets *shall be* bronze. The hooks of the pillars and their bands *shall be* silver. 11 Likewise along the length of the north side *there shall be* hangings one hundred *cubits* long, with its twenty pillars and their twenty sockets of bronze, and the hooks of the pillars and their bands of silver.

12 "And along the width of the court on the west side *shall be* hangings of fifty cubits, with their ten pillars and their ten sockets. 13 The width of the court on the east side *shall be* fifty cubits. 14 The hangings on *one* side *of the gate shall be* fifteen cubits, *with* their three pillars and their three sockets. 15 And on the other side *shall be* hangings of fifteen *cubits, with* their three pillars and their three sockets.

16 "For the gate of the court *there shall be* a screen twenty cubits long, *woven of* blue, purple, and scarlet *thread,* and fine woven linen, made

Gospel Pearls

by a weaver. It *shall have* four pillars and four sockets. 17 All the pillars around the court shall have bands of silver; their hooks *shall be* of silver and their sockets of bronze. 18 The length of the court *shall be* one hundred cubits, the width fifty throughout, and the height five cubits, *made of* fine woven linen, and its sockets of bronze. 19 All the utensils of the tabernacle for all its service, all its pegs, and all the pegs of the court, *shall be* of bronze.

20 "And you shall command the children of Israel that they bring you pure oil of pressed olives for the light, to cause the lamp to burn continually. 21 In the tabernacle of meeting, outside the veil which *is* before the Testimony, Aaron and his sons shall tend it from evening until morning before the LORD. *It shall be* a statute forever to their generations on behalf of the children of Israel.

28 "Now take Aaron your brother, and his sons with him, from among the children of Israel, that he may minister to Me as priest, Aaron *and* Aaron's sons: Nadab, Abihu, Eleazar, and Ithamar. 2 And you shall make holy garments for Aaron your brother, for glory and for beauty. 3 So you shall speak to all *who are* gifted artisans, whom I have filled with the spirit of wisdom, that they may make Aaron's garments, to consecrate him, that he may minister to Me as priest. 4 And these *are* the garments which they shall make: a breastplate, an ephod,^a a robe, a skillfully woven tunic, a turban, and a sash. So they shall make holy garments for Aaron your brother and his sons, that he may minister to Me as priest.

5 "They shall take the gold, blue, purple, and scarlet *thread,* and the fine linen, 6 and they shall make the ephod of gold, blue, purple, *and* scarlet *thread,* and fine woven linen, artistically worked. 7 It shall have two shoulder straps joined at its two edges, and *so* it shall be joined together. 8 And the intricately woven band of the ephod, which *is* on it, shall be of the same workmanship, *made of* gold, blue, purple, and scarlet *thread,* and fine woven linen.

9 "Then you shall take two onyx stones and engrave on them the names of the sons of Israel: 10 six of their names on one stone and six names on the other stone, in order of their birth. 11 With the work of an engraver in stone, *like* the engravings of a signet, you shall engrave the two stones with the names of the sons of Israel. You shall set them in settings of gold. 12 And you shall put the two stones on the shoulders of the ephod *as* memorial stones for the sons of Israel. So Aaron shall bear their names before the LORD on his two shoulders as a memorial. 13 You shall also make settings of gold, 14 and you shall make two chains of pure gold like braided cords, and fasten the braided chains to the settings.

15 "You shall make the breastplate of judgment. Artistically woven according to the workmanship of the ephod you shall make it: of gold, blue, purple, and scarlet *thread,* and fine woven linen, you shall make it. 16 It shall be doubled into a square: a span *shall be* its length, and a span *shall be* its width. 17 And you shall put settings of stones in it, four rows of stones: *The first* row *shall be* a sardius, a topaz, and an emerald; *this shall be* the first row; 18 the second row *shall be* a turquoise, a sapphire, and a diamond; 19 the third row, a jacinth, an agate, and an amethyst; 20 and the fourth row, a beryl, an onyx, and a jasper. They shall be set in gold settings. 21 And the stones shall have the names of the sons of Israel, twelve according to their names, *like* the engravings of a signet, each one with its own name; they shall be according to the twelve tribes.

22 "You shall make chains for the breastplate at the end, like braided cords of pure gold. 23 And you shall make two rings of gold for the breastplate, and put the two rings on the two ends of the breastplate. 24 Then you shall put the two braided *chains* of gold in the two rings which are on the ends of the breastplate; 25 and the *other* two ends of the two braided *chains* you shall fasten to the two settings, and put them on the shoulder straps of the ephod in the front.

26 "You shall make two rings of

28:4 ^aThat is, an ornamented vest

*Y*ou're better off sticking with what God created you to be than substituting that for what some person tries to create. Another person can never create you to be as good as what God has made.

gold, and put them on the two ends of the breastplate, on the edge of it, which is on the inner side of the ephod. 27 And two *other* rings of gold you shall make, and put them on the two shoulder straps, underneath the ephod toward its front, right at the seam above the intricately woven band of the ephod. 28 They shall bind the breastplate by means of its rings to the rings of the ephod, using a blue cord, so that it is above the intricately woven band of the ephod, and so that the breastplate does not come loose from the ephod.

29 "So Aaron shall bear the names of the sons of Israel on the breastplate of judgment over his heart, when he goes into the holy *place,* as a memorial before the LORD continually. 30 And you shall put in the breastplate of judgment the Urim and the Thummim,*ª* and they shall be over Aaron's heart when he goes in before the LORD. So Aaron shall bear the judgment of the children of Israel over his heart before the LORD continually.

31 "You shall make the robe of the ephod all of blue. 32 There shall be an opening for his head in the middle of it; it shall have a woven binding all around its opening, like the opening in a coat of mail, so that it does not tear. 33 And upon its hem you shall make pomegranates of blue, purple, and scarlet, all around its hem, and bells of gold between them all around: 34 a golden bell and a pomegranate, a golden bell and a pomegranate, upon the hem of the robe all around. 35 And it shall be upon Aaron when he ministers, and its sound will be heard when he goes into the holy *place* before the LORD and when he comes out, that he may not die.

36 "You shall also make a plate of pure gold and engrave on it, *like* the engraving of a signet:

HOLINESS TO THE LORD.

37 And you shall put it on a blue cord, that it may be on the turban; it shall be on the front of the turban. 38 So it shall be on Aaron's forehead, that Aaron may bear the iniquity of the holy things which the children of Israel hallow in all their holy gifts;

and it shall always be on his forehead, that they may be accepted before the LORD.

39 "You shall skillfully weave the tunic of fine linen *thread,* you shall make the turban of fine linen, and you shall make the sash of woven work.

40 "For Aaron's sons you shall make tunics, and you shall make sashes for them. And you shall make hats for them, for glory and beauty. 41 So you shall put them on Aaron your brother and on his sons with him. You shall anoint them, consecrate them, and sanctify them, that they may minister to Me as priests. 42 And you shall make for them linen trousers to cover their nakedness; they shall reach from the waist to the thighs. 43 They shall be on Aaron and on his sons when they come into the tabernacle of meeting, or when they come near the altar to minister in the holy *place,* that they do not incur iniquity and die. *It shall be* a statute forever to him and his descendants after him.

29 "And this is what you shall do to them to hallow them for ministering to Me as priests: Take one young bull and two rams without blemish, 2 and unleavened bread, unleavened cakes mixed with oil, and unleavened wafers anointed with oil (you shall make them of wheat flour). 3 You shall put them in one basket and bring them in the basket, with the bull and the two rams.

4 "And Aaron and his sons you shall bring to the door of the tabernacle of meeting, and you shall wash them with water. 5 Then you shall take the garments, put the tunic on Aaron, and the robe of the ephod, the ephod, and the breastplate, and gird him with the intricately woven band of the ephod. 6 You shall put the turban on his head, and put the holy crown on the turban. 7 And you shall take the anointing oil, pour *it* on his head, and anoint him. 8 Then you shall bring his sons and put tunics on them. 9 And you shall gird them with sashes, Aaron and his sons, and put the hats on them. The priesthood shall be theirs for a perpetual statute. So you shall consecrate Aaron and his sons.

28:30 ªLiterally the Lights and the Perfections (compare Leviticus 8:8)

Gospel Pearls

10 "You shall also have the bull brought before the tabernacle of meeting, and Aaron and his sons shall put their hands on the head of the bull. 11 Then you shall kill the bull before the LORD, *by* the door of the tabernacle of meeting. 12 You shall take *some* of the blood of the bull and put *it* on the horns of the altar with your finger, and pour all the blood beside the base of the altar. 13 And you shall take all the fat that covers the entrails, the fatty lobe *attached* to the liver, and the two kidneys and the fat that *is* on them, and burn *them* on the altar. 14 But the flesh of the bull, with its skin and its offal, you shall burn with fire outside the camp. It *is* a sin offering.

15 "You shall also take one ram, and Aaron and his sons shall put their hands on the head of the ram; 16 and you shall kill the ram, and you shall take its blood and sprinkle *it* all around on the altar. 17 Then you shall cut the ram in pieces, wash its entrails and its legs, and put *them* with its pieces and with its head. 18 And you shall burn the whole ram on the altar. It *is* a burnt offering to the LORD; it *is* a sweet aroma, an offering made by fire to the LORD.

19 "You shall also take the other ram, and Aaron and his sons shall put their hands on the head of the ram. 20 Then you shall kill the ram, and take some of its blood and put *it* on the tip of the right ear of Aaron and on the tip of the right ear of his sons, on the thumb of their right hand and on the big toe of their right foot, and sprinkle the blood all around on the altar. 21 And you shall take some of the blood that is on the altar, and some of the anointing oil, and sprinkle *it* on Aaron and on his garments, on his sons and on the garments of his sons with him; and he and his garments shall be hallowed, and his sons and his sons' garments with him.

22 "Also you shall take the fat of the ram, the fat tail, the fat that covers the entrails, the fatty lobe *attached to* the liver, the two kidneys and the fat on them, the right thigh (for it *is* a ram of consecration), 23 one loaf of bread, one cake *made with* oil, and one wafer from the basket of the unleavened bread that *is* before the LORD; 24 and you shall put all these in the hands of Aaron and in the hands of his sons, and you shall wave them *as* a wave offering before the LORD. 25 You shall receive them back from their hands and burn *them* on the altar as a burnt offering, as a sweet aroma before the LORD. It *is* an offering made by fire to the LORD.

26 "Then you shall take the breast of the ram of Aaron's consecration and wave it *as* a wave offering before the LORD; and it shall be your portion. 27 And from the ram of the consecration you shall consecrate the breast of the wave offering which is waved, and the thigh of the heave offering which is raised, of *that* which is for Aaron and of *that* which is for his sons. 28 It shall be from the children of Israel *for* Aaron and his sons by a statute forever. For it is a heave offering; it shall be a heave offering from the children of Israel from the sacrifices of their peace offerings, *that is,* their heave offering to the LORD.

29 "And the holy garments of Aaron shall be his sons' after him, to be anointed in them and to be consecrated in them. 30 That son who becomes priest in his place shall put them on for seven days, when he enters the tabernacle of meeting to minister in the holy *place.*

31 "And you shall take the ram of the consecration and boil its flesh in the holy place. 32 Then Aaron and his sons shall eat the flesh of the ram, and the bread that *is* in the basket, *by* the door of the tabernacle of meeting. 33 They shall eat those things with which the atonement was made, to consecrate *and* to sanctify them; but an outsider shall not eat *them,* because they *are* holy. 34 And if any of the flesh of the consecration offerings, or of the bread, remains until the morning, then you shall burn the remainder with fire. It shall not be eaten, because it *is* holy.

35 "Thus you shall do to Aaron and his sons, according to all that I have commanded you. Seven days you shall consecrate them. 36 And you shall offer a bull every day *as* a sin offering for atonement. You shall cleanse the altar when you make atonement for it, and you shall anoint it to sanctify it. 37 Seven days you shall make atonement for the altar and sanctify it. And the altar shall

be most holy. Whatever touches the altar must be holy.[a]

38 "Now this *is* what you shall offer on the altar: two lambs of the first year, day by day continually. 39 One lamb you shall offer in the morning, and the other lamb you shall offer at twilight. 40 With the one lamb shall be one-tenth *of an ephah* of flour mixed with one-fourth of a hin of pressed oil, and one-fourth of a hin of wine *as* a drink offering. 41 And the other lamb you shall offer at twilight; and you shall offer with it the grain offering and the drink offering, as in the morning, for a sweet aroma, an offering made by fire to the LORD. 42 *This shall be* a continual burnt offering throughout your generations *at* the door of the tabernacle of meeting before the LORD, where I will meet you to speak with you. 43 And there I will meet with the children of Israel, and *the tabernacle* shall be sanctified by My glory. 44 So I will consecrate the tabernacle of meeting and the altar. I will also consecrate both Aaron and his sons to minister to Me as priests. 45 I will dwell among the children of Israel and will be their God. 46 And they shall know that I *am* the LORD their God, who brought them up out of the land of Egypt, that I may dwell among them. I *am* the LORD their God.

30 "You shall make an altar to burn incense on; you shall make it of acacia wood. 2 A cubit *shall be* its length and a cubit its width—it shall be square—and two cubits *shall be* its height. Its horns *shall be* of one piece with it. 3 And you shall overlay its top, its sides all around, and its horns with pure gold; and you shall make for it a molding of gold all around. 4 Two gold rings you shall make for it, under the molding on both its sides. You shall place *them* on its two sides, and they will be holders for the poles with which to bear it. 5 You shall make the poles of acacia wood, and overlay them with gold. 6 And you shall put it before the veil that *is* before the ark of the Testimony, before the mercy seat that *is* over the Testimony, where I will meet with you.

7 "Aaron shall burn on it sweet incense every morning; when he tends the lamps, he shall burn incense on it. 8 And when Aaron lights the lamps at twilight, he shall burn incense on it, a perpetual incense before the LORD throughout your generations. 9 You shall not offer strange incense on it, or a burnt offering, or a grain offering; nor shall you pour a drink offering on it. 10 And Aaron shall make atonement upon its horns once a year with the blood of the sin offering of atonement; once a year he shall make atonement upon it throughout your generations. It *is* most holy to the LORD."

11 Then the LORD spoke to Moses, saying: 12 "When you take the census of the children of Israel for their number, then every man shall give a ransom for himself to the LORD, when you number them, that there may be no plague among them when *you* number them. 13 This is what everyone among those who are numbered shall give: half a shekel according to the shekel of the sanctuary (a shekel *is* twenty gerahs). The half-shekel *shall be* an offering to the LORD. 14 Everyone included among those who are numbered, from twenty years old and above, shall give an offering to the LORD. 15 The rich shall not give more and the poor shall not give less than half a shekel, when *you* give an offering to the LORD, to make atonement for yourselves. 16 And you shall take the atonement money of the children of Israel, and shall appoint it for the service of the tabernacle of meeting, that it may be a memorial for the children of Israel before the LORD, to make atonement for yourselves."

17 Then the LORD spoke to Moses, saying: 18 "You shall also make a laver of bronze, with its base also of bronze, for washing. You shall put it between the tabernacle of meeting and the altar. And you shall put water in it, 19 for Aaron and his sons shall wash their hands and their feet in water from it. 20 When they go into the tabernacle of meeting, or when they come near the altar to minister, to burn an offering made by fire to the LORD, they shall wash with water, lest they die. 21 So they shall wash

29:37 [a]Compare Numbers 4:15 and Haggai 2:11–13

Gospel Pearls

their hands and their feet, lest they die. And it shall be a statute forever to them—to him and his descendants throughout their generations."

22 Moreover the LORD spoke to Moses, saying: 23 "Also take for yourself quality spices—five hundred *shekels* of liquid myrrh, half as much sweet-smelling cinnamon (two hundred and fifty *shekels*), two hundred and fifty *shekels* of sweet-smelling cane, 24 five hundred *shekels* of cassia, according to the shekel of the sanctuary, and a hin of olive oil. 25 And you shall make from these a holy anointing oil, an ointment compounded according to the art of the perfumer. It shall be a holy anointing oil. 26 With it you shall anoint the tabernacle of meeting and the ark of the Testimony; 27 the table and all its utensils, the lampstand and its utensils, and the altar of incense; 28 the altar of burnt offering with all its utensils, and the laver and its base. 29 You shall consecrate them, that they may be most holy; whatever touches them must be holy.*a* 30 And you shall anoint Aaron and his sons, and consecrate them, that *they* may minister to Me as priests.

31 "And you shall speak to the children of Israel, saying: 'This shall be a holy anointing oil to Me throughout your generations. 32 It shall not be poured on man's flesh; nor shall you make *any other* like it, according to its composition. It *is* holy, *and* it shall be holy to you. 33 Whoever compounds *any* like it, or whoever puts *any* of it on an outsider, shall be cut off from his people.'"

34 And the LORD said to Moses: "Take sweet spices, stacte and onycha and galbanum, and pure frankincense with *these* sweet spices; there shall be equal amounts of each. 35 You shall make of these an incense, a compound according to the art of the perfumer, salted, pure, *and* holy. 36 And you shall beat *some* of it very fine, and put some of it before the Testimony in the tabernacle of meeting where I will meet with you. It shall be most holy to you. 37 But *as for* the incense which you shall make, you shall not make any for yourselves, according to its composition. It shall be to you holy for the LORD. 38 Whoever makes *any* like

it, to smell it, he shall be cut off from his people."

31 Then the LORD spoke to Moses, saying: 2 "See, I have called by name Bezalel the son of Uri, the son of Hur, of the tribe of Judah. 3 And I have filled him with the Spirit of God, in wisdom, in understanding, in knowledge, and in all *manner of* workmanship, 4 to design artistic works, to work in gold, in silver, in bronze, 5 in cutting jewels for setting, in carving wood, and to work in all *manner of* workmanship.

6 "And I, indeed I, have appointed with him Aholiab the son of Ahisamach, of the tribe of Dan; and I have put wisdom in the hearts of all the gifted artisans, that they may make all that I have commanded you: 7 the tabernacle of meeting, the ark of the Testimony and the mercy seat that *is* on it, and all the furniture of the tabernacle— 8 the table and its utensils, the pure *gold* lampstand with all its utensils, the altar of incense, 9 the altar of burnt offering with all its utensils, and the laver and its base— 10 the garments of ministry,*a* the holy garments for Aaron the priest and the garments of his sons, to minister as priests, 11 and the anointing oil and sweet incense for the holy *place*. According to all that I have commanded you they shall do."

12 And the LORD spoke to Moses, saying, 13 "Speak also to the children of Israel, saying: 'Surely My Sabbaths you shall keep, for it *is* a sign between Me and you throughout your generations, that *you* may know that I *am* the LORD who sanctifies you. 14 You shall keep the Sabbath, therefore, for *it is* holy to you. Everyone who profanes it shall surely be put to death; for whoever does *any* work on it, that person shall be cut off from among his people. 15 Work shall be done for six days, but the seventh *is* the Sabbath of rest, holy to the LORD. Whoever does *any* work on the Sabbath day, he shall surely be put to death. 16 Therefore the children of Israel shall keep the Sabbath, to observe the Sabbath throughout their generations *as* a perpetual covenant. 17 It *is* a sign between Me and the children of Israel forever; for *in*

30:29 *a*Compare Numbers 4:15 and Haggai 2:11–13   31:10 *a*Or *woven garments*

God calls us *individually*—by name, not by number—to do a specific job and to fill a specific role in His Kingdom. Nobody else will do.

six days the LORD made the heavens and the earth, and on the seventh day He rested and was refreshed.' "

18 And when He had made an end of speaking with him on Mount Sinai, He gave Moses two tablets of the Testimony, tablets of stone, written with the finger of God.

32 Now when the people saw that Moses delayed coming down from the mountain, the people gathered together to Aaron, and said to him, "Come, make us gods that shall go before us; for *as for* this Moses, the man who brought us up out of the land of Egypt, we do not know what has become of him."

2 And Aaron said to them, "Break off the golden earrings which *are* in the ears of your wives, your sons, and your daughters, and bring *them* to me." 3 So all the people broke off the golden earrings which *were* in their ears, and brought *them* to Aaron. 4 And he received *the* gold from their hand, and he fashioned it with an engraving tool, and made a molded calf.

Then they said, "This *is* your god, O Israel, that brought you out of the land of Egypt!"

5 So when Aaron saw *it,* he built an altar before it. And Aaron made a proclamation and said, "Tomorrow *is* a feast to the LORD." 6 Then they rose early on the next day, offered burnt offerings, and brought peace offerings; and the people sat down to eat and drink, and rose up to play.

7 And the LORD said to Moses, "Go, get down! For your people whom you brought out of the land of Egypt have corrupted *themselves.* 8 They have turned aside quickly out of the way which I commanded them. They have made themselves a molded calf, and worshiped it and sacrificed to it, and said, 'This *is* your god, O Israel, that brought you out of the land of Egypt!' " 9 And the LORD said to Moses, "I have seen this people, and indeed it *is* a stiff-necked people! 10 Now therefore, let Me alone, that My wrath may burn hot against them and I may consume them. And I will make of you a great nation."

11 Then Moses pleaded with the LORD his God, and said: "LORD, why does Your wrath burn hot against Your people whom You have

brought out of the land of Egypt with great power and with a mighty hand? 12 Why should the Egyptians speak, and say, 'He brought them out to harm them, to kill them in the mountains, and to consume them from the face of the earth'? Turn from Your fierce wrath, and relent from this harm to Your people. 13 Remember Abraham, Isaac, and Israel, Your servants, to whom You swore by Your own self, and said to them, 'I will multiply your descendants as the stars of heaven; and all this land that I have spoken of I give to your descendants, and they shall inherit *it* forever.' "*a* 14 So the LORD relented from the harm which He said He would do to His people.

15 And Moses turned and went down from the mountain, and the two tablets of the Testimony *were* in his hand. The tablets *were* written on both sides; on the one *side* and on the other they were written. 16 Now the tablets *were* the work of God, and the writing *was* the writing of God engraved on the tablets.

17 And when Joshua heard the noise of the people as they shouted, he said to Moses, "*There is* a noise of war in the camp."

18 But he said:

"*It is* not the noise of the shout of victory,
　　Nor the noise of the cry of defeat,
　　But the sound of singing I hear."

19 So it was, as soon as he came near the camp, that he saw the calf *and* the dancing. So Moses' anger became hot, and he cast the tablets out of his hands and broke them at the foot of the mountain. 20 Then he took the calf which they had made, burned *it* in the fire, and ground *it* to powder; and he scattered *it* on the water and made the children of Israel drink *it*. 21 And Moses said to Aaron, "What did this people do to you that you have brought *so* great a sin upon them?"

22 So Aaron said, "Do not let the anger of my lord become hot. You know the people, that they *are* set on evil. 23 For they said to me, 'Make us gods that shall go before us; *as*

32:13 *a*Genesis 13:15 and 22:17

Gospel
Pearls

for this Moses, the man who brought us out of the land of Egypt, we do not know what has become of him.' 24 And I said to them, 'Whoever has any gold, let them break *it* off.' So they gave *it* to me, and I cast it into the fire, and this calf came out."

25 Now when Moses saw that the people *were* unrestrained (for Aaron had not restrained them, to *their* shame among their enemies), 26 then Moses stood in the entrance of the camp, and said, "Whoever *is* on the LORD's side—*come* to me!" And all the sons of Levi gathered themselves together to him. 27 And he said to them, "Thus says the LORD God of Israel: 'Let every man put his sword on his side, and go in and out from entrance to entrance throughout the camp, and let every man kill his brother, every man his companion, and every man his neighbor.' " 28 So the sons of Levi did according to the word of Moses. And about three thousand men of the people fell that day. 29 Then Moses said, "Consecrate yourselves today to the LORD, that He may bestow on you a blessing this day, for every man has opposed his son and his brother."

30 Now it came to pass on the next day that Moses said to the people, "You have committed a great sin. So now I will go up to the LORD; perhaps I can make atonement for your sin." 31 Then Moses returned to the LORD and said, "Oh, these people have committed a great sin, and have made for themselves a god of gold! 32 Yet now, if You will forgive their sin—but if not, I pray, blot me out of Your book which You have written."

33 And the LORD said to Moses, "Whoever has sinned against Me, I will blot him out of My book. 34 Now therefore, go, lead the people to *the place* of which I have spoken to you. Behold, My Angel shall go before you. Nevertheless, in the day when I visit for punishment, I will visit punishment upon them for their sin."

35 So the LORD plagued the people because of what they did with the calf which Aaron made.

33 Then the LORD said to Moses, "Depart *and* go up from here, you and the people whom you have brought out of the land of Egypt, to the land of which I swore to Abraham, Isaac, and Jacob, saying, 'To your descendants I will give it.' 2 And I will send *My* Angel before you, and I will drive *My* out the Canaanite and the Amorite and the Hittite and the Perizzite and the Hivite and the Jebusite. 3 *Go up* to a land flowing with milk and honey; for I will not go up in your midst, lest I consume you on the way, for you *are* a stiff-necked people."

4 And when the people heard this bad news, they mourned, and no one put on his ornaments. 5 For the LORD had said to Moses, "Say to the children of Israel, 'You *are* a stiff-necked people. I could come up into your midst in one moment and consume you. Now therefore, take off your ornaments, that I may know what to do to you.' " 6 So the children of Israel stripped themselves of their ornaments by Mount Horeb.

7 Moses took his tent and pitched it outside the camp, far from the camp, and called it the tabernacle of meeting. And it came to pass *that* everyone who sought the LORD went out to the tabernacle of meeting which *was* outside the camp. 8 So it was, whenever Moses went out to the tabernacle, *that* all the people rose, and each man stood *at* his tent door and watched Moses until he had gone into the tabernacle. 9 And it came to pass, when Moses entered the tabernacle, that the pillar of cloud descended and stood *at* the door of the tabernacle, and *the* LORD talked with Moses. 10 All the people saw the pillar of cloud standing *at* the tabernacle door, and all the people rose and worshiped, each man *in* his tent door. 11 So the LORD spoke to Moses face to face, as a man speaks to his friend. And he would return to the camp, but his servant Joshua the son of Nun, a young man, did not depart from the tabernacle.

12 Then Moses said to the LORD, "See, You say to me, 'Bring up this people.' But You have not let me know whom You will send with me. Yet You have said, 'I know you by name, and you have also found grace in My sight.' 13 Now therefore, I pray, if I have found grace in Your sight, show me now Your way, that I may know You and that I may find grace in Your sight. And consider that this nation *is* Your people."

God knows what He has put in you. He knows what He desires to come out of you. And He knows how to access what He has put in you and bring it out of you.

Your Call

Exodus 33:12

*I*n the theater world, actors and actresses often audition for roles. After that, the person in charge of the production will schedule callbacks. Certain ones who have auditioned will be asked to come back for a second and sometimes a third or fourth audition before they are either given the part or told that someone else has landed it.

A person in the entertainment world knows that he or she has arrived as a star when a director or producer calls and offers them a part without an audition. The candidate is being chosen to fill a role that the director believes is absolutely perfect for that person and nobody else.

God doesn't deal in auditions and callbacks for His children. He has something for you to do that only you *can* do. No one else can play the part or fill the role or meet the need. Only you.

If you just want to be "a woman," then you have a lot of competition. But when the call goes out for you, you have no competition. Only you can truly be you. The real you is a composite of what is on the inside and what is on the outside, and what is on the inside is the more important part.

Wait for the call that is specifically for you. Don't respond to a blanket call, or a generic call, or a gender call, or a wolf-whistle call. Listen for the call that says, "I don't want anybody but you because only you will do." Then respond.

Wait for that call before you decide to marry someone. Wait for that call before you commit to a friendship. It's the same call God puts on your life. He calls you individually—by name, not by number—to do a very specific job and to fill a very specific role in His Kingdom. Nobody else will do. He has designed you to meet all the qualifications. He hasn't created any other person who will fit the bill like you fit the bill.

You don't need to be jealous of or intimidated by anyone else because when God calls for you, you are the only one who can answer. You have no contenders in His sight. You are the star He has in mind for the role He has written just for you.

14 And He said, "My Presence will go *with you,* and I will give you rest."

15 Then he said to Him, "If Your Presence does not go *with us,* do not bring us up from here. 16 For how then will it be known that Your people and I have found grace in Your sight, except You go with us? So we shall be separate, Your people and I, from all the people who *are* upon the face of the earth."

17 So the LORD said to Moses, "I will also do this thing that you have spoken; for you have found grace in My sight, and I know you by name."

18 And he said, "Please, show me Your glory."

19 Then He said, "I will make all My goodness pass before you, and I will proclaim the name of the LORD before you. I will be gracious to whom I will be gracious, and I will have compassion on whom I will have compassion." 20 But He said, "You cannot see My face; for no man shall see Me, and live." 21 And the LORD said, "Here is a place by Me, and you shall stand on the rock. 22 So it shall be, while My glory passes by, that I will put you in the cleft of the rock, and will cover you with My hand while I pass by. 23 Then I will take away My hand, and you shall see My back; but My face shall not be seen."

34 And the LORD said to Moses, "Cut two tablets of stone like the first *ones,* and I will write on *these* tablets the words that were on the first tablets which you broke. 2 So be ready in the morning, and come up in the morning to Mount Sinai, and present yourself to Me there on the top of the mountain. 3 And no man shall come up with you, and let no man be seen throughout all the mountain; let neither flocks nor herds feed before that mountain."

4 So he cut two tablets of stone like the first *ones.* Then Moses rose early in the morning and went up Mount Sinai, as the LORD had commanded him; and he took in his hand the two tablets of stone.

5 Now the LORD descended in the cloud and stood with him there, and proclaimed the name of the LORD. 6 And the LORD passed before him and proclaimed, "The LORD, the LORD God, merciful and gracious, longsuf-

fering, and abounding in goodness and truth, 7 keeping mercy for thousands, forgiving iniquity and transgression and sin, by no means clearing *the guilty,* visiting the iniquity of the fathers upon the children and the children's children to the third and the fourth generation."

8 So Moses made haste and bowed his head toward the earth, and worshiped. 9 Then he said, "If now I have found grace in Your sight, O Lord, let my Lord, I pray, go among us, even though we *are* a stiff-necked people; and pardon our iniquity and our sin, and take us as Your inheritance."

10 And He said: "Behold, I make a covenant. Before all your people I will do marvels such as have not been done in all the earth, nor in any nation; and all the people among whom you *are* shall see the work of the LORD. For it *is* an awesome thing that I will do with you. 11 Observe what I command you this day. Behold, I am driving out from before you the Amorite and the Canaanite and the Hittite and the Perizzite and the Hivite and the Jebusite. 12 Take heed to yourself, lest you make a covenant with the inhabitants of the land where you are going, lest it be a snare in your midst. 13 But you shall destroy their altars, break their *sacred* pillars, and cut down their wooden images 14 (for you shall worship no other god, for the LORD, whose name *is* Jealous, *is* a jealous God), 15 lest you make a covenant with the inhabitants of the land, and they play the harlot with their gods and make sacrifice to their gods, and *one of them* invites you and you eat of his sacrifice, 16 and you take of his daughters for your sons, and his daughters play the harlot with their gods and make your sons play the harlot with their gods.

17 "You shall make no molded gods for yourselves.

18 "The Feast of Unleavened Bread you shall keep. Seven days you shall eat unleavened bread, as I commanded you, in the appointed time of the month of Abib; for in the month of Abib you came out from Egypt.

19 "All that open the womb *are* Mine, and every male firstborn among your livestock, *whether* ox or sheep. 20 But the firstborn of a don-

---

God has given every woman treasure—something that He intends for her to use in order to fulfill her purpose on earth. And in the process of fulfilling her purpose and God's purpose, she will bring Him glory.

key you shall redeem with a lamb. And if you will not redeem *him*, then you shall break his neck. All the firstborn of your sons you shall redeem.

"And none shall appear before Me empty-handed.

21 "Six days you shall work, but on the seventh day you shall rest; in plowing time and in harvest you shall rest.

22 "And you shall observe the Feast of Weeks, of the firstfruits of wheat harvest, and the Feast of Ingathering at the year's end.

23 "Three times in the year all your men shall appear before the Lord, the LORD God of Israel. 24 For I will cast out the nations before you and enlarge your borders; neither will any man covet your land when you go up to appear before the LORD your God three times in the year.

25 "You shall not offer the blood of My sacrifice with leaven, nor shall the sacrifice of the Feast of the Passover be left until morning.

26 "The first of the firstfruits of your land you shall bring to the house of the LORD your God. You shall not boil a young goat in its mother's milk."

27 Then the LORD said to Moses, "Write these words, for according to the tenor of these words I have made a covenant with you and with Israel."

28 So he was there with the LORD forty days and forty nights; he neither ate bread nor drank water. And He wrote on the tablets the words of the covenant, the Ten Commandments.*a*

29 Now it was so, when Moses came down from Mount Sinai (and the two tablets of the Testimony *were* in Moses' hand when he came down from the mountain), that Moses did not know that the skin of his face shone while he talked with Him. 30 So when Aaron and all the children of Israel saw Moses, behold, the skin of his face shone, and they were afraid to come near him. 31 Then Moses called to them, and Aaron and all the rulers of the congregation returned to him; and Moses talked with them. 32 Afterward all the children of Israel came near, and he gave them as commandments all that the LORD had spoken with him on Mount Sinai. 33 And when Moses had finished

speaking with them, he put a veil on his face. 34 But whenever Moses went in before the LORD to speak with Him, he would take the veil off until he came out; and he would come out and speak to the children of Israel whatever he had been commanded. 35 And whenever the children of Israel saw the face of Moses, that the skin of Moses' face shone, then Moses would put the veil on his face again, until he went in to speak with Him.

35 Then Moses gathered all the congregation of the children of Israel together, and said to them, "These *are* the words which the LORD has commanded *you* to do: 2 Work shall be done for six days, but the seventh day shall be a holy day for you, a Sabbath of rest to the LORD. Whoever does any work on it shall be put to death. 3 You shall kindle no fire throughout your dwellings on the Sabbath day."

4 And Moses spoke to all the congregation of the children of Israel, saying, "This *is* the thing which the LORD commanded, saying: 5 'Take from among you an offering to the LORD. Whoever *is* of a willing heart, let him bring it as an offering to the LORD: gold, silver, and bronze; 6 blue, purple, and scarlet *thread*, fine linen, and goats' *hair*; 7 ram skins dyed red, badger skins, and acacia wood; 8 oil for the light, and spices for the anointing oil and for the sweet incense; 9 onyx stones, and stones to be set in the ephod and in the breastplate.

10 'All *who are* gifted artisans among you shall come and make all that the LORD has commanded: 11 the tabernacle, its tent, its covering, its clasps, its boards, its bars, its pillars, and its sockets; 12 the ark and its poles, *with* the mercy seat, and the veil of the covering; 13 the table and its poles, all its utensils, and the showbread; 14 also the lampstand for the light, its utensils, its lamps, and the oil for the light; 15 the incense altar, its poles, the anointing oil, the sweet incense, and the screen for the door at the entrance of the tabernacle; 16 the altar of burnt offering with its bronze grating, its poles, all its utensils, *and* the laver and its base;

34:28 *a*Literally *Ten Words*

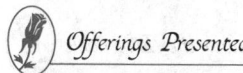

17 the hangings of the court, its pillars, their sockets, and the screen for the gate of the court; 18 the pegs of the tabernacle, the pegs of the court, and their cords; 19 the garments of ministry,ᵃ for ministering in the holy *place*—the holy garments for Aaron the priest and the garments of his sons, to minister as priests.' "

20 And all the congregation of the children of Israel departed from the presence of Moses. 21 Then everyone came whose heart was stirred, and everyone whose spirit was willing, *and* they brought the LORD's offering for the work of the tabernacle of meeting, for all its service, and for the holy garments. 22 They came, both men and women, as many as had a willing heart, *and* brought earrings and nose rings, rings and necklaces, all jewelry of gold, that is, every man who *made* an offering of gold to the LORD. 23 And every man, with whom was found blue, purple, and scarlet *thread*, fine linen, and goats' *hair*, red skins of rams, and badger skins, brought *them*. 24 Everyone who offered an offering of silver or bronze brought the LORD's offering. And everyone with whom was found acacia wood for any work of the service, brought *it*. 25 All the women *who were* gifted artisans spun yarn with their hands, and brought what they had spun, of blue, purple, *and* scarlet, and fine linen. 26 And all the women whose hearts stirred with wisdom spun yarn of goats' *hair*. 27 The rulers brought onyx stones, and the stones to be set in the ephod and in the breastplate, 28 and spices and oil for the light, for the anointing oil, and for the sweet incense. 29 The children of Israel brought a freewill offering to the LORD, all the men and women whose hearts were willing to bring *material* for all kinds of work which the LORD, by the hand of Moses, had commanded to be done.

30 And Moses said to the children of Israel, "See, the LORD has called by name Bezalel the son of Uri, the son of Hur, of the tribe of Judah; 31 and He has filled him with the Spirit of God, in wisdom and understanding, in knowledge and all manner of workmanship, 32 to design artistic works, to work in gold and silver and bronze, 33 in cutting jewels for setting, in carving wood, and to work in all manner of artistic workmanship.

34 "And He has put in his heart the ability to teach, *in* him and Aholiab the son of Ahisamach, of the tribe of Dan. 35 He has filled them with skill to do all manner of work of the engraver and the designer and the tapestry maker, in blue, purple, and scarlet *thread*, and fine linen, and of the weaver—those who do every work and those who design artistic works.

36 "And Bezalel and Aholiab, and every gifted artisan in whom the LORD has put wisdom and understanding, to know how to do all manner of work for the service of the sanctuary, shall do according to all that the LORD has commanded."

2 Then Moses called Bezalel and Aholiab, and every gifted artisan in whose heart the LORD had put wisdom, everyone whose heart was stirred, to come and do the work. 3 And they received from Moses all the offering which the children of Israel had brought for the work of the service of making the sanctuary. So they continued bringing to him freewill offerings every morning. 4 Then all the craftsmen who were doing all the work of the sanctuary came, each from the work he was doing, 5 and they spoke to Moses, saying, "The people bring much more than enough for the service of the work which the LORD commanded *us* to do."

6 So Moses gave a commandment, and they caused it to be proclaimed throughout the camp, saying, "Let neither man nor woman do any more work for the offering of the sanctuary." And the people were restrained from bringing, 7 for the material they had was sufficient for all the work to be done—indeed too much.

8 Then all the gifted artisans among them who worked on the tabernacle made ten curtains woven of fine linen, and of blue, purple, and scarlet *thread; with* artistic designs of cherubim they made them. 9 The length of each curtain *was* twenty-eight cubits, and the width of

35:19 ᵃOr *woven garments*

*B*eing loosed means that the treasure within you has been released. It means that the treasure that has been bound within you has been given an emancipation proclamation. It means that you are free to blossom and bring forth fruit!

each curtain four cubits; the curtains *were* all the same size. 10 And he coupled five curtains to one another, and *the other* five curtains he coupled to one another. 11 He made loops of blue *yarn* on the edge of the curtain on the selvedge of one set; likewise he did on the outer edge of *the other* curtain of the second set. 12 Fifty loops he made on one curtain, and fifty loops he made on the edge of the curtain on the end of the second set; the loops held one *curtain* to another. 13 And he made fifty clasps of gold, and coupled the curtains to one another with the clasps, that it might be one tabernacle.

14 He made curtains of goats' *hair* for the tent over the tabernacle; he made eleven curtains. 15 The length of each curtain *was* thirty cubits, and the width of each curtain four cubits; the eleven curtains *were* the same size. 16 He coupled five curtains by themselves and six curtains by themselves. 17 And he made fifty loops on the edge of the curtain that is outermost in one set, and fifty loops he made on the edge of the curtain of the second set. 18 He also made fifty bronze clasps to couple the tent together, that it might be one. 19 Then he made a covering for the tent of ram skins dyed red, and a covering of badger skins above *that.*

20 For the tabernacle he made boards of acacia wood, standing upright. 21 The length of each board *was* ten cubits, and the width of each board a cubit and a half. 22 Each board had two tenons for binding one to another. Thus he made for all the boards of the tabernacle. 23 And he made boards for the tabernacle, twenty boards for the south side. 24 Forty sockets of silver he made to go under the twenty boards: two sockets under each of the boards for its two tenons. 25 And for the other side of the tabernacle, the north side, he made twenty boards 26 and their forty sockets of silver: two sockets under each of the boards. 27 For the west side of the tabernacle he made six boards. 28 He also made two boards for the two back corners of the tabernacle. 29 And they were coupled at the bottom and coupled together at the top by one ring. Thus he made both of them for the two corners. 30 So there were eight boards and their sockets—sixteen sockets of silver—two sockets under each of the boards.

31 And he made bars of acacia wood: five for the boards on one side of the tabernacle, 32 five bars for the boards on the other side of the tabernacle, and five bars for the boards of the tabernacle on the far side westward. 33 And he made the middle bar to pass through the boards from one end to the other. 34 He overlaid the boards with gold, made their rings of gold *to be* holders for the bars, and overlaid the bars with gold.

35 And he made a veil of blue, purple, and scarlet *thread,* and fine woven linen; it was worked *with* an artistic design of cherubim. 36 He made for it four pillars of acacia *wood,* and overlaid them with gold, with their hooks of gold; and he cast four sockets of silver for them.

37 He also made a screen for the tabernacle door, of blue, purple, and scarlet *thread,* and fine woven linen, made by a weaver, 38 and its five pillars with their hooks. And he overlaid their capitals and their rings with gold, but their five sockets *were* bronze.

37 Then Bezalel made the ark of acacia wood; two and a half cubits *was* its length, a cubit and a half its width, and a cubit and a half its height. 2 He overlaid it with pure gold inside and outside, and made a molding of gold all around it. 3 And he cast for it four rings of gold *to be set* in its four corners: two rings on one side, and two rings on the other side of it. 4 He made poles of acacia wood, and overlaid them with gold. 5 And he put the poles into the rings at the sides of the ark, to bear the ark. 6 He also made the mercy seat of pure gold; two and a half cubits *was* its length and a cubit and a half its width. 7 He made two cherubim of beaten gold; he made them of one piece at the two ends of the mercy seat: 8 one cherub at one end on this side, and the other cherub at the *other* end on that side. He made the cherubim at the two ends *of one piece* with the mercy seat. 9 The cherubim spread out *their* wings above, *and* covered the mercy seat with their wings. They faced one another; the faces of the cherubim were toward the mercy seat.

10 He made the table of acacia wood; two cubits *was* its length, a cubit its width, and a cubit and a half its height. 11 And he overlaid it with pure gold, and made a molding of gold all around it. 12 Also he made a frame of a handbreadth all around it, and made a molding of gold for the frame all around it. 13 And he cast for it four rings of gold, and put the rings on the four corners that *were* at its four legs. 14 The rings were close to the frame, as holders for the poles to bear the table. 15 And he made the poles of acacia wood to bear the table, and overlaid them with gold. 16 He made of pure gold the utensils which were on the table: its dishes, its cups, its bowls, and its pitchers for pouring.

17 He also made the lampstand of pure gold; of hammered work he made the lampstand. Its shaft, its branches, its bowls, its *ornamental* knobs, and its flowers were of the same. piece. 18 And six branches came out of its sides: three branches of the lampstand out of one side, and three branches of the lampstand out of the other side. 19 There were three bowls made like almond *blossoms* on one branch, with an *ornamental* knob and a flower, and three bowls made like almond *blossoms* on the other branch, with an *ornamental* knob and a flower—and so for the six branches coming out of the lampstand. 20 And on the lampstand itself *were* four bowls made like almond *blossoms, each with* its *ornamental* knob and flower. 21 *There was* a knob under the *first* two branches of the same, a knob under the *second* two branches of the same, and a knob under the *third* two branches of the same, according to the six branches extending from it. 22 Their knobs and their branches were of one piece; all of it *was* one hammered piece of pure gold. 23 And he made its seven lamps, its wick-trimmers, and its trays of pure gold. 24 Of a talent of pure gold he made it, with all its utensils.

25 He made the incense altar of acacia wood. Its length *was* a cubit and its width a cubit—*it was* square—and two cubits *was* its height. Its horns were *of one piece* with it. 26 And he overlaid it with pure gold: its top, its sides all around, and its horns. He also made for it a molding of gold all around it. 27 He made two rings of gold for it under its molding, by its two corners on both sides, as holders for the poles with which to bear it. 28 And he made the poles of acacia wood, and overlaid them with gold.

29 He also made the holy anointing oil and the pure incense of sweet spices, according to the work of the perfumer.

38 He made the altar of burnt offering of acacia wood; five cubits *was* its length and five cubits its width—*it was* square—and its height *was* three cubits. 2 He made its horns on its four corners; the horns were *of one piece* with it. And he overlaid it with bronze. 3 He made all the utensils for the altar: the pans, the shovels, the basins, the forks, and the firepans; all its utensils he made of bronze. 4 And he made a grate of bronze network for the altar, under its rim, midway from the bottom. 5 He cast four rings for the four corners of the bronze grating, *as* holders for the poles. 6 And he made the poles of acacia wood, and overlaid them with bronze. 7 Then he put the poles into the rings on the sides of the altar, with which to bear it. He made the altar hollow with boards.

8 He made the laver of bronze and its base of bronze, from the bronze mirrors of the serving women who assembled at the door of the tabernacle of meeting.

9 Then he made the court on the south side; the hangings of the court *were of* fine woven linen, one hundred cubits long. 10 There *were* twenty pillars for them, with twenty bronze sockets. The hooks of the pillars and their bands *were* silver. 11 On the north side *the hangings were* one hundred cubits *long,* with twenty pillars and their twenty bronze sockets. The hooks of the pillars and their bands *were* silver. 12 And on the west side *there were* hangings of fifty cubits, with ten pillars and their ten sockets. The hooks of the pillars and their bands *were* silver. 13 For the east side *the hangings were* fifty cubits. 14 The hangings of one side *of the gate were* fifteen cubits *long, with* their three pillars and their three sockets, 15 and the same for the other side of the court gate; on this side and that

were hangings of fifteen cubits, *with* their three pillars and their three sockets. 16 All the hangings of the court all around *were of* fine woven linen. 17 The sockets for the pillars *were* bronze, the hooks of the pillars and their bands *were* silver, and the overlay of their capitals *was* silver; and all the pillars of the court had bands of silver. 18 The screen for the gate of the court *was* woven of blue, purple, and scarlet *thread,* and of fine woven linen. The length *was* twenty cubits, and the height along its width *was* five cubits, corresponding to the hangings of the court. 19 And *there were* four pillars *with* their four sockets of bronze; their hooks *were* silver, and the overlay of their capitals and their bands *was* silver. 20 All the pegs of the tabernacle, and of the court all around, *were* bronze.

21 This is the inventory of the tabernacle, the tabernacle of the Testimony, which was counted according to the commandment of Moses, for the service of the Levites, by the hand of Ithamar, son of Aaron the priest.

22 Bezalel the son of Uri, the son of Hur, of the tribe of Judah, made all that the Lord had commanded Moses. 23 And with him *was* Aholiab the son of Ahisamach, of the tribe of Dan, an engraver and designer, a weaver of blue, purple, and scarlet *thread,* and of fine linen.

24 All the gold that was used in all the work of the holy *place,* that is, the gold of the offering, was twenty-nine talents and seven hundred and thirty shekels, according to the shekel of the sanctuary. 25 And the silver from those who were numbered of the congregation *was* one hundred talents and one thousand seven hundred and seventy-five shekels, according to the shekel of the sanctuary: 26 a bekah for each man (*that is,* half a shekel, according to the shekel of the sanctuary), for everyone included in the numbering from twenty years old and above, for six hundred and three thousand, five hundred and fifty *men.* 27 And from the hundred talents of silver were cast the sockets of the sanctuary and the bases of the veil: one hundred sockets from the hundred talents, one talent for each socket. 28 Then

from the one thousand seven hundred and seventy-five *shekels* he made hooks for the pillars, overlaid their capitals, and made bands for them.

29 The offering of bronze *was* seventy talents and two thousand four hundred shekels. 30 And with it he made the sockets for the door of the tabernacle of meeting, the bronze altar, the bronze grating for it, and all the utensils for the altar, 31 the sockets for the court all around, the bases for the court gate, all the pegs for the tabernacle, and all the pegs for the court all around.

39 Of the blue, purple, and scarlet *thread* they made garments of ministry,*ᵃ* for ministering in the holy *place,* and made the holy garments for Aaron, as the Lord had commanded Moses.

2 He made the ephod of gold, blue, purple, and scarlet *thread,* and of fine woven linen. 3 And they beat the gold into thin sheets and cut *it into* threads, to work *it* in *with* the blue, purple, and scarlet *thread,* and the fine linen, *into* artistic designs. 4 They made shoulder straps for it to couple *it* together; it was coupled together at its two edges. 5 And the intricately woven band of his ephod that *was* on it *was* of the same workmanship, *woven of* gold, blue, purple, and scarlet *thread,* and of fine woven linen, as the Lord had commanded Moses.

6 And they set onyx stones, enclosed in settings of gold; they were engraved, as signets are engraved, with the names of the sons of Israel. 7 He put them on the shoulders of the ephod *as* memorial stones for the sons of Israel, as the Lord had commanded Moses.

8 And he made the breastplate, artistically woven like the workmanship of the ephod, of gold, blue, purple, and scarlet *thread,* and of fine woven linen. 9 They made the breastplate square by doubling it; a span *was* its length and a span its width when doubled. 10 And they set in it four rows of stones: a row with a sardius, a topaz, and an emerald was the first row; 11 the second row, a turquoise, a sapphire, and a diamond; 12 the third row, a jacinth, an agate,

39:1 *ᵃ*Or *woven garments*

and an amethyst; 13 the fourth row, a beryl, an onyx, and a jasper. *They were* enclosed in settings of gold in their mountings. 14 *There were* twelve stones according to the names of the sons of Israel: according to their names, *engraved like* a signet, each one with its own name according to the twelve tribes. 15 And they made chains for the breastplate at the ends, like braided cords of pure gold. 16 They also made two settings of gold and two gold rings, and put the two rings on the two ends of the breastplate. 17 And they put the two braided *chains* of gold in the two rings on the ends of the breastplate. 18 The two ends of the two braided *chains* they fastened in the two settings, and put them on the shoulder straps of the ephod in the front. 19 And they made two rings of gold and put *them* on the two ends of the breastplate, on the edge of it, which *was* on the inward side of the ephod. 20 They made two *other* gold rings and put them on the two shoulder straps, underneath the ephod toward its front, right at the seam above the intricately woven band of the ephod. 21 And they bound the breastplate by means of its rings to the rings of the ephod with a blue cord, so that it would be above the intricately woven band of the ephod, and that the breastplate would not come loose from the ephod, as the LORD had commanded Moses.

22 He made the robe of the ephod of woven work, all of blue. 23 And *there was* an opening in the middle of the robe, like the opening in a coat of mail, *with* a woven binding all around the opening, so that it would not tear. 24 They made on the hem of the robe pomegranates of blue, purple, and scarlet, and of fine woven *linen*. 25 And they made bells of pure gold, and put the bells between the pomegranates on the hem of the robe all around between the pomegranates: 26 a bell and a pomegranate, a bell and a pomegranate, all around the hem of the robe to minister in, as the LORD had commanded Moses.

27 They made tunics, artistically woven of fine linen, for Aaron and his sons, 28 a turban of fine linen, exquisite hats of fine linen, short trousers of fine woven linen, 29 and a

sash of fine woven linen with blue, purple, and scarlet *thread*, made by a weaver, as the LORD had commanded Moses.

30 Then they made the plate of the holy crown of pure gold, and wrote on it an inscription *like* the engraving of a signet:

HOLINESS TO THE LORD.

31 And they tied to it a blue cord, to fasten *it* above on the turban, as the LORD had commanded Moses.

32 Thus all the work of the tabernacle of the tent of meeting was finished. And the children of Israel did according to all that the LORD had commanded Moses; so they did. 33 And they brought the tabernacle to Moses, the tent and all its furnishings: its clasps, its boards, its bars, its pillars, and its sockets; 34 the covering of ram skins dyed red, the covering of badger skins, and the veil of the covering; 35 the ark of the Testimony with its poles, and the mercy seat; 36 the table, all its utensils, and the showbread; 37 the pure *gold* lampstand with its lamps (the lamps set in order), all its utensils, and the oil for light; 38 the gold altar, the anointing oil, and the sweet incense; the screen for the tabernacle door; 39 the bronze altar, its grate of bronze, its poles, and all its utensils; the laver with its base; 40 the hangings of the court, its pillars and its sockets, the screen for the court gate, its cords, and its pegs; all the utensils for the service of the tabernacle, for the tent of meeting; 41 and the garments of ministry,*ᵃ* to minister in the holy *place:* the holy garments for Aaron the priest, and his sons' garments, to minister as priests.

42 According to all that the LORD had commanded Moses, so the children of Israel did all the work. 43 Then Moses looked over all the work, and indeed they had done it; as the LORD had commanded, just so they had done it. And Moses blessed them.

40 Then the LORD spoke to Moses, saying: 2 "On the first day of the first month you shall set up the tabernacle of the tent of meeting.

39:41 ᵃOr *woven garments*

*T*he day has come for you to forget those things which are past and look toward the future. It's time to look at what talents and gifts and resources are within you that have the power to cause serious damage to what Satan is attempting to do in this world.

3 You shall put in it the ark of the Testimony, and partition off the ark with the veil. 4 You shall bring in the table and arrange the things that are to be set in order on it; and you shall bring in the lampstand and light its lamps. 5 You shall also set the altar of gold for the incense before the ark of the Testimony, and put up the screen for the door of the tabernacle. 6 Then you shall set the altar of the burnt offering before the door of the tabernacle of the tent of meeting. 7 And you shall set the laver between the tabernacle of meeting and the altar, and put water in it. 8 You shall set up the court all around, and hang up the screen at the court gate.

9 "And you shall take the anointing oil, and anoint the tabernacle and all that *is* in it; and you shall hallow it and all its utensils, and it shall be holy. 10 You shall anoint the altar of the burnt offering and all its utensils, and consecrate the altar. The altar shall be most holy. 11 And you shall anoint the laver and its base, and consecrate it.

12 "Then you shall bring Aaron and his sons to the door of the tabernacle of meeting and wash them with water. 13 You shall put the holy garments on Aaron, and anoint him and consecrate him, that he may minister to Me as priest. 14 And you shall bring his sons and clothe them with tunics. 15 You shall anoint them, as you anointed their father, that they may minister to Me as priests; for their anointing shall surely be an everlasting priesthood throughout their generations."

16 Thus Moses did; according to all that the LORD had commanded him, so he did.

17 And it came to pass in the first month of the second year, on the first *day* of the month, *that* the tabernacle was raised up. 18 So Moses raised up the tabernacle, fastened its sockets, set up its boards, put in its bars, and raised up its pillars. 19 And he spread out the tent over the tabernacle and put the covering of the tent on top of it, as the LORD had commanded Moses. 20 He took the Testimony and put *it* into the ark, inserted the poles through the rings of the ark, and put the mercy seat on top of the ark.

21 And he brought the ark into the tabernacle, hung up the veil of the covering, and partitioned off the ark of the Testimony, as the LORD had commanded Moses.

22 He put the table in the tabernacle of meeting, on the north side of the tabernacle, outside the veil; 23 and he set the bread in order upon it before the LORD, as the LORD had commanded Moses. 24 He put the lampstand in the tabernacle of meeting, across from the table, on the south side of the tabernacle; 25 and he lit the lamps before the LORD, as the LORD had commanded Moses. 26 He put the gold altar in the tabernacle of meeting in front of the veil; 27 and he burned sweet incense on it, as the LORD had commanded Moses. 28 He hung up the screen *at* the door of the tabernacle. 29 And he put the altar of burnt offering *before* the door of the tabernacle of the tent of meeting, and offered upon it the burnt offering and the grain offering, as the LORD had commanded Moses. 30 He set the laver between the tabernacle of meeting and the altar, and put water there for washing; 31 and Moses, Aaron, and his sons would wash their hands and their feet *with water* from it. 32 Whenever they went into the tabernacle of meeting, and when they came near the altar, they washed, as the LORD had commanded Moses. 33 And he raised up the court all around the tabernacle and the altar, and hung up the screen of the court gate. So Moses finished the work.

34 Then the cloud covered the tabernacle of meeting, and the glory of the LORD filled the tabernacle. 35 And Moses was not able to enter the tabernacle of meeting, because the cloud rested above it, and the glory of the LORD filled the tabernacle. 36 Whenever the cloud was taken up from above the tabernacle, the children of Israel would go onward in all their journeys. 37 But if the cloud was not taken up, then they did not journey till the day that it was taken up. 38 For the cloud of the LORD *was* above the tabernacle by day, and fire was over it by night, in the sight of all the house of Israel, throughout all their journeys.

Gospel Pearls

LEVITICUS

1 Now the LORD called to Moses, and spoke to him from the tabernacle of meeting, saying, 2 "Speak to the children of Israel, and say to them: 'When any one of you brings an offering to the LORD, you shall bring your offering of the livestock—of the herd and of the flock.

3 'If his offering is a burnt sacrifice of the herd, let him offer a male without blemish; he shall offer it of his own free will at the door of the tabernacle of meeting before the LORD. 4 Then he shall put his hand on the head of the burnt offering, and it will be accepted on his behalf to make atonement for him. 5 He shall kill the bull before the LORD; and the priests, Aaron's sons, shall bring the blood and sprinkle the blood all around on the altar that is by the door of the tabernacle of meeting. 6 And he shall skin the burnt offering and cut it into its pieces. 7 The sons of Aaron the priest shall put fire on the altar, and lay the wood in order on the fire. 8 Then the priests, Aaron's sons, shall lay the parts, the head, and the fat in order on the wood that is on the fire upon the altar; 9 but he shall wash its entrails and its legs with water. And the priest shall burn all on the altar as a burnt sacrifice, an offering made by fire, a sweet aroma to the LORD.

10 'If his offering is of the flocks—of the sheep or of the goats—as a burnt sacrifice, he shall bring a male without blemish. 11 He shall kill it on the north side of the altar before the LORD; and the priests, Aaron's sons, shall sprinkle its blood all around on the altar. 12 And he shall cut it into its pieces, with its head and its fat; and the priest shall lay them in order on the wood that is on the fire upon the altar; 13 but he shall wash the entrails and the legs with water. Then the priest shall bring it all and burn it on the altar; it is a burnt sacrifice, an offering made by fire, a sweet aroma to the LORD.

14 'And if the burnt sacrifice of his offering to the LORD is of birds, then he shall bring his offering of turtledoves or young pigeons. 15 The priest shall bring it to the altar, wring off its head, and burn it on the altar; its blood shall be drained out at the side of the altar. 16 And he shall remove its crop with its feathers and cast it beside the altar on the east side, into the place for ashes. 17 Then he shall split it at its wings, but shall not divide it completely; and the priest shall burn it on the altar, on the wood that is on the fire. It is a burnt sacrifice, an offering made by fire, a sweet aroma to the LORD.

2 'When anyone offers a grain offering to the LORD, his offering shall be of fine flour. And he shall pour oil on it, and put frankincense on it. 2 He shall bring it to Aaron's sons, the priests, one of whom shall take from it his handful of fine flour and oil with all the frankincense. And the priest shall burn it as a memorial on the altar, an offering made by fire, a sweet aroma to the LORD. 3 The rest of the grain offering shall be Aaron's and his sons'. It is most holy of the offerings to the LORD made by fire.

4 'And if you bring as an offering a grain offering baked in the oven, it shall be unleavened cakes of fine flour mixed with oil, or unleavened wafers anointed with oil. 5 But if your offering is a grain offering baked in a pan, it shall be of fine flour, unleavened, mixed with oil. 6 You shall break it in pieces and pour oil on it; it is a grain offering.

7 'If your offering is a grain offering baked in a covered pan, it shall be made of fine flour with oil. 8 You shall bring the grain offering that is made of these things to the LORD. And when it is presented to the priest, he shall bring it to the altar. 9 Then the priest shall take from the grain offering a memorial portion, and burn it on the altar. It is an offering made by fire, a sweet aroma to the LORD. 10 And what is left of the grain offering shall be Aaron's and his sons'. It is most holy of the offerings to the LORD made by fire.

11 'No grain offering which you bring to the LORD shall be made with leaven, for you shall burn no leaven nor any honey in any offering to the LORD made by fire. 12 As for the offering of the firstfruits, you shall offer

Is there an opportunity that you see but you've been afraid to reach out and grab hold of it? It's time for you to bring forth the treasure that God has given you.

them to the LORD, but they shall not be burned on the altar for a sweet aroma. 13 And every offering of your grain offering you shall season with salt; you shall not allow the salt of the covenant of your God to be lacking from your grain offering. With all your offerings you shall offer salt.

14 'If you offer a grain offering of your firstfruits to the LORD, you shall offer for the grain offering of your firstfruits green heads of grain roasted on the fire, grain beaten from full heads. 15 And you shall put oil on it, and lay frankincense on it. It *is* a grain offering. 16 Then the priest shall burn the memorial portion: *part* of its beaten grain and *part* of its oil, with all the frankincense, as an offering made by fire to the LORD.

3 'When his offering *is* a sacrifice of a peace offering, if he offers *it* of the herd, whether male or female, he shall offer it without blemish before the LORD. 2 And he shall lay his hand on the head of his offering, and kill it *at* the door of the tabernacle of meeting; and Aaron's sons, the priests, shall sprinkle the blood all around on the altar. 3 Then he shall offer from the sacrifice of the peace offering an offering made by fire to the LORD. The fat that covers the entrails and all the fat that *is* on the entrails, 4 the two kidneys and the fat that *is* on them by the flanks, and the fatty lobe *attached* to the liver above the kidneys, he shall remove; 5 and Aaron's sons shall burn it on the altar upon the burnt sacrifice, which *is* on the wood that *is* on the fire, *as* an offering made by fire, a sweet aroma to the LORD.

6 'If his offering as a sacrifice of a peace offering to the LORD *is* of the flock, *whether* male or female, he shall offer it without blemish. 7 If he offers a lamb as his offering, then he shall offer it before the LORD. 8 And he shall lay his hand on the head of his offering, and kill it before the tabernacle of meeting; and Aaron's sons shall sprinkle its blood all around on the altar.

9 'Then he shall offer from the sacrifice of the peace offering, as an offering made by fire to the LORD, its fat *and* the whole fat tail which he shall remove close to the backbone. And the fat that covers the entrails and all the fat that *is* on the entrails,

10 the two kidneys and the fat that *is* on them by the flanks, and the fatty lobe *attached* to the liver above the kidneys, he shall remove; 11 and the priest shall burn *them* on the altar *as* food, an offering made by fire to the LORD.

12 'And if his offering *is* a goat, then he shall offer it before the LORD. 13 He shall lay his hand on its head and kill it before the tabernacle of meeting; and the sons of Aaron shall sprinkle its blood all around on the altar. 14 Then he shall offer from it his offering, as an offering made by fire to the LORD. The fat that covers the entrails and all the fat that *is* on the entrails, 15 the two kidneys and the fat that *is* on them by the flanks, and the fatty lobe *attached* to the liver above the kidneys, he shall remove; 16 and the priest shall burn them on the altar *as* food, an offering made by fire for a sweet aroma; all the fat *is* the LORD's.

17 'This shall be a perpetual statute throughout your generations in all your dwellings: you shall eat neither fat nor blood.' "

4 Now the LORD spoke to Moses, saying, 2 "Speak to the children of Israel, saying: 'If a person sins unintentionally against any of the commandments of the LORD *in anything* which ought not to be done, and does any of them, 3 if the anointed priest sins, bringing guilt on the people, then let him offer to the LORD for his sin which he has sinned a young bull without blemish as a sin offering. 4 He shall bring the bull to the door of the tabernacle of meeting before the LORD, lay his hand on the bull's head, and kill the bull before the LORD. 5 Then the anointed priest shall take some of the bull's blood and bring it to the tabernacle of meeting. 6 The priest shall dip his finger in the blood and sprinkle some of the blood seven times before the LORD, in front of the veil of the sanctuary. 7 And the priest shall put some of the blood on the horns of the altar of sweet incense before the LORD, which is in the tabernacle of meeting; and he shall pour the remaining blood of the bull at the base of the altar of the burnt offering, which is at the door of the tabernacle of meeting. 8 He shall take from it all the fat of the bull as the sin offering. The fat

that covers the entrails and all the fat which *is* on the entrails, 9 the two kidneys and the fat that *is* on them by the flanks, and the fatty lobe *attached* to the liver above the kidneys, he shall remove, 10 as it was taken from the bull of the sacrifice of the peace offering; and the priest shall burn them on the altar of the burnt offering. 11 But the bull's hide and all its flesh, with its head and legs, its entrails and offal— 12 the whole bull he shall carry outside the camp to a clean place, where the ashes are poured out, and burn it on wood with fire; where the ashes are poured out it shall be burned.

13 'Now if the whole congregation of Israel sins unintentionally, and the thing is hidden from the eyes of the assembly, and they have done *something against* any of the commandments of the LORD *in anything* which should not be done, and are guilty; 14 when the sin which they have committed becomes known, then the assembly shall offer a young bull for the sin, and bring it before the tabernacle of meeting. 15 And the elders of the congregation shall lay their hands on the head of the bull before the LORD. Then the bull shall be killed before the LORD. 16 The anointed priest shall bring some of the bull's blood to the tabernacle of meeting. 17 Then the priest shall dip his finger in the blood and sprinkle *it* seven times before the LORD, in front of the veil. 18 And he shall put *some* of the blood on the horns of the altar which *is* before the LORD, which *is* in the tabernacle of meeting; and he shall pour the remaining blood at the base of the altar of burnt offering, which is at the door of the tabernacle of meeting. 19 He shall take all the fat from it and burn *it* on the altar. 20 And he shall do with the bull as he did with the bull as a sin offering; thus he shall do with it. So the priest shall make atonement for them, and it shall be forgiven them. 21 Then he shall carry the bull outside the camp, and burn it as he burned the first bull. It *is* a sin offering for the assembly.

22 'When a ruler has sinned, and done *something* unintentionally *against* any of the commandments of the LORD his God *in anything* which should not be done, and is guilty, 23 or if his sin which he has committed comes to his knowledge, he shall bring as his offering a kid of the goats, a male without blemish. 24 And he shall lay his hand on the head of the goat, and kill it at the place where they kill the burnt offering before the LORD. It *is* a sin offering. 25 The priest shall take some of the blood of the sin offering with his finger, put *it* on the horns of the altar of burnt offering, and pour its blood at the base of the altar of burnt offering. 26 And he shall burn all its fat on the altar, like the fat of the sacrifice of the peace offering. So the priest shall make atonement for him concerning his sin, and it shall be forgiven him.

27 'If anyone of the common people sins unintentionally by doing *something against* any of the commandments of the LORD *in anything* which ought not to be done, and is guilty, 28 or if his sin which he has committed comes to his knowledge, then he shall bring as his offering a kid of the goats, a female without blemish, for his sin which he has committed. 29 And he shall lay his hand on the head of the sin offering, and kill the sin offering at the place of the burnt offering. 30 Then the priest shall take *some* of its blood with his finger, put *it* on the horns of the altar of burnt offering, and pour all *the remaining* blood at the base of the altar. 31 He shall remove all its fat, as fat is removed from the sacrifice of the peace offering; and the priest shall burn it on the altar for a sweet aroma to the LORD. So the priest shall make atonement for him, and it shall be forgiven him.

32 'If he brings a lamb as his sin offering, he shall bring a female without blemish. 33 Then he shall lay his hand on the head of the sin offering, and kill it as a sin offering at the place where they kill the burnt offering. 34 The priest shall take *some* of the blood of the sin offering with his finger, put *it* on the horns of the altar of burnt offering, and pour all *the remaining* blood at the base of the altar. 35 He shall remove all its fat, as the fat of the lamb is removed from the sacrifice of the peace offering. Then the priest shall burn it on the altar, according to the offerings made by fire to the LORD. So the priest shall make atonement for his sin that he has committed, and it shall be forgiven him.

*E*ve was created in the man, called out of the man, and then presented to the man. Together, Eve and Adam, woman and man, are a picture of the wholeness of God.

5 'If a person sins in hearing the utterance of an oath, and *is* a witness, whether he has seen or known *of the matter*—if he does not tell *it,* he bears guilt.

2 'Or if a person touches any unclean thing, whether *it is* the carcass of an unclean beast, or the carcass of unclean livestock, or the carcass of unclean creeping things, and he is unaware of it, he also shall be unclean and guilty. 3 Or if he touches human uncleanness—whatever uncleanness with which a man may be defiled, and he is unaware of it—when he realizes *it,* then he shall be guilty.

4 'Or if a person swears, speaking thoughtlessly with *his* lips to do evil or to do good, whatever *it is* that a man may pronounce by an oath, and he is unaware of it—when he realizes *it,* then he shall be guilty in any of these *matters.*

5 'And it shall be, when he is guilty in any of these *matters,* that he shall confess that he has sinned in that *thing;* 6 and he shall bring his trespass offering to the LORD for his sin which he has committed, a female from the flock, a lamb or a kid of the goats as a sin offering. So the priest shall make atonement for him concerning his sin.

7 'If he is not able to bring a lamb, then he shall bring to the LORD, for his trespass which he has committed, two turtledoves or two young pigeons: one as a sin offering and the other as a burnt offering. 8 And he shall bring them to the priest, who shall offer *that* which *is* for the sin offering first, and wring off its head from its neck, but shall not divide *it* completely. 9 Then he shall sprinkle *some* of the blood of the sin offering on the side of the altar, and the rest of the blood shall be drained out at the base of the altar. It *is* a sin offering. 10 And he shall offer the second *as* a burnt offering according to the prescribed manner. So the priest shall make atonement on his behalf for his sin which he has committed, and it shall be forgiven him.

11 'But if he is not able to bring two turtledoves or two young pigeons, then he who sinned shall bring for his offering one-tenth of an ephah of fine flour as a sin offering. He shall put no oil on it, nor shall he put frankincense on it, for it *is* a sin offering. 12 Then he shall bring it to the priest, and the priest shall take his handful of it as a memorial portion, and burn *it* on the altar according to the offerings made by fire to the LORD. It *is* a sin offering. 13 The priest shall make atonement for him, for his sin that he has committed in any of these matters; and it shall be forgiven him. *The rest* shall be the priest's as a grain offering.' "

14 Then the LORD spoke to Moses, saying: 15 "If a person commits a trespass, and sins unintentionally in regard to the holy things of the LORD, then he shall bring to the LORD as his trespass offering a ram without blemish from the flocks, with your valuation in shekels of silver according to the shekel of the sanctuary, as a trespass offering. 16 And he shall make restitution for the harm that he has done in regard to the holy thing, and shall add one-fifth to it and give it to the priest. So the priest shall make atonement for him with the ram of the trespass offering, and it shall be forgiven him.

17 "If a person sins, and commits any of these things which are forbidden to be done by the commandments of the LORD, though he does not know *it,* yet he is guilty and shall bear his iniquity. 18 And he shall bring to the priest a ram without blemish from the flock, with your valuation, as a trespass offering. So the priest shall make atonement for him regarding his ignorance in which he erred and did not know *it,* and it shall be forgiven him. 19 It is a trespass offering; he has certainly trespassed against the LORD."

6 And the LORD spoke to Moses, saying: 2 "If a person sins and commits a trespass against the LORD by lying to his neighbor about what was delivered to him for safekeeping, or about a pledge, or about a robbery, or if he has extorted from his neighbor, 3 or if he has found what was lost and lies concerning it, and swears falsely—in any one of these things that a man may do in which he sins: 4 then it shall be, because he has sinned and is guilty, that he shall restore what he has stolen, or the thing which he has extorted, or what was delivered to him for safekeeping, or the lost thing which he found, 5 or all that about which he has

Gospel Pearls

sworn falsely. He shall restore its full value, add one-fifth more to it, *and* give it to whomever it belongs, on the day of his trespass offering. 6 And he shall bring his trespass offering to the LORD, a ram without blemish from the flock, with your valuation, as a trespass offering, to the priest. 7 So the priest shall make atonement for him before the LORD, and he shall be forgiven for any one of these things that he may have done in which he trespasses."

8 Then the LORD spoke to Moses, saying, 9 "Command Aaron and his sons, saying, 'This *is* the law of the burnt offering: The burnt offering *shall be* on the hearth upon the altar all night until morning, and the fire of the altar shall be kept burning on it. 10 And the priest shall put on his linen garment, and his linen trousers he shall put on his body, and take up the ashes of the burnt offering which the fire has consumed on the altar, and he shall put them beside the altar. 11 Then he shall take off his garments, put on other garments, and carry the ashes outside the camp to a clean place. 12 And the fire on the altar shall be kept burning on it; it shall not be put out. And the priest shall burn wood on it every morning, and lay the burnt offering in order on it; and he shall burn on it the fat of the peace offerings. 13 A fire shall always be burning on the altar; it shall never go out.

14 'This *is* the law of the grain offering: The sons of Aaron shall offer it on the altar before the LORD. 15 He shall take from it his handful of the fine flour of the grain offering, with its oil, and all the frankincense which *is* on the grain offering, and shall burn *it* on the altar *for* a sweet aroma, as a memorial to the LORD. 16 And the remainder of it Aaron and his sons shall eat; with unleavened bread it shall be eaten in a holy place; in the court of the tabernacle of meeting they shall eat it. 17 It shall not be baked with leaven. I have given it *as* their portion of My offerings made by fire; it *is* most holy, like the sin offering and the trespass offering. 18 All the males among the children of Aaron may eat it. *It shall be* a statute forever in your generations con-

cerning the offerings made by fire to the LORD. Everyone who touches them must be holy.'"[a]

19 And the LORD spoke to Moses, saying, 20 "This *is* the offering of Aaron and his sons, which they shall offer to the LORD, *beginning* on the day when he is anointed: one-tenth of an ephah of fine flour as a daily grain offering, half of it in the morning and half of it at night. 21 It shall be made in a pan with oil. *When it is* mixed, you shall bring it in. The baked pieces of the grain offering you shall offer *for* a sweet aroma to the LORD. 22 The priest from among his sons, who is anointed in his place, shall offer it. *It is* a statute forever to the LORD. It shall be wholly burned. 23 For every grain offering for the priest shall be wholly burned. It shall not be eaten."

24 Also the LORD spoke to Moses, saying, 25 "Speak to Aaron and to his sons, saying, 'This *is* the law of the sin offering: In the place where the burnt offering is killed, the sin offering shall be killed before the LORD. It *is* most holy. 26 The priest who offers it for sin shall eat it. In a holy place it shall be eaten, in the court of the tabernacle of meeting. 27 Everyone who touches its flesh must be holy.[a] And when its blood is sprinkled on any garment, you shall wash that on which it was sprinkled, in a holy place. 28 But the earthen vessel in which it is boiled shall be broken. And if it is boiled in a bronze pot, it shall be both scoured and rinsed in water. 29 All the males among the priests may eat it. It *is* most holy. 30 But no sin offering from which *any* of the blood is brought into the tabernacle of meeting, to make atonement in the holy *place*,[a] shall be eaten. It shall be burned in the fire.

7 'Likewise this *is* the law of the trespass offering (it *is* most holy): 2 In the place where they kill the burnt offering they shall kill the trespass offering. And its blood he shall sprinkle all around on the altar. 3 And he shall offer from it all its fat. The fat tail and the fat that covers the entrails, 4 the two kidneys and the fat that *is* on them by the flanks,

---

6:18 ᵃCompare Numbers 4:15 and Haggai 2:11–13   6:27 ᵃCompare Numbers 4:15 and Haggai
2:11–13   6:30 ᵃThe Most Holy Place when capitalized

---

*N*either man nor woman can totally depict God's nature without the other. When we come together, we are able to express the total nature of God to a hurting world.

Soul Secrets
when sacrifice is a struggle

*L*ord, there is only one way to have more of You, and that is to have less of me. The Bible talks about "the sweet aroma of sacrifice." But dying to myself is nearly killing me. I really want to want to sacrifice, but I keep discovering how much I'm holding on to my life, my hopes, my dreams, my stuff. Lord, lead me to the place where I can let go gladly, where I can release everything to You and offer a true sacrifice.

I want to give more than I have and more than I am. I want to learn to give what I'd rather keep. Not a sacrifice of law, but a sacrifice of love. Give me more love than I have so that I can love You more. Give me greater gratitude that I might be more grateful than I am.

I want the sacrifice of my praise to rise before Your throne like the finest perfume. And with every prayer, the pure, sweet fragrance of love. Let my worship be like incense, filling up the halls of heaven.

Lord, I lay my heart upon Your holy altar. You know this heart so well—its flaws, its frailty, its fire. Now send Your fire. Purify me. Make me Yours. Make me a living sacrifice, pleasing and acceptable to You.

and the fatty lobe *attached* to the liver above the kidneys, he shall remove; 5 and the priest shall burn them on the altar *as* an offering made by fire to the LORD. It *is* a trespass offering. 6 Every male among the priests may eat it. It shall be eaten in a holy place. It *is* most holy. 7 The trespass offering *is* like the sin offering; *there is* one law for them both: the priest who makes atonement with it shall have *it.* 8 And the priest who offers anyone's burnt offering, that priest shall have for himself the skin of the burnt offering which he has offered. 9 Also every grain offering that is baked in the oven and all that is prepared in the covered pan, or in a pan, shall be the priest's who offers it. 10 Every grain offering, *whether* mixed with oil or dry, shall belong to all the sons of Aaron, to one *as much* as the other.

11 'This *is* the law of the sacrifice of peace offerings which he shall offer to the LORD: 12 If he offers it for a thanksgiving, then he shall offer, with the sacrifice of thanksgiving, unleavened cakes mixed with oil, unleavened wafers anointed with oil, or cakes of blended flour mixed with oil. 13 Besides the cakes, *as* his offering he shall offer leavened bread with the sacrifice of thanksgiving of his peace offering. 14 And from it he shall offer one cake from each offering *as* a heave offering to the LORD. It shall belong to the priest who sprinkles the blood of the peace offering.

15 'The flesh of the sacrifice of his peace offering for thanksgiving shall be eaten the same day it is offered. He shall not leave any of it until morning. 16 But if the sacrifice of his offering *is* a vow or a voluntary offering, it shall be eaten the same day that he offers his sacrifice; but on the next day the remainder of it also may be eaten; 17 the remainder of the flesh of the sacrifice on the third day must be burned with fire. 18 And if *any* of the flesh of the sacrifice of his peace offering is eaten at all on the third day, it shall not be accepted, nor shall it be imputed to him; it shall be an abomination *to* him who offers it, and the person who eats of it shall bear guilt.

19 'The flesh that touches any unclean thing shall not be eaten. It shall be burned with fire. And as for the *clean* flesh, all who are clean may eat of it. 20 But the person who eats the flesh of the sacrifice of the peace offering that *belongs* to the LORD, while he is unclean, that person shall be cut off from his people. 21 Moreover the person who touches any unclean thing, *such as* human uncleanness, *an* unclean animal, or any abominable unclean thing,ᵃ and who eats the flesh of the sacrifice of the peace offering that *belongs* to the LORD, that person shall be cut off from his people.' "

22 And the LORD spoke to Moses, saying, 23 "Speak to the children of Israel, saying: 'You shall not eat any fat, of ox or sheep or goat. 24 And the fat of an animal that dies *naturally,* and the fat of what is torn by wild beasts, may be used in any other way; but you shall by no means eat it. 25 For whoever eats the fat of the animal of which men offer an offering made by fire to the LORD, the person who eats *it* shall be cut off from his people. 26 Moreover you shall not eat any blood in any of your dwellings, *whether* of bird or beast. 27 Whoever eats any blood, that person shall be cut off from his people.' "

28 Then the LORD spoke to Moses, saying, 29 "Speak to the children of Israel, saying: 'He who offers the sacrifice of his peace offering to the LORD shall bring his offering to the LORD from the sacrifice of his peace offering. 30 His own hands shall bring the offerings made by fire to the LORD. The fat with the breast he shall bring, that the breast may be waved *as* a wave offering before the LORD. 31 And the priest shall burn the fat on the altar, but the breast shall be Aaron's and his sons'. 32 Also the right thigh you shall give to the priest *as* a heave offering from the sacrifices of your peace offerings. 33 He among the sons of Aaron, who offers the blood of the peace offering and the fat, shall have the right thigh for *his* part. 34 For the breast of the wave offering and the thigh of the heave offering I have taken from the children of Israel, from the sacrifices of their peace offerings, and I have given them to Aaron the priest and

---

7:21 ᵃFollowing Masoretic Text, Septuagint, and Vulgate; Samaritan Pentateuch, Syriac, and Targum read *swarming thing* (compare 5:2).

Ⓦhen men and women come together, God allows them to act out who He is—they are privileged to be partners with Him in the creative process of life.

to his sons from the children of Israel by a statute forever.' "

35 This *is* the consecrated portion for Aaron and his sons, from the offerings made by fire to the LORD, on the day when *Moses* presented them to minister to the LORD as priests. 36 The LORD commanded this to be given to them by the children of Israel, on the day that He anointed them, *by* a statute forever throughout their generations.

37 This *is* the law of the burnt offering, the grain offering, the sin offering, the trespass offering, the consecrations, and the sacrifice of the peace offering, 38 which the LORD commanded Moses on Mount Sinai, on the day when He commanded the children of Israel to offer their offerings to the LORD in the Wilderness of Sinai.

8 And the LORD spoke to Moses, saying: 2 "Take Aaron and his sons with him, and the garments, the anointing oil, a bull as the sin offering, two rams, and a basket of unleavened bread; 3 and gather all the congregation together at the door of the tabernacle of meeting."

4 So Moses did as the LORD commanded him. And the congregation was gathered together at the door of the tabernacle of meeting. 5 And Moses said to the congregation, "This *is* what the LORD commanded to be done."

6 Then Moses brought Aaron and his sons and washed them with water. 7 And he put the tunic on him, girded him with the sash, clothed him with the robe, and put the ephod on him; and he girded him with the intricately woven band of the ephod, and with it tied *the ephod* on him. 8 Then he put the breastplate on him, and he put the Urim and the Thummim[a] in the breastplate. 9 And he put the turban on his head. Also on the turban, on its front, he put the golden plate, the holy crown, as the LORD had commanded Moses.

10 Also Moses took the anointing oil, and anointed the tabernacle and all that *was* in it, and consecrated them. 11 He sprinkled some of it on the altar seven times, anointed the altar and all its utensils, and the laver and its base, to consecrate them.

12 And he poured some of the anointing oil on Aaron's head and anointed him, to consecrate him.

13 Then Moses brought Aaron's sons and put tunics on them, girded them with sashes, and put hats on them, as the LORD had commanded Moses.

14 And he brought the bull for the sin offering. Then Aaron and his sons laid their hands on the head of the bull for the sin offering, 15 and Moses killed *it*. Then he took the blood, and put *some* on the horns of the altar all around with his finger, and purified the altar. And he poured the blood at the base of the altar, and consecrated it, to make atonement for it. 16 Then he took all the fat that *was* on the entrails, the fatty lobe *attached to* the liver, and the two kidneys with their fat, and Moses burned *them* on the altar. 17 But the bull, its hide, its flesh, and its offal, he burned with fire outside the camp, as the LORD had commanded Moses.

18 Then he brought the ram as the burnt offering. And Aaron and his sons laid their hands on the head of the ram, 19 and Moses killed *it*. Then he sprinkled the blood all around on the altar. 20 And he cut the ram into pieces; and Moses burned the head, the pieces, and the fat. 21 Then he washed the entrails and the legs in water. And Moses burned the whole ram on the altar. It *was* a burnt sacrifice for a sweet aroma, an offering made by fire to the LORD, as the LORD had commanded Moses.

22 And he brought the second ram, the ram of consecration. Then Aaron and his sons laid their hands on the head of the ram, 23 and Moses killed *it*. Also he took *some* of its blood and put it on the tip of Aaron's right ear, on the thumb of his right hand, and on the big toe of his right foot. 24 Then he brought Aaron's sons. And Moses put *some* of the blood on the tips of their right ears, on the thumbs of their right hands, and on the big toes of their right feet. And Moses sprinkled the blood all around on the altar. 25 Then he took the fat and the fat tail, all the fat that *was* on the entrails, the fatty lobe *attached to* the liver, the two kidneys and their fat, and the right thigh; 26 and from the basket of unleavened bread that was before the LORD he

8:8 [a]Literally *the Lights and the Perfections* (compare Exodus 28:30)

Gospel Pearls

took one unleavened cake, a cake of bread *anointed with* oil, and one wafer, and put *them* on the fat and on the right thigh; 27 and he put all *these* in Aaron's hands and in his sons' hands, and waved them *as* a wave offering before the LORD. 28 Then Moses took them from their hands and burned *them* on the altar, on the burnt offering. They *were* consecration offerings for a sweet aroma. That *was* an offering made by fire to the LORD. 29 And Moses took the breast and waved it *as* a wave offering before the LORD. It was Moses' part of the ram of consecration, as the LORD had commanded Moses.

30 Then Moses took some of the anointing oil and some of the blood which *was* on the altar, and sprinkled *it* on Aaron, on his garments, on his sons, and on the garments of his sons with him; and he consecrated Aaron, his garments, his sons, and the garments of his sons with him.

31 And Moses said to Aaron and his sons, "Boil the flesh *at* the door of the tabernacle of meeting, and eat it there with the bread that *is* in the basket of consecration offerings, as I commanded, saying, 'Aaron and his sons shall eat it.' 32 What remains of the flesh and of the bread you shall burn with fire. 33 And you shall not go outside the door of the tabernacle of meeting *for* seven days, until the days of your consecration are ended. For seven days he shall consecrate you. 34 As he has done this day, *so* the LORD has commanded to do, to make atonement for you. 35 Therefore you shall stay *at* the door of the tabernacle of meeting day and night for seven days, and keep the charge of the LORD, so that you may not die; for so I have been commanded." 36 So Aaron and his sons did all the things that the LORD had commanded by the hand of Moses.

9 It came to pass on the eighth day that Moses called Aaron and his sons and the elders of Israel. 2 And he said to Aaron, "Take for yourself a young bull as a sin offering and a ram as a burnt offering, without blemish, and offer *them* before the LORD. 3 And to the children of Israel you shall speak, saying, 'Take a kid of the goats as a sin offering, and a calf and a lamb, *both* of the first year, without blemish, as a burnt of-

fering, 4 also a bull and a ram as peace offerings, to sacrifice before the LORD, and a grain offering mixed with oil; for today the LORD will appear to you.' "

5 So they brought what Moses commanded before the tabernacle of meeting. And all the congregation drew near and stood before the LORD. 6 Then Moses said, "This *is* the thing which the LORD commanded you to do, and the glory of the LORD will appear to you." 7 And Moses said to Aaron, "Go to the altar, offer your sin offering and your burnt offering, and make atonement for yourself and for the people. Offer the offering of the people, and make atonement for them, as the LORD commanded."

8 Aaron therefore went to the altar and killed the calf of the sin offering, which *was* for himself. 9 Then the sons of Aaron brought the blood to him. And he dipped his finger in the blood, put *it* on the horns of the altar, and poured the blood at the base of the altar. 10 But the fat, the kidneys, and the fatty lobe from the liver of the sin offering he burned on the altar, as the LORD had commanded Moses. 11 The flesh and the hide he burned with fire outside the camp.

12 And he killed the burnt offering; and Aaron's sons presented to him the blood, which he sprinkled all around on the altar. 13 Then they presented the burnt offering to him, with its pieces and head, and he burned *them* on the altar. 14 And he washed the entrails and the legs, and burned *them* with the burnt offering on the altar.

15 Then he brought the people's offering, and took the goat, which *was* the sin offering for the people, and killed it and offered it for sin, like the first one. 16 And he brought the burnt offering and offered it according to the prescribed manner. 17 Then he brought the grain offering, took a handful of it, and burned *it* on the altar, besides the burnt sacrifice of the morning.

18 He also killed the bull and the ram *as* sacrifices of peace offerings, which *were* for the people. And Aaron's sons presented to him the blood, which he sprinkled all around on the altar, 19 and the fat from the bull and the ram—the fatty tail, what covers *the entrails* and the kidneys, and the fatty lobe *attached to* the liver;

20 and they put the fat on the breasts. Then he burned the fat on the altar; 21 but the breasts and the right thigh Aaron waved *as* a wave offering before the LORD, as Moses had commanded.

22 Then Aaron lifted his hand toward the people, blessed them, and came down from offering the sin offering, the burnt offering, and peace offerings. 23 And Moses and Aaron went into the tabernacle of meeting, and came out and blessed the people. Then the glory of the LORD appeared to all the people, 24 and fire came out from before the LORD and consumed the burnt offering and the fat on the altar. When all the people saw *it*, they shouted and fell on their faces.

10 Then Nadab and Abihu, the sons of Aaron, each took his censer and put fire in it, put incense on it, and offered profane fire before the LORD, which He had not commanded them. 2 So fire went out from the LORD and devoured them, and they died before the LORD. 3 And Moses said to Aaron, "This is what the LORD spoke, saying:

'By those who come near Me
I must be regarded as holy;
And before all the people
I must be glorified.' "

So Aaron held his peace.
4 Then Moses called Mishael and Elzaphan, the sons of Uzziel the uncle of Aaron, and said to them, "Come near, carry your brethren from before the sanctuary out of the camp." 5 So they went near and carried them by their tunics out of the camp, as Moses had said.

6 And Moses said to Aaron, and to Eleazar and Ithamar, his sons, "Do not uncover your heads nor tear your clothes, lest you die, and wrath come upon all the people. But let your brethren, the whole house of Israel, bewail the burning which the LORD has kindled. 7 You shall not go out from the door of the tabernacle of meeting, lest you die, for the anointing oil of the LORD *is* upon you." And they did according to the word of Moses.

8 Then the LORD spoke to Aaron, saying: 9 "Do not drink wine or intoxicating drink, you, nor your sons

with you, when you go into the tabernacle of meeting, lest you die. *It shall be* a statute forever throughout your generations, 10 that you may distinguish between holy and unholy, and between unclean and clean, 11 and that you may teach the children of Israel all the statutes which the LORD has spoken to them by the hand of Moses."

12 And Moses spoke to Aaron, and to Eleazar and Ithamar, his sons who were left: "Take the grain offering that remains of the offerings made by fire to the LORD, and eat it without leaven beside the altar; for it *is* most holy. 13 You shall eat it in a holy place, because it *is* your due and your sons' due, of the sacrifices made by fire to the LORD; for so I have been commanded. 14 The breast of the wave offering and the thigh of the heave offering you shall eat in a clean place, you, your sons, and your daughters with you; for they *are* your due and your sons' due, *which* are given from the sacrifices of peace offerings of the children of Israel. 15 The thigh of the heave offering and the breast of the wave offering they shall bring with the offerings of fat made by fire, to offer *as* a wave offering before the LORD. And it shall be yours and your sons' with you, by a statute forever, as the LORD has commanded."

16 Then Moses made careful inquiry about the goat of the sin offering, and there it was—burned up. And he was angry with Eleazar and Ithamar, the sons of Aaron *who were* left, saying, 17 "Why have you not eaten the sin offering in a holy place, since it *is* most holy, and *God* has given it to you to bear the guilt of the congregation, to make atonement for them before the LORD? 18 See! Its blood was not brought inside the holy *place;*ᵃ indeed you should have eaten it in a holy *place,* as I commanded."

19 And Aaron said to Moses, "Look, this day they have offered their sin offering and their burnt offering before the LORD, and such things have befallen me! *If* I had eaten the sin offering today, would it have been accepted in the sight of the LORD?" 20 So when Moses heard *that,* he was content.

10:18 ᵃThe Most Holy Place when capitalized

Gospel Pearls

11 Now the LORD spoke to Moses and Aaron, saying to them, 2 "Speak to the children of Israel, saying, 'These *are* the animals which you may eat among all the animals that *are* on the earth: 3 Among the animals, whatever divides the hoof, having cloven hooves *and* chewing the cud—that you may eat. 4 Nevertheless these you shall not eat among those that chew the cud or those that have cloven hooves: the camel, because it chews the cud but does not have cloven hooves, is unclean to you; 5 the rock hyrax, because it chews the cud but does not have cloven hooves, *is* unclean to you; 6 the hare, because it chews the cud but does not have cloven hooves, *is* unclean to you; 7 and the swine, though it divides the hoof, having cloven hooves, yet does not chew the cud, *is* unclean to you. 8 Their flesh you shall not eat, and their carcasses you shall not touch. They *are* unclean to you.

9 'These you may eat of all that *are* in the water: whatever in the water has fins and scales, whether in the seas or in the rivers—that you may eat. 10 But all in the seas or in the rivers that do not have fins and scales, all that move in the water or any living thing which *is* in the water, they *are* an abomination to you. 11 They shall be an abomination to you; you shall not eat their flesh, but you shall regard their carcasses as an abomination. 12 Whatever in the water does not have fins or scales— that *shall be* an abomination to you.

13 'And these you shall regard as an abomination among the birds; they shall not be eaten, they *are* an abomination: the eagle, the vulture, the buzzard, 14 the kite, and the falcon after its kind; 15 every raven after its kind, 16 the ostrich, the short-eared owl, the seagull, and the hawk after its kind; 17 the little owl, the fisher owl, and the screech owl; 18 the white owl, the jackdaw, and the carrion vulture; 19 the stork, the heron after its kind, the hoopoe, and the bat.

20 'All flying insects that creep on *all* fours *shall be* an abomination to you. 21 Yet these you may eat of every flying insect that creeps on *all* fours: those which have jointed legs above their feet with which to leap on the earth. 22 These you may eat:

the locust after its kind, the destroying locust after its kind, the cricket after its kind, and the grasshopper after its kind. 23 But all *other* flying insects which have four feet *shall be* an abomination to you.

24 'By these you shall become unclean; whoever touches the carcass of any of them shall be unclean until evening; 25 whoever carries part of the carcass of any of them shall wash his clothes and be unclean until evening: 26 *The carcass* of any animal which divides the foot, but is not cloven-hoofed or does not chew the cud, *is* unclean to you. Everyone who touches it shall be unclean. 27 And whatever goes on its paws, among all kinds of animals that go on *all* fours, those *are* unclean to you. Whoever touches any such carcass shall be unclean until evening. 28 Whoever carries *any such* carcass shall wash his clothes and be unclean until evening. It *is* unclean to you.

29 'These also *shall be* unclean to you among the creeping things that creep on the earth: the mole, the mouse, and the large lizard after its kind; 30 the gecko, the monitor lizard, the sand reptile, the sand lizard, and the chameleon. 31 These *are* unclean to you among all that creep. Whoever touches them when they are dead shall be unclean until evening. 32 Anything on which *any* of them falls, when they are dead shall be unclean, whether *it is* any item of wood or clothing or skin or sack, whatever item *it is,* in which *any* work is done, it must be put in water. And it shall be unclean until evening; then it shall be clean. 33 Any earthen vessel into which *any* of them falls you shall break; and whatever *is* in it shall be unclean: 34 in such a vessel, any edible food upon which water falls becomes unclean, and any drink that may be drunk from it becomes unclean. 35 And everything on which *a part* of *any such* carcass falls shall be unclean; *whether it is* an oven or cooking stove, it shall be broken down; *for they are* unclean, and shall be unclean to you. 36 Nevertheless a spring or a cistern, *in which there is* plenty of water, shall be clean, but whatever touches any such carcass becomes unclean. 37 And if a part of *any such* carcass falls on any planting seed which is to be sown, it *remains* clean. 38 But if water is put on

the seed, and if *a part* of *any such* carcass falls on it, it *becomes* unclean to you.

39 'And if any animal which you may eat dies, he who touches its carcass shall be unclean until evening. 40 He who eats of its carcass shall wash his clothes and be unclean until evening. He also who carries its carcass shall wash his clothes and be unclean until evening.

41 'And every creeping thing that creeps on the earth *shall be* an abomination. It shall not be eaten. 42 Whatever crawls on its belly, whatever goes on *all* fours, or whatever has many feet among all creeping things that creep on the earth— these you shall not eat, for they *are* an abomination. 43 You shall not make yourselves abominable with any creeping thing that creeps; nor shall you make yourselves unclean with them, lest you be defiled by them. 44 For I *am* the LORD your God. You shall therefore consecrate yourselves, and you shall be holy; for I *am* holy. Neither shall you defile yourselves with any creeping thing that creeps on the earth. 45 For I *am* the LORD who brings you up out of the land of Egypt, to be your God. You shall therefore be holy, for I *am* holy.

46 'This *is* the law of the animals and the birds and every living creature that moves in the waters, and of every creature that creeps on the earth, 47 to distinguish between the unclean and the clean, and between the animal that may be eaten and the animal that may not be eaten.' "

12 Then the LORD spoke to Moses, saying, 2 "Speak to the children of Israel, saying: 'If a woman has conceived, and borne a male child, then she shall be unclean seven days; as in the days of her customary impurity she shall be unclean. 3 And on the eighth day the flesh of his foreskin shall be circumcised. 4 She shall then continue in the blood of *her* purification thirty-three days. She shall not touch any hallowed thing, nor come into the sanctuary until the days of her purification are fulfilled.

5 'But if she bears a female child, then she shall be unclean two weeks, as in her customary impurity, and she shall continue in the blood of *her* purification sixty-six days.

6 'When the days of her purification are fulfilled, whether for a son or a daughter, she shall bring to the priest a lamb of the first year as a burnt offering, and a young pigeon or a turtledove as a sin offering, to the door of the tabernacle of meeting. 7 Then he shall offer it before the LORD, and make atonement for her. And she shall be clean from the flow of her blood. This *is* the law for her who has borne a male or a female.

8 'And if she is not able to bring a lamb, then she may bring two turtledoves or two young pigeons—one as a burnt offering and the other as a sin offering. So the priest shall make atonement for her, and she will be clean.' "

13 And the LORD spoke to Moses and Aaron, saying: 2 "When a man has on the skin of his body a swelling, a scab, or a bright spot, and it becomes on the skin of his body *like* a leprous[a] sore, then he shall be brought to Aaron the priest or to one of his sons the priests. 3 The priest shall examine the sore on the skin of the body; and if the hair on the sore has turned white, and the sore appears *to be* deeper than the skin of his body, it *is* a leprous sore. Then the priest shall examine him, and pronounce him unclean. 4 But if the bright spot *is* white on the skin of his body, and does not appear *to be* deeper than the skin, and its hair has not turned white, then the priest shall isolate *the one who has* the sore seven days. 5 And the priest shall examine him on the seventh day; and indeed *if* the sore appears to be as it was, *and* the sore has not spread on the skin, then the priest shall isolate him another seven days. 6 Then the priest shall examine him again on the seventh day; and indeed *if* the sore has faded, *and* the sore has not spread on the skin, then the priest shall pronounce him clean; it *is only* a scab, and he shall wash his clothes and be clean. 7 But if the scab should at all spread over the skin, after he has been seen by the priest for his cleansing, he shall be seen by the priest again. 8 And *if* the priest sees

13:2 [a]Hebrew *saraath,* disfiguring skin diseases, including leprosy, and so in verses 2–46 and 14:1–32

*Y*ou can't stand on your strength. By yourself, you are just another Eve. But in the strength of Jesus, you can stand and not give in.

How to Be Holy

Leviticus 11:44

I'm not sure what it would have been like to have been raised in the church, insulated from worldliness and sin. Sometimes I envy those who have been able to live victoriously all of their lives. But most of us have not had that kind of experience.

There are those who define *holiness* as what one wears or eats. For years churches displayed the name holiness because they were monitoring a person's outward appearance. They weren't truly looking at the character on the inside. Often they got sidetracked by how much makeup or jewelry someone wore while thousands of people were destroying themselves with drugs and prostitution.

The Church is a hospital for wounded souls. The staff in a hospital understands that people get sick and need a place to recover. Many of those in Scripture were sick, unholy. The Bible never camouflaged the weaknesses of the people God used. He used David. He used Abraham. Sometimes people break the boundaries, go out of control, and need to be readmitted to the hospital for treatment.

The fact is, we were all born in sin and shaped in iniquity. We have no true badge of righteousness that we can wear on the outside. God concluded that all are in sin so He needed to save us from ourselves (see Galatians 3:22). It wasn't the act of sin, but the state of sin, that brought us into condemnation.

A church that focuses on the externals has lost its passion for souls. When you go into that kind of church, it is possible to walk away feeling like a second-class citizen. Or you may try to be super-spiritual in order to compensate for an embarrassing past. You can't earn deliverance. You have to receive it by faith. Christ is the only righteousness God will accept.

No one person needs any more of the blood of Jesus than anyone else. Jesus died once for all (see Romans 6:10). Each person must come to Him individually. When you come to Him, He will raise you up by the blood of Christ—not because you've done good things.

There is a sanctity of spirit that comes through the blood of the Lord Jesus Christ. It cleans up the innermost part of your being. Once you get cleaned up in your spirit, it will be reflected in your character and conduct. You can't be like Mary, the mother of Jesus, and dress like Mary Magdalene did before she met the Master. The Spirit of the Lord will give you boundaries and teach you how to be holy.

that the scab has indeed spread on the skin, then the priest shall pronounce him unclean. It *is* leprosy.

9 "When the leprous sore is on a person, then he shall be brought to the priest. 10 And the priest shall examine *him;* and indeed *if* the swelling on the skin *is* white, and it has turned the hair white, and *there is* a spot of raw flesh in the swelling, 11 it *is* an old leprosy on the skin of his body. The priest shall pronounce him unclean, and shall not isolate him, for he *is* unclean.

12 "And if leprosy breaks out all over the skin, and the leprosy covers all the skin of *the one who has* the sore, from his head to his foot, wherever the priest looks, 13 then the priest shall consider; and indeed *if* the leprosy has covered all his body, he shall pronounce *him* clean *who has* the sore. It has all turned white. He *is* clean. 14 But when raw flesh appears on him, he shall be unclean. 15 And the priest shall examine the raw flesh and pronounce him to be unclean; *for* the raw flesh *is* unclean. It *is* leprosy. 16 Or if the raw flesh changes and turns white again, he shall come to the priest. 17 And the priest shall examine him; and indeed *if* the sore has turned white, then the priest shall pronounce *him* clean *who has* the sore. He *is* clean.

18 "If the body develops a boil in the skin, and it is healed, 19 and in the place of the boil there comes a white swelling or a bright spot, reddish-white, then it shall be shown to the priest; 20 and *if,* when the priest sees it, it indeed *appears* deeper than the skin, and its hair has turned white, the priest shall pronounce him unclean. It *is* a leprous sore which has broken out of the boil. 21 But if the priest examines it, and indeed *there are* no white hairs in it, and it *is* not deeper than the skin, but has faded, then the priest shall isolate him seven days; 22 and if it should at all spread over the skin, then the priest shall pronounce him unclean. It *is* a leprous sore. 23 But if the bright spot stays in one place, *and* has not spread, it *is* the scar of the boil; and the priest shall pronounce him clean.

24 "Or if the body receives a burn on its skin by fire, and the raw *flesh* of the burn becomes a bright spot, reddish-white or white, 25 then the priest shall examine it; and indeed *if* the hair of the bright spot has turned white, and it appears deeper than the skin, it *is* leprosy broken out in the burn. Therefore the priest shall pronounce him unclean. It *is* a leprous sore. 26 But if the priest examines it, and indeed *there are* no white hairs in the bright spot, and it *is* not deeper than the skin, but has faded, then the priest shall isolate him seven days. 27 And the priest shall examine him on the seventh day. If it has at all spread over the skin, then the priest shall pronounce him unclean. It *is* a leprous sore. 28 But if the bright spot stays in one place, *and* has not spread on the skin, but has faded, *is* a swelling from the burn. The priest shall pronounce him clean, for it *is* the scar from the burn.

29 "If a man or woman has a sore on the head or the beard, 30 then the priest shall examine the sore; and indeed if it appears deeper than the skin, *and there is* in it thin yellow hair, then the priest shall pronounce him unclean. It *is* a scaly leprosy of the head or beard. 31 But if the priest examines the scaly sore, and indeed it does not appear deeper than the skin, and *there is* no black hair in it, then the priest shall isolate *the one who has* the scale seven days. 32 And on the seventh day the priest shall examine the sore; and indeed *if* the scale has not spread, and there is no yellow hair in it, and the scale does not appear deeper than the skin, 33 he shall shave himself, but the scale he shall not shave. And the priest shall isolate *the one who has* the scale another seven days. 34 On the seventh day the priest shall examine the scale; and indeed *if* the scale has not spread over the skin, and does not appear deeper than the skin, then the priest shall pronounce him clean. He shall wash his clothes and be clean. 35 But if the scale should at all spread over the skin after his cleansing, 36 then the priest shall examine him; and indeed *if* the scale has spread over the skin, the priest need not seek for yellow hair. He *is* unclean. 37 But if the scale appears to be at a standstill, and there is black hair grown up in it, the scale has healed. He *is* clean, and the priest shall pronounce him clean.

38 "If a man or a woman has bright spots on the skin of the body, *specifically* white bright spots, 39 then the

Gospel Pearls

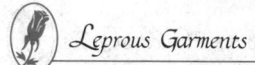

priest shall look; and indeed *if* the bright spots on the skin of the body *are* dull white, it *is* a white spot *that* grows on the skin. He *is* clean.

40 "As for the man whose hair has fallen from his head, he *is* bald, *but* he *is* clean. 41 He whose hair has fallen from his forehead, he *is* bald on the forehead, *but* he *is* clean. 42 And if there is on the bald head or bald forehead a reddish-white sore, it *is* leprosy breaking out on his bald head or his bald forehead. 43 Then the priest shall examine it; and indeed *if* the swelling of the sore *is* reddish-white on his bald head or on his bald forehead, as the appearance of leprosy on the skin of the body, 44 he is a leprous man. He *is* unclean. The priest shall surely pronounce him unclean; his sore *is* on his head.

45 "Now the leper on whom the sore *is*, his clothes shall be torn and his head bare; and he shall cover his mustache, and cry, 'Unclean! Unclean!' 46 He shall be unclean. All the days he has the sore he shall be unclean. He *is* unclean, and he shall dwell alone; his dwelling *shall be* outside the camp.

47 "Also, if a garment has a leprous plague[a] in it, *whether it is* a woolen garment or a linen garment, 48 whether *it is* in the warp or woof of linen or wool, whether in leather or in anything made of leather, 49 and if the plague is greenish or reddish in the garment or in the leather, whether in the warp or in the woof, or in anything made of leather, it *is* a leprous plague and shall be shown to the priest. 50 The priest shall examine the plague and isolate *that which has* the plague seven days. 51 And he shall examine the plague on the seventh day. If the plague has spread in the garment, either in the warp or in the woof, in the leather *or* in anything made of leather, the plague *is* an active leprosy. It *is* unclean. 52 He shall therefore burn that garment in which is the plague, whether warp or woof, in wool or in linen, or anything of leather, for it *is* an active leprosy; *the garment* shall be burned in the fire.

53 "But if the priest examines *it*, and indeed the plague has not spread in the garment, either in the warp or in the woof, or in anything made of leather, 54 then the priest shall command that they wash *the thing* in which *is* the plague; and he shall isolate it another seven days. 55 Then the priest shall examine the plague after it has been washed; and indeed *if* the plague has not changed its color, though the plague has not spread, it *is* unclean, and you shall burn it in the fire; it continues eating away, *whether* the damage *is* outside or inside. 56 If the priest examines *it*, and indeed the plague has faded after washing it, then he shall tear it out of the garment, whether out of the warp or out of the woof, or out of the leather. 57 But if it appears again in the garment, either in the warp or in the woof, or in anything made of leather, it *is* a spreading *plague;* you shall burn with fire that in which is the plague. 58 And if you wash the garment, either warp or woof, or whatever is made of leather, if the plague has disappeared from it, then it shall be washed a second time, and shall be clean.

59 "This *is* the law of the leprous plague in a garment of wool or linen, either in the warp or woof, or in anything made of leather, to pronounce it clean or to pronounce it unclean."

14 Then the LORD spoke to Moses, saying, 2 "This shall be the law of the leper for the day of his cleansing: He shall be brought to the priest. 3 And the priest shall go out of the camp, and the priest shall examine *him*; and indeed, *if* the leprosy is healed in the leper, 4 then the priest shall command to take for him who is to be cleansed two living *and* clean birds, cedar wood, scarlet, and hyssop. 5 And the priest shall command that one of the birds be killed in an earthen vessel over running water. 6 As for the living bird, he shall take it, the cedar wood and the scarlet and the hyssop, and dip them and the living bird in the blood of the bird *that was* killed over the running water. 7 And he shall sprinkle it seven times on him who is to be cleansed from the leprosy, and shall pronounce him clean, and shall let the living bird loose in the open field. 8 He who is to be cleansed shall wash his clothes, shave off all his hair, and wash him-

13:47 *a*A mold, fungus, or similar infestation, and so in verses 47–59

The blood of Jesus Christ has set you free and will continue to uphold you, if you will just stand. On Christ the solid rock we *stand!*

self in water, that he may be clean. After that he shall come into the camp, and shall stay outside his tent seven days. 9 But on the seventh day he shall shave all the hair off his head and his beard and his eyebrows—all his hair he shall shave off. He shall wash his clothes and wash his body in water, and he shall be clean.

10 "And on the eighth day he shall take two male lambs without blemish, one ewe lamb of the first year without blemish, three-tenths *of an ephah* of fine flour mixed with oil as a grain offering, and one log of oil. 11 Then the priest who makes *him* clean shall present the man who is to be made clean, and those things, before the LORD, *at* the door of the tabernacle of meeting. 12 And the priest shall take one male lamb and offer it as a trespass offering, and the log of oil, and wave them *as* a wave offering before the LORD. 13 Then he shall kill the lamb in the place where he kills the sin offering and the burnt offering, in a holy place; for as the sin offering *is* the priest's, so *is* the trespass offering. It *is* most holy. 14 The priest shall take *some* of the blood of the trespass offering, and the priest shall put *it* on the tip of the right ear of him who is to be cleansed, on the thumb of his right hand, and on the big toe of his right foot. 15 And the priest shall take *some* of the log of oil, and pour *it* into the palm of his own left hand. 16 Then the priest shall dip his right finger in the oil that *is* in his left hand, and shall sprinkle some of the oil with his finger seven times before the LORD. 17 And of the rest of the oil in his hand, the priest shall put *some* on the tip of the right ear of him who is to be cleansed, on the thumb of his right hand, and on the big toe of his right foot, on the blood of the trespass offering. 18 The rest of the oil that *is* in the priest's hand he shall put on the head of him who is to be cleansed. So the priest shall make atonement for him before the LORD.

19 "Then the priest shall offer the sin offering, and make atonement for him who is to be cleansed from his uncleanness. Afterward he shall kill the burnt offering. 20 And the priest shall offer the burnt offering and the grain offering on the altar. So the priest shall make atonement for him, and he shall be clean.

21 "But if he *is* poor and cannot afford it, then he shall take one male lamb *as* a trespass offering to be waved, to make atonement for him, one-tenth *of an ephah* of fine flour mixed with oil as a grain offering, a log of oil, 22 and two turtledoves or two young pigeons, such as he is able to afford: one shall be a sin offering and the other a burnt offering. 23 He shall bring them to the priest on the eighth day for his cleansing, to the door of the tabernacle of meeting, before the LORD. 24 And the priest shall take the lamb of the trespass offering and the log of oil, and the priest shall wave them *as* a wave offering before the LORD. 25 Then he shall kill the lamb of the trespass offering, and the priest shall take *some* of the blood of the trespass offering and put *it* on the tip of the right ear of him who is to be cleansed, on the thumb of his right hand, and on the big toe of his right foot. 26 And the priest shall pour some of the oil into the palm of his own left hand. 27 Then the priest shall sprinkle with his right finger *some* of the oil that *is* in his left hand seven times before the LORD. 28 And the priest shall put *some* of the oil that *is* in his hand on the tip of the right ear of him who is to be cleansed, on the thumb of the right hand, and on the big toe of his right foot, on the place of the blood of the trespass offering. 29 The rest of the oil that *is* in the priest's hand he shall put on the head of him who is to be cleansed, to make atonement for him before the LORD. 30 And he shall offer one of the turtledoves or young pigeons, such as he can afford— 31 such as he is able to afford, the one *as* a sin offering and the other *as* a burnt offering, with the grain offering. So the priest shall make atonement for him who is to be cleansed before the LORD. 32 This *is* the law *for one* who had a leprous sore, who cannot afford the usual cleansing."

33 And the LORD spoke to Moses and Aaron, saying: 34 "When you have come into the land of Canaan, which I give you as a possession, and I put the leprous plague[a] in a house in the land of your possession,

14:34 [a]Decomposition by mildew, mold, dry rot, etc., and so in verses 34–53

Gospel Pearls

35 and he who owns the house comes and tells the priest, saying, 'It seems to me that *there is* some plague in the house,' 36 then the priest shall command that they empty the house, before the priest goes *into it* to examine the plague, that all that *is* in the house may not be made unclean; and afterward the priest shall go in to examine the house. 37 And he shall examine the plague; and indeed *if* the plague *is* on the walls of the house with ingrained streaks, greenish or reddish, which appear to be deep in the wall, 38 then the priest shall go out of the house, to the door of the house, and shut up the house seven days. 39 And the priest shall come again on the seventh day and look; and indeed *if* the plague has spread on the walls of the house, 40 then the priest shall command that they take away the stones in which *is* the plague, and they shall cast them into an unclean place outside the city. 41 And he shall cause the house to be scraped inside, all around, and the dust that they scrape off they shall pour out in an unclean place outside the city. 42 Then they shall take other stones and put *them* in the place of *those* stones, and he shall take other mortar and plaster the house.

43 "Now if the plague comes back and breaks out in the house, after he has taken away the stones, after he has scraped the house, and after it is plastered, 44 then the priest shall come and look; and indeed *if* the plague has spread in the house, it *is* an active leprosy in the house. It *is* unclean. 45 And he shall break down the house, its stones, its timber, and all the plaster of the house, and he shall carry *them* outside the city to an unclean place. 46 Moreover he who goes into the house at all while it is shut up shall be unclean until evening. 47 And he who lies down in the house shall wash his clothes, and he who eats in the house shall wash his clothes.

48 "But if the priest comes in and examines *it*, and indeed the plague has not spread in the house after the house was plastered, then the priest shall pronounce the house clean, because the plague is healed. 49 And he shall take, to cleanse the house, two birds, cedar wood, scarlet, and hyssop. 50 Then he shall kill one of the birds in an earthen vessel over running water; 51 and he shall take the cedar wood, the hyssop, the scarlet, and the living bird, and dip them in the blood of the slain bird and in the running water, and sprinkle the house seven times. 52 And he shall cleanse the house with the blood of the bird and the running water and the living bird, with the cedar wood, the hyssop, and the scarlet. 53 Then he shall let the living bird loose outside the city in the open field, and make atonement for the house, and it shall be clean.

54 "This *is* the law for any leprous sore and scale, 55 for the leprosy of a garment and of a house, 56 for a swelling and a scab and a bright spot, 57 to teach when *it is* unclean and when *it is* clean. This *is* the law of leprosy."

15 And the LORD spoke to Moses and Aaron, saying, 2 "Speak to the children of Israel, and say to them: 'When any man has a discharge from his body, his discharge *is* unclean. 3 And this shall be his uncleanness in regard to his discharge—whether his body runs with his discharge, or his body is stopped up by his discharge, it *is* his uncleanness. 4 Every bed is unclean on which he who has the discharge lies, and everything on which he sits shall be unclean. 5 And whoever touches his bed shall wash his clothes and bathe in water, and be unclean until evening. 6 He who sits on anything on which he who has the discharge sat shall wash his clothes and bathe in water, and be unclean until evening. 7 And he who touches the body of him who has the discharge shall wash his clothes and bathe in water, and be unclean until evening. 8 If he who has the discharge spits on him who is clean, then he shall wash his clothes and bathe in water, and be unclean until evening. 9 Any saddle on which he who has the discharge rides shall be unclean. 10 Whoever touches anything that was under him shall be unclean until evening. He who carries *any of* those things shall wash his clothes and bathe in water, and be unclean until evening. 11 And whomever the one who has the discharge touches, and has not rinsed his hands in water, he shall wash his clothes and bathe in water, and be unclean until evening.

Christ doesn't just strengthen us once. He strengthens us again and again and again. He strengthens us every time we face a difficult challenge.

12 The vessel of earth that he who has the discharge touches shall be broken, and every vessel of wood shall be rinsed in water.

13 'And when he who has a discharge is cleansed of his discharge, then he shall count for himself seven days for his cleansing, wash his clothes, and bathe his body in running water; then he shall be clean. 14 On the eighth day he shall take for himself two turtledoves or two young pigeons, and come before the LORD, to the door of the tabernacle of meeting, and give them to the priest. 15 Then the priest shall offer them, the one *as* a sin offering and the other *as* a burnt offering. So the priest shall make atonement for him before the LORD because of his discharge.

16 'If any man has an emission of semen, then he shall wash all his body in water, and be unclean until evening. 17 And any garment and any leather on which there is semen, it shall be washed with water, and be unclean until evening. 18 Also, when a woman lies with a man, and *there is* an emission of semen, they shall bathe in water, and be unclean until evening.

19 'If a woman has a discharge, *and* the discharge from her body is blood, she shall be set apart seven days; and whoever touches her shall be unclean until evening. 20 Everything that she lies on during her impurity shall be unclean; also everything that she sits on shall be unclean. 21 Whoever touches her bed shall wash his clothes and bathe in water, and be unclean until evening. 22 And whoever touches anything that she sat on shall wash his clothes and bathe in water, and be unclean until evening. 23 If *anything* is on *her* bed or on anything on which she sits, when he touches it, he shall be unclean until evening. 24 And if any man lies with her at all, so that her impurity is on him, he shall be unclean seven days; and every bed on which he lies shall be unclean.

25 'If a woman has a discharge of blood for many days, other than at the time of her *customary* impurity, or if it runs beyond her *usual time of* impurity, all the days of her unclean discharge shall be as the days of her *customary* impurity. She *shall be* unclean. 26 Every bed on which she lies all the days of her discharge

shall be to her as the bed of her impurity; and whatever she sits on shall be unclean, as the uncleanness of her impurity. 27 Whoever touches those things shall be unclean; he shall wash his clothes and bathe in water, and be unclean until evening.

28 'But if she is cleansed of her discharge, then she shall count for herself seven days, and after that she shall be clean. 29 And on the eighth day she shall take for herself two turtledoves or two young pigeons, and bring them to the priest, to the door of the tabernacle of meeting. 30 Then the priest shall offer the one *as* a sin offering and the other *as* a burnt offering, and the priest shall make atonement for her before the LORD for the discharge of her uncleanness.

31 'Thus you shall separate the children of Israel from their uncleanness, lest they die in their uncleanness when they defile My tabernacle that *is* among them. 32 This *is* the law for one who has a discharge, and *for him* who emits semen and is unclean thereby, 33 and for her who is indisposed because of her *customary* impurity, and for one who has a discharge, either man or woman, and for him who lies with her who is unclean.' "

16 Now the LORD spoke to Moses after the death of the two sons of Aaron, when they offered *profane fire* before the LORD, and died; 2 and the LORD said to Moses: "Tell Aaron your brother not to come at *just* any time into the Holy *Place* inside the veil, before the mercy seat which *is* on the ark, lest he die; for I will appear in the cloud above the mercy seat.

3 "Thus Aaron shall come into the Holy *Place:* with *the blood of* a young bull as a sin offering, and *of* a ram as a burnt offering. 4 He shall put the holy linen tunic and the linen trousers on his body; he shall be girded with a linen sash, and with the linen turban he shall be attired. These *are* holy garments. Therefore he shall wash his body in water, and put them on. 5 And he shall take from the congregation of the children of Israel two kids of the goats as a sin offering, and one ram as a burnt offering.

Gospel Pearls

6 "Aaron shall offer the bull as a sin offering, which *is* for himself, and make atonement for himself and for his house. 7 He shall take the two goats and present them before the LORD *at* the door of the tabernacle of meeting. 8 Then Aaron shall cast lots for the two goats: one lot for the LORD and the other lot for the scapegoat. 9 And Aaron shall bring the goat on which the LORD's lot fell, and offer it *as* a sin offering. 10 But the goat on which the lot fell to be the scapegoat shall be presented alive before the LORD, to make atonement upon it, *and* to let it go as the scapegoat into the wilderness.

11 "And Aaron shall bring the bull of the sin offering, which is for himself, and make atonement for himself and for his house, and shall kill the bull as the sin offering which *is* for himself. 12 Then he shall take a censer full of burning coals of fire from the altar before the LORD, with his hands full of sweet incense beaten fine, and bring *it* inside the veil. 13 And he shall put the incense on the fire before the LORD, that the cloud of incense may cover the mercy seat that *is* on the Testimony, lest he die. 14 He shall take some of the blood of the bull and sprinkle *it* with his finger on the mercy seat on the east *side;* and before the mercy seat he shall sprinkle some of the blood with his finger seven times.

15 "Then he shall kill the goat of the sin offering, which *is* for the people, bring its blood inside the veil, do with that blood as he did with the blood of the bull, and sprinkle it on the mercy seat and before the mercy seat. 16 So he shall make atonement for the Holy *Place,* because of the uncleanness of the children of Israel, and because of their transgressions, for all their sins; and so he shall do for the tabernacle of meeting which remains among them in the midst of their uncleanness. 17 There shall be no man in the tabernacle of meeting when he goes in to make atonement in the Holy *Place,* until he comes out, that he may make atonement for himself, for his household, and for all the assembly of Israel. 18 And he shall go out to the altar that *is* before the LORD, and make atonement for it, and shall take some of the blood of the bull and some of the blood of the goat, and put it on the horns of the altar all around. 19 Then he shall sprinkle some of the blood on it with his finger seven times, cleanse it, and consecrate it from the uncleanness of the children of Israel.

20 "And when he has made an end of atoning for the Holy *Place,* the tabernacle of meeting, and the altar, he shall bring the live goat. 21 Aaron shall lay both his hands on the head of the live goat, confess over it all the iniquities of the children of Israel, and all their transgressions, concerning all their sins, putting them on the head of the goat, and shall send *it* away into the wilderness by the hand of a suitable man. 22 The goat shall bear on itself all their iniquities to an uninhabited land; and he shall release the goat in the wilderness.

23 "Then Aaron shall come into the tabernacle of meeting, shall take off the linen garments which he put on when he went into the Holy *Place,* and shall leave them there. 24 And he shall wash his body with water in a holy place, put on his garments, come out and offer his burnt offering and the burnt offering of the people, and make atonement for himself and for the people. 25 The fat of the sin offering he shall burn on the altar. 26 And he who released the goat as the scapegoat shall wash his clothes and bathe his body in water, and afterward he may come into the camp. 27 The bull *for* the sin offering and the goat *for* the sin offering, whose blood was brought in to make atonement in the Holy *Place,* shall be carried outside the camp. And they shall burn in the fire their skins, their flesh, and their offal. 28 Then he who burns them shall wash his clothes and bathe his body in water, and afterward he may come into the camp.

29 "*This* shall be a statute forever for you: In the seventh month, on the tenth *day* of the month, you shall afflict your souls, and do no work at all, *whether* a native of your own country or a stranger who dwells among you. 30 For on that day *the priest* shall make atonement for you, to cleanse you, *that* you may be clean from all your sins before the LORD. 31 It *is* a sabbath of solemn rest for you, and you shall afflict your souls. *It is* a statute forever. 32 And the priest, who is anointed and consecrated to minister as priest in his father's place, shall make atonement,

---

*T*he fact is, you can stand if you want to stand. Choose to stand up to the devil today in the strength of Christ Jesus.

and put on the linen clothes, the holy garments; 33 then he shall make atonement for the Holy Sanctuary,*ᵃ* and he shall make atonement for the tabernacle of meeting and for the altar, and he shall make atonement for the priests and for all the people of the assembly. 34 This shall be an everlasting statute for you, to make atonement for the children of Israel, for all their sins, once a year." And he did as the LORD commanded Moses.

17 And the LORD spoke to Moses, saying, 2 "Speak to Aaron, to his sons, and to all the children of Israel, and say to them, 'This *is* the thing which the LORD has commanded, saying: 3 "Whatever man of the house of Israel who kills an ox or lamb or goat in the camp, or who kills *it* outside the camp, 4 and does not bring it to the door of the tabernacle of meeting to offer an offering to the LORD before the tabernacle of the LORD, the guilt of bloodshed shall be imputed to that man. He has shed blood; and that man shall be cut off from among his people, 5 to the end that the children of Israel may bring their sacrifices which they offer in the open field, that they may bring them to the LORD at the door of the tabernacle of meeting, to the priest, and offer them *as* peace offerings to the LORD. 6 And the priest shall sprinkle the blood on the altar of the LORD *at* the door of the tabernacle of meeting, and burn the fat for a sweet aroma to the LORD. 7 They shall no more offer their sacrifices to demons, after whom they have played the harlot. This shall be a statute forever for them throughout their generations." '

8 "Also you shall say to them: 'Whatever man of the house of Israel, or of the strangers who dwell among you, who offers a burnt offering or sacrifice, 9 and does not bring it to the door of the tabernacle of meeting, to offer it to the LORD, that man shall be cut off from among his people.

10 'And whatever man of the house of Israel, or of the strangers who dwell among you, who eats any blood, I will set My face against that person who eats blood, and will cut him off from among his people. 11 For the life of the flesh *is* in the blood, and I have given it to you upon

the altar to make atonement for your souls; for it *is* the blood *that* makes atonement for the soul.' 12 Therefore I said to the children of Israel, 'No one among you shall eat blood, nor shall any stranger who dwells among you eat blood.'

13 "Whatever man of the children of Israel, or of the strangers who dwell among you, who hunts and catches any animal or bird that may be eaten, he shall pour out its blood and cover it with dust; 14 for *it is* the life of all flesh. Its blood sustains its life. Therefore I said to the children of Israel, 'You shall not eat the blood of any flesh, for the life of all flesh is its blood. Whoever eats it shall be cut off.'

15 "And every person who eats what died *naturally* or what was torn *by beasts, whether he is* a native of your own country or a stranger, he shall both wash his clothes and bathe in water, and be unclean until evening. Then he shall be clean. 16 But if he does not wash *them* or bathe his body, then he shall bear his guilt."

18 Then the LORD spoke to Moses, saying, 2 "Speak to the children of Israel, and say to them: 'I am the LORD your God. 3 According to the doings of the land of Egypt, where you dwelt, you shall not do; and according to the doings of the land of Canaan, where I am bringing you, you shall not do; nor shall you walk in their ordinances. 4 You shall observe My judgments and keep My ordinances, to walk in them: I *am* the LORD your God. 5 You shall therefore keep My statutes and My judgments, which if a man does, he shall live by them: I *am* the LORD.

6 'None of you shall approach anyone who is near of kin to him, to uncover his nakedness: I *am* the LORD. 7 The nakedness of your father or the nakedness of your mother you shall not uncover. She *is* your mother; you shall not uncover her nakedness. 8 The nakedness of your father's wife you shall not uncover; it *is* your father's nakedness. 9 The nakedness of your sister, the daughter of your father, or the daughter of your mother, *whether* born at home or elsewhere, their nakedness you shall not un-

16:33 *ᵃ*That is, the Most Holy Place

cover. 10 The nakedness of your son's daughter or your daughter's daughter, their nakedness you shall not uncover; for theirs *is* your own nakedness. 11 The nakedness of your father's wife's daughter, begotten by your father—she *is* your sister—you shall not uncover her nakedness. 12 You shall not uncover the nakedness of your father's sister; she *is* near of kin to your father. 13 You shall not uncover the nakedness of your mother's sister, for she *is* near of kin to your mother. 14 You shall not uncover the nakedness of your father's brother. You shall not approach his wife; she *is* your aunt. 15 You shall not uncover the nakedness of your daughter-in-law—she *is* your son's wife—you shall not uncover her nakedness. 16 You shall not uncover the nakedness of your brother's wife; it *is* your brother's nakedness. 17 You shall not uncover the nakedness of a woman and her daughter, nor shall you take her son's daughter or her daughter's daughter, to uncover her nakedness. They *are* near of kin to her. It *is* wickedness. 18 Nor shall you take a woman as a rival to her sister, to uncover her nakedness while the other is alive.

19 'Also you shall not approach a woman to uncover her nakedness as long as she is in her *customary* impurity. 20 Moreover you shall not lie carnally with your neighbor's wife, to defile yourself with her. 21 And you shall not let any of your descendants pass through *the fire* to Molech, nor shall you profane the name of your God: I *am* the LORD. 22 You shall not lie with a male as with a woman. It *is* an abomination. 23 Nor shall you mate with any animal, to defile yourself with it. Nor shall any woman stand before an animal to mate with it. It *is* perversion. 24 'Do not defile yourselves with any of these things; for by all these the nations are defiled, which I am casting out before you. 25 For the land is defiled; therefore I visit the punishment of its iniquity upon it, and the land vomits out its inhabitants. 26 You shall therefore keep My statutes and My judgments, and shall not commit *any* of these abominations, *either* any of your own nation or any stranger who dwells among you 27 (for all these abominations the

men of the land have done, who *were* before you, and thus the land is defiled), 28 lest the land vomit you out also when you defile it, as it vomited out the nations that *were* before you. 29 For whoever commits any of these abominations, the persons who commit *them* shall be cut off from among their people.

30 'Therefore you shall keep My ordinance, so that *you* do not commit *any* of these abominable customs which were committed before you, and that you do not defile yourselves by them: I *am* the LORD your God.' "

19 And the LORD spoke to Moses, saying, 2 "Speak to all the congregation of the children of Israel, and say to them: 'You shall be holy, for I the LORD your God *am* holy.

3 'Every one of you shall revere his mother and his father, and keep My Sabbaths: I *am* the LORD your God.

4 'Do not turn to idols, nor make for yourselves molded gods: I *am* the LORD your God.

5 'And if you offer a sacrifice of a peace offering to the LORD, you shall offer it of your own free will. 6 It shall be eaten the same day you offer *it,* and on the next day. And if any remains until the third day, it shall be burned in the fire. 7 And if it is eaten at all on the third day, it *is* an abomination. It shall not be accepted. 8 Therefore *everyone* who eats it shall bear his iniquity, because he has profaned the hallowed *offering* of the LORD; and that person shall be cut off from his people.

9 'When you reap the harvest of your land, you shall not wholly reap the corners of your field, nor shall you gather the gleanings of your harvest. 10 And you shall not glean your vineyard, nor shall you gather *every* grape of your vineyard; you shall leave them for the poor and the stranger: I *am* the LORD your God.

11 'You shall not steal, nor deal falsely, nor lie to one another. 12 And you shall not swear by My name falsely, nor shall you profane the name of your God: I *am* the LORD.

13 'You shall not cheat your neighbor, nor rob *him.* The wages of him who is hired shall not remain with you all night until morning. 14 You shall not curse the deaf, nor put a stumblingblock before the blind, but shall fear your God: I *am* the LORD.

Get your praise out. Start praising God for what He has done for you. Celebrate the life He has given you.

15 'You shall do no injustice in judgment. You shall not be partial to the poor, nor honor the person of the mighty. In righteousness you shall judge your neighbor. 16 You shall not go about *as* a talebearer among your people; nor shall you take a stand against the life of your neighbor: I *am* the LORD.

17 'You shall not hate your brother in your heart. You shall surely rebuke your neighbor, and not bear sin because of him. 18 You shall not take vengeance, nor bear any grudge against the children of your people, but you shall love your neighbor as yourself: I *am* the LORD.

19 'You shall keep My statutes. You shall not let your livestock breed with another kind. You shall not sow your field with mixed seed. Nor shall a garment of mixed linen and wool come upon you.

20 'Whoever lies carnally with a woman who *is* betrothed to a man as a concubine, and who has not at all been redeemed nor given her freedom, for this there shall be scourging; *but* they shall not be put to death, because she was not free. 21 And he shall bring his trespass offering to the LORD, to the door of the tabernacle of meeting, a ram as a trespass offering. 22 The priest shall make atonement for him with the ram of the trespass offering before the LORD for his sin which he has committed. And the sin which he has committed shall be forgiven him.

23 'When you come into the land, and have planted all kinds of trees for food, then you shall count their fruit as uncircumcised. Three years it shall be as uncircumcised to you. *It* shall not be eaten. 24 But in the fourth year all its fruit shall be holy, a praise to the LORD. 25 And in the fifth year you may eat its fruit, that it may yield to you its increase: I *am* the LORD your God.

26 'You shall not eat *anything* with the blood, nor shall you practice divination or soothsaying. 27 You shall not shave around the sides of your head, nor shall you disfigure the edges of your beard. 28 You shall not make any cuttings in your flesh for the dead, nor tattoo any marks on you: I *am* the LORD.

29 'Do not prostitute your daughter, to cause her to be a harlot, lest the land fall into harlotry, and the land become full of wickedness.

30 'You shall keep My Sabbaths and reverence My sanctuary: I *am* the LORD.

31 'Give no regard to mediums and familiar spirits; do not seek after them, to be defiled by them: I *am* the LORD your God.

32 'You shall rise before the gray headed and honor the presence of an old man, and fear your God: I *am* the LORD.

33 'And if a stranger dwells with you in your land, you shall not mistreat him. 34 The stranger who dwells among you shall be to you as one born among you, and you shall love him as yourself; for you were strangers in the land of Egypt: I *am* the LORD your God.

35 'You shall do no injustice in judgment, in measurement of length, weight, or volume. 36 You shall have honest scales, honest weights, an honest ephah, and an honest hin: I *am* the LORD your God, who brought you out of the land of Egypt.

37 'Therefore you shall observe all My statutes and all My judgments, and perform them: I *am* the LORD.' "

20 Then the LORD spoke to Moses, saying, 2 "Again, you shall say to the children of Israel: 'Whoever of the children of Israel, or of the strangers who dwell in Israel, who gives *any* of his descendants to Molech, he shall surely be put to death. The people of the land shall stone him with stones. 3 I will set My face against that man, and will cut him off from his people, because he has given *some* of his descendants to Molech, to defile My sanctuary and profane My holy name. 4 And if the people of the land should in any way hide their eyes from the man, when he gives *some* of his descendants to Molech, and they do not kill him, 5 then I will set My face against that man and against his family; and I will cut him off from his people, and all who prostitute themselves with him to commit harlotry with Molech.

6 'And the person who turns to mediums and familiar spirits, to prostitute himself with them, I will set My face against that person and cut him off from his people. 7 Consecrate yourselves therefore, and be holy, for

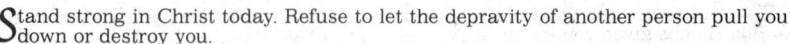

Be Good to Yourself

Leviticus 19:18

When a woman is abused as a child, she grows up with more problems than the pain of that abuse. She also lives with the anger that nobody helped her, nobody intervened on her behalf, nobody stepped in and rescued her. People may have seen, but nobody helped. God said something like this, "You were cast out into the open field, and everybody loathed you" (see Ezekiel 16:5). That's the way a woman feels if she was abused as a child—like a throw-away baby.

But abused women aren't the only ones who feel this way. Divorced women, rejected women, and abandoned women feel this way too. In fact, virtually every woman goes through this experience at some time. When people reject you, it's very difficult for you to feel good about yourself. You start thinking, "Well, if they don't think I'm worth anything, maybe I'm not. If they are willing to throw me aside, I must be of no value."

I beg you not ever to allow another person's view of you to control the way you see yourself. That's too much power to give to another human being. If people don't have the ability to discern the riches of the treasure inside you, that's their problem. But if you sit at home and wallow in self-pity because they have no discernment, then it becomes your problem.

Recognize that those who reject you have no ability to see inside you, to hear the meaning behind your words, to feel the quality of your touch. They have bought a lie—either consciously or unconsciously—that the devil has told them about you. They may believe that lie, but don't you believe it!

If you buy that deception and come to the conclusion that you don't like yourself, you can't like anybody else. In dealing with other people, we reach into the well of our own self-esteem and treat them out of the supply that is in us. If your well is dry, you don't have anything to give anyone else. In Matthew 22:39, Jesus says we are to love other people to the degree that we love ourselves. If we don't love ourselves, then we don't have any love to give to our neighbors.

People who have been treated hatefully become full of hate and can only give hate. People who have been criticized become filled with a critical spirit and can only give criticism. People who have been abused become bitter and angry and can only give abuse.

Refuse to accept the loathing of other people. Don't allow their opinion to creep into your inner person. Refuse to loathe yourself. If no one else has compassion on you, remember that God does and that's reason enough to be good to yourself!

I *am* the LORD your God. 8 And you shall keep My statutes, and perform them: I *am* the LORD who sanctifies you.

9 'For everyone who curses his father or his mother shall surely be put to death. He has cursed his father or his mother. His blood *shall be* upon him.

10 'The man who commits adultery with *another* man's wife, *he* who commits adultery with his neighbor's wife, the adulterer and the adulteress, shall surely be put to death. 11 The man who lies with his father's wife has uncovered his father's nakedness; both of them shall surely be put to death. Their blood *shall be* upon them. 12 If a man lies with his daughter-in-law, both of them shall surely be put to death. They have committed perversion. Their blood *shall be* upon them. 13 If a man lies with a male as he lies with a woman, both of them have committed an abomination. They shall surely be put to death. Their blood *shall be* upon them. 14 If a man marries a woman and her mother, it *is* wickedness. They shall be burned with fire, both he and they, that there may be no wickedness among you. 15 If a man mates with an animal, he shall surely be put to death, and you shall kill the animal. 16 If a woman approaches any animal and mates with it, you shall kill the woman and the animal. They shall surely be put to death. Their blood *is* upon them.

17 'If a man takes his sister, his father's daughter or his mother's daughter, and sees her nakedness and she sees his nakedness, it *is* a wicked thing. And they shall be cut off in the sight of their people. He has uncovered his sister's nakedness. He shall bear his guilt. 18 If a man lies with a woman during her sickness and uncovers her nakedness, he has exposed her flow, and she has uncovered the flow of her blood. Both of them shall be cut off from their people.

19 'You shall not uncover the nakedness of your mother's sister nor of your father's sister, for that would uncover his near of kin. They shall bear their guilt. 20 If a man lies with his uncle's wife, he has uncovered his uncle's nakedness. They shall bear their sin; they shall die childless. 21 If a man takes his brother's wife, it *is* an unclean thing. He has uncovered his brother's nakedness. They shall be childless.

22 'You shall therefore keep all My statutes and all My judgments, and perform them, that the land where I am bringing you to dwell may not vomit you out. 23 And you shall not walk in the statutes of the nation which I am casting out before you; for they commit all these things, and therefore I abhor them. 24 But I have said to you, "You shall inherit their land, and I will give it to you to possess, a land flowing with milk and honey." I *am* the LORD your God, who has separated you from the peoples. 25 You shall therefore distinguish between clean animals and unclean, between unclean birds and clean, and you shall not make yourselves abominable by beast or by bird, or by any kind of living thing that creeps on the ground, which I have separated from you as unclean. 26 And you shall be holy to Me, for I the LORD *am* holy, and have separated you from the peoples, that you should be Mine.

27 'A man or a woman who is a medium, or who has familiar spirits, shall surely be put to death; they shall stone them with stones. Their blood *shall be* upon them.' "

21 And the LORD said to Moses, "Speak to the priests, the sons of Aaron, and say to them: 'None shall defile himself for the dead among his people, 2 except for his relatives who are nearest to him: his mother, his father, his son, his daughter, and his brother; 3 also his virgin sister who is near to him, who has had no husband; for her he may defile himself. 4 *Otherwise* he shall not defile himself, *being* a chief man among his people, to profane himself.

5 'They shall not make any bald *place* on their heads, nor shall they shave the edges of their beards nor make any cuttings in their flesh. 6 They shall be holy to their God and not profane the name of their God, for they offer the offerings of the LORD made by fire, *and* the bread of their God; therefore they shall be holy. 7 They shall not take a wife *who is* a harlot or a defiled woman, nor shall they take a woman divorced

Gospel Pearls

from her husband; for *the priest*[a] is holy to his God. 8 Therefore you shall consecrate him, for he offers the bread of your God. He shall be holy to you, for I the LORD, who sanctify you, *am* holy. 9 The daughter of any priest, if she profanes herself by playing the harlot, she profanes her father. She shall be burned with fire.

10 '*He who is* the high priest among his brethren, on whose head the anointing oil was poured and who is consecrated to wear the garments, shall not uncover his head nor tear his clothes; 11 nor shall he go near any dead body, nor defile himself for his father or his mother; 12 nor shall he go out of the sanctuary, nor profane the sanctuary of his God; for the consecration of the anointing oil of his God *is* upon him: I *am* the LORD. 13 And he shall take a wife in her virginity. 14 A widow or a divorced woman or a defiled woman *or* a harlot—these he shall not marry; but he shall take a virgin of his own people as wife. 15 Nor shall he profane his posterity among his people, for I the LORD sanctify him.' "

16 And the LORD spoke to Moses, saying, 17 "Speak to Aaron, saying: 'No man of your descendants in *succeeding* generations, who has *any* defect, may approach to offer the bread of his God. 18 For any man who has a defect shall not approach: a man blind or lame, who has a marred *face* or any *limb* too long, 19 a man who has a broken foot or broken hand, 20 or is a hunchback or a dwarf, or *a man* who has a defect in his eye, or eczema or scab, or is a eunuch. 21 No man of the descendants of Aaron the priest, who has a defect, shall come near to offer the offerings made by fire to the LORD. He has a defect; he shall not come near to offer the bread of his God. 22 He may eat the bread of his God, *both* the most holy and the holy; 23 only he shall not go near the veil or approach the altar, because he has a defect, lest he profane My sanctuaries; for I the LORD sanctify them.' "

24 And Moses told *it* to Aaron and his sons, and to all the children of Israel.

22 Then the LORD spoke to Moses, saying, 2 "Speak to Aaron and

his sons, that they separate themselves from the holy things of the children of Israel, and that they do not profane My holy name *by* what they dedicate to Me: I *am* the LORD. 3 Say to them: 'Whoever of all your descendants throughout your generations, who goes near the holy things which the children of Israel dedicate to the LORD, while he has uncleanness upon him, that person shall be cut off from My presence: I *am* the LORD.

4 'Whatever man of the descendants of Aaron, who *is* a leper or has a discharge, shall not eat the holy offerings until he is clean. And whoever touches anything made unclean *by* a corpse, or a man who has had an emission of semen, 5 or whoever touches any creeping thing by which he would be made unclean, or any person by whom he would become unclean, whatever his uncleanness may be— 6 the person who has touched any such thing shall be unclean until evening, and shall not eat the holy *offerings* unless he washes his body with water. 7 And when the sun goes down he shall be clean; and afterward he may eat the holy *offerings,* because it *is* his food. 8 Whatever dies *naturally* or is torn *by beasts* he shall not eat, to defile himself with it: I *am* the LORD.

9 'They shall therefore keep My ordinance, lest they bear sin for it and die thereby, if they profane it: I the LORD sanctify them.

10 'No outsider shall eat the holy *offering;* one who dwells with the priest, or a hired servant, shall not eat the holy thing. 11 But if the priest buys a person with his money, he may eat it; and one who is born in his house may eat his food. 12 If the priest's daughter is married to an outsider, she may not eat of the holy offerings. 13 But if the priest's daughter is a widow or divorced, and has no child, and has returned to her father's house as in her youth, she may eat her father's food; but no outsider shall eat it.

14 'And if a man eats the holy *offering* unintentionally, then he shall restore a holy *offering* to the priest, and add one-fifth to it. 15 They shall not profane the holy *offerings* of the children of Israel, which they offer to the

21:7 *a*Literally he

It doesn't matter how young you are, or how old you are. If you are alive today, then God has kept you here for this very hour and He has something more for you.

LORD, 16 or allow them to bear the guilt of trespass when they eat their holy *offerings;* for I the LORD sanctify them.' "

17 And the LORD spoke to Moses, saying, 18 "Speak to Aaron and his sons, and to all the children of Israel, and say to them: 'Whatever man of the house of Israel, or of the strangers in Israel, who offers his sacrifice for any of his vows or for any of his freewill offerings, which they offer to the LORD as a burnt offering— 19 *you shall offer* of your own free will a male without blemish from the cattle, from the sheep, or from the goats. 20 Whatever has a defect, you shall not offer, for it shall not be acceptable on your behalf. 21 And whoever offers a sacrifice of a peace offering to the LORD, to fulfill *his* vow, or a freewill offering from the cattle or the sheep, it must be perfect to be accepted; there shall be no defect in it. 22 Those *that are* blind or broken or maimed, or have an ulcer or eczema or scabs, you shall not offer to the LORD, nor make an offering by fire of them on the altar to the LORD. 23 Either a bull or a lamb that has any limb too long or too short you may offer *as* a freewill offering, but for a vow it shall not be accepted.

24 'You shall not offer to the LORD what is bruised or crushed, or torn or cut; nor shall you make *any offering of them* in your land. 25 Nor from a foreigner's hand shall you offer any of these as the bread of your God, because their corruption *is* in them, *and* defects *are* in them. They shall not be accepted on your behalf.' "

26 And the LORD spoke to Moses, saying: 27 "When a bull or a sheep or a goat is born, it shall be seven days with its mother; and from the eighth day and thereafter it shall be accepted as an offering made by fire to the LORD. 28 *Whether it is* a cow or ewe, do not kill both her and her young on the same day. 29 And when you offer a sacrifice of thanksgiving to the LORD, offer *it* of your own free will. 30 On the same day it shall be eaten; you shall leave none of it until morning: I *am* the LORD.

31 "Therefore you shall keep My commandments, and perform them: I *am* the LORD. 32 You shall not profane My holy name, but I will be hallowed among the children of Israel. I *am* the LORD who sanctifies you,

33 who brought you out of the land of Egypt, to be your God: I *am* the LORD."

23 And the LORD spoke to Moses, saying, 2 "Speak to the children of Israel, and say to them: 'The feasts of the LORD, which you shall proclaim *to be* holy convocations, these *are* My feasts.

3 'Six days shall work be done, but the seventh day *is* a Sabbath of solemn rest, a holy convocation. You shall do no work *on it;* it *is* the Sabbath of the LORD in all your dwellings.

4 'These *are* the feasts of the LORD, holy convocations which you shall proclaim at their appointed times. 5 On the fourteenth *day* of the first month at twilight *is* the LORD's Passover. 6 And on the fifteenth day of the same month *is* the Feast of Unleavened Bread to the LORD; seven days you must eat unleavened bread. 7 On the first day you shall have a holy convocation; you shall do no customary work on it. 8 But you shall offer an offering made by fire to the LORD for seven days. The seventh day *shall be* a holy convocation; you shall do no customary work *on it.*' "

9 And the LORD spoke to Moses, saying, 10 "Speak to the children of Israel, and say to them: 'When you come into the land which I give to you, and reap its harvest, then you shall bring a sheaf of the firstfruits of your harvest to the priest. 11 He shall wave the sheaf before the LORD, to be accepted on your behalf; on the day after the Sabbath the priest shall wave it. 12 And you shall offer on that day, when you wave the sheaf, a male lamb of the first year, without blemish, as a burnt offering to the LORD. 13 Its grain offering *shall be* two-tenths *of an ephah* of fine flour mixed with oil, an offering made by fire to the LORD, for a sweet aroma; and its drink offering *shall be* of wine, one-fourth of a hin. 14 You shall eat neither bread nor parched grain nor fresh grain until the same day that you have brought an offering to your God; *it shall be* a statute forever throughout your generations in all your dwellings.

15 'And you shall count for yourselves from the day after the Sabbath, from the day that you brought the sheaf of the wave offering: seven

Gospel Pearls

Sabbaths shall be completed. 16 Count fifty days to the day after the seventh Sabbath; then you shall offer a new grain offering to the LORD. 17 You shall bring from your dwellings two wave *loaves* of two-tenths *of an ephah.* They shall be of fine flour; they shall be baked with leaven. *They are* the firstfruits to the LORD. 18 And you shall offer with the bread seven lambs of the first year, without blemish, one young bull, and two rams. They shall be *as* a burnt offering to the LORD, with their grain offering and their drink offerings, an offering made by fire for a sweet aroma to the LORD. 19 Then you shall sacrifice one kid of the goats as a sin offering, and two male lambs of the first year as a sacrifice of a peace offering. 20 The priest shall wave them with the bread of the firstfruits *as* a wave offering before the LORD, with the two lambs. They shall be holy to the LORD for the priest. 21 And you shall proclaim on the same day *that* it is a holy convocation to you. You shall do no customary work *on it. It shall be* a statute forever in all your dwellings throughout your generations.

22 'When you reap the harvest of your land, you shall not wholly reap the corners of your field when you reap, nor shall you gather any gleaning from your harvest. You shall leave them for the poor and for the stranger: I *am* the LORD your God.' "

23 Then the LORD spoke to Moses, saying, 24 "Speak to the children of Israel, saying: 'In the seventh month, on the first *day* of the month, you shall have a sabbath-*rest,* a memorial of blowing of trumpets, a holy convocation. 25 You shall do no customary work *on it;* and you shall offer an offering made by fire to the LORD.' "

26 And the LORD spoke to Moses, saying: 27 "Also the tenth *day* of this seventh month *shall be* the Day of Atonement. It shall be a holy convocation for you; you shall afflict your souls, and offer an offering made by fire to the LORD. 28 And you shall do no work on that same day, for it *is* the Day of Atonement, to make atonement for you before the LORD your God. 29 For any person who is not afflicted *in soul* on that same day shall be cut off from his people. 30 And any person who does any

work on that same day, that person I will destroy from among his people. 31 You shall do no manner of work; *it shall be* a statute forever throughout your generations in all your dwellings. 32 It *shall be* to you a sabbath of *solemn* rest, and you shall afflict your souls; on the ninth *day* of the month at evening, from evening to evening, you shall celebrate your sabbath."

33 Then the LORD spoke to Moses, saying, 34 "Speak to the children of Israel, saying: 'The fifteenth day of this seventh month *shall be* the Feast of Tabernacles *for* seven days to the LORD. 35 On the first day *there shall be* a holy convocation. You shall do no customary work *on it.* 36 *For* seven days you shall offer an offering made by fire to the LORD. On the eighth day you shall have a holy convocation, and you shall offer an offering made by fire to the LORD. It *is* a sacred assembly, *and* you shall do no customary work *on it.*

37 'These *are* the feasts of the LORD which you shall proclaim *to be* holy convocations, to offer an offering made by fire to the LORD, a burnt offering and a grain offering, a sacrifice and drink offerings, everything on its day— 38 besides the Sabbaths of the LORD, besides your gifts, besides all your vows, and besides all your freewill offerings which you give to the LORD.

39 'Also on the fifteenth day of the seventh month, when you have gathered in the fruit of the land, you shall keep the feast of the LORD *for* seven days; on the first day *there shall be* a sabbath-*rest,* and on the eighth day a sabbath-*rest.* 40 And you shall take for yourselves on the first day the fruit of beautiful trees, branches of palm trees, the boughs of leafy trees, and willows of the brook; and you shall rejoice before the LORD your God for seven days. 41 You shall keep it as a feast to the LORD for seven days in the year. *It shall be* a statute forever in your generations. You shall celebrate it in the seventh month. 42 You shall dwell in booths for seven days. All who are native Israelites shall dwell in booths, 43 that your generations may know that I made the children of Israel dwell in booths when I brought them out of the land of Egypt: I *am* the LORD your God.' "

I want you to get it into your heart, in your mind, in your spirit: There's a reason for you to go forward. God has something ahead for your future. He has something good planned for you. You aren't dead. You're alive . . . so *live!*

44 So Moses declared to the children of Israel the feasts of the LORD.

24 Then the LORD spoke to Moses, saying: 2 "Command the children of Israel that they bring to you pure oil of pressed olives for the light, to make the lamps burn continually. 3 Outside the veil of the Testimony, in the tabernacle of meeting, Aaron shall be in charge of it from evening until morning before the LORD continually; *it shall be* a statute forever in your generations. 4 He shall be in charge of the lamps on the pure *gold* lampstand before the LORD continually.

5 "And you shall take fine flour and bake twelve cakes with it. Two-tenths *of an ephah* shall be in each cake. 6 You shall set them in two rows, six in a row, on the pure *gold* table before the LORD. 7 And you shall put pure frankincense on *each* row, that it may be on the bread for a memorial, an offering made by fire to the LORD. 8 Every Sabbath he shall set it in order before the LORD continually, *being taken* from the children of Israel by an everlasting covenant. 9 And it shall be for Aaron and his sons, and they shall eat it in a holy place; for it *is* most holy to him from the offerings of the LORD made by fire, by a perpetual statute."

10 Now the son of an Israelite woman, whose father *was* an Egyptian, went out among the children of Israel; and this Israelite *woman's* son and a man of Israel fought each other in the camp. 11 And the Israelite woman's son blasphemed the name *of the* LORD and cursed; and so they brought him to Moses. (His mother's name *was* Shelomith the daughter of Dibri, of the tribe of Dan.) 12 Then they put him in custody, that the mind of the LORD might be shown to them.

13 And the LORD spoke to Moses, saying, 14 "Take outside the camp him who has cursed; then let all who heard *him* lay their hands on his head, and let all the congregation stone him.

15 "Then you shall speak to the children of Israel, saying: 'Whoever curses his God shall bear his sin. 16 And whoever blasphemes the name of the LORD shall surely be put to death. All the congregation shall certainly stone him, the stranger as

well as him who is born in the land. When he blasphemes the name *of the* LORD, he shall be put to death. 17 'Whoever kills any man shall surely be put to death. 18 Whoever kills an animal shall make it good, animal for animal. 19 'If a man causes disfigurement of his neighbor, as he has done, so shall it be done to him— 20 fracture for fracture, eye for eye, tooth for tooth; as he has caused disfigurement of a man, so shall it be done to him. 21 And whoever kills an animal shall restore it; but whoever kills a man shall be put to death. 22 You shall have the same law for the stranger and for one from your own country; for I *am* the LORD your God.' "

23 Then Moses spoke to the children of Israel; and they took outside the camp him who had cursed, and stoned him with stones. So the children of Israel did as the LORD commanded Moses.

25 And the LORD spoke to Moses on Mount Sinai, saying, 2 "Speak to the children of Israel, and say to them: 'When you come into the land which I give you, then the land shall keep a sabbath to the LORD. 3 Six years you shall sow your field, and six years you shall prune your vineyard, and gather its fruit; 4 but in the seventh year there shall be a sabbath of solemn rest for the land, a sabbath to the LORD. You shall neither sow your field nor prune your vineyard. 5 What grows of its own accord of your harvest you shall not reap, nor gather the grapes of your untended vine, *for* it is a year of rest for the land. 6 And the sabbath *produce* of the land shall be food for you: for you, your male and female servants, your hired man, and the stranger who dwells with you, 7 for your livestock and the beasts that *are* in your land—all its produce shall be for food.

8 'And you shall count seven sabbaths of years for yourself, seven times seven years; and the time of the seven sabbaths of years shall be to you forty-nine years. 9 Then you shall cause the trumpet of the Jubilee to sound on the tenth *day* of the seventh month; on the Day of Atonement you shall make the trumpet to

Gospel Pearls

sound throughout all your land. 10 And you shall consecrate the fiftieth year, and proclaim liberty throughout *all* the land to all its inhabitants. It shall be a Jubilee for you; and each of you shall return to his possession, and each of you shall return to his family. 11 That fiftieth year shall be a Jubilee to you; in it you shall neither sow nor reap what grows of its own accord, nor gather *the grapes* of your untended vine. 12 For it *is* the Jubilee; it shall be holy to you; you shall eat its produce from the field.

13 'In this Year of Jubilee, each of you shall return to his possession. 14 And if you sell anything to your neighbor or buy from your neighbor's hand, you shall not oppress one another. 15 According to the number of years after the Jubilee you shall buy from your neighbor, and according to the number of years of crops he shall sell to you. 16 According to the multitude of years you shall increase its price, and according to the fewer number of years you shall diminish its price; for he sells to you *according* to the number *of the years* of the crops. 17 Therefore you shall not oppress one another, but you shall fear your God; for I *am* the LORD your God.

18 'So you shall observe My statutes and keep My judgments, and perform them; and you will dwell in the land in safety. 19 Then the land will yield its fruit, and you will eat your fill, and dwell there in safety. 20 'And if you say, "What shall we eat in the seventh year, since we shall not sow nor gather in our produce?" 21 Then I will command My blessing on you in the sixth year, and it will bring forth produce enough for three years. 22 And you shall sow in the eighth year, and eat old produce until the ninth year; until its produce comes in, you shall eat *of* the old *harvest*.

23 'The land shall not be sold permanently, for the land *is* Mine; for you *are* strangers and sojourners with Me. 24 And in all the land of your possession you shall grant redemption of the land.

25 'If one of your brethren becomes poor, and has sold *some* of his possession, and if his redeeming relative comes to redeem it, then he may redeem what his brother sold.

26 Or if the man has no one to redeem it, but he himself becomes able to redeem it, 27 then let him count the years since its sale, and restore the remainder to the man to whom he sold it, that he may return to his possession. 28 But if he is not able to have *it* restored to himself, then what was sold shall remain in the hand of him who bought it until the Year of Jubilee; and in the Jubilee it shall be released, and he shall return to his possession.

29 'If a man sells a house in a walled city, then he may redeem it within a whole year after it is sold; *within* a full year he may redeem it. 30 But if it is not redeemed within the space of a full year, then the house in the walled city shall belong permanently to him who bought it, throughout his generations. It shall not be released in the Jubilee. 31 However the houses of villages which have no wall around them shall be counted as the fields of the country. They may be redeemed, and they shall be released in the Jubilee. 32 Nevertheless the cities of the Levites, *and* the houses in the cities of their possession, the Levites may redeem at any time. 33 And if a man purchases a house from the Levites, then the house that was sold in the city of his possession shall be released in the Jubilee; for the houses in the cities of the Levites *are* their possession among the children of Israel. 34 But the field of the common-land of their cities may not be sold, for it *is* their perpetual possession.

35 'If one of your brethren becomes poor, and falls into poverty among you, then you shall help him, like a stranger or a sojourner, that he may live with you. 36 Take no usury or interest from him; but fear your God, that your brother may live with you. 37 You shall not lend him your money for usury, nor lend him your food at a profit. 38 I *am* the LORD your God, who brought you out of the land of Egypt, to give you the land of Canaan *and* to be your God.

39 'And if *one of* your brethren *who dwells* by you becomes poor, and sells himself to you, you shall not compel him to serve as a slave. 40 As a hired servant *and* a sojourner he shall be with you, *and* shall serve you until the Year of Jubilee. 41 And *then* he shall depart from

There can be no recovery until a woman is willing to look at herself in the mirror and say, "I messed up." People who blame other people never recover because they live in a state of denial.

you—he and his children with him—and shall return to his own family. He shall return to the possession of his fathers. 42 For they *are* My servants, whom I brought out of the land of Egypt; they shall not be sold as slaves. 43 You shall not rule over him with rigor, but you shall fear your God. 44 And as for your male and female slaves whom you may have—from the nations that are around you, from them you may buy male and female slaves. 45 Moreover you may buy the children of the strangers who dwell among you, and their families who are with you, which they beget in your land; and they shall become your property. 46 And you may take them as an inheritance for your children after you, to inherit *them as* a possession; they shall be your permanent slaves. But regarding your brethren, the children of Israel, you shall not rule over one another with rigor.

47 'Now if a sojourner or stranger close to you becomes rich, and *one of* your brethren *who dwells* by him becomes poor, and sells himself to the stranger *or* sojourner close to you, or to a member of the stranger's family, 48 after he is sold he may be redeemed again. One of his brothers may redeem him; 49 or his uncle or his uncle's son may redeem him; or *anyone* who is near of kin to him in his family may redeem him; or if he is able he may redeem himself. 50 Thus he shall reckon with him who bought him: The price of his release shall be according to the number of years, from the year that he was sold to him until the Year of Jubilee; *it shall be* according to the time of a hired servant for him. 51 If *there are* still many years *remaining*, according to them he shall repay the price of his redemption from the money with which he was bought. 52 And if there remain but a few years until the Year of Jubilee, then he shall reckon with him, *and* according to his years he shall repay him the price of his redemption. 53 He shall be with him as a yearly hired servant, and he shall not rule with rigor over him in your sight. 54 And if he is not redeemed in these *years*, then he shall be released in the Year of Jubilee—he and his children with him. 55 For the children of Israel *are* servants to Me; they *are* My servants

whom I brought out of the land of Egypt: I *am* the LORD your God.

26 'You shall not make idols for yourselves;
neither a carved image nor a *sacred* pillar shall you rear up for yourselves;
nor shall you set up an engraved stone in your land, to bow down to it;
for I *am* the LORD your God.
2 You shall keep My Sabbaths and reverence My sanctuary: I *am* the LORD.

3 'If you walk in My statutes and keep My commandments, and perform them,
4 then I will give you rain in its season, the land shall yield its produce, and the trees of the field shall yield their fruit.
5 Your threshing shall last till the time of vintage, and the vintage shall last till the time of sowing;
you shall eat your bread to the full, and dwell in your land safely.
6 I will give peace in the land, and you shall lie down, and none will make *you* afraid;
I will rid the land of evil beasts, and the sword will not go through your land.
7 You will chase your enemies, and they shall fall by the sword before you.
8 Five of you shall chase a hundred, and a hundred of you shall put ten thousand to flight;
your enemies shall fall by the sword before you.

9 'For I will look on you favorably and make you fruitful, multiply you and confirm My covenant with you.
10 You shall eat the old harvest, and clear out the old because of the new.
11 I will set My tabernacle among you, and My soul shall not abhor you.
12 I will walk among you and be your God, and you shall be My people.
13 I *am* the LORD your God, who

Gospel Pearls

brought you out of the land of Egypt, that *you* should not be their slaves;

I have broken the bands of your yoke and made you walk upright.

14 'But if you do not obey Me, and do not observe all these commandments,

15 and if you despise My statutes, or if your soul abhors My judgments, so that you do not perform all My commandments, *but* break My covenant,

16 I also will do this to you:

I will even appoint terror over you, wasting disease and fever which shall consume the eyes and cause sorrow of heart.

And you shall sow your seed in vain, for your enemies shall eat it.

17 I will set My face against you, and you shall be defeated by your enemies.

Those who hate you shall reign over you, and you shall flee when no one pursues you.

18 'And after all this, if you do not obey Me, then I will punish you seven times more for your sins.

19 I will break the pride of your power;

I will make your heavens like iron and your earth like bronze.

20 And your strength shall be spent in vain;

for your land shall not yield its produce, nor shall the trees of the land yield their fruit.

21 'Then, if you walk contrary to Me, and are not willing to obey Me, I will bring on you seven times more plagues, according to your sins.

22 I will also send wild beasts among you, which shall rob you of your children, destroy your livestock, and make you few in number;

and your highways shall be desolate.

23 'And if by these things you are not reformed by Me, but walk contrary to Me,

24 then I also will walk contrary to you, and I will punish you yet seven times for your sins.

25 And I will bring a sword against you that will execute the vengeance of the covenant;

when you are gathered together within your cities I will send pestilence among you;

and you shall be delivered into the hand of the enemy.

26 When I have cut off your supply of bread, ten women shall bake your bread in one oven, and they shall bring back your bread by weight, and you shall eat and not be satisfied.

27 'And after all this, if you do not obey Me, but walk contrary to Me,

28 then I also will walk contrary to you in fury;

and I, even I, will chastise you seven times for your sins.

29 You shall eat the flesh of your sons, and you shall eat the flesh of your daughters.

30 I will destroy your high places, cut down your incense altars, and cast your carcasses on the lifeless forms of your idols;

and My soul shall abhor you.

31 I will lay your cities waste and bring your sanctuaries to desolation, and I will not smell the fragrance of your sweet aromas.

32 I will bring the land to desolation, and your enemies who dwell in it shall be astonished at it.

33 I will scatter you among the nations and draw out a sword after you;

your land shall be desolate and your cities waste.

34 Then the land shall enjoy its sabbaths as long as it lies desolate and you *are* in your enemies' land;

then the land shall rest and enjoy its sabbaths.

35 As long as *it* lies desolate it shall rest—

for the time it did not rest on your sabbaths when you dwelt in it.

---

*F*ind the Cains in your life and deal with them. Confront the issues. Challenge the lies that the devil will try to speak in your mind when he tells you, "It's not your fault."

36 'And as for those of you who are
    left, I will send faintness into
    their hearts in the lands of
    their enemies;
  the sound of a shaken leaf shall
    cause them to flee;
  they shall flee as though fleeing
    from a sword, and they shall
    fall when no one pursues.
37 They shall stumble over one
    another, as it were before a
    sword, when no one pursues;
  and you shall have no *power*
    to stand before your enemies.
38 You shall perish among the
    nations, and the land of your
    enemies shall eat you up.
39 And those of you who are left
    shall waste away in their
    iniquity in your enemies'
    lands;
  also in their fathers' iniquities,
    which are with them, they
    shall waste away.

40 'But if they confess their
    iniquity and the iniquity of
    their fathers, with their
    unfaithfulness in which they
    were unfaithful to Me, and
    that they also have walked
    contrary to Me,
41 and *that* I also have walked
    contrary to them and have
    brought them into the land of
    their enemies;
  if their uncircumcised hearts
    are humbled, and they accept
    their guilt—
42 then I will remember My
    covenant with Jacob, and My
    covenant with Isaac and My
    covenant with Abraham I
    will remember;
  I will remember the land.
43 The land also shall be left
    empty by them, and will
    enjoy its sabbaths while it
    lies desolate without them;
  they will accept their guilt,
    because they despised My
    judgments and because their
    soul abhorred My statutes.
44 Yet for all that, when they are
    in the land of their enemies,
    I will not cast them away, nor
    shall I abhor them, to utterly
    destroy them and break My
    covenant with them;
  for I *am* the Lord their God.
45 But for their sake I will
    remember the covenant of

their ancestors, whom I
brought out of the land of
Egypt in the sight of the
nations, that I might be their
God:
I *am* the Lord.'"

46 These *are* the statutes and judgments and laws which the Lord made
between Himself and the children of
Israel on Mount Sinai by the hand
of Moses.

27 Now the Lord spoke to Moses,
    saying, 2 "Speak to the chil-
dren of Israel, and say to them:
'When a man consecrates by a vow
certain persons to the Lord, according to your valuation, 3 if your valuation is of a male from twenty years
old up to sixty years old, then your
valuation shall be fifty shekels of silver, according to the shekel of the
sanctuary. 4 If it *is* a female, then
your valuation shall be thirty shekels; 5 and if from five years old up
to twenty years old, then your valuation for a male shall be twenty shekels, and for a female ten shekels;
6 and if from a month old up to five
years old, then your valuation for a
male shall be five shekels of silver,
and for a female your valuation shall
be three shekels of silver; 7 and if
from sixty years old and above, if *it
is* a male, then your valuation shall
be fifteen shekels, and for a female
ten shekels.
  8 'But if he is too poor to pay your
valuation, then he shall present himself before the priest, and the priest
shall set a value for him; according
to the ability of him who vowed, the
priest shall value him.
  9 'If *it is* an animal that men may
bring as an offering to the Lord, all
that *anyone* gives to the Lord shall
be holy. 10 He shall not substitute it
or exchange it, good for bad or bad
for good; and if he at all exchanges
animal for animal, then both it and
the one exchanged for it shall be
holy. 11 If *it is* an unclean animal
which they do not offer as a sacrifice
to the Lord, then he shall present the
animal before the priest; 12 and the
priest shall set a value for it, whether
it is good or bad; as you, the priest,
value it, so it shall be. 13 But if he
wants at all *to* redeem it, then he
must add one-fifth to your valuation.
  14 'And when a man dedicates his

Gospel
Pearls

house *to be* holy to the LORD, then the priest shall set a value for it, whether it is good or bad; as the priest values it, so it shall stand. 15 If he who dedicated it *wants* to redeem his house, then he must add one-fifth of the money of your valuation to it, and it shall be his.

16 'If a man dedicates to the LORD *part* of a field of his possession, then your valuation shall be according to the seed for it. A homer of barley seed *shall be valued* at fifty shekels of silver. 17 If he dedicates his field from the Year of Jubilee, according to your valuation it shall stand. 18 But if he dedicates his field after the Jubilee, then the priest shall reckon to him the money due according to the years that remain till the Year of Jubilee, and it shall be deducted from your valuation. 19 And if he who dedicates the field ever wishes to redeem it, then he must add one-fifth of the money of your valuation to it, and it shall belong to him. 20 But if he does not want to redeem the field, or if he has sold the field to another man, it shall not be redeemed anymore; 21 but the field, when it is released in the Jubilee, shall be holy to the LORD, as a devoted field; it shall be the possession of the priest.

22 'And if a man dedicates to the LORD a field which he has bought, which is not the field of his possession, 23 then the priest shall reckon to him the worth of your valuation, up to the Year of Jubilee, and he shall give your valuation on that day *as a* holy *offering* to the LORD. 24 In the Year of Jubilee the field shall return to him from whom it was bought, to the one who *owned* the land as a possession. 25 And all your valuations shall be according to the shekel of the sanctuary: twenty gerahs to the shekel.

26 'But the firstborn of the animals, which should be the LORD's firstborn, no man shall dedicate; whether *it is* an ox or sheep, it *is* the LORD's. 27 And if *it is* an unclean animal, then he shall redeem *it* according to your valuation, and shall add one-fifth to it; or if it is not redeemed, then it shall be sold according to your valuation.

28 'Nevertheless no devoted *offering* that a man may devote to the LORD of all that he has, *both* man and beast, or the field of his possession, shall be sold or redeemed; every devoted *offering is* most holy to the LORD. 29 No person under the ban, who may become doomed to destruction among men, shall be redeemed, *but* shall surely be put to death. 30 And all the tithe of the land, *whether* of the seed of the land *or* of the fruit of the tree, *is* the LORD's. It *is* holy to the LORD. 31 If a man wants at all to redeem *any* of his tithes, he shall add one-fifth to it. 32 And concerning the tithe of the herd or the flock, of whatever passes under the rod, the tenth one shall be holy to the LORD. 33 He shall not inquire whether it is good or bad, nor shall he exchange it; and if he exchanges it at all, then both it and the one exchanged for it shall be holy; it shall not be redeemed.' "

34 These *are* the commandments which the LORD commanded Moses for the children of Israel on Mount Sinai.

The Fourth Book of Moses Called

NUMBERS

1 Now the LORD spoke to Moses in the Wilderness of Sinai, in the tabernacle of meeting, on the first *day* of the second month, in the second year after they had come out of the land of Egypt, saying: 2 "Take a census of all the congregation of the children of Israel, by their families, by their fathers' houses, according to the number of names, every male individually, 3 from twenty years old and above—all who *are able to* go

---

*I*f you will face up to your own sin and take hold of the hand of our forgiving God, you can overcome anything. You can overcome the past influence of any person . . . the evil of any circumstance. You can live and not die!

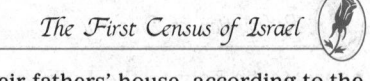

to war in Israel. You and Aaron shall number them by their armies. 4 And with you there shall be a man from every tribe, each one the head of his father's house.

5 "These are the names of the men who shall stand with you: from Reuben, Elizur the son of Shedeur; 6 from Simeon, Shelumiel the son of Zurishaddai; 7 from Judah, Nahshon the son of Amminadab; 8 from Issachar, Nethanel the son of Zuar; 9 from Zebulun, Eliab the son of Helon; 10 from the sons of Joseph: from Ephraim, Elishama the son of Ammihud; from Manasseh, Gamaliel the son of Pedahzur; 11 from Benjamin, Abidan the son of Gideoni; 12 from Dan, Ahiezer the son of Ammishaddai; 13 from Asher, Pagiel the son of Ocran; 14 from Gad, Eliasaph the son of Deuel;*a* 15 from Naphtali, Ahira the son of Enan." 16 These *were* chosen from the congregation, leaders of their fathers' tribes, heads of the divisions in Israel.

17 Then Moses and Aaron took these men who had been mentioned by name, 18 and they assembled all the congregation together on the first *day* of the second month; and they recited their ancestry by families, by their fathers' houses, according to the number of names, from twenty years old and above, each one individually. 19 As the LORD commanded Moses, so he numbered them in the Wilderness of Sinai.

20 Now the children of Reuben, Israel's oldest son, their genealogies by their families, by their fathers' house, according to the number of names, every male individually, from twenty years old and above, all who *were able to* go to war: 21 those who were numbered of the tribe of Reuben *were* forty-six thousand five hundred.

22 From the children of Simeon, their genealogies by their families, by their fathers' house, of those who were numbered, according to the number of names, every male individually, from twenty years old and above, all who *were able to* go to war: 23 those who were numbered of the tribe of Simeon *were* fifty-nine thousand three hundred.

24 From the children of Gad, their genealogies by their families, by their fathers' house, according to the number of names, from twenty years old and above, all who *were able to* go to war: 25 those who were numbered of the tribe of Gad *were* forty-five thousand six hundred and fifty.

26 From the children of Judah, their genealogies by their families, by their fathers' house, according to the number of names, from twenty years old and above, all who *were able to* go to war: 27 those who were numbered of the tribe of Judah *were* seventy-four thousand six hundred.

28 From the children of Issachar, their genealogies by their families, by their fathers' house, according to the number of names, from twenty years old and above, all who *were able to* go to war: 29 those who were numbered of the tribe of Issachar *were* fifty-four thousand four hundred.

30 From the children of Zebulun, their genealogies by their families, by their fathers' house, according to the number of names, from twenty years old and above, all who *were able to* go to war: 31 those who were numbered of the tribe of Zebulun *were* fifty-seven thousand four hundred.

32 From the sons of Joseph, the children of Ephraim, their genealogies by their families, by their fathers' house, according to the number of names, from twenty years old and above, all who *were able to* go to war: 33 those who were numbered of the tribe of Ephraim *were* forty thousand five hundred.

34 From the children of Manasseh, their genealogies by their families, by their fathers' house, according to the number of names, from twenty years old and above, all who *were able to* go to war: 35 those who were numbered of the tribe of Manasseh *were* thirty-two thousand two hundred.

36 From the children of Benjamin, their genealogies by their families, by their fathers' house, according to the number of names, from twenty years old and above, all who *were able to* go to war: 37 those who were numbered of the tribe of Benjamin *were* thirty-five thousand four hundred.

38 From the children of Dan, their

1:14 *a*Spelled *Reuel* in 2:14

Gospel Pearls

genealogies by their families, by their fathers' house, according to the number of names, from twenty years old and above, all who *were able to* go to war: 39 those who were numbered of the tribe of Dan *were* sixty-two thousand seven hundred.

40 From the children of Asher, their genealogies by their families, by their fathers' house, according to the number of names, from twenty years old and above, all who *were able to* go to war: 41 those who were numbered of the tribe of Asher *were* forty-one thousand five hundred.

42 From the children of Naphtali, their genealogies by their families, by their fathers' house, according to the number of names, from twenty years old and above, all who *were able to* go to war: 43 those who were numbered of the tribe of Naphtali *were* fifty-three thousand four hundred.

44 These are the ones who were numbered, whom Moses and Aaron numbered, with the leaders of Israel, twelve men, each one representing his father's house. 45 So all who were numbered of the children of Israel, by their fathers' houses, from twenty years old and above, all who *were able to* go to war in Israel— 46 all who were numbered were six hundred and three thousand five hundred and fifty.

47 But the Levites were not numbered among them by their fathers' tribe; 48 for the LORD had spoken to Moses, saying: 49 "Only the tribe of Levi you shall not number, nor take a census of them among the children of Israel; 50 but you shall appoint the Levites over the tabernacle of the Testimony, over all its furnishings, and over all things that belong to it; they shall carry the tabernacle and all its furnishings; they shall attend to it and camp around the tabernacle. 51 And when the tabernacle is to go forward, the Levites shall take it down; and when the tabernacle is to be set up, the Levites shall set it up. The outsider who comes near shall be put to death. 52 The children of Israel shall pitch their tents, everyone by his own camp, everyone by his own standard, according to their armies; 53 but the Levites shall camp around the tabernacle of the Testi-

mony, that there may be no wrath on the congregation of the children of Israel; and the Levites shall keep charge of the tabernacle of the Testimony."

54 Thus the children of Israel did; according to all that the LORD commanded Moses, so they did.

2 And the LORD spoke to Moses and Aaron, saying: 2 "Everyone of the children of Israel shall camp by his own standard, beside the emblems of his father's house; they shall camp some distance from the tabernacle of meeting. 3 On the east side, toward the rising of the sun, those of the standard of the forces with Judah shall camp according to their armies; and Nahshon the son of Amminadab *shall be* the leader of the children of Judah." 4 And his army was numbered at seventy-four thousand six-hundred.

5 "Those who camp next to him *shall be* the tribe of Issachar, and Nethanel the son of Zuar *shall be* the leader of the children of Issachar." 6 And his army was numbered at fifty-four thousand four hundred.

7 "Then *comes* the tribe of Zebulun, and Eliab the son of Helon *shall be* the leader of the children of Zebulun." 8 And his army was numbered at fifty-seven thousand four hundred. 9 "All who were numbered according to their armies of the forces with Judah, one hundred and eighty-six thousand four hundred—these shall break camp first.

10 "On the south side *shall be* the standard of the forces with Reuben according to their armies, and the leader of the children of Reuben *shall be* Elizur the son of Shedeur." 11 And his army was numbered at forty-six thousand five hundred.

12 "Those who camp next to him *shall be* the tribe of Simeon, and the leader of the children of Simeon *shall be* Shelumiel the son of Zurishaddai." 13 And his army was numbered at fifty-nine thousand three hundred.

14 "Then *comes* the tribe of Gad, and the leader of the children of Gad *shall be* Eliasaph the son of Reuel."[a] 15 And his army was numbered at forty-five thousand six hundred and fifty. 16 "All who were numbered according to their armies of the forces

2:14 [a]Spelled *Deuel* in 1:14 and 7:42

with Reuben, one hundred and fifty-one thousand four hundred and fifty—they shall be the second to break camp.

17 "And the tabernacle of meeting shall move out with the camp of the Levites in the middle of the camps; as they camp, so they shall move out, everyone in his place, by their standards.

18 "On the west side *shall be* the standard of the forces with Ephraim according to their armies, and the leader of the children of Ephraim *shall be* Elishama the son of Ammihud." 19 And his army was numbered at forty thousand five hundred.

20 "Next to him *comes* the tribe of Manasseh, and the leader of the children of Manasseh *shall be* Gamaliel the son of Pedahzur." 21 And his army was numbered at thirty-two thousand two hundred.

22 "Then *comes* the tribe of Benjamin, and the leader of the children of Benjamin *shall be* Abidan the son of Gideoni." 23 And his army was numbered at thirty-five thousand four hundred. 24 "All who were numbered according to their armies of the forces with Ephraim, one hundred and eight thousand one hundred—they shall be the third to break camp.

25 "The standard of the forces with Dan *shall be* on the north side according to their armies, and the leader of the children of Dan *shall be* Ahiezer the son of Ammishaddai." 26 And his army was numbered at sixty-two thousand seven hundred.

27 "Those who camp next to him *shall be* the tribe of Asher, and the leader of the children of Asher *shall be* Pagiel the son of Ocran." 28 And his army was numbered at forty-one thousand five hundred.

29 "Then *comes* the tribe of Naphtali, and the leader of the children of Naphtali *shall be* Ahira the son of Enan." 30 And his army was numbered at fifty-three thousand four hundred. 31 "All who were numbered of the forces with Dan, one hundred and fifty-seven thousand six hundred—they shall break camp last, with their standards."

32 These *are* the ones who were numbered of the children of Israel by their fathers' houses. All who were numbered according to their armies

of the forces *were* six hundred and three thousand five hundred and fifty. 33 But the Levites were not numbered among the children of Israel, just as the LORD commanded Moses.

34 Thus the children of Israel did according to all that the LORD commanded Moses; so they camped by their standards and so they broke camp, each one by his family, according to their fathers' houses.

3 Now these *are* the records of Aaron and Moses when the LORD spoke with Moses on Mount Sinai. 2 And these *are* the names of the sons of Aaron: Nadab, the firstborn, and Abihu, Eleazar, and Ithamar. 3 These *are* the names of the sons of Aaron, the anointed priests, whom he consecrated to minister as priests. 4 Nadab and Abihu had died before the LORD when they offered profane fire before the LORD in the Wilderness of Sinai; and they had no children. So Eleazar and Ithamar ministered as priests in the presence of Aaron their father.

5 And the LORD spoke to Moses, saying: 6 "Bring the tribe of Levi near, and present them before Aaron the priest, that they may serve him. 7 And they shall attend to his needs and the needs of the whole congregation before the tabernacle of meeting, to do the work of the tabernacle. 8 Also they shall attend to all the furnishings of the tabernacle of meeting, and to the needs of the children of Israel, to do the work of the tabernacle. 9 And you shall give the Levites to Aaron and his sons; they *are* given entirely to him[a] from among the children of Israel. 10 So you shall appoint Aaron and his sons, and they shall attend to their priesthood; but the outsider who comes near shall be put to death."

11 Then the LORD spoke to Moses, saying: 12 "Now behold, I Myself have taken the Levites from among the children of Israel instead of every firstborn who opens the womb among the children of Israel. Therefore the Levites shall be Mine, 13 because all the firstborn *are* Mine. On the day that I struck all the firstborn in the land of Egypt, I sanctified to Myself all the firstborn in Israel,

3:9 [a]Samaritan Pentateuch and Septuagint read *Me.*

Gospel Pearls

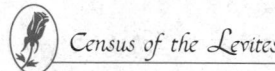

both man and beast. They shall be Mine: I *am* the LORD."

14 Then the LORD spoke to Moses in the Wilderness of Sinai, saying: 15 "Number the children of Levi by their fathers' houses, by their families; you shall number every male from a month old and above."

16 So Moses numbered them according to the word of the LORD, as he was commanded. 17 These were the sons of Levi by their names: Gershon, Kohath, and Merari. 18 And these *are* the names of the sons of Gershon by their families: Libni and Shimei. 19 And the sons of Kohath by their families: Amram, Izehar, Hebron, and Uzziel. 20 And the sons of Merari by their families: Mahli and Mushi. These *are* the families of the Levites by their fathers' houses.

21 From Gershon *came* the family of the Libnites and the family of the Shimites; these *were* the families of the Gershonites. 22 Those who were numbered, according to the number of all the males from a month old and above—of those who were numbered *there were* seven thousand five hundred. 23 The families of the Gershonites were to camp behind the tabernacle westward. 24 And the leader of the father's house of the Gershonites *was* Eliasaph the son of Lael. 25 The duties of the children of Gershon in the tabernacle of meeting *included* the tabernacle, the tent with its covering, the screen for the door of the tabernacle of meeting, 26 the screen for the door of the court, the hangings of the court which *are* around the tabernacle and the altar, and their cords, according to all the work relating to them.

27 From Kohath *came* the family of the Amramites, the family of the Izharites, the family of the Hebronites, and the family of the Uzzielites; these *were* the families of the Kohathites. 28 According to the number of all the males, from a month old and above, *there were* eight thousand six*ª* hundred keeping charge of the sanctuary. 29 The families of the children of Kohath were to camp on the south side of the tabernacle. 30 And the leader of the fathers' house of the families of the Kohathites *was* Elizaphan the son of Uzziel. 31 Their duty *included* the ark, the ta-

ble, the lampstand, the altars, the utensils of the sanctuary with which they ministered, the screen, and all the work relating to them.

32 And Eleazar the son of Aaron the priest *was to be* chief over the leaders of the Levites, *with* oversight of those who kept charge of the sanctuary.

33 From Merari *came* the family of the Mahlites and the family of the Mushites; these *were* the families of Merari. 34 And those who were numbered, according to the number of all the males from a month old and above, *were* six thousand two hundred. 35 The leader of the fathers' house of the families of Merari *was* Zuriel the son of Abihail. These *were* to camp on the north side of the tabernacle. 36 And the appointed duty of the children of Merari *included* the boards of the tabernacle, its bars, its pillars, its sockets, its utensils, all the work relating to them, 37 and the pillars of the court all around, with their sockets, their pegs, and their cords.

38 Moreover those who were to camp before the tabernacle on the east, before the tabernacle of meeting, *were* Moses, Aaron, and his sons, keeping charge of the sanctuary, to meet the needs of the children of Israel; but the outsider who came near was to be put to death. 39 All who were numbered of the Levites, whom Moses and Aaron numbered at the commandment of the LORD, by their families, all the males from a month old and above, *were* twenty-two thousand.

40 Then the LORD said to Moses: "Number all the firstborn males of the children of Israel from a month old and above, and take the number of their names. 41 And you shall take the Levites for Me—I *am* the LORD— instead of all the firstborn among the children of Israel, and the livestock of the Levites instead of all the firstborn among the livestock of the children of Israel." 42 So Moses numbered all the firstborn among the children of Israel, as the LORD commanded him. 43 And all the firstborn males, according to the number of names from a month old and above, of those who were numbered of them, were twenty-two thousand two hundred and seventy-three.

3:28 *ª*Some manuscripts of the Septuagint read *three.*

*K*eep standing. Don't die.

44 Then the LORD spoke to Moses, saying: 45 "Take the Levites instead of all the firstborn among the children of Israel, and the livestock of the Levites instead of their livestock. The Levites shall be Mine: I *am* the LORD. 46 And for the redemption of the two hundred and seventy-three of the firstborn of the children of Israel, who are more than the number of the Levites, 47 you shall take five shekels for each one individually; you shall take *them* in the currency of the shekel of the sanctuary, the shekel of twenty gerahs. 48 And you shall give the money, with which the excess number of them is redeemed, to Aaron and his sons."

49 So Moses took the redemption money from those who were over and above those who were redeemed by the Levites. 50 From the firstborn of the children of Israel he took the money, one thousand three hundred and sixty-five *shekels,* according to the shekel of the sanctuary. 51 And Moses gave their redemption money to Aaron and his sons, according to the word of the LORD, as the LORD commanded Moses.

4 Then the LORD spoke to Moses and Aaron, saying: 2 "Take a census of the sons of Kohath from among the children of Levi, by their families, by their fathers' house, 3 from thirty years old and above, even to fifty years old, all who enter the service to do the work in the tabernacle of meeting.

4 "This *is* the service of the sons of Kohath in the tabernacle of meeting, *relating to* the most holy things: 5 When the camp prepares to journey, Aaron and his sons shall come, and they shall take down the covering veil and cover the ark of the Testimony with it. 6 Then they shall put on it a covering of badger skins, and spread over *that* a cloth entirely of blue; and they shall insert its poles.

7 "On the table of showbread they shall spread a blue cloth, and put on it the dishes, the pans, the bowls, and the pitchers for pouring; and the showbread*a* shall be on it. 8 They shall spread over them a scarlet cloth, and cover the same with a covering of badger skins; and they shall insert its poles. 9 And they shall take

a blue cloth and cover the lampstand of the light, with its lamps, its wick-trimmers, its trays, and all its oil vessels, with which they service it. 10 Then they shall put it with all its utensils in a covering of badger skins, and put *it* on a carrying beam.

11 "Over the golden altar they shall spread a blue cloth, and cover it with a covering of badger skins; and they shall insert its poles. 12 Then they shall take all the utensils of service with which they minister in the sanctuary, put *them* in a blue cloth, cover them with a covering of badger skins, and put *them* on a carrying beam. 13 Also they shall take away the ashes from the altar, and spread a purple cloth over it. 14 They shall put on it all its implements with which they minister there—the firepans, the forks, the shovels, the basins, and all the utensils of the altar—and they shall spread on it a covering of badger skins, and insert its poles. 15 And when Aaron and his sons have finished covering the sanctuary and all the furnishings of the sanctuary, when the camp is set to go, then the sons of Kohath shall come to carry *them;* but they shall not touch any holy thing, lest they die.

"These *are* the things in the tabernacle of meeting which the sons of Kohath are to carry.

16 "The appointed duty of Eleazar the son of Aaron the priest *is* the oil for the light, the sweet incense, the daily grain offering, the anointing oil, the oversight of all the tabernacle, of all that *is* in it, with the sanctuary and its furnishings."

17 Then the LORD spoke to Moses and Aaron, saying: 18 "Do not cut off the tribe of the families of the Kohathites from among the Levites; 19 but do this in regard to them, that they may live and not die when they approach the most holy things: Aaron and his sons shall go in and appoint each of them to his service and his task. 20 But they shall not go in to watch while the holy things are being covered, lest they die."

21 Then the LORD spoke to Moses, saying: 22 "Also take a census of the sons of Gershon, by their fathers' house, by their families. 23 From thirty years old and above, even to fifty years old, you shall number

4:7 *a*Literally the continual bread

Gospel
Pearls

them, all who enter to perform the service, to do the work in the tabernacle of meeting. 24 This *is* the service of the families of the Gershonites, in serving and carrying: 25 They shall carry the curtains of the tabernacle and the tabernacle of meeting *with* its covering, the covering of badger skins that *is* on it, the screen for the door of the tabernacle of meeting, 26 the screen for the door of the gate of the court, the hangings of the court which *are* around the tabernacle and altar, and their cords, all the furnishings for their service and all that is made for these things: so shall they serve.

27 "Aaron and his sons shall assign all the service of the sons of the Gershonites, all their tasks and all their service. And you shall appoint to them all their tasks as their duty. 28 This *is* the service of the families of the sons of Gershon in the tabernacle of meeting. And their duties *shall be* under the authority*ᵃ* of Ithamar the son of Aaron the priest.

29 "As for the sons of Merari, you shall number them by their families and by their fathers' house. 30 From thirty years old and above, even to fifty years old, you shall number them, everyone who enters the service to do the work of the tabernacle of meeting. 31 And this *is* what they must carry as all their service for the tabernacle of meeting: the boards of the tabernacle, its bars, its pillars, its sockets, 32 and the pillars around the court with their sockets, pegs, and cords, with all their furnishings and all their service; and you shall assign *to each man* by name the items he must carry. 33 This *is* the service of the families of the sons of Merari, as all their service for the tabernacle of meeting, under the authority*ᵃ* of Ithamar the son of Aaron the priest."

34 And Moses, Aaron, and the leaders of the congregation numbered the sons of the Kohathites by their families and by their fathers' house, 35 from thirty years old and above, even to fifty years old, everyone who entered the service for work in the tabernacle of meeting; 36 and those who were numbered by their families were two thousand seven hundred and fifty. 37 These *were* the ones who

were numbered of the families of the Kohathites, all who might serve in the tabernacle of meeting, whom Moses and Aaron numbered according to the commandment of the LORD by the hand of Moses.

38 And those who were numbered of the sons of Gershon, by their families and by their fathers' house, 39 from thirty years old and above, even to fifty years old, everyone who entered the service for work in the tabernacle of meeting— 40 those who were numbered by their families, by their fathers' house, were two thousand six hundred and thirty. 41 These *are* the ones who were numbered of the families of the sons of Gershon, of all who might serve in the tabernacle of meeting, whom Moses and Aaron numbered according to the commandment of the LORD.

42 Those of the families of the sons of Merari who were numbered, by their families, by their fathers' house, 43 from thirty years old and above, even to fifty years old, everyone who entered the service for work in the tabernacle of meeting— 44 those who were numbered by their families were three thousand two hundred. 45 These *are* the ones who were numbered of the families of the sons of Merari, whom Moses and Aaron numbered according to the word of the LORD by the hand of Moses.

46 All who were numbered of the Levites, whom Moses, Aaron, and the leaders of Israel numbered, by their families and by their fathers' houses, 47 from thirty years old and above, even to fifty years old, everyone who came to do the work of service and the work of bearing burdens in the tabernacle of meeting— 48 those who were numbered were eight thousand five hundred and eighty.

49 According to the commandment of the LORD they were numbered by the hand of Moses, each according to his service and according to his task; thus were they numbered by him, as the LORD commanded Moses.

5 And the LORD spoke to Moses, saying: 2 "Command the children of Israel that they put out of the camp every leper, everyone who has a discharge, and whoever becomes de-

4:28 *ᵃ*Literally *hand*   4:33 *ᵃ*Literally *hand*

God is about to give you another seed to birth. He's about to open up the windows of heaven to you and pour you out a blessing that will be so great you won't even have room enough to receive it all.

filed by a corpse. 3 You shall put out both male and female; you shall put them outside the camp, that they may not defile their camps in the midst of which I dwell." 4 And the children of Israel did so, and put them outside the camp; as the LORD spoke to Moses, so the children of Israel did.

5 Then the LORD spoke to Moses, saying, 6 "Speak to the children of Israel: 'When a man or woman commits any sin that men commit in unfaithfulness against the LORD, and that person is guilty, 7 then he shall confess the sin which he has committed. He shall make restitution for his trespass in full, plus one-fifth of it, and give *it* to the one he has wronged. 8 But if the man has no relative to whom restitution may be made for the wrong, the restitution for the wrong *must* go to the LORD for the priest, in addition to the ram of the atonement with which atonement is made for him. 9 Every offering of all the holy things of the children of Israel, which they bring to the priest, shall be his. 10 And every man's holy things shall be his; whatever any man gives the priest shall be his.' "

11 And the LORD spoke to Moses, saying, 12 "Speak to the children of Israel, and say to them: 'If any man's wife goes astray and behaves unfaithfully toward him, 13 and a man lies with her carnally, and it is hidden from the eyes of her husband, and it is concealed that she has defiled herself, and *there was* no witness against her, nor was she caught— 14 if the spirit of jealousy comes upon him and he becomes jealous of his wife, who has defiled herself; or if the spirit of jealousy comes upon him and he becomes jealous of his wife, although she has not defiled herself— 15 then the man shall bring his wife to the priest. He shall bring the offering required for her, one-tenth of an ephah of barley meal; he shall pour no oil on it and put no frankincense on it, because it *is* a grain offering of jealousy, an offering for remembering, for bringing iniquity to remembrance.

16 'And the priest shall bring her near, and set her before the LORD. 17 The priest shall take holy water in an earthen vessel, and take some of the dust that is on the floor of the tabernacle and put *it* into the water.

18 Then the priest shall stand the woman before the LORD, uncover the woman's head, and put the offering for remembering in her hands, which *is* the grain offering of jealousy. And the priest shall have in his hand the bitter water that brings a curse. 19 And the priest shall put her under oath, and say to the woman, "If no man has lain with you, and if you have not gone astray to uncleanness *while* under your husband's *authority,* be free from this bitter water that brings a curse. 20 But if you have gone astray *while* under your husband's *authority,* and if you have defiled yourself and some man other than your husband has lain with you"— 21 then the priest shall put the woman under the oath of the curse, and he shall say to the woman—"the LORD make you a curse and an oath among your people, when the LORD makes your thigh rot and your belly swell; 22 and may this water that causes the curse go into your stomach, and make *your* belly swell and *your* thigh rot."

'Then the woman shall say, "Amen, so be it."

23 'Then the priest shall write these curses in a book, and he shall scrape *them* off into the bitter water. 24 And he shall make the woman drink the bitter water that brings a curse, and the water that brings the curse shall enter her *to become* bitter. 25 Then the priest shall take the grain offering of jealousy from the woman's hand, shall wave the offering before the LORD, and bring it to the altar; 26 and the priest shall take a handful of the offering, as its memorial portion, burn *it* on the altar, and afterward make the woman drink the water. 27 When he has made her drink the water, then it shall be, if she has defiled herself and behaved unfaithfully toward her husband, that the water that brings a curse will enter her *and become* bitter, and her belly will swell, her thigh will rot, and the woman will become a curse among her people. 28 But if the woman has not defiled herself, and is clean, then she shall be free and may conceive children.

29 'This *is* the law of jealousy, when a wife, *while* under her husband's *authority,* goes astray and defiles herself, 30 or when the spirit of jealousy comes upon a man, and he becomes

Gospel Pearls

jealous of his wife; then he shall stand the woman before the LORD, and the priest shall execute all this law upon her. 31 Then the man shall be free from iniquity, but that woman shall bear her guilt.' "

6 Then the LORD spoke to Moses, saying, 2 "Speak to the children of Israel, and say to them: 'When either a man or woman consecrates an offering to take the vow of a Nazirite, to separate himself to the LORD, 3 he shall separate himself from wine and *similar* drink; he shall drink neither vinegar made from wine nor vinegar made from *similar* drink; neither shall he drink any grape juice, nor eat fresh grapes or raisins. 4 All the days of his separation he shall eat nothing that is produced by the grapevine, from seed to skin.

5 'All the days of the vow of his separation no razor shall come upon his head; until the days are fulfilled for which he separated himself to the LORD, he shall be holy. *Then* he shall let the locks of the hair of his head grow. 6 All the days that he separates himself to the LORD he shall not go near a dead body. 7 He shall not make himself unclean even for his father or his mother, for his brother or his sister, when they die, because his separation to God *is* on his head. 8 All the days of his separation he shall be holy to the LORD.

9 'And if anyone dies very suddenly beside him, and he defiles his consecrated head, then he shall shave his head on the day of his cleansing; on the seventh day he shall shave it. 10 Then on the eighth day he shall bring two turtledoves or two young pigeons to the priest, to the door of the tabernacle of meeting; 11 and the priest shall offer one as a sin offering and *the* other as a burnt offering, and make atonement for him, because he sinned in regard to the corpse; and he shall sanctify his head that same day. 12 He shall consecrate to the LORD the days of his separation, and bring a male lamb in its first year as a trespass offering; but the former days shall be lost, because his separation was defiled.

13 'Now this *is* the law of the Nazirite: When the days of his separation are fulfilled, he shall be brought to the door of the tabernacle of meeting. 14 And he shall present his offering to the LORD: one male lamb in its first year without blemish as a burnt offering, one ewe lamb in its first year without blemish as a sin offering, one ram without blemish as a peace offering, 15 a basket of unleavened bread, cakes of fine flour mixed with oil, unleavened wafers anointed with oil, and their grain offering with their drink offerings.

16 'Then the priest shall bring *them* before the LORD and offer his sin offering and his burnt offering; 17 and he shall offer the ram as a sacrifice of a peace offering to the LORD, with the basket of unleavened bread; the priest shall also offer its grain offering and its drink offering. 18 Then the Nazirite shall shave his consecrated head *at* the door of the tabernacle of meeting, and shall take the hair from his consecrated head and put *it* on the fire which is under the sacrifice of the peace offering.

19 'And the priest shall take the boiled shoulder of the ram, one unleavened cake from the basket, and one unleavened wafer, and put *them* upon the hands of the Nazirite after he has shaved his consecrated *hair,* 20 and the priest shall wave them as a wave offering before the LORD; they *are* holy for the priest, together with the breast of the wave offering and the thigh of the heave offering. After that the Nazirite may drink wine.'

21 "This is the law of the Nazirite who vows to the LORD the offering for his separation, and besides that, whatever else his hand is able to provide; according to the vow which he takes, so he must do according to the law of his separation."

22 And the LORD spoke to Moses, saying: 23 "Speak to Aaron and his sons, saying, 'This is the way you shall bless the children of Israel. Say to them:

24 "The LORD bless you and keep you;
25 The LORD make His face shine upon you,
And be gracious to you;
26 The LORD lift up His countenance upon you,
And give you peace." '

27 "So they shall put My name on the children of Israel, and I will bless them."

When your trouble is great enough and your desire is strong enough, you will feel that you have nothing to lose and everything to gain by pouring out all your passion to God.

7 Now it came to pass, when Moses had finished setting up the tabernacle, that he anointed it and consecrated it and all its furnishings, and the altar and all its utensils; so he anointed them and consecrated them. 2 Then the leaders of Israel, the heads of their fathers' houses, who *were* the leaders of the tribes and over those who were numbered, made an offering. 3 And they brought their offering before the LORD, six covered carts and twelve oxen, a cart for *every* two of the leaders, and for each one an ox; and they presented them before the tabernacle.

4 Then the LORD spoke to Moses, saying, 5 "Accept *these* from them, that they may be used in doing the work of the tabernacle of meeting; and you shall give them to the Levites, *to* every man according to his service." 6 So Moses took the carts and the oxen, and gave them to the Levites. 7 Two carts and four oxen he gave to the sons of Gershon, according to their service; 8 and four carts and eight oxen he gave to the sons of Merari, according to their service, under the authority[a] of Ithamar the son of Aaron the priest. 9 But to the sons of Kohath he gave none, because theirs *was* the service of the holy things, *which* they carried on their shoulders.

10 Now the leaders offered the dedication *offering* for the altar when it was anointed; so the leaders offered their offering before the altar. 11 For the LORD said to Moses, "They shall offer their offering, one leader each day, for the dedication of the altar."

12 And the one who offered his offering on the first day *was* Nahshon the son of Amminadab, from the tribe of Judah. 13 His offering *was* one silver platter, the weight of which *was* one hundred and thirty *shekels*, and one silver bowl of seventy shekels, according to the shekel of the sanctuary, both of them full of fine flour mixed with oil as a grain offering; 14 one gold pan of ten *shekels*, full of incense; 15 one young bull, one ram, and one male lamb in its first year, as a burnt offering; 16 one kid of the goats as a sin offering; 17 and for the sacrifice of peace offerings: two oxen, five rams, five

male goats, and five male lambs in their first year. This *was* the offering of Nahshon the son of Amminadab.

18 On the second day Nethanel the son of Zuar, leader of Issachar, presented *an offering*. 19 *For* his offering he offered one silver platter, the weight of which *was* one hundred and thirty *shekels*, and one silver bowl of seventy shekels, according to the shekel of the sanctuary, both of them full of fine flour mixed with oil as a grain offering; 20 one gold pan of ten *shekels*, full of incense; 21 one young bull, one ram, and one male lamb in its first year, as a burnt offering; 22 one kid of the goats as a sin offering; 23 and as the sacrifice of peace offerings: two oxen, five rams, five male goats, and five male lambs in their first year. This *was* the offering of Nethanel the son of Zuar.

24 On the third day Eliab the son of Helon, leader of the children of Zebulun, *presented an offering*. 25 His offering *was* one silver platter, the weight of which *was* one hundred and thirty *shekels*, and one silver bowl of seventy shekels, according to the shekel of the sanctuary, both of them full of fine flour mixed with oil as a grain offering; 26 one gold pan of ten *shekels*, full of incense; 27 one young bull, one ram, and one male lamb in its first year, as a burnt offering; 28 one kid of the goats as a sin offering; 29 and for the sacrifice of peace offerings: two oxen, five rams, five male goats, and five male lambs in their first year. This *was* the offering of Eliab the son of Helon.

30 On the fourth day Elizur the son of Shedeur, leader of the children of Reuben, *presented an offering*. 31 His offering *was* one silver platter, the weight of which *was* one hundred and thirty *shekels*, and one silver bowl of seventy shekels, according to the shekel of the sanctuary, both of them full of fine flour mixed with oil as a grain offering; 32 one gold pan of ten *shekels*, full of incense; 33 one young bull, one ram, and one male lamb in its first year, as a burnt offering; 34 one kid of the goats as a sin offering; 35 and as the sacrifice of peace offerings: two oxen, five rams, five male goats, and five male lambs in their first year. This *was* the offering of Elizur the son of Shedeur.

7:8 [a]Literally *hand*

Gospel Pearls

36 On the fifth day Shelumiel the son of Zurishaddai, leader of the children of Simeon, *presented an offering.* 37 His offering *was* one silver platter, the weight of which *was* one hundred and thirty *shekels,* and one silver bowl of seventy shekels, according to the shekel of the sanctuary, both of them full of fine flour mixed with oil as a grain offering; 38 one gold pan of ten *shekels,* full of incense; 39 one young bull, one ram, and one male lamb in its first year, as a burnt offering; 40 one kid of the goats as a sin offering; 41 and as the sacrifice of peace offerings: two oxen, five rams, five male goats, and five male lambs in their first year. This *was* the offering of Shelumiel the son of Zurishaddai.

42 On the sixth day Eliasaph the son of Deuel,[a] leader of the children of Gad, *presented an offering.* 43 His offering *was* one silver platter, the weight of which *was* one hundred and thirty *shekels,* and one silver bowl of seventy shekels, according to the shekel of the sanctuary, both of them full of fine flour mixed with oil as a grain offering; 44 one gold pan of ten *shekels,* full of incense; 45 one young bull, one ram, and one male lamb in its first year, as a burnt offering; 46 one kid of the goats as a sin offering; 47 and as the sacrifice of peace offerings: two oxen, five rams, five male goats, and five male lambs in their first year. This *was* the offering of Eliasaph the son of Deuel.

48 On the seventh day Elishama the son of Ammihud, leader of the children of Ephraim, *presented an offering.* 49 His offering *was* one silver platter, the weight of which *was* one hundred and thirty *shekels,* and one silver bowl of seventy shekels, according to the shekel of the sanctuary, both of them full of fine flour mixed with oil as a grain offering; 50 one gold pan of ten *shekels,* full of incense; 51 one young bull, one ram, and one male lamb in its first year, as a burnt offering; 52 one kid of the goats as a sin offering; 53 and as the sacrifice of peace offerings: two oxen, five rams, five male goats, and five male lambs in their first year. This *was* the offering of Elishama the son of Ammihud.

54 On the eighth day Gamaliel the son of Pedahzur, leader of the children of Manasseh, *presented an offering.* 55 His offering *was* one silver platter, the weight of which *was* one hundred and thirty *shekels,* and one silver bowl of seventy shekels, according to the shekel of the sanctuary, both of them full of fine flour mixed with oil as a grain offering; 56 one gold pan of ten *shekels,* full of incense; 57 one young bull, one ram, and one male lamb in its first year, as a burnt offering; 58 one kid of the goats as a sin offering; 59 and as the sacrifice of peace offerings: two oxen, five rams, five male goats, and five male lambs in their first year. This *was* the offering of Gamaliel the son of Pedahzur.

60 On the ninth day Abidan the son of Gideoni, leader of the children of Benjamin, *presented an offering.* 61 His offering *was* one silver platter, the weight of which *was* one hundred and thirty *shekels,* and one silver bowl of seventy shekels, according to the shekel of the sanctuary, both of them full of fine flour mixed with oil as a grain offering; 62 one gold pan of ten *shekels,* full of incense; 63 one young bull, one ram, and one male lamb in its first year, as a burnt offering; 64 one kid of the goats as a sin offering; 65 and as the sacrifice of peace offerings: two oxen, five rams, five male goats, and five male lambs in their first year. This *was* the offering of Abidan the son of Gideoni.

66 On the tenth day Ahiezer the son of Ammishaddai, leader of the children of Dan, *presented an offering.* 67 His offering *was* one silver platter, the weight of which *was* one hundred and thirty *shekels,* and one silver bowl of seventy shekels, according to the shekel of the sanctuary, both of them full of fine flour mixed with oil as a grain offering; 68 one gold pan of ten *shekels,* full of incense; 69 one young bull, one ram, and one male lamb in its first year, as a burnt offering; 70 one kid of the goats as a sin offering; 71 and as the sacrifice of peace offerings: two oxen, five rams, five male goats, and five male lambs in their first year. This *was* the offering of Ahiezer the son of Ammishaddai.

72 On the eleventh day Pagiel the son of Ocran, leader of the children

7:42 [a]Spelled *Reuel* in 2:14

God wants women who will humble themselves before Him, who will come to Him, who will cry out to Him—without any thought to what other people think or say.

of Asher, *presented an offering.*
73 His offering *was* one silver platter, the weight of which *was* one hundred and thirty *shekels,* and one silver bowl of seventy shekels, according to the shekel of the sanctuary, both of them full of fine flour mixed with oil as a grain offering; 74 one gold pan of ten *shekels,* full of incense; 75 one young bull, one ram, and one male lamb in its first year, as a burnt offering; 76 one kid of the goats as a sin offering; 77 and as the sacrifice of peace offerings: two oxen, five rams, five male goats, and five male lambs in their first year. This *was* the offering of Pagiel the son of Ocran.

78 On the twelfth day Ahira the son of Enan, leader of the children of Naphtali, *presented an offering.*
79 His offering *was* one silver platter, the weight of which *was* one hundred and thirty *shekels,* and one silver bowl of seventy shekels, according to the shekel of the sanctuary, both of them full of fine flour mixed with oil as a grain offering; 80 one gold pan of ten *shekels,* full of incense; 81 one young bull, one ram, and one male lamb in its first year, as a burnt offering; 82 one kid of the goats as a sin offering; 83 and as the sacrifice of peace offerings: two oxen, five rams, five male goats, and five male lambs in their first year. This *was* the offering of Ahira the son of Enan.

84 This *was* the dedication *offering* for the altar from the leaders of Israel, when it was anointed: twelve silver platters, twelve silver bowls, and twelve gold pans. 85 Each silver platter *weighed* one hundred and thirty *shekels* and each bowl seventy *shekels.* All the silver of the vessels *weighed* two thousand four hundred *shekels,* according to the shekel of the sanctuary. 86 The twelve gold pans full of incense *weighed* ten *shekels* apiece, according to the shekel of the sanctuary; all the gold of the pans *weighed* one hundred and twenty *shekels.* 87 All the oxen for the burnt offering *were* twelve young bulls, the rams twelve, the male lambs in their first year twelve, with their grain offering, and the kids of the goats as a sin offering twelve. 88 And all the oxen for the sacrifice of peace offerings *were* twenty-four bulls, the rams sixty, the male goats sixty, and the lambs in their first year sixty. This *was* the dedication *offer-*

ing for the altar after it was anointed.
89 Now when Moses went into the tabernacle of meeting to speak with Him, he heard the voice of One speaking to him from above the mercy seat that *was* on the ark of the Testimony, from between the two cherubim; thus He spoke to him.

8 And the Lord spoke to Moses, saying: 2 "Speak to Aaron, and say to him, 'When you arrange the lamps, the seven lamps shall give light in front of the lampstand.' " 3 And Aaron did so; he arranged the lamps to face toward the front of the lampstand, as the Lord commanded Moses. 4 Now this workmanship of the lampstand *was* hammered gold; from its shaft to its flowers it *was* hammered work. According to the pattern which the Lord had shown Moses, so he made the lampstand.

5 Then the Lord spoke to Moses, saying: 6 "Take the Levites from among the children of Israel and cleanse them *ceremonially.* 7 Thus you shall do to them to cleanse them: Sprinkle water of purification on them, and let them shave all their body, and let them wash their clothes, and *so* make themselves clean. 8 Then let them take a young bull with its grain offering of fine flour mixed with oil, and you shall take another young bull as a sin offering. 9 And you shall bring the Levites before the tabernacle of meeting, and you shall gather together the whole congregation of the children of Israel. 10 So you shall bring the Levites before the Lord, and the children of Israel shall lay their hands on the Levites; 11 and Aaron shall offer the Levites before the Lord *like* a wave offering from the children of Israel, that they may perform the work of the Lord. 12 Then the Levites shall lay their hands on the heads of the young bulls, and you shall offer one as a sin offering and the other as a burnt offering to the Lord, to make atonement for the Levites.

13 "And you shall stand the Levites before Aaron and his sons, and then offer them *like* a wave offering to the Lord. 14 Thus you shall separate the Levites from among the children of Israel, and the Levites shall be Mine. 15 After that the Levites shall go in to service the tabernacle of meeting. So you shall cleanse them and offer

Gospel Pearls

them *like* a wave offering. 16 For they *are* wholly given to Me from among the children of Israel; I have taken them for Myself instead of all who open the womb, the firstborn of all the children of Israel. 17 For all the firstborn among the children of Israel *are* Mine, *both* man and beast; on the day that I struck all the firstborn in the land of Egypt I sanctified them to Myself. 18 I have taken the Levites instead of all the firstborn of the children of Israel. 19 And I have given the Levites as a gift to Aaron and his sons from among the children of Israel, to do the work for the children of Israel in the tabernacle of meeting, and to make atonement for the children of Israel, that there be no plague among the children of Israel when the children of Israel come near the sanctuary."

20 Thus Moses and Aaron and all the congregation of the children of Israel did to the Levites; according to all that the LORD commanded Moses concerning the Levites, so the children of Israel did to them. 21 And the Levites purified themselves and washed their clothes; then Aaron presented them *like* a wave offering before the LORD, and Aaron made atonement for them to cleanse them. 22 After that the Levites went in to do their work in the tabernacle of meeting before Aaron and his sons; as the LORD commanded Moses concerning the Levites, so they did to them.

23 Then the LORD spoke to Moses, saying, 24 "This *is* what *pertains* to the Levites: From twenty-five years old and above one may enter to perform service in the work of the tabernacle of meeting; 25 and at the age of fifty years they must cease performing this work, and shall work no more. 26 They may minister with their brethren in the tabernacle of meeting, to attend to needs, but they *themselves* shall do no work. Thus you shall do to the Levites regarding their duties."

9 Now the LORD spoke to Moses in the Wilderness of Sinai, in the first month of the second year after they had come out of the land of Egypt, saying: 2 "Let the children of Israel keep the Passover at its appointed time. 3 On the fourteenth day of this month, at twilight, you shall keep it at its appointed time. According to all its rites and ceremonies you shall keep it." 4 So Moses told the children of Israel that they should keep the Passover. 5 And they kept the Passover on the fourteenth day of the first month, at twilight, in the Wilderness of Sinai; according to all that the LORD commanded Moses, so the children of Israel did.

6 Now there were *certain* men who were defiled by a human corpse, so that they could not keep the Passover on that day; and they came before Moses and Aaron that day. 7 And those men said to him, "We *became* defiled by a human corpse. Why are we kept from presenting the offering of the LORD at its appointed time among the children of Israel?"

8 And Moses said to them, "Stand still, that I may hear what the LORD will command concerning you."

9 Then the LORD spoke to Moses, saying, 10 "Speak to the children of Israel, saying: 'If anyone of you or your posterity is unclean because of a corpse, or *is* far away on a journey, he may still keep the LORD's Passover. 11 On the fourteenth day of the second month, at twilight, they may keep it. They shall eat it with unleavened bread and bitter herbs. 12 They shall leave none of it until morning, nor break one of its bones. According to all the ordinances of the Passover they shall keep it. 13 But the man who *is* clean and is not on a journey, and ceases to keep the Passover, that same person shall be cut off from among his people, because he did not bring the offering of the LORD at its appointed time; that man shall bear his sin.

14 'And if a stranger dwells among you, and would keep the LORD's Passover, he must do so according to the rite of the Passover and according to its ceremony; you shall have one ordinance, both for the stranger and the native of the land.' "

15 Now on the day that the tabernacle was raised up, the cloud covered the tabernacle, the tent of the Testimony; from evening until morning it was above the tabernacle like the appearance of fire. 16 So it was always: the cloud covered it *by day,* and the appearance of fire by night. 17 Whenever the cloud was taken up from above the tabernacle, after that the children of Israel would journey;

*M*ake a decision that you are going to allow yourself to touch God with intensity. Don't hold anything back. Cry for what you want from Him as if your very life depends upon it.

Soul Secrets
for times
in the wilderness

*L*ord, You are the God of my desert and all my dry places.
I'm stuck here again in the wilderness—helpless, hopeless, friendless—with no home for my heart. It's a
desperate, desolate place. I have visited this wide wasteland
before, feeling trapped between where I am and where I want
to be. Like the children of Israel, I am wandering and wondering, *Will I ever get out of here? Is there even a place beyond
this pain?*

It's not that I don't know how to put one foot in front of
the other. It's that I want to be where I am not. I need the God
of fire by night and cloud by day. I need direction from the
Maker of the stars. There's a Promised Land before me—a
place of provision, a place of plenty. But how do I exchange
my emptiness for Your abundance?

I long for the days of wilderness-walking to end. I want to
go forward with You. Lord, lead me home.

and in the place where the cloud settled, there the children of Israel would pitch their tents. 18 At the command of the LORD the children of Israel would journey, and at the command of the LORD they would camp; as long as the cloud stayed above the tabernacle they remained encamped. 19 Even when the cloud continued long, many days above the tabernacle, the children of Israel kept the charge of the LORD and did not journey. 20 So it was, when the cloud was above the tabernacle a few days: according to the command of the LORD they would remain encamped, and according to the command of the LORD they would journey. 21 So it was, when the cloud remained only from evening until morning: when the cloud was taken up in the morning, then they would journey; whether by day or by night, whenever the cloud was taken up, they would journey. 22 *Whether it was* two days, a month, or a year that the cloud remained above the tabernacle, the children of Israel would remain encamped and not journey; but when it was taken up, they would journey. 23 At the command of the LORD they remained encamped, and at the command of the LORD they journeyed; they kept the charge of the LORD, at the command of the LORD by the hand of Moses.

10 And the LORD spoke to Moses, saying: 2 "Make two silver trumpets for yourself; you shall make them of hammered work; you shall use them for calling the congregation and for directing the movement of the camps. 3 When they blow both of them, all the congregation shall gather before you at the door of the tabernacle of meeting. 4 But if they blow *only* one, then the leaders, the heads of the divisions of Israel, shall gather to you. 5 When you sound the advance, the camps that lie on the east side shall then begin their journey. 6 When you sound the advance the second time, then the camps that lie on the south side shall begin their journey; they shall sound the call for them to begin their journeys. 7 And when the assembly is to be gathered together, you shall blow, but not sound the advance. 8 The sons of Aaron, the priests, shall blow the trumpets; and these shall be to you as an ordinance forever throughout your generations.

9 "When you go to war in your land against the enemy who oppresses you, then you shall sound an alarm with the trumpets, and you will be remembered before the LORD your God, and you will be saved from your enemies. 10 Also in the day of your gladness, in your appointed feasts, and at the beginning of your months, you shall blow the trumpets over your burnt offerings and over the sacrifices of your peace offerings; and they shall be a memorial for you before your God: I *am* the LORD your God."

11 Now it came to pass on the twentieth *day* of the second month, in the second year, that the cloud was taken up from above the tabernacle of the Testimony. 12 And the children of Israel set out from the Wilderness of Sinai on their journeys; then the cloud settled down in the Wilderness of Paran. 13 So they started out for the first time according to the command of the LORD by the hand of Moses.

14 The standard of the camp of the children of Judah set out first according to their armies; over their army was Nahshon the son of Amminadab. 15 Over the army of the tribe of the children of Issachar *was* Nethanel the son of Zuar. 16 And over the army of the tribe of the children of Zebulun *was* Eliab the son of Helon.

17 Then the tabernacle was taken down; and the sons of Gershon and the sons of Merari set out, carrying the tabernacle.

18 And the standard of the camp of Reuben set out according to their armies; over their army *was* Elizur the son of Shedeur. 19 Over the army of the tribe of the children of Simeon *was* Shelumiel the son of Zurishaddai. 20 And over the army of the tribe of the children of Gad *was* Eliasaph the son of Deuel.

21 Then the Kohathites set out, carrying the holy things. (The tabernacle would be prepared for their arrival.)

22 And the standard of the camp of the children of Ephraim set out according to their armies; over their army *was* Elishama the son of Ammihud. 23 Over the army of the tribe of the children of Manasseh *was* Gamaliel the son of Pedahzur.

Rachel said to Jacob, "Give me a child, lest I die." She wanted something so much that if she couldn't have it and live, she would rather die. Go to God with that same attitude.

24 And over the army of the tribe of the children of Benjamin *was* Abidan the son of Gideoni.

25 Then the standard of the camp of the children of Dan (the rear guard of all the camps) set out according to their armies; over their army *was* Ahiezer the son of Ammishaddai. 26 Over the army of the tribe of the children of Asher *was* Pagiel the son of Ocran. 27 And over the army of the tribe of the children of Naphtali *was* Ahira the son of Enan.

28 Thus *was* the order of march of the children of Israel, according to their armies, when they began their journey.

29 Now Moses said to Hobab the son of Reuel*ᵃ* the Midianite, Moses' father-in-law, "We are setting out for the place of which the LORD said, 'I will give it to you.' Come with us, and we will treat you well; for the LORD has promised good things to Israel."

30 And he said to him, "I will not go, but I will depart to my *own* land and to my relatives."

31 So *Moses* said, "Please do not leave, inasmuch as you know how we are to camp in the wilderness, and you can be our eyes. 32 And it shall be, if you go with us—indeed it shall be—that whatever good the LORD will do to us, the same we will do to you."

33 So they departed from the mountain of the LORD on a journey of three days; and the ark of the covenant of the LORD went before them for the three days' journey, to search out a resting place for them. 34 And the cloud of the LORD *was* above them by day when they went out from the camp.

35 So it was, whenever the ark set out, that Moses said:

"Rise up, O LORD!
Let Your enemies be scattered,
And let those who hate You flee before You."

36 And when it rested, he said:

"Return, O LORD,
To the many thousands of Israel."

11 Now *when* the people complained, it displeased the LORD; for the LORD heard *it*, and His anger

was aroused. So the fire of the LORD burned among them, and consumed *some* in the outskirts of the camp. 2 Then the people cried out to Moses, and when Moses prayed to the LORD, the fire was quenched. 3 So he called the name of the place Taberah,*ᵃ* because the fire of the LORD had burned among them.

4 Now the mixed multitude who were among them yielded to intense craving; so the children of Israel also wept again and said: "Who will give us meat to eat? 5 We remember the fish which we ate freely in Egypt, the cucumbers, the melons, the leeks, the onions, and the garlic; 6 but now our whole being *is* dried up; *there is* nothing at all except this manna *before* our eyes!"

7 Now the manna *was* like coriander seed, and its color like the color of bdellium. 8 The people went about and gathered *it,* ground *it* on millstones or beat *it* in the mortar, cooked *it* in pans, and made cakes of it; and its taste was like the taste of pastry prepared with oil. 9 And when the dew fell on the camp in the night, the manna fell on it.

10 Then Moses heard the people weeping throughout their families, everyone at the door of his tent; and the anger of the LORD was greatly aroused; Moses also was displeased. 11 So Moses said to the LORD, "Why have You afflicted Your servant? And why have I not found favor in Your sight, that You have laid the burden of all these people on me? 12 Did I conceive all these people? Did I beget them, that You should say to me, 'Carry them in your bosom, as a guardian carries a nursing child,' to the land which You swore to their fathers? 13 Where am I to get meat to give to all these people? For they weep all over me, saying, 'Give us meat, that we may eat.' 14 I am not able to bear all these people alone, because the burden *is* too heavy for me. 15 If You treat me like this, please kill me here and now—if I have found favor in Your sight—and do not let me see my wretchedness!"

16 So the LORD said to Moses: "Gather to Me seventy men of the elders of Israel, whom you know to be the elders of the people and officers over them; bring them to the tab-

10:29 *ᵃ*Septuagint reads *Raguel* (compare Exodus 2:18).   11:3 *ᵃ*Literally *Burning*

Gospel Pearls

ernacle of meeting, that they may stand there with you. 17 Then I will come down and talk with you there. I will take of the Spirit that *is* upon you and will put *the same* upon them; and they shall bear the burden of the people with you, that you may not bear *it* yourself alone. 18 Then you shall say to the people, 'Consecrate yourselves for tomorrow, and you shall eat meat; for you have wept in the hearing of the LORD, saying, "Who will give us meat to eat? For *it was* well with us in Egypt." Therefore the LORD will give you meat, and you shall eat. 19 You shall eat, not one day, nor two days, nor five days, nor ten days, nor twenty days, 20 but *for* a whole month, until it comes out of your nostrils and becomes loathsome to you, because you have despised the LORD who is among you, and have wept before Him, saying, "Why did we ever come up out of Egypt?" ' "

21 And Moses said, "The people whom I *am* among *are* six hundred thousand men on foot; yet You have said, 'I will give them meat, that they may eat *for* a whole month.' 22 Shall flocks and herds be slaughtered for them, to provide enough for them? Or shall all the fish of the sea be gathered together for them, to provide enough for them?"

23 And the LORD said to Moses, "Has the LORD's arm been shortened? Now you shall see whether what I say will happen to you or not."

24 So Moses went out and told the people the words of the LORD, and he gathered the seventy men of the elders of the people and placed them around the tabernacle. 25 Then the LORD came down in the cloud, and spoke to him, and took of the Spirit that *was* upon him, and placed *the same* upon the seventy elders; and it happened, when the Spirit rested upon them, that they prophesied, although they never did *so* again.[a]

26 But two men had remained in the camp: the name of one *was* Eldad, and the name of the other Medad. And the Spirit rested upon them. Now they *were* among those listed, but who had not gone out to the tabernacle; yet they prophesied in the camp. 27 And a young man ran and told Moses, and said, "Eldad and Me-

dad are prophesying in the camp."

28 So Joshua the son of Nun, Moses' assistant, *one* of his choice men, answered and said, "Moses my lord, forbid them!"

29 Then Moses said to him, "Are you zealous for my sake? Oh, that all the LORD's people were prophets *and* that the LORD would put His Spirit upon them!" 30 And Moses returned to the camp, he and the elders of Israel.

31 Now a wind went out from the LORD, and it brought quail from the sea and left *them* fluttering near the camp, about a day's journey on this side and about a day's journey on the other side, all around the camp, and about two cubits above the surface of the ground. 32 And the people stayed up all that day, all night, and all the next day, and gathered the quail (he who gathered least gathered ten homers); and they spread *them* out for themselves all around the camp. 33 But while the meat *was* still between their teeth, before it was chewed, the wrath of the LORD was aroused against the people, and the LORD struck the people with a very great plague. 34 So he called the name of that place Kibroth Hattaavah,[a] because there they buried the people who had yielded to craving.

35 From Kibroth Hattaavah the people moved to Hazeroth, and camped at Hazeroth.

12 Then Miriam and Aaron spoke against Moses because of the Ethiopian woman whom he had married; for he had married an Ethiopian woman. 2 So they said, "Has the LORD indeed spoken only through Moses? Has He not spoken through us also?" And the LORD heard *it.* 3 (Now the man Moses *was* very humble, more than all men who *were* on the face of the earth.)

4 Suddenly the LORD said to Moses, Aaron, and Miriam, "Come out, you three, to the tabernacle of meeting!" So the three came out. 5 Then the LORD came down in the pillar of cloud and stood *in* the door of the tabernacle, and called Aaron and Miriam. And they both went forward. 6 Then He said, "Hear now My words:

11:25 ªTargum and Vulgate read *did not cease.*   11:34 ªLiterally *Graves of Craving*

God is looking for women who want to see His will done on this earth so much that they will cry for it. He is looking for women who want to see God act on their behalf. He wants women who will cry and not shut up!

"If there is a prophet among you,
I, the LORD, make Myself
known to him in a vision;
I speak to him in a dream.
7 Not so with My servant Moses;
He *is* faithful in all My house.
8 I speak with him face to face,
Even plainly, and not in dark
sayings;
And he sees the form of the
LORD.
Why then were you not afraid
To speak against My servant
Moses?"

9 So the anger of the LORD was aroused against them, and He departed. 10 And when the cloud departed from above the tabernacle, suddenly Miriam *became* leprous, as *white as* snow. Then Aaron turned toward Miriam, and there she was, a leper. 11 So Aaron said to Moses, "Oh, my lord! Please do not lay *this* sin on us, in which we have done foolishly and in which we have sinned. 12 "Please do not let her be as one dead, whose flesh is half consumed when he comes out of his mother's womb!"

13 So Moses cried out to the LORD, saying, "Please heal her, O God, I pray!"

14 Then the LORD said to Moses, "If her father had but spit in her face, would she not be shamed seven days? Let her be shut out of the camp seven days, and afterward she may be received *again*." 15 So Miriam was shut out of the camp seven days, and the people did not journey till Miriam was brought in *again*. 16 And afterward the people moved from Hazeroth and camped in the Wilderness of Paran.

13 And the LORD spoke to Moses, saying, 2 "Send men to spy out the land of Canaan, which I am giving to the children of Israel; from each tribe of their fathers you shall send a man, every one a leader among them."

3 So Moses sent them from the Wilderness of Paran according to the command of the LORD, all of them men who *were* heads of the children of Israel. 4 Now these *were* their names: from the tribe of Reuben, Shammua the son of Zaccur; 5 from the tribe of Simeon, Shaphat the son of Hori; 6 from the tribe of Judah, Caleb the son of Jephunneh; 7 from the tribe of Issachar, Igal the son of Joseph; 8 from the tribe of Ephraim, Hoshea[a] the son of Nun; 9 from the tribe of Benjamin, Palti the son of Raphu; 10 from the tribe of Zebulun, Gaddiel the son of Sodi; 11 from the tribe of Joseph, *that is,* from the tribe of Manasseh, Gaddi the son of Susi; 12 from the tribe of Dan, Ammiel the son of Gemalli; 13 from the tribe of Asher, Sethur the son of Michael; 14 from the tribe of Naphtali, Nahbi the son of Vophsi; 15 from the tribe of Gad, Geuel the son of Machi.

16 These *are* the names of the men whom Moses sent to spy out the land. And Moses called Hoshea[a] the son of Nun, Joshua.

17 Then Moses sent them to spy out the land of Canaan, and said to them, "Go up this *way* into the South, and go up to the mountains, 18 and see what the land is like: whether the people who dwell in it *are* strong or weak, few or many; 19 whether the land they dwell in *is* good or bad; whether the cities they inhabit *are* like camps or strongholds; 20 whether the land *is* rich or poor; and whether there are forests there or not. Be of good courage. And bring some of the fruit of the land." Now the time *was* the season of the first ripe grapes.

21 So they went up and spied out the land from the Wilderness of Zin as far as Rehob, near the entrance of Hamath. 22 And they went up through the South and came to Hebron; Ahiman, Sheshai, and Talmai, the descendants of Anak, *were* there. (Now Hebron was built seven years before Zoan in Egypt.) 23 Then they came to the Valley of Eshcol, and there cut down a branch with one cluster of grapes; they carried it between two of them on a pole. *They* also *brought* some of the pomegranates and figs. 24 The place was called the Valley of Eshcol,[a] because of the cluster which the men of Israel cut down there. 25 And they returned from spying out the land after forty days.

13:8 [a]Septuagint and Vulgate read *Oshea.*   13:16 [a]Septuagint and Vulgate read *Oshea.*
13:24 [a]Literally *Cluster*

Gospel
Pearls

26 Now they departed and came back to Moses and Aaron and all the congregation of the children of Israel in the Wilderness of Paran, at Kadesh; they brought back word to them and to all the congregation, and showed them the fruit of the land. 27 Then they told him, and said: "We went to the land where you sent us. It truly flows with milk and honey, and this *is* its fruit. 28 Nevertheless the people who dwell in the land *are* strong; the cities *are* fortified *and* very large; moreover we saw the descendants of Anak there. 29 The Amalekites dwell in the land of the South; the Hittites, the Jebusites, and the Amorites dwell in the mountains; and the Canaanites dwell by the sea and along the banks of the Jordan."

30 Then Caleb quieted the people before Moses, and said, "Let us go up at once and take possession, for we are well able to overcome it."

31 But the men who had gone up with him said, "We are not able to go up against the people, for they *are* stronger than we." 32 And they gave the children of Israel a bad report of the land which they had spied out, saying, "The land through which we have gone as spies *is* a land that devours its inhabitants, and all the people whom we saw in it *are* men of *great* stature. 33 There we saw the giants*a* (the descendants of Anak came from the giants); and we were like grasshoppers in our own sight, and so we were in their sight."

14 So all the congregation lifted up their voices and cried, and the people wept that night. 2 And all the children of Israel complained against Moses and Aaron, and the whole congregation said to them, "If only we had died in the land of Egypt! Or if only we had died in this wilderness! 3 Why has the LORD brought us to this land to fall by the sword, that our wives and children should become victims? Would it not be better for us to return to Egypt?" 4 So they said to one another, "Let us select a leader and return to Egypt."

5 Then Moses and Aaron fell on their faces before all the assembly of the congregation of the children of Israel.

6 But Joshua the son of Nun and Caleb the son of Jephunneh, *who were* among those who had spied out the land, tore their clothes; 7 and they spoke to all the congregation of the children of Israel, saying: "The land we passed through to spy out *is* an exceedingly good land. 8 If the LORD delights in us, then He will bring us into this land and give it to us, 'a land which flows with milk and honey.'*a* 9 Only do not rebel against the LORD, nor fear the people of the land, for they *are* our bread; their protection has departed from them, and the LORD *is* with us. Do not fear them."

10 And all the congregation said to stone them with stones. Now the glory of the LORD appeared in the tabernacle of meeting before all the children of Israel.

11 Then the LORD said to Moses: "How long will these people reject Me? And how long will they not believe Me, with all the signs which I have performed among them? 12 I will strike them with the pestilence and disinherit them, and I will make of you a nation greater and mightier than they."

13 And Moses said to the LORD: "Then the Egyptians will hear *it*, for by Your might You brought these people up from among them, 14 and they will tell *it* to the inhabitants of this land. They have heard that You, LORD, *are* among these people; that You, LORD, are seen face to face and Your cloud stands above them, and You go before them in a pillar of cloud by day and in a pillar of fire by night. 15 Now *if* You kill these people as one man, then the nations which have heard of Your fame will speak, saying, 16 'Because the LORD was not able to bring this people to the land which He swore to give them, therefore He killed them in the wilderness.' 17 And now, I pray, let the power of my Lord be great, just as You have spoken, saying, 18 'The LORD is longsuffering and abundant in mercy, forgiving iniquity and transgression; but He by no means clears *the guilty*, visiting the iniquity of the fathers on the children to the third and fourth *generation*.'*a* 19 Pardon the iniquity of this people, I pray, according to the great-

13:33 *a*Hebrew *nephilim*   14:8 *a*Exodus 3:8   14:18 *a*Exodus 34:6, 7

*D*on't allow yourself to be intimidated into remaining quiet about what it is that you want God to do for you. Cry for it! God will hear and answer the cry of your heart.

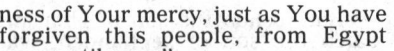
ness of Your mercy, just as You have forgiven this people, from Egypt even until now."

20 Then the LORD said: "I have pardoned, according to your word; 21 but truly, as I live, all the earth shall be filled with the glory of the LORD— 22 because all these men who have seen My glory and the signs which I did in Egypt and in the wilderness, and have put Me to the test now these ten times, and have not heeded My voice, 23 they certainly shall not see the land of which I swore to their fathers, nor shall any of those who rejected Me see it. 24 But My servant Caleb, because he has a different spirit in him and has followed Me fully, I will bring into the land where he went, and his descendants shall inherit it. 25 Now the Amalekites and the Canaanites dwell in the valley; tomorrow turn and move out into the wilderness by the Way of the Red Sea."

26 And the LORD spoke to Moses and Aaron, saying, 27 "How long *shall I bear with* this evil congregation who complain against Me? I have heard the complaints which the children of Israel make against Me. 28 Say to them, 'As I live,' says the LORD, 'just as you have spoken in My hearing, so I will do to you: 29 The carcasses of you who have complained against Me shall fall in this wilderness, all of you who were numbered, according to your entire number, from twenty years old and above. 30 Except for Caleb the son of Jephunneh and Joshua the son of Nun, you shall by no means enter the land which I swore I would make you dwell in. 31 But your little ones, whom you said would be victims, I will bring in, and they shall know the land which you have despised. 32 But *as for* you, your carcasses shall fall in this wilderness. 33 And your sons shall be shepherds in the wilderness forty years, and bear the brunt of your infidelity, until your carcasses are consumed in the wilderness. 34 According to the number of the days in which you spied out the land, forty days, for each day you shall bear your guilt one year, *namely* forty years, and you shall know My rejection. 35 I the LORD have spoken this. I will surely do so to all this evil congregation who are gathered together against Me. In this

wilderness they shall be consumed, and there they shall die.' "

36 Now the men whom Moses sent to spy out the land, who returned and made all the congregation complain against him by bringing a bad report of the land, 37 those very men who brought the evil report about the land, died by the plague before the LORD. 38 But Joshua the son of Nun and Caleb the son of Jephunneh remained alive, of the men who went to spy out the land.

39 Then Moses told these words to all the children of Israel, and the people mourned greatly. 40 And they rose early in the morning and went up to the top of the mountain, saying, "Here we are, and we will go up to the place which the LORD has promised, for we have sinned!"

41 And Moses said, "Now why do you transgress the command of the LORD? For this will not succeed. 42 Do not go up, lest you be defeated by your enemies, for the LORD *is* not among you. 43 For the Amalekites and the Canaanites *are* there before you, and you shall fall by the sword; because you have turned away from the LORD, the LORD will not be with you."

44 But they presumed to go up to the mountaintop. Nevertheless, neither the ark of the covenant of the LORD nor Moses departed from the camp. 45 Then the Amalekites and the Canaanites who dwelt in that mountain came down and attacked them, and drove them back as far as Hormah.

15 And the LORD spoke to Moses, saying, 2 "Speak to the children of Israel, and say to them: 'When you have come into the land you are to inhabit, which I am giving to you, 3 and you make an offering by fire to the LORD, a burnt offering or a sacrifice, to fulfill a vow or as a freewill offering or in your appointed feasts, to make a sweet aroma to the LORD, from the herd or the flock, 4 then he who presents his offering to the LORD shall bring a grain offering of one-tenth *of an ephah* of fine flour mixed with one-fourth of a hin of oil; 5 and one-fourth of a hin of wine as a drink offering you shall prepare with the burnt offering or the sacrifice, for each lamb. 6 Or for a ram you shall prepare as a grain of-

fering two-tenths *of an ephah* of fine flour mixed with one-third of a hin of oil; 7 and as a drink offering you shall offer one-third of a hin of wine as a sweet aroma to the LORD. 8 And when you prepare a young bull as a burnt offering, or as a sacrifice to fulfill a vow, or as a peace offering to the LORD, 9 then shall be offered with the young bull a grain offering of three-tenths *of an ephah* of fine flour mixed with half a hin of oil; 10 and you shall bring as the drink offering half a hin of wine as an offering made by fire, a sweet aroma to the LORD.

11 'Thus it shall be done for each young bull, for each ram, or for each lamb or young goat. 12 According to the number that you prepare, so you shall do with everyone according to their number. 13 All who are native-born shall do these things in this manner, in presenting an offering made by fire, a sweet aroma to the LORD. 14 And if a stranger dwells with you, or whoever *is* among you throughout your generations, and would present an offering made by fire, a sweet aroma to the LORD, just as you do, so shall he do. 15 One ordinance *shall be* for you of the assembly and for the stranger who dwells *with you,* an ordinance forever throughout your generations; as you are, so shall the stranger be before the LORD. 16 One law and one custom shall be for you and for the stranger who dwells with you.' "[a]

17 Again the LORD spoke to Moses, saying, 18 "Speak to the children of Israel, and say to them: 'When you come into the land to which I bring you, 19 then it will be, when you eat of the bread of the land, that you shall offer up a heave offering to the LORD. 20 You shall offer up a cake of the first of your ground meal *as* a heave offering; as a heave offering of the threshing floor, so shall you offer it up. 21 Of the first of your ground meal you shall give to the LORD a heave offering throughout your generations.

22 'If you sin unintentionally, and do not observe all these commandments which the LORD has spoken to Moses— 23 all that the LORD has commanded you by the hand of Moses, from the day the LORD gave com-

mandment and onward throughout your generations— 24 then it will be, if it is unintentionally committed, without the knowledge of the congregation, that the whole congregation shall offer one young bull as a burnt offering, as a sweet aroma to the LORD, with its grain offering and its drink offering, according to the ordinance, and one kid of the goats as a sin offering. 25 So the priest shall make atonement for the whole congregation of the children of Israel, and it shall be forgiven them, for it was unintentional; they shall bring their offering, an offering made by fire to the LORD, and their sin offering before the LORD, for their unintended sin. 26 It shall be forgiven the whole congregation of the children of Israel and the stranger who dwells among them, because all the people *did it* unintentionally.

27 'And if a person sins unintentionally, then he shall bring a female goat in its first year as a sin offering. 28 So the priest shall make atonement for the person who sins unintentionally, when he sins unintentionally before the LORD, to make atonement for him; and it shall be forgiven him. 29 You shall have one law for him who sins unintentionally, *for* him who is native-born among the children of Israel and for the stranger who dwells among them.

30 'But the person who does *anything* presumptuously, *whether he is* native-born or a stranger, that one brings reproach on the LORD, and he shall be cut off from among his people. 31 Because he has despised the word of the LORD, and has broken His commandment, that person shall be completely cut off; his guilt *shall be* upon him.' "

32 Now while the children of Israel were in the wilderness, they found a man gathering sticks on the Sabbath day. 33 And those who found him gathering sticks brought him to Moses and Aaron, and to all the congregation. 34 They put him under guard, because it had not been explained what should be done to him. 35 Then the LORD said to Moses, "The man must surely be put to death; all the congregation shall stone him with stones outside the camp." 36 So, as the LORD com-

15:16 [a]Compare Exodus 12:49

𝒲e will never be entirely free of all problems. And, there are some specific problems from which we may not be entirely freed. But Jesus comes to heal us and deliver us so that the problem ceases to control us, diminish us, hold us back, or keep us down.

manded Moses, all the congregation brought him outside the camp and stoned him with stones, and he died.

37 Again the LORD spoke to Moses, saying, 38 "Speak to the children of Israel: Tell them to make tassels on the corners of their garments throughout their generations, and to put a blue thread in the tassels of the corners. 39 And you shall have the tassel, that you may look upon it and remember all the commandments of the LORD and do them, and that you *may* not follow the harlotry to which your own heart and your own eyes are inclined, 40 and that you may remember and do all My commandments, and be holy for your God. 41 I *am* the LORD your God, who brought you out of the land of Egypt, to be your God: I *am* the LORD your God."

16 Now Korah the son of Izhar, the son of Kohath, the son of Levi, with Dathan and Abiram the sons of Eliab, and On the son of Peleth, sons of Reuben, took *men;* 2 and they rose up before Moses with some of the children of Israel, two hundred and fifty leaders of the congregation, representatives of the congregation, men of renown. 3 They gathered together against Moses and Aaron, and said to them, "*You take* too much upon yourselves, for all the congregation *is* holy, every one of them, and the LORD *is* among them. Why then do you exalt yourselves above the assembly of the LORD?"

4 So when Moses heard *it,* he fell on his face; 5 and he spoke to Korah and all his company, saying, "Tomorrow morning the LORD will show who *is* His and who *is* holy, and will cause *him* to come near to Him. That one whom He chooses He will cause to come near to Him. 6 Do this: Take censers, Korah and all your company; 7 put fire in them and put incense in them before the LORD tomorrow, and it shall be *that* the man whom the LORD chooses *is* the holy one. *You take* too much upon yourselves, you sons of Levi!"

8 Then Moses said to Korah, "Hear now, you sons of Levi: 9 *Is it* a small thing to you that the God of Israel has separated you from the congregation of Israel, to bring you near to Himself, to do the work of the tabernacle of the LORD, and to stand before

the congregation to serve them; 10 and that He has brought you near *to Himself,* you and all your brethren, the sons of Levi, with you? And are you seeking the priesthood also? 11 Therefore you and all your company *are* gathered together against the LORD. And what *is* Aaron that you complain against him?"

12 And Moses sent to call Dathan and Abiram the sons of Eliab, but they said, "We will not come up! 13 *Is it* a small thing that you have brought us up out of a land flowing with milk and honey, to kill us in the wilderness, that you should keep acting like a prince over us? 14 Moreover you have not brought us into a land flowing with milk and honey, nor given us inheritance of fields and vineyards. Will you put out the eyes of these men? We will not come up!"

15 Then Moses was very angry, and said to the LORD, "Do not respect their offering. I have not taken one donkey from them, nor have I hurt one of them."

16 And Moses said to Korah, "Tomorrow, you and all your company be present before the LORD—you and they, as well as Aaron. 17 Let each take his censer and put incense in it, and each of you bring his censer before the LORD, two hundred and fifty censers; both you and Aaron, each *with* his censer." 18 So every man took his censer, put fire in it, laid incense on it, and stood at the door of the tabernacle of meeting with Moses and Aaron. 19 And Korah gathered all the congregation against them at the door of the tabernacle of meeting. Then the glory of the LORD appeared to all the congregation.

20 And the LORD spoke to Moses and Aaron, saying, 21 "Separate yourselves from among this congregation, that I may consume them in a moment."

22 Then they fell on their faces, and said, "O God, the God of the spirits of all flesh, shall one man sin, and You be angry with all the congregation?"

23 So the LORD spoke to Moses, saying, 24 "Speak to the congregation, saying, 'Get away from the tents of Korah, Dathan, and Abiram.'"

25 Then Moses rose and went to Dathan and Abiram, and the elders of Israel followed him. 26 And he spoke to the congregation, saying,

Gospel Pearls

"Depart now from the tents of these wicked men! Touch nothing of theirs, lest you be consumed in all their sins." 27 So they got away from around the tents of Korah, Dathan, and Abiram; and Dathan and Abiram came out and stood at the door of their tents, with their wives, their sons, and their little children.

28 And Moses said: "By this you shall know that the LORD has sent me to do all these works, for *I have* not done *them* of my own will. 29 If these men die naturally like all men, or if they are visited by the common fate of all men, *then* the LORD has not sent me. 30 But if the LORD creates a new thing, and the earth opens its mouth and swallows them up with all that belongs to them, and they go down alive into the pit, then you will understand that these men have rejected the LORD."

31 Now it came to pass, as he finished speaking all these words, that the ground split apart under them, 32 and the earth opened its mouth and swallowed them up, with their households and all the men with Korah, with all *their* goods. 33 So they and all those with them went down alive into the pit; the earth closed over them, and they perished from among the assembly. 34 Then all Israel who *were* around them fled at their cry, for they said, "Lest the earth swallow us up *also!*"

35 And a fire came out from the LORD and consumed the two hundred and fifty men who were offering incense.

36 Then the LORD spoke to Moses, saying: 37 "Tell Eleazar, the son of Aaron the priest, to pick up the censers out of the blaze, for they are holy, and scatter the fire some distance away. 38 The censers of these men who sinned against their own souls, let them be made into hammered plates as a covering for the altar. Because they presented them before the LORD, therefore they are holy; and they shall be a sign to the children of Israel." 39 So Eleazar the priest took the bronze censers, which those who were burned up had presented, and they were hammered out as a covering on the altar, 40 *to be* a memorial to the children of Israel that no outsider, who *is* not a descendant of Aaron, should come near to offer incense before the LORD, that he

might not become like Korah and his companions, just as the LORD had said to him through Moses.

41 On the next day all the congregation of the children of Israel complained against Moses and Aaron, saying, "You have killed the people of the LORD." 42 Now it happened, when the congregation had gathered against Moses and Aaron, that they turned toward the tabernacle of meeting; and suddenly the cloud covered it, and the glory of the LORD appeared. 43 Then Moses and Aaron came before the tabernacle of meeting.

44 And the LORD spoke to Moses, saying, 45 "Get away from among this congregation, that I may consume them in a moment."

And they fell on their faces.

46 So Moses said to Aaron, "Take a censer and put fire in it from the altar, put incense *on it,* and take it quickly to the congregation and make atonement for them; for wrath has gone out from the LORD. The plague has begun." 47 Then Aaron took *it* as Moses commanded, and ran into the midst of the assembly; and already the plague had begun among the people. So he put in the incense and made atonement for the people. 48 And he stood between the dead and the living; so the plague was stopped. 49 Now those who died in the plague were fourteen thousand seven hundred, besides those who died in the Korah incident. 50 So Aaron returned to Moses at the door of the tabernacle of meeting, for the plague had stopped.

17 And the LORD spoke to Moses, saying: 2 "Speak to the children of Israel, and get from them a rod from each father's house, all their leaders according to their fathers' houses—twelve rods. Write each man's name on his rod. 3 And you shall write Aaron's name on the rod of Levi. For there shall be one rod for the head of *each* father's house. 4 Then you shall place them in the tabernacle of meeting before the Testimony, where I meet with you. 5 And it shall be *that* the rod of the man whom I choose will blossom; thus I will rid Myself of the complaints of the children of Israel, which they make against you."

6 So Moses spoke to the children

of Israel, and each of their leaders gave him a rod apiece, for each leader according to their fathers' houses, twelve rods; and the rod of Aaron *was* among their rods. 7 And Moses placed the rods before the LORD in the tabernacle of witness.

8 Now it came to pass on the next day that Moses went into the tabernacle of witness, and behold, the rod of Aaron, of the house of Levi, had sprouted and put forth buds, had produced blossoms and yielded ripe almonds. 9 Then Moses brought out all the rods from before the LORD to all the children of Israel; and they looked, and each man took his rod.

10 And the LORD said to Moses, "Bring Aaron's rod back before the Testimony, to be kept as a sign against the rebels, that you may put their complaints away from Me, lest they die." 11 Thus did Moses; just as the LORD had commanded him, so he did.

12 So the children of Israel spoke to Moses, saying, "Surely we die, we perish, we all perish! 13 Whoever even comes near the tabernacle of the LORD must die. Shall we all utterly die?"

18 Then the LORD said to Aaron: "You and your sons and your father's house with you shall bear the iniquity *related to* the sanctuary, and you and your sons with you shall bear the iniquity *associated with* your priesthood. 2 Also bring with you your brethren of the tribe of Levi, the tribe of your father, that they may be joined with you and serve you while you and your sons *are* with you before the tabernacle of witness. 3 They shall attend to your needs and all the needs of the tabernacle; but they shall not come near the articles of the sanctuary and the altar, lest they die—they and you also. 4 They shall be joined with you and attend to the needs of the tabernacle of meeting, for all the work of the tabernacle; but an outsider shall not come near you. 5 And you shall attend to the duties of the sanctuary and the duties of the altar, that there *may* be no more wrath on the children of Israel. 6 Behold, I Myself have taken your brethren the Levites from among the children of Israel; *they are* a gift to you, given by the LORD, to do the work of the tabernacle of

meeting. 7 Therefore you and your sons with you shall attend to your priesthood for everything at the altar and behind the veil; and you shall serve. I give your priesthood *to you* as a gift for service, but the outsider who comes near shall be put to death."

8 And the LORD spoke to Aaron: "Here, I Myself have also given you charge of My heave offerings, all the holy gifts of the children of Israel; I have given them as a portion to you and your sons, as an ordinance forever. 9 This shall be yours of the most holy things *reserved* from the fire: every offering of theirs, every grain offering and every sin offering and every trespass offering which they render to Me, *shall be* most holy for you and your sons. 10 In a most holy *place* you shall eat it; every male shall eat it. It shall be holy to you.

11 This also *is* yours: the heave offering of their gift, with all the wave offerings of the children of Israel; I have given them to you, and your sons and daughters with you, as an ordinance forever. Everyone who is clean in your house may eat it.

12 "All the best of the oil, all the best of the new wine and the grain, their firstfruits which they offer to the LORD, I have given them to you. 13 Whatever first ripe fruit is in their land, which they bring to the LORD, shall be yours. Everyone who is clean in your house may eat it.

14 "Every devoted thing in Israel shall be yours.

15 "Everything that first opens the womb of all flesh, which they bring to the LORD, whether man or beast, shall be yours; nevertheless the firstborn of man you shall surely redeem, and the firstborn of unclean animals you shall redeem. 16 And those redeemed of the devoted things shall redeem when one month old, according to your valuation, for five shekels of silver, according to the shekel of the sanctuary, which *is* twenty gerahs. 17 But the firstborn of a cow, the firstborn of a sheep, or the firstborn of a goat you shall not redeem; they *are* holy. You shall sprinkle their blood on the altar, and burn their fat *as* an offering made by fire for a sweet aroma to the LORD. 18 And their flesh shall be yours, just as the wave breast and the right thigh are yours.

Gospel Pearls

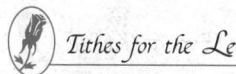
19 "All the heave offerings of the holy things, which the children of Israel offer to the LORD, I have given to you and your sons and daughters with you as an ordinance forever; it *is* a covenant of salt forever before the LORD with you and your descendants with you."

20 Then the LORD said to Aaron: "You shall have no inheritance in their land, nor shall you have any portion among them; I *am* your portion and your inheritance among the children of Israel.

21 "Behold, I have given the children of Levi all the tithes in Israel as an inheritance in return for the work which they perform, the work of the tabernacle of meeting. 22 Hereafter the children of Israel shall not come near the tabernacle of meeting, lest they bear sin and die. 23 But the Levites shall perform the work of the tabernacle of meeting, and they shall bear their iniquity; *it shall be* a statute forever, throughout your generations, that among the children of Israel they shall have no inheritance. 24 For the tithes of the children of Israel, which they offer up *as* a heave offering to the LORD, I have given to the Levites as an inheritance; therefore I have said to them, 'Among the children of Israel they shall have no inheritance.'"

25 Then the LORD spoke to Moses, saying, 26 "Speak thus to the Levites, and say to them: 'When you take from the children of Israel the tithes which I have given you from them as your inheritance, then you shall offer up a heave offering of it to the LORD, a tenth of the tithe. 27 And your heave offering shall be reckoned to you as though *it were* the grain of the threshing floor and as the fullness of the winepress. 28 Thus you shall also offer a heave offering to the LORD from all your tithes which you receive from the children of Israel, and you shall give the LORD's heave offering from it to Aaron the priest. 29 Of all your gifts you shall offer up every heave offering due to the LORD, from all the best of them, the consecrated part of them.' 30 Therefore you shall say to them: 'When you have lifted up the best of it, then *the rest* shall be accounted to the Levites as the produce of the

threshing floor and as the produce of the winepress. 31 You may eat it in any place, you and your households, for it *is* your reward for your work in the tabernacle of meeting. 32 And you shall bear no sin because of it, when you have lifted up the best of it. But you shall not profane the holy gifts of the children of Israel, lest you die.'"

19 Now the LORD spoke to Moses and Aaron, saying, 2 "This *is* the ordinance of the law which the LORD has commanded, saying: 'Speak to the children of Israel, that they bring you a red heifer without blemish, in which there *is* no defect *and* on which a yoke has never come. 3 You shall give it to Eleazar the priest, that he may take it outside the camp, and it shall be slaughtered before him; 4 and Eleazar the priest shall take some of its blood with his finger, and sprinkle some of its blood seven times directly in front of the tabernacle of meeting. 5 Then the heifer shall be burned in his sight: its hide, its flesh, its blood, and its offal shall be burned. 6 And the priest shall take cedar wood and hyssop and scarlet, and cast *them* into the midst of the fire burning the heifer. 7 Then the priest shall wash his clothes, he shall bathe in water, and afterward he shall come into the camp; the priest shall be unclean until evening. 8 And the one who burns it shall wash his clothes in water, bathe in water, and shall be unclean until evening. 9 Then a man *who is* clean shall gather up the ashes of the heifer, and store *them* outside the camp in a clean place; and they shall be kept for the congregation of the children of Israel for the water of purification;*a* *it is* for purifying from sin. 10 And the one who gathers the ashes of the heifer shall wash his clothes, and be unclean until evening. It shall be a statute forever to the children of Israel and to the stranger who dwells among them.

11 'He who touches the dead body of anyone shall be unclean seven days. 12 He shall purify himself with the water on the third day and on the seventh day; *then* he will be clean. But if he does not purify himself on the third day and on the seventh day,

19:9 *a*Literally *impurity*

he will not be clean. 13 Whoever touches the body of anyone who has died, and does not purify himself, defiles the tabernacle of the LORD. That person shall be cut off from Israel. He shall be unclean, because the water of purification was not sprinkled on him; his uncleanness *is* still on him.

14 'This *is* the law when a man dies in a tent: All who come into the tent and all who *are* in the tent shall be unclean seven days; 15 and every open vessel, which has no cover fastened on it, *is* unclean. 16 Whoever in the open field touches one who is slain by a sword or who has died, or a bone of a man, or a grave, shall be unclean seven days.

17 'And for an unclean *person* they shall take some of the ashes of the heifer burnt for purification from sin, and running water shall be put on them in a vessel. 18 A clean person shall take hyssop and dip *it* in the water, sprinkle *it* on the tent, on all the vessels, on the persons who were there, or on the one who touched a bone, the slain, the dead, or a grave. 19 The clean *person* shall sprinkle the unclean on the third day and on the seventh day; and on the seventh day he shall purify himself, wash his clothes, and bathe in water; and at evening he shall be clean.

20 'But the man who is unclean and does not purify himself, that person shall be cut off from among the assembly, because he has defiled the sanctuary of the LORD. The water of purification has not been sprinkled on him; he *is* unclean. 21 It shall be a perpetual statute for them. He who sprinkles the water of purification shall wash his clothes; and he who touches the water of purification shall be unclean until evening. 22 Whatever the unclean *person* touches shall be unclean; and the person who touches *it* shall be unclean until evening.' "

20 Then the children of Israel, the whole congregation, came into the Wilderness of Zin in the first month, and the people stayed in Kadesh; and Miriam died there and was buried there.

2 Now there was no water for the congregation; so they gathered together against Moses and Aaron. 3 And the people contended with Moses and spoke, saying: "If only we had died when our brethren died before the LORD! 4 Why have you brought up the assembly of the LORD into this wilderness, that we and our animals should die here? 5 And why have you made us come up out of Egypt, to bring us to this evil place? It *is* not a place of grain or figs or vines or pomegranates; nor *is* there any water to drink." 6 So Moses and Aaron went from the presence of the assembly to the door of the tabernacle of meeting, and they fell on their faces. And the glory of the LORD appeared to them.

7 Then the LORD spoke to Moses, saying, 8 "Take the rod; you and your brother Aaron gather the congregation together. Speak to the rock before their eyes, and it will yield its water; thus you shall bring water for them out of the rock, and give drink to the congregation and their animals." 9 So Moses took the rod from before the LORD as He commanded him.

10 And Moses and Aaron gathered the assembly together before the rock; and he said to them, "Hear now, you rebels! Must we bring water for you out of this rock?" 11 Then Moses lifted his hand and struck the rock twice with his rod; and water came out abundantly, and the congregation and their animals drank.

12 Then the LORD spoke to Moses and Aaron, "Because you did not believe Me, to hallow Me in the eyes of the children of Israel, therefore you shall not bring this assembly into the land which I have given them."

13 This *was* the water of Meribah,*a* because the children of Israel contended with the LORD, and He was hallowed among them.

14 Now Moses sent messengers from Kadesh to the king of Edom. "Thus says your brother Israel: 'You know all the hardship that has befallen us, 15 how our fathers went down to Egypt, and we dwelt in Egypt a long time, and the Egyptians afflicted us and our fathers. 16 When we cried out to the LORD, He heard our voice and sent the Angel and brought us up out of Egypt; now

20:13 *a*Literally *Contention*

Gospel Pearls

here we are in Kadesh, a city on the edge of your border. 17 Please let us pass through your country. We will not pass through fields or vineyards, nor will we drink water from wells; we will go along the King's Highway; we will not turn aside to the right hand or to the left until we have passed through your territory.' "

18 Then Edom said to him, "You shall not pass through my *land*, lest I come out against you with the sword."

19 So the children of Israel said to him, "We will go by the Highway, and if I or my livestock drink any of your water, then I will pay for it; let me only pass through on foot, nothing *more*."

20 Then he said, "You shall not pass through." So Edom came out against them with many men and with a strong hand. 21 Thus Edom refused to give Israel passage through his territory; so Israel turned away from him.

22 Now the children of Israel, the whole congregation, journeyed from Kadesh and came to Mount Hor. 23 And the LORD spoke to Moses and Aaron in Mount Hor by the border of the land of Edom, saying: 24 "Aaron shall be gathered to his people, for he shall not enter the land which I have given to the children of Israel, because you rebelled against My word at the water of Meribah. 25 Take Aaron and Eleazar his son, and bring them up to Mount Hor; 26 and strip Aaron of his garments and put them on Eleazar his son; for Aaron shall be gathered *to his people* and die there." 27 So Moses did just as the LORD commanded, and they went up to Mount Hor in the sight of all the congregation. 28 Moses stripped Aaron of his garments and put them on Eleazar his son; and Aaron died there on the top of the mountain. Then Moses and Eleazar came down from the mountain. 29 Now when all the congregation saw that Aaron was dead, all the house of Israel mourned for Aaron thirty days.

21 The king of Arad, the Canaanite, who dwelt in the South, heard that Israel was coming on the road to Atharim. Then he fought against Israel and took *some* of them prisoners. 2 So Israel made a vow to the LORD, and said, "If You will indeed deliver this people into my hand, then I will utterly destroy their cities." 3 And the LORD listened to the voice of Israel and delivered up the Canaanites, and they utterly destroyed them and their cities. So the name of that place was called Hormah.*a*

4 Then they journeyed from Mount Hor by the Way of the Red Sea, to go around the land of Edom; and the soul of the people became very discouraged on the way. 5 And the people spoke against God and against Moses: "Why have you brought us up out of Egypt to die in the wilderness? For *there is* no food and no water, and our soul loathes this worthless bread." 6 So the LORD sent fiery serpents among the people, and they bit the people; and many of the people of Israel died.

7 Therefore the people came to Moses, and said, "We have sinned, for we have spoken against the LORD and against you; pray to the LORD that He take away the serpents from us." So Moses prayed for the people.

8 Then the LORD said to Moses, "Make a fiery *serpent*, and set it on a pole; and it shall be that everyone who is bitten, when he looks at it, shall live." 9 So Moses made a bronze serpent, and put it on a pole; and so it was, if a serpent had bitten anyone, when he looked at the bronze serpent, he lived.

10 Now the children of Israel moved on and camped in Oboth. 11 And they journeyed from Oboth and camped at Ije Abarim, in the wilderness which *is* east of Moab, toward the sunrise. 12 From there they moved and camped in the Valley of Zered. 13 From there they moved and camped on the other side of the Arnon, which *is* in the wilderness that extends from the border of the Amorites; for the Arnon *is* the border of Moab, between Moab and the Amorites. 14 Therefore it is said in the Book of the Wars of the LORD:

"Waheb in Suphah,*a*
The brooks of the Arnon,

21:3 *a*Literally *Utter Destruction*   21:14 *a*Ancient unknown places; Vulgate reads *what He did in the Red Sea.*

*I*f for some reason you are left to bring up the children alone, God is able! You can do it but not without the assistance of your heavenly Father, whose wisdom will become a resource center for help and guidance along the way.

15 And the slope of the brooks
That reaches to the dwelling of
Ar,
And lies on the border of
Moab."

16 From there *they went* to Beer,
which *is* the well where the LORD said
to Moses, "Gather the people together, and I will give them water."
17 Then Israel sang this song:

"Spring up, O well!
All of you sing to it—
18 The well the leaders sank,
Dug by the nation's nobles,
By the lawgiver, with their
staves."

And from the wilderness *they went*
to Mattanah, 19 from Mattanah to Nahaliel, from Nahaliel to Bamoth,
20 and from Bamoth, *in* the valley
that *is* in the country of Moab, to the
top of Pisgah which looks down on
the wasteland.*a*
21 Then Israel sent messengers to
Sihon king of the Amorites, saying,
22 "Let me pass through your land.
We will not turn aside into fields or
vineyards; we will not drink water
from wells. We will go by the King's
Highway until we have passed
through your territory." 23 But Sihon
would not allow Israel to pass
through his territory. So Sihon gathered all his people together and went
out against Israel in the wilderness,
and he came to Jahaz and fought
against Israel. 24 Then Israel defeated him with the edge of the
sword, and took possession of his
land from the Arnon to the Jabbok,
as far as the people of Ammon; for
the border of the people of Ammon
was fortified. 25 So Israel took all
these cities, and Israel dwelt in all the
cities of the Amorites, in Heshbon
and in all its villages. 26 For Heshbon
was the city of Sihon king of the Amorites, who had fought against the
former king of Moab, and had taken
all his land from his hand as far as
the Arnon. 27 Therefore those who
speak in proverbs say:

"Come to Heshbon, let it be
built;
Let the city of Sihon be
repaired.

28 "For fire went out from
Heshbon,
A flame from the city of Sihon;
It consumed Ar of Moab,
The lords of the heights of the
Arnon.
29 Woe to you, Moab!
You have perished, O people of
Chemosh!
He has given his sons as
fugitives,
And his daughters into
captivity,
To Sihon king of the Amorites.

30 "But we have shot at them;
Heshbon has perished as far as
Dibon.
Then we laid waste as far as
Nophah,
Which *reaches* to Medeba."

31 Thus Israel dwelt in the land of
the Amorites. 32 Then Moses sent to
spy out Jazer; and they took its villages and drove out the Amorites
who *were* there.
33 And they turned and went up by
the way to Bashan. So Og king of
Bashan went out against them, he
and all his people, to battle at Edrei.
34 Then the LORD said to Moses, "Do
not fear him, for I have delivered him
into your hand, with all his people
and his land; and you shall do to him
as you did to Sihon king of the Amorites, who dwelt at Heshbon."
35 So they defeated him, his sons, and
all his people, until there was no survivor left him; and they took possession of his land.

22 Then the children of Israel
moved, and camped in the
plains of Moab on the side of the Jordan *across from* Jericho.
2 Now Balak the son of Zippor saw
all that Israel had done to the Amorites. 3 And Moab was exceedingly
afraid of the people because they
were many, and Moab was sick with
dread because of the children of Israel. 4 So Moab said to the elders of
Midian, "Now this company will lick
up everything around us, as an ox
licks up the grass of the field." And
Balak the son of Zippor *was* king of
the Moabites at that time. 5 Then he
sent messengers to Balaam the son
of Beor at Pethor, which *is* near the

21:20 *a*Hebrew *Jeshimon*

Gospel
Pearls

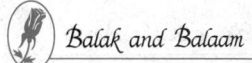
River*a* in the land of the sons of his people,*b* to call him, saying: "Look, a people has come from Egypt. See, they cover the face of the earth, and are settling next to me! 6 Therefore please come at once, curse this people for me, for they *are* too mighty for me. Perhaps I shall be able to defeat them and drive them out of the land, for I know that he whom you bless *is* blessed, and he whom you curse is cursed."

7 So the elders of Moab and the elders of Midian departed with the diviner's fee in their hand, and they came to Balaam and spoke to him the words of Balak. 8 And he said to them, "Lodge here tonight, and I will bring back word to you, as the LORD speaks to me." So the princes of Moab stayed with Balaam.

9 Then God came to Balaam and said, "Who *are* these men with you?" 10 So Balaam said to God, "Balak the son of Zippor, king of Moab, has sent to me, *saying,* 11 'Look, a people has come out of Egypt, and they cover the face of the earth. Come now, curse them for me; perhaps I shall be able to overpower them and drive them out.' "

12 And God said to Balaam, "You shall not go with them; you shall not curse the people, for they *are* blessed."

13 So Balaam rose in the morning and said to the princes of Balak, "Go back to your land, for the LORD has refused to give me permission to go with you."

14 And the princes of Moab rose and went to Balak, and said, "Balaam refuses to come with us."

15 Then Balak again sent princes, more numerous and more honorable than they. 16 And they came to Balaam and said to him, "Thus says Balak the son of Zippor: 'Please let nothing hinder you from coming to me; 17 for I will certainly honor you greatly, and I will do whatever you say to me. Therefore please come, curse this people for me.' "

18 Then Balaam answered and said to the servants of Balak, "Though Balak were to give me his house full of silver and gold, I could not go beyond the word of the LORD my God, to do less or more. 19 Now therefore, please, you also stay here tonight, that I may know what more the LORD will say to me."

20 And God came to Balaam at night and said to him, "If the men come to call you, rise *and* go with them; but only the word which I speak to you—that you shall do." 21 So Balaam rose in the morning, saddled his donkey, and went with the princes of Moab.

22 Then God's anger was aroused because he went, and the Angel of the LORD took His stand in the way as an adversary against him. And he was riding on his donkey, and his two servants *were* with him. 23 Now the donkey saw the Angel of the LORD standing in the way with His drawn sword in His hand, and the donkey turned aside out of the way and went into the field. So Balaam struck the donkey to turn her back onto the road. 24 Then the Angel of the LORD stood in a narrow path between the vineyards, *with* a wall on this side and a wall on that side. 25 And when the donkey saw the Angel of the LORD, she pushed herself against the wall and crushed Balaam's foot against the wall; so he struck her again. 26 Then the Angel of the LORD went further, and stood in a narrow place where there *was* no way to turn either to the right hand or to the left. 27 And when the donkey saw the Angel of the LORD, she lay down under Balaam; so Balaam's anger was aroused, and he struck the donkey with his staff.

28 Then the LORD opened the mouth of the donkey, and she said to Balaam, "What have I done to you, that you have struck me these three times?"

29 And Balaam said to the donkey, "Because you have abused me. I wish there were a sword in my hand, for now I would kill you!"

30 So the donkey said to Balaam, "*Am* I not your donkey on which you have ridden, ever since *I* became yours, to this day? Was I ever disposed to do this to you?"

And he said, "No."

31 Then the LORD opened Balaam's eyes, and he saw the Angel of the LORD standing in the way with His drawn sword in His hand; and he bowed his head and fell flat on his face. 32 And the Angel of the LORD

22:5 *a*That is, the Euphrates   *b*Or *the people of Amau*

I want to recommend the Father who will never leave you nor forsake you. No one can keep you from His favors. He is waiting to give you what you missed. His blood can heal the breach!

said to him, "Why have you struck your donkey these three times? Behold, I have come out to stand against you, because *your* way is perverse before Me. 33 The donkey saw Me and turned aside from Me these three times. If she had not turned aside from Me, surely I would also have killed you by now, and let her live."

34 And Balaam said to the Angel of the LORD, "I have sinned, for I did not know You stood in the way against me. Now therefore, if it displeases You, I will turn back."

35 Then the Angel of the LORD said to Balaam, "Go with the men, but only the word that I speak to you, that you shall speak." So Balaam went with the princes of Balak.

36 Now when Balak heard that Balaam was coming, he went out to meet him at the city of Moab, which *is* on the border at the Arnon, the boundary of the territory. 37 Then Balak said to Balaam, "Did I not earnestly send to you, calling for you? Why did you not come to me? Am I not able to honor you?"

38 And Balaam said to Balak, "Look, I have come to you! Now, have I any power at all to say anything? The word that God puts in my mouth, that I must speak." 39 So Balaam went with Balak, and they came to Kirjath Huzoth. 40 Then Balak offered oxen and sheep, and he sent *some* to Balaam and to the princes who *were* with him.

41 So it was, the next day, that Balak took Balaam and brought him up to the high places of Baal, that from there he might observe the extent of the people.

23 Then Balaam said to Balak, "Build seven altars for me here, and prepare for me here seven bulls and seven rams."

2 And Balak did just as Balaam had spoken, and Balak and Balaam offered a bull and a ram on *each* altar. 3 Then Balaam said to Balak, "Stand by your burnt offering, and I will go; perhaps the LORD will come to meet me, and whatever He shows me I will tell you." So he went to a desolate height. 4 And God met Balaam, and he said to Him, "I have prepared the seven altars, and I have offered on *each* altar a bull and a ram."

5 Then the LORD put a word in Balaam's mouth, and said, "Return to Balak, and thus you shall speak." 6 So he returned to him, and there he was, standing by his burnt offering, he and all the princes of Moab.

7 And he took up his oracle and said:

"Balak the king of Moab has
     brought me from Aram,
From the mountains of the east.
'Come, curse Jacob for me,
     And come, denounce Israel!'

8 "How shall I curse whom God
     has not cursed?
And how shall I denounce
     whom the LORD has not
     denounced?
9 For from the top of the rocks I
     see him,
And from the hills I behold
     him;
There! A people dwelling
     alone,
Not reckoning itself among the
     nations.

10 "Who can count the dust*a* of
     Jacob,
Or number one-fourth of
     Israel?
Let me die the death of the
     righteous,
And let my end be like his!"

11 Then Balak said to Balaam, "What have you done to me? I took you to curse my enemies, and look, you have blessed *them* bountifully!"

12 So he answered and said, "Must I not take heed to speak what the LORD has put in my mouth?"

13 Then Balak said to him, "Please come with me to another place from which you may see them; you shall see only the outer part of them, and shall not see them all; curse them for me from there." 14 So he brought him to the field of Zophim, to the top of Pisgah, and built seven altars, and offered a bull and a ram on *each* altar.

15 And he said to Balak, "Stand here by your burnt offering while I meet*a* the LORD over there."

16 Then the LORD met Balaam, and put a word in his mouth, and said,

23:10 *a*Or *dust cloud*   23:15 *a*Following Masoretic Text, Targum, and Vulgate; Syriac reads *call;* Septuagint reads *go and ask God.*

Gospel Pearls

"Go back to Balak, and thus you shall speak." 17 So he came to him, and there he was, standing by his burnt offering, and the princes of Moab were with him. And Balak said to him, "What has the LORD spoken?"

18 Then he took up his oracle and said:

> "Rise up, Balak, and hear!
> Listen to me, son of Zippor!
>
> 19 "God *is* not a man, that He
>   should lie,
>   Nor a son of man, that He
>   should repent.
>   Has He said, and will He not
>   do?
>   Or has He spoken, and will He
>   not make it good?
> 20 Behold, I have received *a
>   command* to bless;
>   He has blessed, and I cannot
>   reverse it.
>
> 21 "He has not observed iniquity in
>   Jacob,
>   Nor has He seen wickedness in
>   Israel.
>   The LORD his God *is* with him,
>   And the shout of a King *is*
>   among them.
> 22 God brings them out of Egypt;
>   He has strength like a wild ox.
>
> 23 "For *there is* no sorcery against
>   Jacob,
>   Nor any divination against
>   Israel.
>   It now must be said of Jacob
>   And of Israel, 'Oh, what God
>   has done!'
> 24 Look, a people rises like a
>   lioness,
>   And lifts itself up like a lion;
>   It shall not lie down until it
>   devours the prey,
>   And drinks the blood of the
>   slain."

25 Then Balak said to Balaam, "Neither curse them at all, nor bless them at all!"

26 So Balaam answered and said to Balak, "Did I not tell you, saying, 'All that the LORD speaks, that I must do'?"

27 Then Balak said to Balaam, "Please come, I will take you to another place; perhaps it will please God that you may curse them for me

from there." 28 So Balak took Balaam to the top of Peor, that overlooks the wasteland.[a] 29 Then Balaam said to Balak, "Build for me here seven altars, and prepare for me here seven bulls and seven rams." 30 And Balak did as Balaam had said, and offered a bull and a ram on *every* altar.

24 Now when Balaam saw that it pleased the LORD to bless Israel, he did not go as at other times, to seek to use sorcery, but he set his face toward the wilderness. 2 And Balaam raised his eyes, and saw Israel encamped according to their tribes; and the Spirit of God came upon him.

3 Then he took up his oracle and said:

> "The utterance of Balaam the
>   son of Beor,
>   The utterance of the man
>   whose eyes are opened,
> 4   The utterance of him who hears
>   the words of God,
>   Who sees the vision of the
>   Almighty,
>   Who falls down, with eyes wide
>   open:
>
> 5 "How lovely are your tents, O
>   Jacob!
>   Your dwellings, O Israel!
> 6   Like valleys that stretch out,
>   Like gardens by the riverside,
>   Like aloes planted by the LORD,
>   Like cedars beside the waters.
> 7   He shall pour water from his
>   buckets,
>   And his seed *shall be* in many
>   waters.
>
> "His king shall be higher than
>   Agag,
>   And his kingdom shall be
>   exalted.
>
> 8 "God brings him out of Egypt;
>   He has strength like a wild ox;
>   He shall consume the nations,
>   his enemies;
>   He shall break their bones
>   And pierce *them* with his
>   arrows.
> 9 'He bows down, he lies down as
>   a lion;
>   And as a lion, who shall rouse
>   him?'[a]

23:28 ᵃHebrew *Jeshimon*   24:9 ᵃGenesis 49:9

*D*ear daughters of the living God, hear me well. God will not withhold any good thing from you. If it were good, He would have said yes. But either the timing is wrong, or from His position He can see that the future of it is weak.

"Blessed *is* he who blesses you,
And cursed *is* he who curses
you."

10 Then Balak's anger was aroused against Balaam, and he struck his hands together; and Balak said to Balaam, "I called you to curse my enemies, and look, you have bountifully blessed *them* these three times! 11 Now therefore, flee to your place. I said I would greatly honor you, but in fact, the LORD has kept you back from honor."

12 So Balaam said to Balak, "Did I not also speak to your messengers whom you sent to me, saying, 13 'If Balak were to give me his house full of silver and gold, I could not go beyond the word of the LORD, to do good or bad of my own will. What the LORD says, that I must speak'? 14 And now, indeed, I am going to my people. Come, I will advise you what this people will do to your people in the latter days."

15 So he took up his oracle and said:

"The utterance of Balaam the
son of Beor,
And the utterance of the man
whose eyes are opened;
16 The utterance of him who hears
the words of God,
And has the knowledge of the
Most High,
Who sees the vision of the
Almighty,
Who falls down, with eyes wide
open:

17 "I see Him, but not now;
I behold Him, but not near;
A Star shall come out of Jacob;
A Scepter shall rise out of
Israel,
And batter the brow of Moab,
And destroy all the sons of
tumult.*ª*

18 "And Edom shall be a
possession;
Seir also, his enemies, shall be
a possession,
While Israel does valiantly.
19 Out of Jacob One shall have
dominion,

And destroy the remains of the
city."

20 Then he looked on Amalek, and he took up his oracle and said:

"Amalek *was* first among the
nations,
But *shall be* last until he
perishes."

21 Then he looked on the Kenites, and he took up his oracle and said:

"Firm is your dwelling place,
And your nest is set in the rock;
22 Nevertheless Kain shall be
burned.
How long until Asshur carries
you away captive?"

23 Then he took up his oracle and said:

"Alas! Who shall live when God
does this?
24 But ships *shall come* from the
coasts of Cyprus,*ª*
And they shall afflict Asshur
and afflict Eber,
And so shall *Amalek,ᵇ* until he
perishes."

25 So Balaam rose and departed and returned to his place; Balak also went his way.

25 Now Israel remained in Acacia Grove,*ª* and the people began to commit harlotry with the women of Moab. 2 They invited the people to the sacrifices of their gods, and the people ate and bowed down to their gods. 3 So Israel was joined to Baal of Peor, and the anger of the LORD was aroused against Israel.

4 Then the LORD said to Moses, "Take all the leaders of the people and hang the offenders before the LORD, out in the sun, that the fierce anger of the LORD may turn away from Israel."

5 So Moses said to the judges of Israel, "Every one of you kill his men who were joined to Baal of Peor."

6 And indeed, one of the children of Israel came and presented to his brethren a Midianite woman in the sight of Moses and in the sight of all

24:17 *ª*Hebrew *Sheth* (compare Jeremiah 48:45)
25:1 *ª*Hebrew *Shittim*

24:24 *ª*Hebrew *Kittim*   *ᵇ*Literally *he* or *that one*

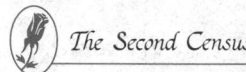
the congregation of the children of Israel, who *were* weeping at the door of the tabernacle of meeting. 7 Now when Phinehas the son of Eleazar, the son of Aaron the priest, saw *it,* he rose from among the congregation and took a javelin in his hand; 8 and he went after the man of Israel into the tent and thrust both of them through, the man of Israel, and the woman through her body. So the plague was stopped among the children of Israel. 9 And those who died in the plague were twenty-four thousand.

10 Then the LORD spoke to Moses, saying: 11 "Phinehas the son of Eleazar, the son of Aaron the priest, has turned back My wrath from the children of Israel, because he was zealous with My zeal among them, so that I did not consume the children of Israel in My zeal. 12 Therefore say, 'Behold, I give to him My covenant of peace; 13 and it shall be to him and his descendants after him a covenant of an everlasting priesthood, because he was zealous for his God, and made atonement for the children of Israel.' "

14 Now the name of the Israelite who was killed, who was killed with the Midianite woman, *was* Zimri the son of Salu, a leader of a father's house among the Simeonites. 15 And the name of the Midianite woman who was killed *was* Cozbi the daughter of Zur; he *was* head of the people of a father's house in Midian.

16 Then the LORD spoke to Moses, saying: 17 "Harass the Midianites, and attack them; 18 for they harassed you with their schemes by which they seduced you in the matter of Peor and in the matter of Cozbi, the daughter of a leader of Midian, their sister, who was killed in the day of the plague because of Peor."

26 And it came to pass, after the plague, that the LORD spoke to Moses and Eleazar the son of Aaron the priest, saying: 2 "Take a census of all the congregation of the children of Israel from twenty years old and above, by their fathers' houses, all who are able to go to war in Israel."

3 So Moses and Eleazar the priest spoke with them in the plains of Moab by the Jordan, *across from* Jericho, saying: 4 "Take a census of the people from twenty years old and above, just as the LORD commanded Moses and the children of Israel who came out of the land of Egypt."

5 Reuben *was* the firstborn of Israel. The children of Reuben *were: of* Hanoch, the family of the Hanochites; *of* Pallu, the family of the Palluites; 6 *of* Hezron, the family of the Hezronites; *of* Carmi, the family of the Carmites. 7 These *are* the families of the Reubenites: those who were numbered of them were forty-three thousand seven hundred and thirty. 8 And the son of Pallu *was* Eliab. 9 The sons of Eliab *were* Nemuel, Dathan, and Abiram. These *are* the Dathan and Abiram, representatives of the congregation, who contended against Moses and Aaron in the company of Korah, when they contended against the LORD; 10 and the earth opened its mouth and swallowed them up together with Korah when that company died, when the fire devoured two hundred and fifty men; and they became a sign. 11 Nevertheless the children of Korah did not die.

12 The sons of Simeon according to their families *were: of* Nemuel,ᵃ the family of the Nemuelites; *of* Jamin, the family of the Jaminites; *of* Jachin,ᵇ the family of the Jachinites; 13 *of* Zerah,ᵃ the family of the Zarhites; *of* Shaul, the family of the Shaulites. 14 These *are* the families of the Simeonites: twenty-two thousand two hundred.

15 The sons of Gad according to their families *were: of* Zephon,ᵃ the family of the Zephonites; *of* Haggi, the family of the Haggites; *of* Shuni, the family of the Shunites; 16 *of* Ozni,ᵃ the family of the Oznites; *of* Eri, the family of the Erites; 17 *of* Arod,ᵃ the family of the Arodites; *of* Areli, the family of the Arelites. 18 These *are* the families of the sons of Gad according to those who were numbered of them: forty thousand five hundred.

19 The sons of Judah *were* Er and Onan; and Er and Onan died in the land of Canaan. 20 And the sons of

26:12 ᵃSpelled *Jemuel* in Genesis 46:10 and Exodus 6:15   ᵇCalled *Jarib* in 1 Chronicles 4:24
26:13 ᵃCalled *Zohar* in Genesis 46:10   26:15 ᵃCalled *Ziphion* in Genesis 46:16   26:16 ᵃCalled *Ezbon* in Genesis 46:16   26:17 ᵃSpelled *Arodi* in Samaritan Pentateuch, Syriac, and Genesis 46:16

I have always believed that people who only thank God for delivering them from what happened are just scraping the surface of praise. The real praise comes when you start thanking Him for what could have happened, but didn't, because of His swift grace!

Judah according to their families were: *of* Shelah, the family of the Shelanites; *of* Perez, the family of the Parzites; *of* Zerah, the family of the Zarhites. 21 And the sons of Perez were: *of* Hezron, the family of the Hezronites; *of* Hamul, the family of the Hamulites. 22 These *are* the families of Judah according to those who were numbered of them: seventy-six thousand five hundred.

23 The sons of Issachar according to their families *were: of* Tola, the family of the Tolaites; of Puah,*a* the family of the Punites;*b* 24 of Jashub, the family of the Jashubites; of Shimron, the family of the Shimronites. 25 These *are* the families of Issachar according to those who were numbered of them: sixty-four thousand three hundred.

26 The sons of Zebulun according to their families *were:* of Sered, the family of the Sardites; of Elon, the family of the Elonites; of Jahleel, the family of the Jahleelites. 27 These *are* the families of the Zebulunites according to those who were numbered of them: sixty thousand five hundred.

28 The sons of Joseph according to their families, by Manasseh and Ephraim, *were:* 29 The sons of Manasseh: of Machir, the family of the Machirites; and Machir begot Gilead; of Gilead, the family of the Gileadites. 30 These *are* the sons of Gilead: *of* Jeezer,*a* the family of the Jeezerites; of Helek, the family of the Helekites; 31 *of* Asriel, the family of the Asrielites; *of* Shechem, the family of the Shechemites; 32 *of* Shemida, the family of the Shemidaites; *of* Hepher, the family of the Hepherites. 33 Now Zelophehad the son of Hepher had no sons, but daughters; and the names of the daughters of Zelophehad *were* Mahlah, Noah, Hoglah, Milcah, and Tirzah. 34 These *are* the families of Manasseh; and those who were numbered of them *were* fifty-two thousand seven hundred.

35 These *are* the sons of Ephraim according to their families: of Shuthelah, the family of the Shuthalhites; of Becher,*a* the family of the Bachrites; of Tahan, the family of the Tahanites. 36 And these *are* the sons of Shuthelah: of Eran, the family of the Eranites. 37 These *are* the families of the sons of Ephraim according to those who were numbered of them: thirty-two thousand five hundred.

These *are* the sons of Joseph according to their families.

38 The sons of Benjamin according to their families were: of Bela, the family of the Belaites; of Ashbel, the family of the Ashbelites; of Ahiram, the family of the Ahiramites; 39 of Shupham,*a* the family of the Shuphamites; of Hupham,*b* the family of the Huphamites. 40 And the sons of Bela were Ard*a* and Naaman: *of* Ard, the family of the Ardites; of Naaman, the family of the Naamites. 41 These *are* the sons of Benjamin according to their families; and those who were numbered of them *were* forty-five thousand six hundred.

42 These *are* the sons of Dan according to their families: of Shuham,*a* the family of the Shuhamites. These *are* the families of Dan according to their families. 43 All the families of the Shuhamites, according to those who were numbered of them, *were* sixty-four thousand four hundred.

44 The sons of Asher according to their families *were:* of Jimna, the family of the Jimnites; of Jesui, the family of the Jesuites; of Beriah, the family of the Beriites. 45 Of the sons of Beriah: of Heber, the family of the Heberites; of Malchiel, the family of the Malchielites. 46 And the name of the daughter of Asher *was* Serah. 47 These *are* the families of the sons of Asher according to those who were numbered of them: fifty-three thousand four hundred.

48 The sons of Naphtali according to their families *were:* of Jahzeel,*a* the family of the Jahzeelites; of Guni, the family of the Gunites; 49 of Jezer, the family of the Jezerites; of Shillem, the family of the Shillemites. 50 These *are* the families of Naphtali according to their families; and those who were numbered of them *were* forty-five thousand four hundred.

51 These *are* those who were num-

26:23 *a*Hebrew *Puvah* (compare Genesis 46:13 and 1 Chronicles 7:1); Samaritan Pentateuch, Septuagint, Syriac, and Vulgate read *Puah.* *b*Samaritan Pentateuch, Septuagint, Syriac, and Vulgate read *Puaites.* 26:30 *a*Called *Abiezer* in Joshua 17:2　26:35 *a*Called *Bered* in 1 Chronicles 7:20　26:39 *a*Masoretic Text reads *Shephupham,* spelled *Shephuphan* in 1 Chronicles 8:5.　*b*Called *Huppim* in Genesis 46:21 26:40 *a*Called *Addar* in 1 Chronicles 8:3　26:42 *a*Called *Hushim* in Genesis 46:23　26:48 *a*Spelled *Jahziel* in 1 Chronicles 7:13

Gospel Pearls

bered of the children of Israel: six hundred and one thousand seven hundred and thirty.

52 Then the LORD spoke to Moses, saying: 53 "To these the land shall be divided as an inheritance, according to the number of names. 54 To a large *tribe* you shall give a larger inheritance, and to a small *tribe* you shall give a smaller inheritance. Each shall be given its inheritance according to those who were numbered of them. 55 But the land shall be divided by lot; they shall inherit according to the names of the tribes of their fathers. 56 According to the lot their inheritance shall be divided between the larger and the smaller."

57 And these *are* those who were numbered of the Levites according to their families: of Gershon, the family of the Gershonites; of Kohath, the family of the Kohathites; of Merari, the family of the Merarites. 58 These *are* the families of the Levites: the family of the Libnites, the family of the Hebronites, the family of the Mahlites, the family of the Mushites, and the family of the Korathites. And Kohath begot Amram. 59 The name of Amram's wife *was* Jochebed the daughter of Levi, who was born to Levi in Egypt; and to Amram she bore Aaron and Moses and their sister Miriam. 60 To Aaron were born Nadab and Abihu, Eleazar and Ithamar. 61 And Nadab and Abihu died when they offered profane fire before the LORD.

62 Now those who were numbered of them were twenty-three thousand, every male from a month old and above; for they were not numbered among the other children of Israel, because there was no inheritance given to them among the children of Israel.

63 These *are* those who were numbered by Moses and Eleazar the priest, who numbered the children of Israel in the plains of Moab by the Jordan, *across from* Jericho. 64 But among these there was not a man of those who were numbered by Moses and Aaron the priest when they numbered the children of Israel in the Wilderness of Sinai. 65 For the LORD had said of them, "They shall surely die in the wilderness." So there was not left a man of them, except Caleb the son of Jephunneh and Joshua the son of Nun.

27 Then came the daughters of Zelophehad the son of Hepher, the son of Gilead, the son of Machir, the son of Manasseh, from the families of Manasseh the son of Joseph; and these *were* the names of his daughters: Mahlah, Noah, Hoglah, Milcah, and Tirzah. 2 And they stood before Moses, before Eleazar the priest, and before the leaders and all the congregation, *by* the doorway of the tabernacle of meeting, saying: 3 "Our father died in the wilderness; but he was not in the company of those who gathered together against the LORD, in company with Korah, but he died in his own sin; and he had no sons. 4 Why should the name of our father be removed from among his family because he had no son? Give us a possession among our father's brothers."

5 So Moses brought their case before the LORD.

6 And the LORD spoke to Moses, saying: 7 "The daughters of Zelophehad speak *what is* right; you shall surely give them a possession of inheritance among their father's brothers, and cause the inheritance of their father to pass to them. 8 And you shall speak to the children of Israel, saying: 'If a man dies and has no son, then you shall cause his inheritance to pass to his daughter. 9 If he has no daughter, then you shall give his inheritance to his brothers. 10 If he has no brothers, then you shall give his inheritance to his father's brothers. 11 And if his father has no brothers, then you shall give his inheritance to the relative closest to him in his family, and he shall possess it.' " And it shall be to the children of Israel a statute of judgment, just as the LORD commanded Moses.

12 Now the LORD said to Moses: "Go up into this Mount Abarim, and see the land which I have given to the children of Israel. 13 And when you have seen it, you also shall be gathered to your people, as Aaron your brother was gathered. 14 For in the Wilderness of Zin, during the strife of the congregation, you rebelled against My command to hallow Me at the waters before their eyes." (These *are* the waters of Meribah, at Kadesh in the Wilderness of Zin.)

15 Then Moses spoke to the LORD, saying: 16 "Let the LORD, the God of

Trusting God transforms calamity into testimony. Knowing that He cares too much for you to abuse you and that He is too wise to be wrong causes a wounded heart to serenade the heavens. When we begin to know Him rather than just serve Him, we can trust His vision, His wisdom and His insight.

Your Father Left You Loaded

Numbers 27:4–8

*T*he Father wants to release the held-up blessing to the pressed-down daughter. You see, ultimately the Father's will is all that matters. So when the daughters of Zelophehad had a problem with their inheritance, Moses asked the Lord what to do.

This was the first case of gender discrimination mentioned in the Scriptures. The court of heaven ruled in the favor of some women who knew how to go after their father's estate!

If you have your Father's favor, no one can stop your blessing. Don't waste your time and energy fighting the opposition. If God is for you, who can be against you (see Romans 8:31)? Just remember who is for you. Your faith will be strengthened through conflict and struggle.

Perhaps there are some things in store for you. Don't be intimidated. Go for it. You may be a single parent. There may not be a "son" to fend for you. Your husband may be long gone. But your blessing doesn't center around a man, or men in general, for that matter. By God's grace and power, you can still receive the inheritance.

Why don't you, as a daughter of God, go after what the Father has willed you? He died for you, and He wants you to have your inheritance. I encourage you as a father would encourage his daughter: Go for all that life has to offer you. Take a large slice of life. Savor every bite. Your Father has willed you good things.

If you have been walking around with a drab spirit and a broken heart, I am talking to you. If you have been in a state of depression that is robbing you of these precious years when you should be thriving and pursuing your destiny, hear this word. Don't waste another day in regret, sleeping away God's mercy, losing your chance to achieve and receive. Get up and get busy. You may have to work it out. You may have to push and shove. But life is worth the struggle.

Now pull off those ragged house shoes and that gingham dress. Take those curlers out of your hair. Take a long, hot, luxurious bath and put on some sweet cologne. If you want it, you can have it. Your Father left you loaded!

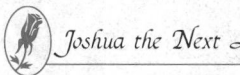

the spirits of all flesh, set a man over the congregation, 17 who may go out before them and go in before them, who may lead them out and bring them in, that the congregation of the LORD may not be like sheep which have no shepherd."

18 And the LORD said to Moses: "Take Joshua the son of Nun with you, a man in whom *is* the Spirit, and lay your hand on him; 19 set him before Eleazar the priest and before all the congregation, and inaugurate him in their sight. 20 And you shall give *some* of your authority to him, that all the congregation of the children of Israel may be obedient. 21 He shall stand before Eleazar the priest, who shall inquire before the LORD for him by the judgment of the Urim. At his word they shall go out, and at his word they shall come in, he and all the children of Israel with him—all the congregation."

22 So Moses did as the LORD commanded him. He took Joshua and set him before Eleazar the priest and before all the congregation. 23 And he laid his hands on him and inaugurated him, just as the LORD commanded by the hand of Moses.

28 Now the LORD spoke to Moses, saying, 2 "Command the children of Israel, and say to them, 'My offering, My food for My offerings made by fire as a sweet aroma to Me, you shall be careful to offer to Me at their appointed time.'

3 "And you shall say to them, 'This *is* the offering made by fire which you shall offer to the LORD: two male lambs in their first year without blemish, day by day, as a regular burnt offering. 4 The one lamb you shall offer in the morning, the other lamb you shall offer in the evening, 5 and one-tenth of an ephah of fine flour as a grain offering mixed with one-fourth of a hin of pressed oil. 6 *It is* a regular burnt offering which was ordained at Mount Sinai for a sweet aroma, an offering made by fire to the LORD. 7 And its drink offering *shall be* one-fourth of a hin for each lamb; in a holy *place* you shall pour out the drink to the LORD as an offering. 8 The other lamb you shall offer in the evening; as the morning grain offering and its drink offering, you shall offer *it* as an offering made by fire, a sweet aroma to the LORD.

9 'And on the Sabbath day two lambs in their first year, without blemish, and two-tenths *of an ephah* of fine flour as a grain offering, mixed with oil, with its drink offering— 10 *this is* the burnt offering for every Sabbath, besides the regular burnt offering with its drink offering.

11 'At the beginnings of your months you shall present a burnt offering to the LORD: two young bulls, one ram, and seven lambs in their first year, without blemish; 12 three-tenths *of an ephah* of fine flour as a grain offering, mixed with oil, for each bull; two-tenths *of an ephah* of fine flour as a grain offering, mixed with oil, for the one ram; 13 and one-tenth *of an ephah* of fine flour, mixed with oil, as a grain offering for each lamb, as a burnt offering of sweet aroma, an offering made by fire to the LORD. 14 Their drink offering shall be half a hin of wine for a bull, one-third of a hin for a ram, and one-fourth of a hin for a lamb; this *is* the burnt offering for each month throughout the months of the year. 15 Also one kid of the goats as a sin offering to the LORD shall be offered, besides the regular burnt offering and its drink offering.

16 'On the fourteenth day of the first month *is* the Passover of the LORD. 17 And on the fifteenth day of this month *is* the feast; unleavened bread shall be eaten for seven days. 18 On the first day *you shall have* a holy convocation. You shall do no customary work. 19 And you shall present an offering made by fire as a burnt offering to the LORD: two young bulls, one ram, and seven lambs in their first year. Be sure they are without blemish. 20 Their grain offering shall be of fine flour mixed with oil: three-tenths *of an ephah* you shall offer for a bull, and two-tenths for a ram; 21 you shall offer one-tenth *of an ephah* for each of the seven lambs; 22 also one goat *as* a sin offering, to make atonement for you. 23 You shall offer these besides the burnt offering of the morning, which *is* for a regular burnt offering. 24 In this manner you shall offer the food of the offering made by fire daily for seven days, as a sweet aroma to the LORD; it shall be offered besides the regular burnt offering and its drink offering. 25 And on the seventh day you shall have a holy

We can readily accept His authority when it is used to perform what we know to be a favor. The real challenge of submission is to submit when the human will would have chosen another way.

convocation. You shall do no customary work.

26 'Also on the day of the firstfruits, when you bring a new grain offering to the LORD at your *Feast of* Weeks, you shall have a holy convocation. You shall do no customary work. 27 You shall present a burnt offering as a sweet aroma to the LORD: two young bulls, one ram, and seven lambs in their first year, 28 with their grain offering of fine flour mixed with oil: three-tenths *of an ephah* for each bull, two-tenths for the one ram, 29 and one-tenth for each of the seven lambs; 30 *also* one kid of the goats, to make atonement for you. 31 Be sure they are without blemish. You shall present *them* with their drink offerings, besides the regular burnt offering with its grain offering.

29 'And in the seventh month, on the first *day* of the month, you shall have a holy convocation. You shall do no customary work. For you it is a day of blowing the trumpets. 2 You shall offer a burnt offering as a sweet aroma to the LORD: one young bull, one ram, *and* seven lambs in their first year, without blemish. 3 Their grain offering *shall be* fine flour mixed with oil: three-tenths *of an ephah* for the bull, two-tenths for the ram, 4 and one-tenth for each of the seven lambs; 5 also one kid of the goats *as* a sin offering, to make atonement for you; 6 besides the burnt offering with its grain offering for the New Moon, the regular burnt offering with its grain offering, and their drink offerings, according to their ordinance, as a sweet aroma, an offering made by fire to the LORD.

7 'On the tenth *day* of this seventh month you shall have a holy convocation. You shall afflict your souls; you shall not do any work. 8 You shall present a burnt offering to the LORD *as* a sweet aroma: one young bull, one ram, *and* seven lambs in their first year. Be sure they are without blemish. 9 Their grain offering *shall be of* fine flour mixed with oil: three-tenths *of an ephah* for the bull, two-tenths for the one ram, 10 and one-tenth for each of the seven lambs; 11 also one kid of the goats *as* a sin offering, besides the sin offering for atonement, the regular

burnt offering with its grain offering, and their drink offerings.

12 'On the fifteenth day of the seventh month you shall have a holy convocation. You shall do no customary work, and you shall keep a feast to the LORD seven days. 13 You shall present a burnt offering, an offering made by fire as a sweet aroma to the LORD: thirteen young bulls, two rams, *and* fourteen lambs in their first year. They shall be without blemish. 14 Their grain offering *shall be of* fine flour mixed with oil: three-tenths *of an ephah* for each of the thirteen bulls, two-tenths for each of the two rams, 15 and one-tenth for each of the fourteen lambs; 16 also one kid of the goats *as* a sin offering, besides the regular burnt offering, its grain offering, and its drink offering.

17 'On the second day *present* twelve young bulls, two rams, fourteen lambs in their first year without blemish, 18 and their grain offering and their drink offerings for the bulls, for the rams, and for the lambs, by their number, according to the ordinance; 19 also one kid of the goats *as* a sin offering, besides the regular burnt offering with its grain offering, and their drink offerings.

20 'On the third day *present* eleven bulls, two rams, fourteen lambs in their first year without blemish, 21 and their grain offering and their drink offerings for the bulls, for the rams, and for the lambs, by their number, according to the ordinance; 22 also one goat *as* a sin offering, besides the regular burnt offering, its grain offering, and its drink offering.

23 'On the fourth day *present* ten bulls, two rams, *and* fourteen lambs in their first year, without blemish, 24 and their grain offering and their drink offerings for the bulls, for the rams, and for the lambs, by their number, according to the ordinance; 25 also one kid of the goats *as* a sin offering, besides the regular burnt offering, its grain offering, and its drink offering.

26 'On the fifth day *present* nine bulls, two rams, *and* fourteen lambs in their first year without blemish, 27 and their grain offering and their drink offerings for the bulls, for the rams, and for the lambs, by their number, according to the ordinance; 28 also one goat *as* a sin offering, besides the regular burnt offering, its

Gospel Pearls

grain offering, and its drink offering.

29 'On the sixth day *present* eight bulls, two rams, *and* fourteen lambs in their first year without blemish, 30 and their grain offering and their drink offerings for the bulls, for the rams, and for the lambs, by their number, according to the ordinance; 31 also one goat *as* a sin offering, besides the regular burnt offering, its grain offering, and its drink offering.

32 'On the seventh day *present* seven bulls, two rams, *and* fourteen lambs in their first year without blemish, 33 and their grain offering and their drink offerings for the bulls, for the rams, and for the lambs, by their number, according to the ordinance; 34 also one goat *as* a sin offering, besides the regular burnt offering, its grain offering, and its drink offering.

35 'On the eighth day you shall have a sacred assembly. You shall do no customary work. 36 You shall present a burnt offering, an offering made by fire as a sweet aroma to the LORD: one bull, one ram, seven lambs in their first year without blemish, 37 and their grain offering and their drink offerings for the bull, for the ram, and for the lambs, by their number, according to the ordinance; 38 also one goat *as* a sin offering, besides the regular burnt offering, its grain offering, and its drink offering.

39 'These you shall present to the LORD at your appointed feasts (besides your vowed offerings and your freewill offerings) as your burnt offerings and your grain offerings, as your drink offerings and your peace offerings.' "

40 So Moses told the children of Israel everything, just as the LORD commanded Moses.

30 Then Moses spoke to the heads of the tribes concerning the children of Israel, saying, "This *is* the thing which the LORD has commanded: 2 If a man makes a vow to the LORD, or swears an oath to bind himself by some agreement, he shall not break his word; he shall do according to all that proceeds out of his mouth.

3 "Or if a woman makes a vow to the LORD, and binds *herself* by some agreement while in her father's house in her youth, 4 and her father hears her vow and the agreement by which she has bound herself, and her father holds his peace, then all her vows shall stand, and every agreement with which she has bound herself shall stand. 5 But if her father overrules her on the day that he hears, then none of her vows nor her agreements by which she has bound herself shall stand; and the LORD will release her, because her father overruled her.

6 "If indeed she takes a husband, while bound by her vows or by a rash utterance from her lips by which she bound herself, 7 and her husband hears *it,* and makes no response to her on the day that he hears, then her vows shall stand, and her agreements by which she bound herself shall stand. 8 But if her husband overrules her on the day that he hears *it,* he shall make void her vow which she took and what she uttered with her lips, by which she bound herself, and the LORD will release her.

9 "Also any vow of a widow or a divorced woman, by which she has bound herself, shall stand against her.

10 "If she vowed in her husband's house, or bound herself by an agreement with an oath, 11 and her husband heard *it,* and made no response to her *and* did not overrule her, then all her vows shall stand, and every agreement by which she bound herself shall stand. 12 But if her husband truly made them void on the day he heard *them,* then whatever proceeded from her lips concerning her vows or concerning the agreement binding her, it shall not stand; her husband has made them void, and the LORD will release her. 13 Every vow and every binding oath to afflict her soul, her husband may confirm it, or her husband may make it void. 14 Now if her husband makes no response whatever to her from day to day, then he confirms all her vows or all the agreements that bind her; he confirms them, because he made no response to her on the day that he heard *them.* 15 But if he does make them void after he has heard *them,* then he shall bear her guilt."

16 These *are* the statutes which the LORD commanded Moses, between a man and his wife, and between a fa-

---

*I*t is significant to understand that the shut door is just as much a move of God as the open one. It is the same mighty hand, it is the same loving heart. It is an action predetermined by the wisdom of a Father who knows what is best.

ther and his daughter in her youth in her father's house.

31 And the LORD spoke to Moses, saying: 2 "Take vengeance on the Midianites for the children of Israel. Afterward you shall be gathered to your people."

3 So Moses spoke to the people, saying, "Arm some of yourselves for war, and let them go against the Midianites to take vengeance for the LORD on Midian. 4 A thousand from each tribe of all the tribes of Israel you shall send to the war."

5 So there were recruited from the divisions of Israel one thousand from *each* tribe, twelve thousand armed for war. 6 Then Moses sent them to the war, one thousand from *each* tribe; he sent them to the war with Phinehas the son of Eleazar the priest, with the holy articles and the signal trumpets in his hand. 7 And they warred against the Midianites, just as the LORD commanded Moses, and they killed all the males. 8 They killed the kings of Midian with *the rest of* those who were killed—Evi, Rekem, Zur, Hur, and Reba, the five kings of Midian. Balaam the son of Beor they also killed with the sword.

9 And the children of Israel took the women of Midian captive, with their little ones, and took as spoil all their cattle, all their flocks, and all their goods. 10 They also burned with fire all the cities where they dwelt, and all their forts. 11 And they took all the spoil and all the booty—of man and beast.

12 Then they brought the captives, the booty, and the spoil to Moses, to Eleazar the priest, and to the congregation of the children of Israel, to the camp in the plains of Moab by the Jordan, *across from* Jericho. 13 And Moses, Eleazar the priest, and all the leaders of the congregation, went to meet them outside the camp. 14 But Moses was angry with the officers of the army, *with* the captains over thousands and captains over hundreds, who had come from the battle.

15 And Moses said to them: "Have you kept all the women alive? 16 Look, these *women* caused the children of Israel, through the counsel of Balaam, to trespass against the LORD in the incident of Peor, and

there was a plague among the congregation of the LORD. 17 Now therefore, kill every male among the little ones, and kill every woman who has known a man intimately. 18 But keep alive for yourselves all the young girls who have not known a man intimately. 19 And as for you, remain outside the camp seven days; whoever has killed any person, and whoever has touched any slain, purify yourselves and your captives on the third day and on the seventh day. 20 Purify every garment, everything made of leather, everything woven of goats' *hair,* and everything made of wood."

21 Then Eleazar the priest said to the men of war who had gone to the battle, "This *is* the ordinance of the law which the LORD commanded Moses: 22 "Only the gold, the silver, the bronze, the iron, the tin, and the lead, 23 everything that can endure fire, you shall put through the fire, and it shall be clean; and it shall be purified with the water of purification. But all that cannot endure fire you shall put through water. 24 And you shall wash your clothes on the seventh day and be clean, and afterward you may come into the camp."

25 Now the LORD spoke to Moses, saying: 26 "Count up the plunder that was taken—of man and beast—you and Eleazar the priest and the chief fathers of the congregation; 27 and divide the plunder into two parts, between those who took part in the war, who went out to battle, and all the congregation. 28 And levy a tribute for the LORD on the men of war who went out to battle: one of every five hundred of the persons, the cattle, the donkeys, and the sheep; 29 take *it* from their half, and give *it* to Eleazar the priest as a heave offering to the LORD. 30 And from the children of Israel's half you shall take one of every fifty, drawn from the persons, the cattle, the donkeys, and the sheep, from all the livestock, and give them to the Levites who keep charge of the tabernacle of the LORD." 31 So Moses and Eleazar the priest did as the LORD commanded Moses.

32 The booty remaining from the plunder, which the men of war had taken, was six hundred and seventy-five thousand sheep, 33 seventy-two thousand cattle, 34 sixty-one thou-

sand donkeys, 35 and thirty-two thousand persons in all, of women who had not known a man intimately. 36 And the half, the portion for those who had gone out to war, was in number three hundred and thirty-seven thousand five hundred sheep; 37 and the LORD's tribute of the sheep was six hundred and seventy-five. 38 The cattle *were* thirty-six thousand, of which the LORD's tribute *was* seventy-two. 39 The donkeys *were* thirty thousand five hundred, of which the LORD's tribute *was* sixty-one. 40 The persons *were* sixteen thousand, of which the LORD's tribute *was* thirty-two persons. 41 So Moses gave the tribute *which was* the LORD's heave offering to Eleazar the priest, as the LORD commanded Moses.

42 And from the children of Israel's half, which Moses separated from the men who fought— 43 now the half belonging to the congregation was three hundred and thirty-seven thousand five hundred sheep, 44 thirty-six thousand cattle, 45 thirty thousand five hundred donkeys, 46 and sixteen thousand persons— 47 and from the children of Israel's half Moses took one of every fifty, drawn from man and beast, and gave them to the Levites, who kept charge of the tabernacle of the LORD, as the LORD commanded Moses.

48 Then the officers who *were* over thousands of the army, the captains of thousands and captains of hundreds, came near to Moses; 49 and they said to Moses, "Your servants have taken a count of the men of war who *are* under our command, and not a man of us is missing. 50 Therefore we have brought an offering for the LORD, what every man found of ornaments of gold: armlets and bracelets and signet rings and earrings and necklaces, to make atonement for ourselves before the LORD." 51 So Moses and Eleazar the priest received the gold from them, all the fashioned ornaments. 52 And all the gold of the offering that they offered to the LORD, from the captains of thousands and captains of hundreds, was sixteen thousand seven hundred and fifty shekels. 53 (The men of war had taken spoil, every man for himself.) 54 And Moses and Eleazar the priest received the gold from the captains of thousands

and of hundreds, and brought it into the tabernacle of meeting as a memorial for the children of Israel before the LORD.

32 Now the children of Reuben and the children of Gad had a very great multitude of livestock; and when they saw the land of Jazer and the land of Gilead, that indeed the region *was* a place for livestock, 2 the children of Gad and the children of Reuben came and spoke to Moses, to Eleazar the priest, and to the leaders of the congregation, saying, 3 "Ataroth, Dibon, Jazer, Nimrah, Heshbon, Elealeh, Shebam, Nebo, and Beon, 4 the country which the LORD defeated before the congregation of Israel, *is* a land for livestock, and your servants have livestock." 5 Therefore they said, "If we have found favor in your sight, let this land be given to your servants as a possession. Do not take us over the Jordan."

6 And Moses said to the children of Gad and to the children of Reuben: "Shall your brethren go to war while you sit here? 7 Now why will you discourage the heart of the children of Israel from going over into the land which the LORD has given them? 8 Thus your fathers did when I sent them away from Kadesh Barnea to see the land. 9 For when they went up to the Valley of Eshcol and saw the land, they discouraged the heart of the children of Israel, so that they did not go into the land which the LORD had given them. 10 So the LORD's anger was aroused on that day, and He swore an oath, saying, 11 'Surely none of the men who came up from Egypt, from twenty years old and above, shall see the land of which I swore to Abraham, Isaac, and Jacob, because they have not wholly followed Me, 12 except Caleb the son of Jephunneh, the Kenizzite, and Joshua the son of Nun, for they have wholly followed the LORD.' 13 So the LORD's anger was aroused against Israel, and He made them wander in the wilderness forty years, until all the generation that had done evil in the sight of the LORD was gone. 14 And look! You have risen in your fathers' place, a brood of sinful men, to increase still more the fierce anger of the LORD against Israel. 15 For if you turn away from following Him,

Young women, whose bright eyes and burning hearts promise to shake nations and capture the hearts of many men, run from the suitors and walk with the Savior. He will not fail you.

He will once again leave them in the wilderness, and you will destroy all these people."

16 Then they came near to him and said: "We will build sheepfolds here for our livestock, and cities for our little ones, 17 but we ourselves will be armed, ready *to* go before the children of Israel until we have brought them to their place; and our little ones will dwell in the fortified cities because of the inhabitants of the land. 18 We will not return to our homes until every one of the children of Israel has received his inheritance. 19 For we will not inherit with them on the other side of the Jordan and beyond, because our inheritance has fallen to us on this eastern side of the Jordan."

20 Then Moses said to them: "If you do this thing, if you arm yourselves before the LORD for the war, 21 and all your armed men cross over the Jordan before the LORD until He has driven out His enemies from before Him, 22 and the land is subdued before the LORD, then afterward you may return and be blameless before the LORD and before Israel; and this land shall be your possession before the LORD. 23 But if you do not do so, then take note, you have sinned against the LORD; and be sure your sin will find you out. 24 Build cities for your little ones and folds for your sheep, and do what has proceeded out of your mouth."

25 And the children of Gad and the children of Reuben spoke to Moses, saying: "Your servants will do as my lord commands. 26 Our little ones, our wives, our flocks, and all our livestock will be there in the cities of Gilead; 27 but your servants will cross over, every man armed for war, before the LORD to battle, just as my lord says."

28 So Moses gave command concerning them to Eleazar the priest, to Joshua the son of Nun, and to the chief fathers of the tribes of the children of Israel. 29 And Moses said to them: "If the children of Gad and the children of Reuben cross over the Jordan with you, every man armed for battle before the LORD, and the land is subdued before you, then you shall give them the land of Gilead as a possession. 30 But if they do not

cross over armed with you, they shall have possessions among you in the land of Canaan."

31 Then the children of Gad and the children of Reuben answered, saying: "As the LORD has said to your servants, so we will do. 32 We will cross over armed before the LORD into the land of Canaan, but the possession of our inheritance *shall remain* with us on this side of the Jordan."

33 So Moses gave to the children of Gad, to the children of Reuben, and to half the tribe of Manasseh the son of Joseph, the kingdom of Sihon king of the Amorites and the kingdom of Og king of Bashan, the land with its cities within the borders, the cities of the surrounding country. 34 And the children of Gad built Dibon and Ataroth and Aroer, 35 Atroth and Shophan and Jazer and Jogbehah, 36 Beth Nimrah and Beth Haran, fortified cities, and folds for sheep. 37 And the children of Reuben built Heshbon and Elealeh and Kirjathaim, 38 Nebo and Baal Meon (*their* names being changed) and Shibmah; and they gave *other* names to the cities which they built.

39 And the children of Machir the son of Manasseh went to Gilead and took it, and dispossessed the Amorites who *were* in it. 40 So Moses gave Gilead to Machir the son of Manasseh, and he dwelt in it. 41 Also Jair the son of Manasseh went and took its small towns, and called them Havoth Jair.ᵃ 42 Then Nobah went and took Kenath and its villages, and he called it Nobah, after his own name.

33 These *are* the journeys of the children of Israel, who went out of the land of Egypt by their armies under the hand of Moses and Aaron. 2 Now Moses wrote down the starting points of their journeys at the command of the LORD. And these *are* their journeys according to their starting points:

3 They departed from Rameses in the first month, on the fifteenth day of the first month; on the day after the Passover the children of Israel went out with boldness in the sight of all the Egyptians. 4 For the Egyptians were burying all *their* firstborn, whom the LORD had killed among

32:41 ᵃLiterally *Towns of Jair*

Gospel Pearls

them. Also on their gods the LORD had executed judgments.

5 Then the children of Israel moved from Rameses and camped at Succoth. 6 They departed from Succoth and camped at Etham, which is on the edge of the wilderness. 7 They moved from Etham and turned back to Pi Hahiroth, which is east of Baal Zephon; and they camped near Migdol. 8 They departed from before Hahiroth[a] and passed through the midst of the sea into the wilderness, went three days' journey in the Wilderness of Etham, and camped at Marah. 9 They moved from Marah and came to Elim. At Elim were twelve springs of water and seventy palm trees; so they camped there.

10 They moved from Elim and camped by the Red Sea. 11 They moved from the Red Sea and camped in the Wilderness of Sin. 12 They journeyed from the Wilderness of Sin and camped at Dophkah. 13 They departed from Dophkah and camped at Alush. 14 They moved from Alush and camped at Rephidim, where there was no water for the people to drink.

15 They departed from Rephidim and camped in the Wilderness of Sinai. 16 They moved from the Wilderness of Sinai and camped at Kibroth Hattaavah. 17 They departed from Kibroth Hattaavah and camped at Hazeroth. 18 They departed from Hazeroth and camped at Rithmah. 19 They departed from Rithmah and camped at Rimmon Perez. 20 They departed from Rimmon Perez and camped at Libnah. 21 They moved from Libnah and camped at Rissah. 22 They journeyed from Rissah and camped at Kehelathah. 23 They went from Kehelathah and camped at Mount Shepher. 24 They moved from Mount Shepher and camped at Haradah. 25 They moved from Haradah and camped at Makheloth. 26 They moved from Makheloth and camped at Tahath. 27 They departed from Tahath and camped at Terah. 28 They moved from Terah and camped at Mithkah. 29 They went from Mithkah and camped at Hashmonah. 30 They departed from Hashmonah and camped at Moseroth. 31 They departed from Moseroth and camped at Bene Jaakan. 32 They moved from

Bene Jaakan and camped at Hor Hagidgad. 33 They went from Hor Hagidgad and camped at Jotbathah. 34 They moved from Jotbathah and camped at Abronah. 35 They departed from Abronah and camped at Ezion Geber. 36 They moved from Ezion Geber and camped in the Wilderness of Zin, which is Kadesh. 37 They moved from Kadesh and camped at Mount Hor, on the boundary of the land of Edom.

38 Then Aaron the priest went up to Mount Hor at the command of the LORD, and died there in the fortieth year after the children of Israel had come out of the land of Egypt, on the first day of the fifth month. 39 Aaron was one hundred and twenty-three years old when he died on Mount Hor.

40 Now the king of Arad, the Canaanite, who dwelt in the South in the land of Canaan, heard of the coming of the children of Israel.

41 So they departed from Mount Hor and camped at Zalmonah. 42 They departed from Zalmonah and camped at Punon. 43 They departed from Punon and camped at Oboth. 44 They departed from Oboth and camped at Ije Abarim, at the border of Moab. 45 They departed from Ijim[a] and camped at Dibon Gad. 46 They moved from Dibon Gad and camped at Almon Diblathaim. 47 They moved from Almon Diblathaim and camped in the mountains of Abarim, before Nebo. 48 They departed from the mountains of Abarim and camped in the plains of Moab by the Jordan, across from Jericho. 49 They camped by the Jordan, from Beth Jesimoth as far as the Abel Acacia Grove[a] in the plains of Moab.

50 Now the LORD spoke to Moses in the plains of Moab by the Jordan, across from Jericho, saying, 51 "Speak to the children of Israel, and say to them: 'When you have crossed the Jordan into the land of Canaan, 52 then you shall drive out all the inhabitants of the land from before you, destroy all their engraved stones, destroy all their molded images, and demolish all their high places; 53 you shall dispossess the inhabitants of the land and dwell in it, for I have given you the land to pos-

---

33:8 [a]Many Hebrew manuscripts, Samaritan Pentateuch, Syriac, Targum, and Vulgate read from Pi Hahiroth (compare verse 7).   33:45 [a]Same as Ije Abarim, verse 44   33:49 [a]Hebrew Abel Shittim

---

*L*ook for the bright days and the rich moments of life. Expect them, and if they don't come, make them happen. Insist on taking a bite out of life and touching heaven. It is your right. You are the daughter of a King.

sess. 54 And you shall divide the land by lot as an inheritance among your families; to the larger you shall give a larger inheritance, and to the smaller you shall give a smaller inheritance; there everyone's *inheritance* shall be whatever falls to him by lot. You shall inherit according to the tribes of your fathers. 55 But if you do not drive out the inhabitants of the land from before you, then it shall be that those whom you let remain *shall be* irritants in your eyes and thorns in your sides, and they shall harass you in the land where you dwell. 56 Moreover it shall be *that* I will do to you as I thought to do to them.' "

34 Then the LORD spoke to Moses, saying, 2 "Command the children of Israel, and say to them: 'When you come into the land of Canaan, this *is* the land that shall fall to you as an inheritance—the land of Canaan to its boundaries. 3 Your southern border shall be from the Wilderness of Zin along the border of Edom; then your southern border shall extend eastward to the end of the Salt Sea; 4 your border shall turn from the southern side of the Ascent of Akrabbim, continue to Zin, and be on the south of Kadesh Barnea; then it shall go on to Hazar Addar, and continue to Azmon; 5 the border shall turn from Azmon to the Brook of Egypt, and it shall end at the Sea.

6 'As for the western border, you shall have the Great Sea for a border; this shall be your western border.

7 'And this shall be your northern border: From the Great Sea you shall mark out your *border* line to Mount Hor; 8 from Mount Hor you shall mark out *your border* to the entrance of Hamath; then the direction of the border shall be toward Zedad; 9 the border shall proceed to Ziphron, and it shall end at Hazar Enan. This shall be your northern border.

10 'You shall mark out your eastern border from Hazar Enan to Shepham; 11 the border shall go down from Shepham to Riblah on the east side of Ain; the border shall go down and reach to the eastern side of the Sea of Chinnereth; 12 the border shall go down along the Jordan, and it shall end at the Salt Sea. This shall be your land with its surrounding boundaries.' "

13 Then Moses commanded the children of Israel, saying: "This *is* the land which you shall inherit by lot, which the LORD has commanded to give to the nine tribes and to the half-tribe. 14 For the tribe of the children of Reuben according to the house of their fathers, and the tribe of the children of Gad according to the house of their fathers, have received *their inheritance;* and the half-tribe of Manasseh has received its inheritance. 15 The two tribes and the half-tribe have received their inheritance on this side of the Jordan, *across from* Jericho eastward, toward the sunrise."

16 And the LORD spoke to Moses, saying, 17 "These *are* the names of the men who shall divide the land among you as an inheritance: Eleazar the priest and Joshua the son of Nun. 18 And you shall take one leader of every tribe to divide the land for the inheritance. 19 These *are* the names of the men: from the tribe of Judah, Caleb the son of Jephunneh; 20 from the tribe of the children of Simeon, Shemuel the son of Ammihud; 21 from the tribe of Benjamin, Elidad the son of Chislon; 22 a leader from the tribe of the children of Dan, Bukki the son of Jogli; 23 from the sons of Joseph: a leader from the tribe of the children of Manasseh, Hanniel the son of Ephod, 24 and a leader from the tribe of the children of Ephraim, Kemuel the son of Shiphtan; 25 a leader from the tribe of the children of Zebulun, Elizaphan the son of Parnach; 26 a leader from the tribe of the children of Issachar, Paltiel the son of Azzan; 27 a leader from the tribe of the children of Asher, Ahihud the son of Shelomi; 28 and a leader from the tribe of the children of Naphtali, Pedahel the son of Ammihud."

29 These *are* the ones the LORD commanded to divide the inheritance among the children of Israel in the land of Canaan.

35 And the LORD spoke to Moses in the plains of Moab by the Jordan *across from* Jericho, saying: 2 "Command the children of Israel that they give the Levites cities to dwell in from the inheritance of their possession, and you shall *also* give the Levites common-land around the cities. 3 They shall have the cities to

Gospel
Pearls

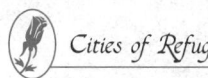
dwell in; and their common-land shall be for their cattle, for their herds, and for all their animals. 4 The common-land of the cities which you will give the Levites *shall extend* from the wall of the city outward a thousand cubits all around. 5 And you shall measure outside the city on the east side two thousand cubits, on the south side two thousand cubits, on the west side two thousand cubits, and on the north side two thousand cubits. The city *shall be* in the middle. This shall belong to them as common-land for the cities.

6 "Now among the cities which you will give to the Levites *you shall appoint* six cities of refuge, to which a manslayer may flee. And to these you shall add forty-two cities. 7 So all the cities you will give to the Levites *shall be* forty-eight; these *you shall give* with their common-land. 8 And the cities which you will give *shall be* from the possession of the children of Israel; from the larger *tribe* you shall give many, from the smaller you shall give few. Each shall give some of its cities to the Levites, in proportion to the inheritance that each receives."

9 Then the LORD spoke to Moses, saying, 10 "Speak to the children of Israel, and say to them: 'When you cross the Jordan into the land of Canaan, 11 then you shall appoint cities to be cities of refuge for you, that the manslayer who kills any person accidentally may flee there. 12 They shall be cities of refuge for you from the avenger, that the manslayer may not die until he stands before the congregation in judgment. 13 And of the cities which you give, you shall have six cities of refuge. 14 You shall appoint three cities on this side of the Jordan, and three cities you shall appoint in the land of Canaan, *which* will be cities of refuge. 15 These six cities shall be for refuge for the children of Israel, for the stranger, and for the sojourner among them, that anyone who kills a person accidentally may flee there.

16 But if he strikes him with an iron implement, so that he dies, he *is* a murderer; the murderer shall surely be put to death. 17 And if he strikes him with a stone in the hand, by which one could die, and he does die, he *is* a murderer; the murderer shall surely be put to death. 18 Or *if* he strikes him with a wooden hand weapon, by which one could die, and he does die, he *is* a murderer; the murderer shall surely be put to death. 19 The avenger of blood himself shall put the murderer to death; when he meets him, he shall put him to death. 20 If he pushes him out of hatred or, while lying in wait, hurls something at him so that he dies, 21 or in enmity he strikes him with his hand so that he dies, the one who struck *him* shall surely be put to death. He *is* a murderer. The avenger of blood shall put the murderer to death when he meets him.

22 However, if he pushes him suddenly without enmity, or throws anything at him without lying in wait, 23 or uses a stone, by which a man could die, throwing *it* at him without seeing *him,* so that he dies, while he was not his enemy or seeking his harm, 24 then the congregation shall judge between the manslayer and the avenger of blood according to these judgments. 25 So the congregation shall deliver the manslayer from the hand of the avenger of blood, and the congregation shall return him to the city of refuge where he had fled, and he shall remain there until the death of the high priest who was anointed with the holy oil. 26 But if the manslayer at any time goes outside the limits of the city of refuge where he fled, 27 and the avenger of blood finds him outside the limits of his city of refuge, and the avenger of blood kills the manslayer, he shall not be guilty of blood, 28 because he should have remained in his city of refuge until the death of the high priest. But after the death of the high priest the manslayer may return to the land of his possession.

29 'And these *things* shall be a statute of judgment to you throughout your generations in all your dwellings. 30 Whoever kills a person, the murderer shall be put to death on the testimony of witnesses; but one witness is not *sufficient* testimony against a person for the death *penalty.* 31 Moreover you shall take no ransom for the life of a murderer who *is* guilty of death, but he shall surely be put to death. 32 And you shall take no ransom for him who has fled to his city of refuge, that he may return to dwell in the land before the death of the priest. 33 So you shall not pol-

Your Right to Be Blessed

Numbers 36:10-12

You have a right to be blessed. The very fact that God has endowed you with ability proves that He has a purpose for you. He gave you the gifting, but you will have to give an account of what you did with it.

Every day is a gift from God. What you do with that day or with your talent is your gift to Him. Have you hidden your talent because someone said you didn't have it? Did they say it was because you are a woman? That's ridiculous. You are only limited by your own creativity and concentration.

Many women have suppressed their God-given ability trying to live up to some negative stereotype—the same stereotype God wants them to shatter. You have neglected a right that the Father gave you at great sacrifice. What a price He has paid to give you your inheritance. It cost the Father His Son's life. It would be like a natural father working all of his life to give his daughter her inheritance, and then have her squander it. Or worse still, refuse to claim it because she is a woman.

Remember the daughters of Zelophehad (see Numbers 27:4-8)? These women challenged the system at a time when women were considered inferior to men. In spite of public opinion, they chose to speak up for their rights, and they got what they wanted.

Many of you are dying from apathy and boredom. You have not challenged life, and life has not challenged you. You need to exercise your potential. Get your blood circulating. Good, spiritual aerobic exercise will start your heart pumping. A stimulating life can even help guard you from mischief and sin. When you're bored, Satan takes the initiative. And you know where that leads.

It is possible to construct an obstacle in your own mind. Don't be limited by your own tendency to settle for less. If you're not careful, you will talk yourself out of living. Speak up and say, "I need more life in my life."

The daughters of Zelophehad refused to be wallflowers when they knew they had the Father's favor. Do likewise. Bloom and blossom and grow in the light of the Father's love.

lute the land where you *are;* for blood defiles the land, and no atonement can be made for the land, for the blood that is shed on it, except by the blood of him who shed it. 34 Therefore do not defile the land which you inhabit, in the midst of which I dwell; for I the LORD dwell among the children of Israel.' "

36 Now the chief fathers of the families of the children of Gilead the son of Machir, the son of Manasseh, of the families of the sons of Joseph, came near and spoke before Moses and before the leaders, the chief fathers of the children of Israel. 2 And they said: "The LORD commanded my lord *Moses* to give the land as an inheritance by lot to the children of Israel, and my lord was commanded by the LORD to give the inheritance of our brother Zelophehad to his daughters. 3 Now if they are married to any of the sons of the *other* tribes of the children of Israel, then their inheritance will be taken from the inheritance of our fathers, and it will be added to the inheritance of the tribe into which they marry; so it will be taken from the lot of our inheritance. 4 And when the Jubilee of the children of Israel comes, then their inheritance will be added to the inheritance of the tribe into which they marry; so their inheritance will be taken away from the inheritance of the tribe of our fathers."

5 Then Moses commanded the children of Israel according to the word of the LORD, saying: "What the tribe of the sons of Joseph speaks is right. 6 This *is* what the LORD commands concerning the daughters of Zelophehad, saying, 'Let them marry whom they think best, but they may marry only within the family of their father's tribe.' 7 So the inheritance of the children of Israel shall not change hands from tribe to tribe, for every one of the children of Israel shall keep the inheritance of the tribe of his fathers. 8 And every daughter who possesses an inheritance in any tribe of the children of Israel shall be the wife of one of the family of her father's tribe, so that the children of Israel each may possess the inheritance of his fathers. 9 Thus no inheritance shall change hands from *one* tribe to another, but every tribe of the children of Israel shall keep its own inheritance."

10 Just as the LORD commanded Moses, so did the daughters of Zelophehad; 11 for Mahlah, Tirzah, Hoglah, Milcah, and Noah, the daughters of Zelophehad, were married to the sons of their father's brothers. 12 They were married into the families of the children of Manasseh the son of Joseph, and their inheritance remained in the tribe of their father's family.

13 These *are* the commandments and the judgments which the LORD commanded the children of Israel by the hand of Moses in the plains of Moab by the Jordan, *across from* Jericho.

The Fifth Book of Moses Called

DEUTERONOMY

1 These *are* the words which Moses spoke to all Israel on this side of the Jordan in the wilderness, in the plain[a] opposite Suph,[b] between Paran, Tophel, Laban, Hazeroth, and Dizahab. 2 *It is* eleven days' *journey* from Horeb by way of Mount Seir to Kadesh Barnea. 3 Now it came to pass in the fortieth year, in the eleventh month, on the first *day* of the month, *that* Moses spoke to the children of Israel according to all that the LORD had given him as commandments to them, 4 after he had killed Sihon king of the Amorites, who dwelt in Heshbon, and Og king of Bashan, who dwelt at Ashtaroth in[a] Edrei.

5 On this side of the Jordan in the land of Moab, Moses began to ex-

1:1 [a]Hebrew *arabah*   [b]One manuscript of the Septuagint, also Targum and Vulgate, read *Red Sea.*
1:4 [a]Septuagint, Syriac, and Vulgate read *and* (compare Joshua 12:4).

God has kissed you with the gentle kiss of a Father's favor whose tenderness would shield you from the traumas of the past. You have been kissed, blessed, touched.

plain this law, saying, 6 "The LORD our God spoke to us in Horeb, saying: 'You have dwelt long enough at this mountain. 7 Turn and take your journey, and go to the mountains of the Amorites, to all the neighboring *places* in the plain,*ᵃ* in the mountains and in the lowland, in the South and on the seacoast, to the land of the Canaanites and to Lebanon, as far as the great river, the River Euphrates. 8 See, I have set the land before you; go in and possess the land which the LORD swore to your fathers—to Abraham, Isaac, and Jacob—to give to them and their descendants after them.'

9 "And I spoke to you at that time, saying: 'I alone am not able to bear you. 10 The LORD your God has multiplied you, and here you *are* today, as the stars of heaven in multitude. 11 May the LORD God of your fathers make you a thousand times more numerous than you are, and bless you as He has promised you! 12 How can I alone bear your problems and your burdens and your complaints? 13 Choose wise, understanding, and knowledgeable men from among your tribes, and I will make them heads over you.' 14 And you answered me and said, 'The thing which you have told *us* to do *is* good.' 15 So I took the heads of your tribes, wise and knowledgeable men, and made them heads over you, leaders of thousands, leaders of hundreds, leaders of fifties, leaders of tens, and officers for your tribes.

16 "Then I commanded your judges at that time, saying, 'Hear *the cases* between your brethren, and judge righteously between a man and his brother or the stranger who is with him. 17 You shall not show partiality in judgment; you shall hear the small as well as the great; you shall not be afraid in any man's presence, for the judgment *is* God's. The case that is too hard for you, bring to me, and I will hear it.' 18 And I commanded you at that time all the things which you should do.

19 "So we departed from Horeb, and went through all that great and terrible wilderness which you saw on the way to the mountains of the Amorites, as the LORD our God had commanded us. Then we came to Kadesh

Barnea. 20 And I said to you, 'You have come to the mountains of the Amorites, which the LORD our God is giving us. 21 Look, the LORD your God has set the land before you; go up *and* possess *it*, as the LORD God of your fathers has spoken to you; do not fear or be discouraged.'

22 "And every one of you came near to me and said, 'Let us send men before us, and let them search out the land for us, and bring back word to us of the way by which we should go up, and of the cities into which we shall come.'

23 "The plan pleased me well; so I took twelve of your men, one man from *each* tribe. 24 And they departed and went up into the mountains, and came to the Valley of Eshcol, and spied it out. 25 They also took *some* of the fruit of the land in their hands and brought *it* down to us; and they brought back word to us, saying, '*It is* a good land which the LORD our God is giving us.'

26 "Nevertheless you would not go up, but rebelled against the command of the LORD your God; 27 and you complained in your tents, and said, 'Because the LORD hates us, He has brought us out of the land of Egypt to deliver us into the hand of the Amorites, to destroy us. 28 Where can we go up? Our brethren have discouraged our hearts, saying, "The people *are* greater and taller than we; the cities *are* great and fortified up to heaven; moreover we have seen the sons of the Anakim there." '

29 "Then I said to you, 'Do not be terrified, or afraid of them. 30 The LORD your God, who goes before you, He will fight for you, according to all He did for you in Egypt before your eyes, 31 and in the wilderness where you saw how the LORD your God carried you, as a man carries his son, in all the way that you went until you came to this place.' 32 Yet, for all that, you did not believe the LORD your God, 33 who went in the way before you to search out a place for you to pitch your tents, to show you the way you should go, in the fire by night and in the cloud by day.

34 "And the LORD heard the sound of your words, and was angry, and took an oath, saying, 35 'Surely not one of these men of this evil genera-

1:7 ᵃHebrew *arabah*

Gospel Pearls

tion shall see that good land of which I swore to give to your fathers, 36 except Caleb the son of Jephunneh; he shall see it, and to him and his children I am giving the land on which he walked, because he wholly followed the LORD.' 37 The LORD was also angry with me for your sakes, saying, 'Even you shall not go in there. 38 Joshua the son of Nun, who stands before you, he shall go in there. Encourage him, for he shall cause Israel to inherit it.

39 'Moreover your little ones and your children, who you say will be victims, who today have no knowledge of good and evil, they shall go in there; to them I will give it, and they shall possess it. 40 But *as for* you, turn and take your journey into the wilderness by the Way of the Red Sea.

41 "Then you answered and said to me, 'We have sinned against the LORD; we will go up and fight, just as the LORD our God commanded us.' And when everyone of you had girded on his weapons of war, you were ready to go up into the mountain.

42 "And the LORD said to me, 'Tell them, "Do not go up nor fight, for I *am* not among you; lest you be defeated before your enemies." '

43 So I spoke to you; yet you would not listen, but rebelled against the command of the LORD, and presumptuously went up into the mountain. 44 And the Amorites who dwelt in that mountain came out against you and chased you as bees do, and drove you back from Seir to Hormah. 45 Then you returned and wept before the LORD, but the LORD would not listen to your voice nor give ear to you.

46 "So you remained in Kadesh many days, according to the days that you spent *there.*

2 "Then we turned and journeyed into the wilderness of the Way of the Red Sea, as the LORD spoke to me, and we skirted Mount Seir for many days.

2 "And the LORD spoke to me, saying: 3 'You have skirted this mountain long enough; turn northward. 4 And command the people, saying, "You *are about to* pass through the territory of your brethren, the descendants of Esau, who live in Seir; and they will be afraid of you. Therefore watch yourselves carefully. 5 Do not meddle with them, for I will not give you *any* of their land, no, not so much as one footstep, because I have given Mount Seir to Esau *as* a possession. 6 You shall buy food from them with money, that you may eat; and you shall also buy water from them with money, that you may drink.

7 "For the LORD your God has blessed you in all the work of your hand. He knows your trudging through this great wilderness. These forty years the LORD your God *has been* with you; you have lacked nothing." '

8 "And when we passed beyond our brethren, the descendants of Esau who dwell in Seir, away from the road of the plain, away from Elath and Ezion Geber, we turned and passed by way of the Wilderness of Moab. 9 Then the LORD said to me, 'Do not harass Moab, nor contend with them in battle, for I will not give you *any* of their land *as* a possession, because I have given Ar to the descendants of Lot *as* a possession.' "

10 (The Emim had dwelt there in times past, a people as great and numerous and tall as the Anakim. 11 They were also regarded as giants,ᵃ like the Anakim, but the Moabites call them Emim. 12 The Horites formerly dwelt in Seir, but the descendants of Esau dispossessed them and destroyed them from before them, and dwelt in their place, just as Israel did to the land of their possession which the LORD gave them.)

13 " 'Now rise and cross over the Valley of the Zered.' So we crossed over the Valley of the Zered. 14 And the time we took to come from Kadesh Barnea until we crossed over the Valley of the Zered *was* thirty-eight years, until all the generation of the men of war was consumed from the midst of the camp, just as the LORD had sworn to them. 15 For indeed the hand of the LORD was against them, to destroy them from the midst of the camp until they were consumed.

16 "So it was, when all the men of war had finally perished from among the people, 17 that the LORD spoke to

2:11 ᵃHebrew *rephaim*

You are kissed by the Father Himself. No wonder Satan has failed to destroy in the night what God has prepared for the light. You have been kissed.

me, saying: 18 'This day you are to cross over at Ar, the boundary of Moab. 19 And *when* you come near the people of Ammon, do not harass them or meddle with them, for I will not give you *any* of the land of the people of Ammon *as* a possession, because I have given it to the descendants of Lot *as* a possession.' "

20 (That was also regarded as a land of giants;*a* giants formerly dwelt there. But the Ammonites call them Zamzummim, 21 a people as great and numerous and tall as the Anakim. But the LORD destroyed them before them, and they dispossessed them and dwelt in their place, 22 just as He had done for the descendants of Esau, who dwelt in Seir, when He destroyed the Horites from before them. They dispossessed them and dwelt in their place, even to this day. 23 And the Avim, who dwelt in villages as far as Gaza—the Caphtorim, who came from Caphtor, destroyed them and dwelt in their place.)

24 " 'Rise, take your journey, and cross over the River Arnon. Look, I have given into your hand Sihon the Amorite, king of Heshbon, and his land. Begin to possess *it*, and engage him in battle. 25 This day I will begin to put the dread and fear of you upon the nations under the whole heaven, who shall hear the report of you, and shall tremble and be in anguish because of you.'

26 "And I sent messengers from the Wilderness of Kedemoth to Sihon king of Heshbon, with words of peace, saying, 27 'Let me pass through your land; I will keep strictly to the road, and I will turn neither to the right nor to the left. 28 You shall sell me food for money, that I may eat, and give me water for money, that I may drink; only let me pass through on foot, 29 just as the descendants of Esau who dwell in Seir and the Moabites who dwell in Ar did for me, until I cross the Jordan to the land which the LORD our God is giving us.'

30 "But Sihon king of Heshbon would not let us pass through, for the LORD your God hardened his spirit and made his heart obstinate, that He might deliver him into your hand, as *it is* this day.

31 "And the LORD said to me, 'See, I have begun to give Sihon and his land over to you. Begin to possess *it*, that you may inherit his land.' 32 Then Sihon and all his people came out against us to fight at Jahaz. 33 And the LORD our God delivered him over to us; so we defeated him, his sons, and all his people. 34 We took all his cities at that time, and we utterly destroyed the men, women, and little ones of every city; we left none remaining. 35 We took only the livestock as plunder for ourselves, with the spoil of the cities which we took. 36 From Aroer, which *is* on the bank of the River Arnon, and *from* the city that *is* in the ravine, as far as Gilead, there was not one city too strong for us; the LORD our God delivered all to us. 37 Only you did not go near the land of the people of Ammon—anywhere along the River Jabbok, or to the cities of the mountains, or wherever the LORD our God had forbidden us.

3 "Then we turned and went up the road to Bashan; and Og king of Bashan came out against us, he and all his people, to battle at Edrei. 2 And the LORD said to me, 'Do not fear him, for I have delivered him and all his people and his land into your hand; you shall do to him as you did to Sihon king of the Amorites, who dwelt at Heshbon.'

3 "So the LORD our God also delivered into our hands Og king of Bashan, with all his people, and we attacked him until he had no survivors remaining. 4 And we took all his cities at that time; there was not a city which we did not take from them: sixty cities, all the region of Argob, the kingdom of Og in Bashan. 5 All these cities *were* fortified with high walls, gates, and bars, besides a great many rural towns. 6 And we utterly destroyed them, as we did to Sihon king of Heshbon, utterly destroying the men, women, and children of every city. 7 But all the livestock and the spoil of the cities we took as booty for ourselves.

8 "And at that time we took the land from the hand of the two kings of the Amorites who *were* on this side of the Jordan, from the River Arnon to Mount Hermon 9 (the Sidonians

2:20 *a*Hebrew *rephaim*

Gospel Pearls

call Hermon Sirion, and the Amorites call it Senir), 10 all the cities of the plain, all Gilead, and all Bashan, as far as Salcah and Edrei, cities of the kingdom of Og in Bashan.

11 "For only Og king of Bashan remained of the remnant of the giants.*ᵃ* Indeed his bedstead *was* an iron bedstead. (*Is* it not in Rabbah of the people of Ammon?) Nine cubits *is* its length and four cubits its width, according to the standard cubit.

12 And this land, *which* we possessed at that time, from Aroer, which *is* by the River Arnon, and half the mountains of Gilead and its cities, I gave to the Reubenites and the Gadites. 13 The rest of Gilead, and all Bashan, the kingdom of Og, I gave to half the tribe of Manasseh. (All the region of Argob, with all Bashan, was called the land of the giants.*ᵃ* 14 Jair the son of Manasseh took all the region of Argob, as far as the border of the Geshurites and the Maachathites, and called Bashan after his own name, Havoth Jair,*ᵃ* to this day.)

15 "Also I gave Gilead to Machir. 16 And to the Reubenites and the Gadites I gave from Gilead as far as the River Arnon, the middle of the river as *the* border, as far as the River Jabbok, the border of the people of Ammon; 17 the plain also, with the Jordan as *the* border, from Chinnereth as far as the east side of the Sea of the Arabah (the Salt Sea), below the slopes of Pisgah.

18 "Then I commanded you at that time, saying: 'The LORD your God has given you this land to possess. All you men of valor shall cross over armed before your brethren, the children of Israel. 19 But your wives, your little ones, and your livestock (I know that you have much livestock) shall stay in your cities which I have given you, 20 until the LORD has given rest to your brethren as to you, and they also possess the land which the LORD your God is giving them beyond the Jordan. Then each of you may return to his possession which I have given you.'

21 And I commanded Joshua at that time, saying, 'Your eyes have seen all that the LORD your God has done to these two kings; so will the LORD do to all the kingdoms through which

you pass. 22 You must not fear them, for the LORD your God Himself fights for you.'

23 "Then I pleaded with the LORD at that time, saying: 24 'O Lord GOD, You have begun to show Your servant Your greatness and Your mighty hand, for what god *is there* in heaven or on earth who can do *anything* like Your works and Your mighty *deeds?* 25 I pray, let me cross over and see the good land beyond the Jordan, those pleasant mountains, and Lebanon.'

26 "But the LORD was angry with me on your account, and would not listen to me. So the LORD said to me: 'Enough of that! Speak no more to Me of this matter. 27 Go up to the top of Pisgah, and lift your eyes toward the west, the north, the south, and the east; behold *it* with your eyes, for you shall not cross over this Jordan. 28 But command Joshua, and encourage him and strengthen him; for he shall go over before this people, and he shall cause them to inherit the land which you will see.'

29 "So we stayed in the valley opposite Beth Peor.

4 "Now, O Israel, listen to the statutes and the judgments which I teach you to observe, that you may live, and go in and possess the land which the LORD God of your fathers is giving you. 2 You shall not add to the word which I command you, nor take from it, that you may keep the commandments of the LORD your God which I command you. 3 Your eyes have seen what the LORD did at Baal Peor; for the LORD your God has destroyed from among you all the men who followed Baal of Peor. 4 But you who held fast to the LORD your God *are* alive today, every one of you.

5 "Surely I have taught you statutes and judgments, just as the LORD my God commanded me, that you should act according *to them* in the land which you go to possess. 6 Therefore be careful to observe *them;* for this *is* your wisdom and your understanding in the sight of the peoples who will hear all these statutes, and say, 'Surely this great nation *is* a wise and understanding people.'

7 "For what great nation *is there*

3:11 *ᵃ*Hebrew *rephaim*   3:13 *ᵃ*Hebrew *rephaim*   3:14 *ᵃ*Literally *Towns of Jair*

*P*recious promises are waiting for loosed women who have made themselves ready to take the kingdom by force. No more forbidden fruit for them; they are taking a bite out of life.

that has God so near to it, as the LORD our God is to us, for whatever *reason* we may call upon Him? 8 And what great nation *is there* that has *such* statutes and righteous judgments as are in all this law which I set before you this day? 9 Only take heed to yourself, and diligently keep yourself, lest you forget the things your eyes have seen, and lest they depart from your heart all the days of your life. And teach them to your children and your grandchildren, 10 *especially concerning* the day you stood before the LORD your God in Horeb, when the LORD said to me, 'Gather the people to Me, and I will let them hear My words, that they may learn to fear Me all the days they live on the earth, and *that* they may teach their children.'

11 "Then you came near and stood at the foot of the mountain, and the mountain burned with fire to the midst of heaven, with darkness, cloud, and thick darkness. 12 And the LORD spoke to you out of the midst of the fire. You heard the sound of the words, but saw no form; *you* only *heard* a voice. 13 So He declared to you His covenant which He commanded you to perform, the Ten Commandments; and He wrote them on two tablets of stone. 14 And the LORD commanded me at that time to teach you statutes and judgments, that you might observe them in the land which you cross over to possess.

15 "Take careful heed to yourselves, for you saw no form when the LORD spoke to you at Horeb out of the midst of the fire, 16 lest you act corruptly and make for yourselves a carved image in the form of any figure: the likeness of male or female, 17 the likeness of any animal that *is* on the earth or the likeness of any winged bird that flies in the air, 18 the likeness of anything that creeps on the ground or the likeness of any fish that *is* in the water beneath the earth. 19 And *take heed,* lest you lift your eyes to heaven, and *when* you see the sun, the moon, and the stars, all the host of heaven, you feel driven to worship them and serve them, which the LORD your God has given to all the peoples under the whole heaven as a heritage. 20 But the LORD has taken you and brought you out of the iron furnace, out of Egypt, to be His people, an in-

heritance, as you are this day. 21 Furthermore the LORD was angry with me for your sakes, and swore that I would not cross over the Jordan, and that I would not enter the good land which the LORD your God is giving you as an inheritance. 22 But I must die in this land, I must not cross over the Jordan; but you shall cross over and possess that good land. 23 Take heed to yourselves, lest you forget the covenant of the LORD your God which He made with you, and make for yourselves a carved image in the form of anything which the LORD your God has forbidden you. 24 For the LORD your God *is* a consuming fire, a jealous God.

25 "When you beget children and grandchildren and have grown old in the land, and act corruptly and make a carved image in the form of anything, and do evil in the sight of the LORD your God to provoke Him to anger, 26 I call heaven and earth to witness against you this day, that you will soon utterly perish from the land which you cross over the Jordan to possess; you will not prolong *your* days in it, but will be utterly destroyed. 27 And the LORD will scatter you among the peoples, and you will be left few in number among the nations where the LORD will drive you. 28 And there you will serve gods, the work of men's hands, wood and stone, which neither see nor hear nor eat nor smell. 29 But from there you will seek the LORD your God, and you will find *Him* if you seek Him with all your heart and with all your soul. 30 When you are in distress, and all these things come upon you in the latter days, when you turn to the LORD your God and obey His voice 31 (for the LORD your God *is* a merciful God), He will not forsake you nor destroy you, nor forget the covenant of your fathers which He swore to them.

32 "For ask now concerning the days that are past, which were before you, since the day that God created man on the earth, and *ask* from one end of heaven to the other, whether *any* great *thing* like this has happened, or *anything* like it has been heard. 33 Did *any* people *ever* hear the voice of God speaking out of the midst of the fire, as you have heard, and live? 34 Or did God *ever* try to go *and* take for Himself a nation from

*T*ell your critics the Father says, "Let My daughter go!" Only the very foolish person would fight a man for his daughter when it is the Father that they will have to fight. You are loosed! Run!

Seek the Lord

Deuteronomy 4:29-31

When you know who you are, you don't have to struggle to live up to what someone else thinks you're supposed to be. That was Jesus' attitude when He met the woman at the well. As she approached, with her water-pot on her shoulder, she was all upset and worried.

Jesus went straight to the heart of her problem: "Whoever drinks of this water will thirst again, but whoever drinks of the water that I shall give him will never thirst" (John 4:13, 14). Jesus went on to tell her all about herself and her five husbands—things that only God could know.

Like this woman, you may be wounded and upset. This kind of hurt can't be healed through human effort. You must get in the presence of God and let Him fill the voids in your life. Follow God's advice in Deuteronomy 4:29-31 and "Seek the LORD your God." You will not settle it by going from friend to friend. This woman had already tried that. She had gone through five men. The answer is not getting another man. It's getting in touch with The Man—Jesus the Lord.

After she met Jesus, the woman at the well didn't even go back home. She threw down her waterpot and ran into the city to tell everyone to come and see the Man who had told her about her life. This woman could never have rid herself of the old man until she met the new Man.

When you meet the new, you find the power to say good-bye to the old. You will never be able to break the grip of those former ways on your life until you know Jesus Christ. You must come to Him just as you are. If something has attached itself to you that is not of God, you won't be able to break it in your own strength. "Submit to God. Resist the devil and he will flee from you" (James 4:7). Knowing Him will give you the power to break away from the old self and the ties that hold you prisoner to your past.

Jesus satisfies. Everyone else may pacify, but He satisfies. Seek His presence. He meets every need and every yearning. He heals every pain and every affliction. He lifts every burden and every trouble in your life. He's The Man!

the midst of *another* nation, by trials, by signs, by wonders, by war, by a mighty hand and an outstretched arm, and by great terrors, according to all that the LORD your God did for you in Egypt before your eyes? 35 To you it was shown, that you might know that the LORD Himself *is* God; *there is* none other besides Him. 36 Out of heaven He let you hear His voice, that He might instruct you; on earth He showed you His great fire, and you heard His words out of the midst of the fire. 37 And because He loved your fathers, therefore He chose their descendants after them; and He brought you out of Egypt with His Presence, with His mighty power, 38 driving out from before you nations greater and mightier than you, to bring you in, to give you their land *as* an inheritance, as *it is* this day. 39 Therefore know this day, and consider *it* in your heart, that the LORD Himself *is* God in heaven above and on the earth beneath; *there is* no other. 40 You shall therefore keep His statutes and His commandments which I command you today, that it may go well with you and with your children after you, and that you may prolong *your* days in the land which the LORD your God is giving you for all time."

41 Then Moses set apart three cities on this side of the Jordan, toward the rising of the sun, 42 that the manslayer might flee there, who kills his neighbor unintentionally, without having hated him in time past, and that by fleeing to one of these cities he might live: 43 Bezer in the wilderness on the plateau for the Reubenites, Ramoth in Gilead for the Gadites, and Golan in Bashan for the Manassites.

44 Now this *is* the law which Moses set before the children of Israel. 45 These *are* the testimonies, the statutes, and the judgments which Moses spoke to the children of Israel after they came out of Egypt, 46 on this side of the Jordan, in the valley opposite Beth Peor, in the land of Sihon king of the Amorites, who dwelt at Heshbon, whom Moses and the children of Israel defeated after they came out of Egypt. 47 And they took possession of his land and the land of Og king of Bashan, two kings of the Amorites, who *were* on this side of the Jordan, toward the rising of the sun, 48 from Aroer, which *is* on the bank of the River Arnon, even to Mount Sion*a* (that is, Hermon), 49 and all the plain on the east side of the Jordan as far as the Sea of the Arabah, below the slopes of Pisgah.

5 And Moses called all Israel, and said to them: "Hear, O Israel, the statutes and judgments which I speak in your hearing today, that you may learn them and be careful to observe them. 2 The LORD our God made a covenant with us in Horeb. 3 The LORD did not make this covenant with our fathers, but with us, those who *are* here today, all of us who *are* alive. 4 The LORD talked with you face to face on the mountain from the midst of the fire. 5 I stood between the LORD and you at that time, to declare to you the word of the LORD; for you were afraid because of the fire, and you did not go up the mountain. '*He* said:

6 'I *am* the LORD your God who brought you out of the land of Egypt, out of the house of bondage.
7 'You shall have no other gods before Me.
8 'You shall not make for yourself a carved image—any likeness *of anything* that *is* in heaven above, or that *is* in the earth beneath, or that *is* in the water under the earth; 9 you shall not bow down to them nor serve them. For I, the LORD your God, *am* a jealous God, visiting the iniquity of the fathers upon the children to the third and fourth *generations* of those who hate Me, 10 but showing mercy to thousands, to those who love Me and keep My commandments.
11 'You shall not take the name of the LORD your God in vain, for the LORD will not hold *him* guiltless who takes His name in vain.
12 'Observe the Sabbath day, to keep it holy, as the LORD your God commanded you. 13 Six days you shall labor

4:48 *a*Syriac reads *Sirion* (compare 3:9).

Gospel Pearls

and do all your work, 14 but the seventh day *is* the Sabbath of the LORD your God. *In it* you shall do no work: you, nor your son, nor your daughter, nor your male servant, nor your female servant, nor your ox, nor your donkey, nor any of your cattle, nor your stranger who *is* within your gates, that your male servant and your female servant may rest as well as you. 15 And remember that you were a slave in the land of Egypt, and the LORD your God brought you out from there by a mighty hand and by an outstretched arm; therefore the LORD your God commanded you to keep the Sabbath day.

16 'Honor your father and your mother, as the LORD your God has commanded you, that your days may be long, and that it may be well with you in the land which the LORD your God is giving you.

17 'You shall not murder.

18 'You shall not commit adultery.

19 'You shall not steal.

20 'You shall not bear false witness against your neighbor.

21 'You shall not covet your neighbor's wife; and you shall not desire your neighbor's house, his field, his male servant, his female servant, his ox, his donkey, or anything that *is* your neighbor's.'

22 "These words the LORD spoke to all your assembly, in the mountain from the midst of the fire, the cloud, and the thick darkness, with a loud voice; and He added no more. And He wrote them on two tablets of stone and gave them to me.

23 "So it was, when you heard the voice from the midst of the darkness, while the mountain was burning with fire, that you came near to me, all the heads of your tribes and your elders. 24 And you said: 'Surely the LORD our God has shown us His glory and His greatness, and we have heard His voice from the midst of the fire. We have seen this day that God speaks with man; yet he *still* lives. 25 Now therefore, why should we die? For this great fire will consume us; if we hear the voice of the LORD our God anymore, then we shall die. 26 For who *is there* of all flesh who has heard the voice of the living God speaking from the midst of the fire, as we *have*, and lived? 27 You go near and hear all that the LORD our God may say, and tell us all that the LORD our God says to you, and we will hear and do *it*.'

28 "Then the LORD heard the voice of your words when you spoke to me, and the LORD said to me: 'I have heard the voice of the words of this people which they have spoken to you. They are right *in* all that they have spoken. 29 Oh, that they had such a heart in them that they would fear Me and always keep all My commandments, that it might be well with them and with their children forever! 30 Go and say to them, "Return to your tents." 31 But as for you, stand here by Me, and I will speak to you all the commandments, the statutes, and the judgments which you shall teach them, that they may observe *them* in the land which I am giving them to possess.'

32 "Therefore you shall be careful to do as the LORD your God has commanded you; you shall not turn aside to the right hand or to the left. 33 You shall walk in all the ways which the LORD your God has commanded you, that you may live and *that it may be* well with you, and *that* you may prolong *your* days in the land which you shall possess.

6 "Now this *is* the commandment, *and these are* the statutes and judgments which the LORD your God has commanded to teach you, that you may observe *them* in the land which you are crossing over to possess, 2 that you may fear the LORD your God, to keep all His statutes and His commandments which I command you, you and your son and your grandson, all the days of your life, and that your days may be prolonged. 3 Therefore hear, O Israel, and be careful to observe *it*, that it may be well with you, and that you may multiply greatly as the LORD God of your fathers has promised

*T*his is your time. It is your moment. This is the hour. God has been waiting to do so much for you. You have been released. It is morning.

you—'a land flowing with milk and honey.'ᵃ

4 "Hear, O Israel: The LORD our God, the LORD *is* one!ᵃ 5 You shall love the LORD your God with all your heart, with all your soul, and with all your strength.

6 "And these words which I command you today shall be in your heart. 7 You shall teach them diligently to your children, and shall talk of them when you sit in your house, when you walk by the way, when you lie down, and when you rise up. 8 You shall bind them as a sign on your hand, and they shall be as frontlets between your eyes. 9 You shall write them on the doorposts of your house and on your gates.

10 "So it shall be, when the LORD your God brings you into the land of which He swore to your fathers, to Abraham, Isaac, and Jacob, to give you large and beautiful cities which you did not build, 11 houses full of all good things, which you did not fill, hewn-out wells which you did not dig, vineyards and olive trees which you did not plant—when you have eaten and are full— 12 *then* beware, lest you forget the LORD who brought you out of the land of Egypt, from the house of bondage. 13 You shall fear the LORD your God and serve Him, and shall take oaths in His name. 14 You shall not go after other gods, the gods of the peoples who *are* all around you 15 (for the LORD your God *is* a jealous God among you), lest the anger of the LORD your God be aroused against you and destroy you from the face of the earth.

16 "You shall not tempt the LORD your God as you tempted *Him* in Massah. 17 You shall diligently keep the commandments of the LORD your God, His testimonies, and His statutes which He has commanded you. 18 And you shall do *what is* right and good in the sight of the LORD, that it may be well with you, and that you may go in and possess the good land of which the LORD swore to your fathers, 19 to cast out all your enemies from before you, as the LORD has spoken.

20 "When your son asks you in time to come, saying, 'What *is the* meaning of the testimonies, the stat-

utes, and the judgments which the LORD our God has commanded you?' 21 then you shall say to your son: 'We were slaves of Pharaoh in Egypt, and the LORD brought us out of Egypt with a mighty hand; 22 and the LORD showed signs and wonders before our eyes, great and severe, against Egypt, Pharaoh, and all his household. 23 Then He brought us out from there, that He might bring us in, to give us the land of which He swore to our fathers. 24 And the LORD commanded us to observe all these statutes, to fear the LORD our God, for our good always, that He might preserve us alive, as *it is* this day. 25 Then it will be righteousness for us, if we are careful to observe all these commandments before the LORD our God, as He has commanded us.'

7 "When the LORD your God brings you into the land which you go to possess, and has cast out many nations before you, the Hittites and the Girgashites and the Amorites and the Canaanites and the Perizzites and the Hivites and the Jebusites, seven nations greater and mightier than you, 2 and when the LORD your God delivers them over to you, you shall conquer them *and* utterly destroy them. You shall make no covenant with them nor show mercy to them. 3 Nor shall you make marriages with them. You shall not give your daughter to their son, nor take their daughter for your son. 4 For they will turn your sons away from following Me, to serve other gods; so the anger of the LORD will be aroused against you and destroy you suddenly. 5 But thus you shall deal with them: you shall destroy their altars, and break down their *sacred* pillars, and cut down their wooden images,ᵃ and burn their carved images with fire.

6 "For you *are* a holy people to the LORD your God; the LORD your God has chosen you to be a people for Himself, a special treasure above all the peoples on the face of the earth. 7 The LORD did not set His love on you nor choose you because you were more in number than any other people, for you were the least of all peoples; 8 but because the LORD loves

6:3 ᵃExodus 3:8   6:4 ᵃOr *The LORD is our God, the LORD alone* (that is, the only one)   7:5 ᵃHebrew *Asherim,* Canaanite deities

Gospel Pearls

you, and because He would keep the oath which He swore to your fathers, the Lord has brought you out with a mighty hand, and redeemed you from the house of bondage, from the hand of Pharaoh king of Egypt.

9 "Therefore know that the Lord your God, He *is* God, the faithful God who keeps covenant and mercy for a thousand generations with those who love Him and keep His commandments; 10 and He repays those who hate Him to their face, to destroy them. He will not be slack with him who hates Him; He will repay him to his face. 11 Therefore you shall keep the commandment, the statutes, and the judgments which I command you today, to observe them.

12 "Then it shall come to pass, because you listen to these judgments, and keep and do them, that the Lord your God will keep with you the covenant and the mercy which He swore to your fathers. 13 And He will love you and bless you and multiply you; He will also bless the fruit of your womb and the fruit of your land, your grain and your new wine and your oil, the increase of your cattle and the offspring of your flock, in the land of which He swore to your fathers to give you. 14 You shall be blessed above all peoples; there shall not be a male or female barren among you or among your livestock. 15 And the Lord will take away from you all sickness, and will afflict you with none of the terrible diseases of Egypt which you have known, but will lay *them* on all those who hate you. 16 Also you shall destroy all the peoples whom the Lord your God delivers over to you; your eye shall have no pity on them; nor shall you serve their gods, for that *will be* a snare to you.

17 "If you should say in your heart, 'These nations are greater than I; how can I dispossess them?'— 18 you shall not be afraid of them, *but* you shall remember well what the Lord your God did to Pharaoh and to all Egypt: 19 the great trials which your eyes saw, the signs and the wonders, the mighty hand and the outstretched arm, by which the Lord your God brought you out. So shall the Lord your God do to all the peoples of whom you are afraid. 20 Moreover the Lord your God will send the hornet among them until

those who are left, who hide themselves from you, are destroyed. 21 You shall not be terrified of them; for the Lord your God, the great and awesome God, *is* among you. 22 And the Lord your God will drive out those nations before you little by little; you will be unable to destroy them at once, lest the beasts of the field become *too* numerous for you. 23 But the Lord your God will deliver them over to you, and will inflict defeat upon them until they are destroyed. 24 And He will deliver their kings into your hand, and you will destroy their name from under heaven; no one shall be able to stand against you until you have destroyed them. 25 You shall burn the carved images of their gods with fire; you shall not covet the silver or gold *that is* on them, nor take *it* for yourselves, lest you be snared by it; for it *is* an abomination to the Lord your God. 26 Nor shall you bring an abomination into your house, lest you be doomed to destruction like it. You shall utterly detest it and utterly abhor it, for it *is* an accursed thing.

8 "Every commandment which I command you today you must be careful to observe, that you may live and multiply, and go in and possess the land of which the Lord swore to your fathers. 2 And you shall remember that the Lord your God led you all the way these forty years in the wilderness, to humble you *and* test you, to know what *was* in your heart, whether you would keep His commandments or not. 3 So He humbled you, allowed you to hunger, and fed you with manna which you did not know nor did your fathers know, that He might make you know that man shall not live by bread alone; but man lives by every *word* that proceeds from the mouth of the Lord. 4 Your garments did not wear out on you, nor did your foot swell these forty years. 5 You should know in your heart that as a man chastens his son, *so* the Lord your God chastens you.

6 "Therefore you shall keep the commandments of the Lord your God, to walk in His ways and to fear Him. 7 For the Lord your God is bringing you into a good land, a land of brooks of water, of fountains and springs, that flow out of valleys and

No matter how foreign this stage in your life may seem, you must know God prepared you for it. When He kissed you, He shielded you, and you are His. Safe and secure, you are to rest in the sanctity and safety of arms that will not fail you.

hills; 8 a land of wheat and barley, of vines and fig trees and pomegranates, a land of olive oil and honey; 9 a land in which you will eat bread without scarcity, in which you will lack nothing; a land whose stones *are* iron and out of whose hills you can dig copper. 10 When you have eaten and are full, then you shall bless the LORD your God for the good land which He has given you.

11 "Beware that you do not forget the LORD your God by not keeping His commandments, His judgments, and His statutes which I command you today, 12 lest—*when* you have eaten and are full, and have built beautiful houses and dwell *in them;* 13 and *when* your herds and your flocks multiply, and your silver and your gold are multiplied, and all that you have is multiplied; 14 when your heart is lifted up, and you forget the LORD your God who brought you out of the land of Egypt, from the house of bondage; 15 who led you through that great and terrible wilderness, *in which were* fiery serpents and scorpions and thirsty land where there was no water; who brought water for you out of the flinty rock; 16 who fed you in the wilderness with manna, which your fathers did not know, that He might humble you and that He might test you, to do you good in the end— 17 then you say in your heart, 'My power and the might of my hand have gained me this wealth.'

18 "And you shall remember the LORD your God, for *it is* He who gives you power to get wealth, that He may establish His covenant which He swore to your fathers, as *it is* this day. 19 Then it shall be, if you by any means forget the LORD your God, and follow other gods, and serve them and worship them, I testify against you this day that you shall surely perish. 20 As the nations which the LORD destroys before you, so you shall perish, because you would not be obedient to the voice of the LORD your God.

9 "Hear, O Israel: You *are* to cross over the Jordan today, and go in to dispossess nations greater and mightier than yourself, cities great and fortified up to heaven, 2 a people great and tall, the descendants of the Anakim, whom you know, and *of whom* you heard *it said,* 'Who can

stand before the descendants of Anak?' 3 Therefore understand today that the LORD your God *is* He who goes over before you *as* a consuming fire. He will destroy them and bring them down before you; so you shall drive them out and destroy them quickly, as the LORD has said to you.

4 "Do not think in your heart, after the LORD your God has cast them out before you, saying, 'Because of my righteousness the LORD has brought me in to possess this land'; but *it is* because of the wickedness of these nations *that* the LORD is driving them out from before you. 5 *It is* not because of your righteousness or the uprightness of your heart *that* you go in to possess their land, but because of the wickedness of these nations *that* the LORD your God drives them out from before you, and that He may fulfill the word which the LORD swore to your fathers, to Abraham, Isaac, and Jacob. 6 Therefore understand that the LORD your God is not giving you this good land to possess because of your righteousness, for you *are* a stiff-necked people.

7 "Remember! Do not forget how you provoked the LORD your God to wrath in the wilderness. From the day that you departed from the land of Egypt until you came to this place, you have been rebellious against the LORD. 8 Also in Horeb you provoked the LORD to wrath, so that the LORD was angry *enough* with you to have destroyed you. 9 When I went up into the mountain to receive the tablets of stone, the tablets of the covenant which the LORD made with you, then I stayed on the mountain forty days and forty nights. I neither ate bread nor drank water. 10 Then the LORD delivered to me two tablets of stone written with the finger of God, and on them *were* all the words which the LORD had spoken to you on the mountain from the midst of the fire in the day of the assembly. 11 And it came to pass, at the end of forty days and forty nights, *that* the LORD gave me the two tablets of stone, the tablets of the covenant.

12 "Then the LORD said to me, 'Arise, go down quickly from here, for your people whom you brought out of Egypt have acted corruptly; they have quickly turned aside from the way which I commanded them;

Gospel Pearls

they have made themselves a molded image.'

13 "Furthermore the LORD spoke to me, saying, 'I have seen this people, and indeed they are a stiff-necked people. 14 Let Me alone, that I may destroy them and blot out their name from under heaven; and I will make of you a nation mightier and greater than they.'

15 "So I turned and came down from the mountain, and the mountain burned with fire; and the two tablets of the covenant *were* in my two hands. 16 And I looked, and behold, you had sinned against the LORD your God—had made for yourselves a molded calf! You had turned aside quickly from the way which the LORD had commanded you. 17 Then I took the two tablets and threw them out of my two hands and broke them before your eyes. 18 And I fell down before the LORD, as at the first, forty days and forty nights; I neither ate bread nor drank water, because of all your sin which you committed in doing wickedly in the sight of the LORD, to provoke Him to anger. 19 For I was afraid of the anger and hot displeasure with which the LORD was angry with you, to destroy you. But the LORD listened to me at that time also. 20 And the LORD was very angry with Aaron *and* would have destroyed him; so I prayed for Aaron also at the same time. 21 Then I took your sin, the calf which you had made, and burned it with fire and crushed it *and* ground *it* very small, until it was as fine as dust; and I threw its dust into the brook that descended from the mountain.

22 "Also at Taberah and Massah and Kibroth Hattaavah you provoked the LORD to wrath. 23 Likewise, when the LORD sent you from Kadesh Barnea, saying, 'Go up and possess the land which I have given you,' then you rebelled against the commandment of the LORD your God, and you did not believe Him nor obey His voice. 24 You have been rebellious against the LORD from the day that I knew you.

25 "Thus I prostrated myself before the LORD; forty days and forty nights I kept prostrating myself, because the LORD had said He would destroy you. 26 Therefore I prayed to the LORD, and said: 'O Lord GOD, do not destroy Your people and Your inheri-

tance whom You have redeemed through Your greatness, whom You have brought out of Egypt with a mighty hand. 27 Remember Your servants, Abraham, Isaac, and Jacob; do not look on the stubbornness of this people, or on their wickedness or their sin, 28 lest the land from which You brought us should say, "Because the LORD was not able to bring them to the land which He promised them, and because He hated them, He has brought them out to kill them in the wilderness." 29 Yet they *are* Your people and Your inheritance, whom You brought out by Your mighty power and by Your outstretched arm.'

10 "At that time the LORD said to me, 'Hew for yourself two tablets of stone like the first, and come up to Me on the mountain and make yourself an ark of wood. 2 And I will write on the tablets the words that were on the first tablets, which you broke; and you shall put them in the ark.'

3 "So I made an ark of acacia wood, hewed two tablets of stone like the first, and went up the mountain, having the two tablets in my hand. 4 And He wrote on the tablets according to the first writing, the Ten Commandments, which the LORD had spoken to you in the mountain from the midst of the fire in the day of the assembly; and the LORD gave them to me. 5 Then I turned and came down from the mountain, and put the tablets in the ark which I had made; and there they are, just as the LORD commanded me."

6 (Now the children of Israel journeyed from the wells of Bene Jaakan to Moserah, where Aaron died, and where he was buried; and Eleazar his son ministered as priest in his stead. 7 From there they journeyed to Gudgodah, and from Gudgodah to Jotbathah, a land of rivers of water. 8 At that time the LORD separated the tribe of Levi to bear the ark of the covenant of the LORD, to stand before the LORD to minister to Him and to bless in His name, to this day. 9 Therefore Levi has no portion nor inheritance with his brethren; the LORD *is* his inheritance, just as the LORD your God promised him.)

10 "As at the first time, I stayed in the mountain forty days and forty

Daybreak is stretching in the fresh hours of a new opportunity just created. It is an empty tomb and a filled manger. It is life, love and hope. Never forget about the breaking of day. It will come.

nights; the LORD also heard me at that time, and the LORD chose not to destroy you. 11 Then the LORD said to me, 'Arise, begin your journey before the people, that they may go in and possess the land which I swore to their fathers to give them.'

12 "And now, Israel, what does the LORD your God require of you, but to fear the LORD your God, to walk in all His ways and to love Him, to serve the LORD your God with all your heart and with all your soul, 13 and to keep the commandments of the LORD and His statutes which I command you today for your good? 14 Indeed heaven and the highest heavens belong to the LORD your God, also the earth with all that is in it. 15 The LORD delighted only in your fathers, to love them; and He chose their descendants after them, you above all peoples, as it is this day. 16 Therefore circumcise the foreskin of your heart, and be stiffnecked no longer. 17 For the LORD your God is God of gods and Lord of lords, the great God, mighty and awesome, who shows no partiality nor takes a bribe. 18 He administers justice for the fatherless and the widow, and loves the stranger, giving him food and clothing. 19 Therefore love the stranger, for you were strangers in the land of Egypt. 20 You shall fear the LORD your God; you shall serve Him, and to Him you shall hold fast, and take oaths in His name. 21 He is your praise, and He is your God, who has done for you these great and awesome things which your eyes have seen. 22 Your fathers went down to Egypt with seventy persons, and now the LORD your God has made you as the stars of heaven in multitude.

11 "Therefore you shall love the LORD your God, and keep His charge, His statutes, His judgments, and His commandments always. 2 Know today that I do not speak with your children, who have not known and who have not seen the chastening of the LORD your God, His greatness and His mighty hand and His outstretched arm— 3 His signs and His acts which He did in the midst of Egypt, to Pharaoh king of Egypt, and to all his land; 4 what He did to the army of Egypt, to their horses and their chariots: how He made the waters of the Red Sea overflow them as they pursued you, and how the LORD has destroyed them to this day; 5 what He did for you in the wilderness until you came to this place; 6 and what He did to Dathan and Abiram the sons of Eliab, the son of Reuben: how the earth opened its mouth and swallowed them up, their households, their tents, and all the substance that was in their possession, in the midst of all Israel— 7 but your eyes have seen every great act of the LORD which He did.

8 "Therefore you shall keep every commandment which I command you today, that you may be strong, and go in and possess the land which you cross over to possess, 9 and that you may prolong your days in the land which the LORD swore to give your fathers, to them and their descendants, 'a land flowing with milk and honey.'ᵃ 10 For the land which you go to possess is not like the land of Egypt from which you have come, where you sowed your seed and watered it by foot, as a vegetable garden; 11 but the land which you cross over to possess is a land of hills and valleys, which drinks water from the rain of heaven, 12 a land for which the LORD your God cares; the eyes of the LORD your God are always on it, from the beginning of the year to the very end of the year.

13 'And it shall be that if you earnestly obey My commandments which I command you today, to love the LORD your God and serve Him with all your heart and with all your soul, 14 then Iᵃ will give you the rain for your land in its season, the early rain and the latter rain, that you may gather in your grain, your new wine, and your oil. 15 And I will send grass in your fields for your livestock, that you may eat and be filled.' 16 Take heed to yourselves, lest your heart be deceived, and you turn aside and serve other gods and worship them, 17 lest the LORD's anger be aroused against you, and He shut up the heavens so that there be no rain, and the land yield no produce, and you per-

---

11:9 ᵃExodus 3:8   11:14 ᵃFollowing Masoretic Text and Targum; Samaritan Pentateuch, Septuagint, and Vulgate read He.

This is your day, and this is your Father's world. He has created it just for you. You are an heir to the universe. Your only boundaries are your own perceptions of potential. You can reach farther than your fingers and leap higher than your doubt.

Married to Jesus

Deuteronomy 10:12, 13

When God picks a wife for one of His royal sons, He will pick her from among the women who are faithful and holy, those who "keep the commandments of the LORD" (Deuteronomy 10:13).

Begin to sanctify yourself. Bring your body before God. Bring your nature before God. Bring your passion to Him. Allow God to strengthen you until you can tell the devil, "My body—my whole body—belongs to God. From the top of my head to the soles of my feet, all that I am belongs to Him. I will seek Him early in the morning. I will lie on my bed at night and call on His name. I'll touch Him and embrace Him. He is the God of my salvation and the Lover of my soul."

Maybe you haven't been living as you should. Maybe your house hasn't been the house of prayer it could have been. Maybe your body has been mauled and pawed over by all sorts of people. But it isn't too late to offer it as a living sacrifice to God (see Romans 12:1). If you can't keep your vow to Him, you would never be able to keep your vow to a man. Give your body to the Lord and sanctify yourself.

The single woman should seek to please God in every way. Understand that while you are waiting for a flesh-and-blood husband, God is your spiritual Husband. Be careful how you treat Him. He thinks He's your man. That's why He does those special favors for you. He has been taking care of you even when you didn't notice His protection. He is the source of every good thing even when you don't recognize His provision. It is He who opens doors for you. He is your Friend and your Companion.

Paul wrote, "Let each one remain [abide] in the same calling in which he was called" (1 Corinthians 7:20). In other words, the single person should be abiding in, not wrestling with singleness. Enjoy it. Rather than spend all your effort trying to change your marital state, you need to learn to develop in the position where He has placed you. The greatest visitation of the Holy Ghost in history happened to an unmarried woman named Mary. Before Joseph had the right, the Holy Ghost came upon her.

That same life-giving anointing wants to come upon you now. Stop murmuring and complaining. His presence is in the room. Worship Him. He is waiting for you.

ish quickly from the good land which the LORD is giving you.

18 "Therefore you shall lay up these words of mine in your heart and in your soul, and bind them as a sign on your hand, and they shall be as frontlets between your eyes. 19 You shall teach them to your children, speaking of them when you sit in your house, when you walk by the way, when you lie down, and when you rise up. 20 And you shall write them on the doorposts of your house and on your gates, 21 that your days and the days of your children may be multiplied in the land of which the LORD swore to your fathers to give them, like the days of the heavens above the earth.

22 "For if you carefully keep all these commandments which I command you to do—to love the LORD your God, to walk in all His ways, and to hold fast to Him— 23 then the LORD will drive out all these nations from before you, and you will dispossess greater and mightier nations than yourselves. 24 Every place on which the sole of your foot treads shall be yours: from the wilderness and Lebanon, from the river, the River Euphrates, even to the Western Sea,[a] shall be your territory. 25 No man shall be able to stand against you; the LORD your God will put the dread of you and the fear of you upon all the land where you tread, just as He has said to you.

26 "Behold, I set before you today a blessing and a curse: 27 the blessing, if you obey the commandments of the LORD your God which I command you today; 28 and the curse, if you do not obey the commandments of the LORD your God, but turn aside from the way which I command you today, to go after other gods which you have not known. 29 Now it shall be, when the LORD your God has brought you into the land which you go to possess, that you shall put the blessing on Mount Gerizim and the curse on Mount Ebal. 30 Are they not on the other side of the Jordan, toward the setting sun, in the land of the Canaanites who dwell in the plain opposite Gilgal, beside the terebinth trees of Moreh? 31 For you will cross over the Jordan and go in to possess the land which the LORD your

God is giving you, and you will possess it and dwell in it. 32 And you shall be careful to observe all the statutes and judgments which I set before you today.

12 "These *are* the statutes and judgments which you shall be careful to observe in the land which the LORD God of your fathers is giving you to possess, all the days that you live on the earth. 2 You shall utterly destroy all the places where the nations which you shall dispossess served their gods, on the high mountains and on the hills and under every green tree. 3 And you shall destroy their altars, break their *sacred* pillars, and burn their wooden images with fire; you shall cut down the carved images of their gods and destroy their names from that place. 4 You shall not worship the LORD your God *with* such *things.*

5 "But you shall seek the place where the LORD your God chooses, out of all your tribes, to put His name for His dwelling place; and there you shall go. 6 There you shall take your burnt offerings, your sacrifices, your tithes, the heave offerings of your hand, your vowed offerings, your freewill offerings, and the firstborn of your herds and flocks. 7 And there you shall eat before the LORD your God, and you shall rejoice in all to which you have put your hand, you and your households, in which the LORD your God has blessed you.

8 "You shall not at all do as we are doing here today—every man doing whatever *is* right in his own eyes— 9 for as yet you have not come to the rest and the inheritance which the LORD your God is giving you. 10 But *when* you cross over the Jordan and dwell in the land which the LORD your God is giving you to inherit, and He gives you rest from all your enemies round about, so that you dwell in safety, 11 then there will be the place where the LORD your God chooses to make His name abide. There you shall bring all that I command you: your burnt offerings, your sacrifices, your tithes, the heave offerings of your hand, and all your choice offerings which you vow to the LORD. 12 And you shall rejoice before the LORD your God, you and your

11:24 aThat is, the Mediterranean

sons and your daughters, your male and female servants, and the Levite who *is* within your gates, since he has no portion nor inheritance with you. 13 Take heed to yourself that you do not offer your burnt offerings in every place that you see; 14 but in the place which the LORD chooses, in one of your tribes, there you shall offer your burnt offerings, and there you shall do all that I command you.

15 "However, you may slaughter and eat meat within all your gates, whatever your heart desires, according to the blessing of the LORD your God which He has given you; the unclean and the clean may eat of it, of the gazelle and the deer alike. 16 Only you shall not eat the blood; you shall pour it on the earth like water. 17 You may not eat within your gates the tithe of your grain or your new wine or your oil, of the firstborn of your herd or your flock, of any of your offerings which you vow, of your freewill offerings, or of the heave offering of your hand. 18 But you must eat them before the LORD your God in the place which the LORD your God chooses, you and your son and your daughter, your male servant and your female servant, and the Levite who *is* within your gates; and you shall rejoice before the LORD your God in all to which you put your hands. 19 Take heed to yourself that you do not forsake the Levite as long as you live in your land.

20 "When the LORD your God enlarges your border as He has promised you, and you say, 'Let me eat meat,' because you long to eat meat, you may eat as much meat as your heart desires. 21 If the place where the LORD your God chooses to put His name is too far from you, then you may slaughter from your herd and from your flock which the LORD has given you, just as I have commanded you, and you may eat within your gates as much as your heart desires. 22 Just as the gazelle and the deer are eaten, so you may eat them; the unclean and the clean alike may eat them. 23 Only be sure that you do not eat the blood, for the blood *is* the life; you may not eat the life with the meat. 24 You shall not eat it; you shall pour it on the earth like water. 25 You shall not eat it, that it may go

well with you and your children after you, when you do *what is* right in the sight of the LORD. 26 Only the holy things which you have, and your vowed offerings, you shall take and go to the place which the LORD chooses. 27 And you shall offer your burnt offerings, the meat and the blood, on the altar of the LORD your God; and the blood of your sacrifices shall be poured out on the altar of the LORD your God, and you shall eat the meat. 28 Observe and obey all these words which I command you, that it may go well with you and your children after you forever, when you do *what is* good and right in the sight of the LORD your God.

29 "When the LORD your God cuts off from before you the nations which you go to dispossess, and you displace them and dwell in their land, 30 take heed to yourself that you are not ensnared to follow them, after they are destroyed from before you, and that you do not inquire after their gods, saying, 'How did these nations serve their gods? I also will do likewise.' 31 You shall not worship the LORD your God in that way; for every abomination to the LORD which He hates they have done to their gods; for they burn even their sons and daughters in the fire to their gods.

32 "Whatever I command you, be careful to observe it; you shall not add to it nor take away from it.

13 "If there arises among you a prophet or a dreamer of dreams, and he gives you a sign or a wonder, 2 and the sign or the wonder comes to pass, of which he spoke to you, saying, 'Let us go after other gods'—which you have not known— 'and let us serve them,' 3 you shall not listen to the words of that prophet or that dreamer of dreams, for the LORD your God is testing you to know whether you love the LORD your God with all your heart and with all your soul. 4 You shall walk after the LORD your God and fear Him, and keep His commandments and obey His voice; you shall serve Him and hold fast to Him. 5 But that prophet or that dreamer of dreams shall be put to death, because he has spoken in order to turn *you* away from the LORD your God, who brought you out of the land of Egypt and redeemed you from the house of bondage, to entice

*N*ever lose that little girl belief in the impossible. The fantasies of the faithful dispel the myths of the frightened.

you from the way in which the LORD your God commanded you to walk. So you shall put away the evil from your midst.

6 "If your brother, the son of your mother, your son or your daughter, the wife of your bosom, or your friend who is as your own soul, secretly entices you, saying, 'Let us go and serve other gods,' which you have not known, neither you nor your fathers, 7 of the gods of the people which *are* all around you, near to you or far off from you, from *one* end of the earth to the *other* end of the earth, 8 you shall not consent to him or listen to him, nor shall your eye pity him, nor shall you spare him or conceal him; 9 but you shall surely kill him; your hand shall be first against him to put him to death, and afterward the hand of all the people. 10 And you shall stone him with stones until he dies, because he sought to entice you away from the LORD your God, who brought you out of the land of Egypt, from the house of bondage. 11 So all Israel shall hear and fear, and not again do such wickedness as this among you.

12 "If you hear someone in one of your cities, which the LORD your God gives you to dwell in, saying, 13 'Corrupt men have gone out from among you and enticed the inhabitants of their city, saying, "Let us go and serve other gods" '—which you have not known— 14 then you shall inquire, search out, and ask diligently. And *if it is* indeed true *and* certain *that* such an abomination was committed among you, 15 you shall surely strike the inhabitants of that city with the edge of the sword, utterly destroying it, all that is in it and its livestock—with the edge of the sword. 16 And you shall gather all its plunder into the middle of the street, and completely burn with fire the city and all its plunder, for the LORD your God. It shall be a heap forever; it shall not be built again. 17 So none of the accursed things shall remain in your hand, that the LORD may turn from the fierceness of His anger and show you mercy, have compassion on you and multiply you, just as He swore to your fathers, 18 because you have listened to the voice of the LORD your

God, to keep all His commandments which I command you today, to do *what is* right in the eyes of the LORD your God.

14 "You *are* the children of the LORD your God; you shall not cut yourselves nor shave the front of your head for the dead. 2 For you *are* a holy people to the LORD your God, and the LORD has chosen you to be a people for Himself, a special treasure above all the peoples who *are* on the face of the earth.

3 "You shall not eat any detestable thing. 4 These *are* the animals which you may eat: the ox, the sheep, the goat, 5 the deer, the gazelle, the roe deer, the wild goat, the mountain goat,*ᵃ* the antelope, and the mountain sheep. 6 And you may eat every animal with cloven hooves, having ⁺the hoof split into two parts, *and that* chews the cud, among the animals. 7 Nevertheless, of those that chew the cud or have cloven hooves, you shall not eat, *such as* these: the camel, the hare, and the rock hyrax; for they chew the cud but do not have cloven hooves; they *are* unclean for you. 8 Also the swine is unclean for you, because it has cloven hooves, yet *does* not *chew* the cud; you shall not eat their flesh or touch their dead carcasses.

9 "These you may eat of all that *are* in the waters: you may eat all that have fins and scales. 10 And whatever does not have fins and scales you shall not eat; it *is* unclean for you.

11 "All clean birds you may eat. 12 But these you shall not eat: the eagle, the vulture, the buzzard, 13 the red kite, the falcon, and the kite after their kinds; 14 every raven after its kind; 15 the ostrich, the short-eared owl, the seagull, and the hawk after their kinds; 16 the little owl, the screech owl, the white owl, 17 the jackdaw, the carrion vulture, the fisher owl, 18 the stork, the heron after its kind, and the hoopoe and the bat.

19 "Also every creeping thing that flies is unclean for you; they shall not be eaten.

20 "You may eat all clean birds.

21 "You shall not eat anything that dies *of itself;* you may give it to the

14:5 *ᵃOr addax*

Gospel Pearls

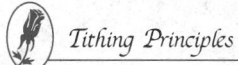

alien who *is* within your gates, that
he may eat it, or you may sell it to a
foreigner; for you *are* a holy people
to the LORD your God.

"You shall not boil a young goat
in its mother's milk.

22 "You shall truly tithe all the increase of your grain that the field
produces year by year. 23 And you
shall eat before the LORD your God,
in the place where He chooses to
make His name abide, the tithe of
your grain and your new wine and
your oil, of the firstborn of your
herds and your flocks, that you may
learn to fear the LORD your God always. 24 But if the journey is too long
for you, so that you are not able to
carry *the tithe, or* if the place where
the LORD your God chooses to put His
name is too far from you, when the
LORD your God has blessed you,
25 then you shall exchange *it* for
money, take the money in your hand,
and go to the place which the LORD
your God chooses. 26 And you shall
spend that money for whatever your
heart desires: for oxen or sheep, for
wine or similar drink, for whatever
your heart desires; you shall eat
there before the LORD your God, and
you shall rejoice, you and your
household. 27 You shall not forsake
the Levite who *is* within your gates,
for he has no part nor inheritance
with you.

28 "At the end of *every* third year
you shall bring out the tithe of your
produce of that year and store *it* up
within your gates. 29 And the Levite,
because he has no portion nor inheritance with you, and the stranger and
the fatherless and the widow who *are*
within your gates, may come and eat
and be satisfied, that the LORD your
God may bless you in all the work
of your hand which you do.

15 "At the end of *every* seven
years you shall grant a release
of debts. 2 And this *is* the form of the
release: Every creditor who has lent
anything to his neighbor shall release *it;* he shall not require *it* of
his neighbor or his brother, because
it is called the LORD's release.
3 Of a foreigner you may require *it;*
but you shall give up your claim to
what is owed by your brother,
4 except when there may be no poor
among you; for the LORD will greatly
bless you in the land which the LORD

your God is giving you to possess *as*
an inheritance— 5 only if you carefully obey the voice of the LORD your
God, to observe with care all these
commandments which I command
you today. 6 For the LORD your God
will bless you just as He promised
you; you shall lend to many nations,
but you shall not borrow; you shall
reign over many nations, but they
shall not reign over you.

7 "If there is among you a poor
man of your brethren, within any of
the gates in your land which the LORD
your God is giving you, you shall not
harden your heart nor shut your
hand from your poor brother,
8 but you shall open your hand wide
to him and willingly lend him sufficient for his need, whatever he needs.
9 Beware lest there be a wicked
thought in your heart, saying, 'The
seventh year, the year of release, is
at hand,' and your eye be evil against
your poor brother and you give him
nothing, and he cry out to the LORD
against you, and it become sin among
you. 10 You shall surely give to him,
and your heart should not be grieved
when you give to him, because for
this thing the LORD your God will
bless you in all your works and in
all to which you put your hand.
11 For the poor will never cease from
the land; therefore I command you,
saying, 'You shall open your hand
wide to your brother, to your poor
and your needy, in your land.'

12 "If your brother, a Hebrew man,
or a Hebrew woman, is sold to you
and serves you six years, then in the
seventh year you shall let him go free
from you. 13 And when you send him
away free from you, you shall not
let him go away empty-handed;
14 you shall supply him liberally from
your flock, from your threshing floor,
and from your winepress. *From what*
the LORD has blessed you with, you
shall give to him. 15 You shall remember that you were a slave in the
land of Egypt, and the LORD your God
redeemed you; therefore I command
you this thing today. 16 And if it happens that he says to you, 'I will not
go away from you,' because he loves
you and your house, since he prospers with you, 17 then you shall take
an awl and thrust *it* through his ear
to the door, and he shall be your servant forever. Also to your female servant you shall do likewise. 18 It shall

This is the truth: I have a friend, and He is for you. Let me tell you about my Friend.
He is stronger than I. He *is* strength. He is Jesus.

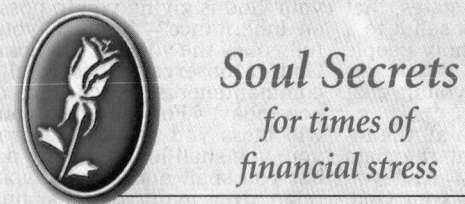

Soul Secrets
for times of
financial stress

*L*ord, you know how strapped we are. You know that there is no way out without Your help. It seems like every time I pick up the phone, there's a bill collector on the other end. I'm not only out of money, I'm out of patience. I never realized how important money was to me until I spent so much more than I had. Now I'm trapped in a cycle of debt that is out of control.

The Bible says that my God "shall supply all my need," so I am calling on You to be my Supplier. I repent of unwise spending choices I have made. I repent of the lack of discipline that got me into this mess. I am calling on You to work a miracle in my finances. I ask You to give me creative ways to make money and the ability to discern how to use it. I commit to walk with You, Lord, until I "owe no one anything except love."

Thank you, Lord, for Your promise of provision and release.

not seem hard to you when you send him away free from you; for he has been worth a double hired servant in serving you six years. Then the LORD your God will bless you in all that you do.

19 "All the firstborn males that come from your herd and your flock you shall sanctify to the LORD your God; you shall do no work with the firstborn of your herd, nor shear the firstborn of your flock. 20 You and your household shall eat *it* before the LORD your God year by year in the place which the LORD chooses. 21 But if there is a defect in it, *if it is* lame or blind *or has* any serious defect, you shall not sacrifice it to the LORD your God. 22 You may eat it within your gates; the unclean and the clean *person* alike *may eat it,* as *if it were* a gazelle or a deer. 23 Only you shall not eat its blood; you shall pour it on the ground like water.

16 "Observe the month of Abib, and keep the Passover to the LORD your God, for in the month of Abib the LORD your God brought you out of Egypt by night. 2 Therefore you shall sacrifice the Passover to the LORD your God, from the flock and the herd, in the place where the LORD chooses to put His name. 3 You shall eat no leavened bread with it; seven days you shall eat unleavened bread with it, *that is,* the bread of affliction (for you came out of the land of Egypt in haste), that you may remember the day in which you came out of the land of Egypt all the days of your life. 4 And no leaven shall be seen among you in all your territory for seven days, nor shall *any* of the meat which you sacrifice the first day at twilight remain overnight until morning.

5 "You may not sacrifice the Passover within any of your gates which the LORD your God gives you; 6 but at the place where the LORD your God chooses to make His name abide, there you shall sacrifice the Passover at twilight, at the going down of the sun, at the time you came out of Egypt. 7 And you shall roast and eat *it* in the place which the LORD your God chooses, and in the morning you shall turn and go to your tents. 8 Six days you shall eat unleavened bread, and on the seventh day there *shall be* a sacred assembly to

the LORD your God. You shall do no work *on it.*

9 "You shall count seven weeks for yourself; begin to count the seven weeks from *the time* you begin *to put* the sickle to the grain. 10 Then you shall keep the Feast of Weeks to the LORD your God with the tribute of a freewill offering from your hand, which you shall give as the LORD your God blesses you. 11 You shall rejoice before the LORD your God, you and your son and your daughter, your male servant and your female servant, the Levite who *is* within your gates, the stranger and the fatherless and the widow who *are* among you, at the place where the LORD your God chooses to make His name abide. 12 And you shall remember that you were a slave in Egypt, and you shall be careful to observe these statutes.

13 "You shall observe the Feast of Tabernacles seven days, when you have gathered from your threshing floor and from your winepress. 14 And you shall rejoice in your feast, you and your son and your daughter, your male servant and your female servant and the Levite, the stranger and the fatherless and the widow, who *are* within your gates. 15 Seven days you shall keep a sacred feast to the LORD your God in the place which the LORD chooses, because the LORD your God will bless you in all your produce and in all the work of your hands, so that you surely rejoice.

16 "Three times a year all your males shall appear before the LORD your God in the place which He chooses: at the Feast of Unleavened Bread, at the Feast of Weeks, and at the Feast of Tabernacles; and they shall not appear before the LORD empty-handed. 17 Every man *shall give* as he is able, according to the blessing of the LORD your God which He has given you.

18 "You shall appoint judges and officers in all your gates, which the LORD your God gives you, according to your tribes, and they shall judge the people with just judgment. 19 You shall not pervert justice; you shall not show partiality, nor take a bribe, for a bribe blinds the eyes of the wise and twists the words of the righteous. 20 You shall follow what is altogether just, that you may live

and inherit the land which the LORD your God is giving you.

21 "You shall not plant for yourself any tree, as a wooden image, near the altar which you build for yourself to the LORD your God. 22 You shall not set up a sacred pillar, which the LORD your God hates.

17 "You shall not sacrifice to the LORD your God a bull or sheep which has any blemish *or* defect, for that *is* an abomination to the LORD your God.

2 "If there is found among you, within any of your gates which the LORD your God gives you, a man or a woman who has been wicked in the sight of the LORD your God, in transgressing His covenant, 3 who has gone and served other gods and worshiped them, either the sun or moon or any of the host of heaven, which I have not commanded, 4 and it is told you, and you hear *of it,* then you shall inquire diligently. And if *it is* indeed true *and* certain that such an abomination has been committed in Israel, 5 then you shall bring out to your gates that man or woman who has committed that wicked thing, and shall stone to death that man or woman with stones. 6 Whoever is deserving of death shall be put to death on the testimony of two or three witnesses; he shall not be put to death on the testimony of one witness. 7 The hands of the witnesses shall be the first against him to put him to death, and afterward the hands of all the people. So you shall put away the evil from among you.

8 "If a matter arises which is too hard for you to judge, between degrees of guilt for bloodshed, between one judgment or another, or between one punishment or another, matters of controversy within your gates, then you shall arise and go up to the place which the LORD your God chooses. 9 And you shall come to the priests, the Levites, and to the judge *there* in those days, and inquire *of them;* they shall pronounce upon you the sentence of judgment. 10 You shall do according to the sentence which they pronounce upon you in that place which the LORD chooses. And you shall be careful to do according to all that they order you. 11 According to the sentence of the law in which they instruct you, ac-

cording to the judgment which they tell you, you shall do; you shall not turn aside *to* the right hand or *to* the left from the sentence which they pronounce upon you. 12 Now the man who acts presumptuously and will not heed the priest who stands to minister there before the LORD your God, or the judge, that man shall die. So you shall put away the evil from Israel. 13 And all the people shall hear and fear, and no longer act presumptuously.

14 "When you come to the land which the LORD your God is giving you, and possess it and dwell in it, and say, 'I will set a king over me like all the nations that *are* around me,' 15 you shall surely set a king over you whom the LORD your God chooses; *one* from among your brethren you shall set as king over you; you may not set a foreigner over you, who *is* not your brother. 16 But he shall not multiply horses for himself, nor cause the people to return to Egypt to multiply horses, for the LORD has said to you, 'You shall not return that way again.' 17 Neither shall he multiply wives for himself, lest his heart turn away; nor shall he greatly multiply silver and gold for himself.

18 "Also it shall be, when he sits on the throne of his kingdom, that he shall write for himself a copy of this law in a book, from *the one* before the priests, the Levites. 19 And it shall be with him, and he shall read it all the days of his life, that he may learn to fear the LORD his God and be careful to observe all the words of this law and these statutes, 20 that his heart may not be lifted above his brethren, that he may not turn aside from the commandment *to* the right hand or *to* the left, and that he may prolong *his* days in his kingdom, he and his children in the midst of Israel.

18 "The priests, the Levites—all the tribe of Levi—shall have no part nor inheritance with Israel; they shall eat the offerings of the LORD made by fire, and His portion. 2 Therefore they shall have no inheritance among their brethren; the LORD is their inheritance, as He said to them.

3 "And this shall be the priest's due from the people, from those who of-

fer a sacrifice, whether *it is* bull or sheep: they shall give to the priest the shoulder, the cheeks, and the stomach. 4 The firstfruits of your grain and your new wine and your oil, and the first of the fleece of your sheep, you shall give him. 5 For the LORD your God has chosen him out of all your tribes to stand to minister in the name of the LORD, him and his sons forever.

6 "So if a Levite comes from any of your gates, from where he dwells among all Israel, and comes with all the desire of his mind to the place which the LORD chooses, 7 then he may serve in the name of the LORD his God as all his brethren the Levites *do,* who stand there before the LORD. 8 They shall have equal portions to eat, besides what comes from the sale of his inheritance.

9 "When you come into the land which the LORD your God is giving you, you shall not learn to follow the abominations of those nations. 10 There shall not be found among you *anyone* who makes his son or his daughter pass through the fire, *or one* who practices witchcraft, *or* a soothsayer, or one who interprets omens, or a sorcerer, 11 or one who conjures spells, or a medium, or a spiritist, or one who calls up the dead. 12 For all who do these things *are* an abomination to the LORD, and because of these abominations the LORD your God drives them out from before you. 13 You shall be blameless before the LORD your God. 14 For these nations which you will dispossess listened to soothsayers and diviners; but as for you, the LORD your God has not appointed such for you.

15 "The LORD your God will raise up for you a Prophet like me from your midst, from your brethren. Him you shall hear, 16 according to all you desired of the LORD your God in Horeb in the day of the assembly, saying, 'Let me not hear again the voice of the LORD my God, nor let me see this great fire anymore, lest I die.' 17 "And the LORD said to me: 'What they have spoken is good. 18 I will raise up for them a Prophet like you from among their brethren, and will put My words in His mouth, and He shall speak to them all that I command Him. 19 And it shall be *that* whoever will not hear My words, which He speaks in My name, I will

require *it* of him. 20 But the prophet who presumes to speak a word in My name, which I have not commanded him to speak, or who speaks in the name of other gods, that prophet shall die.' 21 And if you say in your heart, 'How shall we know the word which the LORD has not spoken?'— 22 when a prophet speaks in the name of the LORD, if the thing does not happen or come to pass, that *is* the thing which the LORD has not spoken; the prophet has spoken it presumptuously; you shall not be afraid of him.

19 "When the LORD your God has cut off the nations whose land the LORD your God is giving you, and you dispossess them and dwell in their cities and in their houses, 2 you shall separate three cities for yourself in the midst of your land which the LORD your God is giving you to possess. 3 You shall prepare roads for yourself, and divide into three parts the territory of your land which the LORD your God is giving you to inherit, that any manslayer may flee there.

4 "And this *is* the case of the manslayer who flees there, that he may live: Whoever kills his neighbor unintentionally, not having hated him in time past— 5 as when *a man* goes to the woods with his neighbor to cut timber, and his hand swings a stroke with the ax to cut down the tree, and the head slips from the handle and strikes his neighbor so that he dies— he shall flee to one of these cities and live; 6 lest the avenger of blood, while his anger is hot, pursue the manslayer and overtake him, because the way is long, and kill him, though he *was* not deserving of death, since he had not hated the victim in time past. 7 Therefore I command you, saying, 'You shall separate three cities for yourself.'

8 "Now if the LORD your God enlarges your territory, as He swore to your fathers, and gives you the land which He promised to give to your fathers, 9 and if you keep all these commandments and do them, which I command you today, to love the LORD your God and to walk always in His ways, then you shall add three more cities for yourself besides these three, 10 lest innocent blood be shed in the midst of your land which the

LORD your God is giving you *as* an inheritance, and *thus* guilt of bloodshed be upon you.

11 "But if anyone hates his neighbor, lies in wait for him, rises against him and strikes him mortally, so that he dies, and he flees to one of these cities, 12 then the elders of his city shall send and bring him from there, and deliver him over to the hand of the avenger of blood, that he may die. 13 Your eye shall not pity him, but you shall put away *the guilt of* innocent blood from Israel, that it may go well with you.

14 "You shall not remove your neighbor's landmark, which the men of old have set, in your inheritance which you will inherit in the land that the LORD your God is giving you to possess.

15 "One witness shall not rise against a man concerning any iniquity or any sin that he commits; by the mouth of two or three witnesses the matter shall be established. 16 If a false witness rises against any man to testify against him of wrongdoing, 17 then both men in the controversy shall stand before the LORD, before the priests and the judges who serve in those days. 18 And the judges shall make careful inquiry, and indeed, *if* the witness *is* a false witness, who has testified falsely against his brother, 19 then you shall do to him as he thought to have done to his brother; so you shall put away the evil from among you. 20 And those who remain shall hear and fear, and hereafter they shall not again commit such evil among you. 21 Your eye shall not pity: life *shall be* for life, eye for eye, tooth for tooth, hand for hand, foot for foot.

20 "When you go out to battle against your enemies, and see horses and chariots *and* people more numerous than you, do not be afraid of them; for the LORD your God *is* with you, who brought you up from the land of Egypt. 2 So it shall be, when you are on the verge of battle, that the priest shall approach and speak to the people. 3 And he shall say to them, 'Hear, O Israel: Today you are on the verge of battle with your enemies. Do not let your heart faint, do not be afraid, and do not tremble or be terrified because of them; 4 for the LORD your God *is* He who goes with you, to fight for you against your enemies, to save you.'

5 "Then the officers shall speak to the people, saying: 'What man *is there* who has built a new house and has not dedicated it? Let him go and return to his house, lest he die in the battle and another man dedicate it. 6 Also what man *is there* who has planted a vineyard and has not eaten of it? Let him go and return to his house, lest he die in the battle and another man eat of it. 7 And what man *is there* who is betrothed to a woman and has not married her? Let him go and return to his house, lest he die in the battle and another man marry her.'

8 "The officers shall speak further to the people, and say, 'What man *is there who is* fearful and fainthearted? Let him go and return to his house, lest the heart of his brethren faint[a] like his heart.' 9 And so it shall be, when the officers have finished speaking to the people, that they shall make captains of the armies to lead the people.

10 "When you go near a city to fight against it, then proclaim an offer of peace to it. 11 And it shall be that if they accept your offer of peace, and open to you, then all the people *who are* found in it shall be placed under tribute to you, and serve you. 12 Now if *the city* will not make peace with you, but war against you, then you shall besiege it. 13 And when the LORD your God delivers it into your hands, you shall strike every male in it with the edge of the sword. 14 But the women, the little ones, the livestock, and all that is in the city, all its spoil, you shall plunder for yourself; and you shall eat the enemies' plunder which the LORD your God gives you. 15 Thus you shall do to all the cities *which are* very far from you, which *are* not of the cities of these nations.

16 "But of the cities of these peoples which the LORD your God gives you *as* an inheritance, you shall let nothing that breathes remain alive, 17 but you shall utterly destroy them:

20:8 ªFollowing Masoretic Text and Targum; Samaritan Pentateuch, Septuagint, Syriac, and Vulgate read *lest he make his brother's heart faint.*

God said, "Arise." You are about to have a resurrection. It will be so strong that your husband should feel it. Your children should feel it. Yes, from the prayer room to the bedroom, a loosed woman is free!

Soul Secrets
of a woman at war
within herself

*L*ord, through the ages You have fought battles for Your
people. Now I need Someone to fight for me. Someone
with tough skin and a tender heart. Someone who
cares that I am daily ambushed and beaten up in the war zones
of work and worry and weariness.

I have no safe place, no shelter, no refuge where I can hide.
And even if I did, I could not call a ceasefire to the war within
my heart. There is such strife and unrest in the deepest parts
of me. And I cry out for You! There's a battle going on in me
between what You say and what I think. I cannot hear Your
still, small voice over the noise that rages inside of me.

King Jesus, win this victory. Be my Bodyguard. Be my Hero.
Even when I'm outnumbered, one word from You can conquer
every conflict, eliminate the enemy, defeat the destroyer. Come
in power, Prince of Peace.

the Hittite and the Amorite and the Canaanite and the Perizzite and the Hivite and the Jebusite, just as the LORD your God has commanded you, 18 lest they teach you to do according to all their abominations which they have done for their gods, and you sin against the LORD your God.

19 "When you besiege a city for a long time, while making war against it to take it, you shall not destroy its trees by wielding an ax against them; if you can eat of them, do not cut them down to use in the siege, for the tree of the field *is* man's *food*. 20 Only the trees which you know *are* not trees for food you may destroy and cut down, to build siegeworks against the city that makes war with you, until it is subdued.

21 "If *anyone* is found slain, lying in the field in the land which the LORD your God is giving you to possess, *and* it is not known who killed him, 2 then your elders and your judges shall go out and measure *the distance* from the slain man to the surrounding cities. 3 And it shall be *that* the elders of the city nearest to the slain man will take a heifer which has not been worked *and* which has not pulled with a yoke. 4 The elders of that city shall bring the heifer down to a valley with flowing water, which is neither plowed nor sown, and they shall break the heifer's neck there in the valley. 5 Then the priests, the sons of Levi, shall come near, for the LORD your God has chosen them to minister to Him and to bless in the name of the LORD; by their word every controversy and every assault shall be *settled*. 6 And all the elders of that city nearest to the slain *man* shall wash their hands over the heifer whose neck was broken in the valley. 7 Then they shall answer and say, 'Our hands have not shed this blood, nor have our eyes seen *it*. 8 Provide atonement, O LORD, for Your people Israel, whom You have redeemed, and do not lay innocent blood to the charge of Your people Israel.' And atonement shall be provided on their behalf for the blood. 9 So you shall put away the *guilt of* innocent blood from among you when you do *what is* right in the sight of the LORD.

10 "When you go out to war against your enemies, and the LORD your God delivers them into your hand, and you take them captive, 11 and you see among the captives a beautiful woman, and desire her and would take her for your wife, 12 then you shall bring her home to your house, and she shall shave her head and trim her nails. 13 She shall put off the clothes of her captivity, remain in your house, and mourn her father and her mother a full month; after that you may go in to her and be her husband, and she shall be your wife. 14 And it shall be, if you have no delight in her, then you shall set her free, but you certainly shall not sell her for money; you shall not treat her brutally, because you have humbled her.

15 "If a man has two wives, one loved and the other unloved, and they have borne him children, *both* the loved and the unloved, and *if* the firstborn son is of her who is unloved, 16 then it shall be, on the day he bequeaths his possessions to his sons, *that* he must not bestow firstborn status on the son of the loved wife in preference to the son of the unloved, the *true* firstborn. 17 But he shall acknowledge the son of the unloved wife *as* the firstborn by giving him a double portion of all that he has, for he *is* the beginning of his strength; the right of the firstborn *is* his.

18 "If a man has a stubborn and rebellious son who will not obey the voice of his father or the voice of his mother, and *who,* when they have chastened him, will not heed them, 19 then his father and his mother shall take hold of him and bring him out to the elders of his city, to the gate of his city. 20 And they shall say to the elders of his city, 'This son of ours is stubborn and rebellious; he will not obey our voice; he is a glutton and a drunkard.' 21 Then all the men of his city shall stone him to death with stones; so you shall put away the evil from among you, and all Israel shall hear and fear.

22 "If a man has committed a sin deserving of death, and he is put to death, and you hang him on a tree, 23 his body shall not remain overnight on the tree, but you shall surely bury him that day, so that you do not defile the land which the LORD your God is giving you *as* an inheritance;

Gospel Pearls

for he who is hanged *is* accursed of God.

22 "You shall not see your brother's ox or his sheep going astray, and hide yourself from them; you shall certainly bring them back to your brother. 2 And if your brother *is* not near you, or if you do not know him, then you shall bring it to your own house, and it shall remain with you until your brother seeks it; then you shall restore it to him. 3 You shall do the same with his donkey, and so shall you do with his garment; with any lost thing of your brother's, which he has lost and you have found, you shall do likewise; you must not hide yourself.

4 "You shall not see your brother's donkey or his ox fall down along the road, and hide yourself from them; you shall surely help him lift *them* up again.

5 "A woman shall not wear anything that pertains to a man, nor shall a man put on a woman's garment, for all who do so *are* an abomination to the LORD your God.

6 "If a bird's nest happens to be before you along the way, in any tree or on the ground, with young ones or eggs, with the mother sitting on the young or on the eggs, you shall not take the mother with the young; 7 you shall surely let the mother go, and take the young for yourself, that it may be well with you and *that* you may prolong *your* days.

8 "When you build a new house, then you shall make a parapet for your roof, that you may not bring guilt of bloodshed on your household if anyone falls from it.

9 "You shall not sow your vineyard with different kinds of seed, lest the yield of the seed which you have sown and the fruit of your vineyard be defiled.

10 "You shall not plow with an ox and a donkey together.

11 "You shall not wear a garment of different sorts, *such as* wool and linen mixed together.

12 "You shall make tassels on the four corners of the clothing with which you cover *yourself*.

13 "If any man takes a wife, and goes in to her, and detests her, 14 and charges her with shameful conduct, and brings a bad name on her, and says, 'I took this woman, and when I came to her I found she *was* not a virgin,' 15 then the father and mother of the young woman shall take and bring out *the evidence of* the young woman's virginity to the elders of the city at the gate. 16 And the young woman's father shall say to the elders, 'I gave my daughter to this man as wife, and he detests her. 17 Now he has charged her with shameful conduct, saying, "I found your daughter *was* not a virgin," and yet these *are the evidences of* my daughter's virginity.' And they shall spread the cloth before the elders of the city. 18 Then the elders of that city shall take that man and punish him; 19 and they shall fine him one hundred *shekels* of silver and give *them* to the father of the young woman, because he has brought a bad name on a virgin of Israel. And she shall be his wife; he cannot divorce her all his days.

20 "But if the thing is true, *and evidences of* virginity are not found for the young woman, 21 then they shall bring out the young woman to the door of her father's house, and the men of her city shall stone her to death with stones, because she has done a disgraceful thing in Israel, to play the harlot in her father's house. So you shall put away the evil from among you.

22 "If a man is found lying with a woman married to a husband, then both of them shall die—the man that lay with the woman, and the woman; so you shall put away the evil from Israel.

23 "If a young woman *who is* a virgin is betrothed to a husband, and a man finds her in the city and lies with her, 24 then you shall bring them both out to the gate of that city, and you shall stone them to death with stones, the young woman because she did not cry out in the city, and the man because he humbled his neighbor's wife; so you shall put away the evil from among you.

25 "But if a man finds a betrothed young woman in the countryside, and the man forces her and lies with her, then only the man who lay with her shall die. 26 But you shall do nothing to the young woman; *there is* in the young woman no sin *deserving* of death, for just as when a man rises against his neighbor and kills him, even so *is* this matter. 27 For he

found her in the countryside, *and* the betrothed young woman cried out, but *there was* no one to save her.

28 "If a man finds a young woman *who is* a virgin, who is not betrothed, and he seizes her and lies with her, and they are found out, 29 then the man who lay with her shall give to the young woman's father fifty *shekels* of silver, and she shall be his wife because he has humbled her; he shall not be permitted to divorce her all his days.

30 "A man shall not take his father's wife, nor uncover his father's bed.

23 "He who is emasculated by crushing or mutilation shall not enter the assembly of the LORD.

2 "One of illegitimate birth shall not enter the assembly of the LORD; even to the tenth generation none of his *descendants* shall enter the assembly of the LORD.

3 "An Ammonite or Moabite shall not enter the assembly of the LORD; even to the tenth generation none of his *descendants* shall enter the assembly of the LORD forever, 4 because they did not meet you with bread and water on the road when you came out of Egypt, and because they hired against you Balaam the son of Beor from Pethor of Mesopotamia,*a* to curse you. 5 Nevertheless the LORD your God would not listen to Balaam, but the LORD your God turned the curse into a blessing for you, because the LORD your God loves you. 6 You shall not seek their peace nor their prosperity all your days forever.

7 "You shall not abhor an Edomite, for he *is* your brother. You shall not abhor an Egyptian, because you were an alien in his land. 8 The children of the third generation born to them may enter the assembly of the LORD.

9 "When the army goes out against your enemies, then keep yourself from every wicked thing. 10 If there is any man among you who becomes unclean by some occurrence in the night, then he shall go outside the camp; he shall not come inside the camp. 11 But it shall be, when evening comes, that he shall wash with water; and when the sun sets, he may come into the camp.

12 "Also you shall have a place outside the camp, where you may go out; 13 and you shall have an implement among your equipment, and when you sit down outside, you shall dig with it and turn and cover your refuse. 14 For the LORD your God walks in the midst of your camp, to deliver you and give your enemies over to you; therefore your camp shall be holy, that He may see no unclean thing among you, and turn away from you.

15 "You shall not give back to his master the slave who has escaped from his master to you. 16 He may dwell with you in your midst, in the place which he chooses within one of your gates, where it seems best to him; you shall not oppress him.

17 "There shall be no *ritual* harlot*a* of the daughters of Israel, or a perverted*b* one of the sons of Israel. 18 You shall not bring the wages of a harlot or the price of a dog to the house of the LORD your God for any vowed offering, for both of these *are* an abomination to the LORD your God.

19 "You shall not charge interest to your brother—interest on money *or* food *or* anything that is lent out at interest. 20 To a foreigner you may charge interest, but to your brother you shall not charge interest, that the LORD your God may bless you in all to which you set your hand in the land which you are entering to possess.

21 "When you make a vow to the LORD your God, you shall not delay to pay it; for the LORD your God will surely require it of you, and it would be sin to you. 22 But if you abstain from vowing, it shall not be sin to you. 23 That which has gone from your lips you shall keep and perform, for you voluntarily vowed to the LORD your God what you have promised with your mouth.

24 "When you come into your neighbor's vineyard, you may eat your fill of grapes at your pleasure, but you shall not put *any* in your container. 25 When you come into your neighbor's standing grain, you may pluck the heads with your hand, but you shall not use a sickle on your neighbor's standing grain.

23:4 *a*Hebrew *Aram Naharaim*   23:17 *a*Hebrew *qedeshah,* feminine of *qadesh* (see note b)   *b*Hebrew *qadesh,* that is, one practicing sodomy and prostitution in religious rituals

Gospel Pearls

24 "When a man takes a wife and marries her, and it happens that she finds no favor in his eyes because he has found some uncleanness in her, and he writes her a certificate of divorce, puts *it* in her hand, and sends her out of his house, 2 when she has departed from his house, and goes and becomes another man's *wife,* 3 *if* the latter husband detests her and writes her a certificate of divorce, puts *it* in her hand, and sends her out of his house, or if the latter husband dies who took her as his wife, 4 *then* her former husband who divorced her must not take her back to be his wife after she has been defiled; for that *is* an abomination before the LORD, and you shall not bring sin on the land which the LORD your God is giving you *as* an inheritance.

5 "When a man has taken a new wife, he shall not go out to war or be charged with any business; he shall be free at home one year, and bring happiness to his wife whom he has taken.

6 "No man shall take the lower or the upper millstone in pledge, for he takes *one's* living in pledge.

7 "If a man is found kidnapping any of his brethren of the children of Israel, and mistreats him or sells him, then that kidnapper shall die; and you shall put away the evil from among you.

8 "Take heed in an outbreak of leprosy, that you carefully observe and do according to all that the priests, the Levites, shall teach you; just as I commanded them, *so* you shall be careful to do. 9 Remember what the LORD your God did to Miriam on the way when you came out of Egypt!

10 "When you lend your brother anything, you shall not go into his house to get his pledge. 11 You shall stand outside, and the man to whom you lend shall bring the pledge out to you. 12 And if the man *is* poor, you shall not keep his pledge overnight. 13 You shall in any case return the pledge to him again when the sun goes down, that he may sleep in his own garment and bless you; and it shall be righteousness to you before the LORD your God.

14 "You shall not oppress a hired servant *who is* poor and needy, *whether* one of your brethren or one of the aliens who *is* in your land within your gates. 15 Each day you shall give *him* his wages, and not let the sun go down on it, for he *is* poor and has set his heart on it; lest he cry out against you to the LORD, and it be sin to you.

16 "Fathers shall not be put to death for *their* children, nor shall children be put to death for *their* fathers; a person shall be put to death for his own sin.

17 "You shall not pervert justice due the stranger or the fatherless, nor take a widow's garment as a pledge. 18 But you shall remember that you were a slave in Egypt, and the LORD your God redeemed you from there; therefore I command you to do this thing.

19 "When you reap your harvest in your field, and forget a sheaf in the field, you shall not go back to get it; it shall be for the stranger, the fatherless, and the widow, that the LORD your God may bless you in all the work of your hands. 20 When you beat your olive trees, you shall not go over the boughs again; it shall be for the stranger, the fatherless, and the widow. 21 When you gather the grapes of your vineyard, you shall not glean *it* afterward; it shall be for the stranger, the fatherless, and the widow. 22 And you shall remember that you were a slave in the land of Egypt; therefore I command you to do this thing.

25 "If there is a dispute between men, and they come to court, that *the judges* may judge them, and they justify the righteous and condemn the wicked, 2 then it shall be, if the wicked man deserves to be beaten, that the judge will cause him to lie down and be beaten in his presence, according to his guilt, with a certain number of blows. 3 Forty blows he may give him *and* no more, lest he should exceed this and beat him with many blows above these, and your brother be humiliated in your sight.

4 "You shall not muzzle an ox while it treads out *the grain.*

5 "If brothers dwell together, and one of them dies and has no son, the widow of the dead man shall not be *married* to a stranger outside *the family;* her husband's brother shall go in to her, take her as his wife, and perform the duty of a husband's

*T*rue spirituality does not exist at the expense of humanity.

brother to her. 6 And it shall be *that* the firstborn son which she bears will succeed to the name of his dead brother, that his name may not be blotted out of Israel. 7 But if the man does not want to take his brother's wife, then let his brother's wife go up to the gate to the elders, and say, 'My husband's brother refuses to raise up a name to his brother in Israel; he will not perform the duty of my husband's brother.' 8 Then the elders of his city shall call him and speak to him. But *if* he stands firm and says, 'I do not want to take her,' 9 then his brother's wife shall come to him in the presence of the elders, remove his sandal from his foot, spit in his face, and answer and say, 'So shall it be done to the man who will not build up his brother's house.' 10 And his name shall be called in Israel, 'The house of him who had his sandal removed.'

11 "If *two* men fight together, and the wife of one draws near to rescue her husband from the hand of the one attacking him, and puts out her hand and seizes him by the genitals, 12 then you shall cut off her hand; your eye shall not pity *her.*

13 "You shall not have in your bag differing weights, a heavy and a light. 14 You shall not have in your house differing measures, a large and a small. 15 You shall have a perfect and just weight, a perfect and just measure, that your days may be lengthened in the land which the LORD your God is giving you. 16 For all who do such things, all who behave unrighteously, *are* an abomination to the LORD your God.

17 "Remember what Amalek did to you on the way as you were coming out of Egypt, 18 how he met you on the way and attacked your rear ranks, all the stragglers at your rear, when you *were* tired and weary; and he did not fear God. 19 Therefore it shall be, when the LORD your God has given you rest from your enemies all around, in the land which the LORD your God is giving you to possess *as* an inheritance, *that* you will blot out the remembrance of Amalek from under heaven. You shall not forget.

26 "And it shall be, when you come into the land which the LORD your God is giving you *as* an inheritance, and you possess it and dwell in it, 2 that you shall take some of the first of all the produce of the ground, which you shall bring from your land that the LORD your God is giving you, and put *it* in a basket and go to the place where the LORD your God chooses to make His name abide. 3 And you shall go to the one who is priest in those days, and say to him, 'I declare today to the LORD your[a] God that I have come to the country which the LORD swore to our fathers to give us.'

4 "Then the priest shall take the basket out of your hand and set it down before the altar of the LORD your God. 5 And you shall answer and say before the LORD your God: 'My father *was* a Syrian,[a] about to perish, and he went down to Egypt and dwelt there, few in number; and there he became a nation, great, mighty, and populous. 6 But the Egyptians mistreated us, afflicted us, and laid hard bondage on us. 7 Then we cried out to the LORD God of our fathers, and the LORD heard our voice and looked on our affliction and our labor and our oppression. 8 So the LORD brought us out of Egypt with a mighty hand and with an outstretched arm, with great terror and with signs and wonders. 9 He has brought us to this place and has given us this land, "a land flowing with milk and honey";[a] 10 and now, behold, I have brought the firstfruits of the land which you, O LORD, have given me.'

"Then you shall set it before the LORD your God, and worship before the LORD your God. 11 So you shall rejoice in every good *thing* which the LORD your God has given to you and your house, you and the Levite and the stranger who *is* among you.

12 "When you have finished laying aside all the tithe of your increase in the third year—the year of tithing—and have given *it* to the Levite, the stranger, the fatherless, and the widow, so that they may eat within your gates and be filled, 13 then you shall say before the LORD your God: 'I have removed the holy *tithe* from *my* house, and also have given them to the Levite, the stranger, the fatherless, and the widow, according to all

26:3 [a]Septuagint reads *my.*   26:5 [a]Or *Aramean*   26:9 [a]Exodus 3:8

Gospel Pearls

Your commandments which You have commanded me; I have not transgressed Your commandments, nor have I forgotten *them.* 14 I have not eaten any of it when in mourning, nor have I removed *any* of it for an unclean *use,* nor given *any* of it for the dead. I have obeyed the voice of the Lord my God, and have done according to all that You have commanded me. 15 Look down from Your holy habitation, from heaven, and bless Your people Israel and the land which You have given us, just as You swore to our fathers, "a land flowing with milk and honey." *'a*

16 "This day the Lord your God commands you to observe these statutes and judgments; therefore you shall be careful to observe them with all your heart and with all your soul. 17 Today you have proclaimed the Lord to be your God, and that you will walk in His ways and keep His statutes, His commandments, and His judgments, and that you will obey His voice. 18 Also today the Lord has proclaimed you to be His special people, just as He promised you, that you should keep all His commandments, 19 and that He will set you high above all nations which He has made, in praise, in name, and in honor, and that you may be a holy people to the Lord your God, just as He has spoken."

27 Now Moses, with the elders of Israel, commanded the people, saying: "Keep all the commandments which I command you today. 2 And it shall be, on the day when you cross over the Jordan to the land which the Lord your God is giving you, that you shall set up for yourselves large stones, and whitewash them with lime. 3 You shall write on them all the words of this law, when you have crossed over, that you may enter the land which the Lord your God is giving you, 'a land flowing with milk and honey,'*a* just as the Lord God of your fathers promised you. 4 Therefore it shall be, when you have crossed over the Jordan, *that* on Mount Ebal you shall set up these stones, which I command you today, and you shall whitewash them with lime. 5 And there you shall build an altar to the Lord your God, an altar of stones; you shall not use an iron *tool* on them. 6 You shall build with whole stones the altar of the Lord your God, and offer burnt offerings on it to the Lord your God. 7 You shall offer peace offerings, and shall eat there, and rejoice before the Lord your God. 8 And you shall write very plainly on the stones all the words of this law."

9 Then Moses and the priests, the Levites, spoke to all Israel, saying, "Take heed and listen, O Israel: This day you have become the people of the Lord your God. 10 Therefore you shall obey the voice of the Lord your God, and observe His commandments and His statutes which I command you today."

11 And Moses commanded the people on the same day, saying, 12 "These shall stand on Mount Gerizim to bless the people, when you have crossed over the Jordan: Simeon, Levi, Judah, Issachar, Joseph, and Benjamin; 13 and these shall stand on Mount Ebal to curse: Reuben, Gad, Asher, Zebulun, Dan, and Naphtali.

14 "And the Levites shall speak with a loud voice and say to all the men of Israel: 15 'Cursed *is* the one who makes a carved or molded image, an abomination to the Lord, the work of the hands of the craftsman, and sets *it* up in secret.'

"And all the people shall answer and say, 'Amen!'

16 'Cursed *is* the one who treats his father or his mother with contempt.'

"And all the people shall say, 'Amen!'

17 'Cursed *is* the one who moves his neighbor's landmark.'

"And all the people shall say, 'Amen!'

18 'Cursed *is* the one who makes the blind to wander off the road.'

"And all the people shall say, 'Amen!'

19 'Cursed *is* the one who perverts the justice due the stranger, the fatherless, and widow.'

"And all the people shall say, 'Amen!'

20 'Cursed *is* the one who lies with his father's wife, because he has uncovered his father's bed.'

"And all the people shall say, 'Amen!'

26:15 *a*Exodus 3:8   27:3 *a*Exodus 3:8

God graces married people to taste the fruit of their relationship in a unique way. He wants you to be creative.

21 'Cursed *is* the one who lies with any kind of animal.'

"And all the people shall say, 'Amen!'

22 'Cursed *is* the one who lies with his sister, the daughter of his father or the daughter of his mother.'

"And all the people shall say, 'Amen!'

23 'Cursed *is* the one who lies with his mother-in-law.'

"And all the people shall say, 'Amen!'

24 'Cursed *is* the one who attacks his neighbor secretly.'

"And all the people shall say, 'Amen!'

25 'Cursed *is* the one who takes a bribe to slay an innocent person.'

"And all the people shall say, 'Amen!'

26 'Cursed *is* the one who does not confirm *all* the words of this law.'

"And all the people shall say, 'Amen!' "

28 "Now it shall come to pass, if you diligently obey the voice of the Lord your God, to observe carefully all His commandments which I command you today, that the Lord your God will set you high above all nations of the earth. 2 And all these blessings shall come upon you and overtake you, because you obey the voice of the Lord your God:

3 "Blessed *shall* you *be* in the city, and blessed *shall* you *be* in the country.

4 "Blessed *shall be* the fruit of your body, the produce of your ground and the increase of your herds, the increase of your cattle and the offspring of your flocks.

5 "Blessed *shall be* your basket and your kneading bowl.

6 "Blessed *shall* you *be* when you come in, and blessed *shall* you *be* when you go out.

7 "The Lord will cause your enemies who rise against you to be defeated before your face; they shall come out against you one way and flee before you seven ways.

8 "The Lord will command the blessing on you in your storehouses and in all to which you set your hand, and He will bless you in the land which the Lord your God is giving you.

9 "The Lord will establish you as a holy people to Himself, just as He has sworn to you, if you keep the commandments of the Lord your God and walk in His ways. 10 Then all peoples of the earth shall see that you are called by the name of the Lord, and they shall be afraid of you. 11 And the Lord will grant you plenty of goods, in the fruit of your body, in the increase of your livestock, and in the produce of your ground, in the land of which the Lord swore to your fathers to give you. 12 The Lord will open to you His good treasure, the heavens, to give the rain to your land in its season, and to bless all the work of your hand. You shall lend to many nations, but you shall not borrow. 13 And the Lord will make you the head and not the tail; you shall be above only, and not be beneath, if you heed the commandments of the Lord your God, which I command you today, and are careful to observe *them.* 14 So you shall not turn aside from any of the words which I command you this day, *to* the right or the left, to go after other gods to serve them.

15 "But it shall come to pass, if you do not obey the voice of the Lord your God, to observe carefully all His commandments and His statutes which I command you today, that all these curses will come upon you and overtake you:

16 "Cursed *shall* you *be* in the city, and cursed *shall* you *be* in the country.

17 "Cursed *shall be* your basket and your kneading bowl.

18 "Cursed *shall be* the fruit of your body and the produce of your land, the increase of your cattle and the offspring of your flocks.

19 "Cursed *shall* you *be* when you come in, and cursed *shall* you *be* when you go out.

20 "The Lord will send on you cursing, confusion, and rebuke in all that you set your hand to do, until you are destroyed and until you perish quickly, because of the wickedness of your doings in which you have forsaken Me. 21 The Lord will make the plague cling to you until He has consumed you from the land which you are going to possess. 22 The Lord will strike you with consumption, with fever, with inflammation, with severe burning fever, with the sword, with scorching, and with mildew; they shall pursue you until you perish.

Gospel Pearls

23 And your heavens which *are* over your head shall be bronze, and the earth which is under you *shall be* iron. 24 The LORD will change the rain of your land to powder and dust; from the heaven it shall come down on you until you are destroyed.

25 "The LORD will cause you to be defeated before your enemies; you shall go out one way against them and flee seven ways before them; and you shall become troublesome to all the kingdoms of the earth. 26 Your carcasses shall be food for all the birds of the air and the beasts of the earth, and no one shall frighten *them* away. 27 The LORD will strike you with the boils of Egypt, with tumors, with the scab, and with the itch, from which you cannot be healed. 28 The LORD will strike you with madness and blindness and confusion of heart. 29 And you shall grope at noonday, as a blind man gropes in darkness; you shall not prosper in your ways; you shall be only oppressed and plundered continually, and no one shall save you.

30 "You shall betroth a wife, but another man shall lie with her; you shall build a house, but you shall not dwell in it; you shall plant a vineyard, but shall not gather its grapes. 31 Your ox *shall be* slaughtered before your eyes, but you shall not eat of it; your donkey *shall be* violently taken away from before you, and shall not be restored to you; your sheep *shall be* given to your enemies, and you shall have no one to rescue *them.* 32 Your sons and your daughters *shall be* given to another people, and your eyes shall look and fail *with longing* for them all day long; and *there shall be* no strength in your hand. 33 A nation whom you have not known shall eat the fruit of your land and the produce of your labor, and you shall be only oppressed and crushed continually. 34 So you shall be driven mad because of the sight which your eyes see. 35 The LORD will strike you in the knees and on the legs with severe boils which cannot be healed, and from the sole of your foot to the top of your head.

36 "The LORD will bring you and the king whom you set over you to a nation which neither you nor your fathers have known, and there you shall serve other gods—wood and stone. 37 And you shall become an astonishment, a proverb, and a byword among all nations where the LORD will drive you.

38 "You shall carry much seed out to the field but gather little in, for the locust shall consume it. 39 You shall plant vineyards and tend *them,* but you shall neither drink *of* the wine nor gather the *grapes;* for the worms shall eat them. 40 You shall have olive trees throughout all your territory, but you shall not anoint *yourself* with the oil; for your olives shall drop off. 41 You shall beget sons and daughters, but they shall not be yours; for they shall go into captivity. 42 Locusts shall consume all your trees and the produce of your land.

43 "The alien who *is* among you shall rise higher and higher above you, and you shall come down lower and lower. 44 He shall lend to you, but you shall not lend to him; he shall be the head, and you shall be the tail.

45 "Moreover all these curses shall come upon you and pursue and overtake you, until you are destroyed, because you did not obey the voice of the LORD your God, to keep His commandments and His statutes which He commanded you. 46 And they shall be upon you for a sign and a wonder, and on your descendants forever.

47 "Because you did not serve the LORD your God with joy and gladness of heart, for the abundance of everything, 48 therefore you shall serve your enemies, whom the LORD will send against you, in hunger, in thirst, in nakedness, and in need of everything; and He will put a yoke of iron on your neck until He has destroyed you. 49 The LORD will bring a nation against you from afar, from the end of the earth, *as swift* as the eagle flies, a nation whose language you will not understand, 50 a nation of fierce countenance, which does not respect the elderly nor show favor to the young. 51 And they shall eat the increase of your livestock and the produce of your land, until you are destroyed; they shall not leave you grain or new wine or oil, *or* the increase of your cattle or the offspring of your flocks, until they have destroyed you.

52 "They shall besiege you at all your gates until your high and fortified walls, in which you trust, come down throughout all your land; and

---

*Y*ou can't use your relationship with God to stay in a state of denial. If something has gone out of your life and your heart, you must believe God for its return.

they shall besiege you at all your gates throughout all your land which the LORD your God has given you. 53 You shall eat the fruit of your own body, the flesh of your sons and your daughters whom the LORD your God has given you, in the siege and desperate straits in which your enemy shall distress you. 54 The sensitive and very refined man among you will be hostile toward his brother, toward the wife of his bosom, and toward the rest of his children whom he leaves behind, 55 so that he will not give any of them the flesh of his children whom he will eat, because he has nothing left in the siege and desperate straits in which your enemy shall distress you at all your gates. 56 The tender and delicate woman among you, who would not venture to set the sole of her foot on the ground because of her delicateness and sensitivity, will refuse,*a* to the husband of her bosom, and to her son and her daughter, 57 her placenta which comes out from between her feet and her children whom she bears; for she will eat them secretly for lack of everything in the siege and desperate straits in which your enemy shall distress you at all your gates.

58 "If you do not carefully observe all the words of this law that are written in this book, that you may fear this glorious and awesome name, THE LORD YOUR GOD, 59 then the LORD will bring upon you and your descendants extraordinary plagues—great and prolonged plagues—and serious and prolonged sicknesses. 60 Moreover He will bring back on you all the diseases of Egypt, of which you were afraid, and they shall cling to you. 61 Also every sickness and every plague, which *is* not written in this Book of the Law, will the LORD bring upon you until you are destroyed. 62 You shall be left few in number, whereas you were as the stars of heaven in multitude, because you would not obey the voice of the LORD your God. 63 And it shall be, *that* just as the LORD rejoiced over you to do you good and multiply you, so the LORD will rejoice over you to destroy you and bring you to nothing; and you shall be plucked from off the land which you go to possess.

64 "Then the LORD will scatter you among all peoples, from one end of the earth to the other, and there you shall serve other gods, which neither you nor your fathers have known—wood and stone. 65 And among those nations you shall find no rest, nor shall the sole of your foot have a resting place; but there the LORD will give you a trembling heart, failing eyes, and anguish of soul. 66 Your life shall hang in doubt before you; you shall fear day and night, and have no assurance of life. 67 In the morning you shall say, 'Oh, that it were evening!' And at evening you shall say, 'Oh, that it were morning!' because of the fear which terrifies your heart, and because of the sight which your eyes see.

68 "And the LORD will take you back to Egypt in ships, by the way of which I said to you, 'You shall never see it again.' And there you shall be offered for sale to your enemies as male and female slaves, but no one will buy *you*."

29 These *are* the words of the covenant which the LORD commanded Moses to make with the children of Israel in the land of Moab, besides the covenant which He made with them in Horeb.

2 Now Moses called all Israel and said to them: "You have seen all that the LORD did before your eyes in the land of Egypt, to Pharaoh and to all his servants and to all his land— 3 the great trials which your eyes have seen, the signs, and those great wonders. 4 Yet the LORD has not given you a heart to perceive and eyes to see and ears to hear, to this *very* day. 5 And I have led you forty years in the wilderness. Your clothes have not worn out on you, and your sandals have not worn out on your feet. 6 You have not eaten bread, nor have you drunk wine or *similar* drink, that you may know that I *am* the LORD your God. 7 And when you came to this place, Sihon king of Heshbon and Og king of Bashan came out against us to battle, and we conquered them. 8 We took their land and gave it as an inheritance to the Reubenites, to the Gadites, and to half the tribe of Manasseh. 9 Therefore keep the words of this

---

28:56 *a*Literally *her eye shall be evil toward*

covenant, and do them, that you may prosper in all that you do.

10 "All of you stand today before the LORD your God: your leaders and your tribes and your elders and your officers, all the men of Israel, 11 your little ones and your wives— also the stranger who *is* in your camp, from the one who cuts your wood to the one who draws your water— 12 that you may enter into covenant with the LORD your God, and into His oath, which the LORD your God makes with you today, 13 that He may establish you today as a people for Himself, and *that* He may be God to you, just as He has spoken to you, and just as He has sworn to your fathers, to Abraham, Isaac, and Jacob.

14 "I make this covenant and this oath, not with you alone, 15 but with *him* who stands here with us today before the LORD our God, as well as with *him* who *is* not here with us today 16 (for you know that we dwelt in the land of Egypt and that we came through the nations which you passed by, 17 and you saw their abominations and their idols which *were* among them—wood and stone and silver and gold); 18 so that there may not be among you man or woman or family or tribe, whose heart turns away today from the LORD our God, to go *and* serve the gods of these nations, and that there may not be among you a root bearing bitterness or wormwood; 19 and so it may not happen, when he hears the words of this curse, that he blesses himself in his heart, saying, 'I shall have peace, even though I follow the dictates*ᵃ* of my heart'—as though the drunkard could be included with the sober.

20 "The LORD would not spare him; for then the anger of the LORD and His jealousy would burn against that man, and every curse that is written in this book would settle on him, and the LORD would blot out his name from under heaven. 21 And the LORD would separate him from all the tribes of Israel for adversity, according to all the curses of the covenant that are written in this Book of the Law, 22 so that the coming generation of your children who rise up after you, and the foreigner who comes

from a far land, would say, when they see the plagues of that land and the sicknesses which the LORD has laid on it:

23 'The whole land *is* brimstone, salt, and burning; it is not sown, nor does it bear, nor does any grass grow there, like the overthrow of Sodom and Gomorrah, Admah, and Zeboiim, which the LORD overthrew in His anger and His wrath.' 24 All nations would say, 'Why has the LORD done so to this land? What does the heat of this great anger mean?' 25 Then *people* would say: 'Because they have forsaken the covenant of the LORD God of their fathers, which He made with them when He brought them out of the land of Egypt; 26 for they went and served other gods and worshiped them, gods that they did not know and that He had not given to them. 27 Then the anger of the LORD was aroused against this land, to bring on it every curse that is written in this book. 28 And the LORD uprooted them from their land in anger, in wrath, and in great indignation, and cast them into another land, as *it is* this day.'

29 "The secret *things belong* to the LORD our God, but those *things which are* revealed *belong* to us and to our children forever, that *we* may do all the words of this law.

30 "Now it shall come to pass, when all these things come upon you, the blessing and the curse which I have set before you, and you call *them* to mind among all the nations where the LORD your God drives you, 2 and you return to the LORD your God and obey His voice, according to all that I command you today, you and your children, with all your heart and with all your soul, 3 that the LORD your God will bring you back from captivity, and have compassion on you, and gather you again from all the nations where the LORD your God has scattered you. 4 If *any* of you are driven out to the farthest *parts* under heaven, from there the LORD your God will gather you, and from there He will bring you. 5 Then the LORD your God will bring you to the land which your fathers possessed, and you shall possess it. He will prosper you and

29:19 *ᵃOr stubbornness*

*J*ust when others have decided you won't be back, here He comes. He comes into your life like a medieval prince, clad in righteousness, dipped in blood. He comes to heal and restore your faith and expectation, your romance and tenderness.

multiply you more than your fathers. 6 And the LORD your God will circumcise your heart and the heart of your descendants, to love the LORD your God with all your heart and with all your soul, that you may live.

7 "Also the LORD your God will put all these curses on your enemies and on those who hate you, who persecuted you. 8 And you will again obey the voice of the LORD and do all His commandments which I command you today. 9 The LORD your God will make you abound in all the work of your hand, in the fruit of your body, in the increase of your livestock, and in the produce of your land for good. For the LORD will again rejoice over you for good as He rejoiced over your fathers, 10 if you obey the voice of the LORD your God, to keep His commandments and His statutes which are written in this Book of the Law, *and* if you turn to the LORD your God with all your heart and with all your soul.

11 "For this commandment which I command you today *is* not *too* mysterious for you, nor *is* it far off. 12 It *is* not in heaven, that you should say, 'Who will ascend into heaven for us and bring it to us, that we may hear it and do it?' 13 Nor *is* it beyond the sea, that you should say, 'Who will go over the sea for us and bring it to us, that we may hear it and do it?' 14 But the word *is* very near you, in your mouth and in your heart, that you may do it.

15 "See, I have set before you today life and good, death and evil, 16 in that I command you today to love the LORD your God, to walk in His ways, and to keep His commandments, His statutes, and His judgments, that you may live and multiply; and the LORD your God will bless you in the land which you go to possess. 17 But if your heart turns away so that you do not hear, and are drawn away, and worship other gods and serve them, 18 I announce to you today that you shall surely perish; you shall not prolong *your* days in the land which you cross over the Jordan to go in and possess. 19 I call heaven and earth as witnesses today against you, *that* I have set before you life and death, blessing and cursing; therefore choose life, that both you and your descendants may live; 20 that you may love

the LORD your God, that you may obey His voice, and that you may cling to Him, for He *is* your life and the length of your days; and that you may dwell in the land which the LORD swore to your fathers, to Abraham, Isaac, and Jacob, to give them."

31 Then Moses went and spoke these words to all Israel. 2 And he said to them: "I *am* one hundred and twenty years old today. I can no longer go out and come in. Also the LORD has said to me, 'You shall not cross over this Jordan.' 3 The LORD your God Himself crosses over before you; He will destroy these nations from before you, and you shall dispossess them. Joshua himself crosses over before you, just as the LORD has said. 4 And the LORD will do to them as He did to Sihon and Og, the kings of the Amorites and their land, when He destroyed them. 5 The LORD will give them over to you, that you may do to them according to every commandment which I have commanded you. 6 Be strong and of good courage, do not fear nor be afraid of them; for the LORD your God, He *is* the One who goes with you. He will not leave you nor forsake you."

7 Then Moses called Joshua and said to him in the sight of all Israel, "Be strong and of good courage, for you must go with this people to the land which the LORD has sworn to their fathers to give them, and you shall cause them to inherit it. 8 And the LORD, He *is* the One who goes before you. He will be with you, He will not leave you nor forsake you; do not fear nor be dismayed."

9 So Moses wrote this law and delivered it to the priests, the sons of Levi, who bore the ark of the covenant of the LORD, and to all the elders of Israel. 10 And Moses commanded them, saying: "At the end of *every* seven years, at the appointed time in the year of release, at the Feast of Tabernacles, 11 when all Israel comes to appear before the LORD your God in the place which He chooses, you shall read this law before all Israel in their hearing. 12 Gather the people together, men and women and little ones, and the stranger who *is* within your gates, that they may hear and that they may learn to fear the LORD your God and carefully observe all

*I*f life has left you disenchanted and aloof, remember Jesus is your knight in shining armor. Do not allow the vicious bandits of misfortune and abuse to rob you of your enthusiasm and vigor for life.

Choose Life

Deuteronomy 30:15-19

Recovery cannot happen until a woman is willing to look at herself in the mirror and say, "I messed up." People who blame other people never recover because they live in a state of denial. Any time you blame another person for your problem, you give that person control of your life. With your blame, you are saying, "I can't get out until you let me out. I can't succeed until you allow me to succeed. I can't move forward in my life until you give me the green light." That's a lie of the devil!

According to Deuteronomy 30:15-19, you make the choice. You must accept responsibility for your own actions. It may not have been all your fault, but you need to accept responsibility for the part that was. You must be able to say to yourself, "I wasn't without fault. I was a contributing factor."

Unless you are able to accept responsibility for your actions, you will be eaten up with unresolved guilt. It will rot inside you and erupt in your life in the form of jealousy and anger and hatred and bitterness. Identify the people you are blaming and deal with them. Confront the issues. Challenge the lies the devil will try to speak in your mind when he tells you, "It's not your fault. It's all his fault. You were right, he was wrong. Things were just out of control. You didn't do anything bad. Somebody else is to blame for all this." No! Accept your share of the responsibility for what has gone wrong and ask God to forgive you.

God is too wise and too loving to put your destiny into the hands of another person. He doesn't want another person's actions to control your future. What you do from this point on is up to you. How you feel and how you react and what you do and what you say and what you choose and how you deal with the past is solely your responsibility. It's your decision.

If you will face up to your own sin and take hold of the hand of our forgiving God, you can overcome anything. You can overcome the past influence of any person, the evil of any circumstance. You can live and not die!

You don't need to live with depression, oppression, or suppression. God wants you to come out of your feelings of failure and rejection and regret. It's time—choose life.

the words of this law, 13 and *that* their children, who have not known it, may hear and learn to fear the LORD your God as long as you live in the land which you cross the Jordan to possess."

14 Then the LORD said to Moses, "Behold, the days approach when you must die; call Joshua, and present yourselves in the tabernacle of meeting, that I may inaugurate him."

So Moses and Joshua went and presented themselves in the tabernacle of meeting. 15 Now the LORD appeared at the tabernacle in a pillar of cloud, and the pillar of cloud stood above the door of the tabernacle.

16 And the LORD said to Moses: "Behold, you will rest with your fathers; and this people will rise and play the harlot with the gods of the foreigners of the land, where they go *to be* among them, and they will forsake Me and break My covenant which I have made with them. 17 Then My anger shall be aroused against them in that day, and I will forsake them, and I will hide My face from them, and they shall be devoured. And many evils and troubles shall befall them, so that they will say in that day, 'Have not these evils come upon us because our God *is* not among us?' 18 And I will surely hide My face in that day because of all the evil which they have done, in that they have turned to other gods.

19 "Now therefore, write down this song for yourselves, and teach it to the children of Israel; put it in their mouths, that this song may be a witness for Me against the children of Israel. 20 When I have brought them to the land flowing with milk and honey, of which I swore to their fathers, and they have eaten and filled themselves and grown fat, then they will turn to other gods and serve them; and they will provoke Me and break My covenant. 21 Then it shall be, when many evils and troubles have come upon them, that this song will testify against them as a witness; for it will not be forgotten in the mouths of their descendants, for I know the inclination of their behavior today, even before I have brought them to the land of which I swore *to give them.*"

22 Therefore Moses wrote this song the same day, and taught it to the children of Israel. 23 Then He inaugurated Joshua the son of Nun, and said, "Be strong and of good courage; for you shall bring the children of Israel into the land of which I swore to them, and I will be with you."

24 So it was, when Moses had completed writing the words of this law in a book, when they were finished, 25 that Moses commanded the Levites, who bore the ark of the covenant of the LORD, saying: 26 "Take this Book of the Law, and put it beside the ark of the covenant of the LORD your God, that it may be there as a witness against you; 27 for I know your rebellion and your stiff neck. *If* today, while I am yet alive with you, you have been rebellious against the LORD, then how much more after my death? 28 Gather to me all the elders of your tribes, and your officers, that I may speak these words in their hearing and call heaven and earth to witness against them. 29 For I know that after my death you will become utterly corrupt, and turn aside from the way which I have commanded you. And evil will befall you in the latter days, because you will do evil in the sight of the LORD, to provoke Him to anger through the work of your hands."

30 Then Moses spoke in the hearing of all the assembly of Israel the words of this song until they were ended:

32 "Give ear, O heavens, and I will speak;
　　And hear, O earth, the words of my mouth.
2　Let my teaching drop as the rain,
　　My speech distill as the dew,
　　As raindrops on the tender herb,
　　And as showers on the grass.
3　For I proclaim the name of the LORD:
　　Ascribe greatness to our God.
4　*He is* the Rock, His work *is* perfect;
　　For all His ways *are* justice,
　　A God of truth and without injustice;
　　Righteous and upright *is* He.

5　"They have corrupted themselves;
　　They are not His children,
　　Because of their blemish:

Gospel Pearls

A perverse and crooked
generation.
6 Do you thus deal with the LORD,
O foolish and unwise people?
Is He not your Father, *who*
bought you?
Has He not made you and
established you?

7 "Remember the days of old,
Consider the years of many
generations.
Ask your father, and he will
show you;
Your elders, and they will tell
you:
8 When the Most High divided
their inheritance to the
nations,
When He separated the sons of
Adam,
He set the boundaries of the
peoples
According to the number of the
children of Israel.
9 For the LORD's portion *is* His
people;
Jacob *is* the place of His
inheritance.

10 "He found him in a desert land
And in the wasteland, a
howling wilderness;
He encircled him, He instructed
him,
He kept him as the apple of His
eye.
11 As an eagle stirs up its nest,
Hovers over its young,
Spreading out its wings, taking
them up,
Carrying them on its wings,
12 *So* the LORD alone led him,
And *there was* no foreign god
with him.

13 "He made him ride in the
heights of the earth,
That he might eat the produce
of the fields;
He made him draw honey from
the rock,
And oil from the flinty rock;
14 Curds from the cattle, and milk
of the flock,
With fat of lambs;
And rams of the breed of
Bashan, and goats,
With the choicest wheat;
And you drank wine, the blood
of the grapes.

15 "But Jeshurun grew fat and
kicked;
You grew fat, you grew thick,
You are obese!
Then he forsook God *who*
made him,
And scornfully esteemed the
Rock of his salvation.
16 They provoked Him to jealousy
with foreign *gods;*
With abominations they
provoked Him to anger.
17 They sacrificed to demons, not
to God,
To gods they did not know,
To new *gods,* new arrivals
That your fathers did not fear.
18 Of the Rock *who* begot you,
you are unmindful,
And have forgotten the God
who fathered you.

19 "And when the LORD saw *it,* He
spurned *them,*
Because of the provocation of
His sons and His daughters.
20 And He said: 'I will hide My
face from them,
I will see what their end *will be,*
For they *are* a perverse
generation,
Children in whom *is* no faith.
21 They have provoked Me to
jealousy by *what* is not God;
They have moved Me to anger
by their foolish idols.
But I will provoke them to
jealousy by *those who are*
not a nation;
I will move them to anger by a
foolish nation.
22 For a fire is kindled in My
anger,
And shall burn to the lowest
hell;
It shall consume the earth with
her increase,
And set on fire the foundations
of the mountains.

23 'I will heap disasters on them;
I will spend My arrows on
them.
24 *They shall be* wasted with
hunger,
Devoured by pestilence and
bitter destruction;
I will also send against them
the teeth of beasts,
With the poison of serpents of
the dust.

I declare to you that when God kissed the first lump of clay and breathed into that
muddy shell the breath of life, He spoke life, and the abstract became vibrant and
alive. The Master's kiss turned a ceramic into a personality.

25 The sword shall destroy
   outside;
   There shall be terror within
   For the young man and virgin,
   The nursing child with the man
   of gray hairs.

26 I would have said, "I will dash
   them in pieces,
   I will make the memory of them
   to cease from among men,"

27 Had I not feared the wrath of
   the enemy,
   Lest their adversaries should
   misunderstand,
   Lest they should say, "Our
   hand *is* high;
   And it is not the LORD who has
   done all this." '

28 "For they *are* a nation void of
   counsel,
   Nor *is there any* understanding
   in them.

29 Oh, that they were wise, *that*
   they understood this,
   That they would consider their
   latter end!

30 How could one chase a
   thousand,
   And two put ten thousand to
   flight,
   Unless their Rock had sold
   them,
   And the LORD had surrendered
   them?

31 For their rock *is* not like our
   Rock,
   Even our enemies themselves
   being judges.

32 For their vine *is* of the vine of
   Sodom
   And of the fields of Gomorrah;
   Their grapes *are* grapes of gall,
   Their clusters *are* bitter.

33 Their wine *is* the poison of
   serpents,
   And the cruel venom of cobras.

34 '*Is* this not laid up in store with
   Me,
   Sealed up among My
   treasures?

35 Vengeance is Mine, and
   recompense;
   Their foot shall slip in *due* time;
   For the day of their calamity *is*
   at hand,
   And the things to come hasten
   upon them.'

36 "For the LORD will judge His
   people
   And have compassion on His
   servants,
   When He sees that *their* power
   is gone,
   And *there is* no one *remaining*,
   bond or free.

37 He will say: 'Where *are* their
   gods,
   The rock in which they sought
   refuge?

38 Who ate the fat of their
   sacrifices,
   And drank the wine of their
   drink offering?
   Let them rise and help you,
   And be your refuge.

39 'Now see that I, *even* I, *am* He,
   And *there is* no God besides
   Me;
   I kill and I make alive;
   I wound and I heal;
   Nor *is there any* who can
   deliver from My hand.

40 For I raise My hand to heaven,
   And say, "*As* I live forever,

41 If I whet My glittering sword,
   And My hand takes hold on
   judgment,
   I will render vengeance to My
   enemies,
   And repay those who hate Me.

42 I will make My arrows drunk
   with blood,
   And My sword shall devour
   flesh,
   With the blood of the slain and
   the captives,
   From the heads of the leaders
   of the enemy." '

43 "Rejoice, O Gentiles, *with* His
   people;*a*
   For He will avenge the blood
   of His servants,
   And render vengeance to His
   adversaries;
   He will provide atonement for
   His land *and* His people."

44 So Moses came with Joshua*a* the
son of Nun and spoke all the words
of this song in the hearing of the people. 45 Moses finished speaking all
these words to all Israel, 46 and he
said to them: "Set your hearts on all
the words which I testify among you

32:43 *a*A Dead Sea Scroll fragment adds *And let all the gods (angels) worship Him* (compare Septuagint
and Hebrews 1:6).   32:44 *a*Hebrew *Hoshea* (compare Numbers 13:8, 16)

today, which you shall command your children to be careful to observe—all the words of this law. 47 For it *is* not a futile thing for you, because it *is* your life, and by this word you shall prolong *your* days in the land which you cross over the Jordan to possess."

48 Then the LORD spoke to Moses that very same day, saying: 49 "Go up this mountain of the Abarim, Mount Nebo, which *is* in the land of Moab, across from Jericho; view the land of Canaan, which I give to the children of Israel as a possession; 50 and die on the mountain which you ascend, and be gathered to your people, just as Aaron your brother died on Mount Hor and was gathered to his people; 51 because you trespassed against Me among the children of Israel at the waters of Meribah Kadesh, in the Wilderness of Zin, because you did not hallow Me in the midst of the children of Israel. 52 Yet you shall see the land before *you,* though you shall not go there, into the land which I am giving to the children of Israel."

33 Now this *is* the blessing with which Moses the man of God blessed the children of Israel before his death. 2 And he said:

"The LORD came from Sinai,
And dawned on them from Seir;
He shone forth from Mount Paran,
And He came with ten thousands of saints;
From His right hand
Came a fiery law for them.
3 Yes, He loves the people;
All His saints *are* in Your hand;
They sit down at Your feet;
Everyone receives Your words.
4 Moses commanded a law for us,
A heritage of the congregation of Jacob.
5 And He was King in Jeshurun,
When the leaders of the people were gathered,
All the tribes of Israel together.

6 "Let Reuben live, and not die,
Nor let his men be few."

7 And this he said of Judah:

"Hear, LORD, the voice of Judah,
And bring him to his people;
Let his hands be sufficient for him,
And may You be a help against his enemies."

8 And of Levi he said:

"*Let* Your Thummim and Your Urim *be* with Your holy one,
Whom You tested at Massah,
And with whom You contended at the waters of Meribah,
9 Who says of his father and mother,
'I have not seen them';
Nor did he acknowledge his brothers,
Or know his own children;
For they have observed Your word
And kept Your covenant.
10 They shall teach Jacob Your judgments,
And Israel Your law.
They shall put incense before You,
And a whole burnt sacrifice on Your altar.
11 Bless his substance, LORD,
And accept the work of his hands;
Strike the loins of those who rise against him,
And of those who hate him, that they rise not again."

12 Of Benjamin he said:

"The beloved of the LORD shall dwell in safety by Him,
Who shelters him all the day long;
And he shall dwell between His shoulders."

13 And of Joseph he said:

"Blessed of the LORD *is* his land,
With the precious things of heaven, with the dew,
And the deep lying beneath,
14 With the precious fruits of the sun,
With the precious produce of the months,
15 With the best things of the ancient mountains,
With the precious things of the everlasting hills,
16 With the precious things of the

God is the Friend of every father who has a daughter he loves and yet cannot always affect. He can do what men cannot do. He can resurrect the cold places in the heart of the woman whose love and life have been rocked to sleep in a cradle of despair.

earth and its fullness,
And the favor of Him who
    dwelt in the bush.
Let *the blessing* come 'on the
    head of Joseph,
And on the crown of the head
    of him *who was* separate
    from his brothers.'*a*

17 His glory *is like* a firstborn bull,
    And his horns *like* the horns of
    the wild ox;
    Together with them
    He shall push the peoples
    To the ends of the earth;
    They *are* the ten thousands of
    Ephraim,
    And they *are* the thousands of
    Manasseh."

18 And of Zebulun he said:

"Rejoice, Zebulun, in your going
    out,
    And Issachar in your tents!
19 They shall call the peoples *to*
    the mountain;
    There they shall offer sacrifices
    of righteousness;
    For they shall partake *of* the
    abundance of the seas
    And *of* treasures hidden in the
    sand."

20 And of Gad he said:

"Blessed *is* he who enlarges
    Gad;
    He dwells as a lion,
    And tears the arm and the
    crown of his head.
21 He provided the first *part* for
    himself,
    Because a lawgiver's portion
    was reserved there.
    He came *with* the heads of the
    people;
    He administered the justice of
    the LORD,
    And His judgments with
    Israel."

22 And of Dan he said:

"Dan *is* a lion's whelp;
    He shall leap from Bashan."

23 And of Naphtali he said:

"O Naphtali, satisfied with
    favor,

And full of the blessing of the
    LORD,
    Possess the west and the
    south."

24 And of Asher he said:

"Asher *is* most blessed of sons;
    Let him be favored by his
    brothers,
    And let him dip his foot in oil.
25 Your sandals *shall be* iron and
    bronze;
    As your days, *so shall* your
    strength *be.*

26 "*There is* no one like the God of
    Jeshurun,
    Who rides the heavens to help
    you,
    And in His excellency on the
    clouds.
27 The eternal God *is your* refuge,
    And underneath *are* the
    everlasting arms;
    He will thrust out the enemy
    from before you,
    And will say, 'Destroy!'
28 Then Israel shall dwell in
    safety,
    The fountain of Jacob alone,
    In a land of grain and new
    wine;
    His heavens shall also drop
    dew.
29 Happy *are* you, O Israel!
    Who *is* like you, a people saved
    by the LORD,
    The shield of your help
    And the sword of your majesty!
    Your enemies shall submit to
    you,
    And you shall tread down their
    high places."

34 Then Moses went up from the
plains of Moab to Mount Nebo,
to the top of Pisgah, which is across
from Jericho. And the LORD showed
him all the land of Gilead as far as
Dan, 2 all Naphtali and the land of
Ephraim and Manasseh, all the land
of Judah as far as the Western Sea,*a*
3 the South, and the plain of the Valley of Jericho, the city of palm trees,
as far as Zoar. 4 Then the LORD said
to him, "This *is* the land of which I
swore to give Abraham, Isaac, and
Jacob, saying, 'I will give it to your

33:16 *a*Genesis 49:26 34:2 *a*That is, the Mediterranean

descendants.' I have caused you to see *it* with your eyes, but you shall not cross over there."

5 So Moses the servant of the LORD died there in the land of Moab, according to the word of the LORD. 6 And He buried him in a valley in the land of Moab, opposite Beth Peor; but no one knows his grave to this day. 7 Moses *was* one hundred and twenty years old when he died. His eyes were not dim nor his natural vigor diminished. 8 And the children of Israel wept for Moses in the plains of Moab thirty days. So the days of weeping *and* mourning for Moses ended.

9 Now Joshua the son of Nun was full of the spirit of wisdom, for Moses had laid his hands on him; so the children of Israel heeded him, and did as the LORD had commanded Moses.

10 But since then there has not arisen in Israel a prophet like Moses, whom the LORD knew face to face, 11 in all the signs and wonders which the LORD sent him to do in the land of Egypt, before Pharaoh, before all his servants, and in all his land, 12 and by all that mighty power and all the great terror which Moses performed in the sight of all Israel.

The Book of

JOSHUA

1 After the death of Moses the servant of the LORD, it came to pass that the LORD spoke to Joshua the son of Nun, Moses' assistant, saying: 2 "Moses My servant is dead. Now therefore, arise, go over this Jordan, you and all this people, to the land which I am giving to them—the children of Israel. 3 Every place that the sole of your foot will tread upon I have given you, as I said to Moses. 4 From the wilderness and this Lebanon as far as the great river, the River Euphrates, all the land of the Hittites, and to the Great Sea toward the going down of the sun, shall be your territory. 5 No man shall *be able to* stand before you all the days of your life; as I was with Moses, *so* I will be with you. I will not leave you nor forsake you. 6 Be strong and of good courage, for to this people you shall divide as an inheritance the land which I swore to their fathers to give them. 7 Only be strong and very courageous, that you may observe to do according to all the law which Moses My servant commanded you; do not turn from it to the right hand or to the left, that you may prosper wherever you go. 8 This Book of the Law shall not depart from your mouth, but you shall meditate in it day and night, that you may observe to do according to all that is written in it. For then you will make your way prosperous, and then you will have good success. 9 Have I not commanded you? Be strong and of good courage; do not be afraid, nor be dismayed, for the LORD your God *is* with you wherever you go."

10 Then Joshua commanded the officers of the people, saying, 11 "Pass through the camp and command the people, saying, 'Prepare provisions for yourselves, for within three days you will cross over this Jordan, to go in to possess the land which the LORD your God is giving you to possess.' "

12 And to the Reubenites, the Gadites, and half the tribe of Manasseh Joshua spoke, saying, 13 "Remember the word which Moses the servant of the LORD commanded you, saying, 'The LORD your God is giving you rest and is giving you this land.' 14 Your wives, your little ones, and your livestock shall remain in the land which Moses gave you on this side of the Jordan. But you shall pass before your brethren armed, all your

*R*evival occurs when that which was dead is revived. It is the waking up of the cast down. You can have a revival in your spiritual life, your personal life, your financial life, or whatever part of you the enemy has rocked to sleep.

Alone, But Never Lonely

Joshua 1:5

Some women secretly carry guilt that they have misappropriated as daughters, thinking it was their fault that their fathers didn't stay with their mothers. If you're one of those women, you are always trying to prove something to yourself. Growing up is hard work. It is even tougher when today's woman is wrestling with yesterday's little girl. Somewhere deep beneath the painted smiles and polished nails is a longing, an aching, a void. Somewhere beneath the symbols of success lurks a feeling of incompleteness.

The emptiness taints your successes and taunts your accomplishments. You are either distrustful of men as a whole or you idealize a man's attention as the epitome of success and fulfillment. You may be afraid to be alone. You may feel as if you have been alone all of your life, and you fight the feeling by adding people to your life. If you were wise, you would know that having people in your life, in your house, or even in your bed doesn't ensure that you will not be lonely. But if you really come to know God, you could be alone and still not be lonely. It is when you understand the gift of being alone that you will really be ready to share your companionship with someone else.

Whenever someone is involved with you, they become a part of what was going on in you before they came around. For some men, that is traumatic because if the woman isn't happy before he comes, she will soon be unhappy with him around. She will go from madly in love to distant and frustrated because she expected him to be all that she hasn't gotten out of life. At first, she is excited. Later, she is disappointed because she realizes that she is still involved with a wound from her past. It is a void that only the Holy Spirit can fill.

Most Christians are seated so high on their perch of self-righteousness that they often fail to minister to the pain behind the sin. They are concerned about the habits of sin. But they don't seem to understand that removing the act doesn't free the heart. It just represses a problem that manifests in cynicism and frustration. People are teachable when they are not in pain. It is like telling a child not to scratch a rash. She will do it even if she does it in her sleep because she is feeling discomfort. But if you can apply a soothing ointment, the habit is easily broken.

I am sorry we live in a world filled with pain and rashes, with imperfections and scars. But, in all of my searching, the only thing I have found that will soothe the itching for affection and the bleeding from scars is Jesus.

mighty men of valor, and help them, 15 until the LORD has given your brethren rest, as He *gave* you, and they also have taken possession of the land which the LORD your God is giving them. Then you shall return to the land of your possession and enjoy it, which Moses the LORD's servant gave you on this side of the Jordan toward the sunrise."

16 So they answered Joshua, saying, "All that you command us we will do, and wherever you send us we will go. 17 Just as we heeded Moses in all things, so we will heed you. Only the LORD your God be with you, as He was with Moses. 18 Whoever rebels against your command and does not heed your words, in all that you command him, shall be put to death. Only be strong and of good courage."

2 Now Joshua the son of Nun sent out two men from Acacia Grove*ᵃ* to spy secretly, saying, "Go, view the land, especially Jericho."

So they went, and came to the house of a harlot named Rahab, and lodged there. 2 And it was told the king of Jericho, saying, "Behold, men have come here tonight from the children of Israel to search out the country."

3 So the king of Jericho sent to Rahab, saying, "Bring out the men who have come to you, who have entered your house, for they have come to search out all the country."

4 Then the woman took the two men and hid them. So she said, "Yes, the men came to me, but I did not know where they *were* from. 5 And it happened as the gate was being shut, when it was dark, that the men went out. Where the men went I do not know; pursue them quickly, for you may overtake them." 6 (But she had brought them up to the roof and hidden them with the stalks of flax, which she had laid in order on the roof.) 7 Then the men pursued them by the road to the Jordan, to the fords. And as soon as those who pursued them had gone out, they shut the gate.

8 Now before they lay down, she came up to them on the roof, 9 and said to the men: "I know that the LORD has given you the land, that the terror of you has fallen on us, and that all the inhabitants of the land are fainthearted because of you. 10 For we have heard how the LORD dried up the water of the Red Sea for you when you came out of Egypt, and what you did to the two kings of the Amorites who *were* on the other side of the Jordan, Sihon and Og, whom you utterly destroyed. 11 And as soon as we heard *these things,* our hearts melted; neither did there remain any more courage in anyone because of you, for the LORD your God, He *is* God in heaven above and on earth beneath. 12 Now therefore, I beg you, swear to me by the LORD, since I have shown you kindness, that you also will show kindness to my father's house, and give me a true token, 13 and spare my father, my mother, my brothers, my sisters, and all that they have, and deliver our lives from death."

14 So the men answered her, "Our lives for yours, if none of you tell this business of ours. And it shall be, when the LORD has given us the land, that we will deal kindly and truly with you."

15 Then she let them down by a rope through the window, for her house *was* on the city wall; she dwelt on the wall. 16 And she said to them, "Get to the mountain, lest the pursuers meet you. Hide there three days, until the pursuers have returned. Afterward you may go your way."

17 So the men said to her: "We *will be* blameless of this oath of yours which you have made us swear, 18 unless, *when* we come into the land, you bind this line of scarlet cord in the window through which you let us down, and unless you bring your father, your mother, your brothers, and all your father's household to your own home. 19 So it shall be *that* whoever goes outside the doors of your house into the street, his blood *shall be* on his own head, and we *will be* guiltless. And whoever is with you in the house, his blood *shall be* on our head if a hand is laid on him. 20 And if you tell this business of ours, then we will be free from your oath which you made us swear."

21 Then she said, "According to your words, so *be* it." And she sent

---

2:1 *ᵃ*Hebrew *Shittim*

---

*J*ust call on the Prince of Peace. His name is Jesus. He is the Prince who revives what life has extinguished. One kiss from Him can restore every area of your life, both natural and spiritual.

them away, and they departed. And she bound the scarlet cord in the window.

22 They departed and went to the mountain, and stayed there three days until the pursuers returned. The pursuers sought *them* all along the way, but did not find *them*. 23 So the two men returned, descended from the mountain, and crossed over; and they came to Joshua the son of Nun, and told him all that had befallen them. 24 And they said to Joshua, "Truly the LORD has delivered all the land into our hands, for indeed all the inhabitants of the country are fainthearted because of us."

3 Then Joshua rose early in the morning; and they set out from Acacia Grove*a* and came to the Jordan, he and all the children of Israel, and lodged there before they crossed over. 2 So it was, after three days, that the officers went through the camp; 3 and they commanded the people, saying, "When you see the ark of the covenant of the LORD your God, and the priests, the Levites, bearing it, then you shall set out from your place and go after it. 4 Yet there shall be a space between you and it, about two thousand cubits by measure. Do not come near it, that you may know the way by which you must go, for you have not passed *this* way before."

5 And Joshua said to the people, "Sanctify yourselves, for tomorrow the LORD will do wonders among you." 6 Then Joshua spoke to the priests, saying, "Take up the ark of the covenant and cross over before the people."

So they took up the ark of the covenant and went before the people.

7 And the LORD said to Joshua, "This day I will begin to exalt you in the sight of all Israel, that they may know that, as I was with Moses, so I will be with you. 8 You shall command the priests who bear the ark of the covenant, saying, 'When you have come to the edge of the water of the Jordan, you shall stand in the Jordan.' "

9 So Joshua said to the children of Israel, "Come here, and hear the words of the LORD your God."

10 And Joshua said, "By this you shall know that the living God *is* among you, and *that* He will without fail drive out from before you the Canaanites and the Hittites and the Hivites and the Perizzites and the Girgashites and the Amorites and the Jebusites: 11 Behold, the ark of the covenant of the Lord of all the earth is crossing over before you into the Jordan. 12 Now therefore, take for yourselves twelve men from the tribes of Israel, one man from every tribe. 13 And it shall come to pass, as soon as the soles of the feet of the priests who bear the ark of the LORD, the Lord of all the earth, shall rest in the waters of the Jordan, *that* the waters of the Jordan shall be cut off, the waters that come down from upstream, and they shall stand as a heap."

14 So it was, when the people set out from their camp to cross over the Jordan, with the priests bearing the ark of the covenant before the people, 15 and as those who bore the ark came to the Jordan, and the feet of the priests who bore the ark dipped in the edge of the water (for the Jordan overflows all its banks during the whole time of harvest), 16 that the waters which came down from upstream stood *still, and* rose in a heap very far away at Adam, the city that *is* beside Zaretan. So the waters that went down into the Sea of the Arabah, the Salt Sea, failed, *and* were cut off; and the people crossed over opposite Jericho. 17 Then the priests who bore the ark of the covenant of the LORD stood firm on dry ground in the midst of the Jordan; and all Israel crossed over on dry ground, until all the people had crossed completely over the Jordan.

4 And it came to pass, when all the people had completely crossed over the Jordan, that the LORD spoke to Joshua, saying: 2 "Take for yourselves twelve men from the people, one man from every tribe, 3 and command them, saying, 'Take for yourselves twelve stones from here, out of the midst of the Jordan, from the place where the priests' feet stood firm. You shall carry them over with you and leave them in the lodging place where you lodge tonight.' "

3:1 *a*Hebrew *Shittim*

Gospel Pearls

4 Then Joshua called the twelve men whom he had appointed from the children of Israel, one man from every tribe; 5 and Joshua said to them: "Cross over before the ark of the LORD your God into the midst of the Jordan, and each one of you take up a stone on his shoulder, according to the number of the tribes of the children of Israel, 6 that this may be a sign among you when your children ask in time to come, saying, 'What do these stones *mean* to you?' 7 Then you shall answer them that the waters of the Jordan were cut off before the ark of the covenant of the LORD; when it crossed over the Jordan, the waters of the Jordan were cut off. And these stones shall be for a memorial to the children of Israel forever."

8 And the children of Israel did so, just as Joshua commanded, and took up twelve stones from the midst of the Jordan, as the LORD had spoken to Joshua, according to the number of the tribes of the children of Israel, and carried them over with them to the place where they lodged, and laid them down there. 9 Then Joshua set up twelve stones in the midst of the Jordan, in the place where the feet of the priests who bore the ark of the covenant stood; and they are there to this day.

10 So the priests who bore the ark stood in the midst of the Jordan until everything was finished that the LORD had commanded Joshua to speak to the people, according to all that Moses had commanded Joshua; and the people hurried and crossed over. 11 Then it came to pass, when all the people had completely crossed over, that the ark of the LORD and the priests crossed over in the presence of the people. 12 And the men of Reuben, the men of Gad, and half the tribe of Manasseh crossed over armed before the children of Israel, as Moses had spoken to them. 13 About forty thousand prepared for war crossed over before the LORD for battle, to the plains of Jericho. 14 On that day the LORD exalted Joshua in the sight of all Israel; and they feared him, as they had feared Moses, all the days of his life.

15 Then the LORD spoke to Joshua, saying, 16 "Command the priests who bear the ark of the Testimony to come up from the Jordan." 17 Joshua therefore commanded the priests, saying, "Come up from the Jordan." 18 And it came to pass, when the priests who bore the ark of the covenant of the LORD had come from the midst of the Jordan, *and* the soles of the priests' feet touched the dry land, that the waters of the Jordan returned to their place and overflowed all its banks as before.

19 Now the people came up from the Jordan on the tenth *day* of the first month, and they camped in Gilgal on the east border of Jericho. 20 And those twelve stones which they took out of the Jordan, Joshua set up in Gilgal. 21 Then he spoke to the children of Israel, saying: "When your children ask their fathers in time to come, saying, 'What *are* these stones?' 22 then you shall let your children know, saying, 'Israel crossed over this Jordan on dry land'; 23 for the LORD your God dried up the waters of the Jordan before you until you had crossed over, as the LORD your God did to the Red Sea, which He dried up before us until we had crossed over, 24 that all the peoples of the earth may know the hand of the LORD, that it *is* mighty, that you may fear the LORD your God forever."

5 So it was, when all the kings of the Amorites who *were* on the west side of the Jordan, and all the kings of the Canaanites who *were* by the sea, heard that the LORD had dried up the waters of the Jordan from before the children of Israel until we[a] had crossed over, that their heart melted; and there was no spirit in them any longer because of the children of Israel.

2 At that time the LORD said to Joshua, "Make flint knives for yourself, and circumcise the sons of Israel again the second time." 3 So Joshua made flint knives for himself, and circumcised the sons of Israel at the hill of the foreskins.[a] 4 And this *is* the reason why Joshua circumcised them: All the people who came out of Egypt *who were* males, all the men of war, had died in the wilderness on

---

5:1 [a]Following Kethib; Qere, some Hebrew manuscripts and editions, Septuagint, Syriac, Targum, and Vulgate read *they.*   5:3 [a]Hebrew *Gibeath Haaraloth*

---

*Y*ou need to be loosed and free. There is another woman who has a key to your destiny. She is courageous and resilient, determined and assertive.

the way, after they had come out of Egypt. 5 For all the people who came out had been circumcised, but all the people born in the wilderness, on the way as they came out of Egypt, had not been circumcised. 6 For the children of Israel walked forty years in the wilderness, till all the people *who were* men of war, who came out of Egypt, were consumed, because they did not obey the voice of the Lord— to whom the Lord swore that He would not show them the land which the Lord had sworn to their fathers that He would give us, "a land flowing with milk and honey."*a* 7 Then Joshua circumcised their sons *whom* He raised up in their place; for they were uncircumcised, because they had not been circumcised on the way.

8 So it was, when they had finished circumcising all the people, that they stayed in their places in the camp till they were healed. 9 Then the Lord said to Joshua, "This day I have rolled away the reproach of Egypt from you." Therefore the name of the place is called Gilgal*a* to this day.

10 Now the children of Israel camped in Gilgal, and kept the Passover on the fourteenth day of the month at twilight on the plains of Jericho. 11 And they ate of the produce of the land on the day after the Passover, unleavened bread and parched grain, on the very same day. 12 Then the manna ceased on the day after they had eaten the produce of the land; and the children of Israel no longer had manna, but they ate the food of the land of Canaan that year.

13 And it came to pass, when Joshua was by Jericho, that he lifted his eyes and looked, and behold, a Man stood opposite him with His sword drawn in His hand. And Joshua went to Him and said to Him, "*Are* You for us or for our adversaries?"

14 So He said, "No, but *as* Commander of the army of the Lord I have now come."

And Joshua fell on his face to the earth and worshiped, and said to Him, "What does my Lord say to His servant?"

15 Then the Commander of the Lord's army said to Joshua, "Take your sandal off your foot, for the place where you stand *is* holy." And Joshua did so.

6 Now Jericho was securely shut up because of the children of Israel; none went out, and none came in. 2 And the Lord said to Joshua: "See! I have given Jericho into your hand, its king, *and* the mighty men of valor. 3 You shall march around the city, all *you* men of war; you shall go all around the city once. This you shall do six days. 4 And seven priests shall bear seven trumpets of rams' horns before the ark. But the seventh day you shall march around the city seven times, and the priests shall blow the trumpets. 5 It shall come to pass, when they make a long *blast* with the ram's horn, *and* when you hear the sound of the trumpet, that all the people shall shout with a great shout; then the wall of the city will fall down flat. And the people shall go up every man straight before him."

6 Then Joshua the son of Nun called the priests and said to them, "Take up the ark of the covenant, and let seven priests bear seven trumpets of rams' horns before the ark of the Lord." 7 And he said to the people, "Proceed, and march around the city, and let him who is armed advance before the ark of the Lord."

8 So it was, when Joshua had spoken to the people, that the seven priests bearing the seven trumpets of rams' horns before the Lord advanced and blew the trumpets, and the ark of the covenant of the Lord followed them. 9 The armed men went before the priests who blew the trumpets, and the rear guard came after the ark, while *the priests* continued blowing the trumpets. 10 Now Joshua had commanded the people, saying, "You shall not shout or make any noise with your voice, nor shall a word proceed out of your mouth, until the day I say to you, 'Shout!' Then you shall shout." 11 So he had the ark of the Lord circle the city, going around *it* once. Then they came into the camp and lodged in the camp.

12 And Joshua rose early in the morning, and the priests took up the ark of the Lord. 13 Then seven priests

Gospel Pearls

bearing seven trumpets of rams' horns before the ark of the LORD went on continually and blew with the trumpets. And the armed men went before them. But the rear guard came after the ark of the LORD, while *the priests* continued blowing the trumpets. 14 And the second day they marched around the city once and returned to the camp. So they did six days.

15 But it came to pass on the seventh day that they rose early, about the dawning of the day, and marched around the city seven times in the same manner. On that day only they marched around the city seven times. 16 And the seventh time it happened, when the priests blew the trumpets, that Joshua said to the people: "Shout, for the LORD has given you the city! 17 Now the city shall be doomed by the LORD to destruction, it and all who *are* in it. Only Rahab the harlot shall live, she and all who *are* with her in the house, because she hid the messengers that we sent. 18 And you, by all means abstain from the accursed things, lest you become accursed when you take of the accursed things, and make the camp of Israel a curse, and trouble it. 19 But all the silver and gold, and vessels of bronze and iron, *are* consecrated to the LORD; they shall come into the treasury of the LORD."

20 So the people shouted when *the priests* blew the trumpets. And it happened when the people heard the sound of the trumpet, and the people shouted with a great shout, that the wall fell down flat. Then the people went up into the city, every man straight before him, and they took the city. 21 And they utterly destroyed all that *was* in the city, both man and woman, young and old, ox and sheep and donkey, with the edge of the sword.

22 But Joshua had said to the two men who had spied out the country, "Go into the harlot's house, and from there bring out the woman and all that she has, as you swore to her." 23 And the young men who had been spies went in and brought out Rahab, her father, her mother, her brothers, and all that she had. So they brought out all her relatives and left them outside the camp of Israel. 24 But they

burned the city and all that *was* in it with fire. Only the silver and gold, and the vessels of bronze and iron, they put into the treasury of the house of the LORD. 25 And Joshua spared Rahab the harlot, her father's household, and all that she had. So she dwells in Israel to this day, because she hid the messengers whom Joshua sent to spy out Jericho.

26 Then Joshua charged *them* at that time, saying, "Cursed *be* the man before the LORD who rises up and builds this city Jericho; he shall lay its foundation with his firstborn, and with his youngest he shall set up its gates."

27 So the LORD was with Joshua, and his fame spread throughout all the country.

7 But the children of Israel committed a trespass regarding the accursed things, for Achan the son of Carmi, the son of Zabdi,*a* the son of Zerah, of the tribe of Judah, took of the accursed things; so the anger of the LORD burned against the children of Israel.

2 Now Joshua sent men from Jericho to Ai, which *is* beside Beth Aven, on the east side of Bethel, and spoke to them, saying, "Go up and spy out the country." So the men went up and spied out Ai. 3 And they returned to Joshua and said to him, "Do not let all the people go up, but let about two or three thousand men go up and attack Ai. Do not weary all the people there, for *the people of Ai are* few." 4 So about three thousand men went up there from the people, but they fled before the men of Ai. 5 And the men of Ai struck down about thirty-six men, for they chased them *from* before the gate as far as Shebarim, and struck them down on the descent; therefore the hearts of the people melted and became like water.

6 Then Joshua tore his clothes, and fell to the earth on his face before the ark of the LORD until evening, he and the elders of Israel; and they put dust on their heads. 7 And Joshua said, "Alas, Lord GOD, why have You brought this people over the Jordan at all—to deliver us into the hand of the Amorites, to destroy us? Oh, that we had been content, and dwelt on

7:1 *a*Called *Zimri* in 1 Chronicles 2:6

God's Word awakens that which should have been awake and puts to sleep some of the issues that should have been retired a long time ago. This is the announcement that releases you from the long night of repression and guilt.

Richest Woman in Town

Rahab was a prostitute who lived in Jericho. The Bible doesn't speak of her having a husband. She had nearly every man in town. Sarah, Abraham's wife, stayed in the tent and knitted socks. She moved wherever her husband went and took care of him. There was no similarity in the lifestyles of these two women; the only similarity they shared was their faith. God saw the faith in Rahab that He had seen in Sarah.

Just before the famous Battle of Jericho, the prostitute decided to take a stand on the side of God's people. She hid their spies. Her decision was based on her faith. Faith is an action. Rahab took action because she believed that God would deliver her when Jericho fell to the Israelites.

Sarah received strength to carry and deliver a child when she was well past childbearing age. She took action because she believed God—that He was faithful to do what He had promised (see Hebrews 11:11).

Regardless of your position or your past, God raises people up equally. No matter how many mistakes you have made, it is your faith God honors. You may have blown it, but God is in the business of restoring broken lives and rebuilding homes. You may have been like Rahab, but if you can believe God, He will save your house. When Jericho fell, He didn't save Rahab alone; He also saved her entire household. All the other homes in Jericho were destroyed. The only house God saved in the whole city was the house where the prostitute lived!

You would have thought He would spare some nice little old lady's house. Maybe some little widow's cottage, with petunias growing outside the door. But God saved the prostitute's house. Was it because He wanted her place? No, it was because He wanted her faith. It is faith that moves God.

If you believe that your background will keep you from moving forward with God, then you don't understand that the thing He is asking from you is faith. Those who live good, clean, separated lives may be proud of how holy they are. But God honors faith. In the Bible, He healed some folks who weren't even saved, because God honors faith.

There was something valuable in Rahab's house. Faith was there. God protected Rahab from the fire because of her faith. But He also saved her stuff. When the fire was over, Rahab was the only woman left who owned any property. She was the richest woman in town.

the other side of the Jordan! 8 O Lord, what shall I say when Israel turns its back before its enemies? 9 For the Canaanites and all the inhabitants of the land will hear *it*, and surround us, and cut off our name from the earth. Then what will You do for Your great name?"

10 So the LORD said to Joshua: "Get up! Why do you lie thus on your face? 11 Israel has sinned, and they have also transgressed My covenant which I commanded them. For they have even taken some of the accursed things, and have both stolen and deceived; and they have also put *it* among their own stuff. 12 Therefore the children of Israel could not stand before their enemies, *but* turned *their* backs before their enemies, because they have become doomed to destruction. Neither will I be with you anymore, unless you destroy the accursed from among you. 13 Get up, sanctify the people, and say, 'Sanctify yourselves for tomorrow, because thus says the LORD God of Israel: *"There is* an accursed thing in your midst, O Israel; you cannot stand before your enemies until you take away the accursed thing from among you." 14 In the morning therefore you shall be brought according to your tribes. And it shall be *that* the tribe which the LORD takes shall come according to families; and the family which the LORD takes shall come by households; and the household which the LORD takes shall come man by man. 15 Then it shall be *that* he who is taken with the accursed thing shall be burned with fire, he and all that he has, because he has transgressed the covenant of the LORD, and because he has done a disgraceful thing in Israel.' "

16 So Joshua rose early in the morning and brought Israel by their tribes, and the tribe of Judah was taken. 17 He brought the clan of Judah, and he took the family of the Zarhites; and he brought the family of the Zarhites man by man, and Zabdi was taken. 18 Then he brought his household man by man, and Achan the son of Carmi, the son of Zabdi, the son of Zerah, of the tribe of Judah, was taken.

19 Now Joshua said to Achan, "My son, I beg you, give glory to the LORD God of Israel, and make confession to Him, and tell me now what you have done; do not hide *it* from me."

20 And Achan answered Joshua and said, "Indeed I have sinned against the LORD God of Israel, and this is what I have done: 21 When I saw among the spoils a beautiful Babylonian garment, two hundred shekels of silver, and a wedge of gold weighing fifty shekels, I coveted them and took them. And there they are, hidden in the earth in the midst of my tent, with the silver under it."

22 So Joshua sent messengers, and they ran to the tent; and there it was, hidden in his tent, with the silver under it. 23 And they took them from the midst of the tent, brought them to Joshua and to all the children of Israel, and laid them out before the LORD. 24 Then Joshua, and all Israel with him, took Achan the son of Zerah, the silver, the garment, the wedge of gold, his sons, his daughters, his oxen, his donkeys, his sheep, his tent, and all that he had, and they brought them to the Valley of Achor. 25 And Joshua said, "Why have you troubled us? The LORD will trouble you this day." So all Israel stoned him with stones; and they burned them with fire after they had stoned them with stones.

26 Then they raised over him a great heap of stones, still there to this day. So the LORD turned from the fierceness of His anger. Therefore the name of that place has been called the Valley of Achor*a* to this day.

8 Now the LORD said to Joshua: "Do not be afraid, nor be dismayed; take all the people of war with you, and arise, go up to Ai. See, I have given into your hand the king of Ai, his people, his city, and his land. 2 And you shall do to Ai and its king as you did to Jericho and its king. Only its spoil and its cattle you shall take as booty for yourselves. Lay an ambush for the city behind it."

3 So Joshua arose, and all the people of war, to go up against Ai; and Joshua chose thirty thousand mighty men of valor and sent them away by night. 4 And he commanded them, saying: "Behold, you shall lie in ambush against the city, behind the city.

7:26 *a*Literally *Trouble*

---

*I*f you never ask for anything, you will never receive anything; the world will assume you are satisfied. Passivity will block you from receiving.

Do not go very far from the city, but all of you be ready. 5 Then I and all the people who *are* with me will approach the city; and it will come about, when they come out against us as at the first, that we shall flee before them. 6 For they will come out after us till we have drawn them from the city, for they will say, 'They *are* fleeing before us as at the first.' Therefore we will flee before them. 7 Then you shall rise from the ambush and seize the city, for the Lord your God will deliver it into your hand. 8 And it will be, when you have taken the city, *that* you shall set the city on fire. According to the commandment of the Lord you shall do. See, I have commanded you."

9 Joshua therefore sent them out; and they went to lie in ambush, and stayed between Bethel and Ai, on the west side of Ai; but Joshua lodged that night among the people. 10 Then Joshua rose up early in the morning and mustered the people, and went up, he and the elders of Israel, before the people to Ai. 11 And all the people of war who *were* with him went up and drew near; and they came before the city and camped on the north side of Ai. Now a valley *lay* between them and Ai. 12 So he took about five thousand men and set them in ambush between Bethel and Ai, on the west side of the city. 13 And when they had set the people, all the army that *was* on the north of the city, and its rear guard on the west of the city, Joshua went that night into the midst of the valley.

14 Now it happened, when the king of Ai saw *it*, that the men of the city hurried and rose early and went out against Israel to battle, he and all his people, at an appointed place before the plain. But he did not know that *there was* an ambush against him behind the city. 15 And Joshua and all Israel made as if they were beaten before them, and fled by the way of the wilderness. 16 So all the people who *were* in Ai were called together to pursue them. And they pursued Joshua and were drawn away from the city. 17 There was not a man left in Ai or Bethel who did not go out after Israel. So they left the city open and pursued Israel.

18 Then the Lord said to Joshua, "Stretch out the spear that *is* in your hand toward Ai, for I will give it into your hand." And Joshua stretched out the spear that *was* in his hand toward the city. 19 So *those in* ambush arose quickly out of their place; they ran as soon as he had stretched out his hand, and they entered the city and took it, and hurried to set the city on fire. 20 And when the men of Ai looked behind them, they saw, and behold, the smoke of the city ascended to heaven. So they had no power to flee this way or that way, and the people who had fled to the wilderness turned back on the pursuers.

21 Now when Joshua and all Israel saw that the ambush had taken the city and that the smoke of the city ascended, they turned back and struck down the men of Ai. 22 Then the others came out of the city against them; so they were *caught* in the midst of Israel, some on this side and some on that side. And they struck them down, so that they let none of them remain or escape. 23 But the king of Ai they took alive, and brought him to Joshua.

24 And it came to pass when Israel had made an end of slaying all the inhabitants of Ai in the field, in the wilderness where they pursued them, and when they all had fallen by the edge of the sword until they were consumed, that all the Israelites returned to Ai and struck it with the edge of the sword. 25 So it was *that* all who fell that day, both men and women, *were* twelve thousand—all the people of Ai. 26 For Joshua did not draw back his hand, with which he stretched out the spear, until he had utterly destroyed all the inhabitants of Ai. 27 Only the livestock and the spoil of that city Israel took as booty for themselves, according to the word of the Lord which He had commanded Joshua. 28 So Joshua burned Ai and made it a heap forever, a desolation to this day. 29 And the king of Ai he hanged on a tree until evening. And as soon as the sun was down, Joshua commanded that they should take his corpse down from the tree, cast it at the entrance of the gate of the city, and raise over it a great heap of stones *that remains* to this day.

30 Now Joshua built an altar to the Lord God of Israel in Mount Ebal, 31 as Moses the servant of the Lord

had commanded the children of Israel, as it is written in the Book of the Law of Moses: "an altar of whole stones over which no man has wielded an iron *tool.*"*ᵃ* And they offered on it burnt offerings to the LORD, and sacrificed peace offerings. 32 And there, in the presence of the children of Israel, he wrote on the stones a copy of the law of Moses, which he had written. 33 Then all Israel, with their elders and officers and judges, stood on either side of the ark before the priests, the Levites, who bore the ark of the covenant of the LORD, the stranger as well as he who was born among them. Half of them *were* in front of Mount Gerizim and half of them in front of Mount Ebal, as Moses the servant of the LORD had commanded before, that they should bless the people of Israel. 34 And afterward he read all the words of the law, the blessings and the cursings, according to all that is written in the Book of the Law. 35 There was not a word of all that Moses had commanded which Joshua did not read before all the assembly of Israel, with the women, the little ones, and the strangers who were living among them.

9 And it came to pass when all the kings who *were* on this side of the Jordan, in the hills and in the lowland and in all the coasts of the Great Sea toward Lebanon—the Hittite, the Amorite, the Canaanite, the Perizzite, the Hivite, and the Jebusite— heard *about it,* 2 that they gathered together to fight with Joshua and Israel with one accord.

3 But when the inhabitants of Gibeon heard what Joshua had done to Jericho and Ai, 4 they worked craftily, and went and pretended to be ambassadors. And they took old sacks on their donkeys, old wineskins torn and mended, 5 old and patched sandals on their feet, and old garments on themselves; and all the bread of their provision was dry *and* moldy. 6 And they went to Joshua, to the camp at Gilgal, and said to him and to the men of Israel, "We have come from a far country; now therefore, make a covenant with us."

7 Then the men of Israel said to the Hivites, "Perhaps you dwell among

us; so how can we make a covenant with you?"

8 But they said to Joshua, "We *are* your servants."

And Joshua said to them, "Who *are* you, and where do you come from?"

9 So they said to him: "From a very far country your servants have come, because of the name of the LORD your God; for we have heard of His fame, and all that He did in Egypt, 10 and all that He did to the two kings of the Amorites who *were* beyond the Jordan—to Sihon king of Heshbon, and Og king of Bashan, who was at Ashtaroth. 11 Therefore our elders and all the inhabitants of our country spoke to us, saying, 'Take provisions with you for the journey, and go to meet them, and say to them, "We *are* your servants; now therefore, make a covenant with us."' 12 This bread of ours we took hot *for* our provision from our houses on the day we departed to come to you. But now look, it is dry and moldy. 13 And these wineskins which we filled *were* new, and see, they are torn; and these our garments and our sandals have become old because of the very long journey."

14 Then the men of Israel took some of their provisions; but they did not ask counsel of the LORD. 15 So Joshua made peace with them, and made a covenant with them to let them live; and the rulers of the congregation swore to them.

16 And it happened at the end of three days, after they had made a covenant with them, that they heard that they *were* their neighbors who dwelt near them. 17 Then the children of Israel journeyed and came to their cities on the third day. Now their cities *were* Gibeon, Chephirah, Beeroth, and Kirjath Jearim. 18 But the children of Israel did not attack them, because the rulers of the congregation had sworn to them by the LORD God of Israel. And all the congregation complained against the rulers. 19 Then all the rulers said to all the congregation, "We have sworn to them by the LORD God of Israel; now therefore, we may not touch them. 20 This we will do to them: We will let them live, lest wrath be upon us because of the oath which we swore to them." 21 And the rulers said to

8:31 ᵃDeuteronomy 27:5, 6

God teaches emphatically the necessity of being an initiator. You must initiate your own blessing. If you don't initiate it, nothing significant will ever occur in your life. It is totally up to you.

them, "Let them live, but let them be woodcutters and water carriers for all the congregation, as the rulers had promised them."

22 Then Joshua called for them, and he spoke to them, saying, "Why have you deceived us, saying, 'We *are* very far from you,' when you dwell near us? 23 Now therefore, you *are* cursed, and none of you shall be freed from being slaves—woodcutters and water carriers for the house of my God."

24 So they answered Joshua and said, "Because your servants were clearly told that the LORD your God commanded His servant Moses to give you all the land, and to destroy all the inhabitants of the land from before you; therefore we were very much afraid for our lives because of you, and have done this thing. 25 And now, here we are, in your hands; do with us as it seems good and right to do to us." 26 So he did to them, and delivered them out of the hand of the children of Israel, so that they did not kill them. 27 And that day Joshua made them woodcutters and water carriers for the congregation and for the altar of the LORD, in the place which He would choose, even to this day.

10 Now it came to pass when Adoni-Zedek king of Jerusalem heard how Joshua had taken Ai and had utterly destroyed it—as he had done to Jericho and its king, so he had done to Ai and its king—and how the inhabitants of Gibeon had made peace with Israel and were among them, 2 that they feared greatly, because Gibeon *was* a great city, like one of the royal cities, and because it *was* greater than Ai, and all its men *were* mighty. 3 Therefore Adoni-Zedek king of Jerusalem sent to Hoham king of Hebron, Piram king of Jarmuth, Japhia king of Lachish, and Debir king of Eglon, saying, 4 "Come up to me and help me, that we may attack Gibeon, for it has made peace with Joshua and with the children of Israel." 5 Therefore the five kings of the Amorites, the king of Jerusalem, the king of Hebron, the king of Jarmuth, the king of Lachish, *and* the king of Eglon, gathered together and went up, they and all their armies, and

camped before Gibeon and made war against it.

6 And the men of Gibeon sent to Joshua at the camp at Gilgal, saying, "Do not forsake your servants; come up to us quickly, save us and help us, for all the kings of the Amorites who dwell in the mountains have gathered together against us."

7 So Joshua ascended from Gilgal, he and all the people of war with him, and all the mighty men of valor. 8 And the LORD said to Joshua, "Do not fear them, for I have delivered them into your hand; not a man of them shall stand before you." 9 Joshua therefore came upon them suddenly, having marched all night from Gilgal. 10 So the LORD routed them before Israel, killed them with a great slaughter at Gibeon, chased them along the road that goes to Beth Horon, and struck them down as far as Azekah and Makkedah. 11 And it happened, as they fled before Israel *and* were on the descent of Beth Horon, that the LORD cast down large hailstones from heaven on them as far as Azekah, and they died. *There were* more who died from the hailstones than the children of Israel killed with the sword.

12 Then Joshua spoke to the LORD in the day when the LORD delivered up the Amorites before the children of Israel, and he said in the sight of Israel:

> "Sun, stand still over Gibeon;
> And Moon, in the Valley of
> Aijalon."
> 13 So the sun stood still,
> And the moon stopped,
> Till the people had revenge
> Upon their enemies.

Is this not written in the Book of Jasher? So the sun stood still in the midst of heaven, and did not hasten to go *down* for about a whole day. 14 And there has been no day like that, before it or after it, that the LORD heeded the voice of a man; for the LORD fought for Israel.

15 Then Joshua returned, and all Israel with him, to the camp at Gilgal.

16 But these five kings had fled and hidden themselves in a cave at Makkedah. 17 And it was told Joshua, saying, "The five kings have been found hidden in the cave at Makkedah."

18 So Joshua said, "Roll large stones against the mouth of the cave, and set men by it to guard them. 19 And do not stay *there* yourselves, *but* pursue your enemies, and attack their rear *guard.* Do not allow them to enter their cities, for the Lord your God has delivered them into your hand." 20 Then it happened, while Joshua and the children of Israel made an end of slaying them with a very great slaughter, till they had finished, that those who escaped entered fortified cities. 21 And all the people returned to the camp, to Joshua at Makkedah, in peace.

No one moved his tongue against any of the children of Israel. 22 Then Joshua said, "Open the mouth of the cave, and bring out those five kings to me from the cave." 23 And they did so, and brought out those five kings to him from the cave: the king of Jerusalem, the king of Hebron, the king of Jarmuth, the king of Lachish, *and* the king of Eglon. 24 So it was, when they brought out those kings to Joshua, that Joshua called for all the men of Israel, and said to the captains of the men of war who went with him, "Come near, put your feet on the necks of these kings." And they drew near and put their feet on their necks. 25 Then Joshua said to them, "Do not be afraid, nor be dismayed; be strong and of good courage, for thus the Lord will do to all your enemies against whom you fight." 26 And afterward Joshua struck them and killed them, and hanged them on five trees; and they were hanging on the trees until evening. 27 So it was at the time of the going down of the sun *that* Joshua commanded, and they took them down from the trees, cast them into the cave where they had been hidden, and laid large stones against the cave's mouth, *which remain* until this very day.

28 On that day Joshua took Makkedah, and struck it and its king with the edge of the sword. He utterly destroyed them*ᵃ*—all the people who *were* in it. He let none remain. He also did to the king of Makkedah as he had done to the king of Jericho. 29 Then Joshua passed from Mak-

kedah, and all Israel with him, to Libnah; and they fought against Libnah. 30 And the Lord also delivered it and its king into the hand of Israel; he struck it and all the people who *were* in it with the edge of the sword. He let none remain in it, but did to its king as he had done to the king of Jericho.

31 Then Joshua passed from Libnah, and all Israel with him, to Lachish; and they encamped against it and fought against it. 32 And the Lord delivered Lachish into the hand of Israel, who took it on the second day, and struck it and all the people who *were* in it with the edge of the sword, according to all that he had done to Libnah. 33 Then Horam king of Gezer came up to help Lachish; and Joshua struck him and his people, until he left him none remaining.

34 From Lachish Joshua passed to Eglon, and all Israel with him; and they encamped against it and fought against it. 35 They took it on that day and struck it with the edge of the sword; all the people who *were* in it he utterly destroyed that day, according to all that he had done to Lachish.

36 So Joshua went up from Eglon, and all Israel with him, to Hebron; and they fought against it. 37 And they took it and struck it with the edge of the sword—its king, all its cities, and all the people who *were* in it; he left none remaining, according to all that he had done to Eglon, but utterly destroyed it and all the people who *were* in it.

38 Then Joshua returned, and all Israel with him, to Debir; and they fought against it. 39 And he took it and its king and all its cities; they struck them with the edge of the sword and utterly destroyed all the people who *were* in it. He left none remaining; as he had done to Hebron, so he did to Debir and its king, as he had done also to Libnah and its king.

40 So Joshua conquered all the land: the mountain country and the South*ᵃ* and the lowland and the wilderness slopes, and all their kings; he left none remaining, but utterly destroyed all that breathed, as the Lord God of Israel had commanded.

10:28 *ᵃ*Following Masoretic Text and most authorities; many Hebrew manuscripts, some manuscripts of the Septuagint, and some manuscripts of the Targum read *it.*   10:40 *ᵃ*Hebrew *Negev,* and so throughout this book

*I*f there is no asking, seeking and knocking, there will be no giving, finding and opening. Many women are living in frustration because they are filled with many wonderful memories and fantasies, but their reality may not be what they desire.

41 And Joshua conquered them from Kadesh Barnea as far as Gaza, and all the country of Goshen, even as far as Gibeon. 42 All these kings and their land Joshua took at one time, because the Lord God of Israel fought for Israel. 43 Then Joshua returned, and all Israel with him, to the camp at Gilgal.

11 And it came to pass, when Jabin king of Hazor heard *these things,* that he sent to Jobab king of Madon, to the king of Shimron, to the king of Achshaph, 2 and to the kings who *were* from the north, in the mountains, in the plain south of Chinneroth, in the lowland, and in the heights of Dor on the west, 3 to the Canaanites in the east and in the west, the Amorite, the Hittite, the Perizzite, the Jebusite in the mountains, and the Hivite below Hermon in the land of Mizpah. 4 So they went out, they and all their armies with them, *as* many people *as* the sand that *is* on the seashore in multitude, with very many horses and chariots. 5 And when all these kings had met together, they came and camped together at the waters of Merom to fight against Israel.

6 But the Lord said to Joshua, "Do not be afraid because of them, for tomorrow about this time I will deliver all of them slain before Israel. You shall hamstring their horses and burn their chariots with fire." 7 So Joshua and all the people of war with him came against them suddenly by the waters of Merom, and they attacked them. 8 And the Lord delivered them into the hand of Israel, who defeated them and chased them to Greater Sidon, to the Brook Misrephoth,[a] and to the Valley of Mizpah eastward; they attacked them until they left none of them remaining. 9 So Joshua did to them as the Lord had told him: he hamstrung their horses and burned their chariots with fire.

10 Joshua turned back at that time and took Hazor, and struck its king with the sword; for Hazor was formerly the head of all those kingdoms. 11 And they struck all the people who *were* in it with the edge of the sword, utterly destroying *them.* There was none left breathing. Then he burned Hazor with fire.

12 So all the cities of those kings, and all their kings, Joshua took and struck with the edge of the sword. He utterly destroyed them, as Moses the servant of the Lord had commanded. 13 But *as for* the cities that stood on their mounds,[a] Israel burned none of them, except Hazor only, *which* Joshua burned. 14 And all the spoil of these cities and the livestock, the children of Israel took as booty for themselves; but they struck every man with the edge of the sword until they had destroyed them, and they left none breathing. 15 As the Lord had commanded Moses his servant, so Moses commanded Joshua, and so Joshua did. He left nothing undone of all that the Lord had commanded Moses.

16 Thus Joshua took all this land: the mountain country, all the South, all the land of Goshen, the lowland, and the Jordan plain[a]—the mountains of Israel and its lowlands, 17 from Mount Halak and the ascent to Seir, even as far as Baal Gad in the Valley of Lebanon below Mount Hermon. He captured all their kings, and struck them down and killed them. 18 Joshua made war a long time with all those kings. 19 There was not a city that made peace with the children of Israel, except the Hivites, the inhabitants of Gibeon. All *the others* they took in battle. 20 For it was of the Lord to harden their hearts, that they should come against Israel in battle, that He might utterly destroy them, *and* that they might receive no mercy, but that He might destroy them, as the Lord had commanded Moses.

21 And at that time Joshua came and cut off the Anakim from the mountains: from Hebron, from Debir, from Anab, from all the mountains of Judah, and from all the mountains of Israel; Joshua utterly destroyed them with their cities. 22 None of the Anakim were left in the land of the children of Israel; they remained only in Gaza, in Gath, and in Ashdod.

23 So Joshua took the whole land, according to all that the Lord had said to Moses; and Joshua gave it as

11:8 aHebrew *Misrephoth Maim*   11:13 aHebrew *tel,* a heap of successive city ruins
11:16 aHebrew *arabah*

Gospel Pearls

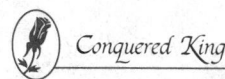

an inheritance to Israel according to their divisions by their tribes. Then the land rested from war.

12 These *are* the kings of the land whom the children of Israel defeated, and whose land they possessed on the other side of the Jordan toward the rising of the sun, from the River Arnon to Mount Hermon, and all the eastern Jordan plain: 2 *One king was* Sihon king of the Amorites, who dwelt in Heshbon *and* ruled half of Gilead, from Aroer, which is on the bank of the River Arnon, from the middle of that river, even as far as the River Jabbok, *which is* the border of the Ammonites, 3 and the eastern Jordan plain from the Sea of Chinneroth as far as the Sea of the Arabah (the Salt Sea), the road to Beth Jeshimoth, and southward below the slopes of Pisgah. 4 *The other king was* Og king of Bashan and his territory, *who was* of the remnant of the giants, who dwelt at Ashtaroth and at Edrei, 5 and reigned over Mount Hermon, over Salcah, over all Bashan, as far as the border of the Geshurites and the Maachathites, and over half of Gilead *to* the border of Sihon king of Heshbon.

6 These Moses the servant of the LORD and the children of Israel had conquered; and Moses the servant of the LORD had given it *as* a possession to the Reubenites, the Gadites, and half the tribe of Manasseh.

7 And these *are* the kings of the country which Joshua and the children of Israel conquered on this side of the Jordan, on the west, from Baal Gad in the Valley of Lebanon as far as Mount Halak and the ascent to Seir, which Joshua gave to the tribes of Israel *as* a possession according to their divisions, 8 in the mountain country, in the lowlands, in the *Jordan* plain, in the slopes, in the wilderness, and in the South—the Hittites, the Amorites, the Canaanites, the Perizzites, the Hivites, and the Jebusites: 9 the king of Jericho, one; the king of Ai, which *is* beside Bethel, one; 10 the king of Jerusalem, one; the king of Hebron, one; 11 the king of Jarmuth, one; the king of Lachish, one; 12 the king of Eglon, one; the king of Gezer, one; 13 the king of De-

bir, one; the king of Geder, one; 14 the king of Hormah, one; the king of Arad, one; 15 the king of Libnah, one; the king of Adullam, one; 16 the king of Makkedah, one; the king of Bethel, one; 17 the king of Tappuah, one; the king of Hepher, one; 18 the king of Aphek, one; the king of Lasharon, one; 19 the king of Madon, one; the king of Hazor, one; 20 the king of Shimron Meron, one; the king of Achshaph, one; 21 the king of Taanach, one; the king of Megiddo, one; 22 the king of Kedesh, one; the king of Jokneam in Carmel, one; 23 the king of Dor in the heights of Dor, one; the king of the people of Gilgal, one; 24 the king of Tirzah, one—all the kings, thirty-one.

13 Now Joshua was old, advanced in years. And the LORD said to him: "You are old, advanced in years, and there remains very much land yet to be possessed. 2 This is the land that yet remains: all the territory of the Philistines and all *that of* the Geshurites, 3 from Sihor, which *is* east of Egypt, as far as the border of Ekron northward (*which* is counted as Canaanite); the five lords of the Philistines—the Gazites, the Ashdodites, the Ashkelonites, the Gittites, and the Ekronites; also the Avites; 4 from the south, all the land of the Canaanites, and Mearah that belongs to the Sidonians as far as Aphek, to the border of the Amorites; 5 the land of the Gebalites,*a* and all Lebanon, toward the sunrise, from Baal Gad below Mount Hermon as far as the entrance to Hamath; 6 all the inhabitants of the mountains from Lebanon as far as the Brook Misrephoth,*a* *and* all the Sidonians—them I will drive out from before the children of Israel; only divide it by lot to Israel as an inheritance, as I have commanded you. 7 Now therefore, divide this land as an inheritance to the nine tribes and half the tribe of Manasseh."

8 With the other half tribe the Reubenites and the Gadites received their inheritance, which Moses had given them, beyond the Jordan eastward, as Moses the servant of the LORD had given them: 9 from Aroer which *is* on the bank of the River Arnon, and the town that *is* in the midst

13:5 *a*Or Giblites   13:6 *a*Hebrew Misrephoth Maim

*M*ost Christians feel that God will do it all. That is not true. If Hannah had not prayed in the spirit for a child (faith) and then slept with Elkanah (works), there would have never been a Samuel (fruit).

of the ravine, and all the plain of Medeba as far as Dibon; 10 all the cities of Sihon king of the Amorites, who reigned in Heshbon, as far as the border of the children of Ammon; 11 Gilead, and the border of the Geshurites and Maachathites, all Mount Hermon, and all Bashan as far as Salcah; 12 all the kingdom of Og in Bashan, who reigned in Ashtaroth and Edrei, who remained of the remnant of the giants; for Moses had defeated and cast out these.

13 Nevertheless the children of Israel did not drive out the Geshurites or the Maachathites, but the Geshurites and the Maachathites dwell among the Israelites until this day.

14 Only to the tribe of Levi he had given no inheritance; the sacrifices of the LORD God of Israel made by fire *are* their inheritance, as He said to them.

15 And Moses had given to the tribe of the children of Reuben *an inheritance* according to their families. 16 Their territory was from Aroer, which *is* on the bank of the River Arnon, and the city that *is* in the midst of the ravine, and all the plain by Medeba; 17 Heshbon and all its cities that *are* in the plain: Dibon, Bamoth Baal, Beth Baal Meon, 18 Jahaza, Kedemoth, Mephaath, 19 Kirjathaim, Sibmah, Zereth Shahar on the mountain of the valley, 20 Beth Peor, the slopes of Pisgah, and Beth Jeshimoth— 21 all the cities of the plain and all the kingdom of Sihon king of the Amorites, who reigned in Heshbon, whom Moses had struck with the princes of Midian: Evi, Rekem, Zur, Hur, and Reba, who *were* princes of Sihon dwelling in the country. 22 The children of Israel also killed with the sword Balaam the son of Beor, the soothsayer, among those who were killed by them. 23 And the border of the children of Reuben was the bank of the Jordan. This *was* the inheritance of the children of Reuben according to their families, the cities and their villages.

24 Moses also had given *an inheritance* to the tribe of Gad, to the children of Gad according to their families. 25 Their territory was Jazer, and all the cities of Gilead, and half the land of the Ammonites as far as Aroer, which *is* before Rabbah, 26 and from Heshbon to Ramath Mizpah and Betonim, and from Ma-

hanaim to the border of Debir, 27 and in the valley Beth Haram, Beth Nimrah, Succoth, and Zaphon, the rest of the kingdom of Sihon king of Heshbon, with the Jordan as *its* border, as far as the edge of the Sea of Chinnereth, on the other side of the Jordan eastward. 28 This *is* the inheritance of the children of Gad according to their families, the cities and their villages.

29 Moses also had given *an inheritance* to half the tribe of Manasseh; it was for half the tribe of the children of Manasseh according to their families: 30 Their territory was from Mahanaim, all Bashan, all the kingdom of Og king of Bashan, and all the towns of Jair which are in Bashan, sixty cities; 31 half of Gilead, and Ashtaroth and Edrei, cities of the kingdom of Og in Bashan, *were* for the children of Machir the son of Manasseh, for half of the children of Machir according to their families.

32 These *are the areas* which Moses had distributed as an inheritance in the plains of Moab on the other side of the Jordan, by Jericho eastward. 33 But to the tribe of Levi Moses had given no inheritance; the LORD God of Israel *was* their inheritance, as He had said to them.

14 These *are the areas* which the children of Israel inherited in the land of Canaan, which Eleazar the priest, Joshua the son of Nun, and the heads of the fathers of the tribes of the children of Israel distributed as an inheritance to them. 2 Their inheritance *was* by lot, as the LORD had commanded by the hand of Moses, for the nine tribes and the half-tribe. 3 For Moses had given the inheritance of the two tribes and the half-tribe on the other side of the Jordan; but to the Levites he had given no inheritance among them. 4 For the children of Joseph were two tribes: Manasseh and Ephraim. And they gave no part to the Levites in the land, except cities to dwell *in,* with their common-lands for their livestock and their property. 5 As the LORD had commanded Moses, so the children of Israel did; and they divided the land.

6 Then the children of Judah came to Joshua in Gilgal. And Caleb the son of Jephunneh the Kenizzite said to him: "You know the word which

Gospel
Pearls

the LORD said to Moses the man of God concerning you and me in Kadesh Barnea. 7 I *was* forty years old when Moses the servant of the LORD sent me from Kadesh Barnea to spy out the land, and I brought back word to him as *it was* in my heart. 8 Nevertheless my brethren who went up with me made the heart of the people melt, but I wholly followed the LORD my God. 9 So Moses swore on that day, saying, 'Surely the land where your foot has trodden shall be your inheritance and your children's forever, because you have wholly followed the LORD my God.' 10 And now, behold, the LORD has kept me alive, as He said, these forty-five years, ever since the LORD spoke this word to Moses while Israel wandered in the wilderness; and now, here I am this day, eighty-five years old. 11 As yet I *am as* strong this day as on the day that Moses sent me; just as my strength *was* then, so now *is* my strength for war, both for going out and for coming in. 12 Now therefore, give me this mountain of which the LORD spoke in that day; for you heard in that day how the Anakim *were* there, and *that* the cities *were* great *and* fortified. It may be that the LORD *will be* with me, and I shall be able to drive them out as the LORD said."

13 And Joshua blessed him, and gave Hebron to Caleb the son of Jephunneh as an inheritance. 14 Hebron therefore became the inheritance of Caleb the son of Jephunneh the Kenizzite to this day, because he wholly followed the LORD God of Israel. 15 And the name of Hebron formerly was Kirjath Arba (*Arba was* the greatest man among the Anakim).

Then the land had rest from war.

15 So *this* was the lot of the tribe of the children of Judah according to their families:

The border of Edom at the Wilderness of Zin southward *was* the extreme southern boundary. 2 And their southern border began at the shore of the Salt Sea, from the bay that faces southward. 3 Then it went out to the southern side of the Ascent of Akrabbim, passed along to Zin, ascended on the south side of Kadesh

Barnea, passed along to Hezron, went up to Adar, and went around to Karkaa. 4 *From there* it passed toward Azmon and went out to the Brook of Egypt; and the border ended at the sea. This shall be your southern border.

5 The east border *was* the Salt Sea as far as the mouth of the Jordan.

And the border on the northern quarter *began* at the bay of the sea at the mouth of the Jordan. 6 The border went up to Beth Hoglah and passed north of Beth Arabah; and the border went up to the stone of Bohan the son of Reuben. 7 Then the border went up toward Debir from the Valley of Achor, and it turned northward toward Gilgal, which *is* before the Ascent of Adummim, which *is* on the south side of the valley. The border continued toward the waters of En Shemesh and ended at En Rogel. 8 And the border went up by the Valley of the Son of Hinnom to the southern slope of the Jebusite *city* (which *is* Jerusalem). The border went up to the top of the mountain that *lies* before the Valley of Hinnom westward, which *is* at the end of the Valley of Rephaim[a] northward. 9 Then the border went around from the top of the hill to the fountain of the water of Nephtoah, and extended to the cities of Mount Ephron. And the border went around to Baalah (which *is* Kirjath Jearim). 10 Then the border turned westward from Baalah to Mount Seir, passed along to the side of Mount Jearim on the north (which *is* Chesalon), went down to Beth Shemesh, and passed on to Timnah. 11 And the border went out to the side of Ekron northward. Then the border went around to Shicron, passed along to Mount Baalah, and extended to Jabneel; and the border ended at the sea.

12 The west border *was* the coastline of the Great Sea. This *is* the boundary of the children of Judah all around according to their families.

13 Now to Caleb the son of Jephunneh he gave a share among the children of Judah, according to the commandment of the LORD to Joshua, *namely*, Kirjath Arba, which *is* Hebron (*Arba was* the father of Anak). 14 Caleb drove out the three sons of Anak from there: Sheshai, Ahiman,

15:8 [a] Literally *Giants*

*I*t is said that this is a man's world. It is not a man's world; it is God's world. He is the only sovereign power. Men may be occupying many seats of authority, but God is in control.

and Talmai, the children of Anak. 15 Then he went up from there to the inhabitants of Debir (formerly the name of Debir was Kirjath Sepher).

16 And Caleb said, "He who attacks Kirjath Sepher and takes it, to him I will give Achsah my daughter as wife." 17 So Othniel the son of Kenaz, the brother of Caleb, took it; and he gave him Achsah his daughter as wife. 18 Now it was so, when she came to him, that she persuaded him to ask her father for a field. So she dismounted from her donkey, and Caleb said to her, "What do you wish?" 19 She answered, "Give me a blessing; since you have given me land in the South, give me also springs of water." So he gave her the upper springs and the lower springs.

20 This was the inheritance of the tribe of the children of Judah according to their families:

21 The cities at the limits of the tribe of the children of Judah, toward the border of Edom in the South, were Kabzeel, Eder, Jagur, 22 Kinah, Dimonah, Adadah, 23 Kedesh, Hazor, Ithnan, 24 Ziph, Telem, Bealoth, 25 Hazor, Hadattah, Kerioth, Hezron (which is Hazor), 26 Amam, Shema, Moladah, 27 Hazar Gaddah, Heshmon, Beth Pelet, 28 Hazar Shual, Beersheba, Bizjothjah, 29 Baalah, Ijim, Ezem, 30 Eltolad, Chesil, Hormah, 31 Ziklag, Madmannah, Sansannah, 32 Lebaoth, Shilhim, Ain, and Rimmon: all the cities are twenty-nine, with their villages.

33 In the lowland: Eshtaol, Zorah, Ashnah, 34 Zanoah, En Gannim, Tappuah, Enam, 35 Jarmuth, Adullam, Socoh, Azekah, 36 Sharaim, Adithaim, Gederah, and Gederothaim: fourteen cities with their villages; 37 Zenan, Hadashah, Migdal Gad, 38 Dilean, Mizpah, Joktheel, 39 Lachish, Bozkath, Eglon, 40 Cabbon, Lahmas,a Kithlish, 41 Gederoth, Beth Dagon, Naamah, and Makkedah: sixteen cities with their villages; 42 Libnah, Ether, Ashan, 43 Jiphtah, Ashnah, Nezib, 44 Keilah, Achzib, and Mareshah: nine cities with their villages; 45 Ekron, with its towns and villages; 46 from Ekron to the sea, all that lay near Ashdod, with their villages; 47 Ashdod with its towns and villages, Gaza with its towns and

villages—as far as the Brook of Egypt and the Great Sea with its coastline.

48 And in the mountain country: Shamir, Jattir, Sochoh, 49 Dannah, Kirjath Sannah (which is Debir), 50 Anab, Eshtemoh, Anim, 51 Goshen, Holon, and Giloh: eleven cities with their villages; 52 Arab, Dumah, Eshean, 53 Janum, Beth Tappuah, Aphekah, 54 Humtah, Kirjath Arba (which is Hebron), and Zior: nine cities with their villages; 55 Maon, Carmel, Ziph, Juttah, 56 Jezreel, Jokdeam, Zanoah, 57 Kain, Gibeah, and Timnah: ten cities with their villages; 58 Halhul, Beth Zur, Gedor, 59 Maarath, Beth Anoth, and Eltekon: six cities with their villages; 60 Kirjath Baal (which is Kirjath Jearim) and Rabbah: two cities with their villages.

61 In the wilderness: Beth Arabah, Middin, Secacah, 62 Nibshan, the City of Salt, and En Gedi: six cities with their villages.

63 As for the Jebusites, the inhabitants of Jerusalem, the children of Judah could not drive them out; but the Jebusites dwell with the children of Judah at Jerusalem to this day.

16 The lot fell to the children of Joseph from the Jordan, by Jericho, to the waters of Jericho on the east, to the wilderness that goes up from Jericho through the mountains to Bethel, 2 then went out from Bethel to Luz,a passed along to the border of the Archites at Ataroth, 3 and went down westward to the boundary of the Japhletites, as far as the boundary of Lower Beth Horon to Gezer; and it ended at the sea.

4 So the children of Joseph, Manasseh and Ephraim, took their inheritance.

5 The border of the children of Ephraim, according to their families, was thus: The border of their inheritance on the east side was Ataroth Addar as far as Upper Beth Horon.

6 And the border went out toward the sea on the north side of Michmethath; then the border went around eastward to Taanath Shiloh, and passed by it on the east of Janohah. 7 Then it went down from Janohah to Ataroth and Naarah,a reached

15:40 aOr Lahmam   16:2 aSeptuagint reads Bethel (that is, Luz).   16:7 aOr Naaran (compare 1 Chronicles 7:28)

*T*he power to get wealth is in your tongue. You shall have whatever you say. Don't sit around murmuring, groaning, and complaining. Open your mouth and speak something good so you can stand up on your feet.

Ask for Your Portion

Joshua 17:3, 4

Notice that the daughters of Zelophehad asked for their portion (see Numbers 27:4). They didn't want their uncle's portion. They just wanted what was rightfully theirs. They wanted property "along with" their father's brothers. They were smart enough to realize they could have it, but they didn't demand it—they requested it. They were not male bashers. Christian women must avoid taking a cue from their secular sisters who have not allowed their bitter experiences to be healed by the love of our Father.

These women never lost their femininity. But they show us that being feminine doesn't mean being a doormat. They didn't tolerate injustice, nor did they become embittered. They used the power of a request. Because Zelophehad's daughters challenged the system without violating the principles, Moses went to God and asked Him for help.

I know it is difficult to be ignored and not become disgruntled. Wise women, however, do not allow their emotions to overrule their ultimate goals and purposes. If there are systems that have ensnared your blessing, they need to be challenged, not attacked.

Maybe no one would have listened to Zelophehad's daughters if they had not initiated a meeting to plead their case. Perhaps you who have struggled need to call a meeting. Get in touch with people in power and demand what you want, or you may not get it. Speak up for yourself.

I believe this is a time when God wants to pour out blessings, not just on His sons, but on His daughters. This is more than an extra check in the mail. It is time for directional changes and life changes. Start expecting a deluge, an outpouring. I don't mean just wait on it. Prepare for it. Expect it. It's going to rain in your life.

Because of the good things He wants to send you, God wants to heal every fear and insecurity and inhibition that would stop you from receiving. Use the power of a request when you ask for your blessing. When it comes, be ready for a downpour.

to Jericho, and came out at the Jordan.

8 The border went out from Tappuah westward to the Brook Kanah, and it ended at the sea. This *was* the inheritance of the tribe of the children of Ephraim according to their families. 9 The separate cities for the children of Ephraim *were* among the inheritance of the children of Manasseh, all the cities with their villages.

10 And they did not drive out the Canaanites who dwelt in Gezer; but the Canaanites dwell among the Ephraimites to this day and have become forced laborers.

17 There was also a lot for the tribe of Manasseh, for he *was* the firstborn of Joseph: *namely* for Machir the firstborn of Manasseh, the father of Gilead, because he was a man of war; therefore he was given Gilead and Bashan. 2 And there was *a lot* for the rest of the children of Manasseh according to their families: for the children of Abiezer,*a* the children of Helek, the children of Asriel, the children of Shechem, the children of Hepher, and the children of Shemida; these *were* the male children of Manasseh the son of Joseph according to their families.

3 But Zelophehad the son of Hepher, the son of Gilead, the son of Machir, the son of Manasseh, had no sons, but only daughters. And these *are* the names of his daughters: Mahlah, Noah, Hoglah, Milcah, and Tirzah. 4 And they came near before Eleazar the priest, before Joshua the son of Nun, and before the rulers, saying, "The LORD commanded Moses to give us an inheritance among our brothers." Therefore, according to the commandment of the LORD, he gave them an inheritance among their father's brothers. 5 Ten shares fell to Manasseh, besides the land of Gilead and Bashan, which *were* on the other side of the Jordan, 6 because the daughters of Manasseh received an inheritance among his sons; and the rest of Manasseh's sons had the land of Gilead.

7 And the territory of Manasseh was from Asher to Michmethath, that *lies* east of Shechem; and the border went along south to the inhabitants of En Tappuah. 8 Manasseh had the land of Tappuah, but Tappuah on the border of Manasseh *belonged* to the children of Ephraim. 9 And the border descended to the Brook Kanah, southward to the brook. These cities of Ephraim *are* among the cities of Manasseh. The border of Manasseh *was* on the north side of the brook; and it ended at the sea.

10 Southward *it was* Ephraim's, northward *it was* Manasseh's, and the sea was its border. Manasseh's territory was adjoining Asher on the north and Issachar on the east. 11 And in Issachar and in Asher, Manasseh had Beth Shean and its towns, Ibleam and its towns, the inhabitants of Dor and its towns, the inhabitants of En Dor and its towns, the inhabitants of Taanach and its towns, and the inhabitants of Megiddo and its towns—three hilly regions. 12 Yet the children of Manasseh could not drive out *the inhabitants of* those cities, but the Canaanites were determined to dwell in that land. 13 And it happened, when the children of Israel grew strong, that they put the Canaanites to forced labor, but did not utterly drive them out.

14 Then the children of Joseph spoke to Joshua, saying, "Why have you given us *only* one lot and one share to inherit, since we *are* a great people, inasmuch as the LORD has blessed us until now?"

15 So Joshua answered them, "If you *are* a great people, *then* go up to the forest *country* and clear a place for yourself there in the land of the Perizzites and the giants, since the mountains of Ephraim are too confined for you."

16 But the children of Joseph said, "The mountain country is not enough for us; and all the Canaanites who dwell in the land of the valley have chariots of iron, *both those* who *are* of Beth Shean and its towns and *those* who *are* of the Valley of Jezreel."

17 And Joshua spoke to the house of Joseph—to Ephraim and Manasseh—saying, "You *are* a great people and have great power; you shall not have *only* one lot, 18 but the mountain country shall be yours. Although it *is* wooded, you shall cut it down, and its farthest extent shall be yours; for

17:2 *a*Called *Jeezer* in Numbers 26:30

Gospel Pearls

you shall drive out the Canaanites, though they have iron chariots *and* are strong."

18 Now the whole congregation of the children of Israel assembled together at Shiloh, and set up the tabernacle of meeting there. And the land was subdued before them. 2 But there remained among the children of Israel seven tribes which had not yet received their inheritance.

3 Then Joshua said to the children of Israel: "How long will you neglect to go and possess the land which the LORD God of your fathers has given you? 4 Pick out from among you three men for *each* tribe, and I will send them; they shall rise and go through the land, survey it according to their inheritance, and come *back* to me. 5 And they shall divide it into seven parts. Judah shall remain in their territory on the south, and the house of Joseph shall remain in their territory on the north. 6 You shall therefore survey the land in seven parts and bring *the survey* here to me, that I may cast lots for you here before the LORD our God. 7 But the Levites have no part among you, for the priesthood of the LORD *is* their inheritance. And Gad, Reuben, and half the tribe of Manasseh have received their inheritance beyond the Jordan on the east, which Moses the servant of the LORD gave them."

8 Then the men arose to go away; and Joshua charged those who went to survey the land, saying, "Go, walk through the land, survey it, and come back to me, that I may cast lots for you here before the LORD in Shiloh." 9 So the men went, passed through the land, and wrote the survey in a book in seven parts by cities; and they came to Joshua at the camp in Shiloh. 10 Then Joshua cast lots for them in Shiloh before the LORD, and there Joshua divided the land to the children of Israel according to their divisions.

11 Now the lot of the tribe of the children of Benjamin came up according to their families, and the territory of their lot came out between the children of Judah and the children of Joseph. 12 Their border on the north side began at the Jordan, and the border went up to the side of Jericho on the north, and went up through the mountains westward; it ended at the Wilderness of Beth Aven. 13 The border went over from there toward Luz, to the side of Luz (which *is* Bethel) southward; and the border descended to Ataroth Addar, near the hill that *lies* on the south side of Lower Beth Horon.

14 Then the border extended around the west side to the south, from the hill that *lies* before Beth Horon southward; and it ended at Kirjath Baal (which *is* Kirjath Jearim), a city of the children of Judah. This *was* the west side.

15 The south side *began* at the end of Kirjath Jearim, and the border extended on the west and went out to the spring of the waters of Nephtoah. 16 Then the border came down to the end of the mountain that *lies* before the Valley of the Son of Hinnom, which *is* in the Valley of the Rephaim[a] on the north, descended to the Valley of Hinnom, to the side of the Jebusite *city* on the south, and descended to En Rogel. 17 And it went around from the north, went out to En Shemesh, and extended toward Geliloth, which is before the Ascent of Adummim, and descended to the stone of Bohan the son of Reuben. 18 Then it passed along toward the north side of Arabah,[a] and went down to Arabah. 19 And the border passed along to the north side of Beth Hoglah; then the border ended at the north bay at the Salt Sea, at the south end of the Jordan. This *was* the southern boundary.

20 The Jordan was its border on the east side. This *was* the inheritance of the children of Benjamin, according to its boundaries all around, according to their families.

21 Now the cities of the tribe of the children of Benjamin, according to their families, were Jericho, Beth Hoglah, Emek Keziz, 22 Beth Arabah, Zemaraim, Bethel, 23 Avim, Parah, Ophrah, 24 Chephar Haammoni, Ophni, and Gaba: twelve cities with their villages; 25 Gibeon, Ramah, Beeroth, 26 Mizpah, Chephirah, Mozah, 27 Rekem, Irpeel, Taralah, 28 Zelah, Eleph, Jebus (which *is* Jerusalem), Gibeath, *and* Kirjath: fourteen cities with their villages. This was the inheritance of the children

---

18:16 ªLiterally *Giants*   18:18 ªOr *Beth Arabah* (compare 15:6 and 18:22)

If God blesses you, do not fear. A blessed woman can survive even in a man's world. The challenge is to receive what is yours without becoming bitter about the times it was withheld from you.

of Benjamin according to their families.

19 The second lot came out for Simeon, for the tribe of the children of Simeon according to their families. And their inheritance was within the inheritance of the children of Judah. 2 They had in their inheritance Beersheba (Sheba), Moladah, 3 Hazar Shual, Balah, Ezem, 4 Eltolad, Bethul, Hormah, 5 Ziklag, Beth Marcaboth, Hazar Susah, 6 Beth Lebaoth, and Sharuhen: thirteen cities and their villages; 7 Ain, Rimmon, Ether, and Ashan: four cities and their villages; 8 and all the villages that were all around these cities as far as Baalath Beer, Ramah of the South. This was the inheritance of the tribe of the children of Simeon according to their families.

9 The inheritance of the children of Simeon was included in the share of the children of Judah, for the share of the children of Judah was too much for them. Therefore the children of Simeon had their inheritance within the inheritance of that people.

10 The third lot came out for the children of Zebulun according to their families, and the border of their inheritance was as far as Sarid. 11 Their border went toward the west and to Maralah, went to Dabbasheth, and extended along the brook that is east of Jokneam. 12 Then from Sarid it went eastward toward the sunrise along the border of Chisloth Tabor, and went out toward Daberath, bypassing Japhia. 13 And from there it passed along on the east of Gath Hepher, toward Eth Kazin, and extended to Rimmon, which borders on Neah. 14 Then the border went around it on the north side of Hannathon, and it ended in the Valley of Jiphthah El. 15 Included were Kattath, Nahallal, Shimron, Idalah, and Bethlehem: twelve cities with their villages. 16 This was the inheritance of the children of Zebulun according to their families, these cities with their villages.

17 The fourth lot came out to Issachar, for the children of Issachar according to their families. 18 And their territory went to Jezreel, and included Chesulloth, Shunem, 19 Haphraim, Shion, Anaharath, 20 Rabbith, Kishion, Abez, 21 Remeth, En Gannim, En Haddah, and Beth Pazzez. 22 And the border reached to Tabor, Shahazimah, and Beth Shemesh; their border ended at the Jordan: sixteen cities with their villages. 23 This was the inheritance of the tribe of the children of Issachar according to their families, the cities and their villages.

24 The fifth lot came out for the tribe of the children of Asher according to their families. 25 And their territory included Helkath, Hali, Beten, Achshaph, 26 Alammelech, Amad, and Mishal; it reached to Mount Carmel westward, along the Brook Shihor Libnath. 27 It turned toward the sunrise to Beth Dagon; and it reached to Zebulun and to the Valley of Jiphthah El, then northward beyond Beth Emek and Neiel, bypassing Cabul which was on the left, 28 including Ebron,ᵃ Rehob, Hammon, and Kanah, as far as Greater Sidon. 29 And the border turned to Ramah and to the fortified city of Tyre; then the border turned to Hosah, and ended at the sea by the region of Achzib. 30 Also Ummah, Aphek, and Rehob were included: twenty-two cities with their villages. 31 This was the inheritance of the tribe of the children of Asher according to their families, these cities with their villages.

32 The sixth lot came out to the children of Naphtali, for the children of Naphtali according to their families. 33 And their border began at Heleph, enclosing the territory from the terebinth tree in Zaanannim, Adami Nekeb, and Jabneel, as far as Lakkum; it ended at the Jordan. 34 From Heleph the border extended westward to Aznoth Tabor, and went out from there toward Hukkok; it adjoined Zebulun on the south side and Asher on the west side, and ended at Judah by the Jordan toward the sunrise. 35 And the fortified cities are Ziddim, Zer, Hammath, Rakkath, Chinnereth, 36 Adamah, Ramah, Hazor, 37 Kedesh, Edrei, En Hazor, 38 Iron, Migdal El, Horem, Beth Anath, and Beth Shemesh: nineteen cities with their villages. 39 This was

19:28 ᵃFollowing Masoretic Text, Targum, and Vulgate; a few Hebrew manuscripts read Abdon (compare 21:30 and 1 Chronicles 6:74).

Gospel Pearls

the inheritance of the tribe of the children of Naphtali according to their families, the cities and their villages.

40 The seventh lot came out for the tribe of the children of Dan according to their families. 41 And the territory of their inheritance was Zorah, Eshtaol, Ir Shemesh, 42 Shaalabbin, Aijalon, Jethlah, 43 Elon, Timnah, Ekron, 44 Eltekeh, Gibbethon, Baalath, 45 Jehud, Bene Berak, Gath Rimmon, 46 Me Jarkon, and Rakkon, with the region near Joppa. 47 And the border of the children of Dan went beyond these, because the children of Dan went up to fight against Leshem and took it; and they struck it with the edge of the sword, took possession of it, and dwelt in it. They called Leshem, Dan, after the name of Dan their father. 48 This *is* the inheritance of the tribe of the children of Dan according to their families, these cities with their villages.

49 When they had made an end of dividing the land as an inheritance according to their borders, the children of Israel gave an inheritance among them to Joshua the son of Nun. 50 According to the word of the LORD they gave him the city which he asked for, Timnath Serah in the mountains of Ephraim; and he built the city and dwelt in it.

51 These *were* the inheritances which Eleazar the priest, Joshua the son of Nun, and the heads of the fathers of the tribes of the children of Israel divided as an inheritance by lot in Shiloh before the LORD, at the door of the tabernacle of meeting. So they made an end of dividing the country.

20 The LORD also spoke to Joshua, saying, 2 "Speak to the children of Israel, saying: 'Appoint for yourselves cities of refuge, of which I spoke to you through Moses, 3 that the slayer who kills a person accidentally *or* unintentionally may flee there; and they shall be your refuge from the avenger of blood. 4 And when he flees to one of those cities, and stands at the entrance of the gate of the city, and declares his case in the hearing of the elders of that city, they shall take him into the city as one of them, and give him a place, that he may dwell among them. 5 Then if the avenger of blood

pursues him, they shall not deliver the slayer into his hand, because he struck his neighbor unintentionally, but did not hate him beforehand. 6 And he shall dwell in that city until he stands before the congregation for judgment, *and* until the death of the one who is high priest in those days. Then the slayer may return and come to his own city and his own house, to the city from which he fled.' "

7 So they appointed Kedesh in Galilee, in the mountains of Naphtali, Shechem in the mountains of Ephraim, and Kirjath Arba (which *is* Hebron) in the mountains of Judah. 8 And on the other side of the Jordan, by Jericho eastward, they assigned Bezer in the wilderness on the plain, from the tribe of Reuben, Ramoth in Gilead, from the tribe of Gad, and Golan in Bashan, from the tribe of Manasseh. 9 These were the cities appointed for all the children of Israel and for the stranger who dwelt among them, that whoever killed a person accidentally might flee there, and not die by the hand of the avenger of blood until he stood before the congregation.

21 Then the heads of the fathers' *houses* of the Levites came near to Eleazar the priest, to Joshua the son of Nun, and to the heads of the fathers' *houses* of the tribes of the children of Israel. 2 And they spoke to them at Shiloh in the land of Canaan, saying, "The LORD commanded through Moses to give us cities to dwell in, with their common-lands for our livestock." 3 So the children of Israel gave to the Levites from their inheritance, at the commandment of the LORD, these cities and their common-lands:

4 Now the lot came out for the families of the Kohathites. And the children of Aaron the priest, *who were* of the Levites, had thirteen cities by lot from the tribe of Judah, from the tribe of Simeon, and from the tribe of Benjamin. 5 The rest of the children of Kohath had ten cities by lot from the families of the tribe of Ephraim, from the tribe of Dan, and from the half-tribe of Manasseh.

6 And the children of Gershon had thirteen cities by lot from the families of the tribe of Issachar, from the tribe of Asher, from the tribe of Naphtali,

and from the half-tribe of Manasseh in Bashan.

7 The children of Merari according to their families had twelve cities from the tribe of Reuben, from the tribe of Gad, and from the tribe of Zebulun.

8 And the children of Israel gave these cities with their common-lands by lot to the Levites, as the LORD had commanded by the hand of Moses.

9 So they gave from the tribe of the children of Judah and from the tribe of the children of Simeon these cities which are designated by name, 10 which were for the children of Aaron, one of the families of the Kohathites, *who were* of the children of Levi; for the lot was theirs first. 11 And they gave them Kirjath Arba (*Arba was* the father of Anak), which *is* Hebron, in the mountains of Judah, with the common-land surrounding it. 12 But the fields of the city and its villages they gave to Caleb the son of Jephunneh as his possession.

13 Thus to the children of Aaron the priest they gave Hebron with its common-land (a city of refuge for the slayer), Libnah with its common-land, 14 Jattir with its common-land, Eshtemoa with its common-land, 15 Holon with its common-land, Debir with its common-land, 16 Ain with its common-land, Juttah with its common-land, and Beth Shemesh with its common-land: nine cities from those two tribes; 17 and from the tribe of Benjamin, Gibeon with its common-land, Geba with its common-land, 18 Anathoth with its common-land, and Almon with its common-land: four cities. 19 All the cities of the children of Aaron, the priests, *were* thirteen cities with their common-lands.

20 And the families of the children of Kohath, the Levites, the rest of the children of Kohath, even they had the cities of their lot from the tribe of Ephraim. 21 For they gave them Shechem with its common-land in the mountains of Ephraim (a city of refuge for the slayer), Gezer with its common-land, 22 Kibzaim with its common-land, and Beth Horon with its common-land: four cities; 23 and from the tribe of Dan, Eltekeh with its common-land, Gibbethon

with its common-land, 24 Aijalon with its common-land, *and* Gath Rimmon with its common-land: four cities; 25 and from the half-tribe of Manasseh, Tanach with its common-land and Gath Rimmon with its common-land: two cities. 26 All the ten cities with their common-lands were for the rest of the families of the children of Kohath.

27 Also to the children of Gershon, of the families of the Levites, from the *other* half-tribe of Manasseh, *they gave* Golan in Bashan with its common-land (a city of refuge for the slayer), and Be Eshterah with its common-land: two cities; 28 and from the tribe of Issachar, Kishion with its common-land, Daberath with its common-land, 29 Jarmuth with its common-land, *and* En Gannim with its common-land: four cities; 30 and from the tribe of Asher, Mishal with its common-land, Abdon with its common-land, 31 Helkath with its common-land, and Rehob with its common-land: four cities; 32 and from the tribe of Naphtali, Kedesh in Galilee with its common-land (a city of refuge for the slayer), Hammoth Dor with its common-land, and Kartan with its common-land: three cities. 33 All the cities of the Gershonites according to their families *were* thirteen cities with their common-lands.

34 And to the families of the children of Merari, the rest of the Levites, from the tribe of Zebulun, Jokneam with its common-land, Kartah with its common-land, 35 Dimnah with its common-land, *and* Nahalal with its common-land: four cities; 36 and from the tribe of Reuben, Bezer with its common-land, Jahaz with its common-land, 37 Kedemoth with its common-land, and Mephaath with its common-land: four cities;[a] 38 and from the tribe of Gad, Ramoth in Gilead with its common-land (a city of refuge for the slayer), Mahanaim with its common-land, 39 Heshbon with its common-land, *and* Jazer with its common-land: four cities in all. 40 So all the cities for the children of Merari according to their families, the rest of the families of the Levites, were *by* their lot twelve cities.

41 All the cities of the Levites

21:37 [a]Following Septuagint and Vulgate (compare 1 Chronicles 6:78, 79); Masoretic Text, Bomberg, and Targum omit verses 36 and 37.

Gospel Pearls

within the possession of the children of Israel *were* forty-eight cities with their common-lands. 42 Every one of these cities had its common-land surrounding it; thus *were* all these cities.

43 So the LORD gave to Israel all the land of which He had sworn to give to their fathers, and they took possession of it and dwelt in it. 44 The LORD gave them rest all around, according to all that He had sworn to their fathers. And not a man of all their enemies stood against them; the LORD delivered all their enemies into their hand. 45 Not a word failed of any good thing which the LORD had spoken to the house of Israel. All came to pass.

22 Then Joshua called the Reubenites, the Gadites, and half the tribe of Manasseh, 2 and said to them: "You have kept all that Moses the servant of the LORD commanded you, and have obeyed my voice in all that I commanded you. 3 You have not left your brethren these many days, up to this day, but have kept the charge of the commandment of the LORD your God. 4 And now the LORD your God has given rest to your brethren, as He promised them; now therefore, return and go to your tents *and* to the land of your possession, which Moses the servant of the LORD gave you on the other side of the Jordan. 5 But take careful heed to do the commandment and the law which Moses the servant of the LORD commanded you, to love the LORD your God, to walk in all His ways, to keep His commandments, to hold fast to Him, and to serve Him with all your heart and with all your soul." 6 So Joshua blessed them and sent them away, and they went to their tents.

7 Now to half the tribe of Manasseh Moses had given a possession in Bashan, but to the *other* half of it Joshua gave *a possession* among their brethren on this side of the Jordan, westward. And indeed, when Joshua sent them away to their tents, he blessed them, 8 and spoke to them, saying, "Return with much riches to your tents, with very much livestock, with silver, with gold, with bronze, with iron, and with very much cloth-

ing. Divide the spoil of your enemies with your brethren."

9 So the children of Reuben, the children of Gad, and half the tribe of Manasseh returned, and departed from the children of Israel at Shiloh, which *is* in the land of Canaan, to go to the country of Gilead, to the land of their possession, which they had obtained according to the word of the LORD by the hand of Moses.

10 And when they came to the region of the Jordan which *is* in the land of Canaan, the children of Reuben, the children of Gad, and half the tribe of Manasseh built an altar there by the Jordan—a great, impressive altar. 11 Now the children of Israel heard *someone* say, "Behold, the children of Reuben, the children of Gad, and half the tribe of Manasseh have built an altar on the frontier of the land of Canaan, in the region of the Jordan—on the children of Israel's side." 12 And when the children of Israel heard *of it,* the whole congregation of the children of Israel gathered together at Shiloh to go to war against them.

13 Then the children of Israel sent Phinehas the son of Eleazar the priest to the children of Reuben, to the children of Gad, and to half the tribe of Manasseh, into the land of Gilead, 14 and with him ten rulers, one ruler each from the chief house of every tribe of Israel; and each one *was* the head of the house of his father among the divisions[a] of Israel. 15 Then they came to the children of Reuben, to the children of Gad, and to half the tribe of Manasseh, to the land of Gilead, and they spoke with them, saying, 16 "Thus says the whole congregation of the LORD: 'What treachery *is* this that you have committed against the God of Israel, to turn away this day from following the LORD, in that you have built for yourselves an altar, that you might rebel this day against the LORD? 17 *Is* the iniquity of Peor not enough for us, from which we are not cleansed till this day, although there was a plague in the congregation of the LORD, 18 but that you must turn away this day from following the LORD? And it shall be, if you rebel today against the LORD, that tomorrow He will be angry with the

22:14 ªLiterally *thousands*

*D*o not allow peer pressure to force you into a role that makes you uncomfortable. Our right, as God's children, is to press toward goals and promises that are as unique and diverse as we ourselves.

whole congregation of Israel. 19 Nevertheless, if the land of your possession *is* unclean, *then* cross over to the land of the possession of the LORD, where the LORD's tabernacle stands, and take possession among us; but do not rebel against the LORD, nor rebel against us, by building yourselves an altar besides the altar of the LORD our God. 20 Did not Achan the son of Zerah commit a trespass in the accursed thing, and wrath fell on all the congregation of Israel? And that man did not perish alone in his iniquity.' "

21 Then the children of Reuben, the children of Gad, and half the tribe of Manasseh answered and said to the heads of the divisions*a* of Israel: 22 "The LORD God of gods, the LORD God of gods, He knows, and let Israel itself know—if *it is* in rebellion, or if in treachery against the LORD, do not save us this day. 23 If we have built ourselves an altar to turn from following the LORD, or if to offer on it burnt offerings or grain offerings, or if to offer peace offerings on it, let the LORD Himself require *an account*. 24 But in fact we have done it for fear, for a reason, saying, 'In time to come your descendants may speak to our descendants, saying, "What have you to do with the LORD God of Israel? 25 For the LORD has made the Jordan a border between you and us, *you* children of Reuben and children of Gad. You have no part in the LORD." So your descendants would make our descendants cease fearing the LORD.' 26 Therefore we said, 'Let us now prepare to build ourselves an altar, not for burnt offering nor for sacrifice, 27 but *that* it *may be* a witness between you and us and our generations after us, that we may perform the service of the LORD before Him with our burnt offerings, with our sacrifices, and with our peace offerings; that your descendants may not say to our descendants in time to come, "You have no part in the LORD." ' 28 Therefore we said that it will be, when they say *this* to us or to our generations in time to come, that we may say, 'Here is the replica of the altar of the LORD which our fathers made, though not for burnt offerings nor for sacrifices; but

it is a witness between you and us.' 29 Far be it from us that we should rebel against the LORD, and turn from following the LORD this day, to build an altar for burnt offerings, for grain offerings, or for sacrifices, besides the altar of the LORD our God which *is* before His tabernacle."

30 Now when Phinehas the priest and the rulers of the congregation, the heads of the divisions*a* of Israel who *were* with him, heard the words that the children of Reuben, the children of Gad, and the children of Manasseh spoke, it pleased them. 31 Then Phinehas the son of Eleazar the priest said to the children of Reuben, the children of Gad, and the children of Manasseh, "This day we perceive that the LORD *is* among us, because you have not committed this treachery against the LORD. Now you have delivered the children of Israel out of the hand of the LORD."

32 And Phinehas the son of Eleazar the priest, and the rulers, returned from the children of Reuben and the children of Gad, from the land of Gilead to the land of Canaan, to the children of Israel, and brought back word to them. 33 So the thing pleased the children of Israel, and the children of Israel blessed God; they spoke no more of going against them in battle, to destroy the land where the children of Reuben and Gad dwelt. 34 The children of Reuben and the children of Gad*a* called the altar, *Witness*, "For *it is* a witness between us that the LORD *is* God."

23 Now it came to pass, a long time after the LORD had given rest to Israel from all their enemies round about, that Joshua was old, advanced in age. 2 And Joshua called for all Israel, for their elders, for their heads, for their judges, and for their officers, and said to them:

"I am old, advanced in age. 3 You have seen all that the LORD your God has done to all these nations because of you, for the LORD your God *is* He who has fought for you. 4 See, I have divided to you by lot these nations that remain, to be an inheritance for your tribes, from the Jordan, with all the nations that

---

22:21 *a*Literally *thousands*   22:30 *a*Literally *thousands*   22:34 *a*Septuagint adds *and half the tribe of Manasseh*

Gospel Pearls

I have cut off, as far as the Great Sea westward. 5 And the LORD your God will expel them from before you and drive them out of your sight. So you shall possess their land, as the LORD your God promised you. 6 Therefore be very courageous to keep and to do all that is written in the Book of the Law of Moses, lest you turn aside from it to the right hand or to the left, 7 *and* lest you go among these nations, these who remain among you. You shall not make mention of the name of their gods, nor cause *anyone* to swear *by them;* you shall not serve them nor bow down to them, 8 but you shall hold fast to the LORD your God, as you have done to this day. 9 For the LORD has driven out from before you great and strong nations; but *as for* you, no one has been able to stand against you to this day. 10 One man of you shall chase a thousand, for the LORD your God *is* He who fights for you, as He promised you. 11 Therefore take careful heed to yourselves, that you love the LORD your God. 12 Or else, if indeed you do go back, and cling to the remnant of these nations—these that remain among you—and make marriages with them, and go in to them and they to you, 13 know for certain that the LORD your God will no longer drive out these nations from before you. But they shall be snares and traps to you, and scourges on your sides and thorns in your eyes, until you perish from this good land which the LORD your God has given you.

14 "Behold, this day I *am* going the way of all the earth. And you know in all your hearts and in all your souls that not one thing has failed of all the good things which the LORD your God spoke concerning you. All have come to pass for you; not one word of them has failed. 15 Therefore it shall come to pass, that as all the good things have come upon you which the LORD your God promised you, so the LORD will bring upon you all harmful things, until He has destroyed you from this good land which the LORD your God has given you. 16 When you have transgressed the covenant of the LORD your God, which He commanded you, and have gone and served other gods, and bowed down to them, then the anger

of the LORD will burn against you, and you shall perish quickly from the good land which He has given you."

24 Then Joshua gathered all the tribes of Israel to Shechem and called for the elders of Israel, for their heads, for their judges, and for their officers; and they presented themselves before God. 2 And Joshua said to all the people, "Thus says the LORD God of Israel: 'Your fathers, *including* Terah, the father of Abraham and the father of Nahor, dwelt on the other side of the River[a] in old times; and they served other gods. 3 Then I took your father Abraham from the other side of the River, led him throughout all the land of Canaan, and multiplied his descendants and gave him Isaac. 4 To Isaac I gave Jacob and Esau. To Esau I gave the mountains of Seir to possess, but Jacob and his children went down to Egypt. 5 Also I sent Moses and Aaron, and I plagued Egypt, according to what I did among them. Afterward I brought you out.

6 'Then I brought your fathers out of Egypt, and you came to the sea; and the Egyptians pursued your fathers with chariots and horsemen to the Red Sea. 7 So they cried out to the LORD; and He put darkness between you and the Egyptians, brought the sea upon them, and covered them. And your eyes saw what I did in Egypt. Then you dwelt in the wilderness a long time. 8 And I brought you into the land of the Amorites, who dwelt on the other side of the Jordan, and they fought with you. But I gave them into your hand, that you might possess their land, and I destroyed them from before you. 9 Then Balak the son of Zippor, king of Moab, arose to make war against Israel, and sent and called Balaam the son of Beor to curse you. 10 But I would not listen to Balaam; therefore he continued to bless you. So I delivered you out of his hand. 11 Then you went over the Jordan and came to Jericho. And the men of Jericho fought against you—*also* the Amorites, the Perizzites, the Canaanites, the Hittites, the Girgashites, the Hivites, and the Jebusites. But I delivered them into your hand. 12 I sent the hornet before you which

24:2 [a]Hebrew *Nahar,* the Euphrates, and so in verses 3, 14, and 15

The very fact that God has endowed you with ability is, after all, indicative of the truth that He has a purpose for you. If He gave you the gifting, you will have to give an account of what you did with what He gave you.

drove them out from before you, *also* the two kings of the Amorites, *but* not with your sword or with your bow. 13 I have given you a land for which you did not labor, and cities which you did not build, and you dwell in them; you eat of the vineyards and olive groves which you did not plant.'

14 "Now therefore, fear the LORD, serve Him in sincerity and in truth, and put away the gods which your fathers served on the other side of the River and in Egypt. Serve the LORD! 15 And if it seems evil to you to serve the LORD, choose for yourselves this day whom you will serve, whether the gods which your fathers served that *were* on the other side of the River, or the gods of the Amorites, in whose land you dwell. But as for me and my house, we will serve the LORD."

16 So the people answered and said: "Far be it from us that we should forsake the LORD to serve other gods; 17 for the LORD our God *is* He who brought us and our fathers up out of the land of Egypt, from the house of bondage, who did those great signs in our sight, and preserved us in all the way that we went and among all the people through whom we passed. 18 And the LORD drove out from before us all the people, including the Amorites who dwelt in the land. We also will serve the LORD, for He *is* our God."

19 But Joshua said to the people, "You cannot serve the LORD, for He *is* a holy God. He *is* a jealous God; He will not forgive your transgressions nor your sins. 20 If you forsake the LORD and serve foreign gods, then He will turn and do you harm and consume you, after He has done you good."

21 And the people said to Joshua, "No, but we will serve the LORD!"

22 So Joshua said to the people, "You *are* witnesses against yourselves that you have chosen the LORD for yourselves, to serve Him." And they said, "*We are* witnesses!"

23 "Now therefore," *he said,* "put away the foreign gods which *are* among you, and incline your heart to the LORD God of Israel."

24 And the people said to Joshua, "The LORD our God we will serve, and His voice we will obey!"

25 So Joshua made a covenant with the people that day, and made for them a statute and an ordinance in Shechem.

26 Then Joshua wrote these words in the Book of the Law of God. And he took a large stone, and set it up there under the oak that *was* by the sanctuary of the LORD. 27 And Joshua said to all the people, "Behold, this stone shall be a witness to us, for it has heard all the words of the LORD which He spoke to us. It shall therefore be a witness to you, lest you deny your God." 28 So Joshua let the people depart, each to his own inheritance.

29 Now it came to pass after these things that Joshua the son of Nun, the servant of the LORD, died, *being* one hundred and ten years old. 30 And they buried him within the border of his inheritance at Timnath Serah, which *is* in the mountains of Ephraim, on the north side of Mount Gaash.

31 Israel served the LORD all the days of Joshua, and all the days of the elders who outlived Joshua, who had known all the works of the LORD which He had done for Israel.

32 The bones of Joseph, which the children of Israel had brought up out of Egypt, they buried at Shechem, in the plot of ground which Jacob had bought from the sons of Hamor the father of Shechem for one hundred pieces of silver, and which had become an inheritance of the children of Joseph.

33 And Eleazar the son of Aaron died. They buried him in a hill *belonging to* Phinehas his son, which was given to him in the mountains of Ephraim.

Gospel Pearls

1 Now after the death of Joshua it came to pass that the children of Israel asked the LORD, saying, "Who shall be first to go up for us against the Canaanites to fight against them?"

2 And the LORD said, "Judah shall go up. Indeed I have delivered the land into his hand."

3 So Judah said to Simeon his brother, "Come up with me to my allotted territory, that we may fight against the Canaanites; and I will likewise go with you to your allotted territory." And Simeon went with him. 4 Then Judah went up, and the LORD delivered the Canaanites and the Perizzites into their hand; and they killed ten thousand men at Bezek. 5 And they found Adoni-Bezek in Bezek, and fought against him; and they defeated the Canaanites and the Perizzites. 6 Then Adoni-Bezek fled, and they pursued him and caught him and cut off his thumbs and big toes. 7 And Adoni-Bezek said, "Seventy kings with their thumbs and big toes cut off used to gather *scraps* under my table; as I have done, so God has repaid me." Then they brought him to Jerusalem, and there he died.

8 Now the children of Judah fought against Jerusalem and took it; they struck it with the edge of the sword and set the city on fire. 9 And afterward the children of Judah went down to fight against the Canaanites who dwelt in the mountains, in the South,*a* and in the lowland. 10 Then Judah went against the Canaanites who dwelt in Hebron. (Now the name of Hebron *was* formerly Kirjath Arba.) And they killed Sheshai, Ahiman, and Talmai.

11 From there they went against the inhabitants of Debir. (The name of Debir *was* formerly Kirjath Sepher.) 12 Then Caleb said, "Whoever attacks Kirjath Sepher and takes it, to him I will give my daughter Achsah as wife." 13 And Othniel the son of Kenaz, Caleb's younger brother, took it; so he gave him his daughter Achsah as wife. 14 Now it happened, when she came *to him,* that she urged him*a* to ask her father for a field. And she dismounted from *her* donkey, and Caleb said to her, "What do you wish?" 15 So she said to him, "Give me a blessing; since you have given me land in the South, give me also springs of water."

And Caleb gave her the upper springs and the lower springs.

16 Now the children of the Kenite, Moses' father-in-law, went up from the City of Palms with the children of Judah into the Wilderness of Judah, which *lies* in the South *near* Arad; and they went and dwelt among the people. 17 And Judah went with his brother Simeon, and they attacked the Canaanites who inhabited Zephath, and utterly destroyed it. So the name of the city was called Hormah. 18 Also Judah took Gaza with its territory, Ashkelon with its territory, and Ekron with its territory. 19 So the LORD was with Judah. And they drove out the mountaineers, but they could not drive out the inhabitants of the lowland, because they had chariots of iron. 20 And they gave Hebron to Caleb, as Moses had said. Then he expelled from there the three sons of Anak. 21 But the children of Benjamin did not drive out the Jebusites who inhabited Jerusalem; so the Jebusites dwell with the children of Benjamin in Jerusalem to this day.

22 And the house of Joseph also went up against Bethel, and the LORD *was* with them. 23 So the house of Joseph sent men to spy out Bethel. (The name of the city *was* formerly Luz.) 24 And when the spies saw a man coming out of the city, they said to him, "Please show us the entrance to the city, and we will show you mercy." 25 So he showed them the entrance to the city, and they struck the city with the edge of the sword; but they let the man and all his family go. 26 And the man went to the land of the Hittites, built a city, and called its name Luz, which *is* its name to this day.

27 However, Manasseh did not drive out *the inhabitants of* Beth Shean and its villages, or Taanach

---

1:9 *a*Hebrew *Negev,* and so throughout this book   1:14 *a*Septuagint and Vulgate read *he urged her.*

I believe that every day is a gift from God. What you do with that day or talent is, in fact, your gift to Him. You are only limited by your own mind's creativity and concentration.

and its villages, or the inhabitants of Dor and its villages, or the inhabitants of Ibleam and its villages, or the inhabitants of Megiddo and its villages; for the Canaanites were determined to dwell in that land. 28 And it came to pass, when Israel was strong, that they put the Canaanites under tribute, but did not completely drive them out.

29 Nor did Ephraim drive out the Canaanites who dwelt in Gezer; so the Canaanites dwelt in Gezer among them.

30 Nor did Zebulun drive out the inhabitants of Kitron or the inhabitants of Nahalol; so the Canaanites dwelt among them, and were put under tribute.

31 Nor did Asher drive out the inhabitants of Acco or the inhabitants of Sidon, or of Ahlab, Achzib, Helbah, Aphik, or Rehob. 32 So the Asherites dwelt among the Canaanites, the inhabitants of the land; for they did not drive them out.

33 Nor did Naphtali drive out the inhabitants of Beth Shemesh or the inhabitants of Beth Anath; but they dwelt among the Canaanites, the inhabitants of the land. Nevertheless the inhabitants of Beth Shemesh and Beth Anath were put under tribute to them.

34 And the Amorites forced the children of Dan into the mountains, for they would not allow them to come down to the valley; 35 and the Amorites were determined to dwell in Mount Heres, in Aijalon, and in Shaalbim;*a* yet when the strength of the house of Joseph became greater, they were put under tribute.

36 Now the boundary of the Amorites *was* from the Ascent of Akrabbim, from Sela, and upward.

2 Then the Angel of the LORD came up from Gilgal to Bochim, and said: "I led you up from Egypt and brought you to the land of which I swore to your fathers; and I said, 'I will never break My covenant with you. 2 And you shall make no covenant with the inhabitants of this land; you shall tear down their altars.' But you have not obeyed My voice. Why have you done this? 3 Therefore I also said, 'I will not drive them out

before you; but they shall be *thorns* in your side,*a* and their gods shall be a snare to you.' " 4 So it was, when the Angel of the LORD spoke these words to all the children of Israel, that the people lifted up their voices and wept.

5 Then they called the name of that place Bochim;*a* and they sacrificed there to the LORD. 6 And when Joshua had dismissed the people, the children of Israel went each to his own inheritance to possess the land.

7 So the people served the LORD all the days of Joshua, and all the days of the elders who outlived Joshua, who had seen all the great works of the LORD which He had done for Israel. 8 Now Joshua the son of Nun, the servant of the LORD, died *when he was* one hundred and ten years old. 9 And they buried him within the border of his inheritance at Timnath Heres, in the mountains of Ephraim, on the north side of Mount Gaash. 10 When all that generation had been gathered to their fathers, another generation arose after them who did not know the LORD nor the work which He had done for Israel.

11 Then the children of Israel did evil in the sight of the LORD, and served the Baals; 12 and they forsook the LORD God of their fathers, who had brought them out of the land of Egypt; and they followed other gods from *among* the gods of the people who *were* all around them, and they bowed down to them; and they provoked the LORD to anger. 13 They forsook the LORD and served Baal and the Ashtoreths.*a* 14 And the anger of the LORD was hot against Israel. So He delivered them into the hands of plunderers who despoiled them; and He sold them into the hands of their enemies all around, so that they could no longer stand before their enemies. 15 Wherever they went out, the hand of the LORD was against them for calamity, as the LORD had said, and as the LORD had sworn to them. And they were greatly distressed.

16 Nevertheless, the LORD raised up judges who delivered them out of the hand of those who plundered them. 17 Yet they would not listen to their judges, but they played the harlot

1:35 *a*Spelled *Shaalabbin* in Joshua 19:42   2:3 *a*Septuagint, Targum, and Vulgate read *enemies to you*.   2:5 *a*Literally *Weeping*   2:13 *a*Canaanite goddesses

Gospel Pearls

with other gods, and bowed down to them. They turned quickly from the way in which their fathers walked, in obeying the commandments of the LORD; they did not do so. 18 And when the LORD raised up judges for them, the LORD was with the judge and delivered them out of the hand of their enemies all the days of the judge; for the LORD was moved to pity by their groaning because of those who oppressed them and harassed them. 19 And it came to pass, when the judge was dead, that they reverted and behaved more corruptly than their fathers, by following other gods, to serve them and bow down to them. They did not cease from their own doings nor from their stubborn way.

20 Then the anger of the LORD was hot against Israel; and He said, "Because this nation has transgressed My covenant which I commanded their fathers, and has not heeded My voice, 21 I also will no longer drive out before them any of the nations which Joshua left when he died, 22 so that through them I may test Israel, whether they will keep the ways of the LORD, to walk in them as their fathers kept *them*, or not." 23 Therefore the LORD left those nations, without driving them out immediately; nor did He deliver them into the hand of Joshua.

3 Now these *are* the nations which the LORD left, that He might test Israel by them, *that is*, all who had not known any of the wars in Canaan 2 (*this was* only so that the generations of the children of Israel might be taught to know war, at least those who had not formerly known it), 3 *namely*, five lords of the Philistines, all the Canaanites, the Sidonians, and the Hivites who dwelt in Mount Lebanon, from Mount Baal Hermon to the entrance of Hamath. 4 And they were *left, that He might* test Israel by them, to know whether they would obey the commandments of the LORD, which He had commanded their fathers by the hand of Moses. 5 Thus the children of Israel dwelt among the Canaanites, the Hittites, the Amorites, the Perizzites, the Hivites, and the Jebusites. 6 And they took their daughters to be their

wives, and gave their daughters to their sons; and they served their gods.

7 So the children of Israel did evil in the sight of the LORD. They forgot the LORD their God, and served the Baals and Asherahs.*ᵃ* 8 Therefore the anger of the LORD was hot against Israel, and He sold them into the hand of Cushan-Rishathaim king of Mesopotamia; and the children of Israel served Cushan-Rishathaim eight years. 9 When the children of Israel cried out to the LORD, the LORD raised up a deliverer for the children of Israel, who delivered them: Othniel the son of Kenaz, Caleb's younger brother. 10 The Spirit of the LORD came upon him, and he judged Israel. He went out to war, and the LORD delivered Cushan-Rishathaim king of Mesopotamia into his hand; and his hand prevailed over Cushan-Rishathaim. 11 So the land had rest for forty years. Then Othniel the son of Kenaz died.

12 And the children of Israel again did evil in the sight of the LORD. So the LORD strengthened Eglon king of Moab against Israel, because they had done evil in the sight of the LORD. 13 Then he gathered to himself the people of Ammon and Amalek, went and defeated Israel, and took possession of the City of Palms. 14 So the children of Israel served Eglon king of Moab eighteen years.

15 But when the children of Israel cried out to the LORD, the LORD raised up a deliverer for them: Ehud the son of Gera, the Benjamite, a left-handed man. By him the children of Israel sent tribute to Eglon king of Moab. 16 Now Ehud made himself a dagger (it was double-edged and a cubit in length) and fastened it under his clothes on his right thigh. 17 So he brought the tribute to Eglon king of Moab. (Now Eglon *was* a very fat man.) 18 And when he had finished presenting the tribute, he sent away the people who had carried the tribute. 19 But he himself turned back from the stone images that *were* at Gilgal, and said, "I have a secret message for you, O king."

He said, "Keep silence!" And all who attended him went out from him.

20 So Ehud came to him (now he

3:7 ᵃName or symbol for Canaanite goddesses

*M*any women have suppressed their God-given ability in order to live up to some negative stereotype. It is that same stereotype God wants them to shatter. You have neglected a right that the Father made great sacrifices to give you!

was sitting upstairs in his cool private chamber). Then Ehud said, "I have a message from God for you." So he arose from *his* seat. 21 Then Ehud reached with his left hand, took the dagger from his right thigh, and thrust it into his belly. 22 Even the hilt went in after the blade, and the fat closed over the blade, for he did not draw the dagger out of his belly; and his entrails came out. 23 Then Ehud went out through the porch and shut the doors of the upper room behind him and locked them.

24 When he had gone out, *Eglon's*ᵃ servants came to look, and *to their* surprise, the doors of the upper room were locked. So they said, "He is probably attending to his needs in the cool chamber." 25 So they waited till they were embarrassed, and still he had not opened the doors of the upper room. Therefore they took the key and opened *them*. And there was their master, fallen dead on the floor.

26 But Ehud had escaped while they delayed, and passed beyond the stone images and escaped to Seirah. 27 And it happened, when he arrived, that he blew the trumpet in the mountains of Ephraim, and the children of Israel went down with him from the mountains; and he led them. 28 Then he said to them, "Follow *me*, for the LORD has delivered your enemies the Moabites into your hand." So they went down after him, seized the fords of the Jordan leading to Moab, and did not allow anyone to cross over. 29 And at that time they killed about ten thousand men of Moab, all stout men of valor; not a man escaped. 30 So Moab was subdued that day under the hand of Israel. And the land had rest for eighty years.

31 After him was Shamgar the son of Anath, who killed six hundred men of the Philistines with an ox goad; and he also delivered Israel.

4 When Ehud was dead, the children of Israel again did evil in the sight of the LORD. 2 So the LORD sold them into the hand of Jabin king of Canaan, who reigned in Hazor. The commander of his army *was* Sisera, who dwelt in Harosheth Hagoyim. 3 And the children of Israel cried out

to the LORD; for Jabin had nine hundred chariots of iron, and for twenty years he had harshly oppressed the children of Israel.

4 Now Deborah, a prophetess, the wife of Lapidoth, was judging Israel at that time. 5 And she would sit under the palm tree of Deborah between Ramah and Bethel in the mountains of Ephraim. And the children of Israel came up to her for judgment. 6 Then she sent and called for Barak the son of Abinoam from Kedesh in Naphtali, and said to him, "Has not the LORD God of Israel commanded, 'Go and deploy *troops* at Mount Tabor; take with you ten thousand men of the sons of Naphtali and of the sons of Zebulun; 7 and against you I will deploy Sisera, the commander of Jabin's army, with his chariots and his multitude at the River Kishon; and I will deliver him into your hand'?"

8 And Barak said to her, "If you will go with me, then I will go; but if you will not go with me, I will not go!"

9 So she said, "I will surely go with you; nevertheless there will be no glory for you in the journey you are taking, for the LORD will sell Sisera into the hand of a woman." Then Deborah arose and went with Barak to Kedesh. 10 And Barak called Zebulun and Naphtali to Kedesh; he went up with ten thousand men under his command,ᵃ and Deborah went up with him.

11 Now Heber the Kenite, of the children of Hobab the father-in-law of Moses, had separated himself from the Kenites and pitched his tent near the terebinth tree at Zaanaim, which *is* beside Kedesh.

12 And they reported to Sisera that Barak the son of Abinoam had gone up to Mount Tabor. 13 So Sisera gathered together all his chariots, nine hundred chariots of iron, and all the people who *were* with him, from Harosheth Hagoyim to the River Kishon.

14 Then Deborah said to Barak, "Up! For this *is* the day in which the LORD has delivered Sisera into your hand. Has not the LORD gone out before you?" So Barak went down from Mount Tabor with ten thousand men following him. 15 And the LORD routed Sisera and all *his* chariots and all *his* army with the edge of the

3:24 ªLiterally *his*   4:10 ªLiterally *at his feet*

---

*M*any of you are dying from apathy and boredom. You have not challenged life, and you are not being challenged by life. Exercise your potential.

Soul Secrets
of a woman
in leadership

*L*ord, it isn't easy to be in the spotlight. It isn't easy to be a lady in leadership. It's often lonely, often scary, often the last place I want to be. So many times I'm tempted to give up. So many times I'm stuck with my nose to the grindstone and my back to the wall. This task is often so far beyond me that there is nothing I can do but throw myself at You.

And yet there's a Deborah anointing upon me. You've called me to a place of responsibility and I want to wield my authority with grace. You've given me a script that only I can act out. Make me strong, O Lord, and give me courage. Send wisdom and revelation and Holy Ghost power. My heart is to lead with Your heart. Lord, give me the love it takes to lead well.

sword before Barak; and Sisera alighted from *his* chariot and fled away on foot. 16 But Barak pursued the chariots and the army as far as Harosheth Hagoyim, and all the army of Sisera fell by the edge of the sword; not a man was left.

17 However, Sisera had fled away on foot to the tent of Jael, the wife of Heber the Kenite; for *there was* peace between Jabin king of Hazor and the house of Heber the Kenite. 18 And Jael went out to meet Sisera, and said to him, "Turn aside, my lord, turn aside to me; do not fear." And when he had turned aside with her into the tent, she covered him with a blanket.

19 Then he said to her, "Please give me a little water to drink, for I am thirsty." So she opened a jug of milk, gave him a drink, and covered him. 20 And he said to her, "Stand at the door of the tent, and if any man comes and inquires of you, and says, 'Is there any man here?' you shall say, 'No.' "

21 Then Jael, Heber's wife, took a tent peg and took a hammer in her hand, and went softly to him and drove the peg into his temple, and it went down into the ground; for he was fast asleep and weary. So he died. 22 And then, as Barak pursued Sisera, Jael came out to meet him, and said to him, "Come, I will show you the man whom you seek." And when he went into her *tent,* there lay Sisera, dead with the peg in his temple.

23 So on that day God subdued Jabin king of Canaan in the presence of the children of Israel. 24 And the hand of the children of Israel grew stronger and stronger against Jabin king of Canaan, until they had destroyed Jabin king of Canaan.

5 Then Deborah and Barak the son of Abinoam sang on that day, saying:

2 "When leaders lead in Israel,
When the people willingly offer themselves,
Bless the Lord!

3 "Hear, O kings! Give ear, O princes!
I, *even* I, will sing to the Lord;
I will sing praise to the Lord God of Israel.

4 "Lord, when You went out from Seir,
When You marched from the field of Edom,
The earth trembled and the heavens poured,
The clouds also poured water;

5 The mountains gushed before the Lord,
This Sinai, before the Lord God of Israel.

6 "In the days of Shamgar, son of Anath,
In the days of Jael,
The highways were deserted,
And the travelers walked along the byways.

7 Village life ceased, it ceased in Israel,
Until I, Deborah, arose,
Arose a mother in Israel.

8 They chose new gods;
Then *there was* war in the gates;
Not a shield or spear was seen among forty thousand in Israel.

9 My heart *is* with the rulers of Israel
Who offered themselves willingly with the people.
Bless the Lord!

10 "Speak, you who ride on white donkeys,
Who sit in judges' attire,
And who walk along the road.

11 Far from the noise of the archers, among the watering places,
There they shall recount the righteous acts of the Lord,
The righteous acts *for* His villagers in Israel;
Then the people of the Lord shall go down to the gates.

12 "Awake, awake, Deborah!
Awake, awake, sing a song!
Arise, Barak, and lead your captives away,
O son of Abinoam!

13 "Then the survivors came down, the people against the nobles;
The Lord came down for me against the mighty.

14 From Ephraim *were* those whose roots were in Amalek.

Gospel Pearls

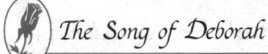

After you, Benjamin, with your
peoples,
From Machir rulers came
down,
And from Zebulun those who
bear the recruiter's staff.
15 And the princes of Issachar*a*
were with Deborah;
As Issachar, so *was* Barak
Sent into the valley under his
command;*b*
Among the divisions of Reuben
There were great resolves of
heart.
16 Why did you sit among the
sheepfolds,
To hear the pipings for the
flocks?
The divisions of Reuben have
great searchings of heart.
17 Gilead stayed beyond the
Jordan,
And why did Dan remain on
ships?*a*
Asher continued at the
seashore,
And stayed by his inlets.
18 Zebulun *is* a people *who*
jeopardized their lives to the
point of death,
Naphtali also, on the heights of
the battlefield.

19 "The kings came *and* fought,
Then the kings of Canaan
fought
In Taanach, by the waters of
Megiddo;
They took no spoils of silver.
20 They fought from the heavens;
The stars from their courses
fought against Sisera.
21 The torrent of Kishon swept
them away,
That ancient torrent, the
torrent of Kishon.
O my soul, march on in
strength!
22 Then the horses' hooves
pounded,
The galloping, galloping of his
steeds.
23 'Curse Meroz,' said the angel*a*
of the LORD,
'Curse its inhabitants bitterly,
Because they did not come to
the help of the LORD,
To the help of the LORD against
the mighty.'

24 "Most blessed among women is
Jael,
The wife of Heber the Kenite;
Blessed is she among women
in tents.
25 He asked for water, she gave
milk;
She brought out cream in a
lordly bowl.
26 She stretched her hand to the
tent peg,
Her right hand to the
workmen's hammer;
She pounded Sisera, she
pierced his head,
She split and struck through
his temple.
27 At her feet he sank, he fell, he
lay still;
At her feet he sank, he fell;
Where he sank, there he fell
dead.

28 "The mother of Sisera looked
through the window,
And cried out through the
lattice,
'Why is his chariot *so* long in
coming?
Why tarries the clatter of his
chariots?'
29 Her wisest ladies answered her,
Yes, she answered herself,
30 'Are they not finding and
dividing the spoil:
To every man a girl *or* two;
For Sisera, plunder of dyed
garments,
Plunder of garments
embroidered and dyed,
Two pieces of dyed embroidery
for the neck of the looter?'

31 "Thus let all Your enemies
perish, O LORD!
But *let* those who love Him *be*
like the sun
When it comes out in full
strength."

So the land had rest for forty years.

6 Then the children of Israel did
evil in the sight of the LORD. So
the LORD delivered them into the
hand of Midian for seven years,
2 and the hand of Midian prevailed

5:15 *a*Following Septuagint, Syriac, Targum, and Vulgate; Masoretic Text reads *And my princes in Issachar.* *b*Literally *at his feet*   5:17 *a*Or *at ease*   5:23 *a*Or *Angel*

*Y*ou need more life in your life. A challenging life can even help keep us from mischief and sin. When we are bored, Satan takes the initiative. You know where that leads.

against Israel. Because of the Midianites, the children of Israel made for themselves the dens, the caves, and the strongholds which *are* in the mountains. 3 So it was, whenever Israel had sown, Midianites would come up; also Amalekites and the people of the East would come up against them. 4 Then they would encamp against them and destroy the produce of the earth as far as Gaza, and leave no sustenance for Israel, neither sheep nor ox nor donkey. 5 For they would come up with their livestock and their tents, coming in as numerous as locusts; both they and their camels were without number; and they would enter the land to destroy it. 6 So Israel was greatly impoverished because of the Midianites, and the children of Israel cried out to the LORD.

7 And it came to pass, when the children of Israel cried out to the LORD because of the Midianites, 8 that the LORD sent a prophet to the children of Israel, who said to them, "Thus says the LORD God of Israel: 'I brought you up from Egypt and brought you out of the house of bondage; 9 and I delivered you out of the hand of the Egyptians and out of the hand of all who oppressed you, and drove them out before you and gave you their land. 10 Also I said to you, "I *am* the LORD your God; do not fear the gods of the Amorites, in whose land you dwell." But you have not obeyed My voice.' "

11 Now the Angel of the LORD came and sat under the terebinth tree which *was* in Ophrah, which *belonged* to Joash the Abiezrite, while his son Gideon threshed wheat in the winepress, in order to hide *it* from the Midianites. 12 And the Angel of the LORD appeared to him, and said to him, "The LORD *is* with you, you mighty man of valor!"

13 Gideon said to Him, "O my lord,*a* if the LORD is with us, why then has all this happened to us? And where *are* all His miracles which our fathers told us about, saying, 'Did not the LORD bring us up from Egypt?' But now the LORD has forsaken us and delivered us into the hands of the Midianites."

14 Then the LORD turned to him and said, "Go in this might of yours, and you shall save Israel from the hand of the Midianites. Have I not sent you?"

15 So he said to Him, "O my Lord,*a* how can I save Israel? Indeed my clan *is* the weakest in Manasseh, and I *am* the least in my father's house."

16 And the LORD said to him, "Surely I will be with you, and you shall defeat the Midianites as one man."

17 Then he said to Him, "If now I have found favor in Your sight, then show me a sign that it is You who talk with me. 18 Do not depart from here, I pray, until I come to You and bring out my offering and set *it* before You."

And He said, "I will wait until you come back."

19 So Gideon went in and prepared a young goat, and unleavened bread from an ephah of flour. The meat he put in a basket, and he put the broth in a pot; and he brought *them* out to Him under the terebinth tree and presented *them*. 20 The Angel of God said to him, "Take the meat and the unleavened bread and lay *them* on this rock, and pour out the broth." And he did so.

21 Then the Angel of the LORD put out the end of the staff that *was* in His hand, and touched the meat and the unleavened bread; and fire rose out of the rock and consumed the meat and the unleavened bread. And the Angel of the LORD departed out of his sight.

22 Now Gideon perceived that He *was* the Angel of the LORD. So Gideon said, "Alas, O Lord GOD! For I have seen the Angel of the LORD face to face."

23 Then the LORD said to him, "Peace *be* with you; do not fear, you shall not die." 24 So Gideon built an altar there to the LORD, and called it The-LORD-Is-Peace.*a* To this day it *is* still in Ophrah of the Abiezrites.

25 Now it came to pass the same night that the LORD said to him, "Take your father's young bull, the second bull of seven years old, and tear down the altar of Baal that your father has, and cut down the wooden image*a* that *is* beside it; 26 and build an altar to the LORD your God on top

6:13 *a*Hebrew *adoni*, used of man   6:15 *a*Hebrew *Adonai*, used of God   6:24 *a*Hebrew *YHWH Shalom*   6:25 *a*Hebrew *Asherah*, a Canaanite goddess

Gospel Pearls

of this rock in the proper arrangement, and take the second bull and offer a burnt sacrifice with the wood of the image which you shall cut down." 27 So Gideon took ten men from among his servants and did as the LORD had said to him. But because he feared his father's household and the men of the city too much to do *it* by day, he did *it* by night.

28 And when the men of the city arose early in the morning, there was the altar of Baal, torn down; and the wooden image that *was* beside it was cut down, and the second bull was being offered on the altar *which had been* built. 29 So they said to one another, "Who has done this thing?" And when they had inquired and asked, they said, "Gideon the son of Joash has done this thing." 30 Then the men of the city said to Joash, "Bring out your son, that he may die, because he has torn down the altar of Baal, and because he has cut down the wooden image that *was* beside it."

31 But Joash said to all who stood against him, "Would you plead for Baal? Would you save him? Let the one who would plead for him be put to death by morning! If he *is* a god, let him plead for himself, because his altar has been torn down!" 32 Therefore on that day he called him Jerubbaal,*a* saying, "Let Baal plead against him, because he has torn down his altar."

33 Then all the Midianites and Amalekites, the people of the East, gathered together; and they crossed over and encamped in the Valley of Jezreel. 34 But the Spirit of the LORD came upon Gideon; then he blew the trumpet, and the Abiezrites gathered behind him. 35 And he sent messengers throughout all Manasseh, who also gathered behind him. He also sent messengers to Asher, Zebulun, and Naphtali; and they came up to meet them.

36 So Gideon said to God, "If You will save Israel by my hand as You have said— 37 look, I shall put a fleece of wool on the threshing floor; if there is dew on the fleece only, and *it is* dry on all the ground, then I shall know that You will save Israel by my hand, as You have said." 38 And it was so. When he rose early the next

morning and squeezed the fleece together, he wrung the dew out of the fleece, a bowlful of water. 39 Then Gideon said to God, "Do not be angry with me, but let me speak just once more: Let me test, I pray, just once more with the fleece; let it now be dry only on the fleece, but on all the ground let there be dew." 40 And God did so that night. It was dry on the fleece only, but there was dew on all the ground.

7 Then Jerubbaal (that *is,* Gideon) and all the people who *were* with him rose early and encamped beside the well of Harod, so that the camp of the Midianites was on the north side of them by the hill of Moreh in the valley.

2 And the LORD said to Gideon, "The people who *are* with you *are* too many for Me to give the Midianites into their hands, lest Israel claim glory for itself against Me, saying, 'My own hand has saved me.' 3 Now therefore, proclaim in the hearing of the people, saying, 'Whoever *is* fearful and afraid, let him turn and depart at once from Mount Gilead.'" And twenty-two thousand of the people returned, and ten thousand remained.

4 But the LORD said to Gideon, "The people *are* still *too* many; bring them down to the water, and I will test them for you there. Then it will be, *that* of whom I say to you, 'This one shall go with you,' the same shall go with you; and of whomever I say to you, 'This one shall not go with you,' the same shall not go." 5 So he brought the people down to the water. And the LORD said to Gideon, "Everyone who laps from the water with his tongue, as a dog laps, you shall set apart by himself; likewise everyone who gets down on his knees to drink." 6 And the number of those who lapped, *putting* their hand to their mouth, was three hundred men; but all the rest of the people got down on their knees to drink water. 7 Then the LORD said to Gideon, "By the three hundred men who lapped I will save you, and deliver the Midianites into your hand. Let all the *other* people go, every man to his place." 8 So the people took provisions and their trumpets in their

6:32 *a*Literally *Let Baal Plead*

*I*t is easier to fight when right is on your side. Always be sure you are right. When right is on your side, then God is on your side. One of the greatest tools you can use in a battle is the blessed assurance that you are right.

hands. And he sent away all *the rest of* Israel, every man to his tent, and retained those three hundred men. Now the camp of Midian was below him in the valley.

9 It happened on the same night that the LORD said to him, "Arise, go down against the camp, for I have delivered it into your hand. 10 But if you are afraid to go down, go down to the camp with Purah your servant, 11 and you shall hear what they say; and afterward your hands shall be strengthened to go down against the camp." Then he went down with Purah his servant to the outpost of the armed men who *were* in the camp. 12 Now the Midianites and Amalekites, all the people of the East, were lying in the valley as numerous as locusts; and their camels *were* without number, as the sand by the seashore in multitude.

13 And when Gideon had come, there was a man telling a dream to his companion. He said, "I have had a dream: *To my* surprise, a loaf of barley bread tumbled into the camp of Midian; it came to a tent and struck it so that it fell and overturned, and the tent collapsed."

14 Then his companion answered and said, "This *is* nothing else but the sword of Gideon the son of Joash, a man of Israel! Into his hand God has delivered Midian and the whole camp."

15 And so it was, when Gideon heard the telling of the dream and its interpretation, that he worshiped. He returned to the camp of Israel, and said, "Arise, for the LORD has delivered the camp of Midian into your hand." 16 Then he divided the three hundred men *into* three companies, and he put a trumpet into every man's hand, with empty pitchers, and torches inside the pitchers. 17 And he said to them, "Look at me and do likewise; watch, and when I come to the edge of the camp you shall do as I do: 18 When I blow the trumpet, I and all who *are* with me, then you also blow the trumpets on every side of the whole camp, and say, 'The sword of the LORD and of Gideon!' "

19 So Gideon and the hundred men who *were* with him came to the outpost of the camp at the beginning of the middle watch, just as they had posted the watch; and they blew the trumpets and broke the pitchers that *were* in their hands. 20 Then the three companies blew the trumpets and broke the pitchers—they held the torches in their left hands and the trumpets in their right hands for blowing—and they cried, "The sword of the LORD and of Gideon!" 21 And every man stood in his place all around the camp; and the whole army ran and cried out and fled. 22 When the three hundred blew trumpets, the LORD set every man's sword against his companion throughout the whole camp; and the army fled to Beth Acacia,*ᵃ* toward Zererah, as far as the border of Abel Meholah, by Tabbath.

23 And the men of Israel gathered together from Naphtali, Asher, and all Manasseh, and pursued the Midianites.

24 Then Gideon sent messengers throughout all the mountains of Ephraim, saying, "Come down against the Midianites, and seize from them the watering places as far as Beth Barah and the Jordan." Then all the men of Ephraim gathered together and seized the watering places as far as Beth Barah and the Jordan. 25 And they captured two princes of the Midianites, Oreb and Zeeb. They killed Oreb at the rock of Oreb, and Zeeb they killed at the winepress of Zeeb. They pursued Midian and brought the heads of Oreb and Zeeb to Gideon on the other side of the Jordan.

8 Now the men of Ephraim said to him, "Why have you done this to us by not calling us when you went to fight with the Midianites?" And they reprimanded him sharply.

2 So he said to them, "What have I done now in comparison with you? *Is* not the gleaning *of the grapes* of Ephraim better than the vintage of Abiezer? 3 God has delivered into your hands the princes of Midian, Oreb and Zeeb. And what was I able to do in comparison with you?" Then their anger toward him subsided when he said that.

4 When Gideon came to the Jordan, he and the three hundred men who *were* with him crossed over, ex-

7:22 ᵃHebrew *Beth Shittah*

Gospel Pearls

hausted but still in pursuit. 5 Then he said to the men of Succoth, "Please give loaves of bread to the people who follow me, for they are exhausted, and I am pursuing Zebah and Zalmunna, kings of Midian."

6 And the leaders of Succoth said, "Are the hands of Zebah and Zalmunna now in your hand, that we should give bread to your army?"

7 So Gideon said, "For this cause, when the LORD has delivered Zebah and Zalmunna into my hand, then I will tear your flesh with the thorns of the wilderness and with briers!" 8 Then he went up from there to Penuel and spoke to them in the same way. And the men of Penuel answered him as the men of Succoth had answered. 9 So he also spoke to the men of Penuel, saying, "When I come back in peace, I will tear down this tower!"

10 Now Zebah and Zalmunna were at Karkor, and their armies with them, about fifteen thousand, all who were left of all the army of the people of the East; for one hundred and twenty thousand men who drew the sword had fallen. 11 Then Gideon went up by the road of those who dwell in tents on the east of Nobah and Jogbehah; and he attacked the army while the camp felt secure. 12 When Zebah and Zalmunna fled, he pursued them; and he took the two kings of Midian, Zebah and Zalmunna, and routed the whole army.

13 Then Gideon the son of Joash returned from battle, from the Ascent of Heres. 14 And he caught a young man of the men of Succoth and interrogated him; and he wrote down for him the leaders of Succoth and its elders, seventy-seven men. 15 Then he came to the men of Succoth and said, "Here are Zebah and Zalmunna, about whom you ridiculed me, saying, 'Are the hands of Zebah and Zalmunna now in your hand, that we should give bread to your weary men?' " 16 And he took the elders of the city, and thorns of the wilderness and briers, and with them he taught the men of Succoth. 17 Then he tore down the tower of Penuel and killed the men of the city.

18 And he said to Zebah and Zalmunna, "What kind of men *were* they whom you killed at Tabor?"

So they answered, "As you *are,* so *were* they; each one resembled the son of a king."

19 Then he said, "They *were* my brothers, the sons of my mother. As the LORD lives, if you had let them live, I would not kill you." 20 And he said to Jether his firstborn, "Rise, kill them!" But the youth would not draw his sword; for he was afraid, because he *was* still a youth.

21 So Zebah and Zalmunna said, "Rise yourself, and kill us; for as a man *is, so is* his strength." So Gideon arose and killed Zebah and Zalmunna, and took the crescent ornaments that *were* on their camels' necks.

22 Then the men of Israel said to Gideon, "Rule over us, both you and your son, and your grandson also; for you have delivered us from the hand of Midian."

23 But Gideon said to them, "I will not rule over you, nor shall my son rule over you; the LORD shall rule over you." 24 Then Gideon said to them, "I would like to make a request of you, that each of you would give me the earrings from his plunder." For they had golden earrings, because they *were* Ishmaelites.

25 So they answered, "We will gladly give *them.*" And they spread out a garment, and each man threw into it the earrings from his plunder. 26 Now the weight of the gold earrings that he requested was one thousand seven hundred *shekels* of gold, besides the crescent ornaments, pendants, and purple robes which *were* on the kings of Midian, and besides the chains that *were* around their camels' necks. 27 Then Gideon made it into an ephod and set it up in his city, Ophrah. And all Israel played the harlot with it there. It became a snare to Gideon and to his house.

28 Thus Midian was subdued before the children of Israel, so that they lifted their heads no more. And the country was quiet for forty years in the days of Gideon.

29 Then Jerubbaal the son of Joash went and dwelt in his own house. 30 Gideon had seventy sons who were his own offspring, for he had many wives. 31 And his concubine who *was* in Shechem also bore him a son, whose name he called Abimelech. 32 Now Gideon the son of Joash died at a good old age, and was bur-

*H*umanism teaches the power of the human spirit. It basically suggests that if you believe anything hard enough, you can make it come to pass. Faith, on the other hand, empowers you to attain what the Father has promised. It hinges on the Father's Word.

ied in the tomb of Joash his father, in Ophrah of the Abiezrites.

33 So it was, as soon as Gideon was dead, that the children of Israel again played the harlot with the Baals, and made Baal-Berith their god. 34 Thus the children of Israel did not remember the LORD their God, who had delivered them from the hands of all their enemies on every side; 35 nor did they show kindness to the house of Jerubbaal (Gideon) in accordance with the good he had done for Israel.

9 Then Abimelech the son of Jerubbaal went to Shechem, to his mother's brothers, and spoke with them and with all the family of the house of his mother's father, saying, 2 "Please speak in the hearing of all the men of Shechem: 'Which is better for you, that all seventy of the sons of Jerubbaal reign over you, or that one reign over you?' Remember that I *am* your own flesh and bone."

3 And his mother's brothers spoke all these words concerning him in the hearing of all the men of Shechem; and their heart was inclined to follow Abimelech, for they said, "He is our brother." 4 So they gave him seventy *shekels* of silver from the temple of Baal-Berith, with which Abimelech hired worthless and reckless men; and they followed him. 5 Then he went to his father's house at Ophrah and killed his brothers, the seventy sons of Jerubbaal, on one stone. But Jotham the youngest son of Jerubbaal was left, because he hid himself. 6 And all the men of Shechem gathered together, all of Beth Millo, and they went and made Abimelech king beside the terebinth tree at the pillar that *was* in Shechem.

7 Now when they told Jotham, he went and stood on top of Mount Gerizim, and lifted his voice and cried out. And he said to them:

"Listen to me, you men of Shechem,
That God may listen to you!

8 "The trees once went forth to anoint a king over them.
And they said to the olive tree, 'Reign over us!'
9 But the olive tree said to them, 'Should I cease giving my oil,

With which they honor God and men,
And go to sway over trees?'

10 "Then the trees said to the fig tree,
'You come *and* reign over us!'
11 But the fig tree said to them, 'Should I cease my sweetness and my good fruit,
And go to sway over trees?'

12 "Then the trees said to the vine, 'You come *and* reign over us!'
13 But the vine said to them, 'Should I cease my new wine,
Which cheers *both* God and men,
And go to sway over trees?'

14 "Then all the trees said to the bramble,
'You come *and* reign over us!'
15 And the bramble said to the trees,
'If in truth you anoint me as king over you,
Then come *and* take shelter in my shade;
But if not, let fire come out of the bramble
And devour the cedars of Lebanon!'

16 "Now therefore, if you have acted in truth and sincerity in making Abimelech king, and if you have dealt well with Jerubbaal and his house, and have done to him as he deserves— 17 for my father fought for you, risked his life, and delivered you out of the hand of Midian; 18 but you have risen up against my father's house this day, and killed his seventy sons on one stone, and made Abimelech, the son of his female servant, king over the men of Shechem, because he is your brother— 19 if then you have acted in truth and sincerity with Jerubbaal and with his house this day, *then* rejoice in Abimelech, and let him also rejoice in you. 20 But if not, let fire come from Abimelech and devour the men of Shechem and Beth Millo; and let fire come from the men of Shechem and from Beth Millo and devour Abimelech!" 21 And Jotham ran away and fled; and he went to Beer and dwelt there, for fear of Abimelech his brother.

22 After Abimelech had reigned over Israel three years, 23 God sent

a spirit of ill will between Abimelech and the men of Shechem; and the men of Shechem dealt treacherously with Abimelech, 24 that the crime *done* to the seventy sons of Jerubbaal might be settled and their blood be laid on Abimelech their brother, who killed them, and on the men of Shechem, who aided him in the killing of his brothers. 25 And the men of Shechem set men in ambush against him on the tops of the mountains, and they robbed all who passed by them along that way; and it was told Abimelech.

26 Now Gaal the son of Ebed came with his brothers and went over to Shechem; and the men of Shechem put their confidence in him. 27 So they went out into the fields, and gathered *grapes* from their vineyards and trod *them*, and made merry. And they went into the house of their god, and ate and drank, and cursed Abimelech. 28 Then Gaal the son of Ebed said, "Who *is* Abimelech, and who *is* Shechem, that we should serve him? *Is he* not the son of Jerubbaal, and *is not* Zebul his officer? Serve the men of Hamor the father of Shechem; but why should we serve him? 29 If only this people were under my authority!*a* I would remove Abimelech." So he*b* said to Abimelech, "Increase your army and come out!"

30 When Zebul, the ruler of the city, heard the words of Gaal the son of Ebed, his anger was aroused. 31 And he sent messengers to Abimelech secretly, saying, "Take note! Gaal the son of Ebed and his brothers have come to Shechem; and here they are, fortifying the city against you. 32 Now therefore, get up by night, you and the people who *are* with you, and lie in wait in the field. 33 And it shall be, as soon as the sun is up in the morning, *that* you shall rise early and rush upon the city; and *when* he and the people who are with him come out against you, you may then do to them as you find opportunity."

34 So Abimelech and all the people who *were* with him rose by night, and lay in wait against Shechem in four companies. 35 When Gaal the son of Ebed went out and stood in the entrance to the city gate, Abimelech and the people who *were* with him rose from lying in wait. 36 And when Gaal saw the people, he said to Zebul, "Look, people are coming down from the tops of the mountains!"

But Zebul said to him, "You see the shadows of the mountains as *if they were* men."

37 So Gaal spoke again and said, "See, people are coming down from the center of the land, and another company is coming from the Diviners'*a* Terebinth Tree."

38 Then Zebul said to him, "Where indeed *is* your mouth now, with which you said, 'Who *is* Abimelech, that we should serve him?' *Are* not these the people whom you despised? Go out, if you will, and fight with them now."

39 So Gaal went out, leading the men of Shechem, and fought with Abimelech. 40 And Abimelech chased him, and he fled from him; and many fell wounded, to the *very* entrance of the gate. 41 Then Abimelech dwelt at Arumah, and Zebul drove out Gaal and his brothers, so that they would not dwell in Shechem.

42 And it came about on the next day that the people went out into the field, and they told Abimelech. 43 So he took his people, divided them into three companies, and lay in wait in the field. And he looked, and there were the people, coming out of the city; and he rose against them and attacked them. 44 Then Abimelech and the company that *was* with him rushed forward and stood at the entrance of the gate of the city; and the *other* two companies rushed upon all who *were* in the fields and killed them. 45 So Abimelech fought against the city all that day; he took the city and killed the people who *were* in it; and he demolished the city and sowed it with salt.

46 Now when all the men of the tower of Shechem had heard *that*, they entered the stronghold of the temple of the god Berith. 47 And it was told Abimelech that all the men of the tower of Shechem were gathered together. 48 Then Abimelech went up to Mount Zalmon, he and all the people who *were* with him.

9:29 *a*Literally *hand*   *b*Following Masoretic Text and Targum; Dead Sea Scrolls read *they;* Septuagint reads *I.*   9:37 *a*Hebrew *Meonenim*

Christian women must avoid taking their cue from their secular sisters who have not allowed their bitter experiences to be healed by the love of our Father, who takes the sting out of life's traumas.

And Abimelech took an ax in his hand and cut down a bough from the trees, and took it and laid *it* on his shoulder; then he said to the people who were with him, "What you have seen me do, make haste *and* do as I *have done.*" 49 So each of the people likewise cut down his own bough and followed Abimelech, put *them* against the stronghold, and set the stronghold on fire above them, so that all the people of the tower of Shechem died, about a thousand men and women.

50 Then Abimelech went to Thebez, and he encamped against Thebez and took it. 51 But there was a strong tower in the city, and all the men and women—all the people of the city— fled there and shut themselves in; then they went up to the top of the tower. 52 So Abimelech came as far as the tower and fought against it; and he drew near the door of the tower to burn it with fire. 53 But a certain woman dropped an upper millstone on Abimelech's head and crushed his skull. 54 Then he called quickly to the young man, his armor- bearer, and said to him, "Draw your sword and kill me, lest men say of me, 'A woman killed him.' " So his young man thrust him through, and he died. 55 And when the men of Is- rael saw that Abimelech was dead, they departed, every man to his place.

56 Thus God repaid the wickedness of Abimelech, which he had done to his father by killing his seventy brothers. 57 And all the evil of the men of Shechem God returned on their own heads, and on them came the curse of Jotham the son of Jerub- baal.

10 After Abimelech there arose to save Israel Tola the son of Puah, the son of Dodo, a man of Is- sachar; and he dwelt in Shamir in the mountains of Ephraim. 2 He judged Israel twenty-three years; and he died and was buried in Shamir.

3 After him arose Jair, a Gileadite; and he judged Israel twenty-two years. 4 Now he had thirty sons who rode on thirty donkeys; they also had thirty towns, which are called "Ha- voth Jair"*ᵃ* to this day, which *are* in

the land of Gilead. 5 And Jair died and was buried in Camon.

6 Then the children of Israel again did evil in the sight of the LORD, and served the Baals and the Ashtoreths, the gods of Syria, the gods of Sidon, the gods of Moab, the gods of the people of Ammon, and the gods of the Philistines; and they forsook the LORD and did not serve Him. 7 So the anger of the LORD was hot against Israel; and He sold them into the hands of the Philistines and into the hands of the people of Ammon. 8 From that year they harassed and oppressed the children of Israel for eighteen years—all the children of Is- rael who *were* on the other side of the Jordan in the land of the Amo- rites, in Gilead. 9 Moreover the peo- ple of Ammon crossed over the Jor- dan to fight against Judah also, against Benjamin, and against the house of Ephraim, so that Israel was severely distressed.

10 And the children of Israel cried out to the LORD, saying, "We have sinned against You, because we have both forsaken our God and served the Baals!"

11 So the LORD said to the children of Israel, "*Did I* not *deliver you* from the Egyptians and from the Amorites and from the people of Ammon and from the Philistines? 12 Also the Si- donians and Amalekites and Maon- ites*ᵃ* oppressed you; and you cried out to Me, and I delivered you from their hand. 13 Yet you have forsaken Me and served other gods. Therefore I will deliver you no more. 14 Go and cry out to the gods which you have chosen; let them deliver you in your time of distress."

15 And the children of Israel said to the LORD, "We have sinned! Do to us whatever seems best to You; only deliver us this day, we pray." 16 So they put away the foreign gods from among them and served the LORD. And His soul could no longer endure the misery of Israel.

17 Then the people of Ammon gath- ered together and encamped in Gilead. And the children of Israel as- sembled together and encamped in Mizpah. 18 And the people, the lead- ers of Gilead, said to one another, "Who *is* the man who will begin the

10:4 ᵃLiterally *Towns of Jair* (compare Numbers 32:41 and Deuteronomy 3:14)   10:12 ᵃSome Septuagint manuscripts read *Midianites.*

Gospel Pearls

fight against the people of Ammon? He shall be head over all the inhabitants of Gilead."

11 Now Jephthah the Gileadite was a mighty man of valor, but he *was* the son of a harlot; and Gilead begot Jephthah. 2 Gilead's wife bore sons; and when his wife's sons grew up, they drove Jephthah out, and said to him, "You shall have no inheritance in our father's house, for you *are* the son of another woman." 3 Then Jephthah fled from his brothers and dwelt in the land of Tob; and worthless men banded together with Jephthah and went out *raiding* with him.

4 It came to pass after a time that the people of Ammon made war against Israel. 5 And so it was, when the people of Ammon made war against Israel, that the elders of Gilead went to get Jephthah from the land of Tob. 6 Then they said to Jephthah, "Come and be our commander, that we may fight against the people of Ammon."

7 So Jephthah said to the elders of Gilead, "Did you not hate me, and expel me from my father's house? Why have you come to me now when you are in distress?"

8 And the elders of Gilead said to Jephthah, "That is why we have turned again to you now, that you may go with us and fight against the people of Ammon, and be our head over all the inhabitants of Gilead."

9 So Jephthah said to the elders of Gilead, "If you take me back home to fight against the people of Ammon, and the Lord delivers them to me, shall I be your head?"

10 And the elders of Gilead said to Jephthah, "The Lord will be a witness between us, if we do not do according to your words." 11 Then Jephthah went with the elders of Gilead, and the people made him head and commander over them; and Jephthah spoke all his words before the Lord in Mizpah.

12 Now Jephthah sent messengers to the king of the people of Ammon, saying, "What do you have against me, that you have come to fight against me in my land?"

13 And the king of the people of Ammon answered the messengers of Jephthah, "Because Israel took away my land when they came up out of Egypt, from the Arnon as far as the Jabbok, and to the Jordan. Now therefore, restore those *lands* peaceably."

14 So Jephthah again sent messengers to the king of the people of Ammon, 15 and said to him, "Thus says Jephthah: 'Israel did not take away the land of Moab, nor the land of the people of Ammon; 16 for when Israel came up from Egypt, they walked through the wilderness as far as the Red Sea and came to Kadesh. 17 Then Israel sent messengers to the king of Edom, saying, "Please let me pass through your land." But the king of Edom would not heed. And in like manner they sent to the king of Moab, but he would not *consent*. So Israel remained in Kadesh. 18 And they went along through the wilderness and bypassed the land of Edom and the land of Moab, came to the east side of the land of Moab, and encamped on the other side of the Arnon. But they did not enter the border of Moab, for the Arnon *was* the border of Moab. 19 Then Israel sent messengers to Sihon king of the Amorites, king of Heshbon; and Israel said to him, "Please let us pass through your land into our place." 20 But Sihon did not trust Israel to pass through his territory. So Sihon gathered all his people together, encamped in Jahaz, and fought against Israel. 21 And the Lord God of Israel delivered Sihon and all his people into the hand of Israel, and they defeated them. Thus Israel gained possession of all the land of the Amorites, who inhabited that country. 22 They took possession of all the territory of the Amorites, from the Arnon to the Jabbok and from the wilderness to the Jordan.

23 'And now the Lord God of Israel has dispossessed the Amorites from before His people Israel; should you then possess it? 24 Will you not possess whatever Chemosh your god gives you to possess? So whatever the Lord our God takes possession of before us, we will possess. 25 And now, *are* you any better than Balak the son of Zippor, king of Moab? Did he ever strive against Israel? Did he ever fight against them? 26 While Israel dwelt in Heshbon and its villages, in Aroer and its villages, and in all the cities along the banks of the Arnon, for three hundred

2 know it is difficult to be ignored and not become disgruntled. But remember that wise women—in fact, wise people—do not allow their emotions to overrule their ultimate goals and purposes.

years, why did you not recover *them* within that time? 27 Therefore I have not sinned against you, but you wronged me by fighting against me. May the LORD, the Judge, render judgment this day between the children of Israel and the people of Ammon.' " 28 However, the king of the people of Ammon did not heed the words which Jephthah sent him.

29 Then the Spirit of the LORD came upon Jephthah, and he passed through Gilead and Manasseh, and passed through Mizpah of Gilead; and from Mizpah of Gilead he advanced *toward* the people of Ammon. 30 And Jephthah made a vow to the LORD, and said, "If You will indeed deliver the people of Ammon into my hands, 31 then it will be that whatever comes out of the doors of my house to meet me, when I return in peace from the people of Ammon, shall surely be the LORD's, and I will offer it up as a burnt offering."

32 So Jephthah advanced toward the people of Ammon to fight against them, and the LORD delivered them into his hands. 33 And he defeated them from Aroer as far as Minnith—twenty cities—and to Abel Kera-mim,*ᵃ* with a very great slaughter. Thus the people of Ammon were subdued before the children of Israel.

34 When Jephthah came to his house at Mizpah, there was his daughter, coming out to meet him with timbrels and dancing; and she *was his* only child. Besides her he had neither son nor daughter. 35 And it came to pass, when he saw her, that he tore his clothes, and said, "Alas, my daughter! You have brought me very low! You are among those who trouble me! For I have given my word to the LORD, and I cannot go back on it."

36 So she said to him, "My father, *if* you have given your word to the LORD, do to me according to what has gone out of your mouth, because the LORD has avenged you of your enemies, the people of Ammon." 37 Then she said to her father, "Let this thing be done for me: let me alone for two months, that I may go and wander on the mountains and bewail my virginity, my friends and I."

38 So he said, "Go." And he sent her away *for* two months; and she went with her friends, and bewailed her virginity on the mountains. 39 And it was so at the end of two months that she returned to her father, and he carried out his vow with her which he had vowed. She knew no man.

And it became a custom in Israel 40 *that* the daughters of Israel went four days each year to lament the daughter of Jephthah the Gileadite.

12 Then the men of Ephraim gathered together, crossed over toward Zaphon, and said to Jephthah, "Why did you cross over to fight against the people of Ammon, and did not call us to go with you? We will burn your house down on you with fire!"

2 And Jephthah said to them, "My people and I were in a great struggle with the people of Ammon; and when I called you, you did not deliver me out of their hands. 3 So when I saw that you would not deliver *me,* I took my life in my hands and crossed over against the people of Ammon; and the LORD delivered them into my hand. Why then have you come up to me this day to fight against me?" 4 Now Jephthah gathered together all the men of Gilead and fought against Ephraim. And the men of Gilead defeated Ephraim, because they said, "You Gileadites *are* fugitives of Ephraim among the Ephraimites *and* among the Manassites." 5 The Gileadites seized the fords of the Jordan before the Ephraimites *arrived.* And when *any* Ephraimite who escaped said, "Let me cross over," the men of Gilead would say to him, "*Are* you an Ephraimite?" If he said, "No," 6 then they would say to him, "Then say, 'Shibboleth'!" And he would say, "Sibboleth," for he could not pronounce *it* right. Then they would take him and kill him at the fords of the Jordan. There fell at that time forty-two thousand Ephraimites.

7 And Jephthah judged Israel six years. Then Jephthah the Gileadite died and was buried among the cities of Gilead.

8 After him, Ibzan of Bethlehem judged Israel. 9 He had thirty sons. And he gave away thirty daughters in marriage, and brought in thirty

11:33 ᵃLiterally *Plain of Vineyards*

Gospel Pearls

daughters from elsewhere for his sons. He judged Israel seven years. 10 Then Ibzan died and was buried at Bethlehem.

11 After him, Elon the Zebulunite judged Israel. He judged Israel ten years. 12 And Elon the Zebulunite died and was buried at Aijalon in the country of Zebulun.

13 After him, Abdon the son of Hillel the Pirathonite judged Israel. 14 He had forty sons and thirty grandsons, who rode on seventy young donkeys. He judged Israel eight years. 15 Then Abdon the son of Hillel the Pirathonite died and was buried in Pirathon in the land of Ephraim, in the mountains of the Amalekites.

13 Again the children of Israel did evil in the sight of the LORD, and the LORD delivered them into the hand of the Philistines for forty years.

2 Now there was a certain man from Zorah, of the family of the Danites, whose name was Manoah; and his wife was barren and had no children. 3 And the Angel of the LORD appeared to the woman and said to her, "Indeed now, you are barren and have borne no children, but you shall conceive and bear a son. 4 Now therefore, please be careful not to drink wine or similar drink, and not to eat anything unclean. 5 For behold, you shall conceive and bear a son. And no razor shall come upon his head, for the child shall be a Nazirite to God from the womb; and he shall begin to deliver Israel out of the hand of the Philistines."

6 So the woman came and told her husband, saying, "A Man of God came to me, and His countenance was like the countenance of the Angel of God, very awesome; but I did not ask Him where He was from, and He did not tell me His name. 7 And He said to me, 'Behold, you shall conceive and bear a son. Now drink no wine or similar drink, nor eat anything unclean, for the child shall be a Nazirite to God from the womb to the day of his death.' "

8 Then Manoah prayed to the LORD, and said, "O my Lord, please let the Man of God whom You sent come to us again and teach us what we shall do for the child who will be born."

9 And God listened to the voice of Manoah, and the Angel of God came to the woman again as she was sitting in the field; but Manoah her husband was not with her. 10 Then the woman ran in haste and told her husband, and said to him, "Look, the Man who came to me the other day has just now appeared to me!"

11 So Manoah arose and followed his wife. When he came to the Man, he said to Him, "Are You the Man who spoke to this woman?"

And He said, "I am."

12 Manoah said, "Now let Your words come to pass! What will be the boy's rule of life, and his work?"

13 So the Angel of the LORD said to Manoah, "Of all that I said to the woman let her be careful. 14 She may not eat anything that comes from the vine, nor may she drink wine or similar drink, nor eat anything unclean. All that I commanded her let her observe."

15 Then Manoah said to the Angel of the LORD, "Please let us detain You, and we will prepare a young goat for You."

16 And the Angel of the LORD said to Manoah, "Though you detain Me, I will not eat your food. But if you offer a burnt offering, you must offer it to the LORD." (For Manoah did not know He was the Angel of the LORD.)

17 Then Manoah said to the Angel of the LORD, "What is Your name, that when Your words come to pass we may honor You?"

18 And the Angel of the LORD said to him, "Why do you ask My name, seeing it is wonderful?"

19 So Manoah took the young goat with the grain offering, and offered it upon the rock to the LORD. And He did a wondrous thing while Manoah and his wife looked on— 20 it happened as the flame went up toward heaven from the altar—the Angel of the LORD ascended in the flame of the altar! When Manoah and his wife saw this, they fell on their faces to the ground. 21 When the Angel of the LORD appeared no more to Manoah and his wife, then Manoah knew that He was the Angel of the LORD.

22 And Manoah said to his wife, "We shall surely die, because we have seen God!"

23 But his wife said to him, "If the LORD had desired to kill us, He would not have accepted a burnt offering

I sense these days as a time when God wants to literally pour out blessings, not just to His sons, but also to His daughters. I want you to start expecting a deluge, an outpouring. I don't mean just wait on it. No, prepare for it and expect it.

and a grain offering from our hands, nor would He have shown us all these *things,* nor would He have told us *such things* as these at this time."

24 So the woman bore a son and called his name Samson; and the child grew, and the LORD blessed him. 25 And the Spirit of the LORD began to move upon him at Mahaneh Dan[a] between Zorah and Eshtaol.

14 Now Samson went down to Timnah, and saw a woman in Timnah of the daughters of the Philistines. 2 So he went up and told his father and mother, saying, "I have seen a woman in Timnah of the daughters of the Philistines; now therefore, get her for me as a wife."

3 Then his father and mother said to him, "*Is there* no woman among the daughters of your brethren, or among all my people, that you must go and get a wife from the uncircumcised Philistines?"

And Samson said to his father, "Get her for me, for she pleases me well."

4 But his father and mother did not know that it was of the LORD—that He was seeking an occasion to move against the Philistines. For at that time the Philistines had dominion over Israel.

5 So Samson went down to Timnah with his father and mother, and came to the vineyards of Timnah.

Now *to his* surprise, a young lion *came* roaring against him. 6 And the Spirit of the LORD came mightily upon him, and he tore the lion apart as one would have torn apart a young goat, though *he had* nothing in his hand. But he did not tell his father or his mother what he had done.

7 Then he went down and talked with the woman; and she pleased Samson well. 8 After some time, when he returned to get her, he turned aside to see the carcass of the lion. And behold, a swarm of bees and honey *were* in the carcass of the lion. 9 He took some of it in his hands and went along, eating. When he came to his father and mother, he gave *some* to them, and they also ate. But he did not tell them that he had

taken the honey out of the carcass of the lion.

10 So his father went down to the woman. And Samson gave a feast there, for young men used to do so. 11 And it happened, when they saw him, that they brought thirty companions to be with him.

12 Then Samson said to them, "Let me pose a riddle to you. If you can correctly solve and explain it to me within the seven days of the feast, then I will give you thirty linen garments and thirty changes of clothing. 13 But if you cannot explain *it* to me, then you shall give me thirty linen garments and thirty changes of clothing."

And they said to him, "Pose your riddle, that we may hear it."

14 So he said to them:

> "Out of the eater came
>   something to eat,
> And out of the strong came
>   something sweet."

Now for three days they could not explain the riddle.

15 But it came to pass on the seventh[a] day that they said to Samson's wife, "Entice your husband, that he may explain the riddle to us, or else we will burn you and your father's house with fire. Have you invited us in order to take what is ours? *Is that* not *so?*"

16 Then Samson's wife wept on him, and said, "You only hate me! You do not love me! You have posed a riddle to the sons of my people, but you have not explained *it* to me."

And he said to her, "Look, I have not explained *it* to my father or my mother; so should I explain *it* to you?" 17 Now she had wept on him the seven days while their feast lasted. And it happened on the seventh day that he told her, because she pressed him so much. Then she explained the riddle to the sons of her people. 18 So the men of the city said to him on the seventh day before the sun went down:

> "What *is* sweeter than honey?
> And what *is* stronger than a
>   lion?"

13:25 aLiterally *Camp of Dan* (compare 18:12)   14:15 aFollowing Masoretic Text, Targum, and Vulgate; Septuagint and Syriac read *fourth.*

Gospel Pearls

And he said to them:

"If you had not plowed with my
    heifer,
You would not have solved my
    riddle!"

19 Then the Spirit of the LORD came upon him mightily, and he went down to Ashkelon and killed thirty of their men, took their apparel, and gave the changes *of clothing* to those who had explained the riddle. So his anger was aroused, and he went back up to his father's house. 20 And Samson's wife was *given* to his companion, who had been his best man.

15 After a while, in the time of wheat harvest, it happened that Samson visited his wife with a young goat. And he said, "Let me go in to my wife, into *her* room." But her father would not permit him to go in.
2 Her father said, "I really thought that you thoroughly hated her; therefore I gave her to your companion. *Is* not her younger sister better than she? Please, take her instead."
3 And Samson said to them, "This time I shall be blameless regarding the Philistines if I harm them!"
4 Then Samson went and caught three hundred foxes; and he took torches, turned *the foxes* tail to tail, and put a torch between each pair of tails. 5 When he had set the torches on fire, he let *the foxes* go into the standing grain of the Philistines, and burned up both the shocks and the standing grain, as well as the vineyards *and* olive groves.
6 Then the Philistines said, "Who has done this?"
And they answered, "Samson, the son-in-law of the Timnite, because he has taken his wife and given her to his companion." So the Philistines came up and burned her and her father with fire.
7 Samson said to them, "Since you would do a thing like this, I will surely take revenge on you, and after that I will cease." 8 So he attacked them hip and thigh with a great slaughter; then he went down and dwelt in the cleft of the rock of Etam.
9 Now the Philistines went up, encamped in Judah, and deployed themselves against Lehi. 10 And the men of Judah said, "Why have you come up against us?"
So they answered, "We have come up to arrest Samson, to do to him as he has done to us."
11 Then three thousand men of Judah went down to the cleft of the rock of Etam, and said to Samson, "Do you not know that the Philistines rule over us? What *is* this you have done to us?"
And he said to them, "As they did to me, so I have done to them."
12 But they said to him, "We have come down to arrest you, that we may deliver you into the hand of the Philistines."
Then Samson said to them, "Swear to me that you will not kill me yourselves."
13 So they spoke to him, saying, "No, but we will tie you securely and deliver you into their hand; but we will surely not kill you." And they bound him with two new ropes and brought him up from the rock.
14 When he came to Lehi, the Philistines came shouting against him. Then the Spirit of the LORD came mightily upon him; and the ropes that *were* on his arms became like flax that is burned with fire, and his bonds broke loose from his hands. 15 He found a fresh jawbone of a donkey, reached out his hand and took it, and killed a thousand men with it. 16 Then Samson said:

"With the jawbone of a donkey,
    Heaps upon heaps,
With the jawbone of a donkey
    I have slain a thousand men!"

17 And so it was, when he had finished speaking, that he threw the jawbone from his hand, and called that place Ramath Lehi.*a*
18 Then he became very thirsty; so he cried out to the LORD and said, "You have given this great deliverance by the hand of Your servant; and now shall I die of thirst and fall into the hand of the uncircumcised?"
19 So God split the hollow place that *is* in Lehi,*a* and water came out, and he drank; and his spirit returned, and he revived. Therefore he called its name En Hakkore,*b* which is in Lehi

15:17 *a*Literally *Jawbone Height*   15:19 *a*Literally *Jawbone* (compare verse 14)   *b*Literally *Spring of the Caller*

God has always had an equal bill of rights for His people. There is no difference between what He will pour out on His sons and what He will pour out on His daughters. He is a good Father. It is His will to bless you.

to this day. 20 And he judged Israel twenty years in the days of the Philistines.

16 Now Samson went to Gaza and saw a harlot there, and went in to her. 2 *When* the Gazites *were told,* "Samson has come here!" they surrounded *the place* and lay in wait for him all night at the gate of the city. They were quiet all night, saying, "In the morning, when it is daylight, we will kill him." 3 And Samson lay *low* till midnight; then he arose at midnight, took hold of the doors of the gate of the city and the two gateposts, pulled them up, bar and all, put *them* on his shoulders, and carried them to the top of the hill that faces Hebron.

4 Afterward it happened that he loved a woman in the Valley of Sorek, whose name *was* Delilah. 5 And the lords of the Philistines came up to her and said to her, "Entice him, and find out where his great strength *lies,* and by what *means* we may overpower him, that we may bind him to afflict him; and every one of us will give you eleven hundred *pieces* of silver."

6 So Delilah said to Samson, "Please tell me where your great strength *lies,* and with what you may be bound to afflict you."

7 And Samson said to her, "If they bind me with seven fresh bowstrings, not yet dried, then I shall become weak, and be like any *other* man."

8 So the lords of the Philistines brought up to her seven fresh bowstrings, not yet dried, and she bound him with them. 9 Now *men were* lying in wait, staying with her in the room. And she said to him, "The Philistines *are* upon you, Samson!" But he broke the bowstrings as a strand of yarn breaks when it touches fire. So the secret of his strength was not known.

10 Then Delilah said to Samson, "Look, you have mocked me and told me lies. Now, please tell me what you may be bound with."

11 So he said to her, "If they bind me securely with new ropes that have never been used, then I shall become weak, and be like any *other* man."

12 Therefore Delilah took new ropes and bound him with them, and said to him, "The Philistines *are* upon you, Samson!" And *men were* lying in wait, staying in the room. But he broke them off his arms like a thread.

13 Delilah said to Samson, "Until now you have mocked me and told me lies. Tell me what you may be bound with."

And he said to her, "If you weave the seven locks of my head into the web of the loom"—

14 So she wove *it* tightly with the batten of the loom, and said to him, "The Philistines *are* upon you, Samson!" But he awoke from his sleep, and pulled out the batten and the web from the loom.

15 Then she said to him, "How can you say, 'I love you,' when your heart *is* not with me? You have mocked me these three times, and have not told me where your great strength *lies.*"

16 And it came to pass, when she pestered him daily with her words and pressed him, *so* that his soul was vexed to death, 17 that he told her all his heart, and said to her, "No razor has ever come upon my head, for I *have been* a Nazirite to God from my mother's womb. If I am shaven, then my strength will leave me, and I shall become weak, and be like any *other* man."

18 When Delilah saw that he had told her all his heart, she sent and called for the lords of the Philistines, saying, "Come up once more, for he has told me all his heart." So the lords of the Philistines came up to her and brought the money in their hand. 19 Then she lulled him to sleep on her knees, and called for a man and had him shave off the seven locks of his head. Then she began to torment him,[a] and his strength left him. 20 And she said, "The Philistines *are* upon you, Samson!" So he awoke from his sleep, and said, "I will go out as before, at other times, and shake myself free!" But he did not know that the LORD had departed from him.

21 Then the Philistines took him and put out his eyes, and brought him down to Gaza. They bound him with bronze fetters, and he became a grinder in the prison. 22 However, the hair of his head began to grow again after it had been shaven.

16:19 [a]Following Masoretic Text, Targum, and Vulgate; Septuagint reads *he began to be weak.*

*T*he Father wants to release the held-up blessing to the pressed-down daughter. You see, ultimately the Father's will is what matters. That is what will be done.

Delilah's Secret

Judges 16:4, 5

Marriage is at its best when both parties can be naked—vulnerable with each other—and not be ashamed. There is no resting place for the man who has to hide in his own house.

In the Garden, God asked Adam, "Where are you?" And Adam displayed the tendency of most men to avoid open confrontation when he confessed: (1) I heard Your voice, (2) I was afraid, (3) I was naked, (4) I hid myself (see Genesis 3:9, 10). When you become confrontational, it's not that your husband doesn't hear you. It's just that when he is afraid of exposure, he has a tendency to hide. Marriage should be transparent. Both you and your spouse need to be able to confess your weaknesses without fear or condemnation. Woe to the man who has no place to lay his head.

Let's stop by Delilah's place (see Judges 16:4-20). Most women would not want to stop at her house; most men would. Most men are not afraid of Delilah; most women don't like her at all. Her morals are inexcusable, but her methods are worth discussing. There are some things that every wife could learn, must learn from Delilah.

What was so powerful about this woman? What was it that caused the Philistine government to put her on the payroll because of what she knew about men? What was it that captured the attention of Israel's mighty man, Samson, and kept him coming back to her bed when he knew all along that she was trying to kill him? He could not leave her alone. It was an Old Testament "fatal attraction."

If your husband is in a high-stress position—if he's powerful and full of purpose, the envy of everyone around—you need to learn from Delilah. Where can the mighty man lay his head? Where can he be vulnerable? Where can he take off his armor and rest for a few hours? Is your home a peaceful place? Is it clean and neat, warm and inviting? If not, Delilah's place is ready. I'm sure she has her own problems, but Samson doesn't have to solve them the minute he walks in the door. She knows he's tired after fighting with the enemy all day, so she says, "Come, lay your head in my lap."

Delilah knows that all men are little boys somewhere deep inside. They are little boys who started their lives being touched by women. A woman sang your husband's first lullaby with her silky voice. A woman gave him his first bath and, when he was tired, he lay his weary head against her warm breast and went to sleep. A woman talked to him and touched him and made him feel safe—not criticized, not ostracized, just safe.

Men respond to praise. Praise will make a weary man perform. A woman who knows what to say to a man is difficult to turn down. For all your husband's tears and all his fears, he needs your arms, your voice, your song.

23 Now the lords of the Philistines gathered together to offer a great sacrifice to Dagon their god, and to rejoice. And they said:

"Our god has delivered into our
  hands
Samson our enemy!"

24 When the people saw him, they praised their god; for they said:

"Our god has delivered into our
  hands our enemy,
The destroyer of our land,
And the one who multiplied our
  dead."

25 So it happened, when their hearts were merry, that they said, "Call for Samson, that he may perform for us." So they called for Samson from the prison, and he performed for them. And they stationed him between the pillars. 26 Then Samson said to the lad who held him by the hand, "Let me feel the pillars which support the temple, so that I can lean on them." 27 Now the temple was full of men and women. All the lords of the Philistines *were* there—about three thousand men and women on the roof watching while Samson performed.

28 Then Samson called to the LORD, saying, "O Lord GOD, remember me, I pray! Strengthen me, I pray, just this once, O God, that I may with one *blow* take vengeance on the Philistines for my two eyes!" 29 And Samson took hold of the two middle pillars which supported the temple, and he braced himself against them, one on his right and the other on his left. 30 Then Samson said, "Let me die with the Philistines!" And he pushed with *all his* might, and the temple fell on the lords and all the people who *were* in it. So the dead that he killed at his death were more than he had killed in his life.

31 And his brothers and all his father's household came down and took him, and brought *him* up and buried him between Zorah and Eshtaol in the tomb of his father Manoah. He had judged Israel twenty years.

17 Now there was a man from the mountains of Ephraim, whose name *was* Micah. 2 And he said to his mother, "The eleven hundred *shekels* of silver that were taken from you, and on which you put a curse, even saying it in my ears—here *is* the silver with me; I took it."

And his mother said, "*May you be* blessed by the LORD, my son!" 3 So when he had returned the eleven hundred *shekels* of silver to his mother, his mother said, "I had wholly dedicated the silver from my hand to the LORD for my son, to make a carved image and a molded image; now therefore, I will return it to you." 4 Thus he returned the silver to his mother. Then his mother took two hundred *shekels* of silver and gave them to the silversmith, and he made it into a carved image and a molded image; and they were in the house of Micah.

5 The man Micah had a shrine, and made an ephod and household idols;[a] and he consecrated one of his sons, who became his priest. 6 In those days *there was* no king in Israel; everyone did *what was* right in his own eyes.

7 Now there was a young man from Bethlehem in Judah, of the family of Judah; he *was* a Levite, and was staying there. 8 The man departed from the city of Bethlehem in Judah to stay wherever he could find *a place*. Then he came to the mountains of Ephraim, to the house of Micah, as he journeyed. 9 And Micah said to him, "Where do you come from?"

So he said to him, "I *am* a Levite from Bethlehem in Judah, and I am on my way to find *a place* to stay."

10 Micah said to him, "Dwell with me, and be a father and a priest to me, and I will give you ten *shekels* of silver per year, a suit of clothes, and your sustenance." So the Levite went in. 11 Then the Levite was content to dwell with the man; and the young man became like one of his sons to him. 12 So Micah consecrated the Levite, and the young man became his priest, and lived in the house of Micah. 13 Then Micah said, "Now I know that the LORD will be good to me, since I have a Levite as priest!"

18 In those days *there was* no king in Israel. And in those days the

17:5 aHebrew *teraphim*

Gospel
Pearls

tribe of the Danites was seeking an inheritance for itself to dwell in; for until that day *their* inheritance among the tribes of Israel had not fallen to them. 2 So the children of Dan sent five men of their family from their territory, men of valor from Zorah and Eshtaol, to spy out the land and search it. They said to them, "Go, search the land." So they went to the mountains of Ephraim, to the house of Micah, and lodged there. 3 While they *were* at the house of Micah, they recognized the voice of the young Levite. They turned aside and said to him, "Who brought you here? What are you doing in this *place*? What do you have here?"

4 He said to them, "Thus and so Micah did for me. He has hired me, and I have become his priest."

5 So they said to him, "Please inquire of God, that we may know whether the journey on which we go will be prosperous."

6 And the priest said to them, "Go in peace. The presence of the LORD *be* with you on your way."

7 So the five men departed and went to Laish. They saw the people who *were* there, how they dwelt safely, in the manner of the Sidonians, quiet and secure. *There were* no rulers in the land who might put *them* to shame for anything. They *were* far from the Sidonians, and they had no ties with anyone.[a]

8 Then *the spies* came back to their brethren at Zorah and Eshtaol, and their brethren said to them, "What *is* your *report*?"

9 So they said, "Arise, let us go up against them. For we have seen the land, and indeed it *is* very good. *Would* you *do* nothing? Do not hesitate to go, *and* enter to possess the land. 10 When you go, you will come to a secure people and a large land. For God has given it into your hands, a place where *there is* no lack of anything that *is* on the earth."

11 And six hundred men of the family of the Danites went from there, from Zorah and Eshtaol, armed with weapons of war. 12 Then they went up and encamped in Kirjath Jearim in Judah. (Therefore they call that place Mahaneh Dan[a] to this day. There *it is*, west of Kirjath Jearim.)

13 And they passed from there to the mountains of Ephraim, and came to the house of Micah.

14 Then the five men who had gone to spy out the country of Laish answered and said to their brethren, "Do you know that there are in these houses an ephod, household idols, a carved image, and a molded image? Now therefore, consider what you should do." 15 So they turned aside there, and came to the house of the young Levite man—to the house of Micah—and greeted him. 16 The six hundred men armed with their weapons of war, who *were* of the children of Dan, stood by the entrance of the gate. 17 Then the five men who had gone to spy out the land went up. Entering there, they took the carved image, the ephod, the household idols, and the molded image. The priest stood at the entrance of the gate with the six hundred men *who were* armed with weapons of war.

18 When these went into Micah's house and took the carved image, the ephod, the household idols, and the molded image, the priest said to them, "What are you doing?"

19 And they said to him, "Be quiet, put your hand over your mouth, and come with us; be a father and a priest to us. *Is it* better for you to be a priest to the household of one man, or that you be a priest to a tribe and a family in Israel?" 20 So the priest's heart was glad; and he took the ephod, the household idols, and the carved image, and took his place among the people.

21 Then they turned and departed, and put the little ones, the livestock, and the goods in front of them. 22 When they were a good way from the house of Micah, the men who *were* in the houses near Micah's house gathered together and overtook the children of Dan. 23 And they called out to the children of Dan. So they turned around and said to Micah, "What ails you, that you have gathered such a company?"

24 So he said, "You have taken away my gods which I made, and the priest, and you have gone away. Now what more do I have? How can you say to me, 'What ails you?'"

25 And the children of Dan said to

18:7 [a]Following Masoretic Text, Targum, and Vulgate; Septuagint reads *with Syria.*   18:12 [a]Literally *Camp of Dan*

---

*I*f you have the favor of your Father, no one can stop you from being blessed. It is important that you don't waste strength fighting the opposition. You see, if God is for you, who can be against you?

him, "Do not let your voice be heard among us, lest angry men fall upon you, and you lose your life, with the lives of your household!" 26 Then the children of Dan went their way. And when Micah saw that they *were* too strong for him, he turned and went back to his house.

27 So they took *the things* Micah had made, and the priest who had belonged to him, and went to Laish, to a people quiet and secure; and they struck them with the edge of the sword and burned the city with fire. 28 *There was* no deliverer, because it *was* far from Sidon, and they had no ties with anyone. It was in the valley that belongs to Beth Rehob. So they rebuilt the city and dwelt there. 29 And they called the name of the city Dan, after the name of Dan their father, who was born to Israel. However, the name of the city formerly *was* Laish.

30 Then the children of Dan set up for themselves the carved image; and Jonathan the son of Gershom, the son of Manasseh,*a* and his sons were priests to the tribe of Dan until the day of the captivity of the land. 31 So they set up for themselves Micah's carved image which he made, all the time that the house of God was in Shiloh.

19 And it came to pass in those days, when *there was* no king in Israel, that there was a certain Levite staying in the remote mountains of Ephraim. He took for himself a concubine from Bethlehem in Judah. 2 But his concubine played the harlot against him, and went away from him to her father's house at Bethlehem in Judah, and was there four whole months. 3 Then her husband arose and went after her, to speak kindly to her *and* bring her back, having his servant and a couple of donkeys with him. So she brought him into her father's house; and when the father of the young woman saw him, he was glad to meet him. 4 Now his father-in-law, the young woman's father, detained him; and he stayed with him three days. So they ate and drank and lodged there.

5 Then it came to pass on the fourth day that they arose early in the morning, and he stood to depart; but the young woman's father said to his son-in-law, "Refresh your heart with a morsel of bread, and afterward go your way."

6 So they sat down, and the two of them ate and drank together. Then the young woman's father said to the man, "Please be content to stay all night, and let your heart be merry." 7 And when the man stood to depart, his father-in-law urged him; so he lodged there again. 8 Then he arose early in the morning on the fifth day to depart, but the young woman's father said, "Please refresh your heart." So they delayed until afternoon; and both of them ate.

9 And when the man stood to depart—he and his concubine and his servant—his father-in-law, the young woman's father, said to him, "Look, the day is now drawing toward evening; please spend the night. See, the day is coming to an end; lodge here, that your heart may be merry. Tomorrow go your way early, so that you may get home."

10 However, the man was not willing to spend that night; so he rose and departed, and came to opposite Jebus (that *is,* Jerusalem). With him were the two saddled donkeys; his concubine *was* also with him. 11 They *were* near Jebus, and the day was far spent; and the servant said to his master, "Come, please, and let us turn aside into this city of the Jebusites and lodge in it."

12 But his master said to him, "We will not turn aside here into a city of foreigners, who *are* not of the children of Israel; we will go on to Gibeah." 13 So he said to his servant, "Come, let us draw near to one of these places, and spend the night in Gibeah or in Ramah." 14 And they passed by and went their way; and the sun went down on them near Gibeah, which belongs to Benjamin. 15 They turned aside there to go in to lodge in Gibeah. And when he went in, he sat down in the open square of the city, for no one would take them into *his* house to spend the night.

16 Just then an old man came in from his work in the field at evening, who also *was* from the mountains of Ephraim; he was staying in Gibeah, whereas the men of the place *were*

18:30 *a*Septuagint and Vulgate read *Moses.*

Gospel
Pearls

Benjamites. 17 And when he raised his eyes, he saw the traveler in the open square of the city; and the old man said, "Where are you going, and where do you come from?"

18 So he said to him, "We *are* passing from Bethlehem in Judah toward the remote mountains of Ephraim; I *am* from there. I went to Bethlehem in Judah; *now* I am going to the house of the LORD. But there *is* no one who will take me into his house, 19 although we have both straw and fodder for our donkeys, and bread and wine for myself, for your female servant, and for the young man *who is* with your servant; *there is* no lack of anything."

20 And the old man said, "Peace *be* with you! However, *let* all your needs *be* my responsibility; only do not spend the night in the open square." 21 So he brought him into his house, and gave fodder to the donkeys. And they washed their feet, and ate and drank.

22 As they were enjoying themselves, suddenly certain men of the city, perverted men,*a* surrounded the house *and* beat on the door. They spoke to the master of the house, the old man, saying, "Bring out the man who came to your house, that we may know him *carnally!*"

23 But the man, the master of the house, went out to them and said to them, "No, my brethren! I beg you, do not act *so* wickedly! Seeing this man has come into my house, do not commit this outrage. 24 Look, *here is* my virgin daughter and *the man's*a concubine; let me bring them out now. Humble them, and do with them as you please; but to this man do not do such a vile thing!" 25 But the man would not heed him. So the man took his concubine and brought *her* out to them. And they knew her and abused her all night until morning; and when the day began to break, they let her go.

26 Then the woman came as the day was dawning, and fell down at the door of the man's house where her master *was*, till it was light.

27 When her master arose in the morning, and opened the doors of the house and went out to go his way, there was his concubine, fallen *at* the door of the house with her hands on

the threshold. 28 And he said to her, "Get up and let us be going." But there was no answer. So the man lifted her onto the donkey; and the man got up and went to his place.

29 When he entered his house he took a knife, laid hold of his concubine, and divided her into twelve pieces, limb by limb,*a* and sent her throughout all the territory of Israel. 30 And so it was that all who saw it said, "No such deed has been done or seen from the day that the children of Israel came up from the land of Egypt until this day. Consider it, confer, and speak up!"

20 So all the children of Israel came out, from Dan to Beersheba, as well as from the land of Gilead, and the congregation gathered together as one man before the LORD at Mizpah. 2 And the leaders of all the people, all the tribes of Israel, presented themselves in the assembly of the people of God, four hundred thousand foot soldiers who drew the sword. 3 (Now the children of Benjamin heard that the children of Israel had gone up to Mizpah.)

Then the children of Israel said, "Tell *us*, how did this wicked deed happen?"

4 So the Levite, the husband of the woman who was murdered, answered and said, "My concubine and I went into Gibeah, which belongs to Benjamin, to spend the night. 5 And the men of Gibeah rose against me, and surrounded the house at night because of me. They intended to kill me, but instead they ravished my concubine so that she died. 6 So I took hold of my concubine, cut her in pieces, and sent her throughout all the territory of the inheritance of Israel, because they committed lewdness and outrage in Israel. 7 "Look! All of you *are* children of Israel; give your advice and counsel here and now!"

8 So all the people arose as one man, saying, "None *of us* will go to his tent, nor will any turn back to his house; 9 but now this *is* the thing which we will do to Gibeah: *We will go up* against it by lot. 10 We will take ten men out of *every* hundred throughout all the tribes of Israel, a

---

19:22 *a*Literally sons of Belial   19:24 *a*Literally his   19:29 *a*Literally with her bones

*P*erhaps there are some things that your Father has for you. Do not be intimidated. In spite of what you don't have, look at what you do have and keep on walking. By God's grace and power you can still receive the inheritance.

hundred out of _every_ thousand, and a thousand out of _every_ ten thousand, to make provisions for the people, that when they come to Gibeah in Benjamin, they may repay all the vileness that they have done in Israel." 11 So all the men of Israel were gathered against the city, united together as one man.

12 Then the tribes of Israel sent men through all the tribe of Benjamin, saying, "What _is_ this wickedness that has occurred among you? 13 Now therefore, deliver up the men, the perverted men*a* who _are_ in Gibeah, that we may put them to death and remove the evil from Israel!" But the children of Benjamin would not listen to the voice of their brethren, the children of Israel. 14 Instead, the children of Benjamin gathered together from their cities to Gibeah, to go to battle against the children of Israel. 15 And from their cities at that time the children of Benjamin numbered twenty-six thousand men who drew the sword, besides the inhabitants of Gibeah, who numbered seven hundred select men. 16 Among all this people _were_ seven hundred select men _who were_ left-handed; every one could sling a stone at a hair's _breadth_ and not miss. 17 Now besides Benjamin, the men of Israel numbered four hundred thousand men who drew the sword; all of these _were_ men of war.

18 Then the children of Israel arose and went up to the house of God*a* to inquire of God. They said, "Which of us shall go up first to battle against the children of Benjamin?"

The LORD said, "Judah first!"

19 So the children of Israel rose in the morning and encamped against Gibeah. 20 And the men of Israel went out to battle against Benjamin, and the men of Israel put themselves in battle array to fight against them at Gibeah. 21 Then the children of Benjamin came out of Gibeah, and on that day cut down to the ground twenty-two thousand men of the Israelites. 22 And the people, that is, the men of Israel, encouraged themselves and again formed the battle line at the place where they had put themselves in array on the first day. 23 Then the children of Israel went up and wept before the LORD until evening, and asked counsel of the LORD, saying, "Shall I again draw near for battle against the children of my brother Benjamin?"

And the LORD said, "Go up against him."

24 So the children of Israel approached the children of Benjamin on the second day. 25 And Benjamin went out against them from Gibeah on the second day, and cut down to the ground eighteen thousand more of the children of Israel; all these drew the sword.

26 Then all the children of Israel, that is, all the people, went up and came to the house of God*a* and wept. They sat there before the LORD and fasted that day until evening; and they offered burnt offerings and peace offerings before the LORD. 27 So the children of Israel inquired of the LORD (the ark of the covenant of God _was_ there in those days, 28 and Phinehas the son of Eleazar, the son of Aaron, stood before it in those days), saying, "Shall I yet again go out to battle against the children of my brother Benjamin, or shall I cease?"

And the LORD said, "Go up, for tomorrow I will deliver them into your hand."

29 Then Israel set men in ambush all around Gibeah. 30 And the children of Israel went up against the children of Benjamin on the third day, and put themselves in battle array against Gibeah as at the other times. 31 So the children of Benjamin went out against the people, _and_ were drawn away from the city. They began to strike down _and_ kill some of the people, as at the other times, in the highways (one of which goes up to Bethel and the other to Gibeah) and in the field, about thirty men of Israel. 32 And the children of Benjamin said, "They _are_ defeated before us, as at first."

But the children of Israel said, "Let us flee and draw them away from the city to the highways." 33 So all the men of Israel rose from their place and put themselves in battle array at Baal Tamar. Then Israel's men in ambush burst forth from their position in the plain of Geba. 34 And ten thousand select men from all Israel came against Gibeah, and the battle was

20:13 *a*Literally _sons of Belial_   20:18 *a*Hebrew _Bethel_   20:26 *a*Hebrew _Bethel_

Gospel Pearls

fierce. But *the Benjamites*ᵃ did not know that disaster *was* upon them. 35 The LORD defeated Benjamin before Israel. And the children of Israel destroyed that day twenty-five thousand one hundred Benjamites; all these drew the sword.

36 So the children of Benjamin saw that they were defeated. The men of Israel had given ground to the Benjamites, because they relied on the men in ambush whom they had set against Gibeah. 37 And the men in ambush quickly rushed upon Gibeah; the men in ambush spread out and struck the whole city with the edge of the sword. 38 Now the appointed signal between the men of Israel and the men in ambush was that they would make a great cloud of smoke rise up from the city, 39 whereupon the men of Israel would turn in battle. Now Benjamin had begun to strike *and* kill about thirty of the men of Israel. For they said, "Surely they are defeated before us, as *in* the first battle." 40 But when the cloud began to rise from the city in a column of smoke, the Benjamites looked behind them, and there was the whole city going up *in smoke* to heaven. 41 And when the men of Israel turned back, the men of Benjamin panicked, for they saw that disaster had come upon them. 42 Therefore they turned *their backs* before the men of Israel in the direction of the wilderness; but the battle overtook them, and whoever *came* out of the cities they destroyed in their midst. 43 They surrounded the Benjamites, chased them, *and* easily trampled them down as far as the front of Gibeah toward the east. 44 And eighteen thousand men of Benjamin fell; all these *were* men of valor. 45 Then theyᵃ turned and fled toward the wilderness to the rock of Rimmon; and they cut down five thousand of them on the highways. Then they pursued them relentlessly up to Gidom, and killed two thousand of them. 46 So all who fell of Benjamin that day were twenty-five thousand men who drew the sword; all these *were* men of valor.

47 But six hundred men turned and fled toward the wilderness to the rock of Rimmon, and they stayed at the rock of Rimmon for four months.

48 And the men of Israel turned back against the children of Benjamin, and struck them down with the edge of the sword—from *every* city, men and beasts, all who were found. They also set fire to all the cities they came to.

21 Now the men of Israel had sworn an oath at Mizpah, saying, "None of us shall give his daughter to Benjamin as a wife." 2 Then the people came to the house of God,ᵃ and remained there before God till evening. They lifted up their voices and wept bitterly, 3 and said, "O LORD God of Israel, why has this come to pass in Israel, that today there should be one tribe *missing* in Israel?"

4 So it was, on the next morning, that the people rose early and built an altar there, and offered burnt offerings and peace offerings. 5 The children of Israel said, "Who *is there* among all the tribes of Israel who did not come up with the assembly to the LORD?" For they had made a great oath concerning anyone who had not come up to the LORD at Mizpah, saying, "He shall surely be put to death." 6 And the children of Israel grieved for Benjamin their brother, and said, "One tribe is cut off from Israel today. 7 What shall we do for wives for those who remain, seeing we have sworn by the LORD that we will not give them our daughters as wives?"

8 And they said, "What one *is there* from the tribes of Israel who did not come up to Mizpah to the LORD?" And, in fact, no one had come to the camp from Jabesh Gilead to the assembly. 9 For when the people were counted, indeed, not one of the inhabitants of Jabesh Gilead *was* there. 10 So the congregation sent out there twelve thousand of their most valiant men, and commanded them, saying, "Go and strike the inhabitants of Jabesh Gilead with the edge of the sword, including the women and children. 11 And this *is* the thing that you shall do: You shall utterly destroy every male, and every woman who has known a man intimately." 12 So they found among the inhabitants of Jabesh Gilead four hundred young virgins who had not known a man intimately; and they brought

20:34 ᵃLiterally *they*   20:45 ᵃSeptuagint reads *the rest.*   21:2 ᵃHebrew *Bethel*

*W*hy don't you, as a woman of God, go after what the Father has willed to you? He died for you, and He wants you to have your inheritance. Every time you experience one of His benefits, thank Him.

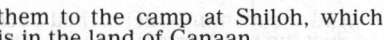

them to the camp at Shiloh, which is in the land of Canaan.

13 Then the whole congregation sent *word* to the children of Benjamin who *were* at the rock of Rimmon, and announced peace to them. 14 So Benjamin came back at that time, and they gave them the women whom they had saved alive of the women of Jabesh Gilead; and yet they had not found enough for them.

15 And the people grieved for Benjamin, because the LORD had made a void in the tribes of Israel.

16 Then the elders of the congregation said, "What shall we do for wives for those who remain, since the women of Benjamin have been destroyed?" 17 And they said, "*There must be* an inheritance for the survivors of Benjamin, that a tribe may not be destroyed from Israel. 18 However, we cannot give them wives from our daughters, for the children of Israel have sworn an oath, saying, 'Cursed *be* the one who gives a wife to Benjamin.'" 19 Then they said, "In fact, *there is* a yearly feast of the LORD in Shiloh, which *is* north of Bethel, on the east side of the highway that goes up from Bethel to Shechem, and south of Lebonah."

20 Therefore they instructed the children of Benjamin, saying, "Go, lie in wait in the vineyards, 21 and watch; and just when the daughters of Shiloh come out to perform their dances, then come out from the vineyards, and every man catch a wife for himself from the daughters of Shiloh; then go to the land of Benjamin. 22 Then it shall be, when their fathers or their brothers come to us to complain, that we will say to them, 'Be kind to them for our sakes, because we did not take a wife for any of them in the war; for *it is* not *as though* you have given the *women* to them at this time, making yourselves guilty of your oath.'"

23 And the children of Benjamin did so; they took enough wives for their number from those who danced, whom they caught. Then they went and returned to their inheritance, and they rebuilt the cities and dwelt in them. 24 So the children of Israel departed from there at that time, every man to his tribe and family; they went out from there, every man to his inheritance.

25 In those days *there was* no king in Israel; everyone did *what was* right in his own eyes.

The Book of

RUTH

1 Now it came to pass, in the days when the judges ruled, that there was a famine in the land. And a certain man of Bethlehem, Judah, went to dwell in the country of Moab, he and his wife and his two sons. 2 The name of the man *was* Elimelech, the name of his wife *was* Naomi, and the names of his two sons *were* Mahlon and Chilion—Ephrathites of Bethlehem, Judah. And they went to the country of Moab and remained there. 3 Then Elimelech, Naomi's husband, died; and she was left, and her two sons. 4 Now they took wives of the women of Moab: the name of the one *was*

Orpah, and the name of the other Ruth. And they dwelt there about ten years. 5 Then both Mahlon and Chilion also died; so the woman survived her two sons and her husband.

6 Then she arose with her daughters-in-law that she might return from the country of Moab, for she had heard in the country of Moab that the LORD had visited His people by giving them bread. 7 Therefore she went out from the place where she was, and her two daughters-in-law with her; and they went on the way to return to the land of Judah. 8 And Naomi said to her two daughters-in-law, "Go, return each to her

Gospel Pearls

mother's house. The LORD deal kindly with you, as you have dealt with the dead and with me. 9 The LORD grant that you may find rest, each in the house of her husband."

So she kissed them, and they lifted up their voices and wept. 10 And they said to her, "Surely we will return with you to your people."

11 But Naomi said, "Turn back, my daughters; why will you go with me? *Are* there still sons in my womb, that they may be your husbands? 12 Turn back, my daughters, go—for I am too old to have a husband. If I should say I have hope, *if* I should have a husband tonight and should also bear sons, 13 would you wait for them till they were grown? Would you restrain yourselves from having husbands? No, my daughters; for it grieves me very much for your sakes that the hand of the LORD has gone out against me!"

14 Then they lifted up their voices and wept again; and Orpah kissed her mother-in-law, but Ruth clung to her.

15 And she said, "Look, your sister-in-law has gone back to her people and to her gods; return after your sister-in-law."

16 But Ruth said:

"Entreat me not to leave you,
   Or to turn back from following
      after you;
   For wherever you go, I will go;
   And wherever you lodge, I will
      lodge;
   Your people *shall be* my
      people,
   And your God, my God.
17 Where you die, I will die,
   And there will I be buried.
   The LORD do so to me, and
      more also,
   If *anything but* death parts you
      and me."

18 When she saw that she was determined to go with her, she stopped speaking to her.

19 Now the two of them went until they came to Bethlehem. And it happened, when they had come to Bethlehem, that all the city was excited because of them; and the women said, "*Is* this Naomi?"

20 But she said to them, "Do not call me Naomi;*a* call me Mara,*b* for the Almighty has dealt very bitterly with me. 21 I went out full, and the LORD has brought me home again empty. Why do you call me Naomi, since the LORD has testified against me, and the Almighty has afflicted me?"

22 So Naomi returned, and Ruth the Moabitess her daughter-in-law with her, who returned from the country of Moab. Now they came to Bethlehem at the beginning of barley harvest.

2 There was a relative of Naomi's husband, a man of great wealth, of the family of Elimelech. His name *was* Boaz. 2 So Ruth the Moabitess said to Naomi, "Please let me go to the field, and glean heads of grain after *him* in whose sight I may find favor."

And she said to her, "Go, my daughter."

3 Then she left, and went and gleaned in the field after the reapers. And she happened to come to the part of the field *belonging* to Boaz, who *was* of the family of Elimelech.

4 Now behold, Boaz came from Bethlehem, and said to the reapers, "The LORD *be* with you!"

And they answered him, "The LORD bless you!"

5 Then Boaz said to his servant who was in charge of the reapers, "Whose young woman *is* this?"

6 So the servant who was in charge of the reapers answered and said, "It *is* the young Moabite woman who came back with Naomi from the country of Moab. 7 And she said, 'Please let me glean and gather after the reapers among the sheaves.' So she came and has continued from morning until now, though she rested a little in the house."

8 Then Boaz said to Ruth, "You will listen, my daughter, will you not? Do not go to glean in another field, nor go from here, but stay close by my young women. 9 *Let* your eyes *be* on the field which they reap, and go after them. Have I not commanded the young men not to touch you? And when you are thirsty, go to the vessels and drink from what the young men have drawn."

1:20 *a*Literally *Pleasant* *b*Literally *Bitter*

---

2 encourage you as a father would his daughter—go for all that life has to offer you. Take a large slice of life. Savor every bite. Your Father has willed you good things.

The Fragrance of Love

Ruth 1:16, 17

We all wonder, *Will I be loved when I am not needed?* If you are the mother of adult children you may harbor this fear. The truth of the matter is the need is still there, but the areas of need have changed. Although your children will always need you, what they need from you will change.

They once needed to be nurtured at your warm breast; they now need to feast on the bounty of your spirit. A mother needs faith enough to quit yearning for yesterday and fearing tomorrow. You can develop a fresh relationship with your daughter or even your son.

Avoid the temptation to attack the people who are a part of your children's adult lives. Many women make the mistake of trading the role of mother for the role of judge. They become critical of people who have influence with their grown children. Jealousy or even genuine disapproval of your children's relationships will not help. Prayer is a better choice than bickering and nagging!

Remember Naomi, who stood by Ruth, her daughter-in-law. Her wisdom and gentle encouragement gave strength and grace to the young girl she influenced. Ruth and Naomi shared life, love, and intimate secrets without Naomi's judgment, criticism, or domination of Ruth. Ultimately Ruth became committed to Naomi's God. The greatest witness we can have is the presence of grace. Be gracious and you will see God move in your life.

You are entitled to your opinion, but once you have offered it, release your children to make their own decisions. Respect their choices and support them as best you can. Do not allow the enemy to rob you of the riches of your investment in your children. It would be foolish to lose all you have deposited in them over someone or something you cannot control.

Mary, Jesus' mother, didn't understand her Son. His decisions led to His death. Yet she supported Him to the end. You must be wise. If not, you will create a cold war that will leave you alone with bitterness and sad memories. Hostility will cause you to be left with Thanksgiving turkeys to eat by yourself. It is not worth it. The fragrance of love is sweet. With wisdom and grace and prayer, you can enjoy it all the days of your life.

10 So she fell on her face, bowed down to the ground, and said to him, "Why have I found favor in your eyes, that you should take notice of me, since I *am* a foreigner?"

11 And Boaz answered and said to her, "It has been fully reported to me, all that you have done for your mother-in-law since the death of your husband, and *how* you have left your father and your mother and the land of your birth, and have come to a people whom you did not know before. 12 The LORD repay your work, and a full reward be given you by the LORD God of Israel, under whose wings you have come for refuge."

13 Then she said, "Let me find favor in your sight, my lord; for you have comforted me, and have spoken kindly to your maidservant, though I am not like one of your maidservants."

14 Now Boaz said to her at mealtime, "Come here, and eat of the bread, and dip your piece of bread in the vinegar." So she sat beside the reapers, and he passed parched *grain* to her; and she ate and was satisfied, and kept some back. 15 And when she rose up to glean, Boaz commanded his young men, saying, "Let her glean even among the sheaves, and do not reproach her. 16 Also let *grain* from the bundles fall purposely for her; leave *it* that she may glean, and do not rebuke her."

17 So she gleaned in the field until evening, and beat out what she had gleaned, and it was about an ephah of barley. 18 Then she took *it* up and went into the city, and her mother-in-law saw what she had gleaned. So she brought out and gave to her what she had kept back after she had been satisfied.

19 And her mother-in-law said to her, "Where have you gleaned today? And where did you work? Blessed be the one who took notice of you."

So she told her mother-in-law with whom she had worked, and said, "The man's name with whom I worked today *is* Boaz."

20 Then Naomi said to her daughter-in-law, "Blessed *be* he of the LORD, who has not forsaken His kindness to the living and the dead!" And Naomi said to her, "This man *is* a re-

lation of ours, one of our close relatives."

21 Ruth the Moabitess said, "He also said to me, 'You shall stay close by my young men until they have finished all my harvest.' "

22 And Naomi said to Ruth her daughter-in-law, "*It is* good, my daughter, that you go out with his young women, and that people do not meet you in any other field." 23 So she stayed close by the young women of Boaz, to glean until the end of barley harvest and wheat harvest; and she dwelt with her mother-in-law.

3 Then Naomi her mother-in-law said to her, "My daughter, shall I not seek security for you, that it may be well with you? 2 Now Boaz, whose young women you were with, *is he* not our relative? In fact, he is winnowing barley tonight at the threshing floor. 3 Therefore wash yourself and anoint yourself, put on your *best* garment and go down to the threshing floor; *but* do not make yourself known to the man until he has finished eating and drinking. 4 Then it shall be, when he lies down, that you shall notice the place where he lies; and you shall go in, uncover his feet, and lie down; and he will tell you what you should do."

5 And she said to her, "All that you say to me I will do."

6 So she went down to the threshing floor and did according to all that her mother-in-law instructed her. 7 And after Boaz had eaten and drunk, and his heart was cheerful, he went to lie down at the end of the heap of grain; and she came softly, uncovered his feet, and lay down.

8 Now it happened at midnight that the man was startled, and turned himself; and there, a woman was lying at his feet. 9 And he said, "Who *are* you?"

So she answered, "I *am* Ruth, your maidservant. Take your maidservant under your wing,[a] for you are a close relative."

10 Then he said, "Blessed *are* you of the LORD, my daughter! For you have shown more kindness at the end than at the beginning, in that you did not go after young men, whether poor or rich. 11 And now, my daugh-

3:9 aOr *Spread the corner of your garment over your maidservant*

*D*on't spend another day wasted in regret, sleeping away your mercy and losing your chance to achieve. Get up and get busy. You may have to work it out. You may have to push and shove. But life is worth the struggle.

ter, do not fear. I will do for you all that you request, for all the people of my town know that you *are* a virtuous woman. 12 Now it is true that I *am* a close relative; however, there is a relative closer than I. 13 Stay this night, and in the morning it shall be *that* if he will perform the duty of a close relative for you—good; let him do it. But if he does not want to perform the duty for you, then I will perform the duty for you, *as* the LORD lives! Lie down until morning."

14 So she lay at his feet until morning, and she arose before one could recognize another. Then he said, "Do not let it be known that the woman came to the threshing floor." 15 Also he said, "Bring the shawl that *is* on you and hold it." And when she held it, he measured six *ephahs* of barley, and laid *it* on her. Then she*a* went into the city.

16 When she came to her mother-in-law, she said, "*Is* that you, my daughter?"

Then she told her all that the man had done for her. 17 And she said, "These six *ephahs* of barley he gave me; for he said to me, 'Do not go empty-handed to your mother-in-law.' "

18 Then she said, "Sit still, my daughter, until you know how the matter will turn out; for the man will not rest until he has concluded the matter this day."

4 Now Boaz went up to the gate and sat down there; and behold, the close relative of whom Boaz had spoken came by. So Boaz said, "Come aside, friend,*a* sit down here." So he came aside and sat down. 2 And he took ten men of the elders of the city, and said, "Sit down here." So they sat down. 3 Then he said to the close relative, "Naomi, who has come back from the country of Moab, sold the piece of land which *belonged* to our brother Elimelech. 4 And I thought to inform you, saying, 'Buy *it* back in the presence of the inhabitants and the elders of my people. If you will redeem *it*, redeem *it;* but if you*a* will not redeem *it, then* tell me, that I may know; for *there is* no one but you to redeem *it*, and I *am* next after you.' "

And he said, "I will redeem *it*."

5 Then Boaz said, "On the day you buy the field from the hand of Naomi, you must also buy *it* from Ruth the Moabitess, the wife of the dead, to perpetuate*a* the name of the dead through his inheritance."

6 And the close relative said, "I cannot redeem *it* for myself, lest I ruin my own inheritance. You redeem my right of redemption for yourself, for I cannot redeem *it*."

7 Now this *was the custom* in former times in Israel concerning redeeming and exchanging, to confirm anything: one man took off his sandal and gave *it* to the other, and this *was* a confirmation in Israel.

8 Therefore the close relative said to Boaz, "Buy *it* for yourself." So he took off his sandal. 9 And Boaz said to the elders and all the people, "You *are* witnesses this day that I have bought all that *was* Elimelech's, and all that *was* Chilion's and Mahlon's, from the hand of Naomi. 10 Moreover, Ruth the Moabitess, the widow of Mahlon, I have acquired as my wife, to perpetuate the name of the dead through his inheritance, that the name of the dead may not be cut off from among his brethren and from his position at the gate.*a* You *are* witnesses this day."

11 And all the people who *were* at the gate, and the elders, said, "*We are* witnesses. The LORD make the woman who is coming to your house like Rachel and Leah, the two who built the house of Israel; and may you prosper in Ephrathah and be famous in Bethlehem. 12 May your house be like the house of Perez, whom Tamar bore to Judah, because of the offspring which the LORD will give you from this young woman."

13 So Boaz took Ruth and she became his wife; and when he went in to her, the LORD gave her conception, and she bore a son. 14 Then the women said to Naomi, "Blessed *be* the LORD, who has not left you this day without a close relative; and may his name be famous in Israel! 15 And may he be to you a restorer of life and a nourisher of your old age; for your daughter-in-law, who loves you, who is better to you than

3:15 *a*Many Hebrew manuscripts, Syriac, and Vulgate read *she;* Masoretic Text, Septuagint, and Targum read *he*.   4:1 *a*Hebrew *peloni almoni;* literally *so and so*   4:4 *a*Following many Hebrew manuscripts, Septuagint, Syriac, Targum, and Vulgate; Masoretic Text reads *he*.   4:5 *a*Literally *raise up*
4:10 *a*Probably his civic office

Gospel
Pearls

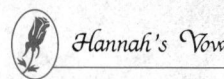

seven sons, has borne him."
16 Then Naomi took the child and laid him on her bosom, and became a nurse to him. 17 Also the neighbor women gave him a name, saying, "There is a son born to Naomi." And they called his name Obed. He *is* the father of Jesse, the father of David.

18 Now this *is* the genealogy of Perez: Perez begot Hezron; 19 Hezron begot Ram, and Ram begot Amminadab; 20 Amminadab begot Nahshon, and Nahshon begot Salmon;[a] 21 Salmon begot Boaz, and Boaz begot Obed; 22 Obed begot Jesse, and Jesse begot David.

4:20 *a*Hebrew *Salmah*

The First Book of

SAMUEL

1 Now there was a certain man of Ramathaim Zophim, of the mountains of Ephraim, and his name *was* Elkanah the son of Jeroham, the son of Elihu,[a] the son of Tohu,[b] the son of Zuph, an Ephraimite. 2 And he had two wives: the name of one *was* Hannah, and the name of the other Peninnah. Peninnah had children, but Hannah had no children. 3 This man went up from his city yearly to worship and sacrifice to the LORD of hosts in Shiloh. Also the two sons of Eli, Hophni and Phinehas, the priests of the LORD, *were* there. 4 And whenever the time came for Elkanah to make an offering, he would give portions to Peninnah his wife and to all her sons and daughters. 5 But to Hannah he would give a double portion, for he loved Hannah, although the LORD had closed her womb. 6 And her rival also provoked her severely, to make her miserable, because the LORD had closed her womb. 7 So it was, year by year, when she went up to the house of the LORD, that she provoked her; therefore she wept and did not eat.

8 Then Elkanah her husband said to her, "Hannah, why do you weep? Why do you not eat? And why is your heart grieved? *Am* I not better to you than ten sons?"

9 So Hannah arose after they had finished eating and drinking in Shiloh. Now Eli the priest was sitting on the seat by the doorpost of the tabernacle[a] of the LORD. 10 And she *was*

in bitterness of soul, and prayed to the LORD and wept in anguish. 11 Then she made a vow and said, "O LORD of hosts, if You will indeed look on the affliction of Your maidservant and remember me, and not forget Your maidservant, but will give Your maidservant a male child, then I will give him to the LORD all the days of his life, and no razor shall come upon his head."

12 And it happened, as she continued praying before the LORD, that Eli watched her mouth. 13 Now Hannah spoke in her heart; only her lips moved, but her voice was not heard. Therefore Eli thought she was drunk. 14 So Eli said to her, "How long will you be drunk? Put your wine away from you!"

15 But Hannah answered and said, "No, my lord, I *am* a woman of sorrowful spirit. I have drunk neither wine nor intoxicating drink, but have poured out my soul before the LORD. 16 Do not consider your maidservant a wicked woman,[a] for out of the abundance of my complaint and grief I have spoken until now."

17 Then Eli answered and said, "Go in peace, and the God of Israel grant your petition which you have asked of Him."

18 And she said, "Let your maidservant find favor in your sight." So the woman went her way and ate, and her face was no longer *sad.*

19 Then they rose early before the morning and worshiped before the

1:1 *a*Spelled *Eliel* in 1 Chronicles 6:34   *b*Spelled *Toah* in 1 Chronicles 6:34   1:9 *a*Hebrew *heykal,* palace or temple   1:16 *a*Literally *daughter of Belial*

*B*eyond yesterday's night there is tomorrow's morning. It is truly morning for those women who have given their hearts to Jesus. If you haven't given your heart to Him, please do it now. He is so much help for those who need a touch.

The Covenant of Motherhood

1 Samuel 1:11

*I*t is easier to give your children back to the Lord if you understand from the beginning that they aren't yours to keep. Hannah was committed to the covenant of motherhood before she ever had a child.

But it is not impossible to gather your faith and turn your children over to God in later years. You are His chosen steward for the children He has given you.

The greatest tragedy is that many mothers end up with resentful children who feel smothered and angry because they are made to feel guilty for growing up. Preserve what you have with your children by allowing the relationship to change in your hand. The caterpillar has been fed in the cocoon of your teaching and has come forth a butterfly. It will never crawl again. It will never need what it once needed, but in every flutter of its lovely wings there is a tribute to the cocoon that permitted the grace of change.

Your authority will change. You will move from the role of diaper-changer, decision-maker and discipline-enforcer to confidante, cheerleader, and champion. That is not promoting disrespect but development. If you respect yesterday's child and recognize that he has become today's adult, he will always love you for your tremendous contribution to that independence.

One of the greatest challenges to this adjustment is redefining boundaries. During this time children must learn to practice independence without being disrespectful. Young people will blunder through the transition from Barbie dolls to beauty shops, from the go-carts to the golf course. But didn't most of us stumble into destiny? Children cannot exist as extensions of their parents.

Look at Luke 2:51, 52. Jesus returned home with His mother and continued to submit to her. But the Scriptures say that from that time He increased in wisdom and stature, and in favor with God and men. He did not disassociate from His mother, whose loyalty followed Him all the way to the Cross. Although their roles changed and He became increasingly independent, His love and care for her continued even to His thirty-third year and the final moments of His life. She was still His mother!

LORD, and returned and came to their house at Ramah. And Elkanah knew Hannah his wife, and the LORD remembered her. 20 So it came to pass in the process of time that Hannah conceived and bore a son, and called his name Samuel,*a* *saying,* "Because I have asked for him from the LORD."

21 Now the man Elkanah and all his house went up to offer to the LORD the yearly sacrifice and his vow. 22 But Hannah did not go up, for she said to her husband, "*Not* until the child is weaned; then I will take him, that he may appear before the LORD and remain there forever."

23 So Elkanah her husband said to her, "Do what seems best to you; wait until you have weaned him. Only let the LORD establish His*a* word." Then the woman stayed and nursed her son until she had weaned him.

24 Now when she had weaned him, she took him up with her, with three bulls,*a* one ephah of flour, and a skin of wine, and brought him to the house of the LORD in Shiloh. And the child *was* young. 25 Then they slaughtered a bull, and brought the child to Eli. 26 And she said, "O my lord! As your soul lives, my lord, I *am* the woman who stood by you here, praying to the LORD. 27 For this child I prayed, and the LORD has granted me my petition which I asked of Him. 28 Therefore I also have lent him to the LORD; as long as he lives he shall be lent to the LORD." So they worshiped the LORD there.

2 And Hannah prayed and said:

"My heart rejoices in the LORD;
My horn*a* is exalted in the LORD.
I smile at my enemies,
Because I rejoice in Your salvation.

2 "No one is holy like the LORD,
For *there is* none besides You,
Nor *is there* any rock like our God.

3 "Talk no more so very proudly;
Let no arrogance come from your mouth,

For the LORD *is* the God of knowledge;
And by Him actions are weighed.

4 "The bows of the mighty men *are* broken,
And those who stumbled are girded with strength.

5 *Those who were* full have hired themselves out for bread,
And the hungry have ceased *to* hunger.
Even the barren has borne seven,
And she who has many children has become feeble.

6 "The LORD kills and makes alive;
He brings down to the grave and brings up.

7 The LORD makes poor and makes rich;
He brings low and lifts up.

8 He raises the poor from the dust
And lifts the beggar from the ash heap,
To set *them* among princes
And make them inherit the throne of glory.

"For the pillars of the earth *are* the LORD's,
And He has set the world upon them.

9 He will guard the feet of His saints,
But the wicked shall be silent in darkness.

"For by strength no man shall prevail.

10 The adversaries of the LORD shall be broken in pieces;
From heaven He will thunder against them.
The LORD will judge the ends of the earth.

"He will give strength to His king,
And exalt the horn of His anointed."

11 Then Elkanah went to his house at Ramah. But the child ministered to the LORD before Eli the priest.

12 Now the sons of Eli *were* corrupt;*a* they did not know the LORD.

1:20 *a*Literally *Heard by God*   1:23 *a*Following Masoretic Text, Targum, and Vulgate; Dead Sea Scrolls, Septuagint, and Syriac read *your*.   1:24 *a*Dead Sea Scrolls, Septuagint, and Syriac read *a three-year-old bull.*   2:1 *a*That is, *strength*   2:12 *a*Literally *sons of Belial*

---

*Y*ou are not alone. Your Father is higher than the stars and yet closer than the air you breathe. No matter how you have suffered or what you have endured, there is something He wants you to know. Without a doubt, the Father loves you.

13 And the priests' custom with the people *was that* when any man offered a sacrifice, the priest's servant would come with a three-pronged fleshhook in his hand while the meat was boiling. 14 Then he would thrust *it* into the pan, or kettle, or caldron, or pot; and the priest would take for himself all that the fleshhook brought up. So they did in Shiloh to all the Israelites who came there. 15 Also, before they burned the fat, the priest's servant would come and say to the man who sacrificed, "Give meat for roasting to the priest, for he will not take boiled meat from you, but raw."

16 And *if* the man said to him, "They should really burn the fat first; *then* you may take *as much as* your heart desires," he would then answer him, "*No*, but you must give *it* now; and if not, I will take *it* by force."

17 Therefore the sin of the young men was very great before the LORD, for men abhorred the offering of the LORD.

18 But Samuel ministered before the LORD, *even as* a child, wearing a linen ephod. 19 Moreover his mother used to make him a little robe, and bring *it* to him year by year when she came up with her husband to offer the yearly sacrifice. 20 And Eli would bless Elkanah and his wife, and say, "The LORD give you descendants from this woman for the loan that was given to the LORD." Then they would go to their own home.

21 And the LORD visited Hannah, so that she conceived and bore three sons and two daughters. Meanwhile the child Samuel grew before the LORD.

22 Now Eli was very old; and he heard everything his sons did to all Israel,[a] and how they lay with the women who assembled at the door of the tabernacle of meeting. 23 So he said to them, "Why do you do such things? For I hear of your evil dealings from all the people. 24 No, my sons! For *it is* not a good report that I hear. You make the LORD's people transgress. 25 If one man sins against another, God will judge him. But if a man sins against the LORD, who will intercede for him?" Nevertheless they did not heed

the voice of their father, because the LORD desired to kill them.

26 And the child Samuel grew in stature, and in favor both with the LORD and men.

27 Then a man of God came to Eli and said to him, "Thus says the LORD: 'Did I not clearly reveal Myself to the house of your father when they were in Egypt in Pharaoh's house? 28 Did I not choose him out of all the tribes of Israel *to be* My priest, to offer upon My altar, to burn incense, and to wear an ephod before Me? And did I not give to the house of your father all the offerings of the children of Israel made by fire? 29 Why do you kick at My sacrifice and My offering which I have commanded *in My* dwelling place, and honor your sons more than Me, to make yourselves fat with the best of all the offerings of Israel My people?' 30 Therefore the LORD God of Israel says: 'I said indeed *that* your house and the house of your father would walk before Me forever.' But now the LORD says: 'Far be it from Me; for those who honor Me I will honor, and those who despise Me shall be lightly esteemed. 31 Behold, the days are coming that I will cut off your arm and the arm of your father's house, so that there will not be an old man in your house. 32 And you will see an enemy *in My* dwelling place, *despite* all the good which God does for Israel. And there shall not be an old man in your house forever. 33 But any of your men *whom* I do not cut off from My altar shall consume your eyes and grieve your heart. And all the descendants of your house shall die in the flower of their age. 34 Now this *shall be* a sign to you that will come upon your two sons, on Hophni and Phinehas: in one day they shall die, both of them. 35 Then I will raise up for Myself a faithful priest *who* shall do according to what *is* in My heart and in My mind. I will build him a sure house, and he shall walk before My anointed forever. 36 And it shall come to pass that everyone who is left in your house will come *and* bow down to him for a piece of silver and a morsel of bread, and say, "Please, put me in one of the priestly posi-

2:22 [a]Following Masoretic Text, Targum, and Vulgate; Dead Sea Scrolls and Septuagint omit the rest of this verse.

Gospel Pearls

tions, that I may eat a piece of bread." ' "

3 Now the boy Samuel ministered to the LORD before Eli. And the word of the LORD was rare in those days; *there was* no widespread revelation. 2 And it came to pass at that time, while Eli *was* lying down in his place, and when his eyes had begun to grow so dim that he could not see, 3 and before the lamp of God went out in the tabernacle*ᵃ* of the LORD where the ark of God *was,* and while Samuel was lying down, 4 that the LORD called Samuel. And he answered, "Here I am!" 5 So he ran to Eli and said, "Here I am, for you called me."

And he said, "I did not call; lie down again." And he went and lay down.

6 Then the LORD called yet again, "Samuel!"

So Samuel arose and went to Eli, and said, "Here I am, for you called me." He answered, "I did not call, my son; lie down again." 7 (Now Samuel did not yet know the LORD, nor was the word of the LORD yet revealed to him.)

8 And the LORD called Samuel again the third time. So he arose and went to Eli, and said, "Here I am, for you did call me."

Then Eli perceived that the LORD had called the boy. 9 Therefore Eli said to Samuel, "Go, lie down; and it shall be, if He calls you, that you must say, 'Speak, LORD, for Your servant hears.' " So Samuel went and lay down in his place.

10 Now the LORD came and stood and called as at other times, "Samuel! Samuel!"

And Samuel answered, "Speak, for Your servant hears."

11 Then the LORD said to Samuel: "Behold, I will do something in Israel at which both ears of everyone who hears it will tingle. 12 In that day I will perform against Eli all that I have spoken concerning his house, from beginning to end. 13 For I have told him that I will judge his house forever for the iniquity which he knows, because his sons made themselves vile, and he did not restrain

them. 14 And therefore I have sworn to the house of Eli that the iniquity of Eli's house shall not be atoned for by sacrifice or offering forever."

15 So Samuel lay down until morning,*ᵃ* and opened the doors of the house of the LORD. And Samuel was afraid to tell Eli the vision. 16 Then Eli called Samuel and said, "Samuel, my son!"

He answered, "Here I am."

17 And he said, "What *is* the word that *the* LORD spoke to you? Please do not hide *it* from me. God do so to you, and more also, if you hide anything from me of all the things that He said to you." 18 Then Samuel told him everything, and hid nothing from him. And he said, "It *is* the LORD. Let Him do what seems good to Him."

19 So Samuel grew, and the LORD was with him and let none of his words fall to the ground. 20 And all Israel from Dan to Beersheba knew that Samuel *had been* established as a prophet of the LORD. 21 Then the LORD appeared again in Shiloh. For the LORD revealed Himself to Samuel in Shiloh by the word of the LORD.

4 And the word of Samuel came to all Israel.*ᵃ*

Now Israel went out to battle against the Philistines, and encamped beside Ebenezer; and the Philistines encamped in Aphek. 2 Then the Philistines put themselves in battle array against Israel. And when they joined battle, Israel was defeated by the Philistines, who killed about four thousand men of the army in the field. 3 And when the people had come into the camp, the elders of Israel said, "Why has the LORD defeated us today before the Philistines? Let us bring the ark of the covenant of the LORD from Shiloh to us, that when it comes among us it may save us from the hand of our enemies." 4 So the people sent to Shiloh, that they might bring from there the ark of the covenant of the LORD of hosts, who dwells *between* the cherubim. And the two sons of Eli, Hophni and Phinehas, *were* there with the ark of the covenant of God.

5 And when the ark of the covenant

3:3 *ᵃ*Hebrew *heykal,* palace or temple   3:15 *ᵃ*Following Masoretic Text, Targum, and Vulgate; Septuagint adds *and he arose in the morning.*   4:1 *ᵃ*Following Masoretic Text and Targum; Septuagint and Vulgate add *And it came to pass in those days that the Philistines gathered themselves together to fight;* Septuagint adds further *against Israel.*

---

*2*f we were only spirit, we would have no need to be loosed of anything once we were born again. But we are not just spirit. We still live in a fleshly body and we have a worldly soul that needs to be transformed.

of the LORD came into the camp, all Israel shouted so loudly that the earth shook. 6 Now when the Philistines heard the noise of the shout, they said, "What *does* the sound of this great shout in the camp of the Hebrews *mean?*" Then they understood that the ark of the LORD had come into the camp. 7 So the Philistines were afraid, for they said, "God has come into the camp!" And they said, "Woe to us! For such a thing has never happened before. 8 Woe to us! Who will deliver us from the hand of these mighty gods? These *are* the gods who struck the Egyptians with all the plagues in the wilderness. 9 Be strong and conduct yourselves like men, you Philistines, that you do not become servants of the Hebrews, as they have been to you. Conduct yourselves like men, and fight!"

10 So the Philistines fought, and Israel was defeated, and every man fled to his tent. There was a very great slaughter, and there fell of Israel thirty thousand foot soldiers. 11 Also the ark of God was captured; and the two sons of Eli, Hophni and Phinehas, died.

12 Then a man of Benjamin ran from the battle line the same day, and came to Shiloh with his clothes torn and dirt on his head. 13 Now when he came, there was Eli, sitting on a seat by the wayside watching,[a] for his heart trembled for the ark of God. And when the man came into the city and told *it,* all the city cried out. 14 When Eli heard the noise of the outcry, he said, "What *does* the sound of this tumult *mean?*" And the man came quickly and told Eli. 15 Eli was ninety-eight years old, and his eyes were so dim that he could not see.

16 Then the man said to Eli, "I *am* he who came from the battle. And I fled today from the battle line."

And he said, "What happened, my son?"

17 So the messenger answered and said, "Israel has fled before the Philistines, and there has been a great slaughter among the people. Also your two sons, Hophni and Phinehas,

are dead; and the ark of God has been captured."

18 Then it happened, when he made mention of the ark of God, that Eli fell off the seat backward by the side of the gate; and his neck was broken and he died, for the man was old and heavy. And he had judged Israel forty years.

19 Now his daughter-in-law, Phinehas' wife, was with child, *due* to be delivered; and when she heard the news that the ark of God was captured, and that her father-in-law and her husband were dead, she bowed herself and gave birth, for her labor pains came upon her. 20 And about the time of her death the women who stood by her said to her, "Do not fear, for you have borne a son." But she did not answer, nor did she regard *it.* 21 Then she named the child Ichabod,[a] saying, "The glory has departed from Israel!" because the ark of God had been captured and because of her father-in-law and her husband. 22 And she said, "The glory has departed from Israel, for the ark of God has been captured."

5 Then the Philistines took the ark of God and brought it from Ebenezer to Ashdod. 2 When the Philistines took the ark of God, they brought it into the house of Dagon[a] and set it by Dagon. 3 And when the people of Ashdod arose early in the morning, there was Dagon, fallen on its face to the earth before the ark of the LORD. So they took Dagon and set it in its place again. 4 And when they arose early the next morning, there was Dagon, fallen on its face to the ground before the ark of the LORD. The head of Dagon and both the palms of its hands *were* broken off on the threshold; only Dagon's torso[a] was left of it. 5 Therefore neither the priests of Dagon nor any who come into Dagon's house tread on the threshold of Dagon in Ashdod to this day.

6 But the hand of the LORD was heavy on the people of Ashdod, and He ravaged them and struck them with tumors,[a] *both* Ashdod and its territory. 7 And when the men of

---

4:13 [a]Following Masoretic Text and Vulgate; Septuagint reads *beside the gate watching the road.*
4:21 [a]Literally *Inglorious*   5:2 [a]A Philistine idol   5:4 [a]Following Septuagint, Syriac, Targum, and Vulgate; Masoretic Text reads *Dagon.*   5:6 [a]Probably bubonic plague. Septuagint and Vulgate add here *And in the midst of their land rats sprang up, and there was a great death panic in the city.*

Gospel Pearls

Ashdod saw how *it was,* they said, "The ark of the God of Israel must not remain with us, for His hand is harsh toward us and Dagon our god." 8 Therefore they sent and gathered to themselves all the lords of the Philistines, and said, "What shall we do with the ark of the God of Israel?"

And they answered, "Let the ark of the God of Israel be carried away to Gath." So they carried the ark of the God of Israel away. 9 So it was, after they had carried it away, that the hand of the LORD was against the city with a very great destruction; and He struck the men of the city, both small and great, and tumors broke out on them.

10 Therefore they sent the ark of God to Ekron. So it was, as the ark of God came to Ekron, that the Ekronites cried out, saying, "They have brought the ark of the God of Israel to us, to kill us and our people!" 11 So they sent and gathered together all the lords of the Philistines, and said, "Send away the ark of the God of Israel, and let it go back to its own place, so that it does not kill us and our people." For there was a deadly destruction throughout all the city; the hand of God was very heavy there. 12 And the men who did not die were stricken with the tumors, and the cry of the city went up to heaven.

6 Now the ark of the LORD was in the country of the Philistines seven months. 2 And the Philistines called for the priests and the diviners, saying, "What shall we do with the ark of the LORD? Tell us how we should send it to its place."

3 So they said, "If you send away the ark of the God of Israel, do not send it empty; but by all means return *it* to Him *with* a trespass offering. Then you will be healed, and it will be known to you why His hand is not removed from you."

4 Then they said, "What *is* the trespass offering which we shall return to Him?"

They answered, "Five golden tumors and five golden rats, *according to* the number of the lords of the Philistines. For the same plague *was* on all of you and on your lords. 5 Therefore you shall make images of your tumors and images of your rats that ravage the land, and you shall

give glory to the God of Israel; perhaps He will lighten His hand from you, from your gods, and from your land. 6 Why then do you harden your hearts as the Egyptians and Pharaoh hardened their hearts? When He did mighty things among them, did they not let the people go, that they might depart? 7 Now therefore, make a new cart, take two milk cows which have never been yoked, and hitch the cows to the cart; and take their calves home, away from them. 8 Then take the ark of the LORD and set it on the cart; and put the articles of gold which you are returning to Him *as a* trespass offering in a chest by its side. Then send it away, and let it go. 9 And watch: if it goes up the road to its own territory, to Beth Shemesh, *then* He has done us this great evil. But if not, then we shall know that *it is* not His hand *that* struck us—it happened to us by chance."

10 Then the men did so; they took two milk cows and hitched them to the cart, and shut up their calves at home. 11 And they set the ark of the LORD on the cart, and the chest with the gold rats and the images of their tumors. 12 Then the cows headed straight for the road to Beth Shemesh, *and* went along the highway, lowing as they went, and did not turn aside to the right hand or the left. And the lords of the Philistines went after them to the border of Beth Shemesh.

13 Now *the people of* Beth Shemesh *were* reaping their wheat harvest in the valley; and they lifted their eyes and saw the ark, and rejoiced to see *it.* 14 Then the cart came into the field of Joshua of Beth Shemesh, and stood there; a large stone *was* there. So they split the wood of the cart and offered the cows as a burnt offering to the LORD. 15 The Levites took down the ark of the LORD and the chest that *was* with it, in which *were* the articles of gold, and put *them* on the large stone. Then the men of Beth Shemesh offered burnt offerings and made sacrifices the same day to the LORD. 16 So when the five lords of the Philistines had seen *it,* they returned to Ekron the same day.

17 These *are* the golden tumors which the Philistines returned *as a* trespass offering to the LORD: one for Ashdod, one for Gaza, one for Ash-

---

God wants you to experience a freedom in Him—a freedom from temptation, sin, guilt, things that are past, relationships that are over—in order that you might *live.*

kelon, one for Gath, one for Ekron; 18 and the golden rats, *according to* the number of all the cities of the Philistines *belonging* to the five lords, *both* fortified cities and country villages, even as far as the large *stone of* Abel on which they set the ark of the LORD, *which stone remains* to this day in the field of Joshua of Beth Shemesh.

19 Then He struck the men of Beth Shemesh, because they had looked into the ark of the LORD. He struck fifty thousand and seventy men*ᵃ* of the people, and the people lamented because the LORD had struck the people with a great slaughter.

20 And the men of Beth Shemesh said, "Who is able to stand before this holy LORD God? And to whom shall it go up from us?" 21 So they sent messengers to the inhabitants of Kirjath Jearim, saying, "The Philistines have brought back the ark of the LORD; come down *and* take it up with you."

7 Then the men of Kirjath Jearim came and took the ark of the LORD, and brought it into the house of Abinadab on the hill, and consecrated Eleazar his son to keep the ark of the LORD.

2 So it was that the ark remained in Kirjath Jearim a long time; it was there twenty years. And all the house of Israel lamented after the LORD.

3 Then Samuel spoke to all the house of Israel, saying, "If you return to the LORD with all your hearts, *then* put away the foreign gods and the Ashtoreths*ᵃ* from among you, and prepare your hearts for the LORD, and serve Him only; and He will deliver you from the hand of the Philistines." 4 So the children of Israel put away the Baals and the Ashtoreths,*ᵃ* and served the LORD only.

5 And Samuel said, "Gather all Israel to Mizpah, and I will pray to the LORD for you." 6 So they gathered together at Mizpah, drew water, and poured *it* out before the LORD. And they fasted that day, and said there, "We have sinned against the LORD." And Samuel judged the children of Israel at Mizpah.

7 Now when the Philistines heard that the children of Israel had gathered together at Mizpah, the lords of the Philistines went up against Israel. And when the children of Israel heard *of it,* they were afraid of the Philistines. 8 So the children of Israel said to Samuel, "Do not cease to cry out to the LORD our God for us, that He may save us from the hand of the Philistines."

9 And Samuel took a suckling lamb and offered *it as* a whole burnt offering to the LORD. Then Samuel cried out to the LORD for Israel, and the LORD answered him. 10 Now as Samuel was offering up the burnt offering, the Philistines drew near to battle against Israel. But the LORD thundered with a loud thunder upon the Philistines that day, and so confused them that they were overcome before Israel. 11 And the men of Israel went out of Mizpah and pursued the Philistines, and drove them back as far as below Beth Car. 12 Then Samuel took a stone and set *it* up between Mizpah and Shen, and called its name Ebenezer,*ᵃ* saying, "Thus far the LORD has helped us."

13 So the Philistines were subdued, and they did not come anymore into the territory of Israel. And the hand of the LORD was against the Philistines all the days of Samuel. 14 Then the cities which the Philistines had taken from Israel were restored to Israel, from Ekron to Gath; and Israel recovered its territory from the hands of the Philistines. Also there was peace between Israel and the Amorites.

15 And Samuel judged Israel all the days of his life. 16 He went from year to year on a circuit to Bethel, Gilgal, and Mizpah, and judged Israel in all those places. 17 But he always returned to Ramah, for his home *was* there. There he judged Israel, and there he built an altar to the LORD.

8 Now it came to pass when Samuel was old that he made his sons judges over Israel. 2 The name of his firstborn was Joel, and the name of his second, Abijah; *they were* judges in Beersheba. 3 But his sons did not walk in his ways; they turned aside after dishonest gain, took bribes, and perverted justice.

6:19 ᵃOr *He struck seventy men of the people and fifty oxen of a man*   7:3 ᵃ*Canaanite goddesses*
7:4 ᵃ*Canaanite goddesses*   7:12 ᵃLiterally *Stone of Help*

Gospel Pearls

4 Then all the elders of Israel gathered together and came to Samuel at Ramah, 5 and said to him, "Look, you are old, and your sons do not walk in your ways. Now make us a king to judge us like all the nations."

6 But the thing displeased Samuel when they said, "Give us a king to judge us." So Samuel prayed to the LORD. 7 And the LORD said to Samuel, "Heed the voice of the people in all that they say to you; for they have not rejected you, but they have rejected Me, that I should not reign over them. 8 According to all the works which they have done since the day that I brought them up out of Egypt, even to this day—with which they have forsaken Me and served other gods—so they are doing to you also. 9 Now therefore, heed their voice. However, you shall solemnly forewarn them, and show them the behavior of the king who will reign over them."

10 So Samuel told all the words of the LORD to the people who asked him for a king. 11 And he said, "This will be the behavior of the king who will reign over you: He will take your sons and appoint *them* for his own chariots and *to be* his horsemen, and *some* will run before his chariots. 12 He will appoint captains over his thousands and captains over his fifties, *will set some* to plow his ground and reap his harvest, and *some* to make his weapons of war and equipment for his chariots. 13 He will take your daughters *to be* perfumers, cooks, and bakers. 14 And he will take the best of your fields, your vineyards, and your olive groves, and give *them* to his servants. 15 He will take a tenth of your grain and your vintage, and give it to his officers and servants. 16 And he will take your male servants, your female servants, your finest young men,[a] and your donkeys, and put *them* to his work. 17 He will take a tenth of your sheep. And you will be his servants. 18 And you will cry out in that day because of your king whom you have chosen for yourselves, and the LORD will not hear you in that day."

19 Nevertheless the people refused to obey the voice of Samuel; and they said, "No, but we will have a king over us, 20 that we also may be like

all the nations, and that our king may judge us and go out before us and fight our battles."

21 And Samuel heard all the words of the people, and he repeated them in the hearing of the LORD. 22 So the LORD said to Samuel, "Heed their voice, and make them a king."

And Samuel said to the men of Israel, "Every man go to his city."

9 There was a man of Benjamin whose name *was* Kish the son of Abiel, the son of Zeror, the son of Bechorath, the son of Aphiah, a Benjamite, a mighty man of power. 2 And he had a choice and handsome son whose name *was* Saul. *There was* not a more handsome person than he among the children of Israel. From his shoulders upward *he was* taller than any of the people.

3 Now the donkeys of Kish, Saul's father, were lost. And Kish said to his son Saul, "Please take one of the servants with you, and arise, go and look for the donkeys." 4 So he passed through the mountains of Ephraim and through the land of Shalisha, but they did not find *them*. Then they passed through the land of Shaalim, and *they were* not *there*. Then he passed through the land of the Benjamites, but they did not find *them*.

5 When they had come to the land of Zuph, Saul said to his servant who *was* with him, "Come, let us return, lest my father cease *caring* about the donkeys and become worried about us."

6 And he said to him, "Look now, *there is* in this city a man of God, and *he is* an honorable man; all that he says surely comes to pass. So let us go there; perhaps he can show us the way that we should go."

7 Then Saul said to his servant, "But look, *if* we go, what shall we bring the man? For the bread in our vessels is all gone, and *there is* no present to bring to the man of God. What do we have?"

8 And the servant answered Saul again and said, "Look, I have here at hand one-fourth of a shekel of silver. I will give *that* to the man of God, to tell us our way." 9 (Formerly in Israel, when a man went to inquire of God, he spoke thus: "Come, let us go to the seer"; for *he who is* now

8:16 *a*Septuagint reads *cattle*.

---

called a prophet was formerly called a seer.)

10 Then Saul said to his servant, "Well said; come, let us go." So they went to the city where the man of God *was.*

11 As they went up the hill to the city, they met some young women going out to draw water, and said to them, "Is the seer here?"

12 And they answered them and said, "Yes, there he is, just ahead of you. Hurry now; for today he came to this city, because there is a sacrifice of the people today on the high place. 13 As soon as you come into the city, you will surely find him before he goes up to the high place to eat. For the people will not eat until he comes, because he must bless the sacrifice; afterward those who are invited will eat. Now therefore, go up, for about this time you will find him."

14 So they went up to the city. As they were coming into the city, there was Samuel, coming out toward them on his way up to the high place.

15 Now the LORD had told Samuel in his ear the day before Saul came, saying, 16 "Tomorrow about this time I will send you a man from the land of Benjamin, and you shall anoint him commander over My people Israel, that he may save My people from the hand of the Philistines; for I have looked upon My people, because their cry has come to Me."

17 So when Samuel saw Saul, the LORD said to him, "There he is, the man of whom I spoke to you. This one shall reign over My people."

18 Then Saul drew near to Samuel in the gate, and said, "Please tell me, where *is* the seer's house?"

19 Samuel answered Saul and said, "I *am* the seer. Go up before me to the high place, for you shall eat with me today; and tomorrow I will let you go and will tell you all that *is* in your heart. 20 But as for your donkeys that were lost three days ago, do not be anxious about them, for they have been found. And on whom *is* all the desire of Israel? *Is it* not on you and on all your father's house?"

21 And Saul answered and said,

"Am I not a Benjamite, of the smallest of the tribes of Israel, and my family the least of all the families of the tribe*ᵃ* of Benjamin? Why then do you speak like this to me?"

22 Now Samuel took Saul and his servant and brought them into the hall, and had them sit in the place of honor among those who were invited; there *were* about thirty persons. 23 And Samuel said to the cook, "Bring the portion which I gave you, of which I said to you, 'Set it apart.' " 24 So the cook took up the thigh with its upper part and set *it* before Saul. And *Samuel* said, "Here it is, what was kept back. *It* was set apart for you. Eat; for until this time it has been kept for you, since I said I invited the people." So Saul ate with Samuel that day.

25 When they had come down from the high place into the city, *Samuel* spoke with Saul on the top of the house.*ᵃ* 26 They arose early; and it was about the dawning of the day that Samuel called to Saul on the top of the house, saying, "Get up, that I may send you on your way." And Saul arose, and both of them went outside, he and Samuel.

27 As they were going down to the outskirts of the city, Samuel said to Saul, "Tell the servant to go on ahead of us." And he went on. "But you stand here awhile, that I may announce to you the word of God."

10 Then Samuel took a flask of oil and poured *it* on his head, and kissed him and said: "*Is it* not because the LORD has anointed you commander over His inheritance?*ᵃ* 2 When you have departed from me today, you will find two men by Rachel's tomb in the territory of Benjamin at Zelzah; and they will say to you, 'The donkeys which you went to look for have been found. And now your father has ceased caring about the donkeys and is worrying about you, saying, "What shall I do about my son?" ' 3 Then you shall go on forward from there and come to the terebinth tree of Tabor. There three men going up to God at Bethel

---

9:21 ᵃLiterally *tribes*   9:25 ᵃFollowing Masoretic Text and Targum; Septuagint omits *He spoke with Saul on top of the house;* Septuagint and Vulgate add *And he prepared a bed for Saul on top of the house, and he slept.*   10:1 ᵃFollowing Masoretic Text, Targum, and Vulgate; Septuagint reads *His people Israel; and you shall rule the people of the Lord;* Septuagint and Vulgate add *And you shall deliver His people from the hands of their enemies all around them. And this shall be a sign to you, that God has anointed you to be prince.*

Gospel Pearls

will meet you, one carrying three young goats, another carrying three loaves of bread, and another carrying a skin of wine. 4 And they will greet you and give you two *loaves* of bread, which you shall receive from their hands. 5 After that you shall come to the hill of God where the Philistine garrison *is*. And it will happen, when you have come there to the city, that you will meet a group of prophets coming down from the high place with a stringed instrument, a tambourine, a flute, and a harp before them; and they will be prophesying. 6 Then the Spirit of the LORD will come upon you, and you will prophesy with them and be turned into another man. 7 And let it be, when these signs come to you, *that* you do as the occasion demands; for God *is* with you. 8 You shall go down before me to Gilgal; and surely I will come down to you to offer burnt offerings *and* make sacrifices of peace offerings. Seven days you shall wait, till I come to you and show you what you should do."

9 So it was, when he had turned his back to go from Samuel, that God gave him another heart; and all those signs came to pass that day. 10 When they came there to the hill, there was a group of prophets to meet him; then the Spirit of God came upon him, and he prophesied among them. 11 And it happened, when all who knew him formerly saw that he indeed prophesied among the prophets, that the people said to one another, "What *is* this *that* has come upon the son of Kish? *Is* Saul also among the prophets?" 12 Then a man from there answered and said, "But who *is* their father?" Therefore it became a proverb: "*Is* Saul also among the prophets?" 13 And when he had finished prophesying, he went to the high place.

14 Then Saul's uncle said to him and his servant, "Where did you go?"

So he said, "To look for the donkeys. When we saw that *they were* nowhere *to be found,* we went to Samuel."

15 And Saul's uncle said, "Tell me, please, what Samuel said to you."

16 So Saul said to his uncle, "He told us plainly that the donkeys had been found." But about the matter of

the kingdom, he did not tell him what Samuel had said.

17 Then Samuel called the people together to the LORD at Mizpah, 18 and said to the children of Israel, "Thus says the LORD God of Israel: 'I brought up Israel out of Egypt, and delivered you from the hand of the Egyptians *and* from the hand of all kingdoms and from those who oppressed you.' 19 But you have today rejected your God, who Himself saved you from all your adversities and your tribulations; and you have said to Him, 'No, set a king over us!' Now therefore, present yourselves before the LORD by your tribes and by your clans."*a*

20 And when Samuel had caused all the tribes of Israel to come near, the tribe of Benjamin was chosen. 21 When he had caused the tribe of Benjamin to come near by their families, the family of Matri was chosen. And Saul the son of Kish was chosen. But when they sought him, he could not be found. 22 Therefore they inquired of the LORD further, "Has the man come here yet?"

And the LORD answered, "There he is, hidden among the equipment."

23 So they ran and brought him from there; and when he stood among the people, he was taller than any of the people from his shoulders upward. 24 And Samuel said to all the people, "Do you see him whom the LORD has chosen, that *there is* no one like him among all the people?"

So all the people shouted and said, "Long live the king!"

25 Then Samuel explained to the people the behavior of royalty, and wrote *it* in a book and laid *it* up before the LORD. And Samuel sent all the people away, every man to his house. 26 And Saul also went home to Gibeah; and valiant *men* went with him, whose hearts God had touched. 27 But some rebels said, "How can this man save us?" So they despised him, and brought him no presents. But he held his peace.

11 Then Nahash the Ammonite came up and encamped against Jabesh Gilead; and all the men of Jabesh said to Nahash, "Make a covenant with us, and we will serve you."

2 And Nahash the Ammonite an-

10:19 *a*Literally *thousands*

God had a plan and purpose for Leah. He had created her for a divine role in His eternal plan and when He saw that Leah was despised by Jacob, He opened her womb and allowed her to bear children.

swered them, "On this *condition* I will make *a* covenant with you, that I may put out all your right eyes, and bring reproach on all Israel."

3 Then the elders of Jabesh said to him, "Hold off for seven days, that we may send messengers to all the territory of Israel. And then, if *there is* no one to save us, we will come out to you."

4 So the messengers came to Gibeah of Saul and told the news in the hearing of the people. And all the people lifted up their voices and wept. 5 Now there was Saul, coming behind the herd from the field; and Saul said, "What *troubles* the people, that they weep?" And they told him the words of the men of Jabesh. 6 Then the Spirit of God came upon Saul when he heard this news, and his anger was greatly aroused. 7 So he took a yoke of oxen and cut them in pieces, and sent *them* throughout all the territory of Israel by the hands of messengers, saying, "Whoever does not go out with Saul and Samuel to battle, so it shall be done to his oxen."

And the fear of the LORD fell on the people, and they came out with one consent. 8 When he numbered them in Bezek, the children of Israel were three hundred thousand, and the men of Judah thirty thousand. 9 And they said to the messengers who came, "Thus you shall say to the men of Jabesh Gilead: 'Tomorrow, by *the time* the sun is hot, you shall have help.'" Then the messengers came and reported *it* to the men of Jabesh, and they were glad. 10 Therefore the men of Jabesh said, "Tomorrow we will come out to you, and you may do with us whatever seems good to you."

11 So it was, on the next day, that Saul put the people in three companies; and they came into the midst of the camp in the morning watch, and killed Ammonites until the heat of the day. And it happened that those who survived were scattered, so that no two of them were left together.

12 Then the people said to Samuel, "Who *is* he who said, 'Shall Saul reign over us?' Bring the men, that we may put them to death."

13 But Saul said, "Not a man shall be put to death this day, for today the LORD has accomplished salvation in Israel."

14 Then Samuel said to the people, "Come, let us go to Gilgal and renew the kingdom there." 15 So all the people went to Gilgal, and there they made Saul king before the LORD in Gilgal. There they made sacrifices of peace offerings before the LORD, and there Saul and all the men of Israel rejoiced greatly.

12 Now Samuel said to all Israel: "Indeed I have heeded your voice in all that you said to me, and have made a king over you. 2 And now here is the king, walking before you; and I am old and grayheaded, and look, my sons *are* with you. I have walked before you from my childhood to this day. 3 Here I am. Witness against me before the LORD and before His anointed: Whose ox have I taken, or whose donkey have I taken, or whom have I cheated? Whom have I oppressed, or from whose hand have I received *any* bribe with which to blind my eyes? I will restore *it* to you."

4 And they said, "You have not cheated us or oppressed us, nor have you taken anything from any man's hand."

5 Then he said to them, "The LORD *is* witness against you, and His anointed *is* witness this day, that you have not found anything in my hand."

And they answered, "*He is* witness."

6 Then Samuel said to the people, "*It is* the LORD who raised up Moses and Aaron, and who brought your fathers up from the land of Egypt. 7 Now therefore, stand still, that I may reason with you before the LORD concerning all the righteous acts of the LORD which He did to you and your fathers: 8 When Jacob had gone into Egypt,[a] and your fathers cried out to the LORD, then the LORD sent Moses and Aaron, who brought your fathers out of Egypt and made them dwell in this place. 9 And when they forgot the LORD their God, He sold them into the hand of Sisera, commander of the army of Hazor, into the hand of the Philistines, and into the hand of the king of Moab; and

---

12:8 [a]Following Masoretic Text, Targum, and Vulgate; Septuagint adds *and the Egyptians afflicted them.*

Gospel Pearls

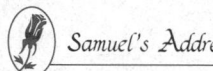
they fought against them. 10 Then they cried out to the LORD, and said, 'We have sinned, because we have forsaken the LORD and served the Baals and Ashtoreths;ᵃ but now deliver us from the hand of our enemies, and we will serve You.' 11 And the LORD sent Jerubbaal,ᵃ Bedan,ᵇ Jephthah, and Samuel,ᶜ and delivered you out of the hand of your enemies on every side; and you dwelt in safety. 12 And when you saw that Nahash king of the Ammonites came against you, you said to me, 'No, but a king shall reign over us,' when the LORD your God *was* your king.

13 "Now therefore, here is the king whom you have chosen *and* whom you have desired. And take note, the LORD has set a king over you. 14 If you fear the LORD and serve Him and obey His voice, and do not rebel against the commandment of the LORD, then both you and the king who reigns over you will continue following the LORD your God. 15 However, if you do not obey the voice of the LORD, but rebel against the commandment of the LORD, then the hand of the LORD will be against you, as *it was* against your fathers.

16 "Now therefore, stand and see this great thing which the LORD will do before your eyes: 17 *Is* today not the wheat harvest? I will call to the LORD, and He will send thunder and rain, that you may perceive and see that your wickedness *is* great, which you have done in the sight of the LORD, in asking a king for yourselves."

18 So Samuel called to the LORD, and the LORD sent thunder and rain that day; and all the people greatly feared the LORD and Samuel.

19 And all the people said to Samuel, "Pray for your servants to the LORD your God, that we may not die; for we have added to all our sins the evil of asking a king for ourselves."

20 Then Samuel said to the people, "Do not fear. You have done all this wickedness; yet do not turn aside from following the LORD, but serve the LORD with all your heart. 21 And do not turn aside; for *then you would* go after empty things which

cannot profit or deliver, for they *are* nothing. 22 For the LORD will not forsake His people, for His great name's sake, because it has pleased the LORD to make you His people. 23 Moreover, as for me, far be it from me that I should sin against the LORD in ceasing to pray for you; but I will teach you the good and the right way. 24 Only fear the LORD, and serve Him in truth with all your heart; for consider what great things He has done for you. 25 But if you still do wickedly, you shall be swept away, both you and your king."

13 Saul reigned one year; and when he had reigned two years over Israel,ᵃ 2 Saul chose for himself three thousand *men* of Israel. Two thousand were with Saul in Michmash and in the mountains of Bethel, and a thousand were with Jonathan in Gibeah of Benjamin. The rest of the people he sent away, every man to his tent.

3 And Jonathan attacked the garrison of the Philistines that *was* in Geba, and the Philistines heard *of it*. Then Saul blew the trumpet throughout all the land, saying, "Let the Hebrews hear!" 4 Now all Israel heard it said *that* Saul had attacked a garrison of the Philistines, and *that* Israel had also become an abomination to the Philistines. And the people were called together to Saul at Gilgal.

5 Then the Philistines gathered together to fight with Israel, thirtyᵃ thousand chariots and six thousand horsemen, and people as the sand which *is* on the seashore in multitude. And they came up and encamped in Michmash, to the east of Beth Aven. 6 When the men of Israel saw that they were in danger (for the people were distressed), then the people hid in caves, in thickets, in rocks, in holes, and in pits. 7 And *some* of the Hebrews crossed over the Jordan to the land of Gad and Gilead.

As for Saul, he *was* still in Gilgal, and all the people followed him trembling. 8 Then he waited seven days, according to the time set by Samuel. But Samuel did not come to Gilgal;

12:10 ᵃCanaanite goddesses   12:11 ᵃSyriac reads *Deborah*; Targum reads *Gideon*.   ᵇSeptuagint and Syriac read *Barak*; Targum reads *Simson*.   ᶜSyriac reads *Simson*.   13:1 ᵃThe Hebrew is difficult (compare 2 Samuel 5:4; 2 Kings 14:2; see also 2 Samuel 2:10; Acts 13:21).   13:5 ᵃFollowing Masoretic Text, Septuagint, Targum, and Vulgate; Syriac and some manuscripts of the Septuagint read *three*.

God sees you. You are not invisible to Him. You are not unknown to Him. You are not a mystery to Him. He *still* has a plan and a purpose for your life. He has something that He has put in you that He desires to bring to fruition.

Free Indeed

I Samuel 12:21, 22

*I*f you are a woman who has been hurt or abused by men, it is time to be loosed. But, you ask, "What do I do?" How can you break free?

First, you need to isolate the problem from the gender. You need to understand that all men are not the same. Isolating the problem brings healing. When you isolate your problem, you put it in quarantine and forbid it to infect all areas of your life. When you isolate it, you stop the enemy from using it to rob you of good moments in the present because of bad moments in the past.

Second, you must allow God's love to pierce through the pain. It must be God's love first, not man's, because God's love is the only love that is perfect enough to pass your stringent test. His love is perfect and will cast out fear (see 1 John 4:18). His love will restore the opportunity for the little girl in you to have a loving relationship with a Father who will not fail. Love is God's gift given against pain. You can come right now and lay your head on His strong breast and be healed. There is no molestation in God; He will not abuse you. You can trust Him. It is with Him that you can learn to unleash the love you have locked up.

But it must not stop with God. When you are whole, you will be able to love others, even others who are imperfect and have flaws, without having flashbacks and associating today with yesterday. Out of the wholeness of your relationship with Jesus, you can regain the courage to experience love and life with others. It is a born-again experience. It is freedom. It is God raising or nurturing a woman who is wrestling with little-girl issues. It is a chance to do it over again and this time get it right.

Out of the wellsprings of her relationship with her heavenly Father, she may be able to mend the breaches and repair the damages that have caused dysfunction to develop in her natural relationships. The wholeness that is reconstructed through her relationship with the Father helps her to understand, appreciate, and develop a comfort zone with men. Beyond having a point of reference that dispels the mystique of the masculine personality, she also has a comfort zone in prayer that is less suspicious and more faith-filled.

One of the greatest things that we are afforded as Christians is the opportunity to receive restoration in our areas of depletion. Thank God that we have a Lord who can be touched by the feeling of our infirmities (Hebrews 4:15)! He is able to minister to the voids in us. This ministry brings us to wholeness. That wholeness in turn makes it possible to live as if the brokenness had never occurred.

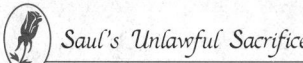

and the people were scattered from him. 9 So Saul said, "Bring a burnt offering and peace offerings here to me." And he offered the burnt offering. 10 Now it happened, as soon as he had finished presenting the burnt offering, that Samuel came; and Saul went out to meet him, that he might greet him.

11 And Samuel said, "What have you done?"

Saul said, "When I saw that the people were scattered from me, and *that* you did not come within the days appointed, and *that* the Philistines gathered together at Michmash, 12 then I said, 'The Philistines will now come down on me at Gilgal, and I have not made supplication to the LORD.' Therefore I felt compelled, and offered a burnt offering."

13 And Samuel said to Saul, "You have done foolishly. You have not kept the commandment of the LORD your God, which He commanded you. For now the LORD would have established your kingdom over Israel forever. 14 But now your kingdom shall not continue. The LORD has sought for Himself a man after His own heart, and the LORD has commanded him *to be* commander over His people, because you have not kept what the LORD commanded you."

15 Then Samuel arose and went up from Gilgal to Gibeah of Benjamin.*ᵃ* And Saul numbered the people present with him, about six hundred men.

16 Saul, Jonathan his son, and the people present with them remained in Gibeah of Benjamin. But the Philistines encamped in Michmash. 17 Then raiders came out of the camp of the Philistines in three companies. One company turned onto the road to Ophrah, to the land of Shual, 18 another company turned to the road *to* Beth Horon, and another company turned *to* the road of the border that overlooks the Valley of Zeboim toward the wilderness.

19 Now there was no blacksmith to be found throughout all the land of Israel, for the Philistines said, "Lest the Hebrews make swords or spears." 20 But all the Israelites would go down to the Philistines to sharpen each man's plowshare, his mattock, his ax, and his sickle; 21 and the charge for a sharpening was a pim*ᵃ* for the plowshares, the mattocks, the forks, and the axes, and to set the points of the goads. 22 So it came about, on the day of battle, that there was neither sword nor spear found in the hand of any of the people who *were* with Saul and Jonathan. But they were found with Saul and Jonathan his son.

23 And the garrison of the Philistines went out to the pass of Michmash.

14 Now it happened one day that Jonathan the son of Saul said to the young man who bore his armor, "Come, let us go over to the Philistines' garrison that *is* on the other side." But he did not tell his father. 2 And Saul was sitting in the outskirts of Gibeah under a pomegranate tree which *is* in Migron. The people who *were* with him *were* about six hundred men. 3 Ahijah the son of Ahitub, Ichabod's brother, the son of Phinehas, the son of Eli, the LORD's priest in Shiloh, was wearing an ephod. But the people did not know that Jonathan had gone.

4 Between the passes, by which Jonathan sought to go over to the Philistines' garrison, *there was* a sharp rock on one side and a sharp rock on the other side. And the name of one *was* Bozez, and the name of the other Seneh. 5 The front of one faced northward opposite Michmash, and the other southward opposite Gibeah.

6 Then Jonathan said to the young man who bore his armor, "Come, let us go over to the garrison of these uncircumcised; it may be that the LORD will work for us. For nothing restrains the LORD from saving by many or by few."

7 So his armorbearer said to him, "Do all that is in your heart. Go then; here I am with you, according to your heart."

8 Then Jonathan said, "Very well, let us cross over to *these* men, and we will show ourselves to them. 9 If they say thus to us, 'Wait until we come to you,' then we will stand

---

13:15 *ᵃFollowing Masoretic Text and Targum; Septuagint and Vulgate add And the rest of the people went up after Saul to meet the people who fought against them, going from Gilgal to Gibeah in the hill of Benjamin.*   13:21 *ᵃAbout two-thirds shekel weight*

God sees you and He intends for others not only to see you but to receive from you the hidden treasure He put inside you.

still in our place and not go up to them. 10 But if they say thus, 'Come up to us,' then we will go up. For the LORD has delivered them into our hand, and this *will be* a sign to us."

11 So both of them showed themselves to the garrison of the Philistines. And the Philistines said, "Look, the Hebrews are coming out of the holes where they have hidden." 12 Then the men of the garrison called to Jonathan and his armorbearer, and said, "Come up to us, and we will show you something."

Jonathan said to his armorbearer, "Come up after me, for the LORD has delivered them into the hand of Israel." 13 And Jonathan climbed up on his hands and knees with his armorbearer after him; and they fell before Jonathan. And as he came after him, his armorbearer killed them. 14 That first slaughter which Jonathan and his armorbearer made was about twenty men within about half an acre of land.*a*

15 And there was trembling in the camp, in the field, and among all the people. The garrison and the raiders also trembled; and the earth quaked, so that it was a very great trembling. 16 Now the watchmen of Saul in Gibeah of Benjamin looked, and *there* was the multitude, melting away; and they went here and there. 17 Then Saul said to the people who *were* with him, "Now call the roll and see who has gone from us." And when they had called the roll, surprisingly, Jonathan and his armorbearer *were* not *there.* 18 And Saul said to Ahijah, "Bring the ark*a* of God here" (for at that time the ark*b* of God was with the children of Israel). 19 Now it happened, while Saul talked to the priest, that the noise which *was* in the camp of the Philistines continued to increase; so Saul said to the priest, "Withdraw your hand." 20 Then Saul and all the people who *were* with him assembled, and they went to the battle; and indeed every man's sword was against his neighbor, *and there was* very great confusion. 21 Moreover the Hebrews *who* were with the Philistines before that time, who went up with them into the camp *from the* sur-

rounding *country,* they also joined the Israelites who *were* with Saul and Jonathan. 22 Likewise all the men of Israel who had hidden in the mountains of Ephraim, *when* they heard that the Philistines fled, they also followed hard after them in the battle. 23 So the LORD saved Israel that day, and the battle shifted to Beth Aven.

24 And the men of Israel were distressed that day, for Saul had placed the people under oath, saying, "Cursed *is* the man who eats *any* food until evening, before I have taken vengeance on my enemies." So none of the people tasted food. 25 Now all *the people* of the land came to a forest; and there was honey on the ground. 26 And when the people had come into the woods, there was the honey, dripping; but no one put his hand to his mouth, for the people feared the oath. 27 But Jonathan had not heard his father charge the people with the oath; therefore he stretched out the end of the rod that *was* in his hand and dipped it in a honeycomb, and put his hand to his mouth; and his countenance brightened. 28 Then one of the people said, "Your father strictly charged the people with an oath, saying, 'Cursed *is* the man who eats food this day.'" And the people were faint.

29 But Jonathan said, "My father has troubled the land. Look now, how my countenance has brightened because I tasted a little of this honey. 30 How much better if the people had eaten freely today of the spoil of their enemies which they found! For now would there not have been a much greater slaughter among the Philistines?"

31 Now they had driven back the Philistines that day from Michmash to Aijalon. So the people were very faint. 32 And the people rushed on the spoil, and took sheep, oxen, and calves, and slaughtered *them* on the ground; and the people ate *them* with the blood. 33 Then they told Saul, saying, "Look, the people are sinning against the LORD by eating with the blood!"

So he said, "You have dealt treacherously; roll a large stone to me this

---

14:14 *a*Literally *half the area plowed by a yoke* (of oxen in a day)   14:18 *a*Following Masoretic Text, Targum, and Vulgate; Septuagint reads *ephod.*   *b*Following Masoretic Text, Targum, and Vulgate; Septuagint reads *ephod.*

Gospel Pearls

day." 34 Then Saul said, "Disperse yourselves among the people, and say to them, 'Bring me here every man's ox and every man's sheep, slaughter *them* here, and eat; and do not sin against the LORD by eating with the blood.' " So every one of the people brought his ox with him that night, and slaughtered *it* there. 35 Then Saul built an altar to the LORD. This was the first altar that he built to the LORD.

36 Now Saul said, "Let us go down after the Philistines by night, and plunder them until the morning light; and let us not leave a man of them."

And they said, "Do whatever seems good to you."

Then the priest said, "Let us draw near to God here."

37 So Saul asked counsel of God, "Shall I go down after the Philistines? Will You deliver them into the hand of Israel?" But He did not answer him that day. 38 And Saul said, "Come over here, all you chiefs of the people, and know and see what this sin was today. 39 For *as* the LORD lives, who saves Israel, though it be in Jonathan my son, he shall surely die." But not a man among all the people answered him. 40 Then he said to all Israel, "You be on one side, and my son Jonathan and I will be on the other side."

And the people said to Saul, "Do what seems good to you."

41 Therefore Saul said to the LORD God of Israel, "Give a perfect *lot.*"*a* So Saul and Jonathan were taken, but the people escaped. 42 And Saul said, "Cast *lots* between my son Jonathan and me." So Jonathan was taken. 43 Then Saul said to Jonathan, "Tell me what you have done."

And Jonathan told him, and said, "I only tasted a little honey with the end of the rod that *was* in my hand. So now I must die!"

44 Saul answered, "God do so and more also; for you shall surely die, Jonathan."

45 But the people said to Saul, "Shall Jonathan die, who has accomplished this great deliverance in Israel? Certainly not! *As* the LORD lives, not one hair of his head shall fall to the ground, for he has worked with God this day." So the people rescued Jonathan, and he did not die.

46 Then Saul returned from pursuing the Philistines, and the Philistines went to their own place.

47 So Saul established his sovereignty over Israel, and fought against all his enemies on every side, against Moab, against the people of Ammon, against Edom, against the kings of Zobah, and against the Philistines. Wherever he turned, he harassed *them.a* 48 And he gathered an army and attacked the Amalekites, and delivered Israel from the hands of those who plundered them.

49 The sons of Saul were Jonathan, Jishui,*a* and Malchishua. And the names of his two daughters *were these:* the name of the firstborn Merab, and the name of the younger Michal. 50 The name of Saul's wife *was* Ahinoam the daughter of Ahimaaz. And the name of the commander of his army *was* Abner son of Ner, Saul's uncle. 51 Kish *was* the father of Saul, and Ner the father of Abner *was* the son of Abiel.

52 Now there was fierce war with the Philistines all the days of Saul. And when Saul saw any strong man or any valiant man, he took him for himself.

15 Samuel also said to Saul, "The LORD sent me to anoint you king over His people, over Israel. Now therefore, heed the voice of the words of the LORD. 2 Thus says the LORD of hosts: 'I will punish Amalek *for* what he did to Israel, how he ambushed him on the way when he came up from Egypt. 3 Now go and attack Amalek, and utterly destroy all that they have, and do not spare them. But kill both man and woman, infant and nursing child, ox and sheep, camel and donkey.' "

4 So Saul gathered the people together and numbered them in Telaim, two hundred thousand foot soldiers and ten thousand men of Judah. 5 And Saul came to a city of Amalek, and lay in wait in the valley.

6 Then Saul said to the Kenites, "Go, depart, get down from among

14:41 *a*Following Masoretic Text and Targum; Septuagint and Vulgate read *Why do You not answer Your servant today? If the injustice is with me or Jonathan my son, O* LORD *God of Israel, give proof; and if You say it is with Your people Israel, give holiness.*   14:47 *a*Septuagint and Vulgate read *prospered.*   14:49 *a*Called *Abinadab* in 1 Chronicles 8:33 and 9:39

A person who manipulates others is a person who says, "I need to con my way into what I don't deserve and cannot earn." The way the curse is broken is to say, "God is capable of using who I am and what I have."

the Amalekites, lest I destroy you with them. For you showed kindness to all the children of Israel when they came up out of Egypt." So the Kenites departed from among the Amalekites. 7 And Saul attacked the Amalekites, from Havilah all the way to Shur, which is east of Egypt. 8 He also took Agag king of the Amalekites alive, and utterly destroyed all the people with the edge of the sword. 9 But Saul and the people spared Agag and the best of the sheep, the oxen, the fatlings, the lambs, and all *that was* good, and were unwilling to utterly destroy them. But everything despised and worthless, that they utterly destroyed.

10 Now the word of the LORD came to Samuel, saying, 11 "I greatly regret that I have set up Saul *as* king, for he has turned back from following Me, and has not performed My commandments." And it grieved Samuel, and he cried out to the LORD all night. 12 So when Samuel rose early in the morning to meet Saul, it was told Samuel, saying, "Saul went to Carmel, and indeed, he set up a monument for himself; and he has gone on around, passed by, and gone down to Gilgal." 13 Then Samuel went to Saul, and Saul said to him, "Blessed *are* you of the LORD! I have performed the commandment of the LORD."

14 But Samuel said, "What then *is* this bleating of the sheep in my ears, and the lowing of the oxen which I hear?"

15 And Saul said, "They have brought them from the Amalekites; for the people spared the best of the sheep and the oxen, to sacrifice to the LORD your God; and the rest we have utterly destroyed."

16 Then Samuel said to Saul, "Be quiet! And I will tell you what the LORD said to me last night."

And he said to him, "Speak on."

17 So Samuel said, "When you *were* little in your own eyes, *were* you not head of the tribes of Israel? And did not the LORD anoint you king over Israel? 18 Now the LORD sent you on a mission, and said, 'Go, and utterly destroy the sinners, the Amalekites, and fight against them until they are consumed.' 19 Why then did you not obey the voice of the LORD? Why did you swoop down on the

spoil, and do evil in the sight of the LORD?"

20 And Saul said to Samuel, "But I have obeyed the voice of the LORD, and gone on the mission on which the LORD sent me, and brought back Agag king of Amalek; I have utterly destroyed the Amalekites. 21 But the people took of the plunder, sheep and oxen, the best of the things which should have been utterly destroyed, to sacrifice to the LORD your God in Gilgal."

22 So Samuel said:

"Has the LORD *as great* delight
   in burnt offerings and
   sacrifices,
As in obeying the voice of the
   LORD?
Behold, to obey is better than
   sacrifice,
And to heed than the fat of
   rams.
23 For rebellion *is as* the sin of
   witchcraft,
And stubbornness *is as* iniquity
   and idolatry.
Because you have rejected the
   word of the LORD,
He also has rejected you from
   being king."

24 Then Saul said to Samuel, "I have sinned, for I have transgressed the commandment of the LORD and your words, because I feared the people and obeyed their voice. 25 Now therefore, please pardon my sin, and return with me, that I may worship the LORD."

26 But Samuel said to Saul, "I will not return with you, for you have rejected the word of the LORD, and the LORD has rejected you from being king over Israel."

27 And as Samuel turned around to go away, *Saul* seized the edge of his robe, and it tore. 28 So Samuel said to him, "The LORD has torn the kingdom of Israel from you today, and has given it to a neighbor of yours, *who is* better than you. 29 And also the Strength of Israel will not lie nor relent. For He *is* not a man, that He should relent."

30 Then he said, "I have sinned; *yet* honor me now, please, before the elders of my people and before Israel, and return with me, that I may worship the LORD your God." 31 So Samuel turned back after Saul, and Saul worshiped the LORD.

Gospel Pearls

32 Then Samuel said, "Bring Agag king of the Amalekites here to me." So Agag came to him cautiously.

And Agag said, "Surely the bitterness of death is past."

33 But Samuel said, "As your sword has made women childless, so shall your mother be childless among women." And Samuel hacked Agag in pieces before the LORD in Gilgal.

34 Then Samuel went to Ramah, and Saul went up to his house at Gibeah of Saul. 35 And Samuel went no more to see Saul until the day of his death. Nevertheless Samuel mourned for Saul, and the LORD regretted that He had made Saul king over Israel.

16 Now the LORD said to Samuel, "How long will you mourn for Saul, seeing I have rejected him from reigning over Israel? Fill your horn with oil, and go; I am sending you to Jesse the Bethlehemite. For I have provided Myself a king among his sons."

2 And Samuel said, "How can I go? If Saul hears it, he will kill me."

But the LORD said, "Take a heifer with you, and say, 'I have come to sacrifice to the LORD.' 3 Then invite Jesse to the sacrifice, and I will show you what you shall do; you shall anoint for Me the one I name to you."

4 So Samuel did what the LORD said, and went to Bethlehem. And the elders of the town trembled at his coming, and said, "Do you come peaceably?"

5 And he said, "Peaceably; I have come to sacrifice to the LORD. Sanctify yourselves, and come with me to the sacrifice." Then he consecrated Jesse and his sons, and invited them to the sacrifice.

6 So it was, when they came, that he looked at Eliab and said, "Surely the LORD's anointed is before Him!"

7 But the LORD said to Samuel, "Do not look at his appearance or at his physical stature, because I have refused him. For the LORD does not see as man sees;a for man looks at the outward appearance, but the LORD looks at the heart."

8 So Jesse called Abinadab, and made him pass before Samuel. And he said, "Neither has the LORD cho-

sen this one." 9 Then Jesse made Shammah pass by. And he said, "Neither has the LORD chosen this one." 10 Thus Jesse made seven of his sons pass before Samuel. And Samuel said to Jesse, "The LORD has not chosen these." 11 And Samuel said to Jesse, "Are all the young men here?" Then he said, "There remains yet the youngest, and there he is, keeping the sheep."

And Samuel said to Jesse, "Send and bring him. For we will not sit downa till he comes here." 12 So he sent and brought him in. Now he was ruddy, with bright eyes, and good-looking. And the LORD said, "Arise, anoint him; for this is the one!"

13 Then Samuel took the horn of oil and anointed him in the midst of his brothers; and the Spirit of the LORD came upon David from that day forward. So Samuel arose and went to Ramah.

14 But the Spirit of the LORD departed from Saul, and a distressing spirit from the LORD troubled him. 15 And Saul's servants said to him, "Surely, a distressing spirit from God is troubling you. 16 Let our master now command your servants, who are before you, to seek out a man who is a skillful player on the harp. And it shall be that he will play it with his hand when the distressing spirit from God is upon you, and you shall be well."

17 So Saul said to his servants, "Provide me now a man who can play well, and bring him to me."

18 Then one of the servants answered and said, "Look, I have seen a son of Jesse the Bethlehemite, who is skillful in playing, a mighty man of valor, a man of war, prudent in speech, and a handsome person; and the LORD is with him."

19 Therefore Saul sent messengers to Jesse, and said, "Send me your son David, who is with the sheep." 20 And Jesse took a donkey loaded with bread, a skin of wine, and a young goat, and sent them by his son David to Saul. 21 So David came to Saul and stood before him. And he loved him greatly, and he became his armorbearer. 22 Then Saul sent to Jesse, saying, "Please let David stand before me, for he has found favor in

16:7 aSeptuagint reads For God does not see as man sees; Targum reads It is not by the appearance of a man; Vulgate reads Nor do I judge according to the looks of a man.   16:11 aFollowing Septuagint and Vulgate; Masoretic Text reads turn around; Targum and Syriac read turn away.

God can take whatever it is that you have—even if it's only a little bit—and multiply it into a miracle. It can be more than enough for you to fulfill what God wants you to do.

my sight." 23 And so it was, whenever the spirit from God was upon Saul, that David would take a harp and play it with his hand. Then Saul would become refreshed and well, and the distressing spirit would depart from him.

17 Now the Philistines gathered their armies together to battle, and were gathered at Sochoh, which belongs to Judah; they encamped between Sochoh and Azekah, in Ephes Dammim. 2 And Saul and the men of Israel were gathered together, and they encamped in the Valley of Elah, and drew up in battle array against the Philistines. 3 The Philistines stood on a mountain on one side, and Israel stood on a mountain on the other side, with a valley between them.

4 And a champion went out from the camp of the Philistines, named Goliath, from Gath, whose height was six cubits and a span. 5 He had a bronze helmet on his head, and he was armed with a coat of mail, and the weight of the coat was five thousand shekels of bronze. 6 And he had bronze armor on his legs and a bronze javelin between his shoulders. 7 Now the staff of his spear was like a weaver's beam, and his iron spearhead weighed six hundred shekels; and a shield-bearer went before him. 8 Then he stood and cried out to the armies of Israel, and said to them, "Why have you come out to line up for battle? Am I not a Philistine, and you the servants of Saul? Choose a man for yourselves, and let him come down to me. 9 If he is able to fight with me and kill me, then we will be your servants. But if I prevail against him and kill him, then you shall be our servants and serve us." 10 And the Philistine said, "I defy the armies of Israel this day; give me a man, that we may fight together." 11 When Saul and all Israel heard these words of the Philistine, they were dismayed and greatly afraid.

12 Now David was the son of that Ephrathite of Bethlehem Judah, whose name was Jesse, and who had eight sons. And the man was old, advanced in years, in the days of Saul. 13 The three oldest sons of Jesse had gone to follow Saul to the battle. The names of his three sons who went to the battle were Eliab the firstborn,

next to him Abinadab, and the third Shammah. 14 David was the youngest. And the three oldest followed Saul. 15 But David occasionally went and returned from Saul to feed his father's sheep at Bethlehem.

16 And the Philistine drew near and presented himself forty days, morning and evening.

17 Then Jesse said to his son David, "Take now for your brothers an ephah of this dried grain and these ten loaves, and run to your brothers at the camp. 18 And carry these ten cheeses to the captain of their thousand, and see how your brothers fare, and bring back news of them." 19 Now Saul and they and all the men of Israel were in the Valley of Elah, fighting with the Philistines.

20 So David rose early in the morning, left the sheep with a keeper, and took the things and went as Jesse had commanded him. And he came to the camp as the army was going out to the fight and shouting for the battle. 21 For Israel and the Philistines had drawn up in battle array, army against army. 22 And David left his supplies in the hand of the supply keeper, ran to the army, and came and greeted his brothers. 23 Then as he talked with them, there was the champion, the Philistine of Gath, Goliath by name, coming up from the armies of the Philistines; and he spoke according to the same words. So David heard them. 24 And all the men of Israel, when they saw the man, fled from him and were dreadfully afraid. 25 So the men of Israel said, "Have you seen this man who has come up? Surely he has come up to defy Israel; and it shall be that the man who kills him the king will enrich with great riches, will give him his daughter, and give his father's house exemption from taxes in Israel."

26 Then David spoke to the men who stood by him, saying, "What shall be done for the man who kills this Philistine and takes away the reproach from Israel? For who is this uncircumcised Philistine, that he should defy the armies of the living God?"

27 And the people answered him in this manner, saying, "So shall it be done for the man who kills him."

28 Now Eliab his oldest brother heard when he spoke to the men; and

Gospel Pearls

Eliab's anger was aroused against David, and he said, "Why did you come down here? And with whom have you left those few sheep in the wilderness? I know your pride and the insolence of your heart, for you have come down to see the battle."

29 And David said, "What have I done now? *Is there* not a cause?" 30 Then he turned from him toward another and said the same thing; and these people answered him as the first ones *did.*

31 Now when the words which David spoke were heard, they reported *them* to Saul; and he sent for him. 32 Then David said to Saul, "Let no man's heart fail because of him; your servant will go and fight with this Philistine."

33 And Saul said to David, "You are not able to go against this Philistine to fight with him; for you *are* a youth, and he a man of war from his youth."

34 But David said to Saul, "Your servant used to keep his father's sheep, and when a lion or a bear came and took a lamb out of the flock, 35 I went out after it and struck it, and delivered *the lamb* from its mouth; and when it arose against me, I caught *it* by its beard, and struck and killed it. 36 Your servant has killed both lion and bear; and this uncircumcised Philistine will be like one of them, seeing he has defied the armies of the living God." 37 Moreover David said, "The LORD, who delivered me from the paw of the lion and from the paw of the bear, He will deliver me from the hand of this Philistine."

And Saul said to David, "Go, and the LORD be with you!"

38 So Saul clothed David with his armor, and he put a bronze helmet on his head; he also clothed him with a coat of mail. 39 David fastened his sword to his armor and tried to walk, for he had not tested *them.* And David said to Saul, "I cannot walk with these, for I have not tested *them.*" So David took them off.

40 Then he took his staff in his hand; and he chose for himself five smooth stones from the brook, and put them in a shepherd's bag, in a pouch which he had, and his sling was in his hand. And he drew near

to the Philistine. 41 So the Philistine came, and began drawing near to David, and the man who bore the shield *went* before him. 42 And when the Philistine looked about and saw David, he disdained him; for he was *only* a youth, ruddy and good-looking. 43 So the Philistine said to David, "*Am* I a dog, that you come to me with sticks?" And the Philistine cursed David by his gods. 44 And the Philistine said to David, "Come to me, and I will give your flesh to the birds of the air and the beasts of the field!"

45 Then David said to the Philistine, "You come to me with a sword, with a spear, and with a javelin. But I come to you in the name of the LORD of hosts, the God of the armies of Israel, whom you have defied. 46 This day the LORD will deliver you into my hand, and I will strike you and take your head from you. And this day I will give the carcasses of the camp of the Philistines to the birds of the air and the wild beasts of the earth, that all the earth may know that there is a God in Israel. 47 Then all this assembly shall know that the LORD does not save with sword and spear; for the battle *is* the LORD's, and He will give you into our hands."

48 So it was, when the Philistine arose and came and drew near to meet David, that David hurried and ran toward the army to meet the Philistine. 49 Then David put his hand in his bag and took out a stone; and he slung *it* and struck the Philistine in his forehead, so that the stone sank into his forehead, and he fell on his face to the earth. 50 So David prevailed over the Philistine with a sling and a stone, and struck the Philistine and killed him. But *there was* no sword in the hand of David. 51 Therefore David ran and stood over the Philistine, took his sword and drew it out of its sheath and killed him, and cut off his head with it.

And when the Philistines saw that their champion was dead, they fled. 52 Now the men of Israel and Judah arose and shouted, and pursued the Philistines as far as the entrance of the valley*a* and to the gates of Ekron. And the wounded of the Philistines

17:52 *a*Following Masoretic Text, Syriac, Targum, and Vulgate; Septuagint reads *Gath.*

God expects us to trust Him with what He has given us—and to use what He has given us—to get what it is that we need and want.

fell along the road to Shaaraim, even as far as Gath and Ekron. 53 Then the children of Israel returned from chasing the Philistines, and they plundered their tents. 54 And David took the head of the Philistine and brought it to Jerusalem, but he put his armor in his tent.

55 When Saul saw David going out against the Philistine, he said to Abner, the commander of the army, "Abner, whose son is this youth?"

And Abner said, "As your soul lives, O king, I do not know."

56 So the king said, "Inquire whose son this young man is."

57 Then, as David returned from the slaughter of the Philistine, Abner took him and brought him before Saul with the head of the Philistine in his hand. 58 And Saul said to him, "Whose son are you, young man?"

So David answered, "I am the son of your servant Jesse the Bethlehemite."

18 Now when he had finished speaking to Saul, the soul of Jonathan was knit to the soul of David, and Jonathan loved him as his own soul. 2 Saul took him that day, and would not let him go home to his father's house anymore. 3 Then Jonathan and David made a covenant, because he loved him as his own soul. 4 And Jonathan took off the robe that was on him and gave it to David, with his armor, even to his sword and his bow and his belt.

5 So David went out wherever Saul sent him, and behaved wisely. And Saul set him over the men of war, and he was accepted in the sight of all the people and also in the sight of Saul's servants. 6 Now it had happened as they were coming home, when David was returning from the slaughter of the Philistine, that the women had come out of all the cities of Israel, singing and dancing, to meet King Saul, with tambourines, with joy, and with musical instruments. 7 So the women sang as they danced, and said:

"Saul has slain his thousands,
And David his ten thousands."

8 Then Saul was very angry, and the saying displeased him; and he said,

"They have ascribed to David ten thousands, and to me they have ascribed only thousands. Now what more can he have but the kingdom?" 9 So Saul eyed David from that day forward.

10 And it happened on the next day that the distressing spirit from God came upon Saul, and he prophesied inside the house. So David played music with his hand, as at other times; but there was a spear in Saul's hand. 11 And Saul cast the spear, for he said, "I will pin David to the wall!" But David escaped his presence twice.

12 Now Saul was afraid of David, because the LORD was with him, but had departed from Saul. 13 Therefore Saul removed him from his presence, and made him his captain over a thousand; and he went out and came in before the people. 14 And David behaved wisely in all his ways, and the LORD was with him. 15 Therefore, when Saul saw that he behaved very wisely, he was afraid of him. 16 But all Israel and Judah loved David, because he went out and came in before them.

17 Then Saul said to David, "Here is my older daughter Merab; I will give her to you as a wife. Only be valiant for me, and fight the LORD's battles." For Saul thought, "Let my hand not be against him, but let the hand of the Philistines be against him."

18 So David said to Saul, "Who am I, and what is my life or my father's family in Israel, that I should be son-in-law to the king?" 19 But it happened at the time when Merab, Saul's daughter, should have been given to David, that she was given to Adriel the Meholathite as a wife.

20 Now Michal, Saul's daughter, loved David. And they told Saul, and the thing pleased him. 21 So Saul said, "I will give her to him, that she may be a snare to him, and that the hand of the Philistines may be against him." Therefore Saul said to David a second time, "You shall be my son-in-law today."

22 And Saul commanded his servants, "Communicate with David secretly, and say, 'Look, the king has delight in you, and all his servants love you. Now therefore, become the king's son-in-law.'"

23 So Saul's servants spoke those

Gospel Pearls

words in the hearing of David. And David said, "Does it seem to you *a* light *thing* to be a king's son-in-law, seeing I *am* a poor and lightly esteemed man?" 24 And the servants of Saul told him, saying, "In this manner David spoke."

25 Then Saul said, "Thus you shall say to David: 'The king does not desire any dowry but one hundred foreskins of the Philistines, to take vengeance on the king's enemies.' " But Saul thought to make David fall by the hand of the Philistines. 26 So when his servants told David these words, it pleased David well to become the king's son-in-law. Now the days had not expired; 27 therefore David arose and went, he and his men, and killed two hundred men of the Philistines. And David brought their foreskins, and they gave them in full count to the king, that he might become the king's son-in-law. Then Saul gave him Michal his daughter as a wife.

28 Thus Saul saw and knew that the LORD *was* with David, and *that* Michal, Saul's daughter, loved him; 29 and Saul was still more afraid of David. So Saul became David's enemy continually. 30 Then the princes of the Philistines went out *to war.* And so it was, whenever they went out, *that* David behaved more wisely than all the servants of Saul, so that his name became highly esteemed.

19 Now Saul spoke to Jonathan his son and to all his servants, that they should kill David; but Jonathan, Saul's son, delighted greatly in David. 2 So Jonathan told David, saying, "My father Saul seeks to kill you. Therefore please be on your guard until morning, and stay in a secret *place* and hide. 3 And I will go out and stand beside my father in the field where you *are,* and I will speak with my father about you. Then what I observe, I will tell you."

4 Thus Jonathan spoke well of David to Saul his father, and said to him, "Let not the king sin against his servant, against David, because he has not sinned against you, and because his works *have been* very good toward you. 5 For he took his life in his hands and killed the Philistine, and the LORD brought about a great deliverance for all Israel. You saw *it* and rejoiced. Why then will you sin

against innocent blood, to kill David without a cause?"

6 So Saul heeded the voice of Jonathan, and Saul swore, "*As the* LORD *lives, he shall not be killed.*" 7 Then Jonathan called David, and Jonathan told him all these things. So Jonathan brought David to Saul, and he was in his presence as in times past.

8 And there was war again; and David went out and fought with the Philistines, and struck them with a mighty blow, and they fled from him.

9 Now the distressing spirit from the LORD came upon Saul as he sat in his house with his spear in his hand. And David was playing *music* with *his* hand. 10 Then Saul sought to pin David to the wall with the spear, but he slipped away from Saul's presence; and he drove the spear into the wall. So David fled and escaped that night.

11 Saul also sent messengers to David's house to watch him and to kill him in the morning. And Michal, David's wife, told him, saying, "If you do not save your life tonight, tomorrow you will be killed." 12 So Michal let David down through a window. And he went and fled and escaped. 13 And Michal took an image and laid *it* in the bed, put a cover of goats' *hair* for his head, and covered *it* with clothes. 14 So when Saul sent messengers to take David, she said, "He *is* sick."

15 Then Saul sent the messengers *back* to see David, saying, "Bring him up to me in the bed, that I may kill him." 16 And when the messengers had come in, there was the image in the bed, with a cover of goats' *hair* for his head. 17 Then Saul said to Michal, "Why have you deceived me like this, and sent my enemy away, so that he has escaped?"

And Michal answered Saul, "He said to me, 'Let me go! Why should I kill you?' "

18 So David fled and escaped, and went to Samuel at Ramah, and told him all that Saul had done to him. And he and Samuel went and stayed in Naioth. 19 Now it was told Saul, saying, "Take note, David *is* at Naioth in Ramah!" 20 Then Saul sent messengers to take David. And when they saw the group of prophets prophesying, and Samuel standing *as* leader over them, the Spirit of God

*E*very time I meet with a group of women, I sense an abundance of treasure that God wants to release. Each one of them has something that God is eager to bless and multiply.

came upon the messengers of Saul, and they also prophesied. 21 And when Saul was told, he sent other messengers, and they prophesied likewise. Then Saul sent messengers again the third time, and they prophesied also. 22 Then he also went to Ramah, and came to the great well that *is* at Sechu. So he asked, and said, "Where *are* Samuel and David?"

And *someone* said, "Indeed *they are* at Naioth in Ramah." 23 So he went there to Naioth in Ramah. Then the Spirit of God was upon him also, and he went on and prophesied until he came to Naioth in Ramah. 24 And he also stripped off his clothes and prophesied before Samuel in like manner, and lay down naked all that day and all that night. Therefore they say, "*Is* Saul also among the prophets?"*a*

20 Then David fled from Naioth in Ramah, and went and said to Jonathan, "What have I done? What *is* my iniquity, and what *is* my sin before your father, that he seeks my life?"

2 So Jonathan said to him, "By no means! You shall not die! Indeed, my father will do nothing either great or small without first telling me. And why should my father hide this thing from me? It *is* not *so!*"

3 Then David took an oath again, and said, "Your father certainly knows that I have found favor in your eyes, and he has said, 'Do not let Jonathan know this, lest he be grieved.' But truly, *as* the LORD lives and *as* your soul lives, *there is* but a step between me and death."

4 So Jonathan said to David, "Whatever you yourself desire, I will do *it* for you."

5 And David said to Jonathan, "Indeed tomorrow *is* the New Moon, and I should not fail to sit with the king to eat. But let me go, that I may hide in the field until the third *day* at evening. 6 If your father misses me at all, then say, 'David earnestly asked *permission* of me that he might run over to Bethlehem, his city, for *there is* a yearly sacrifice there for all the family.' 7 If he says thus: '*It is* well,' your servant will be safe. But if he is very angry, be sure that evil is determined

by him. 8 Therefore you shall deal kindly with your servant, for you have brought your servant into a covenant of the LORD with you. Nevertheless, if there is iniquity in me, kill me yourself, for why should you bring me to your father?"

9 But Jonathan said, "Far be it from you! For if I knew certainly that evil was determined by my father to come upon you, then would I not tell you?"

10 Then David said to Jonathan, "Who will tell me, or what *if* your father answers you roughly?"

11 And Jonathan said to David, "Come, let us go out into the field." So both of them went out into the field. 12 Then Jonathan said to David: "The LORD God of Israel *is* witness! When I have sounded out my father sometime tomorrow, *or* the third *day*, and indeed *there is* good toward David, and if I do not send to you and tell you, 13 may the LORD do so and much more to Jonathan. But if it pleases my father *to do* you evil, then I will report it to you and send you away, that you may go in safety. And the LORD be with you as He has been with my father. 14 And you shall not only show me the kindness of the LORD while I still live, that I may not die; 15 but you shall not cut off your kindness from my house forever, no, not when the LORD has cut off every one of the enemies of David from the face of the earth." 16 So Jonathan made *a covenant* with the house of David, *saying,* "Let the LORD require *it* at the hand of David's enemies."

17 Now Jonathan again caused David to vow, because he loved him; for he loved him as he loved his own soul. 18 Then Jonathan said to David, "Tomorrow *is* the New Moon; and you will be missed, because your seat will be empty. 19 And *when* you have stayed three days, go down quickly and come to the place where you hid on the day of the deed; and remain by the stone Ezel. 20 Then I will shoot three arrows to the side, as though I shot at a target; 21 and there I will send a lad, *saying,* 'Go, find the arrows.' If I expressly say to the lad, 'Look, the arrows *are* on this side of you; get them and come'—then, as the LORD lives, *there is* safety for you and no harm. 22 But if I say thus to

19:24 aCompare 1 Samuel 10:12

God wants each one to recognize what He has given them—even if it's only a little bit—and start working with what they have.

Covenant Friendship

1 Samuel 20:16, 17

Communication happens in unexpected ways between people who need no audible speech. Their language is a quick glance or a soft pat on the shoulder. Their communication is a concerned look when all is not well. They know what you mean before you even say it. If you have ever settled in to the rich lather of a real covenant relationship, you are wealthy.

Biblical covenants were the most binding, the most serious and solemn commitments two people could make. When you are in a covenant friendship, you do not leave. In a true covenant relationship, you are stuck like glue to your friend.

This is the wealth that causes street people to smile in the rain and laugh at a storm. They have no coats to warm them; their only flame may be the friendship of someone who understands their daily struggles. In this regard, many rich people are poor. They have things, but they may lack deep companionship. The greatest blessings of life cannot be bought.

Children understand the rich art of relationship. Their anger flares for an instant, but soon melts in the sunshine of laughter and play. Most adults, however, have been hardened by unforgiveness, created from the remembered pain of what has been spoken against them and stolen from them. Rehearsing offenses prohibits friendship. It's time to be grown up enough to forgive like a child.

Friendship is not a blood relationship, so friends must forge their bond in other ways. It may be through mutual interests, shared passions, or all the lovely little things that bind two hearts together. Friendship is a sanctuary carved out of the jungle of a mad world, where so many people see each other as prey instead of partners. These people never understand the power and commitment of covenant friendship. But you can.

If you already have a covenant friend, savor your days together. If you don't have such a friend, ask God, the Covenant-Maker, to send you a partner of the heart.

the young man, 'Look, the arrows *are* beyond you'—go your way, for the LORD has sent you away. 23 And as for the matter which you and I have spoken of, indeed the LORD *be* between you and me forever."

24 Then David hid in the field. And when the New Moon had come, the king sat down to eat the feast. 25 Now the king sat on his seat, as at other times, on a seat by the wall. And Jonathan arose,*a* and Abner sat by Saul's side, but David's place was empty. 26 Nevertheless Saul did not say anything that day, for he thought, "Something has happened to him; he *is* unclean, surely he *is* unclean." 27 And it happened the next day, the second *day* of the month, that David's place was empty. And Saul said to Jonathan his son, "Why has the son of Jesse not come to eat, either yesterday or today?"

28 So Jonathan answered Saul, "David earnestly asked *permission* of me *to go* to Bethlehem. 29 And he said, 'Please let me go, for our family has a sacrifice in the city, and my brother has commanded me *to be there*. And now, if I have found favor in your eyes, please let me get away and see my brothers.' Therefore he has not come to the king's table."

30 Then Saul's anger was aroused against Jonathan, and he said to him, "You son of a perverse, rebellious *woman!* Do I not know that you have chosen the son of Jesse to your own shame and to the shame of your mother's nakedness? 31 For as long as the son of Jesse lives on the earth, you shall not be established, nor your kingdom. Now therefore, send and bring him to me, for he shall surely die."

32 And Jonathan answered Saul his father, and said to him, "Why should he be killed? What has he done?" 33 Then Saul cast a spear at him to kill him, by which Jonathan knew that it was determined by his father to kill David.

34 So Jonathan arose from the table in fierce anger, and ate no food the second day of the month, for he was grieved for David, because his father had treated him shamefully.

35 And so it was, in the morning, that Jonathan went out into the field

at the time appointed with David, and a little lad *was* with him. 36 Then he said to his lad, "Now run, find the arrows which I shoot." As the lad ran, he shot an arrow beyond him. 37 When the lad had come to the place where the arrow was which Jonathan had shot, Jonathan cried out after the lad and said, "*Is* not the arrow beyond you?" 38 And Jonathan cried out after the lad, "Make haste, hurry, do not delay!" So Jonathan's lad gathered up the arrows and came back to his master. 39 But the lad did not know anything. Only Jonathan and David knew of the matter. 40 Then Jonathan gave his weapons to his lad, and said to him, "Go, carry *them* to the city."

41 As soon as the lad had gone, David arose from *a place* toward the south, fell on his face to the ground, and bowed down three times. And they kissed one another; and they wept together, but David more so. 42 Then Jonathan said to David, "Go in peace, since we have both sworn in the name of the LORD, saying, 'May the LORD be between you and me, and between your descendants and my descendants, forever.' " So he arose and departed, and Jonathan went into the city.

21 Now David came to Nob, to Ahimelech the priest. And Ahimelech was afraid when he met David, and said to him, "Why *are* you alone, and no one is with you?"

2 So David said to Ahimelech the priest, "The king has ordered me on some business, and said to me, 'Do not let anyone know anything about the business on which I send you, or what I have commanded you.' And I have directed *my* young men to such and such a place. 3 Now therefore, what have you on hand? Give *me* five *loaves of* bread in my hand, or whatever can be found."

4 And the priest answered David and said, "*There is* no common bread on hand; but there is holy bread, if the young men have at least kept themselves from women."

5 Then David answered the priest, and said to him, "Truly, women *have been* kept from us about three days since I came out. And the vessels of

20:25 *a*Following Masoretic Text, Syriac, Targum, and Vulgate; Septuagint reads *he sat across from Jonathan.*

Gospel Pearls

the young men are holy, and *the bread is* in effect common, even though it was consecrated in the vessel this day."

6 So the priest gave him holy bread; for there was no bread there but the showbread which had been taken from before the LORD, in order to put hot bread *in its place* on the day when it was taken away.

7 Now a certain man of the servants of Saul *was* there that day, detained before the LORD. And his name *was* Doeg, an Edomite, the chief of the herdsmen who *belonged* to Saul.

8 And David said to Ahimelech, "Is there not here on hand a spear or a sword? For I have brought neither my sword nor my weapons with me, because the king's business required haste."

9 So the priest said, "The sword of Goliath the Philistine, whom you killed in the Valley of Elah, there it is, wrapped in a cloth behind the ephod. If you will take that, take *it*. For *there is* no other except that one here."

And David said, *"There is* none like it; give it to me."

10 Then David arose and fled that day from before Saul, and went to Achish the king of Gath. 11 And the servants of Achish said to him, *"Is* this not David the king of the land? Did they not sing of him to one another in dances, saying:

'Saul has slain his thousands,
And David his ten
    thousands'?"[a]

12 Now David took these words to heart, and was very much afraid of Achish the king of Gath. 13 So he changed his behavior before them, pretended madness in their hands, scratched on the doors of the gate, and let his saliva fall down on his beard. 14 Then Achish said to his servants, "Look, you see the man is insane. Why have you brought him to me? 15 Have I need of madmen, that you have brought this *fellow* to play the madman in my presence? Shall this *fellow* come into my house?"

22 David therefore departed from there and escaped to the cave of Adullam. So when his brothers and all his father's house heard *it*, they went down there to him. 2 And everyone *who was* in distress, everyone who *was* in debt, and everyone *who was* discontented gathered to him. So he became captain over them. And there were about four hundred men with him.

3 Then David went from there to Mizpah of Moab; and he said to the king of Moab, "Please let my father and mother come here with you, till I know what God will do for me." 4 So he brought them before the king of Moab, and they dwelt with him all the time that David was in the stronghold.

5 Now the prophet Gad said to David, "Do not stay in the stronghold; depart, and go to the land of Judah." So David departed and went into the forest of Hereth.

6 When Saul heard that David and the men who *were* with him had been discovered—now Saul was staying in Gibeah under a tamarisk tree in Ramah, with his spear in his hand, and all his servants standing about him— 7 then Saul said to his servants who stood about him, "Hear now, you Benjamites! Will the son of Jesse give every one of you fields and vineyards, *and* make you all captains of thousands and captains of hundreds? 8 All of you have conspired against me, and *there is* no one who reveals to me that my son has made a covenant with the son of Jesse; and *there is* not one of you who is sorry for me or reveals to me that my son has stirred up my servant against me, to lie in wait, as *it is* this day."

9 Then answered Doeg the Edomite, who was set over the servants of Saul, and said, "I saw the son of Jesse going to Nob, to Ahimelech the son of Ahitub. 10 And he inquired of the LORD for him, gave him provisions, and gave him the sword of Goliath the Philistine."

11 So the king sent to call Ahimelech the priest, the son of Ahitub, and all his father's house, the priests who *were* in Nob. And they all came to the king. 12 And Saul said, "Hear now, son of Ahitub!"

He answered, "Here I am, my lord."

13 Then Saul said to him, "Why

21:11 ªCompare 1 Samuel 18:7

*L*oosed women? You had better believe it. They are loosed from the tragedy of a long and dismal night. They are the daughters of Abraham. They are women with a promise.

have you conspired against me, you and the son of Jesse, in that you have given him bread and a sword, and have inquired of God for him, that he should rise against me, to lie in wait, as it is this day?"

14 So Ahimelech answered the king and said, "And who among all your servants *is as* faithful as David, who is the king's son-in-law, who goes at your bidding, and is honorable in your house? 15 Did I then begin to inquire of God for him? Far be it from me! Let not the king impute anything to his servant, *or* to any in the house of my father. For your servant knew nothing of all this, little or much."

16 And the king said, "You shall surely die, Ahimelech, you and all your father's house!" 17 Then the king said to the guards who stood about him, "Turn and kill the priests of the LORD, because their hand also *is* with David, and because they knew when he fled and did not tell it to me." But the servants of the king would not lift their hands to strike the priests of the LORD. 18 And the king said to Doeg, "You turn and kill the priests!" So Doeg the Edomite turned and struck the priests, and killed on that day eighty-five men who wore a linen ephod. 19 Also Nob, the city of the priests, he struck with the edge of the sword, both men and women, children and nursing infants, oxen and donkeys and sheep—with the edge of the sword.

20 Now one of the sons of Ahimelech the son of Ahitub, named Abiathar, escaped and fled after David. 21 And Abiathar told David that Saul had killed the LORD's priests. 22 So David said to Abiathar, "I knew that day, when Doeg the Edomite *was* there, that he would surely tell Saul. I have caused *the death* of all the persons of your father's house. 23 Stay with me; do not fear. For he who seeks my life seeks your life, but with me you *shall be* safe."

23 Then they told David, saying, "Look, the Philistines are fighting against Keilah, and they are robbing the threshing floors."

2 Therefore David inquired of the LORD, saying, "Shall I go and attack these Philistines?"

And the LORD said to David, "Go and attack the Philistines, and save Keilah."

3 But David's men said to him, "Look, we are afraid here in Judah. How much more then if we go to Keilah against the armies of the Philistines?" 4 Then David inquired of the LORD once again.

And the LORD answered him and said, "Arise, go down to Keilah. For I will deliver the Philistines into your hand." 5 And David and his men went to Keilah and fought with the Philistines, struck them with a mighty blow, and took away their livestock. So David saved the inhabitants of Keilah.

6 Now it happened, when Abiathar the son of Ahimelech fled to David at Keilah, *that* he went down *with* an ephod in his hand.

7 And Saul was told that David had gone to Keilah. So Saul said, "God has delivered him into my hand, for he has shut himself in by entering a town that has gates and bars." 8 Then Saul called all the people together for war, to go down to Keilah to besiege David and his men.

9 When David knew that Saul plotted evil against him, he said to Abiathar the priest, "Bring the ephod here." 10 Then David said, "O LORD God of Israel, Your servant has certainly heard that Saul seeks to come to Keilah to destroy the city for my sake. 11 Will the men of Keilah deliver me into his hand? Will Saul come down, as Your servant has heard? O LORD God of Israel, I pray, tell Your servant."

And the LORD said, "He will come down."

12 Then David said, "Will the men of Keilah deliver me and my men into the hand of Saul?"

And the LORD said, "They will deliver *you*."

13 So David and his men, about six hundred, arose and departed from Keilah and went wherever they could go. Then it was told Saul that David had escaped from Keilah; so he halted the expedition.

14 And David stayed in strongholds in the wilderness, and remained in the mountains in the Wilderness of Ziph. Saul sought him every day, but God did not deliver him into his hand. 15 So David saw that Saul had come out to seek his life. And David

Gospel Pearls

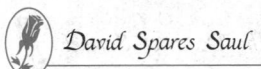

was in the Wilderness of Ziph in a forest.ᵃ 16 Then Jonathan, Saul's son, arose and went to David in the woods and strengthened his hand in God. 17 And he said to him, "Do not fear, for the hand of Saul my father shall not find you. You shall be king over Israel, and I shall be next to you. Even my father Saul knows that." 18 So the two of them made a covenant before the LORD. And David stayed in the woods, and Jonathan went to his own house.

19 Then the Ziphites came up to Saul at Gibeah, saying, "Is David not hiding with us in strongholds in the woods, in the hill of Hachilah, which *is* on the south of Jeshimon? 20 Now therefore, O king, come down according to all the desire of your soul to come down; and our part *shall be* to deliver him into the king's hand."

21 And Saul said, "Blessed *are* you of the LORD, for you have compassion on me. 22 Please go and find out for sure, and see the place where his hideout is, *and* who has seen him there. For I am told he is very crafty. 23 See therefore, and take knowledge of all the lurking places where he hides; and come back to me with certainty, and I will go with you. And it shall be, if he is in the land, that I will search for him throughout all the clansᵃ of Judah."

24 So they arose and went to Ziph before Saul. But David and his men *were* in the Wilderness of Maon, in the plain on the south of Jeshimon. 25 When Saul and his men went to seek *him*, they told David. Therefore he went down to the rock, and stayed in the Wilderness of Maon. And when Saul heard *that*, he pursued David in the Wilderness of Maon. 26 Then Saul went on one side of the mountain, and David and his men on the other side of the mountain. So David made haste to get away from Saul, for Saul and his men were encircling David and his men to take them.

27 But a messenger came to Saul, saying, "Hurry and come, for the Philistines have invaded the land!" 28 Therefore Saul returned from pursuing David, and went against the Philistines; so they called that place the Rock of Escape.ᵃ 29 Then David

went up from there and dwelt in strongholds at En Gedi.

24 Now it happened, when Saul had returned from following the Philistines, that it was told him, saying, "Take note! David *is* in the Wilderness of En Gedi." 2 Then Saul took three thousand chosen men from all Israel, and went to seek David and his men on the Rocks of the Wild Goats. 3 So he came to the sheepfolds by the road, where there *was* a cave; and Saul went in to attend to his needs. (David and his men were staying in the recesses of the cave.) 4 Then the men of David said to him, "This is the day of which the LORD said to you, 'Behold, I will deliver your enemy into your hand, that you may do to him as it seems good to you.'" And David arose and secretly cut off a corner of Saul's robe. 5 Now it happened afterward that David's heart troubled him because he had cut Saul's *robe.* 6 And he said to his men, "The LORD forbid that I should do this thing to my master, the LORD's anointed, to stretch out my hand against him, seeing he *is* the anointed of the LORD." 7 So David restrained his servants with *these* words, and did not allow them to rise against Saul. And Saul got up from the cave and went on *his* way.

8 David also arose afterward, went out of the cave, and called out to Saul, saying, "My lord the king!" And when Saul looked behind him, David stooped with his face to the earth, and bowed down. 9 And David said to Saul: "Why do you listen to the words of men who say, 'Indeed David seeks your harm'? 10 Look, this day your eyes have seen that the LORD delivered you today into my hand in the cave, and *someone* urged *me* to kill you. But *my eye* spared you, and I said, 'I will not stretch out my hand against my lord, for he *is* the LORD's anointed.' 11 Moreover, my father, see! Yes, see the corner of your robe in my hand! For in that I cut off the corner of your robe, and did not kill you, know and see that *there is* neither evil nor rebellion in my hand, and I have not sinned against you. Yet you hunt my life to take it. 12 Let the LORD judge between

23:15 ᵃOr *in Horesh*   23:23 ᵃLiterally *thousands*   23:28 ᵃHebrew *Sela Hammahlekoth*

As much as God is the epitome of fatherhood in His provision and defense of His children, so He is also the epitome of motherhood in His nurture and love.

you and me, and let the LORD avenge me on you. But my hand shall not be against you. 13 As the proverb of the ancients says, 'Wickedness proceeds from the wicked.' But my hand shall not be against you. 14 After whom has the king of Israel come out? Whom do you pursue? A dead dog? A flea? 15 Therefore let the LORD be judge, and judge between you and me, and see and plead my case, and deliver me out of your hand."

16 So it was, when David had finished speaking these words to Saul, that Saul said, "*Is* this your voice, my son David?" And Saul lifted up his voice and wept. 17 Then he said to David: "You *are* more righteous than I; for you have rewarded me with good, whereas I have rewarded you with evil. 18 And you have shown this day how you have dealt well with me; for when the LORD delivered me into your hand, you did not kill me. 19 For if a man finds his enemy, will he let him get away safely? Therefore may the LORD reward you with good for what you have done to me this day. 20 And now I know indeed that you shall surely be king, and that the kingdom of Israel shall be established in your hand. 21 Therefore swear now to me by the LORD that you will not cut off my descendants after me, and that you will not destroy my name from my father's house."

22 So David swore to Saul. And Saul went home, but David and his men went up to the stronghold.

25 Then Samuel died; and the Israelites gathered together and lamented for him, and buried him at his home in Ramah. And David arose and went down to the Wilderness of Paran.*a*

2 Now *there was* a man in Maon whose business *was* in Carmel, and the man *was* very rich. He had three thousand sheep and a thousand goats. And he was shearing his sheep in Carmel. 3 The name of the man *was* Nabal, and the name of his wife Abigail. And *she was* a woman of good understanding and beautiful appearance; but the man *was* harsh and evil in *his* doings. He *was of the house of* Caleb.

4 When David heard in the wilderness that Nabal was shearing his sheep, 5 David sent ten young men; and David said to the young men, "Go up to Carmel, go to Nabal, and greet him in my name. 6 And thus you shall say to him who lives *in prosperity:* 'Peace *be* to you, peace to your house, and peace to all that you have! 7 Now I have heard that you have shearers. Your shepherds were with us, and we did not hurt them, nor was there anything missing from them all the while they were in Carmel. 8 Ask your young men, and they will tell you. Therefore let *my* young men find favor in your eyes, for we come on a feast day. Please give whatever comes to your hand to your servants and to your son David.'"

9 So when David's young men came, they spoke to Nabal according to all these words in the name of David, and waited.

10 Then Nabal answered David's servants, and said, "Who *is* David, and who *is* the son of Jesse? There are many servants nowadays who break away each one from his master. 11 Shall I then take my bread and my water and my meat that I have killed for my shearers, and give *it* to men when I do not know where they *are* from?"

12 So David's young men turned on their heels and went back; and they came and told him all these words. 13 Then David said to his men, "Every man gird on his sword." So every man girded on his sword, and David also girded on his sword. And about four hundred men went with David, and two hundred stayed with the supplies.

14 Now one of the young men told Abigail, Nabal's wife, saying, "Look, David sent messengers from the wilderness to greet our master; and he reviled them. 15 But the men *were* very good to us, and we were not hurt, nor did we miss anything as long as we accompanied them, when we were in the fields. 16 They were a wall to us both by night and day, all the time we were with them keeping the sheep. 17 Now therefore, know and consider what you will do, for harm is determined against our master and against all his household.

25:1 *a*Following Masoretic Text, Syriac, Targum, and Vulgate; Septuagint reads *Maon.*

Gospel Pearls

For he *is such* a scoundrel[a] that *one* cannot speak to him."

18 Then Abigail made haste and took two hundred *loaves* of bread, two skins of wine, five sheep already dressed, five seahs of roasted *grain*, one hundred clusters of raisins, and two hundred cakes of figs, and loaded *them* on donkeys. 19 And she said to her servants, "Go on before me; see, I am coming after you." But she did not tell her husband Nabal.

20 So it was, *as* she rode on the donkey, that she went down under cover of the hill; and there were David and his men, coming down toward her, and she met them. 21 Now David had said, "Surely in vain I have protected all that this *fellow* has in the wilderness, so that nothing was missed of all that *belongs* to him. And he has repaid me evil for good. 22 May God do so, and more also, to the enemies of David, if I leave one male of all who *belong* to him by morning light."

23 Now when Abigail saw David, she dismounted quickly from the donkey, fell on her face before David, and bowed down to the ground. 24 So she fell at his feet and said: "On me, my lord, *on* me *let* this iniquity *be!* And please let your maidservant speak in your ears, and hear the words of your maidservant. 25 Please, let not my lord regard this scoundrel Nabal. For as his name *is,* so *is* he: Nabal[a] *is* his name, and folly *is* with him! But I, your maidservant, did not see the young men of my lord whom you sent. 26 Now therefore, my lord, *as* the LORD lives and *as* your soul lives, since the LORD has held you back from coming to bloodshed and from avenging yourself with your own hand, now then, let your enemies and those who seek harm for my lord be as Nabal. 27 And now this present which your maidservant has brought to my lord, let it be given to the young men who follow my lord. 28 Please forgive the trespass of your maidservant. For the LORD will certainly make for my lord an enduring house, because my lord fights the battles of the LORD, and evil is not found in you throughout your days. 29 Yet a man has risen to pursue you and seek your life, but the life of my

lord shall be bound in the bundle of the living with the LORD your God; and the lives of your enemies He shall sling out, *as from* the pocket of a sling. 30 And it shall come to pass, when the LORD has done for my lord according to all the good that He has spoken concerning you, and has appointed you ruler over Israel, 31 that this will be no grief to you, nor offense of heart to my lord, either that you have shed blood without cause, or that my lord has avenged himself. But when the LORD has dealt well with my lord, then remember your maidservant."

32 Then David said to Abigail: "Blessed *is* the LORD God of Israel, who sent you this day to meet me! 33 And blessed *is* your advice and blessed *are* you, because you have kept me this day from coming to bloodshed and from avenging myself with my own hand. 34 For indeed, *as* the LORD God of Israel lives, who has kept me back from hurting you, unless you had hurried and come to meet me, surely by morning light no males would have been left to Nabal!" 35 So David received from her hand what she had brought him, and said to her, "Go up in peace to your house. See, I have heeded your voice and respected your person."

36 Now Abigail went to Nabal, and there he was, holding a feast in his house, like the feast of a king. And Nabal's heart *was* merry within him, for he *was* very drunk; therefore she told him nothing, little or much, until morning light. 37 So it was, in the morning, when the wine had gone from Nabal, and his wife had told him these things, that his heart died within him, and he became *like* a stone. 38 Then it happened, *after* about ten days, that the LORD struck Nabal, and he died.

39 So when David heard that Nabal was dead, he said, "Blessed *be* the LORD, who has pleaded the cause of my reproach from the hand of Nabal, and has kept His servant from evil! For the LORD has returned the wickedness of Nabal on his own head."

And David sent and proposed to Abigail, to take her as his wife. 40 When the servants of David had come to Abigail at Carmel, they spoke to her saying, "David sent us

25:17 [a]Literally *son of Belial*   25:25 [a]Literally *Fool*

*L*et go of your past so your hands and heart are free for what God has for you *now.*

to you, to ask you to become his wife."

41 Then she arose, bowed her face to the earth, and said, "Here is your maidservant, a servant to wash the feet of the servants of my lord." 42 So Abigail rose in haste and rode on a donkey, attended by five of her maidens; and she followed the messengers of David, and became his wife. 43 David also took Ahinoam of Jezreel, and so both of them were his wives.

44 But Saul had given Michal his daughter, David's wife, to Palti[a] the son of Laish, who was from Gallim.

26 Now the Ziphites came to Saul at Gibeah, saying, "Is David not hiding in the hill of Hachilah, opposite Jeshimon?" 2 Then Saul arose and went down to the Wilderness of Ziph, having three thousand chosen men of Israel with him, to seek David in the Wilderness of Ziph. 3 And Saul encamped in the hill of Hachilah, which is opposite Jeshimon, by the road. But David stayed in the wilderness, and he saw that Saul came after him into the wilderness. 4 David therefore sent out spies, and understood that Saul had indeed come.

5 So David arose and came to the place where Saul had encamped. And David saw the place where Saul lay, and Abner the son of Ner, the commander of his army. Now Saul lay within the camp, with the people encamped all around him. 6 Then David answered, and said to Ahimelech the Hittite and to Abishai the son of Zeruiah, brother of Joab, saying, "Who will go down with me to Saul in the camp?"

And Abishai said, "I will go down with you."

7 So David and Abishai came to the people by night; and there Saul lay sleeping within the camp, with his spear stuck in the ground by his head. And Abner and the people lay all around him. 8 Then Abishai said to David, "God has delivered your enemy into your hand this day. Now therefore, please, let me strike him at once with the spear, right to the earth; and I will not have to strike him a second time!"

9 But David said to Abishai, "Do not destroy him; for who can stretch out his hand against the LORD's anointed, and be guiltless?" 10 David said furthermore, "As the LORD lives, the LORD shall strike him, or his day shall come to die, or he shall go out to battle and perish. 11 The LORD forbid that I should stretch out my hand against the LORD's anointed. But please, take now the spear and the jug of water that are by his head, and let us go." 12 So David took the spear and the jug of water by Saul's head, and they got away; and no man saw or knew it or awoke. For they were all asleep, because a deep sleep from the LORD had fallen on them.

13 Now David went over to the other side, and stood on the top of a hill afar off, a great distance being between them. 14 And David called out to the people and to Abner the son of Ner, saying, "Do you not answer, Abner?"

Then Abner answered and said, "Who are you, calling out to the king?"

15 So David said to Abner, "Are you not a man? And who is like you in Israel? Why then have you not guarded your lord the king? For one of the people came in to destroy your lord the king. 16 This thing that you have done is not good. As the LORD lives, you deserve to die, because you have not guarded your master, the LORD's anointed. And now see where the king's spear is, and the jug of water that was by his head."

17 Then Saul knew David's voice, and said, "Is that your voice, my son David?"

David said, "It is my voice, my lord, O king." 18 And he said, "Why does my lord thus pursue his servant? For what have I done, or what evil is in my hand? 19 Now therefore, please, let my lord the king hear the words of his servant: If the LORD has stirred you up against me, let Him accept an offering. But if it is the children of men, may they be cursed before the LORD, for they have driven me out this day from sharing in the inheritance of the LORD, saying, 'Go, serve other gods.' 20 So now, do not let my blood fall to the earth before the face of the LORD. For the king of Israel has come out to seek a flea,

25:44 [a] Spelled Paltiel in 2 Samuel 3:15

Gospel Pearls

as when one hunts a partridge in the mountains."

21 Then Saul said, "I have sinned. Return, my son David. For I will harm you no more, because my life was precious in your eyes this day. Indeed I have played the fool and erred exceedingly."

22 And David answered and said, "Here is the king's spear. Let one of the young men come over and get it. 23 May the LORD repay every man *for* his righteousness and his faithfulness; for the LORD delivered you into *my* hand today, but I would not stretch out my hand against the LORD's anointed. 24 And indeed, as your life was valued much this day in my eyes, so let my life be valued much in the eyes of the LORD, and let Him deliver me out of all tribulation."

25 Then Saul said to David, "*May* you *be* blessed, my son David! You shall both do great things and also still prevail."

So David went on his way, and Saul returned to his place.

27 And David said in his heart, "Now I shall perish someday by the hand of Saul. *There is* nothing better for me than that I should speedily escape to the land of the Philistines; and Saul will despair of me, to seek me anymore in any part of Israel. So I shall escape out of his hand." 2 Then David arose and went over with the six hundred men who *were* with him to Achish the son of Maoch, king of Gath. 3 So David dwelt with Achish at Gath, he and his men, each man with his household, *and* David with his two wives, Ahinoam the Jezreelitess, and Abigail the Carmelitess, Nabal's widow. 4 And it was told Saul that David had fled to Gath; so he sought him no more.

5 Then David said to Achish, "If I have now found favor in your eyes, let them give me a place in some town in the country, that I may dwell there. For why should your servant dwell in the royal city with you?" 6 So Achish gave him Ziklag that day. Therefore Ziklag has belonged to the kings of Judah to this day. 7 Now the time that David dwelt in the country of the Philistines was one full year and four months.

8 And David and his men went up and raided the Geshurites, the Girzites,ᵃ and the Amalekites. For those nations were the inhabitants of the land from of old, as you go to Shur, even as far as the land of Egypt. 9 Whenever David attacked the land, he left neither man nor woman alive, but took away the sheep, the oxen, the donkeys, the camels, and the apparel, and returned and came to Achish. 10 Then Achish would say, "Where have you made a raid today?" And David would say, "Against the southern *area* of Judah, or against the southern *area* of the Jerahmeelites, or against the southern *area* of the Kenites." 11 David would save neither man nor woman alive, to bring *news* to Gath, saying, "Lest they should inform on us, saying, 'Thus David did.' " And thus *was* his behavior all the time he dwelt in the country of the Philistines. 12 So Achish believed David, saying, "He has made his people Israel utterly abhor him; therefore he will be my servant forever."

28 Now it happened in those days that the Philistines gathered their armies together for war, to fight with Israel. And Achish said to David, "You assuredly know that you will go out with me to battle, you and your men."

2 So David said to Achish, "Surely you know what your servant can do."

And Achish said to David, "Therefore I will make you one of my chief guardians forever."

3 Now Samuel had died, and all Israel had lamented for him and buried him in Ramah, in his own city. And Saul had put the mediums and the spiritists out of the land.

4 Then the Philistines gathered together, and came and encamped at Shunem. So Saul gathered all Israel together, and they encamped at Gilboa. 5 When Saul saw the army of the Philistines, he was afraid, and his heart trembled greatly. 6 And when Saul inquired of the LORD, the LORD did not answer him, either by dreams or by Urim or by the prophets.

7 Then Saul said to his servants, "Find me a woman who is a medium,

27:8 ᵃOr *Gezrites*

God longs to hold us and comfort us and impart to us the strength we need to move forward in our lives. Draw from Him the strength you need to stand.

that I may go to her and inquire of her."

And his servants said to him, "In fact, *there is* a woman who is a medium at En Dor."

8 So Saul disguised himself and put on other clothes, and he went, and two men with him; and they came to the woman by night. And he said, "Please conduct a séance for me, and bring up for me the one I shall name to you."

9 Then the woman said to him, "Look, you know what Saul has done, how he has cut off the mediums and the spiritists from the land. Why then do you lay a snare for my life, to cause me to die?"

10 And Saul swore to her by the LORD, saying, "*As* the LORD lives, no punishment shall come upon you for this thing."

11 Then the woman said, "Whom shall I bring up for you?"

And he said, "Bring up Samuel for me."

12 When the woman saw Samuel, she cried out with a loud voice. And the woman spoke to Saul, saying, "Why have you deceived me? For you *are* Saul!"

13 And the king said to her, "Do not be afraid. What did you see?"

And the woman said to Saul, "I saw a spirit[a] ascending out of the earth."

14 So he said to her, "What *is* his form?"

And she said, "An old man is coming up, and he *is* covered with a mantle." And Saul perceived that it *was* Samuel, and he stooped with *his* face to the ground and bowed down.

15 Now Samuel said to Saul, "Why have you disturbed me by bringing me up?"

And Saul answered, "I am deeply distressed; for the Philistines make war against me, and God has departed from me and does not answer me anymore, neither by prophets nor by dreams. Therefore I have called you, that you may reveal to me what I should do."

16 Then Samuel said: "So why do you ask me, seeing the LORD has departed from you and has become your enemy? 17 And the LORD has done for Himself[a] as He spoke by me. For the LORD has torn the kingdom out of your hand and given it to your neighbor, David. 18 Because you did not obey the voice of the LORD nor execute His fierce wrath upon Amalek, therefore the LORD has done this thing to you this day. 19 Moreover the LORD will also deliver Israel with you into the hand of the Philistines. And tomorrow you and your sons *will be* with me. The LORD will also deliver the army of Israel into the hand of the Philistines."

20 Immediately Saul fell full length on the ground, and was dreadfully afraid because of the words of Samuel. And there was no strength in him, for he had eaten no food all day or all night.

21 And the woman came to Saul and saw that he was severely troubled, and said to him, "Look, your maidservant has obeyed your voice, and I have put my life in my hands and heeded the words which you spoke to me. 22 Now therefore, please, heed also the voice of your maidservant, and let me set a piece of bread before you; and eat, that you may have strength when you go on *your* way."

23 But he refused and said, "I will not eat."

So his servants, together with the woman, urged him; and he heeded their voice. Then he arose from the ground and sat on the bed. 24 Now the woman had a fatted calf in the house, and she hastened to kill it. And she took flour and kneaded *it,* and baked unleavened bread from it. 25 So she brought *it* before Saul and his servants, and they ate. Then they rose and went away that night.

29 Then the Philistines gathered together all their armies at Aphek, and the Israelites encamped by a fountain which *is* in Jezreel. 2 And the lords of the Philistines passed in review by hundreds and by thousands, but David and his men passed in review at the rear with Achish. 3 Then the princes of the Philistines said, "What *are* these Hebrews *doing here?*"

And Achish said to the princes of the Philistines, "*Is* this not David, the servant of Saul king of Israel, who has been with me these days, or these years? And to this day I have found

28:13 [a]Hebrew *elohim*   28:17 [a]Or *him,* that is, David

Gospel Pearls

no fault in him since he defected *to me.*"

4 But the princes of the Philistines were angry with him; so the princes of the Philistines said to him, "Make this fellow return, that he may go back to the place which you have appointed for him, and do not let him go down with us to battle, lest in the battle he become our adversary. For with what could he reconcile himself to his master, if not with the heads of these men? 5 *Is* this not David, of whom they sang to one another in dances, saying:

'Saul has slain his thousands,
And David his ten
thousands'?"*a*

6 Then Achish called David and said to him, "Surely, *as* the LORD lives, you have been upright, and your going out and your coming in with me in the army *is* good in my sight. For to this day I have not found evil in you since the day of your coming to me. Nevertheless the lords do not favor you. 7 Therefore return now, and go in peace, that you may not displease the lords of the Philistines."

8 So David said to Achish, "But what have I done? And to this day what have you found in your servant as long as I have been with you, that I may not go and fight against the enemies of my lord the king?"

9 Then Achish answered and said to David, "I know that you *are* as good in my sight as an angel of God; nevertheless the princes of the Philistines have said, 'He shall not go up with us to the battle.' 10 Now therefore, rise early in the morning with your master's servants who have come with you.*a* And as soon as you are up early in the morning and have light, depart."

11 So David and his men rose early to depart in the morning, to return to the land of the Philistines. And the Philistines went up to Jezreel.

30 Now it happened, when David and his men came to Ziklag, on the third day, that the Amalekites had invaded the South and Ziklag,

attacked Ziklag and burned it with fire, 2 and had taken captive the women and those who *were* there, from small to great; they did not kill anyone, but carried *them* away and went their way. 3 So David and his men came to the city, and there it was, burned with fire; and their wives, their sons, and their daughters had been taken captive. 4 Then David and the people who *were* with him lifted up their voices and wept, until they had no more power to weep. 5 And David's two wives, Ahinoam the Jezreelitess, and Abigail the widow of Nabal the Carmelite, had been taken captive. 6 Now David was greatly distressed, for the people spoke of stoning him, because the soul of all the people was grieved, every man for his sons and his daughters. But David strengthened himself in the LORD his God.

7 Then David said to Abiathar the priest, Ahimelech's son, "Please bring the ephod here to me." And Abiathar brought the ephod to David. 8 So David inquired of the LORD, saying, "Shall I pursue this troop? Shall I overtake them?"

And He answered him, "Pursue, for you shall surely overtake *them* and without fail recover *all.*"

9 So David went, he and the six hundred men who *were* with him, and came to the Brook Besor, where those stayed who were left behind. 10 But David pursued, he and four hundred men; for two hundred stayed *behind,* who were so weary that they could not cross the Brook Besor.

11 Then they found an Egyptian in the field, and brought him to David; and they gave him bread and he ate, and they let him drink water. 12 And they gave him a piece of a cake of figs and two clusters of raisins. So when he had eaten, his strength came back to him; for he had eaten no bread nor drunk water for three days and three nights. 13 Then David said to him, "To whom do you *belong,* and where *are* you from?"

And he said, "I *am* a young man from Egypt, servant of an Amalekite; and my master left me behind, be-

---

29:5 *a*Compare 1 Samuel 18:7   29:10 *a*Following Masoretic Text, Targum, and Vulgate; Septuagint adds *and go to the place which I have selected for you there; and set no bothersome word in your heart, for you are good before me. And rise on your way.*

A ccept your share of the responsibility for what has gone wrong and ask God to forgive you.

cause three days ago I fell sick. 14 We made an invasion of the southern *area* of the Cherethites, in the *territory* which *belongs* to Judah, and of the southern *area* of Caleb; and we burned Ziklag with fire."

15 And David said to him, "Can you take me down to this troop?"

So he said, "Swear to me by God that you will neither kill me nor deliver me into the hands of my master, and I will take you down to this troop."

16 And when he had brought him down, there they were, spread out over all the land, eating and drinking and dancing, because of all the great spoil which they had taken from the land of the Philistines and from the land of Judah. 17 Then David attacked them from twilight until the evening of the next day. Not a man of them escaped, except four hundred young men who rode on camels and fled. 18 So David recovered all that the Amalekites had carried away, and David rescued his two wives. 19 And nothing of theirs was lacking, either small or great, sons or daughters, spoil or anything which they had taken from them; David recovered all. 20 Then David took all the flocks and herds they had driven before those *other* livestock, and said, "This *is* David's spoil."

21 Now David came to the two hundred men who had been so weary that they could not follow David, whom they also had made to stay at the Brook Besor. So they went out to meet David and to meet the people who *were* with him. And when David came near the people, he greeted them. 22 Then all the wicked and worthless men*ᵃ* of those who went with David answered and said, "Because they did not go with us, we will not give them *any* of the spoil that we have recovered, except for every man's wife and children, that they may lead *them* away and depart."

23 But David said, "My brethren, you shall not do so with what the LORD has given us, who has preserved us and delivered into our hand the troop that came against us. 24 For who will heed you in this matter? But as his part *is* who goes down to the battle, so *shall* his part *be* who stays by the supplies; they shall

share alike." 25 So it was, from that day forward; he made it a statute and an ordinance for Israel to this day.

26 Now when David came to Ziklag, he sent *some* of the spoil to the elders of Judah, to his friends, saying, "Here is a present for you from the spoil of the enemies of the LORD"— 27 to *those* who *were* in Bethel, *those* who *were* in Ramoth of the South, *those* who *were* in Jattir, 28 *those* who *were* in Aroer, *those* who *were* in Siphmoth, *those* who *were* in Eshtemoa, 29 *those* who *were* in Rachal, *those* who *were* in the cities of the Jerahmeelites, *those* who *were* in the cities of the Kenites, 30 *those* who *were* in Hormah, *those* who *were* in Chorashan,*ᵃ those* who *were* in Athach, 31 *those* who *were* in Hebron, and to all the places where David himself and his men were accustomed to rove.

31 Now the Philistines fought against Israel; and the men of Israel fled from before the Philistines, and fell slain on Mount Gilboa. 2 Then the Philistines followed hard after Saul and his sons. And the Philistines killed Jonathan, Abinadab, and Malchishua, Saul's sons. 3 The battle became fierce against Saul. The archers hit him, and he was severely wounded by the archers.

4 Then Saul said to his armorbearer, "Draw your sword, and thrust me through with it, lest these uncircumcised men come and thrust me through and abuse me."

But his armorbearer would not, for he was greatly afraid. Therefore Saul took a sword and fell on it. 5 And when his armorbearer saw that Saul was dead, he also fell on his sword, and died with him. 6 So Saul, his three sons, his armorbearer, and all his men died together that same day.

7 And when the men of Israel who *were* on the other side of the valley, and *those* who *were* on the other side of the Jordan, saw that the men of Israel had fled and that Saul and his sons were dead, they forsook the cities and fled; and the Philistines came and dwelt in them. 8 So it happened the next day, when the Philistines came to strip the slain, that they found Saul and his three sons fallen

30:22 *ᵃ*Literally *men of Belial*   30:30 *ᵃ*Or *Borashan*

Gospel
Pearls

on Mount Gilboa. 9 And they cut off his head and stripped off his armor, and sent *word* throughout the land of the Philistines, to proclaim *it in* the temple of their idols and among the people. 10 Then they put his armor in the temple of the Ashtoreths, and they fastened his body to the wall of Beth Shan.*ª*

11 Now when the inhabitants of Ja-besh Gilead heard what the Philistines had done to Saul, 12 all the valiant men arose and traveled all night, and took the body of Saul and the bodies of his sons from the wall of Beth Shan; and they came to Jabesh and burned them there. 13 Then they took their bones and buried *them* under the tamarisk tree at Jabesh, and fasted seven days.

31:10 ªSpelled *Beth Shean* in Joshua 17:11 and elsewhere

The Second Book of
SAMUEL

1 Now it came to pass after the death of Saul, when David had returned from the slaughter of the Amalekites, and David had stayed two days in Ziklag, 2 on the third day, behold, it happened that a man came from Saul's camp with his clothes torn and dust on his head. So it was, when he came to David, that he fell to the ground and prostrated himself.

3 And David said to him, "Where have you come from?"

So he said to him, "I have escaped from the camp of Israel."

4 Then David said to him, "How did the matter go? Please tell me."

And he answered, "The people have fled from the battle, many of the people are fallen and dead, and Saul and Jonathan his son are dead also."

5 So David said to the young man who told him, "How do you know that Saul and Jonathan his son are dead?"

6 Then the young man who told him said, "As I happened by chance *to be* on Mount Gilboa, there was Saul, leaning on his spear; and indeed the chariots and horsemen followed hard after him. 7 Now when he looked behind him, he saw me and called to me. And I answered, 'Here I am.' 8 And he said to me, 'Who *are* you?' So I answered him, 'I *am* an Amalekite.' 9 He said to me again, 'Please stand over me and kill me, for anguish has come upon me, but my life still *remains* in me.' 10 So I stood over him and killed him,

because I was sure that he could not live after he had fallen. And I took the crown that *was* on his head and the bracelet that *was* on his arm, and have brought them here to my lord."

11 Therefore David took hold of his own clothes and tore them, and *so did* all the men who *were* with him. 12 And they mourned and wept and fasted until evening for Saul and for Jonathan his son, for the people of the LORD and for the house of Israel, because they had fallen by the sword.

13 Then David said to the young man who told him, "Where *are* you from?"

And he answered, "I *am* the son of an alien, an Amalekite."

14 So David said to him, "How was it you were not afraid to put forth your hand to destroy the LORD's anointed?" 15 Then David called one of the young men and said, "Go near, *and* execute him!" And he struck him so that he died. 16 So David said to him, "Your blood *is* on your own head, for your own mouth has testified against you, saying, 'I have killed the LORD's anointed.' "

17 Then David lamented with this lamentation over Saul and over Jonathan his son, 18 and he told *them* to teach the children of Judah *the Song of* the Bow; indeed *it is* written in the Book of Jasher:

19 "The beauty of Israel is slain on
    your high places!
  How the mighty have fallen!

20 Tell *it* not in Gath,
Proclaim *it* not in the streets of
Ashkelon—
Lest the daughters of the
Philistines rejoice,
Lest the daughters of the
uncircumcised triumph.

21 "O mountains of Gilboa,
Let there be no dew nor rain
upon you,
Nor fields of offerings.
For the shield of the mighty is
cast away there!
The shield of Saul, not anointed
with oil.
22 From the blood of the slain,
From the fat of the mighty,
The bow of Jonathan did not
turn back,
And the sword of Saul did not
return empty.

23 "Saul and Jonathan *were*
beloved and pleasant in their
lives,
And in their death they were
not divided;
They were swifter than eagles,
They were stronger than lions.

24 "O daughters of Israel, weep
over Saul,
Who clothed you in scarlet,
with luxury;
Who put ornaments of gold on
your apparel.

25 "How the mighty have fallen in
the midst of the battle!
Jonathan *was* slain in your
high places.
26 I am distressed for you, my
brother Jonathan;
You have been very pleasant to
me;
Your love to me was
wonderful,
Surpassing the love of women.

27 "How the mighty have fallen,
And the weapons of war
perished!"

2 It happened after this that David
inquired of the LORD, saying,
"Shall I go up to any of the cities of
Judah?"
And the LORD said to him, "Go up."

David said, "Where shall I go up?"
And He said, "To Hebron."
2 So David went up there, and his
two wives also, Ahinoam the Jezreelitess, and Abigail the widow of Nabal
the Carmelite. 3 And David brought
up the men who *were* with him, every
man with his household. So they
dwelt in the cities of Hebron.
4 Then the men of Judah came, and
there they anointed David king over
the house of Judah. And they told
David, saying, "The men of Jabesh
Gilead *were the ones* who buried
Saul." 5 So David sent messengers to
the men of Jabesh Gilead, and said
to them, "You *are* blessed of the
LORD, for you have shown this kindness to your lord, to Saul, and have
buried him. 6 And now may the LORD
show kindness and truth to you. I
also will repay you this kindness, because you have done this thing.
7 Now therefore, let your hands be
strengthened, and be valiant; for
your master Saul is dead, and also
the house of Judah has anointed me
king over them."
8 But Abner the son of Ner, commander of Saul's army, took Ishbosheth[a] the son of Saul and brought
him over to Mahanaim; 9 and he
made him king over Gilead, over the
Ashurites, over Jezreel, over Ephraim, over Benjamin, and over all Israel. 10 Ishbosheth, Saul's son, *was*
forty years old when he began to
reign over Israel, and he reigned two
years. Only the house of Judah followed David. 11 And the time that
David was king in Hebron over the
house of Judah was seven years and
six months.
12 Now Abner the son of Ner, and
the servants of Ishbosheth the son of
Saul, went out from Mahanaim to
Gibeon. 13 And Joab the son of Zeruiah, and the servants of David, went
out and met them by the pool of
Gibeon. So they sat down, one on one
side of the pool and the other on the
other side of the pool. 14 Then Abner
said to Joab, "Let the young men
now arise and compete before us."
And Joab said, "Let them arise."
15 So they arose and went over by
number, twelve from Benjamin, *followers* of Ishbosheth the son of Saul,
and twelve from the servants of David. 16 And each one grasped his op-

2:8 *a*Called *Esh-Baal* in 1 Chronicles 8:33 and 9:39

Gospel
Pearls

ponent by the head and *thrust* his sword in his opponent's side; so they fell down together. Therefore that place was called the Field of Sharp Swords,ᵃ which *is* in Gibeon. 17 So there was a very fierce battle that day, and Abner and the men of Israel were beaten before the servants of David.

18 Now the three sons of Zeruiah were there: Joab and Abishai and Asahel. And Asahel *was as* fleet of foot as a wild gazelle. 19 So Asahel pursued Abner, and in going he did not turn to the right hand or to the left from following Abner.

20 Then Abner looked behind him and said, "*Are* you Asahel?"

He answered, "I *am.*"

21 And Abner said to him, "Turn aside to your right hand or to your left, and lay hold on one of the young men and take his armor for yourself." But Asahel would not turn aside from following him. 22 So Abner said again to Asahel, "Turn aside from following me. Why should I strike you to the ground? How then could I face your brother Joab?" 23 However, he refused to turn aside. Therefore Abner struck him in the stomach with the blunt end of the spear, so that the spear came out of his back; and he fell down there and died on the spot. So it was *that* as many as came to the place where Asahel fell down and died, stood still.

24 Joab and Abishai also pursued Abner. And the sun was going down when they came to the hill of Ammah, which *is* before Giah by the road to the Wilderness of Gibeon. 25 Now the children of Benjamin gathered together behind Abner and became a unit, and took their stand on top of a hill. 26 Then Abner called to Joab and said, "Shall the sword devour forever? Do you not know that it will be bitter in the latter end? How long will it be then until you tell the people to return from pursuing their brethren?"

27 And Joab said, "As God lives, unless you had spoken, surely then by morning all the people would have given up pursuing their brethren." 28 So Joab blew a trumpet; and all the people stood still and did not pursue Israel anymore, nor did they fight anymore. 29 Then Abner and his men went on all that night through the plain, crossed over the Jordan, and went through all Bithron; and they came to Mahanaim.

30 So Joab returned from pursuing Abner. And when he had gathered all the people together, there were missing of David's servants nineteen men and Asahel. 31 But the servants of David had struck down, of Benjamin and Abner's men, three hundred and sixty men who died. 32 Then they took up Asahel and buried him in his father's tomb, which *was in* Bethlehem. And Joab and his men went all night, and they came to Hebron at daybreak.

3 Now there was a long war between the house of Saul and the house of David. But David grew stronger and stronger, and the house of Saul grew weaker and weaker.

2 Sons were born to David in Hebron: His firstborn was Amnon by Ahinoam the Jezreelitess; 3 his second, Chileab, by Abigail the widow of Nabal the Carmelite; the third, Absalom the son of Maacah, the daughter of Talmai, king of Geshur; 4 the fourth, Adonijah the son of Haggith; the fifth, Shephatiah the son of Abital; 5 and the sixth, Ithream, by David's wife Eglah. These were born to David in Hebron.

6 Now it was so, while there was war between the house of Saul and the house of David, that Abner was strengthening *his hold* on the house of Saul.

7 And Saul had a concubine, whose name *was* Rizpah, the daughter of Aiah. So *Ishbosheth* said to Abner, "Why have you gone in to my father's concubine?"

8 Then Abner became very angry at the words of Ishbosheth, and said, "*Am* I a dog's head that belongs to Judah? Today I show loyalty to the house of Saul your father, to his brothers, and to his friends, and have not delivered you into the hand of David; and you charge me today with a fault concerning this woman? 9 May God do so to Abner, and more also, if I do not do for David as the LORD has sworn to him— 10 to transfer the kingdom from the house of Saul, and set up the throne of David over Israel and over Judah, from Dan

2:16 ᵃHebrew *Helkath Hazzurim*

*W*e were handmade by God in our mother's womb. He custom-designed us to fit a specific role in His sovereign plan for the ages.

to Beersheba." 11 And he could not answer Abner another word, because he feared him.

12 Then Abner sent messengers on his behalf to David, saying, "Whose *is* the land?" saying *also,* "Make your covenant with me, and indeed my hand *shall be* with you to bring all Israel to you."

13 And *David* said, "Good, I will make a covenant with you. But one thing I require of you: you shall not see my face unless you first bring Michal, Saul's daughter, when you come to see my face." 14 So David sent messengers to Ishbosheth, Saul's son, saying, "Give *me* my wife Michal, whom I betrothed to myself for a hundred foreskins of the Philistines." 15 And Ishbosheth sent and took her from *her* husband, from Paltiel[a] the son of Laish. 16 Then her husband went along with her to Bahurim, weeping behind her. So Abner said to him, "Go, return!" And he returned.

17 Now Abner had communicated with the elders of Israel, saying, "In time past you were seeking for David *to be* king over you. 18 Now then, do *it!* For the LORD has spoken of David, saying, 'By the hand of My servant David, I[a] will save My people Israel from the hand of the Philistines and the hand of all their enemies.'" 19 And Abner also spoke in the hearing of Benjamin. Then Abner also went to speak in the hearing of David in Hebron all that seemed good to Israel and the whole house of Benjamin.

20 So Abner and twenty men with him came to David at Hebron. And David made a feast for Abner and the men who *were* with him. 21 Then Abner said to David, "I will arise and go, and gather all Israel to my lord the king, that they may make a covenant with you, and that you may reign over all that your heart desires." So David sent Abner away, and he went in peace.

22 At that moment the servants of David and Joab came from a raid and brought much spoil with them. But Abner *was* not with David in Hebron, for he had sent him away, and he had gone in peace. 23 When Joab and all the troops that *were* with him had come, they told Joab, saying, "Abner the son of Ner came to the king, and he sent him away, and he has gone in peace." 24 Then Joab came to the king and said, "What have you done? Look, Abner came to you; why *is* it *that* you sent him away, and he has already gone? 25 Surely you realize that Abner the son of Ner came to deceive you, to know your going out and your coming in, and to know all that you are doing."

26 And when Joab had gone from David's presence, he sent messengers after Abner, who brought him back from the well of Sirah. But David did not know *it.* 27 Now when Abner had returned to Hebron, Joab took him aside in the gate to speak with him privately, and there stabbed him in the stomach, so that he died for the blood of Asahel his brother.

28 Afterward, when David heard *it,* he said, "My kingdom and I *are* guiltless before the LORD forever of the blood of Abner the son of Ner. 29 Let it rest on the head of Joab and on all his father's house; and let there never fail to be in the house of Joab one who has a discharge or is a leper, who leans on a staff or falls by the sword, or who lacks bread." 30 So Joab and Abishai his brother killed Abner, because he had killed their brother Asahel at Gibeon in the battle.

31 Then David said to Joab and to all the people who were with him, "Tear your clothes, gird yourselves with sackcloth, and mourn for Abner." And King David followed the coffin. 32 So they buried Abner in Hebron; and the king lifted up his voice and wept at the grave of Abner, and all the people wept. 33 And the king sang *a lament* over Abner and said:

"Should Abner die as a fool dies?
34 Your hands were not bound
Nor your feet put into fetters;
As a man falls before wicked men, *so* you fell."

Then all the people wept over him again.

35 And when all the people came to persuade David to eat food while it was still day, David took an oath,

---

3:15 [a]Spelled *Palti* in 1 Samuel 25:44   3:18 [a]Following many Hebrew manuscripts, Septuagint, Syriac, and Targum; Masoretic Text reads *he.*

Gospel Pearls

saying, "God do so to me, and more also, if I taste bread or anything else till the sun goes down!" 36 Now all the people took note *of it,* and it pleased them, since whatever the king did pleased all the people. 37 For all the people and all Israel understood that day that it had not been the king's *intent* to kill Abner the son of Ner. 38 Then the king said to his servants, "Do you not know that a prince and a great man has fallen this day in Israel? 39 And I *am* weak today, though anointed king; and these men, the sons of Zeruiah, *are* too harsh for me. The LORD shall repay the evildoer according to his wickedness."

4 When Saul's son*a* heard that Abner had died in Hebron, he lost heart, and all Israel was troubled. 2 Now Saul's son *had* two men *who were* captains of troops. The name of one *was* Baanah and the name of the other Rechab, the sons of Rimmon the Beerothite, of the children of Benjamin. (For Beeroth also was *part* of Benjamin, 3 because the Beerothites fled to Gittaim and have been sojourners there until this day.)

4 Jonathan, Saul's son, had a son *who was* lame in *his* feet. He was five years old when the news about Saul and Jonathan came from Jezreel; and his nurse took him up and fled. And it happened, as she made haste to flee, that he fell and became lame. His name *was* Mephibosheth.*a*

5 Then the sons of Rimmon the Beerothite, Rechab and Baanah, set out and came at about the heat of the day to the house of Ishbosheth, who was lying on his bed at noon. 6 And they came there, all the way into the house, *as though* to get wheat, and they stabbed him in the stomach. Then Rechab and Baanah his brother escaped. 7 For when they came into the house, he was lying on his bed in his bedroom; then they struck him and killed him, beheaded him and took his head, and were all night escaping through the plain. 8 And they brought the head of Ishbosheth to David at Hebron, and said to the king, "Here is the head of Ishbosheth, the son of Saul your enemy, who sought your life; and the LORD has avenged my lord the king this day of Saul and his descendants."

9 But David answered Rechab and Baanah his brother, the sons of Rimmon the Beerothite, and said to them, "*As* the LORD lives, who has redeemed my life from all adversity, 10 when someone told me, saying, 'Look, Saul is dead,' thinking to have brought good news, I arrested him and had him executed in Ziklag—the one who *thought* I would give him a reward for *his* news. 11 How much more, when wicked men have killed a righteous person in his own house on his bed? Therefore, shall I not now require his blood at your hand and remove you from the earth?" 12 So David commanded his young men, and they executed them, cut off their hands and feet, and hanged *them* by the pool in Hebron. But they took the head of Ishbosheth and buried *it* in the tomb of Abner in Hebron.

5 Then all the tribes of Israel came to David at Hebron and spoke, saying, "Indeed we *are* your bone and your flesh. 2 Also, in time past, when Saul was king over us, you were the one who led Israel out and brought them in; and the LORD said to you, 'You shall shepherd My people Israel, and be ruler over Israel.' " 3 Therefore all the elders of Israel came to the king at Hebron, and King David made a covenant with them at Hebron before the LORD. And they anointed David king over Israel. 4 David *was* thirty years old when he began to reign, *and* he reigned forty years. 5 In Hebron he reigned over Judah seven years and six months, and in Jerusalem he reigned thirty-three years over all Israel and Judah.

6 And the king and his men went to Jerusalem against the Jebusites, the inhabitants of the land, who spoke to David, saying, "You shall not come in here; but the blind and the lame will repel you," thinking, "David cannot come in here." 7 Nevertheless David took the stronghold of Zion (that *is,* the City of David).

8 Now David said on that day, "Whoever climbs up by way of the water shaft and defeats the Jebusites (the lame and the blind, *who are* hated by David's soul), *he shall be*

4:1 *a*That is, Ishbosheth   4:4 *a*Called *Merib-Baal* in 1 Chronicles 8:34 and 9:40

A s a woman, you have a great capacity to express feelings and affections. God gave you that capacity so you could relate more fully to other people and to Him.

chief and captain."ᵃ Therefore they say, "The blind and the lame shall not come into the house."

9 Then David dwelt in the stronghold, and called it the City of David. And David built all around from the Millo*ᵃ* and inward. 10 So David went on and became great, and the LORD God of hosts *was* with him.

11 Then Hiram king of Tyre sent messengers to David, and cedar trees, and carpenters and masons. And they built David a house. 12 So David knew that the LORD had established him as king over Israel, and that He had exalted His kingdom for the sake of His people Israel.

13 And David took more concubines and wives from Jerusalem, after he had come from Hebron. Also more sons and daughters were born to David. 14 Now these *are* the names of those who were born to him in Jerusalem: Shammua,*ᵃ* Shobab, Nathan, Solomon, 15 Ibhar, Elishua,*ᵃ* Nepheg, Japhia, 16 Elishama, Eliada, and Eliphelet.

17 Now when the Philistines heard that they had anointed David king over Israel, all the Philistines went up to search for David. And David heard *of it* and went down to the stronghold. 18 The Philistines also went and deployed themselves in the Valley of Rephaim. 19 So David inquired of the LORD, saying, "Shall I go up against the Philistines? Will You deliver them into my hand?"

And the LORD said to David, "Go up, for I will doubtless deliver the Philistines into your hand."

20 So David went to Baal Perazim, and David defeated them there; and he said, "The LORD has broken through my enemies before me, like a breakthrough of water." Therefore he called the name of that place Baal Perazim.*ᵃ* 21 And they left their images there, and David and his men carried them away.

22 Then the Philistines went up once again and deployed themselves in the Valley of Rephaim. 23 Therefore David inquired of the LORD, and He said, "You shall not go up; circle around behind them, and come upon them in front of the mulberry trees. 24 And it shall be, when you hear the sound of marching in the tops of the mulberry trees, then you shall advance quickly. For then the LORD will go out before you to strike the camp of the Philistines." 25 And David did so, as the LORD commanded him; and he drove back the Philistines from Geba*ᵃ* as far as Gezer.

6 Again David gathered all *the* choice *men* of Israel, thirty thousand. 2 And David arose and went with all the people who *were* with him from Baale Judah to bring up from there the ark of God, whose name is called by the Name,*ᵃ* the LORD of Hosts, who dwells *between* the cherubim. 3 So they set the ark of God on a new cart, and brought it out of the house of Abinadab, which *was* on the hill; and Uzzah and Ahio, the sons of Abinadab, drove the new cart.*ᵃ* 4 And they brought it out of the house of Abinadab, which *was* on the hill, accompanying the ark of God; and Ahio went before the ark. 5 Then David and all the house of Israel played *music* before the LORD on all kinds of *instruments of* fir wood, on harps, on stringed instruments, on tambourines, on sistrums, and on cymbals.

6 And when they came to Nachon's threshing floor, Uzzah put out *his hand* to the ark of God and took hold of it, for the oxen stumbled. 7 Then the anger of the LORD was aroused against Uzzah, and God struck him there for *his* error; and he died there by the ark of God. 8 And David became angry because of the LORD's outbreak against Uzzah; and he called the name of the place Perez Uzzah*ᵃ* to this day.

9 David was afraid of the LORD that day; and he said, "How can the ark of the LORD come to me?" 10 So David would not move the ark of the LORD with him into the City of David; but David took it aside into the house of Obed-Edom the Gittite. 11 The ark of the LORD remained in the house of Obed-Edom the Gittite three months.

5:8 ᵃCompare 1 Chronicles 11:6   5:9 ᵃLiterally *The Landfill*   5:14 ᵃSpelled *Shimea* in 1 Chronicles 3:5   5:15 ᵃSpelled *Elishama* in 1 Chronicles 3:6   5:20 ᵃLiterally *Baal Is Broken*   5:25 ᵃFollowing Masoretic Text, Targum, and Vulgate; Septuagint reads *Gibeon*.   6:2 ᵃSeptuagint, Targum, and Vulgate omit *by the Name;* many Hebrew manuscripts and Syriac read *there.*   6:3 ᵃSeptuagint adds *with the ark.*   6:8 ᵃLiterally *Outburst Against Uzzah*

Gospel Pearls

And the LORD blessed Obed-Edom and all his household.

12 Now it was told King David, saying, "The LORD has blessed the house of Obed-Edom and all that *belongs* to him, because of the ark of God." So David went and brought up the ark of God from the house of Obed-Edom to the City of David with gladness. 13 And so it was, when those bearing the ark of the LORD had gone six paces, that he sacrificed oxen and fatted sheep. 14 Then David danced before the LORD with all *his* might; and David *was* wearing a linen ephod. 15 So David and all the house of Israel brought up the ark of the LORD with shouting and with the sound of the trumpet.

16 Now as the ark of the LORD came into the City of David, Michal, Saul's daughter, looked through a window and saw King David leaping and whirling before the LORD; and she despised him in her heart. 17 So they brought the ark of the LORD, and set it in its place in the midst of the tabernacle that David had erected for it. Then David offered burnt offerings and peace offerings before the LORD. 18 And when David had finished offering burnt offerings and peace offerings, he blessed the people in the name of the LORD of hosts. 19 Then he distributed among all the people, among the whole multitude of Israel, both the women and the men, to everyone a loaf of bread, a piece *of meat*, and a cake of raisins. So all the people departed, everyone to his house.

20 Then David returned to bless his household. And Michal the daughter of Saul came out to meet David, and said, "How glorious was the king of Israel today, uncovering himself today in the eyes of the maids of his servants, as one of the base fellows shamelessly uncovers himself!"

21 So David said to Michal, "*It was* before the LORD, who chose me instead of your father and all his house, to appoint me ruler over the people of the LORD, over Israel. Therefore I will play *music* before the LORD. 22 And I will be even more undignified than this, and will be humble in my own sight. But as for the maidservants of whom you have spoken, by them I will be held in honor."

23 Therefore Michal the daughter of Saul had no children to the day of her death.

7 Now it came to pass when the king was dwelling in his house, and the LORD had given him rest from all his enemies all around, 2 that the king said to Nathan the prophet, "See now, I dwell in a house of cedar, but the ark of God dwells inside tent curtains."

3 Then Nathan said to the king, "Go, do all that *is* in your heart, for the LORD *is* with you."

4 But it happened that night that the word of the LORD came to Nathan, saying, 5 "Go and tell My servant David, 'Thus says the LORD: "Would you build a house for Me to dwell in? 6 For I have not dwelt in a house since the time that I brought the children of Israel up from Egypt, even to this day, but have moved about in a tent and in a tabernacle. 7 Wherever I have moved about with all the children of Israel, have I ever spoken a word to anyone from the tribes of Israel, whom I commanded to shepherd My people Israel, saying, 'Why have you not built Me a house of cedar?' " ' 8 Now therefore, thus shall you say to My servant David, 'Thus says the LORD of hosts: "I took you from the sheepfold, from following the sheep, to be ruler over My people, over Israel. 9 And I have been with you wherever you have gone, and have cut off all your enemies from before you, and have made you a great name, like the name of the great men who *are* on the earth. 10 Moreover I will appoint a place for My people Israel, and will plant them, that they may dwell in a place of their own and move no more; nor shall the sons of wickedness oppress them anymore, as previously, 11 since the time that I commanded judges *to be* over My people Israel, and have caused you to rest from all your enemies. Also the LORD tells you that He will make you a house.ᵃ

12 "When your days are fulfilled and you rest with your fathers, I will set up your seed after you, who will come from your body, and I will establish his kingdom. 13 He shall build a house for My name, and I will establish the throne of his kingdom for-

7:11 ᵃThat is, a royal dynasty

*W*hat is it that you want God to do for you today? Do you want it with all of your heart? Do you want it with passion and intensity?

ever. 14 I will be his Father, and he shall be My son. If he commits iniquity, I will chasten him with the rod of men and with the blows of the sons of men. 15 But My mercy shall not depart from him, as I took *it* from Saul, whom I removed from before you. 16 And your house and your kingdom shall be established forever before you.*a* Your throne shall be established forever." ' "

17 According to all these words and according to all this vision, so Nathan spoke to David.

18 Then King David went in and sat before the LORD; and he said: "Who *am* I, O Lord GOD? And what is my house, that You have brought me this far? 19 And yet this was a small thing in Your sight, O Lord GOD; and You have also spoken of Your servant's house for a great while to come. *Is* this the manner of man, O Lord GOD? 20 Now what more can David say to You? For You, Lord GOD, know Your servant. 21 For Your word's sake, and according to Your own heart, You have done all these great things, to make Your servant know *them*. 22 Therefore You are great, O Lord GOD.*a* For *there is* none like You, nor *is there any* God besides You, according to all that we have heard with our ears. 23 And who *is* like Your people, like Israel, the one nation on the earth whom God went to redeem for Himself as a people, to make for Himself a name—and to do for Yourself great and awesome deeds for Your land—before Your people whom You redeemed for Yourself from Egypt, the nations, and their gods? 24 For You have made Your people Israel Your very own people forever; and You, LORD, have become their God.

25 "Now, O LORD God, the word which You have spoken concerning Your servant and concerning his house, establish *it* forever and do as You have said. 26 So let Your name be magnified forever, saying, 'The LORD of hosts *is* the God over Israel.' And let the house of Your servant David be established before You. 27 For You, O LORD of hosts, God of Israel, have revealed *this* to Your servant, saying, 'I will build you a

house.' Therefore Your servant has found it in his heart to pray this prayer to You. 28 "And now, O Lord GOD, You are God, and Your words are true, and You have promised this goodness to Your servant. 29 Now therefore, let it please You to bless the house of Your servant, that it may continue before You forever; for You, O Lord GOD, have spoken *it*, and with Your blessing let the house of Your servant be blessed forever."

8 After this it came to pass that David attacked the Philistines and subdued them. And David took Metheg Ammah from the hand of the Philistines.

2 Then he defeated Moab. Forcing them down to the ground, he measured them off with a line. With two lines he measured off those to be put to death, and with one full line those to be kept alive. So the Moabites became David's servants, *and* brought tribute.

3 David also defeated Hadadezer the son of Rehob, king of Zobah, as he went to recover his territory at the River Euphrates. 4 David took from him one thousand *chariots,* seven hundred*a* horsemen, and twenty thousand foot soldiers. Also David hamstrung all the chariot horses, except that he spared *enough* of them for one hundred chariots.

5 When the Syrians of Damascus came to help Hadadezer king of Zobah, David killed twenty-two thousand of the Syrians. 6 Then David put garrisons in Syria of Damascus; and the Syrians became David's servants, *and* brought tribute. So the LORD preserved David wherever he went. 7 And David took the shields of gold that had belonged to the servants of Hadadezer, and brought them to Jerusalem. 8 Also from Betah*a* and from Berothai, cities of Hadadezer, King David took a large amount of bronze.

9 When Toi*a* king of Hamath heard that David had defeated all the army of Hadadezer, 10 then Toi sent Joram*a* his son to King David, to greet him and bless him, because he had fought against Hadadezer and de-

---

7:16 *a*Septuagint reads *Me.*   7:22 *a*Targum and Syriac read *O LORD God.*   8:4 *a*Or *seven thousand* (compare 1 Chronicles 18:4)   8:8 *a*Spelled *Tibhath* in 1 Chronicles 18:8   8:9 *a*Spelled *Tou* in 1 Chronicles 18:9   8:10 *a*Spelled *Hadoram* in 1 Chronicles 18:10

Gospel Pearls

feated him (for Hadadezer had been at war with Toi); and *Joram* brought with him articles of silver, articles of gold, and articles of bronze. 11 King David also dedicated these to the LORD, along with the silver and gold that he had dedicated from all the nations which he had subdued— 12 from Syria,*a* from Moab, from the people of Ammon, from the Philistines, from Amalek, and from the spoil of Hadadezer the son of Rehob, king of Zobah.

13 And David made *himself* a name when he returned from killing eighteen thousand Syrians*a* in the Valley of Salt. 14 He also put garrisons in Edom; throughout all Edom he put garrisons, and all the Edomites became David's servants. And the LORD preserved David wherever he went.

15 So David reigned over all Israel; and David administered judgment and justice to all his people. 16 Joab the son of Zeruiah *was* over the army; Jehoshaphat the son of Ahilud *was* recorder; 17 Zadok the son of Ahitub and Ahimelech the son of Abiathar *were* the priests; Seraiah*a* *was* the scribe; 18 Benaiah the son of Jehoiada *was over* both the Cherethites and the Pelethites; and David's sons were chief ministers.

9 Now David said, "Is there still anyone who is left of the house of Saul, that I may show him kindness for Jonathan's sake?"

2 And *there was* a servant of the house of Saul whose name *was* Ziba. So when they had called him to David, the king said to him, "*Are* you Ziba?"

He said, "At your service!"

3 Then the king said, "*Is* there not still someone of the house of Saul, to whom I may show the kindness of God?"

And Ziba said to the king, "There is still a son of Jonathan *who is* lame in *his* feet."

4 So the king said to him, "Where *is* he?"

And Ziba said to the king, "Indeed he *is* in the house of Machir the son of Ammiel, in Lo Debar."

5 Then King David sent and brought him out of the house of Ma-

chir the son of Ammiel, from Lo Debar.

6 Now when Mephibosheth the son of Jonathan, the son of Saul, had come to David, he fell on his face and prostrated himself. Then David said, "Mephibosheth?"

And he answered, "Here is your servant!"

7 So David said to him, "Do not fear, for I will surely show you kindness for Jonathan your father's sake, and will restore to you all the land of Saul your grandfather; and you shall eat bread at my table continually."

8 Then he bowed himself, and said, "What *is* your servant, that you should look upon such a dead dog as I?"

9 And the king called to Ziba, Saul's servant, and said to him, "I have given to your master's son all that belonged to Saul and to all his house. 10 You therefore, and your sons and your servants, shall work the land for him, and you shall bring in *the harvest,* that your master's son may have food to eat. But Mephibosheth your master's son shall eat bread at my table always." Now Ziba had fifteen sons and twenty servants.

11 Then Ziba said to the king, "According to all that my lord the king has commanded his servant, so will your servant do."

"As for Mephibosheth," *said the king,* "he shall eat at my table*a* like one of the king's sons." 12 Mephibosheth had a young son whose name *was* Micha. And all who dwelt in the house of Ziba *were* servants of Mephibosheth. 13 So Mephibosheth dwelt in Jerusalem, for he ate continually at the king's table. And he was lame in both his feet.

10 It happened after this that the king of the people of Ammon died, and Hanun his son reigned in his place. 2 Then David said, "I will show kindness to Hanun the son of Nahash, as his father showed kindness to me."

So David sent by the hand of his servants to comfort him concerning his father. And David's servants

8:12 *a*Septuagint, Syriac, and some Hebrew manuscripts read *Edom.*   8:13 *a*Septuagint, Syriac, and some Hebrew manuscripts read *Edomites* (compare 1 Chronicles 18:12).   8:17 *a*Spelled *Shavsha* in 1 Chronicles 18:16   9:11 *a*Septuagint reads *David's table.*

After you have prayed, speak God's words of life to yourself. Speak them to your problem. Speak them to your circumstance, your situation, your need, your problem, your lack of supply.

No More Dead Dogs

2 Samuel 9:6–10

The Scriptures tell us that "with the heart one believes unto righteousness, and with the mouth confession is made unto salvation" (Romans 10:10). There is a strong tie between what is believed and what is confessed.

You need to allow new meditations to dwell in your heart by faith, for your life will ultimately take on the direction of your thinking. Many weaknesses, such as procrastination and laziness, are just draperies that cover up poor self-esteem and a lack of motivation. They are often symptoms of the subconscious avoiding the risk of failure. Remember that "nothing will be impossible for you" if you will only believe (Matthew 17:20).

Let me remind you of a story from 2 Samuel. King David sent his servant to find any surviving relatives of his friend Jonathan. When his servant returned to his palace from Lo Debar with Mephibosheth, the crippled son of Jonathan, David rolled out the red carpet and invited Mephibosheth to join him for dinner at his royal banquet table. The problem was that Mephibosheth couldn't sit at the table without falling to the floor. He struggled with his position because of his condition. His problem wasn't merely his twisted feet or his crippled body. It was his dysfunctional mentality. Even after he had been raised from the deplorable condition he had lived in for years, he was still so oppressed in his mind that he described himself as a "dead dog" (2 Samuel 9:8). He was a king's kid, but he saw himself as a dead dog.

Perception is everything. Mephibosheth thought of himself as a dead dog, so he lay on the floor like one. Sister, *you have been on the floor long enough!* It is time for a resurrection, and it is going to start in your *mind*. Has God blessed you with something you are afraid of losing? Could it be that you think you are going to lose it because you don't feel worthy? Don't follow Mephibosheth's example.

Understand this one fact: *Just because you've been treated like a dog doesn't mean you are one!* Get up off the floor and take a seat at the Master's table—you are worthy. You have a right to be in the place and position you are in, not because of your goodness, but by virtue of His invitation. I pray that God will heal your thoughts until you are able to enjoy and rest in what He is doing in your life right now!

came into the land of the people of Ammon. 3 And the princes of the people of Ammon said to Hanun their lord, "Do you think that David really honors your father because he has sent comforters to you? Has David not *rather* sent his servants to you to search the city, to spy it out, and to overthrow it?"

4 Therefore Hanun took David's servants, shaved off half of their beards, cut off their garments in the middle, at their buttocks, and sent them away. 5 When they told David, he sent to meet them, because the men were greatly ashamed. And the king said, "Wait at Jericho until your beards have grown, and *then* return."

6 When the people of Ammon saw that they had made themselves repulsive to David, the people of Ammon sent and hired the Syrians of Beth Rehob and the Syrians of Zoba, twenty thousand foot soldiers; and from the king of Maacah one thousand men, and from Ish-Tob twelve thousand men. 7 Now when David heard *of it*, he sent Joab and all the army of the mighty men. 8 Then the people of Ammon came out and put themselves in battle array at the entrance of the gate. And the Syrians of Zoba, Beth Rehob, Ish-Tob, and Maacah *were* by themselves in the field.

9 When Joab saw that the battle line was against him before and behind, he chose some of Israel's best and put *them* in battle array against the Syrians. 10 And the rest of the people he put under the command of Abishai his brother, that he might set *them* in battle array against the people of Ammon. 11 Then he said, "If the Syrians are too strong for me, then you shall help me; but if the people of Ammon are too strong for you, then I will come and help you. 12 Be of good courage, and let us be strong for our people and for the cities of our God. And may the LORD do *what is* good in His sight."

13 So Joab and the people who *were* with him drew near for the battle against the Syrians, and they fled before him. 14 When the people of Ammon saw that the Syrians were fleeing, they also fled before Abishai, and entered the city. So Joab re-

turned from the people of Ammon and went to Jerusalem.

15 When the Syrians saw that they had been defeated by Israel, they gathered together. 16 Then Hadadezer[a] sent and brought out the Syrians who *were* beyond the River,[b] and they came to Helam. And Shobach the commander of Hadadezer's army *went* before them. 17 When it was told David, he gathered all Israel, crossed over the Jordan, and came to Helam. And the Syrians set themselves in battle array against David and fought with him. 18 Then the Syrians fled before Israel; and David killed seven hundred charioteers and forty thousand horsemen of the Syrians, and struck Shobach the commander of their army, who died there. 19 And when all the kings *who were* servants to Hadadezer[a] saw that they were defeated by Israel, they made peace with Israel and served them. So the Syrians were afraid to help the people of Ammon anymore.

11 It happened in the spring of the year, at the time when kings go out *to battle,* that David sent Joab and his servants with him, and all Israel; and they destroyed the people of Ammon and besieged Rabbah. But David remained at Jerusalem.

2 Then it happened one evening that David arose from his bed and walked on the roof of the king's house. And from the roof he saw a woman bathing, and the woman *was* very beautiful to behold. 3 So David sent and inquired about the woman. And *someone* said, "*Is* this not Bathsheba, the daughter of Eliam, the wife of Uriah the Hittite?" 4 Then David sent messengers, and took her; and she came to him, and he lay with her, for she was cleansed from her impurity; and she returned to her house. 5 And the woman conceived; so she sent and told David, and said, "I *am* with child."

6 Then David sent to Joab, *saying,* "Send me Uriah the Hittite." And Joab sent Uriah to David. 7 When Uriah had come to him, David asked how Joab was doing, and how the people were doing, and how the war prospered. 8 And David said to Uriah, "Go down to your house and

---

10:16 ^aHebrew *Hadarezer*   ^bThat is, the Euphrates   10:19 ^aHebrew *Hadarezer*

Quit crying over where you've been. Quit crying over your mistakes and failures. Start looking toward where you are going. Start looking toward what God has for you. Start looking for the way God is going to use what you do have.

wash your feet." So Uriah departed from the king's house, and a gift *of food* from the king followed him. 9 But Uriah slept at the door of the king's house with all the servants of his lord, and did not go down to his house. 10 So when they told David, saying, "Uriah did not go down to his house," David said to Uriah, "Did you not come from a journey? Why did you not go down to your house?"

11 And Uriah said to David, "The ark and Israel and Judah are dwelling in tents, and my lord Joab and the servants of my lord are encamped in the open fields. Shall I then go to my house to eat and drink, and to lie with my wife? *As* you live, and *as* your soul lives, I will not do this thing."

12 Then David said to Uriah, "Wait here today also, and tomorrow I will let you depart." So Uriah remained in Jerusalem that day and the next. 13 Now when David called him, he ate and drank before him; and he made him drunk. And at evening he went out to lie on his bed with the servants of his lord, but he did not go down to his house.

14 In the morning it happened that David wrote a letter to Joab and sent *it* by the hand of Uriah. 15 And he wrote in the letter, saying, "Set Uriah in the forefront of the hottest battle, and retreat from him, that he may be struck down and die." 16 So it was, while Joab besieged the city, that he assigned Uriah to a place where he knew there *were* valiant men. 17 Then the men of the city came out and fought with Joab. And *some* of the people of the servants of David fell; and Uriah the Hittite died also.

18 Then Joab sent and told David all the things concerning the war, 19 and charged the messenger, saying, "When you have finished telling the matters of the war to the king, 20 if it happens that the king's wrath rises, and he says to you: 'Why did you approach so near to the city when you fought? Did you not know that they would shoot from the wall? 21 Who struck Abimelech the son of Jerubbesheth?ᵃ Was it not a woman who cast a piece of a millstone on him from the wall, so that he died in Thebez? Why did you go near the wall?'—then you shall say, 'Your ser-

vant Uriah the Hittite is dead also.' "

22 So the messenger went, and came and told David all that Joab had sent by him. 23 And the messenger said to David, "Surely the men prevailed against us and came out to us in the field; then we drove them back as far as the entrance of the gate. 24 The archers shot from the wall at your servants; and *some* of the king's servants are dead, and your servant Uriah the Hittite is dead also."

25 Then David said to the messenger, "Thus you shall say to Joab: 'Do not let this thing displease you, for the sword devours one as well as another. Strengthen your attack against the city, and overthrow it.' So encourage him."

26 When the wife of Uriah heard that Uriah her husband was dead, she mourned for her husband. 27 And when her mourning was over, David sent and brought her to his house, and she became his wife and bore him a son. But the thing that David had done displeased the LORD.

12 Then the LORD sent Nathan to David. And he came to him, and said to him: "There were two men in one city, one rich and the other poor. 2 The rich *man* had exceedingly many flocks and herds. 3 But the poor *man* had nothing, except one little ewe lamb which he had bought and nourished; and it grew up together with him and with his children. It ate of his own food and drank from his own cup and lay in his bosom; and it was like a daughter to him. 4 And a traveler came to the rich man, who refused to take from his own flock and from his own herd to prepare one for the wayfaring man who had come to him; but he took the poor man's lamb and prepared it for the man who had come to him."

5 So David's anger was greatly aroused against the man, and he said to Nathan, "*As* the LORD lives, the man who has done this shall surely die! 6 And he shall restore fourfold for the lamb, because he did this thing and because he had no pity."

7 Then Nathan said to David, "You *are* the man! Thus says the LORD God of Israel: 'I anointed you king over Israel, and I delivered you from the

11:21 ᵃSame as *Jerubbaal* (Gideon), Judges 6:32ff

Gospel Pearls

hand of Saul. 8 I gave you your master's house and your master's wives into your keeping, and gave you the house of Israel and Judah. And if *that had been* too little, I also would have given you much more! 9 Why have you despised the commandment of the LORD, to do evil in His sight? You have killed Uriah the Hittite with the sword; you have taken his wife *to be* your wife, and have killed him with the sword of the people of Ammon. 10 Now therefore, the sword shall never depart from your house, because you have despised Me, and have taken the wife of Uriah the Hittite to be your wife.' 11 Thus says the LORD: 'Behold, I will raise up adversity against you from your own house; and I will take your wives before your eyes and give *them* to your neighbor, and he shall lie with your wives in the sight of this sun. 12 For you did *it* secretly, but I will do this thing before all Israel, before the sun.' "

13 So David said to Nathan, "I have sinned against the LORD."

And Nathan said to David, "The LORD also has put away your sin; you shall not die. 14 However, because by this deed you have given great occasion to the enemies of the LORD to blaspheme, the child also *who is* born to you shall surely die." 15 Then Nathan departed to his house.

And the LORD struck the child that Uriah's wife bore to David, and it became ill. 16 David therefore pleaded with God for the child, and David fasted and went in and lay all night on the ground. 17 So the elders of his house arose *and went* to him, to raise him up from the ground. But he would not, nor did he eat food with them. 18 Then on the seventh day it came to pass that the child died. And the servants of David were afraid to tell him that the child was dead. For they said, "Indeed, while the child was alive, we spoke to him, and he would not heed our voice. How can we tell him that the child is dead? He may do some harm!"

19 When David saw that his servants were whispering, David perceived that the child was dead. Therefore David said to his servants, "Is the child dead?"

And they said, "He is dead."

20 So David arose from the ground, washed and anointed himself, and changed his clothes; and he went into the house of the LORD and worshiped. Then he went to his own house; and when he requested, they set food before him, and he ate. 21 Then his servants said to him, "What *is* this that you have done? You fasted and wept for the child *while he was* alive, but when the child died, you arose and ate food."

22 And he said, "While the child was alive, I fasted and wept; for I said, 'Who can tell *whether* the LORD[a] will be gracious to me, that the child may live?' 23 But now he is dead; why should I fast? Can I bring him back again? I shall go to him, but he shall not return to me."

24 Then David comforted Bathsheba his wife, and went in to her and lay with her. So she bore a son, and he[a] called his name Solomon. Now the LORD loved him, 25 and He sent *word* by the hand of Nathan the prophet: So he[a] called his name Jedidiah,[b] because of the LORD.

26 Now Joab fought against Rabbah of the people of Ammon, and took the royal city. 27 And Joab sent messengers to David, and said, "I have fought against Rabbah, and I have taken the city's water *supply*. 28 Now therefore, gather the rest of the people together and encamp against the city and take it, lest I take the city and it be called after my name." 29 So David gathered all the people together and went to Rabbah, fought against it, and took it. 30 Then he took their king's crown from his head. Its weight *was* a talent of gold, with precious stones. And it was *set* on David's head. Also he brought out the spoil of the city in great abundance. 31 And he brought out the people who *were* in it, and put *them to work* with saws and iron picks and iron axes, and made them cross over to the brick works. So he did to all the cities of the people of Ammon. Then David and all the people returned to Jerusalem.

13 After this Absalom the son of David had a lovely sister, whose name *was* Tamar; and Amnon

12:22 aA few Hebrew manuscripts and Syriac read *God.*   12:24 aFollowing Kethib, Septuagint, and Vulgate; Qere, a few Hebrew manuscripts, Syriac, and Targum read *she.*   12:25 aQere, some Hebrew manuscripts, Syriac, and Targum read *she.*   bLiterally *Beloved of the LORD*

When the Bible says that we are all born in sin, the word is *sin,* not *sins.* We are born with a sin nature, the state of sin, not as the result of a sinful act or with a host of sins attributed to our account.

the son of David loved her. 2 Amnon was so distressed over his sister Tamar that he became sick; for she *was* a virgin. And it was improper for Amnon to do anything to her. 3 But Amnon had a friend whose name *was* Jonadab the son of Shimeah, David's brother. Now Jonadab *was* a very crafty man. 4 And he said to him, "Why *are* you, the king's son, becoming thinner day after day? Will you not tell me?"

Amnon said to him, "I love Tamar, my brother Absalom's sister."

5 So Jonadab said to him, "Lie down on your bed and pretend to be ill. And when your father comes to see you, say to him, 'Please let my sister Tamar come and give me food, and prepare the food in my sight, that I may see *it* and eat it from her hand.' " 6 Then Amnon lay down and pretended to be ill; and when the king came to see him, Amnon said to the king, "Please let Tamar my sister come and make a couple of cakes for me in my sight, that I may eat from her hand."

7 And David sent home to Tamar, saying, "Now go to your brother Amnon's house, and prepare food for him." 8 So Tamar went to her brother Amnon's house; and he was lying down. Then she took flour and kneaded *it,* made cakes in his sight, and baked the cakes. 9 And she took the pan and placed *them* out before him, but he refused to eat. Then Amnon said, "Have everyone go out from me." And they all went out from him. 10 Then Amnon said to Tamar, "Bring the food into the bedroom, that I may eat from your hand." And Tamar took the cakes which she had made, and brought *them* to Amnon her brother in the bedroom. 11 Now when she had brought *them* to him to eat, he took hold of her and said to her, "Come, lie with me, my sister."

12 But she answered him, "No, my brother, do not force me, for no such thing should be done in Israel. Do not do this disgraceful thing! 13 And I, where could I take my shame? And as for you, you would be like one of the fools in Israel. Now therefore, please speak to the king; for he will not withhold me from you." 14 However, he would not heed her voice; and being stronger than she, he forced her and lay with her.

15 Then Amnon hated her exceedingly, so that the hatred with which he hated her *was* greater than the love with which he had loved her. And Amnon said to her, "Arise, be gone!"

16 So she said to him, "No, indeed! This evil of sending me away *is* worse than the other that you did to me."

But he would not listen to her. 17 Then he called his servant who attended him, and said, "Here! Put this *woman* out, away from me, and bolt the door behind her." 18 Now she had on a robe of many colors, for the king's virgin daughters wore such apparel. And his servant put her out and bolted the door behind her.

19 Then Tamar put ashes on her head, and tore her robe of many colors that *was* on her, and laid her hand on her head and went away crying bitterly. 20 And Absalom her brother said to her, "Has Amnon your brother been with you? But now hold your peace, my sister. He *is* your brother; do not take this thing to heart." So Tamar remained desolate in her brother Absalom's house.

21 But when King David heard of all these things, he was very angry. 22 And Absalom spoke to his brother Amnon neither good nor bad. For Absalom hated Amnon, because he had forced his sister Tamar.

23 And it came to pass, after two full years, that Absalom had sheepshearers in Baal Hazor, which *is* near Ephraim; so Absalom invited all the king's sons. 24 Then Absalom came to the king and said, "Kindly note, your servant has sheepshearers; please, let the king and his servants go with your servant."

25 But the king said to Absalom, "No, my son, let us not all go now, lest we be a burden to you." Then he urged him, but he would not go; and he blessed him.

26 Then Absalom said, "If not, please let my brother Amnon go with us."

And the king said to him, "Why should he go with you?" 27 But Absalom urged him; so he let Amnon and all the king's sons go with him.

28 Now Absalom had commanded his servants, saying, "Watch now, when Amnon's heart is merry with wine, and when I say to you, 'Strike Amnon!' then kill him. Do not be

---

*I*t doesn't matter what you did before you were saved or how bad your life was. God didn't save you because you had accumulated a long list of sinful deeds. He saved you because He loved you and He wanted to *change* your sin nature.

Be a Survivor!

2 Samuel 13:1–20

There are all kinds of rape—emotional, physical, and spiritual. There are many ways to be victimized. The problem is compounded when a woman suffers because of something over which she had no control, when she feels guilty about being a victim.

Tamar was the king's daughter. She was a virgin—a "good girl." She didn't do anything immoral. It is amazing that her own brother would be so driven by desire that he would go to such lengths to destroy his sister. He thought he was in love. It wasn't love. It was lust, a selfish compulsion based on gratification. He craved her so intensely that he lost his appetite for food.

It is frightening to think about the nights Amnon must have stayed awake plotting her destruction. The intensity of his passion for her was overwhelming. So much so, that even his father and his cousin noticed. Tamar's brother was filled with lust—and it showed.

Amnon demonstrates how badly the enemy wants to violate God's children. He is plotting your destruction. He is watching you with wanton eyes. Jesus told Peter, "Satan has asked for you, that he may sift you as wheat. But I have prayed for you, that your faith should not fail" (Luke 22:31–32). Satan craves you with an animal-like passion. He's hiding in the shadows, just waiting for an opportunity to pounce. In addition, he loves to use people to act on the same ravenous desires.

Desire is a powerful motivating force. It can make you do things you never thought you were capable of doing. Lust can make a person break her commitment to herself. It can cause people to reach out for things—or other people—they shouldn't have.

The name *Tamar* means "palm tree." Like the palm, Tamar is a survivor. She stands tall and green in summer, spring, and fall—full of life—able to withstand the chilly winds of winter.

You, too, can be a survivor. Like Peter and Tamar, you may have gone through some horrible times, but Jesus intercedes on your behalf. No matter what struggles you have faced, you can be confident in the ministry of our High Priest. He is praying for you. Faith comes when you recognize that you can't help yourself. Only trust in Christ can bring you through. He will give you the strength to overcome the attacks of Satan and your own human, selfish lust.

afraid. Have I not commanded you? Be courageous and valiant." 29 So the servants of Absalom did to Amnon as Absalom had commanded. Then all the king's sons arose, and each one got on his mule and fled.

30 And it came to pass, while they were on the way, that news came to David, saying, "Absalom has killed all the king's sons, and not one of them is left!" 31 So the king arose and tore his garments and lay on the ground, and all his servants stood by with their clothes torn. 32 Then Jonadab the son of Shimeah, David's brother, answered and said, "Let not my lord suppose they have killed all the young men, the king's sons, for only Amnon is dead. For by the command of Absalom this has been determined from the day that he forced his sister Tamar. 33 Now therefore, let not my lord the king take the thing to his heart, to think that all the king's sons are dead. For only Amnon is dead."

34 Then Absalom fled. And the young man who was keeping watch lifted his eyes and looked, and there, many people were coming from the road on the hillside behind him.ª 35 And Jonadab said to the king, "Look, the king's sons are coming; as your servant said, so it is." 36 So it was, as soon as he had finished speaking, that the king's sons indeed came, and they lifted up their voice and wept. Also the king and all his servants wept very bitterly.

37 But Absalom fled and went to Talmai the son of Ammihud, king of Geshur. And *David* mourned for his son every day. 38 So Absalom fled and went to Geshur, and was there three years. 39 And King David*ª* longed to go to*ᵇ* Absalom. For he had been comforted concerning Amnon, because he was dead.

14 So Joab the son of Zeruiah perceived that the king's heart *was* concerned about Absalom. 2 And Joab sent to Tekoa and brought from there a wise woman, and said to her, "Please pretend to be a mourner, and put on mourning apparel; do not anoint yourself with oil, but act like a woman who has been mourning a long time for the dead. 3 Go to the king and speak to him in this manner." So Joab put the words in her mouth.

4 And when the woman of Tekoa spoke*ª* to the king, she fell on her face to the ground and prostrated herself, and said, "Help, O king!"

5 Then the king said to her, "What troubles you?"

And she answered, "Indeed I *am* a widow, my husband is dead. 6 Now your maidservant had two sons; and the two fought with each other in the field, and *there was* no one to part them, but the one struck the other and killed him. 7 And now the whole family has risen up against your maidservant, and they said, 'Deliver him who struck his brother, that we may execute him for the life of his brother whom he killed; and we will destroy the heir also.' So they would extinguish my ember that is left, and leave to my husband *neither* name nor remnant on the earth."

8 Then the king said to the woman, "Go to your house, and I will give orders concerning you."

9 And the woman of Tekoa said to the king, "My lord, O king, *let* the iniquity *be* on me and on my father's house, and the king and his throne *be* guiltless."

10 So the king said, "Whoever says *anything* to you, bring him to me, and he shall not touch you anymore."

11 Then she said, "Please let the king remember the Lord your God, and do not permit the avenger of blood to destroy anymore, lest they destroy my son."

And he said, "As the Lord lives, not one hair of your son shall fall to the ground."

12 Therefore the woman said, "Please, let your maidservant speak *another* word to my lord the king."

And he said, "Say on."

13 So the woman said: "Why then have you schemed such a thing against the people of God? For the king speaks this thing as one who is

---

13:34 ªSeptuagint adds *And the watchman went and told the king, and said, "I see men from the way of Horonaim, from the regions of the mountains."*   13:39 ªFollowing Masoretic Text, Syriac, and Vulgate; Septuagint reads *the spirit of the king;* Targum reads *the soul of King David.*   ᵇFollowing Masoretic Text and Targum; Septuagint and Vulgate read *ceased to pursue after.*   14:4 ªMany Hebrew manuscripts, Septuagint, Syriac, and Vulgate read *came.*

Gospel Pearls

guilty, *in that* the king does not bring his banished one home again. 14 For we will surely die and *become* like water spilled on the ground, which cannot be gathered up again. Yet God does not take away a life; but He devises means, so that His banished ones are not expelled from Him. 15 Now therefore, I have come to speak of this thing to my lord the king because the people have made me afraid. And your maidservant said, 'I will now speak to the king; it may be that the king will perform the request of his maidservant. 16 For the king will hear and deliver his maidservant from the hand of the man *who would* destroy me and my son together from the inheritance of God.' 17 Your maidservant said, 'The word of my lord the king will now be comforting; for as the angel of God, so *is* my lord the king in discerning good and evil. And may the LORD your God be with you.' "

18 Then the king answered and said to the woman, "Please do not hide from me anything that I ask you."

And the woman said, "Please, let my lord the king speak."

19 So the king said, "*Is* the hand of Joab with you in all this?" And the woman answered and said, "*As* you live, my lord the king, no one can turn to the right hand or to the left from anything that my lord the king has spoken. For your servant Joab commanded me, and he put all these words in the mouth of your maidservant. 20 To bring about this change of affairs your servant Joab has done this thing; but my lord *is* wise, according to the wisdom of the angel of God, to know everything that *is* in the earth."

21 And the king said to Joab, "All right, I have granted this thing. Go therefore, bring back the young man Absalom."

22 Then Joab fell to the ground on his face and bowed himself, and thanked the king. And Joab said, "Today your servant knows that I have found favor in your sight, my lord, O king, in that the king has fulfilled the request of his servant." 23 So Joab arose and went to Geshur, and brought Absalom to Jerusalem. 24 And the king said, "Let him return to his own house, but do not let him see my face." So Absalom returned to his own house, but did not see the king's face.

25 Now in all Israel there was no one who was praised as much as Absalom for his good looks. From the sole of his foot to the crown of his head there was no blemish in him. 26 And when he cut the hair of his head—at the end of every year he cut *it* because it was heavy on him— when he cut it, he weighed the hair of his head at two hundred shekels according to the king's standard. 27 To Absalom were born three sons, and one daughter whose name *was* Tamar. She was a woman of beautiful appearance.

28 And Absalom dwelt two full years in Jerusalem, but did not see the king's face. 29 Therefore Absalom sent for Joab, to send him to the king, but he would not come to him. And when he sent again the second time, he would not come. 30 So he said to his servants, "See, Joab's field is near mine, and he has barley there; go and set it on fire." And Absalom's servants set the field on fire.

31 Then Joab arose and came to Absalom's house, and said to him, "Why have your servants set my field on fire?"

32 And Absalom answered Joab, "Look, I sent to you, saying, 'Come here, so that I may send you to the king, to say, "Why have I come from Geshur? *It would be* better for me *to be* there still." ' Now therefore, let me see the king's face; but if there is iniquity in me, let him execute me."

33 So Joab went to the king and told him. And when he had called for Absalom, he came to the king and bowed himself on his face to the ground before the king. Then the king kissed Absalom.

15 After this it happened that Absalom provided himself with chariots and horses, and fifty men to run before him. 2 Now Absalom would rise early and stand beside the way to the gate. *So* it was, whenever anyone who had a lawsuit came to the king for a decision, that Absalom would call to him and say, "What city *are* you from?" And he would say, "Your servant *is* from such and such a tribe of Israel." 3 Then Absalom would say to him, "Look, your case *is* good and right; but *there is* no deputy of the king to hear you."

Cain represents all those relationships in which a person is present, but not trustworthy or dependable. So many women I know today have "Cains" in their lives. They have unresolved issues, which is exactly what Cain was in Eve's life.

4 Moreover Absalom would say, "Oh, that I were made judge in the land, and everyone who has any suit or cause would come to me; then I would give him justice." 5 And *so* it was, whenever anyone came near to bow down to him, that he would put out his hand and take him and kiss him. 6 In this manner Absalom acted toward all Israel who came to the king for judgment. So Absalom stole the hearts of the men of Israel.

7 Now it came to pass after forty[a] years that Absalom said to the king, "Please, let me go to Hebron and pay the vow which I made to the LORD. 8 For your servant took a vow while I dwelt at Geshur in Syria, saying, 'If the LORD indeed brings me back to Jerusalem, then I will serve the LORD.'" 9 And the king said to him, "Go in peace." So he arose and went to Hebron.

10 Then Absalom sent spies throughout all the tribes of Israel, saying, "As soon as you hear the sound of the trumpet, then you shall say, 'Absalom reigns in Hebron!'" 11 And with Absalom went two hundred men invited from Jerusalem, and they went along innocently and did not know anything. 12 Then Absalom sent for Ahithophel the Gilonite, David's counselor, from his city—from Giloh—while he offered sacrifices. And the conspiracy grew strong, for the people with Absalom continually increased in number.

13 Now a messenger came to David, saying, "The hearts of the men of Israel are with Absalom."

14 So David said to all his servants who *were* with him at Jerusalem, "Arise, and let us flee, or we shall not escape from Absalom. Make haste to depart, lest he overtake us suddenly and bring disaster upon us, and strike the city with the edge of the sword."

15 And the king's servants said to the king, "We *are* your servants, *ready to do* whatever my lord the king commands." 16 Then the king went out with all his household after him. But the king left ten women, concubines, to keep the house. 17 And the king went out with all the people after him, and stopped at the outskirts. 18 Then all his servants passed before him; and all the Cherethites, all the Pelethites, and all the Gittites, six hundred men who had followed him from Gath, passed before the king.

19 Then the king said to Ittai the Gittite, "Why are you also going with us? Return and remain with the king. For you *are* a foreigner and also an exile from your own place. 20 In fact, you came *only* yesterday. Should I make you wander up and down with us today, since I go I know not where? Return, and take your brethren back. Mercy and truth *be* with you."

21 But Ittai answered the king and said, "*As* the LORD lives, and *as* my lord the king lives, surely in whatever place my lord the king shall be, whether in death or life, even there also your servant will be."

22 So David said to Ittai, "Go, and cross over." Then Ittai the Gittite and all his men and all the little ones who *were* with him crossed over. 23 And all the country wept with a loud voice, and all the people crossed over. The king himself also crossed over the Brook Kidron, and all the people crossed over toward the way of the wilderness.

24 There was Zadok also, and all the Levites with him, bearing the ark of the covenant of God. And they set down the ark of God, and Abiathar went up until all the people had finished crossing over from the city. 25 Then the king said to Zadok, "Carry the ark of God back into the city. If I find favor in the eyes of the LORD, He will bring me back and show me *both* it and His dwelling place. 26 But if He says thus: 'I have no delight in you,' here I am, let Him do to me as seems good to Him." 27 The king also said to Zadok the priest, "*Are* you *not* a seer? Return to the city in peace, and your two sons with you, Ahimaaz your son, and Jonathan the son of Abiathar. 28 See, I will wait in the plains of the wilderness until word comes from you to inform me." 29 Therefore Zadok and Abiathar carried the ark of God back to Jerusalem. And they remained there.

30 So David went up by the Ascent of the *Mount of* Olives, and wept as he went up; and he had his head cov-

15:7 [a]Septuagint manuscripts, Syriac, and Josephus read *four.*

Gospel Pearls

ered and went barefoot. And all the people who *were* with him covered their heads and went up, weeping as they went up. 31 Then *someone* told David, saying, "Ahithophel *is* among the conspirators with Absalom." And David said, "O LORD, I pray, turn the counsel of Ahithophel into foolishness!"

32 Now it happened when David had come to the top *of the mountain,* where he worshiped God—there was Hushai the Archite coming to meet him with his robe torn and dust on his head. 33 David said to him, "If you go on with me, then you will become a burden to me. 34 But if you return to the city, and say to Absalom, 'I will be your servant, O king; *as* I *was* your father's servant previously, so I *will* now also *be* your servant,' then you may defeat the counsel of Ahithophel for me. 35 And *do* you not *have* Zadok and Abiathar the priests with you there? Therefore it will be *that* whatever you hear from the king's house, you shall tell to Zadok and Abiathar the priests. 36 Indeed *they have* there with them their two sons, Ahimaaz, Zadok's *son,* and Jonathan, Abiathar's *son;* and by them you shall send me everything you hear."

37 So Hushai, David's friend, went into the city. And Absalom came into Jerusalem.

16 When David was a little past the top *of the mountain,* there was Ziba the servant of Mephibosheth, who met him with a couple of saddled donkeys, and on them two hundred *loaves* of bread, one hundred clusters of raisins, one hundred summer fruits, and a skin of wine. 2 And the king said to Ziba, "What do you mean to do with these?"

So Ziba said, "The donkeys *are* for the king's household to ride on, the bread and summer fruit for the young men to eat, and the wine for those who are faint in the wilderness to drink."

3 Then the king said, "And where *is* your master's son?"

And Ziba said to the king, "Indeed he is staying in Jerusalem, for he said, 'Today the house of Israel will restore the kingdom of my father to me.' "

4 So the king said to Ziba, "Here, all that *belongs* to Mephibosheth *is* yours."

And Ziba said, "I humbly bow before you, *that* I may find favor in your sight, my lord, O king!"

5 Now when King David came to Bahurim, there was a man from the family of the house of Saul, whose name *was* Shimei the son of Gera, coming from there. He came out, cursing continuously as he came. 6 And he threw stones at David and at all the servants of King David. And all the people and all the mighty men *were* on his right hand and on his left. 7 Also Shimei said thus when he cursed: "Come out! Come out! You bloodthirsty man, you rogue! 8 The LORD has brought upon you all the blood of the house of Saul, in whose place you have reigned; and the LORD has delivered the kingdom into the hand of Absalom your son. So now you *are caught* in your own evil, because you are a bloodthirsty man!"

9 Then Abishai the son of Zeruiah said to the king, "Why should this dead dog curse my lord the king? Please, let me go over and take off his head!"

10 But the king said, "What have I to do with you, you sons of Zeruiah? So let him curse, because the LORD has said to him, 'Curse David.' Who then shall say, 'Why have you done so?' "

11 And David said to Abishai and all his servants, "See how my son who came from my own body seeks my life. How much more now *may this* Benjamite? Let him alone, and let him curse; for so the LORD has ordered him. 12 It may be that the LORD will look on my affliction,[a] and that the LORD will repay me with good for his cursing this day." 13 And as David and his men went along the road, Shimei went along the hillside opposite him and cursed as he went, threw stones at him and kicked up dust. 14 Now the king and all the people who *were* with him became weary; so they refreshed themselves there.

15 Meanwhile Absalom and all the people, the men of Israel, came to Je-

16:12 ªFollowing Kethib, Septuagint, Syriac, and Vulgate; Qere reads *my eyes;* Targum reads *tears of my eyes.*

*I*f you don't know where you are, you're confused. And those who are confused find it difficult to get beyond their confusion to see the absolutes and the sovereignty of God.

rusalem; and Ahithophel *was* with him. 16 And so it was, when Hushai the Archite, David's friend, came to Absalom, that Hushai said to Absalom, "*Long* live the king! *Long* live the king!"

17 So Absalom said to Hushai, "*Is* this your loyalty to your friend? Why did you not go with your friend?"

18 And Hushai said to Absalom, "No, but whom the LORD and this people and all the men of Israel choose, his I will be, and with him I will remain. 19 "Furthermore, whom should I serve? *Should I* not *serve* in the presence of his son? As I have served in your father's presence, so will I be in your presence."

20 Then Absalom said to Ahithophel, "Give advice as to what we should do."

21 And Ahithophel said to Absalom, "Go in to your father's concubines, whom he has left to keep the house; and all Israel will hear that you are abhorred by your father. Then the hands of all who are with you will be strong." 22 So they pitched a tent for Absalom on the top of the house, and Absalom went in to his father's concubines in the sight of all Israel.

23 Now the advice of Ahithophel, which he gave in those days, *was* as if one had inquired at the oracle of God. So *was* all the advice of Ahithophel both with David and with Absalom.

17 Moreover Ahithophel said to Absalom, "Now let me choose twelve thousand men, and I will arise and pursue David tonight. 2 I will come upon him while he *is* weary and weak, and make him afraid. And all the people who *are* with him will flee, and I will strike only the king. 3 Then I will bring back all the people to you. When all return except the man whom you seek, all the people will be at peace." 4 And the saying pleased Absalom and all the elders of Israel.

5 Then Absalom said, "Now call Hushai the Archite also, and let us hear what he says too." 6 And when Hushai came to Absalom, Absalom spoke to him, saying, "Ahithophel has spoken in this manner. Shall we do as he says? If not, speak up."

7 So Hushai said to Absalom: "The advice that Ahithophel has given *is* not good at this time. 8 For," said Hushai, "you know your father and his men, that they *are* mighty men, and they *are* enraged in their minds, like a bear robbed of her cubs in the field; and your father *is* a man of war, and will not camp with the people. 9 Surely by now he is hidden in some pit, or in some *other* place. And it will be, when some of them are overthrown at the first, that whoever hears *it* will say, 'There is a slaughter among the people who follow Absalom.' 10 And even he *who is* valiant, whose heart *is* like the heart of a lion, will melt completely. For all Israel knows that your father *is* a mighty man, and *those* who *are* with him *are* valiant men. 11 Therefore I advise that all Israel be fully gathered to you, from Dan to Beersheba, like the sand that *is* by the sea for multitude, and that you go to battle in person. 12 So we will come upon him in some place where he may be found, and we will fall on him as the dew falls on the ground. And of him and all the men who *are* with him there shall not be left so much as one. 13 Moreover, if he has withdrawn into a city, then all Israel shall bring ropes to that city; and we will pull it into the river, until there is not one small stone found there."

14 So Absalom and all the men of Israel said, "The advice of Hushai the Archite *is* better than the advice of Ahithophel." For the LORD had purposed to defeat the good advice of Ahithophel, to the intent that the LORD might bring disaster on Absalom.

15 Then Hushai said to Zadok and Abiathar the priests, "Thus and so Ahithophel advised Absalom and the elders of Israel, and thus and so I have advised. 16 Now therefore, send quickly and tell David, saying, 'Do not spend this night in the plains of the wilderness, but speedily cross over, lest the king and all the people who *are* with him be swallowed up.'"

17 Now Jonathan and Ahimaaz stayed at En Rogel, for they dared not be seen coming into the city; so a female servant would come and tell them, and they would go and tell King David. 18 Nevertheless a lad saw them, and told Absalom. But both of them went away quickly and came to a man's house in Bahurim, who had a well in his court; and they

Gospel
Pearls

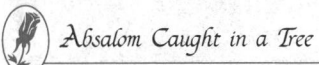

went down into it. 19 Then the woman took and spread a covering over the well's mouth, and spread ground grain on it; and the thing was not known. 20 And when Absalom's servants came to the woman at the house, they said, "Where *are* Ahimaaz and Jonathan?"

So the woman said to them, "They have gone over the water brook."

And when they had searched and could not find *them,* they returned to Jerusalem. 21 Now it came to pass, after they had departed, that they came up out of the well and went and told King David, and said to David, "Arise and cross over the water quickly. For thus has Ahithophel advised against you." 22 So David and all the people who *were* with him arose and crossed over the Jordan. By morning light not one of them was left who had not gone over the Jordan.

23 Now when Ahithophel saw that his advice was not followed, he saddled a donkey, and arose and went home to his house, to his city. Then he put his household in order, and hanged himself, and died; and he was buried in his father's tomb.

24 Then David went to Mahanaim. And Absalom crossed over the Jordan, he and all the men of Israel with him. 25 And Absalom made Amasa captain of the army instead of Joab. This Amasa *was* the son of a man whose name *was* Jithra,[a] an Israelite,[b] who had gone in to Abigail the daughter of Nahash, sister of Zeruiah, Joab's mother. 26 So Israel and Absalom encamped in the land of Gilead.

27 Now it happened, when David had come to Mahanaim, that Shobi the son of Nahash from Rabbah of the people of Ammon, Machir the son of Ammiel from Lo Debar, and Barzillai the Gileadite from Rogelim, 28 brought beds and basins, earthen vessels and wheat, barley and flour, parched *grain* and beans, lentils and parched *seeds,* 29 honey and curds, sheep and cheese of the herd, for David and the people who *were* with him to eat. For they said, "The people are hungry and weary and thirsty in the wilderness."

18 And David numbered the people who *were* with him, and set captains of thousands and captains of hundreds over them. 2 Then David sent out one third of the people under the hand of Joab, one third under the hand of Abishai the son of Zeruiah, Joab's brother, and one third under the hand of Ittai the Gittite. And the king said to the people, "I also will surely go out with you myself."

3 But the people answered, "You shall not go out! For if we flee away, they will not care about us; nor if half of us die, will they care about us. But *you are* worth ten thousand of us now. For you are now more help to us in the city."

4 Then the king said to them, "Whatever seems best to you I will do." So the king stood beside the gate, and all the people went out by hundreds and by thousands. 5 Now the king had commanded Joab, Abishai, and Ittai, saying, "*Deal* gently for my sake with the young man Absalom." And all the people heard when the king gave all the captains orders concerning Absalom.

6 So the people went out into the field of battle against Israel. And the battle was in the woods of Ephraim. 7 The people of Israel were overthrown there before the servants of David, and a great slaughter of twenty thousand took place there that day. 8 For the battle there was scattered over the face of the whole countryside, and the woods devoured more people that day than the sword devoured.

9 Then Absalom met the servants of David. Absalom rode on a mule. The mule went under the thick boughs of a great terebinth tree, and his head caught in the terebinth; so he was left hanging between heaven and earth. And the mule which *was* under him went on. 10 Now a certain man saw *it* and told Joab, and said, "I just saw Absalom hanging in a terebinth tree!"

11 So Joab said to the man who told him, "You just saw *him!* And why did you not strike him there to the ground? I would have given you ten *shekels* of silver and a belt."

17:25 [a]Spelled *Jether* in 1 Chronicles 2:17 and elsewhere   [b]Following Masoretic Text, some manuscripts of the Septuagint, and Targum; some manuscripts of the Septuagint read *Ishmaelite* (compare 1 Chronicles 2:17); Vulgate reads *of Jezrael.*

---

*I*f you are going to be able to receive your next blessing, if you are going to be in a position to experience the next move of God in your life, if you are going to come out of the valley of the shadow of death, you have got to let your past go.

12 But the man said to Joab, "Though I were to receive a thousand *shekels* of silver in my hand, I would not raise my hand against the king's son. For in our hearing the king commanded you and Abishai and Ittai, saying, 'Beware lest anyone *touch* the young man Absalom!'[a] 13 Otherwise I would have dealt falsely against my own life. For there is nothing hidden from the king, and you yourself would have set yourself against *me.*"

14 Then Joab said, "I cannot linger with you." And he took three spears in his hand and thrust them through Absalom's heart, while he was *still* alive in the midst of the terebinth tree. 15 And ten young men who bore Joab's armor surrounded Absalom, and struck and killed him.

16 So Joab blew the trumpet, and the people returned from pursuing Israel. For Joab held back the people. 17 And they took Absalom and cast him into a large pit in the woods, and laid a very large heap of stones over him. Then all Israel fled, everyone to his tent.

18 Now Absalom in his lifetime had taken and set up a pillar for himself, which *is* in the King's Valley. For he said, "I have no son to keep my name in remembrance." He called the pillar after his own name. And to this day it is called Absalom's Monument.

19 Then Ahimaaz the son of Zadok said, "Let me run now and take the news to the king, how the LORD has avenged him of his enemies."

20 And Joab said to him, "You shall not take the news this day, for you shall take the news another day. But today you shall take no news, because the king's son is dead."

21 Then Joab said to the Cushite, "Go, tell the king what you have seen." So the Cushite bowed himself to Joab and ran.

22 And Ahimaaz the son of Zadok said again to Joab, "But whatever happens, please let me also run after the Cushite."

So Joab said, "Why will you run, my son, since you have no news ready?"

23 "But whatever happens," *he said,* "let me run."

So he said to him, "Run." Then Ahimaaz ran by way of the plain, and outran the Cushite.

24 Now David was sitting between the two gates. And the watchman went up to the roof over the gate, to the wall, lifted his eyes and looked, and there was a man, running alone. 25 Then the watchman cried out and told the king. And the king said, "If he *is* alone, *there is* news in his mouth." And he came rapidly and drew near.

26 Then the watchman saw *another* man running, and the watchman called to the gatekeeper and said, "There is *another* man, running alone!"

And the king said, "He also brings news."

27 So the watchman said, "I think the running of the first is like the running of Ahimaaz the son of Zadok."

And the king said, "He *is* a good man, and comes with good news."

28 So Ahimaaz called out and said to the king, "All is well!" Then he bowed down with his face to the earth before the king, and said, "Blessed *be* the LORD your God, who has delivered up the men who raised their hand against my lord the king!"

29 The king said, "Is the young man Absalom safe?"

Ahimaaz answered, "When Joab sent the king's servant and *me* your servant, I saw a great tumult, but I did not know what *it was about.*"

30 And the king said, "Turn aside *and* stand here." So he turned aside and stood still.

31 Just then the Cushite came, and the Cushite said, "There is good news, my lord the king! For the LORD has avenged you this day of all those who rose against you."

32 And the king said to the Cushite, "Is the young man Absalom safe?"

So the Cushite answered, "May the enemies of my lord the king, and all who rise against you to do harm, be like *that* young man!"

33 Then the king was deeply moved, and went up to the chamber over the gate, and wept. And as he went, he said thus: "O my son Absalom—my son, my son Absalom—if only I had died in your place! O Absalom my son, my son!"

18:12 [a]The ancient versions read '*Protect the young man Absalom for me!*'

19 And Joab was told, "Behold, the king is weeping and mourning for Absalom." 2 So the victory that day was *turned* into mourning for all the people. For the people heard it said that day, "The king is grieved for his son." 3 And the people stole back into the city that day, as people who are ashamed steal away when they flee in battle. 4 But the king covered his face, and the king cried out with a loud voice, "O my son Absalom! O Absalom, my son, my son!"

5 Then Joab came into the house to the king, and said, "Today you have disgraced all your servants who today have saved your life, the lives of your sons and daughters, the lives of your wives and the lives of your concubines, 6 in that you love your enemies and hate your friends. For you have declared today that you regard neither princes nor servants; for today I perceive that if Absalom had lived and all of us had died today, then it would have pleased you well. 7 Now therefore, arise, go out and speak comfort to your servants. For I swear by the LORD, if you do not go out, not one will stay with you this night. And that will be worse for you than all the evil that has befallen you from your youth until now." 8 Then the king arose and sat in the gate. And they told all the people, saying, "There is the king, sitting in the gate." So all the people came before the king.

For everyone of Israel had fled to his tent.

9 Now all the people were in a dispute throughout all the tribes of Israel, saying, "The king saved us from the hand of our enemies, he delivered us from the hand of the Philistines, and now he has fled from the land because of Absalom. 10 But Absalom, whom we anointed over us, has died in battle. Now therefore, why do you say nothing about bringing back the king?"

11 So King David sent to Zadok and Abiathar the priests, saying, "Speak to the elders of Judah, saying, 'Why are you the last to bring the king back to his house, since the words of all Israel have come to the king, to his *very* house? 12 You *are* my brethren, you *are* my bone and my flesh. Why then are you the last to bring back the king?' 13 And say to

Amasa, '*Are* you not my bone and my flesh? God do so to me, and more also, if you are not commander of the army before me continually in place of Joab.' " 14 So he swayed the hearts of all the men of Judah, just as *the heart of* one man, so that they sent *this word* to the king: "Return, you and all your servants!"

15 Then the king returned and came to the Jordan. And Judah came to Gilgal, to go to meet the king, to escort the king across the Jordan. 16 And Shimei the son of Gera, a Benjamite, who *was* from Bahurim, hurried and came down with the men of Judah to meet King David. 17 *There were* a thousand men of Benjamin with him, and Ziba the servant of the house of Saul, and his fifteen sons and his twenty servants with him; and they went over the Jordan before the king. 18 Then a ferryboat went across to carry over the king's household, and to do what he thought good.

Now Shimei the son of Gera fell down before the king when he had crossed the Jordan. 19 Then he said to the king, "Do not let my lord impute iniquity to me, or remember what wrong your servant did on the day that my lord the king left Jerusalem, that the king should take *it* to heart. 20 For I, your servant, know that I have sinned. Therefore here I am, the first to come today of all the house of Joseph to go down to meet my lord the king."

21 But Abishai the son of Zeruiah answered and said, "Shall not Shimei be put to death for this, because he cursed the LORD's anointed?"

22 And David said, "What have I to do with you, you sons of Zeruiah, that you should be adversaries to me today? Shall any man be put to death today in Israel? For do I not know that today I *am* king over Israel?" 23 Therefore the king said to Shimei, "You shall not die." And the king swore to him.

24 Now Mephibosheth the son of Saul came down to meet the king. And he had not cared for his feet, nor trimmed his mustache, nor washed his clothes, from the day the king departed until the day he returned in peace. 25 So it was, when he had come to Jerusalem to meet the king, that the king said to him, "Why did you not go with me, Mephibosheth?"

When Jesus said to let the dead bury their dead, He was saying that we shouldn't be overly concerned with that which is over. We should let what is over be over.

26 And he answered, "My lord, O king, my servant deceived me. For your servant said, 'I will saddle a donkey for myself, that I may ride on it and go to the king,' because your servant *is* lame. 27 And he has slandered your servant to my lord the king, but my lord the king *is* like the angel of God. Therefore do *what is* good in your eyes. 28 For all my father's house were but dead men before my lord the king. Yet you set your servant among those who eat at your own table. Therefore what right have I still to cry out anymore to the king?"

29 So the king said to him, "Why do you speak anymore of your matters? I have said, 'You and Ziba divide the land.' "

30 Then Mephibosheth said to the king, "Rather, let him take it all, inasmuch as my lord the king has come back in peace to his own house."

31 And Barzillai the Gileadite came down from Rogelim and went across the Jordan with the king, to escort him across the Jordan. 32 Now Barzillai was a very aged man, eighty years old. And he had provided the king with supplies while he stayed at Mahanaim, for he *was* a very rich man. 33 And the king said to Barzillai, "Come across with me, and I will provide for you while you are with me in Jerusalem."

34 But Barzillai said to the king, "How long have I to live, that I should go up with the king to Jerusalem? 35 I *am* today eighty years old. Can I discern between the good and bad? Can your servant taste what I eat or what I drink? Can I hear any longer the voice of singing men and singing women? Why then should your servant be a further burden to my lord the king? 36 Your servant will go a little way across the Jordan with the king. And why should the king repay me *with* such a reward? 37 Please let your servant turn back again, that I may die in my own city, near the grave of my father and mother. But here is your servant Chimham; let him cross over with my lord the king, and do for him what seems good to you."

38 And the king answered, "Chimham shall cross over with me, and I will do for him what seems good to you. Now whatever you request of me, I will do for you." 39 Then all the people went over the Jordan. And when the king had crossed over, the king kissed Barzillai and blessed him, and he returned to his own place.

40 Now the king went on to Gilgal, and Chimham[a] went on with him. And all the people of Judah escorted the king, and also half the people of Israel. 41 Just then all the men of Israel came to the king, and said to the king, "Why have our brethren, the men of Judah, stolen you away and brought the king, his household, and all David's men with him across the Jordan?"

42 So all the men of Judah answered the men of Israel, "Because the king *is* a close relative of ours. Why then are you angry over this matter? Have we ever eaten at the king's *expense*? Or has he given us any gift?"

43 And the men of Israel answered the men of Judah, and said, "We have ten shares in the king; therefore we also have more *right* to David than you. Why then do you despise us—were we not the first to advise bringing back our king?"

Yet the words of the men of Judah were fiercer than the words of the men of Israel.

20 And there happened to be there a rebel,[a] whose name *was* Sheba the son of Bichri, a Benjamite. And he blew a trumpet, and said:

"We have no share in David,
Nor do we have inheritance in
  the son of Jesse;
Every man to his tents, O
  Israel!"

2 So every man of Israel deserted David, *and* followed Sheba the son of Bichri. But the men of Judah, from the Jordan as far as Jerusalem, remained loyal to their king.

3 Now David came to his house at Jerusalem. And the king took the ten women, his concubines whom he had left to keep the house, and put them in seclusion and supported them, but did not go in to them. So they were shut up to the day of their death, living in widowhood.

19:40 [a]Masoretic Text reads *Chimhan*.   20:1 [a]Literally *man of Belial*

4 And the king said to Amasa, "Assemble the men of Judah for me within three days, and be present here yourself." 5 So Amasa went to assemble *the men of* Judah. But he delayed longer than the set time which David had appointed him. 6 And David said to Abishai, "Now Sheba the son of Bichri will do us more harm than Absalom. Take your lord's servants and pursue him, lest he find for himself fortified cities, and escape us." 7 So Joab's men, with the Cherethites, the Pelethites, and all the mighty men, went out after him. And they went out of Jerusalem to pursue Sheba the son of Bichri. 8 When they *were* at the large stone which *is* in Gibeon, Amasa came before them. Now Joab was dressed in battle armor; on it was a belt *with* a sword fastened in its sheath at his hips; and as he was going forward, it fell out. 9 Then Joab said to Amasa, "*Are* you in health, my brother?" And Joab took Amasa by the beard with his right hand to kiss him. 10 But Amasa did not notice the sword that *was* in Joab's hand. And he struck him with it in the stomach, and his entrails poured out on the ground; and he did not *strike* him again. Thus he died.

Then Joab and Abishai his brother pursued Sheba the son of Bichri. 11 Meanwhile one of Joab's men stood near Amasa, and said, "Whoever favors Joab and whoever *is* for David—follow Joab!" 12 But Amasa wallowed in *his* blood in the middle of the highway. And when the man saw that all the people stood still, he moved Amasa from the highway to the field and threw a garment over him, when he saw that everyone who came upon him halted. 13 When he was removed from the highway, all the people went on after Joab to pursue Sheba the son of Bichri.

14 And he went through all the tribes of Israel to Abel and Beth Maachah and all the Berites. So they were gathered together and also went after Sheba.[a] 15 Then they came and besieged him in Abel of Beth Maachah; and they cast up a siege mound against the city, and it stood by the rampart. And all the people who *were* with Joab battered the wall to throw it down.

16 Then a wise woman cried out from the city, "Hear, hear! Please say to Joab, 'Come nearby, that I may speak with you.' " 17 When he had come near to her, the woman said, "*Are* you Joab?"

He answered, "I *am.*"

Then she said to him, "Hear the words of your maidservant."

And he answered, "I am listening."

18 So she spoke, saying, "They used to talk in former times, saying, 'They shall surely seek *guidance* at Abel,' and so they would end *disputes.* 19 I *am among the* peaceable *and* faithful in Israel. You seek to destroy a city and a mother in Israel. Why would you swallow up the inheritance of the LORD?"

20 And Joab answered and said, "Far be it, far be it from me, that I should swallow up or destroy! 21 That *is* not so. But a man from the mountains of Ephraim, Sheba the son of Bichri by name, has raised his hand against the king, against David. Deliver him only, and I will depart from the city."

So the woman said to Joab, "Watch, his head will be thrown to you over the wall." 22 Then the woman in her wisdom went to all the people. And they cut off the head of Sheba the son of Bichri, and threw *it* out to Joab. Then he blew a trumpet, and they withdrew from the city, every man to his tent. So Joab returned to the king at Jerusalem.

23 And Joab *was* over all the army of Israel; Benaiah the son of Jehoiada *was* over the Cherethites and the Pelethites; 24 Adoram *was* in charge of revenue; Jehoshaphat the son of Ahilud *was* recorder; 25 Sheva *was* scribe; Zadok and Abiathar *were* the priests; 26 and Ira the Jairite was a chief minister under David.

21 Now there was a famine in the days of David for three years, year after year; and David inquired of the LORD. And the LORD answered, "*It is* because of Saul and *his* bloodthirsty house, because he killed the Gibeonites." 2 So the king called the Gibeonites and spoke to them. Now the Gibeonites *were* not of the children of Israel, but of the remnant of the Amorites; the children of Israel had sworn protection to them, but

20:14 [a]Literally *him*

Today is the day to say "good-bye" to what you've lost—both to what you may have buried and to what has gone away from you. It is your day to stop grieving and go forward.

Saul had sought to kill them in his zeal for the children of Israel and Judah.

3 Therefore David said to the Gibeonites, "What shall I do for you? And with what shall I make atonement, that you may bless the inheritance of the LORD?"

4 And the Gibeonites said to him, "We will have no silver or gold from Saul or from his house, nor shall you kill any man in Israel for us."

So he said, "Whatever you say, I will do for you."

5 Then they answered the king, "As for the man who consumed us and plotted against us, *that* we should be destroyed from remaining in any of the territories of Israel, 6 let seven men of his descendants be delivered to us, and we will hang them before the LORD in Gibeah of Saul, *whom* the LORD chose."

And the king said, "I will give *them.*"

7 But the king spared Mephibosheth the son of Jonathan, the son of Saul, because of the LORD's oath that *was* between them, between David and Jonathan the son of Saul. 8 So the king took Armoni and Mephibosheth, the two sons of Rizpah the daughter of Aiah, whom she bore to Saul, and the five sons of Michal[a] the daughter of Saul, whom she brought up for Adriel the son of Barzillai the Meholathite; 9 and he delivered them into the hands of the Gibeonites, and they hanged them on the hill before the LORD. So they fell, *all* seven together, and were put to death in the days of harvest, in the first *days,* in the beginning of barley harvest.

10 Now Rizpah the daughter of Aiah took sackcloth and spread it for herself on the rock, from the beginning of harvest until the late rains poured on them from heaven. And she did not allow the birds of the air to rest on them by day nor the beasts of the field by night.

11 And David was told what Rizpah the daughter of Aiah, the concubine of Saul, had done. 12 Then David went and took the bones of Saul, and the bones of Jonathan his son, from the men of Jabesh Gilead who had stolen them from the street of Beth Shan,[a] where the Philistines had hung them up, after the Philistines had struck down Saul in Gilboa. 13 So he brought up the bones of Saul and the bones of Jonathan his son from there; and they gathered the bones of those who had been hanged. 14 They buried the bones of Saul and Jonathan his son in the country of Benjamin in Zelah, in the tomb of Kish his father. So they performed all that the king commanded. And after that God heeded the prayer for the land.

15 When the Philistines were at war again with Israel, David and his servants with him went down and fought against the Philistines; and David grew faint. 16 Then Ishbi-Benob, who *was* one of the sons of the giant, the weight of whose bronze spear *was* three hundred *shekels,* who was bearing a new *sword,* thought he could kill David. 17 But Abishai the son of Zeruiah came to his aid, and struck the Philistine and killed him. Then the men of David swore to him, saying, "You shall go out no more with us to battle, lest you quench the lamp of Israel."

18 Now it happened afterward that there was again a battle with the Philistines at Gob. Then Sibbechai the Hushathite killed Saph,[a] who *was* one of the sons of the giant. 19 Again there was war at Gob with the Philistines, where Elhanan the son of Jaare-Oregim[a] the Bethlehemite killed *the brother of* Goliath the Gittite, the shaft of whose spear *was* like a weaver's beam.

20 Yet again there was war at Gath, where there was a man of *great* stature, who had six fingers on each hand and six toes on each foot, twenty-four in number; and he also was born to the giant. 21 So when he defied Israel, Jonathan the son of Shimea,[a] David's brother, killed him.

22 These four were born to the giant in Gath, and fell by the hand of David and by the hand of his servants.

22 Then David spoke to the LORD the words of this song, on the day when the LORD had delivered

---

21:8 [a]Or *Merab* (compare 1 Samuel 18:19 and 25:44; 2 Samuel 3:14 and 6:23)   21:12 [a]Spelled *Beth Shean* in Joshua 17:11 and elsewhere   21:18 [a]Spelled *Sippai* in 1 Chronicles 20:4   21:19 [a]Spelled *Jair* in 1 Chronicles 20:5   21:21 [a]Spelled *Shammah* in 1 Samuel 16:9 and elsewhere

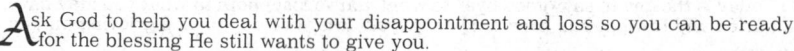

Ask God to help you deal with your disappointment and loss so you can be ready for the blessing He still wants to give you.

Submitted and Committed

2 Samuel 21:8-11

Women are nurturers by nature. They often struggle with submission, so the Holy Spirit challenges women to submit (Ephesians 5:22). Had Eve been submitted to her husband, she would have referred the serpent in the garden to him, her covering. As the church, the submitted bride of Christ, we are told to submit ourselves unto God, resist the devil and he will flee (see James 4:7). Submission brings strength and a submitted vessel gains power to resist. When the enemy meets with real resistance, he will flee. But we must understand that the battle is not ours; it belongs to the One who covers us!

Within a woman the Holy Spirit establishes a nurturing spirit that will not allow her to push away her young but to nurse them and to care for them. Doesn't it make you angry to see how the enemy always wants to pervert good for evil? You see, Satan cannot create. He has to use what is already created. He perverts, corrupts, and even disrupts, but he cannot create. The wise woman learns his devices. Once you learn what he is trying to do, use your strengths for positive purposes. Stop being seduced into using your abilities for what he's trying to grow.

Nurturing a problem not only means you keep it, it also implies that you are feeding it. It is drawing your strength from you, just as an unborn child can only get food from his mother. The enemy cannot live in a blood-washed, regenerated spirit. The enemy can only thrive in your mind if you let him live off your old memories and fears. He is a leech that depends upon your umbilical cord for survival. Cut that cord and watch your fears starve to death.

Like Rizpah, who guarded the bodies of her dead sons until she had gotten the king's attention and arranged a proper burial for them, you have to be careful not to hang around dead issues and keep company with things that ought to be put to death. Rizpah was being faithful to her children, but some of you are hanging around issues that don't belong to you. Recognize those tendencies to walk among the dead as the enemy seeking whom he may devour (see 1 Peter 5:8) and don't let him have you!

him from the hand of all his enemies, and from the hand of Saul. 2 And he said:[a]

"The LORD *is* my rock and my
　　fortress and my deliverer;
3　The God of my strength, in
　　whom I will trust;
　　My shield and the horn of my
　　salvation,
　　My stronghold and my refuge;
　　My Savior, You save me from
　　violence.
4　I will call upon the LORD, *who
　　is worthy* to be praised;
　　So shall I be saved from my
　　enemies.

5　"When the waves of death
　　surrounded me,
　　The floods of ungodliness made
　　me afraid.
6　The sorrows of Sheol
　　surrounded me;
　　The snares of death confronted
　　me.
7　In my distress I called upon the
　　LORD,
　　And cried out to my God;
　　He heard my voice from His
　　temple,
　　And my cry *entered* His ears.

8　"Then the earth shook and
　　trembled;
　　The foundations of heaven[a]
　　quaked and were shaken,
　　Because He was angry.
9　Smoke went up from His
　　nostrils,
　　And devouring fire from His
　　mouth;
　　Coals were kindled by it.
10　He bowed the heavens also,
　　and came down
　　With darkness under His feet.
11　He rode upon a cherub, and
　　flew;
　　And He was seen[a] upon the
　　wings of the wind.
12　He made darkness canopies
　　around Him,
　　Dark waters *and* thick clouds
　　of the skies.
13　From the brightness before
　　Him
　　Coals of fire were kindled.

14　"The LORD thundered from
　　heaven,
　　And the Most High uttered His
　　voice.
15　He sent out arrows and
　　scattered them;
　　Lightning bolts, and He
　　vanquished them.
16　Then the channels of the sea
　　were seen,
　　The foundations of the world
　　were uncovered,
　　At the rebuke of the LORD,
　　At the blast of the breath of His
　　nostrils.

17　"He sent from above, He took
　　me,
　　He drew me out of many
　　waters.
18　He delivered me from my
　　strong enemy,
　　From those who hated me;
　　For they were too strong for
　　me.
19　They confronted me in the day
　　of my calamity,
　　But the LORD was my support.
20　He also brought me out into a
　　broad place;
　　He delivered me because He
　　delighted in me.

21　"The LORD rewarded me
　　according to my
　　righteousness;
　　According to the cleanness of
　　my hands
　　He has recompensed me.
22　For I have kept the ways of the
　　LORD,
　　And have not wickedly
　　departed from my God.
23　For all His judgments *were*
　　before me;
　　And *as for* His statutes, I did
　　not depart from them.
24　I was also blameless before
　　Him,
　　And I kept myself from my
　　iniquity.
25　Therefore the LORD has
　　recompensed me according
　　to my righteousness,
　　According to my cleanness in
　　His eyes.[a]

22:2 [a]Compare Psalm 18   22:8 [a]Following Masoretic Text, Septuagint, and Targum; Syriac and Vulgate read *hills* (compare Psalm 18:7).   22:11 [a]Following Masoretic Text and Septuagint; many Hebrew manuscripts, Syriac, and Vulgate read *He flew* (compare Psalm 18:10); Targum reads *He spoke with power*.   22:25 [a]Septuagint, Syriac, and Vulgate read *the cleanness of my hands in His sight* (compare Psalm 18:24); Targum reads *my cleanness before His word*.

Gospel
Pearls

26 "With the merciful You will
 show Yourself merciful;
 With a blameless man You will
 show Yourself blameless;
27 With the pure You will show
 Yourself pure;
 And with the devious You will
 show Yourself shrewd.
28 You will save the humble
 people;
 But Your eyes *are* on the
 haughty, *that* You may bring
 them down.

29 "For You *are* my lamp, O LORD;
 The LORD shall enlighten my
 darkness.
30 For by You I can run against a
 troop;
 By my God I can leap over a
 wall.
31 *As for* God, His way *is* perfect;
 The word of the LORD *is* proven;
 He *is* a shield to all who trust
 in Him.

32 "For who *is* God, except the
 LORD?
 And who *is* a rock, except our
 God?
33 God *is* my strength *and* power,[a]
 And He makes my[b] way
 perfect.
34 He makes my[a] feet like the *feet*
 of deer,
 And sets me on my high places.
35 He teaches my hands to make
 war,
 So that my arms can bend a
 bow of bronze.

36 "You have also given me the
 shield of Your salvation;
 Your gentleness has made me
 great.
37 You enlarged my path under
 me;
 So my feet did not slip.

38 "I have pursued my enemies and
 destroyed them;
 Neither did I turn back again
 till they were destroyed.
39 And I have destroyed them and
 wounded them,
 So that they could not rise;

They have fallen under my feet.
40 For You have armed me with
 strength for the battle;
 You have subdued under me
 those who rose against me.
41 You have also given me the
 necks of my enemies,
 So that I destroyed those who
 hated me.
42 They looked, but *there was*
 none to save;
 Even to the LORD, but He did
 not answer them.
43 Then I beat them as fine as the
 dust of the earth;
 I trod them like dirt in the
 streets,
 And I spread them out.

44 "You have also delivered me
 from the strivings of my
 people;
 You have kept me as the head
 of the nations.
 A people I have not known
 shall serve me.
45 The foreigners submit to me;
 As soon as they hear, they obey
 me.
46 The foreigners fade away,
 And come frightened[a] from
 their hideouts.

47 "The LORD lives!
 Blessed *be* my Rock!
 Let God be exalted,
 The Rock of my salvation!
48 *It is* God who avenges me,
 And subdues the peoples under
 me;
49 He delivers me from my
 enemies.
 You also lift me up above those
 who rise against me;
 You have delivered me from
 the violent man.
50 Therefore I will give thanks to
 You, O LORD, among the
 Gentiles,
 And sing praises to Your name.

51 *He is* the tower of salvation to
 His king,
 And shows mercy to His
 anointed,
 To David and his descendants
 forevermore."

22:33 [a]Dead Sea Scrolls, Septuagint, Syriac, and Vulgate read *It is God who arms me with strength* (compare Psalm 18:32); Targum reads *It is God who sustains me with strength*. [b]Following Qere, Septuagint, Syriac, Targum, and Vulgate (compare Psalm 18:32); Kethib reads *His*. 22:34 [a]Following Qere, Septuagint, Syriac, Targum, and Vulgate (compare Psalm 18:33); Kethib reads *His*. 22:46 [a]Following Septuagint, Targum, and Vulgate (compare Psalm 18:45); Masoretic Text reads *gird themselves*.

I refuse to glorify anybody but God. I know that all of my needs are met by Him. I know that my identity comes from Him. I know that all my help and all my forgiveness have come from Him.

23 Now these *are* the last words of David.

> *Thus* says David the son of
>   Jesse;
> *Thus* says the man raised up on
>   high,
> The anointed of the God of
>   Jacob,
> And the sweet psalmist of
>   Israel:

2   "The Spirit of the LORD spoke by
>   me,
> And His word *was* on my
>   tongue.
3   The God of Israel said,
> The Rock of Israel spoke to me:
> 'He who rules over men *must
>   be* just,
> Ruling in the fear of God.
4   And *he shall be* like the light
>   of the morning *when* the sun
>   rises,
> A morning without clouds,
> *Like* the tender grass *springing*
>   out of the earth,
> By clear shining after rain.'

5   "Although my house *is* not so
>   with God,
> Yet He has made with me an
>   everlasting covenant,
> Ordered in all *things* and
>   secure.
> For *this is* all my salvation and
>   all *my* desire;
> Will He not make *it* increase?
6   But *the sons* of rebellion *shall*
>   all *be* as thorns thrust away,
> Because they cannot be taken
>   with hands.
7   But the man *who* touches them
> Must be armed with iron and
>   the shaft of a spear,
> And they shall be utterly
>   burned with fire in *their*
>   place."

8 These *are* the names of the mighty men whom David had: Josheb-Basshebeth*ᵃ* the Tachmonite, chief among the captains.*ᵇ* He was called Adino the Eznite, because he had killed eight hundred men at one time. 9 And after him *was* Eleazar the son of Dodo,*ᵃ* the Ahohite, *one* of the three mighty men with David when they defied the Philistines *who* were gathered there for battle, and the men of Israel had retreated. 10 He arose and attacked the Philistines until his hand was weary, and his hand stuck to the sword. The LORD brought about a great victory that day; and the people returned after him only to plunder. 11 And after him *was* Shammah the son of Agee the Hararite. The Philistines had gathered together into a troop where there was a piece of ground full of lentils. So the people fled from the Philistines. 12 But he stationed himself in the middle of the field, defended it, and killed the Philistines. So the LORD brought about a great victory.

13 Then three of the thirty chief men went down at harvest time and came to David at the cave of Adullam. And the troop of Philistines encamped in the Valley of Rephaim. 14 David *was* then in the stronghold, and the garrison of the Philistines *was* then *in* Bethlehem. 15 And David said with longing, "Oh, that someone would give me a drink of the water from the well of Bethlehem, which *is* by the gate!" 16 So the three mighty men broke through the camp of the Philistines, drew water from the well of Bethlehem that *was* by the gate, and took it and brought *it* to David. Nevertheless he would not drink it, but poured it out to the LORD. 17 And he said, "Far be it from me, O LORD, that I should do this! Is *this not* the blood of the men who went in *jeopardy of* their lives?" Therefore he would not drink it.

These things were done by the three mighty men.

18 Now Abishai the brother of Joab, the son of Zeruiah, was chief of *another* three.*ᵃ* He lifted his spear against three hundred *men,* killed *them,* and won a name among *these* three. 19 Was he not the most honored of three? Therefore he became their captain. However, he did not attain to the *first* three.

20 Benaiah *was* the son of Jehoiada, the son of a valiant man from Kabzeel, who had done many deeds. He had killed two lion-like heroes of

Gospel Pearls

Moab. He also had gone down and killed a lion in the midst of a pit on a snowy day. 21 And he killed an Egyptian, a spectacular man. The Egyptian *had* a spear in his hand; so he went down to him with a staff, wrested the spear out of the Egyptian's hand, and killed him with his own spear. 22 These *things* Benaiah the son of Jehoiada did, and won a name among three mighty men. 23 He was more honored than the thirty, but he did not attain to the *first* three. And David appointed him over his guard.

24 Asahel the brother of Joab *was* one of the thirty; Elhanan the son of Dodo of Bethlehem, 25 Shammah the Harodite, Elika the Harodite, 26 Helez the Paltite, Ira the son of Ikkesh the Tekoite, 27 Abiezer the Anathothite, Mebunnai the Hushathite, 28 Zalmon the Ahohite, Maharai the Netophathite, 29 Heleb the son of Baanah (the Netophathite), Ittai the son of Ribai from Gibeah of the children of Benjamin, 30 Benaiah a Pirathonite, Hiddai from the brooks of Gaash, 31 Abi-Albon the Arbathite, Azmaveth the Barhumite, 32 Eliahba the Shaalbonite (of the sons of Jashen), Jonathan, 33 Shammah the Hararite, Ahiam the son of Sharar the Hararite, 34 Eliphelet the son of Ahasbai, the son of the Maachathite, Eliam the son of Ahithophel the Gilonite, 35 Hezrai*ᵃ* the Carmelite, Paarai the Arbite, 36 Igal the son of Nathan of Zobah, Bani the Gadite, 37 Zelek the Ammonite, Naharai the Beerothite (armorbearer of Joab the son of Zeruiah), 38 Ira the Ithrite, Gareb the Ithrite, 39 *and* Uriah the Hittite: thirty-seven in all.

24 Again the anger of the LORD was aroused against Israel, and He moved David against them to say, "Go, number Israel and Judah."

2 So the king said to Joab the commander of the army who *was* with him, "Now go throughout all the tribes of Israel, from Dan to Beersheba, and count the people, that I may know the number of the people."

3 And Joab said to the king, "Now may the LORD your God add to the people a hundred times more than there are, and may the eyes of my lord the king see *it*. But why does my lord the king desire this thing?" 4 Nevertheless the king's word prevailed against Joab and against the captains of the army. Therefore Joab and the captains of the army went out from the presence of the king to count the people of Israel.

5 And they crossed over the Jordan and camped in Aroer, on the right side of the town which *is* in the midst of the ravine of Gad, and toward Jazer. 6 Then they came to Gilead and to the land of Tahtim Hodshi; they came to Dan Jaan and around to Sidon; 7 and they came to the stronghold of Tyre and to all the cities of the Hivites and the Canaanites. Then they went out to South Judah *as far as* Beersheba. 8 So when they had gone through all the land, they came to Jerusalem at the end of nine months and twenty days. 9 Then Joab gave the sum of the number of the people to the king. And there were in Israel eight hundred thousand valiant men who drew the sword, and the men of Judah were five hundred thousand men.

10 And David's heart condemned him after he had numbered the people. So David said to the LORD, "I have sinned greatly in what I have done; but now, I pray, O LORD, take away the iniquity of Your servant, for I have done very foolishly."

11 Now when David arose in the morning, the word of the LORD came to the prophet Gad, David's seer, saying, 12 "Go and tell David, 'Thus says the LORD: "I offer you three *things;* choose one of them for yourself, that I may do *it* to you." ' " 13 So Gad came to David and told him; and he said to him, "Shall seven*ᵃ* years of famine come to you in your land? Or shall you flee three months before your enemies, while they pursue you? Or shall there be three days' plague in your land? Now consider and see what answer I should take back to Him who sent me."

14 And David said to Gad, "I am in great distress. Please let us fall into the hand of the LORD, for His mercies *are* great; but do not let me fall into the hand of man."

15 So the LORD sent a plague upon

23:35 ᵃSpelled *Hezro* in 1 Chronicles 11:37   24:13 ᵃFollowing Masoretic Text, Syriac, Targum, and Vulgate; Septuagint reads *three* (compare 1 Chronicles 21:12).

Father, I stretch my hands to You. I know You will remember me. When others forget and leave me all alone, I know that Jesus, Jesus, Jesus will hear my groan.

Israel from the morning till the appointed time. From Dan to Beersheba seventy thousand men of the people died. 16 And when the angel[a] stretched out His hand over Jerusalem to destroy it, the LORD relented from the destruction, and said to the angel who was destroying the people, "It is enough; now restrain your hand." And the angel of the LORD was by the threshing floor of Araunah[b] the Jebusite.

17 Then David spoke to the LORD when he saw the angel who was striking the people, and said, "Surely I have sinned, and I have done wickedly; but these sheep, what have they done? Let Your hand, I pray, be against me and against my father's house."

18 And Gad came that day to David and said to him, "Go up, erect an altar to the LORD on the threshing floor of Araunah the Jebusite." 19 So David, according to the word of Gad, went up as the LORD commanded. 20 Now Araunah looked, and saw the king and his servants coming toward him. So Araunah went out and bowed before the king with his face to the ground.

21 Then Araunah said, "Why has my lord the king come to his servant?"

And David said, "To buy the threshing floor from you, to build an altar to the LORD, that the plague may be withdrawn from the people."

22 Now Araunah said to David, "Let my lord the king take and offer up whatever *seems* good to him. Look, *here are* oxen for burnt sacrifice, and threshing implements and the yokes of the oxen for wood. 23 All these, O king, Araunah has given to the king."

And Araunah said to the king, "May the LORD your God accept you."

24 Then the king said to Araunah, "No, but I will surely buy *it* from you for a price; nor will I offer burnt offerings to the LORD my God with that which costs me nothing." So David bought the threshing floor and the oxen for fifty shekels of silver. 25 And David built there an altar to the LORD, and offered burnt offerings and peace offerings. So the LORD heeded the prayers for the land, and the plague was withdrawn from Israel.

24:16 [a]Or *Angel*　[b]Spelled *Ornan* in 1 Chronicles 21:15

The First Book of the
KINGS

1 Now King David was old, advanced in years; and they put covers on him, but he could not get warm. 2 Therefore his servants said to him, "Let a young woman, a virgin, be sought for our lord the king, and let her stand before the king, and let her care for him; and let her lie in your bosom, that our lord the king may be warm." 3 So they sought for a lovely young woman throughout all the territory of Israel, and found Abishag the Shunammite, and brought her to the king. 4 The young woman *was* very lovely; and she cared for the king, and served him; but the king did not know her.

5 Then Adonijah the son of Haggith exalted himself, saying, "I will be king"; and he prepared for himself chariots and horsemen, and fifty men to run before him. 6 (And his father had not rebuked him at any time by saying, "Why have you done so?" He *was* also very good-looking. *His mother* had borne him after Absalom.) 7 Then he conferred with Joab the son of Zeruiah and with Abiathar the priest, and they followed and helped Adonijah. 8 But Zadok the

priest, Benaiah the son of Jehoiada, Nathan the prophet, Shimei, Rei, and the mighty men who *belonged* to David were not with Adonijah.

9 And Adonijah sacrificed sheep and oxen and fattened cattle by the stone of Zoheleth, which *is* by En Rogel; he also invited all his brothers, the king's sons, and all the men of Judah, the king's servants. 10 But he did not invite Nathan the prophet, Benaiah, the mighty men, or Solomon his brother.

11 So Nathan spoke to Bathsheba the mother of Solomon, saying, "Have you not heard that Adonijah the son of Haggith has become king, and David our lord does not know *it?* 12 Come, please, let me now give you advice, that you may save your own life and the life of your son Solomon. 13 Go immediately to King David and say to him, 'Did you not, my lord, O king, swear to your maidservant, saying, "Assuredly your son Solomon shall reign after me, and he shall sit on my throne"? Why then has Adonijah become king?' 14 Then, while you are still talking there with the king, I also will come in after you and confirm your words."

15 So Bathsheba went into the chamber to the king. (Now the king was very old, and Abishag the Shunammite was serving the king.) 16 And Bathsheba bowed and did homage to the king. Then the king said, "What is your wish?"

17 Then she said to him, "My lord, you swore by the LORD your God to your maidservant, *saying,* 'Assuredly Solomon your son shall reign after me, and he shall sit on my throne.' 18 So now, look! Adonijah has become king; and now, my lord the king, you do not know about *it.* 19 He has sacrificed oxen and fattened cattle and sheep in abundance, and has invited all the sons of the king, Abiathar the priest, and Joab the commander of the army; but Solomon your servant he has not invited. 20 And as for you, my lord, O king, the eyes of all Israel *are* on you, that you should tell them who will sit on the throne of my lord the king after him. 21 Otherwise it will happen, when my lord the king rests with his fathers, that I and my son Solomon will be counted as offenders."

22 And just then, while she was still talking with the king, Nathan the prophet also came in. 23 So they told the king, saying, "Here is Nathan the prophet." And when he came in before the king, he bowed down before the king with his face to the ground. 24 And Nathan said, "My lord, O king, have you said, 'Adonijah shall reign after me, and he shall sit on my throne'? 25 For he has gone down today, and has sacrificed oxen and fattened cattle and sheep in abundance, and has invited all the king's sons, and the commanders of the army, and Abiathar the priest; and look! They are eating and drinking before him; and they say, 'Long live King Adonijah!' 26 But he has not invited me—me your servant—nor Zadok the priest, nor Benaiah the son of Jehoiada, nor your servant Solomon. 27 Has this thing been done by my lord the king, and you have not told your servant who should sit on the throne of my lord the king after him?"

28 Then King David answered and said, "Call Bathsheba to me." So she came into the king's presence and stood before the king. 29 And the king took an oath and said, "*As* the LORD lives, who has redeemed my life from every distress, 30 just as I swore to you by the LORD God of Israel, saying, 'Assuredly Solomon your son shall be king after me, and he shall sit on my throne in my place,' so I certainly will do this day."

31 Then Bathsheba bowed with *her* face to the earth, and paid homage to the king, and said, "Let my lord King David live forever!"

32 And King David said, "Call to me Zadok the priest, Nathan the prophet, and Benaiah the son of Jehoiada." So they came before the king. 33 The king also said to them, "Take with you the servants of your lord, and have Solomon my son ride on my own mule, and take him down to Gihon. 34 There let Zadok the priest and Nathan the prophet anoint him king over Israel; and blow the horn, and say, 'Long live King Solomon!' 35 Then you shall come up after him, and he shall come and sit on my throne, and he shall be king in my place. For I have appointed him to be ruler over Israel and Judah."

36 Benaiah the son of Jehoiada answered the king and said, "Amen!

---

*W*hen you give all the glory and all the thanks and all the praise to God for delivering you, people may not understand what you are doing or why you are so excited. The main reason is that they don't truly understand how you feel.

May the LORD God of my lord the king say so *too*. 37 As the LORD has been with my lord the king, even so may He be with Solomon, and make his throne greater than the throne of my lord King David."

38 So Zadok the priest, Nathan the prophet, Benaiah the son of Jehoiada, the Cherethites, and the Pelethites went down and had Solomon ride on King David's mule, and took him to Gihon. 39 Then Zadok the priest took a horn of oil from the tabernacle and anointed Solomon. And they blew the horn, and all the people said, "*Long* live King Solomon!" 40 And all the people went up after him; and the people played the flutes and rejoiced with great joy, so that the earth *seemed to* split with their sound.

41 Now Adonijah and all the guests who *were* with him heard *it* as they finished eating. And when Joab heard the sound of the horn, he said, "Why *is* the city in such a noisy uproar?" 42 While he was still speaking, there came Jonathan, the son of Abiathar the priest. And Adonijah said to him, "Come in, for you *are* a prominent man, and bring good news."

43 Then Jonathan answered and said to Adonijah, "No! Our lord King David has made Solomon king. 44 The king has sent with him Zadok the priest, Nathan the prophet, Benaiah the son of Jehoiada, the Cherethites, and the Pelethites; and they have made him ride on the king's mule. 45 So Zadok the priest and Nathan the prophet have anointed him king at Gihon; and they have gone up from there rejoicing, so that the city is in an uproar. This *is* the noise that you have heard. 46 Also Solomon sits on the throne of the kingdom. 47 And moreover the king's servants have gone to bless our lord King David, saying, 'May God make the name of Solomon better than your name, and may He make his throne greater than your throne.' Then the king bowed himself on the bed. 48 Also the king said thus, 'Blessed *be* the LORD God of Israel, who has given *one* to sit on my throne this day, while my eyes see *it!*'"

49 So all the guests who were with Adonijah were afraid, and arose, and each one went his way.

50 Now Adonijah was afraid of Solomon; so he arose, and went and took hold of the horns of the altar. 51 And it was told Solomon, saying, "Indeed Adonijah is afraid of King Solomon; for look, he has taken hold of the horns of the altar, saying, 'Let King Solomon swear to me today that he will not put his servant to death with the sword.'"

52 Then Solomon said, "If he proves himself a worthy man, not one hair of him shall fall to the earth; but if wickedness is found in him, he shall die." 53 So King Solomon sent them to bring him down from the altar. And he came and fell down before King Solomon; and Solomon said to him, "Go to your house."

2 Now the days of David drew near that he should die, and he charged Solomon his son, saying: 2 "I go the way of all the earth; be strong, therefore, and prove yourself a man. 3 And keep the charge of the LORD your God: to walk in His ways, to keep His statutes, His commandments, His judgments, and His testimonies, as it is written in the Law of Moses, that you may prosper in all that you do and wherever you turn; 4 that the LORD may fulfill His word which He spoke concerning me, saying, 'If your sons take heed to their way, to walk before Me in truth with all their heart and with all their soul,' He said, 'you shall not lack a man on the throne of Israel.'

5 "Moreover you know also what Joab the son of Zeruiah did to me, *and* what he did to the two commanders of the armies of Israel, to Abner the son of Ner and Amasa the son of Jether, whom he killed. And he shed the blood of war in peacetime, and put the blood of war on his belt that *was* around his waist, and on his sandals that *were* on his feet. 6 Therefore do according to your wisdom, and do not let him go down to the grave in peace.

7 "But show kindness to the sons of Barzillai the Gileadite, and let them be among those who eat at your table, for so they came to me when I fled from Absalom your brother.

8 "And see, *you have* with you Shimei the son of Gera, a Benjamite from Bahurim, who cursed me with a malicious curse in the day when I went to Mahanaim. But he came down to meet me at the Jordan, and I swore to him by the LORD, saying,

Gospel Pearls

'I will not put you to death with the sword.' 9 Now therefore, do not hold him guiltless, for you *are* a wise man and know what you ought to do to him; but bring his gray hair down to the grave with blood."

10 So David rested with his fathers, and was buried in the City of David. 11 The period that David reigned over Israel *was* forty years; seven years he reigned in Hebron, and in Jerusalem he reigned thirty-three years. 12 Then Solomon sat on the throne of his father David; and his kingdom was firmly established.

13 Now Adonijah the son of Haggith came to Bathsheba the mother of Solomon. So she said, "Do you come peaceably?"

And he said, "Peaceably." 14 Moreover he said, "I have something *to say* to you."

And she said, "Say it."

15 Then he said, "You know that the kingdom was mine, and all Israel had set their expectations on me, that I should reign. However, the kingdom has been turned over, and has become my brother's; for it was his from the LORD. 16 Now I ask one petition of you; do not deny me."

And she said to him, "Say it."

17 Then he said, "Please speak to King Solomon, for he will not refuse you, that he may give me Abishag the Shunammite as wife."

18 So Bathsheba said, "Very well, I will speak for you to the king."

19 Bathsheba therefore went to King Solomon, to speak to him for Adonijah. And the king rose up to meet her and bowed down to her, and sat down on his throne and had a throne set for the king's mother; so she sat at his right hand. 20 Then she said, "I desire one small petition of you; do not refuse me."

And the king said to her, "Ask it, my mother, for I will not refuse you."

21 So she said, "Let Abishag the Shunammite be given to Adonijah your brother as wife."

22 And King Solomon answered and said to his mother, "Now why do you ask Abishag the Shunammite for Adonijah? Ask for him the kingdom also—for he *is* my older brother—for him, and for Abiathar the priest, and for Joab the son of Zeruiah." 23 Then King Solomon swore by the LORD, saying, "May God do so to me, and more also, if Adonijah has not spoken this word against his own life! 24 Now therefore, *as* the LORD lives, who has confirmed me and set me on the throne of David my father, and who has established a house*a* for me, as He promised, Adonijah shall be put to death today!"

25 So King Solomon sent by the hand of Benaiah the son of Jehoiada; and he struck him down, and he died.

26 And to Abiathar the priest the king said, "Go to Anathoth, to your own fields, for you *are* deserving of death; but I will not put you to death at this time, because you carried the ark of the Lord GOD before my father David, and because you were afflicted every time my father was afflicted." 27 So Solomon removed Abiathar from being priest to the LORD, that he might fulfill the word of the LORD which He spoke concerning the house of Eli at Shiloh.

28 Then news came to Joab, for Joab had defected to Adonijah, though he had not defected to Absalom. So Joab fled to the tabernacle of the LORD, and took hold of the horns of the altar. 29 And King Solomon was told, "Joab has fled to the tabernacle of the LORD; there *he is,* by the altar." Then Solomon sent Benaiah the son of Jehoiada, saying, "Go, strike him down." 30 So Benaiah went to the tabernacle of the LORD, and said to him, "Thus says the king, 'Come out!' "

And he said, "No, but I will die here." And Benaiah brought back word to the king, saying, "Thus said Joab, and thus he answered me."

31 Then the king said to him, "Do as he has said, and strike him down and bury him, that you may take away from me and from the house of my father the innocent blood which Joab shed. 32 So the LORD will return his blood on his head, because he struck down two men more righteous and better than he, and killed them with the sword—Abner the son of Ner, the commander of the army of Israel, and Amasa the son of Jether, the commander of the army of Judah—though my father David did not know *it.* 33 Their blood shall

2:24 *a*That is, a royal dynasty

*T*he way you praise God is the way you praise God. You may want to yell or cry or sing or shout or dance! Praise Him the way you want to praise Him.

Soul Secrets
of a woman who needs wisdom

*L*ord, the Bible says You are the "only wise God." I am desperate for wisdom. I've found myself in a situation that human knowledge cannot explain and cannot fix. There is only one way out—through the wisdom of my Father. So send the Spirit of wisdom—Your Holy Spirit—to show me how to walk wisely through these days. Send the Spirit of revelation to help me understand what I can't yet figure out. Only Your wisdom will make a way for me.

As You reveal Your wisdom, Lord, help me to be faithful to do all that You show me to do. Help me to trust You and to remember that the wisdom of this world is foolishness to You. Help me to know the difference between human advice and godly advice and to always choose Your way.

therefore return upon the head of Joab and upon the head of his descendants forever. But upon David and his descendants, upon his house and his throne, there shall be peace forever from the LORD."

34 So Benaiah the son of Jehoiada went up and struck and killed him; and he was buried in his own house in the wilderness. 35 The king put Benaiah the son of Jehoiada in his place over the army, and the king put Zadok the priest in the place of Abiathar.

36 Then the king sent and called for Shimei, and said to him, "Build yourself a house in Jerusalem and dwell there, and do not go out from there anywhere. 37 For it shall be, on the day you go out and cross the Brook Kidron, know for certain you shall surely die; your blood shall be on your own head."

38 And Shimei said to the king, "The saying *is* good. As my lord the king has said, so your servant will do." So Shimei dwelt in Jerusalem many days.

39 Now it happened at the end of three years, that two slaves of Shimei ran away to Achish the son of Maachah, king of Gath. And they told Shimei, saying, "Look, your slaves *are* in Gath!" 40 So Shimei arose, saddled his donkey, and went to Achish at Gath to seek his slaves. And Shimei went and brought his slaves from Gath. 41 And Solomon was told that Shimei had gone from Jerusalem to Gath and had come back. 42 Then the king sent and called for Shimei, and said to him, "Did I not make you swear by the LORD, and warn you, saying, 'Know for certain that on the day you go out and travel anywhere, you shall surely die'? And you said to me, 'The word I have heard *is* good.' 43 Why then have you not kept the oath of the LORD and the commandment that I gave you?" 44 The king said moreover to Shimei, "You know, as your heart acknowledges, all the wickedness that you did to my father David; therefore the LORD will return your wickedness on your own head. 45 But King Solomon *shall be* blessed, and the throne of David shall be established before the LORD forever."

46 So the king commanded Benaiah the son of Jehoiada; and he went out and struck him down, and he died. Thus the kingdom was established in the hand of Solomon.

3 Now Solomon made a treaty with Pharaoh king of Egypt, and married Pharaoh's daughter; then he brought her to the City of David until he had finished building his own house, and the house of the LORD, and the wall all around Jerusalem. 2 Meanwhile the people sacrificed at the high places, because there was no house built for the name of the LORD until those days. 3 And Solomon loved the LORD, walking in the statutes of his father David, except that he sacrificed and burned incense at the high places.

4 Now the king went to Gibeon to sacrifice there, for that *was* the great high place: Solomon offered a thousand burnt offerings on that altar. 5 At Gibeon the LORD appeared to Solomon in a dream by night; and God said, "Ask! What shall I give you?"

6 And Solomon said: "You have shown great mercy to Your servant David my father, because he walked before You in truth, in righteousness, and in uprightness of heart with You; You have continued this great kindness for him, and You have given him a son to sit on his throne, as *it is* this day. 7 Now, O LORD my God, You have made Your servant king instead of my father David, but I *am* a little child; I do not know *how* to go out or come in. 8 And Your servant *is* in the midst of Your people whom You have chosen, a great people, too numerous to be numbered or counted. 9 Therefore give to Your servant an understanding heart to judge Your people, that I may discern between good and evil. For who is able to judge this great people of Yours?"

10 The speech pleased the LORD, that Solomon had asked this thing. 11 Then God said to him: "Because you have asked this thing, and have not asked long life for yourself, nor have asked riches for yourself, nor have asked the life of your enemies, but have asked for yourself understanding to discern justice, 12 behold, I have done according to your words; see, I have given you a wise and understanding heart, so that there has not been anyone like you before you, nor shall any like you arise after you.

*D*on't worry about what other people think of your praise. Get out your praise and give God the glory!

13 And I have also given you what you have not asked: both riches and honor, so that there shall not be anyone like you among the kings all your days. 14 So if you walk in My ways, to keep My statutes and My commandments, as your father David walked, then I will lengthen your days."

15 Then Solomon awoke; and indeed it had been a dream. And he came to Jerusalem and stood before the ark of the covenant of the LORD, offered up burnt offerings, offered peace offerings, and made a feast for all his servants.

16 Now two women who were harlots came to the king, and stood before him. 17 And one woman said, "O my lord, this woman and I dwell in the same house; and I gave birth while she was in the house. 18 Then it happened, the third day after I had given birth, that this woman also gave birth. And we were together; no one was with us in the house, except the two of us in the house. 19 And this woman's son died in the night, because she lay on him. 20 So she arose in the middle of the night and took my son from my side, while your maidservant slept, and laid him in her bosom, and laid her dead child in my bosom. 21 And when I rose in the morning to nurse my son, there he was, dead. But when I had examined him in the morning, indeed, he was not my son whom I had borne."

22 Then the other woman said, "No! But the living one is my son, and the dead one is your son."

And the first woman said, "No! But the dead one is your son, and the living one is my son."

Thus they spoke before the king. 23 And the king said, "The one says, 'This is my son, who lives, and your son is the dead one'; and the other says, 'No! But your son is the dead one, and my son is the living one.'" 24 Then the king said, "Bring me a sword." So they brought a sword before the king. 25 And the king said, "Divide the living child in two, and give half to one, and half to the other."

26 Then the woman whose son was living spoke to the king, for she yearned with compassion for her son; and she said, "O my lord, give her the living child, and by no means kill him!"

But the other said, "Let him be neither mine nor yours, but divide him."

27 So the king answered and said, "Give the first woman the living child, and by no means kill him; she is his mother."

28 And all Israel heard of the judgment which the king had rendered; and they feared the king, for they saw that the wisdom of God was in him to administer justice.

4 So King Solomon was king over all Israel. 2 And these were his officials: Azariah the son of Zadok, the priest; 3 Elihoreph and Ahijah, the sons of Shisha, scribes; Jehoshaphat the son of Ahilud, the recorder; 4 Benaiah the son of Jehoiada, over the army; Zadok and Abiathar, the priests; 5 Azariah the son of Nathan, over the officers; Zabud the son of Nathan, a priest and the king's friend; 6 Ahishar, over the household; and Adoniram the son of Abda, over the labor force.

7 And Solomon had twelve governors over all Israel, who provided food for the king and his household; each one made provision for one month of the year. 8 These are their names: Ben-Hur,a in the mountains of Ephraim; 9 Ben-Deker,a in Makaz, Shaalbim, Beth Shemesh, and Elon Beth Hanan; 10 Ben-Hesed,a in Arubboth; to him belonged Sochoh and all the land of Hepher; 11 Ben-Abinadab,a in all the regions of Dor; he had Taphath the daughter of Solomon as wife; 12 Baana the son of Ahilud, in Taanach, Megiddo, and all Beth Shean, which is beside Zaretan below Jezreel, from Beth Shean to Abel Meholah, as far as the other side of Jokneam; 13 Ben-Geber,a in Ramoth Gilead; to him belonged the towns of Jair the son of Manasseh, in Gilead; to him also belonged the region of Argob in Bashan—sixty large cities with walls and bronze gate-bars; 14 Ahinadab the son of Iddo, in Mahanaim; 15 Ahimaaz, in Naphtali; he also took Basemath the daughter of Solomon as wife; 16 Baanah the son of Hushai, in Asher and Aloth;

4:8 aLiterally Son of Hur   4:9 aLiterally Son of Deker   4:10 aLiterally Son of Hesed   4:11 aLiterally Son of Abinadab   4:13 aLiterally Son of Geber

Gospel Pearls

17 Jehoshaphat the son of Paruah, in Issachar; 18 Shimei the son of Elah, in Benjamin; 19 Geber the son of Uri, in the land of Gilead, *in* the country of Sihon king of the Amorites, and of Og king of Bashan. *He was* the only governor who *was* in the land.

20 Judah and Israel *were* as numerous as the sand by the sea in multitude, eating and drinking and rejoicing. 21 So Solomon reigned over all kingdoms from the River*ᵃ* to the land of the Philistines, as far as the border of Egypt. *They* brought tribute and served Solomon all the days of his life.

22 Now Solomon's provision for one day was thirty kors of fine flour, sixty kors of meal, 23 ten fatted oxen, twenty oxen from the pastures, and one hundred sheep, besides deer, gazelles, roebucks, and fatted fowl.

24 For he had dominion over all *the region* on this side of the River*ᵃ* from Tiphsah even to Gaza, namely over all the kings on this side of the River; and he had peace on every side all around him. 25 And Judah and Israel dwelt safely, each man under his vine and his fig tree, from Dan as far as Beersheba, all the days of Solomon. 26 Solomon had forty*ᵃ* thousand stalls of horses for his chariots, and twelve thousand horsemen. 27 And these governors, each man in his month, provided food for King Solomon and for all who came to King Solomon's table. There was no lack in their supply. 28 They also brought barley and straw to the proper place, for the horses and steeds, each man according to his charge.

29 And God gave Solomon wisdom and exceedingly great understanding, and largeness of heart like the sand on the seashore. 30 Thus Solomon's wisdom excelled the wisdom of all the men of the East and all the wisdom of Egypt. 31 For he was wiser than all men—than Ethan the Ezrahite, and Heman, Chalcol, and Darda, the sons of Mahol; and his fame was in all the surrounding nations. 32 He spoke three thousand proverbs, and his songs were one thousand and five. 33 Also he spoke of trees, from the cedar tree of Lebanon even to the hyssop that springs out of the wall; he spoke also of animals, of birds, of creeping things, and of fish. 34 And men of all nations, from all the kings of the earth who had heard of his wisdom, came to hear the wisdom of Solomon.

5 Now Hiram king of Tyre sent his servants to Solomon, because he heard that they had anointed him king in place of his father, for Hiram had always loved David. 2 Then Solomon sent to Hiram, saying:

3   You know how my father David could not build a house for the name of the LORD his God because of the wars which were fought against him on every side, until the LORD put *his foesᵃ* under the soles of his feet.

4   But now the LORD my God has given me rest on every side; *there is* neither adversary nor evil occurrence.

5   And behold, I propose to build a house for the name of the LORD my God, as the LORD spoke to my father David, saying, "Your son, whom I will set on your throne in your place, he shall build the house for My name."

6   Now therefore, command that they cut down cedars for me from Lebanon; and my servants will be with your servants, and I will pay you wages for your servants according to whatever you say. For you know *there is* none among us who has skill to cut timber like the Sidonians.

7 So it was, when Hiram heard the words of Solomon, that he rejoiced greatly and said,

Blessed *be* the LORD this day, for He has given David a wise son over this great people!

8 Then Hiram sent to Solomon, saying:

I have considered *the message* which you sent me, *and* I will do all you desire concerning the cedar and cypress logs.

4:21 *ᵃ*That is, the Euphrates   4:24 *ᵃ*That is, the Euphrates   4:26 *ᵃ*Following Masoretic Text and most other authorities; some manuscripts of the Septuagint read *four* (compare 2 Chronicles 9:25).   5:3 *ᵃ*Literally *them*

---

*Y*ou must reach the place where you know with certainty that God's love is for *you.* You must reach a place of understanding in which you say, "Yes! A woman with a past can touch a God in the present who is able to change the future."

9 My servants shall bring *them* down from Lebanon to the sea; I will float them in rafts by sea to the place you indicate to me, and will have them broken apart there; then you can take *them* away. And you shall fulfill my desire by giving food for my household.

10 Then Hiram gave Solomon cedar and cypress logs *according to* all his desire. 11 And Solomon gave Hiram twenty thousand kors of wheat *as* food for his household, and twenty[a] kors of pressed oil. Thus Solomon gave to Hiram year by year.

12 So the LORD gave Solomon wisdom, as He had promised him; and there was peace between Hiram and Solomon, and the two of them made a treaty together.

13 Then King Solomon raised up a labor force out of all Israel; and the labor force was thirty thousand men. 14 And he sent them to Lebanon, ten thousand a month in shifts: they were one month in Lebanon *and* two months at home; Adoniram *was* in charge of the labor force. 15 Solomon had seventy thousand who carried burdens, and eighty thousand who quarried *stone* in the mountains, 16 besides three thousand three hundred[a] from the chiefs of Solomon's deputies, who supervised the people who labored in the work. 17 And the king commanded them to quarry large stones, costly stones, *and* hewn stones, to lay the foundation of the temple.[a] 18 So Solomon's builders, Hiram's builders, and the Gebalites quarried *them;* and they prepared timber and stones to build the temple.

6 And it came to pass in the four hundred and eightieth[a] year after the children of Israel had come out of the land of Egypt, in the fourth year of Solomon's reign over Israel, in the month of Ziv, which *is* the second month, that he began to build the house of the LORD. 2 Now the house which King Solomon built for the

LORD, its length *was* sixty cubits, its width twenty, and its height thirty cubits. 3 The vestibule in front of the sanctuary[a] of the house *was* twenty cubits long across the width of the house, *and* the width of *the vestibule*[b] extended ten cubits from the front of the house. 4 And he made for the house windows with beveled frames.

5 Against the wall of the temple he built chambers all around, *against* the walls of the temple, all around the sanctuary and the inner sanctuary.[a] Thus he made side chambers all around it. 6 The lowest chamber *was* five cubits wide, the middle *was* six cubits wide, and the third *was* seven cubits wide; for he made narrow ledges around the outside of the temple, so that *the support beams* would not be fastened into the walls of the temple. 7 And the temple, when it was being built, was built with stone finished at the quarry, so that no hammer or chisel *or* any iron tool was heard in the temple while it was being built. 8 The doorway for the middle story[a] *was* on the right side of the temple. They went up by stairs to the middle *story,* and from the middle to the third.

9 So he built the temple and finished it, and he paneled the temple with beams and boards of cedar. 10 And he built side chambers against the entire temple, each five cubits high; they were attached to the temple with cedar beams.

11 Then the word of the LORD came to Solomon, saying: 12 "Concerning this temple which you are building, if you walk in My statutes, execute My judgments, keep all My commandments, and walk in them, then I will perform My word with you, which I spoke to your father David. 13 And I will dwell among the children of Israel, and will not forsake My people Israel."

14 So Solomon built the temple and finished it. 15 And he built the inside walls of the temple with cedar boards; from the floor of the temple to the ceiling he paneled the inside

5:11 aFollowing Masoretic Text, Targum, and Vulgate; Septuagint and Syriac read *twenty thousand*.
5:16 aFollowing Masoretic Text, Targum, and Vulgate; Septuagint reads *three thousand six hundred*.
5:17 aLiterally *house,* and so frequently throughout this book   6:1 aFollowing Masoretic Text, Targum, and Vulgate; Septuagint reads *fortieth*.   6:3 aHebrew *heykal;* here the main room of the temple, elsewhere called the holy place (compare Exodus 26:33 and Ezekiel 41:1)   bLiterally *it*   6:5 aHebrew *debir;* here the inner room of the temple, elsewhere called the Most Holy Place (compare verse 16)   6:8 aFollowing Masoretic Text and Vulgate; Septuagint reads *upper story;* Targum reads *ground story*.

Gospel Pearls

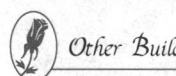

with wood; and he covered the floor of the temple with planks of cypress. 16 Then he built the twenty-cubit room at the rear of the temple, from floor to ceiling, with cedar boards; he built *it* inside as the inner sanctuary, as the Most Holy *Place.* 17 And in front of it the temple sanctuary was forty cubits *long.* 18 The inside of the temple was cedar, carved with ornamental buds and open flowers. All *was* cedar; there was no stone *to be* seen.

19 And he prepared the inner sanctuary inside the temple, to set the ark of the covenant of the LORD there. 20 The inner sanctuary *was* twenty cubits long, twenty cubits wide, and twenty cubits high. He overlaid it with pure gold, and overlaid the altar of cedar. 21 So Solomon overlaid the inside of the temple with pure gold. He stretched gold chains across the front of the inner sanctuary, and overlaid it with gold. 22 The whole temple he overlaid with gold, until he had finished all the temple; also he overlaid with gold the entire altar that *was* by the inner sanctuary.

23 Inside the inner sanctuary he made two cherubim *of* olive wood, *each* ten cubits high. 24 One wing of the cherub *was* five cubits, and the other wing of the cherub five cubits: ten cubits from the tip of one wing to the tip of the other. 25 And the other cherub *was* ten cubits; both cherubim *were* of the same size and shape. 26 The height of one cherub *was* ten cubits, and so *was* the other cherub. 27 Then he set the cherubim inside the inner room;[a] and they stretched out the wings of the cherubim so that the wing of the one touched *one* wall, and the wing of the other cherub touched the other wall. And their wings touched each other in the middle of the room. 28 Also he overlaid the cherubim with gold.

29 Then he carved all the walls of the temple all around, both the inner and outer *sanctuaries,* with carved figures of cherubim, palm trees, and open flowers. 30 And the floor of the temple he overlaid with gold, both the inner and outer *sanctuaries.*

31 For the entrance of the inner sanctuary he made doors *of* olive wood; the lintel *and* doorposts *were* one-fifth *of the wall.* 32 The two doors

were *of* olive wood; and he carved on them figures of cherubim, palm trees, and open flowers, and overlaid *them* with gold; and he spread gold on the cherubim and on the palm trees. 33 So for the door of the sanctuary he also made doorposts *of* olive wood, one-fourth *of the wall.* 34 And the two doors *were of* cypress wood; two panels *comprised* one folding door, and two panels *comprised* the other folding door. 35 Then he carved cherubim, palm trees, and open flowers *on them,* and overlaid *them* with gold applied evenly on the carved work.

36 And he built the inner court with three rows of hewn stone and a row of cedar beams.

37 In the fourth year the foundation of the house of the LORD was laid, in the month of Ziv. 38 And in the eleventh year, in the month of Bul, which is the eighth month, the house was finished in all its details and according to all its plans. So he was seven years in building it.

7 But Solomon took thirteen years to build his own house; so he finished all his house.

2 He also built the House of the Forest of Lebanon; its length *was* one hundred cubits, its width fifty cubits, and its height thirty cubits, with four rows of cedar pillars, and cedar beams on the pillars. 3 And *it was* paneled with cedar above the beams that *were* on forty-five pillars, fifteen *to* a row. 4 *There* were windows *with beveled frames in* three rows, and window *was* opposite window *in* three tiers. 5 And all the doorways and doorposts *had* rectangular frames; and window *was* opposite window *in* three tiers.

6 He also made the Hall of Pillars: its length *was* fifty cubits, and its width thirty cubits; and in front of them *was* a portico with pillars, and a canopy *was* in front of them.

7 Then he made a hall for the throne, the Hall of Judgment, where he might judge; and *it was* paneled with cedar from floor to ceiling.[a]

8 And the house where he dwelt *had* another court inside the hall, of like workmanship. Solomon also made a house like this hall for Pha-

6:27 [a]Literally *house*   7:7 [a]Literally *floor,* that is, of the upper level

*I*t's time to take a look at yourself and declare to the person you see in your own mirror, "It can be done." In spite of your personal history, in spite of the problem, in spite of the circumstances, in spite of what others say, God can be touched by *you.*

raoh's daughter, whom he had taken *as wife.*

9 All these *were of* costly stones cut to size, trimmed with saws, inside and out, from the foundation to the eaves, and also on the outside to the great court. 10 The foundation *was of* costly stones, large stones, some ten cubits and some eight cubits. 11 And above *were* costly stones, hewn to size, and cedar wood. 12 The great court *was* enclosed with three rows of hewn stones and a row of cedar beams. So were the inner court of the house of the LORD and the vestibule of the temple.

13 Now King Solomon sent and brought Huram[a] from Tyre. 14 He *was* the son of a widow from the tribe of Naphtali, and his father *was* a man of Tyre, a bronze worker; he was filled with wisdom and understanding and skill in working with all kinds of bronze work. So he came to King Solomon and did all his work.

15 And he cast two pillars of bronze, each one eighteen cubits high, and a line of twelve cubits measured the circumference of each. 16 Then he made two capitals *of* cast bronze, to set on the tops of the pillars. The height of one capital *was* five cubits, and the height of the other capital *was* five cubits. 17 *He made* a lattice network, with wreaths of chainwork, for the capitals which *were* on top of the pillars: seven chains for one capital and seven for the other capital. 18 So he made the pillars, and two rows of pomegranates above the network all around to cover the capitals that *were* on top; and thus he did for the other capital.

19 The capitals which *were* on top of the pillars in the hall *were* in the shape of lilies, four cubits. 20 The capitals on the two pillars also *had pomegranates* above, by the convex surface which *was* next to the network; and there *were* two hundred such pomegranates in rows on each of the capitals all around.

21 Then he set up the pillars by the vestibule of the temple; he set up the pillar on the right and called its name Jachin, and he set up the pillar on the left and called its name Boaz.

22 The tops of the pillars were in the shape of lilies. So the work of the pillars was finished.

23 And he made the Sea of cast bronze, ten cubits from one brim to the other; *it was* completely round. Its height *was* five cubits, and a line of thirty cubits measured its circumference.

24 Below its brim *were* ornamental buds encircling it all around, ten to a cubit, all the way around the Sea. The ornamental buds *were* cast in two rows when it was cast. 25 It stood on twelve oxen: three looking toward the north, three looking toward the west, three looking toward the south, and three looking toward the east; the Sea *was set* upon them, and all their back parts *pointed* inward. 26 It *was* a handbreadth thick; and its brim was shaped like the brim of a cup, *like* a lily blossom. It contained two thousand[a] baths.

27 He also made ten carts of bronze; four cubits *was* the length of each cart, four cubits its width, and three cubits its height. 28 And this *was* the design of the carts: They had panels, and the panels *were* between frames; 29 on the panels that *were* between the frames *were* lions, oxen, and cherubim. And on the frames *was* a pedestal on top. Below the lions and oxen *were* wreaths of plaited work. 30 Every cart had four bronze wheels and axles of bronze, and its four feet had supports. Under the laver *were* supports of cast *bronze* beside each wreath. 31 Its opening inside the crown at the top *was* one cubit in diameter; and the opening *was* round, shaped *like* a pedestal, one and a half cubits in outside diameter; and also on the opening *were* engravings, but the panels were square, not round. 32 Under the panels *were* the four wheels, and the axles of the wheels *were joined* to the cart. The height of a wheel *was* one and a half cubits. 33 The workmanship of the wheels *was* like the workmanship of a chariot wheel; their axle pins, their rims, their spokes, and their hubs *were* all of cast *bronze.* 34 And *there were* four supports at the four corners of each cart; its supports *were* part of the cart itself. 35 On the top of the

7:13 [a]Hebrew *Hiram* (compare 2 Chronicles 2:13, 14) 4:5)

7:26 [a]Or *three thousand* (compare 2 Chronicles

Gospel Pearls

cart, at the height of half a cubit, *it was* perfectly round. And on the top of the cart, its flanges and its panels *were* of the same casting. 36 On the plates of its flanges and on its panels he engraved cherubim, lions, and palm trees, wherever there was a clear space on each, with wreaths all around. 37 Thus he made the ten carts. All of them were of the same mold, one measure, *and* one shape.

38 Then he made ten lavers of bronze; each laver contained forty baths, *and* each laver *was* four cubits. On each of the ten carts *was* a laver. 39 And he put five carts on the right side of the house, and five on the left side of the house. He set the Sea on the right side of the house, toward the southeast.

40 Huram[a] made the lavers and the shovels and the bowls. So Huram finished doing all the work that he was to do for King Solomon *for* the house of the LORD: 41 the two pillars, the *two* bowl-shaped capitals that *were* on top of the two pillars; the two networks covering the two bowl-shaped capitals which *were* on top of the pillars; 42 four hundred pomegranates for the two networks (two rows of pomegranates for each network, to cover the two bowl-shaped capitals that *were* on top of the pillars); 43 the ten carts, and ten lavers on the carts; 44 one Sea, and twelve oxen under the Sea; 45 the pots, the shovels, and the bowls.

All these articles which Huram[a] made for King Solomon *for* the house of the LORD *were of* burnished bronze. 46 In the plain of Jordan the king had them cast in clay molds, between Succoth and Zaretan. 47 And Solomon did not weigh all the articles, because *there were* so many; the weight of the bronze was not determined.

48 Thus Solomon had all the furnishings made for the house of the LORD: the altar of gold, and the table of gold on which *was* the showbread; 49 the lampstands of pure gold, five on the right *side* and five on the left in front of the inner sanctuary, with the flowers and the lamps and the wick-trimmers of gold; 50 the basins, the trimmers, the bowls, the ladles, and the censers of pure gold; and the

hinges of gold, *both* for the doors of the inner room (the Most Holy *Place*) *and* for the doors of the main hall of the temple.

51 So all the work that King Solomon had done for the house of the LORD was finished; and Solomon brought in the things which his father David had dedicated: the silver and the gold and the furnishings. He put them in the treasuries of the house of the LORD.

8 Now Solomon assembled the elders of Israel and all the heads of the tribes, the chief fathers of the children of Israel, to King Solomon in Jerusalem, that they might bring up the ark of the covenant of the LORD from the City of David, which *is* Zion. 2 Therefore all the men of Israel assembled with King Solomon at the feast in the month of Ethanim, which *is* the seventh month. 3 So all the elders of Israel came, and the priests took up the ark. 4 Then they brought up the ark of the LORD, the tabernacle of meeting, and all the holy furnishings that *were* in the tabernacle. The priests and the Levites brought them up. 5 Also King Solomon, and all the congregation of Israel who were assembled with him, *were* with him before the ark, sacrificing sheep and oxen that could not be counted or numbered for multitude. 6 Then the priests brought in the ark of the covenant of the LORD to its place, into the inner sanctuary of the temple, to the Most Holy *Place*, under the wings of the cherubim. 7 For the cherubim spread *their* two wings over the place of the ark, and the cherubim overshadowed the ark and its poles. 8 The poles extended so that the ends of the poles could be seen from the holy *place*, in front of the inner sanctuary; but they could not be seen from outside. And they are there to this day. 9 Nothing *was* in the ark except the two tablets of stone which Moses put there at Horeb, when the LORD made *a* covenant with the children of Israel, when they came out of the land of Egypt.

10 And it came to pass, when the priests came out of the holy *place*, that the cloud filled the house of the LORD, 11 so that the priests could not

---

7:40 [a]Hebrew *Hiram* (compare 2 Chronicles 2:13, 14)   7:45 [a]Hebrew *Hiram* (compare 2 Chronicles 2:13, 14)

God wants to be touched by you. In spite of your heartache, in spite of your pain, in spite of your depression. You can get to Jesus with the feelings of your infirmities. You can touch Him.

continue ministering because of the cloud; for the glory of the LORD filled the house of the LORD.

12 Then Solomon spoke:

"The LORD said He would dwell
　in the dark cloud.
13 I have surely built You an
　exalted house,
And a place for You to dwell
　in forever."

14 Then the king turned around and blessed the whole assembly of Israel, while all the assembly of Israel was standing. 15 And he said: "Blessed *be* the LORD God of Israel, who spoke with His mouth to my father David, and with His hand has fulfilled *it,* saying, 16 'Since the day that I brought My people Israel out of Egypt, I have chosen no city from any tribe of Israel *in which* to build a house, that My name might be there; but I chose David to be over My people Israel.' 17 Now it was in the heart of my father David to build a temple[a] for the name of the LORD God of Israel. 18 But the LORD said to my father David, 'Whereas it was in your heart to build a temple for My name, you did well that it was in your heart. 19 Nevertheless you shall not build the temple, but your son who will come from your body, he shall build the temple for My name.' 20 So the LORD has fulfilled His word which He spoke; and I have filled the position of my father David, and sit on the throne of Israel, as the LORD promised; and I have built a temple for the name of the LORD God of Israel. 21 And there I have made a place for the ark, in which *is* the covenant of the LORD which He made with our fathers, when He brought them out of the land of Egypt."

22 Then Solomon stood before the altar of the LORD in the presence of all the assembly of Israel, and spread out his hands toward heaven; 23 and he said: "LORD God of Israel, *there is* no God in heaven above or on earth below like You, who keep *Your* covenant and mercy with Your servants who walk before You with all their hearts. 24 You have kept what You promised Your servant David my father; You have both spoken with Your mouth and fulfilled *it* with

Your hand, as *it is* this day. 25 Therefore, LORD God of Israel, now keep what You promised Your servant David my father, saying, 'You shall not fail to have a man sit before Me on the throne of Israel, only if your sons take heed to their way, that they walk before Me as you have walked before Me.' 26 And now I pray, O God of Israel, let Your word come true, which You have spoken to Your servant David my father.

27 "But will God indeed dwell on the earth? Behold, heaven and the heaven of heavens cannot contain You. How much less this temple which I have built! 28 Yet regard the prayer of Your servant and his supplication, O LORD my God, and listen to the cry and the prayer which Your servant is praying before You today: 29 that Your eyes may be open toward this temple night and day, toward the place of which You said, 'My name shall be there,' that You may hear the prayer which Your servant makes toward this place. 30 And may You hear the supplication of Your servant and of Your people Israel, when they pray toward this place. Hear in heaven Your dwelling place; and when You hear, forgive.

31 "When anyone sins against his neighbor, and is forced to take an oath, and comes *and* takes an oath before Your altar in this temple, 32 then hear in heaven, and act, and judge Your servants, condemning the wicked, bringing his way on his head, and justifying the righteous by giving him according to his righteousness.

33 "When Your people Israel are defeated before an enemy because they have sinned against You, and when they turn back to You and confess Your name, and pray and make supplication to You in this temple, 34 then hear in heaven, and forgive the sin of Your people Israel, and bring them back to the land which You gave to their fathers.

35 "When the heavens are shut up and there is no rain because they have sinned against You, when they pray toward this place and confess Your name, and turn from their sin because You afflict them, 36 then hear in heaven, and forgive the sin

8:17 aLiterally *house,* and so in verses 18–20

Gospel
Pearls

of Your servants, Your people Israel, that You may teach them the good way in which they should walk; and send rain on Your land which You have given to Your people as an inheritance.

37 "When there is famine in the land, pestilence *or* blight *or* mildew, locusts *or* grasshoppers; when their enemy besieges them in the land of their cities; whatever plague or whatever sickness *there is;* 38 whatever prayer, whatever supplication is made by anyone, *or* by all Your people Israel, when each one knows the plague of his own heart, and spreads out his hands toward this temple: 39 then hear in heaven Your dwelling place, and forgive, and act, and give to everyone according to all his ways, whose heart You know (for You alone know the hearts of all the sons of men), 40 that they may fear You all the days that they live in the land which You gave to our fathers.

41 "Moreover, concerning a foreigner, who *is* not of Your people Israel, but has come from a far country for Your name's sake 42 (for they will hear of Your great name and Your strong hand and Your outstretched arm), when he comes and prays toward this temple, 43 hear in heaven Your dwelling place, and do according to all for which the foreigner calls to You, that all peoples of the earth may know Your name and fear You, as *do* Your people Israel, and that they may know that this temple which I have built is called by Your name.

44 "When Your people go out to battle against their enemy, wherever You send them, and when they pray to the LORD toward the city which You have chosen and the temple which I have built for Your name, 45 then hear in heaven their prayer and their supplication, and maintain their cause.

46 "When they sin against You (for *there is* no one who does not sin), and You become angry with them and deliver them to the enemy, and they take them captive to the land of the enemy, far or near; 47 *yet* when they come to themselves in the land where they were carried captive, and repent, and make supplication to You in the land of those who took them captive, saying, 'We have sinned and done wrong, we have committed wickedness'; 48 and *when* they return to You with all their heart and with all their soul in the land of their enemies who led them away captive, and pray to You toward their land which You gave to their fathers, the city which You have chosen and the temple which I have built for Your name: 49 then hear in heaven Your dwelling place their prayer and their supplication, and maintain their cause, 50 and forgive Your people who have sinned against You, and all their transgressions which they have transgressed against You; and grant them compassion before those who took them captive, that they may have compassion on them 51 (for they *are* Your people and Your inheritance, whom You brought out of Egypt, out of the iron furnace), 52 that Your eyes may be open to the supplication of Your servant and the supplication of Your people Israel, to listen to them whenever they call to You. 53 For You separated them from among all the peoples of the earth *to be* Your inheritance, as You spoke by Your servant Moses, when You brought our fathers out of Egypt, O Lord GOD."

54 And so it was, when Solomon had finished praying all this prayer and supplication to the LORD, that he arose from before the altar of the LORD, from kneeling on his knees with his hands spread up to heaven. 55 Then he stood and blessed all the assembly of Israel with a loud voice, saying: 56 "Blessed *be* the LORD, who has given rest to His people Israel, according to all that He promised. There has not failed one word of all His good promise, which He promised through His servant Moses. 57 May the LORD our God be with us, as He was with our fathers. May He not leave us nor forsake us, 58 that He may incline our hearts to Himself, to walk in all His ways, and to keep His commandments and His statutes and His judgments, which He commanded our fathers. 59 And may these words of mine, with which I have made supplication before the LORD, be near the LORD our God day and night, that He may maintain the cause of His servant and the cause of His people Israel, as each day may require, 60 that all the peoples of the earth may know that the LORD *is* God; *there is* no

*N*ever let your past reputation or the nature of your problem keep you from going to God and asking for a miracle!

other. 61 Let your heart therefore be loyal to the LORD our God, to walk in His statutes and keep His commandments, as at this day."

62 Then the king and all Israel with him offered sacrifices before the LORD. 63 And Solomon offered a sacrifice of peace offerings, which he offered to the LORD, twenty-two thousand bulls and one hundred and twenty thousand sheep. So the king and all the children of Israel dedicated the house of the LORD. 64 On the same day the king consecrated the middle of the court that was in front of the house of the LORD; for there he offered burnt offerings, grain offerings, and the fat of the peace offerings, because the bronze altar that was before the LORD was too small to receive the burnt offerings, the grain offerings, and the fat of the peace offerings.

65 At that time Solomon held a feast, and all Israel with him, a great assembly from the entrance of Hamath to the Brook of Egypt, before the LORD our God, seven days and seven more days—fourteen days. 66 On the eighth day he sent the people away; and they blessed the king, and went to their tents joyful and glad of heart for all the good that the LORD had done for His servant David, and for Israel His people.

9 And it came to pass, when Solomon had finished building the house of the LORD and the king's house, and all Solomon's desire which he wanted to do, 2 that the LORD appeared to Solomon the second time, as He had appeared to him at Gibeon. 3 And the LORD said to him: "I have heard your prayer and your supplication that you have made before Me; I have consecrated this house which you have built to put My name there forever, and My eyes and My heart will be there perpetually. 4 Now if you walk before Me as your father David walked, in integrity of heart and in uprightness, to do according to all that I have commanded you, and if you keep My statutes and My judgments, 5 then I will establish the throne of your kingdom over Israel forever, as I promised David your father, saying, 'You shall

not fail to have a man on the throne of Israel.' 6 But if you or your sons at all turn from following Me, and do not keep My commandments and My statutes which I have set before you, but go and serve other gods and worship them, 7 then I will cut off Israel from the land which I have given them; and this house which I have consecrated for My name I will cast out of My sight. Israel will be a proverb and a byword among all peoples. 8 And as for this house, which is exalted, everyone who passes by it will be astonished and will hiss, and say, 'Why has the LORD done thus to this land and to this house?' 9 Then they will answer, 'Because they forsook the LORD their God, who brought their fathers out of the land of Egypt, and have embraced other gods, and worshiped them and served them; therefore the LORD has brought all this calamity on them.' "

10 Now it happened at the end of twenty years, when Solomon had built the two houses, the house of the LORD and the king's house 11 (Hiram the king of Tyre had supplied Solomon with cedar and cypress and gold, as much as he desired), that King Solomon then gave Hiram twenty cities in the land of Galilee. 12 Then Hiram went from Tyre to see the cities which Solomon had given him, but they did not please him. 13 So he said, "What kind of cities are these which you have given me, my brother?" And he called them the land of Cabul,ᵃ as they are to this day. 14 Then Hiram sent the king one hundred and twenty talents of gold.

15 And this is the reason for the labor force which King Solomon raised: to build the house of the LORD, his own house, the Millo,ᵃ the wall of Jerusalem, Hazor, Megiddo, and Gezer. 16 (Pharaoh king of Egypt had gone up and taken Gezer and burned it with fire, had killed the Canaanites who dwelt in the city, and had given it as a dowry to his daughter, Solomon's wife.) 17 And Solomon built Gezer, Lower Beth Horon, 18 Baalath, and Tadmor in the wilderness, in the land of Judah, 19 all the storage cities that Solomon had, cities for his chariots and cities for his cavalry, and whatever Solomon desired to build in Jerusalem, in Leba-

9:13 ᵃLiterally Good for Nothing   9:15 ᵃLiterally The Landfill

Gospel Pearls

non, and in all the land of his dominion.

20 All the people *who were* left of the Amorites, Hittites, Perizzites, Hivites, and Jebusites, who *were* not of the children of Israel— 21 that is, their descendants who were left in the land after them, whom the children of Israel had not been able to destroy completely—from these Solomon raised forced labor, as it is to this day. 22 But of the children of Israel Solomon made no forced laborers, because they *were* men of war and his servants: his officers, his captains, commanders of his chariots, and his cavalry.

23 Others *were* chiefs of the officials who *were* over Solomon's work: five hundred and fifty, who ruled over the people who did the work.

24 But Pharaoh's daughter came up from the City of David to her house which *Solomon*ᵃ had built for her. Then he built the Millo.

25 Now three times a year Solomon offered burnt offerings and peace offerings on the altar which he had built for the Lord, and he burned incense with them *on the altar* that *was* before the Lord. So he finished the temple.

26 King Solomon also built a fleet of ships at Ezion Geber, which *is* near Elath*ᵃ* on the shore of the Red Sea, in the land of Edom. 27 Then Hiram sent his servants with the fleet, seamen who knew the sea, to work with the servants of Solomon. 28 And they went to Ophir, and acquired four hundred and twenty talents of gold from there, and brought *it* to King Solomon.

10 Now when the queen of Sheba heard of the fame of Solomon concerning the name of the Lord, she came to test him with hard questions. 2 She came to Jerusalem with a very great retinue, with camels that bore spices, very much gold, and precious stones; and when she came to Solomon, she spoke with him about all that was in her heart. 3 So Solomon answered all her questions; there was nothing so difficult for the king that he could not explain *it* to her. 4 And when the queen of Sheba had seen all the wisdom of Solomon, the

house that he had built, 5 the food on his table, the seating of his servants, the service of his waiters and their apparel, his cupbearers, and his entryway by which he went up to the house of the Lord, there was no more spirit in her. 6 Then she said to the king: "It was a true report which I heard in my own land about your words and your wisdom. 7 However I did not believe the words until I came and saw with my own eyes; and indeed the half was not told me. Your wisdom and prosperity exceed the fame of which I heard. 8 Happy *are* your men and happy *are* these your servants, who stand continually before you *and* hear your wisdom! 9 Blessed be the Lord your God, who delighted in you, setting you on the throne of Israel! Because the Lord has loved Israel forever, therefore He made you king, to do justice and righteousness."

10 Then she gave the king one hundred and twenty talents of gold, spices in great quantity, and precious stones. There never again came such abundance of spices as the queen of Sheba gave to King Solomon. 11 Also, the ships of Hiram, which brought gold from Ophir, brought great *quantities* of almugᵃ wood and precious stones from Ophir. 12 And the king made steps of the almug wood for the house of the Lord and for the king's house, also harps and stringed instruments for singers. There never again came such almug wood, nor has the like been seen to this day.

13 Now King Solomon gave the queen of Sheba all she desired, whatever she asked, besides what Solomon had given her according to the royal generosity. So she turned and went to her own country, she and her servants.

14 The weight of gold that came to Solomon yearly was six hundred and sixty-six talents of gold, 15 besides *that* from the traveling merchants, from the income of traders, from all the kings of Arabia, and from the governors of the country.

16 And King Solomon made two hundred large shields *of* hammered gold; six hundred *shekels* of gold went into each shield. 17 He also

9:24 ᵃLiterally *he* (compare 2 Chronicles 8:11)   9:26 ᵃHebrew *Eloth* (compare 2 Kings 14:22)
10:11 ᵃOr *algum* (compare 2 Chronicles 9:10, 11)

God said that His baby girl wasn't destined to remain a baby. She was intended to grow up and mature and become a mother. His image of her was not of her past, but of her present. He expected her to be a "woman in the now."

made three hundred shields *of* hammered gold; three minas of gold went into each shield. The king put them in the House of the Forest of Lebanon.

18 Moreover the king made a great throne of ivory, and overlaid it with pure gold. 19 The throne had six steps, and the top of the throne *was* round at the back; *there were* armrests on either side of the place of the seat, and two lions stood beside the armrests. 20 Twelve lions stood there, one on each side of the six steps; nothing like *this* had been made for any *other* kingdom.

21 All King Solomon's drinking vessels *were* gold, and all the vessels of the House of the Forest of Lebanon *were* pure gold. Not *one was* silver, for this was accounted as nothing in the days of Solomon. 22 For the king had merchant ships*a* at sea with the fleet of Hiram. Once every three years the merchant ships came bringing gold, silver, ivory, apes, and monkeys.*b* 23 So King Solomon surpassed all the kings of the earth in riches and wisdom.

24 Now all the earth sought the presence of Solomon to hear his wisdom, which God had put in his heart. 25 Each man brought his present: articles of silver and gold, garments, armor, spices, horses, and mules, at a set rate year by year.

26 And Solomon gathered chariots and horsemen; he had one thousand four hundred chariots and twelve thousand horsemen, whom he stationed*a* in the chariot cities and with the king at Jerusalem. 27 The king made silver *as common* in Jerusalem as stones, and he made cedar trees as abundant as the sycamores which *are* in the lowland.

28 Also Solomon had horses imported from Egypt and Keveh; the king's merchants bought them in Keveh at the *current* price. 29 Now a chariot that was imported from Egypt cost six hundred *shekels* of silver, and a horse one hundred and fifty; and thus, through their agents,*a* they exported *them* to all the kings of the Hittites and the kings of Syria.

11 But King Solomon loved many foreign women, as well as the daughter of Pharaoh: women of the Moabites, Ammonites, Edomites, Sidonians, *and* Hittites— 2 from the nations of whom the LORD had said to the children of Israel, "You shall not intermarry with them, nor they with you. Surely they will turn away your hearts after their gods." Solomon clung to these in love. 3 And he had seven hundred wives, princesses, and three hundred concubines; and his wives turned away his heart. 4 For it was so, when Solomon was old, that his wives turned his heart after other gods; and his heart was not loyal to the LORD his God, as *was* the heart of his father David. 5 For Solomon went after Ashtoreth the goddess of the Sidonians, and after Milcom the abomination of the Ammonites. 6 Solomon did evil in the sight of the LORD, and did not fully follow the LORD, as *did* his father David. 7 Then Solomon built a high place for Chemosh the abomination of Moab, on the hill that *is* east of Jerusalem, and for Molech the abomination of the people of Ammon. 8 And he did likewise for all his foreign wives, who burned incense and sacrificed to their gods.

9 So the LORD became angry with Solomon, because his heart had turned from the LORD God of Israel, who had appeared to him twice, 10 and had commanded him concerning this thing, that he should not go after other gods; but he did not keep what the LORD had commanded. 11 Therefore the LORD said to Solomon, "Because you have done this, and have not kept My covenant and My statutes, which I have commanded you, I will surely tear the kingdom away from you and give it to your servant. 12 Nevertheless I will not do it in your days, for the sake of your father David; I will tear it out of the hand of your son. 13 However I will not tear away the whole kingdom; I will give one tribe to your son for the sake of My servant David, and for the sake of Jerusalem which I have chosen."

14 Now the LORD raised up an adversary against Solomon, Hadad the Edomite; he *was* a descendant of the king in Edom. 15 For it happened, when David was in Edom, and Joab

10:22 *a*Literally *ships of Tarshish,* deep-sea vessels   *b*Or *peacocks*   10:26 *a*Following Septuagint, Syriac, Targum, and Vulgate (compare 2 Chronicles 9:25); Masoretic Text reads *led.*   10:29 *a*Literally *by their hands*

Gospel Pearls

the commander of the army had gone up to bury the slain, after he had killed every male in Edom 16 (because for six months Joab remained there with all Israel, until he had cut down every male in Edom), 17 that Hadad fled to go to Egypt, he and certain Edomites of his father's servants with him. Hadad *was* still a little child. 18 Then they arose from Midian and came to Paran; and they took men with them from Paran and came to Egypt, to Pharaoh king of Egypt, who gave him a house, apportioned food for him, and gave him land. 19 And Hadad found great favor in the sight of Pharaoh, so that he gave him as wife the sister of his own wife, that is, the sister of Queen Tahpenes. 20 Then the sister of Tahpenes bore him Genubath his son, whom Tahpenes weaned in Pharaoh's house. And Genubath was in Pharaoh's household among the sons of Pharaoh.

21 So when Hadad heard in Egypt that David rested with his fathers, and that Joab the commander of the army was dead, Hadad said to Pharaoh, "Let me depart, that I may go to my own country."

22 Then Pharaoh said to him, "But what have you lacked with me, that suddenly you seek to go to your own country?"

So he answered, "Nothing, but do let me go anyway."

23 And God raised up *another* adversary against him, Rezon the son of Eliadah, who had fled from his lord, Hadadezer king of Zobah. 24 So he gathered men to him and became captain over a band *of raiders*, when David killed those *of Zobah*. And they went to Damascus and dwelt there, and reigned in Damascus. 25 He was an adversary of Israel all the days of Solomon (besides the trouble that Hadad *caused*); and he abhorred Israel, and reigned over Syria.

26 Then Solomon's servant, Jeroboam the son of Nebat, an Ephraimite from Zereda, whose mother's name *was* Zeruah, a widow, also rebelled against the king. 27 And this *is* what caused him to rebel against the king: Solomon had built the Millo *and* repaired the damages to the City of David his father.

28 The man Jeroboam *was* a mighty man of valor; and Solomon, seeing that the young man was industrious, made him the officer over all the labor force of the house of Joseph.

29 Now it happened at that time, when Jeroboam went out of Jerusalem, that the prophet Ahijah the Shilonite met him on the way; and he had clothed himself with a new garment, and the two *were* alone in the field. 30 Then Ahijah took hold of the new garment that *was* on him, and tore it *into* twelve pieces. 31 And he said to Jeroboam, "Take for yourself ten pieces, for thus says the LORD, the God of Israel: 'Behold, I will tear the kingdom out of the hand of Solomon and will give ten tribes to you 32 (but he shall have one tribe for the sake of My servant David, and for the sake of Jerusalem, the city which I have chosen out of all the tribes of Israel), 33 because they have[a] forsaken Me, and worshiped Ashtoreth the goddess of the Sidonians, Chemosh the god of the Moabites, and Milcom the god of the people of Ammon, and have not walked in My ways to do *what is* right in My eyes and *keep* My statutes and My judgments, as *did* his father David. 34 However I will not take the whole kingdom out of his hand, because I have made him ruler all the days of his life for the sake of My servant David, whom I chose because he kept My commandments and My statutes. 35 But I will take the kingdom out of his son's hand and give it to you— ten tribes. 36 And to his son I will give one tribe, that My servant David may always have a lamp before Me in Jerusalem, the city which I have chosen for Myself, to put My name there. 37 So I will take you, and you shall reign over all your heart desires, and you shall be king over Israel. 38 Then it shall be, if you heed all that I command you, walk in My ways, and do *what is* right in My sight, to keep My statutes and My commandments, as My servant David did, then I will be with you and build for you an enduring house, as I built for David, and will give Israel to you. 39 And I will afflict the descendants of David because of this, but not forever.' "

40 Solomon therefore sought to kill

11:33 [a]Following Masoretic Text and Targum; Septuagint, Syriac, and Vulgate read *he has*.

hat does God desire for every woman who comes to Him as a newborn baby Christian? He wants to raise her up so that she can birth spiritual children and then nurture those spiritual babies so that they grow up in Christ.

Jeroboam. But Jeroboam arose and fled to Egypt, to Shishak king of Egypt, and was in Egypt until the death of Solomon.

41 Now the rest of the acts of Solomon, all that he did, and his wisdom, *are* they not written in the book of the acts of Solomon? 42 And the period that Solomon reigned in Jerusalem over all Israel *was* forty years. 43 Then Solomon rested with his fathers, and was buried in the City of David his father. And Rehoboam his son reigned in his place.

12 And Rehoboam went to Shechem, for all Israel had gone to Shechem to make him king. 2 So it happened, when Jeroboam the son of Nebat heard *it* (he was still in Egypt, for he had fled from the presence of King Solomon and had been dwelling in Egypt), 3 that they sent and called him. Then Jeroboam and the whole assembly of Israel came and spoke to Rehoboam, saying, 4 "Your father made our yoke heavy; now therefore, lighten the burdensome service of your father, and his heavy yoke which he put on us, and we will serve you."

5 So he said to them, "Depart *for* three days, then come back to me." And the people departed.

6 Then King Rehoboam consulted the elders who stood before his father Solomon while he still lived, and he said, "How do you advise *me* to answer these people?"

7 And they spoke to him, saying, "If you will be a servant to these people today, and serve them, and answer them, and speak good words to them, then they will be your servants forever."

8 But he rejected the advice which the elders had given him, and consulted the young men who had grown up with him, who stood before him. 9 And he said to them, "What advice do you give? How should we answer this people who have spoken to me, saying, 'Lighten the yoke which your father put on us'?"

10 Then the young men who had grown up with him spoke to him, saying, "Thus you should speak to this people who have spoken to you, saying, 'Your father made our yoke heavy, but you make *it* lighter on

us'—thus you shall say to them: 'My little *finger* shall be thicker than my father's waist! 11 And now, whereas my father put a heavy yoke on you, I will add to your yoke; my father chastised you with whips, but I will chastise you with scourges!' "[a]

12 So Jeroboam and all the people came to Rehoboam the third day, as the king had directed, saying, "Come back to me the third day." 13 Then the king answered the people roughly, and rejected the advice which the elders had given him; 14 and he spoke to them according to the advice of the young men, saying, "My father made your yoke heavy, but I will add to your yoke; my father chastised you with whips, but I will chastise you with scourges!"[a] 15 So the king did not listen to the people; for the turn *of events* was from the LORD, that He might fulfill His word, which the LORD had spoken by Ahijah the Shilonite to Jeroboam the son of Nebat.

16 Now when all Israel saw that the king did not listen to them, the people answered the king, saying:

"What share have we in David?
    We have no inheritance in the
        son of Jesse.
To your tents, O Israel!
Now, see to your own house,
    O David!"

So Israel departed to their tents. 17 But Rehoboam reigned over the children of Israel who dwelt in the cities of Judah.

18 Then King Rehoboam sent Adoram, who *was* in charge of the revenue; but all Israel stoned him with stones, and he died. Therefore King Rehoboam mounted his chariot in haste to flee to Jerusalem. 19 So Israel has been in rebellion against the house of David to this day.

20 Now it came to pass when all Israel heard that Jeroboam had come back, they sent for him and called him to the congregation, and made him king over all Israel. There was none who followed the house of David, but the tribe of Judah only.

21 And when Rehoboam came to Jerusalem, he assembled all the house of Judah with the tribe of Benjamin, one hundred and eighty thou-

Gospel Pearls

sand chosen *men* who were warriors, to fight against the house of Israel, that he might restore the kingdom to Rehoboam the son of Solomon. 22 But the word of God came to Shemaiah the man of God, saying, 23 "Speak to Rehoboam the son of Solomon, king of Judah, to all the house of Judah and Benjamin, and to the rest of the people, saying, 24 'Thus says the LORD: "You shall not go up nor fight against your brethren the children of Israel. Let every man return to his house, for this thing is from Me." ' " Therefore they obeyed the word of the LORD, and turned back, according to the word of the LORD.

25 Then Jeroboam built Shechem in the mountains of Ephraim, and dwelt there. Also he went out from there and built Penuel. 26 And Jeroboam said in his heart, "Now the kingdom may return to the house of David: 27 If these people go up to offer sacrifices in the house of the LORD at Jerusalem, then the heart of this people will turn back to their lord, Rehoboam king of Judah, and they will kill me and go back to Rehoboam king of Judah."

28 Therefore the king asked advice, made two calves of gold, and said to the people, "It is too much for you to go up to Jerusalem. Here are your gods, O Israel, which brought you up from the land of Egypt!" 29 And he set up one in Bethel, and the other he put in Dan. 30 Now this thing became a sin, for the people went to *worship* before the one as far as Dan. 31 He made shrines[a] on the high places, and made priests from every class of people, who were not of the sons of Levi.

32 Jeroboam ordained a feast on the fifteenth day of the eighth month, like the feast that *was* in Judah, and offered sacrifices on the altar. So he did at Bethel, sacrificing to the calves that he had made. And at Bethel he installed the priests of the high places which he had made. 33 So he made offerings on the altar which he had made at Bethel on the fifteenth day of the eighth month, in the month which he had devised in his own heart. And he ordained a feast for the children of Israel, and offered sacrifices on the altar and burned incense.

13 And behold, a man of God went from Judah to Bethel by the word of the LORD, and Jeroboam stood by the altar to burn incense. 2 Then he cried out against the altar by the word of the LORD, and said, "O altar, altar! Thus says the LORD: 'Behold, a child, Josiah by name, shall be born to the house of David; and on you he shall sacrifice the priests of the high places who burn incense on you, and men's bones shall be burned on you.' " 3 And he gave a sign the same day, saying, "This *is* the sign which the LORD has spoken: Surely the altar shall split apart, and the ashes on it shall be poured out."

4 So it came to pass when King Jeroboam heard the saying of the man of God, who cried out against the altar in Bethel, that he stretched out his hand from the altar, saying, "Arrest him!" Then his hand, which he stretched out toward him, withered, so that he could not pull it back to himself. 5 The altar also was split apart, and the ashes poured out from the altar, according to the sign which the man of God had given by the word of the LORD. 6 Then the king answered and said to the man of God, "Please entreat the favor of the LORD your God, and pray for me, that my hand may be restored to me."

So the man of God entreated the LORD, and the king's hand was restored to him, and became as before. 7 Then the king said to the man of God, "Come home with me and refresh yourself, and I will give you a reward."

8 But the man of God said to the king, "If you were to give me half your house, I would not go in with you; nor would I eat bread nor drink water in this place. 9 For so it was commanded me by the word of the LORD, saying, 'You shall not eat bread, nor drink water, nor return by the same way you came.' " 10 So he went another way and did not return by the way he came to Bethel.

11 Now an old prophet dwelt in Bethel, and his sons came and told him all the works that the man of God had done that day in Bethel; they also told their father the words which he had spoken to the king. 12 And their father said to them,

---

12:31 [a]Literally *a house*

God wants to raise up women who will declare: "The same God who brought me through can bring you through. The same God who helped me can help you. The same God who saved me can save you. The same God who is healing me can heal you."

"Which way did he go?" For his sons had seen[a] which way the man of God went who came from Judah. 13 Then he said to his sons, "Saddle the donkey for me." So they saddled the donkey for him; and he rode on it, 14 and went after the man of God, and found him sitting under an oak. Then he said to him, "*Are* you the man of God who came from Judah?"

And he said, "I *am*."

15 Then he said to him, "Come home with me and eat bread."

16 And he said, "I cannot return with you nor go in with you; neither can I eat bread nor drink water with you in this place. 17 For I have been told by the word of the LORD, 'You shall not eat bread nor drink water there, nor return by going the way you came.'"

18 He said to him, "I too *am* a prophet as you *are,* and an angel spoke to me by the word of the LORD, saying, 'Bring him back with you to your house, that he may eat bread and drink water.'" (He was lying to him.)

19 So he went back with him, and ate bread in his house, and drank water.

20 Now it happened, as they sat at the table, that the word of the LORD came to the prophet who had brought him back; 21 and he cried out to the man of God who came from Judah, saying, "Thus says the LORD: 'Because you have disobeyed the word of the LORD, and have not kept the commandment which the LORD your God commanded you, 22 but you came back, ate bread, and drank water in the place of which *the* LORD said to you, "Eat no bread and drink no water," your corpse shall not come to the tomb of your fathers.'"

23 So it was, after he had eaten bread and after he had drunk, that he saddled the donkey for him, the prophet whom he had brought back. 24 When he was gone, a lion met him on the road and killed him. And his corpse was thrown on the road, and the donkey stood by it. The lion also stood by the corpse. 25 And there, men passed by and saw the corpse thrown on the road, and the lion standing by the corpse. Then they went and told *it* in the city where the old prophet dwelt.

26 Now when the prophet who had brought him back from the way heard *it,* he said, "It *is* the man of God who was disobedient to the word of the LORD. Therefore the LORD has delivered him to the lion, which has torn him and killed him, according to the word of the LORD which He spoke to him." 27 And he spoke to his sons, saying, "Saddle the donkey for me." So they saddled *it.* 28 Then he went and found his corpse thrown on the road, and the donkey and the lion standing by the corpse. The lion had not eaten the corpse nor torn the donkey. 29 And the prophet took up the corpse of the man of God, laid it on the donkey, and brought it back. So the old prophet came to the city to mourn, and to bury him. 30 Then he laid the corpse in his own tomb; and they mourned over him, saying, "Alas, my brother!" 31 So it was, after he had buried him, that he spoke to his sons, saying, "When I am dead, then bury me in the tomb where the man of God *is* buried; lay my bones beside his bones. 32 For the saying which he cried out by the word of the LORD against the altar in Bethel, and against all the shrines[a] on the high places which *are* in the cities of Samaria, will surely come to pass."

33 After this event Jeroboam did not turn from his evil way, but again he made priests from every class of people for the high places; whoever wished, he consecrated him, and he became *one* of the priests of the high places. 34 And this thing was the sin of the house of Jeroboam, so as to exterminate and destroy *it* from the face of the earth.

14 At that time Abijah the son of Jeroboam became sick. 2 And Jeroboam said to his wife, "Please arise, and disguise yourself, that they may not recognize you as the wife of Jeroboam, and go to Shiloh. Indeed, Ahijah the prophet *is* there, who told me that *I would be* king over this people. 3 Also take with you ten loaves, *some* cakes, and a jar of honey, and go to him; he will tell you what will become of the

---

13:12 [a]Septuagint, Syriac, Targum, and Vulgate read *showed him.*   13:32 [a]Literally *houses*

I believe that if you ask Him, God will show you why you had to go through what you went through so you would be who you are right now.

Soul Secrets
to celebrate uniqueness

*L*ord, there have been times when I have felt so different, so weird, so unlike the people I know. It has taken me a while to figure out that I am different by Divine design. I am different because You have made me with gifts and traits and a genetic combination that no one else has. No one in all the ages of the world has ever been me. And no one ever will.

So I celebrate the fact that You have made each tiny part of me unique, one-of-a-kind. Deliver me, Father, from feeling weird. Deliver me from ever wishing I were someone else. Deliver me from envy and jealousy of other people's lives. Help me to discover the wonder of the woman You've created me to be. Help me to enjoy the little things that make me special. Help me to understand what a rare and precious treasure I am to You. Help me to realize that I can give the world some things that no one else can give in the same way.

Thank You, Lord, for the awesome creative work You've done as You've made me who I am!

child." 4 And Jeroboam's wife did so; she arose and went to Shiloh, and came to the house of Ahijah. But Ahijah could not see, for his eyes were glazed by reason of his age.

5 Now the LORD had said to Ahijah, "Here is the wife of Jeroboam, coming to ask you something about her son, for he *is* sick. Thus and thus you shall say to her; for it will be, when she comes in, that she will pretend *to be* another *woman*."

6 And so it was, when Ahijah heard the sound of her footsteps as she came through the door, he said, "Come in, wife of Jeroboam. Why do you pretend *to be* another *person?* For I *have been* sent to you *with* bad news. 7 Go, tell Jeroboam, 'Thus says the LORD God of Israel: "Because I exalted you from among the people, and made you ruler over My people Israel, 8 and tore the kingdom away from the house of David, and gave it to you; and *yet* you have not been as My servant David, who kept My commandments and who followed Me with all his heart, to do only *what was* right in My eyes; 9 but you have done more evil than all who were before you, for you have gone and made for yourself other gods and molded images to provoke Me to anger, and have cast Me behind your back— 10 therefore behold! I will bring disaster on the house of Jeroboam, and will cut off from Jeroboam every male in Israel, bond and free; I will take away the remnant of the house of Jeroboam, as one takes away refuse until it is all gone. 11 The dogs shall eat whoever belongs to Jeroboam and dies in the city, and the birds of the air shall eat whoever dies in the field; for the LORD has spoken!" ' 12 Arise therefore, go to your own house. When your feet enter the city, the child shall die. 13 And all Israel shall mourn for him and bury him, for he is the only one of Jeroboam who shall come to the grave, because in him there is found something good toward the LORD God of Israel in the house of Jeroboam.

14 "Moreover the LORD will raise up for Himself a king over Israel who shall cut off the house of Jeroboam; this is the day. What? Even now!

15 For the LORD will strike Israel, as a reed is shaken in the water. He will uproot Israel from this good land which He gave to their fathers, and will scatter them beyond the River,*a* because they have made their wooden images,*b* provoking the LORD to anger. 16 And He will give Israel up because of the sins of Jeroboam, who sinned and who made Israel sin."

17 Then Jeroboam's wife arose and departed, and came to Tirzah. When she came to the threshold of the house, the child died. 18 And they buried him; and all Israel mourned for him, according to the word of the LORD which He spoke through His servant Ahijah the prophet.

19 Now the rest of the acts of Jeroboam, how he made war and how he reigned, indeed they *are* written in the book of the chronicles of the kings of Israel. 20 The period that Jeroboam reigned *was* twenty-two years. So he rested with his fathers. Then Nadab his son reigned in his place.

21 And Rehoboam the son of Solomon reigned in Judah. Rehoboam *was* forty-one years old when he became king. He reigned seventeen years in Jerusalem, the city which the LORD had chosen out of all the tribes of Israel, to put His name there. His mother's name *was* Naamah, an Ammonitess. 22 Now Judah did evil in the sight of the LORD, and they provoked Him to jealousy with their sins which they committed, more than all that their fathers had done. 23 For they also built for themselves high places, *sacred* pillars, and wooden images on every high hill and under every green tree. 24 And there were also perverted persons*a* in the land. They did according to all the abominations of the nations which the LORD had cast out before the children of Israel.

25 It happened in the fifth year of King Rehoboam *that* Shishak king of Egypt came up against Jerusalem. 26 And he took away the treasures of the house of the LORD and the treasures of the king's house; he took away everything. He also took away all the gold shields which Solomon had made. 27 Then King Rehoboam

14:15 *a*That is, the Euphrates　*b*Hebrew *Asherim*, Canaanite deities　14:24 *a*Hebrew *qadesh*, that is, one practicing sodomy and prostitution in religious rituals

Gospel Pearls

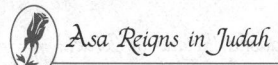
made bronze shields in their place, and committed *them* to the hands of the captains of the guard, who guarded the doorway of the king's house. 28 And whenever the king entered the house of the LORD, the guards carried them, then brought them back into the guardroom.

29 Now the rest of the acts of Rehoboam, and all that he did, *are* they not written in the book of the chronicles of the kings of Judah? 30 And there was war between Rehoboam and Jeroboam all *their* days. 31 So Rehoboam rested with his fathers, and was buried with his fathers in the City of David. His mother's name *was* Naamah, an Ammonitess. Then Abijam*ᵃ* his son reigned in his place.

15 In the eighteenth year of King Jeroboam the son of Nebat, Abijam became king over Judah. 2 He reigned three years in Jerusalem. His mother's name *was* Maachah the granddaughter of Abishalom. 3 And he walked in all the sins of his father, which he had done before him; his heart was not loyal to the LORD his God, as was the heart of his father David. 4 Nevertheless for David's sake the LORD his God gave him a lamp in Jerusalem, by setting up his son after him and by establishing Jerusalem; 5 because David did *what was* right in the eyes of the LORD, and had not turned aside from anything that He commanded him all the days of his life, except in the matter of Uriah the Hittite. 6 And there was war between Rehoboam*ᵃ* and Jeroboam all the days of his life. 7 Now the rest of the acts of Abijam, and all that he did, *are* they not written in the book of the chronicles of the kings of Judah? And there was war between Abijam and Jeroboam.

8 So Abijam rested with his fathers, and they buried him in the City of David. Then Asa his son reigned in his place.

9 In the twentieth year of Jeroboam king of Israel, Asa became king over Judah. 10 And he reigned forty-one years in Jerusalem. His grandmother's name *was* Maachah the grand-

daughter of Abishalom. 11 Asa did *what was* right in the eyes of the LORD, as *did* his father David. 12 And he banished the perverted persons*ᵃ* from the land, and removed all the idols that his fathers had made. 13 Also he removed Maachah his grandmother from *being* queen mother, because she had made an obscene image of Asherah.*ᵃ* And Asa cut down her obscene image and burned *it* by the Brook Kidron. 14 But the high places were not removed. Nevertheless Asa's heart was loyal to the LORD all his days. 15 He also brought into the house of the LORD the things which his father had dedicated, and the things which he himself had dedicated: silver and gold and utensils.

16 Now there was war between Asa and Baasha king of Israel all their days. 17 And Baasha king of Israel came up against Judah, and built Ramah, that he might let none go out or come in to Asa king of Judah. 18 Then Asa took all the silver and gold *that was* left in the treasuries of the house of the LORD and the treasuries of the king's house, and delivered them into the hand of his servants. And King Asa sent them to Ben-Hadad the son of Tabrimmon, the son of Hezion, king of Syria, who dwelt in Damascus, saying, 19 *"Let there be* a treaty between you and me, as there was between my father and your father. See, I have sent you a present of silver and gold. Come and break your treaty with Baasha king of Israel, so that he will withdraw from me."

20 So Ben-Hadad heeded King Asa, and sent the captains of his armies against the cities of Israel. He attacked Ijon, Dan, Abel Beth Maachah, and all Chinneroth, with all the land of Naphtali. 21 Now it happened, when Baasha heard *it,* that he stopped building Ramah, and remained in Tirzah.

22 Then King Asa made a proclamation throughout all Judah; none *was* exempted. And they took away the stones and timber of Ramah, which Baasha had used for building; and with them King Asa built Geba of Benjamin, and Mizpah.

14:31 *ᵃ*Spelled *Abijah* in 2 Chronicles 12:16ff   15:6 *ᵃ*Following Masoretic Text, Septuagint, Targum, and Vulgate; some Hebrew manuscripts and Syriac read *Abijam.*   15:12 *ᵃ*Hebrew *qedeshim,* that is, those practicing sodomy and prostitution in religious rituals   15:13 *ᵃ*A Canaanite goddess

---

I believe that if you desire for Him to tell you, God will reveal to you all that He still has to give to you and all that He wants you to do in ministry to others.

23 The rest of all the acts of Asa, all his might, all that he did, and the cities which he built, *are* they not written in the book of the chronicles of the kings of Judah? But in the time of his old age he was diseased in his feet. 24 So Asa rested with his fathers, and was buried with his fathers in the City of David his father. Then Jehoshaphat his son reigned in his place.

25 Now Nadab the son of Jeroboam became king over Israel in the second year of Asa king of Judah, and he reigned over Israel two years. 26 And he did evil in the sight of the LORD, and walked in the way of his father, and in his sin by which he had made Israel sin.

27 Then Baasha the son of Ahijah, of the house of Issachar, conspired against him. And Baasha killed him at Gibbethon, which *belonged* to the Philistines, while Nadab and all Israel laid siege to Gibbethon. 28 Baasha killed him in the third year of Asa king of Judah, and reigned in his place. 29 And it was so, when he became king, *that* he killed all the house of Jeroboam. He did not leave to Jeroboam anyone that breathed, until he had destroyed him, according to the word of the LORD which He had spoken by His servant Ahijah the Shilonite, 30 because of the sins of Jeroboam, which he had sinned and by which he had made Israel sin, because of his provocation with which he had provoked the LORD God of Israel to anger.

31 Now the rest of the acts of Nadab, and all that he did, *are* they not written in the book of the chronicles of the kings of Israel? 32 And there was war between Asa and Baasha king of Israel all their days.

33 In the third year of Asa king of Judah, Baasha the son of Ahijah became king over all Israel in Tirzah, and *reigned* twenty-four years. 34 He did evil in the sight of the LORD, and walked in the way of Jeroboam, and in his sin by which he had made Israel sin.

16 Then the word of the LORD came to Jehu the son of Hanani, against Baasha, saying: 2 "Inasmuch as I lifted you out of the dust and made you ruler over My people Israel, and you have walked in the way of Jeroboam, and have made My people Israel sin, to provoke Me to anger with their sins, 3 surely I will take away the posterity of Baasha and the posterity of his house, and I will make your house like the house of Jeroboam the son of Nebat. 4 The dogs shall eat whoever belongs to Baasha and dies in the city, and the birds of the air shall eat whoever dies in the fields."

5 Now the rest of the acts of Baasha, what he did, and his might, *are* they not written in the book of the chronicles of the kings of Israel? 6 So Baasha rested with his fathers and was buried in Tirzah. Then Elah his son reigned in his place.

7 And also the word of the LORD came by the prophet Jehu the son of Hanani against Baasha and his house, because of all the evil that he did in the sight of the LORD in provoking Him to anger with the work of his hands, in being like the house of Jeroboam, and because he killed them.

8 In the twenty-sixth year of Asa king of Judah, Elah the son of Baasha became king over Israel, *and reigned* two years in Tirzah. 9 Now his servant Zimri, commander of half *his* chariots, conspired against him as he was in Tirzah drinking himself drunk in the house of Arza, steward of *his* house in Tirzah. 10 And Zimri went in and struck him and killed him in the twenty-seventh year of Asa king of Judah, and reigned in his place.

11 Then it came to pass, when he began to reign, as soon as he was seated on his throne, *that* he killed all the household of Baasha; he did not leave him one male, neither of his relatives nor of his friends. 12 Thus Zimri destroyed all the household of Baasha, according to the word of the LORD, which He spoke against Baasha by Jehu the prophet, 13 for all the sins of Baasha and the sins of Elah his son, by which they had sinned and by which they had made Israel sin, in provoking the LORD God of Israel to anger with their idols.

14 Now the rest of the acts of Elah, and all that he did, *are* they not written in the book of the chronicles of the kings of Israel?

15 In the twenty-seventh year of Asa king of Judah, Zimri had reigned in Tirzah seven days. And the people *were* encamped against Gibbethon,

Gospel Pearls

which *belonged* to the Philistines. 16 Now the people *who were* encamped heard it said, "Zimri has conspired and also has killed the king." So all Israel made Omri, the commander of the army, king over Israel that day in the camp. 17 Then Omri and all Israel with him went up from Gibbethon, and they besieged Tirzah. 18 And it happened, when Zimri saw that the city was taken, that he went into the citadel of the king's house and burned the king's house down upon himself with fire, and died, 19 because of the sins which he had committed in doing evil in the sight of the LORD, in walking in the way of Jeroboam, and in his sin which he had committed to make Israel sin.

20 Now the rest of the acts of Zimri, and the treason he committed, *are* they not written in the book of the chronicles of the kings of Israel?

21 Then the people of Israel were divided into two parts: half of the people followed Tibni the son of Ginath, to make him king, and half followed Omri. 22 But the people who followed Omri prevailed over the people who followed Tibni the son of Ginath. So Tibni died and Omri reigned. 23 In the thirty-first year of Asa king of Judah, Omri became king over Israel, *and reigned* twelve years. Six years he reigned in Tirzah. 24 And he bought the hill of Samaria from Shemer for two talents of silver; then he built on the hill, and called the name of the city which he built, Samaria, after the name of Shemer, owner of the hill. 25 Omri did evil in the eyes of the LORD, and did worse than all who *were* before him. 26 For he walked in all the ways of Jeroboam the son of Nebat, and in his sin by which he had made Israel sin, provoking the LORD God of Israel to anger with their idols.

27 Now the rest of the acts of Omri which he did, and the might that he showed, *are* they not written in the book of the chronicles of the kings of Israel?

28 So Omri rested with his fathers and was buried in Samaria. Then Ahab his son reigned in his place.

29 In the thirty-eighth year of Asa king of Judah, Ahab the son of Omri became king over Israel; and Ahab the son of Omri reigned over Israel in Samaria twenty-two years. 30 Now Ahab the son of Omri did evil in the sight of the LORD, more than all who *were* before him. 31 And it came to pass, as though it had been a trivial thing for him to walk in the sins of Jeroboam the son of Nebat, that he took as wife Jezebel the daughter of Ethbaal, king of the Sidonians; and he went and served Baal and worshiped him. 32 Then he set up an altar for Baal in the temple of Baal, which he had built in Samaria. 33 And Ahab made a wooden image.*ᵃ* Ahab did more to provoke the LORD God of Israel to anger than all the kings of Israel who were before him. 34 In his days Hiel of Bethel built Jericho. He laid its foundation with Abiram his firstborn, and with his youngest *son* Segub he set up its gates, according to the word of the LORD, which He had spoken through Joshua the son of Nun.*ᵃ*

17 And Elijah the Tishbite, of the inhabitants of Gilead, said to Ahab, "*As* the LORD God of Israel lives, before whom I stand, there shall not be dew nor rain these years, except at my word."

2 Then the word of the LORD came to him, saying, 3 "Get away from here and turn eastward, and hide by the Brook Cherith, which flows into the Jordan. 4 And it will be *that* you shall drink from the brook, and I have commanded the ravens to feed you there."

5 So he went and did according to the word of the LORD, for he went and stayed by the Brook Cherith, which flows into the Jordan. 6 The ravens brought him bread and meat in the morning, and bread and meat in the evening; and he drank from the brook. 7 And it happened after a while that the brook dried up, because there had been no rain in the land.

8 Then the word of the LORD came to him, saying, 9 "Arise, go to Zarephath, which *belongs* to Sidon, and dwell there. See, I have commanded a widow there to provide for you." 10 So he arose and went to Zarephath. And when he came to the gate of the city, indeed a widow *was* there gathering sticks. And he called to her

16:33 ᵃHebrew *Asherah*, a Canaanite goddess   16:34 ᵃCompare Joshua 6:26

*N*ow that God has brought you through the crisis and raised you up to maturity, you are ready to enter into the fullness of His destiny for you.

and said, "Please bring me a little water in a cup, that I may drink." 11 And as she was going to get *it*, he called to her and said, "Please bring me a morsel of bread in your hand."

12 So she said, "As the LORD your God lives, I do not have bread, only a handful of flour in a bin, and a little oil in a jar; and see, I *am* gathering a couple of sticks that I may go in and prepare it for myself and my son, that we may eat it, and die."

13 And Elijah said to her, "Do not fear; go *and* do as you have said, but make me a small cake from it first, and bring *it* to me; and afterward make *some* for yourself and your son. 14 For thus says the LORD God of Israel: 'The bin of flour shall not be used up, nor shall the jar of oil run dry, until the day the LORD sends rain on the earth.' "

15 So she went away and did according to the word of Elijah; and she and he and her household ate for *many* days. 16 The bin of flour was not used up, nor did the jar of oil run dry, according to the word of the LORD which He spoke by Elijah.

17 Now it happened after these things *that* the son of the woman who owned the house became sick. And his sickness was so serious that there was no breath left in him. 18 So she said to Elijah, "What have I to do with you, O man of God? Have you come to me to bring my sin to remembrance, and to kill my son?"

19 And he said to her, "Give me your son." So he took him out of her arms and carried him to the upper room where he was staying, and laid him on his own bed. 20 Then he cried out to the LORD and said, "O LORD my God, have You also brought tragedy on the widow with whom I lodge, by killing her son?" 21 And he stretched himself out on the child three times, and cried out to the LORD and said, "O LORD my God, I pray, let this child's soul come back to him." 22 Then the LORD heard the voice of Elijah; and the soul of the child came back to him, and he revived.

23 And Elijah took the child and brought him down from the upper room into the house, and gave him to his mother. And Elijah said, "See, your son lives!"

24 Then the woman said to Elijah, "Now by this I know that you *are* a man of God, *and* that the word of the LORD in your mouth *is* the truth."

18 And it came to pass *after* many days that the word of the LORD came to Elijah, in the third year, saying, "Go, present yourself to Ahab, and I will send rain on the earth."

2 So Elijah went to present himself to Ahab; and *there was* a severe famine in Samaria. 3 And Ahab had called Obadiah, who *was* in charge of *his* house. (Now Obadiah feared the LORD greatly. 4 For so it was, while Jezebel massacred the prophets of the LORD, that Obadiah had taken one hundred prophets and hidden them, fifty to a cave, and had fed them with bread and water.) 5 And Ahab had said to Obadiah, "Go into the land to all the springs of water and to all the brooks; perhaps we may find grass to keep the horses and mules alive, so that we will not have to kill any livestock." 6 So they divided the land between them to explore it; Ahab went one way by himself, and Obadiah went another way by himself.

7 Now as Obadiah was on his way, suddenly Elijah met him; and he recognized him, and fell on his face, and said, "*Is* that you, my lord Elijah?"

8 And he answered him, "*It is* I. Go, tell your master, 'Elijah *is here.*' "

9 So he said, "How have I sinned, that you are delivering your servant into the hand of Ahab, to kill me? 10 *As* the LORD your God lives, there is no nation or kingdom where my master has not sent someone to hunt for you; and when they said, '*He is* not *here,*' he took an oath from the kingdom or nation that they could not find you. 11 And now you say, 'Go, tell your master, "Elijah *is here*" '! 12 And it shall come to pass, *as soon as* I am gone from you, that the Spirit of the LORD will carry you to a place I do not know; so when I go and tell Ahab, and he cannot find you, he will kill me. But I your servant have feared the LORD from my youth. 13 Was it not reported to my lord what I did when Jezebel killed the prophets of the LORD, how I hid one hundred men of the LORD's prophets, fifty to a cave, and fed them with bread and water? 14 And now you say, 'Go, tell your master, "Elijah *is here.*" ' He will kill me!"

15 Then Elijah said, "*As the LORD*

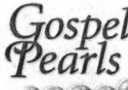

Gospel Pearls

of hosts lives, before whom I stand, I will surely present myself to him today."

16 So Obadiah went to meet Ahab, and told him; and Ahab went to meet Elijah.

17 Then it happened, when Ahab saw Elijah, that Ahab said to him, "*Is that* you, O troubler of Israel?"

18 And he answered, "I have not troubled Israel, but you and your father's house *have*, in that you have forsaken the commandments of the LORD and have followed the Baals. 19 Now therefore, send *and* gather all Israel to me on Mount Carmel, the four hundred and fifty prophets of Baal, and the four hundred prophets of Asherah,*a* who eat at Jezebel's table."

20 So Ahab sent for all the children of Israel, and gathered the prophets together on Mount Carmel. 21 And Elijah came to all the people, and said, "How long will you falter between two opinions? If the LORD *is* God, follow Him; but if Baal, follow him." But the people answered him not a word. 22 Then Elijah said to the people, "I alone am left a prophet of the LORD; but Baal's prophets *are* four hundred and fifty men. 23 Therefore let them give us two bulls; and let them choose one bull for themselves, cut it in pieces, and lay *it* on the wood, but put no fire *under it;* and I will prepare the other bull, and lay *it* on the wood, but put no fire *under it.* 24 Then you call on the name of your gods, and I will call on the name of the LORD; and the God who answers by fire, He is God."

So all the people answered and said, "It is well spoken."

25 Now Elijah said to the prophets of Baal, "Choose one bull for yourselves and prepare *it* first, for you *are* many; and call on the name of your god, but put no fire *under it.*"

26 So they took the bull which was given them, and they prepared *it,* and called on the name of Baal from morning even till noon, saying, "O Baal, hear us!" But *there was* no voice; no one answered. Then they leaped about the altar which they had made.

27 And so it was, at noon, that Elijah mocked them and said, "Cry aloud, for he *is* a god; either he is

meditating, or he is busy, or he is on a journey, *or* perhaps he is sleeping and must be awakened." 28 So they cried aloud, and cut themselves, as was their custom, with knives and lances, until the blood gushed out on them. 29 And when midday was past, they prophesied until the *time* of the offering of the *evening* sacrifice. But *there was* no voice; no one answered, no one paid attention.

30 Then Elijah said to all the people, "Come near to me." So all the people came near to him. And he repaired the altar of the LORD *that was* broken down. 31 And Elijah took twelve stones, according to the number of the tribes of the sons of Jacob, to whom the word of the LORD had come, saying, "Israel shall be your name."*a* 32 Then with the stones he built an altar in the name of the LORD; and he made a trench around the altar large enough to hold two seahs of seed. 33 And he put the wood in order, cut the bull in pieces, and laid *it* on the wood, and said, "Fill four waterpots with water, and pour *it* on the burnt sacrifice and on the wood." 34 Then he said, "Do *it* a second time," and they did *it* a second time; and he said, "Do *it* a third time," and they did *it* a third time. 35 So the water ran all around the altar; and he also filled the trench with water.

36 And it came to pass, at *the time* of the offering of the *evening* sacrifice, that Elijah the prophet came near and said, "LORD God of Abraham, Isaac, and Israel, let it be known this day that You *are* God in Israel and I *am* Your servant, and *that* I have done all these things at your word. 37 Hear me, O LORD, hear me, that this people may know that You *are* the LORD God, and *that* You have turned their hearts back *to You* again."

38 Then the fire of the LORD fell and consumed the burnt sacrifice, and the wood and the stones and the dust, and it licked up the water that *was* in the trench. 39 Now when all the people saw *it,* they fell on their faces; and they said, "The LORD, He *is* God! The LORD, He *is* God!"

40 And Elijah said to them, "Seize the prophets of Baal! Do not let one of them escape!" So they seized

18:19 *a*A Canaanite goddess   18:31 *a*Genesis 32:28

*Y*our eyes have not yet seen; and your ears have not yet heard; and neither has it entered into your heart all the things that God has prepared for you! *Now* is the time to see, to hear, and to believe. *Now* is the time for blessing.

them; and Elijah brought them down to the Brook Kishon and executed them there.

41 Then Elijah said to Ahab, "Go up, eat and drink; for *there is* the sound of abundance of rain." 42 So Ahab went up to eat and drink. And Elijah went up to the top of Carmel; then he bowed down on the ground, and put his face between his knees, 43 and said to his servant, "Go up now, look toward the sea."

So he went up and looked, and said, "*There is* nothing." And seven times he said, "Go again."

44 Then it came to pass the seventh *time,* that he said, "There is a cloud, as small as a man's hand, rising out of the sea!" So he said, "Go up, say to Ahab, 'Prepare *your* chariot, and go down before the rain stops you.' "

45 Now it happened in the meantime that the sky became black with clouds and wind, and there was a heavy rain. So Ahab rode away and went to Jezreel. 46 Then the hand of the LORD came upon Elijah; and he girded up his loins and ran ahead of Ahab to the entrance of Jezreel.

19 And Ahab told Jezebel all that Elijah had done, also how he had executed all the prophets with the sword. 2 Then Jezebel sent a messenger to Elijah, saying, "So let the gods do *to me,* and more also, if I do not make your life as the life of one of them by tomorrow about this time." 3 And when he saw *that,* he arose and ran for his life, and went to Beersheba, which *belongs* to Judah, and left his servant there.

4 But he himself went a day's journey into the wilderness, and came and sat down under a broom tree. And he prayed that he might die, and said, "It is enough! Now, LORD, take my life, for I *am* no better than my fathers!"

5 Then as he lay and slept under a broom tree, suddenly an angel[a] touched him, and said to him, "Arise *and* eat." 6 Then he looked, and there by his head *was* a cake baked on coals, and a jar of water. So he ate and drank, and lay down again. 7 And the angel[a] of the LORD came back the second time, and touched him, and said, "Arise *and* eat, because the journey *is* too great for

you." 8 So he arose, and ate and drank; and he went in the strength of that food forty days and forty nights as far as Horeb, the mountain of God.

9 And there he went into a cave, and spent the night in that place; and behold, the word of the LORD *came* to him, and He said to him, "What are you doing here, Elijah?"

10 So he said, "I have been very zealous for the LORD God of hosts; for the children of Israel have forsaken Your covenant, torn down Your altars, and killed Your prophets with the sword. I alone am left; and they seek to take my life."

11 Then He said, "Go out, and stand on the mountain before the LORD." And behold, the LORD passed by, and a great and strong wind tore into the mountains and broke the rocks in pieces before the LORD, *but* the LORD *was* not in the wind; and after the wind an earthquake, *but* the LORD *was* not in the earthquake; 12 and after the earthquake a fire, *but* the LORD *was* not in the fire; and after the fire a still small voice.

13 So it was, when Elijah heard *it,* that he wrapped his face in his mantle and went out and stood in the entrance of the cave. Suddenly a voice *came* to him, and said, "What are you doing here, Elijah?"

14 And he said, "I have been very zealous for the LORD God of hosts; because the children of Israel have forsaken Your covenant, torn down Your altars, and killed Your prophets with the sword. I alone am left; and they seek to take my life."

15 Then the LORD said to him: "Go, return on your way to the Wilderness of Damascus; and when you arrive, anoint Hazael *as* king over Syria. 16 Also you shall anoint Jehu the son of Nimshi *as* king over Israel. And Elisha the son of Shaphat of Abel Meholah you shall anoint *as* prophet in your place. 17 It shall be *that* whoever escapes the sword of Hazael, Jehu will kill; and whoever escapes the sword of Jehu, Elisha will kill. 18 Yet I have reserved seven thousand in Israel, all whose knees have not bowed to Baal, and every mouth that has not kissed him."

19 So he departed from there, and found Elisha the son of Shaphat, who

19:5 aOr *Angel*   19:7 aOr *Angel*

Gospel Pearls

was plowing *with* twelve yoke *of* oxen before him, and he was with the twelfth. Then Elijah passed by him and threw his mantle on him. 20 And he left the oxen and ran after Elijah, and said, "Please let me kiss my father and my mother, and *then* I will follow you."

And he said to him, "Go back again, for what have I done to you?"

21 So *Elisha* turned back from him, and took a yoke of oxen and slaughtered them and boiled their flesh, using the oxen's equipment, and gave it to the people, and they ate. Then he arose and followed Elijah, and became his servant.

20 Now Ben-Hadad the king of Syria gathered all his forces together; thirty-two kings *were* with him, with horses and chariots. And he went up and besieged Samaria, and made war against it. 2 Then he sent messengers into the city to Ahab king of Israel, and said to him, "Thus says Ben-Hadad: 3 'Your silver and your gold *are* mine; your loveliest wives and children are mine.' "

4 And the king of Israel answered and said, "My lord, O king, just as you say, I and all that I have *are* yours."

5 Then the messengers came back and said, "Thus speaks Ben-Hadad, saying, 'Indeed I have sent to you, saying, "You shall deliver to me your silver and your gold, your wives and your children"; 6 but I will send my servants to you tomorrow about this time, and they shall search your house and the houses of your servants. And it shall be, *that* whatever is pleasant in your eyes, they will put *it* in their hands and take *it*.' "

7 So the king of Israel called all the elders of the land, and said, "Notice, please, and see how this *man* seeks trouble, for he sent to me for my wives, my children, my silver, and my gold; and I did not deny him."

8 And all the elders and all the people said to him, "Do not listen or consent."

9 Therefore he said to the messengers of Ben-Hadad, "Tell my lord the king, 'All that you sent for to your servant the first time I will do, but this thing I cannot do.' "

And the messengers departed and brought back word to him.

10 Then Ben-Hadad sent to him and said, "The gods do so to me, and more also, if enough dust is left of Samaria for a handful for each of the people who follow me."

11 So the king of Israel answered and said, "Tell *him*, 'Let not the one who puts on *his armor* boast like the one who takes *it off*.' "

12 And it happened when *Ben-Hadad* heard this message, as he and the kings *were* drinking at the command post, that he said to his servants, "Get ready." And they got ready to attack the city.

13 Suddenly a prophet approached Ahab king of Israel, saying, "Thus says the LORD: 'Have you seen all this great multitude? Behold, I will deliver it into your hand today, and you shall know that I *am* the LORD.' "

14 So Ahab said, "By whom?"

And he said, "Thus says the LORD: 'By the young leaders of the provinces.' "

Then he said, "Who will set the battle in order?"

And he answered, "You."

15 Then he mustered the young leaders of the provinces, and there were two hundred and thirty-two; and after them he mustered all the people, all the children of Israel—seven thousand.

16 So they went out at noon. Meanwhile Ben-Hadad and the thirty-two kings helping him were getting drunk at the command post. 17 The young leaders of the provinces went out first. And Ben-Hadad sent out *a patrol*, and they told him, saying, "Men are coming out of Samaria!" 18 So he said, "If they have come out for peace, take them alive; and if they have come out for war, take them alive."

19 Then these young leaders of the provinces went out of the city with the army which followed them. 20 And each one killed his man; so the Syrians fled, and Israel pursued them; and Ben-Hadad the king of Syria escaped on a horse with the cavalry. 21 Then the king of Israel went out and attacked the horses and chariots, and killed the Syrians with a great slaughter.

22 And the prophet came to the king of Israel and said to him, "Go, strengthen yourself; take note, and see what you should do, for in the spring of the year the king of Syria will come up against you."

*B*elieve God today for His *now* blessing in your life. Ask Him to reveal to you how you might help and bless others.

23 Then the servants of the king of Syria said to him, "Their gods *are* gods of the hills. Therefore they were stronger than we; but if we fight against them in the plain, surely we will be stronger than they. 24 So do this thing: Dismiss the kings, each from his position, and put captains in their places; 25 and you shall muster an army like the army that you have lost, horse for horse and chariot for chariot. Then we will fight against them in the plain; surely we will be stronger than they."

And he listened to their voice and did so.

26 So it was, in the spring of the year, that Ben-Hadad mustered the Syrians and went up to Aphek to fight against Israel. 27 And the children of Israel were mustered and given provisions, and they went against them. Now the children of Israel encamped before them like two little flocks of goats, while the Syrians filled the countryside.

28 Then a man of God came and spoke to the king of Israel and said, "Thus says the LORD: 'Because the Syrians have said, "The LORD *is* God of the hills, but He *is* not God of the valleys," therefore I will deliver all this great multitude into your hand, and you shall know that I *am* the LORD.' " 29 And they encamped opposite each other for seven days. So it was that on the seventh day the battle was joined; and the children of Israel killed one hundred thousand foot soldiers *of* the Syrians in one day. 30 But the rest fled to Aphek, into the city; then a wall fell on twenty-seven thousand of the men *who were* left.

And Ben-Hadad fled and went into the city, into an inner chamber.

31 Then his servants said to him, "Look now, we have heard that the kings of the house of Israel *are* merciful kings. Please, let us put sackcloth around our waists and ropes around our heads, and go out to the king of Israel; perhaps he will spare your life." 32 So they wore sackcloth around their waists and *put* ropes around their heads, and came to the king of Israel and said, "Your servant Ben-Hadad says, 'Please let me live.' "

And he said, "*Is* he still alive? He *is* my brother."

33 Now the men were watching closely to see whether *any sign of mercy would come* from him; and they quickly grasped *at this word* and said, "Your brother Ben-Hadad."

So he said, "Go, bring him." Then Ben-Hadad came out to him; and he had him come up into the chariot.

34 So *Ben-Hadad* said to him, "The cities which my father took from your father I will restore; and you may set up marketplaces for yourself in Damascus, as my father did in Samaria."

Then *Ahab said,* "I will send you away with this treaty." So he made a treaty with him and sent him away.

35 Now a certain man of the sons of the prophets said to his neighbor by the word of the LORD, "Strike me, please." And the man refused to strike him. 36 Then he said to him, "Because you have not obeyed the voice of the LORD, surely, as soon as you depart from me, a lion shall kill you." And as soon as he left him, a lion found him and killed him.

37 And he found another man, and said, "Strike me, please." So the man struck him, inflicting a wound. 38 Then the prophet departed and waited for the king by the road, and disguised himself with a bandage over his eyes. 39 Now as the king passed by, he cried out to the king and said, "Your servant went out into the midst of the battle; and there, a man came over and brought a man to me, and said, 'Guard this man; if by any means he is missing, your life shall be for his life, or else you shall pay a talent of silver.' 40 While your servant was busy here and there, he was gone."

Then the king of Israel said to him, "So *shall* your judgment *be; you* yourself have decided *it.*"

41 And he hastened to take the bandage away from his eyes; and the king of Israel recognized him as one of the prophets. 42 Then he said to him, "Thus says the LORD: 'Because you have let slip out of *your* hand a man whom I appointed to utter destruction, therefore your life shall go for his life, and your people for his people.' "

43 So the king of Israel went to his house sullen and displeased, and came to Samaria.

21 And it came to pass after these things *that* Naboth the Jezreel-

Gospel
Pearls

ite had a vineyard which *was* in Jezreel, next to the palace of Ahab king of Samaria. 2 So Ahab spoke to Naboth, saying, "Give me your vineyard, that I may have it for a vegetable garden, because it *is* near, next to my house; and for it I will give you a vineyard better than it. *Or*, if it seems good to you, I will give you its worth in money."

3 But Naboth said to Ahab, "The LORD forbid that I should give the inheritance of my fathers to you!"

4 So Ahab went into his house sullen and displeased because of the word which Naboth the Jezreelite had spoken to him; for he had said, "I will not give you the inheritance of my fathers." And he lay down on his bed, and turned away his face, and would eat no food. 5 But Jezebel his wife came to him, and said to him, "Why is your spirit so sullen that you eat no food?"

6 He said to her, "Because I spoke to Naboth the Jezreelite, and said to him, 'Give me your vineyard for money; or else, if it pleases you, I will give you *another* vineyard for it.' And he answered, 'I will not give you my vineyard.' "

7 Then Jezebel his wife said to him, "You now exercise authority over Israel! Arise, eat food, and let your heart be cheerful; I will give you the vineyard of Naboth the Jezreelite."

8 And she wrote letters in Ahab's name, sealed *them* with his seal, and sent the letters to the elders and the nobles who *were* dwelling in the city with Naboth. 9 She wrote in the letters, saying,

> Proclaim a fast, and seat Naboth with high honor among the people; 10 and seat two men, scoundrels, before him to bear witness against him, saying, "You have blasphemed God and the king." *Then* take him out, and stone him, that he may die.

11 So the men of his city, the elders and nobles who were inhabitants of his city, did as Jezebel had sent to them, as it *was* written in the letters which she had sent to them. 12 They proclaimed a fast, and seated

Naboth with high honor among the people. 13 And two men, scoundrels, came in and sat before him; and the scoundrels witnessed against him, against Naboth, in the presence of the people, saying, "Naboth has blasphemed God and the king!" Then they took him outside the city and stoned him with stones, so that he died. 14 Then they sent to Jezebel, saying, "Naboth has been stoned and is dead."

15 And it came to pass, when Jezebel heard that Naboth had been stoned and was dead, that Jezebel said to Ahab, "Arise, take possession of the vineyard of Naboth the Jezreelite, which he refused to give you for money; for Naboth is not alive, but dead." 16 So it was, when Ahab heard that Naboth was dead, that Ahab got up and went down to take possession of the vineyard of Naboth the Jezreelite.

17 Then the word of the LORD came to Elijah the Tishbite, saying, 18 "Arise, go down to meet Ahab king of Israel, who *lives* in Samaria. There *he is*, in the vineyard of Naboth, where he has gone down to take possession of it. 19 You shall speak to him, saying, 'Thus says the LORD: "Have you murdered and also taken possession?" ' And you shall speak to him, saying, 'Thus says the LORD: "In the place where dogs licked the blood of Naboth, dogs shall lick your blood, even yours." ' "

20 So Ahab said to Elijah, "Have you found me, O my enemy?"

And he answered, "I have found *you*, because you have sold yourself to do evil in the sight of the LORD: 21 'Behold, I will bring calamity on you. I will take away your posterity, and will cut off from Ahab every male in Israel, both bond and free. 22 I will make your house like the house of Jeroboam the son of Nebat, and like the house of Baasha the son of Ahijah, because of the provocation with which you have provoked *Me* to anger, and made Israel sin.' 23 And concerning Jezebel the LORD also spoke, saying, 'The dogs shall eat Jezebel by the wall*a* of Jezreel.' 24 The dogs shall eat whoever belongs to Ahab and dies in the city, and the birds of the air

---

21:23 *a*Following Masoretic Text and Septuagint; some Hebrew manuscripts, Syriac, Targum, and Vulgate read *plot of ground* (compare 2 Kings 9:36).

---

*N*ow is your time to enter into His service—no longer as His orphaned baby girl, but as His woman. He has loosed you so that you might loose others in His name.

shall eat whoever dies in the field."

25 But there was no one like Ahab who sold himself to do wickedness in the sight of the Lord, because Jezebel his wife stirred him up. 26 And he behaved very abominably in following idols, according to all *that* the Amorites had done, whom the Lord had cast out before the children of Israel.

27 So it was, when Ahab heard those words, that he tore his clothes and put sackcloth on his body, and fasted and lay in sackcloth, and went about mourning.

28 And the word of the Lord came to Elijah the Tishbite, saying, 29 "See how Ahab has humbled himself before Me? Because he has humbled himself before Me, I will not bring the calamity in his days. In the days of his son I will bring the calamity on his house."

22 Now three years passed without war between Syria and Israel. 2 Then it came to pass, in the third year, that Jehoshaphat the king of Judah went down to *visit* the king of Israel.

3 And the king of Israel said to his servants, "Do you know that Ramoth in Gilead *is* ours, but we hesitate to take it out of the hand of the king of Syria?" 4 So he said to Jehoshaphat, "Will you go with me to fight at Ramoth Gilead?"

Jehoshaphat said to the king of Israel, "I *am* as you *are,* my people as your people, my horses as your horses." 5 Also Jehoshaphat said to the king of Israel, "Please inquire for the word of the Lord today."

6 Then the king of Israel gathered the prophets together, about four hundred men, and said to them, "Shall I go against Ramoth Gilead to fight, or shall I refrain?"

So they said, "Go up, for the Lord will deliver *it* into the hand of the king."

7 And Jehoshaphat said, "*Is there* not still a prophet of the Lord here, that we may inquire of Him?"*a*

8 So the king of Israel said to Jehoshaphat, "*There is* still one man, Micaiah the son of Imlah, by whom we may inquire of the Lord; but I hate him, because he does not prophesy good concerning me, but evil."

And Jehoshaphat said, "Let not the king say such things!"

9 Then the king of Israel called an officer and said, "Bring Micaiah the son of Imlah quickly!"

10 The king of Israel and Jehoshaphat the king of Judah, having put on *their* robes, sat each on his throne, at a threshing floor at the entrance of the gate of Samaria; and all the prophets prophesied before them. 11 Now Zedekiah the son of Chenaanah had made horns of iron for himself; and he said, "Thus says the Lord: 'With these you shall gore the Syrians until they are destroyed.'" 12 And all the prophets prophesied so, saying, "Go up to Ramoth Gilead and prosper, for the Lord will deliver *it* into the king's hand."

13 Then the messenger who had gone to call Micaiah spoke to him, saying, "Now listen, the words of the prophets with one accord encourage the king. Please, let your word be like the word of one of them, and speak encouragement."

14 And Micaiah said, "*As* the Lord lives, whatever the Lord says to me, that I will speak."

15 Then he came to the king; and the king said to him, "Micaiah, shall we go to war against Ramoth Gilead, or shall we refrain?"

And he answered him, "Go and prosper, for the Lord will deliver *it* into the hand of the king!"

16 So the king said to him, "How many times shall I make you swear that you tell me nothing but the truth in the name of the Lord?"

17 Then he said, "I saw all Israel scattered on the mountains, as sheep that have no shepherd. And the Lord said, 'These have no master. Let each return to his house in peace.'"

18 And the king of Israel said to Jehoshaphat, "Did I not tell you he would not prophesy good concerning me, but evil?"

19 Then *Micaiah* said, "Therefore hear the word of the Lord: I saw the Lord sitting on His throne, and all the host of heaven standing by, on His right hand and on His left. 20 And the Lord said, 'Who will persuade Ahab to go up, that he may fall at Ramoth Gilead?' So one spoke in this manner, and another spoke in that manner. 21 Then a spirit came

Gospel Pearls

forward and stood before the LORD, and said, 'I will persuade him.' 22 The LORD said to him, 'In what way?' So he said, 'I will go out and be a lying spirit in the mouth of all his prophets.' And the LORD said, 'You shall persuade *him,* and also prevail. Go out and do so.' 23 Therefore look! The LORD has put a lying spirit in the mouth of all these prophets of yours, and the LORD has declared disaster against you."

24 Now Zedekiah the son of Chenaanah went near and struck Micaiah on the cheek, and said, "Which way did the spirit from the LORD go from me to speak to you?"

25 And Micaiah said, "Indeed, you shall see on that day when you go into an inner chamber to hide!"

26 So the king of Israel said, "Take Micaiah, and return him to Amon the governor of the city and to Joash the king's son; 27 and say, 'Thus says the king: "Put this *fellow* in prison, and feed him with bread of affliction and water of affliction, until I come in peace." ' "

28 But Micaiah said, "If you ever return in peace, the LORD has not spoken by me." And he said, "Take heed, all you people!"

29 So the king of Israel and Jehoshaphat the king of Judah went up to Ramoth Gilead. 30 And the king of Israel said to Jehoshaphat, "I will disguise myself and go into battle; but you put on your robes." So the king of Israel disguised himself and went into battle.

31 Now the king of Syria had commanded the thirty-two captains of his chariots, saying, "Fight with no one small or great, but only with the king of Israel." 32 So it was, when the captains of the chariots saw Jehoshaphat, that they said, "Surely it *is* the king of Israel!" Therefore they turned aside to fight against him, and Jehoshaphat cried out. 33 And it happened, when the captains of the chariots saw that it *was* not the king of Israel, that they turned back from pursuing him. 34 Now a *certain* man drew a bow at random, and struck the king of Israel between the joints of his armor. So he said to the driver of his chariot, "Turn around and take me out of the battle, for I am wounded."

35 The battle increased that day; and the king was propped up in his chariot, facing the Syrians, and died at evening. The blood ran out from the wound onto the floor of the chariot. 36 Then, as the sun was going down, a shout went throughout the army, saying, "Every man to his city, and every man to his own country!"

37 So the king died, and was brought to Samaria. And they buried the king in Samaria. 38 Then *someone* washed the chariot at a pool in Samaria, and the dogs licked up his blood while the harlots bathed,ᵃ according to the word of the LORD which He had spoken.

39 Now the rest of the acts of Ahab, and all that he did, the ivory house which he built and all the cities that he built, *are* they not written in the book of the chronicles of the kings of Israel? 40 So Ahab rested with his fathers. Then Ahaziah his son reigned in his place.

41 Jehoshaphat the son of Asa had become king over Judah in the fourth year of Ahab king of Israel. 42 Jehoshaphat *was* thirty-five years old when he became king, and he reigned twenty-five years in Jerusalem. His mother's name *was* Azubah the daughter of Shilhi. 43 And he walked in all the ways of his father Asa. He did not turn aside from them, doing *what was* right in the eyes of the LORD. Nevertheless the high places were not taken away, *for* the people offered sacrifices and burned incense on the high places. 44 Also Jehoshaphat made peace with the king of Israel.

45 Now the rest of the acts of Jehoshaphat, the might that he showed, and how he made war, *are* they not written in the book of the chronicles of the kings of Judah? 46 And the rest of the perverted persons,ᵃ who remained in the days of his father Asa, he banished from the land. 47 *There was* then no king in Edom, only a deputy of the king.

48 Jehoshaphat made merchant shipsᵃ to go to Ophir for gold; but they never sailed, for the ships were wrecked at Ezion Geber. 49 Then Ahaziah the son of Ahab said to Jehoshaphat, "Let my servants go with

22:38 ᵃSyriac and Targum read *they washed his armor.* 22:46 ᵃHebrew *qadesh,* that is, one practicing sodomy and prostitution in religious rituals 22:48 ᵃOr *ships of Tarshish*

*J*ust because you are not gifted like someone else doesn't mean that you are not gifted. God never made a worthless child. No two of us are meant to be alike.

your servants in the ships." But Jehoshaphat would not.

50 And Jehoshaphat rested with his fathers, and was buried with his fathers in the City of David his father. Then Jehoram his son reigned in his place.

51 Ahaziah the son of Ahab became king over Israel in Samaria in the seventeenth year of Jehoshaphat king of Judah, and reigned two years over Israel. 52 He did evil in the sight of the LORD, and walked in the way of his father and in the way of his mother and in the way of Jeroboam the son of Nebat, who had made Israel sin; 53 for he served Baal and worshiped him, and provoked the LORD God of Israel to anger, according to all that his father had done.

The Second Book of the

KINGS

1 Moab rebelled against Israel after the death of Ahab.

2 Now Ahaziah fell through the lattice of his upper room in Samaria, and was injured; so he sent messengers and said to them, "Go, inquire of Baal-Zebub, the god of Ekron, whether I shall recover from this injury." 3 But the angel*a* of the LORD said to Elijah the Tishbite, "Arise, go up to meet the messengers of the king of Samaria, and say to them, '*Is it* because *there is* no God in Israel *that* you are going to inquire of Baal-Zebub, the god of Ekron?' 4 Now therefore, thus says the LORD: 'You shall not come down from the bed to which you have gone up, but you shall surely die.'" So Elijah departed.

5 And when the messengers returned to him, he said to them, "Why have you come back?"

6 So they said to him, "A man came up to meet us, and said to us, 'Go, return to the king who sent you, and say to him, "Thus says the LORD: '*Is it* because *there is* no God in Israel *that* you are sending to inquire of Baal-Zebub, the god of Ekron? Therefore you shall not come down from the bed to which you have gone up, but you shall surely die.'"'"

7 Then he said to them, "What kind of man *was it* who came up to meet you and told you these words?"

8 So they answered him, "A hairy man wearing a leather belt around his waist."

And he said, "It *is* Elijah the Tishbite."

9 Then the king sent to him a captain of fifty with his fifty men. So he went up to him; and there he was, sitting on the top of a hill. And he spoke to him: "Man of God, the king has said, 'Come down!'"

10 So Elijah answered and said to the captain of fifty, "If I *am* a man of God, then let fire come down from heaven and consume you and your fifty men." And fire came down from heaven and consumed him and his fifty. 11 Then he sent to him another captain of fifty with his fifty men.

And he answered and said to him: "Man of God, thus has the king said, 'Come down quickly!'"

12 So Elijah answered and said to them, "If I *am* a man of God, let fire come down from heaven and consume you and your fifty men." And the fire of God came down from heaven and consumed him and his fifty.

13 Again, he sent a third captain of fifty with his fifty men. And the third captain of fifty went up, and came and fell on his knees before Elijah, and pleaded with him, and said to him: "Man of God, please let my life and the life of these fifty servants of yours be precious in your sight. 14 Look, fire has come down from heaven and burned up the first two captains of fifties with their fifties. But let my life now be precious in your sight."

1:3 *a*Or *Angel*

Gospel Pearls

15 And the angel[a] of the LORD said to Elijah, "Go down with him; do not be afraid of him." So he arose and went down with him to the king. 16 Then he said to him, "Thus says the LORD: 'Because you have sent messengers to inquire of Baal-Zebub, the god of Ekron, *is it* because *there is* no God in Israel to inquire of His word? Therefore you shall not come down from the bed to which you have gone up, but you shall surely die.' "

17 So *Ahaziah* died according to the word of the LORD which Elijah had spoken. Because he had no son, Jehoram[a] became king in his place, in the second year of Jehoram the son of Jehoshaphat, king of Judah. 18 Now the rest of the acts of Ahaziah which he did, *are* they not written in the book of the chronicles of the kings of Israel?

2 And it came to pass, when the LORD was about to take up Elijah into heaven by a whirlwind, that Elijah went with Elisha from Gilgal. 2 Then Elijah said to Elisha, "Stay here, please, for the LORD has sent me on to Bethel."

But Elisha said, "*As* the LORD lives, and *as* your soul lives, I will not leave you!" So they went down to Bethel.

3 Now the sons of the prophets who *were* at Bethel came out to Elisha, and said to him, "Do you know that the LORD will take away your master from over you today?"

And he said, "Yes, I know; keep silent!"

4 Then Elijah said to him, "Elisha, stay here, please, for the LORD has sent me on to Jericho."

But he said, "*As* the LORD lives, and *as* your soul lives, I will not leave you!" So they came to Jericho.

5 Now the sons of the prophets who *were* at Jericho came to Elisha and said to him, "Do you know that the LORD will take away your master from over you today?"

So he answered, "Yes, I know; keep silent!"

6 Then Elijah said to him, "Stay here, please, for the LORD has sent me on to the Jordan."

But he said, "*As* the LORD lives, and *as* your soul lives, I will not leave you!" So the two of them went on.

7 And fifty men of the sons of the prophets went and stood facing *them* at a distance, while the two of them stood by the Jordan. 8 Now Elijah took his mantle, rolled *it* up, and struck the water; and it was divided this way and that, so that the two of them crossed over on dry ground.

9 And so it was, when they had crossed over, that Elijah said to Elisha, "Ask! What may I do for you, before I am taken away from you?"

Elisha said, "Please let a double portion of your spirit be upon me."

10 So he said, "You have asked a hard thing. *Nevertheless,* if you see me *when I am* taken from you, it shall be so for you; but if not, it shall not be *so.*" 11 Then it happened, as they continued on and talked, that suddenly a chariot of fire *appeared* with horses of fire, and separated the two of them; and Elijah went up by a whirlwind into heaven.

12 And Elisha saw *it,* and he cried out, "My father, my father, the chariot of Israel and its horsemen!" So he saw him no more. And he took hold of his own clothes and tore them into two pieces. 13 He also took up the mantle of Elijah that had fallen from him, and went back and stood by the bank of the Jordan. 14 Then he took the mantle of Elijah that had fallen from him, and struck the water, and said, "Where *is* the LORD God of Elijah?" And when he also had struck the water, it was divided this way and that; and Elisha crossed over.

15 Now when the sons of the prophets who *were* from Jericho saw him, they said, "The spirit of Elijah rests on Elisha." And they came to meet him, and bowed to the ground before him. 16 Then they said to him, "Look now, there are fifty strong men with your servants. Please let them go and search for your master, lest perhaps the Spirit of the LORD has taken him up and cast him upon some mountain or into some valley."

And he said, "You shall not send anyone."

17 But when they urged him till he was ashamed, he said, "Send *them!*" Therefore they sent fifty men, and they searched for three days but did not find him. 18 And when they came back to him, for he had stayed in Jeri-

1:15 *a*Or *Angel*   1:17 *a*The son of Ahab king of Israel (compare 3:1)

*I*f you can remember tragic events from your past and not feel the pain they once caused, you have been healed. If you can see that person who wronged or hurt you and you don't feel bitterness, you have been healed.

cho, he said to them, "Did I not say to you, 'Do not go'?"

19 Then the men of the city said to Elisha, "Please notice, the situation of this city is pleasant, as my lord sees; but the water is bad, and the ground barren."

20 And he said, "Bring me a new bowl, and put salt in it." So they brought it to him. 21 Then he went out to the source of the water, and cast in the salt there, and said, "Thus says the LORD: 'I have healed this water; from it there shall be no more death or barrenness.' " 22 So the water remains healed to this day, according to the word of Elisha which he spoke.

23 Then he went up from there to Bethel; and as he was going up the road, some youths came from the city and mocked him, and said to him, "Go up, you baldhead! Go up, you baldhead!"

24 So he turned around and looked at them, and pronounced a curse on them in the name of the LORD. And two female bears came out of the woods and mauled forty-two of the youths.

25 Then he went from there to Mount Carmel, and from there he returned to Samaria.

3 Now Jehoram the son of Ahab became king over Israel at Samaria in the eighteenth year of Jehoshaphat king of Judah, and reigned twelve years. 2 And he did evil in the sight of the LORD, but not like his father and mother; for he put away the sacred pillar of Baal that his father had made. 3 Nevertheless he persisted in the sins of Jeroboam the son of Nebat, who had made Israel sin; he did not depart from them.

4 Now Mesha king of Moab was a sheepbreeder, and he regularly paid the king of Israel one hundred thousand lambs and the wool of one hundred thousand rams. 5 But it happened, when Ahab died, that the king of Moab rebelled against the king of Israel.

6 So King Jehoram went out of Samaria at that time and mustered all Israel. 7 Then he went and sent to Jehoshaphat king of Judah, saying, "The king of Moab has rebelled against me. Will you go with me to fight against Moab?"

And he said, "I will go up; I am as you are, my people as your people, my horses as your horses."

8 Then he said, "Which way shall we go up?"

And he answered, "By way of the Wilderness of Edom."

9 So the king of Israel went with the king of Judah and the king of Edom, and they marched on that roundabout route seven days; and there was no water for the army, nor for the animals that followed them. 10 And the king of Israel said, "Alas! For the LORD has called these three kings together to deliver them into the hand of Moab."

11 But Jehoshaphat said, "Is there no prophet of the LORD here, that we may inquire of the LORD by him?"

So one of the servants of the king of Israel answered and said, "Elisha the son of Shaphat is here, who poured water on the hands of Elijah."

12 And Jehoshaphat said, "The word of the LORD is with him." So the king of Israel and Jehoshaphat and the king of Edom went down to him.

13 Then Elisha said to the king of Israel, "What have I to do with you? Go to the prophets of your father and the prophets of your mother."

But the king of Israel said to him, "No, for the LORD has called these three kings together to deliver them into the hand of Moab."

14 And Elisha said, "As the LORD of hosts lives, before whom I stand, surely were it not that I regard the presence of Jehoshaphat king of Judah, I would not look at you, nor see you. 15 But now bring me a musician."

Then it happened, when the musician played, that the hand of the LORD came upon him. 16 And he said, "Thus says the LORD: 'Make this valley full of ditches.' 17 For thus says the LORD: 'You shall not see wind, nor shall you see rain; yet that valley shall be filled with water, so that you, your cattle, and your animals may drink.' 18 And this is a simple matter in the sight of the LORD; He will also deliver the Moabites into your hand. 19 Also you shall attack every fortified city and every choice city, and shall cut down every good tree, and stop up every spring of water, and ruin every good piece of land with stones."

20 Now it happened in the morning,

Gospel
Pearls

when the grain offering was offered, that suddenly water came by way of Edom, and the land was filled with water.

21 And when all the Moabites heard that the kings had come up to fight against them, all who were able to bear arms and older were gathered; and they stood at the border. 22 Then they rose up early in the morning, and the sun was shining on the water; and the Moabites saw the water on the other side *as* red as blood. 23 And they said, "This is blood; the kings have surely struck swords and have killed one another; now therefore, Moab, to the spoil!"

24 So when they came to the camp of Israel, Israel rose up and attacked the Moabites, so that they fled before them; and they entered *their* land, killing the Moabites. 25 Then they destroyed the cities, and each man threw a stone on every good piece of land and filled it; and they stopped up all the springs of water and cut down all the good trees. But they left the stones of Kir Haraseth *intact.* However the slingers surrounded and attacked it.

26 And when the king of Moab saw that the battle was too fierce for him, he took with him seven hundred men who drew swords, to break through to the king of Edom, but they could not. 27 Then he took his eldest son who would have reigned in his place, and offered him *as* a burnt offering upon the wall; and there was great indignation against Israel. So they departed from him and returned to *their own* land.

4 A certain woman of the wives of the sons of the prophets cried out to Elisha, saying, "Your servant my husband is dead, and you know that your servant feared the LORD. And the creditor is coming to take my two sons to be his slaves."

2 So Elisha said to her, "What shall I do for you? Tell me, what do you have in the house?" And she said, "Your maidservant has nothing in the house but a jar of oil."

3 Then he said, "Go, borrow vessels from everywhere, from all your neighbors—empty vessels; do not gather just a few. 4 And when you have come in, you shall shut the door behind you and your sons; then pour

it into all those vessels, and set aside the full ones."

5 So she went from him and shut the door behind her and her sons, who brought *the vessels* to her; and she poured *it* out. 6 Now it came to pass, when the vessels were full, that she said to her son, "Bring me another vessel."

And he said to her, "*There is* not another vessel." So the oil ceased. 7 Then she came and told the man of God. And he said, "Go, sell the oil and pay your debt; and you *and* your sons live on the rest."

8 Now it happened one day that Elisha went to Shunem, where there *was* a notable woman, and she persuaded him to eat some food. So it was, as often as he passed by, he would turn in there to eat some food. 9 And she said to her husband, "Look now, I know that this *is* a holy man of God, who passes by us regularly. 10 Please, let us make a small upper room on the wall; and let us put a bed for him there, and a table and a chair and a lampstand; so it will be, whenever he comes to us, he can turn in there."

11 And it happened one day that he came there, and he turned in to the upper room and lay down there. 12 Then he said to Gehazi his servant, "Call this Shunammite woman." When he had called her, she stood before him. 13 And he said to him, "Say now to her, 'Look, you have been concerned for us with all this care. What *can I* do for you? Do you want me to speak on your behalf to the king or to the commander of the army?' "

She answered, "I dwell among my own people."

14 So he said, "What then *is* to be done for her?"

And Gehazi answered, "Actually, she has no son, and her husband is old."

15 So he said, "Call her." When he had called her, she stood in the doorway. 16 Then he said, "About this time next year you shall embrace a son."

And she said, "No, my lord. Man of God, do not lie to your maidservant!"

17 But the woman conceived, and bore a son when the appointed time had come, of which Elisha had told her.

*D*on't confuse the outer symptoms with the inner work. The fact that you have a limp does not mean you haven't been healed. The symptoms, the memories, or even the scars do not define you. What God has done in your innermost being is what defines you.

The Wonder of a Mother

2 Kings 4:8-37

O ur families need to be healed and restored. That can start with a godly woman. What is more touching than to see a mother cradling a child? What a wonderfully natural thing it is to see women of all races and religions loving their children. The African woman holding her baby has the same sparkle in her eyes as her Chinese sister. From Hawaii to London, Russia to Italy, there are certain feelings that transcend culture. A mother's love is the love from which truth is spawned. We are all very much alike when it comes to the essentials of life. We need, we love, we touch, we give! When God allows us to parent, He desires us to love.

There is something unique about a woman's natural ability to nurture. In the case of the Shunammite woman whose son fell into his father's arms with a violent headache, it was his mother who refused to accept his impending death. She saddled a donkey and rode to the man of God, demanding that he raise up the now-dead child. She knew the child was dead; she just refused to accept it. She was so convinced he would live that she would not bury him.

This woman is no different from Rizpah, a courageous mother in 2 Samuel 21:8-11, or from Mary and the other women who ran to the tomb expecting to find Jesus' dead body, while the disciples were shut up in a room for fear of the Jews.

When a woman is pregnant, she shares her food and oxygen with a baby she has never seen, much less known. Her warm hands stroke her bulging abdomen as she reaches out to a baby who cannot see her, but shares a bond that exists before birth. Her mineral and protein supplies begin to serve two guests at one table. Her cord carries life to a child whose every need is dependent upon her for fulfillment. Her tender breasts collect milk as they become the place where the baby will be nourished. He need not depart from her; his needs can all be met in her arms.

Men could not create a machine as multifaceted as a mother. What else can feed, clothe, touch, provide intimacy and affection and training? All these needs are met for the child without ever leaving one spot. This is the place of provision. It is the place of excellence.

18 And the child grew. Now it happened one day that he went out to his father, to the reapers. 19 And he said to his father, "My head, my head!"

So he said to a servant, "Carry him to his mother." 20 When he had taken him and brought him to his mother, he sat on her knees till noon, and *then* died. 21 And she went up and laid him on the bed of the man of God, shut *the door* upon him, and went out. 22 Then she called to her husband, and said, "Please send me one of the young men and one of the donkeys, that I may run to the man of God and come back."

23 So he said, "Why are you going to him today? *It is* neither the New Moon nor the Sabbath."

And she said, "*It is* well." 24 Then she saddled a donkey, and said to her servant, "Drive, and go forward; do not slacken the pace for me unless I tell you." 25 And so she departed, and went to the man of God at Mount Carmel.

So it was, when the man of God saw her afar off, that he said to his servant Gehazi, "Look, the Shunammite woman! 26 Please run now to meet her, and say to her, '*Is it* well with you? *Is it* well with your husband? *Is it* well with the child?' "

And she answered, "*It is* well." 27 Now when she came to the man of God at the hill, she caught him by the feet, but Gehazi came near to push her away. But the man of God said, "Let her alone; for her soul *is* in deep distress, and the LORD has hidden *it* from me, and has not told me."

28 So she said, "Did I ask a son of my lord? Did I not say, 'Do not deceive me'?"

29 Then he said to Gehazi, "Get yourself ready, and take my staff in your hand, and be on your way. If you meet anyone, do not greet him; and if anyone greets you, do not answer him; but lay my staff on the face of the child."

30 And the mother of the child said, "*As* the LORD lives, and *as* your soul lives, I will not leave you." So he arose and followed her. 31 Now Gehazi went on ahead of them, and laid the staff on the face of the child; but *there was* neither voice nor hearing. Therefore he went back to meet him, and told him, saying, "The child has not awakened."

32 When Elisha came into the house, there was the child, lying dead on his bed. 33 He went in therefore, shut the door behind the two of them, and prayed to the LORD. 34 And he went up and lay on the child, and put his mouth on his mouth, his eyes on his eyes, and his hands on his hands; and he stretched himself out on the child, and the flesh of the child became warm. 35 He returned and walked back and forth in the house, and again went up and stretched himself out on him; then the child sneezed seven times, and the child opened his eyes. 36 And he called Gehazi and said, "Call this Shunammite woman." So he called her. And when she came in to him, he said, "Pick up your son." 37 So she went in, fell at his feet, and bowed to the ground; then she picked up her son and went out.

38 And Elisha returned to Gilgal, and *there was* a famine in the land. Now the sons of the prophets *were* sitting before him; and he said to his servant, "Put on the large pot, and boil stew for the sons of the prophets." 39 So one went out into the field to gather herbs, and found a wild vine, and gathered from it a lapful of wild gourds, and came and sliced *them* into the pot of stew, though they did not know *what they were.* 40 Then they served it to the men to eat. Now it happened, as they were eating the stew, that they cried out and said, "Man of God, *there is* death in the pot!" And they could not eat *it.*

41 So he said, "Then bring some flour." And he put *it* into the pot, and said, "Serve *it* to the people, that they may eat." And there was nothing harmful in the pot.

42 Then a man came from Baal Shalisha, and brought the man of God bread of the firstfruits, twenty loaves of barley bread, and newly ripened grain in his knapsack. And he said, "Give *it* to the people, that they may eat."

43 But his servant said, "What? Shall I set this before one hundred men?"

He said again, "Give it to the people, that they may eat; for thus says the LORD: 'They shall eat and have *some* left over.' " 44 So he set *it* before them; and they ate and had *some* left over, according to the word of the LORD.

5 Now Naaman, commander of the army of the king of Syria, was a great and honorable man in the eyes of his master, because by him the LORD had given victory to Syria. He was also a mighty man of valor, *but* a leper. 2 And the Syrians had gone out on raids, and had brought back captive a young girl from the land of Israel. She waited on Naaman's wife. 3 Then she said to her mistress, "If only my master *were* with the prophet who *is* in Samaria! For he would heal him of his leprosy." 4 And *Naaman* went in and told his master, saying, "Thus and thus said the girl who *is* from the land of Israel."

5 Then the king of Syria said, "Go now, and I will send a letter to the king of Israel."

So he departed and took with him ten talents of silver, six thousand *shekels* of gold, and ten changes of clothing. 6 Then he brought the letter to the king of Israel, which said,

Now be advised, when this letter comes to you, that I have sent Naaman my servant to you, that you may heal him of his leprosy.

7 And it happened, when the king of Israel read the letter, that he tore his clothes and said, "*Am* I God, to kill and make alive, that this man sends a man to me to heal him of his leprosy? Therefore please consider, and see how he seeks a quarrel with me."

8 So it was, when Elisha the man of God heard that the king of Israel had torn his clothes, that he sent to the king, saying, "Why have you torn your clothes? Please let him come to me, and he shall know that there is a prophet in Israel."

9 Then Naaman went with his horses and chariot, and he stood at the door of Elisha's house. 10 And Elisha sent a messenger to him, saying, "Go and wash in the Jordan seven times, and your flesh shall be restored to you, and *you shall* be clean." 11 But Naaman became furious, and went away and said, "In-

deed, I said to myself, 'He will surely come out *to me,* and stand and call on the name of the LORD his God, and wave his hand over the place, and heal the leprosy.' 12 *Are* not the Abanah*ᵃ* and the Pharpar, the rivers of Damascus, better than all the waters of Israel? Could I not wash in them and be clean?" So he turned and went away in a rage. 13 And his servants came near and spoke to him, and said, "My father, *if* the prophet had told you *to do* something great, would you not have done *it?* How much more then, when he says to you, 'Wash, and be clean'?" 14 So he went down and dipped seven times in the Jordan, according to the saying of the man of God; and his flesh was restored like the flesh of a little child, and he was clean.

15 And he returned to the man of God, he and all his aides, and came and stood before him; and he said, "Indeed, now I know that *there is* no God in all the earth, except in Israel; now therefore, please take a gift from your servant."

16 But he said, "*As* the LORD lives, before whom I stand, I will receive nothing." And he urged him to take *it,* but he refused.

17 So Naaman said, "Then, if not, please let your servant be given two mule-loads of earth; for your servant will no longer offer either burnt offering or sacrifice to other gods, but to the LORD. 18 Yet in this thing may the LORD pardon your servant: when my master goes into the temple of Rimmon to worship there, and he leans on my hand, and I bow down in the temple of Rimmon—when I bow down in the temple of Rimmon, may the LORD please pardon your servant in this thing."

19 Then he said to him, "Go in peace." So he departed from him a short distance.

20 But Gehazi, the servant of Elisha the man of God, said, "Look, my master has spared Naaman this Syrian, while not receiving from his hands what he brought; but *as* the LORD lives, I will run after him and take something from him." 21 So Gehazi pursued Naaman. When Naaman saw *him* running after him, he got down from the chariot to meet him, and said, "*Is* all well?"

5:12 ᵃFollowing Kethib, Septuagint, and Vulgate; Qere, Syriac, and Targum read *Amanah.*

Gospel
Pearls

22 And he said, "All *is* well. My master has sent me, saying, 'Indeed, just now two young men of the sons of the prophets have come to me from the mountains of Ephraim. Please give them a talent of silver and two changes of garments.'"

23 So Naaman said, "Please, take two talents." And he urged him, and bound two talents of silver in two bags, with two changes of garments, and handed *them* to two of his servants; and they carried *them* on ahead of him. 24 When he came to the citadel, he took *them* from their hand, and stored *them* away in the house; then he let the men go, and they departed. 25 Now he went in and stood before his master. Elisha said to him, "Where *did you go,* Gehazi?" And he said, "Your servant did not go anywhere."

26 Then he said to him, "Did not my heart go *with you* when the man turned back from his chariot to meet you? *Is it* time to receive money and to receive clothing, olive groves and vineyards, sheep and oxen, male and female servants? 27 Therefore the leprosy of Naaman shall cling to you and your descendants forever." And he went out from his presence leprous, *as white* as snow.

6 And the sons of the prophets said to Elisha, "See now, the place where we dwell with you is too small for us. 2 Please, let us go to the Jordan, and let every man take a beam from there, and let us make there a place where we may dwell."

So he answered, "Go."

3 Then one said, "Please consent to go with your servants."

And he answered, "I will go." 4 So he went with them. And when they came to the Jordan, they cut down trees. 5 But as one was cutting down a tree, the iron *ax head* fell into the water; and he cried out and said, "Alas, master! For it was borrowed."

6 So the man of God said, "Where did it fall?" And he showed him the place. So he cut off a stick, and threw *it* in there; and he made the iron float. 7 Therefore he said, "Pick *it* up for yourself." So he reached out his hand and took it.

8 Now the king of Syria was making war against Israel; and he consulted with his servants, saying, "My camp *will be* in such and such a place." 9 And the man of God sent to the king of Israel, saying, "Beware that you do not pass this place, for the Syrians are coming down there." 10 Then the king of Israel sent *someone* to the place of which the man of God had told him. Thus he warned him, and he was watchful there, not just once or twice.

11 Therefore the heart of the king of Syria was greatly troubled by this thing; and he called his servants and said to them, "Will you not show me which of us *is* for the king of Israel?"

12 And one of his servants said, "None, my lord, O king; but Elisha, the prophet who *is* in Israel, tells the king of Israel the words that you speak in your bedroom."

13 So he said, "Go and see where he *is,* that I may send and get him." And it was told him, saying, "Surely *he is* in Dothan."

14 Therefore he sent horses and chariots and a great army there, and they came by night and surrounded the city. 15 And when the servant of the man of God arose early and went out, there was an army, surrounding the city with horses and chariots. And his servant said to him, "Alas, my master! What shall we do?"

16 So he answered, "Do not fear, for those who *are* with us *are* more than those who *are* with them." 17 And Elisha prayed, and said, "LORD, I pray, open his eyes that he may see." Then the LORD opened the eyes of the young man, and he saw. And behold, the mountain *was* full of horses and chariots of fire all around Elisha. 18 So when *the Syrians* came down to him, Elisha prayed to the LORD, and said, "Strike this people, I pray, with blindness." And He struck them with blindness according to the word of Elisha.

19 Now Elisha said to them, "This *is* not the way, nor *is* this the city. Follow me, and I will bring you to the man whom you seek." But he led them to Samaria.

20 So it was, when they had come to Samaria, that Elisha said, "LORD, open the eyes of these *men,* that they may see." And the LORD opened their eyes, and they saw; and there *they were,* inside Samaria!

21 Now when the king of Israel saw them, he said to Elisha, "My father, shall I kill *them?* Shall I kill *them?*" 22 But he answered, "You shall not

The greater fact is this: It isn't what people say about you or to you that's going to matter in the long run, it's what you say about yourself to yourself.

kill *them*. Would you kill those whom you have taken captive with your sword and your bow? Set food and water before them, that they may eat and drink and go to their master." 23 Then he prepared a great feast for them; and after they ate and drank, he sent them away and they went to their master. So the bands of Syrian *raiders* came no more into the land of Israel.

24 And it happened after this that Ben-Hadad king of Syria gathered all his army, and went up and besieged Samaria. 25 And there was a great famine in Samaria; and indeed they besieged it until a donkey's head was *sold* for eighty *shekels* of silver, and one-fourth of a kab of dove droppings for five *shekels* of silver.

26 Then, as the king of Israel was passing by on the wall, a woman cried out to him, saying, "Help, my lord, O king!"

27 And he said, "If the LORD does not help you, where can I find help for you? From the threshing floor or from the winepress?" 28 Then the king said to her, "What is troubling you?"

And she answered, "This woman said to me, 'Give your son, that we may eat him today, and we will eat my son tomorrow.' 29 So we boiled my son, and ate him. And I said to her on the next day, 'Give your son, that we may eat him'; but she has hidden her son."

30 Now it happened, when the king heard the words of the woman, that he tore his clothes; and as he passed by on the wall, the people looked, and there underneath *he had* sackcloth on his body. 31 Then he said, "God do so to me and more also, if the head of Elisha the son of Shaphat remains on him today!"

32 But Elisha was sitting in his house, and the elders were sitting with him. And *the king* sent a man ahead of him, but before the messenger came to him, he said to the elders, "Do you see how this son of a murderer has sent someone to take away my head? Look, when the messenger comes, shut the door, and hold him fast at the door. *Is* not the sound of his master's feet behind him?" 33 And while he was still talking with them, there was the messenger, coming down to him; and then *the king* said, "Surely this calamity *is* from

the LORD; why should I wait for the LORD any longer?"

7 Then Elisha said, "Hear the word of the LORD. Thus says the LORD: 'Tomorrow about this time a seah of fine flour *shall be sold* for a shekel, and two seahs of barley for a shekel, at the gate of Samaria.' "

2 So an officer on whose hand the king leaned answered the man of God and said, "Look, *if* the LORD would make windows in heaven, could this thing be?"

And he said, "In fact, you shall see *it* with your eyes, but you shall not eat of it."

3 Now there were four leprous men at the entrance of the gate; and they said to one another, "Why are we sitting here until we die? 4 If we say, 'We will enter the city,' the famine *is* in the city, and we shall die there. And if we sit here, we die also. Now therefore, come, let us surrender to the army of the Syrians. If they keep us alive, we shall live; and if they kill us, we shall only die." 5 And they rose at twilight to go to the camp of the Syrians; and when they had come to the outskirts of the Syrian camp, to their surprise no one *was* there. 6 For the LORD had caused the army of the Syrians to hear the noise of chariots and the noise of horses—the noise of a great army; so they said to one another, "Look, the king of Israel has hired against us the kings of the Hittites and the kings of the Egyptians to attack us!" 7 Therefore they arose and fled at twilight, and left the camp intact—their tents, their horses, and their donkeys—and they fled for their lives. 8 And when these lepers came to the outskirts of the camp, they went into one tent and ate and drank, and carried from it silver and gold and clothing, and went and hid *them;* then they came back and entered another tent, and carried *some* from there *also,* and went and hid *it.*

9 Then they said to one another, "We are not doing right. This day *is* a day of good news, and we remain silent. If we wait until morning light, some punishment will come upon us. Now therefore, come, let us go and tell the king's household." 10 So they went and called to the gatekeepers of the city, and told them, saying,

Gospel Pearls

"We went to the Syrian camp, and surprisingly no one *was* there, not a human sound—only horses and donkeys tied, and the tents intact." 11 And the gatekeeperscalled out, and they told *it* to the king's household inside.

12 So the king arose in the night and said to his servants, "Let me now tell you what the Syrians have done to us. They know that we *are* hungry; therefore they have gone out of the camp to hide themselves in the field, saying, 'When they come out of the city, we shall catch them alive, and get into the city.' "

13 And one of his servants answered and said, "Please, let several *men* take five of the remaining horses which are left in the city. Look, they *may either become* like all the multitude of Israel that are left in it; or indeed, *I say*, they *may become* like all the multitude of Israel left from those who are consumed; so let us send them and see." 14 Therefore they took two chariots with horses; and the king sent them in the direction of the Syrian army, saying, "Go and see." 15 And they went after them to the Jordan; and indeed all the road *was* full of garments and weapons which the Syrians had thrown away in their haste. So the messengers returned and told the king. 16 Then the people went out and plundered the tents of the Syrians. So a seah of fine flour was *sold* for a shekel, and two seahs of barley for a shekel, according to the word of the LORD.

17 Now the king had appointed the officer on whose hand he leaned to have charge of the gate. But the people trampled him in the gate, and he died, just as the man of God had said, who spoke when the king came down to him. 18 So it happened just as the man of God had spoken to the king, saying, "Two seahs of barley for a shekel, and a seah of fine flour for a shekel, shall be *sold* tomorrow about this time in the gate of Samaria."

19 Then that officer had answered the man of God, and said, "Now look, *if* the LORD would make windows in heaven, could such a thing be?"

And he had said, "In fact, you shall see *it* with your eyes, but you shall not eat of it." 20 And so it happened to him, for the people trampled him in the gate, and he died.

8 Then Elisha spoke to the woman whose son he had restored to life, saying, "Arise and go, you and your household, and stay wherever you can; for the LORD has called for a famine, and furthermore, it will come upon the land for seven years." 2 So the woman arose and did according to the saying of the man of God, and she went with her household and dwelt in the land of the Philistines seven years.

3 It came to pass, at the end of seven years, that the woman returned from the land of the Philistines; and she went to make an appealto the king for her house and for her land. 4 Then the king talked with Gehazi, the servant of theman of God, saying, "Tell me, please, all the great things Elisha has done." 5 Now it happened, as he was telling the king how he had restored the dead to life, that there was the woman whose son he had restored to life, appealing to the king for her house and for her land. And Gehazi said, "My lord, O king, this *is* the woman, and this *is* her son whom Elisha restored to life." 6 And when the king asked the woman, she told him.

So the king appointed a certain officer for her, saying, "Restore all that *was* hers, and all the proceeds of the field from the day that she left the land until now."

7 Then Elisha went to Damascus, and Ben-Hadad king of Syria was sick; and it was told him, saying, "The man of God has come here." 8 And the king said to Hazael, "Take a present in your hand, and go to meet the man of God, and inquire of the LORD by him, saying, 'Shall I recover from this disease?' " 9 So Hazael went to meet him and took a present with him, of every good thing of Damascus, forty camel-loads; and he came and stood before him, and said, "Your son Ben-Hadad king of Syria has sent me to you, saying, 'Shall I recover from this disease?' "

10 And Elisha said to him, "Go, say to him, 'You shall certainly recover.' However the LORD has shown me that he will really die." 11 Then he set his countenance in a stare until he was ashamed; and the man of God wept. 12 And Hazael said, "Why is my lord weeping?"

He answered, "Because I know the evil that you will do to the children

---

Restored

2 Kings 8:3-6

While I was in school, I worked at a local paint store. Part of my job was to acquaint myself with the products and procedures. I was intrigued by a refinishing product that restored old furniture to its former luster. So I purchased the product to see if it was as effective as I had been told. I learned right away that the most difficult part of restoring furniture is stripping off the old wax. It takes patience to overcome the effects of years of use and abuse.

If you are not committed to getting back what you once had, you could easily decide that the process is impossible. Nevertheless, I assure you that it is not impossible. David, the psalmist, declares, "He restores my soul" (Psalm 23:3). The term *restores* indicates process. Only God knows what it takes to remove the build-up that may exist in your life. But He specializes in restoring and renewing the human heart.

In the first chapter of Ruth, Naomi almost changed her name to "Mara." She felt that God had dealt bitterly with her. Before it was over, however, everyone agreed that the hand of the Lord was upon her.

You may be challenged by the silent struggles of winter. There are two things that every Naomi can rely upon as she gathers wood for winter days: First, God is a restorer. That is to say, as you sit by the fire sipping coffee, rehearsing your own thoughts, playing old reruns from the scenes in your life—some things He will explain and others He will heal. Restoration doesn't mean that all the lost people who left you will return. It is just that God gives purpose to the years of question marks.

Second, God is a nourisher. This may be a difficult role for you who have clutched babies and husband alike to the warm breast of your sensitivity. You, who have been the source of others' strength, may not welcome this role reversal. But the nourisher must learn to be nourished. El Shaddai, "the Breasted One," gives strength to the feeble and warmth to the cold. There is great comfort in His embrace. Like children, even adults can snuggle into His everlasting arms and hear the heartbeat of a loving God who says, "And you shall eat in plenty and be satisfied, and praise the name of the LORD your God" (Joel 2:26).

Expect God in all His varied forms. He is a master of disguise, a guiding star in the night, a lily left growing in the valley, an answered prayer sent on the breath of an angel.

My sister, set your cup down, take the blanket off your lap, and stand to your feet! Have you not known, have you not heard? For every woman facing winter, there is new life in your old age!

of Israel: Their strongholds you will set on fire, and their young men you will kill with the sword; and you will dash their children, and rip open their women with child."

13 So Hazael said, "But what *is* your servant—a dog, that he should do this gross thing?"

And Elisha answered, "The LORD has shown me that you *will become* king over Syria."

14 Then he departed from Elisha, and came to his master, who said to him, "What did Elisha say to you?" And he answered, "He told me you would surely recover." 15 But it happened on the next day that he took a thick cloth and dipped *it* in water, and spread *it* over his face so that he died; and Hazael reigned in his place.

16 Now in the fifth year of Joram the son of Ahab, king of Israel, Jehoshaphat *having been* king of Judah, Jehoram the son of Jehoshaphat began to reign as king of Judah. 17 He was thirty-two years old when he became king, and he reigned eight years in Jerusalem. 18 And he walked in the way of the kings of Israel, just as the house of Ahab had done, for the daughter of Ahab was his wife; and he did evil in the sight of the LORD. 19 Yet the LORD would not destroy Judah, for the sake of his servant David, as He promised him to give a lamp to him *and* his sons forever.

20 In his days Edom revolted against Judah's authority, and made a king over themselves. 21 So Joram[a] went to Zair, and all his chariots with him. Then he rose by night and attacked the Edomites who had surrounded him and the captains of the chariots; and the troops fled to their tents. 22 Thus Edom has been in revolt against Judah's authority to this day. And Libnah revolted at that time.

23 Now the rest of the acts of Joram, and all that he did, *are* they not written in the book of the chronicles of the kings of Judah? 24 So Joram rested with his fathers, and was buried with his fathers in the City of David. Then Ahaziah his son reigned in his place.

25 In the twelfth year of Joram the son of Ahab, king of Israel, Ahaziah the son of Jehoram, king of Judah, began to reign. 26 Ahaziah *was* twenty-two years old when he became king, and he reigned one year in Jerusalem. His mother's name *was* Athaliah the granddaughter of Omri, king of Israel. 27 And he walked in the way of the house of Ahab, and did evil in the sight of the LORD, like the house of Ahab, for he *was* the son-in-law of the house of Ahab.

28 Now he went with Joram the son of Ahab to war against Hazael king of Syria at Ramoth Gilead; and the Syrians wounded Joram. 29 Then King Joram went back to Jezreel to recover from the wounds which the Syrians had inflicted on him at Ramah, when he fought against Hazael king of Syria. And Ahaziah the son of Jehoram, king of Judah, went down to see Joram the son of Ahab in Jezreel, because he was sick.

9 And Elisha the prophet called one of the sons of the prophets, and said to him, "Get yourself ready, take this flask of oil in your hand, and go to Ramoth Gilead. 2 Now when you arrive at that place, look there for Jehu the son of Jehoshaphat, the son of Nimshi, and go in and make him rise up from among his associates, and take him to an inner room. 3 Then take the flask of oil, and pour *it* on his head, and say, 'Thus says the LORD: "I have anointed you king over Israel." ' Then open the door and flee, and do not delay."

4 So the young man, the servant of the prophet, went to Ramoth Gilead. 5 And when he arrived, there *were* the captains of the army sitting; and he said, "I have a message for you, Commander."

Jehu said, "For which *one* of us?"

And he said, "For you, Commander." 6 Then he arose and went into the house. And he poured the oil on his head, and said to him, "Thus says the LORD God of Israel: 'I have anointed you king over the people of the LORD, over Israel. 7 You shall strike down the house of Ahab your master, that I may avenge the blood of My servants the prophets, and the blood of all the servants of the LORD, at the hand of Jezebel. 8 For the whole house of Ahab shall perish; and I will cut off from Ahab all the

8:21 *a*Spelled *Jehoram* in verse 16

males in Israel, both bond and free. 9 So I will make the house of Ahab like the house of Jeroboam the son of Nebat, and like the house of Baasha the son of Ahijah. 10 The dogs shall eat Jezebel on the plot *of ground* at Jezreel, and *there shall be* none to bury *her.*' " And he opened the door and fled.

11 Then Jehu came out to the servants of his master, and *one* said to him, "*Is* all well? Why did this madman come to you?"

And he said to them, "You know the man and his babble."

12 And they said, "A lie! Tell us now."

So he said, "Thus and thus he spoke to me, saying, 'Thus says the LORD: "I have anointed you king over Israel." ' "

13 Then each man hastened to take his garment and put *it* under him on the top of the steps; and they blew trumpets, saying, "Jehu is king!"

14 So Jehu the son of Jehoshaphat, the son of Nimshi, conspired against Joram. (Now Joram had been defending Ramoth Gilead, he and all Israel, against Hazael king of Syria. 15 But King Joram had returned to Jezreel to recover from the wounds which the Syrians had inflicted on him when he fought with Hazael king of Syria.) And Jehu said, "If you are so minded, let no one leave *or* escape from the city to go and tell *it* in Jezreel." 16 So Jehu rode in a chariot and went to Jezreel, for Joram was laid up there; and Ahaziah king of Judah had come down to see Joram.

17 Now a watchman stood on the tower in Jezreel, and he saw the company of Jehu as he came, and said, "I see a company of men."

And Joram said, "Get a horseman and send him to meet them, and let him say, '*Is* it peace?' "

18 So the horseman went to meet him, and said, "Thus says the king: '*Is* it peace?' "

And Jehu said, "What have you to do with peace? Turn around and follow me."

So the watchman reported, saying, "The messenger went to them, but is not coming back."

19 Then he sent out a second horseman who came to them, and said, "Thus says the king: '*Is* it peace?' "

And Jehu answered, "What have you to do with peace? Turn around and follow me."

20 So the watchman reported, saying, "He went up to them and is not coming back; and the driving *is* like the driving of Jehu the son of Nimshi, for he drives furiously!"

21 Then Joram said, "Make ready." And his chariot was made ready. Then Joram king of Israel and Ahaziah king of Judah went out, each in his chariot; and they went out to meet Jehu, and met him on the property of Naboth the Jezreelite. 22 Now it happened, when Joram saw Jehu, that he said, "*Is it* peace, Jehu?"

So he answered, "What peace, as long as the harlotries of your mother Jezebel and her witchcraft *are so* many?"

23 Then Joram turned around and fled, and said to Ahaziah, "Treachery, Ahaziah!" 24 Now Jehu drew his bow with full strength and shot Jehoram between his arms; and the arrow came out at his heart, and he sank down in his chariot. 25 Then *Jehu* said to Bidkar his captain, "Pick *him* up, *and* throw him into the tract of the field of Naboth the Jezreelite; for remember, when you and I were riding together behind Ahab his father, that the LORD laid this burden upon him: 26 'Surely I saw yesterday the blood of Naboth and the blood of his sons,' says the LORD, 'and I will repay you in this plot,' says the LORD. Now therefore, take *and* throw him on the plot *of ground,* according to the word of the LORD."

27 But when Ahaziah king of Judah saw *this,* he fled by the road to Beth Haggan.[a] So Jehu pursued him, and said, "Shoot him also in the chariot." *And they shot him* at the Ascent of Gur, which is by Ibleam. Then he fled to Megiddo, and died there. 28 And his servants carried him in the chariot to Jerusalem, and buried him in his tomb with his fathers in the City of David. 29 In the eleventh year of Joram the son of Ahab, Ahaziah had become king over Judah.

30 Now when Jehu had come to Jezreel, Jezebel heard *of it;* and she put paint on her eyes and adorned her head, and looked through a window. 31 Then, as Jehu entered at the

9:27 ªLiterally *The Garden House*

Gospel Pearls

gate, she said, "Is it peace, Zimri, murderer of your master?"

32 And he looked up at the window, and said, "Who is on my side? Who?" So two or three eunuchs looked out at him. 33 Then he said, "Throw her down." So they threw her down, and some of her blood spattered on the wall and on the horses; and he trampled her underfoot. 34 And when he had gone in, he ate and drank. Then he said, "Go now, see to this accursed woman, and bury her, for she was a king's daughter." 35 So they went to bury her, but they found no more of her than the skull and the feet and the palms of her hands. 36 Therefore they came back and told him. And he said, "This is the word of the LORD, which He spoke by His servant Elijah the Tishbite, saying, 'On the plot of ground at Jezreel dogs shall eat the flesh of Jezebel;ᵃ 37 and the corpse of Jezebel shall be as refuse on the surface of the field, in the plot at Jezreel, so that they shall not say, "Here lies Jezebel." ' "

10 Now Ahab had seventy sons in Samaria. And Jehu wrote and sent letters to Samaria, to the rulers of Jezreel,ᵃ to the elders, and to those who reared Ahab's sons, saying:

2 Now as soon as this letter comes to you, since your master's sons are with you, and you have chariots and horses, a fortified city also, and weapons, 3 choose the best qualified of your master's sons, set him on his father's throne, and fight for your master's house.

4 But they were exceedingly afraid, and said, "Look, two kings could not stand up to him; how then can we stand?" 5 And he who was in charge of the house, and he who was in charge of the city, the elders also, and those who reared the sons, sent to Jehu, saying, "We are your servants, we will do all you tell us; but we will not make anyone king. Do what is good in your sight." 6 Then he wrote a second letter to them, saying:

If you are for me and will obey my voice, take the heads of the men, your master's sons, and come to me at Jezreel by this time tomorrow.

Now the king's sons, seventy persons, were with the great men of the city, who were rearing them. 7 So it was, when the letter came to them, that they took the king's sons and slaughtered seventy persons, put their heads in baskets and sent them to him at Jezreel.

8 Then a messenger came and told him, saying, "They have brought the heads of the king's sons."

And he said, "Lay them in two heaps at the entrance of the gate until morning."

9 So it was, in the morning, that he went out and stood, and said to all the people, "You are righteous. Indeed I conspired against my master and killed him; but who killed all these? 10 Know now that nothing shall fall to the earth of the word of the LORD which the LORD spoke concerning the house of Ahab; for the LORD has done what He spoke by His servant Elijah." 11 So Jehu killed all who remained of the house of Ahab in Jezreel, and all his great men and his close acquaintances and his priests, until he left him none remaining.

12 And he arose and departed and went to Samaria. On the way, at Beth Ekedᵃ of the Shepherds, 13 Jehu met with the brothers of Ahaziah king of Judah, and said, "Who are you?"

So they answered, "We are the brothers of Ahaziah; we have come down to greet the sons of the king and the sons of the queen mother."

14 And he said, "Take them alive!" So they took them alive, and killed them at the well of Beth Eked, forty-two men; and he left none of them.

15 Now when he departed from there, he met Jehonadab the son of Rechab, coming to meet him; and he greeted him and said to him, "Is your heart right, as my heart is toward your heart?"

And Jehonadab answered, "It is."

Jehu said, "If it is, give me your hand." So he gave him his hand, and he took him up to him into the char-

---

9:36 ᵃ1 Kings 21:23   10:1 ᵃFollowing Masoretic Text, Syriac, and Targum; Septuagint reads Samaria; Vulgate reads city.   10:12 ᵃOr The Shearing House

God put into the feminine spirit some things that a man needs more than anything God put on the feminine body. If a woman knows who she is on the inside, no matter what she looks like, she will have no problem being attractive to a man.

iot. 16 Then he said, "Come with me, and see my zeal for the LORD." So they had him ride in his chariot. 17 And when he came to Samaria, he killed all who remained to Ahab in Samaria, till he had destroyed them, according to the word of the LORD which He spoke to Elijah.

18 Then Jehu gathered all the people together, and said to them, "Ahab served Baal a little, Jehu will serve him much. 19 Now therefore, call to me all the prophets of Baal, all his servants, and all his priests. Let no one be missing, for I have a great sacrifice for Baal. Whoever is missing shall not live." But Jehu acted deceptively, with the intent of destroying the worshipers of Baal. 20 And Jehu said, "Proclaim a solemn assembly for Baal." So they proclaimed *it.* 21 Then Jehu sent throughout all Israel; and all the worshipers of Baal came, so that there was not a man left who did not come. So they came into the temple*a* of Baal, and the temple of Baal was full from one end to the other. 22 And he said to the one in charge of the wardrobe, "Bring out vestments for all the worshipers of Baal." So he brought out vestments for them. 23 Then Jehu and Jehonadab the son of Rechab went into the temple of Baal, and said to the worshipers of Baal, "Search and see that no servants of the LORD are here with you, but only the worshipers of Baal." 24 So they went in to offer sacrifices and burnt offerings. Now Jehu had appointed for himself eighty men on the outside, and had said, "*If* any of the men whom I have brought into your hands escapes, *whoever lets him escape, it shall be* his life for the life of the other."

25 Now it happened, as soon as he had made an end of offering the burnt offering, that Jehu said to the guard and to the captains, "Go in *and* kill them; let no one come out!" And they killed them with the edge of the sword; then the guards and the officers threw *them* out, and went into the inner room of the temple of Baal. 26 And they brought the *sacred* pillars out of the temple of Baal and burned them. 27 Then they broke down the *sacred* pillar of Baal, and tore down the temple of Baal and made it a refuse dump to this day.

28 Thus Jehu destroyed Baal from Israel.

29 However Jehu did not turn away from the sins of Jeroboam the son of Nebat, who had made Israel sin, *that is,* from the golden calves that *were* at Bethel and Dan. 30 And the LORD said to Jehu, "Because you have done well in doing *what is* right in My sight, *and* have done to the house of Ahab all that *was* in My heart, your sons shall sit on the throne of Israel to the fourth *generation.*" 31 But Jehu took no heed to walk in the law of the LORD God of Israel with all his heart; for he did not depart from the sins of Jeroboam, who had made Israel sin.

32 In those days the LORD began to cut off *parts* of Israel; and Hazael conquered them in all the territory of Israel 33 from the Jordan eastward: all the land of Gilead—Gad, Reuben, and Manasseh—from Aroer, which *is* by the River Arnon, including Gilead and Bashan.

34 Now the rest of the acts of Jehu, all that he did, and all his might, *are* they not written in the book of the chronicles of the kings of Israel? 35 So Jehu rested with his fathers, and they buried him in Samaria. Then Jehoahaz his son reigned in his place. 36 And the period that Jehu reigned over Israel in Samaria *was* twenty-eight years.

11 When Athaliah the mother of Ahaziah saw that her son was dead, she arose and destroyed all the royal heirs. 2 But Jehosheba, the daughter of King Joram, sister of Ahaziah, took Joash the son of Ahaziah, and stole him away from among the king's sons *who were* being murdered; and they hid him and his nurse in the bedroom, from Athaliah, so that he was not killed. 3 So he was hidden with her in the house of the LORD for six years, while Athaliah reigned over the land.

4 In the seventh year Jehoiada sent and brought the captains of hundreds—of the bodyguards and the escorts—and brought them into the house of the LORD to him. And he made a covenant with them and took an oath from them in the house of the LORD, and showed them the king's son. 5 Then he commanded

10:21 *a*Literally *house,* and so elsewhere in this chapter

Gospel Pearls

them, saying, "This is what you shall do: One-third of you who come on duty on the Sabbath shall be keeping watch over the king's house, 6 one-third shall be at the gate of Sur, and one-third at the gate behind the escorts. You shall keep the watch of the house, lest it be broken down. 7 The two contingents of you who go off duty on the Sabbath shall keep the watch of the house of the LORD for the king. 8 But you shall surround the king on all sides, every man with his weapons in his hand; and whoever comes within range, let him be put to death. You are to be with the king as he goes out and as he comes in."

9 So the captains of the hundreds did according to all that Jehoiada the priest commanded. Each of them took his men who were to be on duty on the Sabbath, with those who were going off duty on the Sabbath, and came to Jehoiada the priest. 10 And the priest gave the captains of hundreds the spears and shields which had belonged to King David, that were in the temple of the LORD. 11 Then the escorts stood, every man with his weapons in his hand, all around the king, from the right side of the temple to the left side of the temple, by the altar and the house. 12 And he brought out the king's son, put the crown on him, and gave him the Testimony;a they made him king and anointed him, and they clapped their hands and said, "Long live the king!"

13 Now when Athaliah heard the noise of the escorts and the people, she came to the people in the temple of the LORD. 14 When she looked, there was the king standing by a pillar according to custom; and the leaders and the trumpeters were by the king. All the people of the land were rejoicing and blowing trumpets. So Athaliah tore her clothes and cried out, "Treason! Treason!"

15 And Jehoiada the priest commanded the captains of the hundreds, the officers of the army, and said to them, "Take her outside under guard, and slay with the sword whoever follows her." For the priest had said, "Do not let her be killed in the house of the LORD." 16 So they

seized her; and she went by way of the horses' entrance into the king's house, and there she was killed.

17 Then Jehoiada made a covenant between the LORD, the king, and the people, that they should be the LORD's people, and also between the king and the people. 18 And all the people of the land went to the temple of Baal, and tore it down. They thoroughly broke in pieces its altars and images, and killed Mattan the priest of Baal before the altars. And the priest appointed officers over the house of the LORD. 19 Then he took the captains of hundreds, the bodyguards, the escorts, and all the people of the land; and they brought the king down from the house of the LORD, and went by way of the gate of the escorts to the king's house. Then he sat on the throne of the kings. 20 So all the people of the land rejoiced; and the city was quiet, for they had slain Athaliah with the sword in the king's house. 21 Jehoash was seven years old when he became king.

12 In the seventh year of Jehu, Jehoasha became king, and he reigned forty years in Jerusalem. His mother's name was Zibiah of Beersheba. 2 Jehoash did what was right in the sight of the LORD all the days in which Jehoiada the priest instructed him. 3 But the high places were not taken away; the people still sacrificed and burned incense on the high places.

4 And Jehoash said to the priests, "All the money of the dedicated gifts that are brought into the house of the LORD—each man's census money, each man's assessment moneya—and all the money that a man purposes in his heart to bring into the house of the LORD, 5 let the priests take it themselves, each from his constituency; and let them repair the damages of the temple, wherever any dilapidation is found."

6 Now it was so, by the twenty-third year of King Jehoash, that the priests had not repaired the damages of the temple. 7 So King Jehoash called Jehoiada the priest and the other priests, and said to them, "Why have you not repaired the damages

11:12 aThat is, the Law (compare Exodus 25:16, 21 and Deuteronomy 31:9) 12:1 aSpelled Joash in 11:2ff 12:4 aCompare Leviticus 27:2ff

A spirit of infirmity is not a bondage that another person places on your life. It's a bondage on the inside. And you can't walk away from a bondage that is on the inside of you. It will keep you locked up until you quit agreeing with the person who has mistreated you or the event that has crippled you.

of the temple? Now therefore, do not take *more* money from your constituency, but deliver it for repairing the damages of the temple." 8 And the priests agreed that they would neither receive *more* money from the people, nor repair the damages of the temple.

9 Then Jehoiada the priest took a chest, bored a hole in its lid, and set it beside the altar, on the right side as one comes into the house of the LORD; and the priests who kept the door put there all the money brought into the house of the LORD. 10 So it was, whenever they saw that *there was* much money in the chest, that the king's scribe and the high priest came up and put it in bags, and counted the money that was found in the house of the LORD. 11 Then they gave the money, which had been apportioned, into the hands of those who did the work, who had the oversight of the house of the LORD; and they paid it out to the carpenters and builders who worked on the house of the LORD, 12 and to masons and stonecutters, and for buying timber and hewn stone, to repair the damage of the house of the LORD, and for all that was paid out to repair the temple. 13 However there were not made for the house of the LORD basins of silver, trimmers, sprinkling-bowls, trumpets, any articles of gold or articles of silver, from the money brought into the house of the LORD. 14 But they gave that to the workmen, and they repaired the house of the LORD with it. 15 Moreover they did not require an account from the men into whose hand they delivered the money to be paid to workmen, for they dealt faithfully. 16 The money from the trespass offerings and the money from the sin offerings was not brought into the house of the LORD. It belonged to the priests.

17 Hazael king of Syria went up and fought against Gath, and took it; then Hazael set his face to go up to Jerusalem. 18 And Jehoash king of Judah took all the sacred things that his fathers, Jehoshaphat and Jehoram and Ahaziah, kings of Judah, had dedicated, and his own sacred things, and all the gold found in the treasuries of the house of the LORD and in the king's house, and sent *them* to Hazael king of Syria. Then he went away from Jerusalem.

19 Now the rest of the acts of Joash,ᵃ and all that he did, *are* they not written in the book of the chronicles of the kings of Judah? 20 And his servants arose and formed a conspiracy, and killed Joash in the house of the Millo,ᵃ which goes down to Silla. 21 For Jozacharᵃ the son of Shimeath and Jehozabad the son of Shomer,ᵇ his servants, struck him. So he died, and they buried him with his fathers in the City of David. Then Amaziah his son reigned in his place.

13 In the twenty-third year of Joashᵃ the son of Ahaziah, king of Judah, Jehoahaz the son of Jehu became king over Israel in Samaria, *and reigned* seventeen years. 2 And he did evil in the sight of the LORD, and followed the sins of Jeroboam the son of Nebat, who had made Israel sin. He did not depart from them.

3 Then the anger of the LORD was aroused against Israel, and He delivered them into the hand of Hazael king of Syria, and into the hand of Ben-Hadad the son of Hazael, all *their* days. 4 So Jehoahaz pleaded with the LORD, and the LORD listened to him; for He saw the oppression of Israel, because the king of Syria oppressed them. 5 Then the LORD gave Israel a deliverer, so that they escaped from under the hand of the Syrians; and the children of Israel dwelt in their tents as before. 6 Nevertheless they did not depart from the sins of the house of Jeroboam, who had made Israel sin, *but* walked in them; and the wooden imageᵃ also remained in Samaria. 7 For He left of the army of Jehoahaz only fifty horsemen, ten chariots, and ten thousand foot soldiers; for the king of Syria had destroyed them and made them like the dust at threshing.

8 Now the rest of the acts of Jehoahaz, all that he did, and his might, *are* they not written in the book of the chronicles of the kings of Israel?

12:19 ᵃSpelled *Jehoash* in 12:1ff   12:20 ᵃLiterally *The Landfill*   12:21 ᵃCalled *Zabad* in 2 Chronicles 24:26   ᵇCalled *Shimrith* in 2 Chronicles 24:26   13:1 ᵃSpelled *Jehoash* in 12:1ff   13:6 ᵃHebrew *Asherah,* a Canaanite goddess

Gospel
Pearls

9 So Jehoahaz rested with his fathers, and they buried him in Samaria. Then Joash his son reigned in his place.

10 In the thirty-seventh year of Joash king of Judah, Jehoash[a] the son of Jehoahaz became king over Israel in Samaria, *and reigned* sixteen years. 11 And he did evil in the sight of the LORD. He did not depart from all the sins of Jeroboam the son of Nebat, who made Israel sin, *but* walked in them.

12 Now the rest of the acts of Joash, all that he did, and his might with which he fought against Amaziah king of Judah, *are* they not written in the book of the chronicles of the kings of Israel? 13 So Joash rested with his fathers. Then Jeroboam sat on his throne. And Joash was buried in Samaria with the kings of Israel.

14 Elisha had become sick with the illness of which he would die. Then Joash the king of Israel came down to him, and wept over his face, and said, "O my father, my father, the chariots of Israel and their horsemen!"

15 And Elisha said to him, "Take a bow and some arrows." So he took himself a bow and some arrows. 16 Then he said to the king of Israel, "Put your hand on the bow." So he put his hand *on it*, and Elisha put his hands on the king's hands. 17 And he said, "Open the east window"; and he opened *it*. Then Elisha said, "Shoot"; and he shot. And he said, "The arrow of the LORD's deliverance and the arrow of deliverance from Syria; for you must strike the Syrians at Aphek till you have destroyed *them*." 18 Then he said, "Take the arrows"; so he took *them*. And he said to the king of Israel, "Strike the ground"; so he struck three times, and stopped. 19 And the man of God was angry with him, and said, "You should have struck five or six times; then you would have struck Syria till you had destroyed *it!* But now you will strike Syria *only* three times."

20 Then Elisha died, and they buried him. And the *raiding* bands from Moab invaded the land in the spring of the year. 21 So it was, as they were burying a man, that suddenly they spied a band *of raiders;* and they put the man in the tomb of Elisha; and when the man was let down and touched the bones of Elisha, he revived and stood on his feet.

22 And Hazael king of Syria oppressed Israel all the days of Jehoahaz. 23 But the LORD was gracious to them, had compassion on them, and regarded them, because of His covenant with Abraham, Isaac, and Jacob, and would not yet destroy them or cast them from His presence.

24 Now Hazael king of Syria died. Then Ben-Hadad his son reigned in his place. 25 And Jehoash[a] the son of Jehoahaz recaptured from the hand of Ben-Hadad, the son of Hazael, the cities which he had taken out of the hand of Jehoahaz his father by war. Three times Joash defeated him and recaptured the cities of Israel.

14 In the second year of Joash the son of Jehoahaz, king of Israel, Amaziah the son of Joash, king of Judah, became king. 2 He was twenty-five years old when he became king, and he reigned twenty-nine years in Jerusalem. His mother's name was Jehoaddan of Jerusalem. 3 And he did *what was* right in the sight of the LORD, yet not like his father David; he did everything as his father Joash had done. 4 However the high places were not taken away, and the people still sacrificed and burned incense on the high places.

5 Now it happened, as soon as the kingdom was established in his hand, that he executed his servants who had murdered his father the king. 6 But the children of the murderers he did not execute, according to what is written in the Book of the Law of Moses, in which the LORD commanded, saying, "Fathers shall not be put to death for their children, nor shall children be put to death for their fathers; but a person shall be put to death for his own sin."[a]

7 He killed ten thousand Edomites in the Valley of Salt, and took Sela by war, and called its name Joktheel to this day.

8 Then Amaziah sent messengers to Jehoash[a] the son of Jehoahaz, the son of Jehu, king of Israel, saying, "Come, let us face one another *in battle.*" 9 And Jehoash king of Israel

13:10 [a]Spelled *Joash* in verse 9   13:25 [a]Spelled *Joash* in verses 12–14, 25   14:6 [a]Deuteronomy 24:16   14:8 [a]Spelled *Joash* in 13:12ff and 2 Chronicles 25:17ff

---

*T*he wonderful thing about God is that He doesn't meet with a board or a committee before He decides to bless you. He doesn't have to get anyone else's approval before He pours out His love to you. He doesn't consult anybody about you!

sent to Amaziah king of Judah, saying, "The thistle that *was* in Lebanon sent to the cedar that *was* in Lebanon, saying, 'Give your daughter to my son as wife'; and a wild beast that *was* in Lebanon passed by and trampled the thistle. 10 You have indeed defeated Edom, and your heart has lifted you up. Glory *in that,* and stay at home; for why should you meddle with trouble so that you fall—you and Judah with you?"

11 But Amaziah would not heed. Therefore Jehoash king of Israel went out; so he and Amaziah king of Judah faced one another at Beth Shemesh, which *belongs* to Judah. 12 And Judah was defeated by Israel, and every man fled to his tent. 13 Then Jehoash king of Israel captured Amaziah king of Judah, the son of Jehoash, the son of Ahaziah, at Beth Shemesh; and he went to Jerusalem, and broke down the wall of Jerusalem from the Gate of Ephraim to the Corner Gate—four hundred cubits. 14 And he took all the gold and silver, all the articles that were found in the house of the LORD and in the treasuries of the king's house, and hostages, and returned to Samaria.

15 Now the rest of the acts of Jehoash which he did—his might, and how he fought with Amaziah king of Judah—*are* they not written in the book of the chronicles of the kings of Israel? 16 So Jehoash rested with his fathers, and was buried in Samaria with the kings of Israel. Then Jeroboam his son reigned in his place.

17 Amaziah the son of Joash, king of Judah, lived fifteen years after the death of Jehoash the son of Jehoahaz, king of Israel. 18 Now the rest of the acts of Amaziah, *are* they not written in the book of the chronicles of the kings of Judah? 19 And they formed a conspiracy against him in Jerusalem, and he fled to Lachish; but they sent after him to Lachish and killed him there. 20 Then they brought him on horses, and he was buried at Jerusalem with his fathers in the City of David.

21 And all the people of Judah took Azariah,[a] who *was* sixteen years old, and made him king instead of his father Amaziah. 22 He built Elath and

restored it to Judah, after the king rested with his fathers.

23 In the fifteenth year of Amaziah the son of Joash, king of Judah, Jeroboam the son of Joash, king of Israel, became king in Samaria, *and reigned* forty-one years. 24 And he did evil in the sight of the LORD; he did not depart from all the sins of Jeroboam the son of Nebat, who had made Israel sin. 25 He restored the territory of Israel from the entrance of Hamath to the Sea of the Arabah, according to the word of the LORD God of Israel, which He had spoken through His servant Jonah the son of Amittai, the prophet who *was* from Gath Hepher. 26 For the LORD saw *that* the affliction of Israel *was* very bitter; and whether bond or free, there was no helper for Israel. 27 And the LORD did not say that He would blot out the name of Israel from under heaven; but He saved them by the hand of Jeroboam the son of Joash.

28 Now the rest of the acts of Jeroboam, and all that he did—his might, how he made war, and how he recaptured for Israel, from Damascus and Hamath, *what had belonged* to Judah—*are* they not written in the book of the chronicles of the kings of Israel? 29 So Jeroboam rested with his fathers, the kings of Israel. Then Zechariah his son reigned in his place.

15 In the twenty-seventh year of Jeroboam king of Israel, Azariah the son of Amaziah, king of Judah, became king. 2 He was sixteen years old when he became king, and he reigned fifty-two years in Jerusalem. His mother's name *was* Jecholiah of Jerusalem. 3 And he did *what was* right in the sight of the LORD, according to all that his father Amaziah had done, 4 except that the high places were not removed; the people still sacrificed and burned incense on the high places. 5 Then the LORD struck the king, so that he was a leper until the day of his death; so he dwelt in an isolated house. And Jotham the king's son *was* over the *royal* house, judging the people of the land.

6 Now the rest of the acts of Azariah, and all that he did, *are* they not written in the book of the chronicles

14:21 ªCalled *Uzziah* in 2 Chronicles 26:1ff, Isaiah 6:1, and elsewhere

Gospel
Pearls

of the kings of Judah? 7 So Azariah rested with his fathers, and they buried him with his fathers in the City of David. Then Jotham his son reigned in his place.

8 In the thirty-eighth year of Azariah king of Judah, Zechariah the son of Jeroboam reigned over Israel in Samaria six months. 9 And he did evil in the sight of the LORD, as his fathers had done; he did not depart from the sins of Jeroboam the son of Nebat, who had made Israel sin. 10 Then Shallum the son of Jabesh conspired against him, and struck and killed him in front of the people; and he reigned in his place.

11 Now the rest of the acts of Zechariah, indeed they *are* written in the book of the chronicles of the kings of Israel.

12 This *was* the word of the LORD which He spoke to Jehu, saying, "Your sons shall sit on the throne of Israel to the fourth *generation.*"*a* And so it was.

13 Shallum the son of Jabesh became king in the thirty-ninth year of Uzziah*a* king of Judah; and he reigned a full month in Samaria. 14 For Menahem the son of Gadi went up from Tirzah, came to Samaria, and struck Shallum the son of Jabesh in Samaria and killed him; and he reigned in his place.

15 Now the rest of the acts of Shallum, and the conspiracy which he led, indeed they *are* written in the book of the chronicles of the kings of Israel. 16 Then from Tirzah, Menahem attacked Tiphsah, all who *were* there, and its territory. Because they did not surrender, therefore he attacked *it.* All the women there who were with child he ripped open.

17 In the thirty-ninth year of Azariah king of Judah, Menahem the son of Gadi became king over Israel, *and reigned* ten years in Samaria. 18 And he did evil in the sight of the LORD; he did not depart all his days from the sins of Jeroboam the son of Nebat, who had made Israel sin. 19 Pul*a* king of Assyria came against the land; and Menahem gave Pul a thousand talents of silver, that his hand might be with him to strengthen the kingdom under his control. 20 And Menahem exacted

the money from Israel, from all the very wealthy, from each man fifty shekels of silver, to give to the king of Assyria. So the king of Assyria turned back, and did not stay there in the land.

21 Now the rest of the acts of Menahem, and all that he did, *are* they not written in the book of the chronicles of the kings of Israel? 22 So Menahem rested with his fathers. Then Pekahiah his son reigned in his place.

23 In the fiftieth year of Azariah king of Judah, Pekahiah the son of Menahem became king over Israel in Samaria, *and reigned* two years. 24 And he did evil in the sight of the LORD; he did not depart from the sins of Jeroboam the son of Nebat, who had made Israel sin. 25 Then Pekah the son of Remaliah, an officer of his, conspired against him and killed him in Samaria, in the citadel of the king's house, along with Argob and Arieh; and with him were fifty men of Gilead. He killed him and reigned in his place.

26 Now the rest of the acts of Pekahiah, and all that he did, indeed they *are* written in the book of the chronicles of the kings of Israel.

27 In the fifty-second year of Azariah king of Judah, Pekah the son of Remaliah became king over Israel in Samaria, *and reigned* twenty years. 28 And he did evil in the sight of the LORD; he did not depart from the sins of Jeroboam the son of Nebat, who had made Israel sin. 29 In the days of Pekah king of Israel, Tiglath-Pileser king of Assyria came and took Ijon, Abel Beth Maachah, Janoah, Kedesh, Hazor, Gilead, and Galilee, all the land of Naphtali; and he carried them captive to Assyria. 30 Then Hoshea the son of Elah led a conspiracy against Pekah the son of Remaliah, and struck and killed him; so he reigned in his place in the twentieth year of Jotham the son of Uzziah.

31 Now the rest of the acts of Pekah, and all that he did, indeed they *are* written in the book of the chronicles of the kings of Israel.

32 In the second year of Pekah the son of Remaliah, king of Israel, Jotham the son of Uzziah, king of Judah, began to reign. 33 He was

15:12 *a*2 Kings 10:30   15:13 *a*Called *Azariah* in 14:21ff and 15:1ff   15:19 *a*That is, Tiglath-Pileser III (compare verse 29)

---

*I*f people are upset with your deliverance and your praise, consider their "upset-ness" to be their problem. Don't try to explain yourself or justify your praise. Just remain standing and keep praising.

twenty-five years old when he became king, and he reigned sixteen years in Jerusalem. His mother's name was Jerusha*a* the daughter of Zadok. 34 And he did what was right in the sight of the LORD; he did according to all that his father Uzziah had done. 35 However the high places were not removed; the people still sacrificed and burned incense on the high places. He built the Upper Gate of the house of the LORD.

36 Now the rest of the acts of Jotham, and all that he did, are they not written in the book of the chronicles of the kings of Judah? 37 In those days the LORD began to send Rezin king of Syria and Pekah the son of Remaliah against Judah. 38 So Jotham rested with his fathers, and was buried with his fathers in the City of David his father. Then Ahaz his son reigned in his place.

16 In the seventeenth year of Pekah the son of Remaliah, Ahaz the son of Jotham, king of Judah, began to reign. 2 Ahaz was twenty years old when he became king, and he reigned sixteen years in Jerusalem; and he did not do what was right in the sight of the LORD his God, as his father David had done. 3 But he walked in the way of the kings of Israel; indeed he made his son pass through the fire, according to the abominations of the nations whom the LORD had cast out from before the children of Israel. 4 And he sacrificed and burned incense on the high places, on the hills, and under every green tree.

5 Then Rezin king of Syria and Pekah the son of Remaliah, king of Israel, came up to Jerusalem to make war; and they besieged Ahaz but could not overcome him. 6 At that time Rezin king of Syria captured Elath for Syria, and drove the men of Judah from Elath. Then the Edomites*a* went to Elath, and dwell there to this day.

7 So Ahaz sent messengers to Tiglath-Pileser king of Assyria, saying, "I am your servant and your son. Come up and save me from the hand of the king of Syria and from the hand of the king of Israel, who rise up against me." 8 And Ahaz took the

silver and gold that was found in the house of the LORD, and in the treasuries of the king's house, and sent it as a present to the king of Assyria. 9 So the king of Assyria heeded him; for the king of Assyria went up against Damascus and took it, carried its people captive to Kir, and killed Rezin.

10 Now King Ahaz went to Damascus to meet Tiglath-Pileser king of Assyria, and saw an altar that was at Damascus; and King Ahaz sent to Urijah the priest the design of the altar and its pattern, according to all its workmanship. 11 Then Urijah the priest built an altar according to all that King Ahaz had sent from Damascus. So Urijah the priest made it before King Ahaz came back from Damascus. 12 And when the king came back from Damascus, the king saw the altar; and the king approached the altar and made offerings on it. 13 So he burned his burnt offering and his grain offering; and he poured his drink offering and sprinkled the blood of his peace offerings on the altar. 14 He also brought the bronze altar which was before the LORD, from the front of the temple—from between the new altar and the house of the LORD—and put it on the north side of the new altar. 15 Then King Ahaz commanded Urijah the priest, saying, "On the great new altar burn the morning burnt offering, the evening grain offering, the king's burnt sacrifice, and his grain offering, with the burnt offering of all the people of the land, their grain offering, and their drink offerings; and sprinkle on it all the blood of the burnt offering and all the blood of the sacrifice. And the bronze altar shall be for me to inquire by." 16 Thus did Urijah the priest, according to all that King Ahaz commanded.

17 And King Ahaz cut off the panels of the carts, and removed the lavers from them; and he took down the Sea from the bronze oxen that were under it, and put it on a pavement of stones. 18 Also he removed the Sabbath pavilion which they had built in the temple, and he removed the king's outer entrance from the house of the LORD, on account of the king of Assyria.

19 Now the rest of the acts of Ahaz

15:33 *a*Spelled Jerushah in 2 Chronicles 27:1   16:6 *a*Some ancient authorities read Syrians.

---

*I*t's very difficult to do something if you've never seen it done before. It's tough to be a good wife if you've never seen a good wife in action. No wonder Eve went for a walk in the garden. She was probably stressed out!

Soul Secrets
when it's hard to
be submitted

*L*ord, I'm an independent spirit. I've been on my own, made my own choices, and taken care of myself. At times, submission comes easily, but not right now. You have placed authority in my life as a means of protection, not as a means of control. I don't want to be like the stiff-necked people in the Bible, so I need Your help.

I commit those who have authority in my life to You. I ask You to give them supernatural wisdom so that they will make godly decisions. I ask You to fill their lives with love so that I will be glad to submit to them—and even want to. Make them so full of Your Spirit that I cannot help but respect them.

Help me, Lord, to crucify the flesh in me that tries to rebel. Cleanse me of every rebellious thought. Keep me from confusing Your definition of submission with the world's definition. Thank You for bringing me to an understanding of true, holy submission and servanthood.

which he did, *are* they not written in the book of the chronicles of the kings of Judah? 20 So Ahaz rested with his fathers, and was buried with his fathers in the City of David. Then Hezekiah his son reigned in his place.

17 In the twelfth year of Ahaz king of Judah, Hoshea the son of Elah became king of Israel in Samaria, *and he reigned* nine years. 2 And he did evil in the sight of the LORD, but not as the kings of Israel who were before him. 3 Shalmaneser king of Assyria came up against him; and Hoshea became his vassal, and paid him tribute money. 4 And the king of Assyria uncovered a conspiracy by Hoshea; for he had sent messengers to So, king of Egypt, and brought no tribute to the king of Assyria, as *he had done* year by year. Therefore the king of Assyria shut him up, and bound him in prison.

5 Now the king of Assyria went throughout all the land, and went up to Samaria and besieged it for three years. 6 In the ninth year of Hoshea, the king of Assyria took Samaria and carried Israel away to Assyria, and placed them in Halah and by the Habor, the River of Gozan, and in the cities of the Medes.

7 For so it was that the children of Israel had sinned against the LORD their God, who had brought them up out of the land of Egypt, from under the hand of Pharaoh king of Egypt; and they had feared other gods, 8 and had walked in the statutes of the nations whom the LORD had cast out from before the children of Israel, and of the kings of Israel, which they had made. 9 Also the children of Israel secretly did against the LORD their God things that *were* not right, and they built for themselves high places in all their cities, from watchtower to fortified city. 10 They set up for themselves *sacred* pillars and wooden images*a* on every high hill and under every green tree. 11 There they burned incense on all the high places, like the nations whom the LORD had carried away before them; and they did wicked things to provoke the LORD to anger, 12 for they served idols, of which the

LORD had said to them, "You shall not do this thing."

13 Yet the LORD testified against Israel and against Judah, by all of His prophets, every seer, saying, "Turn from your evil ways, and keep My commandments *and* My statutes, according to all the law which I commanded your fathers, and which I sent to you by My servants the prophets." 14 Nevertheless they would not hear, but stiffened their necks, like the necks of their fathers, who did not believe in the LORD their God. 15 And they rejected His statutes and His covenant that He had made with their fathers, and His testimonies which He had testified against them; they followed idols, became idolaters, and *went* after the nations who *were* all around them, *concerning* whom the LORD had charged them that they should not do like them. 16 So they left all the commandments of the LORD their God, made for themselves a molded image *and* two calves, made a wooden image and worshiped all the host of heaven, and served Baal. 17 And they caused their sons and daughters to pass through the fire, practiced witchcraft and soothsaying, and sold themselves to do evil in the sight of the LORD, to provoke Him to anger. 18 Therefore the LORD was very angry with Israel, and removed them from His sight; there was none left but the tribe of Judah alone.

19 Also Judah did not keep the commandments of the LORD their God, but walked in the statutes of Israel which they made. 20 And the LORD rejected all the descendants of Israel, afflicted them, and delivered them into the hand of plunderers, until He had cast them from His sight. 21 For He tore Israel from the house of David, and they made Jeroboam the son of Nebat king. Then Jeroboam drove Israel from following the LORD, and made them commit a great sin. 22 For the children of Israel walked in all the sins of Jeroboam which he did; they did not depart from them, 23 until the LORD removed Israel out of His sight, as He had said by all His servants the prophets. So Israel was carried away from their own land to Assyria, *as it is* to this day.

17:10 *a*Hebrew *Asherim,* Canaanite deities

Gospel Pearls

24 Then the king of Assyria brought *people* from Babylon, Cuthah, Ava, Hamath, and from Sepharvaim, and placed *them* in the cities of Samaria instead of the children of Israel; and they took possession of Samaria and dwelt in its cities. 25 And it was so, at the beginning of their dwelling there, *that* they did not fear the LORD; therefore the LORD sent lions among them, which killed *some* of them. 26 So they spoke to the king of Assyria, saying, "The nations whom you have removed and placed in the cities of Samaria do not know the rituals of the God of the land; therefore He has sent lions among them, and indeed, they are killing them because they do not know the rituals of the God of the land." 27 Then the king of Assyria commanded, saying, "Send there one of the priests whom you brought from there; let him go and dwell there, and let him teach them the rituals of the God of the land." 28 Then one of the priests whom they had carried away from Samaria came and dwelt in Bethel, and taught them how they should fear the LORD.

29 However every nation continued to make gods of its own, and put *them* in the shrines on the high places which the Samaritans had made, *every* nation in the cities where they dwelt. 30 The men of Babylon made Succoth Benoth, the men of Cuth made Nergal, the men of Hamath made Ashima, 31 and the Avites made Nibhaz and Tartak; and the Sepharvites burned their children in fire to Adrammelech and Anammelech, the gods of Sepharvaim. 32 So they feared the LORD, and from every class they appointed for themselves priests of the high places, who sacrificed for them in the shrines of the high places. 33 They feared the LORD, yet served their own gods—according to the rituals of the nations from among whom they were carried away.

34 To this day they continue practicing the former rituals; they do not fear the LORD, nor do they follow their statutes or their ordinances, or the law and commandment which the LORD had commanded the children of Jacob, whom He named Israel, 35 with whom the LORD had made a covenant and charged them, saying: "You shall not fear other gods, nor bow down to them nor serve them nor sacrifice to them; 36 but the LORD, who brought you up from the land of Egypt with great power and an outstretched arm, Him you shall fear, Him you shall worship, and to Him you shall offer sacrifice. 37 And the statutes, the ordinances, the law, and the commandment which He wrote for you, you shall be careful to observe forever; you shall not fear other gods. 38 And the covenant that I have made with you, you shall not forget, nor shall you fear other gods. 39 But the LORD your God you shall fear; and He will deliver you from the hand of all your enemies." 40 However they did not obey, but they followed their former rituals. 41 So these nations feared the LORD, yet served their carved images; also their children and their children's children have continued doing as their fathers did, even to this day.

18 Now it came to pass in the third year of Hoshea the son of Elah, king of Israel, *that* Hezekiah the son of Ahaz, king of Judah, began to reign. 2 He was twenty-five years old when he became king, and he reigned twenty-nine years in Jerusalem. His mother's name *was* Abi*ᵃ* the daughter of Zechariah. 3 And he did *what was* right in the sight of the LORD, according to all that his father David had done.

4 He removed the high places and broke the *sacred* pillars, cut down the wooden image*ᵃ* and broke in pieces the bronze serpent that Moses had made; for until those days the children of Israel burned incense to it, and called it Nehushtan.*ᵇ* 5 He trusted in the LORD God of Israel, so that after him was none like him among all the kings of Judah, nor who were before him. 6 For he held fast to the LORD; he did not depart from following Him, but kept His commandments, which the LORD had commanded Moses. 7 The LORD was with him; he prospered wherever he went. And he rebelled against the king of Assyria and did not serve him. 8 He subdued the Philistines, as

18:2 ᵃCalled *Abijah* in 2 Chronicles 29:1ff   18:4 ᵃHebrew *Asherah*, a Canaanite goddess   ᵇLiterally *Bronze Thing*

*I*n our world today, there are lots of women who have found themselves being women before they had the chance to be girls. They haven't had an opportunity to know what it means to be innocent, to feel free to trust, or to know what it means to receive genuine love.

far as Gaza and its territory, from watchtower to fortified city.

9 Now it came to pass in the fourth year of King Hezekiah, which *was* the seventh year of Hoshea the son of Elah, king of Israel, *that* Shalmaneser king of Assyria came up against Samaria and besieged it. 10 And at the end of three years they took it. In the sixth year of Hezekiah, that *is,* the ninth year of Hoshea king of Israel, Samaria was taken. 11 Then the king of Assyria carried Israel away captive to Assyria, and put them in Halah and by the Habor, the River of Gozan, and in the cities of the Medes, 12 because they did not obey the voice of the LORD their God, but transgressed His covenant *and* all that Moses the servant of the LORD had commanded; and they would neither hear nor do *them.*

13 And in the fourteenth year of King Hezekiah, Sennacherib king of Assyria came up against all the fortified cities of Judah and took them. 14 Then Hezekiah king of Judah sent to the king of Assyria at Lachish, saying, "I have done wrong; turn away from me; whatever you impose on me I will pay." And the king of Assyria assessed Hezekiah king of Judah three hundred talents of silver and thirty talents of gold. 15 So Hezekiah gave *him* all the silver that was found in the house of the LORD and in the treasuries of the king's house. 16 At that time Hezekiah stripped *the* gold *from* the doors of the temple of the LORD, and *from* the pillars which Hezekiah king of Judah had overlaid, and gave it to the king of Assyria.

17 Then the king of Assyria sent *the* Tartan,*ᵃ the* Rabsaris,*ᵇ* and *the* Rabshakehᶜ from Lachish, with a great army against Jerusalem, to King Hezekiah. And they went up and came to Jerusalem. When they had come up, they went and stood by the aqueduct from the upper pool, which *was* on the highway to the Fuller's Field. 18 And when they had called to the king, Eliakim the son of Hilkiah, who *was* over the household, Shebna the scribe, and Joah the son of Asaph, the recorder, came out to them. 19 Then *the* Rabshakeh said to them, "Say now to Hezekiah, 'Thus

says the great king, the king of Assyria: "What confidence *is* this in which you trust? 20 You speak of *having* plans and power for war; but *they are* mere words. And in whom do you trust, that you rebel against me? 21 Now look! You are trusting in the staff of this broken reed, Egypt, on which if a man leans, it will go into his hand and pierce it. So *is* Pharaoh king of Egypt to all who trust in him. 22 But if you say to me, 'We trust in the LORD our God,' *is* it not He whose high places and whose altars Hezekiah has taken away, and said to Judah and Jerusalem, 'You shall worship before this altar in Jerusalem'?" ' 23 Now therefore, I urge you, give a pledge to my master the king of Assyria, and I will give you two thousand horses—if you are able on your part to put riders on them! 24 How then will you repel one captain of the least of my master's servants, and put your trust in Egypt for chariots and horsemen? 25 Have I now come up without the LORD against this place to destroy it? The LORD said to me, 'Go up against this land, and destroy it.' "

26 Then Eliakim the son of Hilkiah, Shebna, and Joah said to *the* Rabshakeh, "Please speak to your servants in Aramaic, for we understand *it;* and do not speak to us in Hebrewᵃ in the hearing of the people who *are* on the wall."

27 But *the* Rabshakeh said to them, "Has my master sent me to your master and to you to speak these words, and not to the men who sit on the wall, who will eat and drink their own waste with you?"

28 Then *the* Rabshakeh stood and called out with a loud voice in Hebrew, and spoke, saying, "Hear the word of the great king, the king of Assyria! 29 Thus says the king: 'Do not let Hezekiah deceive you, for he shall not be able to deliver you from his hand; 30 nor let Hezekiah make you trust in the LORD, saying, "The LORD will surely deliver us; this city shall not be given into the hand of the king of Assyria." ' 31 Do not listen to Hezekiah; for thus says the king of Assyria: 'Make *peace* with me by a present and come out to me; and every one of you eat from his own

18:17 ᵃA title, probably *Commander in Chief*   ᵇA title, probably *Chief Officer*   ᶜA title, probably *Chief of Staff* or *Governor*   18:26 ᵃLiterally *Judean*

Gospel Pearls

vine and every one from his own fig tree, and every one of you drink the waters of his own cistern; 32 until I come and take you away to a land like your own land, a land of grain and new wine, a land of bread and vineyards, a land of olive groves and honey, that you may live and not die. But do not listen to Hezekiah, lest he persuade you, saying, "The LORD will deliver us." 33 Has any of the gods of the nations at all delivered its land from the hand of the king of Assyria? 34 Where *are* the gods of Hamath and Arpad? Where *are* the gods of Sepharvaim and Hena and Ivah? Indeed, have they delivered Samaria from my hand? 35 Who among all the gods of the lands have delivered their countries from my hand, that the LORD should deliver Jerusalem from my hand?' "

36 But the people held their peace and answered him not a word; for the king's commandment was, "Do not answer him." 37 Then Eliakim the son of Hilkiah, who *was* over the household, Shebna the scribe, and Joah the son of Asaph, the recorder, came to Hezekiah with *their* clothes torn, and told him the words of *the* Rabshakeh.

19 And so it was, when King Hezekiah heard *it*, that he tore his clothes, covered himself with sackcloth, and went into the house of the LORD. 2 Then he sent Eliakim, who *was* over the household, Shebna the scribe, and the elders of the priests, covered with sackcloth, to Isaiah the prophet, the son of Amoz. 3 And they said to him, "Thus says Hezekiah: 'This day *is* a day of trouble, and rebuke, and blasphemy; for the children have come to birth, but *there is* no strength to bring them forth. 4 It may be that the LORD your God will hear all the words of *the* Rabshakeh, whom his master the king of Assyria has sent to reproach the living God, and will rebuke the words which the LORD your God has heard. Therefore lift up *your* prayer for the remnant that is left.' "

5 So the servants of King Hezekiah came to Isaiah. 6 And Isaiah said to them, "Thus you shall say to your master, 'Thus says the LORD: "Do not be afraid of the words which you have heard, with which the servants

of the king of Assyria have blasphemed Me. 7 Surely I will send a spirit upon him, and he shall hear a rumor and return to his own land; and I will cause him to fall by the sword in his own land." ' "

8 Then *the* Rabshakeh returned and found the king of Assyria warring against Libnah, for he heard that he had departed from Lachish. 9 And the king heard concerning Tirhakah king of Ethiopia, "Look, he has come out to make war with you." So he again sent messengers to Hezekiah, saying, 10 "Thus you shall speak to Hezekiah king of Judah, saying: 'Do not let your God in whom you trust deceive you, saying, "Jerusalem shall not be given into the hand of the king of Assyria." 11 Look! You have heard what the kings of Assyria have done to all lands by utterly destroying them; and shall you be delivered? 12 Have the gods of the nations delivered those whom my fathers have destroyed, Gozan and Haran and Rezeph, and the people of Eden who *were* in Telassar? 13 Where *is* the king of Hamath, the king of Arpad, and the king of the city of Sepharvaim, Hena, and Ivah?' "

14 And Hezekiah received the letter from the hand of the messengers, and read it; and Hezekiah went up to the house of the LORD, and spread it before the LORD. 15 Then Hezekiah prayed before the LORD, and said: "O LORD God of Israel, *the One* who dwells *between* the cherubim, You are God, You alone, of all the kingdoms of the earth. You have made heaven and earth. 16 Incline Your ear, O LORD, and hear; open Your eyes, O LORD, and see; and hear the words of Sennacherib, which he has sent to reproach the living God. 17 Truly, LORD, the kings of Assyria have laid waste the nations and their lands, 18 and have cast their gods into the fire; for they *were* not gods, but the work of men's hands—wood and stone. Therefore they destroyed them. 19 Now therefore, O LORD our God, I pray, save us from his hand, that all the kingdoms of the earth may know that You *are* the LORD God, You alone."

20 Then Isaiah the son of Amoz sent to Hezekiah, saying, "Thus says the LORD God of Israel: 'Because you have prayed to Me against Sen-

---

Sometimes life can come at us too fast. Sometimes we have our childhoods stripped away from us. The little girl in you may have never had an opportunity to be a little girl. And if that happened, you were robbed of something very precious.

nacherib king of Assyria, I have heard.' 21 This *is* the word which the LORD has spoken concerning him:

'The virgin, the daughter of Zion,
Has despised you, laughed you to scorn;
The daughter of Jerusalem
Has shaken *her* head behind your back!

22 'Whom have you reproached and blasphemed?
Against whom have you raised *your* voice,
And lifted up your eyes on high?
Against the Holy *One* of Israel.
23 By your messengers you have reproached the Lord,
And said: "By the multitude of my chariots
I have come up to the height of the mountains,
To the limits of Lebanon;
I will cut down its tall cedars
And its choice cypress trees;
I will enter the extremity of its borders,
To its fruitful forest.
24 I have dug and drunk strange water,
And with the soles of my feet I have dried up
All the brooks of defense."

25 'Did you not hear long ago
How I made it,
From ancient times that I formed it?
Now I have brought it to pass,
That you should be
For crushing fortified cities *into* heaps of ruins.
26 Therefore their inhabitants had little power;
They were dismayed and confounded;
They were *as* the grass of the field
And the green herb,
As the grass on the housetops
And *grain* blighted before it is grown.

27 'But I know your dwelling place,
Your going out and your coming in,

And your rage against Me.
28 Because your rage against Me and your tumult
Have come up to My ears,
Therefore I will put My hook in your nose
And My bridle in your lips,
And I will turn you back
By the way which you came.

29 'This *shall be* a sign to you:

You shall eat this year such as grows of itself,
And in the second year what springs from the same;
Also in the third year sow and reap,
Plant vineyards and eat the fruit of them.
30 And the remnant who have escaped of the house of Judah
Shall again take root downward,
And bear fruit upward.
31 For out of Jerusalem shall go a remnant,
And those who escape from Mount Zion.
The zeal of the LORD of hosts[a] will do this.'

32 "Therefore thus says the LORD concerning the king of Assyria:

'He shall not come into this city,
Nor shoot an arrow there,
Nor come before it with shield,
Nor build a siege mound against it.
33 By the way that he came,
By the same shall he return;
And he shall not come into this city,'
Says the LORD.
34 'For I will defend this city, to save it
For My own sake and for My servant David's sake.' "

35 And it came to pass on a certain night that the angel[a] of the LORD went out, and killed in the camp of the Assyrians one hundred and eighty-five thousand; and when *people* arose early in the morning, there were the corpses—all dead. 36 So Sennacherib king of Assyria

19:31 [a]Following many Hebrew manuscripts and ancient versions (compare Isaiah 37:32); Masoretic Text omits *of hosts*.   19:35 [a]Or *Angel*

Gospel Pearls

departed and went away, returned *home*, and remained at Nineveh. 37 Now it came to pass, as he was worshiping in the temple of Nisroch his god, that his sons Adrammelech and Sharezer struck him down with the sword; and they escaped into the land of Ararat. Then Esarhaddon his son reigned in his place.

20 In those days Hezekiah was sick and near death. And Isaiah the prophet, the son of Amoz, went to him and said to him, "Thus says the LORD: 'Set your house in order, for you shall die, and not live.' "

2 Then he turned his face toward the wall, and prayed to the LORD, saying, 3 "Remember now, O LORD, I pray, how I have walked before You in truth and with a loyal heart, and have done *what was* good in Your sight." And Hezekiah wept bitterly.

4 And it happened, before Isaiah had gone out into the middle court, that the word of the LORD came to him, saying, 5 "Return and tell Hezekiah the leader of My people, 'Thus says the LORD, the God of David your father: "I have heard your prayer, I have seen your tears; surely I will heal you. On the third day you shall go up to the house of the LORD. 6 And I will add to your days fifteen years. I will deliver you and this city from the hand of the king of Assyria; and I will defend this city for My own sake, and for the sake of My servant David." ' "

7 Then Isaiah said, "Take a lump of figs." So they took and laid *it* on the boil, and he recovered.

8 And Hezekiah said to Isaiah, "What *is* the sign that the LORD will heal me, and that I shall go up to the house of the LORD the third day?"

9 Then Isaiah said, "This is the sign to you from the LORD, that the LORD will do the thing which He has spoken: *shall* the shadow go forward ten degrees or go backward ten degrees?"

10 And Hezekiah answered, "It is an easy thing for the shadow to go down ten degrees; no, but let the shadow go backward ten degrees."

11 So Isaiah the prophet cried out to the LORD, and He brought the shadow ten degrees backward, by which it had gone down on the sundial of Ahaz.

12 At that time Berodach-Baladan*ᵃ* the son of Baladan, king of Babylon, sent letters and a present to Hezekiah, for he heard that Hezekiah had been sick. 13 And Hezekiah was attentive to them, and showed them all the house of his treasures—the silver and gold, the spices and precious ointment, and all*ᵃ* his armory—all that was found among his treasures. There was nothing in his house or in all his dominion that Hezekiah did not show them.

14 Then Isaiah the prophet went to King Hezekiah, and said to him, "What did these men say, and from where did they come to you?"

So Hezekiah said, "They came from a far country, from Babylon."

15 And he said, "What have they seen in your house?"

So Hezekiah answered, "They have seen all that *is* in my house; there is nothing among my treasures that I have not shown them."

16 Then Isaiah said to Hezekiah, "Hear the word of the LORD: 17 'Behold, the days are coming when all that *is* in your house, and what your fathers have accumulated until this day, shall be carried to Babylon; nothing shall be left,' says the LORD. 18 'And they shall take away some of your sons who will descend from you, whom you will beget; and they shall be eunuchs in the palace of the king of Babylon.' "

19 So Hezekiah said to Isaiah, "The word of the LORD which you have spoken *is* good!" For he said, "Will there not be peace and truth at least in my days?"

20 Now the rest of the acts of Hezekiah—all his might, and how he made a pool and a tunnel and brought water into the city—*are* they not written in the book of the chronicles of the kings of Judah? 21 So Hezekiah rested with his fathers. Then Manasseh his son reigned in his place.

21 Manasseh *was* twelve years old when he became king, and he reigned fifty-five years in Jerusalem. His mother's name *was* Hephzibah. 2 And he did evil in the sight of the

20:12 *ᵃ*Spelled *Merodach-Baladan* in Isaiah 39:1 and Targum; Masoretic Text omits *all*.   20:13 *ᵃ*Following many Hebrew manuscripts, Syriac,

*Y*ou must refuse to blame your past for your present and future. The fact is, you can never relive your past. You are not the person you were then and you are never going to be that person again.

LORD, according to the abominations of the nations whom the LORD had cast out before the children of Israel. 3 For he rebuilt the high places which Hezekiah his father had destroyed; he raised up altars for Baal, and made a wooden image,*a* as Ahab king of Israel had done; and he worshiped all the host of heaven*b* and served them. 4 He also built altars in the house of the LORD, of which the LORD had said, "In Jerusalem I will put My name." 5 And he built altars for all the host of heaven in the two courts of the house of the LORD. 6 Also he made his son pass through the fire, practiced soothsaying, used witchcraft, and consulted spiritists and mediums. He did much evil in the sight of the LORD, to provoke *Him* to anger. 7 He even set a carved image of Asherah*a* that he had made, in the house of which the LORD had said to David and to Solomon his son, "In this house and in Jerusalem, which I have chosen out of all the tribes of Israel, I will put My name forever; 8 and I will not make the feet of Israel wander anymore from the land which I gave their fathers—only if they are careful to do according to all that I have commanded them, and according to all the law that My servant Moses commanded them." 9 But they paid no attention, and Manasseh seduced them to do more evil than the nations whom the LORD had destroyed before the children of Israel.

10 And the LORD spoke by His servants the prophets, saying, 11 "Because Manasseh king of Judah has done these abominations (he has acted more wickedly than all the Amorites who *were* before him, and has also made Judah sin with his idols), 12 therefore thus says the LORD God of Israel: 'Behold, *I* am bringing *such* calamity upon Jerusalem and Judah, that whoever hears of it, both his ears will tingle. 13 And I will stretch over Jerusalem the measuring line of Samaria and the plummet of the house of Ahab; I will wipe Jerusalem as *one* wipes a dish, wiping *it* and turning *it* upside down. 14 So I will forsake the remnant of My inheritance and deliver them into the hand of their enemies; and they shall become vic-

tims of plunder to all their enemies, 15 because they have done evil in My sight, and have provoked Me to anger since the day their fathers came out of Egypt, even to this day.' "

16 Moreover Manasseh shed very much innocent blood, till he had filled Jerusalem from one end to another, besides his sin by which he made Judah sin, in doing evil in the sight of the LORD.

17 Now the rest of the acts of Manasseh—all that he did, and the sin that he committed—*are* they not written in the book of the chronicles of the kings of Judah? 18 So Manasseh rested with his fathers, and was buried in the garden of his own house, in the garden of Uzza. Then his son Amon reigned in his place.

19 Amon *was* twenty-two years old when he became king, and he reigned two years in Jerusalem. His mother's name *was* Meshullemeth the daughter of Haruz of Jotbah. 20 And he did evil in the sight of the LORD, as his father Manasseh had done. 21 So he walked in all the ways that his father had walked; and he served the idols that his father had served, and worshiped them. 22 He forsook the LORD God of his fathers, and did not walk in the way of the LORD.

23 Then the servants of Amon conspired against him, and killed the king in his own house. 24 But the people of the land executed all those who had conspired against King Amon. Then the people of the land made his son Josiah king in his place.

25 Now the rest of the acts of Amon which he did, *are* they not written in the book of the chronicles of the kings of Judah? 26 And he was buried in his tomb in the garden of Uzza. Then Josiah his son reigned in his place.

22 Josiah *was* eight years old when he became king, and he reigned thirty-one years in Jerusalem. His mother's name *was* Jedidah the daughter of Adaiah of Bozkath. 2 And he did *what was* right in the sight of the LORD, and walked in all the ways of his father David; he did not turn aside to the right hand or to the left.

21:3 *a*Hebrew *Asherah,* a Canaanite goddess   *b*The gods of the Assyrians   21:7 *a*A Canaanite goddess

3 Now it came to pass, in the eighteenth year of King Josiah, *that* the king sent Shaphan the scribe, the son of Azaliah, the son of Meshullam, to the house of the LORD, saying: 4 "Go up to Hilkiah the high priest, that he may count the money which has been brought into the house of the LORD, which the doorkeepers have gathered from the people. 5 And let them deliver it into the hand of those doing the work, who are the overseers in the house of the LORD; let them give it to those who *are* in the house of the LORD doing the work, to repair the damages of the house— 6 to carpenters and builders and masons—and to buy timber and hewn stone to repair the house. 7 However there need be no accounting made with them of the money delivered into their hand, because they deal faithfully."

8 Then Hilkiah the high priest said to Shaphan the scribe, "I have found the Book of the Law in the house of the LORD." And Hilkiah gave the book to Shaphan, and he read it. 9 So Shaphan the scribe went to the king, bringing the king word, saying, "Your servants have gathered the money that was found in the house, and have delivered it into the hand of those who do the work, who oversee the house of the LORD." 10 Then Shaphan the scribe showed the king, saying, "Hilkiah the priest has given me a book." And Shaphan read it before the king.

11 Now it happened, when the king heard the words of the Book of the Law, that he tore his clothes. 12 Then the king commanded Hilkiah the priest, Ahikam the son of Shaphan, Achbor[a] the son of Michaiah, Shaphan the scribe, and Asaiah a servant of the king, saying, 13 "Go, inquire of the LORD for me, for the people and for all Judah, concerning the words of this book that has been found; for great *is* the wrath of the LORD that is aroused against us, because our fathers have not obeyed the words of this book, to do according to all that is written concerning us."

14 So Hilkiah the priest, Ahikam, Achbor, Shaphan, and Asaiah went to Huldah the prophetess, the wife of Shallum the son of Tikvah, the son of Harhas, keeper of the wardrobe. (She dwelt in Jerusalem in the Second Quarter.) And they spoke with her. 15 Then she said to them, "Thus says the LORD God of Israel, 'Tell the man who sent you to Me, 16 "Thus says the LORD: 'Behold, I will bring calamity on this place and on its inhabitants—all the words of the book which the king of Judah has read— 17 because they have forsaken Me and burned incense to other gods, that they might provoke Me to anger with all the works of their hands. Therefore My wrath shall be aroused against this place and shall not be quenched.' " ' 18 But as for the king of Judah, who sent you to inquire of the LORD, in this manner you shall speak to him, 'Thus says the LORD God of Israel: "Concerning the words which you have heard— 19 because your heart was tender, and you humbled yourself before the LORD when you heard what I spoke against this place and against its inhabitants, that they would become a desolation and a curse, and you tore your clothes and wept before Me, I also have heard you," says the LORD. 20 Surely, therefore, I will gather you to your fathers, and you shall be gathered to your grave in peace; and your eyes shall not see all the calamity which I will bring on this place." ' " So they brought back word to the king.

23 Now the king sent them to gather all the elders of Judah and Jerusalem to him. 2 The king went up to the house of the LORD with all the men of Judah, and with him all the inhabitants of Jerusalem—the priests and the prophets and all the people, both small and great. And he read in their hearing all the words of the Book of the Covenant which had been found in the house of the LORD.

3 Then the king stood by a pillar and made a covenant before the LORD, to follow the LORD and to keep His commandments and His testimonies and His statutes, with all *his* heart and all *his* soul, to perform the words of this covenant that were written in this book. And all the people took a stand for the covenant. 4 And the king commanded Hilkiah the high priest, the priests of the sec-

22:12 ªAbdon the son of Micah in 2 Chronicles 34:20

*Y*ou can't go back into your mother's womb. Your past is your past. It is over! Accept that fact and dismiss your past and move on. Let it go!

ond order, and the doorkeepers, to bring out of the temple of the LORD all the articles that were made for Baal, for Asherah,ᵃ and for all the host of heaven;ᵇ and he burned them outside Jerusalem in the fields of Kidron, and carried their ashes to Bethel. 5 Then he removed the idolatrous priests whom the kings of Judah had ordained to burn incense on the high places in the cities of Judah and in the places all around Jerusalem, and those who burned incense to Baal, to the sun, to the moon, to the constellations, and to all the host of heaven. 6 And he brought out the wooden imageᵃ from the house of the LORD, to the Brook Kidron outside Jerusalem, burned it at the Brook Kidron and ground it to ashes, and threw its ashes on the graves of the common people. 7 Then he tore down the ritual booths of the perverted personsᵃ that were in the house of the LORD, where the women wove hangings for the wooden image. 8 And he brought all the priests from the cities of Judah, and defiled the high places where the priests had burned incense, from Geba to Beersheba; also he broke down the high places at the gates which were at the entrance of the Gate of Joshua the governor of the city, which were to the left of the city gate. 9 Nevertheless the priests of the high places did not come up to the altar of the LORD in Jerusalem, but they ate unleavened bread among their brethren.

10 And he defiled Topheth, which is in the Valley of the Sonᵃ of Hinnom, that no man might make his son or his daughter pass through the fire to Molech. 11 Then he removed the horses that the kings of Judah had dedicated to the sun, at the entrance to the house of the LORD, by the chamber of Nathan-Melech, the officer who was in the court; and he burned the chariots of the sun with fire. 12 The altars that were on the roof, the upper chamber of Ahaz, which the kings of Judah had made, and the altars which Manasseh had made in the two courts of the house of the LORD, the king broke down and pulverized there, and threw

their dust into the Brook Kidron. 13 Then the king defiled the high places that were east of Jerusalem, which were on the south of the Mount of Corruption, which Solomon king of Israel had built for Ashtoreth the abomination of the Sidonians, for Chemosh the abomination of the Moabites, and for Milcom the abomination of the people of Ammon. 14 And he broke in pieces the sacred pillars and cut down the wooden images, and filled their places with the bones of men.

15 Moreover the altar that was at Bethel, and the high place which Jeroboam the son of Nebat, who made Israel sin, had made, both that altar and the high place he broke down; and he burned the high place and crushed it to powder, and burned the wooden image. 16 As Josiah turned, he saw the tombs that were there on the mountain. And he sent and took the bones out of the tombs and burned them on the altar, and defiled it according to the word of the LORD which the man of God proclaimed, who proclaimed these words. 17 Then he said, "What gravestone is this that I see?"

So the men of the city told him, "It is the tomb of the man of God who came from Judah and proclaimed these things which you have done against the altar of Bethel."

18 And he said, "Let him alone; let no one move his bones." So they let his bones alone, with the bones of the prophet who came from Samaria.

19 Now Josiah also took away all the shrines of the high places that were in the cities of Samaria, which the kings of Israel had made to provoke the LORDᵃ to anger; and he did to them according to all the deeds he had done in Bethel. 20 He executed all the priests of the high places who were there, on the altars, and burned men's bones on them; and he returned to Jerusalem.

21 Then the king commanded all the people, saying, "Keep the Passover to the LORD your God, as it is written in this Book of the Covenant." 22 Such a Passover surely had never been held since the days of the judges who judged Israel, nor in all

23:4 ᵃA Canaanite goddess   ᵇThe gods of the Assyrians   23:6 ᵃHebrew Asherah, a Canaanite goddess   23:7 ᵃHebrew qedeshim, that is, those practicing sodomy and prostitution in religious rituals   23:10 ᵃKethib reads Sons.   23:19 ᵃFollowing Septuagint, Syriac, and Vulgate; Masoretic Text and Targum omit the LORD.

Gospel Pearls

the days of the kings of Israel and the kings of Judah. 23 But in the eighteenth year of King Josiah this Passover was held before the LORD in Jerusalem. 24 Moreover Josiah put away those who consulted mediums and spiritists, the household gods and idols, all the abominations that were seen in the land of Judah and in Jerusalem, that he might perform the words of the law which were written in the book that Hilkiah the priest found in the house of the LORD. 25 Now before him there was no king like him, who turned to the LORD with all his heart, with all his soul, and with all his might, according to all the Law of Moses; nor after him did *any* arise like him.

26 Nevertheless the LORD did not turn from the fierceness of His great wrath, with which His anger was aroused against Judah, because of all the provocations with which Manasseh had provoked Him. 27 And the LORD said, "I will also remove Judah from My sight, as I have removed Israel, and will cast off this city Jerusalem which I have chosen, and the house of which I said, 'My name shall be there.' "*ᵃ*

28 Now the rest of the acts of Josiah, and all that he did, *are* they not written in the book of the chronicles of the kings of Judah? 29 In his days Pharaoh Necho king of Egypt went to the aid of the king of Assyria, to the River Euphrates; and King Josiah went against him. And *Pharaoh Necho* killed him at Megiddo when he confronted him. 30 Then his servants moved his body in a chariot from Megiddo, brought him to Jerusalem, and buried him in his own tomb. And the people of the land took Jehoahaz the son of Josiah, anointed him, and made him king in his father's place.

31 Jehoahaz *was* twenty-three years old when he became king, and he reigned three months in Jerusalem. His mother's name *was* Hamutal the daughter of Jeremiah of Libnah. 32 And he did evil in the sight of the LORD, according to all that his fathers had done. 33 Now Pharaoh Necho put him in prison at Riblah in the land of Hamath, that he might not reign in Jerusalem; and he imposed on the land a tribute of one hundred talents of silver and a talent of gold.

34 Then Pharaoh Necho made Eliakim the son of Josiah king in place of his father Josiah, and changed his name to Jehoiakim. And *Pharaoh* took Jehoahaz and went to Egypt, and he*ᵃ* died there.

35 So Jehoiakim gave the silver and gold to Pharaoh; but he taxed the land to give money according to the command of Pharaoh; he exacted the silver and gold from the people of the land, from every one according to his assessment, to give *it* to Pharaoh Necho. 36 Jehoiakim *was* twenty-five years old when he became king, and he reigned eleven years in Jerusalem. His mother's name *was* Zebudah the daughter of Pedaiah of Rumah. 37 And he did evil in the sight of the LORD, according to all that his fathers had done.

24 In his days Nebuchadnezzar king of Babylon came up, and Jehoiakim became his vassal *for* three years. Then he turned and rebelled against him. 2 And the LORD sent against him *raiding* bands of Chaldeans, bands of Syrians, bands of Moabites, and bands of the people of Ammon; He sent them against Judah to destroy it, according to the word of the LORD which He had spoken by His servants the prophets. 3 Surely at the commandment of the LORD *this* came upon Judah, to remove *them* from His sight because of the sins of Manasseh, according to all that he had done, 4 and also because of the innocent blood that he had shed; for he had filled Jerusalem with innocent blood, which the LORD would not pardon.

5 Now the rest of the acts of Jehoiakim, and all that he did, *are* they not written in the book of the chronicles of the kings of Judah? 6 So Jehoiakim rested with his fathers. Then Jehoiachin his son reigned in his place.

7 And the king of Egypt did not come out of his land anymore, for the king of Babylon had taken all that belonged to the king of Egypt from the Brook of Egypt to the River Euphrates.

8 Jehoiachin *was* eighteen years old when he became king, and he reigned in Jerusalem three months. His mother's name *was* Nehushta the

---

23:27 *ᵃ*1 Kings 8:29   23:34 *ᵃ*That is, Jehoahaz

*L*et go of anything that is holding you back, or slowing you down, and keeping you all bound up inside. If you are holding on to your past, it's because there is something about your past that you think you still need.

daughter of Elnathan of Jerusalem. 9 And he did evil in the sight of the LORD, according to all that his father had done.

10 At that time the servants of Nebuchadnezzar king of Babylon came up against Jerusalem, and the city was besieged. 11 And Nebuchadnezzar king of Babylon came against the city, as his servants were besieging it. 12 Then Jehoiachin king of Judah, his mother, his servants, his princes, and his officers went out to the king of Babylon; and the king of Babylon, in the eighth year of his reign, took him prisoner.

13 And he carried out from there all the treasures of the house of the LORD and the treasures of the king's house, and he cut in pieces all the articles of gold which Solomon king of Israel had made in the temple of the LORD, as the LORD had said. 14 Also he carried into captivity all Jerusalem: all the captains and all the mighty men of valor, ten thousand captives, and all the craftsmen and smiths. None remained except the poorest people of the land. 15 And he carried Jehoiachin captive to Babylon. The king's mother, the king's wives, his officers, and the mighty of the land he carried into captivity from Jerusalem to Babylon. 16 All the valiant men, seven thousand, and craftsmen and smiths, one thousand, all *who were* strong *and* fit for war, these the king of Babylon brought captive to Babylon.

17 Then the king of Babylon made Mattaniah, *Jehoiachin's*ᵃ uncle, king in his place, and changed his name to Zedekiah.

18 Zedekiah *was* twenty-one years old when he became king, and he reigned eleven years in Jerusalem. His mother's name *was* Hamutal the daughter of Jeremiah of Libnah. 19 He also did evil in the sight of the LORD, according to all that Jehoiakim had done. 20 For because of the anger of the LORD *this* happened in Jerusalem and Judah, that He finally cast them out from His presence. Then Zedekiah rebelled against the king of Babylon.

25 Now it came to pass in the ninth year of his reign, in the tenth month, on the tenth *day* of the month, *that* Nebuchadnezzar king of Babylon and all his army came against Jerusalem and encamped against it; and they built a siege wall against it all around. 2 So the city was besieged until the eleventh year of King Zedekiah. 3 By the ninth *day* of the *fourth* month the famine had become so severe in the city that there was no food for the people of the land.

4 Then the city wall was broken through, and all the men of war *fled* at night by way of the gate between two walls, which was by the king's garden, even though the Chaldeans *were* still encamped all around against the city. And *the king*ᵃ went by way of the plain.ᵇ 5 But the army of the Chaldeans pursued the king, and they overtook him in the plains of Jericho. All his army was scattered from him. 6 So they took the king and brought him up to the king of Babylon at Riblah, and they pronounced judgment on him. 7 Then they killed the sons of Zedekiah before his eyes, put out the eyes of Zedekiah, bound him with bronze fetters, and took him to Babylon.

8 And in the fifth month, on the seventh *day* of the month (which *was* the nineteenth year of King Nebuchadnezzar king of Babylon), Nebuzaradan the captain of the guard, a servant of the king of Babylon, came to Jerusalem. 9 He burned the house of the LORD and the king's house; all the houses of Jerusalem, that is, all the houses of the great, he burned with fire. 10 And all the army of the Chaldeans who *were with* the captain of the guard broke down the walls of Jerusalem all around.

11 Then Nebuzaradan the captain of the guard carried away captive the rest of the people *who* remained in the city and the defectors who had deserted to the king of Babylon, with the rest of the multitude. 12 But the captain of the guard left *some* of the poor of the land as vinedressers and farmers. 13 The bronze pillars that *were* in the house of the LORD, and the carts and the bronze Sea that *were* in the house of the LORD, the Chaldeans broke in pieces, and carried their bronze to Babylon. 14 They also took away the pots, the

24:17 ªLiterally *his*   25:4 ªLiterally *he*   ᵇOr *Arabah*, that is, the Jordan Valley shovels, the trimmers, the spoons, and all the bronze utensils with which the priests ministered. 15 The firepans and the basins, the things of solid gold and solid silver, the captain of the guard took away. 16 The two pillars, one Sea, and the carts, which Solomon had made for the house of the LORD, the bronze of all these articles was beyond measure. 17 The height of one pillar *was* eighteen cubits, and the capital on it *was* of bronze. The height of the capital was three cubits, and the network and pomegranates all around the capital were all of bronze. The second pillar was the same, with a network.

18 And the captain of the guard took Seraiah the chief priest, Zephaniah the second priest, and the three doorkeepers. 19 He also took out of the city an officer who had charge of the men of war, five men of the king's close associates who were found in the city, the chief recruiting officer of the army, who mustered the people of the land, and sixty men of the people of the land *who were* found in the city. 20 So Nebuzaradan, captain of the guard, took these and brought them to the king of Babylon at Riblah. 21 Then the king of Babylon struck them and put them to death at Riblah in the land of Hamath. Thus Judah was carried away captive from its own land.

22 Then he made Gedaliah the son of Ahikam, the son of Shaphan, governor over the people who remained in the land of Judah, whom Nebuchadnezzar king of Babylon had left. 23 Now when all the captains of the armies, they and *their* men, heard

that the king of Babylon had made Gedaliah governor, they came to Gedaliah at Mizpah—Ishmael the son of Nethaniah, Johanan the son of Careah, Seraiah the son of Tanhumeth the Netophathite, and Jaazaniah[a] the son of a Maachathite, they and their men. 24 And Gedaliah took an oath before them and their men, and said to them, "Do not be afraid of the servants of the Chaldeans. Dwell in the land and serve the king of Babylon, and it shall be well with you."

25 But it happened in the seventh month that Ishmael the son of Nethaniah, the son of Elishama, of the royal family, came with ten men and struck and killed Gedaliah, the Jews, as well as the Chaldeans who were with him at Mizpah. 26 And all the people, small and great, and the captains of the armies, arose and went to Egypt; for they were afraid of the Chaldeans.

27 Now it came to pass in the thirty-seventh year of the captivity of Jehoiachin king of Judah, in the twelfth month, on the twenty-seventh *day* of the month, *that* Evil-Merodach[a] king of Babylon, in the year that he began to reign, released Jehoiachin king of Judah from prison. 28 He spoke kindly to him, and gave him a more prominent seat than those of the kings who *were* with him in Babylon. 29 So Jehoiachin changed from his prison garments, and he ate bread regularly before the king all the days of his life. 30 And as for his provisions, *there was* a regular ration given him by the king, a portion for each day, all the days of his life.

25:23 [a]Spelled *Jezaniah* in Jeremiah 40:8   25:27 [a]Literally *Man of Marduk*

---

*P*eople who don't let go of things easily have little faith. They cling to things because they fear they will never be able to replace them. Develop a large faith and let go.

1 Adam, Seth, Enosh, 2 Cainan,*a* Mahalalel, Jared, 3 Enoch, Methuselah, Lamech, 4 Noah,*a* Shem, Ham, and Japheth.

5 The sons of Japheth *were* Gomer, Magog, Madai, Javan, Tubal, Meshech, and Tiras. 6 The sons of Gomer *were* Ashkenaz, Diphath,*a* and Togarmah. 7 The sons of Javan *were* Elishah, Tarshishah,*a* Kittim, and Rodanim.*b*

8 The sons of Ham *were* Cush, Mizraim, Put, and Canaan. 9 The sons of Cush *were* Seba, Havilah, Sabta,*a* Raama,*b* and Sabtecha. The sons of Raama *were* Sheba and Dedan. 10 Cush begot Nimrod; he began to be a mighty one on the earth. 11 Mizraim begot Ludim, Anamim, Lehabim, Naphtuhim, 12 Pathrusim, Casluhim (from whom came the Philistines and the Caphtorim). 13 Canaan begot Sidon, his firstborn, and Heth; 14 the Jebusite, the Amorite, and the Girgashite; 15 the Hivite, the Arkite, and the Sinite; 16 the Arvadite, the Zemarite, and the Hamathite.

17 The sons of Shem *were* Elam, Asshur, Arphaxad, Lud, Aram, Uz, Hul, Gether, and Meshech.*a* 18 Arphaxad begot Shelah, and Shelah begot Eber. 19 To Eber were born two sons: the name of one *was* Peleg,*a* for in his days the earth was divided; and his brother's name *was* Joktan. 20 Joktan begot Almodad, Sheleph, Hazarmaveth, Jerah, 21 Hadoram, Uzal, Diklah, 22 Ebal,*a* Abimael, Sheba, 23 Ophir, Havilah, and Jobab. All these *were* the sons of Joktan.

24 Shem, Arphaxad, Shelah, 25 Eber, Peleg, Reu, 26 Serug, Nahor, Terah, 27 and Abram, who *is* Abraham. 28 The sons of Abraham *were* Isaac and Ishmael.

29 These *are* their genealogies: The firstborn of Ishmael *was* Nebajoth; then Kedar, Adbeel, Mibsam, 30 Mishma, Dumah, Massa, Hadad,*a* Tema, 31 Jetur, Naphish, and Kedemah. These *were* the sons of Ishmael.

32 Now the sons born to Keturah, Abraham's concubine, *were* Zimran, Jokshan, Medan, Midian, Ishbak, and Shuah. The sons of Jokshan *were* Sheba and Dedan. 33 The sons of Midian *were* Ephah, Epher, Hanoch, Abida, and Eldaah. All these were the children of Keturah.

34 And Abraham begot Isaac. The sons of Isaac *were* Esau and Israel. 35 The sons of Esau *were* Eliphaz, Reuel, Jeush, Jaalam, and Korah. 36 And the sons of Eliphaz *were* Teman, Omar, Zephi,*a* Gatam, *and* Kenaz; and *by* Timna,*b* Amalek. 37 The sons of Reuel *were* Nahath, Zerah, Shammah, and Mizzah.

38 The sons of Seir *were* Lotan, Shobal, Zibeon, Anah, Dishon, Ezer, and Dishan. 39 And the sons of Lotan *were* Hori and Homam; Lotan's sister *was* Timna. 40 The sons of Shobal *were* Alian,*a* Manahath, Ebal, Shephi,*b* and Onam. The sons of Zibeon *were* Ajah and Anah. 41 The son of Anah *was* Dishon. The sons of Dishon *were* Hamran,*a* Eshban, Ithran, and Cheran. 42 The sons of Ezer *were* Bilhan, Zaavan, *and* Jaakan.*a* The sons of Dishan *were* Uz and Aran.

43 Now these *were* the kings who reigned in the land of Edom before a king reigned over the children of Israel: Bela the son of Beor, and the name of his city was Dinhabah. 44 And when Bela died, Jobab the son of Zerah of Bozrah reigned in his place. 45 When Jobab died, Husham of the land of the Temanites reigned in his place. 46 And when Husham died, Hadad the son of Bedad, who attacked Midian in the field of Moab, reigned in his place. The name of his city *was* Avith. 47 When Hadad died, Samlah of Masrekah reigned in his place. 48 And when Samlah died,

---

1:2 *a*Hebrew *Qenan*   1:4 *a*Following Masoretic Text and Vulgate; Septuagint adds *the sons of Noah.*
1:6 *a*Spelled *Riphath* in Genesis 10:3   1:7 *a*Spelled *Tarshish* in Genesis 10:4   *b*Spelled *Dodanim* in
Genesis 10:4   1:9 *a*Spelled *Sabtah* in Genesis 10:7   *b*Spelled *Raamah* in Genesis 10:7   1:17 *a*Spelled
Mash in Genesis 10:23   1:19 *a*Literally *Division*   1:22 *a*Spelled *Obal* in Genesis 10:28   1:30 *a*Spelled
Hadar in Genesis 25:15   1:36 *a*Spelled *Zepho* in Genesis 36:11   *b*Compare Genesis 36:12
1:40 *a*Spelled *Alvan* in Genesis 36:23   *b*Spelled *Shepho* in Genesis 36:23   1:41 *a*Spelled *Hemdan* in
Genesis 36:26   1:42 *a*Spelled *Akan* in Genesis 36:27

---

*D*on't you know that God has more for you? He has something else for you. If you are trusting God for your future, then you have not yet seen your best days. There's more before you than there is behind you.

Keep Your Appointment

*I*t seems that every time I get ready for a major appointment, something comes up to slow me down. People will call and just want to chit-chat. I'll be pacing the floor trying to find a way to get off the phone, but the person will just go on and on. Or I won't be able to find the car keys. Or the gas gauge will read empty. Or the traffic will be heavy. Or an accident will block the highway.

When God has an appointed seed for you to birth, there may be obstacles to overcome and hindrances to hurdle. There may be delays you have to endure. There may be opportunities you have to refuse.

When God appoints a task for you, there's no time for idleness. There's no time for gossip. In order for you to receive what God has for you, you are going to have to hang up on some folks. You are going to have to hang up on some situations. You are going to have to outlast or outmaneuver some circumstances. You are going to have to say no to some activities that would make you late or pull you away from your appointment altogether. You will have no time for foolishness, pity parties, or side shows.

If you are going to hold on to your miracle, your dream, the fulfillment of God's plan for your life, then you are going to have to keep moving, keep moving, keep moving. Always keep moving toward what God has for you.

You may have to crawl to get there, but keep crawling. You may have to cry a lot of tears along the way, but keep walking. You may get knocked down, but get up and get going. Don't let anything keep you from keeping your appointment!

The thing that God has for you must be done. That's the way God feels about His plan for you. Write yourself a note: "I have an appointment. It must be kept."

Eve kept her appointment. Look at the genealogy in 1 Chronicles 1:1, and you'll see that she had a son named Seth, and he had a son named Enosh. The Bible says that it was with the birth of Enosh that Eve's descendants began to "call on the name of the LORD" (Genesis 4:26). That means that they began to trust God with their lives and to identify completely with Him. Seth was God's man. Enosh was God's man. The people of Enosh were God's people.

Eve lived to see her son and her grandson walk in holiness before the Lord. She lived to see her miracle. She lived to see her son and her grandson turn back to God and live in obedience, turning back the tide of disobedience and reversing the curse on her family.

Your curse can be reversed, too, if you will only keep your appointment with God.

Saul of Rehoboth-by-the-River reigned in his place. 49 When Saul died, Baal-Hanan the son of Achbor reigned in his place. 50 And when Baal-Hanan died, Hadad*a* reigned in his place; and the name of his city was Pai.*b* His wife's name was Mehetabel the daughter of Matred, the daughter of Mezahab. 51 Hadad died also. And the chiefs of Edom were Chief Timnah, Chief Aliah,*a* Chief Jetheth, 52 Chief Aholibamah, Chief Elah, Chief Pinon, 53 Chief Kenaz, Chief Teman, Chief Mibzar, 54 Chief Magdiel, and Chief Iram. These *were* the chiefs of Edom.

2 These *were* the sons of Israel: Reuben, Simeon, Levi, Judah, Issachar, Zebulun, 2 Dan, Joseph, Benjamin, Naphtali, Gad, and Asher.

3 The sons of Judah *were* Er, Onan, and Shelah. *These* three were born to him by the daughter of Shua, the Canaanitess. Er, the firstborn of Judah, was wicked in the sight of the LORD; so He killed him. 4 And Tamar, his daughter-in-law, bore him Perez and Zerah. All the sons of Judah *were* five.

5 The sons of Perez *were* Hezron and Hamul. 6 The sons of Zerah *were* Zimri, Ethan, Heman, Calcol, and Dara—five of them in all.

7 The son of Carmi *was* Achar,*a* the troubler of Israel, who transgressed in the accursed thing.

8 The son of Ethan *was* Azariah.

9 Also the sons of Hezron who were born to him *were* Jerahmeel, Ram, and Chelubai.*a* 10 Ram begot Amminadab, and Amminadab begot Nahshon, leader of the children of Judah; 11 Nahshon begot Salma,*a* and Salma begot Boaz; 12 Boaz begot Obed, and Obed begot Jesse; 13 Jesse begot Eliab his firstborn, Abinadab the second, Shimea*a* the third, 14 Nethanel the fourth, Raddai the fifth, 15 Ozem the sixth, *and* David the seventh.

16 Now their sisters *were* Zeruiah and Abigail. And the sons of Zeruiah *were* Abishai, Joab, and Asahel— three. 17 Abigail bore Amasa; and the father of Amasa *was* Jether the Ishmaelite.*a*

18 Caleb the son of Hezron had children by Azubah, *his* wife, and by Jerioth. Now these were her sons: Jesher, Shobab, and Ardon. 19 When Azubah died, Caleb took Ephrath*a* as his wife, who bore him Hur. 20 And Hur begot Uri, and Uri begot Bezalel.

21 Now afterward Hezron went in to the daughter of Machir the father of Gilead, whom he married when he *was* sixty years old; and she bore him Segub. 22 Segub begot Jair, who had twenty-three cities in the land of Gilead. 23 (Geshur and Syria took from them the towns of Jair, with Kenath and its towns—sixty towns.) All these *belonged to* the sons of Machir the father of Gilead. 24 After Hezron died in Caleb Ephrathah, Hezron's wife Abijah bore him Ashhur the father of Tekoa.

25 The sons of Jerahmeel, the firstborn of Hezron, *were* Ram, the firstborn, and Bunah, Oren, Ozem, *and* Ahijah. 26 Jerahmeel had another wife, whose name was Atarah; she was the mother of Onam. 27 The sons of Ram, the firstborn of Jerahmeel, were Maaz, Jamin, and Eker. 28 The sons of Onam were Shammai and Jada. The sons of Shammai *were* Nadab and Abishur.

29 And the name of the wife of Abishur *was* Abihail, and she bore him Ahban and Molid. 30 The sons of Nadab *were* Seled and Appaim; Seled died without children. 31 The son of Appaim *was* Ishi, the son of Ishi *was* Sheshan, and Sheshan's son *was* Ahlai. 32 The sons of Jada, the brother of Shammai, *were* Jether and Jonathan; Jether died without children. 33 The sons of Jonathan *were* Peleth and Zaza. These were the sons of Jerahmeel.

34 Now Sheshan had no sons, only daughters. And Sheshan had an Egyptian servant whose name *was* Jarha. 35 Sheshan gave his daughter to Jarha his servant as wife, and she bore him Attai. 36 Attai begot Nathan, and Nathan begot Zabad; 37 Zabad begot Ephlal, and Ephlal begot Obed; 38 Obed begot Jehu, and Jehu begot Azariah; 39 Azariah begot Helez, and Helez begot Eleasah;

1:50 *a*Spelled *Hadar* in Genesis 36:39   *b*Spelled *Pau* in Genesis 36:39   1:51 *a*Spelled *Alvah* in Genesis 36:40   2:7 *a*Spelled *Achan* in Joshua 7:1 and elsewhere   2:9 *a*Spelled *Caleb* in 2:18, 42   2:11 *a*Spelled *Salmon* in Ruth 4:21 and Luke 3:32   2:13 *a*Spelled *Shammah* in 1 Samuel 16:9 and elsewhere   2:17 *a*Compare 2 Samuel 17:25   2:19 *a*Spelled *Ephrathah* elsewhere

Gospel Pearls

40 Eleasah begot Sismai, and Sismai begot Shallum; 41 Shallum begot Jekamiah, and Jekamiah begot Elishama.

42 The descendants of Caleb the brother of Jerahmeel *were* Mesha, his firstborn, who was the father of Ziph, and the sons of Mareshah the father of Hebron. 43 The sons of Hebron *were* Korah, Tappuah, Rekem, and Shema. 44 Shema begot Raham the father of Jorkoam, and Rekem begot Shammai. 45 And the son of Shammai *was* Maon, and Maon *was* the father of Beth Zur.

46 Ephah, Caleb's concubine, bore Haran, Moza, and Gazez; and Haran begot Gazez. 47 And the sons of Jahdai *were* Regem, Jotham, Geshan, Pelet, Ephah, and Shaaph.

48 Maachah, Caleb's concubine, bore Sheber and Tirhanah. 49 She also bore Shaaph the father of Madmannah, Sheva the father of Machbenah and the father of Gibea. And the daughter of Caleb *was* Achsah.

50 These were the descendants of Caleb: The sons of Hur, the firstborn of Ephrathah, *were* Shobal the father of Kirjath Jearim, 51 Salma the father of Bethlehem, *and* Hareph the father of Beth Gader.

52 And Shobal the father of Kirjath Jearim had descendants: Haroeh, *and* half of the families of Manuhoth.*a* 53 The families of Kirjath Jearim *were* the Ithrites, the Puthites, the Shumathites, and the Mishraites. From these came the Zorathites and the Eshtaolites.

54 The sons of Salma *were* Bethlehem, the Netophathites, Atroth Beth Joab, half of the Manahethites, and the Zorites.

55 And the families of the scribes who dwelt at Jabez *were* the Tirathites, the Shimeathites, *and* the Suchathites. These *were* the Kenites who came from Hammath, the father of the house of Rechab.

3 Now these were the sons of David who were born to him in Hebron: The firstborn *was* Amnon, by Ahinoam the Jezreelitess; the second, Daniel,*a* by Abigail the Carmelitess; 2 the third, Absalom the son of Maacah, the daughter of Talmai, king of Geshur; the fourth, Adonijah the son of Haggith; 3 the fifth, Shephatiah, by Abital; the sixth, Ithream, by his wife Eglah.

4 *These* six were born to him in Hebron. There he reigned seven years and six months, and in Jerusalem he reigned thirty-three years. 5 And these were born to him in Jerusalem: Shimea,*a* Shobab, Nathan, and Solomon—four by Bathshua*b* the daughter of Ammiel.*c* 6 Also *there* were Ibhar, Elishama,*a* Eliphelet,*b* 7 Nogah, Nepheg, Japhia, 8 Elishama, Eliada,*a* and Eliphelet—nine *in all.* 9 *These were* all the sons of David, besides the sons of the concubines, and Tamar their sister.

10 Solomon's son *was* Rehoboam; Abijah*a was* his son, Asa his son, Jehoshaphat his son, 11 Joram*a* his son, Ahaziah his son, Joash*b* his son, 12 Amaziah his son, Azariah*a* his son, Jotham his son, 13 Ahaz his son, Hezekiah his son, Manasseh his son, 14 Amon his son, *and* Josiah his son. 15 The sons of Josiah *were* Johanan the firstborn, the second Jehoiakim, the third Zedekiah, and the fourth Shallum.*a* 16 The sons of Jehoiakim *were* Jeconiah his son *and* Zedekiah*a* his son.

17 And the sons of Jeconiah*a were* Assir,*b* Shealtiel his son, 18 *and* Malchiram, Pedaiah, Shenazzar, Jecamiah, Hoshama, and Nedabiah. 19 The sons of Pedaiah *were* Zerubbabel and Shimei. The sons of Zerubbabel *were* Meshullam, Hananiah, Shelomith their sister, 20 and Hashubah, Ohel, Berechiah, Hasadiah, and Jushab-Hesed—five *in all.*

21 The sons of Hananiah *were* Pelatiah and Jeshaiah, the sons of Rephaiah, the sons of Arnan, the sons of Obadiah, and the sons of Shechaniah. 22 The son of Shechaniah was Shemaiah. The sons of Shemaiah *were* Hattush, Igal, Bariah, Neariah, and Shaphat—six *in all.* 23 The sons of Neariah *were* Elioenai, Hezekiah,

---

2:52 *a*Same as *the Manahethites,* verse 54   3:1 *a*Called *Chileab* in 2 Samuel 3:3   3:5 *a*Spelled *Shammua* in 14:4 and 2 Samuel 5:14   *b*Spelled *Bathsheba* in 2 Samuel 11:3   *c*Called *Eliam* in 2 Samuel 11:3   3:6 *a*Spelled *Elishua* in 14:5 and 2 Samuel 5:15   *b*Spelled *Elpelet* in 14:5   3:8 *a*Spelled *Beeliada* in 14:7   3:10 *a*Spelled *Abijam* in 1 Kings 15:1   3:11 *a*Spelled *Jehoram* in 2 Kings 1:17 and 8:16   *b*Spelled *Jehoash* in 2 Kings 12:1   3:12 *a*Called *Uzziah* in Isaiah 6:1   3:15 *a*Called *Jehoahaz* in 2 Kings 23:31   3:16 *a*Compare 2 Kings 24:17   3:17 *a*Also called *Coniah* in Jeremiah 22:24 and *Jehoiachin* in 2 Kings 24:8   *b*Or *the captive were*

What we want is not to be a slave to our own passions, our own emotions, our own desires, or our own appetites; but to enjoy them and let them serve to glorify God. That is the true nature of deliverance in the vast majority of cases.

and Azrikam—three *in all.* 24 The sons of Elioenai *were* Hodaviah, Eliashib, Pelaiah, Akkub, Johanan, Delaiah, and Anani—seven *in all.*

4 The sons of Judah *were* Perez, Hezron, Carmi, Hur, and Shobal. 2 And Reaiah the son of Shobal begot Jahath, and Jahath begot Ahumai and Lahad. These *were* the families of the Zorathites. 3 These *were* the sons *of the father* of Etam: Jezreel, Ishma, and Idbash; and the name of their sister *was* Hazelelponi; 4 and Penuel *was* the father of Gedor, and Ezer *was the* father of Hushah.

These *were* the sons of Hur, the firstborn of Ephrathah the father of Bethlehem.

5 And Ashhur the father of Tekoa had two wives, Helah and Naarah. 6 Naarah bore him Ahuzzam, Hepher, Temeni, and Haahashtari. These *were* the sons of Naarah. 7 The sons of Helah *were* Zereth, Zohar, and Ethnan; 8 and Koz begot Anub, Zobebah, and the families of Aharhel the son of Harum.

9 Now Jabez was more honorable than his brothers, and his mother called his name Jabez,*a* saying, "Because I bore *him* in pain." 10 And Jabez called on the God of Israel saying, "Oh, that You would bless me indeed, and enlarge my territory, that Your hand would be with me, and that You would keep *me* from evil, that I may not cause pain!" So God granted him what he requested.

11 Chelub the brother of Shuhah begot Mehir, who *was* the father of Eshton. 12 And Eshton begot Beth-Rapha, Paseah, and Tehinnah the father of Ir-Nahash. These *were* the men of Rechah.

13 The sons of Kenaz *were* Othniel and Seraiah. The sons of Othniel *were* Hathath,*a* 14 and Meonothai who begot Ophrah. Seraiah begot Joab the father of Ge Harashim,*a* for they were craftsmen. 15 The sons of Caleb the son of Jephunneh *were* Iru, Elah, and Naam. The son of Elah *was* Kenaz. 16 The sons of Jehallelel *were* Ziph, Ziphah, Tiria, and Asarel. 17 The sons of Ezrah *were* Jether, Mered, Epher, and Jalon. And

Mered's wife*a* bore Miriam, Shammai, and Ishbah the father of Eshtemoa. 18 (His wife Jehudijah*a* bore Jered the father of Gedor, Heber the father of Sochoh, and Jekuthiel the father of Zanoah.) And these *were* the sons of Bithiah the daughter of Pharaoh, whom Mered took.

19 The sons of Hodiah's wife, the sister of Naham, *were* the fathers of Keilah the Garmite and of Eshtemoa the Maachathite. 20 And the sons of Shimon *were* Amnon, Rinnah, Ben-Hanan, and Tilon. And the sons of Ishi *were* Zoheth and Ben-Zoheth.

21 The sons of Shelah the son of Judah *were* Er the father of Lecah, Laadah the father of Mareshah, and the families of the house of the linen workers of the house of Ashbea; 22 also Jokim, the men of Chozeba, and Joash; Saraph, who ruled in Moab, and Jashubi-Lehem. Now the records are ancient. 23 These *were* the potters and those who dwell at Netaim*a* and Gederah;*b* there they dwelt with the king for his work.

24 The sons of Simeon *were* Nemuel, Jamin, Jarib,*a* Zerah,*b* and Shaul, 25 Shallum his son, Mibsam his son, and Mishma his son. 26 And the sons of Mishma *were* Hamuel his son, Zacchur his son, and Shimei his son. 27 Shimei had sixteen sons and six daughters; but his brothers did not have many children, nor did any of their families multiply as much as the children of Judah.

28 They dwelt at Beersheba, Moladah, Hazar Shual, 29 Bilhah, Ezem, Tolad, 30 Bethuel, Hormah, Ziklag, 31 Beth Marcaboth, Hazar Susim, Beth Biri, and at Shaaraim. These *were* their cities until the reign of David. 32 And their villages *were* Etam, Ain, Rimmon, Tochen, and Ashan—five cities— 33 and all the villages that *were* around these cities as far as Baal.*a* These *were* their dwelling places, and they maintained their genealogy: 34 Meshobab, Jamlech, and Joshah the son of Amaziah; 35 Joel, and Jehu the son of Joshibiah, the son of Seraiah, the son of Asiel; 36 Elioenai, Jaakobah, Jeshohaiah, Asaiah, Adiel, Jesimiel, and Benaiah; 37 Ziza the son of Shiphi,

4:9 *a*Literally *He Will Cause Pain*   4:13 *a*Septuagint and Vulgate add *and Meonothai.*   4:14 *a*Literally *Valley of Craftsmen*   4:17 *a*Literally *she*   4:18 *a*Or *His Judean wife*   4:23 *a*Literally *Plants*   *b*Literally *Hedges*   4:24 *a*Called *Jachin* in Genesis 46:10   *b*Called *Zohar* in Genesis 46:10   4:33 *a*Or *Baalath Beer* (compare Joshua 19:8)

Gospel Pearls

the son of Allon, the son of Jedaiah, the son of Shimri, the son of She- maiah— 38 these mentioned by name *were* leaders in their families, and their father's house increased greatly.

39 So they went to the entrance of Gedor, as far as the east side of the valley, to seek pasture for their flocks. 40 And they found rich, good pasture, and the land *was* broad, quiet, and peaceful; for some Ham- ites formerly lived there.

41 These recorded by name came in the days of Hezekiah king of Ju- dah; and they attacked their tents and the Meunites who were found there, and utterly destroyed them, as it is to this day. So they dwelt in their place, because *there was* pasture for their flocks there. 42 Now *some* of them, five hundred men of the sons of Simeon, went to Mount Seir, hav- ing as their captains Pelatiah, Nea- riah, Rephaiah, and Uzziel, the sons of Ishi. 43 And they defeated the rest of the Amalekites who had escaped. They have dwelt there to this day.

5 Now the sons of Reuben the first- born of Israel—he *was* indeed the firstborn, but because he defiled his father's bed, his birthright was given to the sons of Joseph, the son of Is- rael, so that the genealogy is not listed according to the birthright; 2 yet Judah prevailed over his broth- ers, and from him *came* a ruler, al- though the birthright was Joseph's— 3 the sons of Reuben the firstborn of Israel were Hanoch, Pallu, Hezron, and Carmi.

4 The sons of Joel *were* Shemaiah his son, Gog his son, Shimei his son, 5 Micah his son, Reaiah his son, Baal his son, 6 and Beerah his son, whom Tiglath-Pileser[a] king of Assyria car- ried into captivity. He *was* leader of the Reubenites. 7 And his brethren by their families, when the genealogy of their generations was registered: the chief, Jeiel, and Zechariah, 8 and Bela the son of Azaz, the son of Shema, the son of Joel, who dwelt in Aroer, as far as Nebo and Baal Meon. 9 Eastward they settled as far as the entrance of the wilderness this side of the River Euphrates, because their cattle had multiplied in the land of Gilead.

10 Now in the days of Saul they made war with the Hagrites, who fell by their hand; and they dwelt in their tents throughout the entire *area* east of Gilead.

11 And the children of Gad dwelt next to them in the land of Bashan as far as Salcah: 12 Joel *was* the chief, Shapham the next, then Jaanai and Shaphat in Bashan, 13 and their brethren of their father's house: Mi- chael, Meshullam, Sheba, Jorai, Ja- chan, Zia, and Eber—seven *in all.* 14 These *were* the children of Abihail the son of Huri, the son of Jaroah, the son of Gilead, the son of Michael, the son of Jeshishai, the son of Jahdo, the son of Buz; 15 Ahi the son of Abdiel, the son of Guni, *was* chief of their father's house. 16 And *the Gadites* dwelt in Gilead, in Bashan and in its villages, and in all the com- mon-lands of Sharon within their borders. 17 All these were registered by genealogies in the days of Jotham king of Judah, and in the days of Jer- oboam king of Israel.

18 The sons of Reuben, the Gadites, and half the tribe of Manasseh *had* forty-four thousand seven hundred and sixty valiant men, men able to bear shield and sword, to shoot with the bow, and skillful in war, who went to war. 19 They made war with the Hagrites, Jetur, Naphish, and No- dab. 20 And they were helped against them, and the Hagrites were deliv- ered into their hand, and all who *were* with them, for they cried out to God in the battle. He heeded their prayer, because they put their trust in Him. 21 Then they took away their livestock—fifty thousand of their camels, two hundred and fifty thou- sand of their sheep, and two thou- sand of their donkeys—also one hundred thousand of their men; 22 for many fell dead, because the war *was* God's. And they dwelt in their place until the captivity.

23 So the children of the half-tribe of Manasseh dwelt in the land. Their *numbers* increased from Bashan to Baal Hermon, that is, to Senir, or Mount Hermon. 24 These *were* the heads of their fathers' houses: Epher, Ishi, Eliel, Azriel, Jeremiah, Hoda- viah, and Jahdiel. They were mighty men of valor, famous men, *and* heads of their fathers' houses.

5:6 ᵃHebrew *Tilgath-Pilneser*

*J*acob wrestled with an angel of the Lord one night and came out of that experience with two things: the blessing of God and a limp in his walk. Your struggle with sin doesn't mean that you aren't saved in your spirit or healed in your soul. It means only that you still have a limp.

25 And they were unfaithful to the God of their fathers, and played the harlot after the gods of the peoples of the land, whom God had destroyed before them. 26 So the God of Israel stirred up the spirit of Pul king of Assyria, that is, Tiglath-Pileser*a* king of Assyria. He carried the Reubenites, the Gadites, and the half-tribe of Manasseh into captivity. He took them to Halah, Habor, Hara, and the river of Gozan to this day.

6 The sons of Levi *were* Gershon, Kohath, and Merari. 2 The sons of Kohath *were* Amram, Izhar, Hebron, and Uzziel. 3 The children of Amram *were* Aaron, Moses, and Miriam. And the sons of Aaron *were* Nadab, Abihu, Eleazar, and Ithamar. 4 Eleazar begot Phinehas, *and* Phinehas begot Abishua; 5 Abishua begot Bukki, and Bukki begot Uzzi; 6 Uzzi begot Zerahiah, and Zerahiah begot Meraioth; 7 Meraioth begot Amariah, and Amariah begot Ahitub; 8 Ahitub begot Zadok, and Zadok begot Ahimaaz; 9 Ahimaaz begot Azariah, and Azariah begot Johanan; 10 Johanan begot Azariah (it was he who ministered as priest in the temple that Solomon built in Jerusalem); 11 Azariah begot Amariah, and Amariah begot Ahitub; 12 Ahitub begot Zadok, and Zadok begot Shallum; 13 Shallum begot Hilkiah, and Hilkiah begot Azariah; 14 Azariah begot Seraiah, and Seraiah begot Jehozadak. 15 Jehozadak went *into captivity* when the LORD carried Judah and Jerusalem into captivity by the hand of Nebuchadnezzar.

16 The sons of Levi *were* Gershon,*a* Kohath, and Merari. 17 These are the names of the sons of Gershon: Libni and Shimei. 18 The sons of Kohath *were* Amram, Izhar, Hebron, and Uzziel. 19 The sons of Merari *were* Mahli and Mushi. Now these *are* the families of the Levites according to their fathers: 20 Of Gershon *were* Libni his son, Jahath his son, Zimmah his son, 21 Joah his son, Iddo his son, Zerah his son, *and* Jeatherai his son. 22 The sons of Kohath *were* Amminadab his son, Korah his son,

Assir his son, 23 Elkanah his son, Ebiasaph his son, Assir his son, 24 Tahath his son, Uriel his son, Uzziah his son, and Shaul his son. 25 The sons of Elkanah *were* Amasai and Ahimoth. 26 *As for* Elkanah,*a* the sons of Elkanah *were* Zophai*b* his son, Nahath*c* his son, 27 Eliab*a* his son, Jeroham his son, *and* Elkanah his son. 28 The sons of Samuel *were* Joel*a* the firstborn, and Abijah the second.*b* 29 The sons of Merari *were* Mahli, Libni his son, Shimei his son, Uzzah his son, 30 Shimea his son, Haggiah his son, *and* Asaiah his son.

31 Now these are the men whom David appointed over the service of song in the house of the LORD, after the ark came to rest. 32 They were ministering with music before the dwelling place of the tabernacle of meeting, until Solomon had built the house of the LORD in Jerusalem, and they served in their office according to their order.

33 And these *are* the ones who ministered with their sons: Of the sons of the Kohathites *were* Heman the singer, the son of Joel, the son of Samuel, 34 the son of Elkanah, the son of Jeroham, the son of Eliel,*a* the son of Toah,*b* 35 the son of Zuph, the son of Elkanah, the son of Mahath, the son of Amasai, 36 the son of Elkanah, the son of Joel, the son of Azariah, the son of Zephaniah, 37 the son of Tahath, the son of Assir, the son of Ebiasaph, the son of Korah, 38 the son of Izhar, the son of Kohath, the son of Levi, the son of Israel. 39 And his brother Asaph, who stood at his right hand, *was* Asaph the son of Berachiah, the son of Shimea, 40 the son of Michael, the son of Baaseiah, the son of Malchijah, 41 the son of Ethni, the son of Zerah, the son of Adaiah, 42 the son of Ethan, the son of Zimmah, the son of Shimei, 43 the son of Jahath, the son of Gershon, the son of Levi.

44 Their brethren, the sons of Merari, on the left hand, *were* Ethan the son of Kishi, the son of Abdi, the son of Malluch, 45 the son of Hashabiah, the son of Amaziah, the son of Hilkiah, 46 the son of Amzi, the son of

---

Gospel Pearls

Bani, the son of Shamer, 47 the son of Mahli, the son of Mushi, the son of Merari, the son of Levi.

48 And their brethren, the Levites, *were* appointed to every kind of service of the tabernacle of the house of God.

49 But Aaron and his sons offered sacrifices on the altar of burnt offering and on the altar of incense, for all the work of the Most Holy *Place,* and to make atonement for Israel, according to all that Moses the servant of God had commanded. 50 Now these *are* the sons of Aaron: Eleazar his son, Phinehas his son, Abishua his son, 51 Bukki his son, Uzzi his son, Zerahiah his son, 52 Meraioth his son, Amariah his son, Ahitub his son, 53 Zadok his son, *and* Ahimaaz his son.

54 Now these *are* their dwelling places throughout their settlements in their territory, for they were *given* by lot to the sons of Aaron, of the family of the Kohathites: 55 They gave them Hebron in the land of Judah, with its surrounding common-lands. 56 But the fields of the city and its villages they gave to Caleb the son of Jephunneh. 57 And to the sons of Aaron they gave *one of* the cities of refuge, Hebron; also Libnah with its common-lands, Jattir, Eshtemoa with its common-lands, 58 Hilen*a* with its common-lands, Debir with its common-lands, 59 Ashan*a* with its common-lands, and Beth Shemesh with its common-lands. 60 And from the tribe of Benjamin: Geba with its common-lands, Alemeth*a* with its common-lands, and Anathoth with its common-lands. All their cities among their families *were* thirteen.

61 To the rest of the family of the tribe of the Kohathites *they gave* by lot ten cities from half the tribe of Manasseh. 62 And to the sons of Gershon, throughout their families, *they gave* thirteen cities from the tribe of Issachar, from the tribe of Asher, from the tribe of Naphtali, and from the tribe of Manasseh in Bashan. 63 To the sons of Merari, throughout their families, *they gave* twelve cities from the tribe of Reuben, from the tribe of Gad, and from the tribe of Zebulun. 64 So the children of Israel gave *these* cities with their common-

lands to the Levites. 65 And they gave by lot from the tribe of the children of Judah, from the tribe of the children of Simeon, and from the tribe of Benjamin these cities which are called by *their* names.

66 Now some of the families of the sons of Kohath *were given* cities as their territory from the tribe of Ephraim. 67 And they gave them *one of* the cities of refuge, Shechem with its common-lands, in the mountains of Ephraim, also Gezer with its common-lands, 68 Jokmeam with its common-lands, Beth Horon with its common-lands, 69 Aijalon with its common-lands, and Gath Rimmon with its common-lands. 70 And from the half-tribe of Manasseh: Aner with its common-lands and Bileam with its common-lands, for the rest of the family of the sons of Kohath.

71 From the family of the half-tribe of Manasseh the sons of Gershon *were given* Golan in Bashan with its common-lands and Ashtaroth with its common-lands. 72 And from the tribe of Issachar: Kedesh with its common-lands, Daberath with its common-lands, 73 Ramoth with its common-lands, and Anem with its common-lands. 74 And from the tribe of Asher: Mashal with its common-lands, Abdon with its common-lands, 75 Hukok with its common-lands, and Rehob with its common-lands. 76 And from the tribe of Naphtali: Kedesh in Galilee with its common-lands, Hammon with its common-lands, and Kirjathaim with its common-lands.

77 From the tribe of Zebulun the rest of the children of Merari *were given* Rimmon*a* with its common-lands and Tabor with its common-lands. 78 And on the other side of the Jordan, across from Jericho, on the east side of the Jordan, *they were given* from the tribe of Reuben: Bezer in the wilderness with its common-lands, Jahzah with its common-lands, 79 Kedemoth with its common-lands, and Mephaath with its common-lands. 80 And from the tribe of Gad: Ramoth in Gilead with its common-lands, Mahanaim with its common-lands, 81 Heshbon with its common-lands, and Jazer with its common-lands.

6:58 *a*Spelled *Holon* in Joshua 21:15   6:59 *a*Spelled *Ain* in Joshua 21:16   6:60 *a*Spelled *Almon* in Joshua 21:18   6:77 *a*Hebrew *Rimmono,* alternate spelling of *Rimmon;* see 4:32

*D*on't let lingering symptoms fool you. Your deliverance is sure when the pain has been taken away from your heart.

7 The sons of Issachar *were* Tola, Puah,*a* Jashub, and Shimron— four *in all.* 2 The sons of Tola *were* Uzzi, Rephaiah, Jeriel, Jahmai, Jibsam, and Shemuel, heads of their father's house. *The sons* of Tola *were* mighty men of valor in their generations; their number in the days of David *was* twenty-two thousand six hundred. 3 The son of Uzzi *was* Izrahiah, and the sons of Izrahiah *were* Michael, Obadiah, Joel, and Ishiah. All five of them *were* chief men. 4 And with them, by their generations, according to their fathers' houses, *were* thirty-six thousand troops ready for war; for they had many wives and sons.

5 Now their brethren among all the families of Issachar *were* mighty men of valor, listed by their genealogies, eighty-seven thousand in all.

6 *The sons* of Benjamin *were* Bela, Becher, and Jediael—three *in all.* 7 The sons of Bela were Ezbon, Uzzi, Uzziel, Jerimoth, and Iri—five *in all.* They *were* heads of *their* fathers' houses, and they were listed by their genealogies, twenty-two thousand and thirty-four mighty men of valor.

8 The sons of Becher *were* Zemirah, Joash, Eliezer, Elioenai, Omri, Jerimoth, Abijah, Anathoth, and Alemeth. All these *are* the sons of Becher. 9 And they were recorded by genealogy according to their generations, heads of their fathers' houses, twenty thousand two hundred mighty men of valor. 10 The son of Jediael *was* Bilhan, and the sons of Bilhan *were* Jeush, Benjamin, Ehud, Chenaanah, Zethan, Tharshish, and Ahishahar.

11 All these sons of Jediael *were* heads of their fathers' houses; *there were* seventeen thousand two hundred mighty men of valor fit to go out for war *and* battle. 12 Shuppim and Huppim*a were* the sons of Ir, *and* Hushim *was* the son of Aher.

13 The sons of Naphtali *were* Jahziel,*a* Guni, Jezer, and Shallum,*b* the sons of Bilhah.

14 The descendants of Manasseh: his Syrian concubine bore him Machir the father of Gilead, the father of Asriel.*a* 15 Machir took as his wife *the sister* of Huppim and Shuppim,*a* whose name *was* Maachah. The name of *Gilead's* grandson*b was* Zelophehad,*c* but Zelophehad begot only daughters. 16 (Maachah the wife of Machir bore a son, and she called his name Peresh. The name of his brother *was* Sheresh, and his sons *were* Ulam and Rakem. 17 The son of Ulam *was* Bedan.) These *were* the descendants of Gilead the son of Machir, the son of Manasseh.

18 His sister Hammoleketh bore Ishhod, Abiezer, and Mahlah.

19 And the sons of Shemida were Ahian, Shechem, Likhi, and Aniam.

20 The sons of Ephraim *were* Shuthelah, Bered his son, Tahath his son, Eladah his son, Tahath his son, 21 Zabad his son, Shuthelah his son, and Ezer and Elead. The men of Gath who were born in *that* land killed *them* because they came down to take away their cattle. 22 Then Ephraim their father mourned many days, and his brethren came to comfort him.

23 And when he went in to his wife, she conceived and bore a son; and he called his name Beriah,*a* because tragedy had come upon his house. 24 Now his daughter *was* Sheerah, who built Lower and Upper Beth Horon and Uzzen Sheerah; 25 and Rephah *was* his son, *as well as* Resheph, and Telah his son, Tahan his son, 26 Laadan his son, Ammihud his son, Elishama his son, 27 Nun*a* his son, and Joshua his son.

28 Now their possessions and dwelling places *were* Bethel and its towns: to the east Naaran, to the west Gezer and its towns, and Shechem and its towns, as far as Ayyah*a* and its towns; 29 and by the borders of the children of Manasseh *were* Beth Shean and its towns, Taanach and its towns, Megiddo and its towns, Dor and its towns. In these dwelt the children of Joseph, the son of Israel.

30 The sons of Asher *were* Imnah, Ishvah, Ishvi, Beriah, and their sister Serah. 31 The sons of Beriah *were* Heber and Malchiel, who was the father of Birzaith.*a* 32 And Heber begot

---

7:1 *a*Spelled *Puvah* in Genesis 46:13   7:12 *a*Called *Hupham* in Numbers 26:39   7:13 *a*Spelled *Jahzeel* in Genesis 46:24   *b*Spelled *Shillem* in Genesis 46:24   7:14 *a*The son of Gilead (compare Numbers 26:30, 31)   7:15 *a*Compare verse 12   *b*Literally *the second*   *c*Compare Numbers 26:30–33   7:23 *a*Literally *In Tragedy*   7:27 *a*Hebrew *Non*   7:28 *a*Many Hebrew manuscripts, Bomberg, Septuagint, Targum, and Vulgate read *Gazza.*   7:31 *a*Or *Birzavith* or *Birzoth*

Gospel Pearls

Japhlet, Shomer,ᵃ Hotham,ᵇ and their sister Shua. 33 The sons of Japhlet *were* Pasach, Bimhal, and Ashvath. These *were* the children of Japhlet. 34 The sons of Shemer *were* Ahi, Rohgah, Jehubbah, and Aram. 35 And the sons of his brother Helem *were* Zophah, Imna, Shelesh, and Amal. 36 The sons of Zophah *were* Suah, Harnepher, Shual, Beri, Imrah, 37 Bezer, Hod, Shamma, Shilshah, Jithran,ᵃ and Beera. 38 The sons of Jether *were* Jephunneh, Pispah, and Ara. 39 The sons of Ulla *were* Arah, Haniel, and Rizia.

40 All these *were* the children of Asher, heads of *their* fathers' houses, choice men, mighty men of valor, chief leaders. And they were recorded by genealogies among the army fit for battle; their number *was* twenty-six thousand.

8 Now Benjamin begot Bela his firstborn, Ashbel the second, Aharahᵃ the third, 2 Nohah the fourth, and Rapha the fifth. 3 The sons of Bela *were* Addar,ᵃ Gera, Abihud, 4 Abishua, Naaman, Ahoah, 5 Gera, Shephuphan, and Huram.

6 These *are* the sons of Ehud, who were the heads of the fathers' *houses* of the inhabitants of Geba, and who forced them to move to Manahath: 7 Naaman, Ahijah, and Gera who forced them to move. He begot Uzza and Ahihud.

8 Also Shaharaim had children in the country of Moab, after he had sent away Hushim and Baara his wives. 9 By Hodesh his wife he begot Jobab, Zibia, Mesha, Malcam, 10 Jeuz, Sachiah, and Mirmah. These *were* his sons, heads of their fathers' *houses*.

11 And by Hushim he begot Abitub and Elpaal. 12 The sons of Elpaal *were* Eber, Misham, and Shemed, who built Ono and Lod with its towns; 13 and Beriah and Shema, who *were* heads of their fathers' *houses* of the inhabitants of Aijalon, who drove out the inhabitants of Gath. 14 Ahio, Shashak, Jeremoth, 15 Zebadiah, Arad, Eder, 16 Michael, Ispah, and Joha *were* the sons of Be-

riah. 17 Zebadiah, Meshullam, Hizki, Heber, 18 Ishmerai, Jizliah, and Jobab *were* the sons of Elpaal. 19 Jakim, Zichri, Zabdi, 20 Elienai, Zillethai, Eliel, 21 Adaiah, Beraiah, and Shimrath *were* the sons of Shimei. 22 Ishpan, Eber, Eliel, 23 Abdon, Zichri, Hanan, 24 Hananiah, Elam, Antothijah, 25 Iphdeiah, and Penuel *were* the sons of Shashak. 26 Shamsherai, Shehariah, Athaliah, 27 Jaareshiah, Elijah, and Zichri *were* the sons of Jeroham.

28 These *were* heads of the fathers' *houses* by their generations, chief men. These dwelt in Jerusalem.

29 Now the father of Gibeon, whose wife's name *was* Maacah, dwelt at Gibeon. 30 And his firstborn son *was* Abdon, then Zur, Kish, Baal, Nadab, 31 Gedor, Ahio, Zecher, 32 and Mikloth, *who* begot Shimeah.ᵃ They also dwelt alongside their relatives in Jerusalem, with their brethren. 33 Nerᵃ begot Kish, Kish begot Saul, and Saul begot Jonathan, Malchishua, Abinadab,ᵇ and Esh-Baal.ᶜ 34 The son of Jonathan *was* Merib-Baal,ᵃ and Merib-Baal begot Micah. 35 The sons of Micah *were* Pithon, Melech, Tarea, and Ahaz. 36 And Ahaz begot Jehoaddah;ᵃ Jehoaddah begot Alemeth, Azmaveth, and Zimri; and Zimri begot Moza. 37 Moza begot Binea, Raphahᵃ his son, Eleasah his son, *and* Azel his son.

38 Azel had six sons whose names *were* these: Azrikam, Bocheru, Ishmael, Sheariah, Obadiah, and Hanan. All these *were* the sons of Azel. 39 And the sons of Eshek his brother *were* Ulam his firstborn, Jeush the second, and Eliphelet the third.

40 The sons of Ulam were mighty men of valor—archers. *They* had many sons and grandsons, one hundred and fifty *in all*. These *were* all sons of Benjamin.

9 So all Israel was recorded by genealogies, and indeed, they *were* inscribed in the book of the kings of Israel. But Judah was carried away captive to Babylon because of their

---

7:32 ᵃSpelled *Shemer* in verse 34   ᵇSpelled *Helem* in verse 35   7:37 ᵃSpelled *Jether* in verse 38
8:1 ᵃSpelled *Ahiram* in Numbers 26:38   8:3 ᵃCalled *Ard* in Numbers 26:40   8:32 ᵃSpelled *Shimeam* in 9:38   8:33 ᵃAlso the son of Gibeon (compare 9:36, 39)   ᵇCalled *Jishui* in 1 Samuel 14:49   ᶜCalled *Ishbosheth* in 2 Samuel 2:8 and elsewhere   8:34 ᵃCalled *Mephibosheth* in 2 Samuel 4:4   8:36 ᵃSpelled *Jarah* in 9:42   8:37 ᵃSpelled *Rephaiah* in 9:43

---

*N*ever allow another person's actions to control how you see yourself. That's too much power to give to another human being.

unfaithfulness. 2 And the first inhabitants who *dwelt* in their possessions in their cities *were* Israelites, priests, Levites, and the Nethinim.

3 Now in Jerusalem the children of Judah dwelt, and some of the children of Benjamin, and of the children of Ephraim and Manasseh: 4 Uthai the son of Ammihud, the son of Omri, the son of Imri, the son of Bani, of the descendants of Perez, the son of Judah. 5 Of the Shilonites: Asaiah the firstborn and his sons. 6 Of the sons of Zerah: Jeuel, and their brethren— six hundred and ninety. 7 Of the sons of Benjamin: Sallu the son of Meshullam, the son of Hodaviah, the son of Hassenuah; 8 Ibneiah the son of Jeroham; Elah the son of Uzzi, the son of Michri; Meshullam the son of Shephatiah, the son of Reuel, the son of Ibnijah; 9 and their brethren, according to their generations—nine hundred and fifty-six. All these men *were* heads of a father's *house* in their fathers' houses.

10 Of the priests: Jedaiah, Jehoiarib, and Jachin; 11 Azariah the son of Hilkiah, the son of Meshullam, the son of Zadok, the son of Meraioth, the son of Ahitub, the officer over the house of God; 12 Adaiah the son of Jeroham, the son of Pashur, the son of Malchijah; Maasai the son of Adiel, the son of Jahzerah, the son of Meshullam, the son of Meshillemith, the son of Immer; 13 and their brethren, heads of their fathers' houses—one thousand seven hundred and sixty. *They were* very able men for the work of the service of the house of God.

14 Of the Levites: Shemaiah the son of Hasshub, the son of Azrikam, the son of Hashabiah, of the sons of Merari; 15 Bakbakkar, Heresh, Galal, and Mattaniah the son of Micah, the son of Zichri, the son of Asaph; 16 Obadiah the son of Shemaiah, the son of Galal, the son of Jeduthun; and Berechiah the son of Asa, the son of Elkanah, who lived in the villages of the Netophathites.

17 And the gatekeepers *were* Shallum, Akkub, Talmon, Ahiman, and their brethren. Shallum *was* the chief. 18 Until then *they had been* gatekeepers for the camps of the children of Levi at the King's Gate on the east.

19 Shallum the son of Kore, the son of Ebiasaph, the son of Korah, and his brethren, from his father's house, the Korahites, *were* in charge of the work of the service, gatekeepers of the tabernacle. Their fathers had been keepers of the entrance to the camp of the LORD. 20 And Phinehas the son of Eleazar had been the officer over them in time past; the LORD *was* with him. 21 Zechariah the son of Meshelemiah *was* keeper of the door of the tabernacle of meeting.

22 All those chosen as gatekeepers *were* two hundred and twelve. They were recorded by their genealogy, in their villages. David and Samuel the seer had appointed them to their trusted office. 23 So they and their children *were* in charge of the gates of the house of the LORD, the house of the tabernacle, by assignment. 24 The gatekeepers were assigned to the four directions: the east, west, north, and south. 25 And their brethren in their villages *had* to come with them from time to time for seven days. 26 For in this trusted office *were* four chief gatekeepers; they were Levites. And they had charge over the chambers and treasuries of the house of God. 27 And they lodged *all* around the house of God because they *had* the responsibility, and they *were* in charge of opening *it* every morning.

28 Now *some* of them were in charge of the serving vessels, for they brought them in and took them out by count. 29 *Some* of them *were* appointed over the furnishings and over all the implements of the sanctuary, and over the fine flour and the wine and the oil and the incense and the spices. 30 And *some* of the sons of the priests made the ointment of the spices.

31 Mattithiah of the Levites, the firstborn of Shallum the Korahite, had the trusted office over the things that were baked in the pans. 32 And some of their brethren of the sons of the Kohathites *were* in charge of preparing the showbread for every Sabbath.

33 These are the singers, heads of the fathers' *houses* of the Levites, who *lodged* in the chambers, *and* were free *from other duties;* for they were employed in *that* work day and night. 34 These heads of the fathers' *houses* of the Levites *were* heads throughout their generations. They dwelt at Jerusalem.

Gospel Pearls

35 Jeiel the father of Gibeon, whose wife's name *was* Maacah, dwelt at Gibeon. 36 His firstborn son *was* Abdon, then Zur, Kish, Baal, Ner, Nadab, 37 Gedor, Ahio, Zechariah,*a* and Mikloth. 38 And Mikloth begot Shimeam.*a* They also dwelt alongside their relatives in Jerusalem, with their brethren. 39 Ner begot Kish, Kish begot Saul, and Saul begot Jonathan, Malchishua, Abinadab, and Esh-Baal. 40 The son of Jonathan *was* Merib-Baal, and Merib-Baal begot Micah. 41 The sons of Micah *were* Pithon, Melech, Tahrea,*a* *and Ahaz.*b 42 And Ahaz begot Jarah;*a* Jarah begot Alemeth, Azmaveth, and Zimri; and Zimri begot Moza; 43 Moza begot Binea, Rephaiah*a* his son, Eleasah his son, and Azel his son.

44 And Azel had six sons whose names *were* these: Azrikam, Bocheru, Ishmael, Sheariah, Obadiah, and Hanan; these *were* the sons of Azel.

10 Now the Philistines fought against Israel; and the men of Israel fled from before the Philistines, and fell slain on Mount Gilboa. 2 Then the Philistines followed hard after Saul and his sons. And the Philistines killed Jonathan, Abinadab, and Malchishua, Saul's sons. 3 The battle became fierce against Saul. The archers hit him, and he was wounded by the archers. 4 Then Saul said to his armorbearer, "Draw your sword, and thrust me through with it, lest these uncircumcised men come and abuse me." But his armorbearer would not, for he was greatly afraid. Therefore Saul took a sword and fell on it. 5 And when his armorbearer saw that Saul was dead, he also fell on his sword and died. 6 So Saul and his three sons died, and all his house died together. 7 And when all the men of Israel who *were* in the valley saw that they had fled and that Saul and his sons were dead, they forsook their cities and fled; then the Philistines came and dwelt in them.

8 So it happened the next day, when the Philistines came to strip the slain, that they found Saul and his sons fallen on Mount Gilboa.

9 And they stripped him and took his head and his armor, and sent word *throughout* the land of the Philistines to proclaim the news *in the temple* of their idols and among the people. 10 Then they put his armor in the temple of their gods, and fastened his head in the temple of Dagon.

11 And when all Jabesh Gilead heard all that the Philistines had done to Saul, 12 all the valiant men arose and took the body of Saul and the bodies of his sons; and they brought them to Jabesh, and buried their bones under the tamarisk tree at Jabesh, and fasted seven days.

13 So Saul died for his unfaithfulness which he had committed against the LORD, because he did not keep the word of the LORD, and also because he consulted a medium for guidance. 14 But *he* did not inquire of the LORD; therefore He killed him, and turned the kingdom over to David the son of Jesse.

11 Then all Israel came together to David at Hebron, saying, "Indeed we *are* your bone and your flesh. 2 Also, in time past, even when Saul was king, you *were* the one who led Israel out and brought them in; and the LORD your God said to you, 'You shall shepherd My people Israel, and be ruler over My people Israel.' " 3 Therefore all the elders of Israel came to the king at Hebron, and David made a covenant with them at Hebron before the LORD. And they anointed David king over Israel, according to the word of the LORD by Samuel.

4 And David and all Israel went to Jerusalem, which is Jebus, where the Jebusites *were,* the inhabitants of the land. 5 But the inhabitants of Jebus said to David, "You shall not come in here!" Nevertheless David took the stronghold of Zion (that is, the City of David). 6 Now David said, "Whoever attacks the Jebusites first shall be chief and captain." And Joab the son of Zeruiah went up first, and became chief. 7 Then David dwelt in the stronghold; therefore they called it the City of David. 8 And he built the city around it, from the Millo*a* to the surrounding area. Joab repaired

---

9:37 *a*Called *Zecher* in 8:31   9:38 *a*Spelled *Shimeah* in 8:32   9:41 *a*Spelled *Tarea* in 8:35   *b*Following Arabic, Syriac, Targum, and Vulgate (compare 8:35); Masoretic Text and Septuagint omit *and Ahaz.* 9:42 *a*Spelled *Jehoaddah* in 8:36   9:43 *a*Spelled *Raphah* in 8:37   11:8 *a*Literally *The Landfill*

---

*T*here are thousands of Lydias in this country. They have climbed the ladder to success and found that there is little fulfillment on the top rung. They need to know about Jesus and His love.

the rest of the city. 9 So David went on and became great, and the LORD of hosts *was* with him.

10 Now these *were* the heads of the mighty men whom David had, who strengthened themselves with him in his kingdom, with all Israel, to make him king, according to the word of the LORD concerning Israel.

11 And this *is* the number of the mighty men whom David had: Jasho-beam the son of a Hachmonite, chief of the captains;*a* he had lifted up his spear against three hundred, killed *by him* at one time.

12 After him *was* Eleazar the son of Dodo, the Ahohite, who *was one* of the three mighty men. 13 He was with David at Pasdammim. Now there the Philistines were gathered for battle, and there was a piece of ground full of barley. So the people fled from the Philistines. 14 But they stationed themselves in the middle of *that* field, defended it, and killed the Philistines. So the LORD brought about a great victory.

15 Now three of the thirty chief men went down to the rock to David, into the cave of Adullam; and the army of the Philistines encamped in the Valley of Rephaim. 16 David *was* then in the stronghold, and the garrison of the Philistines *was* then in Bethlehem. 17 And David said with longing, "Oh, that someone would give me a drink of water from the well of Bethlehem, which is by the gate!" 18 So the three broke through the camp of the Philistines, drew water from the well of Bethlehem that *was* by the gate, and took *it* and brought *it* to David. Nevertheless David would not drink it, but poured it out to the LORD. 19 And he said, "Far be it from me, O my God, that I should do this! Shall I drink the blood of these men *who have put* their lives *in jeopardy?* For at the risk of their lives they brought it." Therefore he would not drink it. These things were done by the three mighty men.

20 Abishai the brother of Joab was chief of *another* three.*a* He had lifted up his spear against three hundred *men,* killed *them,* and won a name among *these* three. 21 Of the three he was more honored than the other two men. Therefore he became their captain. However he did not attain to the *first* three.

22 Benaiah was the son of Jehoi-ada, the son of a valiant man from Kabzeel, who had done many deeds. He had killed two lion-like heroes of Moab. He also had gone down and killed a lion in the midst of a pit on a snowy day. 23 And he killed an Egyptian, a man of *great* height, five cubits tall. In the Egyptian's hand *there was* a spear like a weaver's beam; and he went down to him with a staff, wrested the spear out of the Egyptian's hand, and killed him with his own spear. 24 These *things* Be-naiah the son of Jehoiada did, and won a name among three mighty men. 25 Indeed he was more honored than the thirty, but he did not attain to the *first* three. And David appointed him over his guard.

26 Also the mighty warriors *were* Asahel the brother of Joab, Elhanan the son of Dodo of Bethlehem, 27 Shammoth the Harorite,*a* Helez the Pelonite,*b* 28 Ira the son of Ikkesh the Tekoite, Abiezer the Anathothite, 29 Sibbechai the Hushathite, Ilai the Ahohite, 30 Maharai the Netopha-thite, Heled*a* the son of Baanah the Netophathite, 31 Ithai*a* the son of Ri-bai of Gibeah, of the sons of Ben-jamin, Benaiah the Pirathonite, 32 Hurai*a* of the brooks of Gaash, Abiel*b* the Arbathite, 33 Azmaveth the Baharumite,*a* Eliahba the Shaal-bonite, 34 the sons of Hashem the Gi-zonite, Jonathan the son of Shageh the Hararite, 35 Ahiam the son of Sa-car the Hararite, Eliphal the son of Ur, 36 Hepher the Mecherathite, Ahi-jah the Pelonite, 37 Hezro the Car-melite, Naarai the son of Ezbai, 38 Joel the brother of Nathan, Mibhar the son of Hagri, 39 Zelek the Am-monite, Naharai the Berothite*a* (the armorbearer of Joab the son of Zeruiah), 40 Ira the Ithrite, Gareb the Ithrite, 41 Uriah the Hittite, Zabad the son of Ahlai, 42 Adina the son of Shiza the Reubenite (a chief of the Reubenites) and thirty with

11:11 *a*Following Qere; Kethib, Septuagint, and Vulgate read *the thirty* (compare 2 Samuel 23:8).
11:20 *a*Following Masoretic Text, Septuagint, and Vulgate; Syriac reads *thirty.*   11:27 *a*Spelled *Harodite* in 2 Samuel 23:25   *b*Called *Paltite* in 2 Samuel 23:26   11:30 *a*Spelled *Heleb* in 2 Samuel 23:29 and *Heldai* in 1 Chronicles 27:15   11:31 *a*Spelled *Ittai* in 2 Samuel 23:29   11:32 *a*Spelled *Hiddai* in 2 Samuel 23:30   *b*Spelled *Abi-Albon* in 2 Samuel 23:31   11:33 *a*Spelled *Barhumite* in 2 Samuel 23:31
11:39 *a*Spelled *Beerothite* in 2 Samuel 23:37

Gospel Pearls

him, 43 Hanan the son of Maachah, Joshaphat the Mithnite, 44 Uzzia the Ashterathite, Shama and Jeiel the sons of Hotham the Aroerite, 45 Jediael the son of Shimri, and Joha his brother, the Tizite, 46 Eliel the Mahavite, Jeribai and Joshaviah the sons of Elnaam, Ithmah the Moabite, 47 Eliel, Obed, and Jaasiel the Mezobaite.

12 Now these *were* the men who came to David at Ziklag while he was still a fugitive from Saul the son of Kish; and they *were* among the mighty men, helpers in the war, 2 armed with bows, using both the right hand and the left in *hurling* stones and *shooting* arrows with the bow. *They were* of Benjamin, Saul's brethren.

3 The chief *was* Ahiezer, then Joash, the sons of Shemaah the Gibeathite; Jeziel and Pelet the sons of Azmaveth; Berachah, and Jehu the Anathothite; 4 Ishmaiah the Gibeonite, a mighty man among the thirty, and over the thirty; Jeremiah, Jahaziel, Johanan, and Jozabad the Gederathite; 5 Eluzai, Jerimoth, Bealiah, Shemariah, and Shephatiah the Haruphite; 6 Elkanah, Jisshiah, Azarel, Joezer, and Jashobeam, the Korahites; 7 and Joelah and Zebadiah the sons of Jeroham of Gedor.

8 *Some* Gadites joined David at the stronghold in the wilderness, mighty men of valor, men trained for battle, who could handle shield and spear, whose faces *were like* the faces of lions, and *were* as swift as gazelles on the mountains: 9 Ezer the first, Obadiah the second, Eliab the third, 10 Mishmannah the fourth, Jeremiah the fifth, 11 Attai the sixth, Eliel the seventh, 12 Johanan the eighth, Elzabad the ninth, 13 Jeremiah the tenth, and Machbanai the eleventh. 14 These *were* from the sons of Gad, captains of the army; the least was over a hundred, and the greatest was over a thousand. 15 These *are* the ones who crossed the Jordan in the first month, when it had overflowed all its banks; and they put to flight all *those* in the valleys, to the east and to the west.

16 Then some of the sons of Benjamin and Judah came to David at the stronghold. 17 And David went out to meet them, and answered and said to them, "If you have come peaceably to me to help me, my heart will be united with you; but if to betray me to my enemies, since *there is* no wrong in my hands, may the God of our fathers look and bring judgment." 18 Then the Spirit came upon Amasai, chief of the captains, *and he said:*

"*We are* yours, O David;
    We *are* on your side, O son of Jesse!
Peace, peace to you,
    And peace to your helpers!
For your God helps you."

So David received them, and made them captains of the troop.

19 And *some* from Manasseh defected to David when he was going with the Philistines to battle against Saul; but they did not help them, for the lords of the Philistines sent him away by agreement, saying, "He may defect to his master Saul *and endanger* our heads." 20 When he went to Ziklag, those of Manasseh who defected to him were Adnah, Jozabad, Jediael, Michael, Jozabad, Elihu, and Zillethai, captains of the thousands who *were* from Manasseh. 21 And they helped David against the bands *of raiders,* for they *were* all mighty men of valor, and they were captains in the army. 22 For at *that* time they came to David day by day to help him, until *it was* a great army, like the army of God.

23 Now these *were* the numbers of the divisions *that were* equipped for war, *and* came to David at Hebron to turn *over* the kingdom of Saul to him, according to the word of the LORD: 24 of the sons of Judah bearing shield and spear, six thousand eight hundred armed for war; 25 of the sons of Simeon, mighty men of valor fit for war, seven thousand one hundred; 26 of the sons of Levi four thousand six hundred; 27 Jehoiada, the leader of the Aaronites, and with him three thousand seven hundred; 28 Zadok, a young man, a valiant warrior, and from his father's house twenty-two captains; 29 of the sons of Benjamin, relatives of Saul, three thousand (until then the greatest part of them had remained loyal to the house of Saul); 30 of the sons of Ephraim twenty thousand eight hundred, mighty men of valor, famous men throughout their father's house;

*I*f people don't have the ability to discern the inner riches of your treasure, that's their problem. But if you sit at home and wallow in self-pity because they have no discernment, that becomes *your* problem.

31 of the half-tribe of Manasseh eighteen thousand, who were designated by name to come and make David king; 32 of the sons of Issachar who had understanding of the times, to know what Israel ought to do, their chiefs were two hundred; and all their brethren were at their command; 33 of Zebulun there were fifty thousand who went out to battle, expert in war with all weapons of war, stouthearted men who could keep ranks; 34 of Naphtali one thousand captains, and with them thirty-seven thousand with shield and spear; 35 of the Danites who could keep battle formation, twenty-eight thousand six hundred; 36 of Asher, those who could go out to war, able to keep battle formation, forty thousand; 37 of the Reubenites and the Gadites and the half-tribe of Manasseh, from the other side of the Jordan, one hundred and twenty thousand armed for battle with every *kind* of weapon of war.

38 All these men of war, who could keep ranks, came to Hebron with a loyal heart, to make David king over all Israel; and all the rest of Israel *were* of one mind to make David king. 39 And they were there with David three days, eating and drinking, for their brethren had prepared for them. 40 Moreover those who were near to them, from as far away as Issachar and Zebulun and Naphtali, were bringing food on donkeys and camels, on mules and oxen—provisions of flour and cakes of figs and cakes of raisins, wine and oil and oxen and sheep abundantly, for *there was* joy in Israel.

13 Then David consulted with the captains of thousands and hundreds, *and* with every leader. 2 And David said to all the assembly of Israel, "If *it seems* good to you, and if it is of the LORD our God, let us send out to our brethren everywhere *who are* left in all the land of Israel, and with them to the priests and Levites *who are* in their cities *and* their common-lands, that they may gather together to us; 3 and let us bring the ark of our God back to us, for we have not inquired at it since the days of Saul." 4 Then all the

assembly said that they would do so, for the thing was right in the eyes of all the people.

5 So David gathered all Israel together, from Shihor in Egypt to as far as the entrance of Hamath, to bring the ark of God from Kirjath Jearim. 6 And David and all Israel went up to Baalah,*a* to Kirjath Jearim, which belonged to Judah, to bring up from there the ark of God the LORD, who dwells *between* the cherubim, where *His* name is proclaimed. 7 So they carried the ark of God on a new cart from the house of Abinadab, and Uzza and Ahio drove the cart. 8 Then David and all Israel played *music* before God with all *their* might, with singing, on harps, on stringed instruments, on tambourines, on cymbals, and with trumpets.

9 And when they came to Chidon's*a* threshing floor, Uzza put out his hand to hold the ark, for the oxen stumbled. 10 Then the anger of the LORD was aroused against Uzza, and He struck him because he put his hand to the ark; and he died there before God. 11 And David became angry because of the LORD's outbreak against Uzza; therefore that place is called Perez Uzza*a* to this day. 12 David was afraid of God that day, saying, "How can I bring the ark of God to me?"

13 So David would not move the ark with him into the City of David, but took it aside into the house of Obed-Edom the Gittite. 14 The ark of God remained with the family of Obed-Edom in his house three months. And the LORD blessed the house of Obed-Edom and all that he had.

14 Now Hiram king of Tyre sent messengers to David, and cedar trees, with masons and carpenters, to build him a house. 2 So David knew that the LORD had established him as king over Israel, for his kingdom was highly exalted for the sake of His people Israel.

3 Then David took more wives in Jerusalem, and David begot more sons and daughters. 4 And these are the names of his children whom he had in Jerusalem: Shammua,*a* Sho-

13:6 *a*Called *Baale Judah* in 2 Samuel 6:2   13:9 *a*Called *Nachon* in 2 Samuel 6:6   13:11 *a*Literally Outburst Against Uzza   14:4 *a*Spelled *Shimea* in 3:5

Gospel Pearls

bab, Nathan, Solomon, 5 Ibhar, Elishua,*ᵃ* Elpelet,*ᵇ* 6 Nogah, Nepheg, Japhia, 7 Elishama, Beeliada,*ᵃ* and Eliphelet.

8 Now when the Philistines heard that David had been anointed king over all Israel, all the Philistines went up to search for David. And David heard *of it* and went out against them. 9 Then the Philistines went and made a raid on the Valley of Rephaim. 10 And David inquired of God, saying, "Shall I go up against the Philistines? Will You deliver them into my hand?"

The LORD said to him, "Go up, for I will deliver them into your hand."

11 So they went up to Baal Perazim, and David defeated them there. Then David said, "God has broken through my enemies by my hand like a breakthrough of water." Therefore they called the name of that place Baal Perazim.*ᵃ* 12 And when they left their gods there, David gave a commandment, and they were burned with fire.

13 Then the Philistines once again made a raid on the valley.

14 Therefore David inquired again of God, and God said to him, "You shall not go up after them; circle around them, and come upon them in front of the mulberry trees. 15 And it shall be, when you hear a sound of marching in the tops of the mulberry trees, then you shall go out to battle, for God has gone out before you to strike the camp of the Philistines." 16 So David did as God commanded him, and they drove back the army of the Philistines from Gibeon as far as Gezer. 17 Then the fame of David went out into all lands, and the LORD brought the fear of him upon all nations.

15 David built houses for himself in the City of David; and he prepared a place for the ark of God, and pitched a tent for it. 2 Then David said, "No one may carry the ark of God but the Levites, for the LORD has chosen them to carry the ark of God and to minister before Him forever." 3 And David gathered all Israel together at Jerusalem, to bring up the ark of the LORD to its place, which he had prepared for it. 4 Then David assembled the children of Aaron and the Levites: 5 of the sons of Kohath, Uriel the chief, and one hundred and twenty of his brethren; 6 of the sons of Merari, Asaiah the chief, and two hundred and twenty of his brethren; 7 of the sons of Gershom, Joel the chief, and one hundred and thirty of his brethren; 8 of the sons of Elizaphan, Shemaiah the chief, and two hundred of his brethren; 9 of the sons of Hebron, Eliel the chief, and eighty of his brethren; 10 of the sons of Uzziel, Amminadab the chief, and one hundred and twelve of his brethren.

11 And David called for Zadok and Abiathar the priests, and for the Levites: for Uriel, Asaiah, Joel, Shemaiah, Eliel, and Amminadab. 12 He said to them, "You *are* the heads of the fathers' *houses* of the Levites; sanctify yourselves, you and your brethren, that you may bring up the ark of the LORD God of Israel to *the place* I have prepared for it. 13 For because you *did* not *do it* the first *time,* the LORD our God broke out against us, because we did not consult Him about the proper order."

14 So the priests and the Levites sanctified themselves to bring up the ark of the LORD God of Israel. 15 And the children of the Levites bore the ark of God on their shoulders, by its poles, as Moses had commanded according to the word of the LORD.

16 Then David spoke to the leaders of the Levites to appoint their brethren *to be* the singers accompanied by instruments of music, stringed instruments, harps, and cymbals, by raising the voice with resounding joy. 17 So the Levites appointed Heman the son of Joel; and of his brethren, Asaph the son of Berechiah; and of their brethren, the sons of Merari, Ethan the son of Kushaiah; 18 and with them their brethren of the second *rank:* Zechariah, Ben,*ᵃ* Jaaziel, Shemiramoth, Jehiel, Unni, Eliab, Benaiah, Maaseiah, Mattithiah, Elipheleh, Mikneiah, Obed-Edom, and Jeiel, the gatekeepers; 19 the singers, Heman, Asaph, and Ethan, *were* to sound the cymbals of bronze; 20 Zechariah, Aziel, Shemiramoth, Jehiel, Unni, Eliab, Maaseiah, and Benaiah, with strings according to Alamoth; 21 Mattithiah, Elipheleh, Mikneiah, Obed-Edom,

---

14:5 *ᵃ*Spelled *Elishama* in 3:6   *ᵇ*Spelled *Eliphelet* in 3:6   14:7 *ᵃ*Spelled *Eliada* in 3:8   14:11 *ᵃ*Literally *Master of Breakthroughs*   15:18 *ᵃ*Following Masoretic Text and Vulgate; Septuagint omits *Ben.*

Recognize that those who reject you have no ability to see inside you. They have no ability to hear the meaning behind your words. They have bought a lie—either willfully or unconsciously—that the devil has told them about you.

Jeiel, and Azaziah, to direct with harps on the Sheminith; 22 Chenaniah, leader of the Levites, was instructor *in charge of* the music, because he *was* skillful; 23 Berechiah and Elkanah *were* doorkeepers for the ark; 24 Shebaniah, Joshaphat, Nethanel, Amasai, Zechariah, Benaiah, and Eliezer, the priests, were to blow the trumpets before the ark of God; and Obed-Edom and Jehiah, doorkeepers for the ark.

25 So David, the elders of Israel, and the captains over thousands went to bring up the ark of the covenant of the LORD from the house of Obed-Edom with joy. 26 And so it was, when God helped the Levites who bore the ark of the covenant of the LORD, that they offered seven bulls and seven rams. 27 David was clothed with a robe of fine linen, as were all the Levites who bore the ark, the singers, and Chenaniah the music master *with* the singers. David also wore a linen ephod. 28 Thus all Israel brought up the ark of the covenant of the LORD with shouting and with the sound of the horn, with trumpets and with cymbals, making music with stringed instruments and harps.

29 And it happened, *as* the ark of the covenant of the LORD came to the City of David, that Michal, Saul's daughter, looked through a window and saw King David whirling and playing music; and she despised him in her heart.

16 So they brought the ark of God, and set it in the midst of the tabernacle that David had erected for it. Then they offered burnt offerings and peace offerings before God. 2 And when David had finished offering the burnt offerings and the peace offerings, he blessed the people in the name of the LORD. 3 Then he distributed to everyone of Israel, both man and woman, to everyone a loaf of bread, a piece *of meat,* and a cake of raisins.

4 And he appointed some of the Levites to minister before the ark of the LORD, to commemorate, to thank, and to praise the LORD God of Israel: 5 Asaph the chief, and next to him Zechariah, *then* Jeiel, Shemiramoth, Jehiel, Mattithiah, Eliab, Benaiah, and Obed-Edom: Jeiel with stringed instruments and harps, but Asaph made music with cymbals; 6 Benaiah

and Jahaziel the priests regularly *blew* the trumpets before the ark of the covenant of God.

7 On that day David first delivered *this psalm* into the hand of Asaph and his brethren, to thank the LORD:

8 Oh, give thanks to the LORD!
   Call upon His name;
   Make known His deeds among the peoples!

9 Sing to Him, sing psalms to Him;
   Talk of all His wondrous works!

10 Glory in His holy name;
    Let the hearts of those rejoice who seek the LORD!

11 Seek the LORD and His strength;
    Seek His face evermore!

12 Remember His marvelous works which He has done,
    His wonders, and the judgments of His mouth,

13 O seed of Israel His servant,
    You children of Jacob, His chosen ones!

14 He *is* the LORD our God;
    His judgments *are* in all the earth.

15 Remember His covenant forever,
    The word which He commanded, for a thousand generations,

16 *The covenant which* He made with Abraham,
    And His oath to Isaac,

17 And confirmed it to Jacob for a statute,
    To Israel *for* an everlasting covenant,

18 Saying, "To you I will give the land of Canaan
    As the allotment of your inheritance,"

19 When you were few in number,
    Indeed very few, and strangers in it.

20 When they went from one nation to another,
    And from *one* kingdom to another people,

21 He permitted no man to do them wrong;
    Yes, He rebuked kings for their sakes,

22 *Saying,* "Do not touch My anointed ones,

*I*f you don't treat yourself well, you won't treat others well. We treat other people out of the well of our own self-esteem. And if your well is dry, you don't have any esteem that you can give to another person. You can't value someone else because you have no value for yourself.

Attitude of Gratitude

1 Chronicles 16:8, 9

*L*ove is eternal. It is not limited by time. When you commit yourself to loving someone, you make your commitment to everything that person is. You are who you are because of your history, because of all that's happened before. To be loved effectively, we have to allow others into our history.

Many couples in a relationship argue over relatively insignificant things. Often the reason these things are important is that they remind one or the other of a past event. How can one person love another if he or she doesn't know the other person's history?

The Church is built on relationship. We must learn to be open and honest. Too many Christians want to keep their attitudes and their histories to themselves. We need to learn how to share, how to "bear one another's burdens" (Galatians 6:2).

Thousands of people are afraid. The Church can give strength to counter that fear. Thousands have built walls around themselves because they don't trust anyone else. The body of Christ can help its members regain trust. Thousands more are codependent and get value from a relationship with another person. The Church can point to God's love as the source of self-worth. We are not valuable because we love God; we are valuable because He loves us.

In Luke 13, Jesus took away the infirm woman's ability to make excuses for herself and gave her the strength to maintain an attitude of gratitude and praise. The Church today is to be that kind of safe haven where those who are wounded may come and find strength in praise.

Gratitude and defensive praise are contagious. Although the Bible does not specifically say so, I imagine that those who saw what was going on the day Jesus healed the infirm woman were caught up in praise as well. Those who missed the great blessing that day were those who decided to argue about religion instead of rejoicing over her release.

The Bible describes Heaven as a place where the angels celebrate one sinner who comes into the faith (see Luke 15:10). They sing and praise God because Jesus heals those who are broken. Likewise, God's people are to rejoice when the brokenhearted and emotionally wounded come to Him.

And do My prophets no
harm."[a]

23 Sing to the LORD, all the earth;
Proclaim the good news of His
salvation from day to day.
24 Declare His glory among the
nations,
His wonders among all
peoples.
25 For the LORD *is* great and
greatly to be praised;
He *is* also to be feared above
all gods.
26 For all the gods of the peoples
are idols,
But the LORD made the
heavens.
27 Honor and majesty *are* before
Him;
Strength and gladness are in
His place.

28 Give to the LORD, O families of
the peoples,
Give to the LORD glory and
strength.
29 Give to the LORD the glory *due*
His name;
Bring an offering, and come
before Him.
Oh, worship the LORD in the
beauty of holiness!
30 Tremble before Him, all the
earth.
The world also is firmly
established,
It shall not be moved.

31 Let the heavens rejoice, and let
the earth be glad;
And let them say among the
nations, "The LORD reigns."
32 Let the sea roar, and all its
fullness;
Let the field rejoice, and all that
is in it.
33 Then the trees of the woods
shall rejoice before the LORD,
For He is coming to judge the
earth.[a]

34 Oh, give thanks to the LORD, for
He is good!
For His mercy *endures*
forever.[a]
35 And say, "Save us, O God of
our salvation;

Gather us together, and deliver
us from the Gentiles,
To give thanks to Your holy
name,
To triumph in Your praise."

36 Blessed *be* the LORD God of
Israel
From everlasting to
everlasting![a]

And all the people said, "Amen!" and
praised the LORD.

37 So he left Asaph and his brothers there before the ark of the covenant of the LORD to minister before
the ark regularly, as every day's
work required; 38 and Obed-Edom
with his sixty-eight brethren, including Obed-Edom the son of Jeduthun,
and Hosah, *to be* gatekeepers;
39 and Zadok the priest and his brethren the priests, before the tabernacle
of the LORD at the high place that *was*
at Gibeon, 40 to offer burnt offerings
to the LORD on the altar of burnt offering regularly morning and evening, and *to do* according to all that
is written in the Law of the LORD
which He commanded Israel;
41 and with them Heman and Jeduthun and the rest who were chosen,
who were designated by name, to
give thanks to the LORD, because His
mercy *endures* forever; 42 and with
them Heman and Jeduthun, to sound
aloud with trumpets and cymbals
and the musical instruments of God.
Now the sons of Jeduthun *were*
gatekeepers.
43 Then all the people departed, every man to his house; and David returned to bless his house.

17 Now it came to pass, when David was dwelling in his house,
that David said to Nathan the
prophet, "See now, I dwell in a house
of cedar, but the ark of the covenant
of the LORD *is* under tent curtains."
2 Then Nathan said to David, "Do
all that *is* in your heart, for God *is*
with you."
3 But it happened that night that
the word of God came to Nathan,
saying, 4 "Go and tell My servant David, 'Thus says the LORD: "You shall
not build Me a house to dwell in.

16:22 [a]Compare verses 8–22 with Psalm 105:1–15
96:1–13   16:34 [a]Compare verse 34 with Psalm 106:1
106:47, 48

16:33 [a]Compare verses 23–33 with Psalm
16:36 [a]Compare verses 35, 36 with Psalm

Gospel
Pearls

5 For I have not dwelt in a house since the time that I brought up Israel, even to this day, but have gone from tent to tent, and from *one* tabernacle *to another.* 6 Wherever I have moved about with all Israel, have I ever spoken a word to any of the judges of Israel, whom I commanded to shepherd My people, saying, 'Why have you not built Me a house of cedar?' " ' 7 Now therefore, thus shall you say to My servant David, 'Thus says the LORD of hosts: "I took you from the sheepfold, from following the sheep, to be ruler over My people Israel. 8 And I have been with you wherever you have gone, and have cut off all your enemies from before you, and have made you a name like the name of the great men who *are* on the earth. 9 Moreover I will appoint a place for My people Israel, and will plant them, that they may dwell in a place of their own and move no more; nor shall the sons of wickedness oppress them anymore, as previously, 10 since the time that I commanded judges *to be* over My people Israel. Also I will subdue all your enemies. Furthermore I tell you that the LORD will build you a house.*a* 11 And it shall be, when your days are fulfilled, when you must go *to be* with your fathers, that I will set up your seed after you, who will be of your sons; and I will establish his kingdom. 12 He shall build Me a house, and I will establish his throne forever. 13 I will be his Father, and he shall be My son; and I will not take My mercy away from him, as I took *it* from *him* who was before you. 14 And I will establish him in My house and in My kingdom forever; and his throne shall be established forever." ' "

15 According to all these words and according to all this vision, so Nathan spoke to David.

16 Then King David went in and sat before the LORD; and he said: "Who *am* I, O LORD God? And what is my house, that You have brought me this far? 17 And *yet* this was a small thing in Your sight, O God; and You have *also* spoken of Your servant's house for a great while to come, and have regarded me according to the rank of a man of high degree, O LORD God.

18 What more can David *say* to You for the honor of Your servant? For You know Your servant. 19 O LORD, for Your servant's sake, and according to Your own heart, You have done all this greatness, in making known all these great things. 20 O LORD, *there is* none like You, nor *is there any* God besides You, according to all that we have heard with our ears. 21 And who *is* like Your people Israel, the one nation on the earth whom God went to redeem for Himself *as* a people—to make for Yourself a name by great and awesome deeds, by driving out nations from before Your people whom You redeemed from Egypt? 22 For You have made Your people Israel Your very own people forever; and You, LORD, have become their God.

23 "And now, O LORD, the word which You have spoken concerning Your servant and concerning his house, *let it* be established forever, and do as You have said. 24 So let it be established, that Your name may be magnified forever, saying, 'The LORD of hosts, the God of Israel, *is* Israel's God.' And let the house of Your servant David be established before You. 25 For You, O my God, have revealed to Your servant that You will build him a house. Therefore Your servant has found it *in his heart* to pray before You. 26 And now, LORD, You are God, and have promised this goodness to Your servant. 27 Now You have been pleased to bless the house of Your servant, that it may continue before You forever; for You have blessed it, O LORD, and *it shall be* blessed forever."

18 After this it came to pass that David attacked the Philistines, subdued them, and took Gath and its towns from the hand of the Philistines. 2 Then he defeated Moab, and the Moabites became David's servants, *and* brought tribute.

3 And David defeated Hadadezer*a* king of Zobah *as far as* Hamath, as he went to establish his power by the River Euphrates. 4 David took from him one thousand chariots, seven thousand*a* horsemen, and twenty thousand foot soldiers. Also David hamstrung all the chariot *horses,* ex-

---

17:10 *a*That is, a royal dynasty   18:3 *a*Hebrew *Hadarezer,* and so throughout chapters 18 and 19
18:4 *a*Or *seven hundred* (compare 2 Samuel 8:4)

---

*L*ive vivaciously, love deeply and pray fervently. Remember to give with simplicity and to serve with humility. Still, observe that meekness does not necessitate weakness. Therefore, when challenged by obstacles, fight with tenacity.

cept that he spared enough of them for one hundred chariots.

5 When the Syrians of Damascus came to help Hadadezer king of Zobah, David killed twenty-two thousand of the Syrians. 6 Then David put *garrisons* in Syria of Damascus; and the Syrians became David's servants, *and* brought tribute. So the LORD preserved David wherever he went. 7 And David took the shields of gold that were on the servants of Hadadezer, and brought them to Jerusalem. 8 Also from Tibhath*ᵃ* and from Chun, cities of Hadadezer, David brought a large amount of bronze, with which Solomon made the bronze Sea, the pillars, and the articles of bronze.

9 Now when Tou*ᵃ* king of Hamath heard that David had defeated all the army of Hadadezer king of Zobah, 10 he sent Hadoram*ᵃ* his son to King David, to greet him and bless him, because he had fought against Hadadezer and defeated him (for Hadadezer had been at war with Tou); and *Hadoram brought with him* all kinds of articles of gold, silver, and bronze. 11 King David also dedicated these to the LORD, along with the silver and gold that he had brought from all *these* nations—from Edom, from Moab, from the people of Ammon, from the Philistines, and from Amalek.

12 Moreover Abishai the son of Zeruiah killed eighteen thousand Edomites*ᵃ* in the Valley of Salt. 13 He also put garrisons in Edom, and all the Edomites became David's servants. And the LORD preserved David wherever he went.

14 So David reigned over all Israel, and administered judgment and justice to all his people. 15 Joab the son of Zeruiah *was* over the army; Jehoshaphat the son of Ahilud *was* recorder; 16 Zadok the son of Ahitub and Abimelech the son of Abiathar *were* the priests; Shavsha*ᵃ was* the scribe; 17 Benaiah the son of Jehoiada *was* over the Cherethites and the Pelethites; and David's sons *were* chief ministers at the king's side.

19 It happened after this that Nahash the king of the people of Ammon died, and his son reigned in his place. 2 Then David said, "I will show kindness to Hanun the son of Nahash, because his father showed kindness to me." So David sent messengers to comfort him concerning his father. And David's servants came to Hanun in the land of the people of Ammon to comfort him.

3 And the princes of the people of Ammon said to Hanun, "Do you think that David really honors your father because he has sent comforters to you? Did his servants not come to you to search and to overthrow and to spy out the land?"

4 Therefore Hanun took David's servants, shaved them, and cut off their garments in the middle, at their buttocks, and sent them away. 5 Then *some* went and told David about the men; and he sent to meet them, because the men were greatly ashamed. And the king said, "Wait at Jericho until your beards have grown, and *then* return."

6 When the people of Ammon saw that they had made themselves repulsive to David, Hanun and the people of Ammon sent a thousand talents of silver to hire for themselves chariots and horsemen from Mesopotamia,*ᵃ* from Syrian Maacah, and from Zobah.*ᵇ* 7 So they hired for themselves thirty-two thousand chariots, with the king of Maacah and his people, who came and encamped before Medeba. Also the people of Ammon gathered together from their cities, and came to battle.

8 Now when David heard *of it*, he sent Joab and all the army of the mighty men. 9 Then the people of Ammon came out and put themselves in battle array before the gate of the city, and the kings who had come *were* by themselves in the field.

10 When Joab saw that the battle line was against him before and behind, he chose some of Israel's best and put *them* in battle array against the Syrians. 11 And the rest of the people he put under the command of Abishai his brother, and they set *themselves* in battle array against the people of Ammon. 12 Then he said, "If the Syrians are too strong for me, then you shall help me; but if the peo-

---

18:8 *ᵃSpelled Betah in 2 Samuel 8:8   18:9 *ᵃSpelled Toi in 2 Samuel 8:9, 10   18:10 *ᵃSpelled Joram in 2 Samuel 8:10   18:12 *ᵃOr Syrians (compare 2 Samuel 8:13)   18:16 *ᵃSpelled Seraiah in 2 Samuel 8:17   19:6 *ᵃHebrew Aram Naharaim   *ᵇSpelled Zoba in 2 Samuel 10:6

Gospel Pearls

ple of Ammon are too strong for you, then I will help you. ¹³ Be of good courage, and let us be strong for our people and for the cities of our God. And may the LORD do *what is* good in His sight."

¹⁴ So Joab and the people who *were* with him drew near for the battle against the Syrians, and they fled before him. ¹⁵ When the people of Ammon saw that the Syrians were fleeing, they also fled before Abishai his brother, and entered the city. So Joab went to Jerusalem.

¹⁶ Now when the Syrians saw that they had been defeated by Israel, they sent messengers and brought the Syrians who were beyond the River,ᵃ and Shophachᵇ the commander of Hadadezer's army *went* before them. ¹⁷ When it was told David, he gathered all Israel, crossed over the Jordan and came upon them, and set up in battle array against them. So when David had set up in *battle* array against the Syrians, they fought with him. ¹⁸ Then the Syrians fled before Israel; and David killed seven thousandᵃ charioteers and forty thousand foot soldiersᵇ of the Syrians, and killed Shophach the commander of the army. ¹⁹ And when the servants of Hadadezer saw that they were defeated by Israel, they made peace with David and became his servants. So the Syrians were not willing to help the people of Ammon anymore.

20 It happened in the spring of the year, at the time kings go out *to battle,* that Joab led out the armed forces and ravaged the country of the people of Ammon, and came and besieged Rabbah. But David stayed at Jerusalem. And Joab defeated Rabbah and overthrew it. ² Then David took their king's crown from his head, and found it to weigh a talent of gold, and *there were* precious stones in it. And it was set on David's head. Also he brought out the spoil of the city in great abundance. ³ And he brought out the people who *were* in it, and put *them* to workᵃ with saws, with iron picks, and with axes. So David did to all the cities

of the people of Ammon. Then David and all the people returned *to* Jerusalem.

⁴ Now it happened afterward that war broke out at Gezer with the Philistines, at which time Sibbechai the Hushathite killed Sippai,ᵃ *who was* one of the sons of the giant. And they were subdued.

⁵ Again there was war with the Philistines, and Elhanan the son of Jairᵃ killed Lahmi the brother of Goliath the Gittite, the shaft of whose spear *was* like a weaver's beam.

⁶ Yet again there was war at Gath, where there was a man of *great* stature, with twenty-four fingers and toes, six *on each hand* and six *on each foot;* and he also was born to the giant. ⁷ So when he defied Israel, Jonathan the son of Shimea,ᵃ David's brother, killed him.

⁸ These were born to the giant in Gath, and they fell by the hand of David and by the hand of his servants.

21 Now Satan stood up against Israel, and moved David to number Israel. ² So David said to Joab and to the leaders of the people, "Go, number Israel from Beersheba to Dan, and bring the number of them to me that I may know *it.*"

³ And Joab answered, "May the LORD make His people a hundred times more than they are. But, my lord the king, *are* they not all my lord's servants? Why then does my lord require this thing? Why should he be a cause of guilt in Israel?"

⁴ Nevertheless the king's word prevailed against Joab. Therefore Joab departed and went throughout all Israel and came to Jerusalem. ⁵ Then Joab gave the sum of the number of the people to David. All Israel *had* one million one hundred thousand men who drew the sword, and Judah *had* four hundred and seventy thousand men who drew the sword. ⁶ But he did not count Levi and Benjamin among them, for the king's word was abominable to Joab.

⁷ And God was displeased with this thing; therefore He struck Israel. ⁸ So David said to God, "I have

---

19:16 ᵃThat is, the Euphrates   ᵇSpelled *Shobach* in 2 Samuel 10:16   19:18 ᵃOr *seven hundred* (compare 2 Samuel 10:18)   ᵇOr *horsemen* (compare 2 Samuel 10:18)   20:3 ᵃSeptuagint reads *cut them.*
20:4 ᵃSpelled *Saph* in 2 Samuel 21:18   20:5 ᵃSpelled *Jaare-Oregim* in 2 Samuel 21:19   20:7 ᵃSpelled *Shimeah* in 2 Samuel 21:21 and *Shammah* in 1 Samuel 16:9

---

*D*o not revel in your failures or play in your past. Overcome every doubt. Sign no treatise with the enemy and take no hostages. Never settle for less than your best or compromise your principles for your pleasures.

sinned greatly, because I have done this thing; but now, I pray, take away the iniquity of Your servant, for I have done very foolishly."

9 Then the LORD spoke to Gad, David's seer, saying, 10 "Go and tell David, saying, 'Thus says the LORD: "I offer you three *things;* choose one of them for yourself, that I may do *it* to you." ' "

11 So Gad came to David and said to him, "Thus says the LORD: 'Choose for yourself, 12 either three^a years of famine, or three months to be defeated by your foes with the sword of your enemies overtaking *you,* or else for three days the sword of the LORD—the plague in the land, with the angel^b of the LORD destroying throughout all the territory of Israel.' Now consider what answer I should take back to Him who sent me."

13 And David said to Gad, "I am in great distress. Please let me fall into the hand of the LORD, for His mercies *are* very great; but do not let me fall into the hand of man."

14 So the LORD sent a plague upon Israel, and seventy thousand men of Israel fell. 15 And God sent an angel to Jerusalem to destroy it. As he^a was destroying, the LORD looked and relented of the disaster, and said to the angel who was destroying, "It is enough; now restrain your^b hand." And the angel of the LORD stood by the threshing floor of Ornan^c the Jebusite.

16 Then David lifted his eyes and saw the angel of the LORD standing between earth and heaven, having in his hand a drawn sword stretched out over Jerusalem. So David and the elders, clothed in sackcloth, fell on their faces. 17 And David said to God, "Was it not I who commanded the people to be numbered? I am the one who has sinned and done evil indeed; but these sheep, what have they done? Let Your hand, I pray, O LORD my God, be against me and my father's house, but not against Your people that they should be plagued."

18 Therefore, the angel of the LORD commanded Gad to say to David that David should go and erect an altar to the LORD on the threshing floor of Ornan the Jebusite. 19 So David went up at the word of Gad, which he had

spoken in the name of the LORD. 20 Now Ornan turned and saw the angel; and his four sons *who were* with him hid themselves, but Ornan continued threshing wheat. 21 So David came to Ornan, and Ornan looked and saw David. And he went out from the threshing floor, and bowed before David with *his* face to the ground. 22 Then David said to Ornan, "Grant me the place of *this* threshing floor, that I may build an altar on it to the LORD. You shall grant it to me at the full price, that the plague may be withdrawn from the people."

23 But Ornan said to David, "Take *it* to yourself, and let my lord the king do *what is* good in his eyes. Look, I *also* give *you* the oxen for burnt offerings, the threshing implements for wood, and the wheat for the grain offering; I give *it* all."

24 Then King David said to Ornan, "No, but I will surely buy *it* for the full price, for I will not take what is yours for the LORD, nor offer burnt offerings with *that which* costs *me* nothing." 25 So David gave Ornan six hundred shekels of gold by weight for the place. 26 And David built there an altar to the LORD, and offered burnt offerings and peace offerings, and called on the LORD; and He answered him from heaven by fire on the altar of burnt offering.

27 So the LORD commanded the angel, and he returned his sword to its sheath.

28 At that time, when David saw that the LORD had answered him on the threshing floor of Ornan the Jebusite, he sacrificed there. 29 For the tabernacle of the LORD and the altar of the burnt offering, which Moses had made in the wilderness, *were* at that time at the high place in Gibeon. 30 But David could not go before it to inquire of God, for he was afraid of the sword of the angel of the LORD.

22 Then David said, "This *is* the house of the LORD God, and this *is* the altar of burnt offering for Israel." 2 So David commanded to gather the aliens who *were* in the land of Israel; and he appointed masons to cut hewn stones to build the house of God. 3 And David prepared

---

21:12 ^aOr *seven* (compare 2 Samuel 24:13)   ^bOr *Angel,* and so elsewhere in this chapter   21:15 ^aOr *He*   ^bOr *Your*   ^cSpelled *Araunah* in 2 Samuel 24:16

Gospel Pearls

iron in abundance for the nails of the doors of the gates and for the joints, and bronze in abundance beyond measure, 4 and cedar trees in abundance; for the Sidonians and those from Tyre brought much cedar wood to David.

5 Now David said, "Solomon my son *is* young and inexperienced, and the house to be built for the LORD *must be* exceedingly magnificent, famous and glorious throughout all countries. I will now make preparation for it." So David made abundant preparations before his death.

6 Then he called for his son Solomon, and charged him to build a house for the LORD God of Israel. 7 And David said to Solomon: "My son, as for me, it was in my mind to build a house to the name of the LORD my God; 8 but the word of the LORD came to me, saying, 'You have shed much blood and have made great wars; you shall not build a house for My name, because you have shed much blood on the earth in My sight. 9 Behold, a son shall be born to you, who shall be a man of rest; and I will give him rest from all his enemies all around. His name shall be Solomon,ᵃ for I will give peace and quietness to Israel in his days. 10 He shall build a house for My name, and he shall be My son, and I *will be* his Father; and I will establish the throne of his kingdom over Israel forever.' 11 Now, my son, may the LORD be with you; and may you prosper, and build the house of the LORD your God, as He has said to you. 12 Only may the LORD give you wisdom and understanding, and give you charge concerning Israel, that you may keep the law of the LORD your God. 13 Then you will prosper, if you take care to fulfill the statutes and judgments with which the LORD charged Moses concerning Israel. Be strong and of good courage; do not fear nor be dismayed. 14 Indeed I have taken much trouble to prepare for the house of the LORD one hundred thousand talents of gold and one million talents of silver, and bronze and iron beyond measure, for it is so abundant. I have prepared timber and stone also, and you may add to them. 15 Moreover *there are* workmen with you in abundance: woodsmen and stonecutters, and all types of skillful men for every kind of work. 16 Of gold and silver and bronze and iron *there is* no limit. Arise and begin working, and the LORD be with you."

17 David also commanded all the leaders of Israel to help Solomon his son, *saying,* 18 "*Is* not the LORD your God with you? And has He *not* given you rest on every side? For He has given the inhabitants of the land into my hand, and the land is subdued before the LORD and before His people. 19 Now set your heart and your soul to seek the LORD your God. Therefore arise and build the sanctuary of the LORD God, to bring the ark of the covenant of the LORD and the holy articles of God into the house that is to be built for the name of the LORD."

23 So when David was old and full of days, he made his son Solomon king over Israel.

2 And he gathered together all the leaders of Israel, with the priests and the Levites. 3 Now the Levites were numbered from the age of thirty years and above; and the number of individual males was thirty-eight thousand. 4 Of these, twenty-four thousand *were* to look after the work of the house of the LORD, six thousand *were* officers and judges, 5 four thousand *were* gatekeepers, and four thousand praised the LORD with *musical* instruments, "which I made," *said David,* "for giving praise."

6 Also David separated them into divisions among the sons of Levi: Gershon, Kohath, and Merari.

7 Of the Gershonites: Laadanᵃ and Shimei. 8 The sons of Laadan: the first Jehiel, then Zetham and Joel—three *in all.* 9 The sons of Shimei: Shelomith, Haziel, and Haran—three *in all.* These were the heads of the fathers' *houses* of Laadan. 10 And the sons of Shimei: Jahath, Zina,ᵃ Jeush, and Beriah. These *were* the four sons of Shimei. 11 Jahath was the first and Zizah the second. But Jeush and Beriah did not have many sons; therefore they were assigned as one father's house.

12 The sons of Kohath: Amram, Izhar, Hebron, and Uzziel—four *in*

22:9 ᵃLiterally *Peaceful*   23:7 ᵃSpelled *Libni* in Exodus 6:17   23:10 ᵃSeptuagint and Vulgate read *Zizah* (compare verse 11).

---

*N*ever doubt that the Father wants His daughters to be blessed! It is His joy to see you flourish and succeed.

all. 13 The sons of Amram: Aaron and Moses; and Aaron was set apart, he and his sons forever, that he should sanctify the most holy things, to burn incense before the LORD, to minister to Him, and to give the blessing in His name forever. 14 Now the sons of Moses the man of God were reckoned to the tribe of Levi. 15 The sons of Moses *were* Gershon*ᵃ* and Eliezer. 16 Of the sons of Gershon, Shebuel*ᵃ* *was* the first. 17 Of the descendants of Eliezer, Rehabiah was the first. And Eliezer had no other sons, but the sons of Rehabiah were very many. 18 Of the sons of Izhar, Shelomith *was* the first. 19 Of the sons of Hebron, Jeriah *was* the first, Amariah the second, Jahaziel the third, and Jekameam the fourth. 20 Of the sons of Uzziel, Michah *was* the first and Jesshiah the second.

21 The sons of Merari *were* Mahli and Mushi. The sons of Mahli *were* Eleazar and Kish. 22 And Eleazar died, and had no sons, but only daughters; and their brethren, the sons of Kish, took them *as wives.* 23 The sons of Mushi *were* Mahli, Eder, and Jeremoth—three *in all.*

24 These *were* the sons of Levi by their fathers' houses—the heads of the fathers' *houses* as they were counted individually by the number of their names, who did the work for the service of the house of the LORD, from the age of twenty years and above.

25 For David said, "The LORD God of Israel has given rest to His people, that they may dwell in Jerusalem forever"; 26 and also to the Levites, "They shall no longer carry the tabernacle, or any of the articles for its service." 27 For by the last words of David the Levites *were* numbered from twenty years old and above; 28 because their duty *was* to help the sons of Aaron in the service of the house of the LORD, in the courts and in the chambers, in the purifying of all holy things and the work of the service of the house of God, 29 both with the showbread and the fine flour for the grain offering, with the unleavened cakes and *what is baked in* the pan, with what is mixed and with all kinds of measures and sizes; 30 to stand every morning to

thank and praise the LORD, and likewise at evening; 31 and at every presentation of a burnt offering to the LORD on the Sabbaths and on the New Moons and on the set feasts, by number according to the ordinance governing them, regularly before the LORD; 32 and that they should attend to the needs of the tabernacle of meeting, the needs of the holy *place,* and the needs of the sons of Aaron their brethren in the work of the house of the LORD.

24 Now *these are* the divisions of the sons of Aaron. The sons of Aaron *were* Nadab, Abihu, Eleazar, and Ithamar. 2 And Nadab and Abihu died before their father, and had no children; therefore Eleazar and Ithamar ministered as priests. 3 Then David with Zadok of the sons of Eleazar, and Ahimelech of the sons of Ithamar, divided them according to the schedule of their service.

4 There were more leaders found of the sons of Eleazar than of the sons of Ithamar, and *thus* they were divided. Among the sons of Eleazar *were* sixteen heads of *their* fathers' houses, and eight heads of their fathers' houses among the sons of Ithamar. 5 Thus they were divided by lot, one group as another, for there were officials of the sanctuary and officials *of the house* of God, from the sons of Eleazar and from the sons of Ithamar. 6 And the scribe, Shemaiah the son of Nethanel, *one of* the Levites, wrote them down before the king, the leaders, Zadok the priest, Ahimelech the son of Abiathar, and the heads of the fathers' *houses* of the priests and Levites, one father's house taken for Eleazar and *one* for Ithamar.

7 Now the first lot fell to Jehoiarib, the second to Jedaiah, 8 the third to Harim, the fourth to Seorim, 9 the fifth to Malchijah, the sixth to Mijamin, 10 the seventh to Hakkoz, the eighth to Abijah, 11 the ninth to Jeshua, the tenth to Shecaniah, 12 the eleventh to Eliashib, the twelfth to Jakim, 13 the thirteenth to Huppah, the fourteenth to Jeshebeab, 14 the fifteenth to Bilgah, the sixteenth to Immer, 15 the seventeenth to Hezir, the eighteenth to Happizzez,*ᵃ* 16 the nineteenth to Pethahiah,

---

23:15 *ᵃ*Hebrew *Gershom* (compare 6:16)   23:16 *ᵃ*Spelled *Shubael* in 24:20   24:15 *ᵃ*Septuagint and Vulgate read *Aphses.*

Gospel Pearls

the twentieth to Jehezekel,[a] 17 the twenty-first to Jachin, the twenty-second to Gamul, 18 the twenty-third to Delaiah, the twenty-fourth to Maaziah.

19 This was the schedule of their service for coming into the house of the LORD according to their ordinance by the hand of Aaron their father, as the LORD God of Israel had commanded him.

20 And the rest of the sons of Levi: of the sons of Amram, Shubael;[a] of the sons of Shubael, Jehdeiah. 21 Concerning Rehabiah, of the sons of Rehabiah, the first was Isshiah. 22 Of the Izharites, Shelomoth;[a] of the sons of Shelomoth, Jahath. 23 Of the sons of Hebron,[a] Jeriah was the first,[b] Amariah the second, Jahaziel the third, and Jekameam the fourth. 24 Of the sons of Uzziel, Michah; of the sons of Michah, Shamir. 25 The brother of Michah, Isshiah; of the sons of Isshiah, Zechariah. 26 The sons of Merari were Mahli and Mushi; the son of Jaaziah, Beno. 27 The sons of Merari by Jaaziah were Beno, Shoham, Zaccur, and Ibri. 28 Of Mahli: Eleazar, who had no sons. 29 Of Kish: the son of Kish, Jerahmeel.

30 Also the sons of Mushi were Mahli, Eder, and Jerimoth. These were the sons of the Levites according to their fathers' houses.

31 These also cast lots just as their brothers the sons of Aaron did, in the presence of King David, Zadok, Ahimelech, and the heads of the fathers' houses of the priests and Levites. The chief fathers did just as their younger brethren.

25 Moreover David and the captains of the army separated for the service some of the sons of Asaph, of Heman, and of Jeduthun, who should prophesy with harps, stringed instruments, and cymbals. And the number of the skilled men performing their service was: 2 Of the sons of Asaph: Zaccur, Joseph, Nethaniah, and Asharelah;[a] the sons of Asaph were under the direction of Asaph, who prophesied according to the order of the king. 3 Of Jeduthun, the sons of Jeduthun: Gedaliah, Zeri,[a] Jeshaiah, Shimei, Hashabiah, and Mattithiah, six,[b] under the direction of their father Jeduthun, who prophesied with a harp to give thanks and to praise the LORD. 4 Of Heman, the sons of Heman: Bukkiah, Mattaniah, Uzziel,[a] Shebuel,[b] Jerimoth,[c] Hananiah, Hanani, Eliathah, Giddalti, Romamti-Ezer, Joshbekashah, Mallothi, Hothir, and Mahazioth. 5 All these were the sons of Heman the king's seer in the words of God, to exalt his horn.[a] For God gave Heman fourteen sons and three daughters.

6 All these were under the direction of their father for the music in the house of the LORD, with cymbals, stringed instruments, and harps, for the service of the house of God. Asaph, Jeduthun, and Heman were under the authority of the king. 7 So the number of them, with their brethren who were instructed in the songs of the LORD, all who were skillful, was two hundred and eighty-eight.

8 And they cast lots for their duty, the small as well as the great, the teacher with the student.

9 Now the first lot for Asaph came out for Joseph; the second for Gedaliah, him with his brethren and sons, twelve; 10 the third for Zaccur, his sons and his brethren, twelve; 11 the fourth for Jizri,[a] his sons and his brethren, twelve; 12 the fifth for Nethaniah, his sons and his brethren, twelve; 13 the sixth for Bukkiah, his sons and his brethren, twelve; 14 the seventh for Jesharelah,[a] his sons and his brethren, twelve; 15 the eighth for Jeshaiah, his sons and his brethren, twelve; 16 the ninth for Mattaniah, his sons and his brethren, twelve; 17 the tenth for Shimei, his sons and his brethren, twelve; 18 the eleventh for Azarel,[a] his sons and his brethren, twelve; 19 the

---

24:16 [a]Masoretic Text reads Jehezkel. 24:20 [a]Spelled Shebuel in 23:16 24:22 [a]Spelled Shelomith in 23:18 24:23 [a]Supplied from 23:19 (following some Hebrew manuscripts and Septuagint manuscripts) [b]Supplied from 23:19 (following some Hebrew manuscripts and Septuagint manuscripts) 25:2 [a]Spelled Jesharelah in verse 14 25:3 [a]Spelled Jizri in verse 11 [b]Shimei, appearing in one Hebrew and several Septuagint manuscripts, completes the total of six sons (compare verse 17). 25:4 [a]Spelled Azarel in verse 18 [b]Spelled Shubael in verse 20 [c]Spelled Jeremoth in verse 22 25:5 [a]That is, to increase his power or influence 25:11 [a]Spelled Zeri in verse 3 25:14 [a]Spelled Asharelah in verse 2 25:18 [a]Spelled Uzziel in verse 4

Do you need a healing? Ask God. He loves you like a father, and He cares about how you feel. He is not some aloof, macho, egotistical God who has no compassion for His children. He loves you, and He wants to bless you now!

twelfth for Hashabiah, his sons and his brethren, twelve; 20 the thirteenth for Shubael,ᵃ his sons and his brethren, twelve; 21 the fourteenth for Mattithiah, his sons and his brethren, twelve; 22 the fifteenth for Jeremoth,ᵃ his sons and his brethren, twelve; 23 the sixteenth for Hananiah, his sons and his brethren, twelve; 24 the seventeenth for Joshbekashah, his sons and his brethren, twelve; 25 the eighteenth for Hanani, his sons and his brethren, twelve; 26 the nineteenth for Mallothi, his sons and his brethren, twelve; 27 the twentieth for Eliathah, his sons and his brethren, twelve; 28 the twenty-first for Hothir, his sons and his brethren, twelve; 29 the twenty-second for Giddalti, his sons and his brethren, twelve; 30 the twenty-third for Mahazioth, his sons and his brethren, twelve; 31 the twenty-fourth for Romamti-Ezer, his sons and his brethren, twelve.

26 Concerning the divisions of the gatekeepers: of the Korahites, Meshelemiah the son of Kore, of the sons of Asaph. 2 And the sons of Meshelemiah *were* Zechariah the firstborn, Jediael the second, Zebadiah the third, Jathniel the fourth, 3 Elam the fifth, Jehohanan the sixth, Eliehoenai the seventh.

4 Moreover the sons of Obed-Edom *were* Shemaiah the firstborn, Jehozabad the second, Joah the third, Sacar the fourth, Nethanel the fifth, 5 Ammiel the sixth, Issachar the seventh, Peulthai the eighth; for God blessed him.

6 Also to Shemaiah his son were sons born who governed their fathers' houses, because they *were* men of great ability. 7 The sons of Shemaiah *were* Othni, Rephael, Obed, and Elzabad, whose brothers Elihu and Semachiah *were* able men.

8 All these *were* of the sons of Obed-Edom, they and their sons and their brethren, able men with strength for the work: sixty-two of Obed-Edom.

9 And Meshelemiah had sons and brethren, eighteen able men.

10 Also Hosah, of the children of Merari, had sons: Shimri the first (for though he was not the firstborn, his father made him the first), 11 Hilkiah the second, Tebaliah the third, Zechariah the fourth; all the sons and brethren of Hosah *were* thirteen.

12 Among these *were* the divisions of the gatekeepers, among the chief men, *having* duties just like their brethren, to serve in the house of the LORD. 13 And they cast lots for each gate, the small as well as the great, according to their father's house. 14 The lot for the East *Gate* fell to Shelemiah. Then they cast lots *for* his son Zechariah, a wise counselor, and his lot came out for the North Gate; 15 to Obed-Edom the South Gate, and to his sons the storehouse.ᵃ 16 To Shuppim and Hosah *the lot came out* for the West Gate, with the Shallecheth Gate on the ascending highway—watchman opposite watchman. 17 On the east were *six* Levites, on the north four each day, on the south four each day, and for the storehouseᵃ two by two. 18 As for the Parbarᵃ on the west, *there were* four on the highway *and* two at the Parbar. 19 These were the divisions of the gatekeepers among the sons of Korah and among the sons of Merari.

20 Of the Levites, Ahijah *was* over the treasuries of the house of God and over the treasuries of the dedicated things. 21 The sons of Laadan, the descendants of the Gershonites of Laadan, heads of their fathers' *houses*, of Laadan the Gershonite: Jehieli. 22 The sons of Jehieli, Zetham and Joel his brother, *were* over the treasuries of the house of the LORD. 23 Of the Amramites, the Izharites, the Hebronites, and the Uzzielites: 24 Shebuel the son of Gershom, the son of Moses, *was* overseer of the treasuries. 25 And his brethren by Eliezer *were* Rehabiah his son, Jeshaiah his son, Joram his son, Zichri his son, and Shelomith his son.

26 This Shelomith and his brethren *were* over all the treasuries of the dedicated things which King David and the heads of fathers' *houses*, the captains over thousands and hundreds, and the captains of the army, had dedicated. 27 Some of the spoils won in battles they dedicated to maintain the house of the LORD.

25:20 ᵃSpelled *Shebuel* in verse 4   25:22 ᵃSpelled *Jerimoth* in verse 4   26:15 ᵃHebrew *asuppim*
26:17 ᵃHebrew *asuppim*   26:18 ᵃProbably a court or colonnade extending west of the temple

Gospel Pearls

28 And all that Samuel the seer, Saul the son of Kish, Abner the son of Ner, and Joab the son of Zeruiah had dedicated, every dedicated *thing,* was under the hand of Shelomith and his brethren.

29 Of the Izharites, Chenaniah and his sons *performed* duties as officials and judges over Israel outside Jerusalem.

30 Of the Hebronites, Hashabiah and his brethren, one thousand seven hundred able men, had the oversight of Israel on the west side of the Jordan for all the business of the LORD, and in the service of the king. 31 Among the Hebronites, Jerijah *was* head of the Hebronites according to his genealogy of the fathers. In the fortieth year of the reign of David they were sought, and there were found among them capable men at Jazer of Gilead. 32 And his brethren *were* two thousand seven hundred able men, heads of fathers' *houses,* whom King David made officials over the Reubenites, the Gadites, and the half-tribe of Manasseh, for every matter pertaining to God and the affairs of the king.

27 And the children of Israel, according to their number, the heads of fathers' *houses,* the captains of thousands and hundreds and their officers, served the king in every matter of the *military* divisions. *These divisions* came in and went out month by month throughout all the months of the year, each division *having* twenty-four thousand.

2 Over the first division for the first month *was* Jashobeam the son of Zabdiel, and in his division *were* twenty-four thousand; 3 *he was* of the children of Perez, and the chief of all the captains of the army for the first month. 4 Over the division of the second month *was* Dodai*ª* an Ahohite, and of his division Mikloth also *was* the leader; in his division *were* twenty-four thousand. 5 The third captain of the army for the third month *was* Benaiah, the son of Jehoiada the priest, who was chief; in his division *were* twenty-four thousand. 6 This was the Benaiah *who* was mighty *among* the thirty, and was over the thirty; in his division *was*

Ammizabad his son. 7 The fourth *captain* for the fourth month *was* Asahel the brother of Joab, and Zebadiah his son after him; in his division *were* twenty-four thousand. 8 The fifth *captain* for the fifth month *was* Shamhuth*ª* the Izrahite; in his division were twenty-four thousand. 9 The sixth *captain* for the sixth month *was* Ira the son of Ikkesh the Tekoite; in his division *were* twenty-four thousand. 10 The seventh *captain* for the seventh month *was* Helez the Pelonite, of the children of Ephraim; in his division *were* twenty-four thousand. 11 The eighth *captain* for the eighth month *was* Sibbechai the Hushathite, of the Zarhites; in his division *were* twenty-four thousand. 12 The ninth *captain* for the ninth month *was* Abiezer the Anathothite, of the Benjamites; in his division *were* twenty-four thousand. 13 The tenth *captain* for the tenth month *was* Maharai the Netophathite, of the Zarhites; in his division *were* twenty-four thousand. 14 The eleventh *captain* for the eleventh month *was* Benaiah the Pirathonite, of the children of Ephraim; in his division *were* twenty-four thousand. 15 The twelfth *captain* for the twelfth month *was* Heldai*ª* the Netophathite, of Othniel; in his division *were* twenty-four thousand.

16 Furthermore, over the tribes of Israel: the officer over the Reubenites *was* Eliezer the son of Zichri; over the Simeonites, Shephatiah the son of Maachah; 17 *over* the Levites, Hashabiah the son of Kemuel; over the Aaronites, Zadok; 18 *over* Judah, Elihu, *one* of David's brothers; *over* Issachar, Omri the son of Michael; 19 *over* Zebulun, Ishmaiah the son of Obadiah; *over* Naphtali, Jerimoth the son of Azriel; 20 *over* the children of Ephraim, Hoshea the son of Azaziah; *over* the half-tribe of Manasseh, Joel the son of Pedaiah; 21 *over* the half-*tribe* of Manasseh in Gilead, Iddo the son of Zechariah; *over* Benjamin, Jaasiel the son of Abner; 22 *over* Dan, Azarel the son of Jeroham. These *were* the leaders of the tribes of Israel.

23 But David did not take the number of those twenty years old and under, because the LORD had said He

27:4 *ª*Hebrew *Dodai,* usually spelled *Dodo* (compare 2 Samuel 23:9)   27:8 *ª*Spelled *Shammoth* in 11:27 and *Shammah* in 2 Samuel 23:11   27:15 *ª*Spelled *Heled* in 11:30 and *Heleb* in 2 Samuel 23:29

*D*on't choose for lust. Don't choose for fortune and fame. Don't choose because of notoriety. All these things will fade. If you are going to marry, choose God's kind of man.

would multiply Israel like the stars of the heavens. 24 Joab the son of Zeruiah began a census, but he did not finish, for wrath came upon Israel because of this census; nor was the number recorded in the account of the chronicles of King David.

25 And Azmaveth the son of Adiel *was* over the king's treasuries; and Jehonathan the son of Uzziah was over the storehouses in the field, in the cities, in the villages, and in the fortresses. 26 Ezri the son of Chelub was over those who did the work of the field for tilling the ground. 27 And Shimei the Ramathite *was* over the vineyards, and Zabdi the Shiphmite was over the produce of the vineyards for the supply of wine. 28 Baal-Hanan the Gederite was over the olive trees and the sycamore trees that *were* in the lowlands, and Joash *was* over the store of oil. 29 And Shitrai the Sharonite *was* over the herds that fed in Sharon, and Shaphat the son of Adlai was over the herds *that were* in the valleys. 30 Obil the Ishmaelite *was* over the camels, Jehdeiah the Meronothite *was* over the donkeys, 31 and Jaziz the Hagrite *was* over the flocks. All these *were* the officials over King David's property.

32 Also Jehonathan, David's uncle, *was* a counselor, a wise man, and a scribe; and Jehiel the son of Hachmoni *was* with the king's sons. 33 Ahithophel *was* the king's counselor, and Hushai the Archite *was* the king's companion. 34 After Ahithophel *was* Jehoiada the son of Benaiah, then Abiathar. And the general of the king's army *was* Joab.

28 Now David assembled at Jerusalem all the leaders of Israel: the officers of the tribes and the captains of the divisions who served the king, the captains over thousands and captains over hundreds, and the stewards over all the substance and possessions of the king and of his sons, with the officials, the valiant men, and all the mighty men of valor. 2 Then King David rose to his feet and said, "Hear me, my brethren and my people: I *had* it in my heart to build a house of rest for the ark of the covenant of the LORD, and for the footstool of our God, and had made preparations to build it. 3 But God said to me, 'You shall not build a house for My name, because you *have been* a man of war and have shed blood.' 4 However the LORD God of Israel chose me above all the house of my father to be king over Israel forever, for He has chosen Judah *to be* the ruler. And of the house of Judah, the house of my father, and among the sons of my father, He was pleased with me to make *me* king over all Israel. 5 And of all my sons (for the LORD has given me many sons) He has chosen my son Solomon to sit on the throne of the kingdom of the LORD over Israel. 6 Now He said to me, 'It is your son Solomon *who* shall build My house and My courts; for I have chosen him *to be* My son, and I will be his Father. 7 Moreover I will establish his kingdom forever, if he is steadfast to observe My commandments and My judgments, as it is this day.' 8 Now therefore, in the sight of all Israel, the assembly of the LORD, and in the hearing of our God, be careful to seek out all the commandments of the LORD your God, that you may possess this good land, and leave *it* as an inheritance for your children after you forever.

9 "As for you, my son Solomon, know the God of your father, and serve Him with a loyal heart and with a willing mind; for the LORD searches all hearts and understands all the intent of the thoughts. If you seek Him, He will be found by you; but if you forsake Him, He will cast you off forever. 10 Consider now, for the LORD has chosen you to build a house for the sanctuary; be strong, and do it."

11 Then David gave his son Solomon the plans for the vestibule, its houses, its treasuries, its upper chambers, its inner chambers, and the place of the mercy seat; 12 and the plans for all that he had by the Spirit, of the courts of the house of the LORD, of all the chambers all around, of the treasuries of the house of God, and of the treasuries for the dedicated things; 13 also for the division of the priests and the Levites, for all the work of the service of the house of the LORD, and for all the articles of service in the house of the LORD. 14 *He* gave gold by weight for *things* of gold, for all articles used in every kind of service; also *silver* for all articles of silver by weight, for all articles used in

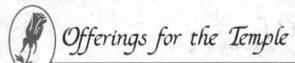

every kind of service; 15 the weight for the lampstands of gold, and their lamps of gold, by weight for each lampstand and its lamps; for the lampstands of silver by weight, for the lampstand and its lamps, according to the use of each lampstand. 16 And by weight *he gave* gold for the tables of the showbread, for each table, and silver for the tables of silver; 17 also pure gold for the forks, the basins, the pitchers of pure gold, and the golden bowls—*he gave gold* by weight for every bowl; and for the silver bowls, *silver* by weight for every bowl; 18 and refined gold by weight for the altar of incense, and for the construction of the chariot, that is, the gold cherubim that spread *their wings* and overshadowed the ark of the covenant of the LORD. 19 "All *this*," said David, "the LORD made me understand in writing, by *His* hand upon me, all the works of these plans."

20 And David said to his son Solomon, "Be strong and of good courage, and do *it;* do not fear nor be dismayed, for the LORD God—my God—*will be* with you. He will not leave you nor forsake you, until you have finished all the work for the service of the house of the LORD. 21 *Here are* the divisions of the priests and the Levites for all the service of the house of God; and every willing craftsman *will be* with you for all manner of workmanship, for every kind of service; also the leaders and all the people *will be* completely at your command."

29 Furthermore King David said to all the assembly: "My son Solomon, whom alone God has chosen, *is* young and inexperienced; and the work *is* great, because the temple*a* is not for man but for the LORD God. 2 Now for the house of my God I have prepared with all my might: gold for *things to be made of* gold, silver for *things of* silver, bronze for *things of* bronze, iron for *things of* iron, wood for *things of* wood, onyx stones, *stones* to be set, glistening stones of various colors, all kinds of precious stones, and marble slabs in abundance. 3 Moreover, because I have set my affection on the house of my God, I have given to the house

of my God, over and above all that I have prepared for the holy house, my own special treasure of gold and silver: 4 three thousand talents of gold, of the gold of Ophir, and seven thousand talents of refined silver, to overlay the walls of the houses; 5 the gold for *things of* gold and the silver for *things of* silver, and for all kinds of work *to be done* by the hands of craftsmen. Who *then* is willing to consecrate himself this day to the LORD?"

6 Then the leaders of the fathers' *houses,* leaders of the tribes of Israel, the captains of thousands and of hundreds, with the officers over the king's work, offered willingly. 7 They gave for the work of the house of God five thousand talents and ten thousand darics of gold, ten thousand talents of silver, eighteen thousand talents of bronze, and one hundred thousand talents of iron. 8 And whoever had *precious* stones gave *them* to the treasury of the house of the LORD, into the hand of Jehiel*a* the Gershonite. 9 Then the people rejoiced, for they had offered willingly, because with a loyal heart they had offered willingly to the LORD; and King David also rejoiced greatly.

10 Therefore David blessed the LORD before all the assembly; and David said:

"Blessed are You, LORD God of Israel, our Father, forever and ever.
11 Yours, O LORD, *is* the greatness, The power and the glory, The victory and the majesty; For all *that is* in heaven and in earth *is Yours;* Yours *is* the kingdom, O LORD, And You are exalted as head over all.
12 Both riches and honor *come* from You, And You reign over all. In Your hand *is* power and might; In Your hand *it is* to make great And to give strength to all.
13 "Now therefore, our God, We thank You And praise Your glorious name.

29:1 *a*Literally *palace*   29:8 *a*Possibly the same as *Jehieli* (compare 26:21, 22)

Know your own strength. If you are going to cope with life, you must know your own strength. Do you have weaknesses? Sure, we all do. But the greatest of all weaknesses is the inability to recognize and capitalize on your own strength and self-reliance.

Fix Your Heart

1 Chronicles 29:18

Your past can cause you to look at life in a way that is less than God's perspective. A little girl who was abused learns to defend herself by not trusting men. A defensive attitude can accompany you into adulthood. If you have successfully protected yourself in a certain way in the past, it is natural to continue that pattern throughout life.

Many people live in co-dependent relationships. Others are anesthetized to their problems because they have had them so long. Perhaps you have become so accustomed to your problem that even when you have a chance to be delivered, you find it hard to let go. Problems can become like a security blanket.

The infirm woman in Luke 13 was completely healed by Jesus' touch. She couldn't help herself no matter how hard she tried. But Jesus unleashed her. He lifted a heavy burden from her shoulders and set her free (see Luke 13:11–12).

Jesus also took away her excuse. Hearing Him say, "Woman, thou art loosed from thine infirmity," required something of her that she hadn't had to deal with before. For eighteen years she had excused herself because she was handicapped. But the moment He told her the problem was gone, she had no excuse.

Before you get out of trouble, you need to straighten out your attitude. Until your attitude is corrected, you can't be corrected. One woman I pastored was rather obnoxious. When I prayed about the matter, God allowed me to meet the woman's husband. Seeing his nasty attitude toward her, I understood why, when she reached down into her reservoir, all she had stored was hostility. That's all she had taken in, so that's all she could give.

You may want everyone to make an allowance for your problem, but the truth is that your problem needs to make an allowance for God. As the Bible says in 1 Chronicles 29:18, you've got to fix your thoughts, your attitude, your whole heart on the living God. You can't expect the whole human race to move over because you had a bad childhood. They won't do it. And you'll just end up depressed, frustrated, and confused.

Jesus Christ wants to separate you from the source of your bitterness until it no longer makes you a carrier of pain. Your attitude is what affects your situation—not other people's attitudes toward you. Let go of your old attitudes, fix your heart on God, and let Him make you whole.

14 But who *am* I, and who *are* my people,
That we should be able to offer so willingly as this?
For all things *come* from You,
And of Your own we have given You.
15 For we *are* aliens and pilgrims before You,
As *were* all our fathers;
Our days on earth *are* as a shadow,
And without hope.

16 "O LORD our God, all this abundance that we have prepared to build You a house for Your holy name is from Your hand, and *is* all Your own. 17 I know also, my God, that You test the heart and have pleasure in uprightness. As for me, in the uprightness of my heart I have willingly offered all these *things;* and now with joy I have seen Your people, who are present here to offer willingly to You. 18 O LORD God of Abraham, Isaac, and Israel, our fathers, keep this forever in the intent of the thoughts of the heart of Your people, and fix their heart toward You. 19 And give my son Solomon a loyal heart to keep Your commandments and Your testimonies and Your statutes, to do all *these things,* and to build the temple*ᵃ* for which I have made provision."

20 Then David said to all the assembly, "Now bless the LORD your God." So all the assembly blessed the LORD God of their fathers, and bowed their heads and prostrated themselves before the LORD and the king.

29:19 ᵃLiterally *palace*

21 And they made sacrifices to the LORD and offered burnt offerings to the LORD on the next day: a thousand bulls, a thousand rams, a thousand lambs, with their drink offerings, and sacrifices in abundance for all Israel. 22 So they ate and drank before the LORD with great gladness on that day. And they made Solomon the son of David king the second time, and anointed *him* before the LORD *to be* the leader, and Zadok *to be* priest. 23 Then Solomon sat on the throne of the LORD as king instead of David his father, and prospered; and all Israel obeyed him. 24 All the leaders and the mighty men, and also all the sons of King David, submitted themselves to King Solomon. 25 So the LORD exalted Solomon exceedingly in the sight of all Israel, and bestowed on him *such* royal majesty as had not been on any king before him in Israel.

26 Thus David the son of Jesse reigned over all Israel. 27 And the period that he reigned over Israel *was* forty years; seven years he reigned in Hebron, and thirty-three *years* he reigned in Jerusalem. 28 So he died in a good old age, full of days and riches and honor; and Solomon his son reigned in his place. 29 Now the acts of King David, first and last, indeed they *are* written in the book of Samuel the seer, in the book of Nathan the prophet, and in the book of Gad the seer, 30 with all his reign and his might, and the events that happened to him, to Israel, and to all the kingdoms of the lands.

The Second Book of the
CHRONICLES

1 Now Solomon the son of David was strengthened in his kingdom, and the LORD his God *was* with him and exalted him exceedingly.
2 And Solomon spoke to all Israel, to the captains of thousands and of hundreds, to the judges, and to every leader in all Israel, the heads of the fathers' *houses.* 3 Then Solomon, and all the assembly with him, went to the high place that *was* at Gibeon; for the tabernacle of meeting with God was there, which Moses the servant of the LORD had made in the wil-

*F*ather, help us to realize that we often contribute to our own storms. We keep alive things that should be released, and we release many things that You wanted us to keep alive.

derness. 4 But David had brought up the ark of God from Kirjath Jearim to *the place* David had prepared for it, for he had pitched a tent for it at Jerusalem. 5 Now the bronze altar that Bezalel the son of Uri, the son of Hur, had made, he put*a* before the tabernacle of the LORD; Solomon and the assembly sought Him *there*. 6 And Solomon went up there to the bronze altar before the LORD, which *was* at the tabernacle of meeting, and offered a thousand burnt offerings on it.

7 On that night God appeared to Solomon, and said to him, "Ask! What shall I give you?"

8 And Solomon said to God: "You have shown great mercy to David my father, and have made me king in his place. 9 Now, O LORD God, let Your promise to David my father be established, for You have made me king over a people like the dust of the earth in multitude. 10 Now give me wisdom and knowledge, that I may go out and come in before this people; for who can judge this great people of Yours?"

11 Then God said to Solomon: "Because this was in your heart, and you have not asked riches or wealth or honor or the life of your enemies, nor have you asked long life—but have asked wisdom and knowledge for yourself, that you may judge My people over whom I have made you king— 12 wisdom and knowledge *are* granted to you; and I will give you riches and wealth and honor, such as none of the kings have had who *were* before you, nor shall any after you have the like."

13 So Solomon came to Jerusalem from the high place that *was* at Gibeon, from before the tabernacle of meeting, and reigned over Israel. 14 And Solomon gathered chariots and horsemen; he had one thousand four hundred chariots and twelve thousand horsemen, whom he stationed in the chariot cities and with the king in Jerusalem. 15 Also the king made silver and gold as common in Jerusalem as stones, and he made cedars as abundant as the sycamores which *are* in the lowland. 16 And Solomon had horses imported from Egypt and Keveh; the king's

merchants bought them in Keveh at the *current* price. 17 They also acquired and imported from Egypt a chariot for six hundred *shekels* of silver, and a horse for one hundred and fifty; thus, through their agents,*a* they exported them to all the kings of the Hittites and the kings of Syria.

2 Then Solomon determined to build a temple for the name of the LORD, and a royal house for himself. 2 Solomon selected seventy thousand men to bear burdens, eighty thousand to quarry *stone* in the mountains, and three thousand six hundred to oversee them.

3 Then Solomon sent to Hiram*a* king of Tyre, saying:

As you have dealt with David my father, and sent him cedars to build himself a house to dwell in, *so deal with me.* 4 Behold, I am building a temple for the name of the LORD my God, to dedicate *it* to Him, to burn before Him sweet incense, for the continual showbread, for the burnt offerings morning and evening, on the Sabbaths, on the New Moons, and on the set feasts of the LORD our God. This *is an ordinance* forever to Israel.

5 And the temple which I build *will be* great, for our God is greater than all gods. 6 But who is able to build Him a temple, since heaven and the heaven of heavens cannot contain Him? Who *am* I then, that I should build Him a temple, except to burn sacrifice before Him?

7 Therefore send me at once a man skillful to work in gold and silver, in bronze and iron, in purple and crimson and blue, who has skill to engrave with the skillful men who are with me in Judah and Jerusalem, whom David my father provided. 8 Also send me cedar and cypress and algum logs from Lebanon, for I know that your servants have skill to cut timber in Lebanon; and indeed

---

1:5 *a*Some authorities read *it was there.*   1:17 *a*Literally *by their hands*   2:3 *a*Hebrew *Huram* (compare 1 Kings 5:1)

my servants *will be* with your servants, 9 to prepare timber for me in abundance, for the temple which I am about to build *shall be* great and wonderful.

10 And indeed I will give to your servants, the woodsmen who cut timber, twenty thousand kors of ground wheat, twenty thousand kors of barley, twenty thousand baths of wine, and twenty thousand baths of oil.

11 Then Hiram king of Tyre answered in writing, which he sent to Solomon:

> Because the LORD loves His people, He has made you king over them.

12 Hiram*a* also said:

> Blessed *be* the LORD God of Israel, who made heaven and earth, for He has given King David a wise son, endowed with prudence and understanding, who will build a temple for the LORD and a royal house for himself!

13 And now I have sent a skillful man, endowed with understanding, Huram*a* my master*b* *craftsman* 14 (the son of a woman of the daughters of Dan, and his father was a man of Tyre), skilled to work in gold and silver, bronze and iron, stone and wood, purple and blue, fine linen and crimson, and to make any engraving and to accomplish any plan which may be given to him, with your skillful men and with the skillful men of my lord David your father.

15 Now therefore, the wheat, the barley, the oil, and the wine which my lord has spoken of, let him send to his servants. 16 And we will cut wood from

Lebanon, as much as you need; we will bring it to you in rafts by sea to Joppa, and you will carry it up to Jerusalem.

17 Then Solomon numbered all the aliens who *were* in the land of Israel, after the census in which David his father had numbered them; and there were found to be one hundred and fifty-three thousand six hundred. 18 And he made seventy thousand of them bearers of burdens, eighty thousand stonecutters in the mountain, and three thousand six hundred overseers to make the people work.

3 Now Solomon began to build the house of the LORD at Jerusalem on Mount Moriah, where *the LORD*a had appeared to his father David, at the place that David had prepared on the threshing floor of Ornan*b* the Jebusite. 2 And he began to build on the second *day* of the second month in the fourth year of his reign.

3 This is the foundation which Solomon laid for building the house of God: The length *was* sixty cubits (by cubits according to the former measure) and the width twenty cubits. 4 And the vestibule that *was* in front *of the sanctuary*a was twenty cubits long across the width of the house, and the height *was* one hundred and*b* twenty. He overlaid the inside with pure gold. 5 The larger room*a* he paneled with cypress which he overlaid with fine gold, and he carved palm trees and chainwork on it. 6 And he decorated the house with precious stones for beauty, and the gold *was* gold from Parvaim. 7 He also overlaid the house—the beams and doorposts, its walls and doors—with gold; and he carved cherubim on the walls.

8 And he made the Most Holy Place. Its length was according to the width of the house, twenty cubits, and its width twenty cubits. He overlaid it with six hundred talents of fine gold. 9 The weight of the nails *was* fifty shekels of gold; and he overlaid the upper area with gold. 10 In the Most Holy Place he made two cherubim, fashioned by carving, and over-

---

2:12 *a*Hebrew *Huram* (compare 1 Kings 5:1)   2:13 *a*Spelled *Hiram* in 1 Kings 7:13   *b*Literally *father* (compare 1 Kings 7:13, 14)   3:1 *a*Literally *He,* following Masoretic Text and Vulgate; Septuagint reads *the LORD;* Targum reads *the Angel of the LORD.*   *b*Spelled *Araunah* in 2 Samuel 24:16ff   3:4 *a*The main room of the temple; elsewhere called the holy place (compare 1 Kings 6:3)   *b*Following Masoretic Text, Septuagint, and Vulgate; Arabic, some manuscripts of the Septuagint, and Syriac omit *one hundred and*. 3:5 *a*Literally *house*

God has called you to serve in a church. It is a place where He wants to realign you and teach you relational skills. It is there that God teaches women how to love, despite their fears and inhibitions, and experience real sisterhood.

laid them with gold. 11 The wings of the cherubim *were* twenty cubits in *overall* length: one wing *of the one cherub was* five cubits, touching the wall of the room, and the other wing *was* five cubits, touching the wing of the other cherub; 12 *one* wing of the other cherub *was* five cubits, touching the wall of the room, and the other wing *also was* five cubits, touching the wing of the other cherub. 13 The wings of these cherubim spanned twenty cubits overall. They stood on their feet, and they faced inward. 14 And he made the veil of blue, purple, crimson, and fine linen, and wove cherubim into it.

15 Also he made in front of the temple*a* two pillars thirty-five*b* cubits high, and the capital that *was* on the top of each of *them* was five cubits. 16 He made wreaths of chainwork, as in the inner sanctuary, and put *them* on top of the pillars; and he made one hundred pomegranates, and put *them* on the wreaths of chainwork. 17 Then he set up the pillars before the temple, one on the right hand and the other on the left; he called the name of the one on the right hand Jachin, and the name of the one on the left Boaz.

4 Moreover he made a bronze altar: twenty cubits was its length, twenty cubits its width, and ten cubits its height. 2 Then he made the Sea of cast *bronze*, ten cubits from one brim to the other; *it was* completely round. Its height *was* five cubits, and a line of thirty cubits measured its circumference. 3 And under it *was* the likeness of oxen encircling it all around, ten to a cubit, all the way around the Sea. The oxen *were* cast in two rows, when it was cast. 4 It stood on twelve oxen: three looking toward the north, three looking toward the west, three looking toward the south, and three looking toward the east; the Sea *was* set upon them, and all their back parts *pointed* inward. 5 It *was* a handbreadth thick; and its brim was shaped like the brim of a cup, *like* a lily blossom. It contained three thousand*a* baths.

6 He also made ten lavers, and put five on the right side and five on the left, to wash in them; such things as they offered for the burnt offering they would wash in them, but the Sea *was* for the priests to wash in. 7 And he made ten lampstands of gold according to their design, and set *them* in the temple, five on the right side and five on the left. 8 He also made ten tables, and placed *them* in the temple, five on the right side and five on the left. And he made one hundred bowls of gold.

9 Furthermore he made the court of the priests, and the great court and doors for the court; and he overlaid these doors with bronze. 10 He set the Sea on the right side, toward the southeast.

11 Then Huram made the pots and the shovels and the bowls. So Huram finished doing the work that he was to do for King Solomon for the house of God: 12 the two pillars and the bowl-shaped capitals *that were* on top of the two pillars; the two networks covering the two bowl-shaped capitals which *were* on top of the pillars; 13 four hundred pomegranates for the two networks (two rows of pomegranates for each network, to cover the two bowl-shaped capitals that *were* on the pillars); 14 he also made carts and the lavers on the carts; 15 one Sea and twelve oxen under it; 16 also the pots, the shovels, the forks—and all their articles Huram his master*a* *craftsman* made of burnished bronze for King Solomon for the house of the LORD.

17 In the plain of Jordan the king had them cast in clay molds, between Succoth and Zeredah.*a* 18 And Solomon had all these articles made in such great abundance that the weight of the bronze was not determined.

19 Thus Solomon had all the furnishings made for the house of God: the altar of gold and the tables on which *was* the showbread; 20 the lampstands with their lamps of pure gold, to burn in the prescribed manner in front of the inner sanctuary, 21 with the flowers and the lamps and the wick-trimmers of gold, of purest gold; 22 the trimmers, the bowls, the ladles, and the censers of pure gold. As for the entry of the sanctuary, its inner doors to the Most Holy *Place*,

---

3:15 *a*Literally *house*   *b*Or *eighteen* (compare 1 Kings 7:15; 2 Kings 25:17; and Jeremiah 52:21)
4:5 *a*Or *two thousand* (compare 1 Kings 7:26)   4:16 *a*Literally *father*   4:17 *a*Spelled *Zaretan* in 1 Kings 7:46

Gospel Pearls

and the doors of the main hall of the temple, *were* gold.

5 So all the work that Solomon had done for the house of the LORD was finished; and Solomon brought in the things which his father David had dedicated: the silver and the gold and all the furnishings. And he put *them* in the treasuries of the house of God.

2 Now Solomon assembled the elders of Israel and all the heads of the tribes, the chief fathers of the children of Israel, in Jerusalem, that they might bring the ark of the covenant of the LORD up from the City of David, which *is* Zion. 3 Therefore all the men of Israel assembled with the king at the feast, which *was* in the seventh month. 4 So all the elders of Israel came, and the Levites took up the ark. 5 Then they brought up the ark, the tabernacle of meeting, and all the holy furnishings that *were* in the tabernacle. The priests and the Levites brought them up. 6 Also King Solomon, and all the congregation of Israel who were assembled with him before the ark, were sacrificing sheep and oxen that could not be counted or numbered for multitude. 7 Then the priests brought in the ark of the covenant of the LORD to its place, into the inner sanctuary of the temple,*ᵃ* to the Most Holy *Place,* under the wings of the cherubim. 8 For the cherubim spread *their* wings over the place of the ark, and the cherubim overshadowed the ark and its poles. 9 The poles extended so that the ends of the poles of the ark could be seen from *the holy place,* in front of the inner sanctuary; but they could not be seen from outside. And they are there to this day. 10 Nothing was in the ark except the two tablets which Moses put *there* at Horeb, when the LORD made *a* covenant with the children of Israel, when they had come out of Egypt.

11 And it came to pass when the priests came out of the *Most* Holy Place (for all the priests who *were* present had sanctified themselves, without keeping to their divisions), 12 and the Levites *who were* the singers, all those of Asaph and Heman and Jeduthun, with their sons and their brethren, stood at the east end of the altar, clothed in white linen, having cymbals, stringed instruments and harps, and with them one hundred and twenty priests sounding with trumpets— 13 indeed it came to pass, when the trumpeters and singers *were* as one, to make one sound to be heard in praising and thanking the LORD, and when they lifted up their voice with the trumpets and cymbals and instruments of music, and praised the LORD, *saying:*

> "*For He is* good,
> For His mercy *endures*
> forever,"*ᵃ*

that the house, the house of the LORD, was filled with a cloud, 14 so that the priests could not continue ministering because of the cloud; for the glory of the LORD filled the house of God.

6 Then Solomon spoke:

> "The LORD said He would dwell
> in the dark cloud.
> 2   I have surely built You an
> exalted house,
> And a place for You to dwell
> in forever."

3 Then the king turned around and blessed the whole assembly of Israel, while all the assembly of Israel was standing. 4 And he said: "Blessed *be* the LORD God of Israel, who has fulfilled with His hands *what* He spoke with His mouth to my father David, saying, 5 'Since the day that I brought My people out of the land of Egypt, I have chosen no city from any tribe of Israel *in which* to build a house, that My name might be there, nor did I choose any man to be a ruler over My people Israel. 6 Yet I have chosen Jerusalem, that My name may be there, and I have chosen David to be over My people Israel.' 7 Now it was in the heart of my father David to build a temple*ᵃ* for the name of the LORD God of Israel. 8 But the LORD said to my father David, 'Whereas it was in your heart to build a temple for My name, you did well in that it was in your heart. 9 Nevertheless you shall not build the temple, but your son who will come from your body, he shall build the temple for My

2 wonder what would happen to the unity and harmony of the ministry if women across the world would meet at the body of Christ and anoint Him together, sister to sister!

name.' 10 So the LORD has fulfilled His word which He spoke, and I have filled the position of my father David, and sit on the throne of Israel, as the LORD promised; and I have built the temple for the name of the LORD God of Israel. 11 And there I have put the ark, in which *is* the covenant of the LORD which He made with the children of Israel."

12 Then *Solomon*ᵃ stood before the altar of the LORD in the presence of all the assembly of Israel, and spread out his hands 13 (for Solomon had made a bronze platform five cubits long, five cubits wide, and three cubits high, and had set it in the midst of the court; and he stood on it, knelt down on his knees before all the assembly of Israel, and spread out his hands toward heaven), 14 and he said: "LORD God of Israel, *there is* no God in heaven or on earth like You, who keep *Your* covenant and mercy with Your servants who walk before You with all their hearts; 15 You have kept what You promised Your servant David my father; You have both spoken with Your mouth and fulfilled *it* with Your hand, as *it is* this day. 16 Therefore, LORD God of Israel, now keep what You promised Your servant David my father, saying, 'You shall not fail to have a man sit before Me on the throne of Israel, only if your sons take heed to their way, that they walk in My law as you have walked before Me.' 17 And now, O LORD God of Israel, let Your word come true, which You have spoken to Your servant David.

18 "But will God indeed dwell with men on the earth? Behold, heaven and the heaven of heavens cannot contain You. How much less this templeᵃ which I have built! 19 Yet regard the prayer of Your servant and his supplication, O LORD my God, and listen to the cry and the prayer which Your servant is praying before You: 20 that Your eyes may be open toward this temple day and night, toward the place where *You* said *You would* put Your name, that You may hear the prayer which Your servant makes toward this place. 21 And may You hear the supplications of Your servant and of Your people Israel, when they pray toward this place. Hear from heaven Your dwelling place, and when You hear, forgive.

22 "If anyone sins against his neighbor, and is forced to take an oath, and comes *and* takes an oath before Your altar in this temple, 23 then hear from heaven, and act, and judge Your servants, bringing retribution on the wicked by bringing his way on his own head, and justifying the righteous by giving him according to his righteousness.

24 "Or if Your people Israel are defeated before an enemy because they have sinned against You, and return and confess Your name, and pray and make supplication before You in this temple, 25 then hear from heaven and forgive the sin of Your people Israel, and bring them back to the land which You gave to them and their fathers.

26 "When the heavens are shut up and there is no rain because they have sinned against You, when they pray toward this place and confess Your name, and turn from their sin because You afflict them, 27 then hear *in* heaven, and forgive the sin of Your servants, Your people Israel, that You may teach them the good way in which they should walk; and send rain on Your land which You have given to Your people as an inheritance.

28 "When there is famine in the land, pestilence or blight or mildew, locusts or grasshoppers; when their enemies besiege them in the land of their cities; whatever plague or whatever sickness *there is;* 29 whatever prayer, whatever supplication is *made* by anyone, or by all Your people Israel, when each one knows his own burden and his own grief, and spreads out his hands to this temple: 30 then hear from heaven Your dwelling place, and forgive, and give to everyone according to all his ways, whose heart You know (for You alone know the hearts of the sons of men), 31 that they may fear You, to walk in Your ways as long as they live in the land which You gave to our fathers.

32 "Moreover, concerning a foreigner, who is not of Your people Israel, but has come from a far country for the sake of Your great name and Your mighty hand and Your outstretched arm, when they come and

6:12 ᵃLiterally *he* (compare 1 Kings 8:22)   6:18 ᵃLiterally *house*

Gospel Pearls

pray in this temple; 33 then hear from heaven Your dwelling place, and do according to all for which the foreigner calls to You, that all peoples of the earth may know Your name and fear You, as *do* Your people Israel, and that they may know that this temple which I have built is called by Your name.

34 "When Your people go out to battle against their enemies, wherever You send them, and when they pray to You toward this city which You have chosen and the temple which I have built for Your name, 35 then hear from heaven their prayer and their supplication, and maintain their cause.

36 "When they sin against You (for *there is* no one who does not sin), and You become angry with them and deliver them to the enemy, and they take them captive to a land far or near; 37 yet when they come to themselves in the land where they were carried captive, and repent, and make supplication to You in the land of their captivity, saying, 'We have sinned, we have done wrong, and have committed wickedness'; 38 and *when* they return to You with all their heart and with all their soul in the land of their captivity, where they have been carried captive, and pray toward their land which You gave to their fathers, the city which You have chosen, and toward the temple which I have built for Your name: 39 then hear from heaven Your dwelling place their prayer and their supplications, and maintain their cause, and forgive Your people who have sinned against You. 40 Now, my God, I pray, let Your eyes be open and *let* Your ears *be* attentive to the prayer *made* in this place.

41 "Now therefore,
Arise, O LORD God, to Your
resting place,
You and the ark of Your
strength.
Let Your priests, O LORD God,
be clothed with salvation,
And let Your saints rejoice in
goodness.

42 "O LORD God, do not turn away
the face of Your Anointed;

Remember the mercies of Your
servant David."*a*

7 When Solomon had finished praying, fire came down from heaven and consumed the burnt offering and the sacrifices; and the glory of the LORD filled the temple.*a* 2 And the priests could not enter the house of the LORD, because the glory of the LORD had filled the LORD's house. 3 When all the children of Israel saw how the fire came down, and the glory of the LORD on the temple, they bowed their faces to the ground on the pavement, and worshiped and praised the LORD, *saying:*

"For *He is* good,
For His mercy *endures*
forever."*a*

4 Then the king and all the people offered sacrifices before the LORD. 5 King Solomon offered a sacrifice of twenty-two thousand bulls and one hundred and twenty thousand sheep. So the king and all the people dedicated the house of God. 6 And the priests attended to their services; the Levites also with instruments of the music of the LORD, which King David had made to praise the LORD, saying, "For His mercy *endures* forever,"*a* whenever David offered praise by their ministry. The priests sounded trumpets opposite them, while all Israel stood.

7 Furthermore Solomon consecrated the middle of the court that *was* in front of the house of the LORD; for there he offered burnt offerings and the fat of the peace offerings, because the bronze altar which Solomon had made was not able to receive the burnt offerings, the grain offerings, and the fat.

8 At that time Solomon kept the feast seven days, and all Israel with him, a very great assembly from the entrance of Hamath to the Brook of Egypt.*a* 9 And on the eighth day they held a sacred assembly, for they observed the dedication of the altar seven days, and the feast seven days. 10 On the twenty-third day of the seventh month he sent the people away to their tents, joyful and glad of heart

---

6:42 *a*Compare Psalm 132:8–10   7:1 *a*Literally *house*   7:3 *a*Compare Psalm 106:1   7:6 *a*Compare Psalm 106:1   7:8 *a*That is, the Shihor (compare 1 Chronicles 13:5)

*W*e have the right to climb mountains and stretch the wings God has given us!

for the good that the LORD had done for David, for Solomon, and for His people Israel. 11 Thus Solomon finished the house of the LORD and the king's house; and Solomon successfully accomplished all that came into his heart to make in the house of the LORD and in his own house.

12 Then the LORD appeared to Solomon by night, and said to him: "I have heard your prayer, and have chosen this place for Myself as a house of sacrifice. 13 When I shut up heaven and there is no rain, or command the locusts to devour the land, or send pestilence among My people, 14 if My people who are called by My name will humble themselves, and pray and seek My face, and turn from their wicked ways, then I will hear from heaven, and will forgive their sin and heal their land. 15 Now My eyes will be open and My ears attentive to prayer *made* in this place. 16 For now I have chosen and sanctified this house, that My name may be there forever; and My eyes and My heart will be there perpetually. 17 As for you, if you walk before Me as your father David walked, and do according to all that I have commanded you, and if you keep My statutes and My judgments, 18 then I will establish the throne of your kingdom, as I covenanted with David your father, saying, 'You shall not fail *to have* a man as ruler in Israel.'

19 "But if you turn away and forsake My statutes and My commandments which I have set before you, and go and serve other gods, and worship them, 20 then I will uproot them from My land which I have given them; and this house which I have sanctified for My name I will cast out of My sight, and will make it a proverb and a byword among all peoples. 21 "And *as for* this house, which is exalted, everyone who passes by it will be astonished and say, 'Why has the LORD done thus to this land and this house?' 22 Then they will answer, 'Because they forsook the LORD God of their fathers, who brought them out of the land of Egypt, and embraced other gods, and worshiped them and served them; therefore He has brought all this calamity on them.' "

8 It came to pass at the end of twenty years, when Solomon had built the house of the LORD and his own house, 2 that the cities which Hiram[a] had given to Solomon, Solomon built them; and he settled the children of Israel there. 3 And Solomon went to Hamath Zobah and seized it. 4 He also built Tadmor in the wilderness, and all the storage cities which he built in Hamath. 5 He built Upper Beth Horon and Lower Beth Horon, fortified cities *with* walls, gates, and bars, 6 also Baalath and all the storage cities that Solomon had, and all the chariot cities and the cities of the cavalry, and all that Solomon desired to build in Jerusalem, in Lebanon, and in all the land of his dominion.

7 All the people *who were* left of the Hittites, Amorites, Perizzites, Hivites, and Jebusites, who *were* not of Israel— 8 that is, their descendants who were left in the land after them, whom the children of Israel did not destroy—from these Solomon raised forced labor, as it is to this day. 9 But Solomon did not make the children of Israel servants for his work. Some *were* men of war, captains of his officers, captains of his chariots, and his cavalry. 10 And others *were* chiefs of the officials of King Solomon: two hundred and fifty, who ruled over the people.

11 Now Solomon brought the daughter of Pharaoh up from the City of David to the house he had built for her, for he said, "My wife shall not dwell in the house of David king of Israel, because *the places* to which the ark of the LORD has come are holy."

12 Then Solomon offered burnt offerings to the LORD on the altar of the LORD which he had built before the vestibule, 13 according to the daily rate, offering according to the commandment of Moses, for the Sabbaths, the New Moons, and the three appointed yearly feasts—the Feast of Unleavened Bread, the Feast of Weeks, and the Feast of Tabernacles. 14 And, according to the order of David his father, he appointed the divisions of the priests for their service, the Levites for their duties (to praise and serve before the priests) as the duty of each day required, and the gatekeepers by their divisions at

8:2 aHebrew *Huram* (compare 2 Chronicles 2:3)

Gospel Pearls

each gate; for so David the man of God had commanded. 15 They did not depart from the command of the king to the priests and Levites concerning any matter or concerning the treasuries.

16 Now all the work of Solomon was well-ordered from*a* the day of the foundation of the house of the LORD until it was finished. So the house of the LORD was completed.

17 Then Solomon went to Ezion Geber and Elath*a* on the seacoast, in the land of Edom. 18 And Hiram sent him ships by the hand of his servants, and servants who knew the sea. They went with the servants of Solomon to Ophir, and acquired four hundred and fifty talents of gold from there, and brought it to King Solomon.

9 Now when the queen of Sheba heard of the fame of Solomon, she came to Jerusalem to test Solomon with hard questions, *having* a very great retinue, camels that bore spices, gold in abundance, and precious stones; and when she came to Solomon, she spoke with him about all that was in her heart. 2 So Solomon answered all her questions; there was nothing so difficult for Solomon that he could not explain it to her. 3 And when the queen of Sheba had seen the wisdom of Solomon, the house that he had built, 4 the food on his table, the seating of his servants, the service of his waiters and their apparel, his cupbearers and their apparel, and his entryway by which he went up to the house of the LORD, there was no more spirit in her.

5 Then she said to the king: "*It was* a true report which I heard in my own land about your words and your wisdom. 6 However I did not believe their words until I came and saw with my own eyes; and indeed the half of the greatness of your wisdom was not told me. You exceed the fame of which I heard. 7 Happy *are* your men and happy *are* these your servants, who stand continually before you and hear your wisdom! 8 Blessed be the LORD your God, who delighted in you, setting you on His throne *to be* king for the LORD your God! Because your God has loved Israel, to establish them forever, therefore He made

you king over them, to do justice and righteousness."

9 And she gave the king one hundred and twenty talents of gold, spices in great abundance, and precious stones; there never were any spices such as those the queen of Sheba gave to King Solomon.

10 Also, the servants of Hiram and the servants of Solomon, who brought gold from Ophir, brought algum*a* wood and precious stones. 11 And the king made walkways *of* the algum*a* wood for the house of the LORD and for the king's house, also harps and stringed instruments for singers; and there were none such *as these* seen before in the land of Judah.

12 Now King Solomon gave to the queen of Sheba all she desired, whatever she asked, *much more* than she had brought to the king. So she turned and went to her own country, she and her servants.

13 The weight of gold that came to Solomon yearly was six hundred and sixty-six talents of gold, 14 besides *what* the traveling merchants and traders brought. And all the kings of Arabia and governors of the country brought gold and silver to Solomon. 15 And King Solomon made two hundred large shields of hammered gold; six hundred *shekels* of hammered gold went into each shield. 16 *He* also *made* three hundred shields of hammered gold; three hundred *shekels*a of gold went into each shield. The king put them in the House of the Forest of Lebanon.

17 Moreover the king made a great throne of ivory, and overlaid it with pure gold. 18 The throne *had* six steps, with a footstool of gold, *which were* fastened to the throne; there were armrests on either side of the place of the seat, and two lions stood beside the armrests. 19 Twelve lions stood there, one on each side of the six steps; nothing like *this* had been made for any *other* kingdom.

20 All King Solomon's drinking vessels *were* gold, and all the vessels of the House of the Forest of Lebanon *were* pure gold. Not *one was* silver, for this was accounted as nothing in the days of Solomon. 21 For the

8:16 *a*Following Septuagint, Syriac, and Vulgate; Masoretic Text reads *as far as*.   8:17 *a*Hebrew *Eloth* (compare 2 Kings 14:22)   9:10 *a*Or *almug* (compare 1 Kings 10:11, 12)   9:11 *a*Or *almug* (compare 1 Kings 10:11, 12)   9:16 *a*Or *three minas* (compare 1 Kings 10:17)

Christ was an obvious emancipator of oppressed women, from the woman taken in adultery to the woman at the well. He was always liberating them and upgrading their standard of living.

king's ships went to Tarshish with the servants of Hiram.[a] Once every three years the merchant ships[b] came, bringing gold, silver, ivory, apes, and monkeys.[c]

22 So King Solomon surpassed all the kings of the earth in riches and wisdom. 23 And all the kings of the earth sought the presence of Solomon to hear his wisdom, which God had put in his heart. 24 Each man brought his present: articles of silver and gold, garments, armor, spices, horses, and mules, at a set rate year by year.

25 Solomon had four thousand stalls for horses and chariots, and twelve thousand horsemen whom he stationed in the chariot cities and with the king at Jerusalem.

26 So he reigned over all the kings from the River[a] to the land of the Philistines, as far as the border of Egypt. 27 The king made silver as common in Jerusalem as stones, and he made cedar trees as abundant as the sycamores which are in the lowland. 28 And they brought horses to Solomon from Egypt and from all lands.

29 Now the rest of the acts of Solomon, first and last, are they not written in the book of Nathan the prophet, in the prophecy of Ahijah the Shilonite, and in the visions of Iddo the seer concerning Jeroboam the son of Nebat? 30 Solomon reigned in Jerusalem over all Israel forty years. 31 Then Solomon rested with his fathers, and was buried in the City of David his father. And Rehoboam his son reigned in his place.

10 And Rehoboam went to Shechem, for all Israel had gone to Shechem to make him king. 2 So it happened, when Jeroboam the son of Nebat heard it (he was in Egypt, where he had fled from the presence of King Solomon), that Jeroboam returned from Egypt. 3 Then they sent for him and called him. And Jeroboam and all Israel came and spoke to Rehoboam, saying, 4 "Your father made our yoke heavy; now therefore, lighten the burdensome service of your father and his heavy yoke which he

put on us, and we will serve you."

5 So he said to them, "Come back to me after three days." And the people departed.

6 Then King Rehoboam consulted the elders who stood before his father Solomon while he still lived, saying, "How do you advise me to answer these people?"

7 And they spoke to him, saying, "If you are kind to these people, and please them, and speak good words to them, they will be your servants forever."

8 But he rejected the advice which the elders had given him, and consulted the young men who had grown up with him, who stood before him. 9 And he said to them, "What advice do you give? How should we answer this people who have spoken to me, saying, 'Lighten the yoke which your father put on us'?"

10 Then the young men who had grown up with him spoke to him, saying, "Thus you should speak to the people who have spoken to you, saying, 'Your father made our yoke heavy, but you make it lighter on us'—thus you shall say to them: 'My little finger shall be thicker than my father's waist! 11 And now, whereas my father put a heavy yoke on you, I will add to your yoke; my father chastised you with whips, but I will chastise you with scourges!' "[a]

12 So Jeroboam and all the people came to Rehoboam on the third day, as the king had directed, saying, "Come back to me the third day." 13 Then the king answered them roughly. King Rehoboam rejected the advice of the elders, 14 and he spoke to them according to the advice of the young men, saying, "My father[a] made your yoke heavy, but I will add to it; my father chastised you with whips, but I will chastise you with scourges!"[b] 15 So the king did not listen to the people; for the turn of events was from God, that the LORD might fulfill His word, which He had spoken by the hand of Ahijah the Shilonite to Jeroboam the son of Nebat.

16 Now when all Israel saw that the king did not listen to them, the people answered the king, saying:

9:21 [a]Hebrew Huram (compare 1 Kings 10:22)   [b]Literally ships of Tarshish (deep-sea vessels) [c]Or peacocks   9:26 [a]That is, the Euphrates   10:11 [a]Literally scorpions   10:14 [a]Following many Hebrew manuscripts, Septuagint, Syriac, and Vulgate (compare verse 10 and 1 Kings 12:14); Masoretic Text reads I.   [b]Literally scorpions

Gospel Pearls

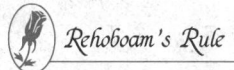

"What share have we in David?
We have no inheritance in the
son of Jesse.
Every man to your tents, O
Israel!
Now see to your own house, O
David!"

So all Israel departed to their tents.
17 But Rehoboam reigned over the
children of Israel who dwelt in the
cities of Judah.
18 Then King Rehoboam sent Hadoram, who *was* in charge of revenue; but the children of Israel stoned
him with stones, and he died. Therefore King Rehoboam mounted *his*
chariot in haste to flee to Jerusalem.
19 So Israel has been in rebellion
against the house of David to this
day.

11 Now when Rehoboam came to
Jerusalem, he assembled from
the house of Judah and Benjamin one
hundred and eighty thousand chosen
men who were warriors, to fight
against Israel, that he might restore
the kingdom to Rehoboam.
2 But the word of the LORD came
to Shemaiah the man of God, saying,
3 "Speak to Rehoboam the son of
Solomon, king of Judah, and to all
Israel in Judah and Benjamin, saying, 4 'Thus says the LORD: "You shall
not go up or fight against your brethren! Let every man return to his
house, for this thing is from Me." ' "
Therefore they obeyed the words of
the LORD, and turned back from attacking Jeroboam.
5 So Rehoboam dwelt in Jerusalem, and built cities for defense in Judah. 6 And he built Bethlehem, Etam,
Tekoa, 7 Beth Zur, Sochoh, Adullam,
8 Gath, Mareshah, Ziph, 9 Adoraim,
Lachish, Azekah, 10 Zorah, Aijalon,
and Hebron, which are in Judah and
Benjamin, fortified cities. 11 And he
fortified the strongholds, and put
captains in them, and stores of food,
oil, and wine. 12 Also in every city *he
put* shields and spears, and made
them very strong, having Judah and
Benjamin on his side.
13 And from all their territories the
priests and the Levites who *were* in
all Israel took their stand with him.
14 For the Levites left their common-

lands and their possessions and came
to Judah and Jerusalem, for Jeroboam and his sons had rejected them
from serving as priests to the LORD.
15 Then he appointed for himself
priests for the high places, for the demons, and the calf idols which he had
made. 16 And after *the Levites left,*ᵃ
those from all the tribes of Israel,
such as set their heart to seek the
LORD God of Israel, came to Jerusalem to sacrifice to the LORD God of
their fathers. 17 So they strengthened
the kingdom of Judah, and made Rehoboam the son of Solomon strong
for three years, because they walked
in the way of David and Solomon for
three years.
18 Then Rehoboam took for himself as wife Mahalath the daughter
of Jerimoth the son of David, *and of*
Abihail the daughter of Eliah the son
of Jesse. 19 And she bore him children: Jeush, Shamariah, and Zaham.
20 After her he took Maachah the
granddaughterᵃ of Absalom; and she
bore him Abijah, Attai, Ziza, and
Shelomith. 21 Now Rehoboam loved
Maachah the granddaughter of Absalom more than all his wives and
his concubines; for he took eighteen
wives and sixty concubines, and begot twenty-eight sons and sixty
daughters. 22 And Rehoboam appointed Abijah the son of Maachah
as chief, *to be* leader among his
brothers; for he *intended* to make
him king. 23 He dealt wisely, and dispersed some of his sons throughout
all the territories of Judah and Benjamin, to every fortified city; and he
gave them provisions in abundance.
He also sought many wives *for them.*

12 Now it came to pass, when Rehoboam had established the
kingdom and had strengthened himself, that he forsook the law of the
LORD, and all Israel along with him.
2 And it happened in the fifth year
of King Rehoboam *that* Shishak king
of Egypt came up against Jerusalem,
because they had transgressed
against the LORD, 3 with twelve hundred chariots, sixty thousand horsemen, and people without number
who came with him out of Egypt—
the Lubim and the Sukkiim and the
Ethiopians. 4 And he took the forti-

11:16 ᵃLiterally *after them*   11:20 ᵃLiterally *daughter,* but in the broader sense of granddaughter (compare
2 Chronicles 13:2)

---

*I*t is time for us to discuss and define oppression in all of its forms. Let us not allow
it to hide as it takes on various forms, and for God's sake we cannot allow it to
separate any of us who have fallen prey to its vicious grip.

fied cities of Judah and came to Jerusalem.

5 Then Shemaiah the prophet came to Rehoboam and the leaders of Judah, who were gathered together in Jerusalem because of Shishak, and said to them, "Thus says the LORD: 'You have forsaken Me, and therefore I also have left you in the hand of Shishak.'"

6 So the leaders of Israel and the king humbled themselves; and they said, "The LORD is righteous."

7 Now when the LORD saw that they humbled themselves, the word of the LORD came to Shemaiah, saying, "They have humbled themselves; therefore I will not destroy them, but I will grant them some deliverance. My wrath shall not be poured out on Jerusalem by the hand of Shishak. 8 Nevertheless they will be his servants, that they may distinguish My service from the service of the kingdoms of the nations."

9 So Shishak king of Egypt came up against Jerusalem, and took away the treasures of the house of the LORD and the treasures of the king's house; he took everything. He also carried away the gold shields which Solomon had made. 10 Then King Rehoboam made bronze shields in their place, and committed *them* to the hands of the captains of the guard, who guarded the doorway of the king's house. 11 And whenever the king entered the house of the LORD, the guard would go and bring them out; then they would take them back into the guardroom. 12 When he humbled himself, the wrath of the LORD turned from him, so as not to destroy *him* completely; and things also went well in Judah.

13 Thus King Rehoboam strengthened himself in Jerusalem and reigned. Now Rehoboam *was* forty-one years old when he became king; and he reigned seventeen years in Jerusalem, the city which the LORD had chosen out of all the tribes of Israel, to put His name there. His mother's name *was* Naamah, an Ammonitess. 14 And he did evil, because he did not prepare his heart to seek the LORD.

15 The acts of Rehoboam, first and last, *are* they not written in the book of Shemaiah the prophet, and of Iddo the seer concerning genealogies?

And *there were* wars between Rehoboam and Jeroboam all their days. 16 So Rehoboam rested with his fathers, and was buried in the City of David. Then Abijah[a] his son reigned in his place.

13 In the eighteenth year of King Jeroboam, Abijah became king over Judah. 2 He reigned three years in Jerusalem. His mother's name *was* Michaiah[a] the daughter of Uriel of Gibeah.

And there was war between Abijah and Jeroboam. 3 Abijah set the battle in order with an army of valiant warriors, four hundred thousand choice men. Jeroboam also drew up in battle formation against him with eight hundred thousand choice men, mighty men of valor.

4 Then Abijah stood on Mount Zemaraim, which *is* in the mountains of Ephraim, and said, "Hear me, Jeroboam and all Israel: 5 Should you not know that the LORD God of Israel gave the dominion over Israel to David forever, to him and his sons, by a covenant of salt? 6 Yet Jeroboam the son of Nebat, the servant of Solomon the son of David, rose up and rebelled against his lord. 7 Then worthless rogues gathered to him, and strengthened themselves against Rehoboam the son of Solomon, when Rehoboam was young and inexperienced and could not withstand them. 8 And now you think to withstand the kingdom of the LORD, which is in the hand of the sons of David; and you *are* a great multitude, and with you are the gold calves which Jeroboam made for you as gods. 9 Have you not cast out the priests of the LORD, the sons of Aaron, and the Levites, and made for yourselves priests, like the peoples of *other* lands, so that whoever comes to consecrate himself with a young bull and seven rams may be a priest of *things that are* not gods? 10 But as for us, the LORD *is* our God, and we have not forsaken Him; and the priests who minister to the LORD *are* the sons of Aaron, and the Levites *attend to their* duties. 11 And they burn to the LORD every morning and every evening burnt sacrifices and sweet incense; *they* also *set* the showbread *in order on* the pure *gold* table, and the lampstand of gold with

12:16 *aSpelled Abijam in 1 Kings 14:31   13:2 *aSpelled Maachah in 11:20, 21 and 1 Kings 15:2

its lamps to burn every evening; for we keep the command of the LORD our God, but you have forsaken Him. 12 Now look, God Himself is with us as *our* head, and His priests with sounding trumpets to sound the alarm against you. O children of Israel, do not fight against the LORD God of your fathers, for you shall not prosper!"

13 But Jeroboam caused an ambush to go around behind them; so they were in front of Judah, and the ambush *was* behind them. 14 And when Judah looked around, to their surprise the battle line *was* at both front and rear; and they cried out to the LORD, and the priests sounded the trumpets. 15 Then the men of Judah gave a shout; and as the men of Judah shouted, it happened that God struck Jeroboam and all Israel before Abijah and Judah. 16 And the children of Israel fled before Judah, and God delivered them into their hand. 17 Then Abijah and his people struck them with a great slaughter; so five hundred thousand choice men of Israel fell slain. 18 Thus the children of Israel were subdued at that time; and the children of Judah prevailed, because they relied on the LORD God of their fathers.

19 And Abijah pursued Jeroboam and took cities from him: Bethel with its villages, Jeshanah with its villages, and Ephrain*ᵃ* with its villages. 20 So Jeroboam did not recover strength again in the days of Abijah; and the LORD struck him, and he died.

21 But Abijah grew mighty, married fourteen wives, and begot twenty-two sons and sixteen daughters. 22 Now the rest of the acts of Abijah, his ways, and his sayings *are* written in the annals of the prophet Iddo.

14 So Abijah rested with his fathers, and they buried him in the City of David. Then Asa his son reigned in his place. In his days the land was quiet for ten years.

2 Asa did *what was* good and right in the eyes of the LORD his God, 3 for he removed the altars of the foreign *gods* and the high places, and broke down the *sacred* pillars and cut down the wooden images. 4 He commanded Judah to seek the LORD

God of their fathers, and to observe the law and the commandment. 5 He also removed the high places and the incense altars from all the cities of Judah, and the kingdom was quiet under him. 6 And he built fortified cities in Judah, for the land had rest; he had no war in those years, because the LORD had given him rest. 7 Therefore he said to Judah, "Let us build these cities and make walls around *them,* and towers, gates, and bars, *while* the land *is* yet before us, because we have sought the LORD our God; we have sought *Him,* and He has given us rest on every side." So they built and prospered. 8 And Asa had an army of three hundred thousand from Judah who carried shields and spears, and from Benjamin two hundred and eighty thousand men who carried shields and drew bows; all these *were* mighty men of valor.

9 Then Zerah the Ethiopian came out against them with an army of a million men and three hundred chariots, and he came to Mareshah. 10 So Asa went out against him, and they set the troops in battle array in the Valley of Zephathah at Mareshah. 11 And Asa cried out to the LORD his God, and said, "LORD, *it is* nothing for You to help, whether with many or with those who have no power; help us, O LORD our God, for we rest on You, and in Your name we go against this multitude. O LORD, You *are* our God; do not let man prevail against You!"

12 So the LORD struck the Ethiopians before Asa and Judah, and the Ethiopians fled. 13 And Asa and the people who *were* with him pursued them to Gerar. So the Ethiopians were overthrown, and they could not recover, for they were broken before the LORD and His army. And they carried away very much spoil. 14 Then they defeated all the cities around Gerar, for the fear of the LORD came upon them; and they plundered all the cities, for there was exceedingly much spoil in them. 15 They also attacked the livestock enclosures, and carried off sheep and camels in abundance, and returned to Jerusalem.

15 Now the Spirit of God came upon Azariah the son of Oded. 2 And he went out to meet Asa, and

13:19 ᵃOr *Ephron*

*T*oday everyone has at one time or another been the victim of some sort of discrimination. Perhaps in some way we can better understand the plight of others when we have experienced it ourselves.

Soul Secrets
of a woman who needs rest

F ather, I have worked so hard and I have given all I've got. I see in the Bible that the Israelites found rest when they sought You "with all of their heart and with all of their soul." There is a place of rest in You that I have not entered into yet. There is an ability to rest in Your presence that I've not yet found. Teach me, Lord, to give You first place in my life. Teach me to seek You with all my heart and with all my soul—and to find Your rest.

Thank You, Lord, for ordaining times of rest for Your people. Thank You for calling me to a season of rest, even in the midst of my hectic life. I am here to learn from You, Lord. Teach me to rest.

said to him: "Hear me, Asa, and all Judah and Benjamin. The LORD *is* with you while you are with Him. If you seek Him, He will be found by you; but if you forsake Him, He will forsake you. 3 For a long time Israel *has been* without the true God, without a teaching priest, and without law; 4 but when in their trouble they turned to the LORD God of Israel, and sought Him, He was found by them. 5 And in those times *there was* no peace to the one who went out, nor to the one who came in, but great turmoil *was* on all the inhabitants of the lands. 6 So nation was destroyed by nation, and city by city, for God troubled them with every adversity. 7 But you, be strong and do not let your hands be weak, for your work shall be rewarded!"

8 And when Asa heard these words and the prophecy of Oded[a] the prophet, he took courage, and removed the abominable idols from all the land of Judah and Benjamin and from the cities which he had taken in the mountains of Ephraim; and he restored the altar of the LORD that *was* before the vestibule of the LORD. 9 Then he gathered all Judah and Benjamin, and those who dwelt with them from Ephraim, Manasseh, and Simeon, for they came over to him in great numbers from Israel when they saw that the LORD his God was with him.

10 So they gathered together at Jerusalem in the third month, in the fifteenth year of the reign of Asa. 11 And they offered to the LORD at that time seven hundred bulls and seven thousand sheep from the spoil they had brought. 12 Then they entered into a covenant to seek the LORD God of their fathers with all their heart and with all their soul; 13 and whoever would not seek the LORD God of Israel was to be put to death, whether small or great, whether man or woman. 14 Then they took an oath before the LORD with a loud voice, with shouting and trumpets and rams' horns. 15 And all Judah rejoiced at the oath, for they had sworn with all their heart and sought Him with all their soul; and He was found by them, and the LORD gave them rest all around.

16 Also he removed Maachah, the mother of Asa the king, from *being* queen mother, because she had made an obscene image of Asherah;[a] and Asa cut down her obscene image, then crushed and burned *it* by the Brook Kidron. 17 But the high places were not removed from Israel. Nevertheless the heart of Asa was loyal all his days. 18 He also brought into the house of God the things that his father had dedicated and that he himself had dedicated: silver and gold and utensils. 19 And there was no war until the thirty-fifth year of the reign of Asa.

16 In the thirty-sixth year of the reign of Asa, Baasha king of Israel came up against Judah and built Ramah, that he might let none go out or come in to Asa king of Judah. 2 Then Asa brought silver and gold from the treasuries of the house of the LORD and of the king's house, and sent to Ben-Hadad king of Syria, who dwelt in Damascus, saying, 3 "*Let there be* a treaty between you and me, as there was between my father and your father. See, I have sent you silver and gold; come, break your treaty with Baasha king of Israel, so that he will withdraw from me."

4 So Ben-Hadad heeded King Asa, and sent the captains of his armies against the cities of Israel. They attacked Ijon, Dan, Abel Maim, and all the storage cities of Naphtali. 5 Now it happened, when Baasha heard *it,* that he stopped building Ramah and ceased his work. 6 Then King Asa took all Judah, and they carried away the stones and timber of Ramah, which Baasha had used for building; and with them he built Geba and Mizpah.

7 And at that time Hanani the seer came to Asa king of Judah, and said to him: "Because you have relied on the king of Syria, and have not relied on the LORD your God, therefore the army of the king of Syria has escaped from your hand. 8 Were the Ethiopians and the Lubim not a huge army with very many chariots and horsemen? Yet, because you relied on the LORD, He delivered them into your

---

15:8 [a]Following Masoretic Text and Septuagint; Syriac and Vulgate read *Azariah the son of Oded* (compare verse 1).   15:16 [a]A Canaanite deity

We cannot get others to purge the innocent blood of captives locked up behind small-mindedness if we ourselves have not exorcised the demons of discontentment that allow us to reject our own.

hand. 9 For the eyes of the LORD run to and fro throughout the whole earth, to show Himself strong on behalf of *those* whose heart *is* loyal to Him. In this you have done foolishly; therefore from now on you shall have wars." 10 Then Asa was angry with the seer, and put him in prison, for *he was* enraged at him because of this. And Asa oppressed *some* of the people at that time.

11 Note that the acts of Asa, first and last, are indeed written in the book of the kings of Judah and Israel. 12 And in the thirty-ninth year of his reign, Asa became diseased in his feet, and his malady was severe; yet in his disease he did not seek the LORD, but the physicians.

13 So Asa rested with his fathers; he died in the forty-first year of his reign. 14 They buried him in his own tomb, which he had made for himself in the City of David; and they laid him in the bed which was filled with spices and various ingredients prepared in a mixture of ointments. They made a very great burning for him.

17 Then Jehoshaphat his son reigned in his place, and strengthened himself against Israel. 2 And he placed troops in all the fortified cities of Judah, and set garrisons in the land of Judah and in the cities of Ephraim which Asa his father had taken. 3 Now the LORD was with Jehoshaphat, because he walked in the former ways of his father David; he did not seek the Baals, 4 but sought the God[a] of his father, and walked in His commandments and not according to the acts of Israel. 5 Therefore the LORD established the kingdom in his hand; and all Judah gave presents to Jehoshaphat, and he had riches and honor in abundance. 6 And his heart took delight in the ways of the LORD; moreover he removed the high places and wooden images from Judah.

7 Also in the third year of his reign he sent his leaders, Ben-Hail, Obadiah, Zechariah, Nethanel, and Michaiah, to teach in the cities of Judah. 8 And with them *he sent* Levites: Shemaiah, Nethaniah, Zebadiah, Asahel, Shemiramoth, Jehonathan,

Adonijah, Tobijah, and Tobadonijah—the Levites; and with them Elishama and Jehoram, the priests. 9 So they taught in Judah, and *had* the Book of the Law of the LORD with them; they went throughout all the cities of Judah and taught the people.

10 And the fear of the LORD fell on all the kingdoms of the lands that *were* around Judah, so that they did not make war against Jehoshaphat. 11 Also *some* of the Philistines brought Jehoshaphat presents and silver as tribute; and the Arabians brought him flocks, seven thousand seven hundred rams and seven thousand seven hundred male goats.

12 So Jehoshaphat became increasingly powerful, and he built fortresses and storage cities in Judah. 13 He had much property in the cities of Judah; and the men of war, mighty men of valor, *were* in Jerusalem. 14 These *are* their numbers, according to their fathers' houses. Of Judah, the captains of thousands: Adnah the captain, and with him three hundred thousand mighty men of valor; 15 and next to him *was* Jehohanan the captain, and with him two hundred and eighty thousand; 16 and next to him *was* Amasiah the son of Zichri, who willingly offered himself to the LORD, and with him two hundred thousand mighty men of valor. 17 Of Benjamin: Eliada a mighty man of valor, and with him two hundred thousand men armed with bow and shield; 18 and next to him *was* Jehozabad, and with him one hundred and eighty thousand prepared for war. 19 These served the king, besides those the king put in the fortified cities throughout all Judah.

18 Jehoshaphat had riches and honor in abundance; and by marriage he allied himself with Ahab. 2 After some years he went down to *visit* Ahab in Samaria; and Ahab killed sheep and oxen in abundance for him and the people who were with him, and persuaded him to go up *with him* to Ramoth Gilead. 3 So Ahab king of Israel said to Jehoshaphat king of Judah, "Will you go with me *against* Ramoth Gilead?"

And he answered him, "I *am* as you *are*, and my people as your peo-

17:4 aSeptuagint reads LORD God.

ple; *we will be* with you in the war."

4 Also Jehoshaphat said to the king of Israel, "Please inquire for the word of the LORD today."

5 Then the king of Israel gathered the prophets together, four hundred men, and said to them, "Shall we go to war against Ramoth Gilead, or shall I refrain?"

So they said, "Go up, for God will deliver it into the king's hand."

6 But Jehoshaphat said, "*Is there* not still a prophet of the LORD here, that we may inquire of Him?"*ᵃ*

7 So the king of Israel said to Jehoshaphat, "*There is* still one man by whom we may inquire of the LORD; but I hate him, because he never prophesies good concerning me, but always evil. He *is* Micaiah the son of Imla."

And Jehoshaphat said, "Let not the king say such things!"

8 Then the king of Israel called one *of his* officers and said, "Bring Micaiah the son of Imla quickly!"

9 The king of Israel and Jehoshaphat king of Judah, clothed in *their* robes, sat each on his throne; and they sat at a threshing floor at the entrance of the gate of Samaria; and all the prophets prophesied before them. 10 Now Zedekiah the son of Chenaanah had made horns of iron for himself; and he said, "Thus says the LORD: 'With these you shall gore the Syrians until they are destroyed.'"

11 And all the prophets prophesied so, saying, "Go up to Ramoth Gilead and prosper, for the LORD will deliver *it* into the king's hand."

12 Then the messenger who had gone to call Micaiah spoke to him, saying, "Now listen, the words of the prophets with one accord encourage the king. Therefore please let your word be like *the word of* one of them, and speak encouragement."

13 And Micaiah said, "*As* the LORD lives, whatever my God says, that I will speak."

14 Then he came to the king; and the king said to him, "Micaiah, shall we go to war against Ramoth Gilead, or shall I refrain?"

And he said, "Go and prosper, and they shall be delivered into your hand!"

15 So the king said to him, "How many times shall I make you swear that you tell me nothing but the truth in the name of the LORD?"

16 Then he said, "I saw all Israel scattered on the mountains, as sheep that have no shepherd. And the LORD said, 'These have no master. Let each return to his house in peace.'"

17 And the king of Israel said to Jehoshaphat, "Did I not tell you he would not prophesy good concerning me, but evil?"

18 Then *Micaiah* said, "Therefore hear the word of the LORD: I saw the LORD sitting on His throne, and all the host of heaven standing on His right hand and His left. 19 And the LORD said, 'Who will persuade Ahab king of Israel to go up, that he may fall at Ramoth Gilead?' So one spoke in this manner, and another spoke in that manner. 20 Then a spirit came forward and stood before the LORD, and said, 'I will persuade him.' The LORD said to him, 'In what way?' 21 So he said, 'I will go out and be a lying spirit in the mouth of all his prophets.' And *the* LORD said, 'You shall persuade *him* and also prevail; go out and do so.' 22 Therefore look! The LORD has put a lying spirit in the mouth of these prophets of yours, and the LORD has declared disaster against you."

23 Then Zedekiah the son of Chenaanah went near and struck Micaiah on the cheek, and said, "Which way did the spirit from the LORD go from me to speak to you?"

24 And Micaiah said, "Indeed you shall see on that day when you go into an inner chamber to hide!"

25 Then the king of Israel said, "Take Micaiah, and return him to Amon the governor of the city and to Joash the king's son; 26 and say, 'Thus says the king: "Put this *fellow* in prison, and feed him with bread of affliction and water of affliction, until I return in peace."' "

27 But Micaiah said, "If you ever return in peace, the LORD has not spoken by me." And he said, "Take heed, all you people!"

28 So the king of Israel and Jehoshaphat the king of Judah went up to Ramoth Gilead. 29 And the king of Israel said to Jehoshaphat, "I will disguise myself and go into battle; but you put on your robes." So the king

18:6 *ᵃOr him*

I challenge you not to allow others to pull you back. If God has given you the grace to go forth, do it. Life is too long to spend it bent down to keep from standing out. And it is too short to wait on people to change their minds before you plunge ahead with your giftings!

of Israel disguised himself, and they went into battle.

30 Now the king of Syria had commanded the captains of the chariots who *were* with him, saying, "Fight with no one small or great, but only with the king of Israel." 31 So it was, when the captains of the chariots saw Jehoshaphat, that they said, "It *is* the king of Israel!" Therefore they surrounded him to attack; but Jehoshaphat cried out, and the LORD helped him, and God diverted them from him. 32 For so it was, when the captains of the chariots saw that it was not the king of Israel, that they turned back from pursuing him. 33 Now a certain man drew a bow at random, and struck the king of Israel between the joints of his armor. So he said to the driver of his chariot, "Turn around and take me out of the battle, for I am wounded." 34 The battle increased that day, and the king of Israel propped *himself* up in *his* chariot facing the Syrians until evening; and about the time of sunset he died.

19 Then Jehoshaphat the king of Judah returned safely to his house in Jerusalem. 2 And Jehu the son of Hanani the seer went out to meet him, and said to King Jehoshaphat, "Should you help the wicked and love those who hate the LORD? Therefore the wrath of the LORD *is* upon you. 3 Nevertheless good things are found in you, in that you have removed the wooden images from the land, and have prepared your heart to seek God."

4 So Jehoshaphat dwelt at Jerusalem; and he went out again among the people from Beersheba to the mountains of Ephraim, and brought them back to the LORD God of their fathers. 5 Then he set judges in the land throughout all the fortified cities of Judah, city by city, 6 and said to the judges, "Take heed to what you are doing, for you do not judge for man but for the LORD, who *is* with you in the judgment. 7 Now therefore, let the fear of the LORD be upon you; take care and do *it*, for *there is* no iniquity with the LORD our God, no partiality, nor taking of bribes."

8 Moreover in Jerusalem, for the judgment of the LORD and for controversies, Jehoshaphat appointed some of the Levites and priests, and some of the chief fathers of Israel, when they returned to Jerusalem.*a* 9 And he commanded them, saying, "Thus you shall act in the fear of the LORD, faithfully and with a loyal heart: 10 Whatever case comes to you from your brethren who dwell in their cities, whether of bloodshed or offenses against law or commandment, against statutes or ordinances, you shall warn them, lest they trespass against the LORD and wrath come upon you and your brethren. Do this, and you will not be guilty. 11 And take notice: Amariah the chief priest *is* over you in all matters of the LORD; and Zebadiah the son of Ishmael, the ruler of the house of Judah, for all the king's matters; also the Levites *will be* officials before you. Behave courageously, and the LORD will be with the good."

20 It happened after this *that* the people of Moab with the people of Ammon, and *others* with them besides the Ammonites,*a* came to battle against Jehoshaphat. 2 Then some came and told Jehoshaphat, saying, "A great multitude is coming against you from beyond the sea, from Syria;*a* and they are in Hazazon Tamar" (which *is* En Gedi). 3 And Jehoshaphat feared, and set himself to seek the LORD, and proclaimed a fast throughout all Judah. 4 So Judah gathered together to ask *help* from the LORD; and from all the cities of Judah they came to seek the LORD.

5 Then Jehoshaphat stood in the assembly of Judah and Jerusalem, in the house of the LORD, before the new court, 6 and said: "O LORD God of our fathers, *are* You not God in heaven, and do You *not* rule over all the kingdoms of the nations, and in Your hand *is there not* power and might, so that no one is able to withstand You? 7 *Are* You not our God, *who* drove out the inhabitants of this land before Your people Israel, and gave it to the descendants of Abraham Your friend forever? 8 And they dwell in it, and have built You a sanc-

---

19:8 *a*Septuagint and Vulgate read *for the inhabitants of Jerusalem.*   20:1 *a*Following Masoretic Text and Vulgate; Septuagint reads *Meunites* (compare 26:7).   20:2 *a*Following Masoretic Text, Septuagint, and Vulgate; some Hebrew manuscripts and Old Latin read *Edom.*

Gospel Pearls

tuary in it for Your name, saying, 9 'If disaster comes upon us—sword, judgment, pestilence, or famine—we will stand before this temple and in Your presence (for Your name *is* in this temple), and cry out to You in our affliction, and You will hear and save.' 10 And now, here are the people of Ammon, Moab, and Mount Seir—whom You would not let Israel invade when they came out of the land of Egypt, but they turned from them and did not destroy them— 11 here they are, rewarding us by coming to throw us out of Your possession which You have given us to inherit. 12 O our God, will You not judge them? For we have no power against this great multitude that is coming against us; nor do we know what to do, but our eyes *are* upon You."

13 Now all Judah, with their little ones, their wives, and their children, stood before the LORD.

14 Then the Spirit of the LORD came upon Jahaziel the son of Zechariah, the son of Benaiah, the son of Jeiel, the son of Mattaniah, a Levite of the sons of Asaph, in the midst of the assembly. 15 And he said, "Listen, all you of Judah and you inhabitants of Jerusalem, and you, King Jehoshaphat! Thus says the LORD to you: 'Do not be afraid nor dismayed because of this great multitude, for the battle *is* not yours, but God's. 16 Tomorrow go down against them. They will surely come up by the Ascent of Ziz, and you will find them at the end of the brook before the Wilderness of Jeruel. 17 You will not *need* to fight in this *battle.* Position yourselves, stand still and see the salvation of the LORD, who is with you, O Judah and Jerusalem!' Do not fear or be dismayed; tomorrow go out against them, for the LORD *is* with you."

18 And Jehoshaphat bowed his head with *his* face to the ground, and all Judah and the inhabitants of Jerusalem bowed before the LORD, worshiping the LORD. 19 Then the Levites of the children of the Kohathites and of the children of the Korahites stood up to praise the LORD God of Israel with voices loud and high.

20 So they rose early in the morning and went out into the Wilderness

of Tekoa; and as they went out, Jehoshaphat stood and said, "Hear me, O Judah and you inhabitants of Jerusalem: Believe in the LORD your God, and you shall be established; believe His prophets, and you shall prosper." 21 And when he had consulted with the people, he appointed those who should sing to the LORD, and who should praise the beauty of holiness, as they went out before the army and were saying:

"Praise the LORD,
    For His mercy *endures*
        forever."[a]

22 Now when they began to sing and to praise, the LORD set ambushes against the people of Ammon, Moab, and Mount Seir, who had come against Judah; and they were defeated. 23 For the people of Ammon and Moab stood up against the inhabitants of Mount Seir to utterly kill and destroy *them.* And when they had made an end of the inhabitants of Seir, they helped to destroy one another.

24 So when Judah came to a place overlooking the wilderness, they looked toward the multitude; and there *were* their dead bodies, fallen on the earth. No one had escaped.

25 When Jehoshaphat and his people came to take away their spoil, they found among them an abundance of valuables on the dead bodies,[a] and precious jewelry, which they stripped off for themselves, more than they could carry away; and they were three days gathering the spoil because there was so much. 26 And on the fourth day they assembled in the Valley of Berachah, for there they blessed the LORD; therefore the name of that place was called The Valley of Berachah[a] until this day. 27 Then they returned, every man of Judah and Jerusalem, with Jehoshaphat in front of them, to go back to Jerusalem with joy, for the LORD had made them rejoice over their enemies. 28 So they came to Jerusalem, with stringed instruments and harps and trumpets, to the house of the LORD. 29 And the fear of God was on all the kingdoms of *those* countries when they heard that the

---

20:21 [a]Compare Psalm 106:1   20:25 [a]A few Hebrew manuscripts, Old Latin, and Vulgate read *garments;* Septuagint reads *armor.*   20:26 [a]Literally *Blessing*

I feel like God is about to loose some precious women who have been struggling with public opinion versus personal ambitions. Oh yes, there is greatness in you that is waiting to be unleashed.

LORD had fought against the enemies of Israel. 30 Then the realm of Jehoshaphat was quiet, for his God gave him rest all around.

31 So Jehoshaphat was king over Judah. *He was* thirty-five years old when he became king, and he reigned twenty-five years in Jerusalem. His mother's name *was* Azubah the daughter of Shilhi. 32 And he walked in the way of his father Asa, and did not turn aside from it, doing *what was* right in the sight of the LORD. 33 Nevertheless the high places were not taken away, for as yet the people had not directed their hearts to the God of their fathers.

34 Now the rest of the acts of Jehoshaphat, first and last, indeed they *are* written in the book of Jehu the son of Hanani, which *is* mentioned in the book of the kings of Israel.

35 After this Jehoshaphat king of Judah allied himself with Ahaziah king of Israel, who acted very wickedly. 36 And he allied himself with him to make ships to go to Tarshish, and they made the ships in Ezion Geber. 37 But Eliezer the son of Dodavah of Mareshah prophesied against Jehoshaphat, saying, "Because you have allied yourself with Ahaziah, the LORD has destroyed your works." Then the ships were wrecked, so that they were not able to go to Tarshish.

21 And Jehoshaphat rested with his fathers, and was buried with his fathers in the City of David. Then Jehoram his son reigned in his place. 2 He had brothers, the sons of Jehoshaphat: Azariah, Jehiel, Zechariah, Azaryahu, Michael, and Shephatiah; all these *were* the sons of Jehoshaphat king of Israel. 3 Their father gave them great gifts of silver and gold and precious things, with fortified cities in Judah; but he gave the kingdom to Jehoram, because he *was* the firstborn.

4 Now when Jehoram was established over the kingdom of his father, he strengthened himself and killed all his brothers with the sword, and also *others* of the princes of Israel.

5 Jehoram *was* thirty-two years old when he became king, and he reigned eight years in Jerusalem. 6 And he walked in the way of the kings of Israel, just as the house of Ahab had done, for he had the daughter of Ahab as a wife; and he did evil in the sight of the LORD. 7 Yet the LORD would not destroy the house of David, because of the covenant that He had made with David, and since He had promised to give a lamp to him and to his sons forever.

8 In his days Edom revolted against Judah's authority, and made a king over themselves. 9 So Jehoram went out with his officers, and all his chariots with him. And he rose by night and attacked the Edomites who had surrounded him and the captains of the chariots. 10 Thus Edom has been in revolt against Judah's authority to this day. At that time Libnah revolted against his rule, because he had forsaken the LORD God of his fathers. 11 Moreover he made high places in the mountains of Judah, and caused the inhabitants of Jerusalem to commit harlotry, and led Judah astray.

12 And a letter came to him from Elijah the prophet, saying,

Thus says the LORD God of your father David:
Because you have not walked in the ways of Jehoshaphat your father, or in the ways of Asa king of Judah, 13 but have walked in the way of the kings of Israel, and have made Judah and the inhabitants of Jerusalem to play the harlot like the harlotry of the house of Ahab, and also have killed your brothers, those of your father's household, *who were* better than yourself, 14 behold, the LORD will strike your people with a serious affliction—your children, your wives, and all your possessions; 15 and you *will become* very sick with a disease of your intestines, until your intestines come out by reason of the sickness, day by day.

16 Moreover the LORD stirred up against Jehoram the spirit of the Philistines and the Arabians who *were* near the Ethiopians. 17 And they came up into Judah and invaded it, and carried away all the possessions that were found in the king's house, and also his sons and his wives, so that there was not a son left to him

except Jehoahaz,ᵃ the youngest of his sons.

18 After all this the LORD struck him in his intestines with an incurable disease. 19 Then it happened in the course of time, after the end of two years, that his intestines came out because of his sickness; so he died in severe pain. And his people made no burning for him, like the burning for his fathers.

20 He was thirty-two years old when he became king. He reigned in Jerusalem eight years and, to no one's sorrow, departed. However they buried him in the City of David, but not in the tombs of the kings.

22 Then the inhabitants of Jerusalem made Ahaziah his youngest son king in his place, for the raiders who came with the Arabians into the camp had killed all the older *sons*. So Ahaziah the son of Jehoram, king of Judah, reigned. 2 Ahaziah *was* forty-twoᵃ years old when he became king, and he reigned one year in Jerusalem. His mother's name *was* Athaliah the granddaughter of Omri. 3 He also walked in the ways of the house of Ahab, for his mother advised him to do wickedly. 4 Therefore he did evil in the sight of the LORD, like the house of Ahab; for they were his counselors after the death of his father, to his destruction. 5 He also followed their advice, and went with Jehoramᵃ the son of Ahab king of Israel to war against Hazael king of Syria at Ramoth Gilead; and the Syrians wounded Joram. 6 Then he returned to Jezreel to recover from the wounds which he had received at Ramah, when he fought against Hazael king of Syria. And Azariahᵃ the son of Jehoram, king of Judah, went down to see Jehoram the son of Ahab in Jezreel, because he was sick.

7 His going to Joram was God's occasion for Ahaziah's downfall; for when he arrived, he went out with Jehoram against Jehu the son of Nimshi, whom the LORD had anointed to cut off the house of Ahab. 8 And it happened, when Jehu was executing judgment on the house of Ahab, and found the princes of Judah and the sons of Ahaziah's brothers

who served Ahaziah, that he killed them. 9 Then he searched for Ahaziah; and they caught him (he was hiding in Samaria), and brought him to Jehu. When they had killed him, they buried him, "because," they said, "he is the son of Jehoshaphat, who sought the LORD with all his heart."

So the house of Ahaziah had no one to assume power over the kingdom.

10 Now when Athaliah the mother of Ahaziah saw that her son was dead, she arose and destroyed all the royal heirs of the house of Judah. 11 But Jehoshabeath,ᵃ the daughter of the king, took Joash the son of Ahaziah, and stole him away from among the king's sons who were being murdered, and put him and his nurse in a bedroom. So Jehoshabeath, the daughter of King Jehoram, the wife of Jehoiada the priest (for she was the sister of Ahaziah), hid him from Athaliah so that she did not kill him. 12 And he was hidden with them in the house of God for six years, while Athaliah reigned over the land.

23 In the seventh year Jehoiada strengthened himself, *and made a* covenant with the captains of hundreds: Azariah the son of Jeroham, Ishmael the son of Jehohanan, Azariah the son of Obed, Maaseiah the son of Adaiah, and Elishaphat the son of Zichri. 2 And they went throughout Judah and gathered the Levites from all the cities of Judah, and the chief fathers of Israel, and they came to Jerusalem.

3 Then all the assembly made a covenant with the king in the house of God. And he said to them, "Behold, the king's son shall reign, as the LORD has said of the sons of David. 4 This *is* what you shall do: One-third of you entering on the Sabbath, of the priests and the Levites, *shall be* keeping watch over the doors; 5 one-third *shall be* at the king's house; and one-third at the Gate of the Foundation. All the people *shall be* in the courts of the house of the LORD. 6 But let no one come into the house of the LORD except the priests

---

21:17 ᵃElsewhere called *Ahaziah* (compare 2 Chronicles 22:1)   22:2 ᵃOr *twenty-two* (compare 2 Kings 8:26)   22:5 ᵃAlso spelled *Joram* (compare verses 5 and 7; 2 Kings 8:28; and elsewhere)   22:6 ᵃSome Hebrew manuscripts, Septuagint, Syriac, Vulgate, and 2 Kings 8:29 read *Ahaziah*.   22:11 ᵃSpelled *Jehosheba* in 2 Kings 11:2

---

*I*t is healthy for all of us to see liberation. It is not at the expense of men that women are released—not if it is done God's way.

and those of the Levites who serve. They may go in, for they *are* holy; but all the people shall keep the watch of the LORD. 7 And the Levites shall surround the king on all sides, every man with his weapons in his hand; and whoever comes into the house, let him be put to death. You are to be with the king when he comes in and when he goes out."

8 So the Levites and all Judah did according to all that Jehoiada the priest commanded. And each man took his men who were to be on duty on the Sabbath, with those who were going *off duty* on the Sabbath; for Jehoiada the priest had not dismissed the divisions. 9 And Jehoiada the priest gave to the captains of hundreds the spears and the large and small shields which *had belonged* to King David, that *were* in the temple of God. 10 Then he set all the people, every man with his weapon in his hand, from the right side of the temple to the left side of the temple, along by the altar and by the temple, all around the king. 11 And they brought out the king's son, put the crown on him, *gave him* the Testimony,*a* and made him king. Then Jehoiada and his sons anointed him, and said, "*Long* live the king!"

12 Now when Athaliah heard the noise of the people running and praising the king, she came to the people *in* the temple of the LORD. 13 *When* she looked, there was the king standing by his pillar at the entrance; and the leaders and the trumpeters *were* by the king. All the people of the land were rejoicing and blowing trumpets, also the singers with musical instruments, and those who led in praise. So Athaliah tore her clothes and said, "Treason! Treason!"

14 And Jehoiada the priest brought out the captains of hundreds who were set over the army, and said to them, "Take her outside under guard, and slay with the sword whoever follows her." For the priest had said, "Do not kill her in the house of the LORD."

15 So they seized her; and she went by way of the entrance of the Horse Gate *into* the king's house, and they killed her there.

16 Then Jehoiada made a covenant between himself, the people, and the king, that they should be the LORD's people. 17 And all the people went to the temple*a* of Baal, and tore it down. They broke in pieces its altars and images, and killed Mattan the priest of Baal before the altars. 18 Also Jehoiada appointed the oversight of the house of the LORD to the hand of the priests, the Levites, whom David had assigned in the house of the LORD, to offer the burnt offerings of the LORD, as *it is* written in the Law of Moses, with rejoicing and with singing, *as it was established* by David. 19 And he set the gatekeepers at the gates of the house of the LORD, so that no one *who was* in any way unclean should enter.

20 Then he took the captains of hundreds, the nobles, the governors of the people, and all the people of the land, and brought the king down from the house of the LORD; and they went through the Upper Gate to the king's house, and set the king on the throne of the kingdom. 21 So all the people of the land rejoiced; and the city was quiet, for they had slain Athaliah with the sword.

24 Joash *was* seven years old when he became king, and he reigned forty years in Jerusalem. His mother's name *was* Zibiah of Beersheba. 2 Joash did *what was* right in the sight of the LORD all the days of Jehoiada the priest. 3 And Jehoiada took two wives for him, and he had sons and daughters.

4 Now it happened after this *that* Joash set his heart on repairing the house of the LORD. 5 Then he gathered the priests and the Levites, and said to them, "Go out to the cities of Judah, and gather from all Israel money to repair the house of your God from year to year, and see that you do it quickly."

However the Levites did not do it quickly. 6 So the king called Jehoiada the chief *priest*, and said to him, "Why have you not required the Levites to bring in from Judah and from Jerusalem the collection, *according to the commandment* of Moses the servant of the LORD and of the assembly of Israel, for the tabernacle of witness?" 7 For the sons of Athaliah, that wicked woman, had broken into

23:11 *a*That is, the Law (compare Exodus 25:16, 21; 31:18)   23:17 *a*Literally *house*

Gospel
Pearls

the house of God, and had also presented all the dedicated things of the house of the LORD to the Baals.

8 Then at the king's command they made a chest, and set it outside at the gate of the house of the LORD. 9 And they made a proclamation throughout Judah and Jerusalem to bring to the LORD the collection *that* Moses the servant of God *had imposed* on Israel in the wilderness. 10 Then all the leaders and all the people rejoiced, brought their contributions, and put *them* into the chest until all had given. 11 So it was, at that time, when the chest was brought to the king's official by the hand of the Levites, and when they saw that *there was* much money, that the king's scribe and the high priest's officer came and emptied the chest, and took it and returned it to its place. Thus they did day by day, and gathered money in abundance.

12 The king and Jehoiada gave it to those who did the work of the service of the house of the LORD; and they hired masons and carpenters to repair the house of the LORD, and also those who worked in iron and bronze to restore the house of the LORD. 13 So the workmen labored, and the work was completed by them; they restored the house of God to its original condition and reinforced it. 14 When they had finished, they brought the rest of the money before the king and Jehoiada; they made from it articles for the house of the LORD, articles for serving and offering, spoons and vessels of gold and silver. And they offered burnt offerings in the house of the LORD continually all the days of Jehoiada.

15 But Jehoiada grew old and was full of days, and he died; *he was* one hundred and thirty years old when he died. 16 And they buried him in the City of David among the kings, because he had done good in Israel, both toward God and His house.

17 Now after the death of Jehoiada the leaders of Judah came and bowed down to the king. And the king listened to them. 18 Therefore they left the house of the LORD God of their fathers, and served wooden images and idols; and wrath came upon Judah and Jerusalem because of their trespass. 19 Yet He sent prophets to them, to bring them back to the LORD; and they testified against them, but they would not listen.

20 Then the Spirit of God came upon Zechariah the son of Jehoiada the priest, who stood above the people, and said to them, "Thus says God: 'Why do you transgress the commandments of the LORD, so that you cannot prosper? Because you have forsaken the LORD, He also has forsaken you.' " 21 So they conspired against him, and at the command of the king they stoned him with stones in the court of the house of the LORD. 22 Thus Joash the king did not remember the kindness which Jehoiada his father had done to him, but killed his son; and as he died, he said, "The LORD look on *it*, and repay!"

23 So it happened in the spring of the year *that* the army of Syria came up against him; and they came to Judah and Jerusalem, and destroyed all the leaders of the people from among the people, and sent all their spoil to the king of Damascus. 24 For the army of the Syrians came with a small company of men; but the LORD delivered a very great army into their hand, because they had forsaken the LORD God of their fathers. So they executed judgment against Joash. 25 And when they had withdrawn from him (for they left him severely wounded), his own servants conspired against him because of the blood of the sons[a] of Jehoiada the priest, and killed him on his bed. So he died. And they buried him in the City of David, but they did not bury him in the tombs of the kings.

26 These are the ones who conspired against him: Zabad[a] the son of Shimeath the Ammonitess, and Jehozabad the son of Shimrith[b] the Moabitess. 27 Now *concerning* his sons, and the many oracles about him, and the repairing of the house of God, indeed they *are* written in the annals of the book of the kings. Then Amaziah his son reigned in his place.

25 Amaziah *was* twenty-five years old *when* he became king, and he reigned twenty-nine years in Jerusalem. His mother's name *was* Jehoaddan of Jerusalem. 2 And he did

24:25 [a]Septuagint and Vulgate read *son* (compare verses 20–22). 24:26 [a]Or *Jozachar* (compare 2 Kings 12:21) [b]Or *Shomer* (compare 2 Kings 12:21)

We impact other people with subtle signals. When they hear us speaking highly of people they will become positive and motivated to speak highly of others also.

what was right in the sight of the LORD, but not with a loyal heart.

3 Now it happened, as soon as the kingdom was established for him, that he executed his servants who had murdered his father the king. 4 However he did not execute their children, but *did* as *it is* written in the Law in the Book of Moses, where the LORD commanded, saying, "The fathers shall not be put to death for their children, nor shall the children be put to death for their fathers; but a person shall die for his own sin."[a]

5 Moreover Amaziah gathered Judah together and set over them captains of thousands and captains of hundreds, according to *their* fathers' houses, throughout all Judah and Benjamin; and he numbered them from twenty years old and above, and found them to be three hundred thousand choice *men, able* to go to war, who could handle spear and shield. 6 He also hired one hundred thousand mighty men of valor from Israel for one hundred talents of silver. 7 But a man of God came to him, saying, "O king, do not let the army of Israel go with you, for the LORD *is* not with Israel—*not with* any of the children of Ephraim. 8 But if you go, be gone! Be strong in battle! *Even so,* God shall make you fall before the enemy; for God has power to help and to overthrow."

9 Then Amaziah said to the man of God, "But what *shall we* do about the hundred talents which I have given to the troops of Israel?"

And the man of God answered, "The LORD is able to give you much more than this." 10 So Amaziah discharged the troops that had come to him from Ephraim, to go back home. Therefore their anger was greatly aroused against Judah, and they returned home in great anger.

11 Then Amaziah strengthened himself, and leading his people, he went to the Valley of Salt and killed ten thousand of the people of Seir. 12 Also the children of Judah took captive ten thousand alive, brought them to the top of the rock, and cast them down from the top of the rock, so that they all were dashed in pieces.

13 But as for the soldiers of the army which Amaziah had discharged, so that they would not go with him to battle, they raided the cities of Judah from Samaria to Beth Horon, killed three thousand in them, and took much spoil.

14 Now it was so, after Amaziah came from the slaughter of the Edomites, that he brought the gods of the people of Seir, set them up *to be* his gods, and bowed down before them and burned incense to them. 15 Therefore the anger of the LORD was aroused against Amaziah, and He sent him a prophet who said to him, "Why have you sought the gods of the people, which could not rescue their own people from your hand?"

16 So it was, as he talked with him, that *the king* said to him, "Have we made you the king's counselor? Cease! Why should you be killed?"

Then the prophet ceased, and said, "I know that God has determined to destroy you, because you have done this and have not heeded my advice."

17 Now Amaziah king of Judah asked advice and sent to Joash[a] the son of Jehoahaz, the son of Jehu, king of Israel, saying, "Come, let us face one another *in battle.*"

18 And Joash king of Israel sent to Amaziah king of Judah, saying, "The thistle that *was* in Lebanon sent to the cedar that was in Lebanon, saying, 'Give your daughter to my son as wife'; and a wild beast that *was* in Lebanon passed by and trampled the thistle. 19 Indeed you say that you have defeated the Edomites, and your heart is lifted up to boast. Stay at home now; why should you meddle with trouble, that you should fall—you and Judah with you?"

20 But Amaziah would not heed, for it *came* from God, that He might give them into the hand *of their enemies,* because they sought the gods of Edom. 21 So Joash king of Israel went out; and he and Amaziah king of Judah faced one another at Beth Shemesh, which *belongs* to Judah. 22 And Judah was defeated by Israel, and every man fled to his tent. 23 Then Joash the king of Israel captured Amaziah king of Judah, the son of Joash, the son of Jehoahaz, at Beth Shemesh; and he brought him to Jerusalem, and broke down the wall of Jerusalem from the Gate of Ephraim to the Corner Gate—four hundred cu-

25:4 [a]Deuteronomy 24:16   25:17 [a]Spelled *Jehoash* in 2 Kings 14:8ff

Gospel Pearls

bits. 24 And *he took* all the gold and silver, all the articles that were found in the house of God with Obed-Edom, the treasures of the king's house, and hostages, and returned to Samaria.

25 Amaziah the son of Joash, king of Judah, lived fifteen years after the death of Joash the son of Jehoahaz, king of Israel. 26 Now the rest of the acts of Amaziah, from first to last, indeed *are* they not written in the book of the kings of Judah and Israel? 27 After the time that Amaziah turned away from following the LORD, they made a conspiracy against him in Jerusalem, and he fled to Lachish; but they sent after him to Lachish and killed him there. 28 Then they brought him on horses and buried him with his fathers in the City of Judah.

26 Now all the people of Judah took Uzziah,*a* who *was* sixteen years old, and made him king instead of his father Amaziah. 2 He built Elath*a* and restored it to Judah, after the king rested with his fathers.

3 Uzziah *was* sixteen years old when he became king, and he reigned fifty-two years in Jerusalem. His mother's name was Jecholiah of Jerusalem. 4 And he did *what was* right in the sight of the LORD, according to all that his father Amaziah had done. 5 He sought God in the days of Zechariah, who had understanding in the visions*a* of God; and as long as he sought the LORD, God made him prosper.

6 Now he went out and made war against the Philistines, and broke down the wall of Gath, the wall of Jabneh, and the wall of Ashdod; and he built cities *around* Ashdod and among the Philistines. 7 God helped him against the Philistines, against the Arabians who lived in Gur Baal, and against the Meunites. 8 Also the Ammonites brought tribute to Uzziah. His fame spread as far as the entrance of Egypt, for he became exceedingly strong.

9 And Uzziah built towers in Jerusalem at the Corner Gate, at the Valley Gate, and at the corner buttress of the wall; then he fortified them. 10 Also he built towers in the desert. He dug many wells, for he had much livestock, both in the lowlands and in the plains; *he also had* farmers and vinedressers in the mountains and in Carmel, for he loved the soil.

11 Moreover Uzziah had an army of fighting men who went out to war by companies, according to the number on their roll as prepared by Jeiel the scribe and Maaseiah the officer, under the hand of Hananiah, *one of* the king's captains. 12 The total number of chief officers*a* of the mighty men of valor *was* two thousand six hundred. 13 And under their authority *was* an army of three hundred and seven thousand five hundred, that made war with mighty power, to help the king against the enemy. 14 Then Uzziah prepared for them, for the entire army, shields, spears, helmets, body armor, bows, and slings *to cast* stones. 15 And he made devices in Jerusalem, invented by skillful men, to be on the towers and the corners, to shoot arrows and large stones. So his fame spread far and wide, for he was marvelously helped till he became strong.

16 But when he was strong his heart was lifted up, to *his* destruction, for he transgressed against the LORD his God by entering the temple of the LORD to burn incense on the altar of incense. 17 So Azariah the priest went in after him, and with him were eighty priests of the LORD—valiant men. 18 And they withstood King Uzziah, and said to him, "*It is* not for you, Uzziah, to burn incense to the LORD, but for the priests, the sons of Aaron, who are consecrated to burn incense. Get out of the sanctuary, for you have trespassed! You *shall have* no honor from the LORD God."

19 Then Uzziah became furious; and he *had* a censer in his hand to burn incense. And while he was angry with the priests, leprosy broke out on his forehead, before the priests in the house of the LORD, beside the incense altar. 20 And Azariah the chief priest and all the priests looked at him, and there, on his forehead, he *was* leprous; so they thrust him out of that place. Indeed he also hurried to get out, because the LORD had struck him.

21 King Uzziah was a leper until the day of his death. He dwelt in an

26:1 *aCalled Azariah in 2 Kings 14:21ff*   26:2 *aHebrew Eloth*   26:5 *aSeveral Hebrew manuscripts, Septuagint, Syriac, Targum, and Arabic read fear.*   26:12 *aLiterally chief fathers*

*Y*ou are truly imprisoned by your own attitude. Your only limit is the lock you place on your own creativity.

isolated house, because he was a leper; for he was cut off from the house of the LORD. Then Jotham his son *was* over the king's house, judging the people of the land.

22 Now the rest of the acts of Uzziah, from first to last, the prophet Isaiah the son of Amoz wrote. 23 So Uzziah rested with his fathers, and they buried him with his fathers in the field of burial which *belonged* to the kings, for they said, "He is a leper." Then Jotham his son reigned in his place.

27 Jotham *was* twenty-five years old when he became king, and he reigned sixteen years in Jerusalem. His mother's name *was* Jerushah[a] the daughter of Zadok. 2 And he did *what was* right in the sight of the LORD, according to all that his father Uzziah had done (although he did not enter the temple of the LORD). But still the people acted corruptly.

3 He built the Upper Gate of the house of the LORD, and he built extensively on the wall of Ophel. 4 Moreover he built cities in the mountains of Judah, and in the forests he built fortresses and towers. 5 He also fought with the king of the Ammonites and defeated them. And the people of Ammon gave him in that year one hundred talents of silver, ten thousand kors of wheat, and ten thousand of barley. The people of Ammon paid this to him in the second and third years also. 6 So Jotham became mighty, because he prepared his ways before the LORD his God.

7 Now the rest of the acts of Jotham, and all his wars and his ways, indeed they *are* written in the book of the kings of Israel and Judah. 8 He was twenty-five years old when he became king, and he reigned sixteen years in Jerusalem. 9 So Jotham rested with his fathers, and they buried him in the City of David. Then Ahaz his son reigned in his place.

28 Ahaz *was* twenty years old when he became king, and he reigned sixteen years in Jerusalem; and he did not do *what was* right in the sight of the LORD, as his father David *had done.* 2 For he walked in the ways of the kings of Israel, and

made molded images for the Baals. 3 He burned incense in the Valley of the Son of Hinnom, and burned his children in the fire, according to the abominations of the nations whom the LORD had cast out before the children of Israel. 4 And he sacrificed and burned incense on the high places, on the hills, and under every green tree.

5 Therefore the LORD his God delivered him into the hand of the king of Syria. They defeated him, and carried away a great multitude of them as captives, and brought *them* to Damascus. Then he was also delivered into the hand of the king of Israel, who defeated him with a great slaughter. 6 For Pekah the son of Remaliah killed one hundred and twenty thousand in Judah in one day, all valiant men, because they had forsaken the LORD God of their fathers. 7 Zichri, a mighty man of Ephraim, killed Maaseiah the king's son, Azrikam the officer over the house, and Elkanah *who was* second to the king. 8 And the children of Israel carried away captive of their brethren two hundred thousand women, sons, and daughters; and they also took away much spoil from them, and brought the spoil to Samaria.

9 But a prophet of the LORD was there, whose name *was* Oded; and he went out before the army that came to Samaria, and said to them: "Look, because the LORD God of your fathers was angry with Judah, He has delivered them into your hand; but you have killed them in a rage *that* reaches up to heaven. 10 And now you propose to force the children of Judah and Jerusalem to be your male and female slaves; *but are* you not also guilty before the LORD your God? 11 Now hear me, therefore, and return the captives, whom you have taken captive from your brethren, for the fierce wrath of the LORD *is* upon you."

12 Then some of the heads of the children of Ephraim, Azariah the son of Johanan, Berechiah the son of Meshillemoth, Jehizkiah the son of Shallum, and Amasa the son of Hadlai, stood up against those who came from the war, 13 and said to them, "You shall not bring the captives here, for we *already* have offended

27:1 [a]Spelled *Jerusha* in 2 Kings 15:33

Gospel Pearls

the LORD. You intend to add to our sins and to our guilt; for our guilt is great, and *there is* fierce wrath against Israel." 14 So the armed men left the captives and the spoil before the leaders and all the assembly. 15 Then the men who were designated by name rose up and took the captives, and from the spoil they clothed all who were naked among them, dressed them and gave them sandals, gave them food and drink, and anointed them; and they let all the feeble ones ride on donkeys. So they brought them to their brethren at Jericho, the city of palm trees. Then they returned to Samaria.

16 At the same time King Ahaz sent to the kings*ᵃ* of Assyria to help him. 17 For again the Edomites had come, attacked Judah, and carried away captives. 18 The Philistines also had invaded the cities of the lowland and of the South of Judah, and had taken Beth Shemesh, Aijalon, Gederoth, Sochoh with its villages, Timnah with its villages, and Gimzo with its villages; and they dwelt there. 19 For the LORD brought Judah low because of Ahaz king of Israel, for he had encouraged moral decline in Judah and had been continually unfaithful to the LORD. 20 Also Tiglath-Pileser*ᵃ* king of Assyria came to him and distressed him, and did not assist him. 21 For Ahaz took part *of the treasures* from the house of the LORD, from the house of the king, and from the leaders, and he gave *it* to the king of Assyria; but he did not help him.

22 Now in the time of his distress King Ahaz became increasingly unfaithful to the LORD. This *is that* King Ahaz. 23 For he sacrificed to the gods of Damascus which had defeated him, saying, "Because the gods of the kings of Syria help them, I will sacrifice to them that they may help me." But they were the ruin of him and of all Israel. 24 So Ahaz gathered the articles of the house of God, cut in pieces the articles of the house of God, shut up the doors of the house of the LORD, and made for himself altars in every corner of Jerusalem. 25 And in every single city of Judah he made high places to burn incense to other gods, and provoked to anger the LORD God of his fathers.

26 Now the rest of his acts and all his ways, from first to last, indeed they *are* written in the book of the kings of Judah and Israel. 27 So Ahaz rested with his fathers, and they buried him in the city, in Jerusalem; but they did not bring him into the tombs of the kings of Israel. Then Hezekiah his son reigned in his place.

29 Hezekiah became king *when he was* twenty-five years old, and he reigned twenty-nine years in Jerusalem. His mother's name *was* Abijah*ᵃ* the daughter of Zechariah. 2 And he did *what was* right in the sight of the LORD, according to all that his father David had done.

3 In the first year of his reign, in the first month, he opened the doors of the house of the LORD and repaired them. 4 Then he brought in the priests and the Levites, and gathered them in the East Square, 5 and said to them: "Hear me, Levites! Now sanctify yourselves, sanctify the house of the LORD God of your fathers, and carry out the rubbish from the holy *place*. 6 For our fathers have trespassed and done evil in the eyes of the LORD our God; they have forsaken Him, have turned their faces away from the dwelling place of the LORD, and turned *their* backs *on Him*. 7 They have also shut up the doors of the vestibule, put out the lamps, and have not burned incense or offered burnt offerings in the holy *place* to the God of Israel. 8 Therefore the wrath of the LORD fell upon Judah and Jerusalem, and He has given them up to trouble, to desolation, and to jeering, as you see with your eyes. 9 For indeed, because of this our fathers have fallen by the sword; and our sons, our daughters, and our wives *are* in captivity.

10 "Now *it is* in my heart to make a covenant with the LORD God of Israel, that His fierce wrath may turn away from us. 11 My sons, do not be negligent now, for the LORD has chosen you to stand before Him, to serve Him, and that you should minister to Him and burn incense."

12 Then these Levites arose: Mahath the son of Amasai and Joel the son of Azariah, of the sons of the Kohathites; of the sons of Merari, Kish

28:16 *ᵃ*Septuagint, Syriac, and Vulgate read *king* (compare verse 20).   28:20 *ᵃ*Hebrew *Tilgath-Pilneser*   29:1 *ᵃ*Spelled *Abi* in 2 Kings 18:2

*I*f you really want to know how you feel about yourself, you may evaluate that by watching the way you treat other people who are like you! You will know you are healed when you respect those around you who are similar to you!

the son of Abdi and Azariah the son of Jehallelel; of the Gershonites, Joah the son of Zimmah and Eden the son of Joah; 13 of the sons of Elizaphan, Shimri and Jeiel; of the sons of Asaph, Zechariah and Mattaniah; 14 of the sons of Heman, Jehiel and Shimei; and of the sons of Jeduthun, Shemaiah and Uzziel.

15 And they gathered their brethren, sanctified themselves, and went according to the commandment of the king, at the words of the LORD, to cleanse the house of the LORD. 16 Then the priests went into the inner part of the house of the LORD to cleanse it, and brought out all the debris that they found in the temple of the LORD to the court of the house of the LORD. And the Levites took it out and carried it to the Brook Kidron.

17 Now they began to sanctify on the first day of the first month, and on the eighth day of the month they came to the vestibule of the LORD. So they sanctified the house of the LORD in eight days, and on the sixteenth day of the first month they finished. 18 Then they went in to King Hezekiah and said, "We have cleansed all the house of the LORD, the altar of burnt offerings with all its articles, and the table of the showbread with all its articles. 19 Moreover all the articles which King Ahaz in his reign had cast aside in his transgression we have prepared and sanctified; and there they are, before the altar of the LORD."

20 Then King Hezekiah rose early, gathered the rulers of the city, and went up to the house of the LORD. 21 And they brought seven bulls, seven rams, seven lambs, and seven male goats for a sin offering for the kingdom, for the sanctuary, and for Judah. Then he commanded the priests, the sons of Aaron, to offer them on the altar of the LORD. 22 So they killed the bulls, and the priests received the blood and sprinkled it on the altar. Likewise they killed the rams and sprinkled the blood on the altar. They also killed the lambs and sprinkled the blood on the altar. 23 Then they brought out the male goats for the sin offering before the king and the assembly, and they laid their hands on them. 24 And the priests killed them; and they presented their blood on the altar as a sin offering to make an atonement for all Israel, for the king commanded that the burnt offering and the sin offering be made for all Israel.

25 And he stationed the Levites in the house of the LORD with cymbals, with stringed instruments, and with harps, according to the commandment of David, of Gad the king's seer, and of Nathan the prophet; for thus was the commandment of the LORD by his prophets. 26 The Levites stood with the instruments of David, and the priests with the trumpets. 27 Then Hezekiah commanded them to offer the burnt offering on the altar. And when the burnt offering began, the song of the LORD also began, with the trumpets and with the instruments of David king of Israel. 28 So all the assembly worshiped, the singers sang, and the trumpeters sounded; all this continued until the burnt offering was finished. 29 And when they had finished offering, the king and all who were present with him bowed and worshiped. 30 Moreover King Hezekiah and the leaders commanded the Levites to sing praise to the LORD with the words of David and of Asaph the seer. So they sang praises with gladness, and they bowed their heads and worshiped.

31 Then Hezekiah answered and said, "Now that you have consecrated yourselves to the LORD, come near, and bring sacrifices and thank offerings into the house of the LORD." So the assembly brought in sacrifices and thank offerings, and as many as were of a willing heart brought burnt offerings. 32 And the number of the burnt offerings which the assembly brought was seventy bulls, one hundred rams, and two hundred lambs; all these were for a burnt offering to the LORD. 33 The consecrated things were six hundred bulls and three thousand sheep. 34 But the priests were too few, so that they could not skin all the burnt offerings; therefore their brethren the Levites helped them until the work was ended and until the other priests had sanctified themselves, for the Levites were more diligent in sanctifying themselves than the priests. 35 Also the burnt offerings were in abundance, with the fat of the peace offerings and with the drink offerings for every burnt offering.

Respect means "to honor and esteem as valuable." This attitude starting in our churches would usher in real healing for women who have had trouble trusting even close friends and relationships.

Soul Secrets
when sudden change occurs

*L*ord, just yesterday everything was so different. I can't believe how suddenly things can change—and how completely. It seems like just moments ago my life was happy and secure. Now I feel as though I've stepped on a land mine. My world is shattered. There is nothing left but You.

Lord, I cannot even articulate everything I need from You. I have to rest in the promise that You know my every need and that You will provide. Send Your Holy Spirit to minister to every aspect of this situation—to bring truth, to bring wisdom, to bring redemption, to bring a vision of what to do next. As I said, there is nothing left but You. And You are all I need. You are my Rock, my one stable Place, my only sure Foundation.

So the service of the house of the LORD was set in order. 36 Then Hezekiah and all the people rejoiced that God had prepared the people, since the events took place so suddenly.

30 And Hezekiah sent to all Israel and Judah, and also wrote letters to Ephraim and Manasseh, that they should come to the house of the LORD at Jerusalem, to keep the Passover to the LORD God of Israel. 2 For the king and his leaders and all the assembly in Jerusalem had agreed to keep the Passover in the second month. 3 For they could not keep it at the regular time,ᵃ because a sufficient number of priests had not consecrated themselves, nor had the people gathered together at Jerusalem. 4 And the matter pleased the king and all the assembly. 5 So they resolved to make a proclamation throughout all Israel, from Beersheba to Dan, that they should come to keep the Passover to the LORD God of Israel at Jerusalem, since they had not done it for a long time in the prescribed manner.

6 Then the runners went throughout all Israel and Judah with the letters from the king and his leaders, and spoke according to the command of the king: "Children of Israel, return to the LORD God of Abraham, Isaac, and Israel; then He will return to the remnant of you who have escaped from the hand of the kings of Assyria. 7 And do not be like your fathers and your brethren, who trespassed against the LORD God of their fathers, so that He gave them up to desolation, as you see. 8 Now do not be stiff-necked, as your fathers were, but yield yourselves to the LORD; and enter His sanctuary, which He has sanctified forever, and serve the LORD your God, that the fierceness of His wrath may turn away from you. 9 For if you return to the LORD, your brethren and your children will be treated with compassion by those who lead them captive, so that they may come back to this land; for the LORD your God is gracious and merciful, and will not turn His face from you if you return to Him."

10 So the runners passed from city to city through the country of Ephraim and Manasseh, as far as Zebulun; but they laughed at them and mocked them. 11 Nevertheless some from Asher, Manasseh, and Zebulun humbled themselves and came to Jerusalem. 12 Also the hand of God was on Judah to give them singleness of heart to obey the command of the king and the leaders, at the word of the LORD.

13 Now many people, a very great assembly, gathered at Jerusalem to keep the Feast of Unleavened Bread in the second month. 14 They arose and took away the altars that were in Jerusalem, and they took away all the incense altars and cast them into the Brook Kidron. 15 Then they slaughtered the Passover lambs on the fourteenth day of the second month. The priests and the Levites were ashamed, and sanctified themselves, and brought the burnt offerings to the house of the LORD. 16 They stood in their place according to their custom, according to the Law of Moses the man of God; the priests sprinkled the blood received from the hand of the Levites. 17 For there were many in the assembly who had not sanctified themselves; therefore the Levites had charge of the slaughter of the Passover lambs for everyone who was not clean, to sanctify them to the LORD. 18 For a multitude of the people, many from Ephraim, Manasseh, Issachar, and Zebulun, had not cleansed themselves, yet they ate the Passover contrary to what was written. But Hezekiah prayed for them, saying, "May the good LORD provide atonement for everyone 19 who prepares his heart to seek God, the LORD God of his fathers, though he is not cleansed according to the purification of the sanctuary." 20 And the LORD listened to Hezekiah and healed the people.

21 So the children of Israel who were present at Jerusalem kept the Feast of Unleavened Bread seven days with great gladness; and the Levites and the priests praised the LORD day by day, singing to the LORD, accompanied by loud instruments. 22 And Hezekiah gave encouragement to all the Levites who taught the good knowledge of the LORD; and they ate throughout the feast seven days, offering peace offerings and

30:3 ᵃThat is, the first month (compare Leviticus 23:5); literally at that time

Gospel
Pearls

making confession to the Lord God of their fathers.

23 Then the whole assembly agreed to keep *the feast* another seven days, and they kept it *another* seven days with gladness. 24 For Hezekiah king of Judah gave to the assembly a thousand bulls and seven thousand sheep, and the leaders gave to the assembly a thousand bulls and ten thousand sheep; and a great number of priests sanctified themselves. 25 The whole assembly of Judah rejoiced, also the priests and Levites, all the assembly that came from Israel, the sojourners who came from the land of Israel, and those who dwelt in Judah. 26 So there was great joy in Jerusalem, for since the time of Solomon the son of David, king of Israel, *there had* been nothing like this in Jerusalem. 27 Then the priests, the Levites, arose and blessed the people, and their voice was heard; and their prayer came *up* to His holy dwelling place, to heaven.

31 Now when all this was finished, all Israel who were present went out to the cities of Judah and broke the sacred pillars in pieces, cut down the wooden images, and threw down the high places and the altars—from all Judah, Benjamin, Ephraim, and Manasseh—until they had utterly destroyed them all. Then all the children of Israel returned to their own cities, every man to his possession.

2 And Hezekiah appointed the divisions of the priests and the Levites according to their divisions, each man according to his service, the priests and Levites for burnt offerings and peace offerings, to serve, to give thanks, and to praise in the gates of the camp*ᵃ* of the Lord. 3 The king also *appointed* a portion of his possessions for the burnt offerings: for the morning and evening burnt offerings, the burnt offerings for the Sabbaths and the New Moons and the set feasts, as *it is* written in the Law of the Lord.

4 Moreover he commanded the people who dwelt in Jerusalem to contribute support for the priests and the Levites, that they might devote themselves to the Law of the Lord. 5 As soon as the commandment

was circulated, the children of Israel brought in abundance the firstfruits of grain and wine, oil and honey, and of all the produce of the field; and they brought in abundantly the tithe of everything. 6 And the children of Israel and Judah, who dwelt in the cities of Judah, brought the tithe of oxen and sheep; also the tithe of holy things which were consecrated to the Lord their God they laid in heaps.

7 In the third month they began laying them in heaps, and they finished in the seventh month. 8 And when Hezekiah and the leaders came and saw the heaps, they blessed the Lord and His people Israel. 9 Then Hezekiah questioned the priests and the Levites concerning the heaps. 10 And Azariah the chief priest, from the house of Zadok, answered him and said, "Since *the people* began to bring the offerings into the house of the Lord, we have had enough to eat and have plenty left, for the Lord has blessed His people; and what is left *is* this great abundance."

11 Now Hezekiah commanded *them* to prepare rooms in the house of the Lord, and they prepared them. 12 Then they faithfully brought in the offerings, the tithes, and the dedicated things; Cononiah the Levite had charge of them, and Shimei his brother *was* the next. 13 Jehiel, Azaziah, Nahath, Asahel, Jerimoth, Jozabad, Eliel, Ismachiah, Mahath, and Benaiah *were* overseers under the hand of Cononiah and Shimei his brother, at the commandment of Hezekiah the king and Azariah the ruler of the house of God. 14 Kore the son of Imnah the Levite, the keeper of the East Gate, *was* over the freewill offerings to God, to distribute the offerings of the Lord and the most holy things. 15 And under him *were* Eden, Miniamin, Jeshua, Shemaiah, Amariah, and Shecaniah, *his* faithful assistants in the cities of the priests, to distribute allotments to their brethren by divisions, to the great as well as the small.

16 Besides those males from three years old and up who were written in the genealogy, they distributed to everyone who entered the house of the Lord his daily portion for the work of his service, by his division,

31:2 *ᵃThat is, the temple

What can you do to bridge the gulf between yourself and other women? You have to rummage through the recreated heart that the Holy Spirit places within you and allow God to use you as a paramedic of mercy.

17 and to the priests who were written in the genealogy according to their father's house, and to the Levites from twenty years old and up according to their work, by their divisions, 18 and to all who were written in the genealogy—their little ones and their wives, their sons and daughters, the whole company of them—for in their faithfulness they sanctified themselves in holiness.

19 Also for the sons of Aaron the priests, *who were* in the fields of the common-lands of their cities, in every single city, *there were* men who were designated by name to distribute portions to all the males among the priests and to all who were listed by genealogies among the Levites.

20 Thus Hezekiah did throughout all Judah, and he did what *was* good and right and true before the LORD his God. 21 And in every work that he began in the service of the house of God, in the law and in the commandment, to seek his God, he did *it* with all his heart. So he prospered.

32 After these deeds of faithfulness, Sennacherib king of Assyria came and entered Judah; he encamped against the fortified cities, thinking to win them over to himself. 2 And when Hezekiah saw that Sennacherib had come, and that his purpose was to make war against Jerusalem, 3 he consulted with his leaders and commanders*a* to stop the water from the springs which *were* outside the city; and they helped him. 4 Thus many people gathered together who stopped all the springs and the brook that ran through the land, saying, "Why should the kings*a* of Assyria come and find much water?" 5 And he strengthened himself, built up all the wall that was broken, raised *it* up to the towers, and *built* another wall outside; also he repaired the Millo*a* *in* the City of David, and made weapons and shields in abundance. 6 Then he set military captains over the people, gathered them together to him in the open square of the city gate, and gave them encouragement, saying, 7 "Be strong and courageous; do not be afraid nor dismayed before the king of Assyria, nor before all the

multitude that *is* with him; for *there are* more with us than with him. 8 With him *is* an arm of flesh; but with us *is* the LORD our God, to help us and to fight our battles." And the people were strengthened by the words of Hezekiah king of Judah.

9 After this Sennacherib king of Assyria sent his servants to Jerusalem (but he and all the forces with him *laid siege* against Lachish), to Hezekiah king of Judah, and to all Judah who *were* in Jerusalem, saying, 10 "Thus says Sennacherib king of Assyria: 'In what do you trust, that you remain under siege in Jerusalem? 11 Does not Hezekiah persuade you to give yourselves over to die by famine and by thirst, saying, "The LORD our God will deliver us from the hand of the king of Assyria"? 12 Has not the same Hezekiah taken away His high places and His altars, and commanded Judah and Jerusalem, saying, "You shall worship before one altar and burn incense on it"? 13 Do you not know what I and my fathers have done to all the peoples of *other* lands? Were the gods of the nations of those lands in any way able to deliver their lands out of my hand? 14 Who *was there* among all the gods of those nations that my fathers utterly destroyed that could deliver his people from my hand, that your God should be able to deliver you from my hand? 15 Now therefore, do not let Hezekiah deceive you or persuade you like this, and do not believe him; for no god of any nation or kingdom was able to deliver his people from my hand or the hand of my fathers. How much less will your God deliver you from my hand?' "

16 Furthermore, his servants spoke against the LORD God and against His servant Hezekiah.

17 He also wrote letters to revile the LORD God of Israel, and to speak against Him, saying, "As the gods of the nations of *other* lands have not delivered their people from my hand, so the God of Hezekiah will not deliver His people from my hand." 18 Then they called out with a loud voice in Hebrew*a* to the people of Jerusalem who *were* on the wall, to frighten them and trouble them, that

---

32:3 *a*Literally *mighty men*   32:4 *a*Following Masoretic Text and Vulgate; Arabic, Septuagint, and Syriac read *king*.   32:5 *a*Literally *The Landfill*   32:18 *a*Literally *Judean*

Gospel Pearls

they might take the city. 19 And they spoke against the God of Jerusalem, as against the gods of the people of the earth—the work of men's hands.

20 Now because of this King Hezekiah and the prophet Isaiah, the son of Amoz, prayed and cried out to heaven. 21 Then the Lord sent an angel who cut down every mighty man of valor, leader, and captain in the camp of the king of Assyria. So he returned shamefaced to his own land. And when he had gone into the temple of his god, some of his own offspring struck him down with the sword there.

22 Thus the Lord saved Hezekiah and the inhabitants of Jerusalem from the hand of Sennacherib the king of Assyria, and from the hand of all *others,* and guided them*a* on every side. 23 And many brought gifts to the Lord at Jerusalem, and presents to Hezekiah king of Judah, so that he was exalted in the sight of all nations thereafter.

24 In those days Hezekiah was sick and near death, and he prayed to the Lord; and He spoke to him and gave him a sign. 25 But Hezekiah did not repay according to the favor *shown* him, for his heart was lifted up; therefore wrath was looming over him and over Judah and Jerusalem. 26 Then Hezekiah humbled himself for the pride of his heart, he and the inhabitants of Jerusalem, so that the wrath of the Lord did not come upon them in the days of Hezekiah.

27 Hezekiah had very great riches and honor. And he made himself treasuries for silver, for gold, for precious stones, for spices, for shields, and for all kinds of desirable items; 28 storehouses for the harvest of grain, wine, and oil; and stalls for all kinds of livestock, and folds for flocks.*a* 29 Moreover he provided cities for himself, and possessions of flocks and herds in abundance; for God had given him very much property. 30 This same Hezekiah also stopped the water outlet of Upper Gihon, and brought the water by tunnel*a* to the west side of the City of David. Hezekiah prospered in all his works.

31 However, *regarding* the ambas-

sadors of the princes of Babylon, whom they sent to him to inquire about the wonder that was *done* in the land, God withdrew from him, in order to test him, that He might know all *that was* in his heart.

32 Now the rest of the acts of Hezekiah, and his goodness, indeed they *are* written in the vision of Isaiah the prophet, the son of Amoz, *and* in the book of the kings of Judah and Israel. 33 So Hezekiah rested with his fathers, and they buried him in the upper tombs of the sons of David; and all Judah and the inhabitants of Jerusalem honored him at his death. Then Manasseh his son reigned in his place.

33 Manasseh *was* twelve years old when he became king, and he reigned fifty-five years in Jerusalem. 2 But he did evil in the sight of the Lord, according to the abominations of the nations whom the Lord had cast out before the children of Israel. 3 For he rebuilt the high places which Hezekiah his father had broken down; he raised up altars for the Baals, and made wooden images; and he worshiped all the host of heaven*a* and served them. 4 He also built altars in the house of the Lord, of which the Lord had said, "In Jerusalem shall My name be forever." 5 And he built altars for all the host of heaven in the two courts of the house of the Lord. 6 Also he caused his sons to pass through the fire in the Valley of the Son of Hinnom; he practiced soothsaying, used witchcraft and sorcery, and consulted mediums and spiritists. He did much evil in the sight of the Lord, to provoke Him to anger. 7 He even set a carved image, the idol which he had made, in the house of God, of which God had said to David and to Solomon his son, "In this house and in Jerusalem, which I have chosen out of all the tribes of Israel, I will put My name forever; 8 and I will not again remove the foot of Israel from the land which I have appointed for your fathers—only if they are careful to do all that I have commanded them, according to the whole law and the statutes and the ordinances by the hand

32:22 *a*Septuagint reads *gave them rest;* Vulgate reads *gave them treasures.*   32:28 *a*Following Septuagint and Vulgate; Arabic and Syriac omit *folds for flocks;* Masoretic Text reads *flocks for sheepfolds.*   32:30 *a*Literally *brought it straight* (compare 2 Kings 20:20)   33:3 *a*The gods of the Assyrians

*Y*ou have to change the world one person at a time.

of Moses." 9 So Manasseh seduced Judah and the inhabitants of Jerusalem to do more evil than the nations whom the LORD had destroyed before the children of Israel.

10 And the LORD spoke to Manasseh and his people, but they would not listen. 11 Therefore the LORD brought upon them the captains of the army of the king of Assyria, who took Manasseh with hooks,ª bound him with bronze *fetters,* and carried him off to Babylon. 12 Now when he was in affliction, he implored the LORD his God, and humbled himself greatly before the God of his fathers, 13 and prayed to Him; and He received his entreaty, heard his supplication, and brought him back to Jerusalem into his kingdom. Then Manasseh knew that the LORD *was* God.

14 After this he built a wall outside the City of David on the west side of Gihon, in the valley, as far as the entrance of the Fish Gate; and *it* enclosed Ophel, and he raised it to a very great height. Then he put military captains in all the fortified cities of Judah. 15 He took away the foreign gods and the idol from the house of the LORD, and all the altars that he had built in the mount of the house of the LORD and in Jerusalem; and he cast *them* out of the city. 16 He also repaired the altar of the LORD, sacrificed peace offerings and thank offerings on it, and commanded Judah to serve the LORD God of Israel. 17 Nevertheless the people still sacrificed on the high places, *but* only to the LORD their God.

18 Now the rest of the acts of Manasseh, his prayer to his God, and the words of the seers who spoke to him in the name of the LORD God of Israel, indeed they *are written* in the bookª of the kings of Israel. 19 Also his prayer and *how* God received his entreaty, and all his sin and trespass, and the sites where he built high places and set up wooden images and carved images, before he was humbled, indeed they *are* written among the sayings of Hozai.ª 20 So Manasseh rested with his fathers, and they buried him in his own house. Then his son Amon reigned in his place.

21 Amon *was* twenty-two years old when he became king, and he reigned two years in Jerusalem. 22 But he did evil in the sight of the LORD, as his father Manasseh had done; for Amon sacrificed to all the carved images which his father Manasseh had made, and served them. 23 And he did not humble himself before the LORD, as his father Manasseh had humbled himself; but Amon trespassed more and more.

24 Then his servants conspired against him, and killed him in his own house. 25 But the people of the land executed all those who had conspired against King Amon. Then the people of the land made his son Josiah king in his place.

34 Josiah *was* eight years old when he became king, and he reigned thirty-one years in Jerusalem. 2 And he did *what was* right in the sight of the LORD, and walked in the ways of his father David; *he* did *not* turn aside to the right hand or to the left.

3 For in the eighth year of his reign, while he was still young, he began to seek the God of his father David; and in the twelfth year he began to purge Judah and Jerusalem of the high places, the wooden images, the carved images, and the molded images. 4 They broke down the altars of the Baals in his presence, and the incense altars which *were* above them he cut down; and the wooden images, the carved images, and the molded images he broke in pieces, and made dust of them and scattered *it* on the graves of those who had sacrificed to them. 5 He also burned the bones of the priests on their altars, and cleansed Judah and Jerusalem. 6 And *so he did* in the cities of Manasseh, Ephraim, and Simeon, as far as Naphtali and all around, with axes.ª 7 When he had broken down the altars and the wooden images, had beaten the carved images into powder, and cut down all the incense altars throughout all the land of Israel, he returned to Jerusalem.

8 In the eighteenth year of his reign, when he had purged the land and the temple,ª he sent Shaphan the son of Azaliah, Maaseiah the gover-

33:11 ªThat is, nose hooks (compare 2 Kings 19:28)   33:18 ªLiterally *words*   33:19 ªSeptuagint reads *the seers.*   34:6 ªLiterally *swords*   34:8 ªLiterally *house*

Gospel Pearls

nor of the city, and Joah the son of Joahaz the recorder, to repair the house of the LORD his God. 9 When they came to Hilkiah the high priest, they delivered the money that was brought into the house of God, which the Levites who kept the doors had gathered from the hand of Manasseh and Ephraim, from all the remnant of Israel, from all Judah and Benjamin, and which they had brought back to Jerusalem. 10 Then they put it in the hand of the foremen who had the oversight of the house of the LORD; and they gave it to the workmen who worked in the house of the LORD, to repair and restore the house. 11 They gave it to the craftsmen and builders to buy hewn stone and timber for beams, and to floor the houses which the kings of Judah had destroyed. 12 And the men did the work faithfully. Their overseers were Jahath and Obadiah the Levites, of the sons of Merari, and Zechariah and Meshullam, of the sons of the Kohathites, to supervise. Others of the Levites, all of whom were skillful with instruments of music, 13 were over the burden bearers and were overseers of all who did work in any kind of service. And some of the Levites were scribes, officers, and gatekeepers.

14 Now when they brought out the money that was brought into the house of the LORD, Hilkiah the priest found the Book of the Law of the LORD given by Moses. 15 Then Hilkiah answered and said to Shaphan the scribe, "I have found the Book of the Law in the house of the LORD." And Hilkiah gave the book to Shaphan. 16 So Shaphan carried the book to the king, bringing the king word, saying, "All that was committed to your servants they are doing. 17 And they have gathered the money that was found in the house of the LORD, and have delivered it into the hand of the overseers and the workmen." 18 Then Shaphan the scribe told the king, saying, "Hilkiah the priest has given me a book." And Shaphan read it before the king.

19 Thus it happened, when the king heard the words of the Law, that he tore his clothes. 20 Then the king commanded Hilkiah, Ahikam the son of Shaphan, Abdon[a] the son of Micah, Shaphan the scribe, and Asaiah a servant of the king, saying, 21 "Go, inquire of the LORD for me, and for those who are left in Israel and Judah, concerning the words of the book that is found; for great is the wrath of the LORD that is poured out on us, because our fathers have not kept the word of the LORD, to do according to all that is written in this book."

22 So Hilkiah and those the king had appointed went to Huldah the prophetess, the wife of Shallum the son of Tokhath,[a] the son of Hasrah,[b] keeper of the wardrobe. (She dwelt in Jerusalem in the Second Quarter.) And they spoke to her to that effect.

23 Then she answered them, "Thus says the LORD God of Israel, 'Tell the man who sent you to Me, 24 Thus says the LORD: 'Behold, I will bring calamity on this place and on its inhabitants, all the curses that are written in the book which they have read before the king of Judah, 25 because they have forsaken Me and burned incense to other gods, that they might provoke Me to anger with all the works of their hands. Therefore My wrath will be poured out on this place, and not be quenched.' " ' 26 But as for the king of Judah, who sent you to inquire of the LORD, in this manner you shall speak to him, 'Thus says the LORD God of Israel: "Concerning the words which you have heard— 27 because your heart was tender, and you humbled yourself before God when you heard His words against this place and against its inhabitants, and you humbled yourself before Me, and you tore your clothes and wept before Me, I also have heard you," says the LORD. 28 Surely I will gather you to your fathers, and you shall be gathered to your grave in peace; and your eyes shall not see all the calamity which I will bring on this place and its inhabitants." ' " So they brought back word to the king.

29 Then the king sent and gathered all the elders of Judah and Jerusalem. 30 The king went up to the house of the LORD, with all the men of Judah and the inhabitants of Jerusalem— the priests and the Levites, and all

34:20 [a]Achbor the son of Michaiah in 2 Kings 22:12   34:22 [a]Spelled Tikvah in 2 Kings 22:14   [b]Spelled Harhas in 2 Kings 22:14

When the Lord does send someone into your life who loves you like you want to be loved, understand that love does not mean you will always get your way. It is a sharing situation with negotiations and compromises for mutual good.

the people, great and small. And he read in their hearing all the words of the Book of the Covenant which had been found in the house of the LORD. 31 Then the king stood in his place and made a covenant before the LORD, to follow the LORD, and to keep His commandments and His testimonies and His statutes with all his heart and all his soul, to perform the words of the covenant that were written in this book. 32 And he made all who were present in Jerusalem and Benjamin take a stand. So the inhabitants of Jerusalem did according to the covenant of God, the God of their fathers. 33 Thus Josiah removed all the abominations from all the country that *belonged* to the children of Israel, and made all who were present in Israel diligently serve the LORD their God. All his days they did not depart from following the LORD God of their fathers.

35 Now Josiah kept a Passover to the LORD in Jerusalem, and they slaughtered the Passover *lambs* on the fourteenth *day* of the first month. 2 And he set the priests in their duties and encouraged them for the service of the house of the LORD. 3 Then he said to the Levites who taught all Israel, who were holy to the LORD: "Put the holy ark in the house which Solomon the son of David, king of Israel, built. *It shall* no longer *be* a burden on *your* shoulders. Now serve the LORD your God and His people Israel. 4 Prepare *yourselves* according to your fathers' houses, according to your divisions, following the written instruction of David king of Israel and the written instruction of Solomon his son. 5 And stand in the holy *place* according to the divisions of the fathers' houses of your brethren the *lay* people, and *according to* the division of the father's house of the Levites. 6 So slaughter the Passover *offerings*, consecrate yourselves, and prepare *them* for your brethren, that *they* may do according to the word of the LORD by the hand of Moses."

7 Then Josiah gave the *lay* people lambs and young goats from the flock, all for Passover *offerings* for all who were present, to the number of thirty thousand, as well as three thousand cattle; these *were* from the king's possessions. 8 And his leaders gave willingly to the people, to the priests, and to the Levites. Hilkiah, Zechariah, and Jehiel, rulers of the house of God, gave to the priests for the Passover *offerings* two thousand six hundred *from the flock,* and three hundred cattle. 9 Also Conaniah, his brothers Shemaiah and Nethanel, and Hashabiah and Jeiel and Jozabad, chief of the Levites, gave to the Levites for Passover *offerings* five thousand *from the flock* and five hundred cattle.

10 So the service was prepared, and the priests stood in their places, and the Levites in their divisions, according to the king's command. 11 And they slaughtered the Passover *offerings;* and the priests sprinkled *the blood* with their hands, while the Levites skinned *the animals.* 12 Then they removed the burnt offerings that *they* might give them to the divisions of the fathers' houses of the *lay* people, to offer to the LORD, as *it is* written in the Book of Moses. And so *they did* with the cattle. 13 Also they roasted the Passover *offerings* with fire according to the ordinance; but the *other* holy *offerings* they boiled in pots, in caldrons, and in pans, and divided *them* quickly among all the *lay* people. 14 Then afterward they prepared portions for themselves and for the priests, because the priests, the sons of Aaron, *were* busy in offering burnt offerings and fat until night; therefore the Levites prepared portions for themselves and for the priests, the sons of Aaron. 15 And the singers, the sons of Asaph, *were* in their places, according to the command of David, Asaph, Heman, and Jeduthun the king's seer. Also the gatekeepers were at each gate; they did not have to leave their position, because their brethren the Levites prepared portions for them.

16 So all the service of the LORD was prepared the same day, to keep the Passover and to offer burnt offerings on the altar of the LORD, according to the command of King Josiah. 17 And the children of Israel who were present kept the Passover at that time, and the Feast of Unleavened Bread for seven days. 18 There had been no Passover kept in Israel like that since the days of Samuel the prophet; and none of the kings of Israel had kept such a Passover as Jo-

Gospel Pearls

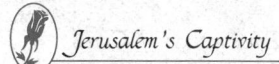

siah kept, with the priests and the Levites, all Judah and Israel who were present, and the inhabitants of Jerusalem. 19 In the eighteenth year of the reign of Josiah this Passover was kept.

20 After all this, when Josiah had prepared the temple, Necho king of Egypt came up to fight against Carchemish by the Euphrates; and Josiah went out against him. 21 But he sent messengers to him, saying, "What have I to do with you, king of Judah? *I have* not *come* against you this day, but against the house with which I have war; for God commanded me to make haste. Refrain *from meddling with* God, who *is* with me, lest He destroy you." 22 Nevertheless Josiah would not turn his face from him, but disguised himself so that he might fight with him, and did not heed the words of Necho from the mouth of God. So he came to fight in the Valley of Megiddo.

23 And the archers shot King Josiah; and the king said to his servants, "Take me away, for I am severely wounded." 24 His servants therefore took him out of that chariot and put him in the second chariot that he had, and they brought him to Jerusalem. So he died, and was buried in *one of* the tombs of his fathers. And all Judah and Jerusalem mourned for Josiah.

25 Jeremiah also lamented for Josiah. And to this day all the singing men and the singing women speak of Josiah in their lamentations. They made it a custom in Israel; and indeed they *are* written in the Laments.

26 Now the rest of the acts of Josiah and his goodness, according to *what was* written in the Law of the Lord, 27 and his deeds from first to last, indeed they *are* written in the book of the kings of Israel and Judah.

36 Then the people of the land took Jehoahaz the son of Josiah, and made him king in his father's place in Jerusalem. 2 Jehoahaz*ᵃ was* twenty-three years old when he became king, and he reigned three months in Jerusalem. 3 Now the king of Egypt deposed him

at Jerusalem; and he imposed on the land a tribute of one hundred talents of silver and a talent of gold. 4 Then the king of Egypt made *Jehoahaz's*ᵃ brother Eliakim king over Judah and Jerusalem, and changed his name to Jehoiakim. And Necho took Jehoahaz*ᵇ* his brother and carried him off to Egypt.

5 Jehoiakim *was* twenty-five years old when he became king, and he reigned eleven years in Jerusalem. And he did evil in the sight of the Lord his God. 6 Nebuchadnezzar king of Babylon came up against him, and bound him in bronze *fetters* to carry him off to Babylon. 7 Nebuchadnezzar also carried off *some* of the articles from the house of the Lord to Babylon, and put them in his temple at Babylon. 8 Now the rest of the acts of Jehoiakim, the abominations which he did, and what was found against him, indeed they *are* written in the book of the kings of Israel and Judah. Then Jehoiachin his son reigned in his place.

9 Jehoiachin *was* eightᵃ years old when he became king, and he reigned in Jerusalem three months and ten days. And he did evil in the sight of the Lord. 10 At the turn of the year King Nebuchadnezzar summoned *him* and took him to Babylon, with the costly articles from the house of the Lord, and made Zedekiah, *Jehoiakim's*ᵃ brother, king over Judah and Jerusalem.

11 Zedekiah *was* twenty-one years old when he became king, and he reigned eleven years in Jerusalem. 12 He did evil in the sight of the Lord his God, *and* did not humble himself before Jeremiah the prophet, *who spoke* from the mouth of the Lord. 13 And he also rebelled against King Nebuchadnezzar, who had made him swear *an oath* by God; but he stiffened his neck and hardened his heart against turning to the Lord God of Israel. 14 Moreover all the leaders of the priests and the people transgressed more and more, *according* to all the abominations of the nations, and defiled the house of the Lord which He had consecrated in Jerusalem.

36:2 ᵃMasoretic Text reads *Joahaz.*   36:4 ᵃLiterally *his*   ᵇMasoretic Text reads *Joahaz.*   36:9 ᵃSome Hebrew manuscripts, Septuagint, Syriac, and 2 Kings 24:8 read *eighteen.*   36:10 ᵃLiterally *his* (compare 2 Kings 24:17)

---

*L*ove is not immature. It is not for the frivolous. Love requires maturity, and it can require discipline and a great deal of trust.

15 And the LORD God of their fathers sent *warnings* to them by His messengers, rising up early and sending *them*, because He had compassion on His people and on His dwelling place. 16 But they mocked the messengers of God, despised His words, and scoffed at His prophets, until the wrath of the LORD arose against His people, till *there was* no remedy.

17 Therefore He brought against them the king of the Chaldeans, who killed their young men with the sword in the house of their sanctuary, and had no compassion on young man or virgin, on the aged or the weak; He gave *them* all into his hand. 18 And all the articles from the house of God, great and small, the treasures of the house of the LORD, and the treasures of the king and of his leaders, all *these* he took to Babylon. 19 Then they burned the house of God, broke down the wall of Jerusalem, burned all its palaces with fire, and destroyed all its precious possessions. 20 And those who es-caped from the sword he carried away to Babylon, where they became servants to him and his sons until the rule of the kingdom of Persia, 21 to fulfill the word of the LORD by the mouth of Jeremiah, until the land had enjoyed her Sabbaths. As long as she lay desolate she kept Sabbath, to fulfill seventy years.

22 Now in the first year of Cyrus king of Persia, that the word of the LORD by the mouth of Jeremiah might be fulfilled, the LORD stirred up the spirit of Cyrus king of Persia, so that he made a proclamation throughout all his kingdom, and also *put it* in writing, saying,

23 Thus says Cyrus king of Persia: All the kingdoms of the earth the LORD God of heaven has given me. And He has commanded me to build Him a house at Jerusalem which is in Judah. Who *is* among you of all His people? May the LORD his God *be* with him, and let him go up!

The Book of

EZRA

1 Now in the first year of Cyrus king of Persia, that the word of the LORD by the mouth of Jeremiah might be fulfilled, the LORD stirred up the spirit of Cyrus king of Persia, so that he made a proclamation throughout all his kingdom, and also *put it* in writing, saying,

2 Thus says Cyrus king of Persia: All the kingdoms of the earth the LORD God of heaven has given me. And He has commanded me to build Him a house at Jerusalem which *is* in Judah. 3 Who *is* among you of all His people? May his God be with him, and let him go up to Jerusalem which *is* in Judah, and build the house of the LORD God of Israel (He *is* God), which *is* in Jerusalem.

4 And whoever is left in any place where he dwells, let the men of his place help him with silver and gold, with goods and livestock, besides the freewill offerings for the house of God which *is* in Jerusalem.

5 Then the heads of the fathers' *houses* of Judah and Benjamin, and the priests and the Levites, with all whose spirits God had moved, arose to go up and build the house of the LORD which *is* in Jerusalem. 6 And all those who *were* around them encouraged them with articles of silver and gold, with goods and livestock, and with precious things, besides all *that* was willingly offered.

7 King Cyrus also brought out the articles of the house of the LORD, which Nebuchadnezzar had taken

Gospel Pearls

from Jerusalem and put in the temple of his gods; 8 and Cyrus king of Persia brought them out by the hand of Mithredath the treasurer, and counted them out to Sheshbazzar the prince of Judah. 9 This *is* the number of them: thirty gold platters, one thousand silver platters, twenty-nine knives, 10 thirty gold basins, four hundred and ten silver basins of a similar *kind, and* one thousand other articles. 11 All the articles of gold and silver *were* five thousand four hundred. All *these* Sheshbazzar took with the captives who were brought from Babylon to Jerusalem.

2 Now*a* these *are* the people of the province who came back from the captivity, of those who had been carried away, whom Nebuchadnezzar the king of Babylon had carried away to Babylon, and who returned to Jerusalem and Judah, everyone to his *own* city.

2 *Those* who came with Zerubbabel *were* Jeshua, Nehemiah, Seraiah, Reelaiah, Mordecai, Bilshan, Mispar,*a* Bigvai, Rehum,*b* *and* Baanah. The number of the men of the people of Israel: 3 the people of Parosh, two thousand one hundred and seventy-two; 4 the people of Shephatiah, three hundred and seventy-two; 5 the people of Arah, seven hundred and seventy-five; 6 the people of Pahath-Moab, of the people of Jeshua *and* Joab, two thousand eight hundred and twelve; 7 the people of Elam, one thousand two hundred and fifty-four; 8 the people of Zattu, nine hundred and forty-five; 9 the people of Zaccai, seven hundred and sixty; 10 the people of Bani,*a* six hundred and forty-two; 11 the people of Bebai, six hundred and twenty-three; 12 the people of Azgad, one thousand two hundred and twenty-two; 13 the people of Adonikam, six hundred and sixty-six; 14 the people of Bigvai, two thousand and fifty-six; 15 the people of Adin, four hundred and fifty-four; 16 the people of Ater of Hezekiah, ninety-eight; 17 the people of Bezai, three hundred and

twenty-three; 18 the people of Jorah,*a* one hundred and twelve; 19 the people of Hashum, two hundred and twenty-three; 20 the people of Gibbar,*a* ninety-five; 21 the people of Bethlehem, one hundred and twenty-three; 22 the men of Netophah, fifty-six; 23 the men of Anathoth, one hundred and twenty-eight; 24 the people of Azmaveth,*a* forty-two; 25 the people of Kirjath Arim,*a* Chephirah, and Beeroth, seven hundred and forty-three; 26 the people of Ramah and Geba, six hundred and twenty-one; 27 the men of Michmas, one hundred and twenty-two; 28 the men of Bethel and Ai, two hundred and twenty-three; 29 the people of Nebo, fifty-two; 30 the people of Magbish, one hundred and fifty-six; 31 the people of the other Elam, one thousand two hundred and fifty-four; 32 the people of Harim, three hundred and twenty; 33 the people of Lod, Hadid, and Ono, seven hundred and twenty-five; 34 the people of Jericho, three hundred and forty-five; 35 the people of Senaah, three thousand six hundred and thirty.

36 The priests: the sons of Jedaiah, of the house of Jeshua, nine hundred and seventy-three; 37 the sons of Immer, one thousand and fifty-two; 38 the sons of Pashhur, one thousand two hundred and forty-seven; 39 the sons of Harim, one thousand and seventeen.

40 The Levites: the sons of Jeshua and Kadmiel, of the sons of Hodaviah,*a* seventy-four.

41 The singers: the sons of Asaph, one hundred and twenty-eight.

42 The sons of the gatekeepers: the sons of Shallum, the sons of Ater, the sons of Talmon, the sons of Akkub, the sons of Hatita, and the sons of Shobai, one hundred and thirty-nine *in* all.

43 The Nethinim: the sons of Ziha, the sons of Hasupha, the sons of Tabbaoth, 44 the sons of Keros, the sons of Siaha,*a* the sons of Padon, 45 the sons of Lebanah, the sons of Hagabah, the sons of Akkub, 46 the sons of Hagab, the sons of Shalmai, the sons of Hanan, 47 the sons

---

2:1 *a*Compare this chapter with Nehemiah 7:6–73.   2:2 *a*Spelled *Mispereth* in Nehemiah 7:7   *b*Spelled *Nehum* in Nehemiah 7:7   2:10 *a*Spelled *Binnui* in Nehemiah 7:15   2:18 *a*Called *Hariph* in Nehemiah 7:24   2:20 *a*Called *Gibeon* in Nehemiah 7:25   2:24 *a*Called *Beth Azmaveth* in Nehemiah 7:28 2:25 *a*Called *Kirjath Jearim* in Nehemiah 7:29   2:40 *a*Spelled *Hodevah* in Nehemiah 7:43   2:44 *a*Spelled *Sia* in Nehemiah 7:47

When life's disappointments come, remember that whenever God says no, it is because He wants what is best for you. He wants that so much that He is willing to see you disappointed today in order to give you His best tomorrow.

of Giddel, the sons of Gahar, the sons of Reaiah, 48 the sons of Rezin, the sons of Nekoda, the sons of Gazzam, 49 the sons of Uzza, the sons of Paseah, the sons of Besai, 50 the sons of Asnah, the sons of Meunim, the sons of Nephusim,*a* 51 the sons of Bakbuk, the sons of Hakupha, the sons of Harhur, 52 the sons of Bazluth,*a* the sons of Mehida, the sons of Harsha, 53 the sons of Barkos, the sons of Sisera, the sons of Tamah, 54 the sons of Neziah, and the sons of Hatipha.

55 The sons of Solomon's servants: the sons of Sotai, the sons of Sophereth, the sons of Peruda,*a* 56 the sons of Jaala, the sons of Darkon, the sons of Giddel, 57 the sons of Shephatiah, the sons of Hattil, the sons of Pochereth of Zebaim, and the sons of Ami.*a* 58 All the Nethinim and the children of Solomon's servants were three hundred and ninety-two.

59 And these *were* the ones who came up from Tel Melah, Tel Harsha, Cherub, Addan,*a* and Immer; but they could not identify their father's house or their genealogy,*b* whether they *were* of Israel: 60 the sons of Delaiah, the sons of Tobiah, and the sons of Nekoda, six hundred and fifty-two; 61 and of the sons of the priests: the sons of Habaiah, the sons of Koz,*a* and the sons of Barzillai, who took a wife of the daughters of Barzillai the Gileadite, and was called by their name. 62 These sought their listing *among* those who were registered by genealogy, but they were not found; therefore they *were* excluded from the priesthood as defiled. 63 And the governor*a* said to them that they should not eat of the most holy things till a priest could consult with the Urim and Thummim.

64 The whole assembly together *was* forty-two thousand three hundred *and* sixty, 65 besides their male and female servants, of whom *there were* seven thousand three hundred and thirty-seven; and they had two hundred men and women singers. 66 Their horses *were* seven hundred and thirty-six, their mules two hundred and forty-five, 67 their camels four hundred and thirty-five, and *their* donkeys six thousand seven hundred and twenty.

68 *Some* of the heads of the fathers' *houses,* when they came to the house of the LORD which *is* in Jerusalem, offered freely for the house of God, to erect it in its place: 69 According to their ability, they gave to the treasury for the work sixty-one thousand gold drachmas, five thousand minas of silver, and one hundred priestly garments.

70 So the priests and the Levites, *some* of the people, the singers, the gatekeepers, and the Nethinim, dwelt in their cities, and all Israel in their cities.

3 And when the seventh month had come, and the children of Israel *were* in the cities, the people gathered together as one man to Jerusalem. 2 Then Jeshua the son of Jozadak*a* and his brethren the priests, and Zerubbabel the son of Shealtiel and his brethren, arose and built the altar of the God of Israel, to offer burnt offerings on it, as *it is* written in the Law of Moses the man of God. 3 Though fear *had come* upon them because of the people of those countries, they set the altar on its bases; and they offered burnt offerings on it to the LORD, *both* the morning and evening burnt offerings. 4 They also kept the Feast of Tabernacles, as *it is* written, and *offered* the daily burnt offerings in the number required by ordinance for each day. 5 Afterwards *they offered* the regular burnt offering, and *those* for New Moons and for all the appointed feasts of the LORD that were consecrated, and *those* of everyone who willingly offered a freewill offering to the LORD. 6 From the first day of the seventh month they began to offer burnt offerings to the LORD, although the foundation of the temple of the LORD had not been laid. 7 They also gave money to the masons and the carpenters, and food, drink, and oil to the people of Sidon and Tyre to bring cedar logs from Lebanon to the sea, to Joppa, according to the permission which they had from Cyrus king of Persia.

2:50 *a*Spelled *Nephishesim* in Nehemiah 7:52   2:52 *a*Spelled *Bazlith* in Nehemiah 7:54   2:55 *a*Spelled *Perida* in Nehemiah 7:57   2:57 *a*Spelled *Amon* in Nehemiah 7:59   2:59 *a*Spelled *Addon* in Nehemiah 7:61   *b*Literally *seed*   2:61 *a*Or *Hakkoz*   2:63 *a*Hebrew *Tirshatha*   3:2 *a*Spelled *Jehozadak* in 1 Chronicles 6:14

Gospel Pearls

8 Now in the second month of the second year of their coming to the house of God at Jerusalem, Zerubbabel the son of Shealtiel, Jeshua the son of Jozadak,*a* and the rest of their brethren the priests and the Levites, and all those who had come out of the captivity to Jerusalem, began *work* and appointed the Levites from twenty years old and above to oversee the work of the house of the LORD. 9 Then Jeshua *with* his sons and brothers, Kadmiel *with* his sons, and the sons of Judah,*a* arose as one to oversee those working on the house of God: the sons of Henadad *with* their sons and their brethren the Levites.

10 When the builders laid the foundation of the temple of the LORD, the priests stood*a* in their apparel with trumpets, and the Levites, the sons of Asaph, with cymbals, to praise the LORD, according to the ordinance of David king of Israel. 11 And they sang responsively, praising and giving thanks to the LORD:

"For *He is* good,
    For His mercy *endures* forever
        toward Israel."*a*

Then all the people shouted with a great shout, when they praised the LORD, because the foundation of the house of the LORD was laid.

12 But many of the priests and Levites and heads of the fathers' *houses,* old men who had seen the first temple, wept with a loud voice when the foundation of this temple was laid before their eyes. Yet many shouted aloud for joy, 13 so that the people could not discern the noise of the shout of joy from the noise of the weeping of the people, for the people shouted with a loud shout, and the sound was heard afar off.

4 Now when the adversaries of Judah and Benjamin heard that the descendants of the captivity were building the temple of the LORD God of Israel, 2 they came to Zerubbabel and the heads of the fathers' *houses,* and said to them, "Let us build with you, for we seek your God as you *do;*

and we have sacrificed to Him since the days of Esarhaddon king of Assyria, who brought us here." 3 But Zerubbabel and Jeshua and the rest of the heads of the fathers' *houses* of Israel said to them, "You may do nothing with us to build a house for our God; but we alone will build to the LORD God of Israel, as King Cyrus the king of Persia has commanded us." 4 Then the people of the land tried to discourage the people of Judah. They troubled them in building, 5 and hired counselors against them to frustrate their purpose all the days of Cyrus king of Persia, even until the reign of Darius king of Persia.

6 In the reign of Ahasuerus, in the beginning of his reign, they wrote an accusation against the inhabitants of Judah and Jerusalem.

7 In the days of Artaxerxes also, Bishlam, Mithredath, Tabel, and the rest of their companions wrote to Artaxerxes king of Persia; and the letter *was* written in Aramaic script, and translated into the Aramaic language. 8 Rehum*a* the commander and Shimshai the scribe wrote a letter against Jerusalem to King Artaxerxes in this fashion:

9   From*a* Rehum the commander,
    Shimshai the scribe, and the
    rest of their companions—
    representatives of the Dinaites,
    the Apharsathchites, the
    Tarpelites, the people of Persia
    and Erech and Babylon and
    Shushan,*b* the Dehavites, the
    Elamites, 10 and the rest of the
    nations whom the great and
    noble Osnapper took captive
    and settled in the cities of
    Samaria and the remainder
    beyond the River*a*—and so
    forth.*b*

11 (This *is* a copy of the letter that they sent him)

    To King Artaxerxes from your
    servants, the men *of the region*
    beyond the River, and so
    forth:*a*

12 Let it be known to the king that
    the Jews who came up from
    you have come to us at

3:8 *a*Spelled *Jehozadak* in 1 Chronicles 6:14   3:9 *a*Or *Hodaviah* (compare 2:40)   3:10 *a*Following Septuagint, Syriac, and Vulgate; Masoretic Text reads *they stationed the priests.*   3:11 *a*Compare Psalm 136:1   4:8 *a*The original language of Ezra 4:8 through 6:18 is Aramaic.   4:9 *a*Literally *Then* *b*Or *Susa*   4:10 *a*That is, the Euphrates   *b*Literally *and now*   4:11 *a*Literally *and now*

---

*O*ut of our own experience we can speak to others who did not have the inner strength or the helpful background to withstand the pain. God wants to use you! Perhaps you can help others to trust when they are disappointed.

Jerusalem, and are building the rebellious and evil city, and are finishing *its* walls and repairing the foundations. 13 Let it now be known to the king that, if this city is built and the walls completed, they will not pay tax, tribute, or custom, and the king's treasury will be diminished. 14 Now because we receive support from the palace, it was not proper for us to see the king's dishonor; therefore we have sent and informed the king, 15 that search may be made in the book of the records of your fathers. And you will find in the book of the records and know that this city *is* a rebellious city, harmful to kings and provinces, and that they have incited sedition within the city in former times, for which cause this city was destroyed.

16 We inform the king that if this city is rebuilt and its walls are completed, the result will be that you will have no dominion beyond the River.

17 The king sent an answer:

To Rehum the commander, *to* Shimshai the scribe, *to* the rest of their companions who dwell in Samaria, and *to* the remainder beyond the River:

Peace, and so forth.*ᵃ*

18 The letter which you sent to us has been clearly read before me. 19 And I gave the command, and a search has been made, and it was found that this city in former times has revolted against kings, and rebellion and sedition have been fostered in it. 20 There have also been mighty kings over Jerusalem, who have ruled over all *the region* beyond the River; and tax, tribute, and custom were paid to them. 21 Now give the command to make these men cease, that this city may not be built until the command is given by me.

22 Take heed now that you do not fail to do this. Why should damage increase to the hurt of the kings?

23 Now when the copy of King Artaxerxes' letter *was* read before Rehum, Shimshai the scribe, and their companions, they went up in haste to Jerusalem against the Jews, and by force of arms made them cease. 24 Thus the work of the house of God which *is* at Jerusalem ceased, and it was discontinued until the second year of the reign of Darius king of Persia.

5 Then the prophet Haggai and Zechariah the son of Iddo, prophets, prophesied to the Jews who *were* in Judah and Jerusalem, in the name of the God of Israel, *who was* over them. 2 So Zerubbabel the son of Shealtiel and Jeshua the son of Jozadak*ᵃ* rose up and began to build the house of God which *is* in Jerusalem; and the prophets of God *were* with them, helping them.

3 At the same time Tattenai the governor of *the region* beyond the River*ᵃ* and Shethar-Boznai and their companions came to them and spoke thus to them: "Who has commanded you to build this temple and finish this wall?" 4 Then, accordingly, we told them the names of the men who were constructing this building. 5 But the eye of their God was upon the elders of the Jews, so that they could not make them cease till a report could go to Darius. Then a written answer was returned concerning this *matter.* 6 This is a copy of the letter that Tattenai sent:

The governor of *the region* beyond the River, and Shethar-Boznai, and his companions, the Persians who *were in the region* beyond the River, to Darius the king.

7 (They sent a letter to him, in which was written thus)

To Darius the king:

All peace.

8 Let it be known to the king that we went into the province of

Gospel Pearls

Judea, to the temple of the great God, which is being built with heavy stones, and timber is being laid in the walls; and this work goes on diligently and prospers in their hands.

9 Then we asked those elders, *and* spoke thus to them: "Who commanded you to build this temple and to finish these walls?" 10 We also asked them their names to inform you, that we might write the names of the men who *were* chief among them.

11 And thus they returned us an answer, saying: "We are the servants of the God of heaven and earth, and we are rebuilding the temple that was built many years ago, which a great king of Israel built and completed. 12 But because our fathers provoked the God of heaven to wrath, He gave them into the hand of Nebuchadnezzar king of Babylon, the Chaldean, *who* destroyed this temple and carried the people away to Babylon. 13 However, in the first year of Cyrus king of Babylon, King Cyrus issued a decree to build this house of God. 14 Also, the gold and silver articles of the house of God, which Nebuchadnezzar had taken from the temple that *was* in Jerusalem and carried into the temple of Babylon— those King Cyrus took from the temple of Babylon, and they were given to one named Sheshbazzar, whom he had made governor. 15 And he said to him, 'Take these articles; go, carry them to the temple *site* that *is* in Jerusalem, and let the house of God be rebuilt on its former site.' 16 Then the same Sheshbazzar came *and* laid the foundation of the house of God which *is* in Jerusalem; but from that time even until now it has been under construction, and it is not finished."

17 Now therefore, if *it seems* good to the king, let a search be made in the king's treasure house, which *is* there in Babylon, whether it is *so* that a decree was issued by King Cyrus to build this house of God at Jerusalem, and let the king send us his pleasure concerning this *matter*.

6 Then King Darius issued a decree, and a search was made in the archives,ᵃ where the treasures were stored in Babylon. 2 And at Achmetha,ᵃ in the palace that *is* in the province of Media, a scroll was found, and in it a record *was* written thus:

3 In the first year of King Cyrus, King Cyrus issued a decree *concerning* the house of God at Jerusalem: "Let the house be rebuilt, the place where they offered sacrifices; and let the foundations of it be firmly laid, its height sixty cubits *and* its width sixty cubits, 4 *with* three rows of heavy stones and one row of new timber. Let the expenses be paid from the king's treasury. 5 Also let the gold and silver articles of the house of God, which Nebuchadnezzar took from the temple which *is* in Jerusalem and brought to Babylon, be restored and taken back to the temple which *is* in Jerusalem, *each* to its place; and deposit *them* in the house of God"—

6 Now *therefore*, Tattenai, governor of *the region* beyond the River, and Shethar-Boznai, and your companions the Persians who *are* beyond the River, keep yourselves far from there. 7 Let the work of this house of God alone; let the governor of the Jews and the elders of the Jews build this house of God on its site.

8 Moreover I issue a decree *as to* what you shall do for the elders of these Jews, for the building of this house of God: Let the cost be paid at the king's expense from taxes *on the*

6:1 ᵃLiterally *house of the scrolls*   6:2 ᵃProbably *Ecbatana,* the ancient capital of Media

God wants to see you blessed. Please don't allow anyone to tell you that being a Christian means you must be poor. God doesn't mind your having money. He minds its having you.

region beyond the River; this is to be given immediately to these men, so that they are not hindered. 9 And whatever they need—young bulls, rams, and lambs for the burnt offerings of the God of heaven, wheat, salt, wine, and oil, according to the request of the priests who *are* in Jerusalem—let it be given them day by day without fail, 10 that they may offer sacrifices of sweet aroma to the God of heaven, and pray for the life of the king and his sons.

11 Also I issue a decree that whoever alters this edict, let a timber be pulled from his house and erected, and let him be hanged on it; and let his house be made a refuse heap because of this. 12 And may the God who causes His name to dwell there destroy any king or people who put their hand to alter it, or to destroy this house of God which is in Jerusalem. I Darius issue a decree; let it be done diligently.

13 Then Tattenai, governor of *the region* beyond the River, Shethar-Boznai, and their companions diligently did according to what King Darius had sent. 14 So the elders of the Jews built, and they prospered through the prophesying of Haggai the prophet and Zechariah the son of Iddo. And they built and finished *it*, according to the commandment of the God of Israel, and according to the command of Cyrus, Darius, and Artaxerxes king of Persia. 15 Now the temple was finished on the third day of the month of Adar, which was in the sixth year of the reign of King Darius. 16 Then the children of Israel, the priests and the Levites and the rest of the descendants of the captivity, celebrated the dedication of this house of God with joy. 17 And they offered sacrifices at the dedication of this house of God, one hundred bulls, two hundred rams, four hundred lambs, and as a sin offering for all Israel twelve male goats, according to the number of the tribes of Israel. 18 They assigned the priests to their divisions and the Levites to their divisions, over the service of God in Jeru-

salem, as it is written in the Book of Moses.

19 And the descendants of the captivity kept the Passover on the fourteenth *day* of the first month. 20 For the priests and the Levites had purified themselves; all of them *were ritually* clean. And they slaughtered the Passover *lambs* for all the descendants of the captivity, for their brethren the priests, and for themselves. 21 Then the children of Israel who had returned from the captivity ate together with all who had separated themselves from the filth of the nations of the land in order to seek the LORD God of Israel. 22 And they kept the Feast of Unleavened Bread seven days with joy; for the LORD made them joyful, and turned the heart of the king of Assyria toward them, to strengthen their hands in the work of the house of God, the God of Israel.

7 Now after these things, in the reign of Artaxerxes king of Persia, Ezra the son of Seraiah, the son of Azariah, the son of Hilkiah, 2 the son of Shallum, the son of Zadok, the son of Ahitub, 3 the son of Amariah, the son of Azariah, the son of Meraioth, 4 the son of Zerahiah, the son of Uzzi, the son of Bukki, 5 the son of Abishua, the son of Phinehas, the son of Eleazar, the son of Aaron the chief priest— 6 this Ezra came up from Babylon; and he *was* a skilled scribe in the Law of Moses, which the LORD God of Israel had given. The king granted him all his request, according to the hand of the LORD his God upon him. 7 *Some* of the children of Israel, the priests, the Levites, the singers, the gatekeepers, and the Nethinim came up to Jerusalem in the seventh year of King Artaxerxes. 8 And Ezra came to Jerusalem in the fifth month, which *was* in the seventh year of the king. 9 On the first *day* of the first month he began *his* journey from Babylon, and on the first *day* of the fifth month he came to Jerusalem, according to the good hand of his God upon him. 10 For Ezra had prepared his heart to seek the Law of the LORD, and to do *it*, and to teach statutes and ordinances in Israel.

11 This *is* a copy of the letter that King Artaxerxes gave Ezra the priest, the scribe, expert in the words

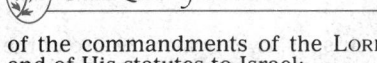

of the commandments of the LORD, and of His statutes to Israel:

12 Artaxerxes,[a] king of kings,

To Ezra the priest, a scribe of the Law of the God of heaven:

Perfect *peace,* and so forth.[b]

13 I issue a decree that all those of the people of Israel and the priests and Levites in my realm, who volunteer to go up to Jerusalem, may go with you. 14 And whereas you are being sent by the king and his seven counselors to inquire concerning Judah and Jerusalem, with regard to the Law of your God which *is* in your hand; 15 and *whereas you are* to carry the silver and gold which the king and his counselors have freely offered to the God of Israel, whose dwelling *is* in Jerusalem; 16 and *whereas* all the silver and gold that you may find in all the province of Babylon, along with the freewill offering of the people and the priests, *are to be* freely offered for the house of their God in Jerusalem— 17 now therefore, be careful to buy with this money bulls, rams, and lambs, with their grain offerings and their drink offerings, and offer them on the altar of the house of your God in Jerusalem.

18 And whatever seems good to you and your brethren to do with the rest of the silver and the gold, do it according to the will of your God. 19 Also the articles that are given to you for the service of the house of your God, deliver in full before the God of Jerusalem. 20 And whatever more may be needed for the house of your God, which you may have occasion to provide, pay *for it* from the king's treasury.

21 And I, *even* I, Artaxerxes the king, issue a decree to all the treasurers who *are* in the region beyond the River, that whatever Ezra the priest, the scribe of the Law of the God of heaven, may require of you, let it be done diligently, 22 up to one hundred talents of silver, one hundred kors of wheat, one hundred baths of wine, one hundred baths of oil, and salt without prescribed limit. 23 Whatever is commanded by the God of heaven, let it diligently be done for the house of the God of heaven. For why should there be wrath against the realm of the king and his sons?

24 Also we inform you that it shall not be lawful to impose tax, tribute, or custom *on* any of the priests, Levites, singers, gatekeepers, Nethinim, or servants of this house of God. 25 And you, Ezra, according to your God-given wisdom, set magistrates and judges who may judge all the people who *are in the region* beyond the River, all such as know the laws of your God; and teach those who do not know *them.* 26 Whoever will not observe the law of your God and the law of the king, let judgment be executed speedily on him, whether *it be* death, or banishment, or confiscation of goods, or imprisonment.

27 Blessed *be* the LORD God of our fathers, who has put *such a thing* as this in the king's heart, to beautify the house of the LORD which *is* in Jerusalem, 28 and has extended mercy to me before the king and his counselors, and before all the king's mighty princes.

So I was encouraged, as the hand of the LORD my God *was* upon me; and I gathered leading men of Israel to go up with me.

8 These *are* the heads of their fathers' *houses,* and *this is* the genealogy of those who went up with me from Babylon, in the reign of King Artaxerxes: 2 of the sons of

---

7:12 [a]The original language of Ezra 7:12–26 is Aramaic.   [b]Literally *and now*

---

*P*overty is a silent prison. Its jailer is despair, and its guards are depression. Flee from it! You are the daughters of a rich man. You are the daughters of God! Don't just dress like the wealthy; secure your future.

Phinehas, Gershom; of the sons of Ithamar, Daniel; of the sons of David, Hattush; 3 of the sons of Shecaniah, of the sons of Parosh, Zechariah; and registered with him *were* one hundred and fifty males; 4 of the sons of Pahath-Moab, Eliehoenai the son of Zerahiah, and with him two hundred males; 5 of the sons of Shechaniah,ᵃ Ben-Jahaziel, and with him three hundred males; 6 of the sons of Adin, Ebed the son of Jonathan, and with him fifty males; 7 of the sons of Elam, Jeshaiah the son of Athaliah, and with him seventy males; 8 of the sons of Shephatiah, Zebadiah the son of Michael, and with him eighty males; 9 of the sons of Joab, Obadiah the son of Jehiel, and with him two hundred and eighteen males; 10 of the sons of Shelomith,ᵃ Ben-Josiphiah, and with him one hundred and sixty males; 11 of the sons of Bebai, Zechariah the son of Bebai, and with him twenty-eight males; 12 of the sons of Azgad, Johanan the son of Hakkatan, and with him one hundred and ten males; 13 of the last sons of Adonikam, whose names *are* these—Eliphelet, Jeiel, and Shemaiah—and with them sixty males; 14 also of the sons of Bigvai, Uthai and Zabbud, and with them seventy males.

15 Now I gathered them by the river that flows to Ahava, and we camped there three days. And I looked among the people and the priests, and found none of the sons of Levi there. 16 Then I sent for Eliezer, Ariel, Shemaiah, Elnathan, Jarib, Elnathan, Nathan, Zechariah, and Meshullam, leaders; also for Joiarib and Elnathan, men of understanding. 17 And I gave them a command for Iddo the chief man at the place Casiphia, and I told them what they should say to Iddo *and* his brethrenᵃ the Nethinim at the place Casiphia—that they should bring us servants for the house of our God. 18 Then, by the good hand of our God upon us, they brought us a man of understanding, of the sons of Mahli the son of Levi, the son of Israel, namely Sherebiah, with his sons and brothers, eighteen men; 19 and Hashabiah, and with him Jeshaiah of the sons of Merari, his brothers and

their sons, twenty men; 20 also of the Nethinim, whom David and the leaders had appointed for the service of the Levites, two hundred and twenty Nethinim. All of them were designated by name.

21 Then I proclaimed a fast there at the river of Ahava, that we might humble ourselves before our God, to seek from Him the right way for us and our little ones and all our possessions. 22 For I was ashamed to request of the king an escort of soldiers and horsemen to help us against the enemy on the road, because we had spoken to the king, saying, "The hand of our God *is* upon all those for good who seek Him, but His power and His wrath *are* against all those who forsake Him." 23 So we fasted and entreated our God for this, and He answered our prayer.

24 And I separated twelve of the leaders of the priests—Sherebiah, Hashabiah, and ten of their brethren with them— 25 and weighed out to them the silver, the gold, and the articles, the offering for the house of our God which the king and his counselors and his princes, and all Israel *who were* present, had offered. 26 I weighed into their hand six hundred and fifty talents of silver, silver articles *weighing* one hundred talents, one hundred talents of gold, 27 twenty gold basins *worth* a thousand drachmas, and two vessels of fine polished bronze, precious as gold. 28 And I said to them, "You *are* holy to the Lᴏʀᴅ; the articles *are* holy also; and the silver and the gold *are* a freewill offering to the Lᴏʀᴅ God of your fathers. 29 Watch and keep *them* until you weigh *them* before the leaders of the priests and the Levites and heads of the fathers' *houses* of Israel in Jerusalem, *in* the chambers of the house of the Lᴏʀᴅ." 30 So the priests and the Levites received the silver and the gold and the articles by weight, to bring *them* to Jerusalem to the house of our God.

31 Then we departed from the river of Ahava on the twelfth *day* of the first month, to go to Jerusalem. And the hand of our God was upon us, and He delivered us from the hand of the enemy and from ambush along

---

8:5 ᵃFollowing Masoretic Text and Vulgate; Septuagint reads *the sons of Zatho, Shechaniah.*
8:10 ᵃFollowing Masoretic Text and Vulgate; Septuagint reads *the sons of Banni, Shelomith.*
8:17 ᵃFollowing Vulgate; Masoretic Text reads *to Iddo his brother;* Septuagint reads *to their brethren.*

Gospel Pearls

the road. 32 So we came to Jerusalem, and stayed there three days.

33 Now on the fourth day the silver and the gold and the articles were weighed in the house of our God by the hand of Meremoth the son of Uriah the priest, and with him *was* Eleazar the son of Phinehas; with them *were* the Levites, Jozabad the son of Jeshua and Noadiah the son of Binnui, 34 with the number *and* weight of everything. All the weight was written down at that time.

35 The children of those who had been carried away captive, who had come from the captivity, offered burnt offerings to the God of Israel: twelve bulls for all Israel, ninety-six rams, seventy-seven lambs, and twelve male goats *as* a sin offering. All *this was* a burnt offering to the LORD.

36 And they delivered the king's orders to the king's satraps and the governors *in the region* beyond the River. So they gave support to the people and the house of God.

9 When these things were done, the leaders came to me, saying, "The people of Israel and the priests and the Levites have not separated themselves from the peoples of the lands, with respect to the abominations of the Canaanites, the Hittites, the Perizzites, the Jebusites, the Ammonites, the Moabites, the Egyptians, and the Amorites. 2 For they have taken some of their daughters *as wives* for themselves and their sons, so that the holy seed is mixed with the peoples of *those* lands. Indeed, the hand of the leaders and rulers has been foremost in this trespass." 3 So when I heard this thing, I tore my garment and my robe, and plucked out some of the hair of my head and beard, and sat down astonished. 4 Then everyone who trembled at the words of the God of Israel assembled to me, because of the transgression of those who had been carried away captive, and I sat astonished until the evening sacrifice.

5 At the evening sacrifice I arose from my fasting; and having torn my garment and my robe, I fell on my knees and spread out my hands to the LORD my God. 6 And I said: "O my God, I am too ashamed and humiliated to lift up my face to You, my God; for our iniquities have risen

higher than *our* heads, and our guilt has grown up to the heavens. 7 Since the days of our fathers to this day we *have been* very guilty, and for our iniquities we, our kings, *and* our priests have been delivered into the hand of the kings of the lands, to the sword, to captivity, to plunder, and to humiliation, as *it is* this day. 8 And now for a little while grace has been *shown* from the LORD our God, to leave us a remnant to escape, and to give us a peg in His holy place, that our God may enlighten our eyes and give us a measure of revival in our bondage. 9 For we *were* slaves. Yet our God did not forsake us in our bondage; but He extended mercy to us in the sight of the kings of Persia, to revive us, to repair the house of our God, to rebuild its ruins, and to give us a wall in Judah and Jerusalem. 10 And now, O our God, what shall we say after this? For we have forsaken Your commandments, 11 which You commanded by Your servants the prophets, saying, 'The land which you are entering to possess is an unclean land, with the uncleanness of the peoples of the lands, with their abominations which have filled it from one end to another with their impurity. 12 Now therefore, do not give your daughters as wives for their sons, nor take their daughters to your sons; and never seek their peace or prosperity, that you may be strong and eat the good of the land, and leave *it* as an inheritance to your children forever.' 13 And after all that has come upon us for our evil deeds and for our great guilt, since You our God have punished us less than our iniquities *deserve,* and have given us *such* deliverance as this, 14 should we again break Your commandments, and join in marriage with the people *committing* these abominations? Would You not be angry with us until You had consumed *us,* so that *there would be* no remnant or survivor? 15 O LORD God of Israel, You *are* righteous, for we are left as a remnant, as *it is* this day. Here we *are* before You, in our guilt, though no one can stand before You because of this!"

10 Now while Ezra was praying, and while he was confessing, weeping, and bowing down before the house of God, a very large assembly of men, women, and children

---

God is raising up women who can be decisive and effective in a board room and still be feminine and sensitive in the bedroom! You can have a career, goals and aspirations and still be a good mother or a good wife.

gathered to him from Israel; for the people wept very bitterly. 2 And Shechaniah the son of Jehiel, *one* of the sons of Elam, spoke up and said to Ezra, "We have trespassed against our God, and have taken pagan wives from the peoples of the land; yet now there is hope in Israel in spite of this. 3 Now therefore, let us make a covenant with our God to put away all these wives and those who have been born to them, according to the advice of my master and of those who tremble at the commandment of our God; and let it be done according to the law. 4 Arise, for *this* matter *is* your *responsibility*. We also *are* with you. Be of good courage, and do *it*."

5 Then Ezra arose, and made the leaders of the priests, the Levites, and all Israel swear an oath that they would do according to this word. So they swore an oath. 6 Then Ezra rose up from before the house of God, and went into the chamber of Jehohanan the son of Eliashib; and *when* he came there, he ate no bread and drank no water, for he mourned because of the guilt of those from the captivity.

7 And they issued a proclamation throughout Judah and Jerusalem to all the descendants of the captivity, that they must gather at Jerusalem, 8 and that whoever would not come within three days, according to the instructions of the leaders and elders, all his property would be confiscated, and he himself would be separated from the assembly of those from the captivity.

9 So all the men of Judah and Benjamin gathered at Jerusalem within three days. It *was* the ninth month, on the twentieth of the month; and all the people sat in the open square of the house of God, trembling because of *this* matter and because of heavy rain. 10 Then Ezra the priest stood up and said to them, "You have transgressed and have taken pagan wives, adding to the guilt of Israel. 11 Now therefore, make confession to the LORD God of your fathers, and do His will; separate yourselves from the peoples of the land, and from the pagan wives."

12 Then all the assembly answered and said with a loud voice, "Yes! As you have said, so we must do.

13 But *there are* many people; *it is* the season for heavy rain, and we are not able to stand outside. Nor *is this* the work of one or two days, for *there are* many of us who have transgressed in this matter. 14 Please, let the leaders of our entire assembly stand; and let all those in our cities who have taken pagan wives come at appointed times, together with the elders and judges of their cities, until the fierce wrath of our God is turned away from us in this matter." 15 Only Jonathan the son of Asahel and Jahaziah the son of Tikvah opposed this, and Meshullam and Shabbethai the Levite gave them support.

16 Then the descendants of the captivity did so. And Ezra the priest, *with* certain heads of the fathers' *households*, were set apart by the fathers' *households*, each of them by name; and they sat down on the first day of the tenth month to examine the matter. 17 By the first day of the first month they finished *questioning* all the men who had taken pagan wives.

18 And among the sons of the priests who had taken pagan wives *the following* were found of the sons of Jeshua the son of Jozadak,*a* and his brothers: Maaseiah, Eliezer, Jarib, and Gedaliah. 19 And they gave their promise that they would put away their wives; and *being* guilty, *they presented* a ram of the flock as their trespass offering.

20 Also of the sons of Immer: Hanani and Zebadiah; 21 of the sons of Harim: Maaseiah, Elijah, Shemaiah, Jehiel, and Uzziah; 22 of the sons of Pashhur: Elioenai, Maaseiah, Ishmael, Nethanel, Jozabad, and Elasah.

23 Also of the Levites: Jozabad, Shimei, Kelaiah (the same *is* Kelita), Pethahiah, Judah, and Eliezer.

24 Also of the singers: Eliashib; and of the gatekeepers: Shallum, Telem, and Uri.

25 And others of Israel: of the sons of Parosh: Ramiah, Jeziah, Malchiah, Mijamin, Eleazar, Malchijah, and Benaiah; 26 of the sons of Elam: Mattaniah, Zechariah, Jehiel, Abdi, Jeremoth, and Eliah; 27 of the sons of Zattu: Elioenai, Eliashib, Mattaniah, Jeremoth, Zabad, and Aziza;

10:18 *a*Spelled *Jehozadak* in 1 Chronicles 6:14

*I*t is God's mercy, and God's plan, to bring people into our lives who are strong in areas where we are weak, and people who are weak in areas where we are strong. That way we can help one another and bring balance to the body of Christ.

Cut the Cord

Ezra 10:11

So often I want to tell women, "Go out and buy yourself a pair of scissors and write on the blades, 'Cut the cord!'" Maybe that would remind them to disassociate themselves from their past. There are things you need to cut away from your life. There are relationships you need to sever. There are habits you need to amputate from your daily routine. Don't allow a guilt trip from the past to strangle you or cling to you or trip you up. Go ahead. Cut the cord!

God wants to free you from cords of manipulation, cords of blackmail, cords of emotional slavery, cords of bondage to someone who seeks to control your life. Cut the cords that tie you to the old mud holes of your life. Let me explain it this way. If a little lamb and a pig fall into the same dirty, oozing mud hole, the pig will wallow in the mud, but the lamb will cry to get out. If you are a child of God and fall into the mud, you'll start to cry, "I don't like this. I want out of this. I'm not really like this. I hate this! Help me!" It's time to cut the cords that tie you to the old mud holes of your life.

Whether you fall into the mud or someone throws you into the mud is not the issue. What you do when you are in the mud is what matters. Realize that there is something in your nature that defies your environment. There *is* something inside of you that is willing and able to cut the cord. Say good-bye to Joe's Bar and Ruby's Lounge. Say good-bye to the pimp and the pusher. Say good-bye to the drinking girls and the gambling friends. Put that addiction, that abortion, that sickness, that divorce, that failure, that loss behind you.

Pronounce your own benediction on your former life. Administer your own last rites to your failures. Conduct your own funeral for the "old person" you were before you were saved. Declare that the old you—the one who existed before God found you, lifted you out of the mud, and cleaned you up—is dead. Declare that the old sinful patterns of your life and the old sin-producing relationships are gone. Declare any dominating evil spirit evicted from your life. Declare that you are a new creature in Christ Jesus. The old you has died and has been buried. The new you is being resurrected!

As you cut the cord, get ready for a new enthusiasm, a new outpouring of faith, a new freshness of anointing. God will release you to live in freedom.

28 of the sons of Bebai: Jehohanan, Hananiah, Zabbai, and Athlai; 29 of the sons of Bani: Meshullam, Malluch, Adaiah, Jashub, Sheal, and Ramoth;ᵃ 30 of the sons of Pahath-Moab: Adna, Chelal, Benaiah, Maaseiah, Mattaniah, Bezalel, Binnui, and Manasseh; 31 of the sons of Harim: Eliezer, Ishijah, Malchijah, Shemaiah, Shimeon, 32 Benjamin, Malluch, and Shemariah; 33 of the sons of Hashum: Mattenai, Mattattah, Zabad, Eliphelet, Jeremai, Manasseh, and Shimei; 34 of the sons of Bani: Maadai, Amram, Uel, 35 Benaiah, Bedeiah, Cheluh,ᵃ 36 Vaniah, Meremoth, Eliashib, 37 Mattaniah, Mattenai, Jaasai,ᵃ 38 Bani, Binnui, Shimei, 39 Shelemiah, Nathan, Adaiah, 40 Machnadebai, Shashai, Sharai, 41 Azarel, Shelemiah, Shemariah, 42 Shallum, Amariah, and Joseph; 43 of the sons of Nebo: Jeiel, Mattithiah, Zabad, Zebina, Jaddai,ᵃ Joel, and Benaiah.

44 All these had taken pagan wives, and some of them had wives by whom they had children.

10:29 ᵃOr Jeremoth　　10:35 ᵃOr Cheluhi, or Cheluhu　　10:37 ᵃOr Jaasu　　10:43 ᵃOr Jaddu

The Book of

NEHEMIAH

1 The words of Nehemiah the son of Hachaliah.

It came to pass in the month of Chislev, in the twentieth year, as I was in Shushanᵃ the citadel, 2 that Hanani one of my brethren came with men from Judah; and I asked them concerning the Jews who had escaped, who had survived the captivity, and concerning Jerusalem. 3 And they said to me, "The survivors who are left from the captivity in the province are there in great distress and reproach. The wall of Jerusalem is also broken down, and its gates are burned with fire."

4 So it was, when I heard these words, that I sat down and wept, and mourned for many days; I was fasting and praying before the God of heaven.

5 And I said: "I pray, LORD God of heaven, O great and awesome God, You who keep Your covenant and mercy with those who love Youᵃ and observe Yourᵇ commandments, 6 please let Your ear be attentive and Your eyes open, that You may hear the prayer of Your servant which I pray before You now, day and night, for the children of Israel Your servants, and confess the sins of the children of Israel which we have sinned against You. Both my father's house and I have sinned. 7 We have acted very corruptly against You, and have not kept the commandments, the statutes, nor the ordinances which You commanded Your servant Moses. 8 Remember, I pray, the word that You commanded Your servant Moses, saying, 'If you are unfaithful, I will scatter you among the nations;ᵃ 9 but if you return to Me, and keep My commandments and do them, though some of you were cast out to the farthest part of the heavens, yet I will gather them from there, and bring them to the place which I have chosen as a dwelling for My name.'ᵃ 10 Now these are Your servants and Your people, whom You have redeemed by Your great power, and by Your strong hand. 11 O Lord, I pray, please let Your ear be attentive to the prayer of Your servant, and to the prayer of Your servants who desire to fear Your name; and let Your servant prosper this day, I pray, and grant him mercy in the sight of this man."

For I was the king's cupbearer.

1:1 ᵃOr Susa　　1:5 ᵃLiterally Him　ᵇLiterally His　　1:8 ᵃLeviticus 26:33　　1:9 ᵃDeuteronomy 30:2–5

*Y*ou can never receive anything without being a person who knows how to ask. That means you can't sit there and stew until you are hysterical. If you alienate the one you have to ask, you have disassociated yourself from the solution, and you are left with the problem.

Naked Prayer

Nehemiah 1:4

*I*n the Word of God, we occasionally read about a place of naked prayer. People who pray in this way have been stripped of their self-consciousness, their concern about the opinions of others, and their pride. Hannah was a woman who prayed like this. When she came to the temple and poured out all her locked-up bitterness, she appeared drunk (see 1 Samuel 1:12–18). Even the priest did not recognize this kind of consuming, passionate prayer.

God is raising up some men and women who will blow the minds of the most religious people! Radical Christians—those who have nothing to lose—are coming to the forefront. Like Christ, they have been laid bare on the cross and are speaking the truth under the threat of nails and spears.

When your options run out, your faith will grow. Think about it. Who needs faith for water when you can turn on a faucet? Who needs faith for the parting of the sea when there are bridges standing strong? Faith is reserved for those times when there are no alternatives, when you must look to the Invisible to do the impossible!

Your crisis is a privilege God has given you to experience a deeper realm of miracle-working power. Get up and start shouting! You have been chosen for a miracle. Faith must have the incubator of impossibility to grow. Don't panic. This trouble is just a test—a test with a reward. So don't stop short of the prize. The greater the conflict, the greater the conquest.

Lay aside every sin that could trip you up. Forgive everyone who ever hurt you or disappointed you. Slip the spirit of heaviness from your shoulders—the old depression that is weighing you down. When you are stripped down to nothing but prayer, let your request be made known to God.

You may have to walk the floor and pray. You may have to confess some issues you have not wanted to confront. You may have to forgive someone who wasn't even courteous enough to ask for forgiveness. Do it anyway. Considering what God has done for you, you can't afford any barriers to prayer.

Let the cool waters of His Word rinse the residue from your past. Spread before Him every issue; He can't cleanse what you will not expose. Bathe your mind in the streams of His mercy. This kind of bathing is as holy as a christening and as refreshing as a shower. It brings the renewal that can only occur in the heart of a woman who has been through enough to open her heart, to board up her past, and to stand in the rain of His grace. The only way you can dress up for God is to undress. Present yourself as a living sacrifice offered on the altar in naked prayer.

2 And it came to pass in the month of Nisan, in the twentieth year of King Artaxerxes, *when* wine *was* before him, that I took the wine and gave it to the king. Now I had never been sad in his presence before. 2 Therefore the king said to me, "Why *is* your face sad, since you *are* not sick? This *is* nothing but sorrow of heart."

So I became dreadfully afraid, 3 and said to the king, "May the king live forever! Why should my face not be sad, when the city, the place of my fathers' tombs, *lies* waste, and its gates are burned with fire?"

4 Then the king said to me, "What do you request?"

So I prayed to the God of heaven. 5 And I said to the king, "If it pleases the king, and if your servant has found favor in your sight, I ask that you send me to Judah, to the city of my fathers' tombs, that I may rebuild it."

6 Then the king said to me (the queen also sitting beside him), "How long will your journey be? And when will you return?" So it pleased the king to send me; and I set him a time.

7 Furthermore I said to the king, "If it pleases the king, let letters be given to me for the governors *of the region* beyond the River,*a* that they must permit me to pass through till I come to Judah, 8 and a letter to Asaph the keeper of the king's forest, that he must give me timber to make beams for the gates of the citadel which *pertains*a* to the temple,*a* for the city wall, and for the house that I will occupy." And the king granted *them* to me according to the good hand of my God upon me.

9 Then I went to the governors *in the region* beyond the River, and gave them the king's letters. Now the king had sent captains of the army and horsemen with me. 10 When Sanballat the Horonite and Tobiah the Ammonite official*a* heard *of it*, they were deeply disturbed that a man had come to seek the well-being of the children of Israel.

11 So I came to Jerusalem and was there three days. 12 Then I arose in the night, I and a few men with me; I told no one what my God had put in my heart to do at Jerusalem; nor was there any animal with me, except the one on which I rode. 13 And I went out by night through the Valley Gate to the Serpent Well and the Refuse Gate, and viewed the walls of Jerusalem which were broken down and its gates which were burned with fire. 14 Then I went on to the Fountain Gate and to the King's Pool, but *there was* no room for the animal under me to pass. 15 So I went up in the night by the valley, and viewed the wall; then I turned back and entered by the Valley Gate, and so returned. 16 And the officials did not know where I had gone or what I had done; I had not yet told the Jews, the priests, the nobles, the officials, or the others who did the work.

17 Then I said to them, "You see the distress that we *are* in, how Jerusalem *lies* waste, and its gates are burned with fire. Come and let us build the wall of Jerusalem, that we may no longer be a reproach." 18 And I told them of the hand of my God which had been good upon me, and also of the king's words that he had spoken to me.

So they said, "Let us rise up and build." Then they set their hands to *this* good *work*.

19 But when Sanballat the Horonite, Tobiah the Ammonite official, and Geshem the Arab heard *of it*, they laughed at us and despised us, and said, "What *is* this thing that you are doing? Will you rebel against the king?"

20 So I answered them, and said to them, "The God of heaven Himself will prosper us; therefore we His servants will arise and build, but you have no heritage or right or memorial in Jerusalem."

3 Then Eliashib the high priest rose up with his brethren the priests and built the Sheep Gate; they consecrated it and hung its doors. They built as far as the Tower of the Hundred,*a and* consecrated it, then as far as the Tower of Hananel. 2 Next to *Eliashib*a* the men of Jericho built. And next to them Zaccur the son of Imri built.

3 Also the sons of Hassenaah built the Fish Gate; they laid its beams and

2:7 *a*That is, the Euphrates, and so elsewhere in this book   2:8 *a*Literally *house*   2:10 *a*Literally *servant,* and so elsewhere in this book   3:1 *a*Hebrew *Hammeah,* also at 12:39   3:2 *a*Literally *On his hand*

Gospel Pearls

hung its doors with its bolts and bars. 4 And next to them Meremoth the son of Urijah, the son of Koz,[a] made repairs. Next to them Meshullam the son of Berechiah, the son of Meshezabel, made repairs. Next to them Zadok the son of Baana made repairs. 5 Next to them the Tekoites made repairs; but their nobles did not put their shoulders[a] to the work of their Lord.

6 Moreover Jehoiada the son of Paseah and Meshullam the son of Besodeiah repaired the Old Gate; they laid its beams and hung its doors, with its bolts and bars. 7 And next to them Melatiah the Gibeonite, Jadon the Meronothite, the men of Gibeon and Mizpah, repaired the residence[a] of the governor *of the region* beyond the River. 8 Next to him Uzziel the son of Harhaiah, one of the goldsmiths, made repairs. Also next to him Hananiah, one[a] of the perfumers, made repairs; and they fortified Jerusalem as far as the Broad Wall. 9 And next to them Rephaiah the son of Hur, leader of half the district of Jerusalem, made repairs. 10 Next to them Jedaiah the son of Harumaph made repairs in front of his house. And next to him Hattush the son of Hashabniah made repairs.

11 Malchijah the son of Harim and Hashub the son of Pahath-Moab repaired another section, as well as the Tower of the Ovens. 12 And next to him was Shallum the son of Hallohesh, leader of half the district of Jerusalem; he and his daughters made repairs.

13 Hanun and the inhabitants of Zanoah repaired the Valley Gate. They built it, hung its doors with its bolts and bars, and *repaired* a thousand cubits of the wall as far as the Refuse Gate.

14 Malchijah the son of Rechab, leader of the district of Beth Haccerem, repaired the Refuse Gate; he built it and hung its doors with its bolts and bars.

15 Shallun the son of Col-Hozeh, leader of the district of Mizpah, repaired the Fountain Gate; he built it, covered it, hung its doors with its bolts and bars, and repaired the wall of the Pool of Shelah by the King's Garden, as far as the stairs that go down from the City of David. 16 After him Nehemiah the son of Azbuk, leader of half the district of Beth Zur, made repairs as far as *the place* in front of the tombs[a] of David, to the man-made pool, and as far as House of the Mighty.

17 After him the Levites, *under* Rehum the son of Bani, made repairs. Next to him Hashabiah, leader of half the district of Keilah, made repairs for his district. 18 After him their brethren, *under* Bavai[a] the son of Henadad, leader of the *other* half of the district of Keilah, made repairs. 19 And next to him Ezer the son of Jeshua, the leader of Mizpah, repaired another section in front of the Ascent to the Armory at the buttress. 20 After him Baruch the son of Zabbai[a] carefully repaired the other section, from the buttress to the door of the house of Eliashib the high priest. 21 After him Meremoth the son of Urijah, the son of Koz,[a] repaired another section, from the door of the house of Eliashib to the end of the house of Eliashib.

22 And after him the priests, the men of the plain, made repairs. 23 After him Benjamin and Hasshub made repairs opposite their house. After them Azariah the son of Maaseiah, the son of Ananiah, made repairs by his house. 24 After him Binnui the son of Henadad repaired another section, from the house of Azariah to the buttress, even as far as the corner. 25 Palal the son of Uzai *made repairs* opposite the buttress, and on the tower which projects from the king's upper house that *was* by the court of the prison. After him Pedaiah the son of Parosh *made repairs.*

26 Moreover the Nethinim who dwelt in Ophel *made repairs* as far as *the place* in front of the Water Gate toward the east, and on the projecting tower. 27 After them the Tekoites repaired another section, next to the great projecting tower, and as far as the wall of Ophel.

28 Beyond the Horse Gate the

3:4 [a]Or *Hakkoz*   3:5 [a]Literally *necks*   3:7 [a]Literally *throne*   3:8 [a]Literally *the son*
3:16 [a]Septuagint, Syriac, and Vulgate read *tomb.*   3:18 [a]Following Masoretic Text and Vulgate; some Hebrew manuscripts, Septuagint, and Syriac read *Binnui* (compare verse 24).   3:20 [a]A few Hebrew manuscripts, Syriac, and Vulgate read *Zaccai.*   3:21 [a]Or *Hakkoz*

---

*W*hen all is said and done, you are a significant part of the pulse beat of God's divine purpose in the earth. Maintain your focus and whatever you do . . . keep moving!

priests made repairs, each in front of his *own* house. 29 After them Zadok the son of Immer made repairs in front of his *own* house. After him Shemaiah the son of Shechaniah, the keeper of the East Gate, made repairs. 30 After him Hananiah the son of Shelemiah, and Hanun, the sixth son of Zalaph, repaired another section. After him Meshullam the son of Berechiah made repairs in front of his dwelling. 31 After him Malchijah, one of the goldsmiths, made repairs as far as the house of the Nethinim and of the merchants, in front of the Miphkad*ᵃ* Gate, and as far as the upper room at the corner. 32 And between the upper room at the corner, as far as the Sheep Gate, the goldsmiths and the merchants made repairs.

4 But it so happened, when Sanballat heard that we were rebuilding the wall, that he was furious and very indignant, and mocked the Jews. 2 And he spoke before his brethren and the army of Samaria, and said, "What are these feeble Jews doing? Will they fortify themselves? Will they offer sacrifices? Will they complete it in a day? Will they revive the stones from the heaps of rubbish— *stones* that are burned?"

3 Now Tobiah the Ammonite *was* beside him, and he said, "Whatever they build, if even a fox goes up *on it,* he will break down their stone wall."

4 Hear, O our God, for we are despised; turn their reproach on their own heads, and give them as plunder to a land of captivity! 5 Do not cover their iniquity, and do not let their sin be blotted out from before You; for they have provoked *You* to anger before the builders.

6 So we built the wall, and the entire wall was joined together up to half its *height,* for the people had a mind to work.

7 Now it happened, when Sanballat, Tobiah, the Arabs, the Ammonites, and the Ashdodites heard that the walls of Jerusalem were being restored and the gaps were beginning to be closed, that they became very angry, 8 and all of them conspired together to come *and* attack Jerusalem and create confusion. 9 Nevertheless we made our prayer to our God, and because of them we set a watch against them day and night.

10 Then Judah said, "The strength of the laborers is failing, and *there is* so much rubbish that we are not able to build the wall."

11 And our adversaries said, "They will neither know nor see anything, till we come into their midst and kill them and cause the work to cease."

12 So it was, when the Jews who dwelt near them came, that they told us ten times, "From whatever place you turn, *they will be* upon us."

13 Therefore I positioned *men* behind the lower parts of the wall, at the openings; and I set the people according to their families, with their swords, their spears, and their bows. 14 And I looked, and arose and said to the nobles, to the leaders, and to the rest of the people, "Do not be afraid of them. Remember the Lord, great and awesome, and fight for your brethren, your sons, your daughters, your wives, and your houses."

15 And it happened, when our enemies heard that it was known to us, and *that* God had brought their plot to nothing, that all of us returned to the wall, everyone to his work. 16 So it was, from that time on, *that* half of my servants worked at construction, while the other half held the spears, the shields, the bows, and *wore* armor; and the leaders *were* behind all the house of Judah. 17 Those who built on the wall, and those who carried burdens, loaded themselves so that with one hand they worked at construction, and with the other held a weapon. 18 Every one of the builders had his sword girded at his side as he built. And the one who sounded the trumpet *was* beside me.

19 Then I said to the nobles, the rulers, and the rest of the people, "The work *is* great and extensive, and we are separated far from one another on the wall. 20 Wherever you hear the sound of the trumpet, rally to us there. Our God will fight for us."

21 So we labored in the work, and half of *the men*ᵃ held the spears from daybreak until the stars appeared. 22 At the same time I also said to the people, "Let each man and his ser-

---

3:31 *ᵃLiterally Inspection* or *Recruiting*   4:21 *ᵃLiterally them*

Gospel Pearls

vant stay at night in Jerusalem, that they may be our guard by night and a working party by day." 23 So neither I, my brethren, my servants, nor the men of the guard who followed me took off our clothes, *except* that everyone took them off for washing.

5 And there was a great outcry of the people and their wives against their Jewish brethren. 2 For there were those who said, "We, our sons, and our daughters *are* many; therefore let us get grain, that we may eat and live."

3 There were also *some* who said, "We have mortgaged our lands and vineyards and houses, that we might buy grain because of the famine."

4 There were also those who said, "We have borrowed money for the king's tax *on* our lands and vineyards. 5 Yet now our flesh *is* as the flesh of our brethren, our children as their children; and indeed we are forcing our sons and our daughters to be slaves, and *some* of our daughters have been brought into slavery. *It is* not in our power *to redeem them,* for other men have our lands and vineyards."

6 And I became very angry when I heard their outcry and these words. 7 After serious thought, I rebuked the nobles and rulers, and said to them, "Each of you is exacting usury from his brother." So I called a great assembly against them. 8 And I said to them, "According to our ability we have redeemed our Jewish brethren who were sold to the nations. Now indeed, will you even sell your brethren? Or should they be sold to us?" Then they were silenced and found nothing *to say.* 9 Then I said, "What you are doing *is* not good. Should you not walk in the fear of our God because of the reproach of the nations, our enemies? 10 I also, *with* my brethren and my servants, am lending them money and grain. Please, let us stop this usury! 11 Restore now to them, even this day, their lands, their vineyards, their olive groves, and their houses, also a hundredth of the money and the grain, the new wine and the oil, that you have charged them."

12 So they said, "We will restore *it,*

and will require nothing from them; we will do as you say."

Then I called the priests, and required an oath from them that they would do according to this promise. 13 Then I shook out the fold of my garment[a] and said, "So may God shake out each man from his house, and from his property, who does not perform this promise. Even thus may he be shaken out and emptied."

And all the assembly said, "Amen!" and praised the LORD. Then the people did according to this promise.

14 Moreover, from the time that I was appointed to be their governor in the land of Judah, from the twentieth year until the thirty-second year of King Artaxerxes, twelve years, neither I nor my brothers ate the governor's provisions. 15 But the former governors who *were* before me laid burdens on the people, and took from them bread and wine, besides forty shekels of silver. Yes, even their servants bore rule over the people, but I did not do so, because of the fear of God. 16 Indeed, I also continued the work on this wall, and we[a] did not buy any land. All my servants *were* gathered there for the work.

17 And at my table *were* one hundred and fifty Jews and rulers, besides those who came to us from the nations around us. 18 Now *that* which was prepared daily *was* one ox *and* six choice sheep. Also fowl were prepared for me, and once every ten days an abundance of all kinds of wine. Yet in spite of this I did not demand the governor's provisions, because the bondage was heavy on this people.

19 Remember me, my God, for good, *according to* all that I have done for this people.

6 Now it happened when Sanballat, Tobiah, Geshem the Arab, and the rest of our enemies heard that I had rebuilt the wall, and *that* there were no breaks left in it (though at that time I had not hung the doors in the gates), 2 that Sanballat and Geshem sent to me, saying, "Come, let us meet together among the villages in the plain of Ono." But they thought to do me harm.

3 So I sent messengers to them,

5:13 [a]Literally *my lap*   5:16 [a]Following Masoretic Text; Septuagint, Syriac, and Vulgate read *I.*

If we have been truly born again, our essence—what I call our "is-ness"—has been changed. We have been given an incorruptible nature in our spirit and we are forever changed.

saying, "I *am* doing a great work, so that I cannot come down. Why should the work cease while I leave it and go down to you?"

4 But they sent me this message four times, and I answered them in the same manner.

5 Then Sanballat sent his servant to me as before, the fifth time, with an open letter in his hand. 6 In it *was* written:

> It is reported among the nations, and Geshem[a] says, *that* you and the Jews plan to rebel; therefore, according to these rumors, you are rebuilding the wall, that you may be their king. 7 And you have also appointed prophets to proclaim concerning you at Jerusalem, saying, "*There is* a king in Judah!" Now these matters will be reported to the king. So come, therefore, and let us consult together.

8 Then I sent to him, saying, "No such things as you say are being done, but you invent them in your own heart."

9 For they all *were trying to* make us afraid, saying, "Their hands will be weakened in the work, and it will not be done."

Now therefore, *O God,* strengthen my hands.

10 Afterward I came to the house of Shemaiah the son of Delaiah, the son of Mehetabel, who *was* a secret informer; and he said, "Let us meet together in the house of God, within the temple, and let us close the doors of the temple, for they are coming to kill you; indeed, at night they will come to kill you."

11 And I said, "Should such a man as I flee? And who *is there* such as I who would go into the temple to save his life? I will not go in!" 12 Then I perceived that God had not sent him at all, but that he pronounced *this* prophecy against me because Tobiah and Sanballat had hired him. 13 For this reason he *was* hired, that I should be afraid and act that way and sin, so *that* they might have *cause* for an evil report, that they might reproach me.

14 My God, remember Tobiah and Sanballat, according to these their works, and the prophetess Noadiah and the rest of the prophets who would have made me afraid.

15 So the wall was finished on the twenty-fifth *day* of Elul, in fifty-two days. 16 And it happened, when all our enemies heard *of it,* and all the nations around us saw *these things,* that they were very disheartened in their own eyes; for they perceived that this work was done by our God.

17 Also in those days the nobles of Judah sent many letters to Tobiah, and *the letters of* Tobiah came to them. 18 For many in Judah were pledged to him, because he was the son-in-law of Shechaniah the son of Arah, and his son Jehohanan had married the daughter of Meshullam the son of Berechiah. 19 Also they reported his good deeds before me, and reported my words to him. Tobiah sent letters to frighten me.

7 Then it was, when the wall was built and I had hung the doors, when the gatekeepers, the singers, and the Levites had been appointed, 2 that I gave the charge of Jerusalem to my brother Hanani, and Hananiah the leader of the citadel, for he *was* a faithful man and feared God more than many.

3 And I said to them, "Do not let the gates of Jerusalem be opened until the sun is hot; and while they stand *guard,* let them shut and bar the doors; and appoint guards from among the inhabitants of Jerusalem, one at his watch station and another in front of his own house."

4 Now the city *was* large and spacious, but the people in it *were* few, and the houses *were* not rebuilt. 5 Then my God put it into my heart to gather the nobles, the rulers, and the people, that they might be registered by genealogy. And I found a register of the genealogy of those who had come up in the first *return,* and found written in it:

> 6 These[a] *are* the people of the province who came back from the captivity, of those who had been carried away, whom Nebuchadnezzar the king of Babylon had carried away, and

6:6 ªHebrew *Gashmu*   7:6 ªCompare verses 6–72 with Ezra 2:1–70

Gospel Pearls

who returned to Jerusalem and Judah, everyone to his city.

7 Those who came with Zerubbabel *were* Jeshua, Nehemiah, Azariah, Raamiah, Nahamani, Mordecai, Bilshan, Mispereth,*a* Bigvai, Nehum, and Baanah.

The number of the men of the people of Israel: 8 the sons of Parosh, two thousand one hundred and seventy-two; 9 the sons of Shephatiah, three hundred and seventy-two; 10 the sons of Arah, six hundred and fifty-two; 11 the sons of Pahath-Moab, of the sons of Jeshua and Joab, two thousand eight hundred and eighteen; 12 the sons of Elam, one thousand two hundred and fifty-four; 13 the sons of Zattu, eight hundred and forty-five; 14 the sons of Zaccai, seven hundred and sixty; 15 the sons of Binnui,*a* six hundred and forty-eight; 16 the sons of Bebai, six hundred and twenty-eight; 17 the sons of Azgad, two thousand three hundred and twenty-two; 18 the sons of Adonikam, six hundred and sixty-seven; 19 the sons of Bigvai, two thousand and sixty-seven; 20 the sons of Adin, six hundred and fifty-five; 21 the sons of Ater of Hezekiah, ninety-eight; 22 the sons of Hashum, three hundred and twenty-eight; 23 the sons of Bezai, three hundred and twenty-four; 24 the sons of Hariph,*a* one hundred and twelve; 25 the sons of Gibeon,*a* ninety-five; 26 the men of Bethlehem and Netophah, one hundred and eighty-eight; 27 the men of Anathoth, one hundred and twenty-eight; 28 the men of Beth Azmaveth,*a* forty-two;

29 the men of Kirjath Jearim, Chephirah, and Beeroth, seven hundred and forty-three; 30 the men of Ramah and Geba, six hundred and twenty-one; 31 the men of Michmas, one hundred and twenty-two; 32 the men of Bethel and Ai, one hundred and twenty-three; 33 the men of the other Nebo, fifty-two; 34 the sons of the other Elam, one thousand two hundred and fifty-four; 35 the sons of Harim, three hundred and twenty; 36 the sons of Jericho, three hundred and forty-five; 37 the sons of Lod, Hadid, and Ono, seven hundred and twenty-one; 38 the sons of Senaah, three thousand nine hundred and thirty.

39 The priests: the sons of Jedaiah, of the house of Jeshua, nine hundred and seventy-three; 40 the sons of Immer, one thousand and fifty-two; 41 the sons of Pashhur, one thousand two hundred and forty-seven; 42 the sons of Harim, one thousand and seventeen.

43 The Levites: the sons of Jeshua, of Kadmiel,
and of the sons of Hodevah,*a*
seventy-four.

44 The singers: the sons of Asaph, one hundred and forty-eight.

45 The gatekeepers: the sons of Shallum,
the sons of Ater,
the sons of Talmon,
the sons of Akkub,
the sons of Hatita,
the sons of Shobai, one hundred and thirty-eight.

46 The Nethinim: the sons of Ziha, the sons of Hasupha,
the sons of Tabbaoth,
47 the sons of Keros,
the sons of Sia,*a*

7:7 *a*Spelled *Mispar* in Ezra 2:2   7:15 *a*Spelled *Bani* in Ezra 2:10   7:24 *a*Called *Jorah* in Ezra 2:18
7:25 *a*Called *Gibbar* in Ezra 2:20   7:28 *a*Called *Azmaveth* in Ezra 2:24   7:43 *a*Spelled *Hodaviah* in
Ezra 2:40   7:47 *a*Spelled *Siaha* in Ezra 2:44

A woman who had hemorrhaged for twelve years made her way to Jesus one day. When she touched the hem of His garment, she was healed just as she had believed she would be. Jesus said to her that her faith had made her whole—not only healed in her body, but fully restored in every area of her life.

the sons of Padon,
48 the sons of Lebana,ᵃ
the sons of Hagaba,ᵇ
the sons of Salmai,ᶜ
49 the sons of Hanan,
the sons of Giddel,
the sons of Gahar,
50 the sons of Reaiah,
the sons of Rezin,
the sons of Nekoda,
51 the sons of Gazzam,
the sons of Uzza,
the sons of Paseah,
52 the sons of Besai,
the sons of Meunim,
the sons of Nephishesim,ᵃ
53 the sons of Bakbuk,
the sons of Hakupha,
the sons of Harhur,
54 the sons of Bazlith,ᵃ
the sons of Mehida,
the sons of Harsha,
55 the sons of Barkos,
the sons of Sisera,
the sons of Tamah,
56 the sons of Neziah,
and the sons of Hatipha.

57 The sons of Solomon's
servants: the sons of Sotai,
the sons of Sophereth,
the sons of Perida,ᵃ
58 the sons of Jaala,
the sons of Darkon,
the sons of Giddel,
59 the sons of Shephatiah,
the sons of Hattil,
the sons of Pochereth of
Zebaim,
and the sons of Amon.ᵃ
60 All the Nethinim, and the
sons of Solomon's servants,
were three hundred and ninety-
two.

61 And these *were* the ones who
came up from Tel Melah, Tel
Harsha, Cherub, Addon,ᵃ and
Immer, but they could not
identify their father's house nor
their lineage, whether they
were of Israel: 62 the sons of
Delaiah,
the sons of Tobiah,
the sons of Nekoda, six
hundred and forty-two;
63 and of the priests: the sons
of Habaiah,

the sons of Koz,ᵃ
the sons of Barzillai, who took
a wife of the daughters of
Barzillai the Gileadite, and was
called by their name.
64 These sought their listing
among those who were
registered by genealogy, but it
was not found; therefore they
were excluded from the
priesthood as defiled. 65 And
the governorᵃ said to them that
they should not eat of the most
holy things till a priest could
consult with the Urim and
Thummim.

66 Altogether the whole assembly
was forty-two thousand three
hundred and sixty, 67 besides
their male and female servants,
of whom *there were* seven
thousand three hundred and
thirty-seven; and they had two
hundred and forty-five men
and women singers. 68 Their
horses were seven hundred and
thirty-six, their mules two
hundred and forty-five,
69 *their* camels four hundred
and thirty-five, *and* donkeys six
thousand seven hundred and
twenty.

70 And some of the heads of the
fathers' houses gave to the
work. The governorᵃ gave to
the treasury one thousand gold
drachmas, fifty basins, and five
hundred and thirty priestly
garments. 71 Some of the heads
of the fathers' *houses* gave to
the treasury of the work twenty
thousand gold drachmas, and
two thousand two hundred
silver minas. 72 And that which
the rest of the people gave *was*
twenty thousand gold
drachmas, two thousand silver
minas, and sixty-seven priestly
garments.

73 So the priests, the Levites, the
gatekeepers, the singers, *some* of the
people, the Nethinim, and all Israel
dwelt in their cities.
When the seventh month came, the
children of Israel *were* in their cities.

7:48 ᵃMasoretic Text reads *Lebanah.*   ᵇMasoretic Text reads *Hogabah.*   ᶜOr *Shalmai,* or *Shamlai*
7:52 ᵃSpelled *Nephusim* in Ezra 2:50   7:54 ᵃSpelled *Bazluth* in Ezra 2:52   7:57 ᵃSpelled *Peruda* in
Ezra 2:55   7:59 ᵃSpelled *Ami* in Ezra 2:57   7:61 ᵃSpelled *Addan* in Ezra 2:59   7:63 ᵃOr *Hakkoz*
7:65 ᵃHebrew *Tirshatha*   7:70 ᵃHebrew *Tirshatha*

Gospel
Pearls

8 Now all the people gathered together as one man in the open square that *was* in front of the Water Gate; and they told Ezra the scribe to bring the Book of the Law of Moses, which the LORD had commanded Israel. 2 So Ezra the priest brought the Law before the assembly of men and women and all who *could* hear with understanding on the first day of the seventh month. 3 Then he read from it in the open square that *was* in front of the Water Gate from morning until midday, before the men and women and those who could understand; and the ears of all the people *were attentive* to the Book of the Law.

4 So Ezra the scribe stood on a platform of wood which they had made for the purpose; and beside him, at his right hand, stood Mattithiah, Shema, Anaiah, Urijah, Hilkiah, and Maaseiah; and at his left hand Pedaiah, Mishael, Malchijah, Hashum, Hashbadana, Zechariah, *and* Meshullam. 5 And Ezra opened the book in the sight of all the people, for he was *standing* above all the people; and when he opened it, all the people stood up. 6 And Ezra blessed the LORD, the great God.

Then all the people answered, "Amen, Amen!" while lifting up their hands. And they bowed their heads and worshiped the LORD with *their* faces to the ground.

7 Also Jeshua, Bani, Sherebiah, Jamin, Akkub, Shabbethai, Hodijah, Maaseiah, Kelita, Azariah, Jozabad, Hanan, Pelaiah, and the Levites, helped the people to understand the Law; and the people *stood* in their place. 8 So they read distinctly from the book, in the Law of God; and they gave the sense, and helped *them* to understand the reading.

9 And Nehemiah, who *was* the governor,ᵃ Ezra the priest *and* scribe, and the Levites who taught the people said to all the people, "This day *is* holy to the LORD your God; do not mourn nor weep." For all the people wept, when they heard the words of the Law.

10 Then he said to them, "Go your way, eat the fat, drink the sweet, and send portions to those for whom nothing is prepared; for *this* day *is* holy to our LORD. Do not sorrow, for the joy of the LORD is your strength."

11 So the Levites quieted all the people, saying, "Be still, for the day *is* holy; do not be grieved." 12 And all the people went their way to eat and drink, to send portions and rejoice greatly, because they understood the words that were declared to them.

13 Now on the second day the heads of the fathers' *houses* of all the people, with the priests and Levites, were gathered to Ezra the scribe, in order to understand the words of the Law. 14 And they found written in the Law, which the LORD had commanded by Moses, that the children of Israel should dwell in booths during the feast of the seventh month, 15 and that they should announce and proclaim in all their cities and in Jerusalem, saying, "Go out to the mountain, and bring olive branches, branches of oil trees, myrtle branches, palm branches, and branches of leafy trees, to make booths, as *it is* written."

16 Then the people went out and brought *them* and made themselves booths, each one on the roof of his house, or in their courtyards or the courts of the house of God, and in the open square of the Water Gate and in the open square of the Gate of Ephraim. 17 So the whole assembly of those who had returned from the captivity made booths and sat under the booths; for since the days of Joshua the son of Nun until that day the children of Israel had not done so. And there was very great gladness. 18 Also day by day, from the first day until the last day, he read from the Book of the Law of God. And they kept the feast seven days; and on the eighth day *there was* a sacred assembly, according to the *prescribed* manner.

9 Now on the twenty-fourth day of this month the children of Israel were assembled with fasting, in sackcloth, and with dust on their heads.ᵃ 2 Then those of Israelite lineage separated themselves from all foreigners; and they stood and confessed their sins and the iniquities of their fathers. 3 And they stood up in their place and read from the Book of the Law of the LORD their God *for one-*

8:9 ᵃHebrew *Tirshatha*   9:1 ᵃLiterally *earth on them*

*E*ven if no one in the entire world has compassion on you ... God does. He will help you if you will only turn to Him for help.

fourth of the day; and *for another* fourth they confessed and worshiped the LORD their God.

4 Then Jeshua, Bani, Kadmiel, Shebaniah, Bunni, Sherebiah, Bani, *and* Chenani stood on the stairs of the Levites and cried out with a loud voice to the LORD their God. 5 And the Levites, Jeshua, Kadmiel, Bani, Hashabniah, Sherebiah, Hodijah, Shebaniah, *and* Pethahiah, said:

"Stand up *and* bless the LORD
　　your God
　Forever and ever!

"Blessed be Your glorious name,
　Which is exalted above all
　　blessing and praise!
6　You alone *are* the LORD;
　You have made heaven,
　The heaven of heavens, with all
　　their host,
　The earth and everything on it,
　The seas and all that is in them,
　And You preserve them all.
　The host of heaven worships
　　You.

7　"You *are* the LORD God,
　Who chose Abram,
　And brought him out of Ur of
　　the Chaldeans,
　And gave him the name
　　Abraham;
8　You found his heart faithful
　　before You,
　And made a covenant with him
　To give the land of the
　　Canaanites,
　The Hittites, the Amorites,
　The Perizzites, the Jebusites,
　And the Girgashites—
　To give *it* to his descendants.
　You have performed Your
　　words,
　For You *are* righteous.

9　"You saw the affliction of our
　　fathers in Egypt,
　And heard their cry by the Red
　　Sea.
10　You showed signs and wonders
　　against Pharaoh,
　Against all his servants,
　And against all the people of
　　his land.
　For You knew that they acted
　　proudly against them.
　So You made a name for
　　Yourself, as *it is* this day.

11　And You divided the sea before
　　them,
　So that they went through the
　　midst of the sea on the dry
　　land;
　And their persecutors You
　　threw into the deep,
　As a stone into the mighty
　　waters.
12　Moreover You led them by day
　　with a cloudy pillar,
　And by night with a pillar of
　　fire,
　To give them light on the road
　Which they should travel.

13　"You came down also on Mount
　　Sinai,
　And spoke with them from
　　heaven,
　And gave them just ordinances
　　and true laws,
　Good statutes and
　　commandments.
14　You made known to them Your
　　holy Sabbath,
　And commanded them
　　precepts, statutes and laws,
　By the hand of Moses Your
　　servant.
15　You gave them bread from
　　heaven for their hunger,
　And brought them water out of
　　the rock for their thirst,
　And told them to go in to
　　possess the land
　Which You had sworn to give
　　them.

16　"But they and our fathers acted
　　proudly,
　Hardened their necks,
　And did not heed Your
　　commandments.
17　They refused to obey,
　And they were not mindful of
　　Your wonders
　That You did among them.
　But they hardened their
　　necks,
　And in their rebellion[a]
　They appointed a leader
　To return to their bondage.
　But You *are* God,
　Ready to pardon,
　Gracious and merciful,
　Slow to anger,
　Abundant in kindness,
　And did not forsake them.

9:17 [a]Following Masoretic Text and Vulgate; Septuagint reads *in Egypt*.

Gospel
Pearls

18 "Even when they made a
   molded calf for themselves,
   And said, 'This *is* your god
   That brought you up out of
      Egypt,'
   And worked great
      provocations.
19 Yet in Your manifold mercies
   You did not forsake them in the
      wilderness.
   The pillar of the cloud did not
      depart from them by day,
   To lead them on the road;
   Nor the pillar of fire by night,
   To show them light,
   And the way they should go.
20 You also gave Your good Spirit
      to instruct them,
   And did not withhold Your
      manna from their mouth,
   And gave them water for their
      thirst.
21 Forty years You sustained
      them in the wilderness;
   They lacked nothing;
   Their clothes did not wear out*ᵃ*
   And their feet did not swell.

22 "Moreover You gave them
      kingdoms and nations,
   And divided them into
      districts.*ᵃ*
   So they took possession of the
      land of Sihon,
   The land of*ᵇ* the king of
      Heshbon,
   And the land of Og king of
      Bashan.
23 You also multiplied their
      children as the stars of
      heaven,
   And brought them into the land
   Which You had told their
      fathers
   To go in and possess.
24 So the people went in
   And possessed the land;
   You subdued before them the
      inhabitants of the land,
   The Canaanites,
   And gave them into their
      hands,
   With their kings
   And the people of the land,
   That they might do with them
      as they wished.
25 And they took strong cities and
      a rich land,
   And possessed houses full of all
      goods,

Cisterns *already* dug,
   vineyards, olive groves,
And fruit trees in abundance.
So they ate and were filled and
   grew fat,
And delighted themselves in
   Your great goodness.

26 "Nevertheless they were
      disobedient
   And rebelled against You,
   Cast Your law behind their
      backs
   And killed Your prophets, who
      testified against them
   To turn them to Yourself;
   And they worked great
      provocations.
27 Therefore You delivered them
      into the hand of their
      enemies,
   Who oppressed them;
   And in the time of their trouble,
   When they cried to You,
   You heard from heaven;
   And according to Your
      abundant mercies
   You gave them deliverers who
      saved them
   From the hand of their
      enemies.

28 "But after they had rest,
   They again did evil before You.
   Therefore You left them in the
      hand of their enemies,
   So that they had dominion over
      them;
   Yet when they returned and
      cried out to You,
   You heard from heaven;
   And many times You delivered
      them according to Your
      mercies,
29 And testified against them,
   That You might bring them
      back to Your law.
   Yet they acted proudly,
   And did not heed Your
      commandments,
   But sinned against Your
      judgments,
   'Which if a man does, he shall
      live by them.'*ᵃ*
   And they shrugged their
      shoulders,
   Stiffened their necks,
   And would not hear.
30 Yet for many years You had
      patience with them,

9:21 *ᵃ*Compare Deuteronomy 29:5   9:22 *ᵃ*Literally *corners*   *ᵇ*Following Masoretic Text and Vulgate;
Septuagint omits *The land of.*   9:29 *ᵃ*Leviticus 18:5

When God delivers you, He wants you to be delivered from the entire environment
in which you were kept cooped up and chained. Go where you can be refreshed
in the Lord and stay there.

And testified against them by
  Your Spirit in Your prophets.
Yet they would not listen;
Therefore You gave them into
  the hand of the peoples of the
  lands.
31 Nevertheless in Your great
    mercy
  You did not utterly consume
    them nor forsake them;
  For You *are* God, gracious and
    merciful.

32 "Now therefore, our God,
  The great, the mighty, and
    awesome God,
  Who keeps covenant and
    mercy:
  Do not let all the trouble seem
    small before You
  That has come upon us,
  Our kings and our princes,
  Our priests and our prophets,
  Our fathers and on all Your
    people,
  From the days of the kings of
    Assyria until this day.
33 However You *are* just in all that
    has befallen us;
  For You have dealt faithfully,
  But we have done wickedly.
34 Neither our kings nor our
    princes,
  Our priests nor our fathers,
  Have kept Your law,
  Nor heeded Your
    commandments and Your
    testimonies,
  With which You testified
    against them.
35 For they have not served You
    in their kingdom,
  Or in the many good *things* that
    You gave them,
  Or in the large and rich land
    which You set before them;
  Nor did they turn from their
    wicked works.

36 "Here we *are*, servants today!
  And the land that You gave to
    our fathers,
  To eat its fruit and its bounty,
  Here we *are*, servants in it!
37 And it yields much increase to
    the kings
  You have set over us,
  Because of our sins;
  Also they have dominion over
    our bodies and our cattle
  At their pleasure;
  And we *are* in great distress.

38 "And because of all this,
  We make a sure *covenant* and
    write *it;*
  Our leaders, our Levites, *and*
    our priests seal *it.*"

10 Now those who placed *their*
   seal on *the document were:*

Nehemiah the governor, the
  son of Hacaliah, and Zedekiah,
2 Seraiah, Azariah, Jeremiah,
3 Pashhur, Amariah,
  Malchijah, 4 Hattush,
  Shebaniah, Malluch,
5 Harim, Meremoth, Obadiah,
6 Daniel, Ginnethon, Baruch,
7 Meshullam, Abijah, Mijamin,
8 Maaziah, Bilgai, *and*
  Shemaiah. These *were* the
  priests.

9 The Levites: Jeshua the son of
  Azaniah, Binnui of the sons of
  Henadad, *and* Kadmiel.

10 Their brethren: Shebaniah,
  Hodijah, Kelita, Pelaiah,
  Hanan, 11 Micha, Rehob,
  Hashabiah, 12 Zaccur,
  Sherebiah, Shebaniah,
13 Hodijah, Bani, *and* Beninu.

14 The leaders of the people:
  Parosh, Pahath-Moab, Elam,
  Zattu, Bani, 15 Bunni, Azgad,
  Bebai, 16 Adonijah, Bigvai,
  Adin, 17 Ater, Hezekiah, Azzur,
18 Hodijah, Hashum, Bezai,
19 Hariph, Anathoth, Nebai,
20 Magpiash, Meshullam,
  Hezir, 21 Meshezabel, Zadok,
  Jaddua, 22 Pelatiah, Hanan,
  Anaiah, 23 Hoshea, Hananiah,
  Hasshub, 24 Hallohesh, Pilha,
  Shobek, 25 Rehum, Hashabnah,
  Maaseiah, 26 Ahijah, Hanan,
  Anan, 27 Malluch, Harim, *and*
  Baanah.

28 Now the rest of the people—the
priests, the Levites, the gatekeepers,
the singers, the Nethinim, and all
those who had separated themselves
from the peoples of the lands to the
Law of God, their wives, their sons,
and their daughters, everyone who
had knowledge and understanding—
29 these joined with their brethren,
their nobles, and entered into a curse
and an oath to walk in God's Law,
which was given by Moses the ser-

Gospel Pearls

vant of God, and to observe and do all the commandments of the LORD our Lord, and His ordinances and His statutes; 30 We would not give our daughters as wives to the peoples of the land, nor take their daughters for our sons; 31 *if* the peoples of the land brought wares or any grain to sell on the Sabbath day, we would not buy it from them on the Sabbath, or on a holy day; and we would forego the seventh year's *produce* and the exacting of every debt.

32 Also we made ordinances for ourselves, to exact from ourselves yearly one-third of a shekel for the service of the house of our God: 33 for the showbread, for the regular grain offering, for the regular burnt offering of the Sabbaths, the New Moons, and the set feasts; for the holy things, for the sin offerings to make atonement for Israel, and all the work of the house of our God. 34 We cast lots among the priests, the Levites, and the people, for *bringing* the wood offering into the house of our God, according to our fathers' houses, at the appointed times year by year, to burn on the altar of the LORD our God as *it is* written in the Law.

35 And *we made ordinances* to bring the firstfruits of our ground and the firstfruits of all fruit of all trees, year by year, to the house of the LORD; 36 to bring the firstborn of our sons and our cattle, as *it is* written in the Law, and the firstborn of our herds and our flocks, to the house of our God, to the priests who minister in the house of our God; 37 to bring the firstfruits of our dough, our offerings, the fruit from all kinds of trees, *the* new wine and oil, to the priests, to the storerooms of the house of our God; and to bring the tithes of our land to the Levites, for the Levites should receive the tithes in all our farming communities. 38 And the priest, the descendant of Aaron, shall be with the Levites when the Levites receive tithes; and the Levites shall bring up a tenth of the tithes to the house of our God, to the rooms of the storehouse.

39 For the children of Israel and the children of Levi shall bring the offering of the grain, of the new wine and the oil, to the storerooms where the articles of the sanctuary *are, where* the priests who minister and the gatekeepers and the singers *are;* and we will not neglect the house of our God.

11 Now the leaders of the people dwelt at Jerusalem; the rest of the people cast lots to bring one out of ten to dwell in Jerusalem, the holy city, and nine-tenths *were to dwell* in *other* cities. 2 And the people blessed all the men who willingly offered themselves to dwell at Jerusalem.

3 These *are* the heads of the province who dwelt in Jerusalem. (But in the cities of Judah everyone dwelt in his own possession in their cities— Israelites, priests, Levites, Nethinim, and descendants of Solomon's servants.) 4 Also in Jerusalem dwelt *some* of the children of Judah and of the children of Benjamin.

The children of Judah: Athaiah the son of Uzziah, the son of Zechariah, the son of Amariah, the son of Shephatiah, the son of Mahalalel, of the children of Perez; 5 and Maaseiah the son of Baruch, the son of Col-Hozeh, the son of Hazaiah, the son of Adaiah, the son of Joiarib, the son of Zechariah, the son of Shiloni. 6 All the sons of Perez who dwelt at Jerusalem *were* four hundred and sixty-eight valiant men.

7 And these are the sons of Benjamin: Sallu the son of Meshullam, the son of Joed, the son of Pedaiah, the son of Kolaiah, the son of Maaseiah, the son of Ithiel, the son of Jeshaiah; 8 and after him Gabbai *and* Sallai, nine hundred and twenty-eight. 9 Joel the son of Zichri *was* their overseer, and Judah the son of Senuah[a] *was* second over the city.

10 Of the priests: Jedaiah the son of Joiarib, and Jachin; 11 Seraiah the son of Hilkiah, the son of Meshullam, the son of Zadok, the son of Meraioth, the son of Ahitub, *was* the leader of the house of God. 12 Their brethren who did the work of the house *were* eight hundred and twenty-two; and Adaiah the son of Jeroham, the son of Pelaliah, the son of Amzi, the son of Zechariah, the son of Pashhur, the son of Malchijah, 13 and his brethren, heads of the fathers' *houses, were* two hundred and

11:9 ^aOr Hassenuah

2 If you agree with the person who rejects you or abuses you, then you put yourself in bondage to that person. When their bad opinion of you becomes your bad opinion of you, a prison is built inside your soul with only one prisoner in it—you.

forty-two; and Amashai the son of Azarel, the son of Ahzai, the son of Meshillemoth, the son of Immer, 14 and their brethren, mighty men of valor, *were* one hundred and twenty-eight. Their overseer *was* Zabdiel the son of *one of* the great men.*a*

15 Also of the Levites: Shemaiah the son of Hasshub, the son of Azrikam, the son of Hashabiah, the son of Bunni; 16 Shabbethai and Jozabad, of the heads of the Levites, *had* the oversight of the business outside of the house of God; 17 Mattaniah the son of Micha,*a* the son of Zabdi, the son of Asaph, the leader *who* began the thanksgiving with prayer; Bakbukiah, the second among his brethren; and Abda the son of Shammua, the son of Galal, the son of Jeduthun. 18 All the Levites in the holy city *were* two hundred and eighty-four.

19 Moreover the gatekeepers, Akkub, Talmon, and their brethren who kept the gates, *were* one hundred and seventy-two.

20 And the rest of Israel, of the priests *and* Levites, *were* in all the cities of Judah, everyone in his inheritance. 21 But the Nethinim dwelt in Ophel. And Ziha and Gishpa *were* over the Nethinim.

22 Also the overseer of the Levites at Jerusalem *was* Uzzi the son of Bani, the son of Hashabiah, the son of Mattaniah, the son of Micha, of the sons of Asaph, the singers in charge of the service of the house of God. 23 For *it was* the king's command concerning them that a certain portion should be for the singers, a quota day by day. 24 Pethahiah the son of Meshezabel, of the children of Zerah the son of Judah, *was* the king's deputy*a* in all matters concerning the people.

25 And as for the villages with their fields, *some* of the children of Judah dwelt in Kirjath Arba and its villages, Dibon and its villages, Jekabzeel and its villages; 26 in Jeshua, Moladah, Beth Pelet, 27 Hazar Shual, and Beersheba and its villages; 28 in Ziklag and Meconah and its villages; 29 in En Rimmon, Zorah, Jarmuth, 30 Zanoah, Adullam, and their villages; in Lachish and its fields; in

Azekah and its villages. They dwelt from Beersheba to the Valley of Hinnom.

31 Also the children of Benjamin from Geba *dwelt* in Michmash, Aija, and Bethel, and their villages; 32 in Anathoth, Nob, Ananiah; 33 in Hazor, Ramah, Gittaim; 34 in Hadid, Zeboim, Neballat; 35 in Lod, Ono, *and* the Valley of Craftsmen. 36 Some of the Judean divisions of Levites *were* in Benjamin.

12 Now these *are* the priests and the Levites who came up with Zerubbabel the son of Shealtiel, and Jeshua: Seraiah, Jeremiah, Ezra, 2 Amariah, Malluch, Hattush, 3 Shechaniah, Rehum, Meremoth, 4 Iddo, Ginnethoi,*a* Abijah, 5 Mijamin, Maadiah, Bilgah, 6 Shemaiah, Joiarib, Jedaiah, 7 Sallu, Amok, Hilkiah, *and* Jedaiah.

These *were* the heads of the priests and their brethren in the days of Jeshua.

8 Moreover the Levites *were* Jeshua, Binnui, Kadmiel, Sherebiah, Judah, *and* Mattaniah *who* led the thanksgiving *psalms,* he and his brethren. 9 Also Bakbukiah and Unni, their brethren, *stood* across from them in *their* duties.

10 Jeshua begot Joiakim, Joiakim begot Eliashib, Eliashib begot Joiada, 11 Joiada begot Jonathan, and Jonathan begot Jaddua.

12 Now in the days of Joiakim, the priests, the heads of the fathers' *houses were:* of Seraiah, Meraiah; of Jeremiah, Hananiah; 13 of Ezra, Meshullam; of Amariah, Jehohanan; 14 of Melichu,*a* Jonathan; of Shebaniah,*b* Joseph; 15 of Harim,*a* Adna; of Meraioth,*b* Helkai; 16 of Iddo, Zechariah; of Ginnethon, Meshullam; 17 of Abijah, Zichri; *the son* of Minjamin;*a* of Moadiah,*b* Piltai; 18 of Bilgah, Shammua; of Shemaiah, Jehonathan; 19 of Joiarib, Mattenai; of Jedaiah, Uzzi; 20 of Sallai,*a* Kallai; of Amok, Eber; 21 of Hilkiah, Hashabiah; *and* of Jedaiah, Nethanel.

22 During the reign of Darius the Persian, a record *was also kept* of the Levites and priests *who had been* heads of their fathers' *houses* in the

Gospel Pearls

days of Eliashib, Joiada, Johanan, and Jaddua. 23 The sons of Levi, the heads of the fathers' *houses* until the days of Johanan the son of Eliashib, *were* written in the book of the chronicles.

24 And the heads of the Levites *were* Hashabiah, Sherebiah, and Jeshua the son of Kadmiel, with their brothers across from them, to praise *and* give thanks, group alternating with group, according to the command of David the man of God. 25 Mattaniah, Bakbukiah, Obadiah, Meshullam, Talmon, and Akkub *were* gatekeepers keeping the watch at the storerooms of the gates. 26 These *lived* in the days of Joiakim the son of Jeshua, the son of Jozadak,ª and in the days of Nehemiah the governor, and of Ezra the priest, the scribe.

27 Now at the dedication of the wall of Jerusalem they sought out the Levites in all their places, to bring them to Jerusalem to celebrate the dedication with gladness, both with thanksgivings and singing, *with* cymbals and stringed instruments and harps. 28 And the sons of the singers gathered together from the countryside around Jerusalem, from the villages of the Netophathites, 29 from the house of Gilgal, and from the fields of Geba and Azmaveth; for the singers had built themselves villages all around Jerusalem. 30 Then the priests and Levites purified themselves, and purified the people, the gates, and the wall.

31 So I brought the leaders of Judah up on the wall, and appointed two large thanksgiving choirs. *One* went to the right hand on the wall toward the Refuse Gate. 32 After them went Hoshaiah and half of the leaders of Judah, 33 and Azariah, Ezra, Meshullam, 34 Judah, Benjamin, Shemaiah, Jeremiah, 35 and some of the priests' sons with trumpets—Zechariah the son of Jonathan, the son of Shemaiah, the son of Mattaniah, the son of Michaiah, the son of Zaccur, the son of Asaph, 36 and his brethren, Shemaiah, Azarel, Milalai, Gilalai, Maai, Nethanel, Judah, *and* Hanani, with the musical instruments of David the man of God. And Ezra the scribe *went* before them. 37 By the Fountain Gate, in front of them, they went up the stairs of the City of David, on the stairway of the wall, beyond the house of David, as far as the Water Gate eastward.

38 The other thanksgiving choir went the opposite *way*, and I *was* behind them with half of the people on the wall, going past the Tower of the Ovens as far as the Broad Wall, 39 and above the Gate of Ephraim, above the Old Gate, above the Fish Gate, the Tower of Hananel, the Tower of the Hundred, as far as the Sheep Gate; and they stopped by the Gate of the Prison.

40 So the two thanksgiving choirs stood in the house of God, likewise I and the half of the rulers with me; 41 and the priests, Eliakim, Maaseiah, Minjamin,ª Michaiah, Elioenai, Zechariah, *and* Hananiah with trumpets; 42 also Maaseiah, Shemaiah, Eleazar, Uzzi, Jehohanan, Malchijah, Elam, and Ezer. The singers sang loudly with Jezrahiah the director.

43 Also that day they offered great sacrifices, and rejoiced, for God had made them rejoice with great joy; the women and the children also rejoiced, so that the joy of Jerusalem was heard afar off.

44 And at the same time some were appointed over the rooms of the storehouse for the offerings, the firstfruits, and the tithes, to gather into them from the fields of the cities the portions specified by the Law for the priests and Levites; for Judah rejoiced over the priests and Levites who ministered. 45 Both the singers and the gatekeepers kept the charge of their God and the charge of the purification, according to the command of David *and* Solomon his son. 46 For in the days of David and Asaph of old *there were* chiefs of the singers, and songs of praise and thanksgiving to God. 47 In the days of Zerubbabel and in the days of Nehemiah all Israel gave the portions for the singers and the gatekeepers, a portion for each day. They also consecrated *holy things* for the Levites, and the Levites consecrated *them* for the children of Aaron.

13 On that day they read from the Book of Moses in the hearing of the people, and in it was found

12:26 ªSpelled *Jehozadak* in 1 Chronicles 6:14   12:41 ªOr *Mijamin* (compare verse 5)

*T*he deliverance you likely need most is not a deliverance from the devil or a deliverance from another person. The deliverance you probably need most is a deliverance from something in your own heart and mind.

written that no Ammonite or Moabite should ever come into the assembly of God, 2 because they had not met the children of Israel with bread and water, but hired Balaam against them to curse them. However, our God turned the curse into a blessing. 3 So it was, when they had heard the Law, that they separated all the mixed multitude from Israel.

4 Now before this, Eliashib the priest, having authority over the storerooms of the house of our God, *was* allied with Tobiah. 5 And he had prepared for him a large room, where previously they had stored the grain offerings, the frankincense, the articles, the tithes of grain, the new wine and oil, which were commanded *to be given* to the Levites and singers and gatekeepers, and the offerings for the priests. 6 But during all this I was not in Jerusalem, for in the thirty-second year of Artaxerxes king of Babylon I had returned to the king. Then after certain days I obtained leave from the king, 7 and I came to Jerusalem and discovered the evil that Eliashib had done for Tobiah, in preparing a room for him in the courts of the house of God. 8 And it grieved me bitterly; therefore I threw all the household goods of Tobiah out of the room. 9 Then I commanded them to cleanse the rooms; and I brought back into them the articles of the house of God, with the grain offering and the frankincense.

10 I also realized that the portions for the Levites had not been given *them;* for each of the Levites and the singers who did the work had gone back to his field. 11 So I contended with the rulers, and said, "Why is the house of God forsaken?" And I gathered them together and set them in their place. 12 Then all Judah brought the tithe of the grain and the new wine and the oil to the storehouse. 13 And I appointed as treasurers over the storehouse Shelemiah the priest and Zadok the scribe, and of the Levites, Pedaiah; and next to them *was* Hanan the son of Zaccur, the son of Mattaniah; for they were considered faithful, and their task *was* to distribute to their brethren.

14 Remember me, O my God, concerning this, and do not wipe out my good deeds that I have done for the house of my God, and for its services!

15 In those days I saw *people* in Judah treading wine presses on the Sabbath, and bringing in sheaves, and loading donkeys with wine, grapes, figs, and all *kinds of* burdens, which they brought into Jerusalem on the Sabbath day. And I warned *them* about the day on which they were selling provisions. 16 Men of Tyre dwelt there also, who brought in fish and all kinds of goods, and sold *them* on the Sabbath to the children of Judah, and in Jerusalem.

17 Then I contended with the nobles of Judah, and said to them, "What evil thing *is* this that you do, by which you profane the Sabbath day? 18 Did not your fathers do thus, and did not our God bring all this disaster on us and on this city? Yet you bring added wrath on Israel by profaning the Sabbath."

19 So it was, at the gates of Jerusalem, as it began to be dark before the Sabbath, that I commanded the gates to be shut, and charged that they must not be opened till after the Sabbath. Then I posted *some* of my servants at the gates, *so that* no burdens would be brought in on the Sabbath day. 20 Now the merchants and sellers of all kinds of wares lodged outside Jerusalem once or twice.

21 Then I warned them, and said to them, "Why do you spend the night around the wall? If you do so again, I will lay hands on you!" From that time on they came no *more* on the Sabbath. 22 And I commanded the Levites that they should cleanse themselves, and that they should go and guard the gates, to sanctify the Sabbath day.

Remember me, O my God, *concerning* this also, and spare me according to the greatness of Your mercy!

23 In those days I also saw Jews *who* had married women of Ashdod, Ammon, *and* Moab. 24 And half of their children spoke the language of Ashdod, and could not speak the language of Judah, but spoke according to the language of one or the other people.

25 So I contended with them and cursed them, struck some of them and pulled out their hair, and made them swear by God, *saying,* "You shall not give your daughters as wives to their sons, nor take their

Gospel Pearls

daughters for your sons or your-selves. 26 Did not Solomon king of Is-rael sin by these things? Yet among many nations there was no king like him, who was beloved of his God; and God made him king over all Is-rael. Nevertheless pagan women caused even him to sin. 27 Should we then hear of your doing all this great evil, transgressing against our God by marrying pagan women?"

28 And *one* of the sons of Joiada, the son of Eliashib the high priest, *was* a son-in-law of Sanballat the Horonite; therefore I drove him from me.

29 Remember them, O my God, be-cause they have defiled the priest-hood and the covenant of the priest-hood and the Levites.

30 Thus I cleansed them of every-thing pagan. I also assigned duties to the priests and the Levites, each to his service, 31 and *to bringing* the wood offering and the firstfruits at appointed times.

Remember me, O my God, for good!

The Book of
ESTHER

1 Now it came to pass in the days of Ahasuerus*a* (this *was* the Ahasuerus who reigned over one hundred and twenty-seven prov-inces, from India to Ethiopia), 2 in those days when King Ahasuerus sat on the throne of his kingdom, which *was* in Shushan*a* the citadel, 3 *that* in the third year of his reign he made a feast for all his officials and servants—the powers of Persia and Media, the nobles, and the princes of the provinces *being* before him— 4 when he showed the riches of his glorious kingdom and the splendor of his excellent majesty for many days, one hundred and eighty days *in all.*

5 And when these days were com-pleted, the king made a feast lasting seven days for all the people who were present in Shushan the citadel, from great to small, in the court of the garden of the king's palace. 6 *There were* white and blue linen *curtains* fastened with cords of fine linen and purple on silver rods and marble pillars; *and the* couches *were* of gold and silver on a *mosaic* pave-ment of alabaster, turquoise, and white and black marble. 7 And they served drinks in golden vessels, each vessel being different from the other, with royal wine in abundance, ac-cording to the generosity of the king. 8 In accordance with the law, the drinking was not compulsory; for so the king had ordered all the officers of his household, that they should do according to each man's pleasure.

9 Queen Vashti also made a feast for the women *in* the royal palace which *belonged* to King Ahasuerus.

10 On the seventh day, when the heart of the king was merry with wine, he commanded Mehuman, Biz-tha, Harbona, Bigtha, Abagtha, Ze-thar, and Carcas, seven eunuchs who served in the presence of King Ahasuerus, 11 to bring Queen Vashti before the king, *wearing* her royal crown, in order to show her beauty to the people and the officials, for she *was* beautiful to behold. 12 But Queen Vashti refused to come at the king's command *brought* by *his* eunuchs; therefore the king was furious, and his anger burned within him.

13 Then the king said to the wise men who understood the times (for this *was* the king's manner toward all who knew law and justice, 14 those closest to him *being* Carshena, Shethar, Admatha, Tar-shish, Meres, Marsena, and Memu-can, the seven princes of Persia and Media, who had access to the king's presence, *and* who ranked highest in

1:1 *a*Generally identified with Xerxes I (485–464 B.C.)   1:2 *a*Or *Susa,* and so throughout this book

*N*ever allow another person's good opinion of you to be your goal. The fact is, they might never like you. They may never approve of you, consider you to be important, or call you good. They may never change their opinion of you.

the kingdom): 15 "What *shall we* do to Queen Vashti, according to law, because she did not obey the command of King Ahasuerus *brought to her* by the eunuchs?"

16 And Memucan answered before the king and the princes: "Queen Vashti has not only wronged the king, but also all the princes, and all the people who *are* in all the provinces of King Ahasuerus. 17 For the queen's behavior will become known to all women, so that they will despise their husbands in their eyes, when they report, 'King Ahasuerus commanded Queen Vashti to be brought in before him, but she did not come.' 18 This very day the *noble* ladies of Persia and Media will say to all the king's officials that they have heard of the behavior of the queen. Thus *there will be* excessive contempt and wrath. 19 If it pleases the king, let a royal decree go out from him, and let it be recorded in the laws of the Persians and the Medes, so that it will not be altered, that Vashti shall come no more before King Ahasuerus; and let the king give her royal position to another who is better than she. 20 When the king's decree which he will make is proclaimed throughout all his empire (for it is great), all wives will honor their husbands, both great and small."

21 And the reply pleased the king and the princes, and the king did according to the word of Memucan. 22 Then he sent letters to all the king's provinces, to each province in its own script, and to every people in their own language, that each man should be master in his own house, and speak in the language of his own people.

2 After these things, when the wrath of King Ahasuerus subsided, he remembered Vashti, what she had done, and what had been decreed against her. 2 Then the king's servants who attended him said: "Let beautiful young virgins be sought for the king; 3 and let the king appoint officers in all the provinces of his kingdom, that they may gather all the beautiful young virgins to Shushan the citadel, into the women's quarters, under the custody of Hegai*ᵃ* the

king's eunuch, custodian of the women. And let beauty preparations be given *them*. 4 Then let the young woman who pleases the king be queen instead of Vashti."

This thing pleased the king, and he did so.

5 In Shushan the citadel there was a certain Jew whose name *was* Mordecai the son of Jair, the son of Shimei, the son of Kish, a Benjamite. 6 *Kish*ᵃ had been carried away from Jerusalem with the captives who had been captured with Jeconiah*ᵇ* king of Judah, whom Nebuchadnezzar the king of Babylon had carried away. 7 And *Mordecai* had brought up Hadassah, that *is*, Esther, his uncle's daughter, for she had neither father nor mother. The young woman *was* lovely and beautiful. When her father and mother died, Mordecai took her as his own daughter.

8 So it was, when the king's command and decree were heard, and when many young women were gathered at Shushan the citadel, *under* the custody of Hegai, that Esther also was taken to the king's palace, into the care of Hegai the custodian of the women. 9 Now the young woman pleased him, and she obtained his favor; so he readily gave beauty preparations to her, besides her allowance. Then seven choice maidservants were provided for her from the king's palace, and he moved her and her maidservants to the best *place* in the house of the women.

10 Esther had not revealed her people or family, for Mordecai had charged her not to reveal *it*. 11 And every day Mordecai paced in front of the court of the women's quarters, to learn of Esther's welfare and what was happening to her.

12 Each young woman's turn came to go in to King Ahasuerus after she had completed twelve months' preparation, according to the regulations for the women, for thus were the days of their preparation apportioned: six months with oil of myrrh, and six months with perfumes and preparations for beautifying women. 13 Thus *prepared, each* young woman went to the king, and she was given whatever she desired to take with her from the women's quarters to the king's palace. 14 In the evening

2:3 ᵃHebrew *Hege*   2:6 ᵃLiterally *Who*   ᵇSame as *Jehoiachin*, 2 Kings 24:6 and elsewhere

Gospel
Pearls

she went, and in the morning she returned to the second house of the women, to the custody of Shaashgaz, the king's eunuch who kept the concubines. She would not go in to the king again unless the king delighted in her and called for her by name.

15 Now when the turn came for Esther the daughter of Abihail the uncle of Mordecai, who had taken her as his daughter, to go in to the king, she requested nothing but what Hegai the king's eunuch, the custodian of the women, advised. And Esther obtained favor in the sight of all who saw her. 16 So Esther was taken to King Ahasuerus, into his royal palace, in the tenth month, which *is* the month of Tebeth, in the seventh year of his reign. 17 The king loved Esther more than all the *other* women, and she obtained grace and favor in his sight more than all the virgins; so he set the royal crown upon her head and made her queen instead of Vashti. 18 Then the king made a great feast, the Feast of Esther, for all his officials and servants; and he proclaimed a holiday in the provinces and gave gifts according to the generosity of a king.

19 When virgins were gathered together a second time, Mordecai sat within the king's gate. 20 *Now* Esther had not revealed her family and her people, just as Mordecai had charged her, for Esther obeyed the command of Mordecai as when she was brought up by him.

21 In those days, while Mordecai sat within the king's gate, two of the king's eunuchs, Bigthan and Teresh, doorkeepers, became furious and sought to lay hands on King Ahasuerus. 22 So the matter became known to Mordecai, who told Queen Esther, and Esther informed the king in Mordecai's name. 23 And when an inquiry was made into the matter, it was confirmed, and both were hanged on a gallows; and it was written in the book of the chronicles in the presence of the king.

3 After these things King Ahasuerus promoted Haman, the son of Hammedatha the Agagite, and advanced him and set his seat above all the princes who *were* with him. 2 And all the king's servants who *were* within the king's gate bowed and paid homage to Haman, for so the king had commanded concerning him. But Mordecai would not bow or pay homage. 3 Then the king's servants who *were* within the king's gate said to Mordecai, "Why do you transgress the king's command?" 4 Now it happened, when they spoke to him daily and he would not listen to them, that they told *it* to Haman, to see whether Mordecai's words would stand; for *Mordecai* had told them that he *was* a Jew. 5 When Haman saw that Mordecai did not bow or pay him homage, Haman was filled with wrath. 6 But he disdained to lay hands on Mordecai alone, for they had told him of the people of Mordecai. Instead, Haman sought to destroy all the Jews who *were* throughout the whole kingdom of Ahasuerus—the people of Mordecai.

7 In the first month, which is the month of Nisan, in the twelfth year of King Ahasuerus, they cast Pur (that *is*, the lot), before Haman to determine the day and the month,[a] until it *fell on the* twelfth *month*,[b] which *is* the month of Adar.

8 Then Haman said to King Ahasuerus, "There is a certain people scattered and dispersed among the people in all the provinces of your kingdom; their laws *are* different from all *other* people's, and they do not keep the king's laws. Therefore it *is* not fitting for the king to let them remain. 9 If it pleases the king, let *a decree* be written that they be destroyed, and I will pay ten thousand talents of silver into the hands of those who do the work, to bring *it* into the king's treasuries."

10 So the king took his signet ring from his hand and gave it to Haman, the son of Hammedatha the Agagite, the enemy of the Jews. 11 And the king said to Haman, "The money and the people *are* given to you, to do with them as seems good to you."

12 Then the king's scribes were called on the thirteenth day of the first month, and *a decree* was written according to all that Haman commanded—to the king's satraps, to the

3:7 [a]Septuagint adds *to destroy the people of Mordecai in one day*; Vulgate adds *the nation of the Jews should be destroyed.* [b]Following Masoretic Text and Vulgate; Septuagint reads *and the lot fell on the fourteenth of the month.*

There's a freedom that comes with deliverance that you must secure for yourself. You must refuse to be put back into a stall that keeps you from the things you need. You must stay close to the water. Stay close to the place where you can be refreshed.

Stand Up Straight

Esther 4:14

You have had enough tragedy. You have been bent over long enough. God will do something good in you. He has kept you alive through all those years of infirmity because He had something greater for you than anything you experienced earlier. You may be like Esther. Who knows, my sister, you may have come to God's kingdom "for such a time as this" (Esther 4:14).

You may have been abused and misused. Perhaps all those you trusted have turned on you and broken your heart. Still God has sustained you. You didn't make it because you were strong. You didn't make it because you were wise. You didn't make it because you were smart. You made it because God's amazing grace kept you. He has more for you today than what you went through yesterday. Don't give up. Don't give in. Hold on. The blessing is on the way.

I dare you to realize that you can do all things through Christ who strengthens you (see Philippians 4:13). Once the infirm woman knew she didn't have to be bent over, she stood up straight. Jesus told the woman at the well to get rid of her old ways of doing things. He wanted her to give up that old pattern of selfishness. Suddenly she realized that she didn't have what she thought she had. The sinful things she had fought to maintain weren't worth as much as she thought they were.

I'm referring to some of those things that have attached themselves to your life and become comfortable for you. Some of those habits you've come to enjoy, some of those relationships you thought you'd found security in, but weren't really profitable. Often we settle for less because we haven't met the best. When you get the best, it gives you the power to let go of the rest.

The infirm woman didn't panic because of her crippling disease. She had been in pain and torment for eighteen years. When she came into the presence of Jesus, she relaxed in Him. She expected that He would take care of her. The result was a wonderful healing.

Rest and Sabbath are the ability to find eternal satisfaction in Jesus. The world will never give us peace and satisfaction. Jesus offers both freely.

If you have struggled, you can find satisfaction. You can find hope for your soul. It is found in the Master of the universe. He will not deny you because of your past. He will not scrutinize your every action. He will take you as you are and give you rest. He will provide a peace that will satisfy the very yearning of your soul.

governors who *were* over each province, to the officials of all people, to every province according to its script, and to every people in their language. In the name of King Ahasuerus it was written, and sealed with the king's signet ring. 13 And the letters were sent by couriers into all the king's provinces, to destroy, to kill, and to annihilate all the Jews, both young and old, little children and women, in one day, on the thirteenth *day* of the twelfth *month,* which *is* the month of Adar, and to plunder their possessions.*a* 14 A copy of the document was to be issued as law in every province, being published for all people, that they should be ready for that day. 15 The couriers went out, hastened by the king's command; and the decree was proclaimed in Shushan the citadel. So the king and Haman sat down to drink, but the city of Shushan was perplexed.

4 When Mordecai learned all that had happened, he tore his clothes and put on sackcloth and ashes, and went out into the midst of the city. He cried out with a loud and bitter cry. 2 He went as far as the front of the king's gate, for no one *might* enter the king's gate clothed with sackcloth. 3 And in every province where the king's command and decree arrived, *there was* great mourning among the Jews, with fasting, weeping, and wailing; and many lay in sackcloth and ashes.

4 So Esther's maids and eunuchs came and told her, and the queen was deeply distressed. Then she sent garments to clothe Mordecai and take his sackcloth away from him, but he would not accept *them.* 5 Then Esther called Hathach, *one* of the king's eunuchs whom he had appointed to attend her, and she gave him a command concerning Mordecai, to learn what and why this *was.* 6 So Hathach went out to Mordecai in the city square that *was* in front of the king's gate. 7 And Mordecai told him all that had happened to him, and the sum of money that Haman had promised to pay into the king's treasuries to destroy the Jews. 8 He also gave him a copy of the written decree for their destruction,

which was given at Shushan, that he might show it to Esther and explain it to her, and that he might command her to go in to the king to make supplication to him and plead before him for her people. 9 So Hathach returned and told Esther the words of Mordecai.

10 Then Esther spoke to Hathach, and gave him a command for Mordecai: 11 "All the king's servants and the people of the king's provinces know that any man or woman who goes into the inner court to the king, who has not been called, *he has* but one law: put *all* to death, except the one to whom the king holds out the golden scepter, that he may live. Yet I myself have not been called to go in to the king these thirty days." 12 So they told Mordecai Esther's words.

13 And Mordecai told *them* to answer Esther: "Do not think in your heart that you will escape in the king's palace any more than all the other Jews. 14 For if you remain completely silent at this time, relief and deliverance will arise for the Jews from another place, but you and your father's house will perish. Yet who knows whether you have come to the kingdom for *such* a time as this?" 15 Then Esther told *them* to reply to Mordecai: 16 "Go, gather all the Jews who are present in Shushan, and fast for me; neither eat nor drink for three days, night or day. My maids and I will fast likewise. And so I will go to the king, which *is* against the law; and if I perish, I perish!"

17 So Mordecai went his way and did according to all that Esther commanded him.*a*

5 Now it happened on the third day that Esther put on *her* royal *robes* and stood in the inner court of the king's palace, across from the king's house, while the king sat on his royal throne in the royal house, facing the entrance of the house.*a* 2 So it was, when the king saw Queen Esther standing in the court, *that* she found favor in his sight, and the king held out to Esther the golden scepter that *was* in his hand. Then Esther went

3:13 *a*Septuagint adds the text of the letter here.   4:17 *a*Septuagint adds a prayer of Mordecai here.
5:1 *a*Septuagint adds many extra details in verses 1 and 2.

*I*f you are going to deal effectively with people in this world, you have got to be able to work right alongside them without allowing yourself to be controlled or governed by their opinion of you.

near and touched the top of the scepter.

3 And the king said to her, "What do you wish, Queen Esther? What is your request? It shall be given to you—up to half the kingdom!"

4 So Esther answered, "If it pleases the king, let the king and Haman come today to the banquet that I have prepared for him."

5 Then the king said, "Bring Haman quickly, that he may do as Esther has said." So the king and Haman went to the banquet that Esther had prepared.

6 At the banquet of wine the king said to Esther, "What is your petition? It shall be granted you. What is your request, up to half the kingdom? It shall be done!"

7 Then Esther answered and said, "My petition and request is this: 8 If I have found favor in the sight of the king, and if it pleases the king to grant my petition and fulfill my request, then let the king and Haman come to the banquet which I will prepare for them, and tomorrow I will do as the king has said."

9 So Haman went out that day joyful and with a glad heart; but when Haman saw Mordecai in the king's gate, and that he did not stand or tremble before him, he was filled with indignation against Mordecai. 10 Nevertheless Haman restrained himself and went home, and he sent and called for his friends and his wife Zeresh. 11 Then Haman told them of his great riches, the multitude of his children, everything in which the king had promoted him, and how he had advanced him above the officials and servants of the king.

12 Moreover Haman said, "Besides, Queen Esther invited no one but me to come in with the king to the banquet that she prepared; and tomorrow I am again invited by her, along with the king. 13 Yet all this avails me nothing, so long as I see Mordecai the Jew sitting at the king's gate."

14 Then his wife Zeresh and all his friends said to him, "Let a gallows be made, fifty cubits high, and in the morning suggest to the king that Mordecai be hanged on it; then go merrily with the king to the banquet."

And the thing pleased Haman; so he had the gallows made.

6 That night the king could not sleep. So one was commanded to bring the book of the records of the chronicles; and they were read before the king. 2 And it was found written that Mordecai had told of Bigthana and Teresh, two of the king's eunuchs, the doorkeepers who had sought to lay hands on King Ahasuerus. 3 Then the king said, "What honor or dignity has been bestowed on Mordecai for this?"

And the king's servants who attended him said, "Nothing has been done for him."

4 So the king said, "Who is in the court?" Now Haman had just entered the outer court of the king's palace to suggest that the king hang Mordecai on the gallows that he had prepared for him.

5 The king's servants said to him, "Haman is there, standing in the court."

And the king said, "Let him come in."

6 So Haman came in, and the king asked him, "What shall be done for the man whom the king delights to honor?"

Now Haman thought in his heart, "Whom would the king delight to honor more than me?" 7 And Haman answered the king, "For the man whom the king delights to honor, 8 let a royal robe be brought which the king has worn, and a horse on which the king has ridden, which has a royal crest placed on its head. 9 Then let this robe and horse be delivered to the hand of one of the king's most noble princes, that he may array the man whom the king delights to honor. Then parade him on horseback through the city square, and proclaim before him: 'Thus shall it be done to the man whom the king delights to honor!'"

10 Then the king said to Haman, "Hurry, take the robe and the horse, as you have suggested, and do so for Mordecai the Jew who sits within the king's gate! Leave nothing undone of all that you have spoken."

11 So Haman took the robe and the horse, arrayed Mordecai and led him on horseback through the city square, and proclaimed before him, "Thus shall it be done to the man whom the king delights to honor!"

12 Afterward Mordecai went back to the king's gate. But Haman hurried

Gospel Pearls

to his house, mourning and with his head covered. 13 When Haman told his wife Zeresh and all his friends everything that had happened to him, his wise men and his wife Zeresh said to him, "If Mordecai, before whom you have begun to fall, is of Jewish descent, you will not prevail against him but will surely fall before him."

14 While they *were* still talking with him, the king's eunuchs came, and hastened to bring Haman to the banquet which Esther had prepared.

7 So the king and Haman went to dine with Queen Esther. 2 And on the second day, at the banquet of wine, the king again said to Esther, "What *is* your petition, Queen Esther? It shall be granted you. And what *is* your request, up to half the kingdom? It shall be done!"

3 Then Queen Esther answered and said, "If I have found favor in your sight, O king, and if it pleases the king, let my life be given me at my petition, and my people at my request. 4 For we have been sold, my people and I, to be destroyed, to be killed, and to be annihilated. Had we been sold as male and female slaves, I would have held my tongue, although the enemy could never compensate for the king's loss."

5 So King Ahasuerus answered and said to Queen Esther, "Who is he, and where is he, who would dare presume in his heart to do such a thing?"

6 And Esther said, "The adversary and enemy *is* this wicked Haman!"

So Haman was terrified before the king and queen.

7 Then the king arose in his wrath from the banquet of wine *and went* into the palace garden; but Haman stood before Queen Esther, pleading for his life, for he saw that evil was determined against him by the king. 8 When the king returned from the palace garden to the place of the banquet of wine, Haman had fallen across the couch where Esther *was*. Then the king said, "Will he also assault the queen while I *am* in the house?"

As the word left the king's mouth, they covered Haman's face. 9 Now Harbonah, one of the eunuchs, said to the king, "Look! The gallows, fifty cubits high, which Haman made for Mordecai, who spoke good on the

king's behalf, is standing at the house of Haman."

Then the king said, "Hang him on it!"

10 So they hanged Haman on the gallows that he had prepared for Mordecai. Then the king's wrath subsided.

8 On that day King Ahasuerus gave Queen Esther the house of Haman, the enemy of the Jews. And Mordecai came before the king, for Esther had told how he *was related* to her. 2 So the king took off his signet ring, which he had taken from Haman, and gave it to Mordecai; and Esther appointed Mordecai over the house of Haman.

3 Now Esther spoke again to the king, fell down at his feet, and implored him with tears to counteract the evil of Haman the Agagite, and the scheme which he had devised against the Jews. 4 And the king held out the golden scepter toward Esther. So Esther arose and stood before the king, 5 and said, "If it pleases the king, and if I have found favor in his sight and the thing *seems* right to the king and I am pleasing in his eyes, let it be written to revoke the letters devised by Haman, the son of Hammedatha the Agagite, which he wrote to annihilate the Jews who *are* in all the king's provinces. 6 For how can I endure to see the evil that will come to my people? Or how can I endure to see the destruction of my countrymen?"

7 Then King Ahasuerus said to Queen Esther and Mordecai the Jew, "Indeed, I have given Esther the house of Haman, and they have hanged him on the gallows because he *tried to* lay his hand on the Jews. 8 You yourselves write *a decree* concerning the Jews, as you please, in the king's name, and seal *it* with the king's signet ring; for whatever is written in the king's name and sealed with the king's signet ring no one can revoke."

9 So the king's scribes were called at that time, in the third month, which *is* the month of Sivan, on the twenty-third *day;* and it was written, according to all that Mordecai commanded, to the Jews, the satraps, the governors, and the princes of the provinces from India to Ethiopia, one hundred and twenty-seven provinces

in all, to every province in its own script, to every people in their own language, and to the Jews in their own script and language. 10 And he wrote in the name of King Ahasuerus, sealed *it* with the king's signet ring, and sent letters by couriers on horseback, riding on royal horses bred from swift steeds.ᵃ

11 By these letters the king permitted the Jews who *were* in every city to gather together and protect their lives—to destroy, kill, and annihilate all the forces of any people or province that would assault them, *both* little children and women, and to plunder their possessions, 12 on one day in all the provinces of King Ahasuerus, on the thirteenth *day* of the twelfth month, which *is* the month of Adar.ᵃ 13 A copy of the document was to be issued as a decree in every province and published for all people, so that the Jews would be ready on that day to avenge themselves on their enemies. 14 The couriers who rode on royal horses went out, hastened and pressed on by the king's command. And the decree was issued in Shushan the citadel.

15 So Mordecai went out from the presence of the king in royal apparel of blue and white, with a great crown of gold and a garment of fine linen and purple; and the city of Shushan rejoiced and was glad. 16 The Jews had light and gladness, joy and honor. 17 And in every province and city, wherever the king's command and decree came, the Jews had joy and gladness, a feast and a holiday. Then many of the people of the land became Jews, because fear of the Jews fell upon them.

9 Now in the twelfth month, that *is,* the month of Adar, on the thirteenth day, *the time* came for the king's command and his decree to be executed. On the day that the enemies of the Jews had hoped to overpower them, the opposite occurred, in that the Jews themselves overpowered those who hated them. 2 The Jews gathered together in their cities throughout all the provinces of King Ahasuerus to lay hands on those who sought their harm. And no one could withstand them, because fear of them fell upon all people.

3 And all the officials of the provinces, the satraps, the governors, and all those doing the king's work, helped the Jews, because the fear of Mordecai fell upon them. 4 For Mordecai *was* great in the king's palace, and his fame spread throughout all the provinces; for this man Mordecai became increasingly prominent. 5 Thus the Jews defeated all their enemies with the stroke of the sword, with slaughter and destruction, and did what they pleased with those who hated them.

6 And in Shushan the citadel the Jews killed and destroyed five hundred men. 7 Also Parshandatha, Dalphon, Aspatha, 8 Poratha, Adalia, Aridatha, 9 Parmashta, Arisai, Aridai, and Vajezatha— 10 the ten sons of Haman the son of Hammedatha, the enemy of the Jews—they killed; but they did not lay a hand on the plunder.

11 On that day the number of those who were killed in Shushan the citadel was brought to the king. 12 And the king said to Queen Esther, "The Jews have killed and destroyed five hundred men in Shushan the citadel, and the ten sons of Haman. What have they done in the rest of the king's provinces? Now what *is* your petition? It shall be granted to you. Or what *is* your further request? It shall be done."

13 Then Esther said, "If it pleases the king, let it be granted to the Jews who *are* in Shushan to do again tomorrow according to today's decree, and let Haman's ten sons be hanged on the gallows."

14 So the king commanded this to be done; the decree was issued in Shushan, and they hanged Haman's ten sons.

15 And the Jews who *were* in Shushan gathered together again on the fourteenth day of the month of Adar and killed three hundred men at Shushan; but they did not lay a hand on the plunder.

16 The remainder of the Jews in the king's provinces gathered together and protected their lives, had rest from their enemies, and killed seventy-five thousand of their enemies; but they did not lay a hand on the plunder. 17 *This was* on the thirteenth day of the month of Adar. And on

8:10 ᵃLiterally *sons of the swift horses*　　8:12 ᵃSeptuagint adds the text of the letter here.

Gospel
Pearls

the fourteenth of *the month*[a] they rested and made it a day of feasting and gladness.

18 But the Jews who *were* at Shushan assembled together on the thirteenth *day*, as well as on the fourteenth; and on the fifteenth of *the month*[a] they rested, and made it a day of feasting and gladness. 19 Therefore the Jews of the villages who dwelt in the unwalled towns celebrated the fourteenth day of the month of Adar *with* gladness and feasting, as a holiday, and for sending presents to one another.

20 And Mordecai wrote these things and sent letters to all the Jews, near and far, who *were* in all the provinces of King Ahasuerus, 21 to establish among them that they should celebrate yearly the fourteenth and fifteenth days of the month of Adar, 22 as the days on which the Jews had rest from their enemies, as the month which was turned from sorrow to joy for them, and from mourning to a holiday; that they should make them days of feasting and joy, of sending presents to one another and gifts to the poor. 23 So the Jews accepted the custom which they had begun, as Mordecai had written to them, 24 because Haman, the son of Hammedatha the Agagite, the enemy of all the Jews, had plotted against the Jews to annihilate them, and had cast Pur (that *is*, the lot), to consume them and destroy them; 25 but when *Esther*[a] came before the king, he commanded by letter that this[b] wicked plot which *Haman* had devised against the Jews should return on his own head, and that he and his sons should be hanged on the gallows.

26 So they called these days Purim, after the name Pur. Therefore, because of all the words of this letter, what they had seen concerning this matter, and what had happened to them, 27 the Jews established and imposed it upon themselves and their descendants and all who would join them, that without fail they should celebrate these two days every year, according to the written *instructions* and according to the *prescribed* time, 28 *that* these days *should be* remembered and kept throughout every generation, every family, every province, and every city, that these days of Purim should not fail *to be observed* among the Jews, and *that* the memory of them should not perish among their descendants.

29 Then Queen Esther, the daughter of Abihail, with Mordecai the Jew, wrote with full authority to confirm this second letter about Purim. 30 And *Mordecai* sent letters to all the Jews, to the one hundred and twenty-seven provinces of the kingdom of Ahasuerus, *with* words of peace and truth, 31 to confirm these days of Purim at their *appointed* time, as Mordecai the Jew and Queen Esther had prescribed for them, and as they had decreed for themselves and their descendants concerning matters of their fasting and lamenting. 32 So the decree of Esther confirmed these matters of Purim, and it was written in the book.

10 And King Ahasuerus imposed tribute on the land and *on* the islands of the sea. 2 Now all the acts of his power and his might, and the account of the greatness of Mordecai, to which the king advanced him, *are* they not written in the book of the chronicles of the kings of Media and Persia? 3 For Mordecai the Jew *was* second to King Ahasuerus, and was great among the Jews and well received by the multitude of his brethren, seeking the good of his people and speaking peace to all his countrymen.[a]

9:17 [a]Literally *it*   9:18 [a]Literally *it*   9:25 [a]Literally *she* or *it*   [b]Literally *his*   10:3 [a]Literally *seed*.
Septuagint and Vulgate add a dream of Mordecai here; Vulgate adds six more chapters.

*P*eople who have been treated with hate become full of hate and can only give hate. Refuse to accept the loathing of other people. Refuse to loathe yourself. Face the reality that if no one has had compassion on you, you can still have compassion on yourself.

The Book of

JOB

1 There was a man in the land of Uz, whose name *was* Job; and that man was blameless and upright, and one who feared God and shunned evil. 2 And seven sons and three daughters were born to him. 3 Also, his possessions were seven thousand sheep, three thousand camels, five hundred yoke of oxen, five hundred female donkeys, and a very large household, so that this man was the greatest of all the people of the East.

4 And his sons would go and feast *in their* houses, each on his *appointed* day, and would send and invite their three sisters to eat and drink with them. 5 So it was, when the days of feasting had run their course, that Job would send and sanctify them, and he would rise early in the morning and offer burnt offerings *according to* the number of them all. For Job said, "It may be that my sons have sinned and cursed[a] God in their hearts." Thus Job did regularly.

6 Now there was a day when the sons of God came to present themselves before the LORD, and Satan[a] also came among them. 7 And the LORD said to Satan, "From where do you come?"

So Satan answered the LORD and said, "From going to and fro on the earth, and from walking back and forth on it."

8 Then the LORD said to Satan, "Have you considered My servant Job, that *there is* none like him on the earth, a blameless and upright man, one who fears God and shuns evil?"

9 So Satan answered the LORD and said, "Does Job fear God for nothing? 10 Have You not made a hedge around him, around his household, and around all that he has on every side? You have blessed the work of his hands, and his possessions have increased in the land. 11 But now, stretch out Your hand and touch all that he has, and he will surely curse You to Your face!"

12 And the LORD said to Satan, "Behold, all that he has *is* in your power; only do not lay a hand on his *person.*"

So Satan went out from the presence of the LORD.

13 Now there was a day when his sons and daughters *were* eating and drinking wine in their oldest brother's house; 14 and a messenger came to Job and said, "The oxen were plowing and the donkeys feeding beside them, 15 when the Sabeans[a] raided *them* and took them away— indeed they have killed the servants with the edge of the sword; and I alone have escaped to tell you!"

16 While he *was* still speaking, another also came and said, "The fire of God fell from heaven and burned up the sheep and the servants, and consumed them; and I alone have escaped to tell you!"

17 While he *was* still speaking, another also came and said, "The Chaldeans formed three bands, raided the camels and took them away, yes, and killed the servants with the edge of the sword; and I alone have escaped to tell you!"

18 While he *was* still speaking, another also came and said, "Your sons and daughters *were* eating and drinking wine in their oldest brother's house, 19 and suddenly a great wind came from across[a] the wilderness and struck the four corners of the house, and it fell on the young people, and they are dead; and I alone have escaped to tell you!"

20 Then Job arose, tore his robe, and shaved his head; and he fell to the ground and worshiped. 21 And he said:

> "Naked I came from my
>   mother's womb,
> And naked shall I return there.
> The LORD gave, and the LORD
>   has taken away;
> Blessed be the name of the
>   LORD."

22 In all this Job did not sin nor charge God with wrong.

1:5 [a]Literally *blessed,* but used here in the evil sense, and so in verse 11 and 2:5, 9   1:6 [a]Literally *the Adversary,* and so throughout this book   1:15 [a]Literally *Sheba* (compare 6:19)   1:19 [a]Septuagint omits *across.*

Gospel Pearls

2 Again there was a day when the sons of God came to present themselves before the LORD, and Satan came also among them to present himself before the LORD. 2 And the LORD said to Satan, "From where do you come?"

Satan answered the LORD and said, "From going to and fro on the earth, and from walking back and forth on it."

3 Then the LORD said to Satan, "Have you considered My servant Job, that *there is* none like him on the earth, a blameless and upright man, one who fears God and shuns evil? And still he holds fast to his integrity, although you incited Me against him, to destroy him without cause."

4 So Satan answered the LORD and said, "Skin for skin! Yes, all that a man has he will give for his life. 5 But stretch out Your hand now, and touch his bone and his flesh, and he will surely curse You to Your face!"

6 And the LORD said to Satan, "Behold, he *is* in your hand, but spare his life."

7 So Satan went out from the presence of the LORD, and struck Job with painful boils from the sole of his foot to the crown of his head. 8 And he took for himself a potsherd with which to scrape himself while he sat in the midst of the ashes.

9 Then his wife said to him, "Do you still hold fast to your integrity? Curse God and die!"

10 But he said to her, "You speak as one of the foolish women speaks. Shall we indeed accept good from God, and shall we not accept adversity?" In all this Job did not sin with his lips.

11 Now when Job's three friends heard of all this adversity that had come upon him, each one came from his own place—Eliphaz the Temanite, Bildad the Shuhite, and Zophar the Naamathite. For they had made an appointment together to come and mourn with him, and to comfort him. 12 And when they raised their eyes from afar, and did not recognize him, they lifted their voices and wept; and each one tore his robe and sprinkled dust on his head toward heaven. 13 So they sat down with him on the ground seven days and seven nights,

and no one spoke a word to him, for they saw that *his* grief was very great.

3 After this Job opened his mouth and cursed the day of his *birth*. 2 And Job spoke, and said:

3 "May the day perish on which I was born,
And the night *in which* it was said,
'A male child is conceived.'
4 May that day be darkness;
May God above not seek it,
Nor the light shine upon it.
5 May darkness and the shadow of death claim it;
May a cloud settle on it;
May the blackness of the day terrify it.
6 *As for* that night, may darkness seize it;
May it not rejoice[a] among the days of the year,
May it not come into the number of the months.
7 Oh, may that night be barren!
May no joyful shout come into it!
8 May those curse it who curse the day,
Those who are ready to arouse Leviathan.
9 May the stars of its morning be dark;
May it look for light, but *have* none,
And not see the dawning of the day;
10 Because it did not shut up the doors of my *mother's* womb,
Nor hide sorrow from my eyes.

11 "Why did I not die at birth?
Why did I *not* perish when I came from the womb?
12 Why did the knees receive me?
Or why the breasts, that I should nurse?
13 For now I would have lain still and been quiet,
I would have been asleep;
Then I would have been at rest
14 With kings and counselors of the earth,
Who built ruins for themselves,
15 Or with princes who had gold,
Who filled their houses *with* silver;

3:6 ªSeptuagint, Syriac, Targum, and Vulgate read *be joined*.

---

*T*he Bible says that we are to love our neighbors as we love ourselves—which means we are to love other people to the degree that we love ourselves. If we don't love ourselves, we don't have any love to give to our neighbors.

16 Or *why* was I not hidden like
   a stillborn child,
   Like infants who never saw
   light?
17 There the wicked cease *from*
   troubling,
   And there the weary are at rest.
18 *There* the prisoners rest
   together;
   They do not hear the voice of
   the oppressor.
19 The small and great are there,
   And the servant *is* free from his
   master.

20 "Why is light given to him who
   is in misery,
   And life to the bitter of soul,
21 Who long for death, but it does
   not *come,*
   And search for it more than
   hidden treasures;
22 Who rejoice exceedingly,
   And are glad when they can
   find the grave?
23 *Why is light given* to a man
   whose way is hidden,
   And whom God has hedged in?
24 For my sighing comes before I
   eat,[a]
   And my groanings pour out
   like water.
25 For the thing I greatly feared
   has come upon me,
   And what I dreaded has
   happened to me.
26 I am not at ease, nor am I quiet;
   I have no rest, for trouble
   comes."

4 Then Eliphaz the Temanite answered and said:

2 "If one attempts a word with
   you, will you become weary?
   But who can withhold himself
   from speaking?
3 Surely you have instructed
   many,
   And you have strengthened
   weak hands.
4 Your words have upheld him
   who was stumbling,
   And you have strengthened the
   feeble knees;
5 But now it comes upon you,
   and you are weary;
   It touches you, and you are
   troubled.

6 *Is* not your reverence your
   confidence?
   And the integrity of your ways
   your hope?

7 "Remember now, who *ever*
   perished being innocent?
   Or where were the upright *ever*
   cut off?
8 Even as I have seen,
   Those who plow iniquity
   And sow trouble reap the same.
9 By the blast of God they perish,
   And by the breath of His anger
   they are consumed.
10 The roaring of the lion,
   The voice of the fierce lion,
   And the teeth of the young
   lions are broken.
11 The old lion perishes for lack
   of prey,
   And the cubs of the lioness are
   scattered.

12 "Now a word was secretly
   brought to me,
   And my ear received a whisper
   of it.
13 In disquieting thoughts from
   the visions of the night,
   When deep sleep falls on men,
14 Fear came upon me, and
   trembling,
   Which made all my bones
   shake.
15 Then a spirit passed before my
   face;
   The hair on my body stood up.
16 It stood still,
   But I could not discern its
   appearance.
   A form *was* before my eyes;
   There was silence;
   Then I heard a voice *saying:*
17 'Can a mortal be more righteous
   than God?
   Can a man be more pure than
   his Maker?
18 If He puts no trust in His
   servants,
   If He charges His angels with
   error,
19 How much more those who
   dwell in houses of clay,
   Whose foundation is in the
   dust,
   Who are crushed before a
   moth?
20 They are broken in pieces from
   morning till evening;

3:24 [a]Literally *my bread*

Gospel
Pearls

They perish forever, with no one regarding.

21 Does not their own excellence go away?
They die, even without wisdom.'

5 "Call out now;
Is there anyone who will answer you?
And to which of the holy ones will you turn?

2 For wrath kills a foolish man,
And envy slays a simple one.

3 I have seen the foolish taking root,
But suddenly I cursed his dwelling place.

4 His sons are far from safety,
They are crushed in the gate,
And *there is* no deliverer.

5 Because the hungry eat up his harvest,
Taking it even from the thorns,[a]
And a snare snatches their substance.[b]

6 For affliction does not come from the dust,
Nor does trouble spring from the ground;

7 Yet man is born to trouble,
As the sparks fly upward.

8 "But as for me, I would seek God,
And to God I would commit my cause—

9 Who does great things, and unsearchable,
Marvelous things without number.

10 He gives rain on the earth,
And sends waters on the fields.

11 He sets on high those who are lowly,
And those who mourn are lifted to safety.

12 He frustrates the devices of the crafty,
So that their hands cannot carry out their plans.

13 He catches the wise in their own craftiness,
And the counsel of the cunning comes quickly upon them.

14 They meet with darkness in the daytime,
And grope at noontime as in the night.

15 But He saves the needy from the sword,
From the mouth of the mighty,
And from their hand.

16 So the poor have hope,
And injustice shuts her mouth.

17 "Behold, happy *is* the man whom God corrects;
Therefore do not despise the chastening of the Almighty.

18 For He bruises, but He binds up;
He wounds, but His hands make whole.

19 He shall deliver you in six troubles,
Yes, in seven no evil shall touch you.

20 In famine He shall redeem you from death,
And in war from the power of the sword.

21 You shall be hidden from the scourge of the tongue,
And you shall not be afraid of destruction when it comes.

22 You shall laugh at destruction and famine,
And you shall not be afraid of the beasts of the earth.

23 For you shall have a covenant with the stones of the field,
And the beasts of the field shall be at peace with you.

24 You shall know that your tent *is* in peace;
You shall visit your dwelling and find nothing amiss.

25 You shall also know that your descendants *shall be* many,
And your offspring like the grass of the earth.

26 You shall come to the grave at a full age,
As a sheaf of grain ripens in its season.

27 Behold, this we have searched out;
It *is* true.
Hear it, and know for yourself."

6 Then Job answered and said:

2 "Oh, that my grief were fully weighed,

5:5 [a]Septuagint reads *They shall not be taken from evil men;* Vulgate reads *And the armed man shall take him by violence.* [b]Septuagint reads *The might shall draw them off;* Vulgate reads *And the thirsty shall drink up their riches.*

Jesus said to the woman with a spirit of infirmity, "Woman, thou art loosed from thine infirmity." He knows about your infirmity, too. His word to you today is, "I'm going to loose you." Get ready for Him to do it.

Soul Secrets
from a widow's heart

O God! My heart hurts with a pain I have never known before! I need hope and I need help. Well-meaning people come with offers of help, lunch invitations and other opportunities for distraction, but even their love cannot reach the pit of my soul that is in so much pain. My loss has left me feeling lost and alone. His death ended what we had together and what we were together—one flesh, one mind, one spirit.

I do not want to face the world by myself. Pull me back to life from the grave of my grief. Heal the aching of my soul. Soften the stabbing pains I feel when everything I see reminds me of the one I loved. Deliver me from feeling guilty over things I wish had been different between us. Help me to realize that he knew the things I wish I had said more often. Speak to me the living words that only You can utter. Send me the kind of comfort that only comes from heaven.

You are the only man in my life now, Lord. I am leaning on Your love. Bring the light of Your presence to this dark place I'm in. Restore me with the tenderness of Your mercy, until I am strong and whole again.

And my calamity laid with it on the scales!

3 For then it would be heavier than the sand of the sea—
Therefore my words have been rash.

4 For the arrows of the Almighty *are* within me;
My spirit drinks in their poison;
The terrors of God are arrayed against me.

5 Does the wild donkey bray when it has grass,
Or does the ox low over its fodder?

6 Can flavorless food be eaten without salt?
Or is there *any* taste in the white of an egg?

7 My soul refuses to touch them;
They *are* as loathsome food to me.

8 "Oh, that I might have my request,
That God would grant *me* the thing that I long for!

9 That it would please God to crush me,
That He would loose His hand and cut me off!

10 Then I would still have comfort;
Though in anguish I would exult,
He will not spare;
For I have not concealed the words of the Holy One.

11 "What strength do I have, that I should hope?
And what *is* my end, that I should prolong my life?

12 *Is* my strength the strength of stones?
Or is my flesh bronze?

13 *Is* my help not within me?
And is success driven from me?

14 "To him who is afflicted, kindness *should be shown* by his friend,
Even though he forsakes the fear of the Almighty.

15 My brothers have dealt deceitfully like a brook,
Like the streams of the brooks that pass away,

16 Which are dark because of the ice,
And into which the snow vanishes.

17 When it is warm, they cease to flow;
When it is hot, they vanish from their place.

18 The paths of their way turn aside,
They go nowhere and perish.

19 The caravans of Tema look,
The travelers of Sheba hope for them.

20 They are disappointed because they were confident;
They come there and are confused.

21 For now you are nothing,
You see terror and are afraid.

22 Did I ever say, 'Bring *something* to me'?
Or, 'Offer a bribe for me from your wealth'?

23 Or, 'Deliver me from the enemy's hand'?
Or, 'Redeem me from the hand of oppressors'?

24 "Teach me, and I will hold my tongue;
Cause me to understand wherein I have erred.

25 How forceful are right words!
But what does your arguing prove?

26 Do you intend to rebuke *my* words,
And the speeches of a desperate one, *which are* as wind?

27 Yes, you overwhelm the fatherless,
And you undermine your friend.

28 Now therefore, be pleased to look at me;
For I would never lie to your face.

29 Yield now, let there be no injustice!
Yes, concede, my righteousness still stands!

30 Is there injustice on my tongue?
Cannot my taste discern the unsavory?

7 "*Is there* not a time of hard service for man on earth?
Are not his days also like the days of a hired man?

2 Like a servant who earnestly desires the shade,
And like a hired man who eagerly looks for his wages,

*D*on't make the mistake of thinking that your deliverance must take a long time. Change can happen in an instant. You can arrive *immediately* at an understanding of the truth.

3 So I have been allotted months
       of futility,
   And wearisome nights have
       been appointed to me.
4 When I lie down, I say, 'When
       shall I arise,
   And the night be ended?'
   For I have had my fill of tossing
       till dawn.
5 My flesh is caked with worms
       and dust,
   My skin is cracked and breaks
       out afresh.

6 "My days are swifter than a
       weaver's shuttle,
   And are spent without hope.
7 Oh, remember that my life *is* a
       breath!
   My eye will never again see
       good.
8 The eye of him who sees me
       will see me no *more;*
   While your *eyes* are upon me,
       I shall no longer *be.*
9 *As* the cloud disappears and
       vanishes away,
   So he who goes down to the
       grave does not come up.
10 He shall never return to his
       house,
   Nor shall his place know him
       anymore.

11 "Therefore I will not restrain my
       mouth;
   I will speak in the anguish of
       my spirit;
   I will complain in the bitterness
       of my soul.
12 *Am* I a sea, or a sea serpent,
   That You set a guard over me?
13 When I say, 'My bed will
       comfort me,
   My couch will ease my
       complaint,'
14 Then You scare me with
       dreams
   And terrify me with visions,
15 So that my soul chooses
       strangling
   And death rather than my
       body.*a*
16 I loathe *my life;*
   I would not live forever.
   Let me alone,
   For my days *are but* a breath.

17 "What *is* man, that You should
       exalt him,
   That You should set Your heart
       on him,
18 That You should visit him
       every morning,
   And test him every moment?
19 How long?
   Will You not look away from
       me,
   And let me alone till I swallow
       my saliva?
20 Have I sinned?
   What have I done to You, O
       watcher of men?
   Why have You set me as Your
       target,
   So that I am a burden to
       myself?*a*
21 Why then do You not pardon
       my transgression,
   And take away my iniquity?
   For now I will lie down in the
       dust,
   And You will seek me
       diligently,
   But I *will* no longer *be.*"

8 Then Bildad the Shuhite answered and said:

2 "How long will you speak these
       things,
   And the words of your mouth
       be like a strong wind?
3 Does God subvert judgment?
   Or does the Almighty pervert
       justice?
4 If your sons have sinned
       against Him,
   He has cast them away for their
       transgression.
5 If you would earnestly seek
       God
   And make your supplication to
       the Almighty,
6 If you *were* pure and upright,
   Surely now He would awake
       for you,
   And prosper your rightful
       dwelling place.
7 Though your beginning was
       small,
   Yet your latter end would
       increase abundantly.

8 "For inquire, please, of the
       former age,
   And consider the things
       discovered by their fathers;

7:15 *a*Literally my bones   7:20 *a*Following Masoretic Text, Targum, and Vulgate; Septuagint and Jewish
tradition read to You.

Gospel
Pearls

9 For we *were born* yesterday,
and know nothing,
Because our days on earth *are*
a shadow.

10 Will they not teach you and tell
you,
And utter words from their
heart?

11 "Can the papyrus grow up
without a marsh?
Can the reeds flourish without
water?

12 While it *is* yet green *and* not cut
down,
It withers before any *other*
plant.

13 So *are* the paths of all who
forget God;
And the hope of the hypocrite
shall perish,

14 Whose confidence shall be cut
off,
And whose trust *is* a spider's
web.

15 He leans on his house, but it
does not stand.
He holds it fast, but it does not
endure.

16 He grows green in the sun,
And his branches spread out in
his garden.

17 His roots wrap around the rock
heap,
And look for a place in the
stones.

18 If he is destroyed from his
place,
Then *it* will deny him, *saying,*
'I have not seen you.'

19 "Behold, this is the joy of His
way,
And out of the earth others will
grow.

20 Behold, God will not cast away
the blameless,
Nor will He uphold the
evildoers.

21 He will yet fill your mouth with
laughing,
And your lips with rejoicing.

22 Those who hate you will be
clothed with shame,
And the dwelling place of the
wicked will come to
nothing."*a*

9 Then Job answered and said:

2 "Truly I know *it is* so,

But how can a man be
righteous before God?

3 If one wished to contend with
Him,
He could not answer Him one
time out of a thousand.

4 *God is* wise in heart and mighty
in strength.
Who has hardened *himself*
against Him and prospered?

5 He removes the mountains, and
they do not know
When He overturns them in His
anger;

6 He shakes the earth out of its
place,
And its pillars tremble;

7 He commands the sun, and it
does not rise;
He seals off the stars;

8 He alone spreads out the
heavens,
And treads on the waves of the
sea;

9 He made the Bear, Orion, and
the Pleiades,
And the chambers of the south;

10 He does great things past
finding out,
Yes, wonders without number.

11 If He goes by me, I do not see
Him;
If He moves past, I do not
perceive Him;

12 If He takes away, who can
hinder Him?
Who can say to Him, 'What are
You doing?'

13 God will not withdraw His
anger,
The allies of the proud*a* lie
prostrate beneath Him.

14 "How then can I answer Him,
And choose my words *to
reason* with Him?

15 For though I were righteous, I
could not answer Him;
I would beg mercy of my Judge.

16 If I called and He answered me,
I would not believe that He was
listening to my voice.

17 For He crushes me with a
tempest,
And multiplies my wounds
without cause.

18 He will not allow me to catch
my breath,
But fills me with bitterness.

8:22 *a*Literally *will not be*   9:13 *a*Hebrew *rahab*

*I*f you pull a plant up out of the ground, it might look good for a day or two, but then
it's going to wither and die. If you isolate a person and put her in an isolation
chamber for very long, she'll curl up in a ball and be totally useless. We all need to
be connected.

19 If *it is a matter* of strength,
indeed *He is* strong;
And if of justice, who will
appoint my day *in court?*
20 Though I were righteous, my
own mouth would condemn
me;
Though I *were* blameless, it
would prove me perverse.

21 "I am blameless, yet I do not
know myself;
I despise my life.
22 It *is* all one *thing;*
Therefore I say, 'He destroys
the blameless and the
wicked.'
23 If the scourge slays suddenly,
He laughs at the plight of the
innocent.
24 The earth is given into the hand
of the wicked.
He covers the faces of its
judges.
If it is not *He,* who else could
it be?

25 "Now my days are swifter than
a runner;
They flee away, they see no
good.
26 They pass by like swift ships,
Like an eagle swooping on its
prey.
27 If I say, 'I will forget my
complaint,
I will put off my sad face and
wear a smile,'
28 I am afraid of all my sufferings;
I know that You will not hold
me innocent.
29 *If* I am condemned,
Why then do I labor in vain?
30 If I wash myself with snow
water,
And cleanse my hands with
soap,
31 Yet You will plunge me into the
pit,
And my own clothes will abhor
me.

32 "For *He is* not a man, as I *am,*
That I may answer Him,
And that we should go to court
together.
33 Nor is there any mediator
between us,
Who may lay his hand on us
both.
34 Let Him take His rod away
from me,

And do not let dread of Him
terrify me.
35 *Then* I would speak and not
fear Him,
But it is not so with me.

10 "My soul loathes my life;
I will give free course to my
complaint,
I will speak in the bitterness of
my soul.
2 I will say to God, 'Do not
condemn me;
Show me why You contend
with me.
3 *Does it* seem good to You that
You should oppress,
That You should despise the
work of Your hands,
And smile on the counsel of the
wicked?
4 Do You have eyes of flesh?
Or do You see as man sees?
5 *Are* Your days like the days of
a mortal man?
Are Your years like the days of
a mighty man,
6 That You should seek for my
iniquity
And search out my sin,
7 Although You know that I am
not wicked,
And *there is* no one who can
deliver from Your hand?

8 'Your hands have made me and
fashioned me,
An intricate unity;
Yet You would destroy me.
9 Remember, I pray, that You
have made me like clay.
And will You turn me into dust
again?
10 Did You not pour me out like
milk,
And curdle me like cheese,
11 Clothe me with skin and flesh,
And knit me together with
bones and sinews?
12 You have granted me life and
favor,
And Your care has preserved
my spirit.

13 'And these *things* You have
hidden in Your heart;
I know that this *was* with You:
14 If I sin, then You mark me,
And will not acquit me of my
iniquity.
15 If I am wicked, woe to me;

Gospel
Pearls

Even *if* I am righteous, I cannot
    lift up my head.
I am full of disgrace;
See my misery!
16 If *my head* is exalted,
    You hunt me like a fierce lion,
    And again You show Yourself
    awesome against me.
17 You renew Your witnesses
    against me,
    And increase Your indignation
    toward me;
    Changes and war are *ever* with
    me.

18 'Why then have You brought
    me out of the womb?
    Oh, that I had perished and no
    eye had seen me!
19 I would have been as though I
    had not been.
    I would have been carried from
    the womb to the grave.
20 Are not my days few?
    Cease! Leave me alone, that I
    may take a little comfort,
21 Before I go *to the place from
    which* I shall not return,
    To the land of darkness and the
    shadow of death,
22 A land as dark as darkness
    itself,
    As the shadow of death,
    without any order,
    Where even the light *is* like
    darkness.' "

11 Then Zophar the Naamathite
    answered and said:

2 "Should not the multitude of
    words be answered?
    And should a man full of talk
    be vindicated?
3 Should your empty talk make
    men hold their peace?
    And when you mock, should no
    one rebuke you?
4 For you have said,
    'My doctrine *is* pure,
    And I am clean in your eyes.'
5 But oh, that God would speak,
    And open His lips against you,
6 That He would show you the
    secrets of wisdom!
    For *they would* double *your*
    prudence.
    Know therefore that God
    exacts from you
    Less than your iniquity
    deserves.

7 "Can you search out the deep
    things of God?
    Can you find out the limits of
    the Almighty?
8 *They are* higher than heaven—
    what can you do?
    Deeper than Sheol—what can
    you know?
9 Their measure *is* longer than
    the earth
    And broader than the sea.

10 "If He passes by, imprisons, and
    gathers *to judgment,*
    Then who can hinder Him?
11 For He knows deceitful men;
    He sees wickedness also.
    Will He not then consider *it?*
12 For an empty-headed man will
    be wise,
    When a wild donkey's colt is
    born a man.

13 "If you would prepare your
    heart,
    And stretch out your hands
    toward Him;
14 If iniquity *were* in your hand,
    and you put it far away,
    And would not let wickedness
    dwell in your tents;
15 Then surely you could lift up
    your face without spot;
    Yes, you could be steadfast,
    and not fear;
16 Because you would forget *your*
    misery,
    And remember *it* as waters
    that have passed away,
17 And *your* life would be brighter
    than noonday.
    Though you were dark, you
    would be like the morning.
18 And you would be secure,
    because there is hope;
    Yes, you would dig *around you,*
    and take your rest in safety.
19 You would also lie down, and
    no one would make *you*
    afraid;
    Yes, many would court your
    favor.
20 But the eyes of the wicked will
    fail,
    And they shall not escape,
    And their hope—loss of life!"

12 Then Job answered and said:

2 "No doubt you *are* the people,
    And wisdom will die with you!

---

*D*on't criticize another person for being too emotional in praise. You haven't walked
in their shoes, so you can't understand why they are now dancing in their shoes.

3   But I have understanding as
    well as you;
    I *am* not inferior to you.
    Indeed, who does not *know*
    such things as these?

4   "I am one mocked by his friends,
    Who called on God, and He
    answered him,
    The just and blameless *who is*
    ridiculed.

5   A lamp*ᵃ* is despised in the
    thought of one who is at ease;
    It is made ready for those
    whose feet slip.

6   The tents of robbers prosper,
    And those who provoke God
    are secure—
    In what God provides by His
    hand.

7   "But now ask the beasts, and
    they will teach you;
    And the birds of the air, and
    they will tell you;

8   Or speak to the earth, and it
    will teach you;
    And the fish of the sea will
    explain to you.

9   Who among all these does not
    know
    That the hand of the LORD has
    done this,

10 In whose hand *is* the life of
    every living thing,
    And the breath of all mankind?

11 Does not the ear test words
    And the mouth taste its food?

12 Wisdom *is* with aged men,
    And with length of days,
    understanding.

13 "With Him *are* wisdom and
    strength,
    He has counsel and
    understanding.

14 If He breaks *a thing* down, it
    cannot be rebuilt;
    If He imprisons a man, there
    can be no release.

15 If He withholds the waters,
    they dry up;
    If He sends them out, they
    overwhelm the earth.

16 With Him *are* strength and
    prudence.
    The deceived and the deceiver
    are His.

17 He leads counselors away
    plundered,

    And makes fools of the judges.

18 He loosens the bonds of kings,
    And binds their waist with a
    belt.

19 He leads princes*ᵃ* away
    plundered,
    And overthrows the mighty.

20 He deprives the trusted ones of
    speech,
    And takes away the
    discernment of the elders.

21 He pours contempt on princes,
    And disarms the mighty.

22 He uncovers deep things out of
    darkness,
    And brings the shadow of
    death to light.

23 He makes nations great, and
    destroys them;
    He enlarges nations, and
    guides them.

24 He takes away the
    understanding*ᵃ* of the chiefs
    of the people of the earth,
    And makes them wander in a
    pathless wilderness.

25 They grope in the dark without
    light,
    And He makes them stagger
    like a drunken *man*.

13 "Behold, my eye has seen all
    this,
    My ear has heard and
    understood it.

2   What you know, I also know;
    I *am* not inferior to you.

3   But I would speak to the
    Almighty,
    And I desire to reason with
    God.

4   But you forgers of lies,
    You *are* all worthless
    physicians.

5   Oh, that you would be silent,
    And it would be your wisdom!

6   Now hear my reasoning,
    And heed the pleadings of my
    lips.

7   Will you speak wickedly for
    God,
    And talk deceitfully for Him?

8   Will you show partiality for
    Him?
    Will you contend for God?

9   Will it be well when He
    searches you out?
    Or can you mock Him as one
    mocks a man?

10 He will surely rebuke you

12:5 *ᵃ*Or *disaster*   12:19 *ᵃ*Literally *priests,* but not in the technical sense   12:24 *ᵃ*Literally *heart*

Don't break your rhythm of praise for anybody. No matter what you hear said about you . . . No matter how people may look at you . . . No matter what happens . . . Keep your praise going!

Fire Inside

Job 12:12

I once had the privilege of entertaining my 90-year-old grandmother, whose robust frame and bountiful body had deteriorated to just a mere shadow of its former presence. Her hair had turned to wisps, reminding me of the angel hair we used to decorate our Christmas tree when I was a child. Nevertheless, her spirit seemed strong and graceful.

In my grandmother's eyes I saw the burning embers of a fire, embers of wisdom buried deep beneath the ashes of her experiences. When I looked beyond her slow steps and brittle bones, I realized that she still possessed more flame in her winter than most people muster in the heat of summer! I recognized her as a woman who had come to the setting of the sun.

I could see that sun still burning beneath her leathery skin and brilliant eyes. It seemed that age had somehow smothered her need to talk. She would lapse into long periods of silence that left me clamoring foolishly through my own conversations. When asked if she was all right, she would assure me that she was greatly enjoying my company. Then she would flee again into the counsel of her own thoughts, coming out occasionally just to humor me.

As I pondered her Indian-like demeanor, I realized that her silence did not indicate boredom. It was, first of all, the mark of someone who had learned how to be alone. It reflected the hours she had spent sitting in a rocking chair, entertaining herself with her own thoughts, and reconciling old accounts that brought the past into balance before the books were presented to the Master Himself. My grandmother had prepared her heart for the God who audits our thoughts in the chambers of His own wisdom, and rewards us according to what He finds hidden within us. She had entered into the state where things that seemed so important when you are young and full of days now seem trivial and unimportant. She was at peace, with the kind of peace that comes from a firm faith and deep sense of resolution and invisible reward.

So I, too, am rewarded. I am rewarded with a friendly reminder from a loving God who speaks through the eyes of an aged relative, telling me to relax and enjoy life. During that visit, I determined to understand two secrets of my grandmother's wisdom. First, I committed to a renewed faith and trust in the ableness of God. Second, I promised to spend more time with myself, to warm myself at the fire of my own thoughts and smile with the contentment of the riches contained therein.

If you secretly show partiality.
11 Will not His excellence make
you afraid,
And the dread of Him fall upon
you?
12 Your platitudes *are* proverbs of
ashes,
Your defenses are defenses of
clay.

13 "Hold your peace with me, and
let me speak,
Then let come on me what *may!*
14 Why do I take my flesh in my
teeth,
And put my life in my hands?
15 Though He slay me, yet will I
trust Him.
Even so, I will defend my own
ways before Him.
16 He also *shall* be my salvation,
For a hypocrite could not come
before Him.
17 Listen carefully to my speech,
And to my declaration with
your ears.
18 See now, I have prepared *my*
case,
I know that I shall be
vindicated.
19 Who *is* he *who* will contend
with me?
If now I hold my tongue, I
perish.
20 "Only two *things* do not do to
me,
Then I will not hide myself
from You:
21 Withdraw Your hand far from
me,
And let not the dread of You
make me afraid.
22 Then call, and I will answer;
Or let me speak, then You
respond to me.
23 How many *are* my iniquities
and sins?
Make me know my
transgression and my sin.
24 Why do You hide Your face,
And regard me as Your enemy?
25 Will You frighten a leaf driven
to and fro?
And will You pursue dry
stubble?
26 For You write bitter things
against me,
And make me inherit the
iniquities of my youth.
27 You put my feet in the stocks,

And watch closely all my paths.
You set a limit[a] for the soles of
my feet.

28 "Man[a] decays like a rotten thing,
Like a garment that is moth-
eaten.

14 "Man *who is* born of woman
Is of few days and full of
trouble.
2 He comes forth like a flower
and fades away;
He flees like a shadow and does
not continue.
3 And do You open Your eyes on
such a one,
And bring me[a] to judgment
with Yourself?
4 Who can bring a clean *thing*
out of an unclean?
No one!
5 Since his days *are* determined,
The number of his months *is*
with You;
You have appointed his limits,
so that he cannot pass.
6 Look away from him that he
may rest,
Till like a hired man he finishes
his day.

7 "For there is hope for a tree,
If it is cut down, that it will
sprout again,
And that its tender shoots will
not cease.
8 Though its root may grow old
in the earth,
And its stump may die in the
ground,
9 *Yet* at the scent of water it will
bud
And bring forth branches like
a plant.
10 But man dies and is laid away;
Indeed he breathes his last
And where *is* he?
11 *As* water disappears from the
sea,
And a river becomes parched
and dries up,
12 So man lies down and does not
rise.
Till the heavens *are* no more,
They will not awake
Nor be roused from their sleep.

13 "Oh, that You would hide me in
the grave,

13:27 [a]Literally *inscribe a print*   13:28 [a]Literally *He*   14:3 [a]Septuagint, Syriac, and Vulgate read *him.*

Gospel
Pearls

That You would conceal me
  until Your wrath is past,
That You would appoint me a
  set time, and remember me!
14 If a man dies, shall he live
  again?
  All the days of my hard service
  I will wait,
  Till my change comes.
15 You shall call, and I will
  answer You;
  You shall desire the work of
  Your hands.
16 For now You number my steps,
  But do not watch over my sin.
17 My transgression *is* sealed up
  in a bag,
  And You cover*ᵃ* my iniquity.

18 "But *as* a mountain falls *and*
  crumbles away,
  And *as* a rock is moved from
  its place;
19 *As* water wears away stones,
  And as torrents wash away the
  soil of the earth;
  So You destroy the hope of
  man.
20 You prevail forever against
  him, and he passes on;
  You change his countenance
  and send him away.
21 His sons come to honor, and he
  does not know *it;*
  They are brought low, and he
  does not perceive *it.*
22 But his flesh will be in pain
  over it,
  And his soul will mourn over
  it."

15 Then Eliphaz the Temanite answered and said:

2 "Should a wise man answer with
  empty knowledge,
  And fill himself with the east
  wind?
3 Should he reason with
  unprofitable talk,
  Or by speeches with which he
  can do no good?
4 Yes, you cast off fear,
  And restrain prayer before
  God.
5 For your iniquity teaches your
  mouth,
  And you choose the tongue of
  the crafty.

6 Your own mouth condemns
  you, and not I;
  Yes, your own lips testify
  against you.

7 "*Are* you the first man *who* was
  born?
  Or were you made before the
  hills?
8 Have you heard the counsel of
  God?
  Do you limit wisdom to
  yourself?
9 What do you know that we do
  not know?
  What do you understand that
  is not in us?
10 Both the gray-haired and the
  aged *are* among us,
  Much older than your father.
11 *Are* the consolations of God too
  small for you,
  And the word *spoken* gently*ᵃ*
  with you?
12 Why does your heart carry you
  away,
  And what do your eyes wink
  at,
13 That you turn your spirit
  against God,
  And let *such* words go out of
  your mouth?

14 "What *is* man, that he could be
  pure?
  And *he who is* born of a
  woman, that he could be
  righteous?
15 If *God* puts no trust in His
  saints,
  And the heavens are not pure
  in His sight,
16 How much less man, *who is*
  abominable and filthy,
  Who drinks iniquity like water!

17 "I will tell you, hear me;
  What I have seen I will declare,
18 What wise men have told,
  Not hiding *anything received*
  from their fathers,
19 To whom alone the land was
  given,
  And no alien passed among
  them:
20 The wicked man writhes with
  pain all *his* days,
  And the number of years is
  hidden from the oppressor.

14:17 ᵃLiterally *plaster over*   15:11 ᵃSeptuagint reads *a secret thing.*

*P*eople may not like your deliverance. But . . . It doesn't matter if some people don't
speak to you any more . . . You have been loosed by God and, therefore, you have
a God-given right to stand straight and praise!

21 Dreadful sounds *are* in his ears;
In prosperity the destroyer
comes upon him.
22 He does not believe that he will
return from darkness,
For a sword is waiting for him.
23 He wanders about for bread,
saying, 'Where *is it?*'
He knows that a day of
darkness is ready at his
hand.
24 Trouble and anguish make him
afraid;
They overpower him, like a
king ready for battle.
25 For he stretches out his hand
against God,
And acts defiantly against the
Almighty,
26 Running stubbornly against
Him
With his strong, embossed
shield.
27 "Though he has covered his face
with his fatness,
And made *his* waist heavy with
fat,
28 He dwells in desolate cities,
In houses which no one
inhabits,
Which are destined to become
ruins.
29 He will not be rich,
Nor will his wealth continue,
Nor will his possessions
overspread the earth.
30 He will not depart from
darkness;
The flame will dry out his
branches,
And by the breath of His mouth
he will go away.
31 Let him not trust in futile
things, deceiving himself,
For futility will be his reward.
32 It will be accomplished before
his time,
And his branch will not be
green.
33 He will shake off his unripe
grape like a vine,
And cast off his blossom like
an olive tree.
34 For the company of hypocrites
will be barren,
And fire will consume the tents
of bribery.
35 They conceive trouble and
bring forth futility;
Their womb prepares deceit."

16:13 *a*Literally *kidneys*

16 Then Job answered and said:

2 "I have heard many such things;
Miserable comforters *are* you
all!
3 Shall words of wind have an
end?
Or what provokes you that you
answer?
4 I also could speak as you *do,*
If your soul were in my soul's
place.
I could heap up words against
you,
And shake my head at you;
5 *But* I would strengthen you
with my mouth,
And the comfort of my lips
would relieve *your grief.*

6 "Though I speak, my grief is not
relieved;
And *if* I remain silent, how am
I eased?
7 But now He has worn me out;
You have made desolate all my
company.
8 You have shriveled me up,
And it is a witness *against
me;*
My leanness rises up against
me
And bears witness to my face.
9 He tears *me* in His wrath, and
hates me;
He gnashes at me with His
teeth;
My adversary sharpens His
gaze on me.
10 They gape at me with their
mouth,
They strike me reproachfully
on the cheek,
They gather together against
me.
11 God has delivered me to the
ungodly,
And turned me over to the
hands of the wicked.
12 I was at ease, but He has
shattered me;
He also has taken *me* by my
neck, and shaken me to
pieces;
He has set me up for His target,
13 His archers surround me.
He pierces my heart*a* and does
not pity;
He pours out my gall on the
ground.

Gospel Pearls

14 He breaks me with wound upon
wound;
He runs at me like a warrior.*a*

15 "I have sewn sackcloth over my
skin,
And laid my head*a* in the dust.
16 My face is flushed from
weeping,
And on my eyelids *is* the
shadow of death;
17 Although no violence *is* in my
hands,
And my prayer *is* pure.

18 "O earth, do not cover my blood,
And let my cry have no *resting*
place!
19 Surely even now my witness *is*
in heaven,
And my evidence *is* on high.
20 My friends scorn me;
My eyes pour out *tears* to God.
21 Oh, that one might plead for a
man with God,
As a man *pleads* for his
neighbor!
22 For when a few years are
finished,
I shall go the way of no return.

17 "My spirit is broken,
My days are extinguished,
The grave *is ready* for me.
2 *Are* not mockers with me?
And does not my eye dwell on
their provocation?

3 "Now put down a pledge for me
with Yourself.
Who *is* he *who* will shake
hands with me?
4 For You have hidden their
heart from understanding;
Therefore You will not exalt
them.
5 He who speaks flattery to *his*
friends,
Even the eyes of his children
will fail.

6 "But He has made me a byword
of the people,
And I have become one in
whose face men spit.
7 My eye has also grown dim
because of sorrow,
And all my members *are* like
shadows.

8 Upright *men* are astonished at
this,
And the innocent stirs himself
up against the hypocrite.
9 Yet the righteous will hold to
his way,
And he who has clean hands
will be stronger and stronger.

10 "But please, come back again,
all of you,*a*
For I shall not find *one* wise
man among you.
11 My days are past,
My purposes are broken off,
Even the thoughts of my heart.
12 They change the night into day;
'The light *is* near,' *they say*, in
the face of darkness.
13 If I wait *for* the grave *as* my
house,
If I make my bed in the
darkness,
14 If I say to corruption, 'You *are*
my father,'
And to the worm, 'You *are* my
mother and my sister,'
15 Where then *is* my hope?
As for my hope, who can see
it?
16 *Will* they go down to the gates
of Sheol?
Shall *we have* rest together in
the dust?"

18 Then Bildad the Shuhite answered and said:

2 "How long *till* you put an end
to words?
Gain understanding, and
afterward we will speak.
3 Why are we counted as beasts,
And regarded as stupid in your
sight?
4 You who tear yourself in anger,
Shall the earth be forsaken for
you?
Or shall the rock be removed
from its place?

5 "The light of the wicked indeed
goes out,
And the flame of his fire does
not shine.
6 The light is dark in his tent,
And his lamp beside him is put
out.

16:14 *a*Vulgate reads *giant.* 16:15 *a*Literally *horn* 17:10 *a*Following some Hebrew manuscripts,
Septuagint, Syriac, and Vulgate; Masoretic Text and Targum read *all of them.*

A re you aware that you have a God-given privilege to praise God as much as you
want? And furthermore, you can be as emotional as you want to be in your praise?
Find a place where you can praise God the way you want to praise Him!

7   The steps of his strength are
      shortened,
    And his own counsel casts him
      down.
8   For he is cast into a net by his
      own feet,
    And he walks into a snare.
9   The net takes *him* by the heel,
    And a snare lays hold of him.
10 A noose *is* hidden for him on
      the ground,
    And a trap for him in the road.
11 Terrors frighten him on every
      side,
    And drive him to his feet.
12 His strength is starved,
    And destruction *is* ready at his
      side.
13 It devours patches of his skin;
    The firstborn of death devours
      his limbs.
14 He is uprooted from the shelter
      of his tent,
    And they parade him before the
      king of terrors.
15 They dwell in his tent *who are*
      none of his;
    Brimstone is scattered on his
      dwelling.
16 His roots are dried out below,
    And his branch withers above.
17 The memory of him perishes
      from the earth,
    And he has no name among the
      renowned.*a*
18 He is driven from light into
      darkness,
    And chased out of the world.
19 He has neither son nor
      posterity among his people,
    Nor any remaining in his
      dwellings.
20 Those in the west are
      astonished at his day,
    As those in the east are
      frightened.
21 Surely such *are* the dwellings
      of the wicked,
    And this *is* the place *of him* who
      does not know God."

19 Then Job answered and said:
2   "How long will you torment my
      soul,
    And break me in pieces with
      words?
3   These ten times you have
      reproached me;

    You are not ashamed *that* you
      have wronged me.*a*
4   And if indeed I have erred,
    My error remains with me.
5   If indeed you exalt *yourselves*
      against me,
    And plead my disgrace against
      me,
6   Know then that God has
      wronged me,
    And has surrounded me with
      His net.

7   "If I cry out concerning wrong,
      I am not heard.
    If I cry aloud, *there is* no
      justice.
8   He has fenced up my way, so
      that I cannot pass;
    And He has set darkness in my
      paths.
9   He has stripped me of my glory,
    And taken the crown *from* my
      head.
10 He breaks me down on every
      side,
    And I am gone;
    My hope He has uprooted like
      a tree.
11 He has also kindled His wrath
      against me,
    And He counts me as *one of* His
      enemies.
12 His troops come together
    And build up their road against
      me;
    They encamp all around my
      tent.

13 "He has removed my brothers
      far from me,
    And my acquaintances are
      completely estranged from
      me.
14 My relatives have failed,
    And my close friends have
      forgotten me.
15 Those who dwell in my house,
      and my maidservants,
    Count me as a stranger;
    I am an alien in their sight.
16 I call my servant, but he gives
      no answer;
    I beg him with my mouth.
17 My breath is offensive to my
      wife,
    And I am repulsive to the
      children of my own body.
18 Even young children despise
      me;

18:17 *a*Literally *before the outside*, meaning distinguished, famous   19:3 *a*A Jewish tradition reads *make
yourselves strange to me.*

I arise, and they speak against me.

19 All my close friends abhor me,
And those whom I love have turned against me.

20 My bone clings to my skin and to my flesh,
And I have escaped by the skin of my teeth.

21 "Have pity on me, have pity on me, O you my friends,
For the hand of God has struck me!

22 Why do you persecute me as God *does,*
And are not satisfied with my flesh?

23 "Oh, that my words were written!
Oh, that they were inscribed in a book!

24 That they were engraved on a rock
With an iron pen and lead, forever!

25 For I know *that* my Redeemer lives,
And He shall stand at last on the earth;

26 And after my skin is destroyed, this *I know,*
That in my flesh I shall see God,

27 Whom I shall see for myself,
And my eyes shall behold, and not another.
How my heart yearns within me!

28 If you should say, 'How shall we persecute him?'—
Since the root of the matter is found in me,

29 Be afraid of the sword for yourselves;
For wrath *brings* the punishment of the sword,
That you may know *there is* a judgment."

20 Then Zophar the Naamathite answered and said:

2 "Therefore my anxious thoughts make me answer,
Because of the turmoil within me.

3 I have heard the rebuke that reproaches me,
And the spirit of my understanding causes me to answer.

4 "Do you *not* know this of old,
Since man was placed on earth,

5 That the triumphing of the wicked is short,
And the joy of the hypocrite is *but* for a moment?

6 Though his haughtiness mounts up to the heavens,
And his head reaches to the clouds,

7 *Yet* he will perish forever like his own refuse;
Those who have seen him will say, 'Where is he?'

8 He will fly away like a dream, and not be found;
Yes, he will be chased away like a vision of the night.

9 The eye *that* saw him will *see him* no more,
Nor will his place behold him anymore.

10 His children will seek the favor of the poor,
And his hands will restore his wealth.

11 His bones are full of his youthful vigor,
But it will lie down with him in the dust.

12 "Though evil is sweet in his mouth,
And he hides it under his tongue,

13 *Though* he spares it and does not forsake it,
But still keeps it in his mouth,

14 *Yet* his food in his stomach turns sour;
It becomes cobra venom within him.

15 He swallows down riches
And vomits them up again;
God casts them out of his belly.

16 He will suck the poison of cobras;
The viper's tongue will slay him.

17 He will not see the streams,
The rivers flowing with honey and cream.

18 He will restore that for which he labored,
And will not swallow *it* down;
From the proceeds of business He will get no enjoyment.

19 For he has oppressed *and* forsaken the poor,
He has violently seized a house which he did not build.

*D*on't worry about what the world says. For that matter, don't worry about what someone in the church says. You have the privilege and right to praise the God of your deliverances—so praise the Lord!

20 "Because he knows no quietness
　　in his heart,ᵃ
　He will not save anything he
　　desires.
21　Nothing is left for him to eat;
　Therefore his well-being will
　　not last.
22　In his self-sufficiency he will be
　　in distress;
　Every hand of misery will come
　　against him.
23　*When* he is about to fill his
　　stomach,
　God will cast on him the fury
　　of His wrath,
　And will rain *it* on him while
　　he is eating.
24　He will flee from the iron
　　weapon;
　A bronze bow will pierce him
　　through.
25　It is drawn, and comes out of
　　the body;
　Yes, the glittering *point comes*
　　out of his gall.
　Terrors *come* upon him;
26　Total darkness *is* reserved for
　　his treasures.
　An unfanned fire will consume
　　him;
　It shall go ill with him who is
　　left in his tent.
27　The heavens will reveal his
　　iniquity,
　And the earth will rise up
　　against him.
28　The increase of his house will
　　depart,
　And his goods will flow away
　　in the day of His wrath.
29　This *is* the portion from God for
　　a wicked man,
　The heritage appointed to him
　　by God."

21 Then Job answered and said:

2　"Listen carefully to my speech,
　And let this be your
　　consolation.
3　Bear with me that I may speak,
　And after I have spoken, keep
　　mocking.

4　"As for me, *is* my complaint
　　against man?
　And if *it were,* why should I not
　　be impatient?
5　Look at me and be astonished;
　Put *your* hand over *your* mouth.

6　Even when I remember I am
　　terrified,
　And trembling takes hold of my
　　flesh.
7　Why do the wicked live *and*
　　become old,
　Yes, become mighty in power?
8　Their descendants are
　　established with them in
　　their sight,
　And their offspring before their
　　eyes.
9　Their houses *are* safe from fear,
　Neither *is* the rod of God upon
　　them.
10　Their bull breeds without
　　failure;
　Their cow calves without
　　miscarriage.
11　They send forth their little ones
　　like a flock,
　And their children dance.
12　They sing to the tambourine
　　and harp,
　And rejoice to the sound of the
　　flute.
13　They spend their days in
　　wealth,
　And in a moment go down to
　　the grave.ᵃ
14　Yet they say to God, 'Depart
　　from us,
　For we do not desire the
　　knowledge of Your ways.
15　Who *is* the Almighty, that we
　　should serve Him?
　And what profit do we have if
　　we pray to Him?'
16　Indeed their prosperity *is* not in
　　their hand;
　The counsel of the wicked is far
　　from me.

17 "How often is the lamp of the
　　wicked put out?
　How often does their
　　destruction come upon them,
　The sorrows *God* distributes in
　　His anger?
18　They are like straw before the
　　wind,
　And like chaff that a storm
　　carries away.
19　*They say,* 'God lays up one'sᵃ
　　iniquity for his children';
　Let Him recompense him, that
　　he may know *it.*
20　Let his eyes see his destruction,
　And let him drink of the wrath
　　of the Almighty.

20:20 ᵃLiterally *belly*　　21:13 ᵃOr *Sheol*　　21:19 ᵃLiterally *his*

Gospel
Pearls

21 For what does he care about his
household after him,
When the number of his
months is cut in half?

22 "Can *anyone* teach God
knowledge,
Since He judges those on high?

23 One dies in his full strength,
Being wholly at ease and
secure;

24 His pails*ᵃ* are full of milk,
And the marrow of his bones
is moist.

25 Another man dies in the
bitterness of his soul,
Never having eaten with
pleasure.

26 They lie down alike in the dust,
And worms cover them.

27 "Look, I know your thoughts,
And the schemes *with which*
you would wrong me.

28 For you say,
'Where *is* the house of the
prince?
And where *is* the tent,*ᵃ*
The dwelling place of the
wicked?'

29 Have you not asked those who
travel the road?
And do you not know their
signs?

30 For the wicked are reserved for
the day of doom;
They shall be brought out on
the day of wrath.

31 Who condemns his way to his
face?
And who repays him *for what*
he has done?

32 Yet he shall be brought to the
grave,
And a vigil kept over the tomb.

33 The clods of the valley shall be
sweet to him;
Everyone shall follow him,
As countless *have gone* before
him.

34 How then can you comfort me
with empty words,
Since falsehood remains in
your answers?"

22 Then Eliphaz the Temanite answered and said:

2 "Can a man be profitable to God,

Though he who is wise may be
profitable to himself?

3 *Is it* any pleasure to the
Almighty that you are
righteous?
Or *is it* gain *to Him* that you
make your ways blameless?

4 "Is it because of your fear of Him
that He corrects you,
And enters into judgment with
you?

5 *Is* not your wickedness great,
And your iniquity without
end?

6 For you have taken pledges
from your brother for no
reason,
And stripped the naked of their
clothing.

7 You have not given the weary
water to drink,
And you have withheld bread
from the hungry.

8 But the mighty man possessed
the land,
And the honorable man dwelt
in it.

9 You have sent widows away
empty,
And the strength of the
fatherless was crushed.

10 Therefore snares *are* all around
you,
And sudden fear troubles you,

11 Or darkness *so that* you cannot
see;
And an abundance of water
covers you.

12 "Is not God in the height of
heaven?
And see the highest stars, how
lofty they are!

13 And you say, 'What does God
know?
Can He judge through the deep
darkness?

14 Thick clouds cover Him, so that
He cannot see,
And He walks above the circle
of heaven.'

15 Will you keep to the old way
Which wicked men have trod,

16 Who were cut down before
their time,
Whose foundations were swept
away by a flood?

21:24 *ᵃ*Septuagint and Vulgate read *bowels;* Syriac reads *sides;* Targum reads *breasts.*   21:28 *ᵃ*Vulgate
omits *the tent.*

While you are praising God today, the Lord is fighting the battle for you in the
heavenlies. He is dealing with the enemy of your soul. He is pulverizing the
demonic powers that sought to oppress you and bind you and keep you from God's
blessings.

17 They said to God, 'Depart from
      us!
   What can the Almighty do to
      them?'[a]
18 Yet He filled their houses with
      good *things;*
   But the counsel of the wicked
      is far from me.

19 "The righteous see *it* and are
      glad,
   And the innocent laugh at
      them:
20 'Surely our adversaries[a] are cut
      down,
   And the fire consumes their
      remnant.'

21 "Now acquaint yourself with
      Him, and be at peace;
   Thereby good will come to you.
22 Receive, please, instruction
      from His mouth,
   And lay up His words in your
      heart.
23 If you return to the Almighty,
      you will be built up;
   You will remove iniquity far
      from your tents.
24 Then you will lay your gold in
      the dust,
   And the *gold* of Ophir among
      the stones of the brooks.
25 Yes, the Almighty will be your
      gold[a]
   And your precious silver;
26 For then you will have your
      delight in the Almighty,
   And lift up your face to God.
27 You will make your prayer to
      Him,
   He will hear you,
   And you will pay your vows.
28 You will also declare a thing,
   And it will be established for
      you;
   So light will shine on your
      ways.
29 When they cast *you* down, and
      you say, 'Exaltation *will
      come!'*
   Then He will save the humble
      person.
30 He will *even* deliver one who
      is not innocent;
   Yes, he will be delivered by the
      purity of your hands."

23 Then Job answered and said:

2 "Even today my complaint is
      bitter;
   My[a] hand is listless because of
      my groaning.
3 Oh, that I knew where I might
      find Him,
   That I might come to His seat!
4 I would present *my* case before
      Him,
   And fill my mouth with
      arguments.
5 I would know the words *which*
      He would answer me,
   And understand what He
      would say to me.
6 Would He contend with me in
      His great power?
   No! But He would take *note* of
      me.
7 There the upright could reason
      with Him,
   And I would be delivered
      forever from my Judge.

8 "Look, I go forward, but He is
      not *there,*
   And backward, but I cannot
      perceive Him;
9 When He works on the left
      hand, I cannot behold *Him;*
   When He turns to the right
      hand, I cannot see *Him.*
10 But He knows the way that I
      take;
   When He has tested me, I shall
      come forth as gold.
11 My foot has held fast to His
      steps;
   I have kept His way and not
      turned aside.
12 I have not departed from the
      commandment of His lips;
   I have treasured the words of
      His mouth
   More than my necessary *food.*

13 "But He *is* unique, and who can
      make Him change?
   And *whatever* His soul desires,
      that He does.
14 For He performs *what is*
      appointed for me,
   And many such *things are* with
      Him.
15 Therefore I am terrified at His
      presence;

22:17 [a]Septuagint and Syriac read *us.*   22:20 [a]Septuagint reads *substance.*   22:25 [a]The ancient
versions suggest *defense;* Hebrew reads *gold* as in verse 24.   23:2 [a]Following Masoretic Text, Targum,
and Vulgate; Septuagint and Syriac read *His.*

*Y*our praise isn't just an expression of your joy. You actually are doing battle in the
   spirit realm. While you are praising God—swoop!—the angels of God are stopping
your enemy in his tracks. Swoop!—the angels of God are scattering your enemy!

When God Says No

Job 23:10

Some of the greatest challenges to our faith are those moments when we must endure the cold blight of a disappointment. The greater the anticipation, the greater the disappointment when we fail to receive what we have anticipated.

I know firsthand the sinking feeling of dejection that comes into your heart when things fall through. It feels almost as though an earthquake has struck in your heart. The very things you were counting on and standing on have slipped from under you, and something inside you begins to sink. The floor gives way, and everything you have planned seems meaningless. The temptation is to have an all-out pity party—complete with candles, cake, and ice cream!

There is no shield that can keep away the days that come to teach our hearts submission to God's will and purpose for us. There are no cards that are so poetic, no roses that are so fragrant that they dismiss the tingling sensations of brokenness that come upon us when we see our expectations cave in. It's a feeling that will bring the most mature person into a fetal position. It comes as if it will not leave, but you can be sure that is not so. It will go, and the sun will come again and rebuke the clouds that have hidden the light of God's purpose from shining through to you.

There is within the human capacity a tenacious survival instinct that kicks in when we are at our lowest. It enables us to succeed through the storms of life. They will come, but they will not overthrow you if you learn to trust God even when you can't trace Him.

He is so wise. He knows the greater truths that can only be realized by eyes that can behold today and tomorrow in one glance. His vision supersedes our nearsighted requests centered around the thirst of the day and not the droughts of the future. He must, as a good Father, deny requests that would insult the greater destiny He has prepared for those who are His. He is a God of tough love. He has the ability to firmly decline a request when you would be endangered by a positive response. In short, He loves you enough to say no! You may not know why you have had to face the chilling winds of despair, but trust His love. Trust God to renew you. And just live on.

When I consider *this*, I am
afraid of Him.
16 For God made my heart weak,
And the Almighty terrifies me;
17 Because I was not cut off from
the presence of darkness,
And He did *not* hide deep
darkness from my face.

24 "*Since* times are not hidden
from the Almighty,
Why do those who know Him
see not His days?

2 "*Some* remove landmarks;
They seize flocks violently and
feed *on them;*
3 They drive away the donkey of
the fatherless;
They take the widow's ox as a
pledge.
4 They push the needy off the
road;
All the poor of the land are
forced to hide.
5 Indeed, *like* wild donkeys in the
desert,
They go out to their work,
searching for food.
The wilderness *yields* food for
them *and* for *their* children.
6 They gather their fodder in the
field
And glean in the vineyard of
the wicked.
7 They spend the night naked,
without clothing,
And have no covering in the
cold.
8 They are wet with the showers
of the mountains,
And huddle around the rock for
want of shelter.

9 "*Some* snatch the fatherless
from the breast,
And take a pledge from the
poor.
10 They cause *the poor* to go
naked, without clothing;
And they take away the
sheaves from the hungry.
11 They press out oil within their
walls,
And tread winepresses, yet
suffer thirst.
12 The dying groan in the city,
And the souls of the wounded
cry out;

Yet God does not charge *them*
with wrong.

13 "There are those who rebel
against the light;
They do not know its ways
Nor abide in its paths.
14 The murderer rises with the
light;
He kills the poor and needy;
And in the night he is like a
thief.
15 The eye of the adulterer waits
for the twilight,
Saying, 'No eye will see me';
And he disguises *his* face.
16 In the dark they break into
houses
Which they marked for
themselves in the daytime;
They do not know the light.
17 For the morning is the same to
them as the shadow of death;
If *someone* recognizes *them,*
They are in the terrors of the
shadow of death.

18 "They *should be* swift on the
face of the waters,
Their portion *should be* cursed
in the earth,
So that no *one would* turn into
the way of their vineyards.
19 As drought and heat consume
the snow waters,
So the grave*ᵃ* *consumes those
who* have sinned.
20 The womb *should* forget him,
The worm *should* feed sweetly
on him;
He *should* be remembered no
more,
And wickedness *should* be
broken like a tree.
21 For he preys on the barren *who*
do not bear,
And does no good for the
widow.

22 "But *God* draws the mighty
away with His power;
He rises up, but no *man* is sure
of life.
23 He gives them security, and
they rely *on it;*
Yet His eyes *are* on their ways.
24 They are exalted for a little
while,
Then they are gone.
They are brought low;

24:19 ᵃOr *Sheol*

Gospel Pearls

They are taken out of the way
like all *others;*
They dry out like the heads of
grain.

25 "Now if *it is* not *so,* who will
prove me a liar,
And make my speech worth
nothing?"

25 Then Bildad the Shuhite answered and said:

2 "Dominion and fear *belong* to
Him;
He makes peace in His high
places.
3 Is there any number to His
armies?
Upon whom does His light not
rise?
4 How then can man be righteous
before God?
Or how can he be pure *who is*
born of a woman?
5 If even the moon does not
shine,
And the stars are not pure in
His sight,
6 How much less man, *who is* a
maggot,
And a son of man, *who is* a
worm?"

26 But Job answered and said:

2 "How have you helped *him who
is* without power?
How have you saved the arm
that has no strength?
3 How have you counseled *one
who has* no wisdom?
And *how* have you declared
sound advice to many?
4 To whom have you uttered
words?
And whose spirit came from
you?

5 "The dead tremble,
Those under the waters and
those inhabiting them.
6 Sheol *is* naked before Him,
And Destruction has no
covering.
7 He stretches out the north over
empty space;
He hangs the earth on nothing.
8 He binds up the water in His
thick clouds,
Yet the clouds are not broken
under it.

9 He covers the face of *His*
throne,
And spreads His cloud over
it.
10 He drew a circular horizon on
the face of the waters,
At the boundary of light and
darkness.
11 The pillars of heaven tremble,
And are astonished at His
rebuke.
12 He stirs up the sea with His
power,
And by His understanding He
breaks up the storm.
13 By His Spirit He adorned the
heavens;
His hand pierced the fleeing
serpent.
14 Indeed these *are* the mere
edges of His ways,
And how small a whisper we
hear of Him!
But the thunder of His power
who can understand?"

27 Moreover Job continued his
discourse, and said:

2 "As God lives, *who* has taken
away my justice,
And the Almighty, *who* has
made my soul bitter,
3 As long as my breath *is* in
me,
And the breath of God in my
nostrils,
4 My lips will not speak
wickedness,
Nor my tongue utter deceit.
5 Far be it from me
That I should say you are right;
Till I die I will not put away my
integrity from me.
6 My righteousness I hold fast,
and will not let it go;
My heart shall not reproach *me*
as long as I live.

7 "May my enemy be like the
wicked,
And he who rises up against me
like the unrighteous.
8 For what is the hope of the
hypocrite,
Though he may gain *much,*
If God takes away his life?
9 Will God hear his cry
When trouble comes upon him?
10 Will he delight himself in the
Almighty?
Will he always call on God?

ave you ever praised God—singing and rejoicing—as you drove your car and suddenly, you felt as if you weren't alone? The fact is, you weren't. God's angels were
there right by your side. You may not see them, but they are there!

11 "I will teach you about the hand
of God;
   What *is* with the Almighty I
will not conceal.
12 Surely all of you have seen *it;*
   Why then do you behave with
complete nonsense?

13 "This is the portion of a wicked
man with God,
   And the heritage of oppressors,
received from the Almighty:
14 If his children are multiplied, *it
is* for the sword;
   And his offspring shall not be
satisfied with bread.
15 Those who survive him shall be
buried in death,
   And their[a] widows shall not
weep,
16 Though he heaps up silver like
dust,
   And piles up clothing like
clay—
17 He may pile *it* up, but the just
will wear *it,*
   And the innocent will divide
the silver.
18 He builds his house like a
moth,[a]
   Like a booth *which* a
watchman makes.
19 The rich man will lie down,
But not be gathered *up;*[a]
   He opens his eyes,
And he *is* no more.
20 Terrors overtake him like a
flood;
   A tempest steals him away in
the night.
21 The east wind carries him
away, and he is gone;
   It sweeps him out of his place.
22 It hurls against him and does
not spare;
   He flees desperately from its
power.
23 *Men* shall clap their hands at
him,
   And shall hiss him out of his
place.

28 "Surely there is a mine for
silver,
   And a place *where* gold is
refined.
2 Iron is taken from the earth,
   And copper *is* smelted *from*
ore.
3 *Man* puts an end to darkness,
   And searches every recess
For ore in the darkness and the
shadow of death.
4 He breaks open a shaft away
from people;
   In places forgotten by feet
They hang far away from men;
They swing to and fro.
5 *As for* the earth, from it comes
bread,
   But underneath it is turned up
as by fire;
6 Its stones *are* the source of
sapphires,
   And it contains gold dust.
7 *That* path no bird knows,
   Nor has the falcon's eye seen
it.
8 The proud lions[a] have not
trodden it,
   Nor has the fierce lion passed
over it.
9 He puts his hand on the flint;
   He overturns the mountains at
the roots.
10 He cuts out channels in the
rocks,
   And his eye sees every precious
thing.
11 He dams up the streams from
trickling;
   What is hidden he brings forth
to light.

12 "But where can wisdom be
found?
   And where *is* the place of
understanding?
13 Man does not know its value,
   Nor is it found in the land of
the living.
14 The deep says, '*It is* not in me';
   And the sea says, '*It is* not with
me.'
15 It cannot be purchased for gold,
   Nor can silver be weighed *for*
its price.
16 It cannot be valued in the gold
of Ophir,
   In precious onyx or sapphire.
17 Neither gold nor crystal can
equal it,
   Nor can it be exchanged for
jewelry of fine gold.

27:15 [a]Literally *his*   27:18 [a]Following Masoretic Text and Vulgate; Septuagint and Syriac read *spider*
(compare 8:14); Targum reads *decay*.   27:19 [a]Following Masoretic Text and Targum; Septuagint and
Syriac read *But shall not add* (that is, do it again); Vulgate reads *But take away nothing*.   28:8 [a]Literally
sons of pride, figurative of the great lions

18 No mention shall be made of
coral or quartz,
For the price of wisdom *is*
above rubies.
19 The topaz of Ethiopia cannot
equal it,
Nor can it be valued in pure
gold.

20 "From where then does wisdom
come?
And where *is* the place of
understanding?
21 It is hidden from the eyes of all
living,
And concealed from the birds
of the air.
22 Destruction and Death say,
'We have heard a report about
it with our ears.'
23 God understands its way,
And He knows its place.
24 For He looks to the ends of the
earth,
And sees under the whole
heavens,
25 To establish a weight for the
wind,
And apportion the waters by
measure.
26 When He made a law for the
rain,
And a path for the thunderbolt,
27 Then He saw wisdom*a* and
declared it;
He prepared it, indeed, He
searched it out.
28 And to man He said,
'Behold, the fear of the Lord,
that *is* wisdom,
And to depart from evil *is*
understanding.' "

29 Job further continued his discourse, and said:

2 "Oh, that I were as *in* months
past,
As *in* the days *when* God
watched over me;
3 When His lamp shone upon my
head,
And when by His light I walked
through darkness;
4 Just as I was in the days of my
prime,
When the friendly counsel of
God *was* over my tent;
5 When the Almighty *was* yet
with me,

When my children *were* around
me;
6 When my steps were bathed
with cream,*a*
And the rock poured out rivers
of oil for me!

7 "When I went out to the gate by
the city,
When I took my seat in the
open square,
8 The young men saw me and
hid,
And the aged arose *and* stood;
9 The princes refrained from
talking,
And put *their* hand on their
mouth;
10 The voice of nobles was
hushed,
And their tongue stuck to the
roof of their mouth.
11 When the ear heard, then it
blessed me,
And when the eye saw, then it
approved me;
12 Because I delivered the poor
who cried out,
The fatherless and *the one who*
had no helper.
13 The blessing of a perishing
man came upon me,
And I caused the widow's heart
to sing for joy.
14 I put on righteousness, and it
clothed me;
My justice *was* like a robe and
a turban.
15 I *was* eyes to the blind,
And I *was* feet to the lame.
16 I *was* a father to the poor,
And I searched out the case
that I did not know.
17 I broke the fangs of the
wicked,
And plucked the victim from
his teeth.

18 "Then I said, 'I shall die in my
nest,
And multiply *my* days as the
sand.
19 My root *is* spread out to the
waters,
And the dew lies all night on
my branch.
20 My glory *is* fresh within me,
And my bow is renewed in my
hand.'

28:27 *a*Literally *it*   29:6 *a*Masoretic Text reads *wrath;* ancient versions and some Hebrew manuscripts read *cream* (compare 20:17).

*D*on't give in to the criticism that other people may offer about your deliverance.
Don't let them hurt your feelings or inhibit you. Sometimes you just have to praise
God in the midst of background noise!

Fear or Fright?

Job 28:28

The Bible is very clear as to how you should feel about God (see Job 28:28). But when you read that you should "fear" Him, you may wonder. Let me explain. The Hebrew term for *fear* means "a strong degree of reverence"—not fright.

There is a great deal of difference between fear and reverence. The term *reverence* means "to respect or revere"; the term *fear* carries with it a certain connotation of terror and intimidation. That kind of fear is not a healthy attitude for a daughter of God to have toward her heavenly Father. In Job 28:28, the term rendered *fear* could be better translated as "respect." Fear will drive man away from God, as it drove Adam to hide in the bushes. Adam said, "I heard Your voice in the garden, and I was afraid" (Genesis 3:10). That's not the reaction a loving father wants from his children. I don't want my children to scatter and hide like mice when I approach! I may not always agree with what they have done, but I will always love who they are.

I remember an occasion when some students from my sons' elementary school saw me for the first time. Because I stand a good 6 feet, 4 inches tall, and weigh over 250 pounds, the little children were completely astonished. "Look how big your Dad is!" one of them said. "I bet he could just about squash you. Aren't you afraid of him?"

My sons quickly responded, "Afraid? Naah, he's not mean. He's our dad!" They were not afraid of my stature because they were secure in our relationship. Does that mean they have never been punished? Of course not! What it does mean is that they have never been abused. My love holds my judgment in check.

As imperfect as I am, if I know how to love my children, then what about God? He may not approve of your conduct, my sister, but He still loves you. In fact, understanding His love will help you improve your conduct (see Romans 2:4).

If this is true (and it is), then we must tell others who need to change their minds about God. I believe the Church has confused conviction with condemnation. The Holy Spirit convicts of sin. Conviction leads to a place of deliverance and change. Condemnation leads to the gallows of despair and hopelessness.

Why have we withheld from so many hurting hearts the good news of the gospel? Too many have replaced this good news with self-righteous rhetoric. But if you're convinced that God is good and loves you—no matter what you've done—then tell somebody else. There is healing for their sin too. The only cure is found in the presence of our loving and forgiving Father. Respect Him. Reverence Him. Fear Him.

21 "Men listened to me and waited,
And kept silence for my
counsel.
22 After my words they did not
speak again,
And my speech settled on them
as dew.
23 They waited for me as for the
rain,
And they opened their mouth
wide as for the spring rain.
24 If I mocked at them, they did
not believe it,
And the light of my
countenance they did not
cast down.
25 I chose the way for them, and
sat as chief;
So I dwelt as a king in the
army,
As one who comforts
mourners.

30 "But now they mock at me,
men younger than I,
Whose fathers I disdained to
put with the dogs of my flock.
2 Indeed, what profit is the
strength of their hands to
me?
Their vigor has perished.
3 They are gaunt from want and
famine,
Fleeing late to the wilderness,
desolate and waste,
4 Who pluck mallow by the
bushes,
And broom tree roots for their
food.
5 They were driven out from
among men,
They shouted at them as at a
thief.
6 They had to live in the clefts of
the valleys,
In caves of the earth and the
rocks.
7 Among the bushes they brayed,
Under the nettles they nestled.
8 They were sons of fools,
Yes, sons of vile men;
They were scourged from the
land.

9 "And now I am their taunting
song;
Yes, I am their byword.
10 They abhor me, they keep far
from me;

They do not hesitate to spit in
my face.
11 Because He has loosed my[a]
bowstring and afflicted me,
They have cast off restraint
before me.
12 At my right hand the rabble
arises;
They push away my feet,
And they raise against me their
ways of destruction.
13 They break up my path,
They promote my calamity;
They have no helper.
14 They come as broad breakers;
Under the ruinous storm they
roll along.
15 Terrors are turned upon me;
They pursue my honor as the
wind,
And my prosperity has passed
like a cloud.

16 "And now my soul is poured out
because of my plight;
The days of affliction take hold
of me.
17 My bones are pierced in me at
night,
And my gnawing pains take no
rest.
18 By great force my garment is
disfigured;
It binds me about as the collar
of my coat.
19 He has cast me into the mire,
And I have become like dust
and ashes.

20 "I cry out to You, but You do
not answer me;
I stand up, and You regard me.
21 But You have become cruel to
me;
With the strength of Your hand
You oppose me.
22 You lift me up to the wind and
cause me to ride on it;
You spoil my success.
23 For I know that You will bring
me to death,
And to the house appointed for
all living.

24 "Surely He would not stretch out
His hand against a heap of
ruins,
If they cry out when He
destroys it.

30:11 [a]Following Masoretic Text, Syriac, and Targum; Septuagint and Vulgate read His.

S tay standing tall. Keep praising. Continue to glorify God regardless of what others
may say.

25 Have I not wept for him who
　　was in trouble?
　　Has *not* my soul grieved for the
　　poor?
26 But when I looked for good,
　　evil came *to me;*
　　And when I waited for light,
　　then came darkness.
27 My heart is in turmoil and
　　cannot rest;
　　Days of affliction confront me.
28 I go about mourning, but not
　　in the sun;
　　I stand up in the assembly *and*
　　cry out for help.
29 I am a brother of jackals,
　　And a companion of ostriches.
30 My skin grows black and falls
　　from me;
　　My bones burn with fever.
31 My harp is *turned* to mourning,
　　And my flute to the voice of
　　those who weep.

31 "I have made a covenant with
　　my eyes;
　　Why then should I look upon
　　a young woman?
2 For what *is* the allotment of
　　God from above,
　　And the inheritance of the
　　Almighty from on high?
3 *Is* it not destruction for the
　　wicked,
　　And disaster for the workers of
　　iniquity?
4 Does He not see my ways,
　　And count all my steps?

5 "If I have walked with
　　falsehood,
　　Or if my foot has hastened to
　　deceit,
6 Let me be weighed on honest
　　scales,
　　That God may know my
　　integrity.
7 If my step has turned from the
　　way,
　　Or my heart walked after my
　　eyes,
　　Or if any spot adheres to my
　　hands,
8 *Then* let me sow, and another
　　eat;
　　Yes, let my harvest be rooted
　　out.

9 "If my heart has been enticed by
　　a woman,

Or *if* I have lurked at my
　　neighbor's door,
10 *Then* let my wife grind for
　　another,
　　And let others bow down over
　　her.
11 For that *would be* wickedness;
　　Yes, it *would be* iniquity
　　deserving of judgment.
12 For that *would be* a fire *that*
　　consumes to destruction,
　　And would root out all my
　　increase.

13 "If I have despised the cause of
　　my male or female servant
　　When they complained against
　　me,
14 What then shall I do when God
　　rises up?
　　When He punishes, how shall
　　I answer Him?
15 Did not He who made me in the
　　womb make them?
　　Did not the same One fashion
　　us in the womb?

16 "If I have kept the poor from
　　their desire,
　　Or caused the eyes of the
　　widow to fail,
17 Or eaten my morsel by myself,
　　So that the fatherless could not
　　eat of it
18 (But from my youth I reared
　　him as a father,
　　And from my mother's womb
　　I guided *the widow*ᵃ);
19 If I have seen anyone perish for
　　lack of clothing,
　　Or any poor *man* without
　　covering,
20 If his heartᵃ has not blessed
　　me,
　　And *if* he was *not* warmed with
　　the fleece of my sheep;
21 If I have raised my hand
　　against the fatherless,
　　When I saw I had help in the
　　gate;
22 *Then* let my arm fall from my
　　shoulder,
　　Let my arm be torn from the
　　socket.
23 For destruction *from* God *is* a
　　terror to me,
　　And because of His
　　magnificence I cannot
　　endure.

31:18 ᵃLiterally *her* (compare verse 16)　　31:20 ᵃLiterally *loins*

Gospel
Pearls

24 "If I have made gold my hope,
Or said to fine gold, '*You are*
my confidence';
25 If I have rejoiced because my
wealth *was* great,
And because my hand had
gained much;
26 If I have observed the sun[a]
when it shines,
Or the moon moving *in*
brightness,
27 So that my heart has been
secretly enticed,
And my mouth has kissed my
hand;
28 This also *would be* an iniquity
deserving of judgment,
For I would have denied God
who is above.

29 "If I have rejoiced at the
destruction of him who hated
me,
Or lifted myself up when evil
found him
30 (Indeed I have not allowed my
mouth to sin
By asking for a curse on his
soul);
31 If the men of my tent have not
said,
'Who is there that has not been
satisfied with his meat?'
32 (*But* no sojourner had to lodge
in the street,
For I have opened my doors to
the traveler[a]);
33 If I have covered my
transgressions as Adam,
By hiding my iniquity in my
bosom,
34 Because I feared the great
multitude,
And dreaded the contempt of
families,
So that I kept silence
And did not go out of the
door—
35 Oh, that I had one to hear me!
Here is my mark.
Oh, that the Almighty would
answer me,
That my Prosecutor had
written a book!
36 Surely I would carry it on my
shoulder,
And bind it on me *like* a crown;
37 I would declare to Him the
number of my steps;

Like a prince I would approach
Him.

38 "If my land cries out against me,
And its furrows weep together;
39 If I have eaten its fruit[a] without
money,
Or caused its owners to lose
their lives;
40 *Then* let thistles grow instead
of wheat,
And weeds instead of barley."

The words of Job are ended.

32 So these three men ceased answering Job, because he *was* righteous in his own eyes. 2 Then the wrath of Elihu, the son of Barachel the Buzite, of the family of Ram, was aroused against Job; his wrath was aroused because he justified himself rather than God. 3 Also against his three friends his wrath was aroused, because they had found no answer, and *yet* had condemned Job. 4 Now because they *were* years older than he, Elihu had waited to speak to Job.[a] 5 When Elihu saw that *there was* no answer in the mouth of these three men, his wrath was aroused.

6 So Elihu, the son of Barachel the Buzite, answered and said:

"I *am* young in years, and you
are very old;
Therefore I was afraid,
And dared not declare my
opinion to you.
7 I said, 'Age[a] should speak,
And multitude of years should
teach wisdom.'
8 But *there is* a spirit in man,
And the breath of the Almighty
gives him understanding.
9 Great men[a] are not *always*
wise,
Nor do the aged *always*
understand justice.

10 "Therefore I say, 'Listen to me,
I also will declare my opinion.'
11 Indeed I waited for your words,
I listened to your reasonings,
while you searched out what
to say.
12 I paid close attention to you;

31:26 [a]Literally *light*   31:32 [a]Following Septuagint, Syriac, Targum, and Vulgate; Masoretic Text reads *road*.   31:39 [a]Literally *its strength*   32:4 [a]Vulgate reads *till Job had spoken*.   32:7 [a]Literally *Days, that is, years*   32:9 [a]Or *Men of many years*

---

*Y*our deliverance does not depend upon the scope of your future usefulness or your future ministry. God delivers you because He loves you.

And surely not one of you
convinced Job,
Or answered his words—
13 Lest you say,
'We have found wisdom';
God will vanquish him, not
man.
14 Now he has not directed *his*
words against me;
So I will not answer him with
your words.

15 "They are dismayed and answer
no more;
Words escape them.
16 And I have waited, because
they did not speak,
Because they stood still *and*
answered no more.
17 I also will answer my part,
I too will declare my opinion.
18 For I am full of words;
The spirit within me compels
me.
19 Indeed my belly *is* like wine
that has no vent;
It is ready to burst like new
wineskins.
20 I will speak, that I may find
relief;
I must open my lips and
answer.
21 Let me not, I pray, show
partiality to anyone;
Nor let me flatter any man.
22 For I do not know how to
flatter,
Else my Maker would soon
take me away.

33 "But please, Job, hear my
speech,
And listen to all my words.
2 Now, I open my mouth;
My tongue speaks in my
mouth.
3 My words *come* from my
upright heart;
My lips utter pure knowledge.
4 The Spirit of God has made me,
And the breath of the Almighty
gives me life.
5 If you can answer me,
Set *your* words in order before
me;
Take your stand.
6 Truly I *am* as your spokesman[a]
before God;
I also have been formed out of
clay.

7 Surely no fear of me will terrify
you,
Nor will my hand be heavy on
you.

8 "Surely you have spoken in my
hearing,
And I have heard the sound of
your words, *saying,*
9 'I *am* pure, without
transgression;
I *am* innocent, and *there is* no
iniquity in me.
10 Yet He finds occasions against
me,
He counts me as His enemy;
11 He puts my feet in the stocks,
He watches all my paths.'

12 "Look, *in* this you are not
righteous.
I will answer you,
For God is greater than man.
13 Why do you contend with Him?
For He does not give an
accounting of any of His
words.
14 For God may speak in one way,
or in another,
Yet man does not perceive it.
15 In a dream, in a vision of the
night,
When deep sleep falls upon
men,
While slumbering on their
beds,
16 Then He opens the ears of men,
And seals their instruction.
17 In order to turn man *from his*
deed,
And conceal pride from man,
18 He keeps back his soul from the
Pit,
And his life from perishing by
the sword.

19 "*Man* is also chastened with
pain on his bed,
And with strong *pain* in many
of his bones,
20 So that his life abhors bread,
And his soul succulent food.
21 His flesh wastes away from
sight,
And his bones stick out *which*
once were not seen.
22 Yes, his soul draws near the
Pit,
And his life to the executioners.

33:6 [a]Literally *as your mouth*

Gospel Pearls

23 "If there is a messenger for him,
   A mediator, one among a
      thousand,
   To show man His uprightness,
24 Then He is gracious to him, and
      says,
   'Deliver him from going down
      to the Pit;
   I have found a ransom';
25 His flesh shall be young like a
      child's,
   He shall return to the days of
      his youth.
26 He shall pray to God, and He
      will delight in him,
   He shall see His face with joy,
   For He restores to man His
      righteousness.
27 Then he looks at men and says,
   'I have sinned, and perverted
      what was right,
   And it did not profit me.'
28 He will redeem his*a* soul from
      going down to the Pit,
   And his*b* life shall see the light.

29 "Behold, God works all these
      things,
   Twice, *in fact,* three *times* with
      a man,
30 To bring back his soul from the
      Pit,
   That he may be enlightened
      with the light of life.

31 "Give ear, Job, listen to me;
   Hold your peace, and I will
      speak.
32 If you have anything to say,
      answer me;
   Speak, for I desire to justify
      you.
33 If not, listen to me;
   Hold your peace, and I will
      teach you wisdom."

34 Elihu further answered and
      said:

2 "Hear my words, you wise *men;*
   Give ear to me, you who have
      knowledge.
3 For the ear tests words
   As the palate tastes food.
4 Let us choose justice for
      ourselves;
   Let us know among ourselves
      what *is* good.

5 "For Job has said, 'I am
      righteous,

But God has taken away my
      justice;
6 Should I lie concerning my
      right?
   My wound *is* incurable, *though
      I am* without transgression.'
7 What man *is* like Job,
   Who drinks scorn like water,
8 Who goes in company with the
      workers of iniquity,
   And walks with wicked men?
9 For he has said, 'It profits a
      man nothing
   That he should delight in God.'

10 "Therefore listen to me, you men
      of understanding:
   Far be it from God *to do*
      wickedness,
   And *from* the Almighty to
      commit iniquity.
11 For He repays man *according
      to* his work,
   And makes man to find a
      reward according to *his* way.
12 Surely God will never do
      wickedly,
   Nor will the Almighty pervert
      justice.
13 Who gave Him charge over the
      earth?
   Or who appointed *Him over* the
      whole world?
14 If He should set His heart on
      it,
   If He should gather to Himself
      His Spirit and His breath,
15 All flesh would perish together,
   And man would return to dust.

16 "If *you have* understanding,
      hear this;
   Listen to the sound of my
      words:
17 Should one who hates justice
      govern?
   Will you condemn *Him who is*
      most just?
18 *Is it fitting* to say to a king,
      'You *are* worthless,'
   And to nobles, '*You are*
      wicked'?
19 Yet He is not partial to princes,
   Nor does He regard the rich
      more than the poor;
   For they *are* all the work of His
      hands.
20 In a moment they die, in the
      middle of the night;

33:28 *a*Or *my* (Kethib) *b*Or *my* (Kethib)

*T*he cord to your past is cut only when you realize that what you need can be found
in a better source. Hold out for the love and forgiveness and healing power of God.
Draw from God a flow of life that will replace and nullify your need for the former life.

The people are shaken and
    pass away;
The mighty are taken away
    without a hand.

21 "For His eyes *are* on the ways
    of man,
And He sees all his steps.
22 There is no darkness nor
    shadow of death
Where the workers of iniquity
    may hide themselves.
23 For He need not further
    consider a man,
That he should go before God
    in judgment.
24 He breaks in pieces mighty
    men without inquiry,
And sets others in their place.
25 Therefore He knows their
    works;
He overthrows *them* in the
    night,
And they are crushed.
26 He strikes them as wicked *men*
    In the open sight of others,
27 Because they turned back from
    Him,
And would not consider any of
    His ways,
28 So that they caused the cry of
    the poor to come to Him;
For He hears the cry of the
    afflicted.
29 When He gives quietness, who
    then can make trouble?
And when He hides *His* face,
    who then can see Him,
Whether *it is* against a nation
    or a man alone?—
30 That the hypocrite should not
    reign,
Lest the people be ensnared.

31 "For has *anyone* said to God,
    'I have borne *chastening;*
I will offend no more;
32 Teach me *what* I do not see;
If I have done iniquity, I will
    do no more'?
33 Should He repay *it* according
    to your *terms,*
Just because you disavow it?
You must choose, and not I;
Therefore speak what you
    know.

34 "Men of understanding say to
    me,
Wise men who listen to me:
35 'Job speaks without knowledge,
His words *are* without wisdom.'

36 Oh, that Job were tried to the
    utmost,
Because *his* answers *are like*
    those of wicked men!
37 For he adds rebellion to his sin;
He claps *his hands* among us,
And multiplies his words
    against God."

35 Moreover Elihu answered and
said:

2 "Do you think this is right?
Do you say,
'My righteousness is more than
    God's'?
3 For you say,
'What advantage will it be to
    You?
What profit shall I have, more
    than *if* I had sinned?'

4 "I will answer you,
And your companions with
    you.
5 Look to the heavens and see;
And behold the clouds—
They are higher than you.
6 If you sin, what do you
    accomplish against Him?
Or, *if* your transgressions are
    multiplied, what do you do to
    Him?
7 If you are righteous, what do
    you give Him?
Or what does He receive from
    your hand?
8 Your wickedness affects a man
    such as you,
And your righteousness a son
    of man.

9 "Because of the multitude of
    oppressions they cry out;
They cry out for help because
    of the arm of the mighty.
10 But no one says, 'Where *is* God
    my Maker,
Who gives songs in the night,
11 Who teaches us more than the
    beasts of the earth,
And makes us wiser than the
    birds of heaven?'
12 There they cry out, but He does
    not answer,
Because of the pride of evil
    men.
13 Surely God will not listen to
    empty *talk,*
Nor will the Almighty regard it.
14 Although you say you do not
    see Him,

Gospel Pearls

Yet justice *is* before Him, and
you must wait for Him.
15 And now, because He has not
punished in His anger,
Nor taken much notice of folly,
16 Therefore Job opens his mouth
in vain;
He multiplies words without
knowledge."

36 Elihu also proceeded and said:
2 "Bear with me a little, and I will
show you
That *there are* yet words to
speak on God's behalf.
3 I will fetch my knowledge from
afar;
I will ascribe righteousness to
my Maker.
4 For truly my words *are* not
false;
One who is perfect in
knowledge *is* with you.

5 "Behold, God *is* mighty, but
despises *no one;*
He is mighty in strength of
understanding.
6 He does not preserve the life of
the wicked,
But gives justice to the
oppressed.
7 He does not withdraw His eyes
from the righteous;
But *they are* on the throne with
kings,
For He has seated them
forever,
And they are exalted.
8 And if *they are* bound in
fetters,
Held in the cords of affliction,
9 Then He tells them their work
and their transgressions—
That they have acted defiantly.
10 He also opens their ear to
instruction,
And commands that they turn
from iniquity.
11 If they obey and serve *Him,*
They shall spend their days in
prosperity,
And their years in pleasures.
12 But if they do not obey,
They shall perish by the sword,
And they shall die without
knowledge.*ᵃ*

13 "But the hypocrites in heart
store up wrath;
They do not cry for help when
He binds them.
14 They die in youth,
And their life *ends* among the
perverted persons.*ᵃ*
15 He delivers the poor in their
affliction,
And opens their ears in
oppression.

16 "Indeed He would have brought
you out of dire distress,
Into a broad place where *there
is* no restraint;
And what is set on your table
would be full of richness.
17 But you are filled with the
judgment due the wicked;
Judgment and justice take hold
of you.
18 Because *there is* wrath, *beware*
lest He take you away with
one blow;
For a large ransom would not
help you avoid *it.*
19 Will your riches,
Or all the mighty forces,
Keep you from distress?
20 Do not desire the night,
When people are cut off in their
place.
21 Take heed, do not turn to
iniquity,
For you have chosen this rather
than affliction.

22 "Behold, God is exalted by His
power;
Who teaches like Him?
23 Who has assigned Him His
way,
Or who has said, 'You have
done wrong'?

24 "Remember to magnify His
work,
Of which men have sung.
25 Everyone has seen it;
Man looks on *it* from afar.

26 "Behold, God *is* great, and we
do not know *Him;*
Nor can the number of His
years *be* discovered.
27 For He draws up drops of
water,

36:12 *ᵃ*Masoretic Text reads *as one without knowledge.*
practicing sodomy and prostitution in religious rituals

36:14 *ᵃ*Hebrew *qedeshim,* that is, those

---

*D*on't allow a guilt trip from the past to strangle you or cling to you or trip you up.
Cut the cord! God wants to free you from cords of manipulation, cords of blackmail,
cords of emotional slavery, cords of bondage to someone who seeks to control your
life.

Which distill as rain from the mist,

28 Which the clouds drop down
And pour abundantly on man.

29 Indeed, can *anyone* understand the spreading of clouds,
The thunder from His canopy?

30 Look, He scatters His light upon it,
And covers the depths of the sea.

31 For by these He judges the peoples;
He gives food in abundance.

32 He covers *His* hands with lightning,
And commands it to strike.

33 His thunder declares it,
The cattle also, concerning the rising *storm.*

37 "At this also my heart trembles,
And leaps from its place.

2 Hear attentively the thunder of His voice,
And the rumbling *that* comes from His mouth.

3 He sends it forth under the whole heaven,
His lightning to the ends of the earth.

4 After it a voice roars;
He thunders with His majestic voice,
And He does not restrain them when His voice is heard.

5 God thunders marvelously with His voice;
He does great things which we cannot comprehend.

6 For He says to the snow, 'Fall *on* the earth';
Likewise to the gentle rain and the heavy rain of His strength.

7 He seals the hand of every man,
That all men may know His work.

8 The beasts go into dens,
And remain in their lairs.

9 From the chamber *of the south* comes the whirlwind,
And cold from the scattering winds *of the north.*

10 By the breath of God ice is given,
And the broad waters are frozen.

11 Also with moisture He saturates the thick clouds;

He scatters His bright clouds.

12 And they swirl about, being turned by His guidance,
That they may do whatever He commands them
On the face of the whole earth.*a*

13 He causes it to come,
Whether for correction,
Or for His land,
Or for mercy.

14 "Listen to this, O Job;
Stand still and consider the wondrous works of God.

15 Do you know when God dispatches them,
And causes the light of His cloud to shine?

16 Do you know how the clouds are balanced,
Those wondrous works of Him who is perfect in knowledge?

17 Why *are* your garments hot,
When He quiets the earth by the south *wind?*

18 With Him, have you spread out the skies,
Strong as a cast metal mirror?

19 "Teach us what we should say to Him,
For we can prepare nothing because of the darkness.

20 Should He be told that I *wish* to speak?
If a man were to speak, surely he would be swallowed up.

21 Even now *men* cannot look at the light *when it is* bright in the skies,
When the wind has passed and cleared them.

22 He comes from the north *as* golden *splendor;*
With God *is* awesome majesty.

23 *As for* the Almighty, we cannot find Him;
He is excellent in power,
In judgment and abundant justice;
He does not oppress.

24 Therefore men fear Him;
He shows no partiality to any who *are* wise of heart."

38 Then the LORD answered Job out of the whirlwind, and said:

2 "Who *is* this who darkens counsel

37:12 *a*Literally *the world of the earth*

Gospel Pearls

By words without knowledge?
3 Now prepare yourself like a
   man;
   I will question you, and you
   shall answer Me.

4 "Where were you when I laid the
   foundations of the earth?
   Tell *Me*, if you have
   understanding.
5 Who determined its
   measurements?
   Surely you know!
   Or who stretched the line upon
   it?
6 To what were its foundations
   fastened?
   Or who laid its cornerstone,
7 When the morning stars sang
   together,
   And all the sons of God shouted
   for joy?

8 "Or *who* shut in the sea with
   doors,
   When it burst forth *and* issued
   from the womb;
9 When I made the clouds its
   garment,
   And thick darkness its
   swaddling band;
10 When I fixed My limit for it,
   And set bars and doors;
11 When I said,
   'This far you may come, but no
   farther,
   And here your proud waves
   must stop!'

12 "Have you commanded the
   morning since your days
   began,
   And caused the dawn to know
   its place,
13 That it might take hold of the
   ends of the earth,
   And the wicked be shaken out
   of it?
14 It takes on form like clay *under*
   a seal,
   And stands out like a garment.
15 From the wicked their light is
   withheld,
   And the upraised arm is
   broken.

16 "Have you entered the springs
   of the sea?
   Or have you walked in search
   of the depths?

17 Have the gates of death been
   revealed to you?
   Or have you seen the doors of
   the shadow of death?
18 Have you comprehended the
   breadth of the earth?
   Tell *Me,* if you know all this.

19 "Where *is* the way *to* the
   dwelling of light?
   And darkness, where *is* its
   place,
20 That you may take it to its
   territory,
   That you may know the paths
   to its home?
21 Do you know *it,* because you
   were born then,
   Or *because* the number of your
   days *is* great?

22 "Have you entered the treasury
   of snow,
   Or have you seen the treasury
   of hail,
23 Which I have reserved for the
   time of trouble,
   For the day of battle and war?
24 By what way is light diffused,
   Or the east wind scattered over
   the earth?

25 "Who has divided a channel for
   the overflowing *water,*
   Or a path for the thunderbolt,
26 To cause it to rain on a land
   where there is no one,
   A wilderness in which *there is*
   no man;
27 To satisfy the desolate waste,
   And cause to spring forth the
   growth of tender grass?
28 Has the rain a father?
   Or who has begotten the drops
   of dew?
29 From whose womb comes the
   ice?
   And the frost of heaven, who
   gives it birth?
30 The waters harden like stone,
   And the surface of the deep is
   frozen.

31 "Can you bind the cluster of the
   Pleiades,
   Or loose the belt of Orion?
32 Can you bring out Mazzaroth*ᵃ*
   in its season?
   Or can you guide the Great
   Bear with its cubs?

38:32 *ᵃ*Literally *Constellations*

*D*eclare that the old sinful patterns of your life, the old sin-producing relationships
in your life are dead and gone. They don't exist for you anymore. Declare any
dominating evil spirit evicted from your life. The only spirit He wants at work in your
life is His Holy Spirit!

33 Do you know the ordinances of
the heavens?
Can you set their dominion
over the earth?

34 "Can you lift up your voice to
the clouds,
That an abundance of water
may cover you?

35 Can you send out lightnings,
that they may go,
And say to you, 'Here we *are*!'?

36 Who has put wisdom in the
mind?*a*
Or who has given
understanding to the heart?

37 Who can number the clouds by
wisdom?
Or who can pour out the bottles
of heaven,

38 When the dust hardens in
clumps,
And the clods cling together?

39 "Can you hunt the prey for the
lion,
Or satisfy the appetite of the
young lions,

40 When they crouch in *their*
dens,
Or lurk in their lairs to lie in
wait?

41 Who provides food for the
raven,
When its young ones cry to
God,
And wander about for lack of
food?

39 "Do you know the time when the
wild mountain goats bear
young?
Or can you mark when the deer
gives birth?

2 Can you number the months
that they fulfill?
Or do you know the time when
they bear young?

3 They bow down,
They bring forth their young,
They deliver their offspring.*a*

4 Their young ones are healthy,
They grow strong with grain;
They depart and do not return
to them.

5 "Who set the wild donkey free?
Who loosed the bonds of the
onager,

6 Whose home I have made the
wilderness,

And the barren land his
dwelling?

7 He scorns the tumult of the city;
He does not heed the shouts of
the driver.

8 The range of the mountains *is*
his pasture,
And he searches after every
green thing.

9 "Will the wild ox be willing to
serve you?
Will he bed by your manger?

10 Can you bind the wild ox in the
furrow with ropes?
Or will he plow the valleys
behind you?

11 Will you trust him because his
strength *is* great?
Or will you leave your labor to
him?

12 Will you trust him to bring
home your grain,
And gather it to your threshing
floor?

13 "The wings of the ostrich wave
proudly,
But are her wings and pinions
like the kindly stork's?

14 For she leaves her eggs on the
ground,
And warms them in the dust;

15 She forgets that a foot may
crush them,
Or that a wild beast may break
them.

16 She treats her young harshly,
as though *they were* not hers;
Her labor is in vain, without
concern,

17 Because God deprived her of
wisdom,
And did not endow her with
understanding.

18 When she lifts herself on high,
She scorns the horse and its
rider.

19 "Have you given the horse
strength?
Have you clothed his neck with
thunder?*a*

20 Can you frighten him like a
locust?
His majestic snorting strikes
terror.

21 He paws in the valley, and
rejoices in *his* strength;

38:36 *a*Literally *inward parts*   39:3 *a*Literally *pangs*, figurative of offspring   39:19 *a*Or *a mane*

Gospel
Pearls

He gallops into the clash of arms.

22 He mocks at fear, and is not frightened;
Nor does he turn back from the sword.

23 The quiver rattles against him,
The glittering spear and javelin.

24 He devours the distance with fierceness and rage;
Nor does he come to a halt because the trumpet *has* sounded.

25 At *the blast of* the trumpet he says, 'Aha!'
He smells the battle from afar,
The thunder of captains and shouting.

26 "Does the hawk fly by your wisdom,
And spread its wings toward the south?

27 Does the eagle mount up at your command,
And make its nest on high?

28 On the rock it dwells and resides,
On the crag of the rock and the stronghold.

29 From there it spies out the prey;
Its eyes observe from afar.

30 Its young ones suck up blood;
And where the slain *are,* there it *is.*"

40 Moreover the LORD answered Job, and said:

2 "Shall the one who contends with the Almighty correct *Him*?
He who rebukes God, let him answer it."

3 Then Job answered the LORD and said:

4 "Behold, I am vile;
What shall I answer You?
I lay my hand over my mouth.

5 Once I have spoken, but I will not answer;
Yes, twice, but I will proceed no further."

6 Then the LORD answered Job out of the whirlwind, and said:

7 "Now prepare yourself like a man;
I will question you, and you shall answer Me:

8 "Would you indeed annul My judgment?
Would you condemn Me that you may be justified?

9 Have you an arm like God?
Or can you thunder with a voice like His?

10 Then adorn yourself *with* majesty and splendor,
And array yourself with glory and beauty.

11 Disperse the rage of your wrath;
Look on everyone *who is* proud, and humble him.

12 Look on everyone *who is* proud, *and* bring him low;
Tread down the wicked in their place.

13 Hide them in the dust together,
Bind their faces in hidden *darkness.*

14 Then I will also confess to you
That your own right hand can save you.

15 "Look now at the behemoth,[a]
which I made *along* with you;
He eats grass like an ox.

16 See now, his strength *is* in his hips,
And his power *is* in his stomach muscles.

17 He moves his tail like a cedar;
The sinews of his thighs are tightly knit.

18 His bones *are like* beams of bronze,
His ribs like bars of iron.

19 He *is* the first of the ways of God;
Only He who made him can bring near His sword.

20 Surely the mountains yield food for him,
And all the beasts of the field play there.

21 He lies under the lotus trees,
In a covert of reeds and marsh.

22 The lotus trees cover him *with* their shade;
The willows by the brook surround him.

23 Indeed the river may rage,
Yet he is not disturbed;

40:15 ᵃA large animal, exact identity unknown

*D*eclare that you are a new creature in Christ Jesus. The old you has died and has been buried. The new you is being resurrected! God will release you to live in freedom.

He is confident, though the
Jordan gushes into his
mouth,

24 *Though* he takes it in his eyes,
Or one pierces *his* nose with a
snare.

41 "Can you draw out Leviathan[a]
with a hook,
Or *snare* his tongue with a line
which you lower?

2 Can you put a reed through his
nose,
Or pierce his jaw with a hook?

3 Will he make many
supplications to you?
Will he speak softly to you?

4 Will he make a covenant with
you?
Will you take him as a servant
forever?

5 Will you play with him as *with*
a bird,
Or will you leash him for your
maidens?

6 Will *your* companions make a
banquet[a] of him?
Will they apportion him among
the merchants?

7 Can you fill his skin with
harpoons,
Or his head with fishing
spears?

8 Lay your hand on him;
Remember the battle—
Never do it again!

9 Indeed, *any* hope of
overcoming him is false;
Shall *one not* be overwhelmed
at the sight of him?

10 No one *is so* fierce that he
would dare stir him up.
Who then is able to stand
against Me?

11 Who has preceded Me, that I
should pay *him*?
Everything under heaven is
Mine.

12 "I will not conceal[a] his limbs,
His mighty power, or his
graceful proportions.

13 Who can remove his outer
coat?
Who can approach *him* with a
double bridle?

14 Who can open the doors of his
face,
With his terrible teeth all
around?

15 *His* rows of scales are *his* pride,
Shut up tightly *as with* a seal;

16 One is so near another
That no air can come between
them;

17 They are joined one to another,
They stick together and cannot
be parted.

18 His sneezings flash forth light,
And his eyes *are* like the
eyelids of the morning.

19 Out of his mouth go burning
lights;
Sparks of fire shoot out.

20 Smoke goes out of his nostrils,
As *from* a boiling pot and
burning rushes.

21 His breath kindles coals,
And a flame goes out of his
mouth.

22 Strength dwells in his neck,
And sorrow dances before him.

23 The folds of his flesh are joined
together;
They are firm on him and
cannot be moved.

24 His heart is as hard as stone,
Even as hard as the lower
millstone.

25 When he raises himself up, the
mighty are afraid;
Because of his crashings they
are beside[a] themselves.

26 *Though* the sword reaches him,
it cannot avail;
Nor does spear, dart, or javelin.

27 He regards iron as straw,
And bronze as rotten wood.

28 The arrow cannot make him
flee;
Slingstones become like
stubble to him.

29 Darts are regarded as straw;
He laughs at the threat of
javelins.

30 His undersides *are* like sharp
potsherds;
He spreads pointed *marks* in
the mire.

31 He makes the deep boil like a
pot;
He makes the sea like a pot of
ointment.

32 He leaves a shining wake
behind him;
One would think the deep had
white hair.

33 On earth there is nothing like
him,

41:1 [a]A large sea creature, exact identity unknown
silent about   41:25 [a]Or *purify themselves*   41:6 [a]Or *bargain over him*   41:12 [a]Literally *keep*

Gospel
Pearls

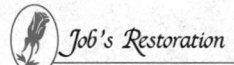

Which is made without fear.
34 He beholds every high *thing;*
He *is* king over all the children
of pride."

42 Then Job answered the LORD
and said:

2 "I know that You can do
everything,
And that no purpose *of Yours*
can be withheld from You.
3 *You asked,* 'Who *is* this who
hides counsel without
knowledge?'
Therefore I have uttered what
I did not understand,
Things too wonderful for me,
which I did not know.
4 Listen, please, and let me
speak;
You said, 'I will question you,
and you shall answer Me.'

5 "I have heard of You by the
hearing of the ear,
But now my eye sees You.
6 Therefore I abhor *myself,*
And repent in dust and ashes."

7 And so it was, after the LORD had
spoken these words to Job, that the
LORD said to Eliphaz the Temanite,
"My wrath is aroused against you
and your two friends, for you have
not spoken of Me *what is* right, as
My servant Job *has.* 8 Now therefore,
take for yourselves seven bulls and
seven rams, go to My servant Job,
and offer up for yourselves a burnt
offering; and My servant Job shall
pray for you. For I will accept him,
lest I deal with you *according to your*
folly; because you have not spoken
of Me *what is* right, as My servant
Job *has.*"

9 So Eliphaz the Temanite and Bildad the Shuhite *and* Zophar the
Naamathite went and did as the LORD
commanded them; for the LORD had
accepted Job. 10 And the LORD restored Job's losses*a* when he prayed
for his friends. Indeed the LORD gave
Job twice as much as he had before.
11 Then all his brothers, all his sisters, and all those who had been his
acquaintances before, came to him
and ate food with him in his house;
and they consoled him and comforted him for all the adversity that
the LORD had brought upon him.
Each one gave him a piece of silver
and each a ring of gold.

12 Now the LORD blessed the latter
days of Job more than his beginning;
for he had fourteen thousand sheep,
six thousand camels, one thousand
yoke of oxen, and one thousand female donkeys. 13 He also had seven
sons and three daughters. 14 And he
called the name of the first Jemimah,
the name of the second Keziah, and
the name of the third Keren-Hap-
puch. 15 In all the land were found
no women *so* beautiful as the daughters of Job; and their father gave
them an inheritance among their
brothers.

16 After this Job lived one hundred
and forty years, and saw his children
and grandchildren *for* four generations. 17 So Job died, old and full of
days.

42:10 *a*Literally *Job's captivity,* that is, what was captured from Job

*B*eing born again means you are out of the womb of sin. Cut the ties that will seek
to draw you back into darkness.

The Book of
PSALMS

Book One   Psalms 1–41

Psalm 1

1 Blessed *is* the man
Who walks not in the counsel of
   the ungodly,
   Nor stands in the path of
    sinners,
   Nor sits in the seat of the
    scornful;
2 But his delight *is* in the law of
   the LORD,
   And in His law he meditates
    day and night.
3 He shall be like a tree
   Planted by the rivers of water,
   That brings forth its fruit in its
    season,
   Whose leaf also shall not
    wither;
   And whatever he does shall
    prosper.

4 The ungodly *are* not so,
   But *are* like the chaff which the
    wind drives away.
5 Therefore the ungodly shall not
   stand in the judgment,
   Nor sinners in the congregation
    of the righteous.

6 For the LORD knows the way of
   the righteous,
   But the way of the ungodly shall
    perish.

Psalm 2

1 Why do the nations rage,
   And the people plot a vain thing?
2 The kings of the earth set
   themselves,
   And the rulers take counsel
    together,
   Against the LORD and against His
    Anointed, *saying,*
3 "Let us break Their bonds in
   pieces
   And cast away Their cords from
    us."

4 He who sits in the heavens shall
   laugh;

The LORD shall hold them in
   derision.
5 Then He shall speak to them in
   His wrath,
   And distress them in His deep
    displeasure:
6 "Yet I have set My King
   On My holy hill of Zion."

7 "I will declare the decree:
   The LORD has said to Me,
  'You *are* My Son,
   Today I have begotten You.
8 Ask of Me, and I will give *You*
   The nations *for* Your inheritance,
   And the ends of the earth *for*
    Your possession.
9 You shall break[a] them with a rod
   of iron;
   You shall dash them to pieces
    like a potter's vessel.' "

10 Now therefore, be wise, O kings;
   Be instructed, you judges of the
    earth.
11 Serve the LORD with fear,
   And rejoice with trembling.
12 Kiss the Son,[a] lest He[b] be angry,
   And you perish *in* the way,
   When His wrath is kindled but a
    little.
   Blessed *are* all those who put
    their trust in Him.

Psalm 3

A Psalm of David when he fled from Absalom
his son.

1 LORD, how they have increased
   who trouble me!
   Many *are* they who rise up
    against me.
2 Many *are* they who say of me,
  "*There is* no help for him in God."
                  Selah

3 But You, O LORD, *are* a shield for
   me,
   My glory and the One who lifts
    up my head.
4 I cried to the LORD with my voice,
   And He heard me from His holy
    hill.   Selah

2:9 [a]Following Masoretic Text and Targum; Septuagint, Syriac, and Vulgate read *rule* (compare Revelation 2:27).   2:12 [a]Septuagint and Vulgate read *Embrace discipline;* Targum reads *Receive instruction.* [b]Septuagint reads *the LORD.*

Gospel Pearls

5 I lay down and slept;
I awoke, for the LORD sustained
me.
6 I will not be afraid of ten
thousands of people
Who have set *themselves* against
me all around.

7 Arise, O LORD;
Save me, O my God!
For You have struck all my
enemies on the cheekbone;
You have broken the teeth of the
ungodly.
8 Salvation *belongs* to the LORD.
Your blessing *is* upon Your
people.   Selah

Psalm 4

To the Chief Musician. With stringed
instruments. A Psalm of David.

1 Hear me when I call, O God of
my righteousness!
You have relieved me in *my*
distress;
Have mercy on me, and hear my
prayer.

2 How long, O you sons of men,
Will you turn my glory to shame?
How long will you love
worthlessness
And seek falsehood?   Selah
3 But know that the LORD has set
apart[a] for Himself him who is
godly;
The LORD will hear when I call
to Him.

4 Be angry, and do not sin.
Meditate within your heart on
your bed, and be still.   Selah
5 Offer the sacrifices of
righteousness,
And put your trust in the LORD.

6 *There are* many who say,
"Who will show us *any* good?"
LORD, lift up the light of Your
countenance upon us.
7 You have put gladness in my
heart,
More than in the season that their
grain and wine increased.
8 I will both lie down in peace, and
sleep;
For You alone, O LORD, make me
dwell in safety.

Psalm 5

To the Chief Musician. With flutes.[a] A Psalm of
David.

1 Give ear to my words, O LORD,
Consider my meditation.
2 Give heed to the voice of my cry,
My King and my God,
For to You I will pray.
3 My voice You shall hear in the
morning, O LORD;
In the morning I will direct *it* to
You,
And I will look up.

4 For You *are* not a God who takes
pleasure in wickedness,
Nor shall evil dwell with You.
5 The boastful shall not stand in
Your sight;
You hate all workers of iniquity.
6 You shall destroy those who
speak falsehood;
The LORD abhors the bloodthirsty
and deceitful man.

7 But as for me, I will come into
Your house in the multitude of
Your mercy;
In fear of You I will worship
toward Your holy temple.
8 Lead me, O LORD, in Your
righteousness because of my
enemies;
Make Your way straight before
my face.

9 For *there is* no faithfulness in
their mouth;
Their inward part *is* destruction;
Their throat *is* an open tomb;
They flatter with their tongue.
10 Pronounce them guilty, O God!
Let them fall by their own
counsels;
Cast them out in the multitude of
their transgressions,
For they have rebelled against
You.

11 But let all those rejoice who put
their trust in You;
Let them ever shout for joy,
because You defend them;
Let those also who love Your
name
Be joyful in You.
12 For You, O LORD, will bless the
righteous;

4:3 [a]Many Hebrew manuscripts, Septuagint, Targum, and Vulgate read *made wonderful*.   5:title [a]Hebrew
nehiloth

*T*he more a woman knows that she is accepted and loved by other women who will
be honest with her and with whom she can be honest, the less she needs to be
handled with kid gloves. When she feels that it's all right to be herself, she will be less
defensive about hiding who she has been or who she really is on the inside.

With favor You will surround
   him as *with* a shield.

Psalm 6

To the Chief Musician. With stringed
instruments. On an eight-stringed harp.*a* A
Psalm of David.

1   O Lᴏʀᴅ, do not rebuke me in
   Your anger,
   Nor chasten me in Your hot
   displeasure.
2   Have mercy on me, O Lᴏʀᴅ, for
   I *am* weak;
   O Lᴏʀᴅ, heal me, for my bones
   are troubled.
3   My soul also is greatly troubled;
   But You, O Lᴏʀᴅ—how long?

4   Return, O Lᴏʀᴅ, deliver me!
   Oh, save me for Your mercies'
   sake!
5   For in death *there is* no
   remembrance of You;
   In the grave who will give You
   thanks?

6   I am weary with my groaning;
   All night I make my bed swim;
   I drench my couch with my tears.
7   My eye wastes away because of
   grief;
   It grows old because of all my
   enemies.

8   Depart from me, all you workers
   of iniquity;
   For the Lᴏʀᴅ has heard the voice
   of my weeping.
9   The Lᴏʀᴅ has heard my
   supplication;
   The Lᴏʀᴅ will receive my prayer.
10   Let all my enemies be ashamed
   and greatly troubled;
   Let them turn back *and* be
   ashamed suddenly.

Psalm 7

A Meditation*a* of David, which he sang to the
Lᴏʀᴅ concerning the words of Cush, a
Benjamite.

1   O Lᴏʀᴅ my God, in You I put my
   trust;
   Save me from all those who
   persecute me;
   And deliver me,
2   Lest they tear me like a lion,
   Rending *me* in pieces, while
   there is none to deliver.

3   O Lᴏʀᴅ my God, if I have done
   this:
   If there is iniquity in my hands,
4   If I have repaid evil to him who
   was at peace with me,
   Or have plundered my enemy
   without cause,
5   Let the enemy pursue me and
   overtake *me;*
   Yes, let him trample my life to
   the earth,
   And lay my honor in the dust.
                  Selah

6   Arise, O Lᴏʀᴅ, in Your anger;
   Lift Yourself up because of the
   rage of my enemies;
   Rise up for me*a to* the judgment
   You have commanded!
7   So the congregation of the
   peoples shall surround You;
   For their sakes, therefore, return
   on high.
8   The Lᴏʀᴅ shall judge the peoples;
   Judge me, O Lᴏʀᴅ, according to
   my righteousness,
   And according to my integrity
   within me.

9   Oh, let the wickedness of the
   wicked come to an end,
   But establish the just;
   For the righteous God tests the
   hearts and minds.
10   My defense *is* of God,
   Who saves the upright in heart.

11   God *is* a just judge,
   And God is angry *with the
   wicked* every day.
12   If he does not turn back,
   He will sharpen His sword;
   He bends His bow and makes it
   ready.
13   He also prepares for Himself
   instruments of death;
   He makes His arrows into fiery
   shafts.

14   Behold, *the wicked* brings forth
   iniquity;
   Yes, he conceives trouble and
   brings forth falsehood.
15   He made a pit and dug it out,
   And has fallen into the ditch
   which he made.
16   His trouble shall return upon his
   own head,

6:title *a*Hebrew *sheminith*   7:title *a*Hebrew *Shiggaion*   7:6 *a*Following Masoretic Text, Targum, and
Vulgate; Septuagint reads *O* Lᴏʀᴅ *my God.*

Gospel
Pearls

And his violent dealing shall
   come down on his own crown.

17 I will praise the LORD according
   to His righteousness,
   And will sing praise to the name
   of the LORD Most High.

Psalm 8

To the Chief Musician. On the instrument of
Gath.[a] A Psalm of David.

1 O LORD, our Lord,
   How excellent *is* Your name in
     all the earth,
   Who have set Your glory above
     the heavens!

2 Out of the mouth of babes and
     nursing infants
   You have ordained strength,
   Because of Your enemies,
   That You may silence the enemy
     and the avenger.

3 When I consider Your heavens,
     the work of Your fingers,
   The moon and the stars, which
     You have ordained,
4 What is man that You are
     mindful of him,
   And the son of man that You visit
     him?
5 For You have made him a little
     lower than the angels,[a]
   And You have crowned him with
     glory and honor.

6 You have made him to have
     dominion over the works of
     Your hands;
   You have put all *things* under his
     feet,
7 All sheep and oxen—
   Even the beasts of the field,
8 The birds of the air,
   And the fish of the sea
   That pass through the paths of
     the seas.

9 O LORD, our Lord,
   How excellent *is* Your name in
     all the earth!

Psalm 9

To the Chief Musician. To *the tune of* "Death
of the Son."[a] A Psalm of David.

1 I will praise *You,* O LORD, with
   my whole heart;

I will tell of all Your marvelous
   works.
2 I will be glad and rejoice in You;
   I will sing praise to Your name,
     O Most High.

3 When my enemies turn back,
   They shall fall and perish at Your
     presence.
4 For You have maintained my
     right and my cause;
   You sat on the throne judging in
     righteousness.
5 You have rebuked the nations,
   You have destroyed the wicked;
   You have blotted out their name
     forever and ever.

6 O enemy, destructions are
     finished forever!
   And you have destroyed cities;
   Even their memory has perished.
7 But the LORD shall endure
     forever;
   He has prepared His throne for
     judgment.
8 He shall judge the world in
     righteousness,
   And He shall administer
     judgment for the peoples in
     uprightness.

9 The LORD also will be a refuge for
     the oppressed,
   A refuge in times of trouble.
10 And those who know Your name
     will put their trust in You;
   For You, LORD, have not forsaken
     those who seek You.

11 Sing praises to the LORD, who
     dwells in Zion!
   Declare His deeds among the
     people.
12 When He avenges blood, He
     remembers them;
   He does not forget the cry of the
     humble.

13 Have mercy on me, O LORD!
   Consider my trouble from those
     who hate me,
   You who lift me up from the gates
     of death,
14 That I may tell of all Your praise
   In the gates of the daughter of
     Zion.
   I will rejoice in Your salvation.

8:title [a]Hebrew *Al Gittith*   8:5 [a]Hebrew *Elohim, God;* Septuagint, Syriac, Targum, and Jewish tradition
translate as *angels.*   9:title [a]Hebrew *Muth Labben*

When we swaddle a newborn Christian, we are to wrap that woman up in our arms of supernatural love and give her a continual dose of God's grace and to give her hope for her life.

Excuse Me

Psalm 8:4, 5

God has made you exactly the woman He wants you to be. He has made you beautiful in His eyes and "crowned you with glory and honor" (see Psalm 8:5). I want to encourage you to be wary about dating somebody or marrying somebody who demands that you change things about yourself to conform to what he thinks you ought to look like, talk like, act like, or dress like. That person doesn't want what God created. He wants to do the creating. You're better off sticking with what God created you to be than to substitute that for what some person tries to create. Another person can never create you to be as good as what God has made.

Now, there are lots of people that I admire. I may admire some of their attributes or think they look wonderful or appreciate the way they do certain things. But I have never met anyone who had anything about them that I found so wonderful or so intimidating that I was willing to give up being me in order to try to be them. No way!

Furthermore, you must develop deep within yourself the capacity and the tenacity to disagree with those who feel differently about you than you do. You must be able to say to another person: "You don't approve of me? You don't like the way I look? You don't like the way I talk? You don't think I'm a quality person? You don't think I have value? You don't think I'm worthy? You don't think I have a purpose and reason for being that's just as important as that of the next person?"

"I disagree!"

You don't have to get mad about it, argue the point, fight over the facts, or spend the rest of your life trying to prove that you're right and they're wrong. You simply disagree. You take the position. And just before you walk away, you simply and calmly say, "You have your opinion, but I also have mine. I disagree with your opinion. I like me. I value me, and I know God does, too."

It's time for you to look yourself and others in the eye, and to say with your attitude, if not your words: "Excuse me, but I have a right to be myself. Excuse me, but I have the right to express myself. Excuse me, but I have the right to have my opinions. Excuse me, but I have the right to use my faith. Excuse me, but I choose to agree with what God has said about me!"

15 The nations have sunk down in
the pit *which* they made;
In the net which they hid, their
own foot is caught.
16 The LORD is known *by* the
judgment He executes;
The wicked is snared in the work
of his own hands.
Meditation.*a* Selah

17 The wicked shall be turned into
hell,
And all the nations that forget
God.
18 For the needy shall not always be
forgotten;
The expectation of the poor shall
not perish forever.

19 Arise, O LORD,
Do not let man prevail;
Let the nations be judged in Your
sight.
20 Put them in fear, O LORD,
That the nations may know
themselves *to be but* men.
Selah

Psalm 10

1 Why do You stand afar off, O
LORD?
Why do You hide in times of
trouble?
2 The wicked in *his* pride
persecutes the poor;
Let them be caught in the plots
which they have devised.

3 For the wicked boasts of his
heart's desire;
He blesses the greedy *and*
renounces the LORD.
4 The wicked in his proud
countenance does not seek
God;
God *is* in none of his thoughts.

5 His ways are always prospering;
Your judgments *are* far above,
out of his sight;
As for all his enemies, he sneers
at them.
6 He has said in his heart, "I shall
not be moved;
I shall never be in adversity."
7 His mouth is full of cursing and
deceit and oppression;
Under his tongue *is* trouble and
iniquity.

8 He sits in the lurking places of
the villages;
In the secret places he murders
the innocent;
His eyes are secretly fixed on the
helpless.
9 He lies in wait secretly, as a lion
in his den;
He lies in wait to catch the poor;
He catches the poor when he
draws him into his net.
10 So he crouches, he lies low,
That the helpless may fall by his
strength.
11 He has said in his heart,
"God has forgotten;
He hides His face;
He will never see."

12 Arise, O LORD!
O God, lift up Your hand!
Do not forget the humble.
13 Why do the wicked renounce
God?
He has said in his heart,
"You will not require an *account*."
14 But You have seen, for You
observe trouble and grief,
To repay *it* by Your hand.
The helpless commits himself to
You;
You are the helper of the
fatherless.
15 Break the arm of the wicked and
the evil *man;*
Seek out his wickedness *until*
You find none.

16 The LORD *is* King forever and
ever;
The nations have perished out of
His land.
17 LORD, You have heard the desire
of the humble;
You will prepare their heart;
You will cause Your ear to hear,
18 To do justice to the fatherless and
the oppressed,
That the man of the earth may
oppress no more.

Psalm 11

To the Chief Musician. A Psalm of David.

1 In the LORD I put my trust;
How can you say to my soul,
"Flee *as* a bird to your mountain"?
2 For look! The wicked bend *their*
bow,

9:16 *a*Hebrew *Higgaion*

*Y*ou can start over. You can be healed. You can start having good things in your
life to replace the bad things.

The Perfect Father

Psalm 10:14

I am sad to remind you that many women are disappointed in their natural fathers. Many men do not treat their daughters as the precious little girls and women that they are. These women have an unhealthy concept of fatherhood.

You see, a man becomes a father through a biological act. Fatherhood is not always the desire of a man's heart. Some men do love their children with a depth you cannot understand. Others do not know how to love and end up hurting their children instead. Whether it happened physically, emotionally, sexually, or otherwise, there are countless women in our world who have been abused. Many have been molested and some ostracized. They come in all colors, ages, and sizes. Many wrap their secrets in furs and dress them up with jewelry. Some are staggering down city streets in tattered clothing. In a guttural voice, they shout obscenities and vulgarities. Both kinds are bitter and in pain. They have never known love and tenderness. Their lives have been a series of disappointments and distresses. When you find them, tell them that there is a Father who does not abuse or rape, rob or demean. Tell them that He is the One who enabled them to survive the dark places. Tell them He is real.

He is the One who enables the broken to break without falling apart. He is the One who holds the feeble and comforts the broken. He is the Father who rocks the street woman to sleep and holds the beaten prostitute through the night. He is the One who stopped the gun from going off. He is the One who eased the addict's pain and gave rest to the nervous and strength to the trembling. He is the Father of the fatherless. They may not know that He got them home many nights when others would have devoured them. He has parented them through circumstances and fed them through the hand of strangers. He hasn't forgotten the less fortunate or the more fearful. He puts His loving ointments on the secrets of their lives.

Tell these women that God is faithful. They should not blame Him for their pain. They should thank Him for their survival. He is the night watchman who saves the wounded hearts of broken daughters and gives them the gift of tomorrow. He is the perfect gentleman, the perfect Father.

They make ready their arrow on
the string,
That they may shoot secretly at
the upright in heart.
3 If the foundations are destroyed,
What can the righteous do?

4 The LORD *is* in His holy temple,
The LORD'S throne *is* in heaven;
His eyes behold,
His eyelids test the sons of men.
5 The LORD tests the righteous,
But the wicked and the one who
loves violence His soul hates.
6 Upon the wicked He will rain
coals;
Fire and brimstone and a burning
wind
Shall be the portion of their cup.

7 For the LORD *is* righteous,
He loves righteousness;
His countenance beholds the
upright.[a]

Psalm 12

To the Chief Musician. On an eight-stringed
harp.[a] A Psalm of David.

1 Help, LORD, for the godly man
ceases!
For the faithful disappear from
among the sons of men.
2 They speak idly everyone with
his neighbor;
With flattering lips *and* a double
heart they speak.

3 May the LORD cut off all flattering
lips,
And the tongue that speaks proud
things,
4 Who have said,
"With our tongue we will prevail;
Our lips *are* our own;
Who *is* lord over us?"

5 "For the oppression of the poor,
for the sighing of the needy,
Now I will arise," says the LORD;
"I will set *him* in the safety for
which he yearns."

6 The words of the LORD *are* pure
words,
Like silver tried in a furnace of
earth,
Purified seven times.
7 You shall keep them, O LORD,
You shall preserve them from
this generation forever.

8 The wicked prowl on every side,
When vileness is exalted among
the sons of men.

Psalm 13

To the Chief Musician. A Psalm of David.

1 How long, O LORD? Will You
forget me forever?
How long will You hide Your
face from me?
2 How long shall I take counsel in
my soul,
Having sorrow in my heart daily?
How long will my enemy be
exalted over me?

3 Consider *and* hear me, O LORD
my God;
Enlighten my eyes,
Lest I sleep the *sleep of* death;
4 Lest my enemy say,
"I have prevailed against him";
Lest those who trouble me
rejoice when I am moved.

5 But I have trusted in Your mercy;
My heart shall rejoice in Your
salvation.
6 I will sing to the LORD,
Because He has dealt bountifully
with me.

Psalm 14

To the Chief Musician. A Psalm of David.

1 The fool has said in his heart,
"There is no God."
They are corrupt,
They have done abominable
works,
There is none who does good.

2 The LORD looks down from
heaven upon the children of
men,
To see if there are any who
understand, who seek God.
3 They have all turned aside,
They have together become
corrupt;
There is none who does good,
No, not one.

4 Have all the workers of iniquity
no knowledge,
Who eat up my people *as* they
eat bread,
And do not call on the LORD?
5 There they are in great fear,

11:7 [a]Or *The upright beholds His countenance*   12:title [a]Hebrew *sheminith*

S waddle yourself by refusing to fill your mind with filth and unrealistic expectations
and lusts. Swaddle yourself with praise music and teaching tapes and videos of
conferences in which God's Word is taught and God's delivering power is manifest.

For God *is* with the generation of
the righteous.
6 You shame the counsel of the
poor,
But the LORD *is* his refuge.

7 Oh, that the salvation of Israel
would come out of Zion!
When the LORD brings back the
captivity of His people,
Let Jacob rejoice *and* Israel be
glad.

Psalm 15

A Psalm of David.
1 LORD, who may abide in Your
tabernacle?
Who may dwell in Your holy hill?

2 He who walks uprightly,
And works righteousness,
And speaks the truth in his
heart;
3 He *who* does not backbite with
his tongue,
Nor does evil to his neighbor,
Nor does he take up a reproach
against his friend;
4 In whose eyes a vile person is
despised,
But he honors those who fear
the LORD;
He *who* swears to his own hurt
and does not change;
5 He *who* does not put out his
money at usury,
Nor does he take a bribe
against the innocent.

He who does these *things* shall
never be moved.

Psalm 16

A Michtam of David.
1 Preserve me, O God, for in You
I put my trust.

2 O *my soul,* you have said to the
LORD,
"You *are* my Lord,
My goodness is nothing apart
from You."
3 As for the saints who *are* on the
earth,
"They are the excellent ones, in
whom is all my delight."

4 Their sorrows shall be multiplied
who hasten *after* another *god;*

Their drink offerings of blood I
will not offer,
Nor take up their names on my
lips.

5 O LORD, *You are* the portion of
my inheritance and my cup;
You maintain my lot.
6 The lines have fallen to me in
pleasant *places;*
Yes, I have a good inheritance.

7 I will bless the LORD who has
given me counsel;
My heart also instructs me in the
night seasons.
8 I have set the LORD always before
me;
Because *He is* at my right hand I
shall not be moved.

9 Therefore my heart is glad, and
my glory rejoices;
My flesh also will rest in hope.
10 For You will not leave my soul
in Sheol,
Nor will You allow Your Holy
One to see corruption.
11 You will show me the path of life;
In Your presence *is* fullness of
joy;
At Your right hand *are* pleasures
forevermore.

Psalm 17

A Prayer of David.
1 Hear a just cause, O LORD,
Attend to my cry;
Give ear to my prayer *which is*
not from deceitful lips.
2 Let my vindication come from
Your presence;
Let Your eyes look on the things
that are upright.

3 You have tested my heart;
You have visited *me* in the night;
You have tried me and have
found nothing;
I have purposed that my mouth
shall not transgress.
4 Concerning the works of men,
By the word of Your lips,
I have kept away from the paths
of the destroyer.
5 Uphold my steps in Your paths,
That my footsteps may not slip.

6 I have called upon You, for You
will hear me, O God;

When the devil tells you that you can't be cleaned up, when he tells you that you
can't be salted, when he tells you that you can't be swaddled, look the enemy in
the eye and say, "Devil, you are a liar!"

Life or Living?

Psalm 16:11

Many people are so tired of trying to "get there" that they don't even want to get there anymore. They are zombies trapped in a state of existence that is neither here nor there. This lukewarm attitude pulls them into the abyss of mediocrity. They get a job, marry, buy a car, accumulate stocks, and have children. But without passion, they are simply going through the motions!

Instead of rising each morning with a song of joy in their hearts, they hum a melody in monotone. They go through their day, mumbling and complaining. These mummies may be mommies or daddies; they may even be preachers or teachers. But they are corpses who aren't quite dead. Their near-comatose condition exempts them from pain, but denies them pleasure. They may be immune to failure, but they are susceptible to all kinds of negative experiences.

What good is life without living? Taste it, live it—even at the risk of occasional failure and adversity. If you are going to stand at the plate, take a swing at the ball! "What if I miss?" you say. Well, I say, "What if you miss out before you've even taken a swing?" Wake up and play! You're not dead! Many things in you may have died, but you are not dead!

Perhaps you have given up. No one knows you've quit, but inside, you have thrown in the towel. You wanted to make a difference, but when you ran into some obstacle, you decided to adjust your expectations to your limitations.

Jesus suffered the loss of His disciples, His earthly ministry, His friends, and even His clothes. They cast lots at His bleeding feet for His seamless robe (see John 19:23, 24), but they could not strip away His passion. Even while He was dying He continued to minister His message. He went through hell to reach the joy set before Him, but when He had finished, He got up with the keys to death and hell! His prize was a Church purchased by the blood He shed. But what is ultimately important is that He accomplished it with His passion.

God has too much for you to do to waste any more time! Get up, breathe deeply of this moment. There will never be another moment in your life like this one. I can't spare you tears, fears, or trauma; each passion has its cost. In fact, it is the cost that validates the enormity of the passion. It is what you endure that expresses the depth of your desire.

Incline Your ear to me, *and* hear my speech.

7 Show Your marvelous lovingkindness by Your right hand,
O You who save those who trust *in You*
From those who rise up *against them.*

8 Keep me as the apple of Your eye;
Hide me under the shadow of Your wings,

9 From the wicked who oppress me,
From my deadly enemies who surround me.

10 They have closed up their fat *hearts;*
With their mouths they speak proudly.

11 They have now surrounded us in our steps;
They have set their eyes, crouching down to the earth,

12 As a lion is eager to tear his prey,
And like a young lion lurking in secret places.

13 Arise, O Lord,
Confront him, cast him down;
Deliver my life from the wicked with Your sword,

14 With Your hand from men, O Lord,
From men of the world *who have* their portion in *this* life,
And whose belly You fill with Your hidden treasure.
They are satisfied with children,
And leave the rest of their *possession* for their babes.

15 As for me, I will see Your face in righteousness;
I shall be satisfied when I awake in Your likeness.

Psalm 18

To the Chief Musician. A Psalm of David the servant of the Lord, who spoke to the Lord the words of this song on the day that the Lord delivered him from the hand of all his enemies and from the hand of Saul. And he said:

1 I will love You, O Lord, my strength.

2 The Lord is my rock and my fortress and my deliverer;

My God, my strength, in whom I will trust;
My shield and the horn of my salvation, my stronghold.

3 I will call upon the Lord, *who is worthy* to be praised;
So shall I be saved from my enemies.

4 The pangs of death surrounded me,
And the floods of ungodliness made me afraid.

5 The sorrows of Sheol surrounded me;
The snares of death confronted me.

6 In my distress I called upon the Lord,
And cried out to my God;
He heard my voice from His temple,
And my cry came before Him, *even* to His ears.

7 Then the earth shook and trembled;
The foundations of the hills also quaked and were shaken,
Because He was angry.

8 Smoke went up from His nostrils,
And devouring fire from His mouth;
Coals were kindled by it.

9 He bowed the heavens also, and came down
With darkness under His feet.

10 And He rode upon a cherub, and flew;
He flew upon the wings of the wind.

11 He made darkness His secret place;
His canopy around Him *was* dark waters
And thick clouds of the skies.

12 From the brightness before Him,
His thick clouds passed with hailstones and coals of fire.

13 The Lord thundered from heaven,
And the Most High uttered His voice,
Hailstones and coals of fire.[a]

14 He sent out His arrows and scattered the foe,
Lightnings in abundance, and He vanquished them.

18:13 [a]Following Masoretic Text, Targum, and Vulgate; a few Hebrew manuscripts and Septuagint omit *Hailstones and coals of fire.*

Gospel Pearls

15 Then the channels of the sea
were seen,
The foundations of the world
were uncovered
At Your rebuke, O LORD,
At the blast of the breath of Your
nostrils.

16 He sent from above, He took me;
He drew me out of many waters.

17 He delivered me from my strong
enemy,
From those who hated me,
For they were too strong for me.

18 They confronted me in the day
of my calamity,
But the LORD was my support.

19 He also brought me out into a
broad place;
He delivered me because He
delighted in me.

20 The LORD rewarded me
according to my righteousness;
According to the cleanness of my
hands
He has recompensed me.

21 For I have kept the ways of the
LORD,
And have not wickedly departed
from my God.

22 For all His judgments *were*
before me,
And I did not put away His
statutes from me.

23 I was also blameless before Him,
And I kept myself from my
iniquity.

24 Therefore the LORD has
recompensed me according to
my righteousness,
According to the cleanness of my
hands in His sight.

25 With the merciful You will show
Yourself merciful;
With a blameless man You will
show Yourself blameless;

26 With the pure You will show
Yourself pure;
And with the devious You will
show Yourself shrewd.

27 For You will save the humble
people,
But will bring down haughty
looks.

28 For You will light my lamp;
The LORD my God will enlighten
my darkness.

29 For by You I can run against a
troop,

By my God I can leap over a wall.

30 *As for* God, His way *is* perfect;
The word of the LORD is proven;
He *is* a shield to all who trust in
Him.

31 For who *is* God, except the LORD?
And who *is* a rock, except our
God?

32 *It is* God who arms me with
strength,
And makes my way perfect.

33 He makes my feet like the *feet
of* deer,
And sets me on my high places.

34 He teaches my hands to make
war,
So that my arms can bend a bow
of bronze.

35 You have also given me the
shield of Your salvation;
Your right hand has held me up,
Your gentleness has made me
great.

36 You enlarged my path under me,
So my feet did not slip.

37 I have pursued my enemies and
overtaken them;
Neither did I turn back again till
they were destroyed.

38 I have wounded them,
So that they could not rise;
They have fallen under my feet.

39 For You have armed me with
strength for the battle;
You have subdued under me
those who rose up against me.

40 You have also given me
the necks of my enemies,
So that I destroyed those who
hated me.

41 They cried out, but *there was*
none to save;
Even to the LORD, but He did not
answer them.

42 Then I beat them as fine as the
dust before the wind;
I cast them out like dirt in the
streets.

43 You have delivered me from the
strivings of the people;
You have made me the head of
the nations;
A people I have not known shall
serve me.

44 As soon as they hear of me they
obey me;
The foreigners submit to me.

45 The foreigners fade away,

God has only one word to speak to you in answer to your depression, your thoughts
of suicide, your feelings of unworthiness. In your state of emergency there is only
one word God could speak to you that will matter. He says to you, *"Live!"*

And come frightened from their
hideouts.

46 The LORD lives!
Blessed *be* my Rock!
Let the God of my salvation be
exalted.
47 *It is* God who avenges me,
And subdues the peoples under
me;
48 He delivers me from my enemies.
You also lift me up above those
who rise against me;
You have delivered me from the
violent man.
49 Therefore I will give thanks to
You, O LORD, among the
Gentiles,
And sing praises to Your name.

50 Great deliverance He gives to His
king,
And shows mercy to His
anointed,
To David and his descendants
forevermore.

Psalm 19

To the Chief Musician. A Psalm of David.
1 The heavens declare the glory of
God;
And the firmament shows His
handiwork.
2 Day unto day utters speech,
And night unto night reveals
knowledge.
3 *There is* no speech nor language
Where their voice is not heard.
4 Their line*a* has gone out through
all the earth,
And their words to the end of the
world.

In them He has set a tabernacle
for the sun,
5 Which *is* like a bridegroom
coming out of his chamber,
And rejoices like a strong man to
run its race.
6 Its rising *is* from one end of
heaven,
And its circuit to the other end;
And there is nothing hidden from
its heat.

7 The law of the LORD *is* perfect,
converting the soul;
The testimony of the LORD *is* sure,
making wise the simple;

8 The statutes of the LORD *are* right,
rejoicing the heart;
The commandment of the LORD
is pure, enlightening the eyes;
9 The fear of the LORD *is* clean,
enduring forever;
The judgments of the LORD *are*
true *and* righteous altogether.
10 More to be desired *are they* than
gold,
Yea, than much fine gold;
Sweeter also than honey and the
honeycomb.
11 Moreover by them Your servant
is warned,
And in keeping them *there is*
great reward.

12 Who can understand *his* errors?
Cleanse me from secret *faults.*
13 Keep back Your servant also
from presumptuous *sins;*
Let them not have dominion over
me.
Then I shall be blameless,
And I shall be innocent of great
transgression.

14 Let the words of my mouth and
the meditation of my heart
Be acceptable in Your sight,
O LORD, my strength and my
Redeemer.

Psalm 20

To the Chief Musician. A Psalm of David.
1 May the LORD answer you in the
day of trouble;
May the name of the God of
Jacob defend you;
2 May He send you help from the
sanctuary,
And strengthen you out of Zion;
3 May He remember all your
offerings,
And accept your burnt sacrifice.
Selah

4 May He grant you according to
your heart's *desire,*
And fulfill all your purpose.
5 We will rejoice in your salvation,
And in the name of our God we
will set up *our* banners!
May the LORD fulfill all your
petitions.

6 Now I know that the LORD saves
His anointed;

19:4 *a*Septuagint, Syriac, and Vulgate read *sound;* Targum reads *business.*

He will answer him from His holy
  heaven
With the saving strength of His
  right hand.

7 Some *trust* in chariots, and some
  in horses;
But we will remember the name
  of the LORD our God.
8 They have bowed down and
  fallen;
But we have risen and stand
  upright.

9 Save, LORD!
May the King answer us when we
  call.

Psalm 21

To the Chief Musician. A Psalm of David.

1 The king shall have joy in Your
  strength, O LORD;
And in Your salvation how
  greatly shall he rejoice!
2 You have given him his heart's
  desire,
And have not withheld the
  request of his lips.   Selah

3 For You meet him with the
  blessings of goodness;
You set a crown of pure gold
  upon his head.
4 He asked life from You, *and* You
  gave *it* to him—
Length of days forever and ever.
5 His glory *is* great in Your
  salvation;
Honor and majesty You have
  placed upon him.
6 For You have made him most
  blessed forever;
You have made him exceedingly
  glad with Your presence.
7 For the king trusts in the LORD,
And through the mercy of the
  Most High he shall not be
  moved.

8 Your hand will find all Your
  enemies;
Your right hand will find those
  who hate You.
9 You shall make them as a fiery
  oven in the time of Your anger;
The LORD shall swallow them up
  in His wrath,
And the fire shall devour them.

10 Their offspring You shall destroy
  from the earth,
And their descendants from
  among the sons of men.
11 For they intended evil against
  You;
They devised a plot *which* they
  are not able *to perform*.
12 Therefore You will make them
  turn their back;
You will make ready *Your
  arrows* on Your string toward
  their faces.

13 Be exalted, O LORD, in Your own
  strength!
We will sing and praise Your
  power.

Psalm 22

To the Chief Musician. Set to "The Deer of the
Dawn."[a] A Psalm of David.

1 My God, My God, why have You
  forsaken Me?
Why are You so far from helping
  Me,
And from the words of My
  groaning?
2 O My God, I cry in the daytime,
  but You do not hear;
And in the night season, and am
  not silent.

3 But You *are* holy,
Enthroned in the praises of
  Israel.
4 Our fathers trusted in You;
They trusted, and You delivered
  them.
5 They cried to You, and were
  delivered;
They trusted in You, and were
  not ashamed.

6 But I *am* a worm, and no man;
A reproach of men, and despised
  by the people.
7 All those who see Me ridicule Me;
They shoot out the lip, they shake
  the head, *saying,*
8 "He trusted[a] in the LORD, let Him
  rescue Him;
Let Him deliver Him, since He
  delights in Him!"

9 But You *are* He who took Me out
  of the womb;

22:title [a]Hebrew *Aijeleth Hashahar*   22:8 [a]Septuagint, Syriac, and Vulgate read *hoped;* Targum reads
praised.

*T*o the part of you that seems to be dying in sorrow or grief right now, God says,
"Live!"

You made Me trust *while* on My
mother's breasts.

10 I was cast upon You from birth.
From My mother's womb
You *have been* My God.

11 Be not far from Me,
For trouble *is* near;
For *there is* none to help.

12 Many bulls have surrounded Me;
Strong *bulls* of Bashan have
encircled Me.

13 They gape at Me *with* their
mouths,
Like a raging and roaring lion.

14 I am poured out like water,
And all My bones are out of joint;
My heart is like wax;
It has melted within Me.

15 My strength is dried up like a
potsherd,
And My tongue clings to My
jaws;
You have brought Me to the dust
of death.

16 For dogs have surrounded Me;
The congregation of the wicked
has enclosed Me.
They pierced[a] My hands and My
feet;

17 I can count all My bones.
They look *and* stare at Me.

18 They divide My garments among
them,
And for My clothing they cast
lots.

19 But You, O LORD, do not be far
from Me;
O My Strength, hasten to help
Me!

20 Deliver Me from the sword,
My precious *life* from the power
of the dog.

21 Save Me from the lion's mouth
And from the horns of the wild
oxen!

You have answered Me.

22 I will declare Your name to My
brethren;
In the midst of the assembly I will
praise You.

23 You who fear the LORD, praise
Him!
All you descendants of Jacob,
glorify Him,

And fear Him, all you offspring
of Israel!

24 For He has not despised nor
abhorred the affliction of the
afflicted;
Nor has He hidden His face from
Him;
But when He cried to Him, He
heard.

25 My praise *shall be* of You in the
great assembly;
I will pay My vows before those
who fear Him.

26 The poor shall eat and be
satisfied;
Those who seek Him will praise
the LORD.
Let your heart live forever!

27 All the ends of the world
Shall remember and turn to the
LORD,
And all the families of the nations
Shall worship before You.[a]

28 For the kingdom *is* the LORD's,
And He rules over the nations.

29 All the prosperous of the earth
Shall eat and worship;
All those who go down to the dust
Shall bow before Him,
Even he who cannot keep himself
alive.

30 A posterity shall serve Him.
It will be recounted of the Lord
to the *next* generation,

31 They will come and declare His
righteousness to a people who
will be born,
That He has done *this*.

Psalm 23

A Psalm of David.

1 The LORD *is* my shepherd;
I shall not want.

2 He makes me to lie down in green
pastures;
He leads me beside the still
waters.

3 He restores my soul;
He leads me in the paths of
righteousness
For His name's sake.

4 Yea, though I walk through the
valley of the shadow of death,

22:16 [a]Following some Hebrew manuscripts, Septuagint, Syriac, Vulgate; Masoretic Text reads *Like a
lion*.   22:27 [a]Following Masoretic Text, Septuagint, and Targum; Arabic, Syriac, and Vulgate read *Him*.

*P*art of your maturity—part of your growing up to be God's woman—is to draw a
line between the unwashed, unsalted, unswaddled, cord-bound baby that you were,
and the mature, ornamented, breasted woman in Christ that you are.

The Restorer
of Your Soul

Psalm 23:3

*I*t is no wonder that God can restore your soul, for He is the Lover of the soul. He can mend the past, the present, and the future. He is the therapist that relieves trauma no matter how it was incurred. Perhaps you have been through a devastating moment. Maybe no one has been able to heal what has been hurt or fill what has been depleted.

There are so many kinds of pain. Some of you have survived the loss of a parent. Some of you have lost children. Some have buried your sons or daughters who died untimely deaths because of AIDS or some other deadly disease. Sadly, some have watched the caskets of their little children lowered in the ground because of a senseless drunk driving accident or drive-by shooting. Some of you are grieving over the death of a relationship. You don't even understand why it died, but you are forced to accept something that you cannot explain.

You have replayed the events like a jury reviews evidence. Accept that your deliberation is pointless. The chance to change the verdict is over. There were moments of rage that bordered on hatred, and then there were the nights of loneliness and the deepest grief you've ever known. Some of you have seen adultery—the saboteur of trust and the executioner of bonding. Some of you have walked into a room and seen an incident that was so shocking you relive it over and over again. It is one thing to be suspicious, but quite another to have a memory to contend with for the rest of your life. You dream about it and wake up in tears. It reruns before you like an old "B" movie that you have seen too many times before. Some of you are still injured over relationships that crumbled before your eyes.

Perhaps you have been haunted by one of these issues or some other crisis. Have you known what it was like to want someone to rescue you from the pain? Well, my sister, let me save you some precious time. Only the Lord can heal deep pain. It does not matter whether your pain comes from a brutal rape kept secret, a fractured promise never fulfilled, or some other gut-wrenching disturbance. He is the Prince of Peace and He rides into the worst situations on the wings of hope. His divine hand over you gives sense to the tragic events that seemed meaningless. He knows how to orchestrate your pain and somehow bring a blessing out of a mess. He is the restorer of your soul.

I will fear no evil;
For You *are* with me;
Your rod and Your staff, they
    comfort me.

5 You prepare a table before me in
    the presence of my enemies;
You anoint my head with oil;
My cup runs over.
6 Surely goodness and mercy shall
    follow me
All the days of my life;
And I will dwell[a] in the house of
    the LORD
Forever.

Psalm 24

A Psalm of David.

1 The earth *is* the LORD's, and all
    its fullness,
The world and those who dwell
    therein.
2 For He has founded it upon the
    seas,
And established it upon the
    waters.

3 Who may ascend into the hill of
    the LORD?
Or who may stand in His holy
    place?
4 He who has clean hands and a
    pure heart,
Who has not lifted up his soul to
    an idol,
Nor sworn deceitfully.
5 He shall receive blessing from
    the LORD,
And righteousness from the God
    of his salvation.
6 This *is* Jacob, the generation of
    those who seek Him,
Who seek Your face.   Selah

7 Lift up your heads, O you gates!
And be lifted up, you everlasting
    doors!
And the King of glory shall come
    in.
8 Who *is* this King of glory?
The LORD strong and mighty,
The LORD mighty in battle.
9 Lift up your heads, O you gates!
Lift up, you everlasting doors!
And the King of glory shall come
    in.
10 Who is this King of glory?
The LORD of hosts,

He *is* the King of glory.
                              Selah

Psalm 25

A Psalm of David.

1 To You, O LORD, I lift up my soul.
2 O my God, I trust in You;
Let me not be ashamed;
Let not my enemies triumph over
    me.
3 Indeed, let no one who waits on
    You be ashamed;
Let those be ashamed who deal
    treacherously without cause.

4 Show me Your ways, O LORD;
Teach me Your paths.
5 Lead me in Your truth and teach
    me,
For You *are* the God of my
    salvation;
On You I wait all the day.

6 Remember, O LORD, Your tender
    mercies and Your
    lovingkindnesses,
For they *are* from of old.
7 Do not remember the sins of my
    youth, nor my transgressions;
According to Your mercy
    remember me,
For Your goodness' sake, O LORD.

8 Good and upright *is* the LORD;
Therefore He teaches sinners in
    the way.
9 The humble He guides in justice,
And the humble He teaches His
    way.
10 All the paths of the LORD *are*
    mercy and truth,
To such as keep His covenant
    and His testimonies.
11 For Your name's sake, O LORD,
Pardon my iniquity, for it *is* great.

12 Who *is* the man that fears the
    LORD?
Him shall He[a] teach in the way
He[a] chooses.
13 He himself shall dwell in
    prosperity,
And his descendants shall inherit
    the earth.
14 The secret of the LORD *is* with
    those who fear Him,

23:6 ᵃFollowing Septuagint, Syriac, Targum, and Vulgate; Masoretic Text reads *return*.   25:12 ᵃOr *he*

And He will show them His covenant.

15 My eyes *are* ever toward the LORD,
For He shall pluck my feet out of the net.

16 Turn Yourself to me, and have mercy on me,
For I *am* desolate and afflicted.

17 The troubles of my heart have enlarged;
Bring me out of my distresses!

18 Look on my affliction and my pain,
And forgive all my sins.

19 Consider my enemies, for they are many;
And they hate me with cruel hatred.

20 Keep my soul, and deliver me;
Let me not be ashamed, for I put my trust in You.

21 Let integrity and uprightness preserve me,
For I wait for You.

22 Redeem Israel, O God,
Out of all their troubles!

Psalm 26

A Psalm of David.

1 Vindicate me, O LORD,
For I have walked in my integrity.
I have also trusted in the LORD;
I shall not slip.

2 Examine me, O LORD, and prove me;
Try my mind and my heart.

3 For Your lovingkindness *is* before my eyes,
And I have walked in Your truth.

4 I have not sat with idolatrous mortals,
Nor will I go in with hypocrites.

5 I have hated the assembly of evildoers,
And will not sit with the wicked.

6 I will wash my hands in innocence;
So I will go about Your altar, O LORD,

7 That I may proclaim with the voice of thanksgiving,
And tell of all Your wondrous works.

8 LORD, I have loved the habitation of Your house,
And the place where Your glory dwells.

9 Do not gather my soul with sinners,
Nor my life with bloodthirsty men,

10 In whose hands *is* a sinister scheme,
And whose right hand is full of bribes.

11 But as for me, I will walk in my integrity;
Redeem me and be merciful to me.

12 My foot stands in an even place;
In the congregations I will bless the LORD.

Psalm 27

A Psalm of David.

1 The LORD *is* my light and my salvation;
Whom shall I fear?
The LORD *is* the strength of my life;
Of whom shall I be afraid?

2 When the wicked came against me
To eat up my flesh,
My enemies and foes,
They stumbled and fell.

3 Though an army may encamp against me,
My heart shall not fear;
Though war may rise against me,
In this I *will be* confident.

4 One *thing* I have desired of the LORD,
That will I seek:
That I may dwell in the house of the LORD
All the days of my life,
To behold the beauty of the LORD,
And to inquire in His temple.

5 For in the time of trouble
He shall hide me in His pavilion;
In the secret place of His tabernacle
He shall hide me;
He shall set me high upon a rock.

6 And now my head shall be lifted up above my enemies all around me;
Therefore I will offer sacrifices of joy in His tabernacle;
I will sing, yes, I will sing praises to the LORD.

7 Hear, O LORD, *when* I cry with my voice!

*Y*ou are alive. You are strong. You made it. You are a survivor of whatever it was that the devil tried to do to you to keep you from God's salvation and take you out of God's plan.

Have mercy also upon me, and
answer me.
8 *When You said,* "Seek My face,"
My heart said to You, "Your face,
LORD, I will seek."
9 Do not hide Your face from me;
Do not turn Your servant away
in anger;
You have been my help;
Do not leave me nor forsake me,
O God of my salvation.
10 When my father and my mother
forsake me,
Then the LORD will take care of
me.

11 Teach me Your way, O LORD,
And lead me in a smooth path,
because of my enemies.
12 Do not deliver me to the will of
my adversaries;
For false witnesses have risen
against me,
And such as breathe out violence.
13 *I would have lost heart,* unless I
had believed
That I would see the goodness of
the LORD
In the land of the living.

14 Wait on the LORD;
Be of good courage,
And He shall strengthen your
heart;
Wait, I say, on the LORD!

Psalm 28

A Psalm of David.

1 To You I will cry, O LORD my
Rock:
Do not be silent to me,
Lest, if You *are* silent to me,
I become like those who go down
to the pit.
2 Hear the voice of my
supplications
When I cry to You,
When I lift up my hands toward
Your holy sanctuary.

3 Do not take me away with the
wicked
And with the workers of iniquity,
Who speak peace to their
neighbors,
But evil *is* in their hearts.
4 Give them according to their
deeds,

And according to the wickedness
of their endeavors;
Give them according to the work
of their hands;
Render to them what they
deserve.
5 Because they do not regard the
works of the LORD,
Nor the operation of His hands,
He shall destroy them
And not build them up.

6 Blessed *be* the LORD,
Because He has heard the voice
of my supplications!
7 The LORD *is* my strength and my
shield;
My heart trusted in Him, and I
am helped;
Therefore my heart greatly
rejoices,
And with my song I will praise
Him.

8 The LORD *is* their strength,[a]
And He *is* the saving refuge of
His anointed.
9 Save Your people,
And bless Your inheritance;
Shepherd them also,
And bear them up forever.

Psalm 29

A Psalm of David.

1 Give unto the LORD, O you mighty
ones,
Give unto the LORD glory and
strength.
2 Give unto the LORD the glory due
to His name;
Worship the LORD in the beauty
of holiness.

3 The voice of the LORD *is* over the
waters;
The God of glory thunders;
The LORD *is* over many waters.
4 The voice of the LORD *is*
powerful;
The voice of the LORD *is* full of
majesty.

5 The voice of the LORD breaks the
cedars,
Yes, the LORD splinters the cedars
of Lebanon.
6 He makes them also skip like a
calf,

28:8 [a]Following Masoretic Text and Targum; Septuagint, Syriac, and Vulgate read *the strength of His people.*

*M*ake a decision today to bury anything that has pulled you down, held you back,
kept you in despair, limited you, deceived you, or made you vulnerable. Throw
it into the coffin. Lower it into the ground. Declare it finished in your life.

The Land of the Living

Psalm 27:13

*L*et me tell you something about the way things work. Just before your seed springs forth, just before your miracle happens, just before your promise is fulfilled ... that's when all hell will seem to break out against you.

Just before you experience the fullness of God's power working in you, that's when the devil will try to break you. Just before the baby arrives, that's when the labor pains reach their peak. But while you're waiting, all the makings of a miracle are growing inside you.

Before I ever wrote a book, I wrote a letter to myself. I said, "Don't die. Don't die. It's going to get better in a minute." I told myself, "You can make it. You can make it. Don't give up." I said, "You've gone through too much to die now. You may cry, but don't die. There's got to be something else for you. There's got to be a reason you feel the way you feel. There's got be a blessing on its way that is better than anything you have ever felt before."

Those are the very words I believe the Lord wants me to say to you: Don't die. Don't die. *Don't die.* Keep standing. Keep standing. *Keep standing.* God is about to give you another seed to birth. He's about to open up the windows of heaven and pour you out a blessing that will be so great you won't even have room enough to receive it all.

When God restores you, He will do it so that you are suddenly walking in the light and can hardly recall how dark your life has been. When you move into the fullness of your appointment with God's destiny, you won't think about your past anymore. You won't have the time or the inclination to dwell on your failures, your mistakes, your former life. You will be so busy raising up your miracle and living in your blessing that all the former things in your life will not only be out of your sight and out of your mind, but out of your heart.

You will be free. You will be loosed at last to do and to be all God has appointed you to do and to be!

Lebanon and Sirion like a young
    wild ox.
7 The voice of the LORD divides the
    flames of fire.

8 The voice of the LORD shakes the
    wilderness;
    The LORD shakes the Wilderness
    of Kadesh.
9 The voice of the LORD makes the
    deer give birth,
    And strips the forests bare;
    And in His temple everyone says,
    "Glory!"

10 The LORD sat *enthroned* at the
    Flood,
    And the LORD sits as King
    forever.
11 The LORD will give strength to His
    people;
    The LORD will bless His people
    with peace.

Psalm 30

A Psalm. A Song at the dedication of the house
of David.

1 I will extol You, O LORD, for You
    have lifted me up,
    And have not let my foes rejoice
    over me.
2 O LORD my God, I cried out to
    You,
    And You healed me.
3 O LORD, You brought my soul up
    from the grave;
    You have kept me alive, that I
    should not go down to the pit.*

4 Sing praise to the LORD, you
    saints of His,
    And give thanks at the
    remembrance of His holy
    name.*
5 For His anger *is but for* a
    moment,
    His favor *is for* life;
    Weeping may endure for a night,
    But joy *comes* in the morning.

6 Now in my prosperity I said,
    "I shall never be moved."
7 LORD, by Your favor You have
    made my mountain stand
    strong;
    You hid Your face, *and* I was
    troubled.

8 I cried out to You, O LORD;
    And to the LORD I made
    supplication:
9 "What profit *is there* in my blood,
    When I go down to the pit?
    Will the dust praise You?
    Will it declare Your truth?
10 Hear, O LORD, and have mercy on
    me;
    LORD, be my helper!"

11 You have turned for me my
    mourning into dancing;
    You have put off my sackcloth
    and clothed me with gladness,
12 To the end that *my* glory may
    sing praise to You and not be
    silent.
    O LORD my God, I will give
    thanks to You forever.

Psalm 31

To the Chief Musician. A Psalm of David.

1 In You, O LORD, I put my trust;
    Let me never be ashamed;
    Deliver me in Your
    righteousness.
2 Bow down Your ear to me,
    Deliver me speedily;
    Be my rock of refuge,
    A fortress of defense to save me.

3 For You *are* my rock and my
    fortress;
    Therefore, for Your name's sake,
    Lead me and guide me.
4 Pull me out of the net which they
    have secretly laid for me,
    For You *are* my strength.
5 Into Your hand I commit my
    spirit;
    You have redeemed me, O LORD
    God of truth.

6 I have hated those who regard
    useless idols;
    But I trust in the LORD.
7 I will be glad and rejoice in Your
    mercy,
    For You have considered my
    trouble;
    You have known my soul in
    adversities,
8 And have not shut me up into the
    hand of the enemy;
    You have set my feet in a wide
    place.

30:3 *Following Qere and Targum; Kethib, Septuagint, Syriac, and Vulgate read *from those who descend
to the pit.*   30:4 *Or *His holiness*

9 Have mercy on me, O LORD, for
   I am in trouble;
My eye wastes away with grief,
   Yes, my soul and my body!
10 For my life is spent with grief,
   And my years with sighing;
My strength fails because of my
   iniquity,
And my bones waste away.
11 I am a reproach among all my
   enemies,
But especially among my
   neighbors,
And *am* repulsive to my
   acquaintances;
Those who see me outside flee
   from me.
12 I am forgotten like a dead man,
   out of mind;
I am like a broken vessel.
13 For I hear the slander of many;
Fear *is* on every side;
While they take counsel together
   against me,
They scheme to take away my
   life.

14 But as for me, I trust in You, O
   LORD;
I say, "You *are* my God."
15 My times *are* in Your hand;
Deliver me from the hand of my
   enemies,
And from those who persecute
   me.
16 Make Your face shine upon Your
   servant;
Save me for Your mercies' sake.
17 Do not let me be ashamed, O
   LORD, for I have called upon
   You;
Let the wicked be ashamed;
Let them be silent in the grave.
18 Let the lying lips be put to
   silence,
Which speak insolent things
   proudly and contemptuously
   against the righteous.

19 Oh, how great *is* Your goodness,
Which You have laid up for those
   who fear You,
Which You have prepared for
   those who trust in You
In the presence of the sons of
   men!
20 You shall hide them in the secret
   place of Your presence
From the plots of man;

You shall keep them secretly in
   a pavilion
From the strife of tongues.
21 Blessed *be* the LORD,
For He has shown me His
   marvelous kindness in a strong
   city!
22 For I said in my haste,
"I am cut off from before Your
   eyes";
Nevertheless You heard the voice
   of my supplications
When I cried out to You.

23 Oh, love the LORD, all you His
   saints!
For the LORD preserves the
   faithful,
And fully repays the proud
   person.
24 Be of good courage,
And He shall strengthen your
   heart,
All you who hope in the LORD.

Psalm 32

A Psalm of David. A Contemplation.[a]

1 Blessed *is he whose*
   transgression *is* forgiven,
Whose sin *is* covered.
2 Blessed *is* the man to whom the
   LORD does not impute iniquity,
And in whose spirit *there is* no
   deceit.

3 When I kept silent, my bones
   grew old
Through my groaning all the day
   long.
4 For day and night Your hand was
   heavy upon me;
My vitality was turned into the
   drought of summer.   Selah
5 I acknowledged my sin to You,
And my iniquity I have not
   hidden.
I said, "I will confess my
   transgressions to the LORD,"
And You forgave the iniquity of
   my sin.   Selah

6 For this cause everyone who is
   godly shall pray to You
In a time when You may be
   found;
Surely in a flood of great waters
They shall not come near him.
7 You *are* my hiding place;

32:title [a]Hebrew *Maschil*

When God saves you, He quickens the eternal part of you. He calls it to come to life and it springs to life in a moment of time. Your spirit is immediately changed by the Holy Ghost and you can never be any more saved than you are in that moment.

You shall preserve me from
trouble;
You shall surround me with
songs of deliverance.   Selah

8 I will instruct you and teach you
in the way you should go;
I will guide you with My eye.
9 Do not be like the horse *or* like
the mule,
Which have no understanding,
Which must be harnessed with
bit and bridle,
Else they will not come near you.

10 Many sorrows *shall be* to the
wicked;
But he who trusts in the LORD,
mercy shall surround him.
11 Be glad in the LORD and rejoice,
you righteous;
And shout for joy, all *you* upright
in heart!

Psalm 33

1 Rejoice in the LORD, O you
righteous!
For praise from the upright is
beautiful.
2 Praise the LORD with the harp;
Make melody to Him with an
instrument of ten strings.
3 Sing to Him a new song;
Play skillfully with a shout of joy.

4 For the word of the LORD *is* right,
And all His work *is done* in truth.
5 He loves righteousness and
justice;
The earth is full of the goodness
of the LORD.

6 By the word of the LORD the
heavens were made,
And all the host of them by the
breath of His mouth.
7 He gathers the waters of the sea
together as a heap;[a]
He lays up the deep in
storehouses.

8 Let all the earth fear the LORD;
Let all the inhabitants of the
world stand in awe of Him.
9 For He spoke, and it was *done;*
He commanded, and it stood fast.

10 The LORD brings the counsel of
the nations to nothing;

He makes the plans of the
peoples of no effect.
11 The counsel of the LORD stands
forever,
The plans of His heart to all
generations.
12 Blessed *is* the nation whose God
is the LORD,
The people He has chosen as His
own inheritance.

13 The LORD looks from heaven;
He sees all the sons of men.
14 From the place of His dwelling
He looks
On all the inhabitants of the
earth;
15 He fashions their hearts
individually;
He considers all their works.

16 No king *is* saved by the multitude
of an army;
A mighty man is not delivered by
great strength.
17 A horse *is* a vain hope for safety;
Neither shall it deliver *any* by its
great strength.

18 Behold, the eye of the LORD *is* on
those who fear Him,
On those who hope in His mercy,
19 To deliver their soul from death,
And to keep them alive in famine.

20 Our soul waits for the LORD;
He *is* our help and our shield.
21 For our heart shall rejoice in Him,
Because we have trusted in His
holy name.
22 Let Your mercy, O LORD, be upon
us,
Just as we hope in You.

Psalm 34

A Psalm of David when he pretended madness
before Abimelech, who drove him away, and he
departed.
1 I will bless the LORD at all times;
His praise *shall* continually *be* in
my mouth.
2 My soul shall make its boast in
the LORD;
The humble shall hear *of it* and
be glad.
3 Oh, magnify the LORD with me,
And let us exalt His name
together.
4 I sought the LORD, and He heard
me,

33:7 [a]Septuagint, Targum, and Vulgate read *in a vessel.*

You are either saved or you aren't. It's a state of being, not a state of becoming. If
you were made alive in Christ, then you are alive in Christ.

Don't Break
Your Rhythm

Psalm 34:1

Don't break your rhythm of praise to the Lord for anybody. No matter what you hear said about yourself, no matter how people may look at you, no matter what happens, keep your praise going. There is power in praise!

In the story of the infirm woman, the woman's deliverance infuriated the ruler of the synagogue (see Luke 13:11–14). This church man even spoke out *against* her miracle. This could happen to you. People may not like your deliverance, either. But it doesn't matter if some folks don't speak to you anymore, or don't come to see you anymore, or don't seem to understand you, or don't call you. You have been loosed by God and that gives you the right to stand straight and praise Him!

Are you aware that you have a God-given privilege to praise Him as much as you can? And, furthermore, that you can be as emotional as you want to be while you're doing it? Find a place where you can praise God the way you want to praise Him!

This is the way it works: While you are praising the Lord, He is fighting your battle in the heavenlies. He is dealing with the enemy of your soul. He is pulverizing the demonic powers that sought to oppress you and bind you and keep you from His blessings.

Your praise isn't just an expression of your joy. It is actual warfare in the spirit realm. While you are praising God—swoop! The angels of the Lord are coming into your hospital room. Swoop! The angels of the Lord are surrounding your children and protecting them. Swoop! The angels of the Lord are stopping the adversary in his tracks. Swoop! The angels of the Lord are scattering your enemies! God's angels *do* encamp around us when we reverence and fear the Lord.

Have you ever praised God—singing and rejoicing—as you were driving your car and, suddenly, you felt as if you weren't alone? You weren't. Swoop! God's angels were there right by your side. You may not have seen them, but they were there! The Bible says that "the angel of the LORD encamps all around those who fear Him, and delivers them" (Psalm 34:7).

Don't pay any attention to anybody's criticism of your deliverance. Don't listen to their protests, their murmuring, their gossip, or their attempts to rationalize what God has done in your life. Don't let them hurt your feelings or inhibit you. Sometimes you just have to praise God in the midst of background noise! Whatever you do, don't break your rhythm.

And delivered me from all my
fears.

5 They looked to Him and were
radiant,
And their faces were not
ashamed.

6 This poor man cried out, and the
LORD heard *him,*
And saved him out of all his
troubles.

7 The angel[a] of the LORD encamps
all around those who fear Him,
And delivers them.

8 Oh, taste and see that the LORD
is good;
Blessed *is* the man *who* trusts in
Him!

9 Oh, fear the LORD, you His saints!
There is no want to those who
fear Him.

10 The young lions lack and suffer
hunger;
But those who seek the LORD
shall not lack any good *thing.*

11 Come, you children, listen to me;
I will teach you the fear of the
LORD.

12 Who *is* the man *who* desires life,
And loves *many* days, that he
may see good?

13 Keep your tongue from evil,
And your lips from speaking
deceit.

14 Depart from evil and do good;
Seek peace and pursue it.

15 The eyes of the LORD *are* on the
righteous,
And His ears *are open* to their
cry.

16 The face of the LORD *is* against
those who do evil,
To cut off the remembrance of
them from the earth.

17 *The righteous* cry out, and the
LORD hears,
And delivers them out of all their
troubles.

18 The LORD *is* near to those who
have a broken heart,
And saves such as have a contrite
spirit.

19 Many *are* the afflictions of the
righteous,
But the LORD delivers him out of
them all.

20 He guards all his bones;
Not one of them is broken.

21 Evil shall slay the wicked,
And those who hate the righteous
shall be condemned.

22 The LORD redeems the soul of His
servants,
And none of those who trust in
Him shall be condemned.

Psalm 35

A Psalm of David.

1 Plead *my cause,* O LORD, with
those who strive with me;
Fight against those who fight
against me.

2 Take hold of shield and buckler,
And stand up for my help.

3 Also draw out the spear,
And stop those who pursue me.
Say to my soul,
"I am your salvation."

4 Let those be put to shame and
brought to dishonor
Who seek after my life;
Let those be turned back and
brought to confusion
Who plot my hurt.

5 Let them be like chaff before the
wind,
And let the angel[a] of the LORD
chase *them.*

6 Let their way be dark and
slippery,
And let the angel of the LORD
pursue them.

7 For without cause they have
hidden their net for me *in* a pit,
Which they have dug without
cause for my life.

8 Let destruction come upon him
unexpectedly,
And let his net that he has hidden
catch himself;
Into that very destruction let him
fall.

9 And my soul shall be joyful in the
LORD;
It shall rejoice in His salvation.

10 All my bones shall say,
"LORD, who *is* like You,
Delivering the poor from him
who is too strong for him,
Yes, the poor and the needy from
him who plunders him?"

34:7 ªOr *Angel*   35:5 ªOr *Angel*

Gospel Pearls

11 Fierce witnesses rise up;
They ask me *things* that I do not
know.
12 They reward me evil for good,
To the sorrow of my soul.
13 But as for me, when they were
sick,
My clothing *was* sackcloth;
I humbled myself with fasting;
And my prayer would return to
my own heart.
14 I paced about as though *he were*
my friend *or* brother;
I bowed down heavily, as one
who mourns *for his* mother.

15 But in my adversity they rejoiced
And gathered together;
Attackers gathered against me,
And I did not know *it;*
They tore *at me* and did not
cease;
16 With ungodly mockers at feasts
They gnashed at me with their
teeth.

17 Lord, how long will You look on?
Rescue me from their
destructions,
My precious *life* from the lions.
18 I will give You thanks in the great
assembly;
I will praise You among many
people.

19 Let them not rejoice over me who
are wrongfully my enemies;
Nor let them wink with the eye
who hate me without a cause.
20 For they do not speak peace,
But they devise deceitful matters
Against *the* quiet ones in the
land.
21 They also opened their mouth
wide against me,
And said, "Aha, aha!
Our eyes have seen *it.*"

22 *This* You have seen, O LORD;
Do not keep silence.
O Lord, do not be far from me.
23 Stir up Yourself, and awake to
my vindication,
To my cause, my God and my
Lord.
24 Vindicate me, O LORD my God,
according to Your
righteousness;
And let them not rejoice over me.
25 Let them not say in their hearts,
"Ah, so we would have it!"
Let them not say, "We have
swallowed him up."

26 Let them be ashamed and
brought to mutual confusion
Who rejoice at my hurt;
Let them be clothed with shame
and dishonor
Who exalt themselves against
me.

27 Let them shout for joy and be
glad,
Who favor my righteous cause;
And let them say continually,
"Let the LORD be magnified,
Who has pleasure in the
prosperity of His servant."
28 And my tongue shall speak of
Your righteousness
And of Your praise all the day
long.

Psalm 36

To the Chief Musician. A Psalm of David the
servant of the LORD.
1 An oracle within my heart
concerning the transgression
of the wicked:
There is no fear of God before his
eyes.
2 For he flatters himself in his own
eyes,
When he finds out his iniquity
and when he hates.
3 The words of his mouth *are*
wickedness and deceit;
He has ceased to be wise *and* to
do good.
4 He devises wickedness on his
bed;
He sets himself in a way *that is*
not good;
He does not abhor evil.

5 Your mercy, O LORD, *is* in the
heavens;
Your faithfulness *reaches* to the
clouds.
6 Your righteousness *is* like the
great mountains;
Your judgments *are* a great deep;
O LORD, You preserve man and
beast.

7 How precious *is* Your
lovingkindness, O God!
Therefore the children of men put
their trust under the shadow of
Your wings.
8 They are abundantly satisfied
with the fullness of Your house,
And You give them drink from
the river of Your pleasures.

Even though your spirit has been saved, you can still have some areas in your mind, your emotions, your appetites, and your desires that need to be healed. In every one of us, there is something that needs to be healed.

9 For with You *is* the fountain of
 life;
 In Your light we see light.

10 Oh, continue Your
 lovingkindness to those who
 know You,
 And Your righteousness to the
 upright in heart.

11 Let not the foot of pride come
 against me,
 And let not the hand of the
 wicked drive me away.

12 There the workers of iniquity
 have fallen;
 They have been cast down and
 are not able to rise.

Psalm 37

A Psalm of David.

1 Do not fret because of evildoers,
 Nor be envious of the workers of
 iniquity.

2 For they shall soon be cut down
 like the grass,
 And wither as the green herb.

3 Trust in the LORD, and do good;
 Dwell in the land, and feed on His
 faithfulness.

4 Delight yourself also in the LORD,
 And He shall give you the desires
 of your heart.

5 Commit your way to the LORD,
 Trust also in Him,
 And He shall bring *it* to pass.

6 He shall bring forth your
 righteousness as the light,
 And your justice as the noonday.

7 Rest in the LORD, and wait
 patiently for Him;
 Do not fret because of him who
 prospers in his way,
 Because of the man who brings
 wicked schemes to pass.

8 Cease from anger, and forsake
 wrath;
 Do not fret—*it* only *causes* harm.

9 For evildoers shall be cut off;
 But those who wait on the LORD,
 They shall inherit the earth.

10 For yet a little while and the
 wicked *shall be* no *more;*
 Indeed, you will look carefully
 for his place,
 But it *shall be* no *more.*

11 But the meek shall inherit the
 earth,

 And shall delight themselves in
 the abundance of peace.

12 The wicked plots against the just,
 And gnashes at him with his
 teeth.

13 The Lord laughs at him,
 For He sees that his day is
 coming.

14 The wicked have drawn the
 sword
 And have bent their bow,
 To cast down the poor and needy,
 To slay those who are of upright
 conduct.

15 Their sword shall enter their own
 heart,
 And their bows shall be broken.

16 A little that a righteous man has
 Is better than the riches of many
 wicked.

17 For the arms of the wicked shall
 be broken,
 But the LORD upholds the
 righteous.

18 The LORD knows the days of the
 upright,
 And their inheritance shall be
 forever.

19 They shall not be ashamed in the
 evil time,
 And in the days of famine they
 shall be satisfied.

20 But the wicked shall perish;
 And the enemies of the LORD,
 Like the splendor of the
 meadows, shall vanish.
 Into smoke they shall vanish
 away.

21 The wicked borrows and does not
 repay,
 But the righteous shows mercy
 and gives.

22 For *those* blessed by Him shall
 inherit the earth,
 But *those* cursed by Him shall be
 cut off.

23 The steps of a *good* man are
 ordered by the LORD,
 And He delights in his way.

24 Though he fall, he shall not be
 utterly cast down;
 For the LORD upholds *him with*
 His hand.

25 I have been young, and *now* am
 old;

Yet I have not seen the righteous
   forsaken,
Nor his descendants begging
   bread.
26 *He is* ever merciful, and lends;
And his descendants *are* blessed.

27 Depart from evil, and do good;
And dwell forevermore.
28 For the LORD loves justice,
And does not forsake His saints;
They are preserved forever,
But the descendants of the
   wicked shall be cut off.
29 The righteous shall inherit the
   land,
And dwell in it forever.

30 The mouth of the righteous
   speaks wisdom,
And his tongue talks of justice.
31 The law of his God *is* in his heart;
None of his steps shall slide.

32 The wicked watches the
   righteous,
And seeks to slay him.
33 The LORD will not leave him in
   his hand,
Nor condemn him when he is
   judged.

34 Wait on the LORD,
And keep His way,
And He shall exalt you to inherit
   the land;
When the wicked are cut off, you
   shall see *it.*
35 I have seen the wicked in great
   power,
And spreading himself like a
   native green tree.
36 Yet he passed away,[a] and behold,
   he *was* no *more;*
Indeed I sought him, but he could
   not be found.

37 Mark the blameless *man,* and
   observe the upright;
For the future of *that* man *is*
   peace.
38 But the transgressors shall be
   destroyed together;
The future of the wicked shall be
   cut off.

39 But the salvation of the righteous
   is from the LORD;
He is their strength in the time
   of trouble.

40 And the LORD shall help them and
   deliver them;
He shall deliver them from the
   wicked,
And save them,
Because they trust in Him.

Psalm 38

A Psalm of David. To bring to remembrance.

1 O LORD, do not rebuke me in
   Your wrath,
Nor chasten me in Your hot
   displeasure!
2 For Your arrows pierce me
   deeply,
And Your hand presses me down.

3 *There is* no soundness in my flesh
Because of Your anger,
Nor *any* health in my bones
Because of my sin.
4 For my iniquities have gone over
   my head;
Like a heavy burden they are too
   heavy for me.
5 My wounds are foul *and* festering
Because of my foolishness.

6 I am troubled, I am bowed down
   greatly;
I go mourning all the day long.
7 For my loins are full of
   inflammation,
And *there is* no soundness in my
   flesh.
8 I am feeble and severely broken;
I groan because of the turmoil of
   my heart.

9 Lord, all my desire *is* before You;
And my sighing is not hidden
   from You.
10 My heart pants, my strength fails
   me;
As for the light of my eyes, it also
   has gone from me.

11 My loved ones and my friends
   stand aloof from my plague,
And my relatives stand afar off.
12 Those also who seek my life lay
   snares *for me;*
Those who seek my hurt speak
   of destruction,
And plan deception all the day
   long.

13 But I, like a deaf *man,* do not
   hear;

37:36 [a]Following Masoretic Text, Septuagint, and Targum; Syriac and Vulgate read *I passed by.*

Wholeness comes when you turn to Him in your weakness, your pain, your suffering, and you allow Him to do for you what no one else can do. Only God can
regenerate the human spirit. And only God can raise a person to spiritual maturity
and wholeness.

And *I am* like a mute *who* does
not open his mouth.
14 Thus I am like a man who does
not hear,
And in whose mouth *is* no
response.

15 For in You, O LORD, I hope;
You will hear, O Lord my God.
16 For I said, *"Hear me,* lest they
rejoice over me,
Lest, when my foot slips, they
exalt *themselves* against me."

17 For I *am* ready to fall,
And my sorrow *is* continually
before me.
18 For I will declare my iniquity;
I will be in anguish over my sin.
19 But my enemies *are* vigorous,
and they are strong;
And those who hate me
wrongfully have multiplied.
20 Those also who render evil for
good,
They are my adversaries,
because I follow *what is* good.

21 Do not forsake me, O LORD;
O my God, be not far from me!
22 Make haste to help me,
O Lord, my salvation!

Psalm 39

To the Chief Musician. To Jeduthun. A Psalm
of David.
1 I said, "I will guard my ways,
Lest I sin with my tongue;
I will restrain my mouth with a
muzzle,
While the wicked are before me."
2 I was mute with silence,
I held my peace *even* from good;
And my sorrow was stirred up.
3 My heart was hot within me;
While I was musing, the fire
burned.
Then I spoke with my tongue:

4 "LORD, make me to know my end,
And what *is* the measure of my
days,
That I may know how frail I *am.*
5 Indeed, You have made my days
as handbreadths,
And my age *is* as nothing before
You;
Certainly every man at his best
state *is* but vapor.   Selah
6 Surely every man walks about
like a shadow;

Surely they busy themselves in
vain;
He heaps up *riches,*
And does not know who will
gather them.

7 "And now, Lord, what do I wait
for?
My hope *is* in You.
8 Deliver me from all my
transgressions;
Do not make me the reproach of
the foolish.
9 I was mute, I did not open my
mouth,
Because it was You who did *it.*
10 Remove Your plague from me;
I am consumed by the blow of
Your hand.
11 When with rebukes You correct
man for iniquity,
You make his beauty melt away
like a moth;
Surely every man *is* vapor.
Selah

12 "Hear my prayer, O LORD,
And give ear to my cry;
Do not be silent at my tears;
For I *am* a stranger with You,
A sojourner, as all my fathers
were.
13 Remove Your gaze from me, that
I may regain strength,
Before I go away and am no
more."

Psalm 40

To the Chief Musician. A Psalm of David.
1 I waited patiently for the LORD;
And He inclined to me,
And heard my cry.
2 He also brought me up out of a
horrible pit,
Out of the miry clay,
And set my feet upon a rock,
And established my steps.
3 He has put a new song in my
mouth—
Praise to our God;
Many will see *it* and fear,
And will trust in the LORD.

4 Blessed *is* that man who makes
the LORD his trust,
And does not respect the proud,
nor such as turn aside to lies.
5 Many, O LORD my God, *are* Your
wonderful works
Which You have done;
And Your thoughts toward us

Gospel
Pearls

Cannot be recounted to You in
order;
If I would declare and speak *of
them,*
They are more than can be
numbered.

6 Sacrifice and offering You did
not desire;
My ears You have opened.
Burnt offering and sin offering
You did not require.

7 Then I said, "Behold, I come;
In the scroll of the book *it is*
written of me.

8 I delight to do Your will, O my
God,
And Your law *is* within my
heart."

9 I have proclaimed the good news
of righteousness
In the great assembly;
Indeed, I do not restrain my lips,
O LORD, You Yourself know.

10 I have not hidden Your
righteousness within my heart;
I have declared Your faithfulness
and Your salvation;
I have not concealed Your
lovingkindness and Your truth
From the great assembly.

11 Do not withhold Your tender
mercies from me, O LORD;
Let Your lovingkindness and
Your truth continually
preserve me.

12 For innumerable evils have
surrounded me;
My iniquities have overtaken me,
so that I am not able to look
up;
They are more than the hairs of
my head;
Therefore my heart fails me.

13 Be pleased, O LORD, to deliver
me;
O LORD, make haste to help me!

14 Let them be ashamed and
brought to mutual confusion
Who seek to destroy my life;
Let them be driven backward and
brought to dishonor
Who wish me evil.

15 Let them be confounded because
of their shame,
Who say to me, "Aha, aha!"

16 Let all those who seek You
rejoice and be glad in You;

Let such as love Your salvation
say continually,
"The LORD be magnified!"

17 But I *am* poor and needy;
Yet the LORD thinks upon me.
You *are* my help and my
deliverer;
Do not delay, O my God.

Psalm 41

To the Chief Musician. A Psalm of David.

1 Blessed *is* he who considers the
poor;
The LORD will deliver him in time
of trouble.

2 The LORD will preserve him and
keep him alive,
And he will be blessed on the
earth;
You will not deliver him to the
will of his enemies.

3 The LORD will strengthen him on
his bed of illness;
You will sustain him on his
sickbed.

4 I said, "LORD, be merciful to me;
Heal my soul, for I have sinned
against You."

5 My enemies speak evil of me:
"When will he die, and his name
perish?"

6 And if he comes to see *me,* he
speaks lies;
His heart gathers iniquity to
itself;
When he goes out, he tells *it.*

7 All who hate me whisper
together against me;
Against me they devise my hurt.

8 "An evil disease," *they say,*
"clings to him.
And *now* that he lies down, he
will rise up no more."

9 Even my own familiar friend in
whom I trusted,
Who ate my bread,
Has lifted up *his* heel against me.

10 But You, O LORD, be merciful to
me, and raise me up,
That I may repay them.

11 By this I know that You are well
pleased with me,
Because my enemy does not
triumph over me.

12 As for me, You uphold me in my
integrity,
And set me before Your face
forever.

*S*tart appreciating yourself. Remind yourself, "I am valuable to God. I am somebody.
Yes, I've been through some bad times. But the Lord touched me and loosed me
and now I'm glorifying God and I'm not going back to where I came from."

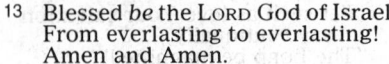
13 Blessed be the LORD God of Israel
From everlasting to everlasting!
Amen and Amen.

Book Two   Psalms 42–72

Psalm 42

To the Chief Musician. A Contemplation[a] of the
sons of Korah.

1 As the deer pants for the water
brooks,
So pants my soul for You, O
God.
2 My soul thirsts for God, for the
living God.
When shall I come and appear
before God?[a]
3 My tears have been my food day
and night,
While they continually say to me,
"Where is your God?"

4 When I remember these things,
I pour out my soul within me.
For I used to go with the
multitude;
I went with them to the house of
God,
With the voice of joy and praise,
With a multitude that kept a
pilgrim feast.

5 Why are you cast down, O my
soul?
And why are you disquieted
within me?
Hope in God, for I shall yet praise
Him
For the help of His countenance.[a]

6 O my God,[a] my soul is cast down
within me;
Therefore I will remember You
from the land of the Jordan,
And from the heights of Hermon,
From the Hill Mizar.
7 Deep calls unto deep at the noise
of Your waterfalls;
All Your waves and billows have
gone over me.
8 The LORD will command His
lovingkindness in the daytime,
And in the night His song shall
be with me—
A prayer to the God of my life.

9 I will say to God my Rock,
"Why have You forgotten me?
Why do I go mourning because
of the oppression of the
enemy?"
10 As with a breaking of my bones,
My enemies reproach me,
While they say to me all day
long,
"Where is your God?"

11 Why are you cast down, O my
soul?
And why are you disquieted
within me?
Hope in God;
For I shall yet praise Him,
The help of my countenance and
my God.

Psalm 43

1 Vindicate me, O God,
And plead my cause against an
ungodly nation;
Oh, deliver me from the deceitful
and unjust man!
2 For You are the God of my
strength;
Why do You cast me off?
Why do I go mourning because
of the oppression of the
enemy?

3 Oh, send out Your light and Your
truth!
Let them lead me;
Let them bring me to Your holy
hill
And to Your tabernacle.
4 Then I will go to the altar of
God,
To God my exceeding joy;
And on the harp I will praise
You,
O God, my God.

5 Why are you cast down, O my
soul?
And why are you disquieted
within me?
Hope in God;
For I shall yet praise Him,
The help of my countenance and
my God.

42:title [a]Hebrew Maschil   42:2 [a]Following Masoretic Text and Vulgate; some Hebrew manuscripts,
Septuagint, Syriac, Targum read I see the face of God.   42:5 [a]Following Masoretic Text and Targum; a
few Hebrew manuscripts, Septuagint, Syriac, and Vulgate read The help of my countenance, my God.
42:6 [a]Following Masoretic Text and Targum; a few Hebrew manuscripts, Septuagint, Syriac, and Vulgate
put my God at the end of verse 5.

Gospel
Pearls

Psalm 44

To the Chief Musician. A Contemplation*a* of the sons of Korah.

1 We have heard with our ears, O God,
Our fathers have told us,
The deeds You did in their days,
In days of old:

2 You drove out the nations with Your hand,
But them You planted;
You afflicted the peoples, and cast them out.

3 For they did not gain possession of the land by their own sword,
Nor did their own arm save them;
But it was Your right hand, Your arm, and the light of Your countenance,
Because You favored them.

4 You are my King, O God;*a*
Command*b* victories for Jacob.

5 Through You we will push down our enemies;
Through Your name we will trample those who rise up against us.

6 For I will not trust in my bow,
Nor shall my sword save me.

7 But You have saved us from our enemies,
And have put to shame those who hated us.

8 In God we boast all day long,
And praise Your name forever.
                       Selah

9 But You have cast *us* off and put us to shame,
And You do not go out with our armies.

10 You make us turn back from the enemy,
And those who hate us have taken spoil for themselves.

11 You have given us up like sheep *intended* for food,
And have scattered us among the nations.

12 You sell Your people for *next to* nothing,
And are not enriched by selling them.

13 You make us a reproach to our neighbors,

14 A scorn and a derision to those all around us.
You make us a byword among the nations,
A shaking of the head among the peoples.

15 My dishonor *is* continually before me,
And the shame of my face has covered me,

16 Because of the voice of him who reproaches and reviles,
Because of the enemy and the avenger.

17 All this has come upon us;
But we have not forgotten You,
Nor have we dealt falsely with Your covenant.

18 Our heart has not turned back,
Nor have our steps departed from Your way;

19 But You have severely broken us in the place of jackals,
And covered us with the shadow of death.

20 If we had forgotten the name of our God,
Or stretched out our hands to a foreign god,

21 Would not God search this out?
For He knows the secrets of the heart.

22 Yet for Your sake we are killed all day long;
We are accounted as sheep for the slaughter.

23 Awake! Why do You sleep, O Lord?
Arise! Do not cast *us* off forever.

24 Why do You hide Your face,
And forget our affliction and our oppression?

25 For our soul is bowed down to the dust;
Our body clings to the ground.

26 Arise for our help,
And redeem us for Your mercies' sake.

Psalm 45

To the Chief Musician. Set to "The Lilies."*a* A Contemplation*b* of the sons of Korah. A Song of Love.

1 My heart is overflowing with a good theme;
I recite my composition concerning the King;

44:title *a*Hebrew *Maschil*   44:4 *a*Following Masoretic Text and Targum; Septuagint and Vulgate read *and my God.*   *b*Following Masoretic Text and Targum; Septuagint, Syriac, and Vulgate read *who commands.*
45:title *a*Hebrew *Shoshannim* *b*Hebrew *Maschil*

*Y*our real value cannot be bought, applied, added on, hung from your ears, or laid on your neck. The real thing that causes a man to need you so desperately he can't leave you is not what is *on* you, but what is *in* you.

My tongue *is* the pen of a ready writer.

2 You are fairer than the sons of men;
Grace is poured upon Your lips;
Therefore God has blessed You forever.

3 Gird Your sword upon *Your* thigh, O Mighty One,
With Your glory and Your majesty.

4 And in Your majesty ride prosperously because of truth, humility, *and* righteousness;
And Your right hand shall teach You awesome things.

5 Your arrows *are* sharp in the heart of the King's enemies;
The peoples fall under You.

6 Your throne, O God, *is* forever and ever;
A scepter of righteousness *is* the scepter of Your kingdom.

7 You love righteousness and hate wickedness;
Therefore God, Your God, has anointed You
With the oil of gladness more than Your companions.

8 All Your garments are scented with myrrh and aloes *and* cassia,
Out of the ivory palaces, by which they have made You glad.

9 Kings' daughters *are* among Your honorable women;
At Your right hand stands the queen in gold from Ophir.

10 Listen, O daughter,
Consider and incline your ear;
Forget your own people also, and your father's house;

11 So the King will greatly desire your beauty;
Because He *is* your Lord, worship Him.

12 And the daughter of Tyre *will come* with a gift;
The rich among the people will seek your favor.

13 The royal daughter *is* all glorious within *the palace;*
Her clothing *is* woven with gold.

14 She shall be brought to the King in robes of many colors;
The virgins, her companions who follow her, shall be brought to You.

15 With gladness and rejoicing they shall be brought;
They shall enter the King's palace.

16 Instead of Your fathers shall be Your sons,
Whom You shall make princes in all the earth.

17 I will make Your name to be remembered in all generations;
Therefore the people shall praise You forever and ever.

Psalm 46

To the Chief Musician. A Psalm of the sons of Korah. A Song for Alamoth.

1 God *is* our refuge and strength,
A very present help in trouble.

2 Therefore we will not fear,
Even though the earth be removed,
And though the mountains be carried into the midst of the sea;

3 *Though* its waters roar *and* be troubled,
Though the mountains shake with its swelling.   Selah

4 *There is* a river whose streams shall make glad the city of God,
The holy *place* of the tabernacle of the Most High.

5 God *is* in the midst of her, she shall not be moved;
God shall help her, just at the break of dawn.

6 The nations raged, the kingdoms were moved;
He uttered His voice, the earth melted.

7 The LORD of hosts *is* with us;
The God of Jacob *is* our refuge.   Selah

8 Come, behold the works of the LORD,
Who has made desolations in the earth.

9 He makes wars cease to the end of the earth;
He breaks the bow and cuts the spear in two;
He burns the chariot in the fire.

10 Be still, and know that I *am* God;
I will be exalted among the nations,
I will be exalted in the earth!

You need to recognize what God has put in you. God, when He made the woman, didn't just decorate the outside. He decorated the inside of the woman. He put beauty in her spirit.

Your Lord

Psalm 45:11

*E*very woman who walks with God walks through storms, winds, and rain. O woman of God, your life is filled with challenges and victories, smiles and tears. You are like a sweet salve mixed by an apothecary. You are a careful blend of life's many spices. Your personality is a potpourri of so many different things that years of knowing you will not reveal everything that makes you who you are. You are carefully concocted and slowly simmered, stirred patiently by the Lord. It is amazing how deliberate God is in preparing you for your destiny. He knows exactly how long it will take. He knows who to send into your life. He knows what events it will take to bring you to a place of maturity in Him. He is your Lord.

It does not take long to realize that though you may have many admirers, friends, and family, none will ever take the place of your Lord. His place in your life is the foundation of every success you will ever enjoy. He will be there in every moment of pain and glory. He is the force that brings all the pieces of your life together. It is His tender love for you that keeps your mind from breaking under the stress of life. And when all is said and done, no one can comfort you or hold you like He can.

You may be prosperous in your business, secure in your relationships, confident in who you are, but it is all because of Him. It is knowing Him that gives you the grace to endure transitions, to withstand opposition, and to deflect the ammunition of the enemy. He enables you to know when the day is at its end. He will watch you through the night and His kiss will bring you out of your sleep come dawn. He is your Lord.

Oh yes, for men it is a privilege to know and love, hold and touch a lady of excellence. It is an honor to be born out of your womb. It is a distinct privilege to take your hand in marriage. It is a joy to hear the laughter that comes from the mouth of a woman whose heart is filled with love and peace. We watch you like admirers in a museum. We appreciate you like connoisseurs of fine cuisine. But, when all is said and done, there is a part of your life that none can touch—but your Lord.

So know Him and love Him and worship Him. Of all the men on earth, no one can ever speak to your spirit or heal your heart like your Lord.

11 The LORD of hosts *is* with us;
   The God of Jacob *is* our refuge.
                          Selah

Psalm 47

To the Chief Musician. A Psalm of the sons of Korah.

1 Oh, clap your hands, all you
   peoples!
   Shout to God with the voice of
   triumph!
2 For the LORD Most High *is*
   awesome;
   He is a great King over all the
   earth.
3 He will subdue the peoples under
   us,
   And the nations under our feet.
4 He will choose our inheritance
   for us,
   The excellence of Jacob whom
   He loves.   Selah

5 God has gone up with a shout,
   The LORD with the sound of a
   trumpet.
6 Sing praises to God, sing
   praises!
   Sing praises to our King, sing
   praises!
7 For God *is* the King of all the
   earth;
   Sing praises with understanding.

8 God reigns over the nations;
   God sits on His holy throne.
9 The princes of the people have
   gathered together,
   The people of the God of
   Abraham.
   For the shields of the earth
   belong to God;
   He is greatly exalted.

Psalm 48

A Song. A Psalm of the sons of Korah.

1 Great *is* the LORD, and greatly to
   be praised
   In the city of our God,
   In His holy mountain.
2 Beautiful in elevation,
   The joy of the whole earth,
   Is Mount Zion *on* the sides of the
   north,
   The city of the great King.
3 God *is* in her palaces;
   He is known as her refuge.

4 For behold, the kings assembled,
   They passed by together.
5 They saw *it, and* so they
   marveled;
   They were troubled, they
   hastened away.
6 Fear took hold of them there,
   And pain, as of a woman in birth
   pangs,
7 *As when* You break the ships of
   Tarshish
   With an east wind.

8 As we have heard,
   So we have seen
   In the city of the LORD of hosts,
   In the city of our God:
   God will establish it forever.
                          Selah

9 We have thought, O God, on
   Your lovingkindness,
   In the midst of Your temple.
10 According to Your name, O God,
   So *is* Your praise to the ends of
   the earth;
   Your right hand is full of
   righteousness.
11 Let Mount Zion rejoice,
   Let the daughters of Judah be
   glad,
   Because of Your judgments.

12 Walk about Zion,
   And go all around her.
   Count her towers;
13 Mark well her bulwarks;
   Consider her palaces;
   That you may tell *it* to the
   generation following.
14 For this *is* God,
   Our God forever and ever;
   He will be our guide
   Even to death.[a]

Psalm 49

To the Chief Musician. A Psalm of the sons of Korah.

1 Hear this, all peoples;
   Give ear, all inhabitants of the
   world,
2 Both low and high,
   Rich and poor together.
3 My mouth shall speak wisdom,
   And the meditation of my heart
   shall give understanding.
4 I will incline my ear to a proverb;
   I will disclose my dark saying on
   the harp.

48:14 [a]Following Masoretic Text and Syriac; Septuagint and Vulgate read *Forever.*

Gospel
Pearls

5 Why should I fear in the days of
evil,
When the iniquity at my heels
surrounds me?
6 Those who trust in their wealth
And boast in the multitude of
their riches,
7 None *of them* can by any means
redeem *his* brother,
Nor give to God a ransom for
him—
8 For the redemption of their souls
is costly,
And it shall cease forever—
9 That he should continue to live
eternally,
And not see the Pit.

10 For he sees wise men die;
Likewise the fool and the
senseless person perish,
And leave their wealth to others.
11 Their inner thought *is that* their
houses *will last* forever,[a]
Their dwelling places to all
generations;
They call *their* lands after their
own names.
12 Nevertheless man, *though* in
honor, does not remain;[a]
He is like the beasts *that* perish.

13 This is the way of those who *are*
foolish,
And of their posterity who
approve their sayings.   Selah
14 Like sheep they are laid in the
grave;
Death shall feed on them;
The upright shall have dominion
over them in the morning;
And their beauty shall be
consumed in the grave, far
from their dwelling.
15 But God will redeem my soul
from the power of the grave,
For He shall receive me.
Selah

16 Do not be afraid when one
becomes rich,
When the glory of his house is
increased;
17 For when he dies he shall carry
nothing away;
His glory shall not descend after
him.

18 Though while he lives he blesses
himself
(For *men* will praise you when
you do well for yourself),
19 He shall go to the generation of
his fathers;
They shall never see light.
20 A man *who is* in honor, yet does
not understand,
Is like the beasts *that* perish.

Psalm 50

A Psalm of Asaph.

1 The Mighty One, God the LORD,
Has spoken and called the earth
From the rising of the sun to its
going down.
2 Out of Zion, the perfection of
beauty,
God will shine forth.
3 Our God shall come, and shall
not keep silent;
A fire shall devour before Him,
And it shall be very tempestuous
all around Him.

4 He shall call to the heavens from
above,
And to the earth, that He may
judge His people:
5 "Gather My saints together to Me,
Those who have made a covenant
with Me by sacrifice."
6 Let the heavens declare His
righteousness,
For God Himself *is* Judge.
Selah

7 "Hear, O My people, and I will
speak,
O Israel, and I will testify against
you;
I *am* God, your God!
8 I will not rebuke you for your
sacrifices
Or your burnt offerings,
Which are continually before Me.
9 I will not take a bull from your
house,
Nor goats out of your folds.
10 For every beast of the forest *is*
Mine,
And the cattle on a thousand
hills.
11 I know all the birds of the
mountains,

49:11 [a]Septuagint, Syriac, Targum, and Vulgate read *Their graves shall be their houses forever.*
49:12 [a]Following Masoretic Text and Targum; Septuagint, Syriac, and Vulgate read *understand* (compare
verse 20).

God gave you the ornament of a meek and quiet spirit that is more valuable than
any other outer form of jewelry. It is worth more than gold. It is more powerful than
sexual ability.

And the wild beasts of the field
   are Mine.

12 "If I were hungry, I would not tell
   you;
   For the world *is* Mine, and all its
   fullness.
13 Will I eat the flesh of bulls,
   Or drink the blood of goats?
14 Offer to God thanksgiving,
   And pay your vows to the Most
   High.
15 Call upon Me in the day of
   trouble;
   I will deliver you, and you shall
   glorify Me."

16 But to the wicked God says:
   "What *right* have you to declare
   My statutes,
   Or take My covenant in your
   mouth,
17 Seeing you hate instruction
   And cast My words behind you?
18 When you saw a thief, you
   consented*ᵃ* with him,
   And have been a partaker with
   adulterers.
19 You give your mouth to evil,
   And your tongue frames deceit.
20 You sit *and* speak against your
   brother;
   You slander your own mother's
   son.
21 These *things* you have done, and
   I kept silent;
   You thought that I was altogether
   like you;
   But I will rebuke you,
   And set *them* in order before
   your eyes.

22 "Now consider this, you who
   forget God,
   Lest I tear *you* in pieces,
   And *there be* none to deliver:
23 Whoever offers praise glorifies
   Me;
   And to him who orders *his*
   conduct *aright*
   I will show the salvation of God."

Psalm 51

To the Chief Musician. A Psalm of David when
Nathan the prophet went to him, after he had
gone in to Bathsheba.

1 Have mercy upon me, O God,
   According to Your
   lovingkindness;

According to the multitude of
   Your tender mercies,
   Blot out my transgressions.
2 Wash me thoroughly from my
   iniquity,
   And cleanse me from my sin.

3 For I acknowledge my
   transgressions,
   And my sin *is* always before me.
4 Against You, You only, have I
   sinned,
   And done *this* evil in Your
   sight—
   That You may be found just when
   You speak,*ᵃ*
   And blameless when You judge.

5 Behold, I was brought forth in
   iniquity,
   And in sin my mother conceived
   me.
6 Behold, You desire truth in the
   inward parts,
   And in the hidden *part* You will
   make me to know wisdom.

7 Purge me with hyssop, and I shall
   be clean;
   Wash me, and I shall be whiter
   than snow.
8 Make me hear joy and gladness,
   That the bones You have broken
   may rejoice.
9 Hide Your face from my sins,
   And blot out all my iniquities.

10 Create in me a clean heart, O
   God,
   And renew a steadfast spirit
   within me.
11 Do not cast me away from Your
   presence,
   And do not take Your Holy Spirit
   from me.

12 Restore to me the joy of Your
   salvation,
   And uphold me *by Your* generous
   Spirit.
13 *Then* I will teach transgressors
   Your ways,
   And sinners shall be converted to
   You.

14 Deliver me from the guilt of
   bloodshed, O God,
   The God of my salvation,

50:18 *ᵃ*Septuagint, Syriac, Targum, and Vulgate read *run.
in Your words.*   51:4 *ᵃ*Septuagint, Targum, and Vulgate read

God is adorning you with glory, power and majesty. He will send people into your
life to appreciate your real beauty, your real essence. It is the kind of beauty that
lasts in a face full of wrinkles, gray hair, fallen arches, crow's feet, and all the pitfalls
that may come your way.

Soul Secrets
when marriage
is difficult

Lord, can there be revival in our marriage? How can something that started out so fresh now seem so stale? I am torn between all the hats I wear. Our intimacy has lost its spontaneity and our love feels canned and uncreative. I need You to break through the veil of politeness that hides our hushed frustration.

Give me the grace to forgive the things that seem insensitive in my husband. Give me strength and creativity, patience and humility. Make my heart race with the passion and affection that once came so freely. Please, Father, teach me how to be a good wife. Bind us together.

As I love him, I must realize that I will always love an imperfect person, and so will he. Maybe I am learning how You really love me as I reach out to this man who doesn't always seem in touch with where I am. I see that You love me when I am out of touch with You.

Most of all, Lord, make me like You. Hover over us. Fashion me for my husband and him for me. Breathe fresh life into our love and allow us to be friends again, to laugh and play again. I miss the way it used to be. Take us back, dear Lord. Take us back. Thank You for knowing what to do with our hearts. I believe there will be change because of You.

And my tongue shall sing aloud
of Your righteousness.
15 O Lord, open my lips,
And my mouth shall show forth
Your praise.
16 For You do not desire sacrifice,
or else I would give *it;*
You do not delight in burnt
offering.
17 The sacrifices of God *are* a
broken spirit,
A broken and a contrite heart—
These, O God, You will not
despise.

18 Do good in Your good pleasure
to Zion;
Build the walls of Jerusalem.
19 Then You shall be pleased with
the sacrifices of righteousness,
With burnt offering and whole
burnt offering;
Then they shall offer bulls on
Your altar.

Psalm 52

To the Chief Musician. A Contemplation*a* of
David when Doeg the Edomite went and told
Saul, and said to him, "David has gone to the
house of Ahimelech."

1 Why do you boast in evil, O
mighty man?
The goodness of God *endures*
continually.
2 Your tongue devises destruction,
Like a sharp razor, working
deceitfully.
3 You love evil more than good,
Lying rather than speaking
righteousness.   Selah
4 You love all devouring words,
You deceitful tongue.

5 God shall likewise destroy you
forever;
He shall take you away, and
pluck you out of *your* dwelling
place,
And uproot you from the land of
the living.   Selah
6 The righteous also shall see and
fear,
And shall laugh at him, *saying,*
7 "Here is the man *who* did not
make God his strength,
But trusted in the abundance of
his riches,
And strengthened himself in his
wickedness."

8 But I *am* like a green olive tree
in the house of God;
I trust in the mercy of God
forever and ever.
9 I will praise You forever,
Because You have done *it;*
And in the presence of Your
saints
I will wait on Your name, for *it
is* good.

Psalm 53

To the Chief Musician. Set to "Mahalath." A
Contemplation*a* of David.

1 The fool has said in his heart,
"*There is* no God."
They are corrupt, and have done
abominable iniquity;
There is none who does good.

2 God looks down from heaven
upon the children of men,
To see if there are *any* who
understand, who seek God.
3 Every one of them has turned
aside;
They have together become
corrupt;
There is none who does good,
No, not one.

4 Have the workers of iniquity no
knowledge,
Who eat up my people *as* they
eat bread,
And do not call upon God?
5 There they are in great fear
Where no fear was,
For God has scattered the bones
of him who encamps against
you;
You have put *them* to shame,
Because God has despised them.

6 Oh, that the salvation of Israel
would come out of Zion!
When God brings back the
captivity of His people,
Let Jacob rejoice *and* Israel be
glad.

Psalm 54

To the Chief Musician. With stringed
instruments.*a* A Contemplation*b* of David when
the Ziphites went and said to Saul, "Is David
not hiding with us?"

1 Save me, O God, by Your name,
And vindicate me by Your
strength.

52:title *a*Hebrew *Maschil*   53:title *a*Hebrew *Maschil*   54:title *a*Hebrew *neginoth*   *b*Hebrew *Maschil*

Gospel
Pearls

2 Hear my prayer, O God;
  Give ear to the words of my
    mouth.
3 For strangers have risen up
    against me,
  And oppressors have sought
    after my life;
  They have not set God before
    them.   Selah

4 Behold, God *is* my helper;
  The Lord *is* with those who
    uphold my life.
5 He will repay my enemies for
    their evil.
  Cut them off in Your truth.

6 I will freely sacrifice to You;
  I will praise Your name, O Lord,
    for *it is* good.
7 For He has delivered me out of
    all trouble;
  And my eye has seen *its desire*
    upon my enemies.

Psalm 55

To the Chief Musician. With stringed
instruments.*a* A Contemplation*b* of David.

1 Give ear to my prayer, O God,
  And do not hide Yourself from
    my supplication.
2 Attend to me, and hear me;
  I am restless in my complaint,
    and moan noisily,
3 Because of the voice of the
    enemy,
  Because of the oppression of the
    wicked;
  For they bring down trouble upon
    me,
  And in wrath they hate me.

4 My heart is severely pained
    within me,
  And the terrors of death have
    fallen upon me.
5 Fearfulness and trembling have
    come upon me,
  And horror has overwhelmed
    me.
6 So I said, "Oh, that I had wings
    like a dove!
  I would fly away and be at rest.
7 Indeed, I would wander far off,
  And remain in the wilderness.
                               Selah
8 I would hasten my escape
  From the windy storm *and*
    tempest."

9 Destroy, O Lord, *and* divide their
    tongues,
  For I have seen violence and
    strife in the city.
10 Day and night they go around it
     on its walls;
   Iniquity and trouble *are* also in
     the midst of it.
11 Destruction *is* in its midst;
   Oppression and deceit do not
     depart from its streets.

12 For *it is* not an enemy *who*
     reproaches me;
   Then I could bear *it.*
   Nor *is it* one *who* hates me who
     has exalted *himself* against me;
   Then I could hide from him.
13 But *it was* you, a man my equal,
   My companion and my
     acquaintance.
14 We took sweet counsel together,
   And walked to the house of God
     in the throng.

15 Let death seize them;
   Let them go down alive into hell,
   For wickedness *is* in their
     dwellings *and* among them.

16 As for me, I will call upon God,
   And the Lord shall save me.
17 Evening and morning and at
     noon
   I will pray, and cry aloud,
   And He shall hear my voice.
18 He has redeemed my soul in
     peace from the battle *that was*
     against me,
   For there were many against me.
19 God will hear, and afflict them,
   Even He who abides from of old.
                               Selah
   Because they do not change,
   Therefore they do not fear God.

20 He has put forth his hands
     against those who were at
     peace with him;
   He has broken his covenant.
21 *The words* of his mouth were
     smoother than butter,
   But war *was* in his heart;
   His words were softer than oil,
   Yet they *were* drawn swords.

22 Cast your burden on the Lord,
   And He shall sustain you;
   He shall never permit the
     righteous to be moved.

55:title *a*Hebrew *neginoth*   *b*Hebrew *Maschil*

*B*eauty comes in many ways. However, true beauty is always on the inside. A faithful
wife is more precious than words can express. The inner beauty that makes you
valuable to God will also make you valuable to others.

23　But You, O God, shall bring them
　　down to the pit of destruction;
　Bloodthirsty and deceitful men
　　shall not live out half their
　　days;
　But I will trust in You.

Psalm 56

To the Chief Musician. Set to "The Silent Dove
in Distant Lands."[a] A Michtam of David when
the Philistines captured him in Gath.

1　Be merciful to me, O God, for
　　man would swallow me up;
　Fighting all day he oppresses me.
2　My enemies would hound *me* all
　　day,
　For *there are* many who fight
　　against me, O Most High.

3　Whenever I am afraid,
　I will trust in You.
4　In God (I will praise His word),
　In God I have put my trust;
　I will not fear.
　What can flesh do to me?

5　All day they twist my words;
　All their thoughts *are* against me
　　for evil.
6　They gather together,
　They hide, they mark my steps,
　When they lie in wait for my life.
7　Shall they escape by iniquity?
　In anger cast down the peoples,
　　O God!

8　You number my wanderings;
　Put my tears into Your bottle;
　Are they not in Your book?
9　When I cry out *to You,*
　Then my enemies will turn back;
　This I know, because God *is* for
　　me.
10　In God (I will praise *His* word),
　In the LORD (I will praise *His*
　　word),
11　In God I have put my trust;
　I will not be afraid.
　What can man do to me?

12　Vows *made* to You *are* binding
　　upon me, O God;
　I will render praises to You,
13　For You have delivered my soul
　　from death.
　Have You not *kept* my feet from
　　falling,
　That I may walk before God
　In the light of the living?

Psalm 57

To the Chief Musician. Set to "Do Not Destroy."[a]
A Michtam of David when he fled from Saul into
the cave.

1　Be merciful to me, O God, be
　　merciful to me!
　For my soul trusts in You;
　And in the shadow of Your wings
　　I will make my refuge,
　Until *these* calamities have
　　passed by.

2　I will cry out to God Most High,
　To God who performs *all things*
　　for me.
3　He shall send from heaven and
　　save me;
　He reproaches the one who
　　would swallow me up.　Selah
　God shall send forth His mercy
　　and His truth.

4　My soul *is* among lions;
　I lie *among* the sons of men
　Who are set on fire,
　Whose teeth *are* spears and
　　arrows,
　And their tongue a sharp sword.
5　Be exalted, O God, above the
　　heavens;
　Let Your glory *be* above all the
　　earth.

6　They have prepared a net for my
　　steps;
　My soul is bowed down;
　They have dug a pit before me;
　Into the midst of it they
　　themselves have fallen.
　　　　　　　　　Selah

7　My heart is steadfast, O God, my
　　heart is steadfast;
　I will sing and give praise.
8　Awake, my glory!
　Awake, lute and harp!
　I will awaken the dawn.

9　I will praise You, O Lord, among
　　the peoples;
　I will sing to You among the
　　nations.
10　For Your mercy reaches unto the
　　heavens,
　And Your truth unto the clouds.

11　Be exalted, O God, above the
　　heavens;

56:title [a]Hebrew *Jonath Elem Rechokim*　　　57:title [a]Hebrew *Al Tashcheth*

Let Your glory *be* above all the earth.

Psalm 58

To the Chief Musician. Set to "Do Not Destroy."*ᵃ*
A Michtam of David.

1 Do you indeed speak
   righteousness, you silent ones?
   Do you judge uprightly, you sons
   of men?
2 No, in heart you work
   wickedness;
   You weigh out the violence of
   your hands in the earth.

3 The wicked are estranged from
   the womb;
   They go astray as soon as they
   are born, speaking lies.
4 Their poison *is* like the poison of
   a serpent;
   They are like the deaf cobra *that*
   stops its ear,
5 Which will not heed the voice of
   charmers,
   Charming ever so skillfully.

6 Break their teeth in their mouth,
   O God!
   Break out the fangs of the young
   lions, O Lord!
7 Let them flow away as waters
   which run continually;
   When he bends *his bow,*
   Let his arrows be as if cut in
   pieces.
8 *Let them be* like a snail which
   melts away as it goes,
   Like a stillborn child of a woman,
   that they may not see the sun.

9 Before your pots can feel *the
   burning* thorns,
   He shall take them away as with
   a whirlwind,
   As in His living and burning
   wrath.
10 The righteous shall rejoice when
   he sees the vengeance;
   He shall wash his feet in the
   blood of the wicked,
11 So that men will say,
   "Surely *there is* a reward for the
   righteous;
   Surely He is God who judges in
   the earth."

Psalm 59

To the Chief Musician. Set to "Do Not Destroy."*ᵃ*
A Michtam of David when Saul sent men, and
they watched the house in order to kill him.

1 Deliver me from my enemies, O
   my God;
   Defend me from those who rise
   up against me.
2 Deliver me from the workers of
   iniquity,
   And save me from bloodthirsty
   men.

3 For look, they lie in wait for my
   life;
   The mighty gather against me,
   Not *for* my transgression nor *for*
   my sin, O Lord.
4 They run and prepare themselves
   through no fault *of mine.*

   Awake to help me, and behold!
5 You therefore, O Lord God of
   hosts, the God of Israel,
   Awake to punish all the nations;
   Do not be merciful to any wicked
   transgressors.   Selah

6 At evening they return,
   They growl like a dog,
   And go all around the city.
7 Indeed, they belch with their
   mouth;
   Swords *are* in their lips;
   For *they say,* "Who hears?"

8 But You, O Lord, shall laugh at
   them;
   You shall have all the nations in
   derision.
9 I will wait for You,
   O You his Strength;*ᵃ*
   For God *is* my defense.
10 My God of mercy*ᵃ* shall come to
   meet me;
   God shall let me see *my desire*
   on my enemies.

11 Do not slay them, lest my people
   forget;
   Scatter them by Your power,
   And bring them down,
   O Lord our shield.
12 *For* the sin of their mouth *and* the
   words of their lips,

58:title *ᵃ*Hebrew *Al Tashcheth*   59:title *ᵃ*Hebrew *Al Tashcheth*   59:9 *ᵃ*Following Masoretic Text and
Syriac; some Hebrew manuscripts, Septuagint, Targum, and Vulgate read *my Strength.*   59:10 *ᵃ*Following
Qere; some Hebrew manuscripts, Septuagint, and Vulgate read *My God, His mercy;* Kethib, some Hebrew
manuscripts and Targum read *O God, my mercy;* Syriac reads *O God, Your mercy.*

---

*B*e careful what you get used to. If you don't watch out, you can become accustomed
to negative things, things the Father never wanted you to have, like pain or abuse.

Let them even be taken in their
pride,
And for the cursing and lying
which they speak.
13 Consume *them* in wrath,
consume *them,*
That they *may* not *be;*
And let them know that God rules
in Jacob
To the ends of the earth.

Selah

14 And at evening they return,
They growl like a dog,
And go all around the city.
15 They wander up and down for
food,
And howl[a] if they are not
satisfied.

16 But I will sing of Your power;
Yes, I will sing aloud of Your
mercy in the morning;
For You have been my defense
And refuge in the day of my
trouble.
17 To You, O my Strength, I will
sing praises;
For God *is* my defense,
My God of mercy.

Psalm 60

To the Chief Musician. Set to "Lily of the
Testimony."[a] A Michtam of David. For teaching.
When he fought against Mesopotamia and Syria
of Zobah, and Joab returned and killed twelve
thousand Edomites in the Valley of Salt.

1 O God, You have cast us off;
You have broken us down;
You have been displeased;
Oh, restore us again!
2 You have made the earth
tremble;
You have broken it;
Heal its breaches, for it is
shaking.
3 You have shown Your people
hard things;
You have made us drink the wine
of confusion.

4 You have given a banner to those
who fear You,
That it may be displayed because
of the truth.   Selah
5 That Your beloved may be
delivered,
Save *with* Your right hand, and
hear me.

6 God has spoken in His holiness:
"I will rejoice;
I will divide Shechem
And measure out the Valley of
Succoth.
7 Gilead *is* Mine, and Manasseh *is*
Mine;
Ephraim also *is* the helmet for
My head;
Judah *is* My lawgiver.
8 Moab *is* My washpot;
Over Edom I will cast My shoe;
Philistia, shout in triumph
because of Me."

9 Who will bring me *to* the strong
city?
Who will lead me to Edom?
10 *Is it* not You, O God, *who* cast
us off?
And You, O God, *who* did not go
out with our armies?
11 Give us help from trouble,
For the help of man *is* useless.
12 Through God we will do
valiantly,
For *it is* He *who* shall tread down
our enemies.[a]

Psalm 61

To the Chief Musician. On a stringed
instrument.[a] A Psalm of David.

1 Hear my cry, O God;
Attend to my prayer.
2 From the end of the earth I will
cry to You,
When my heart is overwhelmed;
Lead me to the rock that is higher
than I.

3 For You have been a shelter for
me,
A strong tower from the enemy.
4 I will abide in Your tabernacle
forever;
I will trust in the shelter of Your
wings.   Selah

5 For You, O God, have heard my
vows;
You have given *me* the heritage
of those who fear Your name.
6 You will prolong the king's life,
His years as many generations.
7 He shall abide before God
forever.
Oh, prepare mercy and truth,
which may preserve him!

59:15 [a]Following Septuagint and Vulgate; Masoretic Text, Syriac, and Targum read *spend the night.*
60:title [a]Hebrew *Shushan Eduth*   60:12 [a]Compare verses 5–12 with 108:6–13   61:title [a]Hebrew
neginah

*T*he real victory occurs when you change your own mind. The power of choice is a
great power. Be careful that you do not give that power away. It is your right to
choose how you want to live. Even God respects that right. He gives you the right.

The Dawning

Psalm 59:16

You are a woman of excellence. You are strong and powerful in your own right. Occasionally, if God so wills, He sends to an excellent woman an excellent husband who has the grace to be a lover and the anointing to be a friend. Occasionally, He will send someone to sing the songs your heart longs to hear. Occasionally, He will send a strong arm to wrap around a weary body and give you a moment of rest and tranquillity. But none of these experiences will ever take the place of the ultimate experience. For the greatest morning you will ever know is the dawning of faith in Jesus, your Lord.

No matter what sorrow life has brought you, don't stop until you see morning, because morning does come. It is at the end of every tragic divorce, but it does come. It is at the end of setbacks, betrayals, delays and denials, but when they're all over, morning does come. I challenge you, my sister and my friend, hold out for the morning. It does come.

Do not allow the tragedies of life to so depress you that you lose your hope. Do not allow the bitter disappointments and losses you face to rob your expectations of daybreak. Wake up singing hallelujah in the morning. Breathe in the fresh air, expel the stale air of your past, and say, "I can feel the breaking of day." And it will come. Overcome obstacles with confidence. Rise above trauma with triumph. Feel solace through sorrow. Know comfort in the midst of crisis. The morning does come!

Some years ago, John Newton penned these words during a crisis in his life. They are words to a hymn that strengthens the heart and rekindles the will to survive. He wrote:

> Amazing grace, how sweet the sound
> That saved a wretch like me;
> I once was lost, but now am found,
> Was blind but now I see.

Isn't that what morning is all about? Stepping out of blindness into seeing? It is my prayer that the darkness will roll back from every issue in your life, like clouds being pushed across the sky by a strong wind. The Lord can do that for you. He will bring you grace. He will help you see. He will watch over you through the night. Morning is dawning!

8 So I will sing praise to Your name
forever,
That I may daily perform my
vows.

Psalm 62

To the Chief Musician. To Jeduthun. A Psalm
of David.

1 Truly my soul silently *waits* for
God;
From Him *comes* my salvation.
2 He only *is* my rock and my
salvation;
He is my defense;
I shall not be greatly moved.

3 How long will you attack a man?
You shall be slain, all of you,
Like a leaning wall and a
tottering fence.
4 They only consult to cast *him*
down from his high position;
They delight in lies;
They bless with their mouth,
But they curse inwardly. Selah

5 My soul, wait silently for God
alone,
For my expectation *is* from Him.
6 He only *is* my rock and my
salvation;
He is my defense;
I shall not be moved.
7 In God *is* my salvation and my
glory;
The rock of my strength,
And my refuge, *is* in God.

8 Trust in Him at all times, you
people;
Pour out your heart before Him;
God *is* a refuge for us.   Selah

9 Surely men of low degree *are* a
vapor,
Men of high degree *are* a lie;
If they are weighed on the scales,
They *are* altogether *lighter* than
vapor.
10 Do not trust in oppression,
Nor vainly hope in robbery;
If riches increase,
Do not set *your* heart *on them.*

11 God has spoken once,
Twice I have heard this:
That power *belongs* to God.
12 Also to You, O Lord, *belongs*
mercy;
For You render to each one
according to his work.

Psalm 63

A Psalm of David when he was in the wilderness
of Judah.

1 O God, You *are* my God;
Early will I seek You;
My soul thirsts for You;
My flesh longs for You
In a dry and thirsty land
Where there is no water.
2 So I have looked for You in the
sanctuary,
To see Your power and Your
glory.

3 Because Your lovingkindness *is*
better than life,
My lips shall praise You.
4 Thus I will bless You while I live;
I will lift up my hands in Your
name.
5 My soul shall be satisfied as with
marrow and fatness,
And my mouth shall praise You
with joyful lips.

6 When I remember You on my
bed,
I meditate on You in the *night*
watches.
7 Because You have been my help,
Therefore in the shadow of Your
wings I will rejoice.
8 My soul follows close behind
You;
Your right hand upholds me.

9 But those *who* seek my life, to
destroy *it,*
Shall go into the lower parts of
the earth.
10 They shall fall by the sword;
They shall be a portion for
jackals.

11 But the king shall rejoice in God;
Everyone who swears by Him
shall glory;
But the mouth of those who
speak lies shall be stopped.

Psalm 64

To the Chief Musician. A Psalm of David.

1 Hear my voice, O God, in my
meditation;
Preserve my life from fear of the
enemy.
2 Hide me from the secret plots of
the wicked,
From the rebellion of the workers
of iniquity,

Gospel Pearls

3 Who sharpen their tongue like a
    sword,
    And bend *their bows to shoot
    their arrows*—bitter words,
4 That they may shoot in secret at
    the blameless;
    Suddenly they shoot at him and
    do not fear.

5 They encourage themselves *in* an
    evil matter;
    They talk of laying snares
    secretly;
    They say, "Who will see them?"
6 They devise iniquities:
    "We have perfected a shrewd
    scheme."
    Both the inward thought and the
    heart of man are deep.

7 But God shall shoot at them *with*
    an arrow;
    Suddenly they shall be wounded.
8 So He will make them stumble
    over their own tongue;
    All who see them shall flee away.
9 All men shall fear,
    And shall declare the work of
    God;
    For they shall wisely consider His
    doing.

10 The righteous shall be glad in the
    LORD, and trust in Him.
    And all the upright in heart shall
    glory.

Psalm 65

To the Chief Musician. A Psalm of David. A
Song.

1 Praise is awaiting You, O God,
    in Zion;
    And to You the vow shall be
    performed.
2 O You who hear prayer,
    To You all flesh will come.
3 Iniquities prevail against me;
    As for our transgressions,
    You will provide atonement for
    them.

4 Blessed *is the man* You choose,
    And cause to approach *You,*
    That he may dwell in Your
    courts.
    We shall be satisfied with the
    goodness of Your house,
    Of Your holy temple.

5 *By* awesome deeds in
    righteousness You will answer
    us,

O God of our salvation,
You who are the confidence of all
    the ends of the earth,
    And of the far-off seas;
6 Who established the mountains
    by His strength,
    Being clothed with power;
7 You who still the noise of the
    seas,
    The noise of their waves,
    And the tumult of the peoples.
8 They also who dwell in the
    farthest parts are afraid of
    Your signs;
    You make the outgoings of the
    morning and evening rejoice.

9 You visit the earth and water it,
    You greatly enrich it;
    The river of God is full of water;
    You provide their grain,
    For so You have prepared it.
10 You water its ridges abundantly,
    You settle its furrows;
    You make it soft with showers,
    You bless its growth.

11 You crown the year with Your
    goodness,
    And Your paths drip *with*
    abundance.
12 They drop *on* the pastures of the
    wilderness,
    And the little hills rejoice on
    every side.
13 The pastures are clothed with
    flocks;
    The valleys also are covered with
    grain;
    They shout for joy, they also sing.

Psalm 66

To the Chief Musician. A Song. A Psalm.

1 Make a joyful shout to God, all
    the earth!
2 Sing out the honor of His name;
    Make His praise glorious.
3 Say to God,
    "How awesome are Your works!
    Through the greatness of Your
    power
    Your enemies shall submit
    themselves to You.
4 All the earth shall worship You
    And sing praises to You;
    They shall sing praises *to* Your
    name."   Selah

5 Come and see the works of God;
    He is awesome *in His* doing
    toward the sons of men.

*I*nstead of asking an abuser if he has had enough, ask yourself if *you* have had
enough. This is always the greater question.

6 He turned the sea into dry *land;*
  They went through the river on
    foot.
  There we will rejoice in Him.
7 He rules by His power forever;
  His eyes observe the nations;
  Do not let the rebellious exalt
    themselves.   Selah

8 Oh, bless our God, you peoples!
  And make the voice of His praise
    to be heard,
9 Who keeps our soul among the
    living,
  And does not allow our feet to be
    moved.
10 For You, O God, have tested us;
   You have refined us as silver is
     refined.
11 You brought us into the net;
   You laid affliction on our backs.
12 You have caused men to ride
     over our heads;
   We went through fire and
     through water;
   But You brought us out to rich
     fulfillment.

13 I will go into Your house with
     burnt offerings;
   I will pay You my vows,
14 Which my lips have uttered
   And my mouth has spoken when
     I was in trouble.
15 I will offer You burnt sacrifices
     of fat animals,
   With the sweet aroma of rams;
   I will offer bulls with goats.
                                   Selah

16 Come *and* hear, all you who fear
     God,
   And I will declare what He has
     done for my soul.
17 I cried to Him with my mouth,
   And He was extolled with my
     tongue.
18 If I regard iniquity in my heart,
   The Lord will not hear.
19 *But* certainly God has heard
     me;
   He has attended to the voice of
     my prayer.

20 Blessed *be* God,
   Who has not turned away my
     prayer,
   Nor His mercy from me!

Psalm 67

To the Chief Musician. On stringed instruments.[a]
A Psalm. A Song.

1 God be merciful to us and bless
     us,
   And cause His face to shine upon
     us,   Selah
2 That Your way may be known on
     earth,
   Your salvation among all
     nations.

3 Let the peoples praise You, O
     God;
   Let all the peoples praise You.
4 Oh, let the nations be glad and
     sing for joy!
   For You shall judge the people
     righteously,
   And govern the nations on earth.
                                   Selah

5 Let the peoples praise You, O
     God;
   Let all the peoples praise You.
6 *Then* the earth shall yield her
     increase;
   God, our own God, shall bless
     us.
7 God shall bless us,
   And all the ends of the earth shall
     fear Him.

Psalm 68

To the Chief Musician. A Psalm of David. A
Song.

1 Let God arise,
   Let His enemies be scattered;
   Let those also who hate Him flee
     before Him.
2 As smoke is driven away,
   So drive *them* away;
   As wax melts before the fire,
   So let the wicked perish at the
     presence of God.
3 But let the righteous be glad;
   Let them rejoice before God;
   Yes, let them rejoice exceedingly.

4 Sing to God, sing praises to His
     name;
   Extol Him who rides on the
     clouds,[a]
   By His name YAH,
   And rejoice before Him.

67:title [a]Hebrew *neginoth*   68:4 [a]Masoretic Text reads *deserts;* Targum reads *heavens* (compare verse
34 and Isaiah 19:1).

*B*y God's rich grace you have the power. Don't forfeit it or forsake it. You can change
your situation whenever you get ready.

Get to Know
Your Father

Psalm 68:5

*I*f you have never known the love of an earthly father, you may have nothing to compare with the heavenly Father's love. His love is more gentle than a mother's breast and stronger than a father's arms at the same time. It is more intimate than a lover's caress. It is more consistent than a child's affection. It is *agape*. It is God's love. If you could ever fathom it—His love alone would heal the aching of your broken heart. He absolutely adores you.

Why are you running from place to place and person to person looking for love? Have you not heard? He has been speaking to you through all of your circumstances. He is the One you need when life has wounded you and you have fallen from your nesting place like a bird. It is His hand that catches the falling soul. Then He casts it to the wind and commands it to fly again.

It is a shame that we as Christians have moved so far away from the masterful plan of salvation. We need to teach again the marvelous plan of salvation—not just the recipe of salvation, the repeat-after-me recipes that soon become canned and cold. We need to teach the chemistry of salvation. An eternal God chose you before you were ever born. His hand-picked bride—that is what you are. You *have been* selected—not *will be*. You *are* selected. You are not running for office. You are chosen.

You need to know your Father. You know so much about the church, and that is great. The church is the mother who held you in her womb and carried you with her grace. She has fed you the sincere milk from her breast. The milk of the Word has caused you to grow (see 1 Peter 2:1-3). That is wonderful, but I am concerned because we have raised up too many children in the kingdom who know so much about their mother. They know when to worship; they know when to sit and when to stand. They know all about the social order and politics. They are full of church history and programs, but they know nothing of their Father.

If the church is your mother, as glorious as she is, you still need to know your Father. He is the One who produced the seed of His Word that caused you to come into being. It is His name you inherit, and your calling upon His name opens up all of heaven. It is He who carries you and delivers you. If you are insecure, it is because you have spent so much time nestled near your mother's tenderness that you have not experienced your Father's strength. He is strong and mighty. He is your Father, and the devil can't stop Him!

5 A father of the fatherless, a
  defender of widows,
  Is God in His holy habitation.
6 God sets the solitary in families;
  He brings out those who are
    bound into prosperity;
  But the rebellious dwell in a dry
    land.

7 O God, when You went out
    before Your people,
  When You marched through the
    wilderness,   Selah
8 The earth shook;
  The heavens also dropped *rain* at
    the presence of God;
  Sinai itself *was moved* at the
    presence of God, the God of
    Israel.
9 You, O God, sent a plentiful rain,
  Whereby You confirmed Your
    inheritance,
  When it was weary.
10 Your congregation dwelt in it;
   You, O God, provided from Your
     goodness for the poor.

11 The Lord gave the word;
   Great *was* the company of those
     who proclaimed *it:*
12 "Kings of armies flee, they flee,
   And she who remains at home
     divides the spoil.
13 Though you lie down among the
     sheepfolds,
   You will be like the wings of a
     dove covered with silver,
   And her feathers with yellow
     gold."
14 When the Almighty scattered
     kings in it,
   It was *white* as snow in Zalmon.

15 A mountain of God *is* the
     mountain of Bashan;
   A mountain *of many* peaks *is* the
     mountain of Bashan.
16 Why do you fume with envy, you
     mountains of *many* peaks?
   This is the mountain *which* God
     desires to dwell in;
   Yes, the LORD will dwell *in it*
     forever.

17 The chariots of God *are* twenty
     thousand,
   Even thousands of thousands;
   The Lord is among them *as in*
     Sinai, in the Holy *Place.*

18 You have ascended on high,
   You have led captivity captive;
   You have received gifts among
     men,
   Even *from* the rebellious,
   That the LORD God might dwell
     there.

19 Blessed *be* the Lord,
   Who daily loads us *with benefits,*
   The God of our salvation!   Selah
20 Our God *is* the God of salvation;
   And to GOD the Lord *belong*
     escapes from death.

21 But God will wound the head of
     His enemies,
   The hairy scalp of the one who
     still goes on in his trespasses.
22 The Lord said, "I will bring back
     from Bashan,
   I will bring *them* back from the
     depths of the sea,
23 That your foot may crush *them*[a]
     in blood,
   And the tongues of your dogs
     may have their portion from
     your enemies."

24 They have seen Your procession,
     O God,
   The procession of my God, my
     King, into the sanctuary.
25 The singers went before, the
     players on instruments
     followed after;
   Among *them were* the maidens
     playing timbrels.
26 Bless God in the congregations,
   The Lord, from the fountain of
     Israel.
27 There *is* little Benjamin, their
     leader,
   The princes of Judah *and* their
     company,
   The princes of Zebulun *and* the
     princes of Naphtali.

28 Your God has commanded[a] your
     strength;
   Strengthen, O God, what You
     have done for us.
29 Because of Your temple at
     Jerusalem,
   Kings will bring presents to You.
30 Rebuke the beasts of the reeds,
   The herd of bulls with the calves
     of the peoples,

68:23 [a]Septuagint, [Syriac], Targum, and Vulgate read *you may dip your foot.*   68:28 [a]Septuagint, [Syriac], Targum, and Vulgate read *Command, O God.*

*Gospel
Pearls*

Till everyone submits himself
with pieces of silver.
Scatter the peoples *who* delight
in war.
31 Envoys will come out of Egypt;
Ethiopia will quickly stretch out
her hands to God.

32 Sing to God, you kingdoms of the
earth;
Oh, sing praises to the Lord,
               Selah
33 To Him who rides on the heaven
of heavens, *which were* of old!
Indeed, He sends out His voice,
a mighty voice.
34 Ascribe strength to God;
His excellence *is* over Israel,
And His strength *is* in the clouds.
35 O God, *You are* more awesome
than Your holy places.
The God of Israel *is* He who gives
strength and power to *His*
people.

Blessed *be* God!

Psalm 69

To the Chief Musician. Set to "The Lilies."ᵃ A
Psalm of David.

1 Save me, O God!
For the waters have come up to
my neck.
2 I sink in deep mire,
Where *there is* no standing;
I have come into deep waters,
Where the floods overflow me.
3 I am weary with my crying;
My throat is dry;
My eyes fail while I wait for my
God.

4 Those who hate me without a
cause
Are more than the hairs of my
head;
They are mighty who would
destroy me,
Being my enemies wrongfully;
Though I have stolen nothing,
I *still* must restore *it.*

5 O God, You know my
foolishness;
And my sins are not hidden from
You.
6 Let not those who wait for You,
O Lord God of hosts, be
ashamed because of me;

Let not those who seek You be
confounded because of me, O
God of Israel.
7 Because for Your sake I have
borne reproach;
Shame has covered my face.
8 I have become a stranger to my
brothers,
And an alien to my mother's
children;
9 Because zeal for Your house has
eaten me up,
And the reproaches of those who
reproach You have fallen on
me.
10 When I wept *and chastened* my
soul with fasting,
That became my reproach.
11 I also made sackcloth my
garment;
I became a byword to them.
12 Those who sit in the gate speak
against me,
And I *am* the song of the
drunkards.

13 But as for me, my prayer *is* to
You,
O Lord, *in* the acceptable time;
O God, in the multitude of Your
mercy,
Hear me in the truth of Your
salvation.
14 Deliver me out of the mire,
And let me not sink;
Let me be delivered from those
who hate me,
And out of the deep waters.
15 Let not the floodwater overflow
me,
Nor let the deep swallow me up;
And let not the pit shut its mouth
on me.

16 Hear me, O Lord, for Your
lovingkindness *is* good;
Turn to me according to the
multitude of Your tender
mercies.
17 And do not hide Your face from
Your servant,
For I am in trouble;
Hear me speedily.
18 Draw near to my soul, *and*
redeem it;
Deliver me because of my
enemies.

19 You know my reproach, my
shame, and my dishonor;

69:title ᵃHebrew *Shoshannim*

When you have Christ, He is all the help you need. He has been there all the time.
Never forget to turn to Him, and never let anyone have His place. If you do, you
will always be disappointed.

My adversaries *are* all before
  You.
20 Reproach has broken my heart,
  And I am full of heaviness;
  I looked *for someone* to take pity,
  but *there was* none;
  And for comforters, but I found
  none.
21 They also gave me gall for my
  food,
  And for my thirst they gave me
  vinegar to drink.

22 Let their table become a snare
  before them,
  And their well-being a trap.
23 Let their eyes be darkened, so
  that they do not see;
  And make their loins shake
  continually.
24 Pour out Your indignation upon
  them,
  And let Your wrathful anger take
  hold of them.
25 Let their dwelling place be
  desolate;
  Let no one live in their tents.
26 For they persecute the *ones* You
  have struck,
  And talk of the grief of those You
  have wounded.
27 Add iniquity to their iniquity,
  And let them not come into Your
  righteousness.
28 Let them be blotted out of the
  book of the living,
  And not be written with the
  righteous.

29 But I *am* poor and sorrowful;
  Let Your salvation, O God, set me
  up on high.
30 I will praise the name of God with
  a song,
  And will magnify Him with
  thanksgiving.
31 *This* also shall please the LORD
  better than an ox *or* bull,
  Which has horns and hooves.
32 The humble shall see *this and* be
  glad;
  And you who seek God, your
  hearts shall live.
33 For the LORD hears the poor,
  And does not despise His
  prisoners.

34 Let heaven and earth praise Him,
  The seas and everything that
  moves in them.

35 For God will save Zion
  And build the cities of Judah,
  That they may dwell there and
  possess it.
36 Also, the descendants of His
  servants shall inherit it,
  And those who love His name
  shall dwell in it.

Psalm 70

To the Chief Musician. *A Psalm* of David. To
bring to remembrance.

1 Make *haste,* O God, to deliver
  me!
  Make haste to help me, O LORD!

2 Let them be ashamed and
  confounded
  Who seek my life;
  Let them be turned back[a] and
  confused
  Who desire my hurt.
3 Let them be turned back because
  of their shame,
  Who say, "Aha, aha!"

4 Let all those who seek You
  rejoice and be glad in You;
  And let those who love Your
  salvation say continually,
  "Let God be magnified!"

5 But I *am* poor and needy;
  Make haste to me, O God!
  You *are* my help and my
  deliverer;
  O LORD, do not delay.

Psalm 71

1 In You, O LORD, I put my trust;
  Let me never be put to shame.
2 Deliver me in Your
  righteousness, and cause me to
  escape;
  Incline Your ear to me, and save
  me.
3 Be my strong refuge,
  To which I may resort
  continually;
  You have given the
  commandment to save me,
  For You *are* my rock and my
  fortress.

4 Deliver me, O my God, out of the
  hand of the wicked,
  Out of the hand of the
  unrighteous and cruel man.

70:2 [a]Following Masoretic Text, Septuagint, Targum, and Vulgate; some Hebrew manuscripts and Syriac
read *be appalled* (compare 40:15).

God is the One who gives you the power to change. With Him on your side you will
always survive. You are empowered by the presence of God.

Mothering God's Way

Psalm 71:6

God grants some women the unique honor and blessing of becoming mothers. When you have children, hold them, love them, care for them, empower them. But understand that you are only temporary stewards. Your children belong to God. They will grow up and leave. They were not meant to be grasped or clung to—as if you really could freeze a moment. No, moments cannot be frozen, but you will be allowed to hold memories. If you are good at mothering, you will hold the memories and release the child. If you cannot do that, you will destroy the memories by corrupting the relationship between you and the little chick whose development has outgrown the shell of your parenting.

Many women come close to losing their relationships with their children. They feel betrayed by the growth of the children they trained. They have trained the children to be productive and then have failed to prepare themselves for that growth—not just the growth of the body but also the growth of the person, the development of personalities and preferences. They feel that their children are belligerent when in truth many of the children are just independent. Of course, there are children who grow to be calloused. I pray that you will be spared the disappointment of that experience. But even if your parenting goes well, there will still be moments when you see your children slipping through your fingers like grains of sand. For many mothers who once struggled to wean the child from tender breasts, it is later a struggle to wean the mother from the child!

Letting go is especially painful when you allow your relationship with your child to become cluttered like an attic stuffed with things that belong somewhere else. Often there are misplaced passions dumped on the child to compensate for loneliness in other areas. Because there was no place to put them, they were shoved into the attic. Often it is love that should have been invested in a spouse, but there was no spouse or no capacity in the spouse to be loved. So the love was dumped on a child. This is not a healthy love; it is obsessive.

Every good mother, sooner or later, must understand she is denied ownership; she is merely granted stewardship. This is so important. This is the understanding you need to mother God's children God's way.

5 For You are my hope, O Lord
    GOD;
    You are my trust from my youth.
6 By You I have been upheld from
    birth;
    You are He who took me out of
    my mother's womb.
    My praise *shall be* continually of
    You.

7 I have become as a wonder to
    many,
    But You *are* my strong refuge.
8 Let my mouth be filled *with* Your
    praise
    And with Your glory all the day.

9 Do not cast me off in the time of
    old age;
    Do not forsake me when my
    strength fails.
10 For my enemies speak against
    me;
    And those who lie in wait for my
    life take counsel together,
11 Saying, "God has forsaken him;
    Pursue and take him, for *there is*
    none to deliver *him.*"

12 O God, do not be far from me;
    O my God, make haste to help
    me!
13 Let them be confounded *and*
    consumed
    Who are adversaries of my life;
    Let them be covered *with*
    reproach and dishonor
    Who seek my hurt.

14 But I will hope continually,
    And will praise You yet more and
    more.
15 My mouth shall tell of Your
    righteousness
    And Your salvation all the day,
    For I do not know *their* limits.
16 I will go in the strength of the
    Lord GOD;
    I will make mention of Your
    righteousness, of Yours only.

17 O God, You have taught me from
    my youth;
    And to this *day* I declare Your
    wondrous works.
18 Now also when *I am* old and
    grayheaded,
    O God, do not forsake me,
    Until I declare Your strength to
    this generation,

Your power to everyone *who* is
    to come.

19 Also Your righteousness, O God,
    is very high,
    You who have done great things;
    O God, who *is* like You?
20 *You,* who have shown me great
    and severe troubles,
    Shall revive me again,
    And bring me up again from the
    depths of the earth.
21 You shall increase my greatness,
    And comfort me on every side.

22 Also with the lute I will praise
    You—
    And Your faithfulness, O my
    God!
    To You I will sing with the harp,
    O Holy One of Israel.
23 My lips shall greatly rejoice when
    I sing to You,
    And my soul, which You have
    redeemed.
24 My tongue also shall talk of Your
    righteousness all the day long;
    For they are confounded,
    For they are brought to shame
    Who seek my hurt.

Psalm 72

A Psalm of Solomon.

1 Give the king Your judgments, O
    God,
    And Your righteousness to the
    king's Son.
2 He will judge Your people with
    righteousness,
    And Your poor with justice.
3 The mountains will bring peace
    to the people,
    And the little hills, by
    righteousness.
4 He will bring justice to the poor
    of the people;
    He will save the children of the
    needy,
    And will break in pieces the
    oppressor.

5 They shall fear You[a]
    As long as the sun and moon
    endure,
    Throughout all generations.
6 He shall come down like rain
    upon the grass before mowing,
    Like showers *that* water the
    earth.

72:5 [a]Following Masoretic Text and Targum; Septuagint and Vulgate read *They shall continue.*

Gospel Pearls

7 In His days the righteous shall
   flourish,
   And abundance of peace,
   Until the moon is no more.

8 He shall have dominion also from
   sea to sea,
   And from the River to the ends
   of the earth.
9 Those who dwell in the
   wilderness will bow before
   Him,
   And His enemies will lick the
   dust.
10 The kings of Tarshish and of the
   isles
   Will bring presents;
   The kings of Sheba and Seba
   Will offer gifts.
11 Yes, all kings shall fall down
   before Him;
   All nations shall serve Him.

12 For He will deliver the needy
   when he cries,
   The poor also, and *him* who has
   no helper.
13 He will spare the poor and needy,
   And will save the souls of the
   needy.
14 He will redeem their life from
   oppression and violence;
   And precious shall be their blood
   in His sight.

15 And He shall live;
   And the gold of Sheba will be
   given to Him;
   Prayer also will be made for Him
   continually,
   And daily He shall be praised.

16 There will be an abundance of
   grain in the earth,
   On the top of the mountains;
   Its fruit shall wave like Lebanon;
   And *those* of the city shall
   flourish like grass of the earth.

17 His name shall endure forever;
   His name shall continue as long
   as the sun.
   And *men* shall be blessed in Him;
   All nations shall call Him
   blessed.

18 Blessed *be* the Lᴏʀᴅ God, the God
   of Israel,
   Who only does wondrous things!

19 And blessed *be* His glorious
   name forever!
   And let the whole earth be filled
   with His glory.
   Amen and Amen.

20 The prayers of David the son of
   Jesse are ended.

Book Three   Psalms 73–89

Psalm 73

A Psalm of Asaph.

1 Truly God *is* good to Israel,
   To such as are pure in heart.
2 But as for me, my feet had almost
   stumbled;
   My steps had nearly slipped.
3 For I *was* envious of the boastful,
   When I saw the prosperity of the
   wicked.

4 For *there are* no pangs in their
   death,
   But their strength *is* firm.
5 They *are* not in trouble *as other*
   men,
   Nor are they plagued like *other*
   men.
6 Therefore pride serves as their
   necklace;
   Violence covers them *like* a
   garment.
7 Their eyes bulge*ᵃ* with
   abundance;
   They have more than heart could
   wish.
8 They scoff and speak wickedly
   concerning oppression;
   They speak loftily.
9 They set their mouth against the
   heavens,
   And their tongue walks through
   the earth.

10 Therefore his people return here,
   And waters of a full *cup* are
   drained by them.
11 And they say, "How does God
   know?
   And is there knowledge in the
   Most High?"
12 Behold, these *are* the ungodly,
   Who are always at ease;
   They increase *in* riches.
13 Surely I have cleansed my heart
   in vain,

73:7 *ᵃ*Targum reads *face bulges;* Septuagint, Syriac, and Vulgate read *iniquity bulges.*

*T*he Father weans us through life's circumstances. He weans us until we get the
strength to make proper choices. He knows how to bring us to a state of security
where we cease to be so dependent on others and their affirmation.

And washed my hands in innocence.

14 For all day long I have been plagued,
And chastened every morning.

15 If I had said, "I will speak thus,"
Behold, I would have been untrue to the generation of Your children.

16 When I thought *how* to understand this,
It *was* too painful for me—

17 Until I went into the sanctuary of God;
Then I understood their end.

18 Surely You set them in slippery places;
You cast them down to destruction.

19 Oh, how they are *brought* to desolation, as in a moment!
They are utterly consumed with terrors.

20 As a dream when *one* awakes,
So, Lord, when You awake,
You shall despise their image.

21 Thus my heart was grieved,
And I was vexed in my mind.

22 I *was* so foolish and ignorant;
I was *like* a beast before You.

23 Nevertheless I *am* continually with You;
You hold *me* by my right hand.

24 You will guide me with Your counsel,
And afterward receive me *to* glory.

25 Whom have I in heaven but *You?*
And *there is* none upon earth *that* I desire besides You.

26 My flesh and my heart fail;
But God *is* the strength of my heart and my portion forever.

27 For indeed, those who are far from You shall perish;
You have destroyed all those who desert You for harlotry.

28 But *it is* good for me to draw near to God;
I have put my trust in the Lord God,
That I may declare all Your works.

Psalm 74

A Contemplation[a] of Asaph.

1 O God, why have You cast *us* off forever?
Why does Your anger smoke against the sheep of Your pasture?

2 Remember Your congregation, *which* You have purchased of old,
The tribe of Your inheritance, *which* You have redeemed—
This Mount Zion where You have dwelt.

3 Lift up Your feet to the perpetual desolations.
The enemy has damaged everything in the sanctuary.

4 Your enemies roar in the midst of Your meeting place;
They set up their banners *for* signs.

5 They seem like men who lift up Axes among the thick trees.

6 And now they break down its carved work, all at once,
With axes and hammers.

7 They have set fire to Your sanctuary;
They have defiled the dwelling place of Your name to the ground.

8 They said in their hearts,
"Let us destroy them altogether."
They have burned up all the meeting places of God in the land.

9 We do not see our signs;
There is no longer any prophet;
Nor *is there* any among us who knows how long.

10 O God, how long will the adversary reproach?
Will the enemy blaspheme Your name forever?

11 Why do You withdraw Your hand, even Your right hand?
Take it out of Your bosom and destroy *them.*

12 For God *is* my King from of old,
Working salvation in the midst of the earth.

13 You divided the sea by Your strength;
You broke the heads of the sea serpents in the waters.

14 You broke the heads of Leviathan in pieces,

74:title [a]Hebrew *Maschil*

Gospel Pearls

And gave him *as* food to the people inhabiting the wilderness.

15 You broke open the fountain and the flood;
You dried up mighty rivers.

16 The day *is* Yours, the night also *is* Yours;
You have prepared the light and the sun.

17 You have set all the borders of the earth;
You have made summer and winter.

18 Remember this, *that* the enemy has reproached, O LORD,
And *that* a foolish people has blasphemed Your name.

19 Oh, do not deliver the life of Your turtledove to the wild beast!
Do not forget the life of Your poor forever.

20 Have respect to the covenant;
For the dark places of the earth are full of the haunts of cruelty.

21 Oh, do not let the oppressed return ashamed!
Let the poor and needy praise Your name.

22 Arise, O God, plead Your own cause;
Remember how the foolish man reproaches You daily.

23 Do not forget the voice of Your enemies;
The tumult of those who rise up against You increases continually.

Psalm 75

To the Chief Musician. Set to "Do Not Destroy."[a] A Psalm of Asaph. A Song.

1 We give thanks to You, O God, we give thanks!
For Your wondrous works declare *that* Your name is near.

2 "When I choose the proper time, I will judge uprightly.

3 The earth and all its inhabitants are dissolved;
I set up its pillars firmly.

Selah

4 "I said to the boastful, 'Do not deal boastfully,'

And to the wicked, 'Do not lift up the horn.

5 Do not lift up your horn on high;
Do *not* speak with a stiff neck.' "

6 For exaltation *comes* neither from the east
Nor from the west nor from the south.

7 But God *is* the Judge:
He puts down one,
And exalts another.

8 For in the hand of the LORD *there is* a cup,
And the wine is red;
It is fully mixed, and He pours it out;
Surely its dregs shall all the wicked of the earth
Drain *and* drink down.

9 But I will declare forever,
I will sing praises to the God of Jacob.

10 "All the horns of the wicked I will also cut off,
But the horns of the righteous shall be exalted."

Psalm 76

To the Chief Musician. On stringed instruments.[a] A Psalm of Asaph. A Song.

1 In Judah God *is* known;
His name *is* great in Israel.

2 In Salem[a] also is His tabernacle,
And His dwelling place in Zion.

3 There He broke the arrows of the bow,
The shield and sword of battle.

Selah

4 You *are* more glorious and excellent
Than the mountains of prey.

5 The stouthearted were plundered;
They have sunk into their sleep;
And none of the mighty men have found the use of their hands.

6 At Your rebuke, O God of Jacob,
Both the chariot and horse were cast into a dead sleep.

7 You, Yourself, *are* to be feared;
And who may stand in Your presence
When once You are angry?

75:title [a]Hebrew *Al Tashcheth*   76:title [a]Hebrew *neginoth*   76:2 [a]That is, Jerusalem

8 You caused judgment to be heard
from heaven;
The earth feared and was still,
9 When God arose to judgment,
To deliver all the oppressed of the
earth.   **Selah**

10 Surely the wrath of man shall
praise You;
With the remainder of wrath You
shall gird Yourself.

11 Make vows to the Lord your God,
and pay *them;*
Let all who are around Him bring
presents to Him who ought to
be feared.
12 He shall cut off the spirit of
princes;
He is awesome to the kings of the
earth.

Psalm 77

To the Chief Musician. To Jeduthun. A Psalm
of Asaph.

1 I cried out to God with my
voice—
To God with my voice;
And He gave ear to me.
2 In the day of my trouble I sought
the Lord;
My hand was stretched out in the
night without ceasing;
My soul refused to be comforted.
3 I remembered God, and was
troubled;
I complained, and my spirit was
overwhelmed.   **Selah**

4 You hold my eyelids *open;*
I am so troubled that I cannot
speak.
5 I have considered the days of old,
The years of ancient times.
6 I call to remembrance my song
in the night;
I meditate within my heart,
And my spirit makes diligent
search.

7 Will the Lord cast off forever?
And will He be favorable no
more?
8 Has His mercy ceased forever?
Has *His* promise failed
forevermore?
9 Has God forgotten to be
gracious?

Has He in anger shut up His
tender mercies?   **Selah**

10 And I said, "This *is* my anguish;
But I will remember the years of
the right hand of the Most
High."
11 I will remember the works of the
Lord;
Surely I will remember Your
wonders of old.
12 I will also meditate on all Your
work,
And talk of Your deeds.
13 Your way, O God, *is* in the
sanctuary;
Who *is* so great a God as *our*
God?
14 You *are* the God who does
wonders;
You have declared Your strength
among the peoples.
15 You have with *Your* arm
redeemed Your people,
The sons of Jacob and Joseph.
    Selah

16 The waters saw You, O God;
The waters saw You, they were
afraid;
The depths also trembled.
17 The clouds poured out water;
The skies sent out a sound;
Your arrows also flashed about.
18 The voice of Your thunder *was*
in the whirlwind;
The lightnings lit up the world;
The earth trembled and shook.
19 Your way *was* in the sea,
Your path in the great waters,
And Your footsteps were not
known.
20 You led Your people like a flock
By the hand of Moses and Aaron.

Psalm 78

A Contemplation[a] of Asaph.

1 Give ear, O my people, *to* my law;
Incline your ears to the words of
my mouth.
2 I will open my mouth in a
parable;
I will utter dark sayings of old,
3 Which we have heard and
known,
And our fathers have told us.
4 We will not hide *them* from their
children,

78:title [a]Hebrew *Maschil*

Gospel Pearls

Telling to the generation to come
the praises of the LORD,
And His strength and His
wonderful works that He has
done.

5 For He established a testimony in
Jacob,
And appointed a law in Israel,
Which He commanded our
fathers,
That they should make them
known to their children;
6 That the generation to come
might know *them,*
The children *who* would be born,
That they may arise and declare
them to their children,
7 That they may set their hope in
God,
And not forget the works of
God,
But keep His commandments;
8 And may not be like their fathers,
A stubborn and rebellious
generation,
A generation *that* did not set its
heart aright,
And whose spirit was not faithful
to God.

9 The children of Ephraim, *being*
armed *and* carrying bows,
Turned back in the day of battle.
10 They did not keep the covenant
of God;
They refused to walk in His law,
11 And forgot His works
And His wonders that He had
shown them.

12 Marvelous things He did in the
sight of their fathers,
In the land of Egypt, *in* the field
of Zoan.
13 He divided the sea and caused
them to pass through;
And He made the waters stand
up like a heap.
14 In the daytime also He led them
with the cloud,
And all the night with a light of
fire.
15 He split the rocks in the
wilderness,
And gave *them* drink in
abundance like the depths.
16 He also brought streams out of
the rock,
And caused waters to run down
like rivers.

17 But they sinned even more
against Him
By rebelling against the Most
High in the wilderness.
18 And they tested God in their
heart
By asking for the food of their
fancy.
19 Yes, they spoke against God:
They said, "Can God prepare a
table in the wilderness?
20 Behold, He struck the rock,
So that the waters gushed out,
And the streams overflowed.
Can He give bread also?
Can He provide meat for His
people? "

21 Therefore the LORD heard *this*
and was furious;
So a fire was kindled against
Jacob,
And anger also came up against
Israel,
22 Because they did not believe in
God,
And did not trust in His salvation.
23 Yet He had commanded the
clouds above,
And opened the doors of
heaven,
24 Had rained down manna on them
to eat,
And given them of the bread of
heaven.
25 Men ate angels' food;
He sent them food to the full.

26 He caused an east wind to blow
in the heavens;
And by His power He brought in
the south wind.
27 He also rained meat on them like
the dust,
Feathered fowl like the sand of
the seas;
28 And He let *them* fall in the midst
of their camp,
All around their dwellings.
29 So they ate and were well filled,
For He gave them their own
desire.
30 They were not deprived of their
craving;
But while their food *was* still in
their mouths,
31 The wrath of God came against
them,
And slew the stoutest of them,
And struck down the choice *men*
of Israel.

*I*t's the knowledge of your liberty that the enemy wants to steal from you. He cannot
take away the *power* to be free. So he tries to steal the *knowledge* of your freedom.

32 In spite of this they still sinned,
    And did not believe in His
        wondrous works.
33 Therefore their days He
        consumed in futility,
    And their years in fear.

34 When He slew them, then they
        sought Him;
    And they returned and sought
        earnestly for God.
35 Then they remembered that God
        was their rock,
    And the Most High God their
        Redeemer.
36 Nevertheless they flattered Him
        with their mouth,
    And they lied to Him with their
        tongue;
37 For their heart was not steadfast
        with Him,
    Nor were they faithful in His
        covenant.
38 But He, *being* full of compassion,
        forgave *their* iniquity,
    And did not destroy *them.*
    Yes, many a time He turned His
        anger away,
    And did not stir up all His wrath;
39 For He remembered that they
        were but flesh,
    A breath that passes away and
        does not come again.

40 How often they provoked Him in
        the wilderness,
    And grieved Him in the desert!
41 Yes, again and again they
        tempted God,
    And limited the Holy One of
        Israel.
42 They did not remember His
        power:
    The day when He redeemed them
        from the enemy,
43 When He worked His signs in
        Egypt,
    And His wonders in the field of
        Zoan;
44 Turned their rivers into blood,
    And their streams, that they
        could not drink.
45 He sent swarms of flies among
        them, which devoured them,
    And frogs, which destroyed
        them.
46 He also gave their crops to the
        caterpillar,
    And their labor to the locust.
47 He destroyed their vines with
        hail,

And their sycamore trees with
    frost.
48 He also gave up their cattle to the
        hail,
    And their flocks to fiery
        lightning.
49 He cast on them the fierceness of
        His anger,
    Wrath, indignation, and trouble,
    By sending angels of destruction
        among them.
50 He made a path for His anger;
    He did not spare their soul from
        death,
    But gave their life over to the
        plague,
51 And destroyed all the firstborn in
        Egypt,
    The first of *their* strength in the
        tents of Ham.
52 But He made His own people go
        forth like sheep,
    And guided them in the
        wilderness like a flock;
53 And He led them on safely, so
        that they did not fear;
    But the sea overwhelmed their
        enemies.
54 And He brought them to His holy
        border,
    This mountain *which* His right
        hand had acquired.
55 He also drove out the nations
        before them,
    Allotted them an inheritance by
        survey,
    And made the tribes of Israel
        dwell in their tents.

56 Yet they tested and provoked the
        Most High God,
    And did not keep His testimonies,
57 But turned back and acted
        unfaithfully like their fathers;
    They were turned aside like a
        deceitful bow.
58 For they provoked Him to anger
        with their high places,
    And moved Him to jealousy with
        their carved images.
59 When God heard *this,* He was
        furious,
    And greatly abhorred Israel,
60 So that He forsook the tabernacle
        of Shiloh,
    The tent He had placed among
        men,
61 And delivered His strength into
        captivity,
    And His glory into the enemy's
        hand.

Gospel
Pearls

62 He also gave His people over to
the sword,
And was furious with His
inheritance.
63 The fire consumed their young
men,
And their maidens were not
given in marriage.
64 Their priests fell by the sword,
And their widows made no
lamentation.

65 Then the Lord awoke as *from*
sleep,
Like a mighty man who shouts
because of wine.
66 And He beat back His enemies;
He put them to a perpetual
reproach.

67 Moreover He rejected the tent of
Joseph,
And did not choose the tribe of
Ephraim,
68 But chose the tribe of Judah,
Mount Zion which He loved.
69 And He built His sanctuary like
the heights,
Like the earth which He has
established forever.
70 He also chose David His servant,
And took him from the
sheepfolds;
71 From following the ewes that had
young He brought him,
To shepherd Jacob His people,
And Israel His inheritance.
72 So he shepherded them
according to the integrity of his
heart,
And guided them by the
skillfulness of his hands.

Psalm 79

A Psalm of Asaph.

1 O God, the nations have come
into Your inheritance;
Your holy temple they have
defiled;
They have laid Jerusalem in
heaps.
2 The dead bodies of Your servants
They have given *as* food for the
birds of the heavens,
The flesh of Your saints to the
beasts of the earth.
3 Their blood they have shed like
water all around Jerusalem,

And *there was* no one to bury
them.
4 We have become a reproach to
our neighbors,
A scorn and derision to those
who are around us.

5 How long, LORD?
Will You be angry forever?
Will Your jealousy burn like fire?
6 Pour out Your wrath on the
nations that do not know You,
And on the kingdoms that do not
call on Your name.
7 For they have devoured Jacob,
And laid waste his dwelling
place.

8 Oh, do not remember former
iniquities against us!
Let Your tender mercies come
speedily to meet us,
For we have been brought very
low.
9 Help us, O God of our salvation,
For the glory of Your name;
And deliver us, and provide
atonement for our sins,
For Your name's sake!
10 Why should the nations say,
"*Where is* their God?"
Let there be known among the
nations in our sight
The avenging of the blood of
Your servants *which has been*
shed.

11 Let the groaning of the prisoner
come before You;
According to the greatness of
Your power
Preserve those who are
appointed to die;
12 And return to our neighbors
sevenfold into their bosom
Their reproach with which they
have reproached You, O Lord.

13 So we, Your people and sheep of
Your pasture,
Will give You thanks forever;
We will show forth Your praise
to all generations.

Psalm 80

To the Chief Musician. Set to "The Lilies."[a] A
Testimony[b] of Asaph. A Psalm.

1 Give ear, O Shepherd of Israel,
You who lead Joseph like a flock;

80:title [a]Hebrew *Shoshannim*   [b]Hebrew *Eduth*

*T*he Father weans us from what we thought we had to have in order to give us what
He has for us. His plans are so much better than ours that it's worth the pain to
make the switch.

You who dwell *between* the
   cherubim, shine forth!
2 Before Ephraim, Benjamin, and
   Manasseh,
Stir up Your strength,
And come *and* save us!

3 Restore us, O God;
Cause Your face to shine,
And we shall be saved!

4 O Lord God of hosts,
How long will You be angry
Against the prayer of Your
   people?
5 You have fed them with the bread
   of tears,
And given them tears to drink in
   great measure.
6 You have made us a strife to our
   neighbors,
And our enemies laugh among
   themselves.

7 Restore us, O God of hosts;
Cause Your face to shine,
And we shall be saved!

8 You have brought a vine out of
   Egypt;
You have cast out the nations,
   and planted it.
9 You prepared *room* for it,
And caused it to take deep root,
And it filled the land.
10 The hills were covered with its
   shadow,
And the mighty cedars with its
   boughs.
11 She sent out her boughs to the
   Sea,[a]
And her branches to the River.[b]

12 Why have You broken down her
   hedges,
So that all who pass by the way
   pluck her *fruit?*
13 The boar out of the woods
   uproots it,
And the wild beast of the field
   devours it.

14 Return, we beseech You, O God
   of hosts;
Look down from heaven and see,
And visit this vine
15 And the vineyard which Your
   right hand has planted,
And the branch *that* You made
   strong for Yourself.

16 *It is* burned with fire, *it is* cut
   down;
They perish at the rebuke of Your
   countenance.
17 Let Your hand be upon the man
   of Your right hand,
Upon the son of man *whom* You
   made strong for Yourself.
18 Then we will not turn back from
   You;
Revive us, and we will call upon
   Your name.

19 Restore us, O Lord God of hosts;
Cause Your face to shine,
And we shall be saved!

Psalm 81

To the Chief Musician. On an instrument of
Gath.[a] A Psalm of Asaph.

1 Sing aloud to God our strength;
Make a joyful shout to the God
   of Jacob.
2 Raise a song and strike the
   timbrel,
The pleasant harp with the lute.

3 Blow the trumpet at the time of
   the New Moon,
At the full moon, on our solemn
   feast day.
4 For this *is* a statute for Israel,
A law of the God of Jacob.
5 This He established in Joseph *as*
   a testimony,
When He went throughout the
   land of Egypt,
Where I heard a language I did
   not understand.

6 "I removed his shoulder from the
   burden;
His hands were freed from the
   baskets.
7 You called in trouble, and I
   delivered you;
I answered you in the secret place
   of thunder;
I tested you at the waters of
   Meribah.   Selah

8 "Hear, O My people, and I will
   admonish you!
O Israel, if you will listen to Me!
9 There shall be no foreign god
   among you;
Nor shall you worship any
   foreign god.
10 I *am* the Lord your God,

80:11 [a]That is, the Mediterranean   [b]That is, the Euphrates   81:title [a]Hebrew *Al Gittith*

Gospel
Pearls

Who brought you out of the land
of Egypt;
Open your mouth wide, and I will
fill it.

11 "But My people would not heed
My voice,
And Israel would *have* none of
Me.
12 So I gave them over to their own
stubborn heart,
To walk in their own counsels.

13 "Oh, that My people would listen
to Me,
That Israel would walk in My
ways!
14 I would soon subdue their
enemies,
And turn My hand against their
adversaries.
15 The haters of the LORD would
pretend submission to Him,
But their fate would endure
forever.
16 He would have fed them also
with the finest of wheat;
And with honey from the rock I
would have satisfied you."

Psalm 82

A Psalm of Asaph.

1 God stands in the congregation
of the mighty;
He judges among the gods.*a*
2 How long will you judge unjustly,
And show partiality to the
wicked?   Selah
3 Defend the poor and fatherless;
Do justice to the afflicted and
needy.
4 Deliver the poor and needy;
Free *them* from the hand of the
wicked.

5 They do not know, nor do they
understand;
They walk about in darkness;
All the foundations of the earth
are unstable.

6 I said, "You *are* gods,*a*
And all of you *are* children of the
Most High.
7 But you shall die like men,
And fall like one of the princes."

8 Arise, O God, judge the earth;
For You shall inherit all nations.

Psalm 83

A Song. A Psalm of Asaph.

1 Do not keep silent, O God!
Do not hold Your peace,
And do not be still, O God!
2 For behold, Your enemies make
a tumult;
And those who hate You have
lifted up their head.
3 They have taken crafty counsel
against Your people,
And consulted together against
Your sheltered ones.
4 They have said, "Come, and let
us cut them off from *being* a
nation,
That the name of Israel may be
remembered no more."

5 For they have consulted together
with one consent;
They form a confederacy against
You:
6 The tents of Edom and the
Ishmaelites;
Moab and the Hagrites;
7 Gebal, Ammon, and Amalek;
Philistia with the inhabitants of
Tyre;
8 Assyria also has joined with
them;
They have helped the children of
Lot.   Selah

9 Deal with them as *with* Midian,
As *with* Sisera,
As *with* Jabin at the Brook
Kishon,
10 Who perished at En Dor,
Who became *as* refuse on the
earth.
11 Make their nobles like Oreb and
like Zeeb,
Yes, all their princes like Zebah
and Zalmunna,
12 Who said, "Let us take for
ourselves
The pastures of God for a
possession."

13 O my God, make them like the
whirling dust,
Like the chaff before the wind!
14 As the fire burns the woods,
And as the flame sets the
mountains on fire,
15 So pursue them with Your
tempest,

82:1 *a*Hebrew *elohim, mighty ones;* that is, the judges
judges
    82:6 *a*Hebrew *elohim, mighty ones;* that is, the

*I*f you have been feeling like you were being driven and not led, if you have been
compelled by some need to prove something or validate yourself, stop it now.

And frighten them with Your
    storm.
16 Fill their faces with shame,
    That they may seek Your name,
    O LORD.
17 Let them be confounded and
    dismayed forever;
    Yes, let them be put to shame and
    perish,
18 That they may know that You,
    whose name alone *is* the LORD,
    Are the Most High over all the
    earth.

Psalm 84

To the Chief Musician. On an instrument of
Gath.[a] A Psalm of the sons of Korah.

1 How lovely *is* Your tabernacle,
    O LORD of hosts!
2 My soul longs, yes, even faints
    For the courts of the LORD;
    My heart and my flesh cry out for
    the living God.

3 Even the sparrow has found a
    home,
    And the swallow a nest for
    herself,
    Where she may lay her young—
    Even Your altars, O LORD of
    hosts,
    My King and my God.
4 Blessed *are* those who dwell in
    Your house;
    They will still be praising You.
                                  Selah

5 Blessed *is* the man whose
    strength *is* in You,
    Whose heart *is* set on pilgrimage.
6 *As they* pass through the Valley
    of Baca,
    They make it a spring;
    The rain also covers it with pools.
7 They go from strength to
    strength;
    Each one appears before God in
    Zion.[a]

8 O LORD God of hosts, hear my
    prayer;
    Give ear, O God of Jacob!
                                  Selah
9 O God, behold our shield,
    And look upon the face of Your
    anointed.

10 For a day in Your courts *is* better
    than a thousand.

I would rather be a doorkeeper
    in the house of my God
    Than dwell in the tents of
    wickedness.
11 For the LORD God *is* a sun and
    shield;
    The LORD will give grace and
    glory;
    No good *thing* will He withhold
    From those who walk uprightly.

12 O LORD of hosts,
    Blessed *is* the man who trusts in
    You!

Psalm 85

To the Chief Musician. A Psalm of the sons of
Korah.

1 LORD, You have been favorable
    to Your land;
    You have brought back the
    captivity of Jacob.
2 You have forgiven the iniquity of
    Your people;
    You have covered all their sin.
                                  Selah
3 You have taken away all Your
    wrath;
    You have turned from the
    fierceness of Your anger.

4 Restore us, O God of our
    salvation,
    And cause Your anger toward us
    to cease.
5 Will You be angry with us
    forever?
    Will You prolong Your anger to
    all generations?
6 Will You not revive us again,
    That Your people may rejoice in
    You?
7 Show us Your mercy, LORD,
    And grant us Your salvation.

8 I will hear what God the LORD
    will speak,
    For He will speak peace
    To His people and to His saints;
    But let them not turn back to
    folly.
9 Surely His salvation *is* near to
    those who fear Him,
    That glory may dwell in our land.

10 Mercy and truth have met
    together;

84:title [a]Hebrew *Al Gittith*   84:7 [a]Septuagint, Syriac, and Vulgate read *The God of gods shall be seen.*

Gospel
Pearls

Righteousness and peace have
   kissed.
11 Truth shall spring out of the
   earth,
   And righteousness shall look
   down from heaven.
12 Yes, the LORD will give *what is*
   good;
   And our land will yield its
   increase.
13 Righteousness will go before
   Him,
   And shall make His footsteps *our*
   pathway.

Psalm 86

A Prayer of David.

1 Bow down Your ear, O LORD,
   hear me;
   For I *am* poor and needy.
2 Preserve my life, for I *am* holy;
   You are my God;
   Save Your servant who trusts in
   You!
3 Be merciful to me, O Lord,
   For I cry to You all day long.
4 Rejoice the soul of Your servant,
   For to You, O Lord, I lift up my
   soul.
5 For You, Lord, *are* good, and
   ready to forgive,
   And abundant in mercy to all
   those who call upon You.

6 Give ear, O LORD, to my prayer;
   And attend to the voice of my
   supplications.
7 In the day of my trouble I will
   call upon You,
   For You will answer me.

8 Among the gods *there is* none
   like You, O Lord;
   Nor *are there any works* like
   Your works.
9 All nations whom You have
   made
   Shall come and worship before
   You, O Lord,
   And shall glorify Your name.
10 For You *are* great, and do
   wondrous things;
   You alone *are* God.

11 Teach me Your way, O LORD;
   I will walk in Your truth;
   Unite my heart to fear Your
   name.
12 I will praise You, O Lord my God,
   with all my heart,

And I will glorify Your name
   forevermore.
13 For great *is* Your mercy toward
   me,
   And You have delivered my soul
   from the depths of Sheol.

14 O God, the proud have risen
   against me,
   And a mob of violent *men* have
   sought my life,
   And have not set You before
   them.
15 But You, O Lord, *are* a God full
   of compassion, and gracious,
   Longsuffering and abundant in
   mercy and truth.

16 Oh, turn to me, and have mercy
   on me!
   Give Your strength to Your
   servant,
   And save the son of Your
   maidservant.
17 Show me a sign for good,
   That those who hate me may see
   it and be ashamed,
   Because You, LORD, have helped
   me and comforted me.

Psalm 87

A Psalm of the sons of Korah. A Song.

1 His foundation *is* in the holy
   mountains.
2 The LORD loves the gates of Zion
   More than all the dwellings of
   Jacob.
3 Glorious things are spoken of
   you,
   O city of God!   Selah

4 "I will make mention of Rahab
   and Babylon to those who
   know Me;
   Behold, O Philistia and Tyre,
   with Ethiopia:
   'This *one* was born there.' "

5 And of Zion it will be said,
   "*This one* and that *one* were born
   in her;
   And the Most High Himself shall
   establish her."
6 The LORD will record,
   When He registers the peoples:
   "This *one* was born there."   Selah

7 Both the singers and the players
   on instruments *say,*
   "All my springs *are* in you."

*Y*ou are not to be driven or compelled, controlled or dominated, not by a person, a
goal or even your own flesh. Jesus died to set you free.

Psalm 88

A Song. A Psalm of the sons of Korah. To the Chief Musician. Set to "Mahalath Leannoth." A Contemplation[a] of Heman the Ezrahite.

1 O LORD, God of my salvation,
   I have cried out day and night
      before You.
2 Let my prayer come before You;
   Incline Your ear to my cry.

3 For my soul is full of troubles,
   And my life draws near to the
      grave.
4 I am counted with those who go
      down to the pit;
   I am like a man *who has* no
      strength,
5 Adrift among the dead,
   Like the slain who lie in the
      grave,
   Whom You remember no more,
   And who are cut off from Your
      hand.

6 You have laid me in the lowest
      pit,
   In darkness, in the depths.
7 Your wrath lies heavy upon me,
   And You have afflicted *me* with
      all Your waves.   Selah
8 You have put away my
      acquaintances far from me;
   You have made me an
      abomination to them;
   I am shut up, and I cannot get
      out;
9 My eye wastes away because of
      affliction.

   LORD, I have called daily upon
      You;
   I have stretched out my hands to
      You.
10 Will You work wonders for the
      dead?
   Shall the dead arise *and* praise
      You?   Selah
11 Shall Your lovingkindness be
      declared in the grave?
   Or Your faithfulness in the place
      of destruction?
12 Shall Your wonders be known in
      the dark?
   And Your righteousness in the
      land of forgetfulness?

13 But to You I have cried out, O
      LORD,
   And in the morning my prayer
      comes before You.

14 LORD, why do You cast off my
      soul?
   Why do You hide Your face from
      me?
15 I *have been* afflicted and ready
      to die from *my* youth;
   I suffer Your terrors;
   I am distraught.
16 Your fierce wrath has gone over
      me;
   Your terrors have cut me off.
17 They came around me all day
      long like water;
   They engulfed me altogether.
18 Loved one and friend You have
      put far from me,
   And my acquaintances into
      darkness.

Psalm 89

A Contemplation[a] of Ethan the Ezrahite.

1 I will sing of the mercies of the
      LORD forever;
   With my mouth will I make
      known Your faithfulness to all
      generations.
2 For I have said, "Mercy shall be
      built up forever;
   Your faithfulness You shall
      establish in the very heavens."

3 "I have made a covenant with My
      chosen,
   I have sworn to My servant
      David:
4 'Your seed I will establish forever,
   And build up your throne to all
      generations.' "   Selah

5 And the heavens will praise Your
      wonders, O LORD;
   Your faithfulness also in the
      assembly of the saints.
6 For who in the heavens can be
      compared to the LORD?
   Who among the sons of the
      mighty can be likened to the
      LORD?
7 God is greatly to be feared in the
      assembly of the saints,
   And to be held in reverence by
      all *those* around Him.
8 O LORD God of hosts,
   Who *is* mighty like You, O LORD?
   Your faithfulness also surrounds
      You.
9 You rule the raging of the sea;
   When its waves rise, You still
      them.

88:title *a*Hebrew *Maschil*   89:title *a*Hebrew *Maschil*

*I*t is a great blessing when you understand that life is full of change. Change is unavoidable: Anything that grows will change.

Child of the Father

Psalm 89:7

Thank God He understands the child within you. He speaks to your blanket-clutching, thumb-sucking need. In spite of your age, your income, your education, or your celebrity, He knows the childhood issues of the maturing heart. This is the ministry that only our Father can give.

Have you ever noticed that to those who brought you into the world, you will never grow up? They will completely disregard your gray hairs, your crow's feet, and your blossoming waistline. No matter how many children call you "Mom," to your parents you are still just a child yourself. They seem to think you have slipped into the closet to try on grown-up clothes and are really just pretending. They must believe that somewhere beneath the lines on your face there is still a child, parading around in her mother's dress and high-heeled shoes.

When the disciples asked Jesus to teach them to pray, the first thing He taught them was to acknowledge the *Fatherhood* of God. When we say, "Our Father," we acknowledge His Fatherhood and declare our sonship. Sonship is the basis for our relationship with Him as it relates to the privilege of belonging to His divine family. Similarly, one of the first words most babies say is "Daddy." Knowing your earthly father helps you understand your own identity as a son or daughter. Greater still is the need to know not only *who* my Father is, but *how He feels about me*.

The Lord looks beyond the facade of maturity and sees the trembling, uncertain places in your life. He knows your innermost needs. No matter how spiritually mature you try to appear, He is aware that lurking in the shadows is some childish desire you just prayed away last night—the lingering evidence of some tiny temptation that only the Father can see within His supposedly "all-grown-up" little child.

Only He can see the very worst in us, yet think the very best of us. It is the unfailing love of the Father whose daughter should have been old enough to receive her inheritance without acting like a child, without wandering off into failure and stumbling into sin. Even then, your Father throws a party for the prodigal and prepares a feast for the foolish. Comprehend with childlike faith the love of the Father you have in God!

10 You have broken Rahab in
   pieces, as one who is slain;
   You have scattered Your enemies
   with Your mighty arm.

11 The heavens *are* Yours, the earth
   also *is* Yours;
   The world and all its fullness,
   You have founded them.

12 The north and the south, You
   have created them;
   Tabor and Hermon rejoice in
   Your name.

13 You have a mighty arm;
   Strong is Your hand, *and* high is
   Your right hand.

14 Righteousness and justice *are* the
   foundation of Your throne;
   Mercy and truth go before Your
   face.

15 Blessed *are* the people who know
   the joyful sound!
   They walk, O LORD, in the light
   of Your countenance.

16 In Your name they rejoice all day
   long,
   And in Your righteousness they
   are exalted.

17 For You *are* the glory of their
   strength,
   And in Your favor our horn is
   exalted.

18 For our shield *belongs* to the
   LORD,
   And our king to the Holy One of
   Israel.

19 Then You spoke in a vision to
   Your holy one,[a]
   And said: "I have given help to
   one who is mighty;
   I have exalted one chosen from
   the people.

20 I have found My servant David;
   With My holy oil I have anointed
   him,

21 With whom My hand shall be
   established;
   Also My arm shall strengthen
   him.

22 The enemy shall not outwit him,
   Nor the son of wickedness afflict
   him.

23 I will beat down his foes before
   his face,
   And plague those who hate him.

24 "But My faithfulness and My
   mercy *shall be* with him,

And in My name his horn shall
be exalted.

25 Also I will set his hand over the
   sea,
   And his right hand over the
   rivers.

26 He shall cry to Me,'You *are* my
   Father,
   My God, and the rock of my
   salvation.'

27 Also I will make him My
   firstborn,
   The highest of the kings of the
   earth.

28 My mercy I will keep for him
   forever,
   And My covenant shall stand
   firm with him.

29 His seed also I will make *to
   endure* forever,
   And his throne as the days of
   heaven.

30 "If his sons forsake My law
   And do not walk in My
   judgments,

31 If they break My statutes
   And do not keep My
   commandments,

32 Then I will punish their
   transgression with the rod,
   And their iniquity with stripes.

33 Nevertheless My lovingkindness
   I will not utterly take from him,
   Nor allow My faithfulness to fail.

34 My covenant I will not break,
   Nor alter the word that has gone
   out of My lips.

35 Once I have sworn by My
   holiness;
   I will not lie to David:

36 His seed shall endure forever,
   And his throne as the sun before
   Me;

37 It shall be established forever like
   the moon,
   Even *like* the faithful witness in
   the sky."   Selah

38 But You have cast off and
   abhorred,
   You have been furious with Your
   anointed.

39 You have renounced the
   covenant of Your servant;
   You have profaned his crown *by
   casting it* to the ground.

40 You have broken down all his
   hedges;

89:19 [a]Following many Hebrew manuscripts; Masoretic Text, Septuagint, Targum, and Vulgate read *holy
ones.*

Gospel
Pearls

You have brought his
strongholds to ruin.
41 All who pass by the way plunder
him;
He is a reproach to his neighbors.
42 You have exalted the right hand
of his adversaries;
You have made all his enemies
rejoice.
43 You have also turned back the
edge of his sword,
And have not sustained him in
the battle.
44 You have made his glory cease,
And cast his throne down to the
ground.
45 The days of his youth You have
shortened;
You have covered him with
shame.   Selah

46 How long, Lord?
Will You hide Yourself forever?
Will Your wrath burn like fire?
47 Remember how short my time is;
For what futility have You
created all the children of men?
48 What man can live and not see
death?
Can he deliver his life from the
power of the grave?   Selah

49 Lord, where *are* Your former
lovingkindnesses,
Which You swore to David in
Your truth?
50 Remember, Lord, the reproach of
Your servants—
How I bear in my bosom *the
reproach of* all the many
peoples,
51 With which Your enemies have
reproached, O Lord,
With which they have
reproached the footsteps of
Your anointed.

52 Blessed *be* the Lord forevermore!
Amen and Amen.

Book Four   Psalms 90–106

Psalm 90

A Prayer of Moses the man of God.

1 Lord, You have been our
dwelling place*ᵃ* in all
generations.
2 Before the mountains were
brought forth,

Or ever You had formed the earth
and the world,
Even from everlasting to
everlasting, You *are* God.

3 You turn man to destruction,
And say, "Return, O children of
men."
4 For a thousand years in Your
sight
Are like yesterday when it is past,
And *like* a watch in the night.
5 You carry them away *like* a flood;
They are like a sleep.
In the morning they are like grass
which grows up:
6 In the morning it flourishes and
grows up;
In the evening it is cut down and
withers.

7 For we have been consumed by
Your anger,
And by Your wrath we are
terrified.
8 You have set our iniquities before
You,
Our secret *sins* in the light of
Your countenance.
9 For all our days have passed
away in Your wrath;
We finish our years like a sigh.
10 The days of our lives *are* seventy
years;
And if by reason of strength *they
are* eighty years,
Yet their boast *is* only labor and
sorrow;
For it is soon cut off, and we fly
away.
11 Who knows the power of Your
anger?
For as the fear of You, *so is* Your
wrath.
12 So teach *us* to number our days,
That we may gain a heart of
wisdom.

13 Return, O Lord!
How long?
And have compassion on Your
servants.
14 Oh, satisfy us early with Your
mercy,
That we may rejoice and be glad
all our days!
15 Make us glad according to the
days *in which* You have
afflicted us,

90:1 *ᵃ*Septuagint, Targum, and Vulgate read *refuge*.

When you have children, hold them, love them, care for them, empower them. But
understand that you are only temporary stewards. They belong to God.

Get to Jesus

Psalm 90:8

One of the main reasons women don't share their problems is this: They are told they shouldn't have problems—especially after they are saved!

In Hebrews 11, we find a list of people who are often called the heroes of the faith. On that list you'll see Noah and Abraham and Sarah and Moses and Rahab and Gideon and David and Samuel and all the prophets. The amazing thing is that every one of these giants of faith had a problem.

The Bible says that some of these heroes were tortured and mocked and scourged and imprisoned and stoned and sawn asunder. It says they were afflicted and tormented, and that some of them wandered in deserts and lived in caves. I've lived in some poor places, but I've never lived in a cave.

God's people have problems. We need to face up to that. It's not a matter of lack of faith or of not being saved. It's a fact of life in a fallen world. Problems come with the turf of a world that has been turned upside down by sin.

The infirm woman's problem was a private problem. It was not a public problem. It was a problem that could be covered up. Oh, we are so good at hiding our problems. I was once in a meeting where the women were wearing silk dresses and diamond jewelry and sequined jackets. They were looking good. But I wasn't fooled. I knew that every imaginable secret was present in that room. That room was filled with private problems.

Sister Rape was present. Sister Child Abuse came along. Sister Crack Cocaine was there. Sister Battered Wife was with her. Sister Lesbian showed up. Sister Oppressed attended. Sister Depressed was sitting right by her side. All the girls were there that night. They are present in any large gathering of women anywhere in our nation at any time. The fact that you have a problem is not what matters. What matters is what you choose to do about it.

This woman made the right choice about where to take her problem. Now, she didn't make the right choice immediately, but she made it ultimately. She had suffered for twelve years and had spent all her money on doctors.

Be careful who you allow to help you. That person who is so eager to treat you may be after your money. Be careful whom you trust with your problem. That person may not be worthy of your trust. Be careful whom you invite into your confidence. That person may gossip about you behind your back. Beware of the counsel of the ungodly. They'll give you plenty of advice, but they can't give you any lasting help.

If you are going to seek out someone to help you, seek out someone who knows the Answer. Find someone who will say to you, "Jesus is on the way. Jesus is coming. Jesus is the Healer. Jesus is the Problem-Solver. Jesus is the One who can plug the problem that is draining you dry. Reach out and touch Him by your faith!"

The years *in which* we have seen evil.

16 Let Your work appear to Your servants,
And Your glory to their children.

17 And let the beauty of the LORD our God be upon us,
And establish the work of our hands for us;
Yes, establish the work of our hands.

Psalm 91

1 He who dwells in the secret place of the Most High
Shall abide under the shadow of the Almighty.

2 I will say of the LORD, *"He is* my refuge and my fortress;
My God, in Him I will trust."

3 Surely He shall deliver you from the snare of the fowler^a
And from the perilous pestilence.

4 He shall cover you with His feathers,
And under His wings you shall take refuge;
His truth *shall be your* shield and buckler.

5 You shall not be afraid of the terror by night,
Nor of the arrow *that* flies by day,

6 *Nor* of the pestilence *that* walks in darkness,
Nor of the destruction *that* lays waste at noonday.

7 A thousand may fall at your side,
And ten thousand at your right hand;
But it shall not come near you.

8 Only with your eyes shall you look,
And see the reward of the wicked.

9 Because you have made the LORD, *who is* my refuge,
Even the Most High, your dwelling place,

10 No evil shall befall you,
Nor shall any plague come near your dwelling;

11 For He shall give His angels charge over you,
To keep you in all your ways.

12 In *their* hands they shall bear you up,
Lest you dash your foot against a stone.

13 You shall tread upon the lion and the cobra,
The young lion and the serpent you shall trample underfoot.

14 "Because he has set his love upon Me, therefore I will deliver him;
I will set him on high, because he has known My name.

15 He shall call upon Me, and I will answer him;
I will be with him in trouble;
I will deliver him and honor him.

16 With long life I will satisfy him,
And show him My salvation."

Psalm 92

A Psalm. A Song for the Sabbath day.

1 *It is* good to give thanks to the LORD,
And to sing praises to Your name, O Most High;

2 To declare Your lovingkindness in the morning,
And Your faithfulness every night,

3 On an instrument of ten strings,
On the lute,
And on the harp,
With harmonious sound.

4 For You, LORD, have made me glad through Your work;
I will triumph in the works of Your hands.

5 O LORD, how great are Your works!
Your thoughts are very deep.

6 A senseless man does not know,
Nor does a fool understand this.

7 When the wicked spring up like grass,
And when all the workers of iniquity flourish,
It is that they may be destroyed forever.

8 But You, LORD, *are* on high forevermore.

9 For behold, Your enemies, O LORD,
For behold, Your enemies shall perish;
All the workers of iniquity shall be scattered.

91:3 ^aThat is, one who catches birds in a trap or snare

*R*efuse to reconnect with your infirmity. When you are loosed, stay loosed. Don't allow yourself to go back into bondage. Once you are free, stay free!

The Covering

Psalm 91:1-13

*I*n the process of creating Eve, the mother of all living, God's timing was crucial. He did not unveil her until everything she needed was provided. From establishment to relationship, all things were in order. Woman was meant to be covered, to be nurtured and protected. Originally, Adam was her covering.

My sister, even as a child, you were made to be covered. If someone "uncovered" you, there is a feeling of being violated. Even when these feelings are suppressed, they are still powerful. I think it is interesting that when the Bible talks about incest, it uses the word *uncovered*. Sexual abuse violates the covering of the family and the responsible persons whom you looked to for guidance. This stripping away of right relationship leaves you exposed and vulnerable to the reality of corrupt, lustful imaginations. Like fruit peeled too soon, it is wrong to uncover what God wished to remain protected.

To molest a child is to uncover her, to leave her feeling unprotected. Do you realize that one of the things the blood of Jesus Christ does is to cover us? Like Noah's sons who covered their father's nakedness, the blood of Jesus will cover the uncovered. He will not allow you to spend the rest of your life exposed and violated.

For the wounded and hurting, God has intensive care. There may be times in your life when God nurtures you through a crisis. On the other hand, you may not even realize the many times He intervenes to relieve the tensions and stresses of everyday living. He knows when the load is overwhelming. And He moves just in the nick of time.

The Bible instructs husbands to dwell with their wives according to knowledge and understanding (see 1 Peter 3:7). It will pay every husband to understand that many women do not deal easily with such stresses as unpaid bills and financial disorder. A feeling of security is a plus in matters of the home. That same principle is just as important when it comes to your relationship with the Lord. He is constantly reassuring you that you have a consolation and a hope for your soul.

Reach out and embrace the fact that God has been watching over you all your life. My sister, He covers you, clothes you, and blesses you. Rejoice in Him in spite of the broken places. God's grace is sufficient for your needs and your scars. He will anoint you with oil. The anointing of the Lord be upon you now!

10 But my horn You have exalted
     like a wild ox;
   I have been anointed with fresh
     oil.
11 My eye also has seen *my desire*
     on my enemies;
   My ears hear *my desire* on the
     wicked
   Who rise up against me.

12 The righteous shall flourish like
     a palm tree,
   He shall grow like a cedar in
     Lebanon.
13 Those who are planted in the
     house of the LORD
   Shall flourish in the courts of our
     God.
14 They shall still bear fruit in old
     age;
   They shall be fresh and
     flourishing,
15 To declare that the LORD is
     upright;
   He is my rock, and *there is* no
     unrighteousness in Him.

Psalm 93

1 The LORD reigns, He is clothed
     with majesty;
   The LORD is clothed,
   He has girded Himself with
     strength.
   Surely the world is established,
     so that it cannot be moved.
2 Your throne *is* established from
     of old;
   You *are* from everlasting.

3 The floods have lifted up, O LORD,
   The floods have lifted up their
     voice;
   The floods lift up their waves.
4 The LORD on high *is* mightier
   Than the noise of many waters,
   Than the mighty waves of the
     sea.

5 Your testimonies are very sure;
   Holiness adorns Your house,
   O LORD, forever.

Psalm 94

1 O LORD God, to whom vengeance
     belongs—
   O God, to whom vengeance
     belongs, shine forth!
2 Rise up, O Judge of the earth;
   Render punishment to the proud.
3 LORD, how long will the wicked,

How long will the wicked
  triumph?

4 They utter speech, *and* speak
     insolent things;
   All the workers of iniquity boast
     in themselves.
5 They break in pieces Your
     people, O LORD,
   And afflict Your heritage.
6 They slay the widow and the
     stranger,
   And murder the fatherless.
7 Yet they say, "The LORD does not
     see,
   Nor does the God of Jacob
     understand."

8 Understand, you senseless
     among the people;
   And *you* fools, when will you be
     wise?
9 He who planted the ear, shall He
     not hear?
   He who formed the eye, shall He
     not see?
10 He who instructs the nations,
     shall He not correct,
   He who teaches man knowledge?
11 The LORD knows the thoughts of
     man,
   That they *are* futile.

12 Blessed *is* the man whom You
     instruct, O LORD,
   And teach out of Your law,
13 That You may give him rest from
     the days of adversity,
   Until the pit is dug for the wicked.
14 For the LORD will not cast off His
     people,
   Nor will He forsake His
     inheritance.
15 But judgment will return to
     righteousness,
   And all the upright in heart will
     follow it.

16 Who will rise up for me against
     the evildoers?
   Who will stand up for me against
     the workers of iniquity?
17 Unless the LORD *had been* my
     help,
   My soul would soon have settled
     in silence.
18 If I say, "My foot slips,"
   Your mercy, O LORD, will hold me
     up.
19 In the multitude of my anxieties
     within me,
   Your comforts delight my soul.

*D*o not give your children the part of your heart that they were not meant to hold.
Do not dump your pain, frustration or even your affection upon them more lavishly
than a good mother should. If you do, you will find yourself bribing your children to
stay with you, and that will cripple them.

20 Shall the throne of iniquity,
    which devises evil by law,
    Have fellowship with You?
21 They gather together against the
    life of the righteous,
    And condemn innocent blood.
22 But the LORD has been my
    defense,
    And my God the rock of my
    refuge.
23 He has brought on them their
    own iniquity,
    And shall cut them off in their
    own wickedness;
    The LORD our God shall cut them
    off.

Psalm 95

1 Oh come, let us sing to the LORD!
    Let us shout joyfully to the Rock
    of our salvation.
2 Let us come before His presence
    with thanksgiving;
    Let us shout joyfully to Him with
    psalms.
3 For the LORD *is* the great God,
    And the great King above all
    gods.
4 In His hand *are* the deep places
    of the earth;
    The heights of the hills *are* His
    also.
5 The sea *is* His, for He made it;
    And His hands formed the dry
    land.

6 Oh come, let us worship and bow
    down;
    Let us kneel before the LORD our
    Maker.
7 For He *is* our God,
    And we *are* the people of His
    pasture,
    And the sheep of His hand.

    Today, if you will hear His voice:
8 "Do not harden your hearts, as in
    the rebellion,*a*
    As *in* the day of trial*b* in the
    wilderness,
9 When your fathers tested Me;
    They tried Me, though they saw
    My work.
10 For forty years I was grieved with
    that generation,
    And said, 'It *is* a people who go
    astray in their hearts,
    And they do not know My ways.'

11 So I swore in My wrath,
    'They shall not enter My rest.' "

Psalm 96

1 Oh, sing to the LORD a new song!
    Sing to the LORD, all the earth.
2 Sing to the LORD, bless His name;
    Proclaim the good news of His
    salvation from day to day.
3 Declare His glory among the
    nations,
    His wonders among all peoples.

4 For the LORD *is* great and greatly
    to be praised;
    He *is* to be feared above all gods.
5 For all the gods of the peoples *are*
    idols,
    But the LORD made the heavens.
6 Honor and majesty *are* before
    Him;
    Strength and beauty *are* in His
    sanctuary.

7 Give to the LORD, O families of
    the peoples,
    Give to the LORD glory and
    strength.
8 Give to the LORD the glory *due*
    His name;
    Bring an offering, and come into
    His courts.
9 Oh, worship the LORD in the
    beauty of holiness!
    Tremble before Him, all the
    earth.

10 Say among the nations, "The
    LORD reigns;
    The world also is firmly
    established,
    It shall not be moved;
    He shall judge the peoples
    righteously."

11 Let the heavens rejoice, and let
    the earth be glad;
    Let the sea roar, and all its
    fullness;
12 Let the field be joyful, and all that
    is in it.
    Then all the trees of the woods
    will rejoice before the LORD.
13 For He is coming, for He is
    coming to judge the earth.
    He shall judge the world with
    righteousness,
    And the peoples with His truth.

95:8 *a*Hebrew *Meribah*   *b*Hebrew *Massah*

*I*t is important that you do not lose your sense of personhood. Don't stop valuing
yourself and your needs. The Word of God doesn't teach us to be selfish, but it does
admonish us to love others as we love ourselves.

Soul Secrets
of a woman
in intimate worship

God, You alone are King of my heart. My Hero, my Helper, my Confidant, my Friend. You are the great and only Lover of my soul. My Solace, my Listener, my Amazing One. Protector, Provider, Supreme Sacrificer, Source of life and love and all good gifts. You are the River that runs through me, the Rock of Ages beneath me, the God of Glory above me, the Spirit of Life within me.

My heart beats for You. Yours is the love that I lean on. Yours is the hand that I reach for. Yours is the breast my tears find their way to. You are Counselor, Comforter, Captain of all my ways. You are the Searcher of my heart, the Keeper of my secrets, the Giver of my dreams. You are all the wonder that is love to me—my most intimate Companion, Dweller in the deepest parts of me.

We walk together now and through all eternity—Father and daughter, King and princess, Savior and saint, Heaven and earth. The most natural conversation of my day is prayer. You are my favorite Friend.

Psalm 97

1 The LORD reigns;
Let the earth rejoice;
Let the multitude of isles be glad!

2 Clouds and darkness surround Him;
Righteousness and justice *are* the foundation of His throne.

3 A fire goes before Him,
And burns up His enemies round about.

4 His lightnings light the world;
The earth sees and trembles.

5 The mountains melt like wax at the presence of the LORD,
At the presence of the Lord of the whole earth.

6 The heavens declare His righteousness,
And all the peoples see His glory.

7 Let all be put to shame who serve carved images,
Who boast of idols.
Worship Him, all *you* gods.

8 Zion hears and is glad,
And the daughters of Judah rejoice
Because of Your judgments, O LORD.

9 For You, LORD, *are* most high above all the earth;
You are exalted far above all gods.

10 You who love the LORD, hate evil!
He preserves the souls of His saints;
He delivers them out of the hand of the wicked.

11 Light is sown for the righteous,
And gladness for the upright in heart.

12 Rejoice in the LORD, you righteous,
And give thanks at the remembrance of His holy name.[a]

Psalm 98

A Psalm.

1 Oh, sing to the LORD a new song!
For He has done marvelous things;
His right hand and His holy arm have gained Him the victory.

2 The LORD has made known His salvation;
His righteousness He has revealed in the sight of the nations.

3 He has remembered His mercy and His faithfulness to the house of Israel;
All the ends of the earth have seen the salvation of our God.

4 Shout joyfully to the LORD, all the earth;
Break forth in song, rejoice, and sing praises.

5 Sing to the LORD with the harp,
With the harp and the sound of a psalm,

6 With trumpets and the sound of a horn;
Shout joyfully before the LORD, the King.

7 Let the sea roar, and all its fullness,
The world and those who dwell in it;

8 Let the rivers clap *their* hands;
Let the hills be joyful together before the LORD,

9 For He is coming to judge the earth.
With righteousness He shall judge the world,
And the peoples with equity.

Psalm 99

1 The LORD reigns;
Let the peoples tremble!
He dwells *between* the cherubim;
Let the earth be moved!

2 The LORD *is* great in Zion,
And He *is* high above all the peoples.

3 Let them praise Your great and awesome name—
He *is* holy.

4 The King's strength also loves justice;
You have established equity;
You have executed justice and righteousness in Jacob.

5 Exalt the LORD our God,
And worship at His footstool—
He *is* holy.

6 Moses and Aaron were among His priests,
And Samuel was among those who called upon His name;

97:12 *a*Or *His holiness*

Gospel Pearls

They called upon the LORD, and
   He answered them.
7 He spoke to them in the cloudy
   pillar;
They kept His testimonies and
   the ordinance He gave them.

8 You answered them, O LORD our
   God;
You were to them God-Who-
   Forgives,
Though You took vengeance on
   their deeds.
9 Exalt the LORD our God,
And worship at His holy hill;
For the LORD our God *is* holy.

Psalm 100

A Psalm of Thanksgiving.

1 Make a joyful shout to the LORD,
   all you lands!
2 Serve the LORD with gladness;
Come before His presence with
   singing.
3 Know that the LORD, He *is* God;
It is He *who* has made us, and
   not we ourselves;[a]
We are His people and the sheep
   of His pasture.

4 Enter into His gates with
   thanksgiving,
And into His courts with praise.
Be thankful to Him, *and* bless His
   name.
5 For the LORD *is* good;
His mercy *is* everlasting,
And His truth *endures* to all
   generations.

Psalm 101

A Psalm of David.

1 I will sing of mercy and justice;
To You, O LORD, I will sing
   praises.

2 I will behave wisely in a perfect
   way.
Oh, when will You come to me?
I will walk within my house with
   a perfect heart.

3 I will set nothing wicked before
   my eyes;
I hate the work of those who fall
   away;
It shall not cling to me.

4 A perverse heart shall depart
   from me;
I will not know wickedness.

5 Whoever secretly slanders his
   neighbor,
Him I will destroy;
The one who has a haughty look
   and a proud heart,
Him I will not endure.

6 My eyes *shall be* on the faithful
   of the land,
That they may dwell with me;
He who walks in a perfect way,
He shall serve me.
7 He who works deceit shall not
   dwell within my house;
He who tells lies shall not
   continue in my presence.
8 Early I will destroy all the wicked
   of the land,
That I may cut off all the
   evildoers from the city of the
   LORD.

Psalm 102

A Prayer of the afflicted, when he is
overwhelmed and pours out his complaint before
the LORD.

1 Hear my prayer, O LORD,
And let my cry come to You.
2 Do not hide Your face from me
   in the day of my trouble;
Incline Your ear to me;
In the day that I call, answer me
   speedily.

3 For my days are consumed like
   smoke,
And my bones are burned like a
   hearth.
4 My heart is stricken and withered
   like grass,
So that I forget to eat my bread.
5 Because of the sound of my
   groaning
My bones cling to my skin.
6 I am like a pelican of the
   wilderness;
I am like an owl of the desert.
7 I lie awake,
And am like a sparrow alone on
   the housetop.

8 My enemies reproach me all day
   long;
Those who deride me swear an
   oath against me.

100:3 [a]Following Kethib, Septuagint, and Vulgate; Qere, many Hebrew manuscripts, and Targum read *we are His.*

Grace empowers us to continue and experience with God's help. Why don't you ask Him for the grace you need to accept the things that you cannot change? When He gives it to you, get on with your life.

9 For I have eaten ashes like bread,
And mingled my drink with
weeping,
10 Because of Your indignation and
Your wrath;
For You have lifted me up and
cast me away.
11 My days *are* like a shadow that
lengthens,
And I wither away like grass.

12 But You, O LORD, shall endure
forever,
And the remembrance of Your
name to all generations.
13 You will arise *and* have mercy on
Zion;
For the time to favor her,
Yes, the set time, has come.
14 For Your servants take pleasure
in her stones,
And show favor to her dust.
15 So the nations shall fear the
name of the LORD,
And all the kings of the earth
Your glory.
16 For the LORD shall build up Zion;
He shall appear in His glory.
17 He shall regard the prayer of the
destitute,
And shall not despise their
prayer.

18 This will be written for the
generation to come,
That a people yet to be created
may praise the LORD.
19 For He looked down from the
height of His sanctuary;
From heaven the LORD viewed
the earth,
20 To hear the groaning of the
prisoner,
To release those appointed to
death,
21 To declare the name of the LORD
in Zion,
And His praise in Jerusalem,
22 When the peoples are gathered
together,
And the kingdoms, to serve the
LORD.

23 He weakened my strength in the
way;
He shortened my days.
24 I said, "O my God,
Do not take me away in the midst
of my days;
Your years *are* throughout all
generations.

25 Of old You laid the foundation of
the earth,
And the heavens *are* the work of
Your hands.
26 They will perish, but You will
endure;
Yes, they will all grow old like a
garment;
Like a cloak You will change
them,
And they will be changed.
27 But You *are* the same,
And Your years will have no end.
28 The children of Your servants
will continue,
And their descendants will be
established before You."

Psalm 103

A Psalm of David.

1 Bless the LORD, O my soul;
And all that is within me, *bless*
His holy name!
2 Bless the LORD, O my soul,
And forget not all His benefits:
3 Who forgives all your iniquities,
Who heals all your diseases,
4 Who redeems your life from
destruction,
Who crowns you with
lovingkindness and tender
mercies,
5 Who satisfies your mouth with
good *things*,
So that your youth is renewed
like the eagle's.

6 The LORD executes righteousness
And justice for all who are
oppressed.
7 He made known His ways to
Moses,
His acts to the children of Israel.
8 The LORD *is* merciful and
gracious,
Slow to anger, and abounding in
mercy.
9 He will not always strive *with us,*
Nor will He keep *His anger*
forever.
10 He has not dealt with us
according to our sins,
Nor punished us according to our
iniquities.

11 For as the heavens are high
above the earth,
So great is His mercy toward
those who fear Him;
12 As far as the east is from the
west,

*E*ach experience has its own value if you do not close your eyes to where you are, trying foolishly to be where you have already been. I know life can feel terribly unstable and vulnerable when you accept change. But I am so glad God ever remains the same. He is the stability that enables us to adjust to the variables of life.

Jesus Calls the Cripple

Psalm 103:1-5

When Jesus encountered the infirm woman of Luke 13, He called out to her. There may have been many fine women present that day, but the Lord didn't call them forward. He reached around all of them and found that crippled woman in the back. He called forth the wounded, hurting woman with a past. He issued the Spirit's call to the one whose value and self-esteem had been destroyed by the intrusion of vicious circumstances.

The infirm woman must have thought, "He wants me. He wants *me*. I'm frayed and worn, but He wants me. I have been through trouble. I have been through trauma, but He wants me!" She may have thought no one would ever want her again. But Jesus wanted her. He had a plan.

She may have known that it would take a while to put her life back together. She had many things to overcome. She was handicapped. She was probably filled with insecurities. Yet Jesus still called her forward to receive His touch.

If you can identify with the feelings of this infirm woman, then know that He's waiting on you because He wants you. He sees your struggle and He knows all about your pain. He knows what happened to you eighteen years ago and ten years ago and last week. With patience He waits for you as the father waited for the prodigal son (see Luke 15:11-32). Jesus says to the hurting and the crippled, "I want you enough to wait for you to hobble your way back home."

Now God says, "I'm going to deliver you and heal you. I'm going to renew and release you. I'm going to tell you who you are. I'm ready to reveal to you why you had to go through what you did to become what you will become." He says, "I'm going to tell you a secret, something just between you and me. No one else knows. Your boyfriend doesn't know. Your first husband doesn't know. Your father, uncle, brother, or whoever abused you doesn't know. This is the secret: You're the daughter of a king. Your Father is the King."

When that woman came to Jesus, He proclaimed her freedom. Now she stands erect for the first time in eighteen years. When you come to Jesus, He will cause you to stand in His strength. You will know how important you are to Him. Part of your recovery is to learn how to stand up and live in the "now" of today instead of the "then" of yesterday.

I proclaim victory to the abused: You will recover the loss you suffered at the hands of your abuser. You will get back every stolen item. You will reclaim your self-esteem, your self-respect, your integrity. There is a healing going into your spirit right now. I speak life to you. I speak deliverance to you. I speak restoration to you. All in the mighty name of Jesus—the invincible, all-powerful, everlasting name of Jesus!

So far has He removed our
transgressions from us.

13 As a father pities *his* children,
So the LORD pities those who fear
Him.

14 For He knows our frame;
He remembers that we *are* dust.

15 *As for* man, his days *are* like
grass;
As a flower of the field, so he
flourishes.

16 For the wind passes over it, and
it is gone,
And its place remembers it no
more.^a

17 But the mercy of the LORD *is* from
everlasting to everlasting
On those who fear Him,
And His righteousness to
children's children,

18 To such as keep His covenant,
And to those who remember His
commandments to do them.

19 The LORD has established His
throne in heaven,
And His kingdom rules over all.

20 Bless the LORD, you His angels,
Who excel in strength, who do
His word,
Heeding the voice of His word.

21 Bless the LORD, all *you* His hosts,
You ministers of His, who do His
pleasure.

22 Bless the LORD, all His works,
In all places of His dominion.

Bless the LORD, O my soul!

Psalm 104

1 Bless the LORD, O my soul!

O LORD my God, You are very
great:
You are clothed with honor and
majesty,

2 Who cover *Yourself* with light as
with a garment,
Who stretch out the heavens like
a curtain.

3 He lays the beams of His upper
chambers in the waters,
Who makes the clouds His
chariot,
Who walks on the wings of the
wind,

4 Who makes His angels spirits,
His ministers a flame of fire.

5 *You who* laid the foundations of
the earth,
So *that* it should not be moved
forever,

6 You covered it with the deep as
with a garment;
The waters stood above the
mountains.

7 At Your rebuke they fled;
At the voice of Your thunder they
hastened away.

8 They went up over the
mountains;
They went down into the valleys,
To the place which You founded
for them.

9 You have set a boundary that
they may not pass over,
That they may not return to cover
the earth.

10 He sends the springs into the
valleys;
They flow among the hills.

11 They give drink to every beast of
the field;
The wild donkeys quench their
thirst.

12 By them the birds of the heavens
have their home;
They sing among the branches.

13 He waters the hills from His
upper chambers;
The earth is satisfied with the
fruit of Your works.

14 He causes the grass to grow for
the cattle,
And vegetation for the service of
man,
That he may bring forth food
from the earth,

15 And wine *that* makes glad the
heart of man,
Oil to make *his* face shine,
And bread *which* strengthens
man's heart.

16 The trees of the LORD are full *of
sap,*
The cedars of Lebanon which He
planted,

17 Where the birds make their
nests;
The stork has her home in the fir
trees.

18 The high hills *are* for the wild
goats;

103:16 ^aCompare Job 7:10

Gospel
Pearls

The cliffs are a refuge for the
    rock badgers.[a]

19 He appointed the moon for
    seasons;
    The sun knows its going down.
20 You make darkness, and it is
    night,
    In which all the beasts of the
    forest creep about.
21 The young lions roar after their
    prey,
    And seek their food from God.
22 When the sun rises, they gather
    together
    And lie down in their dens.
23 Man goes out to his work
    And to his labor until the
    evening.

24 O LORD, how manifold are Your
    works!
    In wisdom You have made them
    all.
    The earth is full of Your
    possessions—
25 This great and wide sea,
    In which are innumerable
    teeming things,
    Living things both small and
    great.
26 There the ships sail about;
    There is that Leviathan
    Which You have made to play
    there.

27 These all wait for You,
    That You may give them their
    food in due season.
28 What You give them they gather
    in;
    You open Your hand, they are
    filled with good.
29 You hide Your face, they are
    troubled;
    You take away their breath, they
    die and return to their dust.
30 You send forth Your Spirit, they
    are created;
    And You renew the face of the
    earth.

31 May the glory of the LORD endure
    forever;
    May the LORD rejoice in His
    works.
32 He looks on the earth, and it
    trembles;
    He touches the hills, and they
    smoke.

33 I will sing to the LORD as long as
    I live;
    I will sing praise to my God while
    I have my being.
34 May my meditation be sweet to
    Him;
    I will be glad in the LORD.
35 May sinners be consumed from
    the earth,
    And the wicked be no more.

Bless the LORD, O my soul!
Praise the LORD!

Psalm 105

1 Oh, give thanks to the LORD!
    Call upon His name;
    Make known His deeds among
    the peoples!
2 Sing to Him, sing psalms to Him;
    Talk of all His wondrous works!
3 Glory in His holy name;
    Let the hearts of those rejoice
    who seek the LORD!
4 Seek the LORD and His strength;
    Seek His face evermore!
5 Remember His marvelous works
    which He has done,
    His wonders, and the judgments
    of His mouth,
6 O seed of Abraham His servant,
    You children of Jacob, His
    chosen ones!

7 He is the LORD our God;
    His judgments are in all the earth.
8 He remembers His covenant
    forever,
    The word which He commanded,
    for a thousand generations,
9 The covenant which He made
    with Abraham,
    And His oath to Isaac,
10 And confirmed it to Jacob for a
    statute,
    To Israel as an everlasting
    covenant,
11 Saying, "To you I will give the
    land of Canaan
    As the allotment of your
    inheritance,"
12 When they were few in number,
    Indeed very few, and strangers in
    it.

13 When they went from one nation
    to another,
    From one kingdom to another
    people,

104:18 [a]Or rock hyrax (compare Leviticus 11:5)

If you recognize areas in your life where you have been guilty of resisting change,
stop right where you are and allow God to cleanse your heart from the fear of
change. Know in your spirit that something good is going to come out of it.

14 He permitted no one to do them wrong;
   Yes, He rebuked kings for their sakes,
15 *Saying,* "Do not touch My anointed ones,
   And do My prophets no harm."

16 Moreover He called for a famine in the land;
   He destroyed all the provision of bread.
17 He sent a man before them—
   Joseph—*who* was sold as a slave.
18 They hurt his feet with fetters,
   He was laid in irons.
19 Until the time that his word came to pass,
   The word of the LORD tested him.
20 The king sent and released him,
   The ruler of the people let him go free.
21 He made him lord of his house,
   And ruler of all his possessions,
22 To bind his princes at his pleasure,
   And teach his elders wisdom.

23 Israel also came into Egypt,
   And Jacob dwelt in the land of Ham.
24 He increased His people greatly,
   And made them stronger than their enemies.
25 He turned their heart to hate His people,
   To deal craftily with His servants.

26 He sent Moses His servant,
   And Aaron whom He had chosen.
27 They performed His signs among them,
   And wonders in the land of Ham.
28 He sent darkness, and made *it* dark;
   And they did not rebel against His word.
29 He turned their waters into blood,
   And killed their fish.
30 Their land abounded with frogs,
   Even in the chambers of their kings.
31 He spoke, and there came swarms of flies,
   And lice in all their territory.
32 He gave them hail for rain,
   And flaming fire in their land.
33 He struck their vines also, and their fig trees,
   And splintered the trees of their territory.
34 He spoke, and locusts came,
   Young locusts without number,
35 And ate up all the vegetation in their land,
   And devoured the fruit of their ground.
36 He also destroyed all the firstborn in their land,
   The first of all their strength.

37 He also brought them out with silver and gold,
   And *there was* none feeble among His tribes.
38 Egypt was glad when they departed,
   For the fear of them had fallen upon them.
39 He spread a cloud for a covering,
   And fire to give light in the night.
40 *The people* asked, and He brought quail,
   And satisfied them with the bread of heaven.
41 He opened the rock, and water gushed out;
   It ran in the dry places *like* a river.

42 For He remembered His holy promise,
   And Abraham His servant.
43 He brought out His people with joy,
   His chosen ones with gladness.
44 He gave them the lands of the Gentiles,
   And they inherited the labor of the nations,
45 That they might observe His statutes
   And keep His laws.

Praise the LORD!

Psalm 106

1 Praise the LORD!

   Oh, give thanks to the LORD, for *He is* good!
   For His mercy *endures* forever.

2 Who can utter the mighty acts of the LORD?
   Who can declare all His praise?
3 Blessed *are* those who keep justice,

And he who does[a] righteousness
at all times!

4 Remember me, O LORD, with the
favor *You have toward* Your
people.
Oh, visit me with Your salvation,
5 That I may see the benefit of
Your chosen ones,
That I may rejoice in the gladness
of Your nation,
That I may glory with Your
inheritance.

6 We have sinned with our fathers,
We have committed iniquity,
We have done wickedly.
7 Our fathers in Egypt did not
understand Your wonders;
They did not remember the
multitude of Your mercies,
But rebelled by the sea—the Red
Sea.

8 Nevertheless He saved them for
His name's sake,
That He might make His mighty
power known.
9 He rebuked the Red Sea also, and
it dried up;
So He led them through the
depths,
As through the wilderness.
10 He saved them from the hand of
him who hated *them,*
And redeemed them from the
hand of the enemy.
11 The waters covered their
enemies;
There was not one of them left.
12 Then they believed His words;
They sang His praise.

13 They soon forgot His works;
They did not wait for His counsel,
14 But lusted exceedingly in the
wilderness,
And tested God in the desert.
15 And He gave them their request,
But sent leanness into their soul.

16 When they envied Moses in the
camp,
And Aaron the saint of the LORD,
17 The earth opened up and
swallowed Dathan,
And covered the faction of
Abiram.
18 A fire was kindled in their
company;
The flame burned up the wicked.

19 They made a calf in Horeb,
And worshiped the molded
image.
20 Thus they changed their glory
Into the image of an ox that eats
grass.
21 They forgot God their Savior,
Who had done great things in
Egypt,
22 Wondrous works in the land of
Ham,
Awesome things by the Red Sea.
23 Therefore He said that He would
destroy them,
Had not Moses His chosen one
stood before Him in the breach,
To turn away His wrath, lest He
destroy *them.*

24 Then they despised the pleasant
land;
They did not believe His word,
25 But complained in their tents,
And did not heed the voice of the
LORD.
26 Therefore He raised His hand *in
an oath* against them,
To overthrow them in the
wilderness,
27 To overthrow their descendants
among the nations,
And to scatter them in the lands.

28 They joined themselves also to
Baal of Peor,
And ate sacrifices made to the
dead.
29 Thus they provoked *Him* to anger
with their deeds,
And the plague broke out among
them.
30 Then Phinehas stood up and
intervened,
And the plague was stopped.
31 And that was accounted to him
for righteousness
To all generations forevermore.

32 They angered *Him* also at the
waters of strife,[a]
So that it went ill with Moses on
account of them;
33 Because they rebelled against His
Spirit,
So that he spoke rashly with his
lips.

34 They did not destroy the peoples,
Concerning whom the LORD had
commanded them,

106:3 [a]Septuagint, Syriac, Targum, and Vulgate read *those who do.*   106:32 [a]Or *Meribah*

*O*ur faith teaches us to trust God. He doesn't change, but His methods of ministering
to you will change over and over again. Do not worry. He will give you what you
need when you need it.

35 But they mingled with the
    Gentiles
    And learned their works;
36 They served their idols,
    Which became a snare to them.
37 They even sacrificed their sons
    And their daughters to demons,
38 And shed innocent blood,
    The blood of their sons and
    daughters,
    Whom they sacrificed to the idols
    of Canaan;
    And the land was polluted with
    blood.
39 Thus they were defiled by their
    own works,
    And played the harlot by their
    own deeds.

40 Therefore the wrath of the LORD
    was kindled against His
    people,
    So that He abhorred His own
    inheritance.
41 And He gave them into the hand
    of the Gentiles,
    And those who hated them ruled
    over them.
42 Their enemies also oppressed
    them,
    And they were brought into
    subjection under their hand.
43 Many times He delivered them;
    But they rebelled in their counsel,
    And were brought low for their
    iniquity.
44 Nevertheless He regarded their
    affliction,
    When He heard their cry;
45 And for their sake He
    remembered His covenant,
    And relented according to the
    multitude of His mercies.
46 He also made them to be pitied
    By all those who carried them
    away captive.

47 Save us, O LORD our God,
    And gather us from among the
    Gentiles,
    To give thanks to Your holy
    name,
    To triumph in Your praise.

48 Blessed *be* the LORD God of
    Israel
    From everlasting to everlasting!
    And let all the people say,
    "Amen!"

    Praise the LORD!

Book Five   Psalms 107–150

Psalm 107

1 Oh, give thanks to the LORD, for
    He is good!
    For His mercy *endures* forever.
2 Let the redeemed of the LORD say
    so,
    Whom He has redeemed from the
    hand of the enemy,
3 And gathered out of the lands,
    From the east and from the west,
    From the north and from the
    south.

4 They wandered in the wilderness
    in a desolate way;
    They found no city to dwell in.
5 Hungry and thirsty,
    Their soul fainted in them.
6 Then they cried out to the LORD
    in their trouble,
    And He delivered them out of
    their distresses.
7 And He led them forth by the
    right way,
    That they might go to a city for
    a dwelling place.
8 Oh, that *men* would give thanks
    to the LORD *for* His goodness,
    And *for* His wonderful works to
    the children of men!
9 For He satisfies the longing soul,
    And fills the hungry soul with
    goodness.

10 Those who sat in darkness and
    in the shadow of death,
    Bound in affliction and irons—
11 Because they rebelled against the
    words of God,
    And despised the counsel of the
    Most High,
12 Therefore He brought down their
    heart with labor;
    They fell down, and *there was*
    none to help.
13 Then they cried out to the LORD
    in their trouble,
    And He saved them out of their
    distresses.
14 He brought them out of darkness
    and the shadow of death,
    And broke their chains in
    pieces.
15 Oh, that *men* would give thanks
    to the LORD *for* His goodness,
    And *for* His wonderful works to
    the children of men!
16 For He has broken the gates of
    bronze,
    And cut the bars of iron in two.

Gospel Pearls

17 Fools, because of their
transgression,
And because of their iniquities,
were afflicted.
18 Their soul abhorred all manner
of food,
And they drew near to the gates
of death.
19 Then they cried out to the LORD
in their trouble,
And He saved them out of their
distresses.
20 He sent His word and healed
them,
And delivered *them* from their
destructions.
21 Oh, that *men* would give thanks
to the LORD *for* His goodness,
And *for* His wonderful works to
the children of men!
22 Let them sacrifice the sacrifices
of thanksgiving,
And declare His works with
rejoicing.

23 Those who go down to the sea
in ships,
Who do business on great
waters,
24 They see the works of the
LORD,
And His wonders in the deep.
25 For He commands and raises the
stormy wind,
Which lifts up the waves of the
sea.
26 They mount up to the heavens,
They go down again to the
depths;
Their soul melts because of
trouble.
27 They reel to and fro, and stagger
like a drunken man,
And are at their wits' end.
28 Then they cry out to the LORD in
their trouble,
And He brings them out of their
distresses.
29 He calms the storm,
So that its waves are still.
30 Then they are glad because they
are quiet;
So He guides them to their
desired haven.
31 Oh, that *men* would give thanks
to the LORD *for* His goodness,
And *for* His wonderful works to
the children of men!
32 Let them exalt Him also in the
assembly of the people,
And praise Him in the company
of the elders.

33 He turns rivers into a wilderness,
And the watersprings into dry
ground;
34 A fruitful land into barrenness,
For the wickedness of those who
dwell in it.
35 He turns a wilderness into pools
of water,
And dry land into watersprings.
36 There He makes the hungry
dwell,
That they may establish a city for
a dwelling place,
37 And sow fields and plant
vineyards,
That they may yield a fruitful
harvest.
38 He also blesses them, and they
multiply greatly;
And He does not let their cattle
decrease.

39 When they are diminished and
brought low
Through oppression, affliction
and sorrow,
40 He pours contempt on princes,
And causes them to wander in
the wilderness *where there is*
no way;
41 Yet He sets the poor on high, far
from affliction,
And makes *their* families like a
flock.
42 The righteous see *it* and rejoice,
And all iniquity stops its
mouth.

43 Whoever *is* wise will observe
these *things,*
And they will understand the
lovingkindness of the LORD.

Psalm 108

A Song. A Psalm of David.

1 O God, my heart is steadfast;
I will sing and give praise, even
with my glory.
2 Awake, lute and harp!
I will awaken the dawn.
3 I will praise You, O LORD, among
the peoples,
And I will sing praises to You
among the nations.
4 For Your mercy *is* great above
the heavens,
And Your truth *reaches* to the
clouds.

5 Be exalted, O God, above the
heavens,

*M*any cling to the past because they are convinced that their better days are behind them. This attitude leads to great depression. If you can accept the challenge to which God is calling you and realize there are new levels of love and life before you, it will be great.

After the Storm

Psalm 107:29

L ife is a series of challenges and tests. It comes fully equipped with pleasure and pain, sunshine and rain. It is a potpourri of every feeling imaginable. I have been in the storm and I have stood by the ones I love in the storm, and I must tell you that the storm does pass after a while. The thunder quits clapping, the rain stops, the clouds clear, and the day breaks. What a blessing it is when the night has been too long, to know that at last—it is morning.

I have held my wife through storms and night seasons, and she has held me. Neither of us is perfect. We are simply two broken people who have made the commitment to hobble home together. It is so nice to know that I do not have to stumble through life alone on crippled feet and twisted knees. My wife and I have decided to walk all the way together—rain or shine, right or wrong, weak or strong.

When my wife goes through a crisis, God is the One who stops her tears, but I am the one who gets to wipe her eyes. Tomorrow, she may have to wipe mine. In our situations and in yours, the wonderful thing is that the lady has her lover, and her lover has the Lord. We have Him for moments that are too deep, too painful, or too complicated for human minds to resolve.

If you are blessed to live a long life, you will see many triumphs and face many challenges. You will laugh with glee and you will wail in pain. You will experience every feeling known to man. You will see good times as well as bad. No one is exempt from bad times. No one can hide from pain. They are realities that knock on the doors of both mansions and shacks. They visit people who have everything and people who have nothing. Yet in the midst of it all, when we are facing situations that seem to have no rhyme or reason, it helps to know that somewhere in and beyond the passion and the pain, there is God.

The Lord Himself gives us new days. He sees us through the storms and the night times. So what about those storms? They will cease. And when they pass, we will be safe in the arms of our Lord, the Master of all seasons.

And Your glory above all the
earth;
6 That Your beloved may be
delivered,
Save *with* Your right hand, and
hear me.

7 God has spoken in His holiness:
"I will rejoice;
I will divide Shechem
And measure out the Valley of
Succoth.
8 Gilead *is* Mine; Manasseh *is*
Mine;
Ephraim also *is* the helmet for
My head;
Judah *is* My lawgiver.
9 Moab *is* My washpot;
Over Edom I will cast My shoe;
Over Philistia I will triumph."

10 Who will bring me *into* the strong
city?
Who will lead me to Edom?
11 *Is it* not *You,* O God, *who* cast
us off?
And *You,* O God, *who* did not go
out with our armies?
12 Give us help from trouble,
For the help of man is useless.
13 Through God we will do
valiantly,
For *it is* He *who* shall tread down
our enemies.[a]

Psalm 109

To the Chief Musician. A Psalm of David.

1 Do not keep silent,
O God of my praise!
2 For the mouth of the wicked and
the mouth of the deceitful
Have opened against me;
They have spoken against me
with a lying tongue.
3 They have also surrounded me
with words of hatred,
And fought against me without a
cause.
4 In return for my love they are my
accusers,
But I *give myself to* prayer.
5 Thus they have rewarded me evil
for good,
And hatred for my love.

6 Set a wicked man over him,
And let an accuser[a] stand at his
right hand.

7 When he is judged, let him be
found guilty,
And let his prayer become sin.
8 Let his days be few,
And let another take his office.
9 Let his children be fatherless,
And his wife a widow.
10 Let his children continually be
vagabonds, and beg;
Let them seek *their bread*[a] also
from their desolate places.
11 Let the creditor seize all that he
has,
And let strangers plunder his
labor.
12 Let there be none to extend
mercy to him,
Nor let there be any to favor his
fatherless children.
13 Let his posterity be cut off,
And in the generation following
let their name be blotted out.
14 Let the iniquity of his fathers be
remembered before the LORD,
And let not the sin of his mother
be blotted out.
15 Let them be continually before
the LORD,
That He may cut off the memory
of them from the earth;
16 Because he did not remember to
show mercy,
But persecuted the poor and
needy man,
That he might even slay the
broken in heart.
17 As he loved cursing, so let it come
to him;
As he did not delight in blessing,
so let it be far from him.
18 As he clothed himself with
cursing as with his garment,
So let it enter his body like water,
And like oil into his bones.
19 Let it be to him like the garment
which covers him,
And for a belt with which he
girds himself continually.
20 *Let this be* the LORD's reward to
my accusers,
And to those who speak evil
against my person.

21 But You, O GOD the Lord,
Deal with me for Your name's
sake;
Because Your mercy *is* good,
deliver me.

108:13 [a]Compare verses 6–13 with 60:5–12   109:6 [a]Hebrew *satan*   109:10 [a]Following Masoretic Text
and Targum; Septuagint and Vulgate read *be cast out.*

*R*enovate your life with love and hope and release bitterness. A woman who can
move on is invincible. Whatever your next assignment in life, you will miss it if you
worship the past and yearn for yesterday. Let it go!

22 For I *am* poor and needy,
   And my heart is wounded within
     me.
23 I am gone like a shadow when it
     lengthens;
   I am shaken off like a locust.
24 My knees are weak through
     fasting,
   And my flesh is feeble from lack
     of fatness.
25 I also have become a reproach to
     them;
   When they look at me, they
     shake their heads.

26 Help me, O LORD my God!
   Oh, save me according to Your
     mercy,
27 That they may know that this *is*
     Your hand—
   That You, LORD, have done it!
28 Let them curse, but You bless;
   When they arise, let them be
     ashamed,
   But let Your servant rejoice.
29 Let my accusers be clothed with
     shame,
   And let them cover themselves
     with their own disgrace as with
     a mantle.

30 I will greatly praise the LORD with
     my mouth;
   Yes, I will praise Him among the
     multitude.
31 For He shall stand at the right
     hand of the poor,
   To save *him* from those who
     condemn him.

Psalm 110

A Psalm of David.
1 The LORD said to my Lord,
   "Sit at My right hand,
   Till I make Your enemies Your
     footstool."
2 The LORD shall send the rod of
     Your strength out of Zion.
   Rule in the midst of Your
     enemies!

3 Your people *shall be* volunteers
   In the day of Your power;
   In the beauties of holiness, from
     the womb of the morning,
   You have the dew of Your youth.
4 The LORD has sworn
   And will not relent,
   "You *are* a priest forever
   According to the order of
     Melchizedek."

5 The Lord *is* at Your right hand;
   He shall execute kings in the day
     of His wrath.
6 He shall judge among the
     nations,
   He shall fill *the places* with dead
     bodies,
   He shall execute the heads of
     many countries.
7 He shall drink of the brook by the
     wayside;
   Therefore He shall lift up the
     head.

Psalm 111

1 Praise the LORD!

   I will praise the LORD with *my*
     whole heart,
   In the assembly of the upright
     and *in* the congregation.

2 The works of the LORD *are* great,
   Studied by all who have pleasure
     in them.
3 His work *is* honorable and
     glorious,
   And His righteousness endures
     forever.
4 He has made His wonderful
     works to be remembered;
   The LORD *is* gracious and full of
     compassion.
5 He has given food to those who
     fear Him;
   He will ever be mindful of His
     covenant.
6 He has declared to His people the
     power of His works,
   In giving them the heritage of the
     nations.

7 The works of His hands *are*
     verity and justice;
   All His precepts *are* sure.
8 They stand fast forever and ever,
   And are done in truth and
     uprightness.
9 He has sent redemption to His
     people;
   He has commanded His covenant
     forever:
   Holy and awesome *is* His name.

10 The fear of the LORD *is* the
     beginning of wisdom;
   A good understanding have all
     those who do *His*
     commandments.
   His praise endures forever.

Gospel
Pearls

Psalm 112

1 Praise the LORD!

Blessed *is* the man *who* fears the LORD,
Who delights greatly in His commandments.

2 His descendants will be mighty on earth;
The generation of the upright will be blessed.

3 Wealth and riches *will be* in his house,
And his righteousness endures forever.

4 Unto the upright there arises light in the darkness;
He is gracious, and full of compassion, and righteous.

5 A good man deals graciously and lends;
He will guide his affairs with discretion.

6 Surely he will never be shaken;
The righteous will be in everlasting remembrance.

7 He will not be afraid of evil tidings;
His heart is steadfast, trusting in the LORD.

8 His heart *is* established;
He will not be afraid,
Until he sees *his desire* upon his enemies.

9 He has dispersed abroad,
He has given to the poor;
His righteousness endures forever;
His horn will be exalted with honor.

10 The wicked will see *it* and be grieved;
He will gnash his teeth and melt away;
The desire of the wicked shall perish.

Psalm 113

1 Praise the LORD!

Praise, O servants of the LORD,
Praise the name of the LORD!

2 Blessed be the name of the LORD
From this time forth and forevermore!

3 From the rising of the sun to its going down
The LORD's name *is* to be praised.

4 The LORD *is* high above all nations,
His glory above the heavens.

5 Who *is* like the LORD our God,
Who dwells on high,

6 Who humbles Himself to behold
The things that are in the heavens and in the earth?

7 He raises the poor out of the dust,
And lifts the needy out of the ash heap,

8 That He may seat *him* with princes—
With the princes of His people.

9 He grants the barren woman a home,
Like a joyful mother of children.

Praise the LORD!

Psalm 114

1 When Israel went out of Egypt,
The house of Jacob from a people of strange language,

2 Judah became His sanctuary,
And Israel His dominion.

3 The sea saw *it* and fled;
Jordan turned back.

4 The mountains skipped like rams,
The little hills like lambs.

5 What ails you, O sea, that you fled?
O Jordan, *that* you turned back?

6 O mountains, *that* you skipped like rams?
O little hills, like lambs?

7 Tremble, O earth, at the presence of the Lord,
At the presence of the God of Jacob,

8 Who turned the rock *into* a pool of water,
The flint into a fountain of waters.

Psalm 115

1 Not unto us, O LORD, not unto us,
But to Your name give glory,
Because of Your mercy,
Because of Your truth.

2 Why should the Gentiles say,
"So where *is* their God?"

3 But our God *is* in heaven;
He does whatever He pleases.

*P*reserve what you have with your children by allowing the relationship to change in your hand. The caterpillar has been fed in the cocoon of your teaching and has come forth a butterfly. In every flap of its lovely wings there is a tribute to the cocoon that allowed it the grace of change.

4 Their idols *are* silver and gold,
The work of men's hands.
5 They have mouths, but they do
not speak;
Eyes they have, but they do not
see;
6 They have ears, but they do not
hear;
Noses they have, but they do not
smell;
7 They have hands, but they do not
handle;
Feet they have, but they do not
walk;
Nor do they mutter through their
throat.
8 Those who make them are like
them;
So is everyone who trusts in
them.

9 O Israel, trust in the LORD;
He *is* their help and their shield.
10 O house of Aaron, trust in the
LORD;
He *is* their help and their shield.
11 You who fear the LORD, trust in
the LORD;
He *is* their help and their shield.

12 The LORD has been mindful of *us;*
He will bless us;
He will bless the house of Israel;
He will bless the house of Aaron.
13 He will bless those who fear the
LORD,
Both small and great.

14 May the LORD give you increase
more and more,
You and your children.
15 *May* you *be* blessed by the LORD,
Who made heaven and earth.

16 The heaven, *even* the heavens,
are the LORD's;
But the earth He has given to the
children of men.
17 The dead do not praise the LORD,
Nor any who go down into
silence.
18 But we will bless the LORD
From this time forth and
forevermore.

Praise the LORD!

Psalm 116

1 I love the LORD, because He has
heard
My voice *and* my supplications.

2 Because He has inclined His ear
to me,
Therefore I will call *upon Him* as
long as I live.
3 The pains of death surrounded
me,
And the pangs of Sheol laid hold
of me;
I found trouble and sorrow.
4 Then I called upon the name of
the LORD:
"O LORD, I implore You, deliver
my soul!"

5 Gracious *is* the LORD, and
righteous;
Yes, our God *is* merciful.
6 The LORD preserves the simple;
I was brought low, and He saved
me.
7 Return to your rest, O my soul,
For the LORD has dealt
bountifully with you.

8 For You have delivered my soul
from death,
My eyes from tears,
And my feet from falling.
9 I will walk before the LORD
In the land of the living.
10 I believed, therefore I spoke,
"I am greatly afflicted."
11 I said in my haste,
"All men *are* liars."

12 What shall I render to the LORD
For all His benefits toward me?
13 I will take up the cup of salvation,
And call upon the name of the
LORD.
14 I will pay my vows to the LORD
Now in the presence of all His
people.

15 Precious in the sight of the LORD
Is the death of His saints.

16 O LORD, truly I *am* Your servant;
I *am* Your servant, the son of
Your maidservant;
You have loosed my bonds.
17 I will offer to You the sacrifice
of thanksgiving,
And will call upon the name of
the LORD.
18 I will pay my vows to the LORD
Now in the presence of all His
people,
19 In the courts of the LORD's house,
In the midst of you, O Jerusalem.

Praise the LORD!

Gospel Pearls

Psalm 117

1 Praise the LORD, all you Gentiles!
  Laud Him, all you peoples!
2 For His merciful kindness is great
    toward us,
  And the truth of the LORD *endures*
    forever.

  Praise the LORD!

Psalm 118

1 Oh, give thanks to the LORD, for
    He is good!
  For His mercy *endures* forever.

2 Let Israel now say,
  "His mercy *endures* forever."
3 Let the house of Aaron now say,
  "His mercy *endures* forever."
4 Let those who fear the LORD now
    say,
  "His mercy *endures* forever."

5 I called on the LORD in distress;
  The LORD answered me *and set
    me* in a broad place.
6 The LORD *is* on my side;
  I will not fear.
  What can man do to me?
7 The LORD is for me among those
    who help me;
  Therefore I shall see *my desire* on
    those who hate me.
8 *It is* better to trust in the LORD
  Than to put confidence in man.
9 *It is* better to trust in the LORD
  Than to put confidence in
    princes.

10 All nations surrounded me,
  But in the name of the LORD I will
    destroy them.
11 They surrounded me,
  Yes, they surrounded me;
  But in the name of the LORD I will
    destroy them.
12 They surrounded me like bees;
  They were quenched like a fire
    of thorns;
  For in the name of the LORD I will
    destroy them.
13 You pushed me violently, that I
    might fall,
  But the LORD helped me.
14 The LORD *is* my strength and
    song,

And He has become my
  salvation.[a]

15 The voice of rejoicing and
    salvation
  Is in the tents of the righteous;
  The right hand of the LORD does
    valiantly.
16 The right hand of the LORD is
    exalted;
  The right hand of the LORD does
    valiantly.
17 I shall not die, but live,
  And declare the works of the
    LORD.
18 The LORD has chastened me
    severely,
  But He has not given me over to
    death.

19 Open to me the gates of
    righteousness;
  I will go through them,
  And I will praise the LORD.
20 This is the gate of the LORD,
  Through which the righteous
    shall enter.

21 I will praise You,
  For You have answered me,
  And have become my salvation.

22 The stone *which* the builders
    rejected
  Has become the chief
    cornerstone.
23 This was the LORD's doing;
  It *is* marvelous in our eyes.
24 This *is* the day the LORD has
    made;
  We will rejoice and be glad in it.

25 Save now, I pray, O LORD;
  O LORD, I pray, send now
    prosperity.
26 Blessed *is* he who comes in the
    name of the LORD!
  We have blessed you from the
    house of the LORD.
27 God *is* the LORD,
  And He has given us light;
  Bind the sacrifice with cords to
    the horns of the altar.
28 You *are* my God, and I will praise
    You;
  You are my God, I will exalt You.

29 Oh, give thanks to the LORD, for
    He is good!
  For His mercy *endures* forever.

118:14 *a*Compare Exodus 15:2

*W*e all wonder if we will be loved when we are not needed? The truth of the matter
is that the need to be loved is still there, but the areas of that need have changed.
Affirm your mother by guiding her to areas where she will always be needed.

Psalm 119

א ALEPH

1 Blessed *are* the undefiled in the
way,
Who walk in the law of the LORD!
2 Blessed *are* those who keep His
testimonies,
Who seek Him with the whole
heart!
3 They also do no iniquity;
They walk in His ways.
4 You have commanded *us*
To keep Your precepts diligently.
5 Oh, that my ways were directed
To keep Your statutes!
6 Then I would not be ashamed,
When I look into all Your
commandments.
7 I will praise You with
uprightness of heart,
When I learn Your righteous
judgments.
8 I will keep Your statutes;
Oh, do not forsake me utterly!

ב BETH

9 How can a young man cleanse
his way?
By taking heed according to Your
word.
10 With my whole heart I have
sought You;
Oh, let me not wander from Your
commandments!
11 Your word I have hidden in my
heart,
That I might not sin against You.
12 Blessed *are* You, O LORD!
Teach me Your statutes.
13 With my lips I have declared
All the judgments of Your mouth.
14 I have rejoiced in the way of Your
testimonies,
As *much as* in all riches.
15 I will meditate on Your precepts,
And contemplate Your ways.
16 I will delight myself in Your
statutes;
I will not forget Your word.

ג GIMEL

17 Deal bountifully with Your
servant,
That I may live and keep Your
word.
18 Open my eyes, that I may see
Wondrous things from Your law.
19 I *am* a stranger in the earth;
Do not hide Your
commandments from me.

20 My soul breaks with longing
For Your judgments at all times.
21 You rebuke the proud—the
cursed,
Who stray from Your
commandments.
22 Remove from me reproach and
contempt,
For I have kept Your testimonies.
23 Princes also sit *and* speak against
me,
But Your servant meditates on
Your statutes.
24 Your testimonies also *are* my
delight
And my counselors.

ד DALETH

25 My soul clings to the dust;
Revive me according to Your
word.
26 I have declared my ways, and
You answered me;
Teach me Your statutes.
27 Make me understand the way of
Your precepts;
So shall I meditate on Your
wonderful works.
28 My soul melts from heaviness;
Strengthen me according to Your
word.
29 Remove from me the way of
lying,
And grant me Your law
graciously.
30 I have chosen the way of truth;
Your judgments I have laid
before me.
31 I cling to Your testimonies;
O LORD, do not put me to shame!
32 I will run the course of Your
commandments,
For You shall enlarge my heart.

ה HE

33 Teach me, O LORD, the way of
Your statutes,
And I shall keep it *to* the end.
34 Give me understanding, and I
shall keep Your law;
Indeed, I shall observe it with *my*
whole heart.
35 Make me walk in the path of
Your commandments,
For I delight in it.
36 Incline my heart to Your
testimonies,
And not to covetousness.
37 Turn away my eyes from looking
at worthless things,

And revive me in Your way.[a]

38 Establish Your word to Your
    servant,
    Who *is devoted* to fearing You.
39 Turn away my reproach which I
    dread,
    For Your judgments *are* good.
40 Behold, I long for Your precepts;
    Revive me in Your righteousness.

ו WAW

41 Let Your mercies come also to
    me, O LORD—
    Your salvation according to Your
    word.
42 So shall I have an answer for him
    who reproaches me,
    For I trust in Your word.
43 And take not the word of truth
    utterly out of my mouth,
    For I have hoped in Your
    ordinances.
44 So shall I keep Your law
    continually,
    Forever and ever.
45 And I will walk at liberty,
    For I seek Your precepts.
46 I will speak of Your testimonies
    also before kings,
    And will not be ashamed.
47 And I will delight myself in Your
    commandments,
    Which I love.
48 My hands also I will lift up to
    Your commandments,
    Which I love,
    And I will meditate on Your
    statutes.

ז ZAYIN

49 Remember the word to Your
    servant,
    Upon which You have caused me
    to hope.
50 This *is* my comfort in my
    affliction,
    For Your word has given me life.
51 The proud have me in great
    derision,
    Yet I do not turn aside from Your
    law.
52 I remembered Your judgments of
    old, O LORD,
    And have comforted myself.
53 Indignation has taken hold of me
    Because of the wicked, who
    forsake Your law.
54 Your statutes have been my
    songs
    In the house of my pilgrimage.

55 I remember Your name in the
    night, O LORD,
    And I keep Your law.
56 This has become mine,
    Because I kept Your precepts.

ח HETH

57 *You are* my portion, O LORD;
    I have said that I would keep
    Your words.
58 I entreated Your favor with *my*
    whole heart;
    Be merciful to me according to
    Your word.
59 I thought about my ways,
    And turned my feet to Your
    testimonies.
60 I made haste, and did not delay
    To keep Your commandments.
61 The cords of the wicked have
    bound me,
    But I have not forgotten Your
    law.
62 At midnight I will rise to give
    thanks to You,
    Because of Your righteous
    judgments.
63 I *am* a companion of all who fear
    You,
    And of those who keep Your
    precepts.
64 The earth, O LORD, is full of Your
    mercy;
    Teach me Your statutes.

ט TETH

65 You have dealt well with Your
    servant,
    O LORD, according to Your word.
66 Teach me good judgment and
    knowledge,
    For I believe Your
    commandments.
67 Before I was afflicted I went
    astray,
    But now I keep Your word.
68 You *are* good, and do good;
    Teach me Your statutes.
69 The proud have forged a lie
    against me,
    But I will keep Your precepts
    with *my* whole heart.
70 Their heart is as fat as grease,
    But I delight in Your law.
71 *It is* good for me that I have been
    afflicted,
    That I may learn Your statutes.
72 The law of Your mouth *is* better
    to me
    Than thousands of *coins of* gold
    and silver.

119:37 [a]Following Masoretic Text, Septuagint, and Vulgate; Targum reads *Your words*.

Avoid the temptation to attack the people who are a part of your children's adult
life. Many mothers make the mistake of releasing the role of mother and replacing
it with the role of judge. No one is attracted to a critic, and without knowing it she
pushes her loved ones away.

א YOD

73 Your hands have made me and
fashioned me;
Give me understanding, that I
may learn Your
commandments.
74 Those who fear You will be glad
when they see me,
Because I have hoped in Your
word.
75 I know, O LORD, that Your
judgments *are* right,
And *that* in faithfulness You
have afflicted me.
76 Let, I pray, Your merciful
kindness be for my comfort,
According to Your word to Your
servant.
77 Let Your tender mercies come to
me, that I may live;
For Your law *is* my delight.
78 Let the proud be ashamed,
For they treated me wrongfully
with falsehood;
But I will meditate on Your
precepts.
79 Let those who fear You turn to
me,
Those who know Your
testimonies.
80 Let my heart be blameless
regarding Your statutes,
That I may not be ashamed.

כ KAPH

81 My soul faints for Your salvation,
But I hope in Your word.
82 My eyes fail *from searching* Your
word,
Saying, "When will You comfort
me?"
83 For I have become like a
wineskin in smoke,
Yet I do not forget Your statutes.
84 How many *are* the days of Your
servant?
When will You execute judgment
on those who persecute me?
85 The proud have dug pits for
me,
Which *is* not according to Your
law.
86 All Your commandments *are*
faithful;
They persecute me wrongfully;
Help me!
87 They almost made an end of me
on earth,
But I did not forsake Your
precepts.
88 Revive me according to Your
lovingkindness,

So that I may keep the testimony
of Your mouth.

ל LAMED

89 Forever, O LORD,
Your word is settled in heaven.
90 Your faithfulness *endures* to all
generations;
You established the earth, and it
abides.
91 They continue this day according
to Your ordinances,
For all *are* Your servants.
92 Unless Your law *had been* my
delight,
I would then have perished in my
affliction.
93 I will never forget Your precepts,
For by them You have given me
life.
94 I *am* Yours, save me;
For I have sought Your precepts.
95 The wicked wait for me to
destroy me,
But I will consider Your
testimonies.
96 I have seen the consummation of
all perfection,
But Your commandment *is*
exceedingly broad.

מ MEM

97 Oh, how I love Your law!
It *is* my meditation all the day.
98 You, through Your
commandments, make me
wiser than my enemies;
For they *are* ever with me.
99 I have more understanding than
all my teachers,
For Your testimonies *are* my
meditation.
100 I understand more than the
ancients,
Because I keep Your precepts.
101 I have restrained my feet from
every evil way,
That I may keep Your word.
102 I have not departed from Your
judgments,
For You Yourself have taught
me.
103 How sweet are Your words to my
taste,
Sweeter than honey to my
mouth!
104 Through Your precepts I get
understanding;
Therefore I hate every false way.

נ NUN

105 Your word *is* a lamp to my feet
And a light to my path.

106 I have sworn and confirmed
That I will keep Your righteous
judgments.
107 I am afflicted very much;
Revive me, O LORD, according to
Your word.
108 Accept, I pray, the freewill
offerings of my mouth, O LORD,
And teach me Your judgments.
109 My life is continually in my hand,
Yet I do not forget Your law.
110 The wicked have laid a snare for
me,
Yet I have not strayed from Your
precepts.
111 Your testimonies I have taken as
a heritage forever,
For they are the rejoicing of my
heart.
112 I have inclined my heart to
perform Your statutes
Forever, to the very end.

ם SAMEK
113 I hate the double-minded,
But I love Your law.
114 You are my hiding place and my
shield;
I hope in Your word.
115 Depart from me, you evildoers,
For I will keep the
commandments of my God!
116 Uphold me according to Your
word, that I may live;
And do not let me be ashamed
of my hope.
117 Hold me up, and I shall be safe,
And I shall observe Your statutes
continually.
118 You reject all those who stray
from Your statutes,
For their deceit is falsehood.
119 You put away all the wicked of
the earth like dross;
Therefore I love Your
testimonies.
120 My flesh trembles for fear of You,
And I am afraid of Your
judgments.

ע AYIN
121 I have done justice and
righteousness;
Do not leave me to my
oppressors.
122 Be surety for Your servant for
good;
Do not let the proud oppress me.
123 My eyes fail from seeking Your
salvation
And Your righteous word.

124 Deal with Your servant
according to Your mercy,
And teach me Your statutes.
125 I am Your servant;
Give me understanding,
That I may know Your
testimonies.
126 It is time for You to act, O LORD,
For they have regarded Your law
as void.
127 Therefore I love Your
commandments
More than gold, yes, than fine
gold!
128 Therefore all Your precepts
concerning all things
I consider to be right;
I hate every false way.

פ PE
129 Your testimonies are wonderful;
Therefore my soul keeps them.
130 The entrance of Your words
gives light;
It gives understanding to the
simple.
131 I opened my mouth and panted,
For I longed for Your
commandments.
132 Look upon me and be merciful
to me,
As Your custom is toward those
who love Your name.
133 Direct my steps by Your word,
And let no iniquity have
dominion over me.
134 Redeem me from the oppression
of man,
That I may keep Your precepts.
135 Make Your face shine upon Your
servant,
And teach me Your statutes.
136 Rivers of water run down from
my eyes,
Because men do not keep Your
law.

צ TSADDE
137 Righteous are You, O LORD,
And upright are Your judgments.
138 Your testimonies, which You
have commanded,
Are righteous and very faithful.
139 My zeal has consumed me,
Because my enemies have
forgotten Your words.
140 Your word is very pure;
Therefore Your servant loves it.
141 I am small and despised,
Yet I do not forget Your precepts.
142 Your righteousness is an
everlasting righteousness,

Ruth and Naomi shared life, love and intimate secrets without Naomi's judging, criticizing or dominating Ruth. Ultimately Ruth became committed to the God of Naomi. The greatest witness we can have is the presence of grace. Be gracious and you will see God move in your life!

And Your law *is* truth.
143 Trouble and anguish have
overtaken me,
Yet Your commandments *are* my
delights.
144 The righteousness of Your
testimonies *is* everlasting;
Give me understanding, and I
shall live.

צ QOPH
145 I cry out with *my* whole heart;
Hear me, O Lord!
I will keep Your statutes.
146 I cry out to You;
Save me, and I will keep Your
testimonies.
147 I rise before the dawning of the
morning,
And cry for help;
I hope in Your word.
148 My eyes are awake through the
night watches,
That I may meditate on Your
word.
149 Hear my voice according to Your
lovingkindness;
O Lord, revive me according to
Your justice.
150 They draw near who follow after
wickedness;
They are far from Your law.
151 You *are* near, O Lord,
And all Your commandments *are*
truth.
152 Concerning Your testimonies,
I have known of old that You
have founded them forever.

ר RESH
153 Consider my affliction and
deliver me,
For I do not forget Your law.
154 Plead my cause and redeem me;
Revive me according to Your
word.
155 Salvation *is* far from the wicked,
For they do not seek Your
statutes.
156 Great *are* Your tender mercies, O
Lord;
Revive me according to Your
judgments.
157 Many *are* my persecutors and my
enemies,
Yet I do not turn from Your
testimonies.
158 I see the treacherous, and am
disgusted,
Because they do not keep Your
word.

159 Consider how I love Your
precepts;
Revive me, O Lord, according to
Your lovingkindness.
160 The entirety of Your word *is*
truth,
And every one of Your righteous
judgments *endures* forever.

ש SHIN
161 Princes persecute me without a
cause,
But my heart stands in awe of
Your word.
162 I rejoice at Your word
As one who finds great treasure.
163 I hate and abhor lying,
But I love Your law.
164 Seven times a day I praise You,
Because of Your righteous
judgments.
165 Great peace have those who love
Your law,
And nothing causes them to
stumble.
166 Lord, I hope for Your salvation,
And I do Your commandments.
167 My soul keeps Your testimonies,
And I love them exceedingly.
168 I keep Your precepts and Your
testimonies,
For all my ways *are* before You.

ת TAU
169 Let my cry come before You, O
Lord;
Give me understanding
according to Your word.
170 Let my supplication come before
You;
Deliver me according to Your
word.
171 My lips shall utter praise,
For You teach me Your statutes.
172 My tongue shall speak of Your
word,
For all Your commandments *are*
righteousness.
173 Let Your hand become my help,
For I have chosen Your precepts.
174 I long for Your salvation, O Lord,
And Your law *is* my delight.
175 Let my soul live, and it shall
praise You;
And let Your judgments help
me.
176 I have gone astray like a lost
sheep;
Seek Your servant,
For I do not forget Your
commandments.

Gospel
Pearls

Psalm 120

A Song of Ascents.

1 In my distress I cried to the LORD,
  And He heard me.
2 Deliver my soul, O LORD, from
    lying lips
  And from a deceitful tongue.

3 What shall be given to you,
  Or what shall be done to you,
  You false tongue?
4 Sharp arrows of the warrior,
  With coals of the broom tree!

5 Woe is me, that I dwell in
    Meshech,
  That I dwell among the tents of
    Kedar!
6 My soul has dwelt too long
  With one who hates peace.
7 I *am for* peace;
  But when I speak, they *are* for
    war.

Psalm 121

A Song of Ascents.

1 I will lift up my eyes to the hills—
  From whence comes my help?
2 My help *comes* from the LORD,
  Who made heaven and earth.

3 He will not allow your foot to be
    moved;
  He who keeps you will not
    slumber.
4 Behold, He who keeps Israel
  Shall neither slumber nor sleep.

5 The LORD *is* your keeper;
  The LORD *is* your shade at your
    right hand.
6 The sun shall not strike you by
    day,
  Nor the moon by night.
7 The LORD shall preserve you from
    all evil;
  He shall preserve your soul.
8 The LORD shall preserve your
    going out and your coming in
  From this time forth, and even
    forevermore.

Psalm 122

A Song of Ascents. Of David.

1 I was glad when they said to me,
  "Let us go into the house of the
    LORD."
2 Our feet have been standing
  Within your gates, O Jerusalem!

3 Jerusalem is built
  As a city that is compact
    together;
4 Where the tribes go up,
  The tribes of the LORD,
  To the Testimony of Israel,
  To give thanks to the name of the
    LORD.
5 For thrones are set there for
    judgment,
  The thrones of the house of
    David.

6 Pray for the peace of Jerusalem:
  "May they prosper who love you.
7 Peace be within your walls,
  Prosperity within your palaces."
8 For the sake of my brethren and
    companions,
  I will now say, "Peace *be* within
    you."
9 Because of the house of the LORD
    our God
  I will seek your good.

Psalm 123

A Song of Ascents.

1 Unto You I lift up my eyes,
  O You who dwell in the heavens.
2 Behold, as the eyes of servants
    look to the hand of their
    masters,
  As the eyes of a maid to the hand
    of her mistress,
  So our eyes *look* to the LORD our
    God,
  Until He has mercy on us.

3 Have mercy on us, O LORD, have
    mercy on us!
  For we are exceedingly filled
    with contempt.
4 Our soul is exceedingly filled
  With the scorn of those who are
    at ease,
  With the contempt of the proud.

Psalm 124

A Song of Ascents. Of David.

1 "If it had not been the LORD who
    was on our side,"
  Let Israel now say—
2 "If it had not been the LORD who
    was on our side,
  When men rose up against us,
3 Then they would have swallowed
    us alive,
  When their wrath was kindled
    against us;

*Y*ou are always entitled to your opinion, but once you have said it, release your
children to make their own decisions. Respect their choices and support them as
best you can. Do not allow the enemy to rob you of the riches of your investment in
your children.

The Father
Who Never Sleeps
Psalm 121:3, 4

I wonder how many women realize that they have a Father who never slumbers nor sleeps. He has assigned angels to compass about you and to ensure your safety. He will spare no expense to insure that you are safe. He will not rest. He will arise with healing in His wings. He will come to you in a flash and stay with you through the night. He is the Everlasting Father. He doesn't leave, He doesn't desert, and He doesn't forsake you. What you must come to understand is that He cares so much for you. He wants you to have all that you need.

A thousand so-called feminists may erase *Father* from the Bible and replace it with a neutered term they find less offensive. If God represents Himself as a Father, perhaps it is because He knows best what a Father's love should represent. The offense taken to the term *father* is born in the heart of someone who has failed to understand that a father is a compliment to a woman and not an insult. Sadly, we have come to a time when the role of the father has been so mutilated that we have lost any real revelation into the breadth and depth of the Father's heart.

I repeat, a good father is not an insult to femininity. A good father is an avid fan of his daughter, a source of insulation from insult and adversity. He is there for her. He nurtures her.

Hear me when I declare to you that the Father loves His girls. His heart cried through the prophet Jeremiah for the healing of His daughters (see Jeremiah 8:21–22). He is broken at the thought of their brokenness. He is longing to restore them and to provide for them. Whatever the need, He longs to see it met. He is Jehovah-Jireh. He is the Father of blessing. He is the giving God who loves to know that all of His children are blessed. He will bless His sons, who are created directly in His image and after His similitude. How much more would He have respect for the woman as the weaker vessel? She is not weak in terms of substandard, but weak in terms of softer. A silk shirt is more delicate than a cotton one. But it is also more valuable. Weaker doesn't mean lesser—just softer, more satin-like.

Rejoice in the softness of your femininity. The Lord is your strong man, your hero, your Father who loves to bless you. And He never goes to sleep.

4 Then the waters would have
  overwhelmed us,
  The stream would have gone
  over our soul;
5 Then the swollen waters
  Would have gone over our soul."

6 Blessed *be* the LORD,
  Who has not given us *as* prey to
  their teeth.
7 Our soul has escaped as a bird
  from the snare of the fowlers;*a*
  The snare is broken, and we have
  escaped.
8 Our help *is* in the name of the
  LORD,
  Who made heaven and earth.

Psalm 125

A Song of Ascents.

1 Those who trust in the LORD
  Are like Mount Zion,
  Which cannot be moved, *but*
  abides forever.
2 As the mountains surround
  Jerusalem,
  So the LORD surrounds His
  people
  From this time forth and forever.

3 For the scepter of wickedness
  shall not rest
  On the land allotted to the
  righteous,
  Lest the righteous reach out their
  hands to iniquity.

4 Do good, O LORD, to *those who
  are* good,
  And to *those who are* upright in
  their hearts.

5 As for such as turn aside to their
  crooked ways,
  The LORD shall lead them away
  With the workers of iniquity.

  Peace *be* upon Israel!

Psalm 126

A Song of Ascents.

1 When the LORD brought back the
  captivity of Zion,
  We were like those who dream.
2 Then our mouth was filled with
  laughter,
  And our tongue with singing.

Then they said among the
  nations,
  "The LORD has done great things
  for them."
3 The LORD has done great things
  for us,
  And we are glad.

4 Bring back our captivity, O LORD,
  As the streams in the South.

5 Those who sow in tears
  Shall reap in joy.
6 He who continually goes forth
  weeping,
  Bearing seed for sowing,
  Shall doubtless come again with
  rejoicing,
  Bringing his sheaves *with him.*

Psalm 127

A Song of Ascents. Of Solomon.

1 Unless the LORD builds the house,
  They labor in vain who build it;
  Unless the LORD guards the city,
  The watchman stays awake in
  vain.
2 *It is* vain for you to rise up early,
  To sit up late,
  To eat the bread of sorrows;
  For so He gives His beloved
  sleep.

3 Behold, children *are* a heritage
  from the LORD,
  The fruit of the womb *is* a reward.
4 Like arrows in the hand of a
  warrior,
  So *are* the children of one's
  youth.
5 Happy *is* the man who has his
  quiver full of them;
  They shall not be ashamed,
  But shall speak with their
  enemies in the gate.

Psalm 128

A Song of Ascents.

1 Blessed *is* every one who fears
  the LORD,
  Who walks in His ways.

2 When you eat the labor of your
  hands,
  You *shall be* happy, and *it shall
  be* well with you.
3 Your wife *shall be* like a fruitful
  vine

124:7 *a*That is, persons who catch birds in a trap or snare

*C*hange is not always an enemy. It can be God's way of saying enough is enough. If
you can remain flexible and face the changes of life with the assurance of God,
you will win. It is God's desire to make you a wise woman.

Broken Arrows

Psalm 127:4

I write to every empty-eyed child with tears and trembling lips who has ever sat in my office struggling to mention the unmentionable. I write to the quavering voice of every midnight caller who has spoken into the telephone a secret they could not keep and would not tell. I write to every husband who holds his wife at night—a child lost in space, a rosebud crushed before he met her, a broken arrow shaking in the quiver. I write to every lady who hides behind silk dresses and leather purses a terrible shame that makeup can't cover and showers will not wash away.

Some call them abused children. Some call them victims. Some call them statistics. But I call them "broken arrows." These splintered, broken arrows come in all colors and forms. Black and white, rich and poor. Often camouflaged behind the walls of otherwise successful lives, people wrestle with secret pain. You may be one of them. You may not bear any outward sign of trauma, but your tragedy may have been severe enough to have destroyed your life if God had not held you together.

Or you may have escaped such horrifying experiences. Let the strong bear the infirmities of the weak. God can greatly use you to restore wholeness to others who walk in varying degrees of brokenness.

Every time you see some insecure, vulnerable, intimidated adult with unnatural fear in her eyes, low self-esteem, or an apologetic posture, you may be seeing a broken arrow. Every time you see a bra-less woman, choosing to act like a man rather than to marry one; every time you see a handsome young man who could have been someone's father, walking like someone's mother, you may be seeing a broken arrow. If you think it's ugly, you're right. If you think it's wrong, you're right again. If you think it can't be fixed, you're dead wrong! If you look closely into these eyes, you will sense something that is weak, hurt, maimed, or disturbed—but fixable.

To every husband who wants to see his wife healed, to every mother who has a little girl with a woman's problem, I say: The power to heal is in the power to care. Compassion is the mother of miracles.

If you yourself are a broken arrow, I say: Allow Someone into your life who can fix what's wrong. The walls you have built to protect yourself have also imprisoned you. Our compassionate Lord wants to loose you from the dungeon of fear. He cares. Rise and be healed in the name of Jesus.

In the very heart of your house,
Your children like olive plants
All around your table.
4 Behold, thus shall the man be
blessed
Who fears the LORD.

5 The LORD bless you out of Zion,
And may you see the good of
Jerusalem
All the days of your life.
6 Yes, may you see your children's
children.

Peace *be* upon Israel!

Psalm 129

A Song of Ascents.

1 "Many a time they have afflicted
me from my youth,"
Let Israel now say—
2 "Many a time they have afflicted
me from my youth;
Yet they have not prevailed
against me.
3 The plowers plowed on my back;
They made their furrows long."
4 The LORD *is* righteous;
He has cut in pieces the cords of
the wicked.

5 Let all those who hate Zion
Be put to shame and turned back.
6 Let them be as the grass *on* the
housetops,
Which withers before it grows
up,
7 With which the reaper does not
fill his hand,
Nor he who binds sheaves, his
arms.
8 Neither let those who pass by
them say,
"The blessing of the LORD *be* upon
you;
We bless you in the name of the
LORD!"

Psalm 130

A Song of Ascents.

1 Out of the depths I have cried to
You, O LORD;
2 Lord, hear my voice!
Let Your ears be attentive
To the voice of my supplications.

3 If You, LORD, should mark
iniquities,
O Lord, who could stand?

132:6 ᵃHebrew *Jaar*

4 But *there is* forgiveness with
You,
That You may be feared.

5 I wait for the LORD, my soul waits,
And in His word I do hope.
6 My soul *waits* for the Lord
More than those who watch for
the morning—
Yes, more than those who watch
for the morning.

7 O Israel, hope in the LORD;
For with the LORD *there is* mercy,
And with Him *is* abundant
redemption.
8 And He shall redeem Israel
From all his iniquities.

Psalm 131

A Song of Ascents. Of David.

1 LORD, my heart is not haughty,
Nor my eyes lofty.
Neither do I concern myself with
great matters,
Nor with things too profound for
me.

2 Surely I have calmed and quieted
my soul,
Like a weaned child with his
mother;
Like a weaned child *is* my soul
within me.

3 O Israel, hope in the LORD
From this time forth and forever.

Psalm 132

A Song of Ascents.

1 LORD, remember David
And all his afflictions;
2 How he swore to the LORD,
And vowed to the Mighty One of
Jacob:
3 "Surely I will not go into the
chamber of my house,
Or go up to the comfort of my
bed;
4 I will not give sleep to my eyes
Or slumber to my eyelids,
5 Until I find a place for the LORD,
A dwelling place for the Mighty
One of Jacob."

6 Behold, we heard of it in
Ephrathah;
We found it in the fields of the
woods.ᵃ

Daughters of the living God, for the many changes you will face on all levels of life,
I recommend Jesus. He does not change. He is an unchanging God in a rapidly
changing world.

7 Let us go into His tabernacle;
  Let us worship at His footstool.
8 Arise, O LORD, to Your resting
    place,
  You and the ark of Your strength.
9 Let Your priests be clothed with
    righteousness,
  And let Your saints shout for joy.

10 For Your servant David's sake,
   Do not turn away the face of
    Your Anointed.

11 The LORD has sworn *in* truth to
   David;
   He will not turn from it:
  "I will set upon your throne the
    fruit of your body.
12 If your sons will keep My
   covenant
   And My testimony which I shall
    teach them,
   Their sons also shall sit upon
    your throne forevermore."

13 For the LORD has chosen Zion;
   He has desired *it* for His dwelling
    place:
14 "This *is* My resting place forever;
   Here I will dwell, for I have
    desired it.
15 I will abundantly bless her
   provision;
   I will satisfy her poor with bread.
16 I will also clothe her priests with
   salvation,
   And her saints shall shout aloud
    for joy.
17 There I will make the horn of
   David grow;
   I will prepare a lamp for My
    Anointed.
18 His enemies I will clothe with
   shame,
   But upon Himself His crown shall
    flourish."

Psalm 133

A Song of Ascents. Of David.
1 Behold, how good and how
  pleasant *it is*
  For brethren to dwell together in
    unity!

2 *It is* like the precious oil upon the
   head,
   Running down on the beard,
   The beard of Aaron,
   Running down on the edge of his
    garments.
3 *It is* like the dew of Hermon,

Descending upon the mountains
  of Zion;
For there the LORD commanded
  the blessing—
Life forevermore.

Psalm 134

A Song of Ascents.
1 Behold, bless the LORD,
  All *you* servants of the LORD,
  Who by night stand in the house
    of the LORD!
2 Lift up your hands *in* the
   sanctuary,
   And bless the LORD.

3 The LORD who made heaven and
   earth
   Bless you from Zion!

Psalm 135

1 Praise the LORD!

  Praise the name of the LORD;
  Praise *Him,* O you servants of the
    LORD!
2 You who stand in the house of
   the LORD,
   In the courts of the house of our
    God,
3 Praise the LORD, for the LORD *is*
   good;
   Sing praises to His name, for *it*
    is pleasant.
4 For the LORD has chosen Jacob
   for Himself,
   Israel for His special treasure.

5 For I know that the LORD *is* great,
   And our Lord *is* above all gods.
6 Whatever the LORD pleases He
   does,
   In heaven and in earth,
   In the seas and in all deep places.
7 He causes the vapors to ascend
   from the ends of the earth;
   He makes lightning for the rain;
   He brings the wind out of His
    treasuries.

8 He destroyed the firstborn of
   Egypt,
   Both of man and beast.
9 He sent signs and wonders into
   the midst of you, O Egypt,
   Upon Pharaoh and all his
    servants.
10 He defeated many nations
   And slew mighty kings—
11 Sihon king of the Amorites,

Gospel
Pearls

Og king of Bashan,
And all the kingdoms of
Canaan—

12 And gave their land *as* a heritage,
A heritage to Israel His people.

13 Your name, O LORD, *endures*
forever,
Your fame, O LORD, throughout
all generations.

14 For the LORD will judge His
people,
And He will have compassion on
His servants.

15 The idols of the nations *are* silver
and gold,
The work of men's hands.

16 They have mouths, but they do
not speak;
Eyes they have, but they do not
see;

17 They have ears, but they do not
hear;
Nor is there *any* breath in their
mouths.

18 Those who make them are like
them;
So is everyone who trusts in
them.

19 Bless the LORD, O house of Israel!
Bless the LORD, O house of
Aaron!

20 Bless the LORD, O house of Levi!
You who fear the LORD, bless the
LORD!

21 Blessed be the LORD out of Zion,
Who dwells in Jerusalem!

Praise the LORD!

Psalm 136

1 Oh, give thanks to the LORD, for
He is good!
For His mercy *endures* forever.

2 Oh, give thanks to the God of
gods!
For His mercy *endures* forever.

3 Oh, give thanks to the Lord of
lords!
For His mercy *endures* forever:

4 To Him who alone does great
wonders,
For His mercy *endures* forever;

5 To Him who by wisdom made the
heavens,
For His mercy *endures* forever;

6 To Him who laid out the earth
above the waters,
For His mercy *endures* forever;

7 To Him who made great lights,
For His mercy *endures*
forever—

8 The sun to rule by day,
For His mercy *endures* forever;

9 The moon and stars to rule by
night,
For His mercy *endures* forever.

10 To Him who struck Egypt in their
firstborn,
For His mercy *endures* forever;

11 And brought out Israel from
among them,
For His mercy *endures* forever;

12 With a strong hand, and with an
outstretched arm,
For His mercy *endures* forever;

13 To Him who divided the Red Sea
in two,
For His mercy *endures* forever;

14 And made Israel pass through the
midst of it,
For His mercy *endures* forever;

15 But overthrew Pharaoh and his
army in the Red Sea,
For His mercy *endures* forever;

16 To Him who led His people
through the wilderness,
For His mercy *endures* forever;

17 To Him who struck down great
kings,
For His mercy *endures* forever;

18 And slew famous kings,
For His mercy *endures*
forever—

19 Sihon king of the Amorites,
For His mercy *endures* forever;

20 And Og king of Bashan,
For His mercy *endures*
forever—

21 And gave their land as a heritage,
For His mercy *endures* forever;

22 A heritage to Israel His servant,
For His mercy *endures* forever.

23 Who remembered us in our lowly
state,
For His mercy *endures* forever;

24 And rescued us from our
enemies,
For His mercy *endures* forever;

25 Who gives food to all flesh,
For His mercy *endures* forever.

26 Oh, give thanks to the God of
heaven!
For His mercy *endures* forever.

Get up every morning and throw aside the curtain of doubt. Brush past the foggy films that would cloud your eyes from seeing what is right in front of you and embrace expectancy. It is the breaking of a new day. It is the establishing of fresh options.

Psalm 137

1 By the rivers of Babylon,
There we sat down, yea, we wept
When we remembered Zion.
2 We hung our harps
Upon the willows in the midst of
it.
3 For there those who carried us
away captive asked of us a
song,
And those who plundered us
requested mirth,
Saying, "Sing us *one* of the songs
of Zion!"

4 How shall we sing the LORD's
song
In a foreign land?
5 If I forget you, O Jerusalem,
Let my right hand forget *its skill!*
6 If I do not remember you,
Let my tongue cling to the roof
of my mouth—
If I do not exalt Jerusalem
Above my chief joy.

7 Remember, O LORD, against the
sons of Edom
The day of Jerusalem,
Who said, "Raze *it,* raze *it,*
To its very foundation!"

8 O daughter of Babylon, who are
to be destroyed,
Happy the one who repays you
as you have served us!
9 Happy the one who takes and
dashes
Your little ones against the rock!

Psalm 138

A *Psalm* of David.

1 I will praise You with my whole
heart;
Before the gods I will sing praises
to You.
2 I will worship toward Your holy
temple,
And praise Your name
For Your lovingkindness and
Your truth;
For You have magnified Your
word above all Your name.
3 In the day when I cried out, You
answered me,
And made me bold *with* strength
in my soul.

4 All the kings of the earth shall
praise You, O LORD,

When they hear the words of
Your mouth.
5 Yes, they shall sing of the ways
of the LORD,
For great *is* the glory of the LORD.
6 Though the LORD *is* on high,
Yet He regards the lowly;
But the proud He knows from
afar.

7 Though I walk in the midst of
trouble, You will revive me;
You will stretch out Your hand
Against the wrath of my enemies,
And Your right hand will save
me.
8 The LORD will perfect *that which*
concerns me;
Your mercy, O LORD, *endures*
forever;
Do not forsake the works of Your
hands.

Psalm 139

For the Chief Musician. A Psalm of David.

1 O LORD, You have searched me
and known *me.*
2 You know my sitting down and
my rising up;
You understand my thought afar
off.
3 You comprehend my path and
my lying down,
And are acquainted with all my
ways.
4 For *there is* not a word on my
tongue,
But behold, O LORD, You know
it altogether.
5 You have hedged me behind and
before,
And laid Your hand upon me.
6 *Such* knowledge *is* too wonderful
for me;
It is high, I cannot *attain* it.

7 Where can I go from Your Spirit?
Or where can I flee from Your
presence?
8 If I ascend into heaven, You *are*
there;
If I make my bed in hell, behold,
You *are there.*
9 *If* I take the wings of the morning,
And dwell in the uttermost parts
of the sea,
10 Even there Your hand shall lead
me,
And Your right hand shall hold
me.

Gospel
Pearls

11 If I say, "Surely the darkness
shall fall[a] on me,"
Even the night shall be light
about me;
12 Indeed, the darkness shall not
hide from You,
But the night shines as the day;
The darkness and the light *are*
both alike *to* You.

13 For You formed my inward parts;
You covered me in my mother's
womb.
14 I will praise You, for I am
fearfully *and* wonderfully
made;[a]
Marvelous are Your works,
And *that* my soul knows very
well.
15 My frame was not hidden from
You,
When I was made in secret,
And skillfully wrought in the
lowest parts of the earth.
16 Your eyes saw my substance,
being yet unformed.
And in Your book they all were
written,
The days fashioned for me,
When *as yet there were* none of
them.

17 How precious also are Your
thoughts to me, O God!
How great is the sum of them!
18 *If* I should count them, they
would be more in number than
the sand;
When I awake, I am still with
You.

19 Oh, that You would slay the
wicked, O God!
Depart from me, therefore, you
bloodthirsty men.
20 For they speak against You
wickedly;
Your enemies take *Your name* in
vain.[a]
21 Do I not hate them, O LORD, who
hate You?
And do I not loathe those who
rise up against You?
22 I hate them with perfect hatred;
I count them my enemies.

23 Search me, O God, and know my
heart;
Try me, and know my anxieties;
24 And see if *there is any* wicked
way in me,
And lead me in the way
everlasting.

Psalm 140

To the Chief Musician. A Psalm of David.

1 Deliver me, O LORD, from evil
men;
Preserve me from violent men,
2 Who plan evil things in *their*
hearts;
They continually gather together
for war.
3 They sharpen their tongues like
a serpent;
The poison of asps *is* under their
lips.   Selah

4 Keep me, O LORD, from the hands
of the wicked;
Preserve me from violent men,
Who have purposed to make my
steps stumble.
5 The proud have hidden a snare
for me, and cords;
They have spread a net by the
wayside;
They have set traps for me.
                            Selah

6 I said to the LORD: "You *are* my
God;
Hear the voice of my
supplications, O LORD.
7 O GOD the Lord, the strength of
my salvation,
You have covered my head in the
day of battle.
8 Do not grant, O LORD, the desires
of the wicked;
Do not further his *wicked*
scheme,
Lest they be exalted.   Selah

9 "*As for* the head of those who
surround me,
Let the evil of their lips cover
them;
10 Let burning coals fall upon them;
Let them be cast into the fire,
Into deep pits, that they rise not
up again.
11 Let not a slanderer be established
in the earth;

139:11 aVulgate and Symmachus read *cover*.   139:14 aFollowing Masoretic Text and Targum; Septuagint,
Syriac, and Vulgate read *You are fearfully wonderful*.   139:20 aSeptuagint and Vulgate read *They take
your cities in vain*.

*T*his is God's gift to you. From the God who cares more than you know, He gave
you today. Enjoy it. It is yours. There will never be another moment like this one.
Savor.

Designer Original

Psalm 139:14

One of the things that makes high-fashion designs so expensive is that they are one-of-a-kind creations. A woman who buys a *haute couture* design knows that she isn't going to see her dress on any other woman. She knows she is going to have a superbly crafted garment. In many cases, it will be hand-stitched and custom-tailored to fit her like a soft leather glove fits a hand. She knows that every aspect of the design of her garment has been carefully conceived and constructed. Women are willing to pay a high price for an original design.

And so it should be when we look at our lives. God has put us together in a way that cannot and should not be replicated. He chose every aspect of our personalities, crafted every gift and talent He bestowed on us, and gave special thought to each one of our features and traits. We were handmade by Him in our mother's womb. He custom-designed us to fit a specific role in His sovereign plan for the ages.

You are a designer original. God made you to be one of a kind. Your fingerprint is different from that of anybody else—living or dead. The same goes for your hand print, footprint, voice print, and your entire genetic code. Nobody else has the combination of physical traits you have. Nobody else has the identical set of genes.

And even if you did have the exact genetic makeup of another person, you would still be unique. Nobody else has been placed by God in exactly your family, your neighborhood, your church, your group of friends and associates. Nobody else has been put on the earth at precisely this moment in history. Nobody else has had the same experiences you've had. Nobody else has the same talents and personality quirks and strengths and weaknesses and abilities and disabilities and skills and training and connections.

Nobody has ever been just like you. And nobody ever will be just like you. You are a designer original. Have you ever celebrated yourself? Have you ever praised God for the way He made you? If not, today is a good day to begin.

Let evil hunt the violent man to
overthrow *him.*"

12 I know that the LORD will
maintain
The cause of the afflicted,
And justice for the poor.
13 Surely the righteous shall give
thanks to Your name;
The upright shall dwell in Your
presence.

Psalm 141

A Psalm of David.

1 LORD, I cry out to You;
Make haste to me!
Give ear to my voice when I cry
out to You.
2 Let my prayer be set before You
as incense,
The lifting up of my hands *as* the
evening sacrifice.

3 Set a guard, O LORD, over my
mouth;
Keep watch over the door of my
lips.
4 Do not incline my heart to any
evil thing,
To practice wicked works
With men who work iniquity;
And do not let me eat of their
delicacies.

5 Let the righteous strike me;
It shall be a kindness.
And let him rebuke me;
It shall be as excellent oil;
Let my head not refuse it.

For still my prayer *is* against the
deeds of the wicked.
6 Their judges are overthrown by
the sides of the cliff,
And they hear my words, for they
are sweet.
7 Our bones are scattered at the
mouth of the grave,
As when one plows and breaks
up the earth.

8 But my eyes *are* upon You, O GOD
the Lord;
In You I take refuge;
Do not leave my soul destitute.
9 Keep me from the snares they
have laid for me,
And from the traps of the
workers of iniquity.

10 Let the wicked fall into their own
nets,
While I escape safely.

Psalm 142

A Contemplation[a] of David. A Prayer when he
was in the cave.

1 I cry out to the LORD with my
voice;
With my voice to the LORD I make
my supplication.
2 I pour out my complaint before
Him;
I declare before Him my trouble.

3 When my spirit was
overwhelmed within me,
Then You knew my path.
In the way in which I walk
They have secretly set a snare for
me.
4 Look on *my* right hand and see,
For *there is* no one who
acknowledges me;
Refuge has failed me;
No one cares for my soul.

5 I cried out to You, O LORD:
I said, "You *are* my refuge,
My portion in the land of the
living.
6 Attend to my cry,
For I am brought very low;
Deliver me from my persecutors,
For they are stronger than I.
7 Bring my soul out of prison,
That I may praise Your name;
The righteous shall surround me,
For You shall deal bountifully
with me."

Psalm 143

A Psalm of David.

1 Hear my prayer, O LORD,
Give ear to my supplications!
In Your faithfulness answer me,
And in Your righteousness.
2 Do not enter into judgment with
Your servant,
For in Your sight no one living
is righteous.

3 For the enemy has persecuted my
soul;
He has crushed my life to the
ground;
He has made me dwell in
darkness,

142:title [a]Hebrew *Maschil*

*H*ow do you want to live your life? That is the question that each of us must ask
ourselves. And after asking the question, we must not complain about the answer.
We can choose how we want to live, and then we must live with the choices we make.

Like those who have long been
dead.
4 Therefore my spirit is
overwhelmed within me;
My heart within me is distressed.

5 I remember the days of old;
I meditate on all Your works;
I muse on the work of Your
hands.
6 I spread out my hands to You;
My soul *longs* for You like a
thirsty land.   Selah

7 Answer me speedily, O Lord;
My spirit fails!
Do not hide Your face from me,
Lest I be like those who go down
into the pit.
8 Cause me to hear Your
lovingkindness in the morning,
For in You do I trust;
Cause me to know the way in
which I should walk,
For I lift up my soul to You.

9 Deliver me, O Lord, from my
enemies;
In You I take shelter.*a*
10 Teach me to do Your will,
For You *are* my God;
Your Spirit *is* good.
Lead me in the land of
uprightness.

11 Revive me, O Lord, for Your
name's sake!
For Your righteousness' sake
bring my soul out of trouble.
12 In Your mercy cut off my
enemies,
And destroy all those who afflict
my soul;
For I *am* Your servant.

Psalm 144

A Psalm of David.
1 Blessed *be* the Lord my Rock,
Who trains my hands for war,
And my fingers for battle—
2 My lovingkindness and my
fortress,
My high tower and my deliverer,
My shield and *the One* in whom
I take refuge,
Who subdues my people*a* under
me.

3 Lord, what *is* man, that You take
knowledge of him?
Or the son of man, that You are
mindful of him?
4 Man is like a breath;
His days *are* like a passing
shadow.

5 Bow down Your heavens, O
Lord, and come down;
Touch the mountains, and they
shall smoke.
6 Flash forth lightning and scatter
them;
Shoot out Your arrows and
destroy them.
7 Stretch out Your hand from
above;
Rescue me and deliver me out of
great waters,
From the hand of foreigners,
8 Whose mouth speaks lying
words,
And whose right hand *is* a right
hand of falsehood.

9 I will sing a new song to You, O
God;
On a harp of ten strings I will sing
praises to You,
10 *The One* who gives salvation to
kings,
Who delivers David His servant
From the deadly sword.

11 Rescue me and deliver me from
the hand of foreigners,
Whose mouth speaks lying
words,
And whose right hand *is* a right
hand of falsehood—
12 That our sons *may be* as plants
grown up in their youth;
That our daughters *may be* as
pillars,
Sculptured in palace style;
13 *That* our barns *may be* full,
Supplying all kinds of produce;
That our sheep may bring forth
thousands
And ten thousands in our fields;
14 *That* our oxen *may be* well-laden;
That there be no breaking in or
going out;
That there be no outcry in our
streets.
15 Happy *are* the people who are in
such a state;

143:9 *a*Septuagint and Vulgate read *To You I flee.*   144:2 *a*Following Masoretic Text, Septuagint, and
Vulgate; Syriac and Targum read *the peoples* (compare 18:47).

When life seems unfair and uncertain, do not be denied and do not be delayed by
nurturing things that should be neutered. Just throw them on your stack of
learning experiences and keep moving on.

Drained of Life

Psalm 143:11

I don't know anything about the woman with the issue of blood. She could have been any woman. She could have been every woman. Perhaps the Lord referred to her in such a generic manner so that any woman could relate to her and put her name in her place.

An issue of blood is normal for a woman. This woman's problem was that her issue of blood lasted too long. It didn't go away.

Have you ever had a problem that stayed around too long? Have you ever said, "I'll surely be over this by such and such a date. I'll have come out of this by then. I'll surely have had children, I will have entered fully into my ministry, I will have accomplished what God created me to do"?

Problems that linger too long are problems that drain away your life. That's what happened to this woman. She had had an issue of blood for twelve years, and her life had drained away from her.

When a problem stays around too long, you end up with two problems instead of one. You've got your original problem, and then you've got the problem that your problem won't go away. The fact that you've had the same problem for so long begins to grate on you.

Your problem will begin to speak to you: "I'm here to stay. You might as well get used to me because I'm not budging. Everything you've tried has failed. Nothing is going to work. I am your problem for the rest of your life!"

Your problem will remind you of a pattern of failure in your life. It will remind you of how you grew up and give you all the details of every negative thing you have ever experienced. That's because it is engineered by the devil. The enemy loves to brag about how long he has been around.

Your issue may not be blood. Whatever it is, however, it is like this woman's problem if it is draining the life out of you, if it's diminishing your vitality, your sparkle, your energy, your enthusiasm for living. If it isn't money, it's the children. If it isn't the children, it's your marriage. If it isn't your marriage, it's your lack of a marriage. If it isn't that, it's something else. Your issue may be a secret—in the family, on the job, in the church, in your past. It may be a secret that involves somebody you want to keep secret.

Your issue today may be a need—a need to touch Jesus for salvation. It may be a need to touch Him for healing in your body, for your marriage, your family, or your ministry.

I don't know what your issue is, but I know this: Every woman has one. There's always something. Look long enough, listen hard enough, be sensitive enough . . . and you'll discover it. You may be in denial about your own problem. Look deep into your own heart, listen to your own talk . . . and you'll find it. It is your life-draining issue that Jesus wants to heal.

Happy *are* the people whose God *is* the LORD!

Psalm 145

A Praise of David.

1 I will extol You, my God, O King;
   And I will bless Your name
   forever and ever.
2 Every day I will bless You,
   And I will praise Your name
   forever and ever.
3 Great *is* the LORD, and greatly to
   be praised;
   And His greatness *is*
   unsearchable.

4 One generation shall praise Your
   works to another,
   And shall declare Your mighty
   acts.
5 I[a] will meditate on the glorious
   splendor of Your majesty,
   And on Your wondrous works.[b]
6 *Men* shall speak of the might of
   Your awesome acts,
   And I will declare Your
   greatness.
7 They shall utter the memory of
   Your great goodness,
   And shall sing of Your
   righteousness.

8 The LORD *is* gracious and full of
   compassion,
   Slow to anger and great in mercy.
9 The LORD *is* good to all,
   And His tender mercies *are* over
   all His works.

10 All Your works shall praise You,
   O LORD,
   And Your saints shall bless You.
11 They shall speak of the glory of
   Your kingdom,
   And talk of Your power,
12 To make known to the sons of
   men His mighty acts,
   And the glorious majesty of His
   kingdom.
13 Your kingdom *is* an everlasting
   kingdom,
   And Your dominion *endures*
   throughout all generations.[a]

14 The LORD upholds all who fall,
   And raises up all *who are* bowed
   down.

15 The eyes of all look expectantly
   to You,
   And You give them their food in
   due season.
16 You open Your hand
   And satisfy the desire of every
   living thing.

17 The LORD *is* righteous in all His
   ways,
   Gracious in all His works.
18 The LORD *is* near to all who call
   upon Him,
   To all who call upon Him in truth.
19 He will fulfill the desire of those
   who fear Him;
   He also will hear their cry and
   save them.
20 The LORD preserves all who love
   Him,
   But all the wicked He will
   destroy.
21 My mouth shall speak the praise
   of the LORD,
   And all flesh shall bless His holy
   name
   Forever and ever.

Psalm 146

1 Praise the LORD!

   Praise the LORD, O my soul!
2 While I live I will praise the LORD;
   I will sing praises to my God
   while I have my being.

3 Do not put your trust in princes,
   Nor in a son of man, in whom
   there is no help.
4 His spirit departs, he returns to
   his earth;
   In that very day his plans perish.

5 Happy *is* he who *has* the God of
   Jacob for his help,
   Whose hope *is* in the LORD his
   God,
6 Who made heaven and earth,
   The sea, and all that *is* in them;
   Who keeps truth forever,
7 Who executes justice for the
   oppressed,
   Who gives food to the hungry.
   The LORD gives freedom to the
   prisoners.

145:5 [a]Following Masoretic Text and Targum; Dead Sea Scrolls, Septuagint, Syriac, and Vulgate read *They*.   [b]Literally *on the words of Your wondrous works*   145:13 [a]Following Masoretic Text and Targum; Dead Sea Scrolls, Septuagint, Syriac, and Vulgate add *The LORD is faithful in all His words, and holy in all His works.*

Gospel
Pearls

8 The LORD opens *the eyes of* the
blind;
The LORD raises those who are
bowed down;
The LORD loves the righteous.
9 The LORD watches over the
strangers;
He relieves the fatherless and
widow;
But the way of the wicked He
turns upside down.

10 The LORD shall reign forever—
Your God, O Zion, to all
generations.

Praise the LORD!

Psalm 147

1 Praise the LORD!
For *it is* good to sing praises to
our God;
For *it is* pleasant, *and* praise is
beautiful.

2 The LORD builds up Jerusalem;
He gathers together the outcasts
of Israel.
3 He heals the brokenhearted
And binds up their wounds.
4 He counts the number of the
stars;
He calls them all by name.
5 Great *is* our Lord, and mighty in
power;
His understanding *is* infinite.
6 The LORD lifts up the humble;
He casts the wicked down to the
ground.

7 Sing to the LORD with
thanksgiving;
Sing praises on the harp to our
God,
8 Who covers the heavens with
clouds,
Who prepares rain for the earth,
Who makes grass to grow on the
mountains.
9 He gives to the beast its food,
And to the young ravens that cry.

10 He does not delight in the
strength of the horse;
He takes no pleasure in the legs
of a man.
11 The LORD takes pleasure in those
who fear Him,
In those who hope in His mercy.

12 Praise the LORD, O Jerusalem!
Praise your God, O Zion!
13 For He has strengthened the bars
of your gates;
He has blessed your children
within you.
14 He makes peace *in* your borders,
And fills you with the finest
wheat.

15 He sends out His command *to the*
earth;
His word runs very swiftly.
16 He gives snow like wool;
He scatters the frost like ashes;
17 He casts out His hail like morsels;
Who can stand before His cold?
18 He sends out His word and melts
them;
He causes His wind to blow, *and*
the waters flow.

19 He declares His word to Jacob,
His statutes and His judgments to
Israel.
20 He has not dealt thus with any
nation;
And *as for His* judgments, they
have not known them.

Praise the LORD!

Psalm 148

1 Praise the LORD!

Praise the LORD from the
heavens;
Praise Him in the heights!
2 Praise Him, all His angels;
Praise Him, all His hosts!
3 Praise Him, sun and moon;
Praise Him, all you stars of light!
4 Praise Him, you heavens of
heavens,
And you waters above the
heavens!

5 Let them praise the name of the
LORD,
For He commanded and they
were created.
6 He also established them forever
and ever;
He made a decree which shall not
pass away.

7 Praise the LORD from the earth,
You great sea creatures and all
the depths;
8 Fire and hail, snow and clouds;
Stormy wind, fulfilling His word;

*T*here is no shield that can keep away the days that come to teach our hearts to
submit to God's will and purpose for us. It comes as if it will not leave, but you can
be sure that is not so. It will go, and the sun will come again and rebuke the clouds
that have hidden the light of God's purpose from shining through to you.

9 Mountains and all hills;
  Fruitful trees and all cedars;
10 Beasts and all cattle;
  Creeping things and flying fowl;
11 Kings of the earth and all
  peoples;
  Princes and all judges of the
  earth;
12 Both young men and maidens;
  Old men and children.

13 Let them praise the name of the
  LORD,
  For His name alone is exalted;
  His glory *is* above the earth and
  heaven.
14 And He has exalted the horn of
  His people,
  The praise of all His saints—
  Of the children of Israel,
  A people near to Him.

  Praise the LORD!

Psalm 149

1 Praise the LORD!

  Sing to the LORD a new song,
  And His praise in the assembly
  of saints.

2 Let Israel rejoice in their Maker;
  Let the children of Zion be joyful
  in their King.
3 Let them praise His name with
  the dance;
  Let them sing praises to Him with
  the timbrel and harp.
4 For the LORD takes pleasure in
  His people;
  He will beautify the humble with
  salvation.

5 Let the saints be joyful in glory;
  Let them sing aloud on their
  beds.
6 *Let* the high praises of God *be*
  in their mouth,
  And a two-edged sword in their
  hand,
7 To execute vengeance on the
  nations,
  And punishments on the peoples;
8 To bind their kings with chains,
  And their nobles with fetters of
  iron;
9 To execute on them the written
  judgment—
  This honor have all His saints.

  Praise the LORD!

Psalm 150

1 Praise the LORD!

  Praise God in His sanctuary;
  Praise Him in His mighty
  firmament!

2 Praise Him for His mighty acts;
  Praise Him according to His
  excellent greatness!

3 Praise Him with the sound of the
  trumpet;
  Praise Him with the lute and
  harp!
4 Praise Him with the timbrel and
  dance;
  Praise Him with stringed
  instruments and flutes!
5 Praise Him with loud cymbals;
  Praise Him with clashing
  cymbals!

6 Let everything that has breath
  praise the LORD.

  Praise the LORD!

The Book of

PROVERBS

1 The proverbs of Solomon the son
 of David, king of Israel:

2 To know wisdom and
  instruction,

  To perceive the words of
  understanding,
3 To receive the instruction of
  wisdom,
  Justice, judgment, and equity;

4 To give prudence to the
   simple,
   To the young man knowledge
   and discretion—
5 A wise *man* will hear and
   increase learning,
   And a man of understanding
   will attain wise counsel,
6 To understand a proverb and
   an enigma,
   The words of the wise and their
   riddles.

7 The fear of the LORD *is* the
   beginning of knowledge,
   But fools despise wisdom and
   instruction.

8 My son, hear the instruction of
   your father,
   And do not forsake the law of
   your mother;
9 For they *will be* a graceful
   ornament on your head,
   And chains about your neck.

10 My son, if sinners entice you,
   Do not consent.
11 If they say, "Come with us,
   Let us lie in wait to *shed* blood;
   Let us lurk secretly for the
   innocent without cause;
12 Let us swallow them alive like
   Sheol,*ᵃ*
   And whole, like those who go
   down to the Pit;
13 We shall find all *kinds* of
   precious possessions,
   We shall fill our houses with
   spoil;
14 Cast in your lot among us,
   Let us all have one purse"—
15 My son, do not walk in the way
   with them,
   Keep your foot from their
   path;
16 For their feet run to evil,
   And they make haste to shed
   blood.
17 Surely, in vain the net is spread
   In the sight of any bird;
18 But they lie in wait for their
   own blood,
   They lurk secretly for their *own*
   lives.
19 So *are* the ways of everyone
   who is greedy for gain;
   It takes away the life of its
   owners.

20 Wisdom calls aloud outside;
   She raises her voice in the open
   squares.
21 She cries out in the chief
   concourses,*ᵃ*
   At the openings of the gates in
   the city
   She speaks her words:
22 "How long, you simple ones, will
   you love simplicity?
   For scorners delight in their
   scorning,
   And fools hate knowledge.
23 Turn at my rebuke;
   Surely I will pour out my spirit
   on you;
   I will make my words known
   to you.
24 Because I have called and you
   refused,
   I have stretched out my hand
   and no one regarded,
25 Because you disdained all my
   counsel,
   And would have none of my
   rebuke,
26 I also will laugh at your
   calamity;
   I will mock when your terror
   comes,
27 When your terror comes like a
   storm,
   And your destruction comes
   like a whirlwind,
   When distress and anguish
   come upon you.

28 "Then they will call on me, but
   I will not answer;
   They will seek me diligently,
   but they will not find me.
29 Because they hated knowledge
   And did not choose the fear of
   the LORD,
30 They would have none of my
   counsel
   And despised my every rebuke.
31 Therefore they shall eat the
   fruit of their own way,
   And be filled to the full with
   their own fancies.
32 For the turning away of the
   simple will slay them,
   And the complacency of fools
   will destroy them;
33 But whoever listens to me will
   dwell safely,
   And will be secure, without
   fear of evil."

1:12 *ᵃ*Or *the grave*   1:21 *ᵃ*Septuagint, Syriac, and Targum read *top of the walls;* Vulgate reads *the head of multitudes.*

*G*od is so wise. He knows the greater truths that can only be realized by eyes that can behold today and tomorrow in one glance. He must, as a good Father, deny requests that would insult the greater destiny He has prepared for those who are His.

2 My son, if you receive my
words,
And treasure my commands
within you,
2 So that you incline your ear to
wisdom,
And apply your heart to
understanding;
3 Yes, if you cry out for
discernment,
And lift up your voice for
understanding,
4 If you seek her as silver,
And search for her as *for*
hidden treasures;
5 Then you will understand the
fear of the LORD,
And find the knowledge of
God.
6 For the LORD gives wisdom;
From His mouth *come*
knowledge and
understanding;
7 He stores up sound wisdom for
the upright;
He is a shield to those who
walk uprightly;
8 He guards the paths of
justice,
And preserves the way of His
saints.
9 Then you will understand
righteousness and justice,
Equity *and* every good path.

10 When wisdom enters your
heart,
And knowledge is pleasant to
your soul,
11 Discretion will preserve you;
Understanding will keep you,
12 To deliver you from the way of
evil,
From the man who speaks
perverse things,
13 From those who leave the paths
of uprightness
To walk in the ways of
darkness;
14 Who rejoice in doing evil,
And delight in the perversity of
the wicked;
15 Whose ways *are* crooked,
And *who are* devious in their
paths;
16 To deliver you from the
immoral woman,
From the seductress *who*
flatters with her words,

17 Who forsakes the companion
of her youth,
And forgets the covenant of her
God.
18 For her house leads down to
death,
And her paths to the dead;
19 None who go to her return,
Nor do they regain the paths of
life—
20 So you may walk in the way
of goodness,
And keep to the paths of
righteousness.
21 For the upright will dwell in the
land,
And the blameless will remain
in it;
22 But the wicked will be cut off
from the earth,
And the unfaithful will be
uprooted from it.

3 My son, do not forget my law,
But let your heart keep my
commands;
2 For length of days and long life
And peace they will add to
you.

3 Let not mercy and truth forsake
you;
Bind them around your neck,
Write them on the tablet of
your heart,
4 *And* so find favor and high
esteem
In the sight of God and man.

5 Trust in the LORD with all your
heart,
And lean not on your own
understanding;
6 In all your ways acknowledge
Him,
And He shall direct[a] your
paths.

7 Do not be wise in your own
eyes;
Fear the LORD and depart from
evil.
8 It will be health to your flesh,[a]
And strength[b] to your bones.

9 Honor the LORD with your
possessions,
And with the firstfruits of all
your increase;

3:6 [a]Or *make smooth* or *straight*   3:8 [a]Literally *navel*, figurative of the body   [b]Literally *drink* or *refreshment*

When He says no, you ought to say yes! He would never interrupt you or embarrass
you before your friends if He didn't see something ahead that necessitated the
answer He gave. You ought to praise Him right now!

It Takes Trust

Proverbs 3:5, 6

The basis of any relationship must be trust. Trusting God with your successes isn't much of a challenge. The real test of trust is sharing your secrets, your inner failures and fears.

Jesus once told the woman at the well, "True worshipers will worship the Father in spirit and truth; for the Father is seeking such [real people, flawed people like you] to worship Him. God is Spirit, and those who worship Him must worship in spirit and truth" (John 4:23, 24).

You have nothing to fear, for your honesty with the Father won't reveal anything He doesn't already know. His intellect is so keen that He doesn't have to wait for you to make a mistake. He knows about your failure before you fail. His knowledge is all-inclusive, spanning the gap between time and incident. He knows your thoughts even as you subconsciously gather them in your own mind.

Once you realize this, all your attempts at silence and secrecy will seem childish and ridiculous. He is "the all-seeing One," and He knows perfectly and completely what is in you. When you pray, and more importantly, when you commune with God, you must have the kind of confidence and assurance that neither requires nor allows deceit. Although my Father abhors my sin, He loves me. His love is incomprehensible, primarily because there is nothing with which to compare it.

There is a balance in the awareness of His holiness, which would condemn you, and His love, which esteems and redeems you. He is far too holy for you to be arrogant about your humanity, yet He is far too loving for you to be frightened by the emotional dysfunction that comes from being raised by a father you could never seem to please.

God does not change; neither does His compassion. One thing we search for at every level of our relationships is to be understood. When I am properly understood, I don't always have to express and explain. *Thank You, Lord, for not asking me to explain what I can scarcely express!*

We quickly grow weary of people who demand that we constantly explain ourselves. We'd rather be around those who are able to read the meaning of a touch, a brief hug, a sigh emitted in the stillness of a moment. Real communion cannot be typed or taught; it must be understood. At this level, there is a communication so intense that those who understand it can clearly speak it, even through closed lips. As with lovers staring at each other across a crowded room, words are unnecessary when there is true understanding. It is with this kind of understanding that God clearly perceives your every need.

10 So your barns will be filled with
plenty,
And your vats will overflow
with new wine.

11 My son, do not despise the
chastening of the LORD,
Nor detest His correction;
12 For whom the LORD loves He
corrects,
Just as a father the son *in
whom* he delights.

13 Happy *is* the man *who* finds
wisdom,
And the man *who* gains
understanding;
14 For her proceeds *are* better
than the profits of silver,
And her gain than fine gold.
15 She *is* more precious than
rubies,
And all the things you may
desire cannot compare with
her.
16 Length of days *is* in her right
hand,
In her left hand riches and
honor.
17 Her ways *are* ways of
pleasantness,
And all her paths *are* peace.
18 She *is* a tree of life to those who
take hold of her,
And happy *are all* who retain
her.

19 The LORD by wisdom founded
the earth;
By understanding He
established the heavens;
20 By His knowledge the depths
were broken up,
And clouds drop down the dew.

21 My son, let them not depart
from your eyes—
Keep sound wisdom and
discretion;
22 So they will be life to your soul
And grace to your neck.
23 Then you will walk safely in
your way,
And your foot will not stumble.
24 When you lie down, you will
not be afraid;
Yes, you will lie down and your
sleep will be sweet.
25 Do not be afraid of sudden
terror,
Nor of trouble from the wicked
when it comes;

26 For the LORD will be your
confidence,
And will keep your foot from
being caught.

27 Do not withhold good from
those to whom it is due,
When it is in the power of your
hand to do *so.*
28 Do not say to your neighbor,
"Go, and come back,
And tomorrow I will give *it,*"
When *you have* it with you.
29 Do not devise evil against your
neighbor,
For he dwells by you for
safety's sake.
30 Do not strive with a man
without cause,
If he has done you no harm.

31 Do not envy the oppressor,
And choose none of his ways;
32 For the perverse *person is* an
abomination to the LORD,
But His secret counsel *is* with
the upright.
33 The curse of the LORD *is* on the
house of the wicked,
But He blesses the home of the
just.
34 Surely He scorns the scornful,
But gives grace to the
humble.
35 The wise shall inherit glory,
But shame shall be the legacy
of fools.

4 Hear, *my* children, the
instruction of a father,
And give attention to know
understanding;
2 For I give you good doctrine:
Do not forsake my law.
3 When I was my father's son,
Tender and the only one in the
sight of my mother,
4 He also taught me, and said to
me:
"Let your heart retain my
words;
Keep my commands, and live.
5 Get wisdom! Get
understanding!
Do not forget, nor turn away
from the words of my mouth.
6 Do not forsake her, and she will
preserve you;
Love her, and she will keep
you.
7 Wisdom *is* the principal thing;
Therefore get wisdom.

And in all your getting, get
understanding.
8 Exalt her, and she will promote
you;
She will bring you honor, when
you embrace her.
9 She will place on your head an
ornament of grace;
A crown of glory she will
deliver to you.''

10 Hear, my son, and receive my
sayings,
And the years of your life will
be many.
11 I have taught you in the way
of wisdom;
I have led you in right paths.
12 When you walk, your steps will
not be hindered,
And when you run, you will not
stumble.
13 Take firm hold of instruction,
do not let go;
Keep her, for she *is* your life.

14 Do not enter the path of the
wicked,
And do not walk in the way of
evil.
15 Avoid it, do not travel on it;
Turn away from it and pass on.
16 For they do not sleep unless
they have done evil;
And their sleep is taken away
unless they make *someone*
fall.
17 For they eat the bread of
wickedness,
And drink the wine of violence.

18 But the path of the just *is* like
the shining sun,[a]
That shines ever brighter unto
the perfect day.
19 The way of the wicked *is* like
darkness;
They do not know what makes
them stumble.

20 My son, give attention to my
words;
Incline your ear to my sayings.
21 Do not let them depart from
your eyes;
Keep them in the midst of your
heart;
22 For they *are* life to those who
find them,
And health to all their flesh.

23 Keep your heart with all
diligence,
For out of it *spring* the issues
of life.
24 Put away from you a deceitful
mouth,
And put perverse lips far from
you.
25 Let your eyes look straight
ahead,
And your eyelids look right
before you.
26 Ponder the path of your feet,
And let all your ways be
established.
27 Do not turn to the right or the
left;
Remove your foot from evil.

5 My son, pay attention to my
wisdom;
Lend your ear to my
understanding.
2 That you may preserve
discretion,
And your lips may keep
knowledge.
3 For the lips of an immoral
woman drip honey,
And her mouth *is* smoother
than oil;
4 But in the end she is bitter as
wormwood,
Sharp as a two-edged sword.
5 Her feet go down to death,
Her steps lay hold of hell.[a]
6 Lest you ponder *her* path of
life—
Her ways are unstable;
You do not know *them*.

7 Therefore hear me now, *my*
children,
And do not depart from the
words of my mouth.
8 Remove your way far from
her,
And do not go near the door
of her house,
9 Lest you give your honor to
others,
And your years to the cruel
one;
10 Lest aliens be filled with your
wealth,
And your labors *go* to the
house of a foreigner;
11 And you mourn at last,
When your flesh and your body
are consumed,

4:18 [a]Literally *light*   5:5 [a]Or *Sheol*

---

*O*nly a praying heart that turns to Him can determine the answer. Hang up the
telephone, cut off the television set and fall down on bended knees. Prayer does
work. If you pray, He does have the key, and He can open the door!

12 And say:
"How I have hated instruction,
And my heart despised
correction!
13 I have not obeyed the voice of
my teachers,
Nor inclined my ear to those
who instructed me!
14 I was on the verge of total ruin,
In the midst of the assembly
and congregation."

15 Drink water from your own
cistern,
And running water from your
own well.
16 Should your fountains be
dispersed abroad,
Streams of water in the streets?
17 Let them be only your own,
And not for strangers with you.
18 Let your fountain be blessed,
And rejoice with the wife of
your youth.
19 *As a* loving deer and a graceful
doe,
Let her breasts satisfy you at
all times;
And always be enraptured with
her love.
20 For why should you, my son,
be enraptured by an immoral
woman,
And be embraced in the arms
of a seductress?

21 For the ways of man *are* before
the eyes of the LORD,
And He ponders all his paths.
22 His own iniquities entrap the
wicked *man,*
And he is caught in the cords
of his sin.
23 He shall die for lack of
instruction,
And in the greatness of his folly
he shall go astray.

6 My son, if you become surety
for your friend,
If you have shaken hands in
pledge for a stranger,
2 You are snared by the words
of your mouth;
You are taken by the words of
your mouth.
3 So do this, my son, and deliver
yourself;
For you have come into the
hand of your friend:

Go and humble yourself;
Plead with your friend.
4 Give no sleep to your eyes,
Nor slumber to your eyelids.
5 Deliver yourself like a gazelle
from the hand *of the hunter,*
And like a bird from the hand
of the fowler.*a*

6 Go to the ant, you sluggard!
Consider her ways and be wise,
7 Which, having no captain,
Overseer or ruler,
8 Provides her supplies in the
summer,
And gathers her food in the
harvest.
9 How long will you slumber, O
sluggard?
When will you rise from your
sleep?
10 A little sleep, a little slumber,
A little folding of the hands to
sleep—
11 So shall your poverty come on
you like a prowler,
And your need like an armed
man.

12 A worthless person, a wicked
man,
Walks with a perverse mouth;
13 He winks with his eyes,
He shuffles his feet,
He points with his fingers;
14 Perversity *is* in his heart,
He devises evil continually,
He sows discord.
15 Therefore his calamity shall
come suddenly;
Suddenly he shall be broken
without remedy.

16 These six *things* the LORD
hates,
Yes, seven *are* an abomination
to Him:
17 A proud look,
A lying tongue,
Hands that shed innocent
blood,
18 A heart that devises wicked
plans,
Feet that are swift in running
to evil,
19 A false witness *who* speaks
lies,
And one who sows discord
among brethren.

6:5 *a*That is, one who catches birds in a trap or snare

Gospel Pearls

20 My son, keep your father's
command,
And do not forsake the law of
your mother.
21 Bind them continually upon
your heart;
Tie them around your neck.
22 When you roam, they[a] will lead
you;
When you sleep, they will keep
you;
And *when* you awake, they will
speak with you.
23 For the commandment *is* a
lamp,
And the law a light;
Reproofs of instruction *are* the
way of life,
24 To keep you from the evil
woman,
From the flattering tongue of a
seductress.
25 Do not lust after her beauty in
your heart,
Nor let her allure you with her
eyelids.
26 For by means of a harlot
A man is reduced to a crust of
bread;
And an adulteress[a] will prey
upon his precious life.
27 Can a man take fire to his
bosom,
And his clothes not be
burned?
28 Can one walk on hot coals,
And his feet not be seared?
29 So *is* he who goes in to his
neighbor's wife;
Whoever touches her shall not
be innocent.

30 *People* do not despise a thief
If he steals to satisfy himself
when he is starving.
31 Yet *when* he is found, he must
restore sevenfold;
He may have to give up all the
substance of his house.
32 Whoever commits adultery
with a woman lacks
understanding;
He *who* does so destroys his
own soul.
33 Wounds and dishonor he will
get,
And his reproach will not be
wiped away.
34 For jealousy *is* a husband's
fury;

Therefore he will not spare in
the day of vengeance.
35 He will accept no recompense,
Nor will he be appeased though
you give many gifts.

7 My son, keep my words,
And treasure my commands
within you.
2 Keep my commands and live,
And my law as the apple of
your eye.
3 Bind them on your fingers;
Write them on the tablet of
your heart.
4 Say to wisdom, "You *are* my
sister,"
And call understanding *your*
nearest kin,
5 That they may keep you from
the immoral woman,
From the seductress *who*
flatters with her words.

6 For at the window of my house
I looked through my lattice,
7 And saw among the simple,
I perceived among the youths,
A young man devoid of
understanding,
8 Passing along the street near
her corner;
And he took the path to her
house
9 In the twilight, in the evening,
In the black and dark night.

10 And there a woman met him,
With the attire of a harlot, and
a crafty heart.
11 She *was* loud and rebellious,
Her feet would not stay at
home.
12 At times *she was* outside, at
times in the open square,
Lurking at every corner.
13 So she caught him and kissed
him;
With an impudent face she said
to him:
14 "*I have* peace offerings with
me;
Today I have paid my vows.
15 So I came out to meet you,
Diligently to seek your face,
And I have found you.
16 I have spread my bed with
tapestry,
Colored coverings of Egyptian
linen.
17 I have perfumed my bed

6:22 [a]Literally *it*   6:26 [a]Literally *a man's wife*, that is, of another

*H*is love is gentler than a mother's breast and stronger than a father's arms at the same time. It is more intimate than a lover's caress. It is more consistent than a child's affection. It is *agape*. It is God's love.

With myrrh, aloes, and
cinnamon.

18 Come, let us take our fill of love
until morning;
Let us delight ourselves with
love.

19 For my husband *is* not at home;
He has gone on a long journey;

20 He has taken a bag of money
with him,
And will come home on the
appointed day."

21 With her enticing speech she
caused him to yield,
With her flattering lips she
seduced him.

22 Immediately he went after her,
as an ox goes to the
slaughter,
Or as a fool to the correction
of the stocks,[a]

23 Till an arrow struck his liver.
As a bird hastens to the snare,
He did not know it *would cost*
his life.

24 Now therefore, listen to me, *my*
children;
Pay attention to the words of
my mouth:

25 Do not let your heart turn aside
to her ways,
Do not stray into her paths;

26 For she has cast down many
wounded,
And all who were slain by her
were strong *men.*

27 Her house *is* the way to hell,[a]
Descending to the chambers of
death.

8 Does not wisdom cry out,
And understanding lift up her
voice?

2 She takes her stand on the top
of the high hill,
Beside the way, where the
paths meet.

3 She cries out by the gates, at
the entry of the city,
At the entrance of the doors:

4 "To you, O men, I call,
And my voice *is* to the sons of
men.

5 O you simple ones, understand
prudence,
And you fools, be of an
understanding heart.

6 Listen, for I will speak of
excellent things,
And from the opening of my
lips *will come* right things;

7 For my mouth will speak truth;
Wickedness *is* an abomination
to my lips.

8 All the words of my mouth *are*
with righteousness;
Nothing crooked or perverse *is*
in them.

9 They *are* all plain to him who
understands,
And right to those who find
knowledge.

10 Receive my instruction, and not
silver,
And knowledge rather than
choice gold;

11 For wisdom *is* better than
rubies,
And all the things one may
desire cannot be compared
with her.

12 "I, wisdom, dwell with
prudence,
And find out knowledge *and*
discretion.

13 The fear of the LORD *is* to hate
evil;
Pride and arrogance and the
evil way
And the perverse mouth I hate.

14 Counsel *is* mine, and sound
wisdom;
I *am* understanding, I have
strength.

15 By me kings reign,
And rulers decree justice.

16 By me princes rule, and nobles,
All the judges of the earth.[a]

17 I love those who love me,
And those who seek me
diligently will find me.

18 Riches and honor *are* with me,
Enduring riches and
righteousness.

19 My fruit *is* better than gold, yes,
than fine gold,
And my revenue than choice
silver.

20 I traverse the way of
righteousness,
In the midst of the paths of
justice,

21 That I may cause those who
love me to inherit wealth,
That I may fill their treasuries.

7:22 [a]Septuagint, Syriac, and Targum read *as a dog to bonds;* Vulgate reads *as a lamb . . . to bonds.*
7:27 [a]Or *Sheol*   8:16 [a]Masoretic Text, Syriac, Targum, and Vulgate read *righteousness;* Bomberg,
Septuagint, and some manuscripts and editions read *earth.*

Gospel
Pearls

22 "The LORD possessed me at the
beginning of His way,
Before His works of old.

23 I have been established from
everlasting,
From the beginning, before
there was ever an earth.

24 When *there were* no depths I
was brought forth,
When *there were* no fountains
abounding with water.

25 Before the mountains were
settled,
Before the hills, I was brought
forth;

26 While as yet He had not made
the earth or the fields,
Or the primal dust of the world.

27 When He prepared the
heavens, I *was* there,
When He drew a circle on the
face of the deep,

28 When He established the
clouds above,
When He strengthened the
fountains of the deep,

29 When He assigned to the sea
its limit,
So that the waters would not
transgress His command,
When He marked out the
foundations of the earth,

30 Then I was beside Him *as* a
master craftsman;[a]
And I was daily *His* delight,
Rejoicing always before Him,

31 Rejoicing in His inhabited
world,
And my delight *was* with the
sons of men.

32 "Now therefore, listen to me, *my*
children,
For blessed *are those who* keep
my ways.

33 Hear instruction and be wise,
And do not disdain *it.*

34 Blessed is the man who listens
to me,
Watching daily at my gates,
Waiting at the posts of my
doors.

35 For whoever finds me finds
life,
And obtains favor from the
LORD;

36 But he who sins against me
wrongs his own soul;
All those who hate me love
death."

9 Wisdom has built her house,
She has hewn out her seven
pillars;

2 She has slaughtered her meat,
She has mixed her wine,
She has also furnished her
table.

3 She has sent out her maidens,
She cries out from the highest
places of the city,

4 "Whoever *is* simple, let him turn
in here!"
As for him who lacks
understanding, she says to
him,

5 "Come, eat of my bread
And drink of the wine I have
mixed.

6 Forsake foolishness and live,
And go in the way of
understanding.

7 "He who corrects a scoffer gets
shame for himself,
And he who rebukes a wicked
man only harms himself.

8 Do not correct a scoffer, lest he
hate you;
Rebuke a wise *man,* and he will
love you.

9 Give *instruction* to a wise *man,*
and he will be still wiser;
Teach a just *man,* and he will
increase in learning.

10 "The fear of the LORD *is* the
beginning of wisdom,
And the knowledge of the Holy
One *is* understanding.

11 For by me your days will be
multiplied,
And years of life will be added
to you.

12 If you are wise, you are wise
for yourself,
And *if* you scoff, you will bear
it alone."

13 A foolish woman is clamorous;
She is simple, and knows
nothing.

14 For she sits at the door of her
house,
On a seat *by* the highest places
of the city,

15 To call to those who pass by,
Who go straight on their way:

16 "Whoever *is* simple, let him turn
in here";
And *as for* him who lacks

8:30 [a] A Jewish tradition reads *one brought up.*

2 f the church is your mother, as glorious as she is, you still need to know your Father.
He is the One who produced the seed of His Word that caused you to come into
being. It is His name you inherit, and your calling upon that name opens up all of
heaven.

9:16 sg.

...inding, she says to

"...ater is sweet,
...ead *eaten* in secret is
...ant."
...e does not know that the
...d *are* there,
... her guests *are* in the
...epths of hell.*a*

10 The proverbs of Solomon:

A wise son makes a glad father,
But a foolish son *is* the grief of
his mother.

2   Treasures of wickedness profit
nothing,
But righteousness delivers
from death.
3   The LORD will not allow the
righteous soul to famish,
But He casts away the desire
of the wicked.

4   He who has a slack hand
becomes poor,
But the hand of the diligent
makes rich.
5   He who gathers in summer *is*
a wise son;
He who sleeps in harvest *is* a
son who causes shame.

6   Blessings *are* on the head of the
righteous,
But violence covers the mouth
of the wicked.
7   The memory of the righteous *is*
blessed,
But the name of the wicked will
rot.

8   The wise in heart will receive
commands,
But a prating fool will fall.

9   He who walks with integrity
walks securely,
But he who perverts his ways
will become known.

10   He who winks with the eye
causes trouble,
But a prating fool will fall.

11   The mouth of the righteous *is*
a well of life,
But violence covers the mouth
of the wicked.

12   Hatred stirs up strife,
But love covers all sins.

13   Wisdom is found on the lips of
him who has understanding,
But a rod *is* for the back of him
who is devoid of
understanding.

14   Wise *people* store up
knowledge,
But the mouth of the foolish *is*
near destruction.

15   The rich man's wealth *is* his
strong city;
The destruction of the poor *is*
their poverty.

16   The labor of the righteous *leads*
to life,
The wages of the wicked to sin.

17   He who keeps instruction *is in*
the way of life,
But he who refuses correction
goes astray.

18   Whoever hides hatred *has*
lying lips,
And whoever spreads slander
is a fool.

19   In the multitude of words sin
is not lacking,
But he who restrains his lips *is*
wise.
20   The tongue of the righteous *is*
choice silver;
The heart of the wicked *is*
worth little.
21   The lips of the righteous feed
many,
But fools die for lack of
wisdom.*a*

22   The blessing of the LORD makes
one rich,
And He adds no sorrow with
it.

23   To do evil *is* like sport to a fool,
But a man of understanding
has wisdom.
24   The fear of the wicked will
come upon him,
And the desire of the righteous
will be granted.
25   When the whirlwind passes by,
the wicked *is* no *more*,

9:18 *a*Or *Sheol*   10:21 *a*Literally *heart*

*Y*ou have been called out and separated by God. You were not created to be popular.
You were not called to cliques or clubs. You were chosen to fit in the hands of God
who has already accepted you.

The Blessing of His Love

Proverbs 10:22

Love at its apex is when you have seen the worst in a person and have not forsaken him. This is the love that your heavenly Father has for you. Why do I want you to know this? Because I don't want you to be one of the foolish women who run from the only answer there is to the questions of life. You need never run from Him. He made up His mind about you before the worlds were framed.

This is not the love that you are to seek from men. You will never find a man like Jesus, the Lover of your soul. This love is the love that God gives to compensate the thirsting heart that has drunk from the waters of men's empty promises. It is the brook you come to when no other has quenched the thirstiness of life. It is the cool, refreshing knowledge of a love that calms your desperate cravings and clingings. You may grope and fight to have the touch of men whose arms can ease no pain. But you don't have to, for I speak to you of the only One whose kiss can curse pain and ease fears.

Do not join the masses of women who are chasing after the affections of some fictional lover whose shiny armor is a mere fantasy that will never be humanly realized. Don't become bitter as you rummage through relationships, looking for divine love from human hearts. Don't fall into the trap of thinking that there is, somewhere beneath the sun's bright light, a hero who isn't tarnished with human flaws. If you are to love a man, understand that he is a man. You will never be disappointed by what you don't expect.

In short, whatever you need, natural or spiritual, God is the source from which your blessings must come. You will not look to men. Blessing may come *through* men, but not *from* them. All of your help will come from the Lord. He will use people from time to time. But your deepest needs He will fill Himself. He alone can give the soul release. Man sets bones, but God causes them to knit together. Man gives love, but God fills voids. Whatever the arena, remember to include Him.

Redeem your treasures through His Word. If they are not from His Word, they are not from Him. You want only the answer that comes from Him. Patience is going to be the real challenge. It is difficult to learn to wait. When you feel that you need something today and God doesn't answer readily, you must learn to trust Him and wait. Anything you provide yourself will only increase the struggle. Wait on His blessings and His timing, and you will have the kind of blessings that add no sorrow.

But the righteous *has* an everlasting foundation.

26 As vinegar to the teeth and smoke to the eyes,
So *is* the lazy *man* to those who send him.

27 The fear of the LORD prolongs days,
But the years of the wicked will be shortened.

28 The hope of the righteous *will be* gladness,
But the expectation of the wicked will perish.

29 The way of the LORD *is* strength for the upright,
But destruction *will come* to the workers of iniquity.

30 The righteous will never be removed,
But the wicked will not inhabit the earth.

31 The mouth of the righteous brings forth wisdom,
But the perverse tongue will be cut out.

32 The lips of the righteous know what is acceptable,
But the mouth of the wicked *what is* perverse.

11 Dishonest scales *are* an abomination to the LORD,
But a just weight *is* His delight.

2 When pride comes, then comes shame;
But with the humble *is* wisdom.

3 The integrity of the upright will guide them,
But the perversity of the unfaithful will destroy them.

4 Riches do not profit in the day of wrath,
But righteousness delivers from death.

5 The righteousness of the blameless will direct*a* his way aright,
But the wicked will fall by his own wickedness.

6 The righteousness of the upright will deliver them,
But the unfaithful will be caught by *their* lust.

7 When a wicked man dies, *his* expectation will perish,
And the hope of the unjust perishes.

8 The righteous is delivered from trouble,
And it comes to the wicked instead.

9 The hypocrite with *his* mouth destroys his neighbor,
But through knowledge the righteous will be delivered.

10 When it goes well with the righteous, the city rejoices;
And when the wicked perish, *there is* jubilation.

11 By the blessing of the upright the city is exalted,
But it is overthrown by the mouth of the wicked.

12 He who is devoid of wisdom despises his neighbor,
But a man of understanding holds his peace.

13 A talebearer reveals secrets,
But he who is of a faithful spirit conceals a matter.

14 Where *there is* no counsel, the people fall;
But in the multitude of counselors *there is* safety.

15 He who is surety for a stranger will suffer,
But one who hates being surety is secure.

16 A gracious woman retains honor,
But ruthless *men* retain riches.

17 The merciful man does good for his own soul,
But *he who is* cruel troubles his own flesh.

18 The wicked *man* does deceptive work,
But he who sows righteousness *will have* a sure reward.

19 As righteousness *leads* to life,
So he who pursues evil *pursues it* to his own death.

20 Those who are of a perverse heart *are* an abomination to the LORD,
But *the* blameless in their ways *are* His delight.

11:5 *a*Or *make smooth or straight*

Gospel Pearls

21 *Though they join* forces,*a* the
wicked will not go
unpunished;
But the posterity of the
righteous will be delivered.

22 *As* a ring of gold in a swine's
snout,
So is a lovely woman who lacks
discretion.

23 The desire of the righteous *is*
only good,
But the expectation of the
wicked *is* wrath.

24 There is *one* who scatters, yet
increases more;
And there is *one* who withholds
more than is right,
But it *leads* to poverty.

25 The generous soul will be made
rich,
And he who waters will also be
watered himself.

26 The people will curse him who
withholds grain,
But blessing *will be* on the head
of him who sells *it.*

27 He who earnestly seeks good
finds favor,
But trouble will come to him
who seeks *evil.*

28 He who trusts in his riches will
fall,
But the righteous will flourish
like foliage.

29 He who troubles his own house
will inherit the wind,
And the fool *will be* servant to
the wise of heart.

30 The fruit of the righteous *is a*
tree of life,
And he who wins souls *is* wise.

31 If the righteous will be
recompensed on the earth,
How much more the ungodly
and the sinner.

12 Whoever loves instruction
loves knowledge,
But he who hates correction *is*
stupid.

2 A good *man* obtains favor from
the LORD,

But a man of wicked intentions
He will condemn.

3 A man is not established by
wickedness,
But the root of the righteous
cannot be moved.

4 An excellent*a* wife *is* the crown
of her husband,
But she who causes shame *is*
like rottenness in his bones.

5 The thoughts of the righteous
are right,
But the counsels of the wicked
are deceitful.

6 The words of the wicked *are,*
"Lie in wait for blood,"
But the mouth of the upright
will deliver them.

7 The wicked are overthrown
and *are* no more,
But the house of the righteous
will stand.

8 A man will be commended
according to his wisdom,
But he who is of a perverse
heart will be despised.

9 Better *is the one* who is slighted
but has a servant,
Than he who honors himself
but lacks bread.

10 A righteous *man* regards the
life of his animal,
But the tender mercies of the
wicked *are* cruel.

11 He who tills his land will be
satisfied with bread,
But he who follows frivolity *is*
devoid of understanding.*a*

12 The wicked covet the catch of
evil *men,*
But the root of the righteous
yields *fruit.*

13 The wicked is ensnared by the
transgression of *his* lips,
But the righteous will come
through trouble.

14 A man will be satisfied with
good by the fruit of *his*
mouth,
And the recompense of a man's

11:21 *a*Literally *hand in hand*   12:4 *a*Literally *A wife of valor*   12:11 *a*Literally *heart*

Some women have never been secure in the love of their natural fathers, and it affects how they view their heavenly Father. But listen to me. There is no doubt about His love. He made the ultimate sacrifice just to prove to you the authenticity of His love.

hands will be rendered to him.

15 The way of a fool *is* right in his own eyes,
But he who heeds counsel *is* wise.

16 A fool's wrath is known at once,
But a prudent *man* covers shame.

17 He *who* speaks truth declares righteousness,
But a false witness, deceit.

18 There is one who speaks like the piercings of a sword,
But the tongue of the wise *promotes* health.

19 The truthful lip shall be established forever,
But a lying tongue *is* but for a moment.

20 Deceit is in the heart of those who devise evil,
But counselors of peace have joy.

21 No grave trouble will overtake the righteous,
But the wicked shall be filled with evil.

22 Lying lips *are* an abomination to the LORD,
But those who deal truthfully *are* His delight.

23 A prudent man conceals knowledge,
But the heart of fools proclaims foolishness.

24 The hand of the diligent will rule,
But the lazy *man* will be put to forced labor.

25 Anxiety in the heart of man causes depression,
But a good word makes it glad.

26 The righteous should choose his friends carefully,
For the way of the wicked leads them astray.

27 The lazy *man* does not roast what he took in hunting,
But diligence *is* man's precious possession.

28 In the way of righteousness *is* life,
And in *its* pathway *there is* no death.

13 A wise son *heeds* his father's instruction,
But a scoffer does not listen to rebuke.

2 A man shall eat well by the fruit of *his* mouth,
But the soul of the unfaithful feeds on violence.

3 He who guards his mouth preserves his life,
But he who opens wide his lips shall have destruction.

4 The soul of a lazy *man* desires, and *has* nothing;
But the soul of the diligent shall be made rich.

5 A righteous *man* hates lying,
But a wicked *man* is loathsome and comes to shame.

6 Righteousness guards *him* whose way is blameless,
But wickedness overthrows the sinner.

7 There is one who makes himself rich, yet *has* nothing;
And one who makes himself poor, yet *has* great riches.

8 The ransom of a man's life *is* his riches,
But the poor does not hear rebuke.

9 The light of the righteous rejoices,
But the lamp of the wicked will be put out.

10 By pride comes nothing but strife,
But with the well-advised *is* wisdom.

11 Wealth *gained by* dishonesty will be diminished,
But he who gathers by labor will increase.

12 Hope deferred makes the heart sick,
But *when* the desire comes, *it* is a tree of life.

13 He who despises the word will be destroyed,
But he who fears the

Gospel Pearls

commandment will be rewarded.

14 The law of the wise *is* a
fountain of life,
To turn *one* away from the
snares of death.

15 Good understanding gains
favor,
But the way of the unfaithful
is hard.

16 Every prudent *man* acts with
knowledge,
But a fool lays open *his* folly.

17 A wicked messenger falls into
trouble,
But a faithful ambassador
brings health.

18 Poverty and shame *will come*
to him who disdains
correction,
But he who regards a rebuke
will be honored.

19 A desire accomplished is sweet
to the soul,
But *it is* an abomination to
fools to depart from evil.

20 He who walks with wise *men*
will be wise,
But the companion of fools will
be destroyed.

21 Evil pursues sinners,
But to the righteous, good shall
be repaid.

22 A good *man* leaves an
inheritance to his children's
children,
But the wealth of the sinner is
stored up for the righteous.

23 Much food *is in* the fallow
ground of the poor,
And for lack of justice there is
waste.[a]

24 He who spares his rod hates his
son,
But he who loves him
disciplines him promptly.

25 The righteous eats to the
satisfying of his soul,
But the stomach of the wicked
shall be in want.

14 The wise woman builds her
house,
But the foolish pulls it down
with her hands.

2 He who walks in his
uprightness fears the LORD,
But *he who is* perverse in his
ways despises Him.

3 In the mouth of a fool *is* a rod
of pride,
But the lips of the wise will
preserve them.

4 Where no oxen *are,* the trough
is clean;
But much increase *comes* by
the strength of an ox.

5 A faithful witness does not lie,
But a false witness will utter
lies.

6 A scoffer seeks wisdom and
does not *find it,*
But knowledge *is* easy to him
who understands.

7 Go from the presence of a
foolish man,
When you do not perceive *in
him* the lips of knowledge.

8 The wisdom of the prudent *is*
to understand his way,
But the folly of fools *is* deceit.

9 Fools mock at sin,
But among the upright *there is*
favor.

10 The heart knows its own
bitterness,
And a stranger does not share
its joy.

11 The house of the wicked will be
overthrown,
But the tent of the upright will
flourish.

12 There is a way *that seems* right
to a man,
But its end *is* the way of death.

13 Even in laughter the heart may
sorrow,
And the end of mirth *may be*
grief.

13:23 ªLiterally *what is swept away*

God loves you when you are wrong. That is what gives you the power to right the
wrongs you've made. He wants desperately to heal the aching heart that has believed the lies of life.

14 The backslider in heart will be
    filled with his own ways,
    But a good man *will be satisfied*
    from above.*a*

15 The simple believes every
    word,
    But the prudent considers well
    his steps.
16 A wise *man* fears and departs
    from evil,
    But a fool rages and is self-
    confident.
17 A quick-tempered *man* acts
    foolishly,
    And a man of wicked
    intentions is hated.
18 The simple inherit folly,
    But the prudent are crowned
    with knowledge.
19 The evil will bow before the
    good,
    And the wicked at the gates of
    the righteous.

20 The poor *man* is hated even by
    his own neighbor,
    But the rich *has* many friends.
21 He who despises his neighbor
    sins;
    But he who has mercy on the
    poor, happy *is* he.
22 Do they not go astray who
    devise evil?
    But mercy and truth *belong* to
    those who devise good.

23 In all labor there is profit,
    But idle chatter*a* *leads* only to
    poverty.

24 The crown of the wise is their
    riches,
    But the foolishness of fools *is*
    folly.

25 A true witness delivers souls,
    But a deceitful *witness* speaks
    lies.

26 In the fear of the LORD *there is*
    strong confidence,
    And His children will have a
    place of refuge.
27 The fear of the LORD *is* a
    fountain of life,
    To turn *one* away from the
    snares of death.

28 In a multitude of people *is* a
    king's honor,
    But in the lack of people *is* the
    downfall of a prince.

29 *He who is* slow to wrath has
    great understanding,
    But *he who is* impulsive*a* exalts
    folly.

30 A sound heart *is* life to the
    body,
    But envy *is* rottenness to the
    bones.

31 He who oppresses the poor
    reproaches his Maker,
    But he who honors Him has
    mercy on the needy.

32 The wicked is banished in his
    wickedness,
    But the righteous has a refuge
    in his death.

33 Wisdom rests in the heart of
    him who has understanding,
    But *what is* in the heart of fools
    is made known.

34 Righteousness exalts a nation,
    But sin *is* a reproach to *any*
    people.

35 The king's favor *is* toward a
    wise servant,
    But his wrath *is against* him
    who causes shame.

15 A soft answer turns away
    wrath,
    But a harsh word stirs up
    anger.
2   The tongue of the wise uses
    knowledge rightly,
    But the mouth of fools pours
    forth foolishness.

3   The eyes of the LORD *are* in
    every place,
    Keeping watch on the evil and
    the good.

4   A wholesome tongue *is* a tree
    of life,
    But perverseness in it breaks
    the spirit.

5   A fool despises his father's
    instruction,

14:14 *a*Literally *from above himself*   14:23 *a*Literally *talk of the lips*   14:29 *a*Literally *short of spirit*

Gospel
Pearls

But he who receives correction is prudent.

6 In the house of the righteous there is much treasure,
But in the revenue of the wicked is trouble.

7 The lips of the wise disperse knowledge,
But the heart of the fool does not do so.

8 The sacrifice of the wicked is an abomination to the LORD,
But the prayer of the upright is His delight.

9 The way of the wicked is an abomination to the LORD,
But He loves him who follows righteousness.

10 Harsh discipline is for him who forsakes the way,
And he who hates correction will die.

11 Hell[a] and Destruction[b] are before the LORD;
So how much more the hearts of the sons of men.

12 A scoffer does not love one who corrects him,
Nor will he go to the wise.

13 A merry heart makes a cheerful countenance,
But by sorrow of the heart the spirit is broken.

14 The heart of him who has understanding seeks knowledge,
But the mouth of fools feeds on foolishness.

15 All the days of the afflicted are evil,
But he who is of a merry heart has a continual feast.

16 Better is a little with the fear of the LORD,
Than great treasure with trouble.

17 Better is a dinner of herbs[a] where love is,
Than a fatted calf with hatred.

18 A wrathful man stirs up strife,
But he who is slow to anger allays contention.

19 The way of the lazy man is like a hedge of thorns,
But the way of the upright is a highway.

20 A wise son makes a father glad,
But a foolish man despises his mother.

21 Folly is joy to him who is destitute of discernment,
But a man of understanding walks uprightly.

22 Without counsel, plans go awry,
But in the multitude of counselors they are established.

23 A man has joy by the answer of his mouth,
And a word spoken in due season, how good it is!

24 The way of life winds upward for the wise,
That he may turn away from hell[a] below.

25 The LORD will destroy the house of the proud,
But He will establish the boundary of the widow.

26 The thoughts of the wicked are an abomination to the LORD,
But the words of the pure are pleasant.

27 He who is greedy for gain troubles his own house,
But he who hates bribes will live.

28 The heart of the righteous studies how to answer,
But the mouth of the wicked pours forth evil.

29 The LORD is far from the wicked,
But He hears the prayer of the righteous.

30 The light of the eyes rejoices the heart,

15:11 [a]Or Sheol   [b]Hebrew Abaddon   15:17 [a]Or vegetables   15:24 [a]Or Sheol

God's arms are outstretched. He is waiting for you in the secret place. He will not fail you. Rise up with a quickened pulse and a gleaming eye. He is all yours, and it is all good.

And a good report makes the bones healthy.[a]

31 The ear that hears the rebukes of life
Will abide among the wise.

32 He who disdains instruction despises his own soul,
But he who heeds rebuke gets understanding.

33 The fear of the Lord *is* the instruction of wisdom,
And before honor *is* humility.

16 The preparations of the heart *belong* to man,
But the answer of the tongue *is* from the Lord.

2 All the ways of a man *are* pure in his own eyes,
But the Lord weighs the spirits.

3 Commit your works to the Lord,
And your thoughts will be established.

4 The Lord has made all for Himself,
Yes, even the wicked for the day of doom.

5 Everyone proud in heart *is* an abomination to the Lord;
Though they join forces,[a] none will go unpunished.

6 In mercy and truth Atonement is provided for iniquity;
And by the fear of the Lord *one* departs from evil.

7 When a man's ways please the Lord,
He makes even his enemies to be at peace with him.

8 Better *is* a little with righteousness,
Than vast revenues without justice.

9 A man's heart plans his way,
But the Lord directs his steps.

10 Divination *is* on the lips of the king;
His mouth must not transgress in judgment.

11 Honest weights and scales *are* the Lord's;
All the weights in the bag *are* His work.

12 *It is* an abomination for kings to commit wickedness,
For a throne is established by righteousness.

13 Righteous lips *are* the delight of kings,
And they love him who speaks *what is* right.

14 As messengers of death *is* the king's wrath,
But a wise man will appease it.

15 In the light of the king's face *is* life,
And his favor *is* like a cloud of the latter rain.

16 How much better to get wisdom than gold!
And to get understanding is to be chosen rather than silver.

17 The highway of the upright *is* to depart from evil;
He who keeps his way preserves his soul.

18 Pride *goes* before destruction,
And a haughty spirit before a fall.

19 Better *to be* of a humble spirit with the lowly,
Than to divide the spoil with the proud.

20 He who heeds the word wisely will find good,
And whoever trusts in the Lord, happy *is* he.

21 The wise in heart will be called prudent,
And sweetness of the lips increases learning.

22 Understanding *is* a wellspring of life to him who has it.
But the correction of fools *is* folly.

23 The heart of the wise teaches his mouth,
And adds learning to his lips.

15:30 *a*Literally *fat*   16:5 *a*Literally *hand in hand*

Gospel Pearls

24 Pleasant words *are like* a
honeycomb,
Sweetness to the soul and
health to the bones.

25 There is a way *that seems* right
to a man,
But its end *is* the way of death.

26 The person who labors, labors
for himself,
For his *hungry* mouth drives
him *on.*

27 An ungodly man digs up evil,
And *it is* on his lips like a
burning fire.

28 A perverse man sows strife,
And a whisperer separates the
best of friends.

29 A violent man entices his
neighbor,
And leads him in a way *that
is* not good.

30 He winks his eye to devise
perverse things;
He purses his lips *and* brings
about evil.

31 The silver-haired head *is* a
crown of glory,
If it is found in the way of
righteousness.

32 *He who is* slow to anger *is*
better than the mighty,
And he who rules his spirit
than he who takes a city.

33 The lot is cast into the lap,
But its every decision *is* from
the LORD.

17 Better *is* a dry morsel with
quietness,
Than a house full of feasting[a]
with strife.

2 A wise servant will rule over a
son who causes shame,
And will share an inheritance
among the brothers.

3 The refining pot *is* for silver
and the furnace for gold,
But the LORD tests the hearts.

4 An evildoer gives heed to false
lips;
A liar listens eagerly to a
spiteful tongue.

5 He who mocks the poor
reproaches his Maker;
He who is glad at calamity will
not go unpunished.

6 Children's children *are* the
crown of old men,
And the glory of children *is*
their father.

7 Excellent speech is not
becoming to a fool,
Much less lying lips to a prince.

8 A present *is* a precious stone
in the eyes of its possessor;
Wherever he turns, he
prospers.

9 He who covers a transgression
seeks love,
But he who repeats a matter
separates friends.

10 Rebuke is more effective for a
wise *man*
Than a hundred blows on a
fool.

11 An evil *man* seeks only
rebellion;
Therefore a cruel messenger
will be sent against him.

12 Let a man meet a bear robbed
of her cubs,
Rather than a fool in his folly.

13 Whoever rewards evil for good,
Evil will not depart from his
house.

14 The beginning of strife *is like*
releasing water;
Therefore stop contention
before a quarrel starts.

15 He who justifies the wicked,
and he who condemns the
just,
Both of them alike *are* an
abomination to the LORD.

16 Why *is there* in the hand of a
fool the purchase price of
wisdom,
Since *he has* no heart *for it?*

17 A friend loves at all times,
And a brother is born for
adversity.

17:1 *a*Or *sacrificial meals*

*H*e is not the kind of Father who would deny a good thing to you. If He is trying to
wrench a little sin toy out of your hand, it is because He knows it will eventually
destroy you, your children or your self-esteem. Let it go.

That's What Friends Are For

Proverbs 17:17

When Mary was expecting the baby who would turn out to be the Savior of the world, she paid a visit to her cousin Elizabeth, who was also pregnant. Her child was to be the forerunner of the Messiah. The two women came together to share their stories and to encourage each other. After Mary arrived, the Bible says that Elizabeth's baby leaped in her womb and she was filled with the Holy Spirit (see Luke 1:41).

When you stop working against other women and come together like Mary and Elizabeth, the things you had stopped believing God for will start leaping in your spirit again. Your babies will leap in your wombs, and the power of the Lord Jesus will do a new thing in your life.

If you are a woman who has had a dream and sensed a promise, reach out to God. Every woman who knows there is another woman inside who hasn't come forth can call out to God, and He will reveal that inner woman. He will replace what was stolen by your suffering and shame. He will take back from the enemy all that was swallowed up in your history. To accomplish this, He may provide a partner of the heart—a sister in Christ.

Don't be surprised if Satan attempts to spoil your plans. He can cause you to doubt your sister's motives. He can plant all kinds of bitter seeds in your relationship. He can even make you jealous of her prayer power. But God is greater. He will build you up in His Spirit so that when you come together, you will be able to cast down the enemy and trample him under your feet.

Jesus Himself said, "If two of you agree on earth concerning anything that they ask, it will be done for them by My Father in heaven. For where two or three are gathered together in My name, I am there in the midst of them" (Matthew 18:19, 20).

God wants to bring sisters together. Every Mary needs an Elizabeth. Stop your bickering and your badmouthing. Drop your guns and your gossip. Throw down your verbal swords and the walls you've built around yourself for protection. God put something in your sister that you need, and He put something in you that she needs. When you come together for prayer and mutual support, powerful things can happen.

18 A man devoid of understanding
　　shakes hands in a pledge,
　　And becomes surety for his
　　friend.

19 He who loves transgression
　　loves strife,
　　And he who exalts his gate
　　seeks destruction.

20 He who has a deceitful heart
　　finds no good,
　　And he who has a perverse
　　tongue falls into evil.

21 He who begets a scoffer *does
　　so* to his sorrow,
　　And the father of a fool has no
　　joy.

22 A merry heart does good, *like*
　　medicine,*ᵃ*
　　But a broken spirit dries the
　　bones.

23 A wicked *man* accepts a bribe
　　behind the back*ᵃ*
　　To pervert the ways of justice.

24 Wisdom *is* in the sight of him
　　who has understanding,
　　But the eyes of a fool *are* on
　　the ends of the earth.

25 A foolish son *is* a grief to his
　　father,
　　And bitterness to her who bore
　　him.

26 Also, to punish the righteous *is*
　　not good,
　　Nor to strike princes for *their*
　　uprightness.

27 He who has knowledge spares
　　his words,
　　And a man of understanding is
　　of a calm spirit.

28 Even a fool is counted wise
　　when he holds his peace;
　　When he shuts his lips, *he is
　　considered* perceptive.

18 A man who isolates himself
　　seeks his own desire;
　　He rages against all wise
　　judgment.

2 A fool has no delight in
　　understanding,
But in expressing his own
　　heart.

3 When the wicked comes,
　　contempt comes also;
　　And with dishonor *comes*
　　reproach.

4 The words of a man's mouth
　　are deep waters;
　　The wellspring of wisdom *is* a
　　flowing brook.

5 *It is* not good to show partiality
　　to the wicked,
　　Or to overthrow the righteous
　　in judgment.

6 A fool's lips enter into
　　contention,
　　And his mouth calls for blows.

7 A fool's mouth *is* his
　　destruction,
　　And his lips *are* the snare of his
　　soul.

8 The words of a talebearer *are*
　　like tasty trifles,*ᵃ*
　　And they go down into the
　　inmost body.

9 He who is slothful in his work
　　Is a brother to him who is a
　　great destroyer.

10 The name of the Lᴏʀᴅ *is* a
　　strong tower;
　　The righteous run to it and are
　　safe.

11 The rich man's wealth *is* his
　　strong city,
　　And like a high wall in his own
　　esteem.

12 Before destruction the heart of
　　a man is haughty,
　　And before honor *is* humility.

13 He who answers a matter
　　before he hears *it,*
　　It *is* folly and shame to him.

14 The spirit of a man will sustain
　　him in sickness,
　　But who can bear a broken
　　spirit?

15 The heart of the prudent
　　acquires knowledge,
　　And the ear of the wise seeks
　　knowledge.

17:22 *ᵃOr makes medicine even better* 　17:23 *ᵃLiterally from the bosom* 　18:8 *ᵃA Jewish tradition reads
wounds.*

*E*very time you resist temptation, whether that temptation is an extramarital affair
or the temptation to be critical and rude to others, you will see that the Father has
rewards for accomplishments.

16 A man's gift makes room for
him,
And brings him before great
men.

17 The first *one* to plead his cause
seems right,
Until his neighbor comes and
examines him.

18 Casting lots causes contentions
to cease,
And keeps the mighty apart.

19 A brother offended *is harder to
win* than a strong city,
And contentions *are* like the
bars of a castle.

20 A man's stomach shall be
satisfied from the fruit of his
mouth;
From the produce of his lips he
shall be filled.

21 Death and life *are* in the power
of the tongue,
And those who love it will eat
its fruit.

22 *He who* finds a wife finds a
good *thing*,
And obtains favor from the
LORD.

23 The poor *man* uses entreaties,
But the rich answers roughly.

24 A man *who has* friends must
himself be friendly,[a]
But there is a friend *who* sticks
closer than a brother.

19 Better *is* the poor who walks in
his integrity
Than *one who is* perverse in his
lips, and is a fool.

2 Also it is not good *for* a soul
to be without knowledge,
And he sins who hastens with
his feet.

3 The foolishness of a man twists
his way,
And his heart frets against the
LORD.

4 Wealth makes many friends,
But the poor is separated from
his friend.

5 A false witness will not go
unpunished,
And *he who* speaks lies will not
escape.

6 Many entreat the favor of the
nobility,
And every man *is* a friend to
one who gives gifts.

7 All the brothers of the poor
hate him;
How much more do his friends
go far from him!
He may pursue *them with*
words, *yet* they abandon
him.

8 He who gets wisdom loves his
own soul;
He who keeps understanding
will find good.

9 A false witness will not go
unpunished,
And *he who* speaks lies shall
perish.

10 Luxury is not fitting for a fool,
Much less for a servant to rule
over princes.

11 The discretion of a man makes
him slow to anger,
And his glory *is* to overlook a
transgression.

12 The king's wrath *is* like the
roaring of a lion,
But his favor *is* like dew on the
grass.

13 A foolish son *is* the ruin of his
father,
And the contentions of a wife
are a continual dripping.

14 Houses and riches *are* an
inheritance from fathers,
But a prudent wife *is* from the
LORD.

15 Laziness casts *one* into a deep
sleep,
And an idle person will suffer
hunger.

16 He who keeps the
commandment keeps his
soul,

18:24 [a]Following Greek manuscripts, Targum, Syriac, and Vulgate; Masoretic Text reads *may come to ruin*

Go quickly into His presence; climb upon His knee; lay your head on His breast. Cry
if you must, but talk to Him. Let Him cleanse you of sin and purge you of pride. He
loves you just as much when He says no as He does when He says yes.

A Good Thing

Proverbs 18:22

How many single women do you know who are almost consumed by the desire to get married? There are so many women who are longing for a relationship they are not ready to receive. If you are going to walk with God, you must understand something: *Timing is everything.* When the Lord has prepared the right man for you and you for him, and that man shows up at the right time, you must be sure that you are in the right place with the right perspective to receive all that God wants to release to you.

Read Proverbs 18:22. The Bible says that "He who finds a wife finds a good thing, and obtains favor from the LORD." Often, because of old issues you haven't dealt with or old wounds that haven't healed, you may find yourself wandering around in a stupor somewhere, emotionally unprepared for a healthy relationship. You will not be able to be the "good thing" you were meant to be in your husband's life. Unless you are healed and whole, your man will not feel that He's enjoying the Lord's favor in his relationship with you.

Ladies, men do not exist to bring the favor of the Lord to your lives, either. You find the favor of the Lord by being the woman He created you to be—by breaking the chains with which the devil had you bound, by knowing the Lord passionately and intimately, by walking in His power and worshiping Him with your life. You must take responsibility for making yourself, with God's help, the good thing He wants you to be.

Notice that the Bible does not say that whoever finds a *woman* finds a good thing. It says that whoever finds a *wife* finds a good thing. But how can you be a wife before you have a husband? You become a wife in your spirit. Yes, you become a wife in your spirit before you ever get married. That way, you will be prepared to be a wife in other ways. If you are not prepared, if you do not have the anointing of the Holy Spirit, you will find yourself dragging your ugly past into what could be the most beautiful relationship of your life.

My sister, do what you need to do in order to be whole. The Lord heals. The Lord mends. The Lord restores. And He will make you a woman of strength and grace and wholeness. When He has done His work in you, you will be such a good thing.

But he who is careless*ᵃ* of his ways will die.

17 He who has pity on the poor lends to the LORD,
And He will pay back what he has given.

18 Chasten your son while there is hope,
And do not set your heart on his destruction.*ᵃ*

19 *A man of* great wrath will suffer punishment;
For if you rescue *him,* you will have to do it again.

20 Listen to counsel and receive instruction,
That you may be wise in your latter days.

21 There are many plans in a man's heart,
Nevertheless the LORD's counsel—that will stand.

22 What is desired in a man is kindness,
And a poor man is better than a liar.

23 The fear of the LORD *leads* to life,
And *he who has it* will abide in satisfaction;
He will not be visited with evil.

24 A lazy *man* buries his hand in the bowl,*ᵃ*
And will not so much as bring it to his mouth again.

25 Strike a scoffer, and the simple will become wary;
Rebuke one who has understanding, *and* he will discern knowledge.

26 He who mistreats *his* father *and* chases away *his* mother
Is a son who causes shame and brings reproach.

27 Cease listening to instruction, my son,
And you will stray from the words of knowledge.

28 A disreputable witness scorns justice,
And the mouth of the wicked devours iniquity.

29 Judgments are prepared for scoffers,
And beatings for the backs of fools.

20 Wine *is* a mocker,
Strong drink *is* a brawler,
And whoever is led astray by it is not wise.

2 The wrath*ᵃ* of a king *is* like the roaring of a lion;
Whoever provokes him to anger sins *against* his own life.

3 *It is* honorable for a man to stop striving,
Since any fool can start a quarrel.

4 The lazy *man* will not plow because of winter;
He will beg during harvest and *have* nothing.

5 Counsel in the heart of man *is like* deep water,
But a man of understanding will draw it out.

6 Most men will proclaim each his own goodness,
But who can find a faithful man?

7 The righteous *man* walks in his integrity;
His children *are* blessed after him.

8 A king who sits on the throne of judgment
Scatters all evil with his eyes.

9 Who can say, "I have made my heart clean,
I am pure from my sin"?

10 Diverse weights *and* diverse measures,
They *are* both alike, an abomination to the LORD.

19:16 *ᵃ*Literally *despises,* figurative of recklessness or carelessness   19:18 *ᵃ*Literally *to put him to death;* a Jewish tradition reads *his crying.*   19:24 *ᵃ*Septuagint and Syriac read *bosom;* Targum and Vulgate read *armpit.*   20:2 *ᵃ*Literally *fear* or *terror* which is produced by the king's wrath

Gospel Pearls

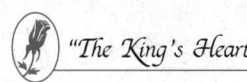

11 Even a child is known by his
deeds,
Whether what he does *is* pure
and right.

12 The hearing ear and the seeing
eye,
The LORD has made them both.

13 Do not love sleep, lest you
come to poverty;
Open your eyes, *and* you will
be satisfied with bread.

14 "*It is* good for nothing,"ᵃ cries
the buyer;
But when he has gone his way,
then he boasts.

15 There is gold and a multitude
of rubies,
But the lips of knowledge *are*
a precious jewel.

16 Take the garment of one who
is surety *for* a stranger,
And hold it as a pledge *when*
it is for a seductress.

17 Bread gained by deceit *is* sweet
to a man,
But afterward his mouth will be
filled with gravel.

18 Plans are established by
counsel;
By wise counsel wage war.

19 He who goes about *as* a
talebearer reveals secrets;
Therefore do not associate with
one who flatters with his lips.

20 Whoever curses his father or
his mother,
His lamp will be put out in deep
darkness.

21 An inheritance gained hastily
at the beginning
Will not be blessed at the end.

22 Do not say, "I will recompense
evil";
Wait for the LORD, and He will
save you.

23 Diverse weights *are* an
abomination to the LORD,

And dishonest scales *are* not
good.

24 A man's steps *are* of the LORD;
How then can a man
understand his own way?

25 *It is* a snare for a man to devote
rashly *something as* holy,
And afterward to reconsider
his vows.

26 A wise king sifts out the
wicked,
And brings the threshing wheel
over them.

27 The spirit of a man *is* the lamp
of the LORD,
Searching all the inner depths
of his heart.ᵃ

28 Mercy and truth preserve the
king,
And by lovingkindness he
upholds his throne.

29 The glory of young men *is* their
strength,
And the splendor of old men *is*
their gray head.

30 Blows that hurt cleanse away
evil,
As *do* stripes the inner depths
of the heart.ᵃ

21 The king's heart *is* in the hand
of the LORD,
Like the rivers of water; He
turns it wherever He wishes.

2 Every way of a man *is* right in
his own eyes,
But the LORD weighs the hearts.

3 To do righteousness and justice
Is more acceptable to the LORD
than sacrifice.

4 A haughty look, a proud heart,
And the plowingᵃ of the wicked
are sin.

5 The plans of the diligent *lead*
surely to plenty,
But *those of* everyone *who is*
hasty, surely to poverty.

20:14 ᵃLiterally *evil, evil*   20:27 ᵃLiterally *the rooms of the belly*   20:30 ᵃLiterally *the rooms of the belly*   21:4 ᵃOr *lamp*

It is important to remember that for every person, there will be a problem. Even more importantly, for every problem, our God has a prescription!

6 Getting treasures by a lying
tongue
Is the fleeting fantasy of those
who seek death.*a*

7 The violence of the wicked will
destroy them,*a*
Because they refuse to do
justice.

8 The way of a guilty man *is*
perverse;*a*
But *as for* the pure, his work
is right.

9 Better to dwell in a corner of a
housetop,
Than in a house shared with a
contentious woman.

10 The soul of the wicked desires
evil;
His neighbor finds no favor in
his eyes.

11 When the scoffer is punished,
the simple is made wise;
But when the wise is instructed,
he receives knowledge.

12 The righteous *God* wisely
considers the house of the
wicked,
Overthrowing the wicked for
their wickedness.

13 Whoever shuts his ears to the
cry of the poor
Will also cry himself and not
be heard.

14 A gift in secret pacifies anger,
And a bribe behind the back,*a*
strong wrath.

15 *It is* a joy for the just to do
justice,
But destruction *will come* to the
workers of iniquity.

16 A man who wanders from the
way of understanding
Will rest in the assembly of the
dead.

17 He who loves pleasure *will be*
a poor man;

He who loves wine and oil will
not be rich.

18 The wicked *shall be* a ransom
for the righteous,
And the unfaithful for the
upright.

19 Better to dwell in the
wilderness,
Than with a contentious and
angry woman.

20 *There is* desirable treasure,
And oil in the dwelling of the
wise,
But a foolish man squanders it.

21 He who follows righteousness
and mercy
Finds life, righteousness and
honor.

22 A wise *man* scales the city of
the mighty,
And brings down the trusted
stronghold.

23 Whoever guards his mouth and
tongue
Keeps his soul from troubles.

24 A proud *and* haughty *man*—
"Scoffer" *is* his name;
He acts with arrogant pride.

25 The desire of the lazy *man* kills
him,
For his hands refuse to labor.

26 He covets greedily all day long,
But the righteous gives and
does not spare.

27 The sacrifice of the wicked *is*
an abomination;
How much more *when* he
brings it with wicked intent!

28 A false witness shall perish,
But the man who hears *him* will
speak endlessly.

29 A wicked man hardens his
face,
But *as for* the upright, he
establishes*a* his way.

21:6 *a*Septuagint reads *Pursue vanity on the snares of death;* Vulgate reads *Is vain and foolish, and shall
stumble on the snares of death;* Targum reads *They shall be destroyed, and they shall fall who seek
death.* 21:7 *a*Literally *drag them away* 21:8 *a*Or *The way of a man is perverse and strange.*
21:14 *a*Literally *in the bosom* 21:29 *a*Qere and Septuagint read *understands.*

Gospel
Pearls

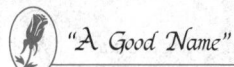

30 *There is* no wisdom or
understanding
Or counsel against the LORD.

31 The horse *is* prepared for the
day of battle,
But deliverance *is* of the LORD.

22 A *good* name is to be chosen
rather than great riches,
Loving favor rather than silver
and gold.

2 The rich and the poor have this
in common,
The LORD *is* the maker of them
all.

3 A prudent *man* foresees evil
and hides himself,
But the simple pass on and are
punished.

4 By humility *and* the fear of the
LORD
Are riches and honor and life.

5 Thorns *and* snares *are* in the
way of the perverse;
He who guards his soul will be
far from them.

6 Train up a child in the way he
should go,
And when he is old he will not
depart from it.

7 The rich rules over the poor,
And the borrower *is* servant to
the lender.

8 He who sows iniquity will reap
sorrow,
And the rod of his anger will
fail.

9 He who has a generous eye will
be blessed,
For he gives of his bread to the
poor.

10 Cast out the scoffer, and
contention will leave;
Yes, strife and reproach will
cease.

11 He who loves purity of heart
And has grace on his lips,
The king *will be* his friend.

12 The eyes of the LORD preserve
knowledge,

But He overthrows the words
of the faithless.

13 The lazy *man* says, "There is
a lion outside!
I shall be slain in the streets!"

14 The mouth of an immoral
woman *is* a deep pit;
He who is abhorred by the
LORD will fall there.

15 Foolishness *is* bound up in the
heart of a child;
The rod of correction will drive
it far from him.

16 He who oppresses the poor to
increase his *riches,*
And he who gives to the rich,
will surely *come* to poverty.

17 Incline your ear and hear the
words of the wise,
And apply your heart to my
knowledge;

18 For *it is* a pleasant thing if you
keep them within you;
Let them all be fixed upon your
lips,

19 So that your trust may be in the
LORD;
I have instructed you today,
even you.

20 Have I not written to you
excellent things
Of counsels and knowledge,

21 That I may make you know the
certainty of the words of
truth,
That you may answer words of
truth
To those who send to you?

22 Do not rob the poor because he
is poor,
Nor oppress the afflicted at the
gate;

23 For the LORD will plead their
cause,
And plunder the soul of those
who plunder them.

24 Make no friendship with an
angry man,
And with a furious man do not
go,

25 Lest you learn his ways
And set a snare for your soul.

26 Do not be one of those who
shakes hands in a pledge,

One of the first things a hurting person needs to do is break the habit of using other people as a narcotic to numb the dull aching of an inner void. The more you medicate the symptoms, the less chance you have of allowing God to heal you.

One of those who is surety for debts;

27 If you have nothing *with which* to pay,
Why should he take away your bed from under you?

28 Do not remove the ancient landmark
Which your fathers have set.

29 Do you see a man *who* excels in his work?
He will stand before kings;
He will not stand before unknown *men.*

23 When you sit down to eat with a ruler,
Consider carefully what *is* before you;

2 And put a knife to your throat
If you *are* a man given to appetite.

3 Do not desire his delicacies,
For they *are* deceptive food.

4 Do not overwork to be rich;
Because of your own understanding, cease!

5 Will you set your eyes on that which is not?
For *riches* certainly make themselves wings;
They fly away like an eagle *toward* heaven.

6 Do not eat the bread of a miser,[a]
Nor desire his delicacies;

7 For as he thinks in his heart, so *is* he.
"Eat and drink!" he says to you,
But his heart is not with you.

8 The morsel you have eaten, you will vomit up,
And waste your pleasant words.

9 Do not speak in the hearing of a fool,
For he will despise the wisdom of your words.

10 Do not remove the ancient landmark,
Nor enter the fields of the fatherless;

11 For their Redeemer *is* mighty;
He will plead their cause against you.

12 Apply your heart to instruction,
And your ears to words of knowledge.

13 Do not withhold correction from a child,
For *if* you beat him with a rod, he will not die.

14 You shall beat him with a rod,
And deliver his soul from hell.[a]

15 My son, if your heart is wise,
My heart will rejoice—indeed, I myself;

16 Yes, my inmost being will rejoice
When your lips speak right things.

17 Do not let your heart envy sinners,
But *be zealous* for the fear of the LORD all the day;

18 For surely there is a hereafter,
And your hope will not be cut off.

19 Hear, my son, and be wise;
And guide your heart in the way.

20 Do not mix with winebibbers,
Or with gluttonous eaters of meat;

21 For the drunkard and the glutton will come to poverty,
And drowsiness will clothe *a man* with rags.

22 Listen to your father who begot you,
And do not despise your mother when she is old.

23 Buy the truth, and do not sell *it,*
Also wisdom and instruction and understanding.

24 The father of the righteous will greatly rejoice,
And he who begets a wise *child* will delight in him.

25 Let your father and your mother be glad,
And let her who bore you rejoice.

23:6 [a]Literally *one who has an evil eye*   23:14 [a]Or *Sheol*

Sometimes we esteem others more important than ourselves. We always become the martyr. It is wonderful to be self-sacrificing but watch out for self-disdain!

You Are What You Think

Proverbs 23:7

We need to continually purge our thoughts because *we become what we think*. It is not just the lust that we must clean out, but also low self-esteem, pride, arrogance, hidden jealousy, and much more. To use a medical metaphor, the mind is the "placenta" of the spirit man. It holds and nurtures the seeds it has been impregnated with until their time of delivery. If you have the seed of a thought in your mind and you don't want the child that that seed will produce, your only recourse is to abort it before it is carried to full term.

If you don't want depression, why do you continue to rehearse those same sickening thoughts that led you there in the first place? You don't need a famous minister to lay hands on you to win the battle over your mind! What you need is the inner discipline required of all disciples to resist evil thoughts before they become evidenced in your life. Abort those seeds that are causing you to miss the mark and press on!

My sister, your mind is continually being reconstructed by the Holy Spirit. He wants to put new thoughts within you that will enable you to soar above your past and fill you with a great sense of destiny.

Most of us come to the Lord damaged—dead spiritually, damaged emotionally, and decaying physically. When He saved you, He made your dead spirit alive. He also promised you a new body. Then He began the massive renovation necessary to repair your damaged thoughts about life, about others, and about yourself.

While we dress and smell nice outwardly, people do not hear the constant hammering and sawing going on inwardly, as the Lord works within us, trying desperately to present us as a newly constructed masterpiece fit for His use.

Beneath our pasted-on smiles and pleasant greetings, we alone hear the rumblings of the midnight shift. God is constantly excommunicating lethal thoughts that hinder us from grasping the many-faceted callings and giftings buried beneath the rubble of our minds.

We all need the Lord to help us with ourselves. We came to Him as condemned buildings, and He reopened the places that Satan thought would never be inhabited. The Holy Spirit moved in. And He brought His hammers and saws with Him.

26 My son, give me your heart,
And let your eyes observe my
ways.
27 For a harlot *is* a deep pit,
And a seductress *is* a narrow
well.
28 She also lies in wait as *for* a
victim,
And increases the unfaithful
among men.

29 Who has woe?
Who has sorrow?
Who has contentions?
Who has complaints?
Who has wounds without
cause?
Who has redness of eyes?
30 Those who linger long at the
wine,
Those who go in search of
mixed wine.
31 Do not look on the wine when
it is red,
When it sparkles in the cup,
When it swirls around
smoothly;
32 At the last it bites like a
serpent,
And stings like a viper.
33 Your eyes will see strange
things,
And your heart will utter
perverse things.
34 Yes, you will be like one who
lies down in the midst of the
sea,
Or like one who lies at the top
of the mast, *saying:*
35 "They have struck me, *but* I was
not hurt;
They have beaten me, but I did
not feel *it.*
When shall I awake, that I may
seek another *drink?*"

24 Do not be envious of evil men,
Nor desire to be with them;
2 For their heart devises
violence,
And their lips talk of
troublemaking.

3 Through wisdom a house is
built,
And by understanding it is
established;
4 By knowledge the rooms are
filled
With all precious and pleasant
riches.

5 A wise man *is* strong,
Yes, a man of knowledge
increases strength;
6 For by wise counsel you will
wage your own war,
And in a multitude of
counselors *there is* safety.

7 Wisdom *is* too lofty for a fool;
He does not open his mouth in
the gate.

8 He who plots to do evil
Will be called a schemer.
9 The devising of foolishness *is*
sin,
And the scoffer *is* an
abomination to men.

10 *If* you faint in the day of
adversity,
Your strength *is* small.

11 Deliver *those who* are drawn
toward death,
And hold back *those* stumbling
to the slaughter.
12 If you say, "Surely we did not
know this,"
Does not He who weighs the
hearts consider *it?*
He who keeps your soul, does
He *not* know *it?*
And will He *not* render to *each*
man according to his deeds?

13 My son, eat honey because *it
is* good,
And the honeycomb *which is*
sweet to your taste;
14 So *shall* the knowledge of
wisdom *be* to your soul;
If you have found *it,* there is a
prospect,
And your hope will not be cut
off.

15 Do not lie in wait, O wicked
man, against the dwelling of
the righteous;
Do not plunder his resting
place;
16 For a righteous *man* may fall
seven times
And rise again,
But the wicked shall fall by
calamity.

17 Do not rejoice when your
enemy falls,
And do not let your heart be
glad when he stumbles;

Gospel Pearls

18 Lest the LORD see *it,* and it
   displease Him,
   And He turn away His wrath
   from him.

19 Do not fret because of
   evildoers,
   Nor be envious of the wicked;
20 For there will be no prospect
   for the evil *man;*
   The lamp of the wicked will be
   put out.

21 My son, fear the LORD and the
   king;
   Do not associate with those
   given to change;
22 For their calamity will rise
   suddenly,
   And who knows the ruin those
   two can bring?

23 These *things* also *belong* to the
wise:

   It is not good to show partiality
   in judgment.
24 He who says to the wicked,
   "You *are* righteous,"
   Him the people will curse;
   Nations will abhor him.
25 But those who rebuke *the*
   wicked will have delight,
   And a good blessing will come
   upon them.

26 He who gives a right answer
   kisses the lips.

27 Prepare your outside work,
   Make it fit for yourself in the
   field;
   And afterward build your
   house.

28 Do not be a witness against
   your neighbor without cause,
   For would you deceive[a] with
   your lips?
29 Do not say, "I will do to him
   just as he has done to me;
   I will render to the man
   according to his work."

30 I went by the field of the lazy
   man,
   And by the vineyard of the man
   devoid of understanding;
31 And there it was, all overgrown
   with thorns;

Its surface was covered with
   nettles;
   Its stone wall was broken
   down.
32 When I saw *it,* I considered *it*
   well;
   I looked on *it and* received
   instruction:
33 A little sleep, a little slumber,
   A little folding of the hands to
   rest;
34 So shall your poverty come *like*
   a prowler,
   And your need like an armed
   man.

25 These also *are* proverbs of Solomon which the men of Hezekiah king of Judah copied:

2 *It is* the glory of God to conceal
   a matter,
   But the glory of kings *is* to
   search out a matter.

3 *As* the heavens for height and
   the earth for depth,
   So the heart of kings *is*
   unsearchable.

4 Take away the dross from
   silver,
   And it will go to the silversmith
   for jewelry.
5 Take away the wicked from
   before the king,
   And his throne will be
   established in righteousness.

6 Do not exalt yourself in the
   presence of the king,
   And do not stand in the place
   of the great;
7 For *it is* better that he say to
   you,
   "Come up here,"
   Than that you should be put
   lower in the presence of the
   prince,
   Whom your eyes have seen.

8 Do not go hastily to court;
   For what will you do in the end,
   When your neighbor has put
   you to shame?
9 Debate your case with your
   neighbor,
   And do not disclose the secret
   to another;

24:28 [a]Septuagint and Vulgate read *Do not deceive.*

---

*D*ivorce is not merely separating; it is the tearing apart of what was once joined
together. Whenever something is torn, it does not heal easily. But Jesus can heal
a broken or torn heart!

10   Lest he who hears *it* expose
        your shame,
        And your reputation be ruined.

11   A word fitly spoken *is like*
        apples of gold
        In settings of silver.
12   *Like* an earring of gold and an
        ornament of fine gold
        Is a wise rebuker to an obedient
        ear.

13   Like the cold of snow in time
        of harvest
        Is a faithful messenger to those
        who send him,
        For he refreshes the soul of his
        masters.

14   Whoever falsely boasts of
        giving
        Is like clouds and wind without
        rain.

15   By long forbearance a ruler is
        persuaded,
        And a gentle tongue breaks a
        bone.

16   Have you found honey?
        Eat only as much as you need,
        Lest you be filled with it and
        vomit.

17   Seldom set foot in your
        neighbor's house,
        Lest he become weary of you
        and hate you.

18   A man who bears false witness
        against his neighbor
        Is like a club, a sword, and a
        sharp arrow.

19   Confidence in an unfaithful
        man in time of trouble
        Is like a bad tooth and a foot
        out of joint.

20   *Like* one who takes away a
        garment in cold weather,
        And like vinegar on soda,
        Is one who sings songs to a
        heavy heart.

21   If your enemy is hungry, give
        him bread to eat;
        And if he is thirsty, give him
        water to drink;
22   For *so* you will heap coals of
        fire on his head,
        And the LORD will reward you.

23   The north wind brings forth
        rain,
        And a backbiting tongue an
        angry countenance.

24   *It is* better to dwell in a corner
        of a housetop,
        Than in a house shared with a
        contentious woman.

25   *As* cold water to a weary soul,
        So *is* good news from a far
        country.

26   A righteous *man* who falters
        before the wicked
        Is like a murky spring and a
        polluted well.

27   *It is* not good to eat much
        honey;
        So to seek one's own glory *is
        not* glory.

28   Whoever *has* no rule over his
        own spirit
        Is like a city broken down,
        without walls.

26 As snow in summer and rain
        in harvest,
        So honor is not fitting for a fool.

2   Like a flitting sparrow, like a
        flying swallow,
        So a curse without cause shall
        not alight.

3   A whip for the horse,
        A bridle for the donkey,
        And a rod for the fool's back.
4   Do not answer a fool according
        to his folly,
        Lest you also be like him.
5   Answer a fool according to his
        folly,
        Lest he be wise in his own eyes.
6   He who sends a message by the
        hand of a fool
        Cuts off *his own* feet *and* drinks
        violence.
7   *Like* the legs of the lame that
        hang limp
        Is a proverb in the mouth of
        fools.
8   Like one who binds a stone in
        a sling
        Is he who gives honor to a fool.
9   *Like* a thorn *that* goes into the
        hand of a drunkard
        Is a proverb in the mouth of
        fools.

10 The great *God* who formed
   everything
   Gives the fool *his* hire and the
   transgressor *his* wages.^a
11 As a dog returns to his own
   vomit,
   So a fool repeats his folly.
12 Do you see a man wise in his
   own eyes?
   There is more hope for a fool
   than for him.

13 The lazy *man* says, "*There is*
   a lion in the road!
   A fierce lion *is* in the streets!"
14 *As* a door turns on its hinges,
   So *does* the lazy *man* on his
   bed.
15 The lazy *man* buries his hand
   in the bowl;^a
   It wearies him to bring it back
   to his mouth.
16 The lazy *man is* wiser in his
   own eyes
   Than seven men who can
   answer sensibly.

17 He who passes by *and* meddles
   in a quarrel not his own
   Is like one who takes a dog by
   the ears.

18 Like a madman who throws
   firebrands, arrows, and
   death,
19 *Is* the man *who* deceives his
   neighbor,
   And says, "I was only joking!"

20 Where *there is* no wood, the
   fire goes out;
   And where *there is* no
   talebearer, strife ceases.
21 *As* charcoal *is* to burning coals,
   and wood to fire,
   So *is* a contentious man to
   kindle strife.
22 The words of a talebearer *are*
   like tasty trifles,
   And they go down into the
   inmost body.

23 Fervent lips with a wicked
   heart
   Are like earthenware covered
   with silver dross.

24 He who hates, disguises *it* with
   his lips,
   And lays up deceit within
   himself;

25 When he speaks kindly, do not
   believe him,
   For *there are* seven
   abominations in his heart;
26 *Though his* hatred is covered
   by deceit,
   His wickedness will be
   revealed before the
   assembly.

27 Whoever digs a pit will fall into
   it,
   And he who rolls a stone will
   have it roll back on him.

28 A lying tongue hates *those who
   are* crushed by it,
   And a flattering mouth works
   ruin.

27 Do not boast about tomorrow,
   For you do not know what a
   day may bring forth.

2 Let another man praise you,
   and not your own mouth;
   A stranger, and not your own
   lips.

3 A stone *is* heavy and sand *is*
   weighty,
   But a fool's wrath *is* heavier
   than both of them.

4 Wrath *is* cruel and anger a
   torrent,
   But who *is* able to stand before
   jealousy?

5 Open rebuke *is* better
   Than love carefully concealed.

6 Faithful *are* the wounds of a
   friend,
   But the kisses of an enemy *are*
   deceitful.

7 A satisfied soul loathes the
   honeycomb,
   But to a hungry soul every
   bitter thing *is* sweet.

8 Like a bird that wanders from
   its nest
   Is a man who wanders from his
   place.

9 Ointment and perfume delight
   the heart,
   And the sweetness of a man's

26:10 ^aThe Hebrew is difficult; ancient and modern translators differ greatly.   26:15 ^aCompare 19:24

*O*ne of the great healing balms of the Holy Spirit is forgiveness. To forgive is to break
the link between you and your past.

friend *gives delight* by hearty counsel.

10 Do not forsake your own friend
   or your father's friend,
   Nor go to your brother's house
   in the day of your calamity;
   Better *is* a neighbor nearby
   than a brother far away.

11 My son, be wise, and make my
   heart glad,
   That I may answer him who
   reproaches me.

12 A prudent *man* foresees evil
   and hides himself;
   The simple pass on *and* are
   punished.

13 Take the garment of him who
   is surety for a stranger,
   And hold it in pledge *when* he
   is surety for a seductress.

14 He who blesses his friend with
   a loud voice, rising early in
   the morning,
   It will be counted a curse to
   him.

15 A continual dripping on a very
   rainy day
   And a contentious woman are
   alike;

16 Whoever restrains her
   restrains the wind,
   And grasps oil with his right
   hand.

17 *As* iron sharpens iron,
   So a man sharpens the
   countenance of his friend.

18 Whoever keeps the fig tree will
   eat its fruit;
   So he who waits on his master
   will be honored.

19 As in water face *reflects* face,
   So a man's heart *reveals* the
   man.

20 Hell*ᵃ* and Destruction*ᵇ* are
   never full;
   So the eyes of man are never
   satisfied.

21 The refining pot *is* for silver
   and the furnace for gold,
   And a man *is valued* by what
   others say of him.

22 Though you grind a fool in a
   mortar with a pestle along
   with crushed grain,
   Yet his foolishness will not
   depart from him.

23 Be diligent to know the state of
   your flocks,
   And attend to your herds;

24 For riches *are* not forever,
   Nor does a crown *endure* to all
   generations.

25 *When* the hay is removed, and
   the tender grass shows itself,
   And the herbs of the mountains
   are gathered in,

26 The lambs *will provide* your
   clothing,
   And the goats the price of a
   field;

27 *You shall have* enough goats'
   milk for your food,
   For the food of your household,
   And the nourishment of your
   maidservants.

28 The wicked flee when no one
   pursues,
   But the righteous are bold as a
   lion.

2 Because of the transgression of
   a land, many *are* its princes;
   But by a man of understanding
   and knowledge
   Right will be prolonged.

3 A poor man who oppresses the
   poor
   Is like a driving rain which
   leaves no food.

4 Those who forsake the law
   praise the wicked,
   But such as keep the law
   contend with them.

5 Evil men do not understand
   justice,
   But those who seek the LORD
   understand all.

6 Better *is* the poor who walks in
   his integrity
   Than one perverse *in his* ways,
   though he *be* rich.

27:20 ᵃOr *Sheol*   ᵇHebrew *Abaddon*

Gospel
Pearls

7 Whoever keeps the law *is* a
    discerning son,
But a companion of gluttons
    shames his father.

8 One who increases his
    possessions by usury and
    extortion
Gathers it for him who will pity
    the poor.

9 One who turns away his ear
    from hearing the law,
Even his prayer *is* an
    abomination.

10 Whoever causes the upright to
    go astray in an evil way,
He himself will fall into his own
    pit;
But the blameless will inherit
    good.

11 The rich man *is* wise in his own
    eyes,
But the poor who has
    understanding searches him
    out.

12 When the righteous rejoice,
    there is great glory;
But when the wicked arise,
    men hide themselves.

13 He who covers his sins will not
    prosper,
But whoever confesses and
    forsakes *them* will have
    mercy.

14 Happy *is* the man who is
    always reverent,
But he who hardens his heart
    will fall into calamity.

15 *Like* a roaring lion and a
    charging bear
Is a wicked ruler over poor
    people.

16 A ruler who lacks
    understanding *is* a great
    oppressor,
But he who hates covetousness
    will prolong *his* days.

17 A man burdened with
    bloodshed will flee into a pit;
Let no one help him.

18 Whoever walks blamelessly
    will be saved,

But *he who is* perverse *in his*
    ways will suddenly fall.

19 He who tills his land will have
    plenty of bread,
But he who follows frivolity
    will have poverty enough!

20 A faithful man will abound
    with blessings,
But he who hastens to be rich
    will not go unpunished.

21 To show partiality *is* not good,
Because for a piece of bread a
    man will transgress.

22 A man with an evil eye hastens
    after riches,
And does not consider that
    poverty will come upon him.

23 He who rebukes a man will find
    more favor afterward
Than he who flatters with the
    tongue.

24 Whoever robs his father or his
    mother,
And says, "*It is* no
    transgression,"
The same *is* companion to a
    destroyer.

25 He who is of a proud heart stirs
    up strife,
But he who trusts in the LORD
    will be prospered.

26 He who trusts in his own heart
    is a fool,
But whoever walks wisely will
    be delivered.

27 He who gives to the poor will
    not lack,
But he who hides his eyes will
    have many curses.

28 When the wicked arise, men
    hide themselves;
But when they perish, the
    righteous increase.

29 He who is often rebuked, *and*
    hardens *his* neck,
Will suddenly be destroyed,
    and that without remedy.

2 When the righteous are in
    authority, the people rejoice;

*R*egardless of who you hold responsible, there is no healing in blame! When you
begin to realize that your past does not necessarily dictate the outcome of your
future, then you can release the hurt.

But when a wicked *man* rules,
the people groan.

3 Whoever loves wisdom makes
his father rejoice,
But a companion of harlots
wastes *his* wealth.

4 The king establishes the land
by justice,
But he who receives bribes
overthrows it.

5 A man who flatters his
neighbor
Spreads a net for his feet.

6 By transgression an evil man is
snared,
But the righteous sings and
rejoices.

7 The righteous considers the
cause of the poor,
But the wicked does not
understand *such* knowledge.

8 Scoffers set a city aflame,
But wise *men* turn away wrath.

9 *If* a wise man contends with a
foolish man,
Whether *the fool* rages or
laughs, *there is* no peace.

10 The bloodthirsty hate the
blameless,
But the upright seek his well-
being.*a*

11 A fool vents all his feelings,*a*
But a wise *man* holds them
back.

12 If a ruler pays attention to lies,
All his servants *become*
wicked.

13 The poor *man* and the
oppressor have this in
common:
The LORD gives light to the eyes
of both.

14 The king who judges the poor
with truth,
His throne will be established
forever.

15 The rod and rebuke give
wisdom,
But a child left *to himself*
brings shame to his mother.

16 When the wicked are
multiplied, transgression
increases;
But the righteous will see their
fall.

17 Correct your son, and he will
give you rest;
Yes, he will give delight to your
soul.

18 Where *there is* no revelation,*a*
the people cast off restraint;
But happy *is* he who keeps the
law.

19 A servant will not be corrected
by mere words;
For though he understands, he
will not respond.

20 Do you see a man hasty in his
words?
There is more hope for a fool
than for him.

21 He who pampers his servant
from childhood
Will have him as a son in the
end.

22 An angry man stirs up strife,
And a furious man abounds in
transgression.

23 A man's pride will bring him
low,
But the humble in spirit will
retain honor.

24 Whoever is a partner with a
thief hates his own life;
He swears to tell the truth,*a* but
reveals nothing.

25 The fear of man brings a snare,
But whoever trusts in the LORD
shall be safe.

26 Many seek the ruler's favor,
But justice for man *comes* from
the LORD.

29:10 *a*Literally *soul*   29:11 *a*Literally *spirit*   29:18 *a*Or *prophetic vision*   29:24 *a*Literally *hears the adjuration*

Gospel
Pearls

27 An unjust man *is* an
   abomination to the righteous,
   And *he who is* upright in the
   way *is* an abomination to the
   wicked.

30 The words of Agur the son of
   Jakeh, *his* utterance. This man
   declared to Ithiel—to Ithiel and Ucal:

2 Surely I *am* more stupid than
   any man,
   And do not have the
   understanding of a man.
3 I neither learned wisdom
   Nor have knowledge of the
   Holy One.

4 Who has ascended into heaven,
   or descended?
   Who has gathered the wind in
   His fists?
   Who has bound the waters in
   a garment?
   Who has established all the
   ends of the earth?
   What *is* His name, and what *is*
   His Son's name,
   If you know?

5 Every word of God *is* pure;
   He *is* a shield to those who put
   their trust in Him.
6 Do not add to His words,
   Lest He rebuke you, and you
   be found a liar.

7 Two *things* I request of You
   (Deprive me not before I die):
8 Remove falsehood and lies far
   from me;
   Give me neither poverty nor
   riches—
   Feed me with the food allotted
   to me;
9 Lest I be full and deny *You,*
   And say, "Who *is* the LORD?"
   Or lest I be poor and steal,
   And profane the name of my
   God.

10 Do not malign a servant to his
   master,
   Lest he curse you, and you be
   found guilty.

11 *There is* a generation *that*
   curses its father,
   And does not bless its mother.

12 *There is* a generation *that is*
   pure in its own eyes,
   Yet is not washed from its
   filthiness.
13 *There is* a generation—oh, how
   lofty are their eyes!
   And their eyelids are lifted up.
14 *There is* a generation whose
   teeth *are like* swords,
   And whose fangs *are like*
   knives,
   To devour the poor from off the
   earth,
   And the needy from *among*
   men.

15 The leech has two daughters—
   Give *and* Give!

   There are three *things that* are
   never satisfied,
   Four never say, "Enough!":
16 The grave,*a*
   The barren womb,
   The earth *that* is not satisfied
   with water—
   And the fire never says,
   "Enough!"

17 The eye *that* mocks *his* father,
   And scorns obedience to *his*
   mother,
   The ravens of the valley will
   pick it out,
   And the young eagles will eat
   it.

18 There are three *things which*
   are too wonderful for me,
   Yes, four *which* I do not
   understand:
19 The way of an eagle in the air,
   The way of a serpent on a rock,
   The way of a ship in the midst
   of the sea,
   And the way of a man with a
   virgin.

20 This *is* the way of an adulterous
   woman:
   She eats and wipes her mouth,
   And says, "I have done no
   wickedness."

21 For three *things* the earth is
   perturbed,
   Yes, for four it cannot bear up:
22 For a servant when he reigns,
   A fool when he is filled with
   food,

30:16 *a*Or *Sheol*

*U*ncover the wounds in God's presence and allow Him to gently heal the injuries.
One woman found healing in the hem of His garment. There is a balm in Gilead!

23 A hateful *woman* when she is
　　married,
　　And a maidservant who
　　succeeds her mistress.

24 There are four *things which* are
　　little on the earth,
　　But they *are* exceedingly wise:
25 The ants *are* a people not
　　strong,
　　Yet they prepare their food in
　　the summer;
26 The rock badgers*ᵃ* are a feeble
　　folk,
　　Yet they make their homes in
　　the crags;
27 The locusts have no king,
　　Yet they all advance in ranks;
28 The spider*ᵃ* skillfully grasps
　　with its hands,
　　And it is in kings' palaces.

29 There are three *things which*
　　are majestic in pace,
　　Yes, four *which* are stately in
　　walk:
30 A lion, *which is* mighty among
　　beasts
　　And does not turn away from
　　any;
31 A greyhound,*ᵃ*
　　A male goat also,
　　And a king *whose* troops *are*
　　with him.*ᵇ*

32 If you have been foolish in
　　exalting yourself,
　　Or if you have devised evil, *put*
　　your hand on *your* mouth.
33 For *as* the churning of milk
　　produces butter,
　　And wringing the nose
　　produces blood,
　　So the forcing of wrath
　　produces strife.

31 The words of King Lemuel, the
　　utterance which his mother
taught him:

2 What, my son?
　　And what, son of my womb?
　　And what, son of my vows?
3 Do not give your strength to
　　women,
　　Nor your ways to that which
　　destroys kings.

4 *It is* not for kings, O Lemuel,
　　It is not for kings to drink wine,
　　Nor for princes intoxicating
　　drink;
5 Lest they drink and forget the
　　law,
　　And pervert the justice of all
　　the afflicted.
6 Give strong drink to him who
　　is perishing,
　　And wine to those who are
　　bitter of heart.
7 Let him drink and forget his
　　poverty,
　　And remember his misery no
　　more.

8 Open your mouth for the
　　speechless,
　　In the cause of all *who are*
　　appointed to die.*ᵃ*
9 Open your mouth, judge
　　righteously,
　　And plead the cause of the poor
　　and needy.
10 Who*ᵃ* can find a virtuous*ᵇ* wife?
　　For her worth *is* far above
　　rubies.
11 The heart of her husband safely
　　trusts her;
　　So he will have no lack of gain.
12 She does him good and not evil
　　All the days of her life.
13 She seeks wool and flax,
　　And willingly works with her
　　hands.
14 She is like the merchant ships,
　　She brings her food from afar.
15 She also rises while it is yet
　　night,
　　And provides food for her
　　household,
　　And a portion for her
　　maidservants.
16 She considers a field and buys
　　it;
　　From her profits she plants a
　　vineyard.
17 She girds herself with strength,
　　And strengthens her arms.
18 She perceives that her
　　merchandise *is* good,
　　And her lamp does not go out
　　by night.
19 She stretches out her hands to
　　the distaff,
　　And her hand holds the
　　spindle.

30:26 *ᵃ*Or *hyraxes*　　30:28 *ᵃ*Or *lizard*　　30:31 *ᵃ*Exact identity unknown　*ᵇ*A Jewish tradition reads *a king*
against whom there is no uprising.　　31:8 *ᵃ*Literally *sons of passing away*　　31:10 *ᵃ*Verses 10 through
31 are an alphabetic acrostic in Hebrew (compare Psalm 119).　*ᵇ*Literally *a wife of valor*, in the sense of
all forms of excellence

We frame our references around our own experiences. If those experiences are
distorted, our ability to comprehend spiritual truths can be off center.

The Modern Woman

Proverbs 31

We all make choices. Some very vibrant and intelligent women trade fame and fortune for peace and quiet. It is a matter of preference. Do not allow peer pressure to force you into a role that makes you uncomfortable. You have a right, as a daughter of the living God, to press toward goals and promises that are as unique and diverse as you can imagine.

Even animals have a strategy for the future. It is crucial that you also prepare a strategy by assessing the environment in which you must survive. Then, begin to make preparations for the changing seasons of life. If the ant has to do it, so do you.

The daughter who aspires to a lofty goal that she is capable of managing emotionally and intellectually should not be restricted purely on the basis of her sex. Likewise, within the gender, other women should not try to belittle her because she has chosen to express her gifting in an arena that may not be traditional in her society. Need I remind you that the virtuous woman in Proverbs 31 was a businesswoman who owned property, produced products, sold goods, and cared for her family? She was a modern woman.

Do not allow even well-meaning Christians to box you in with their personal preferences. You do not have to consult any ladies' luncheon group or sewing circle. A single woman is submitted to her God. A married woman is submitted to her husband. Beyond the submission outlined in Scripture, tell everyone else to stop playing God with your future. In spiritual matters, whether you are married or unmarried, submit to your pastor (see Hebrews 13:17).

Let's look back again at these precious daughters of Zelophehad who went to Moses to challenge the fairness of the "good ol' boys" policy that was in effect (see Numbers 27:1–11). Their actions suggested, "We are women, but we are blessed women." In other words, "We are not cursed, and we have the right to walk as any other blessed person walks." They did it without male bashing or disrespect to authority. They went through proper channels, but bless God, they went through. You don't want to be rebellious, because "rebellion is as the sin of witchcraft" (see 1 Samuel 15:23). Nevertheless, you still want to get what the Father has for you to inherit.

You are a modern woman. You are free to be everything God has gifted you to be. Do not allow the world to define what your womanhood should be. Know God's call to your life and obey it. There has never been a time when women have been more free. So explore, express, and enjoy the opportunities He sets before you.

20 She extends her hand to the
poor,
Yes, she reaches out her hands
to the needy.
21 She is not afraid of snow for
her household,
For all her household *is* clothed
with scarlet.
22 She makes tapestry for herself;
Her clothing *is* fine linen and
purple.
23 Her husband is known in the
gates,
When he sits among the elders
of the land.
24 She makes linen garments and
sells *them,*
And supplies sashes for the
merchants.
25 Strength and honor *are* her
clothing;
She shall rejoice in time to
come.

26 She opens her mouth with
wisdom,
And on her tongue *is* the law
of kindness.
27 She watches over the ways of
her household,
And does not eat the bread of
idleness.
28 Her children rise up and call
her blessed;
Her husband *also,* and he
praises her:
29 "Many daughters have done
well,
But you excel them all."
30 Charm *is* deceitful and beauty
is passing,
But a woman *who* fears the
Lord, she shall be praised.
31 Give her of the fruit of her
hands,
And let her own works praise
her in the gates.

The Book of

ECCLESIASTES

1 The words of the Preacher, the
son of David, king in Jerusalem.

2 "Vanity*a* of vanities," says the
Preacher;
"Vanity of vanities, all *is*
vanity."

3 What profit has a man from all
his labor
In which he toils under the sun?
4 *One* generation passes away,
and *another* generation
comes;
But the earth abides forever.
5 The sun also rises, and the sun
goes down,
And hastens to the place where
it arose.
6 The wind goes toward the
south,
And turns around to the north;
The wind whirls about
continually,
And comes again on its circuit.
7 All the rivers run into the sea,
Yet the sea *is* not full;

To the place from which the
rivers come,
There they return again.
8 All things *are* full of labor;
Man cannot express *it.*
The eye is not satisfied with
seeing,
Nor the ear filled with hearing.

9 That which has been *is* what
will be,
That which *is* done is what will
be done,
And *there is* nothing new under
the sun.
10 Is there anything of which it
may be said,
"See, this *is* new"?
It has already been in ancient
times before us.
11 *There is* no remembrance of
former *things,*
Nor will there be any
remembrance of *things* that
are to come
By *those* who will come
after.

1:2 *a*Or *Absurdity, Frustration, Futility, Nonsense;* and so throughout this book

12 I, the Preacher, was king over Israel in Jerusalem. 13 And I set my heart to seek and search out by wisdom concerning all that is done under heaven; this burdensome task God has given to the sons of man, by which they may be exercised. 14 I have seen all the works that are done under the sun; and indeed, all *is* vanity and grasping for the wind.

15 *What is* crooked cannot be
made straight,
And what is lacking cannot be
numbered.

16 I communed with my heart, saying, "Look, I have attained greatness, and have gained more wisdom than all who were before me in Jerusalem. My heart has understood great wisdom and knowledge." 17 And I set my heart to know wisdom and to know madness and folly. I perceived that this also is grasping for the wind.

18 For in much wisdom *is* much
grief,
And he who increases
knowledge increases sorrow.

2 I said in my heart, "Come now, I will test you with mirth; therefore enjoy pleasure"; but surely, this also *was* vanity. 2 I said of laughter— "Madness!"; and of mirth, "What does it accomplish?" 3 I searched in my heart *how* to gratify my flesh with wine, while guiding my heart with wisdom, and how to lay hold on folly, till I might see what *was* good for the sons of men to do under heaven all the days of their lives.

4 I made my works great, I built myself houses, and planted myself vineyards. 5 I made myself gardens and orchards, and I planted all *kinds* of fruit trees in them. 6 I made myself water pools from which to water the growing trees of the grove. 7 I acquired male and female servants, and had servants born in my house. Yes, I had greater possessions of herds and flocks than all who were in Jerusalem before me. 8 I also gathered for myself silver and gold and the special treasures of kings and of the provinces. I acquired male and female singers, the delights of the sons of

men, *and* musical instruments[a] of all kinds.

9 So I became great and excelled more than all who were before me in Jerusalem. Also my wisdom remained with me.

10 Whatever my eyes desired I did
not keep from them.
I did not withhold my heart
from any pleasure,
For my heart rejoiced in all my
labor;
And this was my reward from
all my labor.
11 Then I looked on all the works
that my hands had done
And on the labor in which I had
toiled;
And indeed all *was* vanity and
grasping for the wind.
There was no profit under the
sun.
12 Then I turned myself to
consider wisdom and
madness and folly;
For what *can* the man *do* who
succeeds the king?—
Only what he has already done.
13 Then I saw that wisdom excels
folly
As light excels darkness.
14 The wise man's eyes *are* in his
head,
But the fool walks in darkness.
Yet I myself perceived
That the same event happens
to them all.

15 So I said in my heart,
"As it happens to the fool,
It also happens to me,
And why was I then more
wise?"
Then I said in my heart,
"This also *is* vanity."
16 For *there is* no more
remembrance of the wise
than of the fool forever,
Since all that now *is* will be
forgotten in the days to come.
And how does a wise *man* die?
As the fool!

17 Therefore I hated life because the work that was done under the sun *was* distressing to me, for all *is* vanity and grasping for the wind. 18 Then I hated all my labor in which I had toiled under the sun, be-

2:8 ᵃExact meaning unknown

*W*hat do you do when you have been poorly programmed by life's events? I've got good news! You can re-program your mind through the Word of God.

cause I must leave it to the man who will come after me. 19 And who knows whether he will be wise or a fool? Yet he will rule over all my labor in which I toiled and in which I have shown myself wise under the sun. This also *is* vanity. 20 Therefore I turned my heart and despaired of all the labor in which I had toiled under the sun. 21 For there is a man whose labor *is* with wisdom, knowledge, and skill; yet he must leave his heritage to a man who has not labored for it. This also *is* vanity and a great evil. 22 For what has man for all his labor, and for the striving of his heart with which he has toiled under the sun? 23 For all his days *are* sorrowful, and his work burdensome; even in the night his heart takes no rest. This also *is* vanity.

24 Nothing *is* better for a man *than* that he should eat and drink, and *that* his soul should enjoy good in his labor. This also, I saw, was from the hand of God. 25 For who can eat, or who can have enjoyment, more than I?*a* 26 For *God* gives wisdom and knowledge and joy to a man who *is* good in His sight; but to the sinner He gives the work of gathering and collecting, that he may give to *him who is* good before God. This also *is* vanity and grasping for the wind.

3 To everything *there is* a season,
A time for every purpose
under heaven:

2 A time to be born,
And a time to die;
A time to plant,
And a time to pluck *what is*
planted;
3 A time to kill,
And a time to heal;
A time to break down,
And a time to build up;
4 A time to weep,
And a time to laugh;
A time to mourn,
And a time to dance;
5 A time to cast away stones,
And a time to gather stones;
A time to embrace,
And a time to refrain from
embracing;
6 A time to gain,
And a time to lose;

A time to keep,
And a time to throw away;
7 A time to tear,
And a time to sew;
A time to keep silence,
And a time to speak;
8 A time to love,
And a time to hate;
A time of war,
And a time of peace.

9 What profit has the worker from that in which he labors? 10 I have seen the God-given task with which the sons of men are to be occupied. 11 He has made everything beautiful in its time. Also He has put eternity in their hearts, except that no one can find out the work that God does from beginning to end.

12 I know that nothing *is* better for them than to rejoice, and to do good in their lives, 13 and also that every man should eat and drink and enjoy the good of all his labor—it *is* the gift of God.

14 I know that whatever God does,
It shall be forever.
Nothing can be added to it,
And nothing taken from it.
God does *it*, that men should
fear before Him.
15 That which is has already been,
And what is to be has already
been;
And God requires an account
of what is past.

16 Moreover I saw under the sun:

In the place of judgment,
Wickedness *was* there;
And *in* the place of
righteousness,
Iniquity *was* there.

17 I said in my heart,

"God shall judge the righteous
and the wicked,
For *there is* a time there for
every purpose and for every
work."

18 I said in my heart, "Concerning the condition of the sons of men, God tests them, that they may see that they themselves are *like* animals."

2:25 *a*Following Masoretic Text, Targum, and Vulgate; some Hebrew manuscripts, Septuagint, and Syriac read *without Him.*

*T*he glory of God is manifested only when there is a balance between grace and truth. Religion doesn't transform. Legalism doesn't transform.

The Last Laugh

Ecclesiastes 3:1

*I*n the summer of her life, all was well with Sarah. At that time she knew little about Jehovah, her husband's God. She only knew that she was in love with a wonderful man. She was the luckiest woman in Ur!

Soon the giddy exuberance of summer began to fade as she wrestled with the harsh realities of following a dreamer to an unknown land. But what was really troubling her was not the strife between the relatives nor the fighting herdsmen; it was her barren womb. When someone said she would have a baby, Sara laughed. "If I'm going to get a miracle, God had better hurry!"

I want to warn you about setting your own watch. God's time is not your time. He may not come when you want Him to, but He will come right on time. Twice it is mentioned that Sarah laughed. The first time she laughed *at* God—at the impossibility of His promise. In the wintertime of her life, she laughed *with* God—because He had been faithful to perform His word.

In between these powerful moments, everything in Sarah was tested. Her love for her husband gave her the courage to leave home, but her love for God brought forth the promised seed. After all, what good is it to appreciate what God has given if we do not appreciate the God who gave it?

Sarah learned that even her beloved husband was only a man. He failed her in a moment of fear and self-indulgence. But God did not! He brought her through in safety, then rewarded her for her faith.

When Hebrews 11 lists the patriarchs and their awesome faith, this winter woman's name is included. Abraham is mentioned for the kind of faith that would leave home and look for a city whose builder and maker is God (see verse 10). But Sarah's faith caused an old woman's barren womb to conceive!

She didn't take faith classes. She just went through her winter clutching the warm hand of a loving God who would not fail. So when you hear Sarah laughing the last time, she is laughing with God. She is holding her baby to her now-wrinkled breast. She understands the miracles that come only to winter women.

19 For what happens to the sons of men also happens to animals; one thing befalls them: as one dies, so dies the other. Surely, they all have one breath; man has no advantage over animals, for all *is* vanity. 20 All go to one place: all are from the dust, and all return to dust. 21 Who knows the spirit of the sons of men, which goes upward, and the spirit of the animal, which goes down to the earth?*a* 22 So I perceived that nothing *is* better than that a man should rejoice in his own works, for that *is* his heritage. For who can bring him to see what will happen after him?

4 Then I returned and considered all the oppression that is done under the sun:

> And look! The tears of the
> oppressed,
> But they have no comforter—
> On the side of their oppressors
> *there is* power,
> But they have no comforter.
> 2 Therefore I praised the dead
> who were already dead,
> More than the living who are
> still alive.
> 3 Yet, better than both *is he* who
> has never existed,
> Who has not seen the evil work
> that is done under the sun.

4 Again, I saw that for all toil and every skillful work a man is envied by his neighbor. This also *is* vanity and grasping for the wind.

> 5 The fool folds his hands
> And consumes his own flesh.
> 6 Better a handful *with* quietness
> Than both hands full, *together
> with* toil and grasping for the
> wind.

7 Then I returned, and I saw vanity under the sun:

> 8 There is one alone, without
> companion:
> He has neither son nor brother.
> Yet *there is* no end to all his
> labors,
> Nor is his eye satisfied with
> riches.

> *But he never asks,*
> "For whom do I toil and deprive
> myself of good?"
> This also *is* vanity and a grave
> misfortune.

> 9 Two *are* better than one,
> Because they have a good
> reward for their labor.
> 10 For if they fall, one will lift up
> his companion.
> But woe to him *who is* alone
> when he falls,
> For *he has* no one to help him
> up.
> 11 Again, if two lie down together,
> they will keep warm;
> But how can one be warm
> *alone?*
> 12 Though one may be
> overpowered by another, two
> can withstand him.
> And a threefold cord is not
> quickly broken.

> 13 Better a poor and wise youth
> Than an old and foolish king
> who will be admonished no
> more.
> 14 For he comes out of prison to
> be king,
> Although he was born poor in
> his kingdom.
> 15 I saw all the living who walk
> under the sun;
> They were with the second
> youth who stands in his
> place.
> 16 *There was* no end of all the
> people over whom he was
> made king;
> Yet those who come afterward
> will not rejoice in him.
> Surely this also *is* vanity and
> grasping for the wind.

5 Walk prudently when you go to the house of God; and draw near to hear rather than to give the sacrifice of fools, for they do not know that they do evil.

> 2 Do not be rash with your
> mouth,
> And let not your heart utter
> anything hastily before God.
> For God *is* in heaven, and you
> on earth;

3:21 *a*Septuagint, Syriac, Targum, and Vulgate read *Who knows whether the spirit . . . goes upward, and whether . . . goes downward to the earth?*

God doesn't have to punish you to heal you. Jesus has already prayed for you.

Your Very
Own Infirmity

Ecclesiastes 4:10

*E*very woman has her very own tailor-made infirmity—her place of weakness. Whoever you are, the enemy has been studying you all of your life—spying on you, checking you out, figuring out which temptation will work best on you. He's not going to bring you ice cream if you like chocolate candy. He knows your weaknesses, maybe better than you do, and he knows what is most likely to tempt you to sin, worry or doubt.

In case you haven't experienced this truth yet, let me tell you that church people are prejudiced when it comes to sin. They tend to classify sin in two categories: acceptable and unacceptable. If they can relate to your sin—if they're guilty of the same thing—it will be labeled acceptable. If not—if your weakness is not the same as theirs—it will be unacceptable. In fact, you'll probably be condemned without benefit of judge, jury, or trial.

We all tend to gravitate toward people who have similar infirmities. And there's a danger in that. If we hang around people who are just like we are, we become comfortable calling right wrong or thinking the abnormal is normal. We feed the sin in them and they feed the sin in us. We help their weakness continue, and they help ours. Instead of healing one another, we make one another worse. In the mercy of God's plan, He brings people into our lives who are strong in areas where we are weak, and people who are weak in areas where we are strong. That way we can truly help one another and bring balance to the body of Christ.

When Satan sends his demons out to oppress you, they already have a full portfolio on you. They know exactly which buttons to push and exactly which order to push them in. They know your particular infirmities. Those demons know if your father never liked you and if your mother was partial to your older sister. If your boyfriend rejected you and started going with your best friend. If a teacher said you were stupid and would never amount to anything. Those demons have an entire profile worked up on you so that they won't have to waste time experimenting on which temptations are going to work best. They know just where you are vulnerable.

In the beautiful old King James Version of the Bible, Jesus said to the woman with a spirit of infirmity, "Woman, thou art loosed from thine infirmity" (Luke 13:12). Jesus knew exactly what was wrong with her. He knew the very weakness that had her bound up and bent over.

He knows about your infirmity, too. His word to you today is, "I'm going to loose you and set you free." Get ready for Him to do it!

Therefore let your words be
few.
3 For a dream comes through
much activity,
And a fool's voice *is known* by
his many words.

4 When you make a vow to God,
do not delay to pay it;
For *He has* no pleasure in fools.
Pay what you have vowed—
5 Better not to vow than to vow
and not pay.

6 Do not let your mouth cause your flesh to sin, nor say before the messenger *of God* that it *was* an error. Why should God be angry at your excuse[a] and destroy the work of your hands? 7 For in the multitude of dreams and many words *there is* also vanity. But fear God.

8 If you see the oppression of the poor, and the violent perversion of justice and righteousness in a province, do not marvel at the matter; for high official watches over high official, and higher officials are over them.

9 Moreover the profit of the land is for all; *even* the king is served from the field.

10 He who loves silver will not be
satisfied with silver;
Nor he who loves abundance,
with increase.
This also *is* vanity.

11 When goods increase,
They increase who eat them;
So what profit have the owners
Except to see *them* with their
eyes?

12 The sleep of a laboring man *is*
sweet,
Whether he eats little or much;
But the abundance of the rich
will not permit him to sleep.

13 There is a severe evil *which* I
have seen under the sun:
Riches kept for their owner to
his hurt.

14 But those riches perish through
misfortune;
When he begets a son, *there is*
nothing in his hand.

15 As he came from his mother's
womb, naked shall he return,
To go as he came;
And he shall take nothing from
his labor
Which he may carry away in
his hand.

16 And this also *is* a severe evil—
Just exactly as he came, so
shall he go.
And what profit has he who has
labored for the wind?

17 All his days he also eats in
darkness,
And *he has* much sorrow and
sickness and anger.

18 Here is what I have seen: *It is* good and fitting *for one* to eat and drink, and to enjoy the good of all his labor in which he toils under the sun all the days of his life which God gives him; for it *is* his heritage. 19 As for every man to whom God has given riches and wealth, and given him power to eat of it, to receive his heritage and rejoice in his labor—this *is* the gift of God. 20 For he will not dwell unduly on the days of his life, because God keeps *him* busy with the joy of his heart.

6 There is an evil which I have seen under the sun, and it *is* common among men: 2 A man to whom God has given riches and wealth and honor, so that he lacks nothing for himself of all he desires; yet God does not give him power to eat of it, but a foreigner consumes it. This *is* vanity, and it *is* an evil affliction. 3 If a man begets a hundred *children* and lives many years, so that the days of his years are many, but his soul is not satisfied with goodness, or indeed he has no burial, I say *that* a stillborn child *is* better than he— 4 for it comes in vanity and departs in darkness, and its name is covered with darkness. 5 Though it has not seen the sun or known *anything,* this has more rest than that man, 6 even if he lives a thousand years twice—but has not seen goodness. Do not all go to one place?

7 All the labor of man *is* for his
mouth,
And yet the soul is not satisfied.

5:6 aLiterally *voice*

Gospel
Pearls

8 For what more has the wise
   man than the fool?
   What does the poor man have,
   Who knows *how* to walk before
   the living?
9 Better *is* the sight of the eyes
   than the wandering of desire.
   This also *is* vanity and grasping
   for the wind.

10 Whatever one is, he has been
    named already,
    For it is known that he *is* man;
    And he cannot contend with
    Him who is mightier than he.
11 Since there are many things
    that increase vanity,
    How *is* man the better?

12 For who knows what *is* good for
man in life, all the days of his vain
life which he passes like a shadow?
Who can tell a man what will happen
after him under the sun?

7 A good name *is* better than
   precious ointment,
   And the day of death than the
   day of one's birth;
2 Better to go to the house of
   mourning
   Than to go to the house of
   feasting,
   For that *is* the end of all men;
   And the living will take *it* to
   heart.
3 Sorrow *is* better than laughter,
   For by a sad countenance the
   heart is made better.
4 The heart of the wise *is* in the
   house of mourning,
   But the heart of fools *is* in the
   house of mirth.
5 *It is* better to hear the rebuke
   of the wise
   Than for a man to hear the
   song of fools.
6 For like the crackling of thorns
   under a pot,
   So *is* the laughter of the fool.
   This also is vanity.
7 Surely oppression destroys a
   wise *man's* reason,
   And a bribe debases the heart.

8 The end of a thing *is* better than
   its beginning;
   The patient in spirit *is* better
   than the proud in spirit.
9 Do not hasten in your spirit to
   be angry,

For anger rests in the bosom of
   fools.
10 Do not say,
    "Why were the former days
    better than these?"
    For you do not inquire wisely
    concerning this.

11 Wisdom *is* good with an
    inheritance,
    And profitable to those who see
    the sun.
12 For wisdom *is* a defense *as*
    money *is* a defense,
    But the excellence of
    knowledge *is that* wisdom
    gives life to those who have
    it.

13 Consider the work of God;
    For who can make straight
    what He has made crooked?
14 In the day of prosperity be
    joyful,
    But in the day of adversity
    consider:
    Surely God has appointed the
    one as well as the other,
    So that man can find out
    nothing *that will come* after
    him.

15 I have seen everything in my
days of vanity:

There is a just *man* who
    perishes in his righteousness,
    And there is a wicked *man* who
    prolongs *life* in his
    wickedness.

16 Do not be overly righteous,
    Nor be overly wise:
    Why should you destroy
    yourself?
17 Do not be overly wicked,
    Nor be foolish:
    Why should you die before
    your time?
18 *It is* good that you grasp this,
    And also not remove your hand
    from the other;
    For he who fears God will
    escape them all.

19 Wisdom strengthens the wise
    More than ten rulers of the city.

20 For *there is* not a just man on
    earth who does good
    And does not sin.

*B*elieve the Word of God and be free. Jesus our Lord was a great emancipator of the
oppressed. It does not matter whether someone has been oppressed socially, sexually or racially; our Lord is an eliminator of distinctions.

21 Also do not take to heart
everything people say,
Lest you hear your servant
cursing you.
22 For many times, also, your own
heart has known
That even you have cursed
others.

23 All this I have proved by
wisdom.
I said, "I will be wise";
But it *was* far from me.
24 As for that which is far off and
exceedingly deep,
Who can find it out?
25 I applied my heart to know,
To search and seek out wisdom
and the reason *of things,*
To know the wickedness of
folly,
Even of foolishness *and*
madness.
26 And I find more bitter than
death
The woman whose heart *is*
snares and nets,
Whose hands *are* fetters.
He who pleases God shall
escape from her,
But the sinner shall be trapped
by her.

27 "Here is what I have found,"
says the Preacher,
"*Adding* one thing to the other
to find out the reason,
28 Which my soul still seeks but I
cannot find:
One man among a thousand I
have found,
But a woman among all these
I have not found.
29 Truly, this only I have found:
That God made man upright,
But they have sought out many
schemes."

8 Who *is* like a wise *man?*
And who knows the
interpretation of a thing?
A man's wisdom makes his
face shine,
And the sternness of his face
is changed.

2 I *say,* "Keep the king's commandment for the sake of your oath to
God. 3 Do not be hasty to go from
his presence. Do not take your stand

for an evil thing, for he does whatever pleases him."

4 Where the word of a king *is,*
there is power;
And who may say to him,
"What are you doing?"
5 He who keeps his command
will experience nothing
harmful;
And a wise man's heart
discerns both time and
judgment,
6 Because for every matter there
is a time and judgment,
Though the misery of man
increases greatly.
7 For he does not know what will
happen;
So who can tell him when it will
occur?
8 No one has power over the
spirit to retain the spirit,
And no one has power in the
day of death.
There is no release from that
war,
And wickedness will not
deliver those who are given
to it.

9 All this I have seen, and applied
my heart to every work that is done
under the sun: *There is* a time in
which one man rules over another to
his own hurt.
10 Then I saw the wicked buried,
who had come and gone from the
place of holiness, and they were forgotten[a] in the city where they had so
done. This also *is* vanity. 11 Because
the sentence against an evil work is
not executed speedily, therefore the
heart of the sons of men is fully set
in them to do evil. 12 Though a sinner
does evil a hundred *times,* and his
days are prolonged, yet I surely know
that it will be well with those who
fear God, who fear before Him.
13 But it will not be well with the
wicked; nor will he prolong *his* days,
which are as a shadow, because he
does not fear before God.
14 There is a vanity which occurs
on earth, that there are just *men* to
whom it happens according to the
work of the wicked; again, there are
wicked *men* to whom it happens according to the work of the righteous.
I said that this also *is* vanity.

8:10 *a*Some Hebrew manuscripts, Septuagint, and Vulgate read *praised.*

Gospel Pearls

15 So I commended enjoyment, because a man has nothing better under the sun than to eat, drink, and be merry; for this will remain with him in his labor *all* the days of his life which God gives him under the sun.

16 When I applied my heart to know wisdom and to see the business that is done on earth, even though one sees no sleep day or night, 17 then I saw all the work of God, that a man cannot find out the work that is done under the sun. For though a man labors to discover *it*, yet he will not find *it;* moreover, though a wise *man* attempts to know *it*, he will not be able to find *it*.

9 For I considered all this in my heart, so that I could declare it all: that the righteous and the wise and their works *are* in the hand of God. People know neither love nor hatred *by* anything *they see* before them. 2 All things *come* alike to all:

> One event *happens* to the righteous and the wicked;
> To the good,*ᵃ* the clean, and the unclean;
> To him who sacrifices and him who does not sacrifice.
> As is the good, so *is* the sinner;
> He who takes an oath as *he* who fears an oath.

3 This *is* an evil in all that is done under the sun: that one thing *happens* to all. Truly the hearts of the sons of men are full of evil; madness *is* in their hearts while they live, and after that *they* go to the dead. 4 But for him who is joined to all the living there is hope, for a living dog is better than a dead lion.

> 5 For the living know that they will die;
> But the dead know nothing,
> And they have no more reward,
> For the memory of them is forgotten.
> 6 Also their love, their hatred, and their envy have now perished;
> Nevermore will they have a share
> In anything done under the sun.

7 Go, eat your bread with j⌐
> And drink your wine with a merry heart;
> For God has already accepted your works.
> 8 Let your garments always be white,
> And let your head lack no oil.

9 Live joyfully with the wife whom you love all the days of your vain life which He has given you under the sun, all your days of vanity; for that *is* your portion in life, and in the labor which you perform under the sun. 10 Whatever your hand finds to do, do *it* with your might; for *there is* no work or device or knowledge or wisdom in the grave where you are going.

11 I returned and saw under the sun that—

> The race *is* not to the swift,
> Nor the battle to the strong,
> Nor bread to the wise,
> Nor riches to men of understanding,
> Nor favor to men of skill;
> But time and chance happen to them all.
> 12 For man also does not know his time:
> Like fish taken in a cruel net,
> Like birds caught in a snare,
> So the sons of men *are* snared in an evil time,
> When it falls suddenly upon them.

13 This wisdom I have also seen under the sun, and it *seemed* great to me: 14 *There was* a little city with few men in it; and a great king came against it, besieged it, and built great snares*ᵃ* around it. 15 Now there was found in it a poor wise man, and he by his wisdom delivered the city. Yet no one remembered that same poor man. 16 Then I said:

> "Wisdom *is* better than strength.
> Nevertheless the poor man's wisdom *is* despised,
> And his words are not heard.
> 17 Words of the wise, *spoken quietly, should be* heard

9:2 *ᵃ*Septuagint, Syriac, and Vulgate read *good and bad.*   9:14 *ᵃ*Septuagint, Syriac, and Vulgate read *bulwarks.*

God is no respecter of persons. He tears down barriers that would promote prejudice and separation in the Body of Christ.

Rather than the shout of a ruler
of fools.
18 Wisdom *is* better than weapons
of war;
But one sinner destroys much
good."

10 Dead flies putrefy[a] the
perfumer's ointment,
And cause it to give off a foul
odor;
So does a little folly to one
respected for wisdom *and*
honor.
2 A wise man's heart *is* at his
right hand,
But a fool's heart at his left.
3 Even when a fool walks along
the way,
He lacks wisdom,
And he shows everyone *that* he
is a fool.
4 If the spirit of the ruler rises
against you,
Do not leave your post;
For conciliation pacifies great
offenses.

5 There is an evil I have seen
under the sun,
As an error proceeding from
the ruler:
6 Folly is set in great dignity,
While the rich sit in a lowly
place.
7 I have seen servants on horses,
While princes walk on the
ground like servants.

8 He who digs a pit will fall into
it,
And whoever breaks through a
wall will be bitten by a
serpent.
9 He who quarries stones may be
hurt by them,
And he who splits wood may
be endangered by it.
10 If the ax is dull,
And one does not sharpen the
edge,
Then he must use more
strength;
But wisdom brings success.

11 A serpent may bite when *it is*
not charmed;
The babbler is no different.
12 The words of a wise man's
mouth *are* gracious,

But the lips of a fool shall
swallow him up;
13 The words of his mouth begin
with foolishness,
And the end of his talk *is* raving
madness.
14 A fool also multiplies words.
No man knows what is to be;
Who can tell him what will be
after him?
15 The labor of fools wearies
them,
For they do not even know how
to go to the city!

16 Woe to you, O land, when your
king *is* a child,
And your princes feast in the
morning!
17 Blessed *are* you, O land, when
your king *is* the son of
nobles,
And your princes feast at the
proper time—
For strength and not for
drunkenness!
18 Because of laziness the
building decays,
And through idleness of hands
the house leaks.
19 A feast is made for laughter,
And wine makes merry;
But money answers everything.

20 Do not curse the king, even in
your thought;
Do not curse the rich, even in
your bedroom;
For a bird of the air may carry
your voice,
And a bird in flight may tell the
matter.

11 Cast your bread upon the
waters,
For you will find it after many
days.
2 Give a serving to seven, and
also to eight,
For you do not know what evil
will be on the earth.

3 If the clouds are full of rain,
They empty *themselves* upon
the earth;
And if a tree falls to the south
or the north,
In the place where the tree
falls, there it shall lie.

10:1 [a]Targum and Vulgate omit *putrefy*.

Gospel
Pearls

4 He who observes the wind will
   not sow,
And he who regards the clouds
   will not reap.

5 As you do not know what *is* the
   way of the wind,[a]
Or how the bones *grow* in the
   womb of her who is with
   child,
So you do not know the works
   of God who makes
   everything.

6 In the morning sow your seed,
And in the evening do not
   withhold your hand;
For you do not know which will
   prosper,
Either this or that,
Or whether both alike *will be*
   good.

7 Truly the light is sweet,
And *it is* pleasant for the eyes
   to behold the sun;

8 But if a man lives many years
And rejoices in them all,
Yet let him remember the days
   of darkness,
For they will be many.
All that is coming *is* vanity.

9 Rejoice, O young man, in your
   youth,
And let your heart cheer you
   in the days of your youth;
Walk in the ways of your heart,
And in the sight of your eyes;
But know that for all these
God will bring you into
   judgment.

10 Therefore remove sorrow from
   your heart,
And put away evil from your
   flesh,
For childhood and youth *are*
   vanity.

12 Remember now your Creator
   in the days of your youth,
Before the difficult days come,
And the years draw near when
   you say,
"I have no pleasure in them":

2 While the sun and the light,
The moon and the stars,
Are not darkened,
And the clouds do not return
   after the rain;

3 In the day when the keepers of
   the house tremble,
And the strong men bow
   down;
When the grinders cease
   because they are few,
And those that look through
   the windows grow dim;

4 When the doors are shut in the
   streets,
And the sound of grinding is
   low;
When one rises up at the sound
   of a bird,
And all the daughters of music
   are brought low.

5 Also they are afraid of
   height,
And of terrors in the way;
When the almond tree
   blossoms,
The grasshopper is a burden,
And desire fails.
For man goes to his eternal
   home,
And the mourners go about the
   streets.

6 *Remember your Creator* before
   the silver cord is loosed,[a]
Or the golden bowl is broken,
Or the pitcher shattered at the
   fountain,
Or the wheel broken at the
   well.

7 Then the dust will return to the
   earth as it was,
And the spirit will return to
   God who gave it.

8 "Vanity of vanities," says the
   Preacher,
"All *is* vanity."

9 And moreover, because the
Preacher was wise, he still taught the
people knowledge; yes, he pondered
and sought out *and* set in order many
proverbs. 10 The Preacher sought to
find acceptable words; and *what was*
written *was* upright—words of truth.
11 The words of the wise are like
goads, and the words of scholars[a] are
like well-driven nails, given by one
Shepherd. 12 And further, my son, be
admonished by these. Of making
many books *there is* no end, and
much study *is* wearisome to the flesh.

11:5 [a]Or *spirit*   12:6 [a]Following Qere and Targum; Kethib reads *removed;* Septuagint and Vulgate read
broken.   12:11 [a]Literally *masters of assemblies*

*M*ale and female are one in Christ. Yet they are unique and that uniqueness is not
to be tampered with. Let the male be masculine and the female be feminine!

13 Let us hear the conclusion of the whole matter:

> Fear God and keep His
>   commandments,

For this is man's all.

14 For God will bring every work
       into judgment,
    Including every secret thing,
    Whether good or evil.

The

SONG OF SOLOMON

1 The song of songs, which *is* Solomon's.

2 Let him kiss me with the kisses
       of his mouth—
    For your[a] love *is* better than
       wine.
3 Because of the fragrance of
       your good ointments,
    Your name *is* ointment poured
       forth;
    Therefore the virgins love you.
4 Draw me away!

We will run after you.[a]

The king has brought me into
    his chambers.

We will be glad and rejoice in
    you.[b]

We will remember your[c] love
    more than wine.

Rightly do they love you.[d]

5 I *am* dark, but lovely,
    O daughters of Jerusalem,
    Like the tents of Kedar,
    Like the curtains of Solomon.
6 Do not look upon me, because
       I *am* dark,
    Because the sun has tanned me.
    My mother's sons were angry
       with me;
    They made me the keeper of
       the vineyards,
    But my own vineyard I have
       not kept.

7 Tell me, O you whom I love,
    Where you feed *your flock,*
    Where you make *it* rest at
       noon.
    For why should I be as one who
       veils herself[a]
    By the flocks of your
       companions?

8 If you do not know, O fairest
       among women,
    Follow in the footsteps of the
       flock,
    And feed your little goats
    Beside the shepherds' tents.
9 I have compared you, my love,
    To my filly among Pharaoh's
       chariots.
10 Your cheeks are lovely with
       ornaments,
    Your neck with chains *of gold.*

11 We will make you[a] ornaments
       of gold
    With studs of silver.

12 While the king *is* at his table,
    My spikenard sends forth its
       fragrance.
13 A bundle of myrrh *is* my
       beloved to me,
    That lies all night between my
       breasts.
14 My beloved *is* to me a cluster
       of henna *blooms*
    In the vineyards of En Gedi.

15 Behold, you *are* fair, my love!
    Behold, you *are* fair!
    You *have* dove's eyes.

1:2 [a]Masculine singular, that is, the Beloved   1:4 [a]Masculine singular, that is, the Beloved   [b]Feminine singular, that is, the Shulamite   [c]Masculine singular, that is, the Beloved   [d]Masculine singular, that is, the Beloved   1:7 [a]Septuagint, Syriac, and Vulgate read *wanders.*   1:11 [a]Feminine singular, that is, the Shulamite

---

God can appreciate our differences and still create unity. Together we produce a sound of harmony that expresses the multifaceted character of God.

The Lord's Kiss

Song of Solomon 1:2

Y ou are greater than your past. You are stronger than any moment of failure. You can rise like smoke up a chimney. You were meant to spiral to the sky. All the chilling drafts of broken promises should not deny you the gift of life. Never forget that you are alive—sometimes weak, sometimes strong, but alive. You will be right some days and wrong some nights, but don't stop waking up in the morning. The morning is God's gift of another chance to pass the exam.

He has kissed you gently, tenderly, but definitely. It is not the urgent kiss of a desperate lover who makes demands in the night. He has kissed you with the gentle kiss of a Father's favor whose tenderness would shield you from the traumas of the past. You have been touched, blessed, kissed. One smooch, gently delivered from heaven's lips to human pain. You have been kissed by the Father Himself. No wonder Satan has failed to destroy in the night what God has prepared for the light. You have been kissed.

This is what you have to know if you are to withstand the darkness. This is what you must rehearse against the goblins of old images and past memories that would assault your dreams and turn them into nightmares. Just as sure as a father's kiss would ease a nervous child trying to rest in a strange place, God's kiss is a sedative for you.

No matter how foreign this place in your life may seem, you must know He prepared you for it. When He kissed you, He shielded you, and you are His. Safe and secure, you may rest in the sanctity and safety of arms that will not fail you. A kiss good night is His way of sealing you till morning. And it will come; it will not tarry. The morning is yours. Spend it well. Use it sparingly. It is a gift.

The morning is for the hopeful, not the regretful. It is expectation. It is wet dew moistening dry ground. It is hummingbirds and honking horns and a city yawning into alertness. Greater still, it is the future lying naked before you. Daybreak is stretching in the fresh hours of a new opportunity just created. It is an empty tomb and a filled manger. It is life, love, and hope. Never forget about the breaking of day. It will come.

Nights will pass, tears will dry, and enemies will leave. But you will arise in the morning.

16 Behold, you *are* handsome, my
    beloved!
    Yes, pleasant!
    Also our bed *is* green.
17 The beams of our houses *are*
    cedar,
    And our rafters of fir.

2 I *am* the rose of Sharon,
    And the lily of the valleys.

2 Like a lily among thorns,
    So is my love among the
    daughters.

3 Like an apple tree among the
    trees of the woods,
    So *is* my beloved among the
    sons.
    I sat down in his shade with
    great delight,
    And his fruit *was* sweet to my
    taste.

4 He brought me to the
    banqueting house,
    And his banner over me *was*
    love.
5 Sustain me with cakes of
    raisins,
    Refresh me with apples,
    For I *am* lovesick.

6 His left hand *is* under my
    head,
    And his right hand embraces
    me.
7 I charge you, O daughters of
    Jerusalem,
    By the gazelles or by the does
    of the field,
    Do not stir up nor awaken love
    Until it pleases.

8 The voice of my beloved!
    Behold, he comes
    Leaping upon the mountains,
    Skipping upon the hills.
9 My beloved is like a gazelle or
    a young stag.
    Behold, he stands behind our
    wall;
    He is looking through the
    windows,
    Gazing through the lattice.

10 My beloved spoke, and said to
    me:
    "Rise up, my love, my fair one,
    And come away.

11 For lo, the winter is past,
    The rain is over *and* gone.
12 The flowers appear on the
    earth;
    The time of singing has come,
    And the voice of the turtledove
    Is heard in our land.
13 The fig tree puts forth her green
    figs,
    And the vines *with* the tender
    grapes
    Give a good smell.
    Rise up, my love, my fair one,
    And come away!

14 "O my dove, in the clefts of the
    rock,
    In the secret *places* of the cliff,
    Let me see your face,
    Let me hear your voice;
    For your voice *is* sweet,
    And your face *is* lovely."

15 Catch us the foxes,
    The little foxes that spoil the
    vines,
    For our vines *have* tender
    grapes.

16 My beloved *is* mine, and I *am*
    his.
    He feeds *his flock* among the
    lilies.

17 Until the day breaks
    And the shadows flee away,
    Turn, my beloved,
    And be like a gazelle
    Or a young stag
    Upon the mountains of Bether.[a]

3 By night on my bed I sought
    the one I love;
    I sought him, but I did not find
    him.
2 "I will rise now," *I said,*
    "And go about the city;
    In the streets and in the squares
    I will seek the one I love."
    I sought him, but I did not find
    him.
3 The watchmen who go about
    the city found me;
    I said,
    "Have you seen the one I love?"

4 Scarcely had I passed by them,
    When I found the one I love.
    I held him and would not let
    him go,

2:17 [a]Literally *Separation*

Gospel Pearls

Until I had brought him to the house of my mother,
And into the chamber of her who conceived me.

5 I charge you, O daughters of Jerusalem,
By the gazelles or by the does of the field,
Do not stir up nor awaken love
Until it pleases.

6 Who *is* this coming out of the wilderness
Like pillars of smoke,
Perfumed with myrrh and frankincense,
With all the merchant's fragrant powders?

7 Behold, it *is* Solomon's couch,
With sixty valiant men around it,
Of the valiant of Israel.

8 They all hold swords,
Being expert in war.
Every man *has* his sword on his thigh
Because of fear in the night.

9 Of the wood of Lebanon
Solomon the King
Made himself a palanquin:[a]

10 He made its pillars *of* silver,
Its support *of* gold,
Its seat *of* purple,
Its interior paved *with* love
By the daughters of Jerusalem.

11 Go forth, O daughters of Zion,
And see King Solomon with the crown
With which his mother crowned him
On the day of his wedding,
The day of the gladness of his heart.

4 Behold, you *are* fair, my love!
Behold, you *are* fair!
You *have* dove's eyes behind your veil.
Your hair *is* like a flock of goats,
Going down from Mount Gilead.

2 Your teeth *are* like a flock of shorn *sheep*
Which have come up from the washing,
Every one of which bears twins,

And none *is* barren among them.

3 Your lips *are* like a strand of scarlet,
And your mouth is lovely.
Your temples behind your veil
Are like a piece of pomegranate.

4 Your neck *is* like the tower of David,
Built for an armory,
On which hang a thousand bucklers,
All shields of mighty men.

5 Your two breasts *are* like two fawns,
Twins of a gazelle,
Which feed among the lilies.

6 Until the day breaks
And the shadows flee away,
I will go my way to the mountain of myrrh
And to the hill of frankincense.

7 You *are* all fair, my love,
And *there is* no spot in you.

8 Come with me from Lebanon, *my* spouse,
With me from Lebanon.
Look from the top of Amana,
From the top of Senir and Hermon,
From the lions' dens,
From the mountains of the leopards.

9 You have ravished my heart,
My sister, *my* spouse;
You have ravished my heart
With one *look* of your eyes,
With one link of your necklace.

10 How fair is your love,
My sister, *my* spouse!
How much better than wine is your love,
And the scent of your perfumes
Than all spices!

11 Your lips, O *my* spouse,
Drip as the honeycomb;
Honey and milk *are* under your tongue;
And the fragrance of your garments
Is like the fragrance of Lebanon.

12 A garden enclosed
Is my sister, *my* spouse,

3:9 *a*A portable enclosed chair

*M*en tend to act out of what they perceive to be facts, while women tend to react out of their emotions. If your actions and moods are not a reaction to the probing of the Holy Spirit, then you are reacting to the subtle taunting of the enemy.

A spring shut up,
A fountain sealed.

13 Your plants *are* an orchard of
    pomegranates
With pleasant fruits,
Fragrant henna with
    spikenard,

14 Spikenard and saffron,
Calamus and cinnamon,
With all trees of frankincense,
Myrrh and aloes,
With all the chief spices—

15 A fountain of gardens,
A well of living waters,
And streams from Lebanon.

16 Awake, O north *wind,*
And come, O south!
Blow upon my garden,
That its spices may flow out.
Let my beloved come to his
    garden
And eat its pleasant fruits.

5 I have come to my garden, my
    sister, *my* spouse;
I have gathered my myrrh with
    my spice;
I have eaten my honeycomb
    with my honey;
I have drunk my wine with my
    milk.

Eat, O friends!
Drink, yes, drink deeply,
O beloved ones!

2 I sleep, but my heart is
    awake;
   It is the voice of my beloved!
He knocks, *saying,*
"Open for me, my sister, my
    love,
My dove, my perfect one;
For my head is covered with
    dew,
My locks with the drops of the
    night."

3 I have taken off my robe;
How can I put it on *again?*
I have washed my feet;
How can I defile them?

4 My beloved put his hand
By the latch *of the door,*
And my heart yearned for
    him.

5 I arose to open for my beloved,
And my hands dripped *with*
    myrrh,
My fingers with liquid myrrh,
On the handles of the lock.

6 I opened for my beloved,
But my beloved had turned
    away *and* was gone.
My heart leaped up when he
    spoke.
I sought him, but I could not
    find him;
I called him, but he gave me no
    answer.

7 The watchmen who went about
    the city found me.
They struck me, they wounded
    me;
The keepers of the walls
Took my veil away from me.

8 I charge you, O daughters of
    Jerusalem,
If you find my beloved,
That you tell him I *am* lovesick!

9 What *is* your beloved
More than *another* beloved,
O fairest among women?
What *is* your beloved
More than *another* beloved,
That you so charge us?

10 My beloved *is* white and ruddy,
Chief among ten thousand.

11 His head *is like* the finest
    gold;
His locks *are* wavy,
And black as a raven.

12 His eyes *are* like doves
By the rivers of waters,
Washed with milk,
And fitly set.

13 His cheeks *are* like a bed of
    spices,
Banks of scented herbs.
His lips *are* lilies,
Dripping liquid myrrh.

14 His hands *are* rods of gold
Set with beryl.
His body *is* carved ivory
Inlaid *with* sapphires.

15 His legs *are* pillars of marble
Set on bases of fine gold.
His countenance *is* like
    Lebanon,
Excellent as the cedars.

16 His mouth *is* most sweet,
Yes, he *is* altogether lovely.
This *is* my beloved,
And this *is* my friend,
O daughters of Jerusalem!

6 Where has your beloved gone,
O fairest among women?
Where has your beloved turned
    aside,

That we may seek him with you?

2 My beloved has gone to his garden,
To the beds of spices,
To feed *his flock* in the gardens,
And to gather lilies.

3 I *am* my beloved's,
And my beloved *is* mine.
He feeds *his flock* among the lilies.

4 O my love, you *are as* beautiful as Tirzah,
Lovely as Jerusalem,
Awesome as *an army* with banners!

5 Turn your eyes away from me,
For they have overcome me.
Your hair *is* like a flock of goats
Going down from Gilead.

6 Your teeth *are* like a flock of sheep
Which have come up from the washing;
Every one bears twins,
And none *is* barren among them.

7 Like a piece of pomegranate
Are your temples behind your veil.

8 There are sixty queens
And eighty concubines,
And virgins without number.

9 My dove, my perfect one,
Is the only one,
The only one of her mother,
The favorite of the one who bore her.
The daughters saw her
And called her blessed,
The queens and the concubines,
And they praised her.

10 Who is she who looks forth as the morning,
Fair as the moon,
Clear as the sun,
Awesome as *an army* with banners?

11 I went down to the garden of nuts
To see the verdure of the valley,
To see whether the vine had budded

And the pomegranates had bloomed.

12 Before I was even aware,
My soul had made me
As the chariots of my noble people.[a]

13 Return, return, O Shulamite;
Return, return, that we may look upon you!

What would you see in the Shulamite—
As it were, the dance of the two camps?[a]

7 How beautiful are your feet in sandals,
O prince's daughter!
The curves of your thighs *are* like jewels,
The work of the hands of a skillful workman.

2 Your navel *is* a rounded goblet;
It lacks no blended beverage.
Your waist *is* a heap of wheat
Set about with lilies.

3 Your two breasts *are* like two fawns,
Twins of a gazelle.

4 Your neck *is* like an ivory tower,
Your eyes *like* the pools in Heshbon
By the gate of Bath Rabbim.
Your nose *is* like the tower of Lebanon
Which looks toward Damascus.

5 Your head *crowns* you like *Mount* Carmel,
And the hair of your head *is* like purple;
A king *is* held captive by *your* tresses.

6 How fair and how pleasant you are,
O love, with your delights!

7 This stature of yours is like a palm tree,
And your breasts *like* its clusters.

8 I said, "I will go up to the palm tree,
I will take hold of its branches."
Let now your breasts be like clusters of the vine,

6:12 ªHebrew *Ammi Nadib*   6:13 ªHebrew *Mahanaim*

*D*on't allow the enemy to plug into you and violate you through his subtle seductions. He is a giver and he is looking for a receiver. You must discern his influence if you are going to rebuke him.

A Woman of Passion

Song of Solomon 7:10-12

Married women, Satan will try to rob you and your husband of the passion God created for you to enjoy. The enemy will try to callous your soft, supple flesh with stress and unforgiveness and leave you with a hard shell that imprisons a broken heart. He is afraid for you to love and give. There is a level of romance and chivalry in marriage that the Father meant for you to enjoy—not just sex, but sensitivity. More than obligation or performance, I am talking to you about the return of passion.

If you are not careful, life will cause you to leak. Your marriage will be drained by the leaking passion and wilted excitement produced by hard times and struggle. Your mommyhood will try to rob you of your womanhood. Satan wants to leave you drab and aloof, hiding behind religious excuses rather than fighting your way out and being the wife and woman you were created to be.

Perhaps you do not need to know this now. But someday when you feel a heavy depression about to descend upon what was once a vibrant love, you will need to turn to God as your Friend. When that day comes, you may suddenly realize that your husband is longing for the woman you used to be. Somewhere beneath your problems there is another woman screaming, "Let me out! I want to love and live." This is the woman who has been trampled by low self-esteem and fear of rejection. She is the woman you were before. Remember her?

She is soft and sensitive, fanciful and frilly. She is bright-eyed and full of mischief, creative and sensual. Your husband has been on a fast, waiting for her to step out of the freezer. If ever there were a time you needed to stop suppressing her and let her loose, it is now.

I can't leave you lying in the bed of despair with your emotions dead, your passion subdued, your attitude cynical, your disposition critical. God says, "Arise." You are about to have a resurrection. It will be so strong that your husband should feel it. Your children should feel it. From the prayer room to the bedroom, a loosed woman is free!

The fragrance of your breath
like apples,

9 And the roof of your mouth like
the best wine.

The wine goes *down* smoothly
for my beloved,
Moving gently the lips of
sleepers.[a]

10 I *am* my beloved's,
And his desire *is* toward me.

11 Come, my beloved,
Let us go forth to the field;
Let us lodge in the villages.

12 Let us get up early to the
vineyards;
Let us see if the vine has
budded,
Whether the grape blossoms
are open,
And the pomegranates are in
bloom.
There I will give you my love.

13 The mandrakes give off a
fragrance,
And at our gates *are* pleasant
fruits,
All manner, new and old,
Which I have laid up for you,
my beloved.

8 Oh, that you were like my
brother,
Who nursed at my mother's
breasts!
If I should find you outside,
I would kiss you;
I would not be despised.

2 I would lead you *and* bring you
Into the house of my mother,
She *who* used to instruct me.
I would cause you to drink of
spiced wine,
Of the juice of my
pomegranate.

3 His left hand *is* under my head,
And his right hand embraces
me.

4 I charge you, O daughters of
Jerusalem,
Do not stir up nor awaken love
Until it pleases.

5 Who *is* this coming up from the
wilderness,
Leaning upon her beloved?
I awakened you under the
apple tree.

There your mother brought you
forth;
There she *who* bore you
brought *you* forth.

6 Set me as a seal upon your
heart,
As a seal upon your arm;
For love *is as* strong as death,
Jealousy *as* cruel as the grave;[a]
Its flames *are* flames of fire,
A most vehement[b] flame.

7 Many waters cannot quench
love,
Nor can the floods drown it.
If a man would give for love
All the wealth of his house,
It would be utterly despised.

8 We have a little sister,
And she has no breasts.
What shall we do for our sister
In the day when she is spoken
for?

9 If she *is* a wall,
We will build upon her
A battlement of silver;
And if she *is* a door,
We will enclose her
With boards of cedar.

10 I *am* a wall,
And my breasts like towers;
Then I became in his eyes
As one who found peace.

11 Solomon had a vineyard at
Baal Hamon;
He leased the vineyard to
keepers;
Everyone was to bring for its
fruit
A thousand silver coins.

12 My own vineyard *is* before me.
You, O Solomon, *may have* a
thousand,
And those who tend its fruit
two hundred.

13 You who dwell in the gardens,
The companions listen for your
voice—
Let me hear it!

14 Make haste, my beloved,
And be like a gazelle
Or a young stag
On the mountains of spices.

7:9 [a]Septuagint, Syriac, and Vulgate read *lips and teeth*.   8:6 [a]Or *Sheol*   [b]Literally *A flame of* Y*AH* (a
poetic form of *YHWH, the* L*ORD*)

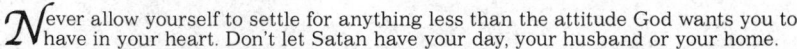

*N*ever allow yourself to settle for anything less than the attitude God wants you to
have in your heart. Don't let Satan have your day, your husband or your home.

Slam the Door!

Song of Solomon 8:9

From the foundations of the world, God chose you. In order to move people from eternity to time, God has only one method—birth through a woman. He is so serious about this law of creation that when He got ready to pour Himself into human flesh and live on this earth, He didn't violate it; rather, He was born of a woman.

Women are the only legal entryway to the earthly realm. If something is going to be born, it is going to be born of a woman. If it is going to come from the realm of eternity into the realm of time, it is going to come through the door of a woman's womb.

This fact is what puts women on the devil's hit list. The enemy is opposed to life. He deals in sickness, destruction, denial, devastation, thievery, and death. The enemy knows that if he is going to be successful, he must conquer the legal entrance to life. So he is waiting at that door!

But, woman, there are other doors in your life. Guard them and lock them. Slam your fence gates shut and chain them tight. Be very careful what you allow to enter you, what you allow to come through you, what you allow to affect you. Be careful what spirit you let loose in your mind, in your emotions, in your family.

Shut the door! Shut the door on that confusion, that depression, that temptation, that evil spirit. When you do, you are shutting the door in the devil's face!

In the Song of Solomon 8:8, 9, the writer was describing an immature sister. He said that if she were "swinging loose," he would teach her how to "keep herself." He would close her in so she didn't give entrance to just any old thing or any old person who happened to come along. But if she proved to be a wall—if she were found to be solid in what she believed and how she behaved—then he would build on her.

Guard the doors of your life, your soul, your spirit. Inside you is precious treasure that needs to be protected. You have the capacity to bear life in many forms. Don't let the enemy steal it from you. Slam the door on the devil today!

The Book of

ISAIAH

1 The vision of Isaiah the son of Amoz, which he saw concerning Judah and Jerusalem in the days of Uzziah, Jotham, Ahaz, *and* Hezekiah, kings of Judah.

2 Hear, O heavens, and give ear, O earth!
For the LORD has spoken:
"I have nourished and brought up children,
And they have rebelled against Me;
3 The ox knows its owner
And the donkey its master's crib;
But Israel does not know,
My people do not consider."

4 Alas, sinful nation,
A people laden with iniquity,
A brood of evildoers,
Children who are corrupters!
They have forsaken the LORD,
They have provoked to anger
The Holy One of Israel,
They have turned away backward.

5 Why should you be stricken again?
You will revolt more and more.
The whole head is sick,
And the whole heart faints.
6 From the sole of the foot even to the head,
There is no soundness in it,
But wounds and bruises and putrefying sores;
They have not been closed or bound up,
Or soothed with ointment.

7 Your country *is* desolate,
Your cities *are* burned with fire;
Strangers devour your land in your presence;
And *it is* desolate, as overthrown by strangers.
8 So the daughter of Zion is left as a booth in a vineyard,
As a hut in a garden of cucumbers,
As a besieged city.
9 Unless the LORD of hosts
Had left to us a very small remnant,
We would have become like Sodom,
We would have been made like Gomorrah.

10 Hear the word of the LORD,
You rulers of Sodom;
Give ear to the law of our God,
You people of Gomorrah:
11 "To what purpose *is* the multitude of your sacrifices to Me?"
Says the LORD.
"I have had enough of burnt offerings of rams
And the fat of fed cattle.
I do not delight in the blood of bulls,
Or of lambs or goats.

12 When you come to appear before Me,
Who has required this from your hand,
To trample My courts?
13 Bring no more futile sacrifices;
Incense is an abomination to Me.
The New Moons, the Sabbaths, and the calling of assemblies—
I cannot endure iniquity and the sacred meeting.
14 Your New Moons and your appointed feasts
My soul hates;
They are a trouble to Me,
I am weary of bearing *them.*
15 When you spread out your hands,
I will hide My eyes from you;
Even though you make many prayers,
I will not hear.
Your hands are full of blood.

16 "Wash yourselves, make yourselves clean;
Put away the evil of your doings from before My eyes.
Cease to do evil,
17 Learn to do good;
Seek justice,
Rebuke the oppressor;*a*

1:17 *a*Some ancient versions read *the oppressed.*

---

*2*t is not enough to reject the enemy's plan. You must nurture the Word of the Lord. You need to draw the promise of God and the vision for the future to your breast.

Defend the fatherless,
Plead for the widow.

18 "Come now, and let us reason
together,"
Says the LORD,
"Though your sins are like
scarlet,
They shall be as white as
snow;
Though they are red like
crimson,
They shall be as wool.
19 If you are willing and obedient,
You shall eat the good of the
land;
20 But if you refuse and rebel,
You shall be devoured by the
sword";
For the mouth of the LORD has
spoken.

21 How the faithful city has
become a harlot!
It was full of justice;
Righteousness lodged in it,
But now murderers.
22 Your silver has become dross,
Your wine mixed with water.
23 Your princes *are* rebellious,
And companions of thieves;
Everyone loves bribes,
And follows after rewards.
They do not defend the
fatherless,
Nor does the cause of the
widow come before them.
24 Therefore the Lord says,
The LORD of hosts, the Mighty
One of Israel,
"Ah, I will rid Myself of My
adversaries,
And take vengeance on My
enemies.
25 I will turn My hand against
you,
And thoroughly purge away
your dross,
And take away all your alloy.
26 I will restore your judges as at
the first,
And your counselors as at the
beginning.
Afterward you shall be called
the city of righteousness, the
faithful city."

27 Zion shall be redeemed with
justice,

And her penitents with
righteousness.
28 The destruction of
transgressors and of sinners
shall be together,
And those who forsake the
LORD shall be consumed.
29 For they*a* shall be ashamed of
the terebinth trees
Which you have desired;
And you shall be embarrassed
because of the gardens
Which you have chosen.
30 For you shall be as a terebinth
whose leaf fades,
And as a garden that has no
water.
31 The strong shall be as tinder,
And the work of it as a spark;
Both will burn together,
And no one shall quench
them.

2 The word that Isaiah the son of
Amoz saw concerning Judah and
Jerusalem.

2 Now it shall come to pass in the
latter days
That the mountain of the
LORD's house
Shall be established on the top
of the mountains,
And shall be exalted above the
hills;
And all nations shall flow to it.
3 Many people shall come and
say,
"Come, and let us go up to the
mountain of the LORD,
To the house of the God of
Jacob;
He will teach us His ways,
And we shall walk in His
paths."
For out of Zion shall go forth
the law,
And the word of the LORD from
Jerusalem.
4 He shall judge between the
nations,
And rebuke many people;
They shall beat their swords
into plowshares,
And their spears into pruning
hooks;
Nation shall not lift up sword
against nation,
Neither shall they learn war
anymore.

1:29 *a*Following Masoretic Text, Septuagint, and Vulgate; some Hebrew manuscripts and Targum read *you.*

Gospel Pearls

5 O house of Jacob, come and let
us walk
In the light of the LORD.

6 For You have forsaken Your
people, the house of Jacob,
Because they are filled with
eastern ways;
They *are* soothsayers like the
Philistines,
And they are pleased with the
children of foreigners.

7 Their land is also full of silver
and gold,
And there is no end to their
treasures;
Their land is also full of horses,
And there is no end to their
chariots.

8 Their land is also full of idols;
They worship the work of their
own hands,
That which their own fingers
have made.

9 People bow down,
And each man humbles
himself;
Therefore do not forgive them.

10 Enter into the rock, and hide in
the dust,
From the terror of the LORD
And the glory of His majesty.

11 The lofty looks of man shall be
humbled,
The haughtiness of men shall
be bowed down,
And the LORD alone shall be
exalted in that day.

12 For the day of the LORD of hosts
Shall come upon everything
proud and lofty,
Upon everything lifted up—
And it shall be brought low—

13 Upon all the cedars of Lebanon
that are high and lifted up,
And upon all the oaks of
Bashan;

14 Upon all the high mountains,
And upon all the hills *that are*
lifted up;

15 Upon every high tower,
And upon every fortified wall;

16 Upon all the ships of Tarshish,
And upon all the beautiful
sloops.

17 The loftiness of man shall be
bowed down,
And the haughtiness of men
shall be brought low;

The LORD alone will be exalted
in that day,

18 But the idols He shall utterly
abolish.

19 They shall go into the holes of
the rocks,
And into the caves of the earth,
From the terror of the LORD
And the glory of His majesty,
When He arises to shake the
earth mightily.

20 In that day a man will cast
away his idols of silver
And his idols of gold,
Which they made, *each* for
himself to worship,
To the moles and bats,

21 To go into the clefts of the
rocks,
And into the crags of the
rugged rocks,
From the terror of the LORD
And the glory of His majesty,
When He arises to shake the
earth mightily.

22 Sever yourselves from such a
man,
Whose breath *is* in his nostrils;
For of what account is he?

3 For behold, the Lord, the LORD
of hosts,
Takes away from Jerusalem
and from Judah
The stock and the store,
The whole supply of bread and
the whole supply of water;

2 The mighty man and the man
of war,
The judge and the prophet,
And the diviner and the elder;

3 The captain of fifty and the
honorable man,
The counselor and the skillful
artisan,
And the expert enchanter.

4 "I will give children *to be* their
princes,
And babes shall rule over them.

5 The people will be oppressed,
Every one by another and
every one by his neighbor;
The child will be insolent
toward the elder,
And the base toward the
honorable."

6 When a man takes hold of his
brother

*T*here is no way you can plan for the future and dwell in the past at the same time.
It is midnight—the turning point of days! It is your time for a change. Praise God
and escape the dungeons of your past.

In the house of his father,
  saying,
 "You have clothing;
 You be our ruler,
 And *let* these ruins *be* under
   your power,"*a*
7 In that day he will protest,
  saying,
 "I cannot cure *your* ills,
 For in my house *is* neither food
  nor clothing;
 Do not make me a ruler of the
  people."

8 For Jerusalem stumbled,
 And Judah is fallen,
 Because their tongue and their
  doings
 Are against the LORD,
 To provoke the eyes of His
  glory.
9 The look on their countenance
  witnesses against them,
 And they declare their sin as
  Sodom;
 They do not hide *it.*
 Woe to their soul!
 For they have brought evil
  upon themselves.

10 "Say to the righteous that *it shall
  be* well *with them,*
 For they shall eat the fruit of
  their doings.
11 Woe to the wicked! *It shall be
  ill with him,*
 For the reward of his hands
  shall be given him.
12 *As for* My people, children *are*
  their oppressors,
 And women rule over them.
 O My people! Those who
  lead you cause *you* to
  err,
 And destroy the way of your
  paths."

13 The LORD stands up to plead,
 And stands to judge the
  people.
14 The LORD will enter into
  judgment
 With the elders of His people
 And His princes:
 "For you have eaten up the
  vineyard;
 The plunder of the poor *is* in
  your houses.
15 What do you mean by crushing
  My people

And grinding the faces of the
  poor?"
 Says the Lord GOD of hosts.

16 Moreover the LORD says:

 "Because the daughters of Zion
  are haughty,
 And walk with outstretched
  necks
 And wanton eyes,
 Walking and mincing *as* they
  go,
 Making a jingling with their
  feet,
17 Therefore the Lord will strike
  with a scab
 The crown of the head of the
  daughters of Zion,
 And the LORD will uncover
  their secret parts."

18 In that day the Lord will take
  away the finery:
 The jingling anklets, the
  scarves, and the crescents;
19 The pendants, the bracelets,
  and the veils;
20 The headdresses, the leg
  ornaments, and the
  headbands;
 The perfume boxes, the
  charms,
21 and the rings;
 The nose jewels,
22 the festal apparel, and the
  mantles;
 The outer garments, the purses,
23 and the mirrors;
 The fine linen, the turbans, and
  the robes.

24 And so it shall be:

 Instead of a sweet smell there
  will be a stench;
 Instead of a sash, a rope;
 Instead of well-set hair,
  baldness;
 Instead of a rich robe, a girding
  of sackcloth;
 And branding instead of
  beauty.
25 Your men shall fall by the
  sword,
 And your mighty in the war.

26 Her gates shall lament and
  mourn,
 And she *being* desolate shall sit
  on the ground.

3:6 *a*Literally *hand*

4 And in that day seven women
shall take hold of one man,
saying,
"We will eat our own food and
wear our own apparel;
Only let us be called by your
name,
To take away our reproach."
2 In that day the Branch of the
LORD shall be beautiful and
glorious;
And the fruit of the earth *shall
be* excellent and appealing
For those of Israel who have
escaped.

3 And it shall come to pass that *he
who is* left in Zion and remains in
Jerusalem will be called holy—everyone who is recorded among the living
in Jerusalem. 4 When the Lord has
washed away the filth of the daughters of Zion, and purged the blood
of Jerusalem from her midst, by the
spirit of judgment and by the spirit
of burning, 5 then the LORD will create above every dwelling place of
Mount Zion, and above her assemblies, a cloud and smoke by day and
the shining of a flaming fire by night.
For over all the glory there *will be* a
covering. 6 And there will be a tabernacle for shade in the daytime from
the heat, for a place of refuge, and
for a shelter from storm and rain.

5 Now let me sing to my Well-
beloved
A song of my Beloved
regarding His vineyard:

My Well-beloved has a
vineyard
On a very fruitful hill.
2 He dug it up and cleared out
its stones,
And planted it with the choicest
vine.
He built a tower in its midst,
And also made a winepress in
it;
So He expected *it* to bring forth
good grapes,
But it brought forth wild
grapes.

3 "And now, O inhabitants of
Jerusalem and men of Judah,
Judge, please, between Me and
My vineyard.
4 What more could have been
done to My vineyard

That I have not done in it?
Why then, when I expected *it*
to bring forth *good* grapes,
Did it bring forth wild grapes?
5 And now, please let Me tell you
what I will do to My
vineyard:
I will take away its hedge, and
it shall be burned;
And break down its wall, and
it shall be trampled down.
6 I will lay it waste;
It shall not be pruned or dug,
But there shall come up briers
and thorns.
I will also command the clouds
That they rain no rain on it."

7 For the vineyard of the LORD of
hosts *is* the house of Israel,
And the men of Judah are His
pleasant plant.
He looked for justice, but
behold, oppression;
For righteousness, but behold,
a cry *for help.*

8 Woe to those who join house
to house;
They add field to field,
Till *there is* no place
Where they may dwell alone in
the midst of the land!
9 In my hearing the LORD of hosts
said,
"Truly, many houses shall be
desolate,
Great and beautiful ones,
without inhabitant.
10 For ten acres of vineyard shall
yield one bath,
And a homer of seed shall yield
one ephah."

11 Woe to those who rise early in
the morning,
That they may follow
intoxicating drink;
Who continue until night, *till*
wine inflames them!
12 The harp and the strings,
The tambourine and flute,
And wine are in their feasts;
But they do not regard the
work of the LORD,
Nor consider the operation of
His hands.

13 Therefore my people have gone
into captivity,

*E*very woman has something she wishes she could forget. Forgetting isn't a memory
lapse; it is a memory release! Like carbon dioxide the body can no longer use,
exhale it and let it go out of your spirit.

Because *they have* no
knowledge;
Their honorable men *are*
famished,
And their multitude dried up
with thirst.

14 Therefore Sheol has enlarged
itself
And opened its mouth beyond
measure;
Their glory and their multitude
and their pomp,
And he who is jubilant, shall
descend into it.

15 People shall be brought down,
Each man shall be humbled,
And the eyes of the lofty shall
be humbled.

16 But the LORD of hosts shall be
exalted in judgment,
And God who is holy shall be
hallowed in righteousness.

17 Then the lambs shall feed in
their pasture,
And in the waste places of the
fat ones strangers shall eat.

18 Woe to those who draw
iniquity with cords of vanity,
And sin as if with a cart rope;

19 That say, "Let Him make speed
and hasten His work,
That we may see *it;*
And let the counsel of the Holy
One of Israel draw near and
come,
That we may know *it.*"

20 Woe to those who call evil
good, and good evil;
Who put darkness for light, and
light for darkness;
Who put bitter for sweet, and
sweet for bitter!

21 Woe to *those who are* wise in
their own eyes,
And prudent in their own sight!

22 Woe to men mighty at drinking
wine,
Woe to men valiant for mixing
intoxicating drink,

23 Who justify the wicked for a
bribe,
And take away justice from the
righteous man!

24 Therefore, as the fire devours
the stubble,
And the flame consumes the
chaff,

So their root will be as
rottenness,
And their blossom will ascend
like dust;
Because they have rejected the
law of the LORD of hosts,
And despised the word of the
Holy One of Israel.

25 Therefore the anger of the
LORD is aroused against His
people;
He has stretched out His hand
against them
And stricken them,
And the hills trembled.
Their carcasses *were* as refuse
in the midst of the streets.

For all this His anger is not
turned away,
But His hand *is* stretched out
still.

26 He will lift up a banner to the
nations from afar,
And will whistle to them from
the end of the earth;
Surely they shall come with
speed, swiftly.

27 No one will be weary or
stumble among them,
No one will slumber or sleep;
Nor will the belt on their loins
be loosed,
Nor the strap of their sandals
be broken;

28 Whose arrows *are* sharp,
And all their bows bent;
Their horses' hooves will seem
like flint,
And their wheels like a
whirlwind.

29 Their roaring *will be* like a lion,
They will roar like young lions;
Yes, they will roar
And lay hold of the prey;
They will carry *it* away safely,
And no one will deliver.

30 In that day they will roar
against them
Like the roaring of the sea.
And if *one* looks to the land,
Behold, darkness *and* sorrow;
And the light is darkened by
the clouds.

6 In the year that King Uzziah died,
I saw the Lord sitting on a throne,
high and lifted up, and the train of
His *robe* filled the temple. 2 Above it
stood seraphim; each one had six
wings: with two he covered his face,

Gospel
Pearls

with two he covered his feet, and with two he flew. 3 And one cried to another and said:

"Holy, holy, holy *is* the LORD of hosts;
The whole earth *is* full of His glory!"

4 And the posts of the door were shaken by the voice of him who cried out, and the house was filled with smoke.

5 So I said:

"Woe *is* me, for I am undone!
Because I *am* a man of unclean lips,
And I dwell in the midst of a people of unclean lips;
For my eyes have seen the King,
The LORD of hosts."

6 Then one of the seraphim flew to me, having in his hand a live coal *which* he had taken with the tongs from the altar. 7 And he touched my mouth *with it,* and said:

"Behold, this has touched your lips;
Your iniquity is taken away,
And your sin purged."

8 Also I heard the voice of the Lord, saying:

"Whom shall I send,
And who will go for Us?"

Then I said, "Here *am* I! Send me."

9 And He said, "Go, and tell this people:

'Keep on hearing, but do not understand;
Keep on seeing, but do not perceive.'

10 "Make the heart of this people dull,
And their ears heavy,
And shut their eyes;
Lest they see with their eyes,
And hear with their ears,
And understand with their heart,
And return and be healed."

11 Then I said, "Lord, how long?"
And He answered:

"Until the cities are laid waste and without inhabitant,
The houses are without a man,
The land is utterly desolate,
12 The LORD has removed men far away,
And the forsaken places *are* many in the midst of the land.
13 But yet a tenth *will be* in it,
And will return and be for consuming,
As a terebinth tree or as an oak,
Whose stump *remains* when it is cut down.
So the holy seed *shall be* its stump."

7 Now it came to pass in the days of Ahaz the son of Jotham, the son of Uzziah, king of Judah, *that* Rezin king of Syria and Pekah the son of Remaliah, king of Israel, went up to Jerusalem to *make* war against it, but could not prevail against it. 2 And it was told to the house of David, saying, "Syria's forces are deployed in Ephraim." So his heart and the heart of his people were moved as the trees of the woods are moved with the wind.

3 Then the LORD said to Isaiah, "Go out now to meet Ahaz, you and Shear-Jashub[a] your son, at the end of the aqueduct from the upper pool, on the highway to the Fuller's Field, 4 and say to him: 'Take heed, and be quiet; do not fear or be fainthearted for these two stubs of smoking firebrands, for the fierce anger of Rezin and Syria, and the son of Remaliah. 5 Because Syria, Ephraim, and the son of Remaliah have plotted evil against you, saying, 6 "Let us go up against Judah and trouble it, and let us make a gap in its wall for ourselves, and set a king over them, the son of Tabel"— 7 thus says the Lord GOD:

"It shall not stand,
Nor shall it come to pass.
8 For the head of Syria *is* Damascus,
And the head of Damascus *is* Rezin.
Within sixty-five years Ephraim will be broken,

7:3 aLiterally *A Remnant Shall Return*

*Y*ou can call upon God even in the middle of the night. Like a 24-hour medical center, you can reach Him at any time. He is touched by the feeling of your infirmity.

Soul Secrets
of a woman needing comfort

*L*ord, You have sent Immanuel. God with us, God with me. You have sent Your Holy Spirit to comfort me. I call upon my Comforter. Visit this place where I am suffering so. I thank You, my God, that just one touch of the Holy Ghost changes everything. Holy Spirit, show Yourself as Comforter to me. Deep is my despair and dark is my night. I need comfort right now in the deepest places of my soul. My heart is weeping, Lord, and only You can touch it and make it whole.

My prayer is simple. Comforter, come. There is no sweeter comfort than Your presence. These is no one I would rather sit with in this hour. Lord, my greatest peace comes from You. Lord, my greatest comfort is You. The quiet of Your presence stills my soul and calms my fears. You are near me now. Let me feel the sure and perfect embrace of God. Let me see the radiance of Your face. It is awesome just to know You look upon me in grace, to know that You are near when I need You, that You welcome me into the holy place where You are. Holy Spirit, comfort me.

So that it will not *be* a people.
9 The head of Ephraim *is*
Samaria,
And the head of Samaria *is*
Remaliah's son.
If you will not believe,
Surely you shall not be
established." ' "

10 Moreover the LORD spoke again to Ahaz, saying, 11 "Ask a sign for yourself from the LORD your God; ask it either in the depth or in the height above."

12 But Ahaz said, "I will not ask, nor will I test the LORD!"

13 Then he said, "Hear now, O house of David! *Is it* a small thing for you to weary men, but will you weary my God also? 14 Therefore the Lord Himself will give you a sign: Behold, the virgin shall conceive and bear a Son, and shall call His name Immanuel.*a* 15 Curds and honey He shall eat, that He may know to refuse the evil and choose the good. 16 For before the Child shall know to refuse the evil and choose the good, the land that you dread will be forsaken by both her kings. 17 The LORD will bring the king of Assyria upon you and your people and your father's house—days that have not come since the day that Ephraim departed from Judah."

18 And it shall come to pass in that day
That the LORD will whistle for the fly
That *is* in the farthest part of the rivers of Egypt,
And for the bee that *is* in the land of Assyria.
19 They will come, and all of them will rest
In the desolate valleys and in the clefts of the rocks,
And on all thorns and in all pastures.

20 In the same day the Lord will shave with a hired razor,
With those from beyond the River,*a* with the king of Assyria,
The head and the hair of the legs,

And will also remove the beard.

21 It shall be in that day
That a man will keep alive a young cow and two sheep;
22 So it shall be, from the abundance of milk they give,
That he will eat curds;
For curds and honey everyone will eat who is left in the land.

23 It shall happen in that day,
That wherever there could be a thousand vines
Worth a thousand *shekels* of silver,
It will be for briers and thorns.
24 With arrows and bows men will come there,
Because all the land will become briers and thorns.

25 And to any hill which could be dug with the hoe,
You will not go there for fear of briers and thorns;
But it will become a range for oxen
And a place for sheep to roam.

8 Moreover the LORD said to me, "Take a large scroll, and write on it with a man's pen concerning Maher-Shalal-Hash-Baz.*a* 2 And I will take for Myself faithful witnesses to record, Uriah the priest and Zechariah the son of Jeberechiah."

3 Then I went to the prophetess, and she conceived and bore a son. Then the LORD said to me, "Call his name Maher-Shalal-Hash-Baz; 4 for before the child shall have knowledge to cry 'My father' and 'My mother,' the riches of Damascus and the spoil of Samaria will be taken away before the king of Assyria."

5 The LORD also spoke to me again, saying:

6 "Inasmuch as these people refused
The waters of Shiloah that flow softly,
And rejoice in Rezin and in Remaliah's son;
7 Now therefore, behold, the Lord brings up over them

7:14 *a*Literally *God-With-Us*   7:20 *a*That is, the Euphrates   8:1 *a*Literally *Speed the Spoil, Hasten the Booty*

---

2 am excited to say that God never loosed anybody that He wasn't going to use mightily. May God reveal healing and purpose as you continue to seek Him.

The waters of the River,^a strong
and mighty—
The king of Assyria and all his
glory;
He will go up over all his
channels
And go over all his banks.
8 He will pass through Judah,
He will overflow and pass over,
He will reach up to the neck;
And the stretching out of his
wings
Will fill the breadth of Your
land, O Immanuel.^a

9 "Be shattered, O you peoples,
and be broken in pieces!
Give ear, all you from far
countries.
Gird yourselves, but be broken
in pieces;
Gird yourselves, but be broken
in pieces.
10 Take counsel together, but it
will come to nothing;
Speak the word, but it will not
stand,
For God *is* with us."^a

11 For the LORD spoke thus to me
with a strong hand, and instructed
me that I should not walk in the way
of this people, saying:

12 "Do not say, 'A conspiracy,'
Concerning all that this people
call a conspiracy,
Nor be afraid of their threats,
nor be troubled.
13 The LORD of hosts, Him you
shall hallow;
Let Him *be* your fear,
And *let* Him *be* your dread.
14 He will be as a sanctuary,
But a stone of stumbling and a
rock of offense
To both the houses of Israel,
As a trap and a snare to the
inhabitants of Jerusalem.
15 And many among them shall
stumble;
They shall fall and be broken,
Be snared and taken."

16 Bind up the testimony,
Seal the law among my
disciples.
17 And I will wait on the LORD,

Who hides His face from the
house of Jacob;
And I will hope in Him.
18 Here am I and the children
whom the LORD has given
me!
We are for signs and wonders
in Israel
From the LORD of hosts,
Who dwells in Mount Zion.

19 And when they say to you,
"Seek those who are mediums and
wizards, who whisper and mutter,"
should not a people seek their God?
Should they seek the dead on behalf
of the living? 20 To the law and to the
testimony! If they do not speak according to this word, *it is* because
there is no light in them.
21 They will pass through it hard
pressed and hungry; and it shall happen, when they are hungry, that they
will be enraged and curse their king
and their God, and look upward.
22 Then they will look to the earth,
and see trouble and darkness, gloom
of anguish; and *they will be* driven
into darkness.

9 Nevertheless the gloom *will
not be* upon her who *is*
distressed,
As when at first He lightly
esteemed
The land of Zebulun and the
land of Naphtali,
And afterward more heavily
oppressed *her,*
By the way of the sea, beyond
the Jordan,
In Galilee of the Gentiles.
2 The people who walked in
darkness
Have seen a great light;
Those who dwelt in the land of
the shadow of death,
Upon them a light has shined.

3 You have multiplied the nation
And increased its joy;^a
They rejoice before You
According to the joy of harvest,
As *men* rejoice when they
divide the spoil.
4 For You have broken the yoke
of his burden
And the staff of his shoulder,

8:7 ^aThat is, the Euphrates   8:8 ^aLiterally *God-With-Us*   8:10 ^aHebrew *Immanuel*   9:3 ^aFollowing
Qere and Targum; Kethib and Vulgate read *not increased joy;* Septuagint reads *Most of the people You
brought down in Your joy.*

Gospel
Pearls

The rod of his oppressor,
As in the day of Midian.
5 For every warrior's sandal
from the noisy battle,
And garments rolled in blood,
Will be used for burning *and*
fuel of fire.

6 For unto us a Child is born,
Unto us a Son is given;
And the government will be
upon His shoulder.
And His name will be called
Wonderful, Counselor, Mighty
God,
Everlasting Father, Prince of
Peace.
7 Of the increase of *His*
government and peace
There will be no end,
Upon the throne of David and
over His kingdom,
To order it and establish it with
judgment and justice
From that time forward, even
forever.
The zeal of the LORD of hosts
will perform this.

8 The LORD sent a word against
Jacob,
And it has fallen on Israel.
9 All the people will know—
Ephraim and the inhabitant of
Samaria—
Who say in pride and
arrogance of heart:
10 "The bricks have fallen down,
But we will rebuild with hewn
stones;
The sycamores are cut down,
But we will replace *them* with
cedars."
11 Therefore the LORD shall set up
The adversaries of Rezin
against him,
And spur his enemies on,
12 The Syrians before and the
Philistines behind;
And they shall devour Israel
with an open mouth.

For all this His anger is not
turned away,
But His hand *is* stretched out
still.

13 For the people do not turn to
Him who strikes them,
Nor do they seek the LORD of
hosts.

14 Therefore the LORD will cut off
head and tail from Israel,
Palm branch and bulrush in
one day.
15 The elder and honorable, he *is*
the head;
The prophet who teaches lies,
he *is* the tail.
16 For the leaders of this people
cause *them* to err,
And *those who are* led by them
are destroyed.
17 Therefore the LORD will have
no joy in their young men,
Nor have mercy on their
fatherless and widows;
For everyone *is* a hypocrite and
an evildoer,
And every mouth speaks folly.

For all this His anger is not
turned away,
But His hand *is* stretched out
still.

18 For wickedness burns as the
fire;
It shall devour the briers and
thorns,
And kindle in the thickets of
the forest;
They shall mount up *like* rising
smoke.
19 Through the wrath of the LORD
of hosts
The land is burned up,
And the people shall be as fuel
for the fire;
No man shall spare his brother.
20 And he shall snatch on the
right hand
And be hungry;
He shall devour on the left
hand
And not be satisfied;
Every man shall eat the flesh
of his own arm.
21 Manasseh *shall devour*
Ephraim, and Ephraim
Manasseh;
Together they *shall be* against
Judah.

For all this His anger is not
turned away,
But His hand *is* stretched out
still.

10 "Woe to those who decree
unrighteous decrees,
Who write misfortune,
Which they have prescribed
2 To rob the needy of justice,

And to take what is right from
  the poor of My people,
That widows may be their prey,
And *that* they may rob the
  fatherless.
3 What will you do in the day of
  punishment,
And in the desolation *which*
  will come from afar?
To whom will you flee for help?
And where will you leave your
  glory?
4 Without Me they shall bow
  down among the prisoners,
And they shall fall among the
  slain.''

For all this His anger is not
  turned away,
But His hand *is* stretched out
  still.

5 "Woe to Assyria, the rod of My
  anger
And the staff in whose hand is
  My indignation.
6 I will send him against an
  ungodly nation,
And against the people of My
  wrath
I will give him charge,
To seize the spoil, to take the
  prey,
And to tread them down like
  the mire of the streets.
7 Yet he does not mean so,
Nor does his heart think so;
But *it is* in his heart to destroy,
And cut off not a few nations.
8 For he says,
'*Are* not my princes altogether
  kings?
9 *Is* not Calno like Carchemish?
Is not Hamath like Arpad?
Is not Samaria like Damascus?
10 As my hand has found the
  kingdoms of the idols,
Whose carved images excelled
  those of Jerusalem and
  Samaria,
11 As I have done to Samaria and
  her idols,
Shall I not do also to Jerusalem
  and her idols?' ''

12 Therefore it shall come to pass,
when the LORD has performed all His
work on Mount Zion and on Jerusalem, *that He will say,* "I will punish
the fruit of the arrogant heart of the

king of Assyria, and the glory of his
haughty looks.''
13 For he says:

"By the strength of my hand I
  have done *it,*
And by my wisdom, for I am
  prudent;
Also I have removed the
  boundaries of the people,
And have robbed their
  treasuries;
So I have put down the
  inhabitants like a valiant
  man.
14 My hand has found like a nest
  the riches of the people,
And as one gathers eggs *that
  are* left,
I have gathered all the earth;
And there was no one who
  moved *his* wing,
Nor opened *his* mouth with
  even a peep.''

15 Shall the ax boast itself against
  him who chops with it?
Or shall the saw exalt itself
  against him who saws with
  it?
As if a rod could wield *itself*
  against those who lift it up,
Or as if a staff could lift up, *as
  if it were* not wood!
16 Therefore the Lord, the Lord[a]
  of hosts,
Will send leanness among his
  fat ones;
And under his glory
He will kindle a burning
Like the burning of a fire.
17 So the Light of Israel will be
  for a fire,
And his Holy One for a flame;
It will burn and devour
His thorns and his briers in one
  day.
18 And it will consume the glory
  of his forest and of his fruitful
  field,
Both soul and body;
And they will be as when a sick
  man wastes away.
19 Then the rest of the trees of his
  forest
Will be so few in number
That a child may write them.
20 And it shall come to pass in that
  day
That the remnant of Israel,

10:16 [a]Following Bomberg; Masoretic Text and Dead Sea Scrolls read *YHWH* (LORD).

And such as have escaped of
  the house of Jacob,
Will never again depend on
  him who defeated them,
But will depend on the LORD,
  the Holy One of Israel, in
  truth.
21 The remnant will return, the
  remnant of Jacob,
  To the Mighty God.
22 For though your people, O
  Israel, be as the sand of the
  sea,
  A remnant of them will return;
The destruction decreed shall
  overflow with righteousness.
23 For the Lord GOD of hosts
Will make a determined end
  In the midst of all the land.

24 Therefore thus says the Lord
GOD of hosts: "O My people, who
dwell in Zion, do not be afraid of the
Assyrian. He shall strike you with a
rod and lift up his staff against you,
in the manner of Egypt. 25 For yet a
very little while and the indignation
will cease, as will My anger in their
destruction." 26 And the LORD of
hosts will stir up a scourge for him
like the slaughter of Midian at the
rock of Oreb; *as* His rod was on the
sea, so will He lift it up in the manner
of Egypt.

27 It shall come to pass in that
  day
  That his burden will be taken
  away from your shoulder,
And his yoke from your neck,
And the yoke will be destroyed
  because of the anointing oil.

28 He has come to Aiath,
He has passed Migron;
  At Michmash he has attended
  to his equipment.
29 They have gone along the
  ridge,
They have taken up lodging at
  Geba.
Ramah is afraid,
  Gibeah of Saul has fled.
30 Lift up your voice,
  O daughter of Gallim!
Cause it to be heard as far as
  Laish—
  O poor Anathoth!*a*
31 Madmenah has fled,

The inhabitants of Gebim seek
  refuge.
32 As yet he will remain at Nob
  that day;
He will shake his fist at the
  mount of the daughter of
  Zion,
  The hill of Jerusalem.

33 Behold, the Lord,
  The LORD of hosts,
Will lop off the bough with
  terror;
Those of high stature *will be*
  hewn down,
And the haughty will be
  humbled.
34 He will cut down the thickets
  of the forest with iron,
And Lebanon will fall by the
  Mighty One.

11 There shall come forth a Rod
  from the stem of Jesse,
And a Branch shall grow out
  of his roots.
2 The Spirit of the LORD shall rest
  upon Him,
The Spirit of wisdom and
  understanding,
The Spirit of counsel and
  might,
The Spirit of knowledge and of
  the fear of the LORD.

3 His delight *is* in the fear of the
  LORD,
And He shall not judge by the
  sight of His eyes,
Nor decide by the hearing of
  His ears;
4 But with righteousness He shall
  judge the poor,
And decide with equity for the
  meek of the earth;
He shall strike the earth with
  the rod of His mouth,
And with the breath of His
  lips He shall slay the
  wicked.
5 Righteousness shall be the belt
  of His loins,
And faithfulness the belt of His
  waist.

6 "The wolf also shall dwell with
  the lamb,
The leopard shall lie down with
  the young goat,

10:30 *a*Following Masoretic Text, Targum, and Vulgate; Septuagint and Syriac read *Listen to her, O Anathoth*.

*T*he Lord wants to loose you out of the dungeon of fear. He does care. We care. No one would take hours away from themselves and from their family praying for you, preaching to you, or even writing this to you if they didn't care. *Rise and be healed in the name of Jesus.*

The calf and the young lion and
    the fatling together;
And a little child shall lead
    them.
7   The cow and the bear shall
    graze;
Their young ones shall lie
    down together;
And the lion shall eat straw like
    the ox.
8   The nursing child shall play by
    the cobra's hole,
And the weaned child shall put
    his hand in the viper's den.
9   They shall not hurt nor destroy
    in all My holy mountain,
For the earth shall be full of the
    knowledge of the LORD
As the waters cover the sea.

10 "And in that day there shall be
    a Root of Jesse,
Who shall stand as a banner to
    the people;
For the Gentiles shall seek Him,
And His resting place shall be
    glorious."

11   It shall come to pass in that day
That the LORD shall set His
    hand again the second time
To recover the remnant of His
    people who are left,
From Assyria and Egypt,
From Pathros and Cush,
From Elam and Shinar,
From Hamath and the islands
    of the sea.

12   He will set up a banner for the
    nations,
And will assemble the outcasts
    of Israel,
And gather together the
    dispersed of Judah
From the four corners of the
    earth.
13   Also the envy of Ephraim shall
    depart,
And the adversaries of Judah
    shall be cut off;
Ephraim shall not envy Judah,
And Judah shall not harass
    Ephraim.
14   But they shall fly down upon
    the shoulder of the
    Philistines toward the west;
Together they shall plunder the
    people of the East;

They shall lay their hand on
    Edom and Moab;
And the people of Ammon shall
    obey them.
15   The LORD will utterly destroy*a*
    the tongue of the Sea of
    Egypt;
With His mighty wind He will
    shake His fist over the River,*b*
And strike it in the seven
    streams,
And make *men* cross over
    dry-shod.
16   There will be a highway for the
    remnant of His people
Who will be left from Assyria,
As it was for Israel
In the day that he came up from
    the land of Egypt.

12 And in that day you will say:

"O LORD, I will praise You;
Though You were angry with
    me,
Your anger is turned away, and
    You comfort me.
2   Behold, God *is* my salvation,
I will trust and not be afraid;
'For YAH, the LORD, *is* my
    strength and song;
He also has become
    salvation.' "*a*

3   Therefore with joy you will
    draw water
From the wells of salvation.

4 And in that day you will say:

"Praise the LORD, call upon His
    name;
Declare His deeds among the
    peoples,
Make mention that His name is
    exalted.
5   Sing to the LORD,
For He has done excellent
    things;
This *is* known in all the earth.
6   Cry out and shout, O inhabitant
    of Zion,
For great *is* the Holy One of
    Israel in your midst!"

13 The burden against Babylon
which Isaiah the son of Amoz
saw.

11:15 *a*Following Masoretic Text and Vulgate; Septuagint, Syriac, and Targum read *dry up.*   *b*That is, the Euphrates   12:2 *a*Exodus 15:2

2 "Lift up a banner on the high
mountain,
Raise your voice to them;
Wave your hand, that they may
enter the gates of the nobles.
3 I have commanded My
sanctified ones;
I have also called My mighty
ones for My anger—
Those who rejoice in My
exaltation."

4 The noise of a multitude in the
mountains,
Like that of many people!
A tumultuous noise of the
kingdoms of nations
gathered together!
The LORD of hosts musters
The army for battle.
5 They come from a far country,
From the end of heaven—
The LORD and His weapons of
indignation,
To destroy the whole land.

6 Wail, for the day of the LORD
is at hand!
It will come as destruction from
the Almighty.
7 Therefore all hands will be
limp,
Every man's heart will melt,
8 And they will be afraid.
Pangs and sorrows will take
hold of *them;*
They will be in pain as a
woman in childbirth;
They will be amazed at one
another;
Their faces *will be like* flames.

9 Behold, the day of the LORD
comes,
Cruel, with both wrath and
fierce anger,
To lay the land desolate;
And He will destroy its sinners
from it.
10 For the stars of heaven and
their constellations
Will not give their light;
The sun will be darkened in its
going forth,
And the moon will not cause its
light to shine.

11 "I will punish the world for *its*
evil,
And the wicked for their
iniquity;

I will halt the arrogance of the
proud,
And will lay low the
haughtiness of the terrible.
12 I will make a mortal more rare
than fine gold,
A man more than the golden
wedge of Ophir.
13 Therefore I will shake the
heavens,
And the earth will move out of
her place,
In the wrath of the LORD of
hosts
And in the day of His fierce
anger.
14 It shall be as the hunted
gazelle,
And as a sheep that no man
takes up;
Every man will turn to his own
people,
And everyone will flee to his
own land.
15 Everyone who is found will be
thrust through,
And everyone who is captured
will fall by the sword.
16 Their children also will be
dashed to pieces before their
eyes;
Their houses will be plundered
And their wives ravished.

17 "Behold, I will stir up the Medes
against them,
Who will not regard silver;
And *as for* gold, they will not
delight in it.
18 Also *their* bows will dash the
young men to pieces,
And they will have no pity on
the fruit of the womb;
Their eye will not spare
children.
19 And Babylon, the glory of
kingdoms,
The beauty of the Chaldeans'
pride,
Will be as when God overthrew
Sodom and Gomorrah.
20 It will never be inhabited,
Nor will it be settled from
generation to generation;
Nor will the Arabian pitch tents
there,
Nor will the shepherds make
their sheepfolds there.
21 But wild beasts of the desert
will lie there,
And their houses will be full of
owls;

*L*et the strong bear the infirmities of the weak. God can greatly use you to restore
wholeness to others who walk in varying degrees of brokenness.

Ostriches will dwell there,
And wild goats will caper there.
22 The hyenas will howl in their
   citadels,
And jackals in their pleasant
   palaces.
Her time *is* near to come,
And her days will not be
   prolonged."

14 For the LORD will have mercy
on Jacob, and will still choose
Israel, and settle them in their own
land. The strangers will be joined
with them, and they will cling to the
house of Jacob. 2 Then people will
take them and bring them to their
place, and the house of Israel will
possess them for servants and maids
in the land of the LORD; they will take
them captive whose captives they
were, and rule over their oppressors.

3 It shall come to pass in the day
the LORD gives you rest from your
sorrow, and from your fear and the
hard bondage in which you were
made to serve, 4 that you will take
up this proverb against the king of
Babylon, and say:

"How the oppressor has ceased,
   The golden*a* city ceased!
5 The LORD has broken the staff
   of the wicked,
   The scepter of the rulers;
6 He who struck the people in
   wrath with a continual
   stroke,
   He who ruled the nations in
   anger,
   Is persecuted *and* no one
   hinders.
7 The whole earth is at rest *and*
   quiet;
   They break forth into singing.
8 Indeed the cypress trees rejoice
   over you,
   And the cedars of Lebanon,
   Saying, 'Since you were cut
   down,
   No woodsman has come up
   against us.'

9 "Hell from beneath is excited
   about you,
   To meet *you* at your coming;
   It stirs up the dead for you,
   All the chief ones of the earth;
   It has raised up from their
   thrones
   All the kings of the nations.

10 They all shall speak and say to
   you:
   'Have you also become as weak
   as we?
   Have you become like us?
11 Your pomp is brought down to
   Sheol,
   And the sound of your stringed
   instruments;
   The maggot is spread under
   you,
   And worms cover you.'

12 "How you are fallen from
   heaven,
   O Lucifer,*a* son of the morning!
   How you are cut down to the
   ground,
   You who weakened the
   nations!
13 For you have said in your heart:
   'I will ascend into heaven,
   I will exalt my throne above the
   stars of God;
   I will also sit on the mount of
   the congregation
   On the farthest sides of the
   north;
14 I will ascend above the heights
   of the clouds,
   I will be like the Most High.'
15 Yet you shall be brought down
   to Sheol,
   To the lowest depths of the Pit.

16 "Those who see you will gaze at
   you,
   And consider you, *saying:*
   '*Is* this the man who made the
   earth tremble,
   Who shook kingdoms,
17 Who made the world as a
   wilderness
   And destroyed its cities,
   Who did not open the house of
   his prisoners?'

18 "All the kings of the nations,
   All of them, sleep in glory,
   Everyone in his own house;
19 But you are cast out of your
   grave
   Like an abominable branch,
   Like the garment of those who
   are slain,
   Thrust through with a sword,
   Who go down to the stones of
   the pit,
   Like a corpse trodden
   underfoot.

14:4 *a*Or *insolent*   14:12 *a*Literally *Day Star*

Gospel
Pearls

20 You will not be joined with
    them in burial,
Because you have destroyed
    your land
And slain your people.
The brood of evildoers shall
    never be named.

21 Prepare slaughter for his
    children
Because of the iniquity of their
    fathers,
Lest they rise up and possess
    the land,
And fill the face of the world
    with cities."

22 "For I will rise up against
    them," says the LORD of
    hosts,
"And cut off from Babylon the
    name and remnant,
And offspring and posterity,"
    says the LORD.

23 "I will also make it a possession
    for the porcupine,
And marshes of muddy water;
I will sweep it with the broom
    of destruction," says the
    LORD of hosts.

24 The LORD of hosts has sworn,
    saying,
"Surely, as I have thought, so it
    shall come to pass,
And as I have purposed, *so* it
    shall stand:

25 That I will break the Assyrian
    in My land,
And on My mountains tread
    him underfoot.
Then his yoke shall be removed
    from them,
And his burden removed from
    their shoulders.

26 This *is* the purpose that is
    purposed against the whole
    earth,
And this *is* the hand that is
    stretched out over all the
    nations.

27 For the LORD of hosts has
    purposed,
And who will annul *it?*
His hand *is* stretched out,
And who will turn it back?"

28 This is the burden which came
in the year that King Ahaz died.

29 "Do not rejoice, all you of
    Philistia,
Because the rod that struck you
    is broken;
For out of the serpent's roots
    will come forth a viper,
And its offspring *will be* a fiery
    flying serpent.

30 The firstborn of the poor will
    feed,
And the needy will lie down in
    safety;
I will kill your roots with
    famine,
And it will slay your remnant.

31 Wail, O gate! Cry, O city!
All you of Philistia *are*
    dissolved;
For smoke will come from the
    north,
And no one *will be* alone in his
    appointed times."

32 What will they answer the
    messengers of the nation?
That the LORD has founded
    Zion,
And the poor of His people
    shall take refuge in it.

15 The burden against Moab.

Because in the night Ar of
    Moab is laid waste
And destroyed,
Because in the night Kir of
    Moab is laid waste
And destroyed,

2 He has gone up to the temple*ᵃ*
    and Dibon,
To the high places to weep.
Moab will wail over Nebo and
    over Medeba;
On all their heads *will be*
    baldness,
And every beard cut off.

3 In their streets they will
    clothe themselves with
    sackcloth;
On the tops of their houses
And in their streets
Everyone will wail, weeping
    bitterly.

4 Heshbon and Elealeh will cry
    out,
Their voice shall be heard as
    far as Jahaz;
Therefore the armed soldiers*ᵃ*
    of Moab will cry out;

15:2 *ᵃ*Hebrew *bayith* (*house*)   15:4 *ᵃ*Following Masoretic Text, Targum, and Vulgate; Septuagint and
Syriac read *loins*.

---

*M*ost of us have had some degree of cracking, tearing or damage. The fact that
we have persevered is a testimony to all who understand themselves to be broken
arrows.

His life will be burdensome to
him.

5 "My heart will cry out for Moab;
His fugitives *shall flee* to Zoar,
Like a three-year-old heifer.*ᵃ*
For by the Ascent of Luhith
They will go up with weeping;
For in the way of Horonaim
They will raise up a cry of
destruction,
6 For the waters of Nimrim will
be desolate,
For the green grass has
withered away;
The grass fails, there is nothing
green.
7 Therefore the abundance they
have gained,
And what they have laid up,
They will carry away to the
Brook of the Willows.
8 For the cry has gone all around
the borders of Moab,
Its wailing to Eglaim
And its wailing to Beer Elim.
9 For the waters of Dimon*ᵃ* will
be full of blood;
Because I will bring more upon
Dimon,*ᵇ*
Lions upon him who escapes
from Moab,
And on the remnant of the
land."

16 Send the lamb to the ruler of
the land,
From Sela to the wilderness,
To the mount of the daughter
of Zion.
2 For it shall be as a wandering
bird thrown out of the nest;
So shall be the daughters of
Moab at the fords of the
Arnon.

3 "Take counsel, execute
judgment;
Make your shadow like the
night in the middle of the
day;
Hide the outcasts,
Do not betray him who
escapes.
4 Let My outcasts dwell with you,
O Moab;
Be a shelter to them from the
face of the spoiler.
For the extortioner is at an end,

Devastation ceases,
The oppressors are consumed
out of the land.
5 In mercy the throne will be
established;
And One will sit on it in truth,
in the tabernacle of David,
Judging and seeking justice
and hastening
righteousness."

6 We have heard of the pride of
Moab—
He is very proud—
Of his haughtiness and his
pride and his wrath;
But his lies *shall* not *be* so.
7 Therefore Moab shall wail for
Moab;
Everyone shall wail.
For the foundations of Kir
Hareseth you shall mourn;
Surely *they are* stricken.

8 For the fields of Heshbon
languish,
And the vine of Sibmah;
The lords of the nations have
broken down its choice
plants,
Which have reached to Jazer
And wandered through the
wilderness.
Her branches are stretched out,
They are gone over the sea.
9 Therefore I will bewail the vine
of Sibmah,
With the weeping of Jazer;
I will drench you with my tears,
O Heshbon and Elealeh;
For battle cries have fallen
Over your summer fruits and
your harvest.

10 Gladness is taken away,
And joy from the plentiful field;
In the vineyards there will be
no singing,
Nor will there be shouting;
No treaders will tread out wine
in the presses;
I have made their shouting
cease.
11 Therefore my heart shall
resound like a harp for Moab,
And my inner being for Kir
Heres.

15:5 *ᵃ*Or *The Third Eglath,* an unknown city (compare Jeremiah 48:34)   15:9 *ᵃ*Following Masoretic Text
and Targum; Dead Sea Scrolls and Vulgate read *Dibon;* Septuagint reads *Rimon.*   *ᵇ*Following Masoretic
Text and Targum; Dead Sea Scrolls and Vulgate read *Dibon;* Septuagint reads *Rimon.*

Gospel Pearls

12 And it shall come to pass,
  When it is seen that Moab is
    weary on the high place,
  That he will come to his
    sanctuary to pray;
  But he will not prevail.

13 This *is* the word which the LORD has spoken concerning Moab since that time. 14 But now the LORD has spoken, saying, "Within three years, as the years of a hired man, the glory of Moab will be despised with all that great multitude, and the remnant *will be* very small *and* feeble."

17 The burden against Damascus.

"Behold, Damascus will cease
    from *being* a city,
  And it will be a ruinous heap.
2 The cities of Aroer *are*
    forsaken;*a*
  They will be for flocks
  Which lie down, and no one
    will make *them* afraid.
3 The fortress also will cease
    from Ephraim,
  The kingdom from Damascus,
  And the remnant of Syria;
  They will be as the glory of the
    children of Israel,"
  Says the LORD of hosts.

4 "In that day it shall come to pass
  That the glory of Jacob will
    wane,
  And the fatness of his flesh
    grow lean.
5 It shall be as when the
    harvester gathers the grain,
  And reaps the heads with his
    arm;
  It shall be as he who gathers
    heads of grain
  In the Valley of Rephaim.
6 Yet gleaning grapes will be left
    in it,
  Like the shaking of an olive
    tree,
  Two *or* three olives at the top
    of the uppermost bough,
  Four *or* five in its most fruitful
    branches,"
  Says the LORD God of Israel.

7 In that day a man will look to
    his Maker,

And his eyes will have respect
    for the Holy One of Israel.
8 He will not look to the altars,
  The work of his hands;
  He will not respect what his
    fingers have made,
  Nor the wooden images*a* nor
    the incense altars.

9 In that day his strong cities will
    be as a forsaken bough*a*
  And an uppermost branch,*b*
  Which they left because of the
    children of Israel;
  And there will be desolation.

10 Because you have forgotten the
    God of your salvation,
  And have not been mindful of
    the Rock of your stronghold,
  Therefore you will plant
    pleasant plants
  And set out foreign seedlings;
11 In the day you will make your
    plant to grow,
  And in the morning you will
    make your seed to flourish;
  But the harvest *will be* a heap
    of ruins
  In the day of grief and
    desperate sorrow.

12 Woe to the multitude of many
    people
  Who make a noise like the roar
    of the seas,
  And to the rushing of nations
  That make a rushing like
    the rushing of mighty
    waters!
13 The nations will rush like the
    rushing of many waters;
  But *God* will rebuke them and
    they will flee far away,
  And be chased like the chaff of
    the mountains before the
    wind,
  Like a rolling thing before the
    whirlwind.
14 Then behold, at eventide,
    trouble!
  And before the morning, he *is*
    no more.
  This *is* the portion of those who
    plunder us,
  And the lot of those who rob
    us.

17:2 *a*Following Masoretic Text and Vulgate; Septuagint reads *It shall be forsaken forever;* Targum reads *Its cities shall be forsaken and desolate.* 17:8 *a*Hebrew *Asherah,* a Canaanite goddess 17:9 *a*Septuagint reads *Hivites;* Targum reads *laid waste;* Vulgate reads *as the ploughs.* *b*Septuagint reads *Amorites;* Targum reads *in ruins;* Vulgate reads *corn.*

I salute all the wonderful people who work with children. Whether through children's church or public school, you have a very high calling. Don't forget to touch their little lives with a word of hope and a smile of encouragement.

18 Woe to the land shadowed with
buzzing wings,
Which *is* beyond the rivers of
Ethiopia,

2   Which sends ambassadors by
sea,
Even in vessels of reed on the
waters, *saying,*
"Go, swift messengers, to a
nation tall and smooth *of
skin,*
To a people terrible from their
beginning onward,
A nation powerful and treading
down,
Whose land the rivers divide."

3   All inhabitants of the world
and dwellers on the
earth:
When he lifts up a banner
on the mountains, you see
it;
And when he blows a trumpet,
you hear *it.*

4   For so the LORD said to me,
"I will take My rest,
And I will look from My
dwelling place
Like clear heat in sunshine,
Like a cloud of dew in the heat
of harvest."

5   For before the harvest, when
the bud is perfect
And the sour grape is ripening
in the flower,
He will both cut off the sprigs
with pruning hooks
And take away *and* cut down
the branches.

6   They will be left together for
the mountain birds of prey
And for the beasts of the earth;
The birds of prey will summer
on them,
And all the beasts of the earth
will winter on them.

7   In that time a present will be
brought to the LORD of hosts
From[a] a people tall and smooth
of skin,
And from a people terrible
from their beginning onward,
A nation powerful and treading
down,
Whose land the rivers divide—

To the place of the name of the
LORD of hosts,
To Mount Zion.

19 The burden against Egypt.

Behold, the LORD rides on a
swift cloud,
And will come into Egypt;
The idols of Egypt will totter at
His presence,
And the heart of Egypt will
melt in its midst.

2   "I will set Egyptians against
Egyptians;
Everyone will fight against his
brother,
And everyone against his
neighbor,
City against city, kingdom
against kingdom.

3   The spirit of Egypt will fail in
its midst;
I will destroy their counsel,
And they will consult the idols
and the charmers,
The mediums and the
sorcerers.

4   And the Egyptians I will give
Into the hand of a cruel master,
And a fierce king will rule over
them,"
Says the Lord, the LORD of
hosts.

5   The waters will fail from the
sea,
And the river will be wasted
and dried up.

6   The rivers will turn foul;
The brooks of defense will be
emptied and dried up;
The reeds and rushes will
wither.

7   The papyrus reeds by the
River,[a] by the mouth of the
River,
And everything sown by the
River,
Will wither, be driven away,
and be no more.

8   The fishermen also will mourn;
All those will lament who cast
hooks into the River,
And they will languish who
spread nets on the waters.

9   Moreover those who work in
fine flax

18:7 [a]Following Dead Sea Scrolls, Septuagint, and Vulgate; Masoretic Text omits *From;* Targum reads
To.   19:7 [a]That is, the Nile

*Gospel
Pearls*

And those who weave fine
fabric will be ashamed;
10 And its foundations will be
broken.
All who make wages *will be*
troubled of soul.

11 Surely the princes of Zoan *are*
fools;
Pharaoh's wise counselors give
foolish counsel.
How do you say to Pharaoh, "I
am the son of the wise,
The son of ancient kings?"
12 Where *are* they?
Where are your wise men?
Let them tell you now,
And let them know what the
LORD of hosts has purposed
against Egypt.
13 The princes of Zoan have
become fools;
The princes of Noph*ᵃ* are
deceived;
They have also deluded Egypt,
Those who are the mainstay of
its tribes.
14 The LORD has mingled a
perverse spirit in her midst;
And they have caused Egypt to
err in all her work,
As a drunken man staggers in
his vomit.
15 Neither will there be *any* work
for Egypt,
Which the head or tail,
Palm branch or bulrush, may
do.*ᵃ*

16 In that day Egypt will be like
women, and will be afraid and fear
because of the waving of the hand
of the LORD of hosts, which He waves
over it. 17 And the land of Judah will
be a terror to Egypt; everyone who
makes mention of it will be afraid in
himself, because of the counsel of the
LORD of hosts which He has determined against it.
18 In that day five cities in the land
of Egypt will speak the language of
Canaan and swear by the LORD of
hosts; one will be called the City of
Destruction.*ᵃ*
19 In that day there will be an altar
to the LORD in the midst of the land
of Egypt, and a pillar to the LORD at
its border. 20 And it will be for a sign

and for a witness to the LORD of hosts
in the land of Egypt; for they will cry
to the LORD because of the oppressors, and He will send them a Savior
and a Mighty One, and He will deliver them. 21 Then the LORD will be
known to Egypt, and the Egyptians
will know the LORD in that day, and
will make sacrifice and offering; yes,
they will make a vow to the LORD and
perform *it*. 22 And the LORD will
strike Egypt, He will strike and heal
it; they will return to the LORD, and
He will be entreated by them and
heal them.
23 In that day there will be a highway from Egypt to Assyria, and the
Assyrian will come into Egypt and
the Egyptian into Assyria, and the
Egyptians will serve with the Assyrians.
24 In that day Israel will be one of
three with Egypt and Assyria—a
blessing in the midst of the land,
25 whom the LORD of hosts shall
bless, saying, "Blessed *is* Egypt My
people, and Assyria the work of My
hands, and Israel My inheritance."

20 In the year that Tartan*ᵃ* came
to Ashdod, when Sargon the
king of Assyria sent him, and he
fought against Ashdod and took it,
2 at the same time the LORD spoke by
Isaiah the son of Amoz, saying, "Go,
and remove the sackcloth from your
body, and take your sandals off your
feet." And he did so, walking naked
and barefoot.
3 Then the LORD said, "Just as My
servant Isaiah has walked naked and
barefoot three years *for* a sign and a
wonder against Egypt and Ethiopia,
4 so shall the king of Assyria lead
away the Egyptians as prisoners and
the Ethiopians as captives, young
and old, naked and barefoot, with
their buttocks uncovered, to the
shame of Egypt. 5 Then they shall be
afraid and ashamed of Ethiopia their
expectation and Egypt their glory.
6 And the inhabitant of this territory
will say in that day, 'Surely such *is*
our expectation, wherever we flee for
help to be delivered from the king of
Assyria; and how shall we escape?' "

21 The burden against the Wilderness of the Sea.

19:13 *ᵃ*That is, ancient Memphis   19:15 *ᵃ*Compare Isaiah 9:14–16   19:18 *ᵃ*Some Hebrew manuscripts,
Arabic, Dead Sea Scrolls, Targum, and Vulgate read *Sun;* Septuagint reads *Asedek* (literally
Righteousness).   20:1 *ᵃ*Or *the Commander in Chief*

---

*H*ow can we be in the presence of a loving God and then not love little ones? When
Jesus blessed the children, He challenged the adults to become as children.

As whirlwinds in the South
  pass through,
So it comes from the desert,
  from a terrible land.
2 A distressing vision is declared
  to me;
The treacherous dealer deals
  treacherously,
And the plunderer plunders.
Go up, O Elam!
Besiege, O Media!
All its sighing I have made to
  cease.

3 Therefore my loins are filled
  with pain;
Pangs have taken hold of me,
  like the pangs of a woman in
  labor.
I was distressed when *I* heard
  it;
I was dismayed when *I* saw
  it.
4 My heart wavered, fearfulness
  frightened me;
The night for which I longed He
  turned into fear for me.
5 Prepare the table,
Set a watchman in the tower,
Eat and drink.
Arise, you princes,
Anoint the shield!

6 For thus has the Lord said to
  me:
"Go, set a watchman,
  Let him declare what he sees."
7 And he saw a chariot *with* a
  pair of horsemen,
A chariot of donkeys, *and* a
  chariot of camels,
And he listened earnestly with
  great care.
8 Then he cried, "A lion,*ᵃ* my
  Lord!
I stand continually on the
  watchtower in the daytime;
I have sat at my post every
  night.
9 And look, here comes a chariot
  of men *with* a pair of
  horsemen!"
Then he answered and said,
"Babylon is fallen, is fallen!
And all the carved images of
  her gods
He has broken to the ground."

10 Oh, my threshing and the grain
  of my floor!

That which I have heard from
  the Lord of hosts,
The God of Israel,
I have declared to you.

11 The burden against Dumah.

He calls to me out of Seir,
"Watchman, what of the night?
Watchman, what of the
  night?"
12 The watchman said,
"The morning comes, and also
  the night.
If you will inquire, inquire;
Return! Come back!"

13 The burden against Arabia.

In the forest in Arabia you will
  lodge,
O you traveling companies of
  Dedanites.
14 O inhabitants of the land of
  Tema,
Bring water to him who is
  thirsty;
With their bread they met him
  who fled.
15 For they fled from the swords,
  from the drawn sword,
From the bent bow, and from
  the distress of war.

16 For thus the Lord has said to me:
"Within a year, according to the year
of a hired man, all the glory of Kedar
will fail; 17 and the remainder of the
number of archers, the mighty men
of the people of Kedar, will be diminished; for the Lord God of Israel has
spoken *it.*"

22 The burden against the Valley
of Vision.

What ails you now, that you
  have all gone up to the
  housetops,
2 You who are full of noise,
A tumultuous city, a joyous
  city?
Your slain *men are* not slain
  with the sword,
Nor dead in battle.
3 All your rulers have fled
  together;
They are captured by the
  archers.
All who are found in you are
  bound together;

21:8 ᵃDead Sea Scrolls read *Then the observer cried.*

Gospel Pearls

They have fled from afar.
4 Therefore I said, "Look away
from me,
I will weep bitterly;
Do not labor to comfort me
Because of the plundering of
the daughter of my people."

5 For *it is* a day of trouble and
treading down and
perplexity
By the Lord GOD of hosts
In the Valley of Vision—
Breaking down the walls
And of crying to the mountain.
6 Elam bore the quiver
With chariots of men *and*
horsemen,
And Kir uncovered the shield.
7 It shall come to pass *that* your
choicest valleys
Shall be full of chariots,
And the horsemen shall set
themselves in array at the
gate.

8 He removed the protection of
Judah.
You looked in that day to the
armor of the House of the
Forest;
9 You also saw the damage to the
city of David,
That it was great;
And you gathered together the
waters of the lower pool.
10 You numbered the houses of
Jerusalem,
And the houses you broke
down
To fortify the wall.
11 You also made a reservoir
between the two walls
For the water of the old pool.
But you did not look to its
Maker,
Nor did you have respect for
Him who fashioned it long
ago.

12 And in that day the Lord GOD
of hosts
Called for weeping and for
mourning,
For baldness and for girding
with sackcloth.
13 But instead, joy and gladness,
Slaying oxen and killing sheep,
Eating meat and drinking wine:

"Let us eat and drink, for
tomorrow we die!"

14 Then it was revealed in my
hearing by the LORD of hosts,
"Surely for this iniquity there
will be no atonement for you,
Even to your death," says the
Lord GOD of hosts.

15 Thus says the Lord GOD of hosts:

"Go, proceed to this steward,
To Shebna, who *is* over the
house, *and say:*
16 'What have you here, and whom
have you here,
That you have hewn a
sepulcher here,
As he who hews himself a
sepulcher on high,
Who carves a tomb for himself
in a rock?
17 Indeed, the LORD will throw
you away violently,
O mighty man,
And will surely seize you.
18 He will surely turn violently
and toss you like a ball
Into a large country;
There you shall die, and there
your glorious chariots
Shall be the shame of your
master's house.
19 So I will drive you out of your
office,
And from your position he will
pull you down.*a*

20 'Then it shall be in that day,
That I will call My servant
Eliakim the son of Hilkiah;
21 I will clothe him with your robe
And strengthen him with your
belt;
I will commit your
responsibility into his hand.
He shall be a father to the
inhabitants of Jerusalem
And to the house of Judah.
22 The key of the house of David
I will lay on his shoulder;
So he shall open, and no one
shall shut;
And he shall shut, and no one
shall open.
23 I will fasten him *as* a peg in a
secure place,
And he will become a glorious
throne to his father's house.

22:19 *a*Septuagint omits *he will pull you down;* Syriac, Targum, and Vulgate read *I will pull you down.*

Sometimes we need to allow the Lord to adjust the damaged places of our past. I am
glad to say that God provides arms that allow adults to climb up like children and
be nurtured through the tragedies of early days.

24 'They will hang on him all the glory of his father's house, the off-spring and the posterity, all vessels of small quantity, from the cups to all the pitchers. 25 In that day,' says the LORD of hosts, 'the peg that is fastened in the secure place will be removed and be cut down and fall, and the burden that *was* on it will be cut off; for the LORD has spoken.' "

23 The burden against Tyre.

Wail, you ships of Tarshish!
For it is laid waste,
So that there is no house, no harbor;
From the land of Cyprus*ᵃ* it is revealed to them.

2 Be still, you inhabitants of the coastland,
You merchants of Sidon,
Whom those who cross the sea have filled.*ᵃ*
3 And on great waters the grain of Shihor,
The harvest of the River,*ᵃ* *is* her revenue;
And she is a marketplace for the nations.

4 Be ashamed, O Sidon;
For the sea has spoken,
The strength of the sea, saying,
"I do not labor, nor bring forth children;
Neither do I rear young men,
Nor bring up virgins."
5 When the report *reaches* Egypt,
They also will be in agony at the report of Tyre.

6 Cross over to Tarshish;
Wail, you inhabitants of the coastland!
7 *Is* this your joyous *city,*
Whose antiquity *is* from ancient days,
Whose feet carried her far off to dwell?
8 Who has taken this counsel against Tyre, the crowning *city,*
Whose merchants *are* princes,
Whose traders *are* the honorable of the earth?

9 The LORD of hosts has purposed it,
To bring to dishonor the pride of all glory,
To bring into contempt all the honorable of the earth.

10 Overflow through your land like the River,*ᵃ*
O daughter of Tarshish;
There is no more strength.
11 He stretched out His hand over the sea,
He shook the kingdoms;
The LORD has given a commandment against Canaan
To destroy its strongholds.
12 And He said, "You will rejoice no more,
O you oppressed virgin daughter of Sidon.
Arise, cross over to Cyprus;
There also you will have no rest."

13 Behold, the land of the Chaldeans,
This people *which* was not;
Assyria founded it for wild beasts of the desert.
They set up its towers,
They raised up its palaces,
And brought it to ruin.

14 Wail, you ships of Tarshish!
For your strength is laid waste.

15 Now it shall come to pass in that day that Tyre will be forgotten seventy years, according to the days of one king. At the end of seventy years it will happen to Tyre as *in* the song of the harlot:

16 "Take a harp, go about the city,
You forgotten harlot;
Make sweet melody, sing many songs,
That you may be remembered."

17 And it shall be, at the end of seventy years, that the LORD will deal with Tyre. She will return to her hire, and commit fornication with all the kingdoms of the world on the face of the earth. 18 Her gain and her pay will be set apart for the LORD; it will not be treasured nor laid up, for her

23:1 *ᵃ*Hebrew *Kittim,* western lands, especially Cyprus   23:2 *ᵃ*Following Masoretic Text and Vulgate; Septuagint and Targum read *passing over the water;* Dead Sea Scrolls read *your messengers passing over the sea.*   23:3 *ᵃ*That is, the Nile   23:10 *ᵃ*That is, the Nile

Gospel Pearls

gain will be for those who dwell before the Lord, to eat sufficiently, and
for fine clothing.

24 Behold, the Lord makes the
earth empty and makes it
waste,
Distorts its surface
And scatters abroad its
inhabitants.
2   And it shall be:
As with the people, so with the
priest;
As with the servant, so with his
master;
As with the maid, so with her
mistress;
As with the buyer, so with the
seller;
As with the lender, so with the
borrower;
As with the creditor, so with
the debtor.
3   The land shall be entirely
emptied and utterly
plundered,
For the Lord has spoken this
word.

4   The earth mourns *and* fades
away,
The world languishes *and* fades
away;
The haughty people of the
earth languish.
5   The earth is also defiled under
its inhabitants,
Because they have
transgressed the laws,
Changed the ordinance,
Broken the everlasting
covenant.
6   Therefore the curse has
devoured the earth,
And those who dwell in it are
desolate.
Therefore the inhabitants of
the earth are burned,
And few men *are* left.

7   The new wine fails, the vine
languishes,
All the merry-hearted sigh.
8   The mirth of the tambourine
ceases,
The noise of the jubilant ends,
The joy of the harp ceases.
9   They shall not drink wine with
a song;
Strong drink is bitter to those
who drink it.

10   The city of confusion is broken
down;
Every house is shut up, so that
none may go in.
11   *There is* a cry for wine in the
streets,
All joy is darkened,
The mirth of the land is gone.
12   In the city desolation is left,
And the gate is stricken with
destruction.
13   When it shall be thus in the
midst of the land among the
people,
It shall be like the shaking of
an olive tree,
Like the gleaning of grapes
when the vintage is done.

14   They shall lift up their voice,
they shall sing;
For the majesty of the Lord
They shall cry aloud from the
sea.
15   Therefore glorify the Lord in
the dawning light,
The name of the Lord God of
Israel in the coastlands of the
sea.
16   From the ends of the earth we
have heard songs:
"Glory to the righteous!"
But I said, "I am ruined, ruined!
Woe to me!
The treacherous dealers have
dealt treacherously,
Indeed, the treacherous dealers
have dealt very
treacherously."

17   Fear and the pit and the snare
Are upon you, O inhabitant of
the earth.
18   And it shall be
That he who flees from the
noise of the fear
Shall fall into the pit,
And he who comes up from the
midst of the pit
Shall be caught in the snare;
For the windows from on high
are open,
And the foundations of the
earth are shaken.

19   The earth is violently broken,
The earth is split open,
The earth is shaken
exceedingly.
20   The earth shall reel to and fro
like a drunkard,

---

*I*n God, we can become children again. Salvation is God giving us a chance to start
over again. He will not abuse the children that come to Him.

And shall totter like a hut;
Its transgression shall be heavy
upon it,
And it will fall, and not rise
again.

21 It shall come to pass in that day
That the LORD will punish on
high the host of exalted ones,
And on the earth the kings of
the earth.
22 They will be gathered together,
As prisoners are gathered in
the pit,
And will be shut up in the
prison;
After many days they will be
punished.
23 Then the moon will be
disgraced
And the sun ashamed;
For the LORD of hosts will reign
On Mount Zion and in
Jerusalem
And before His elders,
gloriously.

25 O LORD, You *are* my God.
I will exalt You,
I will praise Your name,
For You have done wonderful
things;
Your counsels of old *are*
faithfulness and truth.
2 For You have made a city a
ruin,
A fortified city a ruin,
A palace of foreigners to be a
city no more;
It will never be rebuilt.
3 Therefore the strong people
will glorify You;
The city of the terrible nations
will fear You.
4 For You have been a strength
to the poor,
A strength to the needy in his
distress,
A refuge from the storm,
A shade from the heat;
For the blast of the terrible ones
is as a storm *against* the wall.
5 You will reduce the noise of
aliens,
As heat in a dry place;
As heat in the shadow of a
cloud,
The song of the terrible ones
will be diminished.

6 And in this mountain
The LORD of hosts will make for
all people

A feast of choice pieces,
A feast of wines on the lees,
Of fat things full of marrow,
Of well-refined wines on the
lees.
7 And He will destroy on this
mountain
The surface of the covering cast
over all people,
And the veil that is spread over
all nations.
8 He will swallow up death
forever,
And the Lord GOD will wipe
away tears from all faces;
The rebuke of His people
He will take away from all the
earth;
For the LORD has spoken.

9 And it will be said in that day:
"Behold, this *is* our God;
We have waited for Him, and
He will save us.
This *is* the LORD;
We have waited for Him;
We will be glad and rejoice in
His salvation."

10 For on this mountain the hand
of the LORD will rest,
And Moab shall be trampled
down under Him,
As straw is trampled down for
the refuse heap.
11 And He will spread out His
hands in their midst
As a swimmer reaches out to
swim,
And He will bring down their
pride
Together with the trickery of
their hands.
12 The fortress of the high fort of
your walls
He will bring down, lay low,
And bring to the ground, down
to the dust.

26 In that day this song will be
sung in the land of Judah:

"We have a strong city;
God will appoint salvation *for*
walls and bulwarks.
2 Open the gates,
That the righteous nation
which keeps the truth may
enter in.
3 You will keep *him* in perfect
peace,
Whose mind *is* stayed *on You,*

*I*f God says no, thank Him. Some of my greatest moments with God have come
when I said yes to His corrections and decisions. Satan was defeated, and God was
worshiped by my trust in His sovereign will for my life.

The Pain and the Promise

Isaiah 25:8

Birthing—everything you bring forth—comes through sorrow. If you're going to bring forth anything in your career, your marriage or your life; if you're going to develop anything in your character; if you're going to be a fruitful woman, it will come through the things you suffer. You will enter into strength through sorrow.

Sorrow is not the object; it is simply the canal through which the object comes. For every sorrow, for every intense groaning in your spirit, you ought to have something to show for it. Don't let the devil give you sorrow without seed. Any time you have sorrow, it is a sign that God is trying to get something through you and to you.

You are the entrance of all things. You are the door of life. You are a vehicle, an expression of blessing. If there is to be any virtue, any praise, any victory, any deliverance, it has to come through you.

Satan wants to use you as a legal entry into this world or into your family. That's how he attempted to destroy the human race with the first family. Be careful what you allow to come through you. Close the doors to the enemy. Then know that when travail comes into your spirit, it's because you're about to give birth. When you see sorrow multiply, it is a sign that God is getting ready to send something to you.

Don't become so preoccupied with the pain that you forget to push the baby. When the pain is at its peak, that's when you have to push. Push! You don't have time to cry. Push! You don't have time to be suicidal. Push! This is not the time to give up. Push, because God is about to birth a promise through you. Cry if you must, and groan if you have to, but keep on pushing. God has promised that if it is to come into the world, it has to pass through you.

Don't settle for the pain and not receive the benefit. Disregard the pain and hold out for the promise. Understand that God has promised some things to you that He wants you to have, and you've got to stay there on the table until you get to the place where you ought to be in the Lord. Don't become so engrossed with what's hurting you that you're not doing what it takes to produce fruit in your life.

If you're in a financial rut, bring forth. If you're in need of healing for your body, bring forth. If you are seeking deliverance from a besetting sin, bring forth. Understand that it must be brought forth. It doesn't just happen by accident. That's why you have suffered pain. Hang on! After all, the pain is forgotten when the baby is born.

Because he trusts in You.

4 Trust in the LORD forever,
For in YAH, the LORD, *is*
everlasting strength.*ª*

5 For He brings down those who
dwell on high,
The lofty city;
He lays it low,
He lays it low to the ground,
He brings it down to the
dust.

6 The foot shall tread it down—
The feet of the poor
And the steps of the needy."

7 The way of the just *is*
uprightness;
O Most Upright,
You weigh the path of the
just.

8 Yes, in the way of Your
judgments,
O LORD, we have waited for
You;
The desire of *our* soul *is* for
Your name
And for the remembrance of
You.

9 With my soul I have desired
You in the night,
Yes, by my spirit within me I
will seek You early;
For when Your judgments *are*
in the earth,
The inhabitants of the world
will learn righteousness.

10 Let grace be shown to the
wicked,
Yet he will not learn
righteousness;
In the land of uprightness he
will deal unjustly,
And will not behold the
majesty of the LORD.

11 LORD, *when* Your hand is lifted
up, they will not see.
But they will see and be
ashamed
For *their* envy of people;
Yes, the fire of Your enemies
shall devour them.

12 LORD, You will establish peace
for us,
For You have also done all our
works in us.

13 O LORD our God, masters
besides You
Have had dominion over us;

But by You only we make
mention of Your name.

14 *They are* dead, they will not
live;
They are deceased, they will
not rise.
Therefore You have punished
and destroyed them,
And made all their memory to
perish.

15 You have increased the nation,
O LORD,
You have increased the nation;
You are glorified;
You have expanded all the
borders of the land.

16 LORD, in trouble they have
visited You,
They poured out a prayer *when*
Your chastening *was* upon
them.

17 As a woman with child
Is in pain and cries out in her
pangs,
When she draws near the time
of her delivery,
So have we been in Your sight,
O LORD.

18 We have been with child, we
have been in pain;
We have, as it were, brought
forth wind;
We have not accomplished any
deliverance in the earth,
Nor have the inhabitants of the
world fallen.

19 Your dead shall live;
Together with my dead body*ª*
they shall arise.
Awake and sing, you who
dwell in dust;
For your dew *is like* the dew of
herbs,
And the earth shall cast out the
dead.

20 Come, my people, enter your
chambers,
And shut your doors behind
you;
Hide yourself, as it were, for a
little moment,
Until the indignation is past.

21 For behold, the LORD comes out
of His place
To punish the inhabitants of
the earth for their iniquity;

26:4 *ª*Or *Rock of Ages*   26:19 *ª*Following Masoretic Text and Vulgate; Syriac and Targum read *their
dead bodies;* Septuagint reads *those in the tombs.*

Gospel
Pearls

The earth will also disclose her
  blood,
And will no more cover her
  slain.

27 In that day the LORD with His
  severe sword, great and
  strong,
Will punish Leviathan the
  fleeing serpent,
Leviathan that twisted serpent;
And He will slay the reptile that
  is in the sea.

2 In that day sing to her,
  "A vineyard of red wine!*ᵃ*
3 I, the LORD, keep it,
I water it every moment;
Lest any hurt it,
I keep it night and day.
4 Fury *is* not in Me.
Who would set briers *and*
  thorns
Against Me in battle?
I would go through them,
I would burn them together.
5 Or let him take hold of My
  strength,
That he may make peace with
  Me;
And he shall make peace with
  Me."

6 Those who come He shall cause
  to take root in Jacob;
Israel shall blossom and bud,
And fill the face of the world
  with fruit.

7 Has He struck Israel as He
  struck those who struck
  him?
Or has He been slain according
  to the slaughter of those who
  were slain by Him?
8 In measure, by sending it away,
You contended with it.
He removes *it* by His rough
  wind
In the day of the east wind.
9 Therefore by this the iniquity
  of Jacob will be covered;
And this *is* all the fruit of taking
  away his sin:
When he makes all the stones
  of the altar
Like chalkstones that are
  beaten to dust,

Wooden images*ᵃ* and incense
  altars shall not stand.
10 Yet the fortified city *will be*
  desolate,
The habitation forsaken and
  left like a wilderness;
There the calf will feed, and
  there it will lie down
And consume its branches.
11 When its boughs are withered,
  they will be broken off;
The women come *and* set them
  on fire.
For it *is* a people of no
  understanding;
Therefore He who made them
  will not have mercy on
  them,
And He who formed them will
  show them no favor.

12 And it shall come to pass in that
  day
That the LORD will thresh,
From the channel of the River*ᵃ*
  to the Brook of Egypt;
And you will be gathered one
  by one,
O you children of Israel.

13 So it shall be in that day:
The great trumpet will be
  blown;
They will come, who are about
  to perish in the land of
  Assyria,
And they who are outcasts in
  the land of Egypt,
And shall worship the LORD in
  the holy mount at Jerusalem.

28 Woe to the crown of pride, to
  the drunkards of Ephraim,
Whose glorious beauty *is* a
  fading flower
Which *is* at the head of the
  verdant valleys,
To those who are overcome
  with wine!
2 Behold, the Lord has a mighty
  and strong one,
Like a tempest of hail and a
  destroying storm,
Like a flood of mighty waters
  overflowing,
Who will bring *them* down to
  the earth with *His* hand.

27:2 *ᵃ*Following Masoretic Text (Kittel's *Biblia Hebraica*), Bomberg, and Vulgate; Masoretic Text (*Biblia Hebraica Stuttgartensia*), some Hebrew manuscripts, and Septuagint read *delight;* Targum reads *choice vineyard.*   27:9 *ᵃ*Hebrew *Asherim,* Canaanite deities   27:12 *ᵃ*That is, the Euphrates

*I*t is so important that we learn how to worship and adore Him. There is no better way to climb into His arms.

3 The crown of pride, the
    drunkards of Ephraim,
Will be trampled underfoot;
4 And the glorious beauty is a
    fading flower
Which *is* at the head of the
    verdant valley,
Like the first fruit before the
    summer,
Which an observer sees;
He eats it up while it is still in
    his hand.

5 In that day the LORD of hosts
    will be
For a crown of glory and a
    diadem of beauty
To the remnant of His people,
6 For a spirit of justice to him
    who sits in judgment,
And for strength to those who
    turn back the battle at the
    gate.

7 But they also have erred
    through wine,
And through intoxicating drink
    are out of the way;
The priest and the prophet
    have erred through
    intoxicating drink,
They are swallowed up by
    wine,
They are out of the way
    through intoxicating drink;
They err in vision, they stumble
    in judgment.
8 For all tables are full of vomit
    and filth;
No place *is clean.*

9 "Whom will he teach
    knowledge?
And whom will he make to
    understand the message?
Those *just* weaned from milk?
Those *just* drawn from the
    breasts?
10 For precept *must be* upon
    precept, precept upon
    precept,
Line upon line, line upon line,
Here a little, there a little."

11 For with stammering lips and
    another tongue
He will speak to this people,
12 To whom He said, "This *is* the
    rest *with which*
You may cause the weary to
    rest,"

And, "This *is* the refreshing";
Yet they would not hear.
13 But the word of the LORD was
    to them,
"Precept upon precept, precept
    upon precept,
Line upon line, line upon line,
Here a little, there a little,"
That they might go and fall
    backward, and be broken
And snared and caught.

14 Therefore hear the word of the
    LORD, you scornful men,
Who rule this people who *are*
    in Jerusalem,
15 Because you have said, "We
    have made a covenant with
    death,
And with Sheol we are in
    agreement.
When the overflowing scourge
    passes through,
It will not come to us,
For we have made lies our
    refuge,
And under falsehood we have
    hidden ourselves."

16 Therefore thus says the Lord
GOD:

"Behold, I lay in Zion a stone for
    a foundation,
A tried stone, a precious
    cornerstone, a sure
    foundation;
Whoever believes will not act
    hastily.
17 Also I will make justice the
    measuring line,
And righteousness the
    plummet;
The hail will sweep away the
    refuge of lies,
And the waters will overflow
    the hiding place.
18 Your covenant with death will
    be annulled,
And your agreement with
    Sheol will not stand;
When the overflowing scourge
    passes through,
Then you will be trampled
    down by it.
19 As often as it goes out it will
    take you;
For morning by morning it will
    pass over,
And by day and by night;
It will be a terror just to
    understand the report."

Gospel
Pearls

20 For the bed is too short to
stretch out *on*,
And the covering so narrow
that one cannot wrap himself
in it.
21 For the LORD will rise up as *at*
Mount Perazim,
He will be angry as in the
Valley of Gibeon—
That He may do His work, His
awesome work,
And bring to pass His act, His
unusual act.
22 Now therefore, do not be
mockers,
Lest your bonds be made
strong;
For I have heard from the Lord
GOD of hosts,
A destruction determined even
upon the whole earth.

23 Give ear and hear my voice,
Listen and hear my speech.
24 Does the plowman keep
plowing all day to sow?
Does he keep turning his soil
and breaking the clods?
25 When he has leveled its
surface,
Does he not sow the black
cummin
And scatter the cummin,
Plant the wheat in rows,
The barley in the appointed
place,
And the spelt in its place?
26 For He instructs him in right
judgment,
His God teaches him.

27 For the black cummin is not
threshed with a threshing
sledge,
Nor is a cartwheel rolled over
the cummin;
But the black cummin is beaten
out with a stick,
And the cummin with a rod.
28 Bread *flour* must be ground;
Therefore he does not thresh it
forever,
Break *it with* his cartwheel,
Or crush it *with* his horsemen.
29 This also comes from the LORD
of hosts,
Who is wonderful in counsel
and excellent in guidance.

29 "Woe to Ariel,[a] to Ariel, the city
where David dwelt!

29:1 [a]That is, Jerusalem

Add year to year;
Let feasts come around.
2 Yet I will distress Ariel;
There shall be heaviness and
sorrow,
And it shall be to Me as Ariel.
3 I will encamp against you all
around,
I will lay siege against you with
a mound,
And I will raise siegeworks
against you.
4 You shall be brought down,
You shall speak out of the
ground;
Your speech shall be low, out
of the dust;
Your voice shall be like a
medium's, out of the
ground;
And your speech shall whisper
out of the dust.

5 "Moreover the multitude of your
foes
Shall be like fine dust,
And the multitude of the
terrible ones
Like chaff that passes away;
Yes, it shall be in an instant,
suddenly.
6 You will be punished by the
LORD of hosts
With thunder and earthquake
and great noise,
With storm and tempest
And the flame of devouring
fire.
7 The multitude of all the nations
who fight against Ariel,
Even all who fight against her
and her fortress,
And distress her,
Shall be as a dream of a night
vision.
8 It shall even be as when a
hungry man dreams,
And look—he eats;
But he awakes, and his soul is
still empty;
Or as when a thirsty man
dreams,
And look—he drinks;
But he awakes, and indeed *he
is* faint,
And his soul still craves:
So the multitude of all the
nations shall be,
Who fight against Mount
Zion."

Stand in a stream with waters around your ankles. The waters that pass by you at
that moment, you will never see again. So it is with the misery that has challenged
your life: Let it go, let it pass away.

9 Pause and wonder!
Blind yourselves and be blind!
They are drunk, but not with wine;
They stagger, but not with intoxicating drink.
10 For the LORD has poured out on you
The spirit of deep sleep,
And has closed your eyes,
namely, the prophets;
And He has covered your heads, *namely,* the seers.

11 The whole vision has become to you like the words of a book that is sealed, which *men* deliver to one who is literate, saying, "Read this, please."
And he says, "I cannot, for it *is* sealed."
12 Then the book is delivered to one who is illiterate, saying, "Read this, please."
And he says, "I am not literate."
13 Therefore the LORD said:

"Inasmuch as these people draw near with their mouths
And honor Me with their lips,
But have removed their hearts far from Me,
And their fear toward Me is taught by the commandment of men,
14 Therefore, behold, I will again do a marvelous work
Among this people,
A marvelous work and a wonder;
For the wisdom of their wise *men* shall perish,
And the understanding of their prudent *men* shall be hidden."

15 Woe to those who seek deep to hide their counsel far from the LORD,
And their works are in the dark;
They say, "Who sees us?" and, "Who knows us?"
16 Surely you have things turned around!
Shall the potter be esteemed as the clay;
For shall the thing made say of him who made it,
"He did not make me"?
Or shall the thing formed say of him who formed it,
"He has no understanding"?

17 *Is* it not yet a very little while
Till Lebanon shall be turned into a fruitful field,
And the fruitful field be esteemed as a forest?
18 In that day the deaf shall hear the words of the book,
And the eyes of the blind shall see out of obscurity and out of darkness.
19 The humble also shall increase *their* joy in the LORD,
And the poor among men shall rejoice
In the Holy One of Israel.
20 For the terrible one is brought to nothing,
The scornful one is consumed,
And all who watch for iniquity are cut off—
21 Who make a man an offender by a word,
And lay a snare for him who reproves in the gate,
And turn aside the just by empty words.

22 Therefore thus says the LORD, who redeemed Abraham, concerning the house of Jacob:

"Jacob shall not now be ashamed,
Nor shall his face now grow pale;
23 But when he sees his children,
The work of My hands, in his midst,
They will hallow My name,
And hallow the Holy One of Jacob,
And fear the God of Israel.
24 These also who erred in spirit will come to understanding,
And those who complained will learn doctrine."

30 "Woe to the rebellious children," says the LORD,
"Who take counsel, but not of Me,
And who devise plans, but not of My Spirit,
That they may add sin to sin;
2 Who walk to go down to Egypt,
And have not asked My advice,
To strengthen themselves in the strength of Pharaoh,
And to trust in the shadow of Egypt!
3 Therefore the strength of Pharaoh

Gospel Pearls

Shall be your shame,
And trust in the shadow of
   Egypt
Shall be *your* humiliation.
4 For his princes were at Zoan,
And his ambassadors came to
   Hanes.
5 They were all ashamed of a
   people *who* could not benefit
   them,
Or be help or benefit,
But a shame and also a
   reproach."

6 The burden against the beasts of
the South.

Through a land of trouble and
   anguish,
From which *came* the lioness
   and lion,
The viper and fiery flying
   serpent,
They will carry their riches on
   the backs of young donkeys,
And their treasures on the
   humps of camels,
To a people *who* shall not
   profit;
7 For the Egyptians shall help in
   vain and to no purpose.
Therefore I have called her
   Rahab-Hem-Shebeth.*ᵃ*

8 Now go, write it before them on
   a tablet,
And note it on a scroll,
That it may be for time to come,
   Forever and ever:
9 That this *is* a rebellious people,
Lying children,
Children *who* will not hear the
   law of the LORD;
10 Who say to the seers, "Do not
   see,"
And to the prophets, "Do not
   prophesy to us right things;
Speak to us smooth things,
   prophesy deceits.
11 Get out of the way,
Turn aside from the path,
Cause the Holy One of Israel
   To cease from before us."

12 Therefore thus says the Holy
One of Israel:

"Because you despise this word,
And trust in oppression and
   perversity,
And rely on them,

13 Therefore this iniquity shall be
   to you
Like a breach ready to fall,
A bulge in a high wall,
Whose breaking comes
   suddenly, in an instant.
14 And He shall break it like the
   breaking of the potter's
   vessel,
Which is broken in pieces;
He shall not spare.
So there shall not be found
   among its fragments
A shard to take fire from the
   hearth,
Or to take water from the
   cistern."

15 For thus says the Lord GOD, the
Holy One of Israel:

"In returning and rest you shall
   be saved;
In quietness and confidence
   shall be your strength."
But you would not,
16 And you said, "No, for we will
   flee on horses"—
Therefore you shall flee!
And, "We will ride on swift
   horses"—
Therefore those who pursue
   you shall be swift!

17 One thousand *shall flee* at the
   threat of one,
At the threat of five you shall
   flee,
Till you are left as a pole on
   top of a mountain
And as a banner on a hill.
18 Therefore the LORD will wait,
   that He may be gracious to
   you;
And therefore He will be
   exalted, that He may have
   mercy on you.
For the LORD *is* a God of justice;
Blessed *are* all those who wait
   for Him.

19 For the people shall dwell in
   Zion at Jerusalem;
You shall weep no more.
He will be very gracious to you
   at the sound of your cry;
When He hears it, He will
   answer you.
20 And *though* the Lord gives you

30:7 ᵃLiterally *Rahab Sits Idle*

*D*o you realize that one of the things the blood of Jesus Christ does is cover us? The
blood of Jesus will cover the uncovered. He will not allow you to spend the rest of
your life exposed and violated.

The bread of adversity and the
water of affliction,
Yet your teachers will not be
moved into a corner
anymore,
But your eyes shall see your
teachers.
21 Your ears shall hear a word
behind you, saying,
"This *is* the way, walk in it,"
Whenever you turn to the right
hand
Or whenever you turn to the
left.
22 You will also defile the
covering of your images of
silver,
And the ornament of your
molded images of gold.
You will throw them away as
an unclean thing;
You will say to them, "Get
away!"

23 Then He will give the rain for
your seed
With which you sow the
ground,
And bread of the increase of
the earth;
It will be fat and plentiful.
In that day your cattle will feed
In large pastures.
24 Likewise the oxen and the
young donkeys that work the
ground
Will eat cured fodder,
Which has been winnowed
with the shovel and fan.
25 There will be on every high
mountain
And on every high hill
Rivers *and* streams of waters,
In the day of the great
slaughter,
When the towers fall.
26 Moreover the light of the moon
will be as the light of the
sun,
And the light of the sun will be
sevenfold,
As the light of seven days,
In the day that the LORD binds
up the bruise of His people
And heals the stroke of their
wound.

27 Behold, the name of the LORD
comes from afar,
Burning *with* His anger,
And *His* burden *is* heavy;
His lips are full of indignation,

And His tongue like a
devouring fire.
28 His breath is like an
overflowing stream,
Which reaches up to the neck,
To sift the nations with the
sieve of futility;
And *there shall be* a bridle in
the jaws of the people,
Causing *them* to err.

29 You shall have a song
As in the night *when* a holy
festival is kept,
And gladness of heart as when
one goes with a flute,
To come into the mountain of
the LORD,
To the Mighty One of Israel.
30 The LORD will cause His
glorious voice to be heard,
And show the descent of His
arm,
With the indignation of *His*
anger
And the flame of a devouring
fire,
With scattering, tempest, and
hailstones.
31 For through the voice of the
LORD
Assyria will be beaten down,
As He strikes with the rod.
32 And *in* every place where the
staff of punishment passes,
Which the LORD lays on him,
It will be with tambourines and
harps;
And in battles of brandishing
He will fight with it.
33 For Tophet *was* established of
old,
Yes, for the king it is prepared.
He has made *it* deep and large;
Its pyre *is* fire with much
wood;
The breath of the LORD, like a
stream of brimstone,
Kindles it.

31 Woe to those who go down to
Egypt for help,
And rely on horses,
Who trust in chariots because
they are many,
And in horsemen because they
are very strong,
But who do not look to the Holy
One of Israel,
Nor seek the LORD!
2 Yet He also *is* wise and will
bring disaster,

Gospel
Pearls

And will not call back His
words,
But will arise against the house
of evildoers,
And against the help of those
who work iniquity.
3 Now the Egyptians *are* men,
and not God;
And their horses are flesh, and
not spirit.
When the LORD stretches out
His hand,
Both he who helps will fall,
And he who is helped will fall
down;
They all will perish together.

4 For thus the LORD has spoken to
me:

"As a lion roars,
And a young lion over his prey
(When a multitude of
shepherds is summoned
against him,
He will not be afraid of their
voice
Nor be disturbed by their
noise),
So the LORD of hosts will come
down
To fight for Mount Zion and for
its hill.
5 Like birds flying about,
So will the LORD of hosts
defend Jerusalem.
Defending, He will also deliver
it;
Passing over, He will preserve
it."

6 Return *to Him* against whom the
children of Israel have deeply revolted. 7 For in that day every man
shall throw away his idols of silver
and his idols of gold—sin, which your
own hands have made for yourselves.

8 "Then Assyria shall fall by a
sword not of man,
And a sword not of mankind
shall devour him.
But he shall flee from the
sword,
And his young men shall
become forced labor.
9 He shall cross over to his
stronghold for fear,
And his princes shall be afraid
of the banner,"
Says the LORD,

Whose fire *is* in Zion
And whose furnace *is* in
Jerusalem.

32 Behold, a king will reign in
righteousness,
And princes will rule with
justice.
2 A man will be as a hiding place
from the wind,
And a cover from the tempest,
As rivers of water in a dry
place,
As the shadow of a great rock
in a weary land.
3 The eyes of those who see will
not be dim,
And the ears of those who hear
will listen.
4 Also the heart of the rash will
understand knowledge,
And the tongue of the
stammerers will be ready to
speak plainly.
5 The foolish person will no
longer be called generous,
Nor the miser said *to be*
bountiful;
6 For the foolish person will
speak foolishness,
And his heart will work
iniquity:
To practice ungodliness,
To utter error against the LORD,
To keep the hungry unsatisfied,
And he will cause the drink of
the thirsty to fail.
7 Also the schemes of the
schemer *are* evil;
He devises wicked plans
To destroy the poor with lying
words,
Even when the needy speaks
justice.
8 But a generous man devises
generous things,
And by generosity he shall
stand.
9 Rise up, you women who are
at ease,
Hear my voice;
You complacent daughters,
Give ear to my speech.
10 In a year and *some* days
You will be troubled, you
complacent women;
For the vintage will fail,
The gathering will not come.
11 Tremble, you *women* who are
at ease;

---

*R*each out and embrace the fact that God has been watching over you all of your
life. My sister, He covers you, He clothes you, and He blesses you! Rejoice in Him
in spite of the broken places.

Soul Secrets
of a weary woman

*L*ord, I am weary of the loads I'm carrying. The business of living has drained the life out of me. And I am just so tired. I don't think I can face another day. It's not just sleep I need. I need real rest. My body needs to rest; my mind needs to rest; even my spirit needs to rest. I need to be renewed from the inside out. And You say, Wait. "Wait upon the Lord, and He shall renew your strength." I am so weary, Lord, that waiting will take all I've got.

You promise "quiet resting places." You promise "quietness and assurance forever." That is what I need. I need to run and hide and rest. O God, bring the river of Your life to me. Let it flow and refresh every weary, worn-out place in me.

I want to lie down before the throne of Your grace and rest in Your presence, my Lord. You call me away to a peaceful, quiet place in You. God, I thank You for rest. I thank You for rescuing me from my weariness and for renewing me day by day.

Be troubled, you complacent
  ones;
Strip yourselves, make
  yourselves bare,
And gird *sackcloth* on *your*
  waists.

12 People shall mourn upon their
   breasts
  For the pleasant fields, for the
   fruitful vine.
13 On the land of my people will
   come up thorns *and* briers,
  Yes, on all the happy homes *in*
   the joyous city;
14 Because the palaces will be
   forsaken,
  The bustling city will be
   deserted.
  The forts and towers will
   become lairs forever,
  A joy of wild donkeys, a
   pasture of flocks—
15 Until the Spirit is poured upon
   us from on high,
  And the wilderness becomes a
   fruitful field,
  And the fruitful field is counted
   as a forest.

16 Then justice will dwell in the
   wilderness,
  And righteousness remain in
   the fruitful field.
17 The work of righteousness will
   be peace,
  And the effect of righteousness,
   quietness and assurance
   forever.
18 My people will dwell in a
   peaceful habitation,
  In secure dwellings, and in
   quiet resting places,
19 Though hail comes down on
   the forest,
  And the city is brought low in
   humiliation.

20 Blessed *are* you who sow
   beside all waters,
  Who send out freely the feet of
   the ox and the donkey.

33 Woe to you who plunder,
   though you *have* not *been*
   plundered;
  And you who deal
   treacherously, though they
   have not dealt treacherously
   with you!

When you cease plundering,
  You will be plundered;
When you make an end of
  dealing treacherously,
  They will deal treacherously
   with you.

2 O Lᴏʀᴅ, be gracious to us;
  We have waited for You.
  Be their*ᵃ* arm every morning,
  Our salvation also in the time
   of trouble.
3 At the noise of the tumult the
   people shall flee;
  When You lift Yourself up, the
   nations shall be scattered;
4 And Your plunder shall be
   gathered
  Like the gathering of the
   caterpillar;
  As the running to and fro of
   locusts,
  He shall run upon them.

5 The Lᴏʀᴅ is exalted, for He
   dwells on high;
  He has filled Zion with justice
   and righteousness.
6 Wisdom and knowledge will be
   the stability of your times,
  And the strength of salvation;
  The fear of the Lᴏʀᴅ *is* His
   treasure.

7 Surely their valiant ones shall
   cry outside,
  The ambassadors of peace
   shall weep bitterly.
8 The highways lie waste,
  The traveling man ceases.
  He has broken the covenant,
  He has despised the cities,*ᵃ*
  He regards no man.
9 The earth mourns *and*
   languishes,
  Lebanon is shamed *and*
   shriveled;
  Sharon is like a wilderness,
  And Bashan and Carmel shake
   off *their fruits.*

10 "Now I will rise," says the Lᴏʀᴅ;
   "Now I will be exalted,
   Now I will lift Myself up.
11 You shall conceive chaff,
   You shall bring forth stubble;
   Your breath, *as* fire, shall
   devour you.

33:2 *ᵃ*Septuagint omits *their;* Syriac, Targum, and Vulgate read *our.*   **33:8** *ᵃ*Following Masoretic Text and Vulgate; Dead Sea Scrolls read *witnesses;* Septuagint omits *cities;* Targum reads *They have been removed from their cities.*

God's grace is sufficient for your needs and your scars. He will anoint you with oil. *The anointing of the Lord be upon you now!* May it bathe, heal and strengthen you as never before.

12 And the people shall be *like* the
      burnings of lime;
      Like thorns cut up they shall be
      burned in the fire.
13 Hear, you *who are* afar off,
      what I have done;
      And you *who are* near,
      acknowledge My might."

14 The sinners in Zion are afraid;
      Fearfulness has seized the
      hypocrites:
      "Who among us shall dwell with
      the devouring fire?
      Who among us shall dwell with
      everlasting burnings?"
15 He who walks righteously and
      speaks uprightly,
      He who despises the gain of
      oppressions,
      Who gestures with his hands,
      refusing bribes,
      Who stops his ears from
      hearing of bloodshed,
      And shuts his eyes from seeing
      evil:
16 He will dwell on high;
      His place of defense *will be* the
      fortress of rocks;
      Bread will be given him,
      His water *will be* sure.

17 Your eyes will see the King in
      His beauty;
      They will see the land that is
      very far off.
18 Your heart will meditate on
      terror:
      "Where *is* the scribe?
      Where *is* he who weighs?
      Where *is* he who counts the
      towers?"
19 You will not see a fierce people,
      A people of obscure speech,
      beyond perception,
      Of a stammering tongue *that
      you* cannot understand.

20 Look upon Zion, the city of our
      appointed feasts;
      Your eyes will see Jerusalem,
      a quiet home,
      A tabernacle *that* will not be
      taken down,
      Not one of its stakes will ever
      be removed,
      Nor will any of its cords be
      broken.
21 But there the majestic LORD *will
      be* for us
      A place of broad rivers *and*
      streams,

In which no galley with oars
      will sail,
      Nor majestic ships pass by
22 (For the LORD *is* our Judge,
      The LORD *is* our Lawgiver,
      The LORD *is* our King;
      He will save us);
23 Your tackle is loosed,
      They could not strengthen their
      mast,
      They could not spread the sail.

Then the prey of great plunder
      is divided;
      The lame take the prey.
24 And the inhabitant will not say,
      "I am sick";
      The people who dwell in it *will
      be* forgiven *their* iniquity.

34 Come near, you nations, to
      hear;
      And heed, you people!
      Let the earth hear, and all that
      is in it,
      The world and all things that
      come forth from it.
2   For the indignation of the LORD
      is against all nations,
      And *His* fury against all their
      armies;
      He has utterly destroyed them,
      He has given them over to the
      slaughter.
3   Also their slain shall be thrown
      out;
      Their stench shall rise from
      their corpses,
      And the mountains shall be
      melted with their blood.
4   All the host of heaven shall be
      dissolved,
      And the heavens shall be rolled
      up like a scroll;
      All their host shall fall down
      As the leaf falls from the vine,
      And as *fruit* falling from a fig
      tree.

5   "For My sword shall be bathed
      in heaven;
      Indeed it shall come down on
      Edom,
      And on the people of My curse,
      for judgment.
6   The sword of the LORD is filled
      with blood,
      It is made overflowing with
      fatness,
      With the blood of lambs and
      goats,

Gospel
Pearls

With the fat of the kidneys of
rams.
For the LORD has a sacrifice in
Bozrah,
And a great slaughter in the
land of Edom.

7 The wild oxen shall come down
with them,
And the young bulls with the
mighty bulls;
Their land shall be soaked with
blood,
And their dust saturated with
fatness."

8 For *it is* the day of the LORD's
vengeance,
The year of recompense for the
cause of Zion.

9 Its streams shall be turned into
pitch,
And its dust into brimstone;
Its land shall become burning
pitch.

10 It shall not be quenched night
or day;
Its smoke shall ascend forever.
From generation to generation
it shall lie waste;
No one shall pass through it
forever and ever.

11 But the pelican and the
porcupine shall possess it,
Also the owl and the raven
shall dwell in it.
And He shall stretch out over
it
The line of confusion and the
stones of emptiness.

12 They shall call its nobles to the
kingdom,
But none *shall be* there, and all
its princes shall be nothing.

13 And thorns shall come up in its
palaces,
Nettles and brambles in its
fortresses;
It shall be a habitation of
jackals,
A courtyard for ostriches.

14 The wild beasts of the desert
shall also meet with the
jackals,
And the wild goat shall bleat
to its companion;
Also the night creature shall
rest there,
And find for herself a place of
rest.

15 There the arrow snake shall
make her nest and lay *eggs*

And hatch, and gather *them*
under her shadow;
There also shall the hawks be
gathered,
Every one with her mate.

16 "Search from the book of the
LORD, and read:
Not one of these shall fail;
Not one shall lack her mate.
For My mouth has commanded
it, and His Spirit has
gathered them.

17 He has cast the lot for them,
And His hand has divided it
among them with a
measuring line.
They shall possess it forever;
From generation to generation
they shall dwell in it."

35 The wilderness and the
wasteland shall be glad for
them,
And the desert shall rejoice and
blossom as the rose;

2 It shall blossom abundantly
and rejoice,
Even with joy and singing.
The glory of Lebanon shall be
given to it,
The excellence of Carmel and
Sharon.
They shall see the glory of the
LORD,
The excellency of our God.

3 Strengthen the weak hands,
And make firm the feeble
knees.

4 Say to those *who are* fearful-
hearted,

"Be strong, do not fear!
Behold, your God will come
with vengeance,
With the recompense of God;
He will come and save you."

5 Then the eyes of the blind shall
be opened,
And the ears of the deaf shall
be unstopped.

6 Then the lame shall leap like a
deer,
And the tongue of the dumb
sing.
For waters shall burst forth in
the wilderness,
And streams in the desert.

7 The parched ground shall
become a pool,

*T*here will be a time in your life when God nurtures you through a crisis situation.
You may not even realize how many times God has intervened to relieve the tensions
and stresses of day-to-day living.

And the thirsty land springs of
water;
In the habitation of jackals,
where each lay,
There shall be grass with reeds
and rushes.
8   A highway shall be there, and
a road,
And it shall be called the
Highway of Holiness.
The unclean shall not pass over
it,
But it *shall be* for others.
Whoever walks the road,
although a fool,
Shall not go astray.
9   No lion shall be there,
Nor shall *any* ravenous beast
go up on it;
It shall not be found there.
But the redeemed shall walk
there,
10 And the ransomed of the LORD
shall return,
And come to Zion with singing,
With everlasting joy on their
heads.
They shall obtain joy and
gladness,
And sorrow and sighing shall
flee away.

36 Now it came to pass in the fourteenth year of King Hezekiah
that Sennacherib king of Assyria
came up against all the fortified cities
of Judah and took them. 2 Then the
king of Assyria sent *the* Rabshakeh*ᵃ*
with a great army from Lachish to
King Hezekiah at Jerusalem. And he
stood by the aqueduct from the upper
pool, on the highway to the Fuller's
Field. 3 And Eliakim the son of Hilkiah, who was over the household,
Shebna the scribe, and Joah the son
of Asaph, the recorder, came out to
him.
4 Then *the* Rabshakeh said to
them, "Say now to Hezekiah, 'Thus
says the great king, the king of Assyria: "What confidence is this in
which you trust? 5 I say you speak
of having plans and power for war;
but *they are* mere words. Now in
whom do you trust, that you rebel
against me? 6 Look! You are trusting
in the staff of this broken reed, Egypt,
on which if a man leans, it will go
into his hand and pierce it. So *is*

Pharaoh king of Egypt to all who
trust in him.
7 "But if you say to me, 'We trust
in the LORD our God,' *is it* not He
whose high places and whose altars Hezekiah has taken away, and
said to Judah and Jerusalem, 'You
shall worship before this altar'?" '
8 Now therefore, I urge you, give a
pledge to my master the king of Assyria, and I will give you two thousand horses—if you are able on your
part to put riders on them! 9 How
then will you repel one captain of the
least of my master's servants, and
put your trust in Egypt for chariots
and horsemen? 10 Have I now come
up without the LORD against this land
to destroy it? The LORD said to me,
'Go up against this land, and destroy
it.' "
11 Then Eliakim, Shebna, and Joah
said to *the* Rabshakeh, "Please speak
to your servants in Aramaic, for we
understand *it;* and do not speak to
us in Hebrew*ᵃ* in the hearing of the
people who *are* on the wall."
12 But *the* Rabshakeh said, "Has
my master sent me to your master
and to you to speak these words, and
not to the men who sit on the wall,
who will eat and drink their own
waste with you?"
13 Then *the* Rabshakeh stood and
called out with a loud voice in Hebrew, and said, "Hear the words of
the great king, the king of Assyria!
14 Thus says the king: 'Do not let
Hezekiah deceive you, for he will not
be able to deliver you; 15 nor let
Hezekiah make you trust in the LORD,
saying, "The LORD will surely deliver
us; this city will not be given into the
hand of the king of Assyria." '
16 Do not listen to Hezekiah; for thus
says the king of Assyria: 'Make
peace with me *by a* present and come
out to me; and every one of you eat
from his own vine and every one
from his own fig tree, and every one
of you drink the waters of his own
cistern; 17 until I come and take you
away to a land like your own land,
a land of grain and new wine, a land
of bread and vineyards. 18 *Beware*
lest Hezekiah persuade you, saying,
"The LORD will deliver us." Has any
one of the gods of the nations delivered its land from the hand of the
king of Assyria? 19 Where *are* the

36:2 ᵃA title, probably *Chief of Staff* or *Governor*   36:11 ᵃLiterally *Judean*

Gospel
Pearls

gods of Hamath and Arpad? Where *are* the gods of Sepharvaim? Indeed, have they delivered Samaria from my hand? 20 Who among all the gods of these lands have delivered their countries from my hand, that the Lord should deliver Jerusalem from my hand?' "

21 But they held their peace and answered him not a word; for the king's commandment was, "Do not answer him." 22 Then Eliakim the son of Hilkiah, who *was* over the household, Shebna the scribe, and Joah the son of Asaph, the recorder, came to Hezekiah with *their* clothes torn, and told him the words of *the* Rabshakeh.

37 And so it was, when King Hezekiah heard *it*, that he tore his clothes, covered himself with sackcloth, and went into the house of the Lord. 2 Then he sent Eliakim, who *was* over the household, Shebna the scribe, and the elders of the priests, covered with sackcloth, to Isaiah the prophet, the son of Amoz. 3 And they said to him, "Thus says Hezekiah: 'This day *is* a day of trouble and rebuke and blasphemy; for the children have come to birth, but *there is* no strength to bring them forth. 4 It may be that the Lord your God will hear the words of *the* Rabshakeh, whom his master the king of Assyria has sent to reproach the living God, and will rebuke the words which the Lord your God has heard. Therefore lift up *your* prayer for the remnant that is left.' "

5 So the servants of King Hezekiah came to Isaiah. 6 And Isaiah said to them, "Thus you shall say to your master, 'Thus says the Lord: "Do not be afraid of the words which you have heard, with which the servants of the king of Assyria have blasphemed Me. 7 Surely I will send a spirit upon him, and he shall hear a rumor and return to his own land; and I will cause him to fall by the sword in his own land." ' "

8 Then *the* Rabshakeh returned, and found the king of Assyria warring against Libnah, for he heard that he had departed from Lachish. 9 And the king heard concerning Tirhakah king of Ethiopia, "He has come out to make war with you." So when he heard *it*, he sent messengers to Hezekiah, saying, 10 "Thus you

shall speak to Hezekiah king of Judah, saying: 'Do not let your God in whom you trust deceive you, saying, "Jerusalem shall not be given into the hand of the king of Assyria." 11 Look! You have heard what the kings of Assyria have done to all lands by utterly destroying them; and shall you be delivered? 12 Have the gods of the nations delivered those whom my fathers have destroyed, Gozan and Haran and Rezeph, and the people of Eden who *were* in Telassar? 13 Where *is* the king of Hamath, the king of Arpad, and the king of the city of Sepharvaim, Hena, and Ivah?' "

14 And Hezekiah received the letter from the hand of the messengers, and read it; and Hezekiah went up to the house of the Lord, and spread it before the Lord. 15 Then Hezekiah prayed to the Lord, saying: 16 "O Lord of hosts, God of Israel, *the One* who dwells *between* the cherubim, You *are* God, You alone, of all the kingdoms of the earth. You have made heaven and earth. 17 Incline Your ear, O Lord, and hear; open Your eyes, O Lord, and see; and hear all the words of Sennacherib, which he has sent to reproach the living God. 18 Truly, Lord, the kings of Assyria have laid waste all the nations and their lands, 19 and have cast their gods into the fire; for they *were* not gods, but the work of men's hands—wood and stone. Therefore they destroyed them. 20 Now therefore, O Lord our God, save us from his hand, that all the kingdoms of the earth may know that You *are* the Lord, You alone."

21 Then Isaiah the son of Amoz sent to Hezekiah, saying, "Thus says the Lord God of Israel, 'Because you have prayed to Me against Sennacherib king of Assyria, 22 this *is* the word which the Lord has spoken concerning him:

"The virgin, the daughter of Zion,
    Has despised you, laughed you to scorn;
The daughter of Jerusalem
    Has shaken *her* head behind your back!

23 "Whom have you reproached and blasphemed?
    Against whom have you raised *your* voice,

And lifted up your eyes on
high?
Against the Holy One of Israel.
24 By your servants you have
reproached the Lord,
And said, 'By the multitude of
my chariots
I have come up to the height
of the mountains,
To the limits of Lebanon;
I will cut down its tall cedars
And its choice cypress trees;
I will enter its farthest height,
To its fruitful forest.
25 I have dug and drunk water,
And with the soles of my feet I
have dried up
All the brooks of defense.'

26 "Did you not hear long ago
How I made it,
From ancient times that I
formed it?
Now I have brought it to pass,
That you should be
For crushing fortified cities *into*
heaps of ruins.
27 Therefore their inhabitants *had*
little power;
They were dismayed and
confounded;
They were *as* the grass of the
field
And the green herb,
As the grass on the housetops
And grain blighted before it is
grown.

28 "But I know your dwelling place,
Your going out and your
coming in,
And your rage against Me.
29 Because your rage against Me
and your tumult
Have come up to My ears,
Therefore I will put My hook
in your nose
And My bridle in your lips,
And I will turn you back
By the way which you came." '

30 "This *shall be* a sign to you:

You shall eat this year such as
grows of itself,
And the second year what
springs from the same;
Also in the third year sow and
reap,

Plant vineyards and eat the
fruit of them.
31 And the remnant who have
escaped of the house of
Judah
Shall again take root
downward,
And bear fruit upward.
32 For out of Jerusalem shall go
a remnant,
And those who escape from
Mount Zion.
The zeal of the LORD of hosts
will do this.

33 "Therefore thus says the LORD
concerning the king of Assyria:

'He shall not come into this city,
Nor shoot an arrow there,
Nor come before it with shield,
Nor build a siege mound
against it.
34 By the way that he came,
By the same shall he return;
And he shall not come into this
city,'
Says the LORD.
35 'For I will defend this city, to
save it
For My own sake and for My
servant David's sake.' "

36 Then the angel*a* of the LORD went
out, and killed in the camp of the Assyrians one hundred and eighty-five
thousand; and when *people* arose
early in the morning, there were the
corpses—all dead. 37 So Sennacherib
king of Assyria departed and went
away, returned *home,* and remained
at Nineveh. 38 Now it came to pass,
as he was worshiping in the house
of Nisroch his god, that his sons
Adrammelech and Sharezer struck
him down with the sword; and they
escaped into the land of Ararat. Then
Esarhaddon his son reigned in his
place.

38 In those days Hezekiah was
sick and near death. And Isaiah
the prophet, the son of Amoz, went
to him and said to him, "Thus says
the LORD: 'Set your house in order,
for you shall die and not live.' "
2 Then Hezekiah turned his face toward the wall, and prayed to the
LORD, 3 and said, "Remember now, O
LORD, I pray, how I have walked before You in truth and with a loyal

37:36 *a*Or *Angel*

*Gospel
Pearls*

heart, and have done *what is* good in Your sight." And Hezekiah wept bitterly.

4 And the word of the LORD came to Isaiah, saying, 5 "Go and tell Hezekiah, 'Thus says the LORD, the God of David your father: "I have heard your prayer, I have seen your tears; surely I will add to your days fifteen years. 6 I will deliver you and this city from the hand of the king of Assyria, and I will defend this city." ' 7 And this *is* the sign to you from the LORD, that the LORD will do this thing which He has spoken: 8 Behold, I will bring the shadow on the sundial, which has gone down with the sun on the sundial of Ahaz, ten degrees backward." So the sun returned ten degrees on the dial by which it had gone down.

9 This is the writing of Hezekiah king of Judah, when he had been sick and had recovered from his sickness:

10 I said,

"In the prime of my life
  I shall go to the gates of
   Sheol;
I am deprived of the remainder
  of my years."

11 I said,

"I shall not see YAH,
  The LORD^a in the land of the
   living;
I shall observe man no more
  among the inhabitants of the
  world.^b
12 My life span is gone,
  Taken from me like a
   shepherd's tent;
I have cut off my life like a
  weaver.
He cuts me off from the loom;
  From day until night You make
   an end of me.
13 I have considered until
  morning—
Like a lion,
  So He breaks all my bones;
From day until night You make
  an end of me.
14 Like a crane *or* a swallow, so I
  chattered;
I mourned like a dove;

My eyes fail *from looking*
  upward.
O LORD,^a I am oppressed;
  Undertake for me!

15 "What shall I say?
He has both spoken to me,^a
  And He Himself has done *it*.
I shall walk carefully all my
  years
In the bitterness of my soul.
16 O LORD, by these *things men*
  live;
And in all these *things is* the
  life of my spirit;
So You will restore me and
  make me live.
17 Indeed *it was* for *my own* peace
  That I had great bitterness;
But You have lovingly
  delivered my soul from the
  pit of corruption,
For You have cast all my sins
  behind Your back.
18 For Sheol cannot thank You,
  Death cannot praise You;
Those who go down to the pit
  cannot hope for Your truth.
19 The living, the living man, he
  shall praise You,
As I *do* this day;
  The father shall make known
  Your truth to the children.

20 "The LORD *was ready* to save
  me;
Therefore we will sing my
  songs with stringed
  instruments
All the days of our life, in the
  house of the LORD."

21 Now Isaiah had said, "Let them take a lump of figs, and apply *it* as a poultice on the boil, and he shall recover."
22 And Hezekiah had said, "What *is* the sign that I shall go up to the house of the LORD?"

39 At that time Merodach-Baladan^a the son of Baladan, king of Babylon, sent letters and a present to Hezekiah, for he heard that he had been sick and had recovered.
2 And Hezekiah was pleased with

38:11 ^aHebrew YAH, YAH   ^bFollowing some Hebrew manuscripts; Masoretic Text and Vulgate read *rest;* Septuagint omits *among the inhabitants of the world;* Targum reads *land.*   38:14 ^aFollowing Bomberg; Masoretic Text and Dead Sea Scrolls read *Lord.*   38:15 ^aFollowing Masoretic Text and Vulgate; Dead Sea Scrolls and Targum read *And shall I say to Him;* Septuagint omits first half of this verse.   39:1 ^aSpelled *Berodach-Baladan* in 2 Kings 20:12

I pray that you who have been marred, would allow the reconstructing hand of the Potter to mend the broken places in your lives. May the peace and calmness of knowing God cause the birth of fresh dreams.

them, and showed them the house of his treasures—the silver and gold, the spices and precious ointment, and all his armory—all that was found among his treasures. There was nothing in his house or in all his dominion that Hezekiah did not show them.

3 Then Isaiah the prophet went to King Hezekiah, and said to him, "What did these men say, and from where did they come to you?"

So Hezekiah said, "They came to me from a far country, from Babylon."

4 And he said, "What have they seen in your house?"

So Hezekiah answered, "They have seen all that *is* in my house; there is nothing among my treasures that I have not shown them."

5 Then Isaiah said to Hezekiah, "Hear the word of the LORD of hosts: 6 'Behold, the days are coming when all that *is* in your house, and what your fathers have accumulated until this day, shall be carried to Babylon; nothing shall be left,' says the LORD. 7 'And they shall take away *some* of your sons who will descend from you, whom you will beget; and they shall be eunuchs in the palace of the king of Babylon.' "

8 So Hezekiah said to Isaiah, "The word of the LORD which you have spoken *is* good!" For he said, "At least there will be peace and truth in my days."

40 "Comfort, yes, comfort My people!"
Says your God.
2 "Speak comfort to Jerusalem,
    and cry out to her,
That her warfare is ended,
That her iniquity is pardoned;
For she has received from the
    LORD's hand
Double for all her sins."

3 The voice of one crying in the
    wilderness:
"Prepare the way of the LORD;
Make straight in the desert[a]
A highway for our God.
4   Every valley shall be exalted
And every mountain and hill
    brought low;

The crooked places shall be
    made straight
And the rough places smooth;
5   The glory of the LORD shall be
    revealed,
And all flesh shall see *it*
    together;
For the mouth of the LORD has
    spoken."

6   The voice said, "Cry out!"
And he[a] said, "What shall I
    cry?"

"All flesh *is* grass,
And all its loveliness *is* like the
    flower of the field.
7   The grass withers, the flower
    fades,
Because the breath of the LORD
    blows upon it;
Surely the people *are* grass.
8   The grass withers, the flower
    fades,
But the word of our God stands
    forever."

9   O Zion,
You who bring good tidings,
Get up into the high mountain;
O Jerusalem,
You who bring good tidings,
Lift up your voice with
    strength,
Lift *it* up, be not afraid;
Say to the cities of Judah,
    "Behold your God!"

10 Behold, the Lord GOD shall
    come with a strong *hand*,
And His arm shall rule for Him;
Behold, His reward *is* with
    Him,
And His work before Him.
11 He will feed His flock like a
    shepherd;
He will gather the lambs with
    His arm,
And carry *them* in His bosom,
And gently lead those who are
    with young.

12 Who has measured the waters[a]
    in the hollow of His hand,
Measured heaven with a span
And calculated the dust of the
    earth in a measure?

40:3 aFollowing Masoretic Text, Targum, and Vulgate; Septuagint omits *in the desert*. 40:6 aFollowing Masoretic Text and Targum; Dead Sea Scrolls, Septuagint, and Vulgate read *I*. 40:12 aFollowing Masoretic Text, Septuagint, and Vulgate; Dead Sea Scrolls read *waters of the sea;* Targum reads *waters of the world*.

We were all born in sin and shaped in iniquity. We have no true badge of righteousness that we can wear on the outside. God saves us from ourselves.

Soul Secrets
for postpartum blues

F ather, You have just made me a mother. You have granted me the opportunity of partnering with You in the creative act of life. I should feel blessed beyond belief, but I am so depressed I can hardly function. On top of that, I feel so guilty that I'm not rejoicing.

They say it's hormones, but whatever it is, I need Your help. Lord, I need You to move gently with me through these days. Shepherd me as tenderly as You would a little lamb and help me to feel like myself again. Show me softly the tiny wonders of brand new life.

You alone are my joy, my peace. You have always been the One who puts a smile on my face and a twinkle in my eye. I need You very near me now. The responsibility is overwhelming and I am always so tired. Thank You for the promise of Your presence. I cannot do it without You.

Weighed the mountains in
  scales
And the hills in a balance?
13 Who has directed the Spirit of
  the L*ORD*,
Or *as* His counselor has taught
  Him?
14 With whom did He take
  counsel, and *who* instructed
  Him,
And taught Him in the path of
  justice?
Who taught Him knowledge,
And showed Him the way of
  understanding?

15 Behold, the nations *are* as a
  drop in a bucket,
And are counted as the small
  dust on the scales;
Look, He lifts up the isles as a
  very little thing.
16 And Lebanon *is* not sufficient
  to burn,
Nor its beasts sufficient for a
  burnt offering.
17 All nations before Him *are* as
  nothing,
And they are counted by Him
  less than nothing and
  worthless.

18 To whom then will you liken
  God?
Or what likeness will you
  compare to Him?
19 The workman molds an image,
The goldsmith overspreads it
  with gold,
And the silversmith casts silver
  chains.
20 Whoever *is* too impoverished
  for *such* a contribution
Chooses a tree *that* will not rot;
He seeks for himself a skillful
  workman
To prepare a carved image *that*
  will not totter.

21 Have you not known?
Have you not heard?
Has it not been told you from
  the beginning?
Have you not understood from
  the foundations of the earth?
22 *It is* He who sits above the
  circle of the earth,
And its inhabitants *are* like
  grasshoppers,
Who stretches out the heavens
  like a curtain,

And spreads them out like a
  tent to dwell in.
23 He brings the princes to
  nothing;
He makes the judges of the
  earth useless.

24 Scarcely shall they be planted,
Scarcely shall they be sown,
Scarcely shall their stock take
  root in the earth,
When He will also blow on
  them,
And they will wither,
And the whirlwind will take
  them away like stubble.

25 "To whom then will you liken
  Me,
Or *to whom* shall I be equal?"
  says the Holy One.
26 Lift up your eyes on high,
And see who has created these
  things,
Who brings out their host by
  number;
He calls them all by name,
By the greatness of His might
And the strength of *His* power;
Not one is missing.

27 Why do you say, O Jacob,
And speak, O Israel:
"My way is hidden from the
  L*ORD*,
And my just claim is passed
  over by my God"?
28 Have you not known?
Have you not heard?
The everlasting God, the L*ORD*,
The Creator of the ends of the
  earth,
Neither faints nor is weary.
His understanding is
  unsearchable.
29 He gives power to the weak,
And to *those who have* no
  might He increases strength.
30 Even the youths shall faint and
  be weary,
And the young men shall
  utterly fall,
31 But those who wait on the L*ORD*
Shall renew *their* strength;
They shall mount up with
  wings like eagles,
They shall run and not be
  weary,
They shall walk and not faint.

41 "Keep silence before Me, O
  coastlands,

And let the people renew *their*
   strength!
Let them come near, then let
   them speak;
Let us come near together for
   judgment.

2 "Who raised up one from the
   east?
Who in righteousness called
   him to His feet?
Who gave the nations before
   him,
And made *him* rule over kings?
Who gave *them* as the dust *to*
   his sword,
As driven stubble to his bow?
3 Who pursued them, *and* passed
   safely
By the way *that* he had not
   gone with his feet?
4 Who has performed and done
   it,
Calling the generations from
   the beginning?
'I, the LORD, am the first;
And with the last I *am* He.' "

5 The coastlands saw *it* and
   feared,
The ends of the earth were
   afraid;
They drew near and came.
6 Everyone helped his neighbor,
And said to his brother,
Be of good courage!"
7 So the craftsman encouraged
   the goldsmith;
He who smooths *with* the
   hammer *inspired* him who
   strikes the anvil,
Saying, "It *is* ready for the
   soldering";
Then he fastened it with pegs,
That it might not totter.

8 "But you, Israel, *are* My servant,
Jacob whom I have chosen,
The descendants of Abraham
   My friend.
9 *You* whom I have taken from
   the ends of the earth,
And called from its farthest
   regions,
And said to you,
'You *are* My servant,
I have chosen you and have not
   cast you away:
10 Fear not, for I *am* with you;
Be not dismayed, for I *am* your
   God.
I will strengthen you,

Yes, I will help you,
I will uphold you with My
   righteous right hand.'

11 "Behold, all those who were
   incensed against you
Shall be ashamed and
   disgraced;
They shall be as nothing,
And those who strive with you
   shall perish.
12 You shall seek them and not
   find them—
Those who contended with
   you.
Those who war against you
Shall be as nothing,
As a nonexistent thing.
13 For I, the LORD your God, will
   hold your right hand,
Saying to you, 'Fear not, I will
   help you.'

14 "Fear not, you worm Jacob,
You men of Israel!
I will help you," says the LORD
And your Redeemer, the Holy
   One of Israel.
15 "Behold, I will make you into a
   new threshing sledge with
   sharp teeth;
You shall thresh the mountains
   and beat *them* small,
And make the hills like chaff.
16 You shall winnow them, the
   wind shall carry them away,
And the whirlwind shall scatter
   them;
You shall rejoice in the LORD,
And glory in the Holy One of
   Israel.

17 "The poor and needy seek
   water, but *there is* none,
Their tongues fail for thirst.
I, the LORD, will hear them;
I, the God of Israel, will not
   forsake them.
18 I will open rivers in desolate
   heights,
And fountains in the midst of
   the valleys;
I will make the wilderness a
   pool of water,
And the dry land springs of
   water.
19 I will plant in the wilderness
   the cedar and the acacia tree,
The myrtle and the oil tree;
I will set in the desert the
   cypress tree *and* the pine
And the box tree together,

*N*o one person needs more of the blood of Jesus than another. Jesus died once and for
all. Humanity must come to God on equal terms, each individual totally helpless to
earn his or her way to Him.

20 That they may see and know,
And consider and understand
together,
That the hand of the LORD has
done this,
And the Holy One of Israel has
created it.

21 "Present your case," says the
LORD.
"Bring forth your strong
reasons," says the King of
Jacob.
22 "Let them bring forth and show
us what will happen;
Let them show the former
things, what they *were,*
That we may consider them,
And know the latter end of
them;
Or declare to us things to
come.
23 Show the things that are to
come hereafter,
That we may know that you *are*
gods;
Yes, do good or do evil,
That we may be dismayed and
see *it* together.
24 Indeed you *are* nothing,
And your work *is* nothing;
He who chooses you *is* an
abomination.

25 "I have raised up one from the
north,
And he shall come;
From the rising of the sun he
shall call on My name;
And he shall come against
princes as *though* mortar,
As the potter treads clay.
26 Who has declared from the
beginning, that we may
know?
And former times, that we may
say, '*He is* righteous'?
Surely *there is* no one who
shows,
Surely *there is* no one who
declares,
Surely *there is* no one who
hears your words.
27 The first time *I said* to Zion,
'Look, there they are!'
And I will give to Jerusalem
one who brings good tidings.
28 For I looked, and *there was* no
man;

I looked among them, but *there
was* no counselor,
Who, when I asked of them,
could answer a word.
29 Indeed they *are* all worthless;[a]
Their works *are* nothing;
Their molded images *are* wind
and confusion.

42 "Behold! My Servant whom I
uphold,
My Elect One *in whom* My soul
delights!
I have put My Spirit upon
Him;
He will bring forth justice to the
Gentiles.
2 He will not cry out, nor raise
His voice,
Nor cause His voice to be heard
in the street.
3 A bruised reed He will not
break,
And smoking flax He will not
quench;
He will bring forth justice for
truth.
4 He will not fail nor be
discouraged,
Till He has established justice
in the earth;
And the coastlands shall wait
for His law."

5 Thus says God the LORD,
Who created the heavens and
stretched them out,
Who spread forth the earth and
that which comes from it,
Who gives breath to the people
on it,
And spirit to those who walk
on it:
6 "I, the LORD, have called You in
righteousness,
And will hold Your hand;
I will keep You and give You
as a covenant to the people,
As a light to the Gentiles,
7 To open blind eyes,
To bring out prisoners from the
prison,
Those who sit in darkness from
the prison house.
8 I *am* the LORD, that *is* My name;
And My glory I will not give to
another,
Nor My praise to carved
images.

41:29 [a]Following Masoretic Text and Vulgate; Dead Sea Scrolls, Syriac, and Targum read *nothing;* Septuagint
omits the first line.

Gospel Pearls

9 Behold, the former things have
   come to pass,
   And new things I declare;
   Before they spring forth I tell
   you of them."

10 Sing to the LORD a new song,
   And His praise from the ends
   of the earth,
   You who go down to the sea,
   and all that is in it,
   You coastlands and you
   inhabitants of them!
11 Let the wilderness and its cities
   lift up *their voice,*
   The villages *that* Kedar
   inhabits.
   Let the inhabitants of Sela
   sing,
   Let them shout from the top of
   the mountains.
12 Let them give glory to the
   LORD,
   And declare His praise in the
   coastlands.
13 The LORD shall go forth like a
   mighty man;
   He shall stir up *His* zeal like a
   man of war.
   He shall cry out, yes, shout
   aloud;
   He shall prevail against His
   enemies.

14 "I have held My peace a long
   time,
   I have been still and restrained
   Myself.
   Now I will cry like a woman in
   labor,
   I will pant and gasp at once.
15 I will lay waste the mountains
   and hills,
   And dry up all their vegetation;
   I will make the rivers
   coastlands,
   And I will dry up the pools.
16 I will bring the blind by a way
   they did not know;
   I will lead them in paths they
   have not known.
   I will make darkness light
   before them,
   And crooked places straight.
   These things I will do for
   them,
   And not forsake them.
17 They shall be turned back,
   They shall be greatly ashamed,
   Who trust in carved images,
   Who say to the molded images,
   'You *are* our gods.'

18 "Hear, you deaf;
   And look, you blind, that you
   may see.
19 Who *is* blind but My servant,
   Or deaf as My messenger
   whom I send?
   Who *is* blind as *he who is*
   perfect,
   And blind as the LORD's
   servant?
20 Seeing many things, but you do
   not observe;
   Opening the ears, but he does
   not hear."

21 The LORD is well pleased for
   His righteousness' sake;
   He will exalt the law and make
   it honorable.
22 But this *is* a people robbed and
   plundered;
   All of them are snared in holes,
   And they are hidden in prison
   houses;
   They are for prey, and no one
   delivers;
   For plunder, and no one says,
   "Restore!"

23 Who among you will give ear
   to this?
   Who will listen and hear for the
   time to come?
24 Who gave Jacob for plunder,
   and Israel to the robbers?
   Was it not the LORD,
   He against whom we have
   sinned?
   For they would not walk in His
   ways,
   Nor were they obedient to His
   law.
25 Therefore He has poured on
   him the fury of His anger
   And the strength of battle;
   It has set him on fire all around,
   Yet he did not know;
   And it burned him,
   Yet he did not take *it* to heart.

43 But now, thus says the LORD,
   who created you, O Jacob,
   And He who formed you, O
   Israel:
   "Fear not, for I have redeemed
   you;
   I have called *you* by your name;
   You *are* Mine.
2 When you pass through the
   waters, I *will be* with you;
   And through the rivers, they
   shall not overflow you.

He raises us up by the blood of Christ. He doesn't raise us up because we do good
things. He raises us up because we have faith in the finished work on the Cross.

A Princess in His Courts

Isaiah 43:4

Daughters of the King, there will be those who try to demean and belittle you. They will try to discriminate against you because you are women. Fight not for equality but for neutrality. Your distinctions are too valuable to forfeit.

We need distinction. Distinction can exist without discrimination. One of the greatest tragedies occurs when women fight their way to the place of being treated like men. The tragedy becomes apparent as they later realize that the real honor would have been to be recognized and honored as women.

Enjoy who you are. There are some benefits that go along with being who you are and whose you are. Your Father is the King, and you are His daughters, His princesses. You need only ask Him, and He has the power to move in your behalf.

If you would come to Him as your Father and understand that you are His princesses, His daughters, His joy, what a miracle would happen as you lose your inhibitions in the strength of His loving arms. These are the arms that threaten enemies and chase away assailants. But they are also the tender, caring arms of the affectionate Father who is vulnerable to the cry of His seed! Your prayer life will literally explode when you realize that the Father longs to bless you.

When my daughters were small, they would run toward me with soggy diapers. Although sometimes the odors were pungent and the accident hidden in those diapers was strong enough to make me want to put them down, still love would gather them into my arms.

This is the love that God has for you, only a thousand times more real. There will be times you will be afraid to run to Him, knowing that He can easily tell that you have had an accident. Never be afraid of Him. As weak as I am, I loved my daughters enough to hold them until I could wash them. How much greater is His love than mine! This is the love that comes from the Father who knows that the smell of the mistake will pass, but His love for the daughter will last.

When you walk through the
fire, you shall not be burned,
Nor shall the flame scorch you.
3 For I *am* the LORD your God,
The Holy One of Israel, your
Savior;
I gave Egypt for your ransom,
Ethiopia and Seba in your
place.
4 Since you were precious in My
sight,
You have been honored,
And I have loved you;
Therefore I will give men for
you,
And people for your life.
5 Fear not, for I *am* with you;
I will bring your descendants
from the east,
And gather you from the west;
6 I will say to the north, 'Give
them up!'
And to the south, 'Do not keep
them back!'
Bring My sons from afar,
And My daughters from the
ends of the earth—
7 Everyone who is called by My
name,
Whom I have created for My
glory;
I have formed him, yes, I have
made him."

8 Bring out the blind people who
have eyes,
And the deaf who have ears.
9 Let all the nations be gathered
together,
And let the people be
assembled.
Who among them can declare
this,
And show us former things?
Let them bring out their
witnesses, that they may be
justified;
Or let them hear and say, "It
is truth."
10 "You *are* My witnesses," says
the LORD,
"And My servant whom I have
chosen,
That you may know and
believe Me,
And understand that I *am* He.
Before Me there was no God
formed,
Nor shall there be after Me.
11 I, *even* I, *am* the LORD,
And besides Me *there is* no
savior.

12 I have declared and saved,
I have proclaimed,
And *there was* no foreign *god*
among you;
Therefore you *are* My
witnesses,"
Says the LORD, "that I *am* God.
13 Indeed before the day *was*, I *am*
He;
And *there is* no one who can
deliver out of My hand;
I work, and who will reverse
it?"

14 Thus says the LORD, your
Redeemer,
The Holy One of Israel:
"For your sake I will send to
Babylon,
And bring them all down as
fugitives—
The Chaldeans, who rejoice in
their ships.
15 I *am* the LORD, your Holy One,
The Creator of Israel, your
King."

16 Thus says the LORD, who
makes a way in the sea
And a path through the mighty
waters,
17 Who brings forth the chariot
and horse,
The army and the power
(They shall lie down together,
they shall not rise;
They are extinguished, they are
quenched like a wick):
18 "Do not remember the former
things,
Nor consider the things of
old.
19 Behold, I will do a new thing,
Now it shall spring forth;
Shall you not know it?
I will even make a road in the
wilderness
And rivers in the desert.
20 The beast of the field will honor
Me,
The jackals and the ostriches,
Because I give waters in the
wilderness
And rivers in the desert,
To give drink to My people, My
chosen.
21 This people I have formed for
Myself;
They shall declare My praise.

22 "But you have not called upon
Me, O Jacob;

*Y*ou can't earn deliverance. You just have to receive it by faith. Christ is the only
righteousness that God will accept.

Letting Go

Isaiah 43:18, 19

Never forget how to let go. It may be a person, a thing, or a moment that you can never repeat. Nothing challenges our ability to let go like death. It wrenches from our hands a loved one to whom we would cling forever if we could. When you stand over a casket that is being lowered into the ground, truth slaps you in the face. The person you loved is gone.

For Christians, death is a portal that enables us to move from one realm of existence into another. Eventually death will knock on the door no matter who we are. It helps a little to know that it will come. When it does, God will give you grace to accept what cannot be changed. That same grace will empower you as you learn to cope with changes among the living. Grace empowers us to continue and experience with God's help. Why don't you ask Him for the grace you need to accept the things that you cannot change? When He gives it to you, get on with your life.

Each experience has its own value if you do not close your eyes to where you are, trying foolishly to be where you have already been. I know life can feel terribly unstable and vulnerable when you accept change. But I am so glad God ever remains the same. He is the stability that enables us to adjust to the variables of life.

If you recognize areas in your life where you have been guilty of resisting change, stop right where you are and allow God to cleanse your heart from the fear of change. Know in your spirit that something good is going to come out of it. Take it in stride and start planning ways you can enjoy where you are. Maybe you have been neglecting your children, husband, or job. You want to go back to the past. But you are also missing the good things that God has prepared for you today.

Our faith teaches us to trust God. He doesn't change, but His methods of ministering to you will change over and over again. Do not worry. He will give you what you need when you need it. He may not bring it the same way twice. But why do you care *how* He does it as long as you know He does it? Leave the "hows" in the hands of the great One who is able to control the circumstances in your life. Repent of manipulating those with whom you associate. Let them go. You have no right to hold anyone a prisoner in the jail cell of your fears, not even yourself. Let yourself go. You have been imprisoned from what God wants to give you most, a new experience in Christ Jesus!

And you have been weary of
Me, O Israel.
23 You have not brought Me the
sheep for your burnt
offerings,
Nor have you honored Me with
your sacrifices.
I have not caused you to serve
with grain offerings,
Nor wearied you with incense.
24 You have bought Me no sweet
cane with money,
Nor have you satisfied Me with
the fat of your sacrifices;
But you have burdened Me
with your sins,
You have wearied Me with
your iniquities.

25 "I, *even* I, *am* He who blots out
your transgressions for My
own sake;
And I will not remember your
sins.
26 Put Me in remembrance;
Let us contend together;
State your *case*, that you may
be acquitted.
27 Your first father sinned,
And your mediators have
transgressed against Me.
28 Therefore I will profane the
princes of the sanctuary;
I will give Jacob to the curse,
And Israel to reproaches.

44 "Yet hear now, O Jacob My
servant,
And Israel whom I have
chosen.
2 Thus says the LORD who made
you
And formed you from the
womb, *who* will help you:
'Fear not, O Jacob My servant;
And you, Jeshurun, whom I
have chosen.
3 For I will pour water on him
who is thirsty,
And floods on the dry ground;
I will pour My Spirit on your
descendants,
And My blessing on your
offspring;
4 They will spring up among the
grass
Like willows by the
watercourses.'
5 One will say, 'I *am* the LORD's';
Another will call *himself* by the
name of Jacob;

Another will write *with* his
hand, 'The LORD's,'
And name *himself* by the name
of Israel.

6 "Thus says the LORD, the King
of Israel,
And his Redeemer, the LORD of
hosts:
'I *am* the First and I *am* the Last;
Besides Me *there is* no God.
7 And who can proclaim as I do?
Then let him declare it and set
it in order for Me,
Since I appointed the ancient
people.
And the things that are coming
and shall come,
Let them show these to them.
8 Do not fear, nor be afraid;
Have I not told you from that
time, and declared *it*?
You *are* My witnesses.
Is there a God besides Me?
Indeed *there is* no other Rock;
I know not *one*.' "

9 Those who make an image, all
of them *are* useless,
And their precious things shall
not profit;
They *are* their own witnesses;
They neither see nor know, that
they may be ashamed.
10 Who would form a god or mold
an image
That profits him nothing?
11 Surely all his companions
would be ashamed;
And the workmen, they *are*
mere men.
Let them all be gathered
together,
Let them stand up;
Yet they shall fear,
They shall be ashamed
together.

12 The blacksmith with the tongs
works one in the coals,
Fashions it with hammers,
And works it with the strength
of his arms.
Even so, he is hungry, and his
strength fails;
He drinks no water and is faint.

13 The craftsman stretches out *his*
rule,
He marks one out with chalk;
He fashions it with a plane,

*J*esus' actions were massively different from ours. He focused on hurting people.
Every time He saw a hurting person, He reached out and ministered to their need.

He marks it out with the
compass,
And makes it like the figure of
a man,
According to the beauty of a
man, that it may remain in
the house.

14 He cuts down cedars for
himself,
And takes the cypress and the
oak;
He secures *it* for himself
among the trees of the
forest.
He plants a pine, and the rain
nourishes *it.*

15 Then it shall be for a man to
burn,
For he will take some of it and
warm himself;
Yes, he kindles *it* and bakes
bread;
Indeed he makes a god and
worships *it;*
He makes it a carved image,
and falls down to it.

16 He burns half of it in the fire;
With this half he eats meat;
He roasts a roast, and is
satisfied.
He even warms *himself* and
says,
"Ah! I am warm,
I have seen the fire."

17 And the rest of it he makes into
a god,
His carved image.
He falls down before it and
worships *it,*
Prays to it and says,
"Deliver me, for you *are* my
god!"

18 They do not know nor
understand;
For He has shut their eyes, so
that they cannot see,
And their hearts, so that they
cannot understand.

19 And no one considers in his
heart,
Nor *is there* knowledge nor
understanding to say,
"I have burned half of it in the
fire,
Yes, I have also baked bread
on its coals;
I have roasted meat and eaten
it;
And shall I make the rest of it
an abomination?

Shall I fall down before a block
of wood?"

20 He feeds on ashes;
A deceived heart has turned
him aside;
And he cannot deliver his soul,
Nor say, "*Is there* not a lie in
my right hand?"

21 "Remember these, O Jacob,
And Israel, for you *are* My
servant;
I have formed you, you *are* My
servant;
O Israel, you will not be
forgotten by Me!

22 I have blotted out, like a thick
cloud, your transgressions,
And like a cloud, your sins.
Return to Me, for I have
redeemed you."

23 Sing, O heavens, for the LORD
has done *it!*
Shout, you lower parts of the
earth;
Break forth into singing, you
mountains,
O forest, and every tree in it!
For the LORD has redeemed
Jacob,
And glorified Himself in Israel.

24 Thus says the LORD, your
Redeemer,
And He who formed you from
the womb:
"I *am* the LORD, who makes all
things,
Who stretches out the heavens
all alone,
Who spreads abroad the earth
by Myself;

25 Who frustrates the signs of the
babblers,
And drives diviners mad;
Who turns wise men backward,
And makes their knowledge
foolishness;

26 Who confirms the word of His
servant,
And performs the counsel of
His messengers;
Who says to Jerusalem, 'You
shall be inhabited,'
To the cities of Judah, 'You
shall be built,'
And I will raise up her waste
places;

27 Who says to the deep, 'Be
dry!
And I will dry up your rivers';

Gospel
Pearls

28 Who says of Cyrus, 'He is My
shepherd,
And he shall perform all My
pleasure,
Saying to Jerusalem, "You
shall be built,"
And to the temple, "Your
foundation shall be laid." '

45 "Thus says the LORD to His
anointed,
To Cyrus, whose right hand I
have held—
To subdue nations before him
And loose the armor of kings,
To open before him the double
doors,
So that the gates will not be
shut:

2 'I will go before you
And make the crooked places[a]
straight;
I will break in pieces the gates
of bronze
And cut the bars of iron.

3 I will give you the treasures of
darkness
And hidden riches of secret
places,
That you may know that I, the
LORD,
Who call you by your name,
Am the God of Israel.

4 For Jacob My servant's sake,
And Israel My elect,
I have even called you by your
name;
I have named you, though you
have not known Me.

5 I am the LORD, and there is no
other;
There is no God besides Me.
I will gird you, though you have
not known Me,

6 That they may know from the
rising of the sun to its setting
That there is none besides Me.
I am the LORD, and there is no
other;

7 I form the light and create
darkness,
I make peace and create
calamity;
I, the LORD, do all these things.'

8 "Rain down, you heavens, from
above,
And let the skies pour down
righteousness;

Let the earth open, let them
bring forth salvation,
And let righteousness spring
up together.
I, the LORD, have created it.

9 "Woe to him who strives with
his Maker!
Let the potsherd strive with the
potsherds of the earth!
Shall the clay say to him who
forms it, 'What are you
making?'
Or shall your handiwork say,
'He has no hands'?

10 Woe to him who says to his
father, 'What are you
begetting?'
Or to the woman, 'What have
you brought forth?' "

11 Thus says the LORD,
The Holy One of Israel, and his
Maker:
"Ask Me of things to come
concerning My sons;
And concerning the work of
My hands, you command Me.

12 I have made the earth,
And created man on it.
I—My hands—stretched out the
heavens,
And all their host I have
commanded.

13 I have raised him up in
righteousness,
And I will direct all his ways;
He shall build My city
And let My exiles go free,
Not for price nor reward,"
Says the LORD of hosts.

14 Thus says the LORD:

"The labor of Egypt and
merchandise of Cush
And of the Sabeans, men of
stature,
Shall come over to you, and
they shall be yours;
They shall walk behind you,
They shall come over in chains;
And they shall bow down to
you.
They will make supplication to
you, saying, 'Surely God is in
you,
And there is no other;
There is no other God.' "

45:2 aDead Sea Scrolls and Septuagint read mountains; Targum reads I will trample down the walls; Vulgate
reads I will humble the great ones of the earth.

Thank God He calls women with a past. He reaches out and says, "Get up! You can
come to Me." Regardless of what a person has done, or what kind of abuse one has
suffered, He still calls.

15 Truly You *are* God, who hide
    Yourself,
    O God of Israel, the Savior!
16 They shall be ashamed
    And also disgraced, all of
    them;
    They shall go in confusion
    together,
    Who are makers of idols.
17 *But* Israel shall be saved by the
    L{ORD}
    With an everlasting salvation;
    You shall not be ashamed or
    disgraced
    Forever and ever.

18 For thus says the L{ORD},
    Who created the heavens,
    Who is God,
    Who formed the earth and
    made it,
    Who has established it,
    Who did not create it in vain,
    Who formed it to be inhabited:
    "I *am* the L{ORD}, and *there is* no
    other.
19 I have not spoken in secret,
    In a dark place of the earth;
    I did not say to the seed of
    Jacob,
    'Seek Me in vain';
    I, the L{ORD}, speak
    righteousness,
    I declare things that are right.

20 "Assemble yourselves and
    come;
    Draw near together,
    You *who have* escaped from
    the nations.
    They have no knowledge,
    Who carry the wood of their
    carved image,
    And pray to a god *that* cannot
    save.
21 Tell and bring forth *your case*;
    Yes, let them take counsel
    together.
    Who has declared this from
    ancient time?
    Who has told it from that
    time?
    Have not I, the L{ORD}?
    And *there is* no other God
    besides Me,
    A just God and a Savior;
    There is none besides Me.

22 "Look to Me, and be saved,
    All you ends of the earth!
    For I *am* God, and *there is* no
    other.

23 I have sworn by Myself;
    The word has gone out of My
    mouth *in* righteousness,
    And shall not return,
    That to Me every knee shall
    bow,
    Every tongue shall take an
    oath.
24 He shall say,
    'Surely in the L{ORD} I have
    righteousness and strength.
    To Him *men* shall come,
    And all shall be ashamed
    Who are incensed against Him.
25 In the L{ORD} all the descendants
    of Israel
    Shall be justified, and shall
    glory.' "

46 Bel bows down, Nebo stoops;
    Their idols were on the beasts
    and on the cattle.
    Your carriages *were* heavily
    loaded,
    A burden to the weary *beast.*
2 They stoop, they bow down
    together;
    They could not deliver the
    burden,
    But have themselves gone into
    captivity.

3 "Listen to Me, O house of Jacob,
    And all the remnant of the
    house of Israel,
    Who have been upheld *by Me*
    from birth,
    Who have been carried from
    the womb:
4 Even to *your* old age, I *am* He,
    And *even* to gray hairs I will
    carry *you!*
    I have made, and I will bear;
    Even I will carry, and will
    deliver *you.*

5 "To whom will you liken Me,
    and make *Me* equal
    And compare Me, that we
    should be alike?
6 They lavish gold out of the
    bag,
    And weigh silver on the scales;
    They hire a goldsmith, and he
    makes it a god;
    They prostrate themselves, yes,
    they worship.
7 They bear it on the shoulder,
    they carry it
    And set it in its place, and it
    stands;
    From its place it shall not move.

Gospel Pearls

Though *one* cries out to it, yet
   it cannot answer
Nor save him out of his trouble.

8 "Remember this, and show
   yourselves men;
   Recall to mind, O you
   transgressors.
9 Remember the former things of
   old,
   For I *am* God, and *there is* no
   other;
   I am God, and *there is* none like
   Me,
10 Declaring the end from the
   beginning,
   And from ancient times *things*
   that are not *yet* done,
   Saying, 'My counsel shall
   stand,
   And I will do all My pleasure,'
11 Calling a bird of prey from the
   east,
   The man who executes My
   counsel, from a far country.
   Indeed I have spoken *it;*
   I will also bring it to pass.
   I have purposed *it;*
   I will also do it.

12 "Listen to Me, you stubborn-
   hearted,
   Who *are* far from
   righteousness:
13 I bring My righteousness near,
   it shall not be far off;
   My salvation shall not linger.
   And I will place salvation in
   Zion,
   For Israel My glory.

47 "Come down and sit in the
   dust,
   O virgin daughter of Babylon;
   Sit on the ground without a
   throne,
   O daughter of the Chaldeans!
   For you shall no more be
   called
   Tender and delicate.
2 Take the millstones and grind
   meal.
   Remove your veil,
   Take off the skirt,
   Uncover the thigh,
   Pass through the rivers.
3 Your nakedness shall be
   uncovered,
   Yes, your shame will be seen;
   I will take vengeance,
   And I will not arbitrate with a
   man."

4 *As for* our Redeemer, the LORD
   of hosts *is* His name,
   The Holy One of Israel.

5 "Sit in silence, and go into
   darkness,
   O daughter of the Chaldeans;
   For you shall no longer be
   called
   The Lady of Kingdoms.
6 I was angry with My people;
   I have profaned My
   inheritance,
   And given them into your hand.
   You showed them no mercy;
   On the elderly you laid your
   yoke very heavily.
7 And you said, 'I shall be a lady
   forever,'
   So that you did not take these
   things to heart,
   Nor remember the latter end of
   them.

8 "Therefore hear this now, *you*
   who are given to pleasures,
   Who dwell securely,
   Who say in your heart,
   'I *am,* and *there is* no one else
   besides me;
   I shall not sit *as* a widow,
   Nor shall I know the loss of
   children';
9 But these two *things* shall come
   to you
   In a moment, in one day:
   The loss of children, and
   widowhood.
   They shall come upon you in
   their fullness
   Because of the multitude of
   your sorceries,
   For the great abundance of
   your enchantments.

10 "For you have trusted in your
   wickedness;
   You have said, 'No one sees
   me';
   Your wisdom and your
   knowledge have warped you;
   And you have said in your
   heart,
   'I *am,* and *there is* no one else
   besides me.'
11 Therefore evil shall come upon
   you;
   You shall not know from where
   it arises.
   And trouble shall fall upon you;
   You will not be able to put it
   off.

*N*o matter how difficult life seems, people with a past need to make their way to Jesus. Regardless of the obstacles within and without, they must reach Him.

And desolation shall come
upon you suddenly,
Which you shall not know.

12 "Stand now with your
enchantments
And the multitude of your
sorceries,
In which you have labored
from your youth—
Perhaps you will be able to
profit,
Perhaps you will prevail.
13 You are wearied in the
multitude of your counsels;
Let now the astrologers, the
stargazers,
And the monthly
prognosticators
Stand up and save you
From what shall come upon
you.
14 Behold, they shall be as
stubble,
The fire shall burn them;
They shall not deliver
themselves
From the power of the flame;
It shall not *be* a coal to be
warmed by,
Nor a fire to sit before!
15 Thus shall they be to you
With whom you have labored,
Your merchants from your
youth;
They shall wander each one to
his quarter.
No one shall save you.

48 "Hear this, O house of Jacob,
Who are called by the name of
Israel,
And have come forth from the
wellsprings of Judah;
Who swear by the name of the
LORD,
And make mention of the God
of Israel,
But not in truth or in
righteousness;
2 For they call themselves after
the holy city,
And lean on the God of Israel;
The LORD of hosts *is* His name:

3 "I have declared the former
things from the beginning;
They went forth from My
mouth, and I caused them to
hear it.
Suddenly I did *them,* and they
came to pass.

4 Because I knew that you *were*
obstinate,
And your neck *was* an iron
sinew,
And your brow bronze,
5 Even from the beginning I have
declared *it* to you;
Before it came to pass I
proclaimed *it* to you,
Lest you should say, 'My idol
has done them,
And my carved image and my
molded image
Have commanded them.'

6 "You have heard;
See all this.
And will you not declare *it?*
I have made you hear new
things from this time,
Even hidden things, and you
did not know them.
7 They are created now and not
from the beginning;
And before this day you have
not heard them,
Lest you should say, 'Of course
I knew them.'
8 Surely you did not hear,
Surely you did not know;
Surely from long ago your ear
was not opened.
For I knew that you would deal
very treacherously,
And were called a transgressor
from the womb.

9 "For My name's sake I will defer
My anger,
And *for* My praise I will
restrain it from you,
So that I do not cut you off.
10 Behold, I have refined you, but
not as silver;
I have tested you in the furnace
of affliction.
11 For My own sake, for My own
sake, I will do *it;*
For how should *My name* be
profaned?
And I will not give My glory to
another.

12 "Listen to Me, O Jacob,
And Israel, My called:
I *am* He, I *am* the First,
I *am* also the Last.
13 Indeed My hand has laid the
foundation of the earth,
And My right hand has
stretched out the heavens;
When I call to them,
They stand up together.

Gospel
Pearls

14 "All of you, assemble
  yourselves, and hear!
Who among them has declared
  these *things*?
The LORD loves him;
He shall do His pleasure on
  Babylon,
And His arm *shall be against*
  the Chaldeans.
15 I, *even* I, have spoken;
Yes, I have called him,
I have brought him, and his
  way will prosper.

16 "Come near to Me, hear this:
I have not spoken in secret
  from the beginning;
From the time that it was, I *was*
  there.
And now the Lord GOD and His
  Spirit
Have[a] sent Me."

17 Thus says the LORD, your
  Redeemer,
The Holy One of Israel:
"I *am* the LORD your God,
Who teaches you to profit,
Who leads you by the way you
  should go.
18 Oh, that you had heeded My
  commandments!
Then your peace would have
  been like a river,
And your righteousness like
  the waves of the sea.
19 Your descendants also would
  have been like the sand,
And the offspring of your body
  like the grains of sand;
His name would not have been
  cut off
Nor destroyed from before
  Me."

20 Go forth from Babylon!
Flee from the Chaldeans!
With a voice of singing,
Declare, proclaim this,
Utter it to the end of the earth;
Say, "The LORD has redeemed
His servant Jacob!"
21 And they did not thirst
When He led them through the
  deserts;
He caused the waters to flow
  from the rock for them;
He also split the rock, and the
  waters gushed out.

22 "*There is* no peace," says the
  LORD, "for the wicked."

49 "Listen, O coastlands, to Me,
  And take heed, you peoples
    from afar!
The LORD has called Me from
  the womb;
From the matrix of My mother
  He has made mention of My
  name.
2 And He has made My mouth
  like a sharp sword;
In the shadow of His hand He
  has hidden Me,
And made Me a polished shaft;
In His quiver He has hidden
  Me."

3 "And He said to me,
'You *are* My servant, O Israel,
In whom I will be glorified.'
4 Then I said, 'I have labored in
  vain,
I have spent my strength for
  nothing and in vain;
Yet surely my just reward *is*
  with the LORD,
And my work with my God.'"

5 "And now the LORD says,
Who formed Me from the
  womb *to be* His Servant,
To bring Jacob back to Him,
So that Israel is gathered to
  Him[a]
(For I shall be glorious in the
  eyes of the LORD,
And My God shall be My
  strength),
6 Indeed He says,
'It is too small a thing that You
  should be My Servant
To raise up the tribes of Jacob,
And to restore the preserved
  ones of Israel;
I will also give You as a light
  to the Gentiles,
That You should be My
  salvation to the ends of the
  earth.'"

7 Thus says the LORD,
The Redeemer of Israel, their
  Holy One,
To Him whom man despises,
To Him whom the nation
  abhors,
To the Servant of rulers:

48:16 [a]The Hebrew verb is singular.   49:5 [a]Qere, Dead Sea Scrolls, and Septuagint read *is gathered to Him;* Kethib reads *not gathered.*

*T*he blood of Jesus is efficacious, cleansing the woman who feels unclean. Just as He said to the woman then, He proclaims today, "Neither do I condemn thee: go and sin no more."

"Kings shall see and arise,
Princes also shall worship,
Because of the LORD who is
faithful,
The Holy One of Israel;
And He has chosen You."

8 Thus says the LORD:

"In an acceptable time I have
heard You,
And in the day of salvation I
have helped You;
I will preserve You and give
You
As a covenant to the people,
To restore the earth,
To cause them to inherit the
desolate heritages;
9 That You may say to the
prisoners, 'Go forth,'
To those who *are* in darkness,
'Show yourselves.'

"They shall feed along the
roads,
And their pastures *shall be* on
all desolate heights.
10 They shall neither hunger nor
thirst,
Neither heat nor sun shall
strike them;
For He who has mercy on them
will lead them,
Even by the springs of water
He will guide them.
11 I will make each of My
mountains a road,
And My highways shall be
elevated.
12 Surely these shall come from
afar;
Look! Those from the north
and the west,
And these from the land of
Sinim."

13 Sing, O heavens!
Be joyful, O earth!
And break out in singing, O
mountains!
For the LORD has comforted His
people,
And will have mercy on His
afflicted.

14 But Zion said, "The LORD has
forsaken me,
And my Lord has forgotten
me."

15 "Can a woman forget her
nursing child,
And not have compassion on
the son of her womb?
Surely they may forget,
Yet I will not forget you.
16 See, I have inscribed you on the
palms *of My hands;*
Your walls *are* continually
before Me.
17 Your sons[a] shall make haste;
Your destroyers and those who
laid you waste
Shall go away from you.
18 Lift up your eyes, look around
and see;
All these gather together *and*
come to you.
As I live," says the LORD,
"You shall surely clothe
yourselves with them all as
an ornament,
And bind them *on you* as a
bride *does.*

19 "For your waste and desolate
places,
And the land of your
destruction,
Will even now be too small for
the inhabitants;
And those who swallowed you
up will be far away.
20 The children you will have,
After you have lost the others,
Will say again in your ears,
'The place *is* too small for me;
Give me a place where I may
dwell.'
21 Then you will say in your heart,
'Who has begotten these for me,
Since I have lost my children
and am desolate,
A captive, and wandering to
and fro?
And who has brought these up?
There I was, left alone;
But these, where *were* they?' "

22 Thus says the Lord GOD:

"Behold, I will lift My hand in
an oath to the nations,
And set up My standard for the
peoples;
They shall bring your sons in
their arms,
And your daughters shall be
carried on *their* shoulders;
23 Kings shall be your foster
fathers,

49:17 [a]Dead Sea Scrolls, Septuagint, Targum, and Vulgate read *builders.*

And their queens your nursing
mothers;
They shall bow down to you
with *their* faces to the earth,
And lick up the dust of your
feet.
Then you will know that I *am*
the LORD,
For they shall not be ashamed
who wait for Me."

24 Shall the prey be taken from
the mighty,
Or the captives of the
righteous[a] be delivered?

25 But thus says the LORD:

"Even the captives of the mighty
shall be taken away,
And the prey of the terrible be
delivered;
For I will contend with him who
contends with you,
And I will save your children.
26 I will feed those who oppress
you with their own flesh,
And they shall be drunk with
their own blood as with
sweet wine.
All flesh shall know
That I, the LORD, *am* your
Savior,
And your Redeemer, the
Mighty One of Jacob."

50 Thus says the LORD:

"Where *is* the certificate of your
mother's divorce,
Whom I have put away?
Or which of My creditors *is it*
to whom I have sold you?
For your iniquities you have
sold yourselves,
And for your transgressions
your mother has been put
away.
2 Why, when I came, *was there*
no man?
Why, when I called, *was there*
none to answer?
Is My hand shortened at all that
it cannot redeem?
Or have I no power to deliver?
Indeed with My rebuke I dry up
the sea,
I make the rivers a wilderness;

Their fish stink because *there
is* no water,
And die of thirst.
3 I clothe the heavens with
blackness,
And I make sackcloth their
covering."

4 "The Lord GOD has given Me
The tongue of the learned,
That I should know how to
speak
A word in season to *him who
is* weary.
He awakens Me morning by
morning,
He awakens My ear
To hear as the learned.
5 The Lord GOD has opened My
ear;
And I was not rebellious,
Nor did I turn away.
6 I gave My back to those who
struck *Me,*
And My cheeks to those who
plucked out the beard;
I did not hide My face from
shame and spitting.

7 "For the Lord GOD will help Me;
Therefore I will not be
disgraced;
Therefore I have set My face
like a flint,
And I know that I will not be
ashamed.
8 *He is* near who justifies Me;
Who will contend with Me?
Let us stand together.
Who *is* My adversary?
Let him come near Me.
9 Surely the Lord GOD will help
Me;
Who *is* he *who* will condemn
Me?
Indeed they will all grow old
like a garment;
The moth will eat them up.

10 "Who among you fears the
LORD?
Who obeys the voice of His
Servant?
Who walks in darkness
And has no light?
Let him trust in the name of the
LORD
And rely upon his God.
11 Look, all you who kindle a fire,

49:24 [a]Following Masoretic Text and Targum; Dead Sea Scrolls, Syriac, and Vulgate read *the mighty;* Septuagint reads *unjustly.*

---

*J*esus comes to set us free. He is unleashing the women of His Church. He forgives, heals and restores. Women can find the potential of their future because of His wonderful power operating in their lives.

Who encircle *yourselves* with
sparks:
Walk in the light of your fire
and in the sparks you have
kindled—
This you shall have from My
hand:
You shall lie down in torment.

51 "Listen to Me, you who follow
after righteousness,
You who seek the LORD:
Look to the rock *from which*
you were hewn,
And to the hole of the pit *from
which* you were dug.

2 Look to Abraham your father,
And to Sarah *who* bore you;
For I called him alone,
And blessed him and increased
him."

3 For the LORD will comfort Zion,
He will comfort all her waste
places;
He will make her wilderness
like Eden,
And her desert like the garden
of the LORD;
Joy and gladness will be found
in it,
Thanksgiving and the voice of
melody.

4 "Listen to Me, My people;
And give ear to Me, O My
nation:
For law will proceed from Me,
And I will make My justice
rest
As a light of the peoples.

5 My righteousness *is* near,
My salvation has gone forth,
And My arms will judge the
peoples;
The coastlands will wait upon
Me,
And on My arm they will trust.

6 Lift up your eyes to the
heavens,
And look on the earth beneath.
For the heavens will vanish
away like smoke,
The earth will grow old like a
garment,
And those who dwell in it will
die in like manner;
But My salvation will be
forever,
And My righteousness will not
be abolished.

7 "Listen to Me, you who know
righteousness,
You people in whose heart *is*
My law:
Do not fear the reproach of
men,
Nor be afraid of their insults.

8 For the moth will eat them up
like a garment,
And the worm will eat them
like wool;
But My righteousness will be
forever,
And My salvation from
generation to generation."

9 Awake, awake, put on strength,
O arm of the LORD!
Awake as in the ancient days,
In the generations of old.
Are You not *the arm* that cut
Rahab apart,
And wounded the serpent?

10 *Are* You not *the One* who dried
up the sea,
The waters of the great deep;
That made the depths of the sea
a road
For the redeemed to cross over?

11 So the ransomed of the LORD
shall return,
And come to Zion with singing,
With everlasting joy on their
heads.
They shall obtain joy and
gladness;
Sorrow and sighing shall flee
away.

12 "I, *even* I, *am* He who comforts
you.
Who *are* you that you should
be afraid
Of a man *who* will die,
And of the son of a man *who*
will be made like grass?

13 And you forget the LORD your
Maker,
Who stretched out the heavens
And laid the foundations of the
earth;
You have feared continually
every day
Because of the fury of the
oppressor,
When *he has* prepared to
destroy.
And where *is* the fury of the
oppressor?

14 The captive exile hastens, that
he may be loosed,

Gospel
Pearls

That he should not die in the
pit,
And that his bread should not
fail.
15 But I *am* the LORD your
God,
Who divided the sea whose
waves roared—
The LORD of hosts *is* His
name.
16 And I have put My words in
your mouth;
I have covered you with the
shadow of My hand,
That I may plant the heavens,
Lay the foundations of the
earth,
And say to Zion, 'You *are* My
people.' "
17 Awake, awake!
Stand up, O Jerusalem,
You who have drunk at the
hand of the LORD
The cup of His fury;
You have drunk the dregs of
the cup of trembling,
And drained *it* out.
18 *There is* no one to guide her
Among all the sons she has
brought forth;
Nor *is there any* who takes her
by the hand
Among all the sons she has
brought up.
19 These two *things* have come to
you;
Who will be sorry for you?—
Desolation and destruction,
famine and sword—
By whom will I comfort you?
20 Your sons have fainted,
They lie at the head of all the
streets,
Like an antelope in a net;
They are full of the fury of the
LORD,
The rebuke of your God.

21 Therefore please hear this, you
afflicted,
And drunk but not with
wine.
22 Thus says your Lord,
The LORD and your God,
Who pleads the cause of His
people:
"See, I have taken out of your
hand
The cup of trembling,

The dregs of the cup of My
fury;
You shall no longer drink it.
23 But I will put it into the hand
of those who afflict you,
Who have said to you,*a*
'Lie down, that we may walk
over you.'
And you have laid your body
like the ground,
And as the street, for those who
walk over."

52 Awake, awake!
Put on your strength, O Zion;
Put on your beautiful garments,
O Jerusalem, the holy city!
For the uncircumcised and the
unclean
Shall no longer come to you.
2 Shake yourself from the dust,
arise;
Sit down, O Jerusalem!
Loose yourself from the bonds
of your neck,
O captive daughter of Zion!

3 For thus says the LORD:

"You have sold yourselves for
nothing,
And you shall be redeemed
without money."

4 For thus says the Lord GOD:

"My people went down at first
Into Egypt to dwell there;
Then the Assyrian oppressed
them without cause.
5 Now therefore, what have I
here," says the LORD,
"That My people are taken away
for nothing?
Those who rule over them
Make them wail,"*a* says the
LORD,
"And My name *is* blasphemed
continually every day.
6 Therefore My people shall
know My name;
Therefore *they* shall *know* in
that day
That I *am* He who speaks:
'Behold, *it is* I.' "

7 How beautiful upon the
mountains

51:23 *a*Literally *your soul*   52:5 *a*Dead Sea Scrolls read *Mock;* Septuagint reads *Marvel and wail;* Targum
reads *Boast themselves;* Vulgate reads *Treat them unjustly.*

*Y*ou may have gone through some horrible times, but Jesus intercedes on your
behalf. No matter what struggles women have faced, confidence is found in the
ministry of our High Priest. He prays for you.

Are the feet of him who brings
good news,
Who proclaims peace,
Who brings glad tidings of
good *things,*
Who proclaims salvation,
Who says to Zion,
"Your God reigns!"
8 Your watchmen shall lift up
their voices,
With their voices they shall
sing together;
For they shall see eye to eye
When the LORD brings back
Zion.
9 Break forth into joy, sing
together,
You waste places of Jerusalem!
For the LORD has comforted His
people,
He has redeemed Jerusalem.
10 The LORD has made bare His
holy arm
In the eyes of all the nations;
And all the ends of the earth
shall see
The salvation of our God.

11 Depart! Depart! Go out from
there,
Touch no unclean *thing;*
Go out from the midst of her,
Be clean,
You who bear the vessels of the
LORD.
12 For you shall not go out with
haste,
Nor go by flight;
For the LORD will go before
you,
And the God of Israel *will be*
your rear guard.

13 Behold, My Servant shall deal
prudently;
He shall be exalted and
extolled and be very high.
14 Just as many were astonished
at you,
So His visage was marred more
than any man,
And His form more than the
sons of men;
15 So shall He sprinkle[a] many
nations.
Kings shall shut their mouths
at Him;
For what had not been told
them they shall see,
And what they had not heard
they shall consider.

53 Who has believed our report?
And to whom has the arm of
the LORD been revealed?
2 For He shall grow up before
Him as a tender plant,
And as a root out of dry
ground.
He has no form or comeliness;
And when we see Him,
There is no beauty that we
should desire Him.
3 He is despised and rejected by
men,
A Man of sorrows and
acquainted with grief.
And we hid, as it were, *our*
faces from Him;
He was despised, and we did
not esteem Him.

4 Surely He has borne our griefs
And carried our sorrows;
Yet we esteemed Him stricken,
Smitten by God, and afflicted.
5 But He *was* wounded for our
transgressions,
He was bruised for our
iniquities;
The chastisement for our peace
was upon Him,
And by His stripes we are
healed.
6 All we like sheep have gone
astray;
We have turned, every one, to
his own way;
And the LORD has laid on Him
the iniquity of us all.

7 He was oppressed and He was
afflicted,
Yet He opened not His mouth;
He was led as a lamb to the
slaughter,
And as a sheep before its
shearers is silent,
So He opened not His mouth.
8 He was taken from prison and
from judgment,
And who will declare His
generation?
For He was cut off from the
land of the living;
For the transgressions of My
people He was stricken.
9 And they[a] made His grave with
the wicked—
But with the rich at His death,
Because He had done no
violence,

52:15 [a]Or *startle*   53:9 [a]Literally *he* or *He*

*F*aith comes when you recognize that you can't help yourself. Only trust in Christ
can bring you through. Many have suffered mightily, but Jesus gives the strength
to overcome the attacks of Satan and human, selfish lust.

The Ultimate Sacrifice

Isaiah 53:4-12

You have been called out and separated by God. You were not created to be popular. You were not called to cliques or clubs. You were chosen to fit in the hands of God who has already accepted you. Insecurity dissipates in the reality of divine truth. How I want you to know the height and the depth of His unfathomable love for you!

Some women have never been secure in the love of their natural fathers, and it affects how they view their heavenly Father. But listen to me. There is no doubt about His love. He made the ultimate sacrifice just to prove the authenticity of His love for you.

You are so valuable that Satan held you for ransom, knowing that your Father was so rich! He asked of God, "What would you give to see this woman freed?" Your Father sent His Son armed with love and wrapped in flesh. He said, "This is how much I think she is worth." Jesus hung His head between His shoulders and died naked on a tree because you mean so much to Him.

Never again insult His great sacrifice by questioning His love. You may not see it or understand it, but believe it. He absolutely loves you. Not just when you are right. He loves you when you are wrong. That is what gives you the power to right the wrongs you've made. He wants desperately to heal the aching heart that has believed the lies of life. You are special and vibrant, full of potential and possibilities. You are the daughter of a King. He is the King who spared no expense to pay the ransom that delivered you from the things that held you hostage. Get a clue; catch the hint; you are somebody!

These are the truths He wants every believer to know. These are the words I found in the Bible. It is a living love letter to a dying world. It is a statement of intent from a God who wants you to have it all.

His arms are outstretched. He is waiting for you in the secret place. He will not fail you. Rise up, rise up with a quickened pulse and a gleaming eye. He is all yours, and it is all good. A no from Him is as sweet as a yes. It is the evidence of His intense attraction to you and His raging love for you. Your life is about to crescendo into a symphony of praise. When His plan crescendos, you will be glad you didn't settle for your own way. He is up to something. Do not miss it!

Nor *was any* deceit in His
mouth.

10 Yet it pleased the LORD to
bruise Him;
He has put *Him* to grief.
When You make His soul an
offering for sin,
He shall see *His* seed, He shall
prolong *His* days,
And the pleasure of the LORD
shall prosper in His hand.

11 He shall see the labor of His
soul,[a] *and* be satisfied.
By His knowledge My
righteous Servant shall
justify many,
For He shall bear their
iniquities.

12 Therefore I will divide Him a
portion with the great,
And He shall divide the spoil
with the strong,
Because He poured out His soul
unto death,
And He was numbered with the
transgressors,
And He bore the sin of many,
And made intercession for the
transgressors.

54 "Sing, O barren,
You *who* have not borne!
Break forth into singing, and
cry aloud,
You *who* have not labored with
child!
For more *are* the children of the
desolate
Than the children of the
married woman," says the
LORD.

2 "Enlarge the place of your tent,
And let them stretch out the
curtains of your dwellings;
Do not spare;
Lengthen your cords,
And strengthen your stakes.

3 For you shall expand to the
right and to the left,
And your descendants will
inherit the nations,
And make the desolate cities
inhabited.

4 "Do not fear, for you will not be
ashamed;
Neither be disgraced, for you
will not be put to shame;

For you will forget the shame
of your youth,
And will not remember the
reproach of your widowhood
anymore.

5 For your Maker *is* your
husband,
The LORD of hosts *is* His name;
And your Redeemer *is* the Holy
One of Israel;
He is called the God of the
whole earth.

6 For the LORD has called you
Like a woman forsaken and
grieved in spirit,
Like a youthful wife when you
were refused,"
Says your God.

7 "For a mere moment I have
forsaken you,
But with great mercies I will
gather you.

8 With a little wrath I hid My face
from you for a moment;
But with everlasting kindness
I will have mercy on you,"
Says the LORD, your Redeemer.

9 "For this *is* like the waters of
Noah to Me;
For as I have sworn
That the waters of Noah would
no longer cover the earth,
So have I sworn
That I would not be angry with
you, nor rebuke you.

10 For the mountains shall depart
And the hills be removed,
But My kindness shall not
depart from you,
Nor shall My covenant of peace
be removed,"
Says the LORD, who has mercy
on you.

11 "O you afflicted one,
Tossed with tempest, *and* not
comforted,
Behold, I will lay your stones
with colorful gems,
And lay your foundations with
sapphires.

12 I will make your pinnacles of
rubies,
Your gates of crystal,
And all your walls of precious
stones.

13 All your children *shall be*
taught by the LORD,

53:11 [a]Following Masoretic Text, Targum, and Vulgate; Dead Sea Scrolls and Septuagint read *from the labor of His soul He shall see light.*

*J*esus has promised to set you free from every curse of the past. If you have suffered abuse, please know that He will bring you complete healing. He wants the whole person well—in body, emotions and spirit.

The Only Man
Who Can Help

Isaiah 54:5

Many times we fail to go to the Father who can help, and instead we run straight into the arms of someone who cannot help. Understand that you must not marry someone thinking he can save you. Men are not saviors. They have nothing with which to save you. We men are heirs, together with our wives, of the grace of life. We are both eligible for inheritance. We do not *give* the inheritance. We *need* it just like our wives do.

Don't be fooled into looking to the arms of flesh for healings that come only from the arms of God. If you choose to marry, don't marry out of what you need. Marry out of the abundance of what you have to offer. When two people enter into a relationship for what they can receive, they are both disappointed.

No man, no matter how wonderful, can wipe all tears from your eyes. Your life will bring many tears. They are unavoidable. They are a part of existence. Pleasure and pain, sunshine and rain are all intermingled with day-to-day bruises and brokenness that neither your husband nor your natural father can heal. I want you to know where to go when life is too much.

It is honorable to be married if that is your choice. Just understand that whoever God sends into your life will be limited and human. He will give a measure of comfort, but real wholeness comes from God alone. There are some areas in your life that God has reserved for Himself alone. He will heal them and fill them. No one else can.

I recommend Him because He has been my trusted friend and confidant. He has never betrayed me nor divulged my secrets. He is the strong, silent type. He knows when to keep still. When nights are cold and days are dreary, He is a comfort and a peace. He is to the soul what hot tea is to the body. He strengthens and warms the chill of life for those who will trust Him. He is the provision for the problem and the solution to the challenges that life will surely present.

You need not impress Him. He already knows who you are. He has searched you and known you (see Psalm 139:1). There is no need to try to project an image. He has seen you in the raw. He has examined your thoughts and known your imaginations. You feel somewhat vulnerable, realizing that whatever you are trying to discuss with Him, He already knows. But the healing balm flows into the bleeding places of life when you realize that this omniscient knowledge of you has not caused Him to forsake you. He is still there. What a love!

And great *shall be* the peace of
your children.

14 In righteousness you shall be
established;
You shall be far from
oppression, for you shall not
fear;
And from terror, for it shall not
come near you.

15 Indeed they shall surely
assemble, *but* not because of
Me.
Whoever assembles against
you shall fall for your sake.

16 "Behold, I have created the
blacksmith
Who blows the coals in the fire,
Who brings forth an
instrument for his work;
And I have created the spoiler
to destroy.

17 No weapon formed against you
shall prosper,
And every tongue *which* rises
against you in judgment
You shall condemn.
This *is* the heritage of the
servants of the LORD,
And their righteousness *is* from
Me,"
Says the LORD.

55 "Ho! Everyone who thirsts,
Come to the waters;
And you who have no money,
Come, buy and eat.
Yes, come, buy wine and milk
Without money and without
price.

2 Why do you spend money for
what is not bread,
And your wages for *what* does
not satisfy?
Listen carefully to Me, and eat
what is good,
And let your soul delight itself
in abundance.

3 Incline your ear, and come to
Me.
Hear, and your soul shall live;
And I will make an everlasting
covenant with you—
The sure mercies of David.

4 Indeed I have given him *as* a
witness to the people,
A leader and commander for
the people.

5 Surely you shall call a nation
you do not know,
And nations *who* do not know
you shall run to you,

Because of the LORD your God,
And the Holy One of Israel;
For He has glorified you."

6 Seek the LORD while He may
be found,
Call upon Him while He is
near.

7 Let the wicked forsake his
way,
And the unrighteous man his
thoughts;
Let him return to the LORD,
And He will have mercy on
him;
And to our God,
For He will abundantly pardon.

8 "For My thoughts *are* not your
thoughts,
Nor *are* your ways My ways,"
says the LORD.

9 "For *as* the heavens are higher
than the earth,
So are My ways higher than
your ways,
And My thoughts than your
thoughts.

10 "For as the rain comes down,
and the snow from heaven,
And do not return there,
But water the earth,
And make it bring forth and
bud,
That it may give seed to the
sower
And bread to the eater,

11 So shall My word be that goes
forth from My mouth;
It shall not return to Me void,
But it shall accomplish what I
please,
And it shall prosper *in the
thing* for which I sent it.

12 "For you shall go out with joy,
And be led out with peace;
The mountains and the hills
Shall break forth into singing
before you,
And all the trees of the field
shall clap *their* hands.

13 Instead of the thorn shall come
up the cypress tree,
And instead of the brier shall
come up the myrtle tree;
And it shall be to the LORD for
a name,
For an everlasting sign *that*
shall not be cut off."

Gospel
Pearls

56 Thus says the LORD:

"Keep justice, and do
righteousness,
For My salvation *is* about to
come,
And My righteousness to be
revealed.
2 Blessed *is* the man *who* does
this,
And the son of man *who* lays
hold on it;
Who keeps from defiling the
Sabbath,
And keeps his hand from doing
any evil."

3 Do not let the son of the
foreigner
Who has joined himself to the
LORD
Speak, saying,
"The LORD has utterly separated
me from His people";
Nor let the eunuch say,
"Here I am, a dry tree."
4 For thus says the LORD:
"To the eunuchs who keep My
Sabbaths,
And choose what pleases
Me,
And hold fast My covenant,
5 Even to them I will give in My
house
And within My walls a place
and a name
Better than that of sons and
daughters;
I will give them*a* an everlasting
name
That shall not be cut off.

6 "Also the sons of the foreigner
Who join themselves to the
LORD, to serve Him,
And to love the name of the
LORD, to be His servants—
Everyone who keeps from
defiling the Sabbath,
And holds fast My covenant—
7 Even them I will bring to My
holy mountain,
And make them joyful in My
house of prayer.
Their burnt offerings and their
sacrifices
Will be accepted on My altar;
For My house shall be called a
house of prayer for all
nations."

8 The Lord GOD, who gathers the
outcasts of Israel, says,
"Yet I will gather to him
Others besides those who are
gathered to him."

9 All you beasts of the field, come
to devour,
All you beasts in the forest.
10 His watchmen *are* blind,
They are all ignorant;
They *are* all dumb dogs,
They cannot bark;
Sleeping, lying down, loving to
slumber.
11 Yes, *they are* greedy dogs
Which never have enough.
And they *are* shepherds
Who cannot understand;
They all look to their own way,
Every one for his own gain,
From his *own* territory.
12 "Come," *one says,* "I will bring
wine,
And we will fill ourselves with
intoxicating drink;
Tomorrow will be as today,
And much more abundant."

57 The righteous perishes,
And no man takes *it* to heart;
Merciful men *are* taken away,
While no one considers
That the righteous is taken
away from evil.
2 He shall enter into peace;
They shall rest in their beds,
Each one walking *in* his
uprightness.

3 "But come here,
You sons of the sorceress,
You offspring of the adulterer
and the harlot!
4 Whom do you ridicule?
Against whom do you make a
wide mouth
And stick out the tongue?
Are you not children of
transgression,
Offspring of falsehood,
5 Inflaming yourselves with gods
under every green tree,
Slaying the children in the
valleys,
Under the clefts of the rocks?
6 Among the smooth *stones* of
the stream
Is your portion;
They, they, *are* your lot!

56:5 *a*Literally *him*

*T*he Lord is calling the hurting to Him. He will fill that void in your life. He wants
to be that heavenly Father who will mend your heart with a positive role model.

Even to them you have poured
a drink offering,
You have offered a grain
offering.
Should I receive comfort in
these?

7 "On a lofty and high mountain
You have set your bed;
Even there you went up
To offer sacrifice.
8 Also behind the doors and their
posts
You have set up your
remembrance;
For you have uncovered
yourself *to those other* than
Me,
And have gone up to them;
You have enlarged your bed
And made *a covenant* with
them;
You have loved their bed,
Where you saw *their* nudity.*ᵃ*
9 You went to the king with
ointment,
And increased your perfumes;
You sent your messengers far
off,
And *even* descended to
Sheol.
10 You are wearied in the length
of your way;
Yet you did not say, 'There is
no hope.'
You have found the life of your
hand;
Therefore you were not
grieved.

11 "And of whom have you been
afraid, or feared,
That you have lied
And not remembered Me,
Nor taken *it* to your heart?
Is it not because I have held My
peace from of old
That you do not fear Me?
12 I will declare your
righteousness
And your works,
For they will not profit you.
13 When you cry out,
Let your collection *of idols*
deliver you.
But the wind will carry them all
away,
A breath will take *them*.
But he who puts his trust in Me
shall possess the land,

And shall inherit My holy
mountain."

14 And one shall say,
"Heap it up! Heap it up!
Prepare the way,
Take the stumbling block out
of the way of My people."

15 For thus says the High and
Lofty One
Who inhabits eternity, whose
name *is* Holy:
"I dwell in the high and holy
place,
With him *who* has a contrite
and humble spirit,
To revive the spirit of the
humble,
And to revive the heart of the
contrite ones.
16 For I will not contend forever,
Nor will I always be angry;
For the spirit would fail before
Me,
And the souls *which* I have
made.
17 For the iniquity of his
covetousness
I was angry and struck him;
I hid and was angry,
And he went on backsliding in
the way of his heart.
18 I have seen his ways, and will
heal him;
I will also lead him,
And restore comforts to him
And to his mourners.

19 "I create the fruit of the lips:
Peace, peace to *him who is* far
off and to *him who is* near,"
Says the LORD,
"And I will heal him."
20 But the wicked *are* like the
troubled sea,
When it cannot rest,
Whose waters cast up mire and
dirt.

21 "*There is* no peace,"
Says my God, "for the wicked."

58 "Cry aloud, spare not;
Lift up your voice like a
trumpet;
Tell My people their
transgression,
And the house of Jacob their
sins.
2 Yet they seek Me daily,

57:8 *ᵃ*Literally *hand,* a euphemism

Gospel Pearls

And delight to know My ways,
As a nation that did
   righteousness,
And did not forsake the
   ordinance of their God.
They ask of Me the ordinances
   of justice;
They take delight in
   approaching God.
3 'Why have we fasted,' *they say,*
   'and You have not seen?
Why have we afflicted our
   souls, and You take no
   notice?'

"In fact, in the day of your fast
   you find pleasure,
And exploit all your laborers.
4 Indeed you fast for strife and
   debate,
And to strike with the fist of
   wickedness.
You will not fast as *you do* this
   day,
To make your voice heard on
   high.
5 Is it a fast that I have chosen,
A day for a man to afflict his
   soul?
Is it to bow down his head like
   a bulrush,
And to spread out sackcloth
   and ashes?
Would you call this a fast,
And an acceptable day to the
   LORD?

6 "*Is* this not the fast that I have
   chosen:
To loose the bonds of
   wickedness,
To undo the heavy burdens,
To let the oppressed go free,
And that you break every
   yoke?
7 *Is it* not to share your bread
   with the hungry,
And that you bring to your
   house the poor who are cast
   out;
When you see the naked, that
   you cover him,
And not hide yourself from
   your own flesh?
8 Then your light shall break
   forth like the morning,
Your healing shall spring forth
   speedily,
And your righteousness shall
   go before you;
The glory of the LORD shall be
   your rear guard.

9 Then you shall call, and the
   LORD will answer;
You shall cry, and He will say,
   'Here I *am.*'

"If you take away the yoke from
   your midst,
The pointing of the finger, and
   speaking wickedness,
10 *If* you extend your soul to the
   hungry
And satisfy the afflicted soul,
Then your light shall dawn in
   the darkness,
And your darkness shall *be* as
   the noonday.
11 The LORD will guide you
   continually,
And satisfy your soul in
   drought,
And strengthen your bones;
You shall be like a watered
   garden,
And like a spring of water,
   whose waters do not fail.
12 Those from among you
Shall build the old waste
   places;
You shall raise up the
   foundations of many
   generations;
And you shall be called the
   Repairer of the Breach,
The Restorer of Streets to
   Dwell In.

13 "If you turn away your foot from
   the Sabbath,
From doing your pleasure on
   My holy day,
And call the Sabbath a delight,
The holy *day* of the LORD
   honorable,
And shall honor Him, not doing
   your own ways,
Nor finding your own pleasure,
Nor speaking *your own* words,
14 Then you shall delight yourself
   in the LORD;
And I will cause you to ride on
   the high hills of the earth,
And feed you with the heritage
   of Jacob your father.
The mouth of the LORD has
   spoken."

59 Behold, the LORD's hand is not
   shortened,
That it cannot save;
Nor His ear heavy,
That it cannot hear.

*M*illions have longed for a positive hug and nurturing embrace from fathers without ever receiving what they longed for. There is a way to fill that emptiness inside. It is through a relationship with God.

2 But your iniquities have
separated you from your
God;
And your sins have hidden *His*
face from you,
So that He will not hear.
3 For your hands are defiled with
blood,
And your fingers with iniquity;
Your lips have spoken lies,
Your tongue has muttered
perversity.

4 No one calls for justice,
Nor does *any* plead for truth.
They trust in empty words and
speak lies;
They conceive evil and bring
forth iniquity.
5 They hatch vipers' eggs and
weave the spider's web;
He who eats of their eggs dies,
And *from* that which is crushed
a viper breaks out.

6 Their webs will not become
garments,
Nor will they cover themselves
with their works;
Their works *are* works of
iniquity,
And the act of violence *is* in
their hands.
7 Their feet run to evil,
And they make haste to shed
innocent blood;
Their thoughts *are* thoughts of
iniquity;
Wasting and destruction *are* in
their paths.
8 The way of peace they have not
known,
And *there is* no justice in their
ways;
They have made themselves
crooked paths;
Whoever takes that way shall
not know peace.

9 Therefore justice is far from us,
Nor does righteousness
overtake us;
We look for light, but there is
darkness!
For brightness, *but* we walk in
blackness!
10 We grope for the wall like the
blind,
And we grope as if *we had* no
eyes;
We stumble at noonday as at
twilight;

We are as dead *men* in desolate
places.
11 We all growl like bears,
And moan sadly like doves;
We look for justice, but *there
is* none;
For salvation, *but* it is far from
us.
12 For our transgressions are
multiplied before You,
And our sins testify against us;
For our transgressions *are* with
us,
And *as for* our iniquities, we
know them:
13 In transgressing and lying
against the LORD,
And departing from our God,
Speaking oppression and
revolt,
Conceiving and uttering from
the heart words of falsehood.
14 Justice is turned back,
And righteousness stands afar
off;
For truth is fallen in the street,
And equity cannot enter.
15 So truth fails,
And he *who* departs from evil
makes himself a prey.

Then the LORD saw *it,* and it
displeased Him
That *there was* no justice.
16 He saw that *there was* no man,
And wondered that *there was*
no intercessor;
Therefore His own arm
brought salvation for Him;
And His own righteousness, it
sustained Him.
17 For He put on righteousness as
a breastplate,
And a helmet of salvation on
His head;
He put on the garments of
vengeance for clothing,
And was clad with zeal as a
cloak.
18 According to *their* deeds,
accordingly He will repay,
Fury to His adversaries,
Recompense to His enemies;
The coastlands He will fully
repay.
19 So shall they fear
The name of the LORD from the
west,
And His glory from the rising
of the sun;
When the enemy comes in like
a flood,

Gospel Pearls

The Spirit of the Lord will lift
up a standard against him.

20 "The Redeemer will come to
Zion,
And to those who turn from
transgression in Jacob,"
Says the Lord.

21 "As for Me," says the Lord, "this
is My covenant with them: My Spirit
who *is* upon you, and My words
which I have put in your mouth, shall
not depart from your mouth, nor
from the mouth of your descendants,
nor from the mouth of your descendants' descendants," says the Lord,
"from this time and forevermore."

60 Arise, shine;
For your light has come!
And the glory of the Lord is
risen upon you.
2 For behold, the darkness shall
cover the earth,
And deep darkness the
people;
But the Lord will arise over
you,
And His glory will be seen
upon you.
3 The Gentiles shall come to your
light,
And kings to the brightness of
your rising.

4 "Lift up your eyes all around,
and see:
They all gather together, they
come to you;
Your sons shall come from
afar,
And your daughters shall be
nursed at *your* side.
5 Then you shall see and become
radiant,
And your heart shall swell with
joy;
Because the abundance of the
sea shall be turned to you,
The wealth of the Gentiles shall
come to you.
6 The multitude of camels shall
cover your *land,*
The dromedaries of Midian and
Ephah;
All those from Sheba shall
come;
They shall bring gold and
incense,
And they shall proclaim the
praises of the Lord.

7 All the flocks of Kedar shall be
gathered together to you,
The rams of Nebaioth shall
minister to you;
They shall ascend with
acceptance on My altar,
And I will glorify the house of
My glory.

8 "Who *are* these *who* fly like a
cloud,
And like doves to their roosts?
9 Surely the coastlands shall wait
for Me;
And the ships of Tarshish *will
come* first,
To bring your sons from afar,
Their silver and their gold with
them,
To the name of the Lord your
God,
And to the Holy One of Israel,
Because He has glorified you.

10 "The sons of foreigners shall
build up your walls,
And their kings shall minister
to you;
For in My wrath I struck
you,
But in My favor I have had
mercy on you.
11 Therefore your gates shall be
open continually;
They shall not be shut day or
night,
That *men* may bring to you the
wealth of the Gentiles,
And their kings in procession.
12 For the nation and kingdom
which will not serve you shall
perish,
And *those* nations shall be
utterly ruined.

13 "The glory of Lebanon shall
come to you,
The cypress, the pine, and the
box tree together,
To beautify the place of My
sanctuary;
And I will make the place of My
feet glorious.
14 Also the sons of those who
afflicted you
Shall come bowing to you,
And all those who despised you
shall fall prostrate at the
soles of your feet;
And they shall call you The
City of the Lord,
Zion of the Holy One of Israel.

God's people are to nurture and protect one another. It makes no difference how
tempestuous our lives have been. Even in the face of abuse, God still cares.

15 "Whereas you have been
      forsaken and hated,
   So that no one went through
      you,
   I will make you an eternal
      excellence,
   A joy of many generations.
16 You shall drink the milk of the
      Gentiles,
   And milk the breast of kings;
   You shall know that I, the
      LORD, *am* your Savior
   And your Redeemer, the
      Mighty One of Jacob.

17 "Instead of bronze I will bring
      gold,
   Instead of iron I will bring
      silver,
   Instead of wood, bronze,
   And instead of stones, iron.
   I will also make your officers
      peace,
   And your magistrates
      righteousness.
18 Violence shall no longer be
      heard in your land,
   Neither wasting nor
      destruction within your
      borders;
   But you shall call your walls
      Salvation,
   And your gates Praise.

19 "The sun shall no longer be your
      light by day,
   Nor for brightness shall the
      moon give light to you;
   But the LORD will be to you an
      everlasting light,
   And your God your glory.
20 Your sun shall no longer go
      down,
   Nor shall your moon withdraw
      itself;
   For the LORD will be your
      everlasting light,
   And the days of your mourning
      shall be ended.
21 Also your people *shall* all *be*
      righteous;
   They shall inherit the land
      forever,
   The branch of My planting,
   The work of My hands,
   That I may be glorified.
22 A little one shall become a
      thousand,
   And a small one a strong
      nation.
   I, the LORD, will hasten it in its
      time."

61 "The Spirit of the Lord GOD *is*
      upon Me,
   Because the LORD has anointed
      Me
   To preach good tidings to the
      poor;
   He has sent Me to heal the
      brokenhearted,
   To proclaim liberty to the
      captives,
   And the opening of the prison
      to *those who are* bound;
2 To proclaim the acceptable
      year of the LORD,
   And the day of vengeance of
      our God;
   To comfort all who mourn,
3 To console those who mourn in
      Zion,
   To give them beauty for ashes,
   The oil of joy for mourning,
   The garment of praise for the
      spirit of heaviness;
   That they may be called trees
      of righteousness,
   The planting of the LORD, that
      He may be glorified."

4 And they shall rebuild the old
      ruins,
   They shall raise up the former
      desolations,
   And they shall repair the
      ruined cities,
   The desolations of many
      generations.
5 Strangers shall stand and feed
      your flocks,
   And the sons of the foreigner
   Shall be your plowmen and
      your vinedressers.
6 But you shall be named the
      priests of the LORD,
   They shall call you the servants
      of our God.
   You shall eat the riches of the
      Gentiles,
   And in their glory you shall
      boast.
7 Instead of your shame *you shall
      have* double *honor,*
   And *instead of* confusion they
      shall rejoice in their portion.
   Therefore in their land they
      shall possess double;
   Everlasting joy shall be theirs.

8 "For I, the LORD, love justice;
   I hate robbery for burnt
      offering;
   I will direct their work in
      truth,

*L*ove embraces the totality of the other person. It is impossible to completely and
   effectively love someone without being included in that other person's history.

Open the Door

Isaiah 61:3

*E*lizabeth, the wife of the priest Zacharias, was a winter woman with a summer experience (see Luke 1:36). She was pregnant with a promise. In spite of her declining years, she was fulfilling more destiny at that time than she had in her youth. She proved that God blesses us in His own time and on His own terms. She was a living example of Isaiah 61:3. She did indeed receive "beauty for ashes, the oil of joy for mourning, the garment of praise for the spirit of heaviness."

We can only imagine that Elizabeth had spent many years longing for a child. She knew the shame of barrenness in biblical times and, perhaps, had even given up. But God had other plans. At what some might consider an age too old for childbearing, Elizabeth was pregnant. She was also in seclusion. Perhaps it was the attitude of the community. When an older woman is still vibrant and productive, others may be jealous or intimidated. Perhaps it was the silent stillness of her womb that some believe she experienced. Whatever the reason, she hid in her house for six months before she heard a knock at the door.

When Elizabeth lifted her creaking body and dragged her enlarged torso to the door, she saw a young girl, a picture of herself in days gone by. Opening that door changed her life forever. Mary, the future mother of our Savior and Lord, Elizabeth's young cousin, was at the door. The salutation of this young woman, the exposure to her experience, made the baby in Elizabeth's womb leap, and she was filled with the Holy Ghost.

If you have isolated yourself from others, regardless of the reason, I pray that you will hear the knocking of the Lord. He will give you the garment of praise for the spirit of heaviness (see Isaiah 61:3). As you open the door to new relationships and remove the chain from your own fears, God will overwhelm you with new splendor. He will jump-start your heart. He doesn't mean for you to go sit in a chair and die. In Jesus' name, get up and answer the door!

And will make with them an
everlasting covenant.
9 Their descendants shall be
known among the Gentiles,
And their offspring among the
people.
All who see them shall
acknowledge them,
That they *are* the posterity
whom the LORD has blessed."

10 I will greatly rejoice in the
LORD,
My soul shall be joyful in my
God;
For He has clothed me with the
garments of salvation,
He has covered me with the
robe of righteousness,
As a bridegroom decks *himself*
with ornaments,
And as a bride adorns *herself*
with her jewels.
11 For as the earth brings forth its
bud,
As the garden causes the things
that are sown in it to spring
forth,
So the Lord GOD will cause
righteousness and praise to
spring forth before all the
nations.

62 For Zion's sake I will not hold
My peace,
And for Jerusalem's sake I will
not rest,
Until her righteousness goes
forth as brightness,
And her salvation as a lamp
that burns.
2 The Gentiles shall see your
righteousness,
And all kings your glory.
You shall be called by a new
name,
Which the mouth of the LORD
will name.
3 You shall also be a crown of
glory
In the hand of the LORD,
And a royal diadem
In the hand of your God.
4 You shall no longer be termed
Forsaken,
Nor shall your land any more
be termed Desolate;
But you shall be called
Hephzibah,*a* and your land
Beulah;*b*

For the LORD delights in you,
And your land shall be
married.
5 For *as* a young man marries a
virgin,
So shall your sons marry you;
And *as* the bridegroom rejoices
over the bride,
So shall your God rejoice over
you.

6 I have set watchmen on your
walls, O Jerusalem;
They shall never hold their
peace day or night.
You who make mention of the
LORD, do not keep silent,
7 And give Him no rest till He
establishes
And till He makes Jerusalem a
praise in the earth.

8 The LORD has sworn by His
right hand
And by the arm of His strength:
"Surely I will no longer give
your grain
As food for your enemies;
And the sons of the foreigner
shall not drink your new
wine,
For which you have labored.
9 But those who have gathered it
shall eat it,
And praise the LORD;
Those who have brought it
together shall drink it in My
holy courts."

10 Go through,
Go through the gates!
Prepare the way for the people;
Build up,
Build up the highway!
Take out the stones,
Lift up a banner for the
peoples!

11 Indeed the LORD has
proclaimed
To the end of the world:
"Say to the daughter of Zion,
'Surely your salvation is
coming;
Behold, His reward *is* with
Him,
And His work before Him.'"
12 And they shall call them The
Holy People,
The Redeemed of the LORD;

62:4 *a*Literally *My Delight Is in Her*   *b*Literally *Married*

And you shall be called Sought
Out,
A City Not Forsaken.

63 Who *is* this who comes from
Edom,
With dyed garments from
Bozrah,
This *One who is* glorious in His
apparel,
Traveling in the greatness of
His strength?—

"I who speak in righteousness,
mighty to save."

2 Why *is* Your apparel red,
And Your garments like one
who treads in the winepress?

3 "I have trodden the winepress
alone,
And from the peoples no one
was with Me.
For I have trodden them in My
anger,
And trampled them in My fury;
Their blood is sprinkled upon
My garments,
And I have stained all My
robes.
4 For the day of vengeance *is* in
My heart,
And the year of My redeemed
has come.
5 I looked, but *there was* no one
to help,
And I wondered
That *there was* no one to
uphold;
Therefore My own arm brought
salvation for Me;
And My own fury, it sustained
Me.
6 I have trodden down the
peoples in My anger,
Made them drunk in My fury,
And brought down their
strength to the earth."

7 I will mention the
lovingkindnesses of the LORD
And the praises of the LORD,
According to all that the LORD
has bestowed on us,
And the great goodness toward
the house of Israel,
Which He has bestowed on
them according to His
mercies,
According to the multitude of
His lovingkindnesses.

8 For He said, "Surely they *are*
My people,
Children *who* will not lie."
So He became their Savior.
9 In all their affliction He was
afflicted,
And the Angel of His Presence
saved them;
In His love and in His pity He
redeemed them;
And He bore them and carried
them
All the days of old.
10 But they rebelled and grieved
His Holy Spirit;
So He turned Himself against
them as an enemy,
And He fought against them.

11 Then he remembered the days
of old,
Moses *and* his people, *saying:*
"Where *is* He who brought them
up out of the sea
With the shepherd of His flock?
Where *is* He who put His Holy
Spirit within them,
12 Who led *them* by the right
hand of Moses,
With His glorious arm,
Dividing the water before them
To make for Himself an
everlasting name,
13 Who led them through the
deep,
As a horse in the wilderness,
That they might not stumble?"

14 As a beast goes down into the
valley,
And the Spirit of the LORD
causes him to rest,
So You lead Your people,
To make Yourself a glorious
name.

15 Look down from heaven,
And see from Your habitation,
holy and glorious.
Where *are* Your zeal and Your
strength,
The yearning of Your heart and
Your mercies toward me?
Are they restrained?
16 Doubtless You *are* our Father,
Though Abraham was ignorant
of us,
And Israel does not
acknowledge us.
You, O LORD, *are* our Father;
Our Redeemer from
Everlasting *is* Your name.

*T*he images, scars and victories that we live with have shaped us into the people
we have become. We will never know who a person is until we understand where
they have been.

17 O LORD, why have You made
us stray from Your ways,
And hardened our heart from
Your fear?
Return for Your servants' sake,
The tribes of Your inheritance.

18 Your holy people have
possessed *it* but a little
while;
Our adversaries have trodden
down Your sanctuary.

19 We have become *like* those of
old, over whom You never
ruled,
Those who were never called
by Your name.

64 Oh, that You would rend the
heavens!
That You would come down!
That the mountains might
shake at Your presence—

2 As fire burns brushwood,
As fire causes water to boil—
To make Your name known to
Your adversaries,
That the nations may tremble
at Your presence!

3 When You did awesome things
for which we did not look,
You came down,
The mountains shook at Your
presence.

4 For since the beginning of the
world
Men have not heard nor
perceived by the ear,
Nor has the eye seen any God
besides You,
Who acts for the one who waits
for Him.

5 You meet him who rejoices and
does righteousness,
Who remembers You in Your
ways.
You are indeed angry, for we
have sinned—
In these ways we continue;
And we need to be saved.

6 But we are all like an unclean
thing,
And all our righteousnesses *are*
like filthy rags;
We all fade as a leaf,
And our iniquities, like the
wind,
Have taken us away.

7 And *there is* no one who calls
on Your name,
Who stirs himself up to take
hold of You;

For You have hidden Your face
from us,
And have consumed us
because of our iniquities.

8 But now, O LORD,
You *are* our Father;
We *are* the clay, and You our
potter;
And all we *are* the work of
Your hand.

9 Do not be furious, O LORD,
Nor remember iniquity forever;
Indeed, please look—we all *are*
Your people!

10 Your holy cities are a
wilderness,
Zion is a wilderness,
Jerusalem a desolation.

11 Our holy and beautiful temple,
Where our fathers praised
You,
Is burned up with fire;
And all our pleasant things are
laid waste.

12 Will You restrain Yourself
because of these *things,* O
LORD?
Will You hold Your peace, and
afflict us very severely?

65 "I was sought by *those who* did
not ask *for Me;*
I was found by *those who* did
not seek Me.
I said, 'Here I am, here I am,'
To a nation *that* was not called
by My name.

2 I have stretched out My hands
all day long to a rebellious
people,
Who walk in a way *that is* not
good,
According to their own
thoughts;

3 A people who provoke Me to
anger continually to My
face;
Who sacrifice in gardens,
And burn incense on altars of
brick;

4 Who sit among the graves,
And spend the night in the
tombs;
Who eat swine's flesh,
And the broth of abominable
things is *in* their vessels;

5 Who say, 'Keep to yourself,
Do not come near me,
For I am holier than you!'
These *are* smoke in My nostrils,
A fire that burns all the day.

*T*he secret of being transformed from a vulnerable victim to a victorious, loving
person is found in the ability to open your past to someone responsible enough to
share your weaknesses and pains.

Soul Secrets
of a woman who needs a Father

Lord, I am feeling lonely and vulnerable and scared and confused. There is nothing I need more right now than a Daddy. I need strength and wisdom and direction. I need a Protector and a Provider. I have tried to control my own life and I have ended up in a mess. I need help. I have wandered long. And I am ready to come home to You.

It is so good to know that I have a Father, even if I've never had one before. It is so good to know that You are a Father who will love me, nurture me, bring me peace. It is so good to know that the Creator of the universe is the Father of my heart.

Make me like clay in Your hands. Make me a woman You can easily mold into exactly the person You want me to be—pure, strong, gracious, whole, faithful, steadfast. Thank You that I can never be too old to become Your daughter.

6 "Behold, *it is* written before Me:
   I will not keep silence, but will
     repay—
   Even repay into their bosom—
7 Your iniquities and the
    iniquities of your fathers
    together,"
   Says the LORD,
  "Who have burned incense on
    the mountains
   And blasphemed Me on the
    hills;
   Therefore I will measure their
    former work into their
    bosom."

8 Thus says the LORD:

  "As the new wine is found in the
    cluster,
   And *one* says, 'Do not destroy
    it,
   For a blessing *is* in it,'
   So will I do for My servants'
    sake,
   That I may not destroy them
    all.
9 I will bring forth descendants
   from Jacob,
   And from Judah an heir of My
    mountains;
   My elect shall inherit it,
   And My servants shall dwell
    there.
10 Sharon shall be a fold of flocks,
   And the Valley of Achor a place
    for herds to lie down,
   For My people who have
    sought Me.

11 "But you *are* those who forsake
    the LORD,
   Who forget My holy mountain,
   Who prepare a table for Gad,*a*
   And who furnish a drink
    offering for Meni.*b*
12 Therefore I will number you for
    the sword,
   And you shall all bow down to
    the slaughter;
   Because, when I called, you did
    not answer;
   When I spoke, you did not hear,
   But did evil before My eyes,
   And chose *that* in which I do
    not delight."

13 Therefore thus says the Lord
GOD:

  "Behold, My servants shall eat,
   But you shall be hungry;
   Behold, My servants shall
    drink,
   But you shall be thirsty;
   Behold, My servants shall
    rejoice,
   But you shall be ashamed;
14 Behold, My servants shall sing
   for joy of heart,
   But you shall cry for sorrow of
    heart,
   And wail for grief of spirit.
15 You shall leave your name as
   a curse to My chosen;
   For the Lord GOD will slay
    you,
   And call His servants by
    another name;
16 So that he who blesses himself
    in the earth
   Shall bless himself in the God
    of truth;
   And he who swears in the earth
   Shall swear by the God of
    truth;
   Because the former troubles
    are forgotten,
   And because they are hidden
    from My eyes.

17 "For behold, I create new
    heavens and a new earth;
   And the former shall not be
    remembered or come to
    mind.
18 But be glad and rejoice forever
    in what I create;
   For behold, I create Jerusalem
    as a rejoicing,
   And her people a joy.
19 I will rejoice in Jerusalem,
   And joy in My people;
   The voice of weeping shall no
    longer be heard in her,
   Nor the voice of crying.

20 "No more shall an infant from
    there *live but a few* days,
   Nor an old man who has not
    fulfilled his days;
   For the child shall die one
    hundred years old,
   But the sinner *being* one
    hundred years old shall be
    accursed.
21 They shall build houses and
    inhabit *them;*
   They shall plant vineyards and
    eat their fruit.

65:11 *a*Literally *Troop* or *Fortune*, a pagan deity　*b*Literally *Number* or *Destiny*, a pagan deity

Gospel
Pearls

22 They shall not build and
     another inhabit;
   They shall not plant and
     another eat;
   For as the days of a tree, *so
     shall be* the days of My
     people,
   And My elect shall long enjoy
     the work of their hands.
23 They shall not labor in vain,
   Nor bring forth children for
     trouble;
   For they *shall be* the
     descendants of the blessed of
     the LORD,
   And their offspring with them.

24 "It shall come to pass
   That before they call, I will
     answer;
   And while they are still
     speaking, I will hear.
25 The wolf and the lamb shall
     feed together,
   The lion shall eat straw like the
     ox,
   And dust *shall be* the serpent's
     food.
   They shall not hurt nor destroy
     in all My holy mountain,"
   Says the LORD.

66 Thus says the LORD:

   "Heaven *is* My throne,
   And earth *is* My footstool.
   Where *is* the house that you
     will build Me?
   And where *is* the place of My
     rest?
2 For all those *things* My hand
     has made,
   And all those *things* exist,"
   Says the LORD.
   "But on this *one* will I look:
   On *him who is* poor and of a
     contrite spirit,
   And who trembles at My word.

3 "He who kills a bull *is as if* he
     slays a man;
   He who sacrifices a lamb, *as if*
     he breaks a dog's neck;
   He who offers a grain offering,
     as if he offers swine's blood;
   He who burns incense, *as if* he
     blesses an idol.
   Just as they have chosen their
     own ways,
   And their soul delights in their
     abominations,

4 So will I choose their delusions,
   And bring their fears on them;
   Because, when I called, no one
     answered,
   When I spoke they did not
     hear;
   But they did evil before My
     eyes,
   And chose *that* in which I do
     not delight."

5 Hear the word of the LORD,
   You who tremble at His word:
   "Your brethren who hated you,
   Who cast you out for My
     name's sake, said,
   'Let the LORD be glorified,
   That we may see your joy.'
   But they shall be ashamed."

6 The sound of noise from the
     city!
   A voice from the temple!
   The voice of the LORD,
   Who fully repays His enemies!

7 "Before she was in labor, she
     gave birth;
   Before her pain came,
   She delivered a male child.
8 Who has heard such a thing?
   Who has seen such things?
   Shall the earth be made to give
     birth in one day?
   Or shall a nation be born at
     once?
   For as soon as Zion was in
     labor,
   She gave birth to her children.
9 Shall I bring to the time of
     birth, and not cause
     delivery?" says the LORD.
   "Shall I who cause delivery shut
     up *the womb*?" says your
     God.
10 "Rejoice with Jerusalem,
   And be glad with her, all you
     who love her;
   Rejoice for joy with her, all you
     who mourn for her;
11 That you may feed and be
     satisfied
   With the consolation of her
     bosom,
   That you may drink deeply and
     be delighted
   With the abundance of her
     glory."

12 For thus says the LORD:

   "Behold, I will extend peace to
     her like a river,

*T*he Church is a body. No one operates independent of another. We are all in this
walk together, and therefore can build one another up and carry some of the load
with which our sisters are burdened.

And the glory of the Gentiles
  like a flowing stream.
Then you shall feed;
On *her* sides shall you be
  carried,
And be dandled on *her*
  knees.
13 As one whom his mother
  comforts,
So I will comfort you;
And you shall be comforted in
  Jerusalem."

14 When you see *this,* your heart
  shall rejoice,
And your bones shall flourish
  like grass;
The hand of the LORD shall be
  known to His servants,
And *His* indignation to His
  enemies.
15 For behold, the LORD will come
  with fire
And with His chariots, like a
  whirlwind,
To render His anger with
  fury,
And His rebuke with flames of
  fire.
16 For by fire and by His sword
The LORD will judge all flesh;
And the slain of the LORD shall
  be many.

17 "Those who sanctify themselves
  and purify themselves,
To go to the gardens
After an *idol* in the midst,
Eating swine's flesh and
  the abomination and the
  mouse,
Shall be consumed together,"
  says the LORD.

18 "For I *know* their works and
their thoughts. It shall be that I will
gather all nations and tongues; and
they shall come and see My glory.
19 I will set a sign among them; and
those among them who escape I will
send to the nations: *to* Tarshish and
Pul[a] and Lud, who draw the bow, and
Tubal and Javan, *to* the coastlands
afar off who have not heard My fame
nor seen My glory. And they shall
declare My glory among the Gentiles.
20 Then they shall bring all your
brethren for an offering to the LORD
out of all nations, on horses and in
chariots and in litters, on mules and
on camels, to My holy mountain Jerusalem," says the LORD, "as the children of Israel bring an offering in a
clean vessel into the house of the
LORD. 21 And I will also take some of
them for priests *and* Levites," says
the LORD.

22 "For as the new heavens and the
  new earth
Which I will make shall remain
  before Me," says the LORD,
"So shall your descendants and
  your name remain.
23 And it shall come to pass
That from one New Moon to
  another,
And from one Sabbath to
  another,
All flesh shall come to worship
  before Me," says the LORD.

24 "And they shall go forth and
  look
Upon the corpses of the men
Who have transgressed against
  Me.
For their worm does not die,
And their fire is not quenched.
They shall be an abhorrence to
  all flesh."

66:19 *a*Following Masoretic Text and Targum; Septuagint reads *Put* (compare Jeremiah 46:9).

The Book of

JEREMIAH

1 The words of Jeremiah the son of
Hilkiah, of the priests who *were*
in Anathoth in the land of Benjamin,
2 to whom the word of the LORD came
in the days of Josiah the son of
Amon, king of Judah, in the thirteenth year of his reign. 3 It came also
in the days of Jehoiakim the son of

Gospel Pearls

Josiah, king of Judah, until the end of the eleventh year of Zedekiah the son of Josiah, king of Judah, until the carrying away of Jerusalem captive in the fifth month.

4 Then the word of the LORD came to me, saying:

5 "Before I formed you in the
    womb I knew you;
Before you were born I
    sanctified you;
I ordained you a prophet to the
    nations."

6 Then said I:

"Ah, Lord GOD!
Behold, I cannot speak, for I *am*
    a youth."

7 But the LORD said to me:

"Do not say, 'I *am* a youth,'
For you shall go to all to whom
    I send you,
And whatever I command you,
    you shall speak.
8   Do not be afraid of their faces,
For I *am* with you to deliver
    you," says the LORD.

9 Then the LORD put forth His hand and touched my mouth, and the LORD said to me:

"Behold, I have put My words
    in your mouth.
10   See, I have this day set you
    over the nations and over the
    kingdoms,
To root out and to pull down,
To destroy and to throw down,
To build and to plant."

11 Moreover the word of the LORD came to me, saying, "Jeremiah, what do you see?"

And I said, "I see a branch of an almond tree."

12 Then the LORD said to me, "You have seen well, for I am ready to perform My word."

13 And the word of the LORD came to me the second time, saying, "What do you see?"

And I said, "I see a boiling pot, and it is facing away from the north."

14 Then the LORD said to me:

"Out of the north calamity shall
    break forth

On all the inhabitants of the
    land.
15   For behold, I am calling
All the families of the
    kingdoms of the north," says
    the LORD;
"They shall come and each one
    set his throne
At the entrance of the gates of
    Jerusalem,
Against all its walls all around,
And against all the cities of
    Judah.
16   I will utter My judgments
Against them concerning all
    their wickedness,
Because they have forsaken
    Me,
Burned incense to other gods,
And worshiped the works of
    their own hands.

17 "Therefore prepare yourself and
    arise,
And speak to them all that I
    command you.
Do not be dismayed before
    their faces,
Lest I dismay you before them.
18   For behold, I have made you
    this day
A fortified city and an iron
    pillar,
And bronze walls against the
    whole land—
Against the kings of Judah,
Against its princes,
Against its priests,
And against the people of the
    land.
19   They will fight against you,
But they shall not prevail
    against you.
For I *am* with you," says the
    LORD, "to deliver you."

2 Moreover the word of the LORD came to me, saying, 2 "Go and cry in the hearing of Jerusalem, saying, 'Thus says the LORD:

"I remember you,
The kindness of your youth,
The love of your betrothal,
When you went after Me in the
    wilderness,
In a land not sown.
3   Israel *was* holiness to the LORD,
The firstfruits of His increase.
All that devour him will offend;
Disaster will come upon them,"
    says the LORD.' "

There is hope for victims. There is no need to feel weak when one has Jesus Christ. His power is enough to bring about the kinds of changes that will set you free. He is calling, through the work of the Holy Spirit, for you to be set free.

4 Hear the word of the LORD, O house of Jacob and all the families of the house of Israel. 5 Thus says the LORD:

"What injustice have your fathers found in Me,
That they have gone far from Me,
Have followed idols,
And have become idolaters?
6 Neither did they say, 'Where *is* the LORD,
Who brought us up out of the land of Egypt,
Who led us through the wilderness,
Through a land of deserts and pits,
Through a land of drought and the shadow of death,
Through a land that no one crossed
And where no one dwelt?'
7 I brought you into a bountiful country,
To eat its fruit and its goodness.
But when you entered, you defiled My land
And made My heritage an abomination.
8 The priests did not say, 'Where *is* the LORD?'
And those who handle the law did not know Me;
The rulers also transgressed against Me;
The prophets prophesied by Baal,
And walked after *things that* do not profit.

9 "Therefore I will yet bring charges against you," says the LORD,
"And against your children's children I will bring charges.
10 For pass beyond the coasts of Cyprus^a and see,
Send to Kedar^b and consider diligently,
And see if there has been such *a thing*.
11 Has a nation changed *its* gods,
Which *are* not gods?
But My people have changed their Glory
For *what* does not profit.

12 Be astonished, O heavens, at this,
And be horribly afraid;
Be very desolate," says the LORD.
13 "For My people have committed two evils:
They have forsaken Me, the fountain of living waters,
And hewn themselves cisterns—broken cisterns that can hold no water.

14 "*Is* Israel a servant?
Is he a homeborn *slave?*
Why is he plundered?
15 The young lions roared at him, *and* growled;
They made his land waste;
His cities are burned, without inhabitant.
16 Also the people of Noph^a and Tahpanhes
Have broken the crown of your head.
17 Have you not brought this on yourself,
In that you have forsaken the LORD your God
When He led you in the way?
18 And now why take the road to Egypt,
To drink the waters of Sihor?
Or why take the road to Assyria,
To drink the waters of the River?^{a}
19 Your own wickedness will correct you,
And your backslidings will rebuke you.
Know therefore and see that *it is* an evil and bitter *thing*
That you have forsaken the LORD your God,
And the fear of Me *is* not in you,"
Says the Lord GOD of hosts.

20 "For of old I have broken your yoke *and* burst your bonds;
And you said, 'I will not transgress,'
When on every high hill and under every green tree
You lay down, playing the harlot.
21 Yet I had planted you a noble

2:10 ^{a}Hebrew *Kittim,* western lands, especially Cyprus ^{b}In the northern Arabian desert, representative of the eastern cultures   2:16 ^{a}That is, Memphis in ancient Egypt   2:18 ^{a}That is, the Euphrates

vine, a seed of highest
quality.
How then have you turned
before Me
Into the degenerate plant of an
alien vine?
22 For though you wash yourself
with lye, and use much
soap,
Yet your iniquity is marked
before Me," says the Lord
G**od**.

23 "How can you say, 'I am not
polluted,
I have not gone after the
Baals'?
See your way in the valley;
Know what you have done:
You are a swift dromedary
breaking loose in her ways,
24 A wild donkey used to the
wilderness,
That sniffs at the wind in her
desire;
In her time of mating, who can
turn her away?
All those who seek her will not
weary themselves;
In her month they will find her.
25 Withhold your foot from being
unshod, and your throat from
thirst.
But you said, 'There is no hope.
No! For I have loved aliens, and
after them I will go.'

26 "As the thief is ashamed when
he is found out,
So is the house of Israel
ashamed;
They and their kings and their
princes, and their priests and
their prophets.
27 Saying to a tree, 'You *are* my
father,'
And to a stone, 'You gave birth
to me.'
For they have turned *their* back
to Me, and not *their* face.
But in the time of their trouble
They will say, 'Arise and save
us.'
28 But where *are* your gods that
you have made for
yourselves?
Let them arise,
If they can save you in the time
of your trouble;
For *according to* the number of
your cities
Are your gods, O Judah.

29 "Why will you plead with Me?
You all have transgressed
against Me," says the L**ord**.
30 "In vain I have chastened your
children;
They received no correction.
Your sword has devoured your
prophets
Like a destroying lion.

31 "O generation, see the word of
the L**ord**!
Have I been a wilderness to
Israel,
Or a land of darkness?
Why do My people say, 'We are
lords;
We will come no more to You'?
32 Can a virgin forget her
ornaments,
Or a bride her attire?
Yet My people have forgotten
Me days without number.

33 "Why do you beautify your way
to seek love?
Therefore you have also taught
The wicked women your ways.
34 Also on your skirts is found
The blood of the lives of the
poor innocents.
I have not found it by secret
search,
But plainly on all these things.
35 Yet you say, 'Because I am
innocent,
Surely His anger shall turn
from me.'
Behold, I will plead My case
against you,
Because you say, 'I have not
sinned.'
36 Why do you gad about so much
to change your way?
Also you shall be ashamed of
Egypt as you were ashamed
of Assyria.
37 Indeed you will go forth from
him
With your hands on your head;
For the L**ord** has rejected your
trusted allies,
And you will not prosper by
them.

3 "They say, 'If a man divorces his
wife,
And she goes from him
And becomes another man's,
May he return to her again?'
Would not that land be greatly
polluted?

---

*T*here's a call out in the Spirit for hurting women. The Lord says, "I want you." No
matter how many men have told you, "I don't want you," God says, "I want you."

But you have played the harlot
with many lovers;
Yet return to Me," says the
LORD.

2 "Lift up your eyes to the
desolate heights and see:
Where have you not lain *with
men?*
By the road you have sat for
them
Like an Arabian in the
wilderness;
And you have polluted the land
With your harlotries and your
wickedness.
3 Therefore the showers have
been withheld,
And there has been no latter
rain.
You have had a harlot's
forehead;
You refuse to be ashamed.
4 Will you not from this time cry
to Me,
'My Father, You *are* the guide
of my youth?
5 Will He remain angry forever?
Will He keep it to the end?'
Behold, you have spoken and
done evil things,
As you were able."

6 The LORD said also to me in the days of Josiah the king: "Have you seen what backsliding Israel has done? She has gone up on every high mountain and under every green tree, and there played the harlot. 7 And I said, after she had done all these *things,* 'Return to Me.' But she did not return. And her treacherous sister Judah saw it. 8 Then I saw that for all the causes for which backsliding Israel had committed adultery, I had put her away and given her a certificate of divorce; yet her treacherous sister Judah did not fear, but went and played the harlot also. 9 So it came to pass, through her casual harlotry, that she defiled the land and committed adultery with stones and trees. 10 And yet for all this her treacherous sister Judah has not turned to Me with her whole heart, but in pretense," says the LORD.

11 Then the LORD said to me, "Backsliding Israel has shown herself more righteous than treacherous Judah. 12 Go and proclaim these words toward the north, and say:

'Return, backsliding Israel,'
says the LORD;
'I will not cause My anger to fall
on you.
For I *am* merciful,' says the
LORD;
'I will not remain angry forever.
13 Only acknowledge your
iniquity,
That you have transgressed
against the LORD your God,
And have scattered your
charms
To alien deities under every
green tree,
And you have not obeyed My
voice,' says the LORD.

14 "Return, O backsliding children," says the LORD; "for I am married to you. I will take you, one from a city and two from a family, and I will bring you to Zion. 15 And I will give you shepherds according to My heart, who will feed you with knowledge and understanding.

16 Then it shall come to pass, when you are multiplied and increased in the land in those days," says the LORD, "that they will say no more, 'The ark of the covenant of the LORD.' It shall not come to mind, nor shall they remember it, nor shall they visit *it,* nor shall it be made anymore.

17 "At that time Jerusalem shall be called The Throne of the LORD, and all the nations shall be gathered to it, to the name of the LORD, to Jerusalem. No more shall they follow the dictates of their evil hearts.

18 "In those days the house of Judah shall walk with the house of Israel, and they shall come together out of the land of the north to the land that I have given as an inheritance to your fathers.

19 "But I said:

'How can I put you among the
children
And give you a pleasant land,
A beautiful heritage of the
hosts of nations?'

"And I said:

'You shall call Me, "My Father,"
And not turn away from Me.'
20 Surely, *as* a wife treacherously
departs from her husband,
So have you dealt
treacherously with Me,

Gospel
Pearls

O house of Israel," says the
LORD.

21 A voice was heard on the
 desolate heights,
Weeping *and* supplications of
 the children of Israel.
For they have perverted their
 way;
They have forgotten the LORD
 their God.
22 "Return, you backsliding
 children,
And I will heal your
 backslidings."

"Indeed we do come to You,
For You are the LORD our God.
23 Truly, in vain *is salvation
 hoped for* from the hills,
And from the multitude of
 mountains;
Truly, in the LORD our God
Is the salvation of Israel.
24 For shame has devoured
The labor of our fathers from
 our youth—
Their flocks and their herds,
Their sons and their daughters.
25 We lie down in our shame,
And our reproach covers us.
For we have sinned against the
 LORD our God,
We and our fathers,
From our youth even to this
 day,
And have not obeyed the voice
 of the LORD our God."

4 "If you will return, O Israel,"
 says the LORD,
"Return to Me;
And if you will put away your
 abominations out of My
 sight,
Then you shall not be moved.
2 And you shall swear, 'The LORD
 lives,'
In truth, in judgment, and in
 righteousness;
The nations shall bless
 themselves in Him,
And in Him they shall glory."

3 For thus says the LORD to the men
of Judah and Jerusalem:

"Break up your fallow ground,
And do not sow among thorns.
4 Circumcise yourselves to the
 LORD,

And take away the foreskins of
 your hearts,
You men of Judah and
 inhabitants of Jerusalem,
Lest My fury come forth like
 fire,
And burn so that no one can
 quench *it*,
Because of the evil of your
 doings."

5 Declare in Judah and proclaim in
Jerusalem, and say:

"Blow the trumpet in the land;
Cry, 'Gather together,'
And say, 'Assemble yourselves,
And let us go into the fortified
 cities.'
6 Set up the standard toward
 Zion.
Take refuge! Do not delay!
For I will bring disaster from
 the north,
And great destruction."

7 The lion has come up from his
 thicket,
And the destroyer of nations is
 on his way.
He has gone forth from his
 place
To make your land desolate.
Your cities will be laid waste,
Without inhabitant.
8 For this, clothe yourself with
 sackcloth,
Lament and wail.
For the fierce anger of the
 LORD
Has not turned back from us.

9 "And it shall come to pass in that
 day," says the LORD,
"*That* the heart of the king shall
 perish,
And the heart of the princes;
The priests shall be astonished,
And the prophets shall
 wonder."

10 Then I said, "Ah, Lord GOD!
Surely You have greatly
 deceived this people and
 Jerusalem,
Saying, 'You shall have peace,'
Whereas the sword reaches to
 the heart."

11 At that time it will be said
To this people and to
 Jerusalem,

*W*ith patience God waits for you, as the father waited for the prodigal son. Jesus says to the hurting and crippled, "I want you enough to wait for you to hobble your way back home."

"A dry wind of the desolate
heights *blows* in the
wilderness
Toward the daughter of My
people—
Not to fan or to cleanse—
12 A wind too strong for these will
come for Me;
Now I will also speak judgment
against them."

13 "Behold, he shall come up like
clouds,
And his chariots like a
whirlwind.
His horses are swifter than
eagles.
Woe to us, for we are
plundered!"

14 O Jerusalem, wash your heart
from wickedness,
That you may be saved.
How long shall your evil
thoughts lodge within you?
15 For a voice declares from Dan
And proclaims affliction from
Mount Ephraim:
16 "Make mention to the nations,
Yes, proclaim against
Jerusalem,
That watchers come from a far
country
And raise their voice against
the cities of Judah.
17 Like keepers of a field they are
against her all around,
Because she has been
rebellious against Me," says
the LORD.
18 "Your ways and your doings
Have procured these *things* for
you.
This *is* your wickedness,
Because it is bitter,
Because it reaches to your
heart."

19 O my soul, my soul!
I am pained in my very heart!
My heart makes a noise in
me;
I cannot hold my peace,
Because you have heard, O my
soul,
The sound of the trumpet,
The alarm of war.
20 Destruction upon destruction is
cried,
For the whole land is
plundered.

Suddenly my tents are
plundered,
And my curtains in a moment.
21 How long will I see the
standard,
And hear the sound of the
trumpet?

22 "For My people *are* foolish,
They have not known Me.
They *are* silly children,
And they have no
understanding.
They *are* wise to do evil,
But to do good they have no
knowledge."

23 I beheld the earth, and indeed
it was without form, and
void;
And the heavens, they *had* no
light.
24 I beheld the mountains, and
indeed they trembled,
And all the hills moved back
and forth.
25 I beheld, and indeed *there was*
no man,
And all the birds of the heavens
had fled.
26 I beheld, and indeed the fruitful
land *was* a wilderness,
And all its cities were broken
down
At the presence of the LORD,
By His fierce anger.

27 For thus says the LORD:

"The whole land shall be
desolate;
Yet I will not make a full end.
28 For this shall the earth mourn,
And the heavens above be
black,
Because I have spoken.
I have purposed and will not
relent,
Nor will I turn back from it.
29 The whole city shall flee from
the noise of the horsemen
and bowmen.
They shall go into thickets and
climb up on the rocks.
Every city *shall be* forsaken,
And not a man shall dwell in
it.

30 "And *when* you *are* plundered,
What will you do?
Though you clothe yourself
with crimson,

Gospel Pearls

Though you adorn *yourself*
with ornaments of gold,
Though you enlarge your eyes
with paint,
In vain you will make yourself
fair;
Your lovers will despise you;
They will seek your life.

31 "For I have heard a voice as of
a woman in labor,
The anguish as of her who
brings forth her first child,
The voice of the daughter of
Zion bewailing herself;
She spreads her hands, *saying,*
'Woe *is* me now, for my soul is
weary
Because of murderers!'

5 "Run to and fro through the
streets of Jerusalem;
See now and know;
And seek in her open places
If you can find a man,
If there is *anyone* who executes
judgment,
Who seeks the truth,
And I will pardon her.
2 Though they say, 'As the LORD
lives,'
Surely they swear falsely."

3 O LORD, *are* not Your eyes on
the truth?
You have stricken them,
But they have not grieved;
You have consumed them,
But they have refused to
receive correction.
They have made their faces
harder than rock;
They have refused to return.

4 Therefore I said, "Surely these
are poor.
They are foolish;
For they do not know the way
of the LORD,
The judgment of their God.
5 I will go to the great men and
speak to them,
For they have known the way
of the LORD,
The judgment of their God."

But these have altogether
broken the yoke
And burst the bonds.
6 Therefore a lion from the forest
shall slay them,

A wolf of the deserts shall
destroy them;
A leopard will watch over their
cities.
Everyone who goes out from
there shall be torn in pieces,
Because their transgressions
are many;
Their backslidings have
increased.

7 "How shall I pardon you for
this?
Your children have forsaken
Me
And sworn by *those that are*
not gods.
When I had fed them to the full,
Then they committed adultery
And assembled themselves by
troops in the harlots' houses.
8 They were *like* well-fed lusty
stallions;
Every one neighed after his
neighbor's wife.
9 Shall I not punish *them* for
these *things*?" says the LORD.
"And shall I not avenge Myself
on such a nation as this?

10 "Go up on her walls and destroy,
But do not make a complete
end.
Take away her branches,
For they *are* not the LORD's.
11 For the house of Israel and the
house of Judah
Have dealt very treacherously
with Me," says the LORD.

12 They have lied about the LORD,
And said, "*It is* not He.
Neither will evil come upon us,
Nor shall we see sword or
famine.
13 And the prophets become
wind,
For the word *is* not in them.
Thus shall it be done to them."

14 Therefore thus says the LORD
God of hosts:

"Because you speak this word,
Behold, I will make My words
in your mouth fire,
And this people wood,
And it shall devour them.
15 Behold, I will bring a nation
against you from afar,
O house of Israel," says the
LORD.

*N*ow God says, "I'm going to deliver you and heal you. I'm going to tell you who
you really are. Now I'm ready to reveal to you why you had to go through what
you did to become what you shall become."

"It *is* a mighty nation,
It *is* an ancient nation,
A nation whose language you
　do not know,
Nor can you understand what
　they say.
16 Their quiver *is* like an open
　tomb;
They *are* all mighty men.
17 And they shall eat up your
　harvest and your bread,
Which your sons and
　daughters should eat.
They shall eat up your flocks
　and your herds;
They shall eat up your vines
　and your fig trees;
They shall destroy your
　fortified cities,
In which you trust, with the
　sword.

18 "Nevertheless in those days,"
says the LORD, "I will not make a
complete end of you. 19 And it will
be when you say, 'Why does the LORD
our God do all these *things* to us?'
then you shall answer them, 'Just as
you have forsaken Me and served
foreign gods in your land, so you
shall serve aliens in a land *that is*
not yours.'

20 "Declare this in the house of
　Jacob
And proclaim it in Judah,
　saying,
21 'Hear this now, O foolish
　people,
Without understanding,
Who have eyes and see not,
And who have ears and hear
　not:
22 Do you not fear Me?' says the
　LORD.
　'Will you not tremble at My
　presence,
Who have placed the sand as
　the bound of the sea,
By a perpetual decree, that it
　cannot pass beyond it?
And though its waves toss to
　and fro,
Yet they cannot prevail;
Though they roar, yet they
　cannot pass over it.
23 But this people has a defiant
　and rebellious heart;
They have revolted and
　departed.
24 They do not say in their
　heart,

"Let us now fear the LORD our
　God,
Who gives rain, both the
　former and the latter, in its
　season.
He reserves for us the
　appointed weeks of the
　harvest."
25 Your iniquities have turned
　these *things* away,
And your sins have withheld
　good from you.

26 'For among My people are
　found wicked *men;*
They lie in wait as one who sets
　snares;
They set a trap;
They catch men.
27 As a cage is full of birds,
So their houses *are* full of
　deceit.
Therefore they have become
　great and grown rich.
28 They have grown fat, they are
　sleek;
Yes, they surpass the deeds of
　the wicked;
They do not plead the cause,
The cause of the fatherless;
Yet they prosper,
And the right of the needy they
　do not defend.
29 Shall I not punish *them* for
　these *things?*' says the LORD.
　'Shall I not avenge Myself on
　such a nation as this?'

30 "An astonishing and horrible
　thing
Has been committed in the
　land:
31 The prophets prophesy falsely,
And the priests rule by their
　own power;
And My people love *to have it*
　so.
But what will you do in the
　end?

6 "O you children of Benjamin,
Gather yourselves to flee from
　the midst of Jerusalem!
Blow the trumpet in Tekoa,
And set up a signal-fire in Beth
　Haccerem;
For disaster appears out of the
　north,
And great destruction.
2 I have likened the daughter of
　Zion

Gospel Pearls

To a lovely and delicate
woman.
3 The shepherds with their flocks
shall come to her.
They shall pitch *their* tents
against her all around.
Each one shall pasture in his
own place."

4 "Prepare war against her;
Arise, and let us go up at noon.
Woe to us, for the day goes
away,
For the shadows of the evening
are lengthening.
5 Arise, and let us go by night,
And let us destroy her
palaces."

6 For thus has the LORD of hosts
said:

"Cut down trees,
And build a mound against
Jerusalem.
This *is* the city to be punished.
She *is* full of oppression in her
midst.
7 As a fountain wells up with
water,
So she wells up with her
wickedness.
Violence and plundering are
heard in her.
Before Me continually *are* grief
and wounds.
8 Be instructed, O Jerusalem,
Lest My soul depart from you;
Lest I make you desolate,
A land not inhabited."

9 Thus says the LORD of hosts:

"They shall thoroughly glean as
a vine the remnant of Israel;
As a grape-gatherer, put your
hand back into the
branches."

10 To whom shall I speak and give
warning,
That they may hear?
Indeed their ear *is*
uncircumcised,
And they cannot give heed.
Behold, the word of the LORD
is a reproach to them;
They have no delight in it.
11 Therefore I am full of the fury
of the LORD.
I am weary of holding *it* in.

"I will pour it out on the children
outside,
And on the assembly of young
men together;
For even the husband shall be
taken with the wife,
The aged with *him who is* full
of days.
12 And their houses shall be
turned over to others,
Fields and wives together;
For I will stretch out My
hand
Against the inhabitants of the
land," says the LORD.
13 "Because from the least of them
even to the greatest of
them,
Everyone *is* given to
covetousness;
And from the prophet even to
the priest,
Everyone deals falsely.
14 They have also healed the hurt
of My people slightly,
Saying, 'Peace, peace!'
When *there is* no peace.
15 Were they ashamed when they
had committed abomination?
No! They were not at all
ashamed;
Nor did they know how to
blush.
Therefore they shall fall among
those who fall;
At the time I punish them,
They shall be cast down," says
the LORD.

16 Thus says the LORD:

"Stand in the ways and see,
And ask for the old paths,
where the good way *is,*
And walk in it;
Then you will find rest for your
souls.
But they said, 'We will not walk
in it.'
17 Also, I set watchmen over you,
saying,
'Listen to the sound of the
trumpet!'
But they said, 'We will not
listen.'
18 Therefore hear, you nations,
And know, O congregation,
what *is* among them.
19 Hear, O earth!
Behold, I will certainly bring
calamity on this people—
The fruit of their thoughts,

Because they have not heeded
My words
Nor My law, but rejected it.

20 For what purpose to Me
Comes frankincense from
Sheba,
And sweet cane from a far
country?
Your burnt offerings *are* not
acceptable,
Nor your sacrifices sweet to
Me."

21 Therefore thus says the LORD:

"Behold, I will lay stumbling
blocks before this people,
And the fathers and the sons
together shall fall on them.
The neighbor and his friend
shall perish."

22 Thus says the LORD:

"Behold, a people comes from
the north country,
And a great nation will be
raised from the farthest parts
of the earth.
23 They will lay hold on bow and
spear;
They *are* cruel and have no
mercy;
Their voice roars like the sea;
And they ride on horses,
As men of war set in array
against you, O daughter of
Zion."

24 We have heard the report of it;
Our hands grow feeble.
Anguish has taken hold of us,
Pain as of a woman in labor.
25 Do not go out into the field,
Nor walk by the way.
Because of the sword of the
enemy,
Fear *is* on every side.
26 O daughter of my people,
Dress in sackcloth
And roll about in ashes!
Make mourning *as for* an only
son, most bitter lamentation;
For the plunderer will suddenly
come upon us.

27 "I have set you *as* an assayer
and a fortress among My
people,
That you may know and test
their way.

28 They *are* all stubborn rebels,
walking as slanderers.
They are bronze and iron,
They *are* all corrupters;
29 The bellows blow fiercely,
The lead is consumed by the
fire;
The smelter refines in vain,
For the wicked are not drawn
off.
30 *People* will call them rejected
silver,
Because the LORD has rejected
them."

7 The word that came to Jeremiah
from the LORD, saying, 2 "Stand
in the gate of the LORD's house, and
proclaim there this word, and say,
'Hear the word of the LORD, all *you*
of Judah who enter in at these gates
to worship the LORD!' " 3 Thus says
the LORD of hosts, the God of Israel:
"Amend your ways and your doings,
and I will cause you to dwell in this
place. 4 Do not trust in these lying
words, saying, 'The temple of the
LORD, the temple of the LORD, the
temple of the LORD *are* these.'
5 "For if you thoroughly amend
your ways and your doings, if you
thoroughly execute judgment between a man and his neighbor,
6 if you do not oppress the stranger,
the fatherless, and the widow, and do
not shed innocent blood in this place,
or walk after other gods to your hurt,
7 then I will cause you to dwell in this
place, in the land that I gave to your
fathers forever and ever.
8 "Behold, you trust in lying words
that cannot profit. 9 Will you steal,
murder, commit adultery, swear
falsely, burn incense to Baal, and
walk after other gods whom you do
not know, 10 and *then* come and
stand before Me in this house which
is called by My name, and say, 'We
are delivered to do all these abominations'? 11 Has this house, which is
called by My name, become a den of
thieves in your eyes? Behold, I, even
I, have seen *it*," says the LORD.
12 "But go now to My place which
was in Shiloh, where I set My name
at the first, and see what I did to it
because of the wickedness of My
people Israel. 13 And now, because
you have done all these works," says
the LORD, "and I spoke to you, rising
up early and speaking, but you did
not hear, and I called you, but you

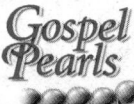

did not answer, 14 therefore I will do to the house which is called by My name, in which you trust, and to this place which I gave to you and your fathers, as I have done to Shiloh. 15 And I will cast you out of My sight, as I have cast out all your brethren— the whole posterity of Ephraim.

16 "Therefore do not pray for this people, nor lift up a cry or prayer for them, nor make intercession to Me; for I will not hear you. 17 Do you not see what they do in the cities of Judah and in the streets of Jerusalem? 18 The children gather wood, the fathers kindle the fire, and the women knead dough, to make cakes for the queen of heaven; and *they* pour out drink offerings to other gods, that they may provoke Me to anger. 19 Do they provoke Me to anger?" says the LORD. "*Do they* not *provoke* themselves, to the shame of their own faces?"

20 Therefore thus says the Lord GOD: "Behold, My anger and My fury will be poured out on this place—on man and on beast, on the trees of the field and on the fruit of the ground. And it will burn and not be quenched."

21 Thus says the LORD of hosts, the God of Israel: "Add your burnt offerings to your sacrifices and eat meat. 22 For I did not speak to your fathers, or command them in the day that I brought them out of the land of Egypt, concerning burnt offerings or sacrifices. 23 But this is what I commanded them, saying, 'Obey My voice, and I will be your God, and you shall be My people. And walk in all the ways that I have commanded you, that it may be well with you.' 24 Yet they did not obey or incline their ear, but followed the counsels *and* the dictates of their evil hearts, and went backward and not forward. 25 Since the day that your fathers came out of the land of Egypt until this day, I have even sent to you all My servants the prophets, daily rising up early and sending *them*. 26 Yet they did not obey Me or incline their ear, but stiffened their neck. They did worse than their fathers.

27 "Therefore you shall speak all these words to them, but they will not obey you. You shall also call to them, but they will not answer you.

28 "So you shall say to them, 'This *is* a nation that does not obey the voice of the LORD their God nor receive correction. Truth has perished and has been cut off from their mouth. 29 Cut off your hair and cast *it* away, and take up a lamentation on the desolate heights; for the LORD has rejected and forsaken the generation of His wrath.' 30 For the children of Judah have done evil in My sight," says the LORD. "They have set their abominations in the house which is called by My name, to pollute it. 31 And they have built the high places of Tophet, which *is* in the Valley of the Son of Hinnom, to burn their sons and their daughters in the fire, which I did not command, nor did it come into My heart.

32 "Therefore behold, the days are coming," says the LORD, "when it will no more be called Tophet, or the Valley of the Son of Hinnom, but the Valley of Slaughter; for they will bury in Tophet until there is no room. 33 The corpses of this people will be food for the birds of the heaven and for the beasts of the earth. And no one will frighten *them away*. 34 Then I will cause to cease from the cities of Judah and from the streets of Jerusalem the voice of mirth and the voice of gladness, the voice of the bridegroom and the voice of the bride. For the land shall be desolate.

8 "At that time," says the LORD, "they shall bring out the bones of the kings of Judah, and the bones of its princes, and the bones of the priests, and the bones of the prophets, and the bones of the inhabitants of Jerusalem, out of their graves. 2 They shall spread them before the sun and the moon and all the host of heaven, which they have loved and which they have served and after which they have walked, which they have sought and which they have worshiped. They shall not be gathered nor buried; they shall be like refuse on the face of the earth. 3 Then death shall be chosen rather than life by all the residue of those who remain of this evil family, who remain in all the places where I have driven them," says the LORD of hosts.

4 "Moreover you shall say to them, 'Thus says the LORD:

"Will they fall and not rise?
Will one turn away and not
        return?

I proclaim to the abused: There is a healing going into your spirit right now. I speak deliverance to you. I speak restoration to you. All in the mighty name of Jesus, in the invincible, all-powerful, everlasting name of Jesus.

5 Why has this people slidden
    back,
  Jerusalem, in a perpetual
    backsliding?
  They hold fast to deceit,
  They refuse to return.
6 I listened and heard,
  But they do not speak aright.
  No man repented of his
    wickedness,
  Saying, 'What have I done?'
  Everyone turned to his own
    course,
  As the horse rushes into the
    battle.

7 "Even the stork in the heavens
  Knows her appointed times;
  And the turtledove, the swift,
    and the swallow
  Observe the time of their
    coming.
  But My people do not know the
    judgment of the LORD.

8 "How can you say, 'We *are* wise,
  And the law of the LORD *is* with
    us'?
  Look, the false pen of the scribe
    certainly works falsehood.
9 The wise men are ashamed,
  They are dismayed and taken.
  Behold, they have rejected the
    word of the LORD;
  So what wisdom do they have?
10 Therefore I will give their wives
    to others,
  And their fields to those who
    will inherit *them;*
  Because from the least even to
    the greatest
  Everyone is given to
    covetousness;
  From the prophet even to the
    priest
  Everyone deals falsely.
11 For they have healed the hurt
    of the daughter of My people
    slightly,
  Saying, 'Peace, peace!'
  When *there is* no peace.
12 Were they ashamed when they
    had committed abomination?
  No! They were not at all
    ashamed,
  Nor did they know how to
    blush.
  Therefore they shall fall among
    those who fall;
  In the time of their punishment
  They shall be cast down," says
    the LORD.

13 "I will surely consume them,"
    says the LORD.
  "No grapes *shall be* on the vine,
  Nor figs on the fig tree,
  And the leaf shall fade;
  And *the things* I have given
    them shall pass away from
    them." ' "

14 "Why do we sit still?
  Assemble yourselves,
  And let us enter the fortified
    cities,
  And let us be silent there.
  For the LORD our God has put
    us to silence
  And given us water of gall to
    drink,
  Because we have sinned
    against the LORD.

15 "*We* looked for peace, but no
    good *came;*
  And for a time of health, and
    there was trouble!
16 The snorting of His horses was
    heard from Dan.
  The whole land trembled at the
    sound of the neighing of His
    strong ones;
  For they have come and
    devoured the land and all
    that is in it,
  The city and those who dwell
    in it."

17 "For behold, I will send serpents
    among you,
  Vipers which cannot be
    charmed,
  And they shall bite you," says
    the LORD.

18 I would comfort myself in
    sorrow;
  My heart *is* faint in me.
19 Listen! The voice,
  The cry of the daughter of my
    people
  From a far country:
  "*Is* not the LORD in Zion?
  Is not her King in her?"

  "Why have they provoked Me to
    anger
  With their carved images—
  With foreign idols?"

20 "The harvest is past,
  The summer is ended,
  And we are not saved!"

21 For the hurt of the daughter of
    my people I am hurt.

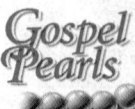

I am mourning;
Astonishment has taken hold
   of me.
22 *Is there* no balm in Gilead,
   Is there no physician there?
Why then is there no recovery
For the health of the daughter
   of my people?

9 Oh, that my head were waters,
   And my eyes a fountain of
      tears,
That I might weep day and
      night
For the slain of the daughter of
      my people!
2 Oh, that I had in the wilderness
   A lodging place for travelers;
That I might leave my people,
   And go from them!
For they *are* all adulterers,
   An assembly of treacherous
      men.

3 "And *like* their bow they have
      bent their tongues *for* lies.
They are not valiant for the
      truth on the earth.
For they proceed from evil to
      evil,
And they do not know Me,"
   says the LORD.
4 "Everyone take heed to his
      neighbor,
And do not trust any brother;
   For every brother will utterly
      supplant,
And every neighbor will walk
      with slanderers.
5 Everyone will deceive his
      neighbor,
And will not speak the truth;
They have taught their tongue
      to speak lies;
They weary themselves to
      commit iniquity.
6 Your dwelling place *is* in the
      midst of deceit;
Through deceit they refuse to
      know Me," says the LORD.

7 Therefore thus says the LORD of
hosts:

   "Behold, I will refine them and
      try them;
   For how shall I deal with the
      daughter of My people?
8 Their tongue *is* an arrow shot
      out;
   It speaks deceit;

One speaks peaceably to his
      neighbor with his mouth,
But in his heart he lies in wait.
9 Shall I not punish them for
   these *things?*" says the LORD.
"Shall I not avenge Myself on
   such a nation as this?"

10 I will take up a weeping and
      wailing for the mountains,
And for the dwelling places of
      the wilderness a lamentation,
Because they are burned up,
   So that no one can pass
      through;
Nor can *men* hear the voice of
      the cattle.
Both the birds of the heavens
      and the beasts have fled;
They are gone.

11 "I will make Jerusalem a heap
      of ruins, a den of jackals.
I will make the cities of Judah
      desolate, without an
      inhabitant."

12 Who *is* the wise man who may understand this? And *who is he* to whom the mouth of the LORD has spoken, that he may declare it? Why does the land perish *and* burn up like a wilderness, so that no one can pass through?
13 And the LORD said, "Because they have forsaken My law which I set before them, and have not obeyed My voice, nor walked according to it, 14 but they have walked according to the dictates of their own hearts and after the Baals, which their fathers taught them," 15 therefore thus says the LORD of hosts, the God of Israel: "Behold, I will feed them, this people, with wormwood, and give them water of gall to drink. 16 I will scatter them also among the Gentiles, whom neither they nor their fathers have known. And I will send a sword after them until I have consumed them."
17 Thus says the LORD of hosts:

   "Consider and call for the
      mourning women,
That they may come;
   And send for skillful wailing
      women,
That they may come.
18 Let them make haste
   And take up a wailing for us,

God will take care of the secrets. He touches the places where you've been assassinated. He knows the woman you would have been, the woman you should have been, the woman you could have been. God is healing and restoring her in you as you call out to Him.

Send for the Women

Jeremiah 9:17–21

Y ou have talents and gifts and resources within you that can do serious damage to what Satan is attempting to do in this world.

When the children of Israel were about to be taken in bondage to Babylon, the prophet Jeremiah said something like this, "Send for the mourning women. Find some women who are not so hateful and bitter that they have become like mannequins, women who are not so downtrodden that they can no longer feel. Send for some women who still have the ability to feel and cry so they might wail against what the devil is doing."

Get a picture of what these women were to do. They were to weep and wail, to mourn in sackcloth and ashes, to wake up everybody around them. They were to call out, "The devil is destroying us! Death is on its way!" They were God's warning shout to His people. They were His alarm system, His tornado signal, His air-raid siren. They were the ones God would use to warn His people of the impending consequences of sin. They were the ones who created a platform from which Jeremiah's words could ring out with stinging conviction.

These women had a God-given destiny to destroy the power of Satan over God's people by waking them up and calling them to a mourning of repentance. These women were instructed to teach their daughters to weep against sin and the assault of the devil.

God has a destiny for women today—a destiny for you. He wants you women loosed to open your mouth and cry out against the evil that the devil has put upon God's people. You have ideas that haven't been voiced. You have energy that hasn't been released. You have abilities that haven't been exercised. You have power that hasn't been loosed. You have spiritual gifts that haven't been given expression.

The day has come for you to forget those things that are past and look toward the future. It's time to look at what you can be and what you can do and what you can say and what you can possess that will bring glory to God and defeat the devil and fulfill your destiny.

That our eyes may run with
    tears,
And our eyelids gush with
    water.
19 For a voice of wailing is heard
    from Zion:
'How we are plundered!
We are greatly ashamed,
Because we have forsaken the
    land,
Because we have been cast out
    of our dwellings.' "

20 Yet hear the word of the LORD,
    O women,
And let your ear receive the
    word of His mouth;
Teach your daughters wailing,
And everyone her neighbor a
    lamentation.
21 For death has come through
    our windows,
Has entered our palaces,
To kill off the children—*no
longer to be* outside!
And the young men—*no longer*
    on the streets!

22 Speak, "Thus says the LORD:

'Even the carcasses of men shall
    fall as refuse on the open
    field,
Like cuttings after the
    harvester,
And no one shall gather
    them.' "

23 Thus says the LORD:

"Let not the wise *man* glory in
    his wisdom,
Let not the mighty *man* glory
    in his might,
Nor let the rich *man* glory in
    his riches;
24 But let him who glories glory
    in this,
That he understands and
    knows Me,
That I *am* the LORD, exercising
    lovingkindness, judgment,
    and righteousness in the
    earth.
For in these I delight," says the
    LORD.

25 "Behold, the days are coming,"
says the LORD, "that I will punish all
who are circumcised with the uncircumcised— 26 Egypt, Judah, Edom,
the people of Ammon, Moab, and all

who are in the farthest corners, who
dwell in the wilderness. For all *these*
nations *are* uncircumcised, and all
the house of Israel *are* uncircumcised
in the heart."

10 Hear the word which the LORD
speaks to you, O house of Israel.
2 Thus says the LORD:

"Do not learn the way of the
    Gentiles;
Do not be dismayed at the signs
    of heaven,
For the Gentiles are dismayed
    at them.
3 For the customs of the peoples
    are futile;
For *one* cuts a tree from the
    forest,
The work of the hands of the
    workman, with the ax.
4 They decorate it with silver and
    gold;
They fasten it with nails and
    hammers
So that it will not topple.
5 They *are* upright, like a palm
    tree,
And they cannot speak;
They must be carried,
Because they cannot go *by
    themselves.*
Do not be afraid of them,
For they cannot do evil,
Nor can they do any good."

6 Inasmuch as *there is* none like
    You, O LORD
(You *are* great, and Your name
    is great in might),
7 Who would not fear You, O
    King of the nations?
For this is Your rightful due.
For among all the wise *men* of
    the nations,
And in all their kingdoms,
There is none like You.
8 But they are altogether dull-
    hearted and foolish;
A wooden idol *is* a worthless
    doctrine.
9 Silver is beaten into plates;
It is brought from Tarshish,
And gold from Uphaz,
The work of the craftsman
And of the hands of the
    metalsmith;
Blue and purple *are* their
    clothing;

The anointing of the living God is reaching out to you. He calls you forth to set you free. When you reach out to Him and allow the Holy Spirit to have His way, His anointing is present to deliver you.

They *are* all the work of skillful
men.
10 But the LORD *is* the true God;
He *is* the living God and the
everlasting King.
At His wrath the earth will
tremble,
And the nations will not be able
to endure His indignation.

11 Thus you shall say to them: "The
gods that have not made the heavens
and the earth shall perish from the
earth and from under these heavens."

12 He has made the earth by His
power,
He has established the world
by His wisdom,
And has stretched out the
heavens at His discretion.
13 When He utters His voice,
There is a multitude of waters
in the heavens:
"And He causes the vapors to
ascend from the ends of the
earth.
He makes lightning for the
rain,
He brings the wind out of His
treasuries."*a*

14 Everyone is dull-hearted,
without knowledge;
Every metalsmith is put to
shame by an image;
For his molded image *is*
falsehood,
And *there is* no breath in them.
15 They *are* futile, a work of
errors;
In the time of their punishment
they shall perish.
16 The Portion of Jacob *is* not like
them,
For He *is* the Maker of all
things,
And Israel *is* the tribe of His
inheritance;
The LORD of hosts *is* His name.
17 Gather up your wares from the
land,
O inhabitant of the fortress!

18 For thus says the LORD:

"Behold, I will throw out at this
time
The inhabitants of the land,

And will distress them,
That they may find *it* so."

19 Woe is me for my hurt!
My wound is severe.
But I say, "Truly this *is* an
infirmity,
And I must bear it."
20 My tent is plundered,
And all my cords are broken;
My children have gone from
me,
And they *are* no more.
There is no one to pitch my tent
anymore,
Or set up my curtains.
21 For the shepherds have become
dull-hearted,
And have not sought the LORD;
Therefore they shall not
prosper,
And all their flocks shall be
scattered.
22 Behold, the noise of the report
has come,
And a great commotion out of
the north country,
To make the cities of Judah
desolate, a den of jackals.
23 O LORD, I know the way of man
is not in himself;
It is not in man who walks to
direct his own steps.
24 O LORD, correct me, but with
justice;
Not in Your anger, lest You
bring me to nothing.
25 Pour out Your fury on the
Gentiles, who do not know
You,
And on the families who do not
call on Your name;
For they have eaten up Jacob,
Devoured him and consumed
him,
And made his dwelling place
desolate.

11 The word that came to Jeremiah from the LORD, saying,
2 "Hear the words of this covenant,
and speak to the men of Judah and
to the inhabitants of Jerusalem;
3 and say to them, 'Thus says the
LORD God of Israel: "Cursed *is* the
man who does not obey the words
of this covenant 4 which I commanded your fathers in the day I
brought them out of the land of
Egypt, from the iron furnace, saying,

10:13 *a*Psalm 135:7

'Obey My voice, and do according to all that I command you; so shall you be My people, and I will be your God,' 5 that I may establish the oath which I have sworn to your fathers, to give them 'a land flowing with milk and honey,'ᵃ as *it is* this day." ' "

And I answered and said, "So be it, LORD."

6 Then the LORD said to me, "Proclaim all these words in the cities of Judah and in the streets of Jerusalem, saying: 'Hear the words of this covenant and do them. 7 For I earnestly exhorted your fathers in the day I brought them up out of the land of Egypt, until this day, rising early and exhorting, saying, "Obey My voice." 8 Yet they did not obey or incline their ear, but everyone followed the dictates of his evil heart; therefore I will bring upon them all the words of this covenant, which I commanded *them* to do, but *which* they have not done.' "

9 And the LORD said to me, "A conspiracy has been found among the men of Judah and among the inhabitants of Jerusalem. 10 They have turned back to the iniquities of their forefathers who refused to hear My words, and they have gone after other gods to serve them; the house of Israel and the house of Judah have broken My covenant which I made with their fathers."

11 Therefore thus says the LORD: "Behold, I will surely bring calamity on them which they will not be able to escape; and though they cry out to Me, I will not listen to them. 12 Then the cities of Judah and the inhabitants of Jerusalem will go and cry out to the gods to whom they offer incense, but they will not save them at all in the time of their trouble. 13 For *according to* the number of your cities were your gods, O Judah; and *according to* the number of the streets of Jerusalem you have set up altars to *that* shameful thing, altars to burn incense to Baal.

14 "So do not pray for this people, or lift up a cry or prayer for them; for I will not hear *them* in the time that they cry out to Me because of their trouble.

15 "What has My beloved to do in My house,

Having done lewd deeds with many?
And the holy flesh has passed from you.
When you do evil, then you rejoice.
16   The LORD called your name,
Green Olive Tree, Lovely *and* of Good Fruit.
With the noise of a great tumult He has kindled fire on it,
And its branches are broken.

17 "For the LORD of hosts, who planted you, has pronounced doom against you for the evil of the house of Israel and of the house of Judah, which they have done against themselves to provoke Me to anger in offering incense to Baal."

18 Now the LORD gave me knowledge *of it*, and I know *it;* for You showed me their doings. 19 But I *was* like a docile lamb brought to the slaughter; and I did not know that they had devised schemes against me, *saying,* "Let us destroy the tree with its fruit, and let us cut him off from the land of the living, that his name may be remembered no more."

20   But, O LORD of hosts,
You who judge righteously,
Testing the mind and the heart,
Let me see Your vengeance on them,
For to You I have revealed my cause.

21 "Therefore thus says the LORD concerning the men of Anathoth who seek your life, saying, 'Do not prophesy in the name of the LORD, lest you die by our hand'— 22 therefore thus says the LORD of hosts: 'Behold, I will punish them. The young men shall die by the sword, their sons and their daughters shall die by famine; 23 and there shall be no remnant of them, for I will bring catastrophe on the men of Anathoth, *even* the year of their punishment.' "

12 Righteous *are* You, O LORD,
when I plead with You;
Yet let me talk with You about *Your* judgments.
Why does the way of the wicked prosper?

11:5 ᵃExodus 3:8

---

*T*hank God for the Church. It's the place where you can come broken and disgusted, and be healed, delivered and set free in the name of Jesus.

Why are those happy who deal
so treacherously?
2 You have planted them, yes,
they have taken root;
They grow, yes, they bear fruit.
You *are* near in their mouth
But far from their mind.

3 But You, O Lord, know me;
You have seen me,
And You have tested my heart
toward You.
Pull them out like sheep for the
slaughter,
And prepare them for the day
of slaughter.
4 How long will the land mourn,
And the herbs of every field
wither?
The beasts and birds are
consumed,
For *the* wickedness of those
who dwell there,
Because they said, "He will not
see our final end."

5 "If you have run with the
footmen, and they have
wearied you,
Then how can you contend
with horses?
And *if* in the land of peace,
In which you trusted, *they
wearied you,*
Then how will you do in the
floodplain*ᵃ* of the Jordan?
6 For even your brothers, the
house of your father,
Even they have dealt
treacherously with you;
Yes, they have called a
multitude after you.
Do not believe them,
Even though they speak
smooth words to you.

7 "I have forsaken My house, I
have left My heritage;
I have given the dearly beloved
of My soul into the hand of
her enemies.
8 My heritage is to Me like a lion
in the forest;
It cries out against Me;
Therefore I have hated it.
9 My heritage *is* to Me *like* a
speckled vulture;
The vultures all around *are*
against her.

Come, assemble all the beasts
of the field,
Bring them to devour!
10 "Many rulers*ᵃ* have destroyed
My vineyard,
They have trodden My portion
underfoot;
They have made My pleasant
portion a desolate
wilderness.
11 They have made it desolate;
Desolate, it mourns to Me;
The whole land is made
desolate,
Because no one takes *it* to
heart.
12 The plunderers have come
On all the desolate heights in
the wilderness,
For the sword of the Lord shall
devour
From *one* end of the land to the
other end of the land;
No flesh shall have peace.
13 They have sown wheat but
reaped thorns;
They have put themselves to
pain *but* do not profit.
But be ashamed of your harvest
Because of the fierce anger of
the Lord."

14 Thus says the Lord: "Against all
My evil neighbors who touch the inheritance which I have caused My
people Israel to inherit—behold, I
will pluck them out of their land and
pluck out the house of Judah from
among them. 15 Then it shall be, after
I have plucked them out, that I will
return and have compassion on them
and bring them back, everyone to his
heritage and everyone to his land.
16 And it shall be, if they will learn
carefully the ways of My people, to
swear by My name, 'As the Lord
lives,' as they taught My people to
swear by Baal, then they shall be established in the midst of My people.
17 But if they do not obey, I will utterly pluck up and destroy that nation," says the Lord.

13 Thus the Lord said to me: "Go
and get yourself a linen sash,
and put it around your waist, but do
not put it in water." 2 So I got a sash
according to the word of the Lord,
and put *it* around my waist.
3 And the word of the Lord came
to me the second time, saying,

12:5 *ᵃOr thicket*   12:10 *ᵃLiterally shepherds or pastors*

Gospel
Pearls

4 "Take the sash that you acquired, which *is* around your waist, and arise, go to the Euphrates,*a* and hide it there in a hole in the rock."
5 So I went and hid it by the Euphrates, as the LORD commanded me.

6 Now it came to pass after many days that the LORD said to me, "Arise, go to the Euphrates, and take from there the sash which I commanded you to hide there." 7 Then I went to the Euphrates and dug, and I took the sash from the place where I had hidden it; and there was the sash, ruined. It was profitable for nothing.

8 Then the word of the LORD came to me, saying, 9 "Thus says the LORD: 'In this manner I will ruin the pride of Judah and the great pride of Jerusalem. 10 This evil people, who refuse to hear My words, who follow the dictates of their hearts, and walk after other gods to serve them and worship them, shall be just like this sash which is profitable for nothing. 11 For as the sash clings to the waist of a man, so I have caused the whole house of Israel and the whole house of Judah to cling to Me,' says the LORD, 'that they may become My people, for renown, for praise, and for glory; but they would not hear.'

12 "Therefore you shall speak to them this word: 'Thus says the LORD God of Israel: "Every bottle shall be filled with wine." '

"And they will say to you, 'Do we not certainly know that every bottle will be filled with wine?'

13 "Then you shall say to them, 'Thus says the LORD: "Behold, I will fill all the inhabitants of this land—even the kings who sit on David's throne, the priests, the prophets, and all the inhabitants of Jerusalem—with drunkenness! 14 And I will dash them one against another, even the fathers and the sons together," says the LORD. "I will not pity nor spare nor have mercy, but will destroy them." ' "

15 Hear and give ear:
Do not be proud,
For the LORD has spoken.
16 Give glory to the LORD your
God
Before He causes darkness,
And before your feet stumble
On the dark mountains,

And while you are looking for
light,
He turns it into the shadow of
death
And makes *it* dense darkness.
17 But if you will not hear it,
My soul will weep in secret for
your pride;
My eyes will weep bitterly
And run down with tears,
Because the LORD's flock has
been taken captive.

18 Say to the king and to the
queen mother,
"Humble yourselves;
Sit down,
For your rule shall collapse, the
crown of your glory."
19 The cities of the South shall be
shut up,
And no one shall open *them;*
Judah shall be carried away
captive, all of it;
It shall be wholly carried away
captive.

20 Lift up your eyes and see
Those who come from the
north.
Where *is* the flock *that* was
given to you,
Your beautiful sheep?
21 What will you say when He
punishes you?
For you have taught them
To be chieftains, to be head
over you.
Will not pangs seize you,
Like a woman in labor?
22 And if you say in your heart,
"Why have these things come
upon me?"
For the greatness of your
iniquity
Your skirts have been
uncovered,
Your heels made bare.
23 Can the Ethiopian change his
skin or the leopard its spots?
Then may you also do good
who are accustomed to do
evil.

24 "Therefore I will scatter them
like stubble
That passes away by the wind
of the wilderness.
25 This is your lot,

13:4 *a*Hebrew *Perath*

*Y*ou may have thought you would never rejoice again. God declares that you can have freedom in Him—now! The joy He brings can be restored to your soul.

The portion of your measures
from Me," says the LORD,
"Because you have forgotten Me
And trusted in falsehood.
26 Therefore I will uncover your
skirts over your face,
That your shame may appear.
27 I have seen your adulteries
And your *lustful* neighings,
The lewdness of your harlotry,
Your abominations on the hills
in the fields.
Woe to you, O Jerusalem!
Will you still not be made
clean?"

14 The word of the LORD that
came to Jeremiah concerning
the droughts.

2 "Judah mourns,
And her gates languish;
They mourn for the land,
And the cry of Jerusalem has
gone up.
3 Their nobles have sent their
lads for water;
They went to the cisterns *and*
found no water.
They returned with their
vessels empty;
They were ashamed and
confounded
And covered their heads.
4 Because the ground is parched,
For there was no rain in the
land,
The plowmen were ashamed;
They covered their heads.
5 Yes, the deer also gave birth in
the field,
But left because there was no
grass.
6 And the wild donkeys stood in
the desolate heights;
They sniffed at the wind like
jackals;
Their eyes failed because *there
was* no grass."

7 O LORD, though our iniquities
testify against us,
Do it for Your name's sake;
For our backslidings are many,
We have sinned against You.
8 O the Hope of Israel, his Savior
in time of trouble,
Why should You be like a
stranger in the land,
And like a traveler *who* turns
aside to tarry for a night?

9 Why should You be like a man
astonished,
Like a mighty one *who* cannot
save?
Yet You, O LORD, *are* in our
midst,
And we are called by Your
name;
Do not leave us!

10 Thus says the LORD to this people:

"Thus they have loved to
wander;
They have not restrained their
feet.
Therefore the LORD does not
accept them;
He will remember their iniquity
now,
And punish their sins."

11 Then the LORD said to me, "Do
not pray for this people, for *their*
good. 12 When they fast, I will not
hear their cry; and when they offer
burnt offering and grain offering, I
will not accept them. But I will consume them by the sword, by the famine, and by the pestilence."
13 Then I said, "Ah, Lord GOD! Behold, the prophets say to them, 'You
shall not see the sword, nor shall you
have famine, but I will give you assured peace in this place.' "
14 And the LORD said to me, "The
prophets prophesy lies in My name.
I have not sent them, commanded
them, nor spoken to them; they
prophesy to you a false vision, divination, a worthless thing, and the deceit of their heart. 15 Therefore thus
says the LORD concerning the prophets who prophesy in My name, whom
I did not send, and who say, 'Sword
and famine shall not be in this
land'—'By sword and famine those
prophets shall be consumed!
16 And the people to whom they
prophesy shall be cast out in the
streets of Jerusalem because of the
famine and the sword; they will have
no one to bury them—them nor their
wives, their sons nor their daughters—for I will pour their wickedness
on them.'
17 "Therefore you shall say this
word to them:

'Let my eyes flow with tears
night and day,

And let them not cease;
For the virgin daughter of my
people
Has been broken with a mighty
stroke, with a very severe
blow.
18 If I go out to the field,
Then behold, those slain with
the sword!
And if I enter the city,
Then behold, those sick from
famine!
Yes, both prophet and priest go
about in a land they do not
know.'"

19 Have You utterly rejected
Judah?
Has Your soul loathed Zion?
Why have You stricken us so
that *there is* no healing for
us?
We looked for peace, but *there
was* no good;
And for the time of healing, and
there was trouble.
20 We acknowledge, O LORD, our
wickedness
And the iniquity of our fathers,
For we have sinned against
You.
21 Do not abhor *us,* for Your
name's sake;
Do not disgrace the throne of
Your glory.
Remember, do not break Your
covenant with us.
22 Are there any among the idols
of the nations that can cause
rain?
Or can the heavens give
showers?
Are You not He, O LORD our
God?
Therefore we will wait for You,
Since You have made all these.

15 Then the LORD said to me,
"*Even* if Moses and Samuel
stood before Me, My mind *would* not
be favorable toward this people. Cast
them out of My sight, and let them
go forth. 2 And it shall be, if they say
to you, 'Where should we go?' then
you shall tell them, 'Thus says the
LORD:

"Such as *are* for death, to death;
And such as *are* for the sword,
to the sword;
And such as *are* for the famine,
to the famine;

And such as *are* for the
captivity, to the captivity."'

3 "And I will appoint over them
four forms *of destruction,*" says the
LORD: "the sword to slay, the dogs
to drag, the birds of the heavens and
the beasts of the earth to devour and
destroy. 4 I will hand them over to
trouble, to all kingdoms of the earth,
because of Manasseh the son of
Hezekiah, king of Judah, for what he
did in Jerusalem.

5 "For who will have pity on you,
O Jerusalem?
Or who will bemoan you?
Or who will turn aside to ask
how you are doing?
6 You have forsaken Me," says
the LORD,
"You have gone backward.
Therefore I will stretch out My
hand against you and destroy
you;
I am weary of relenting!
7 And I will winnow them with
a winnowing fan in the gates
of the land;
I will bereave *them* of children;
I will destroy My people,
Since they do not return from
their ways.
8 Their widows will be increased
to Me more than the sand of
the seas;
I will bring against them,
Against the mother of the
young men,
A plunderer at noonday;
I will cause anguish and terror
to fall on them suddenly.

9 "She languishes who has borne
seven;
She has breathed her last;
Her sun has gone down
While *it was* yet day;
She has been ashamed and
confounded.
And the remnant of them I will
deliver to the sword
Before their enemies," says the
LORD.

10 Woe is me, my mother,
That you have borne me,
A man of strife and a man of
contention to the whole
earth!
I have neither lent for interest,

*O*nce you have called out to Him, you can lift up your hands in praise. No matter
what you have suffered, you can hold up your head. Regardless of who has hurt
you, hold up your head!

Nor have men lent to me for
interest.
Every one of them curses me.

11 The LORD said:

"Surely it will be well with your
remnant;
Surely I will cause the enemy
to intercede with you
In the time of adversity and in
the time of affliction.
12 Can anyone break iron,
The northern iron and the
bronze?
13 Your wealth and your treasures
I will give as plunder without
price,
Because of all your sins,
Throughout your territories.
14 And I will make *you* cross over
with*ᵃ* your enemies
Into a land *which* you do not
know;
For a fire is kindled in My
anger,
Which shall burn upon you."

15 O LORD, You know;
Remember me and visit me,
And take vengeance for me on
my persecutors.
In Your enduring patience, do
not take me away.
Know that for Your sake I have
suffered rebuke.
16 Your words were found, and I
ate them,
And Your word was to me the
joy and rejoicing of my
heart;
For I am called by Your
name,
O LORD God of hosts.
17 I did not sit in the assembly of
the mockers,
Nor did I rejoice;
I sat alone because of Your
hand,
For You have filled me with
indignation.
18 Why is my pain perpetual
And my wound incurable,
Which refuses to be healed?
Will You surely be to me like
an unreliable stream,
As waters *that* fail?

19 Therefore thus says the LORD:

"If you return,
Then I will bring you back;
You shall stand before Me;
If you take out the precious
from the vile,
You shall be as My mouth.
Let them return to you,
But you must not return to
them.
20 And I will make you to this
people a fortified bronze
wall;
And they will fight against
you,
But they shall not prevail
against you;
For I *am* with you to save you
And deliver you," says the
LORD.
21 "I will deliver you from the hand
of the wicked,
And I will redeem you from the
grip of the terrible."

16 The word of the LORD also
came to me, saying, 2 "You
shall not take a wife, nor shall you
have sons or daughters in this place."
3 For thus says the LORD concerning
the sons and daughters who are born
in this place, and concerning their
mothers who bore them and their fathers who begot them in this land:
4 "They shall die gruesome deaths;
they shall not be lamented nor shall
they be buried, *but* they shall be like
refuse on the face of the earth. They
shall be consumed by the sword and
by famine, and their corpses shall be
meat for the birds of heaven and for
the beasts of the earth."

5 For thus says the LORD: "Do not
enter the house of mourning, nor go
to lament or bemoan them; for I have
taken away My peace from this people," says the LORD, "lovingkindness
and mercies. 6 Both the great and the
small shall die in this land. They shall
not be buried; neither shall men lament for them, cut themselves, nor
make themselves bald for them.
7 Nor shall *men* break *bread* in
mourning for them, to comfort them
for the dead; nor shall *men* give them
the cup of consolation to drink for
their father or their mother.
8 Also you shall not go into the house
of feasting to sit with them, to eat and
drink."

15:14 ᵃFollowing Masoretic Text and Vulgate; Septuagint, Syriac, and Targum read *cause you to serve*
(compare 17:4).

Gospel Pearls

9 For thus says the LORD of hosts, the God of Israel: "Behold, I will cause to cease from this place, before your eyes and in your days, the voice of mirth and the voice of gladness, the voice of the bridegroom and the voice of the bride.

10 "And it shall be, when you show this people all these words, and they say to you, 'Why has the LORD pronounced all this great disaster against us? Or what *is* our iniquity? Or what *is* our sin that we have committed against the LORD our God?' 11 then you shall say to them, 'Because your fathers have forsaken Me,' says the LORD; 'they have walked after other gods and have served them and worshiped them, and have forsaken Me and not kept My law. 12 And you have done worse than your fathers, for behold, each one follows the dictates of his own evil heart, so that no one listens to Me. 13 Therefore I will cast you out of this land into a land that you do not know, neither you nor your fathers; and there you shall serve other gods day and night, where I will not show you favor.'

14 "Therefore behold, the days are coming," says the LORD, "that it shall no more be said, 'The LORD lives who brought up the children of Israel from the land of Egypt,' 15 but, 'The LORD lives who brought up the children of Israel from the land of the north and from all the lands where He had driven them.' For I will bring them back into their land which I gave to their fathers.

16 "Behold, I will send for many fishermen," says the LORD, "and they shall fish them; and afterward I will send for many hunters, and they shall hunt them from every mountain and every hill, and out of the holes of the rocks. 17 For My eyes *are* on all their ways; they are not hidden from My face, nor is their iniquity hidden from My eyes. 18 And first I will repay double for their iniquity and their sin, because they have defiled My land; they have filled My inheritance with the carcasses of their detestable and abominable idols."

19   O LORD, my strength and my fortress,

My refuge in the day of affliction,
The Gentiles shall come to You
From the ends of the earth and say,
"Surely our fathers have inherited lies,
Worthlessness and unprofitable *things*."
20   Will a man make gods for himself,
Which *are* not gods?

21 "Therefore behold, I will this once cause them to know,
I will cause them to know
My hand and My might;
And they shall know that My name *is* the LORD.

17 "The sin of Judah *is* written with a pen of iron;
With the point of a diamond *it is* engraved
On the tablet of their heart,
And on the horns of your altars,
2   While their children remember
Their altars and their wooden images[a]
By the green trees on the high hills.
3   O My mountain in the field,
I will give as plunder your wealth, all your treasures,
And your high places of sin within all your borders.
4   And you, even yourself,
Shall let go of your heritage which I gave you;
And I will cause you to serve your enemies
In the land which you do not know;
For you have kindled a fire in My anger *which* shall burn forever."

5 Thus says the LORD:

"Cursed *is* the man who trusts in man
And makes flesh his strength,
Whose heart departs from the LORD.
6   For he shall be like a shrub in the desert,
And shall not see when good comes,

17:2 aHebrew *Asherim,* Canaanite deities

*Y*ou should celebrate your survival. Instead of agonizing over your tragedies, you should celebrate your victory and thank God you made it. I charge you to step over your adversity and walk into the newness.

Close to the Water

Jeremiah 17:7, 8

*I*n Bible days, the ox—one of the strongest animals alive—was used for important labor and was considered very profitable for farmers. The donkey—one of the most stubborn and contentious animals alive—was not considered to be as valuable or as useful. Jesus once said something like this to a man who criticized Him for healing on the Sabbath: "You will loose not only your valuable animal, but your nearly worthless animal on the Sabbath, and yet complain that a human being has been delivered?" (see Luke 13:15, 16).

People seem to get excited when talented folks are delivered. The whole world takes notice when a celebrity gets saved. They don't get as excited when ordinary people are set free from their infirmities. I've got good news for you today: God doesn't make that differentiation. He wants to meet needs for everyone. Your deliverance does not depend upon the scope of your future usefulness in His kingdom or your future ministry. God delivers you because He loves you.

God has delivered countless people who have never written a book about their experience or gone on to lead the choir or sing a solo or chair a committee or teach a Sunday school class. God's deliverance is not contingent upon what you will do after you are delivered. Just remember the infirm woman. She is never mentioned again in the Bible. Jesus delivered her anyway.

Jesus also reminded the people that they kept their oxen and donkeys in stalls, instead of staked near a place where water was flowing freely. If the animals had been able to drink, there would have been no need to loose them on the Sabbath.

Stalls, built by men, are designed to keep animals closed off from each other. There are man-made stalls today, too, used to divide and separate people. These stalls prohibit people from moving into areas where they can get what they need. These stalls keep folks "in their place" so they can be controlled.

When you are delivered by God, you may need to say no to anyone who attempts to keep you in the stall they've built for you. You may have to say, "Now that I'm free, I'm not going back into that cage." You may have to say, "I've decided to stay close to the living water of the Holy Spirit, and I'm not going to be stuck in a place where I can't praise Him."

When God delivers you, He wants you to be delivered from everything that has confined you. Live close to the water of life. Go where you can be refreshed in the Lord—and stay there.

But shall inhabit the parched
  places in the wilderness,
In a salt land *which is* not
  inhabited.

7 "Blessed *is* the man who trusts
    in the LORD,
  And whose hope is the LORD.
8 For he shall be like a tree
    planted by the waters,
  Which spreads out its roots by
    the river,
  And will not fear[a] when heat
    comes;
  But its leaf will be green,
  And will not be anxious in the
    year of drought,
  Nor will cease from yielding
    fruit.

9 "The heart *is* deceitful above all
    things,
  And desperately wicked;
  Who can know it?
10 I, the LORD, search the heart,
  I test the mind,
  Even to give every man
    according to his ways,
  According to the fruit of his
    doings.

11 "*As* a partridge that broods but
    does not hatch,
  So is he who gets riches, but
    not by right;
  It will leave him in the midst
    of his days,
  And at his end he will be a
    fool."

12 A glorious high throne from the
    beginning
  Is the place of our sanctuary.
13 O LORD, the hope of Israel,
  All who forsake You shall be
    ashamed.

  "Those who depart from Me
  Shall be written in the earth,
  Because they have forsaken the
    LORD,
  The fountain of living waters."

14 Heal me, O LORD, and I shall
    be healed;
  Save me, and I shall be saved,
  For You *are* my praise.
15 Indeed they say to me,
  "Where *is* the word of the LORD?
  Let it come now!"

16 As for me, I have not hurried
    away from *being* a shepherd
    who follows You,
  Nor have I desired the woeful
    day;
  You know what came out of my
    lips;
  It was right there before You.
17 Do not be a terror to me;
  You *are* my hope in the day of
    doom.
18 Let them be ashamed who
    persecute me,
  But do not let me be put to
    shame;
  Let them be dismayed,
  But do not let me be dismayed.
  Bring on them the day of doom,
  And destroy them with double
    destruction!

19 Thus the LORD said to me: "Go and stand in the gate of the children of the people, by which the kings of Judah come in and by which they go out, and in all the gates of Jerusalem; 20 and say to them, 'Hear the word of the LORD, you kings of Judah, and all Judah, and all the inhabitants of Jerusalem, who enter by these gates. 21 Thus says the LORD: "Take heed to yourselves, and bear no burden on the Sabbath day, nor bring *it* in by the gates of Jerusalem; 22 nor carry a burden out of your houses on the Sabbath day, nor do any work, but hallow the Sabbath day, as I commanded your fathers. 23 But they did not obey nor incline their ear, but made their neck stiff, that they might not hear nor receive instruction.

24 "And it shall be, if you heed Me carefully," says the LORD, "to bring no burden through the gates of this city on the Sabbath day, but hallow the Sabbath day, to do no work in it, 25 then shall enter the gates of this city kings and princes sitting on the throne of David, riding in chariots and on horses, they and their princes, accompanied by the men of Judah and the inhabitants of Jerusalem; and this city shall remain forever. 26 And they shall come from the cities of Judah and from the places around Jerusalem, from the land of Benjamin and from the lowland, from the mountains and from the South, bringing burnt offerings and sacrifices, grain offerings and in-

17:8 [a]Qere and Targum read *see*.

---

*T*he Holy Spirit is calling for the broken, infirm women to come to Jesus. He will restore and deliver. How do we come to Jesus? We come to His Body, the Church.

cense, bringing sacrifices of praise to the house of the LORD.

27 "But if you will not heed Me to hallow the Sabbath day, such as not carrying a burden when entering the gates of Jerusalem on the Sabbath day, then I will kindle a fire in its gates, and it shall devour the palaces of Jerusalem, and it shall not be quenched." ' "

18 The word which came to Jeremiah from the LORD, saying: 2 "Arise and go down to the potter's house, and there I will cause you to hear My words." 3 Then I went down to the potter's house, and there he was, making something at the wheel. 4 And the vessel that he made of clay was marred in the hand of the potter; so he made it again into another vessel, as it seemed good to the potter to make.

5 Then the word of the LORD came to me, saying: 6 "O house of Israel, can I not do with you as this potter?" says the LORD. "Look, as the clay *is* in the potter's hand, so *are* you in My hand, O house of Israel! 7 The instant I speak concerning a nation and concerning a kingdom, to pluck up, to pull down, and to destroy *it,* 8 if that nation against whom I have spoken turns from its evil, I will relent of the disaster that I thought to bring upon it. 9 And the instant I speak concerning a nation and concerning a kingdom, to build and to plant *it,* 10 if it does evil in My sight so that it does not obey My voice, then I will relent concerning the good with which I said I would benefit it.

11 "Now therefore, speak to the men of Judah and to the inhabitants of Jerusalem, saying, 'Thus says the LORD: "Behold, I am fashioning a disaster and devising a plan against you. Return now every one from his evil way, and make your ways and your doings good." ' "

12 And they said, "That is hopeless! So we will walk according to our own plans, and we will every one obey the dictates of his evil heart."

13 Therefore thus says the LORD:

"Ask now among the Gentiles,
Who has heard such things?

The virgin of Israel has done a
   very horrible thing.
14 Will *a man* leave the snow-
   water of Lebanon,
Which comes from the rock of
   the field?
Will the cold flowing waters be
   forsaken for strange waters?

15 "Because My people have
   forgotten Me,
They have burned incense to
   worthless idols.
And they have caused
   themselves to stumble in
   their ways,
From the ancient paths,
To walk in pathways and not
   on a highway,
16 To make their land desolate
   and a perpetual hissing;
Everyone who passes by it will
   be astonished
And shake his head.
17 I will scatter them as with an
   east wind before the enemy;
I will show them[a] the back and
   not the face
In the day of their calamity."

18 Then they said, "Come and let us devise plans against Jeremiah; for the law shall not perish from the priest, nor counsel from the wise, nor the word from the prophet. Come and let us attack him with the tongue, and let us not give heed to any of his words."

19 Give heed to me, O LORD,
   And listen to the voice of those
    who contend with me!
20 Shall evil be repaid for good?
For they have dug a pit for my
   life.
Remember that I stood before
   You
To speak good for them,
To turn away Your wrath from
   them.
21 Therefore deliver up their
   children to the famine,
And pour out their *blood*
By the force of the *sword;*
Let their wives *become* widows
And bereaved of their children.
Let their men be put to death,
Their young men *be* slain
By the sword in battle.

18:17 [a]Following Septuagint, Syriac, Targum, and Vulgate; Masoretic Text reads *look them in.*

Gospel Pearls

22 Let a cry be heard from their
  houses,
  When You bring a troop
    suddenly upon them;
  For they have dug a pit to take
    me,
  And hidden snares for my feet.
23 Yet, LORD, You know all their
    counsel
  Which is against me, to slay
    me.
  Provide no atonement for their
    iniquity,
  Nor blot out their sin from Your
    sight;
  But let them be overthrown
    before You.
  Deal *thus* with them
  In the time of Your anger.

19 Thus says the LORD: "Go and
  get a potter's earthen flask, and
take some of the elders of the people
and some of the elders of the priests.
2 And go out to the Valley of the Son
of Hinnom, which *is* by the entry of
the Potsherd Gate; and proclaim
there the words that I will tell you,
3 and say, 'Hear the word of the
LORD, O kings of Judah and inhabitants of Jerusalem. Thus says the
LORD of hosts, the God of Israel: "Behold, I will bring such a catastrophe
on this place, that whoever hears of
it, his ears will tingle.

4 "Because they have forsaken Me
and made this an alien place, because
they have burned incense in it to
other gods whom neither they, their
fathers, nor the kings of Judah have
known, and have filled this place
with the blood of the innocents
5 (they have also built the high places
of Baal, to burn their sons with fire
for burnt offerings to Baal, which I
did not command or speak, nor did
it come into My mind), 6 therefore behold, the days are coming," says the
LORD, "that this place shall no more
be called Tophet or the Valley of the
Son of Hinnom, but the Valley of
Slaughter. 7 And I will make void the
counsel of Judah and Jerusalem in
this place, and I will cause them to
fall by the sword before their enemies and by the hands of those who
seek their lives; their corpses I will
give as meat for the birds of the
heaven and for the beasts of the
earth. 8 I will make this city desolate

and a hissing; everyone who passes
by it will be astonished and hiss because of all its plagues. 9 And I will
cause them to eat the flesh of their
sons and the flesh of their daughters,
and everyone shall eat the flesh of
his friend in the siege and in the desperation with which their enemies
and those who seek their lives shall
drive them to despair." '

10 "Then you shall break the flask
in the sight of the men who go with
you, 11 and say to them, 'Thus says
the LORD of hosts: "Even so I will
break this people and this city, as *one*
breaks a potter's vessel, which cannot be made whole again; and they
shall bury *them* in Tophet till *there
is* no place to bury. 12 Thus I will do
to this place," says the LORD, "and
to its inhabitants, and make this city
like Tophet. 13 And the houses of Jerusalem and the houses of the kings
of Judah shall be defiled like the
place of Tophet, because of all the
houses on whose roofs they have
burned incense to all the host of
heaven, and poured out drink offerings to other gods." ' "

14 Then Jeremiah came from Tophet, where the LORD had sent him
to prophesy; and he stood in the
court of the Lord's house and said
to all the people, 15 "Thus says the
LORD of hosts, the God of Israel: 'Behold, I will bring on this city and on
all her towns all the doom that I have
pronounced against it, because they
have stiffened their necks that they
might not hear My words.' "

20 Now Pashhur the son of Immer, the priest who *was* also
chief governor in the house of the
LORD, heard that Jeremiah prophesied these things. 2 Then Pashhur
struck Jeremiah the prophet, and put
him in the stocks that *were* in the
high gate of Benjamin, which *was* by
the house of the LORD.

3 And it happened on the next day
that Pashhur brought Jeremiah out
of the stocks. Then Jeremiah said to
him, "The LORD has not called your
name Pashhur, but Magor-Missabib.*a*
4 For thus says the LORD: 'Behold, I
will make you a terror to yourself
and to all your friends; and they shall
fall by the sword of their enemies,
and your eyes shall see *it*. I will give

20:3 *a*Literally *Fear on Every Side*

*T*he Church gives us strength and nourishment. The Church is to be the place where
we share our burdens and allow others to help us with them. The Spirit calls; the
burdened need only heed the call.

all Judah into the hand of the king of Babylon, and he shall carry them captive to Babylon and slay them with the sword. 5 Moreover I will deliver all the wealth of this city, all its produce, and all its precious things; all the treasures of the kings of Judah I will give into the hand of their enemies, who will plunder them, seize them, and carry them to Babylon. 6 And you, Pashhur, and all who dwell in your house, shall go into captivity. You shall go to Babylon, and there you shall die, and be buried there, you and all your friends, to whom you have prophesied lies.' ''

7　O Lord, You induced me, and I was persuaded;
　　You are stronger than I, and have prevailed.
　　I am in derision daily;
　　Everyone mocks me.
8　For when I spoke, I cried out;
　　I shouted, "Violence and plunder!"
　　Because the word of the Lord was made to me
　　A reproach and a derision daily.
9　Then I said, "I will not make mention of Him,
　　Nor speak anymore in His name."
　　But *His word* was in my heart like a burning fire
　　Shut up in my bones;
　　I was weary of holding *it* back, And I could not.
10　For I heard many mocking: "Fear on every side!"
　　"Report," *they say*, "and we will report it!"
　　All my acquaintances watched for my stumbling, *saying,*
　　"Perhaps he can be induced; Then we will prevail against him,
　　And we will take our revenge on him."

11　But the Lord *is* with me as a mighty, awesome One.
　　Therefore my persecutors will stumble, and will not prevail.
　　They will be greatly ashamed, for they will not prosper.
　　Their everlasting confusion will never be forgotten.
12　But, O Lord of hosts,

　　You who test the righteous,
　　And see the mind and heart,
　　Let me see Your vengeance on them;
　　For I have pleaded my cause before You.

13　Sing to the Lord! Praise the Lord!
　　For He has delivered the life of the poor
　　From the hand of evildoers.

14　Cursed *be* the day in which I was born!
　　Let the day not be blessed in which my mother bore me!
15　Let the man *be* cursed
　　Who brought news to my father, saying,
　　"A male child has been born to you!"
　　Making him very glad.
16　And let that man be like the cities
　　Which the Lord overthrew, and did not relent;
　　Let him hear the cry in the morning
　　And the shouting at noon,
17　Because he did not kill me from the womb,
　　That my mother might have been my grave,
　　And her womb always enlarged *with me.*
18　Why did I come forth from the womb to see labor and sorrow,
　　That my days should be consumed with shame?

21 The word which came to Jeremiah from the Lord when King Zedekiah sent to him Pashhur the son of Melchiah, and Zephaniah the son of Maaseiah, the priest, saying, 2 "Please inquire of the Lord for us, for Nebuchadnezzar*ᵃ* king of Babylon makes war against us. Perhaps the Lord will deal with us according to all His wonderful works, that *the king* may go away from us."

3 Then Jeremiah said to them, "Thus you shall say to Zedekiah, 4 'Thus says the Lord God of Israel: "Behold, I will turn back the weapons of war that *are* in your hands, with which you fight against the king

21:2 *ᵃ*Hebrew *Nebuchadrezzar,* and so elsewhere

Gospel Pearls

of Babylon and the Chaldeans[a] who besiege you outside the walls; and I will assemble them in the midst of this city. 5 I Myself will fight against you with an outstretched hand and with a strong arm, even in anger and fury and great wrath. 6 I will strike the inhabitants of this city, both man and beast; they shall die of a great pestilence. 7 And afterward," says the LORD, "I will deliver Zedekiah king of Judah, his servants and the people, and such as are left in this city from the pestilence and the sword and the famine, into the hand of Nebuchadnezzar king of Babylon, into the hand of their enemies, and into the hand of those who seek their life; and he shall strike them with the edge of the sword. He shall not spare them, or have pity or mercy."'

8 "Now you shall say to this people, 'Thus says the LORD: "Behold, I set before you the way of life and the way of death. 9 He who remains in this city shall die by the sword, by famine, and by pestilence; but he who goes out and defects to the Chaldeans who besiege you, he shall live, and his life shall be as a prize to him. 10 For I have set My face against this city for adversity and not for good," says the LORD. "It shall be given into the hand of the king of Babylon, and he shall burn it with fire."'

11 "And concerning the house of the king of Judah, say, 'Hear the word of the LORD, 12 O house of David! Thus says the LORD:

"Execute judgment in the morning;
And deliver him who is plundered
Out of the hand of the oppressor,
Lest My fury go forth like fire
And burn so that no one can quench it,
Because of the evil of your doings.

13 "Behold, I am against you, O inhabitant of the valley,
And rock of the plain," says the LORD,
"Who say, 'Who shall come down against us?

Or who shall enter our dwellings?'
14 But I will punish you according to the fruit of your doings," says the LORD;
"I will kindle a fire in its forest,
And it shall devour all things around it."''"

22 Thus says the LORD: "Go down to the house of the king of Judah, and there speak this word, 2 and say, 'Hear the word of the LORD, O king of Judah, you who sit on the throne of David, you and your servants and your people who enter these gates! 3 Thus says the LORD: "Execute judgment and righteousness, and deliver the plundered out of the hand of the oppressor. Do no wrong and do no violence to the stranger, the fatherless, or the widow, nor shed innocent blood in this place. 4 For if you indeed do this thing, then shall enter the gates of this house, riding on horses and in chariots, accompanied by servants and people, kings who sit on the throne of David. 5 But if you will not hear these words, I swear by Myself," says the LORD, "that this house shall become a desolation."''"

6 For thus says the LORD to the house of the king of Judah:

"You are Gilead to Me,
The head of Lebanon;
Yet I surely will make you a wilderness,
Cities which are not inhabited.
7 I will prepare destroyers against you,
Everyone with his weapons;
They shall cut down your choice cedars
And cast them into the fire.

8 And many nations will pass by this city; and everyone will say to his neighbor, 'Why has the LORD done so to this great city?' 9 Then they will answer, 'Because they have forsaken the covenant of the LORD their God, and worshiped other gods and served them.'"

10 Weep not for the dead, nor bemoan him;
Weep bitterly for him who goes away,

21:4 aOr Babylonians

Even now, after all you've been through, God has the power to raise you up again! This is the present tense of faith. Walk into your newness even now.

For he shall return no more,
Nor see his native country.

11 For thus says the LORD concerning Shallum[a] the son of Josiah, king of Judah, who reigned instead of Josiah his father, who went from this place: "He shall not return here anymore, 12 but he shall die in the place where they have led him captive, and shall see this land no more.

13 "Woe to him who builds his
      house by unrighteousness
   And his chambers by injustice,
   Who uses his neighbor's
      service without wages
   And gives him nothing for his
      work,
14 Who says, 'I will build myself
      a wide house with spacious
      chambers,
   And cut out windows for it,
   Paneling *it* with cedar
   And painting *it* with vermilion.'

15 "Shall you reign because you
      enclose *yourself* in cedar?
   Did not your father eat and
      drink,
   And do justice and
      righteousness?
   Then *it was* well with him.
16 He judged the cause of the poor
      and needy;
   Then *it was* well.
   Was not this knowing Me?"
      says the LORD.
17 "Yet your eyes and your heart
      are for nothing but your
      covetousness,
   For shedding innocent blood,
   And practicing oppression and
      violence."

18 Therefore thus says the LORD concerning Jehoiakim the son of Josiah, king of Judah:

   "They shall not lament for him,
   Saying, 'Alas, my brother!' or
      'Alas, my sister!'
   They shall not lament for him,
   Saying, 'Alas, master!' or 'Alas,
      his glory!'
19 He shall be buried with the
      burial of a donkey,
   Dragged and cast out beyond
      the gates of Jerusalem.

20 "Go up to Lebanon, and cry out,
   And lift up your voice in
      Bashan;
   Cry from Abarim,
   For all your lovers are
      destroyed.
21 I spoke to you in your
      prosperity,
   But you said, 'I will not hear.'
   This *has been* your manner
      from your youth,
   That you did not obey My
      voice.
22 The wind shall eat up all your
      rulers,
   And your lovers shall go into
      captivity;
   Surely then you will be
      ashamed and humiliated
   For all your wickedness.
23 O inhabitant of Lebanon,
   Making your nest in the cedars,
   How gracious will you be when
      pangs come upon you,
   Like the pain of a woman in
      labor?

24 "*As I live*," says the LORD, "though Coniah[a] the son of Jehoiakim, king of Judah, were the signet on My right hand, yet I would pluck you off; 25 and I will give you into the hand of those who seek your life, and into the hand *of those* whose face you fear—the hand of Nebuchadnezzar king of Babylon and the hand of the Chaldeans. 26 So I will cast you out, and your mother who bore you, into another country where you were not born; and there you shall die. 27 But to the land to which they desire to return, there they shall not return.

28 "Is this man Coniah a despised,
      broken idol—
   A vessel in which *is* no
      pleasure?
   Why are they cast out, he and
      his descendants,
   And cast into a land which they
      do not know?
29 O earth, earth, earth,
   Hear the word of the LORD!
30 Thus says the LORD:
   'Write this man down as
      childless,
   A man *who* shall not prosper
      in his days;

22:11 [a]Also called *Jehoahaz*   22:24 [a]Also called *Jeconiah* and *Jehoiachin*

Gospel
Pearls

For none of his descendants
   shall prosper,
Sitting on the throne of David,
   And ruling anymore in
      Judah.' "

23 "Woe to the shepherds who destroy and scatter the sheep of My pasture!" says the LORD. 2 Therefore thus says the LORD God of Israel against the shepherds who feed My people: "You have scattered My flock, driven them away, and not attended to them. Behold, I will attend to you for the evil of your doings," says the LORD. 3 "But I will gather the remnant of My flock out of all countries where I have driven them, and bring them back to their folds; and they shall be fruitful and increase. 4 I will set up shepherds over them who will feed them; and they shall fear no more, nor be dismayed, nor shall they be lacking," says the LORD.

5 "Behold, *the* days are coming,"
     says the LORD,
  "That I will raise to David a
     Branch of righteousness;
  A King shall reign and prosper,
  And execute judgment and
     righteousness in the earth.
6 In His days Judah will be
     saved,
  And Israel will dwell safely;
  Now this *is* His name by which
     He will be called:

THE LORD OUR
RIGHTEOUSNESS.*a*

7 "Therefore, behold, *the* days are coming," says the LORD, "that they shall no longer say, 'As the LORD lives who brought up the children of Israel from the land of Egypt,' 8 but, 'As the LORD lives who brought up and led the descendants of the house of Israel from the north country and from all the countries where I had driven them.' And they shall dwell in their own land."

9 My heart within me is broken
    Because of the prophets;
  All my bones shake.
  I am like a drunken man,
  And like a man whom wine has
    overcome,

    Because of the LORD,
    And because of His holy words.
10 For the land is full of
    adulterers;
  For because of a curse the land
    mourns.
  The pleasant places of the
    wilderness are dried up.
  Their course of life is evil,
  And their might *is* not right.

11 "For both prophet and priest are
    profane;
  Yes, in My house I have found
    their wickedness," says the
    LORD.
12 "Therefore their way shall be to
    them
  Like slippery *ways;*
  In the darkness they shall be
    driven on
  And fall in them;
  For I will bring disaster on
    them,
  The year of their punishment,"
    says the LORD.
13 "And I have seen folly in the
    prophets of Samaria:
  They prophesied by Baal
  And caused My people Israel to
    err.
14 Also I have seen a horrible
    thing in the prophets of
    Jerusalem:
  They commit adultery and
    walk in lies;
  They also strengthen the hands
    of evildoers,
  So that no one turns back from
    his wickedness.
  All of them are like Sodom to
    Me,
  And her inhabitants like
    Gomorrah.

15 "Therefore thus says the LORD of hosts concerning the prophets:

   'Behold, I will feed them with
    wormwood,
  And make them drink the
    water of gall;
  For from the prophets of
    Jerusalem
  Profaneness has gone out into
    all the land.' "

16 Thus says the LORD of hosts:

23:6 *a*Hebrew *YHWH Tsidkenu*

*T*he woman was made, fashioned out of the man, to be a helpmeet. Through their union, they find wholeness in each other. She helps him meet and accomplish his task.

"Do not listen to the words of the prophets who prophesy to you.
They make you worthless;
They speak a vision of their own heart,
Not from the mouth of the LORD.

17 They continually say to those who despise Me,
'The LORD has said, "You shall have peace" ';
And to everyone who walks according to the dictates of his own heart, they say,
'No evil shall come upon you.' "

18 For who has stood in the counsel of the LORD,
And has perceived and heard His word?
Who has marked His word and heard it?
19 Behold, a whirlwind of the LORD has gone forth in fury—
A violent whirlwind!
It will fall violently on the head of the wicked.
20 The anger of the LORD will not turn back
Until He has executed and performed the thoughts of His heart.
In the latter days you will understand it perfectly.

21 "I have not sent these prophets, yet they ran.
I have not spoken to them, yet they prophesied.
22 But if they had stood in My counsel,
And had caused My people to hear My words,
Then they would have turned them from their evil way
And from the evil of their doings.

23 "Am I a God near at hand," says the LORD,
"And not a God afar off?
24 Can anyone hide himself in secret places,
So I shall not see him?" says the LORD;
"Do I not fill heaven and earth?" says the LORD.

25 "I have heard what the prophets have said who prophesy lies in My name, saying, 'I have dreamed, I have dreamed!' 26 How long will *this* be in the heart of the prophets who prophesy lies? Indeed *they are* prophets of the deceit of their own heart, 27 who try to make My people forget My name by their dreams which everyone tells his neighbor, as their fathers forgot My name for Baal.

28 "The prophet who has a dream, let him tell a dream;
And he who has My word, let him speak My word faithfully.
What *is* the chaff to the wheat?" says the LORD.
29 "*Is* not My word like a fire?" says the LORD,
"And like a hammer *that* breaks the rock in pieces?

30 "Therefore behold, I *am* against the prophets," says the LORD, "who steal My words every one from his neighbor. 31 Behold, I *am* against the prophets," says the LORD, "who use their tongues and say, 'He says.' 32 Behold, I *am* against those who prophesy false dreams," says the LORD, "and tell them, and cause My people to err by their lies and by their recklessness. Yet I did not send them or command them; therefore they shall not profit this people at all," says the LORD.

33 "So when these people or the prophet or the priest ask you, saying, 'What is the oracle of the LORD?' you shall then say to them, 'What oracle?'[a] I will even forsake you," says the LORD. 34 "And *as for* the prophet and the priest and the people who say, 'The oracle of the LORD!' I will even punish that man and his house. 35 Thus every one of you shall say to his neighbor, and every one to his brother, 'What has the LORD answered?' and, 'What has the LORD spoken?' 36 And the oracle of the LORD you shall mention no more. For every man's word will be his oracle, for you have perverted the words of the living God, the LORD of hosts, our God. 37 Thus you shall say to the prophet, 'What has the LORD answered you?' and, 'What has the

23:33 [a]Septuagint, Targum, and Vulgate read '*You are the burden.*'

*J*esus called forth the wounded, hurting woman with a past. He issued the Spirit's call to those who had their value and self-esteem destroyed by the intrusion of vicious circumstances.

God's Operating Table

Jeremiah 23:24

When the Scriptures declare that men "always ought to pray and not lose heart" (Luke 18:1), they are speaking of living in a state of open communication with God, not necessarily jabbering at Him nonstop. Some people ramble on for hours on their knees and end up watching the clock, trying to get in a specified amount of prayer time.

We are called to live in a state of open-hearted communication with the Lord. Complete exposure before Him brings a sense of vulnerability, yet every one of us desperately needs someone to help us, someone who is able to understand our deepest issues.

Since you never think a thought or say a word that God does not hear and know, there is no need for a sanctimonious misrepresentation of who you are. No need for the strain of continual camouflage. You stand naked before Him in the same way a person lies naked on an operating table before a surgeon. The patient is neither boastful nor embarrassed, but understands that her condition is necessary to the relationship. Whatever the doctor finds in her body—either healthy or diseased tissue—is already present, and the patient must rest in the conviction that the doctor possesses the skill to perform the proper procedure.

Before your heart can be pure, God must flush away the corrosion and corruption that blocks the flow of His grace and mercy. The Greek word for purity, *katheros*, is the word from which we derive our English term, *catheterize*. This is a medical procedure used to cleanse, flush, or release fluids from the body. God is continually sending a deluge of His cleansing grace into the hearts of His children. But He can't clean or purify what you hide in the secret corners of your heart and mind.

My sister, you will never worship God in the beauty of His holiness if you live in the shadows, wrestling with unconfessed sin. Whatever you do, find your place in the presence of the Lord. He is always there, waiting to comfort and to heal.

LORD spoken?' 38 But since you say, 'The oracle of the LORD!' therefore thus says the LORD: 'Because you say this word, "The oracle of the LORD!" and I have sent to you, saying, "Do not say, 'The oracle of the LORD!' " 39 therefore behold, I, even I, will utterly forget you and forsake you, and the city that I gave you and your fathers, and *will cast you* out of My presence. 40 And I will bring an everlasting reproach upon you, and a perpetual shame, which shall not be forgotten.' "

24 The LORD showed me, and there were two baskets of figs set before the temple of the LORD, after Nebuchadnezzar king of Babylon had carried away captive Jeconiah the son of Jehoiakim, king of Judah, and the princes of Judah with the craftsmen and smiths, from Jerusalem, and had brought them to Babylon. 2 One basket *had* very good figs, like the figs *that are* first ripe; and the other basket *had* very bad figs which could not be eaten, they were so bad. 3 Then the LORD said to me, "What do you see, Jeremiah?"

And I said, "Figs, the good figs, very good; and the bad, very bad, which cannot be eaten, they are so bad."

4 Again the word of the LORD came to me, saying, 5 "Thus says the LORD, the God of Israel: 'Like these good figs, so will I acknowledge those who are carried away captive from Judah, whom I have sent out of this place for *their own* good, into the land of the Chaldeans. 6 For I will set My eyes on them for good, and I will bring them back to this land; I will build them and not pull *them* down, and I will plant them and not pluck *them* up. 7 Then I will give them a heart to know Me, that I *am* the LORD; and they shall be My people, and I will be their God, for they shall return to Me with their whole heart.

8 'And as the bad figs which cannot be eaten, they are so bad'—surely thus says the LORD—'so will I give up Zedekiah the king of Judah, his princes, the residue of Jerusalem who remain in this land, and those who dwell in the land of Egypt. 9 I will deliver them to trouble into all the kingdoms of the earth, for *their* harm, *to be* a reproach and a byword, a taunt and a curse, in all places where I shall drive them. 10 And I will send the sword, the famine, and the pestilence among them, till they are consumed from the land that I gave to them and their fathers.' "

25 The word that came to Jeremiah concerning all the people of Judah, in the fourth year of Jehoiakim the son of Josiah, king of Judah (which *was* the first year of Nebuchadnezzar king of Babylon), 2 which Jeremiah the prophet spoke to all the people of Judah and to all the inhabitants of Jerusalem, saying: 3 "From the thirteenth year of Josiah the son of Amon, king of Judah, even to this day, this *is* the twenty-third year in which the word of the LORD has come to me; and I have spoken to you, rising early and speaking, but you have not listened. 4 And the LORD has sent to you all His servants the prophets, rising early and sending *them,* but you have not listened nor inclined your ear to hear. 5 They said, 'Repent now everyone of his evil way and his evil doings, and dwell in the land that the LORD has given to you and your fathers forever and ever. 6 Do not go after other gods to serve them and worship them, and do not provoke Me to anger with the works of your hands; and I will not harm you.' 7 Yet you have not listened to Me," says the LORD, "that you might provoke Me to anger with the works of your hands to your own hurt.

8 "Therefore thus says the LORD of hosts: 'Because you have not heard My words, 9 behold, I will send and take all the families of the north,' says the LORD, 'and Nebuchadnezzar the king of Babylon, My servant, and will bring them against this land, against its inhabitants, and against these nations all around, and will utterly destroy them, and make them an astonishment, a hissing, and perpetual desolations. 10 Moreover I will take from them the voice of mirth and the voice of gladness, the voice of the bridegroom and the voice of the bride, the sound of the millstones and the light of the lamp. 11 And this whole land shall be a desolation *and* an astonishment, and these nations shall serve the king of Babylon seventy years.

12 'Then it will come to pass, when seventy years are completed, *that I*

will punish the king of Babylon and that nation, the land of the Chaldeans, for their iniquity,' says the LORD; 'and I will make it a perpetual desolation. 13 So I will bring on that land all My words which I have pronounced against it, all that is written in this book, which Jeremiah has prophesied concerning all the nations. 14 (For many nations and great kings shall be served by them also; and I will repay them according to their deeds and according to the works of their own hands.)' "

15 For thus says the LORD God of Israel to me: "Take this wine cup of fury from My hand, and cause all the nations, to whom I send you, to drink it. 16 And they will drink and stagger and go mad because of the sword that I will send among them."

17 Then I took the cup from the LORD's hand, and made all the nations drink, to whom the LORD had sent me: 18 Jerusalem and the cities of Judah, its kings and its princes, to make them a desolation, an astonishment, a hissing, and a curse, as *it is* this day; 19 Pharaoh king of Egypt, his servants, his princes, and all his people; 20 all the mixed multitude, all the kings of the land of Uz, all the kings of the land of the Philistines (namely, Ashkelon, Gaza, Ekron, and the remnant of Ashdod); 21 Edom, Moab, and the people of Ammon; 22 all the kings of Tyre, all the kings of Sidon, and the kings of the coastlands which *are* across the sea; 23 Dedan, Tema, Buz, and all *who are* in the farthest corners; 24 all the kings of Arabia and all the kings of the mixed multitude who dwell in the desert; 25 all the kings of Zimri, all the kings of Elam, and all the kings of the Medes; 26 all the kings of the north, far and near, one with another; and all the kingdoms of the world which *are* on the face of the earth. Also the king of Sheshach[a] shall drink after them.

27 "Therefore you shall say to them, 'Thus says the LORD of hosts, the God of Israel: "Drink, be drunk, and vomit! Fall and rise no more, because of the sword which I will send among you." ' 28 And it shall be, if they refuse to take the cup from your hand to drink, then you shall say to them, 'Thus says the LORD of hosts:

"You shall certainly drink! 29 For behold, I begin to bring calamity on the city which is called by My name, and should you be utterly unpunished? You shall not be unpunished, for I will call for a sword on all the inhabitants of the earth," says the LORD of hosts.'

30 "Therefore prophesy against them all these words, and say to them:

'The LORD will roar from on
high,
And utter His voice from His
holy habitation;
He will roar mightily against
His fold.
He will give a shout, as those
who tread *the grapes,*
Against all the inhabitants of
the earth.
31 A noise will come to the ends
of the earth—
For the LORD has a controversy
with the nations;
He will plead His case with all
flesh.
He will give those *who are*
wicked to the sword,' says
the LORD."

32 Thus says the LORD of hosts:

"Behold, disaster shall go forth
From nation to nation,
And a great whirlwind shall be
raised up
From the farthest parts of the
earth.

33 "And at that day the slain of the LORD shall be from *one* end of the earth even to the *other* end of the earth. They shall not be lamented, or gathered, or buried; they shall become refuse on the ground.

34 "Wail, shepherds, and cry!
Roll about *in the ashes,*
You leaders of the flock!
For the days of your slaughter
and your dispersions are
fulfilled;
You shall fall like a precious
vessel.
35 And the shepherds will have no
way to flee,
Nor the leaders of the flock to
escape.

25:26 [a]A code word for *Babylon* (compare 51:41)

$\mathcal{W}$omen are open by nature and design. Men are closed. You must be careful what you allow to plug into you and draw strength from you. The wrong plugs may seek your help and then drain your power.

36 A voice of the cry of the
    shepherds,
    And a wailing of the leaders to
    the flock *will be heard.*
    For the LORD has plundered
    their pasture,
37 And the peaceful dwellings are
    cut down
    Because of the fierce anger of
    the LORD.
38 He has left His lair like the lion;
    For their land is desolate
    Because of the fierceness of the
    Oppressor,
    And because of His fierce
    anger."

26 In the beginning of the reign of
Jehoiakim the son of Josiah,
king of Judah, this word came from
the LORD, saying, 2 "Thus says the
LORD: 'Stand in the court of the
LORD's house, and speak to all the cities of Judah, which come to worship
in the LORD's house, all the words
that I command you to speak to them.
Do not diminish a word. 3 Perhaps
everyone will listen and turn from his
evil way, that I may relent concerning the calamity which I purpose to
bring on them because of the evil of
their doings.' 4 And you shall say to
them, 'Thus says the LORD: "If you
will not listen to Me, to walk in My
law which I have set before you,
5 to heed the words of My servants
the prophets whom I sent to you,
both rising up early and sending
them (but you have not heeded),
6 then I will make this house like Shiloh, and will make this city a curse
to all the nations of the earth." ' "

7 So the priests and the prophets
and all the people heard Jeremiah
speaking these words in the house of
the LORD. 8 Now it happened, when
Jeremiah had made an end of speaking all that the LORD had commanded
him to speak to all the people, that
the priests and the prophets and all
the people seized him, saying, "You
will surely die! 9 Why have you
prophesied in the name of the LORD,
saying, 'This house shall be like Shiloh, and this city shall be desolate,
without an inhabitant'?" And all the
people were gathered against Jeremiah in the house of the LORD.

10 When the princes of Judah
heard these things, they came up
from the king's house to the house
of the LORD and sat down in the entry
of the New Gate of the LORD's *house.*
11 And the priests and the prophets
spoke to the princes and all the people, saying, "This man deserves to
die! For he has prophesied against
this city, as you have heard with your
ears."

12 Then Jeremiah spoke to all the
princes and all the people, saying:
"The LORD sent me to prophesy
against this house and against this
city with all the words that you have
heard. 13 Now therefore, amend your
ways and your doings, and obey the
voice of the LORD your God; then the
LORD will relent concerning the doom
that He has pronounced against you.
14 As for me, here I am, in your hand;
do with me as seems good and proper
to you. 15 But know for certain that
if you put me to death, you will surely
bring innocent blood on yourselves,
on this city, and on its inhabitants;
for truly the LORD has sent me to you
to speak all these words in your hearing."

16 So the princes and all the people
said to the priests and the prophets,
"This man does not deserve to die.
For he has spoken to us in the name
of the LORD our God."

17 Then certain of the elders of the
land rose up and spoke to all the assembly of the people, saying:
18 "Micah of Moresheth prophesied
in the days of Hezekiah king of Judah, and spoke to all the people of
Judah, saying, 'Thus says the LORD
of hosts:

"Zion shall be plowed *like* a
    field,
    Jerusalem shall become heaps
    of ruins,
    And the mountain of the
    temple[a]
    Like the bare hills of the
    forest." '[b]

19 Did Hezekiah king of Judah and
all Judah ever put him to death? Did
he not fear the LORD and seek the
LORD's favor? And the Lord relented
concerning the doom which He had
pronounced against them. But we are
doing great evil against ourselves."
20 Now there was also a man who
prophesied in the name of the LORD,

26:18 ªLiterally *house* ᵇCompare Micah 3:12

Gospel Pearls

Urijah the son of Shemaiah of Kirjath Jearim, who prophesied against this city and against this land according to all the words of Jeremiah. 21 And when Jehoiakim the king, with all his mighty men and all the princes, heard his words, the king sought to put him to death; but when Urijah heard *it*, he was afraid and fled, and went to Egypt. 22 Then Jehoiakim the king sent men to Egypt: Elnathan the son of Achbor, and *other* men *who went* with him to Egypt. 23 And they brought Urijah from Egypt and brought him to Jehoiakim the king, who killed him with the sword and cast his dead body into the graves of the common people.

24 Nevertheless the hand of Ahikam the son of Shaphan was with Jeremiah, so that they should not give him into the hand of the people to put him to death.

27 In the beginning of the reign of Jehoiakim*a* the son of Josiah, king of Judah, this word came to Jeremiah from the LORD, saying,*b* 2 "Thus says the LORD to me: 'Make for yourselves bonds and yokes, and put them on your neck, 3 and send them to the king of Edom, the king of Moab, the king of the Ammonites, the king of Tyre, and the king of Sidon, by the hand of the messengers who come to Jerusalem to Zedekiah king of Judah. 4 And command them to say to their masters, "Thus says the LORD of hosts, the God of Israel— thus you shall say to your masters: 5 'I have made the earth, the man and the beast that *are* on the ground, by My great power and by My outstretched arm, and have given it to whom it seemed proper to Me. 6 And now I have given all these lands into the hand of Nebuchadnezzar the king of Babylon, My servant; and the beasts of the field I have also given him to serve him. 7 So all nations shall serve him and his son and his son's son, until the time of his land comes; and then many nations and great kings shall make him serve them. 8 And it shall be, *that* the nation and kingdom which will not serve Nebuchadnezzar the king of Babylon, and which will not put its neck under the yoke of the king of Babylon, that nation I will punish,' says the LORD, 'with the sword, the famine, and the pestilence, until I have consumed them by his hand. 9 Therefore do not listen to your prophets, your diviners, your dreamers, your soothsayers, or your sorcerers, who speak to you, saying, "You shall not serve the king of Babylon." 10 For they prophesy a lie to you, to remove you far from your land; and I will drive you out, and you will perish. 11 But the nations that bring their necks under the yoke of the king of Babylon and serve him, I will let them remain in their own land,' says the LORD, 'and they shall till it and dwell in it.' " ' "

12 I also spoke to Zedekiah king of Judah according to all these words, saying, "Bring your necks under the yoke of the king of Babylon, and serve him and his people, and live! 13 Why will you die, you and your people, by the sword, by the famine, and by the pestilence, as the LORD has spoken against the nation that will not serve the king of Babylon? 14 Therefore do not listen to the words of the prophets who speak to you, saying, 'You shall not serve the king of Babylon,' for they prophesy a lie to you; 15 for I have not sent them," says the LORD, "yet they prophesy a lie in My name, that I may drive you out, and that you may perish, you and the prophets who prophesy to you."

16 Also I spoke to the priests and to all this people, saying, "Thus says the LORD: 'Do not listen to the words of your prophets who prophesy to you, saying, "Behold, the vessels of the LORD's house will now shortly be brought back from Babylon"; for they prophesy a lie to you. 17 Do not listen to them; serve the king of Babylon, and live! Why should this city be laid waste? 18 But if they *are* prophets, and if the word of the LORD is with them, let them now make intercession to the LORD of hosts, that the vessels which are left in the house of the LORD, *in* the house of the king of Judah, and at Jerusalem, do not go to Babylon.'

19 "For thus says the LORD of hosts concerning the pillars, concerning

---

27:1 *a*Following Masoretic Text, Targum, and Vulgate; some Hebrew manuscripts, Arabic, and Syriac read *Zedekiah* (compare 27:3, 12; 28:1). *b*Septuagint omits verse 1.

God never intended for people to have casual sex. His design always included the commitment of a covenant. He purposed that a man who has sexual relations with a woman would be committed to that same woman for life.

the Sea, concerning the carts, and concerning the remainder of the vessels that remain in this city, 20 which Nebuchadnezzar king of Babylon did not take, when he carried away captive Jeconiah the son of Jehoiakim, king of Judah, from Jerusalem to Babylon, and all the nobles of Judah and Jerusalem— 21 yes, thus says the Lord of hosts, the God of Israel, concerning the vessels that remain in the house of the Lord, and in the house of the king of Judah and of Jerusalem: 22 'They shall be carried to Babylon, and there they shall be until the day that I visit them,' says the Lord. 'Then I will bring them up and restore them to this place.' "

28 And it happened in the same year, at the beginning of the reign of Zedekiah king of Judah, in the fourth year *and* in the fifth month, *that* Hananiah the son of Azur the prophet, who *was* from Gibeon, spoke to me in the house of the Lord in the presence of the priests and of all the people, saying, 2 "Thus speaks the Lord of hosts, the God of Israel, saying: 'I have broken the yoke of the king of Babylon. 3 Within two full years I will bring back to this place all the vessels of the Lord's house, that Nebuchadnezzar king of Babylon took away from this place and carried to Babylon. 4 And I will bring back to this place Jeconiah the son of Jehoiakim, king of Judah, with all the captives of Judah who went to Babylon,' says the Lord, 'for I will break the yoke of the king of Babylon.' "

5 Then the prophet Jeremiah spoke to the prophet Hananiah in the presence of the priests and in the presence of all the people who stood in the house of the Lord, 6 and the prophet Jeremiah said, "Amen! The Lord do so; the Lord perform your words which you have prophesied, to bring back the vessels of the Lord's house and all who were carried away captive, from Babylon to this place. 7 Nevertheless hear now this word that I speak in your hearing and in the hearing of all the people: 8 The prophets who have been before me and before you of old prophesied against many countries and great kingdoms—of war and disaster and pestilence. 9 As for the prophet who

prophesies of peace, when the word of the prophet comes to pass, the prophet will be known *as* one whom the Lord has truly sent."

10 Then Hananiah the prophet took the yoke off the prophet Jeremiah's neck and broke it. 11 And Hananiah spoke in the presence of all the people, saying, "Thus says the Lord: 'Even so I will break the yoke of Nebuchadnezzar king of Babylon from the neck of all nations within the space of two full years.' " And the prophet Jeremiah went his way.

12 Now the word of the Lord came to Jeremiah, after Hananiah the prophet had broken the yoke from the neck of the prophet Jeremiah, saying, 13 "Go and tell Hananiah, saying, 'Thus says the Lord: "You have broken the yokes of wood, but you have made in their place yokes of iron." 14 For thus says the Lord of hosts, the God of Israel: "I have put a yoke of iron on the neck of all these nations, that they may serve Nebuchadnezzar king of Babylon; and they shall serve him. I have given him the beasts of the field also." ' "

15 Then the prophet Jeremiah said to Hananiah the prophet, "Hear now, Hananiah, the Lord has not sent you, but you make this people trust in a lie. 16 Therefore thus says the Lord: 'Behold, I will cast you from the face of the earth. This year you shall die, because you have taught rebellion against the Lord.' "

17 So Hananiah the prophet died the same year in the seventh month.

29 Now these *are* the words of the letter that Jeremiah the prophet sent from Jerusalem to the remainder of the elders who were carried away captive—to the priests, the prophets, and all the people whom Nebuchadnezzar had carried away captive from Jerusalem to Babylon. 2 (This happened after Jeconiah the king, the queen mother, the eunuchs, the princes of Judah and Jerusalem, the craftsmen, and the smiths had departed from Jerusalem.) 3 *The letter was sent* by the hand of Elasah the son of Shaphan, and Gemariah the son of Hilkiah, whom Zedekiah king of Judah sent to Babylon, to Nebuchadnezzar king of Babylon, saying,

Gospel Pearls

4 Thus says the LORD of hosts, the God of Israel, to all who were carried away captive, whom I have caused to be carried away from Jerusalem to Babylon:

5 Build houses and dwell *in them;* plant gardens and eat their fruit. 6 Take wives and beget sons and daughters; and take wives for your sons and give your daughters to husbands, so that they may bear sons and daughters—that you may be increased there, and not diminished. 7 And seek the peace of the city where I have caused you to be carried away captive, and pray to the LORD for it; for in its peace you will have peace. 8 For thus says the LORD of hosts, the God of Israel: Do not let your prophets and your diviners who are in your midst deceive you, nor listen to your dreams which you cause to be dreamed. 9 For they prophesy falsely to you in My name; I have not sent them, says the LORD.

10 For thus says the LORD: After seventy years are completed at Babylon, I will visit you and perform My good word toward you, and cause you to return to this place. 11 For I know the thoughts that I think toward you, says the LORD, thoughts of peace and not of evil, to give you a future and a hope. 12 Then you will call upon Me and go and pray to Me, and I will listen to you. 13 And you will seek Me and find *Me,* when you search for Me with all your heart. 14 I will be found by you, says the LORD, and I will bring you back from your captivity; I will gather you from all the nations and from all the places where I have driven you, says the LORD, and I will bring you to the place from which I cause you to be carried away captive.

15 Because you have said, "The LORD has raised up prophets for us in Babylon"— 16 therefore thus says the LORD concerning the king who sits on the throne of David, concerning all the people who dwell in this city, and concerning your brethren who have not gone out with you into captivity— 17 thus says the LORD of hosts: Behold, I will send on them the sword, the famine, and the pestilence, and will make them like rotten figs that cannot be eaten, they are so bad. 18 And I will pursue them with the sword, with famine, and with pestilence; and I will deliver them to trouble among all the kingdoms of the earth—to be a curse, an astonishment, a hissing, and a reproach among all the nations where I have driven them, 19 because they have not heeded My words, says the LORD, which I sent to them by My servants the prophets, rising up early and sending *them;* neither would you heed, says the LORD. 20 Therefore hear the word of the LORD, all you of the captivity, whom I have sent from Jerusalem to Babylon.

21 Thus says the LORD of hosts, the God of Israel, concerning Ahab the son of Kolaiah, and Zedekiah the son of Maaseiah, who prophesy a lie to you in My name: Behold, I will deliver them into the hand of Nebuchadnezzar king of Babylon, and he shall slay them before your eyes. 22 And because of them a curse shall be taken up by all the captivity of Judah who *are* in Babylon, saying, "The LORD make you like Zedekiah and Ahab, whom the king of Babylon roasted in the fire"; 23 because they have done disgraceful things in Israel, have committed adultery with their neighbors' wives, and have spoken lying words in My name, which I have not commanded them. Indeed I know, and *am* a witness, says the LORD.

24 You shall also speak to Shemaiah the Nehelamite, saying, 25 Thus speaks the LORD of hosts, the God of Israel,

God explained that birthing comes through sorrow. Everything you bring forth comes through pain. If it didn't come through pain, it probably wasn't worth much.

Soul Secrets
*of a woman who doesn't
understand her destiny*

God, I know You have a destiny for me. I know that there is more of You and more from You than I have right now. You've gifted me in so many ways, but I can't seem to get those gifts out to a place where they can do some good. What is it You want from me?

I have struggled and groaned until I am finally submitted, finally ready to give You all of me. Now here I am on the altar, trying to figure out where to go and what to do next. And yet I hear You say that there is an altar time—a time of consecration beyond readiness. It's a time to enjoy Your presence without instruction. In the waiting—in the patience—You make me holy, You make me strong, You fill me with purpose.

Show me that this consecrating hour is a choice moment between You and me—a moment that will never be repeated. When You launch me out into my destiny in You, I may not have quiet hours in the same way anymore. When the consecration is complete, the action begins. And to act well, I must know the secrets of the fullness of Your presence in me, the secrets of receiving strategy from You, the secrets of moving at the impulse of Your Spirit. Every moment is, in itself, my destiny. There is greater destiny ahead of me. There is always more in You.

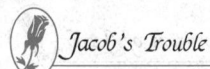

saying: You have sent letters in your name to all the people who *are* at Jerusalem, to Zephaniah the son of Maaseiah the priest, and to all the priests, saying, 26 "The LORD has made you priest instead of Jehoiada the priest, so that there should be officers *in* the house of the LORD over every man *who* is demented and considers himself a prophet, that you should put him in prison and in the stocks. 27 Now therefore, why have you not rebuked Jeremiah of Anathoth who makes himself a prophet to you? 28 For he has sent to us *in* Babylon, saying, 'This *captivity is* long; build houses and dwell *in them*, and plant gardens and eat their fruit.' "

29 Now Zephaniah the priest read this letter in the hearing of Jeremiah the prophet. 30 Then the word of the LORD came to Jeremiah, saying: 31 Send to all those in captivity, saying, Thus says the LORD concerning Shemaiah the Nehelamite: Because Shemaiah has prophesied to you, and I have not sent him, and he has caused you to trust in a lie— 32 therefore thus says the LORD: Behold, I will punish Shemaiah the Nehelamite and his family: he shall not have anyone to dwell among this people, nor shall he see the good that I will do for My people, says the LORD, because he has taught rebellion against the LORD.

30 The word that came to Jeremiah from the LORD, saying, 2 "Thus speaks the LORD God of Israel, saying: 'Write in a book for yourself all the words that I have spoken to you. 3 For behold, the days are coming,' says the LORD, 'that I will bring back from captivity My people Israel and Judah,' says the LORD. 'And I will cause them to return to the land that I gave to their fathers, and they shall possess it.' "

4 Now these *are* the words that the LORD spoke concerning Israel and Judah.

5 "For thus says the LORD:

'We have heard a voice of
    trembling,
Of fear, and not of peace.
6 Ask now, and see,
Whether a man is ever in labor
    with child?
So why do I see every man *with*
    his hands on his loins
Like a woman in labor,
And all faces turned pale?
7 Alas! For that day *is* great,
So that none *is* like it;
And it *is* the time of Jacob's
    trouble,
But he shall be saved out of it.

8 'For it shall come to pass in that
    day,'
Says the LORD of hosts,
'*That* I will break his yoke from
    your neck,
And will burst your bonds;
Foreigners shall no more
    enslave them.
9 But they shall serve the LORD
    their God,
And David their king,
Whom I will raise up for them.

10 'Therefore do not fear, O My
    servant Jacob,' says the
    LORD,
'Nor be dismayed, O Israel;
For behold, I will save you from
    afar,
And your seed from the land of
    their captivity.
Jacob shall return, have rest
    and be quiet,
And no one shall make *him*
    afraid.
11 For I *am* with you,' says the
    LORD, 'to save you;
Though I make a full end of all
    nations where I have
    scattered you,
Yet I will not make a complete
    end of you.
But I will correct you in justice,
And will not let you go
    altogether unpunished.'

12 "For thus says the LORD:

'Your affliction *is* incurable,
Your wound *is* severe.
13 *There is* no one to plead your
    cause,
That you may be bound up;

*F*or every sorrow, for every intense groaning in your spirit, you ought to have something to show for it. Any time you have sorrow, it is a sign that God is trying to get something through you and to you.

You have no healing medicines.

14 All your lovers have forgotten you;
They do not seek you;
For I have wounded you with the wound of an enemy,
With the chastisement of a cruel one,
For the multitude of your iniquities,
Because your sins have increased.

15 Why do you cry about your affliction?
Your sorrow *is* incurable.
Because of the multitude of your iniquities,
Because your sins have increased,
I have done these things to you.

16 'Therefore all those who devour you shall be devoured;
And all your adversaries, every one of them, shall go into captivity;
Those who plunder you shall become plunder,
And all who prey upon you I will make a prey.

17 For I will restore health to you And heal you of your wounds,' says the LORD,
'Because they called you an outcast *saying:*
"This *is* Zion;
No one seeks her." '

18 "Thus says the LORD:

'Behold, I will bring back the captivity of Jacob's tents,
And have mercy on his dwelling places;
The city shall be built upon its own mound,
And the palace shall remain according to its own plan.

19 Then out of them shall proceed thanksgiving
And the voice of those who make merry;
I will multiply them, and they shall not diminish;
I will also glorify them, and they shall not be small.

20 Their children also shall be as before,
And their congregation shall be established before Me;

And I will punish all who oppress them.

21 Their nobles shall be from among them,
And their governor shall come from their midst;
Then I will cause him to draw near,
And he shall approach Me;
For who *is* this who pledged his heart to approach Me?' says the LORD.

22 'You shall be My people,
And I will be your God.' "

23 Behold, the whirlwind of the LORD
Goes forth with fury,
A continuing whirlwind;
It will fall violently on the head of the wicked.

24 The fierce anger of the LORD will not return until He has done it,
And until He has performed the intents of His heart.

In the latter days you will consider it.

31 "At the same time," says the LORD, "I will be the God of all the families of Israel, and they shall be My people."

2 Thus says the LORD:

"The people who survived the sword
Found grace in the wilderness—
Israel, when I went to give him rest."

3 The LORD has appeared of old to me, *saying:*
"Yes, I have loved you with an everlasting love;
Therefore with lovingkindness I have drawn you.

4 Again I will build you, and you shall be rebuilt,
O virgin of Israel!
You shall again be adorned with your tambourines,
And shall go forth in the dances of those who rejoice.

5 You shall yet plant vines on the mountains of Samaria;
The planters shall plant and eat *them* as ordinary food.

6 For there shall be a day

The True Love
of a Father

Jeremiah 31:3

You miss so much of God's power when you parade yourself as self-sufficient. He longs to be your Hero. He longs to open doors you cannot open and move things you cannot move. He would do it just to see the gleam in your eye. He would do it just to hear your voice telling someone else how strong your Father is. He would do it just to express how deeply He is committed to your good! He has the power, and He longs to perform. He is greater than earthly fathers. We make vows we don't keep and promises that we fail to accomplish, but not the heavenly Father. He is able to perform at all times what He has promised in your life.

Yet, this wonderful Father understands how human you are. He knows you will fail. He knows you will stumble, and He will grieve with you when you are hurt or disappointed. He sees you as a clay pot. You are shaped into a doll and painted like a sunset, but you are still a clay pot—a human and a woman. It doesn't matter, He still loves you. You are His daughter! Never run from Him. He knows you inside and out. He already knows who you are, and He will love you when all others forsake you.

This is the Father's love. Do you realize that our Father loves you like that? He already knew you would fail and falter. He always knew you were human. He always knew that you would have struggles. No matter how well you were nurtured, there would still be areas that challenged you. He has sent me to tell you—even after all that has happened to you and with you and in you—that He has not changed His mind. He loves you still!

In this world of broken homes and trembling relationships, it is important that we don't lose complete understanding of a father's love. His strong arms pick you up when you are low. In those arms you nestle as he carries you to bed when sleep has claimed you on the couch. It is on his shoulder you weep when the tears can no longer be contained. His wisdom seems so sovereign, his compassion so pure. A real father is made for your protection. If you do not have that in a man, you do have it in your God. He is your Father.

When the watchmen will cry on
  Mount Ephraim,
'Arise, and let us go up *to* Zion,
To the LORD our God.' "

7 For thus says the LORD:

"Sing with gladness for Jacob,
  And shout among the chief of
    the nations;
Proclaim, give praise, and say,
'O LORD, save Your people,
The remnant of Israel!'
8 Behold, I will bring them from
    the north country,
And gather them from the ends
    of the earth,
Among them the blind and the
    lame,
The woman with child
And the one who labors with
    child, together;
A great throng shall return
    there.
9 They shall come with weeping,
  And with supplications I will
    lead them.
I will cause them to walk by the
    rivers of waters,
In a straight way in which they
    shall not stumble;
For I am a Father to Israel,
And Ephraim *is* My firstborn.

10 "Hear the word of the LORD, O
    nations,
And declare *it* in the isles afar
    off, and say,
'He who scattered Israel will
    gather him,
And keep him as a shepherd
    does his flock.'
11 For the LORD has redeemed
    Jacob,
And ransomed him from the
    hand of one stronger than he.
12 Therefore they shall come and
    sing in the height of Zion,
Streaming to the goodness of
    the LORD—
For wheat and new wine and
    oil,
For the young of the flock and
    the herd;
Their souls shall be like a well-
    watered garden,
And they shall sorrow no more
    at all.

13 "Then shall the virgin rejoice in
    the dance,

And the young men and the
  old, together;
For I will turn their mourning
  to joy,
Will comfort them,
And make them rejoice rather
  than sorrow.
14 I will satiate the soul of the
    priests with abundance,
And My people shall be
  satisfied with My goodness,
says the LORD."

15 Thus says the LORD:

"A voice was heard in Ramah,
Lamentation *and* bitter
  weeping,
Rachel weeping for her
  children,
Refusing to be comforted for
  her children,
Because they *are* no more."

16 Thus says the LORD:

"Refrain your voice from
  weeping,
And your eyes from tears;
For your work shall be
  rewarded, says the LORD,
And they shall come back from
  the land of the enemy.
17 There is hope in your future,
  says the LORD,
That *your* children shall come
  back to their own border.

18 "I have surely heard Ephraim
    bemoaning himself:
'You have chastised me, and I
  was chastised,
Like an untrained bull;
Restore me, and I will return,
For You *are* the LORD my God.
19 Surely, after my turning, I
  repented;
And after I was instructed, I
  struck myself on the thigh;
I was ashamed, yes, even
  humiliated,
Because I bore the reproach of
  my youth.'
20 *Is* Ephraim My dear son?
Is he a pleasant child?
For though I spoke against him,
I earnestly remember him
  still;
Therefore My heart yearns for
  him;
I will surely have mercy on
  him, says the LORD.

Gospel
Pearls

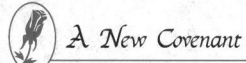

21 "Set up signposts,
Make landmarks;
Set your heart toward the
highway,
The way in *which* you went.
Turn back, O virgin of Israel,
Turn back to these your cities.
22 How long will you gad about,
O you backsliding daughter?
For the LORD has created a new
thing in the earth—
A woman shall encompass a
man."

23 Thus says the LORD of hosts, the God of Israel: "They shall again use this speech in the land of Judah and in its cities, when I bring back their captivity: 'The LORD bless you, O home of justice, *and* mountain of holiness!' 24 And there shall dwell in Judah itself, and in all its cities together, farmers and those going out with flocks. 25 For I have satiated the weary soul, and I have replenished every sorrowful soul."

26 After this I awoke and looked around, and my sleep was sweet to me.

27 "Behold, the days are coming, says the LORD, that I will sow the house of Israel and the house of Judah with the seed of man and the seed of beast. 28 And it shall come to pass, *that* as I have watched over them to pluck up, to break down, to throw down, to destroy, and to afflict, so I will watch over them to build and to plant, says the LORD. 29 In those days they shall say no more:

'The fathers have eaten sour
grapes,
And the children's teeth are set
on edge.'

30 But every one shall die for his own iniquity; every man who eats the sour grapes, his teeth shall be set on edge.

31 "Behold, the days are coming, says the LORD, when I will make a new covenant with the house of Israel and with the house of Judah— 32 not according to the covenant that I made with their fathers in the day *that* I took them by the hand to lead them out of the land of Egypt, My covenant which they broke, though I was a husband to them,^a says the

LORD. 33 But this *is* the covenant that I will make with the house of Israel after those days, says the LORD: I will put My law in their minds, and write it on their hearts; and I will be their God, and they shall be My people. 34 No more shall every man teach his neighbor, and every man his brother, saying, 'Know the LORD,' for they all shall know Me, from the least of them to the greatest of them, says the LORD. For I will forgive their iniquity, and their sin I will remember no more."

35 Thus says the LORD,
Who gives the sun for a light
by day,
The ordinances of the moon
and the stars for a light by
night,
Who disturbs the sea,
And its waves roar
(The LORD of hosts *is* His
name):

36 "If those ordinances depart
From before Me, says the LORD,
Then the seed of Israel shall
also cease
From being a nation before Me
forever."

37 Thus says the LORD:

"If heaven above can be
measured,
And the foundations of the
earth searched out beneath,
I will also cast off all the seed
of Israel
For all that they have done,
says the LORD.

38 "Behold, the days are coming, says the LORD, that the city shall be built for the LORD from the Tower of Hananel to the Corner Gate. 39 The surveyor's line shall again extend straight forward over the hill Gareb; then it shall turn toward Goath. 40 And the whole valley of the dead bodies and of the ashes, and all the fields as far as the Brook Kidron, to the corner of the Horse Gate toward the east, *shall be* holy to the LORD. It shall not be plucked up or thrown down anymore forever."

31:32 ^aFollowing Masoretic Text, Targum, and Vulgate; Septuagint and Syriac read *and I turned away from them.*

*Y*ou are the doors of life. Be careful what you let come through you. Close the doors to the planting of the enemy. Then know that when travail comes into your spirit, it's because you're going to give birth.

32 The word that came to Jeremiah from the LORD in the tenth year of Zedekiah king of Judah, which was the eighteenth year of Nebuchadnezzar. 2 For then the king of Babylon's army besieged Jerusalem, and Jeremiah the prophet was shut up in the court of the prison, which *was* in the king of Judah's house. 3 For Zedekiah king of Judah had shut him up, saying, "Why do you prophesy and say, 'Thus says the LORD: "Behold, I will give this city into the hand of the king of Babylon, and he shall take it; 4 and Zedekiah king of Judah shall not escape from the hand of the Chaldeans, but shall surely be delivered into the hand of the king of Babylon, and shall speak with him face to face,[a] and see him eye to eye; 5 then he shall lead Zedekiah to Babylon, and there he shall be until I visit him," says the LORD; "though you fight with the Chaldeans, you shall not succeed" '?"

6 And Jeremiah said, "The word of the LORD came to me, saying, 7 'Behold, Hanamel the son of Shallum your uncle will come to you, saying, "Buy my field which *is* in Anathoth, for the right of redemption *is* yours to buy *it*." ' 8 Then Hanamel my uncle's son came to me in the court of the prison according to the word of the LORD, and said to me, 'Please buy my field that *is* in Anathoth, which *is* in the country of Benjamin; for the right of inheritance *is* yours, and the redemption yours; buy *it* for yourself.' Then I knew that this was the word of the LORD. 9 So I bought the field from Hanamel, the son of my uncle who *was* in Anathoth, and weighed *out to* him the money—seventeen shekels of silver. 10 And I signed the deed and sealed *it*, took witnesses, and weighed the money on the scales. 11 So I took the purchase deed, *both* that which was sealed *according* to the law and custom, and that which was open; 12 and I gave the purchase deed to Baruch the son of Neriah, son of Mahseiah, in the presence of Hanamel my uncle's *son*, and in the presence of the witnesses who signed the purchase deed, before all the Jews who sat in the court of the prison. 13 "Then I charged Baruch before them, saying, 14 'Thus says the LORD of hosts, the God of Israel: "Take these deeds, both this purchase deed which is sealed and this deed which is open, and put them in an earthen vessel, that they may last many days." 15 For thus says the LORD of hosts, the God of Israel: "Houses and fields and vineyards shall be possessed again in this land." '

16 "Now when I had delivered the purchase deed to Baruch the son of Neriah, I prayed to the LORD, saying: 17 'Ah, Lord GOD! Behold, You have made the heavens and the earth by Your great power and outstretched arm. There is nothing too hard for You. 18 *You* show lovingkindness to thousands, and repay the iniquity of the fathers into the bosom of their children after them—the Great, the Mighty God, whose name *is* the LORD of hosts. 19 *You are* great in counsel and mighty in work, for your eyes *are* open to all the ways of the sons of men, to give everyone according to his ways and according to the fruit of his doings. 20 You have set signs and wonders in the land of Egypt, to this day, and in Israel and among *other* men; and You have made Yourself a name, as it is this day. 21 You have brought Your people Israel out of the land of Egypt with signs and wonders, with a strong hand and an outstretched arm, and with great terror; 22 You have given them this land, of which You swore to their fathers to give them—"a land flowing with milk and honey."[a] 23 And they came in and took possession of it, but they have not obeyed Your voice or walked in Your law. They have done nothing of all that You commanded them to do; therefore You have caused all this calamity to come upon them. 24 'Look, the siege mounds! They have come to the city to take it; and the city has been given into the hand of the Chaldeans who fight against it, because of the sword and famine and pestilence. What You have spoken has happened; there You see *it!* 25 And You have said to me, O Lord GOD, "Buy the field for money, and take witnesses"!—yet the city has been given into the hand of the Chaldeans.' "

26 Then the word of the LORD came to Jeremiah, saying, 27 "Behold, I

32:4 [a]Literally *mouth to mouth*   32:22 [a]Exodus 3:8

Gospel Pearls

am the LORD, the God of all flesh. Is there anything too hard for Me? 28 Therefore thus says the LORD: 'Behold, I will give this city into the hand of the Chaldeans, into the hand of Nebuchadnezzar king of Babylon, and he shall take it. 29 And the Chaldeans who fight against this city shall come and set fire to this city and burn it, with the houses on whose roofs they have offered incense to Baal and poured out drink offerings to other gods, to provoke Me to anger; 30 because the children of Israel and the children of Judah have done only evil before Me from their youth. For the children of Israel have provoked Me only to anger with the work of their hands,' says the LORD. 31 'For this city has been to Me *a provocation of* My anger and My fury from the day that they built it, even to this day; so I will remove it from before My face 32 because of all the evil of the children of Israel and the children of Judah, which they have done to provoke Me to anger—they, their kings, their princes, their priests, their prophets, the men of Judah, and the inhabitants of Jerusalem. 33 And they have turned to Me the back, and not the face; though I taught them, rising up early and teaching *them,* yet they have not listened to receive instruction. 34 But they set their abominations in the house which is called by My name, to defile it. 35 And they built the high places of Baal which *are* in the Valley of the Son of Hinnom, to cause their sons and their daughters to pass through *the fire* to Molech, which I did not command them, nor did it come into My mind that they should do this abomination, to cause Judah to sin.'

36 "Now therefore, thus says the LORD, the God of Israel, concerning this city of which you say, 'It shall be delivered into the hand of the king of Babylon by the sword, by the famine, and by the pestilence: 37 Behold, I will gather them out of all countries where I have driven them in My anger, in My fury, and in great wrath; I will bring them back to this place, and I will cause them to dwell safely. 38 They shall be My people, and I will be their God; 39 then I will give them one heart and one way, that they may

fear Me forever, for the good of them and their children after them. 40 And I will make an everlasting covenant with them, that I will not turn away from doing them good; but I will put My fear in their hearts so that they will not depart from Me. 41 Yes, I will rejoice over them to do them good, and I will assuredly plant them in this land, with all My heart and with all My soul.'

42 "For thus says the LORD: 'Just as I have brought all this great calamity on this people, so I will bring on them all the good that I have promised them. 43 And fields will be bought in this land of which you say, "*It is* desolate, without man or beast; it has been given into the hand of the Chaldeans." 44 Men will buy fields for money, sign deeds and seal *them,* and take witnesses, in the land of Benjamin, in the places around Jerusalem, in the cities of Judah, in the cities of the mountains, in the cities of the lowland, and in the cities of the South; for I will cause their captives to return,' says the LORD."

33 Moreover the word of the LORD came to Jeremiah a second time, while he was still shut up in the court of the prison, saying, 2 "Thus says the LORD who made it, the LORD who formed it to establish it (the LORD *is* His name): 3 'Call to Me, and I will answer you, and show you great and mighty things, which you do not know.'

4 "For thus says the LORD, the God of Israel, concerning the houses of this city and the houses of the kings of Judah, which have been pulled down *to fortify*[a] against the siege mounds and the sword: 5 'They come to fight with the Chaldeans, but *only* to fill their places[a] with the dead bodies of men whom I will slay in My anger and My fury, all for whose wickedness I have hidden My face from this city. 6 Behold, I will bring it health and healing; I will heal them and reveal to them the abundance of peace and truth. 7 And I will cause the captives of Judah and the captives of Israel to return, and will rebuild those places as at the first. 8 I will cleanse them from all their iniquity by which they have sinned against Me, and I will pardon all their

33:4 aCompare Isaiah 22:10   33:5 aCompare 2 Kings 23:14

When you see sorrow multiply, it is a sign that God is getting ready to send something to you. Don't settle for the pain and not get the benefit. Hold out. Disregard the pain and get the promise.

iniquities by which they have sinned and by which they have transgressed against Me. 9 Then it shall be to Me a name of joy, a praise, and an honor before all nations of the earth, who shall hear all the good that I do to them; they shall fear and tremble for all the goodness and all the prosperity that I provide for it.'

10 "Thus says the LORD: 'Again there shall be heard in this place— of which you say, "It *is* desolate, without man and without beast"—in the cities of Judah, in the streets of Jerusalem that are desolate, without man and without inhabitant and without beast, 11 the voice of joy and the voice of gladness, the voice of the bridegroom and the voice of the bride, the voice of those who will say:

> "Praise the LORD of hosts,
> For the LORD *is* good,
> For His mercy *endures*
>   forever"—

and of those *who will* bring the sacrifice of praise into the house of the LORD. For I will cause the captives of the land to return as at the first,' says the LORD.

12 "Thus says the LORD of hosts: 'In this place which is desolate, without man and without beast, and in all its cities, there shall again be a dwelling place of shepherds causing *their* flocks to lie down. 13 In the cities of the mountains, in the cities of the lowland, in the cities of the South, in the land of Benjamin, in the places around Jerusalem, and in the cities of Judah, the flocks shall again pass under the hands of him who counts *them,*' says the LORD.

14 'Behold, the days are coming,' says the LORD, 'that I will perform that good thing which I have promised to the house of Israel and to the house of Judah:

15 'In those days and at that time
   I will cause to grow up to David
   A Branch of righteousness;
   He shall execute judgment and
      righteousness in the earth.
16 In those days Judah will be
      saved,
   And Jerusalem will dwell
      safely.

And this *is the name* by which she will be called:

THE LORD OUR RIGHTEOUSNESS.'ᵃ

17 "For thus says the LORD: 'David shall never lack a man to sit on the throne of the house of Israel; 18 nor shall the priests, the Levites, lack a man to offer burnt offerings before Me, to kindle grain offerings, and to sacrifice continually.' "

19 And the word of the LORD came to Jeremiah, saying, 20 "Thus says the LORD: 'If you can break My covenant with the day and My covenant with the night, so that there will not be day and night in their season, 21 then My covenant may also be broken with David My servant, so that he shall not have a son to reign on his throne, and with the Levites, the priests, My ministers. 22 As the host of heaven cannot be numbered, nor the sand of the sea measured, so will I multiply the descendants of David My servant and the Levites who minister to Me.' "

23 Moreover the word of the LORD came to Jeremiah, saying, 24 "Have you not considered what these people have spoken, saying, 'The two families which the LORD has chosen, He has also cast them off '? Thus they have despised My people, as if they should no more be a nation before them.

25 "Thus says the LORD: 'If My covenant *is* not with day and night, *and if* I have not appointed the ordinances of heaven and earth, 26 then I will cast away the descendants of Jacob and David My servant, *so* that I will not take *any* of his descendants *to be* rulers over the descendants of Abraham, Isaac, and Jacob. For I will cause their captives to return, and will have mercy on them.' "

34 The word which came to Jeremiah from the LORD, when Nebuchadnezzar king of Babylon and all his army, all the kingdoms of the earth under his dominion, and all the people, fought against Jerusalem and all its cities, saying, 2 "Thus says the LORD, the God of Israel: 'Go and speak to Zedekiah king

33:16 ᵃCompare 23:5, 6

Gospel Pearls

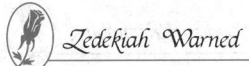
of Judah and tell him, "Thus says the LORD: 'Behold, I will give this city into the hand of the king of Babylon, and he shall burn it with fire. 3 And you shall not escape from his hand, but shall surely be taken and delivered into his hand; your eyes shall see the eyes of the king of Babylon, he shall speak with you face to face,*a* and you shall go to Babylon.' " ' 4 Yet hear the word of the LORD, O Zedekiah king of Judah! Thus says the LORD concerning you: 'You shall not die by the sword. 5 You shall die in peace; as in the ceremonies of your fathers, the former kings who were before you, so they shall burn incense for you and lament for you, *saying*, "Alas, lord!" For I have pronounced the word, says the LORD.' "

6 Then Jeremiah the prophet spoke all these words to Zedekiah king of Judah in Jerusalem, 7 when the king of Babylon's army fought against Jerusalem and all the cities of Judah that were left, against Lachish and Azekah; for *only* these fortified cities remained of the cities of Judah.

8 *This is* the word that came to Jeremiah from the LORD, after King Zedekiah had made a covenant with all the people who *were* at Jerusalem to proclaim liberty to them: 9 that every man should set free his male and female slave—a Hebrew man or woman—that no one should keep a Jewish brother in bondage. 10 Now when all the princes and all the people, who had entered into the covenant, heard that everyone should set free his male and female slaves, that no one should keep them in bondage anymore, they obeyed and let *them* go. 11 But afterward they changed their minds and made the male and female slaves return, whom they had set free, and brought them into subjection as male and female slaves.

12 Therefore the word of the LORD came to Jeremiah from the LORD, saying, 13 "Thus says the LORD, the God of Israel: 'I made a covenant with your fathers in the day that I brought them out of the land of Egypt, out of the house of bondage, saying, 14 "At the end of seven years let every man set free his Hebrew brother, who has been sold to him; and when he has served you six years, you shall let him go free from you." But your fathers did not obey Me nor incline their ear. 15 Then you recently turned and did what was right in My sight—every man proclaiming liberty to his neighbor; and you made a covenant before Me in the house which is called by My name. 16 Then you turned around and profaned My name, and every one of you brought back his male and female slaves, whom he had set at liberty, at their pleasure, and brought them back into subjection, to be your male and female slaves.'

17 "Therefore thus says the LORD: 'You have not obeyed Me in proclaiming liberty, every one to his brother and every one to his neighbor. Behold, I proclaim liberty to you,' says the LORD—'to the sword, to pestilence, and to famine! And I will deliver you to trouble among all the kingdoms of the earth. 18 And I will give the men who have transgressed My covenant, who have not performed the words of the covenant which they made before Me, when they cut the calf in two and passed between the parts of it— 19 the princes of Judah, the princes of Jerusalem, the eunuchs, the priests, and all the people of the land who passed between the parts of the calf— 20 I will give them into the hand of their enemies and into the hand of those who seek their life. Their dead bodies shall be for meat for the birds of the heaven and the beasts of the earth. 21 And I will give Zedekiah king of Judah and his princes into the hand of their enemies, into the hand of those who seek their life, and into the hand of the king of Babylon's army which has gone back from you. 22 Behold, I will command,' says the LORD, 'and cause them to return to this city. They will fight against it and take it and burn it with fire; and I will make the cities of Judah a desolation without inhabitant.' "

35 The word which came to Jeremiah from the LORD in the days of Jehoiakim the son of Josiah, king of Judah, saying, 2 "Go to the house of the Rechabites, speak to them, and bring them into the house of the

34:3 *a*Literally *mouth to mouth*

*Y*ou are holding on to the wrong thing if all you do is concentrate on past pain. Release the pain. Pain doesn't fall off on its own. It's got to be released. *Release* the pain.

LORD, into one of the chambers, and give them wine to drink."

3 Then I took Jaazaniah the son of Jeremiah, the son of Habazziniah, his brothers and all his sons, and the whole house of the Rechabites, 4 and I brought them into the house of the LORD, into the chamber of the sons of Hanan the son of Igdaliah, a man of God, which *was* by the chamber of the princes, above the chamber of Maaseiah the son of Shallum, the keeper of the door. 5 Then I set before the sons of the house of the Rechabites bowls full of wine, and cups; and I said to them, "Drink wine."

6 But they said, "We will drink no wine, for Jonadab the son of Rechab, our father, commanded us, saying, 'You shall drink no wine, you nor your sons, forever. 7 You shall not build a house, sow seed, plant a vineyard, nor have *any of these;* but all your days you shall dwell in tents, that you may live many days in the land where you are sojourners.' 8 Thus we have obeyed the voice of Jonadab the son of Rechab, our father, in all that he charged us, to drink no wine all our days, we, our wives, our sons, or our daughters, 9 nor to build ourselves houses to dwell in; nor do we have vineyard, field, or seed. 10 But we have dwelt in tents, and have obeyed and done according to all that Jonadab our father commanded us. 11 But it came to pass, when Nebuchadnezzar king of Babylon came up into the land, that we said, 'Come, let us go to Jerusalem for fear of the army of the Chaldeans and for fear of the army of the Syrians.' So we dwell at Jerusalem."

12 Then came the word of the LORD to Jeremiah, saying, 13 "Thus says the LORD of hosts, the God of Israel: 'Go and tell the men of Judah and the inhabitants of Jerusalem, "Will you not receive instruction to obey My words?" says the LORD. 14 "The words of Jonadab the son of Rechab, which he commanded his sons, not to drink wine, are performed; for to this day they drink none, and obey their father's commandment. But although I have spoken to you, rising early and speaking, you did not obey Me. 15 I have also sent to you all My servants the prophets, rising up early and sending *them,* saying, 'Turn now everyone from his evil way, amend your doings, and do not go after other gods to serve them; then you will dwell in the land which I have given you and your fathers.' But you have not inclined your ear, nor obeyed Me. 16 Surely the sons of Jonadab the son of Rechab have performed the commandment of their father, which he commanded them, but this people has not obeyed Me." '

17 "Therefore thus says the LORD God of hosts, the God of Israel: 'Behold, I will bring on Judah and on all the inhabitants of Jerusalem all the doom that I have pronounced against them; because I have spoken to them but they have not heard, and I have called to them but they have not answered.' "

18 And Jeremiah said to the house of the Rechabites, "Thus says the LORD of hosts, the God of Israel: 'Because you have obeyed the commandment of Jonadab your father, and kept all his precepts and done according to all that he commanded you, 19 therefore thus says the LORD of hosts, the God of Israel: "Jonadab the son of Rechab shall not lack a man to stand before Me forever." ' "

36 Now it came to pass in the fourth year of Jehoiakim the son of Josiah, king of Judah, *that* this word came to Jeremiah from the LORD, saying: 2 "Take a scroll of a book and write on it all the words that I have spoken to you against Israel, against Judah, and against all the nations, from the day I spoke to you, from the days of Josiah even to this day. 3 It may be that the house of Judah will hear all the adversities which I purpose to bring upon them, that everyone may turn from his evil way, that I may forgive their iniquity and their sin."

4 Then Jeremiah called Baruch the son of Neriah; and Baruch wrote on a scroll of a book, at the instruction of Jeremiah,ᵃ all the words of the LORD which He had spoken to him. 5 And Jeremiah commanded Baruch, saying, "I *am* confined, I cannot go into the house of the LORD. 6 You go, therefore, and read from the scroll which you have written at my in-

36:4 ᵃLiterally *from Jeremiah's mouth*

Gospel Pearls

struction,[a] the words of the LORD, in the hearing of the people in the LORD's house on the day of fasting. And you shall also read them in the hearing of all Judah who come from their cities. 7 It may be that they will present their supplication before the LORD, and everyone will turn from his evil way. For great *is* the anger and the fury that the LORD has pronounced against this people." 8 And Baruch the son of Neriah did according to all that Jeremiah the prophet commanded him, reading from the book the words of the LORD in the LORD's house.

9 Now it came to pass in the fifth year of Jehoiakim the son of Josiah, king of Judah, in the ninth month, *that* they proclaimed a fast before the LORD to all the people in Jerusalem, and to all the people who came from the cities of Judah to Jerusalem. 10 Then Baruch read from the book the words of Jeremiah in the house of the LORD, in the chamber of Gemariah the son of Shaphan the scribe, in the upper court at the entry of the New Gate of the LORD's house, in the hearing of all the people.

11 When Michaiah the son of Gemariah, the son of Shaphan, heard all the words of the LORD from the book, 12 he then went down to the king's house, into the scribe's chamber; and there all the princes were sitting—Elishama the scribe, Delaiah the son of Shemaiah, Elnathan the son of Achbor, Gemariah the son of Shaphan, Zedekiah the son of Hananiah, and all the princes. 13 Then Michaiah declared to them all the words that he had heard when Baruch read the book in the hearing of the people. 14 Therefore all the princes sent Jehudi the son of Nethaniah, the son of Shelemiah, the son of Cushi, to Baruch, saying, "Take in your hand the scroll from which you have read in the hearing of the people, and come." So Baruch the son of Neriah took the scroll in his hand and came to them. 15 And they said to him, "Sit down now, and read it in our hearing." So Baruch read *it* in their hearing.

16 Now it happened, when they had heard all the words, that they looked in fear from one to another, and said to Baruch, "We will surely tell the king of all these words." 17 And they asked Baruch, saying, "Tell us now, how did you write all these words—at his instruction?"[a]

18 So Baruch answered them, "He proclaimed with his mouth all these words to me, and I wrote *them* with ink in the book."

19 Then the princes said to Baruch, "Go and hide, you and Jeremiah; and let no one know where you are."

20 And they went to the king, into the court; but they stored the scroll in the chamber of Elishama the scribe, and told all the words in the hearing of the king. 21 So the king sent Jehudi to bring the scroll, and he took it from Elishama the scribe's chamber. And Jehudi read it in the hearing of the king and in the hearing of all the princes who stood beside the king. 22 Now the king was sitting in the winter house in the ninth month, with *a* fire burning on the hearth before him. 23 And it happened, when Jehudi had read three or four columns, *that the king* cut it with the scribe's knife and cast *it* into the fire that *was* on the hearth, until all the scroll was consumed in the fire that *was* on the hearth. 24 Yet they were not afraid, nor did they tear their garments, the king nor any of his servants who heard all these words. 25 Nevertheless Elnathan, Delaiah, and Gemariah implored the king not to burn the scroll; but he would not listen to them. 26 And the king commanded Jerahmeel the king's[a] son, Seraiah the son of Azriel, and Shelemiah the son of Abdeel, to seize Baruch the scribe and Jeremiah the prophet, but the LORD hid them.

27 Now after the king had burned the scroll with the words which Baruch had written at the instruction of Jeremiah,[a] the word of the LORD came to Jeremiah, saying: 28 "Take yet another scroll, and write on it all the former words that were in the first scroll which Jehoiakim the king of Judah has burned. 29 And you shall say to Jehoiakim king of Judah, 'Thus says the LORD: "You have burned this scroll, saying, 'Why have you written in it that the king of Babylon will certainly come and destroy this land, and cause man

36:6 [a]Literally *from my mouth*   36:17 [a]Literally *with his mouth*   36:26 [a]Hebrew *Hammelech*
36:27 [a]Literally *from Jeremiah's mouth*

*U*ntil the desire to go forward becomes greater than the memories of past pain, you will never hold the power to create again. However, when the desire comes back into your spirit and begins to live in you again, it will release you from the pain.

and beast to cease from here?' "
30 Therefore thus says the LORD concerning Jehoiakim king of Judah: "He shall have no one to sit on the throne of David, and his dead body shall be cast out to the heat of the day and the frost of the night. 31 I will punish him, his family, and his servants for their iniquity; and I will bring on them, on the inhabitants of Jerusalem, and on the men of Judah all the doom that I have pronounced against them; but they did not heed." ' "

32 Then Jeremiah took another scroll and gave it to Baruch the scribe, the son of Neriah, who wrote on it at the instruction of Jeremiah[a] all the words of the book which Jehoiakim king of Judah had burned in the fire. And besides, there were added to them many similar words.

37 Now King Zedekiah the son of Josiah reigned instead of Coniah the son of Jehoiakim, whom Nebuchadnezzar king of Babylon made king in the land of Judah. 2 But neither he nor his servants nor the people of the land gave heed to the words of the LORD which He spoke by the prophet Jeremiah.

3 And Zedekiah the king sent Jehucal the son of Shelemiah, and Zephaniah the son of Maaseiah, the priest, to the prophet Jeremiah, saying, "Pray now to the LORD our God for us." 4 Now Jeremiah was coming and going among the people, for they had not *yet* put him in prison. 5 Then Pharaoh's army came up from Egypt; and when the Chaldeans who were besieging Jerusalem heard news of them, they departed from Jerusalem.

6 Then the word of the LORD came to the prophet Jeremiah, saying, 7 "Thus says the LORD, the God of Israel, 'Thus you shall say to the king of Judah, who sent you to Me to inquire of Me: "Behold, Pharaoh's army which has come up to help you will return to Egypt, to their own land. 8 And the Chaldeans shall come back and fight against this city, and take it and burn it with fire." ' 9 Thus says the LORD: 'Do not deceive yourselves, saying, "The Chaldeans will surely depart from us," for they will not depart. 10 For though you

had defeated the whole army of the Chaldeans who fight against you, and there remained *only* wounded men among them, they would rise up, every man in his tent, and burn the city with fire.' "

11 And it happened, when the army of the Chaldeans left the siege of Jerusalem for fear of Pharaoh's army, 12 that Jeremiah went out of Jerusalem to go into the land of Benjamin to claim his property there among the people. 13 And when he was in the Gate of Benjamin, a captain of the guard *was* there whose name *was* Irijah the son of Shelemiah, the son of Hananiah; and he seized Jeremiah the prophet, saying, "You are defecting to the Chaldeans!"

14 Then Jeremiah said, "False! I am not defecting to the Chaldeans." But he did not listen to him.

So Irijah seized Jeremiah and brought him to the princes. 15 Therefore the princes were angry with Jeremiah, and they struck him and put him in prison in the house of Jonathan the scribe. For they had made that the prison.

16 When Jeremiah entered the dungeon and the cells, and Jeremiah had remained there many days, 17 then Zedekiah the king sent and took him *out*. The king asked him secretly in his house, and said, "Is there *any* word from the LORD?"

And Jeremiah said, "There is." Then he said, "You shall be delivered into the hand of the king of Babylon!"

18 Moreover Jeremiah said to King Zedekiah, "What offense have I committed against you, against your servants, or against this people, that you have put me in prison? 19 Where now *are* your prophets who prophesied to you, saying, 'The king of Babylon will not come against you or against this land?' 20 Therefore please hear now, O my lord the king. Please, let my petition be accepted before you, and do not make me return to the house of Jonathan the scribe, lest I die there."

21 Then Zedekiah the king commanded that they should commit Jeremiah to the court of the prison, and that they should give him daily a piece of bread from the bakers' street, until all the bread in the city

36:32 [a]Literally *from Jeremiah's mouth*

Gospel Pearls

was gone. Thus Jeremiah remained in the court of the prison.

38 Now Shephatiah the son of Mattan, Gedaliah the son of Pashhur, Jucal[a] the son of Shelemiah, and Pashhur the son of Malchiah heard the words that Jeremiah had spoken to all the people, saying, 2 "Thus says the LORD: 'He who remains in this city shall die by the sword, by famine, and by pestilence; but he who goes over to the Chaldeans shall live; his life shall be as a prize to him, and he shall live.'[a] 3 Thus says the LORD: 'This city shall surely be given into the hand of the king of Babylon's army, which shall take it.'"

4 Therefore the princes said to the king, "Please, let this man be put to death, for thus he weakens the hands of the men of war who remain in this city, and the hands of all the people, by speaking such words to them. For this man does not seek the welfare of this people, but their harm." 5 Then Zedekiah the king said, "Look, he is in your hand. For the king can do nothing against you." 6 So they took Jeremiah and cast him into the dungeon of Malchiah the king's[a] son, which was in the court of the prison, and they let Jeremiah down with ropes. And in the dungeon there was no water, but mire. So Jeremiah sank in the mire.

7 Now Ebed-Melech the Ethiopian, one of the eunuchs, who was in the king's house, heard that they had put Jeremiah in the dungeon. When the king was sitting at the Gate of Benjamin, 8 Ebed-Melech went out of the king's house and spoke to the king, saying, 9 "My lord the king, these men have done evil in all that they have done to Jeremiah the prophet, whom they have cast into the dungeon, and he is likely to die from hunger in the place where he is. For there is no more bread in the city." 10 Then the king commanded Ebed-Melech the Ethiopian, saying, "Take from here thirty men with you, and lift Jeremiah the prophet out of the dungeon before he dies." 11 So Ebed-Melech took the men with him and went into the house of the king under the treasury, and took from there old clothes and old rags, and let them down by ropes into the dungeon to

Jeremiah. 12 Then Ebed-Melech the Ethiopian said to Jeremiah, "Please put these old clothes and rags under your armpits, under the ropes." And Jeremiah did so. 13 So they pulled Jeremiah up with ropes and lifted him out of the dungeon. And Jeremiah remained in the court of the prison.

14 Then Zedekiah the king sent and had Jeremiah the prophet brought to him at the third entrance of the house of the LORD. And the king said to Jeremiah, "I will ask you something. Hide nothing from me." 15 Jeremiah said to Zedekiah, "If I declare it to you, will you not surely put me to death? And if I give you advice, you will not listen to me." 16 So Zedekiah the king swore secretly to Jeremiah, saying, "As the LORD lives, who made our very souls, I will not put you to death, nor will I give you into the hand of these men who seek your life."

17 Then Jeremiah said to Zedekiah, "Thus says the LORD, the God of hosts, the God of Israel: 'If you surely surrender to the king of Babylon's princes, then your soul shall live; this city shall not be burned with fire, and you and your house shall live. 18 But if you do not surrender to the king of Babylon's princes, then this city shall be given into the hand of the Chaldeans; they shall burn it with fire, and you shall not escape from their hand.'" 19 And Zedekiah the king said to Jeremiah, "I am afraid of the Jews who have defected to the Chaldeans, lest they deliver me into their hand, and they abuse me." 20 But Jeremiah said, "They shall not deliver you. Please, obey the voice of the LORD which I speak to you. So it shall be well with you, and your soul shall live. 21 But if you refuse to surrender, this is the word that the LORD has shown me: 22 'Now behold, all the women who are left in the king of Judah's house shall be surrendered to the king of Babylon's princes, and those women shall say:

> "Your close friends have set upon you
> And prevailed against you;

38:1 [a]Same as Jehucal (compare 37:3)   38:2 [a]Compare 21:9   38:6 [a]Hebrew Hammelech

---

Vision is the desire to go ahead. Until you have a vision to go ahead, you will always live in yesterday's struggles. God is calling you to today.

Your feet have sunk in the
mire,
And they have turned away
again."

23 'So they shall surrender all your
wives and children to the Chaldeans.
You shall not escape from their hand,
but shall be taken by the hand of the
king of Babylon. And you shall cause
this city to be burned with fire.' "

24 Then Zedekiah said to Jeremiah,
"Let no one know of these words,
and you shall not die. 25 But if the
princes hear that I have talked with
you, and they come to you and say
to you, 'Declare to us now what you
have said to the king, and also what
the king said to you; do not hide *it*
from us, and we will not put you to
death,' 26 then you shall say to them,
'I presented my request before the
king, that he would not make me return to Jonathan's house to die
there.' "

27 Then all the princes came to
Jeremiah and asked him. And he told
them according to all these words
that the king had commanded. So
they stopped speaking with him, for
the conversation had not been heard.
28 Now Jeremiah remained in the
court of the prison until the day that
Jerusalem was taken. And he was
there when Jerusalem was taken.

39 In the ninth year of Zedekiah
king of Judah, in the tenth
month, Nebuchadnezzar king of
Babylon and all his army came
against Jerusalem, and besieged it.
2 In the eleventh year of Zedekiah,
in the fourth month, on the ninth *day*
of the month, the city was pene-
trated.

3 Then all the princes of the king
of Babylon came in and sat in the
Middle Gate: Nergal-Sharezer, Sam-
gar-Nebo, Sarsechim, Rabsaris,ª
Nergal-Sarezer, Rabmag,ᵇ with the
rest of the princes of the king of
Babylon.

4 So it was, when Zedekiah the
king of Judah and all the men of war
saw them, that they fled and went out
of the city by night, by way of the
king's garden, by the gate between
the two walls. And he went out by
way of the plain.ª 5 But the Chaldean

army pursued them and overtook
Zedekiah in the plains of Jericho.
And when they had captured him,
they brought him up to Nebuchadnezzar king of Babylon, to Riblah in
the land of Hamath, where he pronounced judgment on him. 6 Then
the king of Babylon killed the sons
of Zedekiah before his eyes in Riblah; the king of Babylon also killed
all the nobles of Judah. 7 Moreover
he put out Zedekiah's eyes, and
bound him with bronze fetters to
carry him off to Babylon. 8 And the
Chaldeans burned the king's house
and the houses of the people with
fire, and broke down the walls of Jerusalem. 9 Then Nebuzaradan the
captain of the guard carried away
captive to Babylon the remnant of
the people who remained in the city
and those who defected to him, with
the rest of the people who remained.
10 But Nebuzaradan the captain of
the guard left in the land of Judah
the poor people, who had nothing,
and gave them vineyards and fields
at the same time.

11 Now Nebuchadnezzar king of
Babylon gave charge concerning
Jeremiah to Nebuzaradan the captain of the guard, saying, 12 "Take
him and look after him, and do him
no harm; but do to him just as he says
to you." 13 So Nebuzaradan the captain of the guard sent Nebushasban,
Rabsaris, Nergal-Sharezer, Rabmag,
and all the king of Babylon's chief
officers; 14 then they sent *someone* to
take Jeremiah from the court of the
prison, and committed him to Gedaliah the son of Ahikam, the son of
Shaphan, that he should take him
home. So he dwelt among the people.

15 Meanwhile the word of the LORD
had come to Jeremiah while he was
shut up in the court of the prison,
saying, 16 "Go and speak to Ebed-
Melech the Ethiopian, saying, 'Thus
says the LORD of hosts, the God of
Israel: "Behold, I will bring My
words upon this city for adversity
and not for good, and they shall be
performed in that day before you.
17 But I will deliver you in that day,"
says the LORD, "and you shall not be
given into the hand of the men of
whom you *are* afraid. 18 For I will
surely deliver you, and you shall not

39:3 ªtitle, probably *Chief Officer;* also verse 13   ᵇA title, probably *Troop Commander;* also verse 13
39:4 ªOr *the arabah,* that is, the Jordan Valley

Gospel Pearls

fall by the sword; but your life shall be as a prize to you, because you have put your trust in Me," says the LORD.' "

40 The word that came to Jeremiah from the LORD after Nebuzaradan the captain of the guard had let him go from Ramah, when he had taken him bound in chains among all who were carried away captive from Jerusalem and Judah, who were carried away captive to Babylon.

2 And the captain of the guard took Jeremiah and said to him: "The LORD your God has pronounced this doom on this place. 3 Now the LORD has brought *it,* and has done just as He said. Because you *people* have sinned against the LORD, and not obeyed His voice, therefore this thing has come upon you. 4 And now look, I free you this day from the chains that *were* on your hand. If it seems good to you to come with me to Babylon, come, and I will look after you. But if it seems wrong for you to come with me to Babylon, remain here. See, all the land *is* before you; wherever it seems good and convenient for you to go, go there."

5 Now while Jeremiah had not yet gone back, *Nebuzaradan said,* "Go back to Gedaliah the son of Ahikam, the son of Shaphan, whom the king of Babylon has made governor over the cities of Judah, and dwell with him among the people. Or go wherever it seems convenient for you to go." So the captain of the guard gave him rations and a gift and let him go. 6 Then Jeremiah went to Gedaliah the son of Ahikam, to Mizpah, and dwelt with him among the people who were left in the land.

7 And when all the captains of the armies who *were* in the fields, they and their men, heard that the king of Babylon had made Gedaliah the son of Ahikam governor in the land, and had committed to him men, women, children, and the poorest of the land who had not been carried away captive to Babylon, 8 then they came to Gedaliah at Mizpah—Ishmael the son of Nethaniah, Johanan and Jonathan the sons of Kareah, Seraiah the son of Tanhumeth, the sons of Ephai the Netophathite, and Jezaniah[a] the son of a Maachathite, they and their men. 9 And Gedaliah the son of Ahikam, the son of Shaphan, took an oath before them and their men, saying, "Do not be afraid to serve the Chaldeans. Dwell in the land and serve the king of Babylon, and it shall be well with you. 10 As for me, I will indeed dwell at Mizpah and serve the Chaldeans who come to us. But you, gather wine and summer fruit and oil, put *them* in your vessels, and dwell in your cities that you have taken." 11 Likewise, when all the Jews who *were* in Moab, among the Ammonites, in Edom, and who *were* in all the countries, heard that the king of Babylon had left a remnant of Judah, and that he had set over them Gedaliah the son of Ahikam, the son of Shaphan, 12 then all the Jews returned out of all places where they had been driven, and came to the land of Judah, to Gedaliah at Mizpah, and gathered wine and summer fruit in abundance.

13 Moreover Johanan the son of Kareah and all the captains of the forces that *were* in the fields came to Gedaliah at Mizpah, 14 and said to him, "Do you certainly know that Baalis the king of the Ammonites has sent Ishmael the son of Nethaniah to murder you?" But Gedaliah the son of Ahikam did not believe them.

15 Then Johanan the son of Kareah spoke secretly to Gedaliah in Mizpah, saying, "Let me go, please, and I will kill Ishmael the son of Nethaniah, and no one will know *it.* Why should he murder you, so that all the Jews who are gathered to you would be scattered, and the remnant in Judah perish?"

16 But Gedaliah the son of Ahikam said to Johanan the son of Kareah, "You shall not do this thing, for you speak falsely concerning Ishmael."

41 Now it came to pass in the seventh month *that* Ishmael the son of Nethaniah, the son of Elishama, of the royal family and of the officers of the king, came with ten men to Gedaliah the son of Ahikam, at Mizpah. And there they ate bread together in Mizpah. 2 Then Ishmael the son of Nethaniah, and the ten men who were with him, arose and

40:8 *a*Spelled *Jaazaniah* in 2 Kings 25:23

God wants to put desire in the spirit of broken women. There wouldn't be any desire if there weren't any relationship. The very fact that you have a desire is in itself an indication that better days are coming.

struck Gedaliah the son of Ahikam, the son of Shaphan, with the sword, and killed him whom the king of Babylon had made governor over the land. 3 Ishmael also struck down all the Jews who were with him, *that is,* with Gedaliah at Mizpah, and the Chaldeans who were found there, the men of war.

4 And it happened, on the second day after he had killed Gedaliah, when as yet no one knew *it,* 5 that certain men came from Shechem, from Shiloh, and from Samaria, eighty men with their beards shaved and their clothes torn, having cut themselves, with offerings and incense in their hand, to bring *them* to the house of the LORD. 6 Now Ishmael the son of Nethaniah went out from Mizpah to meet them, weeping as he went along; and it happened as he met them that he said to them, "Come to Gedaliah the son of Ahikam!" 7 So it was, when they came into the midst of the city, that Ishmael the son of Nethaniah killed them *and cast them* into the midst of a pit, he and the men who were with him. 8 But ten men were found among them who said to Ishmael, "Do not kill us, for we have treasures of wheat, barley, oil, and honey in the field." So he desisted and did not kill them among their brethren. 9 Now the pit into which Ishmael had cast all the dead bodies of the men whom he had slain, because of Gedaliah, *was* the same one Asa the king had made for fear of Baasha king of Israel. Ishmael the son of Nethaniah filled it with *the* slain. 10 Then Ishmael carried away captive all the rest of the people who *were* in Mizpah, the king's daughters and all the people who remained in Mizpah, whom Nebuzaradan the captain of the guard had committed to Gedaliah the son of Ahikam. And Ishmael the son of Nethaniah carried them away captive and departed to go over to the Ammonites.

11 But when Johanan the son of Kareah and all the captains of the forces that *were* with him heard of all the evil that Ishmael the son of Nethaniah had done, 12 they took all the men and went to fight with Ishmael the son of Nethaniah; and they found him by the great pool that *is* in Gibeon. 13 So it was, when all the people who *were* with Ishmael saw Jo-

hanan the son of Kareah, and all the captains of the forces who *were* with him, that they were glad. 14 Then all the people whom Ishmael had carried away captive from Mizpah turned around and came back, and went to Johanan the son of Kareah. 15 But Ishmael the son of Nethaniah escaped from Johanan with eight men and went to the Ammonites.

16 Then Johanan the son of Kareah, and all the captains of the forces that were with him, took from Mizpah all the rest of the people whom he had recovered from Ishmael the son of Nethaniah after he had murdered Gedaliah the son of Ahikam—the mighty men of war and the women and the children and the eunuchs, whom he had brought back from Gibeon. 17 And they departed and dwelt in the habitation of Chimham, which is near Bethlehem, as they went on their way to Egypt, 18 because of the Chaldeans; for they were afraid of them, because Ishmael the son of Nethaniah had murdered Gedaliah the son of Ahikam, whom the king of Babylon had made governor in the land.

42 Now all the captains of the forces, Johanan the son of Kareah, Jezaniah the son of Hoshaiah, and all the people, from the least to the greatest, came near 2 and said to Jeremiah the prophet, "Please, let our petition be acceptable to you, and pray for us to the LORD your God, for all this remnant (since we are left *but* a few of many, as you can see), 3 that the LORD your God may show us the way in which we should walk and the thing we should do."

4 Then Jeremiah the prophet said to them, "I have heard. Indeed, I will pray to the LORD your God according to your words, and it shall be, *that* whatever the LORD answers you, I will declare *it* to you. I will keep nothing back from you."

5 So they said to Jeremiah, "Let the LORD be a true and faithful witness between us, if we do not do according to everything which the LORD your God sends us by you. 6 Whether *it is* pleasing or displeasing, we will obey the voice of the LORD our God to whom we send you, that it may be well with us when we obey the voice of the LORD our God."

7 And it happened after ten days

You can't receive what God wants for your life by looking back. He is mighty. He is strong enough to bring you out and loose you, deliver you, and set you free.

Soul Secrets
*of a woman seeking
the ways of God*

*L*ord, Your ways are so much higher than mine—ways
You move, ways You walk on the highways of Heaven,
ways You work in hearts, ways that those of us on earth
can never understand. I need Your ways. My own human ways
embarrass and confuse me—but they're all I know.

Just as You talked to the children of Israel through Your
servant Moses, I need You to talk to me and show me Your
ways. Shout Your Name and show Your face so I can know You
better. I want the gentle ways of Jesus to be mine. I want to
follow the paths of love and grace and victory. Call to me
when I'm about to make a wrong move or take the tangled
road that leads to hell.

Teach me how to live in holiness and in righteousness.
Lead me in the ever-loving, everlasting way.

that the word of the LORD came to Jeremiah. 8 Then he called Johanan the son of Kareah, all the captains of the forces which *were* with him, and all the people from the least even to the greatest, 9 and said to them, "Thus says the LORD, the God of Israel, to whom you sent me to present your petition before Him: 10 'If you will still remain in this land, then I will build you and not pull *you* down, and I will plant you and not pluck *you* up. For I relent concerning the disaster that I have brought upon you. 11 Do not be afraid of the king of Babylon, of whom you are afraid; do not be afraid of him,' says the LORD, 'for I *am* with you, to save you and deliver you from his hand. 12 And I will show you mercy, that he may have mercy on you and cause you to return to your own land.'

13 "But if you say, 'We will not dwell in this land,' disobeying the voice of the LORD your God, 14 saying, 'No, but we will go to the land of Egypt where we shall see no war, nor hear the sound of the trumpet, nor be hungry for bread, and there we will dwell'— 15 Then hear now the word of the LORD, O remnant of Judah! Thus says the LORD of hosts, the God of Israel: 'If you wholly set your faces to enter Egypt, and go to dwell there, 16 then it shall be *that* the sword which you feared shall overtake you there in the land of Egypt; the famine of which you were afraid shall follow close after you there *in* Egypt; and there you shall die. 17 So shall it be with all the men who set their faces to go to Egypt to dwell there. They shall die by the sword, by famine, and by pestilence. And none of them shall remain or escape from the disaster that I will bring upon them.'

18 "For thus says the LORD of hosts, the God of Israel: 'As My anger and My fury have been poured out on the inhabitants of Jerusalem, so will My fury be poured out on you when you enter Egypt. And you shall be an oath, an astonishment, a curse, and a reproach; and you shall see this place no more.'

19 "The LORD has said concerning you, O remnant of Judah, 'Do not go to Egypt!' Know certainly that I have admonished you this day. 20 For you were hypocrites in your hearts when you sent me to the LORD your God, saying, 'Pray for us to the LORD our God, and according to all that the LORD your God says, so declare to us and we will do *it*.' 21 And I have this day declared *it* to you, but you have not obeyed the voice of the LORD your God, or anything which He has sent you by me. 22 Now therefore, know certainly that you shall die by the sword, by famine, and by pestilence in the place where you desire to go to dwell."

43 Now it happened, when Jeremiah had stopped speaking to all the people all the words of the LORD their God, for which the LORD their God had sent him to them, all these words, 2 that Azariah the son of Hoshaiah, Johanan the son of Kareah, and all the proud men spoke, saying to Jeremiah, "You speak falsely! The LORD our God has not sent you to say, 'Do not go to Egypt to dwell there.' 3 But Baruch the son of Neriah has set you against us, to deliver us into the hand of the Chaldeans, that they may put us to death or carry us away captive to Babylon." 4 So Johanan the son of Kareah, all the captains of the forces, and all the people would not obey the voice of the LORD, to remain in the land of Judah. 5 But Johanan the son of Kareah and all the captains of the forces took all the remnant of Judah who had returned to dwell in the land of Judah, from all nations where they had been driven— 6 men, women, children, the king's daughters, and every person whom Nebuzaradan the captain of the guard had left with Gedaliah the son of Ahikam, the son of Shaphan, and Jeremiah the prophet and Baruch the son of Neriah. 7 So they went to the land of Egypt, for they did not obey the voice of the LORD. And they went as far as Tahpanhes.

8 Then the word of the LORD came to Jeremiah in Tahpanhes, saying, 9 "Take large stones in your hand, and hide them in the sight of the men of Judah, in the clay in the brick courtyard which *is* at the entrance to Pharaoh's house in Tahpanhes; 10 and say to them, 'Thus says the LORD of hosts, the God of Israel: "Behold, I will send and bring Nebuchadnezzar the king of Babylon, My servant, and will set his throne above

Gospel Pearls

these stones that I have hidden. And he will spread his royal pavilion over them. 11 When he comes, he shall strike the land of Egypt *and deliver* to death *those appointed* for death, and to captivity *those appointed* for captivity, and to the sword *those appointed* for the sword. 12 I*ᵃ* will kindle a fire in the houses of the gods of Egypt, and he shall burn them and carry them away captive. And he shall array himself with the land of Egypt, as a shepherd puts on his garment, and he shall go out from there in peace. 13 He shall also break 'the sacred pillars of Beth Shemesh*ᵃ* that *are* in the land of Egypt; and the houses of the gods of the Egyptians he shall burn with fire." ' "

44 The word that came to Jeremiah concerning all the Jews who dwell in the land of Egypt, who dwell at Migdol, at Tahpanhes, at Noph,*ᵃ* and in the country of Pathros, saying, 2 "Thus says the LORD of hosts, the God of Israel: 'You have seen all the calamity that I have brought on Jerusalem and on all the cities of Judah; and behold, this day they *are* a desolation, and no one dwells in them, 3 because of their wickedness which they have committed to provoke Me to anger, in that they went to burn incense *and* to serve other gods whom they did not know, they nor you nor your fathers. 4 However I have sent to you all My servants the prophets, rising early and sending *them*, saying, "Oh, do not do this abominable thing that I hate!" 5 But they did not listen or incline their ear to turn from their wickedness, to burn no incense to other gods. 6 So My fury and My anger were poured out and kindled in the cities of Judah and in the streets of Jerusalem; and they are wasted *and* desolate, as it is this day.'

7 "Now therefore, thus says the LORD, the God of hosts, the God of Israel: 'Why do you commit *this* great evil against yourselves, to cut off from you man and woman, child and infant, out of Judah, leaving none to remain, 8 in that you provoke Me to wrath with the works of your hands, burning incense to other gods in the land of Egypt where you have gone to dwell, that you may cut yourselves off and be a curse and a reproach among all the nations of the earth? 9 Have you forgotten the wickedness of your fathers, the wickedness of the kings of Judah, the wickedness of their wives, your own wickedness, and the wickedness of your wives, which they committed in the land of Judah and in the streets of Jerusalem? 10 They have not been humbled, to this day, nor have they feared; they have not walked in My law or in My statutes that I set before you and your fathers.'

11 "Therefore thus says the LORD of hosts, the God of Israel: 'Behold, I will set My face against you for catastrophe and for cutting off all Judah. 12 And I will take the remnant of Judah who have set their faces to go into the land of Egypt to dwell there, and they shall all be consumed *and* fall in the land of Egypt. They shall be consumed by the sword *and* by famine. They shall die, from the least to the greatest, by the sword and by famine; and they shall be an oath, an astonishment, a curse and a reproach! 13 For I will punish those who dwell in the land of Egypt, as I have punished Jerusalem, by the sword, by famine, and by pestilence, 14 so that none of the remnant of Judah who have gone into the land of Egypt to dwell there shall escape or survive, lest they return to the land of Judah, to which they desire to return and dwell. For none shall return except those who escape.' "

15 Then all the men who knew that their wives had burned incense to other gods, with all the women who stood by, a great multitude, and all the people who dwelt in the land of Egypt, in Pathros, answered Jeremiah, saying: 16 "*As for* the word that you have spoken to us in the name of the LORD, we will not listen to you! 17 But we will certainly do whatever has gone out of our own mouth, to burn incense to the queen of heaven and pour out drink offerings to her, as we have done, we and our fathers, our kings and our princes, in the cities of Judah and in the streets of Je-

43:12 *ᵃ*Following Masoretic Text and Targum; Septuagint, Syriac, and Vulgate read *He*.   43:13 *ᵃ*Literally *House Of The Sun*, ancient On; later called *Heliopolis*   44:1 *ᵃ*That is, ancient Memphis

*W*omen tend to speak against their bodies, opening the door for sickness and disease. Speak life to your own body. Celebrate who you are. You are the image of God.

rusalem. For *then* we had plenty of food, were well-off, and saw no trouble. 18 But since we stopped burning incense to the queen of heaven and pouring out drink offerings to her, we have lacked everything and have been consumed by the sword and by famine."

19 *The women also said,* "And when we burned incense to the queen of heaven and poured out drink offerings to her, did we make cakes for her, to worship her, and pour out drink offerings to her without our husbands' *permission?*"

20 Then Jeremiah spoke to all the people—the men, the women, and all the people who had given him *that* answer—saying: 21 "The incense that you burned in the cities of Judah and in the streets of Jerusalem, you and your fathers, your kings and your princes, and the people of the land, did not the LORD remember them, and did it *not* come into His mind? 22 So the LORD could no longer bear *it,* because of the evil of your doings *and* because of the abominations which you committed. Therefore your land is a desolation, an astonishment, a curse, and without an inhabitant, as *it is* this day. 23 Because you have burned incense and because you have sinned against the LORD, and have not obeyed the voice of the LORD or walked in His law, in His statutes or in His testimonies, therefore this calamity has happened to you, as *at* this day."

24 Moreover Jeremiah said to all the people and to all the women, "Hear the word of the LORD, all Judah who *are* in the land of Egypt! 25 Thus says the LORD of hosts, the God of Israel, saying: 'You and your wives have spoken with your mouths and fulfilled with your hands, saying, "We will surely keep our vows that we have made, to burn incense to the queen of heaven and pour out drink offerings to her." You will surely keep your vows and perform your vows!' 26 Therefore hear the word of the LORD, all Judah who dwell in the land of Egypt: 'Behold, I have sworn by My great name,' says the LORD, 'that My name shall no more be named in the mouth of any man of Judah in all the land of Egypt, saying, "The Lord GOD lives." 27 Behold, I

will watch over them for adversity and not for good. And all the men of Judah who *are* in the land of Egypt shall be consumed by the sword and by famine, until there is an end to them. 28 Yet a small number who escape the sword shall return from the land of Egypt to the land of Judah; and all the remnant of Judah, who have gone to the land of Egypt to dwell there, shall know whose words will stand, Mine or theirs. 29 And this *shall be* a sign to you,' says the LORD, 'that I will punish you in this place, that you may know that My words will surely stand against you for adversity.'

30 "Thus says the LORD: 'Behold, I will give Pharaoh Hophra king of Egypt into the hand of his enemies and into the hand of those who seek his life, as I gave Zedekiah king of Judah into the hand of Nebuchadnezzar king of Babylon, his enemy who sought his life.' "

45 The word that Jeremiah the prophet spoke to Baruch the son of Neriah, when he had written these words in a book at the instruction of Jeremiah,[a] in the fourth year of Jehoiakim the son of Josiah, king of Judah, saying, 2 "Thus says the LORD, the God of Israel, to you, O Baruch: 3 'You said, "Woe is me now! For the LORD has added grief to my sorrow. I fainted in my sighing, and I find no rest." '

4 "Thus you shall say to him, 'Thus says the LORD: "Behold, what I have built I will break down, and what I have planted I will pluck up, that is, this whole land. 5 And do you seek great things for yourself? Do not seek *them;* for behold, I will bring adversity on all flesh," says the LORD. "But I will give your life to you as a prize in all places, wherever you go." ' "

46 The word of the LORD which came to Jeremiah the prophet against the nations. 2 Against Egypt.

Concerning the army of Pharaoh Necho, king of Egypt, which was by the River Euphrates in Carchemish, and which Nebuchadnezzar king of Babylon defeated in the fourth year of Jehoiakim the son of Josiah, king of Judah:

45:1 aLiterally *from Jeremiah's mouth*

Gospel Pearls

3 "Order the buckler and shield,
And draw near to battle!
4 Harness the horses,
And mount up, you horsemen!
Stand forth with *your* helmets,
Polish the spears,
Put on the armor!
5 Why have I seen them
dismayed *and* turned back?
Their mighty ones are beaten
down;
They have speedily fled,
And did not look back,
For fear *was* all around," says
the LORD.
6 "Do not let the swift flee away,
Nor the mighty man escape;
They will stumble and fall
Toward the north, by the River
Euphrates.

7 "Who *is* this coming up like a
flood,
Whose waters move like the
rivers?
8 Egypt rises up like a flood,
And *its* waters move like the
rivers;
And he says, 'I will go up *and*
cover the earth,
I will destroy the city and its
inhabitants.'
9 Come up, O horses, and rage,
O chariots!
And let the mighty men come
forth:
The Ethiopians and the
Libyans who handle the
shield,
And the Lydians who handle
and bend the bow.
10 For this *is* the day of the Lord
GOD of hosts,
A day of vengeance,
That He may avenge Himself
on His adversaries.
The sword shall devour;
It shall be satiated and made
drunk with their blood;
For the Lord GOD of hosts has
a sacrifice
In the north country by the
River Euphrates.

11 "Go up to Gilead and take balm,
O virgin, the daughter of
Egypt;
In vain you will use many
medicines;
You shall not be cured.

12 The nations have heard of your
shame,
And your cry has filled the
land;
For the mighty man has
stumbled against the mighty;
They both have fallen
together."

13 The word that the LORD spoke
to Jeremiah the prophet, how Nebuchadnezzar king of Babylon would
come *and* strike the land of Egypt.

14 "Declare in Egypt, and proclaim
in Migdol;
Proclaim in Noph*a* and in
Tahpanhes;
Say, 'Stand fast and prepare
yourselves,
For the sword devours all
around you.'
15 Why are your valiant *men*
swept away?
They did not stand
Because the LORD drove them
away.
16 He made many fall;
Yes, one fell upon another.
And they said, 'Arise!
Let us go back to our own
people
And to the land of our nativity
From the oppressing sword.'
17 They cried there,
'Pharaoh, king of Egypt, *is but*
a noise.
He has passed by the appointed
time!'

18 "As I live," says the King,
Whose name *is* the LORD of
hosts,
"Surely as Tabor *is* among the
mountains
And as Carmel by the sea, *so*
he shall come.
19 O you daughter dwelling in
Egypt,
Prepare yourself to go into
captivity!
For Noph*a* shall be waste and
desolate, without inhabitant.

20 "Egypt *is* a very pretty heifer,
But destruction comes, it
comes from the north.
21 Also her mercenaries are in her
midst like fat bulls,
For they also are turned back,

46:14 *a*That is, ancient Memphis   46:19 *a*That is, ancient Memphis

*W*hen we believe God, we are counted as righteous. Righteousness cannot be
earned or merited. It comes only through faith. We can have a good report simply
on the basis of our faith.

They have fled away together.
They did not stand,
For the day of their calamity
had come upon them,
The time of their punishment.
22 Her noise shall go like a
serpent,
For they shall march with an
army
And come against her with
axes,
Like those who chop wood.

23 "They shall cut down her
forest," says the LORD,
"Though it cannot be searched,
Because they *are* innumerable,
And more numerous than
grasshoppers.
24 The daughter of Egypt shall be
ashamed;
She shall be delivered into the
hand
Of the people of the north."

25 The LORD of hosts, the God of
Israel, says: "Behold, I will bring
punishment on Amon[a] of No,[b] and
Pharaoh and Egypt, with their gods
and their kings—Pharaoh and those
who trust in him. 26 And I will deliver
them into the hand of those who seek
their lives, into the hand of Nebuchadnezzar king of Babylon and the
hand of his servants. Afterward it
shall be inhabited as in the days of
old," says the LORD.

27 "But do not fear, O My servant
Jacob,
And do not be dismayed, O
Israel!
For behold, I will save you from
afar,
And your offspring from the
land of their captivity;
Jacob shall return, have rest
and be at ease;
No one shall make *him* afraid.
28 Do not fear, O Jacob My
servant," says the LORD,
"For I *am* with you;
For I will make a complete end
of all the nations
To which I have driven you,
But I will not make a complete
end of you.
I will rightly correct you,
For I will not leave you wholly
unpunished."

47 The word of the LORD that
came to Jeremiah the prophet
against the Philistines, before Pharaoh attacked Gaza.
2 Thus says the LORD:

"Behold, waters rise out of the
north,
And shall be an overflowing
flood;
They shall overflow the land
and all that is in it,
The city and those who dwell
within;
Then the men shall cry,
And all the inhabitants of the
land shall wail.
3 At the noise of the stamping
hooves of his strong horses,
At the rushing of his chariots,
At the rumbling of his
wheels,
The fathers will not look back
for *their* children,
Lacking courage,
4 Because of the day that
comes to plunder all the
Philistines,
To cut off from Tyre and Sidon
every helper who remains;
For the LORD shall plunder the
Philistines,
The remnant of the country of
Caphtor.
5 Baldness has come upon Gaza,
Ashkelon is cut off
With the remnant of their
valley.
How long will you cut yourself?

6 "O you sword of the LORD,
How long until you are quiet?
Put yourself up into your
scabbard,
Rest and be still!
7 How can it be quiet,
Seeing the LORD has given it a
charge
Against Ashkelon and against
the seashore?
There He has appointed it."

48 Against Moab.
Thus says the LORD of hosts,
the God of Israel:

"Woe to Nebo!
For it is plundered,
Kirjathaim is shamed *and*
taken;

The high stronghold[a] is
    shamed and dismayed—
2 No more praise of Moab.
    In Heshbon they have devised
        evil against her:
    'Come, and let us cut her off as
        a nation.'
    You also shall be cut down, O
        Madmen![a]
    The sword shall pursue you;
3 A voice of crying *shall be* from
        Horonaim:
    'Plundering and great
        destruction!'

4 "Moab is destroyed;
    Her little ones have caused a
        cry to be heard;[a]
5 For in the Ascent of Luhith they
        ascend with continual
        weeping;
    For in the descent of Horonaim
        the enemies have heard a cry
        of destruction.

6 "Flee, save your lives!
    And be like the juniper[a] in the
        wilderness.
7 For because you have trusted
        in your works and your
        treasures,
    You also shall be taken.
    And Chemosh shall go forth
        into captivity,
    His priests and his princes
        together.
8 And the plunderer shall come
        against every city;
    No one shall escape.
    The valley also shall perish,
    And the plain shall be
        destroyed,
    As the LORD has spoken.

9 "Give wings to Moab,
    That she may flee and get
        away;
    For her cities shall be desolate,
    Without any to dwell in them.
10 Cursed *is* he who does the work
        of the LORD deceitfully,
    And cursed *is* he who keeps
        back his sword from blood.

11 "Moab has been at ease from
        his[a] youth;
    He has settled on his dregs,
    And has not been emptied from
        vessel to vessel,
    Nor has he gone into captivity.
    Therefore his taste remained in
        him,
    And his scent has not changed.

12 "Therefore behold, the days are
        coming," says the LORD,
    "That I shall send him wine-
        workers
    Who will tip him over
    And empty his vessels
    And break the bottles.
13 Moab shall be ashamed of
        Chemosh,
    As the house of Israel was
        ashamed of Bethel, their
        confidence.

14 "How can you say, 'We *are*
        mighty
    And strong men for the war'?
15 Moab is plundered and gone up
        from her cities;
    Her chosen young men have
        gone down to the slaughter,"
        says the King,
    Whose name *is* the LORD of
        hosts.

16 "The calamity of Moab *is* near
        at hand,
    And his affliction comes
        quickly.
17 Bemoan him, all you who are
        around him;
    And all you who know his
        name,
    Say, 'How the strong staff is
        broken,
    The beautiful rod!'

18 "O daughter inhabiting Dibon,
    Come down from *your* glory,
    And sit in thirst;
    For the plunderer of Moab has
        come against you,
    He has destroyed your
        strongholds.
19 O inhabitant of Aroer,
    Stand by the way and watch;
    Ask him who flees
    And her who escapes;
    Say, 'What has happened?'
20 Moab is shamed, for he is
        broken down.
    Wail and cry!

48:1 [a]Hebrew *Misgab*   48:2 [a]A city of Moab   48:4 [a]Following Masoretic Text, Targum, and Vulgate;
Septuagint reads *Proclaim it in Zoar.*   48:6 [a]Or *Aroer,* a city of Moab   48:11 [a]The Hebrew uses
masculine and feminine pronouns interchangeably in this chapter.

God wants us to understand that just because we can't see it, doesn't mean that He
won't do it. What God wants to do in us begins as a word that gets in the spirit.

Tell it in Arnon, that Moab is
plundered.

21 "And judgment has come on the
plain country:
On Holon and Jahzah and
Mephaath,
22 On Dibon and Nebo and Beth
Diblathaim,
23 On Kirjathaim and Beth Gamul
and Beth Meon,
24 On Kerioth and Bozrah,
On all the cities of the land of
Moab,
Far or near.
25 The horn of Moab is cut off,
And his arm is broken," says
the Lord.

26 "Make him drunk,
Because he exalted *himself*
against the Lord.
Moab shall wallow in his vomit,
And he shall also be in
derision.
27 For was not Israel a derision to
you?
Was he found among thieves?
For whenever you speak of
him,
You shake *your head in scorn.*

28 You who dwell in Moab,
Leave the cities and dwell in
the rock,
And be like the dove *which*
makes her nest
In the sides of the cave's mouth.

29 "We have heard the pride of
Moab
(He *is* exceedingly proud),
Of his loftiness and arrogance
and pride,
And of the haughtiness of his
heart."

30 "I know his wrath," says the
Lord,
"But it *is* not right;
His lies have made nothing
right.
31 Therefore I will wail for Moab,
And I will cry out for all Moab;
I*a* will mourn for the men of Kir
Heres.
32 O vine of Sibmah! I will weep
for you with the weeping of
Jazer.

Your plants have gone over the
sea,
They reach to the sea of Jazer.
The plunderer has fallen on
your summer fruit and your
vintage.
33 Joy and gladness are taken
From the plentiful field
And from the land of Moab;
I have caused wine to fail from
the winepresses;
No one will tread with joyous
shouting—
Not joyous shouting!

34 "From the cry of Heshbon to
Elealeh and to Jahaz
They have uttered their voice,
From Zoar to Horonaim,
Like a three-year-old heifer;*a*
For the waters of Nimrim also
shall be desolate.

35 "Moreover," says the Lord,
"I will cause to cease in Moab
The one who offers *sacrifices* in
the high places
And burns incense to his gods.
36 Therefore My heart shall wail
like flutes for Moab,
And like flutes My heart shall
wail
For the men of Kir Heres.
Therefore the riches they have
acquired have perished.

37 "For every head *shall be* bald,
and every beard clipped;
On all the hands *shall be* cuts,
and on the loins sackcloth—
38 A general lamentation
On all the housetops of Moab,
And in its streets;
For I have broken Moab like a
vessel in which *is* no
pleasure," says the Lord.
39 "They shall wail:
'How she is broken down!
How Moab has turned her back
with shame!'
So Moab shall be a derision
And a dismay to all those about
her."

40 For thus says the Lord:

"Behold, one shall fly like an
eagle,

48:31 *a*Following Dead Sea Scrolls, Septuagint, and Vulgate; Masoretic Text reads *He.*   48:34 *a*Or *The Third Eglath,* an unknown city (compare Isaiah 15:5)

Gospel
Pearls

And spread his wings over
Moab.

41 Kerioth is taken,
And the strongholds are
surprised;
The mighty men's hearts in
Moab on that day shall be
Like the heart of a woman in
birth pangs.

42 And Moab shall be destroyed
as a people,
Because he exalted *himself*
against the LORD.

43 Fear and the pit and the snare
shall be upon you,
O inhabitant of Moab," says the
LORD.

44 He who flees from the fear shall
fall into the pit,
And he who gets out of the pit
shall be caught in the snare.
For upon Moab, upon it I will
bring
The year of their punishment,"
says the LORD.

45 "Those who fled stood under the
shadow of Heshbon
Because of exhaustion.
But a fire shall come out of
Heshbon,
A flame from the midst of
Sihon,
And shall devour the brow of
Moab,
The crown of the head of the
sons of tumult.

46 Woe to you, O Moab!
The people of Chemosh perish;
For your sons have been taken
captive,
And your daughters captive.

47 "Yet I will bring back the
captives of Moab
In the latter days," says the
LORD.

Thus far *is* the judgment of Moab.

49 Against the Ammonites.
Thus says the LORD:

"Has Israel no sons?
Has he no heir?
Why *then* does Milcom[a] inherit
Gad,
And his people dwell in its
cities?

2 Therefore behold, the days are
coming," says the LORD,
"That I will cause to be heard
an alarm of war
In Rabbah of the Ammonites;
It shall be a desolate mound,
And her villages shall be
burned with fire.
Then Israel shall take
possession of his
inheritance," says the LORD.

3 "Wail, O Heshbon, for Ai is
plundered!
Cry, you daughters of Rabbah,
Gird yourselves with sackcloth!
Lament and run to and fro by
the walls;
For Milcom shall go into
captivity
With his priests and his princes
together.

4 Why do you boast in the
valleys,
Your flowing valley, O
backsliding daughter?
Who trusted in her treasures,
saying,
'Who will come against me?'

5 Behold, I will bring fear upon
you,"
Says the Lord GOD of hosts,
"From all those who are around
you;
You shall be driven out,
everyone headlong,
And no one will gather those
who wander off.

6 But afterward I will bring back
The captives of the people of
Ammon," says the LORD.

7 Against Edom.
Thus says the LORD of hosts:

"*Is* wisdom no more in Teman?
Has counsel perished from the
prudent?
Has their wisdom vanished?

8 Flee, turn back, dwell in the
depths, O inhabitants of
Dedan!
For I will bring the calamity of
Esau upon him,
The time *that* I will punish him.

9 If grape-gatherers came to you,
Would they not leave *some*
gleaning grapes?
If thieves by night,

49:1 [a]Hebrew *Malcam*, literally *their king*, a god of the Ammonites; also called *Molech* (compare verse 3)

*Y*ou can't walk with God until you worship God. The first calling is to learn how
to worship God. When you learn how to worship God, then you can develop a
walk with God.

Would they not destroy until
they have enough?

10 But I have made Esau bare;
I have uncovered his secret
places,[a]
And he shall not be able to hide
himself.
His descendants are plundered,
His brethren and his neighbors,
And he is no more.

11 Leave your fatherless children,
I will preserve them alive;
And let your widows trust in
Me."

12 For thus says the LORD: "Behold,
those whose judgment was not to
drink of the cup have assuredly
drunk. And are you the one who will
altogether go unpunished? You shall
not go unpunished, but you shall
surely drink of it. 13 For I have sworn
by Myself," says the LORD, "that
Bozrah shall become a desolation, a
reproach, a waste, and a curse. And
all its cities shall be perpetual
wastes."

14 I have heard a message from
the LORD,
And an ambassador has been
sent to the nations:
"Gather together, come against
her,
And rise up to battle!

15 "For indeed, I will make you
small among nations,
Despised among men.

16 Your fierceness has deceived
you,
The pride of your heart,
O you who dwell in the clefts
of the rock,
Who hold the height of the hill!
Though you make your nest as
high as the eagle,
I will bring you down from
there," says the LORD.[a]

17 "Edom also shall be an
astonishment;
Everyone who goes by it will
be astonished
And will hiss at all its plagues.

18 As in the overthrow of Sodom
and Gomorrah
And their neighbors," says the
LORD,
"No one shall remain there,

Nor shall a son of man dwell
in it.

19 "Behold, he shall come up like
a lion from the floodplain[a] of
the Jordan
Against the dwelling place of
the strong;
But I will suddenly make him
run away from her.
And who is a chosen man that
I may appoint over her?
For who is like Me?
Who will arraign Me?
And who is that shepherd
Who will withstand Me?"

20 Therefore hear the counsel of
the LORD that He has taken
against Edom,
And His purposes that He has
proposed against the
inhabitants of Teman:
Surely the least of the flock
shall draw them out;
Surely He shall make their
dwelling places desolate with
them.

21 The earth shakes at the noise
of their fall;
At the cry its noise is heard at
the Red Sea.

22 Behold, He shall come up and
fly like the eagle,
And spread His wings over
Bozrah;
The heart of the mighty men of
Edom in that day shall be
Like the heart of a woman in
birth pangs.

23 Against Damascus.

"Hamath and Arpad are
shamed,
For they have heard bad news.
They are fainthearted;
There is trouble on the sea;
It cannot be quiet.

24 Damascus has grown feeble;
She turns to flee,
And fear has seized her.
Anguish and sorrows have
taken her like a woman in
labor.

25 Why is the city of praise not
deserted, the city of My joy?

26 Therefore her young men shall
fall in her streets,

49:10 aCompare Obadiah 5, 6   49:16 aCompare Obadiah 3, 4   49:19 aOr thicket

Gospel
Pearls

And all the men of war shall
be cut off in that day," says
the LORD of hosts.
27 "I will kindle a fire in the wall
of Damascus,
And it shall consume the
palaces of Ben-Hadad."*a*

28 Against Kedar and against the
kingdoms of Hazor, which Nebuchadnezzar king of Babylon shall
strike.
Thus says the LORD:

"Arise, go up to Kedar,
And devastate the men of the
East!
29 Their tents and their flocks
they shall take away.
They shall take for themselves
their curtains,
All their vessels and their
camels;
And they shall cry out to them,
'Fear *is* on every side!'

30 "Flee, get far away! Dwell in the
depths,
O inhabitants of Hazor!" says
the LORD.
"For Nebuchadnezzar king of
Babylon has taken counsel
against you,
And has conceived a plan
against you.

31 "Arise, go up to the wealthy
nation that dwells securely,"
says the LORD,
"Which has neither gates nor
bars,
Dwelling alone.
32 Their camels shall be for booty,
And the multitude of their
cattle for plunder.
I will scatter to all winds those
in the farthest corners,
And I will bring their calamity
from all its sides," says the
LORD.
33 "Hazor shall be a dwelling for
jackals, a desolation forever;
No one shall reside there,
Nor son of man dwell in it."

34 The word of the LORD that came
to Jeremiah the prophet against
Elam, in the beginning of the reign
of Zedekiah king of Judah, saying,
35 "Thus says the LORD of hosts:

'Behold, I will break the bow of
Elam,
The foremost of their might.
36 Against Elam I will bring the
four winds
From the four quarters of
heaven,
And scatter them toward all
those winds;
There shall be no nations
where the outcasts of Elam
will not go.
37 For I will cause Elam to be
dismayed before their
enemies
And before those who seek
their life.
I will bring disaster upon them,
My fierce anger,' says the
LORD;
'And I will send the sword after
them
Until I have consumed them.
38 I will set My throne in Elam,
And will destroy from there the
king and the princes,' says
the LORD.

39 'But it shall come to pass in the
latter days:
I will bring back the captives
of Elam,' says the LORD."

50 The word that the LORD spoke
against Babylon *and* against
the land of the Chaldeans by Jeremiah the prophet.

2 "Declare among the nations,
Proclaim, and set up a
standard;
Proclaim—do not conceal *it*—
Say, 'Babylon is taken, Bel is
shamed.
Merodach*a* is broken in pieces;
Her idols are humiliated,
Her images are broken in
pieces.'
3 For out of the north a nation
comes up against her,
Which shall make her land
desolate,
And no one shall dwell therein.
They shall move, they shall
depart,
Both man and beast.

4 "In those days and in that time,"
says the LORD,

49:27 *a*Compare Amos 1:4   50:2 *a*A Babylonian god; sometimes spelled *Marduk*

*E*ach of us needs our own walk with God. Stand back and thank God. Believe God
and know that He is able to do it. Sarah didn't stand on her husband's faith; she
stood on her own.

"The children of Israel shall
    come,
They and the children of Judah
    together;
With continual weeping they
    shall come,
And seek the LORD their
    God.
5 They shall ask the way to
    Zion,
With their faces toward it,
    saying,
'Come and let us join ourselves
    to the LORD
In a perpetual covenant
That will not be forgotten.'

6 "My people have been lost
    sheep.
Their shepherds have led them
    astray;
They have turned them away
    on the mountains.
They have gone from mountain
    to hill;
They have forgotten their
    resting place.
7 All who found them have
    devoured them;
And their adversaries said, 'We
    have not offended,
Because they have sinned
    against the LORD, the
    habitation of justice,
The LORD, the hope of their
    fathers.'

8 "Move from the midst of
    Babylon,
Go out of the land of the
    Chaldeans;
And be like the rams before the
    flocks.
9 For behold, I will raise and
    cause to come up against
    Babylon
An assembly of great nations
    from the north country,
And they shall array
    themselves against her;
From there she shall be
    captured.
Their arrows *shall be* like *those*
    of an expert warrior;[a]
None shall return in vain.
10 And Chaldea shall become
    plunder;
All who plunder her shall be
    satisfied," says the LORD.

11 "Because you were glad,
    because you rejoiced,
You destroyers of My heritage,
Because you have grown fat
    like a heifer threshing grain,
And you bellow like bulls,
12 Your mother shall be deeply
    ashamed;
She who bore you shall be
    ashamed.
Behold, the least of the nations
    shall be a wilderness,
A dry land and a desert.
13 Because of the wrath of the
    LORD
She shall not be inhabited,
But she shall be wholly
    desolate.
Everyone who goes by Babylon
    shall be horrified
And hiss at all her plagues.

14 "Put yourselves in array against
    Babylon all around,
All you who bend the bow;
Shoot at her, spare no arrows,
For she has sinned against the
    LORD.
15 Shout against her all around;
She has given her hand,
Her foundations have fallen,
Her walls are thrown down;
For it *is* the vengeance of the
    LORD.
Take vengeance on her.
As she has done, so do to her.
16 Cut off the sower from
    Babylon,
And him who handles the
    sickle at harvest time.
For fear of the oppressing
    sword
Everyone shall turn to his own
    people,
And everyone shall flee to his
    own land.

17 "Israel *is* like scattered sheep;
The lions have driven *him*
    away.
First the king of Assyria
    devoured him;
Now at last this
    Nebuchadnezzar king of
    Babylon has broken his
    bones."

18 Therefore thus says the LORD of
hosts, the God of Israel:

50:9 [a]Following some Hebrew manuscripts, Septuagint, and Syriac; Masoretic Text, Targum, and Vulgate read *a warrior who makes childless.*

Gospel
Pearls

"Behold, I will punish the king
of Babylon and his land,
As I have punished the king of
Assyria.

19 But I will bring back Israel to
his home,
And he shall feed on Carmel
and Bashan;
His soul shall be satisfied on
Mount Ephraim and Gilead.

20 In those days and in that time,"
says the LORD,
"The iniquity of Israel shall be
sought, but *there shall be*
none;
And the sins of Judah, but they
shall not be found;
For I will pardon those whom
I preserve.

21 "Go up against the land of
Merathaim, against it,
And against the inhabitants of
Pekod.
Waste and utterly destroy
them," says the LORD,
"And do according to all that I
have commanded you.

22 A sound of battle *is* in the
land,
And of great destruction.

23 How the hammer of the whole
earth has been cut apart and
broken!
How Babylon has become a
desolation among the
nations!

I have laid a snare for you;

24 You have indeed been trapped,
O Babylon,
And you were not aware;
You have been found and also
caught,
Because you have contended
against the Lord.

25 The LORD has opened His
armory,
And has brought out the
weapons of His indignation;
For this *is* the work of the Lord
GOD of hosts
In the land of the Chaldeans.

26 Come against her from the
farthest border;
Open her storehouses;
Cast her up as heaps of ruins,
And destroy her utterly;
Let nothing of her be left.

27 Slay all her bulls,

Let them go down to the
slaughter.
Woe to them!
For their day has come, the
time of their punishment.

28 The voice of those who flee and
escape from the land of
Babylon
Declares in Zion the vengeance
of the LORD our God,
The vengeance of His temple.

29 "Call together the archers
against Babylon.
All you who bend the bow,
encamp against it all around;
Let none of them escape.[a]
Repay her according to her
work;
According to all she has done,
do to her;
For she has been proud against
the LORD,
Against the Holy One of Israel.

30 Therefore her young men shall
fall in the streets,
And all her men of war shall
be cut off in that day," says
the LORD.

31 "Behold, I *am* against you,
O most haughty one!" says the
Lord GOD of hosts;
"For your day has come,
The time *that* I will punish
you.[a]

32 The most proud shall stumble
and fall,
And no one will raise him up;
I will kindle a fire in his cities,
And it will devour all around
him."

33 Thus says the LORD of hosts:

"The children of Israel *were*
oppressed,
Along with the children of
Judah;
All who took them captive have
held them fast;
They have refused to let them
go.

34 Their Redeemer *is* strong;
The LORD of hosts *is* His name.
He will thoroughly plead their
case,
That He may give rest to the
land,

50:29 [a]Qere, some Hebrew manuscripts, Septuagint, and Targum add *to her.*   50:31 [a]Following Masoretic
Text and Targum; Septuagint and Vulgate read *The time of your punishment.*

*Y*ou are God's woman. You are not called to sit by the window waiting on God to
send you a husband. You had better have some faith yourself and believe God
down in your own spirit.

And disquiet the inhabitants of
Babylon.

35 "A sword *is* against the
Chaldeans," says the LORD,
"Against the inhabitants of
Babylon,
And against her princes and
her wise men.
36 A sword *is* against the
soothsayers, and they will be
fools.
A sword *is* against her mighty
men, and they will be
dismayed.
37 A sword *is* against their horses,
Against their chariots,
And against all the mixed
peoples who *are* in her midst;
And they will become like
women.
A sword *is* against her
treasures, and they will be
robbed.
38 A drought*a* *is* against her
waters, and they will be dried
up.
For it *is* the land of carved
images,
And they are insane with *their*
idols.

39 "Therefore the wild desert
beasts shall dwell *there* with
the jackals,
And the ostriches shall dwell in
it.
It shall be inhabited no more
forever,
Nor shall it be dwelt in from
generation to generation.
40 As God overthrew Sodom and
Gomorrah
And their neighbors," says the
LORD,
"So no one shall reside there,
Nor son of man dwell in it.

41 "Behold, a people shall come
from the north,
And a great nation and many
kings
Shall be raised up from the
ends of the earth.
42 They shall hold the bow and
the lance;
They *are* cruel and shall not
show mercy.

Their voice shall roar like the
sea;
They shall ride on horses,
Set in array, like a man for the
battle,
Against you, O daughter of
Babylon.

43 "The king of Babylon has heard
the report about them,
And his hands grow feeble;
Anguish has taken hold of him,
Pangs as of a woman in
childbirth.

44 "Behold, he shall come up like
a lion from the floodplain*a* of
the Jordan
Against the dwelling place of
the strong;
But I will make them suddenly
run away from her.
And who *is* a chosen *man that*
I may appoint over her?
For who *is* like Me?
Who will arraign Me?
And who *is* that shepherd
Who will withstand Me?"

45 Therefore hear the counsel of
the LORD that He has taken
against Babylon,
And His purposes that He has
proposed against the land of
the Chaldeans:
Surely the least of the flock
shall draw them out;
Surely He will make their
dwelling place desolate with
them.
46 At the noise of the taking of
Babylon
The earth trembles,
And the cry is heard among the
nations.

51 Thus says the LORD:

"Behold, I will raise up against
Babylon,
Against those who dwell in Leb
Kamai,*a*
A destroying wind.
2 And I will send winnowers to
Babylon,
Who shall winnow her and
empty her land.

50:38 *a*Following Masoretic Text, Targum, and Vulgate; Syriac reads *sword;* Septuagint omits *A drought
is.* 50:44 *a*Or *thicket* 51:1 *a*A code word for *Chaldea* (Babylonia); may be translated *The Midst of
Those Who Rise Up Against Me*

Gospel
Pearls

For in the day of doom
They shall be against her all
    around.
3 Against *her* let the archer bend
    his bow,
And lift himself up against *her*
    in his armor.
Do not spare her young men;
Utterly destroy all her army.
4 Thus the slain shall fall in the
    land of the Chaldeans,
And *those* thrust through in her
    streets.
5 For Israel is not forsaken, nor
    Judah,
By his God, the LORD of hosts,
Though their land was filled
    with sin against the Holy One
    of Israel."

6 Flee from the midst of Babylon,
And every one save his life!
Do not be cut off in her iniquity,
For this *is* the time of the LORD's
    vengeance;
He shall recompense her.
7 Babylon *was* a golden cup in
    the LORD's hand,
That made all the earth drunk.
The nations drank her wine;
Therefore the nations are
    deranged.
8 Babylon has suddenly fallen
    and been destroyed.
Wail for her!
Take balm for her pain;
Perhaps she may be healed.

9 We would have healed
    Babylon,
But she is not healed.
Forsake her, and let us go
    everyone to his own country;
For her judgment reaches to
    heaven and is lifted up to the
    skies.
10 The LORD has revealed our
    righteousness.
Come and let us declare in Zion
    the work of the LORD our
    God.

11 Make the arrows bright!
Gather the shields!
The LORD has raised up the
    spirit of the kings of the
    Medes.
For His plan *is* against Babylon
    to destroy it,

Because it *is* the vengeance of
    the LORD,
The vengeance for His temple.
12 Set up the standard on the
    walls of Babylon;
Make the guard strong,
Set up the watchmen,
Prepare the ambushes.
For the LORD has both devised
    and done
What He spoke against the
    inhabitants of Babylon.
13 O you who dwell by many
    waters,
Abundant in treasures,
Your end has come,
The measure of your
    covetousness.
14 The LORD of hosts has sworn
    by Himself:
"Surely I will fill you with men,
    as with locusts,
And they shall lift up a shout
    against you."

15 He has made the earth by His
    power;
He has established the world
    by His wisdom,
And stretched out the heaven
    by His understanding.
16 When He utters *His* voice—
There is a multitude of waters
    in the heavens:
"He causes the vapors to ascend
    from the ends of the earth;
He makes lightnings for the
    rain;
He brings the wind out of His
    treasuries."*a*

17 Everyone is dull-hearted,
    without knowledge;
Every metalsmith is put to
    shame by the carved image;
For his molded image *is*
    falsehood,
And *there is* no breath in
    them.
18 They *are* futile, a work of
    errors;
In the time of their punishment
    they shall perish.
19 The Portion of Jacob *is* not like
    them,
For He *is* the Maker of all
    things;
And *Israel is* the tribe of His
    inheritance.
The LORD of hosts *is* His name.

51:16 *a*Psalm 135:7

Whatever God gives you, He wants it to be multiplied in the womb of your spirit.
When you bring it forth, it shall be greater than the former.

20 "You *are* My battle-ax *and*
    weapons of war:
For with you I will break the
    nation in pieces;
With you I will destroy
    kingdoms;
21 With you I will break in pieces
    the horse and its rider;
With you I will break in pieces
    the chariot and its rider;
22 With you also I will break in
    pieces man and woman;
With you I will break in pieces
    old and young;
With you I will break in pieces
    the young man and the
    maiden;
23 With you also I will break in
    pieces the shepherd and his
    flock;
With you I will break in pieces
    the farmer and his yoke of
    oxen;
And with you I will break in
    pieces governors and rulers.

24 "And I will repay Babylon
And all the inhabitants of
    Chaldea
For all the evil they have done
In Zion in your sight," says the
    LORD.

25 "Behold, I *am* against you, O
    destroying mountain,
Who destroys all the earth,"
    says the LORD.
"And I will stretch out My hand
    against you,
Roll you down from the rocks,
And make you a burnt
    mountain.
26 They shall not take from you
    a stone for a corner
Nor a stone for a foundation,
But you shall be desolate
    forever," says the LORD.

27 Set up a banner in the land,
Blow the trumpet among the
    nations!
Prepare the nations against
    her,
Call the kingdoms together
    against her:
Ararat, Minni, and Ashkenaz.
Appoint a general against her;
Cause the horses to come up
    like the bristling locusts.
28 Prepare against her the
    nations,
With the kings of the Medes,

Its governors and all its rulers,
All the land of his dominion.
29 And the land will tremble and
    sorrow;
For every purpose of the LORD
    shall be performed against
    Babylon,
To make the land of Babylon
    a desolation without
    inhabitant.
30 The mighty men of Babylon
    have ceased fighting,
They have remained in their
    strongholds;
Their might has failed,
They became *like* women;
They have burned her dwelling
    places,
The bars of her *gate* are
    broken.
31 One runner will run to meet
    another,
And one messenger to meet
    another,
To show the king of Babylon
    that his city is taken on *all*
    sides;
32 The passages are blocked,
The reeds they have burned
    with fire,
And the men of war are
    terrified.

33 For thus says the LORD of hosts,
the God of Israel:

"The daughter of Babylon *is* like
    a threshing floor
When it is time to thresh her;
Yet a little while
And the time of her harvest will
    come."

34 "Nebuchadnezzar the king of
    Babylon
Has devoured me, he has
    crushed me;
He has made me an empty
    vessel,
He has swallowed me up like
    a monster;
He has filled his stomach with
    my delicacies,
He has spit me out.
35 Let the violence *done* to me and
    my flesh *be* upon Babylon,"
The inhabitant of Zion will say;
"And my blood be upon the
    inhabitants of Chaldea!"
Jerusalem will say.

36 Therefore thus says the LORD:

Gospel Pearls

"Behold, I will plead your case
and take vengeance for
you.
I will dry up her sea and make
her springs dry.
37 Babylon shall become a heap,
A dwelling place for jackals,
An astonishment and a hissing,
Without an inhabitant.
38 They shall roar together like
lions,
They shall growl like lions'
whelps.
39 In their excitement I will
prepare their feasts;
I will make them drunk,
That they may rejoice,
And sleep a perpetual sleep
And not awake," says the
LORD.
40 "I will bring them down
Like lambs to the slaughter,
Like rams with male goats.

41 "Oh, how Sheshach*a* is taken!
Oh, how the praise of the whole
earth is seized!
How Babylon has become
desolate among the nations!
42 The sea has come up over
Babylon;
She is covered with the
multitude of its waves.
43 Her cities are a desolation,
A dry land and a wilderness,
A land where no one dwells,
Through which no son of man
passes.
44 I will punish Bel in Babylon,
And I will bring out of his
mouth what he has
swallowed;
And the nations shall not
stream to him anymore.
Yes, the wall of Babylon shall
fall.

45 "My people, go out of the midst
of her!
And let everyone deliver
himself from the fierce anger
of the LORD.
46 And lest your heart faint,
And you fear for the rumor that
will be heard in the land
(A rumor will come *one* year,
And after that, in *another* year
A rumor *will* come,
And violence in the land,
Ruler against ruler),

47 Therefore behold, the days are
coming
That I will bring judgment on
the carved images of
Babylon;
Her whole land shall be
ashamed,
And all her slain shall fall in
her midst.
48 Then the heavens and the earth
and all that *is* in them
Shall sing joyously over
Babylon;
For the plunderers shall come
to her from the north," says
the LORD.

49 As Babylon *has caused* the
slain of Israel to fall,
So at Babylon the slain of all
the earth shall fall.
50 You who have escaped the
sword,
Get away! Do not stand still!
Remember the LORD afar off,
And let Jerusalem come to your
mind.

51 We are ashamed because we
have heard reproach.
Shame has covered our faces,
For strangers have come into
the sanctuaries of the LORD's
house.

52 "Therefore behold, the days are
coming," says the LORD,
"That I will bring judgment on
her carved images,
And throughout all her land the
wounded shall groan.
53 Though Babylon were to mount
up to heaven,
And though she were to fortify
the height of her strength,
Yet from Me plunderers would
come to her," says the LORD.

54 The sound of a cry *comes* from
Babylon,
And great destruction from the
land of the Chaldeans,
55 Because the LORD is plundering
Babylon
And silencing her loud voice,
Though her waves roar like
great waters,
And the noise of their voice is
uttered,

51:41 *a*A code word for *Babylon* (compare Jeremiah 25:26)

*I*n order to move forward, we must be willing to give up yesterday and go on toward
tomorrow. We have to trust God enough to allow Him to come in and plow up our
lives.

56 Because the plunderer comes
  against her, against Babylon,
And her mighty men are taken.
Every one of their bows is
  broken;
For the LORD is the God of
  recompense,
He will surely repay.

57 "And I will make drunk
  Her princes and wise men,
Her governors, her deputies,
  and her mighty men.
And they shall sleep a
  perpetual sleep
And not awake," says the King,
Whose name is the LORD of
  hosts.

58 Thus says the LORD of hosts:

"The broad walls of Babylon
  shall be utterly broken,
And her high gates shall be
  burned with fire;
The people will labor in vain,
And the nations, because of the
  fire;
And they shall be weary."

59 The word which Jeremiah the prophet commanded Seraiah the son of Neriah, the son of Mahseiah, when he went with Zedekiah the king of Judah to Babylon in the fourth year of his reign. And Seraiah was the quartermaster. 60 So Jeremiah wrote in a book all the evil that would come upon Babylon, all these words that are written against Babylon. 61 And Jeremiah said to Seraiah, "When you arrive in Babylon and see it, and read all these words, 62 then you shall say, 'O LORD, You have spoken against this place to cut it off, so that none shall remain in it, neither man nor beast, but it shall be desolate forever.' 63 Now it shall be, when you have finished reading this book, that you shall tie a stone to it and throw it out into the Euphrates. 64 Then you shall say, 'Thus Babylon shall sink and not rise from the catastrophe that I will bring upon her. And they shall be weary.' "
Thus far are the words of Jeremiah.

52 Zedekiah was twenty-one years old when he became

king, and he reigned eleven years in Jerusalem. His mother's name was Hamutal the daughter of Jeremiah of Libnah. 2 He also did evil in the sight of the LORD, according to all that Jehoiakim had done. 3 For because of the anger of the LORD this happened in Jerusalem and Judah, till He finally cast them out from His presence. Then Zedekiah rebelled against the king of Babylon.

4 Now it came to pass in the ninth year of his reign, in the tenth month, on the tenth day of the month, that Nebuchadnezzar king of Babylon and all his army came against Jerusalem and encamped against it; and they built a siege wall against it all around. 5 So the city was besieged until the eleventh year of King Zedekiah. 6 By the fourth month, on the ninth day of the month, the famine had become so severe in the city that there was no food for the people of the land. 7 Then the city wall was broken through, and all the men of war fled and went out of the city at night by way of the gate between the two walls, which was by the king's garden, even though the Chaldeans were near the city all around. And they went by way of the plain.ᵃ

8 But the army of the Chaldeans pursued the king, and they overtook Zedekiah in the plains of Jericho. All his army was scattered from him. 9 So they took the king and brought him up to the king of Babylon at Riblah in the land of Hamath, and he pronounced judgment on him. 10 Then the king of Babylon killed the sons of Zedekiah before his eyes. And he killed all the princes of Judah in Riblah. 11 He also put out the eyes of Zedekiah; and the king of Babylon bound him in bronze fetters, took him to Babylon, and put him in prison till the day of his death.

12 Now in the fifth month, on the tenth day of the month (which was the nineteenth year of King Nebuchadnezzar king of Babylon), Nebuzaradan, the captain of the guard, who served the king of Babylon, came to Jerusalem. 13 He burned the house of the LORD and the king's house; all the houses of Jerusalem, that is, all the houses of the great, he burned with fire. 14 And all the

52:7 ᵃOr the arabah, that is, the Jordan Valley

Gospel Pearls

army of the Chaldeans who *were* with the captain of the guard broke down all the walls of Jerusalem all around. 15 Then Nebuzaradan the captain of the guard carried away captive *some* of the poor people, the rest of the people who remained in the city, the defectors who had deserted to the king of Babylon, and the rest of the craftsmen. 16 But Nebuzaradan the captain of the guard left *some* of the poor of the land as vinedressers and farmers.

17 The bronze pillars that *were* in the house of the LORD, and the carts and the bronze Sea that *were* in the house of the LORD, the Chaldeans broke in pieces, and carried all their bronze to Babylon. 18 They also took away the pots, the shovels, the trimmers, the bowls, the spoons, and all the bronze utensils with which the priests ministered. 19 The basins, the firepans, the bowls, the pots, the lampstands, the spoons, and the cups, whatever *was* solid gold and whatever *was* solid silver, the captain of the guard took away. 20 The two pillars, one Sea, the twelve bronze bulls which *were* under *it, and* the carts, which King Solomon had made for the house of the LORD—the bronze of all these articles was beyond measure. 21 Now *concerning* the pillars: the height of one pillar *was* eighteen cubits, a measuring line of twelve cubits could measure its circumference, and its thickness *was* four fingers; *it was* hollow. 22 A capital of bronze *was* on it; and the height of one capital *was* five cubits, with a network and pomegranates all around the capital, all of bronze. The second pillar, with pomegranates *was* the same. 23 There were ninety-six pomegranates on the sides; all the pomegranates, all around on the network, *were* one hundred.

24 The captain of the guard took Seraiah the chief priest, Zephaniah the second priest, and the three doorkeepers. 25 He also took out of the city an officer who had charge of the men of war, seven men of the king's close associates who were found in the city, the principal scribe of the army who mustered the people of the land, and sixty men of the people of the land who were found in the midst of the city. 26 And Nebuzaradan the captain of the guard took these and brought them to the king of Babylon at Riblah. 27 Then the king of Babylon struck them and put them to death at Riblah in the land of Hamath. Thus Judah was carried away captive from its own land.

28 These *are* the people whom Nebuchadnezzar carried away captive: in the seventh year, three thousand and twenty-three Jews; 29 in the eighteenth year of Nebuchadnezzar he carried away captive from Jerusalem eight hundred and thirty-two persons; 30 in the twenty-third year of Nebuchadnezzar, Nebuzaradan the captain of the guard carried away captive of the Jews seven hundred and forty-five persons. All the persons *were* four thousand six hundred.

31 Now it came to pass in the thirty-seventh year of the captivity of Jehoiachin king of Judah, in the twelfth month, on the twenty-fifth *day* of the month, *that* Evil-Merodach[a] king of Babylon, in the first *year* of his reign, lifted up the head of Jehoiachin king of Judah and brought him out of prison. 32 And he spoke kindly to him and gave him a more prominent seat than those of the kings who *were* with him in Babylon. 33 So Jehoiachin changed from his prison garments, and he ate bread regularly before the king all the days of his life. 34 And as for his provisions, there was a regular ration given him by the king of Babylon, a portion for each day until the day of his death, all the days of his life.

52:31 [a]Or *Awil-Marduk*

God deals directly with the issues of the heart and lets you know you do not have to be afraid. The plans of God are good. He is not like the people who have hurt and abused you. He wants only to help you be completely restored.

LAMENTATIONS

1 How lonely sits the city
That was full of people!
How like a widow is she,
Who *was* great among the
nations!
The princess among the
provinces
Has become a slave!

2 She weeps bitterly in the night,
Her tears *are* on her cheeks;
Among all her lovers
She has none to comfort *her.*
All her friends have dealt
treacherously with her;
They have become her
enemies.

3 Judah has gone into captivity,
Under affliction and hard
servitude;
She dwells among the nations,
She finds no rest;
All her persecutors overtake
her in dire straits.

4 The roads to Zion mourn
Because no one comes to the
set feasts.
All her gates are desolate;
Her priests sigh,
Her virgins are afflicted,
And she *is* in bitterness.

5 Her adversaries have become
the master,
Her enemies prosper;
For the LORD has afflicted her
Because of the multitude of her
transgressions.
Her children have gone into
captivity before the enemy.

6 And from the daughter of Zion
All her splendor has departed.
Her princes have become like
deer
That find no pasture,
That flee without strength
Before the pursuer.

7 In the days of her affliction and
roaming,
Jerusalem remembers all her
pleasant things
That she had in the days of old.

When her people fell into the
hand of the enemy,
With no one to help her,
The adversaries saw her
And mocked at her downfall.[a]

8 Jerusalem has sinned gravely,
Therefore she has become
vile.[a]
All who honored her despise
her
Because they have seen her
nakedness;
Yes, she sighs and turns away.

9 Her uncleanness *is* in her
skirts;
She did not consider her
destiny;
Therefore her collapse was
awesome.
She had no comforter.
"O LORD, behold my affliction,
For *the* enemy is exalted!"

10 The adversary has spread his
hand
Over all her pleasant things;
For she has seen the nations
enter her sanctuary,
Those whom You commanded
Not to enter Your assembly.

11 All her people sigh,
They seek bread;
They have given their
valuables for food to restore
life.
"See, O LORD, and consider,
For I am scorned."

12 "*Is it* nothing to you, all you who
pass by?
Behold and see
If there is any sorrow like my
sorrow,
Which has been brought on me,
Which the LORD has inflicted
In the day of His fierce anger.

13 "From above He has sent fire
into my bones,
And it overpowered them;
He has spread a net for my feet
And turned me back;

1:7 [a]Vulgate reads *her Sabbaths.*   1:8 [a]Septuagint and Vulgate read *moved* or *removed.*

He has made me desolate
And faint all the day.

14 "The yoke of my transgressions
was bound;[a]
They were woven together by
His hands,
And thrust upon my neck.
He made my strength fail;
The Lord delivered me into the
hands of *those whom* I am
not able to withstand.

15 "The Lord has trampled
underfoot all my mighty *men*
in my midst;
He has called an assembly
against me
To crush my young men;
The Lord trampled *as* in a
winepress
The virgin daughter of Judah.

16 "For these *things* I weep;
My eye, my eye overflows with
water;
Because the comforter, who
should restore my life,
Is far from me.
My children are desolate
Because the enemy prevailed."

17 Zion spreads out her hands,
But no one comforts her;
The LORD has commanded
concerning Jacob
That those around him *become*
his adversaries;
Jerusalem has become an
unclean thing among them.

18 "The LORD is righteous,
For I rebelled against His
commandment.
Hear now, all peoples,
And behold my sorrow;
My virgins and my young men
Have gone into captivity.

19 "I called for my lovers,
But they deceived me;
My priests and my elders
Breathed their last in the city,
While they sought food
To restore their life.

20 "See, O LORD, that I *am* in
distress;
My soul is troubled;

My heart is overturned within
me,
For I have been very rebellious.
Outside the sword bereaves,
At home *it is* like death.

21 "They have heard that I sigh,
But no one comforts me.
All my enemies have heard of
my trouble;
They are glad that You have
done *it*.
Bring on the day You have
announced,
That they may become like me.

22 "Let all their wickedness come
before You,
And do to them as You have
done to me
For all my transgressions;
For my sighs *are* many,
And my heart *is* faint."

2 How the Lord has covered the
daughter of Zion
With a cloud in His anger!
He cast down from heaven to
the earth
The beauty of Israel,
And did not remember His
footstool
In the day of His anger.

2 The Lord has swallowed up
and has not pitied
All the dwelling places of
Jacob.
He has thrown down in His
wrath
The strongholds of the
daughter of Judah;
He has brought *them* down to
the ground;
He has profaned the kingdom
and its princes.

3 He has cut off in fierce anger
Every horn of Israel;
He has drawn back His right
hand
From before the enemy.
He has blazed against Jacob
like a flaming fire
Devouring all around.

4 Standing like an enemy, He has
bent His bow;
With His right hand, like an
adversary,

1:14 [a]Following Masoretic Text and Targum; Septuagint, Syriac, and Vulgate read *watched over*.

God is releasing you from fear. You need to allow Him an opportunity in your life.
Then you will start seeing beauty at all different stages of your life.

He has slain all *who were*
pleasing to His eye;
On the tent of the daughter of
Zion,
He has poured out His fury like
fire.

5 The Lord was like an enemy.
He has swallowed up Israel,
He has swallowed up all her
palaces;
He has destroyed her
strongholds,
And has increased mourning
and lamentation
In the daughter of Judah.

6 He has done violence to His
tabernacle,
As if it were a garden;
He has destroyed His place of
assembly;
The LORD has caused
The appointed feasts and
Sabbaths to be forgotten in
Zion.
In His burning indignation He
has spurned the king and the
priest.

7 The Lord has spurned His altar,
He has abandoned His
sanctuary;
He has given up the walls of her
palaces
Into the hand of the enemy.
They have made a noise in the
house of the LORD
As on the day of a set feast.

8 The LORD has purposed to
destroy
The wall of the daughter of
Zion.
He has stretched out a line;
He has not withdrawn His hand
from destroying;
Therefore He has caused the
rampart and wall to lament;
They languished together.

9 Her gates have sunk into the
ground;
He has destroyed and broken
her bars.
Her king and her princes *are*
among the nations;
The Law *is no more*,
And her prophets find no vision
from the LORD.

10 The elders of the daughter of
Zion

Sit on the ground *and* keep
silence;
They throw dust on their heads
And gird themselves with
sackcloth.
The virgins of Jerusalem
Bow their heads to the ground.

11 My eyes fail with tears,
My heart is troubled;
My bile is poured on the ground
Because of the destruction of
the daughter of my people,
Because the children and the
infants
Faint in the streets of the city.

12 They say to their mothers,
"Where *is* grain and wine?"
As they swoon like the
wounded
In the streets of the city,
As their life is poured out
In their mothers' bosom.

13 How shall I console you?
To what shall I liken you,
O daughter of Jerusalem?
What shall I compare with you,
that I may comfort you,
O virgin daughter of Zion?
For your ruin *is* spread wide as
the sea;
Who can heal you?

14 Your prophets have seen for
you
False and deceptive visions;
They have not uncovered your
iniquity,
To bring back your captives,
But have envisioned for you
false prophecies and
delusions.

15 All who pass by clap *their*
hands at you;
They hiss and shake their
heads
At the daughter of Jerusalem:
"*Is* this the city that is called
'The perfection of beauty,
The joy of the whole earth'?"

16 All your enemies have opened
their mouth against you;
They hiss and gnash *their*
teeth.
They say, "We have swallowed
her up!
Surely this *is* the day we have
waited for;

Gospel
Pearls

We have found *it,* we have seen
   it! "

17 The LORD has done what He
   purposed;
He has fulfilled His word
Which He commanded in days
   of old.
He has thrown down and has
   not pitied,
And He has caused an enemy
   to rejoice over you;
He has exalted the horn of your
   adversaries.

18 Their heart cried out to the
   Lord,
"O wall of the daughter of Zion,
Let tears run down like a river
   day and night;
Give yourself no relief;
Give your eyes no rest.

19 "Arise, cry out in the night,
At the beginning of the
   watches;
Pour out your heart like water
   before the face of the Lord.
Lift your hands toward Him
For the life of your young
   children,
Who faint from hunger at the
   head of every street."

20 "See, O LORD, and consider!
To whom have You done this?
Should the women eat their
   offspring,
The children they have
   cuddled?*a*
Should the priest and prophet
   be slain
In the sanctuary of the Lord?

21 "Young and old lie
On the ground in the streets;
My virgins and my young men
Have fallen by the sword;
You have slain *them* in the day
   of Your anger,
You have slaughtered *and* not
   pitied.

22 "You have invited as to a feast
   day
The terrors that surround me.
In the day of the LORD's anger
There was no refugee or
   survivor.

Those whom I have borne and
   brought up
My enemies have destroyed."

3 I *am* the man *who* has seen
   affliction by the rod of His
   wrath.
2 He has led me and made *me*
   walk
In darkness and not *in* light.
3 Surely He has turned His hand
   against me
Time and time again
   throughout the day.

4 He has aged my flesh and my
   skin,
And broken my bones.
5 He has besieged me
And surrounded *me* with
   bitterness and woe.
6 He has set me in dark places
Like the dead of long ago.

7 He has hedged me in so that I
   cannot get out;
He has made my chain heavy.
8 Even when I cry and shout,
He shuts out my prayer.
9 He has blocked my ways with
   hewn stone;
He has made my paths
   crooked.

10 He *has been* to me a bear lying
   in wait,
Like a lion in ambush.
11 He has turned aside my ways
   and torn me in pieces;
He has made me desolate.
12 He has bent His bow
And set me up as a target for
   the arrow.

13 He has caused the arrows of
   His quiver
To pierce my loins.*a*
14 I have become the ridicule of
   all my people—
Their taunting song all the day.
15 He has filled me with
   bitterness,
He has made me drink
   wormwood.
16 He has also broken my teeth
   with gravel,
And covered me with ashes.
17 You have moved my soul far
   from peace;

2:20 *a*Vulgate reads *a span long.*   3:13 *a*Literally *kidneys*

I believe God is bringing health into dry bones, bones that were bowed over, bones that were bent out of shape, bones that made you upset with yourself. All are giving way to the life of the Spirit.

Cry, Baby!

Lamentations 2:19

*A*re you so convinced that your life could be different that you are willing to stagger to the altar and pray while others play?

Do you want something from God so much that you are willing to risk the opinions of those who accuse you of being too emotional in the way you ask God for it? Do you believe so passionately that you are intoxicated with the hope of what God has for you? What dream consumes your thinking, your feeling, your believing? Pray about that, because if your prayer request doesn't move *you,* it probably won't move God.

Use your trouble to fuel your passion. The depth of the trouble you have been experiencing probably equals the depth of the desire that drives you toward God. When your trouble is great enough and your desire is strong enough, you will feel that you have nothing to lose and everything to gain by pouring out all your passion before Him.

There are women who need to stop worrying so much about being Miss Together that they stifle their emotions when they pray. There are women who need to stop weighing everything they do against their need to uphold their reputation. God is not impressed by the right club or the right crowd.

He wants women who will humble themselves, who will come to Him, who will cry out to Him—with no concern for what other people think or say. God is looking for women who want His will done on this earth so much that they will cry for it. He is looking for women who want right to triumph over wrong; good over evil; Jesus over the devil. He is looking for women who want to see Him act on their behalf—and who want it to the extent that they will cry aloud for it and refuse to be silenced. He wants women who will cry and not shut up!

The power of life and death is in your tongue. Refuse to be silenced. Speak life! After you have prayed, speak God's words of life to yourself. Speak them to your problem. Speak them to your circumstance, your situation, your need, your lack of supply. Speak life, life, life.

Don't allow yourself to be intimidated into remaining quiet about what you want God to do for you. Give voice to those things! Go ahead and cry!

I have forgotten prosperity.
18 And I said, "My strength and my hope
Have perished from the LORD."

19 Remember my affliction and roaming,
The wormwood and the gall.
20 My soul still remembers
And sinks within me.
21 This I recall to my mind,
Therefore I have hope.

22 *Through* the LORD's mercies we are not consumed,
Because His compassions fail not.
23 *They are* new every morning;
Great *is* Your faithfulness.
24 "The LORD *is* my portion," says my soul,
"Therefore I hope in Him!"

25 The LORD *is* good to those who wait for Him,
To the soul *who* seeks Him.
26 *It is* good that *one* should hope and wait quietly
For the salvation of the LORD.
27 *It is* good for a man to bear
The yoke in his youth.

28 Let him sit alone and keep silent,
Because *God* has laid *it* on him;
29 Let him put his mouth in the dust—
There may yet be hope.
30 Let him give *his* cheek to the one who strikes him,
And be full of reproach.

31 For the Lord will not cast off forever.
32 Though He causes grief,
Yet He will show compassion
According to the multitude of His mercies.
33 For He does not afflict willingly,
Nor grieve the children of men.

34 To crush under one's feet
All the prisoners of the earth,
35 To turn aside the justice *due* a man
Before the face of the Most High,
36 Or subvert a man in his cause—
The Lord does not approve.

37 Who *is* he *who* speaks and it comes to pass,
When the Lord has not commanded *it?*
38 *Is it* not from the mouth of the Most High
That woe and well-being proceed?
39 Why should a living man complain,
A man for the punishment of his sins?

40 Let us search out and examine our ways,
And turn back to the LORD;
41 Let us lift our hearts and hands
To God in heaven.
42 We have transgressed and rebelled;
You have not pardoned.

43 You have covered *Yourself* with anger
And pursued us;
You have slain *and* not pitied.
44 You have covered Yourself with a cloud,
That prayer should not pass through.
45 You have made us an offscouring and refuse
In the midst of the peoples.

46 All our enemies
Have opened their mouths against us.
47 Fear and a snare have come upon us,
Desolation and destruction.
48 My eyes overflow with rivers of water
For the destruction of the daughter of my people.

49 My eyes flow and do not cease,
Without interruption,
50 Till the LORD from heaven
Looks down and sees.
51 My eyes bring suffering to my soul
Because of all the daughters of my city.

52 My enemies without cause
Hunted me down like a bird.
53 They silenced*a* my life in the pit
And threw stones at me.

3:53 *a*Septuagint reads *put to death.*

God will heal the inner wound and teach you how important you are to Him. You do make a difference. The world would be a different place if it were not for you. You are a part of His divine plan.

The Pen of Hope and the Tablet of Faith

Lamentations 3:24

You would be amazed at the number of people who have decided that they have no options or windows in their lives. They have entombed themselves with guilt. They have embalmed themselves with regret; they exist in a constant state of decomposition.

You will see them on the job. You will see them in the streets. You will even find them in church. Their painted nails are banging keys on the computer. They are dressed in business suits or doctor's frocks, but they are dead. These will be the women you will find with smiling lips but empty eyes. The glow has faded from their cheeks. The bells have ceased to jingle in their voice. They are mannequins, stuck on the stage of life. They are all dressed up and going nowhere. They have rocked their faith to sleep in the cradle of depression, and they are reaping the bitter rewards of negative thinking.

Hear me today: You are not imprisoned; you are empowered. Take control of your circumstances in Jesus' name and arise. You are a daughter of the King, and you can arise by His power without hesitation. Knowing this sets you free.

It's the knowledge of your liberty that the enemy wants to steal from you. He cannot take away the *power* to be free; so he tries to steal the *knowledge* of your freedom. He really laughs when he sees you entrapped behind an open door. There you are crying and frustrated, tormented and afraid. The fact is that two thousand years ago, your God unlocked the door, and you can walk through it at will. You just don't know it!

Moving from imprisonment to empowerment takes some people longer than others. It helps when you have had good, strong childhood affirmation. But even if you haven't, you don't have to limit your future merely because of voids in your past. Close those chapters in your life and write new ones.

Pick up the pen of hope and write on the tablet of faith. Write with grace. Write with flourish. Write with passion. Write with freedom.

54 The waters flowed over my
head;
I said, "I am cut off!"

55 I called on Your name, O LORD,
From the lowest pit.

56 You have heard my voice:
"Do not hide Your ear
From my sighing, from my cry
for help."

57 You drew near on the day I
called on You,
And said, "Do not fear!"

58 O Lord, You have pleaded the
case for my soul;
You have redeemed my life.

59 O LORD, You have seen *how* I
am wronged;
Judge my case.

60 You have seen all their
vengeance,
All their schemes against me.

61 You have heard their reproach,
O LORD,
All their schemes against me,

62 The lips of my enemies
And their whispering against
me all the day.

63 Look at their sitting down and
their rising up;
I *am* their taunting song.

64 Repay them, O LORD,
According to the work of their
hands.

65 Give them a veiled[a] heart;
Your curse *be* upon them!

66 In Your anger,
Pursue and destroy them
From under the heavens of the
LORD.

4 How the gold has become dim!
How changed the fine gold!
The stones of the sanctuary are
scattered
At the head of every street.

2 The precious sons of Zion,
Valuable as fine gold,
How they are regarded as clay
pots,
The work of the hands of the
potter!

3 Even the jackals present their
breasts

To nurse their young;
But the daughter of my people
is cruel,
Like ostriches in the
wilderness.

4 The tongue of the infant clings
To the roof of its mouth for
thirst;
The young children ask for
bread,
But no one breaks *it* for them.

5 Those who ate delicacies
Are desolate in the streets;
Those who were brought up in
scarlet
Embrace ash heaps.

6 The punishment of the iniquity
of the daughter of my people
Is greater than the punishment
of the sin of Sodom,
Which was overthrown in a
moment,
With no hand to help her!

7 Her Nazirites[a] were brighter
than snow
And whiter than milk;
They were more ruddy in body
than rubies,
Like sapphire in their
appearance.

8 *Now* their appearance is
blacker than soot;
They go unrecognized in the
streets;
Their skin clings to their bones,
It has become as dry as wood.

9 *Those* slain by the sword are
better off
Than *those* who die of hunger;
For these pine away,
Stricken *for lack* of the fruits
of the field.

10 The hands of the
compassionate women
Have cooked their own
children;
They became food for them
In the destruction of the
daughter of my people.

11 The LORD has fulfilled His fury,
He has poured out His fierce
anger.

3:65 *a*A Jewish tradition reads *sorrow of.*   4:7 *a*Or *nobles*

---

*T*he Holy Spirit will fill you. He will impregnate you. He will give life to your spirit.
He will put purpose back into you. He will renew you. He will restore you.

He kindled a fire in Zion,
And it has devoured its
    foundations.

12 The kings of the earth,
And all inhabitants of the
    world,
Would not have believed
That the adversary and the
    enemy
Could enter the gates of
    Jerusalem—

13 Because of the sins of her
    prophets
And the iniquities of her
    priests,
Who shed in her midst
The blood of the just.

14 They wandered blind in the
    streets;
They have defiled themselves
    with blood,
So that no one would touch
    their garments.

15 They cried out to them,
"Go away, unclean!
Go away, go away,
Do not touch us!"
When they fled and wandered,
Those among the nations said,
"They shall no longer dwell
    here."

16 The face*ᵃ* of the LORD scattered
    them;
He no longer regards them.
The people do not respect the
    priests
Nor show favor to the elders.

17 Still our eyes failed us,
Watching vainly for our help;
In our watching we watched
For a nation *that* could not
    save *us*.

18 They tracked our steps
So that we could not walk in
    our streets.
Our end was near;
Our days were over,
For our end had come.

19 Our pursuers were swifter
Than the eagles of the heavens.
They pursued us on the
    mountains
And lay in wait for us in the
    wilderness.

20 The breath of our nostrils, the
    anointed of the LORD,
Was caught in their pits,
Of whom we said, "Under his
    shadow
We shall live among the
    nations."

21 Rejoice and be glad, O
    daughter of Edom,
You who dwell in the land of
    Uz!
The cup shall also pass over to
    you
And you shall become drunk
    and make yourself naked.

22 *The punishment of* your
    iniquity is accomplished,
O daughter of Zion;
He will no longer send you into
    captivity.
He will punish your iniquity,
O daughter of Edom;
He will uncover your sins!

5 Remember, O LORD, what has
    come upon us;
Look, and behold our reproach!
2 Our inheritance has been
    turned over to aliens,
And our houses to foreigners.
3 We have become orphans and
    waifs,
Our mothers *are* like widows.

4 We pay for the water we drink,
And our wood comes at a price.
5 *They* pursue at our heels;*ᵃ*
We labor *and* have no rest.
6 We have given our hand *to* the
    Egyptians
And the Assyrians, to be
    satisfied with bread.

7 Our fathers sinned *and are* no
    more,
But we bear their iniquities.
8 Servants rule over us;
There is none to deliver *us* from
    their hand.
9 We get our bread *at the risk*
    of our lives,
Because of the sword in the
    wilderness.
10 Our skin is hot as an oven,
Because of the fever of famine.

4:16 *ᵃTargum reads *anger*.   5:5 *ᵃLiterally *necks*

Gospel Pearls

11 They ravished the women in
Zion,
The maidens in the cities of
Judah.
12 Princes were hung up by their
hands,
And elders were not respected.
13 Young men ground at the
millstones;
Boys staggered under *loads of*
wood.
14 The elders have ceased
gathering at the gate,
And the young men from their
music.

15 The joy of our heart has ceased;
Our dance has turned into
mourning.
16 The crown has fallen *from* our
head.
Woe to us, for we have sinned!

17 Because of this our heart is
faint;
Because of these *things* our
eyes grow dim;
18 Because of Mount Zion which
is desolate,
With foxes walking about on
it.

19 You, O Lord, remain forever;
Your throne from generation to
generation.
20 Why do You forget us
forever,
And forsake us for so long a
time?
21 Turn us back to You, O Lord,
and we will be restored;
Renew our days as of old,
22 Unless You have utterly
rejected us,
And are very angry with us!

The Book of

EZEKIEL

1 Now it came to pass in the thirti-
eth year, in the fourth *month,* on
the fifth *day* of the month, as I *was*
among the captives by the River Chebar, *that* the heavens were opened
and I saw visions[a] of God. 2 On the
fifth *day* of the month, which *was* in
the fifth year of King Jehoiachin's
captivity, 3 the word of the Lord
came expressly to Ezekiel the priest,
the son of Buzi, in the land of the
Chaldeans[a] by the River Chebar; and
the hand of the Lord was upon him
there.

4 Then I looked, and behold, a
whirlwind was coming out of the
north, a great cloud with raging fire
engulfing itself; and brightness *was*
all around it and radiating out of its
midst like the color of amber, out of
the midst of the fire. 5 Also from
within it *came* the likeness of four
living creatures. And this *was* their
appearance: they had the likeness of
a man. 6 Each one had four faces, and
each one had four wings. 7 Their legs

were straight, and the soles of their
feet *were* like the soles of calves' feet.
They sparkled like the color of burnished bronze. 8 The hands of a man
were under their wings on their four
sides; and each of the four had faces
and wings. 9 Their wings touched one
another. *The creatures* did not turn
when they went, but each one went
straight forward.

10 As for the likeness of their faces,
each had the face of a man; each of
the four had the face of a lion on the
right side, each of the four had the
face of an ox on the left side, and
each of the four had the face of an
eagle. 11 Thus *were* their faces. Their
wings stretched upward; two *wings*
of each one touched one another, and
two covered their bodies. 12 And
each one went straight forward; they
went wherever the spirit wanted to
go, and they did not turn when they
went.

13 As for the likeness of the living
creatures, their appearance *was* like

1:1 [a]Following Masoretic Text, Septuagint, and Vulgate; Syriac and Targum read *a vision.* 1:3 [a]Or
Babylonians, and so elsewhere in this book

God's women are to be womb-men. They are to be creative and bring forth new life.
That is exactly what God wants to do with those who are broken and discouraged.

burning coals of fire, like the appearance of torches going back and forth among the living creatures. The fire was bright, and out of the fire went lightning. 14 And the living creatures ran back and forth, in appearance like a flash of lightning.

15 Now as I looked at the living creatures, behold, a wheel *was* on the earth beside each living creature with its four faces. 16 The appearance of the wheels and their workings *was* like the color of beryl, and all four had the same likeness. The appearance of their workings *was*, as it were, a wheel in the middle of a wheel. 17 When they moved, they went toward any one of four directions; they did not turn aside when they went. 18 As for their rims, they were so high they were awesome; and their rims *were* full of eyes, all around the four of them. 19 When the living creatures went, the wheels went beside them; and when the living creatures were lifted up from the earth, the wheels were lifted up. 20 Wherever the spirit wanted to go, they went, *because* there the spirit went; and the wheels were lifted together with them, for the spirit of the living creatures[a] *was* in the wheels. 21 When those went, *these* went; when those stood, *these* stood; and when those were lifted up from the earth, the wheels were lifted up together with them, for the spirit of the living creatures[a] *was* in the wheels. 22 The likeness of the firmament above the heads of the living creatures[a] *was* like the color of an awesome crystal, stretched out over their heads. 23 And under the firmament their wings *spread out* straight, one toward another. Each one had two which covered one side, and each one had two which covered the other side of the body. 24 When they went, I heard the noise of their wings, like the noise of many waters, like the voice of the Almighty, a tumult like the noise of an army; and when they stood still, they let down their wings. 25 A voice came from above the firmament that *was* over their heads; whenever they stood, they let down their wings.

26 And above the firmament over their heads *was* the likeness of a throne, in appearance like a sapphire stone; on the likeness of the throne *was* a likeness with the appearance of a man high above it. 27 Also from the appearance of His waist and upward I saw, as it were, the color of amber with the appearance of fire all around within it; and from the appearance of His waist and downward I saw, as it were, the appearance of fire with brightness all around. 28 Like the appearance of a rainbow in a cloud on a rainy day, so *was* the appearance of the brightness all around it. This *was* the appearance of the likeness of the glory of the LORD.

So when I saw *it*, I fell on my face, and I heard a voice of One speaking.

2 And He said to me, "Son of man, stand on your feet, and I will speak to you." 2 Then the Spirit entered me when He spoke to me, and set me on my feet; and I heard Him who spoke to me. 3 And He said to me: "Son of man, I am sending you to the children of Israel, to a rebellious nation that has rebelled against Me; they and their fathers have transgressed against Me to this very day. 4 For *they are* impudent and stubborn children. I am sending you to them, and you shall say to them, 'Thus says the Lord GOD.' 5 As for them, whether they hear or whether they refuse—for they *are* a rebellious house—yet they will know that a prophet has been among them.

6 "And you, son of man, do not be afraid of them nor be afraid of their words, though briers and thorns *are* with you and you dwell among scorpions; do not be afraid of their words or dismayed by their looks, though they *are* a rebellious house. 7 You shall speak My words to them, whether they hear or whether they refuse, for they *are* rebellious. 8 But you, son of man, hear what I say to you. Do not be rebellious like that rebellious house; open your mouth and eat what I give you."

9 Now when I looked, there was a hand stretched out to me; and behold, a scroll of a book *was* in it. 10 Then He spread it before me; and *there was* writing on the inside and on the outside, and written on it

---

1:20 aLiterally *living creature;* Septuagint and Vulgate read *spirit of life;* Targum reads *creatures.*
1:21 aLiterally *living creature;* Septuagint and Vulgate read *spirit of life;* Targum reads *creatures.*
1:22 aFollowing Septuagint, Targum, and Vulgate; Masoretic Text reads *living creature.*

Gospel Pearls

were lamentations and mourning and woe.

3 Moreover He said to me, "Son of man, eat what you find; eat this scroll, and go, speak to the house of Israel." 2 So I opened my mouth, and He caused me to eat that scroll.

3 And He said to me, "Son of man, feed your belly, and fill your stomach with this scroll that I give you." So I ate, and it was in my mouth like honey in sweetness.

4 Then He said to me: "Son of man, go to the house of Israel and speak with My words to them. 5 For you *are* not sent to a people of unfamiliar speech and of hard language, *but* to the house of Israel, 6 not to many people of unfamiliar speech and of hard language, whose words you cannot understand. Surely, had I sent you to them, they would have listened to you. 7 But the house of Israel will not listen to you, because they will not listen to Me; for all the house of Israel *are* impudent and hardhearted. 8 Behold, I have made your face strong against their faces, and your forehead strong against their foreheads. 9 Like adamant stone, harder than flint, I have made your forehead; do not be afraid of them, nor be dismayed at their looks, though they *are* a rebellious house."

10 Moreover He said to me: "Son of man, receive into your heart all My words that I speak to you, and hear with your ears. 11 And go, get to the captives, to the children of your people, and speak to them and tell them, 'Thus says the Lord GOD,' whether they hear, or whether they refuse."

12 Then the Spirit lifted me up, and I heard behind me a great thunderous voice: "Blessed *is* the glory of the LORD from His place!" 13 *I* also *heard* the noise of the wings of the living creatures that touched one another, and the noise of the wheels beside them, and a great thunderous noise. 14 So the Spirit lifted me up and took me away, and I went in bitterness, in the heat of my spirit; but the hand of the LORD was strong upon me. 15 Then I came to the captives at Tel Abib, who dwelt by the River Chebar; and I sat where they sat, and remained there astonished among them seven days.

16 Now it came to pass at the end of seven days that the word of the LORD came to me, saying, 17 "Son of man, I have made you a watchman for the house of Israel; therefore hear a word from My mouth, and give them warning from Me: 18 When I say to the wicked, 'You shall surely die,' and you give him no warning, nor speak to warn the wicked from his wicked way, to save his life, that same wicked *man* shall die in his iniquity; but his blood I will require at your hand. 19 Yet, if you warn the wicked, and he does not turn from his wickedness, nor from his wicked way, he shall die in his iniquity; but you have delivered your soul.

20 "Again, when a righteous *man* turns from his righteousness and commits iniquity, and I lay a stumbling block before him, he shall die; because you did not give him warning, he shall die in his sin, and his righteousness which he has done shall not be remembered; but his blood I will require at your hand. 21 Nevertheless if you warn the righteous *man* that the righteous should not sin, and he does not sin, he shall surely live because he took warning; also you will have delivered your soul."

22 Then the hand of the LORD was upon me there, and He said to me, "Arise, go out into the plain, and there I shall talk with you."

23 So I arose and went out into the plain, and behold, the glory of the LORD stood there, like the glory which I saw by the River Chebar; and I fell on my face. 24 Then the Spirit entered me and set me on my feet, and spoke with me and said to me: "Go, shut yourself inside your house. 25 And you, O son of man, surely they will put ropes on you and bind you with them, so that you cannot go out among them. 26 I will make your tongue cling to the roof of your mouth, so that you shall be mute and not be one to rebuke them, for they *are* a rebellious house. 27 But when I speak with you, I will open your mouth, and you shall say to them, 'Thus says the Lord GOD.' He who hears, let him hear; and he who refuses, let him refuse; for they *are* a rebellious house.

4 "You also, son of man, take a clay tablet and lay it before you, and portray on it a city, Jerusalem. 2 Lay siege against it, build a siege

wall against it, and heap up a mound against it; set camps against it also, and place battering rams against it all around. 3 Moreover take for yourself an iron plate, and set it *as* an iron wall between you and the city. Set your face against it, and it shall be besieged, and you shall lay siege against it. This *will be* a sign to the house of Israel.

4 "Lie also on your left side, and lay the iniquity of the house of Israel upon it. *According* to the number of the days that you lie on it, you shall bear their iniquity. 5 For I have laid on you the years of their iniquity, according to the number of the days, three hundred and ninety days; so you shall bear the iniquity of the house of Israel. 6 And when you have completed them, lie again on your right side; then you shall bear the iniquity of the house of Judah forty days. I have laid on you a day for each year.

7 "Therefore you shall set your face toward the siege of Jerusalem; your arm *shall be* uncovered, and you shall prophesy against it. 8 And surely I will restrain you so that you cannot turn from one side to another till you have ended the days of your siege.

9 "Also take for yourself wheat, barley, beans, lentils, millet, and spelt; put them into one vessel, and make bread of them for yourself. *During* the number of days that you lie on your side, three hundred and ninety days, you shall eat it. 10 And your food which you eat *shall be* by weight, twenty shekels a day; from time to time you shall eat it. 11 You shall also drink water by measure, one-sixth of a hin; from time to time you shall drink. 12 And you shall eat it *as* barley cakes; and bake it using fuel of human waste in their sight."

13 Then the LORD said, "So shall the children of Israel eat their defiled bread among the Gentiles, where I will drive them."

14 So I said, "Ah, Lord GOD! Indeed I have never defiled myself from my youth till now; I have never eaten what died of itself or was torn by beasts, nor has abominable flesh ever come into my mouth."

15 Then He said to me, "See, I am giving you cow dung instead of human waste, and you shall prepare your bread over it."

16 Moreover He said to me, "Son of man, surely I will cut off the supply of bread in Jerusalem; they shall eat bread by weight and with anxiety, and shall drink water by measure and with dread, 17 that they may lack bread and water, and be dismayed with one another, and waste away because of their iniquity.

5 "And you, son of man, take a sharp sword, take it as a barber's razor, and pass *it* over your head and your beard; then take scales to weigh and divide the hair. 2 You shall burn with fire one-third in the midst of the city, when the days of the siege are finished; then you shall take one-third and strike around *it* with the sword, and one-third you shall scatter in the wind: I will draw out a sword after them. 3 You shall also take a small number of them and bind them in the edge of your *garment.* 4 Then take some of them again and throw them into the midst of the fire, and burn them in the fire. From there a fire will go out into all the house of Israel.

5 "Thus says the Lord GOD: 'This *is* Jerusalem; I have set her in the midst of the nations and the countries all around her. 6 She has rebelled against My judgments by doing wickedness more than the nations, and against My statutes more than the countries that *are* all around her; for they have refused My judgments, and they have not walked in My statutes.' 7 Therefore thus says the Lord GOD: 'Because you have multiplied *disobedience* more than the nations that *are* all around you, have not walked in My statutes nor kept My judgments, nor even done[a] according to the judgments of the nations that *are* all around you'— 8 therefore thus says the Lord GOD: 'Indeed I, even I, *am* against you and will execute judgments in your midst in the sight of the nations. 9 And I will do among you what I have never done, and the like of which I will never do again, because of all your abominations. 10 Therefore fathers

5:7 [a]Following Masoretic Text, Septuagint, Targum, and Vulgate; many Hebrew manuscripts and Syriac read *but have done* (compare 11:12).

Gospel Pearls

shall eat *their* sons in your midst, and sons shall eat their fathers; and I will execute judgments among you, and all of you who remain I will scatter to all the winds.

11 'Therefore, *as* I live,' says the Lord GOD, 'surely, because you have defiled My sanctuary with all your detestable things and with all your abominations, therefore I will also diminish *you;* My eye will not spare, nor will I have any pity. 12 One-third of you shall die of the pestilence, and be consumed with famine in your midst; and one-third shall fall by the sword all around you; and I will scatter another third to all the winds, and I will draw out a sword after them.

13 'Thus shall My anger be spent, and I will cause My fury to rest upon them, and I will be avenged; and they shall know that I, the LORD, have spoken *it* in My zeal, when I have spent My fury upon them. 14 Moreover I will make you a waste and a reproach among the nations that *are* all around you, in the sight of all who pass by.

15 'So it*ᵃ* shall be a reproach, a taunt, a lesson, and an astonishment to the nations that *are* all around you, when I execute judgments among you in anger and in fury and in furious rebukes. I, the LORD, have spoken. 16 When I send against them the terrible arrows of famine which shall be for destruction, which I will send to destroy you, I will increase the famine upon you and cut off your supply of bread. 17 So I will send against you famine and wild beasts, and they will bereave you. Pestilence and blood shall pass through you, and I will bring the sword against you. I, the LORD, have spoken.' "

6 Now the word of the LORD came to me, saying: 2 "Son of man, set your face toward the mountains of Israel, and prophesy against them, 3 and say, 'O mountains of Israel, hear the word of the Lord GOD! Thus says the Lord GOD to the mountains, to the hills, to the ravines, and to the valleys: "Indeed I, *even* I, will bring a sword against you, and I will destroy your high places. 4 Then your altars shall be desolate, your incense altars shall be broken, and I will cast down your slain *men* before your

idols. 5 And I will lay the corpses of the children of Israel before their idols, and I will scatter your bones all around your altars. 6 In all your dwelling places the cities shall be laid waste, and the high places shall be desolate, so that your altars may be laid waste and made desolate, your idols may be broken and made to cease, your incense altars may be cut down, and your works may be abolished. 7 The slain shall fall in your midst, and you shall know that I *am* the LORD.

8 "Yet I will leave a remnant, so that you may have *some* who escape the sword among the nations, when you are scattered through the countries. 9 Then those of you who escape will remember Me among the nations where they are carried captive, because I was crushed by their adulterous heart which has departed from Me, and by their eyes which play the harlot after their idols; they will loathe themselves for the evils which they committed in all their abominations. 10 And they shall know that I *am* the LORD; I have not said in vain that I would bring this calamity upon them."

11 'Thus says the Lord GOD: "Pound your fists and stamp your feet, and say, 'Alas, for all the evil abominations of the house of Israel! For they shall fall by the sword, by famine, and by pestilence. 12 He who is far off shall die by the pestilence, he who is near shall fall by the sword, and he who remains and is besieged shall die by the famine. Thus will I spend My fury upon them. 13 Then you shall know that I *am* the LORD, when their slain are among their idols all around their altars, on every high hill, on all the mountaintops, under every green tree, and under every thick oak, wherever they offered sweet incense to all their idols. 14 So I will stretch out My hand against them and make the land desolate, yes, more desolate than the wilderness toward Diblah, in all their dwelling places. Then they shall know that I *am* the LORD.' " ' "

7 Moreover the word of the LORD came to me, saying, 2 "And you, son of man, thus says the Lord GOD to the land of Israel:

5:15 *ᵃ*Septuagint, Syriac, Targum, and Vulgate read *you.*

*T*he hidden Christ who has been locked up behind your fears, your problems and your insecurity, will come forth in your life. You will see the power of the Lord Jesus do a mighty thing.

'An end! The end has come
upon the four corners of the
land.
3 Now the end *has come* upon
you,
And I will send My anger
against you;
I will judge you according to
your ways,
And I will repay you for all
your abominations.
4 My eye will not spare you,
Nor will I have pity;
But I will repay your ways,
And your abominations will be
in your midst;
Then you shall know that I *am*
the LORD!'

5 "Thus says the Lord GOD:

'A disaster, a singular disaster;
Behold, it has come!
6 An end has come,
The end has come;
It has dawned for you;
Behold, it has come!
7 Doom has come to you, you
who dwell in the land;
The time has come,
A day of trouble *is* near,
And not of rejoicing in the
mountains.
8 Now upon you I will soon pour
out My fury,
And spend My anger upon you;
I will judge you according to
your ways,
And I will repay you for all
your abominations.
9 'My eye will not spare,
Nor will I have pity;
I will repay you according to
your ways,
And your abominations will be
in your midst.
Then you shall know that I *am*
the LORD who strikes.

10 'Behold, the day!
Behold, it has come!
Doom has gone out;
The rod has blossomed,
Pride has budded.
11 Violence has risen up into a rod
of wickedness;
None of them *shall remain,*
None of their multitude,
None of them;
Nor *shall there be* wailing for
them.

12 The time has come,
The day draws near.

'Let not the buyer rejoice,
Nor the seller mourn,
For wrath *is* on their whole
multitude.
13 For the seller shall not return
to what has been sold,
Though he may still be alive;
For the vision concerns the
whole multitude,
And it shall not turn back;
No one will strengthen himself
Who lives in iniquity.

14 'They have blown the trumpet
and made everyone ready,
But no one goes to battle;
For My wrath *is* on all their
multitude.
15 The sword *is* outside,
And the pestilence and famine
within.
Whoever *is* in the field
Will die by the sword;
And whoever *is* in the city,
Famine and pestilence will
devour him.

16 'Those who survive will escape
and be on the mountains
Like doves of the valleys,
All of them mourning,
Each for his iniquity.
17 Every hand will be feeble,
And every knee will be *as* weak
as water.
18 They will also be girded with
sackcloth;
Horror will cover them;
Shame *will be* on every face,
Baldness on all their heads.

19 'They will throw their silver into
the streets,
And their gold will be like
refuse;
Their silver and their gold will
not be able to deliver them
In the day of the wrath of the
LORD;
They will not satisfy their
souls,
Nor fill their stomachs,
Because it became their
stumbling block of iniquity.

20 'As for the beauty of his
ornaments,
He set it in majesty;
But they made from it

Gospel Pearls

The images of their
abominations—
Their detestable things;
Therefore I have made it
Like refuse to them.
21 I will give it as plunder
Into the hands of strangers,
And to the wicked of the earth
as spoil;
And they shall defile it.
22 I will turn My face from them,
And they will defile My secret
place;
For robbers shall enter it and
defile it.

23 'Make a chain,
For the land is filled with
crimes of blood,
And the city is full of violence.
24 Therefore I will bring the worst
of the Gentiles,
And they will possess their
houses;
I will cause the pomp of the
strong to cease,
And their holy places shall be
defiled.
25 Destruction comes;
They will seek peace, but *there
shall be* none.
26 Disaster will come upon
disaster,
And rumor will be upon rumor.
Then they will seek a vision
from a prophet;
But the law will perish from the
priest,
And counsel from the elders.

27 'The king will mourn,
The prince will be clothed with
desolation,
And the hands of the common
people will tremble.
I will do to them according to
their way,
And according to what they
deserve I will judge them;
Then they shall know that I *am*
the LORD!' "

8 And it came to pass in the sixth
year, in the sixth *month,* on the
fifth *day* of the month, as I sat in my
house with the elders of Judah sitting
before me, that the hand of the Lord
GOD fell upon me there. 2 Then I
looked, and there was a likeness, like
the appearance of fire—from the appearance of His waist and downward, fire; and from His waist and

upward, like the appearance of
brightness, like the color of amber.
3 He stretched out the form of a hand,
and took me by a lock of my hair;
and the Spirit lifted me up between
earth and heaven, and brought me
in visions of God to Jerusalem, to the
door of the north gate of the inner
court, where the seat of the image
of jealousy *was,* which provokes to
jealousy. 4 And behold, the glory of
the God of Israel *was* there, like the
vision that I saw in the plain.
5 Then He said to me, "Son of man,
lift your eyes now toward the north."
So I lifted my eyes toward the north,
and there, north of the altar gate, was
this image of jealousy in the entrance.
6 Furthermore He said to me, "Son
of man, do you see what they are doing, the great abominations that the
house of Israel commits here, to
make Me go far away from My sanctuary? Now turn again, you will see
greater abominations." 7 So He
brought me to the door of the court;
and when I looked, there was a hole
in the wall. 8 Then He said to me,
"Son of man, dig into the wall"; and
when I dug into the wall, there was
a door.
9 And He said to me, "Go in, and
see the wicked abominations which
they are doing there." 10 So I went
in and saw, and there—every sort of
creeping thing, abominable beasts,
and all the idols of the house of Israel, portrayed all around on the
walls. 11 And there stood before them
seventy men of the elders of the
house of Israel, and in their midst
stood Jaazaniah the son of Shaphan.
Each man had a censer in his hand,
and a thick cloud of incense went up.
12 Then He said to me, "Son of man,
have you seen what the elders of the
house of Israel do in the dark, every
man in the room of his idols? For they
say, 'The LORD does not see us, the
LORD has forsaken the land.' "
13 And He said to me, "Turn again,
and you will see greater abominations that they are doing." 14 So He
brought me to the door of the north
gate of the LORD's house; and to my
dismay, women were sitting there
weeping for Tammuz.
15 Then He said to me, "Have you
seen *this,* O son of man? Turn again,
you will see greater abominations
than these." 16 So He brought me into

*T*he things you had stopped believing God for can start leaping in your spirit again.
God can renew you. The Holy Ghost can come upon you and restore you.

the inner court of the LORD's house; and there, at the door of the temple of the LORD, between the porch and the altar, *were* about twenty-five men with their backs toward the temple of the LORD and their faces toward the east, and they were worshiping the sun toward the east.

17 And He said to me, "Have you seen *this*, O son of man? Is it a trivial thing to the house of Judah to commit the abominations which they commit here? For they have filled the land with violence; then they have returned to provoke Me to anger. Indeed they put the branch to their nose. 18 Therefore I also will act in fury. My eye will not spare nor will I have pity; and though they cry in My ears with a loud voice, I will not hear them."

9 Then He called out in my hearing with a loud voice, saying, "Let those who have charge over the city draw near, each *with* a deadly weapon in his hand." 2 And suddenly six men came from the direction of the upper gate, which faces north, each with his battle-ax in his hand. One man among them *was* clothed with linen and had a writer's inkhorn at his side. They went in and stood beside the bronze altar.

3 Now the glory of the God of Israel had gone up from the cherub, where it had been, to the threshold of the temple.*a* And He called to the man clothed with linen, who *had* the writer's inkhorn at his side; 4 and the LORD said to him, "Go through the midst of the city, through the midst of Jerusalem, and put a mark on the foreheads of the men who sigh and cry over all the abominations that are done within it."

5 To the others He said in my hearing, "Go after him through the city and kill; do not let your eye spare, nor have any pity. 6 Utterly slay old *and* young men, maidens and little children and women; but do not come near anyone on whom *is* the mark; and begin at My sanctuary." So they began with the elders who *were* before the temple. 7 Then He said to them, "Defile the temple, and fill the courts with the slain. Go out!" And they went out and killed in the city.

8 So it was, that while they were killing them, I was left *alone;* and I fell on my face and cried out, and said, "Ah, Lord GOD! Will You destroy all the remnant of Israel in pouring out Your fury on Jerusalem?"

9 Then He said to me, "The iniquity of the house of Israel and Judah *is* exceedingly great, and the land is full of bloodshed, and the city full of perversity; for they say, 'The LORD has forsaken the land, and the LORD does not see!' 10 And as for Me also, My eye will neither spare, nor will I have pity, *but* I will recompense their deeds on their own head."

11 Just then, the man clothed with linen, who *had* the inkhorn at his side, reported back and said, "I have done as You commanded me."

10 And I looked, and there in the firmament that was above the head of the cherubim, there appeared something like a sapphire stone, having the appearance of the likeness of a throne. 2 Then He spoke to the man clothed with linen, and said, "Go in among the wheels, under the cherub, fill your hands with coals of fire from among the cherubim, and scatter *them* over the city." And he went in as I watched.

3 Now the cherubim were standing on the south side of the temple*a* when the man went in, and the cloud filled the inner court. 4 Then the glory of the LORD went up from the cherub, *and paused* over the threshold of the temple; and the house was filled with the cloud, and the court was full of the brightness of the LORD's glory. 5 And the sound of the wings of the cherubim was heard *even* in the outer court, like the voice of Almighty God when He speaks.

6 Then it happened, when He commanded the man clothed in linen, saying, "Take fire from among the wheels, from among the cherubim," that he went in and stood beside the wheels. 7 And the cherub stretched out his hand from among the cherubim to the fire that *was* among the cherubim, and took *some of it* and put *it* into the hands of the *man* clothed with linen, who took *it* and went out. 8 The cherubim appeared

9:3 *a*Literally *house*   10:3 *a*Literally *house,* also in verses 4 and 18

Gospel Pearls

to have the form of a man's hand under their wings.

9 And when I looked, there were four wheels by the cherubim, one wheel by one cherub and another wheel by each other cherub; the wheels appeared *to have* the color of a beryl stone. 10 As for their appearance, all four looked alike—as it were, a wheel in the middle of a wheel. 11 When they went, they went toward *any of* their four directions; they did not turn aside when they went, but followed in the direction the head was facing. They did not turn aside when they went. 12 And their whole body, with their back, their hands, their wings, and the wheels that the four had, *were* full of eyes all around. 13 As for the wheels, they were called in my hearing, "Wheel."

14 Each one had four faces: the first face *was* the face of a cherub, the second face the face of a man, the third the face of a lion, and the fourth the face of an eagle. 15 And the cherubim were lifted up. This *was* the living creature I saw by the River Chebar. 16 When the cherubim went, the wheels went beside them; and when the cherubim lifted their wings to mount up from the earth, the same wheels also did not turn from beside them. 17 When *the cherubim*[a] stood still, *the wheels* stood still, and when *one*[b] was lifted up, *the other*[c] lifted itself up, for the spirit of the living creature *was* in them.

18 Then the glory of the LORD departed from the threshold of the temple and stood over the cherubim. 19 And the cherubim lifted their wings and mounted up from the earth in my sight. When they went out, the wheels *were* beside them; and they stood at the door of the east gate of the LORD's house, and the glory of the God of Israel *was* above them.

20 This *is* the living creature I saw under the God of Israel by the River Chebar, and I knew they *were* cherubim. 21 Each one had four faces and each one four wings, and the likeness of the hands of a man *was* under their wings. 22 And the likeness of their faces *was* the same *as* the faces which I had seen by the River Chebar, their appearance and their

persons. They each went straight forward.

11 Then the Spirit lifted me up and brought me to the East Gate of the LORD's house, which faces eastward; and there at the door of the gate were twenty-five men, among whom I saw Jaazaniah the son of Azzur, and Pelatiah the son of Benaiah, princes of the people. 2 And He said to me: "Son of man, these *are* the men who devise iniquity and give wicked counsel in this city, 3 who say, 'The time is not near to build houses; this *city is* the caldron, and we *are* the meat.' 4 Therefore prophesy against them, prophesy, O son of man!"

5 Then the Spirit of the LORD fell upon me, and said to me, "Speak! 'Thus says the LORD: "Thus you have said, O house of Israel; for I know the things that come into your mind. 6 You have multiplied your slain in this city, and you have filled its streets with the slain." 7 Therefore thus says the Lord GOD: "Your slain whom you have laid in its midst, they *are* the meat, and this *city is* the caldron; but I shall bring you out of the midst of it. 8 You have feared the sword; and I will bring a sword upon you," says the Lord GOD. 9 "And I will bring you out of its midst, and deliver you into the hands of strangers, and execute judgments on you. 10 You shall fall by the sword. I will judge you at the border of Israel. Then you shall know that I *am* the LORD. 11 This *city* shall not be your caldron, nor shall you be the meat in its midst. I will judge you at the border of Israel. 12 And you shall know that I *am* the LORD; for you have not walked in My statutes nor executed My judgments, but have done according to the customs of the Gentiles which *are* all around you." ' "

13 Now it happened, while I was prophesying, that Pelatiah the son of Benaiah died. Then I fell on my face and cried with a loud voice, and said, "Ah, Lord GOD! Will You make a complete end of the remnant of Israel?"

14 Again the word of the LORD came to me, saying, 15 "Son of man, your brethren, your relatives, your

10:17 aLiterally *they*   bLiterally *they*   cLiterally *they*

---

*T*he fear of abuse can be removed only by the power of the Holy Spirit. There is great potential in women who believe.

countrymen, and all the house of Israel in its entirety, *are* those about whom the inhabitants of Jerusalem have said, 'Get far away from the LORD; this land has been given to us as a possession.' 16 Therefore say, 'Thus says the Lord GOD: "Although I have cast them far off among the Gentiles, and although I have scattered them among the countries, yet I shall be a little sanctuary for them in the countries where they have gone." ' 17 Therefore say, 'Thus says the Lord GOD: "I will gather you from the peoples, assemble you from the countries where you have been scattered, and I will give you the land of Israel." ' 18 And they will go there, and they will take away all its detestable things and all its abominations from there. 19 Then I will give them one heart, and I will put a new spirit within them,*a* and take the stony heart out of their flesh, and give them a heart of flesh, 20 that they may walk in My statutes and keep My judgments and do them; and they shall be My people, and I will be their God. 21 But *as for those* whose hearts follow the desire for their detestable things and their abominations, I will recompense their deeds on their own heads," says the Lord GOD.

22 So the cherubim lifted up their wings, with the wheels beside them, and the glory of the God of Israel *was* high above them. 23 And the glory of the LORD went up from the midst of the city and stood on the mountain, which *is* on the east side of the city.

24 Then the Spirit took me up and brought me in a vision by the Spirit of God into Chaldea,*a* to those in captivity. And the vision that I had seen went up from me. 25 So I spoke to those in captivity of all the things the LORD had shown me.

12 Now the word of the LORD came to me, saying: 2 "Son of man, you dwell in the midst of a rebellious house, which has eyes to see but does not see, and ears to hear but does not hear; for they *are* a rebellious house.

3 "Therefore, son of man, prepare your belongings for captivity, and go into captivity by day in their sight. You shall go from your place into captivity to another place in their sight. It may be that they will consider, though they *are* a rebellious house. 4 By day you shall bring out your belongings in their sight, as though going into captivity; and at evening you shall go in their sight, like those who go into captivity. 5 Dig through the wall in their sight, and carry your belongings out through it. 6 In their sight you shall bear *them* on *your* shoulders *and* carry *them* out at twilight; you shall cover your face, so that you cannot see the ground, for I have made you a sign to the house of Israel."

7 So I did as I was commanded. I brought out my belongings by day, as though going into captivity, and at evening I dug through the wall with my hand. I brought *them* out at twilight, *and* I bore *them* on *my* shoulder in their sight.

8 And in the morning the word of the LORD came to me, saying, 9 "Son of man, has not the house of Israel, the rebellious house, said to you, 'What are you doing?' 10 Say to them, 'Thus says the Lord GOD: "This burden *concerns* the prince in Jerusalem and all the house of Israel who are among them." ' 11 Say, 'I *am* a sign to you. As I have done, so shall it be done to them; they shall be carried away into captivity.' 12 And the prince who *is* among them shall bear *his* belongings on *his* shoulder at twilight and go out. They shall dig through the wall to carry *them* out through it. He shall cover his face, so that he cannot see the ground with *his* eyes. 13 I will also spread My net over him, and he shall be caught in My snare. I will bring him to Babylon, *to* the land of the Chaldeans; yet he shall not see it, though he shall die there. 14 I will scatter to every wind all who *are* around him to help him, and all his troops; and I will draw out the sword after them.

15 "Then they shall know that I *am* the LORD, when I scatter them among the nations and disperse them throughout the countries. 16 But I will spare a few of their men from the sword, from famine, and from pestilence, that they may declare all their abominations among the Gentiles wherever they go. Then they shall know that I *am* the LORD."

11:19 *a*Literally *you*   11:24 *a*Or *Babylon,* and so elsewhere in this book

Gospel Pearls

17 Moreover the word of the LORD came to me, saying, 18 "Son of man, eat your bread with quaking, and drink your water with trembling and anxiety. 19 And say to the people of the land, 'Thus says the Lord GOD to the inhabitants of Jerusalem *and* to the land of Israel: "They shall eat their bread with anxiety, and drink their water with dread, so that her land may be emptied of all who are in it, because of the violence of all those who dwell in it. 20 Then the cities that are inhabited shall be laid waste, and the land shall become desolate; and you shall know that I *am* the LORD." ' "

21 And the word of the LORD came to me, saying, 22 "Son of man, what *is* this proverb *that* you *people* have about the land of Israel, which says, 'The days are prolonged, and every vision fails'? 23 Tell them therefore, 'Thus says the Lord GOD: "I will lay this proverb to rest, and they shall no more use it as a proverb in Israel." But say to them, "The days are at hand, and the fulfillment of every vision. 24 For no more shall there be any false vision or flattering divination within the house of Israel. 25 For I *am* the LORD. I speak, and the word which I speak will come to pass; it will no more be postponed; for in your days, O rebellious house, I will say the word and perform it," says the Lord GOD.' "

26 Again the word of the LORD came to me, saying, 27 "Son of man, look, the house of Israel is saying, 'The vision that he sees *is* for many days *from now,* and he prophesies of times far off.' 28 Therefore say to them, 'Thus says the Lord GOD: "None of My words will be postponed any more, but the word which I speak will be done," says the Lord GOD.' "

13 And the word of the LORD came to me, saying, 2 "Son of man, prophesy against the prophets of Israel who prophesy, and say to those who prophesy out of their own heart, 'Hear the word of the LORD!' "

3 Thus says the Lord GOD: "Woe to the foolish prophets, who follow their own spirit and have seen nothing! 4 O Israel, your prophets are like foxes in the deserts. 5 You have not gone up into the gaps to build a wall for the house of Israel to stand in bat-

tle on the day of the LORD. 6 They have envisioned futility and false divination, saying, 'Thus says the LORD!' But the LORD has not sent them; yet they hope that the word may be confirmed. 7 Have you not seen a futile vision, and have you not spoken false divination? You say, 'The LORD says,' but I have not spoken."

8 Therefore thus says the Lord GOD: "Because you have spoken nonsense and envisioned lies, therefore I *am* indeed against you," says the Lord GOD. 9 "My hand will be against the prophets who envision futility and who divine lies; they shall not be in the assembly of My people, nor be written in the record of the house of Israel, nor shall they enter into the land of Israel. Then you shall know that I *am* the Lord GOD.

10 "Because, indeed, because they have seduced My people, saying, 'Peace!' when *there is* no peace—and one builds a wall, and they plaster it with untempered *mortar*— 11 say to those who plaster *it* with untempered *mortar,* that it will fall. There will be flooding rain, and you, O great hailstones, shall fall; and a stormy wind shall tear *it* down. 12 Surely, when the wall has fallen, will it not be said to you, 'Where *is* the mortar with which you plastered *it?*' "

13 Therefore thus says the Lord GOD: "I will cause a stormy wind to break forth in My fury; and there shall be a flooding rain in My anger, and great hailstones in fury to consume *it.* 14 So I will break down the wall you have plastered with untempered *mortar,* and bring it down to the ground, so that its foundation will be uncovered; it will fall, and you shall be consumed in the midst of it. Then you shall know that I *am* the LORD.

15 "Thus will I accomplish My wrath on the wall and on those who have plastered it with untempered *mortar;* and I will say to you, 'The wall *is* no *more,* nor those who plastered it, 16 *that is,* the prophets of Israel who prophesy concerning Jerusalem, and who see visions of peace for her when *there is* no peace,' " says the Lord GOD.

17 "Likewise, son of man, set your face against the daughters of your people, who prophesy out of their own heart; prophesy against them,

18 and say, 'Thus says the Lord GOD: "Woe to the *women* who sew *magic* charms on their sleeves[a] and make veils for the heads of people of every height to hunt souls! Will you hunt the souls of My people, and keep yourselves alive? 19 And will you profane Me among My people for handfuls of barley and for pieces of bread, killing people who should not die, and keeping people alive who should not live, by your lying to My people who listen to lies?"

20 'Therefore thus says the Lord GOD: "Behold, I *am* against your *magic* charms by which you hunt souls there like birds. I will tear them from your arms, and let the souls go, the souls you hunt like birds. 21 I will also tear off your veils and deliver My people out of your hand, and they shall no longer be as prey in your hand. Then you shall know that I *am* the LORD.

22 "Because with lies you have made the heart of the righteous sad, whom I have not made sad; and you have strengthened the hands of the wicked, so that he does not turn from his wicked way to save his life. 23 Therefore you shall no longer envision futility nor practice divination; for I will deliver My people out of your hand, and you shall know that I *am* the LORD." ' "

14 Now some of the elders of Israel came to me and sat before me. 2 And the word of the LORD came to me, saying, 3 "Son of man, these men have set up their idols in their hearts, and put before them that which causes them to stumble into iniquity. Should I let Myself be inquired of at all by them?

4 "Therefore speak to them, and say to them, 'Thus says the Lord GOD: "Everyone of the house of Israel who sets up his idols in his heart, and puts before him what causes him to stumble into iniquity, and then comes to the prophet, I the LORD will answer him who comes, according to the multitude of his idols, 5 that I may seize the house of Israel by their heart, because they are all estranged from Me by their idols." '

6 "Therefore say to the house of Israel, 'Thus says the Lord GOD: "Repent, turn away from your idols, and turn your faces away from all your abominations. 7 For anyone of the house of Israel, or of the strangers who dwell in Israel, who separates himself from Me and sets up his idols in his heart and puts before him what causes him to stumble into iniquity, then comes to a prophet to inquire of him concerning Me, I the LORD will answer him by Myself. 8 I will set My face against that man and make him a sign and a proverb, and I will cut him off from the midst of My people. Then you shall know that I *am* the LORD.

9 "And if the prophet is induced to speak anything, I the LORD have induced that prophet, and I will stretch out My hand against him and destroy him from among My people Israel. 10 And they shall bear their iniquity; the punishment of the prophet shall be the same as the punishment of the one who inquired, 11 that the house of Israel may no longer stray from Me, nor be profaned anymore with all their transgressions, but that they may be My people and I may be their God," says the Lord GOD.' "

12 The word of the LORD came again to me, saying: 13 "Son of man, when a land sins against Me by persistent unfaithfulness, I will stretch out My hand against it; I will cut off its supply of bread, send famine on it, and cut off man and beast from it. 14 Even *if* these three men, Noah, Daniel, and Job, were in it, they would deliver *only* themselves by their righteousness," says the Lord GOD.

15 "If I cause wild beasts to pass through the land, and they empty it, and make it so desolate that no man may pass through because of the beasts, 16 *even though* these three men *were* in it, *as* I live," says the Lord GOD, "they would deliver neither sons nor daughters; only they would be delivered, and the land would be desolate.

17 "Or *if* I bring a sword on that land, and say, 'Sword, go through the land,' and I cut off man and beast from it, 18 *even though* these three men *were* in it, *as* I live," says the Lord GOD, "they would deliver neither sons nor daughters, but only

---

13:18 [a]Literally *over all the joints of My hands;* Vulgate reads *under every elbow;* Septuagint and Targum read *on all elbows of the hands.*

---

*T*here is nothing wrong with wanting to be married. Simply take care of the Lord while you're waiting. Minister to Him. Let Him heal you and loose you, and worship Him.

Washed, Salted, and Swaddled

Ezekiel 16:4

There are a few things we can do to get a new believer off to a good start in the Body of Christ. First, we must do some washing. The Bible says we are washed by the water of His Word (see Ephesians 5:26). When we give the Word of God to a babe in Christ, we wash that person. The Word of God, spoken in mercy and by the power of the Holy Spirit, regenerates us (see Titus 3:5).

Next, we must do some salting. In Bible times, salt was rubbed into the skin of a newborn baby to heal and toughen the skin and to allow the baby to be handled without bruising. So many people need to be salted today. They are so sensitive that they can't be corrected or admonished without tucking their head and running to hide. When a woman has been salted, nobody has to call her name for her to feel good about herself. Nobody has to compliment her for her to feel loved.

The newborn Christian gets salty by being around salt, and according to Matthew 5:13, established Christians are the salt of the earth. It is our job to accept the new believer in our midst—to make a place for her, surround her, include her, allow her into our circle of friends. The more she feels that she is accepted and loved by other women, the less she will try to hide and the more honest she can be about who she *really* is.

Third, we are to do some swaddling. Some women have been exposed to too much. They've seen too much, heard too much, and experienced too much. When we swaddle a newborn Christian, we wrap that person in our arms of supernatural love and give her a continual dose of God's grace. We intercede on her behalf; and we give her hope for her life.

But what if you are the baby who hasn't been cared for properly? What if you are a woman who needs to be washed, salted, and swaddled, but there is no one to meet your needs?

Then do it yourself. Wash yourself by reading God's Word. Get into a church where you can hear His Word preached with Holy Ghost power. Salt yourself by becoming a part of a group of godly believers. Hang around people who are studying His Word, speaking His Word, and living His Word. Swaddle yourself by refusing to fill your mind with filth and unrealistic expectations and lusts. Instead, listen to praise music and teaching tapes in which God's Word is taught and God's delivering power is manifest.

When you are ready to get cleaned up, God will help you get cleaned up! As you wash yourself, God will wash you with His forgiveness. As you salt yourself, God will salt you with His power and presence. As you swaddle yourself in garments of praise, God will swaddle you in His love.

they themselves would be delivered.

19 "Or *if* I send a pestilence into that land and pour out My fury on it in blood, and cut off from it man and beast, 20 even *though* Noah, Daniel, and Job *were* in it, *as* I live," says the Lord GOD, "they would deliver neither son nor daughter; they would deliver *only* themselves by their righteousness."

21 For thus says the Lord GOD: "How much more it shall be when I send My four severe judgments on Jerusalem—the sword and famine and wild beasts and pestilence—to cut off man and beast from it? 22 Yet behold, there shall be left in it a remnant who will be brought out, *both* sons and daughters; surely they will come out to you, and you will see their ways and their doings. Then you will be comforted concerning the disaster that I have brought upon Jerusalem, all that I have brought upon it. 23 And they will comfort you, when you see their ways and their doings; and you shall know that I have done nothing without cause that I have done in it," says the Lord GOD.

15 Then the word of the LORD came to me, saying: 2 "Son of man, how is the wood of the vine *better* than any other wood, the vine branch which is among the trees of the forest? 3 Is wood taken from it to make any object? Or can *men* make a peg from it to hang any vessel on? 4 Instead, it is thrown into the fire for fuel; the fire devours both ends of it, and its middle is burned. Is it useful for *any* work? 5 Indeed, when it was whole, no object could be made from it. How much less will it be useful for *any* work when the fire has devoured it, and it is burned?

6 "Therefore thus says the Lord GOD: 'Like the wood of the vine among the trees of the forest, which I have given to the fire for fuel, so I will give up the inhabitants of Jerusalem; 7 and I will set My face against them. They will go out from *one* fire, but *another* fire shall devour them. Then you shall know that I *am* the LORD, when I set My face against them. 8 Thus I will make the land desolate, because they have persisted in unfaithfulness,' says the Lord GOD."

16 Again the word of the LORD came to me, saying, 2 "Son of man, cause Jerusalem to know her abominations, 3 and say, 'Thus says the Lord GOD to Jerusalem: "Your birth and your nativity *are* from the land of Canaan; your father *was* an Amorite and your mother a Hittite. 4 *As for* your nativity, on the day you were born your navel cord was not cut, nor were you washed in water to cleanse *you;* you were not rubbed with salt nor wrapped in swaddling cloths. 5 No eye pitied you, to do any of these things for you, to have compassion on you; but you were thrown out into the open field, when you yourself were loathed on the day you were born.

6 "And when I passed by you and saw you struggling in your own blood, I said to you in your blood, 'Live!' Yes, I said to you in your blood, 'Live!' 7 I made you thrive like a plant in the field; and you grew, matured, and became very beautiful. *Your* breasts were formed, your hair grew, but you *were* naked and bare.

8 "When I passed by you again and looked upon you, indeed your time *was* the time of love; so I spread My wing over you and covered your nakedness. Yes, I swore an oath to you and entered into a covenant with you, and you became Mine," says the Lord GOD.

9 "Then I washed you in water; yes, I thoroughly washed off your blood, and I anointed you with oil. 10 I clothed you in embroidered cloth and gave you sandals of badger skin; I clothed you with fine linen and covered you with silk. 11 I adorned you with ornaments, put bracelets on your wrists, and a chain on your neck. 12 And I put a jewel in your nose, earrings in your ears, and a beautiful crown on your head. 13 Thus you were adorned with gold and silver, and your clothing *was of* fine linen, silk, and embroidered cloth. You ate *pastry of* fine flour, honey, and oil. You were exceedingly beautiful, and succeeded to royalty. 14 Your fame went out among the nations because of your beauty, for it *was* perfect through My splendor which I had bestowed on you," says the Lord GOD.

15 "But you trusted in your own beauty, played the harlot because of your fame, and poured out your harlotry on everyone passing by who *would have* it. 16 You took some of

---

*F*aith is more than a fact—faith is an action. If your actions don't change, you might still think you are tied. When you finally understand that you are loose, you will start behaving as if you were set free.

Live!

Ezekiel 16:6

The baby girl in this passage was found lying out in an open field, covered with blood, bruised and raw, strangling on her birth cord.

When God found you, you were in a real mess too. I don't know the circumstances of your life or what drove you to the altar to accept Jesus as your Savior, but it was probably something deplorable. I know you were dying. You had been polluted by life, strangled by sin, bruised and beaten because of the treatment you had received from other people. Your past had left you naked and exposed. You had been cast away.

There was no time for God to tell you all that He wanted to say to you. He had only one word to speak to all of your abuse, all of your trauma, all of your trials, all of your tears, all of your pain, all of your addictions. God had only one word to speak in answer to your depression, your thoughts of suicide, your feelings of unworthiness.

There was no time to teach you Hebrew or Greek or to define for you *redemption, substitution, election, predestination, justification,* or *sanctification.* In your state of emergency, there was only one word God could speak to you that would matter.

He said to you, "Live!"

That's the word we need to speak to those who are suffering or in pain. It's the word we need to hear when we feel the bruising pain of rejection and isolation and abuse. The word is "Live!"

To the woman who has just been told that her husband wants a divorce, God says, "Live!" To the woman who has just been beaten to a pulp by her ex-boyfriend, God says, "Live!" To the woman who has just buried her infant child or her beloved husband of fifty years, God says, "Live!" To the woman who has just been fired from her job, God says, "Live!" To the woman who has just been raped, God says, "Live!" To the woman who is overwhelmed right now by her past, her problems, her inner pain, God says, "Live!"

Whoever you are, whatever your circumstances, God says to you, "Live!"

your garments and adorned multicolored high places for yourself, and played the harlot on them. *Such* things should not happen, nor be. 17 You have also taken your beautiful jewelry from My gold and My silver, which I had given you, and made for yourself male images and played the harlot with them. 18 You took your embroidered garments and covered them, and you set My oil and My incense before them. 19 Also My food which I gave you—the pastry of fine flour, oil, and honey *which* I fed you—you set it before them as sweet incense; and *so* it was," says the Lord God.

20 "Moreover you took your sons and your daughters, whom you bore to Me, and these you sacrificed to them to be devoured. *Were* your *acts* of harlotry a small matter, 21 that you have slain My children and offered them up to them by causing them to pass through *the fire?* 22 And in all your abominations and acts of harlotry you did not remember the days of your youth, when you were naked and bare, struggling in your blood.

23 "Then it was so, after all your wickedness—'Woe, woe to you!' says the Lord God— 24 *that* you also built for yourself a shrine, and made a high place for yourself in every street. 25 You built your high places at the head of every road, and made your beauty to be abhorred. You offered yourself to everyone who passed by, and multiplied your acts of harlotry. 26 You also committed harlotry with the Egyptians, your very fleshly neighbors, and increased your acts of harlotry to provoke Me to anger.

27 "Behold, therefore, I stretched out My hand against you, diminished your allotment, and gave you up to the will of those who hate you, the daughters of the Philistines, who were ashamed of your lewd behavior. 28 You also played the harlot with the Assyrians, because you were insatiable; indeed you played the harlot with them and still were not satisfied. 29 Moreover you multiplied your acts of harlotry as far as the land of the trader, Chaldea; and even then you were not satisfied.

30 "How degenerate is your heart!" says the Lord God, "seeing you do all these *things,* the deeds of a brazen harlot.

31 "You erected your shrine at the head of every road, and built your high place in every street. Yet you were not like a harlot, because you scorned payment. 32 *You are* an adulterous wife, *who* takes strangers instead of her husband. 33 Men make payment to all harlots, but you made your payments to all your lovers, and hired them to come to you from all around for your harlotry. 34 You are the opposite of *other* women in your harlotry, because no one solicited you to be a harlot. In that you gave payment but no payment was given you, therefore you are the opposite."

35 'Now then, O harlot, hear the word of the Lord! 36 Thus says the Lord God: "Because your filthiness was poured out and your nakedness uncovered in your harlotry with your lovers, and with all your abominable idols, and because of the blood of your children which you gave to them, 37 surely, therefore, I will gather all your lovers with whom you took pleasure, all those you loved, *and* all those you hated; I will gather them from all around against you and will uncover your nakedness to them, that they may see all your nakedness. 38 And I will judge you as women who break wedlock or shed blood are judged; I will bring blood upon you in fury and jealousy. 39 I will also give you into their hand, and they shall throw down your shrines and break down your high places. They shall also strip you of your clothes, take your beautiful jewelry, and leave you naked and bare.

40 "They shall also bring up an assembly against you, and they shall stone you with stones and thrust you through with their swords. 41 They shall burn your houses with fire, and execute judgments on you in the sight of many women; and I will make you cease playing the harlot, and you shall no longer hire lovers. 42 So I will lay to rest My fury toward you, and My jealousy shall depart from you. I will be quiet, and be angry no more. 43 Because you did not remember the days of your youth, but agitated Me*a* with all these *things,* surely I will also recompense your deeds on *your own* head," says

16:43 *a*Following Septuagint, Syriac, Targum, and Vulgate; Masoretic Text reads *were agitated with Me.*

Gospel Pearls

the Lord GOD. "And you shall not commit lewdness in addition to all your abominations.

44 "Indeed everyone who quotes proverbs will use *this* proverb against you: 'Like mother, like daughter!' 45 You *are* your mother's daughter, loathing husband and children; and you *are* the sister of your sisters, who loathed their husbands and children; your mother *was* a Hittite and your father an Amorite.

46 "Your elder sister *is* Samaria, who dwells with her daughters to the north of you; and your younger sister, who dwells to the south of you, *is* Sodom and her daughters. 47 You did not walk in their ways nor act according to their abominations; but, as *if that were* too little, you became more corrupt than they in all your ways.

48 "*As* I live," says the Lord GOD, "neither your sister Sodom nor her daughters have done as you and your daughters have done. 49 Look, this was the iniquity of your sister Sodom: She and her daughter had pride, fullness of food, and abundance of idleness; neither did she strengthen the hand of the poor and needy. 50 And they were haughty and committed abomination before Me; therefore I took them away as I saw fit.*a*

51 "Samaria did not commit half of your sins; but you have multiplied your abominations more than they, and have justified your sisters by all the abominations which you have done. 52 You who judged your sisters, bear your own shame also, because the sins which you committed were more abominable than theirs; they are more righteous than you. Yes, be disgraced also, and bear your own shame, because you justified your sisters.

53 "When I bring back their captives, the captives of Sodom and her daughters, and the captives of Samaria and her daughters, then *I will also bring back* the captives of your captivity among them, 54 that you may bear your own shame and be disgraced by all that you did when you comforted them. 55 When your sisters, Sodom and her daughters, return to their former state, and Samaria and her daughters return to their former state, then you and your daughters will return to your former state. 56 For your sister Sodom was not a byword in your mouth in the days of your pride, 57 before your wickedness was uncovered. It was like the time of the reproach of the daughters of Syria*a* and all *those* around her, and of the daughters of the Philistines, who despise you everywhere. 58 You have paid for your lewdness and your abominations," says the LORD. 59 For thus says the Lord GOD: "I will deal with you as you have done, who despised the oath by breaking the covenant.

60 "Nevertheless I will remember My covenant with you in the days of your youth, and I will establish an everlasting covenant with you. 61 Then you will remember your ways and be ashamed, when you receive your older and your younger sisters; for I will give them to you for daughters, but not because of My covenant with you. 62 And I will establish My covenant with you. Then you shall know that I *am* the LORD, 63 that you may remember and be ashamed, and never open your mouth anymore because of your shame, when I provide you an atonement for all you have done," says the Lord GOD.' "

17 And the word of the LORD came to me, saying, 2 "Son of man, pose a riddle, and speak a parable to the house of Israel, 3 and say, 'Thus says the Lord GOD:

"A great eagle with large wings
    and long pinions,
Full of feathers of various
    colors,
Came to Lebanon
And took from the cedar the
    highest branch.
4   He cropped off its topmost
        young twig
    And carried it to a land of
        trade;
    He set it in a city of merchants.
5   Then he took some of the seed
        of the land
    And planted it in a fertile field;

16:50 *a*Vulgate reads *you saw;* Septuagint reads *he saw;* Targum reads *as was revealed to Me.*
16:57 *a*Following Masoretic Text, Septuagint, Targum, and Vulgate; many Hebrew manuscripts and Syriac read *Edom.*

God has a special anointing for the woman who is free to seek Him. Her prayer life should explode in miracles!

He placed *it* by abundant
waters
And set it like a willow tree.
6 And it grew and became a
spreading vine of low
stature;
Its branches turned toward
him,
But its roots were under it.
So it became a vine,
Brought forth branches,
And put forth shoots.

7 "But there was another*a* great
eagle with large wings and
many feathers;
And behold, this vine bent its
roots toward him,
And stretched its branches
toward him,
From the garden terrace where
it had been planted,
That he might water it.
8 It was planted in good soil by
many waters,
To bring forth branches, bear
fruit,
And become a majestic vine." '

9 "Say, 'Thus says the Lord GOD:

"Will it thrive?
Will he not pull up its roots,
Cut off its fruit,
And leave it to wither?
All of its spring leaves will
wither,
And no great power or many
people
Will be needed to pluck it up
by its roots.
10 Behold, *it is* planted,
Will it thrive?
Will it not utterly wither when
the east wind touches it?
It will wither in the garden
terrace where it grew." ' "

11 Moreover the word of the LORD
came to me, saying, 12 "Say now to
the rebellious house: 'Do you not
know what these *things mean?*' Tell
them, 'Indeed the king of Babylon
went to Jerusalem and took its king
and princes, and led them with him
to Babylon. 13 And he took the king's
offspring, made a covenant with him,

and put him under oath. He also took
away the mighty of the land,
14 that the kingdom might be brought
low and not lift itself up, *but* that by
keeping his covenant it might stand.
15 But he rebelled against him by
sending his ambassadors to Egypt,
that they might give him horses and
many people. Will he prosper? Will
he who does such *things* escape? Can
he break a covenant and still be delivered?

16 '*As* I live,' says the Lord GOD,
'surely in the place *where* the king
dwells who made him king, whose
oath he despised and whose covenant he broke—with him in the midst
of Babylon he shall die. 17 Nor will
Pharaoh with *his* mighty army and
great company do anything in the
war, when they heap up a siege
mound and build a wall to cut off
many persons. 18 Since he despised
the oath by breaking the covenant,
and in fact gave his hand and still
did all these *things,* he shall not escape.' "

19 Therefore thus says the Lord
GOD: "*As* I live, surely My oath which
he despised, and My covenant which
he broke, I will recompense on his
own head. 20 I will spread My net
over him, and he shall be taken in
My snare. I will bring him to Babylon
and try him there for the treason
which he committed against Me.
21 All his fugitives*a* with all his troops
shall fall by the sword, and those
who remain shall be scattered to every wind; and you shall know that I,
the LORD, have spoken."

22 Thus says the Lord GOD: "I will
take also *one* of the highest branches
of the high cedar and set *it* out. I will
crop off from the topmost of its
young twigs a tender one, and will
plant *it* on a high and prominent
mountain. 23 On the mountain height
of Israel I will plant it; and it will
bring forth boughs, and bear fruit,
and be a majestic cedar. Under it will
dwell birds of every sort; in the
shadow of its branches they will
dwell. 24 And all the trees of the field
shall know that I, the LORD, have
brought down the high tree and exalted the low tree, dried up the green
tree and made the dry tree flourish;

17:7 *a*Following Septuagint, Syriac, and Vulgate; Masoretic Text and Targum read *one.*   17:21 *a*Following
Masoretic Text and Vulgate; many Hebrew manuscripts and Syriac read *choice men;* Targum reads *mighty
men;* Septuagint omits *All his fugitives.*

I, the LORD, have spoken and have done it."

18 The word of the LORD came to me again, saying, 2 "What do you mean when you use this proverb concerning the land of Israel, saying:

'The fathers have eaten sour grapes,
And the children's teeth are set on edge'?

3 "As I live," says the Lord GOD, "you shall no longer use this proverb in Israel.

4 "Behold, all souls are Mine;
The soul of the father
As well as the soul of the son is Mine;
The soul who sins shall die.
5 But if a man is just
And does what is lawful and right;
6 If he has not eaten on the mountains,
Nor lifted up his eyes to the idols of the house of Israel,
Nor defiled his neighbor's wife,
Nor approached a woman during her impurity;
7 If he has not oppressed anyone,
But has restored to the debtor his pledge;
Has robbed no one by violence,
But has given his bread to the hungry
And covered the naked with clothing;
8 If he has not exacted usury
Nor taken any increase,
But has withdrawn his hand from iniquity
And executed true judgment between man and man;
9 If he has walked in My statutes
And kept My judgments faithfully—
He is just;
He shall surely live!"
Says the Lord GOD.

10 "If he begets a son who is a robber
Or a shedder of blood,
Who does any of these things
11 And does none of those duties,
But has eaten on the mountains
Or defiled his neighbor's wife;

12 If he has oppressed the poor and needy,
Robbed by violence,
Not restored the pledge,
Lifted his eyes to the idols,
Or committed abomination;
13 If he has exacted usury
Or taken increase—
Shall he then live?
He shall not live!
If he has done any of these abominations,
He shall surely die;
His blood shall be upon him.

14 "If, however, he begets a son
Who sees all the sins which his father has done,
And considers but does not do likewise;
15 Who has not eaten on the mountains,
Nor lifted his eyes to the idols of the house of Israel,
Nor defiled his neighbor's wife;
16 Has not oppressed anyone,
Nor withheld a pledge,
Nor robbed by violence,
But has given his bread to the hungry
And covered the naked with clothing;
17 Who has withdrawn his hand from the poor[a]
And not received usury or increase,
But has executed My judgments
And walked in My statutes—
He shall not die for the iniquity of his father;
He shall surely live!

18 "As for his father,
Because he cruelly oppressed,
Robbed his brother by violence,
And did what is not good among his people,
Behold, he shall die for his iniquity.

19 "Yet you say, 'Why should the son not bear the guilt of the father?' Because the son has done what is lawful and right, and has kept all My statutes and observed them, he shall surely live. 20 The soul who sins shall die. The son shall not bear the guilt of the father, nor the father bear the

18:17 [a]Following Masoretic Text, Targum, and Vulgate; Septuagint reads *iniquity* (compare verse 8).

*T*hose who are married seek to please their spouse. Unmarried people seek to please the Lord. There is a special relationship of power between God and the single believer.

guilt of the son. The righteousness of the righteous shall be upon himself, and the wickedness of the wicked shall be upon himself.

21 "But if a wicked man turns from all his sins which he has committed, keeps all My statutes, and does what is lawful and right, he shall surely live; he shall not die. 22 None of the transgressions which he has committed shall be remembered against him; because of the righteousness which he has done, he shall live. 23 Do I have any pleasure at all that the wicked should die?" says the Lord GOD, "*and* not that he should turn from his ways and live?

24 "But when a righteous man turns away from his righteousness and commits iniquity, and does according to all the abominations that the wicked *man* does, shall he live? All the righteousness which he has done shall not be remembered; because of the unfaithfulness of which he is guilty and the sin which he has committed, because of them he shall die.

25 "Yet you say, 'The way of the Lord is not fair.' Hear now, O house of Israel, is it not My way which is fair, and your ways which are not fair? 26 When a righteous *man* turns away from his righteousness, commits iniquity, and dies in it, it is because of the iniquity which he has done that he dies. 27 Again, when a wicked *man* turns away from the wickedness which he committed, and does what is lawful and right, he preserves himself alive. 28 Because he considers and turns away from all the transgressions which he committed, he shall surely live; he shall not die. 29 Yet the house of Israel says, 'The way of the Lord is not fair.' O house of Israel, is it not My ways which are fair, and your ways which are not fair?

30 "Therefore I will judge you, O house of Israel, every one according to his ways," says the Lord GOD. "Repent, and turn from all your transgressions, so that iniquity will not be your ruin. 31 Cast away from you all the transgressions which you have committed, and get yourselves a new heart and a new spirit. For why

should you die, O house of Israel? 32 For I have no pleasure in the death of one who dies," says the Lord GOD. "Therefore turn and live!"

19 "Moreover take up a lamentation for the princes of Israel, 2 and say:

'What *is* your mother? A
   lioness:
She lay down among the lions;
Among the young lions she
   nourished her cubs.
3 She brought up one of her cubs,
And he became a young lion;
He learned to catch prey,
And he devoured men.
4 The nations also heard of him;
He was trapped in their pit,
And they brought him with
   chains to the land of Egypt.

5 'When she saw that she waited,
   that her hope was lost,
She took another of her cubs
   and made him a young lion.
6 He roved among the lions,
And became a young lion;
He learned to catch prey;
He devoured men.
7 He knew their desolate places,[a]
And laid waste their cities;
The land with its fullness was
   desolated
By the noise of his roaring.
8 Then the nations set against
   him from the provinces on
   every side,
And spread their net over him;
He was trapped in their pit.
9 They put him in a cage with
   chains,
And brought him to the king of
   Babylon;
They brought him in nets,
That his voice should no longer
   be heard on the mountains of
   Israel.

10 'Your mother *was* like a vine in
   your bloodline,[a]
Planted by the waters,
Fruitful and full of branches
Because of many waters.
11 She had strong branches for
   scepters of rulers.

19:7 [a]Septuagint reads *He stood in insolence;* Targum reads *He destroyed its palaces;* Vulgate reads *He learned to make widows.*   19:10 [a]Literally *blood.* Following Masoretic Text, Syriac, and Vulgate; Septuagint reads *like a flower on a pomegranate tree;* Targum reads *in your likeness.*

Gospel Pearls

She towered in stature above
the thick branches,
And was seen in her height
amid the dense foliage.
12 But she was plucked up in fury,
She was cast down to the
ground,
And the east wind dried her
fruit.
Her strong branches were
broken and withered;
The fire consumed them.
13 And now she *is* planted in the
wilderness,
In a dry and thirsty land.
14 Fire has come out from a rod
of her branches
And devoured her fruit,
So that she has no strong
branch—a scepter for
ruling.' "

This *is* a lamentation, and has become a lamentation.

20 It came to pass in the seventh
year, in the fifth *month,* on the
tenth *day* of the month, *that* certain
of the elders of Israel came to inquire
of the LORD, and sat before me.
2 Then the word of the LORD came to
me, saying, 3 "Son of man, speak to
the elders of Israel, and say to them,
'Thus says the Lord GOD: "Have you
come to inquire of Me? *As* I live,"
says the Lord GOD, "I will not be inquired of by you." ' 4 Will you judge
them, son of man, will you judge
them? Then make known to them the
abominations of their fathers.
5 "Say to them, 'Thus says the Lord
GOD: "On the day when I chose Israel
and raised My hand in an oath to the
descendants of the house of Jacob,
and made Myself known to them in
the land of Egypt, I raised My hand
in an oath to them, saying, 'I *am* the
LORD your God.' 6 On that day I
raised My hand in an oath to them,
to bring them out of the land of Egypt
into a land that I had searched out
for them, 'flowing with milk and
honey,'*a* the glory of all lands. 7 Then
I said to them, 'Each of you, throw
away the abominations which are before his eyes, and do not defile yourselves with the idols of Egypt. I *am*
the LORD your God.' 8 But they rebelled against Me and would not
obey Me. They did not all cast away

the abominations which were before
their eyes, nor did they forsake the
idols of Egypt. Then I said, 'I will
pour out My fury on them and fulfill
My anger against them in the midst
of the land of Egypt.' 9 But I acted
for My name's sake, that it should
not be profaned before the Gentiles
among whom they *were,* in whose
sight I had made Myself known to
them, to bring them out of the land
of Egypt.
10 "Therefore I made them go out
of the land of Egypt and brought
them into the wilderness. 11 And I
gave them My statutes and showed
them My judgments, 'which, *if* a man
does, he shall live by them.'*a*
12 Moreover I also gave them My
Sabbaths, to be a sign between them
and Me, that they might know that I
am the LORD who sanctifies them.
13 Yet the house of Israel rebelled
against Me in the wilderness; they
did not walk in My statutes; they despised My judgments, 'which, *if* a
man does, he shall live by them';*a*
and they greatly defiled My Sabbaths. Then I said I would pour out
My fury on them in the wilderness,
to consume them. 14 But I acted for
My name's sake, that it should not
be profaned before the Gentiles, in
whose sight I had brought them out.
15 So I also raised My hand in an oath
to them in the wilderness, that I
would not bring them into the land
which I had given *them,* 'flowing
with milk and honey,'*a* the glory of
all lands, 16 because they despised
My judgments and did not walk in
My statutes, but profaned My Sabbaths; for their heart went after their
idols. 17 Nevertheless My eye spared
them from destruction. I did not
make an end of them in the wilderness.
18 "But I said to their children in
the wilderness, 'Do not walk in the
statutes of your fathers, nor observe
their judgments, nor defile yourselves with their idols. 19 I *am* the
LORD your God: Walk in My statutes,
keep My judgments, and do them;
20 hallow My Sabbaths, and they will
be a sign between Me and you, that
you may know that I *am* the LORD
your God.'
21 "Notwithstanding, the children
rebelled against Me; they did not

20:6 *a*Exodus 3:8   20:11 *a*Leviticus 18:5   20:13 *a*Leviticus 18:5   20:15 *a*Exodus 3:8

1 want you to sanctify your body unto the Lord, and give your body as a living
sacrifice to God. If you can't keep your vow to God, you would never be able to keep
your vow to a man. Give your body to God and sanctify yourself.

walk in My statutes, and were not careful to observe My judgments, 'which, *if* a man does, he shall live by them';*a* but they profaned My Sabbaths. Then I said I would pour out My fury on them and fulfill My anger against them in the wilderness. 22 Nevertheless I withdrew My hand and acted for My name's sake, that it should not be profaned in the sight of the Gentiles, in whose sight I had brought them out. 23 Also I raised My hand in an oath to those in the wilderness, that I would scatter them among the Gentiles and disperse them throughout the countries, 24 because they had not executed My judgments, but had despised My statutes, profaned My Sabbaths, and their eyes were fixed on their fathers' idols.

25 "Therefore I also gave them up to statutes *that were* not good, and judgments by which they could not live; 26 and I pronounced them unclean because of their ritual gifts, in that they caused all their firstborn to pass through *the fire,* that I might make them desolate and that they might know that I am the LORD." '

27 "Therefore, son of man, speak to the house of Israel, and say to them, 'Thus says the Lord GOD: "In this too your fathers have blasphemed Me, by being unfaithful to Me. 28 When I brought them into the land *concerning* which I had raised My hand in an oath to give them, and they saw all the high hills and all the thick trees, there they offered their sacrifices and provoked Me with their offerings. There they also sent up their sweet aroma and poured out their drink offerings. 29 Then I said to them, 'What *is* this high place to which you go?' So its name is called Bamah*a* to this day." ' 30 Therefore say to the house of Israel, 'Thus says the Lord GOD: "Are you defiling yourselves in the manner of your fathers, and committing harlotry according to their abominations? 31 For when you offer your gifts and make your sons pass through the fire, you defile yourselves with all your idols, even to this day. So shall I be inquired of by you, O house of Israel? *As* I live," says the Lord GOD, "I will not be inquired of by you. 32 What you have in your mind shall never be,

when you say, 'We will be like the Gentiles, like the families in other countries, serving wood and stone.'

33 "*As* I live," says the Lord GOD, "surely with a mighty hand, with an outstretched arm, and with fury poured out, I will rule over you. 34 I will bring you out from the peoples and gather you out of the countries where you are scattered, with a mighty hand, with an outstretched arm, and with fury poured out. 35 And I will bring you into the wilderness of the peoples, and there I will plead My case with you face to face. 36 Just as I pleaded My case with your fathers in the wilderness of the land of Egypt, so I will plead My case with you," says the Lord GOD.

37 "I will make you pass under the rod, and I will bring you into the bond of the covenant; 38 I will purge the rebels from among you, and those who transgress against Me; I will bring them out of the country where they dwell, but they shall not enter the land of Israel. Then you will know that I *am* the LORD.

39 "As for you, O house of Israel," thus says the Lord GOD: "Go, serve every one of you his idols—and hereafter—if you will not obey Me; but profane My holy name no more with your gifts and your idols. 40 For on My holy mountain, on the mountain height of Israel," says the Lord GOD, "there all the house of Israel, all of them in the land, shall serve Me; there I will accept them, and there I will require your offerings and the firstfruits of your sacrifices, together with all your holy things. 41 I will accept you as a sweet aroma when I bring you out from the peoples and gather you out of the countries where you have been scattered; and I will be hallowed in you before the Gentiles. 42 Then you shall know that I *am* the LORD, when I bring you into the land of Israel, into the country *for* which I raised My hand in an oath to give to your fathers. 43 And there you shall remember your ways and all your doings with which you were defiled; and you shall loathe yourselves in your own sight because of all the evils that you have committed. 44 Then you shall know that I *am* the LORD, when I have

20:21 *a*Leviticus 18:5   20:29 *a*Literally *High Place*

Gospel Pearls

dealt with you for My name's sake, not according to your wicked ways nor according to your corrupt doings, O house of Israel," says the Lord GOD.' "

45 Furthermore the word of the LORD came to me, saying, 46 "Son of man, set your face toward the south; preach against the south and prophesy against the forest land, the South,ᵃ 47 and say to the forest of the South, 'Hear the word of the LORD! Thus says the Lord GOD: "Behold, I will kindle a fire in you, and it shall devour every green tree and every dry tree in you; the blazing flame shall not be quenched, and all faces from the south to the north shall be scorched by it. 48 All flesh shall see that I, the LORD, have kindled it; it shall not be quenched." ' "

49 Then I said, "Ah, Lord GOD! They say of me, 'Does he not speak parables?' "

21 And the word of the LORD came to me, saying, 2 "Son of man, set your face toward Jerusalem, preach against the holy places, and prophesy against the land of Israel; 3 and say to the land of Israel, 'Thus says the LORD: "Behold, I *am* against you, and I will draw My sword out of its sheath and cut off both righteous and wicked from you. 4 Because I will cut off both righteous and wicked from you, therefore My sword shall go out of its sheath against all flesh from south *to* north, 5 that all flesh may know that I, the LORD, have drawn My sword out of its sheath; it shall not return anymore." ' 6 Sigh therefore, son of man, with a breaking heart, and sigh with bitterness before their eyes. 7 And it shall be when they say to you, 'Why are you sighing?' that you shall answer, 'Because of the news; when it comes, every heart will melt, all hands will be feeble, every spirit will faint, and all knees will be weak *as* water. Behold, it is coming and shall be brought to pass,' says the Lord GOD."

8 Again the word of the LORD came to me, saying, 9 "Son of man, prophesy and say, 'Thus says the LORD!' Say:

'A sword, a sword is sharpened
And also polished!

10 Sharpened to make a dreadful
    slaughter,
Polished to flash like lightning!
Should we then make mirth?
It despises the scepter of My
    son,
As it does all wood.
11 And He has given it to be
    polished,
That it may be handled;
This sword is sharpened, and
    it is polished
To be given into the hand of the
    slayer.'

12 "Cry and wail, son of man;
For it will be against My
    people,
Against all the princes of Israel.
Terrors including the sword
    will be against My people;
Therefore strike *your* thigh.

13 "Because *it is* a testing,
And what if *the sword* despises
    even the scepter?
The scepter shall be no *more*,"

says the Lord GOD.

14 "You therefore, son of man,
    prophesy,
And strike *your* hands
    together.
The third time let the sword do
    double *damage*.
It *is* the sword *that* slays,
The sword that slays the great
    men,
That enters their private
    chambers.
15 I have set the point of the sword
    against all their gates,
That the heart may melt and
    many may stumble.
Ah! *It is* made bright;
It is grasped for slaughter:

16 "Swords at the ready!
Thrust right!
Set your blade!
Thrust left—
Wherever your edge is ordered!

17 "I also will beat My fists
    together,
And I will cause My fury to
    rest;
I, the LORD, have spoken."

18 The word of the LORD came to me again, saying: 19 "And son of

20:46 ᵃHebrew *Negev*

---

*B*egin to sanctify yourself. Bring your body before God. Bring your nature before God. Bring your passion to Him. Allow God to plug in to your need.

man, appoint for yourself two ways for the sword of the king of Babylon to go; both of them shall go from the same land. Make a sign; put *it* at the head of the road to the city. 20 Appoint a road for the sword to go to Rabbah of the Ammonites, and to Judah, into fortified Jerusalem. 21 For the king of Babylon stands at the parting of the road, at the fork of the two roads, to use divination: he shakes the arrows, he consults the images, he looks at the liver. 22 In his right hand is the divination for Jerusalem: to set up battering rams, to call for a slaughter, to lift the voice with shouting, to set battering rams against the gates, to heap up a *siege* mound, and to build a wall. 23 And it will be to them like a false divination in the eyes of those who have sworn oaths with them; but he will bring their iniquity to remembrance, that they may be taken.

24 "Therefore thus says the Lord GOD: 'Because you have made your iniquity to be remembered, in that your transgressions are uncovered, so that in all your doings your sins appear—because you have come to remembrance, you shall be taken in hand.

25 'Now to you, O profane, wicked prince of Israel, whose day has come, whose iniquity *shall* end, 26 thus says the Lord GOD:

"Remove the turban, and take off the crown;
Nothing *shall remain* the same.
Exalt the humble, and humble the exalted.
27 Overthrown, overthrown,
I will make it overthrown!
It shall be no *longer,*
Until He comes whose right it is,
And I will give it *to Him.*" '

28 "And you, son of man, prophesy and say, 'Thus says the Lord GOD concerning the Ammonites and concerning their reproach,' and say:

'A sword, a sword *is* drawn,
Polished for slaughter,
For consuming, for flashing—
29 While they see false visions for you,
While they divine a lie to you,
To bring you on the necks of the wicked, the slain

Whose day has come,
Whose iniquity *shall* end.
30 'Return *it* to its sheath.
I will judge you
In the place where you were created,
In the land of your nativity.
31 I will pour out My indignation on you;
I will blow against you with the fire of My wrath,
And deliver you into the hands of brutal men *who are* skillful to destroy.
32 You shall be fuel for the fire;
Your blood shall be in the midst of the land.
You shall not be remembered,
For I the LORD have spoken.' "

22 Moreover the word of the LORD came to me, saying, 2 "Now, son of man, will you judge, will you judge the bloody city? Yes, show her all her abominations! 3 Then say, 'Thus says the Lord GOD: "The city sheds blood in her own midst, that her time may come; and she makes idols within herself to defile herself. 4 You have become guilty by the blood which you have shed, and have defiled yourself with the idols which you have made. You have caused your days to draw near, and have come to *the end of* your years; therefore I have made you a reproach to the nations, and a mockery to all countries. 5 *Those* near and *those* far from you will mock you as infamous *and* full of tumult.

6 "Look, the princes of Israel: each one has used his power to shed blood in you. 7 In you they have made light of father and mother; in your midst they have oppressed the stranger; in you they have mistreated the fatherless and the widow. 8 You have despised My holy things and profaned My Sabbaths. 9 In you are men who slander to cause bloodshed; in you are those who eat on the mountains; in your midst they commit lewdness. 10 In you men uncover their fathers' nakedness; in you they violate women who are set apart during their impurity. 11 One commits abomination with his neighbor's wife; another lewdly defiles his daughter-in-law; and another in you violates his sister, his father's daughter. 12 In you they take bribes to shed

blood; you take usury and increase; you have made profit from your neighbors by extortion, and have forgotten Me," says the Lord GOD.

13 "Behold, therefore, I beat My fists at the dishonest profit which you have made, and at the bloodshed which has been in your midst. 14 Can your heart endure, or can your hands remain strong, in the days when I shall deal with you? I, the LORD, have spoken, and will do *it.* 15 I will scatter you among the nations, disperse you throughout the countries, and remove your filthiness completely from you. 16 You shall defile yourself in the sight of the nations; then you shall know that I *am* the LORD." ' "

17 The word of the LORD came to me, saying, 18 "Son of man, the house of Israel has become dross to Me; they *are* all bronze, tin, iron, and lead, in the midst of a furnace; they have become dross from silver. 19 Therefore thus says the Lord GOD: 'Because you have all become dross, therefore behold, I will gather you into the midst of Jerusalem. 20 *As men* gather silver, bronze, iron, lead, and tin into the midst of a furnace, to blow fire on it, to melt *it;* so I will gather you in My anger and in My fury, and I will leave *you there* and melt you. 21 Yes, I will gather you and blow on you with the fire of My wrath, and you shall be melted in its midst. 22 As silver is melted in the midst of a furnace, so shall you be melted in its midst; then you shall know that I, the LORD, have poured out My fury on you.' "

23 And the word of the LORD came to me, saying, 24 "Son of man, say to her: 'You *are* a land that is not cleansed*ᵃ* or rained on in the day of indignation.' 25 The conspiracy of her prophets*ᵃ* in her midst is like a roaring lion tearing the prey; they have devoured people; they have taken treasure and precious things; they have made many widows in her midst. 26 Her priests have violated My law and profaned My holy things; they have not distinguished between the holy and unholy, nor have they made known *the difference* between the unclean and the clean; and they

have hidden their eyes from My Sabbaths, so that I am profaned among them. 27 Her princes in her midst *are* like wolves tearing the prey, to shed blood, to destroy people, and to get dishonest gain. 28 Her prophets plastered them with untempered *mortar,* seeing false visions, and divining lies for them, saying, 'Thus says the Lord GOD,' when the LORD had not spoken. 29 The people of the land have used oppressions, committed robbery, and mistreated the poor and needy; and they wrongfully oppress the stranger. 30 So I sought for a man among them who would make a wall, and stand in the gap before Me on behalf of the land, that I should not destroy it; but I found no one. 31 Therefore I have poured out My indignation on them; I have consumed them with the fire of My wrath; and I have recompensed their deeds on their own heads," says the Lord GOD.

23 The word of the LORD came again to me, saying:

2 "Son of man, there were two women,
The daughters of one mother.
3 They committed harlotry in Egypt,
They committed harlotry in their youth;
Their breasts were there embraced,
Their virgin bosom was there pressed.
4 Their names: Oholah*ᵃ* the elder and Oholibah*ᵇ* her sister;
They were Mine,
And they bore sons and daughters.
As for their names,
Samaria *is* Oholah, and Jerusalem *is* Oholibah.

5 "Oholah played the harlot even though she was Mine;
And she lusted for her lovers, the neighboring Assyrians,
6 *Who were* clothed in purple, Captains and rulers,
All of them desirable young men,
Horsemen riding on horses.

22:24 *ᵃ*Following Masoretic Text, Syriac, and Vulgate; Septuagint reads *showered upon.*
22:25 *ᵃ*Following Masoretic Text and Vulgate; Septuagint reads *princes;* Targum reads *scribes.*
23:4 *ᵃ*Literally *Her Own Tabernacle* *ᵇ*Literally *My Tabernacle Is in Her*

*F*rom the crown of my head to the soles of my feet, all that I am belongs to God. Early in the morning will I seek His face. I lie upon my bed at night and call on His name. I'll touch Him, embrace Him. He is the God of my salvation.

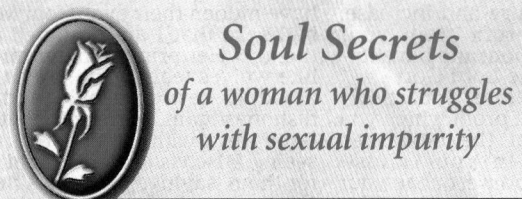

Soul Secrets
of a woman who struggles with sexual impurity

O God, where are You? I need You now. Can You hear me? Do You care? Can You see that I'm down to my last Friend? I've done some awful things. I've taken the body You've given me and used it for cheap thrills and false affection. I'm sick of selling myself for money that is too soon spent. Sick of feeling used instead of loved. Sick of painting a smile on my face when inside I'm screaming. Sick of dressing up a body that has lost its soul.

Lord, I feel so filthy. I just want to be clean. Forgive me for using my beauty to bring out the beast in men. Touch my tears with Your mercy and whisper hope for the future to me. I want to climb up in Your lap and be a little girl again—innocent and new.

They say You are the God of second chances, the God of new beginnings. You're the only One I can count on. From now on, I'm Your woman. I belong to You alone. Be my Hero. Be my Shelter. Be my Man.

7 Thus she committed her
harlotry with them,
All of them choice men of
Assyria;
And with all for whom she
lusted,
With all their idols, she defiled
herself.
8 She has never given up her
harlotry *brought* from Egypt,
For in her youth they had lain
with her,
Pressed her virgin bosom,
And poured out their
immorality upon her.

9 "Therefore I have delivered her
Into the hand of her lovers,
Into the hand of the Assyrians,
For whom she lusted.
10 They uncovered her
nakedness,
Took away her sons and
daughters,
And slew her with the sword;
She became a byword among
women,
For they had executed
judgment on her.

11 "Now although her sister Oholibah saw *this,* she became more corrupt in her lust than she, and in her
harlotry more corrupt than her sister's harlotry.

12 "She lusted for the neighboring
Assyrians,
Captains and rulers,
Clothed most gorgeously,
Horsemen riding on horses,
All of them desirable young
men.
13 Then I saw that she was
defiled;
Both *took* the same way.
14 But she increased her harlotry;
She looked at men portrayed
on the wall,
Images of Chaldeans portrayed
in vermilion,
15 Girded with belts around their
waists,
Flowing turbans on their heads,
All of them looking like
captains,
In the manner of the
Babylonians of Chaldea,
The land of their nativity.
16 As soon as her eyes saw them,
She lusted for them

And sent messengers to them
in Chaldea.

17 "Then the Babylonians came to
her, into the bed of love,
And they defiled her with their
immorality;
So she was defiled by them,
and alienated herself from
them.
18 She revealed her harlotry and
uncovered her nakedness.
Then I alienated Myself from
her,
As I had alienated Myself from
her sister.

19 "Yet she multiplied her harlotry
In calling to remembrance the
days of her youth,
When she had played the
harlot in the land of Egypt.
20 For she lusted for her
paramours,
Whose flesh *is like* the flesh of
donkeys,
And whose issue *is like* the
issue of horses.
21 Thus you called to
remembrance the lewdness
of your youth,
When the Egyptians pressed
your bosom
Because of your youthful
breasts.

22 "Therefore, Oholibah, thus says
the Lord GOD:

'Behold, I will stir up your
lovers against you,
From whom you have alienated
yourself,
And I will bring them against
you from every side:
23 The Babylonians,
All the Chaldeans,
Pekod, Shoa, Koa,
All the Assyrians with them,
All of them desirable young
men,
Governors and rulers,
Captains and men of renown,
All of them riding on horses.
24 And they shall come against
you
With chariots, wagons, and
war-horses,
With a horde of people.
They shall array against you
Buckler, shield, and helmet all
around.

*M*arriage is ministry. If you are single, your ministry is directly unto the Lord. If
you are married, your ministry is through your spouse. Then you learn how to
be devoted to God through the relationship you have with your spouse.

'I will delegate judgment to
them,
And they shall judge you
according to their judgments.
25 I will set My jealousy against
you,
And they shall deal furiously
with you;
They shall remove your nose
and your ears,
And your remnant shall fall by
the sword;
They shall take your sons and
your daughters,
And your remnant shall be
devoured by fire.
26 They shall also strip you of
your clothes
And take away your beautiful
jewelry.

27 'Thus I will make you cease
your lewdness and your
harlotry
Brought from the land of
Egypt,
So that you will not lift your
eyes to them,
Nor remember Egypt
anymore.'

28 "For thus says the Lord GOD:
'Surely I will deliver you into the
hand of those you hate, into the hand
of those from whom you alienated
yourself. 29 They will deal hatefully
with you, take away all you have
worked for, and leave you naked and
bare. The nakedness of your harlotry
shall be uncovered, both your lewdness and your harlotry. 30 I will do
these *things* to you because you have
gone as a harlot after the Gentiles,
because you have become defiled by
their idols. 31 You have walked in the
way of your sister; therefore I will
put her cup in your hand.'
32 "Thus says the Lord GOD:

'You shall drink of your sister's
cup,
The deep and wide one;
You shall be laughed to scorn
And held in derision;
It contains much.
33 You will be filled with
drunkenness and sorrow,
The cup of horror and
desolation,
The cup of your sister Samaria.
34 You shall drink and drain it,
You shall break its shards,

And tear at your own breasts;
For I have spoken,'
Says the Lord GOD.

35 "Therefore thus says the Lord
GOD:

'Because you have forgotten Me
and cast Me behind your
back,
Therefore you shall bear the
penalty
Of your lewdness and your
harlotry.' "

36 The LORD also said to me: "Son
of man, will you judge Oholah and
Oholibah? Then declare to them their
abominations. 37 For they have committed adultery, and blood *is* on their
hands. They have committed adultery with their idols, and even sacrificed their sons whom they bore to
Me, passing them through *the fire,*
to devour *them.* 38 Moreover they
have done this to Me: They have
defiled My sanctuary on the same
day and profaned My Sabbaths.
39 For after they had slain their children for their idols, on the same day
they came into My sanctuary to profane it; and indeed thus they have
done in the midst of My house.
40 "Furthermore you sent for men
to come from afar, to whom a messenger *was* sent; and there they
came. And you washed yourself for
them, painted your eyes, and
adorned yourself with ornaments.
41 You sat on a stately couch, with a
table prepared before it, on which
you had set My incense and My oil.
42 The sound of a carefree multitude
was with her, and Sabeans *were*
brought from the wilderness with
men of the common sort, who put
bracelets on their wrists and beautiful crowns on their heads. 43 Then I
said concerning *her who had grown
old in adulteries,* 'Will they commit
harlotry with her now, and she *with
them?'* 44 Yet they went in to her, as
men go in to a woman who plays the
harlot; thus they went in to Oholah
and Oholibah, the lewd women.
45 But righteous men will judge them
after the manner of adulteresses, and
after the manner of women who shed
blood, because they *are* adulteresses,
and blood *is* on their hands.
46 "For thus says the Lord GOD:
'Bring up an assembly against them,

Gospel
Pearls

give them up to trouble and plunder. 47 The assembly shall stone them with stones and execute them with their swords; they shall slay their sons and their daughters, and burn their houses with fire. 48 Thus I will cause lewdness to cease from the land, that all women may be taught not to practice your lewdness. 49 They shall repay you for your lewdness, and you shall pay for your idolatrous sins. Then you shall know that I *am* the Lord God.' "

24 Again, in the ninth year, in the tenth month, on the tenth *day* of the month, the word of the Lord came to me, saying, 2 "Son of man, write down the name of the day, this very day—the king of Babylon started his siege against Jerusalem this very day. 3 And utter a parable to the rebellious house, and say to them, 'Thus says the Lord God:

"Put on a pot, set *it* on,
And also pour water into it.
4 Gather pieces *of meat* in it,
Every good piece,
The thigh and the shoulder.
Fill *it* with choice cuts;
5 Take the choice of the flock.
Also pile *fuel* bones under it,
Make it boil well,
And let the cuts simmer in it."

6 'Therefore thus says the Lord God:

"Woe to the bloody city,
To the pot whose scum *is* in it,
And whose scum is not gone from it!
Bring it out piece by piece,
On which no lot has fallen.
7 For her blood is in her midst;
She set it on top of a rock;
She did not pour it on the ground,
To cover it with dust.
8 That it may raise up fury and take vengeance,
I have set her blood on top of a rock,
That it may not be covered."

9 'Therefore thus says the Lord God:

"Woe to the bloody city!
I too will make the pyre great.
10 Heap on the wood,

Kindle the fire;
Cook the meat well,
Mix in the spices,
And let the cuts be burned up.
11 "Then set the pot empty on the coals,
That it may become hot and its bronze may burn,
That its filthiness may be melted in it,
That its scum may be consumed.
12 She has grown weary with lies,
And her great scum has not gone from her.
Let her scum *be* in the fire!
13 In your filthiness *is* lewdness.
Because I have cleansed you, and you were not cleansed,
You will not be cleansed of your filthiness anymore,
Till I have caused My fury to rest upon you.
14 I, the Lord, have spoken *it;*
It shall come to pass, and I will do *it;*
I will not hold back,
Nor will I spare,
Nor will I relent;
According to your ways
And according to your deeds
They[a] will judge you,"
Says the Lord God.' "

15 Also the word of the Lord came to me, saying, 16 "Son of man, behold, I take away from you the desire of your eyes with one stroke; yet you shall neither mourn nor weep, nor shall your tears run down. 17 Sigh in silence, make no mourning for the dead; bind your turban on your head, and put your sandals on your feet; do not cover *your* lips, and do not eat man's bread *of sorrow.*"

18 So I spoke to the people in the morning, and at evening my wife died; and the next morning I did as I was commanded.

19 And the people said to me, "Will you not tell us what these *things signify* to us, that you behave so?"

20 Then I answered them, "The word of the Lord came to me, saying, 21 'Speak to the house of Israel, "Thus says the Lord God: 'Behold, I will profane My sanctuary, your arrogant boast, the desire of your eyes, the delight of your soul; and your sons and daughters whom you left

24:14 [a]Septuagint, Syriac, Targum, and Vulgate read *I.*

J esus gave Himself for the Church. So also do husbands and wives give themselves to each another. Marriage is not a place where we seek self-gratification. It is the place where we seek to gratify another.

behind shall fall by the sword. 22 And you shall do as I have done; you shall not cover *your* lips nor eat man's bread *of sorrow.* 23 Your turbans shall be on your heads and your sandals on your feet; you shall neither mourn nor weep, but you shall pine away in your iniquities and mourn with one another. 24 Thus Ezekiel is a sign to you; according to all that he has done you shall do; and when this comes, you shall know that I *am* the Lord God.' "

25 'And you, son of man—*will it* not *be* in the day when I take from them their stronghold, their joy and their glory, the desire of their eyes, and that on which they set their minds, their sons and their daughters: 26 on that day one who escapes will come to you to let *you* hear *it* with *your* ears; 27 on that day your mouth will be opened to him who has escaped; you shall speak and no longer be mute. Thus you will be a sign to them, and they shall know that I *am* the Lord.' "

25 The word of the Lord came to me, saying, 2 "Son of man, set your face against the Ammonites, and prophesy against them. 3 Say to the Ammonites, 'Hear the word of the Lord God! Thus says the Lord God: "Because you said, 'Aha!' against My sanctuary when it was profaned, and against the land of Israel when it was desolate, and against the house of Judah when they went into captivity, 4 indeed, therefore, I will deliver you as a possession to the men of the East, and they shall set their encampments among you and make their dwellings among you; they shall eat your fruit, and they shall drink your milk. 5 And I will make Rabbah a stable for camels and Ammon a resting place for flocks. Then you shall know that I *am* the Lord."

6 'For thus says the Lord God: "Because you clapped *your* hands, stamped your feet, and rejoiced in heart with all your disdain for the land of Israel, 7 indeed, therefore, I will stretch out My hand against you, and give you as plunder to the nations; I will cut you off from the peoples, and I will cause you to perish from the countries; I will destroy you, and you shall know that I *am* the Lord."

8 'Thus says the Lord God: "Because Moab and Seir say, 'Look! The house of Judah *is* like all the nations,' 9 therefore, behold, I will clear the territory of Moab of cities, of the cities on its frontier, the glory of the country, Beth Jeshimoth, Baal Meon, and Kirjathaim. 10 To the men of the East I will give it as a possession, together with the Ammonites, that the Ammonites may not be remembered among the nations. 11 And I will execute judgments upon Moab, and they shall know that I *am* the Lord."

12 'Thus says the Lord God: "Because of what Edom did against the house of Judah by taking vengeance, and has greatly offended by avenging itself on them," 13 therefore thus says the Lord God: "I will also stretch out My hand against Edom, cut off man and beast from it, and make it desolate from Teman; Dedan shall fall by the sword. 14 I will lay My vengeance on Edom by the hand of My people Israel, that they may do in Edom according to My anger and according to My fury; and they shall know My vengeance," says the Lord God.

15 'Thus says the Lord God: "Because the Philistines dealt vengefully and took vengeance with a spiteful heart, to destroy because of the old hatred," 16 therefore thus says the Lord God: "I will stretch out My hand against the Philistines, and I will cut off the Cherethites and destroy the remnant of the seacoast. 17 I will execute great vengeance on them with furious rebukes; and they shall know that I *am* the Lord, when I lay My vengeance upon them." ' "

26 And it came to pass in the eleventh year, on the first *day* of the month, *that* the word of the Lord came to me, saying, 2 "Son of man, because Tyre has said against Jerusalem, 'Aha! She is broken who *was* the gateway of the peoples; now she is turned over to me; I shall be filled; she is laid waste.'

3 "Therefore thus says the Lord God: 'Behold, I *am* against you, O Tyre, and will cause many nations to come up against you, as the sea causes its waves to come up. 4 And they shall destroy the walls of Tyre and break down her towers; I will also scrape her dust from her, and make her like the top of a rock.

Gospel Pearls

5 It shall be *a place for* spreading nets in the midst of the sea, for I have spoken,' says the Lord GOD; 'it shall become plunder for the nations. 6 Also her daughter *villages* which *are* in the fields shall be slain by the sword. Then they shall know that I am the LORD.'

7 "For thus says the Lord GOD: 'Behold, I will bring against Tyre from the north Nebuchadnezzar*ᵃ* king of Babylon, king of kings, with horses, with chariots, and with horsemen, and an army with many people. 8 He will slay with the sword your daughter *villages* in the fields; he will heap up a siege mound against you, build a wall against you, and raise a defense against you. 9 He will direct his battering rams against your walls, and with his axes he will break down your towers. 10 Because of the abundance of his horses, their dust will cover you; your walls will shake at the noise of the horsemen, the wagons, and the chariots, when he enters your gates, as men enter a city that has been breached. 11 With the hooves of his horses he will trample all your streets; he will slay your people by the sword, and your strong pillars will fall to the ground. 12 They will plunder your riches and pillage your merchandise; they will break down your walls and destroy your pleasant houses; they will lay your stones, your timber, and your soil in the midst of the water. 13 I will put an end to the sound of your songs, and the sound of your harps shall be heard no more. 14 I will make you like the top of a rock; you shall be *a place for* spreading nets, and you shall never be rebuilt, for I the LORD have spoken,' says the Lord GOD.

15 "Thus says the Lord GOD to Tyre: 'Will the coastlands not shake at the sound of your fall, when the wounded cry, when slaughter is made in the midst of you? 16 Then all the princes of the sea will come down from their thrones, lay aside their robes, and take off their embroidered garments; they will clothe themselves with trembling; they will sit on the ground, tremble *every* moment, and be astonished at you. 17 And they will take up a lamentation for you, and say to you:

"How you have perished,
    O one inhabited by seafaring men,
    O renowned city,
    Who was strong at sea,
    She and her inhabitants,
    Who caused their terror *to be* on all her inhabitants!
18 Now the coastlands tremble on the day of your fall;
    Yes, the coastlands by the sea are troubled at your departure." '

19 "For thus says the Lord GOD: 'When I make you a desolate city, like cities that are not inhabited, when I bring the deep upon you, and great waters cover you, 20 then I will bring you down with those who descend into the Pit, to the people of old, and I will make you dwell in the lowest part of the earth, in places desolate from antiquity, with those who go down to the Pit, so that you may never be inhabited; and I shall establish glory in the land of the living. 21 I will make you a terror, and you *shall be* no *more;* though you are sought for, you will never be found again,' says the Lord GOD."

27 The word of the LORD came again to me, saying, 2 "Now, son of man, take up a lamentation for Tyre, 3 and say to Tyre, 'You who are situated at the entrance of the sea, merchant of the peoples on many coastlands, thus says the Lord GOD:

"O Tyre, you have said,
    'I *am* perfect in beauty.'
4   Your borders *are* in the midst of the seas.
    Your builders have perfected your beauty.
5   They made all *your* planks of fir trees from Senir;
    They took a cedar from Lebanon to make you a mast.
6   *Of* oaks from Bashan they made your oars;
    The company of Ashurites have inlaid your planks
    With ivory from the coasts of Cyprus.*ᵃ*
7   Fine embroidered linen from

26:7 *ᵃ*Hebrew *Nebuchadrezzar,* and so elsewhere in this book   27:6 *ᵃ*Hebrew *Kittim,* western lands, especially Cyprus

---

*T*he sacredness of marriage is found in the relationship between Christ and the Church. Jesus continues to intercede on behalf of the Church, even after He gave His all for us. He is the greatest advocate of believers.

Egypt was what you spread
for your sail;
Blue and purple from the coasts
of Elishah was what covered
you.

8 "Inhabitants of Sidon and Arvad
were your oarsmen;
Your wise men, O Tyre, were
in you;
They became your pilots.
9 Elders of Gebal and its wise
men
Were in you to caulk your
seams;
All the ships of the sea
And their oarsmen were in you
To market your merchandise.

10 "Those from Persia, Lydia,*a* and
Libya*b*
Were in your army as men of
war;
They hung shield and helmet in
you;
They gave splendor to you.
11 Men of Arvad with your army
were on your walls *all*
around,
And the men of Gammad were
in your towers;
They hung their shields on
your walls *all* around;
They made your beauty
perfect.

12 "Tarshish *was* your merchant
because of your many luxury goods.
They gave you silver, iron, tin, and
lead for your goods. 13 Javan, Tubal,
and Meshech *were* your traders.
They bartered human lives and vessels of bronze for your merchandise.
14 Those from the house of Togarmah
traded for your wares with horses,
steeds, and mules. 15 The men of Dedan *were* your traders; many isles
were the market of your hand. They
brought you ivory tusks and ebony
as payment. 16 Syria *was* your merchant because of the abundance of
goods you made. They gave you for
your wares emeralds, purple, embroidery, fine linen, corals, and rubies. 17 Judah and the land of Israel
were your traders. They traded for
your merchandise wheat of Minnith, millet, honey, oil, and balm.
18 Damascus *was* your merchant because of the abundance of goods you

made, because of your many luxury
items, with the wine of Helbon and
with white wool. 19 Dan and Javan
paid for your wares, traversing back
and forth. Wrought iron, cassia, and
cane were among your merchandise.
20 Dedan *was* your merchant in sad-
dlecloths for riding. 21 Arabia and all
the princes of Kedar *were* your regular merchants. They traded with you
in lambs, rams, and goats. 22 The
merchants of Sheba and Raamah
were your merchants. They traded
for your wares the choicest spices,
all kinds of precious stones, and gold.
23 Haran, Canneh, Eden, the merchants of Sheba, Assyria, *and* Chil-
mad *were* your merchants. 24 These
were your merchants in choice
items—in purple clothes, in embroidered garments, in chests of multicolored apparel, in sturdy woven
cords, which were in your marketplace.

25 "The ships of Tarshish were
carriers of your merchandise.
You were filled and very
glorious in the midst of the
seas.
26 Your oarsmen brought you into
many waters,
But the east wind broke you in
the midst of the seas.

27 "Your riches, wares, and
merchandise,
Your mariners and pilots,
Your caulkers and
merchandisers,
All your men of war who *are*
in you,
And the entire company which
is in your midst,
Will fall into the midst of the
seas on the day of your ruin.
28 The common-land will shake at
the sound of the cry of your
pilots.

29 "All who handle the oar,
The mariners,
All the pilots of the sea
Will come down from their
ships *and* stand on the shore.
30 They will make their voice
heard because of you;
They will cry bitterly and cast
dust on their heads;
They will roll about in ashes;

27:10 *a*Hebrew *Lud* *b*Hebrew *Put*

31 They will shave themselves
completely bald because of
you,
Gird themselves with
sackcloth,
And weep for you
With bitterness of heart *and*
bitter wailing.
32 In their wailing for you
They will take up a
lamentation,
And lament for you:
'What *city is* like Tyre,
Destroyed in the midst of the
sea?
33 'When your wares went out by
sea,
You satisfied many people;
You enriched the kings of the
earth
With your many luxury goods
and your merchandise.
34 But you are broken by the seas
in the depths of the waters;
Your merchandise and the
entire company will fall in
your midst.
35 All the inhabitants of the isles
will be astonished at you;
Their kings will be greatly
afraid,
And *their* countenance will be
troubled.
36 The merchants among the
peoples will hiss at you;
You will become a horror, and
be no more forever.' " ' "

28 The word of the LORD came to
me again, saying, 2 "Son of
man, say to the prince of Tyre, 'Thus
says the Lord GOD:

"Because your heart *is* lifted up,
And you say, 'I *am* a god,
I sit *in* the seat of gods,
In the midst of the seas,'
Yet you *are* a man, and not a
god,
Though you set your heart as
the heart of a god
3 (Behold, you *are* wiser than
Daniel!
There is no secret that can be
hidden from you!
4 With your wisdom and your
understanding
You have gained riches for
yourself,
And gathered gold and silver
into your treasuries;

5 By your great wisdom in trade
you have increased your
riches,
And your heart is lifted up
because of your riches),"

6 'Therefore thus says the Lord
GOD:

"Because you have set your
heart as the heart of a god,
7 Behold, therefore, I will bring
strangers against you,
The most terrible of the
nations;
And they shall draw their
swords against the beauty of
your wisdom,
And defile your splendor.
8 They shall throw you down into
the Pit,
And you shall die the death of
the slain
In the midst of the seas.

9 "Will you still say before him
who slays you,
'I *am* a god'?
But you *shall be* a man, and not
a god,
In the hand of him who slays
you.
10 You shall die the death of the
uncircumcised
By the hand of aliens;
For I have spoken," says the
Lord GOD.' "

11 Moreover the word of the LORD
came to me, saying, 12 "Son of man,
take up a lamentation for the king
of Tyre, and say to him, 'Thus says
the Lord GOD:

"You *were* the seal of perfection,
Full of wisdom and perfect in
beauty.
13 You were in Eden, the garden
of God;
Every precious stone *was* your
covering:
The sardius, topaz, and
diamond,
Beryl, onyx, and jasper,
Sapphire, turquoise, and
emerald with gold.
The workmanship of your
timbrels and pipes
Was prepared for you on the
day you were created.
14 "You *were* the anointed cherub
who covers;

*B*elieve God for your marriage! It will not be your feelings that heal your relationship;
it will be your faith.

I established you;
You were on the holy mountain
of God;
You walked back and forth in
the midst of fiery stones.
15 You *were* perfect in your ways
from the day you were
created,
Till iniquity was found in you.

16 "By the abundance of your
trading
You became filled with
violence within,
And you sinned;
Therefore I cast you as a
profane thing
Out of the mountain of God;
And I destroyed you, O
covering cherub,
From the midst of the fiery
stones.

17 "Your heart was lifted up
because of your beauty;
You corrupted your wisdom for
the sake of your splendor;
I cast you to the ground,
I laid you before kings,
That they might gaze at you.

18 "You defiled your sanctuaries
By the multitude of your
iniquities,
By the iniquity of your trading;
Therefore I brought fire from
your midst;
It devoured you,
And I turned you to ashes upon
the earth
In the sight of all who saw you.
19 All who knew you among the
peoples are astonished at
you;
You have become a horror,
And *shall be* no more
forever." ' "

20 Then the word of the LORD came
to me, saying, 21 "Son of man, set
your face toward Sidon, and prophesy against her, 22 and say, 'Thus
says the Lord GOD:

"Behold, I *am* against you, O
Sidon;
I will be glorified in your midst;
And they shall know that I *am*
the LORD,

When I execute judgments in
her and am hallowed in her.
23 For I will send pestilence upon
her,
And blood in her streets;
The wounded shall be judged
in her midst
By the sword against her on
every side;
Then they shall know that I *am*
the LORD.

24 "And there shall no longer be a
pricking brier or a painful thorn for
the house of Israel from among all
who are around them, who despise
them. Then they shall know that I *am*
the Lord GOD."

25 'Thus says the Lord GOD: "When
I have gathered the house of Israel
from the peoples among whom they
are scattered, and am hallowed in
them in the sight of the Gentiles, then
they will dwell in their own land
which I gave to My servant Jacob.
26 And they will dwell safely there,
build houses, and plant vineyards;
yes, they will dwell securely, when I
execute judgments on all those
around them who despise them. Then
they shall know that I *am* the LORD
their God." ' "

29 In the tenth year, in the tenth
month, on the twelfth *day* of
the month, the word of the LORD
came to me, saying, 2 "Son of man,
set your face against Pharaoh king
of Egypt, and prophesy against him,
and against all Egypt. 3 Speak, and
say, 'Thus says the Lord GOD:

"Behold, I *am* against you,
O Pharaoh king of Egypt,
O great monster who lies in the
midst of his rivers,
Who has said, 'My River*a is* my
own;
I have made *it* for myself.'
4 But I will put hooks in your
jaws,
And cause the fish of your
rivers to stick to your scales;
I will bring you up out of the
midst of your rivers,
And all the fish in your rivers
will stick to your scales.
5 I will leave you in the
wilderness,

29:3 *a*That is, the Nile

Gospel
Pearls

You and all the fish of your
    rivers;
You shall fall on the open field;
You shall not be picked up or
    gathered.*ᵃ*
I have given you as food
To the beasts of the field
And to the birds of the heavens.

6 "Then all the inhabitants of
    Egypt
    Shall know that I *am* the LORD,
    Because they have been a staff
        of reed to the house of Israel.
7   When they took hold of you
    with the hand,
    You broke and tore all their
        shoulders;*ᵃ*
    When they leaned on you,
    You broke and made all their
        backs quiver."

8 'Therefore thus says the Lord
GOD: "Surely I will bring a sword
upon you and cut off from you man
and beast. 9 And the land of Egypt
shall become desolate and waste;
then they will know that I *am* the
LORD, because he said, 'The River *is*
mine, and I have made *it.*' 10 Indeed,
therefore, I *am* against you and
against your rivers, and I will make
the land of Egypt utterly waste and
desolate, from Migdol*ᵃ* to Syene, as
far as the border of Ethiopia.
11 Neither foot of man shall pass
through it nor foot of beast pass
through it, and it shall be uninhabited forty years. 12 I will make the
land of Egypt desolate in the midst
of the countries *that are* desolate;
and among the cities *that are* laid
waste, her cities shall be desolate
forty years; and I will scatter the
Egyptians among the nations and
disperse them throughout the countries."

13 'Yet, thus says the Lord GOD: "At
the end of forty years I will gather
the Egyptians from the peoples
among whom they were scattered.
14 I will bring back the captives of
Egypt and cause them to return to
the land of Pathros, to the land of
their origin, and there they shall be
a lowly kingdom. 15 It shall be the
lowliest of kingdoms; it shall never
again exalt itself above the nations,

for I will diminish them so that they
will not rule over the nations anymore. 16 No longer shall it be the confidence of the house of Israel, but will
remind them of *their* iniquity when
they turned to follow them. Then
they shall know that I *am* the Lord
GOD." ' "

17 And it came to pass in the
twenty-seventh year, in the first
month, on the first *day* of the month,
that the word of the LORD came to
me, saying, 18 "Son of man, Nebuchadnezzar king of Babylon caused
his army to labor strenuously against
Tyre; every head *was* made bald, and
every shoulder rubbed raw; yet neither he nor his army received wages
from Tyre, for the labor which they
expended on it. 19 Therefore thus
says the Lord GOD: 'Surely I will give
the land of Egypt to Nebuchadnezzar
king of Babylon; he shall take away
her wealth, carry off her spoil, and
remove her pillage; and that will be
the wages for his army. 20 I have
given him the land of Egypt *for* his
labor, because they worked for Me,'
says the Lord GOD.

21 'In that day I will cause the horn
of the house of Israel to spring forth,
and I will open your mouth to speak
in their midst. Then they shall know
that I *am* the LORD.' "

30 The word of the LORD came to
    me again, saying, 2 "Son of
man, prophesy and say, 'Thus says
the Lord GOD:

    "Wail, 'Woe to the day!'
3   For the day *is* near,
    Even the day of the LORD *is*
        near;
    It will be a day of clouds, the
        time of the Gentiles.
4   The sword shall come upon
        Egypt,
    And great anguish shall be in
        Ethiopia,
    When the slain fall in Egypt,
    And they take away her wealth,
    And her foundations are
        broken down.

5 "Ethiopia, Libya,*ᵃ* Lydia,*ᵇ* all the
mingled people, Chub, and the men

29:5 *ᵃ*Following Masoretic Text, Septuagint, and Vulgate; some Hebrew manuscripts and Targum read
buried.   29:7 *ᵃ*Following Masoretic Text and Vulgate; Septuagint and Syriac read *hand.*   29:10 *ᵃ*Or
tower   30:5 *ᵃ*Hebrew *Put*   *ᵇ*Hebrew *Lud*

*I*t is terrible to arrest who you are in an attempt to fight fire with fire. The best way
to fight fire is with water! The winning way of a woman is not in her words, it is in
her character.

of the lands who are allied, shall fall with them by the sword."

6 'Thus says the LORD:

> "Those who uphold Egypt shall
>   fall,
> And the pride of her power
>   shall come down.
> From Migdol *to* Syene
> Those within her shall fall by
>   the sword,"
> Says the Lord GOD.

7   "They shall be desolate in the
>   midst of the desolate
>   countries,
> And her cities shall be in the
>   midst of the cities *that are*
>   laid waste.
8   Then they will know that I *am*
>   the LORD,
> When I have set a fire in Egypt
> And all her helpers are
>   destroyed.
9   On that day messengers shall
>   go forth from Me in ships
> To make the careless
>   Ethiopians afraid,
> And great anguish shall come
>   upon them,
> As on the day of Egypt;
> For indeed it is coming!"

10 'Thus says the Lord GOD:

> "I will also make a multitude of
>   Egypt to cease
> By the hand of
>   Nebuchadnezzar king of
>   Babylon.
11 He and his people with him, the
>   most terrible of the nations,
> Shall be brought to destroy the
>   land;
> They shall draw their swords
>   against Egypt,
> And fill the land with the slain.
12 I will make the rivers dry,
> And sell the land into the hand
>   of the wicked;
> I will make the land waste, and
>   all that is in it,
> By the hand of aliens.
> I, the LORD, have spoken."

13 'Thus says the Lord GOD:

> "I will also destroy the idols,
> And cause the images to cease
>   from Noph;*a*
> There shall no longer be
>   princes from the land of
>   Egypt;
> I will put fear in the land of
>   Egypt.
14 I will make Pathros desolate,
> Set fire to Zoan,
> And execute judgments in No.*a*
15 I will pour My fury on Sin,*a* the
>   strength of Egypt;
> I will cut off the multitude of
>   No,
16 And set a fire in Egypt;
> Sin shall have great pain,
> No shall be split open,
> And Noph *shall be in* distress
>   daily.
17 The young men of Aven*a* and
>   Pi Beseth shall fall by the
>   sword,
> And these *cities* shall go into
>   captivity.
18 At Tehaphnehes*a* the day shall
>   also be darkened,*b*
> When I break the yokes of
>   Egypt there.
> And her arrogant strength shall
>   cease in her;
> As for her, a cloud shall cover
>   her,
> And her daughters shall go into
>   captivity.
19 Thus I will execute judgments
>   on Egypt,
> Then they shall know that I *am*
>   the LORD." ' "

20 And it came to pass in the eleventh year, in the first *month,* on the seventh *day* of the month, *that* the word of the LORD came to me, saying, 21 "Son of man, I have broken the arm of Pharaoh king of Egypt; and see, it has not been bandaged for healing, nor a splint put on to bind it, to make it strong enough to hold a sword. 22 Therefore thus says the Lord GOD: 'Surely I *am* against Pharaoh king of Egypt, and will break his arms, both the strong one and the one that was broken; and I will make the sword fall out of his hand. 23 I will scatter the Egyptians among the nations, and disperse them

---

30:13 *a*That is, ancient Memphis   30:14 *a*That is, ancient Thebes   30:15 *a*That is, ancient Pelusium
30:17 *a*That is, ancient On (Heliopolis)   30:18 *a*Spelled *Tahpanhes* in Jeremiah 43:7 and elsewhere
*b*Following many Hebrew manuscripts, Bomberg, Septuagint, Syriac, Targum, and Vulgate; Masoretic Text reads *refrained.*

*Gospel
Pearls*

throughout the countries. 24 I will strengthen the arms of the king of Babylon and put My sword in his hand; but I will break Pharaoh's arms, and he will groan before him with the groanings of a mortally wounded *man*. 25 Thus I will strengthen the arms of the king of Babylon, but the arms of Pharaoh shall fall down; they shall know that I *am* the LORD, when I put My sword into the hand of the king of Babylon and he stretches it out against the land of Egypt. 26 I will scatter the Egyptians among the nations and disperse them throughout the countries. Then they shall know that I *am* the LORD.' "

31 Now it came to pass in the eleventh year, in the third *month,* on the first *day* of the month, *that* the word of the LORD came to me, saying, 2 "Son of man, say to Pharaoh king of Egypt and to his multitude:

'Whom are you like in your
   greatness?
3   Indeed Assyria *was* a cedar in
      Lebanon,
   With fine branches that shaded
      the forest,
   And of high stature;
   And its top was among the
      thick boughs.
4   The waters made it grow;
   Underground waters gave it
      height,
   With their rivers running
      around the place where it
      was planted,
   And sent out rivulets to all the
      trees of the field.

5   'Therefore its height was
      exalted above all the trees of
      the field;
   Its boughs were multiplied,
   And its branches became long
      because of the abundance of
      water,
   As it sent them out.
6   All the birds of the heavens
      made their nests in its
      boughs;
   Under its branches all the
      beasts of the field brought
      forth their young;

   And in its shadow all great
      nations made their home.

7   'Thus it was beautiful in
      greatness and in the length
      of its branches,
   Because its roots reached to
      abundant waters.
8   The cedars in the garden of
      God could not hide it;
   The fir trees were not like its
      boughs,
   And the chestnut[a] trees were
      not like its branches;
   No tree in the garden of God
      was like it in beauty.
9   I made it beautiful with a
      multitude of branches,
   So that all the trees of Eden
      envied it,
   That *were* in the garden of
      God.'

10 "Therefore thus says the Lord GOD: 'Because you have increased in height, and it set its top among the thick boughs, and its heart was lifted up in its height, 11 therefore I will deliver it into the hand of the mighty one of the nations, and he shall surely deal with it; I have driven it out for its wickedness. 12 And aliens, the most terrible of the nations, have cut it down and left it; its branches have fallen on the mountains and in all the valleys; its boughs lie broken by all the rivers of the land; and all the peoples of the earth have gone from under its shadow and left it.

13 'On its ruin will remain all the
      birds of the heavens,
   And all the beasts of the field
      will come to its branches—

14 'So that no trees by the waters may ever again exalt themselves for their height, nor set their tops among the thick boughs, that no tree which drinks water may ever be high enough to reach up to them.

   'For they have all been
      delivered to death,
   To the depths of the earth,
   Among the children of men
      who go down to the Pit.'

15 "Thus says the Lord GOD: 'In the day when it went down to hell, I

31:8 ªHebrew *armon*

*N*o one can do anything to make another person be saved. You can't make them come home. You can't make someone love you. But you can create an atmosphere where your conduct is not undermining your prayers!

caused mourning. I covered the deep because of it. I restrained its rivers, and the great waters were held back. I caused Lebanon to mourn for it, and all the trees of the field wilted because of it. 16 I made the nations shake at the sound of its fall, when I cast it down to hell together with those who descend into the Pit; and all the trees of Eden, the choice and best of Lebanon, all that drink water, were comforted in the depths of the earth. 17 They also went down to hell with it, with those *slain* by the sword; and *those who were* its *strong* arm dwelt in its shadows among the nations.

18 'To which of the trees in Eden will you then be likened in glory and greatness? Yet you shall be brought down with the trees of Eden to the depths of the earth; you shall lie in the midst of the uncircumcised, with *those* slain by the sword. This *is* Pharaoh and all his multitude,' says the Lord GOD."

32 And it came to pass in the twelfth year, in the twelfth *month,* on the first *day* of the month, *that* the word of the LORD came to me, saying, 2 "Son of man, take up a lamentation for Pharaoh king of Egypt, and say to him:

'You are like a young lion among the nations,
And you *are* like a monster in the seas,
Bursting forth in your rivers,
Troubling the waters with your feet,
And fouling their rivers.'

3 "Thus says the Lord GOD:

'I will therefore spread My net over you with a company of many people,
And they will draw you up in My net.
4   Then I will leave you on the land;
I will cast you out on the open fields,
And cause to settle on you all the birds of the heavens.
And with you I will fill the beasts of the whole earth.
5   I will lay your flesh on the mountains,

And fill the valleys with your carcass.

6   'I will also water the land with the flow of your blood,
Even to the mountains;
And the riverbeds will be full of you.
7   When *I* put out your light,
I will cover the heavens, and make its stars dark;
I will cover the sun with a cloud,
And the moon shall not give her light.
8   All the bright lights of the heavens I will make dark over you,
And bring darkness upon your land,'
Says the Lord GOD.

9 'I will also trouble the hearts of many peoples, when I bring your destruction among the nations, into the countries which you have not known. 10 Yes, I will make many peoples astonished at you, and their kings shall be horribly afraid of you when I brandish My sword before them; and they shall tremble *every* moment, every man for his own life, in the day of your fall.'

11 "For thus says the Lord GOD: 'The sword of the king of Babylon shall come upon you. 12 By the swords of the mighty warriors, all of them the most terrible of the nations, I will cause your multitude to fall.

'They shall plunder the pomp of Egypt,
And all its multitude shall be destroyed.
13   Also I will destroy all its animals
From beside its great waters;
The foot of man shall muddy them no more,
Nor shall the hooves of animals muddy them.
14   Then I will make their waters clear,
And make their rivers run like oil,'
Says the Lord GOD.

15   'When I make the land of Egypt desolate,
And the country is destitute of all that once filled it,

When I strike all who dwell in
  it,
Then they shall know that I *am*
  the LORD.

16 'This *is* the lamentation
With which they shall lament
  her;
The daughters of the nations
  shall lament her;
They shall lament for her, for
  Egypt,
And for all her multitude,'
Says the Lord GOD."

17 It came to pass also in the
twelfth year, on the fifteenth *day* of
the month, that the word of the LORD
came to me, saying:

18 "Son of man, wail over the
  multitude of Egypt,
And cast them down to the
  depths of the earth,
Her and the daughters of the
  famous nations,
With those who go down to the
  Pit:
19 'Whom do you surpass in
  beauty?
Go down, be placed with the
  uncircumcised.'

20 "They shall fall in the midst of
  those slain by the sword;
She is delivered to the sword,
Drawing her and all her
  multitudes.
21 The strong among the mighty
Shall speak to him out of the
  midst of hell
With those who help him:
'They have gone down,
They lie with the
  uncircumcised, slain by the
  sword.'

22 "Assyria *is* there, and all her
  company,
With their graves all around
  her,
All of them slain, fallen by the
  sword.
23 Her graves are set in the
  recesses of the Pit,
And her company is all around
  her grave,
All of them slain, fallen by the
  sword,
Who caused terror in the land
  of the living.

24 "There *is* Elam and all her
  multitude,
All around her grave,
All of them slain, fallen by the
  sword,
Who have gone down
  uncircumcised to the lower
  parts of the earth,
Who caused their terror in the
  land of the living;
Now they bear their shame
  with those who go down to
  the Pit.
25 They have set her bed in the
  midst of the slain,
With all her multitude,
With her graves all around it,
All of them uncircumcised,
  slain by the sword,
Though their terror was caused
In the land of the living,
Yet they bear their shame
With those who go down to the
  Pit;
It was put in the midst of the
  slain.

26 "There *are* Meshech and Tubal
  and all their multitudes,
With all their graves around
  it,
All of them uncircumcised,
  slain by the sword,
Though they caused their
  terror in the land of the
  living.
27 They do not lie with the mighty
Who are fallen of the
  uncircumcised,
Who have gone down to hell
  with their weapons of war;
They have laid their swords
  under their heads,
But their iniquities will be on
  their bones,
Because of the terror of the
  mighty in the land of the
  living.
28 Yes, you shall be broken in the
  midst of the uncircumcised,
And lie with *those* slain by the
  sword.

29 "There *is* Edom,
Her kings and all her princes,
Who despite their might
Are laid beside *those* slain by
  the sword;
They shall lie with the
  uncircumcised,
And with those who go down
  to the Pit.

When you approach your husband, do not corner him. Catch him at a time when
he won't feel interrogated. You would be surprised at how men tend to avoid
open confrontation.

30 There *are* the princes of the north,
All of them, and all the Sidonians,
Who have gone down with the slain
In shame at the terror which they caused by their might;
They lie uncircumcised with *those* slain by the sword,
And bear their shame with those who go down to the Pit.

31 "Pharaoh will see them
And be comforted over all his multitude,
Pharaoh and all his army,
Slain by the sword,"
Says the Lord GOD.

32 "For I have caused My terror in the land of the living;
And he shall be placed in the midst of the uncircumcised
With *those* slain by the sword,
Pharaoh and all his multitude,"
Says the Lord GOD.

33 Again the word of the LORD came to me, saying, 2 "Son of man, speak to the children of your people, and say to them: 'When I bring the sword upon a land, and the people of the land take a man from their territory and make him their watchman, 3 when he sees the sword coming upon the land, if he blows the trumpet and warns the people, 4 then whoever hears the sound of the trumpet and does not take warning, if the sword comes and takes him away, his blood shall be on his *own* head. 5 He heard the sound of the trumpet, but did not take warning; his blood shall be upon himself. But he who takes warning will save his life. 6 But if the watchman sees the sword coming and does not blow the trumpet, and the people are not warned, and the sword comes and takes *any* person from among them, he is taken away in his iniquity; but his blood I will require at the watchman's hand.'

7 "So you, son of man: I have made you a watchman for the house of Israel; therefore you shall hear a word from My mouth and warn them for Me. 8 When I say to the wicked, 'O wicked *man*, you shall surely die!' and you do not speak to warn the wicked from his way, that wicked

man shall die in his iniquity; but his blood I will require at your hand. 9 Nevertheless if you warn the wicked to turn from his way, and he does not turn from his way, he shall die in his iniquity; but you have delivered your soul.

10 "Therefore you, O son of man, say to the house of Israel: 'Thus you say, "If our transgressions and our sins *lie* upon us, and we pine away in them, how can we then live?" ' 11 Say to them: 'As I live,' says the Lord GOD, 'I have no pleasure in the death of the wicked, but that the wicked turn from his way and live. Turn, turn from your evil ways! For why should you die, O house of Israel?'

12 "Therefore you, O son of man, say to the children of your people: 'The righteousness of the righteous man shall not deliver him in the day of his transgression; as for the wickedness of the wicked, he shall not fall because of it in the day that he turns from his wickedness; nor shall the righteous be able to live because of *his righteousness* in the day that he sins.' 13 When I say to the righteous *that* he shall surely live, but he trusts in his own righteousness and commits iniquity, none of his righteous works shall be remembered; but because of the iniquity that he has committed, he shall die. 14 Again, when I say to the wicked, 'You shall surely die,' if he turns from his sin and does what is lawful and right, 15 *if* the wicked restores the pledge, gives back what he has stolen, and walks in the statutes of life without committing iniquity, he shall surely live; he shall not die. 16 None of his sins which he has committed shall be remembered against him; he has done what is lawful and right; he shall surely live.

17 "Yet the children of your people say, 'The way of the LORD is not fair.' But it is their way which is not fair! 18 When the righteous turns from his righteousness and commits iniquity, he shall die because of it. 19 But when the wicked turns from his wickedness and does what is lawful and right, he shall live because of it. 20 Yet you say, 'The way of the LORD is not fair.' O house of Israel, I will judge every one of you according to his own ways."

21 And it came to pass in the

Gospel Pearls

twelfth year of our captivity, in the tenth *month,* on the fifth *day* of the month, *that* one who had escaped from Jerusalem came to me and said, "The city has been captured!"

22 Now the hand of the LORD had been upon me the evening before the man came who had escaped. And He had opened my mouth; so when he came to me in the morning, my mouth was opened, and I was no longer mute.

23 Then the word of the LORD came to me, saying: 24 "Son of man, they who inhabit those ruins in the land of Israel are saying, 'Abraham was only one, and he inherited the land. But we *are* many; the land has been given to us as a possession.'

25 "Therefore say to them, 'Thus says the Lord GOD: "You eat *meat* with blood, you lift up your eyes toward your idols, and shed blood. Should you then possess the land? 26 You rely on your sword, you commit abominations, and you defile one another's wives. Should you then possess the land?"'

27 "Say thus to them, 'Thus says the Lord GOD: "*As* I live, surely those who *are* in the ruins shall fall by the sword, and the one who *is* in the open field I will give to the beasts to be devoured, and those who *are* in the strongholds and caves shall die of the pestilence. 28 For I will make the land most desolate, her arrogant strength shall cease, and the mountains of Israel shall be so desolate that no one will pass through. 29 Then they shall know that I *am* the LORD, when I have made the land most desolate because of all their abominations which they have committed."'

30 "As for you, son of man, the children of your people are talking about you beside the walls and in the doors of the houses; and they speak to one another, everyone saying to his brother, 'Please come and hear what the word is that comes from the LORD.' 31 So they come to you as people do, they sit before you *as* My people, and they hear your words, but they do not do them; for with their mouth they show much love, *but* their hearts pursue their *own* gain. 32 Indeed you *are* to them as a very lovely song of one who has a pleasant voice and can play well on an instrument; for they hear your words, but they do not do them. 33 And when

this comes to pass—surely it will come—then they will know that a prophet has been among them."

34 And the word of the LORD came to me, saying, 2 "Son of man, prophesy against the shepherds of Israel, prophesy and say to them, 'Thus says the Lord GOD to the shepherds: "Woe to the shepherds of Israel who feed themselves! Should not the shepherds feed the flocks? 3 You eat the fat and clothe yourselves with the wool; you slaughter the fatlings, *but* you do not feed the flock. 4 The weak you have not strengthened, nor have you healed those who were sick, nor bound up the broken, nor brought back what was driven away, nor sought what was lost; but with force and cruelty you have ruled them. 5 So they were scattered because *there was* no shepherd; and they became food for all the beasts of the field when they were scattered. 6 My sheep wandered through all the mountains, and on every high hill; yes, My flock was scattered over the whole face of the earth, and no one was seeking or searching *for them.*"

7 'Therefore, you shepherds, hear the word of the LORD: 8 "*as* I live," says the Lord GOD, "surely because My flock became a prey, and My flock became food for every beast of the field, because *there was* no shepherd, nor did My shepherds search for My flock, but the shepherds fed themselves and did not feed My flock"— 9 therefore, O shepherds, hear the word of the LORD! 10 Thus says the Lord GOD: "Behold, I *am* against the shepherds, and I will require My flock at their hand; I will cause them to cease feeding the sheep, and the shepherds shall feed themselves no more; for I will deliver My flock from their mouths, that they may no longer be food for them."

11 'For thus says the Lord GOD: "Indeed I Myself will search for My sheep and seek them out. 12 As a shepherd seeks out his flock on the day he is among his scattered sheep, so will I seek out My sheep and deliver them from all the places where they were scattered on a cloudy and dark day. 13 And I will bring them out from the peoples and gather them from the countries, and will bring them to their own land; I will feed them on the mountains of Israel, in

the valleys and in all the inhabited places of the country. 14 I will feed them in good pasture, and their fold shall be on the high mountains of Israel. There they shall lie down in a good fold and feed in rich pasture on the mountains of Israel. 15 I will feed My flock, and I will make them lie down," says the Lord GOD. 16 "I will seek what was lost and bring back what was driven away, bind up the broken and strengthen what was sick; but I will destroy the fat and the strong, and feed them in judgment."

17 'And *as for* you, O My flock, thus says the Lord GOD: "Behold, I shall judge between sheep and sheep, between rams and goats. 18 *Is it* too little for you to have eaten up the good pasture, that you must tread down with your feet the residue of your pasture—and to have drunk of the clear waters, that you must foul the residue with your feet? 19 And *as for* My flock, they eat what you have trampled with your feet, and they drink what you have fouled with your feet."

20 'Therefore thus says the Lord GOD to them: "Behold, I Myself will judge between the fat and the lean sheep. 21 Because you have pushed with side and shoulder, butted all the weak ones with your horns, and scattered them abroad, 22 therefore I will save My flock, and they shall no longer be a prey; and I will judge between sheep and sheep. 23 I will establish one shepherd over them, and he shall feed them—My servant David. He shall feed them and be their shepherd. 24 And I, the LORD, will be their God, and My servant David a prince among them; I, the LORD, have spoken.

25 "I will make a covenant of peace with them, and cause wild beasts to cease from the land; and they will dwell safely in the wilderness and sleep in the woods. 26 I will make them and the places all around My hill a blessing; and I will cause showers to come down in their season; there shall be showers of blessing. 27 Then the trees of the field shall yield their fruit, and the earth shall yield her increase. They shall be safe in their land; and they shall know that I *am* the LORD, when I have broken the bands of their yoke and delivered them from the hand of those

who enslaved them. 28 And they shall no longer be a prey for the nations, nor shall beasts of the land devour them; but they shall dwell safely, and no one shall make *them* afraid. 29 I will raise up for them a garden of renown, and they shall no longer be consumed with hunger in the land, nor bear the shame of the Gentiles anymore. 30 Thus they shall know that I, the LORD their God, *am* with them, and they, the house of Israel, *are* My people," says the Lord GOD.' "

31 "You are My flock, the flock of My pasture; you *are* men, *and* I *am* your God," says the Lord GOD.

35 Moreover the word of the LORD came to me, saying, 2 "Son of man, set your face against Mount Seir and prophesy against it, 3 and say to it, 'Thus says the Lord GOD:

"Behold, O Mount Seir, I *am* against you;
I will stretch out My hand against you,
And make you most desolate;
4 I shall lay your cities waste,
And you shall be desolate.
Then you shall know that I *am* the LORD.

5 "Because you have had an ancient hatred, and have shed *the blood of* the children of Israel by the power of the sword at the time of their calamity, *when* their iniquity *came to an* end, 6 therefore, *as* I live," says the Lord GOD, "I will prepare you for blood, and blood shall pursue you; since you have not hated blood, therefore blood shall pursue you. 7 Thus I will make Mount Seir most desolate, and cut off from it the one who leaves and the one who returns. 8 And I will fill its mountains with the slain; on your hills and in your valleys and in all your ravines those who are slain by the sword shall fall. 9 I will make you perpetually desolate, and your cities shall be uninhabited; then you shall know that I *am* the LORD.

10 "Because you have said, 'These two nations and these two countries shall be mine, and we will possess them,' although the LORD was there, 11 therefore, *as* I live," says the Lord GOD, "I will do according to your anger and according to the envy which

you showed in your hatred against them; and I will make Myself known among them when I judge you. 12 Then you shall know that I *am* the LORD. I have heard all your blasphemies which you have spoken against the mountains of Israel, saying, 'They are desolate; they are given to us to consume.' 13 Thus with your mouth you have boasted against Me and multiplied your words against Me; I have heard *them*."

14 'Thus says the Lord GOD: "The whole earth will rejoice when I make you desolate. 15 As you rejoiced because the inheritance of the house of Israel was desolate, so I will do to you; you shall be desolate, O Mount Seir, as well as all of Edom—all of it! Then they shall know that I *am* the LORD."'

36 "And you, son of man, prophesy to the mountains of Israel, and say, 'O mountains of Israel, hear the word of the LORD! 2 Thus says the Lord GOD: "Because the enemy has said of you, 'Aha! The ancient heights have become our possession,'"' 3 therefore prophesy, and say, 'Thus says the Lord GOD: "Because they made *you* desolate and swallowed you up on every side, so that you became the possession of the rest of the nations, and you are taken up by the lips of talkers and slandered by the people"— 4 therefore, O mountains of Israel, hear the word of the Lord GOD! Thus says the Lord GOD to the mountains, the hills, the rivers, the valleys, the desolate wastes, and the cities that have been forsaken, which became plunder and mockery to the rest of the nations all around— 5 therefore thus says the Lord GOD: "Surely I have spoken in My burning jealousy against the rest of the nations and against all Edom, who gave My land to themselves as a possession, with wholehearted joy *and* spiteful minds, in order to plunder its open country."'

6 "Therefore prophesy concerning the land of Israel, and say to the mountains, the hills, the rivers, and the valleys, 'Thus says the Lord GOD: "Behold, I have spoken in My jealousy and My fury, because you have borne the shame of the nations."

7 Therefore thus says the Lord GOD: "I have raised My hand in an oath that surely the nations that *are* around you shall bear their own shame. 8 But you, O mountains of Israel, you shall shoot forth your branches and yield your fruit to My people Israel, for they are about to come. 9 For indeed I *am* for you, and I will turn to you, and you shall be tilled and sown. 10 I will multiply men upon you, all the house of Israel, all of it; and the cities shall be inhabited and the ruins rebuilt. 11 I will multiply upon you man and beast; and they shall increase and bear young; I will make you inhabited as in former times, and do better *for you* than at your beginnings. Then you shall know that I *am* the LORD. 12 Yes, I will cause men to walk on you, My people Israel; they shall take possession of you, and you shall be their inheritance; no more shall you bereave them *of children*."

13 'Thus says the Lord GOD: "Because they say to you, 'You devour men and bereave your nation *of children*,' 14 therefore you shall devour men no more, nor bereave your nation anymore," says the Lord GOD. 15 Nor will I let you hear the taunts of the nations anymore, nor bear the reproach of the peoples anymore, nor shall you cause your nation to stumble anymore," says the Lord GOD.'"

16 Moreover the word of the LORD came to me, saying: 17 "Son of man, when the house of Israel dwelt in their own land, they defiled it by their own ways and deeds; to Me their way was like the uncleanness of a woman in her customary impurity. 18 Therefore I poured out My fury on them for the blood they had shed on the land, and for their idols *with which* they had defiled it. 19 So I scattered them among the nations, and they were dispersed throughout the countries; I judged them according to their ways and their deeds. 20 When they came to the nations, wherever they went, they profaned My holy name—when they said of them, 'These *are* the people of the LORD, *and* yet they have gone out of His land.' 21 But I had concern for My holy name, which the house of Israel had profaned among the nations wherever they went.

22 "Therefore say to the house of Israel, 'Thus says the Lord GOD: "I do not do *this* for your sake, O house of Israel, but for My holy name's

Marriage needs to be transparent. Fear will not heal, it will only hide. Both you and your spouse need to be able to expose your vulnerabilities without fear or condemnation.

sake, which you have profaned among the nations wherever you went. 23 And I will sanctify My great name, which has been profaned among the nations, which you have profaned in their midst; and the nations shall know that I *am* the LORD," says the Lord GOD, "when I am hallowed in you before their eyes. 24 For I will take you from among the nations, gather you out of all countries, and bring you into your own land. 25 Then I will sprinkle clean water on you, and you shall be clean; I will cleanse you from all your filthiness and from all your idols. 26 I will give you a new heart and put a new spirit within you; I will take the heart of stone out of your flesh and give you a heart of flesh. 27 I will put My Spirit within you and cause you to walk in My statutes, and you will keep My judgments and do *them*. 28 Then you shall dwell in the land that I gave to your fathers; you shall be My people, and I will be your God. 29 I will deliver you from all your uncleannesses. I will call for the grain and multiply it, and bring no famine upon you. 30 And I will multiply the fruit of your trees and the increase of your fields, so that you need never again bear the reproach of famine among the nations. 31 Then you will remember your evil ways and your deeds that *were* not good; and you will loathe yourselves in your own sight, for your iniquities and your abominations. 32 Not for your sake do I do *this*," says the Lord GOD, "let it be known to you. Be ashamed and confounded for your own ways, O house of Israel!"

33 'Thus says the Lord GOD: "On the day that I cleanse you from all your iniquities, I will also enable *you* to dwell in the cities, and the ruins shall be rebuilt. 34 The desolate land shall be tilled instead of lying desolate in the sight of all who pass by. 35 So they will say, 'This land that was desolate has become like the garden of Eden; and the wasted, desolate, and ruined cities *are now* fortified *and* inhabited.' 36 Then the nations which are left all around you shall know that I, the LORD, have rebuilt the ruined places *and* planted what was desolate. I, the LORD, have spoken *it*, and I will do *it*."

37 'Thus says the Lord GOD: "I will also let the house of Israel inquire of Me to do this for them: I will increase their men like a flock. 38 Like a flock *offered as* holy *sacrifices*, like the flock at Jerusalem on its feast days, so shall the ruined cities be filled with flocks of men. Then they shall know that I *am* the LORD." ' "

37 The hand of the LORD came upon me and brought me out in the Spirit of the LORD, and set me down in the midst of the valley; and it *was* full of bones. 2 Then He caused me to pass by them all around, and behold, *there were* very many in the open valley; and indeed *they were* very dry. 3 And He said to me, "Son of man, can these bones live?"

So I answered, "O Lord GOD, You know."

4 Again He said to me, "Prophesy to these bones, and say to them, 'O dry bones, hear the word of the LORD! 5 Thus says the Lord GOD to these bones: "Surely I will cause breath to enter into you, and you shall live. 6 I will put sinews on you and bring flesh upon you, cover you with skin and put breath in you; and you shall live. Then you shall know that I *am* the LORD." ' "

7 So I prophesied as I was commanded; and as I prophesied, there was a noise, and suddenly a rattling; and the bones came together, bone to bone. 8 Indeed, as I looked, the sinews and the flesh came upon them, and the skin covered them over; but *there was* no breath in them.

9 Also He said to me, "Prophesy to the breath, prophesy, son of man, and say to the breath, 'Thus says the Lord GOD: "Come from the four winds, O breath, and breathe on these slain, that they may live." ' " 10 So I prophesied as He commanded me, and breath came into them, and they lived, and stood upon their feet, an exceedingly great army.

11 Then He said to me, "Son of man, these bones are the whole house of Israel. They indeed say, 'Our bones are dry, our hope is lost, and we ourselves are cut off!' 12 Therefore prophesy and say to them, 'Thus says the Lord GOD: "Behold, O My people, I will open your graves and cause you to come up from your graves, and bring you into the land of Israel. 13 Then you shall know that I *am* the LORD, when I have

*M*en, created in the likeness of God, respond to praise. A woman who knows what to say to a man is difficult to withstand. For all men's tears and all their fears, they need your arms, your words, your song.

A Ministry of Hugs

Ezekiel 36:25, 26

*A*ll my life I have had a tremendous compassion for hurting people. Maybe it's because I've had my share of trouble too. When you have suffered, it makes you able to relate to other people's pain.

God has blessed me with three boys and two daughters. As a father, I have found that I have a ministry of hugs. I may not be able to change how other people treat my children. I may not be able to fix what happened at school. I may not be able to make the teacher like them. I can't take away the insults. But I can hug them!

The Church needs to develop a ministry of hugs. The touch of the Master sets us free. The touch of a fellow traveler lets us know we are not alone in our struggle.

The Holy Spirit is calling for broken women to come to Jesus. How do you come to Jesus? One way is by coming to His Body, the Church. The Church can give you strength and nourishment. The Church can be the place where you share your burdens and allow others to help you with them. The Spirit calls; the burdened need only answer.

Maybe you wrestle with guilt. You've been hearing babies crying in your spirit. You feel so dirty. You've had abortions. You've been misused and abused. The devil keeps bringing up your past failures.

But once you have called out to the Lord, He will restore to you all that the cankerworm and the locust ate (see Joel 2:25). He will give it back to you. Then you can lift your hands in praise. No matter what you have suffered, you can hold up your head. Regardless of who has hurt you, hold your head high. Forget how many times you've been married. Put aside thoughts of those who have mistreated you. You may have been a lesbian. You may have been a crack addict. You may have been molested. You can't change where you have been, but you can change where you are going!

You're a survivor. Celebrate your survival. Instead of agonizing over your tragedies, celebrate your victory and thank God you made it. I charge you to step over your adversity and walk into newness. It will be like stepping from the storm into the sunshine. Step into it now.

Then, after you have had some time to heal, use your experience to help bring healing to someone else. Perhaps you, too, will have a ministry of hugs.

opened your graves, O My people, and brought you up from your graves. 14 I will put My Spirit in you, and you shall live, and I will place you in your own land. Then you shall know that I, the Lord, have spoken *it* and performed *it*," says the Lord.' "

15 Again the word of the Lord came to me, saying, 16 "As for you, son of man, take a stick for yourself and write on it: 'For Judah and for the children of Israel, his companions.' Then take another stick and write on it, 'For Joseph, the stick of Ephraim, and *for* all the house of Israel, his companions.' 17 Then join them one to another for yourself into one stick, and they will become one in your hand.

18 "And when the children of your people speak to you, saying, 'Will you not show us what you *mean* by these?'— 19 say to them, 'Thus says the Lord God: "Surely I will take the stick of Joseph, which *is* in the hand of Ephraim, and the tribes of Israel, his companions; and I will join them with it, with the stick of Judah, and make them one stick, and they will be one in My hand." ' 20 And the sticks on which you write will be in your hand before their eyes.

21 "Then say to them, 'Thus says the Lord God: "Surely I will take the children of Israel from among the nations, wherever they have gone, and will gather them from every side and bring them into their own land; 22 and I will make them one nation in the land, on the mountains of Israel; and one king shall be king over them all; they shall no longer be two nations, nor shall they ever be divided into two kingdoms again. 23 They shall not defile themselves anymore with their idols, nor with their detestable things, nor with any of their transgressions; but I will deliver them from all their dwelling places in which they have sinned, and will cleanse them. Then they shall be My people, and I will be their God.

24 "David My servant *shall be* king over them, and they shall all have one shepherd; they shall also walk in My judgments and observe My statutes, and do them. 25 Then they

shall dwell in the land that I have given to Jacob My servant, where your fathers dwelt; and they shall dwell there, they, their children, and their children's children, forever; and My servant David *shall be* their prince forever. 26 Moreover I will make a covenant of peace with them, and it shall be an everlasting covenant with them; I will establish them and multiply them, and I will set My sanctuary in their midst forevermore. 27 My tabernacle also shall be with them; indeed I will be their God, and they shall be My people. 28 The nations also will know that I, the Lord, sanctify Israel, when My sanctuary is in their midst forevermore." ' "

38 Now the word of the Lord came to me, saying, 2 "Son of man, set your face against Gog, of the land of Magog, the prince of Rosh,[a] Meshech, and Tubal, and prophesy against him, 3 and say, 'Thus says the Lord God: "Behold, I *am* against you, O Gog, the prince of Rosh, Meshech, and Tubal. 4 I will turn you around, put hooks into your jaws, and lead you out, with all your army, horses, and horsemen, all splendidly clothed, a great company *with* bucklers and shields, all of them handling swords. 5 Persia, Ethiopia,[a] and Libya[b] are with them, all of them *with* shield and helmet; 6 Gomer and all its troops; the house of Togarmah *from* the far north and all its troops— many people *are* with you.

7 "Prepare yourself and be ready, you and all your companies that are gathered about you; and be a guard for them. 8 After many days you will be visited. In the latter years you will come into the land of those brought back from the sword *and* gathered from many people on the mountains of Israel, which had long been desolate; they were brought out of the nations, and now all of them dwell safely. 9 You will ascend, coming like a storm, covering the land like a cloud, you and all your troops and many peoples with you."

10 'Thus says the Lord God: "On that day it shall come to pass *that* thoughts will arise in your mind, and you will make an evil plan: 11 You will say, 'I will go up against

38:2 [a]Targum, Vulgate, and Aquila read *chief prince of* (also verse 3). 38:5 [a]Hebrew *Cush* [b]Hebrew *Put*

Gospel Pearls

a land of unwalled villages; I will go to a peaceful people, who dwell safely, all of them dwelling without walls, and having neither bars nor gates'— 12 to take plunder and to take booty, to stretch out your hand against the waste places *that are again* inhabited, and against a people gathered from the nations, who have acquired livestock and goods, who dwell in the midst of the land. 13 Sheba, Dedan, the merchants of Tarshish, and all their young lions will say to you, 'Have you come to take plunder? Have you gathered your army to take booty, to carry away silver and gold, to take away livestock and goods, to take great plunder?' " '

14 "Therefore, son of man, prophesy and say to Gog, 'Thus says the Lord GOD: "On that day when My people Israel dwell safely, will you not know *it?* 15 Then you will come from your place out of the far north, you and many peoples with you, all of them riding on horses, a great company and a mighty army. 16 You will come up against My people Israel like a cloud, to cover the land. It will be in the latter days that I will bring you against My land, so that the nations may know Me, when I am hallowed in you, O Gog, before their eyes." 17 Thus says the Lord GOD: "Are *you* he of whom I have spoken in former days by My servants the prophets of Israel, who prophesied for years in those days that I would bring you against them? 18 " ' "And it will come to pass at the same time, when Gog comes against the land of Israel," says the Lord GOD, "*that* My fury will show in My face. 19 For in My jealousy *and* in the fire of My wrath I have spoken: 'Surely in that day there shall be a great earthquake in the land of Israel, 20 so that the fish of the sea, the birds of the heavens, the beasts of the field, all creeping things that creep on the earth, and all men who *are* on the face of the earth shall shake at My presence. The mountains shall be thrown down, the steep places shall fall, and every wall shall fall to the ground.' 21 I will call for a sword against Gog throughout all My mountains," says the Lord GOD. "Every man's sword will be against his

brother. 22 And I will bring him to judgment with pestilence and bloodshed; I will rain down on him, on his troops, and on the many peoples who *are* with him, flooding rain, great hailstones, fire, and brimstone. 23 Thus I will magnify Myself and sanctify Myself, and I will be known in the eyes of many nations. Then they shall know that I *am* the LORD." '

39 "And you, son of man, prophesy against Gog, and say, 'Thus says the Lord GOD: "Behold, I *am* against you, O Gog, the prince of Rosh,[a] Meshech, and Tubal; 2 and I will turn you around and lead you on, bringing you up from the far north, and bring you against the mountains of Israel. 3 Then I will knock the bow out of your left hand, and cause the arrows to fall out of your right hand. 4 You shall fall upon the mountains of Israel, you and all your troops and the peoples who *are* with you; I will give you to birds of prey of every sort and *to* the beasts of the field to be devoured. 5 You shall fall on the open field; for I have spoken," says the Lord GOD. 6 "And I will send fire on Magog and on those who live in security in the coastlands. Then they shall know that I *am* the LORD. 7 So I will make My holy name known in the midst of My people Israel, and I will not *let them* profane My holy name anymore. Then the nations shall know that I *am* the LORD, the Holy One in Israel. 8 Surely it is coming, and it shall be done," says the Lord GOD. "This *is* the day of which I have spoken.

9 "Then those who dwell in the cities of Israel will go out and set on fire and burn the weapons, both the shields and bucklers, the bows and arrows, the javelins and spears; and they will make fires with them for seven years. 10 They will not take wood from the field nor cut down *any* from the forests, because they will make fires with the weapons; and they will plunder those who plundered them, and pillage those who pillaged them," says the Lord GOD.

11 "It will come to pass in that day *that* I will give Gog a burial place there in Israel, the valley of those who pass by east of the sea; and it

39:1 aTargum, Vulgate, and Aquila read *chief prince of.*

Marriage is a ministry. There is much more involved in it than selfish fulfillment. Love is centered around giving, not taking. When you marry someone, you marry everything he is and everything he has been.

will obstruct travelers, because there they will bury Gog and all his multitude. Therefore they will call *it* the Valley of Hamon Gog.*ᵃ* 12 For seven months the house of Israel will be burying them, in order to cleanse the land. 13 Indeed all the people of the land will be burying, and they will gain renown for it on the day that I am glorified," says the Lord GOD. 14 "They will set apart men regularly employed, with the help of a search party,*ᵃ* to pass through the land and bury those bodies remaining on the ground, in order to cleanse it. At the end of seven months they will make a search. 15 The search party will pass through the land; and *when anyone* sees a man's bone, he shall set up a marker by it, till the buriers have buried it in the Valley of Hamon Gog. 16 *The* name of *the* city *will* also *be* Hamonah. Thus they shall cleanse the land." '

17 "And as for you, son of man, thus says the Lord GOD, 'Speak to every sort of bird and to every beast of the field:

"Assemble yourselves and come;
Gather together from all sides
to My sacrificial meal
Which I am sacrificing for you,
A great sacrificial meal on the
mountains of Israel,
That you may eat flesh and
drink blood.
18 You shall eat the flesh of the
mighty,
Drink the blood of the princes
of the earth,
Of rams and lambs,
Of goats and bulls,
All of them fatlings of Bashan.
19 You shall eat fat till you are
full,
And drink blood till you are
drunk,
At My sacrificial meal
Which I am sacrificing for you.
20 You shall be filled at My table
With horses and riders,
With mighty men
And with all the men of war,"
says the Lord GOD.

21 "I will set My glory among the nations; all the nations shall see My judgment which I have executed, and My hand which I have laid on them. 22 So the house of Israel shall know that I *am* the LORD their God from that day forward. 23 The Gentiles shall know that the house of Israel went into captivity for their iniquity; because they were unfaithful to Me, therefore I hid My face from them. I gave them into the hand of their enemies, and they all fell by the sword. 24 According to their uncleanness and according to their transgressions I have dealt with them, and hidden My face from them." '

25 "Therefore thus says the Lord GOD: 'Now I will bring back the captives of Jacob, and have mercy on the whole house of Israel; and I will be jealous for My holy name— 26 after they have borne their shame, and all their unfaithfulness in which they were unfaithful to Me, when they dwelt safely in their *own* land and no one made *them* afraid. 27 When I have brought them back from the peoples and gathered them out of their enemies' lands, and I am hallowed in them in the sight of many nations, 28 then they shall know that I *am* the LORD their God, who sent them into captivity among the nations, but also brought them back to their land, and left none of them captive any longer. 29 And I will not hide My face from them anymore; for I shall have poured out My Spirit on the house of Israel,' says the Lord GOD."

40 In the twenty-fifth year of our captivity, at the beginning of the year, on the tenth *day* of the month, in the fourteenth year after the city was captured, on the very same day the hand of the LORD was upon me; and He took me there. 2 In the visions of God He took me into the land of Israel and set me on a very high mountain; on it toward the south *was* something like the structure of a city. 3 He took me there, and behold, *there was* a man whose appearance *was* like the appearance of bronze. He had a line of flax and a measuring rod in his hand, and he stood in the gateway.

4 And the man said to me, "Son of man, look with your eyes and hear with your ears, and fix your mind on everything I show you; for you *were*

39:11 ᵃLiterally *The Multitude of Gog*   39:14 ᵃLiterally *those who pass through*

Gospel
Pearls

brought here so that I might show *them* to you. Declare to the house of Israel everything you see." 5 Now there was a wall all around the outside of the temple.*a* In the man's hand was a measuring rod six cubits *long, each being a* cubit and a handbreadth; and he measured the width of the wall structure, one rod; and the height, one rod.

6 Then he went to the gateway which faced east; and he went up its stairs and measured the threshold of the gateway, *which was* one rod wide, and the other threshold *was* one rod wide. 7 Each gate chamber *was* one rod long and one rod wide; between the gate chambers *was a space of* five cubits; and the threshold of the gateway by the vestibule of the inside gate *was* one rod. 8 He also measured the vestibule of the inside gate, one rod. 9 Then he measured the vestibule of the gateway, eight cubits; and the gateposts, two cubits. The vestibule of the gate *was* on the inside. 10 In the eastern gateway *were* three gate chambers on one side and three on the other; the three *were* all the same size; also the gateposts were of the same size on this side and that side.

11 He measured the width of the entrance to the gateway, ten cubits; *and* the length of the gate, thirteen cubits. 12 *There was* a space in front of the gate chambers, one cubit *on this side* and one cubit on that side; the gate chambers *were* six cubits on this side and six cubits on that side. 13 Then he measured the gateway from the roof of *one* gate chamber to the roof of the other; the width *was* twenty-five cubits, as door faces door. 14 He measured the gateposts, sixty cubits high, and the court all around the gateway *extended* to the gatepost. 15 *From* the front of the entrance gate to the front of the vestibule of the inner gate *was* fifty cubits. 16 *There were* beveled window *frames* in the gate chambers and in their intervening archways on the inside of the gateway all around, and likewise in the vestibules. *There were* windows all around on the inside. And on each gatepost *were* palm trees.

17 Then he brought me into the outer court; and *there were* chambers and a pavement made all around the court; thirty chambers faced the pavement. 18 The pavement was by the side of the gateways, corresponding to the length of the gateways; *this was* the lower pavement. 19 Then he measured the width from the front of the lower gateway to the front of the inner court exterior, one hundred cubits toward the east and the north.

20 On the outer court was also a gateway facing north, and he measured its length and its width. 21 Its gate chambers, three on this side and three on that side, its gateposts and its archways, had the same measurements as the first gate; its length *was* fifty cubits and its width twenty-five cubits. 22 Its windows and those of its archways, and also its palm trees, *had* the same measurements as the gateway facing east; it was ascended by seven steps, and its archway *was* in front of it. 23 A gate of the inner court was opposite the northern gateway, just as the eastern *gateway;* and he measured from gateway to gateway, one hundred cubits.

24 After that he brought me toward the south, and there a gateway was facing south; and he measured its gateposts and archways according to these same measurements. 25 *There were* windows in it and in its archways all around like those windows; its length *was* fifty cubits and its width twenty-five cubits. 26 Seven steps led up to it, and its archway *was* in front of them; and it had palm trees on its gateposts, one on this side and one on that side. 27 *There was* also a gateway on the inner court, facing south; and he measured from gateway to gateway toward the south, one hundred cubits.

28 Then he brought me to the inner court through the southern gateway; he measured the southern gateway according to these same measurements. 29 Also its gate chambers, its gateposts, and its archways *were* according to these same measurements; *there were* windows in it and in its archways all around; *it was* fifty cubits long and twenty-five cubits wide. 30 *There were* archways all around, twenty-five cubits long and five cubits wide. 31 Its archways faced the outer court, palm trees

40:5 *a*Literally *house,* and so elsewhere in this book

God grants you the grace of ministering to your spouse, to the child in him. Don't be discouraged if you don't see immediate change. Healing is a process and it takes time!

were on its gateposts, and going up to it *were* eight steps.

32 And he brought me into the inner court facing east; he measured the gateway according to these same measurements. 33 Also its gate chambers, its gateposts, and its archways *were* according to these same measurements; and *there were* windows in it and in its archways all around; *it was* fifty cubits long and twenty-five cubits wide. 34 Its archways faced the outer court, and palm trees *were* on its gateposts on this side and on that side; and going up to it *were* eight steps.

35 Then he brought me to the north gateway and measured *it* according to these same measurements— 36 also its gate chambers, its gateposts, and its archways. It had windows all around; its length *was* fifty cubits and its width twenty-five cubits. 37 Its gateposts faced the outer court, palm trees *were* on its gateposts on this side and on that side, and going up to it *were* eight steps.

38 *There was* a chamber and its entrance by the gateposts of the gateway, where they washed the burnt offering. 39 In the vestibule of the gateway *were* two tables on this side and two tables on that side, on which to slay the burnt offering, the sin offering, and the trespass offering. 40 At the outer side of the vestibule, as one goes up to the entrance of the northern gateway, *were* two tables; and on the other side of the vestibule of the gateway *were* two tables. 41 Four tables *were* on this side and four tables on that side, by the side of the gateway, eight tables on which they slaughtered *the sacrifices.* 42 *There were* also four tables of hewn stone for the burnt offering, one cubit and a half long, one cubit and a half wide, and one cubit high; on these they laid the instruments with which they slaughtered the burnt offering and the sacrifice. 43 Inside *were* hooks, a handbreadth wide, fastened all around; and the flesh of the sacrifices *was* on the tables.

44 Outside the inner gate *were* the chambers for the singers in the inner court, one facing south at the side of the northern gateway, and the other

facing north at the side of the southern gateway. 45 Then he said to me, "This chamber which faces south *is* for the priests who have charge of the temple. 46 The chamber which faces north *is* for the priests who have charge of the altar; these *are* the sons of Zadok, from the sons of Levi, who come near the LORD to minister to Him."

47 And he measured the court, one hundred cubits long and one hundred cubits wide, foursquare. The altar *was* in front of the temple. 48 Then he brought me to the vestibule of the temple and measured the doorposts of the vestibule, five cubits on this side and five cubits on that side; and the width of the gateway was three cubits on this side and three cubits on that side. 49 The length of the vestibule *was* twenty cubits, and the width eleven cubits; and by the steps which led up to it *there were* pillars by the doorposts, one on this side and another on that side.

41 Then he brought me into the sanctuary[a] and measured the doorposts, six cubits wide on one side and six cubits wide on the other side—the width of the tabernacle. 2 The width of the entryway *was* ten cubits, and the side walls of the entrance *were* five cubits on this side and five cubits on the other side; and he measured its length, forty cubits, and its width, twenty cubits.

3 Also he went inside and measured the doorposts, two cubits; and the entrance, six cubits *high;* and the width of the entrance, seven cubits. 4 He measured the length, twenty cubits; and the width, twenty cubits, beyond the sanctuary; and he said to me, "This *is* the Most Holy *Place.*"

5 Next, he measured the wall of temple, six cubits. The width of each side chamber all around the temple *was* four cubits on every side. 6 The side chambers *were* in three stories, one above the other, thirty chambers in each story; they rested on ledges which *were* for the side chambers all around, that they might be supported, but not fastened to the wall of the temple. 7 As one went up from story to story, the side chambers became wider all around, be-

41:1 *a*Hebrew *heykal,* here the main room of the temple, sometimes called the *holy place* (compare Exodus 26:33)

Gospel Pearls

cause their supporting ledges in the wall of the temple ascended like steps; therefore the width of the structure increased as one went up *from* the lowest *story* to the highest by way of the middle one. 8 I also saw an elevation all around the temple; it was the foundation of the side chambers, a full rod, *that is,* six cubits *high.* 9 The thickness of the outer wall of the side chambers *was* five cubits, and so also the remaining terrace by the place of the side chambers of the temple. 10 And between *it and* the *wall* chambers was a width of twenty cubits all around the temple on every side. 11 The doors of the side chambers opened on the terrace, one door toward the north and another toward the south; and the width of the terrace *was* five cubits all around.

12 The building that faced the separating courtyard at its western end *was* seventy cubits wide; the wall of the building *was* five cubits thick all around, and its length ninety cubits.

13 So he measured the temple, one hundred cubits long; and the separating courtyard with the building and its walls *was* one hundred cubits long; 14 also the width of the eastern face of the temple, including the separating courtyard, *was* one hundred cubits. 15 He measured the length of the building behind it, facing the separating courtyard, with its galleries on the one side and on the other side, one hundred cubits, as well as the inner temple and the porches of the court, 16 their doorposts and the beveled window frames. And the galleries all around their three stories opposite the threshold were paneled with wood from the ground to the windows—the windows were covered— 17 from the space above the door, even to the inner room,[a] as well as outside, and on every wall all around, inside and outside, by measure.

18 And *it was* made with cherubim and palm trees, a palm tree between cherub and cherub. *Each* cherub had two faces, 19 so that the face of a man *was* toward a palm tree on one side, and the face of a young lion toward a palm tree on the other side; thus *it was* made throughout the temple all around. 20 From the floor to the

space above the door, and on the wall of the sanctuary, cherubim and palm trees *were* carved.

21 The doorposts of the temple *were* square, *as was* the front of the sanctuary; their appearance was similar. 22 The altar *was* of wood, three cubits high, and its length two cubits. Its corners, its length, and its sides *were* of wood; and he said to me, "This *is* the table that *is* before the Lord."

23 The temple and the sanctuary had two doors. 24 The doors had two panels *apiece,* two folding panels: two *panels* for one door and two panels for the other *door.* 25 Cherubim and palm trees *were* carved on the doors of the temple just as they *were* carved on the walls. A wooden canopy *was* on the front of the vestibule outside. 26 *There were* beveled window *frames* and palm trees on one side and on the other, on the sides of the vestibule—also on the side chambers of the temple and on the canopies.

42 Then he brought me out into the outer court, by the way toward the north; and he brought me into the chamber which *was* opposite the separating courtyard, and which *was* opposite the building toward the north. 2 Facing the length, *which was* one hundred cubits (the width was fifty cubits), was the north door. 3 Opposite the inner court of twenty *cubits,* and opposite the pavement of the outer court, *was* gallery against gallery in three *stories.* 4 In front of the chambers, toward the inside, *was* a walk ten cubits wide, at a distance of one cubit; and their doors faced north. 5 Now the upper chambers *were* shorter, because the galleries took away *space* from them more than from the lower and middle stories of the building. 6 For they *were* in three *stories* and did not have pillars like the pillars of the courts; therefore *the upper level* was shortened more than the lower and middle levels from the ground up. 7 And a wall which *was* outside ran parallel to the chambers, at the front of the chambers, toward the outer court; its length *was* fifty cubits. 8 The length of the chambers toward the outer court *was* fifty cubits, whereas that

41:17 aLiterally *house,* here *the Most Holy Place*

*G*od gives the gift of marriage, but you must do your own decorating. Decorate your relationship, or it will become bland for you and for your spouse.

facing the temple *was* one hundred cubits. 9 At the lower chambers *was* the entrance on the east side, as one goes into them from the outer court.

10 Also *there were* chambers in the thickness of the wall of the court toward the east, opposite the separating courtyard and opposite the building. 11 *There was* a walk in front of them also, and their appearance *was* like the chambers which *were* toward the north; they *were* as long and as wide as the others, and all their exits and entrances *were* according to plan. 12 And corresponding to the doors of the chambers that *were* facing south, as one enters them, *there was* a door in front of the walk, the way directly in front of the wall toward the east.

13 Then he said to me, "The north chambers *and* the south chambers, which *are* opposite the separating courtyard, *are* the holy chambers where the priests who approach the LORD shall eat the most holy offerings. There they shall lay the most holy offerings—the grain offering, the sin offering, and the trespass offering—for the place *is* holy. 14 When the priests enter them, they shall not go out of the holy *chamber* into the outer court; but there they shall leave their garments in which they minister, for they *are* holy. They shall put on other garments; then they may approach *that* which *is* for the people."

15 Now when he had finished measuring the inner temple, he brought me out through the gateway that faces toward the east, and measured it all around. 16 He measured the east side with the measuring rod,[a] five hundred rods by the measuring rod all around. 17 He measured the north side, five hundred rods by the measuring rod all around. 18 He measured the south side, five hundred rods by the measuring rod. 19 He came around to the west side *and* measured five hundred rods by the measuring rod. 20 He measured it on the four sides; it had a wall all around, five hundred *cubits* long and five hundred wide, to separate the holy areas from the common.

43 Afterward he brought me to the gate, the gate that faces toward the east. 2 And behold, the glory of the God of Israel came from the way of the east. His voice *was* like the sound of many waters; and the earth shone with His glory. 3 *It was* like the appearance of the vision which I saw—like the vision which I saw when I[a] came to destroy the city. The visions *were* like the vision which I saw by the River Chebar; and I fell on my face. 4 And the glory of the LORD came into the temple by way of the gate which faces toward the east. 5 The Spirit lifted me up and brought me into the inner court; and behold, the glory of the LORD filled the temple.

6 Then I heard *Him* speaking to me from the temple, while a man stood beside me. 7 And He said to me, "Son of man, *this is* the place of My throne and the place of the soles of My feet, where I will dwell in the midst of the children of Israel forever. No more shall the house of Israel defile My holy name, they nor their kings, by their harlotry or with the carcasses of their kings on their high places. 8 When they set their threshold by My threshold, and their doorpost by My doorpost, with a wall between them and Me, they defiled My holy name by the abominations which they committed; therefore I have consumed them in My anger. 9 Now let them put their harlotry and the carcasses of their kings far away from Me, and I will dwell in their midst forever.

10 "Son of man, describe the temple to the house of Israel, that they may be ashamed of their iniquities; and let them measure the pattern. 11 And if they are ashamed of all that they have done, make known to them the design of the temple and its arrangement, its exits and its entrances, its entire design and all its ordinances, all its forms and all its laws. Write *it* down in their sight, so that they may keep its whole design and all its ordinances, and perform them. 12 This *is* the law of the temple: The whole area surrounding the mountaintop *is* most holy. Behold, this *is* the law of the temple.

13 "These are the measurements of the altar in cubits (the *cubit is* one cubit and a handbreadth): the base one cubit high and one cubit wide,

42:16 aCompare 40:5   43:3 aSome Hebrew manuscripts and Vulgate read *He.*

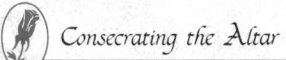

with a rim all around its edge of one span. This *is* the height of the altar: 14 from the base on the ground to the lower ledge, two cubits; the width of the ledge, one cubit; from the smaller ledge to the larger ledge, four cubits; and the width of the ledge, *one* cubit. 15 The altar hearth *is* four cubits high, with four horns extending upward from the hearth. 16 The altar hearth *is* twelve cubits long, twelve wide, square at its four corners; 17 the ledge, fourteen *cubits* long and fourteen wide on its four sides, with a rim of half a cubit around it; its base, one cubit all around; and its steps face toward the east."

18 And He said to me, "Son of man, thus says the Lord GOD: 'These *are* the ordinances for the altar on the day when it is made, for sacrificing burnt offerings on it, and for sprinkling blood on it. 19 You shall give a young bull for a sin offering to the priests, the Levites, who are of the seed of Zadok, who approach Me to minister to Me,' says the Lord GOD. 20 You shall take some of its blood and put *it* on the four horns of the altar, on the four corners of the ledge, and on the rim around it; thus you shall cleanse it and make atonement for it. 21 Then you shall also take the bull of the sin offering, and burn it in the appointed place of the temple, outside the sanctuary. 22 On the second day you shall offer a kid of the goats without blemish for a sin offering; and they shall cleanse the altar, as they cleansed *it* with the bull. 23 When you have finished cleansing *it,* you shall offer a young bull without blemish, and a ram from the flock without blemish. 24 When you offer them before the LORD, the priests shall throw salt on them, and they will offer them up *as* a burnt offering to the LORD. 25 Every day for seven days you shall prepare a goat *for* a sin offering; they shall also prepare a young bull and a ram from the flock, both without blemish. 26 Seven days they shall make atonement for the altar and purify it, and so consecrate *it.* 27 When these days are over it shall be, on the eighth day and thereafter, that the priests shall offer your burnt offerings and your peace offerings on the altar; and I will accept you,' says the Lord GOD."

44 Then He brought me back to the outer gate of the sanctuary which faces toward the east, but it *was* shut. 2 And the LORD said to me, "This gate shall be shut; it shall not be opened, and no man shall enter by it, because the LORD God of Israel has entered by it; therefore it shall be shut. 3 *As for* the prince, *because* he *is* the prince, he may sit in it to eat bread before the LORD; he shall enter by way of the vestibule of the gateway, and go out the same way."

4 Also He brought me by way of the north gate to the front of the temple; so I looked, and behold, the glory of the LORD filled the house of the LORD; and I fell on my face. 5 And the LORD said to me, "Son of man, mark well, see with your eyes and hear with your ears, all that I say to you concerning all the ordinances of the house of the LORD and all its laws. Mark well who may enter the house and all who go out from the sanctuary.

6 "Now say to the rebellious, to the house of Israel, 'Thus says the Lord GOD: "O house of Israel, let Us have no more of all your abominations. 7 When you brought in foreigners, uncircumcised in heart and uncircumcised in flesh, to be in My sanctuary to defile it—My house—and when you offered My food, the fat and the blood, then they broke My covenant because of all your abominations. 8 And you have not kept charge of My holy things, but you have set *others* to keep charge of My sanctuary for you." 9 Thus says the Lord GOD: "No foreigner, uncircumcised in heart or uncircumcised in flesh, shall enter My sanctuary, including any foreigner who *is* among the children of Israel.

10 "And the Levites who went far from Me, when Israel went astray, who strayed away from Me after their idols, they shall bear their iniquity. 11 Yet they shall be ministers in My sanctuary, *as* gatekeepers of the house and ministers of the house; they shall slay the burnt offering and the sacrifice for the people, and they shall stand before them to minister to them. 12 Because they ministered to them before their idols and caused the house of Israel to fall into iniquity, therefore I have raised My hand in an oath against them," says the Lord GOD, "that they shall bear

If you are looking for someone to be your everything, don't look around, look up! God is the only One who can be everything. By expecting perfection from the flesh, you ask more out of someone else than what you can provide yourself.

their iniquity. 13 And they shall not come near Me to minister to Me as priest, nor come near any of My holy things, nor into the Most Holy *Place;* but they shall bear their shame and their abominations which they have committed. 14 Nevertheless I will make them keep charge of the temple, for all its work, and for all that has to be done in it.

15 "But the priests, the Levites, the sons of Zadok, who kept charge of My sanctuary when the children of Israel went astray from Me, they shall come near Me to minister to Me; and they shall stand before Me to offer to Me the fat and the blood," says the Lord GOD. 16 "They shall enter My sanctuary, and they shall come near My table to minister to Me, and they shall keep My charge. 17 And it shall be, whenever they enter the gates of the inner court, that they shall put on linen garments; no wool shall come upon them while they minister within the gates of the inner court or within the house. 18 They shall have linen turbans on their heads and linen trousers on their bodies; they shall not clothe themselves with *anything that causes* sweat. 19 When they go out to the outer court, to the *outer* court to the people, they shall take off their garments in which they have ministered, leave them in the holy chambers, and put on other garments; and in their holy garments they shall not sanctify the people.

20 "They shall neither shave their heads nor let their hair grow long, but they shall keep their hair well trimmed. 21 No priest shall drink wine when he enters the inner court. 22 They shall not take as wife a widow or a divorced woman, but take virgins of the descendants of the house of Israel, or widows of priests.

23 "And they shall teach My people *the difference* between the holy and the unholy, and cause them to discern between the unclean and the clean. 24 In controversy they shall stand as judges, *and* judge it according to My judgments. They shall keep My laws and My statutes in all My appointed meetings, and they shall hallow My Sabbaths.

25 "They shall not defile *themselves* by coming near a dead person.

Only for father or mother, for son or daughter, for brother or unmarried sister may they defile themselves. 26 After he is cleansed, they shall count seven days for him. 27 And on the day that he goes to the sanctuary to minister in the sanctuary, he must offer his sin offering in the inner court," says the Lord GOD.

28 "It shall be, in regard to their inheritance, *that* I *am* their inheritance. You shall give them no possession in Israel, for I *am* their possession. 29 They shall eat the grain offering, the sin offering, and the trespass offering; every dedicated thing in Israel shall be theirs. 30 The best of all firstfruits of any kind, and every sacrifice of any kind from all your sacrifices, shall be the priest's; also you shall give to the priest the first of your ground meal, to cause a blessing to rest on your house. 31 The priests shall not eat anything, bird or beast, that died naturally or was torn *by wild beasts.*

45 "Moreover, when you divide the land by lot into inheritance, you shall set apart a district for the LORD, a holy section of the land; its length *shall be* twenty-five thousand *cubits,* and the width ten thousand. It *shall be* holy throughout its territory all around. 2 Of this there shall be a square plot for the sanctuary, five hundred by five hundred *rods,* with fifty cubits around it for an open space. 3 So this is the district you shall measure: twenty-five thousand *cubits* long and ten thousand wide; in it shall be the sanctuary, the Most Holy *Place.* 4 It shall be a holy *section* of the land, belonging to the priests, the ministers of the sanctuary, who come near to minister to the LORD; it shall be a place for their houses and a holy place for the sanctuary. 5 *An area* twenty-five thousand *cubits* long and ten thousand wide shall belong to the Levites, the ministers of the temple; they shall have twenty chambers as a possession.[a]

6 "You shall appoint as the property of the city *an area* five thousand *cubits* wide and twenty-five thousand long, adjacent to the district of the holy *section; it* shall belong to the whole house of Israel.

45:5 [a]Following Masoretic Text, Targum, and Vulgate; Septuagint reads *a possession, cities of dwelling.*

Gospel Pearls

7 "The prince shall have *a section* on one side and the other of the holy district and the city's property; and bordering on the holy district and the city's property, extending westward on the west side and eastward on the east side, the length *shall be* side by side with one of the *tribal* portions, from the west border to the east border. 8 The land shall be his possession in Israel; and My princes shall no more oppress My people, but they shall give *the rest of* the land to the house of Israel, according to their tribes."

9 'Thus says the Lord God: "Enough, O princes of Israel! Remove violence and plundering, execute justice and righteousness, and stop dispossessing My people," says the Lord God. 10 "You shall have honest scales, an honest ephah, and an honest bath. 11 The ephah and the bath shall be of the same measure, so that the bath contains one-tenth of a homer, and the ephah one-tenth of a homer; their measure shall be according to the homer. 12 The shekel *shall be* twenty gerahs; twenty shekels, twenty-five shekels, *and* fifteen shekels shall be your mina.

13 "This *is* the offering which you shall offer: you shall give one-sixth of an ephah from a homer of wheat, and one-sixth of an ephah from a homer of barley. 14 The ordinance concerning oil, the bath of oil, *is* one-tenth of a bath from a kor. A kor *is* a homer or ten baths, for ten baths *are* a homer. 15 And one lamb shall be given from a flock of two hundred, from the rich pastures of Israel. These shall be for grain offerings, burnt offerings, and peace offerings, to make atonement for them," says the Lord God. 16 "All the people of the land shall give this offering for the prince in Israel. 17 Then it shall be the prince's part *to give* burnt offerings, grain offerings, and drink offerings, at the feasts, the New Moons, the Sabbaths, and at all the appointed seasons of the house of Israel. He shall prepare the sin offering, the grain offering, the burnt offering, and the peace offerings to make atonement for the house of Israel."

18 'Thus says the Lord God: "In the first *month,* on the first *day* of the month, you shall take a young bull without blemish and cleanse the sanctuary. 19 The priest shall take some of the blood of the sin offering and put *it* on the doorposts of the temple, on the four corners of the ledge of the altar, and on the gateposts of the gate of the inner court. 20 And so you shall do on the seventh *day* of the month for everyone who has sinned unintentionally or in ignorance. Thus you shall make atonement for the temple.

21 "In the first *month,* on the fourteenth day of the month, you shall observe the Passover, a feast of seven days; unleavened bread shall be eaten. 22 And on that day the prince shall prepare for himself and for all the people of the land a bull *for* a sin offering. 23 On the seven days of the feast he shall prepare a burnt offering to the Lord, seven bulls and seven rams without blemish, daily for seven days, and a kid of the goats daily *for* a sin offering. 24 And he shall prepare a grain offering of one ephah for each bull and one ephah for each ram, together with a hin of oil for each ephah.

25 "In the seventh *month,* on the fifteenth day of the month, at the feast, he shall do likewise for seven days, according to the sin offering, the burnt offering, the grain offering, and the oil."

46 'Thus says the Lord God: "The gateway of the inner court that faces toward the east shall be shut the six working days; but on the Sabbath it shall be opened, and on the day of the New Moon it shall be opened. 2 The prince shall enter by way of the vestibule of the gateway from the outside, and stand by the gatepost. The priests shall prepare his burnt offering and his peace offerings. He shall worship at the threshold of the gate. Then he shall go out, but the gate shall not be shut until evening. 3 Likewise the people of the land shall worship at the entrance to this gateway before the Lord on the Sabbaths and the New Moons. 4 The burnt offering that the prince offers to the Lord on the Sabbath day *shall be* six lambs without blemish, and a ram without blemish; 5 and the grain offering *shall be one* ephah for a ram, and the grain offering for the lambs, as much as he wants to give, as well as a hin of oil with every ephah. 6 On the day of the

New Moon *it shall be* a young bull without blemish, six lambs, and a ram; they shall be without blemish. 7 He shall prepare a grain offering of an ephah for a bull, an ephah for a ram, as much as he wants to give for the lambs, and a hin of oil with every ephah. 8 When the prince enters, he shall go in by way of the vestibule of the gateway, and go out the same way.

9 "But when the people of the land come before the Lord on the appointed feast days, whoever enters by way of the north gate to worship shall go out by way of the south gate; and whoever enters by way of the south gate shall go out by way of the north gate. He shall not return by way of the gate through which he came, but shall go out through the opposite gate. 10 The prince shall then be in their midst. When they go in, he shall go in; and when they go out, he shall go out. 11 At the festivals and the appointed feast days the grain offering shall be an ephah for a bull, an ephah for a ram, as much as he wants to give for the lambs, and a hin of oil with every ephah.

12 "Now when the prince makes a voluntary burnt offering or voluntary peace offering to the Lord, the gate that faces toward the east shall then be opened for him; and he shall prepare his burnt offering and his peace offerings as he did on the Sabbath day. Then he shall go out, and after he goes out the gate shall be shut.

13 "You shall daily make a burnt offering to the Lord *of* a lamb of the first year without blemish; you shall prepare it every morning. 14 And you shall prepare a grain offering with it every morning, a sixth of an ephah, and a third of a hin of oil to moisten the fine flour. This grain offering is a perpetual ordinance, to be made regularly to the Lord. 15 Thus they shall prepare the lamb, the grain offering, and the oil, *as* a regular burnt offering every morning."

16 'Thus says the Lord God: "If the prince gives a gift *of some* of his inheritance to any of his sons, it shall belong to his sons; it is their possession by inheritance. 17 But if he gives a gift of some of his inheritance to one of his servants, it shall be his until the year of liberty, after which it shall return to the prince. But his inheritance shall belong to his sons; it

shall become theirs. 18 Moreover the prince shall not take any of the people's inheritance by evicting them from their property; he shall provide an inheritance for his sons from his own property, so that none of My people may be scattered from his property." ' "

19 Now he brought me through the entrance, which *was* at the side of the gate, into the holy chambers of the priests which face toward the north; and there a place *was* situated at their extreme western end. 20 And he said to me, "This *is* the place where the priests shall boil the trespass offering and the sin offering, *and* where they shall bake the grain offering, so that they do not bring *them* out into the outer court to sanctify the people."

21 Then he brought me out into the outer court and caused me to pass by the four corners of the court; and in fact, in every corner of the court *there was another* court. 22 In the four corners of the court *were* enclosed courts, forty *cubits* long and thirty wide; all four corners *were* the same size. 23 *There was* a row *of building stones* all around in them, all around the four of them; and cooking hearths were made under the rows of stones all around. 24 And he said to me, "These *are* the kitchens where the ministers of the temple shall boil the sacrifices of the people."

47 Then he brought me back to the door of the temple; and there was water, flowing from under the threshold of the temple toward the east, for the front of the temple faced east; the water was flowing from under the right side of the temple, south of the altar. 2 He brought me out by way of the north gate, and led me around on the outside to the outer gateway that faces east; and there was water, running out on the right side.

3 And when the man went out to the east with the line in his hand, he measured one thousand cubits, and he brought me through the waters; the water *came up to my* ankles. 4 Again he measured one thousand and brought me through the waters; the water *came up to my* knees. Again he measured one thousand and brought me through; the water

Gospel
Pearls

came up to my waist. 5 Again he measured one thousand, *and it was* a river that I could not cross; for the water was too deep, water in which one must swim, a river that could not be crossed. 6 He said to me, "Son of man, have you seen *this?*" Then he brought me and returned me to the bank of the river.

7 When I returned, there, along the bank of the river, *were* very many trees on one side and the other. 8 Then he said to me: "This water flows toward the eastern region, goes down into the valley, and enters the sea. *When it* reaches the sea, *its* waters are healed. 9 And it shall be *that* every living thing that moves, wherever the rivers go, will live. There will be a very great multitude of fish, because these waters go there; for they will be healed, and everything will live wherever the river goes. 10 It shall be *that* fishermen will stand by it from En Gedi to En Eglaim; they will be *places* for spreading their nets. Their fish will be of the same kinds as the fish of the Great Sea, exceedingly many. 11 But its swamps and marshes will not be healed; they will be given over to salt. 12 Along the bank of the river, on this side and that, will grow all *kinds of* trees used for food; their leaves will not wither, and their fruit will not fail. They will bear fruit every month, because their water flows from the sanctuary. Their fruit will be for food, and their leaves for medicine."

13 Thus says the Lord GOD: "These *are* the borders by which you shall divide the land as an inheritance among the twelve tribes of Israel. Joseph *shall have two* portions. 14 You shall inherit it equally with one another; for I raised My hand in an oath to give it to your fathers, and this land shall fall to you as your inheritance.

15 "This *shall be* the border of the land on the north: from the Great Sea, *by* the road to Hethlon, as one goes to Zedad, 16 Hamath, Berothah, Sibraim (which *is* between the border of Damascus and the border of Hamath), to Hazar Hatticon (which *is* on the border of Hauran). 17 Thus the boundary shall be from the Sea to Hazar Enan, the border of Damas-

cus; and as for the north, northward, it is the border of Hamath. *This is* the north side.

18 "On the east side you shall mark out the border from between Hauran and Damascus, and between Gilead and the land of Israel, along the Jordan, and along the eastern side of the sea. *This is* the east side.

19 "The south side, toward the South,ᵃ *shall be* from Tamar to the waters of Meribah by Kadesh, along the brook to the Great Sea. *This is* the south side, toward the South.

20 "The west side *shall be* the Great Sea, from the *southern* boundary until one comes to a point opposite Hamath. This *is* the west side.

21 "Thus you shall divide this land among yourselves according to the tribes of Israel. 22 It shall be that you will divide it by lot as an inheritance for yourselves, and for the strangers who dwell among you and who bear children among you. They shall be to you as native-born among the children of Israel; they shall have an inheritance with you among the tribes of Israel. 23 And it shall be *that* in whatever tribe the stranger dwells, there you shall give *him* his inheritance," says the Lord GOD.

48 "Now these *are* the names of the tribes: From the northern border along the road to Hethlon at the entrance of Hamath, to Hazar Enan, the border of Damascus northward, in the direction of Hamath, *there shall be* one *section for* Dan from its east to its west side; 2 by the border of Dan, from the east side to the west, one *section for* Asher; 3 by the border of Asher, from the east side to the west, one *section for* Naphtali; 4 by the border of Naphtali, from the east side to the west, one *section for* Manasseh; 5 by the border of Manasseh, from the east side to the west, one *section for* Ephraim; 6 by the border of Ephraim, from the east side to the west, one *section for* Reuben; 7 by the border of Reuben, from the east side to the west, one *section for* Judah; 8 by the border of Judah, from the east side to the west, shall be the district which you shall set apart, twenty-five thousand *cubits* in width, and *in* length the same as one of the

47:19 ᵃHebrew *Negev*

God knows how to take a mess and turn it into a miracle. If you're in a mess, don't be too upset about it because God specializes in fixing messes. God is saying some definite things about women being set free and delivered to fulfill their purpose in the Kingdom.

other portions, from the east side to the west, with the sanctuary in the center.

9 "The district that you shall set apart for the LORD *shall be* twenty-five thousand *cubits* in length and ten thousand in width. 10 To these— to the priests—the holy district shall belong: on the north twenty-five thousand *cubits in length,* on the west ten thousand in width, on the east ten thousand in width, and on the south twenty-five thousand in length. The sanctuary of the LORD shall be in the center. 11 *It shall be* for the priests of the sons of Zadok, who are sanctified, who have kept My charge, who did not go astray when the children of Israel went astray, as the Levites went astray. 12 And *this* district of land that is set apart shall be to them a thing most holy by the border of the Levites.

13 "Opposite the border of the priests, the Levites *shall have an area* twenty-five thousand *cubits* in length and ten thousand in width; its entire length *shall be* twenty-five thousand and its width ten thousand. 14 And they shall not sell or exchange any of it; they may not alienate this best *part* of the land, for *it is* holy to the LORD.

15 "The five thousand *cubits* in width that remain, along the edge of the twenty-five thousand, shall be for general use by the city, for dwellings and common-land; and the city shall be in the center. 16 These *shall be* its measurements: the north side four thousand five hundred *cubits,* the south side four thousand five hundred, the east side four thousand five hundred, and the west side four thousand five hundred. 17 The common-land of the city shall be: to the north two hundred and fifty *cubits,* to the south two hundred and fifty, to the east two hundred and fifty, and to the west two hundred and fifty. 18 The rest of the length, alongside the district of the holy *section, shall be* ten thousand *cubits* to the east and ten thousand to the west. It shall be adjacent to the district of the holy *section,* and its produce shall be food for the workers of the city. 19 The workers of the city, from all the tribes of Israel, shall cultivate it. 20 The entire district *shall be* twenty-five thou-

sand *cubits* by twenty-five thousand *cubits,* foursquare. You shall set apart the holy district with the property of the city.

21 "The rest *shall belong* to the prince, on one side and on the other of the holy district and of the city's property, next to the twenty-five thousand *cubits* of the *holy* district as far as the eastern border, and westward next to the twenty-five thousand as far as the western border, adjacent to the *tribal* portions; *it shall belong* to the prince. It shall be the holy district, and the sanctuary of the temple *shall be* in the center. 22 Moreover, apart from the possession of the Levites and the possession of the city *which are* in the midst of what *belongs* to the prince, *the area* between the border of Judah and the border of Benjamin shall belong to the prince.

23 "As for the rest of the tribes, from the east side to the west, Benjamin *shall have* one *section;* 24 by the border of Benjamin, from the east side to the west, Simeon *shall have* one *section;* 25 by the border of Simeon, from the east side to the west, Issachar *shall have* one *section;* 26 by the border of Issachar, from the east side to the west, Zebulun *shall have* one *section;* 27 by the border of Zebulun, from the east side to the west, Gad *shall have* one *section;* 28 by the border of Gad, on the south side, toward the South,[a] the border shall be from Tamar *to* the waters of Meribah *by* Kadesh, along the brook to the Great Sea. 29 This *is* the land which you shall divide by lot as an inheritance among the tribes of Israel, and these *are* their portions," says the Lord GOD.

30 "These *are* the exits of the city. On the north side, measuring four thousand five hundred *cubits* 31 (the gates of the city *shall be* named after the tribes of Israel), the three gates northward: one gate for Reuben, one gate for Judah, and one gate for Levi; 32 on the east side, four thousand five hundred *cubits,* three gates: one gate for Joseph, one gate for Benjamin, and one gate for Dan; 33 on the south side, measuring four thousand five hundred *cubits,* three gates: one gate for Simeon, one gate for Issachar, and one gate for Zebu-

48:28 ªHebrew *Negev*

Gospel Pearls

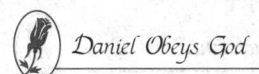

lun; 34 on the west side, four thousand five hundred *cubits* with their three gates: one gate for Gad, one gate for Asher, and one gate for Naphtali. 35 All the way around *shall be* eighteen thousand *cubits;* and the name of the city from *that* day *shall be:* THE LORD *IS* THERE."*a*

48:35 *a*Hebrew *YHWH Shammah*

The Book of

DANIEL

1 In the third year of the reign of Jehoiakim king of Judah, Nebuchadnezzar king of Babylon came to Jerusalem and besieged it. 2 And the Lord gave Jehoiakim king of Judah into his hand, with some of the articles of the house of God, which he carried into the land of Shinar to the house of his god; and he brought the articles into the treasure house of his god.

3 Then the king instructed Ashpenaz, the master of his eunuchs, to bring some of the children of Israel and some of the king's descendants and some of the nobles, 4 young men in whom *there was* no blemish, but good-looking, gifted in all wisdom, possessing knowledge and quick to understand, who *had* ability to serve in the king's palace, and whom they might teach the language and literature of the Chaldeans. 5 And the king appointed for them a daily provision of the king's delicacies and of the wine which he drank, and three years of training for them, so that at the end of *that time* they might serve before the king. 6 Now from among those of the sons of Judah were Daniel, Hananiah, Mishael, and Azariah. 7 To them the chief of the eunuchs gave names: he gave Daniel *the name* Belteshazzar; to Hananiah, Shadrach; to Mishael, Meshach; and to Azariah, Abed-Nego.

8 But Daniel purposed in his heart that he would not defile himself with the portion of the king's delicacies, nor with the wine which he drank; therefore he requested of the chief of the eunuchs that he might not defile himself. 9 Now God had brought Daniel into the favor and goodwill of the chief of the eunuchs. 10 And the chief of the eunuchs said to Daniel, "I fear my lord the king, who has appointed your food and drink. For why should he see your faces looking worse than the young men who *are* your age? Then you would endanger my head before the king."

11 So Daniel said to the steward*a* whom the chief of the eunuchs had set over Daniel, Hananiah, Mishael, and Azariah, 12 "Please test your servants for ten days, and let them give us vegetables to eat and water to drink. 13 Then let our appearance be examined before you, and the appearance of the young men who eat the portion of the king's delicacies; and as you see fit, *so* deal with your servants." 14 So he consented with them in this matter, and tested them ten days.

15 And at the end of ten days their features appeared better and fatter in flesh than all the young men who ate the portion of the king's delicacies. 16 Thus the steward took away their portion of delicacies and the wine that they were to drink, and gave them vegetables.

17 As for these four young men, God gave them knowledge and skill in all literature and wisdom; and Daniel had understanding in all visions and dreams.

18 Now at the end of the days, when the king had said that they should be brought in, the chief of the eunuchs brought them in before Nebuchadnezzar. 19 Then the king interviewed*a* them, and among them all none was found like Daniel, Hananiah, Mishael, and Azariah; therefore they served before the king.

1:11 *a*Hebrew *Melzar*, also in verse 16   1:19 *a*Literally *talked with them*

---

*O*ften we try to separate our personal lives from our spiritual lives. Many see Jesus as a way to Heaven and the solution to spiritual problems, but they fail to see that He is the solution to *all* of life's problems.

20 And in all matters of wisdom *and* understanding about which the king examined them, he found them ten times better than all the magicians *and* astrologers who *were* in all his realm. 21 Thus Daniel continued until the first year of King Cyrus.

2 Now in the second year of Nebuchadnezzar's reign, Nebuchadnezzar had dreams; and his spirit was *so* troubled that his sleep left him. 2 Then the king gave the command to call the magicians, the astrologers, the sorcerers, and the Chaldeans to tell the king his dreams. So they came and stood before the king. 3 And the king said to them, "I have had a dream, and my spirit is anxious to know the dream."

4 Then the Chaldeans spoke to the king in Aramaic,ᵃ "O king, live forever! Tell your servants the dream, and we will give the interpretation."

5 The king answered and said to the Chaldeans, "My decision is firm: if you do not make known the dream to me, and its interpretation, you shall be cut in pieces, and your houses shall be made an ash heap. 6 However, if you tell the dream and its interpretation, you shall receive from me gifts, rewards, and great honor. Therefore tell me the dream and its interpretation."

7 They answered again and said, "Let the king tell his servants the dream, and we will give its interpretation."

8 The king answered and said, "I know for certain that you would gain time, because you see that my decision is firm: 9 if you do not make known the dream to me, *there is only* one decree for you! For you have agreed to speak lying and corrupt words before me till the time has changed. Therefore tell me the dream, and I shall know that you can give me its interpretation."

10 The Chaldeans answered the king, and said, "There is not a man on earth who can tell the king's matter; therefore no king, lord, or ruler has *ever* asked such things of any magician, astrologer, or Chaldean. 11 *It is* a difficult thing that the king requests, and there is no other who can tell it to the king except the gods, whose dwelling is not with flesh."

12 For this reason the king was angry and very furious, and gave the command to destroy all the wise *men* of Babylon. 13 So the decree went out, and they began killing the wise *men;* and they sought Daniel and his companions, to kill *them.*

14 Then with counsel and wisdom Daniel answered Arioch, the captain of the king's guard, who had gone out to kill the wise *men* of Babylon; 15 he answered and said to Arioch the king's captain, "Why is the decree from the king so urgent?" Then Arioch made the decision known to Daniel.

16 So Daniel went in and asked the king to give him time, that he might tell the king the interpretation. 17 Then Daniel went to his house, and made the decision known to Hananiah, Mishael, and Azariah, his companions, 18 that they might seek mercies from the God of heaven concerning this secret, so that Daniel and his companions might not perish with the rest of the wise *men* of Babylon. 19 Then the secret was revealed to Daniel in a night vision. So Daniel blessed the God of heaven.

20 Daniel answered and said:

"Blessed be the name of God
    forever and ever,
For wisdom and might are His.
21 And He changes the times and
    the seasons;
He removes kings and raises up
    kings;
He gives wisdom to the wise
And knowledge to those who
    have understanding.
22 He reveals deep and secret
    things;
He knows what *is* in the
    darkness,
And light dwells with Him.

23 "I thank You and praise You,
    O God of my fathers;
You have given me wisdom
    and might,
And have now made known to
    me what we asked of You,
For You have made known to
    us the king's demand."

24 Therefore Daniel went to Arioch, whom the king had appointed

2:4 ᵃThe original language of Daniel 2:4b through 7:28 is Aramaic.

There's a place in God where the Lord will touch you and provide intimacy in your life when you're not getting it from other places. You must be open to His touch.

Enduring Love

Daniel 2:20, 21

Be prepared for change. Everything changes—people, circumstances, seasons and surroundings. The Bible tells us that God "changes the times and the seasons." It helps when you know that from the beginning. Even love changes. It grows and becomes stronger. It endures the darkest of nights and the brightest of days. It can be as giddy as a giggling girl or as silent as a sunset. It has moments of wonder, moments of passion, moments of glory, moments of pain. Love is dynamic. It will not be tomorrow what it is today. When you are committed, love will endure through its seasons, but it will not stay the same. Sooner or later, and a little bit each day, change will come.

There is no escaping it. The firm breasts that were once small lumps will inflate with child-rearing and deflate in later years. Eyes that burned with fervent love will mellow with time. Arms that once carried you over a threshold will grow weak with the passing of years. The beautiful head of hair you were so proud of will eventually become a crown of gray. But no matter what happens to you physically, you will still be you. You will express yourself in new ways and you may even look different, but the essence of you will always be there.

Love works the same way. It can last for years and years and years. But even long-time love changes in its expression and its manifestation. It endures in many forms. You must be a person who is willing to see that change as a positive and explore each phase as if God has a present locked inside of it for you, because He does. He will show you the many splendors of life if your eyes do not become too fixed on one aspect of its radiance.

If a couple remains married for fifty or sixty years, it is not because the husband sees his wife as the same woman she was on their wedding day. She doesn't look the same, and he doesn't either. They don't love the same. They don't touch the same. It takes them longer to do what they used to do easily. They are together like two travelers exploring the newness and richness of each experience. Beneath leathery skin and crinkled eyes, there are burning embers of wisdom and experience. They still know love, but they express it in changing forms. As it is with them, so it is with change in your own life, whether it is the independence of your children, a new job, or a move.

Determine to keep a positive attitude toward change. Embrace it. Run with it. Be blessed by it.

to destroy the wise *men* of Babylon. He went and said thus to him: "Do not destroy the wise *men* of Babylon; take me before the king, and I will tell the king the interpretation."

25 Then Arioch quickly brought Daniel before the king, and said thus to him, "I have found a man of the captives*ᵃ* of Judah, who will make known to the king the interpretation."

26 The king answered and said to Daniel, whose name *was* Belteshazzar, "Are you able to make known to me the dream which I have seen, and its interpretation?"

27 Daniel answered in the presence of the king, and said, "The secret which the king has demanded, the wise *men*, the astrologers, the magicians, and the soothsayers cannot declare to the king. 28 But there is a God in heaven who reveals secrets, and He has made known to King Nebuchadnezzar what will be in the latter days. Your dream, and the visions of your head upon your bed, were these: 29 As for you, O king, thoughts came *to* your *mind while* on your bed, *about* what would come to pass after this; and He who reveals secrets has made known to you what will be. 30 But as for me, this secret has not been revealed to me because I have more wisdom than anyone living, but for *our* sakes who make known the interpretation to the king, and that you may know the thoughts of your heart.

31 "You, O king, were watching; and behold, a great image! This great image, whose splendor *was* excellent, stood before you; and its form *was* awesome. 32 This image's head *was* of fine gold, its chest and arms of silver, its belly and thighs*ᵃ* of bronze, 33 its legs of iron, its feet partly of iron and partly of clay.*ᵃ* 34 You watched while a stone was cut out without hands, which struck the image on its feet of iron and clay, and broke them in pieces. 35 Then the iron, the clay, the bronze, the silver, and the gold were crushed together, and became like chaff from the summer threshing floors; the wind carried them away so that no trace of them was found. And the stone that struck the image became a great mountain and filled the whole earth.

36 "This *is* the dream. Now we will tell the interpretation of it before the king. 37 You, O king, *are* a king of kings. For the God of heaven has given you a kingdom, power, strength, and glory; 38 and wherever the children of men dwell, or the beasts of the field and the birds of the heaven, He has given *them* into your hand, and has made you ruler over them all—you *are* this head of gold. 39 But after you shall arise another kingdom inferior to yours; then another, a third kingdom of bronze, which shall rule over all the earth. 40 And the fourth kingdom shall be as strong as iron, inasmuch as iron breaks in pieces and shatters everything; and like iron that crushes, *that kingdom* will break in pieces and crush all the others. 41 Whereas you saw the feet and toes, partly of potter's clay and partly of iron, the kingdom shall be divided; yet the strength of the iron shall be in it, just as you saw the iron mixed with ceramic clay. 42 And *as* the toes of the feet *were* partly of iron and partly of clay, *so* the kingdom shall be partly strong and partly fragile. 43 As you saw iron mixed with ceramic clay, they will mingle with the seed of men; but they will not adhere to one another, just as iron does not mix with clay. 44 And in the days of these kings the God of heaven will set up a kingdom which shall never be destroyed; and the kingdom shall not be left to other people; it shall break in pieces and consume all these kingdoms, and it shall stand forever. 45 Inasmuch as you saw that the stone was cut out of the mountain without hands, and that it broke in pieces the iron, the bronze, the clay, the silver, and the gold—the great God has made known to the king what will come to pass after this. The dream is certain, and its interpretation is sure."

46 Then King Nebuchadnezzar fell on his face, prostrate before Daniel, and commanded that they should present an offering and incense to him. 47 The king answered Daniel, and said, "Truly your God *is* the God of gods, the Lord of kings, and a re-

2:25 *ᵃ*Literally *of the sons of the captivity*   2:32 *ᵃ*Or *sides*   2:33 *ᵃ*Or *baked clay,* and so in verses 34, 35, and 42

Gospel Pearls

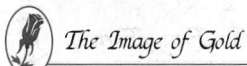
vealer of secrets, since you could reveal this secret." 48 Then the king promoted Daniel and gave him many great gifts; and he made him ruler over the whole province of Babylon, and chief administrator over all the wise *men* of Babylon. 49 Also Daniel petitioned the king, and he set Shadrach, Meshach, and Abed-Nego over the affairs of the province of Babylon; but Daniel *sat* in the gate*ᵃ* of the king.

3 Nebuchadnezzar the king made an image of gold, whose height *was* sixty cubits *and* its width six cubits. He set it up in the plain of Dura, in the province of Babylon. 2 And King Nebuchadnezzar sent *word* to gather together the satraps, the administrators, the governors, the counselors, the treasurers, the judges, the magistrates, and all the officials of the provinces, to come to the dedication of the image which King Nebuchadnezzar had set up. 3 So the satraps, the administrators, the governors, the counselors, the treasurers, the judges, the magistrates, and all the officials of the provinces gathered together for the dedication of the image that King Nebuchadnezzar had set up; and they stood before the image that Nebuchadnezzar had set up. 4 Then a herald cried aloud: "To you it is commanded, O peoples, nations, and languages, 5 *that* at the time you hear the sound of the horn, flute, harp, lyre, *and* psaltery, in symphony with all kinds of music, you shall fall down and worship the gold image that King Nebuchadnezzar has set up; 6 and whoever does not fall down and worship shall be cast immediately into the midst of a burning fiery furnace."

7 So at that time, when all the people heard the sound of the horn, flute, harp, *and* lyre, in symphony with all kinds of music, all the people, nations, and languages fell down *and* worshiped the gold image which King Nebuchadnezzar had set up.

8 Therefore at that time certain Chaldeans came forward and accused the Jews. 9 They spoke and said to King Nebuchadnezzar, "O king, live forever! 10 You, O king,

have made a decree that everyone who hears the sound of the horn, flute, harp, lyre, *and* psaltery, in symphony with all kinds of music, shall fall down and worship the gold image; 11 and whoever does not fall down and worship shall be cast into the midst of a burning fiery furnace. 12 There are certain Jews whom you have set over the affairs of the province of Babylon: Shadrach, Meshach, and Abed-Nego; these men, O king, have not paid due regard to you. They do not serve your gods or worship the gold image which you have set up."

13 Then Nebuchadnezzar, in rage and fury, gave the command to bring Shadrach, Meshach, and Abed-Nego. So they brought these men before the king. 14 Nebuchadnezzar spoke, saying to them, "*Is it* true, Shadrach, Meshach, and Abed-Nego, *that* you do not serve my gods or worship the gold image which I have set up? 15 Now if you are ready at the time you hear the sound of the horn, flute, harp, lyre, *and* psaltery, in symphony with all kinds of music, and you fall down and worship the image which I have made, *good!* But if you do not worship, you shall be cast immediately into the midst of a burning fiery furnace. And who *is* the god who will deliver you from my hands?"

16 Shadrach, Meshach, and Abed-Nego answered and said to the king, "O Nebuchadnezzar, we have no need to answer you in this matter. 17 If that *is the case,* our God whom we serve is able to deliver us from the burning fiery furnace, and He will deliver *us* from your hand, O king. 18 But if not, let it be known to you, O king, that we do not serve your gods, nor will we worship the gold image which you have set up."

19 Then Nebuchadnezzar was full of fury, and the expression on his face changed toward Shadrach, Meshach, and Abed-Nego. He spoke and commanded that they heat the furnace seven times more than it was usually heated. 20 And he commanded certain mighty men of valor who *were* in his army to bind Shadrach, Meshach, and Abed-Nego, *and* cast *them* into the burning fiery furnace. 21 Then these men were bound in their coats, their trousers,

Sometimes pain can become too familiar. Ungodly relationships often become familiar. Sometimes we maintain these relationships because we fear change. However, when we see our value the way Jesus sees us, we muster the courage to break away.

their turbans, and their *other* garments, and were cast into the midst of the burning fiery furnace. 22 Therefore, because the king's command was urgent, and the furnace exceedingly hot, the flame of the fire killed those men who took up Shadrach, Meshach, and Abed-Nego. 23 And these three men, Shadrach, Meshach, and Abed-Nego, fell down bound into the midst of the burning fiery furnace.

24 Then King Nebuchadnezzar was astonished; and he rose in haste *and* spoke, saying to his counselors, "Did we not cast three men bound into the midst of the fire?"

They answered and said to the king, "True, O king."

25 "Look!" he answered, "I see four men loose, walking in the midst of the fire; and they are not hurt, and the form of the fourth is like the Son of God."*a*

26 Then Nebuchadnezzar went near the mouth of the burning fiery furnace *and* spoke, saying, "Shadrach, Meshach, and Abed-Nego, servants of the Most High God, come out, and come *here*." Then Shadrach, Meshach, and Abed-Nego came from the midst of the fire. 27 And the satraps, administrators, governors, and the king's counselors gathered together, and they saw these men on whose bodies the fire had no power; the hair of their head was not singed nor were their garments affected, and the smell of fire was not on them.

28 Nebuchadnezzar spoke, saying, "Blessed be the God of Shadrach, Meshach, and Abed-Nego, who sent His Angel*a* and delivered His servants who trusted in Him, and they have frustrated the king's word, and yielded their bodies, that they should not serve nor worship any god except their own God! 29 Therefore I make a decree that any people, nation, or language which speaks anything amiss against the God of Shadrach, Meshach, and Abed-Nego shall be cut in pieces, and their houses shall be made an ash heap; because there is no other God who can deliver like this."

30 Then the king promoted Shadrach, Meshach, and Abed-Nego in the province of Babylon.

3:25 *a*Or *a son of the gods*   3:28 *a*Or *angel*

4 Nebuchadnezzar the king,

To all peoples, nations, and languages that dwell in all the earth:

Peace be multiplied to you.

2   I thought it good to declare the signs and wonders that the Most High God has worked for me.

3   How great *are* His signs,
And how mighty His wonders!
His kingdom *is* an everlasting kingdom,
And His dominion *is* from generation to generation.

4   I, Nebuchadnezzar, was at rest in my house, and flourishing in my palace. 5 I saw a dream which made me afraid, and the thoughts on my bed and the visions of my head troubled me. 6 Therefore I issued a decree to bring in all the wise *men* of Babylon before me, that they might make known to me the interpretation of the dream. 7 Then the magicians, the astrologers, the Chaldeans, and the soothsayers came in, and I told them the dream; but they did not make known to me its interpretation. 8 But at last Daniel came before me (his name *is* Belteshazzar, according to the name of my god; in him *is* the Spirit of the Holy God), and I told the dream before him, *saying:*
9 "Belteshazzar, chief of the magicians, because I know that the Spirit of the Holy God *is* in you, and no secret troubles you, explain to me the visions of my dream that I have seen, and its interpretation.

10   "These *were* the visions of my head *while* on my bed:

"I was looking, and behold,
A tree in the midst of the earth,
And its height was great.
11   The tree grew and became strong;

Gospel Pearls

Its height reached to the
heavens,
And it could be seen to the ends
of all the earth.
12 Its leaves *were* lovely,
Its fruit abundant,
And in it *was* food for all.
The beasts of the field found
shade under it,
The birds of the heavens dwelt
in its branches,
And all flesh was fed from it.

13 "I saw in the visions of my head
while on my bed, and there was
a watcher, a holy one, coming
down from heaven. 14 He cried
aloud and said thus:

'Chop down the tree and cut off
its branches,
Strip off its leaves and scatter
its fruit.
Let the beasts get out from
under it,
And the birds from its
branches.
15 Nevertheless leave the stump
and roots in the earth,
Bound with a band of iron and
bronze,
In the tender grass of the
field.
Let it be wet with the dew of
heaven,
And *let* him graze with the
beasts
On the grass of the earth.
16 Let his heart be changed from
that of a man,
Let him be given the heart of
a beast,
And let seven times*ª* pass over
him.

17 'This decision *is* by the decree
of the watchers,
And the sentence by the word
of the holy ones,
In order that the living may
know
That the Most High rules in the
kingdom of men,
Gives it to whomever He will,
And sets over it the lowest of
men.'

18 "This dream I, King
Nebuchadnezzar, have seen.

Now you, Belteshazzar, declare
its interpretation, since all the
wise *men* of my kingdom are
not able to make known to me
the interpretation; but you *are*
able, for the Spirit of the Holy
God *is* in you."

19 Then Daniel, whose name was
Belteshazzar, was astonished
for a time, and his thoughts
troubled him. *So* the king
spoke, and said, "Belteshazzar,
do not let the dream or its
interpretation trouble you."
Belteshazzar answered and
said, "My lord, *may* the dream
concern those who hate you,
and its interpretation concern
your enemies!

20 "The tree that you saw, which
grew and became strong,
whose height reached to the
heavens and which *could be
seen* by all the earth, 21 whose
leaves *were* lovely and its fruit
abundant, in which *was* food
for all, under which the beasts
of the field dwelt, and in whose
branches the birds of the
heaven had their home—
22 it *is* you, O king, who have
grown and become strong; for
your greatness has grown and
reaches to the heavens, and
your dominion to the end of the
earth.

23 "And inasmuch as the king saw
a watcher, a holy one, coming
down from heaven and saying,
'Chop down the tree and
destroy it, but leave its stump
and roots in the earth, *bound*
with a band of iron and bronze
in the tender grass of the field;
let it be wet with the dew of
heaven, and let him graze with
the beasts of the field, till seven
times pass over him'; 24 this is
the interpretation, O king, and
this is the decree of the Most
High, which has come upon my
lord the king: 25 They shall
drive you from men, your
dwelling shall be with the
beasts of the field, and they
shall make you eat grass like

4:16 *ª*Possibly *seven years*, and so in verses 23, 25, and 32

*O*nce you realize that you have been unleashed, you will feel a sudden change. When
you come to Jesus, He will motivate you. You will see that other woman in you. You
need to blossom and bring her forth.

oxen. They shall wet you with the dew of heaven, and seven times shall pass over you, till you know that the Most High rules in the kingdom of men, and gives it to whomever He chooses.

26 "And inasmuch as they gave the command to leave the stump *and* roots of the tree, your kingdom shall be assured to you, after you come to know that Heaven rules.
27 Therefore, O king, let my advice be acceptable to you; break off your sins by *being* righteous, and your iniquities by showing mercy to *the* poor. Perhaps there may be a lengthening of your prosperity."

28 All *this* came upon King Nebuchadnezzar. 29 At the end of the twelve months he was walking about the royal palace of Babylon. 30 The king spoke, saying, "Is not this great Babylon, that I have built for a royal dwelling by my mighty power and for the honor of my majesty?"

31 While the word *was still* in the king's mouth, a voice fell from heaven: "King Nebuchadnezzar, to you it is spoken: the kingdom has departed from you! 32 And they shall drive you from men, and your dwelling *shall be* with the beasts of the field. They shall make you eat grass like oxen; and seven times shall pass over you, until you know that the Most High rules in the kingdom of men, and gives it to whomever He chooses."

33 That very hour the word was fulfilled concerning Nebuchadnezzar; he was driven from men and ate grass like oxen; his body was wet with the dew of heaven till his hair had grown like eagles' *feathers* and his nails like birds' *claws.*

34 And at the end of the time[a] I, Nebuchadnezzar, lifted my eyes to heaven, and my understanding returned to me; and I blessed the Most High and praised and honored Him who lives forever:

For His dominion *is* an
  everlasting dominion,
And His kingdom *is* from
  generation to generation.
35 All the inhabitants of the earth
  are reputed as nothing;
He does according to His will
  in the army of heaven
And *among* the inhabitants of
  the earth.
No one can restrain His hand
Or say to Him, "What have You
  done?"

36 At the same time my reason returned to me, and for the glory of my kingdom, my honor and splendor returned to me. My counselors and nobles resorted to me, I was restored to my kingdom, and excellent majesty was added to me. 37 Now I, Nebuchadnezzar, praise and extol and honor the King of heaven, all of whose works *are* truth, and His ways justice. And those who walk in pride He is able to put down.

5 Belshazzar the king made a great feast for a thousand of his lords, and drank wine in the presence of the thousand. 2 While he tasted the wine, Belshazzar gave the command to bring the gold and silver vessels which his father Nebuchadnezzar had taken from the temple which *had been* in Jerusalem, that the king and his lords, his wives, and his concubines might drink from them. 3 Then they brought the gold vessels that had been taken from the temple of the house of God which *had been* in Jerusalem; and the king and his lords, his wives, and his concubines drank from them. 4 They drank wine, and praised the gods of gold and silver, bronze and iron, wood and stone.
5 In the same hour the fingers of a man's hand appeared and wrote opposite the lampstand on the plaster

4:34 aLiterally *days*

Gospel Pearls

of the wall of the king's palace; and the king saw the part of the hand that wrote. 6 Then the king's countenance changed, and his thoughts troubled him, so that the joints of his hips were loosened and his knees knocked against each other. 7 The king cried aloud to bring in the astrologers, the Chaldeans, and the soothsayers. The king spoke, saying to the wise *men* of Babylon, "Whoever reads this writing, and tells me its interpretation, shall be clothed with purple and *have* a chain of gold around his neck; and he shall be the third ruler in the kingdom." 8 Now all the king's wise *men* came, but they could not read the writing, or make known to the king its interpretation. 9 Then King Belshazzar was greatly troubled, his countenance was changed, and his lords were astonished.

10 The queen, because of the words of the king and his lords, came to the banquet hall. The queen spoke, saying, "O king, live forever! Do not let your thoughts trouble you, nor let your countenance change. 11 There is a man in your kingdom in whom *is* the Spirit of the Holy God. And in the days of your father, light and understanding and wisdom, like the wisdom of the gods, were found in him; and King Nebuchadnezzar your father—your father the king—made him chief of the magicians, astrologers, Chaldeans, *and* soothsayers. 12 Inasmuch as an excellent spirit, knowledge, understanding, interpreting dreams, solving riddles, and explaining enigmas[a] were found in this Daniel, whom the king named Belteshazzar, now let Daniel be called, and he will give the interpretation."

13 Then Daniel was brought in before the king. The king spoke, and said to Daniel, "*Are* you that Daniel who is one of the captives[a] from Judah, whom my father the king brought from Judah? 14 I have heard of you, that the Spirit of God *is* in you, and *that* light and understanding and excellent wisdom are found in you. 15 Now the wise *men,* the astrologers, have been brought in before me, that they should read this writing and make known to me its

interpretation, but they could not give the interpretation of the thing. 16 And I have heard of you, that you can give interpretations and explain enigmas. Now if you can read the writing and make known to me its interpretation, you shall be clothed with purple and *have* a chain of gold around your neck, and shall be the third ruler in the kingdom."

17 Then Daniel answered, and said before the king, "Let your gifts be for yourself, and give your rewards to another; yet I will read the writing to the king, and make known to him the interpretation. 18 O king, the Most High God gave Nebuchadnezzar your father a kingdom and majesty, glory and honor. 19 And because of the majesty that He gave him, all peoples, nations, and languages trembled and feared before him. Whomever he wished, he executed; whomever he wished, he kept alive; whomever he wished, he set up; and whomever he wished, he put down. 20 But when his heart was lifted up, and his spirit was hardened in pride, he was deposed from his kingly throne, and they took his glory from him. 21 Then he was driven from the sons of men, his heart was made like the beasts, and his dwelling *was* with the wild donkeys. They fed him with grass like oxen, and his body was wet with the dew of heaven, till he knew that the Most High God rules in the kingdom of men, and appoints over it whomever He chooses.

22 "But you his son, Belshazzar, have not humbled your heart, although you knew all this. 23 And you have lifted yourself up against the Lord of heaven. They have brought the vessels of His house before you, and you and your lords, your wives and your concubines, have drunk wine from them. And you have praised the gods of silver and gold, bronze and iron, wood and stone, which do not see or hear or know; and the God who *holds* your breath in His hand and owns all your ways, you have not glorified. 24 Then the fingers[a] of the hand were sent from Him, and this writing was written. 25 "And this is the inscription that was written:

5:12 [a]Literally *untying knots,* and so in verse 16   5:13 [a]Literally *of the sons of the captivity*
5:24 [a]Literally *palm*

When you approach God, don't worry about the fact that you are a woman. Never become discouraged on that basis when it comes to seeking Him. You will only get as much from God as you can believe Him for.

MENE,ᵃ MENE, TEKEL,ᵇ
UPHARSIN.ᶜ

26 This *is* the interpretation of *each* word. MENE: God has numbered your kingdom, and finished it; 27 TEKEL: You have been weighed in the balances, and found wanting; 28 PERES: Your kingdom has been divided, and given to the Medes and Persians."ᵃ 29 Then Belshazzar gave the command, and they clothed Daniel with purple and *put* a chain of gold around his neck, and made a proclamation concerning him that he should be the third ruler in the kingdom.

30 That very night Belshazzar, king of the Chaldeans, was slain. 31 And Darius the Mede received the kingdom, *being* about sixty-two years old.

6 It pleased Darius to set over the kingdom one hundred and twenty satraps, to be over the whole kingdom; 2 and over these, three governors, of whom Daniel *was* one, that the satraps might give account to them, so that the king would suffer no loss. 3 Then this Daniel distinguished himself above the governors and satraps, because an excellent spirit *was* in him; and the king gave thought to setting him over the whole realm. 4 So the governors and satraps sought to find *some* charge against Daniel concerning the kingdom; but they could find no charge or fault, because he *was* faithful; nor was there any error or fault found in him. 5 Then these men said, "We shall not find any charge against this Daniel unless we find *it* against him concerning the law of his God."

6 So these governors and satraps thronged before the king, and said thus to him: "King Darius, live forever! 7 All the governors of the kingdom, the administrators and satraps, the counselors and advisors, have consulted together to establish a royal statute and to make a firm decree, that whoever petitions any god or man for thirty days, except you, O king, shall be cast into the den of lions. 8 Now, O king, establish the decree and sign the writing, so that it

cannot be changed, according to the law of the Medes and Persians, which does not alter." 9 Therefore King Darius signed the written decree.

10 Now when Daniel knew that the writing was signed, he went home. And in his upper room, with his windows open toward Jerusalem, he knelt down on his knees three times that day, and prayed and gave thanks before his God, as was his custom since early days.

11 Then these men assembled and found Daniel praying and making supplication before his God. 12 And they went before the king, and spoke concerning the king's decree: "Have you not signed a decree that every man who petitions any god or man within thirty days, except you, O king, shall be cast into the den of lions?"

The king answered and said, "The thing *is* true, according to the law of the Medes and Persians, which does not alter."

13 So they answered and said before the king, "That Daniel, who is one of the captivesᵃ from Judah, does not show due regard for you, O king, or for the decree that you have signed, but makes his petition three times a day."

14 And the king, when he heard *these* words, was greatly displeased with himself, and set *his* heart on Daniel to deliver him; and he labored till the going down of the sun to deliver him. 15 Then these men approached the king, and said to the king, "Know, O king, that *it is* the law of the Medes and Persians that no decree or statute which the king establishes may be changed."

16 So the king gave the command, and they brought Daniel and cast *him* into the den of lions. *But* the king spoke, saying to Daniel, "Your God, whom you serve continually, He will deliver you." 17 Then a stone was brought and laid on the mouth of the den, and the king sealed it with his own signet ring and with the signets of his lords, that the purpose concerning Daniel might not be changed.

18 Now the king went to his palace and spent the night fasting; and no

---

5:25 ᵃLiterally *a mina (50 shekels)* from the verb "to number"   ᵇLiterally *a shekel* from the verb "to weigh" ᶜLiterally *and half-shekels* from the verb "to divide"   5:28 ᵃAramaic *Paras,* consonant with *Peres* 6:13 ᵃLiterally *of the sons of the captivity*

Gospel
Pearls

musicians[a] were brought before him. Also his sleep went from him. 19 Then the king arose very early in the morning and went in haste to the den of lions. 20 And when he came to the den, he cried out with a lamenting voice to Daniel. The king spoke, saying to Daniel, "Daniel, servant of the living God, has your God, whom you serve continually, been able to deliver you from the lions?"

21 Then Daniel said to the king, "O king, live forever! 22 My God sent His angel and shut the lions' mouths, so that they have not hurt me, because I was found innocent before Him; and also, O king, I have done no wrong before you."

23 Now the king was exceedingly glad for him, and commanded that they should take Daniel up out of the den. So Daniel was taken up out of the den, and no injury whatever was found on him, because he believed in his God.

24 And the king gave the command, and they brought those men who had accused Daniel, and they cast *them* into the den of lions—them, their children, and their wives; and the lions overpowered them, and broke all their bones in pieces before they ever came to the bottom of the den.

25 Then King Darius wrote:

To all peoples, nations, and languages that dwell in all the earth:

Peace be multiplied to you.

26 I make a decree that in every dominion of my kingdom *men must* tremble and fear before the God of Daniel.

For He *is* the living God,
And steadfast forever;
His kingdom *is the one* which shall not be destroyed,
And His dominion *shall endure* to the end.
27 He delivers and rescues,
And He works signs and wonders
In heaven and on earth,
Who has delivered Daniel from the power of the lions.

28 So this Daniel prospered in the reign of Darius and in the reign of Cyrus the Persian.

7 In the first year of Belshazzar king of Babylon, Daniel had a dream and visions of his head *while* on his bed. Then he wrote down the dream, telling the main facts.[a]

2 Daniel spoke, saying, "I saw in my vision by night, and behold, the four winds of heaven were stirring up the Great Sea. 3 And four great beasts came up from the sea, each different from the other. 4 The first *was* like a lion, and had eagle's wings. I watched till its wings were plucked off; and it was lifted up from the earth and made to stand on two feet like a man, and a man's heart was given to it.

5 "And suddenly another beast, a second, like a bear. It was raised up on one side, and *had* three ribs in its mouth between its teeth. And they said thus to it: 'Arise, devour much flesh!'

6 "After this I looked, and there was another, like a leopard, which had on its back four wings of a bird. The beast also had four heads, and dominion was given to it.

7 "After this I saw in the night visions, and behold, a fourth beast, dreadful and terrible, exceedingly strong. It had huge iron teeth; it was devouring, breaking in pieces, and trampling the residue with its feet. It *was* different from all the beasts that *were* before it, and it had ten horns. 8 I was considering the horns, and there was another horn, a little one, coming up among them, before whom three of the first horns were plucked out by the roots. And there, in this horn, *were* eyes like the eyes of a man, and a mouth speaking pompous words.

9 "I watched till thrones were put in place,
And the Ancient of Days was seated;
His garment *was* white as snow,
And the hair of His head *was* like pure wool.
His throne *was* a fiery flame,
Its wheels a burning fire;
10 A fiery stream issued

*H*e wants you to believe Him. He wants you to personalize the truth that you can do all things through Him. He is trying to teach you so when the time for a real miracle does come, you'll have some faith to draw from.

And came forth from before
    Him.
A thousand thousands
    ministered to Him;
Ten thousand times ten
    thousand stood before Him.
The court*a* was seated,
And the books were opened.

11 "I watched then because of the sound of the pompous words which the horn was speaking; I watched till the beast was slain, and its body destroyed and given to the burning flame. 12 As for the rest of the beasts, they had their dominion taken away, yet their lives were prolonged for a season and a time.

13 "I was watching in the night
        visions,
    And behold, *One* like the Son
        of Man,
    Coming with the clouds of
        heaven!
    He came to the Ancient of
        Days,
    And they brought Him near
        before Him.
14 Then to Him was given
        dominion and glory and a
        kingdom,
    That all peoples, nations, and
        languages should serve Him.
    His dominion *is* an everlasting
        dominion,
    Which shall not pass away,
    And His kingdom *the one*
    Which shall not be destroyed.

15 "I, Daniel, was grieved in my spirit within *my* body, and the visions of my head troubled me. 16 I came near to one of those who stood by, and asked him the truth of all this. So he told me and made known to me the interpretation of these things: 17 'Those great beasts, which are four, *are* four kings*a* which arise out of the earth. 18 But the saints of the Most High shall receive the kingdom, and possess the kingdom forever, even forever and ever.'

19 "Then I wished to know the truth about the fourth beast, which was different from all the others, exceedingly dreadful, *with* its teeth of iron and its nails of bronze, *which* devoured, broke in pieces, and trampled the residue with its feet;

20 and the ten horns that *were* on its head, and the other *horn* which came up, before which three fell, namely, that horn which had eyes and a mouth which spoke pompous words, whose appearance *was* greater than his fellows.
21 "I was watching; and the same horn was making war against the saints, and prevailing against them, 22 until the Ancient of Days came, and a judgment was made *in favor* of the saints of the Most High, and the time came for the saints to possess the kingdom.
23 "Thus he said:

    'The fourth beast shall be
    A fourth kingdom on earth,
    Which shall be different from
        all *other* kingdoms,
    And shall devour the whole
        earth,
    Trample it and break it in
        pieces.
24 The ten horns *are* ten kings
        Who shall arise from this
        kingdom.
    And another shall rise after
        them;
    He shall be different from the
        first *ones*,
    And shall subdue three kings.
25 He shall speak *pompous* words
        against the Most High,
    Shall persecute*a* the saints of
        the Most High,
    And shall intend to change
        times and law.
    Then *the saints* shall be given
        into his hand
    For a time and times and half
        a time.

26 'But the court shall be seated,
    And they shall take away his
        dominion,
    To consume and destroy *it*
        forever.
27 Then the kingdom and
        dominion,
    And the greatness of the
        kingdoms under the whole
        heaven,
    Shall be given to the people, the
        saints of the Most High.
    His kingdom *is* an everlasting
        kingdom,
    And all dominions shall serve
        and obey Him.'

7:10 *a*Or judgment   7:17 *a*Representing their kingdoms (compare verse 23)   7:25 *a*Literally *wear out*

Gospel Pearls

28 "This *is* the end of the account.*ᵃ* As for me, Daniel, my thoughts greatly troubled me, and my countenance changed; but I kept the matter in my heart."

8 In the third year of the reign of King Belshazzar a vision appeared *to* me—to me, Daniel—after the one that appeared to me the first time. 2 I saw in the vision, and it so happened while I was looking, that I was in Shushan, the citadel, which *is* in the province of Elam; and I saw in the vision that I was by the River Ulai. 3 Then I lifted my eyes and saw, and there, standing beside the river, was a ram which had two horns, and the two horns *were* high; but one *was* higher than the other, and the higher *one* came up last. 4 I saw the ram pushing westward, northward, and southward, so that no animal could withstand him; nor *was there any* that could deliver from his hand, but he did according to his will and became great.

5 And as I was considering, suddenly a male goat came from the west, across the surface of the whole earth, without touching the ground; and the goat *had* a notable horn between his eyes. 6 Then he came to the ram that had two horns, which I had seen standing beside the river, and ran at him with furious power. 7 And I saw him confronting the ram; he was moved with rage against him, attacked the ram, and broke his two horns. There was no power in the ram to withstand him, but he cast him down to the ground and trampled him; and there was no one that could deliver the ram from his hand.

8 Therefore the male goat grew very great; but when he became strong, the large horn was broken, and in place of it four notable ones came up toward the four winds of heaven. 9 And out of one of them came a little horn which grew exceedingly great toward the south, toward the east, and toward the Glorious *Land.* 10 And it grew up to the host of heaven; and it cast down *some* of the host and *some* of the stars to the ground, and trampled them. 11 He even exalted *himself* as

high as the Prince of the host; and by him the daily *sacrifices* were taken away, and the place of His sanctuary was cast down. 12 Because of transgression, an army was given over *to the horn* to oppose the daily *sacrifices;* and he cast truth down to the ground. He did *all this* and prospered.

13 Then I heard a holy one speaking; and *another* holy one said to that certain *one* who was speaking, "How long *will* the vision *be, concerning* the daily *sacrifices* and the transgression of desolation, the giving of both the sanctuary and the host to be trampled underfoot?"

14 And he said to me, "For two thousand three hundred days;*ᵃ* then the sanctuary shall be cleansed."

15 Then it happened, when I, Daniel, had seen the vision and was seeking the meaning, that suddenly there stood before me one having the appearance of a man. 16 And I heard a man's voice between *the banks of* the Ulai, who called, and said, "Gabriel, make this *man* understand the vision." 17 So he came near where I stood, and when he came I was afraid and fell on my face; but he said to me, "Understand, son of man, that the vision *refers* to the time of the end."

18 Now, as he was speaking with me, I was in a deep sleep with my face to the ground; but he touched me, and stood me upright. 19 And he said, "Look, I am making known to you what shall happen in the latter time of the indignation; for at the appointed time the end *shall be.* 20 The ram which you saw, having the two horns—*they are* the kings of Media and Persia. 21 And the male goat *is* the kingdom*ᵃ* of Greece. The large horn that *is* between its eyes *is* the first king. 22 As for the broken *horn* and the four that stood up in its place, four kingdoms shall arise out of that nation, but not with its power.

23 "And in the latter time of their
    kingdom,
When the transgressors have
    reached their fullness,
A king shall arise,
Having fierce features,

7:28 *ᵃ*Literally *the word*   8:14 *ᵃ*Literally *evening-mornings*   8:21 *ᵃ*Literally *king,* representing his kingdom (compare 7:17, 23)

God wants your faith to be developed. Regardless of your position and your past, God raises people up equally. Faith is an equal opportunity business.

Who understands sinister
schemes.
24 His power shall be mighty, but
not by his own power;
He shall destroy fearfully,
And shall prosper and thrive;
He shall destroy the mighty,
and *also* the holy people.

25 "Through his cunning
He shall cause deceit to prosper
under his rule;*a*
And he shall exalt *himself* in his
heart.
He shall destroy many in *their*
prosperity.
He shall even rise against the
Prince of princes;
But he shall be broken without
human means.*b*

26 "And the vision of the evenings
and mornings
Which was told is true;
Therefore seal up the vision,
For *it refers* to many days *in
the future."*

27 And I, Daniel, fainted and was
sick for days; afterward I arose and
went about the king's business. I was
astonished by the vision, but no one
understood it.

9 In the first year of Darius the son
of Ahasuerus, of the lineage of the
Medes, who was made king over the
realm of the Chaldeans— 2 in the first
year of his reign I, Daniel, understood by the books the number of the
years *specified* by the word of the
LORD through Jeremiah the prophet,
that He would accomplish seventy
years in the desolations of Jerusalem.
3 Then I set my face toward the
Lord God to make request by prayer
and supplications, with fasting, sackcloth, and ashes. 4 And I prayed to
the LORD my God, and made confession, and said, "O Lord, great and
awesome God, who keeps His covenant and mercy with those who love
Him, and with those who keep His
commandments, 5 we have sinned
and committed iniquity, we have
done wickedly and rebelled, even by
departing from Your precepts and
Your judgments. 6 Neither have we
heeded Your servants the prophets,
who spoke in Your name to our kings

and our princes, to our fathers and
all the people of the land. 7 O Lord,
righteousness *belongs* to You, but to
us shame of face, as *it is* this day—
to the men of Judah, to the inhabitants of Jerusalem and all Israel,
those near and those far off in all the
countries to which You have driven
them, because of the unfaithfulness
which they have committed against
You.
8 "O Lord, to us *belongs* shame of
face, to our kings, our princes, and
our fathers, because we have sinned
against You. 9 To the Lord our God
belong mercy and forgiveness,
though we have rebelled against
Him. 10 We have not obeyed the
voice of the LORD our God, to walk
in His laws, which He set before us
by His servants the prophets.
11 Yes, all Israel has transgressed
Your law, and has departed so as not
to obey Your voice; therefore the
curse and the oath written in the Law
of Moses the servant of God have
been poured out on us, because we
have sinned against Him. 12 And He
has confirmed His words, which He
spoke against us and against our
judges who judged us, by bringing
upon us a great disaster; for under
the whole heaven such has never
been done as what has been done to
Jerusalem.
13 "As *it is* written in the Law of
Moses, all this disaster has come
upon us; yet we have not made our
prayer before the LORD our God, that
we might turn from our iniquities and
understand Your truth. 14 Therefore
the LORD has kept the disaster in
mind, and brought it upon us; for the
LORD our God *is* righteous in all the
works which He does, though we
have not obeyed His voice. 15 And
now, O Lord our God, who brought
Your people out of the land of Egypt
with a mighty hand, and made Yourself a name, as *it is* this day—we have
sinned, we have done wickedly!
16 "O Lord, according to all Your
righteousness, I pray, let Your anger
and Your fury be turned away from
Your city Jerusalem, Your holy
mountain; because for our sins, and
for the iniquities of our fathers, Jerusalem and Your people *are* a reproach to all *those* around us.
17 Now therefore, our God, hear the

8:25 *a*Literally *hand* *b*Literally *hand*

Gospel
Pearls

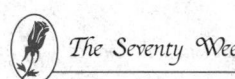

prayer of Your servant, and his supplications, and for the Lord's sake cause Your face to shine on Your sanctuary, which is desolate. 18 O my God, incline Your ear and hear; open Your eyes and see our desolations, and the city which is called by Your name; for we do not present our supplications before You because of our righteous deeds, but because of Your great mercies. 19 O Lord, hear! O Lord, forgive! O Lord, listen and act! Do not delay for Your own sake, my God, for Your city and Your people are called by Your name."

20 Now while I *was* speaking, praying, and confessing my sin and the sin of my people Israel, and presenting my supplication before the LORD my God for the holy mountain of my God, 21 yes, while I *was* speaking in prayer, the man Gabriel, whom I had seen in the vision at the beginning, being caused to fly swiftly, reached me about the time of the evening offering. 22 And he informed *me*, and talked with me, and said, "O Daniel, I have now come forth to give you skill to understand. 23 At the beginning of your supplications the command went out, and I have come to tell *you*, for you *are* greatly beloved; therefore consider the matter, and understand the vision:

24 "Seventy weeks[a] are determined
    For your people and for your
      holy city,
    To finish the transgression,
    To make an end of[b] sins,
    To make reconciliation for
      iniquity,
    To bring in everlasting
      righteousness,
    To seal up vision and prophecy,
    And to anoint the Most Holy.

25 "Know therefore and understand,
    That from the going forth of
      the command
    To restore and build Jerusalem
    Until Messiah the Prince,
    There shall be seven weeks and
      sixty-two weeks;
    The street[a] shall be built again,
      and the wall,[b]
    Even in troublesome times.

26 "And after the sixty-two weeks
    Messiah shall be cut off, but not
      for Himself;
    And the people of the prince
      who is to come
    Shall destroy the city and the
      sanctuary.
    The end of it *shall be* with a
      flood,
    And till the end of the war
      desolations are determined.
27 Then he shall confirm a
      covenant with many for one
      week;
    But in the middle of the
      week
    He shall bring an end to
      sacrifice and offering.
    And on the wing of
      abominations shall be one
      who makes desolate,
    Even until the consummation,
      which is determined,
    Is poured out on the desolate."

10 In the third year of Cyrus king of Persia a message was revealed to Daniel, whose name was called Belteshazzar. The message *was* true, but the appointed time *was* long;[a] and he understood the message, and had understanding of the vision. 2 In those days I, Daniel, was mourning three full weeks. 3 I ate no pleasant food, no meat or wine came into my mouth, nor did I anoint myself at all, till three whole weeks were fulfilled.

4 Now on the twenty-fourth day of the first month, as I was by the side of the great river, that *is*, the Tigris,[a] 5 I lifted my eyes and looked, and behold, a certain man clothed in linen, whose waist *was* girded with gold of Uphaz! 6 His body *was* like beryl, his face like the appearance of lightning, his eyes like torches of fire, his arms and feet like burnished bronze in color, and the sound of his words like the voice of a multitude.

7 And I, Daniel, alone saw the vision, for the men who were with me did not see the vision; but a great terror fell upon them, so that they fled to hide themselves. 8 Therefore I was left alone when I saw this great vision, and no strength remained in me; for my vigor was turned to frailty in me, and I retained no strength.

9:24 [a]Literally *sevens*, and so throughout the chapter   [b]Following Qere, Septuagint, Syriac, and Vulgate; Kethib and Theodotion read *To seal up.*   9:25 [a]Or *open square*   [b]Or *moat*   10:1 [a]Or *and of great conflict*   10:4 [a]Hebrew *Hiddekel*

The thing God is asking from you is faith. Some may live good, clean, separated lives; maybe you are proud of how holy you are. He still honors only faith.

9 Yet I heard the sound of his words; and while I heard the sound of his words I was in a deep sleep on my face, with my face to the ground.

10 Suddenly, a hand touched me, which made me tremble on my knees and *on* the palms of my hands. 11 And he said to me, "O Daniel, man greatly beloved, understand the words that I speak to you, and stand upright, for I have now been sent to you." While he was speaking this word to me, I stood trembling.

12 Then he said to me, "Do not fear, Daniel, for from the first day that you set your heart to understand, and to humble yourself before your God, your words were heard; and I have come because of your words. 13 But the prince of the kingdom of Persia withstood me twenty-one days; and behold, Michael, one of the chief princes, came to help me, for I had been left alone there with the kings of Persia. 14 Now I have come to make you understand what will happen to your people in the latter days, for the vision *refers* to *many* days yet *to come.*"

15 When he had spoken such words to me, I turned my face toward the ground and became speechless. 16 And suddenly, *one* having the likeness of the sons*ᵃ* of men touched my lips; then I opened my mouth and spoke, saying to him who stood before me, "My lord, because of the vision my sorrows have overwhelmed me, and I have retained no strength. 17 For how can this servant of my lord talk with you, my lord? As for me, no strength remains in me now, nor is any breath left in me."

18 Then again, *the one* having the likeness of a man touched me and strengthened me. 19 And he said, "O man greatly beloved, fear not! Peace *be* to you; be strong, yes, be strong!"

So when he spoke to me I was strengthened, and said, "Let my lord speak, for you have strengthened me."

20 Then he said, "Do you know why I have come to you? And now I must return to fight with the prince of Persia; and when I have gone forth, indeed the prince of Greece will come. 21 But I will tell you what is noted in the Scripture of Truth. (No one upholds me against these, except Michael your prince.

11 "Also in the first year of Darius the Mede, I, *even* I, stood up to confirm and strengthen him.) 2 And now I will tell you the truth: Behold, three more kings will arise in Persia, and the fourth shall be far richer than *them* all; by his strength, through his riches, he shall stir up all against the realm of Greece. 3 Then a mighty king shall arise, who shall rule with great dominion, and do according to his will. 4 And when he has arisen, his kingdom shall be broken up and divided toward the four winds of heaven, but not among his posterity nor according to his dominion with which he ruled; for his kingdom shall be uprooted, even for others besides these.

5 "Also the king of the South shall become strong, as well as *one* of his princes; and he shall gain power over him and have dominion. His dominion *shall be* a great dominion. 6 And at the end of *some* years they shall join forces, for the daughter of the king of the South shall go to the king of the North to make an agreement; but she shall not retain the power of her authority, and neither he nor his authority*ᵃ* shall stand; but she shall be given up, with those who brought her, and with him who begot her, and with him who strengthened her in *those* times. 7 But from a branch of her roots *one* shall arise in his place, who shall come with an army, enter the fortress of the king of the North, and deal with them and prevail. 8 And he shall also carry their gods captive to Egypt, with their princes*ᵃ and* their precious articles of silver and gold; and he shall continue *more* years than the king of the North.

9 "Also *the king of the North* shall come to the kingdom of the king of the South, but shall return to his own land. 10 However his sons shall stir up strife, and assemble a multitude of great forces; and *one* shall certainly come and overwhelm and pass through; then he shall return to his fortress and stir up strife.

11 "And the king of the South shall be moved with rage, and go out and

10:16 *ᵃ*Theodotion and Vulgate read *the son;* Septuagint reads *a hand.*   11:6 *ᵃ*Literally *arm*   11:8 *ᵃ*Or *molded images*

fight with him, with the king of the North, who shall muster a great multitude; but the multitude shall be given into the hand of his *enemy.* 12 When he has taken away the multitude, his heart will be lifted up; and he will cast down tens of thousands, but he will not prevail. 13 For the king of the North will return and muster a multitude greater than the former, and shall certainly come at the end of some years with a great army and much equipment.

14 "Now in those times many shall rise up against the king of the South. Also, violent men[a] of your people shall exalt themselves in fulfillment of the vision, but they shall fall. 15 So the king of the North shall come and build a siege mound, and take a fortified city; and the forces[a] of the South shall not withstand *him.* Even his choice troops *shall have* no strength to resist. 16 But he who comes against him shall go according to his own will, and no one shall stand against him. He shall stand in the Glorious Land with destruction in his power.[a]

17 "He shall also set his face to enter with the strength of his whole kingdom, and upright ones[a] with him; thus shall he do. And he shall give him the daughter of women to destroy it; but she shall not stand *with him,* or be for him. 18 After this he shall turn his face to the coastlands, and shall take many. But a ruler shall bring the reproach against them to an end; and with the reproach removed, he shall turn back on him. 19 Then he shall turn his face toward the fortress of his own land; but he shall stumble and fall, and not be found.

20 "There shall arise in his place one who imposes taxes *on* the glorious kingdom; but within a few days he shall be destroyed, but not in anger or in battle. 21 And in his place shall arise a vile person, to whom they will not give the honor of royalty; but he shall come in peaceably, and seize the kingdom by intrigue. 22 With the force[a] of a flood they shall be swept away from before him and be broken, and also the prince of the covenant. 23 And after the league *is made* with him he shall act deceitfully, for he shall come up and become strong with a small *number of* people. 24 He shall enter peaceably, even into the richest places of the province; and he shall do *what* his fathers have not done, nor his forefathers: he shall disperse among them the plunder, spoil, and riches; and he shall devise his plans against the strongholds, but *only* for a time.

25 "He shall stir up his power and his courage against the king of the South with a great army. And the king of the South shall be stirred up to battle with a very great and mighty army; but he shall not stand, for they shall devise plans against him. 26 Yes, those who eat of the portion of his delicacies shall destroy him; his army shall be swept away, and many shall fall down slain. 27 Both these kings' hearts *shall be* bent on evil, and they shall speak lies at the same table; but it shall not prosper, for the end *will* still *be* at the appointed time. 28 While returning to his land with great riches, his heart shall be *moved* against the holy covenant; so he shall do *damage* and return to his own land.

29 "At the appointed time he shall return and go toward the south; but it shall not be like the former or the latter. 30 For ships from Cyprus[a] shall come against him; therefore he shall be grieved, and return in rage against the holy covenant, and do *damage.*

"So he shall return and show regard for those who forsake the holy covenant. 31 And forces[a] shall be mustered by him, and they shall defile the sanctuary fortress; then they shall take away the daily *sacrifices,* and place *there* the abomination of desolation. 32 Those who do wickedly against the covenant he shall corrupt with flattery; but the people who know their God shall be strong, and carry out *great exploits.* 33 And those of the people who understand shall instruct many; yet *for many* days they shall fall by sword and flame, by captivity and plundering. 34 Now when they fall, they shall be aided with a little help; but many shall join with them by intrigue. 35 And *some* of those of understand-

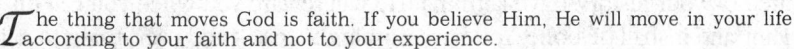

*T*he thing that moves God is faith. If you believe Him, He will move in your life according to your faith and not to your experience.

Breaking the Chain

Daniel 11:32

There is awesome power in women. God has chosen women as the vehicles through which entry is made into this world. He has shared His creativity with them. The enemy wants to destroy God's vehicles of creativity. Satan attacks in many ways—emotionally, physically, and spiritually—and at every age. Little girls are abused and left feeling used and dirty. Young women are deceived into believing that their boyfriends really do love them and that yielding to the demand for sex will prove their love in return. Maybe you were a person who simply wanted to have a good time without considering the consequences.

God has determined your need. He looked down from Heaven and saw your pain and guilt. He evaluated the situation and decided that you needed a Redeemer. He saw that you needed to realize how important you are. It is impossible to know all that was in the mind of God when he looked down on broken humanity, but we know He looked past our broken hearts, our shady histories, and our tendency to sin, and saw our need.

He met that need through Jesus Christ. Jesus took your abuse on Himself on the Cross of Calvary. He paid for your shame. He made a way for you to be clean again. He took your indiscretions and sins upon Himself and died in your place. He saw your desire to please others and feel good. Thus, He took all your sinful desires and crucified them on the Cross.

The abused little girl with all her wounds was healed by the stripes of Jesus (see Isaiah 53:5). The sins of the woman who wanted to fulfill her lusts was crucified on the Cross with Him (see Galatians 2:20). The past is paid for. The wounds may leave scars, but the scars are only there to remind us that we are human.

God recognizes your potential. He also knows that your potential has been bound by your history. Your suffering made you into a different woman from the one He originally intended you to be. The circumstances of your life shaped your way of thinking. Your responses to those circumstances often kept you from living up to your potential.

Hidden inside of you is a great woman who can do great exploits in His name. He wants that woman to be set free. He wants your potential to be unleashed so you can become the person you were created to be.

There is only one way to reach that potential. Listen. He is calling. He is stirring your heart and moving in your life, if you will only respond to His call. When you accept Him, you will be made pure.

Believe that He paid the price for your sin and guilt. Believe that He has washed you and made you clean. Believe that He will satisfy every need created by your history. Have faith that He will reward you when you call on Him, and it shall be done. You have nothing to lose—and everything to gain!

ing shall fall, to refine them, purify *them*, and make *them* white, *until* the time of the end; because *it is* still for the appointed time.

36 "Then the king shall do according to his own will: he shall exalt and magnify himself above every god, shall speak blasphemies against the God of gods, and shall prosper till the wrath has been accomplished; for what has been determined shall be done. 37 He shall regard neither the God[a] of his fathers nor the desire of women, nor regard any god; for he shall exalt himself above *them* all. 38 But in their place he shall honor a god of fortresses; and a god which his fathers did not know he shall honor with gold and silver, with precious stones and pleasant things. 39 Thus he shall act against the strongest fortresses with a foreign god, which he shall acknowledge, *and* advance *its* glory; and he shall cause them to rule over many, and divide the land for gain.

40 "At the time of the end the king of the South shall attack him; and the king of the North shall come against him like a whirlwind, with chariots, horsemen, and with many ships; and he shall enter the countries, overwhelm *them*, and pass through. 41 He shall also enter the Glorious Land, and many *countries* shall be overthrown; but these shall escape from his hand: Edom, Moab, and the prominent people of Ammon. 42 He shall stretch out his hand against the countries, and the land of Egypt shall not escape. 43 He shall have power over the treasures of gold and silver, and over all the precious things of Egypt; also the Libyans and Ethiopians *shall follow* at his heels. 44 But news from the east and the north shall trouble him; therefore he shall go out with great fury to destroy and annihilate many. 45 And he shall plant the tents of his palace between the seas and the glorious holy mountain; yet he shall come to his end, and no one will help him.

12 "At that time Michael shall stand up,
The great prince who stands *watch* over the sons of your people;

And there shall be a time of trouble,
Such as never was since there was a nation,
Even to that time.
And at that time your people shall be delivered,
Every one who is found written in the book.
2 And many of those who sleep in the dust of the earth shall awake,
Some to everlasting life,
Some to shame *and* everlasting contempt.
3 Those who are wise shall shine Like the brightness of the firmament,
And those who turn many to righteousness
Like the stars forever and ever.

4 "But you, Daniel, shut up the words, and seal the book until the time of the end; many shall run to and fro, and knowledge shall increase."

5 Then I, Daniel, looked; and there stood two others, one on this riverbank and the other on that riverbank. 6 And *one* said to the man clothed in linen, who *was* above the waters of the river, "How long shall the fulfillment of these wonders *be?*"

7 Then I heard the man clothed in linen, who *was* above the waters of the river, when he held up his right hand and his left hand to heaven, and swore by Him who lives forever, that *it shall be* for a time, times, and half *a time;* and when the power of the holy people has been completely shattered, all these *things* shall be finished.

8 Although I heard, I did not understand. Then I said, "My lord, what *shall be* the end of these *things?*"

9 And he said, "Go *your way,* Daniel, for the words *are* closed up and sealed till the time of the end. 10 Many shall be purified, made white, and refined, but the wicked shall do wickedly; and none of the wicked shall understand, but the wise shall understand.

11 "And from the time *that* the daily *sacrifice* is taken away, and the abomination of desolation is set up, *there shall be* one thousand two hun-

11:37 [a]Or *gods*

dred and ninety days. 12 Blessed *is* he who waits, and comes to the one thousand three hundred and thirty-five days.

13 "But you, go *your way* till the end; for you shall rest, and will arise to your inheritance at the end of the days."

The Book of
HOSEA

1 The word of the LORD that came to Hosea the son of Beeri, in the days of Uzziah, Jotham, Ahaz, *and* Hezekiah, kings of Judah, and in the days of Jeroboam the son of Joash, king of Israel. 2 When the LORD began to speak by Hosea, the LORD said to Hosea:

> "Go, take yourself a wife of harlotry
> And children of harlotry,
> For the land has committed great harlotry
> *By departing* from the LORD."

3 So he went and took Gomer the daughter of Diblaim, and she conceived and bore him a son. 4 Then the LORD said to him:

> "Call his name Jezreel,
> For in a little *while*
> I will avenge the bloodshed of Jezreel on the house of Jehu,
> And bring an end to the kingdom of the house of Israel.
> 5 It shall come to pass in that day
> That I will break the bow of Israel in the Valley of Jezreel."

6 And she conceived again and bore a daughter. Then *God* said to him:

> "Call her name Lo-Ruhamah,*a*
> For I will no longer have mercy on the house of Israel,
> But I will utterly take them away.*b*
> 7 Yet I will have mercy on the house of Judah,

> Will save them by the LORD their God,
> And will not save them by bow,
> Nor by sword or battle,
> By horses or horsemen."

8 Now when she had weaned Lo-Ruhamah, she conceived and bore a son. 9 Then *God* said:

> "Call his name Lo-Ammi,*a*
> For you *are* not My people,
> And I will not be your *God.*

> 10 "Yet the number of the children of Israel
> Shall be as the sand of the sea,
> Which cannot be measured or numbered.
> And it shall come to pass
> In the place where it was said to them,
> 'You *are* not My people,'*a*
> *There* it shall be said to them,
> '*You are* sons of the living God.'
> 11 Then the children of Judah and the children of Israel
> Shall be gathered together,
> And appoint for themselves one head;
> And they shall come up out of the land,
> For great *will be* the day of Jezreel!

2 "Say to your brethren, 'My people,'*a*
> And to your sisters, 'Mercy*b is shown.'*
> 2 Bring charges against your mother, bring charges;
> For she *is* not My wife, nor *am* I her Husband!

1:6 *a*Literally *No-Mercy*　*b*Or *That I may forgive them at all*　1:9 *a*Literally *Not-My-People*
1:10 *a*Hebrew *lo-ammi* (compare verse 9)　2:1 *a*Hebrew *Ammi* (compare 1:9, 10)　*b*Hebrew *Ruhamah* (compare 1:6)

Gospel Pearls

Let her put away her harlotries
from her sight,
And her adulteries from
between her breasts;
3 Lest I strip her naked
And expose her, as in the day
she was born,
And make her like a
wilderness,
And set her like a dry land,
And slay her with thirst.

4 "I will not have mercy on her
children,
For they *are* the children of
harlotry.
5 For their mother has played the
harlot;
She who conceived them has
behaved shamefully.
For she said, 'I will go after my
lovers,
Who give *me* my bread and my
water,
My wool and my linen,
My oil and my drink.'

6 "Therefore, behold,
I will hedge up your way with
thorns,
And wall her in,
So that she cannot find her
paths.
7 She will chase her lovers,
But not overtake them;
Yes, she will seek them, but not
find *them*.
Then she will say,
'I will go and return to my first
husband,
For then *it was* better for me
than now.'
8 For she did not know
That I gave her grain, new
wine, and oil,
And multiplied her silver and
gold—
Which they prepared for
Baal.

9 "Therefore I will return and take
away
My grain in its time
And My new wine in its season,
And will take back My wool
and My linen,
Given to cover her nakedness.
10 Now I will uncover her
lewdness in the sight of her
lovers,

And no one shall deliver her
from My hand.
11 I will also cause all her mirth
to cease,
Her feast days,
Her New Moons,
Her Sabbaths—
All her appointed feasts.

12 "And I will destroy her vines
and her fig trees,
Of which she has said,
'These *are* my wages that my
lovers have given me.'
So I will make them a forest,
And the beasts of the field shall
eat them.
13 I will punish her
For the days of the Baals to
which she burned incense.
She decked herself with her
earrings and jewelry,
And went after her lovers;
But Me she forgot," says the
LORD.

14 "Therefore, behold, I will allure
her,
Will bring her into the
wilderness,
And speak comfort to her.
15 I will give her her vineyards
from there,
And the Valley of Achor as a
door of hope;
She shall sing there,
As in the days of her youth,
As in the day when she came
up from the land of Egypt.

16 "And it shall be, in that day,"
Says the LORD,
"*That* you will call Me 'My
Husband,'*a*
And no longer call Me 'My
Master,'*b*
17 For I will take from her mouth
the names of the Baals,
And they shall be remembered
by their name no more.
18 In that day I will make a
covenant for them
With the beasts of the field,
With the birds of the air,
And *with* the creeping things
of the ground.
Bow and sword of battle I will
shatter from the earth,
To make them lie down safely.

2:16 *a*Hebrew *Ishi* *b*Hebrew *Baali*

T here is no need to sit around waiting on someone else to get what is yours. Nobody
else is coming. The One who needed to come is already here.

19 "I will betroth you to Me
forever;
Yes, I will betroth you to Me
In righteousness and justice,
In lovingkindness and mercy;
20 I will betroth you to Me in
faithfulness,
And you shall know the LORD.

21 "It shall come to pass in that
day
That I will answer," says the
LORD;
"I will answer the heavens,
And they shall answer the
earth.
22 The earth shall answer
With grain,
With new wine,
And with oil;
They shall answer Jezreel.*a*
23 Then I will sow her for Myself
in the earth,
And I will have mercy on *her*
who had not obtained
mercy;*a*
Then I will say to *those who
were* not My people,*b*
'You *are* My people!'
And they shall say, '*You are* my
God!' "

3 Then the LORD said to me, "Go
again, love a woman *who is* loved
by a lover*a* and is committing adultery, just like the love of the LORD
for the children of Israel, who look
to other gods and love *the* raisin
cakes *of the pagans.*"

2 So I bought her for myself for fifteen *shekels* of silver, and one and
one-half homers of barley. 3 And I
said to her, "You shall stay with me
many days; you shall not play the
harlot, nor shall you have a man—
so, too, *will* I *be* toward you."

4 For the children of Israel shall
abide many days without king or
prince, without sacrifice or sacred
pillar, without ephod or teraphim.
5 Afterward the children of Israel
shall return and seek the LORD their
God and David their king. They shall
fear the LORD and His goodness in
the latter days.

4 Hear the word of the LORD,
You children of Israel,

For the LORD *brings* a charge
against the inhabitants of the
land:

"There is no truth or mercy
Or knowledge of God in the
land.
2 *By* swearing and lying,
Killing and stealing and
committing adultery,
They break all restraint,
With bloodshed upon
bloodshed.
3 Therefore the land will mourn;
And everyone who dwells there
will waste away
With the beasts of the field
And the birds of the air;
Even the fish of the sea will be
taken away.

4 "Now let no man contend, or
rebuke another;
For your people *are* like those
who contend with the
priest.
5 Therefore you shall stumble in
the day;
The prophet also shall stumble
with you in the night;
And I will destroy your mother.
6 My people are destroyed for
lack of knowledge.
Because you have rejected
knowledge,
I also will reject you from being
priest for Me;
Because you have forgotten the
law of your God,
I also will forget your children.

7 "The more they increased,
The more they sinned against
Me;
I will change*a* their glory*b* into
shame.
8 They eat up the sin of My
people;
They set their heart on their
iniquity.
9 And it shall be: like people, like
priest.
So I will punish them for their
ways,
And reward them for their
deeds.
10 For they shall eat, but not have
enough;

2:22 *a*Literally *God Will Sow*   2:23 *a*Hebrew *lo-ruhamah* *b*Hebrew *lo-ammi*   3:1 *a*Literally *friend* or
husband   4:7 *a*Following Masoretic Text, Septuagint, and Vulgate; scribal tradition, Syriac, and Targum
read *They will change.* *b*Following Masoretic Text, Septuagint, Syriac, Targum, and Vulgate; scribal tradition
reads *My glory.*

Gospel
Pearls

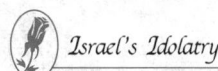
They shall commit harlotry, but
  not increase;
Because they have ceased
  obeying the LORD.

11 "Harlotry, wine, and new wine
  enslave the heart.
12 My people ask counsel from
  their wooden *idols,*
And their staff informs
  them.
For the spirit of harlotry has
  caused *them* to stray,
And they have played the
  harlot against their God.
13 They offer sacrifices on the
  mountaintops,
And burn incense on the
  hills,
Under oaks, poplars, and
  terebinths,
Because their shade *is*
  good.
Therefore your daughters
  commit harlotry,
And your brides commit
  adultery.

14 "I will not punish your
  daughters when they commit
  harlotry,
Nor your brides when they
  commit adultery;
For *the men* themselves go
  apart with harlots,
And offer sacrifices with a
  ritual harlot.*ᵃ*
Therefore people *who* do not
  understand will be trampled.

15 "Though you, Israel, play the
  harlot,
Let not Judah offend.
Do not come up to Gilgal,
Nor go up to Beth Aven,
Nor swear an oath, *saying,* 'As
  the LORD lives'—

16 "For Israel is stubborn
Like a stubborn calf;
Now the LORD will let them
  forage
Like a lamb in open country.

17 "Ephraim *is* joined to idols,
Let him alone.
18 Their drink is rebellion,
They commit harlotry
  continually.
Her rulers dearly love
  dishonor.*ᵃ*

19 The wind has wrapped her up
  in its wings,
And they shall be ashamed
  because of their sacrifices.

5 "Hear this, O priests!
Take heed, O house of Israel!
Give ear, O house of the king!
For yours *is* the judgment,
Because you have been a snare
  to Mizpah
And a net spread on Tabor.
2 The revolters are deeply
  involved in slaughter,
Though I rebuke them all.
3 I know Ephraim,
And Israel is not hidden from
  Me;
For now, O Ephraim, you
  commit harlotry;
Israel is defiled.

4 "They do not direct their deeds
Toward turning to their God,
For the spirit of harlotry is in
  their midst,
And they do not know the
  LORD.
5 The pride of Israel testifies to
  his face;
Therefore Israel and Ephraim
  stumble in their iniquity;
Judah also stumbles with them.

6 "With their flocks and herds
They shall go to seek the LORD,
But they will not find *Him;*
He has withdrawn Himself
  from them.
7 They have dealt treacherously
  with the LORD,
For they have begotten pagan
  children.
Now a New Moon shall devour
  them and their heritage.

8 "Blow the ram's horn in Gibeah,
The trumpet in Ramah!
Cry aloud *at* Beth Aven,
'*Look* behind you, O Benjamin!'
9 Ephraim shall be desolate in
  the day of rebuke;
Among the tribes of Israel I
  make known what is sure.

10 "The princes of Judah are like
  those who remove a
  landmark;

4:14 ᵃCompare Deuteronomy 23:18   4:18 ᵃHebrew is difficult; a Jewish tradition reads *Her rulers
shamefully love, 'Give!'.*

---

*Y*our Father left you an inheritance. If God would bless the sons of Abraham, you
can be sure He would bless the daughters of Abraham.

I will pour out my wrath on
them like water.

11 Ephraim is oppressed *and*
broken in judgment,
Because he willingly walked by
human precept.

12 Therefore I *will be* to Ephraim
like a moth,
And to the house of Judah like
rottenness.

13 "When Ephraim saw his
sickness,
And Judah *saw* his wound,
Then Ephraim went to Assyria
And sent to King Jareb;
Yet he cannot cure you,
Nor heal you of your wound.

14 For I *will be* like a lion to
Ephraim,
And like a young lion to the
house of Judah.
I, *even* I, will tear *them* and go
away;
I will take *them* away, and no
one shall rescue.

15 I will return again to My place
Till they acknowledge their
offense.
Then they will seek My face;
In their affliction they will
earnestly seek Me."

6 Come, and let us return to the
LORD;
For He has torn, but He will
heal us;
He has stricken, but He will
bind us up.

2 After two days He will revive
us;
On the third day He will raise
us up,
That we may live in His sight.

3 Let us know,
Let us pursue the knowledge of
the LORD.
His going forth is established
as the morning;
He will come to us like the rain,
Like the latter *and* former rain
to the earth.

4 "O Ephraim, what shall I do to
you?
O Judah, what shall I do to you?
For your faithfulness is like a
morning cloud,
And like the early dew it goes
away.

5 Therefore I have hewn *them* by
the prophets,
I have slain them by the words
of My mouth;
And your judgments *are like*
light *that* goes forth.

6 For I desire mercy and not
sacrifice,
And the knowledge of
God more than burnt
offerings.

7 "But like men[a] they
transgressed the covenant;
There they dealt treacherously
with Me.

8 Gilead *is* a city of evildoers
And defiled with blood.

9 As bands of robbers lie in wait
for a man,
So the company of priests
murder on the way to
Shechem;
Surely they commit lewdness.

10 I have seen a horrible thing in
the house of Israel:
There *is* the harlotry of
Ephraim;
Israel is defiled.

11 Also, O Judah, a harvest is
appointed for you,
When I return the captives of
My people.

7 "When I would have healed
Israel,
Then the iniquity of Ephraim
was uncovered,
And the wickedness of
Samaria.
For they have committed
fraud;
A thief comes in;
A band of robbers takes spoil
outside.

2 They do not consider in their
hearts
That I remember all their
wickedness;
Now their own deeds have
surrounded them;
They are before My face.

3 They make a king glad with
their wickedness,
And princes with their lies.

4 "They *are* all adulterers.
Like an oven heated by a
baker—

6:7 [a]Or *like Adam*

God's power brings all things up under your feet. Believe Him for your household.
God will deliver. You don't need a sugar daddy. You have the *Jehovah-jireh*, the best
provider this world has ever known.

It's Going to Rain

Hosea 6:3

Lady, your confession is great. You've fought and defended yourself against attackers, and you have seen some increase; but when you allow God to heal your thoughts, you will explode into another dimension. Sometimes we have been strong because we had great struggles. We fought valiantly in the face of life's enemies. However, when sunset falls on the battlefield, and after the troops have gone home, we hang up our gear and wish we really were as valiant as we looked! Perceive and believe what God is doing in you. If you can get that in your head, you can reap it in your life!

The harvest field that God wants to plant is in your head. Amidst all your troubles, hold onto your field of dreams. If you can water your own field when men are trying to command a drought in your life, God will mightily sustain you.

There is still much to be accomplished in the woman who has maintained thoughts of greatness in the midst of degrading dilemmas. These are the smiles that paint the faces of people who know something greater and deeper, who see beyond their circumstances. They look out of the window, but they see far down the road.

If in your thoughts you see something beyond where you are—if you see a dream, a goal, or an aspiration that others would think impossible—you may have to *hold it.* Sometimes you may have to *hide it,* and most of the time you will have to *water it* as a farmer waters his crops to sustain the life in them. But always remember they are your fields. You must eat from the garden of your own thoughts, so don't grow anything you don't want to eat. As you ponder and daydream, receive grace for the hard places and healing for the damaged soil. Just know that whenever your children, your friends, or anyone else comes to the table of your wisdom, you can only feed them *what you have grown in your own fields.* Your wisdom is so flavorful and its texture so rich that it can't be "store bought"; it must be *homegrown.*

A whispering prayer is on my lips: *I pray that this word God has given me be so powerful and personal, so intimate and applicable in your life, that it leaves behind it a barren mind made pregnant. This seed of greatness will explode in your life and harvest in your children, feeding the generations to come and changing the winds of destiny.*

In my heart I smell the indescribable smell of an approaching rain. Moisture is in the air and the clouds have gathered. Our fields have been chosen for the next rain and the wind has already started to blow. Run swiftly into the field with your precious seeds and plant them in the soft ground of your fertile mind. Whatever you plant in the evening will be reaped in the morning. My sister, I am so excited for you. I just heard a clap of thunder ... in just another moment, there'll be rain!

He ceases stirring *the fire* after
    kneading the dough,
Until it is leavened.
5 In the day of our king
Princes have made *him* sick,
    inflamed with wine;
He stretched out his hand with
    scoffers.
6 They prepare their heart like
    an oven,
While they lie in wait;
Their baker[a] sleeps all night;
In the morning it burns like a
    flaming fire.
7 They are all hot, like an
    oven,
And have devoured their
    judges;
All their kings have fallen.
None among them calls upon
    Me.

8 "Ephraim has mixed himself
    among the peoples;
Ephraim is a cake unturned.
9 Aliens have devoured his
    strength,
But he does not know *it;*
Yes, gray hairs are here and
    there on him,
Yet he does not know *it.*
10 And the pride of Israel testifies
    to his face,
But they do not return to the
    LORD their God,
Nor seek Him for all this.

11 "Ephraim also is like a silly
    dove, without sense—
They call to Egypt,
They go to Assyria.
12 Wherever they go, I will spread
    My net on them;
I will bring them down like
    birds of the air;
I will chastise them
According to what their
    congregation has heard.

13 "Woe to them, for they have fled
    from Me!
Destruction to them,
Because they have
    transgressed against Me!
Though I redeemed them,
Yet they have spoken lies
    against Me.

14 They did not cry out to Me with
    their heart
When they wailed upon their
    beds.
"They assemble together for[a]
    grain and new wine,
They rebel against Me;[b]
15 Though I disciplined *and*
    strengthened their arms,
Yet they devise evil against Me;
16 They return, *but* not to the
    Most High;[a]
They are like a treacherous
    bow.
Their princes shall fall by the
    sword
For the cursings of their
    tongue.
This *shall be* their derision in
    the land of Egypt.

8 "*Set* the trumpet[a] to your
    mouth!
He shall come like an eagle
    against the house of the
    LORD,
Because they have
    transgressed My covenant
And rebelled against My law.
2 Israel will cry to Me,
'My God, we know You!'
3 Israel has rejected the good;
The enemy will pursue him.

4 "They set up kings, but not by
    Me;
They made princes, but I did
    not acknowledge *them.*
From their silver and gold
They made idols for
    themselves—
That they might be cut off.
5 Your calf is rejected, O
    Samaria!
My anger is aroused against
    them—
How long until they attain to
    innocence?
6 For from Israel *is* even this:
A workman made it, and it *is*
    not God;
But the calf of Samaria shall be
    broken to pieces.

7 "They sow the wind,
And reap the whirlwind.

7:6 [a]Following Masoretic Text and Vulgate; Syriac and Targum read *Their anger;* Septuagint reads *Ephraim.*   7:14 [a]Following Masoretic Text and Targum; Vulgate reads *thought upon;* Septuagint reads *slashed themselves for* (compare 1 Kings 18:28).   [b]Following Masoretic Text, Syriac, and Targum; Septuagint omits *They rebel against Me;* Vulgate reads *They departed from Me.*   7:16 [a]Or *upward*
8:1 [a]Hebrew *shophar,* ram's horn

Gospel
Pearls

The stalk has no bud;
It shall never produce meal.
If it should produce,
Aliens would swallow it up.
8 Israel is swallowed up;
Now they are among the
Gentiles
Like a vessel in which *is* no
pleasure.
9 For they have gone up to
Assyria,
Like a wild donkey alone by
itself;
Ephraim has hired lovers.
10 Yes, though they have hired
among the nations,
Now I will gather them;
And they shall sorrow a
little,[a]
Because of the burden[b] of the
king of princes.

11 "Because Ephraim has made
many altars for sin,
They have become for him
altars for sinning.
12 I have written for him the great
things of My law,
But they were considered a
strange thing.
13 *For* the sacrifices of My
offerings they sacrifice flesh
and eat *it*,
But the Lord does not accept
them.
Now He will remember their
iniquity and punish their
sins.
They shall return to Egypt.

14 "For Israel has forgotten his
Maker,
And has built temples;[a]
Judah also has multiplied
fortified cities;
But I will send fire upon his
cities,
And it shall devour his
palaces."

9 Do not rejoice, O Israel, with
joy like *other* peoples,
For you have played the harlot
against your God.
You have made love *for* hire on
every threshing floor.
2 The threshing floor and the
winepress
Shall not feed them,

And the new wine shall fail in
her.

3 They shall not dwell in the
Lord's land,
But Ephraim shall return to
Egypt,
And shall eat unclean *things* in
Assyria.
4 They shall not offer wine
offerings to the Lord,
Nor shall their sacrifices be
pleasing to Him.
It shall be like bread of
mourners to them;
All who eat it shall be defiled.
For their bread *shall be* for
their *own* life;
It shall not come into the house
of the Lord.

5 What will you do in the
appointed day,
And in the day of the feast of
the Lord?
6 For indeed they are gone
because of destruction.
Egypt shall gather them up;
Memphis shall bury them.
Nettles shall possess their
valuables of silver;
Thorns *shall be* in their tents.

7 The days of punishment have
come;
The days of recompense have
come.
Israel knows!
The prophet *is* a fool,
The spiritual man *is* insane,
Because of the greatness of
your iniquity and great
enmity.
8 The watchman of Ephraim *is*
with my God;
But the prophet *is* a fowler's[a]
snare in all his ways—
Enmity in the house of his God.
9 They are deeply corrupted,
As in the days of Gibeah.
He will remember their
iniquity;
He will punish their sins.

10 "I found Israel
Like grapes in the wilderness;
I saw your fathers
As the firstfruits on the fig tree
in its first season.

8:10 [a]Or *begin to diminish*   [b]Or *oracle*   8:14 [a]Or *palaces*   9:8 [a]That is, one who catches birds in a trap or snare

Women are just as much children of God as men are. Everything that God will do for a man, He will do for a woman. You are not disadvantaged. You can get an inheritance like any man.

But they went to Baal Peor,
And separated themselves *to
that* shame;
They became an abomination
like the thing they loved.
11 *As for* Ephraim, their glory
shall fly away like a bird—
No birth, no pregnancy, and no
conception!
12 Though they bring up their
children,
Yet I will bereave them to the
last man.
Yes, woe to them when I depart
from them!
13 Just as I saw Ephraim like
Tyre, planted in a pleasant
place,
So Ephraim will bring out his
children to the murderer."

14 Give them, O LORD—
What will You give?
Give them a miscarrying womb
And dry breasts!

15 "All their wickedness *is* in
Gilgal,
For there I hated them.
Because of the evil of their
deeds
I will drive them from My
house;
I will love them no more.
All their princes *are* rebellious.
16 Ephraim is stricken,
Their root is dried up;
They shall bear no fruit.
Yes, were they to bear children,
I would kill the darlings of their
womb."

17 My God will cast them away,
Because they did not obey Him;
And they shall be wanderers
among the nations.

10 Israel empties *his* vine;
He brings forth fruit for
himself.
According to the multitude of
his fruit
He has increased the altars;
According to the bounty of his
land
They have embellished *his*
sacred pillars.
2 Their heart is divided;
Now they are held guilty.

He will break down their altars;
He will ruin their sacred pillars.

3 For now they say,
"We have no king,
Because we did not fear the
LORD.
And as for a king, what would
he do for us?"
4 They have spoken words,
Swearing falsely in making a
covenant.
Thus judgment springs up like
hemlock in the furrows of the
field.

5 The inhabitants of Samaria
fear
Because of the calf*a* of Beth
Aven.
For its people mourn for it,
And its priests shriek for it—
Because its glory has departed
from it.
6 *The idol* also shall be carried
to Assyria
As a present for King Jareb.
Ephraim shall receive shame,
And Israel shall be ashamed of
his own counsel.

7 *As for* Samaria, her king is cut
off
Like a twig on the water.
8 Also the high places of Aven,
the sin of Israel,
Shall be destroyed.
The thorn and thistle shall
grow on their altars;
They shall say to the
mountains, "Cover us!"
And to the hills, "Fall on us!"

9 "O Israel, you have sinned from
the days of Gibeah;
There they stood.
The battle in Gibeah against
the children of iniquity*a*
Did not overtake them.
10 When *it is* My desire, I will
chasten them.
Peoples shall be gathered
against them
When I bind them for their two
transgressions.*a*
11 Ephraim *is* a trained heifer
That loves to thresh *grain*;
But I harnessed her fair neck,

10:5 *a*Literally *calves*   10:9 *a*So read many Hebrew manuscripts, Septuagint, and Vulgate; Masoretic Text
reads *unruliness.*   10:10 *a*Or *in their two habitations*

Gospel
Pearls

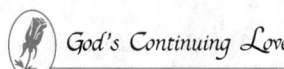
I will make Ephraim pull *a
plow.*
Judah shall plow;
Jacob shall break his clods."

12 Sow for yourselves
righteousness;
Reap in mercy;
Break up your fallow ground,
For *it is* time to seek the LORD,
Till He comes and rains
righteousness on you.

13 You have plowed wickedness;
You have reaped iniquity.
You have eaten the fruit of lies,
Because you trusted in your
own way,
In the multitude of your mighty
men.
14 Therefore tumult shall arise
among your people,
And all your fortresses shall be
plundered
As Shalman plundered Beth
Arbel in the day of battle—
A mother dashed in pieces
upon *her* children.
15 Thus it shall be done to you, O
Bethel,
Because of your great
wickedness.
At dawn the king of Israel
Shall be cut off utterly.

11 "When Israel *was* a child, I loved
him,
And out of Egypt I called My
son.
2 As they called them,*a*
So they went from them;*b*
They sacrificed to the Baals,
And burned incense to carved
images.

3 "I taught Ephraim to walk,
Taking them by their arms;*a*
But they did not know that I
healed them.
4 I drew them with gentle cords,*a*
With bands of love,
And I was to them as those who
take the yoke from their
neck.*b*
I stooped *and* fed them.

5 "He shall not return to the land
of Egypt;

But the Assyrian shall be his
king,
Because they refused to repent.
6 And the sword shall slash in his
cities,
Devour his districts,
And consume *them,*
Because of their own counsels.
7 My people are bent on
backsliding from Me.
Though they call to the Most
High,*a*
None at all exalt *Him.*

8 "How can I give you up,
Ephraim?
How can I hand you over,
Israel?
How can I make you like
Admah?
How can I set you like
Zeboiim?
My heart churns within Me;
My sympathy is stirred.
9 I will not execute the fierceness
of My anger;
I will not again destroy
Ephraim.
For I *am* God, and not man,
The Holy One in your midst;
And I will not come with
terror.*a*

10 "They shall walk after the LORD.
He will roar like a lion.
When He roars,
Then *His* sons shall come
trembling from the west;
11 They shall come trembling like
a bird from Egypt,
Like a dove from the land of
Assyria.
And I will let them dwell in
their houses,"
Says the LORD.

12 "Ephraim has encircled Me with
lies,
And the house of Israel with
deceit;
But Judah still walks with God,
Even with the Holy One*a who
is* faithful.

12 "Ephraim feeds on the wind,
And pursues the east wind;

11:2 *a*Following Masoretic Text and Vulgate; Septuagint reads *Just as I called them;* Targum interprets as
I sent prophets to a thousand of them. *b*Following Masoretic Text, Targum, and Vulgate; Septuagint reads
from My face.   11:3 *a*Some Hebrew manuscripts, Septuagint, Syriac, and Vulgate read *My arms.*
11:4 *a*Literally *cords of a man* *b*Literally *jaws*   11:7 *a*Or *upward*   11:9 *a*Or *I will not enter a city*
11:12 *a*Or *holy ones*

You have put on Christ. There is no reason to be bent over after His touch. You can
walk with respect even when you have past failures.

He daily increases lies and desolation.
Also they make a covenant with the Assyrians,
And oil is carried to Egypt.

2 "The LORD also *brings* a charge against Judah,
And will punish Jacob according to his ways;
According to his deeds He will recompense him.

3 He took his brother by the heel in the womb,
And in his strength he struggled with God.*a*

4 Yes, he struggled with the Angel and prevailed;
He wept, and sought favor from Him.
He found Him *in* Bethel,
And there He spoke to us—

5 That is, the LORD God of hosts.
The LORD *is* His memorable name.

6 So you, by *the help of* your God, return;
Observe mercy and justice,
And wait on your God continually.

7 "A cunning Canaanite!
Deceitful scales *are* in his hand;
He loves to oppress.

8 And Ephraim said,
'Surely I have become rich,
I have found wealth for myself;
In all my labors
They shall find in me no iniquity that *is* sin.'

9 "But I *am* the LORD your God,
Ever since the land of Egypt;
I will again make you dwell in tents,
As in the days of the appointed feast.

10 I have also spoken by the prophets,
And have multiplied visions;
I have given symbols through the witness of the prophets."

11 Though Gilead *has* idols—
Surely they are vanity—
Though they sacrifice bulls in Gilgal,
Indeed their altars *shall be* heaps in the furrows of the field.

12 Jacob fled to the country of Syria;
Israel served for a spouse,
And for a wife he tended *sheep*.

13 By a prophet the LORD brought Israel out of Egypt,
And by a prophet he was preserved.

14 Ephraim provoked *Him* to anger most bitterly;
Therefore his Lord will leave the guilt of his bloodshed upon him,
And return his reproach upon him.

13 When Ephraim spoke, trembling,
He exalted *himself* in Israel;
But when he offended through Baal *worship*, he died.

2 Now they sin more and more,
And have made for themselves molded images,
Idols of their silver, according to their skill;
All of it *is* the work of craftsmen.
They say of them,
"Let the men who sacrifice*a* kiss the calves!"

3 Therefore they shall be like the morning cloud
And like the early dew that passes away,
Like chaff blown off from a threshing floor
And like smoke from a chimney.

4 "Yet I *am* the LORD your God
Ever since the land of Egypt,
And you shall know no God but Me;
For *there is* no savior besides Me.

5 I knew you in the wilderness,
In the land of great drought.

6 When they had pasture, they were filled;
They were filled and their heart was exalted;
Therefore they forgot Me.

7 "So I will be to them like a lion;
Like a leopard by the road I will lurk;

8 I will meet them like a bear deprived *of her cubs;*
I will tear open their rib cage,

13:3 *a*Compare Genesis 32:28   13:2 *a*Or *those who offer human sacrifice*

Gospel Pearls

And there I will devour them
   like a lion.
The wild beast shall tear them.

9 "O Israel, you are destroyed,*a*
   But your help*b* *is* from Me.
10 I will be your King;*a*
   Where *is any other,*
   That he may save you in all
      your cities?
   And your judges to whom you
      said,
   'Give me a king and princes'?
11 I gave you a king in My anger,
   And took *him* away in My
      wrath.

12 "The iniquity of Ephraim *is*
     bound up;
   His sin *is* stored up.
13 The sorrows of a woman in
     childbirth shall come upon
     him.
   He *is* an unwise son,
   For he should not stay long
     where children are born.

14 "I will ransom them from the
     power of the grave;*a*
   I will redeem them from death.
   O Death, I will be your
     plagues!*b*
   O Grave,*c* I will be your
     destruction!*d*
   Pity is hidden from My eyes.

15 Though he is fruitful among *his*
     brethren,
   An east wind shall come;
   The wind of the LORD shall
     come up from the wilderness.
   Then his spring shall become
     dry,
   And his fountain shall be dried
     up.
   He shall plunder the treasury
     of every desirable prize.
16 Samaria is held guilty,*a*
   For she has rebelled against
     her God.
   They shall fall by the sword,
   Their infants shall be dashed in
     pieces,
   And their women with child
     ripped open.

14 O Israel, return to the LORD
     your God,

For you have stumbled because
   of your iniquity;
2 Take words with you,
   And return to the LORD.
   Say to Him,
   "Take away all iniquity;
   Receive *us* graciously,
   For we will offer the sacrifices*a*
     of our lips.
3 Assyria shall not save us,
   We will not ride on horses,
   Nor will we say anymore to the
     work of our hands,
   '*You are* our gods.'
   For in You the fatherless finds
     mercy."

4 "I will heal their backsliding,
   I will love them freely,
   For My anger has turned away
     from him.
5 I will be like the dew to
     Israel;
   He shall grow like the lily,
   And lengthen his roots like
     Lebanon.
6 His branches shall spread;
   His beauty shall be like an olive
     tree,
   And his fragrance like
     Lebanon.
7 Those who dwell under his
     shadow shall return;
   They shall be revived *like*
     grain,
   And grow like a vine.
   Their scent*a* *shall be* like the
     wine of Lebanon.

8 "Ephraim *shall say,*
   'What have I to do anymore
     with idols?'
   I have heard and observed
     him.
   I *am* like a green cypress
     tree;
   Your fruit is found in Me."

9 Who *is* wise?
   Let him understand these
     things.
   Who is prudent?
   Let him know them.
   For the ways of the LORD *are*
     right;
   The righteous walk in them,
   But transgressors stumble in
     them.

13:9 *a*Literally *it* or *he destroyed you* *b*Literally *in your help*   13:10 *a*Septuagint, Syriac, Targum, and Vulgate read *Where is your king?*   13:14 *a*Or *Sheol* *b*Septuagint reads *where is your punishment?* *c*Or *Sheol* *d*Septuagint reads *Where is your sting?*   13:16 *a*Septuagint reads *shall be disfigured* 14:2 *a*Literally *bull calves;* Septuagint reads *fruit.*   14:7 *a*Literally *remembrance*

*R*eal spiritual advantage does not come from the color of your skin. It's not the color of your skin that will bring deliverance and help from God; it's the contents of your heart.

The Book of

JOEL

1 The word of the LORD that came to Joel the son of Pethuel.

2 Hear this, you elders,
And give ear, all you
    inhabitants of the land!
Has *anything like* this
    happened in your days,
Or even in the days of your
    fathers?
3 Tell your children about it,
Let your children *tell* their
    children,
And their children another
    generation.

4 What the chewing locust^a left,
    the swarming locust has
    eaten;
What the swarming locust left,
    the crawling locust has
    eaten;
And what the crawling locust
    left, the consuming locust has
    eaten.

5 Awake, you drunkards, and
    weep;
And wail, all you drinkers of
    wine,
Because of the new wine,
For it has been cut off from
    your mouth.
6 For a nation has come up
    against My land,
Strong, and without number;
His teeth *are* the teeth of a lion,
And he has the fangs of a fierce
    lion.

7 He has laid waste My vine,
And ruined My fig tree;
He has stripped it bare and
    thrown *it* away;
Its branches are made white.

8 Lament like a virgin girded
    with sackcloth
For the husband of her youth.
9 The grain offering and the
    drink offering
Have been cut off from the
    house of the LORD;
The priests mourn, who
    minister to the LORD.
10 The field is wasted,

The land mourns;
For the grain is ruined,
The new wine is dried up,
The oil fails.

11 Be ashamed, you farmers,
Wail, you vinedressers,
For the wheat and the barley;
Because the harvest of the field
    has perished.
12 The vine has dried up,
And the fig tree has withered;
The pomegranate tree,
The palm tree also,
And the apple tree—
All the trees of the field are
    withered;
Surely joy has withered away
    from the sons of men.

13 Gird yourselves and lament,
    you priests;
Wail, you who minister before
    the altar;
Come, lie all night in sackcloth,
You who minister to my God;
For the grain offering and the
    drink offering
Are withheld from the house of
    your God.
14 Consecrate a fast,
Call a sacred assembly;
Gather the elders
And all the inhabitants of the
    land
Into the house of the LORD your
    God,
And cry out to the LORD.

15 Alas for the day!
For the day of the LORD *is* at
    hand;
It shall come as destruction
    from the Almighty.
16 Is not the food cut off before
    our eyes,
Joy and gladness from the
    house of our God?
17 The seed shrivels under the
    clods,
Storehouses are in shambles;
Barns are broken down,
For the grain has withered.
18 How the animals groan!
The herds of cattle are restless,

1:4 ^aExact identity of these locusts is unknown.

Gospel Pearls

Because they have no pasture;
Even the flocks of sheep suffer
punishment.[a]

19 O LORD, to You I cry out;
For fire has devoured the open
pastures,
And a flame has burned all the
trees of the field.
20 The beasts of the field also cry
out to You,
For the water brooks are dried
up,
And fire has devoured the open
pastures.

2 Blow the trumpet in Zion,
And sound an alarm in My holy
mountain!
Let all the inhabitants of the
land tremble;
For the day of the LORD is
coming,
For it is at hand:
2 A day of darkness and
gloominess,
A day of clouds and thick
darkness,
Like the morning *clouds* spread
over the mountains.
A people *come*, great and
strong,
The like of whom has never
been;
Nor will there ever be any *such*
after them,
Even for many successive
generations.

3 A fire devours before them,
And behind them a flame
burns;
The land *is* like the Garden of
Eden before them,
And behind them a desolate
wilderness;
Surely nothing shall escape
them.
4 Their appearance is like the
appearance of horses;
And like swift steeds, so they
run.
5 With a noise like chariots
Over mountaintops they leap,
Like the noise of a flaming fire
that devours the stubble,
Like a strong people set in
battle array.

6 Before them the people writhe
in pain;
All faces are drained of color.[a]
7 They run like mighty men,
They climb the wall like men
of war;
Every one marches in
formation,
And they do not break ranks.
8 They do not push one another;
Every one marches in his own
column.[a]
Though they lunge between the
weapons,
They are not cut down.[b]
9 They run to and fro in the city,
They run on the wall;
They climb into the houses,
They enter at the windows like
a thief.
10 The earth quakes before them,
The heavens tremble;
The sun and moon grow dark,
And the stars diminish their
brightness.
11 The LORD gives voice before
His army,
For His camp is very great;
For strong *is the One* who
executes His word.
For the day of the LORD *is* great
and very terrible;
Who can endure it?

12 "Now, therefore," says the LORD,
"Turn to Me with all your heart,
With fasting, with weeping,
and with mourning."
13 So rend your heart, and not
your garments;
Return to the LORD your God,
For He *is* gracious and
merciful,
Slow to anger, and of great
kindness;
And He relents from doing
harm.
14 Who knows *if* He will turn and
relent,
And leave a blessing behind
Him—
A grain offering and a drink
offering
For the LORD your God?

15 Blow the trumpet in Zion,
Consecrate a fast,
Call a sacred assembly;
16 Gather the people,

1:18 [a]Septuagint and Vulgate read *are made desolate.* 2:6 [a]Septuagint, Targum, and Vulgate read *gather blackness.* 2:8 [a]Literally *his own highway* [b]That is, they are not halted by losses

There is no such thing as a black church. There is no such thing as a white church. It's only one Church, purchased by the blood of the Lamb. We are all one in Christ Jesus.

Sanctify the congregation,
Assemble the elders,
Gather the children and
    nursing babes;
Let the bridegroom go out from
    his chamber,
And the bride from her
    dressing room.
17 Let the priests, who minister to
    the LORD,
Weep between the porch and
    the altar;
Let them say, "Spare Your
    people, O LORD,
And do not give Your heritage
    to reproach,
That the nations should rule
    over them.
Why should they say among
    the peoples,
'Where is their God?' "

18 Then the LORD will be zealous
    for His land,
And pity His people.
19 The LORD will answer and say
    to His people,
"Behold, I will send you grain
    and new wine and oil,
And you will be satisfied by
    them;
I will no longer make you a
    reproach among the nations.

20 "But I will remove far from you
    the northern *army*,
And will drive him away into
    a barren and desolate land,
With his face toward the
    eastern sea
And his back toward the
    western sea;
His stench will come up,
And his foul odor will rise,
Because he has done
    monstrous things."

21 Fear not, O land;
Be glad and rejoice,
For the LORD has done
    marvelous things!
22 Do not be afraid, you beasts of
    the field;
For the open pastures are
    springing up,
And the tree bears its fruit;
The fig tree and the vine yield
    their strength.
23 Be glad then, you children of
    Zion,

And rejoice in the LORD your
    God;
For He has given you the
    former rain faithfully,*a*
And He will cause the rain to
    come down for you—
The former rain,
And the latter rain in the first
    month.
24 The threshing floors shall be
    full of wheat,
And the vats shall overflow
    with new wine and oil.

25 "So I will restore to you the
    years that the swarming
    locust has eaten,
The crawling locust,
The consuming locust,
And the chewing locust,*a*
My great army which I sent
    among you.
26 You shall eat in plenty and be
    satisfied,
And praise the name of the
    LORD your God,
Who has dealt wondrously
    with you;
And My people shall never be
    put to shame.
27 Then you shall know that I *am*
    in the midst of Israel:
I *am* the LORD your God
And there is no other.
My people shall never be put
    to shame.

28 "And it shall come to pass
    afterward
That I will pour out My Spirit
    on all flesh;
Your sons and your daughters
    shall prophesy,
Your old men shall dream
    dreams,
Your young men shall see
    visions.
29 And also on *My* menservants
    and on *My* maidservants
I will pour out My Spirit in
    those days.

30 "And I will show wonders
    in the heavens and in the
    earth:
Blood and fire and pillars of
    smoke.
31 The sun shall be turned into
    darkness,
And the moon into blood,

2:23 *a*Or *the teacher of righteousness*   2:25 *a*Compare 1:4

God doesn't look at your gender. He looks at your heart. He doesn't look at morality and good works. He looks at the faith that lives within. God is looking in your heart.

God's Handmaidens

Joel 2:29

Some of you do not understand the benefits of being single. In reality, while you're not married, you really ought to be involved with God. Single women often forget some very important advantages they have. At five o'clock in the morning, you can lie in bed and pray in the spirit until seven-thirty. You can lie prostrate on the floor and worship the Lord without having to answer to anyone. This time in your life is for you to charge up the battery cells. It's time to pamper—time to take luxurious baths in milk and honey. You can lie there in the bath, praising and worshiping the Lord for as long as you want.

Before you ask the Lord for another man, take care of Him. If you are not ministering to His needs, and yet you are always before Him asking Him to send you one of His princes to minister to, your prayers are not being heard because you are not being faithful to Him. When you become faithful in your singleness, then you will be better prepared to be faithful with a husband.

If you disregard the perfect husband, Jesus, you will certainly disregard the rest of us. The Lord wants you to come home at the end of a day and say, "Lord, I went through so much today. I am so glad You're here. I just couldn't wait to get alone and worship You and praise You and magnify You. Tonight is our night. I'm not so busy that I don't have time for You." If you don't have time for God, you don't have time for a husband.

There is nothing wrong with wanting to be married. Simply take care of the Lord while you're waiting. Minister to Him. Let Him heal you and loose you, and worship Him. Single women ought to be the most consecrated women in the church. You are the ones whose shadows ought to fall on people and they be healed. You are in a position and posture of prayer. The Lord has become your necessary food. While some married women are dependent on their husbands, single women learn to be dependent on the Lord. God told Joel, ". . . and on My maidservants I will pour out My Spirit" (Joel 2:29). There is a special relationship between God and the single believer. God has a special anointing for the woman who is free to seek Him. Her prayer life should explode in miracles!

Before the coming of the great
and awesome day of the
Lord.

32 And it shall come to pass
That whoever calls on the
name of the Lord
Shall be saved.
For in Mount Zion and in
Jerusalem there shall be
deliverance,
As the Lord has said,
Among the remnant whom the
Lord calls.

3 "For behold, in those days and
at that time,
When I bring back the captives
of Judah and Jerusalem,

2 I will also gather all nations,
And bring them down to the
Valley of Jehoshaphat;
And I will enter into judgment
with them there
On account of My people, My
heritage Israel,
Whom they have scattered
among the nations;
They have also divided up My
land.

3 They have cast lots for My
people,
Have given a boy *as payment*
for a harlot,
And sold a girl for wine, that
they may drink.

4 "Indeed, what have you to do
with Me,
O Tyre and Sidon, and all the
coasts of Philistia?
Will you retaliate against Me?
But if you retaliate against
Me,
Swiftly and speedily I will
return your retaliation upon
your own head;

5 Because you have taken My
silver and My gold,
And have carried into your
temples My prized
possessions.

6 Also the people of Judah and
the people of Jerusalem
You have sold to the Greeks,
That you may remove them far
from their borders.

7 "Behold, I will raise them
Out of the place to which you
have sold them,

And will return your retaliation
upon your own head.

8 I will sell your sons and your
daughters
Into the hand of the people of
Judah,
And they will sell them to the
Sabeans,[a]
To a people far off;
For the Lord has spoken."

9 Proclaim this among the
nations:
"Prepare for war!
Wake up the mighty men,
Let all the men of war draw
near,
Let them come up.

10 Beat your plowshares into
swords
And your pruning hooks into
spears;
Let the weak say, 'I *am*
strong.' "

11 Assemble and come, all you
nations,
And gather together all around.
Cause Your mighty ones to go
down there, O Lord.

12 "Let the nations be wakened,
and come up to the Valley of
Jehoshaphat;
For there I will sit to judge all
the surrounding nations.

13 Put in the sickle, for the harvest
is ripe.
Come, go down;
For the winepress is full,
The vats overflow—
For their wickedness *is* great."

14 Multitudes, multitudes in the
valley of decision!
For the day of the Lord *is* near
in the valley of decision.

15 The sun and moon will grow
dark,
And the stars will diminish
their brightness.

16 The Lord also will roar from
Zion,
And utter His voice from
Jerusalem;
The heavens and earth will
shake;
But the Lord will be a shelter
for His people,
And the strength of the
children of Israel.

3:8 *a*Literally *Shebaites* (compare Isaiah 60:6 and Ezekiel 27:22)

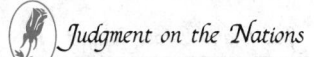

17 "So you shall know that I *am* the
LORD your God,
Dwelling in Zion My holy
mountain.
Then Jerusalem shall be holy,
And no aliens shall ever pass
through her again."

18 And it will come to pass in that
day
That the mountains shall drip
with new wine,
The hills shall flow with milk,
And all the brooks of Judah
shall be flooded with water;
A fountain shall flow from the
house of the LORD

And water the Valley of
Acacias.

19 "Egypt shall be a desolation,
And Edom a desolate
wilderness,
Because of violence *against* the
people of Judah,
For they have shed innocent
blood in their land.
20 But Judah shall abide forever,
And Jerusalem from
generation to generation.
21 For I will acquit them of the
guilt of bloodshed, whom I
had not acquitted;
For the LORD dwells in Zion."

The Book of
AMOS

1 The words of Amos, who was
among the sheepbreeders[a] of
Tekoa, which he saw concerning Israel in the days of Uzziah king of Judah, and in the days of Jeroboam the
son of Joash, king of Israel, two years
before the earthquake.
2 And he said:

"The LORD roars from Zion,
And utters His voice from
Jerusalem;
The pastures of the shepherds
mourn,
And the top of Carmel
withers."

3 Thus says the LORD:

"For three transgressions of
Damascus, and for four,
I will not turn away its
punishment,
Because they have threshed
Gilead with implements of
iron.
4 But I will send a fire into the
house of Hazael,
Which shall devour the palaces
of Ben-Hadad.
5 I will also break the *gate* bar
of Damascus,

And cut off the inhabitant from
the Valley of Aven,
And the one who holds the
scepter from Beth Eden.
The people of Syria shall go
captive to Kir,"
Says the LORD.

6 Thus says the LORD:

"For three transgressions of
Gaza, and for four,
I will not turn away its
punishment,
Because they took captive the
whole captivity
To deliver *them* up to Edom.
7 But I will send a fire upon the
wall of Gaza,
Which shall devour its
palaces.
8 I will cut off the inhabitant from
Ashdod,
And the one who holds the
scepter from Ashkelon;
I will turn My hand against
Ekron,
And the remnant of the
Philistines shall perish,"
Says the Lord GOD.

9 Thus says the LORD:

1:1 ᵃCompare 2 Kings 3:4

2 f you will but dare to believe that you are a daughter of Abraham, you will find the
power to stand up straight and be unleashed. The potential that has been bound
will then truly be set free.

"For three transgressions of
Tyre, and for four,
I will not turn away its
punishment,
Because they delivered up the
whole captivity to Edom,
And did not remember the
covenant of brotherhood.
10 But I will send a fire upon the
wall of Tyre,
Which shall devour its
palaces."

11 Thus says the LORD:

"For three transgressions of
Edom, and for four,
I will not turn away its
punishment,
Because he pursued his brother
with the sword,
And cast off all pity;
His anger tore perpetually,
And he kept his wrath forever.
12 But I will send a fire upon
Teman,
Which shall devour the palaces
of Bozrah."

13 Thus says the LORD:

"For three transgressions of the
people of Ammon, and for
four,
I will not turn away its
punishment,
Because they ripped open the
women with child in Gilead,
That they might enlarge their
territory.
14 But I will kindle a fire in the
wall of Rabbah,
And it shall devour its palaces,
Amid shouting in the day of
battle,
And a tempest in the day of the
whirlwind.
15 Their king shall go into
captivity,
He and his princes together,"
Says the LORD.

2 Thus says the LORD:

"For three transgressions of
Moab, and for four,
I will not turn away its
punishment,
Because he burned the bones
of the king of Edom to lime.

2 But I will send a fire upon
Moab,
And it shall devour the palaces
of Kerioth;
Moab shall die with tumult,
With shouting *and* trumpet
sound.
3 And I will cut off the judge from
its midst,
And slay all its princes with
him,"
Says the LORD.

4 Thus says the LORD:

"For three transgressions of
Judah, and for four,
I will not turn away its
punishment,
Because they have despised the
law of the LORD,
And have not kept His
commandments.
Their lies lead them astray,
Lies which their fathers
followed.
5 But I will send a fire upon
Judah,
And it shall devour the palaces
of Jerusalem."

6 Thus says the LORD:

"For three transgressions of
Israel, and for four,
I will not turn away its
punishment,
Because they sell the righteous
for silver,
And the poor for a pair of
sandals.
7 They pant after[a] the dust of the
earth *which is* on the head of
the poor,
And pervert the way of the
humble.
A man and his father go in to
the *same* girl,
To defile My holy name.
8 They lie down by every
altar on clothes taken in
pledge,
And drink the wine of the
condemned *in* the house of
their god.

9 "Yet *it was* I *who* destroyed the
Amorite before them,
Whose height *was* like the
height of the cedars,

2:7 *a*Or *trample on*

And he *was as* strong as the
oaks;
Yet I destroyed his fruit above
And his roots beneath.
10 Also *it was* I *who* brought you
up from the land of Egypt,
And led you forty years
through the wilderness,
To possess the land of the
Amorite.
11 I raised up some of your sons
as prophets,
And some of your young men
as Nazirites.
Is it not so, O you children of
Israel?"
Says the LORD.
12 "But you gave the Nazirites wine
to drink,
And commanded the prophets
saying,
'Do not prophesy!'

13 "Behold, I am weighed down by
you,
As a cart full of sheaves is
weighed down.
14 Therefore flight shall perish
from the swift,
The strong shall not strengthen
his power,
Nor shall the mighty deliver
himself;
15 He shall not stand who handles
the bow,
The swift of foot shall not
escape,
Nor shall he who rides a horse
deliver himself.
16 The most courageous men of
might
Shall flee naked in that day,"
Says the LORD.

3 Hear this word that the LORD has
spoken against you, O children of
Israel, against the whole family
which I brought up from the land of
Egypt, saying:

2 "You only have I known of all
the families of the earth;
Therefore I will punish you for
all your iniquities."

3 Can two walk together, unless
they are agreed?
4 Will a lion roar in the forest,
when he has no prey?
Will a young lion cry out of his

den, if he has caught
nothing?
5 Will a bird fall into a snare on
the earth, where there is no
trap for it?
Will a snare spring up from the
earth, if it has caught nothing
at all?
6 If a trumpet is blown in a city,
will not the people be
afraid?
If there is calamity in a city,
will not the LORD have done
it?

7 Surely the Lord GOD does
nothing,
Unless He reveals His secret to
His servants the prophets.
8 A lion has roared!
Who will not fear?
The Lord GOD has spoken!
Who can but prophesy?

9 "Proclaim in the palaces at
Ashdod,
And in the palaces in the land
of Egypt, and say:
'Assemble on the mountains of
Samaria;
See great tumults in her midst,
And the oppressed within her.
10 For they do not know to do
right,'
Says the LORD,
'Who store up violence and
robbery in their palaces.' "

11 Therefore thus says the Lord
GOD:

"An adversary *shall be* all
around the land;
He shall sap your strength from
you,
And your palaces shall be
plundered."

12 Thus says the LORD:

"As a shepherd takes from the
mouth of a lion
Two legs or a piece of an ear,
So shall the children of Israel
be taken out
Who dwell in Samaria—
In the corner of a bed and on
the edge^a of a couch!
13 Hear and testify against the
house of Jacob,"

3:12 ^aThe Hebrew is uncertain.

Attitudes affect the way we live our lives. A good attitude can bring success. A
poor attitude can bring destruction.

Says the Lord God, the God of
hosts,

14 "That in the day I punish Israel
for their transgressions,
I will also visit *destruction* on
the altars of Bethel;
And the horns of the altar shall
be cut off
And fall to the ground.

15 I will destroy the winter house
along with the summer
house;
The houses of ivory shall
perish,
And the great houses shall
have an end,"
Says the Lord.

4 Hear this word, you cows of
Bashan, who *are* on the
mountain of Samaria,
Who oppress the poor,
Who crush the needy,
Who say to your husbands,*a*
"Bring *wine,* let us drink!"

2 The Lord God has sworn by His
holiness:
"Behold, the days shall come
upon you
When He will take you away
with fishhooks,
And your posterity with
fishhooks.

3 You will go out *through* broken
walls,
Each one straight ahead of her,
And you will be cast into
Harmon,"
Says the Lord.

4 "Come to Bethel and transgress,
At Gilgal multiply
transgression;
Bring your sacrifices every
morning,
Your tithes every three days.*a*

5 Offer a sacrifice of
thanksgiving with leaven,
Proclaim *and* announce the
freewill offerings;
For this you love,
You children of Israel!"
Says the Lord God.

6 "Also I gave you cleanness of
teeth in all your cities.
And lack of bread in all your
places;
Yet you have not returned to
Me,"
Says the Lord.

7 "I also withheld rain from you,
When *there were* still three
months to the harvest.
I made it rain on one city,
I withheld rain from another
city.
One part was rained upon,
And where it did not rain the
part withered.

8 So two *or* three cities wandered
to another city to drink
water,
But they were not satisfied;
Yet you have not returned to
Me,"
Says the Lord.

9 "I blasted you with blight and
mildew.
When your gardens increased,
Your vineyards,
Your fig trees,
And your olive trees,
The locust devoured *them;*
Yet you have not returned to
Me,"
Says the Lord.

10 "I sent among you a plague after
the manner of Egypt;
Your young men I killed with
a sword,
Along with your captive
horses;
I made the stench of your
camps come up into your
nostrils;
Yet you have not returned to
Me,"
Says the Lord.

11 "I overthrew *some* of you,
As God overthrew Sodom and
Gomorrah,
And you were like a firebrand
plucked from the burning;
Yet you have not returned to
Me,"
Says the Lord.

12 "Therefore thus will I do to you,
O Israel;
Because I will do this to you,
Prepare to meet your God, O
Israel!"

13 For behold,
He who forms mountains,
And creates the wind,
Who declares to man what his*a*
thought *is,*

4:1 *a*Literally *their lords* or *their masters*   4:4 *a*Or *years* (compare Deuteronomy 14:28)   4:13 *a*Or *His*

Gospel
Pearls

And makes the morning
darkness,
Who treads the high places of
the earth—
The LORD God of hosts *is* His
name.

5 Hear this word which I take up
against you, a lamentation, O
house of Israel:

2 The virgin of Israel has fallen;
She will rise no more.
She lies forsaken on her land;
There is no one to raise her up.

3 For thus says the Lord GOD:

"The city that goes out by a
thousand
Shall have a hundred left,
And that which goes out by a
hundred
Shall have ten left to the house
of Israel."

4 For thus says the LORD to the
house of Israel:

"Seek Me and live;
5 But do not seek Bethel,
Nor enter Gilgal,
Nor pass over to Beersheba;
For Gilgal shall surely go into
captivity,
And Bethel shall come to
nothing.
6 Seek the LORD and live,
Lest He break out like fire *in*
the house of Joseph,
And devour *it,*
With no one to quench *it* in
Bethel—
7 You who turn justice to
wormwood,
And lay righteousness to rest
in the earth!"

8 He made the Pleiades and
Orion;
He turns the shadow of death
into morning
And makes the day dark as
night;
He calls for the waters of the
sea
And pours them out on the face
of the earth;
The LORD *is* His name.
9 He rains ruin upon the strong,
So that fury comes upon the
fortress.

10 They hate the one who rebukes
in the gate,
And they abhor the one who
speaks uprightly.
11 Therefore, because you tread
down the poor
And take grain taxes from
him,
Though you have built houses
of hewn stone,
Yet you shall not dwell in them;
You have planted pleasant
vineyards,
But you shall not drink wine
from them.
12 For I know your manifold
transgressions
And your mighty sins:
Afflicting the just *and* taking
bribes;
Diverting the poor *from justice*
at the gate.
13 Therefore the prudent keep
silent at that time,
For it *is* an evil time.

14 Seek good and not evil,
That you may live;
So the LORD God of hosts will
be with you,
As you have spoken.
15 Hate evil, love good;
Establish justice in the gate.
It may be that the LORD God of
hosts
Will be gracious to the remnant
of Joseph.

16 Therefore the LORD God of hosts,
the Lord, says this:

"*There shall be* wailing in all
streets,
And they shall say in all the
highways,
'Alas! Alas!'
They shall call the farmer to
mourning,
And skillful lamenters to
wailing.
17 In all vineyards *there shall be*
wailing,
For I will pass through you,"
Says the LORD.

18 Woe to you who desire the day
of the LORD!
For what good *is* the day of the
LORD to you?
It *will be* darkness, and not
light.

*B*efore you get out of trouble, you need to straighten out your attitude. Until your
attitude is corrected, you can't be corrected.

19 It *will be* as though a man fled
    from a lion,
    And a bear met him!
    Or *as though* he went into the
    house,
    Leaned his hand on the wall,
    And a serpent bit him!
20 *Is* not the day of the LORD
    darkness, and not light?
    Is it not very dark, with no
    brightness in it?

21 "I hate, I despise your feast
    days,
    And I do not savor your sacred
    assemblies.
22 Though you offer Me burnt
    offerings and your grain
    offerings,
    I will not accept *them,*
    Nor will I regard your fattened
    peace offerings.
23 Take away from Me the noise
    of your songs,
    For I will not hear the melody
    of your stringed instruments.
24 But let justice run down like
    water,
    And righteousness like a
    mighty stream.

25 "Did you offer Me sacrifices and
    offerings
    In the wilderness forty years,
    O house of Israel?
26 You also carried Sikkuth[a] your
    king[b]
    And Chiun,[c] your idols,
    The star of your gods,
    Which you made for
    yourselves.
27 Therefore I will send you into
    captivity beyond Damascus,"
    Says the LORD, whose name *is*
    the God of hosts.

6 Woe to you *who are* at ease in
    Zion,
    And trust in Mount Samaria,
    Notable persons in the chief
    nation,
    To whom the house of Israel
    comes!
2 Go over to Calneh and see;
    And from there go to Hamath
    the great;
    Then go down to Gath of the
    Philistines.

Are *you* better than these
    kingdoms?
    Or is their territory greater
    than your territory?

3 *Woe to* you who put far off the
    day of doom,
    Who cause the seat of violence
    to come near;
4 Who lie on beds of ivory,
    Stretch out on your couches,
    Eat lambs from the flock
    And calves from the midst of
    the stall;
5 Who sing idly to the sound of
    stringed instruments,
    And invent for yourselves
    musical instruments like
    David;
6 Who drink wine from bowls,
    And anoint yourselves with the
    best ointments,
    But are not grieved for the
    affliction of Joseph.
7 Therefore they shall now go
    captive as the first of the
    captives,
    And those who recline at
    banquets shall be removed.

8 The Lord GOD has sworn by
    Himself,
    The LORD God of hosts says:
    "I abhor the pride of Jacob,
    And hate his palaces;
    Therefore I will deliver up *the*
    city
    And all that is in it."

9 Then it shall come to pass, that
if ten men remain in one house, they
shall die. 10 And when a relative *of
the dead,* with one who will burn *the
bodies,* picks up the bodies[a] to take
them out of the house, he will say to
one inside the house, "*Are there* any
more with you?"
    Then someone will say, "None."
    And he will say, "Hold your
tongue! For we dare not mention the
name of the LORD."

11 For behold, the LORD gives a
    command:
    He will break the great house
    into bits,
    And the little house into
    pieces.

5:26 aA pagan deity   bSeptuagint and Vulgate read *tabernacle of Moloch.*   cA pagan deity   6:10 aLiterally bones

12 Do horses run on rocks?
Does *one* plow *there* with
oxen?
Yet you have turned justice into
gall,
And the fruit of righteousness
into wormwood,
13 You who rejoice over Lo
Debar,*ᵃ*
Who say, "Have we not taken
Karnaim*ᵇ* for ourselves
By our own strength?"

14 "But, behold, I will raise up a
nation against you,
O house of Israel,"
Says the LORD God of hosts;
"And they will afflict you from
the entrance of Hamath
To the Valley of the Arabah."

7 Thus the Lord GOD showed me:
Behold, He formed locust swarms
at the beginning of the late crop; indeed *it was* the late crop after the
king's mowings. 2 And so it was,
when they had finished eating the
grass of the land, that I said:

"O Lord GOD, forgive, I pray!
Oh, that Jacob may stand,
For he *is* small!"
3 So the LORD relented
concerning this.
"It shall not be," said the LORD.

4 Thus the Lord GOD showed me:
Behold, the Lord GOD called for conflict by fire, and it consumed the
great deep and devoured the territory. 5 Then I said:

"O Lord GOD, cease, I pray!
Oh, that Jacob may stand,
For he *is* small!"
6 So the LORD relented
concerning this.
"This also shall not be," said the
Lord GOD.

7 Thus He showed me: Behold, the
Lord stood on a wall *made* with a
plumb line, with a plumb line in His
hand. 8 And the LORD said to me,
"Amos, what do you see?"
And I said, "A plumb line."
Then the Lord said:

"Behold, I am setting a plumb
line

In the midst of My people
Israel;
I will not pass by them
anymore.
9 The high places of Isaac shall
be desolate,
And the sanctuaries of Israel
shall be laid waste.
I will rise with the sword
against the house of
Jeroboam."

10 Then Amaziah the priest of
Bethel sent to Jeroboam king of Israel, saying, "Amos has conspired
against you in the midst of the house
of Israel. The land is not able to bear
all his words. 11 For thus Amos has
said:

'Jeroboam shall die by the
sword,
And Israel shall surely be led
away captive
From their own land.'"

12 Then Amaziah said to Amos:

"Go, you seer!
Flee to the land of Judah.
There eat bread,
And there prophesy.
13 But never again prophesy at
Bethel,
For it *is* the king's sanctuary,
And it *is* the royal residence."

14 Then Amos answered, and said
to Amaziah:

"I *was* no prophet,
Nor *was* I a son of a prophet,
But I *was* a sheepbreeder*ᵃ*
And a tender of sycamore fruit.
15 Then the LORD took me as I
followed the flock,
And the LORD said to me,
'Go, prophesy to My people
Israel.'
16 Now therefore, hear the word
of the LORD:
You say, 'Do not prophesy
against Israel,
And do not spout against the
house of Isaac.'

17 "Therefore thus says the LORD:

'Your wife shall be a harlot in
the city;

6:13 *ᵃ*Literally *Nothing* *ᵇ*Literally *Horns*, symbol of strength   7:14 *ᵃ*Compare 2 Kings 3:4

Christ wants to separate you from the source of your bitterness until it no longer
gives you the kind of attitude that makes you a carrier of pain.

Your sons and daughters shall
  fall by the sword;
Your land shall be divided by
  survey line;
You shall die in a defiled land;
And Israel shall surely be led
  away captive
From his own land.' "

8 Thus the Lord GOD showed me:
Behold, a basket of summer fruit.
2 And He said, "Amos, what do you
see?"

So I said, "A basket of summer
fruit."

Then the LORD said to me:

"The end has come upon My
  people Israel;
I will not pass by them
  anymore.
3   And the songs of the temple
  Shall be wailing in that day,"
  Says the Lord GOD—
"Many dead bodies everywhere,
They shall be thrown out in
  silence."

4   Hear this, you who swallow up*ᵃ*
  the needy,
  And make the poor of the land
  fail,

5 Saying:

"When will the New Moon be
  past,
That we may sell grain?
And the Sabbath,
That we may trade wheat?
Making the ephah small and
  the shekel large,
Falsifying the scales by
  deceit,
6   That we may buy the poor for
  silver,
  And the needy for a pair of
  sandals—
  Even sell the bad wheat?"

7   The LORD has sworn by the
  pride of Jacob:
"Surely I will never forget any
  of their works.
8   Shall the land not tremble for
  this,
  And everyone mourn who
  dwells in it?

All of it shall swell like the
  River,*ᵃ*
Heave and subside
Like the River of Egypt.

9 "And it shall come to pass in that
  day," says the Lord GOD,
"That I will make the sun go
  down at noon,
And I will darken the earth in
  broad daylight;
10   I will turn your feasts into
  mourning,
  And all your songs into
  lamentation;
I will bring sackcloth on every
  waist,
And baldness on every head;
I will make it like mourning for
  an only *son*,
And its end like a bitter day.

11 "Behold, the days are coming,"
  says the Lord GOD,
"That I will send a famine on the
  land,
Not a famine of bread,
Nor a thirst for water,
But of hearing the words of the
  LORD.
12   They shall wander from sea to
  sea,
  And from north to east;
  They shall run to and fro,
    seeking the word of the LORD,
  But shall not find *it*.

13 "In that day the fair virgins
  And strong young men
  Shall faint from thirst.
14   Those who swear by the sin*ᵃ*
  of Samaria,
  Who say,
'As your god lives, O Dan!'
And, 'As the way of Beersheba
  lives!'
They shall fall and never rise
  again."

9 I saw the Lord standing by the altar, and He said:

"Strike the doorposts, that the
  thresholds may shake,
And break them on the heads
  of them all.
I will slay the last of them with
  the sword.

8:4 *ᵃOr trample on* (compare 2:7)   8:8 *ᵃ*That is, the Nile; some Hebrew manuscripts, Septuagint, Syriac,
Targum, and Vulgate read *River* (compare 9:5); Masoretic Text reads *the light*.   8:14 *ᵃOr Ashima,* a
Syrian goddess

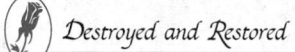

He who flees from them shall
not get away,
And he who escapes from them
shall not be delivered.
2 "Though they dig into hell,*a*
From there My hand shall take
them;
Though they climb up to
heaven,
From there I will bring them
down;
3 And though they hide
themselves on top of Carmel,
From there I will search and
take them;
Though they hide from My
sight at the bottom of the sea,
From there I will command the
serpent, and it shall bite
them;
4 Though they go into captivity
before their enemies,
From there I will command the
sword,
And it shall slay them.
I will set My eyes on them for
harm and not for good."

5 The Lord GOD of hosts,
He who touches the earth and
it melts,
And all who dwell there mourn;
All of it shall swell like the
River,*a*
And subside like the River of
Egypt.
6 He who builds His layers in the
sky,
And has founded His strata in
the earth;
Who calls for the waters of the
sea,
And pours them out on the face
of the earth—
The LORD *is* His name.

7 "*Are* you not like the people of
Ethiopia to Me,
O children of Israel?" says the
LORD.
"Did I not bring up Israel from
the land of Egypt,
The Philistines from Caphtor,
And the Syrians from Kir?

8 "Behold, the eyes of the Lord
GOD *are* on the sinful
kingdom,

And I will destroy it from the
face of the earth;
Yet I will not utterly destroy the
house of Jacob,"
Says the LORD.

9 "For surely I will command,
And will sift the house of Israel
among all nations,
As *grain* is sifted in a sieve;
Yet not the smallest grain shall
fall to the ground.
10 All the sinners of My people
shall die by the sword,
Who say, 'The calamity shall
not overtake nor confront
us.'

11 "On that day I will raise
up
The tabernacle*a* of David,
which has fallen down,
And repair its damages;
I will raise up its ruins,
And rebuild it as in the days of
old;
12 That they may possess the
remnant of Edom,*a*
And all the Gentiles who are
called by My name,"
Says the LORD who does this
thing.

13 "Behold, the days are coming," says the LORD,
"When the plowman shall
overtake the reaper,
And the treader of grapes him
who sows seed;
The mountains shall drip with
sweet wine,
And all the hills shall flow *with
it.*
14 I will bring back the captives
of My people Israel;
They shall build the waste
cities and inhabit *them;*
They shall plant vineyards and
drink wine from them;
They shall also make
gardens and eat fruit from
them.
15 I will plant them in their
land,
And no longer shall they be
pulled up
From the land I have given
them,"
Says the LORD your God.

9:2 *a*Or *Sheol*   9:5 *a*That is, the Nile   9:11 *a*Literally *booth,* figure of a deposed dynasty
9:12 *a*Septuagint reads *mankind.*

When God comes to heal, He wants to heal your emotions also. Sometimes all we pray about is our situation. Fixing circumstances is like applying a Band-Aid ©, though. Healing attitudes set people free to receive wholeness.

The Book of
OBADIAH

1 The vision of Obadiah.

Thus says the Lord GOD
concerning Edom
(We have heard a report from
the LORD,
And a messenger has been
sent among the nations,
saying,
"Arise, and let us rise up against
her for battle"):

2 "Behold, I will make you small
among the nations;
You shall be greatly despised.

3 The pride of your heart has
deceived you,
You who dwell in the clefts of
the rock,
Whose habitation is high;
You who say in your heart,
'Who will bring me down to the
ground?'

4 Though you ascend *as* high as
the eagle,
And though you set your nest
among the stars,
From there I will bring you
down," says the LORD.

5 "If thieves had come to you,
If robbers by night—
Oh, how you will be cut off!—
Would they not have stolen till
they had enough?
If grape-gatherers had come to
you,
Would they not have left *some*
gleanings?

6 "Oh, how Esau shall be searched
out!
How his hidden treasures shall
be sought after!

7 All the men in your
confederacy
Shall force you to the border;
The men at peace with you
Shall deceive you *and* prevail
against you.
Those who eat your bread shall
lay a trap[a] for you.
No one is aware of it.

8 "Will I not in that day," says the
LORD,

"Even destroy the wise *men*
from Edom,
And understanding from the
mountains of Esau?

9 Then your mighty men, O
Teman, shall be dismayed,
To the end that everyone from
the mountains of Esau
May be cut off by slaughter.

10 "For violence against your
brother Jacob,
Shame shall cover you,
And you shall be cut off
forever.

11 In the day that you stood on the
other side—
In the day that strangers
carried captive his forces,
When foreigners entered his
gates
And cast lots for Jerusalem—
Even you *were* as one of
them.

12 "But you should not have
gazed on the day of your
brother
In the day of his captivity;[a]
Nor should you have rejoiced
over the children of Judah
In the day of their destruction;
Nor should you have spoken
proudly
In the day of distress.

13 You should not have entered
the gate of My people
In the day of their calamity.
Indeed, you should not have
gazed on their affliction
In the day of their calamity,
Nor laid *hands* on their
substance
In the day of their calamity.

14 You should not have stood at
the crossroads
To cut off those among them
who escaped;
Nor should you have delivered
up those among them who
remained
In the day of distress.

15 "For the day of the LORD upon
all the nations *is* near;

7 *a*Or *wound*, or *plot*   12 *a*Literally *on the day he became a foreigner*

As you have done, it shall be
done to you;
Your reprisal shall return upon
your own head.
16 For as you drank on my holy
mountain,
So shall all the nations drink
continually;
Yes, they shall drink, and
swallow,
And they shall be as though
they had never been.

17 "But on Mount Zion there shall
be deliverance,
And there shall be holiness;
The house of Jacob shall
possess their
possessions.
18 The house of Jacob shall be a
fire,
And the house of Joseph a
flame;
But the house of Esau *shall be*
stubble;
They shall kindle them and
devour them,

19 The South*a* shall possess the
mountains of Esau,
And the Lowland shall possess
Philistia.
They shall possess the fields of
Ephraim
And the fields of Samaria.
Benjamin *shall possess* Gilead.
20 And the captives of this host of
the children of Israel
Shall possess the land of the
Canaanites
As far as Zarephath.
The captives of Jerusalem who
are in Sepharad
Shall possess the cities of the
South.*a*
21 Then saviors*a* shall come to
Mount Zion
To judge the mountains of
Esau,
And the kingdom shall be the
LORD'S.

And no survivor shall *remain*
of the house of Esau,"
For the LORD has spoken.

19 *a*Hebrew *Negev*   20 *a*Hebrew *Negev*   21 *a*Or *deliverers*

The Book of
JONAH

1 Now the word of the LORD came
to Jonah the son of Amittai, saying, 2 "Arise, go to Nineveh, that
great city, and cry out against it; for
their wickedness has come up before
Me." 3 But Jonah arose to flee to
Tarshish from the presence of the
LORD. He went down to Joppa, and
found a ship going to Tarshish; so
he paid the fare, and went down into
it, to go with them to Tarshish from
the presence of the LORD.

4 But the LORD sent out a great
wind on the sea, and there was a
mighty tempest on the sea, so that
the ship was about to be broken
up.

5 Then the mariners were afraid;
and every man cried out to his god,
and threw the cargo that *was* in the

ship into the sea, to lighten the load.*a*
But Jonah had gone down into the
lowest parts of the ship, had lain
down, and was fast asleep.

6 So the captain came to him, and
said to him, "What do you mean,
sleeper? Arise, call on your God; perhaps your God will consider us, so
that we may not perish."

7 And they said to one another,
"Come, let us cast lots, that we may
know for whose cause this trouble
has come upon us." So they cast lots,
and the lot fell on Jonah. 8 Then they
said to him, "Please tell us! For
whose cause *is* this trouble upon us?
What is your occupation? And where
do you come from? What is your
country? And of what people are
you?"

1:5 *a*Literally *from upon them*

The Lord is your defense. You do not have to defend yourself. When God has delivered you, do not stop what you're doing to answer your accusers. Continue to bless
His name, because you do not want your attitude to become defensive.

9 So he said to them, "I *am* a Hebrew; and I fear the LORD, the God of heaven, who made the sea and the dry *land*."

10 Then the men were exceedingly afraid, and said to him, "Why have you done this?" For the men knew that he fled from the presence of the LORD, because he had told them. 11 Then they said to him, "What shall we do to you that the sea may be calm for us?"—for the sea was growing more tempestuous.

12 And he said to them, "Pick me up and throw me into the sea; then the sea will become calm for you. For I know that this great tempest *is* because of me."

13 Nevertheless the men rowed hard to return to land, but they could not, for the sea continued to grow more tempestuous against them. 14 Therefore they cried out to the LORD and said, "We pray, O LORD, please do not let us perish for this man's life, and do not charge us with innocent blood; for You, O LORD, have done as it pleased You." 15 So they picked up Jonah and threw him into the sea, and the sea ceased from its raging. 16 Then the men feared the LORD exceedingly, and offered a sacrifice to the LORD and took vows.

17 Now the LORD had prepared a great fish to swallow Jonah. And Jonah was in the belly of the fish three days and three nights.

2 Then Jonah prayed to the LORD his God from the fish's belly. 2 And he said:

"I cried out to the LORD because of my affliction,
And He answered me.

"Out of the belly of Sheol I cried,
And You heard my voice.
3   For You cast me into the deep,
Into the heart of the seas,
And the floods surrounded me;
All Your billows and Your
waves passed over me.
4   Then I said, 'I have been cast
out of Your sight;
Yet I will look again toward
Your holy temple.'

5   The waters surrounded me,
even to my soul;
The deep closed around me;
Weeds were wrapped around
my head.
6   I went down to the moorings
of the mountains;
The earth with its bars *closed*
behind me forever;
Yet You have brought up my
life from the pit,
O LORD, my God.

7   "When my soul fainted within
me,
I remembered the LORD;
And my prayer went *up* to You,
Into Your holy temple.

8   "Those who regard worthless
idols
Forsake their own Mercy.
9   But I will sacrifice to You
With the voice of thanksgiving;
I will pay what I have vowed.
Salvation *is* of the LORD."

10 So the LORD spoke to the fish, and it vomited Jonah onto dry *land*.

3 Now the word of the LORD came to Jonah the second time, saying, 2 "Arise, go to Nineveh, that great city, and preach to it the message that I tell you." 3 So Jonah arose and went to Nineveh, according to the word of the LORD. Now Nineveh was an exceedingly great city, a three-day journey[a] *in extent*. 4 And Jonah began to enter the city on the first day's walk. Then he cried out and said, "Yet forty days, and Nineveh shall be overthrown!"

5 So the people of Nineveh believed God, proclaimed a fast, and put on sackcloth, from the greatest to the least of them. 6 Then word came to the king of Nineveh; and he arose from his throne and laid aside his robe, covered *himself* with sackcloth and sat in ashes. 7 And he caused *it* to be proclaimed and published throughout Nineveh by the decree of the king and his nobles, saying,

Let neither man nor beast, herd
nor flock, taste anything; do
not let them eat, or drink water.
8 But let man and beast be
covered with sackcloth, and cry
mightily to God;

3:3 aExact meaning unknown

When you're in trouble, God will reach into the mess and pull you out. However, you must be strong enough not to let people drag you back into it. Once God unleashes you, don't let anyone trap you into some religious fight.

Ouch!

Jonah 2:2

Some people think that real faith means having no feelings. But I believe that life without feelings is like a dry riverbed. Water is what gives the river activity and life. On the other hand, feelings that are out of control are like raging floodwaters. Since the gushing currents can bring death and destruction, they must be held at bay. Just as a river must remain within its banks, you must express your emotions without allowing them to run rampant.

Emotional pain is to the spirit what physical pain is to the body. Physical pain warns you that something in your body is out of order and requires attention, that you are not well. Emotional pain also points to an area where healing or restoration is needed. You dare not ignore these signals, nor should you let them control you.

Like a child who has fallen from his bicycle needs to find a private place where he can honestly say, "Ouch! That hurt more than I let on in front of my friends!" you, too, need a place of honesty. You need to be truthful with yourself. You need a place where you can sit down, reflect, and mourn. After the funeral, there is always a burial. The burial separates the survivor from the deceased, and it is as far as you can go. It is important to come to a place of separation and decide to live on.

It is important to understand the difference between minor and major adjustments. The removal of a person from your life may be painful, but it is not a major adjustment. Whether you realize it or not, people are being born and dying every day. They are coming and going, marrying and divorcing, falling in love and falling out of love. You can survive the loss of people, *but you can't survive without God!* He is the Force that allows you to overcome when people have taken you under. His grace enables you to overcome!

Unfortunately, many people leave their situation bitter and not better. Be careful to bring the richness of the experience to your pain, not the unresolved bitterness. This kind of bitterness is a sign that the healing process in you is not finished. When you have completed the full cycle of survival, the experiences in your life will produce no pain, only peace.

yes, let every one turn from his evil way and from the violence that is in his hands. 9 Who can tell *if* God will turn and relent, and turn away from His fierce anger, so that we may not perish?

10 Then God saw their works, that they turned from their evil way; and God relented from the disaster that He had said He would bring upon them, and He did not do it.

4 But it displeased Jonah exceedingly, and he became angry. 2 So he prayed to the LORD, and said, "Ah, LORD, was not this what I said when I was still in my country? Therefore I fled previously to Tarshish; for I know that You *are* a gracious and merciful God, slow to anger and abundant in lovingkindness, One who relents from doing harm. 3 Therefore now, O LORD, please take my life from me, for *it is* better for me to die than to live!"

4 Then the LORD said, "Is *it* right for you to be angry?"

5 So Jonah went out of the city and sat on the east side of the city. There he made himself a shelter and sat under it in the shade, till he might see what would become of the city. 6 And the LORD God prepared a plant*a* and made it come up over Jonah, that it might be shade for his head to deliver him from his misery. So Jonah was very grateful for the plant. 7 But as morning dawned the next day God prepared a worm, and it *so* damaged the plant that it withered. 8 And it happened, when the sun arose, that God prepared a vehement east wind; and the sun beat on Jonah's head, so that he grew faint. Then he wished death for himself, and said, "It *is* better for me to die than to live."

9 Then God said to Jonah, "Is *it* right for you to be angry about the plant?"

And he said, "It *is* right for me to be angry, even to death!"

10 But the LORD said, "You have had pity on the plant for which you have not labored, nor made it grow, which came up in a night and perished in a night. 11 And should I not pity Nineveh, that great city, in which are more than one hundred and twenty thousand persons who cannot discern between their right hand and their left—and much livestock?"

4:6 *a*Hebrew *kikayon,* exact identity unknown

The Book of

MICAH

1 The word of the LORD that came to Micah of Moresheth in the days of Jotham, Ahaz, *and* Hezekiah, kings of Judah, which he saw concerning Samaria and Jerusalem.

2   Hear, all you peoples!
    Listen, O earth, and all that is in it!
    Let the Lord GOD be a witness against you,
    The Lord from His holy temple.

3   For behold, the LORD is coming out of His place;

    He will come down
    And tread on the high places of the earth.

4   The mountains will melt under Him,
    And the valleys will split
    Like wax before the fire,
    Like waters poured down a steep place.

5   All this is for the transgression of Jacob
    And for the sins of the house of Israel.
    What *is* the transgression of Jacob?
    Is it not Samaria?

Gospel Pearls

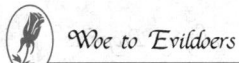

And what *are* the high places
  of Judah?
Are they not Jerusalem?

6 "Therefore I will make Samaria
    a heap of ruins in the field,
  Places for planting a vineyard;
  I will pour down her stones into
    the valley,
  And I will uncover her
    foundations.
7 All her carved images shall be
    beaten to pieces,
  And all her pay as a harlot shall
    be burned with the fire;
  All her idols I will lay desolate,
  For she gathered *it* from the
    pay of a harlot,
  And they shall return to the pay
    of a harlot."

8 Therefore I will wail and howl,
  I will go stripped and naked;
  I will make a wailing like the
    jackals
  And a mourning like the
    ostriches,
9 For her wounds *are* incurable.
  For it has come to Judah;
  It has come to the gate of My
    people—
  To Jerusalem.

10 Tell *it* not in Gath,
   Weep not at all;
   In Beth Aphrah[a]
   Roll yourself in the dust.
11 Pass by in naked shame, you
     inhabitant of Shaphir;
   The inhabitant of Zaanan[a] does
     not go out.
   Beth Ezel mourns;
   Its place to stand is taken away
     from you.

12 For the inhabitant of Maroth
     pined[a] for good,
   But disaster came down from
     the LORD
   To the gate of Jerusalem.
13 O inhabitant of Lachish,
   Harness the chariot to the swift
     steeds
   (She *was* the beginning of sin
     to the daughter of Zion),
   For the transgressions of Israel
     were found in you.

14 Therefore you shall give
     presents to Moresheth
     Gath;[a]
   The houses of Achzib[b] *shall be*
     a lie to the kings of Israel.
15 I will yet bring an heir to you,
     O inhabitant of Mareshah;[a]
   The glory of Israel shall come
     to Adullam.
16 Make yourself bald and cut off
     your hair,
   Because of your precious
     children;
   Enlarge your baldness like an
     eagle,
   For they shall go from you into
     captivity.

2 Woe to those who devise
    iniquity,
  And work out evil on their
    beds!
  At morning light they practice
    it,
  Because it is in the power of
    their hand.
2 They covet fields and take
    them by violence,
  Also houses, and seize *them*.
  So they oppress a man and his
    house,
  A man and his inheritance.

3 Therefore thus says the LORD:

"Behold, against this family I am
    devising disaster,
  From which you cannot remove
    your necks;
  Nor shall you walk haughtily,
  For this *is* an evil time.
4 In that day *one* shall take up a
    proverb against you,
  And lament with a bitter
    lamentation, saying:
  'We are utterly destroyed!
  He has changed the heritage of
    my people;
  How He has removed *it* from
    me!
  To a turncoat He has divided
    our fields.' "

5 Therefore you will have no one
    to determine boundaries[a] by
    lot
  In the assembly of the LORD.

1:10 [a]Literally *House of Dust*   1:11 [a]Literally *Going Out*   1:12 [a]Literally *was sick*   1:14 [a]Literally
Possession of Gath   [b]Literally *Lie*   1:15 [a]Literally *Inheritance*   2:5 [a]Literally *one casting a surveyor's
line*

*T*he Lord wants to speak a word of faith to you. He wants to set you free from every
power that has kept you in bondage. In order for that to be received in your spirit,
you must allow Him to come in and instill faith.

6 "Do not prattle," *you say to*
     those who prophesy.
     So they shall not prophesy to
     you;*a*
     They shall not return insult for
     insult.*b*
7   *You who are* named the house
     of Jacob:
     "Is the Spirit of the LORD
     restricted?
     Are these His doings?
     Do not My words do good
     To him who walks uprightly?

8 "Lately My people have risen up
     as an enemy—
     You pull off the robe with the
     garment
     From those who trust *you,* as
     they pass by,
     Like men returned from war.
9   The women of My people you
     cast out
     From their pleasant houses;
     From their children
     You have taken away My glory
     forever.

10 "Arise and depart,
     For this *is* not *your* rest;
     Because it is defiled, it shall
     destroy,
     Yes, with utter destruction.
11 If a man should walk in a false
     spirit
     And speak a lie, *saying,*
     'I will prophesy to you of wine
     and drink,'
     Even he would be the prattler
     of this people.

12 "I will surely assemble all of
     you, O Jacob,
     I will surely gather the remnant
     of Israel;
     I will put them together like
     sheep of the fold,*a*
     Like a flock in the midst of their
     pasture;
     They shall make a loud noise
     because of *so many* people.
13 The one who breaks open will
     come up before them;
     They will break out,
     Pass through the gate,
     And go out by it;
     Their king will pass before
     them,
     With the LORD at their head."

3 And I said:

     "Hear now, O heads of Jacob,
     And you rulers of the house of
     Israel:
     Is it not for you to know
     justice?
2 You who hate good and love
     evil;
     Who strip the skin from My
     people,*a*
     And the flesh from their bones;
3 Who also eat the flesh of My
     people,
     Flay their skin from them,
     Break their bones,
     And chop *them* in pieces
     Like *meat* for the pot,
     Like flesh in the caldron."

4 Then they will cry to the LORD,
     But He will not hear them;
     He will even hide His face from
     them at that time,
     Because they have been evil in
     their deeds.

5 Thus says the LORD concerning
     the prophets
     Who make my people stray;
     Who chant "Peace"
     While they chew with their
     teeth,
     But who prepare war against
     him
     Who puts nothing into their
     mouths:
6 "Therefore you shall have night
     without vision,
     And you shall have darkness
     without divination;
     The sun shall go down on the
     prophets,
     And the day shall be dark for
     them.
7 So the seers shall be ashamed,
     And the diviners abashed;
     Indeed they shall all cover their
     lips;
     For *there is* no answer from
     God."

8 But truly I am full of power by
     the Spirit of the LORD,
     And of justice and might,
     To declare to Jacob his
     transgression
     And to Israel his sin.
9 Now hear this,

2:6 *a*Literally *to these*   *b*Vulgate reads *He shall not take shame.*   2:12 *a*Hebrew *Bozrah*   3:2 *a*Literally *them*

Gospel Pearls

You heads of the house of
    Jacob
And rulers of the house of
    Israel,
Who abhor justice
And pervert all equity,
10 Who build up Zion with
    bloodshed
And Jerusalem with iniquity:
11 Her heads judge for a bribe,
Her priests teach for pay,
And her prophets divine for
    money.
Yet they lean on the LORD, and
    say,
    "Is not the LORD among us?
No harm can come upon us."
12 Therefore because of you
Zion shall be plowed *like* a
    field,
Jerusalem shall become heaps
    of ruins,
And the mountain of the
    temple*ª*
Like the bare hills of the forest.

4 Now it shall come to pass in the
    latter days
That the mountain of the
    LORD's house
Shall be established on the top
    of the mountains,
And shall be exalted above the
    hills;
And peoples shall flow to it.
2 Many nations shall come and
    say,
    "Come, and let us go up to the
    mountain of the LORD,
To the house of the God of
    Jacob;
He will teach us His ways,
And we shall walk in His
    paths."
For out of Zion the law shall
    go forth,
And the word of the LORD from
    Jerusalem.
3 He shall judge between many
    peoples,
And rebuke strong nations afar
    off;
They shall beat their swords
    into plowshares,
And their spears into pruning
    hooks;
Nation shall not lift up sword
    against nation,
Neither shall they learn war
    anymore.*ª*

4 But everyone shall sit under
    his vine and under his fig
    tree,
And no one shall make *them*
    afraid;
For the mouth of the LORD of
    hosts has spoken.
5 For all people walk each in the
    name of his god,
But we will walk in the name
    of the LORD our God
Forever and ever.

6 "In that day," says the LORD,
    "I will assemble the lame,
I will gather the outcast
And those whom I have
    afflicted;
7 I will make the lame a remnant,
And the outcast a strong
    nation;
So the LORD will reign over
    them in Mount Zion
From now on, even forever.
8 And you, O tower of the
    flock,
The stronghold of the daughter
    of Zion,
To you shall it come,
Even the former dominion shall
    come,
The kingdom of the daughter
    of Jerusalem."

9 Now why do you cry aloud?
Is there no king in your midst?
Has your counselor perished?
For pangs have seized you like
    a woman in labor.
10 Be in pain, and labor to bring
    forth,
O daughter of Zion,
Like a woman in birth pangs.
For now you shall go forth from
    the city,
You shall dwell in the field,
And to Babylon you shall go.
There you shall be delivered;
There the LORD will redeem you
From the hand of your enemies.

11 Now also many nations have
    gathered against you,
Who say, "Let her be defiled,
And let our eye look upon
    Zion."
12 But they do not know the
    thoughts of the LORD,
Nor do they understand His
    counsel;

3:12 *ª*Literally *house*   4:3 *ª*Compare Isaiah 2:2–4

*L*ove is eternal. It is not limited by time. When you commit yourself to loving
someone, you make that commitment to all the person is.

Passion to Continue

Micah 4:10

S ubmit your passions to the Father, just as our Lord submitted everything on the Cross, where He yielded all of His zeal and all of His strength. His passion was aimed at the joy set before Him—being the submitted Son of God. The Father tested the power of His Son's committed passion at Calvary. If it had not been effective, Jesus would have had to buy Joseph's tomb instead of borrow it.

Have you faced some tragedies that have left you in a state of shock? I remember going through a time of complete emptiness in my ministry. I had lost the passion to continue. It was almost as if nothing mattered to me anymore, and I isolated myself from everyone. I became indifferent about details—could care less whether or not things got done. I simply "disconnected." As long as I didn't care, it didn't hurt.

When God spoke to the first woman about childbirth, He spoke of sorrow and travail. He forewarned her of the violent, tempestuous pain of labor. The near-deathlike pains would come faster and harder as she drew closer to delivery.

However, God says that at the end of all this, He will recycle the relationship between the woman and the man by returning desire! He says, "Your desire shall be for your husband" (Genesis 3:16). God knows that there is no cure for past pain like present desire. If the desire is strong enough, the pain of the past will disappear like a shadow at high noon. The wounded and the weary ones will rise victoriously with new desire, and the cycle continues.

My sister, you may have gone through some life-shaking experience. But you can't live the rest of your life in fear and dread. God wants to renew your passion and revive your desire so that you will once again be powerful and productive for Him.

May the passion to be all that God wants you to be sweep across your soul like a gentle breeze. As the Bible says, Jesus "presented Himself alive after His suffering [passion] by many infallible proofs" (Acts 1:3). Do not hide, daughter of God. Show yourself alive with "many infallible proofs." As the passion to continue comes creeping back into your life, resist the temptation to hide behind the fig leaves of your past. Come out of hiding and show yourself!

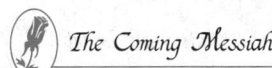

For He will gather them like
sheaves to the threshing
floor.

13 "Arise and thresh, O daughter of
Zion;
For I will make your horn
iron,
And I will make your hooves
bronze;
You shall beat in pieces many
peoples;
I will consecrate their gain to
the LORD,
And their substance to the Lord
of the whole earth."

5 Now gather yourself in troops,
O daughter of troops;
He has laid siege against us;
They will strike the judge of
Israel with a rod on the
cheek.
2 "But you, Bethlehem Ephrathah,
Though you are little among
the thousands of Judah,
Yet out of you shall come forth
to Me
The One to be Ruler in Israel,
Whose goings forth *are* from of
old,
From everlasting."

3 Therefore He shall give them
up,
Until the time *that* she who is
in labor has given birth;
Then the remnant of His
brethren
Shall return to the children of
Israel.
4 And He shall stand and feed
His flock
In the strength of the LORD,
In the majesty of the name of
the LORD His God;
And they shall abide,
For now He shall be great
To the ends of the earth;
5 And this *One* shall be peace.

When the Assyrian comes into
our land,
And when he treads in our
palaces,
Then we will raise against him
Seven shepherds and eight
princely men.
6 They shall waste with the
sword the land of Assyria,

And the land of Nimrod at its
entrances;
Thus He shall deliver *us* from
the Assyrian,
When he comes into our
land
And when he treads within our
borders.

7 Then the remnant of Jacob
Shall be in the midst of many
peoples,
Like dew from the LORD,
Like showers on the grass,
That tarry for no man
Nor wait for the sons of
men.
8 And the remnant of Jacob
Shall be among the Gentiles,
In the midst of many peoples,
Like a lion among the beasts
of the forest,
Like a young lion among flocks
of sheep,
Who, if he passes through,
Both treads down and tears in
pieces,
And none can deliver.
9 Your hand shall be lifted
against your adversaries,
And all your enemies shall be
cut off.

10 "And it shall be in that day,"
says the LORD,
"That I will cut off your horses
from your midst
And destroy your chariots.
11 I will cut off the cities of your
land
And throw down all your
strongholds.
12 I will cut off sorceries from
your hand,
And you shall have no
soothsayers.
13 Your carved images I will also
cut off,
And your sacred pillars from
your midst;
You shall no more worship the
work of your hands;
14 I will pluck your wooden
images[a] from your midst;
Thus I will destroy your
cities.
15 And I will execute vengeance
in anger and fury
On the nations that have not
heard."[a]

5:14 [a]Hebrew *Asherim*, Canaanite deities   5:15 [a]Or *obeyed*

Thousands walk in fear. The Church can give strength to counter that fear. Thousands have built a wall around them because they do not trust anyone else. The Church can help its members learn to trust one another.

6 Hear now what the LORD says:

"Arise, plead your case before
the mountains,
And let the hills hear your
voice.
2 Hear, O you mountains, the
LORD's complaint,
And you strong foundations of
the earth;
For the LORD has a complaint
against His people,
And He will contend with
Israel.

3 "O My people, what have I done
to you?
And how have I wearied you?
Testify against Me.
4 For I brought you up from the
land of Egypt,
I redeemed you from the house
of bondage;
And I sent before you Moses,
Aaron, and Miriam.
5 O My people, remember now
What Balak king of Moab
counseled,
And what Balaam the son of
Beor answered him,
From Acacia Grove[a] to Gilgal,
That you may know the
righteousness of the
LORD."

6 With what shall I come before
the LORD,
And bow myself before the
High God?
Shall I come before Him with
burnt offerings,
With calves a year old?
7 Will the LORD be pleased with
thousands of rams,
Ten thousand rivers of oil?
Shall I give my firstborn *for* my
transgression,
The fruit of my body *for* the sin
of my soul?

8 He has shown you, O man,
what *is* good;
And what does the LORD
require of you
But to do justly,
To love mercy,
And to walk humbly with your
God?

9 The LORD's voice cries to the
city—
Wisdom shall see Your name:

"Hear the rod!
Who has appointed it?
10 Are there yet the treasures of
wickedness
In the house of the wicked,
And the short measure *that is*
an abomination?
11 Shall I count pure *those* with
the wicked scales,
And with the bag of deceitful
weights?
12 For her rich men are full of
violence,
Her inhabitants have spoken
lies,
And their tongue is deceitful in
their mouth.

13 "Therefore I will also make *you*
sick by striking you,
By making *you* desolate
because of your sins.
14 You shall eat, but not be
satisfied;
Hunger[a] *shall be* in your
midst.
You may carry *some* away,[b]
but shall not save *them;*
And what you do rescue I will
give over to the sword.

15 "You shall sow, but not reap;
You shall tread the olives, but
not anoint yourselves with
oil;
And *make* sweet wine, but not
drink wine.
16 For the statutes of Omri are
kept;
All the works of Ahab's house
are done;
And you walk in their counsels,
That I may make you a
desolation,
And your inhabitants a hissing.
Therefore you shall bear the
reproach of My people."[a]

7 Woe is me!
For I am like those who gather
summer fruits,
Like those who glean vintage
grapes;
There is no cluster to eat

6:5 [a]Hebrew *Shittim* (compare Numbers 25:1; Joshua 2:1, 3:1)   6:14 [a]Or *Emptiness* or *Humiliation*
[b]Targum and Vulgate read *You shall take hold.*   6:16 [a]Following Masoretic Text, Targum, and Vulgate;
Septuagint reads *of nations.*

Gospel
Pearls

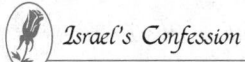

Of the first-ripe fruit *which* my
   soul desires.
2 The faithful *man* has perished
   from the earth,
And *there is* no one upright
   among men.
They all lie in wait for blood;
Every man hunts his brother
   with a net.

3 That they may successfully do
   evil with both hands—
The prince asks *for gifts,*
The judge *seeks* a bribe,
And the great *man* utters his
   evil desire;
So they scheme together.
4 The best of them *is* like a brier;
The most upright *is sharper*
   than a thorn hedge;
The day of your watchman and
   your punishment comes;
Now shall be their perplexity.

5 Do not trust in a friend;
Do not put your confidence in
   a companion;
Guard the doors of your
   mouth
From her who lies in your
   bosom.
6 For son dishonors father,
Daughter rises against her
   mother,
Daughter-in-law against her
   mother-in-law;
A man's enemies *are* the men
   of his own household.
7 Therefore I will look to the
   Lord;
I will wait for the God of my
   salvation;
My God will hear me.

8 Do not rejoice over me, my
   enemy;
When I fall, I will arise;
When I sit in darkness,
The Lord *will be* a light to me.
9 I will bear the indignation of
   the Lord,
Because I have sinned against
   Him,
Until He pleads my case
And executes justice for me.
He will bring me forth to the
   light;
I will see His righteousness.

10 Then *she who is* my enemy will
   see,
And shame will cover her who
   said to me,
"Where is the Lord your God?"
My eyes will see her;
Now she will be trampled down
Like mud in the streets.

11 *In* the day when your walls are
   to be built,
In that day the decree shall go
   far and wide.*a*
12 *In* that day they*a* shall come to
   you
From Assyria and the fortified
   cities,*b*
From the fortress*c* to the River,*d*
From sea to sea,
And mountain *to* mountain.
13 Yet the land shall be desolate
Because of those who dwell in
   it,
And for the fruit of their deeds.

14 Shepherd Your people with
   Your staff,
The flock of Your heritage,
Who dwell solitarily *in* a
   woodland,
In the midst of Carmel;
Let them feed *in* Bashan and
   Gilead,
As in days of old.

15 "As in the days when you came
   out of the land of Egypt,
I will show them*a* wonders."

16 The nations shall see and be
   ashamed of all their might;
They shall put *their* hand over
   their mouth;
Their ears shall be deaf.
17 They shall lick the dust like a
   serpent;
They shall crawl from their
   holes like snakes of the earth.
They shall be afraid of the Lord
   our God,
And shall fear because of
   You.
18 Who *is* a God like You,
Pardoning iniquity
And passing over the
   transgression of the remnant
   of His heritage?

7:11 *a*Or *the boundary shall be extended*   7:12 *a*Literally *he,* collective of the captives *b*Hebrew *arey mazor,* possibly *cities of Egypt* *c*Hebrew *mazor,* possibly *Egypt* *d*That is, the Euphrates   7:15 *a*Literally *him,* collective for the captives

---

*T*he Church can point to God's love as the source for self-worth. We are not valuable
because we love God; we are valuable because He loves us.

He does not retain His anger
    forever,
Because He delights *in* mercy.
19 He will again have compassion
    on us,
    And will subdue our
    iniquities.

7:19 ᵃLiterally *their*

You will cast all our*ᵃ* sins
    Into the depths of the sea.
20 You will give truth to Jacob
    And mercy to Abraham,
    Which You have sworn to our
    fathers
    From days of old.

The Book of
NAHUM

1 The burdenᵃ against Nineveh.
The book of the vision of Nahum
the Elkoshite.

2   God *is* jealous, and the Lord
    avenges;
    The Lord avenges and *is*
    furious.
    The Lord will take vengeance
    on His adversaries,
    And He reserves *wrath* for His
    enemies;
3   The Lord *is* slow to anger and
    great in power,
    And will not at all acquit *the*
    wicked.

    The Lord has His way
    In the whirlwind and in the
    storm,
    And the clouds *are* the dust of
    His feet.
4   He rebukes the sea and makes
    it dry,
    And dries up all the rivers.
    Bashan and Carmel wither,
    And the flower of Lebanon
    wilts.
5   The mountains quake before
    Him,
    The hills melt,
    And the earth heavesᵃ at His
    presence,
    Yes, the world and all who
    dwell in it.

6   Who can stand before His
    indignation?
    And who can endure the
    fierceness of His anger?

1:1 ᵃOr *oracle*   1:5 ᵃTargum reads *burns.*

His fury is poured out like fire,
And the rocks are thrown down
    by Him.

7   The Lord *is* good,
    A stronghold in the day of
    trouble;
    And He knows those who trust
    in Him.
8   But with an overflowing flood
    He will make an utter end of
    its place,
    And darkness will pursue His
    enemies.

9   What do you conspire against
    the Lord?
    He will make an utter end *of*
    it.
    Affliction will not rise up a
    second time.
10   For while tangled *like* thorns,
    And while drunken *like*
    drunkards,
    They shall be devoured like
    stubble fully dried.
11   From you comes forth *one*
    Who plots evil against the
    Lord,
    A wicked counselor.

12 Thus says the Lord:

    "Though *they are* safe, and
    likewise many,
    Yet in this manner they will be
    cut down
    When he passes through.
    Though I have afflicted you,
    I will afflict you no more;

Gospel
Pearls

13 For now I will break off his
yoke from you,
And burst your bonds apart."

14 The LORD has given a command
concerning you:
"Your name shall be
perpetuated no longer.
Out of the house of your gods
I will cut off the carved image
and the molded image.
I will dig your grave,
For you are vile."

15 Behold, on the mountains
The feet of him who brings
good tidings,
Who proclaims peace!
O Judah, keep your appointed
feasts,
Perform your vows.
For the wicked one shall no
more pass through you;
He is utterly cut off.

2 He who scatters*a* has come up
before your face.
Man the fort!
Watch the road!
Strengthen *your* flanks!
Fortify *your* power mightily.

2 For the LORD will restore the
excellence of Jacob
Like the excellence of Israel,
For the emptiers have emptied
them out
And ruined their vine
branches.

3 The shields of his mighty men
are made red,
The valiant men *are* in scarlet.
The chariots *come* with flaming
torches
In the day of his preparation,
And the spears are
brandished.*a*

4 The chariots rage in the streets,
They jostle one another in the
broad roads;
They seem like torches,
They run like lightning.

5 He remembers his nobles;
They stumble in their walk;
They make haste to her walls,
And the defense is prepared.

6 The gates of the rivers are
opened,
And the palace is dissolved.

7 It is decreed:*a*
She shall be led away captive,
She shall be brought up;
And her maidservants shall
lead *her* as with the voice of
doves,
Beating their breasts.

8 Though Nineveh of old *was* like
a pool of water,
Now they flee away.
"Halt! Halt!" *they cry;*
But no one turns back.

9 Take spoil of silver!
Take spoil of gold!
There is no end of treasure,
Or wealth of every desirable
prize.

10 She is empty, desolate, and
waste!
The heart melts, and the knees
shake;
Much pain *is* in every side,
And all their faces are drained
of color.*a*

11 Where *is* the dwelling of the
lions,
And the feeding place of the
young lions,
Where the lion walked, the
lioness *and* lion's cub,
And no one made *them*
afraid?

12 The lion tore in pieces enough
for his cubs,
Killed for his lionesses,
Filled his caves with prey,
And his dens with flesh.

13 "Behold, I *am* against you," says
the LORD of hosts, "I will burn your*a*
chariots in smoke, and the sword
shall devour your young lions; I will
cut off your prey from the earth, and
the voice of your messengers shall
be heard no more."

3 Woe to the bloody city!
It *is* all full of lies *and* robbery.
Its victim never departs.

2 The noise of a whip
And the noise of rattling
wheels,
Of galloping horses,
Of clattering chariots!

2:1 *a*Vulgate reads *he who destroys.*   2:3 *a*Literally *the cypresses are shaken;* Septuagint and Syriac
read *the horses rush about;* Vulgate reads *the drivers are stupefied.*   2:7 *a*Hebrew *Huzzab*
2:10 *a*Compare Joel 2:6   2:13 *a*Literally *her*

*T*he Bible describes Heaven as a place where the angels rejoice over one sinner who
comes into the faith. They rejoice because Jesus heals those who are broken. Likewise God's people are to rejoice because the brokenhearted and emotionally wounded
come to Him.

3 Horsemen charge with
bright sword and glittering
spear.
There is a multitude of slain,
A great number of bodies,
Countless corpses—
They stumble over the
corpses—
4 Because of the multitude of
harlotries of the seductive
harlot,
The mistress of sorceries,
Who sells nations through her
harlotries,
And families through her
sorceries.

5 "Behold, I *am* against you," says
the LORD of hosts;
"I will lift your skirts over your
face,
I will show the nations your
nakedness,
And the kingdoms your shame.
6 I will cast abominable filth
upon you,
Make you vile,
And make you a spectacle.
7 It shall come to pass *that* all
who look upon you
Will flee from you, and say,
'Nineveh is laid waste!
Who will bemoan her?'
Where shall I seek comforters
for you?"

8 Are you better than No Amon[a]
That was situated by the
River,[b]
That had the waters around
her,
Whose rampart *was* the sea,
Whose wall *was* the sea?
9 Ethiopia and Egypt *were* her
strength,
And *it was* boundless;
Put and Lubim were your[a]
helpers.
10 Yet she *was* carried away,
She went into captivity;
Her young children also were
dashed to pieces
At the head of every street;
They cast lots for her
honorable men,
And all her great men were
bound in chains.
11 You also will be drunk;
You will be hidden;

You also will seek refuge from
the enemy.
12 All your strongholds *are* fig
trees with ripened figs:
If they are shaken,
They fall into the mouth of the
eater.
13 Surely, your people in your
midst *are* women!
The gates of your land are wide
open for your enemies;
Fire shall devour the bars of
your *gates*.

14 Draw your water for the siege!
Fortify your strongholds!
Go into the clay and tread the
mortar!
Make strong the brick kiln!
15 There the fire will devour you,
The sword will cut you off;
It will eat you up like a locust.

Make yourself many—like the
locust!
Make yourself many—like the
swarming locusts!
16 You have multiplied your
merchants more than the
stars of heaven.
The locust plunders and flies
away.
17 Your commanders *are* like
swarming locusts,
And your generals like great
grasshoppers,
Which camp in the hedges on
a cold day;
When the sun rises they flee
away,
And the place where they *are*
is not known.

18 Your shepherds slumber, O
king of Assyria;
Your nobles rest *in the* dust.
Your people are scattered on
the mountains,
And no one gathers them.
19 Your injury *has* no healing,
Your wound is severe.
All who hear news of you
Will clap *their* hands over
you,
For upon whom has not your
wickedness passed
continually?

3:8 [a]That is, ancient Thebes; Targum and Vulgate read *populous Alexandria*. [b]Literally *rivers,* that is, the Nile and the surrounding canals 3:9 [a]Septuagint reads *her*.

1 The burden[a] which the prophet Habakkuk saw.

2 O LORD, how long shall I cry,
  And You will not hear?
  Even cry out to You,
    "Violence!"
  And You will not save.
3 Why do You show me iniquity,
  And cause *me* to see trouble?
  For plundering and violence
    are before me;
  There is strife, and contention
    arises.
4 Therefore the law is powerless,
  And justice never goes forth.
  For the wicked surround the
    righteous;
  Therefore perverse judgment
    proceeds.

5 "Look among the nations and
    watch—
  Be utterly astounded!
  For *I will* work a work in your
    days
  Which you would not believe,
    though it were told *you*.
6 For indeed I am raising up the
    Chaldeans,
  A bitter and hasty nation
  Which marches through the
    breadth of the earth,
  To possess dwelling places
    that are not theirs.
7 They are terrible and dreadful;
  Their judgment and their
    dignity proceed from
    themselves.
8 Their horses also are swifter
    than leopards,
  And more fierce than evening
    wolves.
  Their chargers charge ahead;
  Their cavalry comes from afar;
  They fly as the eagle *that*
    hastens to eat.

9 "They all come for violence;
  Their faces are set *like* the east
    wind.
  They gather captives like sand.
10 They scoff at kings,
  And princes are scorned by
    them.
  They deride every stronghold,

  For they heap up earthen
    mounds and seize it.
11 Then *his* mind[a] changes, and he
    transgresses;
  He commits offense,
  Ascribing this power to his
    god."

12 Are You not from everlasting,
  O LORD my God, my Holy
    One?
  We shall not die.
  O LORD, You have appointed
    them for judgment;
  O Rock, You have marked
    them for correction.
13 *You are* of purer eyes than to
    behold evil,
  And cannot look on
    wickedness.
  Why do You look on those who
    deal treacherously,
  And hold Your tongue when
    the wicked devours
  A *person* more righteous than
    he?
14 *Why* do You make men like
    fish of the sea,
  Like creeping things *that have*
    no ruler over them?

15 They take up all of them with
    a hook,
  They catch them in their net,
  And gather them in their
    dragnet.
  Therefore they rejoice and are
    glad.
16 Therefore they sacrifice to their
    net,
  And burn incense to their
    dragnet;
  Because by them their share *is*
    sumptuous
  And their food plentiful.
17 Shall they therefore empty
    their net,
  And continue to slay nations
    without pity?

2 I will stand my watch
  And set myself on the rampart,
  And watch to see what He will
    say to me,
  And what I will answer when
    I am corrected.

1:1 *a*Or *oracle*   1:11 *a*Literally *spirit* or *wind*

R est is for the purpose of restoration. It is not just because you're tired. It is during a time of rest that you replenish or receive back those things that were expended or put out.

2 Then the LORD answered me and said:

"Write the vision
And make *it* plain on tablets,
That he may run who reads it.
3 For the vision *is* yet for an
appointed time;
But at the end it will speak, and
it will not lie.
Though it tarries, wait for it;
Because it will surely come,
It will not tarry.

4 "Behold the proud,
His soul is not upright in him;
But the just shall live by his
faith.

5 "Indeed, because he
transgresses by wine,
He is a proud man,
And he does not stay at home.
Because he enlarges his desire
as hell,*a*
And he *is* like death, and
cannot be satisfied,
He gathers to himself all
nations
And heaps up for himself all
peoples.

6 "Will not all these take up a
proverb against him,
And a taunting riddle against
him, and say,
'Woe to him who increases
What is not his—how long?
And to him who loads himself
with many pledges'?*a*
7 Will not your creditors*a* rise up
suddenly?
Will they not awaken who
oppress you?
And you will become their
booty.
8 Because you have plundered
many nations,
All the remnant of the people
shall plunder you,
Because of men's blood
And the violence of the land
and the city,
And of all who dwell in it.

9 "Woe to him who covets evil
gain for his house,

That he may set his nest on
high,
That he may be delivered from
the power of disaster!
10 You give shameful counsel to
your house,
Cutting off many peoples,
And sin *against* your soul.
11 For the stone will cry out from
the wall,
And the beam from the timbers
will answer it.

12 "Woe to him who builds a town
with bloodshed,
Who establishes a city by
iniquity!
13 Behold, *is it* not of the LORD of
hosts
That the peoples labor to feed
the fire,*a*
And nations weary themselves
in vain?
14 For the earth will be filled
With the knowledge of the
glory of the LORD,
As the waters cover the sea.

15 "Woe to him who gives drink to
his neighbor,
Pressing*a* him *to* your bottle,
Even to make *him* drunk,
That you may look on his
nakedness!
16 You are filled with shame
instead of glory.
You also—drink!
And be exposed as
uncircumcised!*a*
The cup of the LORD's right
hand *will be* turned against
you,
And utter shame *will be* on
your glory.
17 For the violence *done to*
Lebanon will cover you,
And the plunder of beasts
which made them afraid,
Because of men's blood
And the violence of the land
and the city,
And of all who dwell in it.

18 "What profit is the image, that
its maker should carve it,
The molded image, a teacher of
lies,

2:5 *a*Or *Sheol* 2:6 *a*Syriac and Vulgate read *thick clay.* 2:7 *a*Literally *those who bite you*
2:13 *a*Literally *for what satisfies fire,* that is, for what is of no lasting value 2:15 *a*Literally *Attaching* or
Joining 2:16 *a*Dead Sea Scrolls and Septuagint read *And reel!;* Syriac and Vulgate read *And fall fast
asleep!*

God will reward those who persevere in seeking Him. If you will wait on the Lord,
He will strengthen your heart. He will heal you and deliver you.

Faith and Feelings

Habakkuk 2:4

I counsel women all the time who sit with tears streaming down their weary faces and say, "I just can't trust him." I've got news for you. You can't trust yourself either! Your feelings will swing in and out. But your faith will not move.

In Mark 10:7, we read about a man leaving his parents and cleaving to his wife. *Cleaving* implies that you don't want to get away, that you are committed for life. A marriage erodes like the banks of a river—a little each day. Be careful in the little, everyday things of marriage.

There is a certain way a woman treats a man when she is fulfilled. But it takes faith to treat a frustrating relationship with the same respect you would treat a fulfilling relationship. Still, it's worth the effort. When you and your spouse are having problems, don't suppress the gentle side of yourself just to avoid being hurt. If you do, you may fall into depression. And don't fight fire with fire. The best way to fight fire is with water. A woman can win with a gentle, soothing character—like pouring water on blazing coals—not with heated words, which will only fan the flames.

In fact, if you can keep your mouth shut and your feelings under control, you may even be able to lead an unbelieving husband to the Lord (see 1 Peter 3:1). There is great power in words. But there may be times when there is even more power in demonstrating God's unconditional love without words.

You may be in the middle of an awful mess. If so, you might need pastoral care and counseling. But don't forget that the Holy Spirit is your Counselor. His door is open at all times, and He waives His fee for His children.

It is not always a matter of feelings. Romans 1:17 says, "The righteousness of God is revealed from faith to faith; as it is written, '*The just shall live by faith.*'" Believe God for your marriage. It will not be your feelings that heal your relationship. It will be your faith!

The power to unleash your marriage is in your faith. Dare to believe that God will do what He said He would do. Shift your confidence from your own weaknesses or your mate's weaknesses to His power. Trust God. He will soothe your wounds; He will comfort you in your desperate moments. He will resurrect your marriage—no matter how you feel. Believe it!

That the maker of its mold
    should trust in it,
To make mute idols?
19 Woe to him who says to wood,
    'Awake!'
To silent stone, 'Arise! It shall
    teach!'
Behold, it is overlaid with gold
    and silver,
Yet in it there is no breath at
    all.

20 "But the LORD is in His holy
    temple.
Let all the earth keep silence
    before Him."

3 A prayer of Habakkuk the
prophet, on Shigionoth.*a*

2   O LORD, I have heard your
    speech *and* was afraid;
O LORD, revive Your work in
    the midst of the years!
In the midst of the years make
    it known;
In wrath remember mercy.

3   God came from Teman,
The Holy One from Mount
    Paran.   Selah

His glory covered the heavens,
And the earth was full of His
    praise.
4   *His* brightness was like the
    light;
He had rays *flashing* from His
    hand,
And there His power *was*
    hidden.
5   Before Him went pestilence,
And fever followed at His
    feet.

6   He stood and measured the
    earth;
He looked and startled the
    nations.
And the everlasting mountains
    were scattered,
The perpetual hills bowed.
His ways *are* everlasting.
7   I saw the tents of Cushan in
    affliction;
The curtains of the land of
    Midian trembled.

8   O LORD, were *You* displeased
    with the rivers,

Was Your anger against the
    rivers,
Was Your wrath against the
    sea,
That You rode on Your horses,
Your chariots of salvation?
9   Your bow was made quite
    ready;
Oaths were sworn over *Your*
    arrows.*a*   Selah

You divided the earth with
    rivers.
10 The mountains saw You *and*
    trembled;
The overflowing of the water
    passed by.
The deep uttered its voice,
And lifted its hands on high.
11 The sun and moon stood still
    in their habitation;
At the light of Your arrows
    they went,
At the shining of Your
    glittering spear.

12 You marched through the land
    in indignation;
You trampled the nations in
    anger.
13 You went forth for the
    salvation of Your people,
For salvation with Your
    Anointed.
You struck the head from the
    house of the wicked,
By laying bare from foundation
    to neck.   Selah

14 You thrust through with his
    own arrows
The head of his villages.
They came out like a whirlwind
    to scatter me;
Their rejoicing was like
    feasting on the poor in secret.
15 You walked through the sea
    with Your horses,
Through the heap of great
    waters.

16 When I heard, my body
    trembled;
My lips quivered at *the* voice;
Rottenness entered my bones;
And I trembled in myself,
That I might rest in the day of
    trouble.
When he comes up to the
    people,

3:1 *a*Exact meaning unknown   3:9 *a*Literally *rods* or *tribes* (compare verse 14)

*T*here is such a security that comes when we are safe in the arms of God. It is when
we become secure in our relationship with God that we begin to allow the past to
fall from us as a garment. We remember it, but choose not to wear it!

Pat Yourself on the Back

Habakkuk 3:18

D o you ever pat yourself on the back? Have you reached the place in life where you enjoy your own company? Have you taken the time to enjoy your own person-hood? Have you massaged lotion into your own skin, or set the dinner table for yourself? Drive yourself to the mall and spend an afternoon picking out a gift for yourself. These self-affirming ministries can never be given to you by someone else. When other people give it, it reflects their opinion about you. When they leave, you may feel worthless and insignificant. But when you speak comfort and blessings to yourself, that reflects your own opinion about yourself. The best scenario is to enjoy both kinds of affirmation.

There are three reasons to give yourself a standing ovation. The first is the fact that your steps are carefully observed and arranged by God Himself. They are designed to achieve a special purpose in your life. He brings people in and out of your life, but you are the one who is blessed going in and going out (see Deuteronomy 28:6). That is to say, your blessing has not depended and will never depend on someone else's actions. The Bible says, "If God is for us, who can be against us?" (Romans 8:31b). So you must rejoice because you are in step with the beat of Heaven and the purposes of God.

Second, you ought to rejoice because you are pursuing a goal that defies human manipulation. Your blessing rests in accomplishing the will of God. Jesus went to Samaria in John 4 to minister to a hostile, religiously indifferent woman who initially had little appreciation for Him. Yet, He was nourished even by her defensive demeanor because He clearly understood that His purpose for being there was greater than the need of any one woman. Her comments lost their meaning when He weighed them against His purpose. He knew that her struggle to understand and affirm Him was of little consequence because He had a mission, even though she was a part of the plan. He wasn't there to pass the time away. He was there to provoke destiny!

Third, it is wonderful to have a plan, but that means nothing if you have no power to perform the plan and accomplish the purpose. God sends people in and out of your life to exercise your faith and develop your character. When they are gone, they leave you with the knowledge that your God is with you to deliver you wherever you go! Moses died and left Joshua in charge, but God told him, "As I was with Moses, so I will be with you" (see Joshua 1:5). Joshua never would have learned that while Moses was there. You learn this kind of thing when your "Moses" is gone. Power is developed in the absence of human assistance. Then we can see the limits of our resourcefulness and enjoy the tremendous magnitude of the favor of God.

He will invade them with his
troops.

17 Though the fig tree may not
blossom,
Nor fruit be on the vines;
Though the labor of the olive
may fail,
And the fields yield no food;
Though the flock may be cut off
from the fold,
And there be no herd in the
stalls—

3:19 ᵃHebrew YHWH Adonai

18 Yet I will rejoice in the LORD,
I will joy in the God of my
salvation.

19 The LORD Godᵃ is my
strength;
He will make my feet like
deer's *feet,*
And He will make me walk on
my high hills.

To the Chief Musician. With my
stringed instruments.

The Book of
ZEPHANIAH

1 The word of the LORD which came
to Zephaniah the son of Cushi,
the son of Gedaliah, the son of Amariah, the son of Hezekiah, in the days
of Josiah the son of Amon, king of
Judah.

2 "I will utterly consume
everything
From the face of the land,"
Says the LORD;
3 "I will consume man and beast;
I will consume the birds of the
heavens,
The fish of the sea,
And the stumbling blocksᵃ
along with the wicked.
I will cut off man from the face
of the land,"
Says the LORD.

4 "I will stretch out My hand
against Judah,
And against all the inhabitants
of Jerusalem.
I will cut off every trace of Baal
from this place,
The names of the idolatrous
priestsᵃ with the *pagan*
priests—
5 Those who worship the host of
heaven on the housetops;
Those who worship and swear
oaths by the LORD,

But who *also* swear by
Milcom;ᵃ
6 Those who have turned back
from *following* the LORD,
And have not sought the LORD,
nor inquired of Him."

7 Be silent in the presence of the
Lord GOD;
For the day of the LORD *is* at
hand,
For the LORD has prepared a
sacrifice;
He has invitedᵃ His guests.

8 "And it shall be,
In the day of the LORD's
sacrifice,
That I will punish the princes
and the king's children,
And all such as are clothed
with foreign apparel.
9 In the same day I will punish
All those who leap over the
threshold,ᵃ
Who fill their masters' houses
with violence and deceit.

10 "And there shall be on that day,"
says the LORD,
"The sound of a mournful cry
from the Fish Gate,
A wailing from the Second
Quarter,

1:3 ᵃFigurative of idols   1:4 ᵃHebrew *chemarim*   1:5 ᵃOr *Malcam,* an Ammonite god, also called *Molech*
(compare Leviticus 18:21)   1:7 ᵃLiterally *set apart, consecrated*   1:9 ᵃCompare 1 Samuel 5:5

Gospel
Pearls

And a loud crashing from the hills.

11 Wail, you inhabitants of Maktesh!^a
For all the merchant people are cut down;
All those who handle money are cut off.

12 "And it shall come to pass at that time
That I will search Jerusalem with lamps,
And punish the men
Who are settled in complacency,^a
Who say in their heart,
'The Lord will not do good,
Nor will He do evil.'

13 Therefore their goods shall become booty,
And their houses a desolation;
They shall build houses, but not inhabit *them;*
They shall plant vineyards, but not drink their wine."

14 The great day of the Lord *is* near;
It is near and hastens quickly.
The noise of the day of the Lord is bitter;
There the mighty men shall cry out.

15 That day *is* a day of wrath,
A day of trouble and distress,
A day of devastation and desolation,
A day of darkness and gloominess,
A day of clouds and thick darkness,

16 A day of trumpet and alarm
Against the fortified cities
And against the high towers.

17 "I will bring distress upon men,
And they shall walk like blind men,
Because they have sinned against the Lord;
Their blood shall be poured out like dust,
And their flesh like refuse."

18 Neither their silver nor their gold
Shall be able to deliver them
In the day of the Lord's wrath;

But the whole land shall be devoured
By the fire of His jealousy,
For He will make speedy riddance
Of all those who dwell in the land.

2 Gather yourselves together,
yes, gather together,
O undesirable^a nation,

2 Before the decree is issued,
Or the day passes like chaff,
Before the Lord's fierce anger comes upon you,
Before the day of the Lord's anger comes upon you!

3 Seek the Lord, all you meek of the earth,
Who have upheld His justice.
Seek righteousness, seek humility.
It may be that you will be hidden
In the day of the Lord's anger.

4 For Gaza shall be forsaken,
And Ashkelon desolate;
They shall drive out Ashdod at noonday,
And Ekron shall be uprooted.

5 Woe to the inhabitants of the seacoast,
The nation of the Cherethites!
The word of the Lord *is* against you,
O Canaan, land of the Philistines:
"I will destroy you;
So there shall be no inhabitant."

6 The seacoast shall be pastures,
With shelters^a for shepherds and folds for flocks.

7 The coast shall be for the remnant of the house of Judah;
They shall feed *their* flocks there;
In the houses of Ashkelon they shall lie down at evening.
For the Lord their God will intervene for them,
And return their captives.

8 "I have heard the reproach of Moab,
And the insults of the people of Ammon,

1:11 ^aLiterally *Mortar*, a market district of Jerusalem   1:12 ^aLiterally *on their lees*, that is, settled like the dregs of wine   2:1 ^aOr *shameless*   2:6 ^aLiterally *excavations*, either underground huts or cisterns

---

*T*he Sabbath was meant not only for God to rest, but also for God to enjoy His creation with man. The issues are rest and communion.

With which they have
  reproached My people,
And made arrogant threats
  against their borders.
9 Therefore, as I live,"
  Says the LORD of hosts, the God
  of Israel,
"Surely Moab shall be like
  Sodom,
And the people of Ammon like
  Gomorrah—
Overrun with weeds and
  saltpits,
And a perpetual desolation.
The residue of My people shall
  plunder them,
And the remnant of My people
  shall possess them."

10 This they shall have for their
  pride,
Because they have reproached
  and made arrogant threats
Against the people of the LORD
  of hosts.
11 The LORD *will be* awesome to
  them,
For He will reduce to nothing
  all the gods of the earth;
People shall worship Him,
  Each one from his place,
Indeed all the shores of the
  nations.

12 "You Ethiopians also,
You shall be slain by My
  sword."

13 And He will stretch out His
  hand against the north,
Destroy Assyria,
And make Nineveh a
  desolation,
As dry as the wilderness.
14 The herds shall lie down in her
  midst,
Every beast of the nation.
Both the pelican and the
  bittern
Shall lodge on the capitals *of*
  her *pillars;*
Their voice shall sing in the
  windows;
Desolation *shall be* at the
  threshold;
For He will lay bare the cedar
  work.
15 This is the rejoicing city
That dwelt securely,

That said in her heart,
"I *am it,* and *there is* none
  besides me."
How has she become a
  desolation,
A place for beasts to lie down!
Everyone who passes by her
Shall hiss and shake his fist.

3 Woe to her who is rebellious
  and polluted,
To the oppressing city!
2 She has not obeyed *His* voice,
She has not received
  correction;
She has not trusted in the LORD,
She has not drawn near to her
  God.

3 Her princes in her midst *are*
  roaring lions;
Her judges *are* evening wolves
That leave not a bone till
  morning.
4 Her prophets are insolent,
  treacherous people;
Her priests have polluted the
  sanctuary,
They have done violence to the
  law.
5 The LORD *is* righteous in her
  midst,
He will do no unrighteousness.
Every morning He brings His
  justice to light;
He never fails,
But the unjust knows no
  shame.

6 "I have cut off nations,
Their fortresses are devastated;
I have made their streets
  desolate,
With none passing by.
Their cities are destroyed;
There is no one, no inhabitant.
7 I said, 'Surely you will fear Me,
You will receive instruction'—
So that her dwelling would not
  be cut off,
Despite everything for which I
  punished her.
But they rose early and
  corrupted all their deeds.

8 "Therefore wait for Me," says
  the LORD,
"Until the day I rise up for
  plunder;*a*

3:8 *a*Septuagint and Syriac read *for witness;* Targum reads *for the day of My revelation for judgment;*
Vulgate reads *for the day of My resurrection that is to come.*

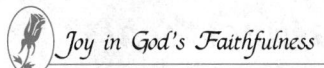

My determination *is* to gather
the nations
To My assembly of kingdoms,
To pour on them My
indignation,
All my fierce anger;
All the earth shall be devoured
With the fire of My jealousy.

9 "For then I will restore to the
peoples a pure language,
That they all may call on the
name of the LORD,
To serve Him with one
accord.
10 From beyond the rivers of
Ethiopia
My worshipers,
The daughter of My dispersed
ones,
Shall bring My offering.
11 In that day you shall not be
shamed for any of your deeds
In which you transgress
against Me;
For then I will take away from
your midst
Those who rejoice in your
pride,
And you shall no longer be
haughty
In My holy mountain.
12 I will leave in your midst
A meek and humble people,
And they shall trust in the
name of the LORD.
13 The remnant of Israel shall do
no unrighteousness
And speak no lies,
Nor shall a deceitful tongue be
found in their mouth;
For they shall feed *their* flocks
and lie down,
And no one shall make *them*
afraid."

14 Sing, O daughter of Zion!
Shout, O Israel!
Be glad and rejoice with all
your heart,
O daughter of Jerusalem!
15 The LORD has taken away your
judgments,
He has cast out your enemy.
The King of Israel, the LORD, *is*
in your midst;
You shall see[a] disaster no
more.

16 In that day it shall be said to
Jerusalem:
"Do not fear;
Zion, let not your hands be
weak.
17 The LORD your God in your
midst,
The Mighty One, will save;
He will rejoice over you with
gladness,
He will quiet *you* with His
love,
He will rejoice over you with
singing."

18 "I will gather those who sorrow
over the appointed assembly,
Who are among you,
To whom its reproach *is* a
burden.
19 Behold, at that time
I will deal with all who afflict
you;
I will save the lame,
And gather those who were
driven out;
I will appoint them for praise
and fame
In every land where they were
put to shame.
20 At that time I will bring you
back,
Even at the time I gather
you;
For I will give you fame and
praise
Among all the peoples of the
earth,
When I return your captives
before your eyes,"
Says the LORD.

3:15 [a]Some Hebrew manuscripts, Septuagint, and Bomberg read *see;* Masoretic Text and Vulgate read *fear.*

When you start murmuring and complaining, the only thing God can focus on is your unbelief. When you start resting in Him, He can focus on your problems and on the areas of your life that need to be touched.

The Father's Heartbeat

Zephaniah 3:17

*P*ut your hand upon your chest and feel the beating of your heart. The rhythm that you feel is steady and consistent. It has a pattern and a direction. So is the Father's love. I want you to know and to feel and to experience deeply a father's heart!

Dear lady, you are the Father's heartbeat. And He loves you so. He will ask you to release and turn from thoughts, actions, conditions of your heart that are not pleasing to Him. He wants you to live and to abide in purity, honor, and love. Please do not break His heart by living in sin. He has a reason for asking you to give up areas that compromise true holiness. He isn't saying no because He is mean. He is saying no because He wants something better for you than this. He is not the kind of Father who would deny a good thing to you. If He is trying to wrench a little sin toy out of your hand, it is because He knows it will eventually destroy you, your children, or your self-esteem. Let it go.

I know how hard it is to confront immorality and weakness. Many are the days I have had to crawl upon His lap and weep, asking Him to help me with myself. I know we have to be weaned from Satan's toys if we are going to be used by the Lord. But it is such a blessing when the foe is conquered, the enemy is defeated, and you look beyond the test and see the joy on the other side. You will see, when you overcome, that the Father has a reward. Every time you resist temptation, whether that temptation is an extramarital affair or the temptation to be critical and rude to others, you will see that the Father has rewards for accomplishments. You may not see them instantly. You may need to apprehend them by faith.

No further excuses. You know the Father is right. Off with you now. Go quickly into His presence; climb upon His knee; lay your head on His breast. Cry if you must, but talk to Him. Let Him cleanse you of sin and purge you of pride. I want you to know He loves you just as much when He says no as He does when He says yes. He loves you as much when He asks you to give up something for Him as He does when He gives everything to you. His heart belongs to you, lovely lady. You are His heartbeat.

The Book of

HAGGAI

1 In the second year of King Darius, in the sixth month, on the first day of the month, the word of the LORD came by Haggai the prophet to Zerubbabel the son of Shealtiel, governor of Judah, and to Joshua the son of Jehozadak, the high priest, saying, 2 "Thus speaks the LORD of hosts, saying: 'This people says, "The time has not come, the time that the LORD's house should be built."'"

3 Then the word of the LORD came by Haggai the prophet, saying, 4 "Is it time for you yourselves to dwell in your paneled houses, and this temple*ª* to lie in ruins?" 5 Now therefore, thus says the LORD of hosts: "Consider your ways!

6 "You have sown much, and
bring in little;
You eat, but do not have
enough;
You drink, but you are not
filled with drink;
You clothe yourselves, but no
one is warm;
And he who earns wages,
Earns wages to put into a bag
with holes."

7 Thus says the LORD of hosts: "Consider your ways! 8 Go up to the mountains and bring wood and build the temple, that I may take pleasure in it and be glorified," says the LORD. 9 "You looked for much, but indeed it came to little; and when you brought it home, I blew it away. Why?" says the LORD of hosts. "Because of My house that is in ruins, while every one of you runs to his own house. 10 Therefore the heavens above you withhold the dew, and the earth withholds its fruit. 11 For I called for a drought on the land and the mountains, on the grain and the new wine and the oil, on whatever the ground brings forth, on men and livestock, and on all the labor of your hands."

12 Then Zerubbabel the son of Shealtiel, and Joshua the son of Jehozadak, the high priest, with all the remnant of the people, obeyed the voice of the LORD their God, and the words of Haggai the prophet, as the LORD their God had sent him; and the people feared the presence of the LORD. 13 Then Haggai, the LORD's messenger, spoke the LORD's message to the people, saying, "I am with you, says the LORD." 14 So the LORD stirred up the spirit of Zerubbabel the son of Shealtiel, governor of Judah, and the spirit of Joshua the son of Jehozadak, the high priest, and the spirit of all the remnant of the people; and they came and worked on the house of the LORD of hosts, their God, 15 on the twenty-fourth day of the sixth month, in the second year of King Darius.

2 In the seventh month, on the twenty-first of the month, the word of the LORD came by Haggai the prophet, saying: 2 "Speak now to Zerubbabel the son of Shealtiel, governor of Judah, and to Joshua the son of Jehozadak, the high priest, and to the remnant of the people, saying: 3 'Who is left among you who saw this temple*ª* in its former glory? And how do you see it now? In comparison with it, is this not in your eyes as nothing? 4 Yet now be strong, Zerubbabel,' says the LORD; 'and be strong, Joshua, son of Jehozadak, the high priest; and be strong, all you people of the land,' says the LORD, 'and work; for I am with you,' says the LORD of hosts. 5 'According to the word that I covenanted with you when you came out of Egypt, so My Spirit remains among you; do not fear!'

6 "For thus says the LORD of hosts: 'Once more (it is a little while) I will shake heaven and earth, the sea and dry land; 7 and I will shake all nations, and they shall come to the Desire of All Nations,*ª* and I will fill this temple with glory,' says the LORD of hosts. 8 'The silver is Mine, and the gold is Mine,' says the LORD of hosts. 9 'The glory of this latter temple shall be greater than the former,' says the LORD of hosts. 'And in this place I

1:4 ªLiterally house, and so in verse 8   2:3 ªLiterally house, and so in verses 7 and 9   2:7 ªOr the desire of all nations

𝒲hen you begin to enter into real worship, that's the best time to have God minister to your needs. That's the time God does restoration in your life.

will give peace,' says the LORD of hosts."

10 On the twenty-fourth *day* of the ninth *month,* in the second year of Darius, the word of the LORD came by Haggai the prophet, saying, 11 "Thus says the LORD of hosts: 'Now, ask the priests *concerning the* law, saying, 12 "If one carries holy meat in the fold of his garment, and with the edge he touches bread or stew, wine or oil, or any food, will it become holy?" ' "

Then the priests answered and said, "No."

13 And Haggai said, "If *one who is* unclean *because* of a dead body touches any of these, will it be unclean?"

So the priests answered and said, "It shall be unclean."

14 Then Haggai answered and said, " 'So is this people, and so is this nation before Me,' says the LORD, 'and so is every work of their hands; and what they offer there is unclean.

15 'And now, carefully consider from this day forward: from before stone was laid upon stone in the temple of the LORD— 16 since those *days,* when *one* came to a heap of twenty ephahs, there were *but* ten; when *one* came to the wine vat to draw out fifty baths from the press, there were *but* twenty. 17 I struck you with blight and mildew and hail in all the labors of your hands; yet you did not *turn* to Me,' says the LORD. 18 'Consider now from this day forward, from the twenty-fourth day of the ninth month, from the day that the foundation of the LORD's temple was laid— consider it: 19 Is the seed still in the barn? As yet the vine, the fig tree, the pomegranate, and the olive tree have not yielded *fruit. But* from this day I will bless *you.' ' "

20 And again the word of the LORD came to Haggai on the twenty-fourth day of the month, saying, 21 "Speak to Zerubbabel, governor of Judah, saying:

'I will shake heaven and
     earth.
22 I will overthrow the throne of
     kingdoms;
I will destroy the strength of
     the Gentile kingdoms.
I will overthrow the chariots
And those who ride in them;
The horses and their riders
     shall come down,
Every one by the sword of his
     brother.

23 'In that day,' says the LORD of hosts, 'I will take you, Zerubbabel My servant, the son of Shealtiel,' says the LORD, 'and will make you like a signet *ring;* for I have chosen you,' says the LORD of hosts."

The Book of

ZECHARIAH

1 In the eighth month of the second year of Darius, the word of the LORD came to Zechariah the son of Berechiah, the son of Iddo the prophet, saying, 2 "The LORD has been very angry with your fathers. 3 Therefore say to them, 'Thus says the LORD of hosts: "Return to Me," says the LORD of hosts, "and I will return to you," says the LORD of hosts. 4 "Do not be like your fathers, to whom the former prophets preached, saying, 'Thus says the LORD of hosts: "Turn now from your evil ways and your evil deeds." ' But they did not hear nor heed Me," says the LORD.

5 "Your fathers, where *are*
     they?
And the prophets, do they live
     forever?
6 Yet surely My words and My
     statutes,
Which I commanded My
     servants the prophets,
Did they not overtake your
     fathers?

"So they returned and said:

Gospel Pearls

'Just as the LORD of hosts
determined to do to us,
According to our ways and
according to our deeds,
So He has dealt with us.' "

7 On the twenty-fourth day of the
eleventh month, which is the month
Shebat, in the second year of Darius,
the word of the LORD came to Zechariah the son of Berechiah, the son of
Iddo the prophet: 8 I saw by night,
and behold, a man riding on a red
horse, and it stood among the myrtle
trees in the hollow; and behind him
were horses: red, sorrel, and white.
9 Then I said, "My lord, what *are*
these?" So the angel who talked with
me said to me, "I will show you what
they *are.*"

10 And the man who stood among
the myrtle trees answered and said,
"These *are the ones* whom the LORD
has sent to walk to and fro throughout the earth."

11 So they answered the Angel of
the LORD, who stood among the myrtle trees, and said, "We have walked
to and fro throughout the earth, and
behold, all the earth is resting quietly."

12 Then the Angel of the LORD answered and said, "O LORD of hosts,
how long will You not have mercy
on Jerusalem and on the cities of Judah, against which You were angry
these seventy years?"

13 And the LORD answered the angel who talked to me, *with* good *and*
comforting words. 14 So the angel
who spoke with me said to me, "Proclaim, saying, 'Thus says the LORD of
hosts:

"I am zealous for Jerusalem
And for Zion with great
zeal.
15 I am exceedingly angry with
the nations at ease;
For I was a little angry,
And they helped—*but* with evil
intent."

16 'Therefore thus says the LORD:

"I am returning to Jerusalem
with mercy;
My house shall be built in it,"
says the LORD of hosts,

"And a *surveyor's* line shall be
stretched out over
Jerusalem." ' "

17 "Again proclaim, saying, 'Thus
says the LORD of hosts:

"My cities shall again spread out
through prosperity;
The LORD will again comfort
Zion,
And will again choose
Jerusalem." ' "

18 Then I raised my eyes and
looked, and there *were* four horns.
19 And I said to the angel who talked
with me, "What *are* these?"

So he answered me, "These *are* the
horns that have scattered Judah, Israel, and Jerusalem."

20 Then the LORD showed me four
craftsmen. 21 And I said, "What are
these coming to do?"

So he said, "These *are* the horns
that scattered Judah, so that no one
could lift up his head; but the
craftsmen[a] are coming to terrify
them, to cast out the horns of the nations that lifted up *their* horn against
the land of Judah to scatter it."

2 Then I raised my eyes and looked,
and behold, a man with a measuring line in his hand. 2 So I said,
"Where are you going?"

And he said to me, "To measure
Jerusalem, to see what *is* its width
and what *is* its length."

3 And there *was* the angel who
talked with me, going out; and another angel was coming out to meet
him, 4 who said to him, "Run, speak
to this young man, saying: 'Jerusalem shall be inhabited *as* towns without walls, because of the multitude
of men and livestock in it. 5 For I,'
says the LORD, 'will be a wall of fire
all around her, and I will be the glory
in her midst.' "

6 "Up, up! Flee from the land of the
north," says the LORD; "for I have
spread you abroad like the four
winds of heaven," says the LORD.
7 Up, Zion! Escape, you who dwell
with the daughter of Babylon."

8 For thus says the LORD of hosts:
"He sent Me after glory, to the nations which plunder you; for he who

1:21 aLiterally *these*

*J*esus Christ is our Sabbath rest. He is the end of our labors. We are saved by grace
through faith and not by works, lest any man should be able to boast.

touches you touches the apple of His eye. 9 For surely I will shake My hand against them, and they shall become spoil for their servants. Then you will know that the LORD of hosts has sent Me.

10 "Sing and rejoice, O daughter of Zion! For behold, I am coming and I will dwell in your midst," says the LORD. 11 Many nations shall be joined to the LORD in that day, and they shall become My people. And I will dwell in your midst. Then you will know that the LORD of hosts has sent Me to you. 12 And the LORD will take possession of Judah as His inheritance in the Holy Land, and will again choose Jerusalem. 13 Be silent, all flesh, before the LORD, for He is aroused from His holy habitation!"

3 Then he showed me Joshua the high priest standing before the Angel of the LORD, and Satan standing at his right hand to oppose him. 2 And the LORD said to Satan, "The LORD rebuke you, Satan! The LORD who has chosen Jerusalem rebuke you! Is this not a brand plucked from the fire?"

3 Now Joshua was clothed with filthy garments, and was standing before the Angel. 4 Then He answered and spoke to those who stood before Him, saying, "Take away the filthy garments from him." And to him He said, "See, I have removed your iniquity from you, and I will clothe you with rich robes."

5 And I said, "Let them put a clean turban on his head."

So they put a clean turban on his head, and they put the clothes on him. And the Angel of the LORD stood by.

6 Then the Angel of the LORD admonished Joshua, saying, 7 "Thus says the LORD of hosts:

'If you will walk in My ways,
And if you will keep My command,
Then you shall also judge My house,
And likewise have charge of My courts;
I will give you places to walk
Among these who stand here.

8 'Hear, O Joshua, the high priest,
You and your companions who sit before you,
For they are a wondrous sign;
For behold, I am bringing forth My Servant the BRANCH.
9 For behold, the stone
That I have laid before Joshua:
Upon the stone are seven eyes.
Behold, I will engrave its inscription,'
Says the LORD of hosts,
'And I will remove the iniquity of that land in one day.
10 In that day,' says the LORD of hosts,
'Everyone will invite his neighbor
Under his vine and under his fig tree.' "

4 Now the angel who talked with me came back and wakened me, as a man who is wakened out of his sleep. 2 And he said to me, "What do you see?"

So I said, "I am looking, and there is a lampstand of solid gold with a bowl on top of it, and on the stand seven lamps with seven pipes to the seven lamps. 3 Two olive trees are by it, one at the right of the bowl and the other at its left." 4 So I answered and spoke to the angel who talked with me, saying, "What are these, my lord?"

5 Then the angel who talked with me answered and said to me, "Do you not know what these are?"

And I said, "No, my lord."

6 So he answered and said to me:

"This is the word of the LORD to Zerubbabel:
'Not by might nor by power, but by My Spirit,'
Says the LORD of hosts.
7 'Who are you, O great mountain?
Before Zerubbabel you shall become a plain!
And he shall bring forth the capstone
With shouts of "Grace, grace to it!" ' "

8 Moreover the word of the LORD came to me, saying:

Gospel Pearls

9 "The hands of Zerubbabel
Have laid the foundation of this
temple;*a*
His hands shall also finish *it.*
Then you will know
That the LORD of hosts has sent
Me to you.
10 For who has despised the day
of small things?
For these seven rejoice to see
The plumb line in the hand of
Zerubbabel.
They are the eyes of the LORD,
Which scan to and fro
throughout the whole
earth."

11 Then I answered and said to
him, "What *are* these two olive
trees—at the right of the lampstand
and at its left?" 12 And I further answered and said to him, "What *are
these* two olive branches that *drip*
into the receptacles*a* of the two gold
pipes from which the golden *oil*
drains?"
13 Then he answered me and said,
"Do you not know what these *are?"*
And I said, "No, my lord."
14 So he said, "These *are* the two
anointed ones, who stand beside the
Lord of the whole earth."

5 Then I turned and raised my
eyes, and saw there a flying
scroll.
2 And he said to me, "What do you
see?"
So I answered, "I see a flying
scroll. Its length *is* twenty cubits and
its width ten cubits."
3 Then he said to me, "This *is* the
curse that goes out over the face of
the whole earth: 'Every thief shall be
expelled,' according *to* this side of
the scroll; and, 'Every perjurer shall
be expelled,' according *to* that side
of it."
4 "I will send out *the curse,"* says
the LORD of hosts;
"It shall enter the house of the
thief
And the house of the one who
swears falsely by My name.
It shall remain in the midst of
his house
And consume it, with its timber
and stones."

5 Then the angel who talked with
me came out and said to me, "Lift
your eyes now, and see what this *is*
that goes forth."
6 So I asked, "What *is* it?" And he
said, "It *is* a basket*a* that is going
forth."
He also said, "This *is* their resem-
blance throughout the earth: 7 Here
is a lead disc lifted up, and this *is* a
woman sitting inside the basket";
8 then he said, "This *is* Wickedness!"
And he thrust her down into the basket, and threw the lead cover*a* over
its mouth. 9 Then I raised my eyes
and looked, and there *were* two
women, coming with the wind in
their wings; for they had wings like
the wings of a stork, and they lifted
up the basket between earth and
heaven.
10 So I said to the angel who talked
with me, "Where are they carrying
the basket?"
11 And he said to me, "To build a
house for it in the land of Shinar;*a*
when it is ready, *the basket* will be
set there on its base."

6 Then I turned and raised my eyes
and looked, and behold, four
chariots *were* coming from between
two mountains, and the mountains
were mountains of bronze. 2 With the
first chariot *were* red horses, with
the second chariot black horses,
3 with the third chariot white horses,
and with the fourth chariot dappled
horses—strong *steeds.* 4 Then I answered and said to the angel who
talked with me, "What *are* these, my
lord?"
5 And the angel answered and said
to me, "These *are* four spirits of
heaven, who go out from *their* station
before the Lord of all the earth.
6 The one with the black horses is going to the north country, the white
are going after them, and the dappled
are going toward the south country."
7 Then the strong *steeds* went out, eager to go, that they might walk to and
fro throughout the earth. And He
said, "Go, walk to and fro throughout
the earth." So they walked to and
fro throughout the earth. 8 And He
called to me, and spoke to me, saying, "See, those who go toward the
north country have given rest

4:9 *a*Literally *house*   4:12 *a*Literally *into the hands of*   5:6 *a*Hebrew *ephah,* a measuring container, and
so elsewhere   5:8 *a*Literally *stone*   5:11 *a*That is, Babylon

*I*f you really want to be set free, and experience restoration, you've got to be in Him,
because your healing comes in the Sabbath rest. Your healing comes in Christ Jesus.

to My Spirit in the north country." 9 Then the word of the LORD came to me, saying: 10 "Receive *the gift* from the captives—from Heldai, Tobijah, and Jedaiah, who have come from Babylon—and go the same day and enter the house of Josiah the son of Zephaniah. 11 Take the silver and gold, make an elaborate crown, and set *it* on the head of Joshua the son of Jehozadak, the high priest. 12 Then speak to him, saying, 'Thus says the LORD of hosts, saying:

> "Behold, the Man whose name
>   *is* the BRANCH!
> From His place He shall branch
>   out,
> And He shall build the temple
>   of the LORD;
> 13 Yes, He shall build the temple
>   of the LORD.
> He shall bear the glory,
> And shall sit and rule on His
>   throne;
> So He shall be a priest on His
>   throne,
> And the counsel of peace shall
>   be between them both." '

14 "Now the elaborate crown shall be for a memorial in the temple of the LORD for Helem,a Tobijah, Jedaiah, and Hen the son of Zephaniah. 15 Even those from afar shall come and build the temple of the LORD. Then you shall know that the LORD of hosts has sent Me to you. And *this* shall come to pass if you diligently obey the voice of the LORD your God."

7 Now in the fourth year of King Darius it came to pass *that* the word of the LORD came to Zechariah, on the fourth day of the ninth month, Chislev, 2 when *the people*a sent Sherezer,b with Regem-Melech and his men, *to* the house of God,c to pray before the LORD, 3 *and* to ask the priests who *were* in the house of the LORD of hosts, and the prophets, saying, "Should I weep in the fifth month and fast as I have done for so many years?"

4 Then the word of the LORD of hosts came to me, saying, 5 "Say to all the people of the land, and to

the priests: 'When you fasted and mourned in the fifth and seventh *months* during those seventy years, did you really fast for Me—for Me? 6 When you eat and when you drink, do you not eat and drink *for yourselves*? 7 *Should you* not *have obeyed* the words which the LORD proclaimed through the former prophets when Jerusalem and the cities around it were inhabited and prosperous, and the Southa and the Lowland were inhabited?' "

8 Then the word of the LORD came to Zechariah, saying, 9 "Thus says the LORD of hosts:

> 'Execute true justice,
> Show mercy and compassion
> Everyone to his brother.
> 10 Do not oppress the widow or
>   the fatherless,
> The alien or the poor.
> Let none of you plan evil in his
>   heart
> Against his brother.'

11 But they refused to heed, shrugged their shoulders, and stopped their ears so that they could not hear. 12 Yes, they made their hearts like flint, refusing to hear the law and the words which the LORD of hosts had sent by His Spirit through the former prophets. Thus great wrath came from the LORD of hosts. 13 Therefore it happened, *that* just as He proclaimed and they would not hear, so they called out and I would not listen," says the LORD of hosts. 14 "But I scattered them with a whirlwind among all the nations which they had not known. Thus the land became desolate after them, so that no one passed through or returned; for they made the pleasant land desolate."

8 Again the word of the LORD of hosts came, saying, 2 "Thus says the LORD of hosts:

> 'I am zealous for Zion with
>   great zeal;
> With great fervor I am zealous
>   for her.'

3 "Thus says the LORD:

6:14 aFollowing Masoretic Text, Targum, and Vulgate; Syriac reads *for Heldai* (compare verse 10); Septuagint reads *for the patient ones.*   7:2 aLiterally *they* (compare verse 5)   bOr *Sar-Ezer*   cHebrew *Bethel*
7:7 aHebrew *Negev*

'I will return to Zion,
And dwell in the midst of
Jerusalem.
Jerusalem shall be called the
City of Truth,
The Mountain of the LORD of
hosts,
The Holy Mountain.'

4 "Thus says the LORD of hosts:

'Old men and old women shall
again sit
In the streets of Jerusalem,
Each one with his staff in his
hand
Because of great age.
5   The streets of the city
Shall be full of boys and girls
Playing in its streets.'

6 "Thus says the LORD of hosts:

'If it is marvelous in the eyes of
the remnant of this people in
these days,
Will it also be marvelous in My
eyes?'
Says the LORD of hosts.

7 "Thus says the LORD of hosts:

'Behold, I will save My people
from the land of the east
And from the land of the west;
8   I will bring them back,
And they shall dwell in the
midst of Jerusalem.
They shall be My people
And I will be their God,
In truth and righteousness.'

9 "Thus says the LORD of hosts:

'Let your hands be strong,
You who have been hearing in
these days
These words by the mouth of
the prophets,
Who spoke in the day the
foundation was laid
For the house of the LORD of
hosts,
That the temple might be built.
10   For before these days
There were no wages for man
nor any hire for beast;
There was no peace from the
enemy for whoever went out
or came in;

For I set all men, everyone,
against his neighbor.

11 'But now I will not treat the remnant of this people as in the former
days,' says the LORD of hosts.

12 'For the seed shall be
prosperous,
The vine shall give its fruit,
The ground shall give her
increase,
And the heavens shall give
their dew—
I will cause the remnant of this
people
To possess all these.
13   And it shall come to pass
That just as you were a curse
among the nations,
O house of Judah and house of
Israel,
So I will save you, and you
shall be a blessing.
Do not fear,
Let your hands be strong.'

14 "For thus says the LORD of hosts:

'Just as I determined to punish
you
When your fathers provoked
Me to wrath,'
Says the LORD of hosts,
'And I would not relent,
15   So again in these days
I am determined to do good
To Jerusalem and to the house
of Judah.
Do not fear.
16   These are the things you shall
do:
Speak each man the truth to his
neighbor;
Give judgment in your gates for
truth, justice, and peace;
17   Let none of you think evil in
your*a* heart against your
neighbor;
And do not love a false oath.
For all these are things that I
hate,'
Says the LORD."

18 Then the word of the LORD of
hosts came to me, saying, 19 "Thus
says the LORD of hosts:

'The fast of the fourth month,
The fast of the fifth,

8:17 aLiterally his

When you meet the new, you get the power to say good-bye to the old. You will
never be able to break the grip on your life that those old ways have until you
know Jesus Christ is the real way.

The fast of the seventh,
And the fast of the tenth,
Shall be joy and gladness and
cheerful feasts
For the house of Judah.
Therefore love truth and
peace.'

20 "Thus says the LORD of hosts:

'Peoples shall yet come,
Inhabitants of many cities;
21 The inhabitants of one *city*
shall go to another, saying,
"Let us continue to go and pray
before the LORD,
And seek the LORD of hosts.
I myself will go also."
22 Yes, many peoples and strong
nations
Shall come to seek the LORD of
hosts in Jerusalem,
And to pray before the LORD.'

23 "Thus says the LORD of hosts: 'In
those days ten men from every language of the nations shall grasp the
sleeve of a Jewish man, saying, "Let
us go with you, for we have heard
that God *is* with you." ' "

9 The burden*a* of the word of the
LORD
Against the land of Hadrach,
And Damascus its resting
place
(For the eyes of men
And all the tribes of Israel
Are on the LORD);
2 Also *against* Hamath, *which*
borders on it,
And *against* Tyre and Sidon,
though they are very wise.

3 For Tyre built herself a tower,
Heaped up silver like the dust,
And gold like the mire of the
streets.
4 Behold, the LORD will cast her
out;
He will destroy her power in
the sea,
And she will be devoured by
fire.

5 Ashkelon shall see *it* and fear;
Gaza also shall be very
sorrowful;
And Ekron, for He dried up her
expectation.

The king shall perish from
Gaza,
And Ashkelon shall not be
inhabited.

6 "A mixed race shall settle in
Ashdod,
And I will cut off the pride of
the Philistines.
7 I will take away the blood from
his mouth,
And the abominations from
between his teeth.
But he who remains, even he
shall be for our God,
And shall be like a leader in
Judah,
And Ekron like a Jebusite.
8 I will camp around My house
Because of the army,
Because of him who passes by
and him who returns.
No more shall an oppressor
pass through them,
For now I have seen with My
eyes.

9 "Rejoice greatly, O daughter of
Zion!
Shout, O daughter of
Jerusalem!
Behold, your King is coming to
you;
He *is* just and having salvation,
Lowly and riding on a donkey,
A colt, the foal of a donkey.
10 I will cut off the chariot from
Ephraim
And the horse from Jerusalem;
The battle bow shall be cut off.
He shall speak peace to the
nations;
His dominion *shall be* 'from sea
to sea,
And from the River to the ends
of the earth.'*a*

11 "As for you also,
Because of the blood of your
covenant,
I will set your prisoners free
from the waterless pit.
12 Return to the stronghold,
You prisoners of hope.
Even today I declare
That I will restore double to
you.
13 For I have bent Judah, My *bow*,
Fitted the bow with Ephraim,

9:1 *a*Or *oracle*   9:10 *a*Psalm 72:8

*Y*ou will never get it straight without Jesus. You must come to Him just as you are.
Knowing Him will give you the power to break away from the old self and the ties
that bind.

Day of Restoration

Zechariah 9:12

ollowing Creation, on the seventh day, God rested. He didn't rest because He was tired. He rested for the purpose of restoring, replenishing, receiving back those things that were expended.

The Sabbath is a day of rest. But it is also a day of restoration. It is during a time of rest that the restoration of your life begins to occur. But watch out! The enemy does not want you to rest in the Lord. He wants you to be anxious. He wants you to be upset. He wants you to be hysterical. He wants you to be suicidal, doubtful, fearful, and neurotic.

It is not mere coincidence that the infirm woman was healed on the Sabbath day. The Sabbath was meant not only for God to rest but for Him to enjoy real communion with the people He created. In fact, in the nation of Israel, God used the Sabbath day as a sign of the covenant. It proved that they were His people.

When you enter into real worship with God, He can minister to your needs. You can never get your needs met by losing your head. When you start murmuring and complaining, God can only focus on your unbelief. When you start resting in Him, He can focus on the areas of your life that need to be touched. When you calm down, God speaks.

The infirm woman was not sitting around complaining. She was not murmuring. She was not hysterical. She had a problem, but she was calm. She was just listening to the words of the Master. She brought her problem with her, but she never allowed her problem to dominate her worship.

What the Sabbath was physically, Jesus Christ is spiritually. He is our Sabbath rest. He is the end of our labors. We are saved by grace through faith, not by works—the good things we do (see Ephesians 2:8, 9).

The rest of the Lord is so complete that when Jesus was dying on the Cross, He said, "It is finished" (John 19:30). For the first time in history, a High Priest sat down in the presence of God without having to run in and out, bringing blood to atone for the sins of man. When Christ entered in once and for all, He offered Himself for us that we might be delivered from sin.

If you really want to be healed, set free, restored, you must be in Him. As you rest in Him, every infirmity, every bent-out-of-shape place will be restored.

And raised up your sons, O
  Zion,
Against your sons, O Greece,
And made you like the sword
  of a mighty man."

14 Then the LORD will be seen over
  them,
And His arrow will go forth like
  lightning.
The Lord GOD will blow the
  trumpet,
And go with whirlwinds from
  the south.
15 The LORD of hosts will defend
  them;
They shall devour and subdue
  with slingstones.
They shall drink *and* roar as if
  with wine;
They shall be filled *with blood*
  like basins,
Like the corners of the altar.
16 The LORD their God will save
  them in that day,
As the flock of His people.
For they *shall be like* the jewels
  of a crown,
Lifted like a banner over His
  land—
17 For how great is its[a] goodness
And how great its[b] beauty!
Grain shall make the young
  men thrive,
And new wine the young
  women.

10 Ask the LORD for rain
In the time of the latter rain.[a]
The LORD will make flashing
  clouds;
He will give them showers of
  rain,
Grass in the field for everyone.

2 For the idols[a] speak delusion;
The diviners envision lies,
And tell false dreams;
They comfort in vain.
Therefore *the people* wend
  their way like sheep;
They are in trouble because
  there is no shepherd.

3 "My anger is kindled against the
  shepherds,
And I will punish the
  goatherds.
For the LORD of hosts will visit
  His flock,

The house of Judah,
And will make them as His
  royal horse in the battle.
4 From him comes the
  cornerstone,
From him the tent peg,
From him the battle bow,
From him every ruler[a] together.
5 They shall be like mighty men,
Who tread down *their enemies*
In the mire of the streets in the
  battle.
They shall fight because the
  LORD is with them,
And the riders on horses shall
  be put to shame.

6 "I will strengthen the house of
  Judah,
And I will save the house of
  Joseph.
I will bring them back,
Because I have mercy on them.
They shall be as though I had
  not cast them aside;
For I *am* the LORD their God,
And I will hear them.
7 *Those of* Ephraim shall be like
  a mighty man,
And their heart shall rejoice as
  if with wine.
Yes, their children shall see *it*
  and be glad;
Their heart shall rejoice in the
  LORD.
8 I will whistle for them and
  gather them,
For I will redeem them;
And they shall increase as they
  once increased.

9 "I will sow them among the
  peoples,
And they shall remember Me
  in far countries;
They shall live, together with
  their children,
And they shall return.
10 I will also bring them back
  from the land of Egypt,
And gather them from Assyria.
I will bring them into the land
  of Gilead and Lebanon,
Until no *more room* is found for
  them.
11 He shall pass through the sea
  with affliction,
And strike the waves of the sea:
All the depths of the River[a]
  shall dry up.

9:17 [a]Or *His*   [b]Or *His*   10:1 [a]That is, spring rain   10:2 [a]Hebrew *teraphim*   10:4 [a]Or *despot*
10:11 [a]That is, the Nile

Then the pride of Assyria shall
be brought down,
And the scepter of Egypt shall
depart.
12 "So I will strengthen them in the
LORD,
And they shall walk up and
down in His name,"
Says the LORD.

11 Open your doors, O Lebanon,
That fire may devour your
cedars.
2 Wail, O cypress, for the cedar
has fallen,
Because the mighty *trees* are
ruined.
Wail, O oaks of Bashan,
For the thick forest has come
down.
3 *There is* the sound of wailing
shepherds!
For their glory is in ruins.
There is the sound of roaring
lions!
For the pride*a* of the Jordan is
in ruins.

4 Thus says the LORD my God,
"Feed the flock for slaughter,
5 whose owners slaughter them and
feel no guilt; those who sell them say,
'Blessed be the LORD, for I am rich';
and their shepherds do not pity them.
6 For I will no longer pity the inhabitants of the land," says the LORD. "But
indeed I will give everyone into his
neighbor's hand and into the hand
of his king. They shall attack the
land, and I will not deliver *them* from
their hand."
7 So I fed the flock for slaughter,
in particular the poor of the flock.*a* I
took for myself two staffs: the one I
called Beauty,*b* and the other I called
Bonds;*c* and I fed the flock. 8 I dismissed the three shepherds in one
month. My soul loathed them, and
their soul also abhorred me.
9 Then I said, "I will not feed you.
Let what is dying die, and what is
perishing perish. Let those that are
left eat each other's flesh." 10 And I
took my staff, Beauty, and cut it in
two, that I might break the covenant
which I had made with all the peoples. 11 So it was broken on that day.
Thus the poor*a* of the flock, who were

watching me, knew that it *was* the
word of the LORD. 12 Then I said to
them, "If it is agreeable to you, give
me my wages; and if not, refrain."
So they weighed out for my wages
thirty *pieces* of silver.
13 And the LORD said to me,
"Throw it to the potter"—that
princely price they set on me. So I
took the thirty *pieces* of silver and
threw them into the house of the
LORD for the potter. 14 Then I cut in
two my other staff, Bonds, that I
might break the brotherhood between Judah and Israel.
15 And the LORD said to me, "Next,
take for yourself the implements of
a foolish shepherd. 16 For indeed I
will raise up a shepherd in the land
who will not care for those who are
cut off, nor seek the young, nor heal
those that are broken, nor feed those
that still stand. But he will eat the
flesh of the fat and tear their hooves
in pieces.

17 "Woe to the worthless shepherd,
Who leaves the flock!
A sword *shall be* against his
arm
And against his right eye;
His arm shall completely
wither,
And his right eye shall be
totally blinded."

12 The burden*a* of the word of the
LORD against Israel. Thus says
the LORD, who stretches out the heavens, lays the foundation of the earth,
and forms the spirit of man within
him: 2 "Behold, I will make Jerusalem a cup of drunkenness to all the
surrounding peoples, when they lay
siege against Judah and Jerusalem.
3 And it shall happen in that day that
I will make Jerusalem a very heavy
stone for all peoples; all who would
heave it away will surely be cut in
pieces, though all nations of the earth
are gathered against it. 4 In that day,"
says the LORD, "I will strike every
horse with confusion, and its rider
with madness; I will open My eyes
on the house of Judah, and will strike
every horse of the peoples with blindness. 5 And the governors of Judah
shall say in their heart, 'The inhabitants of Jerusalem *are* my strength

11:3 *a*Or *floodplain, thicket*   11:7 *a*Following Masoretic Text, Targum, and Vulgate; Septuagint reads *for*
the Canaanites.   *b*Or *Grace,* and so in verse 10   *c*Or *Unity,* and so in verse 14   11:11 *a*Following
Masoretic Text, Targum, and Vulgate; Septuagint reads *the Canaanites.*   12:1 *a*Or *oracle*

*I*f you have something that has attached itself to you that is not of God, you won't
be able to break it through your own strength. Submit yourself unto God, resist the
enemy, and he will flee from you.

Soul Secrets
for the loss of a child

*L*ord, I cannot imagine any grief more consuming than this. O God, my child. I am weary and numb. It is hard for me to realize that this loss is real and that it is permanent. I feel guilty that, as a mother, it is so hard to release my child to You, the Father. But Lord, it is almost more than I can bear.

Lord, bring comfort. Send Your Holy Spirit in a way I've never experienced before. I need You right beside me. I need to cry on Your shoulder. I need to know that You know. You really know.

Lord, give wisdom to those around me who want to help, but feel so inadequate. Equip them to minister to me in ways that will help all of us. But more than that, be my deepest friend. Bring me through these devastating days. Give me grace through all my grief. Help me now to survive, and when it's time, to arise stronger and more compassionate. Remind me that my child is safe with You. And so am I.

in the LORD of hosts, their God.' 6 In that day I will make the governors of Judah like a firepan in the woodpile, and like a fiery torch in the sheaves; they shall devour all the surrounding peoples on the right hand and on the left, but Jerusalem shall be inhabited again in her own place—Jerusalem.

7 "The LORD will save the tents of Judah first, so that the glory of the house of David and the glory of the inhabitants of Jerusalem shall not become greater than that of Judah. 8 In that day the LORD will defend the inhabitants of Jerusalem; the one who is feeble among them in that day shall be like David, and the house of David *shall be* like God, like the Angel of the LORD before them. 9 It shall be in that day *that* I will seek to destroy all the nations that come against Jerusalem.

10 "And I will pour on the house of David and on the inhabitants of Jerusalem the Spirit of grace and supplication; then they will look on Me whom they pierced. Yes, they will mourn for Him as one mourns for *his* only *son*, and grieve for Him as one grieves for a firstborn. 11 In that day there shall be a great mourning in Jerusalem, like the mourning at Hadad Rimmon in the plain of Megiddo.*a* 12 And the land shall mourn, every family by itself: the family of the house of David by itself, and their wives by themselves; the family of the house of Nathan by itself, and their wives by themselves; 13 the family of the house of Levi by itself, and their wives by themselves; the family of Shimei by itself, and their wives by themselves; 14 all the families that remain, every family by itself, and their wives by themselves.

13 "In that day a fountain shall be opened for the house of David and for the inhabitants of Jerusalem, for sin and for uncleanness.

2 "It shall be in that day," says the LORD of hosts, "*that* I will cut off the names of the idols from the land, and they shall no longer be remembered. I will also cause the prophets and the unclean spirit to depart from the land. 3 It shall come to pass *that* if anyone still prophesies, then his fa-

ther and mother who begot him will say to him, 'You shall not live, because you have spoken lies in the name of the LORD.' And his father and mother who begot him shall thrust him through when he prophesies.

4 "And it shall be in that day *that* every prophet will be ashamed of his vision when he prophesies; they will not wear a robe of coarse hair to deceive. 5 But he will say, 'I *am* no prophet, I *am* a farmer; for a man taught me to keep cattle from my youth.' 6 And *one* will say to him, 'What are these wounds between your arms?'*a* Then he will answer, '*Those* with which I was wounded in the house of my friends.'

7 "Awake, O sword, against My Shepherd,
 Against the Man who is My Companion,"
 Says the LORD of hosts.
 "Strike the Shepherd,
 And the sheep will be scattered;
 Then I will turn My hand against the little ones.
8 And it shall come to pass in all the land,"
 Says the LORD,
 "*That* two-thirds in it shall be cut off *and* die,
 But *one*-third shall be left in it:
9 I will bring the *one*-third through the fire,
 Will refine them as silver is refined,
 And test them as gold is tested.
 They will call on My name,
 And I will answer them.
 I will say, 'This *is* My people';
 And each one will say, 'The LORD *is* my God.' "

14 Behold, the day of the LORD is coming,
 And your spoil will be divided in your midst.
2 For I will gather all the nations to battle against Jerusalem;
 The city shall be taken,
 The houses rifled,
 And the women ravished.
 Half of the city shall go into captivity,

12:11 *a*Hebrew *Megiddon* 13:6 *a*Or *hands*

*Y*ou do yourself a disservice until you really come to know Jesus. He satisfies. He can satisfy every need and every yearning. He heals every pain and every affliction. Then He lifts every burden and every trouble in your life.

But the remnant of the people
shall not be cut off from the
city.

3 Then the LORD will go forth
And fight against those
nations,
As He fights in the day of
battle.

4 And in that day His feet will
stand on the Mount of Olives,
Which faces Jerusalem on the
east.
And the Mount of Olives shall
be split in two,
From east to west,
Making a very large valley;
Half of the mountain shall
move toward the north
And half of it toward the south.

5 Then you shall flee *through* My
mountain valley,
For the mountain valley shall
reach to Azal.
Yes, you shall flee
As you fled from the
earthquake
In the days of Uzziah king of
Judah.

Thus the LORD my God will
come,
And all the saints with You.*a*

6 It shall come to pass in that day
That there will be no light;
The lights will diminish.

7 It shall be one day
Which is known to the LORD—
Neither day nor night.
But at evening time it shall
happen
That it will be light.

8 And in that day it shall be
That living waters shall flow
from Jerusalem,
Half of them toward the eastern
sea
And half of them toward the
western sea;
In both summer and winter it
shall occur.

9 And the LORD shall be King
over all the earth.
In that day it shall be—
"The LORD *is* one,"*a*
And His name one.

10 All the land shall be turned into
a plain from Geba to Rimmon south
of Jerusalem. *Jerusalem*ᵃ shall be
raised up and inhabited in her place
from Benjamin's Gate to the place of
the First Gate and the Corner Gate,
and *from* the Tower of Hananel to
the king's winepresses.

11 *The people* shall dwell in it;
And no longer shall there be
utter destruction,
But Jerusalem shall be safely
inhabited.

12 And this shall be the plague with
which the LORD will strike all the people who fought against Jerusalem:

Their flesh shall dissolve while
they stand on their feet,
Their eyes shall dissolve in
their sockets,
And their tongues shall
dissolve in their mouths.

13 It shall come to pass in that day
That a great panic from the
LORD will be among them.
Everyone will seize the hand of
his neighbor,
And raise his hand against his
neighbor's hand;

14 Judah also will fight at
Jerusalem.
And the wealth of all the
surrounding nations
Shall be gathered together:
Gold, silver, and apparel in
great abundance.

15 Such also shall be the plague
On the horse *and* the mule,
On the camel and the donkey,
And on all the cattle that will
be in those camps.
So *shall* this plague *be.*

16 And it shall come to pass *that*
everyone who is left of all the nations
which came against Jerusalem shall
go up from year to year to worship
the King, the LORD of hosts, and to
keep the Feast of Tabernacles.
17 And it shall be *that* whichever of
the families of the earth do not come
up to Jerusalem to worship the King,
the LORD of hosts, on them there will
be no rain. 18 If the family of Egypt

14:5 *a*Or *you;* Septuagint, Targum, and Vulgate read *Him.*   14:9 *a*Compare Deuteronomy 6:4
14:10 *a*Literally *She*

Gospel
Pearls

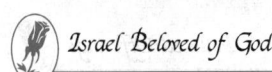

will not come up and enter in, they *shall have* no *rain;* they shall receive the plague with which the LORD strikes the nations who do not come up to keep the Feast of Tabernacles. 19 This shall be the punishment of Egypt and the punishment of all the nations that do not come up to keep the Feast of Tabernacles.

20 In that day "HOLINESS TO THE LORD" shall be *engraved* on the bells of the horses. The pots in the LORD's house shall be like the bowls before the altar. 21 Yes, every pot in Jerusalem and Judah shall be holiness to the LORD of hosts.*a* Everyone who sacrifices shall come and take them and cook in them. In that day there shall no longer be a Canaanite in the house of the LORD of hosts.

14:21 *a*Or *on every pot . . . shall be (engraved)* "HOLINESS TO THE LORD OF HOSTS"

The Book of
MALACHI

1 The burden*a* of the word of the LORD to Israel by Malachi.

2 "I have loved you," says the
   LORD.
   "Yet you say, 'In what way have
      You loved us?'
      Was not Esau Jacob's
      brother?"
   Says the LORD.
   "Yet Jacob I have loved;
3 But Esau I have hated,
   And laid waste his mountains
      and his heritage
   For the jackals of the
      wilderness."

4 Even though Edom has said,
   "We have been impoverished,
   But we will return and build the
      desolate places,"

Thus says the LORD of hosts:

   "They may build, but I will
      throw down;
   They shall be called the
      Territory of Wickedness,
   And the people against whom
      the LORD will have
      indignation forever.
5 Your eyes shall see,
   And you shall say,
   'The LORD is magnified beyond
      the border of Israel.'
6 "A son honors *his* father,
   And a servant *his* master.

If then I am the Father,
   Where *is* My honor?
And if I *am* a Master,
   Where *is* My reverence?
Says the LORD of hosts
To you priests who despise My
   name.
Yet you say, 'In what way have
   we despised Your name?'

7 "You offer defiled food on My
      altar,
   But say,
   'In what way have we defiled
      You?'
   By saying,
   'The table of the LORD is
      contemptible.'
8 And when you offer the blind
      as a sacrifice,
   Is it not evil?
   And when you offer the lame
      and sick,
   Is it not evil?
   Offer it then to your governor!
   Would he be pleased with you?
   Would he accept you
      favorably?"
   Says the LORD of hosts.

9 "But now entreat God's favor,
   That He may be gracious to us.
   While this is being *done* by
      your hands,
   Will He accept you favorably?"
   Says the LORD of hosts.
10 "Who *is there* even among you
      who would shut the doors,

1:1 *a*Or *oracle*

*Y*ou have had enough tragedy. God will do something good in you. God kept you living through all those years of infirmity because He had something greater for you than what you experienced earlier.

So that you would not kindle
fire *on* My altar in vain?
I have no pleasure in you,"
Says the Lord of hosts,
"Nor will I accept an offering
from your hands.
11 For from the rising of the sun,
even to its going down,
My name *shall be* great among
the Gentiles;
In every place incense *shall be*
offered to My name,
And a pure offering;
For My name shall be great
among the nations,"
Says the Lord of hosts.

12 "But you profane it,
In that you say,
'The table of the Lord*ᵃ* is
defiled;
And its fruit, its food, *is*
contemptible.'
13 You also say,
'Oh, what a weariness!'
And you sneer at it,"
Says the Lord of hosts.
"And you bring the stolen, the
lame, and the sick;
Thus you bring an offering!
Should I accept this from your
hand?"
Says the Lord.
14 "But cursed *be* the deceiver
Who has in his flock a male,
And takes a vow,
But sacrifices to the Lord what
is blemished—
For I *am* a great King,"
Says the Lord of hosts,
"And My name *is to be* feared
among the nations.

2 "And now, O priests, this
commandment is for you.
2 If you will not hear,
And if you will not take *it* to
heart,
To give glory to My name,"
Says the Lord of hosts,
"I will send a curse upon you,
And I will curse your blessings.
Yes, I have cursed them
already,
Because you do not take *it* to
heart.

3 "Behold, I will rebuke your
descendants
And spread refuse on your
faces,

The refuse of your solemn
feasts;
And *one* will take you away
with it.
4 Then you shall know that I
have sent this commandment
to you,
That My covenant with Levi
may continue,"
Says the Lord of hosts.
5 "My covenant was with him, *one*
of life and peace,
And I gave them to him *that*
he might fear *Me;*
So he feared Me
And was reverent before My
name.
6 The law of truth*ᵃ* was in his
mouth,
And injustice was not found on
his lips.
He walked with Me in peace
and equity,
And turned many away from
iniquity.

7 "For the lips of a priest should
keep knowledge,
And *people* should seek the law
from his mouth;
For he is the messenger of the
Lord of hosts.
8 But you have departed from the
way;
You have caused many to
stumble at the law.
You have corrupted the
covenant of Levi,"
Says the Lord of hosts.
9 "Therefore I also have made you
contemptible and base
Before all the people,
Because you have not kept My
ways
But have shown partiality in
the law."

10 Have we not all one Father?
Has not one God created us?
Why do we deal treacherously
with one another
By profaning the covenant of
the fathers?
11 Judah has dealt treacherously,
And an abomination has been
committed in Israel and in
Jerusalem,
For Judah has profaned
The Lord's holy *institution*
which He loves:

1:12 *ᵃ*Following Bomberg; Masoretic Text reads *Lord.*   2:6 *ᵃ*Or *true instruction*

Gospel
Pearls

He has married the daughter of
a foreign god.

12 May the LORD cut off from the
tents of Jacob
The man who does this, being
awake and aware,[a]
Yet who brings an offering to
the LORD of hosts!

13 And this is the second thing
you do:
You cover the altar of the LORD
with tears,
With weeping and crying;
So He does not regard the
offering anymore,
Nor receive *it* with goodwill
from your hands.

14 Yet you say, "For what
reason?"
Because the LORD has been
witness
Between you and the wife of
your youth,
With whom you have dealt
treacherously;
Yet she is your companion
And your wife by covenant.

15 But did He not make *them*
one,
Having a remnant of the Spirit?
And why one?
He seeks godly offspring.
Therefore take heed to your
spirit,
And let none deal
treacherously with the wife
of his youth.

16 "For the LORD God of Israel says
That He hates divorce,
For it covers one's garment
with violence,"
Says the LORD of hosts.
"Therefore take heed to your
spirit,
That you do not deal
treacherously."

17 You have wearied the LORD
with your words;
Yet you say,
"In what way have we wearied
Him?"
In that you say,
"Everyone who does evil
Is good in the sight of the LORD,
And He delights in them,"
Or, "Where *is* the God of
justice?"

3 "Behold, I send My messenger,
And he will prepare the way
before Me.
And the Lord, whom you seek,
Will suddenly come to His
temple,
Even the Messenger of the
covenant,
In whom you delight.
Behold, He is coming,"
Says the LORD of hosts.

2 "But who can endure the day of
His coming?
And who can stand when He
appears?
For He *is* like a refiner's fire
And like launderers' soap.

3 He will sit as a refiner and a
purifier of silver;
He will purify the sons of Levi,
And purge them as gold and
silver,
That they may offer to the
LORD
An offering in righteousness.

4 "Then the offering of Judah and
Jerusalem
Will be pleasant to the LORD,
As in the days of old,
As in former years.

5 And I will come near you for
judgment;
I will be a swift witness
Against sorcerers,
Against adulterers,
Against perjurers,
Against those who exploit
wage earners and widows
and orphans,
And against those who turn
away an alien—
Because they do not fear Me,"
Says the LORD of hosts.

6 "For I *am* the LORD, I do not
change;
Therefore you are not
consumed, O sons of Jacob.

7 Yet from the days of your
fathers
You have gone away from My
ordinances
And have not kept *them*.
Return to Me, and I will return
to you,"
Says the LORD of hosts.
"But you said,
'In what way shall we return?'

2:12 [a]Talmud and Vulgate read *teacher and student.*

God has more for you today than what you went through yesterday. Don't give up.
Don't give in. Hold on. The blessing is on the way.

A Mirror of God

Malachi 2:15

Remember Eve in the Book of Genesis? She was not only the first woman and the mother of all living; she is representative of many other firsts as well: the first family, the first marital conflict, the first rekindling of a woman's dream.

Eve was created in the man, called out of the man, and then presented to the man. She was called woman—bone of his bone, flesh of his flesh—created to stand beside man to help meet his need, to help make up the difference. Together, Eve and Adam—woman and man—are a picture of the wholeness of God.

Eve, the woman, was hidden in the "womb" of man. When Adam got to the place where he needed someone, God did not need to reenter the creative process. He simply said, "Adam, I'm going to put you to sleep and pull out of you what I've already created in you. I've already made exactly what you need."

Adam had absolutely no trouble relating to Eve because she *was* Adam. When they came together, they were a picture of total godliness. They were one flesh, a mirror of one God.

Today, when men and women come together in the Spirit, they too are a total picture of all the characteristics of God. That is one of the reasons the enemy wants to do everything he can to divide men and women. That is why he has declared war on marriage. He knows that when we are separated, we do not give a total picture of godliness to the world.

Without the other, neither man nor woman can fully depict God's nature. Men need the gentleness, tenderness, femininity, love, mercy, and compassion of women. Women need men to express the strength, provision, power, protection, and defense of God. When we come together, we are able to express the total nature of God to a hurting world. And the devil doesn't want that to happen.

When men and women come together, God allows them to act out who He is. They are privileged to be partners with Him in the creative process. Their union brings life in the form of children! Just as God breathed His life into Adam, so we men and women are allowed to breathe life into this world as we bear children.

You were created as a woman for a very special purpose—first, to experience wholeness and union with God, and then, to bear children with your husband. That dual purpose is not limited to the natural. It is supernatural. God created you to become the mother of something spiritual that will live forever!

8 "Will a man rob God?
Yet you have robbed Me!
But you say,
'In what way have we robbed
You?'
In tithes and offerings.
9 You are cursed with a
curse,
For you have robbed Me,
Even this whole nation.
10 Bring all the tithes into the
storehouse,
That there may be food in My
house,
And try Me now in this,"
Says the LORD of hosts,
"If I will not open for you the
windows of heaven
And pour out for you *such*
blessing
That *there will* not *be room
enough to receive it.*

11 "And I will rebuke the devourer
for your sakes,
So that he will not destroy the
fruit of your ground,
Nor shall the vine fail to bear
fruit for you in the field,"
Says the LORD of hosts;
12 And all nations will call you
blessed,
For you will be a delightful
land,"
Says the LORD of hosts.

13 "Your words have been harsh
against Me,"
Says the LORD,
"Yet you say,
'What have we spoken against
You?'
14 You have said,
'It is useless to serve God;
What profit *is it* that we have
kept His ordinance,
And that we have walked as
mourners
Before the LORD of hosts?
15 So now we call the proud
blessed,
For those who do wickedness
are raised up;
They even tempt God and go
free.' "

16 Then those who feared the
LORD spoke to one another,
And the LORD listened and
heard *them;*

So a book of remembrance was
written before Him
For those who fear the LORD
And who meditate on His
name.

17 "They shall be Mine," says the
LORD of hosts,
"On the day that I make them
My jewels.*a*
And I will spare them
As a man spares his own son
who serves him."
18 Then you shall again discern
Between the righteous and the
wicked,
Between one who serves God
And one who does not serve
Him.

4 "For behold, the day is coming,
Burning like an oven,
And all the proud, yes, all who
do wickedly will be stubble.
And the day which is coming
shall burn them up,"
Says the LORD of hosts,
"That will leave them neither
root nor branch.
2 But to you who fear My name
The Sun of Righteousness shall
arise
With healing in His wings;
And you shall go out
And grow fat like stall-fed
calves.
3 You shall trample the wicked,
For they shall be ashes under
the soles of your feet
On the day that I do *this,*"
Says the LORD of hosts.

4 "Remember the Law of Moses,
My servant,
Which I commanded him in
Horeb for all Israel,
With the statutes and
judgments.
5 Behold, I will send you Elijah
the prophet
Before the coming of the great
and dreadful day of the LORD.
6 And he will turn
The hearts of the fathers to the
children,
And the hearts of the children
to their fathers,
Lest I come and strike the earth
with a curse."

3:17 *a*Literally *special treasure*

*Y*ou can find hope for your soul. It is found in the Master of the universe. He will
not deny you because of your past. He will take you as you are and give you rest.

The
New Testament

MATTHEW

1 The book of the genealogy of Jesus Christ, the Son of David, the Son of Abraham:

2 Abraham begot Isaac, Isaac begot Jacob, and Jacob begot Judah and his brothers. 3 Judah begot Perez and Zerah by Tamar, Perez begot Hezron, and Hezron begot Ram. 4 Ram begot Amminadab, Amminadab begot Nahshon, and Nahshon begot Salmon. 5 Salmon begot Boaz by Rahab, Boaz begot Obed by Ruth, Obed begot Jesse, 6 and Jesse begot David the king.

David the king begot Solomon by her *who had been the wife*ᵃ of Uriah. 7 Solomon begot Rehoboam, Rehoboam begot Abijah, and Abijah begot Asa.ᵃ 8 Asa begot Jehoshaphat, Jehoshaphat begot Joram, and Joram begot Uzziah. 9 Uzziah begot Jotham, Jotham begot Ahaz, and Ahaz begot Hezekiah. 10 Hezekiah begot Manasseh, Manasseh begot Amon,ᵃ and Amon begot Josiah. 11 Josiah begot Jeconiah and his brothers about the time they were carried away to Babylon.

12 And after they were brought to Babylon, Jeconiah begot Shealtiel, and Shealtiel begot Zerubbabel. 13 Zerubbabel begot Abiud, Abiud begot Eliakim, and Eliakim begot Azor. 14 Azor begot Zadok, Zadok begot Achim, and Achim begot Eliud. 15 Eliud begot Eleazar, Eleazar begot Matthan, and Matthan begot Jacob. 16 And Jacob begot Joseph the husband of Mary, of whom was born Jesus who is called Christ.

17 So all the generations from Abraham to David *are* fourteen generations, from David until the captivity in Babylon *are* fourteen generations, and from the captivity in Babylon until the Christ *are* fourteen generations.

18 Now the birth of Jesus Christ was as follows: After His mother Mary was betrothed to Joseph, before they came together, she was found with child of the Holy Spirit. 19 Then Joseph her husband, being a just *man,* and not wanting to make her a public example, was minded to put her away secretly. 20 But while he thought about these things, behold, an angel of the Lord appeared to him in a dream, saying, "Joseph, son of David, do not be afraid to take to you Mary your wife, for that which is conceived in her is of the Holy Spirit. 21 And she will bring forth a Son, and you shall call His name Jᴇsᴜs, for He will save His people from their sins."

22 So all this was done that it might be fulfilled which was spoken by the Lord through the prophet, saying: 23 *"Behold, the virgin shall be with child, and bear a Son, and they shall call His name Immanuel,"*ᵃ which is translated, "God with us."

24 Then Joseph, being aroused from sleep, did as the angel of the Lord commanded him and took to him his wife, 25 and did not know her till she had brought forth her firstborn Son.ᵃ And he called His name Jᴇsᴜs.

2 Now after Jesus was born in Bethlehem of Judea in the days of Herod the king, behold, wise men from the East came to Jerusalem, 2 saying, "Where is He who has been born King of the Jews? For we have seen His star in the East and have come to worship Him."

3 When Herod the king heard *this,* he was troubled, and all Jerusalem with him. 4 And when he had gathered all the chief priests and scribes of the people together, he inquired of them where the Christ was to be born.

5 So they said to him, "In Bethlehem of Judea, for thus it is written by the prophet:

6 '*But you, Bethlehem, in the land of Judah,
Are not the least among the rulers of Judah;
For out of you shall come a Ruler*

1:6 ᵃWords in italic type have been added for clarity. They are not found in the original Greek.
1:7 ᵃNU-Text reads *Asaph.*   1:10 ᵃNU-Text reads *Amos.*   1:23 ᵃIsaiah 7:14. Words in oblique type in the New Testament are quoted from the Old Testament.   1:25 ᵃNU-Text reads *a Son.*

*Who will shepherd My people
Israel.' "ᵃ*

7 Then Herod, when he had secretly called the wise men, determined from them what time the star
appeared. 8 And he sent them to
Bethlehem and said, "Go and search
carefully for the young Child, and
when you have found *Him,* bring
back word to me, that I may come
and worship Him also."

9 When they heard the king, they
departed; and behold, the star which
they had seen in the East went before them, till it came and stood
over where the young Child was.
10 When they saw the star, they rejoiced with exceedingly great joy.
11 And when they had come into the
house, they saw the young Child with
Mary His mother, and fell down and
worshiped Him. And when they had
opened their treasures, they presented gifts to Him: gold, frankincense, and myrrh.

12 Then, being divinely warned in
a dream that they should not return
to Herod, they departed for their own
country another way.

13 Now when they had departed,
behold, an angel of the Lord appeared to Joseph in a dream, saying,
"Arise, take the young Child and His
mother, flee to Egypt, and stay there
until I bring you word; for Herod will
seek the young Child to destroy
Him."

14 When he arose, he took the
young Child and His mother by night
and departed for Egypt, 15 and was
there until the death of Herod, that
it might be fulfilled which was spoken by the Lord through the prophet,
saying, *"Out of Egypt I called My
Son."ᵃ*

16 Then Herod, when he saw that
he was deceived by the wise men,
was exceedingly angry; and he sent
forth and put to death all the male
children who were in Bethlehem and
in all its districts, from two years old
and under, according to the time
which he had determined from the
wise men. 17 Then was fulfilled what
was spoken by Jeremiah the prophet,
saying:

18 *"A voice was heard in
Ramah,*

*Lamentation, weeping, and
great mourning,
Rachel weeping for her
children,
Refusing to be comforted,
Because they are no more."ᵃ*

19 Now when Herod was dead, behold, an angel of the Lord appeared
in a dream to Joseph in Egypt,
20 saying, "Arise, take the young
Child and His mother, and go to the
land of Israel, for those who sought
the young Child's life are dead."
21 Then he arose, took the young
Child and His mother, and came into
the land of Israel.

22 But when he heard that Arche-
laus was reigning over Judea instead
of his father Herod, he was afraid to
go there. And being warned by God
in a dream, he turned aside into the
region of Galilee. 23 And he came and
dwelt in a city called Nazareth, that
it might be fulfilled which was spoken by the prophets, "He shall be
called a Nazarene."

3 In those days John the Baptist
came preaching in the wilderness
of Judea, 2 and saying, "Repent, for
the kingdom of heaven is at hand!"
3 For this is he who was spoken of
by the prophet Isaiah, saying:

*"The voice of one crying in the
wilderness:
'Prepare the way of the LORD;
Make His paths straight.' "ᵃ*

4 Now John himself was clothed in
camel's hair, with a leather belt
around his waist; and his food was
locusts and wild honey. 5 Then Jerusalem, all Judea, and all the region
around the Jordan went out to him
6 and were baptized by him in the
Jordan, confessing their sins.

7 But when he saw many of the
Pharisees and Sadducees coming to
his baptism, he said to them, "Brood
of vipers! Who warned you to flee
from the wrath to come? 8 Therefore
bear fruits worthy of repentance,
9 and do not think to say to yourselves, 'We have Abraham as *our* father.' For I say to you that God is able
to raise up children to Abraham from
these stones. 10 And even now the ax
is laid to the root of the trees. There-

2:6 ᵃMicah 5:2   2:15 ᵃHosea 11:1   2:18 ᵃJeremiah 31:15   3:3 ᵃIsaiah 40:3

fore every tree which does not bear good fruit is cut down and thrown into the fire. 11 I indeed baptize you with water unto repentance, but He who is coming after me is mightier than I, whose sandals I am not worthy to carry. He will baptize you with the Holy Spirit and fire.*a* 12 His winnowing fan *is* in His hand, and He will thoroughly clean out His threshing floor, and gather His wheat into the barn; but He will burn up the chaff with unquenchable fire."

13 Then Jesus came from Galilee to John at the Jordan to be baptized by him. 14 And John *tried to* prevent Him, saying, "I need to be baptized by You, and are You coming to me?"

15 But Jesus answered and said to him, "Permit *it to be so* now, for thus it is fitting for us to fulfill all righteousness." Then he allowed Him.

16 When He had been baptized, Jesus came up immediately from the water; and behold, the heavens were opened to Him, and He*a* saw the Spirit of God descending like a dove and alighting upon Him. 17 And suddenly a voice *came* from heaven, saying, "This is My beloved Son, in whom I am well pleased."

4 Then Jesus was led up by the Spirit into the wilderness to be tempted by the devil. 2 And when He had fasted forty days and forty nights, afterward He was hungry. 3 Now when the tempter came to Him, he said, "If You are the Son of God, command that these stones become bread."

4 But He answered and said, "It is written, '*Man shall not live by bread alone, but by every word that proceeds from the mouth of God.*'"*a*

5 Then the devil took Him up into the holy city, set Him on the pinnacle of the temple, 6 and said to Him, "If You are the Son of God, throw Yourself down. For it is written:

'*He shall give His angels charge over you,*'

and,

'*In their hands they shall bear you up,*

Lest you dash your foot against a stone.'"*a*

7 Jesus said to him, "It is written again, '*You shall not tempt the LORD your God.*'"*a*

8 Again, the devil took Him up on an exceedingly high mountain, and showed Him all the kingdoms of the world and their glory. 9 And he said to Him, "All these things I will give You if You will fall down and worship me."

10 Then Jesus said to him, "Away with you,*a* Satan! For it is written, '*You shall worship the LORD your God, and Him only you shall serve.*'"*b*

11 Then the devil left Him, and behold, angels came and ministered to Him.

12 Now when Jesus heard that John had been put in prison, He departed to Galilee. 13 And leaving Nazareth, He came and dwelt in Capernaum, which is by the sea, in the regions of Zebulun and Naphtali, 14 that it might be fulfilled which was spoken by Isaiah the prophet, saying:

15 "*The land of Zebulun and the land of Naphtali,*
By the way of the sea, beyond the Jordan,
Galilee of the Gentiles:
16 *The people who sat in darkness have seen a great light,*
And upon those who sat in the region and shadow of death Light has dawned."*a*

17 From that time Jesus began to preach and to say, "Repent, for the kingdom of heaven is at hand."

18 And Jesus, walking by the Sea of Galilee, saw two brothers, Simon called Peter, and Andrew his brother, casting a net into the sea; for they were fishermen. 19 Then He said to them, "Follow Me, and I will make you fishers of men." 20 They immediately left *their* nets and followed Him.

21 Going on from there, He saw two other brothers, James *the son of* Zebedee, and John his brother, in the boat with Zebedee their father, mending their nets. He called them, 22 and immediately they left the boat

No matter what age you are, you have never seen it all. There are no graduations from the school of life other than death. No one knows how God will end His book, but He does tend to save the best for last.

and their father, and followed Him.

23 And Jesus went about all Galilee, teaching in their synagogues, preaching the gospel of the kingdom, and healing all kinds of sickness and all kinds of disease among the people. 24 Then His fame went throughout all Syria; and they brought to Him all sick people who were afflicted with various diseases and torments, and those who were demonpossessed, epileptics, and paralytics; and He healed them. 25 Great multitudes followed Him—from Galilee, and *from* Decapolis, Jerusalem, Judea, and beyond the Jordan.

5 And seeing the multitudes, He went up on a mountain, and when He was seated His disciples came to Him. 2 Then He opened His mouth and taught them, saying:

3 "Blessed *are* the poor in spirit,
  For theirs is the kingdom of
    heaven.
4 Blessed *are* those who mourn,
  For they shall be comforted.
5 Blessed *are* the meek,
  For they shall inherit the
    earth.
6 Blessed *are* those who hunger
    and thirst for
    righteousness,
  For they shall be filled.
7 Blessed *are* the merciful,
  For they shall obtain mercy.
8 Blessed *are* the pure in heart,
  For they shall see God.
9 Blessed *are* the peacemakers,
  For they shall be called sons
    of God.
10 Blessed are those who are
    persecuted for
    righteousness' sake,
  For theirs is the kingdom of
    heaven.

11 "Blessed are you when they revile and persecute you, and say all kinds of evil against you falsely for My sake. 12 Rejoice and be exceedingly glad, for great *is* your reward in heaven, for so they persecuted the prophets who were before you.

13 "You are the salt of the earth; but if the salt loses its flavor, how shall it be seasoned? It is then good for nothing but to be thrown out and trampled underfoot by men.

14 "You are the light of the world. A city that is set on a hill cannot be hidden. 15 Nor do they light a lamp and put it under a basket, but on a lampstand, and it gives light to all *who are* in the house. 16 Let your light so shine before men, that they may see your good works and glorify your Father in heaven.

17 "Do not think that I came to destroy the Law or the Prophets. I did not come to destroy but to fulfill. 18 For assuredly, I say to you, till heaven and earth pass away, one jot or one tittle will by no means pass from the law till all is fulfilled. 19 Whoever therefore breaks one of the least of these commandments, and teaches men so, shall be called least in the kingdom of heaven; but whoever does and teaches *them*, he shall be called great in the kingdom of heaven. 20 For I say to you, that unless your righteousness exceeds *the righteousness* of the scribes and Pharisees, you will by no means enter the kingdom of heaven.

21 "You have heard that it was said to those of old, 'You shall not murder,*a* and whoever murders will be in danger of the judgment.' 22 But I say to you that whoever is angry with his brother without a cause*a* shall be in danger of the judgment. And whoever says to his brother, 'Raca!' shall be in danger of the council. But whoever says, 'You fool!' shall be in danger of hell fire. 23 Therefore if you bring your gift to the altar, and there remember that your brother has something against you, 24 leave your gift there before the altar, and go your way. First be reconciled to your brother, and then come and offer your gift. 25 Agree with your adversary quickly, while you are on the way with him, lest your adversary deliver you to the judge, the judge hand you over to the officer, and you be thrown into prison. 26 Assuredly, I say to you, you will by no means get out of there till you have paid the last penny.

27 "You have heard that it was said to those of old,*a* 'You shall not commit adultery.'*b* 28 But I say to you that whoever looks at a woman to lust for her has already committed adultery with her in her heart. 29 If your right

5:21 *a*Exodus 20:13; Deuteronomy 5:17   5:22 *a*NU-Text omits *without a cause.*   5:27 *a*NU-Text and M-Text omit *to those of old.*   *b*Exodus 20:14; Deuteronomy 5:18

God has the strangest way of restoring purpose to your life. It is dangerous to keep sending people away. The very one you are trying to send away may have the key to restoring purpose and fulfillment to your life.

Robbed, But Still Rich

Matthew 5:11, 12

Have you ever had anything happen to you that changed your life forever? You survived, but you knew you would never be the same. You may have spent every day of your life since then all bent over—not able to lift your head. In public, you may shout, you may sing, you may even dance. But when no one is looking, when the crowd is gone and the lights are out, you are nothing but a trembling, bleeding, weeping mass of pain.

The worst part about the story of Amnon and Tamar is that after Amnon abused his sister, he didn't want her (see 2 Samuel 13:16). He messed up her life and spoiled what she was proud of. He assassinated her future and damaged her prospects. He destroyed her integrity and her self-esteem. He robbed her of her greatest treasure. And afterward, he didn't even want her. Tamar said, "What you're doing to me now is worse than what you did to me at first."

Maybe you've gone through a divorce, an adulterous relationship, or some other kind of tragedy, and you feel unwanted. You can't shout over that sort of thing. You can't leap over that kind of wall. Something in you has been injured, and it will change the way you relate to others for the rest of your life.

Although Tamar fought to save the last remnant of her femininity, the Bible says that Amnon hated her with a greater intensity than that with which he had loved her before (see 2 Samuel 13:15). He hated her so much that he instructed his servant not only to throw her out, but to lock the door!

She lay on the ground and cried. Then she ripped her cape of many colors—the sign of her virginity—the cape she had been planning to give to her husband one day. In that moment she was saying, "I have no future. It wasn't just that he robbed me of my body. He robbed me of my dreams. He stole my value."

What do you do when you're trapped, with the door slammed and locked behind you? You're left, torn and trembling and intimidated. What do you do when you don't know what to do? Maybe you've been physically or emotionally raped and robbed. You survived, but you left a substantial degree of your self-esteem in Amnon's bed.

Remember, this isn't the end of the story. There's a call out for you. The Lord is saying, "I want you." No matter how many men like Amnon have told you, "I don't want you," God says, "I want you. I saw what happened to you. I've seen you at your worst moments, and I still want you." God has not changed His mind. He loves with an everlasting love. What a rich inheritance.

eye causes you to sin, pluck it out and cast *it* from you; for it is more profitable for you that one of your members perish, than for your whole body to be cast into hell. 30 And if your right hand causes you to sin, cut it off and cast *it* from you; for it is more profitable for you that one of your members perish, than for your whole body to be cast into hell.

31 "Furthermore it has been said, 'Whoever divorces his wife, let him give her a certificate of divorce.' 32 But I say to you that whoever divorces his wife for any reason except sexual immorality*ᵃ* causes her to commit adultery; and whoever marries a woman who is divorced commits adultery.

33 "Again you have heard that it was said to those of old, 'You shall not swear falsely, but shall perform your oaths to the Lord.' 34 But I say to you, do not swear at all: neither by heaven, for it is God's throne; 35 nor by the earth, for it is His footstool; nor by Jerusalem, for it is the city of the great King. 36 Nor shall you swear by your head, because you cannot make one hair white or black. 37 But let your 'Yes' be 'Yes,' and your 'No,' 'No.' For whatever is more than these is from the evil one.

38 "You have heard that it was said, *'An eye for an eye and a tooth for a tooth.'ᵃ* 39 But I tell you not to resist an evil person. But whoever slaps you on your right cheek, turn the other to him also. 40 If anyone wants to sue you and take away your tunic, let him have *your* cloak also. 41 And whoever compels you to go one mile, go with him two. 42 Give to him who asks you, and from him who wants to borrow from you do not turn away.

43 "You have heard that it was said, *'You shall love your neighborᵃ* and hate your enemy.' 44 But I say to you, love your enemies, bless those who curse you, do good to those who hate you, and pray for those who spitefully use you and persecute you,*ᵃ* 45 that you may be sons of your Father in heaven; for He makes His sun rise on the evil and on the good, and sends rain on the just and on the

unjust. 46 For if you love those who love you, what reward have you? Do not even the tax collectors do the same? 47 And if you greet your brethren*ᵃ* only, what do you do more *than others?* Do not even the tax collectors*ᵇ* do so? 48 Therefore you shall be perfect, just as your Father in heaven is perfect.

6 "Take heed that you do not do your charitable deeds before men, to be seen by them. Otherwise you have no reward from your Father in heaven. 2 Therefore, when you do a charitable deed, do not sound a trumpet before you as the hypocrites do in the synagogues and in the streets, that they may have glory from men. Assuredly, I say to you, they have their reward. 3 But when you do a charitable deed, do not let your left hand know what your right hand is doing, 4 that your charitable deed may be in secret; and your Father who sees in secret will Himself reward you openly.*ᵃ*

5 "And when you pray, you shall not be like the hypocrites. For they love to pray standing in the synagogues and on the corners of the streets, that they may be seen by men. Assuredly, I say to you, they have their reward. 6 But you, when you pray, go into your room, and when you have shut your door, pray to your Father who *is* in the secret *place;* and your Father who sees in secret will reward you openly.*ᵃ* 7 And when you pray, do not use vain repetitions as the heathen *do.* For they think that they will be heard for their many words.

8 "Therefore do not be like them. For your Father knows the things you have need of before you ask Him. 9 In this manner, therefore, pray:

> Our Father in heaven,
> Hallowed be Your name.
> 10 Your kingdom come.
> Your will be done
> On earth as *it is* in heaven.
> 11 Give us this day our daily
> bread.
> 12 And forgive us our debts,
> As we forgive our debtors.

5:32 *ᵃ*Or *fornication*   5:38 *ᵃ*Exodus 21:24; Leviticus 24:20; Deuteronomy 19:21   5:43 *ᵃ*Compare Leviticus 19:18   5:44 *ᵃ*NU-Text omits three clauses from this verse, leaving, *"But I say to you, love your enemies and pray for those who persecute you."*   5:47 *ᵃ*M-Text reads *friends.*   *ᵇ*NU-Text reads *Gentiles.*   6:4 *ᵃ*NU-Text omits *openly.*   6:6 *ᵃ*NU-Text omits *openly.*

---

*I*f you have isolated yourself from others, regardless of the reason, I pray you will hear the knocking of the Lord. He will give you the garment of praise to clothe the spirit of heaviness.

The Daughters
God Wants to Loose

Matthew 6:9

My mother used to say that a burned child dreads fire. Her illustration is applicable because we dread things from the past that we associate with discomfort and pain. It keeps us from being whole and confident. When you consider a need to be healed or loosed from trauma, it would be a God-given gift to live as if what happened had not happened. God gives us grace not only to overcome the things we face, but also to overcome the *effects* of the things we face.

Satan doesn't want you to be able to run to your heavenly Father and be healed, because you will then live as if the trauma had never occurred. Therefore, even when it comes to approaching God, the enemy will try to make you a little uncomfortable when you kneel down and say, "Our Father." That term, *Father,* may not give you the comfort that it gives to others. You may be tormented by a memory. You may be wrestling with a distrust that aborts your faith and destroys your confidence.

"Our Father." What is that? To you, a father may be someone who left and did not return. Or a father may be someone who touched you inappropriately. Or he may be the one who lied to your mother and betrayed the family trust. When you hear the word *father,* you may smell liquor or hear heavy breathing and slurred speech. You may hear grunting and recall gropings and secrets. You remember secret smiles and lewd looks stolen at the dinner table while Mother was looking in another direction. You feel no closeness, and you have no trust. You are just afraid.

You associate the problem with the gender rather than with the person who inflicted the pain. You feel as if all men are the same. This is a prejudice that we have never marched about. There is no legislation against this prejudice. Yet homes all over America are being destroyed by prejudiced concepts, where abused and mistreated persons have survived an injury but are scarred with a stereotyped definition of what men are all about. Many a good husband has lost the wife he loves to memories that have tormented her all of her life. She couldn't quite seem to trust him or anyone else who looked like the one who hurt her. She is a woman whom God wants to loose! He wants to loose her so that she can be free to love herself, her husband, her life, and even her God.

13 And do not lead us into
    temptation,
    But deliver us from the evil one.
For Yours is the kingdom and
    the power and the glory
    forever. Amen.[a]

14 "For if you forgive men their trespasses, your heavenly Father will also forgive you. 15 But if you do not forgive men their trespasses, neither will your Father forgive your trespasses.

16 "Moreover, when you fast, do not be like the hypocrites, with a sad countenance. For they disfigure their faces that they may appear to men to be fasting. Assuredly, I say to you, they have their reward. 17 But you, when you fast, anoint your head and wash your face, 18 so that you do not appear to men to be fasting, but to your Father who *is* in the secret *place;* and your Father who sees in secret will reward you openly.[a]

19 "Do not lay up for yourselves treasures on earth, where moth and rust destroy and where thieves break in and steal; 20 but lay up for yourselves treasures in heaven, where neither moth nor rust destroys and where thieves do not break in and steal. 21 For where your treasure is, there your heart will be also.

22 "The lamp of the body is the eye. If therefore your eye is good, your whole body will be full of light. 23 But if your eye is bad, your whole body will be full of darkness. If therefore the light that is in you is darkness, how great *is* that darkness!

24 "No one can serve two masters; for either he will hate the one and love the other, or else he will be loyal to the one and despise the other. You cannot serve God and mammon.

25 "Therefore I say to you, do not worry about your life, what you will eat or what you will drink; nor about your body, what you will put on. Is not life more than food and the body more than clothing? 26 Look at the birds of the air, for they neither sow nor reap nor gather into barns; yet your heavenly Father feeds them. Are you not of more value than they? 27 Which of you by worrying can add one cubit to his stature? 28 "So why do you worry about clothing? Consider the lilies of the field, how they grow: they neither toil nor spin; 29 and yet I say to you that even Solomon in all his glory was not arrayed like one of these. 30 Now if God so clothes the grass of the field, which today is, and tomorrow is thrown into the oven, *will He* not much more *clothe* you, O you of little faith?

31 "Therefore do not worry, saying, 'What shall we eat?' or 'What shall we drink?' or 'What shall we wear?' 32 For after all these things the Gentiles seek. For your heavenly Father knows that you need all these things. 33 But seek first the kingdom of God and His righteousness, and all these things shall be added to you. 34 Therefore do not worry about tomorrow, for tomorrow will worry about its own things. Sufficient for the day *is* its own trouble.

7 "Judge not, that you be not judged. 2 For with what judgment you judge, you will be judged; and with the measure you use, it will be measured back to you. 3 And why do you look at the speck in your brother's eye, but do not consider the plank in your own eye? 4 Or how can you say to your brother, 'Let me remove the speck from your eye'; and look, a plank *is* in your own eye? 5 Hypocrite! First remove the plank from your own eye, and then you will see clearly to remove the speck from your brother's eye.

6 "Do not give what is holy to the dogs; nor cast your pearls before swine, lest they trample them under their feet, and turn and tear you in pieces.

7 "Ask, and it will be given to you; seek, and you will find; knock, and it will be opened to you. 8 For everyone who asks receives, and he who seeks finds, and to him who knocks it will be opened. 9 Or what man is there among you who, if his son asks for bread, will give him a stone? 10 Or if he asks for a fish, will he give him a serpent? 11 If you then, being evil, know how to give good gifts to your children, how much more will your Father who is in heaven give good things to those who ask Him! 12 Therefore, whatever you want men to do to you, do also to them,

---

6:13 [a]NU-Text omits *For Yours* through *Amen.*   6:18 [a]NU-Text and M-Text omit *openly.*

As you open the door to new relationships and remove the chain from your own fears, God will overwhelm you with new splendor.

Initiate Your Blessing

Matthew 7:7

Y ou must initiate your blessing. Go to God with the facts of your situation and lay them out in a systematic order, not with wild wailings and flailings. Never allow the enemy to use your emotions against you!

If you never ask for anything, you will never receive anything. Many people are so passive that they hang around life as limp as old rag dolls and never stand up to circumstances or enforce change. At the other extreme are the people who argue about everything. They are bitter and mean, priding themselves on being overbearing and outspoken.

Neither is effective. Overbearing women isolate themselves because men find them so obnoxious that they had rather hide from them than confront them. Passive women are taken for granted and abused because they feel powerless to provoke change. God wants women who will speak up without ranting and raving. The trick is to balance the two extremes.

However, even God will not release blessings to someone who will not speak up. He teaches emphatically the necessity of being an initiator. If you don't initiate it, nothing significant will ever occur in your life. It is totally up to you. If there is no asking, seeking, and knocking, there will be no giving, finding, and opening. Can you see why many women are living in frustration? They are filled with wonderful memories and fantasies, but their reality may not be what they desire.

Too many people sit around and wish something would happen. This will make you stagnant and miserable. If you have dreams and aspirations, move toward those goals with vigor and precision. Most Christians feel that God will do it all. That's not true. If Hannah had not prayed in the spirit for a child (faith) and then slept with Elkanah (works), there would have never been a Samuel (fruit). You can find this story in 1 Samuel 1:20.

You have to make your actions line up with your convictions, or you will live a fruitless life. What is even worse is the fact that in your old age, you will have to eat the fruit of what you did in your youth. Be careful what you cook! Initiate your blessing.

for this is the Law and the Prophets.

13 "Enter by the narrow gate; for wide *is* the gate and broad *is* the way that leads to destruction, and there are many who go in by it. 14 Because[a] narrow *is* the gate and difficult *is* the way which leads to life, and there are few who find it.

15 "Beware of false prophets, who come to you in sheep's clothing, but inwardly they are ravenous wolves. 16 You will know them by their fruits. Do men gather grapes from thornbushes or figs from thistles? 17 Even so, every good tree bears good fruit, but a bad tree bears bad fruit. 18 A good tree cannot bear bad fruit, nor *can* a bad tree bear good fruit. 19 Every tree that does not bear good fruit is cut down and thrown into the fire. 20 Therefore by their fruits you will know them.

21 "Not everyone who says to Me, 'Lord, Lord,' shall enter the kingdom of heaven, but he who does the will of My Father in heaven. 22 Many will say to Me in that day, 'Lord, Lord, have we not prophesied in Your name, cast out demons in Your name, and done many wonders in Your name?' 23 And then I will declare to them, 'I never knew you; depart from Me, you who practice lawlessness!'

24 "Therefore whoever hears these sayings of Mine, and does them, I will liken him to a wise man who built his house on the rock: 25 and the rain descended, the floods came, and the winds blew and beat on that house; and it did not fall, for it was founded on the rock.

26 "But everyone who hears these sayings of Mine, and does not do them, will be like a foolish man who built his house on the sand: 27 and the rain descended, the floods came, and the winds blew and beat on that house; and it fell. And great was its fall."

28 And so it was, when Jesus had ended these sayings, that the people were astonished at His teaching, 29 for He taught them as one having authority, and not as the scribes.

8 When He had come down from the mountain, great multitudes followed Him. 2 And behold, a leper came and worshiped Him, saying, "Lord, if You are willing, You can make me clean."

3 Then Jesus put out *His* hand and touched him, saying, "I am willing; be cleansed." Immediately his leprosy was cleansed.

4 And Jesus said to him, "See that you tell no one; but go your way, show yourself to the priest, and offer the gift that Moses commanded, as a testimony to them."

5 Now when Jesus had entered Capernaum, a centurion came to Him, pleading with Him, 6 saying, "Lord, my servant is lying at home paralyzed, dreadfully tormented."

7 And Jesus said to him, "I will come and heal him."

8 The centurion answered and said, "Lord, I am not worthy that You should come under my roof. But only speak a word, and my servant will be healed. 9 For I also am a man under authority, having soldiers under me. And I say to this *one,* 'Go,' and he goes; and to another, 'Come,' and he comes; and to my servant, 'Do this,' and he does *it.*"

10 When Jesus heard *it,* He marveled, and said to those who followed, "Assuredly, I say to you, I have not found such great faith, not even in Israel! 11 And I say to you that many will come from east and west, and sit down with Abraham, Isaac, and Jacob in the kingdom of heaven. 12 But the sons of the kingdom will be cast out into outer darkness. There will be weeping and gnashing of teeth." 13 Then Jesus said to the centurion, "Go your way; and as you have believed, *so* let it be done for you." And his servant was healed that same hour.

14 Now when Jesus had come into Peter's house, He saw his wife's mother lying sick with a fever. 15 So He touched her hand, and the fever left her. And she arose and served them.[a]

16 When evening had come, they brought to Him many who were demon-possessed. And He cast out the spirits with a word, and healed all who were sick, 17 that it might be fulfilled which was spoken by Isaiah the prophet, saying:

7:14 aNU-Text and M-Text read *How . . . !*   8:15 aNU-Text and M-Text read *Him.*

*"He Himself took our
infirmities
And bore our sicknesses."ᵃ*

18 And when Jesus saw great multitudes about Him, He gave a command to depart to the other side. 19 Then a certain scribe came and said to Him, "Teacher, I will follow You wherever You go."

20 And Jesus said to him, "Foxes have holes and birds of the air have nests, but the Son of Man has nowhere to lay His head."

21 Then another of His disciples said to Him, "Lord, let me first go and bury my father."

22 But Jesus said to him, "Follow Me, and let the dead bury their own dead."

23 Now when He got into a boat, His disciples followed Him. 24 And suddenly a great tempest arose on the sea, so that the boat was covered with the waves. But He was asleep. 25 Then His disciples came to *Him* and awoke Him, saying, "Lord, save us! We are perishing!"

26 But He said to them, "Why are you fearful, O you of little faith?" Then He arose and rebuked the winds and the sea, and there was a great calm. 27 So the men marveled, saying, "Who can this be, that even the winds and the sea obey Him?"

28 When He had come to the other side, to the country of the Gergesenes,ᵃ there met Him two demon-possessed *men,* coming out of the tombs, exceedingly fierce, so that no one could pass that way. 29 And suddenly they cried out, saying, "What have we to do with You, Jesus, You Son of God? Have You come here to torment us before the time?"

30 Now a good way off from them there was a herd of many swine feeding. 31 So the demons begged Him, saying, "If You cast us out, permit us to go awayᵃ into the herd of swine."

32 And He said to them, "Go." So when they had come out, they went into the herd of swine. And suddenly the whole herd of swine ran violently down the steep place into the sea, and perished in the water.

33 Then those who kept *them* fled; and they went away into the city and told everything, including what *had happened* to the demon-possessed *men.* 34 And behold, the whole city came out to meet Jesus. And when they saw Him, they begged *Him* to depart from their region.

9 So He got into a boat, crossed over, and came to His own city. 2 Then behold, they brought to Him a paralytic lying on a bed. When Jesus saw their faith, He said to the paralytic, "Son, be of good cheer; your sins are forgiven you."

3 And at once some of the scribes said within themselves, "This Man blasphemes!"

4 But Jesus, knowing their thoughts, said, "Why do you think evil in your hearts? 5 For which is easier, to say, 'Your sins are forgiven you,' or to say, 'Arise and walk'? 6 But that you may know that the Son of Man has power on earth to forgive sins"—then He said to the paralytic, "Arise, take up your bed, and go to your house." 7 And he arose and departed to his house.

8 Now when the multitudes saw *it,* they marveledᵃ and glorified God, who had given such power to men.

9 As Jesus passed on from there, He saw a man named Matthew sitting at the tax office. And He said to him, "Follow Me." So he arose and followed Him.

10 Now it happened, as Jesus sat at the table in the house, *that* behold, many tax collectors and sinners came and sat down with Him and His disciples. 11 And when the Pharisees saw *it,* they said to His disciples, "Why does your Teacher eat with tax collectors and sinners?"

12 When Jesus heard *that,* He said to them, "Those who are well have no need of a physician, but those who are sick. 13 But go and learn what *this* means: *'I desire mercy and not sacrifice.'ᵃ* For I did not come to call the righteous, but sinners, to repentance."ᵇ

14 Then the disciples of John came to Him, saying, "Why do we and the Pharisees fast often,ᵃ but Your disciples do not fast?"

15 And Jesus said to them, "Can the

8:17 ᵃIsaiah 53:4   8:28 ᵃNU-Text reads *Gadarenes.*   8:31 ᵃNU-Text reads *send us.*   9:8 ᵃNU-Text reads *were afraid.*   9:13 ᵃHosea 6:6   ᵇNU-Text omits *to repentance.*   9:14 ᵃNU-Text brackets *often* as disputed.

---

*D*avid, the psalmist, declares, "He restores my soul." Only God knows what it takes to remove the build-up that may be existing in your life. But He specializes in restoring and renewing the human heart.

friends of the bridegroom mourn as long as the bridegroom is with them? But the days will come when the bridegroom will be taken away from them, and then they will fast. 16 No one puts a piece of unshrunk cloth on an old garment; for the patch pulls away from the garment, and the tear is made worse. 17 Nor do they put new wine into old wineskins, or else the wineskins break, the wine is spilled, and the wineskins are ruined. But they put new wine into new wineskins, and both are preserved."

18 While He spoke these things to them, behold, a ruler came and worshiped Him, saying, "My daughter has just died, but come and lay Your hand on her and she will live." 19 So Jesus arose and followed him, and so *did* His disciples.

20 And suddenly, a woman who had a flow of blood for twelve years came from behind and touched the hem of His garment. 21 For she said to herself, "If only I may touch His garment, I shall be made well." 22 But Jesus turned around, and when He saw her He said, "Be of good cheer, daughter; your faith has made you well." And the woman was made well from that hour.

23 When Jesus came into the ruler's house, and saw the flute players and the noisy crowd wailing, 24 He said to them, "Make room, for the girl is not dead, but sleeping." And they ridiculed Him. 25 But when the crowd was put outside, He went in and took her by the hand, and the girl arose. 26 And the report of this went out into all that land.

27 When Jesus departed from there, two blind men followed Him, crying out and saying, "Son of David, have mercy on us!"

28 And when He had come into the house, the blind men came to Him. And Jesus said to them, "Do you believe that I am able to do this?"

They said to Him, "Yes, Lord."

29 Then He touched their eyes, saying, "According to your faith let it be to you." 30 And their eyes were opened. And Jesus sternly warned them, saying, "See *that* no one

knows *it*." 31 But when they had departed, they spread the news about Him in all that country.

32 As they went out, behold, they brought to Him a man, mute and demon-possessed. 33 And when the demon was cast out, the mute spoke. And the multitudes marveled, saying, "It was never seen like this in Israel!"

34 But the Pharisees said, "He casts out demons by the ruler of the demons."

35 Then Jesus went about all the cities and villages, teaching in their synagogues, preaching the gospel of the kingdom, and healing every sickness and every disease among the people.*a* 36 But when He saw the multitudes, He was moved with compassion for them, because they were weary*a* and scattered, like sheep having no shepherd. 37 Then He said to His disciples, "The harvest truly *is* plentiful, but the laborers *are* few. 38 Therefore pray the Lord of the harvest to send out laborers into His harvest."

10 And when He had called His twelve disciples to *Him*, He gave them power *over* unclean spirits, to cast them out, and to heal all kinds of sickness and all kinds of disease. 2 Now the names of the twelve apostles are these: first, Simon, who is called Peter, and Andrew his brother; James the *son* of Zebedee, and John his brother; 3 Philip and Bartholomew; Thomas and Matthew the tax collector; James the *son* of Alphaeus, and Lebbaeus, whose surname was*a* Thaddaeus; 4 Simon the Cananite,*a* and Judas Iscariot, who also betrayed Him.

5 These twelve Jesus sent out and commanded them, saying: "Do not go into the way of the Gentiles, and do not enter a city of the Samaritans. 6 But go rather to the lost sheep of the house of Israel. 7 And as you go, preach, saying, 'The kingdom of heaven is at hand.' 8 Heal the sick, cleanse the lepers, raise the dead,*a* cast out demons. Freely you have received, freely give. 9 Provide neither gold nor silver nor copper in your money belts, 10 nor bag for *your* journey, nor two tunics, nor sandals, nor

---

9:35 *a*NU-Text omits *among the people.*   9:36 *a*NU-Text and M-Text read *harassed.*   10:3 *a*NU-Text omits *Lebbaeus, whose surname was.*   10:4 *a*NU-Text reads *Cananaean.*   10:8 *a*NU-Text reads *raise the dead, cleanse the lepers;* M-Text omits *raise the dead.*

Trust Him to see you through days that may be different from the ones you encountered earlier. You are being challenged with the silent struggles of winter.

Seize Your Miracle Moment

Matthew 9:20-22

I like the woman with the issue of blood. She knew how to seize the moment.

Each of us needs to learn how to seize the moment in the spirit realm. If you miss the moment, you may miss out on the miracle you need. There are too many things I need God to do for me to sit back in my seat when the anointing of God starts to fall. I want to jump right in. I can't afford for any of my miracles to pass me by.

This woman knew she was at the end of the line. She was out of health, out of money, out of physicians, out of people who could minister to her. But she wasn't out of faith. She had run out of everything in her life but the one thing she needed. She had her belief that if she could only touch the hem of Jesus' garment, she'd be made whole.

This woman did not have any other human being to help her. Nobody was counseling her. Nobody was lobbying for her. Nobody was running interference for her. Nobody was ministering to her. She had nobody. She had only one person who could preach to her—herself. This sick, bleeding, wounded woman—weak in her body, but not in her spirit—began to preach to herself. She said, "If I may but touch . . ."

When the Bible says that she "said," the tense of that word means that she said and she said and she said. She kept on talking to herself. She told herself over and over and over again, "If I may but touch His clothes, I shall be whole." She kept saying, "I can't die yet. I've got to touch Him. I can't give up yet. I've got to touch Him. I can't lie down and surrender yet. I've got to touch Him. And if I can touch Him—if I can only touch His clothes—I shall be whole!"

She may have had a little doubt about whether she had the strength to get through that crowd. She may have had a question about whether she could get close enough to touch Him. She may have had some self-doubts. But she had no doubt about Jesus. She knew that if she could get to Him, He would heal her. If she could only make contact, she would be well. She didn't need any other physician, any other counselor, any other helper, any other person to minister to her . . . if she could just get to Jesus.

Let there be no doubt in your heart today. Jesus is the One. He is the Healer. He is the Deliverer. Touching Jesus is all that matters!

staffs; for a worker is worthy of his food.

11 "Now whatever city or town you enter, inquire who in it is worthy, and stay there till you go out. 12 And when you go into a household, greet it. 13 If the household is worthy, let your peace come upon it. But if it is not worthy, let your peace return to you. 14 And whoever will not receive you nor hear your words, when you depart from that house or city, shake off the dust from your feet. 15 Assuredly, I say to you, it will be more tolerable for the land of Sodom and Gomorrah in the day of judgment than for that city!

16 "Behold, I send you out as sheep in the midst of wolves. Therefore be wise as serpents and harmless as doves. 17 But beware of men, for they will deliver you up to councils and scourge you in their synagogues. 18 You will be brought before governors and kings for My sake, as a testimony to them and to the Gentiles. 19 But when they deliver you up, do not worry about how or what you should speak. For it will be given to you in that hour what you should speak; 20 for it is not you who speak, but the Spirit of your Father who speaks in you.

21 "Now brother will deliver up brother to death, and a father *his* child; and children will rise up against parents and cause them to be put to death. 22 And you will be hated by all for My name's sake. But he who endures to the end will be saved. 23 When they persecute you in this city, flee to another. For assuredly, I say to you, you will not have gone through the cities of Israel before the Son of Man comes.

24 "A disciple is not above *his* teacher, nor a servant above his master. 25 It is enough for a disciple that he be like his teacher, and a servant like his master. If they have called the master of the house Beelzebub,*ª* how much more *will they call* those of his household! 26 Therefore do not fear them. For there is nothing covered that will not be revealed, and hidden that will not be known.

27 "Whatever I tell you in the dark, speak in the light; and what you hear in the ear, preach on the housetops. 28 And do not fear those who kill the body but cannot kill the soul. But rather fear Him who is able to destroy both soul and body in hell. 29 Are not two sparrows sold for a copper coin? And not one of them falls to the ground apart from your Father's will. 30 But the very hairs of your head are all numbered. 31 Do not fear therefore; you are of more value than many sparrows.

32 "Therefore whoever confesses Me before men, him I will also confess before My Father who is in heaven. 33 But whoever denies Me before men, him I will also deny before My Father who is in heaven.

34 "Do not think that I came to bring peace on earth. I did not come to bring peace but a sword. 35 For I have come to *'set a man against his father, a daughter against her mother, and a daughter-in-law against her mother-in-law'*; 36 and *'a man's enemies will be those of his own household.'ª* 37 He who loves father or mother more than Me is not worthy of Me. And he who loves son or daughter more than Me is not worthy of Me. 38 And he who does not take his cross and follow after Me is not worthy of Me. 39 He who finds his life will lose it, and he who loses his life for My sake will find it.

40 "He who receives you receives Me, and he who receives Me receives Him who sent Me. 41 He who receives a prophet in the name of a prophet shall receive a prophet's reward. And he who receives a righteous man in the name of a righteous man shall receive a righteous man's reward. 42 And whoever gives one of these little ones only a cup of cold *water* in the name of a disciple, assuredly, I say to you, he shall by no means lose his reward."

11 Now it came to pass, when Jesus finished commanding His twelve disciples, that He departed from there to teach and to preach in their cities.

2 And when John had heard in prison about the works of Christ, he sent two of*ª* his disciples 3 and said to Him, "Are You the Coming One, or do we look for another?"

4 Jesus answered and said to them, "Go and tell John the things which you hear and see: 5 *The* blind see

10:25 *ª*NU-Text and M-Text read *Beelzebul.*   10:36 *ª*Micah 7:6   11:2 *ª*NU-Text reads *by* for *two of.*

Gospel Pearls

and *the* lame walk; *the* lepers are cleansed and *the* deaf hear; *the* dead are raised up and *the* poor have the gospel preached to them. 6 And blessed is he who is not offended because of Me."

7 As they departed, Jesus began to say to the multitudes concerning John: "What did you go out into the wilderness to see? A reed shaken by the wind? 8 But what did you go out to see? A man clothed in soft garments? Indeed, those who wear soft *clothing* are in kings' houses. 9 But what did you go out to see? A prophet? Yes, I say to you, and more than a prophet. 10 For this is *he* of whom it is written:

'Behold, I send My messenger
before Your face,
Who will prepare Your way
before You.'ᵃ

11 "Assuredly, I say to you, among those born of women there has not risen one greater than John the Baptist; but he who is least in the kingdom of heaven is greater than he. 12 And from the days of John the Baptist until now the kingdom of heaven suffers violence, and the violent take it by force. 13 For all the prophets and the law prophesied until John. 14 And if you are willing to receive *it*, he is Elijah who is to come. 15 He who has ears to hear, let him hear!

16 "But to what shall I liken this generation? It is like children sitting in the marketplaces and calling to their companions, 17 and saying:

'We played the flute for you,
And you did not dance;
We mourned to you,
And you did not lament.'

18 For John came neither eating nor drinking, and they say, 'He has a demon.' 19 The Son of Man came eating and drinking, and they say, 'Look, a glutton and a winebibber, a friend of tax collectors and sinners!' But wisdom is justified by her children."ᵃ

20 Then He began to rebuke the cities in which most of His mighty works had been done, because they did not repent: 21 "Woe to you, Cho-

razin! Woe to you, Bethsaida! For if the mighty works which were done in you had been done in Tyre and Sidon, they would have repented long ago in sackcloth and ashes. 22 But I say to you, it will be more tolerable for Tyre and Sidon in the day of judgment than for you. 23 And you, Capernaum, who are exalted to heaven, will beᵃ brought down to Hades; for if the mighty works which were done in you had been done in Sodom, it would have remained until this day. 24 But I say to you that it shall be more tolerable for the land of Sodom in the day of judgment than for you."

25 At that time Jesus answered and said, "I thank You, Father, Lord of heaven and earth, that You have hidden these things from *the* wise and prudent and have revealed them to babes. 26 Even so, Father, for so it seemed good in Your sight. 27 All things have been delivered to Me by My Father, and no one knows the Son except the Father. Nor does anyone know the Father except the Son, and *the one* to whom the Son wills to reveal *Him.* 28 Come to Me, all *you* who labor and are heavy laden, and I will give you rest. 29 Take My yoke upon you and learn from Me, for I am gentle and lowly in heart, and you will find rest for your souls. 30 For My yoke *is* easy and My burden is light."

12 At that time Jesus went through the grainfields on the Sabbath. And His disciples were hungry, and began to pluck heads of grain and to eat. 2 And when the Pharisees saw *it,* they said to Him, "Look, Your disciples are doing what is not lawful to do on the Sabbath!"

3 But He said to them, "Have you not read what David did when he was hungry, he and those who were with him: 4 how he entered the house of God and ate the showbread which was not lawful for him to eat, nor for those who were with him, but only for the priests? 5 Or have you not read in the law that on the Sabbath the priests in the temple profane the Sabbath, and are blameless? 6 Yet I say to you that in this place there is *One* greater than the temple.

God is a restorer. That is to say, as you sit by the fire sipping coffee, rehearsing your own thoughts, playing old reruns from the scenes in your life—some things He will explain and others He will heal.

7 But if you had known what *this* means, '*I desire mercy and not sacrifice,*'*ᵃ* you would not have condemned the guiltless. 8 For the Son of Man is Lord even*ᵃ* of the Sabbath."

9 Now when He had departed from there, He went into their synagogue. 10 And behold, there was a man who had a withered hand. And they asked Him, saying, "Is it lawful to heal on the Sabbath?"—that they might accuse Him.

11 Then He said to them, "What man is there among you who has one sheep, and if it falls into a pit on the Sabbath, will not lay hold of it and lift *it* out? 12 Of how much more value then is a man than a sheep? Therefore it is lawful to do good on the Sabbath." 13 Then He said to the man, "Stretch out your hand." And he stretched *it* out, and it was restored as whole as the other. 14 Then the Pharisees went out and plotted against Him, how they might destroy Him.

15 But when Jesus knew *it*, He withdrew from there. And great multitudes*ᵃ* followed Him, and He healed them all. 16 Yet He warned them not to make Him known, 17 that it might be fulfilled which was spoken by Isaiah the prophet, saying:

18 "Behold! My Servant whom I
   have chosen,
   My Beloved in whom My soul
   is well pleased!
   I will put My Spirit upon Him,
   And He will declare justice to
   the Gentiles.
19 He will not quarrel nor cry
   out,
   Nor will anyone hear His voice
   in the streets.
20 A bruised reed He will not
   break,
   And smoking flax He will not
   quench,
   Till He sends forth justice to
   victory;
21 And in His name Gentiles will
   trust." *ᵃ*

22 Then one was brought to Him who was demon-possessed, blind and mute; and He healed him, so that the blind and*ᵃ* mute man both spoke and saw. 23 And all the multitudes were amazed and said, "Could this be the Son of David?"

24 Now when the Pharisees heard *it* they said, "This *fellow* does not cast out demons except by Beelzebub,*ᵃ* the ruler of the demons."

25 But Jesus knew their thoughts, and said to them: "Every kingdom divided against itself is brought to desolation, and every city or house divided against itself will not stand. 26 If Satan casts out Satan, he is divided against himself. How then will his kingdom stand? 27 And if I cast out demons by Beelzebub, by whom do your sons cast *them* out? Therefore they shall be your judges. 28 But if I cast out demons by the Spirit of God, surely the kingdom of God has come upon you. 29 Or how can one enter a strong man's house and plunder his goods, unless he first binds the strong man? And then he will plunder his house. 30 He who is not with Me is against Me, and he who does not gather with Me scatters abroad.

31 "Therefore I say to you, every sin and blasphemy will be forgiven men, but the blasphemy *against* the Spirit will not be forgiven men. 32 Anyone who speaks a word against the Son of Man, it will be forgiven him; but whoever speaks against the Holy Spirit, it will not be forgiven him, either in this age or in the *age* to come.

33 "Either make the tree good and its fruit good, or else make the tree bad and its fruit bad; for a tree is known by *its* fruit. 34 Brood of vipers! How can you, being evil, speak good things? For out of the abundance of the heart the mouth speaks. 35 A good man out of the good treasure of his heart*ᵃ* brings forth good things, and an evil man out of the evil treasure brings forth evil things. 36 But I say to you that for every idle word men may speak, they will give account of it in the day of judgment. 37 For by your words you will be justified, and by your words you will be condemned."

38 Then some of the scribes and Pharisees answered, saying,

12:7 *ᵃ*Hosea 6:6   12:8 *ᵃ*NU-Text and M-Text omit *even*.   12:15 *ᵃ*NU-Text brackets *multitudes* as disputed.   12:21 *ᵃ*Isaiah 42:1–4   12:22 *ᵃ*NU-Text omits *blind and*.   12:24 *ᵃ*NU-Text and M-Text read *Beelzebul*.   12:35 *ᵃ*NU-Text and M-Text omit *of his heart*.

Gospel Pearls

"Teacher, we want to see a sign from You."

39 But He answered and said to them, "An evil and adulterous generation seeks after a sign, and no sign will be given to it except the sign of the prophet Jonah. 40 For as Jonah was three days and three nights in the belly of the great fish, so will the Son of Man be three days and three nights in the heart of the earth. 41 The men of Nineveh will rise up in the judgment with this generation and condemn it, because they repented at the preaching of Jonah; and indeed a greater than Jonah *is* here. 42 The queen of the South will rise up in the judgment with this generation and condemn it, for she came from the ends of the earth to hear the wisdom of Solomon; and indeed a greater than Solomon *is* here.

43 "When an unclean spirit goes out of a man, he goes through dry places, seeking rest, and finds none. 44 Then he says, 'I will return to my house from which I came.' And when he comes, he finds *it* empty, swept, and put in order. 45 Then he goes and takes with him seven other spirits more wicked than himself, and they enter and dwell there; and the last *state* of that man is worse than the first. So shall it also be with this wicked generation."

46 While He was still talking to the multitudes, behold, His mother and brothers stood outside, seeking to speak with Him. 47 Then one said to Him, "Look, Your mother and Your brothers are standing outside, seeking to speak with You."

48 But He answered and said to the one who told Him, "Who is My mother and who are My brothers?" 49 And He stretched out His hand toward His disciples and said, "Here are My mother and My brothers! 50 For whoever does the will of My Father in heaven is My brother and sister and mother."

13 On the same day Jesus went out of the house and sat by the sea. 2 And great multitudes were gathered together to Him, so that He got into a boat and sat; and the whole multitude stood on the shore. 3 Then He spoke many things to them in parables, saying: "Behold, a sower went out to sow. 4 And as he sowed, some *seed* fell by the wayside; and the birds came and devoured them. 5 Some fell on stony places, where they did not have much earth; and they immediately sprang up because they had no depth of earth. 6 But when the sun was up they were scorched, and because they had no root they withered away. 7 And some fell among thorns, and the thorns sprang up and choked them. 8 But others fell on good ground and yielded a crop: some a hundredfold, some sixty, some thirty. 9 He who has ears to hear, let him hear!"

10 And the disciples came and said to Him, "Why do You speak to them in parables?"

11 He answered and said to them, "Because it has been given to you to know the mysteries of the kingdom of heaven, but to them it has not been given. 12 For whoever has, to him more will be given, and he will have abundance; but whoever does not have, even what he has will be taken away from him. 13 Therefore I speak to them in parables, because seeing they do not see, and hearing they do not hear, nor do they understand. 14 And in them the prophecy of Isaiah is fulfilled, which says:

'Hearing you will hear and shall
 not understand,
And seeing you will see and not
 perceive;
15 For the hearts of this people
 have grown dull.
Their ears are hard of hearing,
And their eyes they have
 closed,
Lest they should see with their
 eyes and hear with their ears,
Lest they should understand
 with their hearts and turn,
So that I should[a] heal them.'[b]

16 But blessed *are* your eyes for they see, and your ears for they hear; 17 for assuredly, I say to you that many prophets and righteous *men* desired to see what you see, and did not see *it,* and to hear what you hear, and did not hear *it.*

18 "Therefore hear the parable of the sower: 19 When anyone hears the word of the kingdom, and does not

13:15 [a]NU-Text and M-Text read *would.* [b]Isaiah 6:9, 10

*M*any women pray more earnestly as intercessors for others than for themselves. That is wonderful, but there ought to be a time when you desire certain things for yourself.

understand *it*, then the wicked *one* comes and snatches away what was sown in his heart. This is he who received seed by the wayside. 20 But he who received the seed on stony places, this is he who hears the word and immediately receives it with joy; 21 yet he has no root in himself, but endures only for a while. For when tribulation or persecution arises because of the word, immediately he stumbles. 22 Now he who received seed among the thorns is he who hears the word, and the cares of this world and the deceitfulness of riches choke the word, and he becomes unfruitful. 23 But he who received seed on the good ground is he who hears the word and understands *it*, who indeed bears fruit and produces: some a hundredfold, some sixty, some thirty."

24 Another parable He put forth to them, saying: "The kingdom of heaven is like a man who sowed good seed in his field; 25 but while men slept, his enemy came and sowed tares among the wheat and went his way. 26 But when the grain had sprouted and produced a crop, then the tares also appeared. 27 So the servants of the owner came and said to him, 'Sir, did you not sow good seed in your field? How then does it have tares?' 28 He said to them, 'An enemy has done this.' The servants said to him, 'Do you want us then to go and gather them up?' 29 But he said, 'No, lest while you gather up the tares you also uproot the wheat with them. 30 Let both grow together until the harvest, and at the time of harvest I will say to the reapers, "First gather together the tares and bind them in bundles to burn them, but gather the wheat into my barn." ' "

31 Another parable He put forth to them, saying: "The kingdom of heaven is like a mustard seed, which a man took and sowed in his field, 32 which indeed is the least of all the seeds; but when it is grown it is greater than the herbs and becomes a tree, so that the birds of the air come and nest in its branches."

33 Another parable He spoke to them: "The kingdom of heaven is like leaven, which a woman took and hid in three measures[a] of meal till it was all leavened."

34 All these things Jesus spoke to the multitude in parables; and without a parable He did not speak to them, 35 that it might be fulfilled which was spoken by the prophet, saying:

"I will open My mouth in
parables;
I will utter things kept secret
from the foundation of the
world."[a]

36 Then Jesus sent the multitude away and went into the house. And His disciples came to Him, saying, "Explain to us the parable of the tares of the field."
37 He answered and said to them: "He who sows the good seed is the Son of Man. 38 The field is the world, the good seeds are the sons of the kingdom, but the tares are the sons of the wicked *one*. 39 The enemy who sowed them is the devil, the harvest is the end of the age, and the reapers are the angels. 40 Therefore as the tares are gathered and burned in the fire, so it will be at the end of this age. 41 The Son of Man will send out His angels, and they will gather out of His kingdom all things that offend, and those who practice lawlessness, 42 and will cast them into the furnace of fire. There will be wailing and gnashing of teeth. 43 Then the righteous will shine forth as the sun in the kingdom of their Father. He who has ears to hear, let him hear!
44 "Again, the kingdom of heaven is like treasure hidden in a field, which a man found and hid; and for joy over it he goes and sells all that he has and buys that field.
45 "Again, the kingdom of heaven is like a merchant seeking beautiful pearls, 46 who, when he had found one pearl of great price, went and sold all that he had and bought it.
47 "Again, the kingdom of heaven is like a dragnet that was cast into the sea and gathered some of every kind, 48 which, when it was full, they drew to shore; and they sat down and gathered the good into vessels, but threw the bad away. 49 So it will be at the end of the age. The angels will come forth, separate the wicked from among the just, 50 and cast them into

13:33 [a]Greek *sata,* approximately two pecks in all   13:35 [a]Psalm 78:2

There is great comfort in His arms. Like children, even adults can snuggle into His everlasting arms and hear the heartbeat of a loving God who says, "And you shall eat plenty, and be satisfied, and praise the name of your God."

Get It Neutered

Matthew 13:24-30

When I see women who are hurting, I often ask them, "Don't you ever wonder where all your pain comes from?" I also think of the parable in Matthew 13:24-30.

These women don't seem to realize that Satan sowed his tares into their good fields and used their nurturing instincts against them. Some of you have had wasted years of productivity trying to recapture and revive something that wasn't worth the effort. You should have cut the cord years ago. You can actually nurture something that sucks the life out of you. No matter how it wears you down, you keep pouring more of yourself into it. You end up nurturing something that needs to be neutered—a bad relationship, an unhealthy lifestyle, or any other negative situation.

Many women find it difficult to confront these issues because, as nurturers, they always put the comfort of others above their own. It sounds like the unselfish thing to do, but many times you are only putting a nice dress over a low self-esteem. I am challenging you to neuter the things that would limit you because neutering an issue renders it powerless to reproduce in your life. To neuter is to leave the issue impotent. It may still exist, but it is powerless to reproduce in your life. You may remember the event, but the pain is removed like a stinger from a bee. The bee may still buzz, but he is not a threat because his ability to sting is gone. No one would be afraid of being raped by a castrated man who is impotent to harm you. His threat is destroyed. God wants to castrate your doubts and fears. He wants them impotent.

There will be no offspring or side effects of your traumatic events when you have neutered them. They are gone from you like ashes in the wind. They are tossed into the sea of forgetfulness. It is finished!

With these powerful words from the Cross, Jesus died to the things that were tormenting Him. The nails were still there, as was the Cross, but their power over Him was destroyed. He had moved into another realm. So should you, my friend. When life seems unfair and uncertain, do not be delayed by nurturing things that should be neutered. Keep moving on.

the furnace of fire. There will be wailing and gnashing of teeth."

51 Jesus said to them,[a] "Have you understood all these things?"

They said to Him, "Yes, Lord."[b]

52 Then He said to them, "Therefore every scribe instructed concerning[a] the kingdom of heaven is like a householder who brings out of his treasure *things* new and old."

53 Now it came to pass, when Jesus had finished these parables, that He departed from there. 54 When He had come to His own country, He taught them in their synagogue, so that they were astonished and said, "Where did this *Man* get this wisdom and *these* mighty works? 55 Is this not the carpenter's son? Is not His mother called Mary? And His brothers James, Joses,[a] Simon, and Judas? 56 And His sisters, are they not all with us? Where then did this *Man* get all these things?" 57 So they were offended at Him.

But Jesus said to them, "A prophet is not without honor except in his own country and in his own house." 58 Now He did not do many mighty works there because of their unbelief.

14 At that time Herod the tetrarch heard the report about Jesus 2 and said to his servants, "This is John the Baptist; he is risen from the dead, and therefore these powers are at work in him." 3 For Herod had laid hold of John and bound him, and put *him* in prison for the sake of Herodias, his brother Philip's wife. 4 Because John had said to him, "It is not lawful for you to have her." 5 And although he wanted to put him to death, he feared the multitude, because they counted him as a prophet.

6 But when Herod's birthday was celebrated, the daughter of Herodias danced before them and pleased Herod. 7 Therefore he promised with an oath to give her whatever she might ask.

8 So she, having been prompted by her mother, said, "Give me John the Baptist's head here on a platter."

9 And the king was sorry; nevertheless, because of the oaths and because of those who sat with him, he commanded *it* to be given *to her.*

10 So he sent and had John beheaded in prison. 11 And his head was brought on a platter and given to the girl, and she brought *it* to her mother. 12 Then his disciples came and took away the body and buried it, and went and told Jesus.

13 When Jesus heard *it,* He departed from there by boat to a deserted place by Himself. But when the multitudes heard it, they followed Him on foot from the cities. 14 And when Jesus went out He saw a great multitude; and He was moved with compassion for them, and healed their sick. 15 When it was evening, His disciples came to Him, saying, "This is a deserted place, and the hour is already late. Send the multitudes away, that they may go into the villages and buy themselves food."

16 But Jesus said to them, "They do not need to go away. You give them something to eat."

17 And they said to Him, "We have here only five loaves and two fish."

18 He said, "Bring them here to Me." 19 Then He commanded the multitudes to sit down on the grass. And He took the five loaves and the two fish, and looking up to heaven, He blessed and broke and gave the loaves to the disciples; and the disciples gave to the multitudes. 20 So they all ate and were filled, and they took up twelve baskets full of the fragments that remained. 21 Now those who had eaten were about five thousand men, besides women and children.

22 Immediately Jesus made His disciples get into the boat and go before Him to the other side, while He sent the multitudes away. 23 And when He had sent the multitudes away, He went up on the mountain by Himself to pray. Now when evening came, He was alone there. 24 But the boat was now in the middle of the sea,[a] tossed by the waves, for the wind was contrary.

25 Now in the fourth watch of the night Jesus went to them, walking on the sea. 26 And when the disciples saw Him walking on the sea, they were troubled, saying, "It is a ghost!" And they cried out for fear.

27 But immediately Jesus spoke to

13:51 aNU-Text omits *Jesus said to them.* bNU-Text omits *Lord.* 13:52 aOr *for.* 13:55 aNU-Text reads *Joseph.* 14:24 aNU-Text reads *many furlongs away from the land.*

Gospel Pearls

them, saying, "Be of good cheer! It is I; do not be afraid."

28 And Peter answered Him and said, "Lord, if it is You, command me to come to You on the water."

29 So He said, "Come." And when Peter had come down out of the boat, he walked on the water to go to Jesus. 30 But when he saw that the wind *was* boisterous,*ᵃ* he was afraid; and beginning to sink he cried out, saying, "Lord, save me!"

31 And immediately Jesus stretched out *His* hand and caught him, and said to him, "O you of little faith, why did you doubt?" 32 And when they got into the boat, the wind ceased.

33 Then those who were in the boat came and*ᵃ* worshiped Him, saying, "Truly You are the Son of God."

34 When they had crossed over, they came to the land of*ᵃ* Gennesaret. 35 And when the men of that place recognized Him, they sent out into all that surrounding region, brought to Him all who were sick, 36 and begged Him that they might only touch the hem of His garment. And as many as touched *it* were made perfectly well.

15 Then the scribes and Pharisees who were from Jerusalem came to Jesus, saying, 2 "Why do Your disciples transgress the tradition of the elders? For they do not wash their hands when they eat bread."

3 He answered and said to them, "Why do you also transgress the commandment of God because of your tradition? 4 For God commanded, saying, 'Honor your father and your mother';*ᵃ* and, 'He who curses father or mother, let him be put to death.'*ᵇ* 5 But you say, 'Whoever says to his father or mother, "Whatever profit you might have received from me *is* a gift to God"— 6 then he need not honor his father or mother.'*ᵃ* Thus you have made the commandment*ᵇ* of God of no effect by your tradition. 7 Hypocrites! Well did Isaiah prophesy about you, saying:

8 'These people draw near to Me with their mouth,
And*ᵃ* honor Me with their lips,
But their heart is far from Me.
9 And in vain they worship Me,
Teaching as doctrines the commandments of men.' "*ᵃ*

10 When He had called the multitude to *Himself*, He said to them, "Hear and understand: 11 Not what goes into the mouth defiles a man; but what comes out of the mouth, this defiles a man."

12 Then His disciples came and said to Him, "Do You know that the Pharisees were offended when they heard this saying?"

13 But He answered and said, "Every plant which My heavenly Father has not planted will be uprooted. 14 Let them alone. They are blind leaders of the blind. And if the blind leads the blind, both will fall into a ditch."

15 Then Peter answered and said to Him, "Explain this parable to us."

16 So Jesus said, "Are you also still without understanding? 17 Do you not yet understand that whatever enters the mouth goes into the stomach and is eliminated? 18 But those things which proceed out of the mouth come from the heart, and they defile a man. 19 For out of the heart proceed evil thoughts, murders, adulteries, fornications, thefts, false witness, blasphemies. 20 These are *the things* which defile a man, but to eat with unwashed hands does not defile a man."

21 Then Jesus went out from there and departed to the region of Tyre and Sidon. 22 And behold, a woman of Canaan came from that region and cried out to Him, saying, "Have mercy on me, O Lord, Son of David! My daughter is severely demon-possessed."

23 But He answered her not a word.

And His disciples came and urged Him, saying, "Send her away, for she cries out after us."

24 But He answered and said, "I was not sent except to the lost sheep of the house of Israel."

14:30 *ᵃ*NU-Text brackets *that* and *boisterous* as disputed. 14:33 *ᵃ*NU-Text omits *came and*. 14:34 *ᵃ*NU-Text reads *came to land at*. 15:4 *ᵃ*Exodus 20:12; Deuteronomy 5:16 *ᵇ*Exodus 21:17 15:6 *ᵃ*NU-Text omits *or mother*. *ᵇ*NU-Text reads *word*. 15:8 *ᵃ*NU-Text omits *draw near to Me with their mouth, And*. 15:9 *ᵃ*Isaiah 29:13

---

*E*xpect God in all His varied forms. He is a master of disguise, a guiding star in the night, a lily left growing in the valley, or an answered prayer sent on the breath of an angel.

25 Then she came and worshiped Him, saying, "Lord, help me!"

26 But He answered and said, "It is not good to take the children's bread and throw it to the little dogs."

27 And she said, "Yes, Lord, yet even the little dogs eat the crumbs which fall from their masters' table."

28 Then Jesus answered and said to her, "O woman, great is your faith! Let it be to you as you desire." And her daughter was healed from that very hour.

29 Jesus departed from there, skirted the Sea of Galilee, and went up on the mountain and sat down there. 30 Then great multitudes came to Him, having with them the lame, blind, mute, maimed, and many others; and they laid them down at Jesus' feet, and He healed them. 31 So the multitude marveled when they saw the mute speaking, the maimed made whole, the lame walking, and the blind seeing; and they glorified the God of Israel.

32 Now Jesus called His disciples to Himself and said, "I have compassion on the multitude, because they have now continued with Me three days and have nothing to eat. And I do not want to send them away hungry, lest they faint on the way."

33 Then His disciples said to Him, "Where could we get enough bread in the wilderness to fill such a great multitude?"

34 Jesus said to them, "How many loaves do you have?"

And they said, "Seven, and a few little fish."

35 So He commanded the multitude to sit down on the ground. 36 And He took the seven loaves and the fish and gave thanks, broke them and gave them to His disciples; and the disciples gave to the multitude. 37 So they all ate and were filled, and they took up seven large baskets full of the fragments that were left. 38 Now those who ate were four thousand men, besides women and children. 39 And He sent away the multitude, got into the boat, and came to the region of Magdala.[a]

16 Then the Pharisees and Sadducees came, and testing Him asked that He would show them a sign from heaven. 2 He answered and said to them, "When it is evening you say, 'It will be fair weather, for the sky is red'; 3 and in the morning, 'It will be foul weather today, for the sky is red and threatening.' Hypocrites![a] You know how to discern the face of the sky, but you cannot discern the signs of the times. 4 A wicked and adulterous generation seeks after a sign, and no sign shall be given[a] to it except the sign of the prophet[a] Jonah." And He left them and departed.

5 Now when His disciples had come to the other side, they had forgotten to take bread. 6 Then Jesus said to them, "Take heed and beware of the leaven of the Pharisees and the Sadducees."

7 And they reasoned among themselves, saying, "It is because we have taken no bread."

8 But Jesus, being aware of it, said to them, "O you of little faith, why do you reason among yourselves because you have brought no bread?[a] 9 Do you not yet understand, or remember the five loaves of the five thousand and how many baskets you took up? 10 Nor the seven loaves of the four thousand and how many large baskets you took up? 11 How is it you do not understand that I did not speak to you concerning bread?—but to beware of the leaven of the Pharisees and Sadducees." 12 Then they understood that He did not tell them to beware of the leaven of bread, but of the doctrine of the Pharisees and Sadducees.

13 When Jesus came into the region of Caesarea Philippi, He asked His disciples, saying, "Who do men say that I, the Son of Man, am?"

14 So they said, "Some say John the Baptist, some Elijah, and others Jeremiah or one of the prophets."

15 He said to them, "But who do you say that I am?"

16 Simon Peter answered and said, "You are the Christ, the Son of the living God."

17 Jesus answered and said to him, "Blessed are you, Simon Bar-Jonah, for flesh and blood has not revealed this to you, but My Father who is in heaven. 18 And I also say to you that you are Peter, and on this rock I will

15:39 aNU-Text reads *Magadan.* 16:3 aNU-Text omits *Hypocrites.* 16:4 aNU-Text omits *the prophet.* 16:8 aNU-Text reads *you have no bread.*

build My church, and the gates of Hades shall not prevail against it. 19 And I will give you the keys of the kingdom of heaven, and whatever you bind on earth will be bound in heaven, and whatever you loose on earth will be loosed*a* in heaven."

20 Then He commanded His disciples that they should tell no one that He was Jesus the Christ.

21 From that time Jesus began to show to His disciples that He must go to Jerusalem, and suffer many things from the elders and chief priests and scribes, and be killed, and be raised the third day.

22 Then Peter took Him aside and began to rebuke Him, saying, "Far be it from You, Lord; this shall not happen to You!"

23 But He turned and said to Peter, "Get behind Me, Satan! You are an offense to Me, for you are not mindful of the things of God, but the things of men."

24 Then Jesus said to His disciples, "If anyone desires to come after Me, let him deny himself, and take up his cross, and follow Me. 25 For whoever desires to save his life will lose it, but whoever loses his life for My sake will find it. 26 For what profit is it to a man if he gains the whole world, and loses his own soul? Or what will a man give in exchange for his soul? 27 For the Son of Man will come in the glory of His Father with His angels, and then He will reward each according to his works. 28 Assuredly, I say to you, there are some standing here who shall not taste death till they see the Son of Man coming in His kingdom."

17 Now after six days Jesus took Peter, James, and John his brother, led them up on a high mountain by themselves; 2 and He was transfigured before them. His face shone like the sun, and His clothes became as white as the light. 3 And behold, Moses and Elijah appeared to them, talking with Him. 4 Then Peter answered and said to Jesus, "Lord, it is good for us to be here; if You wish, let us*a* make here three tabernacles: one for You, one for Moses, and one for Elijah."

5 While he was still speaking, behold, a bright cloud overshadowed them; and suddenly a voice came out of the cloud, saying, "This is My beloved Son, in whom I am well pleased. Hear Him!" 6 And when the disciples heard *it*, they fell on their faces and were greatly afraid. 7 But Jesus came and touched them and said, "Arise, and do not be afraid." 8 When they had lifted up their eyes, they saw no one but Jesus only.

9 Now as they came down from the mountain, Jesus commanded them, saying, "Tell the vision to no one until the Son of Man is risen from the dead."

10 And His disciples asked Him, saying, "Why then do the scribes say that Elijah must come first?"

11 Jesus answered and said to them, "Indeed, Elijah is coming first*a* and will restore all things. 12 But I say to you that Elijah has come already, and they did not know him but did to him whatever they wished. Likewise the Son of Man is also about to suffer at their hands." 13 Then the disciples understood that He spoke to them of John the Baptist.

14 And when they had come to the multitude, a man came to Him, kneeling down to Him and saying, 15 "Lord, have mercy on my son, for he is an epileptic*a* and suffers severely; for he often falls into the fire and often into the water. 16 So I brought him to Your disciples, but they could not cure him."

17 Then Jesus answered and said, "O faithless and perverse generation, how long shall I be with you? How long shall I bear with you? Bring him here to Me." 18 And Jesus rebuked the demon, and it came out of him; and the child was cured from that very hour.

19 Then the disciples came to Jesus privately and said, "Why could we not cast it out?"

20 So Jesus said to them, "Because of your unbelief;*a* for assuredly, I say to you, if you have faith as a mustard seed, you will say to this mountain, 'Move from here to there,' and it will move; and nothing will be impossible for you. 21 However, this kind does

16:19 *a*Or *will have been bound . . . will have been loosed*   17:4 *a*NU-Text reads *I will.*
17:11 *a*NU-Text omits *first.*   17:15 *a*Literally *moonstruck*   17:20 *a*NU-Text reads *little faith.*

*F*or every woman in crisis, there is an angel! For every lonely night and forgotten mother, there is an angel. For every lost young girl wandering the concrete jungle of an inner city, there is an angel.

not go out except by prayer and fasting."[a]

22 Now while they were staying[a] in Galilee, Jesus said to them, "The Son of Man is about to be betrayed into the hands of men, 23 and they will kill Him, and the third day He will be raised up." And they were exceedingly sorrowful.

24 When they had come to Capernaum,[a] those who received the *temple* tax came to Peter and said, "Does your Teacher not pay the *temple* tax?"

25 He said, "Yes."

And when he had come into the house, Jesus anticipated him, saying, "What do you think, Simon? From whom do the kings of the earth take customs or taxes, from their sons or from strangers?"

26 Peter said to Him, "From strangers."

Jesus said to him, "Then the sons are free. 27 Nevertheless, lest we offend them, go to the sea, cast in a hook, and take the fish that comes up first. And when you have opened its mouth, you will find a piece of money;[a] take that and give it to them for Me and you."

18 At that time the disciples came to Jesus, saying, "Who then is greatest in the kingdom of heaven?" 2 Then Jesus called a little child to Him, set him in the midst of them, 3 and said, "Assuredly, I say to you, unless you are converted and become as little children, you will by no means enter the kingdom of heaven. 4 Therefore whoever humbles himself as this little child is the greatest in the kingdom of heaven. 5 Whoever receives one little child like this in My name receives Me.

6 "But whoever causes one of these little ones who believe in Me to sin, it would be better for him if a millstone were hung around his neck, and he were drowned in the depth of the sea. 7 Woe to the world because of offenses! For offenses must come, but woe to that man by whom the offense comes!

8 "If your hand or foot causes you to sin, cut it off and cast *it* from you. It is better for you to enter into life lame or maimed, rather than having two hands or two feet, to be cast into the everlasting fire. 9 And if your eye causes you to sin, pluck it out and cast *it* from you. It is better for you to enter into life with one eye, rather than having two eyes, to be cast into hell fire.

10 "Take heed that you do not despise one of these little ones, for I say to you that in heaven their angels always see the face of My Father who is in heaven. 11 For the Son of Man has come to save that which was lost.[a]

12 "What do you think? If a man has a hundred sheep, and one of them goes astray, does he not leave the ninety-nine and go to the mountains to seek the one that is straying? 13 And if he should find it, assuredly, I say to you, he rejoices more over that *sheep* than over the ninety-nine that did not go astray. 14 Even so it is not the will of your Father who is in heaven that one of these little ones should perish.

15 "Moreover if your brother sins against you, go and tell him his fault between you and him alone. If he hears you, you have gained your brother. 16 But if he will not hear, take with you one or two more, that 'by the mouth of two or three witnesses every word may be established.'[a] 17 And if he refuses to hear them, tell *it* to the church. But if he refuses even to hear the church, let him be to you like a heathen and a tax collector.

18 "Assuredly, I say to you, whatever you bind on earth will be bound in heaven, and whatever you loose on earth will be loosed in heaven.

19 "Again I say[a] to you that if two of you agree on earth concerning anything that they ask, it will be done for them by My Father in heaven. 20 For where two or three are gathered together in My name, I am there in the midst of them."

21 Then Peter came to Him and said, "Lord, how often shall my brother sin against me, and I forgive him? Up to seven times?"

22 Jesus said to him, "I do not say to you, up to seven times, but up to seventy times seven. 23 Therefore the

17:21 [a]NU-Text omits this verse.   17:22 [a]NU-Text reads *gathering together.*   17:24 [a]NU-Text reads *Capharnaum* (here and elsewhere).   17:27 [a]Greek *stater,* the exact amount to pay the temple tax (didrachma) for two.   18:11 [a]NU-Text omits this verse.   18:16 [a]Deuteronomy 19:15   18:19 [a]NU-Text and M-Text read *Again, assuredly, I say.*

*T*ake courage! Just because Satan has set a snare doesn't mean you can't escape. The God we serve is able. His word to you is, "Woman, thou art loosed."

Soul Secrets
*when it's hard
to forgive*

*L*ord, there is nothing harder than trying to forgive when you've been desperately wounded. It's worse when the offenders show no remorse, but gloat over the pain they have brought to your life. And that's where I am. I do not want to forgive.

But I know enough to understand that the command of Your Holy Word is forgiveness—no matter what. You have not given me an option.

Help me to realize that unforgiveness can kill. It can kill my friendships, my joy, even my body. So Lord, I am choosing today to forgive all those who have stolen from me, all who have broken my heart, all who have wounded my body or my soul, all who have haunted me for years. In the name of Jesus, I forgive.

Thank You, Lord, for strength to walk out this forgiveness in my life. Thank You for using it as a testimony to the power of Your love. And thank You that, as I choose to forgive moment by moment, the feelings will follow.

kingdom of heaven is like a certain king who wanted to settle accounts with his servants. 24 And when he had begun to settle accounts, one was brought to him who owed him ten thousand talents. 25 But as he was not able to pay, his master commanded that he be sold, with his wife and children and all that he had, and that payment be made. 26 The servant therefore fell down before him, saying, 'Master, have patience with me, and I will pay you all.' 27 Then the master of that servant was moved with compassion, released him, and forgave him the debt.

28 "But that servant went out and found one of his fellow servants who owed him a hundred denarii; and he laid hands on him and took *him* by the throat, saying, 'Pay me what you owe!' 29 So his fellow servant fell down at his feet*a* and begged him, saying, 'Have patience with me, and I will pay you all.'*b* 30 And he would not, but went and threw him into prison till he should pay the debt. 31 So when his fellow servants saw what had been done, they were very grieved, and came and told their master all that had been done. 32 Then his master, after he had called him, said to him, 'You wicked servant! I forgave you all that debt because you begged me. 33 Should you not also have had compassion on your fellow servant, just as I had pity on you?' 34 And his master was angry, and delivered him to the torturers until he should pay all that was due to him.

35 "So My heavenly Father also will do to you if each of you, from his heart, does not forgive his brother his trespasses."*a*

19 Now it came to pass, when Jesus had finished these sayings, *that* He departed from Galilee and came to the region of Judea beyond the Jordan. 2 And great multitudes followed Him, and He healed them there.

3 The Pharisees also came to Him, testing Him, and saying to Him, "Is it lawful for a man to divorce his wife for *just* any reason?"

4 And He answered and said to them, "Have you not read that He who made*a* them at the beginning *'made them male and female,'*b* 5 and said, *'For this reason a man shall leave his father and mother and be joined to his wife, and the two shall become one flesh'?*a* 6 So then, they are no longer two but one flesh. Therefore what God has joined together, let not man separate."

7 They said to Him, "Why then did Moses command to give a certificate of divorce, and to put her away?"

8 He said to them, "Moses, because of the hardness of your hearts, permitted you to divorce your wives, but from the beginning it was not so. 9 And I say to you, whoever divorces his wife, except for sexual immorality,*a* and marries another, commits adultery; and whoever marries her who is divorced commits adultery."

10 His disciples said to Him, "If such is the case of the man with *his* wife, it is better not to marry."

11 But He said to them, "All cannot accept this saying, but only *those* to whom it has been given: 12 For there are eunuchs who were born thus from *their* mother's womb, and there are eunuchs who were made eunuchs by men, and there are eunuchs who have made themselves eunuchs for the kingdom of heaven's sake. He who is able to accept *it,* let him accept *it.*"

13 Then little children were brought to Him that He might put *His* hands on them and pray, but the disciples rebuked them. 14 But Jesus said, "Let the little children come to Me, and do not forbid them; for of such is the kingdom of heaven." 15 And He laid *His* hands on them and departed from there.

16 Now behold, one came and said to Him, "Good*a* Teacher, what good thing shall I do that I may have eternal life?"

17 So He said to him, "Why do you call Me good?*a* No one *is* good but One, *that is,* God.*b* But if you want to enter into life, keep the commandments."

18 He said to Him, "Which ones?"

Jesus said, *"'You shall not murder,' 'You shall not commit adultery,' 'You shall not steal,' 'You shall not bear*

18:29 *a*NU-Text omits *at his feet.*   *b*NU-Text and M-Text omit *all.*   18:35 *a*NU-Text omits *his trespasses.*   19:4 *a*NU-Text reads *created.*   *b*Genesis 1:27; 5:2   19:5 *a*Genesis 2:24   19:9 *a*Or *fornication*   19:16 *a*NU-Text omits *Good.*   19:17 *a*NU-Text reads *Why do you ask Me about what is good?*   *b*NU-Text reads *There is One who is good.*

---

*T*here is awesome power in women. God has chosen that women serve as the vehicles through which entry is made into this world. He has shared His creativity with women.

Table for Two

Matthew 19:5, 6

Marriage is having someone to curl up against when the world seems cold and life uncertain. It is having someone who is as concerned as you are when the children are sick. It is having a hand that keeps checking your forehead for fever when you're not well. To be married is to have someone's shoulder to cry on as they lower your parent's body into the ground. It is wrapping wrinkled knees in warm blankets and giggling without teeth!

To the person you marry, you are saying, "When my time comes to leave this world, and the chilly wind of eternity blows away my birthdays, and my future stands cold and dark in the night, it's your face I want to kiss good-bye. It is your hand I want to squeeze as I slip from time into eternity. As the curtain closes on all I have attempted to do and be, I want to look into your eyes and see that I mattered. Not what I looked like. Not what I did or how much money I made. Not how talented I was. I want to look into the teary eyes of someone who loves me and see—I mattered!"

If you are looking for someone to be your everything, don't look around, look up! God is the only One who can be everything. By expecting perfection from the flesh, you ask more out of someone else than you are able to provide yourself. To be married is to have a partner—someone who can look up with you.

Like a suede jacket, the imperfection of your marriage adds to its uniqueness. It is a mixing of good days, sad days, and all the challenges of life. A truly good relationship is a spicy meal served on a shaky table, filled with dreams and pain and tender moments. Moments that, in those split-second flashbacks, make you smile secret smiles in the middle of the day. Moments so strong they never die, yet so fragile they vanish like bubbles in a glass.

Cherish the moments. Lift the glass and drink deeply of life. If you can look back and catch a few of those moments, or trace a smile back to a memory, you are blessed. You could have been anywhere doing anything, but instead the Maitre d' seated you at a table for two!

false witness,' 19 *'Honor your father and your mother,'ª* and, *'You shall love your neighbor as yourself.'"ᵇ*

20 The young man said to Him, "All these things I have kept from my youth.ª What do I still lack?"

21 Jesus said to him, "If you want to be perfect, go, sell what you have and give to the poor, and you will have treasure in heaven; and come, follow Me."

22 But when the young man heard that saying, he went away sorrowful, for he had great possessions.

23 Then Jesus said to His disciples, "Assuredly, I say to you that it is hard for a rich man to enter the kingdom of heaven. 24 And again I say to you, it is easier for a camel to go through the eye of a needle than for a rich man to enter the kingdom of God."

25 When His disciples heard *it*, they were greatly astonished, saying, "Who then can be saved?"

26 But Jesus looked at *them* and said to them, "With men this is impossible, but with God all things are possible."

27 Then Peter answered and said to Him, "See, we have left all and followed You. Therefore what shall we have?"

28 So Jesus said to them, "Assuredly I say to you, that in the regeneration, when the Son of Man sits on the throne of His glory, you who have followed Me will also sit on twelve thrones, judging the twelve tribes of Israel. 29 And everyone who has left houses or brothers or sisters or father or mother or wifeª or children or lands, for My name's sake, shall receive a hundredfold, and inherit eternal life. 30 But many *who are* first will be last, and the last first.

20 "For the kingdom of heaven is like a landowner who went out early in the morning to hire laborers for his vineyard. 2 Now when he had agreed with the laborers for a denarius a day, he sent them into his vineyard. 3 And he went out about the third hour and saw others standing idle in the marketplace, 4 and said to them, 'You also go into the vineyard, and whatever is right I will give you.'

So they went. 5 Again he went out about the sixth and the ninth hour, and did likewise. 6 And about the eleventh hour he went out and found others standing idle,ª and said to them, 'Why have you been standing here idle all day?' 7 They said to him, 'Because no one hired us.' He said to them, 'You also go into the vineyard, and whatever is right you will receive.'ª

8 "So when evening had come, the owner of the vineyard said to his steward, 'Call the laborers and give them *their* wages, beginning with the last to the first.' 9 And when those came who *were hired* about the eleventh hour, they each received a denarius. 10 But when the first came, they supposed that they would receive more; and they likewise received each a denarius. 11 And when they had received *it*, they complained against the landowner, 12 saying, 'These last *men* have worked *only* one hour, and you made them equal to us who have borne the burden and the heat of the day.' 13 But he answered one of them and said, 'Friend, I am doing you no wrong. Did you not agree with me for a denarius? 14 Take *what is* yours and go your way. I wish to give to this last man *the same* as to you. 15 Is it not lawful for me to do what I wish with my own things? Or is your eye evil because I am good?' 16 So the last will be first, and the first last. For many are called, but few chosen."ª

17 Now Jesus, going up to Jerusalem, took the twelve disciples aside on the road and said to them, 18 "Behold, we are going up to Jerusalem, and the Son of Man will be betrayed to the chief priests and to the scribes; and they will condemn Him to death, 19 and deliver Him to the Gentiles to mock and to scourge and to crucify. And the third day He will rise again."

20 Then the mother of Zebedee's sons came to Him with her sons, kneeling down and asking something from Him.

21 And He said to her, "What do you wish?"

She said to Him, "Grant that these

19:19 ªExodus 20:12–16; Deuteronomy 5:16–20   ᵇLeviticus 19:18   19:20 ªNU-Text omits *from my youth.*   19:29 ªNU-Text omits *or wife.*   20:6 ªNU-Text omits *idle.*   20:7 ªNU-Text omits the last clause of this verse.   20:16 ªNU-Text omits the last sentence of this verse.

God has determined your need. He looked down from Heaven and saw your pain and guilt. He evaluated the situation and decided that you needed a Redeemer.

Soul Secrets
for an impossible situation

Lord, I am in an impossible situation. I don't even know how I got here, but I can't see any way out. I am battling circumstances that I cannot defeat. There is nothing anyone can do.

I am left with You, my Lord. I have no one but You, the God who will never forsake me. I need to feel Your presence in this impossible place. I need the encouragement of Your Spirit. I need to be reminded that all things are possible with You. Victory is possible. Healing is possible. Freedom is possible. Life is possible.

So I declare that my God is able. Yes, my God, You are able! Bring the powerful possibilities of heaven to this earthly situation. Touch it with Your grace and might. It looks impossible, but You are the God who created all things from nothing. You made a way through the sea when You rolled the waters back. You made it possible for the blind to see, the lame to walk, the deaf to hear. Indeed, my Lord, all things are possible with You. And I thank You.

two sons of mine may sit, one on Your right hand and the other on the left, in Your kingdom."

22 But Jesus answered and said, "You do not know what you ask. Are you able to drink the cup that I am about to drink, and be baptized with the baptism that I am baptized with?"*a*

They said to Him, "We are able."

23 So He said to them, "You will indeed drink My cup, and be baptized with the baptism that I am baptized with;*a* but to sit on My right hand and on My left is not Mine to give, but *it is for those* for whom it is prepared by My Father."

24 And when the ten heard *it*, they were greatly displeased with the two brothers. 25 But Jesus called them to *Himself* and said, "You know that the rulers of the Gentiles lord it over them, and those who are great exercise authority over them. 26 Yet it shall not be so among you; but whoever desires to become great among you, let him be your servant. 27 And whoever desires to be first among you, let him be your slave— 28 just as the Son of Man did not come to be served, but to serve, and to give His life a ransom for many."

29 Now as they went out of Jericho, a great multitude followed Him. 30 And behold, two blind men sitting by the road, when they heard that Jesus was passing by, cried out, saying, "Have mercy on us, O Lord, Son of David!"

31 Then the multitude warned them that they should be quiet; but they cried out all the more, saying, "Have mercy on us, O Lord, Son of David!"

32 So Jesus stood still and called them, and said, "What do you want Me to do for you?"

33 They said to Him, "Lord, that our eyes may be opened." 34 So Jesus had compassion and touched their eyes. And immediately their eyes received sight, and they followed Him.

21 Now when they drew near Jerusalem, and came to Bethphage,*a* at the Mount of Olives, then Jesus sent two disciples, 2 saying to them, "Go into the village opposite you, and immediately you will find a donkey tied, and a colt with her. Loose *them* and bring *them* to Me. 3 And if anyone says anything to you, you shall say, 'The Lord has need of them,' and immediately he will send them."

4 All*a* this was done that it might be fulfilled which was spoken by the prophet, saying:

5   *"Tell the daughter of Zion,*
     'Behold, your King is coming to you,
     Lowly, and sitting on a donkey,
     A colt, the foal of a donkey.' "a

6 So the disciples went and did as Jesus commanded them. 7 They brought the donkey and the colt, laid their clothes on them, and set *Him*a on them. 8 And a very great multitude spread their clothes on the road; others cut down branches from the trees and spread *them* on the road. 9 Then the multitudes who went before and those who followed cried out, saying:

     "Hosanna to the Son of David!
     '*Blessed is He who comes in the name of the* LORD*!'a*
     Hosanna in the highest!"

10 And when He had come into Jerusalem, all the city was moved, saying, "Who is this?"

11 So the multitudes said, "This is Jesus, the prophet from Nazareth of Galilee."

12 Then Jesus went into the temple of God*a* and drove out all those who bought and sold in the temple, and overturned the tables of the money changers and the seats of those who sold doves. 13 And He said to them, "It is written, '*My house shall be called a house of prayer,'a* but you have made it a '*den of thieves.' "b*

14 Then *the* blind and *the* lame came to Him in the temple, and He healed them. 15 But when the chief priests and scribes saw the wonderful things that He did, and the children crying out in the temple and saying, "Hosanna to the Son of David!" they were indignant 16 and said

---

20:22 *a*NU-Text omits *and be baptized with the baptism that I am baptized with.*   20:23 *a*NU-Text omits *and be baptized with the baptism that I am baptized with.*   21:1 *a*M-Text reads *Bethsphage.*
21:4 *a*NU-Text omits *All.*   21:5 *a*Zechariah 9:9   21:7 *a*NU-Text reads *and He sat.*   21:9 *a*Psalm 118:26   21:12 *a*NU-Text omits *of God.*   21:13 *a*Isaiah 56:7   *b*Jeremiah 7:11

Gospel Pearls

to Him, "Do You hear what these are saying?"

And Jesus said to them, "Yes. Have you never read,

'Out of the mouth of babes and
nursing infants
You have perfected praise'? "[a]

17 Then He left them and went out of the city to Bethany, and He lodged there.

18 Now in the morning, as He returned to the city, He was hungry. 19 And seeing a fig tree by the road, He came to it and found nothing on it but leaves, and said to it, "Let no fruit grow on you ever again." Immediately the fig tree withered away.

20 And when the disciples saw it, they marveled, saying, "How did the fig tree wither away so soon?"

21 So Jesus answered and said to them, "Assuredly, I say to you, if you have faith and do not doubt, you will not only do what was done to the fig tree, but also if you say to this mountain, 'Be removed and be cast into the sea,' it will be done. 22 And whatever things you ask in prayer, believing, you will receive."

23 Now when He came into the temple, the chief priests and the elders of the people confronted Him as He was teaching, and said, "By what authority are You doing these things? And who gave You this authority?"

24 But Jesus answered and said to them, "I also will ask you one thing, which if you tell Me, I likewise will tell you by what authority I do these things: 25 The baptism of John— where was it from? From heaven or from men?"

And they reasoned among themselves, saying, "If we say, 'From heaven,' He will say to us, 'Why then did you not believe him?' 26 But if we say, 'From men,' we fear the multitude, for all count John as a prophet."

27 So they answered Jesus and said, "We do not know."

And He said to them, "Neither will I tell you by what authority I do these things.

28 "But what do you think? A man had two sons, and he came to the first and said, 'Son, go, work today in my vineyard.' 29 He answered and said,

'I will not,' but afterward he regretted it and went. 30 Then he came to the second and said likewise. And he answered and said, 'I go, sir,' but he did not go. 31 Which of the two did the will of *his* father?"

They said to Him, "The first."

Jesus said to them, "Assuredly, I say to you that tax collectors and harlots enter the kingdom of God before you. 32 For John came to you in the way of righteousness, and you did not believe him; but tax collectors and harlots believed him; and when you saw *it*, you did not afterward relent and believe him.

33 "Hear another parable: There was a certain landowner who planted a vineyard and set a hedge around it, dug a winepress in it and built a tower. And he leased it to vinedressers and went into a far country. 34 Now when vintage-time drew near, he sent his servants to the vinedressers, that they might receive its fruit. 35 And the vinedressers took his servants, beat one, killed one, and stoned another. 36 Again he sent other servants, more than the first, and they did likewise to them. 37 Then last of all he sent his son to them, saying, 'They will respect my son.' 38 But when the vinedressers saw the son, they said among themselves, 'This is the heir. Come, let us kill him and seize his inheritance.' 39 So they took him and cast *him* out of the vineyard and killed *him*.

40 "Therefore, when the owner of the vineyard comes, what will he do to those vinedressers?"

41 They said to Him, "He will destroy those wicked men miserably, and lease *his* vineyard to other vinedressers who will render to him the fruits in their seasons."

42 Jesus said to them, "Have you never read in the Scriptures:

'The stone which the builders
rejected
Has become the chief
cornerstone.
This was the LORD's doing,
And it is marvelous in our
eyes'?[a]

43 "Therefore I say to you, the kingdom of God will be taken from you and given to a nation bearing the

21:16 [a]Psalm 8:2   21:42 [a]Psalm 118:22, 23

*I*t is impossible to know all that was in the mind of God when He looked down on broken humanity, but we know He looked past our broken hearts, wounded histories, and our tendency to sin, and saw our need.

Fasten Your Seat Belt

Matthew 21:42

Normally, any time there is a collision, there is damage—either to persons or to things. If one vehicle collides with another, everything associated with both vehicles may be affected. In the same way, when a relationship crashes—whether it is in a corporate office, a ministry, or a family—it impacts everyone involved. The jarring and jolting will do varying degrees of damage, depending upon the nature of the relationship.

Remember, though, you don't have to die in the crashes and collisions of life. Annoying as it may be, a seat belt can save your life! A seat belt is not a restraint that forces you to live like a mannequin, but a protective device that will support you in an emergency. Similarly, we need spiritual and emotional seat belts as well.

Inner assurance is the seat belt that keeps you from going through the roof when you are humiliated; that holds you together when you are disappointed or downright rejected. It is the confidence that God is in control and that what He has determined no one can disregard.

If He told you He was going to bless you, then ignore the mess and believe the God who cannot lie. The rubbish can be cleared and the bruises will heal. Just be sure that when the smoke clears, you are still standing. You're too important to the purposes of God to be destroyed by a situation that was only meant to build character and give you direction. No matter how crushed or devastated you may be, you are still here. Praise God! He will use the cornerstone developed through rejection and failed relationships to perfect what He has prepared.

Lift your voice above the screaming sirens and alarms of panicky people. Lift your eyes above the billowing smoke and spiraling emotions. Pull yourself together. That incident could have killed you, but it didn't. Announce to yourself and everyone else, "I am alive. I can laugh. I can cry, and by God's grace, I can survive!"

fruits of it. 44 And whoever falls on this stone will be broken; but on whomever it falls, it will grind him to powder."

45 Now when the chief priests and Pharisees heard His parables, they perceived that He was speaking of them. 46 But when they sought to lay hands on Him, they feared the multitudes, because they took Him for a prophet.

22 And Jesus answered and spoke to them again by parables and said: 2 "The kingdom of heaven is like a certain king who arranged a marriage for his son, 3 and sent out his servants to call those who were invited to the wedding; and they were not willing to come. 4 Again, he sent out other servants, saying, 'Tell those who are invited, "See, I have prepared my dinner; my oxen and fatted cattle *are* killed, and all things *are* ready. Come to the wedding." ' 5 But they made light of it and went their ways, one to his own farm, another to his business. 6 And the rest seized his servants, treated *them* spitefully, and killed *them.* 7 But when the king heard *about it,* he was furious. And he sent out his armies, destroyed those murderers, and burned up their city. 8 Then he said to his servants, 'The wedding is ready, but those who were invited were not worthy. 9 Therefore go into the highways, and as many as you find, invite to the wedding.' 10 So those servants went out into the highways and gathered together all whom they found, both bad and good. And the wedding *hall* was filled with guests.

11 "But when the king came in to see the guests, he saw a man there who did not have on a wedding garment. 12 So he said to him, 'Friend, how did you come in here without a wedding garment?' And he was speechless. 13 Then the king said to the servants, 'Bind him hand and foot, take him away, and*a* cast *him* into outer darkness; there will be weeping and gnashing of teeth.'

14 "For many are called, but few *are* chosen."

15 Then the Pharisees went and plotted how they might entangle Him in *His* talk. 16 And they sent to Him

their disciples with the Herodians, saying, "Teacher, we know that You are true, and teach the way of God in truth; nor do You care about anyone, for You do not regard the person of men. 17 Tell us, therefore, what do You think? Is it lawful to pay taxes to Caesar, or not?"

18 But Jesus perceived their wickedness, and said, "Why do you test Me, *you* hypocrites? 19 Show Me the tax money."

So they brought Him a denarius.

20 And He said to them, "Whose image and inscription *is* this?"

21 They said to Him, "Caesar's."

And He said to them, "Render therefore to Caesar the things that are Caesar's, and to God the things that are God's." 22 When they had heard *these words,* they marveled, and left Him and went their way.

23 The same day the Sadducees, who say there is no resurrection, came to Him and asked Him, 24 saying: "Teacher, Moses said that if a man dies, having no children, his brother shall marry his wife and raise up offspring for his brother. 25 Now there were with us seven brothers. The first died after he had married, and having no offspring, left his wife to his brother. 26 Likewise the second also, and the third, even to the seventh. 27 Last of all the woman died also. 28 Therefore, in the resurrection, whose wife of the seven will she be? For they all had her."

29 Jesus answered and said to them, "You are mistaken, not knowing the Scriptures nor the power of God. 30 For in the resurrection they neither marry nor are given in marriage, but are like angels of God*a* in heaven. 31 But concerning the resurrection of the dead, have you not read what was spoken to you by God, saying, 32 *'I am the God of Abraham, the God of Isaac, and the God of Jacob'?a* God is not the God of the dead, but of the living." 33 And when the multitudes heard *this,* they were astonished at His teaching.

34 But when the Pharisees heard that He had silenced the Sadducees, they gathered together. 35 Then one of them, a lawyer, asked *Him a question,* testing Him, and saying, 36 "Teacher, which *is* the great commandment in the law?"

22:13 *a*NU-Text omits *take him away, and.*   22:30 *a*NU-Text omits *of God.*   22:32 *a*Exodus 3:6, 15

Jesus took your abuse on Himself on the Cross of Calvary. He paid for your shame. He made a way for you to be clean again. He took all your sinful desires and crucified them on the Cross.

37 Jesus said to him, " *'You shall love the* LORD *your God with all your heart, with all your soul, and with all your mind.'ᵃ* 38 This is *the* first and great commandment. 39 And *the* second *is* like it: *'You shall love your neighbor as yourself.'ᵃ* 40 On these two commandments hang all the Law and the Prophets."

41 While the Pharisees were gathered together, Jesus asked them, 42 saying, "What do you think about the Christ? Whose Son is He?"

They said to Him, *"The Son* of David."

43 He said to them, "How then does David in the Spirit call Him *'Lord,'* saying:

44 *'The* LORD *said to my Lord,*
" *Sit at My right hand,*
Till I make Your enemies Your footstool' ' ' ?ᵃ

45 If David then calls Him *'Lord,'* how is He his Son?" 46 And no one was able to answer Him a word, nor from that day on did anyone dare question Him anymore.

23 Then Jesus spoke to the multitudes and to His disciples, 2 saying: "The scribes and the Pharisees sit in Moses' seat. 3 Therefore whatever they tell you to observe,ᵃ *that* observe and do, but do not do according to their works; for they say, and do not do. 4 For they bind heavy burdens, hard to bear, and lay *them* on men's shoulders; but they *themselves* will not move them with one of their fingers. 5 But all their works they do to be seen by men. They make their phylacteries broad and enlarge the borders of their garments. 6 They love the best places at feasts, the best seats in the synagogues, 7 greetings in the marketplaces, and to be called by men, 'Rabbi, Rabbi.' 8 But you, do not be called 'Rabbi'; for One is your Teacher, the Christ,ᵃ and you are all brethren. 9 Do not call anyone on earth your father; for One is your Father, He who is in heaven. 10 And do not be called teachers; for One is your Teacher, the Christ. 11 But he who is greatest among you shall be

your servant. 12 And whoever exalts himself will be humbled, and he who humbles himself will be exalted.

13 "But woe to you, scribes and Pharisees, hypocrites! For you shut up the kingdom of heaven against men; for you neither go in yourselves, nor do you allow those who are entering to go in. 14 Woe to you, scribes and Pharisees, hypocrites! For you devour widows' houses, and for a pretense make long prayers. Therefore you will receive greater condemnation.ᵃ

15 "Woe to you, scribes and Pharisees, hypocrites! For you travel land and sea to win one proselyte, and when he is won, you make him twice as much a son of hell as yourselves.

16 "Woe to you, blind guides, who say, 'Whoever swears by the temple, it is nothing; but whoever swears by the gold of the temple, he is obliged *to perform it.'* 17 Fools and blind! For which is greater, the gold or the temple that sanctifiesᵃ the gold? 18 And, 'Whoever swears by the altar, it is nothing; but whoever swears by the gift that is on it, he is obliged *to perform it.'* 19 Fools and blind! For which is greater, the gift or the altar that sanctifies the gift? 20 Therefore he who swears by the altar, swears by it and by all things on it. 21 He who swears by the temple, swears by it and by Him who dwellsᵃ in it. 22 And he who swears by heaven, swears by the throne of God and by Him who sits on it.

23 "Woe to you, scribes and Pharisees, hypocrites! For you pay tithe of mint and anise and cummin, and have neglected the weightier *matters* of the law: justice and mercy and faith. These you ought to have done, without leaving the others undone. 24 Blind guides, who strain out a gnat and swallow a camel!

25 "Woe to you, scribes and Pharisees, hypocrites! For you cleanse the outside of the cup and dish, but inside they are full of extortion and self-indulgence.ᵃ 26 Blind Pharisee, first cleanse the inside of the cup and dish, that the outside of them may be clean also.

27 "Woe to you, scribes and Pharisees, hypocrites! For you are like

---

22:37 ᵃDeuteronomy 6:5   22:39 ᵃLeviticus 19:18   22:44 ᵃPsalm 110:1   23:3 ᵃNU-Text omits *to observe.*   23:8 ᵃNU-Text omits *the Christ.*   23:14 ᵃNU-Text omits this verse.   23:17 ᵃNU-Text reads *sanctified.*   23:21 ᵃM-Text reads *dwelt.*   23:25 ᵃM-Text reads *unrighteousness.*

Gospel Pearls

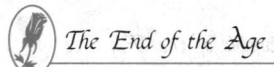

whitewashed tombs which indeed appear beautiful outwardly, but inside are full of dead *men's* bones and all uncleanness. 28 Even so you also outwardly appear righteous to men, but inside you are full of hypocrisy and lawlessness.

29 "Woe to you, scribes and Pharisees, hypocrites! Because you build the tombs of the prophets and adorn the monuments of the righteous, 30 and say, 'If we had lived in the days of our fathers, we would not have been partakers with them in the blood of the prophets.'

31 "Therefore you are witnesses against yourselves that you are sons of those who murdered the prophets. 32 Fill up, then, the measure of your fathers' guilt. 33 Serpents, brood of vipers! How can you escape the condemnation of hell? 34 Therefore, indeed, I send you prophets, wise men, and scribes: *some* of them you will kill and crucify, and *some* of them you will scourge in your synagogues and persecute from city to city, 35 that on you may come all the righteous blood shed on the earth, from the blood of righteous Abel to the blood of Zechariah, son of Berechiah, whom you murdered between the temple and the altar. 36 Assuredly, I say to you, all these things will come upon this generation.

37 "O Jerusalem, Jerusalem, the one who kills the prophets and stones those who are sent to her! How often I wanted to gather your children together, as a hen gathers her chicks under *her* wings, but you were not willing! 38 See! Your house is left to you desolate; 39 for I say to you, you shall see Me no more till you say, '*Blessed is He who comes in the name of the* LORD!' "*a*

24 Then Jesus went out and departed from the temple, and His disciples came up to show Him the buildings of the temple. 2 And Jesus said to them, "Do you not see all these things? Assuredly, I say to you, not *one* stone shall be left here upon another, that shall not be thrown down."

3 Now as He sat on the Mount of Olives, the disciples came to Him privately, saying, "Tell us, when will

these things be? And what *will be* the sign of Your coming, and of the end of the age?"

4 And Jesus answered and said to them: "Take heed that no one deceives you. 5 For many will come in My name, saying, 'I am the Christ,' and will deceive many. 6 And you will hear of wars and rumors of wars. See that you are not troubled; for all*a these things* must come to pass, but the end is not yet. 7 For nation will rise against nation, and kingdom against kingdom. And there will be famines, pestilences,*a* and earthquakes in various places. 8 All these *are* the beginning of sorrows.

9 "Then they will deliver you up to tribulation and kill you, and you will be hated by all nations for My name's sake. 10 And then many will be offended, will betray one another, and will hate one another. 11 Then many false prophets will rise up and deceive many. 12 And because lawlessness will abound, the love of many will grow cold. 13 But he who endures to the end shall be saved. 14 And this gospel of the kingdom will be preached in all the world as a witness to all the nations, and then the end will come.

15 "Therefore when you see the '*abomination of desolation,'a* spoken of by Daniel the prophet, standing in the holy place" (whoever reads, let him understand), 16 "then let those who are in Judea flee to the mountains. 17 Let him who is on the housetop not go down to take anything out of his house. 18 And let him who is in the field not go back to get his clothes. 19 But woe to those who are pregnant and to those who are nursing babies in those days! 20 And pray that your flight may not be in winter or on the Sabbath. 21 For then there will be great tribulation, such as has not been since the beginning of the world until this time, no, nor ever shall be. 22 And unless those days were shortened, no flesh would be saved; but for the elect's sake those days will be shortened.

23 "Then if anyone says to you, 'Look, here *is* the Christ!' or 'There!' do not believe *it.* 24 For false christs and false prophets will rise and show great signs and wonders to deceive,

23:39 *a*Psalm 118:26   24:6 *a*NU-Text omits *all.*   24:7 *a*NU-Text omits *pestilences.*   24:15 *a*Daniel 11:31; 12:11

W hen you accept Him, you become clean and holy. You are made pure. Don't think you were alone though; everyone struggles with the same kinds of sin as you do, whether they show it on the outside or not.

if possible, even the elect. 25 See, I have told you beforehand.

26 "Therefore if they say to you, 'Look, He is in the desert!' do not go out; *or* 'Look, *He is* in the inner rooms!' do not believe *it.* 27 For as the lightning comes from the east and flashes to the west, so also will the coming of the Son of Man be. 28 For wherever the carcass is, there the eagles will be gathered together.

29 "Immediately after the tribulation of those days the sun will be darkened, and the moon will not give its light; the stars will fall from heaven, and the powers of the heavens will be shaken. 30 Then the sign of the Son of Man will appear in heaven, and then all the tribes of the earth will mourn, and they will see the Son of Man coming on the clouds of heaven with power and great glory. 31 And He will send His angels with a great sound of a trumpet, and they will gather together His elect from the four winds, from one end of heaven to the other.

32 "Now learn this parable from the fig tree: When its branch has already become tender and puts forth leaves, you know that summer *is* near. 33 So you also, when you see all these things, know that it*a* is near—at the doors! 34 Assuredly, I say to you, this generation will by no means pass away till all these things take place. 35 Heaven and earth will pass away, but My words will by no means pass away.

36 "But of that day and hour no one knows, not even the angels of heaven,*a* but My Father only. 37 But as the days of Noah *were,* so also will the coming of the Son of Man be. 38 For as in the days before the flood, they were eating and drinking, marrying and giving in marriage, until the day that Noah entered the ark, 39 and did not know until the flood came and took them all away, so also will the coming of the Son of Man be. 40 Then two *men* will be in the field: one will be taken and the other left. 41 Two *women will be* grinding at the mill: one will be taken and the other left. 42 Watch therefore, for you do not know what hour*a* your Lord is coming. 43 But know this, that if the master of the house

had known what hour the thief would come, he would have watched and not allowed his house to be broken into. 44 Therefore you also be ready, for the Son of Man is coming at an hour you do not expect.

45 "Who then is a faithful and wise servant, whom his master made ruler over his household, to give them food in due season? 46 Blessed *is* that servant whom his master, when he comes, will find so doing. 47 Assuredly, I say to you that he will make him ruler over all his goods. 48 But if that evil servant says in his heart, 'My master is delaying his coming,'*a* 49 and begins to beat *his* fellow servants, and to eat and drink with the drunkards, 50 the master of that servant will come on a day when he is not looking for *him* and at an hour that he is not aware of, 51 and will cut him in two and appoint *him* his portion with the hypocrites. There shall be weeping and gnashing of teeth.

25 "Then the kingdom of heaven shall be likened to ten virgins who took their lamps and went out to meet the bridegroom. 2 Now five of them were wise, and five *were* foolish. 3 Those who *were* foolish took their lamps and took no oil with them, 4 but the wise took oil in their vessels with their lamps. 5 But while the bridegroom was delayed, they all slumbered and slept.

6 "And at midnight a cry was *heard:* 'Behold, the bridegroom is coming;*a* go out to meet him!' 7 Then all those virgins arose and trimmed their lamps. 8 And the foolish said to the wise, 'Give us *some* of your oil, for our lamps are going out.' 9 But the wise answered, saying, 'No, lest there should not be enough for us and you; but go rather to those who sell, and buy for yourselves.' 10 And while they went to buy, the bridegroom came, and those who were ready went in with him to the wedding; and the door was shut.

11 "Afterward the other virgins came also, saying, 'Lord, Lord, open to us!' 12 But he answered and said, 'Assuredly, I say to you, I do not know you.' 13 "Watch therefore, for you know

---

24:33 *a*Or He his coming. 24:36 *a*NU-Text adds *nor the Son.* 25:6 *a*NU-Text omits *is coming.* 24:42 *a*NU-Text reads *day.* 24:48 *a*NU-Text omits

*H*idden inside of you is a great woman who can do great exploits in His name. God wants that woman to be set free. He wants the potential within you to be unleashed so you can become the person you were created to be.

The Bridegroom
Is Coming

Matthew 25:6–8

Get ready to hear the shrill sound of a trumpet declaring the breaking of day. You cannot wait until you see the light to start preparing for the day, for midnight announces to the waiting soul that the night is fading and the day is dawning. Midnight is the turning point of every night. It is the time when the sun begins to ascend and the darkness of night gives way to the brightness of expectation. Be prepared! Your night is coming to a close, and daybreak awaits you. It is time to get up, go out, and meet your destiny.

The Bridegroom is coming! Go out to meet Him. This is no time to lie around in the bed of despair—no matter how long the night, no matter how black the darkness. Whatever you've been going through, it's over. Day is dawning, and the Bridegroom is coming.

Throughout the Bible, oil symbolizes the Holy Spirit. My sister, don't be foolish and allow life to steal your oil. You need the oil of the Holy Spirit now more than ever, for now is the time to trim your lamp, get yourself together, organize your dreams, and go out to meet Him (see Matthew 25:6).

This parable speaks of Jesus, the Bridegroom, but I believe it translates well to a woman's marriage experience.

A man likes a woman who will meet him halfway. Maybe you couldn't go out to meet him before because you were in too much pain. If you had gone, it would have been for the wrong reason. You were looking for a healing. Now you can bring healing with you. You must be prepared to establish this moment in your life as a new era with Christ. You are His chosen vessel. Meet Him. He is waiting to usher you out of your past and into your future.

You have to know that something or someone is waiting for you on the other side of your test. Your children are waiting. Your family is waiting. Your husband is waiting to be the lover of your life. The Lord would not have brought you through if He didn't have more for you. God is your Lord, but your husband is your lover. God created love. He has given you someone to love. Like Eve who woke up and found that God already had a man waiting for her, you are the answer to some Adam's prayer. Don't keep him waiting too long!

neither the day nor the hour[a] in which the Son of Man is coming.

14 "For *the kingdom of heaven is* like a man traveling to a far country, *who* called his own servants and delivered his goods to them. 15 And to one he gave five talents, to another two, and to another one; to each according to his own ability; and immediately he went on a journey. 16 Then he who had received the five talents went and traded with them, and made another five talents. 17 And likewise he who *had received* two gained two more also. 18 But he who had received one went and dug in the ground, and hid his lord's money. 19 After a long time the lord of those servants came and settled accounts with them.

20 "So he who had received five talents came and brought five other talents, saying, 'Lord, you delivered to me five talents; look, I have gained five more talents besides them.' 21 His lord said to him, 'Well *done*, good and faithful servant; you were faithful over a few things, I will make you ruler over many things. Enter into the joy of your lord.' 22 He also who had received two talents came and said, 'Lord, you delivered to me two talents; look, I have gained two more talents besides them.' 23 His lord said to him, 'Well *done*, good and faithful servant; you have been faithful over a few things, I will make you ruler over many things. Enter into the joy of your lord.'

24 "Then he who had received the one talent came and said, 'Lord, I knew you to be a hard man, reaping where you have not sown, and gathering where you have not scattered seed. 25 And I was afraid, and went and hid your talent in the ground. Look, *there* you have *what is* yours.' 26 "But his lord answered and said to him, 'You wicked and lazy servant, you knew that I reap where I have not sown, and gather where I have not scattered seed. 27 So you ought to have deposited my money with the bankers, and at my coming I would have received back my own with interest. 28 Therefore take the talent from him, and give *it* to him who has ten talents.

29 'For to everyone who has, more will be given, and he will have abundance; but from him who does not have, even what he has will be taken away. 30 And cast the unprofitable servant into the outer darkness. There will be weeping and gnashing of teeth.'

31 "When the Son of Man comes in His glory, and all the holy[a] angels with Him, then He will sit on the throne of His glory. 32 All the nations will be gathered before Him, and He will separate them one from another, as a shepherd divides *his* sheep from the goats. 33 And He will set the sheep on His right hand, but the goats on the left. 34 Then the King will say to those on His right hand, 'Come, you blessed of My Father, inherit the kingdom prepared for you from the foundation of the world: 35 for I was hungry and you gave Me food; I was thirsty and you gave Me drink; I was a stranger and you took Me in; 36 I *was* naked and you clothed Me; I was sick and you visited Me; I was in prison and you came to Me.'

37 "Then the righteous will answer Him, saying, 'Lord, when did we see You hungry and feed *You*, or thirsty and give *You* drink? 38 When did we see You a stranger and take *You* in, or naked and clothe *You*? 39 Or when did we see You sick, or in prison, and come to You?' 40 And the King will answer and say to them, 'Assuredly, I say to you, inasmuch as you did *it* to one of the least of these My brethren, you did *it* to Me.'

41 "Then He will also say to those on the left hand, 'Depart from Me, you cursed, into the everlasting fire prepared for the devil and his angels: 42 for I was hungry and you gave Me no food; I was thirsty and you gave Me no drink; 43 I was a stranger and you did not take Me in, naked and you did not clothe Me, sick and in prison and you did not visit Me.'

44 "Then they also will answer Him,[a] saying, 'Lord, when did we see You hungry or thirsty or a stranger or naked or sick or in prison, and did not minister to You?' 45 Then He will answer them, saying, 'Assuredly, I say to you, inasmuch as you did not do *it* to one of the least of these, you did not do *it* to Me.' 46 And these will

---

Gospel
Pearls

go away into everlasting punishment, but the righteous into eternal life."

26 Now it came to pass, when Jesus had finished all these sayings, *that* He said to His disciples, 2 "You know that after two days is the Passover, and the Son of Man will be delivered up to be crucified."

3 Then the chief priests, the scribes,ᵃ and the elders of the people assembled at the palace of the high priest, who was called Caiaphas, 4 and plotted to take Jesus by trickery and kill *Him*. 5 But they said, "Not during the feast, lest there be an uproar among the people."

6 And when Jesus was in Bethany at the house of Simon the leper, 7 a woman came to Him having an alabaster flask of very costly fragrant oil, and she poured *it* on His head as He sat *at the table*. 8 But when His disciples saw *it*, they were indignant, saying, "Why this waste? 9 For this fragrant oil might have been sold for much and given to *the* poor."

10 But when Jesus was aware of *it*, He said to them, "Why do you trouble the woman? For she has done a good work for Me. 11 For you have the poor with you always, but Me you do not have always. 12 For in pouring this fragrant oil on My body, she did *it* for My burial. 13 Assuredly, I say to you, wherever this gospel is preached in the whole world, what this woman has done will also be told as a memorial to her."

14 Then one of the twelve, called Judas Iscariot, went to the chief priests 15 and said, "What are you willing to give me if I deliver Him to you?" And they counted out to him thirty pieces of silver. 16 So from that time he sought opportunity to betray Him.

17 Now on the first *day of the Feast* of Unleavened Bread the disciples came to Jesus, saying to Him, "Where do You want us to prepare for You to eat the Passover?"

18 And He said, "Go into the city to a certain man, and say to him, 'The Teacher says, "My time is at hand; I will keep the Passover at your house with My disciples." ' "

19 So the disciples did as Jesus had directed them; and they prepared the Passover.

20 When evening had come, He sat down with the twelve. 21 Now as they were eating, He said, "Assuredly, I say to you, one of you will betray Me."

22 And they were exceedingly sorrowful, and each of them began to say to Him, "Lord, is it I?"

23 He answered and said, "He who dipped *his* hand with Me in the dish will betray Me. 24 The Son of Man indeed goes just as it is written of Him, but woe to that man by whom the Son of Man is betrayed! It would have been good for that man if he had not been born."

25 Then Judas, who was betraying Him, answered and said, "Rabbi, is it I?"

He said to him, "You have said it."

26 And as they were eating, Jesus took bread, blessedᵃ and broke *it*, and gave *it* to the disciples and said, "Take, eat; this is My body."

27 Then He took the cup, and gave thanks, and gave *it* to them, saying, "Drink from it, all of you. 28 For this is My blood of the newᵃ covenant, which is shed for many for the remission of sins. 29 But I say to you, I will not drink of this fruit of the vine from now on until that day when I drink it new with you in My Father's kingdom."

30 And when they had sung a hymn, they went out to the Mount of Olives.

31 Then Jesus said to them, "All of you will be made to stumble because of Me this night, for it is written:

'I will strike the Shepherd,
    And the sheep of the flock will
        be scattered.'ᵃ

32 But after I have been raised, I will go before you to Galilee."

33 Peter answered and said to Him, "Even if all are made to stumble because of You, I will never be made to stumble."

34 Jesus said to him, "Assuredly, I say to you that this night, before the rooster crows, you will deny Me three times."

35 Peter said to Him, "Even if I

26:3 ᵃNU-Text omits *the scribes.*   26:26 ᵃM-Text reads *gave thanks for.*   26:28 ᵃNU-Text omits *new.*   26:31 ᵃZechariah 13:7

God is calling you. He will spiritually stir your heart and let you know that He is moving in your life, if you will only respond to His call.

have to die with You, I will not deny You!"

And so said all the disciples.

36 Then Jesus came with them to a place called Gethsemane, and said to the disciples, "Sit here while I go and pray over there." 37 And He took with Him Peter and the two sons of Zebedee, and He began to be sorrowful and deeply distressed. 38 Then He said to them, "My soul is exceedingly sorrowful, even to death. Stay here and watch with Me."

39 He went a little farther and fell on His face, and prayed, saying, "O My Father, if it is possible, let this cup pass from Me; nevertheless, not as I will, but as You *will*."

40 Then He came to the disciples and found them sleeping, and said to Peter, "What! Could you not watch with Me one hour? 41 Watch and pray, lest you enter into temptation. The spirit indeed *is* willing, but the flesh *is* weak."

42 Again, a second time, He we away and prayed, saying, "O My Father, if this cup cannot pass away from Me unless[a] I drink it, Your will be done." 43 And He came and found them asleep again, for their eyes were heavy.

44 So He left them, went away again, and prayed the third time, saying the same words. 45 Then He came to His disciples and said to them, "Are *you* still sleeping and resting? Behold, the hour is at hand, and the Son of Man is being betrayed into the hands of sinners. 46 Rise, let us be going. See, My betrayer is at hand."

47 And while He was still speaking, behold, Judas, one of the twelve, with a great multitude with swords and clubs, came from the chief priests and elders of the people. 48 Now His betrayer had given them a sign, saying, "Whomever I kiss, He is the One; seize Him." 49 Immediately he went up to Jesus and said, "Greetings, Rabbi!" and kissed Him.

50 But Jesus said to him, "Friend, why have you come?"

Then they came and laid hands on Jesus and took Him. 51 And suddenly, one of those *who were* with Jesus stretched out *his* hand and drew his sword, struck the servant of the high priest, and cut off his ear.

52 But Jesus said to him, "Put your sword in its place, for all who take the sword will perish[a] by the sword. 53 Or do you think that I cannot now pray to My Father, and He will provide Me with more than twelve legions of angels? 54 How then could the Scriptures be fulfilled, that it must happen thus?"

55 In that hour Jesus said to the multitudes, "Have you come out, as against a robber, with swords and clubs to take Me? I sat daily with you, teaching in the temple, and you did not seize Me. 56 But all this was done that the Scriptures of the prophets might be fulfilled."

Then all the disciples forsook Him and fled.

57 And those who had laid hold of Jesus led *Him* away to Caiaphas the high priest, where the scribes and the elders were assembled. 58 But Peter followed Him at a distance to the high priest's courtyard. And he went in and sat with the servants to see the end.

59 Now the chief priests, the elders,[a] and all the council sought false testimony against Jesus to put Him to death, 60 but found none. Even though many false witnesses came forward, they found none.[a] But at last two false witnesses[b] came forward 61 and said, "This *fellow* said, 'I am able to destroy the temple of God and to build it in three days.'"

62 And the high priest arose and said to Him, "Do You answer nothing? What *is it* these men testify against You?" 63 But Jesus kept silent. And the high priest answered and said to Him, "I put You under oath by the living God: Tell us if You are the Christ, the Son of God!"

64 Jesus said to him, "*It is as* you said. Nevertheless, I say to you, hereafter you will see the Son of Man sitting at the right hand of the Power, and coming on the clouds of heaven."

65 Then the high priest tore his clothes, saying, "He has spoken blasphemy! What further need do we have of witnesses? Look, now you have heard His blasphemy! 66 What do you think?"

26:42 aNU-Text reads *if this may not pass away unless.* 26:52 aM-Text reads *die.* 26:59 aNU-Text omits *the elders.* 26:60 aNU-Text puts a comma after *but found none,* does not capitalize *Even,* and omits *they found none.* bNU-Text omits *false witnesses.*

Gospel Pearls

They answered and said, "He is deserving of death."

67 Then they spat in His face and beat Him; and others struck *Him* with the palms of their hands, 68 saying, "Prophesy to us, Christ! Who is the one who struck You?"

69 Now Peter sat outside in the courtyard. And a servant girl came to him, saying, "You also were with Jesus of Galilee."

70 But he denied it before *them* all, saying, "I do not know what you are saying."

71 And when he had gone out to the gateway, another *girl* saw him and said to those *who were* there, "This *fellow* also was with Jesus of Nazareth."

72 But again he denied with an oath, "I do not know the Man!"

73 And a little later those who stood by came up and said to Peter, "Surely you also are *one* of them, for your speech betrays you."

74 Then he began to curse and swear, *saying,* "I do not know the Man!"

Immediately a rooster crowed. 75 And Peter remembered the word of Jesus who had said to him, "Before the rooster crows, you will deny Me three times." So he went out and wept bitterly.

27 When morning came, all the chief priests and elders of the people plotted against Jesus to put Him to death. 2 And when they had bound Him, they led Him away and delivered Him to Pontius*a* Pilate the governor.

3 Then Judas, His betrayer, seeing that He had been condemned, was remorseful and brought back the thirty pieces of silver to the chief priests and elders, 4 saying, "I have sinned by betraying innocent blood."

And they said, "What *is that* to us? You see *to it!*"

5 Then he threw down the pieces of silver in the temple and departed, and went and hanged himself.

6 But the chief priests took the silver pieces and said, "It is not lawful to put them into the treasury, because they are the price of blood." 7 And they consulted together and bought with them the potter's field,

to bury strangers in. 8 Therefore that field has been called the Field of Blood to this day.

9 Then was fulfilled what was spoken by Jeremiah the prophet, saying, *"And they took the thirty pieces of silver, the value of Him who was priced,* whom they of the children of Israel priced, 10 *and gave them for the potter's field, as the* LORD *directed me."a*

11 Now Jesus stood before the governor. And the governor asked Him, saying, "Are You the King of the Jews?"

Jesus said to him, *"It is as* you say." 12 And while He was being accused by the chief priests and elders, He answered nothing.

13 Then Pilate said to Him, "Do You not hear how many things they testify against You?" 14 But He answered him not one word, so that the governor marveled greatly.

15 Now at the feast the governor was accustomed to releasing to the multitude one prisoner whom they wished. 16 And at that time they had a notorious prisoner called Barabbas.*a* 17 Therefore, when they had gathered together, Pilate said to them, "Whom do you want me to release to you? Barabbas, or Jesus who is called Christ?" 18 For he knew that they had handed Him over because of envy.

19 While he was sitting on the judgment seat, his wife sent to him, saying, "Have nothing to do with that just Man, for I have suffered many things today in a dream because of Him."

20 But the chief priests and elders persuaded the multitudes that they should ask for Barabbas and destroy Jesus. 21 The governor answered and said to them, "Which of the two do you want me to release to you?"

They said, "Barabbas!"

22 Pilate said to them, "What then shall I do with Jesus who is called Christ?"

They all said to him, "Let Him be crucified!"

23 Then the governor said, "Why, what evil has He done?"

But they cried out all the more, saying, "Let Him be crucified!"

24 When Pilate saw that he could

27:2 *a*NU-Text omits *Pontius.*   27:10 *a*Jeremiah 32:6–9   27:16 *a*NU-Text reads *Jesus Barabbas.*

*T*he power to unleash you is in your faith. Dare to believe that He will do what He said He would do. Shift your confidence from your own weaknesses to His power. Trust in Him rather than in yourself.

not prevail at all, but rather *that* a tumult was rising, he took water and washed *his* hands before the multitude, saying, "I am innocent of the blood of this just Person.*ᵃ* You see *to it.*"

25 And all the people answered and said, "His blood *be* on us and on our children."

26 Then he released Barabbas to them; and when he had scourged Jesus, he delivered *Him* to be crucified.

27 Then the soldiers of the governor took Jesus into the Praetorium and gathered the whole garrison around Him. 28 And they stripped Him and put a scarlet robe on Him. 29 When they had twisted a crown of thorns, they put *it* on His head, and a reed in His right hand. And they bowed the knee before Him and mocked Him, saying, "Hail, King of the Jews!" 30 Then they spat on Him, and took the reed and struck Him on the head. 31 And when they had mocked Him, they took the robe off Him, put His *own* clothes on Him, and led Him away to be crucified.

32 Now as they came out, they found a man of Cyrene, Simon by name. Him they compelled to bear His cross. 33 And when they had come to a place called Golgotha, that is to say, Place of a Skull, 34 they gave Him sour*ᵃ* wine mingled with gall to drink. But when He had tasted *it*, He would not drink.

35 Then they crucified Him, and divided His garments, casting lots,*ᵃ* that it might be fulfilled which was spoken by the prophet:

> "They divided My garments
>   among them,
> And for My clothing they cast
>   lots."*ᵇ*

36 Sitting down, they kept watch over Him there. 37 And they put up over His head the accusation written against Him:

THIS IS JESUS
THE KING OF THE JEWS.

38 Then two robbers were crucified with Him, one on the right and another on the left.

39 And those who passed by blasphemed Him, wagging their heads 40 and saying, "You who destroy the temple and build *it* in three days, save Yourself! If You are the Son of God, come down from the cross."

41 Likewise the chief priests also, mocking with the scribes and elders,*ᵃ* said, 42 "He saved others; Himself He cannot save. If He is the King of Israel,*ᵃ* let Him now come down from the cross, and we will believe Him.*ᵇ* 43 He trusted in God; let Him deliver Him now if He will have Him; for He said, 'I am the Son of God.'"

44 Even the robbers who were crucified with Him reviled Him with the same thing.

45 Now from the sixth hour until the ninth hour there was darkness over all the land. 46 And about the ninth hour Jesus cried out with a loud voice, saying, "Eli, Eli, lama sabachthani?" that is, *"My God, My God, why have You forsaken Me?"ᵃ*

47 Some of those who stood there, when they heard *that*, said, "This Man is calling for Elijah!" 48 Immediately one of them ran and took a sponge, filled *it* with sour wine and put *it* on a reed, and offered it to Him to drink.

49 The rest said, "Let Him alone; let us see if Elijah will come to save Him."

50 And Jesus cried out again with a loud voice, and yielded up His spirit.

51 Then, behold, the veil of the temple was torn in two from top to bottom; and the earth quaked, and the rocks were split, 52 and the graves were opened; and many bodies of the saints who had fallen asleep were raised; 53 and coming out of the graves after His resurrection, they went into the holy city and appeared to many.

54 So when the centurion and those with him, who were guarding Jesus, saw the earthquake and the things that had happened, they feared greatly, saying, "Truly this was the Son of God!"

55 And many women who followed Jesus from Galilee, ministering to Him, were there looking on from

---

27:24 *ᵃ*NU-Text omits *just.*   27:34 *ᵃ*NU-Text omits *sour.*   27:35 *ᵃ*NU-Text and M-Text omit the rest of this verse. *ᵇ*Psalm 22:18   27:41 *ᵃ*M-Text reads *with the scribes, the Pharisees, and the elders.*
27:42 *ᵃ*NU-Text reads *He is the King of Israel!* *ᵇ*NU-Text and M-Text read *we will believe in Him.*
27:46 *ᵃ*Psalm 22:1

Gospel Pearls

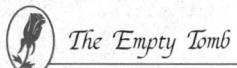

afar, 56 among whom were Mary Magdalene, Mary the mother of James and Joses,ᵃ and the mother of Zebedee's sons.

57 Now when evening had come, there came a rich man from Arimathea, named Joseph, who himself had also become a disciple of Jesus. 58 This man went to Pilate and asked for the body of Jesus. Then Pilate commanded the body to be given to him. 59 When Joseph had taken the body, he wrapped it in a clean linen cloth, 60 and laid it in his new tomb which he had hewn out of the rock; and he rolled a large stone against the door of the tomb, and departed. 61 And Mary Magdalene was there, and the other Mary, sitting opposite the tomb.

62 On the next day, which followed the Day of Preparation, the chief priests and Pharisees gathered together to Pilate, 63 saying, "Sir, we remember, while He was still alive, how that deceiver said, 'After three days I will rise.' 64 Therefore command that the tomb be made secure until the third day, lest His disciples come by nightᵃ and steal Him *away*, and say to the people, 'He has risen from the dead.' So the last deception will be worse than the first."

65 Pilate said to them, "You have a guard; go your way, make *it* as secure as you know how." 66 So they went and made the tomb secure, sealing the stone and setting the guard.

28 Now after the Sabbath, as the first *day* of the week began to dawn, Mary Magdalene and the other Mary came to see the tomb. 2 And behold, there was a great earthquake; for an angel of the Lord descended from heaven, and came and rolled back the stone from the door,ᵃ and sat on it. 3 His countenance was like lightning, and his clothing as white as snow. 4 And the guards shook for fear of him, and became like dead *men*.

5 But the angel answered and said to the women, "Do not be afraid, for I know that you seek Jesus who was crucified. 6 He is not here; for He is risen, as He said. Come, see the place where the Lord lay. 7 And go quickly and tell His disciples that He is risen from the dead, and indeed He is going before you into Galilee; there you will see Him. Behold, I have told you."

8 So they went out quickly from the tomb with fear and great joy, and ran to bring His disciples word.

9 And as they went to tell His disciples,ᵃ behold, Jesus met them, saying, "Rejoice!" So they came and held Him by the feet and worshiped Him. 10 Then Jesus said to them, "Do not be afraid. Go *and* tell My brethren to go to Galilee, and there they will see Me."

11 Now while they were going, behold, some of the guard came into the city and reported to the chief priests all the things that had happened. 12 When they had assembled with the elders and consulted together, they gave a large sum of money to the soldiers, 13 saying, "Tell them, 'His disciples came at night and stole Him *away* while we slept.' 14 And if this comes to the governor's ears, we will appease him and make you secure." 15 So they took the money and did as they were instructed; and this saying is commonly reported among the Jews until this day.

16 Then the eleven disciples went away into Galilee, to the mountain which Jesus had appointed for them. 17 When they saw Him, they worshiped Him; but some doubted.

18 And Jesus came and spoke to them, saying, "All authority has been given to Me in heaven and on earth. 19 Go thereforeᵃ and make disciples of all the nations, baptizing them in the name of the Father and of the Son and of the Holy Spirit, 20 teaching them to observe all things that I have commanded you; and lo, I am with you always, *even* to the end of the age." Amen.ᵃ

27:56 ᵃNU-Text reads *Joseph.*   27:64 ᵃNU-Text omits *by night.*   28:2 ᵃNU-Text omits *from the door.* 28:9 ᵃNU-Text omits the first clause of this verse.   28:19 ᵃM-Text omits *therefore.*   28:20 ᵃNU-Text omits *Amen.*

A nyone who comes to Christ will find deliverance and healing. He will soothe your wounds. He will comfort you in your desperate moments. He will raise you up.

MARK

1 The beginning of the gospel of Jesus Christ, the Son of God. 2 As it is written in the Prophets:*a*

> *"Behold, I send My messenger*
>   *before Your face,*
> *Who will prepare Your way*
>   *before You."* *b*
> 3 *"The voice of one crying in the*
>   *wilderness:*
> *'Prepare the way of the LORD;*
> *Make His paths straight.' "a*

4 John came baptizing in the wilderness and preaching a baptism of repentance for the remission of sins. 5 Then all the land of Judea, and those from Jerusalem, went out to him and were all baptized by him in the Jordan River, confessing their sins.

6 Now John was clothed with camel's hair and with a leather belt around his waist, and he ate locusts and wild honey. 7 And he preached, saying, "There comes One after me who is mightier than I, whose sandal strap I am not worthy to stoop down and loose. 8 I indeed baptized you with water, but He will baptize you with the Holy Spirit."

9 It came to pass in those days *that* Jesus came from Nazareth of Galilee, and was baptized by John in the Jordan. 10 And immediately, coming up from*a* the water, He saw the heavens parting and the Spirit descending upon Him like a dove. 11 Then a voice came from heaven, "You are My beloved Son, in whom I am well pleased."

12 Immediately the Spirit drove Him into the wilderness. 13 And He was there in the wilderness forty days, tempted by Satan, and was with the wild beasts; and the angels ministered to Him.

14 Now after John was put in prison, Jesus came to Galilee, preaching the gospel of the kingdom*a* of God, 15 and saying, "The time is fulfilled, and the kingdom of God is at hand. Repent, and believe in the gospel."

16 And as He walked by the Sea of Galilee, He saw Simon and Andrew his brother casting a net into the sea; for they were fishermen. 17 Then Jesus said to them, "Follow Me, and I will make you become fishers of men." 18 They immediately left their nets and followed Him.

19 When He had gone a little farther from there, He saw James the *son* of Zebedee, and John his brother, who also *were* in the boat mending their nets. 20 And immediately He called them, and they left their father Zebedee in the boat with the hired servants, and went after Him.

21 Then they went into Capernaum, and immediately on the Sabbath He entered the synagogue and taught. 22 And they were astonished at His teaching, for He taught them as one having authority, and not as the scribes.

23 Now there was a man in their synagogue with an unclean spirit. And he cried out, 24 saying, "Let *us* alone! What have we to do with You, Jesus of Nazareth? Did You come to destroy us? I know who You are— the Holy One of God!"

25 But Jesus rebuked him, saying, "Be quiet, and come out of him!" 26 And when the unclean spirit had convulsed him and cried out with a loud voice, he came out of him. 27 Then they were all amazed, so that they questioned among themselves, saying, "What is this? What new doctrine *is* this? For with authority*a* He commands even the unclean spirits, and they obey Him." 28 And immediately His fame spread throughout all the region around Galilee.

29 Now as soon as they had come out of the synagogue, they entered the house of Simon and Andrew, with James and John. 30 But Simon's wife's mother lay sick with a fever, and they told Him about her at once. 31 So He came and took her by the hand and lifted her up, and immediately the fever left her. And she served them.

32 At evening, when the sun had

1:2 *a*NU-Text reads *Isaiah the prophet.* *b*Malachi 3:1   1:3 *a*Isaiah 40:3   1:10 *a*NU-Text reads *out of.*   1:14 *a*NU-Text omits *of the kingdom.*   1:27 *a*NU-Text reads *What is this? A new doctrine with authority.*

Gospel Pearls

set, they brought to Him all who were sick and those who were demon-possessed. 33 And the whole city was gathered together at the door. 34 Then He healed many who were sick with various diseases, and cast out many demons; and He did not allow the demons to speak, because they knew Him.

35 Now in the morning, having risen a long while before daylight, He went out and departed to a solitary place; and there He prayed. 36 And Simon and those who were with Him searched for Him. 37 When they found Him, they said to Him, "Everyone is looking for You."

38 But He said to them, "Let us go into the next towns, that I may preach there also, because for this purpose I have come forth."

39 And He was preaching in their synagogues throughout all Galilee, and casting out demons.

40 Now a leper came to Him, imploring Him, kneeling down to Him and saying to Him, "If You are willing, You can make me clean."

41 Then Jesus, moved with compassion, stretched out *His* hand and touched him, and said to him, "I am willing; be cleansed." 42 As soon as He had spoken, immediately the leprosy left him, and he was cleansed. 43 And He strictly warned him and sent him away at once, 44 and said to him, "See that you say nothing to anyone; but go your way, show yourself to the priest, and offer for your cleansing those things which Moses commanded, as a testimony to them."

45 However, he went out and began to proclaim *it* freely, and to spread the matter, so that Jesus could no longer openly enter the city, but was outside in deserted places; and they came to Him from every direction.

2 And again He entered Capernaum after *some* days, and it was heard that He was in the house. 2 Immediately[a] many gathered together, so that there was no longer room to receive *them,* not even near the door. And He preached the word to them. 3 Then they came to Him, bringing a paralytic who was carried by four *men.* 4 And when they could

not come near Him because of the crowd, they uncovered the roof where He was. So when they had broken through, they let down the bed on which the paralytic was lying.

5 When Jesus saw their faith, He said to the paralytic, "Son, your sins are forgiven you."

6 And some of the scribes were sitting there and reasoning in their hearts, 7 "Why does this *Man* speak blasphemies like this? Who can forgive sins but God alone?"

8 But immediately, when Jesus perceived in His spirit that they reasoned thus within themselves, He said to them, "Why do you reason about these things in your hearts? 9 Which is easier, to say to the paralytic, '*Your* sins are forgiven you,' or to say, 'Arise, take up your bed and walk'? 10 But that you may know that the Son of Man has power on earth to forgive sins"—He said to the paralytic, 11 "I say to you, arise, take up your bed, and go to your house." 12 Immediately he arose, took up the bed, and went out in the presence of them all, so that all were amazed and glorified God, saying, "We never saw *anything* like this!"

13 Then He went out again by the sea; and all the multitude came to Him, and He taught them. 14 As He passed by, He saw Levi the *son* of Alphaeus sitting at the tax office. And He said to him, "Follow Me." So he arose and followed Him.

15 Now it happened, as He was dining in *Levi's* house, that many tax collectors and sinners also sat together with Jesus and His disciples; for there were many, and they followed Him. 16 And when the scribes and[a] Pharisees saw Him eating with the tax collectors and sinners, they said to His disciples, "How *is it* that He eats and drinks with tax collectors and sinners?"

17 When Jesus heard *it,* He said to them, "Those who are well have no need of a physician, but those who are sick. I did not come to call *the* righteous, but sinners, to repentance."[a]

18 The disciples of John and of the Pharisees were fasting. Then they came and said to Him, "Why do the disciples of John and of the Pharisees fast, but Your disciples do not fast?"

2:2 [a]NU-Text omits *Immediately.*   2:16 [a]NU-Text reads *of the.*   2:17 [a]NU-Text omits *to repentance.*

---

*B*elieve that He paid the price for your sin and guilt. Believe that He has washed you and made you clean. Have faith that He will reward you when you call on Him and it shall be done.

Don't Let the Enemy Win

Mark 2:1-12

*H*ell gets very confused when Jesus delivers a person from a spirit of infirmity. Satan has a file that is supposed to predict precisely which of his tactics will work on you. If it isn't effective, there's confusion.

Satan starts grilling his demons: "Did you not catch her at a weak moment? Did you not make the temptation enticing enough? Did you not make the accusation powerful enough? Did you not use strong enough chains to bind that spirit of infirmity to her?" To all of his questions the demons reply, "Yes. But this time it just didn't work."

Once you have been set free, Satan will keep trying to bind you. But now the weapons he used effectively on you in the past don't hurt you anymore. You have been loosed from their ability to wound or incapacitate you.

In Mark 2:1-12, we read about a man who had palsy. Four friends brought him to Jesus and lowered him through the ceiling so Jesus could heal him. Jesus said to him, "Arise, take up your bed, and go to your house" (Mark 2:11). This man was lying on his bed when they carried him to Jesus. After Jesus spoke to him, he carried his bed back home. The two—the man and the bed—traded places!

You are never going to be entirely free from problems. But Jesus comes to heal and deliver you so that the problems cease to diminish you, hold you back, or keep you down. Instead of the problem's controlling you, you control it, in Jesus' name.

I believe that many people have been taught incorrectly about deliverance. As a result, they have unrealistic expectations. They expect to walk through a prayer line and have somebody lay hands on them with such power that the devil will never be able to say another word to them for the rest of their lives. They think that if they go to the right church or sit under the right ministry, they will become so mature in Christ, they will never be tempted again. It'll never happen because it isn't about making the devil impotent; it's about making people strong and free.

Deliverance means that you now control what used to control you. Deliverance means that the thing that sat on the throne of your heart and ruled with ruthless power over your life has been dethroned and replaced by Jesus Christ. It still exists, but it isn't in charge.

Every now and then, Satan will attempt a coup. He'll try to usurp the throne of your life. At that point, it is up to you to resist his efforts, trust in God, and exert control with your will. Satan will not stop trying, but deliverance will put you in position to keep him from succeeding!

19 And Jesus said to them, "Can the friends of the bridegroom fast while the bridegroom is with them? As long as they have the bridegroom with them they cannot fast. 20 But the days will come when the bridegroom will be taken away from them, and then they will fast in those days. 21 No one sews a piece of unshrunk cloth on an old garment; or else the new piece pulls away from the old, and the tear is made worse. 22 And no one puts new wine into old wineskins; or else the new wine bursts the wineskins, the wine is spilled, and the wineskins are ruined. But new wine must be put into new wineskins."

23 Now it happened that He went through the grainfields on the Sabbath; and as they went His disciples began to pluck the heads of grain. 24 And the Pharisees said to Him, "Look, why do they do what is not lawful on the Sabbath?"

25 But He said to them, "Have you never read what David did when he was in need and hungry, he and those with him: 26 how he went into the house of God *in the days* of Abiathar the high priest, and ate the showbread, which is not lawful to eat except for the priests, and also gave some to those who were with him?"

27 And He said to them, "The Sabbath was made for man, and not man for the Sabbath. 28 Therefore the Son of Man is also Lord of the Sabbath."

3 And He entered the synagogue again, and a man was there who had a withered hand. 2 So they watched Him closely, whether He would heal him on the Sabbath, so that they might accuse Him. 3 And He said to the man who had the withered hand, "Step forward." 4 Then He said to them, "Is it lawful on the Sabbath to do good or to do evil, to save life or to kill?" But they kept silent. 5 And when He had looked around at them with anger, being grieved by the hardness of their hearts, He said to the man, "Stretch out your hand." And he stretched *it* out, and his hand was restored as whole as the other.*a* 6 Then the Pharisees went out and immediately plotted with the Herodians against Him, how they might destroy Him.

7 But Jesus withdrew with His disciples to the sea. And a great multitude from Galilee followed Him, and from Judea 8 and Jerusalem and Idumea and beyond the Jordan; and those from Tyre and Sidon, a great multitude, when they heard how many things He was doing, came to Him. 9 So He told His disciples that a small boat should be kept ready for Him because of the multitude, lest they should crush Him. 10 For He healed many, so that as many as had afflictions pressed about Him to touch Him. 11 And the unclean spirits, whenever they saw Him, fell down before Him and cried out, saying, "You are the Son of God." 12 But He sternly warned them that they should not make Him known.

13 And He went up on the mountain and called to *Him* those He Himself wanted. And they came to Him. 14 Then He appointed twelve,*a* that they might be with Him and that He might send them out to preach, 15 and to have power to heal sicknesses and*a* to cast out demons: 16 Simon,*a* to whom He gave the name Peter; 17 James the *son* of Zebedee and John the brother of James, to whom He gave the name Boanerges, that is, "Sons of Thunder"; 18 Andrew, Philip, Bartholomew, Matthew, Thomas, James the *son* of Alphaeus, Thaddaeus, Simon the Cananite; 19 and Judas Iscariot, who also betrayed Him. And they went into a house.

20 Then the multitude came together again, so that they could not so much as eat bread. 21 But when His own people heard *about this,* they went out to lay hold of Him, for they said, "He is out of His mind."

22 And the scribes who came down from Jerusalem said, "He has Beelzebub," and, "By the ruler of the demons He casts out demons."

23 So He called them to *Himself* and said to them in parables: "How can Satan cast out Satan? 24 If a kingdom is divided against itself, that kingdom cannot stand. 25 And if a house is divided against itself, that

3:5 *a*NU-Text omits *as whole as the other.* 3:14 *a*NU-Text adds *whom He also named apostles.*
3:15 *a*NU-Text omits *to heal sicknesses and.* 3:16 *a*NU-Text reads *and He appointed the twelve:*
Simon . . . .

Jesus will straighten the crooked places in your heart and make you completely whole. When you allow Him access to every broken area of your life, you will never be the same broken person again.

He Calls You Anyway

Mark 3:1-5

*J*esus didn't associate with the upper echelon of His community. He surrounded Himself with broken, bleeding, dirty people. He sat with prostitutes and winos. Even though He was criticized for hanging out with questionable characters, the rejects of society followed Him everywhere He went. They knew that He offered mercy and forgiveness.

Every time Jesus saw a hurting person, He reached out and ministered to the need. Once when He was preaching to a crowd, He saw a man with a withered hand and immediately healed him (see Mark 3:1-5). Another time He called a crippled woman to Him. She had been coming to church, sitting in the synagogue for years and years. But nobody had noticed her until Jesus spoke to her that day.

When I first read this passage, I wondered why Jesus didn't just speak the word and heal her in her seat. Why did He call her out, crippled as she was?

Perhaps God wants to see us moving toward Him. Perhaps we need to invest in our own deliverance. To bring a testimony out of a test. To give others the strength to overcome their handicap.

We can't know how long it took that woman to get up to the front. Handicapped people don't move as fast as others do. And believers who have been suffering for a long time don't grow as fast as other people. They've been incapacitated. What is simple for one person may be extremely difficult for another. But Jesus challenged this woman's limitations. He called her anyway.

Thank God He calls women with a past. He reaches out and says, "Get up! You can come to Me. Regardless of what you have done or what kind of abuse you have suffered, I want you to come."

You may think your secret is worse than anyone else's secret. Rest assured that Jesus knows all about it. He will give you a miracle. Many will say, "Is this the same woman who was bent over and wounded? The one who's been coming to church for years?" Others may think, "Is this the same woman who had one foot in the church and the other in an affair?"

People with a past need to make their way to Jesus. Regardless of the obstacles within or without, they must reach Him. You may have a baby out of wedlock cradled in your arms, but keep pressing on. You may have been abused and molested and have never been able to talk to anyone about it, but don't stop reaching out to Him. You don't have to tell everyone your entire story. But you may be sure your secret will be safe with Jesus.

Just know that He calls, on purpose, women with a past. He knows your history, but He's calling you anyway.

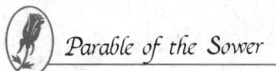

house cannot stand. 26 And if Satan has risen up against himself, and is divided, he cannot stand, but has an end. 27 No one can enter a strong man's house and plunder his goods, unless he first binds the strong man. And then he will plunder his house.

28 "Assuredly, I say to you, all sins will be forgiven the sons of men, and whatever blasphemies they may utter; 29 but he who blasphemes against the Holy Spirit never has forgiveness, but is subject to eternal condemnation"— 30 because they said, "He has an unclean spirit."

31 Then His brothers and His mother came, and standing outside they sent to Him, calling Him. 32 And a multitude was sitting around Him; and they said to Him, "Look, Your mother and Your brothers*ᵃ* are outside seeking You."

33 But He answered them, saying, "Who is My mother, or My brothers?" 34 And He looked around in a circle at those who sat about Him, and said, "Here are My mother and My brothers! 35 For whoever does the will of God is My brother and My sister and mother."

4 And again He began to teach by the sea. And a great multitude was gathered to Him, so that He got into a boat and sat *in it* on the sea; and the whole multitude was on the land facing the sea. 2 Then He taught them many things by parables, and said to them in His teaching: 3 "Listen! Behold, a sower went out to sow. 4 And it happened, as he sowed, *that* some *seed* fell by the wayside; and the birds of the air*ᵃ* came and devoured it. 5 Some fell on stony ground, where it did not have much earth; and immediately it sprang up because it had no depth of earth. 6 But when the sun was up it was scorched, and because it had no root it withered away. 7 And some *seed* fell among thorns; and the thorns grew up and choked it, and it yielded no crop. 8 But other *seed* fell on good ground and yielded a crop that sprang up, increased and produced: some thirtyfold, some sixty, and some a hundred."

9 And He said to them,*ᵃ*"He who has ears to hear, let him hear!"

10 But when He was alone, those around Him with the twelve asked Him about the parable. 11 And He said to them, "To you it has been given to know the mystery of the kingdom of God; but to those who are outside, all things come in parables, 12 so that

'Seeing they may see and not
  perceive,
And hearing they may hear and
  not understand;
Lest they should turn,
And their sins be forgiven
  them.'"*ᵃ*

13 And He said to them, "Do you not understand this parable? How then will you understand all the parables? 14 The sower sows the word. 15 And these are the ones by the wayside where the word is sown. When they hear, Satan comes immediately and takes away the word that was sown in their hearts. 16 These likewise are the ones sown on stony ground who, when they hear the word, immediately receive it with gladness; 17 and they have no root in themselves, and so endure only for a time. Afterward, when tribulation or persecution arises for the word's sake, immediately they stumble. 18 Now these are the ones sown among thorns; *they are* the ones who hear the word, 19 and the cares of this world, the deceitfulness of riches, and the desires for other things entering in choke the word, and it becomes unfruitful. 20 But these are the ones sown on good ground, those who hear the word, accept *it*, and bear fruit: some thirtyfold, some sixty, and some a hundred."

21 Also He said to them,"Is a lamp brought to be put under a basket or under a bed? Is it not to be set on a lampstand? 22 For there is nothing hidden which will not be revealed, nor has anything been kept secret but that it should come to light. 23 If anyone has ears to hear, let him hear."

24 Then He said to them, "Take heed what you hear. With the same measure you use, it will be measured to you; and to you who hear, more will be given. 25 For whoever has, to

---

3:32 *ᵃ*NU-Text and M-Text add *and Your sisters.*   4:4 *ᵃ*NU-Text and M-Text omit *of the air.*
4:9 *ᵃ*NU-Text and M-Text omit *to them.*   4:12 *ᵃ*Isaiah 6:9, 10

---

*A*ppreciate the ornaments of God. Let God give you a new attitude. Let Him wash everything out of your spirit that is against Him. Let go of anger, hate, frustration and bitterness. God wants you unleashed.

him more will be given; but whoever does not have, even what he has will be taken away from him."

26 And He said, "The kingdom of God is as if a man should scatter seed on the ground, 27 and should sleep by night and rise by day, and the seed should sprout and grow, he himself does not know how. 28 For the earth yields crops by itself: first the blade, then the head, after that the full grain in the head. 29 But when the grain ripens, immediately he puts in the sickle, because the harvest has come."

30 Then He said, "To what shall we liken the kingdom of God? Or with what parable shall we picture it? 31 *It is* like a mustard seed which, when it is sown on the ground, is smaller than all the seeds on earth; 32 but when it is sown, it grows up and becomes greater than all herbs, and shoots out large branches, so that the birds of the air may nest under its shade."

33 And with many such parables He spoke the word to them as they were able to hear *it.* 34 But without a parable He did not speak to them. And when they were alone, He explained all things to His disciples.

35 On the same day, when evening had come, He said to them, "Let us cross over to the other side." 36 Now when they had left the multitude, they took Him along in the boat as He was. And other little boats were also with Him. 37 And a great windstorm arose, and the waves beat into the boat, so that it was already filling. 38 But He was in the stern, asleep on a pillow. And they awoke Him and said to Him, "Teacher, do You not care that we are perishing?" 39 Then He arose and rebuked the wind, and said to the sea, "Peace, be still!" And the wind ceased and there was a great calm. 40 But He said to them, "Why are you so fearful? How is it that you have no faith?"*a* 41 And they feared exceedingly, and said to one another, "Who can this be, that even the wind and the sea obey Him!"

5 Then they came to the other side of the sea, to the country of the Gadarenes.*a* 2 And when He had come out of the boat, immediately there met Him out of the tombs a man with an unclean spirit, 3 who had *his* dwelling among the tombs; and no one could bind him,*a* not even with chains, 4 because he had often been bound with shackles and chains. And the chains had been pulled apart by him, and the shackles broken in pieces; neither could anyone tame him. 5 And always, night and day, he was in the mountains and in the tombs, crying out and cutting himself with stones.

6 When he saw Jesus from afar, he ran and worshiped Him. 7 And he cried out with a loud voice and said, "What have I to do with You, Jesus, Son of the Most High God? I implore You by God that You do not torment me."

8 For He said to him, "Come out of the man, unclean spirit!" 9 Then He asked him, "What *is* your name?"

And he answered, saying, "My name *is* Legion; for we are many." 10 Also he begged Him earnestly that He would not send them out of the country.

11 Now a large herd of swine was feeding there near the mountains. 12 So all the demons begged Him, saying, "Send us to the swine, that we may enter them." 13 And at once Jesus*a* gave them permission. Then the unclean spirits went out and entered the swine (there were about two thousand); and the herd ran violently down the steep place into the sea, and drowned in the sea.

14 So those who fed the swine fled, and they told *it* in the city and in the country. And they went out to see what it was that had happened. 15 Then they came to Jesus, and saw the one *who had been* demon-possessed and had the legion, sitting and clothed and in his right mind. And they were afraid. 16 And those who saw *it* told them how it happened to him *who had been* demon-possessed, and about the swine. 17 Then they began to plead with Him to depart from their region.

18 And when He got into the boat, he who had been demon-possessed begged Him that he might be with Him. 19 However, Jesus did not per-

4:40 *a*NU-Text reads *Have you still no faith?*   5:1 *a*NU-Text reads *Gerasenes.*   5:3 *a*NU-Text adds *anymore.*   5:13 *a*NU-Text reads *And He gave.*

Gospel Pearls

mit him, but said to him, "Go home to your friends, and tell them what great things the Lord has done for you, and how He has had compassion on you." 20 And he departed and began to proclaim in Decapolis all that Jesus had done for him; and all marveled.

21 Now when Jesus had crossed over again by boat to the other side, a great multitude gathered to Him; and He was by the sea. 22 And behold, one of the rulers of the synagogue came, Jairus by name. And when he saw Him, he fell at His feet 23 and begged Him earnestly, saying, "My little daughter lies at the point of death. Come and lay Your hands on her, that she may be healed, and she will live." 24 So *Jesus* went with him, and a great multitude followed Him and thronged Him.

25 Now a certain woman had a flow of blood for twelve years, 26 and had suffered many things from many physicians. She had spent all that she had and was no better, but rather grew worse. 27 When she heard about Jesus, she came behind *Him* in the crowd and touched His garment. 28 For she said, "If only I may touch His clothes, I shall be made well."

29 Immediately the fountain of her blood was dried up, and she felt in *her* body that she was healed of the affliction. 30 And Jesus, immediately knowing in Himself that power had gone out of Him, turned around in the crowd and said, "Who touched My clothes?"

31 But His disciples said to Him, "You see the multitude thronging You, and You say, 'Who touched Me?'"

32 And He looked around to see her who had done this thing. 33 But the woman, fearing and trembling, knowing what had happened to her, came and fell down before Him and told Him the whole truth. 34 And He said to her, "Daughter, your faith has made you well. Go in peace, and be healed of your affliction."

35 While He was still speaking, *some* came from the ruler of the synagogue's *house* who said, "Your daughter is dead. Why trouble the Teacher any further?"

36 As soon as Jesus heard the word that was spoken, He said to the ruler of the synagogue, "Do not be afraid; only believe." 37 And He permitted no one to follow Him except Peter, James, and John the brother of James. 38 Then He came to the house of the ruler of the synagogue, and saw a tumult and those who wept and wailed loudly. 39 When He came in, He said to them, "Why make this commotion and weep? The child is not dead, but sleeping."

40 And they ridiculed Him. But when He had put them all outside, He took the father and the mother of the child, and those *who were* with Him, and entered where the child was lying. 41 Then He took the child by the hand, and said to her, "Talitha, cumi," which is translated, "Little girl, I say to you, arise." 42 Immediately the girl arose and walked, for she was twelve years *of age.* And they were overcome with great amazement. 43 But He commanded them strictly that no one should know it, and said that *something* should be given her to eat.

6 Then He went out from there and came to His own country, and His disciples followed Him. 2 And when the Sabbath had come, He began to teach in the synagogue. And many hearing *Him* were astonished, saying, "Where *did* this Man *get* these things? And what wisdom *is* this which is given to Him, that such mighty works are performed by His hands! 3 Is this not the carpenter, the Son of Mary, and brother of James, Joses, Judas, and Simon? And are not His sisters here with us?" So they were offended at Him.

4 But Jesus said to them, "A prophet is not without honor except in his own country, among his own relatives, and in his own house." 5 Now He could do no mighty work there, except that He laid His hands on a few sick people and healed *them.* 6 And He marveled because of their unbelief. Then He went about the villages in a circuit, teaching.

7 And He called the twelve to *Himself,* and began to send them out two *by* two, and gave them power over unclean spirits. 8 He commanded them to take nothing for the journey except a staff—no bag, no bread, no copper in *their* money belts— 9 but to wear sandals, and not to put on two tunics.

10 Also He said to them, "In what-

---

*L*earn the art of rejoicing when God says no. Rejoice when things don't go the way you planned. Rejoice, because if Satan is at work, your attitude will make his efforts futile.

Your Knight in Shining Armor

Mark 5:41, 42

*I*n the true tradition of ancient chivalry, when there were princes, drawbridges, damsels in distress, and villains in pursuit, Jairus, the ruler of the synagogue, had a daughter who was sick. And he sent for Jesus. But Jesus was busy ministering to the woman with the issue of blood, and by the time He had healed her, Jairus's daughter had died. She was laid on a bed in the upper chamber of her house, and neighbors came to mourn the passing of the little girl.

Nothing could be done. The whole family gathered around and wept. Hope was gone.

Perhaps people have gathered around you to weep and mourn, thinking your life is over. It may look like you've forgotten how to love, like your creativity and passion have succumbed to some spiritual affliction.

But, daughter of God, Jairus's Friend would not allow them to commit the child to the ground. Jesus came for her. He came with all the gallantry of a prince. He came with the courage of a mighty man destined to save a damsel in distress. His shiny armor was the glory of the Lord. His sword was in His mouth. He came in the room and put the doubters out.

There can be no doubter crying in your ear—not when you are trying to resurrect a relationship, not when you are trying to revive a part of you that Satan wants to kill. You can't use your relationship with God to stay in a state of denial. If something has gone out of your life and your heart, you must believe God for its return.

Just when they thought Jairus's daughter could not be brought back to life, here came Jesus. Likewise, just when others have decided you won't be back, here He comes. He comes into your life like a medieval prince, clad in righteousness, dipped in blood. He comes to heal and restore your faith and expectation, your romance and tenderness. He longs to be your Hero. He longs to open things you cannot open and move things you cannot move. If life has left you disenchanted and aloof, remember He is your Knight in shining armor.

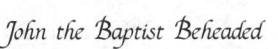

ever place you enter a house, stay there till you depart from that place. 11 And whoever[a] will not receive you nor hear you, when you depart from there, shake off the dust under your feet as a testimony against them.[b] Assuredly, I say to you, it will be more tolerable for Sodom and Gomorrah in the day of judgment than for that city!"

12 So they went out and preached that *people* should repent. 13 And they cast out many demons, and anointed with oil many who were sick, and healed *them*.

14 Now King Herod heard *of Him*, for His name had become well known. And he said, "John the Baptist is risen from the dead, and therefore these powers are at work in him."

15 Others said, "It is Elijah."

And others said, "It is the Prophet, or[a] like one of the prophets."

16 But when Herod heard, he said, "This is John, whom I beheaded; he has been raised from the dead!" 17 For Herod himself had sent and laid hold of John, and bound him in prison for the sake of Herodias, his brother Philip's wife; for he had married her. 18 Because John had said to Herod, "It is not lawful for you to have your brother's wife."

19 Therefore Herodias held it against him and wanted to kill him, but she could not; 20 for Herod feared John, knowing that he *was* a just and holy man, and he protected him. And when he heard him, he did many things, and heard him gladly.

21 Then an opportune day came when Herod on his birthday gave a feast for his nobles, the high officers, and the chief *men* of Galilee. 22 And when Herodias' daughter herself came in and danced, and pleased Herod and those who sat with him, the king said to the girl, "Ask me whatever you want, and I will give *it* to you." 23 He also swore to her, "Whatever you ask me, I will give you, up to half my kingdom."

24 So she went out and said to her mother, "What shall I ask?"

And she said, "The head of John the Baptist!"

25 Immediately she came in with haste to the king and asked, saying, "I want you to give me at once the head of John the Baptist on a platter."

26 And the king was exceedingly sorry; *yet*, because of the oaths and because of those who sat with him, he did not want to refuse her. 27 Immediately the king sent an executioner and commanded his head to be brought. And he went and beheaded him in prison, 28 brought his head on a platter, and gave it to the girl; and the girl gave it to her mother. 29 When his disciples heard *of it*, they came and took away his corpse and laid it in a tomb.

30 Then the apostles gathered to Jesus and told Him all things, both what they had done and what they had taught. 31 And He said to them, "Come aside by yourselves to a deserted place and rest a while." For there were many coming and going, and they did not even have time to eat. 32 So they departed to a deserted place in the boat by themselves.

33 But the multitudes[a] saw them departing, and many knew Him and ran there on foot from all the cities. They arrived before them and came together to Him. 34 And Jesus, when He came out, saw a great multitude and was moved with compassion for them, because they were like sheep not having a shepherd. So He began to teach them many things. 35 When the day was now far spent, His disciples came to Him and said, "This is a deserted place, and already the hour *is* late. 36 Send them away, that they may go into the surrounding country and villages and buy themselves bread;[a] for they have nothing to eat."

37 But He answered and said to them, "You give them something to eat."

And they said to Him, "Shall we go and buy two hundred denarii worth of bread and give them *something* to eat?"

38 But He said to them, "How many loaves do you have? Go and see."

And when they found out they said, "Five, and two fish."

39 Then He commanded them to

6:11 [a]NU-Text reads *whatever place*. [b]NU-Text omits the rest of this verse.   6:15 [a]NU-Text and M-Text omit *or*.   6:33 [a]NU-Text and M-Text read *they*.   6:36 [a]NU-Text reads *something to eat* and omits the rest of verse.

An eternal God chose you before you were ever born. His hand-picked bride, that is what you are. You *have been* selected—not *will be*. You *are* selected. You are not on trial. You are chosen.

make them all sit down in groups on the green grass. 40 So they sat down in ranks, in hundreds and in fifties. 41 And when He had taken the five loaves and the two fish, He looked up to heaven, blessed and broke the loaves, and gave *them* to His disciples to set before them; and the two fish He divided among *them* all. 42 So they all ate and were filled. 43 And they took up twelve baskets full of fragments and of the fish. 44 Now those who had eaten the loaves were about*a* five thousand men.

45 Immediately He made His disciples get into the boat and go before Him to the other side, to Bethsaida, while He sent the multitude away. 46 And when He had sent them away, He departed to the mountain to pray. 47 Now when evening came, the boat was in the middle of the sea; and He *was* alone on the land. 48 Then He saw them straining at rowing, for the wind was against them. Now about the fourth watch of the night He came to them, walking on the sea, and would have passed them by. 49 And when they saw Him walking on the sea, they supposed it was a ghost, and cried out; 50 for they all saw Him and were troubled. But immediately He talked with them and said to them, "Be of good cheer! It is I; do not be afraid." 51 Then He went up into the boat to them, and the wind ceased. And they were greatly amazed in themselves beyond measure, and marveled. 52 For they had not understood about the loaves, because their heart was hardened.

53 When they had crossed over, they came to the land of Gennesaret and anchored there. 54 And when they came out of the boat, immediately the people recognized Him, 55 ran through that whole surrounding region,and began to carry about on beds those who were sick to wherever they heard He was. 56 Wherever He entered, into villages, cities, or the country, they laid the sick in the marketplaces, and begged Him that they might just touch the hem of His garment. And as many as touched Him were made well.

7 Then the Pharisees and some of the scribes came together to Him, having come from Jerusalem. 2 Now when*a* they saw some of His disciples eat bread with defiled, that is, with unwashed hands, they found fault. 3 For the Pharisees and all the Jews do not eat unless they wash *their* hands in a special way, holding the tradition of the elders. 4 *When they come* from the marketplace, they do not eat unless they wash. And there are many other things which they have received and hold, *like* the washing of cups, pitchers, copper vessels, and couches.

5 Then the Pharisees and scribes asked Him, "Why do Your disciples not walk according to the tradition of the elders, but eat bread with unwashed hands?"

6 He answered and said to them, "Well did Isaiah prophesy of you hypocrites, as it is written:

'This people honors Me with
    their lips,
    But their heart is far from Me.
7   And in vain they worship Me,
    Teaching as doctrines the
    commandments of men.'*a*

8 For laying aside the commandment of God, you hold the tradition of men*a*—the washing of pitchers and cups, and many other such things you do."

9 He said to them, "*All too* well you reject the commandment of God, that you may keep your tradition. 10 For Moses said, 'Honor your father and your mother';*a* and, 'He who curses father or mother, let him be put to death.'*b* 11 But you say, 'If a man says to his father or mother, "Whatever profit you might have received from me *is* Corban"—' (that is, a gift *to* God), 12 then you no longer let him do anything for his father or his mother, 13 making the word of God of no effect through your tradition which you have handed down. And many such things you do."

14 When He had called all the multitude to *Himself,* He said to them, "Hear Me, everyone, and understand: 15 There is nothing that enters

6:44 *a*NU-Text and M-Text omit *about.*   7:2 *a*NU-Text omits *when* and *they found fault.*   7:7 *a*Isaiah 29:13   7:8 *a*NU-Text omits the rest of this verse.   7:10 *a*Exodus 20:12; Deuteronomy 5:16   *b*Exodus 21:17

Gospel Pearls

a man from outside which can defile him; but the things which come out of him, those are the things that defile a man. 16 If anyone has ears to hear, let him hear!"ᵃ

17 When He had entered a house away from the crowd, His disciples asked Him concerning the parable. 18 So He said to them, "Are you thus without understanding also? Do you not perceive that whatever enters a man from outside cannot defile him, 19 because it does not enter his heart but his stomach, and is eliminated, *thus* purifying all foods?"ᵃ 20 And He said, "What comes out of a man, that defiles a man. 21 For from within, out of the heart of men, proceed evil thoughts, adulteries, fornications, murders, 22 thefts, covetousness, wickedness, deceit, lewdness, an evil eye, blasphemy, pride, foolishness. 23 All these evil things come from within and defile a man."

24 From there He arose and went to the region of Tyre and Sidon.ᵃ And He entered a house and wanted no one to know *it,* but He could not be hidden. 25 For a woman whose young daughter had an unclean spirit heard about Him, and she came and fell at His feet. 26 The woman was a Greek, a Syro-Phoenician by birth, and she kept asking Him to cast the demon out of her daughter. 27 But Jesus said to her, "Let the children be filled first, for it is not good to take the children's bread and throw *it* to the little dogs."

28 And she answered and said to Him, "Yes, Lord, yet even the little dogs under the table eat from the children's crumbs."

29 Then He said to her, "For this saying go your way; the demon has gone out of your daughter."

30 And when she had come to her house, she found the demon gone out, and her daughter lying on the bed.

31 Again, departing from the region of Tyre and Sidon, He came through the midst of the region of Decapolis to the Sea of Galilee. 32 Then they brought to Him one who was deaf and had an impediment in his speech, and they begged Him to put His hand on him. 33 And He took him aside from the multitude, and put His fingers in his ears, and He spat and touched his tongue. 34 Then, looking up to heaven, He sighed, and said to him, "Ephphatha," that is, "Be opened."

35 Immediately his ears were opened, and the impediment of his tongue was loosed, and he spoke plainly. 36 Then He commanded them that they should tell no one; but the more He commanded them, the more widely they proclaimed *it.* 37 And they were astonished beyond measure, saying, "He has done all things well. He makes both the deaf to hear and the mute to speak."

8 In those days, the multitude being very great and having nothing to eat, Jesus called His disciples *to Him* and said to them, 2 "I have compassion on the multitude, because they have now continued with Me three days and have nothing to eat. 3 And if I send them away hungry to their own houses, they will faint on the way; for some of them have come from afar."

4 Then His disciples answered Him, "How can one satisfy these people with bread here in the wilderness?"

5 He asked them, "How many loaves do you have?"

And they said, "Seven."

6 So He commanded the multitude to sit down on the ground. And He took the seven loaves and gave thanks, broke *them* and gave *them* to His disciples to set before *them;* and they set *them* before the multitude. 7 They also had a few small fish; and having blessed them, He said to set them also before *them.* 8 So they ate and were filled, and they took up seven large baskets of leftover fragments. 9 Now those who had eaten were about four thousand. And He sent them away, 10 immediately got into the boat with His disciples, and came to the region of Dalmanutha.

11 Then the Pharisees came out and began to dispute with Him, seeking from Him a sign from heaven, testing Him. 12 But He sighed deeply in His spirit, and said, "Why does this gen-

7:16 ᵃNU-Text omits this verse.   7:19 ᵃNU-Text ends quotation with *eliminated,* setting off the final clause as Mark's comment that Jesus has declared all foods clean.   7:24 ᵃNU-Text omits *and Sidon.*

*Y*ou are the daughter of a King. He is the King who spared no expense to pay the ransom that delivered you from the things that held you hostage. Get a clue; catch a hint; you are somebody!

eration seek a sign? Assuredly, I say to you, no sign shall be given to this generation."

13 And He left them, and getting into the boat again, departed to the other side. 14 Now the disciples*ᵃ* had forgotten to take bread, and they did not have more than one loaf with them in the boat. 15 Then He charged them, saying, "Take heed, beware of the leaven of the Pharisees and the leaven of Herod."

16 And they reasoned among themselves, saying, "*It is* because we have no bread."

17 But Jesus, being aware of *it*, said to them, "Why do you reason because you have no bread? Do you not yet perceive nor understand? Is your heart still*ᵃ* hardened? 18 Having eyes, do you not see? And having ears, do you not hear? And do you not remember? 19 When I broke the five loaves for the five thousand, how many baskets full of fragments did you take up?"

They said to Him, "Twelve."

20 "Also, when I broke the seven for the four thousand, how many large baskets full of fragments did you take up?"

And they said, "Seven."

21 So He said to them, "How *is it* you do not understand?"

22 Then He came to Bethsaida; and they brought a blind man to Him, and begged Him to touch him. 23 So He took the blind man by the hand and led him out of the town. And when He had spit on his eyes and put His hands on him, He asked him if he saw anything.

24 And he looked up and said, "I see men like trees, walking."

25 Then He put *His* hands on his eyes again and made him look up. And he was restored and saw everyone clearly. 26 Then He sent him away to his house, saying, "Neither go into the town, nor tell anyone in the town."*ᵃ*

27 Now Jesus and His disciples went out to the towns of Caesarea Philippi; and on the road He asked His disciples, saying to them, "Who do men say that I am?"

28 So they answered, "John the Baptist; but some *say,* Elijah; and others, one of the prophets."

29 He said to them, "But who do you say that I am?"

Peter answered and said to Him, "You are the Christ."

30 Then He strictly warned them that they should tell no one about Him.

31 And He began to teach them that the Son of Man must suffer many things, and be rejected by the elders and chief priests and scribes, and be killed, and after three days rise again. 32 He spoke this word openly. Then Peter took Him aside and began to rebuke Him. 33 But when He had turned around and looked at His disciples, He rebuked Peter, saying, "Get behind Me, Satan! For you are not mindful of the things of God, but the things of men."

34 When He had called the people to *Himself,* with His disciples also, He said to them, "Whoever desires to come after Me, let him deny himself, and take up his cross, and follow Me. 35 For whoever desires to save his life will lose it, but whoever loses his life for My sake and the gospel's will save it. 36 For what will it profit a man if he gains the whole world, and loses his own soul? 37 Or what will a man give in exchange for his soul? 38 For whoever is ashamed of Me and My words in this adulterous and sinful generation, of him the Son of Man also will be ashamed when He comes in the glory of His Father with the holy angels."

9 And He said to them, "Assuredly, I say to you that there are some standing here who will not taste death till they see the kingdom of God present with power."

2 Now after six days Jesus took Peter, James, and John, and led them up on a high mountain apart by themselves; and He was transfigured before them. 3 His clothes became shining, exceedingly white, like snow, such as no launderer on earth can whiten them. 4 And Elijah appeared to them with Moses, and they were talking with Jesus. 5 Then Peter answered and said to Jesus, "Rabbi, it is good for us to be here; and let us make three tabernacles: one for You, one for Moses, and one for Elijah"— 6 because he did not know

---

8:14 *ᵃ*NU-Text and M-Text read *they.*   8:17 *ᵃ*NU-Text omits *still.*   8:26 *ᵃ*NU-Text reads *"Do not even go into the town."*

Gospel Pearls

what to say, for they were greatly afraid.

7 And a cloud came and overshadowed them; and a voice came out of the cloud, saying, "This is My beloved Son. Hear Him!" 8 Suddenly, when they had looked around, they saw no one anymore, but only Jesus with themselves.

9 Now as they came down from the mountain, He commanded them that they should tell no one the things they had seen, till the Son of Man had risen from the dead. 10 So they kept this word to themselves, questioning what the rising from the dead meant.

11 And they asked Him, saying, "Why do the scribes say that Elijah must come first?"

12 Then He answered and told them, "Indeed, Elijah is coming first and restores all things. And how is it written concerning the Son of Man, that He must suffer many things and be treated with contempt? 13 But I say to you that Elijah has also come, and they did to him whatever they wished, as it is written of him."

14 And when He came to the disciples, He saw a great multitude around them, and scribes disputing with them. 15 Immediately, when they saw Him, all the people were greatly amazed, and running to Him, greeted Him. 16 And He asked the scribes, "What are you discussing with them?"

17 Then one of the crowd answered and said, "Teacher, I brought You my son, who has a mute spirit. 18 And wherever it seizes him, it throws him down; he foams at the mouth, gnashes his teeth, and becomes rigid. So I spoke to Your disciples, that they should cast it out, but they could not."

19 He answered him and said, "O faithless generation, how long shall I be with you? How long shall I bear with you? Bring him to Me." 20 Then they brought him to Him. And when he saw Him, immediately the spirit convulsed him, and he fell on the ground and wallowed, foaming at the mouth.

21 So He asked his father, "How long has this been happening to him?"

And he said, "From childhood.

22 And often he has thrown him both into the fire and into the water to destroy him. But if You can do anything, have compassion on us and help us."

23 Jesus said to him, "If you can believe,ᵃ all things are possible to him who believes."

24 Immediately the father of the child cried out and said with tears, "Lord, I believe; help my unbelief!"

25 When Jesus saw that the people came running together, He rebuked the unclean spirit, saying to it, "Deaf and dumb spirit, I command you, come out of him and enter him no more!" 26 Then the spirit cried out, convulsed him greatly, and came out of him. And he became as one dead, so that many said, "He is dead." 27 But Jesus took him by the hand and lifted him up, and he arose.

28 And when He had come into the house, His disciples asked Him privately, "Why could we not cast it out?"

29 So He said to them, "This kind can come out by nothing but prayer and fasting."ᵃ

30 Then they departed from there and passed through Galilee, and He did not want anyone to know it. 31 For He taught His disciples and said to them, "The Son of Man is being betrayed into the hands of men, and they will kill Him. And after He is killed, He will rise the third day." 32 But they did not understand this saying, and were afraid to ask Him.

33 Then He came to Capernaum. And when He was in the house He asked them, "What was it you disputed among yourselves on the road?" 34 But they kept silent, for on the road they had disputed among themselves who would be the greatest. 35 And He sat down, called the twelve, and said to them, "If anyone desires to be first, he shall be last of all and servant of all." 36 Then He took a little child and set him in the midst of them. And when He had taken him in His arms, He said to them, 37 "Whoever receives one of these little children in My name receives Me; and whoever receives Me, receives not Me but Him who sent Me."

38 Now John answered Him, saying, "Teacher, we saw someone who

9:23 ᵃNU-Text reads "If You can! All things. . . ." 9:29 ᵃNU-Text omits and fasting.

After you have analyzed the condition, after you have understood its origin, it will still take the authority of God's Word to put the past under your feet!

does not follow us casting out demons in Your name, and we forbade him because he does not follow us."

39 But Jesus said, "Do not forbid him, for no one who works a miracle in My name can soon afterward speak evil of Me. 40 For he who is not against us is on our*a* side. 41 For whoever gives you a cup of water to drink in My name, because you belong to Christ, assuredly, I say to you, he will by no means lose his reward.

42 "But whoever causes one of these little ones who believe in Me to stumble, it would be better for him if a millstone were hung around his neck, and he were thrown into the sea. 43 If your hand causes you to sin, cut it off. It is better for you to enter into life maimed, rather than having two hands, to go to hell, into the fire that shall never be quenched— 44 where

'Their worm does not die,
And the fire is not quenched.'a

45 And if your foot causes you to sin, cut it off. It is better for you to enter life lame, rather than having two feet, to be cast into hell, into the fire that shall never be quenched— 46 where

'Their worm does not die,
And the fire is not quenched.'a

47 And if your eye causes you to sin, pluck it out. It is better for you to enter the kingdom of God with one eye, rather than having two eyes, to be cast into hell fire— 48 where

'Their worm does not die,
And the fire is not quenched.'a

49 "For everyone will be seasoned with fire,*a* and every sacrifice will be seasoned with salt. 50 Salt *is* good, but if the salt loses its flavor, how will you season it? Have salt in yourselves, and have peace with one another."

10 Then He arose from there and came to the region of Judea by the other side of the Jordan. And multitudes gathered to Him again, and as He was accustomed, He taught them again.

2 The Pharisees came and asked Him, "Is it lawful for a man to divorce *his* wife?" testing Him.

3 And He answered and said to them, "What did Moses command you?"

4 They said, "Moses permitted *a man* to write a certificate of divorce, and to dismiss *her.*"

5 And Jesus answered and said to them, "Because of the hardness of your heart he wrote you this precept. 6 But from the beginning of the creation, God *'made them male and female.'a* 7 *'For this reason a man shall leave his father and mother and be joined to his wife,* 8 *and the two shall become one flesh';a* so then they are no longer two, but one flesh. 9 Therefore what God has joined together, let not man separate."

10 In the house His disciples also asked Him again about the same *matter.* 11 So He said to them, "Whoever divorces his wife and marries another commits adultery against her. 12 And if a woman divorces her husband and marries another, she commits adultery."

13 Then they brought little children to Him, that He might touch them; but the disciples rebuked those who brought *them.* 14 But when Jesus saw *it,* He was greatly displeased and said to them, "Let the little children come to Me, and do not forbid them; for of such is the kingdom of God. 15 Assuredly, I say to you, whoever does not receive the kingdom of God as a little child will by no means enter it." 16 And He took them up in His arms, laid *His* hands on them, and blessed them.

17 Now as He was going out on the road, one came running, knelt before Him, and asked Him, "Good Teacher, what shall I do that I may inherit eternal life?"

18 So Jesus said to him, "Why do you call Me good? No one *is* good but One, *that is,* God. 19 You know the commandments: *'Do not commit adultery,' 'Do not murder,' 'Do not steal,' 'Do not bear false witness,' 'Do*

9:40 *a*M-Text reads *against you is on your side.*   9:44 *a*NU-Text omits this verse.   9:46 *a*NU-Text omits the last clause of verse 45 and all of verse 46.   9:48 *a*Isaiah 66:24   9:49 *a*NU-Text omits the rest of this verse.   10:6 *a*Genesis 1:27; 5:2   10:8 *a*Genesis 2:24

Although the problem may be rooted in the past, the prescription is a present word from God! The Word is the same yesterday, today and forevermore! That is to say, the Word you are hearing today is able to heal your yesterday!

Second Childhood

Mark 10:13-16

When Jesus blessed the children, He stopped in the middle of His message to carry out His mission. Imagine tiny hands outstretched, little faces upturned, children perching like sparrows on His knee. He held them with His loving arms. He touched them with His sensitive hands. But most of all, He blessed them with His compassionate heart.

They came to get a touch, but He always gives more than expected. He challenged the adults present to become as little children.

Oh, to be a child again! To allow yourself the kind of relationship with God you may have missed as a child. To toddle into His presence and let Him hold you in His arms. To climb up in His lap and be nurtured through the tragedies of earlier days. You can do that by accepting Him as Savior and Lord and learning how to praise Him.

Salvation is God giving you a chance to start over. He will not abuse the children who come to Him. Through praise, you may approach Him on unskilled legs. In worship, you may kiss His face and be held in the embrace of His anointing. He has no ulterior motives, for His caress is safe and wholesome. There is such security when you are safe in the arms of Jesus. It is when you become secure in your relationship with Him that you begin to allow the past to fall from you as a garment. You may remember it, but you can choose not to wear it!

To forget is not to develop amnesia. It is to reach a place where the misery is pulled from the memory like a stinger is pulled out of an insect bite. Once the stinger is gone, healing is inevitable. The memory will be as "waters that pass away" (see Job 11:16). David must have understood the after-effects of such deliverance when he said, "Weeping may endure for a night, but joy comes in the morning" (see Psalm 30:5b).

Stand in a stream with waters around your ankles. The water that passes by you at that moment, you will never see again. So it is with the misery that has plagued your life. Let it go, let it pass away. Resting in your relationship with God will heal you from feelings of vulnerability.

Even if you were exposed to grown-up situations when you were a child, God can reverse what you've been through. In His presence, the grown-up you can experience the joy of being a child again.

not defraud,' *'Honor your father and your mother.'"*[a]

20 And he answered and said to Him, "Teacher, all these things I have kept from my youth."

21 Then Jesus, looking at him, loved him, and said to him, "One thing you lack: Go your way, sell whatever you have and give to the poor, and you will have treasure in heaven; and come, take up the cross, and follow Me."

22 But he was sad at this word, and went away sorrowful, for he had great possessions.

23 Then Jesus looked around and said to His disciples, "How hard it is for those who have riches to enter the kingdom of God!" 24 And the disciples were astonished at His words. But Jesus answered again and said to them, "Children, how hard it is for those who trust in riches[a] to enter the kingdom of God! 25 It is easier for a camel to go through the eye of a needle than for a rich man to enter the kingdom of God."

26 And they were greatly astonished, saying among themselves, "Who then can be saved?"

27 But Jesus looked at them and said, "With men *it is* impossible, but not with God; for with God all things are possible."

28 Then Peter began to say to Him, "See, we have left all and followed You."

29 So Jesus answered and said, "Assuredly, I say to you, there is no one who has left house or brothers or sisters or father or mother or wife[a] or children or lands, for My sake and the gospel's, 30 who shall not receive a hundredfold now in this time—houses and brothers and sisters and mothers and children and lands, with persecutions—and in the age to come, eternal life. 31 But many *who are* first will be last, and the last first."

32 Now they were on the road, going up to Jerusalem, and Jesus was going before them; and they were amazed. And as they followed they were afraid. Then He took the twelve aside again and began to tell them the things that would happen to Him: 33 "Behold, we are going up to Jerusalem, and the Son of Man will be betrayed to the chief priests and to the scribes; and they will condemn Him to death and deliver Him to the Gentiles; 34 and they will mock Him, and scourge Him, and spit on Him, and kill Him. And the third day He will rise again."

35 Then James and John, the sons of Zebedee, came to Him, saying, "Teacher, we want You to do for us whatever we ask."

36 And He said to them, "What do you want Me to do for you?"

37 They said to Him, "Grant us that we may sit, one on Your right hand and the other on Your left, in Your glory."

38 But Jesus said to them, "You do not know what you ask. Are you able to drink the cup that I drink, and be baptized with the baptism that I am baptized with?"

39 They said to Him, "We are able."

So Jesus said to them, "You will indeed drink the cup that I drink, and with the baptism I am baptized with you will be baptized; 40 but to sit on My right hand and on My left is not Mine to give, but *it is for those* for whom it is prepared."

41 And when the ten heard *it,* they began to be greatly displeased with James and John. 42 But Jesus called them to *Himself* and said to them, "You know that those who are considered rulers over the Gentiles lord it over them, and their great ones exercise authority over them. 43 Yet it shall not be so among you; but whoever desires to become great among you shall be your servant. 44 And whoever of you desires to be first shall be slave of all. 45 For even the Son of Man did not come to be served, but to serve, and to give His life a ransom for many."

46 Now they came to Jericho. As He went out of Jericho with His disciples and a great multitude, blind Bartimaeus, the son of Timaeus, sat by the road begging. 47 And when he heard that it was Jesus of Nazareth, he began to cry out and say, "Jesus, Son of David, have mercy on me!"

48 Then many warned him to be quiet; but he cried out all the more, "Son of David, have mercy on me!"

49 So Jesus stood still and commanded him to be called.

10:19 [a]Exodus 20:12–16; Deuteronomy 5:16–20   10:24 [a]NU-Text omits *for those who trust in riches.*
10:29 [a]NU-Text omits *or wife.*

Gospel Pearls

Then they called the blind man, saying to him, "Be of good cheer. Rise, He is calling you."

50 And throwing aside his garment, he rose and came to Jesus.

51 So Jesus answered and said to him, "What do you want Me to do for you?"

The blind man said to Him, "Rabboni, that I may receive my sight."

52 Then Jesus said to him, "Go your way; your faith has made you well." And immediately he received his sight and followed Jesus on the road.

11 Now when they drew near Jerusalem, to Bethphage*a* and Bethany, at the Mount of Olives, He sent two of His disciples; 2 and He said to them, "Go into the village opposite you; and as soon as you have entered it you will find a colt tied, on which no one has sat. Loose it and bring *it.* 3 And if anyone says to you, 'Why are you doing this?' say, 'The Lord has need of it,' and immediately he will send it here."

4 So they went their way, and found the*a* colt tied by the door outside on the street, and they loosed it. 5 But some of those who stood there said to them, "What are you doing, loosing the colt?"

6 And they spoke to them just as Jesus had commanded. So they let them go. 7 Then they brought the colt to Jesus and threw their clothes on it, and He sat on it. 8 And many spread their clothes on the road, and others cut down leafy branches from the trees and spread *them* on the road. 9 Then those who went before and those who followed cried out, saying:

"Hosanna!
'Blessed *is* He who comes in the name of the Lord!'*a*
10 Blessed *is* the kingdom of our father David
That comes in the name of the Lord!*a*
Hosanna in the highest!"

11 And Jesus went into Jerusalem and into the temple. So when He had looked around at all things, as the hour was already late, He went out to Bethany with the twelve.

12 Now the next day, when they had come out from Bethany, He was hungry. 13 And seeing from afar a fig tree having leaves, He went to see if perhaps He would find something on it. When He came to it, He found nothing but leaves, for it was not the season for figs. 14 In response Jesus said to it, "Let no one eat fruit from you ever again."

And His disciples heard *it.*

15 So they came to Jerusalem. Then Jesus went into the temple and began to drive out those who bought and sold in the temple, and overturned the tables of the money changers and the seats of those who sold doves. 16 And He would not allow anyone to carry wares through the temple. 17 Then He taught, saying to them, "Is it not written, *'My house shall be called a house of prayer for all nations'?a* But you have made it a *'den of thieves.'"b*

18 And the scribes and chief priests heard it and sought how they might destroy Him; for they feared Him, because all the people were astonished at His teaching. 19 When evening had come, He went out of the city.

20 Now in the morning, as they passed by, they saw the fig tree dried up from the roots. 21 And Peter, remembering, said to Him, "Rabbi, look! The fig tree which You cursed has withered away."

22 So Jesus answered and said to them, "Have faith in God. 23 For assuredly, I say to you, whoever says to this mountain, 'Be removed and be cast into the sea,' and does not doubt in his heart, but believes that those things he says will be done, he will have whatever he says. 24 Therefore I say to you, whatever things you ask when you pray, believe that you receive *them,* and you will have *them.*

25 "And whenever you stand praying, if you have anything against anyone, forgive him, that your Father in heaven may also forgive you your trespasses. 26 But if you do not forgive, neither will your Father in heaven forgive your trespasses."*a*

27 Then they came again to Jerusa-

11:1 *a*M-Text reads *Bethsphage.*   11:4 *a*NU-Text and M-Text read *a.*   11:9 *a*Psalm 118:26
11:10 *a*NU-Text omits *in the name of the Lord.*   11:17 *a*Isaiah 56:7   *b*Jeremiah 7:11   11:26 *a*NU-Text omits this verse.

*J*esus said, "Woman, thou art loosed." He did not call her by name. He wasn't speaking to her just as a person. He spoke to her femininity. He spoke to the song in her. He spoke to the lace in her.

lem. And as He was walking in the temple, the chief priests, the scribes, and the elders came to Him. 28 And they said to Him, "By what authority are You doing these things? And who gave You this authority to do these things?"

29 But Jesus answered and said to them, "I also will ask you one question; then answer Me, and I will tell you by what authority I do these things: 30 The baptism of John—was it from heaven or from men? Answer Me."

31 And they reasoned among themselves, saying, "If we say, 'From heaven,' He will say, 'Why then did you not believe him?' 32 But if we say, 'From men'"—they feared the people, for all counted John to have been a prophet indeed. 33 So they answered and said to Jesus, "We do not know."

And Jesus answered and said to them, "Neither will I tell you by what authority I do these things."

12 Then He began to speak to them in parables: "A man planted a vineyard and set a hedge around *it,* dug *a place for* the wine vat and built a tower. And he leased it to vinedressers, and went into a far country. 2 Now at vintage-time he sent a servant to the vinedressers, that he might receive some of the fruit of the vineyard from the vinedressers. 3 And they took *him* and beat him and sent *him* away empty-handed. 4 Again he sent them another servant, and at him they threw stones,*a* wounded *him* in the head, and sent *him* away shamefully treated. 5 And again he sent another, and him they killed; and many others, beating some and killing some. 6 Therefore still having one son, his beloved, he also sent him to them last, saying, 'They will respect my son.' 7 But those vinedressers said among themselves, 'This is the heir. Come, let us kill him, and the inheritance will be ours.' 8 So they took him and killed *him* and cast *him* out of the vineyard.

9 "Therefore what will the owner of the vineyard do? He will come and destroy the vinedressers, and give the vineyard to others. 10 Have you not even read this Scripture:

> 'The stone which the builders rejected
> Has become the chief cornerstone.
> 11 This was the LORD's doing,
> And it is marvelous in our eyes'?"*a*

12 And they sought to lay hands on Him, but feared the multitude, for they knew He had spoken the parable against them. So they left Him and went away.

13 Then they sent to Him some of the Pharisees and the Herodians, to catch Him in *His* words. 14 When they had come, they said to Him, "Teacher, we know that You are true, and care about no one; for You do not regard the person of men, but teach the way of God in truth. Is it lawful to pay taxes to Caesar, or not? 15 Shall we pay, or shall we not pay?"

But He, knowing their hypocrisy, said to them, "Why do you test Me? Bring Me a denarius that I may see *it.*" 16 So they brought *it.*

And He said to them, "Whose image and inscription *is* this?" They said to Him, "Caesar's."

17 And Jesus answered and said to them, "Render to Caesar the things that are Caesar's, and to God the things that are God's."

And they marveled at Him.

18 Then *some* Sadducees, who say there is no resurrection, came to Him; and they asked Him, saying: 19 "Teacher, Moses wrote to us that if a man's brother dies, and leaves *his* wife behind, and leaves no children, his brother should take his wife and raise up offspring for his brother. 20 Now there were seven brothers. The first took a wife; and dying, he left no offspring. 21 And the second took her, and he died; nor did he leave any offspring. And the third likewise. 22 So the seven had her and left no offspring. Last of all the woman died also. 23 Therefore, in the resurrection, when they rise, whose wife will she be? For all seven had her as wife."

24 Jesus answered and said to them, "Are you not therefore mistaken, because you do not know the Scriptures nor the power of God?

12:4 *a*NU-Text omits *and at him they threw stones.*   12:11 *a*Psalm 118:22, 23

Gospel Pearls

25 For when they rise from the dead, they neither marry nor are given in marriage, but are like angels in heaven. 26 But concerning the dead, that they rise, have you not read in the book of Moses, in the *burning bush passage*, how God spoke to him, saying, *'I am the God of Abraham, the God of Isaac, and the God of Jacob'?ᵃ* 27 He is not the God of the dead, but the God of the living. You are therefore greatly mistaken."

28 Then one of the scribes came, and having heard them reasoning together, perceivingᵃ that He had answered them well, asked Him, "Which is the first commandment of all?"

29 Jesus answered him, "The first of all the commandments *is*: 'Hear, O Israel, the LORD our God, the LORD is one. 30 And you shall love the LORD your God with all your heart, with all your soul, with all your mind, and with all your strength.'ᵃ This *is* the first commandment.ᵇ 31 And the second, like *it, is* this: 'You shall love your neighbor as yourself.'ᵃ There is no other commandment greater than these."

32 So the scribe said to Him, "Well said, Teacher. You have spoken the truth, for there is one God, and there is no other but He. 33 And to love Him with all the heart, with all the understanding, with all the soul,ᵃ and with all the strength, and to love one's neighbor as oneself, is more than all the whole burnt offerings and sacrifices."

34 Now when Jesus saw that he answered wisely, He said to him, "You are not far from the kingdom of God."

But after that no one dared question Him.

35 Then Jesus answered and said, while He taught in the temple, "How *is it* that the scribes say that the Christ is the Son of David? 36 For David himself said by the Holy Spirit:

'The LORD said to my Lord,
"Sit at My right hand,
Till I make Your enemies Your
footstool." 'ᵃ

37 Therefore David himself calls Him '*Lord*'; how is He *then* his Son?"

And the common people heard Him gladly.

38 Then He said to them in His teaching, "Beware of the scribes, who desire to go around in long robes, *love* greetings in the marketplaces, 39 the best seats in the synagogues, and the best places at feasts, 40 who devour widows' houses, and for a pretense make long prayers. These will receive greater condemnation."

41 Now Jesus sat opposite the treasury and saw how the people put money into the treasury. And many *who were* rich put in much. 42 Then one poor widow came and threw in two mites,ᵃ which make a quadrans. 43 So He called His disciples to *Himself* and said to them, "Assuredly, I say to you that this poor widow has put in more than all those who have given to the treasury; 44 for they all put in out of their abundance, but she out of her poverty put in all that she had, her whole livelihood."

13 Then as He went out of the temple, one of His disciples said to Him, "Teacher, see what manner of stones and what buildings *are here!*"

2 And Jesus answered and said to him, "Do you see these great buildings? Not *one* stone shall be left upon another, that shall not be thrown down."

3 Now as He sat on the Mount of Olives opposite the temple, Peter, James, John, and Andrew asked Him privately, 4 "Tell us, when will these things be? And what *will be* the sign when all these things will be fulfilled?"

5 And Jesus, answering them, began to say: "Take heed that no one deceives you. 6 For many will come in My name, saying, 'I am *He*,' and will deceive many. 7 But when you hear of wars and rumors of wars, do not be troubled; for *such things* must happen, but the end *is* not yet. 8 For nation will rise against nation, and kingdom against kingdom. And there will be earthquakes in various places, and there will be famines and

12:26 ᵃExodus 3:6, 15   12:28 ᵃNU-Text reads *seeing.*   12:30 ᵃDeuteronomy 6:4, 5   ᵇNU-Text omits this sentence.   12:31 ᵃLeviticus 19:18   12:33 ᵃNU-Text omits *with all the soul.*   12:36 ᵃPsalm 110:1   12:42 ᵃGreek *lepta*, very small copper coins worth a fraction of a penny

Avoid addictive, obsessive relationships. If you are becoming increasingly dependent upon anything other than God to create a sense of wholeness in your life, then you are abusing your relationships.

troubles.*a* These *are* the beginnings of sorrows.

9 "But watch out for yourselves, for they will deliver you up to councils, and you will be beaten in the synagogues. You will be brought*a* before rulers and kings for My sake, for a testimony to them. 10 And the gospel must first be preached to all the nations. 11 But when they arrest *you* and deliver you up, do not worry beforehand, or premeditate*a* what you will speak. But whatever is given you in that hour, speak that; for it is not you who speak, but the Holy Spirit. 12 Now brother will betray brother to death, and a father *his* child; and children will rise up against parents and cause them to be put to death. 13 And you will be hated by all for My name's sake. But he who endures to the end shall be saved.

14 "So when you see the *'abomination of desolation,'a* spoken of by Daniel the prophet,*b* standing where it ought not" (let the reader understand), "then let those who are in Judea flee to the mountains. 15 Let him who is on the housetop not go down into the house, nor enter to take anything out of his house. 16 And let him who is in the field not go back to get his clothes. 17 But woe to those who are pregnant and to those who are nursing babies in those days! 18 And pray that your flight may not be in winter. 19 For *in* those days there will be tribulation, such as has not been since the beginning of the creation which God created until this time, nor ever shall be. 20 And unless the Lord had shortened those days, no flesh would be saved; but for the elect's sake, whom He chose, He shortened the days.

21 "Then if anyone says to you, 'Look, here *is* the Christ!' or, 'Look, He *is* there!' do not believe it. 22 For false christs and false prophets will rise and show signs and wonders to deceive, if possible, even the elect. 23 But take heed; see, I have told you all things beforehand.

24 "But in those days, after that tribulation, the sun will be darkened, and the moon will not give its light; 25 the stars of heaven will fall, and the powers in the heavens will be shaken. 26 Then they will see the Son of Man coming in the clouds with great power and glory. 27 And then He will send His angels, and gather together His elect from the four winds, from the farthest part of earth to the farthest part of heaven.

28 "Now learn this parable from the fig tree: When its branch has already become tender, and puts forth leaves, you know that summer is near. 29 So you also, when you see these things happening, know that it*a* is near—at the doors! 30 Assuredly, I say to you, this generation will by no means pass away till all these things take place. 31 Heaven and earth will pass away, but My words will by no means pass away.

32 "But of that day and hour no one knows, not even the angels in heaven, nor the Son, but only the Father. 33 Take heed, watch and pray; for you do not know when the time is. 34 *It is* like a man going to a far country, who left his house and gave authority to his servants, and to each his work, and commanded the doorkeeper to watch. 35 Watch therefore, for you do not know when the master of the house is coming—in the evening, at midnight, at the crowing of the rooster, or in the morning— 36 lest, coming suddenly, he find you sleeping. 37 And what I say to you, I say to all: Watch!"

14 After two days it was the Passover and *the Feast* of Unleavened Bread. And the chief priests and the scribes sought how they might take Him by trickery and put *Him* to death. 2 But they said, "Not during the feast, lest there be an uproar of the people."

3 And being in Bethany at the house of Simon the leper, as He sat at the table, a woman came having an alabaster flask of very costly oil of spikenard. Then she broke the flask and poured *it* on His head. 4 But there were some who were indignant among themselves, and said, "Why was this fragrant oil wasted? 5 For it might have been sold for

13:8 *a*NU-Text omits *and troubles.*   13:9 *a*NU-Text and M-Text read *will stand.*   13:11 *a*NU-Text omits *or premeditate.*   13:14 *a*Daniel 11:31; 12:11   *b*NU-Text omits *spoken of by Daniel the prophet.* 13:29 *a*Or He

Gospel Pearls

more than three hundred denarii and given to the poor." And they criticized her sharply.

6 But Jesus said, "Let her alone. Why do you trouble her? She has done a good work for Me. 7 For you have the poor with you always, and whenever you wish you may do them good; but Me you do not have always. 8 She has done what she could. She has come beforehand to anoint My body for burial. 9 Assuredly, I say to you, wherever this gospel is preached in the whole world, what this woman has done will also be told as a memorial to her."

10 Then Judas Iscariot, one of the twelve, went to the chief priests to betray Him to them. 11 And when they heard *it*, they were glad, and promised to give him money. So he sought how he might conveniently betray Him.

12 Now on the first day of Unleavened Bread, when they killed the Passover *lamb*, His disciples said to Him, "Where do You want us to go and prepare, that You may eat the Passover?"

13 And He sent out two of His disciples and said to them, "Go into the city, and a man will meet you carrying a pitcher of water; follow him. 14 Wherever he goes in, say to the master of the house, 'The Teacher says, "Where is the guest room in which I may eat the Passover with My disciples?"' 15 Then he will show you a large upper room, furnished *and* prepared; there make ready for us."

16 So His disciples went out, and came into the city, and found it just as He had said to them; and they prepared the Passover.

17 In the evening He came with the twelve. 18 Now as they sat and ate, Jesus said, "Assuredly, I say to you, one of you who eats with Me will betray Me."

19 And they began to be sorrowful, and to say to Him one by one, "*Is it I*?" And another *said*, "*Is it I*?"*a*

20 He answered and said to them, "*It is* one of the twelve, who dips with Me in the dish. 21 The Son of Man indeed goes just as it is written of Him, but woe to that man by whom the Son of Man is betrayed! It would

have been good for that man if he had never been born."

22 And as they were eating, Jesus took bread, blessed and broke *it*, and gave *it* to them and said, "Take, eat;*a* this is My body."

23 Then He took the cup, and when He had given thanks He gave *it* to them, and they all drank from it. 24 And He said to them, "This is My blood of the new*a* covenant, which is shed for many. 25 Assuredly, I say to you, I will no longer drink of the fruit of the vine until that day when I drink it new in the kingdom of God."

26 And when they had sung a hymn, they went out to the Mount of Olives.

27 Then Jesus said to them, "All of you will be made to stumble because of Me this night,*a* for it is written:

> '*I will strike the Shepherd,*
> *And the sheep will be*
> *scattered.*'*b*

28 "But after I have been raised, I will go before you to Galilee."

29 Peter said to Him, "Even if all are made to stumble, yet I *will* not *be*."

30 Jesus said to him, "Assuredly, I say to you that today, *even* this night, before the rooster crows twice, you will deny Me three times."

31 But he spoke more vehemently, "If I have to die with You, I will not deny You!"

And they all said likewise.

32 Then they came to a place which was named Gethsemane; and He said to His disciples, "Sit here while I pray." 33 And He took Peter, James, and John with Him, and He began to be troubled and deeply distressed. 34 Then He said to them, "My soul is exceedingly sorrowful, *even* to death. Stay here and watch."

35 He went a little farther, and fell on the ground, and prayed that if it were possible, the hour might pass from Him. 36 And He said, "Abba, Father, all things *are* possible for You. Take this cup away from Me; nevertheless, not what I will, but what You *will*."

37 Then He came and found them

14:19 *a*NU-Text omits this sentence.   14:22 *a*NU-Text omits *eat*.   14:24 *a*NU-Text omits *new*.
14:27 *a*NU-Text omits *because of Me this night*.   *b*Zechariah 13:7

---

*L*ove is giving. God is love. God proved His love not by His need of us, but by His giving to us.

sleeping, and said to Peter, "Simon, are you sleeping? Could you not watch one hour? 38 Watch and pray, lest you enter into temptation. The spirit indeed *is* willing, but the flesh *is* weak."

39 Again He went away and prayed, and spoke the same words. 40 And when He returned, He found them asleep again, for their eyes were heavy; and they did not know what to answer Him.

41 Then He came the third time and said to them, "Are you still sleeping and resting? It is enough! The hour has come; behold, the Son of Man is being betrayed into the hands of sinners. 42 Rise, let us be going. See, My betrayer is at hand."

43 And immediately, while He was still speaking, Judas, one of the twelve, with a great multitude with swords and clubs, came from the chief priests and the scribes and the elders. 44 Now His betrayer had given them a signal, saying, "Whomever I kiss, He is the One; seize Him and lead *Him* away safely."

45 As soon as He had come, immediately he went up to Him and said to Him, "Rabbi, Rabbi!" and kissed Him.

46 Then they laid their hands on Him and took Him. 47 And one of those who stood by drew his sword and struck the servant of the high priest, and cut off his ear.

48 Then Jesus answered and said to them, "Have you come out, as against a robber, with swords and clubs to take Me? 49 I was daily with you in the temple teaching, and you did not seize Me. But the Scriptures must be fulfilled."

50 Then they all forsook Him and fled.

51 Now a certain young man followed Him, having a linen cloth thrown around *his* naked *body*. And the young men laid hold of him, 52 and he left the linen cloth and fled from them naked.

53 And they led Jesus away to the high priest; and with him were assembled all the chief priests, the elders, and the scribes. 54 But Peter followed Him at a distance, right into the courtyard of the high priest. And he sat with the servants and warmed himself at the fire.

55 Now the chief priests and all the council sought testimony against Jesus to put Him to death, but found none. 56 For many bore false witness against Him, but their testimonies did not agree.

57 Then some rose up and bore false witness against Him, saying, 58 "We heard Him say, 'I will destroy this temple made with hands, and within three days I will build another made without hands.' " 59 But not even then did their testimony agree.

60 And the high priest stood up in the midst and asked Jesus, saying, "Do You answer nothing? What *is it* these men testify against You?" 61 But He kept silent and answered nothing.

Again the high priest asked Him, saying to Him, "Are You the Christ, the Son of the Blessed?"

62 Jesus said, "I am. And you will see the Son of Man sitting at the right hand of the Power, and coming with the clouds of heaven."

63 Then the high priest tore his clothes and said, "What further need do we have of witnesses? 64 You have heard the blasphemy! What do you think?"

And they all condemned Him to be deserving of death.

65 Then some began to spit on Him, and to blindfold Him, and to beat Him, and to say to Him, "Prophesy!" And the officers struck Him with the palms of their hands.*a*

66 Now as Peter was below in the courtyard, one of the servant girls of the high priest came. 67 And when she saw Peter warming himself, she looked at him and said, "You also were with Jesus of Nazareth."

68 But he denied it, saying, "I neither know nor understand what you are saying." And he went out on the porch, and a rooster crowed.

69 And the servant girl saw him again, and began to say to those who stood by, "This is one of them." 70 But he denied it again.

And a little later those who stood by said to Peter again, "Surely you are *one* of them; for you are a Galilean, and your speech shows *it*."*a*

71 Then he began to curse and swear, "I do not know this Man of whom you speak!"

14:65 *a*NU-Text reads *received Him with slaps.*   14:70 *a*NU-Text omits *and your speech shows it.*

Gospel Pearls

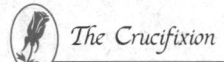
72 A second time *the* rooster crowed. Then Peter called to mind the word that Jesus had said to him, "Before the rooster crows twice, you will deny Me three times." And when he thought about it, he wept.

15 Immediately, in the morning, the chief priests held a consultation with the elders and scribes and the whole council; and they bound Jesus, led *Him* away, and delivered *Him* to Pilate. 2 Then Pilate asked Him, "Are You the King of the Jews?"

He answered and said to him, "*It is as* you say."

3 And the chief priests accused Him of many things, but He answered nothing. 4 Then Pilate asked Him again, saying, "Do You answer nothing? See how many things they testify against You!"*a* 5 But Jesus still answered nothing, so that Pilate marveled.

6 Now at the feast he was accustomed to releasing one prisoner to them, whomever they requested. 7 And there was one named Barabbas, *who was* chained with his fellow rebels; they had committed murder in the rebellion. 8 Then the multitude, crying aloud,*a* began to ask *him to do* just as he had always done for them. 9 But Pilate answered them, saying, "Do you want me to release to you the King of the Jews?" 10 For he knew that the chief priests had handed Him over because of envy.

11 But the chief priests stirred up the crowd, so that he should rather release Barabbas to them. 12 Pilate answered and said to them again, "What then do you want me to do *with Him* whom you call the King of the Jews?"

13 So they cried out again, "Crucify Him!"

14 Then Pilate said to them, "Why, what evil has He done?"

But they cried out all the more, "Crucify Him!"

15 So Pilate, wanting to gratify the crowd, released Barabbas to them; and he delivered Jesus, after he had scourged *Him,* to be crucified.

16 Then the soldiers led Him away into the hall called Praetorium, and they called together the whole garrison. 17 And they clothed Him with purple; and they twisted a crown of thorns, put it on His *head,* 18 and began to salute Him, "Hail, King of the Jews!" 19 Then they struck Him on the head with a reed and spat on Him; and bowing the knee, they worshiped Him. 20 And when they had mocked Him, they took the purple off Him, put His own clothes on Him, and led Him out to crucify Him.

21 Then they compelled a certain man, Simon a Cyrenian, the father of Alexander and Rufus, as he was coming out of the country and passing by, to bear His cross. 22 And they brought Him to the place Golgotha, which is translated, Place of a Skull. 23 Then they gave Him wine mingled with myrrh to drink, but He did not take *it.* 24 And when they crucified Him, they divided His garments, casting lots for them to determine what every man should take.

25 Now it was the third hour, and they crucified Him. 26 And the inscription of His accusation was written above:

THE KING OF THE JEWS.

27 With Him they also crucified two robbers, one on His right and the other on His left. 28 So the Scripture was fulfilled*a* which says, *"And He was numbered with the transgressors."b*

29 And those who passed by blasphemed Him, wagging their heads and saying, "Aha! *You* who destroy the temple and build *it* in three days, 30 save Yourself, and come down from the cross!"

31 Likewise the chief priests also, mocking among themselves with the scribes, said, "He saved others; Himself He cannot save. 32 Let the Christ, the King of Israel, descend now from the cross, that we may see and believe."*a*

Even those who were crucified with Him reviled Him.

33 Now when the sixth hour had come, there was darkness over the whole land until the ninth hour. 34 And at the ninth hour Jesus cried out with a loud voice, saying, "Eloi,

15:4 *a*NU-Text reads *of which they accuse You.* 15:8 *a*NU-Text reads *going up.* 15:28 *a*Isaiah 53:12 *b*NU-Text omits this verse. 15:32 *a*M-Text reads *believe Him.*

When a woman is abused as a child, she grows up not only with the pain of that abuse, but with the anger that nobody helped her, nobody intervened on her behalf, nobody stepped in and rescued her.

Eloi, lama sabachthani?" which is translated, *"My God, My God, why have You forsaken Me?"*[a]

35 Some of those who stood by, when they heard *that,* said, "Look, He is calling for Elijah!" 36 Then someone ran and filled a sponge full of sour wine, put *it* on a reed, and offered *it* to Him to drink, saying, "Let Him alone; let us see if Elijah will come to take Him down."

37 And Jesus cried out with a loud voice, and breathed His last.

38 Then the veil of the temple was torn in two from top to bottom. 39 So when the centurion, who stood opposite Him, saw that He cried out like this and breathed His last,[a] he said, "Truly this Man was the Son of God!"

40 There were also women looking on from afar, among whom were Mary Magdalene, Mary the mother of James the Less and of Joses, and Salome, 41 who also followed Him and ministered to Him when He was in Galilee, and many other women who came up with Him to Jerusalem.

42 Now when evening had come, because it was the Preparation Day, that is, the day before the Sabbath, 43 Joseph of Arimathea, a prominent council member, who was himself waiting for the kingdom of God, coming and taking courage, went in to Pilate and asked for the body of Jesus. 44 Pilate marveled that He was already dead; and summoning the centurion, he asked him if He had been dead for some time. 45 So when he found out from the centurion, he granted the body to Joseph. 46 Then he bought fine linen, took Him down, and wrapped Him in the linen. And he laid Him in a tomb which had been hewn out of the rock, and rolled a stone against the door of the tomb. 47 And Mary Magdalene and Mary *the mother* of Joses observed where He was laid.

16 Now when the Sabbath was past, Mary Magdalene, Mary *the mother* of James, and Salome bought spices, that they might come and anoint Him. 2 Very early in the morning, on the first *day* of the week, they came to the tomb when the sun had risen. 3 And they said among themselves, "Who will roll away the stone from the door of the tomb for us?" 4 But when they looked up, they saw that the stone had been rolled away—for it was very large. 5 And entering the tomb, they saw a young man clothed in a long white robe sitting on the right side; and they were alarmed.

6 But he said to them, "Do not be alarmed. You seek Jesus of Nazareth, who was crucified. He is risen! He is not here. See the place where they laid Him. 7 But go, tell His disciples—and Peter—that He is going before you into Galilee; there you will see Him, as He said to you."

8 So they went out quickly[a] and fled from the tomb, for they trembled and were amazed. And they said nothing to anyone, for they were afraid.

9 Now when *He* rose early on the first *day* of the week, He appeared first to Mary Magdalene, out of whom He had cast seven demons. 10 She went and told those who had been with Him, as they mourned and wept. 11 And when they heard that He was alive and had been seen by her, they did not believe.

12 After that, He appeared in another form to two of them as they walked and went into the country. 13 And they went and told *it* to the rest, *but* they did not believe them either.

14 Later He appeared to the eleven as they sat at the table; and He rebuked their unbelief and hardness of heart, because they did not believe those who had seen Him after He had risen. 15 And He said to them, "Go into all the world and preach the gospel to every creature. 16 He who believes and is baptized will be saved; but he who does not believe will be condemned. 17 And these signs will follow those who believe: In My name they will cast out demons; they will speak with new tongues; 18 they[a] will take up serpents; and if they drink anything deadly, it will by no means hurt them; they will lay hands on the sick, and they will recover."

15:34 [a]Psalm 22:1　　15:39 [a]NU-Text reads *that He thus breathed His last.*　　16:8 [a]NU-Text and M-Text omit *quickly.*　　16:18 [a]NU-Text reads *and in their hands they will.*

Gospel Pearls

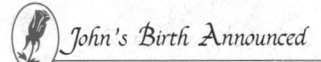
19 So then, after the Lord had spoken to them, He was received up into heaven, and sat down at the right hand of God. 20 And they went out and preached everywhere, the Lord working with *them* and confirming the word through the accompanying signs. Amen.ᵃ

16:20 ᵃVerses 9–20 are bracketed in NU-Text as not original. They are lacking in Codex Sinaiticus and Codex Vaticanus, although nearly all other manuscripts of Mark contain them.

The Gospel According to

LUKE

1 Inasmuch as many have taken in hand to set in order a narrative of those things which have been fulfilledᵃ among us, 2 just as those who from the beginning were eyewitnesses and ministers of the word delivered them to us, 3 it seemed good to me also, having had perfect understanding of all things from the very first, to write to you an orderly account, most excellent Theophilus, 4 that you may know the certainty of those things in which you were instructed.

5 There was in the days of Herod, the king of Judea, a certain priest named Zacharias, of the division of Abijah. His wife *was* of the daughters of Aaron, and her name *was* Elizabeth. 6 And they were both righteous before God, walking in all the commandments and ordinances of the Lord blameless. 7 But they had no child, because Elizabeth was barren, and they were both well advanced in years.

8 So it was, that while he was serving as priest before God in the order of his division, 9 according to the custom of the priesthood, his lot fell to burn incense when he went into the temple of the Lord. 10 And the whole multitude of the people was praying outside at the hour of incense. 11 Then an angel of the Lord appeared to him, standing on the right side of the altar of incense. 12 And when Zacharias saw *him,* he was troubled, and fear fell upon him. 13 But the angel said to him, "Do not be afraid, Zacharias, for your prayer is heard; and your wife Elizabeth will bear you a son, and you shall call his name John. 14 And you will have joy and gladness, and many will rejoice at his birth. 15 For he will be great in the sight of the Lord, and shall drink neither wine nor strong drink. He will also be filled with the Holy Spirit, even from his mother's womb. 16 And he will turn many of the children of Israel to the Lord their God. 17 He will also go before Him in the spirit and power of Elijah, *'to turn the hearts of the fathers to the children,'ᵃ* and the disobedient to the wisdom of the just, to make ready a people prepared for the Lord."

18 And Zacharias said to the angel, "How shall I know this? For I am an old man, and my wife is well advanced in years."

19 And the angel answered and said to him, "I am Gabriel, who stands in the presence of God, and was sent to speak to you and bring you these glad tidings. 20 But behold, you will be mute and not able to speak until the day these things take place, because you did not believe my words which will be fulfilled in their own time."

21 And the people waited for Zacharias, and marveled that he lingered so long in the temple. 22 But when he came out, he could not speak to them; and they perceived that he had seen a vision in the temple, for he beckoned to them and remained speechless.

23 So it was, as soon as the days of his service were completed, that

1:1 ᵃOr *are most surely believed*   1:17 ᵃMalachi 4:5, 6

*T*here's a difference between being cast away privately and being cast away into an open field. It's much more difficult to overcome the shame that attaches itself to you when you are publicly cast away.

he departed to his own house. 24 Now after those days his wife Elizabeth conceived; and she hid herself five months, saying, 25 "Thus the Lord has dealt with me, in the days when He looked on *me,* to take away my reproach among people."

26 Now in the sixth month the angel Gabriel was sent by God to a city of Galilee named Nazareth, 27 to a virgin betrothed to a man whose name was Joseph, of the house of David. The virgin's name *was* Mary. 28 And having come in, the angel said to her, "Rejoice, highly favored *one,* the Lord *is* with you; blessed *are* you among women!"*a*

29 But when she saw *him,a* she was troubled at his saying, and considered what manner of greeting this was. 30 Then the angel said to her, "Do not be afraid, Mary, for you have found favor with God. 31 And behold, you will conceive in your womb and bring forth a Son, and shall call His name JESUS. 32 He will be great, and will be called the Son of the Highest; and the Lord God will give Him the throne of His father David. 33 And He will reign over the house of Jacob forever, and of His kingdom there will be no end."

34 Then Mary said to the angel, "How can this be, since I do not know a man?"

35 And the angel answered and said to her, "*The* Holy Spirit will come upon you, and the power of the Highest will overshadow you; therefore, also, that Holy One who is to be born will be called the Son of God. 36 Now indeed, Elizabeth your relative has also conceived a son in her old age; and this is now the sixth month for her who was called barren. 37 For with God nothing will be impossible."

38 Then Mary said, "Behold the maidservant of the Lord! Let it be to me according to your word." And the angel departed from her.

39 Now Mary arose in those days and went into the hill country with haste, to a city of Judah, 40 and entered the house of Zacharias and greeted Elizabeth. 41 And it happened, when Elizabeth heard the greeting of Mary, that the babe leaped in her womb; and Elizabeth was filled with the Holy Spirit.

42 Then she spoke out with a loud voice and said, "Blessed *are* you among women, and blessed *is* the fruit of your womb! 43 But why *is* this granted to me, that the mother of my Lord should come to me? 44 For indeed, as soon as the voice of your greeting sounded in my ears, the babe leaped in my womb for joy. 45 Blessed *is* she who believed, for there will be a fulfillment of those things which were told her from the Lord."

46 And Mary said:

"My soul magnifies the Lord,
47   And my spirit has rejoiced in
         God my Savior.
48   For He has regarded the lowly
         state of His maidservant;
      For behold, henceforth all
         generations will call me
         blessed.
49   For He who is mighty has done
         great things for me,
      And holy *is* His name.
50   And His mercy *is* on those who
         fear Him
      From generation to generation.
51   He has shown strength with
         His arm;
      He has scattered *the* proud in
         the imagination of their
         hearts.
52   He has put down the mighty
         from *their* thrones,
      And exalted *the* lowly.
53   He has filled *the* hungry with
         good things,
      And *the* rich He has sent away
         empty.
54   He has helped His servant
         Israel,
      In remembrance of *His* mercy,
55   As He spoke to our fathers,
      To Abraham and to his seed
         forever."

56 And Mary remained with her about three months, and returned to her house.

57 Now Elizabeth's full time came for her to be delivered, and she brought forth a son. 58 When her neighbors and relatives heard how the Lord had shown great mercy to her, they rejoiced with her.

59 So it was, on the eighth day, that they came to circumcise the child; and they would have called him by

---

1:28 *a*NU-Text omits *blessed are you among women.*   1:29 *a*NU-Text omits *when she saw him.*

*W*hen people reject you, it's very difficult for you to feel good about yourself. You start thinking, "If they are willing to throw me aside, I must be of no value."

Mary's Baby

Luke 1:34-38

When the angel came to Mary and told her what God was going to do in her life, she questioned how it could be possible (see Luke 1:34). Maybe God has been telling you something He wants to do in your life, but you have wondered how. Maybe you lack the strength to accomplish the task alone. Perhaps, like Mary, you're thinking only in the natural—that you must have a man to do God's will.

If you have been wondering how God will bring impossible things to pass in your life, remember that He Himself will accomplish the task. No man will get the credit for your deliverance. God told Mary, "The Holy Spirit will come upon you" (verse 35).

I believe the same is true of godly women today. The Holy Spirit will fill you. He will impregnate you. He will give life to your spirit. He will restore your purpose. He will renew you.

God had a special plan for Mary. She brought forth Jesus. He has a special plan for you too. God's women are to be womb-men. They are to be creative and bring forth new life. That is exactly what He wants to do for those who are broken and discouraged. If great things came from those who never suffered, we might think they had accomplished those things on their own. When a broken person submits to God, He gets the glory for the wonderful things He accomplishes—no matter how far that person has previously fallen.

After the angel spoke to Mary, do you know what she said? She said, "Behold the maidservant of the Lord! Let it be to me according to your word" (verse 38). She didn't say, "Let it be … according to my marital status." She didn't say, "Let it be … according to my job." She didn't say, "Let it be … according to what I deserve." She said, "Let it be … according to your word." Mary knew enough to believe God and to submit to Him. But she was taking a big risk. To be pregnant and unmarried in those days brought dire consequences. Yet she willingly gave herself to the Lord.

If you are willing, the Holy Spirit will overshadow you, and the hidden Christ—who's been locked up behind your problems, your fears, and your insecurities—will come forth. You will see the power of Jesus do mighty things in your life.

the name of his father, Zacharias. 60 His mother answered and said, "No; he shall be called John."

61 But they said to her, "There is no one among your relatives who is called by this name." 62 So they made signs to his father—what he would have him called.

63 And he asked for a writing tablet, and wrote, saying, "His name is John." So they all marveled. 64 Immediately his mouth was opened and his tongue *loosed,* and he spoke, praising God. 65 Then fear came on all who dwelt around them; and all these sayings were discussed throughout all the hill country of Judea. 66 And all those who heard *them* kept *them* in their hearts, saying, "What kind of child will this be?" And the hand of the Lord was with him.

67 Now his father Zacharias was filled with the Holy Spirit, and prophesied, saying:

68 "Blessed *is* the Lord God of
    Israel,
    For He has visited and
      redeemed His people,
69 And has raised up a horn of
      salvation for us
    In the house of His servant
      David,
70 As He spoke by the mouth of
      His holy prophets,
    Who *have been* since the world
      began,
71 That we should be saved from
      our enemies
    And from the hand of all who
      hate us,
72 To perform the mercy *promised*
      to our fathers
    And to remember His holy
      covenant,
73 The oath which He swore to
      our father Abraham:
74 To grant us that we,
    Being delivered from the hand
      of our enemies,
    Might serve Him without fear,
75 In holiness and righteousness
      before Him all the days of our
      life.
76 And you, child, will be called
      the prophet of the Highest;
    For you will go before the face
      of the Lord to prepare His
      ways,

77 To give knowledge of salvation
      to His people
    By the remission of their sins,
78 Through the tender mercy of
      our God,
    With which the Dayspring
      from on high has visited[a] us;
79 To give light to those who sit
      in darkness and the shadow
      of death,
    To guide our feet into the way
      of peace."

80 So the child grew and became strong in spirit, and was in the deserts till the day of his manifestation to Israel.

2 And it came to pass in those days *that* a decree went out from Caesar Augustus that all the world should be registered. 2 This census first took place while Quirinius was governing Syria. 3 So all went to be registered, everyone to his own city.

4 Joseph also went up from Galilee, out of the city of Nazareth, into Judea, to the city of David, which is called Bethlehem, because he was of the house and lineage of David, 5 to be registered with Mary, his betrothed wife,[a] who was with child. 6 So it was, that while they were there, the days were completed for her to be delivered. 7 And she brought forth her firstborn Son, and wrapped Him in swaddling cloths, and laid Him in a manger, because there was no room for them in the inn.

8 Now there were in the same country shepherds living out in the fields, keeping watch over their flock by night. 9 And behold,[a] an angel of the Lord stood before them, and the glory of the Lord shone around them, and they were greatly afraid. 10 Then the angel said to them, "Do not be afraid, for behold, I bring you good tidings of great joy which will be to all people. 11 For there is born to you this day in the city of David a Savior, who is Christ the Lord. 12 And this *will be* the sign to you: You will find a Babe wrapped in swaddling cloths, lying in a manger."

13 And suddenly there was with the angel a multitude of the heavenly host praising God and saying:

1:78 [a]NU-Text reads *shall visit.*   2:5 [a]NU-Text omits *wife.*   2:9 [a]NU-Text omits *behold.*

Gospel Pearls

14 "Glory to God in the highest,
   And on earth peace, goodwill
      toward men!"[a]

15 So it was, when the angels had gone away from them into heaven, that the shepherds said to one another, "Let us now go to Bethlehem and see this thing that has come to pass, which the Lord has made known to us." 16 And they came with haste and found Mary and Joseph, and the Babe lying in a manger. 17 Now when they had seen Him, they made widely[a] known the saying which was told them concerning this Child. 18 And all those who heard it marveled at those things which were told them by the shepherds. 19 But Mary kept all these things and pondered them in her heart. 20 Then the shepherds returned, glorifying and praising God for all the things that they had heard and seen, as it was told them.

21 And when eight days were completed for the circumcision of the Child,[a] His name was called JESUS, the name given by the angel before He was conceived in the womb.

22 Now when the days of her purification according to the law of Moses were completed, they brought Him to Jerusalem to present Him to the Lord 23 (as it is written in the law of the Lord, "Every male who opens the womb shall be called holy to the LORD"),[a] 24 and to offer a sacrifice according to what is said in the law of the Lord, "A pair of turtledoves or two young pigeons."[a]

25 And behold, there was a man in Jerusalem whose name was Simeon, and this man was just and devout, waiting for the Consolation of Israel, and the Holy Spirit was upon him. 26 And it had been revealed to him by the Holy Spirit that he would not see death before he had seen the Lord's Christ. 27 So he came by the Spirit into the temple. And when the parents brought in the Child Jesus, to do for Him according to the custom of the law, 28 he took Him up in his arms and blessed God and said:

29 "Lord, now You are letting Your
      servant depart in peace,
   According to Your word;
30 For my eyes have seen Your
      salvation
31 Which You have prepared
      before the face of all peoples,
32 A light to bring revelation to
      the Gentiles,
   And the glory of Your people
      Israel."

33 And Joseph and His mother[a] marveled at those things which were spoken of Him. 34 Then Simeon blessed them, and said to Mary His mother, "Behold, this Child is destined for the fall and rising of many in Israel, and for a sign which will be spoken against 35 (yes, a sword will pierce through your own soul also), that the thoughts of many hearts may be revealed."

36 Now there was one, Anna, a prophetess, the daughter of Phanuel, of the tribe of Asher. She was of a great age, and had lived with a husband seven years from her virginity; 37 and this woman was a widow of about eighty-four years,[a] who did not depart from the temple, but served God with fastings and prayers night and day. 38 And coming in that instant she gave thanks to the Lord,[a] and spoke of Him to all those who looked for redemption in Jerusalem.

39 So when they had performed all things according to the law of the Lord, they returned to Galilee, to their own city, Nazareth. 40 And the Child grew and became strong in spirit,[a] filled with wisdom; and the grace of God was upon Him.

41 His parents went to Jerusalem every year at the Feast of the Passover. 42 And when He was twelve years old, they went up to Jerusalem according to the custom of the feast. 43 When they had finished the days, as they returned, the Boy Jesus lingered behind in Jerusalem. And Joseph and His mother[a] did not know it; 44 but supposing Him to have been in the company, they went a day's journey, and sought Him among their relatives and acquaintances. 45 So when they did not find Him,

2:14 [a]NU-Text reads toward men of goodwill.   2:17 [a]NU-Text omits widely.   2:21 [a]NU-Text reads for His circumcision.   2:23 [a]Exodus 13:2, 12, 15   2:24 [a]Leviticus 12:8   2:33 [a]NU-Text reads And His father and mother.   2:37 [a]NU-Text reads a widow until she was eighty-four.   2:38 [a]NU-Text reads to God.   2:40 [a]NU-Text omits in spirit.   2:43 [a]NU-Text reads And His parents.

The Bible says that a man is to love and nurture and care for his wife just as he loves, nurtures, and cares for his own body. How can he nurture anything inside his mate if he doesn't nurture anything inside himself? It can't be done.

they returned to Jerusalem, seeking Him. 46 Now so it was *that* after three days they found Him in the temple, sitting in the midst of the teachers, both listening to them and asking them questions. 47 And all who heard Him were astonished at His understanding and answers. 48 So when they saw Him, they were amazed; and His mother said to Him, "Son, why have You done this to us? Look, Your father and I have sought You anxiously."

49 And He said to them, "Why did you seek Me? Did you not know that I must be about My Father's business?" 50 But they did not understand the statement which He spoke to them.

51 Then He went down with them and came to Nazareth, and was subject to them, but His mother kept all these things in her heart. 52 And Jesus increased in wisdom and stature, and in favor with God and men.

3 Now in the fifteenth year of the reign of Tiberius Caesar, Pontius Pilate being governor of Judea, Herod being tetrarch of Galilee, his brother Philip tetrarch of Iturea and the region of Trachonitis, and Lysanias tetrarch of Abilene, 2 while Annas and Caiaphas were high priests,*ᵃ* the word of God came to John the son of Zacharias in the wilderness. 3 And he went into all the region around the Jordan, preaching a baptism of repentance for the remission of sins, 4 as it is written in the book of the words of Isaiah the prophet, saying:

> "The voice of one crying in the wilderness:
> 'Prepare the way of the LORD;
> Make His paths straight.
> 5 Every valley shall be filled
> And every mountain and hill brought low;
> The crooked places shall be made straight
> And the rough ways smooth;
> 6 And all flesh shall see the salvation of God.' "*ᵃ*

7 Then he said to the multitudes that came out to be baptized by him, "Brood of vipers! Who warned you to flee from the wrath to come? 8 Therefore bear fruits worthy of repentance, and do not begin to say to yourselves, 'We have Abraham as *our* father.' For I say to you that God is able to raise up children to Abraham from these stones. 9 And even now the ax is laid to the root of the trees. Therefore every tree which does not bear good fruit is cut down and thrown into the fire."

10 So the people asked him, saying, "What shall we do then?"

11 He answered and said to them, "He who has two tunics, let him give to him who has none; and he who has food, let him do likewise."

12 Then tax collectors also came to be baptized, and said to him, "Teacher, what shall we do?"

13 And he said to them, "Collect no more than what is appointed for you."

14 Likewise the soldiers asked him, saying, "And what shall we do?"

So he said to them, "Do not intimidate anyone or accuse falsely, and be content with your wages."

15 Now as the people were in expectation, and all reasoned in their hearts about John, whether he was the Christ or not, 16 John answered, saying to all, "I indeed baptize you with water; but One mightier than I is coming, whose sandal strap I am not worthy to loose. He will baptize you with the Holy Spirit and fire. 17 His winnowing fan *is* in His hand, and He will thoroughly clean out His threshing floor, and gather the wheat into His barn; but the chaff He will burn with unquenchable fire."

18 And with many other exhortations he preached to the people. 19 But Herod the tetrarch, being rebuked by him concerning Herodias, his brother Philip's wife,*ᵃ* and for all the evils which Herod had done, 20 also added this, above all, that he shut John up in prison.

21 When all the people were baptized, it came to pass that Jesus also was baptized; and while He prayed, the heaven was opened. 22 And the Holy Spirit descended in bodily form like a dove upon Him, and a voice came from heaven which said, "You are My beloved Son; in You I am well pleased."

3:2 ᵃNU-Text and M-Text read *in the high priesthood of Annas and Caiaphas.*   3:6 ᵃIsaiah 40:3–5
3:19 ᵃNU-Text reads *his brother's wife.*

---

*I*f God delivers you from an addiction, He desires to deliver you from the entire environment that contributed to your addiction in the first place. You're going to have to move out of that circle, that environment, maybe even that neighborhood.

Always a Mother

Luke 2:48, 49

*I*t takes faith to let go of the former things. Many people cling to the past because they are convinced their better days are behind them. This attitude leads to great depression. The truth is that if you can accept the challenge to which God is calling you and realize that there are new levels of love and life before you, you set yourself up for a wonderful future. Renovate your life with love and hope, and release bitterness.

A woman who can move on is invincible. She may be an Esther, a Deborah, a Naomi, or an Anna. Whatever your next assignment in life, you will miss it if you worship the past and yearn for yesterday. Let it go. Look ahead. And start walking.

A tremendous tragedy occurs when a mother finds herself with resentful adult children who feel smothered and angry because they were made to feel guilty for growing up. Preserve what you have with your children by allowing your relationship with them to change in your hand. Each child, like a caterpillar, has been fed in the cocoon of your teaching and has come forth as a beautiful butterfly. The butterfly will never crawl again. It will never need what it once needed, but every flutter of its lovely wings is a tribute to the cocoon that allowed it the grace of change.

As a mother, your authority changes when your children are grown. You move from a sovereign to an advisor. That is growth and development for you. Your word may not be law to your children anymore, and they may not wear the clothes you'd prefer; but if you respect yesterday's child and recognize that he has become today's adult, he will always love you for the enormous contribution you made to that independence.

A major challenge of this adjustment is the redefining of boundaries. While the lines are being re-drawn, the child must understand that he can be independent without being disrespectful. Young people struggle to know their role in life and they may blunder in the process of reaching their goals. But didn't most of us stumble into destiny? Children cannot exist as extensions of their parents. The weaning experience can be challenging, but it is also necessary for both parents and children.

Look at Luke 2:48, 49. The young Jesus returned home with His mother and continued to submit to her. But the Scriptures say that from that time He "increased in wisdom and stature, and in favor with God and men" (Luke 2:52). It is important to recognize that He did not disassociate from His mother, whose loyalty followed Him all the way to the Cross. Although their roles changed and He became increasingly independent, His love and care for her continued even to His thirty-third year and to the final moments of His life. She was always His mother!

23 Now Jesus Himself began *His ministry at* about thirty years of age, being (as was supposed) *the* son of Joseph, *the son* of Heli, 24 *the son* of Matthat,*ᵃ the son* of Levi, *the son* of Melchi, *the son* of Janna, *the son* of Joseph, 25 *the son* of Mattathiah, *the son* of Amos, *the son* of Nahum, *the son* of Esli, *the son* of Naggai, 26 *the son* of Maath, *the son* of Mattathiah, *the son* of Semei, *the son* of Joseph, *the son* of Judah, 27 *the son* of Joannas, *the son* of Rhesa, *the son* of Zerubbabel, *the son* of Shealtiel, *the son* of Neri, 28 *the son* of Melchi, *the son* of Addi, *the son* of Cosam, *the son* of Elmodam, *the son* of Er, 29 *the son* of Jose, *the son* of Eliezer, *the son* of Jorim, *the son* of Matthat, *the son* of Levi, 30 *the son* of Simeon, *the son* of Judah, *the son* of Joseph, *the son* of Jonan, *the son* of Eliakim, 31 *the son* of Melea, *the son* of Menan, *the son* of Mattathah, *the son* of Nathan, *the son* of David, 32 *the son* of Jesse, *the son* of Obed, *the son* of Boaz, *the son* of Salmon, *the son* of Nahshon, 33 *the son* of Amminadab, *the son* of Ram, *the son* of Hezron, *the son* of Perez, *the son* of Judah, 34 *the son* of Jacob, *the son* of Isaac, *the son* of Abraham, *the son* of Terah, *the son* of Nahor, 35 *the son* of Serug, *the son* of Reu, *the son* of Peleg, *the son* of Eber, *the son* of Shelah, 36 *the son* of Cainan, *the son* of Arphaxad, *the son* of Shem, *the son* of Noah, *the son* of Lamech, 37 *the son* of Methuselah, *the son* of Enoch, *the son* of Jared, *the son* of Mahalalel, *the son* of Cainan, 38 *the son* of Enosh, *the son* of Seth, *the son* of Adam, *the son* of God.

4 Then Jesus, being filled with the Holy Spirit, returned from the Jordan and was led by the Spirit into*ᵃ* the wilderness, 2 being tempted for forty days by the devil. And in those days He ate nothing, and afterward, when they had ended, He was hungry.
3 And the devil said to Him, "If You are the Son of God, command this stone to become bread."

4 But Jesus answered him, saying,*ᵃ* "It is written, *'Man shall not live by bread alone, but by every word of God.' 'ᵇ*
5 Then the devil, taking Him up on a high mountain, showed Him*ᵃ* all the kingdoms of the world in a moment of time. 6 And the devil said to Him, "All this authority I will give You, and their glory; for *this* has been delivered to me, and I give it to whomever I wish. 7 Therefore, if You will worship before me, all will be Yours."
8 And Jesus answered and said to him, "Get behind Me, Satan!*ᵃ* For*ᵇ* it is written, *'You shall worship the* Lord *your God, and Him only you shall serve.' 'ᶜ*
9 Then he brought Him to Jerusalem, set Him on the pinnacle of the temple, and said to Him, "If You are the Son of God, throw Yourself down from here. 10 For it is written:

'He shall give His angels charge over you,
To keep you,'

11 and,

'In their hands they shall bear you up,
Lest you dash your foot against a stone.' 'ᵃ

12 And Jesus answered and said to him, "It has been said, *'You shall not tempt the* Lord *your God.' 'ᵃ*
13 Now when the devil had ended every temptation, he departed from Him until an opportune time.
14 Then Jesus returned in the power of the Spirit to Galilee, and news of Him went out through all the surrounding region. 15 And He taught in their synagogues, being glorified by all.
16 So He came to Nazareth, where He had been brought up. And as His custom was, He went into the synagogue on the Sabbath day, and stood up to read. 17 And He was handed the book of the prophet Isaiah. And when He had opened the book, He found the place where it was written:

3:24 ᵃThis and several other names in the genealogy are spelled somewhat differently in the NU-Text. Since the New King James Version uses the Old Testament spelling for persons mentioned in the New Testament, these variations, which come from the Greek, have not been footnoted.   4:1 ᵃNU-Text reads *in.*   4:4 ᵃDeuteronomy 8:3   ᵇNU-Text omits *but by every word of God.*   4:5 ᵃNU-Text reads *And taking Him up, he showed Him.*   4:8 ᵃNU-Text omits *Get behind Me, Satan.*   ᵇNU-Text and M-Text omit *For.*   ᶜDeuteronomy 6:13   4:11 ᵃPsalm 91:11, 12   4:12 ᵃDeuteronomy 6:16

Gospel Pearls

18 "The Spirit of the LORD is upon
      Me,
   Because He has anointed Me
   To preach the gospel to the
      poor;
   He has sent Me to heal the
      brokenhearted,ᵃ
   To proclaim liberty to the
      captives
   And recovery of sight to the
      blind,
   To set at liberty those who are
      oppressed;
19   To proclaim the acceptable
      year of the LORD.''ᵃ

20 Then He closed the book, and gave
it back to the attendant and sat
down. And the eyes of all who were
in the synagogue were fixed on Him.
21 And He began to say to them, "Today this Scripture is fulfilled in your
hearing." 22 So all bore witness to
Him, and marveled at the gracious
words which proceeded out of His
mouth. And they said, "Is this not Joseph's son?"
23 He said to them, "You will surely
say this proverb to Me, 'Physician,
heal yourself! Whatever we have
heard done in Capernaum,ᵃ do also
here in Your country.' " 24 Then He
said, "Assuredly, I say to you, no
prophet is accepted in his own country. 25 But I tell you truly, many widows were in Israel in the days of Elijah, when the heaven was shut up
three years and six months, and
there was a great famine throughout
all the land; 26 but to none of them
was Elijah sent except to Zarephath,ᵃ
in the region of Sidon, to a woman
who was a widow. 27 And many lepers were in Israel in the time of Elisha
the prophet, and none of them was
cleansed except Naaman the Syrian."
28 So all those in the synagogue,
when they heard these things, were
filled with wrath, 29 and rose up and
thrust Him out of the city; and they
led Him to the brow of the hill on
which their city was built, that they
might throw Him down over the cliff.
30 Then passing through the midst of
them, He went His way.
31 Then He went down to Capernaum, a city of Galilee, and was

teaching them on the Sabbaths.
32 And they were astonished at His
teaching, for His word was with authority. 33 Now in the synagogue
there was a man who had a spirit of
an unclean demon. And he cried out
with a loud voice, 34 saying, "Let us
alone! What have we to do with You,
Jesus of Nazareth? Did You come to
destroy us? I know who You are—
the Holy One of God!"
35 But Jesus rebuked him, saying,
"Be quiet, and come out of him!" And
when the demon had thrown him in
their midst, it came out of him and
did not hurt him. 36 Then they were
all amazed and spoke among themselves, saying, "What a word this is!
For with authority and power He
commands the unclean spirits, and
they come out." 37 And the report
about Him went out into every place
in the surrounding region.
38 Now He arose from the synagogue and entered Simon's house.
But Simon's wife's mother was sick
with a high fever, and they made
request of Him concerning her.
39 So He stood over her and rebuked
the fever, and it left her. And immediately she arose and served them.
40 When the sun was setting, all
those who had any that were sick
with various diseases brought them
to Him; and He laid His hands on every one of them and healed them.
41 And demons also came out of
many, crying out and saying, "You
are the Christ,ᵃ the Son of God!"
And He, rebuking them, did not allow them to speak, for they knew
that He was the Christ.
42 Now when it was day, He departed and went into a deserted
place. And the crowd sought Him
and came to Him, and tried to keep
Him from leaving them; 43 but He
said to them, "I must preach the kingdom of God to the other cities also,
because for this purpose I have been
sent." 44 And He was preaching in
the synagogues of Galilee.ᵃ

5 So it was, as the multitude
   pressed about Him to hear the
word of God, that He stood by the
Lake of Gennesaret, 2 and saw two
boats standing by the lake; but the

4:18 ᵃNU-Text omits to heal the brokenhearted.   4:19 ᵃIsaiah 61:1, 2   4:23 ᵃHere and elsewhere the
NU-Text spelling is Capharnaum.   4:26 ᵃGreek Sarepta   4:41 ᵃNU-Text omits the Christ.
4:44 ᵃNU-Text reads Judea.

Are you prepared to deal with the fact that the person you've spent your entire life
trying to impress may never be impressed? Are you prepared to face the reality
that, from God's perspective, it doesn't matter one way or the other?

fishermen had gone from them and were washing *their* nets. 3 Then He got into one of the boats, which was Simon's, and asked him to put out a little from the land. And He sat down and taught the multitudes from the boat.

4 When He had stopped speaking, He said to Simon, "Launch out into the deep and let down your nets for a catch."

5 But Simon answered and said to Him, "Master, we have toiled all night and caught nothing; nevertheless at Your word I will let down the net." 6 And when they had done this, they caught a great number of fish, and their net was breaking. 7 So they signaled to *their* partners in the other boat to come and help them. And they came and filled both the boats, so that they began to sink. 8 When Simon Peter saw *it*, he fell down at Jesus' knees, saying, "Depart from me, for I am a sinful man, O Lord!"

9 For he and all who were with him were astonished at the catch of fish which they had taken; 10 and so also *were* James and John, the sons of Zebedee, who were partners with Simon. And Jesus said to Simon, "Do not be afraid. From now on you will catch men." 11 So when they had brought their boats to land, they forsook all and followed Him.

12 And it happened when He was in a certain city, that behold, a man who was full of leprosy saw Jesus; and he fell on *his* face and implored Him, saying, "Lord, if You are willing, You can make me clean."

13 Then He put out *His* hand and touched him, saying, "I am willing; be cleansed." Immediately the leprosy left him. 14 And He charged him to tell no one, "But go and show yourself to the priest, and make an offering for your cleansing, as a testimony to them, just as Moses commanded."

15 However, the report went around concerning Him all the more; and great multitudes came together to hear, and to be healed by Him of their infirmities. 16 So He Himself *often* withdrew into the wilderness and prayed.

17 Now it happened on a certain day, as He was teaching, that there were Pharisees and teachers of the law sitting by, who had come out of every town of Galilee, Judea, and Jerusalem. And the power of the Lord was *present* to heal them.*a* 18 Then behold, men brought on a bed a man who was paralyzed, whom they sought to bring in and lay before Him. 19 And when they could not find how they might bring him in, because of the crowd, they went up on the housetop and let him down with *his* bed through the tiling into the midst before Jesus.

20 When He saw their faith, He said to him, "Man, your sins are forgiven you."

21 And the scribes and the Pharisees began to reason, saying, "Who is this who speaks blasphemies? Who can forgive sins but God alone?"

22 But when Jesus perceived their thoughts, He answered and said to them, "Why are you reasoning in your hearts? 23 Which is easier, to say, 'Your sins are forgiven you,' or to say, 'Rise up and walk'? 24 But that you may know that the Son of Man has power on earth to forgive sins" —He said to the man who was paralyzed, "I say to you, arise, take up your bed, and go to your house."

25 Immediately he rose up before them, took up what he had been lying on, and departed to his own house, glorifying God. 26 And they were all amazed, and they glorified God and were filled with fear, saying, "We have seen strange things today!"

27 After these things He went out and saw a tax collector named Levi, sitting at the tax office. And He said to him, "Follow Me." 28 So he left all, rose up, and followed Him.

29 Then Levi gave Him a great feast in his own house. And there were a great number of tax collectors and others who sat down with them. 30 And their scribes and the Pharisees*a* complained against His disciples, saying, "Why do You eat and drink with tax collectors and sinners?"

31 Jesus answered and said to them, "Those who are well have no need of a physician, but those who are sick. 32 I have not come to call

5:17 *a*NU-Text reads *present with Him to heal.*   5:30 *a*NU-Text reads *But the Pharisees and their scribes.*

*Y*ou won't get anywhere by worshipping a person, which is what you are doing if you are seeking that person's approval as the most defining opinion about your life.

Real Ministry
for the Needy

Luke 5:31

eal ministry comes to the needy. Many women today have found themselves in a state of single parenting— one person doing the job of two! They did not request such an assignment, nor do they prefer it, but it happened and they must deal with the realities it brings.

If you are a single mother, God gives you the grace to survive. He helps and assists you as only He can. You may have endured desertion, death, or the tragedy of divorce and have been left to raise your children alone.

Please, please hear me. Today, many women are choosing to become mothers without fathers for their children. Some of these women without husbands are deciding to have children because they want them. Non-traditional families are becoming more and more fashionable. I wonder how they could bring babies into the world knowing that those children will grow up with a tremendous daddy-shaped void in their lives.

It is arrogant to think you are so perfect that you can rear a child and give him or her both aspects of parenting. You may be a wonderful, successful, intelligent woman. You might be the bionic mother. But, no matter what, you are not a father. Whether our society wants to admit it or not, God gives children for marriage. The man and the woman in the Garden of Eden were jointly challenged to "be fruitful and multiply" (see Genesis 1:28). It takes both male and female to procreate, and it works best when both contribute to the development of the fruit. Don't rob your children of that wonderful experience of wholeness.

A father's love is essential to good, healthy development. You may be able to do it alone. But there are going to be some challenges you will face in bringing balance—too many challenges for you to willingly choose this plight for yourself. But, if you are left to bring up the children alone, God is able! You can do it, but not without the assistance of your heavenly Father, whose wisdom will become a resource center for help and guidance along the way.

If you are not a Christian, stop right now and give your life to Jesus before you allow your pain to pollute the way you influence your children. If you have been the victim of any kind of abuse, or if your secret childhood wounds are still bleeding, I recommend the Father who will never leave you nor forsake you (see Joshua 1:5).

the righteous, but sinners, to repentance."

33 Then they said to Him, "Why do*ᵃ* the disciples of John fast often and make prayers, and likewise those of the Pharisees, but Yours eat and drink?"

34 And He said to them, "Can you make the friends of the bridegroom fast while the bridegroom is with them? 35 But the days will come when the bridegroom will be taken away from them; then they will fast in those days."

36 Then He spoke a parable to them: "No one puts a piece from a new garment on an old one;*ᵃ* otherwise the new makes a tear, and also the piece that was *taken* out of the new does not match the old. 37 And no one puts new wine into old wineskins; or else the new wine will burst the wineskins and be spilled, and the wineskins will be ruined. 38 But new wine must be put into new wineskins, and both are preserved.*ᵃ* 39 And no one, having drunk old *wine,* immediately*ᵃ* desires new; for he says, 'The old is better.' "*ᵇ*

6 Now it happened on the second Sabbath after the first*ᵃ* that He went through the grainfields. And His disciples plucked the heads of grain and ate *them,* rubbing *them* in *their* hands. 2 And some of the Pharisees said to them, "Why are you doing what is not lawful to do on the Sabbath?"

3 But Jesus answering them said, "Have you not even read this, what David did when he was hungry, he and those who were with him: 4 how he went into the house of God, took and ate the showbread, and also gave some to those with him, which is not lawful for any but the priests to eat?" 5 And He said to them, "The Son of Man is also Lord of the Sabbath."

6 Now it happened on another Sabbath, also, that He entered the synagogue and taught. And a man was there whose right hand was withered. 7 So the scribes and Pharisees watched Him closely, whether He would heal on the Sabbath, that they might find an accusation against Him. 8 But He knew their thoughts, and said to the man who had the withered hand, "Arise and stand here." And he arose and stood. 9 Then Jesus said to them, "I will ask you one thing: Is it lawful on the Sabbath to do good or to do evil, to save life or to destroy?"*ᵃ* 10 And when He had looked around at them all, He said to the man,*ᵃ* "Stretch out your hand." And he did so, and his hand was restored as whole as the other.*ᵇ* 11 But they were filled with rage, and discussed with one another what they might do to Jesus.

12 Now it came to pass in those days that He went out to the mountain to pray, and continued all night in prayer to God. 13 And when it was day, He called His disciples to *Himself;* and from them He chose twelve whom He also named apostles: 14 Simon, whom He also named Peter, and Andrew his brother; James and John; Philip and Bartholomew; 15 Matthew and Thomas; James the *son* of Alphaeus, and Simon called the Zealot; 16 Judas *the son* of James, and Judas Iscariot who also became a traitor.

17 And He came down with them and stood on a level place with a crowd of His disciples and a great multitude of people from all Judea and Jerusalem, and from the seacoast of Tyre and Sidon, who came to hear Him and be healed of their diseases, 18 as well as those who were tormented with unclean spirits. And they were healed. 19 And the whole multitude sought to touch Him, for power went out from Him and healed *them* all.

20 Then He lifted up His eyes toward His disciples, and said:

"Blessed *are you* poor,
    For yours is the kingdom of
        God.
21 Blessed *are you* who hunger
        now,
    For you shall be filled.
    Blessed *are you* who weep now,
        For you shall laugh.
22 Blessed are you when men hate
        you,

5:33 *ᵃ*NU-Text omits *Why do,* making the verse a statement.   5:36 *ᵃ*NU-Text reads *No one tears a piece from a new garment and puts it on an old one.*   5:38 *ᵃ*NU-Text omits *and both are preserved.*
5:39 *ᵃ*NU-Text omits *immediately.*   *ᵇ*NU-Text reads *good.*   6:1 *ᵃ*NU-Text reads *on a Sabbath.*
6:9 *ᵃ*M-Text reads *to kill.*   6:10 *ᵃ*NU-Text and M-Text read *to him.*   *ᵇ*NU-Text omits *as whole as the other.*

*Gospel
Pearls*

And when they exclude you,
And revile *you*, and cast out
your name as evil,
For the Son of Man's sake.
23 Rejoice in that day and leap for
joy!
For indeed your reward *is*
great in heaven,
For in like manner their
fathers did to the prophets.
24 "But woe to you who are rich,
For you have received your
consolation.
25 Woe to you who are full,
For you shall hunger.
Woe to you who laugh now,
For you shall mourn and
weep.
26 Woe to you*a* when all*b* men
speak well of you,
For so did their fathers to the
false prophets.

27 "But I say to you who hear: Love
your enemies, do good to those who
hate you, 28 bless those who curse
you, and pray for those who spitefully use you. 29 To him who strikes
you on the *one* cheek, offer the other
also. And from him who takes away
your cloak, do not withhold *your*
tunic either. 30 Give to everyone who
asks of you. And from him who takes
away your goods do not ask *them*
back. 31 And just as you want men
to do to you, you also do to them likewise.
32 "But if you love those who love
you, what credit is that to you? For
even sinners love those who love
them. 33 And if you do good to those
who do good to you, what credit is
that to you? For even sinners do the
same. 34 And if you lend *to those*
from whom you hope to receive back,
what credit is that to you? For even
sinners lend to sinners to receive as
much back. 35 But love your enemies,
do good, and lend, hoping for nothing in return; and your reward will
be great, and you will be sons of the
Most High. For He is kind to the unthankful and evil. 36 Therefore be
merciful, just as your Father also is
merciful.
37 "Judge not, and you shall not be
judged. Condemn not, and you shall
not be condemned. Forgive, and you
will be forgiven. 38 Give, and it will

be given to you: good measure,
pressed down, shaken together, and
running over will be put into your bosom. For with the same measure that
you use, it will be measured back to
you."
39 And He spoke a parable to them:
"Can the blind lead the blind? Will
they not both fall into the ditch?
40 A disciple is not above his teacher,
but everyone who is perfectly trained
will be like his teacher. 41 And why
do you look at the speck in your
brother's eye, but do not perceive the
plank in your own eye? 42 Or how
can you say to your brother, 'Brother,
let me remove the speck that *is* in
your eye,' when you yourself do not
see the plank that *is* in your own eye?
Hypocrite! First remove the plank
from your own eye, and then you will
see clearly to remove the speck that
is in your brother's eye.
43 "For a good tree does not bear
bad fruit, nor does a bad tree bear
good fruit. 44 For every tree is known
by its own fruit. For *men* do not
gather figs from thorns, nor do they
gather grapes from a bramble bush.
45 A good man out of the good treasure of his heart brings forth good;
and an evil man out of the evil treasure of his heart*a* brings forth evil.
For out of the abundance of the heart
his mouth speaks.
46 "But why do you call Me 'Lord,
Lord,' and not do the things which I
say? 47 Whoever comes to Me, and
hears My sayings and does them, I
will show you whom he is like:
48 He is like a man building a house,
who dug deep and laid the foundation on the rock. And when the flood
arose, the stream beat vehemently
against that house, and could not
shake it, for it was founded on the
rock.*a* 49 But he who heard and did
nothing is like a man who built a
house on the earth without a foundation, against which the stream beat
vehemently; and immediately it fell.*a*
And the ruin of that house was
great."

7 Now when He concluded all His
sayings in the hearing of the
people, He entered Capernaum.
2 And a certain centurion's servant,
who was dear to him, was sick and

6:26 *a*NU-Text and M-Text omit *to you.* *b*M-Text omits *all.* 6:45 *a*NU-Text omits *treasure of his heart.*
6:48 *a*NU-Text reads *for it was well built.* 6:49 *a*NU-Text reads *collapsed.*

---

*W*e all tend to gravitate toward people who have infirmities that are similar to
ours. And that's dangerous. If we hang around people who have our set of infirmities, we become codependent.

ready to die. 3 So when he heard about Jesus, he sent elders of the Jews to Him, pleading with Him to come and heal his servant. 4 And when they came to Jesus, they begged Him earnestly, saying that the one for whom He should do this was deserving, 5 "for he loves our nation, and has built us a synagogue."

6 Then Jesus went with them. And when He was already not far from the house, the centurion sent friends to Him, saying to Him, "Lord, do not trouble Yourself, for I am not worthy that You should enter under my roof. 7 Therefore I did not even think myself worthy to come to You. But say the word, and my servant will be healed. 8 For I also am a man placed under authority, having soldiers under me. And I say to one, 'Go,' and he goes; and to another, 'Come,' and he comes; and to my servant, 'Do this,' and he does it."

9 When Jesus heard these things, He marveled at him, and turned around and said to the crowd that followed Him, "I say to you, I have not found such great faith, not even in Israel!" 10 And those who were sent, returning to the house, found the servant well who had been sick.ª

11 Now it happened, the day after, that He went into a city called Nain; and many of His disciples went with Him, and a large crowd. 12 And when He came near the gate of the city, behold, a dead man was being carried out, the only son of his mother; and she was a widow. And a large crowd from the city was with her. 13 When the Lord saw her, He had compassion on her and said to her, "Do not weep." 14 Then He came and touched the open coffin, and those who carried him stood still. And He said, "Young man, I say to you, arise." 15 So he who was dead sat up and began to speak. And He presented him to his mother.

16 Then fear came upon all, and they glorified God, saying, "A great prophet has risen up among us"; and, "God has visited His people." 17 And this report about Him went throughout all Judea and all the surrounding region.

18 Then the disciples of John reported to him concerning all these things. 19 And John, calling two of his disciples to him, sent them to Jesus,ª saying, "Are You the Coming One, or do we look for another?"

20 When the men had come to Him, they said, "John the Baptist has sent us to You, saying, 'Are You the Coming One, or do we look for another?' "

21 And that very hour He cured many of infirmities, afflictions, and evil spirits; and to many blind He gave sight. 22 Jesus answered and said to them, "Go and tell John the things you have seen and heard: that the blind see, the lame walk, the lepers are cleansed, the deaf hear, the dead are raised, the poor have the gospel preached to them. 23 And blessed is he who is not offended because of Me."

24 When the messengers of John had departed, He began to speak to the multitudes concerning John: "What did you go out into the wilderness to see? A reed shaken by the wind? 25 But what did you go out to see? A man clothed in soft garments? Indeed those who are gorgeously appareled and live in luxury are in kings' courts. 26 But what did you go out to see? A prophet? Yes, I say to you, and more than a prophet. 27 This is he of whom it is written:

> 'Behold, I send My messenger
>   before Your face,
> Who will prepare Your way
>   before You.'ª

28 For I say to you, among those born of women there is not a greater prophet than John the Baptist;ª but he who is least in the kingdom of God is greater than he."

29 And when all the people heard Him, even the tax collectors justified God, having been baptized with the baptism of John. 30 But the Pharisees and lawyers rejected the will of God for themselves, not having been baptized by him.

31 And the Lord said,ª "To what then shall I liken the men of this generation, and what are they like? 32 They are like children sitting in the

---

7:10 ªNU-Text omits who had been sick.   7:19 ªNU-Text reads the Lord.   7:27 ªMalachi 3:1
7:28 ªNU-Text reads there is none greater than John.   7:31 ªNU-Text and M-Text omit And the Lord said.

Gospel
Pearls

marketplace and calling to one another, saying:

'We played the flute for you,
    And you did not dance;
We mourned to you,
    And you did not weep.'

33 For John the Baptist came neither eating bread nor drinking wine, and you say, 'He has a demon.' 34 The Son of Man has come eating and drinking, and you say, 'Look, a glutton and a winebibber, a friend of tax collectors and sinners!' 35 But wisdom is justified by all her children."

36 Then one of the Pharisees asked Him to eat with him. And He went to the Pharisee's house, and sat down to eat. 37 And behold, a woman in the city who was a sinner, when she knew that *Jesus* sat at the table in the Pharisee's house, brought an alabaster flask of fragrant oil, 38 and stood at His feet behind Him weeping; and she began to wash His feet with her tears, and wiped *them* with the hair of her head; and she kissed His feet and anointed *them* with the fragrant oil. 39 Now when the Pharisee who had invited Him saw *this*, he spoke to himself, saying, "This man, if He were a prophet, would know who and what manner of woman *this is* who is touching Him, for she is a sinner."

40 And Jesus answered and said to him, "Simon, I have something to say to you."

So he said, "Teacher, say it."

41 "There was a certain creditor who had two debtors. One owed five hundred denarii, and the other fifty. 42 And when they had nothing with which to repay, he freely forgave them both. Tell Me, therefore, which of them will love him more?"

43 Simon answered and said, "I suppose the *one* whom he forgave more."

And He said to him, "You have rightly judged." 44 Then He turned to the woman and said to Simon, "Do you see this woman? I entered your house; you gave Me no water for My feet, but she has washed My feet with her tears and wiped *them* with the hair of her head. 45 You gave Me no kiss, but this woman has not ceased to kiss My feet since the time I came

in: 46 You did not anoint My head with oil, but this woman has anointed My feet with fragrant oil. 47 Therefore I say to you, her sins, *which are* many, are forgiven, for she loved much. But to whom little is forgiven, *the same* loves little."

48 Then He said to her, "Your sins are forgiven."

49 And those who sat at the table with Him began to say to themselves, "Who is this who even forgives sins?"

50 Then He said to the woman, "Your faith has saved you. Go in peace."

8 Now it came to pass, afterward, that He went through every city and village, preaching and bringing the glad tidings of the kingdom of God. And the twelve *were* with Him, 2 and certain women who had been healed of evil spirits and infirmities— Mary called Magdalene, out of whom had come seven demons, 3 and Joanna the wife of Chuza, Herod's steward, and Susanna, and many others who provided for Him[a] from their substance.

4 And when a great multitude had gathered, and they had come to Him from every city, He spoke by a parable: 5 "A sower went out to sow his seed. And as he sowed, some fell by the wayside; and it was trampled down, and the birds of the air devoured it. 6 Some fell on rock; and as soon as it sprang up, it withered away because it lacked moisture. 7 And some fell among thorns, and the thorns sprang up with it and choked it. 8 But others fell on good ground, sprang up, and yielded a crop a hundredfold." When He had said these things He cried, "He who has ears to hear, let him hear!"

9 Then His disciples asked Him, saying, "What does this parable mean?"

10 And He said, "To you it has been given to know the mysteries of the kingdom of God, but to the rest *it is given* in parables, that

'Seeing they may not see,
    And hearing they may not
        understand.'[a]

11 "Now the parable is this: The seed is the word of God. 12 Those by

8:3 ªNU-Text and M-Text read *them*.   8:10 ªIsaiah 6:9

Change means you were—and now you aren't. Period. You can leave an ungodly affair whether your partner agrees or disagrees, whether he's around or not. When you unhook from him inside yourself, you're free.

Shock Treatment

Luke 7:38

Women are more emotional than men because emotions are the language of relationship. In fact, the more relationship-oriented you are, the more emotional you are likely to be.

There's nothing wrong with being emotional. Emotions are a necessary component of our makeup. What's wrong is when we allow our emotions to be more important or to carry more weight than our spirits.

Men are often conditioned to suppress their emotions. They are taught from an early age to stifle their feelings. I've seen mothers tell their eighteen-month-old sons, "Stop crying and be a man!" When that little boy grows up to be a fifty-year-old man, he's likely to have trouble hugging his wife or raising his hands in praise.

Don't let anyone convince you that you need to hold in or deny your emotions. Don't let anything make you so cold you lose your ability to love. As a woman, you have a great capacity to express feelings and affections. God gave you that capacity so you could relate more fully to other people and to Him.

Some women are in shock. They've lost their sensitivity, their femininity, their ability to feel. When that happens, they often adopt the male tendency to shut down emotionally. They lose part of their identity, the part that makes them uniquely feminine. In fact, when a woman begins to display masculine behavior or appearance, I consider that something has put her femininity into shock.

A person in shock sometimes seems to have passed out. She has withdrawn and lost touch with the reality around her. She needs to be warmed and helped and comforted. She needs to be encouraged.

Some women go into shock because they have been mistreated. Some women go into shock because they have been abused. Some women go into shock because they have been hurt or rejected. A person in shock is immobilized. She has let a part of herself become paralyzed. She has let her emotions die.

If you are such a woman, the time has come for you to come out of it! Allow yourself to feel again. Allow yourself to cry again. Allow yourself to call out to God again. It's time!

the wayside are the ones who hear; then the devil comes and takes away the word out of their hearts, lest they should believe and be saved. 13 But the ones on the rock *are those* who, when they hear, receive the word with joy; and these have no root, who believe for a while and in time of temptation fall away. 14 Now the ones *that* fell among thorns are those who, when they have heard, go out and are choked with cares, riches, and pleasures of life, and bring no fruit to maturity. 15 But the ones *that* fell on the good ground are those who, having heard the word with a noble and good heart, keep *it* and bear fruit with patience.

16 "No one, when he has lit a lamp, covers it with a vessel or puts *it* under a bed, but sets *it* on a lampstand, that those who enter may see the light. 17 For nothing is secret that will not be revealed, nor *anything* hidden that will not be known and come to light. 18 Therefore take heed how you hear. For whoever has, to him *more* will be given; and whoever does not have, even what he seems to have will be taken from him."

19 Then His mother and brothers came to Him, and could not approach Him because of the crowd. 20 And it was told Him *by some,* who said, "Your mother and Your brothers are standing outside, desiring to see You."

21 But He answered and said to them, "My mother and My brothers are these who hear the word of God and do it."

22 Now it happened, on a certain day, that He got into a boat with His disciples. And He said to them, "Let us cross over to the other side of the lake." And they launched out. 23 But as they sailed He fell asleep. And a windstorm came down on the lake, and they were filling *with water,* and were in jeopardy. 24 And they came to Him and awoke Him, saying, "Master, Master, we are perishing!"

Then He arose and rebuked the wind and the raging of the water. And they ceased, and there was a calm. 25 But He said to them, "Where is your faith?"

And they were afraid, and marveled, saying to one another, "Who can this be? For He commands even the winds and water, and they obey Him!"

26 Then they sailed to the country of the Gadarenes,*a* which is opposite Galilee. 27 And when He stepped out on the land, there met Him a certain man from the city who had demons for a long time. And he wore no clothes,*a* nor did he live in a house but in the tombs. 28 When he saw Jesus, he cried out, fell down before Him, and with a loud voice said, "What have I to do with You, Jesus, Son of the Most High God? I beg You, do not torment me!" 29 For He had commanded the unclean spirit to come out of the man. For it had often seized him, and he was kept under guard, bound with chains and shackles; and he broke the bonds and was driven by the demon into the wilderness.

30 Jesus asked him, saying, "What is your name?"

And he said, "Legion," because many demons had entered him. 31 And they begged Him that He would not command them to go out into the abyss.

32 Now a herd of many swine was feeding there on the mountain. So they begged Him that He would permit them to enter them. And He permitted them. 33 Then the demons went out of the man and entered the swine, and the herd ran violently down the steep place into the lake and drowned.

34 When those who fed *them* saw what had happened, they fled and told *it* in the city and in the country. 35 Then they went out to see what had happened, and came to Jesus, and found the man from whom the demons had departed, sitting at the feet of Jesus, clothed and in his right mind. And they were afraid. 36 They also who had seen *it* told them by what means he who had been demon-possessed was healed. 37 Then the whole multitude of the surrounding region of the Gadarenes*a* asked Him to depart from them, for they were seized with great fear. And He got into the boat and returned.

8:26 *a*NU-Text reads *Gerasenes.*   8:27 *a*NU-Text reads *who had demons and for a long time wore no clothes.*   8:37 *a*NU-Text reads *Gerasenes.*

*O*nce you are delivered, don't hang around ungodly people. Get moving and get out. Get as far as you can, as fast as you can. Just leave.

38 Now the man from whom the demons had departed begged Him that he might be with Him. But Jesus sent him away, saying, 39 "Return to your own house, and tell what great things God has done for you." And he went his way and proclaimed throughout the whole city what great things Jesus had done for him.

40 So it was, when Jesus returned, that the multitude welcomed Him, for they were all waiting for Him. 41 And behold, there came a man named Jairus, and he was a ruler of the synagogue. And he fell down at Jesus' feet and begged Him to come to his house, 42 for he had an only daughter about twelve years of age, and she was dying.

But as He went, the multitudes thronged Him. 43 Now a woman, having a flow of blood for twelve years, who had spent all her livelihood on physicians and could not be healed by any, 44 came from behind and touched the border of His garment. And immediately her flow of blood stopped.

45 And Jesus said, "Who touched Me?"

When all denied it, Peter and those with him*a* said, "Master, the multitudes throng and press You, and You say, 'Who touched Me?' "*b*

46 But Jesus said, "Somebody touched Me, for I perceived power going out from Me." 47 Now when the woman saw that she was not hidden, she came trembling; and falling down before Him, she declared to Him in the presence of all the people the reason she had touched Him and how she was healed immediately.

48 And He said to her, "Daughter, be of good cheer;*a* your faith has made you well. Go in peace."

49 While He was still speaking, someone came from the ruler of the synagogue's *house,* saying to him, "Your daughter is dead. Do not trouble the Teacher."*a*

50 But when Jesus heard *it,* He answered him, saying, "Do not be afraid; only believe, and she will be made well." 51 When He came into the house, He permitted no one to go in*a* except Peter, James, and John,*b* and the father and mother of the girl.

52 Now all wept and mourned for her; but He said, "Do not weep; she is not dead, but sleeping." 53 And they ridiculed Him, knowing that she was dead.

54 But He put them all outside,*a* took her by the hand and called, saying, "Little girl, arise." 55 Then her spirit returned, and she arose immediately. And He commanded that she be given *something* to eat. 56 And her parents were astonished, but He charged them to tell no one what had happened.

9 Then He called His twelve disciples together and gave them power and authority over all demons, and to cure diseases. 2 He sent them to preach the kingdom of God and to heal the sick. 3 And He said to them, "Take nothing for the journey, neither staffs nor bag nor bread nor money; and do not have two tunics apiece.

4 "Whatever house you enter, stay there, and from there depart. 5 And whoever will not receive you, when you go out of that city, shake off the very dust from your feet as a testimony against them."

6 So they departed and went through the towns, preaching the gospel and healing everywhere.

7 Now Herod the tetrarch heard of all that was done by Him; and he was perplexed, because it was said by some that John had risen from the dead, 8 and by some that Elijah had appeared, and by others that one of the old prophets had risen again. 9 Herod said, "John I have beheaded, but who is this of whom I hear such things?" So he sought to see Him.

10 And the apostles, when they had returned, told Him all that they had done. Then He took them and went aside privately into a deserted place belonging to the city called Bethsaida. 11 But when the multitudes knew *it,* they followed Him; and He received them and spoke to them about the kingdom of God, and healed those who had need of healing. 12 When the day began to wear away, the twelve came and said to Him, "Send the multitude away, that they may go into the surrounding

8:45 *a*NU-Text omits *and those with him.*   *b*NU-Text omits *and You say, 'Who touched Me?'*
8:48 *a*NU-Text omits *be of good cheer.*   8:49 *a*NU-Text adds *anymore.*   8:51 *a*NU-Text adds *with Him.*   *b*NU-Text and M-Text read *Peter, John, and James.*   8:54 *a*NU-Text omits *put them all outside.*

If God looses you from an infirmity and you aren't reconnected to something good and positive in your life, you are likely to seek out any old reconnection. You might even go back to the thing to which you were originally connected just because it's familiar.

Press On

Luke 8:43-46

The woman with the issue of blood faced two major challenges. One was the challenge of confronting her own self-doubt, wondering: *Can a woman like me touch a God like that?* The answer to that question is always yes.

The second challenge she faced was getting through the crowd. Once you make up your mind to get to Jesus, the devil will do everything he can to put obstacles in your way. There's always the flesh realm that you have to break through to get to God in the spirit realm. You have to say to those who doubt what you are doing, "Excuse me, but I'm on my way to Jesus, no matter what you say." You have to say to those who offer you their expert but ungodly opinions, "Excuse me, but I know where I'm going and if you'll just step out of my path, I'll be on my way." You have to say to those who want you to stop and stroke their egos, "Excuse me, but I don't have time for your games. I'm on my way to Jesus."

Don't let anything stand in your way. Step right over everything of the flesh that the devil puts before you and keep pushing forward to Jesus. When justice says you can't get to Him, God's mercy lets you by. When the law tries to stop you, God's grace opens up a door. When the world says, "Don't go," the Spirit of God says, "Come on." Our part is to press on. God's part is to make a way, to open up a path.

The enemy may be telling you that it is impossible for you to get up, get out, or get on with your life. I'm here to tell you that the devil is a liar! This woman pressed through the crowd. She pressed through the naysayers and the doomsayers. She pressed through the doctor's report and the pile of bills and the laws that were intended to shut her out. She made her way through the crowd of doubters and discouragers and the bad-news reporters. She pressed right on through the drug dealers on her doorstep, the pimps on her corner, and the gang circling her car. She pressed through!

When this woman with an issue of blood touched Jesus, she touched His life. His life poured into every area of her body where life had been draining away to nothing. His life filled up her lack of life. And His life will fill up your lack of life when you touch Him today.

towns and country, and lodge and get provisions; for we are in a deserted place here."

13 But He said to them, "You give them something to eat."

And they said, "We have no more than five loaves and two fish, unless we go and buy food for all these people." 14 For there were about five thousand men.

Then He said to His disciples, "Make them sit down in groups of fifty." 15 And they did so, and made them all sit down.

16 Then He took the five loaves and the two fish, and looking up to heaven, He blessed and broke *them,* and gave *them* to the disciples to set before the multitude. 17 So they all ate and were filled, and twelve baskets of the leftover fragments were taken up by them.

18 And it happened, as He was alone praying, *that* His disciples joined Him, and He asked them, saying, "Who do the crowds say that I am?"

19 So they answered and said, "John the Baptist, but some *say* Elijah; and others *say* that one of the old prophets has risen again."

20 He said to them, "But who do you say that I am?"

Peter answered and said, "The Christ of God."

21 And He strictly warned and commanded them to tell this to no one, 22 saying, "The Son of Man must suffer many things, and be rejected by the elders and chief priests and scribes, and be killed, and be raised the third day."

23 Then He said to *them* all, "If anyone desires to come after Me, let him deny himself, and take up his cross daily,*a* and follow Me. 24 For whoever desires to save his life will lose it, but whoever loses his life for My sake will save it. 25 For what profit is it to a man if he gains the whole world, and is himself destroyed or lost? 26 For whoever is ashamed of Me and My words, of him the Son of Man will be ashamed when He comes in His *own* glory, and *in His* Father's, and of the holy angels. 27 But I tell you truly, there are some standing here who shall not taste death till they see the kingdom of God."

28 Now it came to pass, about eight days after these sayings, that He took Peter, John, and James and went up on the mountain to pray. 29 As He prayed, the appearance of His face was altered, and His robe *became* white *and* glistening. 30 And behold, two men talked with Him, who were Moses and Elijah, 31 who appeared in glory and spoke of His decease which He was about to accomplish at Jerusalem. 32 But Peter and those with him were heavy with sleep; and when they were fully awake, they saw His glory and the two men who stood with Him. 33 Then it happened, as they were parting from Him, *that* Peter said to Jesus, "Master, it is good for us to be here; and let us make three tabernacles: one for You, one for Moses, and one for Elijah"— not knowing what he said.

34 While he was saying this, a cloud came and overshadowed them; and they were fearful as they entered the cloud. 35 And a voice came out of the cloud, saying, "This is My beloved Son.*a* Hear Him!" 36 When the voice had ceased, Jesus was found alone. But they kept quiet, and told no one in those days any of the things they had seen.

37 Now it happened on the next day, when they had come down from the mountain, that a great multitude met Him. 38 Suddenly a man from the multitude cried out, saying, "Teacher, I implore You, look on my son, for he is my only child. 39 And behold, a spirit seizes him, and he suddenly cries out; it convulses him so that he foams *at the mouth;* and it departs from him with great difficulty, bruising him. 40 So I implored Your disciples to cast it out, but they could not."

41 Then Jesus answered and said, "O faithless and perverse generation, how long shall I be with you and bear with you? Bring your son here." 42 And as he was still coming, the demon threw him down and convulsed *him.* Then Jesus rebuked the unclean spirit, healed the child, and gave him back to his father.

43 And they were all amazed at the majesty of God.

But while everyone marveled at all the things which Jesus did, He said to His disciples, 44 "Let these words

9:23 *a*M-Text omits *daily.*   9:35 *a*NU-Text reads *This is My Son, the Chosen One.*

Gospel Pearls

sink down into your ears, for the Son of Man is about to be betrayed into the hands of men." 45 But they did not understand this saying, and it was hidden from them so that they did not perceive it; and they were afraid to ask Him about this saying.

46 Then a dispute arose among them as to which of them would be greatest. 47 And Jesus, perceiving the thought of their heart, took a little child and set him by Him, 48 and said to them, "Whoever receives this little child in My name receives Me; and whoever receives Me receives Him who sent Me. For he who is least among you all will be great."

49 Now John answered and said, "Master, we saw someone casting out demons in Your name, and we forbade him because he does not follow with us."

50 But Jesus said to him, "Do not forbid *him,* for he who is not against us*a* is on our*b* side."

51 Now it came to pass, when the time had come for Him to be received up, that He steadfastly set His face to go to Jerusalem, 52 and sent messengers before His face. And as they went, they entered a village of the Samaritans, to prepare for Him. 53 But they did not receive Him, because His face was *set* for the journey to Jerusalem. 54 And when His disciples James and John saw *this,* they said, "Lord, do You want us to command fire to come down from heaven and consume them, just as Elijah did?"*a*

55 But He turned and rebuked them,*a* and said, "You do not know what manner of spirit you are of. 56 For the Son of Man did not come to destroy men's lives but to save *them.*"*a* And they went to another village.

57 Now it happened as they journeyed on the road, *that* someone said to Him, "Lord, I will follow You wherever You go."

58 And Jesus said to him, "Foxes have holes and birds of the air *have* nests, but the Son of Man has nowhere to lay *His* head."

59 Then He said to another, "Follow Me."

But he said, "Lord, let me first go and bury my father."

60 Jesus said to him, "Let the dead bury their own dead, but you go and preach the kingdom of God."

61 And another also said, "Lord, I will follow You, but let me first go *and* bid them farewell who are at my house."

62 But Jesus said to him, "No one, having put his hand to the plow, and looking back, is fit for the kingdom of God."

10 After these things the Lord appointed seventy others also,*a* and sent them two by two before His face into every city and place where He Himself was about to go. 2 Then He said to them, "The harvest truly *is* great, but the laborers *are* few; therefore pray the Lord of the harvest to send out laborers into His harvest. 3 Go your way; behold, I send you out as lambs among wolves. 4 Carry neither money bag, knapsack, nor sandals; and greet no one along the road. 5 But whatever house you enter, first say, 'Peace to this house.' 6 And if a son of peace is there, your peace will rest on it; if not, it will return to you. 7 And remain in the same house, eating and drinking such things as they give, for the laborer is worthy of his wages. Do not go from house to house. 8 Whatever city you enter, and they receive you, eat such things as are set before you. 9 And heal the sick there, and say to them, 'The kingdom of God has come near to you.' 10 But whatever city you enter, and they do not receive you, go out into its streets and say, 11 'The very dust of your city which clings to us*a* we wipe off against you. Nevertheless know this, that the kingdom of God has come near you.' 12 But*a* I say to you that it will be more tolerable in that Day for Sodom than for that city.

13 "Woe to you, Chorazin! Woe to you, Bethsaida! For if the mighty works which were done in you had been done in Tyre and Sidon, they would have repented long ago, sitting in sackcloth and ashes. 14 But it will be more tolerable for Tyre and Si-

---

9:50 *a*NU-Text reads you. *b*NU-Text reads your. 9:54 *a*NU-Text omits *just as Elijah did.*
9:55 *a*NU-Text omits the rest of this verse. 9:56 *a*NU-Text omits the first sentence of this verse.
10:1 *a*NU-Text reads *seventy-two others.* 10:11 *a*NU-Text reads *our feet.* 10:12 *a*NU-Text and M-Text omit *But.*

*Y*our praise is likely to be related directly to your former pain. The greater the pain, the greater your praise. If you have never been bound, you have no idea how good it feels to be free.

In the Now

Luke 9:60–62

People often talk about a woman being "in the know." I like to talk about a woman being "in the now."

There comes a time when you have to draw a line between now and then, between this and that. There comes a time when you must say, "That was then. This is now. I used to do that. Now I do this. I used to be that. Now I am this."

Part of your maturity—part of your growing up to be God's woman—is drawing a line between the unwashed, unsalted, unswaddled, cord-bound baby you used to be and the mature, ornamented woman in Christ that you are now.

There will come a time when you must declare that the crisis in your life is over. You didn't die. You didn't lose your mind. You didn't fall off the end of the earth. You didn't crumble into a heap. You are alive. You are strong. You are a survivor. You made it!

There will come a time when you must get rid of the rotting, decaying, dead bodies that you have been carrying around. Some women have been dragging around old relationships and old experiences so long that they've become accustomed to the stench of them. God says those things are dead. It's time for you to bury them so you can get on with the resurrection He has planned for you.

Make a decision today to bury anything that has pulled you down, held you back, kept you in despair, limited you, deceived you, or made you vulnerable. Throw it into the coffin and lower it into the ground. Declare "over" in your life everything you can't change and can't fix. Every childhood trauma. Every secret disgrace. Every memory of abuse. Every instance of rejection. Every addiction. Every fear. Every failure. All these must be buried in Christ Jesus!

Commit these things to the Lord once and for all. Give them to Him. Seal them in a grave forever. And arise. You have been cleaned up, freed, clothed, loved, and raised to maturity in Christ. It's time for you to experience His resurrection and live in the now.

don at the judgment than for you. 15 And you, Capernaum, who are exalted to heaven, will be brought down to Hades.*a* 16 He who hears you hears Me, he who rejects you rejects Me, and he who rejects Me rejects Him who sent Me."

17 Then the seventy*a* returned with joy, saying, "Lord, even the demons are subject to us in Your name."

18 And He said to them, "I saw Satan fall like lightning from heaven. 19 Behold, I give you the authority to trample on serpents and scorpions, and over all the power of the enemy, and nothing shall by any means hurt you. 20 Nevertheless do not rejoice in this, that the spirits are subject to you, but rather*a* rejoice because your names are written in heaven."

21 In that hour Jesus rejoiced in the Spirit and said, "I thank You, Father, Lord of heaven and earth, that You have hidden these things from *the* wise and prudent and revealed them to babes. Even so, Father, for so it seemed good in Your sight. 22 All*a* things have been delivered to Me by My Father, and no one knows who the Son is except the Father, and who the Father is except the Son, and *the one* to whom the Son wills to reveal *Him.*"

23 Then He turned to *His* disciples and said privately, "Blessed *are* the eyes which see the things you see; 24 for I tell you that many prophets and kings have desired to see what you see, and have not seen *it,* and to hear what you hear, and have not heard *it.*"

25 And behold, a certain lawyer stood up and tested Him, saying, "Teacher, what shall I do to inherit eternal life?"

26 He said to him, "What is written in the law? What is your reading *of it?*"

27 So he answered and said, "'*You shall love the* LORD *your God with all your heart, with all your soul, with all your strength, and with all your mind,'a* and '*your neighbor as yourself.*'*b*"

28 And He said to him, "You have answered rightly; do this and you will live."

29 But he, wanting to justify himself, said to Jesus, "And who is my neighbor?"

30 Then Jesus answered and said: "A certain *man* went down from Jerusalem to Jericho, and fell among thieves, who stripped him of his clothing, wounded *him,* and departed, leaving *him* half dead. 31 Now by chance a certain priest came down that road. And when he saw him, he passed by on the other side. 32 Likewise a Levite, when he arrived at the place, came and looked, and passed by on the other side. 33 But a certain Samaritan, as he journeyed, came where he was. And when he saw him, he had compassion. 34 So he went to *him* and bandaged his wounds, pouring on oil and wine; and he set him on his own animal, brought him to an inn, and took care of him. 35 On the next day, when he departed,*a* he took out two denarii, gave *them* to the innkeeper, and said to him, 'Take care of him; and whatever more you spend, when I come again, I will repay you.' 36 So which of these three do you think was neighbor to him who fell among the thieves?"

37 And he said, "He who showed mercy on him."

Then Jesus said to him, "Go and do likewise."

38 Now it happened as they went that He entered a certain village; and a certain woman named Martha welcomed Him into her house. 39 And she had a sister called Mary, who also sat at Jesus'*a* feet and heard His word. 40 But Martha was distracted with much serving, and she approached Him and said, "Lord, do You not care that my sister has left me to serve alone? Therefore tell her to help me."

41 And Jesus*a* answered and said to her, "Martha, Martha, you are worried and troubled about many things. 42 But one thing is needed, and Mary has chosen that good part, which will not be taken away from her."

11 Now it came to pass, as He was praying in a certain place,

10:15 *a*NU-Text reads *will you be exalted to heaven? You will be thrust down to Hades!*
10:17 *a*NU-Text reads *seventy-two.* 10:20 *a*NU-Text and M-Text omit *rather.* 10:22 *a*M-Text reads *And turning to the disciples He said, "All . . . .* 10:27 *a*Deuteronomy 6:5 *b*Leviticus 19:18 10:35 *a*NU-Text omits *when he departed.* 10:39 *a*NU-Text reads *the Lord's.* 10:41 *a*NU-Text reads *the Lord.*

*T*here's an undercurrent of criticism that always coexists with praise. There will always be somebody in every praise service who is sitting in the corner criticizing the praise. Don't pay attention to them.

Soul Secrets
of a single woman

*L*ord, it seems I've been through it all—desperation for a man, contentment in You, wondering if I'll *ever* get married, and being a bridesmaid more times than I can count.

I know what it is for a dream to be delayed, but I trust Your perfect timing for my life. What I want is Your very best. I submit to You and to the work of Your hand in my life. I rejoice that, in my singleness, You are my only love. You are the One I share my secrets with, the One who knows me better than I know myself.

All my tender touches come from You and that is an amazing blessing. My whole heart is Yours and You have sanctified me for this season. Lord, You are the greatest Lover of all. I belong to You.

when He ceased, *that* one of His disciples said to Him, "Lord, teach us to pray, as John also taught his disciples."

2 So He said to them, "When you pray, say:

> Our Father in heaven,*a*
> Hallowed be Your name.
> Your kingdom come.*b*
> Your will be done
> On earth as *it is* in heaven.
> 3 Give us day by day our daily
>   bread.
> 4 And forgive us our sins,
>   For we also forgive everyone
>   who is indebted to us.
>   And do not lead us into
>   temptation,
>   But deliver us from the evil
>   one."*a*

5 And He said to them, "Which of you shall have a friend, and go to him at midnight and say to him, 'Friend, lend me three loaves; 6 for a friend of mine has come to me on his journey, and I have nothing to set before him'; 7 and he will answer from within and say, 'Do not trouble me; the door is now shut, and my children are with me in bed; I cannot rise and give to you'? 8 I say to you, though he will not rise and give to him because he is his friend, yet because of his persistence he will rise and give him as many as he needs.

9 "So I say to you, ask, and it will be given to you; seek, and you will find; knock, and it will be opened to you. 10 For everyone who asks receives, and he who seeks finds, and to him who knocks it will be opened. 11 If a son asks for bread*a* from any father among you, will he give him a stone? Or if *he asks* for a fish, will he give him a serpent instead of a fish? 12 Or if he asks for an egg, will he offer him a scorpion? 13 If you then, being evil, know how to give good gifts to your children, how much more will *your* heavenly Father give the Holy Spirit to those who ask Him!"

14 And He was casting out a demon, and it was mute. So it was, when the demon had gone out, that the mute spoke; and the multitudes marveled. 15 But some of them said, "He casts out demons by Beelzebub,*a* the ruler of the demons."

16 Others, testing *Him,* sought from Him a sign from heaven. 17 But He, knowing their thoughts, said to them: "Every kingdom divided against itself is brought to desolation, and a house *divided* against a house falls. 18 If Satan also is divided against himself, how will his kingdom stand? Because you say I cast out demons by Beelzebub. 19 And if I cast out demons by Beelzebub, by whom do your sons cast *them* out? Therefore they will be your judges. 20 But if I cast out demons with the finger of God, surely the kingdom of God has come upon you. 21 When a strong man, fully armed, guards his own palace, his goods are in peace. 22 But when a stronger than he comes upon him and overcomes him, he takes from him all his armor in which he trusted, and divides his spoils. 23 He who is not with Me is against Me, and he who does not gather with Me scatters.

24 "When an unclean spirit goes out of a man, he goes through dry places, seeking rest; and finding none, he says, 'I will return to my house from which I came.' 25 And when he comes, he finds *it* swept and put in order. 26 Then he goes and takes with *him* seven other spirits more wicked than himself, and they enter and dwell there; and the last *state* of that man is worse than the first."

27 And it happened, as He spoke these things, that a certain woman from the crowd raised her voice and said to Him, "Blessed *is* the womb that bore You, and *the* breasts which nursed You!"

28 But He said, "More than that, blessed *are* those who hear the word of God and keep it!"

29 And while the crowds were thickly gathered together, He began to say, "This is an evil generation. It seeks a sign, and no sign will be given to it except the sign of Jonah the prophet.*a* 30 For as Jonah became a sign to the Ninevites, so also the Son of Man will be to this generation. 31 The queen of the South will rise

---

11:2 *a*NU-Text omits *Our* and *in heaven.*   *b*NU-Text omits the rest of this verse.   11:4 *a*NU-Text omits *But deliver us from the evil one.*   11:11 *a*NU-Text omits the words from *bread* through *for* in the next sentence.   11:15 *a*NU-Text and M-Text read *Beelzebul.*   11:29 *a*NU-Text omits *the prophet.*

*P*eople seem to get very excited when talented folks are delivered. They don't get as excited when ordinary people are set free from their infirmities. I've got good news for you today—God doesn't make that differentiation. He desires to see needs met for everyone.

up in the judgment with the men of this generation and condemn them, for she came from the ends of the earth to hear the wisdom of Solomon; and indeed a greater than Solomon *is* here. 32 The men of Nineveh will rise up in the judgment with this generation and condemn it, for they repented at the preaching of Jonah; and indeed a greater than Jonah *is* here.

33 "No one, when he has lit a lamp, puts *it* in a secret place or under a basket, but on a lampstand, that those who come in may see the light. 34 The lamp of the body is the eye. Therefore, when your eye is good, your whole body also is full of light. But when *your eye* is bad, your body also *is* full of darkness. 35 Therefore take heed that the light which is in you is not darkness. 36 If then your whole body *is* full of light, having no part dark, *the* whole *body* will be full of light, as when the bright shining of a lamp gives you light."

37 And as He spoke, a certain Pharisee asked Him to dine with him. So He went in and sat down to eat. 38 When the Pharisee saw *it*, he marveled that He had not first washed before dinner.

39 Then the Lord said to him, "Now you Pharisees make the outside of the cup and dish clean, but your inward part is full of greed and wickedness. 40 Foolish ones! Did not He who made the outside make the inside also? 41 But rather give alms of such things as you have; then indeed all things are clean to you.

42 "But woe to you Pharisees! For you tithe mint and rue and all manner of herbs, and pass by justice and the love of God. These you ought to have done, without leaving the others undone. 43 Woe to you Pharisees! For you love the best seats in the synagogues and greetings in the marketplaces. 44 Woe to you, scribes and Pharisees, hypocrites!*a* For you are like graves which are not seen, and the men who walk over *them* are not aware *of them*."

45 Then one of the lawyers answered and said to Him, "Teacher, by saying these things You reproach us also."

46 And He said, "Woe to you also,

lawyers! For you load men with burdens hard to bear, and you yourselves do not touch the burdens with one of your fingers. 47 Woe to you! For you build the tombs of the prophets, and your fathers killed them. 48 In fact, you bear witness that you approve the deeds of your fathers; for they indeed killed them, and you build their tombs. 49 Therefore the wisdom of God also said, 'I will send them prophets and apostles, and *some* of them they will kill and persecute,' 50 that the blood of all the prophets which was shed from the foundation of the world may be required of this generation, 51 from the blood of Abel to the blood of Zechariah who perished between the altar and the temple. Yes, I say to you, it shall be required of this generation.

52 "Woe to you lawyers! For you have taken away the key of knowledge. You did not enter in yourselves, and those who were entering in you hindered."

53 And as He said these things to them,*a* the scribes and the Pharisees began to assail *Him* vehemently, and to cross-examine Him about many things, 54 lying in wait for Him, and seeking to catch Him in something He might say, that they might accuse Him.*a*

12 In the meantime, when an innumerable multitude of people had gathered together, so that they trampled one another, He began to say to His disciples first *of all,* "Beware of the leaven of the Pharisees, which is hypocrisy. 2 For there is nothing covered that will not be revealed, nor hidden that will not be known. 3 Therefore whatever you have spoken in the dark will be heard in the light, and what you have spoken in the ear in inner rooms will be proclaimed on the housetops.

4 "And I say to you, My friends, do not be afraid of those who kill the body, and after that have no more that they can do. 5 But I will show you whom you should fear: Fear Him who, after He has killed, has power to cast into hell; yes, I say to you, fear Him!

6 "Are not five sparrows sold for

11:44 *a*NU-Text omits *scribes and Pharisees, hypocrites.*   11:53 *a*NU-Text reads *And when He left there.*   11:54 *a*NU-Text omits *and seeking* and *that they might accuse Him.*

Gospel Pearls

two copper coins?[a] And not one of them is forgotten before God. 7 But the very hairs of your head are all numbered. Do not fear therefore; you are of more value than many sparrows.

8 "Also I say to you, whoever confesses Me before men, him the Son of Man also will confess before the angels of God. 9 But he who denies Me before men will be denied before the angels of God.

10 "And anyone who speaks a word against the Son of Man, it will be forgiven him; but to him who blasphemes against the Holy Spirit, it will not be forgiven.

11 "Now when they bring you to the synagogues and magistrates and authorities, do not worry about how or what you should answer, or what you should say. 12 For the Holy Spirit will teach you in that very hour what you ought to say."

13 Then one from the crowd said to Him, "Teacher, tell my brother to divide the inheritance with me."

14 But He said to him, "Man, who made Me a judge or an arbitrator over you?" 15 And He said to them, "Take heed and beware of covetousness,[a] for one's life does not consist in the abundance of the things he possesses."

16 Then He spoke a parable to them, saying: "The ground of a certain rich man yielded plentifully. 17 And he thought within himself, saying, 'What shall I do, since I have no room to store my crops?' 18 So he said, 'I will do this: I will pull down my barns and build greater, and there I will store all my crops and my goods. 19 And I will say to my soul, "Soul, you have many goods laid up for many years; take your ease; eat, drink, *and* be merry." ' 20 But God said to him, 'Fool! This night your soul will be required of you; then whose will those things be which you have provided?'

21 "So *is* he who lays up treasure for himself, and is not rich toward God."

22 Then He said to His disciples, "Therefore I say to you, do not worry about your life, what you will eat; nor about the body, what you will put on. 23 Life is more than food, and the body *is more* than clothing. 24 Consider the ravens, for they neither sow nor reap, which have neither storehouse nor barn; and God feeds them. Of how much more value are you than the birds? 25 And which of you by worrying can add one cubit to his stature? 26 If you then are not able to do *the* least, why are you anxious for the rest? 27 Consider the lilies, how they grow: they neither toil nor spin; and yet I say to you, even Solomon in all his glory was not arrayed like one of these. 28 If then God so clothes the grass, which today is in the field and tomorrow is thrown into the oven, how much more *will He clothe* you, O *you* of little faith?

29 "And do not seek what you should eat or what you should drink, nor have an anxious mind. 30 For all these things the nations of the world seek after, and your Father knows that you need these things. 31 But seek the kingdom of God, and all these things[a] shall be added to you.

32 "Do not fear, little flock, for it is your Father's good pleasure to give you the kingdom. 33 Sell what you have and give alms; provide yourselves money bags which do not grow old, a treasure in the heavens that does not fail, where no thief approaches nor moth destroys. 34 For where your treasure is, there your heart will be also.

35 "Let your waist be girded and *your* lamps burning; 36 and you yourselves be like men who wait for their master, when he will return from the wedding, that when he comes and knocks they may open to him immediately. 37 Blessed *are* those servants whom the master, when he comes, will find watching. Assuredly, I say to you that he will gird himself and have them sit down *to eat,* and will come and serve them. 38 And if he should come in the second watch, or come in the third watch, and find *them* so, blessed are those servants. 39 But know this, that if the master of the house had known what hour the thief would come, he would have watched and[a] not allowed his house to be broken into. 40 Therefore you also be ready, for the Son of Man is coming at an hour you do not expect."

12:6 [a]Greek *assarion,* a coin of very small value   12:15 [a]NU-Text reads *all covetousness.*
12:31 [a]NU-Text reads *His kingdom, and these things.*   12:39 [a]NU-Text reads *he would not have allowed.*

God has delivered countless people who have never written a book about their experience, or who have never gone on to lead the choir or sing a solo or chair a committee or teach a Sunday school class. God's deliverance is not contingent upon what you will do after you're delivered.

The God Who Loves to Give

Luke 12:32

A real father is giving and generous. He is wise in that he will not give to the point of destruction. He doesn't want to damage the character of his children, but he longs, nevertheless, to lavish gifts upon them. In fact, most men express love through giving. If you ask a man, "Do you love me?," he will almost always make reference to what he gives you. The giving of things is one of the ways we men express affection and ascribe value. I realize that there are other gifts, such as time and attention, that may seem more beneficial to you. But remember, if a man is not dysfunctional or disadvantaged, he loves to give.

Giving opens for us an avenue of expressing affection without being encumbered with words. If you knew your Father's love, you would run to Him. He gets as much out of giving as you get from receiving.

It is sad to say that many girls will never experience firsthand the love of an earthly father. Somehow they have been denied the privilege of cultivating a wholesome relationship with their natural father. However, even they will recapture what they lost as they come to know their heavenly Father.

Do you know Him? I mean, really know Him? Or is He a stranger, a foreign concept with no point of reference from your past by which He may define Himself? If you don't know your heavenly Father, you are missing a wonderful chance to touch a loving Father. He is not irresponsible. Neither is He insensitive nor selfish. Curl up in His arms. I know you will be, as the old hymn says, "safe and secure from all alarms."

It is wonderful to realize that the Father stands ready to reveal His love in your life. He is the real Father whom the rest of us imitate poorly at best, and probably frustrate as we stumble through our machismo trying to achieve the gift of relationship! He is the reality of which an earthly father can only be abstract. If you have had a good father, He is all of that and more. If your dad has failed, blame him—not God. He never fails!

41 Then Peter said to Him, "Lord, do You speak this parable *only* to us, or to all *people?*"

42 And the Lord said, "Who then is that faithful and wise steward, whom *his* master will make ruler over his household, to give *them their* portion of food in due season? 43 Blessed *is* that servant whom his master will find so doing when he comes. 44 Truly, I say to you that he will make him ruler over all that he has. 45 But if that servant says in his heart, 'My master is delaying his coming,' and begins to beat the male and female servants, and to eat and drink and be drunk, 46 the master of that servant will come on a day when he is not looking for *him,* and at an hour when he is not aware, and will cut him in two and appoint *him* his portion with the unbelievers. 47 And that servant who knew his master's will, and did not prepare *himself* or do according to his will, shall be beaten with many *stripes.* 48 But he who did not know, yet committed things deserving of stripes, shall be beaten with few. For everyone to whom much is given, from him much will be required; and to whom much has been committed, of him they will ask the more.

49 "I came to send fire on the earth, and how I wish it were already kindled! 50 But I have a baptism to be baptized with, and how distressed I am till it is accomplished! 51 Do *you* suppose that I came to give peace on earth? I tell you, not at all, but rather division. 52 For from now on five in one house will be divided: three against two, and two against three. 53 Father will be divided against son and son against father, mother against daughter and daughter against mother, mother-in-law against her daughter-in-law and daughter-in-law against her mother-in-law."

54 Then He also said to the multitudes, "Whenever *you see* a cloud rising out of the west, immediately you say, 'A shower is coming'; and so it is. 55 And when you see the south wind blow, you say, 'There will be hot weather'; and there is. 56 Hypocrites! You can discern the face of the sky and of the earth, but how *is it* you do not discern this time?

57 "Yes, and why, even of yourselves, do you not judge what is right? 58 When you go with your adversary to the magistrate, make every effort along the way to settle with him, lest he drag you to the judge, the judge deliver you to the officer, and the officer throw you into prison. 59 I tell you, you shall not depart from there till you have paid the very last mite."

13 There were present at that season some who told Him about the Galileans whose blood Pilate had mingled with their sacrifices. 2 And Jesus answered and said to them, "Do you suppose that these Galileans were worse sinners than all *other* Galileans, because they suffered such things? 3 I tell you, no; but unless you repent you will all likewise perish. 4 Or those eighteen on whom the tower in Siloam fell and killed them, do you think that they were worse sinners than all *other* men who dwelt in Jerusalem? 5 I tell you, no; but unless you repent you will all likewise perish."

6 He also spoke this parable: "A certain *man* had a fig tree planted in his vineyard, and he came seeking fruit on it and found none. 7 Then he said to the keeper of his vineyard, 'Look, for three years I have come seeking fruit on this fig tree and find none. Cut it down; why does it use up the ground?' 8 But he answered and said to him, 'Sir, let it alone this year also, until I dig around it and fertilize *it.* 9 And if it bears fruit, *well.* But if not, after that[a] you can cut it down.'"

10 Now He was teaching in one of the synagogues on the Sabbath. 11 And behold, there was a woman who had a spirit of infirmity eighteen years, and was bent over and could in no way raise *herself* up. 12 But when Jesus saw her, He called *her* to *Him* and said to her, "Woman, you are loosed from your infirmity." 13 And He laid *His* hands on her, and immediately she was made straight, and glorified God.

14 But the ruler of the synagogue answered with indignation, because Jesus had healed on the Sabbath; and he said to the crowd, "There are six days on which men ought to work;

13:9 [a]NU-Text reads *And if it bears fruit after that, well. But if not, you can cut it down.*

*P*eople try to keep other people "in their place" so they can control them—so they can lead them to what it is that they want them to have, and to nothing else. When you are delivered by God, you may need to say no to those who have kept you in a stall of their own making.

The Infirm Woman

Luke 13:11, 12

This woman's dilemma is her own, but perhaps you will find some point of relativity between her case history and your own. There are three major characters in this story: the person, the problem, and the prescription. It is important to remember that for every person, there will be a problem. Even more importantly, for every problem, our God has a prescription.

This woman was suffering as a result of something that had attacked her eighteen years earlier. Can you relate to that kind of trauma? Although a problem may be rooted in the past, the prescription is a present word from God. God's Word is the same yesterday, today, and forever (Hebrews 13:8). That is to say, the word you hear today is able to heal your yesterday!

Jesus said, "Woman, thou art loosed." He did not call her by name. He wasn't speaking to her just as a person. He spoke to her femininity. He spoke to the song in her. He spoke to the lace in her. I believe that the Lord spoke to the twinkle that existed in her eye when she was a child, to the girlish glow that makeup can never seem to recapture. He spoke to her God-given uniqueness.

This woman had a problem—a physical infirmity—for eighteen years. She had a personal war waging inside of her. You may have a physical problem, like this woman did. Or you may be suffering from an emotional trauma, which can be just as challenging. Many things can engender physical and emotional troubles. In this woman's case, a spirit of infirmity had gripped her life. A spirit can manifest itself in many forms. For some, it may be low self-esteem caused by abuse, rape, or divorce, among other things. I realize that these are natural problems, but they are rooted in spiritual ailments. And only the Master can heal spiritual hurts.

One of the greatest healing balms of the Holy Spirit is forgiveness. Forgiveness breaks the link between you and your past. Whatever you do, refuse to blame and choose to forgive. There is no healing in blame. When you begin to realize that your past does not necessarily dictate your future, then you can release your hurt. It is impossible to inhale new fresh air until you exhale the old. Get rid of that old air. There is more for you.

I remember, as a child, when my mother would take the bandage off a cut or scrape, wash it, and say, "Things that are covered don't heal well." She was right. Perhaps Jesus was thinking along these lines when he called the infirm woman to come forward. The Lord is the Great Physician who pours healing oil on all our wounds. Uncover your wounds in His presence and allow Him to gently heal you.

therefore come and be healed on them, and not on the Sabbath day."

15 The Lord then answered him and said, "Hypocrite!ᵃ Does not each one of you on the Sabbath loose his ox or donkey from the stall, and lead *it* away to water it? 16 So ought not this woman, being a daughter of Abraham, whom Satan has bound— think of it—for eighteen years, be loosed from this bond on the Sabbath?" 17 And when He said these things, all His adversaries were put to shame; and all the multitude rejoiced for all the glorious things that were done by Him.

18 Then He said, "What is the kingdom of God like? And to what shall I compare it? 19 It is like a mustard seed, which a man took and put in his garden; and it grew and became a largeᵃ tree, and the birds of the air nested in its branches."

20 And again He said, "To what shall I liken the kingdom of God? 21 It is like leaven, which a woman took and hid in three measuresᵃ of meal till it was all leavened."

22 And He went through the cities and villages, teaching, and journeying toward Jerusalem. 23 Then one said to Him, "Lord, are there few who are saved?"

And He said to them, 24 "Strive to enter through the narrow gate, for many, I say to you, will seek to enter and will not be able. 25 When once the Master of the house has risen up and shut the door, and you begin to stand outside and knock at the door, saying, 'Lord, Lord, open for us,' and He will answer and say to you, 'I do not know you, where you are from,' 26 then you will begin to say, 'We ate and drank in Your presence, and You taught in our streets.' 27 But He will say, 'I tell you I do not know you, where you are from. Depart from Me, all you workers of iniquity.' 28 There will be weeping and gnashing of teeth, when you see Abraham and Isaac and Jacob and all the prophets in the kingdom of God, and yourselves thrust out. 29 They will come from the east and the west, from the north and the south, and sit down in the kingdom of God. 30 And indeed there are last who will

be first, and there are first who will be last."

31 On that very dayᵃ some Pharisees came, saying to Him, "Get out and depart from here, for Herod wants to kill You."

32 And He said to them, "Go, tell that fox, 'Behold, I cast out demons and perform cures today and tomorrow, and the third *day* I shall be perfected.' 33 Nevertheless I must journey today, tomorrow, and the *day* following; for it cannot be that a prophet should perish outside of Jerusalem.

34 "O Jerusalem, Jerusalem, the one who kills the prophets and stones those who are sent to her! How often I wanted to gather your children together, as a hen *gathers* her brood under *her* wings, but you were not willing! 35 See! Your house is left to you desolate; and assuredly,ᵃ I say to you, you shall not see Me until *the time* comes when you say, '*Blessed is He who comes in the name of the LORD!*'"ᵇ

14 Now it happened, as He went into the house of one of the rulers of the Pharisees to eat bread on the Sabbath, that they watched Him closely. 2 And behold, there was a certain man before Him who had dropsy. 3 And Jesus, answering, spoke to the lawyers and Pharisees, saying, "Is it lawful to heal on the Sabbath?"ᵃ

4 But they kept silent. And He took *him* and healed him, and let him go. 5 Then He answered them, saying, "Which of you, having a donkeyᵃ or an ox that has fallen into a pit, will not immediately pull him out on the Sabbath day?" 6 And they could not answer Him regarding these things.

7 So He told a parable to those who were invited, when He noted how they chose the best places, saying to them: 8 "When you are invited by anyone to a wedding feast, do not sit down in the best place, lest one more honorable than you be invited by him; 9 and he who invited you and him come and say to you, 'Give place to this man,' and then you begin with shame to take the lowest place. 10 But when you are invited, go and

---

13:15 ᵃNU-Text and M-Text read *Hypocrites*.   13:19 ᵃNU-Text omits *large*.   13:21 ᵃGreek *sata*, approximately two pecks in all   13:31 ᵃNU-Text reads *In that very hour*.   13:35 ᵃNU-Text and M-Text omit *assuredly*.   ᵇPsalm 118:26   14:3 ᵃNU-Text adds *or not*.   14:5 ᵃNU-Text and M-Text read *son*.

---

*I*f you are a child of God and you fall in the mud, you'll start to cry. Whether you fall into the mud or someone throws you into the mud is not the issue. What you do when you are in the mud is what matters.

sit down in the lowest place, so that when he who invited you comes he may say to you, 'Friend, go up higher.' Then you will have glory in the presence of those who sit at the table with you. 11 For whoever exalts himself will be humbled, and he who humbles himself will be exalted.''

12 Then He also said to him who invited Him, ''When you give a dinner or a supper, do not ask your friends, your brothers, your relatives, nor rich neighbors, lest they also invite you back, and you be repaid. 13 But when you give a feast, invite *the* poor, *the* maimed, *the* lame, *the* blind. 14 And you will be blessed, because they cannot repay you; for you shall be repaid at the resurrection of the just.''

15 Now when one of those who sat at the table with Him heard these things, he said to Him, ''Blessed *is* he who shall eat bread*ᵃ* in the kingdom of God!''

16 Then He said to him, ''A certain man gave a great supper and invited many, 17 and sent his servant at supper time to say to those who were invited, 'Come, for all things are now ready.' 18 But they all with one *accord* began to make excuses. The first said to him, 'I have bought a piece of ground, and I must go and see it. I ask you to have me excused.' 19 And another said, 'I have bought five yoke of oxen, and I am going to test them. I ask you to have me excused.' 20 Still another said, 'I have married a wife, and therefore I cannot come.' 21 So that servant came and reported these things to his master. Then the master of the house, being angry, said to his servant, 'Go out quickly into the streets and lanes of the city, and bring in here *the* poor and *the* maimed and *the* lame and *the* blind.' 22 And the servant said, 'Master, it is done as you commanded, and still there is room.' 23 Then the master said to the servant, 'Go out into the highways and hedges, and compel *them* to come in, that my house may be filled. 24 For I say to you that none of those men who were invited shall taste my supper.' ''

25 Now great multitudes went with Him. And He turned and said to them, 26 ''If anyone comes to Me and does not hate his father and mother, wife and children, brothers and sisters, yes, and his own life also, he cannot be My disciple. 27 And whoever does not bear his cross and come after Me cannot be My disciple. 28 For which of you, intending to build a tower, does not sit down first and count the cost, whether he has *enough* to finish *it*— 29 lest, after he has laid the foundation, and is not able to finish, all who see *it* begin to mock him, 30 saying, 'This man began to build and was not able to finish.' 31 Or what king, going to make war against another king, does not sit down first and consider whether he is able with ten thousand to meet him who comes against him with twenty thousand? 32 Or else, while the other is still a great way off, he sends a delegation and asks conditions of peace. 33 So likewise, whoever of you does not forsake all that he has cannot be My disciple.

34 ''Salt *is* good; but if the salt has lost its flavor, how shall it be seasoned? 35 It is neither fit for the land nor for the dunghill, *but* men throw it out. He who has ears to hear, let him hear!''

15 Then all the tax collectors and the sinners drew near to Him to hear Him. 2 And the Pharisees and scribes complained, saying, ''This Man receives sinners and eats with them.'' 3 So He spoke this parable to them, saying:

4 ''What man of you, having a hundred sheep, if he loses one of them, does not leave the ninety-nine in the wilderness, and go after the one which is lost until he finds it? 5 And when he has found *it,* he lays *it* on his shoulders, rejoicing. 6 And when he comes home, he calls together *his* friends and neighbors, saying to them, 'Rejoice with me, for I have found my sheep which was lost!' 7 I say to you that likewise there will be more joy in heaven over one sinner who repents than over ninety-nine just persons who need no repentance.

8 ''Or what woman, having ten silver coins,*ᵃ* if she loses one coin, does not light a lamp, sweep the house,

---

14:15 *ᵃ*M-Text reads *dinner.*   15:8 *ᵃ*Greek *drachma,* a valuable coin often worn in a ten-piece garland by married women

Gospel
Pearls

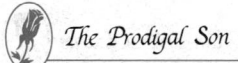

and search carefully until she finds *it*? 9 And when she has found *it*, she calls *her* friends and neighbors together, saying, 'Rejoice with me, for I have found the piece which I lost!' 10 Likewise, I say to you, there is joy in the presence of the angels of God over one sinner who repents."

11 **Then He said:** "A certain man had two sons. 12.And the younger of them said to *his* father, 'Father, give me the portion of goods that falls *to me*.' So he divided to them *his* livelihood. 13 And not many days after, the younger son gathered all together, journeyed to a far country, and there wasted his possessions with prodigal living. 14 But when he had spent all, there arose a severe famine in that land, and he began to be in want. 15 Then he went and joined himself to a citizen of that country, and he sent him into his fields to feed swine. 16 And he would gladly have filled his stomach with the pods that the swine ate, and no one gave him *anything*.

17 "But when he came to himself, he said, 'How many of my father's hired servants have bread enough and to spare, and I perish with hunger! 18 I will arise and go to my father, and will say to him, "Father, I have sinned against heaven and before you, 19 and I am no longer worthy to be called your son. Make me like one of your hired servants." '

20 "And he arose and came to his father. But when he was still a great way off, his father saw him and had compassion, and ran and fell on his neck and kissed him. 21 And the son said to him, 'Father, I have sinned against heaven and in your sight, and am no longer worthy to be called your son.'

22 "But the father said to his servants, 'Bring*a* out the best robe and put *it* on him, and put a ring on his hand and sandals on *his* feet. 23 And bring the fatted calf here and kill *it*, and let us eat and be merry; 24 for this my son was dead and is alive again; he was lost and is found.' And they began to be merry.

25 "Now his older son was in the field. And as he came and drew near to the house, he heard music and dancing. 26 So he called one of the servants and asked what these things

meant. 27 And he said to him, 'Your brother has come, and because he has received him safe and sound, your father has killed the fatted calf.'

28 "But he was angry and would not go in. Therefore his father came out and pleaded with him. 29 So he answered and said to *his* father, 'Lo, these many years I have been serving you; I never transgressed your commandment at any time; and yet you never gave me a young goat, that I might make merry with my friends. 30 But as soon as this son of yours came, who has devoured your livelihood with harlots, you killed the fatted calf for him.'

31 "And he said to him, 'Son, you are always with me, and all that I have is yours. 32 It was right that we should make merry and be glad, for your brother was dead and is alive again, and was lost and is found.' "

16 He also said to His disciples: "There was a certain rich man who had a steward, and an accusation was brought to him that this man was wasting his goods. 2 So he called him and said to him, 'What is this I hear about you? Give an account of your stewardship, for you can no longer be steward.'

3 "Then the steward said within himself, 'What shall I do? For my master is taking the stewardship away from me. I cannot dig; I am ashamed to beg. 4 I have resolved what to do, that when I am put out of the stewardship, they may receive me into their houses.'

5 "So he called every one of his master's debtors to *him*, and said to the first, 'How much do you owe my master?' 6 And he said, 'A hundred measures*a* of oil.' So he said to him, 'Take your bill, and sit down quickly and write fifty.' 7 Then he said to another, 'And how much do you owe?' So he said, 'A hundred measures*a* of wheat.' And he said to him, 'Take your bill, and write eighty.' 8 So the master commended the unjust steward because he had dealt shrewdly. For the sons of this world are more shrewd in their generation than the sons of light.

9 "And I say to you, make friends for yourselves by unrighteous mam-

15:22 *a*NU-Text reads *Quickly bring.*   16:6 *a*Greek *batos,* eight or nine gallons each (Old Testament *bath*)   16:7 *a*Greek *koros,* ten or twelve bushels each (Old Testament *kor*)

Conduct your own funeral for the "old person" you were before you were saved. Declare that the old you—the you who existed before God found you and cleaned you up and grew you up to be His woman—is dead. She doesn't exist anymore.

mon, that when you fail,[a] they may receive you into an everlasting home. 10 He who *is* faithful in *what is* least is faithful also in much; and he who is unjust in *what is* least is unjust also in much. 11 Therefore if you have not been faithful in the unrighteous mammon, who will commit to your trust the true *riches*? 12 And if you have not been faithful in what is another man's, who will give you what is your own?

13 "No servant can serve two masters; for either he will hate the one and love the other, or else he will be loyal to the one and despise the other. You cannot serve God and mammon."

14 Now the Pharisees, who were lovers of money, also heard all these things, and they derided Him. 15 And He said to them, "You are those who justify yourselves before men, but God knows your hearts. For what is highly esteemed among men is an abomination in the sight of God.

16 "The law and the prophets *were* until John. Since that time the kingdom of God has been preached, and everyone is pressing into it. 17 And it is easier for heaven and earth to pass away than for one tittle of the law to fail.

18 "Whoever divorces his wife and marries another commits adultery; and whoever marries her who is divorced from *her* husband commits adultery.

19 "There was a certain rich man who was clothed in purple and fine linen and fared sumptuously every day. 20 But there was a certain beggar named Lazarus, full of sores, who was laid at his gate, 21 desiring to be fed with the crumbs which fell[a] from the rich man's table. Moreover the dogs came and licked his sores. 22 So it was that the beggar died, and was carried by the angels to Abraham's bosom. The rich man also died and was buried. 23 And being in torments in Hades, he lifted up his eyes and saw Abraham afar off, and Lazarus in his bosom.

24 "Then he cried and said, 'Father Abraham, have mercy on me, and send Lazarus that he may dip the tip of his finger in water and cool my tongue; for I am tormented in this flame.' 25 But Abraham said, 'Son, remember that in your lifetime you received your good things, and likewise Lazarus evil things; but now he is comforted and you are tormented. 26 And besides all this, between us and you there is a great gulf fixed, so that those who want to pass from here to you cannot, nor can those from there pass to us.'

27 "Then he said, 'I beg you therefore, father, that you would send him to my father's house, 28 for I have five brothers, that he may testify to them, lest they also come to this place of torment.' 29 Abraham said to him, 'They have Moses and the prophets; let them hear them.' 30 And he said, 'No, father Abraham; but if one goes to them from the dead, they will repent.' 31 But he said to him, 'If they do not hear Moses and the prophets, neither will they be persuaded though one rise from the dead.' "

17 Then He said to the disciples, "It is impossible that no offenses should come, but woe *to him* through whom they do come! 2 It would be better for him if a millstone were hung around his neck, and he were thrown into the sea, than that he should offend one of these little ones. 3 Take heed to yourselves. If your brother sins against you,[a] rebuke him; and if he repents, forgive him. 4 And if he sins against you seven times in a day, and seven times in a day returns to you,[a] saying, 'I repent,' you shall forgive him."

5 And the apostles said to the Lord, "Increase our faith."

6 So the Lord said, "If you have faith as a mustard seed, you can say to this mulberry tree, 'Be pulled up by the roots and be planted in the sea,' and it would obey you. 7 And which of you, having a servant plowing or tending sheep, will say to him when he has come in from the field, 'Come at once and sit down to eat'? 8 But will he not rather say to him, 'Prepare something for my supper, and gird yourself and serve me till I have eaten and drunk, and afterward you will eat and drink'? 9 Does he thank that servant because he did the things that were commanded him? I think not.[a] 10 So like-

---

16:9 [a]NU-Text reads *it fails.*   16:21 [a]NU-Text reads *with what fell.*   17:3 [a]NU-Text omits *against you.*   17:4 [a]M-Text omits *to you.*   17:9 [a]NU-Text ends verse with *commanded;* M-Text omits *him.*

Gospel Pearls

wise you, when you have done all those things which you are commanded, say, 'We are unprofitable servants. We have done what was our duty to do.' "

11 Now it happened as He went to Jerusalem that He passed through the midst of Samaria and Galilee. 12 Then as He entered a certain village, there met Him ten men who were lepers, who stood afar off. 13 And they lifted up *their* voices and said, "Jesus, Master, have mercy on us!"

14 So when He saw *them,* He said to them, "Go, show yourselves to the priests." And so it was that as they went, they were cleansed.

15 And one of them, when he saw that he was healed, returned, and with a loud voice glorified God, 16 and fell down on *his* face at His feet, giving Him thanks. And he was a Samaritan.

17 So Jesus answered and said, "Were there not ten cleansed? But where *are* the nine? 18 Were there not any found who returned to give glory to God except this foreigner?" 19 And He said to him, "Arise, go your way. Your faith has made you well."

20 Now when He was asked by the Pharisees when the kingdom of God would come, He answered them and said, "The kingdom of God does not come with observation; 21 nor will they say, 'See here!' or 'See there!'*a* For indeed, the kingdom of God is within you."

22 Then He said to the disciples, "The days will come when you will desire to see one of the days of the Son of Man, and you will not see *it.* 23 And they will say to you, 'Look here!' or 'Look there!'*a* Do not go after *them* or follow *them.* 24 For as the lightning that flashes out of one *part* under heaven shines to the other *part* under heaven, so also the Son of Man will be in His day. 25 But first He must suffer many things and be rejected by this generation. 26 And as it was in the days of Noah, so it will be also in the days of the Son of Man: 27 They ate, they drank, they married wives, they were given in marriage, until the day that Noah entered the ark, and the flood came and de-

stroyed them all. 28 Likewise as it was also in the days of Lot: They ate, they drank, they bought, they sold, they planted, they built; 29 but on the day that Lot went out of Sodom it rained fire and brimstone from heaven and destroyed *them* all. 30 Even so will it be in the day when the Son of Man is revealed.

31 "In that day, he who is on the housetop, and his goods *are* in the house, let him not come down to take them away. And likewise the one who is in the field, let him not turn back. 32 Remember Lot's wife. 33 Whoever seeks to save his life will lose it, and whoever loses his life will preserve it. 34 I tell you, in that night there will be two *men* in one bed: the one will be taken and the other will be left. 35 Two *women* will be grinding together: the one will be taken and the other left. 36 Two *men* will be in the field: the one will be taken and the other left."*a*

37 And they answered and said to Him, "Where, Lord?"

So He said to them, "Wherever the body is, there the eagles will be gathered together."

18

Then He spoke a parable to them, that men always ought to pray and not lose heart, 2 saying: "There was in a certain city a judge who did not fear God nor regard man. 3 Now there was a widow in that city; and she came to him, saying, 'Get justice for me from my adversary.' 4 And he would not for a while; but afterward he said within himself, 'Though I do not fear God nor regard man, 5 yet because this widow troubles me I will avenge her, lest by her continual coming she weary me.' "

6 Then the Lord said, "Hear what the unjust judge said. 7 And shall God not avenge His own elect who cry out day and night to Him, though He bears long with them? 8 I tell you that He will avenge them speedily. Nevertheless, when the Son of Man comes, will He really find faith on the earth?"

9 Also He spoke this parable to some who trusted in themselves that they were righteous, and despised others: 10 "Two men went up to the

17:21 *a*NU-Text reverses *here* and *there.*   17:23 *a*NU-Text reverses *here* and *there.*   17:36 *a*NU-Text and M-Text omit verse 36.

When a person has been salted, nobody has to call her name for her to feel good about herself. Nobody has to acknowledge her for her to know she's worthy. Nobody has to compliment her in order for her to feel loved.

temple to pray, one a Pharisee and the other a tax collector. 11 The Pharisee stood and prayed thus with himself, 'God, I thank You that I am not like other men—extortioners, unjust, adulterers, or even as this tax collector. 12 I fast twice a week; I give tithes of all that I possess.' 13 And the tax collector, standing afar off, would not so much as raise *his* eyes to heaven, but beat his breast, saying, 'God, be merciful to me a sinner!' 14 I tell you, this man went down to his house justified *rather* than the other; for everyone who exalts himself will be humbled, and he who humbles himself will be exalted."

15 Then they also brought infants to Him that He might touch them; but when the disciples saw *it,* they rebuked them. 16 But Jesus called them to *Him* and said, "Let the little children come to Me, and do not forbid them; for of such is the kingdom of God. 17 Assuredly, I say to you, whoever does not receive the kingdom of God as a little child will by no means enter it."

18 Now a certain ruler asked Him, saying, "Good Teacher, what shall I do to inherit eternal life?"

19 So Jesus said to him, "Why do you call Me good? No one *is* good but One, *that is,* God. 20 You know the commandments: *'Do not commit adultery,' 'Do not murder,' 'Do not steal,' 'Do not bear false witness,' 'Honor your father and your mother.'"*[a]

21 And he said, "All these things I have kept from my youth."

22 So when Jesus heard these things, He said to him, "You still lack one thing. Sell all that you have and distribute to the poor, and you will have treasure in heaven; and come, follow Me."

23 But when he heard this, he became very sorrowful, for he was very rich.

24 And when Jesus saw that he became very sorrowful, He said, "How hard it is for those who have riches to enter the kingdom of God! 25 For it is easier for a camel to go through the eye of a needle than for a rich man to enter the kingdom of God."

26 And those who heard it said, "Who then can be saved?"

27 But He said, "The things which

are impossible with men are possible with God."

28 Then Peter said, "See, we have left all[a] and followed You."

29 So He said to them, "Assuredly, I say to you, there is no one who has left house or parents or brothers or wife or children, for the sake of the kingdom of God, 30 who shall not receive many times more in this present time, and in the age to come eternal life."

31 Then He took the twelve aside and said to them, "Behold, we are going up to Jerusalem, and all things that are written by the prophets concerning the Son of Man will be accomplished. 32 For He will be delivered to the Gentiles and will be mocked and insulted and spit upon. 33 They will scourge *Him* and kill Him. And the third day He will rise again."

34 But they understood none of these things; this saying was hidden from them, and they did not know the things which were spoken.

35 Then it happened, as He was coming near Jericho, that a certain blind man sat by the road begging. 36 And hearing a multitude passing by, he asked what it meant. 37 So they told him that Jesus of Nazareth was passing by. 38 And he cried out, saying, "Jesus, Son of David, have mercy on me!"

39 Then those who went before warned him that he should be quiet; but he cried out all the more, "Son of David, have mercy on me!"

40 So Jesus stood still and commanded him to be brought to Him. And when he had come near, He asked him, 41 saying, "What do you want Me to do for you?"

He said, "Lord, that I may receive my sight."

42 Then Jesus said to him, "Receive your sight; your faith has made you well." 43 And immediately he received his sight, and followed Him, glorifying God. And all the people, when they saw *it,* gave praise to God.

19 Then *Jesus* entered and passed through Jericho. 2 Now behold, *there was* a man named Zacchaeus who was a chief tax collector, and he was rich. 3 And he sought to see

18:20 [a]Exodus 20:12–16; Deuteronomy 5:16–20   18:28 [a]NU-Text reads *our own.*

*J*esus said that His followers were the salt of the earth. The newborn Christian gets salty by being around salt. It is our job to accept that new believer into our midst— to make a place for her, to surround her, to include her, to allow her into our circle of friends.

Soul Secrets
for times when
no one understands

God, there's not a living soul who understands me right now. I've tried to explain time and again, and I'm always met with the same blank stares. It's not that they don't want to understand; it's that they can't. You've given me gifts of seeing and knowing and understanding. And you've given them gifts that are equally puzzling to me. This is how the Body of Christ is supposed to work.

But there's a loneliness that comes with not being understood that surpasses every loneliness I've ever known. There is a place of weeping in the pit of my heart that has never wept before. And as frustrated as I am, I still say yes to You. I still say yes to Jesus—who knows better than anyone how it feels to be misunderstood.

Help me, Lord, to overcome my desire to be understood. Help me walk this lonely road with confidence in You, with the courage that comes from knowing I am Yours. Help me cling to my convictions. Help me love the ones who are so baffled. Keep me far from anger and close to Your heart. And though it is an uphill climb, take my hand, light my way, and help me to walk on.

who Jesus was, but could not because of the crowd, for he was of
short stature. 4 So he ran ahead and
climbed up into a sycamore tree to
see Him, for He was going to pass
that *way.* 5 And when Jesus came to
the place, He looked up and saw
him,*a* and said to him, "Zacchaeus,
make haste and come down, for today I must stay at your house."
6 So he made haste and came down,
and received Him joyfully. 7 But
when they saw *it,* they all complained, saying, "He has gone to be
a guest with a man who is a sinner."

8 Then Zacchaeus stood and said
to the Lord, "Look, Lord, I give half
of my goods to the poor; and if I have
taken anything from anyone by false
accusation, I restore fourfold."

9 And Jesus said to him, "Today
salvation has come to this house, because he also is a son of Abraham;
10 for the Son of Man has come to
seek and to save that which was
lost."

11 Now as they heard these things,
He spoke another parable, because
He was near Jerusalem and because
they thought the kingdom of God
would appear immediately.
12 Therefore He said: "A certain nobleman went into a far country to receive for himself a kingdom and to
return. 13 So he called ten of his servants, delivered to them ten minas,*a*
and said to them, 'Do business till I
come.' 14 But his citizens hated him,
and sent a delegation after him, saying, 'We will not have this *man* to
reign over us.'

15 "And so it was that when he returned, having received the kingdom,
he then commanded these servants,
to whom he had given the money, to
be called to him, that he might know
how much every man had gained by
trading. 16 Then came the first, saying, 'Master, your mina has earned
ten minas.' 17 And he said to him,
'Well *done,* good servant; because
you were faithful in a very little, have
authority over ten cities.' 18 And the
second came, saying, 'Master, your
mina has earned five minas.'
19 Likewise he said to him, 'You also
be over five cities.'

20 "Then another came, saying,
'Master, here is your mina, which I
have kept put away in a handkerchief. 21 For I feared you, because
you are an austere man. You collect
what you did not deposit, and reap
what you did not sow.' 22 And he said
to him, 'Out of your own mouth I will
judge you, *you* wicked servant. You
knew that I was an austere man, collecting what I did not deposit and
reaping what I did not sow. 23 Why
then did you not put my money in
the bank, that at my coming I might
have collected it with interest?'

24 "And he said to those who stood
by, 'Take the mina from him, and
give *it* to him who has ten minas.'
25 ("But they said to him, 'Master, he
has ten minas.') 26 For I say to you,
that to everyone who has will be
given; and from him who does not
have, even what he has will be taken
away from him. 27 But bring here
those enemies of mine, who did not
want me to reign over them, and slay
them before me.' "

28 When He had said this, He went
on ahead, going up to Jerusalem.
29 And it came to pass, when He drew
near to Bethphage*a* and Bethany, at
the mountain called Olivet, *that* He
sent two of His disciples, 30 saying,
"Go into the village opposite *you,*
where as you enter you will find a
colt tied, on which no one has ever
sat. Loose it and bring *it* here.
31 And if anyone asks you, 'Why are
you loosing *it?*' thus you shall say to
him, 'Because the Lord has need of
it.' "

32 So those who were sent went
their way and found *it* just as He had
said to them. 33 But as they were
loosing the colt, the owners of it said
to them, "Why are you loosing the
colt?"

34 And they said, "The Lord has
need of him." 35 Then they brought
him to Jesus. And they threw their
own clothes on the colt, and they set
Jesus on him. 36 And as He went,
many spread their clothes on the
road.

37 Then, as He was now drawing
near the descent of the Mount of Olives, the whole multitude of the disciples began to rejoice and praise God
with a loud voice for all the mighty
works they had seen, 38 saying:

19:5 *a*NU-Text omits *and saw him.*   19:13 *a*The *mina* (Greek *mna,* Hebrew *minah*) was worth about three
months' salary.   19:29 *a*M-Text reads *Bethsphage.*

*Gospel
Pearls*

" 'Blessed is the King who
   comes in the name of the
   LORD!'^a
   Peace in heaven and glory in
   the highest!"

39 And some of the Pharisees called
to Him from the crowd, "Teacher, rebuke Your disciples."

40 But He answered and said to
them, "I tell you that if these should
keep silent, the stones would immediately cry out."

41 Now as He drew near, He saw
the city and wept over it, 42 saying,
"If you had known, even you, especially in this your day, the things *that
make* for your peace! But now they
are hidden from your eyes. 43 For
days will come upon you when your
enemies will build an embankment
around you, surround you and close
you in on every side, 44 and level you,
and your children within you, to the
ground; and they will not leave in
you one stone upon another, because
you did not know the time of your
visitation."

45 Then He went into the temple
and began to drive out those who
bought and sold in it,^a 46 saying to
them, "It is written, *'My house is^a a
house of prayer,'^b* but you have made
it a *'den of thieves.'*"^c

47 And He was teaching daily in the
temple. But the chief priests, the
scribes, and the leaders of the people
sought to destroy Him, 48 and were
unable to do anything; for all the
people were very attentive to hear
Him.

20 Now it happened on one of
those days, as He taught the
people in the temple and preached
the gospel, *that* the chief priests and
the scribes, together with the elders,
confronted *Him* 2 and spoke to Him,
saying, "Tell us, by what authority
are You doing these things? Or who
is he who gave You this authority?"

3 But He answered and said to
them, "I also will ask you one thing,
and answer Me: 4 The baptism of
John—was it from heaven or from
men?"

5 And they reasoned among themselves, saying, "If we say, 'From
heaven,' He will say, 'Why then^a did

you not believe him?' 6 But if we say,
'From men,' all the people will stone
us, for they are persuaded that John
was a prophet." 7 So they answered
that they did not know where *it was*
from.

8 And Jesus said to them, "Neither
will I tell you by what authority I do
these things."

9 Then He began to tell the people
this parable: "A certain man planted
a vineyard, leased it to vinedressers,
and went into a far country for a long
time. 10 Now at vintage-time he sent
a servant to the vinedressers, that
they might give him some of the fruit
of the vineyard. But the vinedressers
beat him and sent *him* away empty-
handed. 11 Again he sent another servant; and they beat him also, treated
him shamefully, and sent *him* away
empty-handed. 12 And again he sent
a third; and they wounded him also
and cast *him* out.

13 "Then the owner of the vineyard
said, 'What shall I do? I will send my
beloved son. Probably they will respect *him* when they see him.'
14 But when the vinedressers saw
him, they reasoned among themselves, saying, 'This is the heir.
Come, let us kill him, that the inheritance may be ours.' 15 So they cast
him out of the vineyard and killed
him. Therefore what will the owner
of the vineyard do to them? 16 He
will come and destroy those vinedressers and give the vineyard to
others."

And when they heard *it* they said,
"Certainly not!"

17 Then He looked at them and
said, "What then is this that is written:

'The stone which the builders
   rejected
   Has become the chief
   cornerstone' ?^a

18 Whoever falls on that stone will
be broken; but on whomever it falls,
it will grind him to powder."

19 And the chief priests and the
scribes that very hour sought to lay
hands on Him, but they feared the
people^a—for they knew He had spoken this parable against them.
20 So they watched *Him*, and sent

19:38 ^aPsalm 118:26   19:45 ^aNU-Text reads *those who were selling.*   19:46 ^aNU-Text reads *shall
be.*   ^bIsaiah 56:7   ^cJeremiah 7:11   20:5 ^aNU-Text and M-Text omit *then.*   20:17 ^aPsalm 118:22
20:19 ^aM-Text reads *but they were afraid.*

Wash yourself by reading God's Word. Get into a church where you can hear His
Word preached with Holy Ghost power. Get around people who are studying
God's Word and speaking His Word and living His Word.

spies who pretended to be righteous, that they might seize on His words, in order to deliver Him to the power and the authority of the governor. 21 Then they asked Him, saying, "Teacher, we know that You say and teach rightly, and You do not show personal favoritism, but teach the way of God in truth: 22 Is it lawful for us to pay taxes to Caesar or not?"

23 But He perceived their craftiness, and said to them, "Why do you test Me?[a] 24 Show Me a denarius. Whose image and inscription does it have?"

They answered and said, "Caesar's."

25 And He said to them, "Render therefore to Caesar the things that are Caesar's, and to God the things that are God's."

26 But they could not catch Him in His words in the presence of the people. And they marveled at His answer and kept silent.

27 Then some of the Sadducees, who deny that there is a resurrection, came to *Him* and asked Him, 28 saying: "Teacher, Moses wrote to us *that* if a man's brother dies, having a wife, and he dies without children, his brother should take his wife and raise up offspring for his brother. 29 Now there were seven brothers. And the first took a wife, and died without children. 30 And the second[a] took her as wife, and he died childless. 31 Then the third took her, and in like manner the seven also; and they left no children,[a] and died. 32 Last of all the woman died also. 33 Therefore, in the resurrection, whose wife does she become? For all seven had her as wife."

34 Jesus answered and said to them, "The sons of this age marry and are given in marriage. 35 But those who are counted worthy to attain that age, and the resurrection from the dead, neither marry nor are given in marriage; 36 nor can they die anymore, for they are equal to the angels and are sons of God, being sons of the resurrection. 37 But even Moses showed in the *burning bush* passage that the dead are raised, when he called the Lord 'the God of Abraham, the God of Isaac, and the God of Jacob.'[a] 38 For He is not the God of the dead but of the living, for all live to Him."

39 Then some of the scribes answered and said, "Teacher, You have spoken well." 40 But after that they dared not question Him anymore.

41 And He said to them, "How can they say that the Christ is the Son of David? 42 Now David himself said in the Book of Psalms:

'The LORD said to my Lord,
"Sit at My right hand,
43 Till I make Your enemies Your
footstool." '[a]

44 Therefore David calls Him 'Lord'; how is He then his Son?"

45 Then, in the hearing of all the people, He said to His disciples, 46 "Beware of the scribes, who desire to go around in long robes, love greetings in the marketplaces, the best seats in the synagogues, and the best places at feasts, 47 who devour widows' houses, and for a pretense make long prayers. These will receive greater condemnation."

21 And He looked up and saw the rich putting their gifts into the treasury, 2 and He saw also a certain poor widow putting in two mites. 3 So He said, "Truly I say to you that this poor widow has put in more than all; 4 for all these out of their abundance have put in offerings for God,[a] but she out of her poverty put in all the livelihood that she had."

5 Then, as some spoke of the temple, how it was adorned with beautiful stones and donations, He said, 6 "These things which you see—the days will come in which not *one* stone shall be left upon another that shall not be thrown down."

7 So they asked Him, saying, "Teacher, but when will these things be? And what sign *will there be* when these things are about to take place?"

8 And He said: "Take heed that you not be deceived. For many will come in My name, saying, 'I am *He*,' and, 'The time has drawn near.' Therefore[a] do not go after them. 9 But when you hear of wars and commotions, do not be terrified; for these things

20:23 [a]NU-Text omits *Why do you test Me?*   20:30 [a]NU-Text ends verse 30 here.   20:31 [a]NU-Text and M-Text read *the seven also left no children.*   20:37 [a]Exodus 3:6, 15   20:43 [a]Psalm 110:1   21:4 [a]NU-Text omits *for God.*   21:8 [a]NU-Text omits *Therefore.*

Gospel
Pearls

must come to pass first, but the end *will not come* immediately."

10 Then He said to them, "Nation will rise against nation, and kingdom against kingdom. 11 And there will be great earthquakes in various places, and famines and pestilences; and there will be fearful sights and great signs from heaven. 12 But before all these things, they will lay their hands on you and persecute *you*, delivering *you* up to the synagogues and prisons. You will be brought before kings and rulers for My name's sake. 13 But it will turn out for you as an occasion for testimony. 14 Therefore settle *it* in your hearts not to meditate beforehand on what you will answer; 15 for I will give you a mouth and wisdom which all your adversaries will not be able to contradict or resist. 16 You will be betrayed even by parents and brothers, relatives and friends; and they will put *some* of you to death. 17 And you will be hated by all for My name's sake. 18 But not a hair of your head shall be lost. 19 By your patience possess your souls.

20 "But when you see Jerusalem surrounded by armies, then know that its desolation is near. 21 Then let those who are in Judea flee to the mountains, let those who are in the midst of her depart, and let not those who are in the country enter her. 22 For these are the days of vengeance, that all things which are written may be fulfilled. 23 But woe to those who are pregnant and to those who are nursing babies in those days! For there will be great distress in the land and wrath upon this people. 24 And they will fall by the edge of the sword, and be led away captive into all nations. And Jerusalem will be trampled by Gentiles until the times of the Gentiles are fulfilled.

25 "And there will be signs in the sun, in the moon, and in the stars; and on the earth distress of nations, with perplexity, the sea and the waves roaring; 26 men's hearts failing them from fear and the expectation of those things which are coming on the earth, for the powers of the heavens will be shaken. 27 Then they will see the Son of Man coming in a cloud with power and great glory.

28 Now when these things begin to happen, look up and lift up your heads, because your redemption draws near."

29 Then He spoke to them a parable: "Look at the fig tree, and all the trees. 30 When they are already budding, you see and know for yourselves that summer is now near. 31 So you also, when you see these things happening, know that the kingdom of God is near. 32 Assuredly, I say to you, this generation will by no means pass away till all things take place. 33 Heaven and earth will pass away, but My words will by no means pass away.

34 "But take heed to yourselves, lest your hearts be weighed down with carousing, drunkenness, and cares of this life, and that Day come on you unexpectedly. 35 For it will come as a snare on all those who dwell on the face of the whole earth. 36 Watch therefore, and pray always that you may be counted worthy[a] to escape all these things that will come to pass, and to stand before the Son of Man."

37 And in the daytime He was teaching in the temple, but at night He went out and stayed on the mountain called Olivet. 38 Then early in the morning all the people came to Him in the temple to hear Him.

22 Now the Feast of Unleavened Bread drew near, which is called Passover. 2 And the chief priests and the scribes sought how they might kill Him, for they feared the people.

3 Then Satan entered Judas, surnamed Iscariot, who was numbered among the twelve. 4 So he went his way and conferred with the chief priests and captains, how he might betray Him to them. 5 And they were glad, and agreed to give him money. 6 So he promised and sought opportunity to betray Him to them in the absence of the multitude.

7 Then came the Day of Unleavened Bread, when the Passover must be killed. 8 And He sent Peter and John, saying, "Go and prepare the Passover for us, that we may eat."

9 So they said to Him, "Where do You want us to prepare?"

10 And He said to them, "Behold,

21:36 ᵃNU-Text reads *may have strength.*

As you wash yourself, He will wash you with His forgiveness. As you salt yourself, God will salt you with His power and presence. As you swaddle yourself in garments of praise, God will swaddle you in His love. Ask God today to provide for you the exact nurture and care that you need.

when you have entered the city, a man will meet you carrying a pitcher of water; follow him into the house which he enters. 11 Then you shall say to the master of the house, 'The Teacher says to you, "Where is the guest room where I may eat the Passover with My disciples?"' 12 Then he will show you a large, furnished upper room; there make ready."

13 So they went and found it just as He had said to them, and they prepared the Passover.

14 When the hour had come, He sat down, and the twelve*a* apostles with Him. 15 Then He said to them, "With *fervent* desire I have desired to eat this Passover with you before I suffer; 16 for I say to you, I will no longer eat of it until it is fulfilled in the kingdom of God."

17 Then He took the cup, and gave thanks, and said, "Take this and divide *it* among yourselves; 18 for I say to you,*a* I will not drink of the fruit of the vine until the kingdom of God comes."

19 And He took bread, gave thanks and broke *it,* and gave *it* to them, saying, "This is My body which is given for you; do this in remembrance of Me."

20 Likewise He also *took* the cup after supper, saying, "This cup *is* the new covenant in My blood, which is shed for you. 21 But behold, the hand of My betrayer *is* with Me on the table. 22 And truly the Son of Man goes as it has been determined, but woe to that man by whom He is betrayed!"

23 Then they began to question among themselves, which of them it was who would do this thing.

24 Now there was also a dispute among them, as to which of them should be considered the greatest. 25 And He said to them, "The kings of the Gentiles exercise lordship over them, and those who exercise authority over them are called 'benefactors.' 26 But not so *among* you; on the contrary, he who is greatest among you, let him be as the younger, and he who governs as he who serves. 27 For who *is* greater, he who sits at the table, or he who serves? *Is* it not he who sits at the table? Yet I am among you as the One who serves.

28 "But you are those who have continued with Me in My trials. 29 And I bestow upon you a kingdom, just as My Father bestowed *one* upon Me, 30 that you may eat and drink at My table in My kingdom, and sit on thrones judging the twelve tribes of Israel."

31 And the Lord said,*a* "Simon, Simon! Indeed, Satan has asked for you, that he may sift *you* as wheat. 32 But I have prayed for you, that your faith should not fail; and when you have returned to *Me,* strengthen your brethren."

33 But he said to Him, "Lord, I am ready to go with You, both to prison and to death."

34 Then He said, "I tell you, Peter, the rooster shall not crow this day before you will deny three times that you know Me."

35 And He said to them, "When I sent you without money bag, knapsack, and sandals, did you lack anything?"

So they said, "Nothing."

36 Then He said to them, "But now, he who has a money bag, let him take *it,* and likewise a knapsack; and he who has no sword, let him sell his garment and buy one. 37 For I say to you that this which is written must still be accomplished in Me: 'And He was numbered with the transgressors.'*a* For the things concerning Me have an end."

38 So they said, "Lord, look, here *are* two swords."

And He said to them, "It is enough."

39 Coming out, He went to the Mount of Olives, as He was accustomed, and His disciples also followed Him. 40 When He came to the place, He said to them, "Pray that you may not enter into temptation."

41 And He was withdrawn from them about a stone's throw, and He knelt down and prayed, 42 saying, "Father, if it is Your will, take this cup away from Me; nevertheless not My will, but Yours, be done." 43 Then an angel appeared to Him from heaven, strengthening Him. 44 And being in agony, He prayed more earnestly. Then His sweat be-

---

22:14 *a*NU-Text omits *twelve.*   22:18 *a*NU-Text adds *from now on.*   22:31 *a*NU-Text omits *And the Lord said.*   22:37 *a*Isaiah 53:12

Gospel Pearls

came like great drops of blood falling down to the ground.*a*

45 When He rose up from prayer, and had come to His disciples, He found them sleeping from sorrow. 46 Then He said to them, "Why do you sleep? Rise and pray, lest you enter into temptation."

47 And while He was still speaking, behold, a multitude; and he who was called Judas, one of the twelve, went before them and drew near to Jesus to kiss Him. 48 But Jesus said to him, "Judas, are you betraying the Son of Man with a kiss?"

49 When those around Him saw what was going to happen, they said to Him, "Lord, shall we strike with the sword?" 50 And one of them struck the servant of the high priest and cut off his right ear.

51 But Jesus answered and said, "Permit even this." And He touched his ear and healed him.

52 Then Jesus said to the chief priests, captains of the temple, and the elders who had come to Him, "Have you come out, as against a robber, with swords and clubs? 53 When I was with you daily in the temple, you did not try to seize Me. But this is your hour, and the power of darkness."

54 Having arrested Him, they led *Him* and brought Him into the high priest's house. But Peter followed at a distance. 55 Now when they had kindled a fire in the midst of the courtyard and sat down together, Peter sat among them. 56 And a certain servant girl, seeing him as he sat by the fire, looked intently at him and said, "This man was also with Him."

57 But he denied Him,*a* saying, "Woman, I do not know Him."

58 And after a little while another saw him and said, "You also are of them."

But Peter said, "Man, I am not!"

59 Then after about an hour had passed, another confidently affirmed, saying, "Surely this *fellow* also was with Him, for he is a Galilean."

60 But Peter said, "Man, I do not know what you are saying!" Immediately, while he was still speaking, the rooster*a* crowed.

61 And the Lord turned and looked at Peter. Then Peter remembered the word of the Lord, how He had said to him, "Before the rooster crows,*a* you will deny Me three times." 62 So Peter went out and wept bitterly.

63 Now the men who held Jesus mocked Him and beat Him. 64 And having blindfolded Him, they struck Him on the face and asked Him,*a* saying, "Prophesy! Who is the one who struck You?" 65 And many other things they blasphemously spoke against Him.

66 As soon as it was day, the elders of the people, both chief priests and scribes, came together and led Him into their council, saying, 67 "If You are the Christ, tell us."

But He said to them, "If I tell you, you will by no means believe. 68 And if I also ask *you,* you will by no means answer Me or let *Me* go.*a* 69 Hereafter the Son of Man will sit on the right hand of the power of God."

70 Then they all said, "Are You then the Son of God?"

So He said to them, "You *rightly* say that I am."

71 And they said, "What further testimony do we need? For we have heard it ourselves from His own mouth."

23 Then the whole multitude of them arose and led Him to Pilate. 2 And they began to accuse Him, saying, "We found this *fellow* perverting the*a* nation, and forbidding to pay taxes to Caesar, saying that He Himself is Christ, a King."

3 Then Pilate asked Him, saying, "Are You the King of the Jews?"

He answered him and said, "*It is as* you say."

4 So Pilate said to the chief priests and the crowd, "I find no fault in this Man."

5 But they were the more fierce, saying, "He stirs up the people, teaching throughout all Judea, beginning from Galilee to this place."

6 When Pilate heard of Galilee,*a* he asked if the Man were a Galilean. 7 And as soon as he knew that He

22:44 *a*NU-Text brackets verses 43 and 44 as not in the original text. 22:57 *a*NU-Text reads *denied it.* 22:60 *a*NU-Text and M-Text read *a rooster.* 22:61 *a*NU-Text adds *today.* 22:64 *a*NU-Text reads *And having blindfolded Him, they asked Him.* 22:68 *a*NU-Text omits *also* and *Me or let Me go.* 23:2 *a*NU-Text reads *our.* 23:6 *a*NU-Text omits *of Galilee.*

God knew all along that His baby girl would become a woman. He expected it to happen. He helped it to happen. And it did. He says, "Now when I see you, I don't see you as you were. I see you only as you are." Focus on that word *now*.

Your Friend Judas

Luke 22:47

Judas was no mistake. He was handpicked and set aside. His role was crucial to the death and resurrection of Jesus Christ. No one helped Jesus reach his goal like Judas. Considering the part he played, though, you'd probably rather have a friend like John, whose character and personality traits won Jesus' heart. Or you might prefer a Peter, bold and brassy and ready to fight anyone and everyone who threatened his beloved Master. Peter even challenged Jesus Himself, rebuking Him for His determination to die for mankind. The truth of the matter is, Jesus could have accomplished His purpose without either Peter or John; but without Judas, He would never have reached the hope of His calling.

God can bless you through the worst of relationships. Learn to accept even the painful or negative ones. The time, effort, and tears invested will not be wasted, because God knows how to turn adversity into opportunity. In short, the bleeding trail of broken hearts and wounded relationships will lead you to the richness of God's purpose.

Periodically, you may hear a knock at the door. It is the knock of your old friend Judas, whose cold kiss and calloused heart will usher you into the will of God. To be sure, these betrayals will call forth bloody tears and nail you to a cruel cross. Nevertheless, the kiss of betrayal can never abort the precious promises of God. The challenge is to sit at the table with Judas on one side and John on the other and, being distinctly aware of each one's identity and agenda, treat one no differently from the other!

If you have been betrayed or wounded by someone you brought too close, please forgive him or her. That person was really a blessing—a friend in disguise. Persecution strengthens you. Trials and trauma build perseverance. You will only be better when you cease to be bitter.

So leave my Judas alone. I need him in my life. He is my mysterious friend, the one who helps me without even knowing it. His assaults send me to my knees and cause me to lean on Jesus—my ultimate Friend.

belonged to Herod's jurisdiction, he sent Him to Herod, who was also in Jerusalem at that time. 8 Now when Herod saw Jesus, he was exceedingly glad; for he had desired for a long *time* to see Him, because he had heard many things about Him, and he hoped to see some miracle done by Him. 9 Then he questioned Him with many words, but He answered him nothing. 10 And the chief priests and scribes stood and vehemently accused Him. 11 Then Herod, with his men of war, treated Him with contempt and mocked *Him*, arrayed Him in a gorgeous robe, and sent Him back to Pilate. 12 That very day Pilate and Herod became friends with each other, for previously they had been at enmity with each other.

13 Then Pilate, when he had called together the chief priests, the rulers, and the people, 14 said to them, "You have brought this Man to me, as one who misleads the people. And indeed, having examined *Him* in your presence, I have found no fault in this Man concerning those things of which you accuse Him; 15 no, neither did Herod, for I sent you back to him;*a* and indeed nothing deserving of death has been done by Him. 16 I will therefore chastise Him and release *Him*" 17 (for it was necessary for him to release one to them at the feast).*a*

18 And they all cried out at once, saying, "Away with this *Man*, and release to us Barabbas"— 19 who had been thrown into prison for a certain rebellion made in the city, and for murder.

20 Pilate, therefore, wishing to release Jesus, again called out to them. 21 But they shouted, saying, "Crucify *Him*, crucify Him!"

22 Then he said to them the third time, "Why, what evil has He done? I have found no reason for death in Him. I will therefore chastise Him and let *Him* go."

23 But they were insistent, demanding with loud voices that He be crucified. And the voices of these men and of the chief priests prevailed.*a* 24 So Pilate gave sentence that it should be as they requested. 25 And

he released to them*a* the one they requested, who for rebellion and murder had been thrown into prison; but he delivered Jesus to their will.

26 Now as they led Him away, they laid hold of a certain man, Simon a Cyrenian, who was coming from the country, and on him they laid the cross that he might bear *it* after Jesus.

27 And a great multitude of the people followed Him, and women who also mourned and lamented Him. 28 But Jesus, turning to them, said, "Daughters of Jerusalem, do not weep for Me, but weep for yourselves and for your children. 29 For indeed the days are coming in which they will say, 'Blessed *are* the barren, wombs that never bore, and breasts which never nursed!' 30 Then they will begin 'to say to the mountains, "Fall on us!" and to the hills, "Cover us!" '*a* 31 For if they do these things in the green wood, what will be done in the dry?"

32 There were also two others, criminals, led with Him to be put to death. 33 And when they had come to the place called Calvary, there they crucified Him, and the criminals, one on the right hand and the other on the left. 34 Then Jesus said, "Father, forgive them, for they do not know what they do."*a*

And they divided His garments and cast lots. 35 And the people stood looking on. But even the rulers with them sneered, saying, "He saved others; let Him save Himself if He is the Christ, the chosen of God."

36 The soldiers also mocked Him, coming and offering Him sour wine, 37 and saying, "If You are the King of the Jews, save Yourself."

38 And an inscription also was written over Him in letters of Greek, Latin, and Hebrew:*a*

THIS IS THE KING
OF THE JEWS.

39 Then one of the criminals who were hanged blasphemed Him, saying, "If You are the Christ,*a* save Yourself and us."

40 But the other, answering, rebuked him, saying, "Do you not even

---

23:15 *a*NU-Text reads *for he sent Him back to us.*   23:17 *a*NU-Text omits verse 17.   23:23 *a*NU-Text omits *and of the chief priests.*   23:25 *a*NU-Text and M-Text omit *to them.*   23:30 *a*Hosea 10:8
23:34 *a*NU-Text brackets the first sentence as a later addition.   23:38 *a*NU-Text omits *written* and *in letters of Greek, Latin, and Hebrew.*   23:39 *a*NU-Text reads *Are You not the Christ?*

---

*T*here comes a time when you have to draw a line between then and now, between that and this. There comes a time when you must say, "That was then. Now is now. I used to do that. Now I do this. I used to be that. Now I am this."

fear God, seeing you are under the same condemnation? 41 And we indeed justly, for we receive the due reward of our deeds; but this Man has done nothing wrong." 42 Then he said to Jesus, "Lord,ᵃ remember me when You come into Your kingdom."

43 And Jesus said to him, "Assuredly, I say to you, today you will be with Me in Paradise."

44 Now it wasᵃ about the sixth hour, and there was darkness over all the earth until the ninth hour. 45 Then the sun was darkened,ᵃ and the veil of the temple was torn in two. 46 And when Jesus had cried out with a loud voice, He said, "Father, 'into Your hands I commit My spirit.'"ᵃ Having said this, He breathed His last.

47 So when the centurion saw what had happened, he glorified God, saying, "Certainly this was a righteous Man!"

48 And the whole crowd who came together to that sight, seeing what had been done, beat their breasts and returned. 49 But all His acquaintances, and the women who followed Him from Galilee, stood at a distance, watching these things.

50 Now behold, there was a man named Joseph, a council member, a good and just man. 51 He had not consented to their decision and deed. He was from Arimathea, a city of the Jews, who himself was also waitingᵃ for the kingdom of God. 52 This man went to Pilate and asked for the body of Jesus. 53 Then he took it down, wrapped it in linen, and laid it in a tomb that was hewn out of the rock, where no one had ever lain before. 54 That day was the Preparation, and the Sabbath drew near.

55 And the women who had come with Him from Galilee followed after, and they observed the tomb and how His body was laid. 56 Then they returned and prepared spices and fragrant oils. And they rested on the Sabbath according to the commandment.

24 Now on the first day of the week, very early in the morning, they, and certain other women with them,ᵃ came to the tomb bringing the spices which they had prepared. 2 But they found the stone rolled away from the tomb. 3 Then they went in and did not find the body of the Lord Jesus. 4 And it happened, as they were greatlyᵃ perplexed about this, that behold, two men stood by them in shining garments. 5 Then, as they were afraid and bowed their faces to the earth, they said to them, "Why do you seek the living among the dead? 6 He is not here, but is risen! Remember how He spoke to you when He was still in Galilee, 7 saying, 'The Son of Man must be delivered into the hands of sinful men, and be crucified, and the third day rise again.'"

8 And they remembered His words. 9 Then they returned from the tomb and told all these things to the eleven and to all the rest. 10 It was Mary Magdalene, Joanna, Mary the mother of James, and the other women with them, who told these things to the apostles. 11 And their words seemed to them like idle tales, and they did not believe them. 12 But Peter arose and ran to the tomb; and stooping down, he saw the linen cloths lyingᵃ by themselves; and he departed, marveling to himself at what had happened.

13 Now behold, two of them were traveling that same day to a village called Emmaus, which was seven milesᵃ from Jerusalem. 14 And they talked together of all these things which had happened. 15 So it was, while they conversed and reasoned, that Jesus Himself drew near and went with them. 16 But their eyes were restrained, so that they did not know Him.

17 And He said to them, "What kind of conversation is this that you have with one another as you walk and are sad?"ᵃ

18 Then the one whose name was Cleopas answered and said to Him, "Are You the only stranger in Jerusalem, and have You not known the things which happened there in these days?"

23:42 ᵃNU-Text reads And he said, "Jesus, remember me.   23:44 ᵃNU-Text adds already.
23:45 ᵃNU-Text reads obscured.   23:46 ᵃPsalm 31:5   23:51 ᵃNU-Text reads who was waiting.
24:1 ᵃNU-Text omits and certain other women with them.   24:4 ᵃNU-Text omits greatly.
24:12 ᵃNU-Text omits lying.   24:13 ᵃLiterally sixty stadia   24:17 ᵃNU-Text reads as you walk?
And they stood still, looking sad.

Gospel Pearls

19 And He said to them, "What things?"

So they said to Him, "The things concerning Jesus of Nazareth, who was a Prophet mighty in deed and word before God and all the people, 20 and how the chief priests and our rulers delivered Him to be condemned to death, and crucified Him. 21 But we were hoping that it was He who was going to redeem Israel. Indeed, besides all this, today is the third day since these things happened. 22 Yes, and certain women of our company, who arrived at the tomb early, astonished us. 23 When they did not find His body, they came saying that they had also seen a vision of angels who said He was alive. 24 And certain of those *who were* with us went to the tomb and found *it* just as the women had said; but Him they did not see."

25 Then He said to them, "O foolish ones, and slow of heart to believe in all that the prophets have spoken! 26 Ought not the Christ to have suffered these things and to enter into His glory?" 27 And beginning at Moses and all the Prophets, He expounded to them in all the Scriptures the things concerning Himself.

28 Then they drew near to the village where they were going, and He indicated that He would have gone farther. 29 But they constrained Him, saying, "Abide with us, for it is toward evening, and the day is far spent." And He went in to stay with them.

30 Now it came to pass, as He sat at the table with them, that He took bread, blessed and broke *it*, and gave it to them. 31 Then their eyes were opened and they knew Him; and He vanished from their sight. 32 And they said to one another, "Did not our heart burn within us while He talked with us on the road, and while He opened the Scriptures to us?" 33 So they rose up that very hour and returned to Jerusalem, and found the eleven and those *who were* with them gathered together, 34 saying, "The Lord is risen indeed, and has appeared to Simon!" 35 And they told about the things *that had happened* on the road, and how He was known to them in the breaking of bread.

36 Now as they said these things, Jesus Himself stood in the midst of them, and said to them, "Peace to you." 37 But they were terrified and frightened, and supposed they had seen a spirit. 38 And He said to them, "Why are you troubled? And why do doubts arise in your hearts? 39 Behold My hands and My feet, that it is I Myself. Handle Me and see, for a spirit does not have flesh and bones as you see I have."

40 When He had said this, He showed them His hands and His feet.*a* 41 But while they still did not believe for joy, and marveled, He said to them, "Have you any food here?" 42 So they gave Him a piece of a broiled fish and some honeycomb.*a* 43 And He took *it* and ate in their presence.

44 Then He said to them, "These *are* the words which I spoke to you while I was still with you, that all things must be fulfilled which were written in the Law of Moses and *the* Prophets and *the* Psalms concerning Me." 45 And He opened their understanding, that they might comprehend the Scriptures.

46 Then He said to them, "Thus it is written, and thus it was necessary for the Christ to suffer and to rise*a* from the dead the third day, 47 and that repentance and remission of sins should be preached in His name to all nations, beginning at Jerusalem. 48 And you are witnesses of these things. 49 Behold, I send the Promise of My Father upon you; but tarry in the city of Jerusalem*a* until you are endued with power from on high."

50 And He led them out as far as Bethany, and He lifted up His hands and blessed them. 51 Now it came to pass, while He blessed them, that He was parted from them and carried up into heaven. 52 And they worshiped Him, and returned to Jerusalem with great joy, 53 and were continually in the temple praising and*a* blessing God. Amen.*b*

24:40 *a*Some printed New Testaments omit this verse. It is found in nearly all Greek manuscripts.
24:42 *a*NU-Text omits *and some honeycomb.* 24:46 *a*NU-Text reads *written, that the Christ should suffer and rise.* 24:49 *a*NU-Text omits *of Jerusalem.* 24:53 *a*NU-Text omits *praising and.* *b*NU-Text omits *Amen.*

Some women have been carrying around old relationships and old experiences so long that they've become accustomed to the stench of them. God declares that thing to be dead in your life. It's time for you to bury it so you can get on with the resurrection.

JOHN

1 In the beginning was the Word, and the Word was with God, and the Word was God. 2 He was in the beginning with God. 3 All things were made through Him, and without Him nothing was made that was made. 4 In Him was life, and the life was the light of men. 5 And the light shines in the darkness, and the darkness did not comprehend[a] it.

6 There was a man sent from God, whose name *was* John. 7 This man came for a witness, to bear witness of the Light, that all through him might believe. 8 He was not that Light, but *was sent* to bear witness of that Light. 9 That was the true Light which gives light to every man coming into the world.[a]

10 He was in the world, and the world was made through Him, and the world did not know Him. 11 He came to His own,[a] and His own[b] did not receive Him. 12 But as many as received Him, to them He gave the right to become children of God, to those who believe in His name: 13 who were born, not of blood, nor of the will of the flesh, nor of the will of man, but of God.

14 And the Word became flesh and dwelt among us, and we beheld His glory, the glory as of the only begotten of the Father, full of grace and truth.

15 John bore witness of Him and cried out, saying, "This was He of whom I said, 'He who comes after me is preferred before me, for He was before me.' "

16 And[a] of His fullness we have all received, and grace for grace. 17 For the law was given through Moses, *but* grace and truth came through Jesus Christ. 18 No one has seen God at any time. The only begotten Son,[a] who is in the bosom of the Father, He has declared *Him.*

19 Now this is the testimony of John, when the Jews sent priests and Levites from Jerusalem to ask him, "Who are you?"

20 He confessed, and did not deny, but confessed, "I am not the Christ."

21 And they asked him, "What then? Are you Elijah?"

He said, "I am not."

"Are you the Prophet?"

And he answered, "No."

22 Then they said to him, "Who are you, that we may give an answer to those who sent us? What do you say about yourself?"

23 He said: "I *am*

'The voice of one crying in the wilderness:
"Make straight the way of the LORD," '[a]

as the prophet Isaiah said."

24 Now those who were sent were from the Pharisees. 25 And they asked him, saying, "Why then do you baptize if you are not the Christ, nor Elijah, nor the Prophet?"

26 John answered them, saying, "I baptize with water, but there stands One among you whom you do not know. 27 It is He who, coming after me, is preferred before me, whose sandal strap I am not worthy to loose."

28 These things were done in Bethabara[a] beyond the Jordan, where John was baptizing.

29 The next day John saw Jesus coming toward him, and said, "Behold! The Lamb of God who takes away the sin of the world! 30 This is He of whom I said, 'After me comes a Man who is preferred before me, for He was before me.' 31 I did not know Him; but that He should be revealed to Israel, therefore I came baptizing with water."

32 And John bore witness, saying, "I saw the Spirit descending from heaven like a dove, and He remained upon Him. 33 I did not know Him, but He who sent me to baptize with water said to me, 'Upon whom you see the Spirit descending, and remaining on Him, this is He who baptizes with the Holy Spirit.' 34 And I have seen and testified that this is the Son of God."

1:5 [a]Or *overcome*   1:9 [a]Or *That was the true Light which, coming into the world, gives light to every man.*   1:11 [a]That is, His own things or domain   [b]That is, His own people   1:16 [a]NU-Text reads *For.*
1:18 [a]NU-Text reads *only begotten God.*   1:23 [a]Isaiah 40:3   1:28 [a]NU-Text and M-Text read *Bethany.*

Gospel Pearls

35 Again, the next day, John stood with two of his disciples. 36 And looking at Jesus as He walked, he said, "Behold the Lamb of God!"

37 The two disciples heard him speak, and they followed Jesus. 38 Then Jesus turned, and seeing them following, said to them, "What do you seek?"

They said to Him, "Rabbi" (which is to say, when translated, Teacher), "where are You staying?"

39 He said to them, "Come and see." They came and saw where He was staying, and remained with Him that day (now it was about the tenth hour).

40 One of the two who heard John *speak,* and followed Him, was Andrew, Simon Peter's brother. 41 He first found his own brother Simon, and said to him, "We have found the Messiah" (which is translated, the Christ). 42 And he brought him to Jesus.

Now when Jesus looked at him, He said, "You are Simon the son of Jonah.*ª* You shall be called Cephas" (which is translated, A Stone).

43 The following day Jesus wanted to go to Galilee, and He found Philip and said to him, "Follow Me." 44 Now Philip was from Bethsaida, the city of Andrew and Peter. 45 Philip found Nathanael and said to him, "We have found Him of whom Moses in the law, and also the prophets, wrote—Jesus of Nazareth, the son of Joseph."

46 And Nathanael said to him, "Can anything good come out of Nazareth?"

Philip said to him, "Come and see."

47 Jesus saw Nathanael coming toward Him, and said of him, "Behold, an Israelite indeed, in whom is no deceit!"

48 Nathanael said to Him, "How do You know me?"

Jesus answered and said to him, "Before Philip called you, when you were under the fig tree, I saw you."

49 Nathanael answered and said to Him, "Rabbi, You are the Son of God! You are the King of Israel!"

50 Jesus answered and said to him, "Because I said to you, 'I saw you under the fig tree,' do you believe? You will see greater things than these." 51 And He said to him, "Most assuredly, I say to you, hereafter*ª* you shall see heaven open, and the angels of God ascending and descending upon the Son of Man."

2 On the third day there was a wedding in Cana of Galilee, and the mother of Jesus was there. 2 Now both Jesus and His disciples were invited to the wedding. 3 And when they ran out of wine, the mother of Jesus said to Him, "They have no wine."

4 Jesus said to her, "Woman, what does your concern have to do with Me? My hour has not yet come."

5 His mother said to the servants, "Whatever He says to you, do *it.*"

6 Now there were set there six waterpots of stone, according to the manner of purification of the Jews, containing twenty or thirty gallons apiece. 7 Jesus said to them, "Fill the waterpots with water." And they filled them up to the brim. 8 And He said to them, "Draw *some* out now, and take *it* to the master of the feast." And they took *it.* 9 When the master of the feast had tasted the water that was made wine, and did not know where it came from (but the servants who had drawn the water knew), the master of the feast called the bridegroom. 10 And he said to him, "Every man at the beginning sets out the good wine, and when the *guests* have well drunk, then the inferior. You have kept the good wine until now!"

11 This beginning of signs Jesus did in Cana of Galilee, and manifested His glory; and His disciples believed in Him.

12 After this He went down to Capernaum, He, His mother, His brothers, and His disciples; and they did not stay there many days.

13 Now the Passover of the Jews was at hand, and Jesus went up to Jerusalem. 14 And He found in the temple those who sold oxen and sheep and doves, and the money changers doing business. 15 When He had made a whip of cords, He drove them all out of the temple, with the sheep and the oxen, and poured out the changers' money and overturned the tables. 16 And He said to those who sold doves, "Take these things away! Do not make My Father's house a house of merchandise!"

1:42 *ª*NU-Text reads *John.*   1:51 *ª*NU-Text omits *hereafter.*

---

*E*very addiction . . . every fear . . . every failure . . . must be buried in Christ Jesus! Commit those things to the Lord once and for all. Give them to Him. Seal them up in a grave forever. And arise.

17 Then His disciples remembered that it was written, *"Zeal for Your house has eaten^a Me up."^b*

18 So the Jews answered and said to Him, "What sign do You show to us, since You do these things?"

19 Jesus answered and said to them, "Destroy this temple, and in three days I will raise it up."

20 Then the Jews said, "It has taken forty-six years to build this temple, and will You raise it up in three days?"

21 But He was speaking of the temple of His body. 22 Therefore, when He had risen from the dead, His disciples remembered that He had said this to them;^a and they believed the Scripture and the word which Jesus had said.

23 Now when He was in Jerusalem at the Passover, during the feast, many believed in His name when they saw the signs which He did. 24 But Jesus did not commit Himself to them, because He knew all *men,* 25 and had no need that anyone should testify of man, for He knew what was in man.

3 There was a man of the Pharisees named Nicodemus, a ruler of the Jews. 2 This man came to Jesus by night and said to Him, "Rabbi, we know that You are a teacher come from God; for no one can do these signs that You do unless God is with him."

3 Jesus answered and said to him, "Most assuredly, I say to you, unless one is born again, he cannot see the kingdom of God."

4 Nicodemus said to Him, "How can a man be born when he is old? Can he enter a second time into his mother's womb and be born?"

5 Jesus answered, "Most assuredly, I say to you, unless one is born of water and the Spirit, he cannot enter the kingdom of God. 6 That which is born of the flesh is flesh, and that which is born of the Spirit is spirit. 7 Do not marvel that I said to you, 'You must be born again.' 8 The wind blows where it wishes, and you hear the sound of it, but cannot tell where it comes from and where it goes. So is everyone who is born of the Spirit."

9 Nicodemus answered and said to Him, "How can these things be?"

10 Jesus answered and said to him, "Are you the teacher of Israel, and do not know these things? 11 Most assuredly, I say to you, We speak what We know and testify what We have seen, and you do not receive Our witness. 12 If I have told you earthly things and you do not believe, how will you believe if I tell you heavenly things? 13 No one has ascended to heaven but He who came down from heaven, *that is,* the Son of Man who is in heaven.^a 14 And as Moses lifted up the serpent in the wilderness, even so must the Son of Man be lifted up, 15 that whoever believes in Him should not perish but^a have eternal life. 16 For God so loved the world that He gave His only begotten Son, that whoever believes in Him should not perish but have everlasting life. 17 For God did not send His Son into the world to condemn the world, but that the world through Him might be saved.

18 "He who believes in Him is not condemned; but he who does not believe is condemned already, because he has not believed in the name of the only begotten Son of God. 19 And this is the condemnation, that the light has come into the world, and men loved darkness rather than light, because their deeds were evil. 20 For everyone practicing evil hates the light and does not come to the light, lest his deeds should be exposed. 21 But he who does the truth comes to the light, that his deeds may be clearly seen, that they have been done in God."

22 After these things Jesus and His disciples came into the land of Judea, and there He remained with them and baptized. 23 Now John also was baptizing in Aenon near Salim, because there was much water there. And they came and were baptized. 24 For John had not yet been thrown into prison.

25 Then there arose a dispute between *some* of John's disciples and the Jews about purification. 26 And they came to John and said to him, "Rabbi, He who was with you beyond the Jordan, to whom you have testified—behold, He is bap-

---

2:17 ^aNU-Text and M-Text read *will eat.* ^bPsalm 69:9   2:22 ^aNU-Text and M-Text omit *to them.*
3:13 ^aNU-Text omits *who is in heaven.*   3:15 ^aNU-Text omits *not perish but.*

---

*T*here's a difference between being saved and being healed until you are whole. Salvation happens instantly. Healing can be a lifelong process.

Born "Unclean"

John 3:5

Before my first experience in the delivery room, the only newborn babies I had seen were the ones on television—the ones who are born looking like those adorable infants in baby-food commercials.

When my daughter was born, she didn't look anything like I expected. She was a mess. Her appearance wasn't her fault, of course. The fact is— she looked exactly like what she had just been through!

Unfortunately for women, it seems the church has a special desire for its female babies to look like Gerber babies. A double standard has developed. A man can come into the church with a long string of sins trailing behind him and the prevailing attitude is, "Well, boys will be boys. Naughty, naughty. He finally quit sowing his wild oats, praise God." But if a woman has had two or three babies by different men and then she comes into the church and word of her past gets out, people treat her as if she has leprosy.

We have placed a veil over the feminine heart in our churches. We insist that women smile and look good and say, "I'm living a victorious life in Christ." We allow them no opportunity to say, "I'm hurting. I'm wounded. I'm struggling."

They are forced to keep a secret because no platform has been established to allow women to be real with one another without fear of being "stoned" to death. The secrets that lie untold in women's hearts are killing a vital part of the church.

Can you imagine a woman coming into your church and saying during a testimony service, "I was abused as a child. I was the victim of incest and then when I got a little older, I was raped. I've had four children now by three different husbands. I've had about twenty-nine boyfriends in my life, and I'm presently divorced and trying hard to raise my kids. I know the Lord has saved me and here I am. I'm struggling, but I know I'm saved."

It's time to get real. It's time that people heard your real testimony. What drove you to the altar? What nightmarish experience caused you to fall upon His mercy and cry out to God? Nobody cries, "Save me!" unless they are drowning. It's time that we start looking at each other with an eye toward seeing what others have been through. It's time we see their brokenness and their heartache. It's time we see their tenacity, their ability, their faith. It's time to look inside ourselves and inside one another and admit, "We are all born 'unclean.' "

tizing, and all are coming to Him!"
27 John answered and said, "A man can receive nothing unless it has been given to him from heaven. 28 You yourselves bear me witness, that I said, 'I am not the Christ,' but, 'I have been sent before Him.' 29 He who has the bride is the bridegroom; but the friend of the bridegroom, who stands and hears him, rejoices greatly because of the bridegroom's voice. Therefore this joy of mine is fulfilled. 30 He must increase, but I *must* decrease. 31 He who comes from above is above all; he who is of the earth is earthly and speaks of the earth. He who comes from heaven is above all. 32 And what He has seen and heard, that He testifies; and no one receives His testimony. 33 He who has received His testimony has certified that God is true. 34 For He whom God has sent speaks the words of God, for God does not give the Spirit by measure. 35 The Father loves the Son, and has given all things into His hand. 36 He who believes in the Son has everlasting life; and he who does not believe the Son shall not see life, but the wrath of God abides on him."

4 Therefore, when the Lord knew that the Pharisees had heard that Jesus made and baptized more disciples than John 2 (though Jesus Himself did not baptize, but His disciples), 3 He left Judea and departed again to Galilee. 4 But He needed to go through Samaria.
5 So He came to a city of Samaria which is called Sychar, near the plot of ground that Jacob gave to his son Joseph. 6 Now Jacob's well was there. Jesus therefore, being wearied from *His* journey, sat thus by the well. It was about the sixth hour.
7 A woman of Samaria came to draw water. Jesus said to her, "Give Me a drink." 8 For His disciples had gone away into the city to buy food.
9 Then the woman of Samaria said to Him, "How is it that You, being a Jew, ask a drink from me, a Samaritan woman?" For Jews have no dealings with Samaritans.
10 Jesus answered and said to her, "If you knew the gift of God, and who it is who says to you, 'Give Me a drink,' you would have asked Him, and He would have given you living water."

11 The woman said to Him, "Sir, You have nothing to draw with, and the well is deep. Where then do You get that living water? 12 Are You greater than our father Jacob, who gave us the well, and drank from it himself, as well as his sons and his livestock?"
13 Jesus answered and said to her, "Whoever drinks of this water will thirst again, 14 but whoever drinks of the water that I shall give him will never thirst. But the water that I shall give him will become in him a fountain of water springing up into everlasting life."
15 The woman said to Him, "Sir, give me this water, that I may not thirst, nor come here to draw."
16 Jesus said to her, "Go, call your husband, and come here."
17 The woman answered and said, "I have no husband."
Jesus said to her, "You have well said, 'I have no husband,' 18 for you have had five husbands, and the one whom you now have is not your husband; in that you spoke truly."
19 The woman said to Him, "Sir, I perceive that You are a prophet. 20 Our fathers worshiped on this mountain, and you *Jews* say that in Jerusalem is the place where one ought to worship."
21 Jesus said to her, "Woman, believe Me, the hour is coming when you will neither on this mountain, nor in Jerusalem, worship the Father. 22 You worship what you do not know; we know what we worship, for salvation is of the Jews. 23 But the hour is coming, and now is, when the true worshipers will worship the Father in spirit and truth; for the Father is seeking such to worship Him. 24 God *is* Spirit, and those who worship Him must worship in spirit and truth."
25 The woman said to Him, "I know that Messiah is coming" (who is called Christ). "When He comes, He will tell us all things."
26 Jesus said to her, "I who speak to you am *He*."
27 And at this *point* His disciples came, and they marveled that He talked with a woman; yet no one said, "What do You seek?" or, "Why are You talking with her?"
28 The woman then left her waterpot, went her way into the city, and said to the men, 29 "Come, see a Man

There are those who will tell you, "If you were really saved, you wouldn't sin like that." Lapses into error have nothing to do with the salvation of your spirit. They have nothing to do with the healing of your soul or the fact that you are not yet whole.

True Worship

John 4:23, 24

rue worship is born when true sacrifice occurs—laying upon the altar something you'd hoped to keep for yourself. You can never be really anointed until you personally experience a situation that calls you to lay aside your garments. Tears of worship fall down a face that has been unveiled and laid bare before God. Who can help but worship Him when we see Him with unclouded vision?

It is what you have left behind and laid aside that seasons you as a true worshiper. How much does it cost to be the "real" you? What have you left behind to follow Him? Whatever it is determines the effectiveness of your ability to touch the world and speak to its heart.

Jesus, in one final blaze of teaching excellence, acted out an unforgettable sermon. He showed the disciples that they would never be able to change the atmosphere around them or wash anybody's feet until they were willing to drop their defenses and endure risk and rejection.

Laying aside your garments requires you to say, "Here are my grudges and my unforgiveness. Here is my need to impress and be acknowledged. Here's my time and my overtime. Here is anything that I may be wrapped up in that hinders me from receiving new glory. You will never have to take these things, Lord. You will not have to snatch them from my clenched fist as I wrestle in rebellion. I have heard the soft brush of Your voice like wind across my face. I will give You whatever it takes to be who You want me to be. Even if I'm the only one who stands in crowds of religious indifference, I will lay aside my garments!"

When people are stripped bare, there is no difference between the executive and the janitor, between the pew-sitter and the pastor. Is that why we're so afraid to let anyone see who we really are? Have we become so addicted to our distinctions that we have lost our commonality?

Come down from your lofty perch of superiority and wash the feet of some hurting person. There is no difference between those feet and the feet of the one who washes them. Your ministry begins to count when you know that there is precious little difference between the people you serve and yourself. Then and only then will you prove that you have truly laid aside your garments.

who told me all things that I ever did. Could this be the Christ?" 30 Then they went out of the city and came to Him.

31 In the meantime His disciples urged Him, saying, "Rabbi, eat."

32 But He said to them, "I have food to eat of which you do not know."

33 Therefore the disciples said to one another, "Has anyone brought Him *anything* to eat?"

34 Jesus said to them, "My food is to do the will of Him who sent Me, and to finish His work. 35 Do you not say, 'There are still four months and *then* comes the harvest'? Behold, I say to you, lift up your eyes and look at the fields, for they are already white for harvest! 36 And he who reaps receives wages, and gathers fruit for eternal life, that both he who sows and he who reaps may rejoice together. 37 For in this the saying is true: 'One sows and another reaps.' 38 I sent you to reap that for which you have not labored; others have labored, and you have entered into their labors."

39 And many of the Samaritans of that city believed in Him because of the word of the woman who testified, "He told me all that I *ever* did." 40 So when the Samaritans had come to Him, they urged Him to stay with them; and He stayed there two days. 41 And many more believed because of His own word.

42 Then they said to the woman, "Now we believe, not because of what you said, for we ourselves have heard *Him* and we know that this is indeed the Christ,ª the Savior of the world."

43 Now after the two days He departed from there and went to Galilee. 44 For Jesus Himself testified that a prophet has no honor in his own country. 45 So when He came to Galilee, the Galileans received Him, having seen all the things He did in Jerusalem at the feast; for they also had gone to the feast.

46 So Jesus came again to Cana of Galilee where He had made the water wine. And there was a certain nobleman whose son was sick at Capernaum. 47 When he heard that Jesus had come out of Judea into Galilee, he went to Him and implored Him

to come down and heal his son, for he was at the point of death. 48 Then Jesus said to him, "Unless you *people* see signs and wonders, you will by no means believe."

49 The nobleman said to Him, "Sir, come down before my child dies!"

50 Jesus said to him, "Go your way; your son lives." So the man believed the word that Jesus spoke to him, and he went his way. 51 And as he was now going down, his servants met him and told *him,* saying, "Your son lives!"

52 Then he inquired of them the hour when he got better. And they said to him, "Yesterday at the seventh hour the fever left him." 53 So the father knew that *it was* at the same hour in which Jesus said to him, "Your son lives." And he himself believed, and his whole household.

54 This again *is* the second sign Jesus did when He had come out of Judea into Galilee.

5 After this there was a feast of the Jews, and Jesus went up to Jerusalem. 2 Now there is in Jerusalem by the Sheep *Gate* a pool, which is called in Hebrew, Bethesda,ª having five porches. 3 In these lay a great multitude of sick people, blind, lame, paralyzed, waiting for the moving of the water. 4 For an angel went down at a certain time into the pool and stirred up the water; then whoever stepped in first, after the stirring of the water, was made well of whatever disease he had.ª 5 Now a certain man was there who had an infirmity thirty-eight years. 6 When Jesus saw him lying there, and knew that he already had been *in that condition* a long time, He said to him, "Do you want to be made well?"

7 The sick man answered Him, "Sir, I have no man to put me into the pool when the water is stirred up; but while I am coming, another steps down before me."

8 Jesus said to him, "Rise, take up your bed and walk." 9 And immediately the man was made well, took up his bed, and walked.

And that day was the Sabbath. 10 The Jews therefore said to him who was cured, "It is the Sabbath;

4:42 ªNU-Text omits *the Christ.*   5:2 ªNU-Text reads *Bethzatha.*   5:4 ªNU-Text omits *waiting for the moving of the water* at the end of verse 3, and all of verse 4.

Gospel Pearls

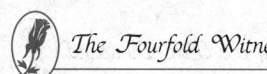

it is not lawful for you to carry your bed."

11 He answered them, "He who made me well said to me, 'Take up your bed and walk.' "

12 Then they asked him, "Who is the Man who said to you, 'Take up your bed and walk'?" 13 But the one who was healed did not know who it was, for Jesus had withdrawn, a multitude being in *that* place. 14 Afterward Jesus found him in the temple, and said to him, "See, you have been made well. Sin no more, lest a worse thing come upon you."

15 The man departed and told the Jews that it was Jesus who had made him well.

16 For this reason the Jews persecuted Jesus, and sought to kill Him,*a* because He had done these things on the Sabbath. 17 But Jesus answered them, "My Father has been working until now, and I have been working."

18 Therefore the Jews sought all the more to kill Him, because He not only broke the Sabbath, but also said that God was His Father, making Himself equal with God. 19 Then Jesus answered and said to them, "Most assuredly, I say to you, the Son can do nothing of Himself, but what He sees the Father do; for whatever He does, the Son also does in like manner. 20 For the Father loves the Son, and shows Him all things that He Himself does; and He will show Him greater works than these, that you may marvel. 21 For as the Father raises the dead and gives life to *them,* even so the Son gives life to whom He will. 22 For the Father judges no one, but has committed all judgment to the Son, 23 that all should honor the Son just as they honor the Father. He who does not honor the Son does not honor the Father who sent Him.

24 "Most assuredly, I say to you, he who hears My word and believes in Him who sent Me has everlasting life, and shall not come into judgment, but has passed from death into life. 25 Most assuredly, I say to you, the hour is coming, and now is, when the dead will hear the voice of the Son of God; and those who hear will live. 26 For as the Father has life in Himself, so He has granted the Son to have life in Himself, 27 and has given

Him authority to execute judgment also, because He is the Son of Man. 28 Do not marvel at this; for the hour is coming in which all who are in the graves will hear His voice 29 and come forth—those who have done good, to the resurrection of life, and those who have done evil, to the resurrection of condemnation. 30 I can of Myself do nothing. As I hear, I judge; and My judgment is righteous, because I do not seek My own will but the will of the Father who sent Me.

31 "If I bear witness of Myself, My witness is not true. 32 There is another who bears witness of Me, and I know that the witness which He witnesses of Me is true. 33 You have sent to John, and he has borne witness to the truth. 34 Yet I do not receive testimony from man, but I say these things that you may be saved. 35 He was the burning and shining lamp, and you were willing for a time to rejoice in his light. 36 But I have a greater witness than John's; for the works which the Father has given Me to finish—the very works that I do—bear witness of Me, that the Father has sent Me. 37 And the Father Himself, who sent Me, has testified of Me. You have neither heard His voice at any time, nor seen His form. 38 But you do not have His word abiding in you, because whom He sent, Him you do not believe. 39 You search the Scriptures, for in them you think you have eternal life; and these are they which testify of Me. 40 But you are not willing to come to Me that you may have life.

41 "I do not receive honor from men. 42 But I know you, that you do not have the love of God in you. 43 I have come in My Father's name, and you do not receive Me; if another comes in his own name, him you will receive. 44 How can you believe, who receive honor from one another, and do not seek the honor that *comes* from the only God? 45 Do not think that I shall accuse you to the Father; there is *one* who accuses you—Moses, in whom you trust. 46 For if you believed Moses, you would believe Me; for he wrote about Me. 47 But if you do not believe his writings, how will you believe My words?"

5:16 *a*NU-Text omits *and sought to kill Him.*

6 After these things Jesus went over the Sea of Galilee, which is *the Sea* of Tiberias. 2 Then a great multitude followed Him, because they saw His signs which He performed on those who were diseased. 3 And Jesus went up on the mountain, and there He sat with His disciples. 4 Now the Passover, a feast of the Jews, was near. 5 Then Jesus lifted up *His* eyes, and seeing a great multitude coming toward Him, He said to Philip, "Where shall we buy bread, that these may eat?" 6 But this He said to test him, for He Himself knew what He would do.

7 Philip answered Him, "Two hundred denarii worth of bread is not sufficient for them, that every one of them may have a little."

8 One of His disciples, Andrew, Simon Peter's brother, said to Him, 9 "There is a lad here who has five barley loaves and two small fish, but what are they among so many?"

10 Then Jesus said, "Make the people sit down." Now there was much grass in the place. So the men sat down, in number about five thousand. 11 And Jesus took the loaves, and when He had given thanks He distributed *them* to the disciples, and the disciples[a] to those sitting down; and likewise of the fish, as much as they wanted. 12 So when they were filled, He said to His disciples, "Gather up the fragments that remain, so that nothing is lost." 13 Therefore they gathered *them* up, and filled twelve baskets with the fragments of the five barley loaves which were left over by those who had eaten. 14 Then those men, when they had seen the sign that Jesus did, said, "This is truly the Prophet who is to come into the world."

15 Therefore when Jesus perceived that they were about to come and take Him by force to make Him king, He departed again to the mountain by Himself alone.

16 Now when evening came, His disciples went down to the sea, 17 got into the boat, and went over the sea toward Capernaum. And it was already dark, and Jesus had not come to them. 18 Then the sea arose because a great wind was blowing.

19 So when they had rowed about three or four miles,[a] they saw Jesus walking on the sea and drawing near the boat; and they were afraid. 20 But He said to them, "It is I; do not be afraid." 21 Then they willingly received Him into the boat, and immediately the boat was at the land where they were going.

22 On the following day, when the people who were standing on the other side of the sea saw that there was no other boat there, except that one which His disciples had entered,[a] and that Jesus had not entered the boat with His disciples, but His disciples had gone away alone— 23 however, other boats came from Tiberias, near the place where they ate bread after the Lord had given thanks— 24 when the people therefore saw that Jesus was not there, nor His disciples, they also got into boats and came to Capernaum, seeking Jesus. 25 And when they found Him on the other side of the sea, they said to Him, "Rabbi, when did You come here?"

26 Jesus answered them and said, "Most assuredly, I say to you, you seek Me, not because you saw the signs, but because you ate of the loaves and were filled. 27 Do not labor for the food which perishes, but for the food which endures to everlasting life, which the Son of Man will give you, because God the Father has set His seal on Him."

28 Then they said to Him, "What shall we do, that we may work the works of God?"

29 Jesus answered and said to them, "This is the work of God, that you believe in Him whom He sent."

30 Therefore they said to Him, "What sign will You perform then, that we may see it and believe You? What work will You do? 31 Our fathers ate the manna in the desert; as it is written, *'He gave them bread from heaven to eat.'*[a]

32 Then Jesus said to them, "Most assuredly, I say to you, Moses did not give you the bread from heaven, but My Father gives you the true bread from heaven. 33 For the bread of God is He who comes down from heaven and gives life to the world."

6:11 [a]NU-Text omits *to the disciples, and the disciples.* 6:19 [a]Literally *twenty-five or thirty stadia*
6:22 [a]NU-Text omits *that* and *which His disciples had entered.* 6:31 [a]Exodus 16:4; Nehemiah 9:15; Psalm 78:24

Gospel Pearls

34 Then they said to Him, "Lord, give us this bread always."

35 And Jesus said to them, "I am the bread of life. He who comes to Me shall never hunger, and he who believes in Me shall never thirst. 36 But I said to you that you have seen Me and yet do not believe. 37 All that the Father gives Me will come to Me, and the one who comes to Me I will by no means cast out. 38 For I have come down from heaven, not to do My own will, but the will of Him who sent Me. 39 This is the will of the Father who sent Me, that of all He has given Me I should lose nothing, but should raise it up at the last day. 40 And this is the will of Him who sent Me, that everyone who sees the Son and believes in Him may have everlasting life; and I will raise him up at the last day."

41 The Jews then complained about Him, because He said, "I am the bread which came down from heaven." 42 And they said, "Is not this Jesus, the son of Joseph, whose father and mother we know? How is it then that He says, 'I have come down from heaven'?"

43 Jesus therefore answered and said to them, "Do not murmur among yourselves. 44 No one can come to Me unless the Father who sent Me draws him; and I will raise him up at the last day. 45 It is written in the prophets, *'And they shall all be taught by God.'*[a] Therefore everyone who has heard and learned[b] from the Father comes to Me. 46 Not that anyone has seen the Father, except He who is from God; He has seen the Father. 47 Most assuredly, I say to you, he who believes in Me[a] has everlasting life. 48 I am the bread of life. 49 Your fathers ate the manna in the wilderness, and are dead. 50 This is the bread which comes down from heaven, that one may eat of it and not die. 51 I am the living bread which came down from heaven. If anyone eats of this bread, he will live forever; and the bread that I shall give is My flesh, which I shall give for the life of the world."

52 The Jews therefore quarreled among themselves, saying, "How can this Man give us *His* flesh to eat?"

53 Then Jesus said to them, "Most assuredly, I say to you, unless you eat the flesh of the Son of Man and drink His blood, you have no life in you. 54 Whoever eats My flesh and drinks My blood has eternal life, and I will raise him up at the last day. 55 For My flesh is food indeed,[a] and My blood is drink indeed. 56 He who eats My flesh and drinks My blood abides in Me, and I in him. 57 As the living Father sent Me, and I live because of the Father, so he who feeds on Me will live because of Me. 58 This is the bread which came down from heaven—not as your fathers ate the manna, and are dead. He who eats this bread will live forever."

59 These things He said in the synagogue as He taught in Capernaum.

60 Therefore many of His disciples, when they heard *this*, said, "This is a hard saying; who can understand it?"

61 When Jesus knew in Himself that His disciples complained about this, He said to them, "Does this offend you? 62 *What* then if you should see the Son of Man ascend where He was before? 63 It is the Spirit who gives life; the flesh profits nothing. The words that I speak to you are spirit, and *they* are life. 64 But there are some of you who do not believe." For Jesus knew from the beginning who they were who did not believe, and who would betray Him. 65 And He said, "Therefore I have said to you that no one can come to Me unless it has been granted to him by My Father."

66 From that *time* many of His disciples went back and walked with Him no more. 67 Then Jesus said to the twelve, "Do you also want to go away?"

68 But Simon Peter answered Him, "Lord, to whom shall we go? You have the words of eternal life. 69 Also we have come to believe and know that You are the Christ, the Son of the living God."[a]

70 Jesus answered them, "Did I not choose you, the twelve, and one of you is a devil?" 71 He spoke of Judas Iscariot, *the son* of Simon, for it was he who would betray Him, being one of the twelve.

6:45 [a]Isaiah 54:13   [b]M-Text reads *hears and has learned.*   6:47 [a]NU-Text omits *in Me.*
6:55 [a]NU-Text reads *true food* and *true drink.*   6:69 [a]NU-Text reads *You are the Holy One of God.*

We must learn to thank God for who we are. Don't be a silly woman watching television and crying because she doesn't look like the girl who opened up the window in the game show. If God had wanted you to look like that, He would have made you like that.

7 After these things Jesus walked in Galilee; for He did not want to walk in Judea, because the Jews^a sought to kill Him. 2 Now the Jews' Feast of Tabernacles was at hand. 3 His brothers therefore said to Him, "Depart from here and go into Judea, that Your disciples also may see the works that You are doing. 4 For no one does anything in secret while he himself seeks to be known openly. If You do these things, show Yourself to the world." 5 For even His brothers did not believe in Him.

6 Then Jesus said to them, "My time has not yet come, but your time is always ready. 7 The world cannot hate you, but it hates Me because I testify of it that its works are evil. 8 You go up to this feast. I am not yet^a going up to this feast, for My time has not yet fully come." 9 When He had said these things to them, He remained in Galilee.

10 But when His brothers had gone up, then He also went up to the feast, not openly, but as it were in secret. 11 Then the Jews sought Him at the feast, and said, "Where is He?" 12 And there was much complaining among the people concerning Him. Some said, "He is good"; others said, "No, on the contrary, He deceives the people." 13 However, no one spoke openly of Him for fear of the Jews.

14 Now about the middle of the feast Jesus went up into the temple and taught. 15 And the Jews marveled, saying, "How does this Man know letters, having never studied?" 16 Jesus^a answered them and said, "My doctrine is not Mine, but His who sent Me. 17 If anyone wills to do His will, he shall know concerning the doctrine, whether it is from God or *whether* I speak on My own *authority.* 18 He who speaks from himself seeks his own glory; but He who seeks the glory of the One who sent Him is true, and no unrighteousness is in Him. 19 Did not Moses give you the law, yet none of you keeps the law? Why do you seek to kill Me?"

20 The people answered and said, "You have a demon. Who is seeking to kill You?"

21 Jesus answered and said to them, "I did one work, and you all marvel. 22 Moses therefore gave you circumcision (not that it is from Moses, but from the fathers), and you circumcise a man on the Sabbath. 23 If a man receives circumcision on the Sabbath, so that the law of Moses should not be broken, are you angry with Me because I made a man completely well on the Sabbath? 24 Do not judge according to appearance, but judge with righteous judgment."

25 Now some of them from Jerusalem said, "Is this not He whom they seek to kill? 26 But look! He speaks boldly, and they say nothing to Him. Do the rulers know indeed that this is truly^a the Christ? 27 However, we know where this Man is from; but when the Christ comes, no one knows where He is from."

28 Then Jesus cried out, as He taught in the temple, saying, "You both know Me, and you know where I am from; and I have not come of Myself, but He who sent Me is true, whom you do not know. 29 But^a I know Him, for I am from Him, and He sent Me."

30 Therefore they sought to take Him; but no one laid a hand on Him, because His hour had not yet come. 31 And many of the people believed in Him, and said, "When the Christ comes, will He do more signs than these which this *Man* has done?"

32 The Pharisees heard the crowd murmuring these things concerning Him, and the Pharisees and the chief priests sent officers to take Him. 33 Then Jesus said to them,^a "I shall be with you a little while longer, and *then* I go to Him who sent Me. 34 You will seek Me and not find *Me,* and where I am you cannot come."

35 Then the Jews said among themselves, "Where does He intend to go that we shall not find Him? Does He intend to go to the Dispersion among the Greeks and teach the Greeks? 36 What is this thing that He said, 'You will seek Me and not find Me, and where I am you cannot come'?"

37 On the last day, that great *day* of the feast, Jesus stood and cried out, saying, "If anyone thirsts, let him come to Me and drink. 38 He who believes in Me, as the Scripture has

---

7:1 ^aThat is, the ruling authorities   7:8 ^aNU-Text omits *yet.*   7:16 ^aNU-Text and M-Text read *So Jesus.*   7:26 ^aNU-Text omits *truly.*   7:29 ^aNU-Text and M-Text omit *But.*   7:33 ^aNU-Text and M-Text omit *to them.*

Gospel Pearls

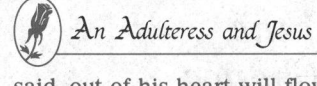

said, out of his heart will flow rivers of living water." 39 But this He spoke concerning the Spirit, whom those believing[a] in Him would receive; for the Holy[b] Spirit was not yet *given*, because Jesus was not yet glorified.

40 Therefore many[a] from the crowd, when they heard this saying, said, "Truly this is the Prophet." 41 Others said, "This is the Christ."

But some said, "Will the Christ come out of Galilee? 42 Has not the Scripture said that the Christ comes from the seed of David and from the town of Bethlehem, where David was?" 43 So there was a division among the people because of Him. 44 Now some of them wanted to take Him, but no one laid hands on Him.

45 Then the officers came to the chief priests and Pharisees, who said to them, "Why have you not brought Him?"

46 The officers answered, "No man ever spoke like this Man!"

47 Then the Pharisees answered them, "Are you also deceived? 48 Have any of the rulers or the Pharisees believed in Him? 49 But this crowd that does not know the law is accursed."

50 Nicodemus (he who came to Jesus by night,[a] being one of them) said to them, 51 "Does our law judge a man before it hears him and knows what he is doing?"

52 They answered and said to him, "Are you also from Galilee? Search and look, for no prophet has arisen[a] out of Galilee."

53 And everyone went to his *own* house.[a]

8 But Jesus went to the Mount of Olives.

2 Now early[a] in the morning He came again into the temple, and all the people came to Him; and He sat down and taught them. 3 Then the scribes and Pharisees brought to Him a woman caught in adultery. And when they had set her in the midst, 4 they said to Him, "Teacher, this woman was caught[a] in adultery, in the very act. 5 Now Moses, in the law, commanded[a] us that such should be stoned.[b] But what do You say?"[c] 6 This they said, testing Him, that they might have *something* of which to accuse Him. But Jesus stooped down and wrote on the ground with *His* finger, as though He did not hear.[a]

7 So when they continued asking Him, He raised Himself up[a] and said to them, "He who is without sin among you, let him throw a stone at her first." 8 And again He stooped down and wrote on the ground. 9 Then those who heard *it*, being convicted by *their* conscience,[a] went out one by one, beginning with the oldest *even* to the last. And Jesus was left alone, and the woman standing in the midst. 10 When Jesus had raised Himself up and saw no one but the woman, He said to her,[a] "Woman, where are those accusers of yours?[b] Has no one condemned you?"

11 She said, "No one, Lord."

And Jesus said to her, "Neither do I condemn you; go and[a] sin no more."

12 Then Jesus spoke to them again, saying, "I am the light of the world. He who follows Me shall not walk in darkness, but have the light of life."

13 The Pharisees therefore said to Him, "You bear witness of Yourself; Your witness is not true."

14 Jesus answered and said to them, "Even if I bear witness of Myself, My witness is true, for I know where I came from and where I am going; but you do not know where I come from and where I am going. 15 You judge according to the flesh; I judge no one. 16 And yet if I do judge, My judgment is true; for I am not alone, but I *am* with the Father who sent Me. 17 It is also written in your law that the testimony of two men is true. 18 I am One who bears witness of Myself, and the Father who sent Me bears witness of Me."

7:39 [a]NU-Text reads *who believed*.	[b]NU-Text omits *Holy*.	7:40 [a]NU-Text reads *some*.
7:50 [a]NU-Text reads *before*.	7:52 [a]NU-Text reads *is to rise*.	7:53 [a]The words *And everyone* through *sin no more* (8:11) are bracketed by NU-Text as not original. They are present in over 900 manuscripts.	8:2 [a]M-Text reads *very early*.	8:4 [a]M-Text reads *we found this woman*.
8:5 [a]M-Text reads *in our law Moses commanded*.	[b]NU-Text and M-Text read *to stone such*.	[c]M-Text adds *about her*.	8:6 [a]NU-Text and M-Text omit *as though He did not hear*.	8:7 [a]M-Text reads *He looked up*.	8:9 [a]NU-Text and M-Text omit *being convicted by their conscience*.	8:10 [a]NU-Text omits *and saw no one but the woman*; M-Text reads *He saw her and said*.	[b]NU-Text and M-Text omit *of yours*.	8:11 [a]NU-Text and M-Text add *from now on*.

A woman's beauty and strength are not on the outside. There is more to you than clothes. There's more to you than gold. There's more to you than a great hairdo.

Lord of the
Second Chance

John 8:3–11

*I*n this passage, Jesus dealt with an issue raised by a group of religious leaders who had caught a woman in the very act of adultery. There was no question that she was guilty. And the law was clear: Adulterers must be stoned to death. But adultery takes two. Have you ever wondered where the man was who had been committing adultery with this woman? Surely the eyewitnesses knew who he was.

Clearly Jesus saw the foolish religious pride in the hearts of these accusers. He was not condoning the sin of adultery. He simply understood the need to meet people where they were and minister to their need. He saw the pride in the Pharisees and ministered correction to that pride. He saw the wounded woman and ministered forgiveness. Justice demanded that she be stoned to death. Mercy threw the case out of court.

Even today there seems to be a double standard when it comes to sexual sin. We often look down on a woman because of her past, but overlook who she has become. Jesus, however, knew the power of a second chance.

People with a past have always been able to come to Jesus. He makes them into something fresh and beautiful, something new. It is said that Mary Magdalene was a prostitute. But Christ was moved with compassion for her and forgave her, and she became one of His most devoted followers.

You may be like these women. You may have come into the church. Perhaps you have made a strong commitment to Christ and have the very Spirit of God living within you. Yet you walk as a cripple. You have been stoned and ridiculed. You may not be physically broken and bowed, but you are wounded within.

The chains that bind you may be from events over which you had no control. Or you may have willfully lived a life that has brought bondage and pain. Regardless of the source, Jesus has come to set you free. He is unleashing the women of His church. He forgives, heals, and restores. You can find the potential of a wonderful future because of His power operating in your life.

The blood of Jesus is efficacious, cleansing the woman who feels unclean. How can we reject what He has cleansed and made whole? Just as He said to the woman then, He proclaims today, "Neither do I condemn you; go and sin no more" (John 8:11).

19 Then they said to Him, "Where is Your Father?"

Jesus answered, "You know neither Me nor My Father. If you had known Me, you would have known My Father also."

20 These words Jesus spoke in the treasury, as He taught in the temple; and no one laid hands on Him, for His hour had not yet come.

21 Then Jesus said to them again, "I am going away, and you will seek Me, and will die in your sin. Where I go you cannot come."

22 So the Jews said, "Will He kill Himself, because He says, 'Where I go you cannot come?'"

23 And He said to them, "You are from beneath; I am from above. You are of this world; I am not of this world. 24 Therefore I said to you that you will die in your sins; for if you do not believe that I am He, you will die in your sins."

25 Then they said to Him, "Who are You?"

And Jesus said to them, "Just what I have been saying to you from the beginning. 26 I have many things to say and to judge concerning you, but He who sent Me is true; and I speak to the world those things which I heard from Him."

27 They did not understand that He spoke to them of the Father.

28 Then Jesus said to them, "When you lift up the Son of Man, then you will know that I am He, and that I do nothing of Myself; but as My Father taught Me, I speak these things. 29 And He who sent Me is with Me. The Father has not left Me alone, for I always do those things that please Him." 30 As He spoke these words, many believed in Him.

31 Then Jesus said to those Jews who believed Him, "If you abide in My word, you are My disciples indeed. 32 And you shall know the truth, and the truth shall make you free."

33 They answered Him, "We are Abraham's descendants, and have never been in bondage to anyone. How can you say, 'You will be made free'?"

34 Jesus answered them, "Most assuredly, I say to you, whoever commits sin is a slave of sin. 35 And a slave does not abide in the house for-

ever, but a son abides forever. 36 Therefore if the Son makes you free, you shall be free indeed.

37 "I know that you are Abraham's descendants, but you seek to kill Me, because My word has no place in you. 38 I speak what I have seen with My Father, and you do what you have seen with*a* your father."

39 They answered and said to Him, "Abraham is our father."

Jesus said to them, "If you were Abraham's children, you would do the works of Abraham. 40 But now you seek to kill Me, a Man who has told you the truth which I heard from God. Abraham did not do this. 41 You do the deeds of your father."

Then they said to Him, "We were not born of fornication; we have one Father—God."

42 Jesus said to them, "If God were your Father, you would love Me, for I proceeded forth and came from God; nor have I come of Myself, but He sent Me. 43 Why do you not understand My speech? Because you are not able to listen to My word. 44 You are of *your* father the devil, and the desires of your father you want to do. He was a murderer from the beginning, and *does not* stand in the truth, because there is no truth in him. When he speaks a lie, he speaks from his own *resources*, for he is a liar and the father of it. 45 But because I tell the truth, you do not believe Me. 46 Which of you convicts Me of sin? And if I tell the truth, why do you not believe Me? 47 He who is of God hears God's words; therefore you do not hear, because you are not of God."

48 Then the Jews answered and said to Him, "Do we not say rightly that You are a Samaritan and have a demon?"

49 Jesus answered, "I do not have a demon; but I honor My Father, and you dishonor Me. 50 And I do not seek My *own* glory; there is One who seeks and judges. 51 Most assuredly, I say to you, if anyone keeps My word he shall never see death."

52 Then the Jews said to Him, "Now we know that You have a demon! Abraham is dead, and the prophets; and You say, 'If anyone keeps My word he shall never taste death.' 53 Are You greater than our

8:38 *a*NU-Text reads *heard from.*

*I*f you are married, you can enrich your marriage through inner beauty. It's not the twists you put in your hair. It's something that God puts in your heart that actually affects the man.

father Abraham, who is dead? And the prophets are dead. Who do You make Yourself out to be?"

54 Jesus answered, "If I honor Myself, My honor is nothing. It is My Father who honors Me, of whom you say that He is your*a* God. 55 Yet you have not known Him, but I know Him. And if I say, 'I do not know Him,' I shall be a liar like you; but I do know Him and keep His word. 56 Your father Abraham rejoiced to see My day, and he saw *it* and was glad."

57 Then the Jews said to Him, "You are not yet fifty years old, and have You seen Abraham?"

58 Jesus said to them, "Most assuredly, I say to you, before Abraham was, I AM."

59 Then they took up stones to throw at Him; but Jesus hid Himself and went out of the temple,*a* going through the midst of them, and so passed by.

9 Now as *Jesus* passed by, He saw a man who was blind from birth. 2 And His disciples asked Him, saying, "Rabbi, who sinned, this man or his parents, that he was born blind?"

3 Jesus answered, "Neither this man nor his parents sinned, but that the works of God should be revealed in him. 4 I*a* must work the works of Him who sent Me while it is day; *the* night is coming when no one can work. 5 As long as I am in the world, I am the light of the world."

6 When He had said these things, He spat on the ground and made clay with the saliva; and He anointed the eyes of the blind man with the clay. 7 And He said to him, "Go, wash in the pool of Siloam" (which is translated, Sent). So he went and washed, and came back seeing.

8 Therefore the neighbors and those who previously had seen that he was blind*a* said, "Is not this he who sat and begged?"

9 Some said, "This is he." Others *said,* "He is like him."*a*

He said, "I am *he.*"

10 Therefore they said to him, "How were your eyes opened?"

11 He answered and said, "A Man called Jesus made clay and anointed

my eyes and said to me, 'Go to the pool of*a* Siloam and wash.' So I went and washed, and I received sight."

12 Then they said to him, "Where is He?"

He said, "I do not know."

13 They brought him who formerly was blind to the Pharisees. 14 Now it was a Sabbath when Jesus made the clay and opened his eyes. 15 Then the Pharisees also asked him again how he had received his sight. He said to them, "He put clay on my eyes, and I washed, and I see."

16 Therefore some of the Pharisees said, "This Man is not from God, because He does not keep the Sabbath."

Others said, "How can a man who is a sinner do such signs?" And there was a division among them.

17 They said to the blind man again, "What do you say about Him because He opened your eyes?"

He said, "He is a prophet."

18 But the Jews did not believe concerning him, that he had been blind and received his sight, until they called the parents of him who had received his sight. 19 And they asked them, saying, "Is this your son, who you say was born blind? How then does he now see?"

20 His parents answered them and said, "We know that this is our son, and that he was born blind; 21 but by what means he now sees we do not know, or who opened his eyes we do not know. He is of age; ask him. He will speak for himself." 22 His parents said these *things* because they feared the Jews, for the Jews had agreed already that if anyone confessed *that* He *was* Christ, he would be put out of the synagogue. 23 Therefore his parents said, "He is of age; ask him."

24 So they again called the man who was blind, and said to him, "Give God the glory! We know that this Man is a sinner."

25 He answered and said, "Whether He is a sinner *or not* I do not know. One thing I know: that though I was blind, now I see."

26 Then they said to him again, "What did He do to you? How did He open your eyes?"

8:54 *a*NU-Text and M-Text read *our.*   8:59 *a*NU-Text omits the rest of this verse.   9:4 *a*NU-Text reads *We.*   9:8 *a*NU-Text reads *a beggar.*   9:9 *a*NU-Text reads *"No, but he is like him."*   9:11 *a*NU-Text omits *the pool of.*

Gospel Pearls

27 He answered them, "I told you already, and you did not listen. Why do you want to hear *it* again? Do you also want to become His disciples?"

28 Then they reviled him and said, "You are His disciple, but we are Moses' disciples. 29 We know that God spoke to Moses; *as for* this *fellow,* we do not know where He is from."

30 The man answered and said to them, "Why, this is a marvelous thing, that you do not know where He is from; yet He has opened my eyes! 31 Now we know that God does not hear sinners; but if anyone is a worshiper of God and does His will, He hears him. 32 Since the world began it has been unheard of that anyone opened the eyes of one who was born blind. 33 If this Man were not from God, He could do nothing."

34 They answered and said to him, "You were completely born in sins, and are you teaching us?" And they cast him out.

35 Jesus heard that they had cast him out; and when He had found him, He said to him, "Do you believe in the Son of God?"*a*

36 He answered and said, "Who is He, Lord, that I may believe in Him?"

37 And Jesus said to him, "You have both seen Him and it is He who is talking with you."

38 Then he said, "Lord, I believe!" And he worshiped Him.

39 And Jesus said, "For judgment I have come into this world, that those who do not see may see, and that those who see may be made blind."

40 Then *some* of the Pharisees who were with Him heard these words, and said to Him, "Are we blind also?"

41 Jesus said to them, "If you were blind, you would have no sin; but now you say, 'We see.' Therefore your sin remains.

10 "Most assuredly, I say to you, he who does not enter the sheepfold by the door, but climbs up some other way, the same is a thief and a robber. 2 But he who enters by the door is the shepherd of the sheep. 3 To him the doorkeeper opens, and the sheep hear his voice; and he calls his own sheep by name and leads them out. 4 And when he brings out his own sheep, he goes before them;

and the sheep follow him, for they know his voice. 5 Yet they will by no means follow a stranger, but will flee from him, for they do not know the voice of strangers." 6 Jesus used this illustration, but they did not understand the things which He spoke to them.

7 Then Jesus said to them again, "Most assuredly, I say to you, I am the door of the sheep. 8 All who *ever* came before Me*a* are thieves and robbers, but the sheep did not hear them. 9 I am the door. If anyone enters by Me, he will be saved, and will go in and out and find pasture. 10 The thief does not come except to steal, and to kill, and to destroy. I have come that they may have life, and that they may have *it* more abundantly.

11 "I am the good shepherd. The good shepherd gives His life for the sheep. 12 But a hireling, *he who is* not the shepherd, one who does not own the sheep, sees the wolf coming and leaves the sheep and flees; and the wolf catches the sheep and scatters them. 13 The hireling flees because he is a hireling and does not care about the sheep. 14 I am the good shepherd; and I know My *sheep,* and am known by My own. 15 As the Father knows Me, even so I know the Father; and I lay down My life for the sheep. 16 And other sheep I have which are not of this fold; them also I must bring, and they will hear My voice; and there will be one flock *and* one shepherd.

17 "Therefore My Father loves Me, because I lay down My life that I may take it again. 18 No one takes it from Me, but I lay it down of Myself. I have power to lay it down, and I have power to take it again. This command I have received from My Father."

19 Therefore there was a division again among the Jews because of these sayings. 20 And many of them said, "He has a demon and is mad. Why do you listen to Him?"

21 Others said, "These are not the words of one who has a demon. Can a demon open the eyes of the blind?"

22 Now it was the Feast of Dedication in Jerusalem, and it was winter. 23 And Jesus walked in the temple, in Solomon's porch. 24 Then the Jews surrounded Him and said to Him,

---

9:35 *a*NU-Text reads *Son of Man.*   10:8 *a*M-Text omits *before Me.*

---

*J*esus called the infirm woman. He unleashed a daughter of Abraham. If you can stay calm in a storm, if you can praise God under pressure, if you can worship in the midst of critics and criticism, God says you are Sarah's daughter.

"How long do You keep us in doubt? If You are the Christ, tell us plainly." 25 Jesus answered them, "I told you, and you do not believe. The works that I do in My Father's name, they bear witness of Me. 26 But you do not believe, because you are not of My sheep, as I said to you.*ᵃ* 27 My sheep hear My voice, and I know them, and they follow Me. 28 And I give them eternal life, and they shall never perish; neither shall anyone snatch them out of My hand. 29 My Father, who has given *them* to Me, is greater than all; and no one is able to snatch *them* out of My Father's hand. 30 I and *My* Father are one."

31 Then the Jews took up stones again to stone Him. 32 Jesus answered them, "Many good works I have shown you from My Father. For which of those works do you stone Me?"

33 The Jews answered Him, saying, "For a good work we do not stone You, but for blasphemy, and because You, being a Man, make Yourself God."

34 Jesus answered them, "Is it not written in your law, *'I said, "You are gods" '?ᵃ* 35 If He called them gods, to whom the word of God came (and the Scripture cannot be broken), 36 do you say of Him whom the Father sanctified and sent into the world, 'You are blaspheming,' because I said, 'I am the Son of God'? 37 If I do not do the works of My Father, do not believe Me; 38 but if I do, though you do not believe Me, believe the works, that you may know and believeᵃ that the Father *is* in Me, and I in Him." 39 Therefore they sought again to seize Him, but He escaped out of their hand.

40 And He went away again beyond the Jordan to the place where John was baptizing at first, and there He stayed. 41 Then many came to Him and said, "John performed no sign, but all the things that John spoke about this Man were true." 42 And many believed in Him there.

11 Now a certain *man* was sick, Lazarus of Bethany, the town of Mary and her sister Martha. 2 It was *that* Mary who anointed the Lord with fragrant oil and wiped His feet with her hair, whose brother Lazarus was sick. 3 Therefore the sisters sent to Him, saying, "Lord, behold, he whom You love is sick."

4 When Jesus heard *that,* He said, "This sickness is not unto death, but for the glory of God, that the Son of God may be glorified through it."

5 Now Jesus loved Martha and her sister and Lazarus. 6 So, when He heard that he was sick, He stayed two more days in the place where He was. 7 Then after this He said to *the* disciples, "Let us go to Judea again."

8 *The* disciples said to Him, "Rabbi, lately the Jews sought to stone You, and are You going there again?"

9 Jesus answered, "Are there not twelve hours in the day? If anyone walks in the day, he does not stumble, because he sees the light of this world. 10 But if one walks in the night, he stumbles, because the light is not in him." 11 These things He said, and after that He said to them, "Our friend Lazarus sleeps, but I go that I may wake him up."

12 Then His disciples said, "Lord, if he sleeps he will get well." 13 However, Jesus spoke of his death, but they thought that He was speaking about taking rest in sleep.

14 Then Jesus said to them plainly, "Lazarus is dead. 15 And I am glad for your sakes that I was not there, that you may believe. Nevertheless let us go to him."

16 Then Thomas, who is called the Twin, said to his fellow disciples, "Let us also go, that we may die with Him."

17 So when Jesus came, He found that he had already been in the tomb four days. 18 Now Bethany was near Jerusalem, about two milesᵃ away. 19 And many of the Jews had joined the women around Martha and Mary, to comfort them concerning their brother.

20 Then Martha, as soon as she heard that Jesus was coming, went and met Him, but Mary was sitting in the house. 21 Now Martha said to Jesus, "Lord, if You had been here, my brother would not have died. 22 But even now I know that what-

---

10:26 ᵃNU-Text omits *as I said to you.*   10:34 ᵃPsalm 82:6   10:38 ᵃNU-Text reads *understand.*
11:18 ᵃLiterally *fifteen stadia*

Gospel Pearls

ever You ask of God, God will give You."

23 Jesus said to her, "Your brother will rise again."

24 Martha said to Him, "I know that he will rise again in the resurrection at the last day."

25 Jesus said to her, "I am the resurrection and the life. He who believes in Me, though he may die, he shall live. 26 And whoever lives and believes in Me shall never die. Do you believe this?"

27 She said to Him, "Yes, Lord, I believe that You are the Christ, the Son of God, who is to come into the world."

28 And when she had said these things, she went her way and secretly called Mary her sister, saying, "The Teacher has come and is calling for you." 29 As soon as she heard *that,* she arose quickly and came to Him. 30 Now Jesus had not yet come into the town, but was*ᵃ* in the place where Martha met Him. 31 Then the Jews who were with her in the house, and comforting her, when they saw that Mary rose up quickly and went out, followed her, saying, "She is going to the tomb to weep there."*ᵃ*

32 Then, when Mary came where Jesus was, and saw Him, she fell down at His feet, saying to Him, "Lord, if You had been here, my brother would not have died."

33 Therefore, when Jesus saw her weeping, and the Jews who came with her weeping, He groaned in the spirit and was troubled. 34 And He said, "Where have you laid him?"

They said to Him, "Lord, come and see."

35 Jesus wept. 36 Then the Jews said, "See how He loved him!"

37 And some of them said, "Could not this Man, who opened the eyes of the blind, also have kept this man from dying?"

38 Then Jesus, again groaning in Himself, came to the tomb. It was a cave, and a stone lay against it. 39 Jesus said, "Take away the stone."

Martha, the sister of him who was dead, said to Him, "Lord, by this time there is a stench, for he has been *dead* four days."

40 Jesus said to her, "Did I not say

to you that if you would believe you would see the glory of God?" 41 Then they took away the stone *from the place* where the dead man was lying.*ᵃ* And Jesus lifted up *His* eyes and said, "Father, I thank You that You have heard Me. 42 And I know that You always hear Me, but because of the people who are standing by I said *this,* that they may believe that You sent Me." 43 Now when He had said these things, He cried with a loud voice, "Lazarus, come forth!" 44 And he who had died came out bound hand and foot with graveclothes, and his face was wrapped with a cloth. Jesus said to them, "Loose him, and let him go."

45 Then many of the Jews who had come to Mary, and had seen the things Jesus did, believed in Him. 46 But some of them went away to the Pharisees and told them the things Jesus did. 47 Then the chief priests and the Pharisees gathered a council and said, "What shall we do? For this Man works many signs. 48 If we let Him alone like this, everyone will believe in Him, and the Romans will come and take away both our place and nation."

49 And one of them, Caiaphas, being high priest that year, said to them, "You know nothing at all, 50 nor do you consider that it is expedient for us*ᵃ* that one man should die for the people, and not that the whole nation should perish." 51 Now this he did not say on his own *authority;* but being high priest that year he prophesied that Jesus would die for the nation, 52 and not for that nation only, but also that He would gather together in one the children of God who were scattered abroad.

53 Then, from that day on, they plotted to put Him to death. 54 Therefore Jesus no longer walked openly among the Jews, but went from there into the country near the wilderness, to a city called Ephraim, and there remained with His disciples.

55 And the Passover of the Jews was near, and many went from the country up to Jerusalem before the

---

11:30 *ᵃ*NU-Text adds *still.*　　　11:31 *ᵃ*NU-Text reads *supposing that she was going to the tomb to weep there.*　　　11:41 *ᵃ*NU-Text omits *from the place where the dead man was lying.*　　　11:50 *ᵃ*NU-Text reads *you.*

---

*D*on't you see that you don't have to spend your life on a quest to find someone to help you? When you have Christ, He is all the help you need. He has been there all the time. Never forget to turn to Him, and never let anyone have His place.

Passover, to purify themselves. 56 Then they sought Jesus, and spoke among themselves as they stood in the temple, "What do you think—that He will not come to the feast?" 57 Now both the chief priests and the Pharisees had given a command, that if anyone knew where He was, he should report *it*, that they might seize Him.

12 Then, six days before the Passover, Jesus came to Bethany, where Lazarus was who had been dead,*a* whom He had raised from the dead. 2 There they made Him a supper; and Martha served, but Lazarus was one of those who sat at the table with Him. 3 Then Mary took a pound of very costly oil of spikenard, anointed the feet of Jesus, and wiped His feet with her hair. And the house was filled with the fragrance of the oil.

4 But one of His disciples, Judas Iscariot, Simon's *son*, who would betray Him, said, 5 "Why was this fragrant oil not sold for three hundred denarii*a* and given to the poor?" 6 This he said, not that he cared for the poor, but because he was a thief, and had the money box; and he used to take what was put in it.

7 But Jesus said, "Let her alone; she has kept*a* this for the day of My burial. 8 For the poor you have with you always, but Me you do not have always."

9 Now a great many of the Jews knew that He was there; and they came, not for Jesus' sake only, but that they might also see Lazarus, whom He had raised from the dead. 10 But the chief priests plotted to put Lazarus to death also, 11 because on account of him many of the Jews went away and believed in Jesus.

12 The next day a great multitude that had come to the feast, when they heard that Jesus was coming to Jerusalem, 13 took branches of palm trees and went out to meet Him, and cried out:

"Hosanna!
'Blessed is He who comes in the name of the LORD!'*a*
The King of Israel!"

14 Then Jesus, when He had found a young donkey, sat on it; as it is written:

15 *"Fear not, daughter of Zion;*
Behold, your King is coming,
*Sitting on a donkey's colt."*a*

16 His disciples did not understand these things at first; but when Jesus was glorified, then they remembered that these things were written about Him and *that* they had done these things to Him.

17 Therefore the people, who were with Him when He called Lazarus out of his tomb and raised him from the dead, bore witness. 18 For this reason the people also met Him, because they heard that He had done this sign. 19 The Pharisees therefore said among themselves, "You see that you are accomplishing nothing. Look, the world has gone after Him!"

20 Now there were certain Greeks among those who came up to worship at the feast. 21 Then they came to Philip, who was from Bethsaida of Galilee, and asked him, saying, "Sir, we wish to see Jesus." 22 Philip came and told Andrew, and in turn Andrew and Philip told Jesus.

23 But Jesus answered them, saying, "The hour has come that the Son of Man should be glorified. 24 Most assuredly, I say to you, unless a grain of wheat falls into the ground and dies, it remains alone; but if it dies, it produces much grain. 25 He who loves his life will lose it, and he who hates his life in this world will keep it for eternal life. 26 If anyone serves Me, let him follow Me; and where I am, there My servant will be also. If anyone serves Me, him My Father will honor.

27 "Now My soul is troubled, and what shall I say? 'Father, save Me from this hour'? But for this purpose I came to this hour. 28 "Father, glorify Your name."

Then a voice came from heaven, saying, "I have both glorified *it* and will glorify *it* again."

29 Therefore the people who stood by and heard *it* said that it had thundered. Others said, "An angel has spoken to Him."

12:1 *a*NU-Text omits *who had been dead.*   12:5 *a*About one year's wages for a worker.
12:7 *a*NU-Text reads *that she may keep.*   12:13 *a*Psalm 118:26   12:15 *a*Zechariah 9:9

Gospel Pearls

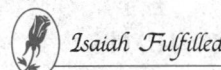

30 Jesus answered and said, "This voice did not come because of Me, but for your sake. 31 Now is the judgment of this world; now the ruler of this world will be cast out. 32 And I, if I am lifted up from the earth, will draw all *peoples* to Myself." 33 This He said, signifying by what death He would die.

34 The people answered Him, "We have heard from the law that the Christ remains forever; and how *can* You say, 'The Son of Man must be lifted up'? Who is this Son of Man?"

35 Then Jesus said to them, "A little while longer the light is with you. Walk while you have the light, lest darkness overtake you; he who walks in darkness does not know where he is going. 36 While you have the light, believe in the light, that you may become sons of light." These things Jesus spoke, and departed, and was hidden from them.

37 But although He had done so many signs before them, they did not believe in Him, 38 that the word of Isaiah the prophet might be fulfilled, which he spoke:

> "Lord, who has believed our
> report?
> And to whom has the arm of
> the Lord been revealed?"[a]

39 Therefore they could not believe, because Isaiah said again:

40 *"He has blinded their eyes and*
hardened their hearts,
Lest they should see with their
eyes,
Lest they should understand
with their hearts and turn,
So that I should heal them." [a]

41 These things Isaiah said when[a] he saw His glory and spoke of Him.

42 Nevertheless even among the rulers many believed in Him, but because of the Pharisees they did not confess *Him*, lest they should be put out of the synagogue; 43 for they loved the praise of men more than the praise of God.

44 Then Jesus cried out and said, "He who believes in Me, believes not in Me but in Him who sent Me. 45 And he who sees Me sees Him who

sent Me. 46 I have come *as* a light into the world, that whoever believes in Me should not abide in darkness. 47 And if anyone hears My words and does not believe,[a] I do not judge him; for I did not come to judge the world but to save the world. 48 He who rejects Me, and does not receive My words, has that which judges him— the word that I have spoken will judge him in the last day. 49 For I have not spoken on My own *authority;* but the Father who sent Me gave Me a command, what I should say and what I should speak. 50 And I know that His command is everlasting life. Therefore, whatever I speak, just as the Father has told Me, so I speak."

13 Now before the feast of the Passover, when Jesus knew that His hour had come that He should depart from this world to the Father, having loved His own who were in the world, He loved them to the end.

2 And supper being ended,[a] the devil having already put it into the heart of Judas Iscariot, Simon's *son,* to betray Him, 3 Jesus, knowing that the Father had given all things into His hands, and that He had come from God and was going to God, 4 rose from supper and laid aside His garments, took a towel and girded Himself. 5 After that, He poured water into a basin and began to wash the disciples' feet, and to wipe *them* with the towel with which He was girded. 6 Then He came to Simon Peter. And *Peter* said to Him, "Lord, are You washing my feet?"

7 Jesus answered and said to him, "What I am doing you do not understand now, but you will know after this."

8 Peter said to Him, "You shall never wash my feet!"

Jesus answered him, "If I do not wash you, you have no part with Me."

9 Simon Peter said to Him, "Lord, not my feet only, but also *my* hands and *my* head!"

10 Jesus said to him, "He who is bathed needs only to wash *his* feet, but is completely clean; and you are clean, but not all of you." 11 For He

12:38 [a]Isaiah 53:1   12:40 [a]Isaiah 6:10   12:41 [a]NU-Text reads *because.*   12:47 [a]NU-Text reads *keep them.*   13:2 [a]NU-Text reads *And during supper.*

There you are crying and frustrated, tormented and afraid. The fact is that two thousand years ago your God unlocked the door, and you can walk through it at will. You just don't know it!

Lay Aside Your Garments

John 13:3–5

When Jesus launched His ministry on earth, He laid aside His garments. That's what ministry is all about. It requires you to lay aside your personal ambitions and visions of grandeur. Unfortunately, gifted people tend to be some of the most egotistical, eccentric individuals in the world. That's why "being gifted" in itself will never deliver anybody.

True ministry is birthed when you are stripped down to your heart's desire, when something inside says, "I want my life to count for God." It is the kind of prayer that pleads, "O God, don't let me try to impress anyone but the One to whom I give my life."

Have you given your life to the Lord? If you work in the Kingdom trying to bring souls to God, you need to be sure you've given yourself to the God you teach about. If you have, then why are you still standing around the table, arguing over who is going to sit on the left and who is going to sit on the right?! Why have you not laid aside your garments. Your garments are the personal agendas you have set for yourself. Like the fig leaves sewn together in the garden, you have contrived your own coverings. The terrible tragedy of it all is that, sooner or later, whatever you have sewn together will ultimately be stripped away.

The Lord often uses trials to realign us with His plan. Everyone who finds real purpose will, sooner or later, go through some adversity that will cause them to let go of the temporal and cleave to the eternal. Some will awaken in hospital rooms and discover that many of the things that seemed important are now meaningless. Left with nothing but the simplicity of a second chance, they lie there—their certificates of deposit in the bank, their cars in the garage, and their clothes crammed into their closets.

Job discusses this terrible stripping that seems to be characteristic of the call. He goes through a brief but painful period that yanks away everything that appeared to be important in his life. Once a successful city official, he is now weak and sick. His home is in shambles, his marriage is a joke, and his children—his precious children—are all dead (see Job 19:14-20).

What word of wisdom falls from his parched lips? What comfort does he offer himself? His only shade beneath the blistering sun of adverse circumstances is the fact that he can only be stripped down to what he started with before—nothing more. He can be stripped of the temporal, but not of the eternal.

It is possible to lose your money, your health, your friends, and your social status. But these are mere imitations of life. It is your character, your class, and your Christianity that will survive.

knew who would betray Him; therefore He said, "You are not all clean."

12 So when He had washed their feet, taken His garments, and sat down again, He said to them, "Do you know what I have done to you? 13 You call Me Teacher and Lord, and you say well, for so I am. 14 If I then, your Lord and Teacher, have washed your feet, you also ought to wash one another's feet. 15 For I have given you an example, that you should do as I have done to you. 16 Most assuredly, I say to you, a servant is not greater than his master; nor is he who is sent greater than he who sent him. 17 If you know these things, blessed are you if you do them.

18 "I do not speak concerning all of you. I know whom I have chosen; but that the Scripture may be fulfilled, 'He who eats bread with Me*a* has lifted up his heel against Me.'*b* 19 Now I tell you before it comes, that when it does come to pass, you may believe that I am He. 20 Most assuredly, I say to you, he who receives whomever I send receives Me; and he who receives Me receives Him who sent Me."

21 When Jesus had said these things, He was troubled in spirit, and testified and said, "Most assuredly, I say to you, one of you will betray Me." 22 Then the disciples looked at one another, perplexed about whom He spoke.

23 Now there was leaning on Jesus' bosom one of His disciples, whom Jesus loved. 24 Simon Peter therefore motioned to him to ask who it was of whom He spoke.

25 Then, leaning back*a* on Jesus' breast, he said to Him, "Lord, who is it?"

26 Jesus answered, "It is he to whom I shall give a piece of bread when I have dipped it." And having dipped the bread, He gave it to Judas Iscariot, the son of Simon. 27 Now after the piece of bread, Satan entered him. Then Jesus said to him, "What you do, do quickly." 28 But no one at the table knew for what reason He said this to him. 29 For some thought, because Judas had the money box,

that Jesus had said to him, "Buy those things we need for the feast," or that he should give something to the poor.

30 Having received the piece of bread, he then went out immediately. And it was night.

31 So, when he had gone out, Jesus said, "Now the Son of Man is glorified, and God is glorified in Him. 32 If God is glorified in Him, God will also glorify Him in Himself, and glorify Him immediately. 33 Little children, I shall be with you a little while longer. You will seek Me; and as I said to the Jews, 'Where I am going, you cannot come,' so now I say to you. 34 A new commandment I give to you, that you love one another; as I have loved you, that you also love one another. 35 By this all will know that you are My disciples, if you have love for one another."

36 Simon Peter said to Him, "Lord, where are You going?"

Jesus answered him, "Where I am going you cannot follow Me now, but you shall follow Me afterward."

37 Peter said to Him, "Lord, why can I not follow You now? I will lay down my life for Your sake."

38 Jesus answered him, "Will you lay down your life for My sake? Most assuredly, I say to you, the rooster shall not crow till you have denied Me three times.

14 "Let not your heart be troubled; you believe in God, believe also in Me. 2 In My Father's house are many mansions;*a* if it were not so, I would have told you. I go to prepare a place for you.*b* 3 And if I go and prepare a place for you, I will come again and receive you to Myself; that where I am, there you may be also. 4 And where I go you know, and the way you know."

5 Thomas said to Him, "Lord, we do not know where You are going, and how can we know the way?"

6 Jesus said to him, "I am the way, the truth, and the life. No one comes to the Father except through Me.

7 "If you had known Me, you would have known My Father also; and

13:18 *a*NU-Text reads My bread. *b*Psalm 41:9   13:25 *a*NU-Text and M-Text add thus.   14:2 *a*Literally dwellings *b*NU-Text adds a word which would cause the text to read either if it were not so, would I have told you that I go to prepare a place for you? or if it were not so I would have told you; for I go to prepare a place for you.

*P*reaching to you doesn't set you free; it just announces to you that you are free. It is a declaration of independence. It is God's word showing you step by step how to click your heels and get away from the enemy!

from now on you know Him and have seen Him."

8 Philip said to Him, "Lord, show us the Father, and it is sufficient for us."

9 Jesus said to him, "Have I been with you so long, and yet you have not known Me, Philip? He who has seen Me has seen the Father; so how can you say, 'Show us the Father'? 10 Do you not believe that I am in the Father, and the Father in Me? The words that I speak to you I do not speak on My own *authority*; but the Father who dwells in Me does the works. 11 Believe Me that I *am* in the Father and the Father in Me, or else believe Me for the sake of the works themselves.

12 "Most assuredly, I say to you, he who believes in Me, the works that I do he will do also; and greater *works* than these he will do, because I go to My Father. 13 And whatever you ask in My name, that I will do, that the Father may be glorified in the Son. 14 If you ask*a* anything in My name, I will do *it*.

15 "If you love Me, keep*a* My commandments. 16 And I will pray the Father, and He will give you another Helper, that He may abide with you forever— 17 the Spirit of truth, whom the world cannot receive, because it neither sees Him nor knows Him; but you know Him, for He dwells with you and will be in you. 18 I will not leave you orphans; I will come to you.

19 "A little while longer and the world will see Me no more, but you will see Me. Because I live, you will live also. 20 At that day you will know that I *am* in My Father, and you in Me, and I in you. 21 He who has My commandments and keeps them, it is he who loves Me. And he who loves Me will be loved by My Father, and I will love him and manifest Myself to him."

22 Judas (not Iscariot) said to Him, "Lord, how is it that You will manifest Yourself to us, and not to the world?"

23 Jesus answered and said to him, "If anyone loves Me, he will keep My word; and My Father will love him, and We will come to him and make Our home with him. 24 He who does

not love Me does not keep My words; and the word which you hear is not Mine but the Father's who sent Me.

25 "These things I have spoken to you while being present with you. 26 But the Helper, the Holy Spirit, whom the Father will send in My name, He will teach you all things, and bring to your remembrance all things that I said to you. 27 Peace I leave with you, My peace I give to you; not as the world gives do I give to you. Let not your heart be troubled, neither let it be afraid. 28 You have heard Me say to you, 'I am going away and coming *back* to you.' If you loved Me, you would rejoice because I said,*a* 'I am going to the Father,' for My Father is greater than I.

29 "And now I have told you before it comes, that when it does come to pass, you may believe. 30 I will no longer talk much with you, for the ruler of this world is coming, and he has nothing in Me. 31 But that the world may know that I love the Father, and as the Father gave Me commandment, so I do. Arise, let us go from here.

15 "I am the true vine, and My Father is the vinedresser. 2 Every branch in Me that does not bear fruit He takes away;*a* and every *branch* that bears fruit He prunes, that it may bear more fruit. 3 You are already clean because of the word which I have spoken to you. 4 Abide in Me, and I in you. As the branch cannot bear fruit of itself, unless it abides in the vine, neither can you, unless you abide in Me.

5 "I am the vine, you *are* the branches. He who abides in Me, and I in him, bears much fruit; for without Me you can do nothing. 6 If anyone does not abide in Me, he is cast out as a branch and is withered; and they gather them and throw *them* into the fire, and they are burned. 7 If you abide in Me, and My words abide in you, you will*a* ask what you desire, and it shall be done for you. 8 By this My Father is glorified, that you bear much fruit; so you will be My disciples.

9 "As the Father loved Me, I also have loved you; abide in My love.

14:14 *a*NU-Text adds *Me*.   14:15 *a*NU-Text reads *you will keep*.   14:28 *a*NU-Text omits *I said*.
15:2 *a*Or *lifts up*   15:7 *a*NU-Text omits *you will*.

*M*oving from imprisonment to empowerment takes some people longer than others. It helps when you have had good, strong childhood affirmation. But even if you haven't, you don't have to limit your future merely because of voids in your past. Close those chapters in your life and write new ones.

Your Father Is Rich

John 14:2, 3

*I*f you have faith, you are a daughter of Abraham. You stand to inherit all that your Father has for you. So why should you sit there and be in need when your Father has left you everything? Your Father is rich, and He left His entire estate to you.

But you will not get your inheritance until you ask for it. Demand what your Father left you. That college degree has your name on it. That promotion has your name on it. That financial breakthrough has your name on it.

There is no need to sit around waiting for someone else to go get what is yours and bring it to you. Nobody else is coming. The One who needed to come is already here. Jesus said, "I have come that they may have life, and that they may have it more abundantly" (John 10:10). That's all you need.

The power to get wealth is in your tongue. You will have whatever you say. Don't sit around murmuring, groaning, and complaining. You may be destroying yourself with your words. Open your mouth and say something good. Don't speak against the other women around you. Open your mouth now and begin to speak deliverance and power. God will answer your prayers. "And whatever things you ask in prayer, believing, you will receive" (Matthew 21:22).

God willed you something. Your Father left you an inheritance. If He would bless the sons of Abraham, surely He would bless the daughters of Abraham. Women are just as much children of God as men are. At one time in history, women were not allowed to own property or to have an inheritance except through their husbands. Everything God will do for a man, He will do for a woman. You are not disadvantaged. You are due your inheritance.

Abraham's daughters have worth. God's power brings all things under your feet. He will make you the head and not the tail (see Deuteronomy 28:13). Believe Him for your household. He will deliver. You don't need a sugar daddy. You have Jehovah-Jireh, the best Provider this world has ever known. If you want the enemy to release you, remind him whose daughter you are!

10 If you keep My commandments, you will abide in My love, just as I have kept My Father's commandments and abide in His love.

11 "These things I have spoken to you, that My joy may remain in you, and *that* your joy may be full. 12 This is My commandment, that you love one another as I have loved you. 13 Greater love has no one than this, than to lay down one's life for his friends. 14 You are My friends if you do whatever I command you. 15 No longer do I call you servants, for a servant does not know what his master is doing; but I have called you friends, for all things that I heard from My Father I have made known to you. 16 You did not choose Me, but I chose you and appointed you that you should go and bear fruit, and *that* your fruit should remain, that whatever you ask the Father in My name He may give you. 17 These things I command you, that you love one another.

18 "If the world hates you, you know that it hated Me before *it hated* you. 19 If you were of the world, the world would love its own. Yet because you are not of the world, but I chose you out of the world, therefore the world hates you. 20 Remember the word that I said to you, 'A servant is not greater than his master.' If they persecuted Me, they will also persecute you. If they kept My word, they will keep yours also. 21 But all these things they will do to you for My name's sake, because they do not know Him who sent Me. 22 If I had not come and spoken to them, they would have no sin, but now they have no excuse for their sin. 23 He who hates Me hates My Father also. 24 If I had not done among them the works which no one else did, they would have no sin; but now they have seen and also hated both Me and My Father. 25 But *this happened* that the word might be fulfilled which is written in their law, 'They hated Me without a cause.'*a*

26 "But when the Helper comes, whom I shall send to you from the Father, the Spirit of truth who proceeds from the Father, He will testify of Me. 27 And you also will bear wit-

ness, because you have been with Me from the beginning.

16 "These things I have spoken to you, that you should not be made to stumble. 2 They will put you out of the synagogues; yes, the time is coming that whoever kills you will think that he offers God service. 3 And these things they will do to you*a* because they have not known the Father nor Me. 4 But these things I have told you, that when the*a* time comes, you may remember that I told you of them.

"And these things I did not say to you at the beginning, because I was with you.

5 "But now I go away to Him who sent Me, and none of you asks Me, 'Where are You going?' 6 But because I have said these things to you, sorrow has filled your heart. 7 Nevertheless I tell you the truth. It is to your advantage that I go away; for if I do not go away, the Helper will not come to you; but if I depart, I will send Him to you. 8 And when He has come, He will convict the world of sin, and of righteousness, and of judgment: 9 of sin, because they do not believe in Me; 10 of righteousness, because I go to My Father and you see Me no more; 11 of judgment, because the ruler of this world is judged.

12 "I still have many things to say to you, but you cannot bear *them* now. 13 However, when He, the Spirit of truth, has come, He will guide you into all truth; for He will not speak on His own *authority*, but whatever He hears He will speak; and He will tell you things to come. 14 He will glorify Me, for He will take of what is Mine and declare *it* to you. 15 All things that the Father has are Mine. Therefore I said that He will take of Mine and declare *it* to you.*a*

16 "A little while, and you will not see Me; and again a little while, and you will see Me, because I go to the Father."

17 Then *some* of His disciples said among themselves, "What is this that He says to us, 'A little while, and you will not see Me; and again a little while, and you will see Me'; and, 'because I go to the Father'?" 18 They

15:25 *a*Psalm 69:4   16:3 *a*NU-Text and M-Text omit *to you*.   16:4 *a*NU-Text reads *their*.
16:15 *a*NU-Text and M-Text read *He takes of Mine and will declare it to you.*

Gospel Pearls

said therefore, "What is this that He says, 'A little while'? We do not know what He is saying."

19 Now Jesus knew that they desired to ask Him, and He said to them, "Are you inquiring among yourselves about what I said, 'A little while, and you will not see Me; and again a little while, and you will see Me'? 20 Most assuredly, I say to you that you will weep and lament, but the world will rejoice; and you will be sorrowful, but your sorrow will be turned into joy. 21 A woman, when she is in labor, has sorrow because her hour has come; but as soon as she has given birth to the child, she no longer remembers the anguish, for joy that a human being has been born into the world. 22 Therefore you now have sorrow; but I will see you again and your heart will rejoice, and your joy no one will take from you.

23 "And in that day you will ask Me nothing. Most assuredly, I say to you, whatever you ask the Father in My name He will give you. 24 Until now you have asked nothing in My name. Ask, and you will receive, that your joy may be full.

25 "These things I have spoken to you in figurative language; but the time is coming when I will no longer speak to you in figurative language, but I will tell you plainly about the Father. 26 In that day you will ask in My name, and I do not say to you that I shall pray the Father for you; 27 for the Father Himself loves you, because you have loved Me, and have believed that I came forth from God. 28 I came forth from the Father and have come into the world. Again, I leave the world and go to the Father."

29 His disciples said to Him, "See, now You are speaking plainly, and using no figure of speech! 30 Now we are sure that You know all things, and have no need that anyone should question You. By this we believe that You came forth from God."

31 Jesus answered them, "Do you now believe? 32 Indeed the hour is coming, yes, has now come, that you will be scattered, each to his own, and will leave Me alone. And yet I am not alone, because the Father is with Me. 33 These things I have spoken to you, that in Me you may have peace. In the world you will[a] have tribulation; but be of good cheer, I have overcome the world."

17 Jesus spoke these words, lifted up His eyes to heaven, and said: "Father, the hour has come. Glorify Your Son, that Your Son also may glorify You, 2 as You have given Him authority over all flesh, that He should[a] give eternal life to as many as You have given Him. 3 And this is eternal life, that they may know You, the only true God, and Jesus Christ whom You have sent. 4 I have glorified You on the earth. I have finished the work which You have given Me to do. 5 And now, O Father, glorify Me together with Yourself, with the glory which I had with You before the world was.

6 "I have manifested Your name to the men whom You have given Me out of the world. They were Yours, You gave them to Me, and they have kept Your word. 7 Now they have known that all things which You have given Me are from You. 8 For I have given to them the words which You have given Me; and they have received *them,* and have known surely that I came forth from You; and they have believed that You sent Me.

9 "I pray for them. I do not pray for the world but for those whom You have given Me, for they are Yours. 10 And all Mine are Yours, and Yours are Mine, and I am glorified in them. 11 Now I am no longer in the world, but these are in the world, and I come to You. Holy Father, keep through Your name those whom You have given Me,[a] that they may be one as We *are.* 12 While I was with them in the world,[a] I kept them in Your name. Those whom You gave Me I have kept;[b] and none of them is lost except the son of perdition, that the Scripture might be fulfilled. 13 But now I come to You, and these things I speak in the world, that they may have My joy fulfilled in themselves. 14 I have given them Your word; and the world has hated them because they are not of the world, just as I am not of the world. 15 I do not pray

---

16:33 [a]NU-Text and M-Text omit *will.*   17:2 [a]M-Text reads *shall.*   17:11 [a]NU-Text and M-Text read *keep them through Your name which You have given Me.*   17:12 [a]NU-Text omits *in the world.*
[b]NU-Text reads *in Your name which You gave Me. And I guarded them* (or *it*).

*D*on't you realize you can worship things or people by paying them too much attention? You can worship them by dedicating your life to impressing them, or by allowing their opinion to determine your self-worth or esteem. Those things are idols in your life.

Soul Secrets
for harried, hurried times

*L*ord, everything is in a panic! Everybody wants a piece of me, there's far too much to do, and there are never enough hours in the day. My head is cluttered with all kinds of junk, and my heart is about ready to break. So where are You when I need You? Are You asleep?

I feel like those disciples on the Sea of Galilee when the storm came up, and the winds and the waves rocked their boat. My cry is the same as theirs: "Somebody go get Jesus! He's asleep in the back of the boat, and we're about to drown out here!"

The storms of my life have all but sunk my ship. I can't take much more. I'm a woman who needs You, my Prince of Peace. I need You, my Father who never slumbers, never sleeps. I need the peace that comes only by the Spirit of the Living God. Lord, speak to my storm. Just say the words, "Peace, be still." Let me find in You a still and quiet place—a place where the gentle breezes of Your love blow softly across my face, a place where just one touch from You takes all my tensions away, a place where I can rest my head upon Your breast, hear Your holy heartbeat—and be at peace.

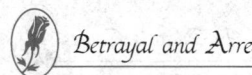
that You should take them out of the world, but that You should keep them from the evil one. 16 They are not of the world, just as I am not of the world. 17 Sanctify them by Your truth. Your word is truth. 18 As You sent Me into the world, I also have sent them into the world. 19 And for their sakes I sanctify Myself, that they also may be sanctified by the truth.

20 "I do not pray for these alone, but also for those who will*a* believe in Me through their word; 21 that they all may be one, as You, Father, *are* in Me, and I in You; that they also may be one in Us, that the world may believe that You sent Me. 22 And the glory which You gave Me I have given them, that they may be one just as We are one: 23 I in them, and You in Me; that they may be made perfect in one, and that the world may know that You have sent Me, and have loved them as You have loved Me.

24 "Father, I desire that they also whom You gave Me may be with Me where I am, that they may behold My glory which You have given Me; for You loved Me before the foundation of the world. 25 O righteous Father! The world has not known You, but I have known You; and these have known that You sent Me. 26 And I have declared to them Your name, and will declare *it,* that the love with which You loved Me may be in them, and I in them."

18 When Jesus had spoken these words, He went out with His disciples over the Brook Kidron, where there was a garden, which He and His disciples entered. 2 And Judas, who betrayed Him, also knew the place; for Jesus often met there with His disciples. 3 Then Judas, having received a detachment *of troops,* and officers from the chief priests and Pharisees, came there with lanterns, torches, and weapons. 4 Jesus therefore, knowing all things that would come upon Him, went forward and said to them, "Whom are you seeking?"

5 They answered Him, "Jesus of Nazareth."

Jesus said to them, "I am *He.*" And Judas, who betrayed Him, also stood with them. 6 Now when He said to them, "I am *He,*" they drew back and fell to the ground.

7 Then He asked them again, "Whom are you seeking?"

And they said, "Jesus of Nazareth."

8 Jesus answered, "I have told you that I am *He.* Therefore, if you seek Me, let these go their way," 9 that the saying might be fulfilled which He spoke, "Of those whom You gave Me I have lost none."

10 Then Simon Peter, having a sword, drew it and struck the high priest's servant, and cut off his right ear. The servant's name was Malchus.

11 So Jesus said to Peter, "Put your sword into the sheath. Shall I not drink the cup which My Father has given Me?"

12 Then the detachment *of troops* and the captain and the officers of the Jews arrested Jesus and bound Him. 13 And they led Him away to Annas first, for he was the father-in-law of Caiaphas who was high priest that year. 14 Now it was Caiaphas who advised the Jews that it was expedient that one man should die for the people.

15 And Simon Peter followed Jesus, and so *did* another*a* disciple. Now that disciple was known to the high priest, and went with Jesus into the courtyard of the high priest. 16 But Peter stood at the door outside. Then the other disciple, who was known to the high priest, went out and spoke to her who kept the door, and brought Peter in. 17 Then the servant girl who kept the door said to Peter, "You are not also *one* of this Man's disciples, are you?"

He said, "I am not."

18 Now the servants and officers who had made a fire of coals stood there, for it was cold, and they warmed themselves. And Peter stood with them and warmed himself.

19 The high priest then asked Jesus about His disciples and His doctrine.

20 Jesus answered him, "I spoke openly to the world. I always taught in synagogues and in the temple, where the Jews always meet,*a* and in secret I have said nothing. 21 Why do

---

17:20 *a*NU-Text and M-Text omit *will.*   18:15 *a*M-Text reads *the other.*   18:20 *a*NU-Text reads *where all the Jews meet.*

---

*L*ord, restore to Your daughter the joy of having You, the joy of being at peace within. I rebuke that spirit that drives and torments her—stealing precious moments from her. In Jesus' name, be loosed!

you ask Me? Ask those who have heard Me what I said to them. Indeed they know what I said."

22 And when He had said these things, one of the officers who stood by struck Jesus with the palm of his hand, saying, "Do You answer the high priest like that?"

23 Jesus answered him, "If I have spoken evil, bear witness of the evil; but if well, why do you strike Me?"

24 Then Annas sent Him bound to Caiaphas the high priest.

25 Now Simon Peter stood and warmed himself. Therefore they said to him, "You are not also *one* of His disciples, are you?"

He denied *it* and said, "I am not!"

26 One of the servants of the high priest, a relative *of him* whose ear Peter cut off, said, "Did I not see you in the garden with Him?" 27 Peter then denied again; and immediately a rooster crowed.

28 Then they led Jesus from Caiaphas to the Praetorium, and it was early morning. But they themselves did not go into the Praetorium, lest they should be defiled, but that they might eat the Passover. 29 Pilate then went out to them and said, "What accusation do you bring against this Man?"

30 They answered and said to him, "If He were not an evildoer, we would not have delivered Him up to you."

31 Then Pilate said to them, "You take Him and judge Him according to your law."

Therefore the Jews said to him, "It is not lawful for us to put anyone to death," 32 that the saying of Jesus might be fulfilled which He spoke, signifying by what death He would die.

33 Then Pilate entered the Praetorium again, called Jesus, and said to Him, "Are You the King of the Jews?"

34 Jesus answered him, "Are you speaking for yourself about this, or did others tell you this concerning Me?"

35 Pilate answered, "Am I a Jew? Your own nation and the chief priests have delivered You to me. What have You done?"

36 Jesus answered, "My kingdom is not of this world. If My kingdom were of this world, My servants would fight, so that I should not be delivered to the Jews; but now My kingdom is not from here."

37 Pilate therefore said to Him, "Are You a king then?"

Jesus answered, "You say *rightly* that I am a king. For this cause I was born, and for this cause I have come into the world, that I should bear witness to the truth. Everyone who is of the truth hears My voice."

38 Pilate said to Him, "What is truth?" And when he had said this, he went out again to the Jews, and said to them, "I find no fault in Him at all.

39 "But you have a custom that I should release someone to you at the Passover. Do you therefore want me to release to you the King of the Jews?"

40 Then they all cried again, saying, "Not this Man, but Barabbas!" Now Barabbas was a robber.

19 So then Pilate took Jesus and scourged *Him.* 2 And the soldiers twisted a crown of thorns and put *it* on His head, and they put on Him a purple robe. 3 Then they said,ᵃ "Hail, King of the Jews!" And they struck Him with their hands.

4 Pilate then went out again, and said to them, "Behold, I am bringing Him out to you, that you may know that I find no fault in Him."

5 Then Jesus came out, wearing the crown of thorns and the purple robe. And *Pilate* said to them, "Behold the Man!"

6 Therefore, when the chief priests and officers saw Him, they cried out, saying, "Crucify *Him,* crucify *Him!*"

Pilate said to them, "You take Him and crucify *Him,* for I find no fault in Him."

7 The Jews answered him, "We have a law, and according to ourᵃ law He ought to die, because He made Himself the Son of God."

8 Therefore, when Pilate heard that saying, he was the more afraid, 9 and went again into the Praetorium, and said to Jesus, "Where are You from?" But Jesus gave him no answer.

10 Then Pilate said to Him, "Are You not speaking to me? Do You not know that I have power to cru-

19:3 ᵃNU-Text reads *And they came up to Him and said.*   19:7 ᵃNU-Text reads *the law.*

Gospel Pearls

cify You, and power to release You?"
11 Jesus answered, "You could have no power at all against Me unless it had been given you from above. Therefore the one who delivered Me to you has the greater sin."

12 From then on Pilate sought to release Him, but the Jews cried out, saying, "If you let this Man go, you are not Caesar's friend. Whoever makes himself a king speaks against Caesar."

13 When Pilate therefore heard that saying, he brought Jesus out and sat down in the judgment seat in a place that is called *The* Pavement, but in Hebrew, Gabbatha. 14 Now it was the Preparation Day of the Passover, and about the sixth hour. And he said to the Jews, "Behold your King!"

15 But they cried out, "Away with *Him,* away with *Him!* Crucify Him!"

Pilate said to them, "Shall I crucify your King?"

The chief priests answered, "We have no king but Caesar!"

16 Then he delivered Him to them to be crucified. Then they took Jesus and led *Him* away.[a]

17 And He, bearing His cross, went out to a place called the *Place* of a Skull, which is called in Hebrew, Golgotha, 18 where they crucified Him, and two others with Him, one on either side, and Jesus in the center. 19 Now Pilate wrote a title and put *it* on the cross. And the writing was:

JESUS OF NAZARETH,
THE KING OF THE JEWS.

20 Then many of the Jews read this title, for the place where Jesus was crucified was near the city; and it was written in Hebrew, Greek, *and* Latin.

21 Therefore the chief priests of the Jews said to Pilate, "Do not write, 'The King of the Jews,' but, 'He said, "I am the King of the Jews." ' "

22 Pilate answered, "What I have written, I have written."

23 Then the soldiers, when they had crucified Jesus, took His garments and made four parts, to each soldier a part, and also the tunic. Now the tunic was without seam, woven from the top in one piece. 24 They said therefore among themselves, "Let us not tear it, but cast lots for it, whose it shall be," that the Scripture might be fulfilled which says:

"They divided My garments
  among them,
And for My clothing they cast
  lots."[a]

Therefore the soldiers did these things.

25 Now there stood by the cross of Jesus His mother, and His mother's sister, Mary the *wife* of Clopas, and Mary Magdalene. 26 When Jesus therefore saw His mother, and the disciple whom He loved standing by, He said to His mother, "Woman, behold your son!" 27 Then He said to the disciple, "Behold your mother!" And from that hour that disciple took her to his own *home.*

28 After this, Jesus, knowing[a] that all things were now accomplished, that the Scripture might be fulfilled, said, "I thirst!" 29 Now a vessel full of sour wine was sitting there; and they filled a sponge with sour wine, put *it* on hyssop, and put *it* to His mouth. 30 So when Jesus had received the sour wine, He said, "It is finished!" And bowing His head, He gave up His spirit.

31 Therefore, because it was the Preparation *Day,* that the bodies should not remain on the cross on the Sabbath (for that Sabbath was a high day), the Jews asked Pilate that their legs might be broken, and *that* they might be taken away. 32 Then the soldiers came and broke the legs of the first and of the other who was crucified with Him. 33 But when they came to Jesus and saw that He was already dead, they did not break His legs. 34 But one of the soldiers pierced His side with a spear, and immediately blood and water came out. 35 And he who has seen has testified, and his testimony is true; and he knows that he is telling the truth, so that you may believe. 36 For these things were done that the Scripture should be fulfilled, *"Not one of His bones shall be broken."*[a] 37 And again another Scripture says, *"They shall look on Him whom they pierced."*[a]

38 After this, Joseph of Arimathea,

19:16 [a]NU-Text omits *and led Him away.*   19:24 [a]Psalm 22:18   19:28 [a]M-Text reads *seeing.*
19:36 [a]Exodus 12:46; Numbers 9:12; Psalm 34:20   19:37 [a]Zechariah 12:10

My advice for you is to be prepared for change. Everything will do it—people, circumstances, and situations. It helps when you know that from the beginning.

being a disciple of Jesus, but secretly, for fear of the Jews, asked Pilate that he might take away the body of Jesus; and Pilate gave *him* permission. So he came and took the body of Jesus. 39 And Nicodemus, who at first came to Jesus by night, also came, bringing a mixture of myrrh and aloes, about a hundred pounds. 40 Then they took the body of Jesus, and bound it in strips of linen with the spices, as the custom of the Jews is to bury. 41 Now in the place where He was crucified there was a garden, and in the garden a new tomb in which no one had yet been laid. 42 So there they laid Jesus, because of the Jews' Preparation *Day*, for the tomb was nearby.

20 Now the first *day* of the week Mary Magdalene went to the tomb early, while it was still dark, and saw *that* the stone had been taken away from the tomb. 2 Then she ran and came to Simon Peter, and to the other disciple, whom Jesus loved, and said to them, "They have taken away the Lord out of the tomb, and we do not know where they have laid Him."

3 Peter therefore went out, and the other disciple, and were going to the tomb. 4 So they both ran together, and the other disciple outran Peter and came to the tomb first. 5 And he, stooping down and looking in, saw the linen cloths lying *there;* yet he did not go in. 6 Then Simon Peter came, following him, and went into the tomb; and he saw the linen cloths lying *there,* 7 and the handkerchief that had been around His head, not lying with the linen cloths, but folded together in a place by itself. 8 Then the other disciple, who came to the tomb first, went in also; and he saw and believed. 9 For as yet they did not know the Scripture, that He must rise again from the dead. 10 Then the disciples went away again to their own homes.

11 But Mary stood outside by the tomb weeping, and as she wept she stooped down *and looked* into the tomb. 12 And she saw two angels in white sitting, one at the head and the other at the feet, where the body of Jesus had lain. 13 Then they said to her, "Woman, why are you weeping?"

She said to them, "Because they have taken away my Lord, and I do not know where they have laid Him."

14 Now when she had said this, she turned around and saw Jesus standing *there,* and did not know that it was Jesus. 15 Jesus said to her, "Woman, why are you weeping? Whom are you seeking?"

She, supposing Him to be the gardener, said to Him, "Sir, if You have carried Him away, tell me where You have laid Him, and I will take Him away."

16 Jesus said to her, "Mary!"

She turned and said to Him,^a "Rabboni!" (which is to say, Teacher).

17 Jesus said to her, "Do not cling to Me, for I have not yet ascended to My Father; but go to My brethren and say to them, 'I am ascending to My Father and your Father, and *to* My God and your God.' "

18 Mary Magdalene came and told the disciples that she had seen the Lord,^a and *that* He had spoken these things to her.

19 Then, the same day at evening, being the first *day* of the week, when the doors were shut where the disciples were assembled,^a for fear of the Jews, Jesus came and stood in the midst, and said to them, "Peace *be* with you." 20 When He had said this, He showed them *His* hands and His side. Then the disciples were glad when they saw the Lord.

21 So Jesus said to them again, "Peace to you! As the Father has sent Me, I also send you." 22 And when He had said this, He breathed on *them,* and said to them, "Receive the Holy Spirit. 23 If you forgive the sins of any, they are forgiven them; if you retain the *sins* of any, they are retained."

24 Now Thomas, called the Twin, one of the twelve, was not with them when Jesus came. 25 The other disciples therefore said to him, "We have seen the Lord."

So he said to them, "Unless I see in His hands the print of the nails, and put my finger into the print of the nails, and put my hand into His side, I will not believe."

26 And after eight days His disci-

20:16 ^aNU-Text adds *in Hebrew.*   20:18 ^aNU-Text reads *disciples, "I have seen the Lord," . . .*
20:19 ^aNU-Text omits *assembled.*

Gospel Pearls

ples were again inside, and Thomas with them. Jesus came, the doors being shut, and stood in the midst, and said, "Peace to you!" 27 Then He said to Thomas, "Reach your finger here, and look at My hands; and reach your hand *here,* and put *it* into My side. Do not be unbelieving, but believing."

28 And Thomas answered and said to Him, "My Lord and my God!"

29 Jesus said to him, "Thomas,ᵃ because you have seen Me, you have believed. Blessed *are* those who have not seen and *yet* have believed."

30 And truly Jesus did many other signs in the presence of His disciples, which are not written in this book; 31 but these are written that you may believe that Jesus is the Christ, the Son of God, and that believing you may have life in His name.

21 After these things Jesus showed Himself again to the disciples at the Sea of Tiberias, and in this way He showed *Himself:* 2 Simon Peter, Thomas called the Twin, Nathanael of Cana in Galilee, the *sons* of Zebedee, and two others of His disciples were together. 3 Simon Peter said to them, "I am going fishing."

They said to him, "We are going with you also." They went out and immediatelyᵃ got into the boat, and that night they caught nothing. 4 But when the morning had now come, Jesus stood on the shore; yet the disciples did not know that it was Jesus. 5 Then Jesus said to them, "Children, have you any food?"

They answered Him, "No."

6 And He said to them, "Cast the net on the right side of the boat, and you will find *some.*" So they cast, and now they were not able to draw it in because of the multitude of fish.

7 Therefore that disciple whom Jesus loved said to Peter, "It is the Lord!" Now when Simon Peter heard that it was the Lord, he put on *his* outer garment (for he had removed it), and plunged into the sea. 8 But the other disciples came in the little boat (for they were not far from land, but about two hundred cubits), dragging the net with fish. 9 Then, as soon as they had come to land, they saw a fire of coals there, and fish laid on it, and bread. 10 Jesus said to them, "Bring some of the fish which you have just caught."

11 Simon Peter went up and dragged the net to land, full of large fish, one hundred and fifty-three; and although there were so many, the net was not broken. 12 Jesus said to them, "Come *and* eat breakfast." Yet none of the disciples dared ask Him, "Who are You?"—knowing that it was the Lord. 13 Jesus then came and took the bread and gave it to them, and likewise the fish.

14 This *is* now the third time Jesus showed Himself to His disciples after He was raised from the dead.

15 So when they had eaten breakfast, Jesus said to Simon Peter, "Simon, *son* of Jonah,ᵃ do you love Me more than these?"

He said to Him, "Yes, Lord; You know that I love You."

He said to him, "Feed My lambs."

16 He said to him again a second time, "Simon, *son* of Jonah,ᵃ do you love Me?"

He said to Him, "Yes, Lord; You know that I love You."

He said to him, "Tend My sheep."

17 He said to him the third time, "Simon, *son* of Jonah,ᵃ do you love Me?" Peter was grieved because He said to him the third time, "Do you love Me?"

And he said to Him, "Lord, You know all things; You know that I love You."

Jesus said to him, "Feed My sheep. 18 Most assuredly, I say to you, when you were younger, you girded yourself and walked where you wished; but when you are old, you will stretch out your hands, and another will gird you and carry *you* where you do not wish." 19 This He spoke, signifying by what death he would glorify God. And when He had spoken this, He said to him, "Follow Me."

20 Then Peter, turning around, saw the disciple whom Jesus loved following, who also had leaned on His breast at the supper, and said, "Lord, who is the one who betrays You?" 21 Peter, seeing him, said to Jesus, "But Lord, what *about* this man?"

22 Jesus said to him, "If I will that

20:29 ᵃNU-Text and M-Text omit *Thomas.* 21:3 ᵃNU-Text omits *immediately.* 21:15 ᵃNU-Text reads *John.* 21:16 ᵃNU-Text reads *John.* 21:17 ᵃNU-Text reads *John.*

*F*or Christians, death is a portal that enables us to move from one realm of existence into another. Eventually death will knock on the door, no matter who we are. It helps a little to know that he will come. When he does, God will give you grace to accept what cannot be changed.

he remain till I come, what *is that* to you? You follow Me."

23 Then this saying went out among the brethren that this disciple would not die. Yet Jesus did not say to him that he would not die, but, "If I will that he remain till I come, what *is that* to you?"

24 This is the disciple who testifies of these things, and wrote these things; and we know that his testimony is true.

25 And there are also many other things that Jesus did, which if they were written one by one, I suppose that even the world itself could not contain the books that would be written. Amen.

THE ACTS of the Apostles

1 The former account I made, O Theophilus, of all that Jesus began both to do and teach, 2 until the day in which He was taken up, after He through the Holy Spirit had given commandments to the apostles whom He had chosen, 3 to whom He also presented Himself alive after His suffering by many infallible proofs, being seen by them during forty days and speaking of the things pertaining to the kingdom of God.

4 And being assembled together with *them,* He commanded them not to depart from Jerusalem, but to wait for the Promise of the Father, "which," *He said,* "you have heard from Me; 5 for John truly baptized with water, but you shall be baptized with the Holy Spirit not many days from now." 6 Therefore, when they had come together, they asked Him, saying, "Lord, will You at this time restore the kingdom to Israel?" 7 And He said to them, "It is not for you to know times or seasons which the Father has put in His own authority. 8 But you shall receive power when the Holy Spirit has come upon you; and you shall be witnesses to Me*a* in Jerusalem, and in all Judea and Samaria, and to the end of the earth."

9 Now when He had spoken these things, while they watched, He was taken up, and a cloud received Him out of their sight. 10 And while they looked steadfastly toward heaven as He went up, behold, two men stood by them in white apparel, 11 who also said, "Men of Galilee, why do you stand gazing up into heaven? This *same* Jesus, who was taken up from you into heaven, will so come in like manner as you saw Him go into heaven."

12 Then they returned to Jerusalem from the mount called Olivet, which is near Jerusalem, a Sabbath day's journey. 13 And when they had entered, they went up into the upper room where they were staying: Peter, James, John, and Andrew; Philip and Thomas; Bartholomew and Matthew; James *the son* of Alphaeus and Simon the Zealot; and Judas *the son* of James. 14 These all continued with one accord in prayer and supplication,*a* with the women and Mary the mother of Jesus, and with His brothers.

15 And in those days Peter stood up in the midst of the disciples*a* (altogether the number of names was about a hundred and twenty), and said, 16 "Men *and* brethren, this Scripture had to be fulfilled, which the Holy Spirit spoke before by the mouth of David concerning Judas, who became a guide to those who arrested Jesus; 17 for he was numbered with us and obtained a part in this ministry."

18 (Now this man purchased a field with the wages of iniquity; and falling headlong, he burst open in the middle and all his entrails gushed out. 19 And it became known to all those dwelling in Jerusalem; so that field is called in their own language, Akel Dama, that is, Field of Blood.)

20 "For it is written in the book of Psalms:

1:8 *a*NU-Text reads *My witnesses.*   1:14 *a*NU-Text omits *and supplication.*   1:15 *a*NU-Text reads brethren.

Gospel Pearls

'Let his dwelling place be
desolate,
And let no one live in it';ᵃ

and,

'Letᵇ another take his office.'ᶜ

21 "Therefore, of these men who
have accompanied us all the time
that the Lord Jesus went in and out
among us, 22 beginning from the baptism of John to that day when He was
taken up from us, one of these must
become a witness with us of His resurrection."
23 And they proposed two: Joseph
called Barsabas, who was surnamed
Justus, and Matthias. 24 And they
prayed and said, "You, O Lord, who
know the hearts of all, show which
of these two You have chosen
25 to take part in this ministry and
apostleship from which Judas by
transgression fell, that he might go
to his own place." 26 And they cast
their lots, and the lot fell on Matthias.
And he was numbered with the
eleven apostles.

2 When the Day of Pentecost had
fully come, they were all with one
accordᵃ in one place. 2 And suddenly
there came a sound from heaven, as
of a rushing mighty wind, and it filled
the whole house where they were sitting. 3 Then there appeared to them
divided tongues, as of fire, and one
sat upon each of them. 4 And they
were all filled with the Holy Spirit
and began to speak with other
tongues, as the Spirit gave them utterance.
5 And there were dwelling in Jerusalem Jews, devout men, from every
nation under heaven. 6 And when
this sound occurred, the multitude
came together, and were confused,
because everyone heard them speak
in his own language. 7 Then they
were all amazed and marveled, saying to one another, "Look, are not
all these who speak Galileans?
8 And how is it that we hear, each
in our own language in which we
were born? 9 Parthians and Medes
and Elamites, those dwelling in Mesopotamia, Judea and Cappadocia,
Pontus and Asia, 10 Phrygia and
Pamphylia, Egypt and the parts of

Libya adjoining Cyrene, visitors
from Rome, both Jews and prose-
lytes, 11 Cretans and Arabs—we hear
them speaking in our own tongues
the wonderful works of God."
12 So they were all amazed and perplexed, saying to one another,
"Whatever could this mean?"
13 Others mocking said, "They are
full of new wine."
14 But Peter, standing up with the
eleven, raised his voice and said to
them, "Men of Judea and all who
dwell in Jerusalem, let this be known
to you, and heed my words.
15 For these are not drunk, as you
suppose, since it is only the third
hour of the day. 16 But this is what
was spoken by the prophet Joel:

17 'And it shall come to pass in the
last days, says God,
That I will pour out of My Spirit
on all flesh;
Your sons and your daughters
shall prophesy,
Your young men shall see
visions,
Your old men shall dream
dreams.
18 And on My menservants and
on My maidservants
I will pour out My Spirit in
those days;
And they shall prophesy.
19 I will show wonders in heaven
above
And signs in the earth beneath:
Blood and fire and vapor of
smoke.
20 The sun shall be turned into
darkness,
And the moon into blood,
Before the coming of the great
and awesome day of the
LORD.
21 And it shall come to pass
That whoever calls on the
name of the LORD
Shall be saved.'ᵃ

22 "Men of Israel, hear these
words: Jesus of Nazareth, a Man at-
tested by God to you by miracles,
wonders, and signs which God did
through Him in your midst, as you
yourselves also know— 23 Him, being delivered by the determined purpose and foreknowledge of God, you
have takenᵃ by lawless hands, have

1:20 ᵃPsalm 69:25 ᵇPsalm 109:8 ᶜGreek episkopen 2:1 ᵃNU-Text reads together.
2:21 ᵃJoel 2:28–32 2:23 ᵃNU-Text omits have taken.

God has sustained you in this life because you are needed. Perhaps it is not a need
that requires a clean bandage on an old cut. But you are needed. Be careful that
you do not hold those things around you captive. You must love enough to let go.

crucified, and put to death; 24 whom God raised up, having loosed the pains of death, because it was not possible that He should be held by it. 25 For David says concerning Him:

'I foresaw the LORD always
   before my face,
For He is at my right hand, that
   I may not be shaken.
26 Therefore my heart rejoiced,
   and my tongue was glad;
Moreover my flesh also will
   rest in hope.
27 For You will not leave my soul
   in Hades,
Nor will You allow Your Holy
   One to see corruption.
28 You have made known to me
   the ways of life;
You will make me full of joy
   in Your presence.'a

29 "Men and brethren, let me speak freely to you of the patriarch David, that he is both dead and buried, and his tomb is with us to this day. 30 Therefore, being a prophet, and knowing that God had sworn with an oath to him that of the fruit of his body, according to the flesh, He would raise up the Christ to sit on his throne,a 31 he, foreseeing this, spoke concerning the resurrection of the Christ, that His soul was not left in Hades, nor did His flesh see corruption. 32 This Jesus God has raised up, of which we are all witnesses. 33 Therefore being exalted to the right hand of God, and having received from the Father the promise of the Holy Spirit, He poured out this which you now see and hear. 34 "For David did not ascend into the heavens, but he says himself:

'The LORD said to my Lord,
   "Sit at My right hand,
35 Till I make Your enemies Your
   footstool." 'a

36 "Therefore let all the house of Israel know assuredly that God has made this Jesus, whom you crucified, both Lord and Christ."

37 Now when they heard this, they were cut to the heart, and said to Peter and the rest of the apostles, "Men

and brethren, what shall we do?" 38 Then Peter said to them, "Repent, and let every one of you be baptized in the name of Jesus Christ for the remission of sins; and you shall receive the gift of the Holy Spirit. 39 For the promise is to you and to your children, and to all who are afar off, as many as the Lord our God will call."

40 And with many other words he testified and exhorted them, saying, "Be saved from this perverse generation." 41 Then those who gladlya received his word were baptized; and that day about three thousand souls were added to them. 42 And they continued steadfastly in the apostles' doctrine and fellowship, in the breaking of bread, and in prayers. 43 Then fear came upon every soul, and many wonders and signs were done through the apostles. 44 Now all who believed were together, and had all things in common, 45 and sold their possessions and goods, and divided them among all, as anyone had need.

46 So continuing daily with one accord in the temple, and breaking bread from house to house, they ate their food with gladness and simplicity of heart, 47 praising God and having favor with all the people. And the Lord added to the churcha daily those who were being saved.

3 Now Peter and John went up together to the temple at the hour of prayer, the ninth hour. 2 And a certain man lame from his mother's womb was carried, whom they laid daily at the gate of the temple which is called Beautiful, to ask alms from those who entered the temple; 3 who, seeing Peter and John about to go into the temple, asked for alms. 4 And fixing his eyes on him, with John, Peter said, "Look at us." 5 So he gave them his attention, expecting to receive something from them. 6 Then Peter said, "Silver and gold I do not have, but what I do have I give you: In the name of Jesus Christ of Nazareth, rise up and walk." 7 And he took him by the right hand and lifted him up, and immediately his feet and ankle bones re-

2:28 aPsalm 16:8–11   2:30 aNU-Text omits according to the flesh, He would raise up the Christ and completes the verse with He would seat one on his throne.   2:35 aPsalm 110:1   2:41 aNU-Text omits gladly.   2:47 aNU-Text omits to the church.

Gospel
Pearls

ceived strength. 8 So he, leaping up, stood and walked and entered the temple with them—walking, leaping, and praising God. 9 And all the people saw him walking and praising God. 10 Then they knew that it was he who sat begging alms at the Beautiful Gate of the temple; and they were filled with wonder and amazement at what had happened to him.

11 Now as the lame man who was healed held on to Peter and John, all the people ran together to them in the porch which is called Solomon's, greatly amazed. 12 So when Peter saw it, he responded to the people: "Men of Israel, why do you marvel at this? Or why look so intently at us, as though by our own power or godliness we had made this man walk? 13 The God of Abraham, Isaac, and Jacob, the God of our fathers, glorified His Servant Jesus, whom you delivered up and denied in the presence of Pilate, when he was determined to let *Him* go. 14 But you denied the Holy One and the Just, and asked for a murderer to be granted to you, 15 and killed the Prince of life, whom God raised from the dead, of which we are witnesses. 16 And His name, through faith in His name, has made this man strong, whom you see and know. Yes, the faith which *comes* through Him has given him this perfect soundness in the presence of you all.

17 "Yet now, brethren, I know that you did *it* in ignorance, as *did* also your rulers. 18 But those things which God foretold by the mouth of all His prophets, that the Christ would suffer, He has thus fulfilled. 19 Repent therefore and be converted, that your sins may be blotted out, so that times of refreshing may come from the presence of the Lord, 20 and that He may send Jesus Christ, who was preached to you before,*a* 21 whom heaven must receive until the times of restoration of all things, which God has spoken by the mouth of all His holy prophets since the world began. 22 For Moses truly said to the fathers, 'The LORD your God will raise up for you a Prophet like me from your brethren. Him you shall hear in all things, whatever He says to you. 23 And it shall be that every soul who will not hear that Prophet shall be utterly destroyed from among the people.'*a* 24 Yes, and all the prophets, from Samuel and those who follow, as many as have spoken, have also foretold*a* these days. 25 You are sons of the prophets, and of the covenant which God made with our fathers, saying to Abraham, 'And in your seed all the families of the earth shall be blessed.'*a* 26 To you first, God, having raised up His Servant Jesus, sent Him to bless you, in turning away every one of you from your iniquities."*

4 Now as they spoke to the people, the priests, the captain of the temple, and the Sadducees came upon them, 2 being greatly disturbed that they taught the people and preached in Jesus the resurrection from the dead. 3 And they laid hands on them, and put *them* in custody until the next day, for it was already evening. 4 However, many of those who heard the word believed; and the number of the men came to be about five thousand.

5 And it came to pass, on the next day, that their rulers, elders, and scribes, 6 as well as Annas the high priest, Caiaphas, John, and Alexander, and as many as were of the family of the high priest, were gathered together at Jerusalem. 7 And when they had set them in the midst, they asked, "By what power or by what name have you done this?"

8 Then Peter, filled with the Holy Spirit, said to them, "Rulers of the people and elders of Israel: 9 If we this day are judged for a good deed *done* to a helpless man, by what means he has been made well, 10 let it be known to you all, and to all the people of Israel, that by the name of Jesus Christ of Nazareth, whom you crucified, whom God raised from the dead, by Him this man stands here before you whole. 11 This is the *'stone which was rejected by you builders, which has become the chief cornerstone.'a* 12 Nor is there salvation in any other, for there is no other name under heaven

---

3:20 *a*NU-Text and M-Text read *Christ Jesus, who was ordained for you before.* 3:23 *a*Deuteronomy 18:15, 18, 19 3:24 *a*NU-Text and M-Text read *proclaimed.* 3:25 *a*Genesis 22:18; 26:4; 28:14 4:11 *a*Psalm 118:22

*M*ary, the mother of Jesus, didn't understand her Son. His decisions led Him to His death. Yet she supported Him to the end. You must be wise! If not, you will create a cold war which will leave you alone with bitterness and sad memories.

No Secrets in the Secret Place

Acts 3:19

*A*cts 3:19 tells us that "times of refreshing . . . come from the presence of the Lord." Yet we shuffle into His presence like children who have been instructed not to disturb their Father, although God isn't sleepy, and He doesn't have to go to work. He is alive and awake, and He is well. We blare like trumpets announcing our successes, but we whisper our failures through parched lips in the shadows of our relationships with Him.

It is the nature of fallen man to hide from God. If you will remember, Adam also hid from God. After he was cornered by his Father, Adam said, "I heard Your voice in the garden, and I was afraid because I was naked; and I hid myself" (Genesis 3:10).

How ridiculous to think that we can hide from God! When a woman hides from God, she loses herself. That loss causes a desperation that produces sin and separation.

Adam's meager attempt at morality drove him to sew together a few leaves into a figgy little apron that was dying even while he was sewing it. Why would a lost man cover himself with leaves? Adam said it was because he was afraid. Fear separated this son from his Father. Fear caused him to conspire to deceive his only Solution. This fear was not reverence; it was desperation. If Adam had only run toward God instead of away from Him, he could have been delivered!

Many Christians feel just as uncomfortable with their heavenly Father. Some do not feel accepted. Others are intimidated by His holiness. I'll admit that God's holiness exposes our flawed, soiled personhood, but His grace allows us to approach Him through skins soaked with Christ's blood.

We are properly dressed to come into the presence of a Holy God only because His Son, Jesus Christ, has wrapped us in His own identity. Like Adam, we are draped in a bloody sacrifice that has made it possible to approach our Father, and live!

It is futile to try to hide from your Father. His intelligence—also called *omniscience*—will expose you. You cannot change His ability to see right through you, so you need to learn to trust Him enough to be comfortable with Him. Who else knows you like God does? If you hide from His perfect love, you will never experience the indescribable joy of sitting in His lap.

given among men by which we must be saved."

13 Now when they saw the boldness of Peter and John, and perceived that they were uneducated and untrained men, they marveled. And they realized that they had been with Jesus. 14 And seeing the man who had been healed standing with them, they could say nothing against it. 15 But when they had commanded them to go aside out of the council, they conferred among themselves, 16 saying, "What shall we do to these men? For, indeed, that a notable miracle has been done through them *is* evident to all who dwell in Jerusalem, and we cannot deny *it*. 17 But so that it spreads no further among the people, let us severely threaten them, that from now on they speak to no man in this name."

18 So they called them and commanded them not to speak at all nor teach in the name of Jesus. 19 But Peter and John answered and said to them, "Whether it is right in the sight of God to listen to you more than to God, you judge. 20 For we cannot but speak the things which we have seen and heard." 21 So when they had further threatened them, they let them go, finding no way of punishing them, because of the people, since they all glorified God for what had been done. 22 For the man was over forty years old on whom this miracle of healing had been performed.

23 And being let go, they went to their own *companions* and reported all that the chief priests and elders had said to them. 24 So when they heard that, they raised their voice to God with one accord and said: "Lord, You *are* God, who made heaven and earth and the sea, and all that is in them, 25 who by the mouth of Your servant David*ᵃ* have said:

'Why did the nations rage,
  And the people plot vain
    things?
26 The kings of the earth took
    their stand,
  And the rulers were gathered
    together
  Against the LORD and against
    His Christ.'*ᵃ*

27 "For truly against Your holy Servant Jesus, whom You anointed, both Herod and Pontius Pilate, with the Gentiles and the people of Israel, were gathered together 28 to do whatever Your hand and Your purpose determined before to be done. 29 Now, Lord, look on their threats, and grant to Your servants that with all boldness they may speak Your word, 30 by stretching out Your hand to heal, and that signs and wonders may be done through the name of Your holy Servant Jesus."

31 And when they had prayed, the place where they were assembled together was shaken; and they were all filled with the Holy Spirit, and they spoke the word of God with boldness.

32 Now the multitude of those who believed were of one heart and one soul; neither did anyone say that any of the things he possessed was his own, but they had all things in common. 33 And with great power the apostles gave witness to the resurrection of the Lord Jesus. And great grace was upon them all. 34 Nor was there anyone among them who lacked; for all who were possessors of lands or houses sold them, and brought the proceeds of the things that were sold, 35 and laid *them* at the apostles' feet; and they distributed to each as anyone had need.

36 And Joses,*ᵃ* who was also named Barnabas by the apostles (which is translated Son of Encouragement), a Levite of the country of Cyprus, 37 having land, sold *it*, and brought the money and laid *it* at the apostles' feet.

5 But a certain man named Ananias, with Sapphira his wife, sold a possession. 2 And he kept back *part* of the proceeds, his wife also being aware *of it*, and brought a certain part and laid *it* at the apostles' feet. 3 But Peter said, "Ananias, why has Satan filled your heart to lie to the Holy Spirit and keep back *part* of the price of the land for yourself? 4 While it remained, was it not your own? And after it was sold, was it not in your own control? Why have you conceived this thing in your heart? You have not lied to men but to God."

4:25 *ᵃ*NU-Text reads who through the Holy Spirit, by the mouth of our father, Your servant David.
4:26 *ᵃ*Psalm 2:1, 2   4:36 *ᵃ*NU-Text reads Joseph.

We are all alike when it comes to the essentials of life. We need, we love, we touch, we give! What else can we do but love what God has allowed us to parent?

5 Then Ananias, hearing these words, fell down and breathed his last. So great fear came upon all those who heard these things. 6 And the young men arose and wrapped him up, carried *him* out, and buried *him*.

7 Now it was about three hours later when his wife came in, not knowing what had happened. 8 And Peter answered her, "Tell me whether you sold the land for so much?"

She said, "Yes, for so much."

9 Then Peter said to her, "How is it that you have agreed together to test the Spirit of the Lord? Look, the feet of those who have buried your husband *are* at the door, and they will carry you out." 10 Then immediately she fell down at his feet and breathed her last. And the young men came in and found her dead, and carrying *her* out, buried *her* by her husband. 11 So great fear came upon all the church and upon all who heard these things.

12 And through the hands of the apostles many signs and wonders were done among the people. And they were all with one accord in Solomon's Porch. 13 Yet none of the rest dared join them, but the people esteemed them highly. 14 And believers were increasingly added to the Lord, multitudes of both men and women, 15 so that they brought the sick out into the streets and laid *them* on beds and couches, that at least the shadow of Peter passing by might fall on some of them. 16 Also a multitude gathered from the surrounding cities to Jerusalem, bringing sick people and those who were tormented by unclean spirits, and they were all healed.

17 Then the high priest rose up, and all those who *were* with him (which is the sect of the Sadducees), and they were filled with indignation, 18 and laid their hands on the apostles and put them in the common prison. 19 But at night an angel of the Lord opened the prison doors and brought them out, and said, 20 "Go, stand in the temple and speak to the people all the words of this life."

21 And when they heard *that*, they entered the temple early in the morning and taught. But the high priest and those with him came and called the council together, with all the elders of the children of Israel, and sent to the prison to have them brought.

22 But when the officers came and did not find them in the prison, they returned and reported, 23 saying, "Indeed we found the prison shut securely, and the guards standing outside[a] before the doors; but when we opened them, we found no one inside!" 24 Now when the high priest,[a] the captain of the temple, and the chief priests heard these things, they wondered what the outcome would be. 25 So one came and told them, saying,[a] "Look, the men whom you put in prison are standing in the temple and teaching the people!"

26 Then the captain went with the officers and brought them without violence, for they feared the people, lest they should be stoned. 27 And when they had brought them, they set *them* before the council. And the high priest asked them, 28 saying, "Did we not strictly command you not to teach in this name? And look, you have filled Jerusalem with your doctrine, and intend to bring this Man's blood on us!"

29 But Peter and the *other* apostles answered and said: "We ought to obey God rather than men. 30 The God of our fathers raised up Jesus whom you murdered by hanging on a tree. 31 Him God has exalted to His right hand *to be* Prince and Savior, to give repentance to Israel and forgiveness of sins. 32 And we are His witnesses to these things, and *so* also *is* the Holy Spirit whom God has given to those who obey Him."

33 When they heard *this*, they were furious and plotted to kill them. 34 Then one in the council stood up, a Pharisee named Gamaliel, a teacher of the law held in respect by all the people, and commanded them to put the apostles outside for a little while. 35 And he said to them: "Men of Israel, take heed to yourselves what you intend to do regarding these men. 36 For some time ago Theudas rose up, claiming to be somebody. A number of men, about four hundred, joined him. He was slain, and all who obeyed him were

5:23 [a]NU-Text and M-Text omit *outside*.   5:24 [a]NU-Text omits *the high priest*.   5:25 [a]NU-Text and M-Text omit *saying*.

Gospel Pearls

scattered and came to nothing. 37 After this man, Judas of Galilee rose up in the days of the census, and drew away many people after him. He also perished, and all who obeyed him were dispersed. 38 And now I say to you, keep away from these men and let them alone; for if this plan or this work is of men, it will come to nothing; 39 but if it is of God, you cannot overthrow it—lest you even be found to fight against God."

40 And they agreed with him, and when they had called for the apostles and beaten *them,* they commanded that they should not speak in the name of Jesus, and let them go. 41 So they departed from the presence of the council, rejoicing that they were counted worthy to suffer shame for His[a] name. 42 And daily in the temple, and in every house, they did not cease teaching and preaching Jesus *as* the Christ.

6 Now in those days, when *the number of* the disciples was multiplying, there arose a complaint against the Hebrews by the Hellenists,[a] because their widows were neglected in the daily distribution. 2 Then the twelve summoned the multitude of the disciples and said, "It is not desirable that we should leave the word of God and serve tables. 3 Therefore, brethren, seek out from among you seven men of *good* reputation, full of the Holy Spirit and wisdom, whom we may appoint over this business; 4 but we will give ourselves continually to prayer and to the ministry of the word."

5 And the saying pleased the whole multitude. And they chose Stephen, a man full of faith and the Holy Spirit, and Philip, Prochorus, Nicanor, Timon, Parmenas, and Nicolas, a proselyte from Antioch, 6 whom they set before the apostles; and when they had prayed, they laid hands on them.

7 Then the word of God spread, and the number of the disciples multiplied greatly in Jerusalem, and a great many of the priests were obedient to the faith.

8 And Stephen, full of faith[a] and power, did great wonders and signs

among the people. 9 Then there arose some from what is called the Synagogue of the Freedmen (Cyrenians, Alexandrians, and those from Cilicia and Asia), disputing with Stephen. 10 And they were not able to resist the wisdom and the Spirit by which he spoke. 11 Then they secretly induced men to say, "We have heard him speak blasphemous words against Moses and God." 12 And they stirred up the people, the elders, and the scribes; and they came upon *him,* seized him, and brought *him* to the council. 13 They also set up false witnesses who said, "This man does not cease to speak blasphemous[a] words against this holy place and the law; 14 for we have heard him say that this Jesus of Nazareth will destroy this place and change the customs which Moses delivered to us." 15 And all who sat in the council, looking steadfastly at him, saw his face as the face of an angel.

7 Then the high priest said, "Are these things so?"

2 And he said, "Brethren and fathers, listen: The God of glory appeared to our father Abraham when he was in Mesopotamia, before he dwelt in Haran, 3 and said to him, *'Get out of your country and from your relatives, and come to a land that I will show you.'*[a] 4 Then he came out of the land of the Chaldeans and dwelt in Haran. And from there, when his father was dead, He moved him to this land in which you now dwell. 5 And *God* gave him no inheritance in it, not even *enough* to set his foot on. But even when *Abraham* had no child, He promised to give it to him for a possession, and to his descendants after him. 6 But God spoke in this way: that his descendants would dwell in a foreign land, and that they would bring them into bondage and oppress *them* four hundred years. 7 *'And the nation to whom they will be in bondage I will judge,'*[a] said God, *'and after that they shall come out and serve Me in this place.'*[b] 8 Then He gave him the covenant of circumcision; and so *Abraham* begot Isaac and circumcised him on the eighth day; and Isaac

---

5:41 [a]NU-Text reads *the name;* M-Text reads *the name of Jesus.* 6:1 [a]That is, Greek-speaking Jews.
6:8 [a]NU-Text reads *grace.*   6:13 [a]NU-Text omits *blasphemous.*   7:3 [a]Genesis 12:1
7:7 [a]Genesis 15:14   [b]Exodus 3:12

*I*f you are carrying old pain, old scars, dead relationships, or even a torch for someone who has moved on, I counsel you to abort anything that is draining your life and blurring your vision.

Necessary Passion

Acts 5:41

There can be no fulfillment where there is no passion. The passion that will cause you to achieve must be strong enough to make you uncomfortable. Simply stated, you must want something—a good marriage, a ministry, a business—badly enough to survive the process required to attain it. There will always be hindrances to overcome. But the force of your personal passion will provide the power to break through anything that stands between you and the object of your passion.

Between Jesus and His goal was a cross. The Cross was not the end; it was the means. He didn't enjoy the means, but He endured it. What gave Him the power to endure the Cross was His passion.

The desire that has ignited your heart and burns in your thoughts becomes the fuel that will enable you to withstand whatever life sends your way. Jesus' suffering was more than a groping in the gross darkness. It was the suffering of our passionate Lord!

Have you ever noticed that some of the most wretched sinners have become the greatest ministers? These people, accustomed to pursuing their passion, were people who dared to desire. Although misdirected at one time, their burning desire, when bridled and properly channeled, caused them to accomplish their goals.

My sister, if you are driven by intense feelings and often wrestle with your ambitious nature, hear me and hear me well: Don't try to kill your passion; redirect it toward the dream God has given you. Satan wants you because he knows that if you ever line up your passion with God's purpose, you will become a spiritual dynamo. There will be no stopping you!

Don't resent your passion. Control it, yes, but please don't kill it. Without it, you would be limp and lifeless, moving through your days like a robot. God created you to be full of zest and enthusiasm. Misdirected passions can drain your life away. But God can recycle your zeal and transform it into something useful for Him.

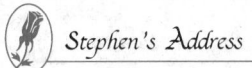

begot Jacob, and Jacob *begot* the twelve patriarchs.

9 "And the patriarchs, becoming envious, sold Joseph into Egypt. But God was with him 10 and delivered him out of all his troubles, and gave him favor and wisdom in the presence of Pharaoh, king of Egypt; and he made him governor over Egypt and all his house. 11 Now a famine and great trouble came over all the land of Egypt and Canaan, and our fathers found no sustenance. 12 But when Jacob heard that there was grain in Egypt, he sent out our fathers first. 13 And the second *time* Joseph was made known to his brothers, and Joseph's family became known to the Pharaoh. 14 Then Joseph sent and called his father Jacob and all his relatives to *him*, seventy-five*ᵃ* people. 15 So Jacob went down to Egypt; and he died, he and our fathers. 16 And they were carried back to Shechem and laid in the tomb that Abraham bought for a sum of money from the sons of Hamor, *the father* of Shechem.

17 "But when the time of the promise drew near which God had sworn to Abraham, the people grew and multiplied in Egypt 18 till another king arose who did not know Joseph. 19 This man dealt treacherously with our people, and oppressed our forefathers, making them expose their babies, so that they might not live. 20 At this time Moses was born, and was well pleasing to God; and he was brought up in his father's house for three months. 21 But when he was set out, Pharaoh's daughter took him away and brought him up as her own son. 22 And Moses was learned in all the wisdom of the Egyptians, and was mighty in words and deeds.

23 "Now when he was forty years old, it came into his heart to visit his brethren, the children of Israel. 24 And seeing one of *them* suffer wrong, he defended and avenged him who was oppressed, and struck down the Egyptian. 25 For he supposed that his brethren would have understood that God would deliver them by his hand, but they did not understand. 26 And the next day he appeared to two of them as they were fighting, and *tried to* reconcile them, saying,

'Men, you are brethren; why do you wrong one another?' 27 But he who did his neighbor wrong pushed him away, saying, '*Who made you a ruler and a judge over us? 28 Do you want to kill me as you did the Egyptian yesterday?'ᵃ* 29 Then, at this saying, Moses fled and became a dweller in the land of Midian, where he had two sons.

30 "And when forty years had passed, an Angel of the Lord*ᵃ* appeared to him in a flame of fire in a bush, in the wilderness of Mount Sinai. 31 When Moses saw *it*, he marveled at the sight; and as he drew near to observe, the voice of the Lord came to him, 32 *saying, 'I am the God of your fathers—the God of Abraham, the God of Isaac, and the God of Jacob.'ᵃ* And Moses trembled and dared not look. 33 '*Then the* LORD *said to him, "Take your sandals off your feet, for the place where you stand is holy ground. 34 I have surely seen the oppression of My people who are in Egypt; I have heard their groaning and have come down to deliver them. And now come, I will send you to Egypt."'ᵃ*

35 "This Moses whom they rejected, saying, '*Who made you a ruler and a judge?'ᵃ* is the one God sent *to be* a ruler and a deliverer by the hand of the Angel who appeared to him in the bush. 36 He brought them out, after he had shown wonders and signs in the land of Egypt, and in the Red Sea, and in the wilderness forty years.

37 "This is that Moses who said to the children of Israel,*ᵃ 'The* LORD *your God will raise up for you a Prophet like me from your brethren. Him you shall hear.'ᵇ*

38 "This is he who was in the congregation in the wilderness with the Angel who spoke to him on Mount Sinai, and *with* our fathers, the one who received the living oracles to give to us, 39 whom our fathers would not obey, but rejected. And in their hearts they turned back to Egypt, 40 saying to Aaron, '*Make us gods to go before us; as for this Moses who brought us out of the land of Egypt, we do not know what has become of him.'ᵃ* 41 And they made a calf in those days, offered sacrifices to the

While you have esteemed all things around you, God is very focused in His interest. He says, "Throw down the thing that has become a solicitude in your life, because I esteem nothing above My interest in you."

idol, and rejoiced in the works of their own hands. 42 Then God turned and gave them up to worship the host of heaven, as it is written in the book of the Prophets:

'Did you offer Me slaughtered
　　animals and sacrifices during
　　forty years in the wilderness,
　　O house of Israel?
43　You also took up the tabernacle
　　of Moloch,
　　And the star of your god
　　Remphan,
　　Images which you made to
　　worship;
　　And I will carry you away
　　beyond Babylon.'ª

44 "Our fathers had the tabernacle of witness in the wilderness, as He appointed, instructing Moses to make it according to the pattern that he had seen, 45 which our fathers, having received it in turn, also brought with Joshua into the land possessed by the Gentiles, whom God drove out before the face of our fathers until the days of David, 46 who found favor before God and asked to find a dwelling for the God of Jacob. 47 But Solomon built Him a house.

48 "However, the Most High does not dwell in temples made with hands, as the prophet says:

49 'Heaven is My throne,
　　And earth is My footstool.
　　What house will you build for
　　Me? says the LORD,
　　Or what is the place of My rest?
50　Has My hand not made all
　　these things?'ª

51 "You stiff-necked and uncircumcised in heart and ears! You always resist the Holy Spirit; as your fathers did, so do you. 52 Which of the prophets did your fathers not persecute? And they killed those who foretold the coming of the Just One, of whom you now have become the betrayers and murderers, 53 who have received the law by the direction of angels and have not kept it."

54 When they heard these things they were cut to the heart, and they gnashed at him with their teeth. 55 But he, being full of the Holy Spirit, gazed into heaven and saw the glory of God, and Jesus standing at the right hand of God, 56 and said, "Look! I see the heavens opened and the Son of Man standing at the right hand of God!"

57 Then they cried out with a loud voice, stopped their ears, and ran at him with one accord; 58 and they cast him out of the city and stoned him. And the witnesses laid down their clothes at the feet of a young man named Saul. 59 And they stoned Stephen as he was calling on God and saying, "Lord Jesus, receive my spirit." 60 Then he knelt down and cried out with a loud voice, "Lord, do not charge them with this sin." And when he had said this, he fell asleep.

8 Now Saul was consenting to his death.
　At that time a great persecution arose against the church which was at Jerusalem; and they were all scattered throughout the regions of Judea and Samaria, except the apostles. 2 And devout men carried Stephen to his burial, and made great lamentation over him.

3 As for Saul, he made havoc of the church, entering every house, and dragging off men and women, committing them to prison.

4 Therefore those who were scattered went everywhere preaching the word. 5 Then Philip went down to theª city of Samaria and preached Christ to them. 6 And the multitudes with one accord heeded the things spoken by Philip, hearing and seeing the miracles which he did. 7 For unclean spirits, crying with a loud voice, came out of many who were possessed; and many who were paralyzed and lame were healed. 8 And there was great joy in that city.

9 But there was a certain man called Simon, who previously practiced sorcery in the city and astonished the people of Samaria, claiming that he was someone great, 10 to whom they all gave heed, from the least to the greatest, saying, "This man is the great power of God." 11 And they heeded him because he had astonished them with his sorceries for a long time. 12 But when they believed Philip as he preached the

7:43 ªAmos 5:25–27　　7:50 ªIsaiah 66:1, 2　　8:5 ªOr a

Gospel Pearls

things concerning the kingdom of God and the name of Jesus Christ, both men and women were baptized. 13 Then Simon himself also believed; and when he was baptized he continued with Philip, and was amazed, seeing the miracles and signs which were done.

14 Now when the apostles who were at Jerusalem heard that Samaria had received the word of God, they sent Peter and John to them, 15 who, when they had come down, prayed for them that they might receive the Holy Spirit. 16 For as yet He had fallen upon none of them. They had only been baptized in the name of the Lord Jesus. 17 Then they laid hands on them, and they received the Holy Spirit.

18 And when Simon saw that through the laying on of the apostles' hands the Holy Spirit was given, he offered them money, 19 saying, "Give me this power also, that anyone on whom I lay hands may receive the Holy Spirit."

20 But Peter said to him, "Your money perish with you, because you thought that the gift of God could be purchased with money! 21 You have neither part nor portion in this matter, for your heart is not right in the sight of God. 22 Repent therefore of this your wickedness, and pray God if perhaps the thought of your heart may be forgiven you. 23 For I see that you are poisoned by bitterness and bound by iniquity."

24 Then Simon answered and said, "Pray to the Lord for me, that none of the things which you have spoken may come upon me."

25 So when they had testified and preached the word of the Lord, they returned to Jerusalem, preaching the gospel in many villages of the Samaritans.

26 Now an angel of the Lord spoke to Philip, saying, "Arise and go toward the south along the road which goes down from Jerusalem to Gaza." This is desert. 27 So he arose and went. And behold, a man of Ethiopia, a eunuch of great authority under Candace the queen of the Ethiopians, who had charge of all her treasury, and had come to Jerusalem to worship, 28 was returning. And sitting in his chariot, he was reading Isaiah the prophet. 29 Then the Spirit said to Philip, "Go near and overtake this chariot."

30 So Philip ran to him, and heard him reading the prophet Isaiah, and said, "Do you understand what you are reading?"

31 And he said, "How can I, unless someone guides me?" And he asked Philip to come up and sit with him. 32 The place in the Scripture which he read was this:

> "He was led as a sheep to the slaughter;
> And as a lamb before its shearer is silent,
> So He opened not His mouth.
> 33 In His humiliation His justice was taken away,
> And who will declare His generation?
> For His life is taken from the earth."[a]

34 So the eunuch answered Philip and said, "I ask you, of whom does the prophet say this, of himself or of some other man?" 35 Then Philip opened his mouth, and beginning at this Scripture, preached Jesus to him. 36 Now as they went down the road, they came to some water. And the eunuch said, "See, *here is* water. What hinders me from being baptized?"

37 Then Philip said, "If you believe with all your heart, you may."

And he answered and said, "I believe that Jesus Christ is the Son of God."[a]

38 So he commanded the chariot to stand still. And both Philip and the eunuch went down into the water, and he baptized him. 39 Now when they came up out of the water, the Spirit of the Lord caught Philip away, so that the eunuch saw him no more; and he went on his way rejoicing. 40 But Philip was found at Azotus. And passing through, he preached in all the cities till he came to Caesarea.

9 Then Saul, still breathing threats and murder against the disciples of the Lord, went to the high priest 2 and asked letters from him to the synagogues of Damascus, so that if

---

8:33 [a]Isaiah 53:7, 8   8:37 [a]NU-Text and M-Text omit this verse. It is found in Western texts, including the Latin tradition.

It is my prayer that you would allow the light to shine brightly upon you as a channel of expression for someone who needs encouragement. It is a habit well worth forming.

he found any who were of the Way, whether men or women, he might bring them bound to Jerusalem.

3 As he journeyed he came near Damascus, and suddenly a light shone around him from heaven. 4 Then he fell to the ground, and heard a voice saying to him, "Saul, Saul, why are you persecuting Me?"

5 And he said, "Who are You, Lord?"

Then the Lord said, "I am Jesus, whom you are persecuting.a It is hard for you to kick against the goads."

6 So he, trembling and astonished, said, "Lord, what do You want me to do?"

Then the Lord said to him, "Arise and go into the city, and you will be told what you must do."

7 And the men who journeyed with him stood speechless, hearing a voice but seeing no one. 8 Then Saul arose from the ground, and when his eyes were opened he saw no one. But they led him by the hand and brought him into Damascus. 9 And he was three days without sight, and neither ate nor drank.

10 Now there was a certain disciple at Damascus named Ananias; and to him the Lord said in a vision, "Ananias."

And he said, "Here I am, Lord."

11 So the Lord said to him, "Arise and go to the street called Straight, and inquire at the house of Judas for one called Saul of Tarsus, for behold, he is praying. 12 And in a vision he has seen a man named Ananias coming in and putting his hand on him, so that he might receive his sight."

13 Then Ananias answered, "Lord, I have heard from many about this man, how much harm he has done to Your saints in Jerusalem. 14 And here he has authority from the chief priests to bind all who call on Your name."

15 But the Lord said to him, "Go, for he is a chosen vessel of Mine to bear My name before Gentiles, kings, and the children of Israel. 16 For I will show him how many things he must suffer for My name's sake."

17 And Ananias went his way and entered the house; and laying his hands on him he said, "Brother Saul, the Lord Jesus,a who appeared to you

on the road as you came, has sent me that you may receive your sight and be filled with the Holy Spirit." 18 Immediately there fell from his eyes something like scales, and he received his sight at once; and he arose and was baptized.

19 So when he had received food, he was strengthened. Then Saul spent some days with the disciples at Damascus.

20 Immediately he preached the Christa in the synagogues, that He is the Son of God.

21 Then all who heard were amazed, and said, "Is this not he who destroyed those who called on this name in Jerusalem, and has come here for that purpose, so that he might bring them bound to the chief priests?"

22 But Saul increased all the more in strength, and confounded the Jews who dwelt in Damascus, proving that this Jesus is the Christ.

23 Now after many days were past, the Jews plotted to kill him. 24 But their plot became known to Saul. And they watched the gates day and night, to kill him. 25 Then the disciples took him by night and let him down through the wall in a large basket.

26 And when Saul had come to Jerusalem, he tried to join the disciples; but they were all afraid of him, and did not believe that he was a disciple. 27 But Barnabas took him and brought him to the apostles. And he declared to them how he had seen the Lord on the road, and that He had spoken to him, and how he had preached boldly at Damascus in the name of Jesus. 28 So he was with them at Jerusalem, coming in and going out. 29 And he spoke boldly in the name of the Lord Jesus and disputed against the Hellenists, but they attempted to kill him. 30 When the brethren found out, they brought him down to Caesarea and sent him out to Tarsus.

31 Then the churchesa throughout all Judea, Galilee, and Samaria had peace and were edified. And walking in the fear of the Lord and in the comfort of the Holy Spirit, they were multiplied.

32 Now it came to pass, as Peter

9:5 aNU-Text and M-Text omit the last sentence of verse 5 and begin verse 6 with But arise and go.
9:17 aM-Text omits Jesus.   9:20 aNU-Text reads Jesus.   9:31 aNU-Text reads church . . . was edified.

Gospel Pearls

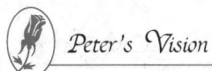

went through all *parts of the country,* that he also came down to the saints who dwelt in Lydda. 33 There he found a certain man named Aeneas, who had been bedridden eight years and was paralyzed. 34 And Peter said to him, "Aeneas, Jesus the Christ heals you. Arise and make your bed." Then he arose immediately. 35 So all who dwelt at Lydda and Sharon saw him and turned to the Lord.

36 At Joppa there was a certain disciple named Tabitha, which is translated Dorcas. This woman was full of good works and charitable deeds which she did. 37 But it happened in those days that she became sick and died. When they had washed her, they laid *her* in an upper room. 38 And since Lydda was near Joppa, and the disciples had heard that Peter was there, they sent two men to him, imploring *him* not to delay in coming to them. 39 Then Peter arose and went with them. When he had come, they brought *him* to the upper room. And all the widows stood by him weeping, showing the tunics and garments which Dorcas had made while she was with them. 40 But Peter put them all out, and knelt down and prayed. And turning to the body he said, "Tabitha, arise." And she opened her eyes, and when she saw Peter she sat up. 41 Then he gave her *his* hand and lifted her up; and when he had called the saints and widows, he presented her alive. 42 And it became known throughout all Joppa, and many believed on the Lord. 43 So it was that he stayed many days in Joppa with Simon, a tanner.

10 There was a certain man in Caesarea called Cornelius, a centurion of what was called the Italian Regiment, 2 a devout *man* and one who feared God with all his household, who gave alms generously to the people, and prayed to God always. 3 About the ninth hour of the day he saw clearly in a vision an angel of God coming in and saying to him, "Cornelius!"

4 And when he observed him, he was afraid, and said, "What is it, lord?"

So he said to him, "Your prayers and your alms have come up for a memorial before God. 5 Now send men to Joppa, and send for Simon whose surname is Peter. 6 He is lodging with Simon, a tanner, whose house is by the sea.ᵃ He will tell you what you must do." 7 And when the angel who spoke to him had departed, Cornelius called two of his household servants and a devout soldier from among those who waited on him continually. 8 So when he had explained all *these* things to them, he sent them to Joppa.

9 The next day, as they went on their journey and drew near the city, Peter went up on the housetop to pray, about the sixth hour. 10 Then he became very hungry and wanted to eat; but while they made ready, he fell into a trance 11 and saw heaven opened and an object like a great sheet bound at the four corners, descending to him and let down to the earth. 12 In it were all kinds of four-footed animals of the earth, wild beasts, creeping things, and birds of the air. 13 And a voice came to him, "Rise, Peter; kill and eat."

14 But Peter said, "Not so, Lord! For I have never eaten anything common or unclean."

15 And a voice *spoke* to him again the second time, "What God has cleansed you must not call common." 16 This was done three times. And the object was taken up into heaven again.

17 Now while Peter wondered within himself what this vision which he had seen meant, behold, the men who had been sent from Cornelius had made inquiry for Simon's house, and stood before the gate. 18 And they called and asked whether Simon, whose surname was Peter, was lodging there.

19 While Peter thought about the vision, the Spirit said to him, "Behold, three men are seeking you. 20 Arise therefore, go down and go with them, doubting nothing; for I have sent them."

21 Then Peter went down to the men who had been sent to him from Cornelius,ᵃ and said, "Yes, I am he whom you seek. For what reason have you come?"

22 And they said, "Cornelius *the*

10:6 ᵃNU-Text and M-Text omit the last sentence of this verse.   10:21 ᵃNU-Text and M-Text omit *who had been sent to him from Cornelius.*

*W*hy are you running from place to place and person to person looking for love? Have you not heard? He has been speaking to you through all of your circumstances. He is the One you need when life has wounded you and you have fallen from your nesting place like a bird.

centurion, a just man, one who fears God and has a good reputation among all the nation of the Jews, was divinely instructed by a holy angel to summon you to his house, and to hear words from you." 23 Then he invited them in and lodged *them.*

On the next day Peter went away with them, and some brethren from Joppa accompanied him.

24 And the following day they entered Caesarea. Now Cornelius was waiting for them, and had called together his relatives and close friends. 25 As Peter was coming in, Cornelius met him and fell down at his feet and worshiped *him.* 26 But Peter lifted him up, saying, "Stand up; I myself am also a man." 27 And as he talked with him, he went in and found many who had come together. 28 Then he said to them, "You know how unlawful it is for a Jewish man to keep company with or go to one of another nation. But God has shown me that I should not call any man common or unclean. 29 Therefore I came without objection as soon as I was sent for. I ask, then, for what reason have you sent for me?"

30 So Cornelius said, "Four days ago I was fasting until this hour; and at the ninth hour[a] I prayed in my house, and behold, a man stood before me in bright clothing, 31 and said, 'Cornelius, your prayer has been heard, and your alms are remembered in the sight of God. 32 Send therefore to Joppa and call Simon here, whose surname is Peter. He is lodging in the house of Simon, a tanner, by the sea.[a] When he comes, he will speak to you.' 33 So I sent to you immediately, and you have done well to come. Now therefore, we are all present before God, to hear all the things commanded you by God."

34 Then Peter opened *his* mouth and said: "In truth I perceive that God shows no partiality. 35 But in every nation whoever fears Him and works righteousness is accepted by Him. 36 The word which *God* sent to the children of Israel, preaching peace through Jesus Christ—He is Lord of all— 37 that word you know, which was proclaimed throughout all Judea, and began from Galilee after

the baptism which John preached: 38 how God anointed Jesus of Nazareth with the Holy Spirit and with power, who went about doing good and healing all who were oppressed by the devil, for God was with Him. 39 And we are witnesses of all things which He did both in the land of the Jews and in Jerusalem, whom they[a] killed by hanging on a tree. 40 Him God raised up on the third day, and showed Him openly, 41 not to all the people, but to witnesses chosen before by God, *even* to us who ate and drank with Him after He arose from the dead. 42 And He commanded us to preach to the people, and to testify that it is He who was ordained by God *to be* Judge of the living and the dead. 43 To Him all the prophets witness that, through His name, whoever believes in Him will receive remission of sins."

44 While Peter was still speaking these words, the Holy Spirit fell upon all those who heard the word. 45 And those of the circumcision who believed were astonished, as many as came with Peter, because the gift of the Holy Spirit had been poured out on the Gentiles also. 46 For they heard them speak with tongues and magnify God.

Then Peter answered, 47 "Can anyone forbid water, that these should not be baptized who have received the Holy Spirit just as we *have?*" 48 And he commanded them to be baptized in the name of the Lord. Then they asked him to stay a few days.

11 Now the apostles and brethren who were in Judea heard that the Gentiles had also received the word of God. 2 And when Peter came up to Jerusalem, those of the circumcision contended with him, 3 saying, "You went in to uncircumcised men and ate with them!"

4 But Peter explained *it* to them in order from the beginning, saying: 5 "I was in the city of Joppa praying; and in a trance I saw a vision, an object descending like a great sheet, let down from heaven by four corners; and it came to me. 6 When I observed it intently and considered, I saw four-footed animals of the earth, wild

---

10:30 [a]NU-Text reads *Four days ago to this hour, at the ninth hour.*   10:32 [a]NU-Text omits the last sentence of this verse.   10:39 [a]NU-Text and M-Text add *also.*

beasts, creeping things, and birds of the air. 7 And I heard a voice saying to me, 'Rise, Peter; kill and eat.' 8 But I said, 'Not so, Lord! For nothing common or unclean has at any time entered my mouth.' 9 But the voice answered me again from heaven, 'What God has cleansed you must not call common.' 10 Now this was done three times, and all were drawn up again into heaven. 11 At that very moment, three men stood before the house where I was, having been sent to me from Caesarea. 12 Then the Spirit told me to go with them, doubting nothing. Moreover these six brethren accompanied me, and we entered the man's house. 13 And he told us how he had seen an angel standing in his house, who said to him, 'Send men to Joppa, and call for Simon whose surname is Peter, 14 who will tell you words by which you and all your household will be saved.' 15 And as I began to speak, the Holy Spirit fell upon them, as upon us at the beginning. 16 Then I remembered the word of the Lord, how He said, 'John indeed baptized with water, but you shall be baptized with the Holy Spirit.' 17 If therefore God gave them the same gift as *He gave* us when we believed on the Lord Jesus Christ, who was I that I could withstand God?''

18 When they heard these things they became silent; and they glorified God, saying, "Then God has also granted to the Gentiles repentance to life."

19 Now those who were scattered after the persecution that arose over Stephen traveled as far as Phoenicia, Cyprus, and Antioch, preaching the word to no one but the Jews only. 20 But some of them were men from Cyprus and Cyrene, who, when they had come to Antioch, spoke to the Hellenists, preaching the Lord Jesus. 21 And the hand of the Lord was with them, and a great number believed and turned to the Lord.

22 Then news of these things came to the ears of the church in Jerusalem, and they sent out Barnabas to go as far as Antioch. 23 When he came and had seen the grace of God, he was glad, and encouraged them all that with purpose of heart they should continue with the Lord.

24 For he was a good man, full of the Holy Spirit and of faith. And a great many people were added to the Lord.

25 Then Barnabas departed for Tarsus to seek Saul. 26 And when he had found him, he brought him to Antioch. So it was that for a whole year they assembled with the church and taught a great many people. And the disciples were first called Christians in Antioch.

27 And in these days prophets came from Jerusalem to Antioch. 28 Then one of them, named Agabus, stood up and showed by the Spirit that there was going to be a great famine throughout all the world, which also happened in the days of Claudius Caesar. 29 Then the disciples, each according to his ability, determined to send relief to the brethren dwelling in Judea. 30 This they also did, and sent it to the elders by the hands of Barnabas and Saul.

12 Now about that time Herod the king stretched out *his* hand to harass some from the church. 2 Then he killed James the brother of John with the sword. 3 And because he saw that it pleased the Jews, he proceeded further to seize Peter also. Now it was *during* the Days of Unleavened Bread. 4 So when he had arrested him, he put *him* in prison, and delivered *him* to four squads of soldiers to keep him, intending to bring him before the people after Passover.

5 Peter was therefore kept in prison, but constant[a] prayer was offered to God for him by the church. 6 And when Herod was about to bring him out, that night Peter was sleeping, bound with two chains between two soldiers; and the guards before the door were keeping the prison. 7 Now behold, an angel of the Lord stood by *him*, and a light shone in the prison; and he struck Peter on the side and raised him up, saying, "Arise quickly!" And his chains fell off *his* hands. 8 Then the angel said to him, "Gird yourself and tie on your sandals"; and so he did. And he said to him, "Put on your garment and follow me." 9 So he went out and followed him, and did not know that what was done by the angel was real, but thought he was seeing a vision.

12:5 [a]NU-Text reads *constantly* (or *earnestly*).

*L*et Him be revealed in your heart right now! It is not just a man thing. It is a God thing, the creator of man. He is the epitome of masculinity. He is omnipotent, not impotent. He is the Everlasting Father.

10 When they were past the first and the second guard posts, they came to the iron gate that leads to the city, which opened to them of its own accord; and they went out and went down one street, and immediately the angel departed from him.

11 And when Peter had come to himself, he said, "Now I know for certain that the Lord has sent His angel, and has delivered me from the hand of Herod and *from* all the expectation of the Jewish people."

12 So, when he had considered *this*, he came to the house of Mary, the mother of John whose surname was Mark, where many were gathered together praying. 13 And as Peter knocked at the door of the gate, a girl named Rhoda came to answer. 14 When she recognized Peter's voice, because of *her* gladness she did not open the gate, but ran in and announced that Peter stood before the gate. 15 But they said to her, "You are beside yourself!" Yet she kept insisting that it was so. So they said, "It is his angel."

16 Now Peter continued knocking; and when they opened *the door* and saw him, they were astonished. 17 But motioning to them with his hand to keep silent, he declared to them how the Lord had brought him out of the prison. And he said, "Go, tell these things to James and to the brethren." And he departed and went to another place.

18 Then, as soon as it was day, there was no small stir among the soldiers about what had become of Peter. 19 But when Herod had searched for him and not found him, he examined the guards and commanded that *they* should be put to death.

And he went down from Judea to Caesarea, and stayed *there*.

20 Now Herod had been very angry with the people of Tyre and Sidon; but they came to him with one accord, and having made Blastus the king's personal aide their friend, they asked for peace, because their country was supplied with food by the king's *country*.

21 So on a set day Herod, arrayed in royal apparel, sat on his throne and gave an oration to them. 22 And the people kept shouting, "The voice of a god and not of a man!" 23 Then immediately an angel of the Lord struck him, because he did not give glory to God. And he was eaten by worms and died.

24 But the word of God grew and multiplied.

25 And Barnabas and Saul returned from*ᵃ* Jerusalem when they had fulfilled *their* ministry, and they also took with them John whose surname was Mark.

13 Now in the church that was at Antioch there were certain prophets and teachers: Barnabas, Simeon who was called Niger, Lucius of Cyrene, Manaen who had been brought up with Herod the tetrarch, and Saul. 2 As they ministered to the Lord and fasted, the Holy Spirit said, "Now separate to Me Barnabas and Saul for the work to which I have called them." 3 Then, having fasted and prayed, and laid hands on them, they sent *them* away.

4 So, being sent out by the Holy Spirit, they went down to Seleucia, and from there they sailed to Cyprus. 5 And when they arrived in Salamis, they preached the word of God in the synagogues of the Jews. They also had John as *their* assistant.

6 Now when they had gone through the island*ᵃ* to Paphos, they found a certain sorcerer, a false prophet, a Jew whose name *was* Bar-Jesus, 7 who was with the proconsul, Sergius Paulus, an intelligent man. This man called for Barnabas and Saul and sought to hear the word of God. 8 But Elymas the sorcerer (for so his name is translated) withstood them, seeking to turn the proconsul away from the faith. 9 Then Saul, who also *is called* Paul, filled with the Holy Spirit, looked intently at him 10 and said, "O full of all deceit and all fraud, *you* son of the devil, *you* enemy of all righteousness, will you not cease perverting the straight ways of the Lord? 11 And now, indeed, the hand of the Lord *is* upon you, and you shall be blind, not seeing the sun for a time."

And immediately a dark mist fell on him, and he went around seeking someone to lead him by the hand. 12 Then the proconsul believed, when he saw what had been done, being

12:25 *ᵃ*NU-Text and M-Text read *to.*   13:6 *ᵃ*NU-Text reads *the whole island.*

Gospel Pearls

astonished at the teaching of the Lord.

13 Now when Paul and his party set sail from Paphos, they came to Perga in Pamphylia; and John, departing from them, returned to Jerusalem. 14 But when they departed from Perga, they came to Antioch in Pisidia, and went into the synagogue on the Sabbath day and sat down. 15 And after the reading of the Law and the Prophets, the rulers of the synagogue sent to them, saying, "Men *and* brethren, if you have any word of exhortation for the people, say on."

16 Then Paul stood up, and motioning with *his* hand said, "Men of Israel, and you who fear God, listen: 17 The God of this people Israel*a* chose our fathers, and exalted the people when they dwelt as strangers in the land of Egypt, and with an uplifted arm He brought them out of it. 18 Now for a time of about forty years He put up with their ways in the wilderness. 19 And when He had destroyed seven nations in the land of Canaan, He distributed their land to them by allotment.

20 "After that He gave *them* judges for about four hundred and fifty years, until Samuel the prophet. 21 And afterward they asked for a king; so God gave them Saul the son of Kish, a man of the tribe of Benjamin, for forty years. 22 And when He had removed him, He raised up for them David as king, to whom also He gave testimony and said, *'I have found David*a* the son of Jesse, a man after My own heart,* who will do all My will.'*b* 23 From this man's seed, according to *the* promise, God raised up for Israel a Savior—Jesus—*a* 24 after John had first preached, before His coming, the baptism of repentance to all the people of Israel. 25 And as John was finishing his course, he said, 'Who do you think I am? I am not *He.* But behold, there comes One after me, the sandals of whose feet I am not worthy to loose.'

26 "Men *and* brethren, sons of the family of Abraham, and those among you who fear God, to you the word of this salvation has been sent. 27 For those who dwell in Jerusalem, and their rulers, because they did not know Him, nor even the voices of the Prophets which are read every Sabbath, have fulfilled *them* in condemning *Him.* 28 And though they found no cause for death *in Him,* they asked Pilate that He should be put to death. 29 Now when they had fulfilled all that was written concerning Him, they took *Him* down from the tree and laid *Him* in a tomb. 30 But God raised Him from the dead. 31 He was seen for many days by those who came up with Him from Galilee to Jerusalem, who are His witnesses to the people. 32 And we declare to you glad tidings—that promise which was made to the fathers. 33 God has fulfilled this for us their children, in that He has raised up Jesus. As it is also written in the second Psalm:

> *'You are My Son,*
> *Today I have begotten*
> *You.'*a

34 "And that He raised Him from the dead, no more to return to corruption, He has spoken thus:

> *'I will give you the sure mercies*
> *of David.'*a

35 "Therefore He also says in another *Psalm:*

> *'You will not allow Your Holy*
> *One to see corruption.'*a

36 "For David, after he had served his own generation by the will of God, fell asleep, was buried with his fathers, and saw corruption; 37 but He whom God raised up saw no corruption. 38 Therefore let it be known to you, brethren, that through this Man is preached to you the forgiveness of sins; 39 and by Him everyone who believes is justified from all things from which you could not be justified by the law of Moses. 40 Beware therefore, lest what has been spoken in the prophets come upon you:

41 *'Behold, you despisers,*
> *Marvel and perish!*
> *For I work a work in your*
> *days,*

13:17 *a*M-Text omits *Israel.*   13:22 *a*Psalm 89:20   *b*1 Samuel 13:14   13:23 *a*M-Text reads *for Israel salvation.*   13:33 *a*Psalm 2:7   13:34 *a*Isaiah 55:3   13:35 *a*Psalm 16:10

*L*ady, you are the Father's heartbeat, and He loves you so. He has a reason for asking you to give up areas that compromise true holiness. He isn't saying no because He is mean. He is saying no because He wants something better for you than this.

A work which you will by no
means believe,
Though one were to declare it
to you.'"ᵃ

42 So when the Jews went out of
the synagogue,ᵃ the Gentiles begged
that these words might be preached
to them the next Sabbath. 43 Now
when the congregation had broken
up, many of the Jews and devout pro-
selytes followed Paul and Barnabas,
who, speaking to them, persuaded
them to continue in the grace of God.
44 On the next Sabbath almost the
whole city came together to hear the
word of God. 45 But when the Jews
saw the multitudes, they were filled
with envy; and contradicting and
blaspheming, they opposed the
things spoken by Paul. 46 Then Paul
and Barnabas grew bold and said, "It
was necessary that the word of God
should be spoken to you first; but
since you reject it, and judge yourselves unworthy of everlasting life,
behold, we turn to the Gentiles.
47 For so the Lord has commanded
us:

'I have set you as a light to the
Gentiles,
That you should be for
salvation to the ends of the
earth.'"ᵃ

48 Now when the Gentiles heard
this, they were glad and glorified the
word of the Lord. And as many as
had been appointed to eternal life believed.
49 And the word of the Lord was
being spread throughout all the region. 50 But the Jews stirred up the
devout and prominent women and
the chief men of the city, raised up
persecution against Paul and Barnabas, and expelled them from their region. 51 But they shook off the dust
from their feet against them, and
came to Iconium. 52 And the disciples
were filled with joy and with the Holy
Spirit.

14 Now it happened in Iconium
that they went together to the
synagogue of the Jews, and so spoke
that a great multitude both of the
Jews and of the Greeks believed.

2 But the unbelieving Jews stirred
up the Gentiles and poisoned their
minds against the brethren. 3 Therefore they stayed there a long time,
speaking boldly in the Lord, who
was bearing witness to the word of
His grace, granting signs and wonders to be done by their hands.
4 But the multitude of the city was
divided: part sided with the Jews,
and part with the apostles. 5 And
when a violent attempt was made by
both the Gentiles and Jews, with
their rulers, to abuse and stone them,
6 they became aware of it and fled
to Lystra and Derbe, cities of Lycao-
nia, and to the surrounding region.
7 And they were preaching the gospel
there.
8 And in Lystra a certain man without strength in his feet was sitting, a
cripple from his mother's womb, who
had never walked. 9 This man heard
Paul speaking. Paul, observing him
intently and seeing that he had faith
to be healed, 10 said with a loud
voice, "Stand up straight on your
feet!" And he leaped and walked.
11 Now when the people saw what
Paul had done, they raised their
voices, saying in the Lycaonian language, "The gods have come down
to us in the likeness of men!"
12 And Barnabas they called Zeus,
and Paul, Hermes, because he was
the chief speaker. 13 Then the priest
of Zeus, whose temple was in front
of their city, brought oxen and gar-
lands to the gates, intending to sacrifice with the multitudes.
14 But when the apostles Barnabas
and Paul heard this, they tore their
clothes and ran in among the multitude, crying out 15 and saying, "Men,
why are you doing these things? We
also are men with the same nature
as you, and preach to you that you
should turn from these useless things
to the living God, who made the
heaven, the earth, the sea, and all
things that are in them, 16 who in
bygone generations allowed all nations to walk in their own ways.
17 Nevertheless He did not leave
Himself without witness, in that He
did good, gave us rain from heaven
and fruitful seasons, filling our hearts
with food and gladness." 18 And with
these sayings they could scarcely re-

13:41 ᵃHabakkuk 1:5   13:42 ᵃOr And when they went out of the synagogue of the Jews; NU-Text reads
And when they went out of the synagogue, they begged.   13:47 ᵃIsaiah 49:6

Gospel
Pearls

strain the multitudes from sacrificing to them.

19 Then Jews from Antioch and Iconium came there; and having persuaded the multitudes, they stoned Paul *and* dragged *him* out of the city, supposing him to be dead. 20 However, when the disciples gathered around him, he rose up and went into the city. And the next day he departed with Barnabas to Derbe.

21 And when they had preached the gospel to that city and made many disciples, they returned to Lystra, Iconium, and Antioch, 22 strengthening the souls of the disciples, exhorting *them* to continue in the faith, and *saying,* "We must through many tribulations enter the kingdom of God." 23 So when they had appointed elders in every church, and prayed with fasting, they commended them to the Lord in whom they had believed. 24 And after they had passed through Pisidia, they came to Pamphylia. 25 Now when they had preached the word in Perga, they went down to Attalia. 26 From there they sailed to Antioch, where they had been commended to the grace of God for the work which they had completed.

27 Now when they had come and gathered the church together, they reported all that God had done with them, and that He had opened the door of faith to the Gentiles. 28 So they stayed there a long time with the disciples.

15 And certain *men* came down from Judea and taught the brethren, "Unless you are circumcised according to the custom of Moses, you cannot be saved." 2 Therefore, when Paul and Barnabas had no small dissension and dispute with them, they determined that Paul and Barnabas and certain others of them should go up to Jerusalem, to the apostles and elders, about this question.

3 So, being sent on their way by the church, they passed through Phoenicia and Samaria, describing the conversion of the Gentiles; and they caused great joy to all the brethren. 4 And when they had come to Jerusalem, they were received by the church and the apostles and the elders; and they reported all things that God had done with them. 5 But some of the sect of the Pharisees who believed rose up, saying, "It is necessary to circumcise them, and to command *them* to keep the law of Moses."

6 Now the apostles and elders came together to consider this matter. 7 And when there had been much dispute, Peter rose up and said to them: "Men and brethren, you know that a good while ago God chose among us, that by my mouth the Gentiles should hear the word of the gospel and believe. 8 So God, who knows the heart, acknowledged them by giving them the Holy Spirit, just as *He did* to us, 9 and made no distinction between us and them, purifying their hearts by faith. 10 Now therefore, why do you test God by putting a yoke on the neck of the disciples which neither our fathers nor we were able to bear? 11 But we believe that through the grace of the Lord Jesus Christ[a] we shall be saved in the same manner as they."

12 Then all the multitude kept silent and listened to Barnabas and Paul declaring how many miracles and wonders God had worked through them among the Gentiles. 13 And after they had become silent, James answered, saying, "Men *and* brethren, listen to me: 14 Simon has declared how God at the first visited the Gentiles to take out of them a people for His name. 15 And with this the words of the prophets agree, just as it is written:

16 '*After this I will return*
　　And will rebuild the tabernacle
　　　of David, which has fallen
　　　down;
　　I will rebuild its ruins,
　　And I will set it up;
17 *So that the rest of mankind*
　　may seek the Lord,
　　Even all the Gentiles who are
　　　called by My name,
　　Says the Lord *who does all*
　　　these things.'[a]

18 "Known to God from eternity are all His works.[a] 19 Therefore I judge that we should not trouble

15:11 [a]NU-Text and M-Text omit *Christ.*　　15:17 [a]Amos 9:11, 12　　15:18 [a]NU-Text reads *Says the Lord, who makes these things known from eternity (of old).*

---

*D*o you realize that broken women find it difficult to maintain relationships? They are always looking for someone who can carry the weight of their pain.

those from among the Gentiles who are turning to God, 20 but that we write to them to abstain from things polluted by idols, *from* sexual immorality,*a from* things strangled, and *from* blood. 21 For Moses has had throughout many generations those who preach him in every city, being read in the synagogues every Sabbath."

22 Then it pleased the apostles and elders, with the whole church, to send chosen men of their own company to Antioch with Paul and Barnabas, *namely*, Judas who was also named Barsabas,*a* and Silas, leading men among the brethren. 23 They wrote this *letter* by them:

The apostles, the elders, and the brethren,

To the brethren who are of the Gentiles in Antioch, Syria, and Cilicia:

Greetings.

24 Since we have heard that some who went out from us have troubled you with words, unsettling your souls, saying, "*You must* be circumcised and keep the law"*a*—to whom we gave no *such* commandment— 25 it seemed good to us, being assembled with one accord, to send chosen men to you with our beloved Barnabas and Paul, 26 men who have risked their lives for the name of our Lord Jesus Christ. 27 We have therefore sent Judas and Silas, who will also report the same things by word of mouth. 28 For it seemed good to the Holy Spirit, and to us, to lay upon you no greater burden than these necessary things: 29 that you abstain from things offered to idols, from blood, from things strangled, and from sexual immorality.*a* If you keep yourselves from these, you will do well.

Farewell.

30 So when they were sent off, they came to Antioch; and when they had

gathered the multitude together, they delivered the letter. 31 When they had read it, they rejoiced over its encouragement. 32 Now Judas and Silas, themselves being prophets also, exhorted and strengthened the brethren with many words. 33 And after they had stayed *there* for a time, they were sent back with greetings from the brethren to the apostles.*a*

34 However, it seemed good to Silas to remain there.*a* 35 Paul and Barnabas also remained in Antioch, teaching and preaching the word of the Lord, with many others also.

36 Then after some days Paul said to Barnabas, "Let us now go back and visit our brethren in every city where we have preached the word of the Lord, *and see* how they are doing." 37 Now Barnabas was determined to take with them John called Mark. 38 But Paul insisted that they should not take with them the one who had departed from them in Pamphylia, and had not gone with them to the work. 39 Then the contention became so sharp that they parted from one another. And so Barnabas took Mark and sailed to Cyprus; 40 but Paul chose Silas and departed, being commended by the brethren to the grace of God. 41 And he went through Syria and Cilicia, strengthening the churches.

16 Then he came to Derbe and Lystra. And behold, a certain disciple was there, named Timothy, *the* son of a certain Jewish woman who believed, but his father *was* Greek. 2 He was well spoken of by the brethren who were at Lystra and Iconium. 3 Paul wanted to have him go on with him. And he took *him* and circumcised him because of the Jews who were in that region, for they all knew that his father was Greek. 4 And as they went through the cities, they delivered to them the decrees to keep, which were determined by the apostles and elders at Jerusalem. 5 So the churches were strengthened in the faith, and increased in number daily.

6 Now when they had gone through Phrygia and the region of Galatia, they were forbidden by the Holy

---

15:20 *a*Or *fornication*   15:22 *a*NU-Text and M-Text read *Barsabbas*.   15:24 *a*NU-Text omits *saying,*
"*You must be circumcised and keep the law*".   15:29 *a*Or *fornication*   15:33 *a*NU-Text reads *to those who had sent them.*   15:34 *a*NU-Text and M-Text omit this verse.

*I*f you are losing life, and leaking love, you need to allow Christ to heal the broken pieces of your life. He can stop the oozing out of what others have tried to give and then give you water, so that you thirst not.

Soul Secrets
of a businesswoman

*L*ord, they often tell me it's a man's world. But I declare that it is Your world. And You have given me a place of influence and authority in my job. I thank You, Lord, for the unique combination of gifts and talents You have given me that enable me to serve well as a leader. Make me an asset to my company and my industry. Make me a woman of wisdom and excellence for all to see.

Lord, I go from the bedroom to the boardroom and everywhere in between. The business world can be cruel and the workload makes me weary. Help me to maintain the gentle side of me and to be tender as I have to be tough. Help me, through every meeting, every negotiation, every tough call, to be not just a lady, but to be the Lord's lady on the job.

Spirit to preach the word in Asia. 7 After they had come to Mysia, they tried to go into Bithynia, but the Spiritᵃ did not permit them. 8 So passing by Mysia, they came down to Troas. 9 And a vision appeared to Paul in the night. A man of Macedonia stood and pleaded with him, saying, "Come over to Macedonia and help us." 10 Now after he had seen the vision, immediately we sought to go to Macedonia, concluding that the Lord had called us to preach the gospel to them.

11 Therefore, sailing from Troas, we ran a straight course to Samothrace, and the next *day* came to Neapolis, 12 and from there to Philippi, which is the foremost city of that part of Macedonia, a colony. And we were staying in that city for some days. 13 And on the Sabbath day we went out of the city to the riverside, where prayer was customarily made; and we sat down and spoke to the women who met *there.* 14 Now a certain woman named Lydia heard *us.* She was a seller of purple from the city of Thyatira, who worshiped God. The Lord opened her heart to heed the things spoken by Paul. 15 And when she and her household were baptized, she begged *us,* saying, "If you have judged me to be faithful to the Lord, come to my house and stay." So she persuaded us.

16 Now it happened, as we went to prayer, that a certain slave girl possessed with a spirit of divination met us, who brought her masters much profit by fortune-telling. 17 This girl followed Paul and us, and cried out, saying, "These men are the servants of the Most High God, who proclaim to us the way of salvation." 18 And this she did for many days.

But Paul, greatly annoyed, turned and said to the spirit, "I command you in the name of Jesus Christ to come out of her." And he came out that very hour. 19 But when her masters saw that their hope of profit was gone, they seized Paul and Silas and dragged *them* into the marketplace to the authorities.

20 And they brought them to the magistrates, and said, "These men, being Jews, exceedingly trouble our city; 21 and they teach customs which are not lawful for us, being Romans,

to receive or observe." 22 Then the multitude rose up together against them; and the magistrates tore off their clothes and commanded *them* to be beaten with rods. 23 And when they had laid many stripes on them, they threw *them* into prison, commanding the jailer to keep them securely. 24 Having received such a charge, he put them into the inner prison and fastened their feet in the stocks.

25 But at midnight Paul and Silas were praying and singing hymns to God, and the prisoners were listening to them. 26 Suddenly there was a great earthquake, so that the foundations of the prison were shaken; and immediately all the doors were opened and everyone's chains were loosed. 27 And the keeper of the prison, awaking from sleep and seeing the prison doors open, supposing the prisoners had fled, drew his sword and was about to kill himself. 28 But Paul called with a loud voice, saying, "Do yourself no harm, for we are all here."

29 Then he called for a light, ran in, and fell down trembling before Paul and Silas. 30 And he brought them out and said, "Sirs, what must I do to be saved?"

31 So they said, "Believe on the Lord Jesus Christ, and you will be saved, you and your household." 32 Then they spoke the word of the Lord to him and to all who were in his house. 33 And he took them the same hour of the night and washed *their* stripes. And immediately he and all his family were baptized. 34 Now when he had brought them into his house, he set food before them; and he rejoiced, having believed in God with all his household.

35 And when it was day, the magistrates sent the officers, saying, "Let those men go."

36 So the keeper of the prison reported these words to Paul, saying, "The magistrates have sent to let you go. Now therefore depart, and go in peace."

37 But Paul said to them, "They have beaten us openly, uncondemned Romans, *and* have thrown *us* into prison. And now do they put us out secretly? No indeed! Let them come themselves and get us out."

16:7 ᵃNU-Text adds *of Jesus.*

God hears the wailing of the muted voice. He hears the faint groan that seeps out in the night, like seeping sewage from a broken pipe. It is a mystery to most men but it is the key that is necessary to start healing and understanding.

Defensive Praise

Acts 16:22-26

When you first read about the woman who was healed of her eighteen-year-long infirmity, you might have thought that the greatest deliverance was her physical healing. The Bible says that when the Lord laid His hand on her, she was made straight. Now that's physical deliverance.

But I want to point out an even greater deliverance: Her attitude changed. She entered into praise and thanksgiving and began to worship the Lord. This woman started leaping and rejoicing and magnifying God and shouting the victory like anybody who has been delivered from an old infirmity should. While she was glorifying God over here, though, the enemy was stirring up strife over there. She just kept on glorifying God. She didn't stop praising God to answer the accusers.

My sister, the Lord is your defense. You do not have to defend yourself. When God has delivered you, do not stop what you're doing to answer your accusers. Continue to bless His name because you do not want your attitude to become defensive. When you have been through difficult times, you cannot afford to play around with moods and attitudes. Depression and defensiveness may make you vulnerable to the devil.

This woman had to protect herself by entering into defensive praise. This was not just praise or thanksgiving, but a strategy and a posture of spiritual warfare that says, "I will not allow my attitude to crumble and fall."

When you get to the point that you quit defending yourself or attacking others, you open a door for the Lord to fight for you. When Paul and Silas began to praise the Lord, the prison doors were opened. When this woman began to bless God, she built walls around her own deliverance. She decided to keep the kind of attitude that would enable the deliverance of God to be maintained in her life.

Can you imagine what would have happened if she had stopped glorifying God and started arguing? If an argument had gotten through her doors, this whole scene would have ended in a fight. But she was thankful and determined to express her gratitude.

When you're in trouble, God will reach into the mess and pull you out. Then you must be strong enough not to let yourself be dragged back into it. Once God unleashes you, don't let anyone trap you into some religious squabble. Keep praising Him!

38 And the officers told these words to the magistrates, and they were afraid when they heard that they were Romans. 39 Then they came and pleaded with them and brought *them* out, and asked *them* to depart from the city. 40 So they went out of the prison and entered *the house of* Lydia; and when they had seen the brethren, they encouraged them and departed.

17 Now when they had passed through Amphipolis and Apollonia, they came to Thessalonica, where there was a synagogue of the Jews. 2 Then Paul, as his custom was, went in to them, and for three Sabbaths reasoned with them from the Scriptures, 3 explaining and demonstrating that the Christ had to suffer and rise again from the dead, and *saying,* "This Jesus whom I preach to you is the Christ." 4 And some of them were persuaded; and a great multitude of the devout Greeks, and not a few of the leading women, joined Paul and Silas.

5 But the Jews who were not persuaded, becoming envious,[a] took some of the evil men from the marketplace, and gathering a mob, set all the city in an uproar and attacked the house of Jason, and sought to bring them out to the people. 6 But when they did not find them, they dragged Jason and some brethren to the rulers of the city, crying out, "These who have turned the world upside down have come here too. 7 Jason has harbored them, and these are all acting contrary to the decrees of Caesar, saying there is another king—Jesus." 8 And they troubled the crowd and the rulers of the city when they heard these things. 9 So when they had taken security from Jason and the rest, they let them go.

10 Then the brethren immediately sent Paul and Silas away by night to Berea. When they arrived, they went into the synagogue of the Jews. 11 These were more fair-minded than those in Thessalonica, in that they received the word with all readiness, and searched the Scriptures daily *to find out* whether these things were so. 12 Therefore many of them believed, and also not a few of the Greeks, prominent women as well as men. 13 But when the Jews from Thessalonica learned that the word of God was preached by Paul at Berea, they came there also and stirred up the crowds. 14 Then immediately the brethren sent Paul away, to go to the sea; but both Silas and Timothy remained there. 15 So those who conducted Paul brought him to Athens; and receiving a command for Silas and Timothy to come to him with all speed, they departed.

16 Now while Paul waited for them at Athens, his spirit was provoked within him when he saw that the city was given over to idols. 17 Therefore he reasoned in the synagogue with the Jews and with the *Gentile* worshipers, and in the marketplace daily with those who happened to be there. 18 Then[a] certain Epicurean and Stoic philosophers encountered him. And some said, "What does this babbler want to say?"

Others said, "He seems to be a proclaimer of foreign gods," because he preached to them Jesus and the resurrection.

19 And they took him and brought him to the Areopagus, saying, "May we know what this new doctrine *is* of which you speak? 20 For you are bringing some strange things to our ears. Therefore we want to know what these things mean." 21 For all the Athenians and the foreigners who were there spent their time in nothing else but either to tell or to hear some new thing.

22 Then Paul stood in the midst of the Areopagus and said, "Men of Athens, I perceive that in all things you are very religious; 23 for as I was passing through and considering the objects of your worship, I even found an altar with this inscription:

TO THE UNKNOWN GOD.

Therefore, the One whom you worship without knowing, Him I proclaim to you: 24 God, who made the world and everything in it, since He is Lord of heaven and earth, does not dwell in temples made with hands. 25 Nor is He worshiped with men's hands, as though He needed anything, since He gives to all life,

17:5 [a]NU-Text omits *who were not persuaded;* M-Text omits *becoming envious.*   17:18 [a]NU-Text and M-Text add *also.*

Gospel Pearls

breath, and all things. 26 And He has made from one blood*a* every nation of men to dwell on all the face of the earth, and has determined their preappointed times and the boundaries of their dwellings, 27 so that they should seek the Lord, in the hope that they might grope for Him and find Him, though He is not far from each one of us; 28 for in Him we live and move and have our being, as also some of your own poets have said, 'For we are also His offspring.' 29 Therefore, since we are the offspring of God, we ought not to think that the Divine Nature is like gold or silver or stone, something shaped by art and man's devising. 30 Truly, these times of ignorance God overlooked, but now commands all men everywhere to repent, 31 because He has appointed a day on which He will judge the world in righteousness by the Man whom He has ordained. He has given assurance of this to all by raising Him from the dead."

32 And when they heard of the resurrection of the dead, some mocked, while others said, "We will hear you again on this *matter*." 33 So Paul departed from among them. 34 However, some men joined him and believed, among them Dionysius the Areopagite, a woman named Damaris, and others with them.

18 After these things Paul departed from Athens and went to Corinth. 2 And he found a certain Jew named Aquila, born in Pontus, who had recently come from Italy with his wife Priscilla (because Claudius had commanded all the Jews to depart from Rome); and he came to them. 3 So, because he was of the same trade, he stayed with them and worked; for by occupation they were tentmakers. 4 And he reasoned in the synagogue every Sabbath, and persuaded both Jews and Greeks.

5 When Silas and Timothy had come from Macedonia, Paul was compelled by the Spirit, and testified to the Jews *that* Jesus *is* the Christ. 6 But when they opposed him and blasphemed, he shook *his* garments and said to them, "Your blood *be* upon your *own* heads; I *am* clean. From now on I will go to the Gen-

tiles." 7 And he departed from there and entered the house of a certain *man* named Justus,*a* one who worshiped God, whose house was next door to the synagogue. 8 Then Crispus, the ruler of the synagogue, believed on the Lord with all his household. And many of the Corinthians, hearing, believed and were baptized.

9 Now the Lord spoke to Paul in the night by a vision, "Do not be afraid, but speak, and do not keep silent; 10 for I am with you, and no one will attack you to hurt you; for I have many people in this city." 11 And he continued *there* a year and six months, teaching the word of God among them.

12 When Gallio was proconsul of Achaia, the Jews with one accord rose up against Paul and brought him to the judgment seat, 13 saying, "This *fellow* persuades men to worship God contrary to the law."

14 And when Paul was about to open *his* mouth, Gallio said to the Jews, "If it were a matter of wrongdoing or wicked crimes, O Jews, there would be reason why I should bear with you. 15 But if it is a question of words and names and your own law, look *to it* yourselves; for I do not want to be a judge of such *matters*." 16 And he drove them from the judgment seat. 17 Then all the Greeks*a* took Sosthenes, the ruler of the synagogue, and beat *him* before the judgment seat. But Gallio took no notice of these things.

18 So Paul still remained a good while. Then he took leave of the brethren and sailed for Syria, and Priscilla and Aquila *were* with him. He had *his* hair cut off at Cenchrea, for he had taken a vow. 19 And he came to Ephesus, and left them there; but he himself entered the synagogue and reasoned with the Jews. 20 When they asked *him* to stay a longer time with them, he did not consent, 21 but took leave of them, saying, "I must by all means keep this coming feast in Jerusalem;*a* but I will return again to you, God willing." And he sailed from Ephesus.

22 And when he had landed at Caesarea, and gone up and greeted the church, he went down to Antioch. 23 After he had spent some time

---

17:26 *a*NU-Text omits *blood*.　18:7 *a*NU-Text reads *Titius Justus*.　18:17 *a*NU-Text reads *they all*. 18:21 *a*NU-Text omits *I must* through *Jerusalem*.

*I*f we are going to reach our children, we had better speak up loud and clear. We have divorced one another, but we cannot divorce our responsibility to our own children.

there, he departed and went over the region of Galatia and Phrygia in order, strengthening all the disciples.

24 Now a certain Jew named Apollos, born at Alexandria, an eloquent man *and* mighty in the Scriptures, came to Ephesus. 25 This man had been instructed in the way of the Lord; and being fervent in spirit, he spoke and taught accurately the things of the Lord, though he knew only the baptism of John. 26 So he began to speak boldly in the synagogue. When Aquila and Priscilla heard him, they took him aside and explained to him the way of God more accurately. 27 And when he desired to cross to Achaia, the brethren wrote, exhorting the disciples to receive him; and when he arrived, he greatly helped those who had believed through grace; 28 for he vigorously refuted the Jews publicly, showing from the Scriptures that Jesus is the Christ.

19 And it happened, while Apollos was at Corinth, that Paul, having passed through the upper regions, came to Ephesus. And finding some disciples 2 he said to them, "Did you receive the Holy Spirit when you believed?"

So they said to him, "We have not so much as heard whether there is a Holy Spirit."

3 And he said to them, "Into what then were you baptized?"

So they said, "Into John's baptism."

4 Then Paul said, "John indeed baptized with a baptism of repentance, saying to the people that they should believe on Him who would come after him, that is, on Christ Jesus."

5 When they heard *this,* they were baptized in the name of the Lord Jesus. 6 And when Paul had laid hands on them, the Holy Spirit came upon them, and they spoke with tongues and prophesied. 7 Now the men were about twelve in all.

8 And he went into the synagogue and spoke boldly for three months, reasoning and persuading concerning the things of the kingdom of God. 9 But when some were hardened and did not believe, but spoke evil of the Way before the multitude, he departed from them and withdrew the disciples, reasoning daily in the school of Tyrannus. 10 And this continued for two years, so that all who dwelt in Asia heard the word of the Lord Jesus, both Jews and Greeks.

11 Now God worked unusual miracles by the hands of Paul, 12 so that even handkerchiefs or aprons were brought from his body to the sick, and the diseases left them and the evil spirits went out of them. 13 Then some of the itinerant Jewish exorcists took it upon themselves to call the name of the Lord Jesus over those who had evil spirits, saying, "We^a exorcise you by the Jesus whom Paul preaches." 14 Also there were seven sons of Sceva, a Jewish chief priest, who did so.

15 And the evil spirit answered and said, "Jesus I know, and Paul I know; but who are you?"

16 Then the man in whom the evil spirit was leaped on them, overpowered^a them, and prevailed against them,^{b} so that they fled out of that house naked and wounded. 17 This became known both to all Jews and Greeks dwelling in Ephesus; and fear fell on them all, and the name of the Lord Jesus was magnified. 18 And many who had believed came confessing and telling their deeds. 19 Also, many of those who had practiced magic brought their books together and burned *them* in the sight of all. And they counted up the value of them, and *it* totaled fifty thousand *pieces* of silver. 20 So the word of the Lord grew mightily and prevailed.

21 When these things were accomplished, Paul purposed in the Spirit, when he had passed through Macedonia and Achaia, to go to Jerusalem, saying, "After I have been there, I must also see Rome." 22 So he sent into Macedonia two of those who ministered to him, Timothy and Erastus, but he himself stayed in Asia for a time.

23 And about that time there arose a great commotion about the Way. 24 For a certain man named Demetrius, a silversmith, who made silver shrines of Diana,^{a} brought no small profit to the craftsmen. 25 He called

19:13 ^{a}NU-Text reads *I.*   19:16 ^{a}M-Text reads *and they overpowered.* ^{b}NU-Text reads *both of them.*
19:24 ^{a}Greek *Artemis*

Gospel Pearls

them together with the workers of similar occupation, and said: "Men, you know that we have our prosperity by this trade. 26 Moreover you see and hear that not only at Ephesus, but throughout almost all Asia, this Paul has persuaded and turned away many people, saying that they are not gods which are made with hands. 27 So not only is this trade of ours in danger of falling into disrepute, but also the temple of the great goddess Diana may be despised and her magnificence destroyed,*a* whom all Asia and the world worship."

28 Now when they heard *this,* they were full of wrath and cried out, saying, "Great *is* Diana of the Ephesians!" 29 So the whole city was filled with confusion, and rushed into the theater with one accord, having seized Gaius and Aristarchus, Macedonians, Paul's travel companions. 30 And when Paul wanted to go in to the people, the disciples would not allow him. 31 Then some of the officials of Asia, who were his friends, sent to him pleading that he would not venture into the theater. 32 Some therefore cried one thing and some another, for the assembly was confused, and most of them did not know why they had come together. 33 And they drew Alexander out of the multitude, the Jews putting him forward. And Alexander motioned with his hand, and wanted to make his defense to the people. 34 But when they found out that he was a Jew, all with one voice cried out for about two hours, "Great *is* Diana of the Ephesians!"

35 And when the city clerk had quieted the crowd, he said: "Men of Ephesus, what man is there who does not know that the city of the Ephesians is temple guardian of the great goddess Diana, and of the *image* which fell down from Zeus? 36 Therefore, since these things cannot be denied, you ought to be quiet and do nothing rashly. 37 For you have brought these men here who are neither robbers of temples nor blasphemers of your*a* goddess. 38 Therefore, if Demetrius and his fellow craftsmen have a case against anyone, the courts are open and there are proconsuls. Let them bring charges against one another. 39 But if you have any other inquiry to make, it shall be determined in the lawful assembly. 40 For we are in danger of being called in question for today's uproar, there being no reason which we may give to account for this disorderly gathering." 41 And when he had said these things, he dismissed the assembly.

20 After the uproar had ceased, Paul called the disciples to himself, embraced *them,* and departed to go to Macedonia. 2 Now when he had gone over that region and encouraged them with many words, he came to Greece 3 and stayed three months. And when the Jews plotted against him as he was about to sail to Syria, he decided to return through Macedonia. 4 And Sopater of Berea accompanied him to Asia—also Aristarchus and Secundus of the Thessalonians, and Gaius of Derbe, and Timothy, and Tychicus and Trophimus of Asia. 5 These men, going ahead, waited for us at Troas. 6 But we sailed away from Philippi after the Days of Unleavened Bread, and in five days joined them at Troas, where we stayed seven days.

7 Now on the first *day* of the week, when the disciples came together to break bread, Paul, ready to depart the next day, spoke to them and continued his message until midnight. 8 There were many lamps in the upper room where they*a* were gathered together. 9 And in a window sat a certain young man named Eutychus, who was sinking into a deep sleep. He was overcome by sleep; and as Paul continued speaking, he fell down from the third story and was taken up dead. 10 But Paul went down, fell on him, and embracing *him* said, "Do not trouble yourselves, for his life is in him." 11 Now when he had come up, had broken bread and eaten, and talked a long while, even till daybreak, he departed. 12 And they brought the young man in alive, and they were not a little comforted.

13 Then we went ahead to the ship and sailed to Assos, there intending to take Paul on board; for so he had given orders, intending himself to go

19:27 *a*NU-Text reads *she be deposed from her magnificence.*   19:37 *a*NU-Text reads *our.*
20:8 *a*NU-Text and M-Text read *we.*

We must be louder than the wild voices that are dancing in the streets. The message that reaches this generation cannot be coy. It must be relevant and pointed. It must be relative and effective.

on foot. 14 And when he met us at Assos, we took him on board and came to Mitylene. 15 We sailed from there, and the next *day* came opposite Chios. The following *day* we arrived at Samos and stayed at Trogyllium. The next *day* we came to Miletus. 16 For Paul had decided to sail past Ephesus, so that he would not have to spend time in Asia; for he was hurrying to be at Jerusalem, if possible, on the Day of Pentecost.

17 From Miletus he sent to Ephesus and called for the elders of the church. 18 And when they had come to him, he said to them: "You know, from the first day that I came to Asia, in what manner I always lived among you, 19 serving the Lord with all humility, with many tears and trials which happened to me by the plotting of the Jews; 20 how I kept back nothing that was helpful, but proclaimed it to you, and taught you publicly and from house to house, 21 testifying to Jews, and also to Greeks, repentance toward God and faith toward our Lord Jesus Christ. 22 And see, now I go bound in the spirit to Jerusalem, not knowing the things that will happen to me there, 23 except that the Holy Spirit testifies in every city, saying that chains and tribulations await me. 24 But none of these things move me; nor do I count my life dear to myself,*a* so that I may finish my race with joy, and the ministry which I received from the Lord Jesus, to testify to the gospel of the grace of God.

25 "And indeed, now I know that you all, among whom I have gone preaching the kingdom of God, will see my face no more. 26 Therefore I testify to you this day that I *am* innocent of the blood of all *men.* 27 For I have not shunned to declare to you the whole counsel of God. 28 Therefore take heed to yourselves and to all the flock, among which the Holy Spirit has made you overseers, to shepherd the church of God*a* which He purchased with His own blood. 29 For I know this, that after my departure savage wolves will come in among you, not sparing the flock. 30 Also from among yourselves men will rise up, speaking perverse

things, to draw away the disciples after themselves. 31 Therefore watch, and remember that for three years I did not cease to warn everyone night and day with tears.

32 "So now, brethren, I commend you to God and to the word of His grace, which is able to build you up and give you an inheritance among all those who are sanctified. 33 I have coveted no one's silver or gold or apparel. 34 Yes,*a* you yourselves know that these hands have provided for my necessities, and for those who were with me. 35 I have shown you in every way, by laboring like this, that you must support the weak. And remember the words of the Lord Jesus, that He said, 'It is more blessed to give than to receive.' "

36 And when he had said these things, he knelt down and prayed with them all. 37 Then they all wept freely, and fell on Paul's neck and kissed him, 38 sorrowing most of all for the words which he spoke, that they would see his face no more. And they accompanied him to the ship.

21 Now it came to pass, that when we had departed from them and set sail, running a straight course we came to Cos, the following *day* to Rhodes, and from there to Patara. 2 And finding a ship sailing over to Phoenicia, we went aboard and set sail. 3 When we had sighted Cyprus, we passed it on the left, sailed to Syria, and landed at Tyre; for there the ship was to unload her cargo. 4 And finding disciples,*a* we stayed there seven days. They told Paul through the Spirit not to go up to Jerusalem. 5 When we had come to the end of those days, we departed and went on our way; and they all accompanied us, with wives and children, till *we were* out of the city. And we knelt down on the shore and prayed. 6 When we had taken our leave of one another, we boarded the ship, and they returned home.

7 And when we had finished *our* voyage from Tyre, we came to Ptolemais, greeted the brethren, and stayed with them one day. 8 On the next *day* we who were Paul's companions*a* departed and came to Cae-

20:24 *a*NU-Text reads *But I do not count my life of any value or dear to myself.*   20:28 *a*M-Text reads *of the Lord and God.*   20:34 *a*NU-Text and M-Text omit *Yes.*   21:4 *a*NU-Text reads *the disciples.*   21:8 *a*NU-Text omits *who were Paul's companions.*

sarea, and entered the house of Philip the evangelist, who was *one* of the seven, and stayed with him. 9 Now this man had four virgin daughters who prophesied. 10 And as we stayed many days, a certain prophet named Agabus came down from Judea. 11 When he had come to us, he took Paul's belt, bound his *own* hands and feet, and said, "Thus says the Holy Spirit, 'So shall the Jews at Jerusalem bind the man who owns this belt, and deliver *him* into the hands of the Gentiles.' "

12 Now when we heard these things, both we and those from that place pleaded with him not to go up to Jerusalem. 13 Then Paul answered, "What do you mean by weeping and breaking my heart? For I am ready not only to be bound, but also to die at Jerusalem for the name of the Lord Jesus."

14 So when he would not be persuaded, we ceased, saying, "The will of the Lord be done."

15 And after those days we packed and went up to Jerusalem. 16 Also some of the disciples from Caesarea went with us and brought with them a certain Mnason of Cyprus, an early disciple, with whom we were to lodge.

17 And when we had come to Jerusalem, the brethren received us gladly. 18 On the following *day* Paul went in with us to James, and all the elders were present. 19 When he had greeted them, he told in detail those things which God had done among the Gentiles through his ministry. 20 And when they heard *it*, they glorified the Lord. And they said to him, "You see, brother, how many myriads of Jews there are who have believed, and they are all zealous for the law; 21 but they have been informed about you that you teach all the Jews who are among the Gentiles to forsake Moses, saying that they ought not to circumcise *their* children nor to walk according to the customs. 22 What then? The assembly must certainly meet, for they will*a* hear that you have come. 23 Therefore do what we tell you: We have four men who have taken a vow. 24 Take them and be purified with them, and pay their expenses so that

they may shave *their* heads, and that all may know that those things of which they were informed concerning you are nothing, but *that* you yourself also walk orderly and keep the law. 25 But concerning the Gentiles who believe, we have written *and* decided that they should observe no such thing,*a* except that they should keep themselves from *things* offered to idols, from blood, from things strangled, and from sexual immorality."

26 Then Paul took the men, and the next day, having been purified with them, entered the temple to announce the expiration of the days of purification, at which time an offering should be made for each one of them.

27 Now when the seven days were almost ended, the Jews from Asia, seeing him in the temple, stirred up the whole crowd and laid hands on him, 28 crying out, "Men of Israel, help! This is the man who teaches all *men* everywhere against the people, the law, and this place; and furthermore he also brought Greeks into the temple and has defiled this holy place." 29 (For they had previously*a* seen Trophimus the Ephesian with him in the city, whom they supposed that Paul had brought into the temple.)

30 And all the city was disturbed; and the people ran together, seized Paul, and dragged him out of the temple; and immediately the doors were shut. 31 Now as they were seeking to kill him, news came to the commander of the garrison that all Jerusalem was in an uproar. 32 He immediately took soldiers and centurions, and ran down to them. And when they saw the commander and the soldiers, they stopped beating Paul. 33 Then the commander came near and took him, and commanded *him* to be bound with two chains; and he asked who he was and what he had done. 34 And some among the multitude cried one thing and some another.

So when he could not ascertain the truth because of the tumult, he commanded him to be taken into the barracks. 35 When he reached the stairs, he had to be carried by the soldiers

21:22 *a*NU-Text reads *What then is to be done? They will certainly.* 21:25 *a*NU-Text omits *that they should observe no such thing, except.* 21:29 *a*M-Text omits *previously.*

*Y*ou don't have to be poor to be broken. There are many people who are sitting in a hot tub contemplating suicide. There are many famous, wealthy people who never hear about Christ. Jesus is not just the God of the welfare mother. He is the God of the middle class and of the affluent too.

because of the violence of the mob. 36 For the multitude of the people followed after, crying out, "Away with him!"

37 Then as Paul was about to be led into the barracks, he said to the commander, "May I speak to you?"

He replied, "Can you speak Greek? 38 Are you not the Egyptian who some time ago stirred up a rebellion and led the four thousand assassins out into the wilderness?"

39 But Paul said, "I am a Jew from Tarsus, in Cilicia, a citizen of no mean city; and I implore you, permit me to speak to the people."

40 So when he had given him permission, Paul stood on the stairs and motioned with his hand to the people. And when there was a great silence, he spoke to *them* in the Hebrew language, saying,

22 "Brethren and fathers, hear my defense before you now." 2 And when they heard that he spoke to them in the Hebrew language, they kept all the more silent.

Then he said: 3 "I am indeed a Jew, born in Tarsus of Cilicia, but brought up in this city at the feet of Gamaliel, taught according to the strictness of our fathers' law, and was zealous toward God as you all are today. 4 I persecuted this Way to the death, binding and delivering into prisons both men and women, 5 as also the high priest bears me witness, and all the council of the elders, from whom I also received letters to the brethren, and went to Damascus to bring in chains even those who were there to Jerusalem to be punished.

6 "Now it happened, as I journeyed and came near Damascus at about noon, suddenly a great light from heaven shone around me. 7 And I fell to the ground and heard a voice saying to me, 'Saul, Saul, why are you persecuting Me?' 8 So I answered, 'Who are You, Lord?' And He said to me, 'I am Jesus of Nazareth, whom you are persecuting.'

9 "And those who were with me indeed saw the light and were afraid,[a] but they did not hear the voice of Him who spoke to me. 10 So I said, 'What shall I do, Lord?' And the Lord said to me, 'Arise and go into Damascus, and there you will be told all things

which are appointed for you to do.' 11 And since I could not see for the glory of that light, being led by the hand of those who were with me, I came into Damascus.

12 "Then a certain Ananias, a devout man according to the law, having a good testimony with all the Jews who dwelt *there*, 13 came to me; and he stood and said to me, 'Brother Saul, receive your sight.' And at that same hour I looked up at him. 14 Then he said, 'The God of our fathers has chosen you that you should know His will, and see the Just One, and hear the voice of His mouth. 15 For you will be His witness to all men of what you have seen and heard. 16 And now why are you waiting? Arise and be baptized, and wash away your sins, calling on the name of the Lord.'

17 "Now it happened, when I returned to Jerusalem and was praying in the temple, that I was in a trance 18 and saw Him saying to me, 'Make haste and get out of Jerusalem quickly, for they will not receive your testimony concerning Me.' 19 So I said, 'Lord, they know that in every synagogue I imprisoned and beat those who believe on You. 20 And when the blood of Your martyr Stephen was shed, I also was standing by consenting to his death,[a] and guarding the clothes of those who were killing him.' 21 Then He said to me, 'Depart, for I will send you far from here to the Gentiles.' "

22 And they listened to him until this word, and *then* they raised their voices and said, "Away with such a *fellow* from the earth, for he is not fit to live!" 23 Then, as they cried out and tore off *their* clothes and threw dust into the air, 24 the commander ordered him to be brought into the barracks, and said that he should be examined under scourging, so that he might know why they shouted so against him. 25 And as they bound him with thongs, Paul said to the centurion who stood by, "Is it lawful for you to scourge a man who is a Roman, and uncondemned?"

26 When the centurion heard *that*, he went and told the commander, saying, "Take care what you do, for this man is a Roman."

27 Then the commander came and

22:9 [a]NU-Text omits *and were afraid.*   22:20 [a]NU-Text omits *to his death.*

Gospel
Pearls

said to him, "Tell me, are you a Roman?"

He said, "Yes."

28 The commander answered, "With a large sum I obtained this citizenship."

And Paul said, "But I was born *a citizen*."

29 Then immediately those who were about to examine him withdrew from him; and the commander was also afraid after he found out that he was a Roman, and because he had bound him.

30 The next day, because he wanted to know for certain why he was accused by the Jews, he released him from *his* bonds, and commanded the chief priests and all their council to appear, and brought Paul down and set him before them.

23 Then Paul, looking earnestly at the council, said, "Men *and* brethren, I have lived in all good conscience before God until this day." 2 And the high priest Ananias commanded those who stood by him to strike him on the mouth. 3 Then Paul said to him, "God will strike you, *you* whitewashed wall! For you sit to judge me according to the law, and do you command me to be struck contrary to the law?"

4 And those who stood by said, "Do you revile God's high priest?"

5 Then Paul said, "I did not know, brethren, that he was the high priest; for it is written, '*You shall not speak evil of a ruler of your people.*' "ª

6 But when Paul perceived that one part were Sadducees and the other Pharisees, he cried out in the council, "Men *and* brethren, I am a Pharisee, the son of a Pharisee; concerning the hope and resurrection of the dead I am being judged!"

7 And when he had said this, a dissension arose between the Pharisees and the Sadducees; and the assembly was divided. 8 For Sadducees say that there is no resurrection—and no angel or spirit; but the Pharisees confess both. 9 Then there arose a loud outcry. And the scribes of the Pharisees' party arose and protested, saying, "We find no evil in this man; but if a spirit or an angel has spoken to him, let us not fight against God."ª

10 Now when there arose a great dissension, the commander, fearing lest Paul might be pulled to pieces by them, commanded the soldiers to go down and take him by force from among them, and bring *him* into the barracks.

11 But the following night the Lord stood by him and said, "Be of good cheer, Paul; for as you have testified for Me in Jerusalem, so you must also bear witness at Rome."

12 And when it was day, some of the Jews banded together and bound themselves under an oath, saying that they would neither eat nor drink till they had killed Paul. 13 Now there were more than forty who had formed this conspiracy. 14 They came to the chief priests and elders, and said, "We have bound ourselves under a great oath that we will eat nothing until we have killed Paul. 15 Now you, therefore, together with the council, suggest to the commander that he be brought down to you tomorrow,ª as though you were going to make further inquiries concerning him; but we are ready to kill him before he comes near."

16 So when Paul's sister's son heard of their ambush, he went and entered the barracks and told Paul. 17 Then Paul called one of the centurions to *him* and said, "Take this young man to the commander, for he has something to tell him." 18 So he took him and brought *him* to the commander and said, "Paul the prisoner called me to *him* and asked *me* to bring this young man to you. He has something to say to you."

19 Then the commander took him by the hand, went aside, and asked privately, "What is it that you have to tell me?"

20 And he said, "The Jews have agreed to ask that you bring Paul down to the council tomorrow, as though they were going to inquire more fully about him. 21 But do not yield to them, for more than forty of them lie in wait for him, men who have bound themselves by an oath that they will neither eat nor drink till they have killed him; and now they are ready, waiting for the promise from you."

22 So the commander let the young

23:5 ªExodus 22:28   23:9 ªNU-Text omits last clause and reads *what if a spirit or an angel has spoken to him?*   23:15 ªNU-Text omits *tomorrow*.

*L*ydia is an excellent example of a progressive Christian woman who is still affluent and successful. She has a heart for ministry. She sowed into ministry out of her resources, and God has blessed her all the more.

man depart, and commanded *him,* "Tell no one that you have revealed these things to me."

23 And he called for two centurions, saying, "Prepare two hundred soldiers, seventy horsemen, and two hundred spearmen to go to Caesarea at the third hour of the night; 24 and provide mounts to set Paul on, and bring *him* safely to Felix the governor." 25 He wrote a letter in the following manner:

26 Claudius Lysias,

To the most excellent governor Felix:

Greetings.

27 This man was seized by the Jews and was about to be killed by them. Coming with the troops I rescued him, having learned that he was a Roman. 28 And when I wanted to know the reason they accused him, I brought him before their council. 29 I found out that he was accused concerning questions of their law, but had nothing charged against him deserving of death or chains. 30 And when it was told me that the Jews lay in wait for the man,*a* I sent him immediately to you, and also commanded his accusers to state before you the charges against him.

Farewell.

31 Then the soldiers, as they were commanded, took Paul and brought *him* by night to Antipatris. 32 The next day they left the horsemen to go on with him, and returned to the barracks. 33 When they came to Caesarea and had delivered the letter to the governor, they also presented Paul to him. 34 And when the governor had read *it,* he asked what province he was from. And when he understood that *he was* from Cilicia, 35 he said, "I will hear you when your accusers also have come." And he commanded him to be kept in Herod's Praetorium.

24 Now after five days Ananias the high priest came down with the elders and a certain orator *named* Tertullus. These gave evidence to the governor against Paul.

2 And when he was called upon, Tertullus began his accusation, saying: "Seeing that through you we enjoy great peace, and prosperity is being brought to this nation by your foresight, 3 we accept *it* always and in all places, most noble Felix, with all thankfulness. 4 Nevertheless, not to be tedious to you any further, I beg you to hear, by your courtesy, a few words from us. 5 For we have found this man a plague, a creator of dissension among all the Jews throughout the world, and a ringleader of the sect of the Nazarenes. 6 He even tried to profane the temple, and we seized him,*a* and wanted to judge him according to our law. 7 But the commander Lysias came by and with great violence took *him* out of our hands, 8 commanding his accusers to come to you. By examining him yourself you may ascertain all these things of which we accuse him." 9 And the Jews also assented,*a* maintaining that these things were so.

10 Then Paul, after the governor had nodded to him to speak, answered: "Inasmuch as I know that you have been for many years a judge of this nation, I do the more cheerfully answer for myself, 11 because you may ascertain that it is no more than twelve days since I went up to Jerusalem to worship. 12 And they neither found me in the temple disputing with anyone nor inciting the crowd, either in the synagogues or in the city. 13 Nor can they prove the things of which they now accuse me. 14 But this I confess to you, that according to the Way which they call a sect, so I worship the God of my fathers, believing all things which are written in the Law and in the Prophets. 15 I have hope in God, which they themselves also accept, that there will be a resurrection of the dead,*a* both of *the* just and *the*

23:30 *a*NU-Text reads *there would be a plot against the man.*   24:6 *a*NU-Text ends the sentence here and omits the rest of verse 6, all of verse 7, and the first clause of verse 8.   24:9 *a*NU-Text and M-Text read *joined the attack.*   24:15 *a*NU-Text omits *of the dead.*

Gospel Pearls

unjust. 16 This *being* so, I myself always strive to have a conscience without offense toward God and men.

17 "Now after many years I came to bring alms and offerings to my nation, 18 in the midst of which some Jews from Asia found me purified in the temple, neither with a mob nor with tumult. 19 They ought to have been here before you to object if they had anything against me. 20 Or else let those who are *here* themselves say if they found any wrongdoing[a] in me while I stood before the council, 21 unless *it is* for this one statement which I cried out, standing among them, 'Concerning the resurrection of the dead I am being judged by you this day.'"

22 But when Felix heard these things, having more accurate knowledge of *the* Way, he adjourned the proceedings and said, "When Lysias the commander comes down, I will make a decision on your case." 23 So he commanded the centurion to keep Paul and to let *him* have liberty, and told him not to forbid any of his friends to provide for or visit him.

24 And after some days, when Felix came with his wife Drusilla, who was Jewish, he sent for Paul and heard him concerning the faith in Christ. 25 Now as he reasoned about righteousness, self-control, and the judgment to come, Felix was afraid and answered, "Go away for now; when I have a convenient time I will call for you." 26 Meanwhile he also hoped that money would be given him by Paul, that he might release him.[a] Therefore he sent for him more often and conversed with him.

27 But after two years Porcius Festus succeeded Felix; and Felix, wanting to do the Jews a favor, left Paul bound.

25 Now when Festus had come to the province, after three days he went up from Caesarea to Jerusalem. 2 Then the high priest[a] and the chief men of the Jews informed him against Paul; and they petitioned him, 3 asking a favor against him, that he would summon him to Jerusalem—while *they* lay in ambush

along the road to kill him. 4 But Festus answered that Paul should be kept at Caesarea, and that he himself was going *there* shortly. 5 "Therefore," he said, "let those who have authority among you go down with *me* and accuse this man, to see if there is any fault in him."

6 And when he had remained among them more than ten days, he went down to Caesarea. And the next day, sitting on the judgment seat, he commanded Paul to be brought. 7 When he had come, the Jews who had come down from Jerusalem stood about and laid many serious complaints against Paul, which they could not prove, 8 while he answered for himself, "Neither against the law of the Jews, nor against the temple, nor against Caesar have I offended in anything at all."

9 But Festus, wanting to do the Jews a favor, answered Paul and said, "Are you willing to go up to Jerusalem and there be judged before me concerning these things?"

10 So Paul said, "I stand at Caesar's judgment seat, where I ought to be judged. To the Jews I have done no wrong, as you very well know. 11 For if I am an offender, or have committed anything deserving of death, I do not object to dying; but if there is nothing in these things of which these men accuse me, no one can deliver me to them. I appeal to Caesar."

12 Then Festus, when he had conferred with the council, answered, "You have appealed to Caesar? To Caesar you shall go!"

13 And after some days King Agrippa and Bernice came to Caesarea to greet Festus. 14 When they had been there many days, Festus laid Paul's case before the king, saying: "There is a certain man left a prisoner by Felix, 15 about whom the chief priests and the elders of the Jews informed *me*, when I was in Jerusalem, asking for a judgment against him. 16 To them I answered, 'It is not the custom of the Romans to deliver any man to destruction[a] before the accused meets the accusers face to face, and has opportunity to answer for himself concerning the

24:20 [a]NU-Text and M-Text read *say what wrongdoing they found.*   24:26 [a]NU-Text omits *that he might release him.*   25:2 [a]NU-Text reads *chief priests.*   25:16 [a]NU-Text omits *to destruction,* although it is implied.

*P*ain is an equal opportunity dilemma. It attacks little boys and little girls and is looking for another generation. It will find them if the real witnesses hide behind the images of success and scramble to the top only to find that the top is filled with empty people full of empty stares and the absence of real meaning!

charge against him.' 17 Therefore when they had come together, without any delay, the next day I sat on the judgment seat and commanded the man to be brought in. 18 When the accusers stood up, they brought no accusation against him of such things as I supposed, 19 but had some questions against him about their own religion and about a certain Jesus, who had died, whom Paul affirmed to be alive. 20 And because I was uncertain of such questions, I asked whether he was willing to go to Jerusalem and there be judged concerning these matters. 21 But when Paul appealed to be reserved for the decision of Augustus, I commanded him to be kept till I could send him to Caesar."

22 Then Agrippa said to Festus, "I also would like to hear the man myself."

"Tomorrow," he said, "you shall hear him."

23 So the next day, when Agrippa and Bernice had come with great pomp, and had entered the auditorium with the commanders and the prominent men of the city, at Festus' command Paul was brought in. 24 And Festus said: "King Agrippa and all the men who are here present with us, you see this man about whom the whole assembly of the Jews petitioned me, both at Jerusalem and here, crying out that he was not fit to live any longer. 25 But when I found that he had committed nothing deserving of death, and that he himself had appealed to Augustus, I decided to send him. 26 I have nothing certain to write to my lord concerning him. Therefore I have brought him out before you, and especially before you, King Agrippa, so that after the examination has taken place I may have something to write. 27 For it seems to me unreasonable to send a prisoner and not to specify the charges against him."

26 Then Agrippa said to Paul, "You are permitted to speak for yourself."

So Paul stretched out his hand and answered for himself: 2 "I think myself happy, King Agrippa, because today I shall answer for myself before you concerning all the things of which I am accused by the Jews, 3 especially because you are expert in all customs and questions which have to do with the Jews. Therefore I beg you to hear me patiently.

4 "My manner of life from my youth, which was spent from the beginning among my own nation at Jerusalem, all the Jews know. 5 They knew me from the first, if they were willing to testify, that according to the strictest sect of our religion I lived a Pharisee. 6 And now I stand and am judged for the hope of the promise made by God to our fathers. 7 To this *promise* our twelve tribes, earnestly serving God night and day, hope to attain. For this hope's sake, King Agrippa, I am accused by the Jews. 8 Why should it be thought incredible by you that God raises the dead?

9 "Indeed, I myself thought I must do many things contrary to the name of Jesus of Nazareth. 10 This I also did in Jerusalem, and many of the saints I shut up in prison, having received authority from the chief priests; and when they were put to death, I cast my vote against *them*. 11 And I punished them often in every synagogue and compelled *them* to blaspheme; and being exceedingly enraged against them, I persecuted *them* even to foreign cities.

12 "While thus occupied, as I journeyed to Damascus with authority and commission from the chief priests, 13 at midday, O king, along the road I saw a light from heaven, brighter than the sun, shining around me and those who journeyed with me. 14 And when we all had fallen to the ground, I heard a voice speaking to me and saying in the Hebrew language, 'Saul, Saul, why are you persecuting Me? *It is* hard for you to kick against the goads.' 15 So I said, 'Who are You, Lord?' And He said, 'I am Jesus, whom you are persecuting. 16 But rise and stand on your feet; for I have appeared to you for this purpose, to make you a minister and a witness both of the things which you have seen and of the things which I will yet reveal to you. 17 I will deliver you from the *Jewish* people, as well as *from* the Gentiles, to whom I now*ᵃ* send you, 18 to open

26:17 ᵃNU-Text and M-Text omit *now*.

their eyes, *in order* to turn *them* from darkness to light, and *from* the power of Satan to God, that they may receive forgiveness of sins and an inheritance among those who are sanctified by faith in Me.'

19 "Therefore, King Agrippa, I was not disobedient to the heavenly vision, 20 but declared first to those in Damascus and in Jerusalem, and throughout all the region of Judea, and *then* to the Gentiles, that they should repent, turn to God, and do works befitting repentance. 21 For these reasons the Jews seized me in the temple and tried to kill *me.* 22 Therefore, having obtained help from God, to this day I stand, witnessing both to small and great, saying no other things than those which the prophets and Moses said would come— 23 that the Christ would suffer, that He would be the first to rise from the dead, and would proclaim light to the *Jewish* people and to the Gentiles."

24 Now as he thus made his defense, Festus said with a loud voice, "Paul, you are beside yourself! Much learning is driving you mad!"

25 But he said, "I am not mad, most noble Festus, but speak the words of truth and reason. 26 For the king, before whom I also speak freely, knows these things; for I am convinced that none of these things escapes his attention, since this thing was not done in a corner. 27 King Agrippa, do you believe the prophets? I know that you do believe."

28 Then Agrippa said to Paul, "You almost persuade me to become a Christian."

29 And Paul said, "I would to God that not only you, but also all who hear me today, might become both almost and altogether such as I am, except for these chains."

30 When he had said these things, the king stood up, as well as the governor and Bernice and those who sat with them; 31 and when they had gone aside, they talked among themselves, saying, "This man is doing nothing deserving of death or chains."

32 Then Agrippa said to Festus, "This man might have been set free if he had not appealed to Caesar."

27

And when it was decided that we should sail to Italy, they delivered Paul and some other prisoners to *one* named Julius, a centurion of the Augustan Regiment. 2 So, entering a ship of Adramyttium, we put to sea, meaning to sail along the coasts of Asia. Aristarchus, a Macedonian of Thessalonica, was with us. 3 And the next *day* we landed at Sidon. And Julius treated Paul kindly and gave *him* liberty to go to his friends and receive care. 4 When we had put to sea from there, we sailed under *the shelter of* Cyprus, because the winds were contrary. 5 And when we had sailed over the sea which is off Cilicia and Pamphylia, we came to Myra, *a city* of Lycia. 6 There the centurion found an Alexandrian ship sailing to Italy, and he put us on board.

7 When we had sailed slowly many days, and arrived with difficulty off Cnidus, the wind not permitting us to proceed, we sailed under *the shelter of* Crete off Salmone. 8 Passing it with difficulty, we came to a place called Fair Havens, near the city *of* Lasea.

9 Now when much time had been spent, and sailing was now dangerous because the Fast was already over, Paul advised them, 10 saying, "Men, I perceive that this voyage will end with disaster and much loss, not only of the cargo and ship, but also our lives." 11 Nevertheless the centurion was more persuaded by the helmsman and the owner of the ship than by the things spoken by Paul. 12 And because the harbor was not suitable to winter in, the majority advised to set sail from there also, if by any means they could reach Phoenix, a harbor of Crete opening toward the southwest and northwest, *and* winter *there.*

13 When the south wind blew softly, supposing that they had obtained *their* desire, putting out to sea, they sailed close by Crete. 14 But not long after, a tempestuous head wind arose, called Euroclydon.*ᵃ* 15 So when the ship was caught, and could not head into the wind, we let *her* drive. 16 And running under *the shelter of* an island called Clauda,*ᵃ* we secured the skiff with difficulty. 17 When they had taken it on board,

27:14 *ᵃNU-Text reads* Euraquilon. 27:16 *ᵃNU-Text reads* Cauda.

Some little girl needs to know your recipe for survival. Somewhere in the streets there is someone dying because she does not know that it is possible to survive what you have already endured. You are a precious commodity. You are the cure to her crisis.

"I Won't Let You Kill Me"

Acts 26:21, 22

*A*ll kinds of families today are marked by murder, including God's family, the church. In fact, you haven't really been killed until you've been killed by a brother or sister in the church! I know some women who've made it through the worst possible life on the streets only to be driven half crazy by saints.

It's time to say to those in your family—both your natural family and your spiritual family—"I love you, I'm related to you, I care about you . . . but I won't let you kill me."

You had better adopt that attitude toward every person in your life—your husband, your children, your friends, your boss, the people you work with, the members of your church. You need to say to them, "Jesus died for me. That's all the dying that needs to be done. I'm going to hide myself in Him. I won't let you kill me."

I'm not talking about your physical body. I'm talking about your spirit and your soul. I'm talking about resisting people who will attempt murder in your emotions, your attitude, your inner life. They'll try to get you to sin with them, or to give in to your own temptation. They'll say to you, "It's all right. It won't matter if you do it just this once. It's no big deal."

Others might say to you, "Nothing is going to get better. You might as well give up and sit down in your ashes because nothing is ever going to change and nothing is ever going to be right in your life."

Those who say such things to you are agents of death, creeping up on you and coming at you in disguise. Don't let them kill you! Stand up to them in the strength of Jesus Christ and say, "I'm not going to let you drive me crazy with your lies and your temptations. I'm not going to let you lead me into sin. I refuse to let you assassinate what God has birthed in me!"

Start praising God for what He has done for you. Celebrate the life He has given you. Declare to God and to every person who speaks death: "My life isn't over. God still has more for me to do and to say and to be. I am loose."

Say no to those drugs. Say no to that sinful relationship. Say no to that evil desire. Say no to those thoughts of depression and suicide. Say no to that thing or that person who is trying to lead you straight back to a life of dying instead of living. Don't let yourself be killed. Live!

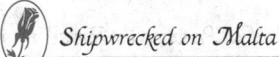

they used cables to undergird the ship; and fearing lest they should run aground on the Syrtis*ᵃ* *Sands*, they struck sail and so were driven. 18 And because we were exceedingly tempest-tossed, the next *day* they lightened the ship. 19 On the third *day* we threw the ship's tackle overboard with our own hands. 20 Now when neither sun nor stars appeared for many days, and no small tempest beat on *us*, all hope that we would be saved was finally given up.

21 But after long abstinence from food, then Paul stood in the midst of them and said, "Men, you should have listened to me, and not have sailed from Crete and incurred this disaster and loss. 22 And now I urge you to take heart, for there will be no loss of life among you, but only of the ship. 23 For there stood by me this night an angel of the God to whom I belong and whom I serve, 24 saying, 'Do not be afraid, Paul; you must be brought before Caesar; and indeed God has granted you all those who sail with you.' 25 Therefore take heart, men, for I believe God that it will be just as it was told me. 26 However, we must run aground on a certain island."

27 Now when the fourteenth night had come, as we were driven up and down in the Adriatic *Sea*, about midnight the sailors sensed that they were drawing near some land. 28 And they took soundings and found *it* to be twenty fathoms; and when they had gone a little farther, they took soundings again and found *it* to be fifteen fathoms. 29 Then, fearing lest we should run aground on the rocks, they dropped four anchors from the stern, and prayed for day to come. 30 And as the sailors were seeking to escape from the ship, when they had let down the skiff into the sea, under pretense of putting out anchors from the prow, 31 Paul said to the centurion and the soldiers, "Unless these men stay in the ship, you cannot be saved." 32 Then the soldiers cut away the ropes of the skiff and let it fall off.

33 And as day was about to dawn, Paul implored *them* all to take food, saying, "Today is the fourteenth day you have waited and continued without food, and eaten nothing.

34 Therefore I urge you to take nourishment, for this is for your survival, since not a hair will fall from the head of any of you." 35 And when he had said these things, he took bread and gave thanks to God in the presence of them all; and when he had broken *it* he began to eat. 36 Then they were all encouraged, and also took food themselves. 37 And in all we were two hundred and seventy-six persons on the ship. 38 So when they had eaten enough, they lightened the ship and threw out the wheat into the sea.

39 When it was day, they did not recognize the land; but they observed a bay with a beach, onto which they planned to run the ship if possible. 40 And they let go the anchors and left *them* in the sea, meanwhile loosing the rudder ropes; and they hoisted the mainsail to the wind and made for shore. 41 But striking a place where two seas met, they ran the ship aground; and the prow stuck fast and remained immovable, but the stern was being broken up by the violence of the waves.

42 And the soldiers' plan was to kill the prisoners, lest any of them should swim away and escape. 43 But the centurion, wanting to save Paul, kept them from *their* purpose, and commanded that those who could swim should jump *overboard* first and get to land, 44 and the rest, some on boards and some on *parts* of the ship. And so it was that they all escaped safely to land.

28 Now when they had escaped, they then found out that the island was called Malta. 2 And the natives showed us unusual kindness; for they kindled a fire and made us all welcome, because of the rain that was falling and because of the cold. 3 But when Paul had gathered a bundle of sticks and laid *them* on the fire, a viper came out because of the heat, and fastened on his hand. 4 So when the natives saw the creature hanging from his hand, they said to one another, "No doubt this man is a murderer, whom, though he has escaped the sea, yet justice does not allow to live." 5 But he shook off the creature into the fire and suffered no harm. 6 However, they were expecting that

27:17 *ᵃ*M-Text reads *Syrtes*.

*L*ook at Jesus. He was giving life while He was dying. He healed the pained because of His pain. He was wounded for our transgressions. Could it be that you went through all you went through so that you could help someone else?

he would swell up or suddenly fall down dead. But after they had looked for a long time and saw no harm come to him, they changed their minds and said that he was a god.

7 In that region there was an estate of the leading citizen of the island, whose name was Publius, who received us and entertained us courteously for three days. 8 And it happened that the father of Publius lay sick of a fever and dysentery. Paul went in to him and prayed, and he laid his hands on him and healed him. 9 So when this was done, the rest of those on the island who had diseases also came and were healed. 10 They also honored us in many ways; and when we departed, they provided such things as were necessary.

11 After three months we sailed in an Alexandrian ship whose figurehead was the Twin Brothers, which had wintered at the island. 12 And landing at Syracuse, we stayed three days. 13 From there we circled round and reached Rhegium. And after one day the south wind blew; and the next day we came to Puteoli, 14 where we found brethren, and were invited to stay with them seven days. And so we went toward Rome. 15 And from there, when the brethren heard about us, they came to meet us as far as Appii Forum and Three Inns. When Paul saw them, he thanked God and took courage.

16 Now when we came to Rome, the centurion delivered the prisoners to the captain of the guard; but Paul was permitted to dwell by himself with the soldier who guarded him.

17 And it came to pass after three days that Paul called the leaders of the Jews together. So when they had come together, he said to them: "Men *and* brethren, though I have done nothing against our people or the customs of our fathers, yet I was delivered as a prisoner from Jerusalem into the hands of the Romans, 18 who, when they had examined me, wanted to let *me* go, because there was no cause for putting me to death. 19 But when the Jews[a] spoke against *it*, I was compelled to appeal to Caesar, not that I had anything of which to accuse my nation. 20 For this reason therefore I have called for you, to see *you* and speak with *you*, because for the hope of Israel I am bound with this chain."

21 Then they said to him, "We neither received letters from Judea concerning you, nor have any of the brethren who came reported or spoken any evil of you. 22 But we desire to hear from you what you think; for concerning this sect, we know that it is spoken against everywhere."

23 So when they had appointed him a day, many came to him at *his* lodging, to whom he explained and solemnly testified of the kingdom of God, persuading them concerning Jesus from both the Law of Moses and the Prophets, from morning till evening. 24 And some were persuaded by the things which were spoken, and some disbelieved. 25 So when they did not agree among themselves, they departed after Paul had said one word: "The Holy Spirit spoke rightly through Isaiah the prophet to our[a] fathers, 26 saying,

> 'Go to this people and say:
> "Hearing you will hear, and
>   shall not understand;
> And seeing you will see, and
>   not perceive;
> 27 For the hearts of this people
>   have grown dull.
> Their ears are hard of hearing,
> And their eyes they have
>   closed,
> Lest they should see with their
>   eyes and hear with their
>   ears,
> Lest they should understand
>   with their hearts and turn,
> So that I should heal them." '[a]

28 "Therefore let it be known to you that the salvation of God has been sent to the Gentiles, and they will hear it!" 29 And when he had said these words, the Jews departed and had a great dispute among themselves.[a]

30 Then Paul dwelt two whole years in his own rented house, and received all who came to him, 31 preaching the kingdom of God and teaching the things which concern the Lord Jesus Christ with all confidence, no one forbidding him.

28:19 [a]That is, the ruling authorities　　28:25 [a]NU-Text reads *your.*　　28:27 [a]Isaiah 6:9, 10
28:29 [a]NU-Text omits this verse.

Gospel Pearls

The Epistle of Paul the Apostle to the

ROMANS

1 Paul, a bondservant of Jesus Christ, called *to be* an apostle, separated to the gospel of God 2 which He promised before through His prophets in the Holy Scriptures, 3 concerning His Son Jesus Christ our Lord, who was born of the seed of David according to the flesh, 4 *and* declared *to be* the Son of God with power according to the Spirit of holiness, by the resurrection from the dead. 5 Through Him we have received grace and apostleship for obedience to the faith among all nations for His name, 6 among whom you also are the called of Jesus Christ;

7 To all who are in Rome, beloved of God, called *to be* saints:

Grace to you and peace from God our Father and the Lord Jesus Christ.

8 First, I thank my God through Jesus Christ for you all, that your faith is spoken of throughout the whole world. 9 For God is my witness, whom I serve with my spirit in the gospel of His Son, that without ceasing I make mention of you always in my prayers, 10 making request if, by some means, now at last I may find a way in the will of God to come to you. 11 For I long to see you, that I may impart to you some spiritual gift, so that you may be established— 12 that is, that I may be encouraged together with you by the mutual faith both of you and me.

13 Now I do not want you to be unaware, brethren, that I often planned to come to you (but was hindered until now), that I might have some fruit among you also, just as among the other Gentiles. 14 I am a debtor both to Greeks and to barbarians, both to wise and to unwise. 15 So, as much as is in me, *I am* ready to preach the gospel to you who are in Rome also.

16 For I am not ashamed of the gospel of Christ,[a] for it is the power of God to salvation for everyone who believes, for the Jew first and also for the Greek. 17 For in it the righteousness of God is revealed from faith to faith; as it is written, *"The just shall live by faith."*[a]

18 For the wrath of God is revealed from heaven against all ungodliness and unrighteousness of men, who suppress the truth in unrighteousness, 19 because what may be known of God is manifest in them, for God has shown *it* to them. 20 For since the creation of the world His invisible *attributes* are clearly seen, being understood by the things that are made, *even* His eternal power and Godhead, so that they are without excuse, 21 because, although they knew God, they did not glorify *Him* as God, nor were thankful, but became futile in their thoughts, and their foolish hearts were darkened. 22 Professing to be wise, they became fools, 23 and changed the glory of the incorruptible God into an image made like corruptible man—and birds and four-footed animals and creeping things.

24 Therefore God also gave them up to uncleanness, in the lusts of their hearts, to dishonor their bodies among themselves, 25 who exchanged the truth of God for the lie, and worshiped and served the creature rather than the Creator, who is blessed forever. Amen.

26 For this reason God gave them up to vile passions. For even their women exchanged the natural use for what is against nature. 27 Likewise also the men, leaving the natural use of the woman, burned in their lust for one another, men with men committing what is shameful, and receiving in themselves the penalty of their error which was due.

28 And even as they did not like to retain God in *their* knowledge, God gave them over to a debased mind, to do those things which are not fitting; 29 being filled with all unrighteousness, sexual immorality,[a] wickedness, covetousness, maliciousness; full of envy, murder, strife, deceit, evil-mindedness; *they are* whisperers, 30 backbiters, haters of God, violent, proud, boasters, inventors of evil things, disobedient to parents,

---

1:16 aNU-Text omits *of Christ.*   1:17 aHabakkuk 2:4   1:29 aNU-Text omits *sexual immorality.*

---

*T*he best people to help others are not just those who studied life in a book. It is those who lived it out on the stage of reality. You will never be healed until you use your pain to heal someone else.

31 undiscerning, untrustworthy, un-loving, unforgiving,[a] unmerciful; 32 who, knowing the righteous judgment of God, that those who practice such things are deserving of death, not only do the same but also approve of those who practice them.

2 Therefore you are inexcusable, O man, whoever you are who judge, for in whatever you judge another you condemn yourself; for you who judge practice the same things. 2 But we know that the judgment of God is according to truth against those who practice such things. 3 And do you think this, O man, you who judge those practicing such things, and doing the same, that you will escape the judgment of God? 4 Or do you despise the riches of His goodness, forbearance, and longsuffering, not knowing that the goodness of God leads you to repentance? 5 But in accordance with your hardness and your impenitent heart you are treasuring up for yourself wrath in the day of wrath and revelation of the righteous judgment of God, 6 who *will render to each one according to his deeds*:[a] 7 eternal life to those who by patient continuance in doing good seek for glory, honor, and immortality; 8 but to those who are self-seeking and do not obey the truth, but obey unrighteousness—indignation and wrath, 9 tribulation and anguish, on every soul of man who does evil, of the Jew first and also of the Greek; 10 but glory, honor, and peace to everyone who works what is good, to the Jew first and also to the Greek. 11 For there is no partiality with God.

12 For as many as have sinned without law will also perish without law, and as many as have sinned in the law will be judged by the law 13 (for not the hearers of the law *are* just in the sight of God, but the doers of the law will be justified; 14 for when Gentiles, who do not have the law, by nature do the things in the law, these, although not having the law, are a law to themselves, 15 who show the work of the law written in their hearts, their conscience also bearing witness, and between themselves *their* thoughts accusing or else excusing *them*) 16 in the day when God will judge the secrets of men by Jesus Christ, according to my gospel.

17 Indeed[a] you are called a Jew, and rest on the law, and make your boast in God, 18 and know *His* will, and approve the things that are excellent, being instructed out of the law, 19 and are confident that you yourself are a guide to the blind, a light to those who are in darkness, 20 an instructor of the foolish, a teacher of babes, having the form of knowledge and truth in the law. 21 You, therefore, who teach another, do you not teach yourself? You who preach that a man should not steal, do you steal? 22 You who say, "Do not commit adultery," do you commit adultery? You who abhor idols, do you rob temples? 23 You who make your boast in the law, do you dishonor God through breaking the law? 24 For *"the name of God is blasphemed among the Gentiles because of you,"*[a] as it is written.

25 For circumcision is indeed profitable if you keep the law; but if you are a breaker of the law, your circumcision has become uncircumcision. 26 Therefore, if an uncircumcised man keeps the righteous requirements of the law, will not his uncircumcision be counted as circumcision? 27 And will not the physically uncircumcised, if he fulfills the law, judge you who, *even* with *your* written *code* and circumcision, *are* a transgressor of the law? 28 For he is not a Jew who *is one* outwardly, nor *is* circumcision that which *is* outward in the flesh; 29 but *he is* a Jew who *is one* inwardly; and circumcision *is that* of the heart, in the Spirit, not in the letter; whose praise *is* not from men but from God.

3 What advantage then has the Jew, or what *is* the profit of circumcision? 2 Much in every way! Chiefly because to them were committed the oracles of God. 3 For what if some did not believe? Will their unbelief make the faithfulness of God without effect? 4 Certainly not! Indeed, let God be true but every man a liar. As it is written:

1:31 [a]NU-Text omits *unforgiving*.   2:6 [a]Psalm 62:12; Proverbs 24:12   2:17 [a]NU-Text reads *But if*.
2:24 [a]Isaiah 52:5; Ezekiel 36:22

Commit the past to the ground. Throw the dirt of helping others on it and it will die before your eyes. Somebody needs you right now. This is an emergency. Stop feeling sorry for yourself and get involved.

The Greatness
of God's Goodness

Romans 2:4

*I*t may sound mushy, and to the religious zealot, sappy and simplistic, but it is the goodness of God that leads to repentance (see Romans 2:4). Repentance doesn't come because of the scare tactics and threats of ministers who need mercy for themselves. Repentance comes through the unfailing love of a perfect God who cares for the cracked vases that others would have discarded long ago. It is His great love that calls you to live for Him.

There is no way you can feel Him standing with you when all others have forsaken you, and not want to please Him. There is no way you can survive a storm, protected by His love, and not say, "I am Yours, O Lord." One experience with His holiness will bring the convicted sinner to her knees. In other words, God is too good for you to experience His love and then abuse that love.

Once you have made a commitment to God, it is natural to want to reach out to others like yourself. Accepting the rejected is not a weakness of the gospel; it is its strength. Neither can we shelter hardened criminals who are content to live as outlaws from the Word of the Lord. There is a great deal of difference between the cold callousness of a rebellious heart and the deeply troubled heart of a sincere Christian whose desperate prayer is, "God, save me from myself."

To the survivors of wrecked lives and damaged homes, we hold out our arms. As we do, they will come—the halt and the lame, the deaf and the dumb. They will need much exposure to the Word and much time before their self-images improve and their marriages cease to tremble. They will have flashbacks and relapses and require intensive care. Yet we swing wide the doors of ministry and admit, with cautious candor, that most of our doctors have at one time been patients themselves. Still we say, "Come. It is Jesus Christ who is the Cure."

To the overlooked and the castaway, to the downtrodden and the wayfaring, we cry, "Come into this shelter. Come out of the cold."

To the wounded and the weary—uptown sophisticate and downtown derelict—we guarantee a welcome. You are accepted in the Beloved.

*"That You may be justified in
Your words,
And may overcome when You
are judged."*[a]

5 But if our unrighteousness demonstrates the righteousness of God, what shall we say? *Is* God unjust who inflicts wrath? (I speak as a man.) 6 Certainly not! For then how will God judge the world?

7 For if the truth of God has increased through my lie to His glory, why am I also still judged as a sinner? 8 And *why* not *say,* "Let us do evil that good may come"?—as we are slanderously reported and as some affirm that we say. Their condemnation is just.

9 What then? Are we better *than they?* Not at all. For we have previously charged both Jews and Greeks that they are all under sin. 10 As it is written:

*"There is none righteous, no, not
one;
11　There is none who
understands;
There is none who seeks after
God.
12　They have all turned aside;
They have together become
unprofitable;
There is none who does good,
no, not one."*[a]
13 *"Their throat is an open tomb;
With their tongues they have
practiced deceit";*[a]
*"The poison of asps is under
their lips";*[b]
14 *"Whose mouth is full of cursing
and bitterness."*[a]
15 *"Their feet are swift to shed
blood;
16　Destruction and misery are in
their ways;
17　And the way of peace they have
not known."*[a]
18 *"There is no fear of God before
their eyes."*[a]

19 Now we know that whatever the law says, it says to those who are under the law, that every mouth may be stopped, and all the world may become guilty before God. 20 Therefore by the deeds of the law no flesh will

be justified in His sight, for by the law *is* the knowledge of sin.

21 But now the righteousness of God apart from the law is revealed, being witnessed by the Law and the Prophets, 22 even the righteousness of God, through faith in Jesus Christ, to all and on all[a] who believe. For there is no difference; 23 for all have sinned and fall short of the glory of God, 24 being justified freely by His grace through the redemption that is in Christ Jesus, 25 whom God set forth *as* a propitiation by His blood, through faith, to demonstrate His righteousness, because in His forbearance God had passed over the sins that were previously committed, 26 to demonstrate at the present time His righteousness, that He might be just and the justifier of the one who has faith in Jesus.

27 Where *is* boasting then? It is excluded. By what law? Of works? No, but by the law of faith. 28 Therefore we conclude that a man is justified by faith apart from the deeds of the law. 29 Or *is* He the God of the Jews only? *Is* He not also the God of the Gentiles? Yes, of the Gentiles also, 30 since *there is* one God who will justify the circumcised by faith and the uncircumcised through faith. 31 Do we then make void the law through faith? Certainly not! On the contrary, we establish the law.

4 What then shall we say that Abraham our father has found according to the flesh?[a] 2 For if Abraham was justified by works, he has *something* to boast about, but not before God. 3 For what does the Scripture say? *"Abraham believed God, and it was accounted to him for righteousness."*[a] 4 Now to him who works, the wages are not counted as grace but as debt.

5 But to him who does not work but believes on Him who justifies the ungodly, his faith is accounted for righteousness, 6 just as David also describes the blessedness of the man to whom God imputes righteousness apart from works:

7 *"Blessed are those whose
lawless deeds are forgiven,*

3:4 [a]Psalm 51:4　　3:12 [a]Psalms 14:1–3; 53:1–3; Ecclesiastes 7:20　　3:13 [a]Psalm 5:9　　[b]Psalm 140:3
3:14 [a]Psalm 10:7　　3:17 [a]Isaiah 59:7, 8　　3:18 [a]Psalm 36:1　　3:22 [a]NU-Text omits *and on all.*
4:1 [a]Or Abraham our (fore)father according to the flesh has found?　　4:3 [a]Genesis 15:6

*Gospel
Pearls*

And whose sins are covered;
8 Blessed is the man to whom the
LORD shall not impute sin."[a]

9 Does this blessedness then *come*
upon the circumcised *only,* or upon
the uncircumcised also? For we say
that faith was accounted to Abraham
for righteousness. 10 How then was
it accounted? While he was circumcised, or uncircumcised? Not while
circumcised, but while uncircumcised. 11 And he received the sign of
circumcision, a seal of the righteousness of the faith which *he had while
still* uncircumcised, that he might be
the father of all those who believe,
though they are uncircumcised, that
righteousness might be imputed to
them also, 12 and the father of circumcision to those who not only *are*
of the circumcision, but who also
walk in the steps of the faith which
our father Abraham *had while still*
uncircumcised.

13 For the promise that he would
be the heir of the world *was* not to
Abraham or to his seed through the
law, but through the righteousness of
faith. 14 For if those who are of the
law *are* heirs, faith is made void and
the promise made of no effect,
15 because the law brings about
wrath; for where there is no law
there is no transgression.

16 Therefore *it is* of faith that *it
might be* according to grace, so that
the promise might be sure to all the
seed, not only to those who are of
the law, but also to those who are of
the faith of Abraham, who is the father of us all 17 (as it is written, *"I
have made you a father of many nations"*[a]) in the presence of Him
whom he believed—God, who gives
life to the dead and calls those things
which do not exist as though they
did; 18 who, contrary to hope, in hope
believed, so that he became the father of many nations, according to
what was spoken, *"So shall your descendants be."*[a] 19 And not being
weak in faith, he did not consider his
own body, already dead (since he
was about a hundred years old), and
the deadness of Sarah's womb.
20 He did not waver at the promise
of God through unbelief, but was
strengthened in faith, giving glory to
God, 21 and being fully convinced
that what He had promised He was
also able to perform. 22 And therefore *"it was accounted to him for
righteousness."*[a]

23 Now it was not written for his
sake alone that it was imputed to
him, 24 but also for us. It shall be imputed to us who believe in Him who
raised up Jesus our Lord from the
dead, 25 who was delivered up because of our offenses, and was raised
because of our justification.

5 Therefore, having been justified
by faith, we have[a] peace with God
through our Lord Jesus Christ,
2 through whom also we have access
by faith into this grace in which we
stand, and rejoice in hope of the
glory of God. 3 And not only *that,* but
we also glory in tribulations, knowing that tribulation produces perseverance; 4 and perseverance, character; and character, hope. 5 Now hope
does not disappoint, because the love
of God has been poured out in our
hearts by the Holy Spirit who was
given to us.

6 For when we were still without
strength, in due time Christ died for
the ungodly. 7 For scarcely for a righteous man will one die; yet perhaps
for a good man someone would even
dare to die. 8 But God demonstrates
His own love toward us, in that while
we were still sinners, Christ died for
us. 9 Much more then, having now
been justified by His blood, we shall
be saved from wrath through Him.
10 For if when we were enemies we
were reconciled to God through the
death of His Son, much more, having
been reconciled, we shall be saved
by His life. 11 And not only *that,* but
we also rejoice in God through our
Lord Jesus Christ, through whom we
have now received the reconciliation.

12 Therefore, just as through one
man sin entered the world, and death
through sin, and thus death spread
to all men, because all sinned—
13 (For until the law sin was in the
world, but sin is not imputed when
there is no law. 14 Nevertheless death
reigned from Adam to Moses, even
over those who had not sinned according to the likeness of the transgression of Adam, who is a type of

4:8 [a]Psalm 32:1, 2   4:17 [a]Genesis 17:5   4:18 [a]Genesis 15:5   4:22 [a]Genesis 15:6   5:1 [a]Another
ancient reading is, *let us have peace.*

*H*ave you ever seen a broken woman? If you ever encounter her, it will change the
whole scope of your ministry. She is a vase that has been cracked, leaking life,
losing love. It seems that relationships slip through her fingers like sand held too
tightly.

Him who was to come. 15 But the free gift *is* not like the offense. For if by the one man's offense many died, much more the grace of God and the gift by the grace of the one Man, Jesus Christ, abounded to many. 16 And the gift *is* not like *that which came* through the one who sinned. For the judgment *which came* from one *offense resulted* in condemnation, but the free gift *which came* from many offenses *resulted* in justification. 17 For if by the one man's offense death reigned through the one, much more those who receive abundance of grace and of the gift of righteousness will reign in life through the One, Jesus Christ.)

18 Therefore, as through one man's offense *judgment* came to all men, resulting in condemnation, even so through one Man's righteous act *the free gift came* to all men, resulting in justification of life. 19 For as by one man's disobedience many were made sinners, so also by one Man's obedience many will be made righteous.

20 Moreover the law entered that the offense might abound. But where sin abounded, grace abounded much more, 21 so that as sin reigned in death, even so grace might reign through righteousness to eternal life through Jesus Christ our Lord.

6 What shall we say then? Shall we continue in sin that grace may abound? 2 Certainly not! How shall we who died to sin live any longer in it? 3 Or do you not know that as many of us as were baptized into Christ Jesus were baptized into His death? 4 Therefore we were buried with Him through baptism into death, that just as Christ was raised from the dead by the glory of the Father, even so we also should walk in newness of life.

5 For if we have been united together in the likeness of His death, certainly we also shall be *in the likeness* of *His* resurrection, 6 knowing this, that our old man was crucified with *Him*, that the body of sin might be done away with, that we should no longer be slaves of sin. 7 For he who has died has been freed from sin. 8 Now if we died with Christ, we believe that we shall also live with Him, 9 knowing that Christ, having been raised from the dead, dies no more. Death no longer has dominion

over Him. 10 For *the death* that He died, He died to sin once for all; but *the life* that He lives, He lives to God. 11 Likewise you also, reckon yourselves to be dead indeed to sin, but alive to God in Christ Jesus our Lord.

12 Therefore do not let sin reign in your mortal body, that you should obey it in its lusts. 13 And do not present your members *as* instruments of unrighteousness to sin, but present yourselves to God as being alive from the dead, and your members *as* instruments of righteousness to God. 14 For sin shall not have dominion over you, for you are not under law but under grace.

15 What then? Shall we sin because we are not under law but under grace? Certainly not! 16 Do you not know that to whom you present yourselves slaves to obey, you are that one's slaves whom you obey, whether of sin *leading* to death, or of obedience *leading* to righteousness? 17 But God be thanked that *though* you were slaves of sin, yet you obeyed from the heart that form of doctrine to which you were delivered. 18 And having been set free from sin, you became slaves of righteousness. 19 I speak in human *terms* because of the weakness of your flesh. For just as you presented your members *as* slaves of uncleanness, and of lawlessness *leading* to *more* lawlessness, so now present your members *as* slaves *of* righteousness for holiness.

20 For when you were slaves of sin, you were free in regard to righteousness. 21 What fruit did you have then in the things of which you are now ashamed? For the end of those things *is* death. 22 But now having been set free from sin, and having become slaves of God, you have your fruit to holiness, and the end, everlasting life. 23 For the wages of sin *is* death, but the gift of God *is* eternal life in Christ Jesus our Lord.

7 Or do you not know, brethren (for I speak to those who know the law), that the law has dominion over a man as long as he lives? 2 For the woman who has a husband is bound by the law to *her* husband as long as he lives. But if the husband dies, she is released from the law of *her* husband. 3 So then if, while *her* husband lives, she marries another man, band lives, she marries another man,

The only man I know who is attracted to carrying others' pain is Jesus. All others give out, get tired and run out, if you put too much weight on them. No one is attracted to a problem except a problem-solver. Jesus is your Problem-Solver!

Liberated Woman

Romans 6:22

*J*esus was the only one who truly knew the woman in Luke 13. He touched her and healed her. He unleashed the potential that had been bound up for eighteen years. He can do the same for you.

You can accomplish anything once you have been called to Jesus. From that moment on, you become invincible. The enemy, however, would love to destroy you. He will try anything. He will use your own words against you; you may have been defeated by the power of what you've said. He will use your strength against you; you may have twisted your own back. The enemy has pitted you against you until you have believed you are crippled. Reverse his plan. If you had enough force to bend yourself over, you have enough force to straighten yourself back up.

The Lord told this woman the truth about herself. He told her that she was loosed and set free. He saw the truth in spite of what everyone else saw.

The religious critics didn't like what Jesus had done. His power revealed the powerlessness of their religion. They accused Him of breaking the law by performing a miracle on the Sabbath day. Jesus exposed their hypocrisy by using an everyday occurrence to illustrate His point. Since they all valued their livestock, which one of them would not loose his donkey on the Sabbath so it could get a drink? Surely this woman was more valuable than any animal. She could be loosed from her pain and sickness, no matter what day it was.

Pain can become too familiar. Ungodly relationships can become familiar. Change doesn't come easily. Habits are hard to break. It is often more comfortable to hang on to old habits than to let them go, because you're afraid of change.

When you begin to see yourself as Jesus sees you, you will muster the courage to break away. He is your defense. He will defend you before your critics. Now is the time for you to focus on receiving the miraculous and getting the water you could not reach before. He is loosing you to be refreshed. You haven't had any water in eighteen years, but now you are free to get a drink.

You may have been a beast of burden. You may have been somebody's pack horse. People have dumped on you. You've had to grit your teeth. But now Someone sees your true value, and He's liberating you to find the Living Water.

she will be called an adulteress; but if her husband dies, she is free from that law, so that she is no adulteress, though she has married another man. 4 Therefore, my brethren, you also have become dead to the law through the body of Christ, that you may be married to another—to Him who was raised from the dead, that we should bear fruit to God. 5 For when we were in the flesh, the sinful passions which were aroused by the law were at work in our members to bear fruit to death. 6 But now we have been delivered from the law, having died to what we were held by, so that we should serve in the newness of the Spirit and not *in* the oldness of the letter.

7 What shall we say then? *Is* the law sin? Certainly not! On the contrary, I would not have known sin except through the law. For I would not have known covetousness unless the law had said, *"You shall not covet."ᵃ* 8 But sin, taking opportunity by the commandment, produced in me all *manner of evil* desire. For apart from the law sin *was* dead. 9 I was alive once without the law, but when the commandment came, sin revived and I died. 10 And the commandment, which *was* to *bring* life, I found to *bring* death. 11 For sin, taking occasion by the commandment, deceived me, and by it killed *me.* 12 Therefore the law *is* holy, and the commandment holy and just and good.

13 Has then what is good become death to me? Certainly not! But sin, that it might appear sin, was producing death in me through what is good, so that sin through the commandment might become exceedingly sinful. 14 For we know that the law is spiritual, but I am carnal, sold under sin. 15 For what I am doing, I do not understand. For what I will to do, that I do not practice; but what I hate, that I do. 16 If, then, I do what I will not to do, I agree with the law that *it is* good. 17 But now, *it is* no longer I who do it, but sin that dwells in me. 18 For I know that in me (that is, in my flesh) nothing good dwells; for to will is present with me, but *how* to perform what is good I do not find. 19 For the good that I will *to do,* I do not do; but the evil I will not *to do,* that I practice. 20 Now if I do what I will not *to do,* it is no longer I who do it, but sin that dwells in me.

21 I find then a law, that evil is present with me, the one who wills to do good. 22 For I delight in the law of God according to the inward man. 23 But I see another law in my members, warring against the law of my mind, and bringing me into captivity to the law of sin which is in my members. 24 O wretched man that I am! Who will deliver me from this body of death? 25 I thank God—through Jesus Christ our Lord!

So then, with the mind I myself serve the law of God, but with the flesh the law of sin.

8 *There is* therefore now no condemnation to those who are in Christ Jesus,ᵃ who do not walk according to the flesh, but according to the Spirit. 2 For the law of the Spirit of life in Christ Jesus has made me free from the law of sin and death. 3 For what the law could not do in that it was weak through the flesh, God *did* by sending His own Son in the likeness of sinful flesh, on account of sin: He condemned sin in the flesh, 4 that the righteous requirement of the law might be fulfilled in us who do not walk according to the flesh but according to the Spirit. 5 For those who live according to the flesh set their minds on the things of the flesh, but those *who live* according to the Spirit, the things of the Spirit. 6 For to be carnally minded *is* death, but to be spiritually minded *is* life and peace. 7 Because the carnal mind *is* enmity against God; for it is not subject to the law of God, nor indeed can be. 8 So then, those who are in the flesh cannot please God.

9 But you are not in the flesh but in the Spirit, if indeed the Spirit of God dwells in you. Now if anyone does not have the Spirit of Christ, he is not His. 10 And if Christ *is* in you, the body *is* dead because of sin, but the Spirit *is* life because of righteousness. 11 But if the Spirit of Him who raised Jesus from the dead dwells in you, He who raised Christ from the dead will also give life to your mortal bodies through His Spirit who dwells in you.

12 Therefore, brethren, we are debtors—not to the flesh, to live accord-

7:7 ᵃExodus 20:17; Deuteronomy 5:21   8:1 ᵃNU-Text omits the rest of this verse.

Gospel Pearls

ing to the flesh. 13 For if you live according to the flesh you will die; but if by the Spirit you put to death the deeds of the body, you will live. 14 For as many as are led by the Spirit of God, these are sons of God. 15 For you did not receive the spirit of bondage again to fear, but you received the Spirit of adoption by whom we cry out, "Abba, Father." 16 The Spirit Himself bears witness with our spirit that we are children of God, 17 and if children, then heirs—heirs of God and joint heirs with Christ, if indeed we suffer with *Him,* that we may also be glorified together.

18 For I consider that the sufferings of this present time are not worthy *to be compared* with the glory which shall be revealed in us. 19 For the earnest expectation of the creation eagerly waits for the revealing of the sons of God. 20 For the creation was subjected to futility, not willingly, but because of Him who subjected *it* in hope; 21 because the creation itself also will be delivered from the bondage of corruption into the glorious liberty of the children of God. 22 For we know that the whole creation groans and labors with birth pangs together until now. 23 Not only *that,* but we also who have the firstfruits of the Spirit, even we ourselves groan within ourselves, eagerly waiting for the adoption, the redemption of our body. 24 For we were saved in this hope, but hope that is seen is not hope; for why does one still hope for what he sees? 25 But if we hope for what we do not see, we eagerly wait for *it* with perseverance.

26 Likewise the Spirit also helps in our weaknesses. For we do not know what we should pray for as we ought, but the Spirit Himself makes intercession for us[a] with groanings which cannot be uttered. 27 Now He who searches the hearts knows what the mind of the Spirit *is,* because He makes intercession for the saints according to *the will of* God.

28 And we know that all things work together for good to those who love God, to those who are the called according to *His* purpose. 29 For whom He foreknew, He also predestined *to be* conformed to the image of His Son, that He might be the

firstborn among many brethren. 30 Moreover whom He predestined, these He also called; whom He called, these He also justified; and whom He justified, these He also glorified.

31 What then shall we say to these things? If God *is* for us, who *can be* against us? 32 He who did not spare His own Son, but delivered Him up for us all, how shall He not with Him also freely give us all things? 33 Who shall bring a charge against God's elect? *It is* God who justifies. 34 Who *is* he who condemns? *It is* Christ who died, and furthermore is also risen, who is even at the right hand of God, who also makes intercession for us. 35 Who shall separate us from the love of Christ? *Shall* tribulation, or distress, or persecution, or famine, or nakedness, or peril, or sword? 36 As it is written:

> "For Your sake we are killed all
>   day long;
> We are accounted as sheep for
>   the slaughter."[a]

37 Yet in all these things we are more than conquerors through Him who loved us. 38 For I am persuaded that neither death nor life, nor angels nor principalities nor powers, nor things present nor things to come, 39 nor height nor depth, nor any other created thing, shall be able to separate us from the love of God which is in Christ Jesus our Lord.

9 I tell the truth in Christ, I am not lying, my conscience also bearing me witness in the Holy Spirit, 2 that I have great sorrow and continual grief in my heart. 3 For I could wish that I myself were accursed from Christ for my brethren, my countrymen[a] according to the flesh, 4 who are Israelites, to whom *pertain* the adoption, the glory, the covenants, the giving of the law, the service *of God,* and the promises; 5 of whom *are* the fathers and from whom, according to the flesh, Christ came, who is over all, *the* eternally blessed God. Amen.

6 But it is not that the word of God has taken no effect. For they *are* not all Israel who *are* of Israel, 7 nor *are they* all children because they are the

8:26 [a]NU-Text omits *for us.*   8:36 [a]Psalm 44:22   9:3 [a]Or *relatives*

Wouldn't it be great to enter into a relationship without being so thirsty for love that you cannot trust your own discernment? When you are not so thirsty for love, you can make better decisions.

Night Watch

Romans 8:26

It is late in the evening. The sufferer walks the floor with her passion, her goals, and her ambitions. Silence envelops the house like a warm blanket around cold feet. There is a gentle caress of tranquillity holding the house in an interlude of submissive bliss. The solace of the evening has crept onto the faces of the sleeping family, softly illuminated by the moon's quiet beams.

While others sleep, there are those who walk the floor as a mother with a suckling child. While others enter into the bliss of calmness and lie in the warmth of peaceful beds, there are those who have a conversation where there are no ears to hear. There are those who find no solace in ordinary things in the middle of the night. They have a restlessness, almost an anticipation, that something is about to happen.

Rising like smoke from a chimney, thoughts float and ascend into the conscious mind with all the grace of a ballerina. Who can log the moment when thought becomes prayer? Sometimes it changes in the middle of a sentence. These nightwalkers move across their rooms and stare blankly out of their windows into the dark. They see something beyond vision. They speak the inaudible to the Intangible, birthing a prayer—fleeting vaporous thoughts whose pattern defies words.

Real prayer was not made for human ears. If you have a problem that can be easily prayed through in public, then it is not a problem. When we earnestly pray, we are surprised at how inner feelings we didn't even know we had come to the surface. In that regard, prayer is a nausea of the mind. It brings up the unresolved past that swirls around and around inside us.

Who of us would want others to hear us as we release our inner groanings before the throne? Religion and its images do not relieve the heart of its brokenness. True prayer is a deep cry for divine assistance! Often what we convey around others is more like a plastic-covered superficial replica of what real prayer is all about. It is a dressed up, Sunday-go-to-meeting counterfeit that is impressive, but completely inconsequential!

Now understand, *nothing fuels prayer like need*. Neither the tranquil mood of a calming organ nor a dimly lit room with hallowed walls can promote the power of prayer like the aching of a heart that says, "I need Thee every hour." The presence of need will produce the power of prayer.

Prayer is the confession, "I do not have it all." It is the humbling experience of the most arrogant mind admitting, "There are still some things I cannot resolve."

The presence of prayer is, in itself, the birthplace of praise. Prayer is your acknowledging the sovereign authority of a God "who can!" You ask, "Can what?" God can do whatever He wants to do, whenever He wants to do it. What a subliminal solace to know the sovereignty of God!

seed of Abraham; but, *"In Isaac your seed shall be called."*[a] 8 That is, those who *are* the children of the flesh, these *are* not the children of God; but the children of the promise are counted as the seed. 9 For this *is* the word of promise: *"At this time I will come and Sarah shall have a son."*[a]

10 And not only *this,* but when Rebecca also had conceived by one man, *even* by our father Isaac 11 (for *the children* not yet being born, nor having done any good or evil, that the purpose of God according to election might stand, not of works but of Him who calls), 12 it was said to her, *"The older shall serve the younger."*[a] 13 As it is written, *"Jacob I have loved, but Esau I have hated."*[a]

14 What shall we say then? *Is there* unrighteousness with God? Certainly not! 15 For He says to Moses, *"I will have mercy on whomever I will have mercy, and I will have compassion on whomever I will have compassion."*[a] 16 So then *it is* not of him who wills, nor of him who runs, but of God who shows mercy. 17 For the Scripture says to the Pharaoh, *"For this very purpose I have raised you up, that I may show My power in you, and that My name may be declared in all the earth."*[a] 18 Therefore He has mercy on whom He wills, and whom He wills He hardens.

19 You will say to me then, "Why does He still find fault? For who has resisted His will?" 20 But indeed, O man, who are you to reply against God? Will the thing formed say to him who formed *it,* "Why have you made me like this?" 21 Does not the potter have power over the clay, from the same lump to make one vessel for honor and another for dishonor? 22 *What* if God, wanting to show His wrath and to make His power known, endured with much longsuffering the vessels of wrath prepared for destruction, 23 and that He might make known the riches of His glory on the vessels of mercy, which He had prepared beforehand for glory, 24 *even* us whom He called, not of the Jews only, but also of the Gentiles?

25 As He says also in Hosea:

> *"I will call them My people, who were not My people,*
> *And her beloved, who was not beloved."*[a]
> 26 *"And it shall come to pass in the place where it was said to them,*
> *'You are not My people,'*
> *There they shall be called sons of the living God."*[a]

27 Isaiah also cries out concerning Israel:[a]

> *"Though the number of the children of Israel be as the sand of the sea,*
> *The remnant will be saved.*
> 28 *For He will finish the work and cut it short in righteousness,*
> *Because the LORD will make a short work upon the earth."*[a]

29 And as Isaiah said before:

> *"Unless the LORD of Sabaoth*[a] *had left us a seed,*
> *We would have become like Sodom,*
> *And we would have been made like Gomorrah."*[b]

30 What shall we say then? That Gentiles, who did not pursue righteousness, have attained to righteousness, even the righteousness of faith; 31 but Israel, pursuing the law of righteousness, has not attained to the law of righteousness.[a] 32 Why? Because *they did* not *seek it* by faith, but as it were, by the works of the law.[a] For they stumbled at that stumbling stone. 33 As it is written:

> *"Behold, I lay in Zion a stumbling stone and rock of offense,*
> *And whoever believes on Him will not be put to shame."*[a]

10 Brethren, my heart's desire and prayer to God for Israel[a] is that they may be saved. 2 For I bear them

9:7 [a]Genesis 21:12   9:9 [a]Genesis 18:10, 14   9:12 [a]Genesis 25:23   9:13 [a]Malachi 1:2, 3   9:15 [a]Exodus 33:19   9:17 [a]Exodus 9:16   9:25 [a]Hosea 2:23   9:26 [a]Hosea 1:10   9:27 [a]Isaiah 10:22, 23   9:28 [a]NU-Text reads *For the Lord will finish the work and cut it short upon the earth.*   9:29 [a]Literally, in Hebrew, *Hosts*   [b]Isaiah 1:9   9:31 [a]NU-Text omits *of righteousness.*   9:32 [a]NU-Text reads *by works.*   9:33 [a]Isaiah 8:14; 28:16   10:1 [a]NU-Text reads *them.*

I have found that many of the broken people in our society are the harsh results of tragic secrets. They are the sad consequences of a generation that has gotten too busy to raise its children. These are the casualties of a generation who are left home alone.

witness that they have a zeal for God, but not according to knowledge. 3 For they being ignorant of God's righteousness, and seeking to establish their own righteousness, have not submitted to the righteousness of God. 4 For Christ *is* the end of the law for righteousness to everyone who believes.

5 For Moses writes about the righteousness which is of the law, *"The man who does those things shall live by them."*[a] 6 But the righteousness of faith speaks in this way, *"Do not say in your heart, 'Who will ascend into heaven?'"*[a] (that is, to bring Christ down *from above*) 7 or, *"'Who will descend into the abyss?'"*[a] (that is, to bring Christ up from the dead). 8 But what does it say? *"The word is near you, in your mouth and in your heart"*[a] (that is, the word of faith which we preach): 9 that if you confess with your mouth the Lord Jesus and believe in your heart that God has raised Him from the dead, you will be saved. 10 For with the heart one believes unto righteousness, and with the mouth confession is made unto salvation. 11 For the Scripture says, *"Whoever believes on Him will not be put to shame."*[a] 12 For there is no distinction between Jew and Greek, for the same Lord over all is rich to all who call upon Him. 13 For *"whoever calls on the name of the LORD shall be saved."*[a]

14 How then shall they call on Him in whom they have not believed? And how shall they believe in Him of whom they have not heard? And how shall they hear without a preacher? 15 And how shall they preach unless they are sent? As it is written:

> "How beautiful are the feet of
> those who preach the gospel
> of peace,[a]
> Who bring glad tidings of good
> things!"[b]

16 But they have not all obeyed the gospel. For Isaiah says, *"Lord, who has believed our report?"*[a] 17 So then faith *comes* by hearing, and hearing by the word of God.

18 But I say, have they not heard? Yes indeed:

> "Their sound has gone out to all
> the earth,
> And their words to the ends of
> the world."[a]

19 But I say, did Israel not know? First Moses says:

> "I will provoke you to jealousy
> by those who are not a
> nation,
> I will move you to anger by a
> foolish nation."[a]

20 But Isaiah is very bold and says:

> "I was found by those who did
> not seek Me;
> I was made manifest to those
> who did not ask for Me."[a]

21 But to Israel he says:

> "All day long I have stretched
> out My hands
> To a disobedient and contrary
> people."[a]

11 I say then, has God cast away His people? Certainly not! For I also am an Israelite, of the seed of Abraham, *of* the tribe of Benjamin. 2 God has not cast away His people whom He foreknew. Or do you not know what the Scripture says of Elijah, how he pleads with God against Israel, saying, 3 *"LORD, they have killed Your prophets and torn down Your altars, and I alone am left, and they seek my life"*? [a] 4 But what does the divine response say to him? *"I have reserved for Myself seven thousand men who have not bowed the knee to Baal."*[a] 5 Even so then, at this present time there is a remnant according to the election of grace. 6 And if by grace, then *it is* no longer of works; otherwise grace is no longer grace.[a] But if *it is* of works, it is no longer grace; otherwise work is no longer work.

7 What then? Israel has not obtained what it seeks; but the elect

10:5 aLeviticus 18:5   10:6 aDeuteronomy 30:12   10:7 aDeuteronomy 30:13   10:8 aDeuteronomy 30:14   10:11 aIsaiah 28:16   10:13 aJoel 2:32   10:15 aNU-Text omits *preach the gospel of peace, Who.*   bIsaiah 52:7; Nahum 1:15   10:16 aIsaiah 53:1   10:18 aPsalm 19:4   10:19 aDeuteronomy 32:21   10:20 aIsaiah 65:1   10:21 aIsaiah 65:2   11:3 a1 Kings 19:10, 14   11:4 a1 Kings 19:18   11:6 aNU-Text omits the rest of this verse.

We permit pain to hide behind money. We let it hide because we believe, in the United States, that success cures pain. We do not minister to the wealthy. We only minister to the homeless. We should help the poor. But do not stop with them.

The Lifeline

Romans 10:17

We need to renew our minds daily in God's presence, for I believe that *as we hear the thoughts of God, His thinking becomes increasingly contagious*. It is so important that we have a relationship with Him. His Word is like a lifeline thrown to a woman who would otherwise drown in the swirling whirlpool of her own thoughts. Peter was so addicted to hearing Jesus speak that when other men walked away, Peter said, "Lord, to whom shall we go? You have the words of eternal life" (John 6:68).

Peter recognized his need to keep hearing the Word of God. Many years before Peter, Job said that he esteemed God's Word more than his necessary food (see Job 23:12). As for me, God is my counselor. He talks with me about my deepest, darkest issues; He comforts the raging tide of my fears and inhibitions. Where would we be if He would wax silent and cease to guide us through this perilous maze of mental mania? His soft words turn away the wrath of our nagging memories. When He speaks to me, His words are symphonies of enlightenment falling on my heart like soft rain on a tin roof. They give rest and peace.

God's Word will accomplish what it is sent out to do. God says, "I won't stop in the middle of the job. I will not give up on you. I will keep hammering until you are balanced in your thinking and whole in your judgments." The greatest part is, no one would ever believe that you were initially in such a deplorable state! He covers you with His precious blood even while His Word works on you. The benefit is that you are simultaneously *privileged with privacy* and *challenged to change*.

In a world where people seem void of commitment and so easily become distracted, it is comforting to know that God won't give up on you. He will persevere and labor with you until His will is accomplished in your life. If anybody ought to praise the Lord, it ought to be those who have a deep appreciation for His unfailing love. It is to them He has spoken His word and changed their thoughts and directions.

Human thoughts are healed by the Word of God. We must, at all cost, maintain an appetite for preaching. Why? "So then faith [a change of mind] comes by hearing, and hearing by the word of God" (Romans 10:17). It amazes secular scholars to see the power of God's Word transforming dysfunctional members of our society into productive parts of our community.

God delivers us (or is in the process of delivering us) while we maintain a veil of secrecy to protect our reputations. The secular scholars would be appalled if they knew how many of us were in serious trouble when we came to our wit's end and submitted to the redemptive work of the Lord. *He* delivered us from the stress and the strain of our crises. His Word gives us the grace to seize the opportunity to escape and go on with our lives!

have obtained it, and the rest were blinded. 8 Just as it is written:

> "God has given them a spirit of
>   stupor,
> Eyes that they should not see
> And ears that they should not
>   hear,
> To this very day."[a]

9 And David says:

> "Let their table become a snare
>   and a trap,
> A stumbling block and a
>   recompense to them.
> 10 Let their eyes be darkened, so
>   that they do not see,
> And bow down their back
>   always."[a]

11 I say then, have they stumbled that they should fall? Certainly not! But through their fall, to provoke them to jealousy, salvation has come to the Gentiles. 12 Now if their fall is riches for the world, and their failure riches for the Gentiles, how much more their fullness!

13 For I speak to you Gentiles; inasmuch as I am an apostle to the Gentiles, I magnify my ministry, 14 if by any means I may provoke to jealousy those who are my flesh and save some of them. 15 For if their being cast away is the reconciling of the world, what will their acceptance be but life from the dead?

16 For if the firstfruit is holy, the lump is also holy; and if the root is holy, so are the branches. 17 And if some of the branches were broken off, and you, being a wild olive tree, were grafted in among them, and with them became a partaker of the root and fatness of the olive tree, 18 do not boast against the branches. But if you do boast, remember that you do not support the root, but the root supports you.

19 You will say then, "Branches were broken off that I might be grafted in." 20 Well said. Because of unbelief they were broken off, and you stand by faith. Do not be haughty, but fear. 21 For if God did not spare the natural branches, He may not spare you either.

22 Therefore consider the goodness and severity of God: on those who fell, severity; but toward you, goodness,[a] if you continue in His goodness. Otherwise you also will be cut off. 23 And they also, if they do not continue in unbelief, will be grafted in, for God is able to graft them in again. 24 For if you were cut out of the olive tree which is wild by nature, and were grafted contrary to nature into a cultivated olive tree, how much more will these, who are natural branches, be grafted into their own olive tree?

25 For I do not desire, brethren, that you should be ignorant of this mystery, lest you should be wise in your own opinion, that blindness in part has happened to Israel until the fullness of the Gentiles has come in. 26 And so all Israel will be saved,[a] as it is written:

> "The Deliverer will come out of
>   Zion,
> And He will turn away
>   ungodliness from Jacob;
> 27 For this is My covenant with
>   them,
> When I take away their sins."[a]

28 Concerning the gospel they are enemies for your sake, but concerning the election they are beloved for the sake of the fathers. 29 For the gifts and the calling of God are irrevocable. 30 For as you were once disobedient to God, yet have now obtained mercy through their disobedience, 31 even so these also have now been disobedient, that through the mercy shown you they also may obtain mercy. 32 For God has committed them all to disobedience, that He might have mercy on all.

33 Oh, the depth of the riches both of the wisdom and knowledge of God! How unsearchable are His judgments and His ways past finding out!

> 34 "For who has known the mind
>   of the LORD?
> Or who has become His
>   counselor?"[a]
> 35 "Or who has first given to Him
>   And it shall be repaid to him?"[a]

11:8 [a]Deuteronomy 29:4; Isaiah 29:10   11:10 [a]Psalm 69:22, 23   11:22 [a]NU-Text adds of God.
11:26 [a]Or delivered   11:27 [a]Isaiah 59:20, 21   11:34 [a]Isaiah 40:13; Jeremiah 23:18   11:35 [a]Job 41:11

---

*I*f you were raised to think that all you had to do to be happy was marry money or finish school and move to the east side of town, I have a news flash. Pain doesn't just confine itself to the projects. It is alive and well in Beverly Hills.

Change Your Mind

Romans 12:2

When I was a child, I was taught that it is a woman's prerogative to change her mind. If you have become accustomed to a thought or habit you should get rid of, stop what you are doing and change your mind. I know it isn't easy, but it is so necessary. It will help you immeasurably to speak to yourself and say, "I am better than this!" You don't have to change the other person's mind. You just need to change your own.

Be careful what you get used to. If you don't watch out, you can become accustomed to negative things, things the Father never wanted you to have, like pain or abuse. Some people have become used to poverty. Some have become used to fighting. They feel at home in pain. They cleave to it because they understand it.

Maybe you've made your life's goal to win someone you may never win. Or perhaps you've spent years trying to change the mind of someone who may not ever change. The real victory occurs when you change your own mind. The power of choice is a great power. Be careful that you do not give that power away. It is your right to choose how you want to live. Even God respects that right. He gives you that right.

Instead of asking an abuser if he has had enough, you must ask yourself if *you* have had enough. This is always the greater question. Others may not ever get their fill of abusing you. If you have judged within yourself that abuse is not God's will for you, why are you asking someone else to choose? The greater question still is, "Do you, as a daughter of the King, want to live in this circumstance?" God can change the other person's heart, and many women have survived to see that wonderful miracle happen. Others have not.

Don't you see that you don't have to spend your life on a quest to find someone to help you? When you have Christ, He is all the help you need. He has been there all the time. Never forget to turn to Him, and never let anyone have His place in your life. If you do, you will always be disappointed. He is the One who gives you the power to change. With Him on your side, you will always survive. You are empowered by the presence of God.

By His rich grace, you have the power to see a miracle. Don't forfeit it or forsake it. You can change your situation whenever you get ready.

36 For of Him and through Him and to Him *are* all things, to whom *be* glory forever. Amen.

12 I beseech you therefore, brethren, by the mercies of God, that you present your bodies a living sacrifice, holy, acceptable to God, *which is* your reasonable service. 2 And do not be conformed to this world, but be transformed by the renewing of your mind, that you may prove what *is* that good and acceptable and perfect will of God.

3 For I say, through the grace given to me, to everyone who is among you, not to think *of himself* more highly than he ought to think, but to think soberly, as God has dealt to each one a measure of faith. 4 For as we have many members in one body, but all the members do not have the same function, 5 so we, *being* many, are one body in Christ, and individually members of one another. 6 Having then gifts differing according to the grace that is given to us, *let us use them:* if prophecy, *let us prophesy* in proportion to our faith; 7 or ministry, *let us use it* in *our* ministering; he who teaches, in teaching; 8 he who exhorts, in exhortation; he who gives, with liberality; he who leads, with diligence; he who shows mercy, with cheerfulness.

9 *Let* love *be* without hypocrisy. Abhor what is evil. Cling to what is good. 10 *Be* kindly affectionate to one another with brotherly love, in honor giving preference to one another; 11 not lagging in diligence, fervent in spirit, serving the Lord; 12 rejoicing in hope, patient in tribulation, continuing steadfastly in prayer; 13 distributing to the needs of the saints, given to hospitality.

14 Bless those who persecute you; bless and do not curse. 15 Rejoice with those who rejoice, and weep with those who weep. 16 Be of the same mind toward one another. Do not set your mind on high things, but associate with the humble. Do not be wise in your own opinion.

17 Repay no one evil for evil. Have regard for good things in the sight of all men. 18 If it is possible, as much as depends on you, live peaceably with all men. 19 Beloved, do not avenge yourselves, but *rather* give place to wrath; for it is written, *"Vengeance is Mine, I will repay,"*[a] says the Lord. 20 Therefore

> *"If your enemy is hungry, feed him;*
> *If he is thirsty, give him a drink;*
> *For in so doing you will heap coals of fire on his head."*[a]

21 Do not be overcome by evil, but overcome evil with good.

13 Let every soul be subject to the governing authorities. For there is no authority except from God, and the authorities that exist are appointed by God. 2 Therefore whoever resists the authority resists the ordinance of God, and those who resist will bring judgment on themselves. 3 For rulers are not a terror to good works, but to evil. Do you want to be unafraid of the authority? Do what is good, and you will have praise from the same. 4 For he is God's minister to you for good. But if you do evil, be afraid; for he does not bear the sword in vain; for he is God's minister, an avenger to *execute* wrath on him who practices evil. 5 Therefore *you* must be subject, not only because of wrath but also for conscience' sake. 6 For because of this you also pay taxes, for they are God's ministers attending continually to this very thing. 7 Render therefore to all their due: taxes to whom taxes *are due,* customs to whom customs, fear to whom fear, honor to whom honor.

8 Owe no one anything except to love one another, for he who loves another has fulfilled the law. 9 For the commandments, *"You shall not commit adultery," "You shall not murder," "You shall not steal," "You shall not bear false witness,"*[a] *"You shall not covet,"*[b] and if *there is* any other commandment, are *all* summed up in this saying, namely, *"You shall love your neighbor as yourself."*[c] 10 Love does no harm to a neighbor; therefore love *is* the fulfillment of the law.

11 And *do* this, knowing the time,

12:19 *a*Deuteronomy 32:35   12:20 *a*Proverbs 25:21, 22   13:9 *a*NU-Text omits *"You shall not bear false witness." b*Exodus 20:13–15, 17; Deuteronomy 5:17–19, 21   *c*Leviticus 19:18

*L*ydia had traditions from her religion and finances from her business, but when she heard Paul's ministry she realized that she had everything to be a blessing except the blessing itself. She needed Christ to complete her faith.

Daughter of the Morning

Romans 13:11, 12

R evival is more than a long meeting in a crowded church. People can meet for weeks and not experience revival. Revival occurs when that which was dead is brought back to life. It is the waking up of the cast down. You can have a revival in your spiritual life, your personal life, your financial life, or whatever part of you the enemy has rocked to sleep. Just call on the Prince of Peace. His name is Jesus.

He is the Prince who ignites what life has extinguished. His kiss can awaken the sleeping beauty. One kiss from Him can restore every area of your life, both natural and supernatural. He is the One who can walk into a room and speak to the romance that the enemy is trying to kill. He says, "Damsel, arise!"

If you are in a catatonic state, it affects everyone with whom you are associated. They are waiting to see that there is another woman in you. She is neither timid nor afraid. She is not angry or insecure. She is whole. It is she who must be awakened. There is another woman in you, a gentler, softer, more loving, more giving woman who has been repressed by circumstances.

You need to be loosed and set free. There is another woman who has a key to your destiny. She is courageous and resilient, determined and assertive. The Word awakens that which should have been awake and puts to sleep some of the issues that should have retired a long time ago. This is the announcement that your soul has been waiting for. This is the announcement that releases you from the long night of repression and guilt. This is the announcement that the nation will feel. It is the blaring sound of an alarm clock shaking with the intensity of its convictions.

To all of you who almost overslept, to all of you who have shed tears and thought you'd missed your chance, to all of you who have ever felt that you were too deeply entrenched in sin, to the damsel whose hair has grayed and whose steps have faltered, to the college student whose willowy arms are full of books and whose heart is full of questions, to all lovely women, young and old, black and white, simply said, but firmly meant, *Talitha cumi!* "Arise, little darling." It is morning!

that now *it is* high time to awake out of sleep; for now our salvation *is* nearer than when we *first* believed. 12 The night is far spent, the day is at hand. Therefore let us cast off the works of darkness, and let us put on the armor of light. 13 Let us walk properly, as in the day, not in revelry and drunkenness, not in lewdness and lust, not in strife and envy. 14 But put on the Lord Jesus Christ, and make no provision for the flesh, to *fulfill its* lusts.

14 Receive one who is weak in the faith, *but* not to disputes over doubtful things. 2 For one believes he may eat all things, but he who is weak eats *only* vegetables. 3 Let not him who eats despise him who does not eat, and let not him who does not eat judge him who eats; for God has received him. 4 Who are you to judge another's servant? To his own master he stands or falls. Indeed, he will be made to stand, for God is able to make him stand.

5 One person esteems *one* day above another; another esteems every day *alike.* Let each be fully convinced in his own mind. 6 He who observes the day, observes *it* to the Lord;*a* and he who does not observe the day, to the Lord he does not observe *it.* He who eats, eats to the Lord, for he gives God thanks; and he who does not eat, to the Lord he does not eat, and gives God thanks. 7 For none of us lives to himself, and no one dies to himself. 8 For if we live, we live to the Lord; and if we die, we die to the Lord. Therefore, whether we live or die, we are the Lord's. 9 For to this end Christ died and rose*a* and lived again, that He might be Lord of both the dead and the living. 10 But why do you judge your brother? Or why do you show contempt for your brother? For we shall all stand before the judgment seat of Christ.*a* 11 For it is written:

"As I live, says the Lord,
Every knee shall bow to Me,
And every tongue shall confess
to God."*a*

12 So then each of us shall give account of himself to God. 13 Therefore let us not judge one another anymore, but rather resolve this, not to put a stumbling block or a cause to fall in *our* brother's way.

14 I know and am convinced by the Lord Jesus that *there is* nothing unclean of itself; but to him who considers anything to be unclean, to him *it is* unclean. 15 Yet if your brother is grieved because of *your* food, you are no longer walking in love. Do not destroy with your food the one for whom Christ died. 16 Therefore do not let your good be spoken of as evil; 17 for the kingdom of God is not eating and drinking, but righteousness and peace and joy in the Holy Spirit. 18 For he who serves Christ in these things*a is* acceptable to God and approved by men.

19 Therefore let us pursue the things *which make* for peace and the things by which one may edify another. 20 Do not destroy the work of God for the sake of food. All things indeed *are* pure, but *it is* evil for the man who eats with offense. 21 *It is* good neither to eat meat nor drink wine nor *do anything* by which your brother stumbles or is offended or is made weak.*a* 22 Do you have faith?*a* Have *it* to yourself before God. Happy *is* he who does not condemn himself in what he approves. 23 But he who doubts is condemned if he eats, because *he does* not *eat* from faith; for whatever *is* not from faith is sin.*a*

15 We then who are strong ought to bear with the scruples of the weak, and not to please ourselves. 2 Let each of us please *his* neighbor for *his* good, leading to edification. 3 For even Christ did not please Himself; but as it is written, *"The reproaches of those who reproached You fell on Me."a* 4 For whatever things were written before were written for our learning, that we through the patience and comfort of the Scriptures might have hope. 5 Now may the God of patience and comfort grant you to be like-minded toward one another, according to

---

14:6 *a*NU-Text omits the rest of this sentence.   14:9 *a*NU-Text omits *and rose.*   14:10 *a*NU-Text reads *of God.*   14:11 *a*Isaiah 45:23   14:18 *a*NU-Text reads *this.*   14:21 *a*NU-Text omits *or is offended or is made weak.*   14:22 *a*NU-Text reads *The faith which you have—have.*   14:23 *a*M-Text puts Romans 16:25–27 here.   15:3 *a*Psalm 69:9

Christ Jesus, 6 that you may with one mind *and* one mouth glorify the God and Father of our Lord Jesus Christ.

7 Therefore receive one another, just as Christ also received us,ᵃ to the glory of God. 8 Now I say that Jesus Christ has become a servant to the circumcision for the truth of God, to confirm the promises *made* to the fathers, 9 and that the Gentiles might glorify God for *His* mercy, as it is written:

"For this reason I will confess
    to You among the Gentiles,
    And sing to Your name."ᵃ

10 And again he says:

"Rejoice, O Gentiles, with His
    people!"ᵃ

11 And again:

"Praise the LORD, all you
    Gentiles!
    Laud Him, all you peoples!"ᵃ

12 And again, Isaiah says:

"There shall be a root of Jesse;
    And He who shall rise to reign
        over the Gentiles,
    In Him the Gentiles shall
        hope."ᵃ

13 Now may the God of hope fill you with all joy and peace in believing, that you may abound in hope by the power of the Holy Spirit.

14 Now I myself am confident concerning you, my brethren, that you also are full of goodness, filled with all knowledge, able also to admonish one another.ᵃ 15 Nevertheless, brethren, I have written more boldly to you on *some* points, as reminding you, because of the grace given to me by God, 16 that I might be a minister of Jesus Christ to the Gentiles, ministering the gospel of God, that the offering of the Gentiles might be acceptable, sanctified by the Holy Spirit. 17 Therefore I have reason to glory in Christ Jesus in the things *which pertain* to God. 18 For I will not dare to speak of any of those things which Christ has not accomplished

through me, in word and deed, to make the Gentiles obedient— 19 in mighty signs and wonders, by the power of the Spirit of God, so that from Jerusalem and round about to Illyricum I have fully preached the gospel of Christ. 20 And so I have made it my aim to preach the gospel, not where Christ was named, lest I should build on another man's foundation, 21 but as it is written:

"To whom He was not
    announced, they shall see;
    And those who have not heard
        shall understand."ᵃ

22 For this reason I also have been much hindered from coming to you. 23 But now no longer having a place in these parts, and having a great desire these many years to come to you, 24 whenever I journey to Spain, I shall come to you.ᵃ For I hope to see you on my journey, and to be helped on my way there by you, if first I may enjoy your *company* for a while. 25 But now I am going to Jerusalem to minister to the saints. 26 For it pleased those from Macedonia and Achaia to make a certain contribution for the poor among the saints who are in Jerusalem. 27 It pleased them indeed, and they are their debtors. For if the Gentiles have been partakers of their spiritual things, their duty is also to minister to them in material things. 28 Therefore, when I have performed this and have sealed to them this fruit, I shall go by way of you to Spain. 29 But I know that when I come to you, I shall come in the fullness of the blessing of the gospelᵃ of Christ.

30 Now I beg you, brethren, through the Lord Jesus Christ, and through the love of the Spirit, that you strive together with me in prayers to God for me, 31 that I may be delivered from those in Judea who do not believe, and that my service for Jerusalem may be acceptable to the saints, 32 that I may come to you with joy by the will of God, and may be refreshed together with you. 33 Now the God of peace *be* with you all. Amen.

15:7 ᵃNU-Text and M-Text read *you*.   15:9 ᵃ2 Samuel 22:50; Psalm 18:49   15:10 ᵃDeuteronomy 32:43   15:11 ᵃPsalm 117:1   15:12 ᵃIsaiah 11:10   15:14 ᵃM-Text reads *others*.   15:21 ᵃIsaiah 52:15   15:24 ᵃNU-Text omits *I shall come to you* (and joins *Spain* with the next sentence). 15:29 ᵃNU-Text omits *of the gospel*.

Anything that comes, any mood that is not in agreement with God's Word, is Satan trying to plug into the earthly realm through your life. He wants you to believe that you cannot change.

Bruise His Head

Romans 16:20

Why is it so important for a woman to give birth to what God has put within her? Because the woman holds the key to deliverance. It is the seed of woman that God appointed to rise up and bruise the heel of Satan. After Adam and Eve sinned, God cursed the serpent that had tempted Eve. He declared enmity between Satan and people from that moment on, saying that Eve's seed would bruise his head (see Genesis 3:15).

God trusted the woman with deliverance in her womb. The devil has had a special hatred for women ever since. He doesn't want you to bring forth what God has put inside you. Why? Because what you produce has the potential to bruise his head!

The devil has tried to take you out more than once. But God has let you go through everything you've been through so you might come to the place of crying out against the particular evils you've encountered. He knows that in the process of crying out, you will bruise the devil's head. God expects you to give birth to the treasure in you so you can turn the tables on the devil!

Were you abused as a child? God wants you to cry out against abuse. He has put something in you that can crush the head of Satan the abuser. Were you raped by a boyfriend who said he loved you, but only wanted to use you? God wants you to cry out against rape. He has put something in you that can crush the head of Satan the rapist. Were you pushed into a prison of failure as a child so that you became so afraid to take any risks that you have become a doormat for society? God wants you to cry out against fear and failure and the loss of self-respect. He has put something in you that can crush the head of Satan the intimidator.

I don't know how God intends for you to defeat the devil. It may be a new business, a new ministry, or a volunteer position you are to fill. I don't know what specifically is within you, but I know it is great. I don't know what opportunity He has given you, but I know it will be perfect for you. Use what God has put within you! The devil can't stand up against it.

Is there an idea you've had for years, but never pursued? Is there a dream you've held, but been afraid to voice? Is there a drive that wells up in you from time to time, but you've never put it into motion? It's time to bring forth the treasure that God has given you.

So many women have spent years, even decades, locked up in a prison of worry over what people will say about them. The result is that they have failed to give birth to those things they could have done, and would have done, and should have done. Today is your day! Bruise his head!

16 I commend to you Phoebe our sister, who is a servant of the church in Cenchrea, 2 that you may receive her in the Lord in a manner worthy of the saints, and assist her in whatever business she has need of you; for indeed she has been a helper of many and of myself also.

3 Greet Priscilla and Aquila, my fellow workers in Christ Jesus, 4 who risked their own necks for my life, to whom not only I give thanks, but also all the churches of the Gentiles. 5 Likewise *greet* the church that is in their house.

Greet my beloved Epaenetus, who is the firstfruits of Achaia*a* to Christ. 6 Greet Mary, who labored much for us. 7 Greet Andronicus and Junia, my countrymen and my fellow prisoners, who are of note among the apostles, who also were in Christ before me.

8 Greet Amplias, my beloved in the Lord. 9 Greet Urbanus, our fellow worker in Christ, and Stachys, my beloved. 10 Greet Apelles, approved in Christ. Greet those who are of the *household* of Aristobulus. 11 Greet Herodion, my countryman.*a* Greet those who are of the *household* of Narcissus who are in the Lord.

12 Greet Tryphena and Tryphosa, who have labored in the Lord. Greet the beloved Persis, who labored much in the Lord. 13 Greet Rufus, chosen in the Lord, and his mother and mine. 14 Greet Asyncritus, Phlegon, Hermas, Patrobas, Hermes, and the brethren who are with them. 15 Greet Philologus and Julia, Nereus and his sister, and Olympas, and all the saints who are with them.

16 Greet one another with a holy kiss. The*a* churches of Christ greet you.

17 Now I urge you, brethren, note those who cause divisions and offenses, contrary to the doctrine which you learned, and avoid them. 18 For those who are such do not serve our Lord Jesus*a* Christ, but their own belly, and by smooth words and flattering speech deceive the hearts of the simple. 19 For your obedience has become known to all. Therefore I am glad on your behalf; but I want you to be wise in what is good, and simple concerning evil. 20 And the God of peace will crush Satan under your feet shortly.

The grace of our Lord Jesus Christ *be* with you. Amen.

21 Timothy, my fellow worker, and Lucius, Jason, and Sosipater, my countrymen, greet you.

22 I, Tertius, who wrote *this* epistle, greet you in the Lord.

23 Gaius, my host and *the* host of the whole church, greets you. Erastus, the treasurer of the city, greets you, and Quartus, a brother. 24 The grace of our Lord Jesus Christ *be* with you all. Amen.*a*

25 Now to Him who is able to establish you according to my gospel and the preaching of Jesus Christ, according to the revelation of the mystery kept secret since the world began 26 but now has been made manifest, and by the prophetic Scriptures has been made known to all nations, according to the commandment of the everlasting God, for obedience to the faith— 27 to God, alone wise, *be* glory through Jesus Christ forever. Amen.*a*

16:5 *a*NU-Text reads *Asia.*   16:11 *a*Or *relative*   16:16 *a*NU-Text reads *All the churches.*
16:18 *a*NU-Text and M-Text omit *Jesus.*   16:24 *a*NU-Text omits this verse.   16:27 *a*M-Text puts Romans 16:25–27 after Romans 14:23.

The First Epistle of Paul the Apostle to the

CORINTHIANS

1 Paul, called *to be* an apostle of Jesus Christ through the will of God, and Sosthenes *our* brother,

2 To the church of God which is at Corinth, to those who are sanctified in Christ Jesus, called *to be* saints, with all who in every place call on

*L*ydia represents not only God's ability to heal the affluent but she also dispels the stereotype that Christianity is oppressive to women. To the contrary. It is the emancipator of intelligence and the liberator of excellence.

the name of Jesus Christ our Lord, both theirs and ours:

3 Grace to you and peace from God our Father and the Lord Jesus Christ. 4 I thank my God always concerning you for the grace of God which was given to you by Christ Jesus, 5 that you were enriched in everything by Him in all utterance and all knowledge, 6 even as the testimony of Christ was confirmed in you, 7 so that you come short in no gift, eagerly waiting for the revelation of our Lord Jesus Christ, 8 who will also confirm you to the end, *that you may be* blameless in the day of our Lord Jesus Christ. 9 God *is* faithful, by whom you were called into the fellowship of His Son, Jesus Christ our Lord.

10 Now I plead with you, brethren, by the name of our Lord Jesus Christ, that you all speak the same thing, and *that* there be no divisions among you, but *that* you be perfectly joined together in the same mind and in the same judgment. 11 For it has been declared to me concerning you, my brethren, by those of Chloe's *household*, that there are contentions among you. 12 Now I say this, that each of you says, "I am of Paul," or "I am of Apollos," or "I am of Cephas," or "I am of Christ." 13 Is Christ divided? Was Paul crucified for you? Or were you baptized in the name of Paul?

14 I thank God that I baptized none of you except Crispus and Gaius, 15 lest anyone should say that I had baptized in my own name. 16 Yes, I also baptized the household of Stephanas. Besides, I do not know whether I baptized any other. 17 For Christ did not send me to baptize, but to preach the gospel, not with wisdom of words, lest the cross of Christ should be made of no effect.

18 For the message of the cross is foolishness to those who are perishing, but to us who are being saved it is the power of God. 19 For it is written:

"I will destroy the wisdom of the wise,
And bring to nothing the

understanding of the prudent."ᵃ

20 Where *is* the wise? Where *is* the scribe? Where *is* the disputer of this age? Has not God made foolish the wisdom of this world? 21 For since, in the wisdom of God, the world through wisdom did not know God, it pleased God through the foolishness of the message preached to save those who believe. 22 For Jews request a sign, and Greeks seek after wisdom; 23 but we preach Christ crucified, to the Jews a stumbling block and to the Greeksᵃ foolishness, 24 but to those who are called, both Jews and Greeks, Christ the power of God and the wisdom of God. 25 Because the foolishness of God is wiser than men, and the weakness of God is stronger than men.

26 For you see your calling, brethren, that not many wise according to the flesh, not many mighty, not many noble, *are called.* 27 But God has chosen the foolish things of the world to put to shame the wise, and God has chosen the weak things of the world to put to shame the things which are mighty; 28 and the base things of the world and the things which are despised God has chosen, and the things which are not, to bring to nothing the things that are, 29 that no flesh should glory in His presence. 30 But of Him you are in Christ Jesus, who became for us wisdom from God—and righteousness and sanctification and redemption— 31 that, as it is written, *"He who glories, let him glory in the LORD."ᵃ*

2 And I, brethren, when I came to you, did not come with excellence of speech or of wisdom declaring to you the testimonyᵃ of God. 2 For I determined not to know anything among you except Jesus Christ and Him crucified. 3 I was with you in weakness, in fear, and in much trembling. 4 And my speech and my preaching *were* not with persuasive words of humanᵃ wisdom, but in demonstration of the Spirit and of power, 5 that your faith should not be in the wisdom of men but in the power of God.

1:19 ᵃIsaiah 29:14   1:23 ᵃNU-Text reads *Gentiles.* mystery.   2:4 ᵃNU-Text omits *human.*   1:31 ᵃJeremiah 9:24   2:1 ᵃNU-Text reads

6 However, we speak wisdom among those who are mature, yet not the wisdom of this age, nor of the rulers of this age, who are coming to nothing. 7 But we speak the wisdom of God in a mystery, the hidden *wisdom* which God ordained before the ages for our glory, 8 which none of the rulers of this age knew; for had they known, they would not have crucified the Lord of glory.

9 But as it is written:

"Eye has not seen, nor ear
    heard,
Nor have entered into the heart
    of man
The things which God has
    prepared for those who love
    Him."*a*

10 But God has revealed *them* to us through His Spirit. For the Spirit searches all things, yes, the deep things of God. 11 For what man knows the things of a man except the spirit of the man which is in him? Even so no one knows the things of God except the Spirit of God. 12 Now we have received, not the spirit of the world, but the Spirit who is from God, that we might know the things that have been freely given to us by God.

13 These things we also speak, not in words which man's wisdom teaches but which the Holy*a* Spirit teaches, comparing spiritual things with spiritual. 14 But the natural man does not receive the things of the Spirit of God, for they are foolishness to him; nor can he know *them*, because they are spiritually discerned. 15 But he who is spiritual judges all things, yet he himself is *rightly* judged by no one. 16 For *"who has known the mind of the LORD that he may instruct Him?"a* But we have the mind of Christ.

3 And I, brethren, could not speak to you as to spiritual *people* but as to carnal, as to babes in Christ. 2 I fed you with milk and not with solid food; for until now you were not able *to receive it*, and even now you are still not able; 3 for you are still carnal. For where *there are* envy, strife, and divisions among you, are you not carnal and behaving like

mere men? 4 For when one says, "I am of Paul," and another, "I *am* of Apollos," are you not carnal?

5 Who then is Paul, and who *is* Apollos, but ministers through whom you believed, as the Lord gave to each one? 6 I planted, Apollos watered, but God gave the increase. 7 So then neither he who plants is anything, nor he who waters, but God who gives the increase. 8 Now he who plants and he who waters are one, and each one will receive his own reward according to his own labor.

9 For we are God's fellow workers; you are God's field, *you are* God's building. 10 According to the grace of God which was given to me, as a wise master builder I have laid the foundation, and another builds on it. But let each one take heed how he builds on it. 11 For no other foundation can anyone lay than that which is laid, which is Jesus Christ. 12 Now if anyone builds on this foundation *with* gold, silver, precious stones, wood, hay, straw, 13 each one's work will become clear; for the Day will declare it, because it will be revealed by fire; and the fire will test each one's work, of what sort it is. 14 If anyone's work which he has built on *it* endures, he will receive a reward. 15 If anyone's work is burned, he will suffer loss; but he himself will be saved, yet so as through fire.

16 Do you not know that you are the temple of God and *that* the Spirit of God dwells in you? 17 If anyone defiles the temple of God, God will destroy him. For the temple of God is holy, which *temple* you are.

18 Let no one deceive himself. If anyone among you seems to be wise in this age, let him become a fool that he may become wise. 19 For the wisdom of this world is foolishness with God. For it is written, *"He catches the wise in their own craftiness";a* 20 and again, *"The LORD knows the thoughts of the wise, that they are futile."a* 21 Therefore let no one boast in men. For all things are yours: 22 whether Paul or Apollos or Cephas, or the world or life or death, or things present or things to come—

2:9 *a*Isaiah 64:4   2:13 *a*NU-Text omits *Holy*.   2:16 *a*Isaiah 40:13   3:19 *a*Job 5:13   3:20 *a*Psalm 94:11

God can reach from one extreme all the way to the other. There is no difference in the price of redemption required for the affluent and the impoverished.

Womb-Man

1 Corinthians 3:16, 17

When Adam saw Eve for the first time, he called her "womb-man." She would bring forth life.

What you need is a seed that you believe is enough to produce an embryo. You must be willing to feed that embryo for it to grow and become visible. When it will not be hidden any longer, it will break forth in life as answered prayer. No matter how hard others try to hold it back, it will break forth.

Put the truth in your spirit and feed it, nurture it, and allow it to grow. Quit telling yourself, "You're too fat, too old, too late, or too ignorant." Stop feeding yourself that garbage. It is unwise to speak against your own body. Women who speak against their bodies open the door for sickness and disease. Speak life to your body. Celebrate who you are. You are the image of God. The Scriptures remind us that we are "fearfully and wonderfully made" (Psalm 139:14). The truth will allow life to well up within you.

The devil wants you to live in yesterday. He's always telling you what you cannot do or be. His method is to bring up your past and turn your attention backward.

God is calling you to today. He wants to sow desire into the spirit of broken women. Until you have a vision to move ahead, you will always live in yesterday's struggles. The very fact that you have a desire is in itself an indication that better days are coming.

When I was a boy, we had a dog named Pup. Don't let the name fool you, though. He was a mean and ferocious animal. We had him chained in the back of the house to a four-by-four post. The chain was huge. We never imagined that he could possibly tear himself loose from that post. He would chase something just out of his reach, and the chain would snap him back.

One day Pup saw something he really wanted. It was just out of his reach. However, the motivation before him became more important than what was behind him. He pulled that chain to the limit. All at once, instead of drawing him back, the chain broke, and Pup was loose to pursue his prey.

That's what God will do for you. The thing that used to pull you back will snap, and you will be liberated because God has put greatness before you and within you. God is powerful enough to destroy the yoke of the enemy. He is strong enough to deliver what He has put in you, and set you free.

all are yours. 23 And you *are* Christ's, and Christ *is* God's.

4 Let a man so consider us, as servants of Christ and stewards of the mysteries of God. 2 Moreover it is required in stewards that one be found faithful. 3 But with me it is a very small thing that I should be judged by you or by a human court.*ᵃ* In fact, I do not even judge myself. 4 For I know of nothing against myself, yet I am not justified by this; but He who judges me is the Lord. 5 Therefore judge nothing before the time, until the Lord comes, who will both bring to light the hidden things of darkness and reveal the counsels of the hearts. Then each one's praise will come from God.

6 Now these things, brethren, I have figuratively transferred to myself and Apollos for your sakes, that you may learn in us not to think beyond what is written, that none of you may be puffed up on behalf of one against the other. 7 For who makes you differ *from another?* And what do you have that you did not receive? Now if you did indeed receive *it,* why do you boast as if you had not received *it?*

8 You are already full! You are already rich! You have reigned as kings without us—and indeed I could wish you did reign, that we also might reign with you! 9 For I think that God has displayed us, the apostles, last, as men condemned to death; for we have been made a spectacle to the world, both to angels and to men. 10 We *are* fools for Christ's sake, but you *are* wise in Christ! We *are* weak, but you *are* strong! You *are* distinguished, but we *are* dishonored! 11 To the present hour we both hunger and thirst, and we are poorly clothed, and beaten, and homeless. 12 And we labor, working with our own hands. Being reviled, we bless; being persecuted, we endure; 13 being defamed, we entreat. We have been made as the filth of the world, the offscouring of all things until now.

14 I do not write these things to shame you, but as my beloved children I warn you. 15 For though you might have ten thousand instructors in Christ, yet *you* do not *have* many fathers; for in Christ Jesus I have begotten you through the gospel. 16 Therefore I urge you, imitate me. 17 For this reason I have sent Timothy to you, who is my beloved and faithful son in the Lord, who will remind you of my ways in Christ, as I teach everywhere in every church.

18 Now some are puffed up, as though I were not coming to you. 19 But I will come to you shortly, if the Lord wills, and I will know, not the word of those who are puffed up, but the power. 20 For the kingdom of God *is* not in word but in power. 21 What do you want? Shall I come to you with a rod, or in love and a spirit of gentleness?

5 It is actually reported that *there is* sexual immorality among you, and such sexual immorality as is not even named*ᵃ* among the Gentiles— that a man has his father's wife! 2 And you are puffed up, and have not rather mourned, that he who has done this deed might be taken away from among you. 3 For I indeed, as absent in body but present in spirit, have already judged (as though I were present) him who has so done this deed. 4 In the name of our Lord Jesus Christ, when you are gathered together, along with my spirit, with the power of our Lord Jesus Christ, 5 deliver such a one to Satan for the destruction of the flesh, that his spirit may be saved in the day of the Lord Jesus.*ᵃ*

6 Your glorying *is* not good. Do you not know that a little leaven leavens the whole lump? 7 Therefore purge out the old leaven, that you may be a new lump, since you truly are unleavened. For indeed Christ, our Passover, was sacrificed for us.*ᵃ* 8 Therefore let us keep the feast, not with old leaven, nor with the leaven of malice and wickedness, but with the unleavened *bread* of sincerity and truth.

9 I wrote to you in my epistle not to keep company with sexually immoral people. 10 Yet *I* certainly *did* not *mean* with the sexually immoral people of this world, or with the covetous, or extortioners, or idolaters, since then you would need to go out

4:3 *ᵃ*Literally *day*   5:1 *ᵃ*NU-Text omits *named.*   5:5 *ᵃ*NU-Text omits *Jesus.*   5:7 *ᵃ*NU-Text omits *for us.*

*M*inistry gives purpose to pain. It widens the gulf between then and now and announces to the perpetrator, "I am healed." We never talk about things that are still gnawing at our guts.

of the world. 11 But now I have written to you not to keep company with anyone named a brother, who is sexually immoral, or covetous, or an idolater, or a reviler, or a drunkard, or an extortioner—not even to eat with such a person.

12 For what *have* I *to do* with judging those also who are outside? Do you not judge those who are inside? 13 But those who are outside God judges. Therefore *"put away from yourselves the evil person."*[a]

6 Dare any of you, having a matter against another, go to law before the unrighteous, and not before the saints? 2 Do you not know that the saints will judge the world? And if the world will be judged by you, are you unworthy to judge the smallest matters? 3 Do you not know that we shall judge angels? How much more, things that pertain to this life? 4 If then you have judgments concerning things pertaining to this life, do you appoint those who are least esteemed by the church to judge? 5 I say this to your shame. Is it so, that there is not a wise man among you, not even one, who will be able to judge between his brethren? 6 But brother goes to law against brother, and that before unbelievers!

7 Now therefore, it is already an utter failure for you that you go to law against one another. Why do you not rather accept wrong? Why do you not rather *let yourselves* be cheated? 8 No, you yourselves do wrong and cheat, and *you do* these things *to your* brethren! 9 Do you not know that the unrighteous will not inherit the kingdom of God? Do not be deceived. Neither fornicators, nor idolaters, nor adulterers, nor homosexuals,[a] nor sodomites, 10 nor thieves, nor covetous, nor drunkards, nor revilers, nor extortioners will inherit the kingdom of God. 11 And such were some of you. But you were washed, but you were sanctified, but you were justified in the name of the Lord Jesus and by the Spirit of our God.

12 All things are lawful for me, but all things are not helpful. All things are lawful for me, but I will not be brought under the power of any.

13 Foods for the stomach and the stomach for foods, but God will destroy both it and them. Now the body *is* not for sexual immorality but for the Lord, and the Lord for the body. 14 And God both raised up the Lord and will also raise us up by His power.

15 Do you not know that your bodies are members of Christ? Shall I then take the members of Christ and make *them* members of a harlot? Certainly not! 16 Or do you not know that he who is joined to a harlot is one body *with her*? For *"the two,"* He says, *"shall become one flesh."*[a] 17 But he who is joined to the Lord is one spirit *with Him*.

18 Flee sexual immorality. Every sin that a man does is outside the body, but he who commits sexual immorality sins against his own body. 19 Or do you not know that your body is the temple of the Holy Spirit *who is* in you, whom you have from God, and you are not your own? 20 For you were bought at a price; therefore glorify God in your body[a] and in your spirit, which are God's.

7 Now concerning the things of which you wrote to me:

It is good for a man not to touch a woman. 2 Nevertheless, because of sexual immorality, let each man have his own wife, and let each woman have her own husband. 3 Let the husband render to his wife the affection due her, and likewise also the wife to her husband. 4 The wife does not have authority over her own body, but the husband *does*. And likewise the husband does not have authority over his own body, but the wife *does*. 5 Do not deprive one another except with consent for a time, that you may give yourselves to fasting and prayer; and come together again so that Satan does not tempt you because of your lack of self-control. 6 But I say this as a concession, not as a commandment. 7 For I wish that all men were even as I myself. But each one has his own gift from God, one in this manner and another in that.

8 But I say to the unmarried and to the widows: It is good for them if they remain even as I am; 9 but if

5:13 *a*Deuteronomy 17:7; 19:19; 22:21, 24; 24:7   6:9 *a*That is, catamites   6:16 *a*Genesis 2:24
6:20 *a*NU-Text ends the verse at *body*.

they cannot exercise self-control, let them marry. For it is better to marry than to burn *with passion.*

10 Now to the married I command, *yet* not I but the Lord: A wife is not to depart from *her* husband. 11 But even if she does depart, let her remain unmarried or be reconciled to *her* husband. And a husband is not to divorce *his* wife.

12 But to the rest I, not the Lord, say: If any brother has a wife who does not believe, and she is willing to live with him, let him not divorce her. 13 And a woman who has a husband who does not believe, if he is willing to live with her, let her not divorce him. 14 For the unbelieving husband is sanctified by the wife, and the unbelieving wife is sanctified by the husband; otherwise your children would be unclean, but now they are holy. 15 But if the unbeliever departs, let him depart; a brother or a sister is not under bondage in such *cases.* But God has called us to peace. 16 For how do you know, O wife, whether you will save *your* husband? Or how do you know, O husband, whether you will save *your* wife?

17 But as God has distributed to each one, as the Lord has called each one, so let him walk. And so I ordain in all the churches. 18 Was anyone called while circumcised? Let him not become uncircumcised. Was anyone called while uncircumcised? Let him not be circumcised. 19 Circumcision is nothing and uncircumcision is nothing, but keeping the commandments of God *is what matters.* 20 Let each one remain in the same calling in which he was called. 21 Were you called *while* a slave? Do not be concerned about it; but if you can be made free, rather use *it.* 22 For he who is called in the Lord *while* a slave is the Lord's freedman. Likewise he who is called *while* free is Christ's slave. 23 You were bought at a price; do not become slaves of men. 24 Brethren, let each one remain with God in that *state* in which he was called.

25 Now concerning virgins: I have no commandment from the Lord; yet I give judgment as one whom the Lord in His mercy *has made* trustworthy. 26 I suppose therefore that this is good because of the present distress—that *it is* good for a man to remain as he is: 27 Are you bound to a wife? Do not seek to be loosed. Are you loosed from a wife? Do not seek a wife. 28 But even if you do marry, you have not sinned; and if a virgin marries, she has not sinned. Nevertheless such will have trouble in the flesh, but I would spare you.

29 But this I say, brethren, the time *is* short, so that from now on even those who have wives should be as though they had none, 30 those who weep as though they did not weep, those who rejoice as though they did not rejoice, those who buy as though they did not possess, 31 and those who use this world as not misusing it. For the form of this world is passing away.

32 But I want you to be without care. He who is unmarried cares for the things of the Lord—how he may please the Lord. 33 But he who is married cares about the things of the world—how he may please *his* wife. 34 There is^a a difference between a wife and a virgin. The unmarried woman cares about the things of the Lord, that she may be holy both in body and in spirit. But she who is married cares about the things of the world—how she may please *her* husband. 35 And this I say for your own profit, not that I may put a leash on you, but for what is proper, and that you may serve the Lord without distraction.

36 But if any man thinks he is behaving improperly toward his virgin, if she is past the flower of youth, and thus it must be, let him do what he wishes. He does not sin; let them marry. 37 Nevertheless he who stands steadfast in his heart, having no necessity, but has power over his own will, and has so determined in his heart that he will keep his virgin,^a does well. 38 So then he who gives her^a in marriage does well, but he who does not give *her* in marriage does better.

39 A wife is bound by law as long as her husband lives; but if her husband dies, she is at liberty to be married to whom she wishes, only in the Lord. 40 But she is happier if she remains as she is, according to my judgment—and I think I also have the Spirit of God.

7:34 ^aM-Text adds *also.*   7:37 ^aOr *virgin daughter*   7:38 ^aNU-Text reads *his own virgin.*

*Y*ou have the authority to release the past in the name of the Lord, and today you must move on to what lies ahead! It is knowing when the past is dead that liberates us to help others. The testimony is what you have left when the test is over.

Marriage Is a Ministry

1 Corinthians 7:34

Marriage is not about selfish fulfillment. Marriage is giving, not taking. When you marry someone, you marry everything he is and everything he has been. You inherit his strengths, his fears, and his weaknesses. It is impossible to pick the parts you want and leave the parts you don't. Marriage is a package deal.

God grants you the grace of ministering to your spouse, to the child in him. Be patient. You may not see immediate change. It takes time for even a small cut to heal. Healing is a process. God will give you the oil of compassion and the sweet wine of sincere love to pour into your husband's wounds.

The apostle Paul teaches the married woman not to be so spiritual that she is unavailable for the ministry of marriage (see 1 Corinthians 7:33, 34). God says, "I want the married woman to be concerned about pleasing her husband, and vice versa." Your ministry, as a wife, is not in the mall, not in the nursing home, but in your own home and to your own spouse. Your priorities need to start there and then spread to career, vocation, and other ministerial pursuits.

God builds the house of marriage, but you must do your own decorating. In effect, God says, "I release the married woman from the level of consecration I expect from the single woman so that she will be able to spend time decorating her relationship."

I can hear you saying, "But I need to spend time with the Lord." True. The Bible doesn't release you from your relationship with the Lord; it just sets some priorities. You are called to be committed to God and a companion to your spouse.

God has ascribed honor to marriage. Your bed is undefiled (see Hebrews 13:4). Decorate your relationship with holiness, but do not neglect each other in the name of being spiritual (see 1 Corinthians 7:3-5). For the godly woman who truly cares, God will anoint you to be successful in the ministry of marriage. Pursue God together!

8 Now concerning things offered to idols: We know that we all have knowledge. Knowledge puffs up, but love edifies. 2 And if anyone thinks that he knows anything, he knows nothing yet as he ought to know. 3 But if anyone loves God, this one is known by Him.

4 Therefore concerning the eating of things offered to idols, we know that an idol *is* nothing in the world, and that *there is* no other God but one. 5 For even if there are so-called gods, whether in heaven or on earth (as there are many gods and many lords), 6 yet for us *there is* one God, the Father, of whom *are* all things, and we for Him; and one Lord Jesus Christ, through whom *are* all things, and through whom we *live.*

7 However, *there is* not in everyone that knowledge; for some, with consciousness of the idol, until now eat it as a thing offered to an idol; and their conscience, being weak, is defiled. 8 But food does not commend us to God; for neither if we eat are we the better, nor if we do not eat are we the worse.

9 But beware lest somehow this liberty of yours become a stumbling block to those who are weak. 10 For if anyone sees you who have knowledge eating in an idol's temple, will not the conscience of him who is weak be emboldened to eat those things offered to idols? 11 And because of your knowledge shall the weak brother perish, for whom Christ died? 12 But when you thus sin against the brethren, and wound their weak conscience, you sin against Christ. 13 Therefore, if food makes my brother stumble, I will never again eat meat, lest I make my brother stumble.

9 Am I not an apostle? Am I not free? Have I not seen Jesus Christ our Lord? Are you not my work in the Lord? 2 If I am not an apostle to others, yet doubtless I am to you. For you are the seal of my apostleship in the Lord.

3 My defense to those who examine me is this: 4 Do we have no right to eat and drink? 5 Do we have no right to take along a believing wife, as *do* also the other apostles, the brothers

of the Lord, and Cephas? 6 Or *is it* only Barnabas and I *who* have no right to refrain from working? 7 Who ever goes to war at his own expense? Who plants a vineyard and does not eat of its fruit? Or who tends a flock and does not drink of the milk of the flock?

8 Do I say these things as a *mere* man? Or does not the law say the same also? 9 For it is written in the law of Moses, *"You shall not muzzle an ox while it treads out the grain."[a]* Is it oxen God is concerned about? 10 Or does He say *it* altogether for our sakes? For our sakes, no doubt, *this* is written, that he who plows should plow in hope, and he who threshes in hope should be partaker of his hope. 11 If we have sown spiritual things for you, *is it* a great thing if we reap your material things? 12 If others are partakers of *this* right over you, *are* we not even more?

Nevertheless we have not used this right, but endure all things lest we hinder the gospel of Christ. 13 Do you not know that those who minister the holy things eat *of the things* of the temple, and those who serve at the altar partake of *the offerings of* the altar? 14 Even so the Lord has commanded that those who preach the gospel should live from the gospel.

15 But I have used none of these things, nor have I written these things that it should be done so to me; for it *would be* better for me to die than that anyone should make my boasting void. 16 For if I preach the gospel, I have nothing to boast of, for necessity is laid upon me; yes, woe is me if I do not preach the gospel! 17 For if I do this willingly, I have a reward; but if against my will, I have been entrusted with a stewardship. 18 What is my reward then? That when I preach the gospel, I may present the gospel of Christ[a] without charge, that I may not abuse my authority in the gospel.

19 For though I am free from all *men,* I have made myself a servant to all, that I might win the more; 20 and to the Jews I became as a Jew, that I might win Jews; to those *who are* under the law, as under the law,[a]

9:9 [a]Deuteronomy 25:4   9:18 [a]NU-Text omits *of Christ.*   9:20 [a]NU-Text adds *though not being myself under the law.*

On the other side of your silence there is a fountain that quenches the wounded souls of broken humanity. You may not choose to share details. It is just important that you help others who are struggling with what you are surviving from.

that I might win those *who are* under the law; 21 to those *who are* without law, as without law (not being without law toward God,[a] but under law toward Christ[b]), that I might win those *who are* without law; 22 to the weak I became as[a] weak, that I might win the weak. I have become all things to all *men,* that I might by all means save some. 23 Now this I do for the gospel's sake, that I may be partaker of it with you.

24 Do you not know that those who run in a race all run, but one receives the prize? Run in such a way that you may obtain *it.* 25 And everyone who competes *for the prize* is temperate in all things. Now they *do it* to obtain a perishable crown, but we *for* an imperishable *crown.* 26 Therefore I run thus: not with uncertainty. Thus I fight: not as *one who* beats the air. 27 But I discipline my body and bring *it* into subjection, lest, when I have preached to others, I myself should become disqualified.

10 Moreover, brethren, I do not want you to be unaware that all our fathers were under the cloud, all passed through the sea, 2 all were baptized into Moses in the cloud and in the sea, 3 all ate the same spiritual food, 4 and all drank the same spiritual drink. For they drank of that spiritual Rock that followed them, and that Rock was Christ. 5 But with most of them God was not well pleased, for *their bodies* were scattered in the wilderness.

6 Now these things became our examples, to the intent that we should not lust after evil things as they also lusted. 7 And do not become idolaters as *were* some of them. As it is written, *"The people sat down to eat and drink, and rose up to play."*[a] 8 Nor let us commit sexual immorality, as some of them did, and in one day twenty-three thousand fell; 9 nor let us tempt Christ, as some of them also tempted, and were destroyed by serpents; 10 nor complain, as some of them also complained, and were destroyed by the destroyer. 11 Now all[a] these things happened to them as examples, and they were written for our admonition, upon

whom the ends of the ages have come.

12 Therefore let him who thinks he stands take heed lest he fall. 13 No temptation has overtaken you except such as is common to man; but God *is* faithful, who will not allow you to be tempted beyond what you are able, but with the temptation will also make the way of escape, that you may be able to bear *it.*

14 Therefore, my beloved, flee from idolatry. 15 I speak as to wise men; judge for yourselves what I say. 16 The cup of blessing which we bless, is it not the communion of the blood of Christ? The bread which we break, is it not the communion of the body of Christ? 17 For we, *though* many, are one bread *and* one body; for we all partake of that one bread.

18 Observe Israel after the flesh: Are not those who eat of the sacrifices partakers of the altar? 19 What am I saying then? That an idol is anything, or what is offered to idols is anything? 20 Rather, that the things which the Gentiles sacrifice they sacrifice to demons and not to God, and I do not want you to have fellowship with demons. 21 You cannot drink the cup of the Lord and the cup of demons; you cannot partake of the Lord's table and of the table of demons. 22 Or do we provoke the Lord to jealousy? Are we stronger than He?

23 All things are lawful for me,[a] but not all things are helpful; all things are lawful for me,[b] but not all things edify. 24 Let no one seek his own, but each one the other's *well-being.*

25 Eat whatever is sold in the meat market, asking no questions for conscience' sake; 26 for *"the earth is the Lord's, and all its fullness."*[a]

27 If any of those who do not believe invites you *to dinner,* and you desire to go, eat whatever is set before you, asking no question for conscience' sake. 28 But if anyone says to you, "This was offered to idols," do not eat it for the sake of the one who told you, and for conscience' sake;[a] for *"the earth is the Lord's, and all its fullness."*[b] 29 "Conscience," I say, not your own, but that of the other. For why is my lib-

---

9:21 [a]NU-Text reads *God's law.* [b]NU-Text reads *Christ's law.* 9:22 [a]NU-Text omits *as.*
10:7 [a]Exodus 32:6 10:11 [a]NU-Text omits *all.* 10:23 [a]NU-Text omits *for me.* [b]NU-Text omits *for me.* 10:26 [a]Psalm 24:1 10:28 [a]NU-Text omits the rest of this verse. [b]Psalm 24:1

erty judged by another *man's* conscience? 30 But if I partake with thanks, why am I evil spoken of for *the food* over which I give thanks?

31 Therefore, whether you eat or drink, or whatever you do, do all to the glory of God. 32 Give no offense, either to the Jews or to the Greeks or to the church of God, 33 just as I also please all *men* in all *things,* not seeking my own profit, but the *profit* of many, that they may be saved.

11 Imitate me, just as I also *imitate* Christ.

2 Now I praise you, brethren, that you remember me in all things and keep the traditions just as I delivered *them* to you. 3 But I want you to know that the head of every man is Christ, the head of woman *is* man, and the head of Christ *is* God. 4 Every man praying or prophesying, having *his* head covered, dishonors his head. 5 But every woman who prays or prophesies with *her* head uncovered dishonors her head, for that is one and the same as if her head were shaved. 6 For if a woman is not covered, let her also be shorn. But if it is shameful for a woman to be shorn or shaved, let her be covered. 7 For a man indeed ought not to cover *his* head, since he is the image and glory of God; but woman is the glory of man. 8 For man is not from woman, but woman from man. 9 Nor was man created for the woman, but woman for the man. 10 For this reason the woman ought to have *a symbol of* authority on *her* head, because of the angels. 11 Nevertheless, neither *is* man independent of woman, nor woman independent of man, in the Lord. 12 For as woman *came* from man, even so man also *comes* through woman; but all things are from God.

13 Judge among yourselves. Is it proper for a woman to pray to God with her head uncovered? 14 Does not even nature itself teach you that if a man has long hair, it is a dishonor to him? 15 But if a woman has long hair, it is a glory to her; for *her* hair is given to her*a* for a covering. 16 But if anyone seems to be conten-

tious, we have no such custom, nor *do* the churches of God.

17 Now in giving these instructions I do not praise *you,* since you come together not for the better but for the worse. 18 For first of all, when you come together as a church, I hear that there are divisions among you, and in part I believe it. 19 For there must also be factions among you, that those who are approved may be recognized among you. 20 Therefore when you come together in one place, it is not to eat the Lord's Supper. 21 For in eating, each one takes his own supper ahead of *others;* and one is hungry and another is drunk. 22 What! Do you not have houses to eat and drink in? Or do you despise the church of God and shame those who have nothing? What shall I say to you? Shall I praise you in this? I do not praise *you.*

23 For I received from the Lord that which I also delivered to you: that the Lord Jesus on the *same* night in which He was betrayed took bread; 24 and when He had given thanks, He broke *it* and said, "Take, eat;*a* this is My body which is broken*b* for you; do this in remembrance of Me." 25 In the same manner *He* also *took* the cup after supper, saying, "This cup is the new covenant in My blood. This do, as often as you drink *it,* in remembrance of Me."

26 For as often as you eat this bread and drink this cup, you proclaim the Lord's death till He comes.

27 Therefore whoever eats this bread or drinks *this* cup of the Lord in an unworthy manner will be guilty of the body and blood*a* of the Lord. 28 But let a man examine himself, and so let him eat of the bread and drink of the cup. 29 For he who eats and drinks in an unworthy manner*a* eats and drinks judgment to himself, not discerning the Lord's*b* body. 30 For this reason many *are* weak and sick among you, and many sleep. 31 For if we would judge ourselves, we would not be judged. 32 But when we are judged, we are chastened by the Lord, that we may not be condemned with the world.

33 Therefore, my brethren, when you come together to eat, wait for

---

11:15 *a*M-Text omits *to her.*   11:24 *a*NU-Text omits *Take, eat.*   *b*NU-Text omits *broken.*
11:27 *a*NU-Text and M-Text read *the blood.*   11:29 *a*NU-Text omits *in an unworthy manner.*
*b*NU-Text omits *Lord's.*

---

*M*any women also wrestle with infirmities in emotional traumas. These infirmities can be just as challenging as a physical affliction. Many times such emotional handicaps will spawn a series of unhealthy relationships.

one another. 34 But if anyone is hungry, let him eat at home, lest you come together for judgment. And the rest I will set in order when I come.

12 Now concerning spiritual *gifts,* brethren, I do not want you to be ignorant: 2 You know that*ᵃ* you were Gentiles, carried away to these dumb idols, however you were led. 3 Therefore I make known to you that no one speaking by the Spirit of God calls Jesus accursed, and no one can say that Jesus is Lord except by the Holy Spirit.

4 There are diversities of gifts, but the same Spirit. 5 There are differences of ministries, but the same Lord. 6 And there are diversities of activities, but it is the same God who works all in all. 7 But the manifestation of the Spirit is given to each one for the profit *of all:* 8 for to one is given the word of wisdom through the Spirit, to another the word of knowledge through the same Spirit, 9 to another faith by the same Spirit, to another gifts of healings by the same*ᵃ* Spirit, 10 to another the working of miracles, to another prophecy, to another discerning of spirits, to another *different* kinds of tongues, to another the interpretation of tongues. 11 But one and the same Spirit works all these things, distributing to each one individually as He wills.

12 For as the body is one and has many members, but all the members of that one body, being many, are one body, so also *is* Christ. 13 For by one Spirit we were all baptized into one body—whether Jews or Greeks, whether slaves or free—and have all been made to drink into*ᵃ* one Spirit. 14 For in fact the body is not one member but many.

15 If the foot should say, "Because I am not a hand, I am not of the body," is it therefore not of the body? 16 And if the ear should say, "Because I am not an eye, I am not of the body," is it therefore not of the body? 17 If the whole body *were* an eye, where *would be* the hearing? If the whole *were* hearing, where *would be* the smelling? 18 But now God has set the members, each one of them, in the body just as He pleased.

19 And if they *were* all one member, where *would* the body *be*?

20 But now indeed *there are* many members, yet one body. 21 And the eye cannot say to the hand, "I have no need of you"; nor again the head to the feet, "I have no need of you." 22 No, much rather, those members of the body which seem to be weaker are necessary. 23 And those *members* of the body which we think to be less honorable, on these we bestow greater honor; and our unpresentable *parts* have greater modesty, 24 but our presentable *parts* have no need. But God composed the body, having given greater honor to that *part* which lacks it, 25 that there should be no schism in the body, but *that* the members should have the same care for one another. 26 And if one member suffers, all the members suffer with *it;* or if one member is honored, all the members rejoice with *it.*

27 Now you are the body of Christ, and members individually. 28 And God has appointed these in the church: first apostles, second prophets, third teachers, after that miracles, then gifts of healings, helps, administrations, varieties of tongues. 29 *Are* all apostles? *Are* all prophets? *Are* all teachers? *Are* all workers of miracles? 30 Do all have gifts of healings? Do all speak with tongues? Do all interpret? 31 But earnestly desire the best*ᵃ* gifts. And yet I show you a more excellent way.

13 Though I speak with the tongues of men and of angels, but have not love, I have become sounding brass or a clanging cymbal. 2 And though I have *the gift of* prophecy, and understand all mysteries and all knowledge, and though I have all faith, so that I could remove mountains, but have not love, I am nothing. 3 And though I bestow all my goods to feed *the poor,* and though I give my body to be burned,*ᵃ* but have not love, it profits me nothing.

4 Love suffers long *and* is kind; love does not envy; love does not parade itself, is not puffed up; 5 does not behave rudely, does not seek its own, is not provoked, thinks

---

12:2 *ᵃ*NU-Text and M-Text add *when.*   12:9 *ᵃ*NU-Text reads *one.*   12:13 *ᵃ*NU-Text omits *into.*
12:31 *ᵃ*NU-Text reads *greater.*   13:3 *ᵃ*NU-Text reads *so I may boast.*

Gospel Pearls

no evil; 6 does not rejoice in iniquity, but rejoices in the truth; 7 bears all things, believes all things, hopes all things, endures all things.

8 Love never fails. But whether *there are* prophecies, they will fail; whether *there are* tongues, they will cease; whether *there is* knowledge, it will vanish away. 9 For we know in part and we prophesy in part. 10 But when that which is perfect has come, then that which is in part will be done away.

11 When I was a child, I spoke as a child, I understood as a child, I thought as a child; but when I became a man, I put away childish things. 12 For now we see in a mirror, dimly, but then face to face. Now I know in part, but then I shall know just as I also am known.

13 And now abide faith, hope, love, these three; but the greatest of these *is* love.

14 Pursue love, and desire spiritual *gifts,* but especially that you may prophesy. 2 For he who speaks in a tongue does not speak to men but to God, for no one understands *him;* however, in the spirit he speaks mysteries. 3 But he who prophesies speaks edification and exhortation and comfort to men. 4 He who speaks in a tongue edifies himself, but he who prophesies edifies the church. 5 I wish you all spoke with tongues, but even more that you prophesied; for*a* he who prophesies *is* greater than he who speaks with tongues, unless indeed he interprets, that the church may receive edification.

6 But now, brethren, if I come to you speaking with tongues, what shall I profit you unless I speak to you either by revelation, by knowledge, by prophesying, or by teaching? 7 Even things without life, whether flute or harp, when they make a sound, unless they make a distinction in the sounds, how will it be known what is piped or played? 8 For if the trumpet makes an uncertain sound, who will prepare for battle? 9 So likewise you, unless you utter by the tongue words easy to understand, how will it be known what is spoken? For you will be speaking into the air. 10 There are, it

may be, so many kinds of languages in the world, and none of them *is* without significance. 11 Therefore, if I do not know the meaning of the language, I shall be a foreigner to him who speaks, and he who speaks *will be* a foreigner to me. 12 Even so you, since you are zealous for spiritual *gifts, let it be* for the edification of the church *that* you seek to excel.

13 Therefore let him who speaks in a tongue pray that he may interpret. 14 For if I pray in a tongue, my spirit prays, but my understanding is unfruitful. 15 What is *the conclusion* then? I will pray with the spirit, and I will also pray with the understanding. I will sing with the spirit, and I will also sing with the understanding. 16 Otherwise, if you bless with the spirit, how will he who occupies the place of the uninformed say "Amen" at your giving of thanks, since he does not understand what you say? 17 For you indeed give thanks well, but the other is not edified.

18 I thank my God I speak with tongues more than you all; 19 yet in the church I would rather speak five words with my understanding, that I may teach others also, than ten thousand words in a tongue.

20 Brethren, do not be children in understanding; however, in malice be babes, but in understanding be mature.

21 In the law it is written:

> "With men of other tongues and
> other lips
> I will speak to this people;
> And yet, for all that, they will
> not hear Me,"*a*

says the Lord.

22 Therefore tongues are for a sign, not to those who believe but to unbelievers; but prophesying is not for unbelievers but for those who believe. 23 Therefore if the whole church comes together in one place, and all speak with tongues, and there come in *those who are* uninformed or unbelievers, will they not say that you are out of your mind? 24 But if all prophesy, and an unbeliever or an uninformed person comes in, he is convinced by all, he is convicted by all. 25 And thus*a* the secrets of his heart are revealed; and so, falling

14:5 *a*NU-Text reads *and.*   14:21 *a*Isaiah 28:11, 12   14:25 *a*NU-Text omits *And thus.*

Clinging to people is far different from loving them. Clinging is not so much a statement of your love for them as it is a crying out of your need for them. Like lust, it is intensely selfish. It is taking and not giving.

Let Go

When Eve awakened on the very first morning of her life on planet Earth, she was a wife! Can you imagine waking up beside a man when you've never even seen one? It was the ultimate "sink-or-swim" situation.

It's difficult to do something that's never been done before. Eve didn't have a mother or a grandmother or a female mentor to teach her the basics of marriage. How could she have possibly known how to be a good wife? She didn't even know what a good wife was! No wonder she went for a walk in the garden. She was probably stressed out!

Eve was created without a childhood, without having had the opportunity to be a little girl. She never had to grow up. She stepped right into being a wife and then a mother. She started out not as a baby girl, but as a woman. Now in Eve's case, that may have been all right. God had a plan, and He did things His way. But in our world today, there are lots of women who have found themselves being women before they had a chance to be girls. They haven't known what it means to be innocent, to feel free to trust, to receive genuine love.

Life can come at you too fast. Your childhood can be stripped away from you too soon. If the little girl in you has never had the opportunity to be a child, you've been robbed of something precious.

I can't believe what I see when I look around—mothers dressing up their little girls to look like women, with their hair all done up and earrings in their ears and lipstick on their mouths . . . even at four months of age! I tell my daughters, "Be little girls as long as you can."

Whether you had a girlhood or not, you must not use the past as an excuse. You must refuse to blame your past for your present or to let it ruin your future. You can never relive your past. You can't go back and make it different. You are not the person you were then and you are never going to be that person again. You can't go back into your mother's womb. You can't relive your first marriage. Your past is past. Accept that fact; dismiss what used to be; and move on. Let go of anything that is holding you back, slowing you down, or keeping you all bound up inside.

People often hold on to their past because there is something about the past that they think they still need. People who don't let go of things easily have little faith. They cling to things because they fear they will never be able to replace them. They won't give you their last twenty-dollar bill because they're afraid they won't ever have another one.

Don't you know that God has more for you? If you are trusting God for your future, then you have not seen your best days. There's more ahead of you than there is behind you. Let go and move on!

down on *his* face, he will worship God and report that God is truly among you.

26 How is it then, brethren? Whenever you come together, each of you has a psalm, has a teaching, has a tongue, has a revelation, has an interpretation. Let all things be done for edification. 27 If anyone speaks in a tongue, *let there be* two or at the most three, *each* in turn, and let one interpret. 28 But if there is no interpreter, let him keep silent in church, and let him speak to himself and to God. 29 Let two or three prophets speak, and let the others judge. 30 But if *anything* is revealed to another who sits by, let the first keep silent. 31 For you can all prophesy one by one, that all may learn and all may be encouraged. 32 And the spirits of the prophets are subject to the prophets. 33 For God is not *the author* of confusion but of peace, as in all the churches of the saints.

34 Let your*ᵃ* women keep silent in the churches, for they are not permitted to speak; but *they are* to be submissive, as the law also says. 35 And if they want to learn something, let them ask their own husbands at home; for it is shameful for women to speak in church.

36 Or did the word of God come *originally* from you? Or *was it* you only that it reached? 37 If anyone thinks himself to be a prophet or spiritual, let him acknowledge that the things which I write to you are the commandments of the Lord. 38 But if anyone is ignorant, let him be ignorant.*ᵃ*

39 Therefore, brethren, desire earnestly to prophesy, and do not forbid to speak with tongues. 40 Let all things be done decently and in order.

15 Moreover, brethren, I declare to you the gospel which I preached to you, which also you received and in which you stand, 2 by which also you are saved, if you hold fast that word which I preached to you—unless you believed in vain.

3 For I delivered to you first of all that which I also received: that Christ died for our sins according to the Scriptures, 4 and that He was buried, and that He rose again the third day according to the Scriptures, 5 and that He was seen by Cephas, then by the twelve. 6 After that He was seen by over five hundred brethren at once, of whom the greater part remain to the present, but some have fallen asleep. 7 After that He was seen by James, then by all the apostles. 8 Then last of all He was seen by me also, as by one born out of due time.

9 For I am the least of the apostles, who am not worthy to be called an apostle, because I persecuted the church of God. 10 But by the grace of God I am what I am, and His grace toward me was not in vain; but I labored more abundantly than they all, yet not I, but the grace of God *which was* with me. 11 Therefore, whether *it was* I or they, so we preach and so you believed.

12 Now if Christ is preached that He has been raised from the dead, how do some among you say that there is no resurrection of the dead? 13 But if there is no resurrection of the dead, then Christ is not risen. 14 And if Christ is not risen, then our preaching *is* empty and your faith *is* also empty. 15 Yes, and we are found false witnesses of God, because we have testified of God that He raised up Christ, whom He did not raise up—if in fact the dead do not rise. 16 For if *the* dead do not rise, then Christ is not risen. 17 And if Christ is not risen, your faith *is* futile; you are still in your sins! 18 Then also those who have fallen asleep in Christ have perished. 19 If in this life only we have hope in Christ, we are of all men the most pitiable.

20 But now Christ is risen from the dead, *and* has become the firstfruits of those who have fallen asleep. 21 For since by man *came* death, by Man also *came* the resurrection of the dead. 22 For as in Adam all die, even so in Christ all shall be made alive. 23 But each one in his own order: Christ the firstfruits, afterward those *who are* Christ's at His coming. 24 Then *comes* the end, when He delivers the kingdom to God the Father, when He puts an end to all rule and all authority and power. 25 For He must reign till He has put all enemies under His feet. 26 The last enemy

14:34 ᵃNU-Text omits *your.*   14:38 ᵃNU-Text reads *If anyone does not recognize this, he is not recognized.*

Soul Secrets
for the death
of someone you love

O Lord, I have lived this day to bury one I love. My gratitude is as full as my grief, and my peace is as deep as my pain—all because of You. I need You as never before. Shepherd my soul through these dry and heavy days.

You send us to this earth for a season, and then You receive us again unto Yourself. I understand this cycle, but I wasn't quite as ready to let go of this one as I thought I'd be. All my life I've known that someday this would happen, but the finality and reality of it are piercing. One thing I know, that death cannot kill love and human hands can't bury it. On this, my loved one's resurrection day, I give You praise for a life lived well.

that will be destroyed *is* death. 27 For *"He has put all things under His feet."ᵃ* But when He says "all things are put under Him," *it is* evident that He who put all things under Him is excepted. 28 Now when all things are made subject to Him, then the Son Himself will also be subject to Him who put all things under Him, that God may be all in all.

29 Otherwise, what will they do who are baptized for the dead, if the dead do not rise at all? Why then are they baptized for the dead? 30 And why do we stand in jeopardy every hour? 31 I affirm, by the boasting in you which I have in Christ Jesus our Lord, I die daily. 32 If, in the manner of men, I have fought with beasts at Ephesus, what advantage *is it* to me? If *the* dead do not rise, *"Let us eat and drink, for tomorrow we die!"ᵃ*

33 Do not be deceived: "Evil company corrupts good habits." 34 Awake to righteousness, and do not sin; for some do not have the knowledge of God. I speak *this* to your shame.

35 But someone will say, "How are the dead raised up? And with what body do they come?" 36 Foolish one, what you sow is not made alive unless it dies. 37 And what you sow, you do not sow that body that shall be, but mere grain—perhaps wheat or some other *grain.* 38 But God gives it a body as He pleases, and to each seed its own body.

39 All flesh *is* not the same flesh, but *there is* one *kind of* fleshᵃ of men, another flesh of animals, another of fish, *and* another of birds.

40 *There are* also celestial bodies and terrestrial bodies; but the glory of the celestial *is* one, and the *glory* of the terrestrial *is* another. 41 *There is* one glory of the sun, another glory of the moon, and another glory of the stars; for *one* star differs from *another* star in glory.

42 So also *is* the resurrection of the dead. *The body* is sown in corruption, it is raised in incorruption. 43 It is sown in dishonor, it is raised in glory. It is sown in weakness, it is raised in power. 44 It is sown a natural body,

it is raised a spiritual body. There is a natural body, and there is a spiritual body. 45 And so it is written, *"The first man Adam became a living being."ᵃ* The last Adam *became* a life-giving spirit.

46 However, the spiritual is not first, but the natural, and afterward the spiritual. 47 The first man *was* of the earth, *made* of dust; the second Man *is* the Lordᵃ from heaven. 48 As *was* the *man* of dust, so also *are* those *who are made* of dust; and as *is* the heavenly *Man,* so also *are* those *who are* heavenly. 49 And as we have borne the image of the *man* of dust, we shall also bearᵃ the image of the heavenly *Man.*

50 Now this I say, brethren, that flesh and blood cannot inherit the kingdom of God; nor does corruption inherit incorruption. 51 Behold, I tell you a mystery: We shall not all sleep, but we shall all be changed— 52 in a moment, in the twinkling of an eye, at the last trumpet. For the trumpet will sound, and the dead will be raised incorruptible, and we shall be changed. 53 For this corruptible must put on incorruption, and this mortal *must* put on immortality. 54 So when this corruptible has put on incorruption, and this mortal has put on immortality, then shall be brought to pass the saying that is written: *"Death is swallowed up in victory."ᵃ*

55 *"O Death, where is your sting?ᵃ O Hades, where is your victory?"ᵇ*

56 The sting of death *is* sin, and the strength of sin *is* the law. 57 But thanks *be* to God, who gives us the victory through our Lord Jesus Christ.

58 Therefore, my beloved brethren, be steadfast, immovable, always abounding in the work of the Lord, knowing that your labor is not in vain in the Lord.

16 Now concerning the collection for the saints, as I have given orders to the churches of Galatia, so you must do also: 2 On the first *day*

15:27 ᵃPsalm 8:6   15:32 ᵃIsaiah 22:13   15:39 ᵃNU-Text and M-Text omit *of flesh.*   15:45 ᵃGenesis 2:7   15:47 ᵃNU-Text omits *the Lord.*   15:49 ᵃM-Text reads *let us also bear.*   15:54 ᵃIsaiah 25:8   15:55 ᵃHosea 13:14   ᵇNU-Text reads *O Death, where is your victory? O Death, where is your sting?*

---

*I*t is impossible to inhale new air until you exhale the old. I pray that God would give the grace of releasing where you have been so you can receive what God has for you now. Exhale, then inhale; there is more for you.

of the week let each one of you lay something aside, storing up as he may prosper, that there be no collections when I come. 3 And when I come, whomever you approve by *your* letters I will send to bear your gift to Jerusalem. 4 But if it is fitting that I go also, they will go with me.

5 Now I will come to you when I pass through Macedonia (for I am passing through Macedonia). 6 And it may be that I will remain, or even spend the winter with you, that you may send me on my journey, wherever I go. 7 For I do not wish to see you now on the way; but I hope to stay a while with you, if the Lord permits.

8 But I will tarry in Ephesus until Pentecost. 9 For a great and effective door has opened to me, and *there are* many adversaries.

10 And if Timothy comes, see that he may be with you without fear; for he does the work of the Lord, as I also *do*. 11 Therefore let no one despise him. But send him on his journey in peace, that he may come to me; for I am waiting for him with the brethren.

12 Now concerning *our* brother Apollos, I strongly urged him to come to you with the brethren, but

he was quite unwilling to come at this time; however, he will come when he has a convenient time.

13 Watch, stand fast in the faith, be brave, be strong. 14 Let all *that* you *do* be done with love.

15 I urge you, brethren—you know the household of Stephanas, that it is the firstfruits of Achaia, and *that* they have devoted themselves to the ministry of the saints— 16 that you also submit to such, and to everyone who works and labors with *us*.

17 I am glad about the coming of Stephanas, Fortunatus, and Achaicus, for what was lacking on your part they supplied. 18 For they refreshed my spirit and yours. Therefore acknowledge such men.

19 The churches of Asia greet you. Aquila and Priscilla greet you heartily in the Lord, with the church that is in their house. 20 All the brethren greet you.

Greet one another with a holy kiss.

21 The salutation with my own hand—Paul's.

22 If anyone does not love the Lord Jesus Christ, let him be accursed.[a] O Lord, come![b]

23 The grace of our Lord Jesus Christ *be* with you. 24 My love *be* with you all in Christ Jesus. Amen.

16:22 [a]Greek *anathema*   [b]Aramaic *Maranatha*

The Second Epistle of Paul the Apostle to the

CORINTHIANS

1 Paul, an apostle of Jesus Christ by the will of God, and Timothy *our* brother,

To the church of God which is at Corinth, with all the saints who are in all Achaia:

2 Grace to you and peace from God our Father and the Lord Jesus Christ.

3 Blessed *be* the God and Father of our Lord Jesus Christ, the Father of mercies and God of all comfort, 4 who comforts us in all our tribula-

tion, that we may be able to comfort those who are in any trouble, with the comfort with which we ourselves are comforted by God. 5 For as the sufferings of Christ abound in us, so our consolation also abounds through Christ. 6 Now if we are afflicted, *it is* for your consolation and salvation, which is effective for enduring the same sufferings which we also suffer. Or if we are comforted, *it is* for your consolation and salvation. 7 And our hope for you *is* steadfast, because we know that as you are partakers of the sufferings, so

2 It takes a lot of courage even in church today to receive ministry in sensitive areas. The Lord, though, is the kind of physician who can pour on the healing oil.

God of All Comfort

2 Corinthians 1:3, 4

One of the many names for the Lord is *Comforter*. What a perfect description! His presence can make you comfortable in the most uncomfortable situations. He can unravel the dark shroud of grief and release the beautiful heart held captive within. He can pull you out of every situation you thought you'd be stuck in forever. He has the ability to bring peace to every trauma. In fact, this God of all comfort even catches your tears and collects your pain. He is with you when it hurts and He will *always* be there for you.

You will live and love and experience loss before your life is over. Losing some things will help you appreciate what you still have. It is the bitter taste of poverty that makes prosperity so sweet. How can you celebrate victory if you have never faced defeat?

You will live each day not knowing what the next one will bring. You will not always be able to see what tomorrow holds, but it is a great comfort to know that your God holds all your tomorrows. Tomorrow is not in the hands of your boss, your children, your husband or anyone else. It is not yours to manipulate or to dominate. Tomorrow is in the hands of the Lord. Whatever you do, take time to get to know Him, because you will need Him. Speak to the God of all comfort, for His comfort is sure for every tomorrow.

He will be there when husbands, friends, children, jobs, and money are all gone. He is there for all your dark places. Now take courage, my sister, and understand that "Weeping may endure for a night, but joy comes in the morning" (Psalm 30:5). Your night may seem long, but when it is over, there will always be morning.

No matter how dark the night, you've always lived to see the light. Understand that it is God's grace that has protected you and provided for you, brought you through and secured you, calmed you and comforted you. Times change and seasons change, but not God. He is always the same. He is the same God who brought you through your past and promises you your future. The God of all comfort has come. Be comforted now, my sister. You will arise.

also *you will partake* of the consolation.

8 For we do not want you to be ignorant, brethren, of our trouble which came to us in Asia: that we were burdened beyond measure, above strength, so that we despaired even of life. 9 Yes, we had the sentence of death in ourselves, that we should not trust in ourselves but in God who raises the dead, 10 who delivered us from so great a death, and does*ᵃ* deliver us; in whom we trust that He will still deliver us, 11 you also helping together in prayer for us, that thanks may be given by many persons on our*ᵃ* behalf for the gift *granted* to us through many.

12 For our boasting is this: the testimony of our conscience that we conducted ourselves in the world in simplicity and godly sincerity, not with fleshly wisdom but by the grace of God, and more abundantly toward you. 13 For we are not writing any other things to you than what you read or understand. Now I trust you will understand, even to the end 14 (as also you have understood us in part), that we are your boast as you also *are* ours, in the day of the Lord Jesus.

15 And in this confidence I intended to come to you before, that you might have a second benefit— 16 to pass by way of you to Macedonia, to come again from Macedonia to you, and be helped by you on my way to Judea. 17 Therefore, when I was planning this, did I do it lightly? Or the things I plan, do I plan according to the flesh, that with me there should be Yes, Yes, and No, No? 18 But as God *is* faithful, our word to you was not Yes and No. 19 For the Son of God, Jesus Christ, who was preached among you by us—by me, Silvanus, and Timothy—was not Yes and No, but in Him was Yes. 20 For all the promises of God in Him *are* Yes, and in Him Amen, to the glory of God through us. 21 Now He who establishes us with you in Christ and has anointed us *is* God, 22 who also has sealed us and given us the Spirit in our hearts as a guarantee.

23 Moreover I call God as witness against my soul, that to spare you I came no more to Corinth. 24 Not that we have dominion over your faith, but are fellow workers for your joy; for by faith you stand.

2 But I determined this within myself, that I would not come again to you in sorrow. 2 For if I make you sorrowful, then who is he who makes me glad but the one who is made sorrowful by me?

3 And I wrote this very thing to you, lest, when I came, I should have sorrow over those from whom I ought to have joy, having confidence in you all that my joy is *the joy* of you all. 4 For out of much affliction and anguish of heart I wrote to you, with many tears, not that you should be grieved, but that you might know the love which I have so abundantly for you.

5 But if anyone has caused grief, he has not grieved me, but all of you to some extent—not to be too severe. 6 This punishment which *was inflicted* by the majority *is* sufficient for such a man, 7 so that, on the contrary, you *ought* rather to forgive and comfort *him,* lest perhaps such a one be swallowed up with too much sorrow. 8 Therefore I urge you to reaffirm *your* love to him. 9 For to this end I also wrote, that I might put you to the test, whether you are obedient in all things. 10 Now whom you forgive anything, I also *forgive.* For if indeed I have forgiven anything, I have forgiven*ᵃ* that one for your sakes in the presence of Christ, 11 lest Satan should take advantage of us; for we are not ignorant of his devices.

12 Furthermore, when I came to Troas to *preach* Christ's gospel, and a door was opened to me by the Lord, 13 I had no rest in my spirit, because I did not find Titus my brother; but taking my leave of them, I departed for Macedonia.

14 Now thanks *be* to God who always leads us in triumph in Christ, and through us diffuses the fragrance of His knowledge in every place. 15 For we are to God the fragrance of Christ among those who are being saved and among those who are perishing. 16 To the one *we are* the aroma of death *leading* to death, and to the other the aroma of life *leading*

1:10 *ᵃ*NU-Text reads *shall.*   1:11 *ᵃ*M-Text reads *your behalf.*   2:10 *ᵃ*NU-Text reads *indeed, what I have forgiven, if I have forgiven anything, I did it for your sakes.*

Gospel Pearls

to life. And who *is* sufficient for these things? 17 For we are not, as so many,*ᵃ* peddling the word of God; but as of sincerity, but as from God, we speak in the sight of God in Christ.

3 Do we begin again to commend ourselves? Or do we need, as some *others*, epistles of commendation to you or *letters* of commendation from you? 2 You are our epistle written in our hearts, known and read by all men; 3 clearly *you are* an epistle of Christ, ministered by us, written not with ink but by the Spirit of the living God, not on tablets of stone but on tablets of flesh, *that is,* of the heart.

4 And we have such trust through Christ toward God. 5 Not that we are sufficient of ourselves to think of anything as *being* from ourselves, but our sufficiency *is* from God, 6 who also made us sufficient as ministers of the new covenant, not of the letter but of the Spirit;*ᵃ* for the letter kills, but the Spirit gives life.

7 But if the ministry of death, written *and* engraved on stones, was glorious, so that the children of Israel could not look steadily at the face of Moses because of the glory of his countenance, which *glory* was passing away, 8 how will the ministry of the Spirit not be more glorious? 9 For if the ministry of condemnation *had* glory, the ministry of righteousness exceeds much more in glory. 10 For even what was made glorious had no glory in this respect, because of the glory that excels. 11 For if what is passing away *was* glorious, what remains *is* much more glorious.

12 Therefore, since we have such hope, we use great boldness of speech— 13 unlike Moses, *who* put a veil over his face so that the children of Israel could not look steadily at the end of what was passing away. 14 But their minds were blinded. For until this day the same veil remains unlifted in the reading of the Old Testament, because the *veil* is taken away in Christ. 15 But even to this day, when Moses is read, a veil lies on their heart. 16 Nevertheless when one turns to the Lord, the veil is taken away. 17 Now the Lord is the Spirit; and where the Spirit of the Lord *is*, there *is* liberty. 18 But we all,

with unveiled face, beholding as in a mirror the glory of the Lord, are being transformed into the same image from glory to glory, just as by the Spirit of the Lord.

4 Therefore, since we have this ministry, as we have received mercy, we do not lose heart. 2 But we have renounced the hidden things of shame, not walking in craftiness nor handling the word of God deceitfully, but by manifestation of the truth commending ourselves to every man's conscience in the sight of God. 3 But even if our gospel is veiled, it is veiled to those who are perishing, 4 whose minds the god of this age has blinded, who do not believe, lest the light of the gospel of the glory of Christ, who is the image of God, should shine on them. 5 For we do not preach ourselves, but Christ Jesus the Lord, and ourselves your bondservants for Jesus' sake. 6 For it is the God who commanded light to shine out of darkness, who has shone in our hearts to *give* the light of the knowledge of the glory of God in the face of Jesus Christ.

7 But we have this treasure in earthen vessels, that the excellence of the power may be of God and not of us. 8 *We are* hard pressed on every side, yet not crushed; *we are* perplexed, but not in despair; 9 persecuted, but not forsaken; struck down, but not destroyed— 10 always carrying about in the body the dying of the Lord Jesus, that the life of Jesus also may be manifested in our body. 11 For we who live are always delivered to death for Jesus' sake, that the life of Jesus also may be manifested in our mortal flesh. 12 So then death is working in us, but life in you.

13 And since we have the same spirit of faith, according to what is written, *"I believed and therefore I spoke,"ᵃ* we also believe and therefore speak, 14 knowing that He who raised up the Lord Jesus will also raise us up with Jesus, and will present *us* with you. 15 For all things *are* for your sakes, that grace, having spread through the many, may cause thanksgiving to abound to the glory of God.

16 Therefore we do not lose heart.

2:17 *ᵃ*M-Text reads *the rest.*   3:6 *ᵃ*Or *spirit*   4:13 *ᵃ*Psalm 116:10

I am telling you that when your desire for the future peaks, you can break out of prison. I challenge you to sit down and write thirty things you would like to do with your life and scratch them off, one by one, as you accomplish them.

Treasure Within You

2 Corinthians 4:7

Something inside of you has been locked up. God wants to unlock it. He knows what gifts and abilities and dreams He has put in you. He knows how to touch them and how to bring them out.

When you get beyond your low self-esteem and stop comparing yourself to other people, and you begin to accept what God has given you, then you are in a position for Him to bring to birth all He has created you to be.

There are things in you that have been overlooked by you, ignored by others, perhaps even ridiculed by some, but God calls those traits His treasure. And He wants to bring it forth!

Every woman alive is a treasure chest. Each one holds something God intends for her to use in fulfilling His purpose for her life. And in the process, she will bring Him glory. My sister, find out what treasure God has hidden in you, because the devil is going to fight you for it. He knows the treasure is there and he wants it for his purposes. He wants it bad.

So many women today are fighting the devil and don't even know why. It's because they haven't discovered the treasure that lies within them. The devil knows it's there. God knows it's there. So the fight is on.

Your treasure is powerful in God's service, and the devil knows it. What he doesn't know is that your treasure is also a weapon you can use to defeat him in your life. The devil will do anything he can to sabotage your self-esteem. He doesn't want you developing your assets because he doesn't want you to give birth to what God has put within you. Being loosed means that your treasure has been released. It means that the gift that has been bound within you has been issued an emancipation proclamation. It means that you are free to blossom and bring forth fruit! When the treasure within you is loosed, you are at liberty to deliver God's purpose in your life.

Now giving birth may require intense effort on your part. You may have to push like a woman in labor. You may have to fill your cheeks with air and push with all your might. So get ready, daughter of the living God, and soon you'll hold a treasure in your arms.

Even though our outward man is perishing, yet the inward *man* is being renewed day by day. 17 For our light affliction, which is but for a moment, is working for us a far more exceeding *and* eternal weight of glory, 18 while we do not look at the things which are seen, but at the things which are not seen. For the things which are seen *are* temporary, but the things which are not seen *are* eternal.

5 For we know that if our earthly house, *this* tent, is destroyed, we have a building from God, a house not made with hands, eternal in the heavens. 2 For in this we groan, earnestly desiring to be clothed with our habitation which is from heaven, 3 if indeed, having been clothed, we shall not be found naked. 4 For we who are in *this* tent groan, being burdened, not because we want to be unclothed, but further clothed, that mortality may be swallowed up by life. 5 Now He who has prepared us for this very thing *is* God, who also has given us the Spirit as a guarantee.

6 So *we are* always confident, knowing that while we are at home in the body we are absent from the Lord. 7 For we walk by faith, not by sight. 8 We are confident, yes, well pleased rather to be absent from the body and to be present with the Lord. 9 Therefore we make it our aim, whether present or absent, to be well pleasing to Him. 10 For we must all appear before the judgment seat of Christ, that each one may receive the things *done* in the body, according to what he has done, whether good or bad. 11 Knowing, therefore, the terror of the Lord, we persuade men; but we are well known to God, and I also trust are well known in your consciences.

12 For we do not commend ourselves again to you, but give you opportunity to boast on our behalf, that you may have *an answer* for those who boast in appearance and not in heart. 13 For if we are beside ourselves, *it is* for God; or if we are of sound mind, *it is* for you. 14 For the love of Christ compels us, because we judge thus: that if One died for all, then all died; 15 and He died for all, that those who live should live no longer for themselves, but for Him who died for them and rose again.

16 Therefore, from now on, we regard no one according to the flesh. Even though we have known Christ according to the flesh, yet now we know *Him thus* no longer. 17 Therefore, if anyone *is* in Christ, *he is* a new creation; old things have passed away; behold, all things have become new. 18 Now all things *are* of God, who has reconciled us to Himself through Jesus Christ, and has given us the ministry of reconciliation, 19 that is, that God was in Christ reconciling the world to Himself, not imputing their trespasses to them, and has committed to us the word of reconciliation.

20 Now then, we are ambassadors for Christ, as though God were pleading through us: we implore *you* on Christ's behalf, be reconciled to God. 21 For He made Him who knew no sin *to be* sin for us, that we might become the righteousness of God in Him.

6 We then, *as* workers together with *Him* also plead with *you* not to receive the grace of God in vain. 2 For He says:

> "In an acceptable time I have heard you,
> And in the day of salvation I have helped you."[a]

Behold, now *is* the accepted time; behold, now *is* the day of salvation.

3 We give no offense in anything, that our ministry may not be blamed. 4 But in all *things* we commend ourselves as ministers of God: in much patience, in tribulations, in needs, in distresses, 5 in stripes, in imprisonments, in tumults, in labors, in sleeplessness, in fastings; 6 by purity, by knowledge, by longsuffering, by kindness, by the Holy Spirit, by sincere love, 7 by the word of truth, by the power of God, by the armor of righteousness on the right hand and on the left, 8 by honor and dishonor, by evil report and good report; as deceivers, and *yet* true; 9 as unknown, and *yet* well known; as dying, and behold we live; as chastened, and *yet* not killed; 10 as sorrowful, yet always

6:2 [a]Isaiah 49:8

In the name of our High Priest, Jesus Christ, I curse the infirmity that has bowed the backs of God's women. I pray that the Holy Spirit would roll you into the recovery room where you can fully realize that the trauma is over.

Celebrate Now!

2 Corinthians 5:17

*H*ave you allowed God to stand in the bow of your ship and speak peace to the thing that once terrified you? You can only benefit from issues that have been resolved. If you keep your pain active, your power is never activated because your past remains unresolved. If you want to see God's power come from the pain of an experience, you must allow the process of healing to take you far beyond bitterness into a resolution that releases you and sets you free.

God's healing sets you free to taste life again, free to trust again, and free to live without the restrictive force of threatening fears. Someone may say, "I don't want to trust again." That is only because that person is not healed. To never trust again is to live on the pinnacle of a tower—safe from life's threatening grasp, but so detached from life that you soon lose consciousness of people, places, dates, and events. Keeping your distance locks you into a time warp. When you always talk about the past, you do it because *you stopped living years ago*. Listen to your speech. You discuss the past as if it were the present because the past has stolen the present right out of your hand! In the name of Jesus, get it back!

Celebration is in order. Yes, it is time to celebrate—regardless of whether you've lost a marriage, a partnership, or a personal friend. Celebration is in order because you were split from your Siamese twin and you are not dead. You are still alive! (Or at least you will be the moment you *decide* to be.) Are you ready to live, or do you still need to subject all your friends to a history class? Will you continue your incessant raging and blubbering about that which no one can change—the past?

Step into the present. Your friends will celebrate—and so will your own mind! It has been locked down, tightly tied to dead issues, and it wants to be creative and inspired again! Could it be possible that there are still those around you who want to be a part of your life, now that you have chosen to stop dwelling among the dead and in the tombs?

Perhaps I have been hard on you, but I am only trying to jump-start your heart and put you back into the presence of a real experience, far from the dark valley of regret and remorse. Celebration is available to you. Celebrate now!

rejoicing; as poor, yet making many rich; as having nothing, and *yet* possessing all things.

11 O Corinthians! We have spoken openly to you, our heart is wide open. 12 You are not restricted by us, but you are restricted by your *own* affections. 13 Now in return for the same (I speak as to children), you also be open.

14 Do not be unequally yoked together with unbelievers. For what fellowship has righteousness with lawlessness? And what communion has light with darkness? 15 And what accord has Christ with Belial? Or what part has a believer with an unbeliever? 16 And what agreement has the temple of God with idols? For you*ᵃ* are the temple of the living God. As God has said:

> "I will dwell in them
> And walk among them.
> I will be their God,
> And they shall be My people."*ᵇ*

17 Therefore

> "Come out from among them
> And be separate, says the Lord.
> Do not touch what is unclean,
> And I will receive you."*ᵃ*
> 18 "I will be a Father to you,
> And you shall be My sons and
> daughters,
> Says the Lᴏʀᴅ Almighty."*ᵃ*

7 Therefore, having these promises, beloved, let us cleanse ourselves from all filthiness of the flesh and spirit, perfecting holiness in the fear of God.

2 Open *your hearts* to us. We have wronged no one, we have corrupted no one, we have cheated no one. 3 I do not say *this* to condemn; for I have said before that you are in our hearts, to die together and to live together. 4 Great *is* my boldness of speech toward you, great *is* my boasting on your behalf. I am filled with comfort. I am exceedingly joyful in all our tribulation.

5 For indeed, when we came to Macedonia, our bodies had no rest, but we were troubled on every side. Outside *were* conflicts, inside *were* fears. 6 Nevertheless God, who comforts the downcast, comforted us by the coming of Titus, 7 and not only by his coming, but also by the consolation with which he was comforted in you, when he told us of your earnest desire, your mourning, your zeal for me, so that I rejoiced even more.

8 For even if I made you sorry with my letter, I do not regret it; though I did regret it. For I perceive that the same epistle made you sorry, though only for a while. 9 Now I rejoice, not that you were made sorry, but that your sorrow led to repentance. For you were made sorry in a godly manner, that you might suffer loss from us in nothing. 10 For godly sorrow produces repentance *leading* to salvation, not to be regretted; but the sorrow of the world produces death. 11 For observe this very thing, that you sorrowed in a godly manner: What diligence it produced in you, *what* clearing *of yourselves, what* indignation, *what* fear, *what* vehement desire, *what* zeal, *what* vindication! In all *things* you proved yourselves to be clear in this matter. 12 Therefore, although I wrote to you, *I* did not *do it* for the sake of him who had done the wrong, nor for the sake of him who suffered wrong, but that our care for you in the sight of God might appear to you.

13 Therefore we have been comforted in your comfort. And we rejoiced exceedingly more for the joy of Titus, because his spirit has been refreshed by you all. 14 For if in anything I have boasted to him about you, I am not ashamed. But as we spoke all things to you in truth, even so our boasting to Titus was found true. 15 And his affections are greater for you as he remembers the obedience of you all, how with fear and trembling you received him. 16 Therefore I rejoice that I have confidence in you in everything.

8 Moreover, brethren, we make known to you the grace of God bestowed on the churches of Macedonia: 2 that in a great trial of affliction the abundance of their joy and their deep poverty abounded in the riches of their liberality. 3 For I bear witness that according to *their* ability, yes, and beyond *their* ability,

---

6:16 *ᵃ*NU-Text reads *we.*   *ᵇ*Leviticus 26:12; Jeremiah 32:38; Ezekiel 37:27   6:17 *ᵃ*Isaiah 52:11; Ezekiel 20:34, 41   6:18 *ᵃ*2 Samuel 7:14

---

*M*any have more faith in a textbook written by a person whose eyes may be clouded by their own secrets, than rely upon the Word of a God who knows the end from the beginning.

they *were* freely willing, 4 imploring us with much urgency that we would receive[a] the gift and the fellowship of the ministering to the saints. 5 And not *only* as we had hoped, but they first gave themselves to the Lord, and *then* to us by the will of God. 6 So we urged Titus, that as he had begun, so he would also complete this grace in you as well. 7 But as you abound in everything— in faith, in speech, in knowledge, in all diligence, and in your love for us—*see* that you abound in this grace also.

8 I speak not by commandment, but I am testing the sincerity of your love by the diligence of others. 9 For you know the grace of our Lord Jesus Christ, that though He was rich, yet for your sakes He became poor, that you through His poverty might become rich.

10 And in this I give advice: It is to your advantage not only to be doing what you began and were desiring to do a year ago; 11 but now you also must complete the doing of *it;* that as *there was* a readiness to desire *it,* so *there* also *may be* a completion out of what *you* have. 12 For if there is first a willing mind, *it is* accepted according to what one has, *and* not according to what he does not have.

13 For *I do* not *mean* that others should be eased and you burdened; 14 but by an equality, *that* now at this time your abundance *may supply* their lack, that their abundance also may supply your lack—that there may be equality. 15 As it is written, *"He who gathered much had nothing left over, and he who gathered little had no lack."*[a]

16 But thanks *be* to God who puts[a] the same earnest care for you into the heart of Titus. 17 For he not only accepted the exhortation, but being more diligent, he went to you of his own accord. 18 And we have sent with him the brother whose praise *is* in the gospel throughout all the churches, 19 and not only *that,* but who was also chosen by the churches to travel with us with this gift, which is administered by us to the glory of the Lord Himself and *to show* your

ready mind, 20 avoiding this: that anyone should blame us in this lavish gift which is administered by us— 21 providing honorable things, not only in the sight of the Lord, but also in the sight of men.

22 And we have sent with them our brother whom we have often proved diligent in many things, but now much more diligent, because of the great confidence which *we have* in you. 23 If *anyone inquires* about Titus, *he is* my partner and fellow worker concerning you. Or if our brethren *are inquired about, they are* messengers of the churches, the glory of Christ. 24 Therefore show to them, and[a] before the churches the proof of your love and of our boasting on your behalf.

9 Now concerning the ministering to the saints, it is superfluous for me to write to you; 2 for I know your willingness, about which I boast of you to the Macedonians, that Achaia was ready a year ago; and your zeal has stirred up the majority. 3 Yet I have sent the brethren, lest our boasting of you should be in vain in this respect, that, as I said, you may be ready; 4 lest if *some* Macedonians come with me and find you unprepared, we (not to mention you!) should be ashamed of this confident boasting.[a] 5 Therefore I thought it necessary to exhort the brethren to go to you ahead of time, and prepare your generous gift beforehand, which *you had* previously promised, that it may be ready as *a matter of* generosity and not as a grudging obligation.

6 But this *I say:* He who sows sparingly will also reap sparingly, and he who sows bountifully will also reap bountifully. 7 So let each one *give* as he purposes in his heart, not grudgingly or of necessity; for God loves a cheerful giver. 8 And God *is* able to make all grace abound toward you, that you, always having all sufficiency in all *things,* may have an abundance for every good work. 9 As it is written:

*"He has dispersed abroad,
He has given to the poor;*

8:4 [a]NU-Text and M-Text omit *that we would receive,* thus changing text to *urgency for the favor and fellowship* . . . .   8:15 [a]Exodus 16:18   8:16 [a]NU-Text reads *has put.*   8:24 [a]NU-Text and M-Text omit *and.*   9:4 [a]NU-Text reads *this confidence.*

*T*o every husband who wants to see his wife healed, to every mother who has a little girl with a woman's problem: The power to heal is in the power to care.

Grab a Towel

2 Corinthians 8:9

*J*esus loved His little band of disciples so much that He didn't wait for them to make the first move. He taught them by going first. He rose up, laid aside His garments, and washed their feet. If you are going to change things in the body of Christ, you must be willing to be a trendsetter. You must be naked and not ashamed.

In the Upper Room, the disciples witnessed their Master stepping down to become one of them (see John 13:3–17). He laid aside His garments—not only for those twelve men, but for us all. He came to earth, stripped of the glory He had enjoyed with the Father before the foundations of the world.

This was no time for form or fashion. Real ministry is done with a complete loss of distinction. If Jesus were to leave a lasting impact on these men in the Upper Room—this little ragged band of disciples—He must cover Himself in humility.

The Prince of Peace stripped Himself of His deity to appear before His disciples in only a common towel. As He knelt down on the floor and began to wash their feet, Peter was embarrassed for his Lord. To think that his Master would allow Himself to be seen in such a demeaning light. One moment He was standing before them as stately as a prince; the next, He was kneeling as a common servant.

The final touch of God was delivered through a Man who humbled Himself. He was dressed like a servant, ready to help the hurting. His ministry was best seen when wrapped in a towel.

If you believe that God would exalt you; if you believe that you have the ability to wash the dusty sands of life from the feet of this world, then please don't join the spiritual elitists who are impressed with their own speech. Lay aside your garments—every distraction, every distinction—and put on the warm towel of servanthood. You may be the only one at your table who knows that the hour has come and the supper is ended. Wait no longer! Lay aside your garments—and serve!

His righteousness endures forever."[a]

10 Now may[a] He who supplies seed to the sower, and bread for food, supply and multiply the seed you have *sown* and increase the fruits of your righteousness, 11 while *you are* enriched in everything for all liberality, which causes thanksgiving through us to God. 12 For the administration of this service not only supplies the needs of the saints, but also is abounding through many thanksgivings to God, 13 while, through the proof of this ministry, they glorify God for the obedience of your confession to the gospel of Christ, and for *your* liberal sharing with them and all *men*, 14 and by their prayer for you, who long for you because of the exceeding grace of God in you. 15 Thanks *be* to God for His indescribable gift!

10 Now I, Paul, myself am pleading with you by the meekness and gentleness of Christ—who in presence *am* lowly among you, but being absent am bold toward you. 2 But I beg *you* that when I am present I may not be bold with that confidence by which I intend to be bold against some, who think of us as if we walked according to the flesh. 3 For though we walk in the flesh, we do not war according to the flesh. 4 For the weapons of our warfare *are* not carnal but mighty in God for pulling down strongholds, 5 casting down arguments and every high thing that exalts itself against the knowledge of God, bringing every thought into captivity to the obedience of Christ, 6 and being ready to punish all disobedience when your obedience is fulfilled.

7 Do you look at things according to the outward appearance? If anyone is convinced in himself that he is Christ's, let him again consider this in himself, that just as he *is* Christ's, even so we *are* Christ's.[a] 8 For even if I should boast somewhat more about our authority, which the Lord gave us[a] for edification and not for your destruction, I shall not be ashamed— 9 lest I seem to terrify you

by letters. 10 "For *his* letters," they say, "*are* weighty and powerful, but *his* bodily presence *is* weak, and *his* speech contemptible." 11 Let such a person consider this, that what we are in word by letters when we are absent, such *we will* also *be* in deed when we are present.

12 For we dare not class ourselves or compare ourselves with those who commend themselves. But they, measuring themselves by themselves, and comparing themselves among themselves, are not wise. 13 We, however, will not boast beyond measure, but within the limits of the sphere which God appointed us—a sphere which especially includes you. 14 For we are not overextending ourselves (as though *our authority* did not extend to you), for it was to you that we came with the gospel of Christ; 15 not boasting of things beyond measure, *that is,* in other men's labors, but having hope, *that* as your faith is increased, we shall be greatly enlarged by you in our sphere, 16 to preach the gospel in the *regions* beyond you, *and* not to boast in another man's sphere of accomplishment.

17 But *"he who glories, let him glory in the* LORD.*"*[a] 18 For not he who commends himself is approved, but whom the Lord commends.

11 Oh, that you would bear with me in a little folly—and indeed you do bear with me. 2 For I am jealous for you with godly jealousy. For I have betrothed you to one husband, that I may present *you as* a chaste virgin to Christ. 3 But I fear, lest somehow, as the serpent deceived Eve by his craftiness, so your minds may be corrupted from the simplicity[a] that is in Christ. 4 For if he who comes preaches another Jesus whom we have not preached, or *if* you receive a different spirit which you have not received, or a different gospel which you have not accepted—you may well put up with it!

5 For I consider that I am not at all inferior to the most eminent apostles. 6 Even though *I am* untrained in speech, yet *I am* not in knowledge.

9:9 [a]Psalm 112:9   9:10 [a]NU-Text reads *Now He who supplies . . . will supply . . . .*   10:7 [a]NU-Text reads *even as we are.*   10:8 [a]NU-Text omits *us.*   10:17 [a]Jeremiah 9:24   11:3 [a]NU-Text adds *and purity.*

Gospel Pearls

But we have been thoroughly manifested[a] among you in all things.

7 Did I commit sin in humbling myself that you might be exalted, because I preached the gospel of God to you free of charge? 8 I robbed other churches, taking wages *from them* to minister to you. 9 And when I was present with you, and in need, I was a burden to no one, for what I lacked the brethren who came from Macedonia supplied. And in everything I kept myself from being burdensome to you, and so I will keep *myself.* 10 As the truth of Christ is in me, no one shall stop me from this boasting in the regions of Achaia. 11 Why? Because I do not love you? God knows!

12 But what I do, I will also continue to do, that I may cut off the opportunity from those who desire an opportunity to be regarded just as we are in the things of which they boast. 13 For such *are* false apostles, deceitful workers, transforming themselves into apostles of Christ. 14 And no wonder! For Satan himself transforms himself into an angel of light. 15 Therefore *it is* no great thing if his ministers also transform themselves into ministers of righteousness, whose end will be according to their works.

16 I say again, let no one think me a fool. If otherwise, at least receive me as a fool, that I also may boast a little. 17 What I speak, I speak not according to the Lord, but as it were, foolishly, in this confidence of boasting. 18 Seeing that many boast according to the flesh, I also will boast. 19 For you put up with fools gladly, since you *yourselves* are wise! 20 For you put up with it if one brings you into bondage, if one devours *you,* if one takes *from you,* if one exalts himself, if one strikes you on the face. 21 To *our* shame I say that we were too weak for that! But in whatever anyone is bold—I speak foolishly—I am bold also.

22 Are they Hebrews? So *am* I. Are they Israelites? So *am* I. Are they the seed of Abraham? So *am* I. 23 Are they ministers of Christ?—I speak as a fool—I *am* more: in labors more abundant, in stripes above measure, in prisons more frequently, in deaths often. 24 From the Jews five times I received forty *stripes* minus one. 25 Three times I was beaten with rods; once I was stoned; three times I was shipwrecked; a night and a day I have been in the deep; 26 *in* journeys often, *in* perils of waters, *in* perils of robbers, *in* perils of *my own* countrymen, *in* perils of the Gentiles, *in* perils in the city, *in* perils in the wilderness, *in* perils in the sea, *in* perils among false brethren; 27 in weariness and toil, in sleeplessness often, in hunger and thirst, in fastings often, in cold and nakedness— 28 besides the other things, what comes upon me daily: my deep concern for all the churches. 29 Who is weak, and I am not weak? Who is made to stumble, and I do not burn *with* indignation?

30 If I must boast, I will boast in the things which concern my infirmity. 31 The God and Father of our Lord Jesus Christ, who is blessed forever, knows that I am not lying. 32 In Damascus the governor, under Aretas the king, was guarding the city of the Damascenes with a garrison, desiring to arrest me; 33 but I was let down in a basket through a window in the wall, and escaped from his hands.

12 It is doubtless[a] not profitable for me to boast. I will come to visions and revelations of the Lord: 2 I know a man in Christ who fourteen years ago—whether in the body I do not know, or whether out of the body I do not know, God knows— such a one was caught up to the third heaven. 3 And I know such a man— whether in the body or out of the body I do not know, God knows— 4 how he was caught up into Paradise and heard inexpressible words, which it is not lawful for a man to utter. 5 Of such a one I will boast; yet of myself I will not boast, except in my infirmities. 6 For though I might desire to boast, I will not be a fool; for I will speak the truth. But I refrain, lest anyone should think of me above what he sees me *to be* or hears from me.

7 And lest I should be exalted above measure by the abundance of the revelations, a thorn in the flesh was given to me, a messenger of Satan to buffet me, lest I be exalted

---

11:6 [a]NU-Text omits *been.*   12:1 [a]NU-Text reads *necessary, though not profitable, to boast.*

We can build all the churches we want. We can decorate them with fine tapestry and ornate artifacts, but if people cannot find a loving voice within our hallowed walls, they will pass through unaltered by our clichés and religious rhetoric.

above measure. 8 Concerning this thing I pleaded with the Lord three times that it might depart from me. 9 And He said to me, "My grace is sufficient for you, for My strength is made perfect in weakness." Therefore most gladly I will rather boast in my infirmities, that the power of Christ may rest upon me. 10 Therefore I take pleasure in infirmities, in reproaches, in needs, in persecutions, in distresses, for Christ's sake. For when I am weak, then I am strong.

11 I have become a fool in boasting;[a] you have compelled me. For I ought to have been commended by you; for in nothing was I behind the most eminent apostles, though I am nothing. 12 Truly the signs of an apostle were accomplished among you with all perseverance, in signs and wonders and mighty deeds. 13 For what is it in which you were inferior to other churches, except that I myself was not burdensome to you? Forgive me this wrong!

14 Now for the third time I am ready to come to you. And I will not be burdensome to you; for I do not seek yours, but you. For the children ought not to lay up for the parents, but the parents for the children. 15 And I will very gladly spend and be spent for your souls; though the more abundantly I love you, the less I am loved.

16 But be that as it may, I did not burden you. Nevertheless, being crafty, I caught you by cunning. 17 Did I take advantage of you by any of those whom I sent to you? 18 I urged Titus, and sent our brother with him. Did Titus take advantage of you? Did we not walk in the same spirit? Did we not walk in the same steps?

19 Again, do you think[a] that we excuse ourselves to you? We speak before God in Christ. But we do all things, beloved, for your edification. 20 For I fear lest, when I come, I shall not find you such as I wish, and that I shall be found by you such as you do not wish; lest there be contentions, jealousies, outbursts of wrath, selfish ambitions, backbitings, whisperings, conceits, tumults; 21 lest,

when I come again, my God will humble me among you, and I shall mourn for many who have sinned before and have not repented of the uncleanness, fornication, and lewdness which they have practiced.

13 This will be the third time I am coming to you. "By the mouth of two or three witnesses every word shall be established."[a] 2 I have told you before, and foretell as if I were present the second time, and now being absent I write[a] to those who have sinned before, and to all the rest, that if I come again I will not spare— 3 since you seek a proof of Christ speaking in me, who is not weak toward you, but mighty in you. 4 For though He was crucified in weakness, yet He lives by the power of God. For we also are weak in Him, but we shall live with Him by the power of God toward you.

5 Examine yourselves as to whether you are in the faith. Test yourselves. Do you not know yourselves, that Jesus Christ is in you?— unless indeed you are disqualified. 6 But I trust that you will know that we are not disqualified.

7 Now I[a] pray to God that you do no evil, not that we should appear approved, but that you should do what is honorable, though we may seem disqualified. 8 For we can do nothing against the truth, but for the truth. 9 For we are glad when we are weak and you are strong. And this also we pray, that you may be made complete. 10 Therefore I write these things being absent, lest being present I should use sharpness, according to the authority which the Lord has given me for edification and not for destruction.

11 Finally, brethren, farewell. Become complete. Be of good comfort, be of one mind, live in peace; and the God of love and peace will be with you.

12 Greet one another with a holy kiss.

13 All the saints greet you.

14 The grace of the Lord Jesus Christ, and the love of God, and the communion of the Holy Spirit be with you all. Amen.

12:11 aNU-Text omits in boasting. 12:19 aNU-Text reads You have been thinking for a long time. . . .
13:1 aDeuteronomy 19:15 13:2 aNU-Text omits I write. 13:7 aNU-Text reads we.

Gospel
Pearls

GALATIANS

1 Paul, an apostle (not from men nor through man, but through Jesus Christ and God the Father who raised Him from the dead), 2 and all the brethren who are with me,

To the churches of Galatia:

3 Grace to you and peace from God the Father and our Lord Jesus Christ, 4 who gave Himself for our sins, that He might deliver us from this present evil age, according to the will of our God and Father, 5 to whom *be* glory forever and ever. Amen.

6 I marvel that you are turning away so soon from Him who called you in the grace of Christ, to a different gospel, 7 which is not another; but there are some who trouble you and want to pervert the gospel of Christ. 8 But even if we, or an angel from heaven, preach any other gospel to you than what we have preached to you, let him be accursed. 9 As we have said before, so now I say again, if anyone preaches any other gospel to you than what you have received, let him be accursed.

10 For do I now persuade men, or God? Or do I seek to please men? For if I still pleased men, I would not be a bondservant of Christ.

11 But I make known to you, brethren, that the gospel which was preached by me is not according to man. 12 For I neither received it from man, nor was I taught *it,* but *it came* through the revelation of Jesus Christ.

13 For you have heard of my former conduct in Judaism, how I persecuted the church of God beyond measure and *tried to* destroy it. 14 And I advanced in Judaism beyond many of my contemporaries in my own nation, being more exceedingly zealous for the traditions of my fathers.

15 But when it pleased God, who separated me from my mother's womb and called *me* through His grace, 16 to reveal His Son in me, that I might preach Him among the Gentiles, I did not immediately confer with flesh and blood, 17 nor did I go up to Jerusalem to those *who were* apostles before me; but I went to Arabia, and returned again to Damascus.

18 Then after three years I went up to Jerusalem to see Peter,[a] and remained with him fifteen days. 19 But I saw none of the other apostles except James, the Lord's brother. 20 (Now *concerning* the things which I write to you, indeed, before God, I do not lie.)

21 Afterward I went into the regions of Syria and Cilicia. 22 And I was unknown by face to the churches of Judea which *were* in Christ. 23 But they were hearing only, "He who formerly persecuted us now preaches the faith which he once *tried to* destroy." 24 And they glorified God in me.

2 Then after fourteen years I went up again to Jerusalem with Barnabas, and also took Titus with *me.* 2 And I went up by revelation, and communicated to them that gospel which I preach among the Gentiles, but privately to those who were of reputation, lest by any means I might run, or had run, in vain. 3 Yet not even Titus who *was* with me, being a Greek, was compelled to be circumcised. 4 And *this occurred* because of false brethren secretly brought in (who came in by stealth to spy out our liberty which we have in Christ Jesus, that they might bring us into bondage), 5 to whom we did not yield submission even for an hour, that the truth of the gospel might continue with you.

6 But from those who seemed to be something—whatever they were, it makes no difference to me; God shows personal favoritism to no man—for those who seemed *to be something* added nothing to me. 7 But on the contrary, when they saw that the gospel for the uncircumcised had been committed to me, as *the gospel* for the circumcised *was* to Peter 8 (for He who worked effectively in Peter for the apostleship to the circumcised also worked effectively in me toward the Gentiles), 9 and when James, Cephas, and John, who

1:18 aNU-Text reads *Cephas.*

2 am convinced that resting in the relationship that we have with God heals us from the feelings of vulnerability. It is a shame that many Christians have not yet rested in the promise of God. Everyone needs reassurance.

Bondage on the Inside

Galatians 1:10

Long after I was saved, I still thought I needed to be delivered from the devil. The popular phrase at the time was, "The devil made me do it." Well, I didn't want the devil to make me do anything, so I prayed hard to be delivered from him.

After a while I realized that the devil wasn't the problem. I stopped wasting my time praying about him. I changed my prayer to, "Lord, save me from me. Please don't let me destroy Your promises with my predicaments. Please don't let me do myself in. Deliver me from my own evil tendencies."

Some people don't blame the devil, but they blame other people or a specific person or a group of people. The real issue is this: What matters in the long run is not what people say about you or to you. It's what you say *about* yourself *to* yourself.

A spirit of infirmity may not always represent a bondage that another person places on your life. It may represent a bondage on the inside. And you can't walk away from that kind of bondage. It will keep you locked up—until you quit agreeing with the person who has mistreated you or the event that crippled you.

So many people have made it their life's work to change somebody's opinion about them. They are determined to prove that they are valuable in that other person's eyes. Their consuming ambition is to show somebody that they are good, that they are fine Christians, that they are important.

Never allow another person's opinion of you to become your goal. The fact is, some folks might never like you. They may never approve of you or think you're good. They may never change their opinion of you.

If you agree with the person who rejects you or abuses you, then you put yourself into bondage to that person. If you say, "You were right to hit me—I deserved to be hit. You were right to leave me—I deserved to be left. You were right to hurt me—I deserved to be hurt" . . . then you are tying yourself up with their opinion of you rather than tying yourself in to God's opinion of you. When their opinion of you becomes *your* bad opinion of you, you've built a prison inside your soul with only one prisoner—you. Are you prepared to deal with the fact that the person you've spent your entire life trying to impress may never be impressed? Are you prepared to face the reality that, from God's perspective, it doesn't matter?

If you are going to deal effectively with people in this world, you must be able to work right alongside others without allowing yourself to be controlled by them or governed by their opinion of you. Likely, the deliverance you need most is not a deliverance from the devil or a deliverance from another person. The deliverance you probably need most is a deliverance from some faulty notion you have in your own heart and mind. Be loosed!

seemed to be pillars, perceived the grace that had been given to me, they gave me and Barnabas the right hand of fellowship, that we *should go* to the Gentiles and they to the circumcised. 10 *They desired* only that we should remember the poor, the very thing which I also was eager to do.

11 Now when Peter*a* had come to Antioch, I withstood him to his face, because he was to be blamed; 12 for before certain men came from James, he would eat with the Gentiles; but when they came, he withdrew and separated himself, fearing those who were of the circumcision. 13 And the rest of the Jews also played the hypocrite with him, so that even Barnabas was carried away with their hypocrisy.

14 But when I saw that they were not straightforward about the truth of the gospel, I said to Peter before *them* all, "If you, being a Jew, live in the manner of Gentiles and not as the Jews, why do you*a* compel Gentiles to live as Jews?*b* 15 We *who are* Jews by nature, and not sinners of the Gentiles, 16 knowing that a man is not justified by the works of the law but by faith in Jesus Christ, even we have believed in Christ Jesus, that we might be justified by faith in Christ and not by the works of the law; for by the works of the law no flesh shall be justified.

17 "But if, while we seek to be justified by Christ, we ourselves also are found sinners, *is* Christ therefore a minister of sin? Certainly not! 18 For if I build again those things which I destroyed, I make myself a transgressor. 19 For I through the law died to the law that I might live to God. 20 I have been crucified with Christ; it is no longer I who live, but Christ lives in me; and the *life* which I now live in the flesh I live by faith in the Son of God, who loved me and gave Himself for me. 21 I do not set aside the grace of God; for if righteousness *comes* through the law, then Christ died in vain."

3 O foolish Galatians! Who has bewitched you that you should not obey the truth,*a* before whose eyes Jesus Christ was clearly portrayed among you*b* as crucified? 2 This only I want to learn from you: Did you receive the Spirit by the works of the law, or by the hearing of faith? 3 Are you so foolish? Having begun in the Spirit, are you now being made perfect by the flesh? 4 Have you suffered so many things in vain—if indeed *it was* in vain?

5 Therefore He who supplies the Spirit to you and works miracles among you, *does He do it* by the works of the law, or by the hearing of faith?— 6 just as Abraham *"believed God, and it was accounted to him for righteousness."a* 7 Therefore know that *only* those who are of faith are *sons* of Abraham. 8 And the Scripture, foreseeing that God would justify the Gentiles by faith, preached the gospel to Abraham beforehand, *saying, "In you all the nations shall be blessed."a* 9 So then those who *are* of faith are blessed with believing Abraham.

10 For as many as are of the works of the law are under the curse; for it is written, *"Cursed is everyone who does not continue in all things which are written in the book of the law, to do them."a* 11 But that no one is justified by the law in the sight of God is evident, for *"the just shall live by faith."a* 12 Yet the law is not of faith, but *"the man who does them shall live by them."a*

13 Christ has redeemed us from the curse of the law, having become a curse for us (for it is written, *"Cursed is everyone who hangs on a tree"a*), 14 that the blessing of Abraham might come upon the Gentiles in Christ Jesus, that we might receive the promise of the Spirit through faith.

15 Brethren, I speak in the manner of men: Though *it is* only a man's covenant, yet *if it is* confirmed, no one annuls or adds to it. 16 Now to Abraham and his Seed were the promises made. He does not say, "And to seeds," as of many, but as of one, *"And to your Seed,"a* who is Christ. 17 And this I say, *that* the law, which was four hundred and thirty years later, cannot annul the cove-

2:11 *a*NU-Text reads *Cephas.* 2:14 *a*NU-Text reads *how can you.* *b*Some interpreters stop the quotation here. 3:1 *a*NU-Text omits *that you should not obey the truth.* *b*NU-Text omits *among you.*
3:6 *a*Genesis 15:6 3:8 *a*Genesis 12:3; 18:18; 22:18; 26:4; 28:14 3:10 *a*Deuteronomy 27:26
3:11 *a*Habakkuk 2:4 3:12 *a*Leviticus 18:5 3:13 *a*Deuteronomy 21:23 3:16 *a*Genesis 12:7; 13:15; 24:7

A feeling of security is a plus, especially in reference to the home. That same principle is important when it comes to your relationship with God. He is constantly reassuring us that we might have a consolation and a hope for the soul, the mind and emotions, steadfast and immovable.

nant that was confirmed before by God in Christ,[a] that it should make the promise of no effect. 18 For if the inheritance *is* of the law, *it is* no longer of promise; but God gave *it* to Abraham by promise.

19 What purpose then *does* the law serve? It was added because of transgressions, till the Seed should come to whom the promise was made; *and it was* appointed through angels by the hand of a mediator. 20 Now a mediator does not *mediate* for one *only,* but God is one.

21 *Is* the law then against the promises of God? Certainly not! For if there had been a law given which could have given life, truly righteousness would have been by the law. 22 But the Scripture has confined all under sin, that the promise by faith in Jesus Christ might be given to those who believe. 23 But before faith came, we were kept under guard by the law, kept for the faith which would afterward be revealed. 24 Therefore the law was our tutor *to bring us* to Christ, that we might be justified by faith. 25 But after faith has come, we are no longer under a tutor.

26 For you are all sons of God through faith in Christ Jesus. 27 For as many of you as were baptized into Christ have put on Christ. 28 There is neither Jew nor Greek, there is neither slave nor free, there is neither male nor female; for you are all one in Christ Jesus. 29 And if you *are* Christ's, then you are Abraham's seed, and heirs according to the promise.

4 Now I say *that* the heir, as long as he is a child, does not differ at all from a slave, though he is master of all, 2 but is under guardians and stewards until the time appointed by the father. 3 Even so we, when we were children, were in bondage under the elements of the world. 4 But when the fullness of the time had come, God sent forth His Son, born[a] of a woman, born under the law, 5 to redeem those who were under the law, that we might receive the adoption as sons.

6 And because you are sons, God has sent forth the Spirit of His Son into your hearts, crying out, "Abba, Father!" 7 Therefore you are no longer a slave but a son, and if a son, then an heir of[a] God through Christ.

8 But then, indeed, when you did not know God, you served those which by nature are not gods. 9 But now after you have known God, or rather are known by God, how *is* it *that* you turn again to the weak and beggarly elements, to which you desire again to be in bondage? 10 You observe days and months and seasons and years. 11 I am afraid for you, lest I have labored for you in vain.

12 Brethren, I urge you to become like me, for I *became* like you. You have not injured me at all. 13 You know that because of physical infirmity I preached the gospel to you at the first. 14 And my trial which was in my flesh you did not despise or reject, but you received me as an angel of God, *even* as Christ Jesus. 15 What[a] then was the blessing you *enjoyed?* For I bear you witness that, if possible, you would have plucked out your own eyes and given them to me. 16 Have I therefore become your enemy because I tell you the truth?

17 They zealously court you, *but* for no good; yes, they want to exclude you, that you may be zealous for them. 18 But it is good to be zealous in a good thing always, and not only when I am present with you. 19 My little children, for whom I labor in birth again until Christ is formed in you, 20 I would like to be present with you now and to change my tone; for I have doubts about you.

21 Tell me, you who desire to be under the law, do you not hear the law? 22 For it is written that Abraham had two sons: the one by a bondwoman, the other by a freewoman. 23 But he *who was* of the bondwoman was born according to the flesh, and he of the freewoman through promise, 24 which things are symbolic. For these are the[a] two covenants: the one from Mount Sinai which gives birth to bondage, which is Hagar— 25 for this Hagar is Mount Sinai in Arabia, and corresponds to Jerusalem which now is, and is in bondage with her children— 26 but the Jerusa-

---

3:17 [a]NU-Text omits *in Christ.*   4:4 [a]Or *made*   4:7 [a]NU-Text reads *through God* and omits *through Christ.*   4:15 [a]NU-Text reads *Where.*   4:24 [a]NU-Text and M-Text omit *the.*

There is a sanctity of your spirit that comes through the blood of the Lord Jesus Christ and sanctifies the innermost part of your being. Once you get cleaned up in your spirit, it will be reflected in your character and in your conduct.

Color Blind

Galatians 3:28

Real spiritual advantage does not come from the color of your skin. It's not the color of your skin that brings deliverance and help from God; it's the contents of your heart.

Some of us have certain problems because of where we came from. You may say, "My people came over on a boat and picked cotton on a plantation." But God says, "There is neither Greek nor Jew." He says there is no such thing as a black church. There is no such thing as a white church. There is only one church, purchased by the blood of the Lamb. We are all one in Christ Jesus.

You may have been born with a silver spoon in your mouth, but that doesn't make any difference to God. In His Kingdom, social status doesn't mean a thing.

God doesn't look at your gender. He says, "There is neither male nor female" (Galatians 3:28). You are spirit, and spirits are sexless. (That's why angels don't have sexes. Don't think of angels in terms of gender. They can manifest themselves as men, but they are really ministering spirits.) He doesn't even look at your morality and good works. Rahab was a harlot until she found faith. Once she had faith, she no longer returned to her old profession. In fact, Rahab can be mentioned right next to Sarah because she believed, and God blessed.

Faith is the only thing in this world where there is true equal opportunity. God looks at the faith that lives within your heart. You can walk with your head held high even when you have past failures. It's not what people say about you that makes a difference. It's what you say about yourself and what your God says about you that really matters.

Jesus saw the worth of the infirm woman because she was a daughter of Abraham (see Luke 13:11–16). She had faith. Jesus will unleash you, too, from the pain you have struggled with and the frustrations that have plagued you. If you will dare to believe that you are a daughter of Abraham, you will find the power to stand up straight. The potential that has been bound in you will then truly be set free.

lem above is free, which is the mother of us all. 27 For it is written:

> "Rejoice, O barren,
> You who do not bear!
> Break forth and shout,
> You who are not in labor!
> For the desolate has many
> more children
> Than she who has a husband."[a]

28 Now we, brethren, as Isaac *was,* are children of promise. 29 But, as he who was born according to the flesh then persecuted him *who was born* according to the Spirit, even so *it is* now. 30 Nevertheless what does the Scripture say? *"Cast out the bondwoman and her son, for the son of the bondwoman shall not be heir with the son of the freewoman."*[a] 31 So then, brethren, we are not children of the bondwoman but of the free.

5 Stand fast therefore in the liberty by which Christ has made us free,[a] and do not be entangled again with a yoke of bondage. 2 Indeed I, Paul, say to you that if you become circumcised, Christ will profit you nothing. 3 And I testify again to every man who becomes circumcised that he is a debtor to keep the whole law. 4 You have become estranged from Christ, you who *attempt to* be justified by law; you have fallen from grace. 5 For we through the Spirit eagerly wait for the hope of righteousness by faith. 6 For in Christ Jesus neither circumcision nor uncircumcision avails anything, but faith working through love.

7 You ran well. Who hindered you from obeying the truth? 8 This persuasion does not *come* from Him who calls you. 9 A little leaven leavens the whole lump. 10 I have confidence in you, in the Lord, that you will have no other mind; but he who troubles you shall bear his judgment, whoever he is.

11 And I, brethren, if I still preach circumcision, why do I still suffer persecution? Then the offense of the cross has ceased. 12 I could wish that those who trouble you would even cut themselves off!

13 For you, brethren, have been called to liberty; only do not *use* liberty as an opportunity for the flesh, but through love serve one another. 14 For all the law is fulfilled in one word, *even* in this: *"You shall love your neighbor as yourself."*[a] 15 But if you bite and devour one another, beware lest you be consumed by one another!

16 I say then: Walk in the Spirit, and you shall not fulfill the lust of the flesh. 17 For the flesh lusts against the Spirit, and the Spirit against the flesh; and these are contrary to one another, so that you do not do the things that you wish. 18 But if you are led by the Spirit, you are not under the law.

19 Now the works of the flesh are evident, which are: adultery,[a] fornication, uncleanness, lewdness, 20 idolatry, sorcery, hatred, contentions, jealousies, outbursts of wrath, selfish ambitions, dissensions, heresies, 21 envy, murders,[a] drunkenness, revelries, and the like; of which I tell you beforehand, just as I also told *you* in time past, that those who practice such things will not inherit the kingdom of God.

22 But the fruit of the Spirit is love, joy, peace, longsuffering, kindness, goodness, faithfulness, 23 gentleness, self-control. Against such there is no law. 24 And those *who are* Christ's have crucified the flesh with its passions and desires. 25 If we live in the Spirit, let us also walk in the Spirit. 26 Let us not become conceited, provoking one another, envying one another.

6 Brethren, if a man is overtaken in any trespass, you who *are* spiritual restore such a one in a spirit of gentleness, considering yourself lest you also be tempted. 2 Bear one another's burdens, and so fulfill the law of Christ. 3 For if anyone thinks himself to be something, when he is nothing, he deceives himself. 4 But let each one examine his own work, and then he will have rejoicing in himself alone, and not in another. 5 For each one shall bear his own load.

6 Let him who is taught the word

4:27 [a]Isaiah 54:1   4:30 [a]Genesis 21:10   5:1 [a]NU-Text reads *For freedom Christ has made us free; stand fast therefore.*   5:14 [a]Leviticus 19:18   5:19 [a]NU-Text omits *adultery.*   5:21 [a]NU-Text omits *murders.*

You don't have to tell everyone your entire history. Just know that Jesus calls, on purpose, women with a past. He knows your history, but He calls you anyway.

Blow Me a Trumpet

Galatians 5:1

T his is your day, and this is your Father's world. He created it just for you. You are an heir to the universe. Your only boundaries are your own perceptions of potential. You can reach farther than your fingers and leap higher than your doubt. If you lift your head and raise your hands, the clouds will run away. You are kissed. Didn't you know it? Haven't you realized? That's why you are alive to show it. So show up and show off and show out. It is morning!

Never lose that little-girl belief in the impossible. The fantasies of the faithful dispel the myths of the frightened. Somebody blow me a trumpet! The races are about to begin, and the daughters of God are all dressed up. They have stripped themselves of the cares of this world. They have washed away the abuse of their childhood. They have demanded their inheritance, nursed their own babies, strengthened themselves, and prepared their feet to run.

They are sisters of the Cross, survivors of the secrets. They have lain awake trembling and even cried through the night. Some have screamed from bruised lips, assaulted bodies, broken hearts, betrayed trust! But what of the night? That's right, what of it? Haven't you heard? It is morning. Sound the alarm.

Tell the executive to make room for black pumps and tweed skirts on the elevator. They are moving from the poor house to the White House. Fresh out of fear, God's women are on the move.

Loosed women? You'd better believe it. They are loosed from the tragedy of a long and dismal night. They are the daughters of Abraham. They are women with a promise. Precious promises are waiting for loosed women who have made themselves ready to take the kingdom by force. No more forbidden fruit for them; they are taking a bite out of life. No more restrictions or inhibitions. Many have been held back by the fear of failure and rejection. Tell the critics the Father says, "Let My daughter go!" Only a foolish person would fight a man for his daughter when it is God the Father he will have to fight.

The trumpet has sounded. You are loosed!

share in all good things with him who teaches.

7 Do not be deceived, God is not mocked; for whatever a man sows, that he will also reap. 8 For he who sows to his flesh will of the flesh reap corruption, but he who sows to the Spirit will of the Spirit reap everlasting life. 9 And let us not grow weary while doing good, for in due season we shall reap if we do not lose heart. 10 Therefore, as we have opportunity, let us do good to all, especially to those who are of the household of faith.

11 See with what large letters I have written to you with my own hand! 12 As many as desire to make a good showing in the flesh, these *would* compel you to be circumcised, only that they may not suffer perse-

cution for the cross of Christ. 13 For not even those who are circumcised keep the law, but they desire to have you circumcised that they may boast in your flesh. 14 But God forbid that I should boast except in the cross of our Lord Jesus Christ, by whom*ᵃ* the world has been crucified to me, and I to the world. 15 For in Christ Jesus neither circumcision nor uncircumcision avails anything, but a new creation.

16 And as many as walk according to this rule, peace and mercy *be* upon them, and upon the Israel of God.

17 From now on let no one trouble me, for I bear in my body the marks of the Lord Jesus.

18 Brethren, the grace of our Lord Jesus Christ *be* with your spirit. Amen.

6:14 *ᵃ*Or *by which* (the cross)

The Epistle of Paul the Apostle to the

EPHESIANS

1 Paul, an apostle of Jesus Christ by the will of God,

To the saints who are in Ephesus, and faithful in Christ Jesus:

2 Grace to you and peace from God our Father and the Lord Jesus Christ.

3 Blessed *be* the God and Father of our Lord Jesus Christ, who has blessed us with every spiritual blessing in the heavenly *places* in Christ, 4 just as He chose us in Him before the foundation of the world, that we should be holy and without blame before Him in love, 5 having predestined us to adoption as sons by Jesus Christ to Himself, according to the good pleasure of His will, 6 to the praise of the glory of His grace, by which He made us accepted in the Beloved.

7 In Him we have redemption through His blood, the forgiveness of sins, according to the riches of His grace 8 which He made to abound to-

ward us in all wisdom and prudence, 9 having made known to us the mystery of His will, according to His good pleasure which He purposed in Himself, 10 that in the dispensation of the fullness of the times He might gather together in one all things in Christ, both*ᵃ* which are in heaven and which are on earth—in Him. 11 In Him also we have obtained an inheritance, being predestined according to the purpose of Him who works all things according to the counsel of His will, 12 that we who first trusted in Christ should be to the praise of His glory.

13 In Him you also *trusted,* after you heard the word of truth, the gospel of your salvation; in whom also, having believed, you were sealed with the Holy Spirit of promise, 14 who*ᵃ* is the guarantee of our inheritance until the redemption of the purchased possession, to the praise of His glory.

15 Therefore I also, after I heard of

1:10 *ᵃ*NU-Text and M-Text omit *both.*   1:14 *ᵃ*NU-Text reads *which.*

*M*uch of the history and greatness of Jesus would be lost to us were it not for Jesus calling Matthew, a man with a past. We must maintain a strong line of demarcation between a person's past and a person's present.

God's Good Idea

Ephesians 1:3, 4

You were created in the mind of God before you were conceived in a womb. You were God's idea. And God is the One who made you for a specific time and place on this earth. You aren't an accident, a mistake, an error, an incident, or a mishap.

You were fashioned and made by *Elohim*—the Lord God Almighty, Creator of heaven and earth. You were meticulously made by the Master. Many people today grew up hearing that they weren't wanted by their parents. They were told that they were the result of a "careless moment." If you have been told that, you need to know the truth.

Your mother and father didn't create you. God created you. Your mother and father set up a circumstance in which God had the option to make you then or to wait and make you at another moment in time. But it is God who made you. You are His creation. And God doesn't make mistakes.

It doesn't matter if you were conceived during an act of date rape and born to a welfare mother who had thirteen other children by ten different men. God is the One who ordained and authorized your birth. He created you for His purposes and His glory.

He didn't allow you to be aborted or miscarried. He didn't allow you to be stillborn or to die of crib death. He didn't allow any number of childhood accidents or diseases to take you out. From the instant He had the idea of you, He intended that you should live and participate in His plan and accomplish His purposes.

He never took His hand off your life. It doesn't matter if you were abused as a child. God brought you through that experience alive, and He is the One who kept you from losing your sanity. He is the One who brought you to an understanding of Jesus Christ as your Savior and raised you up so that you could still fulfill His purposes and reflect His glory in spite of every effort of the enemy to destroy you, diminish you, defame you, or discourage you.

The fact is, if you hadn't gone through everything you have gone through, you wouldn't be the person you are today. And God knows that! He has been in the process of creating you, fashioning you, molding you, designing you, refining you, and perfecting you since the moment before the foundations of the earth when He first thought of you!

He gave you your own personality, your own abilities, your own spiritual gifts, and your own identity in Christ so that you, and you alone, might praise Him the way you praise, give what you give, minister like you minister, and love as you love.

Oh, yes! When God thought of you, He had a good idea!

your faith in the Lord Jesus and your love for all the saints, 16 do not cease to give thanks for you, making mention of you in my prayers: 17 that the God of our Lord Jesus Christ, the Father of glory, may give to you the spirit of wisdom and revelation in the knowledge of Him, 18 the eyes of your understanding*ᵃ* being enlightened; that you may know what is the hope of His calling, what are the riches of the glory of His inheritance in the saints, 19 and what *is* the exceeding greatness of His power toward us who believe, according to the working of His mighty power 20 which He worked in Christ when He raised Him from the dead and seated *Him* at His right hand in the heavenly *places,* 21 far above all principality and power and might and dominion, and every name that is named, not only in this age but also in that which is to come.

22 And He put all *things* under His feet, and gave Him *to be* head over all *things* to the church, 23 which is His body, the fullness of Him who fills all in all.

2 And you *He made alive,* who were dead in trespasses and sins, 2 in which you once walked according to the course of this world, according to the prince of the power of the air, the spirit who now works in the sons of disobedience, 3 among whom also we all once conducted ourselves in the lusts of our flesh, fulfilling the desires of the flesh and of the mind, and were by nature children of wrath, just as the others. 4 But God, who is rich in mercy, because of His great love with which He loved us, 5 even when we were dead in trespasses, made us alive together with Christ (by grace you have been saved), 6 and raised *us* up together, and made *us* sit together in the heavenly *places* in Christ Jesus, 7 that in the ages to come He might show the exceeding riches of His grace in *His* kindness toward us in Christ Jesus. 8 For by grace you have been saved through faith, and that not of yourselves; *it is* the gift of God, 9 not of works, lest anyone should boast. 10 For we are His workmanship, created in Christ Jesus for good works, which God prepared before-

hand that we should walk in them.

11 Therefore remember that you, once Gentiles in the flesh—who are called Uncircumcision by what is called the Circumcision made in the flesh by hands— 12 that at that time you were without Christ, being aliens from the commonwealth of Israel and strangers from the covenants of promise, having no hope and without God in the world. 13 But now in Christ Jesus you who once were far off have been brought near by the blood of Christ.

14 For He Himself is our peace, who has made both one, and has broken down the middle wall of separation, 15 having abolished in His flesh the enmity, *that is,* the law of commandments *contained* in ordinances, so as to create in Himself one new man *from* the two, *thus* making peace, 16 and that He might reconcile them both to God in one body through the cross, thereby putting to death the enmity. 17 And He came and preached peace to you who were afar off and to those who were near. 18 For through Him we both have access by one Spirit to the Father.

19 Now, therefore, you are no longer strangers and foreigners, but fellow citizens with the saints and members of the household of God, 20 having been built on the foundation of the apostles and prophets, Jesus Christ Himself being the chief corner*stone,* 21 in whom the whole building, being fitted together, grows into a holy temple in the Lord, 22 in whom you also are being built together for a dwelling place of God in the Spirit.

3 For this reason I, Paul, the prisoner of Christ Jesus for you Gentiles— 2 if indeed you have heard of the dispensation of the grace of God which was given to me for you, 3 how that by revelation He made known to me the mystery (as I have briefly written already, 4 by which, when you read, you may understand my knowledge in the mystery of Christ), 5 which in other ages was not made known to the sons of men, as it has now been revealed by the Spirit to His holy apostles and prophets: 6 that the Gentiles should be fellow heirs, of the same body, and partak-

---

1:18 *ᵃ*NU-Text and M-Text read *hearts.*

*P*eople with a past have always been able to come to Jesus. He makes them into something wonderful and marvelous. It is said that Mary Magdalene was a prostitute. Christ was moved with compassion for even this base kind of human existence.

Only You!

Ephesians 2:10

You are unique, dear woman. That is what makes you priceless. The Lord will never, ever replace you. Though He has millions more children, each one wonderful, none is exactly like you! Never give up your uniqueness in order to be what you admire in someone else. Glean all you can from everyone, but duplicate none. You are too priceless as an original to be reduced to a cheap copy!

Perhaps you do not understand what an amazing jewel of a woman you are. The Lord created you for a purpose that only you can fulfill. Pay attention now! Have you yet realized how intensely God loves you? In spite of your afflictions, He loves you. The Father sweeps you up into His arms and clutches you. He holds your head to His breast, your ear to His heart. He has held you through the rough places, trusting the strength of His arms to keep you through the pains of life. It has been a long ride, but He is still holding on.

Perhaps you have asked the Father for something, and He didn't do what you thought He should have done. Perhaps you are disappointed that He didn't show up in the way you thought He would. Before you feel unloved, take a moment and think. Isn't there evidence in your life that, from time to time, He has brought you through a storm? Don't you dare act as if the Father doesn't love you just because He doesn't always cater to you. Perhaps you should be glad for the love He has already shown and the night rides He has already carried you through. That love constantly affirms your uniqueness.

You see, our society has spent so much time criticizing differences that we fail to see God in diversity. He never made two snowflakes alike. He wants us to be different. Different doesn't mean less than or more than—just different.

If God hadn't made you as He did, you wouldn't have been able to persevere as you have. There are many people who couldn't take what you have been through. God wants to use you in a unique way to be a blessing to those around you. Remember, people are blessed when you are sincere—not perfect, just sincere.

Don't let anyone manipulate you into forsaking your own uniqueness. Those people weren't built for your life's destiny, and they can't play your role. Aren't you glad that God prepared you for life instead of preparing life for you? So, whether life is ready for you or not, you are ready for it! Just tell the world, "Get ready, get ready, get ready!"

ers of His promise in Christ through the gospel, 7 of which I became a minister according to the gift of the grace of God given to me by the effective working of His power.

8 To me, who am less than the least of all the saints, this grace was given, that I should preach among the Gentiles the unsearchable riches of Christ, 9 and to make all see what *is* the fellowship*a* of the mystery, which from the beginning of the ages has been hidden in God who created all things through Jesus Christ;*b* 10 to the intent that now the manifold wisdom of God might be made known by the church to the principalities and powers in the heavenly *places,* 11 according to the eternal purpose which He accomplished in Christ Jesus our Lord, 12 in whom we have boldness and access with confidence through faith in Him. 13 Therefore I ask that you do not lose heart at my tribulations for you, which is your glory.

14 For this reason I bow my knees to the Father of our Lord Jesus Christ,*a* 15 from whom the whole family in heaven and earth is named, 16 that He would grant you, according to the riches of His glory, to be strengthened with might through His Spirit in the inner man, 17 that Christ may dwell in your hearts through faith; that you, being rooted and grounded in love, 18 may be able to comprehend with all the saints what *is* the width and length and depth and height— 19 to know the love of Christ which passes knowledge; that you may be filled with all the fullness of God.

20 Now to Him who is able to do exceedingly abundantly above all that we ask or think, according to the power that works in us, 21 to Him *be* glory in the church by Christ Jesus to all generations, forever and ever. Amen.

4 I, therefore, the prisoner of the Lord, beseech you to walk worthy of the calling with which you were called, 2 with all lowliness and gentleness, with longsuffering, bearing with one another in love, 3 endeavoring to keep the unity of the Spirit in the bond of peace. 4 *There is* one body and one Spirit, just as you were called in one hope of your calling; 5 one Lord, one faith, one baptism; 6 one God and Father of all, who *is* above all, and through all, and in you*a* all.

7 But to each one of us grace was given according to the measure of Christ's gift. 8 Therefore He says:

"When He ascended on high,
He led captivity captive,
*And gave gifts to men."*a*

9 (Now this, *"He ascended"*—what does it mean but that He also first*a* descended into the lower parts of the earth? 10 He who descended is also the One who ascended far above all the heavens, that He might fill all things.)

11 And He Himself gave some *to be* apostles, some prophets, some evangelists, and some pastors and teachers, 12 for the equipping of the saints for the work of ministry, for the edifying of the body of Christ, 13 till we all come to the unity of the faith and of the knowledge of the Son of God, to a perfect man, to the measure of the stature of the fullness of Christ; 14 that we should no longer be children, tossed to and fro and carried about with every wind of doctrine, by the trickery of men, in the cunning craftiness of deceitful plotting, 15 but, speaking the truth in love, may grow up in all things into Him who is the head—Christ— 16 from whom the whole body, joined and knit together by what every joint supplies, according to the effective working by which every part does its share, causes growth of the body for the edifying of itself in love.

17 This I say, therefore, and testify in the Lord, that you should no longer walk as the rest of the*a* Gentiles walk, in the futility of their mind, 18 having their understanding darkened, being alienated from the life of God, because of the ignorance that is in them, because of the blindness of their heart; 19 who, being past feeling, have given themselves over to lewdness, to work all uncleanness with greediness.

3:9 *a*NU-Text and M-Text read *stewardship (dispensation).*   *b*NU-Text omits *through Jesus Christ.*
3:14 *a*NU-Text omits *of our Lord Jesus Christ.*   4:6 *a*NU-Text omits *you;* M-Text reads *us.*   4:8 *a*Psalm 68:18   4:9 *a*NU-Text omits *first.*   4:17 *a*NU-Text omits *rest of the.*

Gospel
Pearls

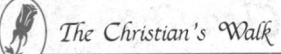

20 But you have not so learned Christ, 21 if indeed you have heard Him and have been taught by Him, as the truth is in Jesus: 22 that you put off, concerning your former conduct, the old man which grows corrupt according to the deceitful lusts, 23 and be renewed in the spirit of your mind, 24 and that you put on the new man which was created according to God, in true righteousness and holiness.

25 Therefore, putting away lying, *"Let each one of you speak truth with his neighbor,"ª* for we are members of one another. 26 *"Be angry, and do not sin":ª* do not let the sun go down on your wrath, 27 nor give place to the devil. 28 Let him who stole steal no longer, but rather let him labor, working with *his* hands what is good, that he may have something to give him who has need. 29 Let no corrupt word proceed out of your mouth, but what is good for necessary edification, that it may impart grace to the hearers. 30 And do not grieve the Holy Spirit of God, by whom you were sealed for the day of redemption. 31 Let all bitterness, wrath, anger, clamor, and evil speaking be put away from you, with all malice. 32 And be kind to one another, tenderhearted, forgiving one another, even as God in Christ forgave you.

5 Therefore be imitators of God as dear children. 2 And walk in love, as Christ also has loved us and given Himself for us, an offering and a sacrifice to God for a sweet-smelling aroma.

3 But fornication and all uncleanness or covetousness, let it not even be named among you, as is fitting for saints; 4 neither filthiness, nor foolish talking, nor coarse jesting, which are not fitting, but rather giving of thanks. 5 For this you know,ª that no fornicator, unclean person, nor covetous man, who is an idolater, has any inheritance in the kingdom of Christ and God. 6 Let no one deceive you with empty words, for because of these things the wrath of God comes upon the sons of disobedience. 7 Therefore do not be partakers with them.

8 For you were once darkness, but now *you are* light in the Lord. Walk as children of light 9 (for the fruit of the Spiritª *is* in all goodness, righteousness, and truth), 10 finding out what is acceptable to the Lord. 11 And have no fellowship with the unfruitful works of darkness, but rather expose *them.* 12 For it is shameful even to speak of those things which are done by them in secret. 13 But all things that are exposed are made manifest by the light, for whatever makes manifest is light. 14 Therefore He says:

"Awake, you who sleep,
Arise from the dead,
And Christ will give you light."

15 See then that you walk circumspectly, not as fools but as wise, 16 redeeming the time, because the days are evil.

17 Therefore do not be unwise, but understand what the will of the Lord *is.* 18 And do not be drunk with wine, in which is dissipation; but be filled with the Spirit, 19 speaking to one another in psalms and hymns and spiritual songs, singing and making melody in your heart to the Lord, 20 giving thanks always for all things to God the Father in the name of our Lord Jesus Christ, 21 submitting to one another in the fear of God.ª

22 Wives, submit to your own husbands, as to the Lord. 23 For the husband is head of the wife, as also Christ is head of the church; and He is the Savior of the body. 24 Therefore, just as the church is subject to Christ, so *let* the wives *be* to their own husbands in everything.

25 Husbands, love your wives, just as Christ also loved the church and gave Himself for her, 26 that He might sanctify and cleanse her with the washing of water by the word, 27 that He might present her to Himself a glorious church, not having spot or wrinkle or any such thing, but that she should be holy and without blemish. 28 So husbands ought to love their own wives as their own bodies; he who loves his wife loves himself. 29 For no one ever hated his own flesh, but nourishes and cherishes it, just as the Lord *does* the church. 30 For we are members of His

---

4:25 ªZechariah 8:16   4:26 ªPsalm 4:4   5:5 ªNU-Text reads *For know this.*   5:9 ªNU-Text reads *light.*   5:21 ªNU-Text reads *Christ.*

Although David longed to follow God, some of his passions and lust were inherited by his children. That is a tendency we must resist. We ought not repeat the failure of our fathers. We are most vulnerable, however, to our father's weaknesses.

Leaving and Cleaving

Ephesians 5:31

The first female mentioned in the Bible was created without a childhood or an example to define her role and her relationship to her husband. The first female was a full-grown woman, fashioned while Adam was asleep. She was God's gift to him. I believe it would be better if we still allowed God to bring us what He has for us.

When God wanted to be praised, He created man in His own likeness or image. Likewise, God gave man someone like himself. Adam called her "womb-man" or woman. Like the Church of Christ, Eve was his body and his bride. They were made of the same material. Adam said, "This is now bone of my bones and flesh of my flesh" (Genesis 2:23). He says nothing of her size or body build or hair color. These superficial components are like placing a product in an attractive container. The packaging may get the consumer to try the product, but only the product itself will keep the consumer coming back for more.

When you find a person with whom you are compatible, there is a bonding that consummates marriage and it has nothing to do with sex. Let's face it, everyone you meet isn't bone of your bones. It is important that you do not allow anyone to manipulate you into choosing someone with whom you have no bond. Every woman must pray and discern if this man is the one she could cleave to for the rest of her life.

The Bible says, "For this reason a man shall leave his father and mother and be joined [cleave] to his wife, and the two shall become one flesh" (Ephesians 5:31). The term *cleave* is translated from a Hebrew word that means "to cling or adhere to; to catch by pursuit or follow close after." There is a great need in most of our lives to cleave, to feel that this is where we belong. It is sad to realize that our society has become so promiscuous that many have mistaken the thrill of a weekend fling for the knitting together of two thirsty hearts at the oasis of a loving commitment.

The secret to *cleaving* is *leaving*. If you enter into marriage and still leave other options open, whether mental, emotional, or physical, your marriage will never work. When the tugging of adversity tries the bonds of your matrimony, you will fall apart. You must leave everyone else and cleave to your husband. It is unhealthy to cleave to someone other than your spouse for support. No other friendship, however wholesome, should have more influence over you than your spouse. Some of you could save your marriages if you would leave some of these extramarital ties and cleave to your companion!

body,[a] of His flesh and of His bones. 31 *"For this reason a man shall leave his father and mother and be joined to his wife, and the two shall become one flesh."*[a] 32 This is a great mystery, but I speak concerning Christ and the church. 33 Nevertheless let each one of you in particular so love his own wife as himself, and let the wife *see* that she respects *her* husband.

6 Children, obey your parents in the Lord, for this is right. 2 *"Honor your father and mother,"*[a] which is the first commandment with promise: 3 *"that it may be well with you and you may live long on the earth."*

4 And you, fathers, do not provoke your children to wrath, but bring them up in the training and admonition of the Lord.

5 Bondservants, be obedient to those who are your masters according to the flesh, with fear and trembling, in sincerity of heart, as to Christ; 6 not with eyeservice, as menpleasers, but as bondservants of Christ, doing the will of God from the heart, 7 with good will doing service, as to the Lord, and not to men, 8 knowing that whatever good anyone does, he will receive the same from the Lord, whether *he is* a slave or free.

9 And you, masters, do the same things to them, giving up threatening, knowing that your own Master also[a] is in heaven, and there is no partiality with Him.

10 Finally, my brethren, be strong in the Lord and in the power of His might. 11 Put on the whole armor of God, that you may be able to stand against the wiles of the devil. 12 For we do not wrestle against flesh and blood, but against principalities, against powers, against the rulers of the darkness of this age,[a] against spiritual *hosts* of wickedness in the heavenly *places.* 13 Therefore take up the whole armor of God, that you may be able to withstand in the evil day, and having done all, to stand.

14 Stand therefore, having girded your waist with truth, having put on the breastplate of righteousness, 15 and having shod your feet with the preparation of the gospel of peace; 16 above all, taking the shield of faith with which you will be able to quench all the fiery darts of the wicked one. 17 And take the helmet of salvation, and the sword of the Spirit, which is the word of God; 18 praying always with all prayer and supplication in the Spirit, being watchful to this end with all perseverance and supplication for all the saints— 19 and for me, that utterance may be given to me, that I may open my mouth boldly to make known the mystery of the gospel, 20 for which I am an ambassador in chains; that in it I may speak boldly, as I ought to speak.

21 But that you also may know my affairs *and* how I am doing, Tychicus, a beloved brother and faithful minister in the Lord, will make all things known to you; 22 whom I have sent to you for this very purpose, that you may know our affairs, and *that* he may comfort your hearts.

23 Peace to the brethren, and love with faith, from God the Father and the Lord Jesus Christ. 24 Grace *be* with all those who love our Lord Jesus Christ in sincerity. Amen.

5:30 [a]NU-Text omits the rest of this verse. 5:31 [a]Genesis 2:24 6:2 [a]Deuteronomy 5:16
6:9 [a]NU-Text reads *He who is both their Master and yours.* 6:12 [a]NU-Text reads *rulers of this darkness.*

*T*here are a whole lot of different types of brokenness. They do not always focus on being impoverished. There are those among us who have not been ministered to because our society suggests that when you are famous or affluent you must be fulfilled. But ask Lydia whose life was so changed that she became a major supporter of ministry.

Stand

Ephesians 6:13, 14

S ince we are born with all sorts of human weaknesses, what are we to do when the devil comes along?

The Bible says, "having done all . . . Stand therefore" (Ephesians 6:13, 14). In Romans 14:4, we read, "God is able to make [you] stand." Not in your strength, but in the strength of Jesus Christ. You can't stand in your own strength. All by yourself, you're just another Eve. But in the strength of Jesus, you can stand and not give in.

God's way isn't always easy. It may be the perfect way, the ideal way, the truly "natural" way according to His creation, but you still may have to work at it. Just because something is right doesn't mean it's easy. Some days you need a little more strength than on other days. Every time you need help, run to the Breasted One. He has what you need. He longs to hold you and comfort you and impart to you the strength you need to move forward.

Your tremors of temptation, your moods and attitudes toward sin, will pass if you will only stand up to them in His name. The blood of Jesus Christ has set you free and will continue to uphold you, if you will just stand on Christ the solid rock!

When the devil shows up with his temptations, announce that you are going to stand in Christ. You're going to stand until the shaking quits, until the thunder stops rolling, until midnight passes into dawn, until you feel peace again, until the wave of loneliness passes, until your marriage is restored, until you come out of debt, until your struggle is over!

When you do the standing, God does the strengthening. Paul said, "I can do all things through Christ who strengthens me" (Philippians 4:13). Christ doesn't strengthen you just once. He will strengthen you again and again and again. He will strengthen you every time you face a difficult challenge, every time a memory comes back to haunt you, every time you're reminded of your imperfect past, every time you face a decision.

Drawing from God the strength you need to stand up to the devil may take effort. It may take your praise, your prayer, your getting into His Word with an intensity you've never had before.

But the fact is, you can stand if you want to. So, stand!

The Epistle of Paul the Apostle to the

PHILIPPIANS

1 Paul and Timothy, bondservants of Jesus Christ,

To all the saints in Christ Jesus who are in Philippi, with the bishops*a* and deacons:

2 Grace to you and peace from God our Father and the Lord Jesus Christ.

3 I thank my God upon every remembrance of you, 4 always in every prayer of mine making request for you all with joy, 5 for your fellowship in the gospel from the first day until now, 6 being confident of this very thing, that He who has begun a good work in you will complete *it* until the day of Jesus Christ; 7 just as it is right for me to think this of you all, because I have you in my heart, inasmuch as both in my chains and in the defense and confirmation of the gospel, you all are partakers with me of grace. 8 For God is my witness, how greatly I long for you all with the affection of Jesus Christ.

9 And this I pray, that your love may abound still more and more in knowledge and all discernment, 10 that you may approve the things that are excellent, that you may be sincere and without offense till the day of Christ, 11 being filled with the fruits of righteousness which *are* by Jesus Christ, to the glory and praise of God.

12 But I want you to know, brethren, that the things *which happened* to me have actually turned out for the furtherance of the gospel, 13 so that it has become evident to the whole palace guard, and to all the rest, that my chains are in Christ; 14 and most of the brethren in the Lord, having become confident by my chains, are much more bold to speak the word without fear.

15 Some indeed preach Christ even from envy and strife, and some also from goodwill: 16 The former*a* preach Christ from selfish ambition, not sincerely, supposing to add affliction to my chains; 17 but the latter out of love, knowing that I am appointed for the defense of the gospel. 18 What then? Only *that* in every way, whether in pretense or in truth, Christ is preached; and in this I rejoice, yes, and will rejoice.

19 For I know that this will turn out for my deliverance through your prayer and the supply of the Spirit of Jesus Christ, 20 according to my earnest expectation and hope that in nothing I shall be ashamed, but with all boldness, as always, so now also Christ will be magnified in my body, whether by life or by death. 21 For to me, to live *is* Christ, and to die *is* gain. 22 But if *I* live on in the flesh, this *will mean* fruit from *my* labor; yet what I shall choose I cannot tell. 23 For*a* I am hard pressed between the two, having a desire to depart and be with Christ, *which is* far better. 24 Nevertheless to remain in the flesh *is* more needful for you. 25 And being confident of this, I know that I shall remain and continue with you all for your progress and joy of faith, 26 that your rejoicing for me may be more abundant in Jesus Christ by my coming to you again.

27 Only let your conduct be worthy of the gospel of Christ, so that whether I come and see you or am absent, I may hear of your affairs, that you stand fast in one spirit, with one mind striving together for the faith of the gospel, 28 and not in any way terrified by your adversaries, which is to them a proof of perdition, but to you of salvation,*a* and that from God. 29 For to you it has been granted on behalf of Christ, not only to believe in Him, but also to suffer for His sake, 30 having the same conflict which you saw in me and now hear *is* in me.

2 Therefore if *there is* any consolation in Christ, if any comfort of love, if any fellowship of the Spirit, if any affection and mercy, 2 fulfill my joy by being like-minded, having the same love, *being* of one accord, of one mind. 3 *Let* nothing *be done* through selfish ambition or conceit,

---

1:1 *a*Literally *overseers* and M-Text read *But.*   1:16 *a*NU-Text reverses the contents of verses 16 and 17.   1:23 *a*NU-Text and M-Text read *But.*   1:28 *a*NU-Text reads *of your salvation.*

---

*T*here can be no argument that David frequently allowed his passions to lead him into moral failure. However, he was a man who recognized his failures and repented. He was a man who sought God's heart.

but in lowliness of mind let each esteem others better than himself. 4 Let each of you look out not only for his own interests, but also for the interests of others.

5 Let this mind be in you which was also in Christ Jesus, 6 who, being in the form of God, did not consider it robbery to be equal with God, 7 but made Himself of no reputation, taking the form of a bondservant, *and* coming in the likeness of men. 8 And being found in appearance as a man, He humbled Himself and became obedient to *the point of* death, even the death of the cross. 9 Therefore God also has highly exalted Him and given Him the name which is above every name, 10 that at the name of Jesus every knee should bow, of those in heaven, and of those on earth, and of those under the earth, 11 and *that* every tongue should confess that Jesus Christ *is* Lord, to the glory of God the Father.

12 Therefore, my beloved, as you have always obeyed, not as in my presence only, but now much more in my absence, work out your own salvation with fear and trembling; 13 for it is God who works in you both to will and to do for *His* good pleasure.

14 Do all things without complaining and disputing, 15 that you may become blameless and harmless, children of God without fault in the midst of a crooked and perverse generation, among whom you shine as lights in the world, 16 holding fast the word of life, so that I may rejoice in the day of Christ that I have not run in vain or labored in vain.

17 Yes, and if I am being poured out *as a drink offering* on the sacrifice and service of your faith, I am glad and rejoice with you all. 18 For the same reason you also be glad and rejoice with me.

19 But I trust in the Lord Jesus to send Timothy to you shortly, that I also may be encouraged when I know your state. 20 For I have no one like-minded, who will sincerely care for your state. 21 For all seek their own, not the things which are of Christ Jesus. 22 But you know his proven character, that as a son with

his father he served with me in the gospel. 23 Therefore I hope to send him at once, as soon as I see how it goes with me. 24 But I trust in the Lord that I myself shall also come shortly.

25 Yet I considered it necessary to send to you Epaphroditus, my brother, fellow worker, and fellow soldier, but your messenger and the one who ministered to my need; 26 since he was longing for you all, and was distressed because you had heard that he was sick. 27 For indeed he was sick almost unto death; but God had mercy on him, and not only on him but on me also, lest I should have sorrow upon sorrow. 28 Therefore I sent him the more eagerly, that when you see him again you may rejoice, and I may be less sorrowful. 29 Receive him therefore in the Lord with all gladness, and hold such men in esteem; 30 because for the work of Christ he came close to death, not regarding his life, to supply what was lacking in your service toward me.

3 Finally, my brethren, rejoice in the Lord. For me to write the same things to you *is* not tedious, but for you *it is* safe.

2 Beware of dogs, beware of evil workers, beware of the mutilation! 3 For we are the circumcision, who worship God in the Spirit,*a* rejoice in Christ Jesus, and have no confidence in the flesh, 4 though I also might have confidence in the flesh. If anyone else thinks he may have confidence in the flesh, I more so: 5 circumcised the eighth day, of the stock of Israel, *of* the tribe of Benjamin, a Hebrew of the Hebrews; concerning the law, a Pharisee; 6 concerning zeal, persecuting the church; concerning the righteousness which is in the law, blameless.

7 But what things were gain to me, these I have counted loss for Christ. 8 Yet indeed I also count all things loss for the excellence of the knowledge of Christ Jesus my Lord, for whom I have suffered the loss of all things, and count them as rubbish, that I may gain Christ 9 and be found in Him, not having my own righteousness, which *is* from the law, but

3:3 *a*NU-Text and M-Text read *who worship in the Spirit of God.*

*T*he Church needs to develop a ministry of hugs. The touch of the Master sets us free. The touch of a fellow pilgrim lets us know we are not alone in our plight.

Push!

Philippians 3:13, 14

The apostle Paul talks about pressing "toward the goal for the prize of the upward call of God in Christ Jesus" (Philippians 3:14). Pressing is pushing.

When you commit to bring forth all that God has for you, you may have to push against everything anybody ever did to you or said about you. You may have to battle years of suppression, oppression, and depression. You may have to push with all your might to release the treasure God has put within you, but He wants to bring it to birth. He put the treasure there. He'll help you bring the treasure out. But it is up to you to push. In fact, it may not happen if you don't!

But what do you push against? You don't push against other people. This isn't a battle in the natural. It is a battle in the spirit. You have to push against the opposition of the devil in its many forms. His opposition attacks you in subtle, but debilitating ways, such as bad memories, low self-esteem, or feelings of unworthiness. The devil may have spent years pushing you aside, pulling you back, and putting you down. But now the Lord says to you, "I want to open you up. I want you to give birth to that which I put in you."

It is time to say to yourself and to the world, "It's my turn to conceive. It's time for the treasure that God put inside me to come forth. It's time for me to be loosed to do what God created me to do."

When a baby is born, everything in the family changes. The same is true for you. When you give birth to the treasure God has put in you, everything around you will be different—your marriage, your relationship with your children, your place in your church, your neighborhood, and your work-place. God's blessing is an overflowing blessing, and it touches every area of your life.

Every woman knows when she is pregnant. In fact, a woman often has an inner knowing long before she feels the baby moving inside her womb. The same is true in the spiritual realm. I'm talking about giving birth to the gifts and talents and powers and the ministries of the Holy Spirit inside you. I don't know what specific thing God wants to birth in you, but you do. Like an expectant mother, you have a knowing deep inside.

Don't fail today to give birth to what God put in you. Now is the time for the baby—that treasure—to be born. Go for it. Push!

that which *is* through faith in Christ, the righteousness which is from God by faith; 10 that I may know Him and the power of His resurrection, and the fellowship of His sufferings, being conformed to His death, 11 if, by any means, I may attain to the resurrection from the dead.

12 Not that I have already attained, or am already perfected; but I press on, that I may lay hold of that for which Christ Jesus has also laid hold of me. 13 Brethren, I do not count myself to have apprehended; but one thing *I do,* forgetting those things which are behind and reaching forward to those things which are ahead, 14 I press toward the goal for the prize of the upward call of God in Christ Jesus.

15 Therefore let us, as many as are mature, have this mind; and if in anything you think otherwise, God will reveal even this to you. 16 Nevertheless, to *the degree* that we have already attained, let us walk by the same rule,*a* let us be of the same mind.

17 Brethren, join in following my example, and note those who so walk, as you have us for a pattern. 18 For many walk, of whom I have told you often, and now tell you even weeping, *that they are* the enemies of the cross of Christ: 19 whose end *is* destruction, whose god *is their* belly, and *whose* glory *is* in their shame—who set their mind on earthly things. 20 For our citizenship is in heaven, from which we also eagerly wait for the Savior, the Lord Jesus Christ, 21 who will transform our lowly body that it may be conformed to His glorious body, according to the working by which He is able even to subdue all things to Himself.

4 Therefore, my beloved and longed-for brethren, my joy and crown, so stand fast in the Lord, beloved.

2 I implore Euodia and I implore Syntyche to be of the same mind in the Lord. 3 And*a* I urge you also, true companion, help these women who labored with me in the gospel, with Clement also, and the rest of my fellow workers, whose names *are* in the Book of Life.

4 Rejoice in the Lord always. Again I will say, rejoice!

5 Let your gentleness be known to all men. The Lord *is* at hand.

6 Be anxious for nothing, but in everything by prayer and supplication, with thanksgiving, let your requests be made known to God; 7 and the peace of God, which surpasses all understanding, will guard your hearts and minds through Christ Jesus.

8 Finally, brethren, whatever things are true, whatever things *are* noble, whatever things *are* just, whatever things *are* pure, whatever things *are* lovely, whatever things *are* of good report, if *there is* any virtue and if *there is* anything praiseworthy—meditate on these things. 9 The things which you learned and received and heard and saw in me, these do, and the God of peace will be with you.

10 But I rejoiced in the Lord greatly that now at last your care for me has flourished again; though you surely did care, but you lacked opportunity. 11 Not that I speak in regard to need, for I have learned in whatever state I am, to be content: 12 I know how to be abased, and I know how to abound. Everywhere and in all things I have learned both to be full and to be hungry, both to abound and to suffer need. 13 I can do all things through Christ*a* who strengthens me.

14 Nevertheless you have done well that you shared in my distress. 15 Now you Philippians know also that in the beginning of the gospel, when I departed from Macedonia, no church shared with me concerning giving and receiving but you only. 16 For even in Thessalonica you sent *aid* once and again for my necessities. 17 Not that I seek the gift, but I seek the fruit that abounds to your account. 18 Indeed I have all and abound. I am full, having received from Epaphroditus the things *sent* from you, a sweet-smelling aroma, an acceptable sacrifice, well pleasing to God. 19 And my God shall supply all your need according to His riches in glory by

---

3:16 *a*NU-Text omits *rule* and the rest of verse.   4:3 *a*NU-Text and M-Text read *Yes.*   4:13 *a*NU-Text reads *Him who.*

If you're going to bring forth anything in your career, your marriage, or your life; if you're going to develop anything in your character; if you're going to be a fruitful woman, it will come through the things you suffer. You will enter into strength through sorrow.

Look to God

Philippians 4:19, 20

Look to God when there are needs in your life. He satisfies. Like calm sheep grazing in the afternoon sun, you will find fulfillment for your soul and contentment with yourself.

There is a difference between wants and needs. There are many things that you will want and some that you will intensely desire. That doesn't necessarily mean you will have them. There will be many desires that are born in your heart through other sources. Some will come from your peers and friends. Some will come from your age and stage in life. There will be times when things as inanimate as a television set will influence what you feel you need. Amidst all of these influences, God will not grant to you everything you suggest. A good father doesn't give in to every whim. He decides carefully what is best for his daughters.

It is going to require faith, but you must with maturity begin to conclude that if God doesn't grant it, you don't need it. You may want it; but if it were a need, He would have supplied it. He promised. You don't have to beg or plead. You don't have to manipulate or pout. If God has promised, His Word is sure. That means that when there is a discrepancy between what you think you need and what is being supplied, God cannot lie. If it were for your good—if it were a need, emotionally, physically, or spiritually—He would supply it.

Remember that you are to prosper and be in good health as your soul prospers (see 3 John 2). If your soul is not prospering, that is the primary need. Nothing should be of greater concern that that. Every other supply is going to flow "as your soul prospers." That is why you must be sure that you maintain a healthy heart for God and a sound mind. For what would it profit you as a woman to gain this whole world and lose your soul (see Mark 8:36)?

Don't lose your soul (mind, memory, and affections) over things. Don't stress out or burn out, become jealous or enter into warfare over things. They will not profit if your values are misconstrued. Keep your head in the right place. Seek His kingdom and His righteousness, and all these things, whatever they are, shall be added unto you (see Matthew 6:33). Why? Because they will come to you as your soul prospers.

If you are reading this page, and your whole life has been ransacked, the very first thing you should do is make sure you are in a right relationship with Jesus Christ. It does matter. When you are in right standing with Him, you have a guarantee that if something is a need, He will supply it. It may not come when you think you should have it, but it will come when you need it most.

Christ Jesus. 20 Now to our God and Father *be* glory forever and ever. Amen.

21 Greet every saint in Christ Jesus. The brethren who are with me greet you. 22 All the saints greet you, but especially those who are of Caesar's household.

23 The grace of our Lord Jesus Christ be with you all.*a* Amen.

4:23 *a*NU-Text reads *your spirit.*

The Epistle of Paul the Apostle to the

COLOSSIANS

1 Paul, an apostle of Jesus Christ by the will of God, and Timothy our brother,

2 To the saints and faithful brethren in Christ *who are* in Colosse:

Grace to you and peace from God our Father and the Lord Jesus Christ.*a*

3 We give thanks to the God and Father of our Lord Jesus Christ, praying always for you, 4 since we heard of your faith in Christ Jesus and of your love for all the saints; 5 because of the hope which is laid up for you in heaven, of which you heard before in the word of the truth of the gospel, 6 which has come to you, as *it has* also in all the world, and is bringing forth fruit,*a* as *it is* also among you since the day you heard and knew the grace of God in truth; 7 as you also learned from Epaphras, our dear fellow servant, who is a faithful minister of Christ on your behalf, 8 who also declared to us your love in the Spirit.

9 For this reason we also, since the day we heard it, do not cease to pray for you, and to ask that you may be filled with the knowledge of His will in all wisdom and spiritual understanding; 10 that you may walk worthy of the Lord, fully pleasing *Him,* being fruitful in every good work and increasing in the knowledge of God; 11 strengthened with all might, according to His glorious power, for all patience and longsuffering with joy; 12 giving thanks to the Father who has qualified us to be partakers of the inheritance of the saints in the light. 13 He has delivered us from the power of darkness and conveyed *us* into the kingdom of the Son of His love, 14 in whom we have redemption through His blood,*a* the forgiveness of sins.

15 He is the image of the invisible God, the firstborn over all creation. 16 For by Him all things were created that are in heaven and that are on earth, visible and invisible, whether thrones or dominions or principalities or powers. All things were created through Him and for Him. 17 And He is before all things, and in Him all things consist. 18 And He is the head of the body, the church, who is the beginning, the firstborn from the dead, that in all things He may have the preeminence.

19 For it pleased *the Father that* in Him all the fullness should dwell, 20 and by Him to reconcile all things to Himself, by Him, whether things on earth or things in heaven, having made peace through the blood of His cross.

21 And you, who once were alienated and enemies in your mind by wicked works, yet now He has reconciled 22 in the body of His flesh through death, to present you holy, and blameless, and above reproach in His sight— 23 if indeed you continue in the faith, grounded and steadfast, and are not moved away from the hope of the gospel which you heard, which was preached to every creature under heaven, of which I, Paul, became a minister.

24 I now rejoice in my sufferings for

1:2 *a*NU-Text omits *and the Lord Jesus Christ.*   1:6 *a*NU-Text and M-Text add *and growing.*
1:14 *a*NU-Text and M-Text omit *through His blood.*

*P*ut the truth in your spirit and feed, nurture, and allow it to grow. Quit telling yourself, "You're too fat, too old, too late, or too ignorant." Stop feeding yourself that garbage.

Beautiful Package, Beautiful Gift

Colossians 1:9-11

The greater part of your attractiveness—the part that draws or attracts other people to you—is on the inside, not on your flesh. Our society spends billions of dollars a year to convince you to buy hundreds, even thousands of dollars worth of clothes and makeup in order to fix up something that doesn't really matter all that much. We spend countless hours at beauty salons and spas and malls in order to buy, acquire, or create the things we think will draw other people to us, but which actually have very little drawing power. What you create or design on the outside of yourself may turn a head or two, but it is powerless to turn a mind or a heart.

You are bombarded daily with messages that tell you that if you will only go to the right weight-loss center and get down to the right size, dye your hair the right shade, go to the right spa, use the right toothpaste, put on the right makeup, wear the right outfit at the right time, and be seen in the right places with the right people, then you will most certainly be able to attract the right man and have the right children and live in the right neighborhood and enjoy the right kind of life!

When we do this and nothing "right" happens for us, we are puzzled. We sit back and ask, "What went wrong?" This is what went wrong: We became the merchandise for those who tried to sell us the merchandise. We've been had! The average woman, Christians included, will spend thousands of dollars this year on hats and hair color, earrings and evening dresses. Sadly, they will make no real investment to build up or support those inner qualities that truly attract others to us and to Jesus Christ our Savior.

If you are only concerned with what you look like, you are going to be a very shallow, superficial person. People are going to find that once they have quit playing with you, the box you came in was beautifully wrapped, but empty.

Go back to the source of your attractiveness—the Holy Spirit of God. He is the One who woos and wins the heart. When you are His woman, He will draw you to the right people for the right purposes at just the right time.

you, and fill up in my flesh what is lacking in the afflictions of Christ, for the sake of His body, which is the church, 25 of which I became a minister according to the stewardship from God which was given to me for you, to fulfill the word of God, 26 the mystery which has been hidden from ages and from generations, but now has been revealed to His saints. 27 To them God willed to make known what are the riches of the glory of this mystery among the Gentiles: which*a* is Christ in you, the hope of glory. 28 Him we preach, warning every man and teaching every man in all wisdom, that we may present every man perfect in Christ Jesus. 29 To this *end* I also labor, striving according to His working which works in me mightily.

2 For I want you to know what a great conflict I have for you and those in Laodicea, and *for* as many as have not seen my face in the flesh, 2 that their hearts may be encouraged, being knit together in love, and *attaining* to all riches of the full assurance of understanding, to the knowledge of the mystery of God, both of the Father and*a* of Christ, 3 in whom are hidden all the treasures of wisdom and knowledge.

4 Now this I say lest anyone should deceive you with persuasive words. 5 For though I am absent in the flesh, yet I am with you in spirit, rejoicing to see your *good* order and the steadfastness of your faith in Christ.

6 As you therefore have received Christ Jesus the Lord, so walk in Him, 7 rooted and built up in Him and established in the faith, as you have been taught, abounding in it*a* with thanksgiving.

8 Beware lest anyone cheat you through philosophy and empty deceit, according to the tradition of men, according to the basic principles of the world, and not according to Christ. 9 For in Him dwells all the fullness of the Godhead bodily; 10 and you are complete in Him, who is the head of all principality and power.

11 In Him you were also circumcised with the circumcision made without hands, by putting off the body of the sins*a* of the flesh, by the circumcision of Christ, 12 buried with Him in baptism, in which you also were raised with *Him* through faith in the working of God, who raised Him from the dead. 13 And you, being dead in your trespasses and the uncircumcision of your flesh, He has made alive together with Him, having forgiven you all trespasses, 14 having wiped out the handwriting of requirements that was against us, which was contrary to us. And He has taken it out of the way, having nailed it to the cross. 15 Having disarmed principalities and powers, He made a public spectacle of them, triumphing over them in it.

16 So let no one judge you in food or in drink, or regarding a festival or a new moon or sabbaths, 17 which are a shadow of things to come, but the substance is of Christ. 18 Let no one cheat you of your reward, taking delight in *false* humility and worship of angels, intruding into those things which he has not*a* seen, vainly puffed up by his fleshly mind, 19 and not holding fast to the Head, from whom all the body, nourished and knit together by joints and ligaments, grows with the increase *that is* from God.

20 Therefore,*a* if you died with Christ from the basic principles of the world, why, as *though* living in the world, do you subject yourselves to regulations— 21 "Do not touch, do not taste, do not handle," 22 which all concern things which perish with the using—according to the commandments and doctrines of men? 23 These things indeed have an appearance of wisdom in self-imposed religion, *false* humility, and neglect of the body, *but are* of no value against the indulgence of the flesh.

3 If then you were raised with Christ, seek those things which are above, where Christ is, sitting at the right hand of God. 2 Set your mind on things above, not on things on the earth. 3 For you died, and your life is hidden with Christ in God. 4 When Christ *who is* our life ap-

---

1:27 *a*M-Text reads *who*.   2:2 *a*NU-Text omits *both of the Father and*.   2:7 *a*NU-Text omits *in it*.
2:11 *a*NU-Text omits *of the sins*.   2:18 *a*NU-Text omits *not*.   2:20 *a*NU-Text and M-Text omit *Therefore*.

Gospel Pearls

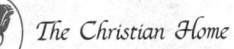
pears, then you also will appear with Him in glory.

5 Therefore put to death your members which are on the earth: fornication, uncleanness, passion, evil desire, and covetousness, which is idolatry. 6 Because of these things the wrath of God is coming upon the sons of disobedience, 7 in which you yourselves once walked when you lived in them.

8 But now you yourselves are to put off all these: anger, wrath, malice, blasphemy, filthy language out of your mouth. 9 Do not lie to one another, since you have put off the old man with his deeds, 10 and have put on the new *man* who is renewed in knowledge according to the image of Him who created him, 11 where there is neither Greek nor Jew, circumcised nor uncircumcised, barbarian, Scythian, slave *nor* free, but Christ *is* all and in all.

12 Therefore, as *the* elect of God, holy and beloved, put on tender mercies, kindness, humility, meekness, longsuffering; 13 bearing with one another, and forgiving one another, if anyone has a complaint against another; even as Christ forgave you, so you also *must do.* 14 But above all these things put on love, which is the bond of perfection. 15 And let the peace of God rule in your hearts, to which also you were called in one body; and be thankful. 16 Let the word of Christ dwell in you richly in all wisdom, teaching and admonishing one another in psalms and hymns and spiritual songs, singing with grace in your hearts to the Lord. 17 And *whatever* you do in word or deed, *do* all in the name of the Lord Jesus, giving thanks to God the Father through Him.

18 Wives, submit to your own husbands, as is fitting in the Lord.

19 Husbands, love your wives and do not be bitter toward them.

20 Children, obey your parents in all things, for this is well pleasing to the Lord.

21 Fathers, do not provoke your children, lest they become discouraged.

22 Bondservants, obey in all things your masters according to the flesh, not with eyeservice, as men-pleasers, but in sincerity of heart, fearing God. 23 And whatever you do, do it heartily, as to the Lord and not to men, 24 knowing that from the Lord you will receive the reward of the inheritance; for[a] you serve the Lord Christ. 25 But he who does wrong will be repaid for what he has done, and there is no partiality.

4 Masters, give your bondservants what is just and fair, knowing that you also have a Master in heaven.

2 Continue earnestly in prayer, being vigilant in it with thanksgiving; 3 meanwhile praying also for us, that God would open to us a door for the word, to speak the mystery of Christ, for which I am also in chains, 4 that I may make it manifest, as I ought to speak.

5 Walk in wisdom toward those *who are* outside, redeeming the time. 6 *Let* your speech always *be* with grace, seasoned with salt, that you may know how you ought to answer each one.

7 Tychicus, a beloved brother, faithful minister, and fellow servant in the Lord, will tell you all the news about me. 8 I am sending him to you for this very purpose, that he[a] may know your circumstances and comfort your hearts, 9 with Onesimus, a faithful and beloved brother, who is *one* of you. They will make known to you all things which *are happening* here.

10 Aristarchus my fellow prisoner greets you, with Mark the cousin of Barnabas (about whom you received instructions: if he comes to you, welcome him), 11 and Jesus who is called Justus. These *are my* only fellow workers for the kingdom of God who are of the circumcision; they have proved to be a comfort to me.

12 Epaphras, who is *one* of you, a bondservant of Christ, greets you, always laboring fervently for you in prayers, that you may stand perfect and complete[a] in all the will of God. 13 For I bear him witness that he has a great zeal[a] for you, and those who are in Laodicea, and those in Hierapolis. 14 Luke the beloved physician and Demas greet you. 15 Greet the

---

3:24 [a]NU-Text omits *for.*   4:8 [a]NU-Text reads *you may know our circumstances and he may.*
4:12 [a]NU-Text reads *fully assured.*   4:13 [a]NU-Text reads *concern.*

---

*E*verything that is tangible started as an intangible. It was a dream, a thought, a word of God. In the same way, what man has invented began as a concept in someone's mind. So just because we don't see it, doesn't mean we won't get it.

Soul Secrets
of a frustrated mother

*L*ord, I am finally bringing this pain to You. I do not know what to do. Parenting is tough! Forgive me for criticizing my parents. I never knew how difficult their job was. Now, all my ideas about children and parenting have shipwrecked. I'm sorting through the debris of my mistakes, looking for Your direction.

At times, I have acted more childish than the children. I have not been a witness behind closed doors. My temper and my attitudes have not reflected You. My lack of control and other shortcomings have come back to haunt me through my children, and I do not like it.

I know that You are the Master Parent. You have such patience and such wisdom with me. Help me to reflect those same graces as I raise my children. You are great at loving damaged children who often fail. Make me the kind of parent to my children that You are to me.

I am through trying to control things that are in Your hands. I repent of my worry and I trust You now to strengthen our relationship with each other and with You. Help me to appreciate the good things and good times we do have. I know that, in the end, things will work out. I claim the promise of the Scripture that says "all things work together for good" to those who love the Lord. Thank You for being my Daddy. I leave my troubles in the lap of Your love.

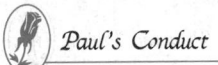

brethren who are in Laodicea, and Nymphas and the church that *is* in his*a* house.

16 Now when this epistle is read among you, see that it is read also in the church of the Laodiceans, and that you likewise read the epistle

from Laodicea. 17 And say to Archippus, "Take heed to the ministry which you have received in the Lord, that you may fulfill it."

18 This salutation by my own hand—Paul. Remember my chains. Grace *be* with you. Amen.

4:15 *a*NU-Text reads *Nympha . . . her house.*

The First Epistle of Paul the Apostle to the
THESSALONIANS

1 Paul, Silvanus, and Timothy,

To the church of the Thessalonians in God the Father and the Lord Jesus Christ:

Grace to you and peace from God our Father and the Lord Jesus Christ.*a*

2 We give thanks to God always for you all, making mention of you in our prayers, 3 remembering without ceasing your work of faith, labor of love, and patience of hope in our Lord Jesus Christ in the sight of our God and Father, 4 knowing, beloved brethren, your election by God. 5 For our gospel did not come to you in word only, but also in power, and in the Holy Spirit and in much assurance, as you know what kind of men we were among you for your sake.

6 And you became followers of us and of the Lord, having received the word in much affliction, with joy of the Holy Spirit, 7 so that you became examples to all in Macedonia and Achaia who believe. 8 For from you the word of the Lord has sounded forth, not only in Macedonia and Achaia, but also in every place. Your faith toward God has gone out, so that we do not need to say anything. 9 For they themselves declare concerning us what manner of entry we had to you, and how you turned to God from idols to serve the living and true God, 10 and to wait for His Son from heaven, whom He raised from

the dead, *even* Jesus who delivers us from the wrath to come.

2 For you yourselves know, brethren, that our coming to you was not in vain. 2 But even*a* after we had suffered before and were spitefully treated at Philippi, as you know, we were bold in our God to speak to you the gospel of God in much conflict. 3 For our exhortation *did* not *come* from error or uncleanness, nor *was it* in deceit.

4 But as we have been approved by God to be entrusted with the gospel, even so we speak, not as pleasing men, but God who tests our hearts. 5 For neither at any time did we use flattering words, as you know, nor a cloak for covetousness—God *is* witness. 6 Nor did we seek glory from men, either from you or from others, when we might have made demands as apostles of Christ. 7 But we were gentle among you, just as a nursing *mother* cherishes her own children. 8 So, affectionately longing for you, we were well pleased to impart to you not only the gospel of God, but also our own lives, because you had become dear to us. 9 For you remember, brethren, our labor and toil; for laboring night and day, that we might not be a burden to any of you, we preached to you the gospel of God.

10 You *are* witnesses, and God *also,* how devoutly and justly and blamelessly we behaved ourselves among you who believe; 11 as you know how

1:1 *a*NU-Text omits *from God our Father and the Lord Jesus Christ.* 2:2 *a*NU-Text and M-Text omit *even.*

*R*ecognize that where life has seemed irrational and out of control, He will turn it around. When trouble was breaking loose in my life, and I thought I couldn't take it anymore, God intervened and broke every chain that held me back. He will do no less for you.

we exhorted, and comforted, and charged[a] every one of you, as a father *does* his own children, 12 that you would walk worthy of God who calls you into His own kingdom and glory.

13 For this reason we also thank God without ceasing, because when you received the word of God which you heard from us, you welcomed *it* not *as* the word of men, but as it is in truth, the word of God, which also effectively works in you who believe. 14 For you, brethren, became imitators of the churches of God which are in Judea in Christ Jesus. For you also suffered the same things from your own countrymen, just as they *did* from the Judeans, 15 who killed both the Lord Jesus and their own prophets, and have persecuted us; and they do not please God and are contrary to all men, 16 forbidding us to speak to the Gentiles that they may be saved, so as always to fill up *the measure of* their sins; but wrath has come upon them to the uttermost.

17 But we, brethren, having been taken away from you for a short time in presence, not in heart, endeavored more eagerly to see your face with great desire. 18 Therefore we wanted to come to you—even I, Paul, time and again—but Satan hindered us. 19 For what *is* our hope, or joy, or crown of rejoicing? *Is it* not even you in the presence of our Lord Jesus Christ at His coming? 20 For you are our glory and joy.

3 Therefore, when we could no longer endure it, we thought it good to be left in Athens alone, 2 and sent Timothy, our brother and minister of God, and our fellow laborer in the gospel of Christ, to establish you and encourage you concerning your faith, 3 that no one should be shaken by these afflictions; for you yourselves know that we are appointed to this. 4 For, in fact, we told you before when we were with you that we would suffer tribulation, just as it happened, and you know. 5 For this reason, when I could no longer endure it, I sent to know your faith, lest by some means the tempter had tempted you, and our labor might be in vain.

6 But now that Timothy has come to us from you, and brought us good news of your faith and love, and that you always have good remembrance of us, greatly desiring to see us, as we also *to see* you— 7 therefore, brethren, in all our affliction and distress we were comforted concerning you by your faith. 8 For now we live, if you stand fast in the Lord.

9 For what thanks can we render to God for you, for all the joy with which we rejoice for your sake before our God, 10 night and day praying exceedingly that we may see your face and perfect what is lacking in your faith?

11 Now may our God and Father Himself, and our Lord Jesus Christ, direct our way to you. 12 And may the Lord make you increase and abound in love to one another and to all, just as we *do* to you, 13 so that He may establish your hearts blameless in holiness before our God and Father at the coming of our Lord Jesus Christ with all His saints.

4 Finally then, brethren, we urge and exhort in the Lord Jesus that you should abound more and more, just as you received from us how you ought to walk and to please God; 2 for you know what commandments we gave you through the Lord Jesus.

3 For this is the will of God, your sanctification: that you should abstain from sexual immorality; 4 that each of you should know how to possess his own vessel in sanctification and honor, 5 not in passion of lust, like the Gentiles who do not know God; 6 that no one should take advantage of and defraud his brother in this matter, because the Lord *is* the avenger of all such, as we also forewarned you and testified. 7 For God did not call us to uncleanness, but in holiness. 8 Therefore he who rejects *this* does not reject man, but God, who has also given[a] us His Holy Spirit.

9 But concerning brotherly love you have no need that I should write to you, for you yourselves are taught by God to love one another; 10 and indeed you do so toward all the brethren who are in all Macedonia. But we urge you, brethren, that you increase more and more; 11 that you also aspire to lead a quiet life, to mind your own business, and

2:11 [a]NU-Text and M-Text read *implored.* 4:8 [a]NU-Text reads *who also gives.*

Gospel Pearls

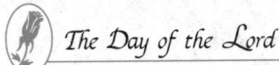
to work with your own hands, as we commanded you, 12 that you may walk properly toward those who are outside, and *that* you may lack nothing.

13 But I do not want you to be ignorant, brethren, concerning those who have fallen asleep, lest you sorrow as others who have no hope. 14 For if we believe that Jesus died and rose again, even so God will bring with Him those who sleep in Jesus.*a*

15 For this we say to you by the word of the Lord, that we who are alive *and* remain until the coming of the Lord will by no means precede those who are asleep. 16 For the Lord Himself will descend from heaven with a shout, with the voice of an archangel, and with the trumpet of God. And the dead in Christ will rise first. 17 Then we who are alive *and* remain shall be caught up together with them in the clouds to meet the Lord in the air. And thus we shall always be with the Lord. 18 Therefore comfort one another with these words.

5 But concerning the times and the seasons, brethren, you have no need that I should write to you. 2 For you yourselves know perfectly that the day of the Lord so comes as a thief in the night. 3 For when they say, "Peace and safety!" then sudden destruction comes upon them, as labor pains upon a pregnant woman. And they shall not escape. 4 But you, brethren, are not in darkness, so that this Day should overtake you as a thief. 5 You are all sons of light and sons of the day. We are not of the night nor of darkness. 6 Therefore let us not sleep, as others *do*, but let us watch and be sober. 7 For those who sleep, sleep at night, and those who get drunk are drunk at night.

8 But let us who are of the day be sober, putting on the breastplate of faith and love, and *as* a helmet the hope of salvation. 9 For God did not appoint us to wrath, but to obtain salvation through our Lord Jesus Christ, 10 who died for us, that whether we wake or sleep, we should live together with Him.

11 Therefore comfort each other and edify one another, just as you also are doing.

12 And we urge you, brethren, to recognize those who labor among you, and are over you in the Lord and admonish you, 13 and to esteem them very highly in love for their work's sake. Be at peace among yourselves.

14 Now we exhort you, brethren, warn those who are unruly, comfort the fainthearted, uphold the weak, be patient with all. 15 See that no one renders evil for evil to anyone, but always pursue what is good both for yourselves and for all.

16 Rejoice always, 17 pray without ceasing, 18 in everything give thanks; for this is the will of God in Christ Jesus for you.

19 Do not quench the Spirit. 20 Do not despise prophecies. 21 Test all things; hold fast what is good. 22 Abstain from every form of evil.

23 Now may the God of peace Himself sanctify you completely; and may your whole spirit, soul, and body be preserved blameless at the coming of our Lord Jesus Christ. 24 He who calls you *is* faithful, who also will do *it.*

25 Brethren, pray for us.

26 Greet all the brethren with a holy kiss.

27 I charge you by the Lord that this epistle be read to all the holy*a* brethren.

28 The grace of our Lord Jesus Christ *be* with you. Amen.

4:14 *a*Or *those who through Jesus sleep*   5:27 *a*NU-Text omits *holy.*

Although we must be careful not to become trapped by the past, we should look back and thank God for how He has kept us through the struggles. Celebrate who you have become through His assistance. In every circumstance, rejoice that He was with you in it.

Get Emotional About It!

1 Thessalonians 5:23

We must understand the difference between our spirits and our emotions. They are linked, yet they are separate. In our spirits, we have God-consciousness. The spirit realm is the realm in which we relate to God intimately and fully. In our bodies, we have world-consciousness, an awareness of our physical world. In our souls, we have self-consciousness. Our emotions are part of our soul realm.

To tell a person not to be emotional is to tell a person not to be human. It is to deny that person's God-given right and privilege to enter into full relationship with the Creator. It is to deny the soul realm. Don't ever try to tell me that God doesn't care about how I feel. I know He does.

Because of the uniqueness of a woman's femininity and her ability to express emotions, there were times in history that God specifically called for women. For example, Jeremiah said, "Send for skillful wailing women, that they may come" (Jeremiah 9:17). God wanted to see tears and brokenness on the altar. He wanted to hear expressions of sorrow over the fact that His people were being carried away into bondage. He said, "Find Me some women and tell them to weep."

God knows the power of tears, of feelings. Jesus said about prayer, "Whatever things you ask when you pray, believe that you receive them, and you will have them" (Mark 11:24). When you desire something, you don't just "want" it. To desire something is to want it with passion. Jesus said, "Make known to Me the things you can't do without, the things you want passionately."

Man looks on the outward appearance, but God looks on the heart. He is looking to see what we desire with all of our hearts, not to see the whims or fleeting ideas of our minds. Is there something today that you want so much you are willing to lie on the altar and cry for it? Is there a desire to see God move in your life—a desire that burns in your innermost being with such passion that you can't forget it, can't escape it, can't dismiss it, and can't ignore it? Is there something you want so desperately to see God do that you wake up in the middle of the night thinking about it? Is there something you feel so certain God wants to do and will do that you just know it is going to be done. Are you convinced, even when everything around you says otherwise?

That is your desire. It arises from your spirit, and it's meant to be expressed by your soul. God expects you to get emotional about it!

The Second Epistle of Paul the Apostle to the

THESSALONIANS

1 Paul, Silvanus, and Timothy,

To the church of the Thessalonians in God our Father and the Lord Jesus Christ:

2 Grace to you and peace from God our Father and the Lord Jesus Christ. 3 We are bound to thank God always for you, brethren, as it is fitting, because your faith grows exceedingly, and the love of every one of you all abounds toward each other, 4 so that we ourselves boast of you among the churches of God for your patience and faith in all your persecutions and tribulations that you endure, 5 *which is* manifest evidence of the righteous judgment of God, that you may be counted worthy of the kingdom of God, for which you also suffer; 6 since *it is* a righteous thing with God to repay with tribulation those who trouble you, 7 and to *give* you who are troubled rest with us when the Lord Jesus is revealed from heaven with His mighty angels, 8 in flaming fire taking vengeance on those who do not know God, and on those who do not obey the gospel of our Lord Jesus Christ. 9 These shall be punished with everlasting destruction from the presence of the Lord and from the glory of His power, 10 when He comes, in that Day, to be glorified in His saints and to be admired among all those who believe,[a] because our testimony among you was believed.

11 Therefore we also pray always for you that our God would count you worthy of *this* calling, and fulfill all the good pleasure of *His* goodness and the work of faith with power, 12 that the name of our Lord Jesus Christ may be glorified in you, and you in Him, according to the grace of our God and the Lord Jesus Christ.

2 Now, brethren, concerning the coming of our Lord Jesus Christ and our gathering together to Him, we ask you, 2 not to be soon shaken in mind or troubled, either by spirit or by word or by letter, as if from us, as though the day of Christ[a] had come. 3 Let no one deceive you by any means; for *that Day will not come* unless the falling away comes first, and the man of sin[a] is revealed, the son of perdition, 4 who opposes and exalts himself above all that is called God or that is worshiped, so that he sits as God[a] in the temple of God, showing himself that he is God.

5 Do you not remember that when I was still with you I told you these things? 6 And now you know what is restraining, that he may be revealed in his own time. 7 For the mystery of lawlessness is already at work; only He[a] who now restrains *will do so* until He[b] is taken out of the way. 8 And then the lawless one will be revealed, whom the Lord will consume with the breath of His mouth and destroy with the brightness of His coming. 9 The coming of the *lawless one* is according to the working of Satan, with all power, signs, and lying wonders, 10 and with all unrighteous deception among those who perish, because they did not receive the love of the truth, that they might be saved. 11 And for this reason God will send them strong delusion, that they should believe the lie, 12 that they all may be condemned who did not believe the truth but had pleasure in unrighteousness.

13 But we are bound to give thanks to God always for you, brethren beloved by the Lord, because God from the beginning chose you for salvation through sanctification by the Spirit and belief in the truth, 14 to which He called you by our gospel, for the obtaining of the glory of our Lord Jesus Christ. 15 Therefore, brethren, stand fast and hold the traditions which you were taught, whether by word or our epistle.

16 Now may our Lord Jesus Christ Himself, and our God and Father, who has loved us and given *us* everlasting consolation and good hope by grace, 17 comfort your hearts and es-

---

1:10 [a]NU-Text and M-Text read *have believed.*   2:2 [a]NU-Text reads *the Lord.*   2:3 [a]NU-Text reads *lawlessness.*   2:4 [a]NU-Text omits *as God.*   2:7 [a]Or *he*   [b]Or *he*

---

2 f you are a woman who has had a dream and sensed a promise, reach out to Him. He will restore what was stolen by your suffering and abuse. He will take back from the enemy what was swallowed up in your history.

Don't Be Deceived

2 Thessalonians 2:9, 10

The number of cases of violence within relationships is growing at an alarming rate. The incidence of date rape is reaching epidemic proportions. The fastest-growing form of murder occurs within marriage. Women have resorted to murder in order to escape the constant violence of an abusive spouse. Husbands and wives and girlfriends and boyfriends are killing one another!

One of the things that makes women particularly vulnerable to abuse and manipulation is their maternal instinct. Wicked men frequently capitalize on this tendency in order to have their way. Women are instinctively nurturers, desiring to reach out to nurture, love, and help. All too often, these healthy desires are exploited by men who are determined to gratify their own selfish lusts.

When Tamar came into that ancient Israeli bedroom, her brother took advantage of her maternal instincts. He told her that he needed help. He sought her sympathy. Once she gave in to his requests for help, he raped her (see 2 Samuel 13:1-20).

The kind of violent act Amnon performed that night was more than an offense against a young woman. He offended God and society by committing incest. And it's still happening today.

Another form of abuse is even more subtle. There are men who coerce women into sexual relationships by claiming to love them. Deception is emotional rape. A deceiver may promise that he will leave his wife for his lover, never intending to keep that promise. He may make every kind of excuse for taking advantage of the woman, and she, because of her vulnerability, may follow along blindly until she's trapped in the relationship. Men who have sex with women without being committed are just as guilty of abuse as rapists.

Some women are victims and don't even know it. Perhaps every time something goes wrong, you think it's your fault. It is not your fault if you are being abused in this way; it is your fault if you don't allow God's Word to arrest sin and weakness in your life. It is time to let go of every ungodly relationship. Do it now!

The effects of abuse may linger for years. Some never find deliverance because they never allow Christ to come into the dark places of their lives. Let Him in. Jesus has promised to set you free from every curse of the past. If you have suffered abuse, please know that He will bring you complete healing. He wants the whole person well—body, emotions, and spirit. He will deliver you from all the damage inflicted on you by the evil people of this world.

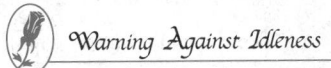

tablish you in every good word and work.

3 Finally, brethren, pray for us, that the word of the Lord may run *swiftly* and be glorified, just as *it is* with you, 2 and that we may be delivered from unreasonable and wicked men; for not all have faith.

3 But the Lord is faithful, who will establish you and guard *you* from the evil one. 4 And we have confidence in the Lord concerning you, both that you do and will do the things we command you.

5 Now may the Lord direct your hearts into the love of God and into the patience of Christ.

6 But we command you, brethren, in the name of our Lord Jesus Christ, that you withdraw from every brother who walks disorderly and not according to the tradition which he[a] received from us. 7 For you yourselves know how you ought to follow us, for we were not disorderly among you; 8 nor did we eat anyone's bread free of charge, but worked with labor and toil night and day, that we might not be a burden to any of you,

9 not because we do not have authority, but to make ourselves an example of how you should follow us.

10 For even when we were with you, we commanded you this: If anyone will not work, neither shall he eat. 11 For we hear that there are some who walk among you in a disorderly manner, not working at all, but are busybodies. 12 Now those who are such we command and exhort through our Lord Jesus Christ that they work in quietness and eat their own bread.

13 But *as for* you, brethren, do not grow weary *in* doing good. 14 And if anyone does not obey our word in this epistle, note that person and do not keep company with him, that he may be ashamed. 15 Yet do not count *him* as an enemy, but admonish *him* as a brother.

16 Now may the Lord of peace Himself give you peace always in every way. The Lord *be* with you all.

17 The salutation of Paul with my own hand, which is a sign in every epistle; so I write.

18 The grace of our Lord Jesus Christ *be* with you all. Amen.

3:6 [a]NU-Text and M-Text read *they.*

The First Epistle of Paul the Apostle to

TIMOTHY

1 Paul, an apostle of Jesus Christ, by the commandment of God our Savior and the Lord Jesus Christ, our hope,

2 To Timothy, a true son in the faith:

Grace, mercy, *and* peace from God our Father and Jesus Christ our Lord.

3 As I urged you when I went into Macedonia—remain in Ephesus that you may charge some that they teach no other doctrine, 4 nor give heed to fables and endless genealogies, which cause disputes rather than godly edification which is in faith. 5 Now the purpose of the commandment is love from a pure heart, *from*

a good conscience, and *from* sincere faith, 6 from which some, having strayed, have turned aside to idle talk, 7 desiring to be teachers of the law, understanding neither what they say nor the things which they affirm.

8 But we know that the law *is* good if one uses it lawfully, 9 knowing this: that the law is not made for a righteous person, but for *the* lawless and insubordinate, for *the* ungodly and for sinners, for *the* unholy and profane, for murderers of fathers and murderers of mothers, for manslayers, 10 for fornicators, for sodomites, for kidnappers, for liars, for perjurers, and if there is any other thing that is contrary to sound doctrine,

---

*T*he woman who is single needs to recognize her position and seek to please God in every way. "Single" means to be "whole." Enjoy being a whole person.

11 according to the glorious gospel of the blessed God which was committed to my trust.

12 And I thank Christ Jesus our Lord who has enabled me, because He counted me faithful, putting *me* into the ministry, 13 although I was formerly a blasphemer, a persecutor, and an insolent man; but I obtained mercy because I did *it* ignorantly in unbelief. 14 And the grace of our Lord was exceedingly abundant, with faith and love which are in Christ Jesus. 15 This *is* a faithful saying and worthy of all acceptance, that Christ Jesus came into the world to save sinners, of whom I am chief. 16 However, for this reason I obtained mercy, that in me first Jesus Christ might show all longsuffering, as a pattern to those who are going to believe on Him for everlasting life. 17 Now to the King eternal, immortal, invisible, to God who alone is wise,*a* *be* honor and glory forever and ever. Amen.

18 This charge I commit to you, son Timothy, according to the prophecies previously made concerning you, that by them you may wage the good warfare, 19 having faith and a good conscience, which some having rejected, concerning the faith have suffered shipwreck, 20 of whom are Hymenaeus and Alexander, whom I delivered to Satan that they may learn not to blaspheme.

2 Therefore I exhort first of all that supplications, prayers, intercessions, *and* giving of thanks be made for all men, 2 for kings and all who are in authority, that we may lead a quiet and peaceable life in all godliness and reverence. 3 For this *is* good and acceptable in the sight of God our Savior, 4 who desires all men to be saved and to come to the knowledge of the truth. 5 For *there is* one God and one Mediator between God and men, *the* Man Christ Jesus, 6 who gave Himself a ransom for all, to be testified in due time, 7 for which I was appointed a preacher and an apostle—I am speaking the truth in Christ*a* *and* not lying—a teacher of the Gentiles in faith and truth.

8 I desire therefore that the men pray everywhere, lifting up holy hands, without wrath and doubting; 9 in like manner also, that the women adorn themselves in modest apparel, with propriety and moderation, not with braided hair or gold or pearls or costly clothing, 10 but, which is proper for women professing godliness, with good works. 11 Let a woman learn in silence with all submission. 12 And I do not permit a woman to teach or to have authority over a man, but to be in silence. 13 For Adam was formed first, then Eve. 14 And Adam was not deceived, but the woman being deceived, fell into transgression. 15 Nevertheless she will be saved in childbearing if they continue in faith, love, and holiness, with self-control.

3 This *is* a faithful saying: If a man desires the position of a bishop,*a* he desires a good work. 2 A bishop then must be blameless, the husband of one wife, temperate, soberminded, of good behavior, hospitable, able to teach; 3 not given to wine, not violent, not greedy for money,*a* but gentle, not quarrelsome, not covetous; 4 one who rules his own house well, having *his* children in submission with all reverence 5 (for if a man does not know how to rule his own house, how will he take care of the church of God?); 6 not a novice, lest being puffed up with pride he fall into the *same* condemnation as the devil. 7 Moreover he must have a good testimony among those who are outside, lest he fall into reproach and the snare of the devil.

8 Likewise deacons *must be* reverent, not double-tongued, not given to much wine, not greedy for money, 9 holding the mystery of the faith with a pure conscience. 10 But let these also first be tested; then let them serve as deacons, being *found* blameless. 11 Likewise, *their* wives *must be* reverent, not slanderers, temperate, faithful in all things. 12 Let deacons be the husbands of one wife, ruling *their* children and their own houses well. 13 For those who have served well as deacons obtain for themselves a good standing and great boldness in the faith which is in Christ Jesus.

14 These things I write to you,

1:17 *a*NU-Text reads *to the only God.*   2:7 *a*NU-Text omits *in Christ.*   3:1 *a*Literally *overseer*
3:3 *a*NU-Text omits *not greedy for money.*

Gospel Pearls

though I hope to come to you shortly; 15 but if I am delayed, *I write* so that you may know how you ought to conduct yourself in the house of God, which is the church of the living God, the pillar and ground of the truth. 16 And without controversy great is the mystery of godliness:

> God[a] was manifested in the flesh,
> Justified in the Spirit,
> Seen by angels,
> Preached among the Gentiles,
> Believed on in the world,
> Received up in glory.

4 Now the Spirit expressly says that in latter times some will depart from the faith, giving heed to deceiving spirits and doctrines of demons, 2 speaking lies in hypocrisy, having their own conscience seared with a hot iron, 3 forbidding to marry, *and commanding* to abstain from foods which God created to be received with thanksgiving by those who believe and know the truth. 4 For every creature of God *is* good, and nothing is to be refused if it is received with thanksgiving; 5 for it is sanctified by the word of God and prayer.

6 If you instruct the brethren in these things, you will be a good minister of Jesus Christ, nourished in the words of faith and of the good doctrine which you have carefully followed. 7 But reject profane and old wives' fables, and exercise yourself toward godliness. 8 For bodily exercise profits a little, but godliness is profitable for all things, having promise of the life that now is and of that which is to come. 9 This *is* a faithful saying and worthy of all acceptance. 10 For to this *end* we both labor and suffer reproach,[a] because we trust in the living God, who is *the* Savior of all men, especially of those who believe. 11 These things command and teach.

12 Let no one despise your youth, but be an example to the believers in word, in conduct, in love, in spirit,[a] in faith, in purity. 13 Till I come, give attention to reading, to exhortation, to doctrine. 14 Do not neglect the gift that is in you, which was given to you by prophecy with the laying on of the hands of the eldership. 15 Meditate on these things; give yourself entirely to them, that your progress may be evident to all. 16 Take heed to yourself and to the doctrine. Continue in them, for in doing this you will save both yourself and those who hear you.

5 Do not rebuke an older man, but exhort *him* as a father, younger men as brothers, 2 older women as mothers, younger women as sisters, with all purity.

3 Honor widows who are really widows. 4 But if any widow has children or grandchildren, let them first learn to show piety at home and to repay their parents; for this is good and[a] acceptable before God. 5 Now she who is really a widow, and left alone, trusts in God and continues in supplications and prayers night and day. 6 But she who lives in pleasure is dead while she lives. 7 And these things command, that they may be blameless. 8 But if anyone does not provide for his own, and especially for those of his household, he has denied the faith and is worse than an unbeliever.

9 Do not let a widow under sixty years old be taken into the number, *and not unless* she has been the wife of one man, 10 well reported for good works: if she has brought up children, if she has lodged strangers, if she has washed the saints' feet, if she has relieved the afflicted, if she has diligently followed every good work.

11 But refuse *the* younger widows; for when they have begun to grow wanton against Christ, they desire to marry, 12 having condemnation because they have cast off their first faith. 13 And besides they learn *to be* idle, wandering about from house to house, and not only idle but also gossips and busybodies, saying things which they ought not. 14 Therefore I desire that *the* younger *widows* marry, bear children, manage the house, give no opportunity to the adversary to speak reproachfully. 15 For some have already turned aside after Satan. 16 If any believing man or[a] woman has widows, let them relieve them, and do not let the

---

3:16 [a]NU-Text reads *Who.*   4:10 [a]NU-Text reads *we labor and strive.*   4:12 [a]NU-Text omits *in spirit.*   5:4 [a]NU-Text and M-Text omit *good and.*   5:16 [a]NU-Text omits *man or.*

*M*any married women who spend a great deal of time fellowshipping with single women do not realize that their perspective and availability should be different. Your ministry, as a wife, begins not in the mall, not in the nursing home, but in your own home and to your own spouse.

church be burdened, that it may relieve those who are really widows.

17 Let the elders who rule well be counted worthy of double honor, especially those who labor in the word and doctrine. 18 For the Scripture says, *"You shall not muzzle an ox while it treads out the grain,"*[a] and, "The laborer *is* worthy of his wages."[b] 19 Do not receive an accusation against an elder except from two or three witnesses. 20 Those who are sinning rebuke in the presence of all, that the rest also may fear.

21 I charge *you* before God and the Lord Jesus Christ and the elect angels that you observe these things without prejudice, doing nothing with partiality. 22 Do not lay hands on anyone hastily, nor share in other people's sins; keep yourself pure.

23 No longer drink only water, but use a little wine for your stomach's sake and your frequent infirmities.

24 Some men's sins are clearly evident, preceding *them* to judgment, but those of some *men* follow later. 25 Likewise, the good works *of some* are clearly evident, and those that are otherwise cannot be hidden.

6 Let as many bondservants as are under the yoke count their own masters worthy of all honor, so that the name of God and *His* doctrine may not be blasphemed. 2 And those who have believing masters, let them not despise *them* because they are brethren, but rather serve *them* because those who are benefited are believers and beloved. Teach and exhort these things.

3 If anyone teaches otherwise and does not consent to wholesome words, *even* the words of our Lord Jesus Christ, and to the doctrine which accords with godliness, 4 he is proud, knowing nothing, but is obsessed with disputes and arguments over words, from which come envy, strife, reviling, evil suspicions, 5 useless wranglings[a] of men of corrupt minds and destitute of the truth, who suppose that godliness is a *means of* gain. From such withdraw yourself.[b]

6 Now godliness with contentment is great gain. 7 For we brought nothing into *this* world, *and it is* certain[a] we can carry nothing out. 8 And having food and clothing, with these we shall be content. 9 But those who desire to be rich fall into temptation and a snare, and *into* many foolish and harmful lusts which drown men in destruction and perdition. 10 For the love of money is a root of all *kinds of* evil, for which some have strayed from the faith in their greediness, and pierced themselves through with many sorrows.

11 But you, O man of God, flee these things and pursue righteousness, godliness, faith, love, patience, gentleness. 12 Fight the good fight of faith, lay hold on eternal life, to which you were also called and have confessed the good confession in the presence of many witnesses. 13 I urge you in the sight of God who gives life to all things, and *before* Christ Jesus who witnessed the good confession before Pontius Pilate, 14 that you keep *this* commandment without spot, blameless until our Lord Jesus Christ's appearing, 15 which He will manifest in His own time, *He who is* the blessed and only Potentate, the King of kings and Lord of lords, 16 who alone has immortality, dwelling in unapproachable light, whom no man has seen or can see, to whom *be* honor and everlasting power. Amen.

17 Command those who are rich in this present age not to be haughty, nor to trust in uncertain riches but in the living God, who gives us richly all things to enjoy. 18 *Let them* do good, that they be rich in good works, ready to give, willing to share, 19 storing up for themselves a good foundation for the time to come, that they may lay hold on eternal life.

20 O Timothy! Guard what was committed to your trust, avoiding the profane *and* idle babblings and contradictions of what is falsely called knowledge— 21 by professing it some have strayed concerning the faith.

Grace *be* with you. Amen.

5:18 [a]Deuteronomy 25:4   [b]Luke 10:7   6:5 [a]NU-Text and M-Text read *constant friction.*   [b]NU-Text omits this sentence.   6:7 [a]NU-Text omits *and it is certain.*

God has ascribed honor to marriage. Your bed is undefiled. However you choose to decorate your relationship is holy. Do not neglect each other in the name of being spiritual. God wants you to be together!

The Gift of Contentment

1 Timothy 6:6

Contentment comes from within. It destroys jealousy and celebrates success in others. It doesn't matter what you accomplish, if you never master contentment you will die miserable. Whether you are famous or infamous, educated or illiterate, if you never learn contentment, you will never be free.

The great gain of the Bible is godliness, which is to continually be our goal; and contentment, which must become the nesting place where greatness is spawned. To be content is to appreciate what God has already given you. Then your gift will bud and blossom, and we will all eat from the fruit of your wholeness!

We are all students now in the school of life. Heaven is our only diploma. You will learn from everyone. The discerning person learns wisdom from the idiot and folly from the intelligent. You must have the perception to look deeply into life and then apply what you see. You will see that every incident, every feeling, every fear is a class.

I encourage you to learn all that you can. At the same time, understand that you must learn from others without losing the core of who you are. Your essence may be cultivated, but do not allow anyone to mutilate the woman you were created to be. Don't get lost in the maze of life and end up being something different from what you were designed to be. You are a daughter of the King!

Find people who enhance you rather than inhibit you. Surround yourself with those persons who celebrate you. When you have been with people of quality, they will leave your sails full of air.

You were born like a blank sheet of paper waiting to be written on. You are the canvas on which time will create a collage of experience and faith. You are a melody waiting to be sung. You are prose whose lines are being formed and whose thoughts are yet being gathered. Be careful whose hand etches on your heart and writes in your life.

Nevertheless, I realize that you are not exempt from challenges and distresses. Be prepared for life's little unexpected events. Whether your challenge comes through failed marriage, moral or physical afflictions, you can still overcome. You are strong and creative, endowed and enabled. Never allow anyone or anything to deplete your confidence in your God. He is a loving Father, and He cares for you. His love is not contingent upon your performance. He has loved you without restriction. And in that love, you can be perfectly content.

The Second Epistle of Paul the Apostle to

TIMOTHY

1 Paul, an apostle of Jesus Christ*a* by the will of God, according to the promise of life which is in Christ Jesus,

2 To Timothy, a beloved son:

Grace, mercy, *and* peace from God the Father and Christ Jesus our Lord.

3 I thank God, whom I serve with a pure conscience, as *my* forefathers *did,* as without ceasing I remember you in my prayers night and day, 4 greatly desiring to see you, being mindful of your tears, that I may be filled with joy, 5 when I call to remembrance the genuine faith that is in you, which dwelt first in your grandmother Lois and your mother Eunice, and I am persuaded is in you also. 6 Therefore I remind you to stir up the gift of God which is in you through the laying on of my hands. 7 For God has not given us a spirit of fear, but of power and of love and of a sound mind.

8 Therefore do not be ashamed of the testimony of our Lord, nor of me His prisoner, but share with me in the sufferings for the gospel according to the power of God, 9 who has saved us and called *us* with a holy calling, not according to our works, but according to His own purpose and grace which was given to us in Christ Jesus before time began, 10 but has now been revealed by the appearing of our Savior Jesus Christ, *who* has abolished death and brought life and immortality to light through the gospel, 11 to which I was appointed a preacher, an apostle, and a teacher of the Gentiles.*a* 12 For this reason I also suffer these things; nevertheless I am not ashamed, for I know whom I have believed and am persuaded that He is able to keep what I have committed to Him until that Day.

13 Hold fast the pattern of sound words which you have heard from me, in faith and love which are in Christ Jesus. 14 That good thing which was committed to you, keep by the Holy Spirit who dwells in us.

15 This you know, that all those in Asia have turned away from me, among whom are Phygellus and Hermogenes. 16 The Lord grant mercy to the household of Onesiphorus, for he often refreshed me, and was not ashamed of my chain; 17 but when he arrived in Rome, he sought me out very zealously and found *me.* 18 The Lord grant to him that he may find mercy from the Lord in that Day—and you know very well how many ways he ministered *to me*a at Ephesus.

2 You therefore, my son, be strong in the grace that is in Christ Jesus. 2 And the things that you have heard from me among many witnesses, commit these to faithful men who will be able to teach others also. 3 You therefore must endure*a* hardship as a good soldier of Jesus Christ. 4 No one engaged in warfare entangles himself with the affairs of *this* life, that he may please him who enlisted him as a soldier. 5 And also anyone competes in athletics, he is not crowned unless he competes according to the rules. 6 The hardworking farmer must be first to partake of the crops. 7 Consider what I say, and may*a* the Lord give you understanding in all things.

8 Remember that Jesus Christ, of the seed of David, was raised from the dead according to my gospel, 9 for which I suffer trouble as an evildoer, *even* to the point of chains; but the word of God is not chained. 10 Therefore I endure all things for the sake of the elect, that they also may obtain the salvation which is in Christ Jesus with eternal glory.

11 *This is* a faithful saying:

For if we died with *Him,*
We shall also live with *Him.*
12 If we endure,
We shall also reign with *Him.*
If we deny *Him,*
He also will deny us.

1:1 *a*NU-Text and M-Text read *Christ Jesus.*   1:11 *a*NU-Text omits *of the Gentiles.*   1:18 *aTo me* is from the Vulgate and a few Greek manuscripts.   2:3 *a*NU-Text reads *You must share.*   2:7 *a*NU-Text reads *the Lord will give you.*

God will not move because you cry and act melancholy. That works with men, but not with God. God only accepts faith, not just feminine rhetoric, not hysteria—just plain old faith in God.

Winter Woman

2 Timothy 1:5

This morning when I arose, the land was still asleep. I watched the miracle of beginnings from the veranda of my hotel. If I had not stayed perched on my window's edge, I might have misjudged the day. I might have thought the morning, or perhaps the bustling sun-drenched afternoon, was the most beautiful part of the day.

But just before I cast my ballot, the wisdom of the evening slipped up on the stage. How had I not noticed that the sun had changed her sun dress to an evening gown, full of color and grandeur? The grace of a closing day is far greater than the uncertainty of morning. Yes, the most beautiful part of the day—as in a woman's life—is at the setting of the sun.

I write this with my mother in mind. Her hair has changed colors before my eyes. Like the afterthought of an artist, lines have been etched upon her brow. Her arms are much weaker now and her gait much slower, but she is somehow warmer at life's winter age than she was in the summer days. All of life's tragedy has been wrestled to the mat, and still she stands to attest to the authenticity of her goals, dreams, and ambitions.

If you are a winter woman, consider this: Just because the glare of summer does not beat upon your face doesn't mean there is nothing left for you to do. Whose presence will stand as a witness that God will see you through? Who will be there to see your children run their race or to catch them when they fall beneath the weight of their day? God never extends days beyond purpose.

We need to teach women to prepare for the winter. Be like Lois and Eunice. Be a woman of genuine faith. Notice that Paul says that faith *dwelt* in Lois, the winter woman, and in Eunice. Faith—genuine, indwelling faith, faith that has lived in you through every season of your life—is the secret power of preparation for every winter woman.

Don't allow changing times to change who you are. It is dangerous to lose your identity in your circumstances. Circumstances change and when they do, the older woman can feel empty and unfulfilled. God knows there are many things only a woman who is full of years and experience can contribute. Just because the demands have changed doesn't mean your life is over.

Redefine your purpose, gather your assets, and keep on living and giving. No matter what age you are, you haven't seen it all. No one knows how God will end His book, but He does tend to save the best for last.

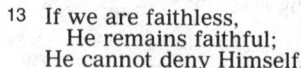

13 If we are faithless,
    He remains faithful;
    He cannot deny Himself.

14 Remind *them* of these things, charging *them* before the Lord not to strive about words to no profit, to the ruin of the hearers. 15 Be diligent to present yourself approved to God, a worker who does not need to be ashamed, rightly dividing the word of truth. 16 But shun profane *and* idle babblings, for they will increase to more ungodliness. 17 And their message will spread like cancer. Hymenaeus and Philetus are of this sort, 18 who have strayed concerning the truth, saying that the resurrection is already past; and they overthrow the faith of some. 19 Nevertheless the solid foundation of God stands, having this seal: "The Lord knows those who are His," and, "Let everyone who names the name of Christ[a] depart from iniquity."

20 But in a great house there are not only vessels of gold and silver, but also of wood and clay, some for honor and some for dishonor. 21 Therefore if anyone cleanses himself from the latter, he will be a vessel for honor, sanctified and useful for the Master, prepared for every good work. 22 Flee also youthful lusts; but pursue righteousness, faith, love, peace with those who call on the Lord out of a pure heart. 23 But avoid foolish and ignorant disputes, knowing that they generate strife. 24 And a servant of the Lord must not quarrel but be gentle to all, able to teach, patient, 25 in humility correcting those who are in opposition, if God perhaps will grant them repentance, so that they may know the truth, 26 and *that* they may come to their senses *and escape* the snare of the devil, having been taken captive by him to *do* his will.

3 But know this, that in the last days perilous times will come: 2 For men will be lovers of themselves, lovers of money, boasters, proud, blasphemers, disobedient to parents, unthankful, unholy, 3 unloving, unforgiving, slanderers, without self-control, brutal, despisers of good, 4 traitors, headstrong, haughty, lovers of pleasure rather than lovers of God, 5 having a form of godliness but denying its power. And from such people turn away! 6 For of this sort are those who creep into households and make captives of gullible women loaded down with sins, led away by various lusts, 7 always learning and never able to come to the knowledge of the truth. 8 Now as Jannes and Jambres resisted Moses, so do these also resist the truth: men of corrupt minds, disapproved concerning the faith; 9 but they will progress no further, for their folly will be manifest to all, as theirs also was.

10 But you have carefully followed my doctrine, manner of life, purpose, faith, longsuffering, love, perseverance, 11 persecutions, afflictions, which happened to me at Antioch, at Iconium, at Lystra—what persecutions I endured. And out of *them* all the Lord delivered me. 12 Yes, and all who desire to live godly in Christ Jesus will suffer persecution. 13 But evil men and impostors will grow worse and worse, deceiving and being deceived. 14 But you must continue in the things which you have learned and been assured of, knowing from whom you have learned *them,* 15 and that from childhood you have known the Holy Scriptures, which are able to make you wise for salvation through faith which is in Christ Jesus.

16 All Scripture *is* given by inspiration of God, and *is* profitable for doctrine, for reproof, for correction, for instruction in righteousness, 17 that the man of God may be complete, thoroughly equipped for every good work.

4 I charge you therefore before God and the Lord Jesus Christ, who will judge the living and the dead at[a] His appearing and His kingdom: 2 Preach the word! Be ready in season *and* out of season. Convince, rebuke, exhort, with all longsuffering and teaching. 3 For the time will come when they will not endure sound doctrine, but according to their own desires, *because* they have itching ears, they will heap up for themselves teachers; 4 and they will turn *their* ears away from the truth, and be turned aside to fables.

2:19 [a]NU-Text and M-Text read *the Lord.*   4:1 [a]NU-Text omits *therefore* and reads *and by* for *at.*

God wants you to believe Him. Make a decision and stand on it. Rahab decided to take a stand on the side of God's people. She hid the spies—a decision based on nothing but her faith.

Get Loosed, Get Lost

2 Timothy 2:22

Don't make the mistake of thinking your deliverance must take a long time. Change can happen in an instant. In one moment of Holy Ghost revelation, you can arrive immediately at an understanding of the truth. It's as if a light comes on. Change means that once you *were*—and now you *aren't*. Period.

You can leave an ungodly affair whether your partner agrees or disagrees. When you are loosed from the problem that drove you to that affair, you don't need to get together with that person and try to figure things out with him. When you unhook from that relationship, you're free inside yourself. You can just walk away and say, "I'm finished with that. I'm not vulnerable in that way anymore."

There doesn't need to be any long, drawn-out discussion or any major confrontation or any redefining of the relationship. You're better off without any of that. Just say, "I'm outta here" and be gone.

Now I'm not talking about husbands and wives. I'm talking about your association with ungodly people who have hurt you, rejected you, abused you, or used you. Once you're delivered, don't hang around. Get moving and get out. Get as far away as you can, as fast as you can. As some people say, just "get lost." People who have abused or used you will not take kindly to your wanting to redefine your relationship. They've been on a power trip and they won't be interested in you if they can't control you. They aren't going to like the fact that you're suddenly not willing to be manipulated. Just leave.

Recognize, too, that any time God looses you from something, He has something else to which He wants you to become attached. Things that are completely loosed—totally on their own without any connection—wither and die. Nothing can exist on its own and remain vital and alive, especially people.

If you pull a plant up out of the ground, it might look fine for a day or two, but then it's going to shrivel up and die. If you put a person in an isolation chamber for very long, she'll curl up into a ball and be totally useless. We all need to be connected to the right things.

If God looses you from an infirmity and you aren't reconnected to something good and positive, you are likely to seek out any old reconnection. You might even go back to that old sin just because it's familiar.

Refuse to reconnect with your infirmity. When you are loosed, stay loosed. Once you are free, stay free!

5 But you be watchful in all things, endure afflictions, do the work of an evangelist, fulfill your ministry.

6 For I am already being poured out as a drink offering, and the time of my departure is at hand. 7 I have fought the good fight, I have finished the race, I have kept the faith. 8 Finally, there is laid up for me the crown of righteousness, which the Lord, the righteous Judge, will give to me on that Day, and not to me only but also to all who have loved His appearing.

9 Be diligent to come to me quickly; 10 for Demas has forsaken me, having loved this present world, and has departed for Thessalonica—Crescens for Galatia, Titus for Dalmatia. 11 Only Luke is with me. Get Mark and bring him with you, for he is useful to me for ministry. 12 And Tychicus I have sent to Ephesus. 13 Bring the cloak that I left with Carpus at Troas when you come—and the books, especially the parchments.

14 Alexander the coppersmith did me much harm. May the Lord repay him according to his works. 15 You also must beware of him, for he has greatly resisted our words.

16 At my first defense no one stood with me, but all forsook me. May it not be charged against them.

17 But the Lord stood with me and strengthened me, so that the message might be preached fully through me, and *that* all the Gentiles might hear. Also I was delivered out of the mouth of the lion. 18 And the Lord will deliver me from every evil work and preserve *me* for His heavenly kingdom. To Him *be* glory forever and ever. Amen!

19 Greet Prisca and Aquila, and the household of Onesiphorus. 20 Erastus stayed in Corinth, but Trophimus I have left in Miletus sick.

21 Do your utmost to come before winter.

Eubulus greets you, as well as Pudens, Linus, Claudia, and all the brethren.

22 The Lord Jesus Christ*ᵃ* be with your spirit. Grace be with you. Amen.

4:22 *ᵃNU-Text omits Jesus Christ.*

The Epistle of Paul the Apostle to

TITUS

1 Paul, a bondservant of God and an apostle of Jesus Christ, according to the faith of God's elect and the acknowledgment of the truth which accords with godliness, 2 in hope of eternal life which God, who cannot lie, promised before time began, 3 but has in due time manifested His word through preaching, which was committed to me according to the commandment of God our Savior;

4 To Titus, a true son in *our* common faith:

Grace, mercy, *and* peace from God the Father and the Lord Jesus Christ*ᵃ* our Savior.

5 For this reason I left you in Crete, that you should set in order the things that are lacking, and appoint elders in every city as I commanded you— 6 if a man is blameless, the husband of one wife, having faithful children not accused of dissipation or insubordination. 7 For a bishop*ᵃ* must be blameless, as a steward of God, not self-willed, not quick-tempered, not given to wine, not violent, not greedy for money, 8 but hospitable, a lover of what is good, soberminded, just, holy, self-controlled, 9 holding fast the faithful word as he has been taught, that he may be able, by sound doctrine, both to exhort and convict those who contradict.

10 For there are many insubordi-

1:4 *ᵃNU-Text reads and Christ Jesus.*   1:7 *ᵃLiterally overseer*

Gospel Pearls

nate, both idle talkers and deceivers, especially those of the circumcision, 11 whose mouths must be stopped, who subvert whole households, teaching things which they ought not, for the sake of dishonest gain. 12 One of them, a prophet of their own, said, "Cretans *are* always liars, evil beasts, lazy gluttons." 13 This testimony is true. Therefore rebuke them sharply, that they may be sound in the faith, 14 not giving heed to Jewish fables and commandments of men who turn from the truth. 15 To the pure all things are pure, but to those who are defiled and unbelieving nothing is pure; but even their mind and conscience are defiled. 16 They profess to know God, but in works they deny Him, being abominable, disobedient, and disqualified for every good work.

2 But as for you, speak the things which are proper for sound doctrine: 2 that the older men be sober, reverent, temperate, sound in faith, in love, in patience; 3 the older women likewise, that they be reverent in behavior, not slanderers, not given to much wine, teachers of good things— 4 that they admonish the young women to love their husbands, to love their children, 5 to be discreet, chaste, homemakers, good, obedient to their own husbands, that the word of God may not be blasphemed.

6 Likewise, exhort the young men to be sober-minded, 7 in all things showing yourself *to be* a pattern of good works; in doctrine *showing* integrity, reverence, incorruptibility,*a* 8 sound speech that cannot be condemned, that one who is an opponent may be ashamed, having nothing evil to say of you.*a*

9 *Exhort* bondservants to be obedient to their own masters, to be well pleasing in all *things,* not answering back, 10 not pilfering, but showing all good fidelity, that they may adorn the doctrine of God our Savior in all things.

11 For the grace of God that brings salvation has appeared to all men, 12 teaching us that, denying ungodliness and worldly lusts, we should live soberly, righteously, and godly in the present age, 13 looking for the blessed hope and glorious appearing of our great God and Savior Jesus Christ, 14 who gave Himself for us, that He might redeem us from every lawless deed and purify for Himself *His* own special people, zealous for good works.

15 Speak these things, exhort, and rebuke with all authority. Let no one despise you.

3 Remind them to be subject to rulers and authorities, to obey, to be ready for every good work, 2 to speak evil of no one, to be peaceable, gentle, showing all humility to all men. 3 For we ourselves were also once foolish, disobedient, deceived, serving various lusts and pleasures, living in malice and envy, hateful and hating one another. 4 But when the kindness and the love of God our Savior toward man appeared, 5 not by works of righteousness which we have done, but according to His mercy He saved us, through the washing of regeneration and renewing of the Holy Spirit, 6 whom He poured out on us abundantly through Jesus Christ our Savior, 7 that having been justified by His grace we should become heirs according to the hope of eternal life.

8 This is a faithful saying, and these things I want you to affirm constantly, that those who have believed in God should be careful to maintain good works. These things are good and profitable to men.

9 But avoid foolish disputes, genealogies, contentions, and strivings about the law; for they are unprofitable and useless. 10 Reject a divisive man after the first and second admonition, 11 knowing that such a person is warped and sinning, being self-condemned.

12 When I send Artemas to you, or Tychicus, be diligent to come to me at Nicopolis, for I have decided to spend the winter there. 13 Send Zenas the lawyer and Apollos on their journey with haste, that they may lack nothing. 14 And let our *people* also learn to maintain good works, to *meet* urgent needs, that they may not be unfruitful.

15 All who *are* with me greet you. Greet those who love us in the faith.

Grace *be* with you all. Amen.

2:7 *a*NU-Text omits *incorruptibility*.   2:8 *a*NU-Text and M-Text read *us*.

*Y*ou need to marry someone who will hold you, help you, strengthen you, build you up, and be with you when the storms of life are raging. If you want a cute guy, buy a photograph. If you want some help, marry a godly man.

PHILEMON

1 Paul, a prisoner of Christ Jesus, and Timothy *our* brother,

To Philemon our beloved *friend* and fellow laborer, 2 to the beloved*ᵃ* Apphia, Archippus our fellow soldier, and to the church in your house:

3 Grace to you and peace from God our Father and the Lord Jesus Christ.

4 I thank my God, making mention of you always in my prayers, 5 hearing of your love and faith which you have toward the Lord Jesus and toward all the saints, 6 that the sharing of your faith may become effective by the acknowledgment of every good thing which is in you*ᵃ* in Christ Jesus. 7 For we have*ᵃ* great joy*ᵇ* and consolation in your love, because the hearts of the saints have been refreshed by you, brother.

8 Therefore, though I might be very bold in Christ to command you what is fitting, 9 *yet* for love's sake I rather appeal *to you*—being such a one as Paul, the aged, and now also a prisoner of Jesus Christ— 10 I appeal to you for my son Onesimus, whom I have begotten *while* in my chains, 11 who once was unprofitable to you, but now is profitable to you and to me.

12 I am sending him back.*ᵃ* You therefore receive him, that is, my own heart, 13 whom I wished to keep with me, that on your behalf he might minister to me in my chains for the gospel. 14 But without your consent I wanted to do nothing, that your good deed might not be by compulsion, as it were, but voluntary.

15 For perhaps he departed for a while for this *purpose,* that you might receive him forever, 16 no longer as a slave but more than a slave—a beloved brother, especially to me but how much more to you, both in the flesh and in the Lord.

17 If then you count me as a partner, receive him as *you would* me. 18 But if he has wronged you or owes anything, put that on my account. 19 I, Paul, am writing with my own hand. I will repay—not to mention to you that you owe me even your own self besides. 20 Yes, brother, let me have joy from you in the Lord; refresh my heart in the Lord.

21 Having confidence in your obedience, I write to you, knowing that you will do even more than I say. 22 But, meanwhile, also prepare a guest room for me, for I trust that through your prayers I shall be granted to you.

23 Epaphras, my fellow prisoner in Christ Jesus, greets you, 24 *as do* Mark, Aristarchus, Demas, Luke, my fellow laborers.

25 The grace of our Lord Jesus Christ *be* with your spirit. Amen.

2 *ᵃ*NU-Text reads *to our sister Apphia.*   6 *ᵃ*NU-Text and M-Text read *us.*   7 *ᵃ*NU-Text reads *had.*
*ᵇ*M-Text reads *thanksgiving.*   12 *ᵃ*NU-Text reads *back to you in person, that is, my own heart.*

The Epistle to the

HEBREWS

1 God, who at various times and in various ways spoke in time past to the fathers by the prophets, 2 has in these last days spoken to us by *His* Son, whom He has appointed heir of all things, through whom also He made the worlds; 3 who being the brightness of *His* glory and the express image of His person, and upholding all things by the word of His power, when He had by Himself[a] purged our[b] sins, sat down at the right hand of the Majesty on high, 4 having become so much better than the angels, as He has by inheritance obtained a more excellent name than they.

5 For to which of the angels did He ever say:

"You are My Son,
Today I have begotten You"?[a]

And again:

"I will be to Him a Father,
And He shall be to Me a Son"?[b]

6 But when He again brings the firstborn into the world, He says:

"Let all the angels of God
worship Him."[a]

7 And of the angels He says:

"Who makes His angels spirits
And His ministers a flame of
fire."[a]

8 But to the Son He says:

"Your throne, O God, is forever
and ever;
A scepter of righteousness is
the scepter of Your kingdom.
9   You have loved righteousness
and hated lawlessness;
Therefore God, Your God, has
anointed You
With the oil of gladness more
than Your companions."[a]

10 And:

"You, LORD, in the beginning
laid the foundation of the
earth,
And the heavens are the work
of Your hands.
11   They will perish, but You
remain;
And they will all grow old like
a garment;
12   Like a cloak You will fold them
up,
And they will be changed.

But You are the same,
And Your years will not fail."[a]

13 But to which of the angels has He ever said:

"Sit at My right hand,
Till I make Your enemies Your
footstool"?[a]

14 Are they not all ministering spirits sent forth to minister for those who will inherit salvation?

2 Therefore we must give the more earnest heed to the things we have heard, lest we drift away. 2 For if the word spoken through angels proved steadfast, and every transgression and disobedience received a just reward, 3 how shall we escape if we neglect so great a salvation, which at the first began to be spoken by the Lord, and was confirmed to us by those who heard Him, 4 God also bearing witness both with signs and wonders, with various miracles, and gifts of the Holy Spirit, according to His own will?

5 For He has not put the world to come, of which we speak, in subjection to angels. 6 But one testified in a certain place, saying:

"What is man that You are
mindful of him,
Or the son of man that You
take care of him?
7   You have made him a little
lower than the angels;
You have crowned him with
glory and honor,[a]
And set him over the works of
Your hands.
8   You have put all things in
subjection under his feet."[a]

For in that He put all in subjection under him, He left nothing that is not put under him. But now we do not yet see all things put under him. 9 But we see Jesus, who was made a little lower than the angels, for the suffering of death crowned with glory and honor, that He, by the grace of God, might taste death for everyone.

1:3 [a]NU-Text omits by Himself.   [b]NU-Text omits our.   1:5 [a]Psalm 2:7   [b]2 Samuel 7:14
1:6 [a]Deuteronomy 32:43 (Septuagint, Dead Sea Scrolls); Psalm 97:7   1:7 [a]Psalm 104:4   1:9 [a]Psalm
45:6, 7   1:12 [a]Psalm 102:25–27   1:13 [a]Psalm 110:1   2:7 [a]NU-Text and M-Text omit the rest of
verse 7.   2:8 [a]Psalm 8:4–6

---

*P*lease understand that rest and restoration are related concepts. You need the calmness of Sabbath rest because it is through the resting of your spirit that the restoration of your life begins to occur.

10 For it was fitting for Him, for whom *are* all things and by whom *are* all things, in bringing many sons to glory, to make the captain of their salvation perfect through sufferings. 11 For both He who sanctifies and those who are being sanctified *are* all of one, for which reason He is not ashamed to call them brethren, 12 saying:

> "I will declare Your name to My brethren;
> In the midst of the assembly I will sing praise to You."*a*

13 And again:

> "I will put My trust in Him."*a*

And again:

> "Here am I and the children whom God has given Me."*b*

14 Inasmuch then as the children have partaken of flesh and blood, He Himself likewise shared in the same, that through death He might destroy him who had the power of death, that is, the devil, 15 and release those who through fear of death were all their lifetime subject to bondage. 16 For indeed He does not give aid to angels, but He does give aid to the seed of Abraham. 17 Therefore, in all things He had to be made like *His* brethren, that He might be a merciful and faithful High Priest in things *pertaining* to God, to make propitiation for the sins of the people. 18 For in that He Himself has suffered, being tempted, He is able to aid those who are tempted.

3 Therefore, holy brethren, partakers of the heavenly calling, consider the Apostle and High Priest of our confession, Christ Jesus, 2 who was faithful to Him who appointed Him, as Moses also *was faithful* in all His house. 3 For this One has been counted worthy of more glory than Moses, inasmuch as He who built the house has more honor than the house. 4 For every house is built by someone, but He who built all things *is* God. 5 And Moses indeed *was* faithful in all His house as a servant, for a testimony of those things which would be spoken *afterward*, 6 but Christ as a Son over His own house, whose house we are if we hold fast the confidence and the rejoicing of the hope firm to the end.*a*

7 Therefore, as the Holy Spirit says:

> "Today, if you will hear His voice,
> 8 Do not harden your hearts as in the rebellion,
> In the day of trial in the wilderness,
> 9 Where your fathers tested Me, tried Me,
> And saw My works forty years.
> 10 Therefore I was angry with that generation,
> And said, 'They always go astray in their heart,
> And they have not known My ways.'
> 11 So I swore in My wrath, 'They shall not enter My rest.' "*a*

12 Beware, brethren, lest there be in any of you an evil heart of unbelief in departing from the living God; 13 but exhort one another daily, while it is called *"Today,"* lest any of you be hardened through the deceitfulness of sin. 14 For we have become partakers of Christ if we hold the beginning of our confidence steadfast to the end, 15 while it is said:

> "Today, if you will hear His voice,
> Do not harden your hearts as in the rebellion."*a*

16 For who, having heard, rebelled? Indeed, *was it* not all who came out of Egypt, *led* by Moses? 17 Now with whom was He angry forty years? *Was it* not with those who sinned, whose corpses fell in the wilderness? 18 And to whom did He swear that they would not enter His rest, but to those who did not obey? 19 So we see that they could not enter in because of unbelief.

4 Therefore, since a promise remains of entering His rest, let us fear lest any of you seem to have

2:12 *a*Psalm 22:22   2:13 *a*2 Samuel 22:3; Isaiah 8:17   *b*Isaiah 8:18   3:6 *a*NU-Text omits *firm to the end*.   3:11 *a*Psalm 95:7–11   3:15 *a*Psalm 95:7, 8

Some of those habits you have come to enjoy, some of those relationships you thought you found security in, were not profitable. Often we settle for less because we didn't meet the best. When you get the best, it gives you the power to let go of the rest.

Soul Secrets
of a woman
with an empty nest

God, I miss them more than I thought I would. The last child is gone—off to chase his dreams, out to sail the uncertain waters of adulthood. In days gone by, I cried out for peace and quiet, but this silence, this stillness, is more deafening than any children's noise.

It's a new day in my house now, Father. A new season in the life You've given me. It is time for us—this lady and her Lord. It is time for me to know You in ways I couldn't when children and teenagers were pulling on me. It is time to worship, time to seek Your face, time to find a brand new intimate place in You.

It is time for this home to belong to You in ways it never has before. Come and fill the empty rooms. Where songs of children once were heard, now let my heart sing to You. Where little voices gasped and giggled, now let me find wonder and delight in the Lover of my soul.

Lord, I welcome this time, even with its challenges. And I welcome You in me as never before.

come short of it. 2 For indeed the gospel was preached to us as well as to them; but the word which they heard did not profit them,*a* not being mixed with faith in those who heard *it*. 3 For we who have believed do enter that rest, as He has said:

"*So I swore in My wrath,
'They shall not enter My rest,' "a*

although the works were finished from the foundation of the world. 4 For He has spoken in a certain place of the seventh *day* in this way: "*And God rested on the seventh day from all His works*";*a* 5 and again in this *place*: "*They shall not enter My rest.*"*a*

6 Since therefore it remains that some *must* enter it, and those to whom it was first preached did not enter because of disobedience, 7 again He designates a certain day, saying in David, "*Today,*" after such a long time, as it has been said:

"*Today, if you will hear His voice,
Do not harden your hearts.*"*a*

8 For if Joshua had given them rest, then He would not afterward have spoken of another day. 9 There remains therefore a rest for the people of God. 10 For he who has entered His rest has himself also ceased from his works as God *did* from His.

11 Let us therefore be diligent to enter that rest, lest anyone fall according to the same example of disobedience. 12 For the word of God *is* living and powerful, and sharper than any two-edged sword, piercing even to the division of soul and spirit, and of joints and marrow, and is a discerner of the thoughts and intents of the heart. 13 And there is no creature hidden from His sight, but all things *are* naked and open to the eyes of Him to whom we *must give* account.

14 Seeing then that we have a great High Priest who has passed through the heavens, Jesus the Son of God, let us hold fast *our* confession. 15 For we do not have a High Priest who cannot sympathize with our weaknesses, but was in all *points*

tempted as *we are, yet* without sin. 16 Let us therefore come boldly to the throne of grace, that we may obtain mercy and find grace to help in time of need.

5 For every high priest taken from among men is appointed for men in things *pertaining* to God, that he may offer both gifts and sacrifices for sins. 2 He can have compassion on those who are ignorant and going astray, since he himself is also subject to weakness. 3 Because of this he is required as for the people, so also for himself, to offer *sacrifices* for sins. 4 And no man takes this honor to himself, but he who is called by God, just as Aaron *was*.

5 So also Christ did not glorify Himself to become High Priest, *but it* was He who said to Him:

"*You are My Son,
Today I have begotten You.*"*a*

6 As *He* also *says* in another *place*:

"*You are a priest forever
According to the order of Melchizedek*";*a*

7 who, in the days of His flesh, when He had offered up prayers and supplications, with vehement cries and tears to Him who was able to save Him from death, and was heard because of His godly fear, 8 though He was a Son, *yet* He learned obedience by the things which He suffered. 9 And having been perfected, He became the author of eternal salvation to all who obey Him, 10 called by God as High Priest "*according to the order of Melchizedek,*" 11 of whom we have much to say, and hard to explain, since you have become dull of hearing.

12 For though by this time you ought to be teachers, you need *someone* to teach you again the first principles of the oracles of God; and you have come to need milk and not solid food. 13 For everyone who partakes *only* of milk *is* unskilled in the word of righteousness, for he is a babe. 14 But solid food belongs to those who are of full age, *that is*, those who

---

4:2 *a*NU-Text and M-Text read *profit them, since they were not united by faith with those who heeded it.*
4:3 *a*Psalm 95:11   4:4 *a*Genesis 2:2   4:5 *a*Psalm 95:11   4:7 *a*Psalm 95:7, 8   5:5 *a*Psalm 2:7
5:6 *a*Psalm 110:4

Just because the glare of summer doesn't beat upon your face doesn't mean that there is nothing left for you to do. God doesn't discriminate against the elderly. He never extends days beyond purpose.

Soul Secrets
when I don't feel
good enough

Lord, I stagger to Your throne today. Sometimes I think that I'm no use, that I can't do anything right, that nothing I do is good enough. And then I remember—when You look at who I am and who I can be, You see Jesus. And He *is* good enough.

It is good enough that He shed His precious blood just to cover my unworthiness. Good enough that He has already paid the price for every sin I'll ever commit. Good enough that He is perfecting me each day. Good enough that I'm the righteousness of God in Christ. Good enough that He has made the perfect sacrifice. Good enough that He is interceding now for me. Good enough that He has washed me clean and made me whole. Good enough that His love is sure.

Thank You, Lord, that everything Jesus does is good enough and that, in Him, even I am good enough.

by reason of use have their senses exercised to discern both good and evil.

6 Therefore, leaving the discussion of the elementary *principles* of Christ, let us go on to perfection, not laying again the foundation of repentance from dead works and of faith toward God, 2 of the doctrine of baptisms, of laying on of hands, of resurrection of the dead, and of eternal judgment. 3 And this we will*a* do if God permits.

4 For *it is* impossible for those who were once enlightened, and have tasted the heavenly gift, and have become partakers of the Holy Spirit, 5 and have tasted the good word of God and the powers of the age to come, 6 if they fall away,*a* to renew them again to repentance, since they crucify again for themselves the Son of God, and put *Him* to an open shame.

7 For the earth which drinks in the rain that often comes upon it, and bears herbs useful for those by whom it is cultivated, receives blessing from God; 8 but if it bears thorns and briers, *it is* rejected and near to being cursed, whose end *is* to be burned.

9 But, beloved, we are confident of better things concerning you, yes, things that accompany salvation, though we speak in this manner. 10 For God *is* not unjust to forget your work and labor of*a* love which you have shown toward His name, *in that* you have ministered to the saints, and do minister. 11 And we desire that each one of you show the same diligence to the full assurance of hope until the end, 12 that you do not become sluggish, but imitate those who through faith and patience inherit the promises.

13 For when God made a promise to Abraham, because He could swear by no one greater, He swore by Himself, 14 saying, *"Surely blessing I will bless you, and multiplying I will multiply you."*a* 15 And so, after he had patiently endured, he obtained the promise. 16 For men indeed swear by the greater, and an oath for confirmation *is* for them an end of all dispute. 17 Thus God, determining to show more abundantly to the heirs

of promise the immutability of His counsel, confirmed *it* by an oath, 18 that by two immutable things, in which it *is* impossible for God to lie, we might*a* have strong consolation, who have fled for refuge to lay hold of the hope set before *us.*

19 This *hope* we have as an anchor of the soul, both sure and steadfast, and which enters the Presence *behind* the veil, 20 where the forerunner has entered for us, *even* Jesus, having become High Priest forever according to the order of Melchizedek.

7 For this Melchizedek, king of Salem, priest of the Most High God, who met Abraham returning from the slaughter of the kings and blessed him, 2 to whom also Abraham gave a tenth part of all, first being translated "king of righteousness," and then also king of Salem, meaning "king of peace," 3 without father, without mother, without genealogy, having neither beginning of days nor end of life, but made like the Son of God, remains a priest continually.

4 Now consider how great this man *was,* to whom even the patriarch Abraham gave a tenth of the spoils. 5 And indeed those who are of the sons of Levi, who receive the priesthood, have a commandment to receive tithes from the people according to the law, that is, from their brethren, though they have come from the loins of Abraham; 6 but he whose genealogy is not derived from them received tithes from Abraham and blessed him who had the promises. 7 Now beyond all contradiction the lesser is blessed by the better. 8 Here mortal men receive tithes, but there he *receives them,* of whom it is witnessed that he lives. 9 Even Levi, who receives tithes, paid tithes through Abraham, so to speak, 10 for he was still in the loins of his father when Melchizedek met him.

11 Therefore, if perfection were through the Levitical priesthood (for under it the people received the law), what further need *was there* that another priest should rise according to the order of Melchizedek, and not be called according to the order of

---

6:3 *a*M-Text reads *let us do.*   6:6 *a*Or *and have fallen away.*   6:10 *a*NU-Text omits *labor of.*
6:14 *a*Genesis 22:17   6:18 *a*M-Text omits *might.*

---

*I*t is dangerous to be prejudiced against God. Prejudice is to prejudge. People, even believers, have often prejudged God. The truth is, He isn't finished yet.

The Flame of Feeling

Hebrews 6:11, 12

There are many things that God expects us to do. But there are many other things that only He can do. And God expects us to call upon Him to do those things that are His "job." He even invites us to "come boldly to the throne of grace" (Hebrews 4:16).

God gave you feelings so that you could light the altar of incense, so that you might burn about something to the point that when you add your believing to your feeling, it's like putting a match to incense. Your prayer then floats up to God as a sweet-smelling savor!

No two blends of incense smell the same. And the same is true for your prayer. The way you pray and the words you use and the intent of your heart are all about you. Don't pray someone else's prayer. Don't say to yourself, "Well, that prayer worked for her. Maybe it will work for me." God is looking for a prayer that comes up out of your passion, your desire, your emotions, your soul!

Do you really want to see God move? Really? Then touch God with your passion. Touch Him with your feelings, with your getting up in the middle of the night and pacing the floor, with your tears that flow like a flood, with your groanings and wailings.

He is not swayed by your need. You may be broke, busted, and disgusted, but those conditions won't sway Him. He is moved by a depth of your desire that is matched by the depth of your faith! It takes both.

If there are any ashes still smoldering in your heart, any flickers of faith still burning in your spirit, blow on those coals. Fan them into a flame of desire, and call out to God.

Can you still feel? Then God can still be moved on your behalf. You may be weak. You may have failed. You may have sinned. But if you still have feeling toward God and you still have a desire in your heart to see Him move on your behalf, then God can still be moved.

You may not have what someone else has. You may not look like that other person looks. You may not have one woman's talents or another woman's skills. But none of that matters. None of that moves God. He is moved by the feelings of your infirmities.

God is not moved by what you have. He is moved by how you feel about what you don't have and by what you need. He is moved by what you are believing for with your faith. Put the flame of feeling to the incense of your prayers, and keep crying out to God!

Aaron? 12 For the priesthood being changed, of necessity there is also a change of the law. 13 For He of whom these things are spoken belongs to another tribe, from which no man has officiated at the altar.

14 For *it is* evident that our Lord arose from Judah, of which tribe Moses spoke nothing concerning priesthood.*a* 15 And it is yet far more evident if, in the likeness of Melchizedek, there arises another priest 16 who has come, not according to the law of a fleshly commandment, but according to the power of an endless life. 17 For He testifies:*a*

> "You are a priest forever
> According to the order of
> Melchizedek."*b*

18 For on the one hand there is an annulling of the former commandment because of its weakness and unprofitableness, 19 for the law made nothing perfect; on the other hand, *there is the* bringing in of a better hope, through which we draw near to God.

20 And inasmuch as *He was* not *made priest* without an oath 21 (for they have become priests without an oath, but He with an oath by Him who said to Him:

> "The LORD has sworn
> And will not relent,
> 'You are a priest forever*a*
> According to the order of
> Melchizedek' "),*b*

22 by so much more Jesus has become a surety of a better covenant.

23 Also there were many priests, because they were prevented by death from continuing. 24 But He, because He continues forever, has an unchangeable priesthood. 25 Therefore He is also able to save to the uttermost those who come to God through Him, since He always lives to make intercession for them.

26 For such a High Priest was fitting for us, *who is* holy, harmless, undefiled, separate from sinners, and has become higher than the heavens; 27 who does not need daily, as those high priests, to offer up sacrifices, first for His own sins and then for

the people's, for this He did once for all when He offered up Himself. 28 For the law appoints as high priests men who have weakness, but the word of the oath, which came after the law, *appoints* the Son who has been perfected forever.

8 Now *this is* the main point of the things we are saying: We have such a High Priest, who is seated at the right hand of the throne of the Majesty in the heavens, 2 a Minister of the sanctuary and of the true tabernacle which the Lord erected, and not man.

3 For every high priest is appointed to offer both gifts and sacrifices. Therefore *it is* necessary that this One also have something to offer. 4 For if He were on earth, He would not be a priest, since there are priests who offer the gifts according to the law; 5 who serve the copy and shadow of the heavenly things, as Moses was divinely instructed when he was about to make the tabernacle. For He said, "See that you make all things according to the pattern shown you on the mountain."*a* 6 But now He has obtained a more excellent ministry, inasmuch as He is also Mediator of a better covenant, which was established on better promises.

7 For if that first *covenant* had been faultless, then no place would have been sought for a second. 8 Because finding fault with them, He says: "Behold, the days are coming, says the LORD, when I will make a new covenant with the house of Israel and with the house of Judah— 9 not according to the covenant that I made with their fathers in the day when I took them by the hand to lead them out of the land of Egypt; because they did not continue in My covenant, and I disregarded them, says the LORD. 10 For this is the covenant that I will make with the house of Israel after those days, says the LORD: I will put My laws in their mind and write them on their hearts; and I will be their God, and they shall be My people. 11 None of them shall teach his neighbor, and none his brother, saying, 'Know the LORD,' for all shall know Me, from the least of them to

---

7:14 *a*NU-Text reads *priests.*   7:17 *a*NU-Text reads *it is testified.*   *b*Psalm 110:4   7:21 *a*NU-Text ends the quotation here.   *b*Psalm 110:4   8:5 *a*Exodus 25:40

the greatest of them. 12 For I will be merciful to their unrighteousness, and their sins and their lawless deeds*a* I will remember no more."*b*

13 In that He says, "A new covenant," He has made the first obsolete. Now what is becoming obsolete and growing old is ready to vanish away.

9 Then indeed, even the first *covenant* had ordinances of divine service and the earthly sanctuary. 2 For a tabernacle was prepared: the first *part*, in which *was* the lampstand, the table, and the showbread, which is called the sanctuary; 3 and behind the second veil, the part of the tabernacle which is called the Holiest of All, 4 which had the golden censer and the ark of the covenant overlaid on all sides with gold, in which *were* the golden pot that had the manna, Aaron's rod that budded, and the tablets of the covenant; 5 and above it were the cherubim of glory overshadowing the mercy seat. Of these things we cannot now speak in detail.

6 Now when these things had been thus prepared, the priests always went into the first part of the tabernacle, performing *the services.* 7 But into the second part the high priest *went* alone once a year, not without blood, which he offered for himself and *for* the people's sins *committed* in ignorance; 8 the Holy Spirit indicating this, that the way into the Holiest of All was not yet made manifest while the first tabernacle was still standing. 9 It *was* symbolic for the present time in which both gifts and sacrifices are offered which cannot make him who performed the service perfect in regard to the conscience— 10 *concerned* only with foods and drinks, various washings, and fleshly ordinances imposed until the time of reformation.

11 But Christ came *as* High Priest of the good things to come,*a* with the greater and more perfect tabernacle not made with hands, that is, not of this creation. 12 Not with the blood of goats and calves, but with His own blood He entered the Most Holy Place once for all, having obtained eternal redemption. 13 For if the blood of bulls and goats and the ashes of a heifer, sprinkling the unclean, sanctifies for the purifying of the flesh, 14 how much more shall the blood of Christ, who through the eternal Spirit offered Himself without spot to God, cleanse your conscience from dead works to serve the living God? 15 And for this reason He is the Mediator of the new covenant, by means of death, for the redemption of the transgressions under the first covenant, that those who are called may receive the promise of the eternal inheritance.

16 For where there is a testament, there must also of necessity be the death of the testator. 17 For a testament is in force after men are dead, since it has no power at all while the testator lives. 18 Therefore not even the first *covenant* was dedicated without blood. 19 For when Moses had spoken every precept to all the people according to the law, he took the blood of calves and goats, with water, scarlet wool, and hyssop, and sprinkled both the book itself and all the people, 20 saying, *"This is the blood of the covenant which God has commanded you."a* 21 Then likewise he sprinkled with blood both the tabernacle and all the vessels of the ministry. 22 And according to the law almost all things are purified with blood, and without shedding of blood there is no remission.

23 Therefore it was necessary that the copies of the things in the heavens should be purified with these, but the heavenly things themselves with better sacrifices than these. 24 For Christ has not entered the holy places made with hands, *which are* copies of the true, but into heaven itself, now to appear in the presence of God for us; 25 not that He should offer Himself often, as the high priest enters the Most Holy Place every year with blood of another— 26 He then would have had to suffer often since the foundation of the world; but now, once at the end of the ages, He has appeared to put away sin by the sacrifice of Himself. 27 And as it is appointed for men to die once, but after this the judgment, 28 so Christ was offered once to bear the sins of many. To those who ea-

8:12 *a*NU-Text omits *and their lawless deeds.* *b*Jeremiah 31:31–34 9:11 *a*NU-Text reads *that have come.* 9:20 *a*Exodus 24:8

*H*ow many times have you been able to look back and say, "If I hadn't gone through that, I wouldn't have known or received this." Simply said, "He'll make it up to you." He restores the ravages of the years of turmoil.

gerly wait for Him He will appear a second time, apart from sin, for salvation.

10 For the law, having a shadow of the good things to come, *and* not the very image of the things, can never with these same sacrifices, which they offer continually year by year, make those who approach perfect. 2 For then would they not have ceased to be offered? For the worshipers, once purified, would have had no more consciousness of sins. 3 But in those *sacrifices there is* a reminder of sins every year. 4 For it is not possible that the blood of bulls and goats could take away sins.

5 Therefore, when He came into the world, He said:

"Sacrifice and offering You did
    not desire,
But a body You have prepared
    for Me.
6   In burnt offerings and
        sacrifices for sin
    You had no pleasure.
7   Then I said, 'Behold, I have
        come—
    In the volume of the book it is
        written of Me—
    To do Your will, O God.' "a

8 Previously saying, "Sacrifice and offering, burnt offerings, and offerings for sin You did not desire, nor had pleasure in them" (which are offered according to the law), 9 then He said, "Behold, I have come to do Your will, O God."a He takes away the first that He may establish the second. 10 By that will we have been sanctified through the offering of the body of Jesus Christ once *for all*.

11 And every priest stands ministering daily and offering repeatedly the same sacrifices, which can never take away sins. 12 But this Man, after He had offered one sacrifice for sins forever, sat down at the right hand of God, 13 from that time waiting till His enemies are made His footstool. 14 For by one offering He has perfected forever those who are being sanctified.

15 But the Holy Spirit also witnesses to us; for after He had said before,

16 "This is the covenant that I will make with them after those days, says the LORD: I will put My laws into their hearts, and in their minds I will write them,"a 17 then He adds, "Their sins and their lawless deeds I will remember no more."a 18 Now where there is remission of these, *there is* no longer an offering for sin.

19 Therefore, brethren, having boldness to enter the Holiest by the blood of Jesus, 20 by a new and living way which He consecrated for us, through the veil, that is, His flesh, 21 and *having* a High Priest over the house of God, 22 let us draw near with a true heart in full assurance of faith, having our hearts sprinkled from an evil conscience and our bodies washed with pure water. 23 Let us hold fast the confession of our hope without wavering, for He who promised *is* faithful. 24 And let us consider one another in order to stir up love and good works, 25 not forsaking the assembling of ourselves together, as *is* the manner of some, but exhorting *one another*, and so much the more as you see the Day approaching.

26 For if we sin willfully after we have received the knowledge of the truth, there no longer remains a sacrifice for sins, 27 but a certain fearful expectation of judgment, and fiery indignation which will devour the adversaries. 28 Anyone who has rejected Moses' law dies without mercy on the testimony of two or three witnesses. 29 Of how much worse punishment, do you suppose, will he be thought worthy who has trampled the Son of God underfoot, counted the blood of the covenant by which he was sanctified a common thing, and insulted the Spirit of grace? 30 For we know Him who said, "Vengeance is Mine, I will repay,"a says the Lord.b And again, "The LORD will judge His people."c 31 It is a fearful thing to fall into the hands of the living God.

32 But recall the former days in which, after you were illuminated, you endured a great struggle with sufferings: 33 partly while you were made a spectacle both by reproaches

10:7 aPsalm 40:6–8   10:9 aNU-Text and M-Text omit *O God.*   10:16 aJeremiah 31:33
10:17 aJeremiah 31:34   10:30 aDeuteronomy 32:35   bNU-Text omits *says the Lord.*   cDeuteronomy
32:36

The sins of the woman who wanted to fulfill her lusts were crucified on the Cross with Him. The past is paid for. The wounds may leave scars, but the scars are only there to remind us that we are human.

God's Cedar Chest

*I*s your heart broken because of immoral relationships—perhaps incest—that took place in your home when you were young and vulnerable? Women who have a desperate need for male attention have usually come from a situation where there have been no positive male role models in the home. Since they didn't get enough nurturing as girls, they find it easy to compromise and agree to do anything to gain male acceptance and love.

Millions of women have longed for a loving embrace from fathers who walked out on them or were never around. If you're one of those women, there is a way to fill the emptiness inside. The Lord will fill that void in your life. He wants to be the heavenly Father who will mend your heart. Through His Spirit, He wants to hold you. He wants to give you a hug.

Look for His helpers in the Church. Many men are learning that a woman who is not their wife is to be treated as a sister. Big brothers protect their little sisters; they do not take advantage of them. A brotherly and sisterly love does not include sexual intimacy or self-gratification.

The Song of Solomon shows a progression of the relationship between the writer and his wife. She was his "sister" before she was his bride. Solomon wrote of protecting a little sister: "Enclose her with boards of cedar" (see Song of Solomon 8:9). The Church is God's cedar chest!

God's people are to nurture and protect one another. It makes no difference how turbulent your past life has been, God still cares. Allow Him the privilege of doing what Absalom did for Tamar. When Tamar lay outside Amnon's door—broken and brutally violated—Absalom took her in and cared for her (see 2 Samuel 13:19–20).

The secret of being transformed from a vulnerable victim to a victorious, loving person is found in the ability to open your past to someone responsible enough to share your weakness and pain. There can be no better first step toward deliverance than to find a Christian counselor or pastor, and come out of hiding. If you seek God's guidance and the help of competent leadership, you will find someone who can help you work through your pain and suffering. The Church is a body. No one operates independent of another. We are all in this together.

and tribulations, and partly while you became companions of those who were so treated; 34 for you had compassion on me[a] in my chains, and joyfully accepted the plundering of your goods, knowing that you have a better and an enduring possession for yourselves in heaven.[b] 35 Therefore do not cast away your confidence, which has great reward. 36 For you have need of endurance, so that after you have done the will of God, you may receive the promise:

37 *"For yet a little while,*
     And He[a] who is coming will come and will not tarry.
38   *Now the[a] just shall live by faith;*
     But if anyone draws back, My soul has no pleasure in him."[b]

39 But we are not of those who draw back to perdition, but of those who believe to the saving of the soul.

11 Now faith is the substance of things hoped for, the evidence of things not seen. 2 For by it the elders obtained a *good* testimony.

3 By faith we understand that the worlds were framed by the word of God, so that the things which are seen were not made of things which are visible.

4 By faith Abel offered to God a more excellent sacrifice than Cain, through which he obtained witness that he was righteous, God testifying of his gifts; and through it he being dead still speaks.

5 By faith Enoch was taken away so that he did not see death, *"and was not found, because God had taken him";[a]* for before he was taken he had this testimony, that he pleased God. 6 But without faith *it is* impossible to please *Him,* for he who comes to God must believe that He is, and *that* He is a rewarder of those who diligently seek Him.

7 By faith Noah, being divinely warned of things not yet seen, moved with godly fear, prepared an ark for the saving of his household, by which he condemned the world and became

heir of the righteousness which is according to faith.

8 By faith Abraham obeyed when he was called to go out to the place which he would receive as an inheritance. And he went out, not knowing where he was going. 9 By faith he dwelt in the land of promise as *in* a foreign country, dwelling in tents with Isaac and Jacob, the heirs with him of the same promise; 10 for he waited for the city which has foundations, whose builder and maker *is* God.

11 By faith Sarah herself also received strength to conceive seed, and she bore a child[a] when she was past the age, because she judged Him faithful who had promised. 12 Therefore from one man, and him as good as dead, were born *as many* as the stars of the sky in multitude— innumerable as the sand which is by the seashore.

13 These all died in faith, not having received the promises, but having seen them afar off were assured of them,[a] embraced *them* and confessed that they were strangers and pilgrims on the earth. 14 For those who say such things declare plainly that they seek a homeland. 15 And truly if they had called to mind that *country* from which they had come out, they would have had opportunity to return. 16 But now they desire a better, that is, a heavenly *country.* Therefore God is not ashamed to be called their God, for He has prepared a city for them.

17 By faith Abraham, when he was tested, offered up Isaac, and he who had received the promises offered up his only begotten *son,* 18 of whom it was said, *"In Isaac your seed shall be called,"[a]* 19 concluding that God *was* able to raise *him* up, even from the dead, from which he also received him in a figurative sense.

20 By faith Isaac blessed Jacob and Esau concerning things to come.

21 By faith Jacob, when he was dying, blessed each of the sons of Joseph, and worshiped, *leaning* on the top of his staff.

22 By faith Joseph, when he was dying, made mention of the depar-

---

10:34 [a]NU-Text reads *the prisoners* instead of *me in my chains.*   [b]NU-Text omits *in heaven.*
10:37 [a]*Or that which*   10:38 [a]NU-Text reads *my just one.*   [b]Habakkuk 2:3, 4   11:5 [a]Genesis 5:24
11:11 [a]NU-Text omits *she bore a child.*   11:13 [a]NU-Text and M-Text omit *were assured of them.*
11:18 [a]Genesis 21:12

What good is it to appreciate what God gave us if we do not appreciate the God who gave it to us? If age should do nothing else, it should help us put things in proper perspective. There is nothing like time to show us that we have misplaced priorities.

The Promise Keeper

Hebrews 11:6

God will reward those who keep on seeking Him. He may not come when you want Him to, but He will be right on time. If you will wait on the Lord, He will strengthen your heart. He will heal you and deliver you. He will lift you up and break your chains. He will give you the garment of praise for the spirit of heaviness (see Isaiah 61:3). He will keep all His promises.

But you have a part to play. And that part is faith. When we believe God's promises, we are counted as righteous. Righteousness cannot be earned or merited. It comes only through faith. "By faith we understand that the worlds were framed by the word of God, so that the things which are seen were not made of things which are visible" (Hebrews 11:3). God wants us to understand that just because we can't see it, doesn't mean He won't do it.

By faith Sarah believed that she could conceive a baby even though she was past childbearing age. She believed that God was capable of giving her a child regardless of what the circumstances looked like. From the natural perspective, it was impossible. The enemy certainly didn't want it to happen. But God kept His promise.

Abraham received many promises from God regarding his descendants. God told Abraham that his seed would be as the sands of the sea and the stars of heaven (see Genesis 22:17). The first promise represents the natural, physical nation of Israel. These were the people of the Old Covenant. But God didn't stop there. He also promised that Abraham's seed would be as the stars of heaven. These are the people of the New Covenant. That's the Church. We, too, are seed of Abraham. We are the stars of heaven. The only thing between the seed and the stars was the woman. Can you see why Sarah had to receive strength to conceive a seed when she was old? When she believed and conceived, God multiplied her blessings.

Whatever God gives you, He wants it to be multiplied in the womb of your spirit. When you bring it forth, it shall be greater than what you had.

The enemy wants to multiply fear in your life. God wants to set you free from fear and fill you with faith. You must learn to trust God enough to allow Him to come in and plow up your life. He may need to root out closet skeletons and replace them with new attitudes.

Satan has assigned fear to block up your womb and cause you to be less productive than God wants you to be. Don't be afraid. You are God's woman. No matter the desire or the blessing that you seek, God has promised to give you the desires of your heart (see Psalm 37:4), and He always keeps His promises!

ture of the children of Israel, and gave instructions concerning his bones.

23 By faith Moses, when he was born, was hidden three months by his parents, because they saw *he was* a beautiful child; and they were not afraid of the king's command.

24 By faith Moses, when he became of age, refused to be called the son of Pharaoh's daughter, 25 choosing rather to suffer affliction with the people of God than to enjoy the passing pleasures of sin, 26 esteeming the reproach of Christ greater riches than the treasures in*ª* Egypt; for he looked to the reward.

27 By faith he forsook Egypt, not fearing the wrath of the king; for he endured as seeing Him who is invisible. 28 By faith he kept the Passover and the sprinkling of blood, lest he who destroyed the firstborn should touch them.

29 By faith they passed through the Red Sea as by dry *land, whereas* the Egyptians, attempting *to do* so, were drowned.

30 By faith the walls of Jericho fell down after they were encircled for seven days. 31 By faith the harlot Rahab did not perish with those who did not believe, when she had received the spies with peace.

32 And what more shall I say? For the time would fail me to tell of Gideon and Barak and Samson and Jephthah, also *of* David and Samuel and the prophets: 33 who through faith subdued kingdoms, worked righteousness, obtained promises, stopped the mouths of lions, 34 quenched the violence of fire, escaped the edge of the sword, out of weakness were made strong, became valiant in battle, turned to flight the armies of the aliens. 35 Women received their dead raised to life again.

Others were tortured, not accepting deliverance, that they might obtain a better resurrection. 36 Still others had trial of mockings and scourgings, yes, and of chains and imprisonment. 37 They were stoned, they were sawn in two, were tempted,*ª* were slain with the sword. They wandered about in sheepskins and goatskins, being destitute, af-

flicted, tormented— 38 of whom the world was not worthy. They wandered in deserts and mountains, *in* dens and caves of the earth.

39 And all these, having obtained a good testimony through faith, did not receive the promise, 40 God having provided something better for us, that they should not be made perfect apart from us.

12 Therefore we also, since we are surrounded by so great a cloud of witnesses, let us lay aside every weight, and the sin which so easily ensnares *us,* and let us run with endurance the race that is set before us, 2 looking unto Jesus, the author and finisher of *our* faith, who for the joy that was set before Him endured the cross, despising the shame, and has sat down at the right hand of the throne of God.

3 For consider Him who endured such hostility from sinners against Himself, lest you become weary and discouraged in your souls. 4 You have not yet resisted to bloodshed, striving against sin. 5 And you have forgotten the exhortation which speaks to you as to sons:

> "My son, do not despise the chastening of the LORD,
> Nor be discouraged when you are rebuked by Him;
> 6 For whom the LORD loves He chastens,
> And scourges every son whom He receives."*ª*

7 If*ª* you endure chastening, God deals with you as with sons; for what son is there whom a father does not chasten? 8 But if you are without chastening, of which all have become partakers, then you are illegitimate and not sons. 9 Furthermore, we have had human fathers who corrected *us,* and we paid *them* respect. Shall we not much more readily be in subjection to the Father of spirits and live? 10 For they indeed for a few days chastened *us* as seemed *best* to them, but He for *our* profit, that *we* may be partakers of His holiness. 11 Now no chastening seems to be joyful for the present, but painful; nevertheless, afterward it yields the peace

11:26 *ª*NU-Text and M-Text read *of.*   11:37 *ª*NU-Text omits *were tempted.*   12:6 *ª*Proverbs 3:11, 12
12:7 *ª*NU-Text and M-Text read *It is for discipline that you endure; God.*

Gospel Pearls

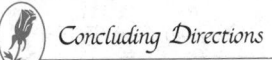
able fruit of righteousness to those who have been trained by it.

12 Therefore strengthen the hands which hang down, and the feeble knees, 13 and make straight paths for your feet, so that what is lame may not be *dislocated*, but rather be healed.

14 Pursue peace with all *people*, and holiness, without which no one will see the Lord: 15 looking carefully lest anyone fall short of the grace of God; lest any root of bitterness springing up cause trouble, and by this many become defiled; 16 lest there *be* any fornicator or profane person like Esau, who for one morsel of food sold his birthright. 17 For you know that afterward, when he wanted to inherit the blessing, he was rejected, for he found no place for repentance, though he sought it diligently with tears.

18 For you have not come to the mountain that*ᵃ* may be touched and that burned with fire, and to blackness and darkness*ᵇ* and tempest, 19 and the sound of a trumpet and the voice of words, so that those who heard *it* begged that the word should not be spoken to them anymore. 20 (For they could not endure what was commanded: *"And if so much as a beast touches the mountain, it shall be stoned*ᵃ *or shot with an arrow."*ᵇ 21 And so terrifying was the sight *that* Moses said, *"I am exceedingly afraid* and trembling."*ᵃ*)

22 But you have come to Mount Zion and to the city of the living God, the heavenly Jerusalem, to an innumerable company of angels, 23 to the general assembly and church of the firstborn *who are* registered in heaven, to God the Judge of all, to the spirits of just men made perfect, 24 to Jesus the Mediator of the new covenant, and to the blood of sprinkling that speaks better things than *that* of Abel.

25 See that you do not refuse Him who speaks. For if they did not escape who refused Him who spoke on earth, much more *shall we not escape* if we turn away from Him who *speaks* from heaven, 26 whose voice then shook the earth; but now He has

promised, saying, *"Yet once more I shake*ᵃ *not only the earth, but also heaven."*ᵇ 27 Now this, *"Yet once more,"* indicates the removal of those things that are being shaken, as of things that are made, that the things which cannot be shaken may remain.

28 Therefore, since we are receiving a kingdom which cannot be shaken, let us have grace, by which we may*ᵃ* serve God acceptably with reverence and godly fear. 29 For our God *is* a consuming fire.

13 Let brotherly love continue. 2 Do not forget to entertain strangers, for by so *doing* some have unwittingly entertained angels. 3 Remember the prisoners as if chained with them—those who are mistreated—since you yourselves are in the body also.

4 Marriage *is* honorable among all, and the bed undefiled; but fornicators and adulterers God will judge.

5 *Let your* conduct *be* without covetousness; *be* content with such things as you have. For He Himself has said, *"I will never leave you nor forsake you."*ᵃ 6 So we may boldly say:

> *"The LORD is my helper;*
> *I will not fear.*
> *What can man do to me?"*ᵃ

7 Remember those who rule over you, who have spoken the word of God to you, whose faith follow, considering the outcome of *their* conduct. 8 Jesus Christ *is* the same yesterday, today, and forever. 9 Do not be carried about*ᵃ* with various and strange doctrines. For *it is* good that the heart be established by grace, not with foods which have not profited those who have been occupied with them.

10 We have an altar from which those who serve the tabernacle have no right to eat. 11 For the bodies of those animals, whose blood is brought into the sanctuary by the high priest for sin, are burned outside the camp. 12 Therefore Jesus also,

12:18 ᵃNU-Text reads *to that which.*   ᵇNU-Text reads *gloom.*   12:20 ᵃNU-Text and M-Text omit the rest of this verse.   ᵇExodus 19:12, 13   12:21 ᵃDeuteronomy 9:19   12:26 ᵃNU-Text reads *will shake.* ᵇHaggai 2:6   12:28 ᵃM-Text omits *may.*   13:5 ᵃDeuteronomy 31:6, 8; Joshua 1:5   13:6 ᵃPsalm 118:6   13:9 ᵃNU-Text and M-Text read *away.*

I am convinced that the things that worry us would not, if we knew the faithfulness of God. He cares for you! Look over your past and remember His faithfulness. Look at your future and trust Him now!

that He might sanctify the people with His own blood, suffered outside the gate. 13 Therefore let us go forth to Him, outside the camp, bearing His reproach. 14 For here we have no continuing city, but we seek the one to come. 15 Therefore by Him let us continually offer the sacrifice of praise to God, that is, the fruit of *our* lips, giving thanks to His name. 16 But do not forget to do good and to share, for with such sacrifices God is well pleased.

17 Obey those who rule over you, and be submissive, for they watch out for your souls, as those who must give account. Let them do so with joy and not with grief, for that would be unprofitable for you.

18 Pray for us; for we are confident that we have a good conscience, in all things desiring to live honorably. 19 But I especially urge *you* to do this,

13:21 *a*NU-Text and M-Text read *us.*

that I may be restored to you the sooner.

20 Now may the God of peace who brought up our Lord Jesus from the dead, that great Shepherd of the sheep, through the blood of the everlasting covenant, 21 make you complete in every good work to do His will, working in you*a* what is well pleasing in His sight, through Jesus Christ, to whom *be* glory forever and ever. Amen.

22 And I appeal to you, brethren, bear with the word of exhortation, for I have written to you in few words. 23 Know that *our* brother Timothy has been set free, with whom I shall see you if he comes shortly.

24 Greet all those who rule over you, and all the saints. Those from Italy greet you.

25 Grace *be* with you all. Amen.

The Epistle of

JAMES

1 James, a bondservant of God and of the Lord Jesus Christ,

To the twelve tribes which are scattered abroad:

Greetings.

2 My brethren, count it all joy when you fall into various trials, 3 knowing that the testing of your faith produces patience. 4 But let patience have *its* perfect work, that you may be perfect and complete, lacking nothing. 5 If any of you lacks wisdom, let him ask of God, who gives to all liberally and without reproach, and it will be given to him. 6 But let him ask in faith, with no doubting, for he who doubts is like a wave of the sea driven and tossed by the wind. 7 For let not that man suppose that he will receive anything from the Lord; 8 *he is* a double-minded man, unstable in all his ways.

9 Let the lowly brother glory in his exaltation, 10 but the rich in his hu-

miliation, because as a flower of the field he will pass away. 11 For no sooner has the sun risen with a burning heat than it withers the grass; its flower falls, and its beautiful appearance perishes. So the rich man also will fade away in his pursuits.

12 Blessed *is* the man who endures temptation; for when he has been approved, he will receive the crown of life which the Lord has promised to those who love Him. 13 Let no one say when he is tempted, "I am tempted by God"; for God cannot be tempted by evil, nor does He Himself tempt anyone. 14 But each one is tempted when he is drawn away by his own desires and enticed. 15 Then, when desire has conceived, it gives birth to sin; and sin, when it is full-grown, brings forth death.

16 Do not be deceived, my beloved brethren. 17 Every good gift and every perfect gift is from above, and comes down from the Father of lights, with whom there is no varia-

*W*e must understand that modern medicine can heal many afflictions of the body, and can even treat the tumors that sometimes attach themselves to the brain. But only God Himself can heal the mind.

Making Friends with Change

James 1:17

Change is not always an enemy. It can be God's way of saying enough is enough. He will promote you from one task to another. If you can remain flexible and face the changes of life with the assurance of God, you will win. It is God's desire to make you a wise woman. What I am trying to tell you is life has a middle name, and the name is change. Anything that grows will change.

My sisters, for the many changes you will face on all levels of life, I recommend Jesus. He does not change. He is an unchanging God in a rapidly changing world. If you are going to survive, you must learn how to accept change, whether it involves your marriage, your children, your job or your ministry. Do not be tormented by something that was once wonderful. When it is time to move on, do not look back. Know when it is time for new discoveries.

Even in the cold crispness of winter there will be sunny days. Early in the morning when icicles hang from eaves, there are still the glowing, glistening rays of morning sun. Though the wind has howled all night, and the gusts beat vehemently against the house, there will be a morning. Expect it in every season of life. Get up and throw aside the curtain of doubt. Brush past the foggy film that would cloud your eyes from seeing what is right in front of you and embrace expectancy. It is the breaking of a new day. It is the establishing of fresh options.

No two days will be the same. They were not designed to be duplicated. Each one is a new expression of a multifaceted God whose being cannot be defined in just one circumstance. Every day we will behold a new wonder of His glory. A splendor, a slice, a sliver of His radiance will dispel the fear of the future. Now, stop crying and fretting over this and that. You will create your own rain.

Get up rejoicing in a day that someone else missed. While you slept someone gasped a final sigh and slipped from time into eternity without seeing this day. But you are still here. This is God's gift to you. From the God who cares enough to give the very best, He gave you today. Enjoy it. It is yours. Change will come soon enough. There will never be another moment like this one.

tion or shadow of turning. 18 Of His own will He brought us forth by the word of truth, that we might be a kind of firstfruits of His creatures.

19 So then,*a* my beloved brethren, let every man be swift to hear, slow to speak, slow to wrath; 20 for the wrath of man does not produce the righteousness of God.

21 Therefore lay aside all filthiness and overflow of wickedness, and receive with meekness the implanted word, which is able to save your souls.

22 But be doers of the word, and not hearers only, deceiving yourselves. 23 For if anyone is a hearer of the word and not a doer, he is like a man observing his natural face in a mirror; 24 for he observes himself, goes away, and immediately forgets what kind of man he was. 25 But he who looks into the perfect law of liberty and continues *in it,* and is not a forgetful hearer but a doer of the work, this one will be blessed in what he does.

26 If anyone among you*a* thinks he is religious, and does not bridle his tongue but deceives his own heart, this one's religion *is* useless. 27 Pure and undefiled religion before God and the Father is this: to visit orphans and widows in their trouble, *and* to keep oneself unspotted from the world.

2 My brethren, do not hold the faith of our Lord Jesus Christ, *the Lord* of glory, with partiality. 2 For if there should come into your assembly a man with gold rings, in fine apparel, and there should also come in a poor man in filthy clothes, 3 and you pay attention to the one wearing the fine clothes and say to him, "You sit here in a good place," and say to the poor man, "You stand there," or, "Sit here at my footstool," 4 have you not shown partiality among yourselves, and become judges with evil thoughts?

5 Listen, my beloved brethren: Has God not chosen the poor of this world *to be* rich in faith and heirs of the kingdom which He promised to those who love Him? 6 But you have dishonored the poor man. Do not the rich oppress you and drag you into the courts? 7 Do they not blaspheme that noble name by which you are called?

8 If you really fulfill *the* royal law according to the Scripture, *"You shall love your neighbor as yourself,"a* you do well; 9 but if you show partiality, you commit sin, and are convicted by the law as transgressors. 10 For whoever shall keep the whole law, and yet stumble in one *point,* he is guilty of all. 11 For He who said, *"Do not commit adultery,"a* also said, *"Do not murder."b* Now if you do not commit adultery, but you do murder, you have become a transgressor of the law. 12 So speak and so do as those who will be judged by the law of liberty. 13 For judgment is without mercy to the one who has shown no mercy. Mercy triumphs over judgment.

14 What *does it* profit, my brethren, if someone says he has faith but does not have works? Can faith save him? 15 If a brother or sister is naked and destitute of daily food, 16 and one of you says to them, "Depart in peace, be warmed and filled," but you do not give them the things which are needed for the body, what *does it* profit? 17 Thus also faith by itself, if it does not have works, is dead.

18 But someone will say, "You have faith, and I have works." Show me your faith without your*a* works, and I will show you my faith by my*b* works. 19 You believe that there is one God. You do well. Even the demons believe—and tremble! 20 But do you want to know, O foolish man, that faith without works is dead?*a* 21 Was not Abraham our father justified by works when he offered Isaac his son on the altar? 22 Do you see that faith was working together with his works, and by works faith was made perfect? 23 And the Scripture was fulfilled which says, *"Abraham believed God, and it was accounted to him for righteousness."a* And he was called the friend of God. 24 You see then that a man is justified by works, and not by faith only.

25 Likewise, was not Rahab the harlot also justified by works when

1:19 *a*NU-Text reads *Know (this)* or *(This) you know.*   1:26 *a*NU-Text omits *among you.*   2:8 *a*Leviticus 19:18   2:11 *a*Exodus 20:14; Deuteronomy 5:18   *b*Exodus 20:13; Deuteronomy 5:17   2:18 *a*NU-Text omits *your.*   *b*NU-Text omits *my.*   2:20 *a*NU-Text reads *useless.*   2:23 *a*Genesis 15:6

Gospel Pearls

she received the messengers and sent *them* out another way?

26 For as the body without the spirit is dead, so faith without works is dead also.

3 My brethren, let not many of you become teachers, knowing that we shall receive a stricter judgment. 2 For we all stumble in many things. If anyone does not stumble in word, he *is* a perfect man, able also to bridle the whole body. 3 Indeed,*a* we put bits in horses' mouths that they may obey us, and we turn their whole body. 4 Look also at ships: although they are so large and are driven by fierce winds, they are turned by a very small rudder wherever the pilot desires. 5 Even so the tongue is a little member and boasts great things.

See how great a forest a little fire kindles! 6 And the tongue *is* a fire, a world of iniquity. The tongue is so set among our members that it defiles the whole body, and sets on fire the course of nature; and it is set on fire by hell. 7 For every kind of beast and bird, of reptile and creature of the sea, is tamed and has been tamed by mankind. 8 But no man can tame the tongue. *It is* an unruly evil, full of deadly poison. 9 With it we bless our God and Father, and with it we curse men, who have been made in the similitude of God. 10 Out of the same mouth proceed blessing and cursing. My brethren, these things ought not to be so. 11 Does a spring send forth fresh *water* and bitter from the same opening? 12 Can a fig tree, my brethren, bear olives, or a grapevine bear figs? Thus no spring yields both salt water and fresh.*a*

13 Who *is* wise and understanding among you? Let him show by good conduct *that* his works *are* done in the meekness of wisdom. 14 But if you have bitter envy and self-seeking in your hearts, do not boast and lie against the truth. 15 This wisdom does not descend from above, but *is* earthly, sensual, demonic. 16 For where envy and self-seeking *exist,* confusion and every evil thing *are* there. 17 But the wisdom that is from above is first pure, then peaceable, gentle, willing to yield, full of mercy and good fruits, without partiality and without hypocrisy. 18 Now the fruit of righteousness is sown in peace by those who make peace.

4 Where do wars and fights *come* from among you? Do *they* not *come* from your *desires for* pleasure that war in your members? 2 You lust and do not have. You murder and covet and cannot obtain. You fight and war. Yet*a* you do not have because you do not ask. 3 You ask and do not receive, because you ask amiss, that you may spend *it* on your pleasures. 4 Adulterers and*a* adulteresses! Do you not know that friendship with the world is enmity with God? Whoever therefore wants to be a friend of the world makes himself an enemy of God. 5 Or do you think that the Scripture says in vain, "The Spirit who dwells in us yearns jealously"?

6 But He gives more grace. Therefore He says:

> "God resists the proud,
> But gives grace to the
> humble."*a*

7 Therefore submit to God. Resist the devil and he will flee from you. 8 Draw near to God and He will draw near to you. Cleanse *your* hands, *you* sinners; and purify *your* hearts, *you* double-minded. 9 Lament and mourn and weep! Let your laughter be turned to mourning and *your* joy to gloom. 10 Humble yourselves in the sight of the Lord, and He will lift you up.

11 Do not speak evil of one another, brethren. He who speaks evil of a brother and judges his brother, speaks evil of the law and judges the law. But if you judge the law, you are not a doer of the law but a judge. 12 There is one Lawgiver,*a* who is able to save and to destroy. Who*b* are you to judge another?*c*

13 Come now, you who say, "Today or tomorrow we will*a* go to such and such a city, spend a year there, buy and sell, and make a profit"; 14 whereas you do not know what

---

3:3 *a*NU-Text reads *Now if.*   3:12 *a*NU-Text reads *Neither can a salty spring produce fresh water.*
4:2 *a*NU-Text and M-Text omit *Yet.*   4:4 *a*NU-Text omits *Adulterers and.*   4:6 *a*Proverbs 3:34
4:12 *a*NU-Text adds *and Judge.*   *b*NU-Text and M-Text read *But who.*   *c*NU-Text reads *a neighbor.*
4:13 *a*M-Text reads *let us.*

---

*R*esist the temptation to allow what happened in the past to determine who you are today. Begin to declare: "I endured what happened yesterday. I survived what happened. But I am not what happened yesterday."

No Passion, No Power

James 4:7, 8

Where there is no passion, there is no power. The enemy will attempt either to steal your passion or to smother it beneath the fear of failure and rejection. Without passion, you will become passive, unable to achieve the purpose of God in your life.

A woman never dies with a twinkle in her eye or a vision in her heart. When you meet a visionary, you'll recognize her by her sense of expectancy, her confidence, her ability to see what no one else can. She can bounce back, and she can hang in there. If Satan can steal your passion, he will gain your power!

The enemy is trying to steal something from you that you cannot see. Any time the invisible is stolen, you may not notice that it's gone at first. What day did passion leave the marriage? On which morning did you lose interest in your job? At what moment did your children grow up?

Enthusiasm leaks out of a life like air seeping out of a tire. The thief siphons vitality from you like a tiny cut flattens a tire. Suddenly you realize how gradually your energy has left you.

The only solution lies in the absolute, committed guarding of the heart (see Proverbs 4:23). Your greatest treasure isn't your bank account. It isn't your retirement fund, or your stocks and bonds. Your greatest treasure is in the strength of the passion that is locked in the deepest places of your heart. Out of the heart flow the issues of life.

You can't spend the rest of your life trying to protect yourself from the struggles of life. They are unavoidable. All people face struggles and the seasons of life, regardless of their economical, spiritual, or sociological persuasion! If you become intimidated by that fact, it will cause you to live your life in an emotional incubator—insulated but isolated. Having declared that, we must no longer focus on protecting ourselves, but we must be willing to live and to risk and to dare.

Stay vigilant and refuse to be overwhelmed. Wrap your godly virtue tightly around your heart, like a warm coat on a winter night. It is the wellspring that gives you the strength to keep on living and giving!

will happen tomorrow. For what *is* your life? It is even a vapor that appears for a little time and then vanishes away. 15 Instead you *ought* to say, "If the Lord wills, we shall live and do this or that." 16 But now you boast in your arrogance. All such boasting is evil.

17 Therefore, to him who knows to do good and does not do *it*, to him it is sin.

5 Come now, *you* rich, weep and howl for your miseries that are coming upon *you!* 2 Your riches are corrupted, and your garments are moth-eaten. 3 Your gold and silver are corroded, and their corrosion will be a witness against you and will eat your flesh like fire. You have heaped up treasure in the last days. 4 Indeed the wages of the laborers who mowed your fields, which you kept back by fraud, cry out; and the cries of the reapers have reached the ears of the Lord of Sabaoth.*a* 5 You have lived on the earth in pleasure and luxury; you have fattened your hearts as*a* in a day of slaughter. 6 You have condemned, you have murdered the just; he does not resist you.

7 Therefore be patient, brethren, until the coming of the Lord. See *how* the farmer waits for the precious fruit of the earth, waiting patiently for it until it receives the early and latter rain. 8 You also be patient. Establish your hearts, for the coming of the Lord is at hand.

9 Do not grumble against one another, brethren, lest you be condemned.*a* Behold, the Judge is standing at the door! 10 My brethren, take the prophets, who spoke in the name of the Lord, as an example of suffering and patience. 11 Indeed we count them blessed who endure. You have heard of the perseverance of Job and seen the end *intended by* the Lord— that the Lord is very compassionate and merciful.

12 But above all, my brethren, do not swear, either by heaven or by earth or with any other oath. But let your "Yes" be "Yes," and *your* "No," "No," lest you fall into judgment.*a*

13 Is anyone among you suffering? Let him pray. Is anyone cheerful? Let him sing psalms. 14 Is anyone among you sick? Let him call for the elders of the church, and let them pray over him, anointing him with oil in the name of the Lord. 15 And the prayer of faith will save the sick, and the Lord will raise him up. And if he has committed sins, he will be forgiven. 16 Confess *your* trespasses*a* to one another, and pray for one another, that you may be healed. The effective, fervent prayer of a righteous man avails much. 17 Elijah was a man with a nature like ours, and he prayed earnestly that it would not rain; and it did not rain on the land for three years and six months. 18 And he prayed again, and the heaven gave rain, and the earth produced its fruit.

19 Brethren, if anyone among you wanders from the truth, and someone turns him back, 20 let him know that he who turns a sinner from the error of his way will save a soul*a* from death and cover a multitude of sins.

5:4 *a*Literally, in Hebrew, *Hosts*   5:5 *a*NU-Text omits *as*.   5:9 *a*NU-Text and M-Text read *judged*.
5:12 *a*M-Text reads *hypocrisy*.   5:16 *a*NU-Text reads *Therefore confess your sins*.   5:20 *a*NU-Text reads *his soul*.

The First Epistle of

PETER

1 Peter, an apostle of Jesus Christ, To the pilgrims of the Dispersion in Pontus, Galatia, Cappadocia, Asia, and Bithynia, 2 elect according to the foreknowledge of God the Father, in sanctification of the Spirit, for obedience and sprinkling of the blood of Jesus Christ:

*Y*ou must choose what you are going to meditate upon. Choose carefully, though, for you will ultimately become whatever it is you meditate upon. The enemy knows this, so when he wants to destroy your morality, he starts with a thought.

Grace to you and peace be multiplied.

3 Blessed be the God and Father of our Lord Jesus Christ, who according to His abundant mercy has begotten us again to a living hope through the resurrection of Jesus Christ from the dead, 4 to an inheritance incorruptible and undefiled and that does not fade away, reserved in heaven for you, 5 who are kept by the power of God through faith for salvation ready to be revealed in the last time.

6 In this you greatly rejoice, though now for a little while, if need be, you have been grieved by various trials, 7 that the genuineness of your faith, being much more precious than gold that perishes, though it is tested by fire, may be found to praise, honor, and glory at the revelation of Jesus Christ, 8 whom having not seen[a] you love. Though now you do not see Him, yet believing, you rejoice with joy inexpressible and full of glory, 9 receiving the end of your faith—the salvation of your souls.

10 Of this salvation the prophets have inquired and searched carefully, who prophesied of the grace that would come to you, 11 searching what, or what manner of time, the Spirit of Christ who was in them was indicating when He testified beforehand the sufferings of Christ and the glories that would follow. 12 To them it was revealed that, not to themselves, but to us[a] they were ministering the things which now have been reported to you through those who have preached the gospel to you by the Holy Spirit sent from heaven—things which angels desire to look into.

13 Therefore gird up the loins of your mind, be sober, and rest your hope fully upon the grace that is to be brought to you at the revelation of Jesus Christ; 14 as obedient children, not conforming yourselves to the former lusts, as in your ignorance; 15 but as He who called you is holy, you also be holy in all your conduct, 16 because it is written, "Be holy, for I am holy."[a]

17 And if you call on the Father,

who without partiality judges according to each one's work, conduct yourselves throughout the time of your stay here in fear; 18 knowing that you were not redeemed with corruptible things, like silver or gold, from your aimless conduct received by tradition from your fathers, 19 but with the precious blood of Christ, as of a lamb without blemish and without spot. 20 He indeed was foreordained before the foundation of the world, but was manifest in these last times for you 21 who through Him believe in God, who raised Him from the dead and gave Him glory, so that your faith and hope are in God.

22 Since you have purified your souls in obeying the truth through the Spirit[a] in sincere love of the brethren, love one another fervently with a pure heart, 23 having been born again, not of corruptible seed but incorruptible, through the word of God which lives and abides forever,[a] 24 because

"All flesh is as grass,
    And all the glory of man[a] as the
        flower of the grass.
    The grass withers,
    And its flower falls away,
25   But the word of the LORD
        endures forever."[a]

Now this is the word which by the gospel was preached to you.

2 Therefore, laying aside all malice, all deceit, hypocrisy, envy, and all evil speaking, 2 as newborn babes, desire the pure milk of the word, that you may grow thereby,[a] 3 if indeed you have tasted that the Lord is gracious.

4 Coming to Him as to a living stone, rejected indeed by men, but chosen by God and precious, 5 you also, as living stones, are being built up a spiritual house, a holy priesthood, to offer up spiritual sacrifices acceptable to God through Jesus Christ. 6 Therefore it is also contained in the Scripture,

"Behold, I lay in Zion
    A chief cornerstone, elect,
        precious,

1:8 [a]M-Text reads known.   1:12 [a]NU-Text and M-Text read you.   1:16 [a]Leviticus 11:44, 45; 19:2; 20:7   1:22 [a]NU-Text omits through the Spirit.   1:23 [a]NU-Text omits forever.   1:24 [a]NU-Text reads all its glory.   1:25 [a]Isaiah 40:6–8   2:2 [a]NU-Text adds up to salvation.

Evil thoughts impede progress and destroy morals. They are as dangerous as the act of sin itself. Thoughts are previews of coming attractions. If an evil thought is not aborted, if it is savored long enough, it will be acted upon!

The Bishop
of Your Soul

1 Peter 2:25

The beautiful old King James Version of the Bible calls the Lord "the Bishop of your souls" (1 Peter 2:25, KJV).

I love that. Who is the bishop of your soul? Is he a portly, kind gentleman walking around a sanctuary in robes, reciting prayers? No. That is an ecclesiastical definition of a man who has churches under his charge. He is like a general in the governmental order of various denominations; others prefer the term *superintendent* or *president*. But this is not an ecclesiastical definition. It is a theological one, and it refers also to oversight—not the oversight of churches but the oversight of souls!

As we see in the New King James Version, the Lord is the Overseer, the Protector of your soul. He watches out for you like a lifeguard at a pool. Imagine that a lifeguard, seated upon his perch far above swimmers—whose only interest was in the thrills and chills of play—sees someone about to be engulfed by impending danger. Because he cares, he leaps from his perch and dives into the very waters where he sensed danger. He makes swift strokes toward the victim, whose next move would send her into the abyss of true destruction.

Just before the cold grasp of disaster devours its victim, the lifeguard swoops her out of danger. Did he interrupt the continuity of the festivities? Yes, he did. Did he perhaps bruise a rib while rescuing her? Perhaps. She may even be embarrassed and humiliated. But the real truth of the matter is that he saw something she didn't see—and rescued her.

This is the kind of Bishop you have. He watches out for you, and His eyes are keen. When He says no, you ought to say yes! He would never interrupt you or embarrass you before your friends if He didn't see something ahead that necessitated the answer He gave. You ought to praise Him right now—on the beach, ribs bruised, head spinning, out of breath, people staring, but alive! The Bishop of your soul has saved you! Trust His swift grace to always accomplish His best for your life.

Trusting God transforms calamity into testimony. He cares too much for you to abuse you and He is too wise to be wrong. When we begin to know Him rather than just serve Him, we can trust His vision, His wisdom, and His insight.

And he who believes on Him
will by no means be put to
shame."[a]

7 Therefore, to you who believe, *He
is* precious; but to those who are disobedient,[a]

"The stone which the builders
rejected
Has become the chief
cornerstone,"[b]

8 and

"A stone of stumbling
And a rock of offense."[a]

They stumble, being disobedient to
the word, to which they also were appointed.

9 But you *are* a chosen generation,
a royal priesthood, a holy nation, His
own special people, that you may
proclaim the praises of Him who
called you out of darkness into His
marvelous light; 10 who once *were*
not a people but *are* now the people
of God, who had not obtained mercy
but now have obtained mercy.

11 Beloved, I beg *you* as sojourners
and pilgrims, abstain from fleshly
lusts which war against the soul,
12 having your conduct honorable
among the Gentiles, that when they
speak against you as evildoers, they
may, by *your* good works which they
observe, glorify God in the day of visitation.

13 Therefore submit yourselves to
every ordinance of man for the
Lord's sake, whether to the king as
supreme, 14 or to governors, as to
those who are sent by him for the
punishment of evildoers and *for the*
praise of those who do good. 15 For
this is the will of God, that by doing
good you may put to silence the
ignorance of foolish men— 16 as
free, yet not using liberty as a
cloak for vice, but as bondservants
of God. 17 Honor all *people.* Love the
brotherhood. Fear God. Honor the
king.

18 Servants, *be* submissive to *your*
masters with all fear, not only to the
good and gentle, but also to the
harsh. 19 For this *is* commendable, if

because of conscience toward God
one endures grief, suffering wrongfully. 20 For what credit *is it* if, when
you are beaten for your faults, you
take it patiently? But when you do
good and suffer, if you take it patiently, this *is* commendable before
God. 21 For to this you were called,
because Christ also suffered for us,[a]
leaving us[b] an example, that you
should follow His steps:

22 "Who committed no sin,
Nor was deceit found in His
mouth";[a]

23 who, when He was reviled, did not
revile in return; when He suffered,
He did not threaten, but committed
Himself to Him who judges righteously; 24 who Himself bore our sins
in His own body on the tree, that we,
having died to sins, might live for
righteousness—by whose stripes you
were healed. 25 For you were like
sheep going astray, but have now returned to the Shepherd and Overseer[a] of your souls.

3 Wives, likewise, *be* submissive to
your own husbands, that even if
some do not obey the word, they,
without a word, may be won by the
conduct of their wives, 2 when they
observe your chaste conduct *accompanied* by fear. 3 Do not let your
adornment be *merely* outward—ar-
ranging the hair, wearing gold, or
putting on *fine* apparel— 4 rather *let
it be* the hidden person of the heart,
with the incorruptible *beauty* of a
gentle and quiet spirit, which is very
precious in the sight of God.
5 For in this manner, in former times,
the holy women who trusted in God
also adorned themselves, being submissive to their own husbands,
6 as Sarah obeyed Abraham, calling
him lord, whose daughters you are
if you do good and are not afraid with
any terror.

7 Husbands, likewise, dwell with
them with understanding, giving
honor to the wife, as to the weaker
vessel, and as *being* heirs together of
the grace of life, that your prayers
may not be hindered.

8 Finally, all *of you be* of one mind,

2:6 [a]Isaiah 28:16   2:7 [a]NU-Text reads *to those who disbelieve.*   [b]Psalm 118:22   2:8 [a]Isaiah 8:14
2:21 [a]NU-Text reads *you.*   [b]NU-Text and M-Text read *you.*   2:22 [a]Isaiah 53:9   2:25 [a]Greek *Episkopos*

*Most of us come to the Lord damaged—dead spiritually, deficient emotionally, and
decaying physically. While you may dress and smell nice on the outside, others
do not hear the hammering and sawing continually going on inside as the Lord works
to present you as a newly constructed dwelling fit for the Master's use.*

The Beauty of the Spirit

1 Peter 3:3, 4

When a designer sends a model down a fashion runway, he or she is concerned with the model's total look. The model isn't just wearing the designer's garment. The designer has usually spent a great deal of time and effort in selecting the proper accessories, instructing the models in how to walk, turn, and carry themselves, and creating the overall environment in which to show off the designs.

And so it is with our great God. He created you as a composite. He gave you certain talents, features, and personality traits. Then He added a variety of emotional responses and spiritual gifts. He was concerned with the overall, total you. He designed you to be a vibrant, thinking, feeling, fully functioning person with a unique attractiveness. He decorated you with far more than physical attributes.

God made you with flesh—an outer appearance. God has blessed you with creativity and an appreciation for beauty. You can and should recognize your appearance as an area in which you can express yourself to the glory of God.

But the outer you doesn't replace the need for the inner you. The inner you doesn't negate the need for the outer you. You must have balance. Remember that your inner qualities are eternal and, therefore, more important. The inner qualities should give rise to the outer ones. In other words, it is who you are on the inside that should define what you choose to do with your outside.

The woman who is confident in the Lord might choose to wear a $1.50 dress she finds at the local thrift shop or a $150 dress she buys at an upscale department store. She is confident either way. Her looks don't determine her character.

The greater part of your beauty cannot be bought, taken off a rack, applied like lipstick, or put on like a hat. The greater part of your attractiveness lies within; it wells up from the inside and finds an appropriate creative expression on the outside. That's what Peter meant when he wrote that "the incorruptible beauty of a gentle and quiet spirit" has a great price in the sight of God (see 1 Peter 3:4). God sees what no one else can see. And it's that part of you that He values most.

having compassion for one another; love as brothers, *be* tenderhearted, *be* courteous;*a* 9 not returning evil for evil or reviling for reviling, but on the contrary blessing, knowing that you were called to this, that you may inherit a blessing. 10 For

> "He who would love life
> And see good days,
> Let him refrain his tongue from
> evil,
> And his lips from speaking
> deceit.
> 11 Let him turn away from evil
> and do good;
> Let him seek peace and pursue
> it.
> 12 For the eyes of the LORD are on
> the righteous,
> And His ears are open to their
> prayers;
> But the face of the LORD is
> against those who do
> evil."*a*

13 And who *is* he who will harm you if you become followers of what is good? 14 But even if you should suffer for righteousness' sake, *you are* blessed. *"And do not be afraid of their threats, nor be troubled."a* 15 But sanctify the Lord God*a* in your hearts, and always *be* ready to *give* a defense to everyone who asks you a reason for the hope that is in you, with meekness and fear; 16 having a good conscience, that when they defame you as evildoers, those who revile your good conduct in Christ may be ashamed. 17 For *it is* better, if it is the will of God, to suffer for doing good than for doing evil.

18 For Christ also suffered once for sins, the just for the unjust, that He might bring us*a* to God, being put to death in the flesh but made alive by the Spirit, 19 by whom also He went and preached to the spirits in prison, 20 who formerly were disobedient, when once the Divine longsuffering waited*a* in the days of Noah, while *the* ark was being prepared, in which a few, that is, eight souls, were saved through water. 21 There is also an antitype which now saves us—baptism (not the removal of the filth of the

flesh, but the answer of a good conscience toward God), through the resurrection of Jesus Christ, 22 who has gone into heaven and is at the right hand of God, angels and authorities and powers having been made subject to Him.

4 Therefore, since Christ suffered for us*a* in the flesh, arm yourselves also with the same mind, for he who has suffered in the flesh has ceased from sin, 2 that he no longer should live the rest of *his* time in the flesh for the lusts of men, but for the will of God. 3 For we *have spent* enough of our past lifetime*a* in doing the will of the Gentiles—when we walked in lewdness, lusts, drunkenness, revelries, drinking parties, and abominable idolatries. 4 In regard to these, they think it strange that you do not run with *them* in the same flood of dissipation, speaking evil of *you.* 5 They will give an account to Him who is ready to judge the living and the dead. 6 For this reason the gospel was preached also to those who are dead, that they might be judged according to men in the flesh, but live according to God in the spirit.

7 But the end of all things is at hand; therefore be serious and watchful in your prayers. 8 And above all things have fervent love for one another, for *"love will cover a multitude of sins."a* 9 *Be* hospitable to one another without grumbling. 10 As each one has received a gift, minister it to one another, as good stewards of the manifold grace of God. 11 If anyone speaks, *let him speak* as the oracles of God. If anyone ministers, *let him do it* as with the ability which God supplies, that in all things God may be glorified through Jesus Christ, to whom belong the glory and the dominion forever and ever. Amen.

12 Beloved, do not think it strange concerning the fiery trial which is to try you, as though some strange thing happened to you; 13 but rejoice to the extent that you partake of Christ's sufferings, that when His glory is revealed, you may also be glad with exceeding joy. 14 If you are

---

3:8 *a*NU-Text reads *humble.*   3:12 *a*Psalm 34:12–16   3:14 *a*Isaiah 8:12   3:15 *a*NU-Text reads *Christ as Lord.*   3:18 *a*NU-Text and M-Text read *you.*   3:20 *a*NU-Text and M-Text read *when the longsuffering of God waited patiently.*   4:1 *a*NU-Text omits *for us.*   4:3 *a*NU-Text reads *time.*   4:8 *a*Proverbs 10:12

We need to renew our minds daily in God's presence. His thinking is contagious. As you meditate on Him, His Word becomes a lifeline thrown to a woman who would otherwise drown in the swirling whirlpool of her own thoughts.

Throw It Down

1 Peter 5:7

*I*f you are carrying old pain, old scars, dead relationships, or even a torch for someone who has moved on, I recommend that you cast away anything that is draining the life out of you and blurring your vision. Let it go, in Jesus' name! The Word literally instructs us to cast our cares on Him (see 1 Peter 5:7). Now, no one casts away anything they care about. We wouldn't cast away a baby, a china dish, or a family heirloom. Yet we are instructed to cast our cares on Him. Whatever you are caring about—whatever is worrying you or holding you back—cast it on the Lord!

The word used for *care* is better translated "solicitudes." Solicitudes are those things that we are anxious or concerned about. The Bible uses the word *epirhippto* for "casting." Literally, it means "to throw upon!" That's right, "throw," as if the care had no value at all. Have no regard for it. Dismiss it totally.

Why does God ask us to be so radical about our solicitudes? Because "He cares for you!" While you are caring for it, He is caring for you. He loves you too much to see you twisted with pain because of something you should have cast away long ago. God has no problem making that thing leave you alone. The struggle is getting you to loose your grip on it. So He speaks to you, not to the thing bothering you. He speaks directly to you and says, "Throw it down!"

Can you do it? You must. If not, it will continue to live off your strength, sucking your joy like the hungry mouth of a nursing child. Now can you see what God is saying? You are nursing your enemy, giving strength to your own emotional nightmare. In the name of Jesus, throw it down!

Peter says, "For He cares for you." The verb form of the word *cares* indicates a perpetual, continual, ongoing attitude of God. It literally means He is "concerned" about or "interested" in you. You are His only interest and His major concern. While you have esteemed all things around you, God is very focused in His interest. He says, "Throw down the thing that has become a solicitude in your life, because I esteem nothing above My interest in you." Gather up everything that concerns you or weighs you down and throw it. I mean, take those cares and hurl them to the Lord, catapult them from your mind, and send them screeching to a halt before the throne of grace. And watch what God will do!

reproached for the name of Christ, blessed *are you,* for the Spirit of glory and of God rests upon you.ᵃ On their part He is blasphemed, but on your part He is glorified. 15 But let none of you suffer as a murderer, a thief, an evildoer, or as a busybody in other people's matters. 16 Yet if *anyone suffers* as a Christian, let him not be ashamed, but let him glorify God in this matter.ᵃ

17 For the time *has come* for judgment to begin at the house of God; and if *it begins* with us first, what will *be* the end of those who do not obey the gospel of God? 18 Now

> *"If the righteous one is scarcely*
> *saved,*
> *Where will the ungodly and the*
> *sinner appear?"ᵃ*

19 Therefore let those who suffer according to the will of God commit their souls *to Him* in doing good, as to a faithful Creator.

5 The elders who are among you I exhort, I who am a fellow elder and a witness of the sufferings of Christ, and also a partaker of the glory that will be revealed: 2 Shepherd the flock of God which is among you, serving as overseers, not by compulsion but willingly,ᵃ not for dishonest gain but eagerly; 3 nor as being lords over those entrusted to you, but being examples to the flock; 4 and when the Chief Shepherd appears, you will receive

the crown of glory that does not fade away.

5 Likewise you younger people, submit yourselves to *your* elders. Yes, all of *you* be submissive to one another, and be clothed with humility, for

> *"God resists the proud,*
> *But gives grace to the*
> *humble."ᵃ*

6 Therefore humble yourselves under the mighty hand of God, that He may exalt you in due time, 7 casting all your care upon Him, for He cares for you.

8 Be sober, be vigilant; becauseᵃ your adversary the devil walks about like a roaring lion, seeking whom he may devour. 9 Resist him, steadfast in the faith, knowing that the same sufferings are experienced by your brotherhood in the world. 10 But mayᵃ the God of all grace, who called usᵇ to His eternal glory by Christ Jesus, after you have suffered a while, perfect, establish, strengthen, and settle *you.* 11 To Him *be* the glory and the dominion forever and ever. Amen.

12 By Silvanus, our faithful brother as I consider him, I have written to you briefly, exhorting and testifying that this is the true grace of God in which you stand.

13 She who is in Babylon, elect together with *you,* greets you; and *so does* Mark my son. 14 Greet one another with a kiss of love.

Peace to you all who are in Christ Jesus. Amen.

4:14 ᵃNU-Text omits the rest of this verse.   4:16 ᵃNU-Text reads *name.*   4:18 ᵃProverbs 11:31
5:2 ᵃNU-Text adds *according to God.*   5:5 ᵃProverbs 3:34   5:8 ᵃNU-Text and M-Text omit *because.*   5:10 ᵃNU-Text reads *But the God of all grace . . . will perfect, establish, strengthen, and settle you.*   ᵇNU-Text and M-Text read *you.*

The Second Epistle of

PETER

1 Simon Peter, a bondservant and apostle of Jesus Christ,

To those who have obtained like precious faith with us by the righ-

teousness of our God and Savior Jesus Christ:

2 Grace and peace be multiplied to you in the knowledge of God and of

Jesus our Lord, 3 as His divine power has given to us all things that *pertain* to life and godliness, through the knowledge of Him who called us by glory and virtue, 4 by which have been given to us exceedingly great and precious promises, that through these you may be partakers of the divine nature, having escaped the corruption *that is* in the world through lust.

5 But also for this very reason, giving all diligence, add to your faith virtue, to virtue knowledge, 6 to knowledge self-control, to self-control perseverance, to perseverance godliness, 7 to godliness brotherly kindness, and to brotherly kindness love. 8 For if these things are yours and abound, *you will be* neither barren nor unfruitful in the knowledge of our Lord Jesus Christ. 9 For he who lacks these things is shortsighted, even to blindness, and has forgotten that he was cleansed from his old sins.

10 Therefore, brethren, be even more diligent to make your call and election sure, for if you do these things you will never stumble; 11 for so an entrance will be supplied to you abundantly into the everlasting kingdom of our Lord and Savior Jesus Christ.

12 For this reason I will not be negligent to remind you always of these things, though you know and are established in the present truth. 13 Yes, I think it is right, as long as I am in this tent, to stir you up by reminding you, 14 knowing that shortly I *must* put off my tent, just as our Lord Jesus Christ showed me. 15 Moreover I will be careful to ensure that you always have a reminder of these things after my decease.

16 For we did not follow cunningly devised fables when we made known to you the power and coming of our Lord Jesus Christ, but were eyewitnesses of His majesty. 17 For He received from God the Father honor and glory when such a voice came to Him from the Excellent Glory: "This is My beloved Son, in whom I am well pleased." 18 And we heard this voice which came from heaven when we were with Him on the holy mountain.

19 And so we have the prophetic word confirmed,[a] which you do well to heed as a light that shines in a dark place, until the day dawns and the morning star rises in your hearts; 20 knowing this first, that no prophecy of Scripture is of any private interpretation,[a] 21 for prophecy never came by the will of man, but holy men of God[a] spoke *as they were* moved by the Holy Spirit.

2 But there were also false prophets among the people, even as there will be false teachers among you, who will secretly bring in destructive heresies, even denying the Lord who bought them, *and* bring on themselves swift destruction. 2 And many will follow their destructive ways, because of whom the way of truth will be blasphemed. 3 By covetousness they will exploit you with deceptive words; for a long time their judgment has not been idle, and their destruction does[a] not slumber.

4 For if God did not spare the angels who sinned, but cast *them* down to hell and delivered *them* into chains of darkness, to be reserved for judgment; 5 and did not spare the ancient world, but saved Noah, *one of* eight *people,* a preacher of righteousness, bringing in the flood on the world of the ungodly; 6 and turning the cities of Sodom and Gomorrah into ashes, condemned *them* to destruction, making *them* an example to those who afterward would live ungodly; 7 and delivered righteous Lot, *who was* oppressed by the filthy conduct of the wicked 8 (for that righteous man, dwelling among them, tormented *his* righteous soul from day to day by seeing and hearing *their* lawless deeds)— 9 *then* the Lord knows how to deliver the godly out of temptations and to reserve the unjust under punishment for the day of judgment, 10 and especially those who walk according to the flesh in the lust of uncleanness and despise authority. *They are* presumptuous, self-willed. They are not afraid to speak evil of dignitaries, 11 whereas angels, who are greater in power and might, do not bring a reviling accusation against them before the Lord.

12 But these, like natural brute

1:19 [a]Or *We also have the more sure prophetic word.* *spoke from God.*   2:3 [a]M-Text reads *will not.*   1:20 [a]Or *origin*   1:21 [a]NU-Text reads *but men*

God's Word will accomplish what it is sent out to do. He says, "I will not give up on you. I will keep hammering until you are balanced in your thinking and whole in your judgments."

beasts made to be caught and destroyed, speak evil of the things they do not understand, and will utterly perish in their own corruption, 13 *and* will receive the wages of unrighteousness, *as* those who count it pleasure to carouse in the daytime. *They are* spots and blemishes, carousing in their own deceptions while they feast with you, 14 having eyes full of adultery and that cannot cease from sin, enticing unstable souls. *They have* a heart trained in covetous practices, *and are* accursed children. 15 They have forsaken the right way and gone astray, following the way of Balaam the *son* of Beor, who loved the wages of unrighteousness; 16 but he was rebuked for his iniquity: a dumb donkey speaking with a man's voice restrained the madness of the prophet.

17 These are wells without water, clouds*a* carried by a tempest, for whom is reserved the blackness of darkness forever.*b*

18 For when they speak great swelling *words* of emptiness, they allure through the lusts of the flesh, through lewdness, the ones who have actually escaped*a* from those who live in error. 19 While they promise them liberty, they themselves are slaves of corruption; for by whom a person is overcome, by him also he is brought into bondage. 20 For if, after they have escaped the pollutions of the world through the knowledge of the Lord and Savior Jesus Christ, they are again entangled in them and overcome, the latter end is worse for them than the beginning. 21 For it would have been better for them not to have known the way of righteousness, than having known *it,* to turn from the holy commandment delivered to them. 22 But it has happened to them according to the true proverb: *"A dog returns to his own vomit,"a* and, "a sow, having washed, to her wallowing in the mire."

3 Beloved, I now write to you this second epistle (in *both of* which I stir up your pure minds by way of reminder), 2 that you may be mindful of the words which were spoken before by the holy prophets, and of the commandment of us,*a* the apostles of the Lord and Savior, 3 knowing this first: that scoffers will come in the last days, walking according to their own lusts, 4 and saying, "Where is the promise of His coming? For since the fathers fell asleep, all things continue as *they were* from the beginning of creation." 5 For this they willfully forget: that by the word of God the heavens were of old, and the earth standing out of water and in the water, 6 by which the world *that* then existed perished, being flooded with water. 7 But the heavens and the earth *which* are now preserved by the same word, are reserved for fire until the day of judgment and perdition of ungodly men.

8 But, beloved, do not forget this one thing, that with the Lord one day *is* as a thousand years, and a thousand years as one day. 9 The Lord is not slack concerning *His* promise, as some count slackness, but is longsuffering toward us,*a* not willing that any should perish but that all should come to repentance.

10 But the day of the Lord will come as a thief in the night, in which the heavens will pass away with a great noise, and the elements will melt with fervent heat; both the earth and the works that are in it will be burned up.*a* 11 Therefore, since all these things will be dissolved, what manner *of persons* ought you to be in holy conduct and godliness, 12 looking for and hastening the coming of the day of God, because of which the heavens will be dissolved, being on fire, and the elements will melt with fervent heat? 13 Nevertheless we, according to His promise, look for new heavens and a new earth in which righteousness dwells.

14 Therefore, beloved, looking forward to these things, be diligent to be found by Him in peace, without spot and blameless; 15 and consider *that* the longsuffering of our Lord *is* salvation—as also our beloved brother Paul, according to the wisdom given to him, has written to you, 16 as also in all his epistles, speaking in them of these things, in which are

---

2:17 *a*NU-Text reads *and mists.* *b*NU-Text omits *forever.*   2:18 *a*NU-Text reads *are barely escaping.*
2:22 *a*Proverbs 26:11   3:2 *a*NU-Text and M-Text read *commandment of the apostles of your Lord and Savior* or *commandment of your apostles of the Lord and Savior.*   3:9 *a*NU-Text reads *you.*
3:10 *a*NU-Text reads *laid bare* (literally *found*).

Gospel
Pearls

some things hard to understand, which untaught and unstable *people* twist to their own destruction, as *they do* also the rest of the Scriptures.

17 You therefore, beloved, since you know *this* beforehand, beware lest you also fall from your own steadfastness, being led away with the error of the wicked; 18 but grow in the grace and knowledge of our Lord and Savior Jesus Christ.

To Him *be* the glory both now and forever. Amen.

The First Epistle of
JOHN

1 That which was from the beginning, which we have heard, which we have seen with our eyes, which we have looked upon, and our hands have handled, concerning the Word of life— 2 the life was manifested, and we have seen, and bear witness, and declare to you that eternal life which was with the Father and was manifested to us— 3 that which we have seen and heard we declare to you, that you also may have fellowship with us; and truly our fellowship *is* with the Father and with His Son Jesus Christ. 4 And these things we write to you that your*ᵃ* joy may be full.

5 This is the message which we have heard from Him and declare to you, that God is light and in Him is no darkness at all. 6 If we say that we have fellowship with Him, and walk in darkness, we lie and do not practice the truth. 7 But if we walk in the light as He is in the light, we have fellowship with one another, and the blood of Jesus Christ His Son cleanses us from all sin.

8 If we say that we have no sin, we deceive ourselves, and the truth is not in us. 9 If we confess our sins, He is faithful and just to forgive us *our* sins and to cleanse us from all unrighteousness. 10 If we say that we have not sinned, we make Him a liar, and His word is not in us.

2 My little children, these things I write to you, so that you may not sin. And if anyone sins, we have an Advocate with the Father, Jesus Christ the righteous. 2 And He Himself is the propitiation for our sins, and not for ours only but also for the whole world.

3 Now by this we know that we know Him, if we keep His commandments. 4 He who says, "I know Him," and does not keep His commandments, is a liar, and the truth is not in him. 5 But whoever keeps His word, truly the love of God is perfected in him. By this we know that we are in Him. 6 He who says he abides in Him ought himself also to walk just as He walked.

7 Brethren,*ᵃ* I write no new commandment to you, but an old commandment which you have had from the beginning. The old commandment is the word which you heard from the beginning.*ᵇ* 8 Again, a new commandment I write to you, which thing is true in Him and in you, because the darkness is passing away, and the true light is already shining.

9 He who says he is in the light, and hates his brother, is in darkness until now. 10 He who loves his brother abides in the light, and there is no cause for stumbling in him. 11 But he who hates his brother is in darkness and walks in darkness, and does not know where he is going, because the darkness has blinded his eyes.

12 I write to you, little children,
Because your sins are
forgiven you for His
name's sake.

1:4 *ᵃNU-Text and M-Text read* our. 2:7 *ᵃNU-Text reads* Beloved. *ᵇNU-Text omits* from the beginning.

God covers you with His precious blood even while His Word is working on you. The benefit is that you are simultaneously privileged with privacy and challenged to change. He will persevere until His will is accomplished in your life.

The Answer

God knows how to take a mess and turn it into a miracle. If you're in a mess, don't be too upset because God specializes in cleaning up messes. God is saying some definite things about women being set free and delivered to fulfill their purpose in the Kingdom.

When the Lord gets through working on you, all your adversaries will be ashamed. All your accusers will have to take it back. All the people who contributed to your sense of low self-esteem will have to admit they were wrong. When God gets through unleashing you, you won't have to prove anything. God will prove it. When He gets through showing that you've done the right thing and come to the right place, all the naysayers will drop their heads.

The infirm woman in Luke 13:10–17 was so bound by Satan for eighteen years that she could not even straighten herself up. She had a past that tormented her, but she had a Jesus who set her free. Satan had bound her, but Jesus unleashed her potential.

Many women in the Church have not really seen Jesus as the answer to their dilemma. They go to church, they love the Lord, they want to go to Heaven when they die, but they still do not see Him as the solution to their problems.

Can you imagine how hard life was for that woman who was bowed over? Because of her problem, she had to struggle to come to Jesus. Jesus could have walked over to where the woman was, but He chose not to. He wanted her to make her way to Him.

Few of us are crippled in the same way, but we all face crippling limitations. We can be bowed over financially. We can be bowed over emotionally. We can be bowed over with lack of self-esteem. Take that first step. He wants to see you making the effort to reach Him. He wants you to want Him enough to overcome obstacles and push in His direction.

When you see a hunched-over person crawling through the crowd, you will know that person really wants help. That kind of desire is what it takes to change your life. Jesus is the answer.

I may seek help by going from one person to another, but only Jesus is the answer. I may be sick in my body, but Jesus is the answer. My son may be dead, or insane, or hooked on drugs, but Jesus is the answer. If my son is dead, Jesus is the resurrection. If I am having family problems, Jesus has the solution. It doesn't matter what the problem is, Jesus is the answer!

13 I write to you, fathers,
Because you have known
Him *who is* from the
beginning.
I write to you, young men,
Because you have overcome
the wicked one.
I write to you, little children,
Because you have known the
Father.
14 I have written to you, fathers,
Because you have known
Him *who is* from the
beginning.
I have written to you, young
men,
Because you are strong, and
the word of God abides in
you,
And you have overcome the
wicked one.

15 Do not love the world or the things in the world. If anyone loves the world, the love of the Father is not in him. 16 For all that *is* in the world—the lust of the flesh, the lust of the eyes, and the pride of life—is not of the Father but is of the world. 17 And the world is passing away, and the lust of it; but he who does the will of God abides forever.

18 Little children, it is the last hour; and as you have heard that the*a* Antichrist is coming, even now many antichrists have come, by which we know that it is the last hour. 19 They went out from us, but they were not of us; for if they had been of us, they would have continued with us; but *they went out* that they might be made manifest, that none of them were of us.

20 But you have an anointing from the Holy One, and you know all things.*a* 21 I have not written to you because you do not know the truth, but because you know it, and that no lie is of the truth.

22 Who is a liar but he who denies that Jesus is the Christ? He is antichrist who denies the Father and the Son. 23 Whoever denies the Son does not have the Father either; he who acknowledges the Son has the Father also.

24 Therefore let that abide in you which you heard from the beginning. If what you heard from the beginning

abides in you, you also will abide in the Son and in the Father. 25 And this is the promise that He has promised us—eternal life.

26 These things I have written to you concerning those who *try to* deceive you. 27 But the anointing which you have received from Him abides in you, and you do not need that anyone teach you; but as the same anointing teaches you concerning all things, and is true, and is not a lie, and just as it has taught you, you will*a* abide in Him.

28 And now, little children, abide in Him, that when*a* He appears, we may have confidence and not be ashamed before Him at His coming. 29 If you know that He is righteous, you know that everyone who practices righteousness is born of Him.

3 Behold what manner of love the Father has bestowed on us, that we should be called children of God!*a* Therefore the world does not know us,*b* because it did not know Him. 2 Beloved, now we are children of God; and it has not yet been revealed what we shall be, but we know that when He is revealed, we shall be like Him, for we shall see Him as He is. 3 And everyone who has this hope in Him purifies himself, just as He is pure.

4 Whoever commits sin also commits lawlessness, and sin is lawlessness. 5 And you know that He was manifested to take away our sins, and in Him there is no sin. 6 Whoever abides in Him does not sin. Whoever sins has neither seen Him nor known Him.

7 Little children, let no one deceive you. He who practices righteousness is righteous, just as He is righteous. 8 He who sins is of the devil, for the devil has sinned from the beginning. For this purpose the Son of God was manifested, that He might destroy the works of the devil. 9 Whoever has been born of God does not sin, for His seed remains in him; and he cannot sin, because he has been born of God.

10 In this the children of God and the children of the devil are manifest: Whoever does not practice righteousness is not of God, nor *is* he who does

2:18 *a*NU-Text omits *the.*   2:20 *a*NU-Text reads *you all know.*   2:27 *a*NU-Text reads *you abide.*
2:28 *a*NU-Text reads *if.*   3:1 *a*NU-Text adds *And we are.*   *b*M-Text reads *you.*

*H*uman thoughts are healed by the Word of God. He filters into the dark places of our diseased or oppressed minds and reconstructs thought patterns by sharing His own mind with us.

The Father's Touch

I John 3:1, 2

Dear daughters of the Father, I have a word for you from Him. It is His word whether you are the daughter of a president or the daughter of an accident. He loves you just the same.

Anyone who knows anything about love will tell you that it cannot be copied, duplicated, repeated, or forced. Each feeling is unique, just as the dripping colors of finger painting bear the uniqueness of the artist's own fingerprints. It is shaped into a moment and mood that could never be recaptured in quite the same way.

Perhaps the daughters of Zion would stop their weeping if they knew how dear they were to their Father. Perhaps they would rise up out of the ashes and cast their fears to the wind if they knew that the Father assigns angels to their charge and gives such attention to details that He has numbered every strand of hair that is caught in their combs.

I know there are many women across this land whose hearts have been broken by the absence of a father. Some have been torn by the hands of the father they had. I'm sorry. Yet we cannot stay there.

Beyond yesterday's night is tomorrow's morning. It is truly morning for those women who have given their hearts to Jesus. If you haven't given your heart to Him, please do it now. He is so much help for those who need a healing.

If something in your heart turns over whenever you see a father holding a child, or an older man walking with his daughter in the park, and you miss the father who slipped away from you, be encouraged. You are not alone. Your Father is higher than the stars and yet closer than your breath, and He sent me to tell women of all ages and stages to come and sit safely on the lap of His love. No matter how you have suffered or what you have endured, there is something He wants you to know. Without a doubt, your Father loves you.

So live vivaciously, love deeply, and pray fervently. Remember to give with simplicity and serve with humility. Still, observe that meekness does not necessitate weakness. Therefore, when challenged by obstacles, fight with tenacity.

Do not revel in your failures nor play in your past. Overcome every doubt, sign no treaties with the enemy and take no hostages. The Father's touch sets you free and makes you strong. I'll say it again. The Father loves you.

not love his brother. 11 For this is the message that you heard from the beginning, that we should love one another, 12 not as Cain *who* was of the wicked one and murdered his brother. And why did he murder him? Because his works were evil and his brother's righteous.

13 Do not marvel, my brethren, if the world hates you. 14 We know that we have passed from death to life, because we love the brethren. He who does not love *his* brother[a] abides in death. 15 Whoever hates his brother is a murderer, and you know that no murderer has eternal life abiding in him.

16 By this we know love, because He laid down His life for us. And we also ought to lay down *our* lives for the brethren. 17 But whoever has this world's goods, and sees his brother in need, and shuts up his heart from him, how does the love of God abide in him?

18 My little children, let us not love in word or in tongue, but in deed and in truth. 19 And by this we know[a] that we are of the truth, and shall assure our hearts before Him. 20 For if our heart condemns us, God is greater than our heart, and knows all things. 21 Beloved, if our heart does not condemn us, we have confidence toward God. 22 And whatever we ask we receive from Him, because we keep His commandments and do those things that are pleasing in His sight. 23 And this is His commandment: that we should believe on the name of His Son Jesus Christ and love one another, as He gave us[a] commandment.

24 Now he who keeps His commandments abides in Him, and He in him. And by this we know that He abides in us, by the Spirit whom He has given us.

4 Beloved, do not believe every spirit, but test the spirits, whether they are of God; because many false prophets have gone out into the world. 2 By this you know the Spirit of God: Every spirit that confesses that Jesus Christ has come in the flesh is of God, 3 and every spirit that does not confess that Jesus Christ

has come in the flesh[a] is not of God. And this is the *spirit* of the Antichrist, which you have heard was coming, and is now already in the world.

4 You are of God, little children, and have overcome them, because He who is in you is greater than he who is in the world. 5 They are of the world. Therefore they speak *as* of the world, and the world hears them. 6 We are of God. He who knows God hears us; he who is not of God does not hear us. By this we know the spirit of truth and the spirit of error.

7 Beloved, let us love one another, for love is of God; and everyone who loves is born of God and knows God. 8 He who does not love does not know God, for God is love. 9 In this the love of God was manifested toward us, that God has sent His only begotten Son into the world, that we might live through Him. 10 In this is love, not that we loved God, but that He loved us and sent His Son *to be* the propitiation for our sins. 11 Beloved, if God so loved us, we also ought to love one another.

12 No one has seen God at any time. If we love one another, God abides in us, and His love has been perfected in us. 13 By this we know that we abide in Him, and He in us, because He has given us of His Spirit. 14 And we have seen and testify that the Father has sent the Son *as* Savior of the world. 15 Whoever confesses that Jesus is the Son of God, God abides in him, and he in God. 16 And we have known and believed the love that God has for us. God is love, and he who abides in love abides in God, and God in him.

17 Love has been perfected among us in this: that we may have boldness in the day of judgment; because as He is, so are we in this world. 18 There is no fear in love; but perfect love casts out fear, because fear involves torment. But he who fears has not been made perfect in love. 19 We love Him[a] because He first loved us.

20 If someone says, "I love God," and hates his brother, he is a liar; for he who does not love his brother whom he has seen, how can[a] he love God whom he has not seen? 21 And

---

3:14 [a]NU-Text omits *his brother.*   3:19 [a]NU-Text reads *we shall know.*   3:23 [a]M-Text omits *us.*
4:3 [a]NU-Text omits *that* and *Christ has come in the flesh.*   4:19 [a]NU-Text omits *Him.*   4:20 [a]NU-Text reads *he cannot.*

---

*A*llow new meditations to dwell in your heart by faith, for your life will ultimately take on the direction of your thinking. Many weaknesses, such as procrastination and laziness, are just draperies that cover up poor self-esteem and lack of motivation.

this commandment we have from Him: that he who loves God *must* love his brother also.

5 Whoever believes that Jesus is the Christ is born of God, and everyone who loves Him who begot also loves him who is begotten of Him. 2 By this we know that we love the children of God, when we love God and keep His commandments. 3 For this is the love of God, that we keep His commandments. And His commandments are not burdensome. 4 For whatever is born of God overcomes the world. And this is the victory that has overcome the world— our*a* faith. 5 Who is he who overcomes the world, but he who believes that Jesus is the Son of God?

6 This is He who came by water and blood—Jesus Christ; not only by water, but by water and blood. And it is the Spirit who bears witness, because the Spirit is truth. 7 For there are three that bear witness in heaven: the Father, the Word, and the Holy Spirit; and these three are one. 8 And there are three that bear witness on earth:*a* the Spirit, the water, and the blood; and these three agree as one.

9 If we receive the witness of men, the witness of God is greater; for this is the witness of God which*a* He has testified of His Son. 10 He who believes in the Son of God has the witness in himself; he who does not believe God has made Him a liar, because he has not believed the testimony that God has given of His Son. 11 And this is the testimony: that God has given us eternal life, and this life is in His Son. 12 He who has the Son has life; he who does not have the Son of God does not have life. 13 These things I have written to you who believe in the name of the Son of God, that you may know that you have eternal life,*a* and that you may *continue to* believe in the name of the Son of God.

14 Now this is the confidence that we have in Him, that if we ask anything according to His will, He hears us. 15 And if we know that He hears us, whatever we ask, we know that we have the petitions that we have asked of Him.

16 If anyone sees his brother sinning a sin *which does* not *lead* to death, he will ask, and He will give him life for those who commit sin not *leading* to death. There is sin *leading* to death. I do not say that he should pray about that. 17 All unrighteousness is sin, and there is sin not *leading* to death.

18 We know that whoever is born of God does not sin; but he who has been born of God keeps himself,*a* and the wicked one does not touch him.

19 We know that we are of God, and the whole world lies *under the sway of* the wicked one.

20 And we know that the Son of God has come and has given us an understanding, that we may know Him who is true; and we are in Him who is true, in His Son Jesus Christ. This is the true God and eternal life.

21 Little children, keep yourselves from idols. Amen.

5:4 *a*M-Text reads *your.*   5:8 *a*NU-Text and M-Text omit the words from *in heaven* (verse 7) through *on earth* (verse 8). Only four or five very late manuscripts contain these words in Greek.   5:9 *a*NU-Text reads *God, that.*   5:13 *a*NU-Text omits the rest of this verse.   5:18 *a*NU-Text reads *him.*

The Second Epistle of

JOHN

1 The Elder,

To the elect lady and her children, whom I love in truth, and not only I, but also all those who have known the truth, 2 because of the truth which abides in us and will be with us forever:

*M*ay the Spirit reveal the areas where you need Him to heal your thinking so you can possess what God wants you to have. Many people don't enjoy the blessing because they have conquered every foe except the enemy within!

True Friends

2 John 5

Different from family love, which is not chosen but accepted, friendship develops like moss on the slippery edges of a creek. It emerges without warning. There is no date to remember. It just grows until one day acquaintance graduates into friendship. Love is the diploma.

This chosen love is real and powerful, bitter and sweet. It is warm enough to wrap up in against the chill of an aloof world. It is bright enough to shine through all the night seasons of your life. Only occasionally in the course of a lifetime will you meet the kind of friend who becomes more than an acquaintance.

Real relationship is hard work. Don't let anybody fool you; contouring your heart to beat with another requires extensive whittling to trim away self-centeredness and distrust. It is like riding the bus. If you're going to have company riding with you, you must be willing to scoot over and rearrange yourself to accommodate another person and the baggage she brings. As you make room for a friend, you show how important the other person is.

Every relationship undergoes adjustments. The reason one relationship becomes more valuable than another is in its ability to survive circumstances and endure realignment. We never know how strong a relationship is until it is threatened. It takes a powerful bond to withstand the pressure and not be weakened by outside forces.

Isn't that what you really want from a relationship? To know that you won't be abandoned—no matter what? To be yourself—hiding nothing, not even your worst imperfection—and know your friend won't run out on you?

Natural blood ties don't always wear as well as heart ties. The Bible says there is a friend "who sticks closer than a brother" (Proverbs 18:24). This is why we must not allow our friendships to be uprooted—not only in our individual lives, but in the Body of Christ. Too often we have thrown away good people who did a bad thing. Have you ever done that? Have you decided that a relationship cannot be repaired? If so, then how can God love you? If He forgave you of your debts as you forgave your debtors, could you stand?

A true friend is one who stands by you, honoring and affirming you and your marriage and family. A true friend should desire to see you prosper in your marriage, in your finances, in your health, and in your relationship with the Lord. With these virtues, you can hurdle personal imperfection and indiscretion.

A true friend really is one of the best gifts God will ever give you. Commit to stay; commit to be strong; and commit to celebrate all He has given you in your friend.

3 Grace, mercy, *and* peace will be with you[a] from God the Father and from the Lord Jesus Christ, the Son of the Father, in truth and love.

4 I rejoiced greatly that I have found *some* of your children walking in truth, as we received commandment from the Father. 5 And now I plead with you, lady, not as though I wrote a new commandment to you, but that which we have had from the beginning: that we love one another. 6 This is love, that we walk according to His commandments. This is the commandment, that as you have heard from the beginning, you should walk in it.

7 For many deceivers have gone out into the world who do not confess Jesus Christ *as* coming in the flesh. This is a deceiver and an antichrist. 8 Look to yourselves, that we[a] do not lose those things we worked for, but that we[b] may receive a full reward.

9 Whoever transgresses[a] and does not abide in the doctrine of Christ does not have God. He who abides in the doctrine of Christ has both the Father and the Son. 10 If anyone comes to you and does not bring this doctrine, do not receive him into your house nor greet him; 11 for he who greets him shares in his evil deeds.

12 Having many things to write to you, I did not wish *to do so* with paper and ink; but I hope to come to you and speak face to face, that our joy may be full.

13 The children of your elect sister greet you. Amen.

3 [a]NU-Text and M-Text read *us*.　8 [a]NU-Text reads *you*.　[b]NU-Text reads *you*.　9 [a]NU-Text reads *goes ahead*.

The Third Epistle of

JOHN

1 The Elder,

To the beloved Gaius, whom I love in truth:

2 Beloved, I pray that you may prosper in all things and be in health, just as your soul prospers. 3 For I rejoiced greatly when brethren came and testified of the truth *that is* in you, just as you walk in the truth. 4 I have no greater joy than to hear that my children walk in truth.[a]

5 Beloved, you do faithfully whatever you do for the brethren and[a] for strangers, 6 who have borne witness of your love before the church. *If* you send them forward on their journey in a manner worthy of God, you will do well, 7 because they went forth for His name's sake, taking nothing from the Gentiles. 8 We therefore ought to receive[a] such, that we may become fellow workers for the truth.

9 I wrote to the church, but Dio- trephes, who loves to have the preeminence among them, does not receive us. 10 Therefore, if I come, I will call to mind his deeds which he does, prating against us with malicious words. And not content with that, he himself does not receive the brethren, and forbids those who wish to, putting *them* out of the church.

11 Beloved, do not imitate what is evil, but what is good. He who does good is of God, but[a] he who does evil has not seen God.

12 Demetrius has a *good* testimony from all, and from the truth itself. And we also bear witness, and you know that our testimony is true.

13 I had many things to write, but I do not wish to write to you with pen and ink; 14 but I hope to see you shortly, and we shall speak face to face.

Peace to you. Our friends greet you. Greet the friends by name.

4 [a]NU-Text reads *the truth*.　5 [a]NU-Text adds *especially*.　8 [a]NU-Text reads *support*.　11 [a]NU-Text and M-Text omit *but*.

Gospel Pearls

The Epistle of
JUDE

1 Jude, a bondservant of Jesus Christ, and brother of James,

To those who are called, sanctified[a] by God the Father, and preserved in Jesus Christ:

2 Mercy, peace, and love be multiplied to you.

3 Beloved, while I was very diligent to write to you concerning our common salvation, I found it necessary to write to you exhorting you to contend earnestly for the faith which was once for all delivered to the saints. 4 For certain men have crept in unnoticed, who long ago were marked out for this condemnation, ungodly men, who turn the grace of our God into lewdness and deny the only Lord God[a] and our Lord Jesus Christ.

5 But I want to remind you, though you once knew this, that the Lord, having saved the people out of the land of Egypt, afterward destroyed those who did not believe. 6 And the angels who did not keep their proper domain, but left their own abode, He has reserved in everlasting chains under darkness for the judgment of the great day; 7 as Sodom and Gomorrah, and the cities around them in a similar manner to these, having given themselves over to sexual immorality and gone after strange flesh, are set forth as an example, suffering the vengeance of eternal fire.

8 Likewise also these dreamers defile the flesh, reject authority, and speak evil of dignitaries. 9 Yet Michael the archangel, in contending with the devil, when he disputed about the body of Moses, dared not bring against him a reviling accusation, but said, "The Lord rebuke you!" 10 But these speak evil of whatever they do not know; and whatever they know naturally, like brute beasts, in these things they corrupt themselves. 11 Woe to them! For they have gone in the way of Cain, have run greedily in the error of Balaam for profit, and perished in the rebellion of Korah.

12 These are spots in your love feasts, while they feast with you without fear, serving only themselves. They are clouds without water, carried about[a] by the winds; late autumn trees without fruit, twice dead, pulled up by the roots; 13 raging waves of the sea, foaming up their own shame; wandering stars for whom is reserved the blackness of darkness forever.

14 Now Enoch, the seventh from Adam, prophesied about these men also, saying, "Behold, the Lord comes with ten thousands of His saints, 15 to execute judgment on all, to convict all who are ungodly among them of all their ungodly deeds which they have committed in an ungodly way, and of all the harsh things which ungodly sinners have spoken against Him."

16 These are grumblers, complainers, walking according to their own lusts; and they mouth great swelling words, flattering people to gain advantage. 17 But you, beloved, remember the words which were spoken before by the apostles of our Lord Jesus Christ: 18 how they told you that there would be mockers in the last time who would walk according to their own ungodly lusts. 19 These are sensual persons, who cause divisions, not having the Spirit.

20 But you, beloved, building yourselves up on your most holy faith, praying in the Holy Spirit, 21 keep yourselves in the love of God, looking for the mercy of our Lord Jesus Christ unto eternal life.

22 And on some have compassion, making a distinction;[a] 23 but others save with fear, pulling them out of the fire,[a] hating even the garment defiled by the flesh.

24 Now to Him who is able to keep you[a] from stumbling,

---

1 [a]NU-Text reads beloved.   4 [a]NU-Text omits God.   12 [a]NU-Text and M-Text read along.
22 [a]NU-Text reads who are doubting (or making distinctions).   23 [a]NU-Text adds and on some have mercy with fear and omits with fear in first clause.   24 [a]M-Text reads them.

Just because you've been treated like a dog doesn't make you one! You have a right to be in the place and position you are in—not because of your goodness, but by virtue of His invitation.

Becoming Whole

Jude 24

Birth and growth are two different processes, both naturally and spiritually. There's a difference between being saved and being healed until you are whole. Salvation happens instantly. Healing can be a lifelong process.

When God saves you, He quickens the eternal part of you. He calls it forth, and it springs to life in an instant. Your spirit is immediately changed by the Holy Ghost, and you can never be any more saved than you are in that moment.

If you compare a person who has just died to a person who died twenty years ago, there's no difference in their state of "deadness." They are equally dead. The same principle holds for your salvation. You are either saved or you aren't. It's a state of being, not a state of becoming. If you were made alive in Christ, then you are alive in Christ. Your salvation was a supernatural impartation of God in your most secret place—your spirit.

Even though your spirit has been saved, you can still have areas that need to be healed—in your mind, your emotions, your appetites, and your desires. And until they are healed, you will continue to fall back into the same cesspool of sinful behavior again and again.

Don't let people tell you, "If you were really saved, you wouldn't act like that. You wouldn't want to do that. You wouldn't sin like that." Lapses into error have nothing to do with the salvation of your spirit. They have to do with the healing of your soul and the fact that you are not yet whole. As a preacher friend of mine once said, "Sin is not the real issue. Sin is merely the way people seek to medicate their problems."

In other words, one reason people keep sinning after they are saved is that they are still hurting. A familiar sinful action is one of the ways they numb their pain. They go to the marketplace because they need intimacy and come home after paying for sex. They go to the marketplace looking for peace and come home with a fifth of alcohol.

Your answer does not lie in people or in things. It lies in the presence of God. Wholeness comes when you turn to Him in your weakness, your pain, your suffering, and you allow Him to do for you what no one else can do. Only God can regenerate the human spirit. And only God can raise a person to spiritual maturity. El Shaddai—the breasted one—can grow you up into a woman of grace and wisdom and wholeness.

And to present *you* faultless
Before the presence of His
    glory with exceeding
    joy,
25 To God our Savior,[a]

Who alone is wise,[b]
Be glory and majesty,
Dominion and power,[c]
Both now and forever.
Amen.

25 [a]NU-Text reads *To the only God, our Savior* and omits *wise.*   [b]NU-Text adds *through Jesus Christ our Lord.*   [c]NU-Text adds *Before all time.*

THE REVELATION
of Jesus Christ

1 The Revelation of Jesus Christ, which God gave Him to show His servants—things which must shortly take place. And He sent and signified *it* by His angel to His servant John, 2 who bore witness to the word of God, and to the testimony of Jesus Christ, to all things that he saw. 3 Blessed *is* he who reads and those who hear the words of this prophecy, and keep those things which are written in it; for the time *is* near.

4 John, to the seven churches which are in Asia:

Grace to you and peace from Him who is and who was and who is to come, and from the seven Spirits who are before His throne, 5 and from Jesus Christ, the faithful witness, the firstborn from the dead, and the ruler over the kings of the earth.

To Him who loved us and washed[a] us from our sins in His own blood, 6 and has made us kings[a] and priests to His God and Father, to Him *be* glory and dominion forever and ever. Amen.

7 Behold, He is coming with clouds, and every eye will see Him, even they who pierced Him. And all the tribes of the earth will mourn because of Him. Even so, Amen.

8 "I am the Alpha and the Omega, *the* Beginning and *the* End," says the Lord,[b] "who is and who was and who is to come, the Almighty."

9 I, John, both[a] your brother and companion in the tribulation and kingdom and patience of Jesus Christ, was on the island that is called Patmos for the word of God and for the testimony of Jesus Christ. 10 I was in the Spirit on the Lord's Day, and I heard behind me a loud voice, as of a trumpet, 11 saying, "I am the Alpha and the Omega, the First and the Last," and,[a] "What you see, write in a book and send *it* to the seven churches which are in Asia:[b] to Ephesus, to Smyrna, to Pergamos, to Thyatira, to Sardis, to Philadelphia, and to Laodicea."

12 Then I turned to see the voice that spoke with me. And having turned I saw seven golden lampstands, 13 and in the midst of the seven lampstands *One* like the Son of Man, clothed with a garment down to the feet and girded about the chest with a golden band. 14 His head and hair *were* white like wool, as white as snow, and His eyes like a flame of fire; 15 His feet *were* like fine brass, as if refined in a furnace, and His voice as the sound of many waters; 16 He had in His right hand seven stars, out of His mouth went a sharp two-edged sword, and His countenance *was* like the sun shining in its strength. 17 And when I saw Him, I fell at His feet as dead. But He laid His right hand on me, saying to me,[a] "Do not be afraid; I am the First and the Last. 18 I *am* He who lives, and was dead, and behold, I am alive forevermore. Amen. And I have

1:5 [a]NU-Text reads *loves us and freed;* M-Text reads *loves us and washed.*   1:6 [a]NU-Text and M-Text read *a kingdom.*   1:8 [a]NU-Text and M-Text omit *the Beginning and the End.*   [b]NU-Text and M-Text add *God.*   1:9 [a]NU-Text and M-Text omit *both.*   1:11 [a]NU-Text and M-Text omit *I am* through third *and.*   [b]NU-Text and M-Text omit *which are in Asia.*   1:17 [a]NU-Text and M-Text omit *to me.*

*T*he harvest God wants to plant is in your head. Hold on to your field of dreams. If you can water your own field when others are trying to command a drought in your life, God will mightily sustain you.

the keys of Hades and of Death.
19 Write[a] the things which you have
seen, and the things which are, and
the things which will take place after
this. 20 The mystery of the seven
stars which you saw in My right
hand, and the seven golden lampstands: The seven stars are the angels of the seven churches, and the
seven lampstands which you saw[a]
are the seven churches.

2 "To the angel of the church of
Ephesus write,
'These things says He who holds
the seven stars in His right hand, who
walks in the midst of the seven
golden lampstands: 2 "I know your
works, your labor, your patience, and
that you cannot bear those who are
evil. And you have tested those who
say they are apostles and are not, and
have found them liars; 3 and you
have persevered and have patience,
and have labored for My name's
sake and have not become weary.
4 Nevertheless I have *this* against
you, that you have left your first love.
5 Remember therefore from where
you have fallen; repent and do the
first works, or else I will come to you
quickly and remove your lampstand
from its place—unless you repent.
6 But this you have, that you hate the
deeds of the Nicolaitans, which I also
hate.
7 "He who has an ear, let him hear
what the Spirit says to the churches.
To him who overcomes I will give
to eat from the tree of life, which
is in the midst of the Paradise of
God." '
8 "And to the angel of the church
in Smyrna write,
'These things says the First and the
Last, who was dead, and came to life:
9 "I know your works, tribulation,
and poverty (but you are rich); and
I *know* the blasphemy of those who
say they are Jews and are not, but
are a synagogue of Satan. 10 Do not
fear any of those things which you
are about to suffer. Indeed, the devil
is about to throw *some* of you into
prison, that you may be tested, and
you will have tribulation ten days. Be

faithful until death, and I will give
you the crown of life.
11 "He who has an ear, let him hear
what the Spirit says to the churches.
He who overcomes shall not be hurt
by the second death." '
12 "And to the angel of the church
in Pergamos write,
'These things says He who has the
sharp two-edged sword: 13 "I know
your works, and where you dwell,
where Satan's throne *is*. And you
hold fast to My name, and did not
deny My faith even in the days in
which Antipas *was* My faithful martyr, who was killed among you,
where Satan dwells. 14 But I have a
few things against you, because you
have there those who hold the doctrine of Balaam, who taught Balak to
put a stumbling block before the children of Israel, to eat things sacrificed
to idols, and to commit sexual immorality. 15 Thus you also have those
who hold the doctrine of the Nicolaitans, which thing I hate.[a] 16 Repent,
or else I will come to you quickly and
will fight against them with the
sword of My mouth.
17 "He who has an ear, let him hear
what the Spirit says to the churches.
To him who overcomes I will give
some of the hidden manna to eat.
And I will give him a white stone,
and on the stone a new name written
which no one knows except him who
receives *it*." '
18 "And to the angel of the church
in Thyatira write,
'These things says the Son of God,
who has eyes like a flame of fire, and
His feet like fine brass: 19 I know
your works, love, service, faith,[a] and
your patience; and *as* for your works,
the last *are* more than the first.
20 Nevertheless I have a few things
against you, because you allow[a] that
woman[b] Jezebel, who calls herself a
prophetess, to teach and seduce[c] My
servants to commit sexual immorality and eat things sacrificed to idols.
21 And I gave her time to repent of
her sexual immorality, and she did
not repent.[a] 22 Indeed I will cast her
into a sickbed, and those who commit adultery with her into great tribu-

---

1:19 [a]NU-Text and M-Text read *Therefore, write.*   1:20 [a]NU-Text and M-Text omit *which you saw.*
2:15 [a]NU-Text and M-Text read *likewise* for *which thing I hate.*   2:19 [a]NU-Text and M-Text read *faith,
service.*   2:20 [a]NU-Text and M-Text read *I have against you that you tolerate.*   [b]M-Text reads *your wife
Jezebel.*   [c]NU-Text and M-Text read *and teaches and seduces.*   2:21 [a]NU-Text and M-Text read *time
to repent, and she does not want to repent of her sexual immorality.*

**Gospel
Pearls**

lation, unless they repent of their[a] deeds. 23 I will kill her children with death, and all the churches shall know that I am He who searches the minds and hearts. And I will give to each one of you according to your works.

24 "Now to you I say, and[a] to the rest in Thyatira, as many as do not have this doctrine, who have not known the depths of Satan, as they say, I will[b] put on you no other burden. 25 But hold fast what you have till I come. 26 And he who overcomes, and keeps My works until the end, to him I will give power over the nations—

27 'He shall rule them with a rod
of iron;
They shall be dashed to pieces
like the potter's vessels'[a]—

as I also have received from My Father; 28 and I will give him the morning star.

29 "He who has an ear, let him hear what the Spirit says to the churches." '

3 "And to the angel of the church in Sardis write,

'These things says He who has the seven Spirits of God and the seven stars: "I know your works, that you have a name that you are alive, but you are dead. 2 Be watchful, and strengthen the things which remain, that are ready to die, for I have not found your works perfect before God.[a] 3 Remember therefore how you have received and heard; hold fast and repent. Therefore if you will not watch, I will come upon you as a thief, and you will not know what hour I will come upon you. 4 You[a] have a few names even in Sardis who have not defiled their garments; and they shall walk with Me in white, for they are worthy. 5 He who overcomes shall be clothed in white garments, and I will not blot out his name from the Book of Life; but I will confess his name before My Father and before His angels.

6 "He who has an ear, let him

hear what the Spirit says to the churches." '

7 "And to the angel of the church in Philadelphia write,

'These things says He who is holy, He who is true, *"He who has the key of David, He who opens and no one shuts, and shuts and no one opens":*[a] 8 I know your works. See, I have set before you an open door, and no one can shut it;[a] for you have a little strength, have kept My word, and have not denied My name. 9 Indeed I will make *those* of the synagogue of Satan, who say they are Jews and are not, but lie—indeed I will make them come and worship before your feet, and to know that I have loved you. 10 Because you have kept My command to persevere, I also will keep you from the hour of trial which shall come upon the whole world, to test those who dwell on the earth. 11 Behold,[a] I am coming quickly! Hold fast what you have, that no one may take your crown. 12 He who overcomes, I will make him a pillar in the temple of My God, and he shall go out no more. I will write on him the name of My God and the name of the city of My God, the New Jerusalem, which comes down out of heaven from My God. And *I will write on him* My new name.

13 "He who has an ear, let him hear what the Spirit says to the churches." '

14 "And to the angel of the church of the Laodiceans[a] write,

'These things says the Amen, the Faithful and True Witness, the Beginning of the creation of God: 15 "I know your works, that you are neither cold nor hot. I could wish you were cold or hot. 16 So then, because you are lukewarm, and neither cold nor hot,[a] I will vomit you out of My mouth. 17 Because you say, 'I am rich, have become wealthy, and have need of nothing'—and do not know that you are wretched, miserable, poor, blind, and naked— 18 I counsel you to buy from Me gold refined in the fire, that you may be rich; and white garments, that you may be clothed, *that* the shame of your

---

2:22 [a]NU-Text and M-Text read *her.*   2:24 [a]NU-Text and M-Text omit *and.*   [b]NU-Text and M-Text omit *will.*   2:27 [a]Psalm 2:9   3:2 [a]NU-Text and M-Text read *My God.*   3:4 [a]NU-Text and M-Text read *Nevertheless you have a few names in Sardis.*   3:7 [a]Isaiah 22:22   3:8 [a]NU-Text and M-Text read *which no one can shut.*   3:11 [a]NU-Text and M-Text omit *Behold.*   3:14 [a]NU-Text and M-Text read *in Laodicea.*   3:16 [a]NU-Text and M-Text read *hot nor cold.*

---

*F*riendship is different from family love, which is not chosen but accepted. Friendship develops like moss on the slippery edges of a creek. It is real and powerful, sweet and bitter. Kindred spirits, warm and fitting as a pair of old house shoes.

The Power
of a Shut Door

Revelation 3:7

*I*n Revelation 3:7, God alludes to the power of the shut door. It is significant to understand that the shut door is just as much a move of God as the open one. It is the same mighty hand, and it is the same loving heart. It is an action predetermined by the wisdom of a Father who knows what is best. He does emphatically shut doors. We have not taught enough about the shut door. The mention of the "key of David" in this verse implies that the door is not just shut, but also locked. This is amplified when we see also that no one can open it. There is no purpose in trying to pray open, work open, or pry open what God has shut.

You know you're up against a shut door when it will not open. I know this seems obvious, because we often have to pray to get a door open when the enemy is trying to discourage us. Here's a simple way to tell the difference: If the door is just closed by the enemy, and he is trying to get you to give up on your dream, prayer and praise will unlock it. But if the door is closed by a sovereign decision of an all-wise God, and prayer and praise do not open it, then you must accept His decision.

That doesn't mean the door cannot be opened. It just means that no human can open it. If God doesn't open the door, it cannot be opened. If He doesn't do it, you don't want it to be done. By now you should know that He does what is best for you. There is a difference between a door Satan has jammed and a door God has locked.

The closed door is a blessing. Many people rejoice about the opening of doors. I guess that is a blessing, especially if you needed the door open and only God could do it. I can understand why the heart sings when the hand of God moves the obstacle out of the way. The eye can see the way made, and the feet begin to dance toward a brighter future.

But I want to challenge you to go a step further into understanding the deeper sovereign truth of a closed door. We can readily accept His authority when it is used to perform what we know to be a favor. The real challenge of submission is to submit when your human will wants to choose another way. This is the graduation exercise of faith and the commencement service of a trust for those whose dependency and reliance is upon the manifold wisdom of God. Never underestimate the power of a shut door!

nakedness may not be revealed; and anoint your eyes with eye salve, that you may see. 19 As many as I love, I rebuke and chasten. Therefore be zealous and repent. 20 Behold, I stand at the door and knock. If anyone hears My voice and opens the door, I will come in to him and dine with him, and he with Me. 21 To him who overcomes I will grant to sit with Me on My throne, as I also overcame and sat down with My Father on His throne.

22 "He who has an ear, let him hear what the Spirit says to the churches." ' "

4 After these things I looked, and behold, a door *standing* open in heaven. And the first voice which I heard *was* like a trumpet speaking with me, saying, "Come up here, and I will show you things which must take place after this."

2 Immediately I was in the Spirit; and behold, a throne set in heaven, and *One* sat on the throne. 3 And He who sat there was[a] like a jasper and a sardius stone in appearance; and *there was* a rainbow around the throne, in appearance like an emerald. 4 Around the throne *were* twenty-four thrones, and on the thrones I saw twenty-four elders sitting, clothed in white robes; and they had crowns[a] of gold on their heads. 5 And from the throne proceeded lightnings, thunderings and voices.[a] Seven lamps of fire *were* burning before the throne, which are the[b] seven Spirits of God.

6 Before the throne *there was*[a] a sea of glass, like crystal. And in the midst of the throne, and around the throne, *were* four living creatures full of eyes in front and in back. 7 The first living creature *was* like a lion, the second living creature like a calf, the third living creature had a face like a man, and the fourth living creature *was* like a flying eagle. 8 *The* four living creatures, each having six wings, were full of eyes around and within. And they do not rest day or night, saying:

"Holy, holy, holy,[a]
Lord God Almighty,
Who was and is and is to come!"

9 Whenever the living creatures give glory and honor and thanks to Him who sits on the throne, who lives forever and ever, 10 the twenty-four elders fall down before Him who sits on the throne and worship Him who lives forever and ever, and cast their crowns before the throne, saying:

11 "You are worthy, O Lord,[a]
To receive glory and honor and power;
For You created all things,
And by Your will they exist[b]
and were created."

5 And I saw in the right *hand* of Him who sat on the throne a scroll written inside and on the back, sealed with seven seals. 2 Then I saw a strong angel proclaiming with a loud voice, "Who is worthy to open the scroll and to loose its seals?" 3 And no one in heaven or on the earth or under the earth was able to open the scroll, or to look at it.

4 So I wept much, because no one was found worthy to open and read[a] the scroll, or to look at it. 5 But one of the elders said to me, "Do not weep. Behold, the Lion of the tribe of Judah, the Root of David, has prevailed to open the scroll and to loose[a] its seven seals."

6 And I looked, and behold,[a] in the midst of the throne and of the four living creatures, and in the midst of the elders, stood a Lamb as though it had been slain, having seven horns and seven eyes, which are the seven Spirits of God sent out into all the earth. 7 Then He came and took the scroll out of the right hand of Him who sat on the throne.

8 Now when He had taken the scroll, the four living creatures and the twenty-four elders fell down before the Lamb, each having a harp, and golden bowls full of incense, which are the prayers of the saints. 9 And they sang a new song, saying:

4:3 [a]M-Text omits And He who sat there was (which makes the description in verse 3 modify the throne rather than God).   4:4 [a]NU-Text and M-Text read *robes, with crowns.*   4:5 [a]NU-Text and M-Text read *voices, and thunderings.* [b]M-Text omits *the.*   4:6 [a]NU-Text and M-Text add *something like.* 4:8 [a]M-Text has *holy* nine times.   4:11 [a]NU-Text and M-Text read *our Lord and God.* [b]NU-Text and M-Text read *existed.*   5:4 [a]NU-Text and M-Text omit *and read.*   5:5 [a]NU-Text and M-Text omit *to loose.*   5:6 [a]NU-Text and M-Text read *I saw in the midst . . . a Lamb standing.*

---

*R*eal relationship is hard work. It is like riding the bus. You must be willing to scoot over and rearrange yourself to accommodate another person and the many parcels that she brings.

"You are worthy to take the
scroll,
And to open its seals;
For You were slain,
And have redeemed us to God
by Your blood
Out of every tribe and tongue
and people and nation,
10 And have made us[a] kings[b] and
priests to our God;
And we[c] shall reign on the
earth."

11 Then I looked, and I heard the voice of many angels around the throne, the living creatures, and the elders; and the number of them was ten thousand times ten thousand, and thousands of thousands, 12 saying with a loud voice:

"Worthy is the Lamb who was
slain
To receive power and riches
and wisdom,
And strength and honor and
glory and blessing!"

13 And every creature which is in heaven and on the earth and under the earth and such as are in the sea, and all that are in them, I heard saying:

"Blessing and honor and glory
and power
Be to Him who sits on the
throne,
And to the Lamb, forever and
ever!"[a]

14 Then the four living creatures said, "Amen!" And the twenty-four[a] elders fell down and worshiped Him who lives forever and ever.[b]

6 Now I saw when the Lamb opened one of the seals;[a] and I heard one of the four living creatures saying with a voice like thunder, "Come and see." 2 And I looked, and behold, a white horse. He who sat on it had a bow; and a crown was given to him, and he went out conquering and to conquer.
3 When He opened the second seal,

I heard the second living creature saying, "Come and see."[a] 4 Another horse, fiery red, went out. And it was granted to the one who sat on it to take peace from the earth, and that *people* should kill one another; and there was given to him a great sword.

5 When He opened the third seal, I heard the third living creature say, "Come and see." So I looked, and behold, a black horse, and he who sat on it had a pair of scales in his hand.
6 And I heard a voice in the midst of the four living creatures saying, "A quart[a] of wheat for a denarius,[b] and three quarts of barley for a denarius; and do not harm the oil and the wine."

7 When He opened the fourth seal, I heard the voice of the fourth living creature saying, "Come and see." 8 So I looked, and behold, a pale horse. And the name of him who sat on it was Death, and Hades followed with him. And power was given to them over a fourth of the earth, to kill with sword, with hunger, with death, and by the beasts of the earth.
9 When He opened the fifth seal, I saw under the altar the souls of those who had been slain for the word of God and for the testimony which they held. 10 And they cried with a loud voice, saying, "How long, O Lord, holy and true, until You judge and avenge our blood on those who dwell on the earth?" 11 Then a white robe was given to each of them; and it was said to them that they should rest a little while longer, until both *the number of* their fellow servants and their brethren, who would be killed as they *were*, was completed.
12 I looked when He opened the sixth seal, and behold,[a] there was a great earthquake; and the sun became black as sackcloth of hair, and the moon[b] became like blood. 13 And the stars of heaven fell to the earth, as a fig tree drops its late figs when it is shaken by a mighty wind. 14 Then the sky receded as a scroll when it is rolled up, and every mountain and island was moved out of its place. 15 And the kings of the earth, the great men, the rich men, the com-

5:10 [a]NU-Text and M-Text read *them.* [b]NU-Text reads *a kingdom.* [c]NU-Text and M-Text read *they.*
5:13 [a]M-Text adds *Amen.*   5:14 [a]NU-Text and M-Text omit *twenty-four.* [b]NU-Text and M-Text omit *Him who lives forever and ever.*   6:1 [a]NU-Text and M-Text read *seven seals.*   6:3 [a]NU-Text and M-Text omit *and see.*   6:6 [a]Greek *choinix;* that is, approximately one quart [b]This was approximately one day's wage for a worker.   6:12 [a]NU-Text and M-Text omit *behold.* [b]NU-Text and M-Text read *the whole moon.*

Gospel Pearls

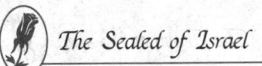
manders,ᵃ the mighty men, every slave and every free man, hid themselves in the caves and in the rocks of the mountains, 16 and said to the mountains and rocks, "Fall on us and hide us from the face of Him who sits on the throne and from the wrath of the Lamb! 17 For the great day of His wrath has come, and who is able to stand?"

7 After these things I saw four angels standing at the four corners of the earth, holding the four winds of the earth, that the wind should not blow on the earth, on the sea, or on any tree. 2 Then I saw another angel ascending from the east, having the seal of the living God. And he cried with a loud voice to the four angels to whom it was granted to harm the earth and the sea, 3 saying, "Do not harm the earth, the sea, or the trees till we have sealed the servants of our God on their foreheads." 4 And I heard the number of those who were sealed. One hundred *and* forty-four thousand of all the tribes of the children of Israel *were* sealed:

5 of the tribe of Judah twelve
   thousand *were* sealed;ᵃ
   of the tribe of Reuben twelve
   thousand *were* sealed;
   of the tribe of Gad twelve
   thousand *were* sealed;
6 of the tribe of Asher twelve
   thousand *were* sealed;
   of the tribe of Naphtali twelve
   thousand *were* sealed;
   of the tribe of Manasseh twelve
   thousand *were* sealed;
7 of the tribe of Simeon twelve
   thousand *were* sealed;
   of the tribe of Levi twelve
   thousand *were* sealed;
   of the tribe of Issachar twelve
   thousand *were* sealed;
8 of the tribe of Zebulun twelve
   thousand *were* sealed;
   of the tribe of Joseph twelve
   thousand *were* sealed;
   of the tribe of Benjamin twelve
   thousand *were* sealed.

9 After these things I looked, and behold, a great multitude which no one could number, of all nations, tribes, peoples, and tongues, standing before the throne and before the Lamb, clothed with white robes, with palm branches in their hands, 10 and crying out with a loud voice, saying, "Salvation *belongs* to our God who sits on the throne, and to the Lamb!" 11 All the angels stood around the throne and the elders and the four living creatures, and fell on their faces before the throne and worshiped God, 12 saying:

"Amen! Blessing and glory and
   wisdom,
Thanksgiving and honor and
   power and might,
Be to our God forever and ever.
Amen."

13 Then one of the elders answered, saying to me, "Who are these arrayed in white robes, and where did they come from?"

14 And I said to him, "Sir,ᵃ you know."

So he said to me, "These are the ones who come out of the great tribulation, and washed their robes and made them white in the blood of the Lamb. 15 Therefore they are before the throne of God, and serve Him day and night in His temple. And He who sits on the throne will dwell among them. 16 They shall neither hunger anymore nor thirst anymore; the sun shall not strike them, nor any heat; 17 for the Lamb who is in the midst of the throne will shepherd them and lead them to living fountains of waters.ᵃ And God will wipe away every tear from their eyes."

8 When He opened the seventh seal, there was silence in heaven for about half an hour. 2 And I saw the seven angels who stand before God, and to them were given seven trumpets. 3 Then another angel, having a golden censer, came and stood at the altar. He was given much incense, that he should offer *it* with the prayers of all the saints upon the golden altar which was before the throne. 4 And the smoke of the incense, with the prayers of the saints, ascended before God from the angel's hand. 5 Then the angel took the

---

6:15 ᵃNU-Text and M-Text read *the commanders, the rich men.*   7:5 ᵃIn NU-Text and M-Text *were sealed* is stated only in verses 5a and 8c; the words are understood in the remainder of the passage.
7:14 ᵃNU-Text and M-Text read *My lord.*   7:17 ᵃNU-Text and M-Text read *to fountains of the waters of life.*

God sees every imperfection we have, yet He maintains His commitment to love the unlovely. Isn't that why we love Him so much? We are completely vulnerable to Him. He knows us, yet He understands and loves us.

censer, filled it with fire from the altar, and threw *it* to the earth. And there were noises, thunderings, lightnings, and an earthquake.

6 So the seven angels who had the seven trumpets prepared themselves to sound.

7 The first angel sounded: And hail and fire followed, mingled with blood, and they were thrown to the earth.[a] And a third of the trees were burned up, and all green grass was burned up.

8 Then the second angel sounded: And *something* like a great mountain burning with fire was thrown into the sea, and a third of the sea became blood. 9 And a third of the living creatures in the sea died, and a third of the ships were destroyed.

10 Then the third angel sounded: And a great star fell from heaven, burning like a torch, and it fell on a third of the rivers and on the springs of water. 11 The name of the star is Wormwood. A third of the waters became wormwood, and many men died from the water, because it was made bitter.

12 Then the fourth angel sounded: And a third of the sun was struck, a third of the moon, and a third of the stars, so that a third of them were darkened. A third of the day did not shine, and likewise the night.

13 And I looked, and I heard an angel[a] flying through the midst of heaven, saying with a loud voice, "Woe, woe, woe to the inhabitants of the earth, because of the remaining blasts of the trumpet of the three angels who are about to sound!"

9 Then the fifth angel sounded: And I saw a star fallen from heaven to the earth. To him was given the key to the bottomless pit. 2 And he opened the bottomless pit, and smoke arose out of the pit like the smoke of a great furnace. So the sun and the air were darkened because of the smoke of the pit. 3 Then out of the smoke locusts came upon the earth. And to them was given power, as the scorpions of the earth have power. 4 They were commanded not to harm the grass of the earth, or any green thing, or any tree, but only those men who do not have the seal

of God on their foreheads. 5 And they were not given *authority* to kill them, but to torment them *for* five months. Their torment *was* like the torment of a scorpion when it strikes a man. 6 In those days men will seek death and will not find it; they will desire to die, and death will flee from them.

7 The shape of the locusts was like horses prepared for battle. On their heads were crowns of something like gold, and their faces *were* like the faces of men. 8 They had hair like women's hair, and their teeth were like lions' *teeth.* 9 And they had breastplates like breastplates of iron, and the sound of their wings *was* like the sound of chariots with many horses running into battle. 10 They had tails like scorpions, and there were stings in their tails. Their power *was* to hurt men five months. 11 And they had as king over them the angel of the bottomless pit, whose name in Hebrew *is* Abaddon, but in Greek he has the name Apollyon.

12 One woe is past. Behold, still two more woes are coming after these things.

13 Then the sixth angel sounded: And I heard a voice from the four horns of the golden altar which is before God, 14 saying to the sixth angel who had the trumpet, "Release the four angels who are bound at the great river Euphrates." 15 So the four angels, who had been prepared for the hour and day and month and year, were released to kill a third of mankind. 16 Now the number of the army of the horsemen *was* two hundred million; I heard the number of them. 17 And thus I saw the horses in the vision: those who sat on them had breastplates of fiery red, hyacinth blue, and sulfur yellow; and the heads of the horses *were* like the heads of lions; and out of their mouths came fire, smoke, and brimstone. 18 By these three *plagues* a third of mankind was killed—by the fire and the smoke and the brimstone which came out of their mouths. 19 For their power[a] is in their mouth and in their tails; for their tails *are* like serpents, having heads; and with them they do harm.

20 But the rest of mankind, who were not killed by these plagues, did

8:7 [a]NU-Text and M-Text add *And a third of the earth was burned up.* 8:13 [a]NU-Text and M-Text read *eagle.* 9:19 [a]NU-Text and M-Text read *the power of the horses.*

Gospel Pearls

not repent of the works of their hands, that they should not worship demons, and idols of gold, silver, brass, stone, and wood, which can neither see nor hear nor walk. 21 And they did not repent of their murders or their sorceries*a* or their sexual immorality or their thefts.

10 I saw still another mighty angel coming down from heaven, clothed with a cloud. And a rainbow *was* on his head, his face *was* like the sun, and his feet like pillars of fire. 2 He had a little book open in his hand. And he set his right foot on the sea and *his* left *foot* on the land, 3 and cried with a loud voice, as *when* a lion roars. When he cried out, seven thunders uttered their voices. 4 Now when the seven thunders uttered their voices,*a* I was about to write; but I heard a voice from heaven saying to me,*b* "Seal up the things which the seven thunders uttered, and do not write them."

5 The angel whom I saw standing on the sea and on the land raised up his hand*a* to heaven 6 and swore by Him who lives forever and ever, who created heaven and the things that are in it, the earth and the things that are in it, and the sea and the things that are in it, that there should be delay no longer, 7 but in the days of the sounding of the seventh angel, when he is about to sound, the mystery of God would be finished, as He declared to His servants the prophets.

8 Then the voice which I heard from heaven spoke to me again and said, "Go, take the little book which is open in the hand of the angel who stands on the sea and on the earth."

9 So I went to the angel and said to him, "Give me the little book."

And he said to me, "Take and eat it; and it will make your stomach bitter, but it will be as sweet as honey in your mouth."

10 Then I took the little book out of the angel's hand and ate it, and it was as sweet as honey in my mouth. But when I had eaten it, my stomach became bitter. 11 And he*a* said to me, "You must prophesy again about many peoples, nations, tongues, and kings."

11 Then I was given a reed like a measuring rod. And the angel stood,*a* saying, "Rise and measure the temple of God, the altar, and those who worship there. 2 But leave out the court which is outside the temple, and do not measure it, for it has been given to the Gentiles. And they will tread the holy city underfoot *for* forty-two months. 3 And I will give *power* to my two witnesses, and they will prophesy one thousand two hundred and sixty days, clothed in sackcloth."

4 These are the two olive trees and the two lampstands standing before the God*a* of the earth. 5 And if anyone wants to harm them, fire proceeds from their mouth and devours their enemies. And if anyone wants to harm them, he must be killed in this manner. 6 These have power to shut heaven, so that no rain falls in the days of their prophecy; and they have power over waters to turn them to blood, and to strike the earth with all plagues, as often as they desire.

7 When they finish their testimony, the beast that ascends out of the bottomless pit will make war against them, overcome them, and kill them. 8 And their dead bodies *will lie* in the street of the great city which spiritually is called Sodom and Egypt, where also our*a* Lord was crucified. 9 Then *those* from the peoples, tribes, tongues, and nations will see their dead bodies three-and-a-half days, and not allow*a* their dead bodies to be put into graves. 10 And those who dwell on the earth will rejoice over them, make merry, and send gifts to one another, because these two prophets tormented those who dwell on the earth.

11 Now after the three-and-a-half days the breath of life from God entered them, and they stood on their feet, and great fear fell on those who saw them. 12 And they*a* heard a loud voice from heaven saying to them, "Come up here." And they ascended to heaven in a cloud, and their enemies saw them. 13 In the same hour

9:21 *a*NU-Text and M-Text read *drugs*.   10:4 *a*NU-Text and M-Text read *sounded*.   *b*NU-Text and M-Text omit *to me*.   10:5 *a*NU-Text and M-Text read *right hand*.   10:11 *a*NU-Text and M-Text read *they*.   11:1 *a*NU-Text and M-Text omit *And the angel stood*.   11:4 *a*NU-Text and M-Text read *Lord*. 11:8 *a*NU-Text and M-Text read *their*.   11:9 *a*NU-Text and M-Text read *nations see . . . and will not allow*.   11:12 *a*M-Text reads *I*.

We must not allow our friendships to be easily uprooted. Have you ever thrown away a good person who did a bad thing? The tragedy is in forgetting the good a friend has done and dwelling only on the one bad thing.

there was a great earthquake, and a tenth of the city fell. In the earthquake seven thousand people were killed, and the rest were afraid and gave glory to the God of heaven.

14 The second woe is past. Behold, the third woe is coming quickly.

15 Then the seventh angel sounded: And there were loud voices in heaven, saying, "The kingdoms[a] of this world have become *the kingdoms* of our Lord and of His Christ, and He shall reign forever and ever!" 16 And the twenty-four elders who sat before God on their thrones fell on their faces and worshiped God, 17 saying:

> "We give You thanks, O Lord
>   God Almighty,
> The One who is and who was
>   and who is to come,[a]
> Because You have taken Your
>   great power and reigned.
> 18 The nations were angry, and
>   Your wrath has come,
> And the time of the dead, that
>   they should be judged,
> And that You should reward
>   Your servants the prophets
>   and the saints,
> And those who fear Your
>   name, small and great,
> And should destroy those who
>   destroy the earth."

19 Then the temple of God was opened in heaven, and the ark of His covenant[a] was seen in His temple. And there were lightnings, noises, thunderings, an earthquake, and great hail.

12 Now a great sign appeared in heaven: a woman clothed with the sun, with the moon under her feet, and on her head a garland of twelve stars. 2 Then being with child, she cried out in labor and in pain to give birth.

3 And another sign appeared in heaven: behold, a great, fiery red dragon having seven heads and ten horns, and seven diadems on his heads. 4 His tail drew a third of the stars of heaven and threw them to the earth. And the dragon stood before the woman who was ready to give birth, to devour her Child as soon as it was born. 5 She bore a male Child who was to rule all nations with a rod of iron. And her Child was caught up to God and His throne. 6 Then the woman fled into the wilderness, where she has a place prepared by God, that they should feed her there one thousand two hundred and sixty days.

7 And war broke out in heaven: Michael and his angels fought with the dragon; and the dragon and his angels fought, 8 but they did not prevail, nor was a place found for them[a] in heaven any longer. 9 So the great dragon was cast out, that serpent of old, called the Devil and Satan, who deceives the whole world; he was cast to the earth, and his angels were cast out with him.

10 Then I heard a loud voice saying in heaven, "Now salvation, and strength, and the kingdom of our God, and the power of His Christ have come, for the accuser of our brethren, who accused them before our God day and night, has been cast down. 11 And they overcame him by the blood of the Lamb and by the word of their testimony, and they did not love their lives to the death. 12 Therefore rejoice, O heavens, and you who dwell in them! Woe to the inhabitants of the earth and the sea! For the devil has come down to you, having great wrath, because he knows that he has a short time."

13 Now when the dragon saw that he had been cast to the earth, he persecuted the woman who gave birth to the male *Child*. 14 But the woman was given two wings of a great eagle, that she might fly into the wilderness to her place, where she is nourished for a time and times and half a time, from the presence of the serpent. 15 So the serpent spewed water out of his mouth like a flood after the woman, that he might cause her to be carried away by the flood. 16 But the earth helped the woman, and the earth opened its mouth and swallowed up the flood which the dragon had spewed out of his mouth. 17 And the dragon was enraged with the woman, and he went to make war with the rest of her offspring, who keep the commandments of God and have the testimony of Jesus Christ.[a]

11:15 [a]NU-Text and M-Text read *kingdom . . . has become. is to come.* 11:19 [a]M-Text reads *the covenant of the Lord.* 12:17 [a]NU-Text and M-Text omit *Christ.* 11:17 [a]NU-Text and M-Text omit *and who* 12:8 [a]M-Text reads *him.*

Gospel Pearls

13 Then I*ᵃ* stood on the sand of the sea. And I saw a beast rising up out of the sea, having seven heads and ten horns,*ᵇ* and on his horns ten crowns, and on his heads a blasphemous name. 2 Now the beast which I saw was like a leopard, his feet were like *the feet of* a bear, and his mouth like the mouth of a lion. The dragon gave him his power, his throne, and great authority. 3 And *I saw* one of his heads as if it had been mortally wounded, and his deadly wound was healed. And all the world marveled and followed the beast. 4 So they worshiped the dragon who gave authority to the beast; and they worshiped the beast, saying, "Who *is* like the beast? Who is able to make war with him?"

5 And he was given a mouth speaking great things and blasphemies, and he was given authority to continue*ᵃ* for forty-two months. 6 Then he opened his mouth in blasphemy against God, to blaspheme His name, His tabernacle, and those who dwell in heaven. 7 It was granted to him to make war with the saints and to overcome them. And authority was given him over every tribe,*ᵃ* tongue, and nation. 8 All who dwell on the earth will worship him, whose names have not been written in the Book of Life of the Lamb slain from the foundation of the world.

9 If anyone has an ear, let him hear. 10 He who leads into captivity shall go into captivity; he who kills with the sword must be killed with the sword. Here is the patience and the faith of the saints.

11 Then I saw another beast coming up out of the earth, and he had two horns like a lamb and spoke like a dragon. 12 And he exercises all the authority of the first beast in his presence, and causes the earth and those who dwell in it to worship the first beast, whose deadly wound was healed. 13 He performs great signs, so that he even makes fire come down from heaven on the earth in the sight of men. 14 And he deceives those*ᵃ* who dwell on the earth by those signs which he was granted to do in the

sight of the beast, telling those who dwell on the earth to make an image to the beast who was wounded by the sword and lived. 15 He was granted *power* to give breath to the image of the beast, that the image of the beast should both speak and cause as many as would not worship the image of the beast to be killed. 16 He causes all, both small and great, rich and poor, free and slave, to receive a mark on their right hand or on their foreheads, 17 and that no one may buy or sell except one who has the mark or*ᵃ* the name of the beast, or the number of his name. 18 Here is wisdom. Let him who has understanding calculate the number of the beast, for it is the number of a man: His number *is* 666.

14 Then I looked, and behold, a*ᵃ* Lamb standing on Mount Zion, and with Him one hundred *and* forty-four thousand, having*ᵇ* His Father's name written on their foreheads. 2 And I heard a voice from heaven, like the voice of many waters, and like the voice of loud thunder. And I heard the sound of harpists playing their harps. 3 They sang as it were a new song before the throne, before the four living creatures, and the elders; and no one could learn that song except the hundred *and* forty-four thousand who were redeemed from the earth. 4 These are the ones who were not defiled with women, for they are virgins. These are the ones who follow the Lamb wherever He goes. These were redeemed*ᵃ* from *among* men, *being* firstfruits to God and to the Lamb. 5 And in their mouth was found no deceit,*ᵃ* for they are without fault before the throne of God.*ᵇ*

6 Then I saw another angel flying in the midst of heaven, having the everlasting gospel to preach to those who dwell on the earth—to every nation, tribe, tongue, and people— 7 saying with a loud voice, "Fear God and give glory to Him, for the hour of His judgment has come; and worship Him who made heaven and earth, the sea and springs of water."

13:1 *ᵃ*NU-Text reads he. *ᵇ*NU-Text and M-Text read *ten horns and seven heads.* 13:5 *ᵃ*M-Text reads *make war.* 13:7 *ᵃ*NU-Text and M-Text add *and people.* 13:14 *ᵃ*M-Text reads *my own people.* 13:17 *ᵃ*NU-Text and M-Text omit *or.* 14:1 *ᵃ*NU-Text and M-Text read *the.* *ᵇ*NU-Text and M-Text add *His name and.* 14:4 *ᵃ*M-Text adds *by Jesus.* 14:5 *ᵃ*NU-Text and M-Text read *falsehood.* *ᵇ*NU-Text and M-Text omit *before the throne of God.*

A true friend is one who stands by you, honoring and affirming you. A true friend should desire to see you prosper in your marriage, in your finances, in your health, and in your spirituality.

8 And another angel followed, saying, "Babylon[a] is fallen, is fallen, that great city, because she has made all nations drink of the wine of the wrath of her fornication."

9 Then a third angel followed them, saying with a loud voice, "If anyone worships the beast and his image, and receives *his* mark on his forehead or on his hand, 10 he himself shall also drink of the wine of the wrath of God, which is poured out full strength into the cup of His indignation. He shall be tormented with fire and brimstone in the presence of the holy angels and in the presence of the Lamb. 11 And the smoke of their torment ascends forever and ever; and they have no rest day or night, who worship the beast and his image, and whoever receives the mark of his name."

12 Here is the patience of the saints; here *are* those[a] who keep the commandments of God and the faith of Jesus.

13 Then I heard a voice from heaven saying to me,[a] "Write: 'Blessed *are* the dead who die in the Lord from now on.'"

"Yes," says the Spirit, "that they may rest from their labors, and their works follow them."

14 Then I looked, and behold, a white cloud, and on the cloud sat *One* like the Son of Man, having on His head a golden crown, and in His hand a sharp sickle. 15 And another angel came out of the temple, crying with a loud voice to Him who sat on the cloud, "Thrust in Your sickle and reap, for the time has come for You[a] to reap, for the harvest of the earth is ripe." 16 So He who sat on the cloud thrust in His sickle on the earth, and the earth was reaped.

17 Then another angel came out of the temple which is in heaven, he also having a sharp sickle.

18 And another angel came out from the altar, who had power over fire, and he cried with a loud cry to him who had the sharp sickle, saying, "Thrust in your sharp sickle and gather the clusters of the vine of the earth, for her grapes are fully ripe."

19 So the angel thrust his sickle into the earth and gathered the vine of the earth, and threw *it* into the great winepress of the wrath of God. 20 And the winepress was trampled outside the city, and blood came out of the winepress, up to the horses' bridles, for one thousand six hundred furlongs.

15 Then I saw another sign in heaven, great and marvelous: seven angels having the seven last plagues, for in them the wrath of God is complete.

2 And I saw *something* like a sea of glass mingled with fire, and those who have the victory over the beast, over his image and over his mark[a] *and* over the number of his name, standing on the sea of glass, having harps of God. 3 They sing the song of Moses, the servant of God, and the song of the Lamb, saying:

"Great and marvelous *are* Your works,
    Lord God Almighty!
Just and true *are* Your ways,
    O King of the saints![a]
4 Who shall not fear You, O Lord, and glorify Your name?
For *You* alone *are* holy.
For all nations shall come and worship before You,
For Your judgments have been manifested."

5 After these things I looked, and behold,[a] the temple of the tabernacle of the testimony in heaven was opened. 6 And out of the temple came the seven angels having the seven plagues, clothed in pure bright linen, and having their chests girded with golden bands. 7 Then one of the four living creatures gave to the seven angels seven golden bowls full of the wrath of God who lives forever and ever. 8 The temple was filled with smoke from the glory of God and from His power, and no one was able to enter the temple till the seven plagues of the seven angels were completed.

14:8 [a]NU-Text reads *Babylon the great is fallen, is fallen, which has made;* M-Text reads *Babylon the great is fallen. She has made.*   14:12 [a]NU-Text and M-Text omit *here are those.*   14:13 [a]NU-Text and M-Text omit *to me.*   14:15 [a]NU-Text and M-Text omit *for You.*   15:2 [a]NU-Text and M-Text omit *over his mark.*   15:3 [a]NU-Text and M-Text read *nations.*   15:5 [a]NU-Text and M-Text omit *behold.*

Gospel Pearls

16 Then I heard a loud voice from the temple saying to the seven angels, "Go and pour out the bowls[a] of the wrath of God on the earth."

2 So the first went and poured out his bowl upon the earth, and a foul and loathsome sore came upon the men who had the mark of the beast and those who worshiped his image.

3 Then the second angel poured out his bowl on the sea, and it became blood as of a dead *man;* and every living creature in the sea died.

4 Then the third angel poured out his bowl on the rivers and springs of water, and they became blood. 5 And I heard the angel of the waters saying:

"You are righteous, O Lord,[a]
The One who is and who was
    and who is to be,[b]
Because You have judged these
    things.
6   For they have shed the blood
        of saints and prophets,
    And You have given them
        blood to drink.
    For[a] it is their just due."

7 And I heard another from[a] the altar saying, "Even so, Lord God Almighty, true and righteous *are* Your judgments."

8 Then the fourth angel poured out his bowl on the sun, and power was given to him to scorch men with fire. 9 And men were scorched with great heat, and they blasphemed the name of God who has power over these plagues; and they did not repent and give Him glory.

10 Then the fifth angel poured out his bowl on the throne of the beast, and his kingdom became full of darkness; and they gnawed their tongues because of the pain. 11 They blasphemed the God of heaven because of their pains and their sores, and did not repent of their deeds.

12 Then the sixth angel poured out his bowl on the great river Euphrates, and its water was dried up, so that the way of the kings from the east might be prepared. 13 And I saw three unclean spirits like frogs *coming* out of the mouth of the dragon, out of the mouth of the beast, and out of the mouth of the false prophet. 14 For they are spirits of demons, performing signs, *which* go out to the kings of the earth and[a] of the whole world, to gather them to the battle of that great day of God Almighty.

15 "Behold, I am coming as a thief. Blessed *is* he who watches, and keeps his garments, lest he walk naked and they see his shame."

16 And they gathered them together to the place called in Hebrew, Armageddon.[a]

17 Then the seventh angel poured out his bowl into the air, and a loud voice came out of the temple of heaven, from the throne, saying, "It is done!" 18 And there were noises and thunderings and lightnings; and there was a great earthquake, such a mighty and great earthquake as had not occurred since men were on the earth. 19 Now the great city was divided into three parts, and the cities of the nations fell. And great Babylon was remembered before God, to give her the cup of the wine of the fierceness of His wrath. 20 Then every island fled away, and the mountains were not found. 21 And great hail from heaven fell upon men, *each hailstone* about the weight of a talent. Men blasphemed God because of the plague of the hail, since that plague was exceedingly great.

17 Then one of the seven angels who had the seven bowls came and talked with me, saying to me,[a] "Come, I will show you the judgment of the great harlot who sits on many waters, 2 with whom the kings of the earth committed fornication, and the inhabitants of the earth were made drunk with the wine of her fornication."

3 So he carried me away in the Spirit into the wilderness. And I saw a woman sitting on a scarlet beast *which was* full of names of blasphemy, having seven heads and ten horns. 4 The woman was arrayed in purple and scarlet, and adorned with gold and precious stones and pearls, having in her hand a golden cup full

16:1 [a]NU-Text and M-Text read *seven bowls.*   16:5 [a]NU-Text and M-Text omit *O Lord.*   [b]NU-Text and M-Text read *who was, the Holy One.*   16:6 [a]NU-Text and M-Text omit *For.*   16:7 [a]NU-Text and M-Text omit *another from.*   16:14 [a]NU-Text and M-Text omit *of the earth and.*   16:16 [a]M-Text reads *Megiddo.*   17:1 [a]NU-Text and M-Text omit *to me.*

*W*ords are not necessary between friends. True friends need no audible speech. Their communication is a quick glance, a soft pat on the shoulder, a concerned look when all is not well.

of abominations and the filthiness of her fornication.*a* 5 And on her forehead a name *was* written:

MYSTERY,
BABYLON THE GREAT,
THE MOTHER OF HARLOTS
AND OF THE ABOMINATIONS
OF THE EARTH.

6 I saw the woman, drunk with the blood of the saints and with the blood of the martyrs of Jesus. And when I saw her, I marveled with great amazement.

7 But the angel said to me, "Why did you marvel? I will tell you the mystery of the woman and of the beast that carries her, which has the seven heads and the ten horns. 8 The beast that you saw was, and is not, and will ascend out of the bottomless pit and go to perdition. And those who dwell on the earth will marvel, whose names are not written in the Book of Life from the foundation of the world, when they see the beast that was, and is not, and yet is.*a*

9 "Here *is* the mind which has wisdom: The seven heads are seven mountains on which the woman sits. 10 There are also seven kings. Five have fallen, one is, *and* the other has not yet come. And when he comes, he must continue a short time. 11 The beast that was, and is not, is himself also the eighth, and is of the seven, and is going to perdition.

12 "The ten horns which you saw are ten kings who have received no kingdom as yet, but they receive authority for one hour as kings with the beast. 13 These are of one mind, and they will give their power and authority to the beast. 14 These will make war with the Lamb, and the Lamb will overcome them, for He is Lord of lords and King of kings; and those *who are* with Him *are* called, chosen, and faithful."

15 Then he said to me, "The waters which you saw, where the harlot sits, are peoples, multitudes, nations, and tongues. 16 And the ten horns which you saw on*a* the beast, these will hate the harlot, make her desolate and

naked, eat her flesh and burn her with fire. 17 For God has put it into their hearts to fulfill His purpose, to be of one mind, and to give their kingdom to the beast, until the words of God are fulfilled. 18 And the woman whom you saw is that great city which reigns over the kings of the earth."

18 After these things I saw another angel coming down from heaven, having great authority, and the earth was illuminated with his glory. 2 And he cried mightily*a* with a loud voice, saying, "Babylon the great is fallen, is fallen, and has become a dwelling place of demons, a prison for every foul spirit, and a cage for every unclean and hated bird! 3 For all the nations have drunk of the wine of the wrath of her fornication, the kings of the earth have committed fornication with her, and the merchants of the earth have become rich through the abundance of her luxury."

4 And I heard another voice from heaven saying, "Come out of her, my people, lest you share in her sins, and lest you receive of her plagues. 5 For her sins have reached*a* to heaven, and God has remembered her iniquities. 6 Render to her just as she rendered to you,*a* and repay her double according to her works; in the cup which she has mixed, mix double for her. 7 In the measure that she glorified herself and lived luxuriously, in the same measure give her torment and sorrow; for she says in her heart, 'I sit *as* queen, and am no widow, and will not see sorrow.' 8 Therefore her plagues will come in one day—death and mourning and famine. And she will be utterly burned with fire, for strong *is* the Lord God who judges*a* her.

9 "The kings of the earth who committed fornication and lived luxuriously with her will weep and lament for her, when they see the smoke of her burning, 10 standing at a distance for fear of her torment, saying, 'Alas, alas, that great city Babylon, that mighty city! For in one hour your judgment has come.'

17:4 *a*M-Text reads *the filthiness of the fornication of the earth.*   17:8 *a*NU-Text and M-Text read *and shall be present.*   17:16 *a*NU-Text and M-Text read *saw, and the beast.*   18:2 *a*NU-Text and M-Text omit *mightily.*   18:5 *a*NU-Text and M-Text read *have been heaped up.*   18:6 *a*NU-Text and M-Text omit *to you.*   18:8 *a*NU-Text and M-Text read *has judged.*

Gospel
Pearls

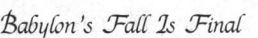

11 "And the merchants of the earth will weep and mourn over her, for no one buys their merchandise anymore: 12 merchandise of gold and silver, precious stones and pearls, fine linen and purple, silk and scarlet, every kind of citron wood, every kind of object of ivory, every kind of object of most precious wood, bronze, iron, and marble; 13 and cinnamon and incense, fragrant oil and frankincense, wine and oil, fine flour and wheat, cattle and sheep, horses and chariots, and bodies and souls of men. 14 The fruit that your soul longed for has gone from you, and all the things which are rich and splendid have gone from you,*a* and you shall find them no more at all. 15 The merchants of these things, who became rich by her, will stand at a distance for fear of her torment, weeping and wailing, 16 and saying, 'Alas, alas, that great city that was clothed in fine linen, purple, and scarlet, and adorned with gold and precious stones and pearls! 17 For in one hour such great riches came to nothing.' Every shipmaster, all who travel by ship, sailors, and as many as trade on the sea, stood at a distance 18 and cried out when they saw the smoke of her burning, saying, 'What *is* like this great city?'

19 "They threw dust on their heads and cried out, weeping and wailing, and saying, 'Alas, alas, that great city, in which all who had ships on the sea became rich by her wealth! For in one hour she is made desolate.'

20 "Rejoice over her, O heaven, and *you* holy apostles*a* and prophets, for God has avenged you on her!"

21 Then a mighty angel took up a stone like a great millstone and threw *it* into the sea, saying, "Thus with violence the great city Babylon shall be thrown down, and shall not be found anymore. 22 The sound of harpists, musicians, flutists, and trumpeters shall not be heard in you anymore. No craftsman of any craft shall be found in you anymore, and the sound of a millstone shall not be heard in you anymore. 23 The light of a lamp shall not shine in you anymore, and the voice of bridegroom and bride shall not be heard in you

anymore. For your merchants were the great men of the earth, for by your sorcery all the nations were deceived. 24 And in her was found the blood of prophets and saints, and of all who were slain on the earth."

19 After these things I heard*a* a loud voice of a great multitude in heaven, saying, "Alleluia! Salvation and glory and honor and power *belong* to the Lord*b* our God! 2 For true and righteous *are* His judgments, because He has judged the great harlot who corrupted the earth with her fornication; and He has avenged on her the blood of His servants *shed* by her." 3 Again they said, "Alleluia! Her smoke rises up forever and ever!" 4 And the twenty-four elders and the four living creatures fell down and worshiped God who sat on the throne, saying, "Amen! Alleluia!" 5 Then a voice came from the throne, saying, "Praise our God, all you His servants and those who fear Him, both*a* small and great!"

6 And I heard, as it were, the voice of a great multitude, as the sound of many waters and as the sound of mighty thunderings, saying, "Alleluia! For the*a* Lord God Omnipotent reigns! 7 Let us be glad and rejoice and give Him glory, for the marriage of the Lamb has come, and His wife has made herself ready." 8 And to her it was granted to be arrayed in fine linen, clean and bright, for the fine linen is the righteous acts of the saints.

9 Then he said to me, "Write: 'Blessed *are* those who are called to the marriage supper of the Lamb!'" And he said to me, "These are the true sayings of God." 10 And I fell at his feet to worship him. But he said to me, "See *that you do* not *do that!* I am your fellow servant, and of your brethren who have the testimony of Jesus. Worship God! For the testimony of Jesus is the spirit of prophecy."

11 Now I saw heaven opened, and behold, a white horse. And He who sat on him *was* called Faithful and True, and in righteousness He judges and makes war. 12 His eyes *were* like a flame of fire, and on His head *were*

18:14 *a*NU-Text and M-Text read *been lost to you.* 18:20 *a*NU-Text and M-Text read *saints and apostles.* 19:1 *a*NU-Text and M-Text add *something like.* *b*NU-Text and M-Text omit *the Lord.* 19:5 *a*NU-Text and M-Text omit *both.* 19:6 *a*NU-Text and M-Text read *our.*

---

*M*any wealthy people are impoverished. They possess things, but they may lack camaraderie. The greatest blessings—like the gift of friendship—are often inexpensive, yet provide precious memories that enrich all of life.

many crowns. He had[a] a name written that no one knew except Himself. 13 He *was* clothed with a robe dipped in blood, and His name is called The Word of God. 14 And the armies in heaven, clothed in fine linen, white and clean,[a] followed Him on white horses. 15 Now out of His mouth goes a sharp[a] sword, that with it He should strike the nations. And He Himself will rule them with a rod of iron. He Himself treads the winepress of the fierceness and wrath of Almighty God. 16 And He has on *His* robe and on His thigh a name written:

KING OF KINGS AND LORD OF LORDS.

17 Then I saw an angel standing in the sun; and he cried with a loud voice, saying to all the birds that fly in the midst of heaven, "Come and gather together for the supper of the great God,[a] 18 that you may eat the flesh of kings, the flesh of captains, the flesh of mighty men, the flesh of horses and of those who sit on them, and the flesh of all *people,* free[a] and slave, both small and great."

19 And I saw the beast, the kings of the earth, and their armies, gathered together to make war against Him who sat on the horse and against His army. 20 Then the beast was captured, and with him the false prophet who worked signs in his presence, by which he deceived those who received the mark of the beast and those who worshiped his image. These two were cast alive into the lake of fire burning with brimstone. 21 And the rest were killed with the sword which proceeded from the mouth of Him who sat on the horse. And all the birds were filled with their flesh.

20 Then I saw an angel coming down from heaven, having the key to the bottomless pit and a great chain in his hand. 2 He laid hold of the dragon, that serpent of old, who is *the* Devil and Satan, and bound him for a thousand years; 3 and he cast him into the bottomless pit, and shut him up, and set a seal on him, so that he should deceive the nations no more till the thousand years were finished. But after these things he must be released for a little while.

4 And I saw thrones, and they sat on them, and judgment was committed to them. Then *I saw* the souls of those who had been beheaded for their witness to Jesus and for the word of God, who had not worshiped the beast or his image, and had not received *his* mark on their foreheads or on their hands. And they lived and reigned with Christ for a[a] thousand years. 5 But the rest of the dead did not live again until the thousand years were finished. This *is* the first resurrection. 6 Blessed and holy *is* he who has part in the first resurrection. Over such the second death has no power, but they shall be priests of God and of Christ, and shall reign with Him a thousand years.

7 Now when the thousand years have expired, Satan will be released from his prison 8 and will go out to deceive the nations which are in the four corners of the earth, Gog and Magog, to gather them together to battle, whose number *is* as the sand of the sea. 9 They went up on the breadth of the earth and surrounded the camp of the saints and the beloved city. And fire came down from God out of heaven and devoured them. 10 The devil, who deceived them, was cast into the lake of fire and brimstone where[a] the beast and the false prophet *are.* And they will be tormented day and night forever and ever.

11 Then I saw a great white throne and Him who sat on it, from whose face the earth and the heaven fled away. And there was found no place for them. 12 And I saw the dead, small and great, standing before God,[a] and books were opened. And another book was opened, which is *the Book* of Life. And the dead were judged according to their works, by the things which were written in the books. 13 The sea gave up the dead who were in it, and Death and Hades delivered up the dead who were in them. And they were judged, each

19:12 [a]M-Text adds *names written, and.*   19:14 [a]NU-Text and M-Text read *pure white linen.*
19:15 [a]M-Text adds *two-edged.*   19:17 [a]NU-Text and M-Text read *the great supper of God.*
19:18 [a]NU-Text and M-Text read *both free.*   20:4 [a]M-Text reads *the.*   20:10 [a]NU-Text and M-Text add *also.*   20:12 [a]NU-Text and M-Text read *the throne.*

Gospel Pearls

one according to his works.
14 Then Death and Hades were cast into the lake of fire. This is the second death.ᵃ 15 And anyone not found written in the Book of Life was cast into the lake of fire.

21 Now I saw a new heaven and a new earth, for the first heaven and the first earth had passed away. Also there was no more sea. 2 Then I, John,ᵃ saw the holy city, New Jerusalem, coming down out of heaven from God, prepared as a bride adorned for her husband. 3 And I heard a loud voice from heaven saying, "Behold, the tabernacle of God *is* with men, and He will dwell with them, and they shall be His people. God Himself will be with them *and be* their God. 4 And God will wipe away every tear from their eyes; there shall be no more death, nor sorrow, nor crying. There shall be no more pain, for the former things have passed away."

5 Then He who sat on the throne said, "Behold, I make all things new." And He said to me,ᵃ "Write, for these words are true and faithful."

6 And He said to me, "It is done!ᵃ I am the Alpha and the Omega, the Beginning and the End. I will give of the fountain of the water of life freely to him who thirsts. 7 He who overcomes shall inherit all things,ᵃ and I will be his God and he shall be My son. 8 But the cowardly, unbelieving,ᵃ abominable, murderers, sexually immoral, sorcerers, idolaters, and all liars shall have their part in the lake which burns with fire and brimstone, which is the second death."

9 Then one of the seven angels who had the seven bowls filled with the seven last plagues came to meᵃ and talked with me, saying, "Come, I will show you the bride, the Lamb's wife."ᵇ 10 And he carried me away in the Spirit to a great and high mountain, and showed me the great city, the holyᵃ Jerusalem, descending out of heaven from God, 11 having the glory of God. Her light *was* like a most precious stone, like a jasper stone, clear as crystal. 12 Also she had a great and high wall with twelve gates, and twelve angels at the gates, and names written on them, which are *the names* of the twelve tribes of the children of Israel: 13 three gates on the east, three gates on the north, three gates on the south, and three gates on the west.

14 Now the wall of the city had twelve foundations, and on them were the namesᵃ of the twelve apostles of the Lamb. 15 And he who talked with me had a gold reed to measure the city, its gates, and its wall. 16 The city is laid out as a square; its length is as great as its breadth. And he measured the city with the reed: twelve thousand furlongs. Its length, breadth, and height are equal. 17 Then he measured its wall: one hundred *and* forty-four cubits, *according* to the measure of a man, that is, of an angel. 18 The construction of its wall was *of* jasper; and the city *was* pure gold, like clear glass. 19 The foundations of the wall of the city *were* adorned with all kinds of precious stones: the first foundation *was* jasper, the second sapphire, the third chalcedony, the fourth emerald, 20 the fifth sardonyx, the sixth sardius, the seventh chrysolite, the eighth beryl, the ninth topaz, the tenth chrysoprase, the eleventh jacinth, and the twelfth amethyst. 21 The twelve gates *were* twelve pearls: each individual gate was of one pearl. And the street of the city *was* pure gold, like transparent glass.

22 But I saw no temple in it, for the Lord God Almighty and the Lamb are its temple. 23 The city had no need of the sun or of the moon to shine in it,ᵃ for the gloryᵇ of God illuminated it. The Lamb *is* its light. 24 And the nations of those who are savedᵃ shall walk in its light, and the kings of the earth bring their glory and honor into it.ᵇ 25 Its gates shall not be shut at all by day (there shall be no night there). 26 And they shall

20:14 ᵃNU-Text and M-Text add *the lake of fire.*   21:2 ᵃNU-Text and M-Text omit *John.*
21:5 ᵃNU-Text and M-Text omit *to me.*   21:6 ᵃM-Text omits *It is done.*   21:7 ᵃM-Text reads *overcomes,*
I shall give him these things.   21:8 ᵃM-Text adds *and sinners.*   21:9 ᵃNU-Text and M-Text omit *to*
me.   ᵇM-Text reads *I will show you the woman, the Lamb's bride.*   21:10 ᵃNU-Text and M-Text omit
the great and read *the holy city, Jerusalem.*   21:14 ᵃNU-Text and M-Text read *twelve names.*
21:23 ᵃNU-Text and M-Text omit *in it.*   ᵇM-Text reads *the very glory.*   21:24 ᵃNU-Text and M-Text omit
of those who are saved.   ᵇM-Text reads *the glory and honor of the nations to Him.*

Are you surrounded—by coworkers and even family members—yet feel alone? Have you become a professional actor on the stage of life, not allowing anyone to get close, lest you be disappointed again? Dare to be transparent. Love is worth the risk.

Arise!

Revelation 21:3, 4

Many women have been through so much that they exist like empty houses on crowded streets. They are standing amid the activity of life, but there is no light in them. Oh, yes, their exteriors are beautiful, but there is a strange feeling of vacancy that keeps real beauty from shining through. Some may not notice, but a discerning eye cannot help but see the evidence of a deserted heart and a forsaken smile.

It is to these haunted houses I write. These are the women who have ceased to celebrate. They have lost the iridescent shimmer that suggests life and love. They have stopped lovemaking and life-making. They are just holding on. They have fallen into the lethargy of those who aren't expecting company. But God says, "Arise." Touch yourself and know in your heart, Jesus is coming!

Some might say, "I am too old." Others might say, "It is too late." Still others might say, "I am too busy." Some would even dare to suggest that they are too spiritual. But I declare to you that when God kissed the first lump of clay and breathed into that muddy shell the breath of life, He spoke life, and the abstract became vibrant and alive. The Master's kiss turned a ceramic into a personality. He breathed upon the vessel, and in one breath He blew blood and bone, thought and idea, attraction and affection, romance and revival. He blew so hard that He blew reproduction into the frame. He blew generations of destiny into Adam. You and I are still sucking in that breath and feeling it flood our frame with life. We are alive, the greatest computer ever witnessed. What a kiss!

These are the lips of a loving Master whose caress rebukes death. The same lips that blew upon the clay spoke to the daughter of Jairus, the ruler of the synagogue. I call Him my Friend. He is the Friend of every father who has a daughter he loves and yet cannot always affect. He can do what men cannot do. He can resurrect the cold places in the heart of the woman whose love and life have been rocked to sleep in a cradle of despair. I commend you—and all the women of the world who have ever fallen asleep in the middle of life—to Him.

bring the glory and the honor of the nations into it.*ᵃ* 27 But there shall by no means enter it anything that defiles, or causes*ᵃ* an abomination or a lie, but only those who are written in the Lamb's Book of Life.

22 And he showed me a pure*ᵃ* river of water of life, clear as crystal, proceeding from the throne of God and of the Lamb. 2 In the middle of its street, and on either side of the river, *was* the tree of life, which bore twelve fruits, each *tree* yielding its fruit every month. The leaves of the tree *were* for the healing of the nations. 3 And there shall be no more curse, but the throne of God and of the Lamb shall be in it, and His servants shall serve Him. 4 They shall see His face, and His name *shall be* on their foreheads. 5 There shall be no night there: They need no lamp nor light of the sun, for the Lord God gives them light. And they shall reign forever and ever.

6 Then he said to me, "These words *are* faithful and true." And the Lord God of the holy*ᵃ* prophets sent His angel to show His servants the things which must shortly take place.

7 "Behold, I am coming quickly! Blessed *is* he who keeps the words of the prophecy of this book."

8 Now I, John, saw and heard*ᵃ* these things. And when I heard and saw, I fell down to worship before the feet of the angel who showed me these things.

9 Then he said to me, "See *that you do* not *do that.* For*ᵃ* I am your fellow servant, and of your brethren the prophets, and of those who keep the words of this book. Worship God."

10 And he said to me, "Do not seal the words of the prophecy of this book, for the time is at hand. 11 He who is unjust, let him be unjust still; he who is filthy, let him be filthy still; he who is righteous, let him be righteous*ᵃ* still; he who is holy, let him be holy still."

12 "And behold, I am coming quickly, and My reward *is* with Me, to give to every one according to his work. 13 I am the Alpha and the Omega, *the* Beginning and *the* End, the First and the Last."*ᵃ*

14 Blessed *are* those who do His commandments,*ᵃ* that they may have the right to the tree of life, and may enter through the gates into the city. 15 But*ᵃ* outside *are* dogs and sorcerers and sexually immoral and murderers and idolaters, and whoever loves and practices a lie.

16 "I, Jesus, have sent My angel to testify to you these things in the churches. I am the Root and the Offspring of David, the Bright and Morning Star."

17 And the Spirit and the bride say, "Come!" And let him who hears say, "Come!" And let him who thirsts come. Whoever desires, let him take the water of life freely.

18 For*ᵃ* I testify to everyone who hears the words of the prophecy of this book: If anyone adds to these things, God will add*ᵇ* to him the plagues that are written in this book; 19 and if anyone takes away from the words of the book of this prophecy, God shall take away*ᵃ* his part from the Book*ᵇ* of Life, from the holy city, and *from* the things which are written in this book.

20 He who testifies to these things says, "Surely I am coming quickly." Amen. Even so, come, Lord Jesus!

21 The grace of our Lord Jesus Christ *be* with you all.*ᵃ* Amen.

If you understand anything about God, then you know that He can bring direction out of rejection. It was Judas's ministry that brought Christ to the Cross. Although this betrayal was painful, it was an essential part of His destiny.

About the
New King James Version

Purpose

In the preface to the 1611 edition, the translators of the Authorized Version, known popularly as the King James Bible, state that it was not their purpose "to make a new translation . . . but to make a good one better." Indebted to the earlier work of William Tyndale and others, they saw their best contribution to consist in revising and enhancing the excellence of the English versions which had sprung from the Reformation of the sixteenth century. In harmony with the purpose of the King James scholars, the translators and editors of the present work have not pursued a goal of innovation. They have perceived the Holy Bible, New King James Version, as a continuation of the labors of the earlier translators, thus unlocking for today's readers the spiritual treasures found especially in the Authorized Version of the Holy Scriptures.

A Living Legacy

For nearly four hundred years, and throughout several revisions of its English form, the King James Bible has been deeply revered among the English-speaking peoples of the world. The precision of translation for which it is historically renowned, and its majesty of style, have enabled that monumental version of the Word of God to become the mainspring of the religion, language, and legal foundations of our civilization.

Complete Equivalence in Translation

Where new translation has been necessary in the New King James Version, the most complete representation of the original has been rendered by considering the history of usage and etymology of words in their contexts. This principle of complete equivalence seeks to preserve *all* of the information in the text, while presenting it in good literary form. Dynamic equivalence, a recent procedure in Bible translation, commonly results in paraphrasing where a more literal rendering is needed to reflect a specific and vital sense. For example, complete equivalence truly renders the original text in expressions such as "lifted her voice and wept" (Gen. 21:16); "I gave you cleanness of teeth" (Amos 4:6); "Jesus met them, saying, 'Rejoice!'" (Matt. 28:9); and "'Woman, what does your concern have to do with Me?'" (John 2:4). Complete equivalence translates fully, in order to provide an English text that is both accurate and readable.

The Style

Students of the Bible applaud the timeless devotional character of our historic Bible. Yet it is also universally understood that our language, like all living languages, has undergone profound change since 1611. Subsequent revisions of the King James Bible have sought to keep abreast of changes in English speech. The present work is a further step toward this objective. Where obsolescence and other reading difficulties exist, present-day vocabulary, punctuation, and grammar have been carefully integrated. Words representing ancient objects, such as *chariot* and *phylactery*, have no modern substitutes and are therefore retained.

A special feature of the New King James Version is its conformity to the thought flow of the 1611 Bible. The reader discovers that the sequence and selection of words, phrases, and clauses of the new edition, while much clearer, are so close to the traditional that there is remarkable ease in listening to the reading of either edition while following with the other.

In the discipline of translating biblical and other ancient languages, a standard method of transliteration, that is, the English spelling of untranslated words, such as names of persons and places, has never been commonly adopted. In keeping with the design of the present work, the King James spelling of untranslated words is retained, although made uniform throughout. For example, instead of the spellings *Isaiah* and *Elijah* in the Old Testament, and *Esaias* and *Elias* in the New Testament, *Isaiah* and *Elijah* now appear in both Testaments.

King James doctrinal and theological terms, for example, *propitiation*, *justification*, and *sanctification*, are generally familiar to English-speaking peoples.

Such terms have been retained except where the original language indicates need for a more precise translation.

Readers of the Authorized Version will immediately be struck by the absence of several pronouns: *thee, thou,* and *ye* are replaced by the simple *you,* while *your* and *yours* are substituted for *thy* and *thine* as applicable. *Thee, thou, thy* and *thine* were once forms of address to express a special relationship to human as well as divine persons. These pronouns are no longer part of our language. However, reverence for God in the present work is preserved by capitalizing pronouns, including *You, Your,* and *Yours,* which refer to Him. Additionally, capitalization of these pronouns benefits the reader by clearly distinguishing divine and human persons referred to in a passage. Without such capitalization the distinction is often obscure, because the antecedent of a pronoun is not always clear in the English translation.

In addition to the pronoun usages of the seventeenth century, the *-eth* and *-est* verb endings, so familiar in the earlier King James editions, are now obsolete. Unless a speaker is schooled in these verb endings, there is common difficulty in selecting the correct form to be used with a given subject of the verb in vocal prayer. That is, should we use *love, loveth,* or *lovest? do, doeth, doest,* or *dost? have, hath,* or *hast?* Because these forms are obsolete, contemporary English usage has been substituted for the previous verb endings.

In older editions of the King James Version, the frequency of the connective *and* far exceeded the limits of present English usage. Also, biblical linguists agree that the Hebrew and Greek original words for this conjunction may commonly be translated otherwise, depending on the immediate context. Therefore, instead of *and,* alternatives such as *also, but, however, now, so, then,* and *thus* are accordingly rendered in the present edition, when the original language permits.

The real character of the Authorized Version does not reside in its archaic pronouns or verbs or other grammatical forms of the seventeenth century, but rather in the care taken by its scholars to impart the letter and spirit of the original text in a majestic and reverent style.

The Format

The format of the New King James Version is designed to enhance the vividness and devotional quality of the Holy Scriptures:

* Words or phrases in *italics* indicate expressions in the original language which require clarification by additional English words, as also done throughout the history of the King James Bible.
* *Oblique type* in the New Testament indicates a quotation from the Old Testament.
* Poetry is structured as contemporary verse to reflect the poetic form and beauty of the passage in the original language.
* The covenant name of God was usually translated from the Hebrew as "LORD" or "GOD" (using capital letters as shown) in the King James Old Testament. This tradition is maintained. In the present edition the name is so capitalized whenever the covenant name is quoted in the New Testament from a passage in the Old Testament.
* Significant explanatory notes, alternate translations, and cross-references, as well as New Testament citations of Old Testament passages, are supplied in footnotes.

The Old Testament Text

The Hebrew Bible has come down to us through the scrupulous care of ancient scribes who copied the original text in successive generations. By the sixth century A.D. the scribes were succeeded by a group known as the Masoretes, who continued to preserve the sacred Scriptures for another five hundred years in a form known as the Masoretic Text. Babylonia, Palestine, and Tiberias were the main centers of Masoretic activity; but by the tenth century A.D. the Masoretes of Tiberias, led by the family of ben Asher, gained the ascendancy. Through subsequent editions, the ben Asher text became in the twelfth century the only recognized form of the Hebrew Scriptures.

Daniel Bomberg printed the first Rabbinic Bible in 1516–17; that work was followed in 1524–25 by a second edition prepared by Jacob ben Chayyim and also published by Bomberg. The text of ben Chayyim was adopted in most subsequent Hebrew Bibles, including those used by the King James translators. The ben Chayyim text was also used for the first two editions of Rudolph Kittel's *Biblia Hebraica* of 1906 and 1912. In 1937 Paul Kahle published a third edition of *Biblia Hebraica*. This edition was based on the oldest dated manuscript of the ben Asher text, the Leningrad Manuscript B19a (A.D. 1008), which Kahle regarded as superior to that used by ben Chayyim.

For the New King James Version the text used was the 1967/1977 Stuttgart edition of the *Biblia Hebraica*, with frequent comparisons being made with the Bomberg edition of 1524–25. The Septuagint (Greek) Version of the Old Testament and the Latin Vulgate also were consulted. In addition to referring to a variety of ancient versions of the Hebrew Scriptures, the New King James Version draws on the resources of relevant manuscripts from the Dead Sea caves. In the few places where the Hebrew was so obscure that the 1611 King James was compelled to follow one of the versions, but where information is now available to resolve the problems, the New King James Version follows the Hebrew text. Significant variations are recorded in the footnotes.

The New Testament Text

There is more manuscript support for the New Testament than for any other body of ancient literature. Over five thousand Greek, eight thousand Latin, and many more manuscripts in other languages attest the integrity of the New Testament. There is only one basic New Testament used by Protestants, Roman Catholics, and Orthodox, by conservatives and liberals. Minor variations in hand copying have appeared through the centuries, before mechanical printing began about A.D. 1450.

Some variations exist in the spelling of Greek words, in word order, and in similar details. These ordinarily do not show up in translation and do not affect the sense of the text in any way.

Other manuscript differences such as omission or inclusion of a word or a clause, and two paragraphs in the Gospels, should not overshadow the overwhelming degree of *agreement* which exists among the ancient records. Bible readers may be assured that the most im-

portant differences in English New Testaments of today are due, not to manuscript divergence, but to the way in which translators view the task of translation: How literally should the text be rendered? How does the translator view the matter of biblical inspiration? Does the translator adopt a paraphrase when a literal rendering would be quite clear and more to the point? The New King James Version follows the historic precedent of the Authorized Version in maintaining a literal approach to translation, except where the idiom of the original language cannot be translated directly into our tongue.

The King James New Testament was based on the traditional text of the Greek-speaking churches, first published in 1516, and later called the Textus Receptus or Received Text. Although based on the relatively few available manuscripts, these were representative of many more which existed at the time but only became known later. In the late nineteenth century, B. Westcott and F. Hort taught that this text had been officially edited by the fourth-century church, but a total lack of historical evidence for this event has forced a revision of the theory. It is now widely held that the Byzantine Text that largely supports the Textus Receptus has as much right as the Alexandrian or any other tradition to be weighed in determining the text of the New Testament. Those readings in the Textus Receptus which have weak support are indicated in the footnotes as being opposed by both Critical and Majority Texts (see "Footnotes").

Since the 1880s most contemporary translations of the New Testament have relied upon a relatively few manuscripts discovered chiefly in the late nineteenth and early twentieth centuries. Such translations depend primarily on two manuscripts, Codex Vaticanus and Codex Sinaiticus, because of their greater age. The Greek text obtained by using these sources and the related papyri (our most ancient manuscripts) is known as the Alexandrian Text. However, some scholars have grounds for doubting the faithfulness of Vaticanus and Sinaiticus, since they often disagree with one another, and Sinaiticus exhibits excessive omission.

A third viewpoint of New Testament scholarship holds that the best text is based on the consensus of the majority of existing Greek manuscripts. This text is called the Majority Text. Most of these manuscripts are in substantial agreement. Even though many are late, and none is earlier than the fifth century, usually their readings are verified by papyri, ancient versions, quotations from the early church fathers, or a combination of these. The Majority Text is similar to the Textus Receptus, but it corrects those readings which have little or no support in the Greek manuscript tradition.

Today, scholars agree that the science of New Testament textual criticism is in a state of flux. Very few scholars still favor the Textus Receptus as such, and then often for its historical prestige as the text of Luther, Calvin, Tyndale, and the King James Version. For about a century most have followed a Critical Text (so called because it is edited according to specific principles of textual criticism) which depends heavily upon the Alexandrian type of text. More recently many have abandoned this Critical Text (which is quite similar to the one edited by Westcott and Hort) for one that is more eclectic. Finally, a small but growing number of scholars prefer the Majority Text, which is close to the traditional text except in the Revelation.

In light of these facts, and also because the New King James Version is the fifth revision of a historic document translated from specific Greek texts, the editors decided to retain the traditional text in the body of the New Testament and to indicate major Critical and Majority Text variant readings in the footnotes. Although these variations are duly indicated in the footnotes of the present edition, it is most important to emphasize that fully eighty-five percent of the New Testament text is the same in the Textus Receptus, the Alexandrian Text, and the Majority Text.

Footnotes

Significant explanatory notes, alternate translations, and cross-references, as well as New Testament citations of Old Testament passages, are supplied in footnotes to the text.

Important textual variants in the Old Testament are identified in a standard form.

The textual notes in the present edition of the New Testament make no evaluation of readings, but do clearly indicate the manuscript sources of readings. They objectively present the facts without such tendentious remarks as "the best manuscripts omit" or "the most reliable manuscripts read." Such notes are value judgments that differ according to varying viewpoints on the text. By giving a clearly defined set of variants the New King James Version benefits readers of all textual persuasions.

Where significant variations occur in the New Testament Greek manuscripts, textual notes are classified as follows:

1. NU-Text
   These variations from the traditional text generally represent the Alexandrian or Egyptian type of text described previously in "The New Testament Text." They are found in the Critical Text published in the Twenty-sixth edition of the Nestle-Aland Greek New Testament (N) and in the United Bible Societies' third edition (U), hence the acronym, "NU-text."

2. M-Text
   This symbol indicates points of variation in the Majority Text from the traditional text, as also previously discussed in "The New Testament Text." It should be noted that M stands for whatever reading is printed in the published *Greek New Testament According to the Majority Text*, whether supported by overwhelming, strong, or only a divided majority textual tradition.

The textual notes reflect the scholarship of the past 150 years and will assist the reader to observe the variations between the different manuscript traditions of the New Testament. Such information is generally not available in English translations of the New Testament.

CONCORDANCE

A

ABASED
I know how to be *a* .....Phil 4:12

ABBA
And He said, "A ...... Mark 14:36
whom we cry out, "A ... Rom 8:15

ABHOR
Therefore I *a* myself .....Job 42:6

ABHORRED
a His own inheritance ..Ps 106:40

ABIDE
the Most High Shall *a* ....Ps 91:1
Him, "If you *a* ....John 8:31
"If you *a* in Me ....John 15:7
a in My love ....John 15:9

ABIDES
He who *a* in Me ....John 15:5
will of God *a* forever .1 John 2:17

ABIDING
not have His word *a* ....John 5:38

ABILITY
to his own *a* ....Matt 25:15
a which God supplies ..1 Pet 4:11

ABLE
shall give as he is *a* ..Deut 16:17
whom we serve is *a* .....Dan 3:17
God is *a* to raise up .....Matt 3:9
fear Him who is *a* .....Matt 10:28
you *a* to drink the .....Matt 20:22
that He is *a* ....2 Tim 1:12
learning and never *a* ..2 Tim 3:7
that God was *a* to .....Heb 11:19

ABOLISHED
having *a* in His flesh ....Eph 2:15
Christ, who has *a* .....2 Tim 1:10

ABOMINABLE
deny Him, being *a* ...Titus 1:16
unbelieving, *a* ....Rev 21:8

ABOMINATION
Yes, seven are an *a* ..Prov 6:16
the scoffer is an *a* ...Prov 24:9
prayer is an *a* ....Prov 28:9
and place there the *a* ..Dan 11:31
the *a* of desolation ....Dan 12:11
the '*a* of desolation,' ..Matt 24:15

ABOMINATIONS
delights in their *a* ......Is 66:3
a golden cup full of *a* ....Rev 17:4

ABOUND
the offense might *a* .....Rom 5:20
sin that grace may *a* .....Rom 6:1
to make all grace *a* .....2 Cor 9:8
and I know how to *a* ....Phil 4:12

ABOUNDED
But where sin *a* ....Rom 5:20

ABOUNDING
immovable, always *a* .1 Cor 15:58

ABOVE
that is in heaven *a* ....Ex 20:4
A it stood seraphim ....Is 6:2
"He who comes from *a* . John 3:31
I am from *a* ....John 8:23
given you from *a* .....John 19:11
things which are *a* ....Col 3:1
perfect gift is from *a* ..James 1:17

ABSENT
in the body we are *a* ....2 Cor 5:6

ABSTAIN
we write to them to *a* ..Acts 15:20
A from every form ..1 Thess 5:22

ABUNDANCE
put in out of their *a* ...Mark 12:44
not consist in the *a* ...Luke 12:15

ABUNDANT
in labors more *a* ......2 Cor 11:23

ABUNDANTLY
a satisfied with the .....Ps 36:8
may have it more *a* ...John 10:10
to do exceedingly *a* .....Eph 3:20

ACCEPT
offering, I will not *a* ....Jer 14:12
Should I *a* this from .....Mal 1:13

ACCEPTABLE
a time I have heard .....Is 49:8
proclaim the *a* year ....Is 61:2
proclaim the a year ....Luke 4:19
is that good and *a* ......Rom 12:2

ACCEPTABLY
we may serve God *a* ...Heb 12:28

ACCEPTED
Behold, now is the *a* ....2 Cor 6:2
which He made us *a* .....Eph 1:6

ACCESS
whom also we have *a* ....Rom 5:2

ACCOMPLISHED
all things were now *a* .John 19:28

ACCORD
continued with one *a* ...Acts 1:14

ACCOUNT
they will give *a* ....Matt 12:36
put that on my *a* ....Philem 18

ACCOUNTED
in the LORD, and He *a* ...Gen 15:6
his faith is *a* ....Rom 4:5
God, and it was a ....Gal 3:6
God, and it was a .....James 2:23

ACCURSED
not know the law is *a* ..John 7:49
of God calls Jesus *a* ...1 Cor 12:3
to you, let him be *a* ......Gal 1:8

ACCUSATION
over His head the *a* ....Matt 27:37
they might find an *a* ....Luke 6:7

ACCUSE
they began to *a* Him ...Luke 23:2

ACCUSED
while He was being *a* ..Matt 27:12

ACCUSER
a of our brethren ....Rev 12:10

ACCUSING
their thoughts *a* ....Rom 2:15

ACKNOWLEDGE
a my transgressions ......Ps 51:3
In all your ways *a* ....Prov 3:6

ACKNOWLEDGES
a the Son has the .....1 John 2:23

ACQUAINT
a yourself with Him ....Job 22:21

ACQUAINTED
A Man of sorrows and *a* ...Is 53:3

ACQUIT
at all *a* the wicked ....Nah 1:3

ACT
in the very *a* ....John 8:4

ACTIONS
by Him *a* are weighed ..1 Sam 2:3

ACTS
of Your awesome *a* ......Ps 145:6

ADD
Do not *a* to His words ..Prov 30:6

ADDED
And the Lord *a* to the ...Acts 2:47
It was *a* because of ......Gal 3:19

ADMONISH
a him as a ....2 Thess 3:15

ADMONITION
written for our *a* .....1 Cor 10:11
in the training and *a* .....Eph 6:4

ADOPTION
the Spirit of *a* ....Rom 8:15
waiting for the *a* ....Rom 8:23
to whom pertain the *a* ...Rom 9:4

ADORN
also, that the women *a* ..1 Tim 2:9

ADORNED
God also *a* themselves ...1 Pet 3:5
prepared as a bride *a* ....Rev 21:2

ADRIFT
A among the dead ....Ps 88:5

ADULTERER
The eye of the *a* ....Job 24:15

ADULTERERS
nor idolaters, nor *a* .....1 Cor 6:9
a God will judge ....Heb 13:4

ADULTEROUS
a generation ....Matt 12:39

ADULTERY
You shall not commit *a* ..Ex 20:14
already committed *a* ....Matt 5:28

ADVANTAGE

is divorced commits *a* ..Matt 5:32
another commits *a* ....Mark 10:11
those who commit *a* ....Rev 2:22

ADVANTAGE

a that I go away ....John 16:7
Satan should take *a* ...2 Cor 2:11

ADVERSARIES

and there are many *a* ..1 Cor 16:9
terrified by your *a* ......Phil 1:28

ADVERSARY

"Agree with your *a* ....Matt 5:25
opportunity to the *a* ...1 Tim 5:14
a the devil walks ....1 Pet 5:8

ADVERSITY

I shall never be in *a* ......Ps 10:6
the day of *a* consider ....Eccl 7:14

ADVICE

in this I give my *a* .....2 Cor 8:10

ADVOCATE

sins, we have an *A* ....1 John 2:1

AFAR

and not a God *a* ....Jer 23:23
to you who were *a* ......Eph 2:17
having seen them *a* ....Heb 11:13

AFFAIRS

himself with the *a* ......2 Tim 2:4

AFFECTION

to his wife the *a* ....1 Cor 7:3

AFFECTIONATE

Be kindly *a* to one .....Rom 12:10

AFFIRM

you to *a* constantly ......Titus 3:8

AFFLICT

a Your heritage ....Ps 94:5
For He does not *a* ......Lam 3:33

AFFLICTED

To him who is *a* ....Job 6:14
hears the cry of the *a* ...Job 34:28
days of the *a* are evil ..Prov 15:15
Smitten by God, and *a* ....Is 53:4
"O you *a* one ....Is 54:11
being destitute, *a* ......Heb 11:37

AFFLICTING

A the just and taking ..Amos 5:12

AFFLICTION

is, the bread of *a* ....Deut 16:3
a take hold of me ......Job 30:16
and it is an evil *a* ....Eccl 6:2
For our light *a* ....2 Cor 4:17
supposing to add *a* ......Phil 1:16

AFRAID

garden, and I was *a* .....Gen 3:10
saying, "Do not be *a* ....Gen 15:1
none will make you *a* ....Lev 26:6
ungodliness made me *a* ...Ps 18:4
Whenever I am *a* ....Ps 56:3
one will make them *a* .....Is 17:2
do not be *a* ....Matt 14:27
if you do evil, be *a* .....Rom 13:4
do good and are not *a* ...1 Pet 3:6

AFTERWARD

a receive me to glory ...Ps 73:24
you shall follow Me *a* .John 13:36

AGAIN

'You must be born *a* ....John 3:7
having been born *a* ....1 Pet 1:23

AGAINST

come to 'set a man *a* ..Matt 10:35
or house divided *a* ....Matt 12:25
Me is *a* Me ....Matt 12:30
a the Spirit will not ....Matt 12:31
lifted up *his heel a* ....John 13:18
LORD and *a* His Christ ..Acts 4:26
to kick *a* the goads ......Acts 9:5
a the promises of God ...Gal 3:21
we do not wrestle *a* .....Eph 6:12
I have a few things *a* ....Rev 2:20

AGE

the grave at a full *a* .....Job 5:26
and in the *a* to come ..Mark 10:30

AGED

a one as Paul, the *a* .....Philem 9

AGES

ordained before the *a* ...1 Cor 2:7

AGONY

And being in *a* ....Luke 22:44

AGREE

that if two of you *a* ....Matt 18:19

AGREED

unless they are *a* ....Amos 3:3

AGREEMENT

what *a* has the temple .2 Cor 6:16

AIR

the birds of the *a* ....Gen 1:26
of the *a* have nests .....Luke 9:58
of the power of the *a* .....Eph 2:2
the Lord in the *a* ....1 Thess 4:17

ALIENATED

darkened, being *a* ....Eph 4:18
you, who once were *a* ....Col 1:21

ALIENS

A have devoured his .....Hos 7:9
Christ, being *a* ....Eph 2:12

ALIKE

esteems every day *a* ....Rom 14:5

ALIVE

I kill and I make *a* ....Deut 32:39
dead and is *a* ....Luke 15:24
presented Himself *a* .....Acts 1:3
indeed to sin, but *a* .....Rom 6:11
all shall be made *a* ...1 Cor 15:22
that we who are *a* ...1 Thess 4:15
and behold, I am *a* ......Rev 1:18
These two were cast *a* ..Rev 19:20

ALLELUIA

Again they said, "*A* .....Rev 19:3

ALLOW

a Your Holy One ....Ps 16:10
a My faithfulness ....Ps 89:33
a Your Holy One ....Acts 2:27

ALLURE

of emptiness, they *a* ....2 Pet 2:18

ALMOND

a tree blossoms ....Eccl 12:5

ALMOST

a persuade me to ......Acts 26:28

ALOES

of myrrh and *a* ....John 19:39

ALPHA

"I am the *A* and the ......Rev 1:8
"I am the *A* and the ....Rev 22:13

ALTAR

Then Noah built an *a* ...Gen 8:20
'An *a* of earth you ......Ex 20:24
it to you upon the *a* ....Lev 17:11
your gift to the *a* ....Matt 5:23
swears by the *a* ......Matt 23:18
I even found an *a* .....Acts 17:23
We have an *a* from .....Heb 13:10

ALTARS

Even Your *a*, O LORD .....Ps 84:3
and torn down Your a ..Rom 11:3

ALTERED

of His face was *a* .....Luke 9:29

ALWAYS

delight, Rejoicing *a* .....Prov 8:30
the poor with you *a* ...Matt 26:11
lo, I am with you *a* ...Matt 28:20
to them, that men *a* ....Luke 18:1
immovable, *a* ....1 Cor 15:58
Rejoice in the Lord *a* .....Phil 4:4
thus we shall *a* ......1 Thess 4:17
a be ready to give a ....1 Pet 3:15

AM

to Moses, "I *A* WHO I ....Ex 3:14
First and I *a* the Last ......Is 44:6
in My name, I *a* ....Matt 18:20
a the bread of life ......John 6:35
a the light of the ......John 8:12
I *a* from above ....John 8:23
Abraham was, I *A* .....John 8:58
"I *a* the door ....John 10:9
a the good shepherd ...John 10:11
a the resurrection ....John 11:25
to him, "I *a* the way ...John 14:6
of God I *a* what I *a* ...1 Cor 15:10

AMBASSADOR

for which I am an *a* .....Eph 6:20

AMBASSADORS

we are *a* for Christ ....2 Cor 5:20

AMBITION

Christ from selfish *a* ....Phil 1:16

AMEN

are Yes, and in Him *A* .2 Cor 1:20
creatures said, "*A* ....Rev 5:14

ANCHOR

hope we have as an *a* ...Heb 6:19

ANCIENT

Do not remove the *a* ..Prov 23:10
"until the *A* of Days ....Dan 7:22

ANGEL

"Behold, I send an *A* ....Ex 23:20
Manoah said to the *A* .Judg 13:17
the *A* of His Presence .....Is 63:9
things, behold, an *a* ....Matt 1:20
for an *a* of the Lord ....Matt 28:2
Then an *a* of the Lord ..Luke 1:11
And behold, an *a* ....Luke 2:9
a appeared to Him ....Luke 22:43
For an *a* went down at ...John 5:4
a has spoken to Him ..John 12:29
But at night an *a* ......Acts 5:19
A who appeared to him .Acts 7:35
immediately an *a* ......Acts 12:23
himself into an *a* .....2 Cor 11:14
even if we, or an *a* ....Gal 1:8
Then I saw a strong *a* ....Rev 5:2
Jesus, have sent My *a* .Rev 22:16

ANGELS

If He charges His *a* .....Job 4:18
lower than the *a* ....Ps 8:5
He shall give His *a* .....Ps 91:11
He shall give His a .....Matt 4:6
not even the *a* ....Matt 24:36

ANGER

and all the holy *a* . . . . . Matt 25:31
twelve legions of *a* . . . . Matt 26:53
And she saw two *a* . . . . John 20:12
and worship of *a* . . . . Col 2:18
much better than the *a* . . . Heb 1:4
entertained *a* . . . . Heb 13:2
things which *a* desire . . 1 Pet 1:12
did not spare the *a* . . . . . 2 Pet 2:4
a who did not keep . . . . Jude 6

ANGER

For His *a* is but for a . . . . . Ps 30:5
gracious, Slow to *a* . . . . . . Ps 103:8
Nor will He keep His *a* . . Ps 103:9
around at them with *a* . . Mark 3:5
bitterness, wrath, *a* . . . . . Eph 4:31

ANGRY

Cain, "Why are you *a* . . . . Gen 4:6
"Let not the Lord be *a* . Gen 18:30
the Son, lest He be *a* . . . . . Ps 2:12
a man stirs up strife . . . Prov 29:22
right for you to be *a* . . . . . Jon 4:4
you that whoever is *a* . . Matt 5:22
"Be *a*, and do not . . . . . . Eph 4:26

ANGUISH

remembers the *a* . . . . . John 16:21
tribulation and *a* . . . . Rom 2:9

ANIMAL

of every clean *a* . . . . Gen 7:2
set him on his own *a* . . Luke 10:34

ANIMALS

of *a* after their kind . . . . Gen 6:20
of four-footed *a* . . . . Acts 10:12

ANNUL

years later, cannot *a* . . . . . Gal 3:17

ANNULS

is confirmed, no one *a* . . . Gal 3:15

ANOINT

a my head with oil . . . . Ps 23:5
when you fast, *a* . . . . Matt 6:17
a My body for burial . . Mark 14:8
a your eyes with eye . . . . Rev 3:18

ANOINTED

"Surely the LORD's *a* . . 1 Sam 16:6
destroy the LORD's *a* . . 2 Sam 1:14
"Do not touch My *a* . . 1 Chr 16:22
Because He has a . . . . . . Luke 4:18
but this woman has *a* . . Luke 7:46
a the eyes of the *a* . . . . . John 9:6
that Mary who *a* . . . . . . John 11:2
Jesus, whom You *a* . . . . Acts 4:27
and has *a* us is God . . . 2 Cor 1:21

ANOINTING

But you have an *a* . . . . 1 John 2:20

ANOTHER

that you love one *a* . . . . John 13:34

ANSWER

Call, and I will *a* . . . . Job 13:22
How shall I *a* Him . . . . . . Job 31:14
the day that I call, *a* . . . . . Ps 102:2
In Your faithfulness *a* . . . Ps 143:1
a turns away wrath . . . . Prov 15:1
a a fool according . . . . . Prov 26:4
or what you should *a* . Luke 12:11
you may have an *a* . . . . 2 Cor 5:12

ANT

Go to the *a* . . . . Prov 6:6

ANTICHRIST

heard that the *A* . . . . . . 1 John 2:18
a who denies the . . . . . 1 John 2:22
is a deceiver and an *a* . . . 2 John 7

ANTITYPE

a which now saves us . . 1 Pet 3:21

ANXIETIES

the multitude of my *a* . . . . Ps 94:19

ANXIETY

A in the heart of man . . Prov 12:25

ANXIOUS

Be *a* for nothing . . . . Phil 4:6

APART

justified by faith *a* . . . . . . Rom 3:28

APOSTLE

called to be an *a* . . . . Rom 1:1
consider the *A* . . . . Heb 3:1

APOSTLES

of the twelve *a* . . . . Matt 10:2
He also named *a* . . . . . . Luke 6:13
am the least of the *a* . . . 1 Cor 15:9
none of the other *a* . . . . . . Gal 1:19
gave some to be *a* . . . . . . Eph 4:11

APOSTLESHIP

in this ministry and *a* . . . Acts 1:25
are the seal of my *a* . . . . 1 Cor 9:2

APPAREL

gold rings, in fine *a* . . . . James 2:2
or putting on fine *a* . . . . . 1 Pet 3:3

APPEAL

love's sake I rather *a* . . . . Philem 9

APPEAR

and let the dry land *a* . . . . Gen 1:9
also outwardly *a* . . . . . Matt 23:28
God would *a* . . . . Luke 19:11
For we must all *a* . . . . . . 2 Cor 5:10

APPEARANCE

Do not look at his *a* . . . 1 Sam 16:7
judge according to *a* . . . John 7:24
those who boast in *a* . . . 2 Cor 5:12
found in *a* as a man . . . . . . Phil 2:8

APPEARED

an angel of the Lord *a* . Luke 1:11
who *a* in glory and . . . . . Luke 9:31
brings salvation has *a* . . . Titus 2:11
of the ages, He has *a* . . . Heb 9:26

APPEARING

Lord Jesus Christ's *a* . . 1 Tim 6:14
and the dead at His *a* . . . 2 Tim 4:1
who have loved His *a* . . . 2 Tim 4:8

APPEARS

can stand when He *a* . . . . Mal 3:2
who is our life *a* . . . . Col 3:4
the Chief Shepherd *a* . . . 1 Pet 5:4
that when He *a* . . . . . . 1 John 2:28

APPETITE

are a man given to *a* . . . Prov 23:2

APPLE

And my law as the *a* . . . . Prov 7:2

APPLES

fitly spoken is like *a* . . . Prov 25:11

APPLIED

a my heart to know . . . . . Eccl 7:25

APPOINT

For God did not *a* . . . . 1 Thess 5:9

APPOINTED

And as it is *a* for men . . . Heb 9:27

APPROACH

year, make those who *a* . Heb 10:1

APPROACHING

as you see the Day *a* . . . Heb 10:25

APPROVE

do the same but also *a* . . Rom 1:32

APPROVED

to God and *a* by men . . Rom 14:18
to present yourself *a* . . 2 Tim 2:15

ARBITRATOR

Me a judge or an *a* . . . . Luke 12:14

ARCHANGEL

the voice of an *a* . . . . 1 Thess 4:16

ARGUMENTS

casting down *a* and . . . . 2 Cor 10:5

ARISE

A, shine . . . . Is 60:1
But the LORD will *a* . . . . Is 60:2
you who sleep, *A* . . . . Eph 5:14

ARK

"Make yourself an *a* . . . . Gen 6:14
him, she took an *a* . . . . Ex 2:3
Bezalel made the *a* . . . . . . Ex 37:1
in heaven, and the *a* . . . Rev 11:19

ARM

with an outstretched *a* . . . . Ex 6:6
Have you an *a* like God . . Job 40:9
strength with His *a* . . . . . Luke 1:51
a yourselves also with . . . 1 Pet 4:1

ARMED

a strong man, fully *a* . . Luke 11:21

ARMIES

And he sent out his *a* . . . Matt 22:7
surrounded by *a* . . . . . . Luke 21:20
And the *a* in heaven . . . Rev 19:14
the earth, and their *a* . . . Rev 19:19

ARMOR

Put on the whole *a* . . . . . . Eph 6:11

ARMS

are the everlasting *a* . . Deut 33:27
took Him up in his *a* . . . Luke 2:28

AROMA

the one we are the *a* . . . 2 Cor 2:16
for a sweet-smelling *a* . . . . Eph 5:2

AROUSED

LORD was greatly *a* . . . . Num 11:10
Then Joseph, being *a* . . . Matt 1:24

ARRAYED

his glory was not *a* . . . . . Matt 6:29
"Who are these *a* . . . . Rev 7:13

ARROGANCE

Pride and *a* and the . . . . Prov 8:13

ARROW

a that flies by day . . . . Ps 91:5

ARROWS

a pierce me deeply . . . . . . Ps 38:2
Like *a* in the hand of . . . . Ps 127:4

ASCEND

Who may *a* into the . . . . . . Ps 24:3
If I *a* into heaven . . . . Ps 139:8
'I will *a* into heaven . . . . . Is 14:13
see the Son of Man . . . John 6:62

ASCENDED

You have *a* on high .....Ps 68:18
"No one has *a* ....John 3:13
"When He *a* on high .....Eph 4:8

ASCENDING

the angels of God *a* ....John 1:51

ASCRIBE

A strength to God ....Ps 68:34

ASHAMED

Let me not be *a* ....Ps 25:2
And Israel shall be *a* ....Hos 10:6
For whoever is *a* .....Mark 8:38
am not *a* of the gospel ..Rom 1:16
Therefore God is not *a* .Heb 11:16

ASHES

become like dust and *a* .Job 30:19
in sackcloth and *a* ....Luke 10:13

ASIDE

lay something *a* ....1 Cor 16:2
lay *a* all filthiness .....James 1:21
Therefore, laying *a* ......1 Pet 2:1

ASK

when your children *a* ....Josh 4:6
"*A* a sign for yourself .....Is 7:11
whatever things you *a* .Matt 21:22
a, and it will be ....Luke 11:9
that whatever You *a* ....John 11:22
a anything in My .....John 14:14
in that day you will *a* ..John 16:23
above all that we *a* .....Eph 3:20
wisdom, let him *a* .....James 1:5
But let him *a* in faith ...James 1:6
because you do not *a* ...James 4:2

ASKS

For everyone who *a* .....Matt 7:8
you who, if his son *a* ....Matt 7:9
Or if he *a* for a fish ...Luke 11:11

ASLEEP

But He was *a* ....Matt 8:24
some have fallen *a* ....1 Cor 15:6
those who are *a* .....1 Thess 4:15

ASSEMBLING

not forsaking the *a* ....Heb 10:25

ASSEMBLY

a I will praise You ....Ps 22:22
fast, Call a sacred *a* ....Joel 1:14
a I will sing praise ......Heb 2:12
to the general *a* ....Heb 12:23

ASSURANCE

riches of the full *a* ....Col 2:2
Spirit and in much *a* ..1 Thess 1:5
to the full *a* of hope .....Heb 6:11

ASSURE

a our hearts before ...1 John 3:19

ASSURED

learned and been *a* ....2 Tim 3:14

ASTONISHED

Just as many were *a* .....Is 52:14
who heard Him were *a* .Luke 2:47

ASTRAY

one of them goes *a* ....Matt 18:12
like sheep going *a* .....1 Pet 2:25

ATONEMENT

the blood that makes *a* .Lev 17:11
for it is the Day of *A* ..Lev 23:28
there will be no *a* ....Is 22:14

ATTAIN

It is high, I cannot *a* .....Ps 139:6

worthy to *a* that age ..Luke 20:35
by any means, I may *a* ..Phil 3:11

ATTENTION

My son, give *a* to my ...Prov 4:20

ATTENTIVE

Let Your ears be *a* ......Ps 130:2

ATTESTED

a Man *a* by God to you .Acts 2:22

AUSTERE

because you are an *a* .Luke 19:21

AUTHOR

For God is not the *a* ..1 Cor 14:33
unto Jesus, the *a* ....Heb 12:2

AUTHORITIES

a that exist are ....Rom 13:1

AUTHORITY

them as one having *a* ...Matt 7:29
"All *a* has been given ..Matt 28:18
a I will give You ....Luke 4:6
and has given Him *a* ....John 5:27
You have given Him *a* ...John 17:2
the flesh, reject *a* ....Jude 8

AUTUMN

a trees without fruit ......Jude 12

AVAILS

of a righteous man *a* ..James 5:16

AVENGE

Beloved, do not *a* .....Rom 12:19
a our blood on those ....Rev 6:10

AVENGER

the Lord is the *a* ......1 Thess 4:6

AWAKE

be satisfied when I *a* ....Ps 17:15
it is high time to *a* .....Rom 13:11
A to righteousness ....1 Cor 15:34

AWAY

the wind drives *a* ....Ps 1:4
Do not cast me *a* ....Ps 51:11
A time to cast *a* ....Eccl 3:5
fair one, And come *a* ...Song 2:10
minded to put her *a* .....Matt 1:19
and earth will pass *a* ..Matt 24:35
"I am going *a* ....John 8:21
they cried out, "*A* .....John 19:15
unless the falling *a* ...2 Thess 2:3
in Asia have turned *a* ..2 Tim 1:15
heard, lest we drift *a* .....Heb 2:1
if they fall *a* ....Heb 6:6
can never take *a* ....Heb 10:11
world is passing *a* ....1 John 2:17
if anyone takes *a* ......Rev 22:19

AWESOME

a is this place ....Gen 28:17
God, the great and *a* ....Deut 7:21
By *a* deeds in ....Ps 65:5
O God, You are more *a* ..Ps 68:35
Your great and *a* name ...Ps 99:3

AWL

his ear with an *a* ....Ex 21:6

AX

If the *a* is dull ....Eccl 10:10
And even now the *a* ....Matt 3:10

B

BABBLER

"What does this *b* .....Acts 17:18

BABBLINGS

the profane and idle *b* .1 Tim 6:20

BABE

the *b* leaped in my .....Luke 1:44
You will find a *B* ......Luke 2:12
for he is a *b* ....Heb 5:13

BABES

Out of the mouth of *b* ......Ps 8:2
revealed them to *b* ....Matt 11:25
of the mouth of b .....Matt 21:16
as to carnal, as to *b* ....1 Cor 3:1
as newborn *b* ....1 Pet 2:2

BACK

for the fool's *b* ....Prov 26:3
I gave My *b* to those ......Is 50:6
plow, and looking *b* ....Luke 9:62
of those who draw *b* ...Heb 10:39
someone turns him *b* ..James 5:19

BACKBITERS

b, haters of God ....Rom 1:30

BACKBITING

b tongue an angry .....Prov 25:23

BACKSLIDER

The *b* in heart will be ..Prov 14:14

BACKSLIDINGS

And I will heal your *b* ....Jer 3:22

BACKWARD

ten degrees *b* ....2 Kin 20:11

BAD

b trees bears *b* fruit ....Matt 7:17

BAG

"nor *b* for your ....Matt 10:10

BAKED

b unleavened cakes .....Ex 12:39

BAKER

the butler and the *b* .....Gen 40:1

BALANCES

Falsifying the *b* ....Amos 8:5

BALD

every head shall be *b* ...Jer 48:37

BALDHEAD

Go up, you *b* ....2 Kin 2:23

BALM

no *b* in Gilead ....Jer 8:22

BANDAGED

and *b* his wounds .....Luke 10:34

BANKERS

my money with the *b* ..Matt 25:27

BANNERS

we will set up our *b* ......Ps 20:5
as an army with *b* ....Song 6:4

BANQUET

b that I have prepared ...Esth 5:4

BANQUETING

He brought me to the *b* ..Song 2:4

BAPTISM

coming to his *b* ....Matt 3:7
b that I am baptized ...Matt 20:22
"But I have a *b* ....Luke 12:50
said, "Into John's *b* .....Acts 19:3
Lord, one faith, one *b* ....Eph 4:5
buried with Him in *b* ....Col 2:12

BAPTISMS
of the doctrine of *b* . . . . Heb 6:2

BAPTIZE
"I indeed *b* you with . . . . Matt 3:11
Himself did not *b* . . . . John 4:2

BAPTIZED
b will be saved . . . . . . Mark 16:16
every one of you be *b* . . . Acts 2:38
all his family were *b* . . . Acts 16:33
Arise and be *b* . . . . Acts 22:16
were *b* into Christ . . . . . . Rom 6:3
I thank God that I *b* . . . 1 Cor 1:14
Spirit we were all . . . 1 Cor 12:13

BAPTIZING
b them in the name of . Matt 28:19

BARBARIAN
nor uncircumcised, *b* . . . . Col 3:11

BARLEY
here who has five *b* . . . . . John 6:9

BARN
the wheat into my *b* . . . Matt 13:30

BARNS
reap nor gather into *b* . . Matt 6:26
I will pull down my *b* . . Luke 12:18

BARREN
But Sarai was *b* . . . . Gen 11:30
"Sing, O *b* . . . . Is 54:1

BASE
and the *b* things of . . . . 1 Cor 1:28

BASIN
poured water into a *b* . . John 13:5

BASKET
and put it under a *b* . . . . Matt 5:15
I was let down in a *b* . 2 Cor 11:33

BASKETS
they took up twelve *b* . Matt 14:20

BATHED
to him, "He who is *b* . . John 13:10

BATS
To the moles and *b* . . . . Is 2:20

BATTLE
b is the LORD's . . . . 1 Sam 17:47
the *b* to the strong . . . . . . Eccl 9:11
became valiant in *b* . . . . Heb 11:34

BEAR
greater than I can *b* . . . . Gen 4:13
whom Sarah shall *b* . . . Gen 17:21
not *b* false witness . . . . . . Ex 20:16
b their iniquities . . . . Is 53:11
child, and *b* a Son . . . . . Matt 1:23
A good tree cannot *b* . . Matt 7:18
how long shall I *b* . . . . Matt 17:17
by, to *b* His cross . . . . Mark 15:21
whoever does not *b* . . . Luke 14:27
are strong ought to *b* . . . Rom 15:1
b one another's . . . . Gal 6:2
b the sins of many . . . . . . Heb 9:28

BEARD
the edges of your *b* . . . . Lev 19:27
Running down on the *b* . . Ps 133:2

BEARING
goes forth weeping, *B* . . . Ps 126:6
And He, *b* His cross . . . John 19:17
b His reproach . . . . Heb 13:13

BEARS
Every branch that *b* . . . . John 15:2

BEAST
You preserve man and *b* . . Ps 36:6
And I saw a *b* rising . . . . Rev 13:1
the mark of the *b* . . . . . . Rev 19:20

BEASTS
like brute *b* . . . . Jude 10

BEAT
b their swords into . . . . Is 2:4
spat in His face and *b* . Matt 26:67

BEATEN
Three times I was *b* . . 2 Cor 11:25

BEAUTIFUL
B in elevation . . . . Ps 48:2
has made everything *b* . . Eccl 3:11
my love, you are as *b* . . . Song 6:4
How *b* upon the . . . . Is 52:7
indeed appear *b* . . . . Matt 23:27

BEAUTIFY
b the place of My . . . . Is 60:13

BEAUTY
"The *b* of Israel is . . . . 2 Sam 1:19
To behold the *b* . . . . Ps 27:4
see the King in His *b* . . . . Is 33:17
no *b* that we should . . . . . . Is 53:2

BECAME
b a living being . . . . Gen 2:7
to the Jews I *b* . . . . 1 Cor 9:20

BED
I remember You on my *b* . Ps 63:6
if I make my *b* in hell . . . . Ps 139:8
"Arise, take up your *b* . . . Matt 9:6
be two men in one *b* . . Luke 17:34
and the *b* undefiled . . . . . Heb 13:4

BEDS
sing aloud on their *b* . . . . Ps 149:5

BEFOREHAND
up, do not worry *b* . . . . Mark 13:11
told you all things *b* . . Mark 13:23
when He testified *b* . . . . 1 Pet 1:11

BEG
b you as sojourners . . . . 1 Pet 2:11

BEGAN
since the world *b* . . . . . . Luke 1:70

BEGGAR
there was a certain *b* . . Luke 16:20

BEGGARLY
weak and *b* elements . . . . . Gal 4:9

BEGINNING
b God created the . . . . Gen 1:1
In the *b* was the Word . . . John 1:1
a murderer from the *b* . . John 8:44
True Witness, the *B* . . . . Rev 3:14
and the Omega, the *B* . . . Rev 21:6

BEGOTTEN
I have *b* You . . . . Ps 2:7
glory as of the only *b* . . . John 1:14
loves him who is *b* . . . . 1 John 5:1

BEGUILING
b unstable souls . . . . 2 Pet 2:14

BEGUN
Having *b* in the Spirit . . . . Gal 3:3

BEHALF
you on Christ's *b* . . . . . . 2 Cor 5:20

BEHAVE
does not *b* rudely . . . . . . 1 Cor 13:5

BEHAVED
blamelessly we *b* . . . . 1 Thess 2:10

BEHAVIOR
of good *b*, hospitable . . . 1 Tim 3:2

BEHEADED
and had John *b* . . . . Matt 14:10

BEHOLD
B, the virgin shall . . . . Is 7:14
Judah, "*B* your God . . . . . . Is 40:9
"*B* the Lamb of God . . . John 1:36
to them, "*B* the Man . . . John 19:5
B what manner of . . . . . 1 John 3:1

BEHOLDING
with unveiled face, *b* . . 2 Cor 3:18

BEING
move and have our *b* . Acts 17:28
who, *b* in the form of . . . . . Phil 2:6

BELIEVE
tears, "Lord, I *b* . . . . Mark 9:24
have no root, who *b* . . . . Luke 8:13
slow of heart to *b* . . . . Luke 24:25
to those who *b* . . . . John 1:12
this, that they may *b* . . John 11:42
that you may *b* . . . . John 20:31
the Lord Jesus and *b* . . . Rom 10:9
Christ, not only to *b* . . . . Phil 1:29
comes to God must *b* . . . Heb 11:6
b that there is one . . . . James 2:19
Even the demons *b* . . . James 2:19

BELIEVED
And he *b* in the LORD . . . Gen 15:6
Who has *b* our report . . . . Is 53:1
seen Me, you have *b* . . John 20:29
"Abraham *b* God . . . . Rom 4:3
whom I have *b* . . . . 2 Tim 1:12

BELIEVERS
example to the *b* . . . . . . 1 Tim 4:12

BELIEVES
The simple *b* every . . . . Prov 14:15
that whoever *b* in Him . John 3:16
"He who *b* in the Son . John 3:36
with the heart one *b* . . Rom 10:10

BELIEVING
you ask in prayer, *b* . . Matt 21:22

BELLY
On your *b* you shall go . Gen 3:14
and Jonah was in the *b* . . Jon 1:17
whose god is their *b* . . . . Phil 3:19

BELOVED
so He gives His *b* . . . . . . Ps 127:2
My *b* is mine . . . . Song 2:16
"This is My *b* . . . . Matt 3:17
us accepted in the *B* . . . . . Eph 1:6
Luke the *b* physician . . . . Col 4:14
"This is My *b* . . . . 2 Pet 1:17

BELT
with a leather *b* . . . . Matt 3:4

BEND
The wicked *b* their bow . . . Ps 11:2

BENEATH
"You are from *b* . . . . John 8:23

BENEFACTORS
them are called '*b* . . . . Luke 22:25

BENEFIT
have a second *b* . . . . 2 Cor 1:15

BESEECH

b you therefore ....Rom 12:1

BESIDE

He leads me *b* the ....Ps 23:2
"Paul, you are *b* ......Acts 26:24

BEST

desire the *b* ....1 Cor 12:31

BESTOWED

love the Father has *b* .. 1 John 3:1

BETRAY

you, one of you will *b* . Matt 26:21

BETRAYED

Man is about to be *b* .. Matt 17:22

BETRAYER

See, My *b* is at ....Matt 26:46

BETRAYING

"Judas, are you *b* .....Luke 22:48

BETRAYS

who is the one who *b* . John 21:20

BETROTH

"I will *b* you to Me ......Hos 2:19

BETROTHED

to a virgin *b* to a man .. Luke 1:27

BETTER

b than sacrifice ......1 Sam 15:22
It is *b* to trust in ....Ps 118:8
For it is *b* to marry .....1 Cor 7:9
Christ, which is far *b* ....Phil 1:23
b than the angels ....Heb 1:4
b things concerning ......Heb 6:9

BEWARE

"*B* of false prophets ....Matt 7:15

BEWITCHED

b you that you should ....Gal 3:1

BEYOND

advanced in Judaism *b* .. Gal 1:14

BILLOWS

b have gone over me .....Ps 42:7

BIND

and whatever you *b* ...Matt 16:19
'*B* him hand and foot .. Matt 22:13

BIRD

soul, "Flee as a *b* ....Ps 11:1

BIRDS

b make their nests ......Ps 104:17
"Look at the *b* ....Matt 6:26
have holes and *b* ....Matt 8:20

BIRTH

the day of one's *b* ....Eccl 7:1
Now the *b* of Jesus ....Matt 1:18
will rejoice at his *b* ....Luke 1:14
conceived, it gives *b* ...James 1:15

BIRTHDAY

was Pharaoh's *b* ......Gen 40:20

BIRTHRIGHT

Esau despised his *b* ....Gen 25:34

BISHOP

the position of a *b* ......1 Tim 3:1
b must be blameless .....Titus 1:7

BIT

and they *b* the people .. Num 21:6

BITE

A serpent may *b* ....Eccl 10:11
But if you *b* and ....Gal 5:15

BITTER

b herbs they ....Ex 12:8
and do not be *b* ....Col 3:19
But if you have *b* .....James 3:14

BITTERLY

And Hezekiah wept *b* .. 2 Kin 20:3
went out and wept *b* ... Matt 26:75

BITTERNESS

you are poisoned by *b* .. Acts 8:23
b springing up cause ...Heb 12:15

BLACK

one hair white or *b* .....Matt 5:36
a *b* horse ....Rev 6:5
and the sun became *b* ... Rev 6:12

BLACKNESS

whom is reserved the *b* ...Jude 13

BLACKSMITH

I have created the *b* ......Is 54:16

BLADE

first the *b* ....Mark 4:28

BLAME

be holy and without *b* ....Eph 1:4

BLAMELESS

and that man was *b* ......Job 1:1
body be preserved *b* . 1 Thess 5:23

BLAMELESSLY

b we behaved ....1 Thess 2:10

BLASPHEME

b Your name forever ....Ps 74:10
compelled them to *b* ...Acts 26:11
b that noble name .....James 2:7

BLASPHEMED

who passed by *b* Him . Matt 27:39
great heat, and they *b* ... Rev 16:9

BLASPHEMER

I was formerly a *b* ....1 Tim 1:13

BLASPHEMES

b the name of the ......Lev 24:16
"This Man *b* ....Matt 9:3

BLASPHEMIES

is this who speaks *b* ....Luke 5:21

BLASPHEMY

but the *b* against ......Matt 12:31
was full of names of *b* ... Rev 17:3

BLEATING

"What then is this *b* . 1 Sam 15:14

BLEMISH

be holy and without *b* ...Eph 5:27
as of a lamb without *b* . 1 Pet 1:19

BLEMISHED

to the Lord what is *b* ... Mal 1:14

BLESS

b those who *b* you ......Gen 12:3
You go unless You *b* ... Gen 32:26
"The LORD *b* you and ... Num 6:24
b the LORD at all ....Ps 34:1
b You while I live ....Ps 63:4
b His holy name ....Ps 103:1
b those who curse .....Luke 6:28
B those who ....Rom 12:14
Being reviled, we *b* ....1 Cor 4:12

BLESSED

B is the man who walks ....Ps 1:1
B is the man to whom ....Ps 32:2
B is the nation whose ....Ps 33:12
B is he who comes ....Ps 118:26
rise up and call her *b* .. Prov 31:28
"*B* are the poor in ....Matt 5:3
B are those who mourn .. Matt 5:4
B are the meek ....Matt 5:5
B are those who hunger . Matt 5:6
B are the merciful ......Matt 5:7
B are the pure in ....Matt 5:8
B are the peacemakers .. Matt 5:9
B are those who are ....Matt 5:10
B is He who comes .....Matt 21:9
'It is more *b* to give ....Acts 20:35
B be the God and ....Eph 1:3
"*B* are the dead who ...Rev 14:13

BLESSING

And you shall be a *b* ....Gen 12:2
before you today a *b* .. Deut 11:26
shall be showers of *b* .. Ezek 34:26
and you shall be a *b* ....Zech 8:13
that the *b* of Abraham ...Gal 3:14
with every spiritual *b* ....Eph 1:3

BLIND

To open *b* eyes ....Is 42:7
His watchmen are *b* ......Is 56:10
b leads the *b* ....Matt 15:14
to Him, "Are we *b* .....John 9:40
miserable, poor, *b* ....Rev 3:17

BLINDED

and the rest were *b* .....Rom 11:7

BLINDS

a bribe, for a bribe *b* .. Deut 16:19

BLOOD

of your brother's *b* ......Gen 4:10
b shall be shed ....Gen 9:6
b that makes ....Lev 17:11
hands are full of *b* ....Is 1:15
And the moon into *b* ....Joel 2:31
For this is My *b* ....Matt 26:28
"His *b* be on us and ... Matt 27:25
covenant in My *b* .....Luke 22:20
were born, not of *b* .....John 1:13
b has eternal life ....John 6:54
with His own *b* ....Acts 20:28
propitiation by His *b* ...Rom 3:25
justified by His *b* ....Rom 5:9
through His *b* ....Eph 1:7
brought near by the *b* .. Eph 2:13
against flesh and *b* .....Eph 6:12
peace through the *b* .....Col 1:20
with the precious *b* .....1 Pet 1:19
b of Jesus Christ His ... 1 John 1:7
our sins in His own *b* ...Rev 1:5
us to God by Your *b* ...Rev 5:9
them white in the *b* .....Rev 7:14
overcame him by the *b* . Rev 12:11
a robe dipped in *b* ....Rev 19:13

BLOODSHED

me from the guilt of *b* ...Ps 51:14

BLOODTHIRSTY

The LORD abhors the *b* .....Ps 5:6

BLOSSOM

and *b* as the rose ....Is 35:1

BLOT

from my sins, and *b* ......Ps 51:9
and I will not *b* ....Rev 3:5

BLOTTED

your sins may be *b* .....Acts 3:19

BLOW

with a very severe *b* ....Jer 14:17

BLOWS

"The wind *b* where it .... John 3:8

BOAST

puts on his armor *b* ... 1 Kin 20:11
and make your *b* ...... Rom 2:17
lest anyone should *b* ..... Eph 2:9

BOASTERS

God, violent, proud, *b* .. Rom 1:30

BOASTING

Where is *b* then .... Rom 3:27

BODIES

b a living sacrifice ...... Rom 12:1
not know that your *b* .. 1 Cor 6:15
wives as their own *b* .... Eph 5:28

BODILY

b form like a dove ..... Luke 3:22
of the Godhead *b* .... Col 2:9

BODY

of the *b* is the eye ...... Matt 6:22
those who kill the *b* ... Matt 10:28
this is My *b* .... Matt 26:26
of the temple of His *b* .. John 2:21
deliver me from this *b* .. Rom 7:24
redemption of our *b* .... Rom 8:23
members in one *b* ...... Rom 12:4
But I discipline my *b* .. 1 Cor 9:27
b which is broken .... 1 Cor 11:24
baptized into one *b* .... 1 Cor 12:13
are the *b* of Christ .... 1 Cor 12:27
though I give my *b* .... 1 Cor 13:3
It is sown a natural *b* .. 1 Cor 15:44
in the *b* of His flesh ...... Col 1:22
our sins in His own *b* .. 1 Pet 2:24

BOILS

Job with painful *b* .... Job 2:7

BOLDLY

therefore come *b* .... Heb 4:16

BOLDNESS

in whom we have *b* ..... Eph 3:12
that we may have *b* ... 1 John 4:17

BOND

love, which is the *b* ...... Col 3:14

BONDAGE

out of the house of *b* .... Ex 13:14
again with a yoke of *b* .... Gal 5:1

BONDS

"Let us break Their *b* ...... Ps 2:3

BONDSERVANTS

B, be obedient to .... Eph 6:5
Masters, give your *b* ...... Col 4:1

BONDWOMAN

the one by a *b* .... Gal 4:22

BONE

b clings to my skin ..... Job 19:20

BONES

I can count all My *b* .... Ps 22:17
and my *b* waste away .. Ps 31:10
I kept silent, my *b* .... Ps 32:3
the wind, Or how the *b* . Eccl 11:5
say to them, 'O dry *b* .. Ezek 37:4
of dead men's *b* .... Matt 23:27
b shall be broken ..... John 19:36

BOOK

are written in the b ...... Gal 3:10
in the Lamb's *B* .... Rev 21:27
the prophecy of this *b* .. Rev 22:18

BOOKS

b there is no end ...... Eccl 12:12
not contain the *b* ...... John 21:25
and *b* were opened ..... Rev 20:12

BOOTH

of Zion is left as a *b* .... Is 1:8

BORDERS

and enlarge the *b* .... Matt 23:5

BORE

And to Sarah who *b* .... Is 51:2
b the sin of many .... Is 53:12
b our sicknesses .... Matt 8:17
Himself *b* our sins ..... 1 Pet 2:24
b a male Child who was . Rev 12:5

BORN

A time to be *b* .... Eccl 3:2
unto us a Child is *b* .... Is 9:6
b Jesus who is called .. Matt 1:16
unless one is *b* again .... John 3:3
"That which is *b* .... John 3:6
having been *b* again ... 1 Pet 1:23
who loves is *b* of God .. 1 John 4:7

BORROWER

b is servant to the ...... Prov 22:7

BORROWS

The wicked *b* and does .. Ps 37:21

BOSOM

to Abraham's *b* .... Luke 16:22
Son, who is in the *b* .... John 1:18

BOTTOMLESS

ascend out of the *b* ...... Rev 17:8
the key to the *b* .... Rev 20:1

BOUGHT

b the threshing floor . 2 Sam 24:24
all that he had and *b* .. Matt 13:46
For you were *b* at a .... 1 Cor 6:20
denying the Lord who *b* . 2 Pet 2:1

BOUND

on earth will be *b* ..... Matt 16:19
And see, now I go *b* ... Acts 20:22
who has a husband is *b* .. Rom 7:2
Are you *b* to a wife .... 1 Cor 7:27
Devil and Satan, and *b* .. Rev 20:2

BOUNTIFULLY

and he who sows *b* ..... 2 Cor 9:6

BOW

"You shall not *b* .... Ex 23:24
let us worship and *b* ...... Ps 95:6
who sat on it had a *b* ..... Rev 6:2

BOWED

stood all around and *b* .. Gen 37:7
And they *b* the knee ... Matt 27:29

BOWL

and poured out his *b* .... Rev 16:2

BOWLS

Go and pour out the *b* ... Rev 16:1

BOX

had the money *b* ...... John 13:29

BOYS

Shall be full of *b* .... Zech 8:5

BRAIDED

not with *b* hair or ...... 1 Tim 2:9

BRANCH

raise to David a *B* .... Jer 23:5

forth My Servant the *B* .. Zech 3:8
b that bears fruit He .... John 15:2

BRANCHES

vine, you are the *b* ..... John 15:5

BRASS

become sounding *b* .... 1 Cor 13:1

BRAVE

in the faith, be *b* ...... 1 Cor 16:13

BREAD

brought out *b* .... Gen 14:18
shall eat unleavened *b* .. Ex 23:15
not live by *b* alone ..... Deut 8:3
b eaten in secret is .... Prov 9:17
B gained by deceit is .. Prov 20:17
Cast your *b* upon the .... Eccl 11:1
for what is not *b* .... Is 55:2
these stones become *b* ... Matt 4:3
not live by b alone .... Matt 4:4
this day our daily *b* .... Matt 6:11
eating, Jesus took *b* ... Matt 26:26
"I am the *b* of life ...... John 6:48
betrayed took *b* ...... 1 Cor 11:23

BREADTH

is as great as its *b* .... Rev 21:16

BREAK

covenant I will not *b* .... Ps 89:34
together to *b* bread ..... Acts 20:7

BREAKING

in the *b* of bread .... Acts 2:42
b bread from house to .. Acts 2:46

BREAKS

Until the day *b* .... Song 2:17

BREAST

back on Jesus' *b* ...... John 13:25

BREASTPLATE

righteousness as a *b* ..... Is 59:17
having put on the *b* .... Eph 6:14

BREASTS

Your two *b* are like ..... Song 4:5
b which nursed You ... Luke 11:27

BREATH

nostrils the *b* of life ...... Gen 2:7
that there was no *b* ... 1 Kin 17:17
Man is like a *b* .... Ps 144:4
everything that has *b* ... Ps 150:6
"Surely I will cause *b* .. Ezek 37:5
gives to all life, *b* ...... Acts 17:25
power to give *b* .... Rev 13:15

BREATHES

indeed he *b* his last .... Job 14:10

BRETHREN

and you are all ...... Matt 23:8
least of these My *b* .... Matt 25:40
among many *b* .... Rom 8:29
thus sin against the *b* .. 1 Cor 8:12
over five hundred *b* .... 1 Cor 15:6
perils among false *b* .. 2 Cor 11:26
sincere love of the *b* ... 1 Pet 1:22
we love the *b* .... 1 John 3:14
our lives for the *b* .... 1 John 3:16

BRIBE

you shall take no *b* ...... Ex 23:8
b blinds the eyes ...... Deut 16:19

BRIBES

hand is full of *b* .... Ps 26:10

BRICK

people straw to make *b* .... Ex 5:7

BRICKS
"Come, let us make *b* ...Gen 11:3

BRIDE
I will show you the *b* ....Rev 21:9
the Spirit and the *b* ....Rev 22:17

BRIDEGROOM
And as the *b* rejoices ......Is 62:5
mourn as long as the *b* .Matt 9:15
went out to meet the *b* .Matt 25:1
the friend of the *b* ......John 3:29

BRIDLE
b the whole body ......James 3:2

BRIER
b shall come up the ......Is 55:13

BRIERS
there shall come up *b* ......Is 5:6

BRIGHTER
a light from heaven, *b* .Acts 26:13

BRIGHTNESS
And kings to the *b* ....Is 60:3
who being the *b* ....Heb 1:3

BRIMSTONE
the lake of fire and *b* ...Rev 20:10

BRING
b back his soul ....Job 33:30
b My righteousness ......Is 46:13
Who shall *b* a charge ....Rom 8:33
b Christ down from ....Rom 10:6
even so God will *b* ...1 Thess 4:14

BROAD
b is the way that ......Matt 7:13

BROKE
b them at the foot of ....Ex 32:19
He blessed and *b* ......Matt 14:19
b the legs of the ......John 19:32

BROKEN
this stone will be *b* ....Matt 21:44
Scripture cannot be *b* .John 10:35
body which is *b* ......1 Cor 11:24

BROKENHEARTED
He heals the *b* And ......Ps 147:3

BRONZE
So Moses made a *b* ....Num 21:9
b walls against the ......Jer 1:18
a third kingdom of *b* ....Dan 2:39

BROOD
"*B* of vipers ....Matt 12:34
hen gathers her *b* .....Luke 13:34

BROOK
disciples over the *B* ....John 18:1

BROOKS
for the water *b* ....Ps 42:1

BROTHER
"Where is Abel your *b* ...Gen 4:9
b offended is harder ...Prov 18:19
b will deliver up ......Matt 10:21
how often shall my *b* ..Matt 18:21
b will rise again ......John 11:23
b goes to law against ...1 Cor 6:6
Whoever hates his *b* ..1 John 3:15

BROTHERHOOD
Love the *b* ....1 Pet 2:17

BROTHERLY
b love continue ....Heb 13:1

BROTHER'S
Am I my *b* keeper ....Gen 4:9
at the speck in your *b* ...Matt 7:3

BROTHERS
is My mother, or My *b* .Mark 3:33
b are these who hear ...Luke 8:21

BRUISE
He shall *b* your head ....Gen 3:15
the LORD to *b* Him ....Is 53:10

BRUISED
He was *b* for our ....Is 53:5
b reed He will not .....Matt 12:20

BUCKLER
be your shield and *b* ......Ps 91:4

BUFFET
of Satan to *b* me ......2 Cor 12:7

BUILD
b ourselves a city ......Gen 11:4
"Would you *b* a house .2 Sam 7:5
labor in vain who *b* ....Ps 127:1
down, And a time to *b* ...Eccl 3:3
'This man began to *b* .Luke 14:30
What house will you *b* ..Acts 7:49
"For if I *b* again ....Gal 2:18

BUILDER
foundations, whose *b* ...Heb 11:10

BUILDING
in whom the whole *b* ....Eph 2:21

BUILDS
take heed how he *b* ....1 Cor 3:10

BUILT
has *b* her house ....Prov 9:1
to a wise man who *b* ...Matt 7:24
having been *b* on the ....Eph 2:20

BULLS
For if the blood of *b* .....Heb 9:13

BULWARKS
Mark well her *b* ....Ps 48:13

BUNDLE
man's *b* of money ......Gen 42:35

BURDEN
Cast your *b* on the ......Ps 55:22
easy and My *b* is light .Matt 11:30
we might not be a *b* ..1 Thess 2:9
on you no other *b* ....Rev 2:24

BURDENS
"For they bind heavy *b* .Matt 23:4
Bear one another's *b* .....Gal 6:2

BURDENSOME
I myself was not *b* ....2 Cor 12:13
are not *b* ....1 John 5:3

BURIAL
she did it for My *b* ....Matt 26:12
for the day of My *b* ....John 12:7

BURIED
Therefore we were *b* ....Rom 6:4
and that He was *b* .....1 Cor 15:4
b with Him in baptism ...Col 2:12

BURN
the bush does not *b* ....Ex 3:3
"Did not our heart *b* ..Luke 24:32

BURNED
If anyone's work is *b* ..1 Cor 3:15
my body to be *b* ....1 Cor 13:3

BURNING
b torch that passed ....Gen 15:17
b fire shut up in my ......Jer 20:9
plucked from the *b* ....Amos 4:11

BURNT
lamb for a *b* offering ....Gen 22:7
delight in *b* offering .....Ps 51:16

BURST
the new wine will *b* ....Luke 5:37

BURY
and let the dead *b* ......Matt 8:22

BUSH
from the midst of a *b* ......Ex 3:2

BUSINESS
about My Father's *b* ....Luke 2:49

BUSYBODIES
at all, but are *b* ......2 Thess 3:11

BUTLER
b did not remember ....Gen 40:23

BUTTER
were smoother than *b* ...Ps 55:21

BUY
Yes, come, *b* wine and ....Is 55:1
"I counsel you to *b* ......Rev 3:18
and that no one may *b* .Rev 13:17

BUYS
has and *b* that field ....Matt 13:44

BYWORD
has made me a *b* ....Job 17:6

C

CAGE
foul spirit, and a *c* ......Rev 18:2

CAKE
Ephraim is a *c* ....Hos 7:8

CAKES
and love the raisin *c* .....Hos 3:1

CALAMITY
will laugh at your *c* ....Prov 1:26

CALCULATED
c the dust of the ....Is 40:12

CALDRON
this city is the *c* ....Ezek 11:3

CALF
and made a molded *c* ....Ex 32:4
bring the fatted *c* .....Luke 15:23

CALL
C upon Him while He ......Is 55:6
c His name JESUS ....Matt 1:21
c the righteous ....Matt 9:13
Lord our God will *c* ....Acts 2:39
c them My people ......Rom 9:25
c and election sure .....2 Pet 1:10

CALLED
c the light Day ....Gen 1:5
c his wife's name Eve ...Gen 3:20
I have *c* you by your ......Is 43:1
"Out of Egypt I *c* ......Matt 2:15
city *c* Nazareth ....Matt 2:23
For many are *c* ....Matt 20:16
to those who are the *c* ..Rom 8:28
these He also *c* ....Rom 8:30
c children of God ......1 John 3:1

CALLING
the gifts and the c .....Rom 11:29
For you see your c ....1 Cor 1:26
remain in the same c ..1 Cor 7:20

CALLS
c them all by name .....Ps 147:4
David himself c .....Mark 12:37
c his own sheep ....John 10:3

CALM
there was a great c .....Matt 8:26

CAMEL
it is easier for a c .....Matt 19:24

CAMP
to Him, outside the c ...Heb 13:13

CAN
I c do all things ....Phil 4:13

CANCER
will spread like c .....2 Tim 2:17

CANOPY
His c around Him was ...Ps 18:11

CAPSTONE
bring forth the c ....Zech 4:7

CAPTAIN
Which, having no c .....Prov 6:7

CAPTIVE
and be led away c ....Luke 21:24
He led captivity c ....Eph 4:8

CAPTIVES
and make c ....2 Tim 3:6

CAPTIVITY
every thought into c ...2 Cor 10:5

CARCASS
"For wherever the c ...Matt 24:28

CARE
"Lord, do You not c ...Luke 10:40
how will he take c ......1 Tim 3:5

CARED
he said, not that he c ...John 12:6

CAREFULLY
I shall walk c all my .....Is 38:15

CARELESS
But he who is c ......Prov 19:16

CARES
No one c for my soul ....Ps 142:4
for He c for you ....1 Pet 5:7

CARNAL
c mind is enmity ....Rom 8:7

CARNALLY
c minded is death ....Rom 8:6

CAROUSE
count it pleasure to c ...2 Pet 2:13

CARPENTER
"Is this not the c ....Mark 6:3

CARRIED
And c our sorrows ....Is 53:4

CARRY
for you to c your bed ...John 5:10
it is certain we can c ....1 Tim 6:7

CARRYING
will meet you c ....Mark 14:13

CASE
Festus laid Paul's c ....Acts 25:14

CASSIA
myrrh and aloes and c ....Ps 45:8

CAST
Why are you c down .....Ps 42:5
whole body to be c .....Matt 5:29
My name they will c ..Mark 16:17
by no means c out .....John 6:37
c their crowns before ....Rev 4:10
the great dragon was c ..Rev 12:9

CASTING
c down arguments .....2 Cor 10:5
c all your care ....1 Pet 5:7

CASTS
perfect love c out .....1 John 4:18

CATCH
c Him in His words ...Mark 12:13
now on you will c .....Luke 5:10

CATCHES
and the wolf c the .....John 10:12
c the wise in their .....1 Cor 3:19

CAUGHT
him was a ram c ....Gen 22:13
her Child was c up ......Rev 12:5

CAUSE
hated Me without a c ..John 15:25
For this c I was born ..John 18:37

CAVES
in dens and c of the ....Heb 11:38

CEASE
and night Shall not c ....Gen 8:22
He makes wars c ....Ps 46:9
tongues, they will c ....1 Cor 13:8

CEASING
pray without c ......1 Thess 5:17

CEDAR
dwell in a house of c ...2 Sam 7:2

CEDARS
the LORD breaks the c .....Ps 29:5

CELESTIAL
but the glory of the c .1 Cor 15:40

CENSER
Aaron, each took his c ...Lev 10:1

CERTAINTY
you may know the c ....Luke 1:4

CERTIFICATE
a man to write a c .....Mark 10:4

CHAFF
be chased like the c ......Is 17:13
He will burn up the c ...Matt 3:12

CHAIN
pit and a great c ....Rev 20:1

CHAINED
of God is not c ....2 Tim 2:9

CHAINS
And his c fell off ....Acts 12:7
am, except for these c .Acts 26:29

CHAMBERS
brought me into his c ....Song 1:4

CHAMPION
And a c went out .....1 Sam 17:4

CHANGE
now to c my tone ...Gal 4:20
there is also a c ....Heb 7:12

CHANGED
c the glory of the ......Rom 1:23
but we shall all be c ..1 Cor 15:51

CHANGERS'
and poured out the c ...John 2:15

CHANGES
c the times and the .....Dan 2:21

CHANNELS
c of the sea were seen ...Ps 18:15

CHARIOT
that suddenly a c ......2 Kin 2:11

CHARIOTS
Some trust in c ....Ps 20:7

CHARITABLE
you do not do your c ....Matt 6:1
c deeds which she ......Acts 9:36

CHARM
C is deceitful and .....Prov 31:30

CHARMS
who sew magic c .....Ezek 13:18

CHASE
Five of you shall c ....Lev 26:8

CHASTE
present you as a c .....2 Cor 11:2

CHASTEN
a father does not c ......Heb 12:7
I love, I rebuke and c ....Rev 3:19

CHASTENED
c us as seemed best ....Heb 12:10

CHASTENING
do not despise the c .....Job 5:17
Now no c seems to be ..Heb 12:11

CHASTENS
the LORD loves He c .....Heb 12:6

CHASTISEMENT
The c for our peace ....Is 53:5

CHATTER
c leads only to ....Prov 14:23

CHEAT
Beware lest anyone c .....Col 2:8

CHEATED
let yourselves be c ......1 Cor 6:7

CHEEK
on your right c ....Matt 5:39

CHEEKBONE
my enemies on the c ....Ps 3:7

CHEEKS
His c are like a bed ....Song 5:13

CHEER
"Son, be of good c ......Matt 9:2

CHEERFUL
for God loves a c ....2 Cor 9:7

CHEERFULNESS
shows mercy, with c .... Rom 12:8

CHEESE
And curdle me like c ... Job 10:10

CHERISHES
but nourishes and c ..... Eph 5:29

CHERUBIM
above it were the c .... Heb 9:5

CHIEF
of whom I am c .... 1 Tim 1:15
Zion a c cornerstone .... 1 Pet 2:6

CHILD
Train up a c in the ..... Prov 22:6
For unto us a C .... Is 9:6
virgin shall be with c ... Matt 1:23
of God as a little c .... Mark 10:15
So the c grew and ..... Luke 1:80
When I was a c .... 1 Cor 13:11
She bore a male C ...... Rev 12:5

CHILDBEARING
she will be saved in c .. 1 Tim 2:15

CHILDBIRTH
pain as a woman in c ..... Is 13:8

CHILDHOOD
c you have known ..... 2 Tim 3:15

CHILDLESS
give me, seeing I go c ... Gen 15:2
this man down as c ..... Jer 22:30

CHILDREN
c are a heritage .... Ps 127:3
c rise up and call her .. Prov 31:28
and become as little c ... Matt 18:3
"Let the little c .... Matt 19:14
the right to become c ... John 1:12
now we are c of God .. 1 John 3:2

CHOOSE
therefore c life .... Deut 30:19
"You did not c .... John 15:16

CHOSE
just as He c us in Him .... Eph 1:4

CHOSEN
servant whom I have c ... Is 43:10
whom I have c .... John 13:18
c the foolish things .... 1 Cor 1:27
Has God not c the ..... James 2:5

CHRIST
Jesus who is called C ... Matt 1:16
"You are the C .... Matt 16:16
a Savior, who is C .... Luke 2:11
It is C who died .... Rom 8:34
to be justified by C .... Gal 2:17
been crucified with C .... Gal 2:20
C is head of the ...... Eph 5:23
to me, to live is C ...... Phil 1:21
which is C in you .... Col 1:27
C who is our .... Col 3:4
Jesus C is the same ..... Heb 13:8
C His Son cleanses us . 1 John 1:7
that Jesus is the C ..... 1 John 5:1

CHRISTIAN
anyone suffers as a C .. 1 Pet 4:16

CHRISTIANS
were first called C ..... Acts 11:26

CHRISTS
"For false c and ...... Matt 24:24

CHURCH
rock I will build My c . Matt 16:18

c daily those who were . Acts 2:47
Himself a glorious c .... Eph 5:27
as the Lord does the c ... Eph 5:29
body, which is the c ..... Col 1:24
assembly and c .... Heb 12:23

CHURCHES
these things in the c .... Rev 22:16

CIRCLE
who sits above the c ..... Is 40:22

CIRCUMCISE
is necessary to c them .. Acts 15:5

CIRCUMCISED
among you shall be c .. Gen 17:10
who will justify the c ... Rom 3:30
if you become c .... Gal 5:2

CIRCUMCISION
c is that of the heart .... Rom 2:29
C is nothing and ...... 1 Cor 7:19
Christ Jesus neither c .... Gal 5:6

CIRCUMSPECTLY
then that you walk c .... Eph 5:15

CISTERN
from your own c .... Prov 5:15

CITIES
He overthrew those c .. Gen 19:25
three parts, and the c ... Rev 16:19

CITIZEN
But I was born a c ..... Acts 22:28

CITIZENS
but fellow c with the .... Eph 2:19

CITIZENSHIP
For our c is in heaven ... Phil 3:20

CITY
shall make glad the c ..... Ps 46:4
c has become a harlot ..... Is 1:21
How lonely sits the c .... Lam 1:1
that is set on a .... Matt 5:14
He has prepared a c ... Heb 11:16
have no continuing c ... Heb 13:14
John, saw the holy c ... Rev 21:2

CLAP
of the field shall c .... Is 55:12

CLAY
pit, out of the miry c ...... Ps 40:2
We are the c .... Is 64:8
blind man with the c .... John 9:6
have power over the c .. Rom 9:21

CLEAN
He who has c hands and .. Ps 24:4
make yourselves c .... Is 1:16
c out His threshing ..... Matt 3:12
You can make me c ..... Matt 8:2
"You are not all c ..... John 13:11
"You are already c ..... John 15:3

CLEANSE
C me from secret .... Ps 19:12
And c me from my sin .... Ps 51:2
How can a young man c . Ps 119:9
might sanctify and c .... Eph 5:26
us our sins and to c .... 1 John 1:9

CLEANSED
"Were there not ten c . Luke 17:17

CLEANSES
Christ His Son c .... 1 John 1:7

CLEAR
of life, c as crystal ...... Rev 22:1

CLIFF
secret places of the c ... Song 2:14

CLIMBS
c up some other way ... John 10:1

CLING
C to what is good ...... Rom 12:9

CLINGS
And My tongue c .... Ps 22:15

CLOAK
let him have your c ..... Matt 5:40
using liberty as a c ..... 1 Pet 2:16

CLODS
The c of the valley ..... Job 21:33

CLOSE
c friends abhor me ..... Job 19:19

CLOSED
The deep c around me .... Jon 2:5

CLOTH
a piece of unshrunk c ... Matt 9:16

CLOTHE
He not much more c .... Matt 6:30

CLOTHED
of skin, and c them ..... Gen 3:21
A man c in soft .... Matt 11:8
naked and you c ...... Matt 25:36
legion, sitting and c .... Mark 5:15
desiring to be c .... 2 Cor 5:2
that you may be c .... Rev 3:18

CLOTHES
c became shining ...... Mark 9:3
many spread their c ... Luke 19:36
a poor man in filthy c .. James 2:2

CLOTHING
c they cast lots .... Ps 22:18
do you worry about c .. Matt 6:28
to you in sheep's c ..... Matt 7:15
c they cast lots .... John 19:24

CLOTHS
in swaddling c .... Luke 2:12

CLOUD
My rainbow in the c .... Gen 9:13
day in a pillar of c ...... Ex 13:21
He led them with the c ... Ps 78:14
behold, a bright c ...... Matt 17:5
of Man coming in a c .. Luke 21:27
c received Him out of .... Acts 1:9
by so great a c .... Heb 12:1

CLOUDS
Man coming on the c .. Matt 24:30
with them in the c ... 1 Thess 4:17
are c without water ...... Jude 12
He is coming with c ...... Rev 1:7

CLOUDY
them by day with a c .... Neh 9:12

CLOVEN
chew the cud or have c . Deut 14:7

CLUSTER
beloved is to me a c .... Song 1:14

COAL
in his hand a live c .... Is 6:6

COALS
doing you will heap c .. Rom 12:20

COBRA
the lion and the c . . . . Ps 91:13

COBRA'S
shall play by the c . . . . Is 11:8

COFFIN
and he was put in a c . . Gen 50:26
touched the open c . . . . . Luke 7:14

COIN
if she loses one c . . . . . . Luke 15:8

COLD
and harvest, C and . . . . . . Gen 8:22
of many will grow c . . . Matt 24:12
that you are neither c . . . Rev 3:15

COLLECTION
concerning the c . . . . . . 1 Cor 16:1

COLT
on a donkey, A c . . . . Zech 9:9
on a donkey, A c . . . . Matt 21:5

COME
He will c and save you . . . . Is 35:4
who have no money, C . . . . Is 55:1
Your kingdom c . . . . Matt 6:10
"C to Me . . . . Matt 11:28
I have c in My . . . . John 5:43
thirsts, let him c . . . . John 7:37
c as a light into the . . . . John 12:46
O Lord, c . . . . 1 Cor 16:22
the door, I will c . . . . Rev 3:20

COMELINESS
He has no form or c . . . . Is 53:2

COMES
Lord's death till He c . 1 Cor 11:26

COMFORT
and Your staff, they c . . . . . Ps 23:4
yes, c My people . . . . Is 40:1
c each other . . . . 1 Thess 5:11

COMFORTED
So Isaac was c after . . . Gen 24:67
Refusing to be c . . . . Jer 31:15

COMFORTER
She had no c . . . . Lam 1:9

COMFORTS
I, even I, am He who c . . . Is 51:12

COMING
see the Son of Man c . Mark 13:26
mightier than I is c . . . . Luke 3:16
are Christ's at His c . . 1 Cor 15:23
Behold, I am c . . . . Rev 3:11
"Surely I am c . . . . Rev 22:20

COMMAND
c I have received . . . . . . John 10:18
and I know that His c . John 12:50
if you do whatever I c . John 15:14

COMMANDED
not endure what was c . Heb 12:20

COMMANDMENT
c of the LORD is pure . . . . . . Ps 19:8
which is the great c . . . Matt 22:36
"A new c I give to . . . . . John 13:34
which is the first c . . . . . . Eph 6:2
And this is His c . . . . . 1 John 3:23

COMMANDMENTS
covenant, the Ten C . . . . . Ex 34:28
as doctrines the c . . . . . Matt 15:9
c hang all the Law . . . . Matt 22:40
"He who has My c . . . . John 14:21

COMMANDS
with authority He c . . . . Mark 1:27

COMMEND
But food does not c . . . . . 1 Cor 8:8

COMMENDABLE
patiently, this is c . . . . . . 1 Pet 2:20

COMMENDED
c the unjust steward . . . . Luke 16:8

COMMENDS
but whom the Lord c . 2 Cor 10:18

COMMIT
"You shall not c . . . . Ex 20:14
into Your hands I c . . . Luke 23:46

COMMITS
sin also c lawlessness . . 1 John 3:4

COMMITTED
c Himself to Him who . . 1 Pet 2:23

COMMON
c people heard Him . . . Mark 12:37
had all things in c . . . . . . Acts 2:44
concerning our c . . . . Jude 3

COMMOTION
there arose a great c . . . Acts 19:23

COMMUNED
I c with my heart . . . . Eccl 1:16

COMMUNION
c of the Holy Spirit . . . 2 Cor 13:14

COMPANION
a man my equal, My c . . . Ps 55:13

COMPANIONS
while you became c . . . . Heb 10:33

COMPANY
Great was the c . . . . Ps 68:11
to an innumerable c . . . . Heb 12:22

COMPARE
c ourselves with . . . . . . 2 Cor 10:12

COMPARED
are not worthy to be c . . Rom 8:18

COMPASSION
are a God full of c . . . . . . Ps 86:15
He was moved with c . . . Matt 9:36
whomever I will have c . Rom 9:15
He can have c on those . . Heb 5:2

COMPASSIONATE
the Lord is very c . . . . . James 5:11

COMPASSIONS
because His c fail not . . . Lam 3:22

COMPEL
c them to come in . . . . Luke 14:23

COMPELS
the love of Christ c . . . . 2 Cor 5:14

COMPLAINED
some of them also c . . 1 Cor 10:10

COMPLAINERS
These are grumblers, c . . . Jude 16

COMPLAINING
all things without c . . . . . Phil 2:14

COMPLAINT
For the LORD has a c . . . . . Mic 6:2

COMPLETE
work in you will c . . . . . . Phil 1:6
and you are c in Him . . . . Col 2:10
of God may be c . . . . . . 2 Tim 3:17

COMPLETELY
sanctify you c . . . . 1 Thess 5:23

COMPOSED
But God c the body . . . 1 Cor 12:24

COMPREHEND
which we cannot c . . . . . . Job 37:5
the darkness did not c . . . John 1:5

CONCEAL
of God to c a matter . . . . Prov 25:2

CONCEALED
Than love carefully c . . . Prov 27:5

CONCEIT
selfish ambition or c . . . . . Phil 2:3

CONCEITED
Let us not become c . . . . . Gal 5:26

CONCEIVE
the virgin shall c . . . . Is 7:14
And behold, you will c . Luke 1:31

CONCEIVED
in sin my mother c . . . . Ps 51:5

CONCERN
Neither do I c myself . . . . Ps 131:1

CONCERNED
Is it oxen God is c . . . . . . 1 Cor 9:9

CONCESSION
But I say this as a c . . . . . 1 Cor 7:6

CONCLUSION
Let us hear the c . . . . . . Eccl 12:13

CONDEMN
world to c the world . . . . John 3:17

CONDEMNATION
can you escape the c . . Matt 23:33
"And this is the c . . . . . . John 3:19
Their c is just . . . . Rom 3:8
therefore now no c . . . . . . Rom 8:1

CONDEMNED
does not believe is c . . . . John 3:18
c sin in the flesh . . . . Rom 8:3

CONDEMNS
Who is he who c . . . . Rom 8:34

CONDUCT
from your aimless c . . . . 1 Pet 1:8
may be won by the c . . . . 1 Pet 3:1

CONFESS
c my transgressions . . . . . . Ps 32:5
that if you c with . . . . . . Rom 10:9
every tongue shall c . . . Rom 14:11
If we c our sins . . . . 1 John 1:9

CONFESSED
c that He was Christ . . . John 9:22

CONFESSES
c that Jesus is the . . . . 1 John 4:15

CONFESSION
with the mouth c . . . . . . Rom 10:10
High Priest of our c . . . . . . Heb 3:1
let us hold fast our c . . . . . Heb 4:14

CONFIDENCE
c shall be your . . . . Is 30:15
Jesus, and have no c . . . . . Phil 3:3

CONFINED
the Scripture has c . . . . . . Gal 3:22

CONFIRM
who will also c . . . . 1 Cor 1:8

CONFIRMED
covenant that was c . . . . . Gal 3:17
c it by an oath . . . . Heb 6:17

CONFIRMING
c the word through . . . Mark 16:20

CONFLICT
to know what a great c . . . Col 2:1

CONFLICTS
Outside were c . . . . 2 Cor 7:5

CONFORMED
predestined to be c . . . . . Rom 8:29
And do not be c . . . . Rom 12:2

CONFUSE
c their language . . . . Gen 11:7

CONFUSED
the assembly was c . . . . Acts 19:32

CONGREGATION
Nor sinners in the c . . . . Ps 1:5
God stands in the c . . . . . . Ps 82:1

CONQUER
conquering and to c . . . . . . Rev 6:2

CONQUERORS
we are more than c . . . . Rom 8:37

CONSCIENCE
convicted by their c . . . . . John 8:9
strive to have a c . . . . . . Acts 24:16

CONSECRATED
c this house which you . . 1 Kin 9:3

CONSENT
and does not c to . . . . 1 Tim 6:3

CONSENTED
He had not c to their . . Luke 23:51

CONSENTING
Now Saul was c to his . . . Acts 8:1

CONSIDER
When I c Your heavens . . . . Ps 8:3
My people do not c . . . . Is 1:3
C the lilies of the . . . . . . Matt 6:28
"C the ravens . . . . Luke 12:24
c Him who endured . . . . . Heb 12:3

CONSIST
in Him all things c . . . . Col 1:17

CONSOLATION
if there is any c . . . . Phil 2:1
us everlasting c . . . 2 Thess 2:16

CONSOLE
c those who mourn . . . . Is 61:3

CONSTANT
c prayer was . . . . Acts 12:5

CONSUME
whom the Lord will c . 2 Thess 2:8

CONSUMED
but the bush was not c . . . . Ex 3:2

mercies we are not c . . . . Lam 3:22
beware lest you be c . . . . . Gal 5:15

CONSUMING
our God is a c fire . . . . . Heb 12:29

CONTAIN
of heavens cannot c . . . . 2 Chr 2:6
c the books that . . . . . . John 21:25

CONTEMPT
and be treated with c . . Mark 9:12

CONTEMPTIBLE
and his speech c . . . . . 2 Cor 10:10

CONTEND
c earnestly for the . . . . Jude 3

CONTENT
state I am, to be c . . . . Phil 4:11
covetousness; be c . . . . . . Heb 13:5

CONTENTIONS
sorcery, hatred, c . . . . Gal 5:20

CONTENTIOUS
anyone seems to be c . 1 Cor 11:16

CONTENTMENT
c is great gain . . . . 1 Tim 6:6

CONTINUAL
a merry heart has a c . . Prov 15:15
c coming she weary . . . . Luke 18:5

CONTINUALLY
heart was only evil c . . . . . Gen 6:5
will give ourselves c . . . . . Acts 6:4
remains a priest c . . . . Heb 7:3

CONTINUE
Shall we c in sin that . . . . Rom 6:1
C earnestly in prayer . . . . . Col 4:2
Let brotherly love c . . . . . Heb 13:1

CONTINUED
c steadfastly in the . . . . . Acts 2:42

CONTRADICTIONS
idle babble and c . . . . . . 1 Tim 6:20

CONTRARY
to worship God c . . . . . . Acts 18:13

CONTRIBUTION
to make a certain c . . . . Rom 15:26

CONTRITE
A broken and a c . . . . Ps 51:17
poor and of a c spirit . . . . . . Is 66:2

CONTROVERSY
For the Lord has a c . . . . Jer 25:31

CONVERSION
describing the c . . . . Acts 15:3

CONVERTED
unless you are c . . . . Matt 18:3

CONVICT
He has come, He will c . John 16:8

CONVICTS
"Which of you c . . . . John 8:46

CONVINCED
Let each be fully c . . . . . Rom 14:5

COOKED
c their own children . . . . Lam 4:10

COOL
and c my tongue . . . . . . Luke 16:24

COPIES
necessary that the c . . . . . Heb 9:23

COPPER
sold for two c coins . . . . Luke 12:6

COPPERSMITH
c did me much harm . . 2 Tim 4:14

COPY
who serve the c . . . . Heb 8:5

CORD
this line of scarlet c . . . . Josh 2:18

CORDS
had made a whip of c . . John 2:15

CORNER
was not done in a c . . . . Acts 26:26

CORNERSTONE
become the chief c . . . . Matt 21:42
in Zion A chief c . . . . 1 Pet 2:6

CORRECT
C your son . . . . Prov 29:17

CORRECTED
human fathers who c . . . . Heb 12:9

CORRECTION
Do not withhold c . . . . . Prov 23:13
for reproof, for c . . . . . . 2 Tim 3:16

CORRECTS
the Lord loves He c . . . . Prov 3:12

CORRODED
and silver are c . . . . James 5:3

CORRUPT
in these things they c . . . . Jude 10

CORRUPTED
for all flesh had c . . . . . . Gen 6:12
Your riches are c . . . . . . James 5:2

CORRUPTIBLE
redeemed with c . . . . . . 1 Pet 1:18

CORRUPTION
Your Holy One to see c . Ps 16:10
c inherit incorruption . 1 Cor 15:50
having escaped the c . . . 2 Pet 1:4

COST
and count the c . . . . . . Luke 14:28

COULD
c remove mountains . . . 1 Cor 13:2
which no one c number . . Rev 7:9

COUNCILS
deliver you up to c . . . . Mark 13:9

COUNSEL
Who walks not in the c . . . . Ps 1:1
We took sweet c . . . . Ps 55:14
guide me with Your c . . . . Ps 73:24
according to the c . . . . . . Eph 1:11
immutability of His c . . . . Heb 6:17
"I c you to buy from . . . . Rev 3:18

COUNSELOR
be called Wonderful, C . . . . . Is 9:6

COUNSELORS
c there is safety . . . . . . Prov 11:14

COUNT
c my life dear to . . . . . . Acts 20:24
His promise, as some c . . 2 Pet 3:9

COUNTED

Even a fool is c ...... Prov 17:28
who rule well be c .... 1 Tim 5:17

COUNTENANCE

The LORD lift up His c .. Num 6:26
with a sad c .... Matt 6:16
His c was like .... Matt 28:3
of the glory of his c ..... 2 Cor 3:7

COUNTRY

"Get out of your c ...... Gen 12:1
that is, a heavenly c .... Heb 11:16

COUNTRYMEN

for my brethren, my c ... Rom 9:3

COURAGE

strong and of good c .. Deut 31:6

COURT

They zealously c .... Gal 4:17

COURTEOUS

be tenderhearted, be c ... 1 Pet 3:8

COURTS

and into His c .... Ps 100:4

COVENANT

I will establish My c .... Gen 6:18
the LORD made a c ..... Gen 15:18
will show them His c .... Ps 25:14
sons will keep My c ... Ps 132:12
I will make a new c ..... Jer 31:31
the Messenger of the c .. Mal 3:1
cup in the new c ...... Luke 22:20
He says, "A new c ..... Heb 8:13
Mediator of the new c .. Heb 12:24
of the everlasting c .... Heb 13:20

COVENANTS

the glory, the c .... Rom 9:4

COVER

He shall c you with .... Ps 91:4
c a multitude of sins .. James 5:20

COVERED

Whose sin is c .... Ps 32:1
c all their sin .... Ps 85:2
For there is nothing c .. Matt 10:26

COVERING

spread a cloud for a c .. Ps 105:39

COVERINGS

and made themselves c ... Gen 3:7

COVET

"You shall not c .... Ex 20:17

COVETED

c no one's silver ...... Acts 20:33

COVETOUS

nor thieves, nor c ..... 1 Cor 6:10

COVETOUSNESS

heed and beware of c . Luke 12:15

COWARDLY

the c, unbelieving .... Rev 21:8

CRAFTILY

His people, to deal c .... Ps 105:25

CRAFTINESS

deceived Eve by his c .. 2 Cor 11:3
in the cunning c .... Eph 4:14

CRAFTSMAN

instructor of every c .... Gen 4:22

CRAFTY

the devices of the c ...... Job 5:12
Nevertheless, being c . 2 Cor 12:16

CREAM

were bathed with c ...... Job 29:6

CREATE

peace and c calamity ...... Is 45:7

CREATED

So God c man in His ... Gen 1:27
Has not one God c ..... Mal 2:10
c in Christ Jesus .... Eph 2:10
new man which was c ... Eph 4:24

CREATION

know that the whole c .. Rom 8:22
Christ, he is a new c ... 2 Cor 5:17
anything, but a new c .... Gal 6:15

CREATOR

Remember now your C . Eccl 12:1
God, the LORD, The C .... Is 40:28
rather than the C .... Rom 1:25

CREATURE

the gospel to every c .. Mark 16:15

CREATURES

firstfruits of His c ..... James 1:18

CREDIT

For what c is it if ...... 1 Pet 2:20

CREDITOR

There was a certain c .. Luke 7:41

CREEP

sort are those who c .... 2 Tim 3:6

CREEPING

c thing and beast of ..... Gen 1:24

CREPT

For certain men have c .... Jude 4

CRIB

donkey its master's c .... Is 1:3

CRIED

the poor who c out ..... Job 29:12
of the depths I have c .... Ps 130:1

CRIES

your brother's blood c ... Gen 4:10

CRIMES

land is filled with c ..... Ezek 7:23

CRIMINALS

also two others, c ..... Luke 23:32

CROOKED

c places shall be made .... Is 40:4
in the midst of a c .... Phil 2:15

CROSS

does not take his c .... Matt 10:38
to bear His c .... Matt 27:32
down from the c ...... Matt 27:40
lest the c of Christ ..... 1 Cor 1:17
boast except in the c ... Gal 6:14
the enemies of the c ... Phil 3:18
Him endured the c ...... Heb 12:2
shall not follow a c ...... Ex 23:2

CROWN

c the year with Your .... Ps 65:11
they had twisted a c ... Matt 27:29
obtain a perishable c .. 1 Cor 9:25
laid up for me the c .... 2 Tim 4:8
on His head a golden c . Rev 14:14

CROWNED

angels, And You have c .... Ps 8:5
athletics, he is not c .... 2 Tim 2:5

CROWNS

His head were many c .. Rev 19:12

CRUCIFIED

"Let Him be c .... Matt 27:22
Calvary, there they c .. Luke 23:33
lawless hands, have c ... Acts 2:23
that our old man was c .. Rom 6:6
Jesus Christ and Him c . 1 Cor 2:2
"I have been c .... Gal 2:20

CRUCIFY

out again, "C Him .... Mark 15:13

CRUEL

hate me with c hatred ... Ps 25:19

CRUELTY

the haunts of c .... Ps 74:20

CRUSH

of peace will c .... Rom 16:20

CRUSHED

every side, yet not c .... 2 Cor 4:8

CRUST

man is reduced to a c ... Prov 6:26

CRY

and their c came up to .... Ex 2:23
Does not wisdom c ...... Prov 8:1
at midnight a c .... Matt 25:6
His own elect who c.... Luke 18:7

CRYING

nor sorrow, nor c .... Rev 21:4

CRYSTAL

a sea of glass, like c ...... Rev 4:6

CUBIT

can add one c .... Matt 6:27

CUNNING

the serpent was more c .. Gen 3:1
c craftiness of deceitful .. Eph 4:14

CUP

My c runs over .... Ps 23:5
Then He took the c .... Matt 26:27
possible, let this c ..... Matt 26:39
c is the new covenant . Luke 22:20
cannot drink the c .... 1 Cor 10:21
c is the new .... 1 Cor 11:25

CURE

and to c diseases .... Luke 9:1

CURES

and perform c .... Luke 13:32

CURSE

c the ground for man's .. Gen 8:21
C God and die .... Job 2:9
"I will send a c .... Mal 2:2
law are under the c ...... Gal 3:10

CURSED

c more than all cattle .... Gen 3:14
from Me, you c .... Matt 25:41

CURSES

I will curse him who c ... Gen 12:3

CURTAIN

the heavens like a c ..... Ps 104:2

CUSTOM

according to the c ...... Acts 15:1

CUT

evildoers shall be c .... Ps 37:9
the wicked will be c .... Prov 2:22

CYMBAL

or a clanging c .... 1 Cor 13:1

D

DAILY

Give us this day our d .. Matt 6:11
take up his cross d ..... Luke 9:23
the Scriptures d .... Acts 17:11

DANCE

mourn, And a time to d .. Eccl 3:4
And you did not d ..... Matt 11:17

DANCED

Then David d before .. 2 Sam 6:14

DANCING

saw the calf and the d ... Ex 32:19
he heard music and d . Luke 15:25

DARE

someone would even d ... Rom 5:7

DARK

I tell you in the d ..... Matt 10:27
shines in a d place ..... 2 Pet 1:19

DARKENED

their understanding d .. Eph 4:18

DARKNESS

d He called Night .... Gen 1:5
Those who sat in d .... Ps 107:10
d Have seen a .... Is 9:2
And deep d the people .... Is 60:2
body will be full of d ... Matt 6:23
cast out into outer d ... Matt 8:12
d rather than light ..... John 3:19
For you were once d .... Eph 5:8
called you out of d ..... 1 Pet 2:9
d is reserved .... 2 Pet 2:17
and in Him is no d .... 1 John 1:5
d is passing away ..... 1 John 2:8

DARTS

quench all the fiery d .. Eph 6:16

DASH

You shall d them to .... Ps 2:9
Lest you d your foot ..... Matt 4:6

DASHED

infants shall be d ...... Hos 13:16

DAUGHTER

"Rejoice greatly, O d .... Zech 9:9
"Fear not, d of Zion ... John 12:15
the son of Pharaoh's d . Heb 11:24

DAUGHTERS

of God saw the d .... Gen 6:2
d shall prophesy .... Acts 2:17

DAY

God called the light D ... Gen 1:5
And d and night .... Gen 8:22
the Sabbath d .... Ex 20:8
For a d in Your courts ... Ps 84:10
d the LORD has .... Ps 118:24
not strike you by d ..... Ps 121:6
For the d of the LORD .... Joel 2:11
who can endure the d ... Mal 3:2
d our daily bread .... Matt 6:11
sent Me while it is d ... John 9:4
person esteems one d ... Rom 14:5
D will declare it .... 1 Cor 3:13
again the third d ...... 1 Cor 15:4
with the Lord one d ..... 2 Pet 3:8

DAYS

d are swifter than a .... Job 7:6
of woman Is of few d .... Job 14:1
The d of our lives are ... Ps 90:10
Before the difficult d .... Eccl 12:1
shortened those d .... Mark 13:20
raise it up in three d .... John 2:20

DAYSPRING

With which the D ...... Luke 1:78

DEACONS

with the bishops and d ... Phil 1:1
d must be reverent ..... 1 Tim 3:8
d be the husbands ..... 1 Tim 3:12

DEAD

But the d know nothing .. Eccl 9:5
d bury their own d ..... Matt 8:22
not the God of the d ... Matt 22:32
this my son was d .... Luke 15:24
d will hear the voice .... John 5:25
was raised from the d.... Rom 6:4
yourselves to be d ..... Rom 6:11
be Lord of both the d ... Rom 14:9
resurrection of the d . 1 Cor 15:12
And the d in Christ .. 1 Thess 4:16
without works is d .... James 2:26
And the d were judged . Rev 20:12

DEADLY

drink anything d .... Mark 16:18
evil, full of d poison .... James 3:8

DEADNESS

the d of Sarah's womb .. Rom 4:19

DEAF

d shall be unstopped ...... Is 35:5
are cleansed and the d .. Matt 11:5

DEAL

My Servant shall d .... Is 52:13

DEATH

d parts you and me .... Ruth 1:17
and the shadow of d .... Job 10:21
I sleep the sleep of d ..... Ps 13:3
of the shadow of d .... Ps 23:4
house leads down to d . Prov 2:18
who hate me love d .... Prov 8:36
swallow up d forever ...... Is 25:8
no pleasure in the .... Ezek 18:32
who shall not taste d .. Matt 16:28
but has passed from d .. John 5:24
Nevertheless d reigned . Rom 5:14
D no longer has .... Rom 6:9
the wages of sin is d .... Rom 6:23
the Lord's d .... 1 Cor 11:26
since by man came d .. 1 Cor 15:21
D is swallowed up in . 1 Cor 15:54
The sting of d is sin .. 1 Cor 15:56
is sin leading to d .... 1 John 5:16
Be faithful until d .... Rev 2:10
shall be no more d ...... Rev 21:4
which is the second d ... Rev 21:8

DEBTOR

I am a d both to .... Rom 1:14
that he is a d to keep ..... Gal 5:3

DEBTORS

as we forgive our d ..... Matt 6:12
of his master's d ...... Luke 16:5
brethren, we are d ..... Rom 8:12

DECEIT

Nor was any d in His ... Is 53:9
philosophy and empty d .. Col 2:8
no sin, nor was d ...... 1 Pet 2:22
mouth was found no d ... Rev 14:5

DECEITFUL

deliver me from the d ..... Ps 43:1

"The heart is d .... Jer 17:9
are false apostles, d .. 2 Cor 11:13

DECEITFULLY

an idol, Nor sworn d ..... Ps 24:4
the word of God .... 2 Cor 4:2

DECEITFULNESS

this world and the d ... Matt 13:22

DECEIVE

rise up and d many .... Matt 24:11
Let no one d you with .... Eph 5:6
we have no sin, we d .. 1 John 1:8

DECEIVED

"The serpent d .... Gen 3:13
the commandment, d ... Rom 7:11
deceiving and being d . 2 Tim 3:13

DECEIVER

how that d said ...... Matt 27:63
This is a d and an .... 2 John 7

DECEIVES

heed that no one d ..... Matt 24:4

DECENTLY

all things be done d ... 1 Cor 14:40

DECEPTIVE

you with d words .... 2 Pet 2:3

DECISION

in the valley of d .... Joel 3:14

DECLARE

The heavens d the .... Ps 19:1
d Your name to My ..... Ps 22:22
seen and heard we d .. 1 John 1:3

DECLARED

and d to be the Son of ... Rom 1:4

DECREE

"I will declare the d .... Ps 2:7
in those days that a d ... Luke 2:1

DEDICATION

it was the Feast of D .. John 10:22

DEED

you do in word or d ..... Col 3:17

DEEDS

because their d .... John 3:19
"You do the d .... John 8:41
one according to his d ... Rom 2:6
you put to death the d .. Rom 8:13

DEEP

LORD God caused a d .... Gen 2:21
d uttered its voice .... Hab 3:10
"Launch out into the d .. Luke 5:4
I have been in the d .. 2 Cor 11:25

DEEPER

D than Sheol .... Job 11:8

DEEPLY

But He sighed d .... Mark 8:12

DEER

As the d pants for the ..... Ps 42:1
shall leap like a d .... Is 35:6

DEFEATED

and Israel was d ...... 1 Sam 4:10

DEFEND

D the fatherless .... Is 1:17

DEFENSE

For wisdom is a d .... Eccl 7:12

DEFILE

am appointed for the *d* . . Phil 1:17
be ready to give a *d* . . . . 1 Pet 3:15

DEFILE

also these dreamers *d* . . . . . Jude 8

DEFILED

lest they should be *d* . . . John 18:28
and conscience are *d* . . . Titus 1:15

DEFILES

mouth, this *d* a man . . . Matt 15:11
it anything that *d* . . . . . . Rev 21:27

DEFRAUD

d his brother in this . . . 1 Thess 4:6

DEGREES

go forward ten *d* . . . . . . 2 Kin 20:9

DELICACIES

of the king's *d* . . . . Dan 1:5

DELICATE

a lovely and *d* woman . . . . . Jer 6:2

DELIGHT

But his *d* is in the . . . . Ps 1:2
I *d* to do Your will . . . . Ps 40:8
And I was daily His *d* . . . Prov 8:30
And let your soul *d* . . . . . . Is 55:2
call the Sabbath a *d* . . . . . . Is 58:13
For I *d* in the law of . . . . Rom 7:22

DELIGHTS

For the LORD *d* in you . . . . . Is 62:4

DELIVER

Let Him *d* Him . . . . Ps 22:8
I will *d* him and honor . . . Ps 91:15
into temptation, But *d* . . Matt 6:13
let Him *d* Him now if . . Matt 27:43
And the Lord will *d* . . . 2 Tim 4:18
d the godly out of . . . . 2 Pet 2:9

DELIVERANCE

not accepting *d* . . . . Heb 11:35

DELIVERED

who was *d* up because . . Rom 4:25
was once for all *d* . . . . Jude 3

DELIVERER

D will come out of . . . . Rom 11:26

DELIVERS

even Jesus who *d* . . . . 1 Thess 1:10

DELUSION

send them strong *d* . . 2 Thess 2:11

DEMON

Jesus rebuked the *d* . . . Matt 17:18
and have a *d* . . . . John 8:48

DEMONIC

is earthly, sensual, *d* . . James 3:15

DEMONS

authority over all *d* . . . . . Luke 9:1
the *d* are subject . . . . Luke 10:17
Even the *d* believe . . . . James 2:19

DEMONSTRATE

faith, to *d* His . . . . Rom 3:25

DEMONSTRATES

d His own love toward . . . Rom 5:8

DEN

cast him into the *d* . . . . . Dan 6:16
it a '*d* of thieves* . . . . . . Matt 21:13

DENARIUS

the laborers for a *d* . . . . . Matt 20:2

DENIED

before men will be *d* . . . Luke 12:9
Peter then *d* again . . . . John 18:27
d the Holy One and the . Acts 3:14
things cannot be *d* . . . . Acts 19:36
household, he has *d* . . . . 1 Tim 5:8

DENIES

But whoever *d* . . . . Matt 10:33
d that Jesus is the . . . . 1 John 2:22

DENY

let him *d* himself . . . . . . Matt 16:24
He cannot *d* Himself . . . 2 Tim 2:13

DENYING

but *d* its power . . . . 2 Tim 3:5
d the Lord who bought . . 2 Pet 2:1

DEPART

scepter shall not *d* . . . . Gen 49:10
on the left hand, '*D* . . Matt 25:41
will *d* from the faith . . . . 1 Tim 4:1

DEPARTING

heart of unbelief in *d* . . . . Heb 3:12

DEPARTURE

d savage wolves will . . . Acts 20:29
and the time of my *d* . . . 2 Tim 4:6

DEPRESSION

of man causes *d* . . . . . . Prov 12:25

DEPTH

nor height nor *d* . . . . Rom 8:39
Oh, the *d* of the . . . . . . Rom 11:33

DEPTHS

our sins Into the *d* . . . . . . Mic 7:19

DERISION

shall hold them in *d* . . . . . . Ps 2:4

DESCEND

d now from the cross . Mark 15:32
Lord Himself will *d* . . 1 Thess 4:16

DESCENDANTS

"We are Abraham's *d* . . John 8:33

DESCENDED

He who *d* is also the . . . . Eph 4:10

DESCENDING

God ascending and *d* . . . John 1:51
the holy Jerusalem, *d* . . . Rev 21:10

DESERT

d shall rejoice . . . . Is 35:1
'Look, He is in the *d* . . . Matt 24:26

DESERTED

d place by Himself . . . . Matt 14:13

DESERTS

They wandered in *d* . . . . Heb 11:38

DESIGN

with an artistic *d* . . . . Ex 26:31

DESIRABLE

the eyes, and a tree *d* . . . . Gen 3:6

DESIRE

d shall be for your . . . . . . Gen 3:16
Behold, You *d* truth in . . . Ps 51:6
"Father, I *d* that . . . . John 17:24
all manner of evil *d* . . . . . Rom 7:8
Brethren, my heart's *d* . . Rom 10:1

d the best gifts . . . . 1 Cor 12:31
the two, having a *d* . . . . . Phil 1:23

DESIRED

d are they than gold . . . . . Ps 19:10
One thing I have *d* . . . . Ps 27:4

DESIRES

shall give you the *d* . . . . . . Ps 37:4
the devil, and the *d* . . . John 8:44
not come from your *d* . . James 4:1

DESOLATE

any more be termed *D* . . . . Is 62:4
house is left to you *d* . . Matt 23:38

DESOLATION

the '*abomination of d* . . Matt 24:15

DESPAIRED

strength, so that we *d* . . . 2 Cor 1:8

DESPISE

one and *d* the other . . . . Matt 6:24
d the riches of His . . . . . . Rom 2:4

DESPISED

He is *d* and rejected . . . . . . Is 53:3
the things which are *d* . 1 Cor 1:28

DESPISES

d his neighbor sins . . . . Prov 14:21

DESPISING

the cross, *d* the shame . . . Heb 12:2

DESTITUTE

of corrupt minds and *d* . 1 Tim 6:5

DESTROY

Why should you *d* . . . . . . Eccl 7:16
shall not hurt nor *d* . . . . . . Is 11:9
I did not come to *d* . . . . . Matt 5:17
Him who is able to *d* . . Matt 10:28
Barabbas and *d* Jesus . Matt 27:20
to save life or to *d* . . . . . . Luke 6:9
d men's lives but to . . . Luke 9:56
d the wisdom of the . . . 1 Cor 1:19
able to save and to *d* . . James 4:12

DESTROYED

d all living things . . . . . . Gen 7:23
house, this tent, is *d* . . . . 2 Cor 5:1

DESTRUCTION

You turn man to *d* . . . . Ps 90:3
d that lays waste . . . . Ps 91:6
your life from *d* . . . . Ps 103:4
Pride goes before *d* . . . Prov 16:18
whose end is *d* . . . . Phil 3:19
with everlasting *d* . . . . 2 Thess 1:9

DESTRUCTIVE

bring in *d* heresies . . . . . . 2 Pet 2:1

DETERMINED

d their preappointed . . . Acts 17:26
For I *d* not to know . . . . . 1 Cor 2:2

DEVICE

there is no work or *d* . . . Eccl 9:10

DEVICES

not ignorant of his *d* . . . 2 Cor 2:11

DEVIL

to be tempted by the *d* . . Matt 4:1
prepared for the *d* . . . . . Matt 25:41
of your father the *d* . . . . John 8:44
give place to the *d* . . . . . Eph 4:27
the snare of the *d* . . . . . 2 Tim 2:26
the works of the *d* . . . . . 1 John 3:8

DEVIOUS

And who are *d* . . . . Prov 2:15

DEVISES
d wickedness on his ......Ps 36:4
But a generous man *d* .....Is 32:8

DEVOID
who is *d* of wisdom ....Prov 11:12

DEVOTED
Your servant, who is *d* ..Ps 119:38

DEVOUR
For you *d* widows' ....Matt 23:14
bite and *d* one another ...Gal 5:15
whom he may *d* ....1 Pet 5:8
d her Child as ....Rev 12:4

DEVOURED
wild beast has *d* ......Gen 37:20
birds came and *d* them .Matt 13:4
of heaven and *d* them ...Rev 20:9

DEVOUT
man was just and *d* ....Luke 2:25
d soldier from among ...Acts 10:7

DEW
God give you Of the *d* ..Gen 27:28

DIADEMS
ten horns, and seven *d* ..Rev 12:3

DIAMOND
d it is engraved ....Jer 17:1

DICTATES
according to the *d* ......Jer 23:17

DIE
it you shall surely *d* .....Gen 2:17
but a person shall *d* ...2 Chr 25:4
I shall not *d* ....Ps 118:17
born, And a time to *d* ...Eccl 3:2
eat of it and not *d* ......John 6:50
to you that you will *d* ...John 8:24
though he may *d* .....John 11:25
one man should *d* .....John 11:50
the flesh you will *d* ....Rom 8:13
For as in Adam all *d* ..1 Cor 15:22
and to *d* is gain ....Phil 1:21
for men to *d* once ....Heb 9:27
are the dead who *d* .....Rev 14:13

DIED
And all flesh *d* ....Gen 7:21
in due time Christ *d* .....Rom 5:6
Christ *d* for us ....Rom 5:8
Now if we *d* with ......Rom 6:8
and He *d* for all ....2 Cor 5:15
for if we *d* with Him ...2 Tim 2:11

DIES
alive unless it *d* ......1 Cor 15:36

DIFFERS
for one star *d* from ...1 Cor 15:41

DILIGENCE
d it produced in you ...2 Cor 7:11

DILIGENT
d makes rich ....Prov 10:4

DILIGENTLY
d lest anyone fall ......Heb 12:15

DIM
His eyes were not *d* ....Deut 34:7

DIMLY
we see in a mirror, *d* .1 Cor 13:12

DINE
come in to him and *d* ....Rev 3:20

DINNER
invites you to *d* ....1 Cor 10:27

DIP
d your piece of bread ...Ruth 2:14

DIPPED
clothed with a robe *d* ..Rev 19:13

DIRECT
Now may the Lord *d* ..2 Thess 3:5

DIRT
cast up mire and *d* ....Is 57:20

DISARMED
d principalities ....Col 2:15

DISASTER
will end with *d* ....Acts 27:10

DISCERN
d the face of the sky ....Matt 16:3
senses exercised to *d* ....Heb 5:14

DISCERNED
they are spiritually *d* ..1 Cor 2:14

DISCERNER
d of the thoughts ....Heb 4:12

DISCERNS
a wise man's heart *d* .....Eccl 8:5

DISCIPLE
he cannot be My *d* ....Luke 14:26
d whom Jesus loved ....John 21:7

DISCIPLES
word, you are My *d* ....John 8:31
but we are Moses' *d* ....John 9:28

DISCIPLINES
he who loves him *d* ....Prov 13:24

DISCORD
And one who sows *d* ...Prov 6:19

DISCOURAGED
lest they become *d* ......Col 3:21
become weary and *d* ....Heb 12:3

DISCRETION
D will preserve you ....Prov 2:11

DISFIGURE
d their faces that ....Matt 6:16

DISGUISES
And he *d* his face ......Job 24:15

DISHONOR
Father, and you *d* Me ...John 8:49
d their bodies among ...Rom 1:24
It is sown in *d* ....1 Cor 15:43

DISHONORED
But you have *d* the .....James 2:6

DISHONORS
For son *d* father ....Mic 7:6

DISOBEDIENT
out My hands To a *d* ..Rom 10:21

DISORDERLY
for this *d* gathering ....Acts 19:40

DISPENSATION
d of the fullness of ......Eph 1:10

DISPERSION
the pilgrims of the *D* ....1 Pet 1:1

DISPLEASE
LORD see it, and it *d* ...Prov 24:18

DISPLEASED
they were greatly *d* ....Matt 20:24
it, He was greatly *d* ...Mark 10:14

DISPUTE
there was also a *d* ....Luke 22:24

DISPUTER
Where is the *d* of this ..1 Cor 1:20

DISPUTES
But avoid foolish *d* ......Titus 3:9

DISQUALIFIED
should become *d* ......1 Cor 9:27

DISQUIETED
And why are you *d* ....Ps 42:5

DISSENSION
had no small *d* and .....Acts 15:2

DISSIPATION
not accused of *d* ....Titus 1:6

DISSOLVED
the heavens will be *d* ...2 Pet 3:12

DISTINCTION
compassion, making a *d* ..Jude 22

DISTRESS
d them in His deep ....Ps 2:5
tribulation, or *d* ....Rom 8:35

DISTRESSED
and deeply *d* ....Mark 14:33

DISTRESSES
Bring me out of my *d* ....Ps 25:17

DISTRIBUTED
and they *d* to each as ...Acts 4:35

DISTRIBUTING
d to the needs of the ...Rom 12:13

DITCH
will fall into a *d* ....Matt 15:14

DIVERSITIES
There are *d* ....1 Cor 12:4

DIVIDE
d the spoil with the ....Prov 16:19
"Take this and *d* ......Luke 22:17

DIVIDED
and the waters were *d* ...Ex 14:21
they were not *d* ....2 Sam 1:23
"Every kingdom *d* ....Matt 12:25
Is Christ *d* ....1 Cor 1:13

DIVIDES
at home the *d* spoil ......Ps 68:12

DIVIDING
rightly *d* the word of ..2 Tim 2:15

DIVINATION
shall you practice *d* ....Lev 19:26
a spirit of *d* met us ....Acts 16:16

DIVINE
d service and the ....Heb 9:1

DIVISION
So there was a *d* ......John 7:43

DIVISIONS
those who cause *d* .....Rom 16:17
persons, who cause *d* ....Jude 19

DIVISIVE
Reject a *d* man after ...Titus 3:10

DIVORCE
her a certificate of *d* ...Deut 24:1
a certificate of *d* ...Mark 10:4

DO
men to *d* to you, *d* ...Matt 7:12
He sees the Father *d* ...John 5:19
without Me you can *d* ...John 15:5
"Sirs, what must I *d* ...Acts 16:30
d evil that good may ...Rom 3:8
or whatever you *d*, *d* ...1 Cor 10:31

DOCTRINE
What new *d* is this ...Mark 1:27
"My *d* is not Mine ...John 7:16
with every wind of *d* ...Eph 4:14
is contrary to sound *d* .1 Tim 1:10
is profitable for *d* ...2 Tim 3:16
not endure sound *d* ...2 Tim 4:3

DOCTRINES
commandments and *d* ...Col 2:22
various and strange *d* ...Heb 13:9

DOERS
But be *d* of the word ..James 1:22

DOG
d is better than a ...Eccl 9:4
d returns to his own ...2 Pet 2:22

DOGS
what is holy to the *d* ...Matt 7:6
d eat the crumbs ...Matt 15:27
But outside are *d* ...Rev 22:15

DOMINION
let them have *d* ...Gen 1:26
d is an everlasting ...Dan 4:34
sin shall not have *d* ...Rom 6:14
glory and majesty, *D* ...Jude 25

DONKEY
d its master's crib ...Is 1:3
and riding on a *d* ...Zech 9:9
colt, the foal of a d ...Matt 21:5
d speaking with a ...2 Pet 2:16

DOOM
for the day of *d* ...Prov 16:4

DOOR
stone against the *d* ...Matt 27:60
to you, I am the *d* ...John 10:7
before you an open *d* ...Rev 3:8
I stand at the *d* ...Rev 3:20

DOORKEEPER
I would rather be a *d* ...Ps 84:10

DOORPOSTS
write them on the *d* ...Deut 6:9

DOORS
up, you everlasting *d* ...Ps 24:7

DOUBLE
from the LORD's hand *D* ...Is 40:2
worthy of *d* honor ...1 Tim 5:17

DOUBLE-MINDED
he is a *d* man ...James 1:8

DOUBT
faith, why did you *d* ...Matt 14:31

DOUBTING
in faith, with no *d* ...James 1:6

DOUBTS
why do *d* arise in ...Luke 24:38
for I have *d* about you ...Gal 4:20

DOVE
d found no resting ...Gen 8:9
descending like a *d* ...Matt 3:16

DOVES
and harmless as *d* ...Matt 10:16

DOWNCAST
who comforts the *d* ...2 Cor 7:6

DRAGNET
d that was cast ...Matt 13:47

DRAGON
they worshiped the *d* ...Rev 13:4
He laid hold of the *d* ...Rev 20:2

DRAINED
All faces are *d* ...Joel 2:6

DRANK
them, and they all *d* ..Mark 14:23

DRAW
d honey from the ...Deut 32:13
me to *d* near to God ...Ps 73:28
And the years *d* ...Eccl 12:1
will *d* all peoples ...John 12:32
D near to God and He ..James 4:8

DRAWS
your redemption *d* ...Luke 21:28

DREAM
Now Joseph had a *d* ...Gen 37:5
Your old men shall *d* ...Joel 2:28
to Joseph in a *d* ...Matt 2:13
things today in a *d* ...Matt 27:19

DREAMERS
d defile the flesh ...Jude 8

DREAMS
Nebuchadnezzar had *d* ...Dan 2:1

DRIED
of her blood was *d* ...Mark 5:29
saw the fig tree *d* ...Mark 11:20

DRIFT
have heard, lest we *d* ...Heb 2:1

DRINK
gave me vinegar to *d* ...Ps 69:21
Lest they *d* and forget ..Prov 31:5
follow intoxicating *d* ...Is 5:11
d the milk of the ...Is 60:16
bosom, That you may *d* ..Is 66:11
"Bring wine, let us *d* ...Amos 4:1
that day when I *d* ...Matt 26:29
mingled with gall to *d* .Matt 27:34
with myrrh to *d* ...Mark 15:23
to her, "Give Me a *d* ...John 4:7
him come to Me and *d* ..John 7:37
do, as often as you *d* ..1 Cor 11:25
No longer *d* only ...1 Tim 5:23

DRINKS
to her, "Whoever *d* ...John 4:13
d My blood has ...John 6:54
he who eats and *d* ...1 Cor 11:29

DRIPPING
His lips are lilies, *D* ...Song 5:13

DROSS
purge away your *d* ...Is 1:25

DROUGHT
in the year of *d* ...Jer 17:8
"For I called for a *d* ...Hag 1:11

DROVE
So He *d* out the man ...Gen 3:24
temple of God and *d* ...Matt 21:12

DROWN
Nor can the floods *d* ...Song 8:7
harmful lusts which *d* ...1 Tim 6:9

DROWSINESS
d will clothe a ...Prov 23:21

DRUNK
of the wine and was *d* ...Gen 9:21
the guests have well *d* ..John 2:10
"For these are not *d* ...Acts 2:15
and another is *d* ...1 Cor 11:21
I saw the woman, *d* ...Rev 17:6

DRUNKARD
to and fro like a *d* ...Is 24:20
or a reviler, or a *d* ...1 Cor 5:11

DRUNKEN
I am like a *d* man ...Jer 23:9

DRUNKENNESS
will be filled with *d* ...Ezek 23:33
not in revelry and *d* ...Rom 13:13
envy, murders, *d* ...Gal 5:21

DRY
place, and let the *d* ...Gen 1:9
made the sea into *d* ...Ex 14:21
It was *d* on the fleece ..Judg 6:40
will be done in the *d* ..Luke 23:31

DUE
pay all that was *d* ...Matt 18:34
d time Christ died ...Rom 5:6
d season we shall ...Gal 6:9
exalt you in *d* time ...1 Pet 5:6

DULL
heart of this people *d* ...Is 6:10
people have grown d ..Matt 13:15

DUMB
the tongue of the *d* ...Is 35:6

DUST
formed man of the *d* ...Gen 2:7
d you shall return ...Gen 3:19
And repent in *d* ...Job 42:6
that we are *d* ...Ps 103:14
counted as the small *d* ...Is 40:15
city, shake off the *d* ...Matt 10:14
of the man of *d* ...1 Cor 15:49

DUTY
done what was our *d* ..Luke 17:10

DWELL
Who may *d* in Your holy ..Ps 15:1
"I *d* in the high and ...Is 57:15
"I will d in them ...2 Cor 6:16
that Christ may *d* ...Eph 3:17
men, and He will *d* ...Rev 21:3

DWELLING
built together for a *d* ...Eph 2:22
a foreign country, *d* ...Heb 11:9

DWELLS
He who in the secret ...Ps 91:1
but the Father who *d* ..John 14:10
d all the fullness ...Col 2:9
which righteousness *d* ..2 Pet 3:13
you, where Satan *d* ...Rev 2:13

DWELT
became flesh and *d* ...John 1:14
By faith he *d* in the ...Heb 11:9

DYING
in the body the *d* ...2 Cor 4:10

E

EAGLE
fly away like an *e* ...Prov 23:5

EAGLES

The way of an *e* ......Prov 30:19
like a flying *e* ....Rev 4:7

EAGLES

up with wings like *e* ......Is 40:31
e will be gathered .....Matt 24:28

EAGLES'

how I bore you on *e* ......Ex 19:4

EAR

shall pierce his *e* ....Ex 21:6
And the *e* of the wise ..Prov 18:15
e is uncircumcised ....Jer 6:10
you hear in the *e* .....Matt 10:27
cut off his right *e* ......John 18:10
not seen, nor e heard ...1 Cor 2:9
"He who has an *e* ....Rev 2:7

EARLY

Very *e* in the morning .Mark 16:2
arrived at the tomb *e* ..Luke 24:22

EARNESTLY

He prayed more *e* ....Luke 22:44
e that it would not ....James 5:17
you to contend *e* ....Jude 3

EARS

And hear with their *e* .....Is 6:10
"He who has *e* ....Matt 11:15
they have itching *e* .....2 Tim 4:3

EARTH

to judge the *e* ....1 Chr 16:33
foundations of the *e* .....Job 38:4
e is the LORD's............Ps 24:1
You had formed the *e* ....Ps 90:2
there was ever an *e* ...Prov 8:23
e abides forever ....Eccl 1:4
for the meek of the *e* ......Is 11:4
e is My footstool ....Is 66:1
I will darken the *e* .....Amos 8:9
shall inherit the *e* ......Matt 5:5
heaven and *e* pass ......Matt 5:18
e as it is in heaven ....Matt 6:10
treasures on *e* ....Matt 6:19
then shook the *e* ....Heb 12:26
heaven and a new *e* .....Rev 21:1

EARTHLY

"If I have told you *e* ....John 3:12
that if our *e* house ....2 Cor 5:1
their mind on *e* things ...Phil 3:19
from above, but is *e* ..James 3:15

EARTHQUAKE

after the wind an *e* ...1 Kin 19:11
there was a great *e* .....Matt 28:2

EARTHQUAKES

And there will be *e* ....Mark 13:8

EASIER

"Which is *e*, to say .....Mark 2:9
"It is *e* for a camel ....Mark 10:25

EAST

goes toward the *e* ....Gen 2:14
wise men from the *E* ....Matt 2:1
many will come from *e* .Matt 8:11
will come from the *e* ...Luke 13:29

EAT

you may freely *e* ....Gen 2:16
'You shall not *e* ....Gen 3:17
e this scroll ....Ezek 3:1
life, what you will *e* ...Matt 6:25
give us His flesh to *e* ...John 6:52
one believes he may *e* ...Rom 14:2
e meat nor drink wine ...Rom 14:21
I will never again *e* ....1 Cor 8:13
neither shall he *e* ....2 Thess 3:10

EATEN

Have you *e* from the ....Gen 3:11
he was *e* by worms ....Acts 12:23

EATS

receives sinners and *e* ..Luke 15:2
"Whoever *e* My flesh ...John 6:54
e this bread will live ....John 6:58
He who *e*, *e* to the ......Rom 14:6
unworthy manner *e* ...1 Cor 11:29

EDIFICATION

has given me for *e* ....2 Cor 13:10
rather than godly *e* .....1 Tim 1:4

EDIFIES

puffs up, but love *e* .....1 Cor 8:1

EDIFY

but not all things *e* ...1 Cor 10:23

EDIFYING

of the body for the *e* ....Eph 4:16

ELDER

against an *e* except ....1 Tim 5:19

ELDERS

the tradition of the *e* ....Matt 15:2
be rejected by the *e* ....Luke 9:22
they had appointed *e* ..Acts 14:23
e who rule well be ....1 Tim 5:17
lacking, and appoint *e* ...Titus 1:5
e obtained a good ......Heb 11:2
e who are among you I ..1 Pet 5:1
I saw twenty-four *e* ......Rev 4:4

ELDERSHIP

of the hands of the *e* ..1 Tim 4:14

ELECT

gather together His *e* ..Matt 24:31
e have obtained it ......Rom 11:7
e according to the ....1 Pet 1:2
A chief cornerstone, e ..1 Pet 2:6

ELECTION

call and *e* sure ....2 Pet 1:10

ELEMENTS

weak and beggarly *e* .....Gal 4:9
e will melt with ....2 Pet 3:10

ELEVEN

numbered with the *e* ....Acts 1:26

ELOQUENT

an *e* man and mighty ..Acts 18:24

EMBALM

to *e* his father ....Gen 50:2

ENCOURAGED

is, that I may be *e* ......Rom 1:12
and all may be *e* .....1 Cor 14:31

END

make me to know my *e* ...Ps 39:4
shall keep it to the *e* ....Ps 119:33
e is the way of death ...Prov 14:12
Declaring the *e* ....Is 46:10
what shall be the *e* .....Dan 12:8
the harvest is the *e* ....Matt 13:39
always, even to the *e* ...Matt 28:20
He loved them to the *e* ...John 13:1
For Christ is the *e* .....Rom 10:4
But the *e* of all ....1 Pet 4:7
the latter *e* is worse ....2 Pet 2:20
My works until the *e* ....Rev 2:26
Beginning and the *E* ...Rev 22:13

ENDLESS

and *e* genealogies ....1 Tim 1:4
to the power of an *e* ....Heb 7:16

ENDURANCE

e the race that ....Heb 12:1

ENDURE

as the sun and moon *e* ....Ps 72:5
His name shall *e* ....Ps 72:17
persecuted, we *e* ......1 Cor 4:12

ENDURED

he had patiently *e* ....Heb 6:15
e as seeing Him who ....Heb 11:27
consider Him who *e* .....Heb 12:3

ENDURES

And His truth *e* ....Ps 100:5
For His mercy *e* ....Ps 136:1
But he who *e* to the ...Matt 10:22
e only for a while ......Matt 13:21
for the food which *e* ....John 6:27
he has built on it *e* .....1 Cor 3:14
hopes all things, *e* .....1 Cor 13:7
word of the LORD e .....1 Pet 1:25

ENDURING

the LORD is clean, *e* ....Ps 19:9

ENEMIES

the presence of my *e* .....Ps 23:5
e will lick the dust ....Ps 72:9
to you, love your *e* .....Matt 5:44
e will be those ....Matt 10:36
e we were reconciled ...Rom 5:10
till He has put all *e* ...1 Cor 15:25
were alienated and *e* ....Col 1:21
His *e* are made His ....Heb 10:13

ENEMY

If your *e* is hungry ....Prov 25:21
rejoice over me, my *e* .....Mic 7:8
and hate your *e* ....Matt 5:43
last *e* that will be ....1 Cor 15:26
become your *e* because ..Gal 4:16
count him as an *e* ....2 Thess 3:15
makes himself an *e* ....James 4:4

ENJOY

richly all things to *e* ...1 Tim 6:17
than to *e* the passing ...Heb 11:25

ENJOYMENT

So I commended *e* ......Eccl 8:15

ENLIGHTEN

E my eyes ....Ps 13:3

ENLIGHTENED

those who were once *e* ...Heb 6:4

ENMITY

And I will put *e* ....Gen 3:15
the carnal mind is *e* .....Rom 8:7
in His flesh the *e* ....Eph 2:15

ENRAPTURED

And always be *e* ....Prov 5:19

ENRICHED

while you are *e* ....2 Cor 9:11

ENSNARED

The wicked is *e* ....Prov 12:13

ENSNARES

sin which so easily *e* ....Heb 12:1

ENTER

E into His gates ....Ps 100:4
you will by no means *e* .Matt 5:20
"E by the narrow ....Matt 7:13
e the kingdom of God ..Matt 19:24
E into the joy of your ..Matt 25:21
and pray, lest you *e* ...Matt 26:41
"Strive to *e* through ...Luke 13:24
who have believed do *e* .Heb 4:3
e the temple till the .....Rev 15:8

ENTERED

Then Satan *e* Judas .... Luke 22:3
through one man sin *e* . . Rom 5:12
ear heard, Nor have *e* ... 1 Cor 2:9
the forerunner has *e* .... Heb 6:20
e the Most Holy Place ... Heb 9:12

ENTERS

If anyone *e* by Me ...... John 10:9

ENTHRONED

You are holy, *E* in .... Ps 22:3

ENTIRELY

give yourself *e* .... 1 Tim 4:15

ENTREAT

being defamed, we *e* ... 1 Cor 4:13

ENTREATED

e our God for this ...... Ezra 8:23

ENVIOUS

patriarchs, becoming *e* ... Acts 7:9

ENVY

e slays a simple .... Job 5:2
e is rottenness .... Prov 14:30
not let your heart *e* .... Prov 23:17
full of *e* .... Rom 1:29
not in strife and *e* ...... Rom 13:13
love does not *e* .... 1 Cor 13:4
e, murders .... Gal 5:21
living in malice and *e* ... Titus 3:3

EPISTLE

You are our *e* written ... 2 Cor 3:2

EPISTLES

as also in all his *e* ...... 2 Pet 3:16

ERR

My people Israel to *e* .... Jer 23:13

ERROR

a sinner from the *e* ... James 5:20
led away with the *e* ... 2 Pet 3:17
run greedily in the *e* ..... Jude 11

ERRORS

can understand his *e* .... Ps 19:12

ESCAPE

e all these things ..... Luke 21:36
same, that you will *e* .... Rom 2:3
make the way of *e* .... 1 Cor 10:13
how shall we *e* if we ..... Heb 2:3

ESCAPED

after they have *e* .... 2 Pet 2:20

ESTABLISH

seeking to *e* their own .. Rom 10:3
faithful, who will *e* .... 2 Thess 3:3
E your hearts .... James 5:8
a while, perfect, *e* ...... 1 Pet 5:10

ESTABLISHED

Your throne is .... Ps 93:2
built up in Him and *e* ..... Col 2:7
covenant, which was *e* ... Heb 8:6

ESTEEM

and we did not *e* .... Is 53:3
e others better than ...... Phil 2:3

ESTEEMED

For what is highly *e* ... Luke 16:15

ESTEEMS

One person *e* one day .. Rom 14:5

ETERNAL

e God is your refuge .. Deut 33:27

For man goes to his *e* ... Eccl 12:5
and inherit *e* life ...... Matt 19:29
in the age to come, *e* . Mark 10:30
not perish but have *e* .. John 3:15
you think you have *e* ... John 5:39
I give them *e* life ...... John 10:28
"And this is *e* life ...... John 17:3
the gift of God is *e* ...... Rom 6:23
are not seen are *e* ..... 2 Cor 4:18
lay hold on *e* life .... 1 Tim 6:12
e life which was .... 1 John 1:2

ETERNITY

Also He has put *e* ...... Eccl 3:11
One who inhabits *e* ...... Is 57:15

EUNUCH

of Ethiopia, a *e* .... Acts 8:27

EUNUCHS

made themselves *e* .... Matt 19:12

EVANGELIST

of Philip the *e* .... Acts 21:8
do the work of an *e* .... 2 Tim 4:5

EVANGELISTS

some prophets, some *e* .. Eph 4:11

EVERLASTING

from *E* is Your name ..... Is 63:16
awake, Some to *e* life ... Dan 12:2
not perish but have *e* ... John 3:16
who sent Me has *e* ..... John 5:24
endures to *e* life .... John 6:27
in Him may have *e* ..... John 6:40
believes in Me has *e* ... John 6:47
e destruction from .... 2 Thess 1:9

EVIDENCE

e of things not seen ..... Heb 11:1

EVIDENT

e that our Lord arose .... Heb 7:14

EVIL

of good and *e* .... Gen 2:9
knowing good and *e* ..... Gen 3:5
his heart was only *e* ..... Gen 6:5
I will fear no *e* .... Ps 23:4
e more than good .... Ps 52:3
To do *e* is like sport ... Prov 10:23
e will bow before the ... Prov 14:19
Keeping watch on the *e* . Prov 15:3
e All the days of her ... Prov 31:12
to those who call *e* .... Is 5:20
of peace and not *e* .... Jer 29:11
Seek good and not *e* ... Amos 5:14
deliver us from the *e* .... Matt 6:13
"If you then, being *e* ... Matt 7:11
e treasure brings .... Matt 12:35
everyone practicing *e* ... John 3:20
done any good or *e* ..... Rom 9:11
Repay no one *e* for .... Rom 12:17
provoked, thinks no *e* . 1 Cor 13:5

EVILDOER

"If He were not an *e* .. John 18:30
suffer trouble as an *e* ... 2 Tim 2:9

EVILDOERS

e shall be cut off .... Ps 37:9
from me, you *e* ...... Ps 119:115
iniquity, A brood of *e* ..... Is 1:4
against you as *e* .... 1 Pet 2:12

EXALT

e His name together ..... Ps 34:3
E the humble .... Ezek 21:26
And he shall *e* himself .. Dan 8:25

EXALTATION

who rejoice in My *e* ...... Is 13:3
brother glory in his *e* ... James 1:9

EXALTED

Let God be *e* .... 2 Sam 22:47
I will be *e* among the .... Ps 46:10
You are *e* far above ...... Ps 97:9
His name alone is *e* ... Ps 148:13
valley shall be *e* .... Is 40:4
"Him God has *e* .... Acts 5:31
And lest I should be *e* . 2 Cor 12:7
also has highly *e* .... Phil 2:9

EXALTS

Righteousness *e* .... Prov 14:34
high thing that *e* ...... 2 Cor 10:5
e himself above all .... 2 Thess 2:4

EXAMINE

But let a man *e* .... 1 Cor 11:28
But let each one *e* .... Gal 6:4

EXAMPLE

to make her a public *e* .. Matt 1:19
I have given you *e* . John 13:15
youth, but be an *e* ..... 1 Tim 4:12
us, leaving us an *e* ..... 1 Pet 2:21
are set forth as an *e* .... Jude 7

EXAMPLES

to them as *e* .... 1 Cor 10:11
to you, but being *e* ...... 1 Pet 5:3

EXCHANGE

give in *e* for his soul ... Matt 16:26

EXCHANGED

Nor can it be *e* .... Job 28:17
e the truth of God for ... Rom 1:25

EXCUSE

now they have no *e* ... John 15:22
they are without *e* ...... Rom 1:20

EXCUSES

began to make *e* ...... Luke 14:18

EXECUTE

e judgment also .... John 5:27
e wrath on him who .... Rom 13:4

EXECUTES

e justice for me .... Mic 7:9

EXERCISE

e yourself toward .... 1 Tim 4:7

EXHORT

e him as a father .... 1 Tim 5:1
Speak these things, *e* ... Titus 2:15
e one another .... Heb 3:13

EXHORTATION

he who exhorts, in *e* .... Rom 12:8
to reading, to *e* .... 1 Tim 4:13

EXHORTED

know how we *e* ..... 1 Thess 2:11

EXIST

by Your will they *e* ..... Rev 4:11

EXPECT

an hour you do not *e* .. Luke 12:40

EXPECTATION

the people were in *e* .... Luke 3:15
a certain fearful *e* ...... Heb 10:27

EXPLAIN

no one who could *e* .... Gen 41:24
"*E* this parable to us ... Matt 15:15
to say, and hard to *e* .... Heb 5:11

EXPLAINED

He *e* all things to His .. Mark 4:34

EXPOSED
his deeds should be *e* ...John 3:20

EXPOUNDED
He *e* to them in all ....Luke 24:27

EXPRESS
of His glory and the *e* ....Heb 1:3

EXTORTION
they are full of *e* ......Matt 23:25

EXTORTIONERS
e will inherit ....1 Cor 6:10

EYE
the ear, But now my *e* ...Job 42:5
guide you with My *e* ......Ps 32:8
e is not satisfied ....Eccl 1:8
the apple of His *e* ......Zech 2:8
if your right *e* ....Matt 5:29
it was said, 'An *e* ......Matt 5:38
plank in your own *e* ....Matt 7:3
e causes you to sin .....Matt 18:9
Or is your *e* evil ......Matt 20:15
the *e* of a needle .....Luke 18:25
the twinkling of an *e* .1 Cor 15:52
every *e* will see Him ......Rev 1:7
your eyes with *e* salve ...Rev 3:18

EYES
e will be opened ....Gen 3:5
And my *e* shall behold ..Job 19:27
e are ever toward the ....Ps 25:15
The *e* of the LORD are ...Ps 34:15
I will lift up my *e* ....Ps 121:1
but the *e* of a fool ....Prov 17:24
be wise in his own *e* ....Prov 26:5
You have dove's *e* .....Song 1:15
e have seen the King ......Is 6:5
Who have *e* and see ....Jer 5:21
rims were full of *e* .....Ezek 1:18
You are of purer *e* ......Hab 1:13
blessed are your *e* ....Matt 13:16
"He put clay on my *e* ...John 9:15
e they have closed ....Acts 28:27
E that they should not ..Rom 11:8
have seen with our *e* ..1 John 1:1
the lust of the *e* ......1 John 2:16
as snow, and His *e* ....Rev 1:14
creatures full of *e* ......Rev 4:6
horns and seven *e* ....Rev 5:6

EYESERVICE
not with *e* ....Eph 6:6

EYEWITNESSES
the beginning were *e* ...Luke 1:2
e of His majesty ......2 Pet 1:16

F

FABLES
nor give heed to *f* ......1 Tim 1:4
cunningly devised *f* ....2 Pet 1:16

FACE
"For I have seen God *f* .Gen 32:30
f shone while he ....Ex 34:29
sins have hidden His *f* ....Is 59:2
f shone like the sun .....Matt 17:2
dimly, but then *f* .....1 Cor 13:12
with unveiled *f* ....2 Cor 3:18
withstood him to his *f* ...Gal 2:11
They shall see His *f* .....Rev 22:4

FADE
We all *f* as a leaf ....Is 64:6
rich man also will *f* ...James 1:11
and that does not *f* ......1 Pet 1:4

FADES
withers, the flower *f* ....Is 40:7

FAIL
tittle of the law to *f* ...Luke 16:17
faith should not *f* .....Luke 22:32
they will *f* ....1 Cor 13:8
Your years will not f ....Heb 1:12

FAILING
"men's hearts *f* ....Luke 21:26

FAILS
Love never *f* ....1 Cor 13:8

FAINT
shall walk and not *f* ......Is 40:31

FAINTS
My soul *f* for Your .....Ps 119:81
And the whole heart *f* ......Is 1:5
the earth, Neither *f* ......Is 40:28

FAITH
shall live by his *f* ....Hab 2:4
you, O you of little *f* ....Matt 6:30
not found such great *f* ..Matt 8:10
that you have no *f* .....Mark 4:40
"Increase our *f* ....Luke 17:5
will He really find *f* ....Luke 18:8
are sanctified by *f* ....Acts 26:18
God is revealed from *f* ..Rom 1:17
f apart from the deeds ..Rom 3:28
his *f* is accounted for ....Rom 4:5
those who are of the *f* ..Rom 4:16
f which we preach ......Rom 10:8
f comes by hearing ....Rom 10:17
and you stand by *f* .....Rom 11:20
in proportion to our *f* ...Rom 12:6
Do you have *f* ....Rom 14:22
though I have all *f* .....1 Cor 13:2
And now abide *f* .....1 Cor 13:13
For we walk by *f* ......2 Cor 5:7
the flesh I live by *f* .....Gal 2:20
f are sons of Abraham ...Gal 3:7
But after *f* has come ....Gal 3:25
of the household of *f* ....Gal 6:10
been saved through *f* ....Eph 2:8
one Lord, one *f* ....Eph 4:5
taking the shield of *f* ....Eph 6:16
your work of *f* ....1 Thess 1:3
for not all have *f* ......2 Thess 3:2
the mystery of the *f* .....1 Tim 3:9
I have kept the *f* ....2 Tim 4:7
in our common *f* ....Titus 1:4
not being mixed with *f* ...Heb 4:2
f is the substance ......Heb 11:1
without *f* it is ....Heb 11:6
says he has *f* ....James 2:14
Show me your *f* ......James 2:18
and not by *f* only .....James 2:24
f will save the sick ....James 5:15
add to your *f* virtue .....2 Pet 1:5
the patience and the *f* ..Rev 13:10

FAITHFUL
God, He is God, the *f* ....Deut 7:9
LORD preserves the *f* .....Ps 31:23
eyes shall be on the *f* ...Ps 101:6
But who can find a *f* ....Prov 20:6
the Holy One who is *f* ...Hos 11:12
"Who then is a *f* ......Matt 24:45
good and *f* servant ....Matt 25:23
"He who is *f* in what ...Luke 16:10
judged me to be *f* .....Acts 16:15
God is *f* ....1 Cor 1:9
is my beloved and *f* ....1 Cor 4:17
But as God is *f* ....2 Cor 1:18
f brethren in Christ ....Col 1:2
who calls you is *f* ....1 Thess 5:24
This is a *f* saying and ..1 Tim 1:15
f High Priest in ....Heb 2:17
He who promised is *f* ...Heb 10:23
He is *f* and just to .....1 John 1:9
Be *f* until death ....Rev 2:10
words are true and *f* ....Rev 21:5

FAITHFULNESS
I have declared Your *f* ...Ps 40:10
Your *f* also surrounds .....Ps 89:8
f endures to all ....Ps 119:90
Great is Your *f* ....Lam 3:23
unbelief make the *f* ......Rom 3:3

FAITHLESS
"O *f* generation ....Mark 9:19
If we are *f* ....2 Tim 2:13

FALL
a deep sleep to *f* ....Gen 2:21
Let them *f* by their ......Ps 5:10
righteous man may *f* ..Prov 24:16
But the wicked shall *f* .Prov 24:16
the blind, both will *f* ...Matt 15:14
the stars will *f* ....Matt 24:29
"I saw Satan *f* ....Luke 10:18
take heed lest he *f* ....1 Cor 10:12
if they *f* away ....Heb 6:6
lest anyone *f* short of ..Heb 12:15
and rocks, "F on us .....Rev 6:16

FALLEN
"Babylon is *f* ....Is 21:9
you have *f* from grace ....Gal 5:4
"Babylon is *f* ....Rev 14:8

FALLING
great drops of blood *f* .Luke 22:44
f away comes first ....2 Thess 2:3

FALSE
"You shall not bear *f* ....Ex 20:16
I hate every *f* way .....Ps 119:104
f witness shall perish ..Prov 21:28
"Beware of *f* prophets ..Matt 7:15
f christs and *f* ....Matt 24:24
and we are found *f* ...1 Cor 15:15
of *f* brethren ....Gal 2:4
f prophets have gone ..1 John 4:1
mouth of the *f* prophet .Rev 16:13

FALSEHOOD
For their deceit is *f* ....Ps 119:118
Offspring of *f* ....Is 57:4

FALSELY
of evil against you *f* ....Matt 5:11
f called knowledge ....1 Tim 6:20

FAMILIES
in you all the *f* ....Gen 12:3
the God of all the *f* ......Jer 31:1
in your seed all the f ....Acts 3:25

FAMILY
shall mourn, every *f* ...Zech 12:12
f were baptized ....Acts 16:33

FAMINES
And there will be *f* .....Matt 24:7

FAMISH
righteous soul to *f* ......Prov 10:3

FAMISHED
honorable men are *f* ....Is 5:13

FAR
Your judgments are *f* .....Ps 10:5
Be not *f* from Me ....Ps 22:11
The LORD is *f* from ....Prov 15:29
their heart is f from ....Matt 15:8
going to a *f* country ...Mark 13:34
though He is not *f* .....Acts 17:27
you who once were *f* ....Eph 2:13

FARMER
The hard-working *f* .....2 Tim 2:6
See how the *f* waits ....James 5:7

FASHIONED
have made me and *f* .....Job 10:8

FASHIONS

He f their hearts . . . . Ps 33:15

FAST

f as you do this day . . . . Is 58:4
f that I have chosen . . . . . . Is 58:5
"Moreover, when you f . Matt 6:16
disciples do not f . . . . . . Matt 9:14
'I f twice a week . . . . . . Luke 18:12

FASTED

'When you f and . . . . Zech 7:5
And when He had f . . . . . Matt 4:2

FASTING

by prayer and f . . . . Matt 17:21
give yourselves to f . . . . 1 Cor 7:5

FASTINGS

in sleeplessness, in f . . 2 Cor 6:5

FAT

and you will eat the f . . Gen 45:18
f is the LORD's . . . . Lev 3:16

FATHER

man shall leave his f . . . . Gen 2:24
and you shall be a f . . . . Gen 17:4
I was a f to the poor . . . . Job 29:16
A f of the fatherless . . . . . Ps 68:5
f pities his children . . . . Ps 103:13
God, Everlasting F . . . . Is 9:6
You, O LORD, are our F . . Is 63:16
time cry to Me, 'My F . . . . Jer 3:4
For I am a F to Israel . . . Jer 31:9
"A son honors his f . . . . . . Mal 1:6
Have we not all one F . . Mal 2:10
Our F in heaven . . . . . . Matt 6:9
"He who loves f . . . . . . Matt 10:37
know the F . . . . Matt 11:27
'He who curses f . . . . . . Matt 15:4
for One is your F . . . . . . Matt 23:9
"F will be divided . . . . Luke 12:53
F loves the Son . . . . John 3:35
F raises the dead . . . . . . John 5:21
F judges no one . . . . John 5:22
He has seen the F . . . . . . John 6:46
F who sent Me bears . . John 8:18
we have one F . . . . John 8:41
of your f the devil . . . . . John 8:44
"I and My F are one . . John 10:30
'I am going to the F . . John 14:28
came forth from the F . John 16:28
that he might be the f . . Rom 4:11
one God and F of all . . . . Eph 4:6
"I will be to Him a F . . . . Heb 1:5
down from the F . . . . . James 1:17
if you call on the F . . . 1 Pet 1:17
and testify that the F . 1 John 4:14

FATHERLESS

the helper of the f . . . . . . Ps 10:14
He relieves the f . . . . . . Ps 146:9
do not defend the f . . . . . . Is 1:23
they may rob the f . . . . . Is 10:2
You the f finds mercy . . . Hos 14:3

FATHER'S

you in My F kingdom . Matt 26:29
I must be about My F . . Luke 2:49
F house are many . . . . . John 14:2
that a man has his f . . . . 1 Cor 5:1

FATHERS

the LORD God of our f . . . Ezra 7:27
f trusted in You . . . . Ps 22:4
our ears, O God, our f . . . . Ps 44:1
f ate the manna . . . . John 6:31
of whom are the f . . . . . . Rom 9:5
unaware that all our f . . 1 Cor 10:1

FATNESS

of the root and f . . . . . . Rom 11:17

FAULT

I have found no f . . . . . Luke 23:14
does He still find f . . . . . . Rom 9:19
of God without f . . . . Phil 2:15

FAULTLESS

covenant had been f . . . . . Heb 8:7
to present you f . . . . Jude 24

FAULTS

"I remember my f . . . . . Gen 41:9
me from secret f . . . . Ps 19:12

FAVOR

granted me life and f . . . Job 10:12
His f is for life . . . . Ps 30:5
A good man obtains f . . . Prov 12:2
and stature, and in f . . . . Luke 2:52
God and having f . . . . . . Acts 2:47

FAVORED

"Rejoice, highly f . . . . . Luke 1:28

FAVORITISM

not show personal f . . . Luke 20:21
God shows personal f . . . . Gal 2:6

FEAR

live, for I f God . . . . Gen 42:18
to put the dread and f . . Deut 2:25
said, "Does Job f . . . . Job 1:9
Yes, you cast off f . . . . . . Job 15:4
The f of the LORD is . . . . . . Ps 19:9
of death, I will f . . . . Ps 23:4
Whom shall I f . . . . Ps 27:1
Oh, f the LORD . . . . Ps 34:9
There is no f of God . . . . . Ps 36:1
The f of the LORD is . . . . Ps 111:10
The f of man brings a . Prov 29:25
F God and keep His . . . . Eccl 12:13
Let Him be your f . . . . Is 8:13
"Be strong, do not f . . . . . Is 35:4
who would not f . . . . Jer 10:7
f Him who is able . . . . Matt 10:28
"Do not f . . . . Luke 12:32
"Do you not even f . . . Luke 23:40
And walking in the f . . . . Acts 9:31
given us a spirit of f . . . . 2 Tim 1:7
those who through f . . . . Heb 2:15
because of His godly f . . . Heb 5:7
F God . . . . 1 Pet 2:17
love casts out f . . . . . . 1 John 4:18

FEARED

He is also to be f . . . . 1 Chr 16:25
f God more than . . . . Neh 7:2
Yourself, are to be f . . . . . Ps 76:7
Then those who f . . . . Mal 3:16

FEARFUL

It is a f thing to . . . . Heb 10:31

FEARFULLY

f and wonderfully . . . . . . Ps 139:14

FEARING

sincerity of heart, f . . . . . Col 3:22
forsook Egypt, not f . . . . Heb 11:27

FEARS

upright man, one who f . . . Job 1:8
me from all my f . . . . Ps 34:4
nation whoever f . . . . . Acts 10:35
f has not been made . . 1 John 4:18

FEAST

and you shall keep a f . Num 29:12
hate, I despise your f . . Amos 5:21
every year at the f . . . . . Luke 2:41
when you give a f . . . . . Luke 14:13
Now the Passover, a f . . . John 6:4
great day of the f . . . . . . John 7:37

FEASTING

go to the house of f . . . . . . Eccl 7:2

FEASTS

the best places at f . . . Luke 20:46
spots in your love f . . . . . . Jude 12

FED

and f you with manna . . . Deut 8:3
f you with milk and . . . . . 1 Cor 3:2

FEEBLE

strengthened the f . . . . Job 4:4
And there was none f . . . Ps 105:37
And my flesh is f . . . . . . Ps 109:24
hang down, and the f . . Heb 12:12

FEED

ravens to f you there . . . 1 Kin 17:4
and f your flocks . . . . Is 61:5
to him, "F My lambs . . John 21:15
your enemy hungers, f . Rom 12:20
goods to f the poor . . . . 1 Cor 13:3

FEEDS

your heavenly Father f . . Matt 6:26

FEET

all things under his f . . . . . . Ps 8:6
He makes my f like the . . Ps 18:33
You have set my f . . . . Ps 31:8
For their f run to . . . . Prov 1:16
Her f go down to death . . Prov 5:5
mountains Are the f . . . . . Is 52:7
place of My f glorious . . . . Is 60:13
in that day His f . . . . . . Zech 14:4
two hands or two f . . . . . Matt 18:8
began to wash His f . . . Luke 7:38
wash the disciples' f . . . John 13:5
f are swift to shed . . . . . Rom 3:15
beautiful are the f . . . . . Rom 10:15
things under His f . . . . 1 Cor 15:27
and having shod your f . . Eph 6:15
fell at His f as dead . . . . Rev 1:17

FELLOW

begins to beat his f . . . Matt 24:49
f citizens with the . . . . . . Eph 2:19
Gentiles should be f . . . . . Eph 3:6
I am your f servant . . . . . Rev 19:10

FELLOWSHIP

doctrine and f . . . . Acts 2:42
were called into the f . . . 1 Cor 1:9
f has righteousness . . . . 2 Cor 6:14
the right hand of f . . . . Gal 2:9
And have no f with the . . Eph 5:11
of love, if any f . . . . Phil 2:1
and the f of His . . . . Phil 3:10
we say that we have f . . 1 John 1:6
the light, we have f . . . . 1 John 1:7

FERVENT

f prayer of a . . . . James 5:16
will melt with f . . . . 2 Pet 3:10

FERVENTLY

love one another f . . . . . 1 Pet 1:22

FEW

let your words be f . . . . . . Eccl 5:2
and there are f . . . . Matt 7:14
but the laborers are f . . . Matt 9:37
called, but f chosen . . . . Matt 20:16
"Lord, are there f . . . . . Luke 13:23

FIDELITY

but showing all good f . Titus 2:10

FIELD

Let the f be joyful . . . . . . Ps 96:12
"The f is the world . . . . Matt 13:38
and buys that f . . . . Matt 13:44
you are God's f . . . . 1 Cor 3:9

FIERY

Lord sent *f* serpents .... Num 21:6
shall make them as a *f* .... Ps 21:9
burning *f* furnace .... Dan 3:6
concerning the *f* .... 1 Pet 4:12

FIG

f leaves together .... Gen 3:7
"Look at the *f* .... Luke 21:29
'I saw you under the *f* .. John 1:50

FIGHT

"The Lord will *f* .... Ex 14:14
Our God will *f* for us .... Neh 4:20
My servants would *f*...John 18:36
to him, let us not *f* ..... Acts 23:9
F the good *f*.......... 1 Tim 6:12
have fought the good *f* .. 2 Tim 4:7

FIGHTS

your God is He who *f* .. Josh 23:10
because my lord *f* .... 1 Sam 25:28
f come from among ....James 4:1

FIGS

thornbushes or *f*........ Matt 7:16
or a grapevine bear *f* .. James 3:12

FILL

f the earth and subdue .. Gen 1:28
"Do I not *f* heaven ..... Jer 23:24
f this temple with ...... Hag 2:7
"F the waterpots .... John 2:7
that He might *f* .... Eph 4:10

FILLED

the whole earth be *f* ..... Ps 72:19
For they shall be *f* .... Matt 5:6
"Let the children be *f* .. Mark 7:27
would gladly have *f* ... Luke 15:16
being *f* with all .... Rom 1:29
but be *f* with the .... Eph 5:18
be warmed and *f*...... James 2:16

FILTHY

with *f* garments .... Zech 3:3
poor man in *f* clothes ... James 2:2
oppressed by the *f* ...... 2 Pet 2:7
let him be *f* .... Rev 22:11

FIND

sure your sin will *f* .... Num 32:23
waters, For you will *f* .... Eccl 11:1
seek, and you will *f*...... Matt 7:7
f a Babe wrapped ...... Luke 2:12
f no fault in this Man .. Luke 23:4
f grace to help in .... Heb 4:16

FINDS

f me *f* life .... Prov 8:35
f a wife *f* a good .... Prov 18:22
and he who seeks *f* ...... Matt 7:8
f his life will lose ...... Matt 10:39
and he who seeks *f* ... Luke 11:10

FINGER

written with the *f* .... Ex 31:18
dip the tip of his *f* ..... Luke 16:24
"Reach your *f*........ John 20:27

FINISH

he has enough to *f* .... Luke 14:28
has given Me to *f* ...... John 5:36

FINISHED

f the work which You .. John 17:4
He said, "It is *f*........ John 19:30
I have *f* the race .... 2 Tim 4:7

FIRE

rained brimstone and *f* . Gen 19:24
to him in a flame of *f* ...... Ex 3:2
who answers by *f* .... 1 Kin 18:24
Lord was not in the *f* . 1 Kin 19:12

We went through *f* ...... Ps 66:12
f goes before Him .... Ps 97:3
burns as the *f* .... Is 9:18
you walk through the *f* .... Is 43:2
f that burns all the .... Is 65:5
He break out like *f* ..... Amos 5:6
for conflict by *f*........ Amos 7:4
like a refiner's *f* .... Mal 3:2
the Holy Spirit and *f* .... Matt 3:11
f is not quenched ..... Mark 9:44
"I came to send *f* ..... Luke 12:49
tongues, as of *f* .... Acts 2:3
f taking vengeance .... 2 Thess 1:8
and that burned with *f* . Heb 12:18
And the tongue is a *f* ... James 3:6
vengeance of eternal *f* ..... Jude 7
into the lake of *f* ...... Rev 20:14

FIRM

of the hope *f* to the .... Heb 3:6

FIRMAMENT

Thus God made the *f* ..... Gen 1:7
f shows His handiwork ... Ps 19:1

FIRST

f father sinned .... Is 43:27
desires to be *f* .... Matt 20:27
f shall be slave .... Mark 10:44
the gospel must *f* ..... Mark 13:10
evil, of the Jew *f*........ Rom 2:9
f man Adam became .. 1 Cor 15:45
that we who *f* trusted ... Eph 1:12
Him because He *f* .... 1 John 4:19
I am the *F* and the ...... Rev 1:17
you have left your *f* ...... Rev 2:4
is the *f* resurrection ..... Rev 20:5

FIRSTBORN

Lord struck all the *f*..... Ex 12:29
brought forth her *f* ..... Matt 1:25
that He might be the *f* .. Rom 8:29
invisible God, the *f* ...... Col 1:15
the beginning, the *f* ..... Col 1:18
witness, the *f* from .... Rev 1:5

FIRSTFRUITS

also who have the *f* ..... Rom 8:23
and has become the *f* . 1 Cor 15:20
Christ the *f* .... 1 Cor 15:23

FISH

had prepared a great *f* ... Jon 1:17
belly of the great *f* .... Matt 12:40
five loaves and two *f* .. Matt 14:17
and likewise the *f* ..... John 21:13

FISHERS

and I will make you *f* ... Matt 4:19

FIVE

f smooth stones ...... 1 Sam 17:40
about *f* thousand men .. Matt 14:21
and *f* were foolish ...... Matt 25:2

FIXED

is a great gulf *f* ...... Luke 16:26

FLAME

appeared to him in a *f* ..... Ex 3:2
tormented in this *f* .... Luke 16:24
and His ministers a f ..... Heb 1:7
and His eyes like a *f* .... Rev 1:14

FLAMES

the Lord divides the *f* .... Ps 29:7

FLAMING

f sword which turned ... Gen 3:24
in *f* fire taking .... 2 Thess 1:8

FLATTER

They *f* with their .... Ps 5:9

FLATTERED

Nevertheless they *f* ...... Ps 78:36

FLATTERING

f speech deceive .... Rom 16:18
swelling words, *f*........ Jude 16

FLATTERS

f his neighbor Spreads .. Prov 29:5

FLATTERY

shall corrupt with *f* .... Dan 11:32

FLAVOR

the salt loses its *f*...... Matt 5:13

FLAX

f He will not quench ... Matt 12:20

FLEE

Or where can I *f*........ Ps 139:7
And the shadows *f* ..... Song 2:17
who are in Judea *f* ..... Matt 24:16
F sexual immorality ... 1 Cor 6:18
f these things and ..... 1 Tim 6:11
devil and he will *f* ...... James 4:7

FLESH

bone of my bones And *f* . Gen 2:23
shall become one *f* ...... Gen 2:24
f had corrupted their .... Gen 6:12
f I shall see God .... Job 19:26
My *f* also will rest in ...... Ps 16:9
is wearisome to the *f* ... Eccl 12:12
And all *f* shall see it .... Is 40:5
"All *f* is grass .... Is 40:6
out My Spirit on all *f* .... Joel 2:28
two shall become one *f* . Matt 19:5
were shortened, no *f* ... Matt 24:22
shall become one f .... Mark 10:8
the Word became *f* ..... John 1:14
I shall give is My *f* ..... John 6:51
f profits nothing .... John 6:63
of God, but with the *f* .... Rom 7:25
on the things of the *f* .... Rom 8:5
to the *f* you will die ..... Rom 8:13
f should glory in His ... 1 Cor 1:29
"shall become one *f* .... 1 Cor 6:16
For the *f* lusts .... Gal 5:17
have crucified the *f* ...... Gal 5:24
may boast in your *f* ...... Gal 6:13
the lust of the *f* .... 1 John 2:16
has come in the *f* ...... 1 John 4:2

FLESHLY

f wisdom but by the ... 2 Cor 1:12
f lusts which .... 1 Pet 2:11

FLIES

Dead *f* putrefy the ...... Eccl 10:1

FLOAT

and he made the iron *f* .. 2 Kin 6:6

FLOCK

lead Joseph like a *f* .... Ps 80:1
He will feed His *f* .... Is 40:11
you do not feed the *f* ... Ezek 34:3
my God, "Feed the *f* ... Zech 11:4
sheep of the f .... Matt 26:31
"Do not fear, little *f* ... Luke 12:32
there will be one *f* ..... John 10:16
Shepherd the *f* of God ... 1 Pet 5:2
examples to the *f*........ 1 Pet 5:3

FLOOD

the waters of the *f* ...... Gen 7:10
them away like a *f*........ Ps 90:5
the days before the *f* .. Matt 24:38
bringing in the *f* .... 2 Pet 2:5
of his mouth like a *f* .... Rev 12:15

FLOODS

me, And the *f* of .... Ps 18:4

FLOURISH

f on the dry ground . . . . Is 44:3
rain descended, the *f* . . Matt 7:25

FLOURISH

the righteous shall *f* . . . . . Ps 72:7

FLOW

of his heart will *f* . . . . . . John 7:38

FLOWER

As a *f* of the field . . . . Ps 103:15
beauty is a fading *f* . . . . . . Is 28:4
grass withers, the *f* . . . . Is 40:7
of man as the f . . . . 1 Pet 1:24

FLOWERS

f appear on the earth . . . Song 2:12

FLOWING

'a land *f* with milk . . . . . . Deut 6:3
the Gentiles like a *f* . . . . . Is 66:12

FLUTE

play the harp and *f* . . . . . Gen 4:21

FLUTES

instruments and *f* . . . . Ps 150:4

FLUTISTS

harpists, musicians, *f* . . Rev 18:22

FLY

soon cut off, and we *f* . . . . Ps 90:10

FOLLOW

f You wherever You go . Matt 8:19
He said to him, "*F* . . . . . . Matt 9:9
up his cross, and *f* . . . . . Mark 8:34
will by no means *f* . . . . . John 10:5
serves Me, let him *f* . . . John 12:26
that you should *f* . . . . 1 Pet 2:21
the Lamb wherever . . . . Rev 14:4
and their works *f* . . . . . . Rev 14:13

FOLLOWED

f the LORD my God . . . . . Josh 14:8
we have left all and *f* . Mark 10:28

FOLLOWS

f Me shall not walk . . . . John 8:12

FOLLY

taken much notice of *f* . . Job 35:15
not turn back to *f* . . . . Ps 85:8
F is joy to him who is . Prov 15:21
F is set in great . . . . Eccl 10:6

FOOD

you it shall be for *f* . . . . . Gen 1:29
that lives shall be *f* . . . . . . Gen 9:3
f which you eat shall . . . Ezek 4:10
the fields yield no *f* . . . . . Hab 3:17
That there may be *f* . . . . . Mal 3:10
to give them *f* . . . . Matt 24:45
and you gave Me *f* . . . Matt 25:35
and he who has *f* . . . . . . Luke 3:11
have you any *f* . . . . John 21:5
they ate their *f* . . . . Acts 2:46
our hearts with *f* . . . . . Acts 14:17
destroy with your *f* . . . . Rom 14:15
f makes my brother . . . . 1 Cor 8:13
the same spiritual *f* . . . . 1 Cor 10:3
sower, and bread for *f* . 2 Cor 9:10
And having *f* and . . . . 1 Tim 6:8
and not solid *f* . . . . Heb 5:12
But solid *f* belongs to . . . Heb 5:14
of *f* sold his . . . . Heb 12:16
destitute of daily *f* . . . . James 2:15

FOODS

f which God . . . . 1 Tim 4:3

FOOL

f has said in his . . . . Ps 14:1
is like sport to a *f* . . . . . Prov 10:23

FOOLISH

f is right in his own . . . . Prov 12:15
is too lofty for a *f* . . . . . . Prov 24:7
whoever says, 'You *f* . . Matt 5:22
I have become a *f* . . . . 2 Cor 12:11

FOOLISH

I was so *f* and . . . . Ps 73:22
f pulls it down with . . . Prov 14:1
f man squanders it . . . Prov 21:20
Has not God made *f* . . . 1 Cor 1:20
O *f* Galatians . . . . Gal 3:1
were also once *f* . . . . Titus 3:3
But avoid *f* disputes . . . . Titus 3:9

FOOLISHLY

I speak *f* . . . . 2 Cor 11:21

FOOLISHNESS

F is bound up in the . . . Prov 22:15
devising of *f* is sin . . . . . Prov 24:9
of the cross is *f* . . . . 1 Cor 1:18
Because the *f* of God . . . 1 Cor 1:25

FOOLS

f despise wisdom . . . . Prov 1:7
folly of *f* is deceit . . . . . Prov 14:8
F mock at sin . . . . Prov 14:9
We are *f* for Christ's . . . 1 Cor 4:10

FOOT

will not allow your *f* . . . . Ps 121:3
f will not stumble . . . . . . Prov 3:23
From the sole of the *f* . . . . Is 1:6
f causes you to sin . . . . . Matt 18:8
you dash your f . . . . Luke 4:11
If the *f* should say . . . . 1 Cor 12:15

FOOTSTOOL

Your enemies Your *f* . . . . Ps 110:1
Your enemies Your f . . Matt 22:44

FORBID

said, "Do not *f* . . . . Mark 9:39
"Can anyone *f* . . . . Acts 10:47
f that I should boast . . . . . Gal 6:14

FORBIDDING

f to marry . . . . 1 Tim 4:3

FOREFATHERS

conscience, as my *f* . . . . 2 Tim 1:3

FOREHEADS

put a mark on the *f* . . . . . Ezek 9:4
seal of God on their *f* . . . Rev 9:4
his mark on their *f* . . . . . Rev 20:4

FOREIGNER

"I am a *f* and a . . . . Gen 23:4
of me, since I am a *f* . . . . Ruth 2:10
to God except this *f* . . . Luke 17:18

FOREIGNERS

f who were there . . . . . . Acts 17:21
longer strangers and *f* . . . Eph 2:19

FOREKNEW

For whom He *f* . . . . Rom 8:29
His people whom He *f* . . Rom 11:2

FOREKNOWLEDGE

purpose and *f* of God . . . Acts 2:23

FOREORDAINED

He indeed was *f* . . . . . . 1 Pet 1:20

FORESAW

'*I f the LORD* . . . . Acts 2:25

FORESEEING

f that God would . . . . Gal 3:8

FORESEES

A prudent man *f* . . . . . . Prov 22:3

FORETOLD

have also *f* these days . . . Acts 3:24
killed those who *f* . . . . . . Acts 7:52

FOREVER

and eat, and live *f* . . . . . . Gen 3:22
to our children *f* . . . . . . Deut 29:29
LORD sits as King *f* . . . . . Ps 29:10
Do not cast us off *f* . . . . . Ps 44:23
throne, O God, is *f* . . . . . . Ps 45:6
"You are a priest *f* . . . . . Ps 110:4
His mercy endures *f* . . . . Ps 136:1
of our God stands *f* . . . . . . Is 40:8
My salvation will be *f* . . . . Is 51:6
will not cast off *f* . . . . . . Lam 3:31
Like the stars *f* . . . . Dan 12:3
and the glory *f* . . . . Matt 6:13
the Christ remains *f* . . John 12:34
who is blessed *f* . . . . . 2 Cor 11:31
to whom be glory *f* . . . . . . Gal 1:5
generation, *f* and ever . . Eph 3:21
and Father be glory *f* . . . Phil 4:20
throne, O God, is f . . . . . . Heb 1:8
lives and abides *f* . . . . . . 1 Pet 1:23
of darkness *f* . . . . Jude 13
power, Both now and *f* . . Jude 25
And they shall reign *f* . . Rev 22:5

FOREVERMORE

Blessed be the LORD *f* . . . . Ps 89:52
this time forth and *f* . . . . Ps 113:2
behold, I am alive *f* . . . . . Rev 1:18

FORGAVE

to repay, he freely *f* . . . Luke 7:42
God in Christ *f* . . . . Eph 4:32
even as Christ *f* . . . . Col 3:13

FORGET

f the LORD who . . . . Deut 6:12
I will not *f* Your word . . Ps 119:16
If I *f* you . . . . Ps 137:5
My son, do not *f* . . . . Prov 3:1
f the LORD your Maker . . . Is 51:13
f your work and labor . . . Heb 6:10

FORGETFULNESS

in the land of *f* . . . . Ps 88:12

FORGETS

and immediately *f* . . . . James 1:24

FORGETTING

f those things which . . . . . Phil 3:13

FORGIVE

f their sin and heal . . . . 2 Chr 7:14
good, and ready to *f* . . . . . Ps 86:5
And *f* us our debts . . . . . Matt 6:12
Father will also *f* . . . . . . Matt 6:14
his heart, does not *f* . . . Matt 18:35
Who can *f* sins but God . Mark 2:7
f the sins of any . . . . . . John 20:23
you ought rather to *f* . . . 2 Cor 2:7
F me this wrong . . . . . . 2 Cor 12:13
f us our sins and to . . . . 1 John 1:9

FORGIVEN

sins be *f* them . . . . Mark 4:12
to whom little is *f* . . . . . Luke 7:47
f you all trespasses . . . . . Col 2:13
your sins are *f* . . . . 1 John 2:12

FORGIVENESS

But there is *f* with . . . . . Ps 130:4
preached to you the *f* . . Acts 13:38
they may receive *f* . . . . Acts 26:18
His blood, the *f* . . . . Eph 1:7

FORGIVES

f all your iniquities . . . . . Ps 103:3
is this who even *f* . . . . . Luke 7:49

FORGIVING

tenderhearted, *f* ....Eph 4:32
and *f* one another ....Col 3:13

FORGOT

Joseph, but *f* ....Gen 40:23
They soon *f* His works ..Ps 106:13

FORGOTTEN

f the God who ....Deut 32:18
not one of them is *f* ....Luke 12:6
f the exhortation ....Heb 12:5
f that he was ....2 Pet 1:9

FORM

earth was without *f* ......Gen 1:2
Who would *f* a god or ....Is 44:10
f the light and create ......Is 45:7
descended in bodily *f* ...Luke 3:22
time, nor seen His *f* ....John 5:37
For the *f* of this ....1 Cor 7:31
who, being in the *f* ......Phil 2:6
having a *f* of ....2 Tim 3:5

FORMED

And the LORD God *f* .....Gen 2:7
f my inward parts ......Ps 139:13
say of him who *f* ....Is 29:16
"Before I *f* you in ......Jer 1:5
Will the thing *f* ....Rom 9:20
until Christ is *f* ....Gal 4:19

FORMER

f days better than ....Eccl 7:10
f rain to the earth ....Hos 6:3
f prophets preached .....Zech 1:4
your *f* conduct ....Eph 4:22
f things have passed ....Rev 21:4

FORMS

clay say to him who *f* .....Is 45:9
f the spirit of man ......Zech 12:1

FORNICATION

"We were not born of *f* . John 8:41
of the wrath of her *f* .....Rev 14:8

FORNICATOR

you know, that no *f* ......Eph 5:5
lest there be any *f* ....Heb 12:16

FORNICATORS

but *f* and adulterers .....Heb 13:4

FORSAKE

But I did not *f* ....Ps 119:87
father, And do not *f* .....Prov 1:8
of you does not *f* ......Luke 14:33
never leave you nor f ....Heb 13:5

FORSAKEN

My God, why have You *f* .Ps 22:1
seen the righteous *f* ....Ps 37:25
a mere moment I have *f* ..Is 54:7
God, why have You f ...Matt 27:46
persecuted, but not *f* ....2 Cor 4:9
for Demas has *f* ....2 Tim 4:10

FORSAKING

f the assembling ....Heb 10:25

FORSOOK

f God who made him ..Deut 32:15
all the disciples *f* ......Matt 26:56
with me, but all *f* ......2 Tim 4:16

FORTRESS

is my rock, my *f* ......2 Sam 22:2
my rock of refuge, a *f* .....Ps 31:2

FOUND

f a helper comparable ...Gen 2:20
a thousand I have *f* .....Eccl 7:28
LORD while He may be *f* ..Is 55:6
fruit on it and *f* none ...Luke 13:6

---

he was lost and is *f* ...Luke 15:24
f the Messiah" (which ..John 1:41
and be *f* in Him ....Phil 3:9

FOUNDATION

Of old You laid the *f* ....Ps 102:25
the earth without a *f* ...Luke 6:49
loved Me before the *f* ..John 17:24
I have laid the *f* ....1 Cor 3:10
f can anyone lay than .. 1 Cor 3:11
us in Him before the *f* ....Eph 1:4
not laying again the *f* ....Heb 6:1
Lamb slain from the *f* ...Rev 13:8

FOUNDATIONS

when I laid the *f* ....Job 38:4
And the *f* of the wall ...Rev 21:19

FOUNTAIN

will become in him a *f* ..John 4:14

FOUNTAINS

on that day all the *f* .....Gen 7:11
lead them to living *f* .....Rev 7:17

FRAGRANCE

was filled with the *f* ....John 12:3
we are to God the *f* ....2 Cor 2:15

FREE

'You will be made *f* ....John 8:33
And having been set *f* ..Rom 6:18
Jesus has made me *f* .....Rom 8:2
is neither slave nor *f* ....Gal 3:28
Christ has made us *f* .....Gal 5:1
he is a slave or *f* ....Eph 6:8

FREED

has died has been *f* ......Rom 6:7

FREEDMAN

slave is the Lord's *f* ....1 Cor 7:22

FREELY

the garden you may *f* ...Gen 2:16
F you have received ....Matt 10:8
f give us all ....Rom 8:32
the water of life *f* ......Rev 22:17

FRIEND

of Abraham Your *f* ....2 Chr 20:7
f who sticks closer ....Prov 18:24
a *f* of tax collectors ....Matt 11:19
of you shall have a *f* ....Luke 11:5
f Lazarus sleeps ....John 11:11
he was called the *f* ....James 2:23
wants to be a *f* ....James 4:4

FRIENDS

My *f* scorn me ....Job 16:20
the rich has many *f* ....Prov 14:20
one's life for his *f* ......John 15:13
I have called you *f* .....John 15:15
to forbid any of his *f* ...Acts 24:23

FROGS

your territory with *f* ....Ex 8:2
f coming out of the .....Rev 16:13

FRUIT

showed them the *f* ....Num 13:26
brings forth its *f* ....Ps 1:3
f is better than gold ....Prov 8:19
with good by the *f* .....Prov 12:14
like the first *f* ....Is 28:4
does not bear good *f* ....Matt 3:10
good tree bears good *f* ..Matt 7:17
not drink of this *f* .....Matt 26:29
and blessed is the *f* ....Luke 1:42
life, and bring no *f* .....Luke 8:14
and he came seeking *f* .Luke 13:6
'And if it bears *f* ......Luke 13:9
branch that bears *f* .....John 15:2
that you bear much *f* ...John 15:8
should go and bear *f* ..John 15:16

God, you have your *f* ...Rom 6:22
that we should bear *f* ....Rom 7:4
But the *f* of the ....Gal 5:22
yields the peaceable *f* ..Heb 12:11
Now the *f* of ....James 3:18
autumn trees without *f* ...Jude 12
tree yielding its *f* ....Rev 22:2

FRUITFUL

them, saying, "Be *f* .....Gen 1:22
wife shall be like a *f* .....Ps 128:3
pleasing Him, being *f* ....Col 1:10

FRUITS

Therefore bear *f* ....Matt 3:8
know them by their *f* ...Matt 7:16
of mercy and good *f* ..James 3:17
which bore twelve *f* .....Rev 22:2

FULFILL

for us to *f* all ....Matt 3:15
f the law of Christ ....Gal 6:2
f my joy by being ....Phil 2:2
and *f* all the good ....2 Thess 1:11
If you really *f* ....James 2:8

FULFILLED

the law till all is *f* ......Matt 5:18
of the Gentiles are *f* ...Luke 21:24
all things must be *f* ...Luke 24:44
of the law might be *f* ....Rom 8:4
loves another has *f* .....Rom 13:8
For all the law is *f* ....Gal 5:14

FULFILLMENT

love is the *f* of the .....Rom 13:10

FULL

and it was *f* of bones ...Ezek 37:1
whole body will be *f* ....Matt 6:22
your joy may be *f* ....John 15:11
You are already *f* ....1 Cor 4:8
learned both to be *f* .....Phil 4:12

FULLNESS

f we have all received ..John 1:16
But when the *f* of the .....Gal 4:4
filled with all the *f* .....Eph 3:19
Him dwells all the *f* ....Col 2:9

FURNACE

you out of the iron *f* ....Deut 4:20
of a burning fiery *f* ....Dan 3:6
cast them into the *f* ....Matt 13:42
the smoke of a great *f* ....Rev 9:2

FURY

Thus will I spend My *f* .Ezek 6:12
in anger and *f* On the ....Mic 5:15

G

GAIN

and to die is *g* ....Phil 1:21
rubbish, that I may *g* .....Phil 3:8
is a means of *g* ....1 Tim 6:5
contentment is great *g* ..1 Tim 6:6
for dishonest *g* ....1 Pet 5:2

GAINED

g five more talents ....Matt 25:20

GAINS

g the whole world .....Matt 16:26

GALL

They also gave me *g* .....Ps 69:21
wine mingled with *g* ..Matt 27:34

GAP

and stand in the *g* ....Ezek 22:30

GARDEN

LORD God planted a *g* ....Gen 2:8

GARMENT (cont.)

g enclosed Is my ...... Song 4:12
Eden, the g of God .... Ezek 28:13
where there was a g .... John 18:1
g a new tomb in ...... John 19:41

GARMENT

the hem of His g ...... Matt 9:20
on a wedding g .... Matt 22:11
cloth on an old g ...... Mark 2:21
all grow old like a g ... Heb 1:11
hating even the g .... Jude 23

GARMENTS

g did not wear out on .... Deut 8:4
They divide My .... Ps 22:18
from Edom, With dyed g .. Is 63:1
"Take away the filthy g . Zech 3:4
man clothed in soft g ... Matt 11:8
spread their g on the ... Matt 21:8
and divided His g ..... Matt 27:35
by them in shining .. Luke 24:4
g are moth-eaten .... James 5:2
be clothed in white g ..... Rev 3:5

GATE

by the narrow g .... Matt 7:13
by the Sheep G a pool ... John 5:2
laid daily at the g .... Acts 3:2
suffered outside the g . Heb 13:12

GATES

up your heads, O you g ... Ps 24:7
The LORD loves the g ....Ps 87:2
is known in the g ..... Prov 31:23
Go through the g .... Is 62:10
and the g of Hades ... Matt 16:18
wall with twelve g .... Rev 21:12
g were twelve pearls .. Rev 21:21
g shall not be shut ... Rev 21:25

GATHER

And a time to g stones ... Eccl 3:5
g the lambs within His ... Is 40:11
g His wheat into the .... Matt 3:12
sow nor reap nor g .... Matt 6:26
Do men g grapes from .. Matt 7:16
g where I have not ... Matt 25:26
g together His .... Mark 13:27

GATHERED

g some of every kind .. Matt 13:47
the nations will be g ... Matt 25:32

GATHERING

g together of the .... Gen 1:10
g together to Him ..... 2 Thess 2:1

GATHERS

The Lord GOD, who g .... Is 56:8
together, as a hen g ... Matt 23:37

GAVE

to be with me, she g .... Gen 3:12
g You this authority .... Matt 21:23
that He g His only ..... John 3:16
Those whom You g ... John 17:12
but God g the increase .. 1 Cor 3:6
g Himself for our sins ... Gal 1:4
g Himself for me .... Gal 2:20
g Himself for it .... Eph 5:25

GENERATION

One g passes away ...... Eccl 1:4
who will declare His g .... Is 53:8
and adulterous g .... Matt 12:39
this g will by no ...... Matt 24:34
from this perverse g ... Acts 2:40
But you are a chosen g . 1 Pet 2:9

GENERATIONS

be remembered in all g . Ps 45:17
g will call me blessed .. Luke 1:48

GENEROUS

no longer be called g ..... Is 32:5

GENTILES

G were separated ...... Gen 10:5
As a light to the G .... Is 42:6
G shall come to your ...... Is 60:3
all these things the G ... Matt 6:32
into the way of the G ... Matt 10:5
revelation to the G .... Luke 2:32
G are fulfilled .... Luke 21:24
My name before G ...... Acts 9:15
poured out on the G ... Acts 10:45
a light to the G .... Acts 13:47
also the God of the G ... Rom 3:29
mystery among the G .... Col 1:27
a teacher of the G ...... 1 Tim 2:7

GENTLE

from Me, for I am g ... Matt 11:29
we were g among ..... 1 Thess 2:7
to be peaceable, g .... Titus 3:2
only to the good and g . 1 Pet 2:18
ornament of a g .... 1 Pet 3:4

GENTLENESS

love and a spirit of g ... 1 Cor 4:21
g, self-control .... Gal 5:23
all lowliness and g ...... Eph 4:2
Let your g be known to .. Phil 4:5
love, patience, g .... 1 Tim 6:11

GHOST

supposed it was a g .... Mark 6:49

GIFT

it is the g of God .... Eccl 3:13
"If you knew the g ..... John 4:10
but the g of God is ..... Rom 6:23
each one has his own g . 1 Cor 7:7
though I have the g ... 1 Cor 13:2
it is the g of God .... Eph 2:8
Do not neglect the g ... 1 Tim 4:14
you to stir up the g ..... 2 Tim 1:6
tasted the heavenly g .... Heb 6:4
Every good g and ..... James 1:17

GIFTS

You have received g ..... Ps 68:18
and Seba Will offer g .... Ps 72:10
how to give good g .... Matt 7:11
rich putting their g .... Luke 21:1
g differing .... Rom 12:6
are diversities of g ..... 1 Cor 12:4
and desire spiritual g . 1 Cor 14:1
captive, And gave g ..... Eph 4:8

GIRD

G Your sword upon Your . Ps 45:3
and another will g .... John 21:18
Therefore g up the ..... 1 Pet 1:13

GIRDED

a towel and g Himself .. John 13:4

GIVE

g you the desires .... Ps 37:4
Yes, the LORD will g ..... Ps 85:12
G me understanding ... Ps 119:34
"G to him who asks .... Matt 5:42
G us this day our ...... Matt 6:11
what you have and g ... Matt 19:21
authority I will g .... Luke 4:6
g them eternal life .... John 10:28
commandment I g ..... John 13:34
but what I do have I g ... Acts 3:6
g us all things .... Rom 8:32
G no offense .... 1 Cor 10:32
g him who has need .... Eph 4:28
g thanks to God ..... 2 Thess 2:13
g yourself entirely ..... 1 Tim 4:15

GIVEN

to him more will be g .. Matt 13:12
has, more will be g .... Matt 25:29
to whom much is g ... Luke 12:48

g Me I should lose ..... John 6:39
Spirit was not yet g .... John 7:39

GIVES

g life to the world ...... John 6:33
"All that the Father g . John 6:37
The good shepherd g .. John 10:11
not as the world g ..... John 14:27
g us richly all things ... 1 Tim 6:17
who g to all liberally ... James 1:5
g grace to the humble . James 4:6

GLAD

streams shall make g .... Ps 46:4
I was g when they said .. Ps 122:1
make merry and be g . Luke 15:32
he saw it and was g ... John 8:56

GLADNESS

me hear joy and g ...... Ps 51:8
Serve the LORD with g ... Ps 100:2

GLORIFIED

and they g the God of . Matt 15:31
Jesus was not yet g .... John 7:39
when Jesus was g ..... John 12:16
this My Father is g ..... John 15:8
"I have g You on the ... John 17:4
g His Servant Jesus .... Acts 3:13
these He also g .... Rom 8:30
things God may be g . 1 Pet 4:11

GLORIFY

g your Father in .... Matt 5:16
"Father, g Your name . John 12:28
"He will g Me .... John 16:14
"And now, O Father, g . John 17:5
death he would g ..... John 21:19
therefore g God in ..... 1 Cor 6:20
also Christ did not g ..... Heb 5:5
ashamed, but let him g . 1 Pet 4:16

GLORIOUS

G things are spoken ...... Ps 87:3
g splendor of Your ..... Ps 145:5
habitation, holy and g .... Is 63:15
it to Himself a g .... Eph 5:27
be conformed to His g ... Phil 3:21
g appearing of our ..... Titus 2:13

GLORY

show me Your g .... Ex 33:18
g has departed from .. 1 Sam 4:21
Who is this King of g ..... Ps 24:8
Your power and Your g .. Ps 63:2
wise shall inherit g ..... Prov 3:35
It is the g of God to ..... Prov 25:2
g I will not give .... Is 42:8
that they may have g .... Matt 6:2
the power and the g ..... Matt 6:13
g was not arrayed ...... Matt 6:29
will come in the g ..... Matt 16:27
power and great g ..... Matt 24:30
"G to God in the .... Luke 2:14
and we beheld His g ... John 1:14
and manifested His g ... John 2:11
not seek My own g .... John 8:50
"Give God the g .... John 9:24
g which I had with ... John 17:5
g which You gave Me . John 17:22
he did not give g ...... Acts 12:23
doing good seek for g .... Rom 2:7
fall short of the g ...... Rom 3:23
in faith, giving g ...... Rom 4:20
the adoption, the g ..... Rom 9:4
the riches of His g ..... Rom 9:23
God, alone wise, be g . Rom 16:27
who glories, let him g . 1 Cor 1:31
to His riches in g .... Phil 4:19
appear with Him in g .... Col 3:4
For you are our g .... 1 Thess 2:20
many sons to g .... Heb 2:10
grass, And all the g . 1 Pet 1:24
to whom belong the g . 1 Pet 4:11
for the Spirit of g ...... 1 Pet 4:14

GLORYING

the presence of His *g* ..... Jude 24
O Lord, to receive *g* ..... Rev 4:11
g of God illuminated ... Rev 21:23

GLORYING

Your *g* is not good ...... 1 Cor 5:6

GLUTTON

you say, 'Look, a *g* ... Luke 7:34

GLUTTONS

g shames his .... Prov 28:7
evil beasts, lazy *g* ...... Titus 1:12

GNASHING

will be weeping and *g* .. Matt 8:12

GO

'Let My people *g* .... Ex 5:1
For wherever you *g* .... Ruth 1:16
Those who *g* down to .. Ps 107:23
Where can I *g* from .... Ps 139:7
to whom shall we *g* ... John 6:68
g you cannot come ..... John 8:21
I *g* to prepare place ... John 14:2
shall *g* out no more ..... Rev 3:12

GOADS

to kick against the *g* ..... Acts 9:5

GOAL

I press toward the *g* ..... Phil 3:14

GOATS

his sheep from the *g* ... Matt 25:32
with the blood of *g* ..... Heb 9:12
g could take away ...... Heb 10:4

GOD

G created the heavens .... Gen 1:1
Abram of *G* Most ...... Gen 14:19
and I will be their *G* .... Gen 17:8
"I am the LORD your *G* ... Ex 20:2
G is a consuming fire ... Deut 4:24
If the LORD is *G* ...... 1 Kin 18:21
G is greater than all .... 2 Chr 2:5
You have been My *G* .. Ps 22:10
G is our refuge .... Ps 46:1
G is in the midst of .... Ps 46:5
me a clean heart, O *G* .. Ps 51:10
Our *G* is the *G* .... Ps 68:20
Who is so great a *G* ... Ps 77:13
Restore us, O *G* .... Ps 80:7
You alone are *G* .... Ps 86:10
Exalt the LORD our *G* ... Ps 99:9
Yes, our *G* is merciful .. Ps 116:5
For *G* in heaven ...... Eccl 5:2
Counselor, Mighty *G* ..... Is 9:6
G is my salvation .... Is 12:2
stricken, Smitten by *G* .... Is 53:4
"*G* with us .... Matt 1:23
in *G* my Savior .... Luke 1:47
the Word was with *G* ... John 1:1
"For *G* so loved the .... John 3:16
"*G* is Spirit .... John 4:24
"My Lord and my *G* ... John 20:28
Christ is the Son of *G* .. Acts 8:37
Indeed, let *G* be true ... Rom 3:4
If *G* is for us .... Rom 8:31
G is faithful .... 1 Cor 1:9
G shall supply all ...... Phil 4:19
and I will be their G .... Heb 8:10
G is a consuming fire .. Heb 12:29
for *G* is love .... 1 John 4:8
No one has seen *G* .... 1 John 4:12
G Himself will be ...... Rev 21:3
and I will be his *G* ...... Rev 21:7

GODDESS

after Ashtoreth the *g* .. 1 Kin 11:5
of the great *g* Diana ... Acts 19:35

GODHEAD

eternal power and *G* .... Rom 1:20
the fullness of the *G* ...... Col 2:9

GODLINESS

is the mystery of *g* .... 1 Tim 3:16
g with contentment ..... 1 Tim 6:6
having a form of *g* ... 2 Tim 3:5
to perseverance *g* ...... 2 Pet 1:6

GODLY

who desire to live *g* ... 2 Tim 3:12
reverence and *g* fear ... Heb 12:28
to deliver the *g* .... 2 Pet 2:9

GODS

God is God of *g* ...... Deut 10:17
I said, "You are *g* .... Ps 82:6
yourselves with *g* .... Is 57:5
If He called them *g* .... John 10:35
g have come down to .. Acts 14:11

GOLD

g I do not have .... Acts 3:6
with braided hair or *g* .. 1 Tim 2:9
a man with *g* rings .... James 2:2
Your *g* and silver are ... James 5:3
more precious than *g* .... 1 Pet 1:7
like silver or *g* .... 1 Pet 1:18
of the city was pure *g* .. Rev 21:21

GONE

like sheep have *g* .... Is 53:6

GOOD

God saw that it was *g* ... Gen 1:10
but God meant it for *g* . Gen 50:20
indeed accept *g* .... Job 2:10
is none who does *g* ...... Ps 14:1
Truly God is *g* to .... Ps 73:1
g word makes it glad ... Prov 12:25
on the evil and the *g* .... Prov 15:3
A merry heart does *g* .. Prov 17:22
Learn to do *g* .... Is 1:17
talked to me, with *g* ... Zech 1:13
they may see your *g* ... Matt 5:16
"A *g* man out of the ... Matt 12:35
No one is *g* but One .. Matt 19:17
For she has done a *g* .. Matt 26:10
g works I have shown .. John 10:32
went about doing *g* .... Acts 10:38
g man someone would ... Rom 5:7
in my flesh) nothing *g* .. Rom 7:18
overcome evil with *g* .. Rom 12:21
Jesus for *g* works ...... Eph 2:10
fruitful in every *g* .... Col 1:10
know that the law is *g* .. 1 Tim 1:8
For this is *g* and ...... 1 Tim 2:3
bishop, he desires a *g* ... 1 Tim 3:1
for this is *g* and .... 1 Tim 5:4
prepared for every *g* .. 2 Tim 2:21
Every *g* gift and ...... James 1:17

GOODNESS

"I will make all My *g* ... Ex 33:19
and abounding in *g* .... Ex 34:6
"You are my Lord, My *g* .. Ps 16:2
Surely *g* and mercy ...... Ps 23:6
That I would see the *g* .. Ps 27:13
the riches of His *g* ...... Rom 2:4
consider the *g* and .... Rom 11:22
kindness, *g* .... Gal 5:22

GOSPEL

The beginning of the *g* . Mark 1:1
and believe in the *g* ... Mark 1:15
g must first be .... Mark 13:10
separated to the *g* .... Rom 1:1
not ashamed of the *g* .. Rom 1:16
to a different *g* .... Gal 1:6
the everlasting *g* .... Rev 14:6

GOVERNMENT

And the *g* will be upon ..... Is 9:6

GRACE

But Noah found *g* .... Gen 6:8
G is poured upon Your .. Ps 45:2

The LORD will give *g* ..... Ps 84:11
the Spirit of *g* .... Zech 12:10
and the *g* of God was .. Luke 2:40
g and truth came ...... John 1:17
And great *g* was upon .. Acts 4:33
receive abundance of *g* .. Rom 5:17
g is no longer *g* .... Rom 11:6
For you know the *g* ..... 2 Cor 8:9
g is sufficient .... 2 Cor 12:9
The *g* of the Lord ... 2 Cor 13:14
you have fallen from *g* ... Gal 5:4
to the riches of His *g* ..... Eph 1:7
g you have been .... Eph 2:8
g was given according .... Eph 4:7
G be with all those ..... Heb 12:28
shaken, let us have *g* ... Heb 12:28
But He gives more *g* .. James 4:6
but grow in the *g* ...... 2 Pet 3:18

GRACIOUS

he said, "God be *g* ..... Gen 43:29
I will be *g* to whom I .... Ex 33:19
at the *g* words which ... Luke 4:22
that the Lord is *g* .... 1 Pet 2:3

GRAFTED

in unbelief, will be *g* ... Rom 11:23

GRAIN

it treads out the *g* ..... Deut 25:4
be revived like *g* .... Hos 14:7
to pluck heads of *g* .... Matt 12:1
unless a *g* of wheat .... John 12:24

GRAPES

brought forth wild *g* .... Is 5:2
have eaten sour *g* ...... Ezek 18:2
Do men gather *g* ...... Matt 7:16
g are fully ripe .... Rev 14:18

GRASS

The *g* withers .... Is 40:7
so clothes the *g* .... Matt 6:30
"*All flesh is as g* .... 1 Pet 1:24

GRAVE

my soul up from the *g* .... Ps 30:3
And they made His *g* ...... Is 53:9
the power of the *g* ...... Hos 13:14

GRAVES

g were opened .... Matt 27:52
g which are not .... Luke 11:44
g will hear His voice ... John 5:28

GRAY

the man of *g* hairs .... Deut 32:25

GREAT

and make your name *g* .. Gen 12:2
For the LORD is *g* ..... 1 Chr 16:25
Who does *g* things .... Job 5:9
g is the Holy One .... Is 12:6
G is Your faithfulness .. Lam 3:23
he shall be called *g* .... Matt 5:19
one pearl of *g* price .... Matt 13:46
desires to become *g* ... Matt 20:26
g drops of blood ...... Luke 22:44
appearing of our *g* ..... Titus 2:13
g men, the rich men ... Rev 6:15
Mystery, Babylon the *G* . Rev 17:5
the dead, small and *g* ... Rev 20:12

GREATER

of heaven is *g* .... Matt 11:11
place there is One *g* ... Matt 12:6
g than Jonah is here ... Matt 12:41
g than Solomon is ..... Matt 12:42
a servant is not *g* ..... John 13:16
"*G* love has no one ... John 15:13
'A servant is not *g* .... John 15:20
who prophesies is *g* ... 1 Cor 14:5
God is *g* .... 1 John 3:20
witness of God is *g* .... 1 John 5:9

GREATEST

little child is the *g* ......Matt 18:4
but the *g* of these is ... 1 Cor 13:13

GREATNESS

is the exceeding *g* ......Eph 1:19

GREED

part is full of *g* ......Luke 11:39

GREEDINESS

all uncleanness with *g* ...Eph 4:19

GREEDY

of everyone who is *g* ...Prov 1:19
not violent, not *g* ......1 Tim 3:3

GREEK

written in Hebrew, *G* ..John 19:20
and also for the *G* ......Rom 1:16
is neither Jew not *G* ......Gal 3:28

GREEN

lie down in *g* pastures ....Ps 23:2

GRIEF

and acquainted with *g* .....Is 53:3
joy and not with *g* .....Heb 13:17

GRIEVE

g the Holy Spirit ....Eph 4:30

GRIEVED

earth, and He was *g* ......Gen 6:6
g His Holy Spirit ....Is 63:10
with anger, being *g* ....Mark 3:5

GROAN

even we ourselves *g* ....Rom 8:23
who are in this tent *g* ...2 Cor 5:4

GROANING

I am weary with my *g* .....Ps 6:6
Then Jesus, again *g* ...John 11:38

GROANINGS

g which cannot ....Rom 8:26

GROUND

"Cursed is the *g* ....Gen 3:17
you stand is holy *g* ......Ex 3:5
up your fallow *g* ....Jer 4:3
others fell on good *g* ....Matt 13:8
bought a piece of *g* .. Luke 14:18
God, the pillar and *g* .. 1 Tim 3:15

GROUNDED

being rooted and *g* .....Eph 3:17

GROW

truth in love, may *g* .....Eph 4:15
but *g* in the grace and ..2 Pet 3:18

GRUDGINGLY

in his heart, not *g* ......2 Cor 9:7

GUARANTEE

in our hearts as a *g* ....2 Cor 1:22
us the Spirit as a *g* ....2 Cor 5:5
who is the *g* of our ......Eph 1:14

GUIDE

He will be our *g* ....Ps 48:14
g our feet into the .....Luke 1:79
has come, He will *g* ...John 16:13

GUIDES

to you, blind *g* ....Matt 23:16

GUILT

of your fathers' *g* ......Matt 23:32

GUILTLESS

g who takes His name ....Ex 20:7
have condemned the *g* .. Matt 12:7

GUILTY

"We are truly *g* ....Gen 42:21
world may become *g* ...Rom 3:19
in one point, he is *g* ...James 2:10

GULF

you there is a great *g* . Luke 16:26

H

HABITATION

Is God in His holy *h* ......Ps 68:5
but He blesses the *h* ....Prov 3:33
Jerusalem, a quiet *h* ......Is 33:20
from His holy *h* ....Zech 2:13
be clothed with our *h* ...2 Cor 5:2

HADES

be brought down to *H* . Matt 11:23
H shall not ....Matt 16:18
in torments in *H* ......Luke 16:23
not leave my soul in H .. Acts 2:27
I have the keys of *H* ....Rev 1:18
H were cast into the ....Rev 20:14

HAIL

of the plague of the *h* . Rev 16:21

HAIR

you cannot make one *h* . Matt 5:36
"But not a *h* of your .. Luke 21:18
not with braided *h* ......1 Tim 2:9
h like women's *h* ....Rev 9:8

HAIRS

"But the very *h* ....Matt 10:30

HALLOWED

the Sabbath day and *h* .. Ex 20:11
who is holy shall be *h* ......Is 5:16
heaven, *H* be Your name . Matt 6:9

HAND

the *h* of God was .....1 Sam 5:11
My times are in Your *h* .. Ps 31:15
"Sit at My right *h* ....Ps 110:1
heart is in the *h* ......Prov 21:1
Whatever your *h* ......Eccl 9:10
is at his right *h* ....Eccl 10:2
do not withhold your *h* . Eccl 11:6
My *h* has laid the ....Is 48:13
Behold, the LORD's *h* ......Is 59:1
are the work of Your *h* ....Is 64:8
"Am I a God near at *h* ..Jer 23:23
of heaven is at *h* ....Matt 3:2
if your right *h* ....Matt 5:30
do not let your left *h* ......Matt 6:3
h causes you to sin ....Mark 9:43
sitting at the right *h* .. Mark 14:62
at the right *h* of God ....Acts 7:55
The Lord is at *h* ....Phil 4:5
"Sit at My right h ......Heb 1:13
down at the right *h* ....Heb 10:12

HANDIWORK

firmament shows His *h* ...Ps 19:1

HANDLE

H Me and see ....Luke 24:39
do not taste, do not *h* ....Col 2:21

HANDLED

and our hands have *h* .. 1 John 1:1

HANDS

took his life in his *h* ...1 Sam 19:5
but His *h* make whole ...Job 5:18
They pierced My *h* ......Ps 22:16
h formed the dry land ....Ps 95:5
than having two *h* ......Matt 18:8
"Behold My *h* and ....Luke 24:39
h the print of the ......John 20:25

HANDWRITING

having wiped out the *h* ..Col 2:14

HANGED

went and *h* himself .....Matt 27:5

HANGS

h the earth on nothing ...Job 26:7
is everyone who h ....Gal 3:13

HAPPY

H is the man who has ...Ps 127:5

HARD

I knew you to be a *h* ...Matt 25:24
"This is a *h* saying .....John 6:60
are some things *h* ......2 Pet 3:16

HARDEN

But I will *h* his heart .....Ex 4:21
h your hearts as ....Heb 3:8

HARDENED

But Pharaoh *h* his ....Ex 8:32
their heart was *h* .....Mark 6:52
and h their hearts .....John 12:40
lest any of you be *h* .....Heb 3:13

HARDENS

whom He wills He *h* ....Rom 9:18

HARDSHIP

h as a good soldier .....2 Tim 2:3

HARLOT

of a *h* named Rahab ....Josh 2:1
h is one body with .....1 Cor 6:16
of the great *h* who ......Rev 17:1

HARLOTRIES

Let her put away her *h* ...Hos 2:2

HARLOTRY

are the children of *h* ....Hos 2:4
For the spirit of *h* ....Hos 5:4

HARLOTS

h enter the ....Matt 21:31
Great, The Mother of *H* . Rev 17:5

HARP

Lamb, each having a *h* ...Rev 5:8

HARPS

We hung our *h* Upon the . Ps 137:2

HARVEST

Seedtime and *h* ....Gen 8:22
"The *h* is past ....Jer 8:20
h truly is plentiful ......Matt 9:37
sickle, because the *h* ...Mark 4:29
already white for *h* .....John 4:35

HASTENS

and he sins who *h* ......Prov 19:2

HASTILY

utter anything *h* ....Eccl 5:2

HASTY

Do you see a man *h* ...Prov 29:20

HATE

love the LORD, *h* evil .....Ps 97:10
h every false way .....Ps 119:104
h the double-minded .. Ps 119:113
I *h* and abhor lying .....Ps 119:163
love, And a time to *h* .....Eccl 3:8
You who *h* good and .....Mic 3:2
either he will *h* ....Matt 6:24

HATED

But Esau I have h . . . . Mal 1:3
"And you will be h . . . . Matt 10:22
have seen and also h . . John 15:24
but Esau I have h . . . . . . Rom 9:13
For no one ever h . . . . Eph 5:29

HATEFUL

h woman when she is . Prov 30:23
in malice and envy, h . . . Titus 3:3

HATERS

backbiters, h of God . . . . Rom 1:30

HATES

six things the LORD h . . . Prov 6:16
lose it, and he who h . . . John 12:25
"If the world h . . . . John 15:18
h his brother is . . . . 1 John 2:11

HAUGHTY

bring down h looks . . . . . . Ps 18:27
my heart is not h . . . . Ps 131:1
h spirit before a fall . . . Prov 16:18

HEAD

He shall bruise your h . . . Gen 3:15
and gave Him to be h . . . Eph 1:22
For the husband is h . . . Eph 5:23

HEAL

O LORD, h me . . . . Ps 6:2
h your backslidings . . . . . . Jer 3:22
torn, but He will h . . . . . . Hos 6:1
"H the sick . . . . Matt 10:8
So that I should h . . . . Matt 13:15
sent Me to h the . . . . . . Luke 4:18
Physician, h yourself . . . Luke 4:23

HEALED

And return and be h . . . . . . Is 6:10
His stripes we are h . . . . . . Is 53:5
"When I would have h . . . Hos 7:1
and He h them . . . . Matt 4:24
that you may be h . . . . James 5:16
his deadly wound was h . Rev 13:3

HEALING

shall arise With h . . . . Mal 4:2
and h all kinds of . . . . . . Matt 4:23
tree were for the h . . . . . Rev 22:2

HEALINGS

to another gifts of h . . 1 Cor 12:9

HEALS

h all your diseases . . . . Ps 103:3
Jesus the Christ h . . . . . . Acts 9:34

HEALTH

all things and be in h . . . . 3 John 2

HEAR

"H, O Israel . . . . Deut 6:4
Him you shall h . . . . Deut 18:15
H me when I call . . . . Ps 4:1
O You who h prayer . . . . . Ps 65:2
ear, shall He not h . . . . . . Ps 94:9
h rather than to give . . . . . Eccl 5:1
'*Hearing you will h* . . . Matt 13:14
heed what you h . . . . Mark 4:24
that God does not h . . . . John 9:31
And how shall they h . . . Rom 10:14
man be swift to h . . . . . James 1:19
h what the Spirit says . . . . Rev 2:7

HEARD

h their cry because of . . . . . Ex 3:7
that they will be h . . . . . . Matt 6:7
h the word believed . . . . Acts 4:4
not seen, nor ear h . . . . 1 Cor 2:9
things that you have h . . 2 Tim 2:2
the word which they h . . . Heb 4:2

which we have h . . . . . . 1 John 1:1
Lord's Day, and I h . . . . . Rev 1:10

HEARER

if anyone is a h . . . . James 1:23

HEARERS

for not the h of the . . . . . Rom 2:13
the word, and not h . . . James 1:22

HEARING

'Keep on h . . . . Is 6:9
h they do not . . . . Matt 13:13
h they may hear . . . . Mark 4:12
or by the h of faith . . . . Gal 3:2

HEARS

out, and the LORD h . . . . . . Ps 34:17
of God in God's words . . John 8:47
"And if anyone h . . . . . John 12:47
who is of the truth h . . . John 18:37
He who knows God h . . 1 John 4:6
And let him who h . . . . . Rev 22:17

HEART

h was only evil . . . . Gen 6:5
h rejoices in the LORD . . 1 Sam 2:1
gave him another h . . . 1 Sam 10:9
LORD looks at the h . . . 1 Sam 16:7
his wives turned his h . . 1 Kin 11:4
He pierces my h . . . . Job 16:13
My h also instructs me . . . . Ps 16:7
h is overflowing . . . . Ps 45:1
h shall depart from me . . Ps 101:4
look and a proud h . . . . . Ps 101:5
with my whole h . . . . Ps 111:1
as he thinks in his h . . . Prov 23:7
h reveals the man . . . . . Prov 27:19
trusts in his own h . . . . Prov 28:26
The h of the wise is . . . . . . Eccl 7:4
And a wise man's h . . . . . Eccl 8:5
h yearned for him . . . . . . Song 5:4
And the whole h . . . . Is 1:5
The yearning of Your h . . Is 63:15
h is deceitful above . . . . . Jer 17:9
I will give them a h . . . . . Jer 24:7
and take the stony h . . Ezek 11:19
yourselves a new h . . . Ezek 18:31
are the pure in h . . . . . . Matt 5:8
is, there your h . . . . Matt 6:21
of the h proceed evil . . Matt 15:19
h will flow rivers . . . . . . John 7:38
"Let not your h . . . . John 14:1
Satan filled your h . . . . . Acts 5:3
h that God has raised . . . Rom 10:9
refresh my h in the . . . Philem 20
and shuts up his h . . . . 1 John 3:17

HEARTILY

you do, do it h . . . . Col 3:23

HEARTS

God tests the h . . . . Ps 7:9
And he will turn The h . . . Mal 4:6
h failing them from . . . Luke 21:26
will guard your h . . . . Phil 4:7
of God rule in your h . . . Col 3:15

HEATHEN

repetitions as the h . . . . . Matt 6:7

HEAVEN

called the firmament H . . . Gen 1:8
LORD looks down from h . . Ps 14:2
word is settled in h . . . . Ps 119:89
For God is in h . . . . Eccl 5:2
"H is My throne . . . . Is 66:1
for the kingdom of h . . . Matt 3:2
your Father in h . . . . . . Matt 5:16
On earth as it is in h . . . Matt 6:10
"H and earth will . . . . . Matt 24:35
Him a sign from h . . . . . Mark 8:11
have sinned against h . Luke 15:18
you shall see h . . . . John 1:51
one has ascended to h . . John 3:13

the true bread from h . . John 6:32
a voice came from h . . . John 12:28
sheet, let down from h . . Acts 11:5
laid up for you in h . . . . . . Col 1:5
there was silence in h . . . . Rev 8:1
Now I saw a new h . . . . . Rev 21:1

HEAVENLY

your h Father will . . . . . Matt 6:14
h host praising God . . . . Luke 2:13
if I tell you h things . . . . John 3:12
blessing in the h . . . . Eph 1:3
a better, that is, a h . . . . Heb 11:16
the living God, the h . . . Heb 12:22

HEAVENS

and the highest h . . . . . Deut 10:14
h cannot contain . . . . . . 1 Kin 8:27
h declare the glory . . . . . . Ps 19:1
For as the h are high . . . Ps 103:11
behold, I create new h . . . . Is 65:17
and behold, the h . . . . . Matt 3:16
h will be shaken . . . . . . Matt 24:29
h are the work of Your . . Heb 1:10
h will pass away . . . . . . 2 Pet 3:10

HEEDS

h counsel is wise . . . . . Prov 12:15

HEEL

you shall bruise His h . . . Gen 3:15
has lifted up his h . . . . Ps 41:9
Me has lifted up his h . John 13:18

HEIGHT

nor h nor depth . . . . . . Rom 8:39
length and depth and h . . Eph 3:18

HEIR

He has appointed h . . . . . Heb 1:2
world and became h . . . . Heb 11:7

HEIRS

if children, then h . . . . . Rom 8:17
should be fellow h . . . . . . Eph 3:6

HELL

shall be turned into h . . . . . Ps 9:17
go down alive into h . . . . . Ps 55:15
H and Destruction are . Prov 27:20
be in danger of h fire . . Matt 5:22
to be cast into h . . . . Matt 18:9
condemnation of h . . . Matt 23:33
power to cast into h . . . Luke 12:5

HELMET

And take the h of . . . . Eph 6:17
and love, and as a h . . 1 Thess 5:8

HELP

May He send you h . . . . . Ps 20:2
A very present h . . . . Ps 46:1
He is their h and . . . . Ps 115:9
Our h is in the name . . . . Ps 124:8
h my unbelief . . . . Mark 9:24
and find grace to h . . . . Heb 4:16

HELPED

fall, but the LORD h . . . . Ps 118:13
of salvation I have h . . . . . Is 49:8
h His servant Israel . . . Luke 1:54

HELPER

I will make him a h . . . . Gen 2:18
Behold, God is my h . . . . Ps 54:4
give you another H . . . John 14:16
"But when the H . . . . . John 15:26
"The LORD is my h . . . . Heb 13:6

HELPFUL

all things are not h . . . . 1 Cor 6:12

HELPS

the Spirit also h . . . . . . Rom 8:26

HEM
and touched the *h* . . . . . . Matt 9:20

HERE
Then I said, "*H* am I . . . . Is 6:8

HERESIES
dissensions, *h* . . . . Gal 5:20

HERITAGE
for that is his *h* . . . . Eccl 3:22
This is the *h* of the . . . . . . Is 54:17
of My people, My *h* . . . . . Joel 3:2
The flock of Your *h* . . . . Mic 7:14

HIDDEN
And my sins are not *h* . . . . Ps 69:5
Your word I have *h* . . . . Ps 119:11
h that will not . . . . Matt 10:26
the *h* wisdom which . . . . 1 Cor 2:7
bring to light the *h* . . . . . 1 Cor 4:5
have renounced the *h* . . . 2 Cor 4:2
rather let it be the *h* . . . 1 Pet 3:4
give some of the *h* . . . . . . Rev 2:17

HIDE
H me under the shadow . . Ps 17:8
You shall *h* them in . . . . . Ps 31:20
You *h* Your face . . . . Ps 104:29
darkness shall not *h* . . . Ps 139:12
You are God, who *h* . . . . . Is 45:15
"Fall on us and *h* . . . . . . Rev 6:16

HIDES
He *h* His face . . . . Ps 10:11

HIDING
You are my *h* place . . . . . . Ps 32:7

HIGH
priest of God Most *H* . . . Gen 14:18
For the LORD Most *H* . . . Ps 47:2
"I dwell in the *h* . . . . Is 57:15
know That the Most *H* . . Dan 4:17
up on a *h* mountain by . . Matt 17:1
your mind on *h* things . Rom 12:16
h thing that exalts . . . . . 2 Cor 10:5
and faithful *H* Priest . . . . Heb 2:17

HIGHER
you, 'Friend, go up *h* . . Luke 14:10

HIGHWAY
in the desert A *h* . . . . Is 40:3

HIGHWAYS
h shall be elevated . . . . Is 49:11
go into the *h* . . . . Matt 22:9

HILL
My King on My holy *h* . . . . Ps 2:6
h cannot be hidden . . . . . Matt 5:14
and h brought low . . . . . . Luke 3:5

HILLS
of the everlasting *h* . . . . Gen 49:26
of the *h* are His also . . . . . Ps 95:4
up my eyes to the *h* . . . . . Ps 121:1

HINDER
all things lest we *h* . . . . 1 Cor 9:12

HINDERED
Who *h* you from obeying . Gal 5:7
prayers may not be *h* . . . 1 Pet 3:7

HOLD
right hand shall *h* . . . . . . Ps 139:10
h fast that word . . . . 1 Cor 15:2
h fast and repent . . . . Rev 3:3

HOLIER
near me, For I am *h* . . . . . . Is 65:5

HOLIEST
the way into the *H* . . . . Heb 9:8

HOLINESS
You, glorious in *h* . . . . . . Ex 15:11
I have sworn by My *h* . . . Ps 89:35
the Highway of *H* . . . . Is 35:8
to the Spirit of *h* . . . . Rom 1:4
spirit, perfecting *h* . . . . . 2 Cor 7:1
uncleanness, but in *h* . . 1 Thess 4:7
be partakers of His *h* . . Heb 12:10

HOLY
where you stand is *h* . . . . . Ex 3:5
day, to keep it *h* . . . . Ex 20:8
LORD your God am *h* . . . . Lev 19:2
h seed is mixed . . . . Ezra 9:2
God sits on His *h* . . . . Ps 47:8
God, in His *h* mountain . . Ps 48:1
"*H, h, h* . . . . Is 6:3
child of the *H* Spirit . . . . Matt 1:18
baptize you with the *H* . . Mark 1:8
who speak, but the *H* . Mark 13:11
H Spirit will come . . . . . Luke 1:35
H Spirit descended . . . . . Luke 3:22
Father give the *H* . . . . . Luke 11:13
H Spirit will teach . . . . . Luke 12:12
H Spirit was not . . . . John 7:39
H Spirit has come . . . . . . Acts 1:8
all filled with the *H* . . . . . Acts 2:4
receive the *H* Spirit . . . . . Acts 19:2
joy in the *H* . . . . Rom 14:17
H Spirit teaches . . . . 1 Cor 2:13
that we should be *h* . . . . . Eph 1:4
were sealed with the *H* . . Eph 1:13
partakers of the *H* . . . . . . Heb 6:4
H Spirit sent from . . . . . . 1 Pet 1:12
it is written, "Be *h* . . . . . 1 Pet 1:16
moved by the *H* Spirit . . 2 Pet 1:21
anointing from the *H* . 1 John 2:20
says He who is *h* . . . . Rev 3:7
For You alone are *h* . . . . Rev 15:4
is *h*, let him be *h* . . . . . Rev 22:11

HOME
sparrow has found a *h* . . . . Ps 84:3
to his eternal *h* . . . . Eccl 12:5
that while we are at *h* . . 2 Cor 5:6
to show piety at *h* . . . . . 1 Tim 5:4

HOMEMAKERS
be discreet, chaste, *h* . . . . Titus 2:5

HONEY
and with *h* from the . . . . . Ps 81:16
was locusts and wild *h* . . . Matt 3:4

HONEYCOMB
than honey and the *h* . . . Ps 19:10
fish and some *h* . . . . . . Luke 24:42

HONOR
"*H* your father and your . Ex 20:12
will deliver him and *h* . . Ps 91:15
H and majesty are . . . . . . Ps 96:6
H the LORD with your . . Prov 3:9
before *h* is humility . . . Prov 15:33
spirit will retain *h* . . . . Prov 29:23
Father, where is My *h* . . . . Mal 1:6
is not without *h* . . . . Matt 13:57
'*H* your father and . . . . . Matt 15:4
h the Son just as they . . John 5:23
"I do not receive *h* . . . . . John 5:41
but I *h* My Father . . . . . . John 8:49
"If I *h* Myself . . . . John 8:54
him My Father will *h* . . John 12:26
to whom fear, ... Rom 13:7
sanctification and *h* . . 1 Thess 4:4
alone is wise, be *h* . . . . . 1 Tim 1:17
and clay, some for *h* . . . 2 Tim 2:20
no man takes this *h* . . . . . Heb 5:4
from God the Father . 2 Pet 1:17
give glory and *h* . . . . Rev 4:9

HONORABLE
His work is *h* and . . . . Ps 111:3
holy day of the LORD *h* . . . Is 58:13
providing *h* things . . . . 2 Cor 8:21
Marriage is *h* among . . . Heb 13:4
having your conduct *h* . 1 Pet 2:12

HONORS
'This people *h* Me . . . . . . Mark 7:6
It is My Father who *h* . . John 8:54

HOPE
h He has uprooted . . . . . Job 19:10
also will rest in *h* . . . . Ps 16:9
My *h* is in You . . . . Ps 39:7
For You are my *h* . . . . Ps 71:5
I *h* in Your word . . . . . . Ps 119:147
good that one should *h* . Lam 3:26
to *h*, in *h* believed . . . . Rom 4:18
h does not disappoint . . . Rom 5:5
were saved in this *h* . . . . Rom 8:24
now abide faith, *h* . . . . 1 Cor 13:13
life only we have *h* . . . 1 Cor 15:19
may know what is the *h* . Eph 1:18
were called in one *h* . . . . . Eph 4:4
Christ in you, the *h* . . . . . Col 1:27
Jesus Christ, our *h* . . . . 1 Tim 1:1
for the blessed *h* . . . . Titus 2:13
to lay hold of the *h* . . . . Heb 6:18
in of a better *h* . . . . Heb 7:19
who has this *h* in Him . 1 John 3:3

HOPED
substance of things *h* . . . Heb 11:1

HORSE
and behold, a white *h* . . . Rev 6:2
and behold, a white *h* . . Rev 19:11

HOSANNA
H in the highest . . . . . . Matt 21:9

HOSPITABLE
Be *h* to one another . . . . 1 Pet 4:9

HOSTS
The LORD of *h* is with . . . . Ps 46:7
Praise Him, all His *h* . . . Ps 148:2
against spiritual *h* . . . . . Eph 6:12

HOUR
is coming at an *h* . . . . . Matt 24:44
"But the *h* is coming . . . John 4:23
save Me from this *h* . . . John 12:27
keep you from the *h* . . . . Rev 3:10

HOUSE
as for me and my *h* . . . Josh 24:15
Through wisdom a *h* . . Prov 24:3
better to go to the *h* . . . . Eccl 7:2
h was filled with . . . . Is 6:4
h divided against . . . . . Matt 12:25
h shall be called a . . . . . Matt 21:13
make My Father's *h* . . . John 2:16
h are many mansions . John 14:2
publicly and from *h* . . . Acts 20:20
who rules his own *h* . . . . 1 Tim 3:4
the church in your *h* . . . Philem 2
For every *h* is built . . . . . Heb 3:4
His own *h*, whose *h* . . . Heb 3:6

HOUSEHOLD
the ways of her *h* . . . . Prov 31:27
be those of his own *h* . Matt 10:36
h were baptized . . . . . . Acts 16:15
saved, you and your *h* . Acts 16:31
who are of Caesar's *h* . . Phil 4:22

HOUSEHOLDER
h who brings out of . . . Matt 13:52

HOUSES
H and riches are an . . Prov 19:14
who has left *h* or . . . . . Matt 19:29
you devour widows' *h* . Matt 23:14

HOVERING

Spirit of God was *h* ......Gen 1:2

HUMBLE

man Moses was very *h* . Num 12:3
the cry of the *h* ....Ps 9:12
h shall hear of it and .....Ps 34:2
contrite and *h* spirit ......Is 57:15
A meek and *h* people ...Zeph 3:12
associate with the *h* ...Rom 12:16
gives grace to the *h* ...James 4:6
H yourselves in the ...James 4:10
gives grace to the *h* .....1 Pet 5:5
h yourselves under the ..1 Pet 5:6

HUMBLED

as a man, He *h* Himself ...Phil 2:8

HUMBLES

h Himself to behold .....Ps 113:6

HUMILITY

the Lord with all *h* ....Acts 20:19
delight in false *h* ....Col 2:18
mercies, kindness, *h* ....Col 3:12
h correcting those .....2 Tim 2:25
gentle, showing all *h* ....Titus 3:2
and be clothed with *h* ...1 Pet 5:5

HUNGER

They shall neither *h* ......Is 49:10
are those who *h* ....Matt 5:6
for you shall *h* ....Luke 6:25
to Me shall never *h* ....John 6:35
hour we both *h* ....1 Cor 4:11
"They shall neither *h* ...Rev 7:16

HUNGRY

and fills the *h* ....Ps 107:9
gives food to the *h* ......Ps 146:7
'for I was *h* and you ...Matt 25:35
did we see You *h* ......Matt 25:37
to be full and to be *h* ....Phil 4:12

HUNTER

Nimrod the mighty *h* ....Gen 10:9
Esau was a skillful *h* ...Gen 25:27

HURT

h a woman with child ...Ex 21:22
but I was not *h* ....Prov 23:35
another to his own *h* .....Eccl 8:9
They shall not *h* ....Is 11:9
it will by no means *h* .Mark 16:18
shall not be *h* by the ....Rev 2:11

HUSBAND

She also gave to her *h* ....Gen 3:6
h safely trusts her .....Prov 31:11
your Maker is your *h* ......Is 54:5
now have is not your *h* .John 4:18
you will save your *h* ...1 Cor 7:16
the *h* of one wife ....1 Tim 3:2

HUSBANDS

H, love your wives ......Eph 5:25
Let deacons be the *h* ..1 Tim 3:12

HYMN

they had sung a *h* ....Matt 26:30

HYMNS

praying and singing *h* .Acts 16:25
in psalms and *h* ....Eph 5:19

HYPOCRISY

you are full of *h* ......Matt 23:28
Pharisees, which is *h* ...Luke 12:1
Let love be without *h* ...Rom 12:9
away with their *h* ......Gal 2:13
and without *h* ....James 3:17
malice, all deceit, *h* ....1 Pet 2:1

HYPOCRITE

and the joy of the *h* .....Job 20:5
For everyone is a *h* ....Is 9:17
also played the *h* ....Gal 2:13

HYPOCRITES

not be like the *h* ....Matt 6:5
do you test Me, you *h* .Matt 22:18
and Pharisees, *h* ......Matt 23:13

I

IDLE

i person will suffer ....Prov 19:15
i word men may ....Matt 12:36
saw others standing *i* ...Matt 20:3
they learn to be *i* ......1 Tim 5:13

IDOL

thing offered to an *i* ....1 Cor 8:7
That an *i* is anything . 1 Cor 10:19

IDOLATER

or covetous, or an *i* ...1 Cor 5:11

IDOLATERS

fornicators, nor *i* ....1 Cor 6:9
and murderers and *i* ....Rev 22:15

IDOLATRIES

and abominable *i* ....1 Pet 4:3

IDOLATRY

beloved, flee from *i* ...1 Cor 10:14
i, sorcery ....Gal 5:20

IDOLS

land is also full of *i* ....Is 2:8
in the room of his *i* ....Ezek 8:12
who regard worthless *i* ...Jon 2:8
You who abhor *i* ......Rom 2:22
yourselves from *i* ...1 John 5:21
worship demons, and *i* ..Rev 9:20

IGNORANCE

that you did it in *i* ......Acts 3:17
i God overlooked ......Acts 17:30
sins committed in *i* ......Heb 9:7

IGNORANTLY

because I did it *i* ......1 Tim 1:13

ILLUMINATED

after you were *i* ....Heb 10:32
and the earth was *i* ......Rev 18:1
for the glory of God *i* ...Rev 21:23

IMAGE

Us make man in Our *i* ...Gen 1:26
since he is the *i* ....1 Cor 11:7
He is the *i* of the ......Col 1:15
and not the very *i* ....Heb 10:1
the beast and his *i* ......Rev 14:9

IMAGINATION

the proud in the *i* ......Luke 1:51

IMITATE

as I also *i* Christ ....1 Cor 11:1

IMMANUEL

shall call His name *I* ......Is 7:14
shall call His name I ....Matt 1:23

IMMORAL

murderers, sexually *i* ....Rev 21:8

IMMORALITY

except sexual *i* ....Matt 5:32
abstain from sexual *i* . 1 Thess 4:3

IMMORTAL

to the King eternal, *i* ..1 Tim 1:17

IMMORTALITY

mortal must put on *i* . 1 Cor 15:53
who alone has *i* ....1 Tim 6:16

IMMOVABLE

be steadfast, *i* ....1 Cor 15:58

IMMUTABLE

that by two *i* things .....Heb 6:18

IMPART

that it may *i* grace ......Eph 4:29

IMPENITENT

i heart you are ....Rom 2:5

IMPOSSIBLE

God nothing will be *i* ...Luke 1:37
without faith it is *i* .....Heb 11:6

IMPUTE

the Lord does not *i* ....Ps 32:2

IMPUTED

might be *i* to them ......Rom 4:11
but sin is not *i* ....Rom 5:13

IMPUTES

i righteousness apart ....Rom 4:6

INCORRUPTIBLE

the glory of the *i* ....Rom 1:23
dead will be raised *i* ..1 Cor 15:52
to an inheritance *i* ......1 Pet 1:4

INCORRUPTION

corruption inherit *i* ...1 Cor 15:50

INCREASE

Of the *i* of His ....Is 9:7
Lord, "*I* our faith .....Luke 17:5
"He must *i* ....John 3:30
but God gave the *i* .....1 Cor 3:6

INCREASES

who have no might He *i* ..Is 40:29

INCURABLE

Your sorrow is *i* ....Jer 30:15

INDIGNATION

i which will devour ....Heb 10:27
into the cup of His *i* ...Rev 14:10

INEXCUSABLE

Therefore you are *i* ......Rom 2:1

INEXPRESSIBLE

Paradise and heard *i* ...2 Cor 12:4
you rejoice with joy *i* ....1 Pet 1:8

INFALLIBLE

suffering by many *i* ......Acts 1:3

INFIRMITIES

"*He Himself took our i* ..Matt 8:17

INHERIT

love me to *i* wealth .....Prov 8:21
i the kingdom ....Matt 25:34
unrighteous will not *i* ...1 Cor 6:9
who overcomes shall *i* ...Rev 21:7

INHERITANCE

"You shall have no *i* ..Num 18:20
is the place of His *i* .....Deut 32:9
the portion of my *i* ......Ps 16:5
i shall be forever ....Ps 37:18
He will choose our *i* ......Ps 47:4
will arise to your *i* .....Dan 12:13
God gave him no *i* ....Acts 7:5
and give you an *i* ......Acts 20:32
For if the *i* is of the ......Gal 3:18
we have obtained an *i* ...Eph 1:11

INIQUITIES

be partakers of the *i* . . . . Col 1:12
receive as an *i* . . . . Heb 11:8
i incorruptible . . . . 1 Pet 1:4

INIQUITIES

i have overtaken me . . . . . Ps 40:12
forgives all your *i* . . . . . . Ps 103:3
LORD, should mark *i* . . . . . Ps 130:3
was bruised for our *i* . . . . Is 53:5
He shall bear their *i* . . . . . Is 53:11
i have separated you . . . . . . Is 59:2

INIQUITY

God, visiting the *i* of the . . Ex 20:5
was brought forth in *i* . . . . Ps 51:5
If I regard *i* in my . . . . Ps 66:18
i have dominion . . . . Ps 119:133
i will reap sorrow . . . . . . Prov 22:8
A people laden with *i* . . . . . . Is 1:4
i is taken away . . . . Is 6:7
has laid on Him the *i* . . . . . . Is 53:6
will remember their *i* . . . . . Hos 9:9
to those who devise *i* . . . . Mic 2:1
like You, Pardoning *i* . . . . Mic 7:18
all you workers of *i* . . . Luke 13:27
a fire, a world of *i* . . . . . James 3:6

INJUSTICE

i have your fathers . . . . Jer 2:5

INN

room for them in the *i* . . . Luke 2:7
brought him to an *i* . . . Luke 10:34

INNOCENCE

washed my hands in *i* . . Ps 73:13

INNOCENT

because I was found *i* . . . Dan 6:22
saying, "I am *i* . . . . . Matt 27:24
this day that I am *i* . . . Acts 20:26

INQUIRED

Therefore David *i* . . . . 1 Sam 23:2
the prophets have *i* . . . . 1 Pet 1:10

INQUIRY

shall make careful *i* . . . Deut 19:18

INSANE

images, And they are *i* . . Jer 50:38

INSPIRATION

is given by *i* of God . . . 2 Tim 3:16

INSTRUCT

I will *i* you and teach . . . . . Ps 32:8
LORD that he may *i* . . . . 1 Cor 2:16

INSTRUCTED

This man had been *i* . . . Acts 18:25
are excellent, being *i* . . . Rom 2:18
Moses was divinely *i* . . . . . Heb 8:5

INSTRUCTION

seeing you hate *i* . . . . Ps 50:17
Hear *i* and be wise . . . . . Prov 8:33
Give *i* to a wise man . . . . . Prov 9:9
for correction, for *i* . . . . 2 Tim 3:16

INSTRUCTS

My heart also *i* . . . . Ps 16:7

INSTRUMENTS

your members as *i* . . . . . Rom 6:13

INSUBORDINATE

for the lawless and *i* . . . . 1 Tim 1:9

INSUBORDINATION

of dissipation or *i* . . . . Titus 1:6

INSULTED

will be mocked and *i* . . Luke 18:32
i the Spirit of grace . . . . Heb 10:29

INSULTS

nor be afraid of their *i* . . . . . Is 51:7

INTEGRITY

In the *i* of my heart . . . . . Gen 20:5
in doctrine showing *i* . . . . Titus 2:7

INTERCEDE

the LORD, who will *i* . . 1 Sam 2:25

INTERCESSION

of many, And made *i* . . . . . Is 53:12
Spirit Himself makes *i* . . Rom 8:26
always lives to make *i* . . . Heb 7:25

INTERCESSOR

that there was no *i* . . . . . . Is 59:16

INTEREST

collected it with *i* . . . . . Luke 19:23

INTERPRET

Do all *i*? . . . . 1 Cor 12:30
pray that he may *i* . . . . 1 Cor 14:13

INTERPRETATION

to another the *i* . . . . 1 Cor 12:10
of any private *i* . . . . 2 Pet 1:20

INTERPRETATIONS

"Do not *i* belong to . . . . . Gen 40:8

INVISIBLE

of the world His *i* . . . . . . Rom 1:20
is the image of the *i* . . . . . Col 1:15
eternal, immortal, *i* . . . . 1 Tim 1:17
as seeing Him who is *i* . . Heb 11:27

INWARD

You have formed my *i* . . Ps 139:13
God according to the *i* . . Rom 7:22
i man is being . . . . 2 Cor 4:16

INWARDLY

i they are . . . . Matt 7:15
is a Jew who is one *i* . . . Rom 2:29

IRON

i sharpens *i* . . . . Prov 27:17
its feet partly of *i* . . . . . . Dan 2:33

ISRAEL

"Hear, O *I* . . . . Deut 6:4
For they are not all *I* . . . . Rom 9:6
and upon the *I* of God . . . Gal 6:16

ITCHING

they have *i* ears . . . . 2 Tim 4:3

J

JEALOUS

God, am a *j* God . . . . Ex 20:5
a consuming fire, a *j* . . . . Deut 4:24
For I am *j* for you . . . . . 2 Cor 11:2

JEALOUSY

provoked Him to *j* . . . . . Deut 32:16
as strong as death, *j* . . . Song 8:6
for you with godly *j* . . . 2 Cor 11:2

JEOPARDY

stand in *j* every hour . 1 Cor 15:30

JESTING

talking, nor coarse *j* . . . . . Eph 5:4

JESUS

J Christ was as . . . . Matt 1:18
shall call His name *J* . . . Matt 1:21
J was led up by the . . . . . . Matt 4:1
and laid hands on *J* . . . Matt 26:50

JUDGES

and destroy *J* . . . . Matt 27:20
J withdrew with His . . . Mark 3:7
J went into . . . . Mark 11:11
they were eating, *J* . . . Mark 14:22
and he delivered *J* . . . . Mark 15:15
truth came through *J* . . John 1:17
J lifted up His eyes . . . . . John 6:5
J wept . . . . John 11:35
J was crucified . . . . John 19:20
"This *J* God has raised . . Acts 2:32
of Your holy Servant *J* . . Acts 4:30
believed on the Lord *J* . Acts 11:17
your mouth the Lord *J* . . Rom 10:9
among you except *J* . . . 1 Cor 2:2
perfect in Christ *J* . . . . . . Col 1:28
But we see *J* . . . . Heb 2:9
looking unto *J* . . . . Heb 12:2
Revelation of *J* Christ . . . Rev 1:1
so, come, Lord *J* . . . . . . Rev 22:20

JOIN

of the rest dared *j* . . . . . . Acts 5:13

JOINED

and mother and be *j* . . . . Gen 2:24
what God has *j* . . . . Matt 19:6
the whole body, *j* . . . . . . Eph 4:16

JOINT

j as He wrestled . . . . . . Gen 32:25
My bones are out of *j* . . . Ps 22:14
j heirs with Christ . . . . . . Rom 8:17

JOINTS

and knit together by *j* . . . Col 2:19
and spirit, and of *j* . . . . . Heb 4:12

JOT

one *j* or one tittle . . . . . . Matt 5:18

JOY

is fullness of *j* . . . . Ps 16:11
j comes in the morning . . . Ps 30:5
j you will draw . . . . Is 12:3
ashes, The oil of *j* . . . . Is 61:3
shall sing for *j* . . . . Is 65:14
receives it with *j* . . . . . Matt 13:20
Enter into the *j* . . . . Matt 25:21
in my womb for *j* . . . . . . Luke 1:44
there will be more *j* . . . . Luke 15:7
did not believe for *j* . . . Luke 24:41
My *j* may remain in . . . John 15:11
they may have My *j* . . . John 17:13
the Spirit is love, *j* . . . . . Gal 5:22
are our glory and *j* . . 1 Thess 2:20
j that was set before . . . . Heb 12:2
count it all *j* . . . . James 1:2
with exceeding *j* . . . . . . 1 Pet 4:13

JOYFUL

Make a *j* shout to the . . . . Ps 100:1
And make them *j* . . . . Is 56:7

JUDGE

The LORD *j* between . . . . . Gen 16:5
coming to *j* the earth . 1 Chr 16:33
sword The LORD will *j* . . . . Is 66:16
deliver you to the *j* . . . . . Matt 5:25
"*J* not . . . . Matt 7:1
who made Me a *j* . . . . . Luke 12:14
j who did not fear God . Luke 18:2
As I hear, I *j* . . . . John 5:30
"Do not *j* according . . . . John 7:24
I *j* no one . . . . John 8:15
j the world but to . . . . . John 12:47
this, O man, you who *j* . . Rom 2:3
Therefore let us not *j* . . . Rom 14:13
Christ, who will *j* . . . . . . 2 Tim 4:1
But if you *j* the law . . . James 4:11

JUDGES

He makes the *j* of the . . . . Is 40:23
For the Father *j* . . . . John 5:22
he who is spiritual *j* . . . 1 Cor 2:15
j me is the Lord . . . . 1 Cor 4:4
Him who *j* righteously . . 1 Pet 2:23

JUDGMENT

Teach me good *j* . . . . Ps 119:66
from prison and from *j* . . . . Is 53:8
be in danger of the *j* . . . . Matt 5:21
shall not come into *j* . . . . John 5:24
and My *j* is righteous . . . John 5:30
if I do judge, My *j* . . . . . . John 8:16
"Now is the *j* . . . . John 12:31
the righteous *j* . . . . Rom 1:32
j which came from one . Rom 5:16
appear before the *j* . . . . 2 Cor 5:10
after this the *j* . . . . Heb 9:27
time has come for *j* . . . . 1 Pet 4:17
a long time their *j* . . . . . . 2 Pet 2:3
darkness for the *j* . . . . Jude 6

JUDGMENTS

The *j* of the LORD are . . . . . Ps 19:9
unsearchable are His *j* . Rom 11:33

JUST

Noah was a *j* man . . . . Gen 6:9
j man who perishes . . . . . Eccl 7:15
j shall live by his . . . . Hab 2:4
her husband, being a *j* . . Matt 1:19
resurrection of the *j* . . Luke 14:14
j persons who need no . Luke 15:7
the Holy One and the *J* . Acts 3:14
dead, both of the *j* . . . . Acts 24:15
j shall live by faith . . . . . . Rom 1:17
that He might be *j* . . . . . . Rom 3:26
j men made perfect . . . . Heb 12:23
have murdered the *j* . . . James 5:6
He is faithful and *j* . . 1 John 1:9

JUSTICE

j as the noonday . . . . Ps 37:6
And Your poor with *j* . . . . Ps 72:2
j the measuring line . . . . Is 28:17
the LORD is a God of *j* . . . Is 30:18
He will bring forth *j* . . . . . . Is 42:1
J is turned back . . . . Is 59:14
I, the LORD, love *j* . . . . . . Is 61:8
truth, and His ways *j* . . . Dan 4:37
'Execute true *j* . . . . Zech 7:9
"Where is the God of *j* . . Mal 2:17
And He will declare j . . Matt 12:18
His humiliation His j . . . . Acts 8:33

JUSTIFICATION

because of our *j* . . . . Rom 4:25
offenses resulted in *j* . . . Rom 5:16

JUSTIFIED

Me that you may be *j* . . . . Job 40:8
words you will be *j* . . . Matt 12:37
"But wisdom is *j* . . . . . . Luke 7:35
j rather than the . . . . . . Luke 18:14
who believes is *j* . . . . . . Acts 13:39
"That You may be j . . . . Rom 3:4
law no flesh will be *j* . . . Rom 3:20
j freely by His grace . . . . Rom 3:24
having been *j* by . . . . Rom 5:1
these He also *j* . . . . Rom 8:30
that we might be *j* . . . . . . Gal 2:16
no flesh shall be *j* . . . . . . Gal 2:16
the harlot also *j* . . . . . . James 2:25

JUSTIFIES

He who *j* the wicked . . . Prov 17:15
It is God who *j* . . . . Rom 8:33

JUSTIFY

wanting to *j* himself . . . Luke 10:29
"You are those who *j* . Luke 16:15
is one God who will *j* . . . Rom 3:30

K

KEEP

k you wherever you . . . . Gen 28:15
day, to *k* it holy . . . . Ex 20:8

Let all the earth *k* . . . . . . Hab 2:20
k the commandments . . Matt 19:17
"If you love Me, *k* . . . . . John 14:15
k through Your name . John 17:11
orderly and *k* the law . . Acts 21:24
k the unity of the . . . . Eph 4:3
k His commandments . . 1 John 2:3

KEEPER

Am I my brother's *k* . . . . . Gen 4:9
The LORD is your *k* . . . . . . Ps 121:5

KEEPS

k truth forever . . . . Ps 146:6
k the commandment . . . Prov 19:16
none of you *k* the law . . . John 7:19
born of God *k* . . . . 1 John 5:18
and *k* his garments . . . . . Rev 16:15

KEPT

For I have *k* the . . . . . 2 Sam 22:22
these things I have *k* . . Matt 19:20
love, just as I have *k* . . . John 15:10
k back part of the . . . . . . Acts 5:2
I have *k* the faith . . . . 2 Tim 4:7
who are *k* by the power . 1 Pet 1:5

KEY

taken away the *k* . . . . . Luke 11:52
"He who has the k . . . . . . Rev 3:7

KEYS

I will give you the *k* . . . Matt 16:19
And I have the *k* . . . . Rev 1:18

KILL

k the Passover . . . . Ex 12:21
I *k* and I make alive . . . Deut 32:39
"Am I God, to *k* . . . . 2 Kin 5:7
A time to *k* . . . . Eccl 3:3
of them they will *k* . . . . Luke 11:49
afraid of those who *k* . . Luke 12:4
Why do you seek to *k* . . John 7:19
k and eat . . . . Acts 10:13

KILLED

Abel his brother and *k* . . . Gen 4:8
for Your sake we are *k* . . Ps 44:22
and scribes, and be *k* . . Matt 16:21
Siloam fell and *k* them . Luke 13:4
k the Prince of life . . . . . . Acts 3:15
Your sake we are k . . . . Rom 8:36
k both the Lord . . . . . 1 Thess 2:15

KILLS

the one who *k* the . . . . . Matt 23:37
for the letter *k* . . . . 2 Cor 3:6

KIND

animals after their *k* . . . . Gen 6:20
k can come out by . . . . . Mark 9:29
suffers long and is *k* . . . 1 Cor 13:4
And be *k* to one . . . . Eph 4:32

KINDLY

Julius treated Paul *k* . . . Acts 27:3
k affectionate to one . . . Rom 12:10

KINDNESS

For His merciful *k* . . . . . . Ps 117:2
k shall not depart . . . . Is 54:10
I remember you, The *k* . . . Jer 2:2
by longsuffering, by *k* . . 2 Cor 6:6
longsuffering, *k* . . . . Gal 5:22
and to brotherly *k* . . . . . . 2 Pet 1:7

KING

"Yet I have set My *K* . . . . . Ps 2:6
The LORD is *K* forever . . . Ps 10:16
And the *K* of glory . . . . . Ps 24:7
For God is my *K* . . . . Ps 74:12
when your *k* is a child . Eccl 10:16
and the everlasting *K* . . . Jer 10:10
the LORD shall be *K* . . . . Zech 14:9
who has been born *K* . . . . Matt 2:2

This Is Jesus The *K* . . . . Matt 27:37
"Behold your *K* . . . . John 19:14
Now to the *K* eternal . . 1 Tim 1:17
only Potentate, the *K* . . 1 Tim 6:15
this Melchizedek, *k* . . . . . . Heb 7:1
K of Kings and Lord . . . Rev 19:16

KINGDOM

Yours is the *k* . . . . 1 Chr 29:11
k is the LORD's . . . . Ps 22:28
the scepter of Your *k* . . . . Ps 45:6
is an everlasting *k* . . . . Ps 145:13
k which shall never be . . Dan 2:44
High rules in the *k* . . . . . . Dan 4:17
"Repent, for the *k* . . . . . . Matt 3:2
for Yours is the *k* . . . . . . Matt 6:13
"But seek first the *k* . . . . Matt 6:33
the mysteries of the *k* . Matt 13:11
are the sons of the *k* . . . Matt 13:38
of such is the *k* . . . . Matt 19:14
back, is fit for the *k* . . . . Luke 9:62
against nation, and *k* . . Luke 21:10
he cannot see the *k* . . . . . John 3:3
he cannot enter the *k* . . . John 3:5
If My *k* were of this . . . John 18:36
for the *k* of God is . . . . . Rom 14:17
will not inherit the *k* . . . . Gal 5:21
the scepter of Your k . . . . Heb 1:8
we are receiving a *k* . . . Heb 12:28

KINGDOMS

the *k* were moved . . . . Ps 46:6
showed Him all the *k* . . . Matt 4:8
have become the *k* . . . . . Rev 11:15

KINGS

The *k* of the earth set . . . . . . Ps 2:2
By me *k* reign . . . . Prov 8:15
governors and *k* . . . . . . Matt 10:18
k have desired to see . . Luke 10:24
You have reigned as *k* . . 1 Cor 4:8
and has made us *k* . . . . . . Rev 1:6
that the way of the *k* . . . Rev 16:12

KISS

K the Son . . . . Ps 2:12
"You gave Me no *k* . . . . Luke 7:45
one another with a *k* . . . 1 Pet 5:14

KISSED

they *k* one another . . . 1 Sam 20:41
and *k* Him . . . . Matt 26:49
and she *k* His feet and . Luke 7:38

KNEE

That to Me every *k* . . . . . . Is 45:23
have not bowed the k . . . Rom 11:4
of Jesus every *k* . . . . Phil 2:10

KNEES

make firm the feeble *k* . . . . Is 35:3
this reason I bow my *k* . . Eph 3:14
and the feeble *k* . . . . . . Heb 12:12

KNEW

in the womb I *k* . . . . Jer 1:5
to them, 'I never *k* . . . . . Matt 7:23
k what was in man . . . . John 2:25
He made Him who *k* . . . 2 Cor 5:21

KNIT

be encouraged, being *k* . . . Col 2:2

KNOCK

k, and it will be . . . . Matt 7:7
at the door and *k* . . . . . . Rev 3:20

KNOW

k good and evil . . . . Gen 3:22
k that I am the LORD . . . . . Ex 6:7
k that my Redeemer . . . . Job 19:25
make me to *k* wisdom . . . Ps 51:6
Who can *k* it . . . . Jer 17:9
saying, '*K* the LORD . . . . . Jer 31:34
k what hour your . . . . . Matt 24:42

an oath, "I do not *k* ...Matt 26:72
the world did not *k* .....John 1:10
We speak what We *k* ...John 3:11
k that You are ....John 6:69
My voice, and I *k* ...John 10:27
If you *k* these things ...John 13:17
k whom I have ....John 13:18
are sure that You *k* ....John 16:30
k that I love You .....John 21:15
k times or seasons ....Acts 1:7
and said, "Jesus I *k* ....Acts 19:15
wisdom did not *k* ......1 Cor 1:21
nor can he *k* them .....1 Cor 2:14
For we *k* in part and ...1 Cor 13:9
k the love of Christ .....Eph 3:19
k whom I have ....2 Tim 1:12
we *k* that we *k* Him ...1 John 2:3
and you *k* all things ..1 John 2:20
By this we *k* love ....1 John 3:16
k that He abides ......1 John 3:24
k that we are of God ..1 John 5:19
"I *k* your works ....Rev 2:2

KNOWLEDGE

and the tree of the *k* .....Gen 2:9
unto night reveals *k* ......Ps 19:2
k is too wonderful ....Ps 139:6
people store up *k* ......Prov 10:14
k spares his words .....Prov 17:27
and he who increases *k* .Eccl 1:18
k is that wisdom ......Eccl 7:12
k shall increase ....Dan 12:4
more accurate *k* ......Acts 24:22
having the form of *k* ....Rom 2:20
law is the *k* of sin .....Rom 3:20
whether there is *k* ....1 Cor 13:8
Christ which passes *k* ..Eph 3:19
is falsely called *k* ......1 Tim 6:20
in the grace and *k* .....2 Pet 3:18

KNOWN

If you had *k* Me ....John 8:19
My sheep, and am *k* ...John 10:14
The world has not *k* ...John 17:25
peace they have not *k* .Rom 3:17
"For who has *k* ......Rom 11:34
after you have *k* ....Gal 4:9
requests be made *k* .....Phil 4:6
k the Holy Scriptures ..2 Tim 3:15

KNOWS

"For God *k* that in ......Gen 3:5
k what is in the ....Dan 2:22
k the things you have ....Matt 6:8
and hour no one *k* ....Matt 24:36
God *k* your hearts ...Luke 16:15
searches the hearts *k* ...Rom 8:27
k the things of God ....1 Cor 2:11
k those who are His ...2 Tim 2:19
to him who *k* to do ....James 4:17
and *k* all things ......1 John 3:20

L

LABOR

Six days you shall *l* ......Ex 20:9
things are full of *l* ....Eccl 1:8
has man for all his *l* ....Eccl 2:22
He shall see the *l* ......Is 53:11
to Me, all you who *l* ...Matt 11:28
"Do not *l* for the .....John 6:27
knowing that your *l* ..1 Cor 15:58
but rather let him *l* ......Eph 4:28
mean fruit from my *l* ...Phil 1:22
your work of faith, *l* ..1 Thess 1:3
forget your work and *l* ..Heb 6:10
your works, your *l* ......Rev 2:2

LABORED

l more abundantly ....1 Cor 15:10
for you, lest I have *l* .....Gal 4:11

LABORERS

but the *l* are few ....Matt 9:37

LABORING

l night and day ....1 Thess 2:9

LABORS

entered into their *l* ....John 4:38
creation groans and *l* ...Rom 8:22
l more abundant .....2 Cor 11:23
may rest from their *l* ...Rev 14:13

LACK

What do I still *l* ....Matt 19:20
"One thing you *l* .....Mark 10:21

LADDER

and behold, a *l* ....Gen 28:12

LAID

the place where they *l* .Mark 16:6
"Where have you *l* ....John 11:34

LAKE

cast alive into the *l* .....Rev 19:20

LAMB

but where is the *l* .....Gen 22:7
He was led as a *l* ....Is 53:7
The *L* of God who .....John 1:29
the elders, stood a *L* .....Rev 5:6
"Worthy is the *L* ....Rev 5:12
by the blood of the *L* ..Rev 12:11

LAME

l shall leap like a ....Is 35:6
blind see and the *l* .....Matt 11:5
And a certain man *l* .....Acts 3:2

LAMENTATION

was heard in Ramah, l ..Matt 2:18
and made great *l* ....Acts 8:2

LAMP

Your word is a *l* ....Ps 119:105
the *l* of the wicked .....Prov 13:9
his *l* will be put out ....Prov 20:20
"Nor do they light a *l* ...Matt 5:15
"The *l* of the body ......Matt 6:22
when he has lit a *l* ....Luke 8:16
l gives you light ......Luke 11:36
does not light a *l* ....Luke 15:8
burning and shining *l* ..John 5:35

LAMPS

he made its seven *l* ......Ex 37:23
and trimmed their *l* ....Matt 25:7

LAMPSTAND

branches of the *l* ....Ex 25:32
a basket, but on a *l* .....Matt 5:15
and remove your *l* ....Rev 2:5

LAND

l that I will show you ....Gen 12:1
l flowing with milk ....Ex 3:8
They will see the *l* .....Is 33:17
Bethlehem, in the l .....Matt 2:6

LANGUAGE

whole earth had one *l* ...Gen 11:1
speak in his own *l* ......Acts 2:6
blasphemy, filthy *l* ....Col 3:8

LANGUAGES

according to their *l* ....Gen 10:20

LAST

He shall stand at *l* .....Job 19:25
First and I am the *L* .....Is 44:6
l will be first ....Matt 20:16
the First and the *L* .....Rev 1:11

LATTER

l times some will ....1 Tim 4:1

LAUGH

"Why did Sarah *l* ......Gen 18:13
Woe to you who *l* .....Luke 6:25

LAUGHS

The Lord *l* at him ....Ps 37:13

LAUGHTER

your *l* be turned to .....James 4:9

LAW

stones a copy of the *l* ...Josh 8:32
The *l* of the LORD is ....Ps 19:7
I delight in Your *l* ......Ps 119:70
Oh, how I love Your *l* ...Ps 119:97
And Your *l* is truth ....Ps 119:142
l will proceed from Me ....Is 51:4
in whose heart 's My *l* ....Is 51:7
The *L* is no more ....Lam 2:9
The *l* of truth was in ....Mal 2:6
to destroy the *L* ....Matt 5:17
for this is the *L* ....Matt 7:12
hang all the *L* and the .Matt 22:40
"The *l* and the ....Luke 16:16
l was given through ....John 1:17
"Does our *l* judge a ....John 7:51
l is the knowledge .....Rom 3:20
because the *l* brings ....Rom 4:15
when there is no *l* ......Rom 5:13
you are not under *l* .....Rom 6:14
For what the *l* could ....Rom 8:3
l that I might live ....Gal 2:19
under guard by the *l* .....Gal 3:23
born under the *l* ....Gal 4:4
l is fulfilled in one ......Gal 5:14
into the perfect *l* ......James 1:25
fulfill the royal *l* ......James 2:8

LAWFUL

Is it *l* to pay taxes .....Matt 22:17
All things are *l* ....1 Cor 6:12

LAWGIVER

There is one *L* ....James 4:12

LAWLESS

l one will be revealed .2 Thess 2:8

LAWLESSNESS

Me, you who practice *l* ..Matt 7:23
l is already at work ...2 Thess 2:7

LAWYERS

"Woe to you also, *l* ...Luke 11:46

LAY

nowhere to *l* His head ..Matt 8:20
l hands may receive ....Acts 8:19

LAZINESS

l the building decays ...Eccl 10:18

LAZY

l man will be put to ....Prov 12:24
wicked and *l* servant ..Matt 25:26
liars, evil beasts, *l* ......Titus 1:12

LEAD

L me in Your truth and ...Ps 25:5
And do not *l* us into ....Matt 6:13
"Can the blind *l* ....Luke 6:39

LEADS

He *l* me in the paths ......Ps 23:3
And if the blind *l* ......Matt 15:14

LEAF

plucked olive *l* ....Gen 8:11

LEAN

all your heart, And *l* .....Prov 3:5

LEAP

Then the lame shall *l* ......Is 35:6

LEARN

L to do good . . . . Is 1:17
yoke upon you and *l* . . . Matt 11:29

LEARNED

Me The tongue of the *l* . . . . Is 50:4
have not so *l* Christ . . . . . Eph 4:20
in all things I have *l* . . . . . Phil 4:12

LEARNING

l is driving you mad . . . Acts 26:24

LEAST

so, shall be called *l* . . . . . Matt 5:19

LEAVE

a man shall *l* his . . . . Gen 2:24
For You will not *l* . . . . Ps 16:10
"*I* will never *l* . . . . Heb 13:5

LEAVEN

of heaven is like *l* . . . Matt 13:33
l leavens the whole . . . . Gal 5:9

LEAVES

and they sewed fig *l* . . . . . . Gen 3:7
The *l* of the tree . . . . Rev 22:2

LED

l them forth by the . . . . . . Ps 107:7
For as many as are *l* . . . . Rom 8:14

LEFT

l hand know what your . . Matt 6:3

LEND

"And if you *l* . . . . Luke 6:34

LENDER

is servant to the *l* . . . . Prov 22:7

LENDS

ever merciful, and *l* . . . . . . Ps 37:26

LENGTH

is your life and the *l* . . . Deut 30:20

LEOPARD

or the *l* its spots . . . . Jer 13:23

LEPERS

"And many *l* were in . . . Luke 4:27

LET

"*L* there be light . . . . Gen 1:3

LETTER

for the *l* kills . . . . 2 Cor 3:6
or by word or by *l* . . . 2 Thess 2:2

LETTERS

does this Man know *l* . . John 7:15

LEVIATHAN

"Can you draw out *L* . . . . Job 41:1

LEVITE

"Likewise a *L* . . . . Luke 10:32

LEWDNESS

wickedness, deceit, *l* . . . Mark 7:22

LIAR

for he is a *l* and the . . . . John 8:44
but every man a *l* . . . . Rom 3:4
we make Him a *l* . . . . . 1 John 1:10
his brother, he is a *l* . . 1 John 4:20

LIARS

"All men are *l* . . . . Ps 116:11
l shall have their . . . . Rev 21:8

LIBERALITY

he who gives, with *l* . . . . Rom 12:8

LIBERALLY

who gives to all *l* . . . . . . James 1:5

LIBERTY

year, and proclaim *l* . . . . Lev 25:10
'*To proclaim l to the* . . . Luke 4:18
into the glorious *l* . . . . . . Rom 8:21
Lord is, there is *l* . . . . . . 2 Cor 3:17
therefore in the *l* . . . . Gal 5:1

LIE

Do not *l* to one . . . . Col 3:9
God, who cannot *l* . . . . . Titus 1:2
an abomination or a *l* . . Rev 21:27

LIED

You have not *l* to men . . . Acts 5:4

LIES

sin *l* at the door . . . . Gen 4:7
speaking *l* in . . . . 1 Tim 4:2

LIFE

the breath of *l* . . . . Gen 2:7
'For the *l* of the . . . . Lev 17:11
before you today *l* . . . . Deut 30:15
He will redeem their *l* . . Ps 72:14
word has given me *l* . . . Ps 119:50
She is a tree of *l* . . . . Prov 3:18
finds me finds *l* . . . . Prov 8:35
L is more than . . . . Luke 12:23
l was the light . . . . John 1:4
so the Son gives *l* . . . . . John 5:21
spirit, and they are *l* . . . John 6:63
have the light of *l* . . . . . John 8:12
and I lay down My *l* . . . John 10:15
resurrection and the *l* . John 11:25
you lay down your *l* . . . John 13:38
l which I now live . . . . . . Gal 2:20
l is hidden with . . . . Col 3:3
For what is your *l* . . . . . James 4:14
l was manifested . . . . . . 1 John 1:2
and the pride of *l* . . . . . 1 John 2:16
has given us eternal *l* . 1 John 5:11
the Lamb's Book of *L* . . Rev 21:27
right to the tree of *l* . . . Rev 22:14
the water of *l* freely . . . Rev 22:17
from the Book of *L* . . . . Rev 22:19

LIFT

I will *l* up my eyes to . . . . Ps 121:1
Lord, and He will *l* . . . . James 4:10

LIFTED

your heart is *l* . . . . Ezek 28:2
in Hades, he *l* up his . . Luke 16:23
the Son of Man be *l* . . . John 3:14
"And I, if I am *l* . . . . . . John 12:32

LIGHT

"Let there be *l* . . . . Gen 1:3
The Lord is my *l* . . . . Ps 27:1
and a *l* to my path . . . . Ps 119:105
The *l* of the righteous . . . Prov 13:9
The Lord gives *l* . . . . . . Prov 29:13
Truly the *l* is sweet . . . . . Eccl 11:7
let us walk in the *l* . . . . . . Is 2:5
l shall break forth . . . . Is 58:8
"You are the *l* . . . . Matt 5:14
"Let your *l* so shine . . . Matt 5:16
than the sons of *l* . . . . . Luke 16:8
and the life was the *l* . . John 1:4
darkness rather than *l* . John 3:19
saying, "I am the *l* . . . . John 8:12
God who commanded *l* . 2 Cor 4:6
Walk as children of *l* . . Eph 5:8
You are all sons of *l* . . 1 Thess 5:5
into His marvelous *l* . . . 1 Pet 2:9
to you, that God is *l* . . 1 John 1:5
l as He is in the . . . . . . 1 John 1:7
says he is in the *l* . . . . . 1 John 2:9
The Lamb is its *l* . . . . . . Rev 21:23

LIBERALLY

LIGHTNING

"For as the *l* . . . . Matt 24:27
countenance was like *l* . . Matt 28:3

LIGHTNINGS

the throne proceeded *l* . . . . Rev 4:5

LIGHTS

"Let there be *l* . . . . Gen 1:14
whom you shine as *l* . . . . Phil 2:15

LIKENESS

according to Our *l* . . . . . . Gen 1:26
carved image—any *l* . . . . . Ex 20:4
when I awake in Your *l* . . Ps 17:15
and coming in the *l* . . . . . . Phil 2:7

LILY

the *l* of the valleys . . . . . . Song 2:1

LIMIT

to the sea its *l* . . . . Prov 8:29

LINE

upon precept, *L* upon . . . . Is 28:10
I am setting a plumb *l* . . Amos 7:8

LINEN

wrapped Him in the *l* . Mark 15:46

LINGER

salvation shall not *l* . . . . . Is 46:13

LION

l shall eat straw . . . . Is 11:7

LIONS

the mouths of *l* . . . . Heb 11:33

LIPS

off all flattering *l* . . . . Ps 12:3
The *l* of the righteous . . Prov 10:21
But the *l* of . . . . Prov 20:15
am a man of unclean *l* . . . . Is 6:5
other l I will speak . . . 1 Cor 14:21
from evil, And his l . . . . 1 Pet 3:10

LISTEN

you are not able to *l* . . . John 8:43
you who fear God, *l* . . . Acts 13:16

LISTENS

But whoever *l* to me . . . . Prov 1:33

LITTLE

Though you are *l* . . . . Mic 5:2
l ones only a cup . . . . . . Matt 10:42
"O you of *l* faith . . . . . . Matt 14:31
to whom *l* is forgiven . . . Luke 7:47
faithful in a very *l* . . . . Luke 19:17

LIVE

eat, and *l* forever . . . . Gen 3:22
a man does, he shall *l* . . . Lev 18:5
"Seek Me and *l* . . . . Amos 5:4
But the just shall *l* . . . . . . Hab 2:4
l by bread alone . . . . Matt 4:4
"for in Him we *l* . . . . . . Acts 17:28
l peaceably with all . . . Rom 12:18
the life which I now . . . . . Gal 2:20
If we *l* in the Spirit . . . . . Gal 5:25
to me, to *l* is Christ . . . . Phil 1:21

LIVED

died and rose and *l* . . . . Rom 14:9
And they *l* and reigned . . Rev 20:4

LIVES

but man *l* by every . . . . . Deut 8:3
but Christ *l* in me . . . . . . Gal 2:20
to lay down our *l* . . . . . 1 John 3:16
"I am He who *l* . . . . Rev 1:18

LIVING

and man became a *l* . . . . Gen 2:7
in the light of the *l* . . . . . Ps 56:13

LOATHSOME

the dead, but of the *l* . . Matt 22:32
do you seek the *l* . . . . . Luke 24:5
the word of God is *l* . . . . Heb 4:12
l creature was like a . . . . . . Rev 4:7

LOATHSOME

But a wicked man is *l* . . Prov 13:5

LOAVES

have here only five *l* . . . Matt 14:17
you ate of the *l* . . . . John 6:26

LOCUST

What the chewing *l* . . . . . . Joel 1:4

LOCUSTS

and his food was *l* . . . . Matt 3:4

LOFTY

Wisdom is too *l* . . . . Prov 24:7

LONG

your days may be *l* . . . . . Deut 5:16
Who *l* for death . . . . Job 3:21
I *l* for Your salvation . . Ps 119:174
go around in *l* robes . . Mark 12:38

LONGSUFFERING

is love, joy, peace, *l* . . . . . Gal 5:22
and gentleness, with *l* . . . Eph 4:2
for all patience and *l* . . . . Col 1:11
might show all *l* . . . . . . 1 Tim 1:16
once the Divine *l* . . . . . . 1 Pet 3:20
and consider that the *l* . 2 Pet 3:15

LOOK

A proud *l* . . . . Prov 6:17
"*L* to Me . . . . Is 45:22
l on Me whom they . . Zech 12:10
say to you, '*L* here . . . Luke 17:23
while we do not *l* . . . . . 2 Cor 4:18

LOOKED

For He *l* down from . . . . Ps 102:19
He *l* for justice . . . . Is 5:7
the Lord turned and *l* . . Luke 22:61
for he *l* to the reward . . Heb 11:26

LOOKING

the plow, and *l* back . . . Luke 9:62
l for the blessed hope . . Titus 2:13
l unto Jesus . . . . Heb 12:2
l carefully lest . . . . Heb 12:15
l for the mercy of . . . . Jude 21

LOOKS

The lofty *l* of man . . . . Is 2:11
to you that whoever *l* . . . Matt 5:28

LOOSE

and whatever you *l* . . . . Matt 16:19
said to them, "*L* him . . John 11:44

LOOSED

the silver cord is *l* . . . . . . Eccl 12:6

LORD

L is my strength . . . . Ex 15:2
L our God, the *L* . . . . Deut 6:4
You alone are the *L* . . . . . . Neh 9:6
The *L* of hosts . . . . Ps 24:10
Gracious is the *L* . . . . Ps 116:5
L surrounds His people . . Ps 125:2
The *L* is righteous . . . . . . Ps 129:4
L is near to all who . . . . . Ps 145:18
L is a God of justice . . . . . Is 30:18
L Our Righteousness . . . Jer 23:6
"The *L* is one . . . . Zech 14:9
shall not tempt the L . . . . Matt 4:7
shall worship the L . . . . Matt 4:10
Son of Man is also *L* . . Mark 2:28
who is Christ the *L* . . . Luke 2:11
L is risen indeed . . . . . Luke 24:34
Me Teacher and *L* . . . . John 13:13
He is *L* of all . . . . Acts 10:36

with your mouth the *L* . . Rom 10:9
say that Jesus is *L* . . . . 1 Cor 12:3
second Man is the *L* . . 1 Cor 15:47
the Spirit of the *L* . . . . . 2 Cor 3:17
that Jesus Christ is *L* . . . . Phil 2:11
and deny the only *L* . . . . . . Jude 4
L God Omnipotent . . . . . . Rev 19:6

LORDS

for He is Lord of *l* . . . . . . Rev 17:14

LOSE

save his life will *l* . . . . . Matt 16:25

LOSES

but if the salt *l* . . . . Matt 5:13
and *l* his own soul . . . . Matt 16:26

LOSS

count all things *l* . . . . Phil 3:8

LOST

save that which was *l* . . Matt 18:11
and none of them is *l* . . John 17:12
You gave Me I have *l* . . . John 18:9

LOTS

garments, casting *l* . . . Mark 15:24
And they cast their *l* . . . . Acts 1:26

LOUD

cried out with a *l* . . . . . Matt 27:46
I heard behind me a *l* . . . Rev 1:10

LOVE

l your neighbor as . . . . . Lev 19:18
l the LORD your God . . . . Deut 6:5
Oh, *l* the LORD . . . . Ps 31:23
he has set his *l* . . . . Ps 91:14
Oh, how I *l* Your law . . Ps 119:97
l covers all sins . . . . . . Prov 10:12
A time to *l* . . . . Eccl 3:8
banner over me was *l* . . . Song 2:4
l is as strong as . . . . Song 8:6
do justly, To *l* mercy . . . . . Mic 6:8
to you, '*l* your enemies . . Matt 5:44
which of them will *l* . . . . Luke 7:42
you do not have the *l* . . John 5:42
if you have *l* for one . . . John 13:35
"If you *l* Me . . . . John 14:15
and My Father will *l* . . . John 14:23
l one another as I . . . . . John 15:12
I has no one than this . . John 15:13
because the *l* of God . . . . Rom 5:5
to *l* one another . . . . Rom 13:8
L suffers long and is . . 1 Cor 13:4
L never fails . . . . 1 Cor 13:8
greatest of these is *l* . . 1 Cor 13:13
For the *l* of Christ . . . . 2 Cor 5:14
of the Spirit is *l* . . . . Gal 5:22
Husbands, *l* your wives . . Eph 5:25
the commandment is *l* . . 1 Tim 1:5
For the *l* of money is . . 1 Tim 6:10
Let brotherly *l* . . . . Heb 13:1
having not seen you *l* . . 1 Pet 1:8
for "*l* will cover a . . . . . . 1 Pet 4:8
brotherly kindness *l* . . . 2 Pet 1:7
By this we know *l* . . . 1 John 3:16
Beloved, let us *l* . . . . . 1 John 4:7
for God is *l* . . . . 1 John 4:8
There is no fear in *l* . . 1 John 4:18
l Him because He . . . . 1 John 4:19
loves God must *l* . . . . 1 John 4:21
For this is the *l* . . . . . . 1 John 5:3
have left your first *l* . . . . Rev 2:4

LOVED

L one and friend You . . . Ps 88:18
Yet Jacob I have *l* . . . . . . Mal 1:2
forgiven, for she *l* . . . . . Luke 7:47
so *l* the world that . . . . . John 3:16
whom Jesus *l* . . . . John 13:23
"As the Father *l* . . . . . . John 15:9
l them as You have . . . John 17:23
the Son of God, who *l* . . Gal 2:20

l the church and gave . . . Eph 5:25
Beloved, if God so *l* . . 1 John 4:11
To Him who *l* us and . . . . Rev 1:5

LOVELY

he is altogether *l* . . . . . . Song 5:16
whatever things are *l* . . . . Phil 4:8

LOVES

"He who *l* father or . . . . Matt 10:37
l his life will lose . . . . . John 12:25
l Me will be loved . . . . John 14:21
l a cheerful giver . . . . . . 2 Cor 9:7
If anyone *l* the world . 1 John 2:15
l God must love his . . . 1 John 4:21

LOVINGKINDNESS

To declare Your *l* . . . . Ps 92:2

LOWER

made him a little *l* . . . . Heb 2:7

LOWLINESS

with all *l* and . . . . Eph 4:2

LOWLY

for I am gentle and *l* . . Matt 11:29
in presence am *l* . . . . . . 2 Cor 10:1
l brother glory . . . . James 1:9

LUKEWARM

because you are *l* . . . . . . Rev 3:16

LUST

looks at a woman to *l* . . Matt 5:28
not fulfill the *l* . . . . Gal 5:16
You *l* and do not have . . James 4:2
the *l* of the flesh . . . . . . 1 John 2:16

LUSTS

to fulfill its *l* . . . . Rom 13:14
also youthful *l* . . . . 2 Tim 2:22
and worldly *l* . . . . Titus 2:12
to the former *l* . . . . 1 Pet 1:14
abstain from fleshly *l* . . 1 Pet 2:11
to their own ungodly *l* . . . Jude 18

LUTE

Praise Him with the *l* . . . Ps 150:3

LUXURY

in pleasure and *l* . . . . . . James 5:5
the abundance of her *l* . . Rev 18:3

LYING

I hate and abhor *l* . . . . . Ps 119:163
righteous man hates *l* . . . Prov 13:5
not trust in these *l* . . . . Jer 7:4
signs, and *l* wonders . . 2 Thess 2:9

M

MADE

m the stars also . . . . Gen 1:16
things My hand has *m* . . . . Is 66:2
All things were *m* . . . . . . John 1:3

MADNESS

m is in their hearts . . . . . . Eccl 9:3

MAGIC

m brought their books . Acts 19:19

MAGNIFIED

let Your name be *m* . . 2 Sam 7:26
the Lord Jesus was *m* . . Acts 19:17
also Christ will be *m* . . . . Phil 1:20

MAGNIFIES

"My soul *m* the Lord . . . Luke 1:46

MAGNIFY

m the LORD with me . . . . . . Ps 34:3

MAIDSERVANT
"Behold the m ....Luke 1:38

MAIDSERVANTS
m I will pour out My ....Acts 2:18

MAJESTY
right hand of the M ......Heb 1:3
eyewitnesses of His m ..2 Pet 1:16
wise, Be glory and m .....Jude 25

MAKE
"Let Us m man in Our ..Gen 1:26
m you a great nation ....Gen 12:2
"You shall not m ....Ex 20:4
m Our home with .....John 14:23

MAKER
M is your husband ....Is 54:5
has forgotten his M ....Hos 8:14
builder and m is God ..Heb 11:10

MALICE
in m be babes ....1 Cor 14:20
laying aside all m ....1 Pet 2:1

MAN
"Let Us make m ....Gen 1:26
m that You are mindful ....Ps 8:4
of the Son of M ....Matt 24:27
"Behold the M ....John 19:5
by m came death .....1 Cor 15:21
our outward m ....2 Cor 4:16
the m of God may .....2 Tim 3:17
is the number of a m ...Rev 13:18

MANGER
and laid Him in a m .....Luke 2:7

MANIFEST
m Myself to him ......John 14:21

MANIFESTATION
But the m of the ....1 Cor 12:7

MANIFESTED
"I have m Your name ..John 17:6
God was m in the .....1 Tim 3:16
the life was m ....1 John 1:2

MANIFOLD
the m wisdom of God ...Eph 3:10

MANNA
of Israel ate m ....Ex 16:35
"Our fathers ate the m .John 6:31

MANNER
Is this the m of man ..2 Sam 7:19
in an unworthy m ....1 Cor 11:27
what m of love ....1 John 3:1

MANSIONS
house are many m .....John 14:2

MANTLE
Then he took the m ..2 Kin 2:14

MARK
And the LORD set a m ...Gen 4:15
receives the m ....Rev 14:11

MARRED
So His visage was m .....Is 52:14

MARRIAGE
M is honorable among ..Heb 13:4

MARRIED
But he who is m ....1 Cor 7:33

MARRY
they neither m nor ....Matt 22:30
forbidding to m ....1 Tim 4:3

MARRYING
and drinking, m ....Matt 24:38

MARTYRS
the blood of the m ......Rev 17:6

MARVELED
Jesus heard it, He m ....Matt 8:10
so that Pilate m ....Mark 15:5

MARVELOUS
It is m in our eyes ......Ps 118:23
of darkness into His m ..1 Pet 2:9

MASTER
a servant like his m ...Matt 10:25
greater than his m ....John 15:20
and useful for the M ..2 Tim 2:21

MASTERS
can serve two m ......Luke 16:13
who have believing m ..1 Tim 6:2

MATTERS
the weightier m ....Matt 23:23

MATURE
understanding be m ..1 Cor 14:20
us, as many as are m ....Phil 3:15

MEANT
but God m it for good ..Gen 50:20

MEASURE
a perfect and just m ...Deut 25:15
give the Spirit by m ....John 3:34
to each one a m ....Rom 12:3

MEASURED
m the waters in the .....Is 40:12
you use, it will be m .....Matt 7:2

MEASURES
house differing m .....Deut 25:14

MEASURING
behold, a man with a m ..Zech 2:1
m themselves by .....2 Cor 10:12

MEAT
will never again eat m .1 Cor 8:13

MEDIATOR
by the hand of a m .....Gal 3:19
is one God and one M ..1 Tim 2:5
to Jesus the M of the ..Heb 12:24

MEDICINE
does good, like m .....Prov 17:22

MEDICINES
you will use many m ...Jer 46:11

MEDITATE
but you shall m ....Josh 1:8
M within your heart on ....Ps 4:4
I will m on Your ......Ps 119:15
m beforehand on .....Luke 21:14
m on these things ....Phil 4:8

MEDITATES
in His law he m ....Ps 1:2

MEDITATION
of my mouth and the m ..Ps 19:14
It is my m all the day ...Ps 119:97

MEDIUM
a woman who is a m ...Lev 20:27

MEDIUM'S
shall be like a m ....Is 29:4

MEDIUMS
"Seek those who are m ....Is 8:19

MEEK
with equity for the m ......Is 11:4
Blessed are the m ....Matt 5:5

MEEKNESS
are done in the m .....James 3:13

MEET
prepare to m your .....Amos 4:12
m the Lord in the ....1 Thess 4:17

MELODY
singing and making m ..Eph 5:19

MELT
the elements will m ....2 Pet 3:10

MEMBER
body is not one m ....1 Cor 12:14

MEMBERS
you that one of your m .Matt 5:29
do not present your m ..Rom 6:13
neighbor, for we are m ..Eph 4:25

MEMORIAL
and this is My m ....Ex 3:15
also be told as a m ....Matt 26:13

MEMORY
The m of the righteous .Prov 10:7

MEN
m began to call on the ..Gen 4:26
make you fishers of m ..Matt 4:19
goodwill toward m .....Luke 2:14
heaven or from m .....Luke 20:4
Likewise also the m ....Rom 1:27
the Lord, and not to m ...Eph 6:7
between God and m ....1 Tim 2:5

MENSERVANTS
And also on My m ......Joel 2:29
And on My m and on ...Acts 2:18

MERCHANDISE
house a house of m ....John 2:16

MERCIES
give you the sure m ...Acts 13:34

MERCIFUL
LORD, the LORD God, m ..Ex 34:6
He is ever m ....Ps 37:26
Blessed are the m ....Matt 5:7
saying, 'God be m ....Luke 18:13
"For I will be m ....Heb 8:12

MERCY
but showing m to ....Ex 20:6
and abundant in m ....Num 14:18
m endures forever ....1 Chr 16:34
M and truth have met ....Ps 85:10
m is everlasting ....Ps 100:5
Let not m and truth ......Prov 3:3
For I desire m and not ....Hos 6:6
do justly, To love m ......Mic 6:8
'I desire m and not ......Matt 9:13
And His m is on those ..Luke 1:50
"I will have m ....Rom 9:15
that He might have m .Rom 11:32
m has made ....1 Cor 7:25
as we have received m ..2 Cor 4:1
God, who is rich in m ....Eph 2:4
but I obtained m ....1 Tim 1:13
that he may find m ....2 Tim 1:18
to His m He saved us ....Titus 3:5
that we may obtain m ...Heb 4:16

MERRY
m heart makes a ......Prov 15:13
we should make m ....Luke 15:32

MESSENGER
"Behold, I send My m ....Mal 3:1
'Behold, I send My m ..Matt 11:10

MESSIAH
Until M the Prince ......Dan 9:25
"We have found the M ..John 1:41

MIDST
God is in the m ....Ps 46:5
I am there in the m ....Matt 18:20

MIGHT
'My power and the m ...Deut 8:17
'Not by m nor by ....Zech 4:6
in the power of His m ...Eph 6:10
honor and power and m .Rev 7:12

MIGHTIER
coming after me is m ....Matt 3:11

MIGHTY
He was a m hunter ......Gen 10:9
m have fallen ....2 Sam 1:19
The LORD m in battle .....Ps 24:8
their Redeemer is m ...Prov 23:11
m has done great ......Luke 1:49
the flesh, not many m .1 Cor 1:26
the working of His m ...Eph 1:19

MILK
come, buy wine and m ....Is 55:1
shall flow with m ......Joel 3:18
have come to need m ...Heb 5:12
desire the pure m ......1 Pet 2:2

MILLSTONE
m were hung around ...Matt 18:6
a stone like a great m ..Rev 18:21

MIND
put wisdom in the m ....Job 38:36
perfect state, Whose m ...Is 26:3
have an anxious m ....Luke 12:29
m I myself serve the ....Rom 7:25
who has known the m .Rom 11:34
Be of the same m .....Rom 12:16
in his own m ....Rom 14:5
has known the m ......1 Cor 2:16
are out of your m ....1 Cor 14:23
Let this m be in you ......Phil 2:5
love and of a sound m ..2 Tim 1:7

MINDFUL
is man that You are m .....Ps 8:4
for you are not m .....Matt 16:23
is man that You are m ...Heb 2:6

MINDS
put My law in their m ...Jer 31:33
I stir up your pure m ....2 Pet 3:1

MINISTER
For he is God's m ......Rom 13:4
you will be a good m ...1 Tim 4:6

MINISTERS
for they are God's m ...Rom 13:6
If anyone m ....1 Pet 4:11

MINISTRIES
are differences of m ...1 Cor 12:5

MINISTRY
But if the m of death ....2 Cor 3:7
since we have this m ....2 Cor 4:1
has given us the m ....2 Cor 5:18
for the work of m ......Eph 4:12
fulfill your m ....2 Tim 4:5
a more excellent m ....Heb 8:6

MIRACLE
one who works a m ....Mark 9:39

MIRACLES
worked unusual m ....Acts 19:11
the working of m .....1 Cor 12:10

MISERY
And remember his m ...Prov 31:7

MITES
putting in two m ....Luke 21:2

MOCK
Fools m at sin ....Prov 14:9
to the Gentiles to m ...Matt 20:19

MOCKED
noon, that Elijah m ...1 Kin 18:27
deceived, God is not m ....Gal 6:7

MOCKER
Wine is a m ....Prov 20:1

MOCKS
He who m the poor .....Prov 17:5

MODERATION
with propriety and m ...1 Tim 2:9

MOMENT
In a m they die ....Job 34:20
in a m, in the ....1 Cor 15:52

MONEY
be redeemed without m ...Is 52:3
And you who have no m ...Is 55:1
and hid his lord's m ...Matt 25:18
to give him m ....Mark 14:11
"Carry neither m ....Luke 22:35
I sent you without m ..Luke 22:35
be purchased with m ...Acts 8:20
not greedy for m ......1 Tim 3:3
m is a root of all ......1 Tim 6:10

MONEYCHANGERS
the tables of the m ....Matt 21:12

MOON
until the m is no more ....Ps 72:7
m will not give its ....Mark 13:24

MORNING
Evening and m and at ..Ps 55:17
Lucifer, son of the m .....Is 14:12
very early in the m ....Luke 24:1
the Bright and M Star ..Rev 22:16

MORTAL
sin reign in your m .....Rom 6:12
and this m must put ..1 Cor 15:53

MORTALITY
m may be swallowed ...2 Cor 5:4

MOTH
where m and rust ......Matt 6:19

MOTHER
because she was the m .Gen 3:20
leave his father and m ..Matt 19:5
"Behold your m ....John 19:27
The M of Harlots ....Rev 17:5

MOUNT
come up to M Sinai .....Ex 19:23
They shall m up with .....Is 40:31

MOUNTAIN
to Horeb, the m ....Ex 3:1
let us go up to the m ......Is 2:3
became a great m ......Dan 2:35
are you, O great m ......Zech 4:7
you will say to this m ..Matt 17:20
Him on the holy m ....2 Pet 1:18

MOUNTAINS
m were brought forth .....Ps 90:2
m shall depart And the ...Is 54:10
in Judea flee to the m .Matt 24:16
that I could remove m .1 Cor 13:2

MOURN
A time to m ....Eccl 3:4
are those who m ....Matt 5:4
of the earth will m ....Rev 1:7

MOURNED
and have not rather m ..1 Cor 5:2

MOURNING
shall be a great m .....Zech 12:11
be turned to m and ....James 4:9

MOUTH
"Who has made man's m ..Ex 4:11
Out of the m of babes ......Ps 8:2
knowledge, But the m .Prov 10:14
The m of an immoral ..Prov 22:14
And a flattering m ....Prov 26:28
m speaking pompous ....Dan 7:8
m defiles a man ....Matt 15:11
m I will judge you ....Luke 19:22
I will give you a m ....Luke 21:15
m confession is made ..Rom 10:10
m great swelling words ...Jude 16
vomit you out of My m ..Rev 3:16

MOVED
she shall not be m ....Ps 46:5
spoke as they were m ..2 Pet 1:21

MUCH
m study is ....Eccl 12:12
to whom m is given ...Luke 12:48

MULTIPLIED
of the disciples m ....Acts 6:7
of God grew and m ....Acts 12:24

MULTIPLY
"Be fruitful and m ......Gen 1:22
m the descendants ......Jer 33:22

MULTITUDE
stars of heaven in m ....Deut 1:10
In the m of words sin ..Prov 10:19
compassion on the m ..Matt 15:32
with the angel a m ....Luke 2:13
"love will cover a m ...1 Pet 4:8
and behold, a great m ....Rev 7:9

MURDER
"You shall not m ......Ex 20:13
'You shall not m ......Matt 5:21
You m and covet and ...James 4:2

MURDERED
up Jesus whom you m ..Acts 5:30

MURDERER
He was a m from the ...John 8:44
his brother is a m ....1 John 3:15

MURDERERS
and profane, for m .....1 Tim 1:9
abominable, m ....Rev 21:8

MURDERS
evil thoughts, m ....Matt 15:19

MUSING
while I was m ....Ps 39:3

MUTILATION
beware of the m ....Phil 3:2

MUZZLE
"You shall not m ......1 Tim 5:18

MYSTERIES

to you to know the *m* ..Matt 13:11
and understand all *m* ..1 Cor 13:2

MYSTERY

given to know the *m* ...Mark 4:11
wisdom of God in a *m* ..1 Cor 2:7
I tell you a *m* ....1 Cor 15:51
made known to us the *m* .Eph 1:9
the *m* of godliness .....1 Tim 3:16

N

NAILED

n it to the cross ....Col 2:14

NAKED

And they were both *n* ...Gen 2:25
knew that they were *n*...Gen 3:7
"*N* I came from my ......Job 1:21
'I was *n* and you ......Matt 25:36
but all things are *n* ......Heb 4:13
brother or sister is *n* ..James 2:15
poor, blind, and *n* .....Rev 3:17

NAKEDNESS

or famine, or *n* ....Rom 8:35
n may not be revealed ...Rev 3:18

NAME

Abram called on the *n* ..Gen 13:4
Israel shall be your *n* ..Gen 35:10
This is My *n* forever ....Ex 3:15
shall not take the *n* ......Ex 20:7
and awesome *n* ....Deut 28:58
excellent is Your *n* ....Ps 8:1
n will put their trust ......Ps 9:10
be His glorious *n* ....Ps 72:19
do not call on Your *n* .....Ps 79:6
to Your *n* give glory ....Ps 115:1
above all Your *n* ....Ps 138:2
A good *n* is to be ....Prov 22:1
what is His Son's *n* .....Prov 30:4
be called by a new *n* ......Is 62:2
Everlasting is Your *n* .....Is 63:16
They will call on My *n* .Zech 13:9
to you who fear My *n* ....Mal 4:2
Hallowed be Your *n* .....Matt 6:9
prophesied in Your *n* ...Matt 7:22
n Gentiles will trust ...Matt 12:21
together in My *n* ......Matt 18:20
will come in My *n* .....Matt 24:5
who believe in His *n* ...John 1:12
comes in his own *n* ....John 5:43
his own sheep by *n* .....John 10:3
through faith in His *n* ..Acts 3:16
there is no other *n* .....Acts 4:12
which is above every *n* .Phil 2:9
deed, do all in the *n* .....Col 3:17
a more excellent *n* ......Heb 1:4
you hold fast to My *n* ..Rev 2:13
n that you are alive ......Rev 3:1
having His Father's *n*...Rev 14:1
and glorify Your *n* .....Rev 15:4
n written that no one ...Rev 19:12

NAMED

I have *n* you ....Is 45:4

NAME'S

saved them for His *n* ....Ps 106:8

NARROW

"Enter by the *n* gate ....Matt 7:13

NATION

make you a great *n* .....Gen 12:2
exalts a *n* ....Prov 14:34
n that was not called ......Is 65:1
make them one *n* .....Ezek 37:22
since there was a *n* .....Dan 12:1
n will rise against ......Matt 24:7
"for he loves our *n* ......Luke 7:5

those who are *not* a *n* .Rom 10:19
tribe, tongue, and *n* .....Rev 13:7

NATIONS

Why do the *n* rage ....Ps 2:1
I will give You the *n* ....Ps 2:8
n shall serve Him ....Ps 72:11
disciples of all the *n* ..Matt 28:19
who was to rule all *n* ....Rev 12:5
the healing of the *n* .....Rev 22:2

NATURAL

exchanged the *n* ......Rom 1:26
the men, leaving the *n* ..Rom 1:27
did not spare the *n* ...Rom 11:21
n man does not ....1 Cor 2:14
It is sown a *n* body ...1 Cor 15:44

NATURE

"We who are Jews by *n* .Gal 2:15
by *n* children of wrath ....Eph 2:3
of the divine *n* ....2 Pet 1:4

NEAR

the word is very *n* .....Deut 30:14
upon Him while He is *n* ...Is 55:6
know that it is *n* .....Matt 24:33
kingdom of God is *n* .Luke 21:31
"*The word is n* ....Rom 10:8
to those who were *n* ....Eph 2:17
for the time is *n* ....Rev 1:3

NEARER

now our salvation is *n* .Rom 13:11

NEED

the things you have *n* ....Matt 6:8
supply all your *n* ....Phil 4:19
to help in time of *n* .....Heb 4:16

NEGLECT

if we *n* so great a ....Heb 2:3

NEGLECTED

n the weightier ....Matt 23:23

NEIGHBOR

'you shall love your *n* ...Lev 19:18
"You shall love your *n* ..Matt 5:43
"And who is my *n* ....Luke 10:29
"You shall love your *n* ..Rom 13:9

NEVER

in Me shall *n* thirst ....John 6:35
in Me shall *n* die .....John 11:26
Love *n* fails ....1 Cor 13:8
n take away sins ....Heb 10:11
"*I will n leave you* .....Heb 13:5
prophecy *n* came by ....2 Pet 1:21

NEW

And there is nothing *n* ...Eccl 1:9
"For behold, I create *n* ...Is 65:17
n every morning ......Lam 3:23
wine into *n* wineskins ..Matt 9:17
of the *n* covenant ....Matt 26:28
n commandment I .....John 13:34
he is a *n* creation ......2 Cor 5:17
when I will make a n .....Heb 8:8
n heavens and a *n* ......2 Pet 3:13
n name written which ....Rev 2:17
And they sang a *n* ....Rev 5:9
And I saw a *n* heaven ...Rev 21:1
I make all things *n* ......Rev 21:5

NEWNESS

also should walk in *n* ....Rom 6:4

NIGHT

darkness He called *N* ....Gen 1:5
It is a *n* of solemn ....Ex 12:42
pillar of fire by *n* ....Ex 13:22
gives songs in the *n* ....Job 35:10
and continued all *n* ....Luke 6:12
man came to Jesus by *n* .John 3:2

n is coming when no ....John 9:4
came to Jesus by *n* ....John 19:39
as a thief in the *n* .....1 Thess 5:2
there shall be no *n* .....Rev 21:25

NINETY-NINE

he not leave the *n* .....Matt 18:12

NOTHING

"I can of Myself do *n* ...John 5:30
Me you can do *n* ....John 15:5
men, it will come to *n* ...Acts 5:38
have not love, I am *n* ..1 Cor 13:2
Be anxious for *n* ....Phil 4:6
For we brought *n* ....1 Tim 6:7

NOURISHED

"I have *n* and ....Is 1:2

NOURISHES

n and cherishes it ....Eph 5:29

NUMBER

if a man could *n* ......Gen 13:16
teach us to *n* our days ...Ps 90:12
which no one could *n* ....Rev 7:9
His *n* is 666 ....Rev 13:18

O

OATH

for the sake of your *o* ....Eccl 8:2
he denied with an *o* ...Matt 26:72
o which He swore ......Luke 1:73

OATHS

shall perform your *o* ....Matt 5:33

OBEDIENCE

o many will be made ...Rom 5:19
captivity to the *o* ......2 Cor 10:5
yet He learned *o* ....Heb 5:8

OBEDIENT

you are willing and *o* ....Is 1:19
of the priests were *o* ....Acts 6:7
make the Gentiles *o* ...Rom 15:18
Himself and became *o* ....Phil 2:8
as *o* children ....1 Pet 1:14

OBEY

God and *o* His voice ....Deut 4:30
His voice we will *o* ....Josh 24:24
o is better than ......1 Sam 15:22
o God rather than men ..Acts 5:29
and do not *o* the truth ....Rom 2:8
yourselves slaves to *o* ..Rom 6:16
o your parents in all ....Col 3:20
Bondservants, *o* in all ....Col 3:22
those who do not *o* ....2 Thess 1:8
O those who rule .....Heb 13:17

OBEYED

of sin, yet you *o* ....Rom 6:17
they have not all *o* ....Rom 10:16
By faith Abraham *o* .....Heb 11:8

OBSERVATION

does not come with *o* .Luke 17:20

OBSERVE

teaching them to *o* all .Matt 28:20

OBTAIN

also may *o* mercy .....Rom 11:31
o salvation through ...1 Thess 5:9

OBTAINED

o a part in this ....Acts 1:17
yet have now *o* mercy .Rom 11:30
endured, he *o* the ....Heb 6:15

OBTAINS

o favor from the LORD ..Prov 8:35

OFFEND

lest we o them .... Matt 17:27
than that he should o .. Luke 17:2
them, "Does this o ..... John 6:61

OFFENDED

they were o at Him .... Matt 13:57

OFFENSE

and a rock of o .... Is 8:14
You are an o to Me .... Matt 16:23
by the one man's o ..... Rom 5:17
the o of the cross .... Gal 5:11
sincere and without o ... Phil 1:10
And a rock of o .... 1 Pet 2:8

OFFENSES

For o must come .... Matt 18:7
impossible that no o .... Luke 17:1

OFFER

come and o your gift .. Matt 5:24
let us continually o .... Heb 13:15

OFFERED

to eat those things o ... 1 Cor 8:10
so Christ was o .... Heb 9:28
o one sacrifice .... Heb 10:12

OFFERING

o You did not require ..... Ps 40:6
You make His soul an o .. Is 53:10
Himself for us, an o ...... Eph 5:2
o You did not .... Heb 10:5
o He has perfected ..... Heb 10:14

OFFERINGS

and offered burnt o ..... Gen 8:20
In burnt o .... Heb 10:6

OFFICE

sitting at the tax o .... Matt 9:9

OFFSPRING

wife and raise up o .... Matt 22:24
we are also His o ...... Acts 17:28
am the Root and the O . Rev 22:16

OFTEN

o I wanted to gather .. Luke 13:34
as o as you eat this ... 1 Cor 11:26

OIL

a bin, and a little o ... 1 Kin 17:12
very costly fragrant o .. Matt 26:7
anointing him with o .. James 5:14
and do not harm the o .. Rev 6:6

OLD

young, and now am o .... Ps 37:25
was said to those of o ... Matt 5:21
but when you are o .. John 21:18
Your o men shall dream Acts 2:17
o man was crucified ..... Rom 6:6
o things have passed .. 2 Cor 5:17
have put off the o man .. Col 3:9
that serpent of o .... Rev 20:2

OLDER

o shall serve the .... Gen 25:23
not rebuke an o man ... 1 Tim 5:1

OLDEST

beginning with the o .... John 8:9

OLIVE

a freshly plucked o ..... Gen 8:11
o tree which is wild ... Rom 11:24

OMNIPOTENT

For the Lord God O ..... Rev 19:6

ONCE

died, He died to sin o ... Rom 6:10

for men to die o .... Heb 9:27
also suffered o .... 1 Pet 3:18

ONE

"O thing you lack .... Mark 10:21
o thing is needed ..... Luke 10:42
I and My Father are o .. John 10:30
that they may be o .... John 17:11
o accord in the temple .. Acts 2:46
for you are all o .... Gal 3:28
to create in Himself o ... Eph 2:15
o Lord .... Eph 4:5
o faith .... Eph 4:5
o baptism .... Eph 4:5
o God and Father of .... Eph 4:6
For there is o God and .. 1 Tim 2:5
o Mediator between .... 1 Tim 2:5
a thousand years as o ... 2 Pet 3:8

OPENED

o not His mouth .... Is 53:7
o the Scriptures ...... Luke 24:32
o their understanding . Luke 24:45
Now I saw heaven o ... Rev 19:11

OPENS

him the doorkeeper o .. John 10:3
and shuts and no one o .. Rev 3:7

OPINION

be wise in your own o . Rom 11:25

OPINIONS

falter between two o .. 1 Kin 18:21

OPPORTUNITY

But sin, taking o .... Rom 7:8
as we have o .... Gal 6:10
but you lacked o .... Phil 4:10

OPPRESS

he loves to o .... Hos 12:7
o the widow or the ..... Zech 7:10
Do not the rich o ..... James 2:6

OPPRESSED

for all who are o .... Ps 103:6
The tears of the o .... Eccl 4:1
He was o and He was ..... Is 53:7
all who were o .... Acts 10:38

OPPRESSES

o the poor reproaches . Prov 14:31

OPPRESSION

have surely seen the o ..... Ex 3:7
their life from o .... Ps 72:14
brought low through o .. Ps 107:39
me from the o .... Ps 119:134
considered all the o ...... Eccl 4:1
o destroys a wise .... Eccl 7:7
justice, but behold, o .... Is 5:7
surely seen the o .... Acts 7:34

ORACLES

received the living o .... Acts 7:38
were committed the o .... Rom 3:2
principles of the o ...... Heb 5:12

ORDAINED

o you a prophet .... Jer 1:5
whom He has o .... Acts 17:31

ORDER

decently and in o ..... 1 Cor 14:40

ORDERS

o his conduct aright I .... Ps 50:23

ORDINANCE

resists the o of God .... Rom 13:2

ORDINANCES

and fleshly o imposed ... Heb 9:10

ORPHANS

will not leave you o ... John 14:18
to visit o and widows . James 1:27

OUGHT

These you o to have ... Matt 23:23
pray for as we o .... Rom 8:26
persons o you to be .... 2 Pet 3:11

OUTCAST

they called you an o ... Jer 30:17

OUTCASTS

will assemble the o .... Is 11:12

OUTRAN

the other disciple o ..... John 20:4

OUTSIDE

and dish, that the o .... Matt 23:26
Pharisees make the o . Luke 11:39
toward those who are o ... Col 4:5
to Him, o the camp .... Heb 13:13
But o are dogs and ..... Rev 22:15

OUTSTRETCHED

and with an o arm ..... Deut 26:8

OUTWARD

at the o appearance ... 1 Sam 16:7
adornment be merely o .. 1 Pet 3:3

OUTWARDLY

not a Jew who is one o . Rom 2:28

OVERCAME

My throne, as I also o ... Rev 3:21
"And they o him by .... Rev 12:11

OVERCOME

good cheer, I have o ... John 16:33
and the Lamb will o .... Rev 17:14

OVERCOMES

of God o the world .... 1 John 5:4
o I will give to eat .... Rev 2:7
o shall not be hurt ...... Rev 2:11
o shall inherit all .... Rev 21:7

OVERSEER

to the Shepherd and O . 1 Pet 2:25

OVERSEERS

you, serving as o .... 1 Pet 5:2

OVERSHADOW

of the Highest will o ... Luke 1:35

OVERTHREW

As God o Sodom and ... Jer 50:40

OVERTHROW

o the faith of some .... 2 Tim 2:18

OVERTHROWN

and Nineveh shall be o ... Jon 3:4

OVERTHROWS

And o the mighty ...... Job 12:19
o them in the night .... Job 34:25
o the words of the ..... Prov 22:12

OVERWHELM

o the fatherless .... Job 6:27

OVERWHELMED

and my spirit was o ...... Ps 77:3
my spirit is within ..... Ps 143:4

OVERWORK

Do not o to be rich ..... Prov 23:4

OWE

O no one anything ..... Rom 13:8

OWED

o him ten thousand .... Matt 18:24

OWN

He came to His o ...... John 1:11
having loved His o .... John 13:1
would love its o ...... John 15:19
you are not your o .... 1 Cor 6:19
But each one has his o .. 1 Cor 7:7
For all seek their o ...... Phil 2:21
from our sins in His o .... Rev 1:5

OX

shall not muzzle an o ... Deut 25:4
o knows its owner .... Is 1:3
Sabbath loose his o ... Luke 13:15
shall not muzzle an o ... 1 Cor 9:9

P

PACIFIES

A gift in secret p ...... Prov 21:14

PAIN

p you shall bring .... Gen 3:16
p as a woman in .... Is 13:8
Why is my p perpetual .. Jer 15:18
shall be no more p ...... Rev 21:4

PAINED

My heart is severely p .... Ps 55:4
I am p in my very .... Jer 4:19

PAINFUL

for the present, but p ... Heb 12:11

PAINS

The p of death .... Ps 116:3
having loosed the p .... Acts 2:24

PAINT

your eyes with p .... Jer 4:30

PALACE

enter the King's p ...... Ps 45:15
guards his own p ..... Luke 11:21
evident to the whole p ... Phil 1:13

PALACES

Out of the ivory p ...... Ps 45:8

PALE

behold, a p horse .... Rev 6:8

PALM

p branches in their ...... Rev 7:9

PALMS

struck Him with the p . Matt 26:67

PAMPERS

p his servant from ..... Prov 29:21

PANGS

The p of death .... Ps 18:4
labors with birth p ..... Rom 8:22

PARABLE

do You speak this p ... Luke 12:41

PARABLES

rest it is given in p ..... Luke 8:10

PARADISE

will be with Me in P .. Luke 23:43
in the midst of the P ...... Rev 2:7

PARDON

He will abundantly p ...... Is 55:7
p all their iniquities ...... Jer 33:8

PARDONING

is a God like You, p ..... Mic 7:18

PARENTS

will rise up against p .. Matt 10:21
has left house or p .... Luke 18:29
disobedient to p .... Rom 1:30

PART

chosen that good p .... Luke 10:42
you, you have no p ..... John 13:8
For we know in p ..... 1 Cor 13:9
shall take away his p ... Rev 22:19

PARTAKE

for we all p of that .... 1 Cor 10:17

PARTAKER

in hope should be p .... 1 Cor 9:10
Christ, and also a p ..... 1 Pet 5:1

PARTAKERS

Gentiles have been p .. Rom 15:27
know that as you are p . 2 Cor 1:7
qualified us to be p ...... Col 1:12

PARTIAL

You shall not be p ..... Lev 19:15

PARTIALITY

that God shows no p .. Acts 10:34
doing nothing with p .. 1 Tim 5:21
good fruits, without p . James 3:17

PASS

I will p over you .... Ex 12:13
When you p through the .. Is 43:2
and earth will p .... Matt 24:35

PASSED

forbearance God had p . Rom 3:25
High Priest who has p ... Heb 4:14
know that we have p . 1 John 3:14

PASSES

of Christ which p .... Eph 3:19

PASSION

uncleanness, p .... Col 3:5

PASSIONS

gave them up to vile p .. Rom 1:26

PASSOVER

It is the LORD's P .... Ex 12:11
I will keep the P ...... Matt 26:18
indeed Christ, our P .... 1 Cor 5:7
By faith he kept the P .. Heb 11:28

PASTORS

and some p and .... Eph 4:11

PASTURE

the sheep of Your p .... Ps 74:1
in and out and find p ... John 10:9

PASTURES

to lie down in green p .... Ps 23:2

PATH

You will show me the p .. Ps 16:11

PATHS

He leads me in the p .... Ps 23:3
Make His p straight ..... Matt 3:3
and make straight p .... Heb 12:13

PATIENCE

'Master, have p ...... Matt 18:26
and bear fruit with p .. Luke 8:15
labor of love, and p ... 1 Thess 1:3
faith, love, p .... 1 Tim 6:11
your faith produces p .. James 1:3
p have its perfect ...... James 1:4
in the kingdom and p .... Rev 1:9

PATIENT

rejoicing in hope, p .... Rom 12:12
the weak, be p ...... 1 Thess 5:14

PATIENTLY

if you take it p .... 1 Pet 2:20

PATRIARCHS

begot the twelve p ...... Acts 7:8

PATTERN

p which you were ...... Ex 26:30
as you have us for a p .. Phil 3:17
p shown you on the ...... Heb 8:5

PEACE

you, And give you p .... Num 6:26
both lie down in p ...... Ps 4:8
p have those who ..... Ps 119:165
I am for p .... Ps 120:7
war, And a time of p ..... Eccl 3:8
Father, Prince of P ...... Is 9:6
keep him in perfect p ..... Is 26:3
p they have not .... Is 59:8
slightly, Saying, 'P ..... Jer 6:14
place I will give p .... Hag 2:9
is worthy, let your p ... Matt 10:13
that I came to bring p . Matt 10:34
And on earth p .... Luke 2:14
if a son of p is there .... Luke 10:6
that make for your p .. Luke 19:42
leave with you, My p ... John 14:27
Me you may have p ... John 16:33
Grace to you and p ..... Rom 1:7
by faith, we have p ...... Rom 5:1
God has called us to p . 1 Cor 7:15
p will be with you .... 2 Cor 13:11
Spirit is love, joy, p ..... Gal 5:22
He Himself is our p ..... Eph 2:14
and the p of God .... Phil 4:7
And let the p of God .... Col 3:15
faith, love, p .... 2 Tim 2:22
meaning "king of p," .... Heb 7:2

PEACEABLE

is first pure, then p .... James 3:17

PEACEABLY

on you, live p .... Rom 12:18

PEACEFUL

in a p habitation .... Is 32:18

PEACEMAKERS

Blessed are the p ...... Matt 5:9

PEARL

had found one p ..... Matt 13:46

PEARLS

nor cast your p .... Matt 7:6
gates were twelve p .... Rev 21:21

PENTECOST

P had fully come .... Acts 2:1

PEOPLE

will take you as My p ..... Ex 6:7
p shall be my p ...... Ruth 1:16
p who know the joyful .. Ps 89:15
We are His p and the .... Ps 100:3
"Blessed is Egypt My p ... Is 19:25
to make ready a p ..... Luke 1:17
take out of them a p ... Acts 15:14
who were not My p .... Rom 9:25
they shall be My p ... 2 Cor 6:16
LORD will judge His p .. Heb 10:30
but are now the p ..... 1 Pet 2:10
tribe and tongue and p .. Rev 5:9
they shall be His p ...... Rev 21:3

PERCEIVE

seeing, but do not p .... Is 6:9
may see and not p ..... Mark 4:12

PERDITION

except the son of p ....John 17:12
revealed, the son of p .2 Thess 2:3
who draw back to p ....Heb 10:39

PERFECT

Noah was a just man, p ..Gen 6:9
Father in heaven is p ...Matt 5:48
they may be made p ...John 17:23
and p will of God .....Rom 12:2
when that which is p .1 Cor 13:10
present every man p .....Col 1:28
good gift and every p .James 1:17
in word, he is a p .....James 3:2
p love casts out fear ..1 John 4:18

PERFECTED

third day I shall be p ..Luke 13:32
or am already p ....Phil 3:12
Son who has been p ....Heb 7:28

PERFECTION

let us go on to p ....Heb 6:1

PERISH

so that we may not p .....Jon 1:6
little ones should p ....Matt 18:14
in Him should not p ....John 3:16
they shall never p ....John 10:28
among those who p ..2 Thess 2:10
that any should p ....2 Pet 3:9

PERISHABLE

do it to obtain a p .....1 Cor 9:25

PERISHED

Truth has p and has ....Jer 7:28

PERISHING

We are p ....Matt 8:25

PERMIT

do not p a woman .....1 Tim 2:12

PERMITS

we will do if God p ....Heb 6:3

PERMITTED

p no one to do them ....Ps 105:14
we are p ....2 Cor 4:8

PERSECUTE

when they revile and p .Matt 5:11

PERSECUTED

If they p Me ....John 15:20
p, but not forsaken .....2 Cor 4:9

PERSECUTES

wicked in his pride p .....Ps 10:2

PERSECUTION

p arises because of ....Matt 13:21
At that time a great p ....Acts 8:1
do I still suffer p ....Gal 5:11

PERSECUTOR

a blasphemer, a p .....1 Tim 1:13

PERSEVERANCE

tribulation produces p ...Rom 5:3

PERSEVERE

kept My command to p ..Rev 3:10

PERSISTENCE

p he will rise and ......Luke 11:8

PERSON

do not regard the p ....Matt 22:16
express image of His p ...Heb 1:3

PERSUADE

"You almost p me .....Acts 26:28

PERSUADED

neither will they be p .Luke 16:31
p that He is able ......2 Tim 1:12

PERSUASIVE

p words of human ......1 Cor 2:4

PERVERSE

your way is p ....Num 22:32
p man sows strife .....Prov 16:28
from this p generation ..Acts 2:40

PERVERT

"You shall not p ......Deut 16:19
p the gospel of Christ .....Gal 1:7

PERVERTING

will you not cease p ...Acts 13:10

PERVERTS

p his ways will become .Prov 10:9

PESTILENCE

from the perilous p ....Ps 91:3
Before Him went p ....Hab 3:5

PESTILENCES

will be famines, p ......Matt 24:7

PETITIONS

p that we have asked .1 John 5:15

PHARISEE

to pray, one a P ......Luke 18:10

PHILOSOPHERS

p encountered him ....Acts 17:18

PHILOSOPHY

cheat you through p ......Col 2:8

PHYSICIAN

have no need of a p ....Matt 9:12

PHYSICIANS

her livelihood on p .....Luke 8:43

PIECES

they took the thirty p ...Matt 27:9

PIERCE

a sword will p ....Luke 2:35

PIERCED

p My hands and My feet .Ps 22:16
whom they have p ....Zech 12:10
of the soldiers p ......John 19:34
p themselves through ..1 Tim 6:10
and they also who p ......Rev 1:7

PIERCING

p even to the division ...Heb 4:12

PILGRIMAGE

heart is set on p ....Ps 84:5
In the house of my p ....Ps 119:54

PILGRIMS

we are aliens and p ...1 Chr 29:15
were strangers and p ..Heb 11:13

PILLAR

and she became a p ....Gen 19:26
and by night in a p ......Ex 13:21
the living God, the p ...1 Tim 3:15

PILLARS

break their sacred p .....Ex 34:13
Blood and fire and p ....Joel 2:30
and his feet like p ....Rev 10:1

PIT

who go down to the p ....Ps 28:1
a harlot is a deep p ....Prov 23:27
my life in the p ....Lam 3:53

up my life from the p .....Jon 2:6
into the bottomless p ....Rev 20:3

PITIABLE

of all men the most p .1 Cor 15:19

PITS

The proud have dug p ..Ps 119:85

PITY

for someone to take p ...Ps 69:20
p He redeemed them ...Is 63:9
just as I had p ....Matt 18:33

PLACE

Come, see the p ....Matt 28:6
My word has no p .....John 8:37
I go to prepare a p .....John 14:2
might go to his own p ...Acts 1:25

PLACES

And the rough p ....Is 40:4
They love the best p ....Matt 23:6
in the heavenly p ....Eph 1:3

PLAGUE

bring yet one more p .....Ex 11:1

PLAGUES

p that are written ......Rev 22:18

PLANK

First remove the p ....Matt 7:5

PLANS

He makes the p of the ...Ps 33:10
that devises wicked p ...Prov 6:18

PLANT

A time to p ....Eccl 3:2
Him as a tender p ....Is 53:2
p of an alien vine ....Jer 2:21
p which My heavenly ..Matt 15:13

PLANTED

shall be like a tree p ....Ps 1:3
by the roots and be p ..Luke 17:6
I p, Apollos watered ....1 Cor 3:6

PLANTS

neither he who p ....1 Cor 3:7

PLATTER

head here on a p ....Matt 14:8

PLEASANT

food, that it was p ....Gen 3:6
how good and how p ....Ps 133:1

PLEASANTNESS

ways are ways of p .....Prov 3:17

PLEASE

in the flesh cannot p .....Rom 8:8
p his neighbor for his ...Rom 15:2
he may p the Lord .....1 Cor 7:32
is impossible to p Him ..Heb 11:6

PLEASED

Then You shall be p .....Ps 51:19
in whom I am well p ....Matt 3:17
God was not well p ....1 Cor 10:5
testimony, that he p ....Heb 11:5

PLEASES

Whatever the Lord p ....Ps 135:6

PLEASING

sacrifice, well p ....Phil 4:18
for this is well p ....Col 3:20
in you what is well p ...Heb 13:21

PLEASURE

Do good in Your good p .Ps 51:18
p will be a poor man ..Prov 21:17

PLEASURES

shall perform all My p .... Is 44:28
your Father's good p .. Luke 12:32
to the good p of His .... Eph 1:5
for sin You had no p .... Heb 10:6
My soul has no p ...... Heb 10:38
p that war in your ..... James 4:1

PLEASURES

Your right hand are p .. Ps 16:11
cares, riches, and p .... Luke 8:14
to enjoy the passing p .. Heb 11:25

PLOW

put his hand to the p ... Luke 9:62

PLOWED

You have p .... Hos 10:13

PLOWMAN

p shall overtake the ... Amos 9:13

PLUCK

p the heads of grain ... Mark 2:23

PLUCKED

cheeks to those who p ... Is 50:6
And His disciples p ..... Luke 6:1
you would have p .... Gal 4:15

PLUNDER

p the Egyptians .... Ex 3:22
The p of the poor is ...... Is 3:14
house and p his goods . Matt 12:29

PLUNDERED

a people robbed and p .... Is 42:22
"And when you are p .... Jer 4:30

PLUNDERING

me Because of the p ...... Is 22:4
accepted the p of your . Heb 10:34

POETS

some of your own p ... Acts 17:28

POISON

"The p of asps is ...... Rom 3:13

POISONED

p by bitterness .... Acts 8:23

POLLUTIONS

have escaped the p ..... 2 Pet 2:20

POMP

had come with great p . Acts 25:23

POMPOUS

and a mouth speaking p .. Dan 7:8

PONDER

P the path of your ...... Prov 4:26

PONDERED

p them in her heart .... Luke 2:19

PONDERS

p all his paths .... Prov 5:21

POOR

p will never cease ..... Deut 15:11
So the p have hope ..... Job 5:16
I delivered the p .... Job 29:12
p shall eat and be ...... Ps 22:26
But I am p and needy .... Ps 40:17
Let the p and needy ..... Ps 74:21
He raises the p .... Ps 113:7
slack hand becomes p .. Prov 10:4
p man is hated even ... Prov 14:20
has mercy on the p .... Prov 14:21
who oppresses the p ... Prov 14:31
p reproaches his .... Prov 17:5
Do not rob the p ...... Prov 22:22
that same p man .... Eccl 9:15
The alien or the p ...... Zech 7:10

"Blessed are the p ...... Matt 5:3
p have the gospel ...... Matt 11:5
"For you have the p ... Matt 26:11
sakes He became p .... 2 Cor 8:9
should remember the p .. Gal 2:10
God not chosen the p .. James 2:5
wretched, miserable, p .. Rev 3:17

PORTION

O Lord, You, are the p ... Ps 16:5
heart and my p forever .. Ps 73:26
You are my p .... Ps 119:57
I will divide Him a p ..... Is 53:12
rejoice in their p .... Is 61:7
The *P* of Jacob is not ... Jer 10:16
"The Lord is my p ..... Lam 3:24
and appoint him his p . Matt 24:51
to give them their p ... Luke 12:42
give me the p .... Luke 15:12

POSSESS

descendants shall p .... Gen 22:17
p the land which ...... Josh 1:11
"By your patience p .. Luke 21:19
p his own vessel ...... 1 Thess 4:4

POSSESSED

"The Lord p me at ..... Prov 8:22

POSSESSING

and yet p all things .... 2 Cor 6:10

POSSESSION

as an everlasting p ..... Gen 17:8
and an enduring p ..... Heb 10:34

POSSESSIONS

and sold their p .... Acts 2:45

POSSIBLE

God all things are p .. Matt 19:26
p that the blood .... Heb 10:4

POUR

p My Spirit on your ...... Is 44:3
P out Your fury .... Jer 10:25
That I will p out My ..... Joel 2:28
"And I will p .... Zech 12:10
angels, "Go and p ...... Rev 16:1

POURED

I am p out like water .... Ps 22:14
grace is p upon Your ..... Ps 45:2
strong, Because He p ..... Is 53:12
and My fury will be p .... Jer 7:20
broke the flask and p .. Mark 14:3
I am already being p .... 2 Tim 4:6
whom He p out on us ... Titus 3:6

POVERTY

leads only to p .... Prov 14:23
p put in all the .... Luke 21:4
and their deep p ...... 2 Cor 8:2
p might become rich .... 2 Cor 8:9
tribulation, and p .... Rev 2:9

POWER

that I may show My p ... Ex 9:16
him who is without p .... Job 26:2
p who can understand .. Job 26:14
p belongs to God .... Ps 62:11
P Your enemies shall ... Ps 66:3
gives strength and p ... Ps 68:35
a king is, there is p ...... Eccl 8:4
No one has p over the .... Eccl 8:8
'Not by might nor by p .. Zech 4:6
the kingdom and the p .. Matt 6:13
the Son of Man has p ... Matt 9:6
Scriptures nor the p ... Matt 22:29
p went out from Him ... Luke 6:19
are endued with p .... Luke 24:49
I have p to lay it ...... John 10:18
"You could have no p . John 19:11
you shall receive p ...... Acts 1:8
though by our own p ... Acts 3:12

---

man is the great p ...... Acts 8:10
"Give me this p .... Acts 8:19
for it is the p .... Rom 1:16
saved it is the p .... 1 Cor 1:18
Greeks, Christ the p ... 1 Cor 1:24
that the p of Christ ... 2 Cor 12:9
greatness of His p ..... Eph 1:19
the Lord and in the p ... Eph 6:10
to His glorious p .... Col 1:11
the glory of His p .... 2 Thess 1:9
of fear, but of p .... 2 Tim 1:7
by the word of His p ... Heb 1:3
p of death, that .... Heb 2:14
as His divine p .... 2 Pet 1:3
Dominion and p .... Jude 25
to him I will give p ..... Rev 2:26
honor and glory and p .. Rev 5:13

POWERFUL

of the Lord is p .... Ps 29:4
of God is living and p .. Heb 4:12

POWERS

principalities and p .... Col 2:15
word of God and the p ... Heb 6:5

PRAISE

p shall be of You in ..... Ps 22:25
the people shall p ...... Ps 45:17
P is awaiting You .... Ps 65:1
Let all the peoples p ...... Ps 67:3
p shall be continually ... Ps 71:6
And the heavens will p ... Ps 89:5
Seven times a day I p ... Ps 119:164
that has breath p .... Ps 150:6
Let another man p ..... Prov 27:2
let her own works p ... Prov 31:31
And your gates *P* .... Is 60:18
He makes Jerusalem a p .. Is 62:7
For You are my p ...... Jer 17:14
Me a name of joy, and p .. Jer 33:9
give you fame and p ... Zeph 3:20
You have perfected p .. Matt 21:16
men more than the p .. John 12:43
p is not from men but .. Rom 2:29
Then each one's p ...... 1 Cor 4:5
should be to the p ...... Eph 1:12
to the glory and p ...... Phil 1:11
I will sing p to You ..... Heb 2:12
the sacrifice of p .... Heb 13:15
and for the p of those .. 1 Pet 2:14
saying, "*P* our God ...... Rev 19:5

PRAISED

daily He shall be p ..... Ps 72:15
Lord's name is to be p ... Ps 113:3
and greatly to be p ...... Ps 145:3
the Most High and p .... Dan 4:34

PRAISES

it is good to sing p ...... Ps 147:1
and he p .... Prov 31:28

PRAISEWORTHY

if there is anything p ..... Phil 4:8

PRAISING

They will still be p .... Ps 84:4
of the heavenly host p .. Luke 2:13
in the temple p .... Luke 24:53

PRAY

at noon I will p .... Ps 55:17
who hate you, and p .... Matt 5:44
"And when you p ...... Matt 6:5
manner, therefore, p ..... Matt 6:9
"Watch and p .... Matt 26:41
"Lord, teach us to p ... Luke 11:1
"And I will p .... John 14:16
I do not p for the ...... John 17:9
"I do not p for ...... John 17:20
p without ceasing .... 1 Thess 5:17
Brethren, p for us ... 1 Thess 5:25
Let him p .... James 5:13

PRAYED

to one another, and *p* . James 5:16
say that he should *p* . . 1 John 5:16

PRAYED

p more earnestly . . . . . Luke 22:44
p earnestly that it . . . . . James 5:17

PRAYER

p made in this place . . . 2 Chr 7:15
And my *p* is pure . . . . . . Job 16:17
A *p* to the God of my . . . Ps 42:8
P also will be made . . . . . . Ps 72:15
He shall regard the *p* . . . Ps 102:17
to the LORD, But the *p* . . Prov 15:8
go out except by *p* . . . . Matt 17:21
all night in *p* to God . . . . Luke 6:12
continually to *p* . . . . Acts 6:4
where *p* was . . . . Acts 16:13
steadfastly in *p* . . . . Rom 12:12
to fasting and *p* . . . . 1 Cor 7:5
always with all *p* . . . . . . Eph 6:18
but in everything by *p* . . . Phil 4:6
the word of God and *p* . . 1 Tim 4:5
And the *p* of faith . . . . . James 5:15

PRAYERS

though You make many *p* . Is 1:15
pretense make long *p* . . Matt 23:14
fervently for you in *p* . . . . Col 4:12
p may not be hindered . . 1 Pet 3:7
which are the *p* . . . . Rev 5:8

PREACH

time Jesus began to *p* . . Matt 4:17
you hear in the ear, *p* . . Matt 10:27
P *the gospel to the* . . . . . Luke 4:18
And how shall they *p* . . . Rom 10:15
p Christ crucified . . . . . . 1 Cor 1:23
I or they, so we *p* . . . . 1 Cor 15:11
P the word . . . . 2 Tim 4:2

PREACHED

p that people . . . . Mark 6:12
out and *p* . . . . Mark 16:20
of sins should be *p* . . . . Luke 24:47
p Christ to them . . . . Acts 8:5
lest, when I have *p* . . . . 1 Cor 9:27
than what we have *p* . . . . Gal 1:8
the gospel was *p* . . . . Heb 4:2
also He went and *p* . . . . 1 Pet 3:19

PREACHER

they hear without a *p* . . Rom 10:14
I was appointed a *p* . . . . 1 Tim 2:7

PREACHES

the Jesus whom Paul *p* Acts 19:13
p another Jesus . . . . 2 Cor 11:4
p any other gospel . . . . Gal 1:9
p the faith which he . . . . . Gal 1:23

PREACHING

p Jesus as the . . . . Acts 5:42
not risen, then our *p* . . 1 Cor 15:14

PRECEPTS

all His *p* are sure . . . . Ps 111:7
how I love Your *p* . . . . . Ps 119:159

PRECIOUS

P in the sight of the . . . . Ps 116:15
She is more *p* than . . . . . Prov 3:15
p things shall not . . . . Is 44:9
if you take out the *p* . . . . Jer 15:19
farmer waits for the *p* . . James 5:7
more *p* than gold . . . . 1 Pet 1:7
who believe, He is *p* . . . 1 Pet 2:7
p in the sight of . . . . 1 Pet 3:4

PREDESTINED

foreknew, He also *p* . . . Rom 8:29
having *p* us to . . . . Eph 1:5
inheritance, being *p* . . . . Eph 1:11

PREEMINENCE

He may have the *p* . . . . Col 1:18
loves to have the *p* . . . . . 3 John 9

PREFERENCE

in honor giving *p* . . . . . . Rom 12:10

PREJUDICE

these things without *p* . 1 Tim 5:21

PREMEDITATE

p what you will . . . . . . Mark 13:11

PREPARATION

Now it was the P . . . . . . John 19:14
your feet with the *p* . . . . . Eph 6:15

PREPARE

p a table before me in . . Ps 23:5
P *the way of the LORD* . . . Mark 1:3
p a place for you . . . . John 14:2

PREPARED

for whom it is *p* . . . . . . Matt 20:23
Which You have *p* . . . . . Luke 2:31
mercy, which He had *p* . Rom 9:23
things which God has p . 1 Cor 2:9
Now He who has *p* . . . . . 2 Cor 5:5
p beforehand that we* . . . Eph 2:10
God, for He has *p* . . . . . Heb 11:16

PRESENCE

themselves from the *p* . . . Gen 3:8
went out from the *p* . . . . Gen 4:16
P will go with you . . . . . . Ex 33:14
afraid in any man's *p* . . . Deut 1:17
p is fullness of joy . . . . . . Ps 16:11
shall dwell in Your *p* . . . Ps 140:13
not tremble at My *p* . . . . . Jer 5:22
shall shake at My *p* . . . Ezek 38:20
and drank in Your *p* . . Luke 13:26
full of joy in Your p . . . . Acts 2:28
but his bodily *p* . . . . . . 2 Cor 10:10
obeyed, not as in my *p* . . Phil 2:12

PRESENT

we are all *p* before . . . . Acts 10:33
evil is *p* with me . . . . Rom 7:21
p your bodies a living . . . Rom 12:1
or death, or things *p* . . . 1 Cor 3:22
absent in body but *p* . . . 1 Cor 5:3
that He might *p* . . . . Eph 5:27
p you faultless . . . . Jude 24

PRESERVE

He shall *p* your soul . . . Ps 121:7
The LORD shall *p* . . . . . . Ps 121:8
loses his life will *p* . . . Luke 17:33
every evil work and *p* . 2 Tim 4:18

PRESERVED

soul, and body be *p* . 1 Thess 5:23

PRESERVES

For the LORD *p* the . . . . . Ps 31:23
p the souls of His . . . . . . Ps 97:10
who keeps his way *p* . . Prov 16:17

PRETENSE

p make long prayers . . Matt 23:14

PRICE

one pearl of great *p* . . . Matt 13:46
were bought at a *p* . . . . 1 Cor 6:20

PRIDE

p serves as . . . . Ps 73:6
By *p* comes nothing . . . Prov 13:10
P goes before . . . . Prov 16:18
her daughter had *p* . . . Ezek 16:49
was hardened in *p* . . . . . Dan 5:20
For the *p* of the . . . . Zech 11:3
evil eye, blasphemy, *p* . Mark 7:22
p he fall into the . . . . 1 Tim 3:6
eyes, and the *p* . . . . . . 1 John 2:16

PRIEST

he was the *p* of God . . . Gen 14:18

PROFANE

and priest are *p* . . . . Jer 23:11
tried to *p* the temple . . . . Acts 24:6
But reject *p* and old . . . . 1 Tim 4:7

PROFANED

and *p* My Sabbaths . . . Ezek 22:8

PROFANENESS

of Jerusalem *p* has . . . . Jer 23:15

PROFANING

p the covenant of the . . . Mal 2:10

---

p forever According . . . . . Ps 110:4
So He shall be a *p* . . . . . Zech 6:13
and faithful High P . . . . . Heb 2:17
we have a great High P . Heb 4:14
p forever according . . . . . . Heb 5:6
Christ came as High P . . Heb 9:11

PRIESTHOOD

p being changed . . . . Heb 7:12
has an unchangeable *p* . . Heb 7:24
generation, a royal *p* . . . 1 Pet 2:9

PRIESTS

to Me a kingdom of *p* . . . . Ex 19:6
Her *p* teach for pay . . . . . Mic 3:11
made us kings and *p* . . . . Rev 1:6

PRINCE

is the house of the *p* . . . Job 21:28
Everlasting Father, P . . . . . . Is 9:6
Until Messiah the P . . . . Dan 9:25
days without king or *p* . . Hos 3:4
P asks for gifts . . . . Mic 7:3
"and killed the P . . . . . . Acts 3:15
His right hand to be P . Acts 5:31
the *p* of the power . . . . Eph 2:2

PRINCES

to put confidence in *p* . . . Ps 118:9
He brings the *p* . . . . Is 40:23

PRISON

and put him into the *p* . Gen 39:20
Bring my soul out of *p* . . Ps 142:7
in darkness from the *p* . . . Is 42:7
the opening of the *p* . . . . Is 61:1
John had heard in *p* . . . . Matt 11:2
I was in *p* and you . . . . Matt 25:36

PRIZE

the goal for the *p* . . . . . . Phil 3:14

PROCEED

of the same mouth *p* . James 3:10

PROCEEDED

for I *p* forth . . . . John 8:42

PROCEEDS

by every word that *p* . . . . Deut 8:3
by every word that p . . . . Matt 4:4
Spirit of truth who *p* . . John 15:26

PROCLAIM

began to *p* it freely . . . . Mark 1:45
knowing, Him I *p* . . . . . . Acts 17:23
drink this cup, you *p* . 1 Cor 11:26

PROCLAIMED

p the good news . . . . Ps 40:9
he went his way and *p* . Luke 8:39

PROCLAIMER

"He seems to be a *p* . . . Acts 17:18

PROCLAIMS

good news, Who *p* . . . . Is 52:7

PRODIGAL

with *p* living . . . . Luke 15:13

PROFESS

They *p* to know God . . . Titus 1:16

PROFIT

For what *p* is it to . . . . . Matt 16:26
"For what will it *p* . . . . . Mark 8:36
"For what *p* is it to . . . . . Luke 9:25
her masters much *p* . . . Acts 16:16
brought no small *p* . . . Acts 19:24
what is the *p* of . . . . Rom 3:1
seeking my own *p* . . . 1 Cor 10:33
Christ will *p* you . . . . Gal 5:2
about words to no *p* . . . 2 Tim 2:14
them, but He for our *p* . Heb 12:10
What does it *p* . . . . James 2:14
sell, and make a *p* . . . . James 4:13

PROFITABLE

It is doubtless not *p* . . . 2 Cor 12:1
of God, and is *p* . . . . 2 Tim 3:16

PROFITS

have not love, it *p* . . . . . 1 Cor 13:3

PROMISE

"Behold, I send the *P* . Luke 24:49
but to wait for the *P* . . . . . Acts 1:4
"For the *p* is to you . . . . . Acts 2:39
for the hope of the *p* . . . Acts 26:6
p might be sure . . . . Rom 4:16
Therefore, since a *p* . . . . . Heb 4:1
to the heirs of the *p* . . . . Heb 6:17
did not receive the *p* . . . Heb 11:39

PROMISED

faithful who had *p* . . . . . Heb 11:11

PROMISES

For all the *p* of God . . . . 2 Cor 1:20
his Seed were the *p* . . . . . Gal 3:16
having received the *p* . . Heb 11:13
great and precious *p* . . . . 2 Pet 1:4

PROPER

you, but for what is *p* . . 1 Cor 7:35
but, which is *p* . . . . 1 Tim 2:10

PROPERLY

Let us walk *p* . . . . Rom 13:13

PROPHECY

to another *p* . . . . 1 Cor 12:10
for *p* never came by . . . 2 Pet 1:21
is the spirit of *p* . . . . Rev 19:10
of the book of this *p* . . . Rev 22:19

PROPHESIED

Lord, have we not *p* . . . . Matt 7:22
and the law *p* . . . . Matt 11:13

PROPHESIES

p edifies the church . . . . 1 Cor 14:4

PROPHESY

prophets, "Do not *p* . . . . . . Is 30:10
The prophets *p* falsely . . . . Jer 5:31
your daughters shall *p* . . Joel 2:28
Who can but *p* . . . . Amos 3:8
saying, "*P* to us . . . . . . Matt 26:68
your daughters shall *p* . . Acts 2:17
in part and we *p* . . . . . . 1 Cor 13:9

PROPHET

raise up for you a *P* . . . . Deut 18:15
"I alone am left a *p* . . . 1 Kin 18:22
I ordained you a *p* . . . . Jer 1:5
The *p* is a fool . . . . Hos 9:7
Nor was I a son of a *p* . Amos 7:14
send you Elijah the *p* . . . . Mal 4:5
p shall receive a . . . . . . Matt 10:41
p is not without honor . Matt 13:57
by Daniel the *p* . . . . . . Mark 13:14
is not a greater *p* . . . . . . Luke 7:28
it cannot be that a *p* . . Luke 13:33

who was a *P* . . . . Luke 24:19
"Are you the *P* . . . . John 1:21
"This is truly the *P* . . . . John 6:14
with him the false *p* . . . . Rev 19:20

PROPHETIC

p word confirmed . . . . . . 2 Pet 1:19

PROPHETS

the Law or the *P* . . . . Matt 5:17
is the Law and the *P* . . . . Matt 7:12
or one of the *p* . . . . Matt 16:14
the tombs of the *p* . . . . . Matt 23:29
indeed, I send you *p* . . . Matt 23:34
one who kills the *p* . . . . . Matt 23:37
Then many false *p* . . . . . Matt 24:11
Moses and the *p* . . . . . . Luke 16:29
are sons of the *p* . . . . Acts 3:25
p did your fathers not . . . Acts 7:52
"To Him all the *p* . . . . . . Acts 10:43
do you believe the *p* . . . Acts 26:27
by the Law and the *P* . . . . Rom 3:21
have killed Your *p* . . . . . Rom 11:3
to be apostles, some *p* . . . Eph 4:11
this salvation the *p* . . . . . 1 Pet 1:10
because many false *p* . . 1 John 4:1
found the blood of *p* . . . . Rev 18:24

PROPITIATION

set forth as a *p* . . . . Rom 3:25
to God, to make *p* . . . . . . Heb 2:17
He Himself is the *p* . . . 1 John 2:2
His Son to be the *p* . . . 1 John 4:10

PROPRIETY

modest apparel, with *p* . 1 Tim 2:9

PROSPER

they *p* who love you . . . . . Ps 122:6
of the LORD shall *p* . . . . . . Is 53:10
against you shall *p* . . . . . . Is 54:17
up as he may *p* . . . . 1 Cor 16:2
I pray that you may *p* . . 3 John 2

PROSPERED

since the LORD has *p* . . . Gen 24:56

PROSPERING

His ways are always *p* . . . . Ps 10:5

PROSPERITY

p all your days . . . . Deut 23:6
the destroyer . . . . Job 15:21
Now in my *p* I said . . . . Ps 30:6
has pleasure in the *p* . . . . . Ps 35:27
When I saw the *p* . . . . Ps 73:3
I pray, send now *p* . . . . . Ps 118:25
that we have our *p* . . . . Acts 19:25

PROSPEROUS

will make your way *p* . . . Josh 1:8

PROSPERS

just as your soul *p* . . . . . . 3 John 2

PROUD

tongue that speaks *p* . . . . . Ps 12:3
And fully repays the *p* . . . Ps 31:23
does not respect the *p* . . . . Ps 40:4
a haughty look and a *p* . . . Ps 101:5
p He knows from afar . . . Ps 138:6
Everyone *p* . . . . Prov 16:5
by wine, He is a *p* . . . . . . Hab 2:5
He has scattered the *p* . Luke 1:51
"*God resists the* *p* . . . . . . 1 Pet 5:5

PROVERB

of a drunkard Is a *p* . . . Prov 26:9
one shall take up a *p* . . . . . Mic 2:4
to the true *p* . . . . 2 Pet 2:22

PROVERBS

three thousand *p* . . . . . . 1 Kin 4:32
in order many *p* . . . . Eccl 12:9

PROVIDE

"My son, God will *p* . . . Gen 22:8
"*P* neither gold nor . . . . . Matt 10:9
if anyone does not *p* . . . . 1 Tim 5:8

PROVIDED

these hands have *p* . . . . Acts 20:34
p something better . . . . . Heb 11:40

PROVISION

no *p* for the flesh . . . . . . Rom 13:14

PROVOKE

"Do they *p* Me to . . . . Jer 7:19
you, fathers, do not *p* . . . . Eph 6:4

PROVOKED

p the Most High . . . . Ps 78:56
his spirit was *p* . . . . Acts 17:16
seek its own, is not *p* . . 1 Cor 13:5

PRUDENCE

To give *p* to the . . . . Prov 1:4
wisdom, dwell with *p* . . . Prov 8:12
us in all wisdom and *p* . . . Eph 1:8

PRUDENT

p man covers shame . . . Prov 12:16
A *p* man conceals . . . . Prov 12:23
The wisdom of the *p* . . . . Prov 14:8
p considers well . . . . . . Prov 14:15
heart will be called *p* . . Prov 16:21
p man foresees evil . . . . . Prov 22:3
Therefore the *p* . . . . Amos 5:13
from the wise and *p* . . . Matt 11:25

PRUDENTLY

Servant shall deal *p* . . . . . Is 52:13

PRUNES

that bears fruit He *p* . . . John 15:2

PSALM

each of you has a *p* . . . 1 Cor 14:26

PSALMIST

And the sweet *p* . . . . . . 2 Sam 23:1

PSALMS

to one another in *p* . . . . . Eph 5:19
Let him sing *p* . . . . James 5:13

PUNISH

p the righteous is . . . . . . Prov 17:26
Shall I not *p* them for . . . . . Jer 5:9

PUNISHED

p them often in every . . Acts 26:11
These shall be *p* . . . . . . 2 Thess 1:9

PUNISHES

will you say when He *p* . Jer 13:21

PUNISHMENT

p is greater than I . . . . Gen 4:13
you do in the day of *p* . . . . . Is 10:3
p they shall perish . . . . . Jer 10:15
not turn away its *p* . . . . . Amos 1:3
into everlasting *p* . . . . Matt 25:46
p which was inflicted . . . 2 Cor 2:6
Of how much worse *p* . . Heb 10:29
sent by him for the *p* . . 1 Pet 2:14
the unjust under *p* . . . . . 2 Pet 2:9

PURE

a mercy seat of *p* gold . . . Ex 25:17
'My doctrine is *p* . . . . Job 11:4
that he could be *p* . . . . . Job 15:14
of the LORD are *p* . . . . Ps 12:6
ways of a man are *p* . . . . Prov 16:2
a generation that is *p* . . Prov 30:12
things indeed are *p* . . . . Rom 14:20
whatever things are *p* . . . . Phil 4:8
keep yourself *p* . . . . 1 Tim 5:22

PURER

p all things are *p* ...... Titus 1:15
above is first *p* .... James 3:17
babes, desire the *p* ..... 1 Pet 2:2
just as He is *p* .... 1 John 3:3

PURER

p eyes than to behold ... Hab 1:13

PURGE

P me with hyssop .... Ps 51:7

PURGED

away, And your sin *p* ...... Is 6:7

PURIFICATION

with the water of *p* .... Num 31:23

PURIFIED

all things are *p* .... Heb 9:22
Since you have *p* ...... 1 Pet 1:22

PURIFIES

hope in Him *p* himself . 1 John 3:3

PURIFY

and *p* your hearts ...... James 4:8

PURIFYING

p their hearts by .... Acts 15:9
sanctifies for the *p* ...... Heb 9:13

PURIM

called these days *P* ..... Esth 9:26

PURITY

spirit, in faith, in *p* .... 1 Tim 4:12

PURPOSE

A time for every *p* ...... Eccl 3:1
But for this *p* I came .. John 12:27
by the determined *p* .. Acts 2:23
to fulfill His *p* .... Rev 17:17

PURSUE

p righteousness .... Rom 9:30
P love .... 1 Cor 14:1

PURSUES

flee when no one *p* ..... Prov 28:1

Q

QUAIL

and it brought *q* ...... Num 11:31

QUARREL

He will not *q* nor cry .. Matt 12:19
the Lord must not *q* .. 2 Tim 2:24

QUARRELSOME

but gentle, not *q* .... 1 Tim 3:3

QUEEN

heart, 'I sit as *q* .... Rev 18:7

QUENCH

Many waters cannot *q* ... Song 8:7
flax He will not *q* ..... Matt 12:20
q all the fiery .... Eph 6:16
Do not *q* the Spirit .. 1 Thess 5:19

QUENCHED

that shall never be *q* ... Mark 9:43

QUESTIONS

and asking them *q* .... Luke 2:46

QUICKLY

with your adversary *q* .. Matt 5:25
"Surely I am coming *q* . Rev 22:20

QUIET

aspire to lead a *q* .... 1 Thess 4:11
a gentle and *q* spirit ..... 1 Pet 3:4

QUIETNESS

a handful with *q* .... Eccl 4:6
In *q* and confidence .... Is 30:15
of righteousness, *q* ...... Is 32:17
that they work in *q* ..2 Thess 3:12

R

RABBI

be called by men, 'R ... Matt 23:7

RACA

to his brother, 'R ...... Matt 5:22

RACE

man to run its *r* .... Ps 19:5
r is not to the swift ..... Eccl 9:11
I have finished the *r* .... 2 Tim 4:7
with endurance the *r* .... Heb 12:1

RAGE

Why do the nations *r* ...... Ps 2:1
'Why did the nations *r* .. Acts 4:25

RAIN

had not caused it to *r* .... Gen 2:5
And the *r* was on the .... Gen 7:12
I will *r* down on him .. Ezek 38:22
given you the former *r* .. Joel 2:23
the good, and sends *r* ... Matt 5:45
"and the *r* descended .. Matt 7:25
r that often comes .... Heb 6:7
that it would not *r* .... James 5:17

RAINBOW

"I set My *r* in the .... Gen 9:13
and there was a *r* .... Rev 4:3

RAINED

r fire and brimstone ... Luke 17:29

RAINS

r righteousness .... Hos 10:12

RAISE

third day He will *r* ...... Hos 6:2
in three days I will *r* .... John 2:19
and I will *r* him up at .. John 6:40
and the Lord will *r* .... James 5:15

RAISED

be killed, and be *r* ..... Matt 16:21
just as Christ was *r* ...... Rom 6:4
Spirit of Him who *r* .... Rom 8:11
"How are the dead *r* .. 1 Cor 15:35
the dead will be *r* ..... 1 Cor 15:52
and *r* us up together ..... Eph 2:6

RAISES

"For as the Father *r* .... John 5:21
but in God who *r* ...... 2 Cor 1:9

RAN

You *r* well .... Gal 5:7

RANSOM

to give His life a *r* .... Mark 10:45
who gave Himself a *r* ... 1 Tim 2:6

RANSOMED

And the *r* of the LORD .... Is 35:10
redeemed Jacob, And *r* .. Jer 31:11

RASH

Do not be *r* with your .... Eccl 5:2

RASHLY

and do nothing *r* ...... Acts 19:36

RAVENOUS

inwardly they are *r* ..... Matt 7:15

RAVENS

"Consider the *r* .... Luke 12:24

REACHING

r forward to those .... Phil 3:13

READ

day, and stood up to *r* .. Luke 4:16
hearts, known and *r* .... 2 Cor 3:2

READER

the *r* understand ..... Mark 13:14

READINESS

the word with all *r* .... Acts 17:11

READING

r the prophet Isaiah .... Acts 8:30

READS

Blessed is he who *r* .... Rev 1:3

READY

and those who were *r* . Matt 25:10
"Lord, I am *r* .... Luke 22:33
Be *r* in season and out ..2 Tim 4:2
and always be *r* .... 1 Pet 3:15

REAP

they neither sow nor *r* .. Matt 6:26
you knew that I *r* ...... Matt 25:26

REAPED

You have *r* iniquity ... Hos 10:13

REAPERS

r are the angels .... Matt 13:39

REAPING

r what I did not .... Luke 19:22

REAPS

sows and another *r* ..... John 4:37

REASON

"Come now, and let us *r* ... Is 1:18
who asks you a *r* ...... 1 Pet 3:15

REASONED

for three Sabbaths *r* .... Acts 17:2

REBEL

if you refuse and *r* .... Is 1:20

REBELLING

more against Him By *r* .. Ps 78:17

REBELLION

hearts as in the *r* .... Heb 3:8

REBELLIOUS

day long to a *r* people ..... Is 65:2

REBUILD

God, to *r* its ruins ...... Ezra 9:9
r it as in the days of ... Amos 9:11

REBUKE

Turn at my *r* .... Prov 1:23
R a wise man .... Prov 9:8
r is better Than love ... Prov 27:5
R the oppressor .... Is 1:17
sins against you, *r* ..... Luke 17:3
Do not *r* an older man .. 1 Tim 5:1
who are sinning *r* ..... 1 Tim 5:20
"The Lord *r* you .... Jude 9
"As many as I love, I *r* .. Rev 3:19

REBUKED

r the winds and the ..... Matt 8:26
r their unbelief ...... Mark 16:14
but he was *r* for his ... 2 Pet 2:16

REBUKES

ear that hears the *r* ... Prov 15:31

RECEIVE

believing, you will *r* ...Matt 21:22
and His own did not *r* ..John 1:11
will come again and *r* ..John 14:3
the world cannot *r* ....John 14:17
Ask, and you will *r* ....John 16:24
"*R* the Holy Spirit ....John 20:22
"Lord Jesus, *r* ....Acts 7:59
r the Holy Spirit ....Acts 19:2
R one who is weak .....Rom 14:1
r the Spirit by the ....Gal 3:2
suppose that he will *r* ..James 1:7

RECEIVED

But as many as *r* ......John 1:12
for God has *r* him .....Rom 14:3
For I *r* from the Lord .1 Cor 11:23
r Christ ....Col 2:6
R up in glory ....1 Tim 3:16

RECEIVES

r you *r* Me ....Matt 10:40
and whoever *r* Me .....Mark 9:37

RECONCILE

and that He might *r* .....Eph 2:16

RECONCILED

First be *r* to your ....Matt 5:24
we were *r* ....Rom 5:10
Christ's behalf, be *r* ....2 Cor 5:20

RECONCILIATION

now received the *r* .....Rom 5:11
to us the word of *r* ....2 Cor 5:19

RECONCILING

cast away is the *r* .....Rom 11:15
God was in Christ *r* ....2 Cor 5:19

REDEEM

But God will *r* my soul ...Ps 49:15
r their life from ....Ps 72:14
was going to *r* Israel ..Luke 24:21
r those who were ....Gal 4:5
us, that He might *r* .....Titus 2:14

REDEEMED

Let the *r* of the LORD ....Ps 107:2
r shall walk there ....Is 35:9
sea a road For the *r* ....Is 51:10
And you shall be *r* ....Is 52:3
and *r* His people ......Luke 1:68
Christ has *r* us from ....Gal 3:13
that you were not *r* ....1 Pet 1:18
were slain, And have *r* ...Rev 5:9

REDEEMER

For I know that my *R* ...Job 19:25
Our *R* from Everlasting ...Is 63:16

REDEEMING

r the time ....Eph 5:16

REDEMPTION

those who looked for *r* .Luke 2:38
your *r* draws near ....Luke 21:28
grace through the *r* ....Rom 3:24
the adoption, the *r* .....Rom 8:23
sanctification and *r* ....1 Cor 1:30
In Him we have *r* ......Eph 1:7
for the day of *r* ....Eph 4:30
obtained eternal *r* ......Heb 9:12

REED

r He will not break ....Is 42:3
r shaken by the wind ...Matt 11:7

REFINED

us as silver is *r* ....Ps 66:10

REFINER

He will sit as a *r* ....Mal 3:3

REFORMATION

until the time of *r* ....Heb 9:10

REFRESH

r my heart in the Lord .Philem 20

REFRESHED

his spirit has been *r* ...2 Cor 7:13
for he often *r* ....2 Tim 1:16

REFRESHES

r the soul of his ....Prov 25:13

REFRESHING

r may come from the ...Acts 3:19

REFUGE

eternal God is your *r* ..Deut 33:27
God is our *r* and ....Ps 46:1
who have fled for *r* .....Heb 6:18

REGARD

r iniquity in my heart ....Ps 66:18
did not fear God nor *r* ..Luke 18:2

REGARDED

my hand and no one *r* ..Prov 1:24
r the lowly state ....Luke 1:48

REGARDS

r a rebuke will be .....Prov 13:18

REGENERATION

to you, that in the *r* ....Matt 19:28
the washing of *r* ....Titus 3:5

REGISTERED

So all went to be *r* ......Luke 2:3

REGRETTED

but afterward he *r* .....Matt 21:29

REGULATIONS

yourselves to *r* ....Col 2:20

REIGN

"And He will *r* ....Luke 1:33
righteousness will *r* ....Rom 5:17
so grace might *r* ....Rom 5:21
do not let sin *r* ....Rom 6:12
For He must *r* till He ..1 Cor 15:25
of Christ, and shall *r* ....Rev 20:6

REIGNED

so that as sin *r* ....Rom 5:21
You have *r* as kings ....1 Cor 4:8
And they lived and *r* ....Rev 20:4

REIGNS

to Zion, "Your God *r* ......Is 52:7
Lord God Omnipotent *r* .Rev 19:6

REJECT

"All too well may *r* .....Mark 7:9
R a divisive man ....Titus 3:10

REJECTED

He is despised and *r* ......Is 53:3
r Has become the .....Matt 21:42
many things and be *r* .Luke 17:25
Moses whom they *r* .....Acts 7:35
to a living stone, *r* ....1 Pet 2:4

REJECTION

you shall know My *r* ..Num 14:34

REJECTS

he who *r* Me *r* ....Luke 10:16

REJOICE

R in the LORD ....Ps 33:1
of Your wings I will *r* .....Ps 63:7
Let them *r* before God ...Ps 68:3
Let the heavens *r* ....Ps 96:11

Let the earth *r* ....Ps 97:1
We will *r* and be glad ...Ps 118:24
She shall *r* in time to ..Prov 31:25
R, O young man ....Eccl 11:9
your heart shall *r* ....Is 66:14
Do not *r* over me ....Mic 7:8
do not *r* ....Luke 10:20
you would *r* ....John 14:28
but the world will *r* ....John 16:20
and your heart will *r* ..John 16:22
R with those who ......Rom 12:15
and in this I *r* ....Phil 1:18
faith, I am glad and *r* ....Phil 2:17
R in the Lord always .....Phil 4:4
R always ....1 Thess 5:16
yet believing, you *r* ......1 Pet 1:8

REJOICED

And my spirit has *r* ....Luke 1:47
In that hour Jesus *r* ...Luke 10:21
Abraham *r* ....John 8:56

REJOICES

glad, and my glory *r* .....Ps 16:9
but *r* in the truth ......1 Cor 13:6

REJOICING

come again with *r* ....Ps 126:6
he went on his way *r* ...Acts 8:39
confidence and the *r* .....Heb 3:6

RELENT

sworn And will not *r* ....Ps 110:4
sworn And will not r ....Heb 7:21

RELENTED

and God *r* from the ......Jon 3:10

RELENTING

I am weary of *r* ....Jer 15:6

RELIGION

in self-imposed *r* ....Col 2:23
and undefiled *r* ....James 1:27

RELIGIOUS

things you are very *r* ..Acts 17:22

REMAIN

that My joy may *r* ....John 15:11
your fruit should *r* ....John 15:16
"If I will that he *r* ....John 21:22
the greater part *r* ......1 Cor 15:6
are alive and *r* ......1 Thess 4:15
the things which *r* ......Rev 3:2

REMAINS

"While the earth *r* ......Gen 8:22
Therefore your sin *r* ....John 9:41
There *r* therefore a ......Heb 4:9

REMEMBER

"*R* the Sabbath day ......Ex 20:8
But we will *r* the name ....Ps 20:7
r Your name in the .....Ps 119:55
R now your Creator ....Eccl 12:1
r the former things ......Is 43:18
and their sin I will *r* ....Jer 31:34
In wrath *r* mercy ....Hab 3:2
And to *r* His holy ......Luke 1:72
"*R* Lot's wife ....Luke 17:32
r the words of the .....Acts 20:35
R that Jesus Christ .....2 Tim 2:8
R those who rule ....Heb 13:7

REMEMBERED

Then God *r* Noah ....Gen 8:1
r His covenant with .....Ex 2:24
r His covenant forever ...Ps 105:8
yea, we wept When we *r* .Ps 137:1
And Peter *r* the word ...Matt 26:75
r the word of the Lord .Acts 11:16

REMEMBRANCE

r my song in the night ....Ps 77:6
Put Me in *r* ....Is 43:26

REMISSION (cont.)
do this in r of Me .....Luke 22:19
do this in r of Me .....1 Cor 11:24

REMISSION
for the r.................Mark 1:4
Jesus Christ for the r ...Acts 2:38
where there is r........Heb 10:18

REMNANT
The r will return ....Is 10:21
time there is a r........Rom 11:5

REMORSEFUL
condemned, was r .....Matt 27:3

REMOVE
r this cup from Me ....Luke 22:42
r your lampstand ....Rev 2:5

REMOVED
Though the earth be r ....Ps 46:2
And the hills be r ....Is 54:10
this mountain, 'Be r ...Matt 21:21

REND
So r your heart ....Joel 2:13

RENDER
What shall I r to the ....Ps 116:12
"R therefore to Caesar .Matt 22:21

RENEW
r a steadfast ....Ps 51:10
on the LORD Shall r ....Is 40:31

RENEWED
that your youth is r .....Ps 103:5
inward man is being r .2 Cor 4:16
and be r in the spirit ....Eph 4:23

RENEWING
transformed by the r ...Rom 12:2

RENOWN
were of old, men of r .....Gen 6:4

REPAID
Shall evil by r ....Jer 18:20

REPAY
again, I will r ....Luke 10:35
they cannot r ....Luke 14:14
R no one evil for evil .Rom 12:17
is Mine, I will r........Rom 12:19
r their parents ....1 Tim 5:4

REPAYS
the LORD, Who fully r .....Is 66:6

REPENT
I abhor myself, And r ...Job 42:6
"R, for the kingdom ....Matt 3:2
you r you will all ......Luke 13:3
said to them, "R ......Acts 2:38
men everywhere to r...Acts 17:30
be zealous and r ....Rev 3:19

REPENTANCE
you with water unto r ...Matt 3:11
a baptism of r for the ...Mark 1:4
persons who need no r .Luke 15:7
renew them again to r ....Heb 6:6
found no place for r ....Heb 12:17
all should come to r .....2 Pet 3:9

REPENTED
it, because they r ......Matt 12:41

REPETITIONS
r as the heathen do ......Matt 6:7

REPORT
Who has believed our r ....Is 53:1
things are of good r ......Phil 4:8

REPROACH
R has broken my heart ..Ps 69:20
with dishonor comes r ..Prov 18:3
not remember the r ......Is 54:4
Because I bore the r .....Jer 31:19
these things You r ....Luke 11:45
lest he fall into r........1 Tim 3:7
esteeming the r ....Heb 11:26
and without r ....James 1:5

REPROACHED
If you are r for the .....1 Pet 4:14

REPROACHES
is not an enemy who r ..Ps 55:12
in infirmities, in r .....2 Cor 12:10

REPROOF
for doctrine, for r ......2 Tim 3:16

REPROOFS
R of instruction are ....Prov 6:23

REPUTATION
seven men of good r .....Acts 6:3
made Himself of no r ....Phil 2:7

REQUEST
He gave them their r....Ps 106:15
For Jews r a sign ......1 Cor 1:22

REQUESTS
r be made known ....Phil 4:6

REQUIRE
offering You did not r ...Ps 40:6
what does the LORD ....Mic 6:8

REQUIRED
your soul will be r ....Luke 12:20
him much will be r....Luke 12:48

REQUIREMENTS
keeps the righteous r ...Rom 2:26
r that was against us ....Col 2:14

RESERVED
"I have r for Myself ....Rom 11:4
r in heaven for you ......1 Pet 1:4
habitation, He has r ....Jude 6

RESIST
r an evil person ....Matt 5:39
r the Holy Spirit ....Acts 7:51
R the devil and he .....James 4:7

RESISTED
For who has r His will ..Rom 9:19
for he has greatly r ....2 Tim 4:15
You have not yet r ......Heb 12:4

RESISTS
"God r the proud ......James 4:6
for "God r the proud ....1 Pet 5:5

RESPECT
of the law held in r .....Acts 5:34
and we paid them r .....Heb 12:9

RESPECTED
And the LORD r Abel .....Gen 4:4

REST
is the Sabbath of r ......Ex 31:15
to build a house of r ...1 Chr 28:2
R in the LORD ....Ps 37:7
fly away and be at r .....Ps 55:6
"This is the r ....Is 28:12
is the place of My r ....Is 66:1
and I will give you r ...Matt 11:28
shall not enter My r .....Heb 3:11
remains therefore a r .....Heb 4:9

that they should r ....Rev 6:11
"that they may r ....Rev 14:13
But the r of the dead ....Rev 20:5

RESTED
He had done, and He r ...Gen 2:2
"And God r on the ....Heb 4:4

RESTORATION
until the times of r .....Acts 3:21

RESTORE
R to me the joy ....Ps 51:12
"So I will r to you ....Joel 2:25
and will r all things ....Matt 17:11
You at this time r ....Acts 1:6
who are spiritual r ....Gal 6:1

RESTORES
He r my soul ....Ps 23:3

RESTRAINS
only He who now r ...2 Thess 2:7

RESTRAINT
They break all r ....Hos 4:2

RESTS
r quietly in the heart ..Prov 14:33

RESURRECTION
to her, "I am the r ....John 11:25
them Jesus and the r ...Acts 17:18
the likeness of His r ....Rom 6:5
say that there is no r .1 Cor 15:12
and the power of His r ..Phil 3:10
obtain a better r ......Heb 11:35
This is the first r ....Rev 20:5

RETAIN
r the sins of any ......John 20:23

RETURN
womb, naked shall he r ..Eccl 5:15
Let him r to the LORD .....Is 55:7
me, and I will r ....Jer 31:18
"R to Me ....Zech 1:3
he says, 'I will r ....Matt 12:44

RETURNED
astray, but have now r .1 Pet 2:25

RETURNING
r evil for evil or ....1 Pet 3:9

RETURNS
As a dog r to his own ..Prov 26:11
"A dog r to his own ....2 Pet 2:22

REVEAL
the Son wills to r Him .Matt 11:27
r His Son in me ....Gal 1:16

REVEALED
things which are r ....Deut 29:29
righteousness to be r ....Is 56:1
the Son of Man is r ...Luke 17:30
the wrath of God is r ...Rom 1:18
glory which shall be r ..Rom 8:18
the Lord Jesus is r ....2 Thess 1:7
lawless one will be r ..2 Thess 2:8
ready to be r in the .....1 Pet 1:5
when His glory is r ....1 Pet 4:13
r what we shall be .....1 John 3:2

REVEALER
Lord of kings, and a r ...Dan 2:47

REVEALING
waits for the r ....Rom 8:19

REVEALS
as a talebearer r.......Prov 20:19
r His secret to His ......Amos 3:7

REVELATION

Where there is no r ...Prov 29:18
it came through the r ....Gal 1:12
spirit of wisdom and r ...Eph 1:17
r He made known to .....Eph 3:3
and glory at the r ....1 Pet 1:7

REVERENCE

and r My sanctuary ....Lev 19:30
God acceptably with r ..Heb 12:28

REVERENT

man who is always r ..Prov 28:14
their wives must be r ..1 Tim 3:11

REVILE

are you when they r ....Matt 5:11
r God's high priest ......Acts 23:4

REVILED

crucified with Him r ..Mark 15:32
who, when He was r ....1 Pet 2:23

REVIVAL

give us a measure of r ...Ezra 9:8

REVIVE

Will You not r us ....Ps 85:6
two days He will r ....Hos 6:2

REVIVED

came, sin r and I died ....Rom 7:9

REWARD

exceedingly great r ....Gen 15:1
look, And see the r ....Ps 91:8
Behold, His r is with .....Is 40:10
for great is your r ......Matt 5:12
you, they have their r ....Matt 6:2
no means lose his r ...Matt 10:42
we receive the due r ..Luke 23:41
will receive his own r ...1 Cor 3:8
cheat you of your r ......Col 2:18
for he looked to the r ..Heb 11:26
quickly, and My r ......Rev 22:12

REWARDS

Whoever r evil for .....Prov 17:13
And follows after r ....Is 1:23

RICH

Abram was very r ....Gen 13:2
The r and the poor .....Prov 22:2
r rules over the poor ...Prov 22:7
r man is wise in his ....Prov 28:11
Do not curse the r ...Eccl 10:20
it is hard for a r ....Matt 19:23
to you who are r ......Luke 6:24
the r man's table ....Luke 16:21
for he was very r .....Luke 18:23
You are already r .....1 Cor 4:8
though He was r ....2 Cor 8:9
who desire to be r .....1 Tim 6:9
of this world to be r ...James 2:5
you say, 'I am r ....Rev 3:17

RICHES

R and honor are ......Prov 8:18
R do not profit ....Prov 11:4
in his r will fall ....Prov 11:28
of the wise is their r ..Prov 14:24
and r are an ....Prov 19:14
of the LORD Are r .....Prov 22:4
r are not forever .....Prov 27:24
do you despise the r ....Rom 2:4
make known the r .....Rom 9:23
what are the r ....Eph 1:18
show the exceeding r ...Eph 2:7
the unsearchable r ......Eph 3:8
r than the treasures ...Heb 11:26
To receive power and r ..Rev 5:12

RICHLY

Christ dwell in you r ....Col 3:16
God, who gives us r ...1 Tim 6:17

RIGHT

the r of the firstborn ...Deut 21:17
"Is your heart r ......2 Kin 10:15
Lord, "Sit at My r ......Ps 110:1
a way which seems r ..Prov 14:12
clothed and in his r ...Mark 5:15
to them He gave the r ..John 1:12
your heart is not r ......Acts 8:21
seven stars in His r ....Rev 2:1

RIGHTEOUS

also destroy the r ......Gen 18:23
and they justify the r ...Deut 25:1
that he could be r ......Job 15:14
"The r see it and ......Job 22:19
r shows mercy and ......Ps 37:21
I have not seen the r .....Ps 37:25
The LORD loves the r ....Ps 146:8
r is a well of life ......Prov 10:11
r will be gladness .....Prov 10:28
r will be delivered .....Prov 11:21
r will be recompensed .Prov 11:31
the prayer of the r .....Prov 15:29
r are bold as a lion .....Prov 28:1
r considers the cause ..Prov 29:7
Do not be overly r ......Eccl 7:16
event happens to the r ...Eccl 9:2
with My r right hand ...Is 41:10
By His knowledge My r ...Is 53:11
The r perishes ....Is 57:1
they sell the r ....Amos 2:6
not come to call the r ...Matt 9:13
r men desired to see ...Matt 13:17
r will shine forth as ...Matt 13:43
that they were r ....Luke 18:9
this was a r ....Luke 23:47
"There is none r ......Rom 3:10
r man will one die ......Rom 5:7
Jesus Christ the r ....1 John 2:1

RIGHTEOUSLY

should live soberly, r ...Titus 2:12
to Him who judges r ...1 Pet 2:23

RIGHTEOUSNESS

it to him for r ....Gen 15:6
I put on r ....Job 29:14
I call, O God of my r ......Ps 4:1
from the LORD, And r .....Ps 24:5
shall speak of Your r ....Ps 35:28
the good news of r ......Ps 40:9
heavens declare His r ...Ps 50:6
R and peace have ....Ps 85:10
R will go before Him ....Ps 85:13
r endures forever ......Ps 111:3
r delivers from death ...Prov 10:2
The r of the blameless ..Prov 11:5
the way of r is life ....Prov 12:28
R exalts a nation ......Prov 14:34
He who follows r ......Prov 21:21
R lodged in it ....Is 1:21
in the LORD I have r .....Is 45:24
r will be forever ....Is 51:8
I will declare your r ......Is 57:12
r as a breastplate .....Is 59:17
r goes forth as ....Is 62:1
The Lord Our R ......Jer 23:6
to David A Branch of r ..Jer 33:15
The r of the righteous .Ezek 18:20
who turn many to r ....Dan 12:3
to fulfill all r ....Matt 3:15
exceeds the r of the ....Matt 5:20
to you in the way of r .Matt 21:32
For in it the r ....Rom 1:17
even the r of God ......Rom 3:22
accounted to him for r ..Rom 4:22
r will reign in life .....Rom 5:17
might reign through r ..Rom 5:21
ignorant of God's r ....Rom 10:3
might become the r ....2 Cor 5:21
the breastplate of r .....Eph 6:14
not having my own r .....Phil 3:9
r which we have ....Titus 3:5
not produce the r .....James 1:20

a preacher of r ....2 Pet 2:5
a new earth in which r .2 Pet 3:13
who practices r ....1 John 2:29
He who practices r ....1 John 3:7

RIGHTLY

wise uses knowledge r ..Prov 15:2
r dividing the word ....2 Tim 2:15

RISE

for He makes His sun r .Matt 5:45
third day He will r .....Matt 20:19
third day He will r .....Luke 18:33
be the first to r ....Acts 26:23
in Christ will r ......1 Thess 4:16

RISEN

there has not r ....Matt 11:11
disciples that He is r ....Matt 28:7
"The Lord is r ....Luke 24:34
then Christ is not r ...1 Cor 15:13
if Christ is not r .....1 Cor 15:17
But now Christ is r ...1 Cor 15:20

RIVER

peace to her like a r ....Is 66:12
he showed me a pure r ..Rev 22:1

RIVERS

By the r of Babylon .....Ps 137:1
All the r run into the .....Eccl 1:7
his heart will flow r ...John 7:38

ROAR

The LORD also will r ....Joel 3:16

ROARING

and the waves r ......Luke 21:25
walks about like a r .....1 Pet 5:8

ROARS

"The LORD r from ......Amos 1:2
as when a lion r.........Rev 10:3

ROB

"Will a man r God ....Mal 3:8

ROBBED

r other churches ....2 Cor 11:8

ROBBER

is a thief and a r ....John 10:1
Barabbas was a r .....John 18:40

ROBBERS

also crucified two r ...Mark 15:27
Me are thieves and r ...John 10:8

ROBBERY

did not consider it r ......Phil 2:6

ROBE

'Bring out the best r ...Luke 15:22
on Him a purple r .....John 19:2
Then a white r was .....Rev 6:11

ROBES

have stained all My r ......Is 63:3
go around in long r ....Luke 20:46
clothed with white r ......Rev 7:9

ROCK

you shall strike the r .....Ex 17:6
and struck the r ......Num 20:11
For their r is not ......Deut 32:31
"The LORD is my r ....2 Sam 22:2
And who is a r ......2 Sam 22:32
Blessed be my R .....2 Sam 22:47
For You are my r ....Ps 31:3
r that is higher than ......Ps 61:2
been mindful of the R ....Is 17:10
shadow of a great r ......Is 32:2
his house on the r ....Matt 7:24
r I will build My ....Matt 16:18

stumbling stone and r . . Rom 9:33
R that followed them . . 1 Cor 10:4

ROD
Your r and Your staff . . . . . Ps 23:4
shall come forth a R . . . . . . Is 11:1
rule them with a r . . . . . . Rev 2:27

ROOM
you a large upper r . . . Mark 14:15
no r for them in the . . . . . Luke 2:7
into the upper r . . . . Acts 1:13

ROOT
day there shall be a R . . . . Is 11:10
because they had no r . . Matt 13:6
of money is a r . . . . 1 Tim 6:10
lest any r of . . . . Heb 12:15
I am the R and the . . . . . Rev 22:16

ROOTED
r and built up in Him . . . . . Col 2:7

ROSE
end Christ died and r . . . Rom 14:9
buried, and that He r . . 1 Cor 15:4
Jesus died and r . . . . 1 Thess 4:14

RULE
And he shall r . . . . Gen 3:16
puts an end to all r . . . 1 Cor 15:24
let the peace of God r . . . Col 3:15
Let the elders who r . . . 1 Tim 5:17
Remember those who r . . Heb 13:7

RULER
to Me The One to be r . . . . Mic 5:2
by Beelzebub, the r . . . . Matt 12:24
the r of this world . . . John 12:31
'Who made you a r . . . . Acts 7:27

RULERS
And the r take counsel . . . . Ps 2:2
"You know that the r . . Matt 20:25
which none of the r . . . . . 1 Cor 2:8
powers, against the r . . . . Eph 6:12

RULES
That the Most High r . . . Dan 4:17
that the Most High r . . . Dan 4:32
r his own house well . . . . 1 Tim 3:4

RULING
r their children . . . . 1 Tim 3:12

RUMORS
hear of wars and r . . . . . Matt 24:6

RUN
r and not be weary . . . . . Is 40:31
us, and let us r . . . . Heb 12:1

S

SABAOTH
S had left us a . . . . Rom 9:29
ears of the Lord of S . . James 5:4

SABBATH
"Remember the S . . . . Ex 20:8
S was made for man . . . Mark 2:27

SABBATHS
S you shall keep . . . . Ex 31:13

SACRIFICE
to the LORD than s . . . . . Prov 21:3
For the LORD has a s . . . . . Is 34:6
of My offerings they s . . . Hos 8:13
LORD has prepared a s . . . Zeph 1:7
desire mercy and not s . . Matt 9:13
an offering and a s . . . . . . Eph 5:2
put away sin by the s . . . Heb 9:26

no longer remains a s . Heb 10:26
offer the s of praise . . . . Heb 13:15

SACRIFICED
s their sons And their . . . Ps 106:37

SACRIFICES
The s of God are a . . . . . . Ps 51:17
multitude of your s . . . . Is 1:11
priests, to offer up s . . . . Heb 7:27
s God is well pleased . . . Heb 13:16

SAFE
he has received him s . Luke 15:27

SAFELY
make them lie down s . . . Hos 2:18

SAFETY
say, "Peace and s . . . . . 1 Thess 5:3

SAINTS
s who are on the earth . . . Ps 16:3
does not forsake His s . . Ps 37:28
Is the death of His s . . . Ps 116:15
war against the s . . . . . . Dan 7:21
Jesus, called to be s . . . . 1 Cor 1:2
be glorified in His s . . 2 Thess 1:10
all delivered to the s . . . . . Jude 3
shed the blood of s . . . . . Rev 16:6

SALT
shall season with s . . . . . Lev 2:13
"You are the s . . . . Matt 5:13
s loses its flavor . . . . . . Mark 9:50

SALVATION
still, and see the s . . . . . . Ex 14:13
S belongs to the LORD . . . . Ps 3:8
is my light and my s . . . . . Ps 27:1
God is the God of s . . . . . Ps 68:20
joy in the God of my s . . . Hab 3:18
raised up a horn of s . . . Luke 1:69
"Nor is there s . . . . Acts 4:12
the power of God to s . . . Rom 1:16
now is the day of s . . . . . 2 Cor 6:2
work out your own s . . . . Phil 2:12
chose you for s . . . . . 2 Thess 2:13
neglect so great a s . . . . . Heb 2:3

SAMARITAN
a drink from me, a S . . . John 4:9

SANCTIFICATION
will of God, your s . . . 1 Thess 4:3

SANCTIFIED
they also may be s . . . . John 17:19
but you were s . . . . 1 Cor 6:11
for it is s by the . . . . 1 Tim 4:5

SANCTIFIES
For both He who s . . . . . Heb 2:11

SANCTIFY
s My great name . . . . . Ezek 36:23
"S them by Your . . . . . John 17:17
that He might s . . . . Eph 5:26

SANCTUARY
let them make Me a s . . . Ex 25:8
and the earthly s . . . . Heb 9:1

SAND
descendants as the s . . . Gen 32:12
innumerable as the s . . . Heb 11:12

SAT
into heaven, and S . . . Mark 16:19
And He who s there was . . Rev 4:3

SATAN
before the LORD, and S . . . Job 1:6
"Away with you, S . . . . . Matt 4:10

"Get behind Me, S . . . . Matt 16:23
"How can S cast out . . . Mark 3:23
S has asked for you . . . Luke 22:31
to the working of S . . . 2 Thess 2:9
known the depths of S . . Rev 2:24
years have expired, S . . . Rev 20:7

SATIATED
s the weary soul . . . . Jer 31:25

SATISFIED
I shall be s when I . . . . . Ps 17:15
that are never s . . . . . . Prov 30:15
of His soul, and be s . . . . Is 53:11

SATISFIES
s the longing soul . . . . . . Ps 107:9

SATISFY
s us early with Your . . . . . Ps 90:14
long life I will s . . . . Ps 91:16
for what does not s . . . . . . Is 55:2

SAVE
Oh, s me for Your . . . . Ps 6:4
s the children of the . . . . . Ps 72:4
s the souls of the . . . . . . Ps 72:13
That it cannot s . . . . Is 59:1
s you And deliver you . . . Jer 15:20
other, That he may s . . . Hos 13:10
JESUS, for He will s . . . Matt 1:21
s his life will . . . . Matt 16:25
s that which was . . . . . Matt 18:11
let Him s Himself if . . . Luke 23:35
but to s the world . . . . John 12:47
the world to s sinners . 1 Tim 1:15

SAVED
"He s others . . . . Matt 27:42
That we should be s . . . Luke 1:71
"Your faith has s . . . . . Luke 7:50
might be s . . . . John 3:17
them, saying, "Be s . . . Acts 2:40
what must I do to be s . Acts 16:30
which also you are s . . 1 Cor 15:2
grace you have been s . . . Eph 2:8
to His mercy He s . . . . . Titus 3:5
of those who are s . . . . Rev 21:24

SAVES
antitype which now s . . 1 Pet 3:21

SAVIOR
I, the LORD, am your S . . . Is 60:16
rejoiced in God my S . . . Luke 1:47
the city of David a S . . . Luke 2:11
up for Israel a S . . . . . Acts 13:23
God, who is the S . . . . . 1 Tim 4:10
and S Jesus Christ . . . . . Titus 2:13

SAWN
stoned, they were s . . . Heb 11:37

SAY
"But I s to you that . . . . Matt 5:22
"But who do you s . . . . Matt 16:15

SAYING
This is a faithful s . . . . . 1 Tim 1:15

SAYINGS
whoever hears these s . . Matt 7:24

SCALES
on it had a pair of s . . . . . Rev 6:5

SCARLET
your sins are like s . . . . Is 1:18

SCATTER
I will s you among the . . Lev 26:33

SCATTERED
"Israel is like s sheep . . . Jer 50:17
the sheep will be s . . . . Mark 14:27

SCATTERS
not gather with Me s ..Matt 12:30

SCEPTER
s shall not depart ......Gen 49:10

SCHEMER
Will be called a s ....Prov 24:8

SCHEMES
sought out many s ......Eccl 7:29

SCHISM
there should be no s ..1 Cor 12:25

SCHOOL
daily in the s of ....Acts 19:9

SCOFF
They s at kings ....Hab 1:10

SCOFFER
"He who corrects a s ....Prov 9:7
s is an abomination ....Prov 24:9

SCOFFERS
s will come in the ....2 Pet 3:3

SCORCHED
And men were s with ....Rev 16:9

SCORN
My friends s me ....Job 16:20

SCORNS
He s the scornful ....Prov 3:34

SCORPIONS
on serpents and s .....Luke 10:19
They had tails like s ....Rev 9:10

SCOURGE
will mock Him, and s . Mark 10:34

SCOURGES
s every son whom ......Heb 12:6

SCRIBES
"Beware of the s .....Mark 12:38

SCRIPTURE
S cannot be broken ...John 10:35
All S is given by ......2 Tim 3:16

SCRIPTURES
S must be fulfilled ....Mark 14:49

SCROLL
eat this s ....Ezek 3:1
the sky receded as a s ...Rev 6:14

SEA
drowned in the Red S ....Ex 15:4
who go down to the s ..Ps 107:23
and the s obey Him .....Matt 8:27
throne there was a s ......Rev 4:6
there was no more s ....Rev 21:1

SEAL
stands, having this s ...2 Tim 2:19

SEALED
by whom you were s ....Eph 4:30

SEAM
tunic was without s ...John 19:23

SÉANCE
"Please conduct a s ...1 Sam 28:8

SEARCH
glory of kings is to s ....Prov 25:2
s the Scriptures ....John 5:39

SEARCHED
s the Scriptures ....Acts 17:11

SEARCHES
For the Spirit s ....1 Cor 2:10

SEASON
Be ready in s and out ...2 Tim 4:2

SEASONED
how shall it be s ....Matt 5:13

SEASONS
the times and the s ...1 Thess 5:1

SEAT
shall make a mercy s ....Ex 25:17
before the judgment s .2 Cor 5:10

SEATS
at feasts, the best s .....Matt 23:6

SECRET
s things belong ....Deut 29:29
In the s place of His ......Ps 27:5
Father who is in the s ....Matt 6:6

SECRETLY
He lies in wait s ....Ps 10:9

SECRETS
For He knows the s ......Ps 44:21
God will judge the s ....Rom 2:16

SECT
to the strictest s ....Acts 26:5

SECURELY
nation that dwells s .....Jer 49:31

SEDUCED
flattering lips she s .....Prov 7:21

SEE
in my flesh I shall s ....Job 19:26
For they shall s God ....Matt 5:8
seeing they do not s ...Matt 13:13
rejoiced to s My day ....John 8:56
They shall s His face ....Rev 22:4

SEED
He shall see His s ....Is 53:10
S were the promises ....Gal 3:16
you are Abraham's s ....Gal 3:29

SEEDS
the good s are the .....Matt 13:38

SEEK
pray and s My face ....2 Chr 7:14
S the LORD while He ......Is 55:6
s, and you will find ......Matt 7:7
of Man has come to s .Luke 19:10
"You will s Me and ....John 7:34
For all s their own ......Phil 2:21
s those things which ......Col 3:1

SEEKING
like a roaring lion, s .....1 Pet 5:8

SEEKS
There is none who s ....Rom 3:11

SEEMS
is a way which s ......Prov 14:12

SEEN
s God face to face .....Gen 32:30
No one has s God at ....John 1:18
s Me has s the ....John 14:9
things which are not s .2 Cor 4:18

SEES
s his brother in need ..1 John 3:17

SELF-CONFIDENT
a fool rages and is s ...Prov 14:16

SELF-CONTROL
gentleness, s ....Gal 5:23
to knowledge s ....2 Pet 1:6

SELF-CONTROLLED
just, holy, s ....Titus 1:8

SELF-SEEKING
envy and s exist ......James 3:16

SELL
s whatever you have .. Mark 10:21

SEND
"Behold, I s you out ...Matt 10:16
has sent Me, I also s ...John 20:21

SENSES
of use have their s ......Heb 5:14

SENSIBLY
who can answer s .....Prov 26:16

SENSUAL
but is earthly, s ....James 3:15

SENT
unless they are s ......Rom 10:15

SEPARATED
it pleased God, who s ....Gal 1:15

SEPARATES
who repeats a matter s . Prov 17:9

SEPARATION
the middle wall of s .....Eph 2:14

SERAPHIM
Above it stood s ....Is 6:2

SERIOUS
therefore be s and ....1 Pet 4:7

SERPENT
s was more cunning ......Gen 3:1
"Make a fiery s ....Num 21:8
Moses lifted up the s ...John 3:14

SERPENTS
be wise as s ....Matt 10:16

SERVANT
s will rule over a son ...Prov 17:2
good and faithful s ....Matt 25:21

SERVANTS
are unprofitable s .....Luke 17:10

SERVE
to be served, but to s ..Matt 20:28
but through love s ....Gal 5:13

SERVES
"If anyone s Me ....John 12:26

SERVICE
is your reasonable s ....Rom 12:1
with good will doing s ....Eph 6:7

SERVING
fervent in spirit, s .....Rom 12:11

SET
"See, I have s ....Deut 30:15
s aside the grace ....Gal 2:21

SETTLE
"Therefore s it in .....Luke 21:14

SETTLED
O LORD, Your word is s . Ps 119:89

51

SEVEN
s churches which are . . . . . Rev 1:4

SEVENTY
"S weeks are . . . . Dan 9:24

SEVERE
not to be too s . . . . 2 Cor 2:5

SEVERITY
the goodness and s . . . . Rom 11:22

SHADE
may nest under its s . . . Mark 4:32

SHADOW
In the s of His hand . . . . Is 49:2
the law, having a s . . . . . . Heb 10:1

SHAKE
s the earth . . . . Is 2:19
I will s all nations . . . . Hag 2:7

SHAKEN
not to be soon s . . . . . . 2 Thess 2:2

SHAKES
s the Wilderness . . . . Ps 29:8

SHAME
never be put to s . . . . Joel 2:26
to put to s the wise . . . . 1 Cor 1:27
glory is in their s . . . . Phil 3:19

SHAMEFUL
For it is s even to . . . . Eph 5:12

SHARE
to do good and to s . . . . Heb 13:16

SHARING
for your liberal s . . . . . . 2 Cor 9:13

SHARP
S as a two-edged sword . . Prov 5:4

SHARPEN
s their tongue like a . . . . . . Ps 64:3

SHARPENS
My adversary s His . . . . . . Job 16:9

SHARPNESS
I should use s . . . . 2 Cor 13:10

SHEATH
your sword into the s . . John 18:11

SHEAVES
Bringing his s . . . . Ps 126:6
gather them like s . . . . Mic 4:12

SHED
which is s for many . . . Matt 26:28

SHEDDING
blood, and without s . . . . Heb 9:22

SHEEP
s will be scattered . . . . . . Zech 13:7
having a hundred s . . . . Luke 15:4
and I know My s . . . . . John 10:14
"He was led as a s . . . . . . Acts 8:32

SHEEPFOLDS
lie down among the s . . . Ps 68:13

SHEET
object like a great s . . . . Acts 10:11

SHELTER
the LORD will be a s . . . . . Joel 3:16

SHELTERS
s him all the day long . Deut 33:12

SHEOL
not leave my soul in S . . Ps 16:10
the belly of S I cried . . . . . . Jon 2:2

SHEPHERD
The LORD is my s . . . . Ps 23:1
His flock like a s . . . . Is 40:11
'I will strike the S . . . . . Matt 26:31
"I am the good s . . . . John 10:11
the dead, that great S . . Heb 13:20
S the flock of God . . . . 1 Pet 5:2
when the Chief S . . . . 1 Pet 5:4

SHEPHERDS
"And I will give you s . . . . Jer 3:15
s have led them astray . . . Jer 50:6

SHIELD
I am your s . . . . Gen 15:1
truth shall be your s . . . . . . Ps 91:4
all, taking the s . . . . Eph 6:16

SHINE
LORD make His face s . . Num 6:25
among whom you s . . . . . Phil 2:15

SHINED
them a light has s . . . . Is 9:2

SHINES
heed as a light that s . . . 2 Pet 1:19

SHINING
light is already s . . . . . . 1 John 2:8

SHIPS
down to the sea in s . . . . Ps 107:23

SHIPWRECK
faith have suffered s . . . 1 Tim 1:19

SHOOT
They s out the lip . . . . Ps 22:7

SHORT
have sinned and fall s . . . Rom 3:23

SHORTENED
those days were s . . . . . Matt 24:22

SHOUT
heaven with a s . . . . . 1 Thess 4:16

SHOW
a land that I will s . . . . . . Gen 12:1
s Him greater works . . . John 5:20

SHOWBREAD
s which was not lawful . Matt 12:4

SHOWERS
make it soft with s . . . . . . Ps 65:10

SHREWDLY
because he had dealt s . Luke 16:8

SHRINES
who made silver s . . . . . Acts 19:24

SHRIVELED
You have s me up . . . . Job 16:8

SHUFFLES
with his eyes, He s . . . . . Prov 6:13

SHUNNED
feared God and s evil . . . . . Job 1:1

SHUT
For you s up the . . . . . . Matt 23:13

SHUTS
s his eyes from seeing . . . . Is 33:15
who opens and no one s . . Rev 3:7

SICK
I was s and you . . . . . . Matt 25:36
faith will save the s . . James 5:15

SICKLE
"Thrust in Your s . . . . . . Rev 14:15

SICKNESS
will sustain him in s . . . Prov 18:14
"This s is not unto . . . . John 11:4

SICKNESSES
And bore our s . . . . Matt 8:17

SIDE
The LORD is on my s . . . . . Ps 118:6

SIFT
s the nations with the . . . . Is 30:28

SIGH
our years like a s . . . . Ps 90:9

SIGHING
For my s comes before . . . Job 3:24

SIGHT
and see this great s . . . . Ex 3:3
by faith, not by s . . . . . . 2 Cor 5:7

SIGN
will give you a s . . . . Is 7:14
seeks after a s . . . . Matt 12:39
For Jews request a s . . . 1 Cor 1:22

SIGNS
and let them be for s . . . . Gen 1:14
cannot discern the s . . . Matt 16:3
did many other s . . . . . . John 20:30

SILENCE
That You may s . . . . Ps 8:2
seal, there was s . . . . Rev 8:1

SILENT
season, and am not s . . . . . Ps 22:2

SILK
covered you with s . . . . Ezek 16:10

SILLY
They are s children . . . . . . Jer 4:22

SILVER
may buy the poor for s . . Amos 8:6
him thirty pieces of s . . Matt 26:15

SIMILITUDE
been made in the s . . . . . James 3:9

SIMPLE
making wise the s . . . . Ps 19:7

SIMPLICITY
corrupted from the s . . . 2 Cor 11:3

SIN
and be sure your s . . . . Num 32:23
Be angry, and do not s . . . . Ps 4:4
s is always before me . . . . . Ps 51:3
soul an offering for s . . . . . Is 53:10
And He bore the s . . . . Is 53:12
who takes away the s . . John 1:29
"He who is without s . . . . John 8:7
convict the world of s . . John 16:8
s entered the world . . . . . Rom 5:12
s is not imputed . . . . Rom 5:13
s shall not have . . . . Rom 6:14
Shall we sin because we . . Rom 6:15
Him who knew no s . . . 2 Cor 5:21

SINCERE
man of *s* is revealed .. 2 Thess 2:3
we are, yet without *s* .... Heb 4:15
do it, to him it is *s* .... James 4:17
say that we have no *s* .. 1 John 1:8
and he cannot *s* .... 1 John 3:9

SINCERE
and from *s* faith .... 1 Tim 1:5

SINCERITY
simplicity and godly *s* . 2 Cor 1:12

SINFUL
from me, for I am a *s* .... Luke 5:8
become exceedingly *s* .. Rom 7:13

SING
Let him *s* psalms ..... James 5:13

SINGERS
The *s* went before .... Ps 68:25

SINGING
His presence with *s* .... Ps 100:2
and spiritual songs, *s* .... Eph 5:19

SINISTER
Who understands *s* ..... Dan 8:23

SINK
I *s* in deep mire .... Ps 69:2
to *s* he cried out .... Matt 14:30

SINNED
You only, have I *s* .... Ps 51:4
"Father, I have *s* ..... Luke 15:18
for all have *s* and ...... Rom 3:23
that we have not *s* .... 1 John 1:10

SINNER
s who repents than .... Luke 15:7
the ungodly and the s . 1 Pet 4:18

SINNERS
in the path of *s* .... Ps 1:1
the righteous, but *s* .... Matt 9:13
while we were still *s* .... Rom 5:8
many were made *s* .... Rom 5:19
the world to save *s* .... 1 Tim 1:15
such hostility from *s* .... Heb 12:3

SINS
from presumptuous *s* .... Ps 19:13
You, Our secret *s* .... Ps 90:8
The soul who *s* shall ... Ezek 18:4
if your brother *s* ...... Matt 18:15
s according to the ..... 1 Cor 15:3
the forgiveness of *s* .... Eph 1:7
If we confess our *s* .... 1 John 1:9
propitiation for our *s* .. 1 John 2:2

SISTER
is My brother and *s* ... Matt 12:50

SIT
but to *s* on My right ... Matt 20:23
"*S* at My right hand ..... Heb 1:13
I will grant to *s* .... Rev 3:21

SITS
It is He who *s* above ..... Is 40:22
so that he *s* as God ... 2 Thess 2:4

SITTING
where Christ is, *s* .... Col 3:1

SKILL
hand forget its *s* .... Ps 137:5

SKILLFULNESS
guided them by the *s* .... Ps 78:72

SKIN
God made tunics of *s* .... Gen 3:21

LORD and said, "*S* .... Job 2:4
Ethiopian change his *s* .. Jer 13:23

SKIP
He makes them also *s* .... Ps 29:6

SKIPPING
upon the mountains, *S* .. Song 2:8

SKULL
to say, Place of a *S* .... Matt 27:33

SKY
s receded as a scroll ..... Rev 6:14

SLACK
The Lord is not *s* .... 2 Pet 3:9

SLAIN
is the Lamb who was *s* . Rev 5:12

SLANDER
whoever spreads *s* .... Prov 10:18

SLANDERERS
be reverent, not *s* ..... 1 Tim 3:11

SLANDEROUSLY
as we are *s* reported ..... Rom 3:8

SLAUGHTER
led as a lamb to the *s* ..... Is 53:7
as sheep for the s ...... Rom 8:36

SLAVE
commits sin is a *s* ...... John 8:34

SLAVES
should no longer be *s* .... Rom 6:6

SLAY
s the righteous .... Gen 18:25

SLEEP
God caused a deep *s* .... Gen 2:21
neither slumber nor *s* ... Ps 121:4
He gives His beloved *s* .. Ps 127:2
and many *s* .... 1 Cor 11:30
We shall not all *s* ..... 1 Cor 15:51

SLEEPERS
gently the lips of *s* ...... Song 7:9

SLEEPING
"Are you still *s* .... Matt 26:45

SLEEPLESSNESS
in labors, in *s* .... 2 Cor 6:5

SLEEPS
"Our friend Lazarus *s* . John 11:11

SLEPT
I lay down and *s* .... Ps 3:5

SLIGHTED
is the one who is *s* ..... Prov 12:9

SLING
he had, and his *s* .... 1 Sam 17:40

SLIP
Their foot shall *s* ...... Deut 32:35

SLIPPERY
set them in *s* places ..... Ps 73:18

SLOOPS
all the beautiful *s* .... Is 2:16

SLOW
hear, *s* to speak, *s* .... James 1:19

SLUGGARD
will you slumber, O *s* .... Prov 6:9

SLUMBERING
upon men, While *s* ..... Job 33:15

SMALL
And I saw the dead, *s* .. Rev 20:12

SMELL
and he smelled the *s* ... Gen 27:27

SMELLS
s the battle from afar ... Job 39:25

SMITTEN
Him stricken, *S* .... Is 53:4

SMOKE
was filled with *s* .... Rev 15:8

SMOOTH
And the rough places *s* .... Is 40:4

SMOOTH-SKINNED
man, and I am a *s* ..... Gen 27:11

SNAIL
s which melts away as .... Ps 58:8

SNARE
is a fowler's *s* .... Hos 9:8
it will come as a *s* .... Luke 21:35
and escape the *s* ...... 2 Tim 2:26

SNARED
All of them are *s* .... Is 42:22

SNARES
who seek my life lay *s* ... Ps 38:12

SNATCH
neither shall anyone *s* . John 10:28

SNATCHES
s away what was ...... Matt 13:19

SNEER
And you *s* at it .... Mal 1:13

SNIFFED
They *s* at the wind .... Jer 14:6

SNORTING
s strikes terror .... Job 39:20

SNOW
shall be whiter than *s* ..... Ps 51:7
shall be as white as *s* ...... Is 1:18

SOAKED
Their land shall be *s* ...... Is 34:7

SOAP
lye, and use much *s* ...... Jer 2:22

SOBER
the older men be *s* ...... Titus 2:2

SOBERLY
think, but to think *s* .... Rom 12:3

SODA
And like vinegar on *s* .. Prov 25:20

SODOMITES
nor homosexuals, nor *s* . 1 Cor 6:9

SOJOURNER
no *s* had to lodge .... Job 31:32

SOJOURNERS
are strangers and *s* ..... Lev 25:23

SOLD
s his birthright .... Gen 25:33

SOLDIER
s all that he had ...... Matt 13:46
but I am carnal, s ...... Rom 7:14

SOLDIER
hardship as a good s .... 2 Tim 2:3

SOLDIERS
s twisted a crown ...... John 19:2

SOLITARILY
heritage, Who dwell s ... Mic 7:14

SOLITARY
God sets the s in .... Ps 68:6

SOMEBODY
up, claiming to be s ..... Acts 5:36

SOMETHING
thinks himself to be s ..... Gal 6:3

SON
Me, 'You are My S .... Ps 2:7
is born, Unto us a S .... Is 9:6
fourth is like the S ...... Dan 3:25
will bring forth a S ...... Matt 1:21
"This is My beloved S .. Matt 3:17
Jesus, You S of God .... Matt 8:29
are the Christ, the S .. Matt 16:16
Whose S is He .... Matt 22:42
of the S of Man .... Matt 24:37
'I am the S of God .... Matt 27:43
of Jesus Christ, the S ... Mark 1:1
out, the only s .... Luke 7:12
The only begotten S .... John 1:18
that this is the S ...... John 1:34
of the only begotten S .. John 3:18
S can do nothing .... John 5:19
s abides forever .... John 8:35
you believe in the S ..... John 9:35
I said, 'I am the S ..... John 10:36
behold your s .... John 19:26
Jesus Christ is the S .... Acts 8:37
by sending His own S ... Rom 8:3
not spare His own S ... Rom 8:32
live by faith in the S ... Gal 2:20
God sent forth His S ... Gal 4:4
the knowledge of the S .. Eph 4:13
"You are My S .... Heb 1:5
though He was a S ...... Heb 5:8
but made like the S ..... Heb 7:3
"This is My beloved S .. 2 Pet 1:17
denies the S .... 1 John 2:23
One like the S of Man ... Rev 1:13

SONG
Sing to Him a new s ...... Ps 33:3
He has put a new s ...... Ps 40:3
I will sing a new s ...... Ps 144:9
they sang a new s .... Rev 5:9

SONGS
my Maker, Who gives s .. Job 35:10
and spiritual s .... Eph 5:19

SONS
s shall come from afar .... Is 60:4
He will purify the s ...... Mal 3:3
you may become s .... John 12:36
who are of faith are s .... Gal 3:7
the adoption as s .... Gal 4:5
in bringing many s ..... Heb 2:10
speaks to you as to s .... Heb 12:5

SOON
For it is s cut off .... Ps 90:10

SOOTHED
or bound up, Or s .... Is 1:6

SORCERER
But Elymas the s ...... Acts 13:8

SORCERERS
outside are dogs and s .. Rev 22:15

SORCERESS
shall not permit a s ..... Ex 22:18

SORCERY
idolatry, s .... Gal 5:20

SORES
and putrefying s .... Is 1:6

SORROW
multiply your s .... Gen 3:16
s is continually .... Ps 38:17
And He adds no s ..... Prov 10:22
Your s is incurable ..... Jer 30:15
them sleeping from s .. Luke 22:45
s will be turned ...... John 16:20
s produces repentance . 2 Cor 7:10
s as others who ..... 1 Thess 4:13
no more death, nor s .... Rev 21:4

SORROWFUL
But I am poor and s ..... Ps 69:29
he went away s ...... Matt 19:22
soul is exceedingly s .. Matt 26:38
and I may be less s ...... Phil 2:28

SORROWS
s shall be multiplied ...... Ps 16:4
by men, A Man of s .... Is 53:3
are the beginning of s .. Matt 24:8

SORRY
s that He had made man . Gen 6:6
For you were made s ... 2 Cor 7:9

SOUGHT
I s the LORD .... Ps 34:4
s what was lost .... Ezek 34:4

SOUL
with all your s .... Deut 6:5
"My s loathes my life .... Job 10:1
s draws near the Pit .... Job 33:22
will not leave my s ...... Ps 16:10
converting the s .... Ps 19:7
He restores my s .... Ps 23:3
you cast down, O my s .... Ps 42:5
Let my s live .... Ps 119:175
No one cares for my s ... Ps 142:4
me wrongs his own s ... Prov 8:36
When You make His s ... Is 53:10
s delight itself .... Is 55:2
The s of the father As .. Ezek 18:4
able to destroy both s . Matt 10:28
and loses his own s .... Matt 16:26
with all your s .... Matt 22:37
your whole spirit, s .. 1 Thess 5:23
to the saving of the s ... Heb 10:39
his way will save a s .. James 5:20
health, just as your s .... 3 John 2

SOULS
And will save the s ...... Ps 72:13
And he who wins s ... Prov 11:30
unsettling your s ...... Acts 15:24
is able to save your s . James 1:21

SOUND
voice was like the s .... Ezek 43:2
do not s a trumpet ...... Matt 6:2
s words which you .... 2 Tim 1:13

SOUNDNESS
him this perfect s ...... Acts 3:16

SOUNDS
a distinction in the s ... 1 Cor 14:7

SOW
s trouble reap .... Job 4:8
Those who s in tears .. Ps 126:5
Blessed are you who s .... Is 32:20
"They s the wind........ Hos 8:7
s is not made alive .... 1 Cor 15:36

SOWER
"Behold, a s went ...... Matt 13:3

SOWN
s spiritual things ...... 1 Cor 9:11
of righteousness is s .. James 3:18

SOWS
s the good seed is the .. Matt 13:37
'One s and another ..... John 4:37
for whatever a man s ..... Gal 6:7

SPARE
He who did not s ...... Rom 8:32
if God did not s .... 2 Pet 2:4

SPARES
s his rod hates his .... Prov 13:24

SPARK
the work of it as a s .... Is 1:31

SPARKLES
it is red, When it s .... Prov 23:31

SPARKS
to trouble, As the s ...... Job 5:7

SPARROW
s has found a home .... Ps 84:3

SPARROWS
than many s .... Matt 10:31

SPAT
Then they s on Him ... Matt 27:30

SPEAK
only the word that I s .. Num 22:35
oh, that God would s .... Job 11:5
And a time to s .... Eccl 3:7
s anymore in His name .. Jer 20:9
or what you should s .. Matt 10:19
to you when all men s .. Luke 6:26
s what I have seen .... John 8:38
He hears He will s .... John 16:13
Spirit and began to s .... Acts 2:4

SPEAKING
envy, and all evil s ..... 1 Pet 2:1

SPEAKS
to face, as a man s .... Ex 33:11
God has sent s .... John 3:34
When he s a lie .... John 8:44
he being dead still s .... Heb 11:4
of sprinkling that s .... Heb 12:24

SPEAR
His side with a s ...... John 19:34

SPEARS
And their s into .... Is 2:4

SPECK
do you look at the s ..... Matt 7:3

SPECTACLE
you were made a s ..... Heb 10:33

SPEECH
one language and one s .. Gen 11:1
his s contemptible .... 2 Cor 10:10
s always be with grace .... Col 4:6

SPEECHLESS
your mouth for the s ... Prov 31:8

SPEED
they shall come with s .... Is 5:26

SPEEDILY
I call, answer me s ...... Ps 102:2

SPEND
you s money for .... Is 55:2
amiss, that you may s .. James 4:3

SPENT
"But when he had s ... Luke 15:14

SPEW
nor hot, I will s .... Rev 3:16

SPIDER
s skillfully grasps ..... Prov 30:28

SPIES
men who had been s .... Josh 6:23

SPIN
neither toil nor s .... Matt 6:28

SPINDLE
her hand holds the s ... Prov 31:19

SPIRIT
And the S of God was .... Gen 1:2
S shall not strive .... Gen 6:3
S that is upon you .... Num 11:17
portion of your s .... 2 Kin 2:9
Then a s passed .... Job 4:15
hand I commit my s ...... Ps 31:5
The s of a man is the .. Prov 20:27
s will return to God .. Eccl 12:7
S has gathered them ..... Is 34:16
I have put My S .... Is 42:1
"The S of the Lord .... Is 61:1
S entered me when He .. Ezek 2:2
and a new s .... Ezek 18:31
"I will put My S .... Ezek 36:27
walk in a false s .... Mic 2:11
and He saw the S ..... Matt 3:16
I will put My S ...... Matt 12:18
S descending upon .... Mark 1:10
s indeed is willing .... Mark 14:38
go before Him in the s . Luke 1:17
manner of s you are of . Luke 9:55
hands I commit My s .. Luke 23:46
they had been a s ..... Luke 24:37
"God is S .... John 4:24
I speak to you are s .... John 6:63
"the S of truth .... John 14:17
but if a s or an angel .... Acts 23:9
the flesh but in the S .... Rom 8:9
does not have the S ..... Rom 8:9
s that we are children .. Rom 8:16
what the mind of the S . Rom 8:27
to us through His S .... 1 Cor 2:10
gifts, but the same S ... 1 Cor 12:4
but the S gives life ...... 2 Cor 3:6
Now the Lord is the S . 2 Cor 3:17
Having begun in the S .... Gal 3:3
has sent forth the S ...... Gal 4:6
with the Holy S ...... Eph 1:13
the unity of the S .... Eph 4:3
stand fast in one s ..... Phil 1:27
S expressly says that ... 1 Tim 4:1
S who dwells in us .... James 4:5
made alive by the S ... 1 Pet 3:18
do not believe every s .. 1 John 4:1
you know the S ...... 1 John 4:2
has given us of His S . 1 John 4:13
S who bears witness ... 1 John 5:6
not having the S .... Jude 19
I was in the S on the .... Rev 1:10
him hear what the S ..... Rev 2:7
And the S and the ...... Rev 22:17

SPIRITS
Who makes His angels s . Ps 104:4
heed to deceiving s ..... 1 Tim 4:1

SPIRITUAL
s judges all things ..... 1 Cor 2:15
However, the s is not . 1 Cor 15:46
s restore such a one ...... Gal 6:1

SPIRITUALLY
s minded is life .... Rom 8:6

SPITEFULLY
for those who s .... Matt 5:44

SPITTING
face from shame and s .... Is 50:6

SPLENDOR
on the glorious s .... Ps 145:5

SPOIL
He shall divide the s ... Is 53:12

SPOILER
I have created the s ...... Is 54:16

SPOKE
"No man ever s .... John 7:46
I was a child, I s ...... 1 Cor 13:11
in various ways s .... Heb 1:1
s as they were moved .. 2 Pet 1:21

SPOKEN
I have not s in secret ..... Is 45:19
why am I evil s .... 1 Cor 10:30

SPOKESMAN
"So he shall be your s .... Ex 4:16

SPONGE
them ran and took a s . Matt 27:48

SPOT
church, not having s .... Eph 5:27
Himself without s .... Heb 9:14

SPOTS
These are s in your ...... Jude 12

SPREAD
Then the word of God s .. Acts 6:7

SPREADS
s them out like a tent ..... Is 40:22

SPRING
Truth shall s out of ...... Ps 85:11
s send forth fresh ..... James 3:11

SPRINGING
a fountain of water s ... John 4:14

SPRINGS
And the thirsty land s ..... Is 35:7

SPRINKLE
"Then I will s .... Ezek 36:25

SPRINKLED
having our hearts s .... Heb 10:22

SPRINKLING
s that speaks .... Heb 12:24

SPROUT
and the seed should s .. Mark 4:27

SQUARES
voice in the open s ..... Prov 1:20

STAFF
this Jordan with my s .. Gen 32:10
Your rod and Your s ..... Ps 23:4
on the top of his s ..... Heb 11:21

STAGGER
they will drink and s .. Jer 25:16

STAGGERS
As a drunken man s ...... Is 19:14

STAKES
s will ever be removed ... Is 33:20

STALLS
be no herd in the s ...... Hab 3:17

STAMMERERS
s will be ready .... Is 32:4

STAMMERING
s tongue that you .... Is 33:19

STAMPING
At the noise of the s ..... Jer 47:3

STAND
one shall be able to s ... Deut 7:24
lives, And He shall s .... Job 19:25
ungodly shall not s .... Ps 1:5
not lack a man to s .... Jer 35:19
And who can s when He .. Mal 3:2
that kingdom cannot s . Mark 3:24
he will be made to s .... Rom 14:4
Watch, s fast in the ... 1 Cor 16:13
for by faith you s ...... 2 Cor 1:24
having done all, to s .... Eph 6:13
S therefore .... Eph 6:14
of God in which you s . 1 Pet 5:12
"Behold, I s at the ...... Rev 3:20

STANDARD
Lord will lift up a s ...... Is 59:19

STANDING
they love to pray s ...... Matt 6:5
and the Son of Man s ... Acts 7:56

STANDS
him who thinks he s .. 1 Cor 10:12

STAR
For we have seen His s .. Matt 2:2
Bright and Morning S .. Rev 22:16

STARS
He made the s also ...... Gen 1:16
born as many as the s .. Heb 11:12

STATE
learned in whatever s ... Phil 4:11

STATURE
in wisdom and s .... Luke 2:52

STATUTE
shall be a perpetual s .... Lev 3:17

STATUTES
the s of the Lord are ..... Ps 19:8
Teach me Your s .... Ps 119:12

STAY
S here and watch ..... Matt 26:38

STEADFAST
brethren, be s .... 1 Cor 15:58
soul, both sure and s ... Heb 6:19
Resist him, s in the ...... 1 Pet 5:9

STEADFASTLY
s set His face to go .... Luke 9:51
And they continued ... Acts 2:42

STEADFASTNESS
good order and the s ..... Col 2:5

STEADILY
could not look s .... 2 Cor 3:13

STEADY
and his hands were s .... Ex 17:12

STEAL
"You shall not s .... Ex 20:15

STEM

thieves break in and *s* . . Matt 6:19
night and *s* Him away . Matt 27:64

STEM

forth a Rod from the *s* . . . . Is 11:1

STENCH

there will be a *s* . . . . Is 3:24
this time there is a *s* . . . John 11:39

STEP

s has turned from the . . . . Job 31:7

STEPS

The *s* of a good man . . . . . Ps 37:23
And established my *s* . . . . . Ps 40:2
the LORD directs his *s* . . . Prov 16:9
should follow His *s* . . . . 1 Pet 2:21

STEWARD

be blameless, as a *s* . . . . . Titus 1:7

STEWARDS

of Christ and *s* . . . . 1 Cor 4:1

STEWARDSHIP

entrusted with a *s* . . . . . 1 Cor 9:17

STICK

'For Joseph, the *s* . . . . . Ezek 37:16

STICKS

a man gathering *s* . . . . . Num 15:32

STIFF

rebellion and your *s* . . . Deut 31:27

STIFF-NECKED

"You *s* and . . . . Acts 7:51

STILL

When I awake, I am *s* . . Ps 139:18
sea, "Peace, be *s* . . . . . . Mark 4:39

STILLBORN

burial, I say that a *s* . . . . . . Eccl 6:3

STINGS

like a serpent, And *s* . . Prov 23:32

STIR

I remind you to *s* . . . . 2 Tim 1:6

STIRRED

So the LORD *s* up the . . . . Hag 1:14

STIRS

It *s* up the dead for . . . . Is 14:9

STOCKS

s that were in the . . . . Jer 20:2

STOIC

and *S* philosophers . . . . Acts 17:18

STOMACH

Foods for the *s* . . . . 1 Cor 6:13

STOMACH'S

little wine for your *s* . . . 1 Tim 5:23

STONE

him, a pillar of *s* . . . . Gen 35:14
s shall be a witness . . . . Josh 24:27
s which the builders . . . . Ps 118:22
I lay in Zion a *s* . . . . Is 28:16
take the heart of *s* . . . . Ezek 36:26
will give him a *s* . . . . Matt 7:9
s will be broken . . . . . . Matt 21:44
s which the builders . . Luke 20:17
those works do you *s* . . John 10:32
Him as to a living *s* . . . . . 1 Pet 2:4

STONED

s Stephen as he was . . . . Acts 7:59
They were *s* . . . . Heb 11:37

STONES

Abraham from these . . . Matt 3:9
command that these *s* . . . Matt 4:3

STONY

fell on *s* ground . . . . Mark 4:5

STOOPED

And again He *s* down . . . John 8:8

STOPPED

her flow of blood *s* . . . . . Luke 8:44

STORE

exist are kept in *s* . . . . 2 Pet 3:7

STORK

s has her home in the . . . Ps 104:17

STORM

He calms the *s* . . . . Ps 107:29
for a shelter from *s* . . . . Is 4:6

STRAIGHT

Make *s* in the desert A . . . . Is 40:3
and make *s* paths for . . Heb 12:13

STRAIGHTFORWARD

that they were not *s* . . . . . Gal 2:14

STRAIN

"Blind guides, who *s* . . Matt 23:24

STRAITS

and desperate *s* . . . . Deut 28:53

STRANGE

s thing happened . . . . . . 1 Pet 4:12

STRANGER

and loves the *s* . . . . Deut 10:18
I was a *s* and you . . . . . Matt 25:35

STRANGERS

know the voice of *s* . . . . John 10:5
you are no longer *s* . . . . . Eph 2:19

STRANGLING

that my soul chooses *s* . . . Job 7:15

STRAP

than I, whose sandal *s* . . Mark 1:7

STRAW

stones, wood, hay, *s* . . . 1 Cor 3:12

STRAY

Who make my people *s* . . Mic 3:5

STRAYED

Yet I have not *s* . . . . . . Ps 119:110
some have *s* . . . . 1 Tim 6:10

STREAM

like a flowing *s* . . . . Is 66:12

STREAMS

He also brought *s* . . . . . . Ps 78:16

STREET

In the middle of its *s* . . . . Rev 22:2

STREETS

You taught in our *s* . . . Luke 13:26

STRENGTH

s no man shall . . . . 1 Sam 2:9
The LORD is the *s* . . . . Ps 27:1
is our refuge and *s* . . . . . . Ps 46:1
They go from *s* to . . . . . . Ps 84:7
S and honor are her . . . Prov 31:25
might He increases *s* . . . . Is 40:29
O LORD, my *s* and my . . . Jer 16:19

were still without *s* . . . . . Rom 5:6
s is made perfect . . . . . . 2 Cor 12:9

STRENGTHEN

And He shall *s* . . . . Ps 27:14
S the weak hands . . . . Is 35:3
s your brethren . . . . . . Luke 22:32
s the things . . . . Rev 3:2

STRENGTHENED

unbelief, but was *s* . . . . . Rom 4:20
stood with me and *s* . . . 2 Tim 4:17

STRENGTHENING

s the souls of the . . . . . . Acts 14:22

STRENGTHENS

through Christ who *s* . . . Phil 4:13

STRETCH

are old, you will *s* . . . . . John 21:18

STRETCHED

I have *s* out my hands . . . . Ps 88:9
"All day long I have *s* . Rom 10:21

STRETCHES

For he *s* out his hand . . . Job 15:25

STRICKEN

of My people He was *s* . . . . Is 53:8

STRIFE

man stirs up *s* . . . . Prov 15:18
even from envy and . . . Phil 1:15
which come envy, *s* . . . . 1 Tim 6:4

STRIKE

The sun shall not *s* . . . . . Ps 121:6
"*S* the Shepherd . . . . . . Zech 13:7
'I will *s* the Shepherd . . Matt 26:31

STRINGED

of your *s* instruments . . Amos 5:23

STRIP

S yourselves . . . . Is 32:11

STRIPES

s we are healed . . . . Is 53:5
s you were healed . . . . . 1 Pet 2:24

STRIVE

"My Spirit shall not *s* . . . . Gen 6:3
"*S* to enter through . . . Luke 13:24
the Lord not to *s* . . . . . . 2 Tim 2:14

STRIVING

for a man to stop *s* . . . . . Prov 20:3

STROKE

with a mighty *s* . . . . Jer 14:17

STRONG

The LORD *s* and mighty . . Ps 24:8
S is Your hand . . . . Ps 89:13
"When a *s* man . . . . . . Luke 11:21
We then who are *s* . . . . . Rom 15:1
weak, then I am *s* . . . . 2 Cor 12:10
my brethren, be *s* . . . . . . Eph 6:10
were made *s* . . . . Heb 11:34

STRONGHOLD

of my salvation, my *s* . . . . . Ps 18:2

STRUCK

s the rock twice . . . . Num 20:11
the hand of God has *s* . . Job 19:21
Behold, He *s* the rock . . . Ps 78:20
in My wrath I *s* . . . . Is 60:10
s the head from the . . . . Hab 3:13
took the reed and *s* . . . . Matt 27:30

STUBBLE

do wickedly will be *s* . . . . . Mal 4:1

STUBBORN
"If a man has a s . . . . . . Deut 21:18

STUBBORN-HEARTED
"Listen to Me, you s . . . . . . Is 46:12

STUBBORNNESS
do not look on the s . . . . Deut 9:27

STUDIED
having never s . . . . John 7:15

STUMBLE
have caused many to s . . . Mal 2:8
you will be made to s . . Matt 26:31
immediately they s . . . . Mark 4:17
who believe in Me to s . Mark 9:42
For we all s in many . . . James 3:2

STUMBLED
s that they should . . . . . Rom 11:11

STUMBLES
immediately he s . . . . . . Matt 13:21

STUMBLING
the deaf, nor put a s . . . . Lev 19:14
But a stone of s . . . . Is 8:14
Behold, I will lay s . . . . Jer 6:21
I lay in Zion a s . . . . Rom 9:33
this, not to put a s . . . . . Rom 14:13
of yours become a s . . . . 1 Cor 8:9
and "A stone of s . . . . 1 Pet 2:8
to keep you from s . . . . Jude 24

STUPID
hates correction is s . . . . Prov 12:1

SUBDUE
s all things to . . . . Phil 3:21

SUBJECT
for it is not s . . . . Rom 8:7
Let every soul be s . . . . Rom 13:1
all their lifetime s . . . . Heb 2:15

SUBJECTED
because of Him who s . . Rom 8:20

SUBJECTION
put all things in s . . . . Heb 2:8

SUBMISSION
his children in s . . . . 1 Tim 3:4

SUBMISSIVE
Yes, all of you be s . . . . . . 1 Pet 5:5

SUBMIT
Therefore s to God . . . . . James 4:7
s yourselves to every . . . 1 Pet 2:13

SUBSIDED
and the waters s . . . . Gen 8:1

SUBSTANCE
Bless his s . . . . Deut 33:11

SUCCESS
please give me s . . . . Gen 24:12
But wisdom brings s . . . Eccl 10:10

SUCCESSFUL
Joseph, and he was a s . . Gen 39:2

SUDDENLY
s there was with the . . . . Luke 2:13

SUE
s you and take away . . . . Matt 5:40

SUFFER
for the Christ to s . . . . . Luke 24:46
Christ, if indeed we s . . . Rom 8:17
in Him, but also to s . . . . Phil 1:29

SUFFERED
s these things and to . . Luke 24:26
for whom I have s . . . . Phil 3:8
after you have s . . . . 1 Pet 5:10

SUFFERING
anyone among you s . . James 5:13

SUFFERINGS
I consider that the s . . . Rom 8:18
perfect through s . . . . Heb 2:10

SUFFERS
Love s long and is . . . . . 1 Cor 13:4

SUFFICIENCY
but our s is from God . . . 2 Cor 3:5

SUFFICIENT
S for the day is its . . . . . . Matt 6:34

SUM
How great is the s . . . . . . Ps 139:17

SUMMER
and heat, Winter and s . . Gen 8:22

SUMPTUOUSLY
fine linen and fared s . Luke 16:19

SUN
So the s stood still . . . . Josh 10:13
s shall not strike you . . . . Ps 121:6
s returned ten degrees . . . . . Is 38:8
The s and moon grow . . . Joel 2:10
s shall go down on the . . . . Mic 3:6
for He makes His s . . . . . Matt 5:45
the s was darkened . . . Luke 23:45
do not let the s . . . . Eph 4:26
s became black as . . . . . . Rev 6:12
had no need of the s . . . . Rev 21:23

SUPPER
to eat the Lord's S . . . . 1 Cor 11:20
took the cup after s . . . 1 Cor 11:25
together for the s . . . . . . Rev 19:17

SUPPLICATION
by prayer and s . . . . Phil 4:6

SUPPLIES
by what every joint s . . . . Eph 4:16

SUPPLY
And my God shall s . . . . . Phil 4:19

SUPPORT
this, that you must s . . . Acts 20:35

SUPREME
to the king as s . . . . 1 Pet 2:13

SURE
s your sin will find . . . . Num 32:23
call and election s . . . . . . 2 Pet 1:10

SURETY
Be s for Your servant . . Ps 119:122
Jesus has become a s . . . Heb 7:22

SURROUND
LORD, mercy shall s . . . . . . Ps 32:10

SURROUNDED
also, since we are s . . . . . Heb 12:1

SURVIVOR
was no refugee or s . . . . Lam 2:22

SUSPICIONS
reviling, evil s . . . . 1 Tim 6:4

SUSTAIN
S me with cakes of . . . . . . Song 2:5

SWADDLING
Him in s cloths . . . . Luke 2:7

SWALLOW
a gnat and s a camel . . Matt 23:24

SWEAR
'You shall not s . . . . Matt 5:33
began to curse and s . . Matt 26:74

SWEARING
By s and lying . . . . Hos 4:2

SWEARS
but whoever s by the . . Matt 23:18

SWEAT
His s became like . . . . . Luke 22:44

SWEET
s are Your words . . . . . . Ps 119:103
but it will be as s . . . . Rev 10:9

SWEETNESS
mouth like honey in s . . . Ezek 3:3

SWELLING
they speak great s . . . . . 2 Pet 2:18

SWIFT
let every man be s . . . . James 1:19

SWIM
night I make my bed s . . . . . Ps 6:6

SWOON
As they s like the . . . . Lam 2:12

SWORD
s which turned every . . . . Gen 3:24
The s of the LORD is . . . . Is 34:6
'A s is sharpened . . . . . . Ezek 21:9
Bow and s of battle I . . . . Hos 2:18
to bring peace but a s . . Matt 10:34
for all who take the s . . Matt 26:52
the s of the Spirit . . . . Eph 6:17
than any two-edged s . . . Heb 4:12
mouth goes a sharp s . . . Rev 19:15

SWORDS
shall beat their s . . . . Is 2:4

SWORE
So I s in My wrath . . . . . . Heb 3:11

SWORN
"By Myself I have s . . . . Gen 22:16
"The LORD has s . . . . Heb 7:21

SYMBOLIC
which things are s . . . . Gal 4:24

SYMPATHIZE
Priest who cannot s . . . . . Heb 4:15

SYMPATHY
My s is stirred . . . . Hos 11:8

SYNAGOGUE
but are a s of Satan . . . . . . Rev 2:9

T

TABERNACLE
t He shall hide me . . . . Ps 27:5
I will abide in Your t . . . . . Ps 61:4
And will rebuild the t . . Acts 15:16
and more perfect t . . . . . . Heb 9:11

TABERNACLES
Feast of T was at hand . . John 7:2

TABLE
prepare a t before me . . . Ps 23:5

TABLES

dogs under the *t* . . . . . . Mark 7:28
of the Lord's *t* . . . . 1 Cor 10:21

TABLES

and overturned the *t* . . Matt 21:12

TABLET

is engraved On the *t* . . . Jer 17:1

TAIL

t drew a third of the . . . . . Rev 12:4

TAKE

t Your Holy Spirit . . . . Ps 51:11
"*T* My yoke upon . . . . . Matt 11:29
and *t* up his cross . . . . . Mark 8:34
My life that I may *t* . . . John 10:17

TAKEN

He was *t* from prison . . . . . Is 53:8
one will be *t* and the . . Matt 24:40
until He is *t* out of . . . . 2 Thess 2:7

TALEBEARER

t reveals secrets . . . . Prov 11:13

TALENT

went and hid your *t* . . . . Matt 25:25

TALK

shall *t* of them when . . . . Deut 6:7

TALKED

within us while He *t* . . Luke 24:32

TALKERS

both idle *t* and . . . . Titus 1:10

TAMBOURINE

The mirth of the *t* . . . . Is 24:8

TARES

the *t* also appeared . . . . Matt 13:26

TARGET

You set me as Your *t* . . . . Job 7:20

TARRY

come and will not *t* . . . . Heb 10:37

TASK

this burdensome *t* . . . . . . Eccl 1:13

TASTE

Oh, *t* and see that the . . . . . Ps 34:8
might *t* death for . . . . Heb 2:9

TASTED

t the heavenly gift . . . . Heb 6:4

TAUGHT

as His counselor has *t* . . . . Is 40:13
from man, nor was I *t* . . . Gal 1:12

TAUNT

and a byword, a *t* . . . . Jer 24:9

TAX

t collectors do the . . . . . . Matt 5:46

TAXES

t to whom *t* . . . . Rom 13:7

TEACH

"Can anyone *t* . . . . Job 21:22
T me Your paths . . . . Ps 25:4
t you the fear of the . . . . . Ps 34:11
t transgressors Your . . . Ps 51:13
So *t* us to number our . . . Ps 90:12
t you again the first . . . . . Heb 5:12

TEACHER

for One is your *T* . . . . Matt 23:8

know that You are a *t* . . . John 3:2
named Gamaliel, a *t* . . . . Acts 5:34
a *t* of the Gentiles in . . . . 1 Tim 2:7

TEACHERS

than all my *t* . . . . Ps 119:99
prophets, third *t* . . . . . . 1 Cor 12:28
and some pastors and *t* . Eph 4:11
desiring to be *t* . . . . 1 Tim 1:7
there will be false *t* . . . . . 2 Pet 2:1

TEACHES

the Holy Spirit *t* . . . . 1 Cor 2:13
the same anointing *t* . . 1 John 2:27

TEACHING

"*t* them to observe all . Matt 28:20
t every man in all . . . . Col 1:28

TEAR

I, even I, will *t* . . . . Hos 5:14
will wipe away every *t* . . Rev 21:4

TEARS

my couch with my *t* . . . . . . Ps 6:6
mindful of your *t* . . . . . . 2 Tim 1:4
it diligently with *t* . . . . . Heb 12:17

TEETH

You have broken the *t* . . . . . Ps 3:7

TELL

"Who can *t* if God . . . . Jon 3:9
t him his fault . . . . Matt 18:15
whatever they *t* . . . . Matt 23:3
He comes, He will *t* . . . . John 4:25

TEMPERATE

prize is *t* in all . . . . 1 Cor 9:25
husband of one wife, *t* . . 1 Tim 3:2

TEMPEST

And suddenly a great *t* . Matt 8:24

TEMPLE

So Solomon built the *t* . 1 Kin 6:14
Lord is in His holy *t* . . . . . . Ps 11:4
One greater than the *t* . . Matt 12:6
"Destroy this *t* . . . . John 2:19
your body is the *t* . . . . . 1 Cor 6:19
grows into a holy *t* . . . . . Eph 2:21
sits as God in the *t* . . . . 2 Thess 2:4
and the Lamb are its *t* . . Rev 21:22

TEMPLES

t made with hands . . . . . Acts 7:48

TEMPORARY

which are seen are *t* . . . 2 Cor 4:18

TEMPT

t the Lord your God . . . . . Matt 4:7
does He Himself *t* . . . . James 1:13

TEMPTATION

do not lead us into *t* . . . . Matt 6:13
man who endures . . . . James 1:12

TEMPTED

forty days, *t* by Satan . . Mark 1:13
lest you also be *t* . . . . Gal 6:1
in all points *t* . . . . Heb 4:15

TEMPTER

Now when the *t* came . . . Matt 4:3

TENDER

your heart was *t* . . . . . 2 Kin 22:19

TENDERHEARTED

to one another, *t* . . . . Eph 4:32

TENDS

t a flock and does not . . . 1 Cor 9:7

TENT

earthly house, this *t* . . . . 2 Cor 5:1

TENTMAKERS

occupation they were *t* . . Acts 18:3

TENTS

Than to dwell in the *t* . . . . . Ps 84:10

TERRESTRIAL

bodies and *t* bodies . . . 1 Cor 15:40

TERRIBLE

is great and very *t* . . . . . . Joel 2:11

TERRIFIED

and not in any way *t* . . . . Phil 1:28

TERRIFY

me with dreams And *t* . . . Job 7:14

TERRIFYING

t was the sight . . . . Heb 12:21

TERROR

are nothing, You see *t* . . . Job 6:21
not be afraid of the *t* . . . . . Ps 91:5

TERRORS

consumed with *t* . . . . Ps 73:19

TEST

said, "Why do you *t* . . . Matt 22:18
T all things . . . . 1 Thess 5:21
but *t* the spirits . . . . 1 John 4:1

TESTAMENT

where there is a *t* . . . . Heb 9:16

TESTED

God *t* Abraham . . . . Gen 22:1
Where your fathers t . . . . . Heb 3:9
though it is *t* by fire . . . . . 1 Pet 1:7

TESTIFIED

who has seen has *t* . . . . John 19:35
which He has *t* . . . . 1 John 5:9

TESTIFIES

that the Holy Spirit *t* . . Acts 20:23

TESTIFY

t what We have . . . . John 3:11
t that the Father . . . . . . 1 John 4:14

TESTIFYING

was righteous, God *t* . . . . Heb 11:4

TESTIMONIES

those who keep His *t* . . . . Ps 119:2
t are my meditation . . . . Ps 119:99

TESTIMONY

two tablets of the *T* . . . . . Ex 31:18
under your feet as a *t* . . Mark 6:11
no one receives His *t* . . . John 3:32
not believed the *t* . . . . . 1 John 5:10
For the *t* of Jesus is . . . . Rev 19:10

TESTING

came to Him, *t* Him . . . . Matt 19:3

TESTS

men, but God who *t* . . 1 Thess 2:4

THANK

"I *t* You, Father . . . . Matt 11:25
t You that I am not . . . . Luke 18:11

THANKFUL

as God, nor were *t* . . . . . . Rom 1:21

THANKFULNESS

Felix, with all *t* . . . . Acts 24:3

THANKS

the cup, and gave t .... Matt 26:27
T be to God for His .... 2 Cor 9:15

THANKSGIVING

His presence with t .... Ps 95:2
into His gates with t ..... Ps 100:4
supplication, with t ...... Phil 4:6

THEATER

and rushed into the t .. Acts 19:29

THIEF

do not despise a t ...... Prov 6:30
because he was a t ..... John 12:6
Lord will come as a t .. 2 Pet 3:10

THIEVES

And companions of t ...... Is 1:23

THINGS

in heaven give good t ... Matt 7:11
kept all these t .... Luke 2:51
share in all good t .... Gal 6:6

THINK

t you have eternal ..... John 5:39
not to t of himself ...... Rom 12:3

THINKS

Yet the LORD t upon me . Ps 40:17
For as he t in his .... Prov 23:7
t he stands take heed . 1 Cor 10:12

THIRST

those who hunger and t . Matt 5:6
in Me shall never t ..... John 6:35
anymore nor t anymore . Rev 7:16

THIRSTS

My soul t for God .... Ps 42:2
saying, "If anyone t .... John 7:37
freely to him who t ..... Rev 21:6

THIRSTY

I was t and you gave .. Matt 25:35

THISTLES

or figs from t .... Matt 7:16

THORN

a t in the flesh was .... 2 Cor 12:7

THORNBUSHES

gather grapes from t .... Matt 7:16

THORNS

Both t and thistles it .... Gen 3:18
some fell among t ..... Matt 13:7
wearing the crown of t . John 19:5

THOUGHT

You understand my t .... Ps 139:2
I t as a child .... 1 Cor 13:11

THOUGHTS

The LORD knows the t ... Ps 94:11
unrighteous man his t ..... Is 55:7
"For My t are not your .... Is 55:8
Jesus, knowing their t ... Matt 9:4
heart proceed evil t .... Matt 15:19
The LORD knows the t . 1 Cor 3:20

THREAT

shall flee at the t .... Is 30:17

THREATEN

suffered, He did not t .. 1 Pet 2:23

THREATENING

to them, giving up t ...... Eph 6:9

THREATS

still breathing t .... Acts 9:1

THREE

hope, love, these t .... 1 Cor 13:13

THRESH

it is time to t her .... Jer 51:33

THRESHING

t shall last till the .... Lev 26:5

THROAT

t is an open tomb ...... Rom 3:13

THRONE

Your t, O God, is .... Ps 45:6
Lord sitting on a t .... Is 6:1
"Heaven is My t .... Is 66:1
for it is God's t .... Matt 5:34
will give Him the t ..... Luke 1:32
"Your t, O God, is ...... Heb 1:8
come boldly to the t .... Heb 4:16
My Father on His t ..... Rev 3:21
I saw a great white t ... Rev 20:11

THRONES

invisible, whether t ...... Col 1:16

THRONG

house of God in the t .... Ps 55:14

THROW

t Yourself down .... Matt 4:6

THROWN

neck, and he were t .... Mark 9:42

THRUST

and rose up and t ...... Luke 4:29

THUNDER

The voice of Your t ...... Ps 77:18
the voice of loud t ...... Rev 14:2

THUNDERED

"The LORD t from ... 2 Sam 22:14

THUNDERINGS

the sound of mighty t ... Rev 19:6

THUNDERS

The God of glory t .... Ps 29:3

TIDINGS

I bring you good t ..... Luke 2:10

TILL

no man to t the ground ... Gen 2:5

TILLER

but Cain was a t .... Gen 4:2

TILLS

t his land will have .... Prov 28:19

TIME

pray to You In a t .... Ps 32:6
for the t is near .... Rev 1:3

TIMES

the signs of the t ...... Matt 16:3
not for you to know t .... Acts 1:7
last days perilous t ..... 2 Tim 3:1

TITHE

And he gave him a t ... Gen 14:20
For you pay t of mint .. Matt 23:23

TITHES

and to bring the t ...... Neh 10:37
Bring all the t .... Mal 3:10

TITHING

the year of t .... Deut 26:12

TITLE

Now Pilate wrote a t .. John 19:19

TITTLE

away, one jot or one t .. Matt 5:18

TODAY

T I have begotten You ..... Ps 2:7
t you will be with Me . Luke 23:43
"T, if you will hear ...... Heb 3:7
the same yesterday, t ... Heb 13:8

TOIL

t you shall eat of .... Gen 3:17

TOILED

"Master, we have t ...... Luke 5:5

TOLD

Behold, I have t .... Matt 28:7
so, I would have t ...... John 14:2

TOLERABLE

you, it will be more t .. Matt 10:15

TOMB

in the garden a new t . John 19:41

TOMBS

like whitewashed t .... Matt 23:27

TOMORROW

drink, for t we die .... Is 22:13
do not worry about t ... Matt 6:34
what will happen t ... James 4:14

TONGUE

remember you, Let my t . Ps 137:6
forever, But a lying t .. Prov 12:19
t breaks a bone ...... Prov 25:15
t should confess that .... Phil 2:11
does not bridle his t .. James 1:26
no man can tame the t . James 3:8
every nation, tribe, t .... Rev 14:6

TONGUES

From the strife of t ...... Ps 31:20
speak with new t ..... Mark 16:17
divided t, as of fire ...... Acts 2:3
I speak with the t ..... 1 Cor 13:1

TOOTH

eye for an eye and a t .. Matt 5:38

TOPHET

the high places of T ...... Jer 7:31

TORCH

and like a fiery t .... Zech 12:6

TORCHES

When he had set the t .. Judg 15:5
come with flaming t ..... Nah 2:3

TORMENT

You come here to t ..... Matt 8:29
t ascends forever ...... Rev 14:11

TORMENTED

And they will be t ...... Rev 20:10

TORMENTS

"And being in t .... Luke 16:23

TORN

of the temple was t .... Matt 27:51

TORTURED

Others were t .... Heb 11:35

TOSSED

t to and fro and .... Eph 4:14

TOTTER

drunkard, And shall t .... Is 24:20

TOUCH
"If only I may *t* ....Matt 9:21

TOUCHED
t my mouth with it ....Is 6:7

TOUCHES
He *t* the hills ....Ps 104:32

TOWER
t whose top is in the ....Gen 11:4
a watchman in the ....Is 21:5

TRACKED
t our steps So that we ..Lam 4:18

TRADERS
are princes, Whose *t* ......Is 23:8

TRADITION
transgress the *t* ....Matt 15:2
according to the *t* ....Col 2:8

TRAIN
T up a child in the ....Prov 22:6

TRAINED
those who have been *t* . Heb 12:11

TRAINING
bring them up in the *t* ....Eph 6:4

TRAITOR
also became a *t* ....Luke 6:16

TRAITORS
t, headstrong ....2 Tim 3:4

TRAMPLE
serpent you shall *t* ......Ps 91:13
swine, lest they *t* ....Matt 7:6

TRAMPLED
t the Son of God ....Heb 10:29
the winepress was *t* ....Rev 14:20

TRANCE
t I saw a vision ....Acts 11:5

TRANSFIGURED
and was *t* before them ..Matt 17:2

TRANSFORMED
this world, but be *t* .....Rom 12:2

TRANSGRESS
do Your disciples *t* .....Matt 15:2

TRANSGRESSED
"Yes, all Israel has *t* ....Dan 9:11
t your commandment . Luke 15:29

TRANSGRESSES
Whoever *t* and does not .2 John 9

TRANSGRESSION
no law there is no *t* ....Rom 4:15
deceived, fell into *t* ....1 Tim 2:14

TRANSGRESSIONS
mercies, Blot out my *t* ....Ps 51:1
For I acknowledge my *t* ...Ps 51:3
was wounded for our *t* ....Is 53:5
For the *t* of My people ....Is 53:8

TRANSGRESSOR
I make myself a *t* ....Gal 2:18

TRANSGRESSORS
Then I will teach *t* ....Ps 51:13
numbered with the *t* .....Is 53:12

TRAP
of Israel, As a *t* ....Is 8:14

TRAPS
for me, And from the *t* ..Ps 141:9

TRAVEL
you *t* land and sea ....Matt 23:15

TRAVELER
t who turns aside ....Jer 14:8

TRAVELING
lie waste, The *t* ....Is 33:8

TREACHEROUS
are insolent, *t* ....Zeph 3:4

TREACHEROUSLY
"This man dealt *t* ....Acts 7:19

TREAD
You shall *t* upon the .....Ps 91:13

TREADS
an ox while it *t* ....1 Tim 5:18
t the winepress ....Rev 19:15

TREASURE
and you will have *t* ....Matt 19:21
he who lays up *t* ......Luke 12:21
But we have this *t* ......2 Cor 4:7

TREASURED
t the words of His ......Job 23:12

TREASURER
Erastus, the *t* of the ...Rom 16:23

TREASURES
it more than hidden *t* ....Job 3:21
I will give you the *t* ....Is 45:3
for yourselves *t* ....Matt 6:19
are hidden all the *t* ....Col 2:3
riches than the *t* ....Heb 11:26

TREATY
Now Solomon made a *t* .1 Kin 3:1

TREE
you eaten from the *t* ....Gen 3:11
t Planted by the ....Ps 1:3
like a native green *t* ....Ps 37:35
t bears good fruit ......Matt 7:17
His own body on the *t* .1 Pet 2:24
the river, was the *t* ......Rev 22:2

TREES
late autumn *t* without ....Jude 12
the sea, or the *t* ....Rev 7:3

TREMBLE
That the nations may *t* ....Is 64:2
they shall fear and *t* .....Jer 33:9

TREMBLED
Then everyone who *t* ....Ezra 9:4
the earth shook and *t* .....Ps 18:7
and indeed they *t* ....Jer 4:24

TREMBLING
in fear, and in much *t* ...1 Cor 2:3
t you received ....2 Cor 7:15
flesh, with fear and *t* .....Eph 6:5

TRENCH
and he made a *t* ......1 Kin 18:32

TRESPASSES
forgive men their *t* .....Matt 6:14
not imputing their *t* ....2 Cor 5:19
who were dead in *t* ......Eph 2:1

TRIAL
concerning the fiery *t* ..1 Pet 4:12

TRIBE
the Lion of the *t* ....Rev 5:5
blood Out of every *t* ......Rev 5:9

TRIBES
t which are scattered ...James 1:1

TRIBULATION
there will be great *t* ...Matt 24:21
world you will have *t* ..John 16:33
with her into great *t* ....Rev 2:22
out of the great *t* ....Rev 7:14

TRIBULATIONS
t enter the kingdom ...Acts 14:22
but we also glory in *t* ....Rom 5:3
t that you endure .....2 Thess 1:4

TRIED
A *t* stone, a precious .....Is 28:16

TRIMMED
and *t* their lamps ....Matt 25:7

TRIUMPH
always leads us in *t* ...2 Cor 2:14

TRIUMPHED
the Lord, For He has *t*....Ex 15:1

TRODDEN
t the winepress alone .....Is 63:3

TROUBLE
few days and full of *t* ....Job 14:1
t He shall hide me ....Ps 27:5
not in *t* as other men .....Ps 73:5
will be with him in *t* .....Ps 91:15
Savior in time of *t* ....Jer 14:8
there are some who *t* .....Gal 1:7

TROUBLED
worried and *t* ....Luke 10:41
shaken in mind or *t* ...2 Thess 2:2

TROUBLES
Out of all their *t* ....Ps 25:22
will be famines and *t* ..Mark 13:8
him out of all his *t* ......Acts 7:10

TROUBLING
wicked cease from *t* .....Job 3:17

TRUE
He who sent Me is *t* ....John 7:28
Indeed, let God be *t* ......Rom 3:4
whatever things are *t* ....Phil 4:8
Him who is *t* ....1 John 5:20
for these words are *t* ....Rev 21:5

TRUMPET
deed, do not sound a *t* ...Matt 6:2
t makes an uncertain ..1 Cor 14:8
For the *t* will sound ...1 Cor 15:52

TRUST
T in the Lord ....Ps 37:3
T in the Lord with all ....Prov 3:5
Do not *t* in a friend ....Mic 7:5
who *t* in riches ....Mark 10:24

TRUSTED
"He *t* in the Lord ....Ps 22:8
"He *t* in God ....Matt 27:43

TRUSTS
But he who *t* in the ......Ps 32:10

TRUTH
led me in the way of *t*..Gen 24:48
Behold, You desire *t* ......Ps 51:6
t shall be your shield .....Ps 91:4
And Your law is *t* .....Ps 119:142

TRY

t is fallen in the ....Is 59:14
called the City of *T* ......Zech 8:3
you shall know the *t* ...John 8:32
"I am the way, the *t* ....John 14:6
He, the Spirit of *t* .....John 16:13
to Him, "What is *t* ...John 18:38
who suppress the *t* .....Rom 1:18
but, speaking the *t* ....Eph 4:15
your waist with *t* ......Eph 6:14
I am speaking the *t* .....1 Tim 2:7
they may know the *t* ..2 Tim 2:25
the knowledge of the *t* ..2 Tim 3:7
that we are of the *t* ...1 John 3:19
the Spirit is *t* ....1 John 5:6

TRY

which is to *t* you ....1 Pet 4:12

TUMULT

Your enemies make a *t* ...Ps 83:2

TUNIC

Also he made him a *t* ...Gen 37:3

TUNICS

the Lord God made *t* ...Gen 3:21

TURBAN

"Remove the *t* ....Ezek 21:26

TURN

you shall not *t* ....Deut 17:11
"Repent, *t* away from ..Ezek 14:6
on your right cheek, *t* ..Matt 5:39
t them from darkness ..Acts 26:18

TURNED

The wicked shall be *t* .....Ps 9:17
of Israel, They have *t* ......Is 1:4
and how you *t* ....1 Thess 1:9

TURNING

marvel that you are *t* .....Gal 1:6
or shadow of *t* ....James 1:17

TURNS

A soft answer *t* ....Prov 15:1
that he who *t* ....James 5:20

TURTLEDOVE

t Is heard in our land ..Song 2:12

TUTOR

the law was our *t* ....Gal 3:24

TWIST

unstable people *t* to ....2 Pet 3:16

TWO

T are better than one ....Eccl 4:9
t shall become one .....Matt 19:5
new man from the *t* .....Eph 2:15

TYPE

of Adam, who is a *t* ....Rom 5:14

U

UNAFRAID

Do you want to be *u* ....Rom 13:3

UNBELIEF

because of their *u* .....Matt 13:58
help my *u* ....Mark 9:24
did it ignorantly in *u* ..1 Tim 1:13
enter in because of *u* ....Heb 3:19

UNBELIEVERS

yoked together with *u* ..2 Cor 6:14

UNBELIEVING

Do not be *u* ....John 20:27

u nothing is pure ......Titus 1:15
"But the cowardly, *u* ....Rev 21:8

UNCIRCUMCISED

not the physically *u* ....Rom 2:27

UNCLEAN

I am a man of *u* lips ....Is 6:5
man common or *u* .....Acts 10:28
there is nothing *u* ......Rom 14:14
that no fornicator, *u* ....Eph 5:5

UNCLEANNESS

men's bones and all *u* ..Matt 23:27
flesh in the lust of *u* ....2 Pet 2:10

UNCLOTHED

we want to be *u* ....2 Cor 5:4

UNCOVERS

u deep things out of ....Job 12:22

UNDEFILED

incorruptible and *u* ......1 Pet 1:4

UNDERMINE

And you *u* your friend ...Job 6:27

UNDERSTAND

if there are any who *u* ....Ps 14:2
hearing, but do not *u* ....Is 6:9
"Why do you not *u* .....John 8:43
lest they should *u* .....Acts 28:27
some things hard to *u* ..2 Pet 3:16

UNDERSTANDING

His *u* is infinite ....Ps 147:5
lean not on your own *u* ..Prov 3:5
u will find good ....Prov 19:8
His *u* is unsearchable ....Is 40:28
also still without *u* ....Matt 15:16
also pray with the *u* ..1 Cor 14:15
the Lord give you *u* ....2 Tim 2:7
Who is wise and *u* ....James 3:13

UNDERSTANDS

There is none who u ....Rom 3:11

UNDERSTOOD

Then I *u* their end ......Ps 73:17
clearly seen, being *u* ....Rom 1:20

UNDESIRABLE

gather together, O *u* ....Zeph 2:1

UNDIGNIFIED

I will be even more *u* .2 Sam 6:22

UNDISCERNING

u, untrustworthy ....Rom 1:31

UNDONE

"Woe is me, for I am *u* .....Is 6:5

UNEDUCATED

that they were *u* ....Acts 4:13

UNFAITHFUL

way of the *u* is hard ...Prov 13:15

UNFAITHFULLY

back and acted *u* ....Ps 78:57

UNFORGIVING

unloving, *u* ....Rom 1:31

UNFORMED

substance, being yet *u* ..Ps 139:16

UNFRUITFUL

and it becomes *u* ......Mark 4:19

UNGODLINESS

heaven against all *u* ....Rom 1:18

UNGODLY

u shall not stand ....Ps 1:5
Christ died for the *u* .....Rom 5:6

UNHOLY

the holy and *u* ....Ezek 22:26

UNINFORMED

the place of the *u* ....1 Cor 14:16

UNINTENTIONALLY

kills his neighbor *u* .....Deut 4:42

UNITE

U my heart to fear ......Ps 86:11

UNITY

to dwell together in *u* ...Ps 133:1
to keep the *u* of the ......Eph 4:3

UNJUST

commended the *u* ......Luke 16:8
of the just and the *u* ...Acts 24:15
For God is not *u* ....Heb 6:10

UNJUSTLY

long will you judge *u* .....Ps 82:2

UNKNOWN

To The *U* God ....Acts 17:23

UNLEAVENED

the Feast of *U* Bread ....Ex 12:17

UNLOVING

untrustworthy, *u* ....Rom 1:31

UNMERCIFUL

unforgiving, *u* ....Rom 1:31

UNPREPARED

with me and find you *u* .2 Cor 9:4

UNPRESENTABLE

u parts have greater ..1 Cor 12:23

UNPROFITABLE

'We are *u* servants ....Luke 17:10
for that would be *u* ....Heb 13:17

UNPUNISHED

wicked will not go *u* ...Prov 11:21

UNQUENCHABLE

up the chaff with *u* .....Matt 3:12

UNRESTRAINED

that the people were *u* ...Ex 32:25

UNRIGHTEOUS

u man his thoughts ....Is 55:7
u will not inherit the ....1 Cor 6:9

UNRIGHTEOUSNESS

all ungodliness and *u* ...Rom 1:18
cleanse us from all *u* ..1 John 1:9
All *u* is sin ....1 John 5:17

UNRULY

those who are *u* .....1 Thess 5:14

UNSEARCHABLE

u are His judgments ...Rom 11:33

UNSKILLED

only of milk is *u* ....Heb 5:13

UNSPOTTED

to keep oneself *u* .....James 1:27

UNSTABLE

U as water ....Gen 49:4

UNSTOPPED
of the deaf shall be *u* ......Is 35:5

UNTAUGHT
which *u* and unstable ..2 Pet 3:16

UNTRUSTWORTHY
undiscerning, *u* ....Rom 1:31

UNWASHED
eat bread with *u* hands ..Mark 7:5

UNWISE
Therefore do not be *u* ...Eph 5:17

UNWORTHY
u manner will be .....1 Cor 11:27

UPHOLD
U me according to ....Ps 119:116

UPHOLDING
u all things by the ....Heb 1:3

UPHOLDS
LORD *u* all who fall .....Ps 145:14

UPPER
show you a large *u* ...Mark 14:15

UPRIGHT
u is His delight ....Prov 15:8

UPRIGHTNESS
princes for their *u* .....Prov 17:26

UPROOT
u the wheat with ......Matt 13:29

URIM
Thummim and Your *U* ..Deut 33:8

US
"God with *u* ....Matt 1:23
If God is for *u* ....Rom 8:31
of them were of *u* ....1 John 2:19

USE
who spitefully *u* you ....Matt 5:44
u liberty as an ....Gal 5:13

USELESS
one's religion is *u* .....James 1:26

USES
if one *u* it lawfully ......1 Tim 1:8

USING
u liberty as a ....1 Pet 2:16

USURY
'Take no *u* or ....Lev 25:36

UTTER
u dark sayings of old .....Ps 78:2

UTTERANCE
the Spirit gave them *u* ...Acts 2:4

UTTERED
which cannot be *u* .....Rom 8:26

UTTERMOST
u those who come ......Heb 7:25

UTTERS
Day unto day *u* speech ....Ps 19:2

V

VAGABOND
v you shall be on the ....Gen 4:12

VAIN
the people plot a *v* ....Ps 2:1
you believed in *v* ......1 Cor 15:2

VALIANT
They are not *v* for the .....Jer 9:3

VALIANTLY
God we will do *v* ....Ps 60:12

VALLEY
v shall be exalted ....Is 40:4

VALOR
a mighty man of *v* ...1 Sam 16:18

VALUE
of more *v* than they ....Matt 6:26

VALUED
It cannot be *v* in the ....Job 28:16

VANISH
knowledge, it will *v* ...1 Cor 13:8

VANISHED
and He *v* from their ...Luke 24:31

VANITY
of vanities, all is *v* ....Eccl 1:2

VAPOR
best state is but *v* ....Ps 39:5
It is even a *v* that .....James 4:14

VARIATION
whom there is no *v* ...James 1:17

VEGETABLES
and let them give us *v* ...Dan 1:12
is weak eats only *v* .....Rom 14:2

VEHEMENT
of fire, A most *v* ....Song 8:6

VEIL
v of the temple was ....Matt 27:51
Presence behind the *v* ...Heb 6:19

VENGEANCE
V is Mine ....Deut 32:35

VENOM
It becomes cobra *v* .....Job 20:14

VESSEL
like a potter's *v* ....Ps 2:9
for he is a chosen *v* .....Acts 9:15

VESSELS
treasure in earthen *v* ....2 Cor 4:7

VEXED
grieved, and I was *v* .....Ps 73:21

VICE
as a cloak for *v* ....1 Pet 2:16

VICTIM
And plucked the *v* ......Job 29:17

VICTORY
v that has overcome ...1 John 5:4

VIEW
"Go, *v* the land ....Josh 2:1

VIGILANT
Be sober, be *v* ....1 Pet 5:8

VIGOR
nor his natural *v* .....Deut 34:7

VILE
them up to *v* passions ..Rom 1:26

VINDICATED
know that I shall be *v* ..Job 13:18

VINDICATION
Let my *v* come from ......Ps 17:2

VINE
"I am the true *v* ....John 15:1

VINEDRESSER
and My Father is the *v* .John 15:1

VINEGAR
As *v* to the teeth and ..Prov 10:26

VINES
foxes that spoil the *v* ...Song 2:15

VINEYARD
Who plants a *v* and .....1 Cor 9:7

VIOLENCE
was filled with *v* ....Gen 6:11
of heaven suffers *v* ....Matt 11:12

VIOLENT
haters of God, *v* ....Rom 1:30

VIPER
And stings like a *v* ....Prov 23:32

VIPERS
to them, "Brood of *v* .....Matt 3:7

VIRGIN
v shall conceive ....Is 7:14
"Behold, the *v* shall ....Matt 1:23

VIRGINS
v who took their lamps .Matt 25:1

VIRTUE
to your faith *v* ....2 Pet 1:5

VISAGE
v was marred more than .Is 52:14

VISIBLE
that are on earth, *v* ......Col 1:16

VISION
in a trance I saw a *v* ....Acts 11:5
to the heavenly *v* ......Acts 26:19

VISIONS
young men shall see *v* ...Joel 2:28

VISIT
v orphans and ....James 1:27

VISITATION
God in the day of *v* ....1 Pet 2:12

VISITED
Israel, for He has *v* ....Luke 1:68

VISITING
v the iniquity of the ......Ex 20:5

VISITOR
am a foreigner and a *v* ..Gen 23:4

VITALITY
v was turned into the .....Ps 32:4

VOICE
fire a still small *v* .....1 Kin 19:12
if you will hear His *v* .....Ps 95:7
"The *v* of one crying ....Matt 3:3
And suddenly a *v* ....Matt 3:17
for they know his *v* ....John 10:4

VOICES

the truth hears My *v* . . John 18:37
If anyone hears My *v* . . . . Rev 3:20

VOICES

And there were loud *v* . . Rev 11:15

VOID

they are a nation *v* . . . . Deut 32:28
heirs, faith is made *v* . . . Rom 4:14

VOLUME

in the *v* of the book . . . . . Heb 10:7

VOLUNTEERS

Your people shall be *v* . . . Ps 110:3

VOMIT

returns to his own *v* . . . . 2 Pet 2:22

VOW

for he had taken a *v* . . . Acts 18:18

VOWS

to reconsider his *v* . . . . Prov 20:25

W

WAGE

w the good warfare . . . . 1 Tim 1:18

WAGES

For the *w* of sin is . . . . . . Rom 6:23
Indeed the *w* of the . . . . James 5:4

WAIL

"Son of man, *w* . . . . Ezek 32:18

WAILING

There will be *w* . . . . Matt 13:42

WAIT

w patiently for Him . . . . Ps 37:7
those who *w* on the . . . . . . Is 40:31
To those who eagerly *w* . Heb 9:28

WAITED

w patiently for the . . . . Ps 40:1
Divine longsuffering *w* . 1 Pet 3:20

WAITING

ourselves, eagerly *w* . . . . Rom 8:23
from that time *w* . . . . Heb 10:13

WAITS

the creation eagerly *w* . . Rom 8:19

WAKE

that whether we *w* . . . 1 Thess 5:10

WALK

w before Me and be . . . . . Gen 17:1
Yea, though I *w* . . . . Ps 23:4
W prudently when you . . . Eccl 5:1
"This is the way, *w* . . . . . . Is 30:21
be weary, they shall *w* . . Is 40:31
w humbly with your God . Mic 6:8
W while you have the . John 12:35
so we also should *w* . . . . Rom 6:4
For we *w* by faith . . . . . . 2 Cor 5:7
W in the Spirit . . . . Gal 5:16
And *w* in love . . . . Eph 5:2
that you may *w* worthy . . Col 1:10
and they shall *w* . . . . Rev 3:4

WALKED

Methuselah, Enoch *w* . . . Gen 5:22
The people who *w* . . . . Is 9:2
in which you once *w* . . . . . Eph 2:2

WALKING

not *w* in craftiness . . . . . . 2 Cor 4:2

WALKS

the LORD your God *w* . . Deut 23:14
is the man Who *w* . . . . Ps 1:1
he who *w* in darkness . John 12:35
adversary the devil *w* . . . 1 Pet 5:8

WALL

then the *w* of the city . . . . Josh 6:5
you whitewashed *w* . . . . Acts 23:3
a window in the *w* . . . 2 Cor 11:33
Now the *w* of the city . . Rev 21:14

WALLS

By faith the *w* of . . . . Heb 11:30

WANDER

they have loved to *w* . . . . Jer 14:10

WANDERED

They *w* in deserts and . Heb 11:38

WANDERERS

And they shall be *w* . . . . . Hos 9:17

WANDERING

w stars for whom is . . . . . . Jude 13

WANDERS

among you *w* . . . . James 5:19

WANT

I shall not *w* . . . . Ps 23:1

WANTING

balances, and found *w* . . Dan 5:27

WANTON

have begun to grow *w* . 1 Tim 5:11

WAR

"There is a noise of *w* . . . Ex 32:17
w may rise against . . . . Ps 27:3
shall they learn *w* . . . . Is 2:4
going to make *w* . . . . . Luke 14:31
You fight and *w* . . . . . . James 4:2
fleshly lusts which *w* . . . 1 Pet 2:11
judges and makes *w* . . . . Rev 19:11

WARFARE

to her, That her *w* . . . . Is 40:2
w entangles . . . . 2 Tim 2:4

WARMED

in peace, be *w* . . . . James 2:16

WARMING

she saw Peter *w* . . . . . . Mark 14:67

WARMS

w them in the dust . . . . . Job 39:14

WARN

w those who are . . . . . 1 Thess 5:14

WARNED

Then, being divinely *w* . Matt 2:12
Who *w* you to flee . . . . Matt 3:7

WARNING

w every man and . . . . Col 1:28

WARPED

such a person is *w* . . . . . Titus 3:11

WARRING

w against the law of . . . . Rom 7:23

WARRIOR

He runs at me like a *w* . Job 16:14

WARS

you will hear of *w* . . . . . . Matt 24:6
Where do *w* and fights . James 4:1

WASH

w myself with snow . . . . . Job 9:30
W me thoroughly . . . . Ps 51:2
w His feet with her . . . . Luke 7:38
said to him, "Go, *w* . . . . . John 9:7
w the disciples' . . . . John 13:5
w away your sins . . . . . Acts 22:16

WASHED

w his hands before . . . . Matt 27:24
But you were *w* . . . . 1 Cor 6:11
Him who loved us and *w* . Rev 1:5

WASHING

us, through the *w* . . . . Titus 3:5

WASHINGS

and drinks, various *w* . . . Heb 9:10

WASTE

the cities are laid *w* . . . . . . Is 6:11
"Why this *w* . . . . Matt 26:8

WASTED

this fragrant oil *w* . . . . . Mark 14:4

WASTELAND

w shall be glad . . . . Is 35:1

WASTING

that this man was *w* . . . . Luke 16:1

WATCH

is past, And like a *w* . . . . Ps 90:4
"*W* therefore . . . . Matt 24:42

WATCHED

he would have *w* . . . . . . Matt 24:43

WATCHES

Blessed is he who *w* . . . . Rev 16:15

WATCHFUL

But you be *w* in all . . . . . 2 Tim 4:5

WATCHING

he comes, will find *w* . Luke 12:37

WATCHMAN

I have made you a *w* . . . Ezek 3:17

WATCHMEN

I have set *w* on your . . . . . . Is 62:6

WATER

Eden to *w* the garden . . . Gen 2:10
I am poured out like *w* . . . Ps 22:14
For I will pour *w* . . . . Is 44:3
given you living *w* . . . . . John 4:10
rivers of living *w* . . . . . . John 7:38
can yield both salt *w* . . James 3:12
the Spirit, the *w* . . . . 1 John 5:8
are clouds without *w* . . . . Jude 12
let him take the *w* . . . . . Rev 22:17

WATERED

I planted, Apollos *w* . . . . 1 Cor 3:6

WATERS

me beside the still *w* . . . . . Ps 23:2
Though its *w* roar and . . . . Ps 46:3
your bread upon the *w* . . Eccl 11:1
thirsts, Come to the *w* . . . . Is 55:1
fountain of living *w* . . . . . Jer 2:13
living fountains of *w* . . . . Rev 7:17

WAVE

Its fruit shall *w* . . . . Ps 72:16

WAVER

He did not *w* at the . . . . . Rom 4:20

WAVERING

of our hope without *w* . Heb 10:23

WAVES
sea, tossed by the w ...Matt 14:24

WAX
My heart is like w ....Ps 22:14

WAY
As for God, His w ...2 Sam 22:31
the LORD knows the w .....Ps 1:6
Teach me Your w ......Ps 27:11
in the w everlasting ....Ps 139:24
w that seems right ....Prov 14:12
The w of the just is ....Is 26:7
wicked forsake his w ......Is 55:7
And pervert the w ......Amos 2:7
he will prepare the w .....Mal 3:1
and broad is the w ......Matt 7:13
will prepare Your w ...Matt 11:10
to him, "I am the w ....John 14:6
to him he w ....Acts 18:26
to have known the w ...2 Pet 2:21

WAYS
For all His w are ....Deut 32:4
transgressors Your w ...Ps 51:13
w please the LORD ......Prov 16:7
"Stand in the w ....Jer 6:16
and owns all your w ....Dan 5:23
w are everlasting ....Hab 3:6
unstable in all his w ....James 1:8
and true are Your w ....Rev 15:3

WEAK
gives power to the w .....Is 40:29
knee will be as w ......Ezek 7:17
but the flesh is w ......Matt 26:41
Receive one who is w ...Rom 14:1
God has chosen the w .1 Cor 1:27
We are w ....1 Cor 4:10
w I became as w ......1 Cor 9:22
For when I am w .....2 Cor 12:10

WEAKENED
w my strength in the ...Ps 102:23

WEAKENS
w the hands of the men ..Jer 38:4

WEAKER
the wife, as to the w .....1 Pet 3:7

WEAKNESS
w were made strong ...Heb 11:34

WEAKNESSES
also helps in our w .....Rom 8:26

WEALTH
W gained by ....Prov 13:11

WEALTHY
rich, have become w ....Rev 3:17

WEANED
w child shall put his ....Is 11:8

WEAPON
w formed against you ....Is 54:17

WEAPONS
For the w of our ....2 Cor 10:4

WEAR
'What shall we w ....Matt 6:31

WEARIED
You have w Me with .....Is 43:24
therefore, being w ....John 4:6

WEARINESS
say, 'Oh, what a w ......Mal 1:13

WEARISOME
and much study is w ...Eccl 12:12

WEARY
shall run and not be w ...Is 40:31
And let us not grow w ....Gal 6:9
do not grow w in ....2 Thess 3:13

WEATHER
'It will be fair w ....Matt 16:2

WEDDING
day there was a w ....John 2:1

WEEK
the first day of the w ...Matt 28:1

WEEKS
w are determined ......Dan 9:24

WEEP
A time to w ....Eccl 3:4
You shall w no more .....Is 30:19
are you who w ....Luke 6:21
do not w ....Luke 23:28
w with those who w ....Rom 12:15

WEEPING
the noise of the w ......Ezra 3:13
They shall come with w ..Jer 31:9
There will be w ....Matt 8:12
by the tomb w ....John 20:11

WEIGH
O Most Upright, You w ....Is 26:7

WEIGHED
You have been w ....Dan 5:27

WEIGHS
eyes, But the LORD w ...Prov 16:2

WEIGHT
us lay aside every w ....Heb 12:1

WEIGHTIER
have neglected the w ..Matt 23:23

WELFARE
does not seek the w ......Jer 38:4

WELL
have done w ....Prov 31:29
wheel broken at the w ...Eccl 12:6
"Those who are w ......Matt 9:12
said to him, 'W done ..Matt 25:21

WELLS
These are w without ...2 Pet 2:17

WENT
They w out from us ...1 John 2:19

WEPT
out and w bitterly .....Matt 26:75
saw the city and w ....Luke 19:41
Jesus w ....John 11:35

WET
his body was w with ....Dan 4:33

WHEAT
w falls into the ....John 12:24

WHEEL
in the middle of a w ....Ezek 1:16

WHEELS
noise of rattling w ......Nah 3:2

WHERE
not knowing w he was ..Heb 11:8

WHIP
A w for the horse ......Prov 26:3

WHIRLWIND
Job out of the w ....Job 38:1
has His way In the w ....Nah 1:3

WHISPER
my ear received a w .....Job 4:12

WHISPERER
w separates the best ...Prov 16:28

WHISPERERS
they are w ....Rom 1:29

WHISPERINGS
backbitings, w ....2 Cor 12:20

WHITE
clothed in w garments ....Rev 3:5
behold, a w horse ....Rev 6:2
and made them w ....Rev 7:14

WHOLE
w body were an eye ..1 Cor 12:17

WHOLESOME
not consent to w words .1 Tim 6:3

WHOLLY
w followed the LORD ....Deut 1:36

WICKED
w shall be silent ....1 Sam 2:9
w shall be no more ....Ps 37:10
if there is any w ....Ps 139:24
w forsake his way ....Is 55:7
And desperately w ......Jer 17:9
the sway of the w ....1 John 5:19

WICKEDLY
God will never do w ....Job 34:12

WICKEDNESS
LORD saw that the w .....Gen 6:5
in the tents of w ....Ps 84:10
man repented of his w ....Jer 8:6
is full of greed and w .Luke 11:39
sexual immorality, w ...Rom 1:29
and overflow of w ....James 1:21

WIDE
open your hand w ......Deut 15:8
w is the gate and ....Matt 7:13
to you, our heart is w ..2 Cor 6:11

WIDOW
the fatherless and w ....Ps 146:9
How like a w is she ......Lam 1:1
Then one poor w .....Mark 12:42
w has children or ....1 Tim 5:4

WIDOW'S
And I caused the w ....Job 29:13

WIDOWS
w were neglected ....Acts 6:1
visit orphans and w ...James 1:27

WIFE
and be joined to his w ...Gen 2:24
w finds a good thing ...Prov 18:22
But a prudent w ....Prov 19:14
"Go, take yourself a w ...Hos 1:2
divorces his w ....Mark 10:11
'I have married a w ...Luke 14:20
"Remember Lot's w ...Luke 17:32
so love his own w ....Eph 5:33
the husband of one w ...Titus 1:6
bride, the Lamb's w ....Rev 21:9

WILD
olive tree which is w ..Rom 11:24

WILDERNESS
I will make the w ....Is 41:18

WILES

of one crying in the w ...Matt 3:3
the serpent in the w ....John 3:14

WILES

to stand against the w ...Eph 6:11

WILL

w be done On earth as ..Matt 6:10
but he who does the w ..Matt 7:21
not My w ....Luke 22:42
flesh, nor of the w .....John 1:13
not to do My own w ....John 6:38
w is present with me ...Rom 7:18
and perfect w of God ...Rom 12:2
works in you both to w ..Phil 2:13
according to His own w ..Heb 2:4
work to do His w ......Heb 13:21

WILLFULLY

For if we sin w ....Heb 10:26
For this they w ....2 Pet 3:5

WILLING

If you are w and ....Is 1:19
The spirit indeed is w .Matt 26:41
w that any should ....2 Pet 3:9

WILLINGLY

by compulsion but w ....1 Pet 5:2

WILLOWS

our harps Upon the w ...Ps 137:2

WILLS

to whom the Son w ....Matt 11:27
it is not of him who w ..Rom 9:16
say, "If the Lord w ....James 4:15

WIN

to all, that I might w ...1 Cor 9:19

WIND

the chaff which the w ......Ps 1:4
reed shaken by the w ...Matt 11:7
"The w blows where ....John 3:8
of a rushing mighty w ...Acts 2:2

WINDOWS

not open for you the w ..Mal 3:10

WINDS

be, that even the w .....Matt 8:27

WINDSTORM

And a great w arose ...Mark 4:37

WINE

W is a mocker ....Prov 20:1
love is better than w ....Song 1:2
Yes, come, buy w ....Is 55:1
they gave Him sour w .Matt 27:34
do not be drunk with w .Eph 5:18
not given to much w ....Titus 2:3

WINEBIBBERS

Do not mix with w ....Prov 23:20

WINEPRESS

"I have trodden the w .....Is 63:3
into the great w ....Rev 14:19
Himself treads the w ..Rev 19:15

WINESKINS

new wine into old w ....Matt 9:17

WING

One w of the cherub ...1 Kin 6:24

WINGS

the shadow of Your w ....Ps 36:7
With healing in His w ...Mal 4:2

WINNOW

You shall w them ....Is 41:16

WINS

w souls is wise ....Prov 11:30

WINTER

For lo, the w is past ....Song 2:11
flight may not be in w .Matt 24:20

WIPE

w away every tear ......Rev 21:4

WISDOM

for this is your w ....Deut 4:6
man who finds w ....Prov 3:13
Get w ....Prov 4:5
is the beginning of w ...Prov 9:10
w is justified by her ...Matt 11:19
Jesus increased in w ...Luke 2:52
riches both of the w ...Rom 11:33
the gospel, not with w .1 Cor 1:17
w of this world ....1 Cor 3:19
not with fleshly w .....2 Cor 1:12
all the treasures of w .....Col 2:3
If any of you lacks w ...James 1:5
power and riches and w .Rev 5:12

WISE

Do not be w in your .....Prov 3:7
who wins souls is w ...Prov 11:30
Therefore be w as .....Matt 10:16
five of them were w ....Matt 25:2
to God, alone w ....Rom 16:27
Where is the w ....1 Cor 1:20
not as fools but as w ....Eph 5:15
able to make you w ...2 Tim 3:15

WISELY

you do not inquire w ....Eccl 7:10

WISER

he was w than all men .1 Kin 4:31
of God is w than men ..1 Cor 1:25

WISH

w it were already .....Luke 12:49

WISHED

Then he w death for ......Jon 4:8

WITCHCRAFT

is as the sin of w .....1 Sam 15:23

WITHDRAW

From such w yourself ...1 Tim 6:5

WITHER

also shall not w ....Ps 1:3

WITHERS

The grass w ....Is 40:7
The grass w ....1 Pet 1:24

WITHHELD

And your sins have w ....Jer 5:25

WITHHOLD

good thing will He w ....Ps 84:11

WITHOUT

pray w ceasing ......1 Thess 5:17
w works is dead ......James 2:26

WITHSTAND

you may be able to w ...Eph 6:13

WITHSTOOD

I w him to his face ......Gal 2:11

WITNESS

all the world as a w ...Matt 24:14
This man came for a w ..John 1:7
do not receive Our w ...John 3:11
Christ, the faithful w ....Rev 1:5
beheaded for their w ....Rev 20:4

WITNESSED

is revealed, being w ....Rom 3:21

WITNESSES

"You are My w ....Is 43:10
presence of many w ...1 Tim 6:12
so great a cloud of w ....Heb 12:1

WIVES

Husbands, love your w ..Eph 5:25
w must be reverent ....1 Tim 3:11

WOLF

The w and the lamb ......Is 65:25

WOLVES

out as lambs among w .Luke 10:3
savage w ....Acts 20:29

WOMAN

She shall be called W ...Gen 2:23
whoever looks at a w ...Matt 5:28
Then the w of Samaria ..John 4:9
"W, behold your ......John 19:26
natural use of the w ....Rom 1:27
His Son, born of a w ......Gal 4:4
w being deceived ......1 Tim 2:14
w clothed with the sun ..Rev 12:1

WOMB

nations are in your w ..Gen 25:23
in the w I knew you ....Jer 1:5
is the fruit of your w ...Luke 1:42

WOMEN

O fairest among w ......Song 1:8
w will be grinding .....Matt 24:41
are you among w ....Luke 1:28
admonish the young w ..Titus 2:4
times, the holy w ....1 Pet 3:5

WONDER

marvelous work and a w .Is 29:14

WONDERFUL

Things too w for me .....Job 42:3
name will be called W ......Is 9:6

WONDERFULLY

fearfully and w made ...Ps 139:14

WONDERS

"And I will show w .....Joel 2:30
signs, and lying w ....2 Thess 2:9

WONDROUS

w works declare that .....Ps 75:1

WONDROUSLY

God, Who has dealt w ..Joel 2:26

WOOD

precious stones, w .....1 Cor 3:12

WOODCUTTERS

but let them be w ....Josh 9:21

WOOL

They shall be as w ....Is 1:18
hair were white like w ..Rev 1:14

WORD

w is very near you ....Deut 30:14
w I have hidden ....Ps 119:11
w is a lamp to my feet .Ps 119:105
Every w of God is pure .Prov 30:5
the w of our God ....Is 40:8
for every idle w ......Matt 12:36
The seed is the w ......Luke 8:11
beginning was the W ....John 1:1
W became flesh and ....John 1:14
Your w is truth ....John 17:17
Let the w of Christ ......Col 3:16
to you in w only ......1 Thess 1:5

WORDS

by the *w* of His power ....Heb 1:3
For the *w* of God is .....Heb 4:12
does not stumble in *w* ...James 3:2
through the *w* of God ..1 Pet 1:23
let us not love in *w* ...1 John 3:18
name is called The *W* ..Rev 19:13

WORDS

Let the *w* of my mouth ..Ps 19:14
The *w* of the wise are ..Eccl 12:11
pass away, but My *w* ..Matt 24:35
You have the *w* of .....John 6:68
not with wisdom of *w* ..1 Cor 1:17
those who hear the *w* ....Rev 1:3

WORK

day God ended His *w* ....Gen 2:2
people had a mind to *w* ..Neh 4:6
the *w* of Your fingers ......Ps 8:3
Man goes out to his *w* ..Ps 104:23
w is honorable and ......Ps 111:3
will bring every *w* ....Eccl 12:14
For I will *w* a *w* ....Hab 1:5
could do no mighty *w* ..Mark 6:5
"This is the *w* of God ...John 6:29
"I must *w* the works ....John 9:4
w which You have ....John 17:4
know that all things *w* ..Rom 8:28
w is no longer *w* ......Rom 11:6
Do not destroy the *w* ..Rom 14:20
abounding in the *w* ...1 Cor 15:58
If anyone will not *w* .2 Thess 3:10
but a doer of the *w* ...James 1:25

WORKED

which He *w* in Christ ...Eph 1:20

WORKER

w is worthy of his .....Matt 10:10
w who does not need ..2 Tim 2:15

WORKERS

we are God's fellow *w* ..1 Cor 3:9

WORKING

Father has been *w* .....John 5:17
through faith in the *w* ....Col 2:12

WORKMANSHIP

For we are His *w* ....Eph 2:10

WORKS

are Your wonderful *w* ....Ps 40:5
And let her own *w* ....Prov 31:31
"For I know their *w* .....Is 66:18
show Him greater *w* ....John 5:20
w that I do he will do .John 14:12
might stand, not of *w* ...Rom 9:11
same God who *w* ......1 Cor 12:6
not justified by the *w* ....Gal 2:16
Now the *w* of the flesh ...Gal 5:19
not of *w*, lest anyone .....Eph 2:9
for it is God who *w* ......Phil 2:13
but does not have *w* ...James 2:14
also justified by *w* ....James 2:25
"I know your *w* ....Rev 2:2
their *w* follow them ....Rev 14:13
according to their *w* ....Rev 20:12

WORLD

"The field is the *w* ....Matt 13:38
He was in the *w* ....John 1:10
God so loved the *w* ....John 3:16
His Son into the *w* ....John 3:17
w cannot hate you ......John 7:7
You are of this *w* ......John 8:23
overcome the *w* ......John 16:33
w may become guilty ...Rom 3:19
be conformed to this *w* ..Rom 12:2
loved this present *w* ...2 Tim 4:10
Do not love the *w* ....1 John 2:15
w is passing away ....1 John 2:17

WORLDS

also He made the *w* ....Heb 1:2

WORM

But I am a *w* ....Ps 22:6
w does not die ....Mark 9:44

WORMS

he was eaten by *w* ....Acts 12:23

WORMWOOD

of the star is *W* ....Rev 8:11

WORRY

to you, do not *w* ....Matt 6:25

WORRYING

w can add one ....Matt 6:27

WORSE

w than their fathers ......Jer 7:26

WORSHIP

come to *w* Him ....Matt 2:2
w what you do not .....John 4:22
the angels of God w ......Heb 1:6

WORSHIPED

on their faces and *w* ....Rev 11:16

WORSHIPER

if anyone is a *w* ....John 9:31

WORTH

make my speech *w* .....Job 24:25

WORTHLESS

Indeed they are all *w* ....Is 41:29

WORTHLESSNESS

long will you love *w* ....Ps 4:2

WORTHY

present time are not *w* ..Rom 8:18
to walk *w* ....Eph 4:1
the world was not *w* ..Heb 11:38
"*W* is the Lamb who ....Rev 5:12

WOUND

And my *w* incurable ....Jer 15:18
and his deadly *w* ....Rev 13:3

WOUNDED

But He was *w* for our .....Is 53:5

WOUNDING

killed a man for *w* ......Gen 4:23

WOUNDS

Faithful are the *w* ......Prov 27:6

WRANGLINGS

useless *w* of men of ....1 Tim 6:5

WRATH

speak to them in His *w* ....Ps 2:5
Surely the *w* of man .....Ps 76:10
So I swore in My *w* ......Ps 95:11
W is cruel and anger a .Prov 27:4
in My *w* I struck you .....Is 60:10
w remember mercy ......Hab 3:2
For the *w* of God is .....Rom 1:18
up for yourself *w* ......Rom 2:5
nature children of *w* ......Eph 2:3
sun go down on your *w* .Eph 4:26
Let all bitterness, *w* .....Eph 4:31
holy hands, without *w* ..1 Tim 2:8
So I swore in My w .....Heb 3:11
not fearing the *w* ......Heb 11:27
for the *w* of man ......James 1:20
of the wine of the *w* .....Rev 14:8

for in them the *w* ....Rev 15:1
fierceness of His *w* .....Rev 16:19

WRATHFUL

w man stirs up strife ..Prov 15:18

WRESTLE

For we do not *w* ....Eph 6:12

WRETCHED

w man that I am ....Rom 7:24
know that you are *w* ....Rev 3:17

WRETCHEDNESS

let me see my *w* ......Num 11:15

WRINGING

w the nose produces ...Prov 30:33

WRINKLE

not having spot or *w* ....Eph 5:27

WRITE

w them on their hearts ..Heb 8:10

WRITING

the *w* was the *w* ....Ex 32:16

WRITINGS

do not believe his *w* ....John 5:47

WRITTEN

tablets of stone, *w* ....Ex 31:18
your names are *w* ....Luke 10:20
"What I have *w* ....John 19:22

WRONG

done nothing *w* ....Luke 23:41
But he who does *w* ......Col 3:25

WRONGED

We have *w* no one ......2 Cor 7:2

WRONGS

me *w* his own soul .....Prov 8:36

WROTE

stooped down and *w* ....John 8:6

WROUGHT

And skillfully *w* ....Ps 139:15

Y

YEAR

the acceptable *y* ....Is 61:2
of sins every *y* ....Heb 10:3

YEARS

and for days and *y* ......Gen 1:14
lives are seventy *y* .....Ps 90:10
when He was twelve *y* .Luke 2:42
with Him a thousand *y* ..Rev 20:6

YES

let your 'Y' be 'Y,' ......Matt 5:37

YESTERDAY

For we were born *y* ....Job 8:9

YOKE

"Take My *y* upon you ..Matt 11:29

YOKED

Do not be unequally *y* .2 Cor 6:14

YOUNG

I have been *y* ....Ps 37:25
she may lay her *y* ....Ps 84:3
I write to you, *y* ......1 John 2:13

YOUNGER

Likewise you *y* people ...1 Pet 5:5

YOURS

the battle is not y ....2 Chr 20:15
Y is the kingdom ......Matt 6:13
all Mine are Y ....John 17:10
for I do not seek y ....2 Cor 12:14

YOUTH

the sins of my y ....Ps 25:7

and y are vanity ....Eccl 11:10
I have kept from my y .Matt 19:20

YOUTHFUL

Flee also y lusts ....2 Tim 2:22

YOUTHS

y shall faint and be ....Is 40:30

Z

ZEAL

The z of the LORD of ..2 Kin 19:31
"Z for Your house has .John 2:17
that they have a z ......Rom 10:2

ZEALOUS

z for good works ......Titus 2:14